The Riverside Anthology of Children's Literature

Formerly Published as

Anthology of Children's Literature

Edna Johnson
Evelyn R. Sickels
Frances Clarke Sayers
Carolyn Horovitz

THE Riverside Anthology OF Children's Literature
SIXTH EDITION

Judith Saltman

University of British Columbia

HOUGHTON MIFFLIN COMPANY   BOSTON

Dallas   Geneva, Illinois   Lawrenceville, New Jersey   Palo Alto

Cover art by Stephen Harvard.

Acknowledgments appear on pp. 1339–47.

Printed in the U.S.A.

Library of Congress Catalog Card Number: 84-81344

ISBN: 0-395-35773-X

GHIJ-RM-96543210

To Sheila Egoff

To the faculty of the Center for the Study of Children's Literature, Simmons College

To the children and the children's librarians of the Toronto Public Library, the Vancouver Public Library, and the West Vancouver Memorial Library

To my parents, Ruth and Harry Saltman

Contents

I Children's Poetry: A Chorus of Voices

Street and Game Lore: Singing Games, Jingles, Chants, and Counting-Out Rhymes

Riddles, Puzzles, and Tongue Twisters

Lullabies and Folk Songs

2   Voices of Nonsense

Introduction 64

3 Voices of Childhood

The Voice of the Storyteller
Traditional Ballads

Narrative Poetry

The Lyric Voice
Poems of the Child's World

Poems of Reflection

The Voices of Children

IV Fiction: The Storied World

Introduction **665**

V *Nonfiction: The Real and Changing World*

VI *Readings on Children's Literature*

Illustrators and Illustrations

Color Section   (following page 162)

John Burningham, from *John Burningham's ABC*

John Burningham, from *Mr. Gumpy's Outing*

Alois Carigiet, from *The Pear Tree, the Birch Tree, and the Barberry Bush*

Ezra Jack Keats, from *The Snowy Day*

William Kurelek, from *A Prairie Boy's Winter*

Celestino Piatti, from *Celestino Piatti's Animal ABC*

Brian Wildsmith, from *Brian Wildsmith's ABC*

Margot Zemach, from *Mommy, Buy Me a China Doll*

Preface

The Riverside Anthology of Children's Literature is the direct descendant of the five editions of the Anthology of Children's Literature, published by Houghton Mifflin Company since 1935. Although the changes from the fifth edition of the Anthology of Children's Literature have been extensive, the Riverside rests upon a bedrock of work done by the previous editors. The current editor shares with the previous editors a dedication to the proposition that children deserve the very best literature we can give them.

Criteria for inclusion in The Riverside Anthology of Children's Literature have been those of literary and artistic excellence. The selections have been chosen to introduce the spectrum of genres in children's literature, to present an overview of the literature, and to provide a balance among acknowledged classics, traditional literature, and the most distinguished of contemporary writing for children. Although the Riverside is intended as a resource for students, parents, and general readers, the selections may certainly be used with children, for they are, after all, the primary audience for this literature.

The organization of selections has been altered from the fifth edition to parallel the chronological development of children's reading interests and skills. Children's first response to literature is aural, through the music of language in nursery rhymes and lullabies, and accordingly the Riverside begins with the voices of the nursery and continues through more mature poetry to picture books, folktales and legends, fiction, and informational books. Each part, however, is self-contained, and instructors may teach the parts in the order they find best.

In expanding and revising the anthology, an effort has been made to cover a wider range of literature, to include more international and contemporary material, and to achieve a broader ethnic representation. New illustrations have been added throughout the text, and a selection from a complete picture book, with both text and accompanying illustrations, has been added. The picture-book selection provides an example of the picture-book genre and may be treated as an artistic whole.

The poetry selections have been reorganized; in Chapter 3, the poems have been arranged by genre and theme, and a section of poetry written by children has been added. The chapter on myths and legends in the fifth edition has been expanded to include sacred writings as well, and science fiction selections have been added to the fiction section. An entirely new part, "Readings on Children's Literature," has been added: a collection of selected readings by significant critics and writers in the field.

In the appendix, the listing of children's book awards has been revised and updated. It also has been expanded to include English-language awards from countries other than the United States. *The Riverside Anthology of Children's Literature* contains updated, revised, and expanded bibliographies, giving broader international coverage. Most titles listed are in print, but important out-of-print titles are also included since they are generally available in libraries. A subject index has been added.

Although a certain amount of introductory and headnote material has been retained from the fifth edition with little alteration, most of this material has been revised and rewritten; many introductions and headnotes were written specifically for the *Riverside*. The introductory material is intended to be substantively critical and informative; to help clarify contemporary trends, issues, and controversies in children's literature; to direct readers to primary critical sources; and to explore the changing image of children and their books in our society.

The substantial amount of work involved in preparing *The Riverside Anthology of Children's Literature* could not have been accomplished without a small but energetic support staff: David Archer, William Barringer, Jeneva Shaw, and research assistant Liora Beder. Many of my colleagues in the field — in particular, Sheila Egoff, Sarah Ellis, Sriani Fernando — provided invaluable advice, and Kit Pearson offered consultative assistance on the fiction section. I especially would like to thank Keith Maillard, who assisted in research, writing, and editing. Terry Clark, Corinne Durston, and Ken Roberts helped in locating materials, and Irene Aubrey, chief of the Children's Literature Service of the National Library of Canada, aided in checking the Canadian bibliographic references and suggested further inclusions. I would also like to recognize the work of the team of people at Houghton Mifflin Company who worked on the *Riverside* and the support of the School of Library, Archival, and Information Studies of the University of British Columbia, and I would like to acknowledge the inspiration and ideas generated by the courses of study and institutes offered by the Center for the Study of Children's Literature at Simmons College.

Finally, I would like to thank the following individuals, who made helpful suggestions about revising this text: William D. Adamson, University of Minnesota, Twin Cities; Marlene Anne Birkman, Webster University, Missouri; Leona Classen, University of Minnesota at Morris; Patricia S. Dolan, Community College of Allegheny County, Pennsylvania; Maryellen Hains, Western Michigan University; Ann Hildebrand, Kent State University; Donald Holliday, Southwest Missouri State University; Glenna L. Howell, East Texas State University; John Knapp II, State University of New York at Oswego; John Lovas, De Anza College, California; Wilma Marshall, Abilene Christian University, Texas; Thérèse McVicar, Mercy College, New York; Harold Nelson, Minot State College, North Dakota; Lee Galda, University of Georgia; Barbara Pilon, Worcester State College, Massachusetts; Sally S. Rumbaugh, San Diego Mesa College, California;

Jacob H. Schuhle, State University of New York at Cortland; John W. Stewig, University of Wisconsin, Milwaukee; Loraine Webster, University of South Dakota; and Bernice Zelditch, Foothill College, California.

One of the most difficult problems in compiling an anthology is that of excerpting from living literature without violating the artistic whole. A platonic ideal of a children's literature anthology — an entire library of the best children's books — might be the anthologist's dream, but in the practical world such ideals are unobtainable. I hope that *The Riverside Anthology of Children's Literature* will offer an introduction to the range, excitement, and vitality of children's literature, provide a historical and critical context for the assessment and study of this literature, and engender in readers a desire to continue their journey through the platonic library, searching out the best literature for children.

Judith Saltman
University of British Columbia

From birth stayned, with Adams
sinfull fact;
From thence I 'gan to sin, as soon
as act.
A perverse will, a love to what's forbid:
A serpents sting in pleasing face
lay hid.
A lying tongue as soon as it
could speak,
And fift Commandement do daily
break.[1]   (1650)

Not in entire forgetfulness,
And not in utter nakedness,
But trailing clouds of glory do
we come
From God, who is our home:
Heaven lies about us in our
infancy![2]   (1807)

Introduction:
"Trade and Plumb-Cake Forever"

I t is impossible to understand fully the children's literature of any period
without closely examining the society that produced it. As Sheila Egoff
writes, "Because children require direction from adults and because they
are much more open to influence than adults, fiction intended for them
has often been invested with very strong moral and social values, along with
heavy doses of information. . . . What children read is too important in its potential for society's good or ill to be made a matter of purely aesthetic consideration.
Thus writing for children has tended, more than most other branches of literature,
to be very much a reflection (although in miniature) of prevailing social concepts
and conditions, and it is in the history of society itself that one must look for

1. Anne Bradstreet, "The Four Ages of Man," stanza 2, lines 59–64, in *The Complete Works of Anne
Bradstreet,* ed. Joseph R. McElrath, Jr., and Allan P. Robb (Twayne, 1981), p. 38.
2. William Wordsworth, "Ode: Intimations of Immortality from Recollections of Early Childhood,"
stanza 5, lines 63–67.

I

the roots of children's literature and its role in reflecting changing values."[3] The most important of these changing values for the student of children's literature is the concept of childhood itself.

Before the seventeenth century, children were considered smaller versions of adults. In those difficult times of high infant mortality and short life spans, children were drawn into the adult world as quickly as possible. No special entertainment was provided for them; children and adults alike enjoyed myths and folktales, ballads and stories, courtly romances, and embroidered histories of their families, neighbors, or regions. At a time when most people were not literate, these stories were shared orally; Sir Philip Sidney, writing in the sixteenth century, describes them as tales "which holdeth children from play and old men from the chimney corner."[4]

Certainly, a society that did not see childhood as a separate state did not create literature specifically for children. John Rowe Townsend states flatly: "I do not know of any survival from the age of manuscript that can be called a children's story. But there were manuscripts that embodied *lessons* for children."[5]   The fifteenth-century courtesy books for children contained instructions, admonitions, and exhortations. Townsend quotes a sample:

> Child, over men's houses no stones fling
> Nor at glass windows no stones sling,
> Nor make no crying, jokes nor plays
> In holy Church on holy days.[6]

We see already the two streams that will continue to run uneasily, side by side, through children's literature: that of *entertainment* (the tale that holdeth children from their play, and holdeth everyone else within listening distance) and that of *didacticism* (the stern adult voice, warning "Child, over men's houses no stones fling"). The first stream received impetus from William Caxton, the first English printer, who published tales from the oral tradition in the fifteenth century. These tales continued to appear in printed form as cheap booklets (called chapbooks), sold by itinerant peddlers, and flourished in collections and retellings by scholars and artists such as those by Charles Perrault in 1697 and Jakob and Wilhelm Grimm in the 1820s.

The other stream became a torrent in the seventeenth century with the advent of Puritanism and the "good godly books" of religious training and moral admonition: didacticism epitomized. The Puritans, in their concern for the child's immortal soul, recognized children as quite distinct from adults. They felt that children were filled with sin—they were conceived and born in sin, would grow to maturity in sin, and would die in sin—unless something were done. The Puritans saw to it that something *was* done and created, in their zeal, the first literature (other than the early courtesy books) specifically for children. This famous stanza pro-

3. Sheila A. Egoff, *Thursday's Child: Trends and Patterns in Contemporary Children's Literature* (American Library Association, 1981), p. 2.
4. Sir Philip Sidney, "An Apology for Poetry," in *English Critical Essays: Sixteenth through Eighteenth Centuries,* ed. E. D. Jones (Oxford University Press, 1922), p. 22.
5. John Rowe Townsend, *Written for Children: An Outline of English-language Children's Literature* (Horn Book, 1974), p. 17.
6. "Symon's Lesson of Wisdom for All Manner Children," in *The Babees' Book,* ed. F. J. Furnivall (Trubner, 1868), as quoted in Townsend, p. 18.

vides an example of the sort of material they gave children. It is taken from a book by James Janeway entitled *A Token for Children: Being an Exact Account of the Conversion, Holy and Exemplary Lives, and Joyful Deaths of Several Young Children* (1671):

> When by spectators I am told
> What beauty doth adorn me,
> Or in a glass when I behold
> How sweetly God did form me—
> Hath God such comliness bestowed
> And on me made to dwell—
> What pity such a pretty maid
> As I should go to Hell!

Offered such fare, children naturally turned to an imaginative allegory written for adults—*Pilgrim's Progress* (1678) by John Bunyan—reading it as a fairy tale full of marvels and adventures. As fairy and folktales continued under attack from the Puritan era into the 1700s, and moral and religious themes were all too often repeated, children claimed two more treasures not intended for them: Daniel Defoe's *Robinson Crusoe* (1719) and Jonathan Swift's *Gulliver's Travels* (1726).

Not long after this, books specifically designed for children began for the first time to offer them delight and entertainment as well as instruction. The best known and most important of these were published by John Newbery, a bustling, energetic bookseller and publisher; his shop was located at the sign of the Bible and Sun in St. Paul's Churchyard, London, and his engaging slogan, "Trade and Plumb-cake for ever, Huzza!" rang out for children and their books. Newbery was not the first publisher to court the children of the rising middle class, but he displayed a unique flair in his *A Little Pretty Pocket-Book* of 1744. A pleasure to behold, covered in gilt paper imported from Holland, it fit comfortably in the pocket and was easily held in a child's hand. The famous *Mother Goose's Melody* (circa 1765), a collection of English folk rhymes with some songs from Shakespeare, came from his press, as did the popular *History of Little Goody Two-Shoes* (1765). Newbery's books combined instruction with amusement, even enlisting the aid of Jack the Giant Killer; yet, ever the man of business, he incorporated as well ingenious references to Dr. James's Fever Powder, a patent medicine to which he held the rights.

Even before Newbery's time, however, adult attitudes toward children had begun to change, largely as a result of the writings of John Locke. In *Some Thoughts Concerning Education* (1690), Locke urged that children be led gently to learning rather than whipped into submission and made to learn by rote. At the same time he deplored the use of fairy tales and stories from old ballads; he could recommend only Aesop's *Fables* and the beast epic *Reynard the Fox* as having any moral value. Newbery, not a man to let fine distinctions stand in the way of making money, later included a quotation from Locke along with the fairy tales and ballads he printed.

Another powerful influence on children's books came from the theories of Jean Jacques Rousseau, as set forth in *Émile* (1762). The eighteenth and nineteenth centuries were affected by Rousseau's belief that children were the hope of humanity, provided they were not contaminated by the world. With the out-of-doors as a schoolroom, children were to learn from experience through their instincts and feelings. They were to have no books before age twelve; instead, they were to be closely associated with a mature person, such as a parent or tutor, who was qualified to answer all their questions and to help solve their problems—but who would never direct their actions. In the literature that followed this theory, learning from experience (with adult interpretation) summoned the plot, cast the characters, and determined the dialogue. Thomas Day's three-volume work, *Sandford and Merton* (1795–98), provided a perfect example of Rousseau's theories at work. Harry Sandford, the awful example of goodness, and naughty, snobbish Tommy Merton are about six years old. Their guide is Mr. Barlow, a priggish bore, who helps them acquire facts in physical geography, lets them look through a telescope at the moon, and shows them informational magic-lantern pictures. He tells them historical tales or lets them read fables—all quoted in full—that give rise to long discussions about vices and virtues. In the end, Tommy, conscious of all his faults, is reformed entirely by the paragon Harry.

With this as an example and inspiration, writers such as Mary Wollstonecraft and Hannah More presented lessons in story form, generally referred to as the "Moral Tale and Matter-of-Fact Tale." The most gifted of Thomas Day's disciples was Maria Edgeworth, whose natural powers of characterization and dialogue could not be wholly submerged beneath this formula. One of Edgeworth's child characters, Rosamund, in "The Purple Jar" (1796), is drawn with a sensitivity that prefigures the high-spirited, authentic children found in later children's books.

The Sunday School Movement, begun in 1780 by publisher Robert Raikes, developed indirectly from Rousseau's theories on education and provided a further influence on children's books. Its basic concept—educating slum children on Sundays to keep them from misbehaving—spread rapidly and led to a demand for stories embodying the Sunday school educational theories. *Hymns in Prose for Children* (1781), by Letitia Aikin Barbauld, attempted to lead the child through nature to God. "A Child," Barbauld says in her introduction to the book, "to feel the full force of the idea of God ought never to remember when he had no such idea. It must come early and with no insistence upon dogma, in association with all that he sees and all that he hears, all that affects his mind with wonder and delight." Mrs. Barbauld's book is marked by poetic beauty and a mystical sense of God, but it found little favor with Charles Lamb. Indicating yet another modulation of the concept of childhood, he wrote to Coleridge: *"Goody Two-Shoes* is almost out of print. Mrs. Barbauld's stuff has banished all the old classics of the nursery. . . . Science has succeeded to Poetry no less in the little walks of children than with men—: Is there no possibility of averting this sore evil? Think what you would have been now, if instead of being fed with Tales and old wives fables in childhood, you had been crammed with Geography and Natural History!"[7]

A striking trend away from children's books of moral and religious edification began under the influence of the Romantic movement and the new Victorian middle class. The public concept of childhood was changing profoundly. If the Puritans discovered *the child,* then the Victorians discovered *childhood.* Children were no longer considered to be either miniature adults or tiny sinners to be saved from damnation; they were people, separate from adults, living their

---

7. Quoted in F. J. Harvey Darton, *Children's Books in England: Five Centuries of Social Life,* rev. Brian Alderson, 3d ed. (Cambridge University Press, 1982), p. 129.

own lives and deserving of their own literature. Although idealized and sentimental, the Victorian image of childhood as a time of life with a unique character—a time of innocence and natural goodness to be cherished, sheltered, and prolonged—survived well into the twentieth century. Its influence is, in fact, still felt. This was the beginning of the first "Golden Age" of children's literature, during which many accomplished writers turned toward this new child audience and created a literature of exuberant energy and original art.

In 1823, Edgar Taylor's translation was published, with drawings by George Cruikshank, of *The Household Tales,* German folktales originally collected and published by Jakob and Wilhelm Grimm. Andersen's *Fairy Tales* appeared in 1846 in a translation by Mary Howitt, and, in the same year, Edward Lear published his first *Nonsense Book.* The world of the imagination is the child's natural sphere, and neither the literature of the Rousseau cult nor that of the Sunday School Movement could withstand such a rush of imaginative stories. Although Sunday school stories lived a shadowy life for many years, they never regained their former power and popularity; the stream of didactic literature for children was reduced to a trickle—at least for a time.

In fact, Charles Lutwidge Dodgson, an Oxford don and teacher of mathematics and logic, dropped the didactic tradition down a rabbit-hole. It is doubtful that Dodgson knew he was taking a revolutionary step on the afternoon in 1862 when, rowing on the river with another adult and the three daughters of a colleague, he began to entertain himself and his young friends by telling a story. From its startling opening, in which a rabbit, about to descend into a hole in the ground, expresses the typical Victorian concern about being on time, *Alice's Adventures in Wonderland* (1865) was free as no other children's story had been before of adult self-consciousness about suitable fare for children. Dodgson's ingenious juxtaposition of fantasy and logic, his absurd inventions, more illuminating and reasonable than reality, were presented to his young listeners in a spirit of complete equality. The story, he said, had "no moral," but it also contained no condescension and no adult posturing—qualities that Dodgson was unable to duplicate after he became known as Lewis Carroll and tried to write for an eager publisher.

The age of *Alice* was a time of refreshing and creative fantasies, such as the works of George MacDonald and Charles Kingsley, and stories of high adventure and romance, such as Robert Louis Stevenson's *Treasure Island* (1883). In the United States, authors such as Mark Twain and Louisa May Alcott were writing spirited stories of child and family life with strikingly realistic characters. The late Victorian and Edwardian eras were also times of remarkable accidental creations, creations springing from writers writing as people, not theorists. They wrote from their inner urgencies and complexities, not from the expectations of any current school of thought. Stevenson seized on his stepson's request for a good yarn as an excuse to write for the boy in himself. *Treasure Island* is filled with Stevenson's own being—his delight in colorful apparel, his ear for a robust rhythm in language, and his penchant for deeds of braggadocio, cunning, and deceit. All the art he could muster was called up as he, the chief actor, spun out the story that has held listeners and attracted readers ever since. Kenneth Grahame, telling bedtime stories to his young son, was also entertaining himself with inventions set on his beloved river. *The Wind in the Willows* (1908) is more than a story: It holds the essence of a man who felt free to share his observation and wit with a receptive yet demanding audience. Rudyard Kipling also was responding to the sympathetic receptiveness of his own children when he told them what later became the *Just So Stories* (1902). Hugh Lofting, writing from the trenches of World War I, wanted to give his young son a gift—an enchantment that would banish the worry and crushing reality of a father away at war—and so he wrote him letters about a man called Doctor Dolittle.

The attraction that such works have for children is not the result of their writers' intensive theoretical knowledge about the nature of childhood; it stems simply from a channeling of the childhood responses in each writer toward those elements in which generations of children have delighted. This is the nature of literature—it is a direct sounding of the human. That Alcott would write a family story, Stevenson an adventure, Carroll a fantasy of nonsense, L. M. Montgomery a story of sentiment and humor, or Frances Hodgson Burnett a romance of character and setting was determined by the nature of each writer's individual experience and sensibilities. The true distinction between the first "Golden Age" of children's literature and preceding eras lies in the marked differences among its writers. The emergence of strong individual voices is indicative of a genuine literature.

Depth of individuality, integrity of spirit, and far-ranging diversity in form and philosophy remained hallmarks of writing for children to the end of the 1950s. Themes of playful nonsense or deep moral significance were treated with equal seriousness by such literary stylists as E. Nesbit, J. M. Barrie, A. A. Milne, J. R. R. Tolkien, E. B. White, and Laura Ingalls Wilder. In all genres of children's literature, the emphasis was on literary merit: the creation of lifelike, three-dimensional characters; inventive, well-paced plots; beautifully crafted language; and a tone of warm humanity reflecting the vital memory of what it is like to be a child. The books of this time were entertainments in the best sense of the word. Their authors succeeded in engaging emotions, invoking empathy and delight, and kindling the imagination in such works as Arthur Ransome's *Swallows and Amazons* (1930); P. L. Travers's *Mary Poppins* (1934); J. R. R. Tolkien's *The Hobbit* (1937); Eleanor Estes's *The Moffats* (1941); C. S. Lewis's Narnia books (1950–56); E. B. White's *Charlotte's Web* (1952); Rosemary Sutcliff's *The Eagle of the Ninth* (1954); Philippa Pearce's *Tom's Midnight Garden* (1958); and Scott O'Dell's *Island of the Blue Dolphins* (1960).

These writers, from what has been called the "Second Golden Age" of children's literature (approximately the 1940s to the 1960s), followed a conservative literary tradition in which children's literature was viewed as a nondidactic source of aesthetic enrichment, a field in which to explore imaginative and moral visions, sentiment, and creative play—all set into a framework of safety and stability. This tradition continues to the present day in the works of Lloyd Alexander, Leon Garfield, Ursula K. Le Guin, Penelope Lively, Joan Aiken, Susan Cooper, Natalie Babbitt, and Jill Paton Walsh.

"But," Sheila Egoff asks, "was there a tarnish on the Second Golden Age? In retrospect it can be seen that the social outlook in these books (taken as a whole) was perhaps too safe, too tranquil, and too predictable."[8] While the writers in the literary tradition that was rooted in the Victorian and Edwardian eras continued to write of children living in a secure world of extended childhood, enormous social changes were taking place: the cataclysm of the Second World War, the economic expansion of the 1940s and 1950s, the increased mobility

8. Egoff, p. 11.

brought about by the automobile, and the coming of television. By the 1960s society's concept of childhood had changed once again. Childhood was no longer considered a preserve of innocence and freedom from adult cares, a time to be extended as long as possible; rather, as prior to the seventeenth century, children were regarded as miniature adults. Children came to share the sociological and psychological anxieties, moral and ethical ambiguities, and responsibilities of the contemporary adult world. They rushed out of childhood as quickly as possible in order to arrive in the newly emphasized state of adolescence. This rapid and unsettling social change caused a parallel upheaval in writing for children.

This altered attitude toward childhood is typified by Louise Fitzhugh's seminal, ground-breaking *Harriet the Spy* (1964)—a book that attracted child readers with the voice of their own time but that disturbed many adults with its satirical depiction of society and its iconoclastic, defiant protagonist. Maurice Sendak's *Where the Wild Things Are* (1963) had a similar impact in the field of picture books. Adults responded with ambivalence to Sendak's intense interpretation of a child's use of fantasy to resolve turbulent, often unconscious, emotions that are as strong, frightening, and disruptive as those of adults. In the time since their publication, both books have become widely accepted, and they are now considered to be classics.

A new style of children's literature developed, which has been referred to by John Rowe Townsend as "didacticism in modern dress." Earnest and apparently candid, this new realism examines modern life with the intention of informing children, commenting on social phenomena, and rectifying social ills by influencing children's moral and social perceptions. Publishers, with their eye on the vast potential market of newly affluent adolescents, invented a new category of writing designed to appeal to them: young adult fiction. Most of the issue-centered problem novels of the new realism, books intended for teenagers but frequently read by children, have been published in this category. Critic Paul Heins has characterized the 1970s and 1980s as an "era one is tempted to call the Age of Judy Blume"; this "new kind of realism," he says, is "unrestricted by taboos and conventions and propriety of subject matter, and it deals freely with sexual as well as with social and racial topics."[9]

A parallel critical stance toward children's books has developed; called an issues or values approach, this point of view analyzes literature for the messages it contains about topics such as families, divorce, death, old age, war, sex, blacks, native Americans, and women. This approach sees books as cures to be prescribed for a given sociological, political, or emotional problem. This latest wave of didacticism has given rise to a great deal of controversy, much of it more heated than enlightening. Many critics have applauded the explicitness, therapeutic potential, and social relevance of this new realism (as it appears, for example, in the works of Judy Blume and Norma Klein); they praise its recognition of the difficulties and complexities of the lives of contemporary children. Others have objected to the harsh naturalism, faddishness, cliché-ridden plots, flat tone, polemical nature, or just plain bad writing in many of these books. But an important point is often missed: It is possible to object to works of the new realism on literary grounds without advocating either a socially unresponsive aestheticism or a return to a Golden Age of childhood.

9. Paul Heins, "Literary Criticism and Children's Books," *The Quarterly Journal of the Library of Congress*, 38 (1981), 261.

Fortunately, this new broadening of subject matter and treatment has not served merely to attract a host of interchangeable writers to a series of repetitive issues and problems. It has enabled first-class writers to investigate for children mature themes and serious topics in a way that would have been impossible twenty years ago. Writers such as Katherine Paterson in *Bridge to Terabithia* (1977), Virginia Hamilton in *The Planet of Junior Brown* (1971), and Robert Cormier in *The Chocolate War* (published in the young adult category, 1974) have created works with the literary integrity, emotional realism, and craftsmanship that distinguish the best writing for children from earlier years. And more light-hearted writers, such as Lois Lowry in *Anastasia Krupnik* (1979), have also succeeded equally well in capturing the flavor of our age.

One result of more than a decade of the new realism has been a reaction against the genre, which may be seen in the resurgence of children's formula fiction such as the *Nancy Drew* and *Hardy Boys* books (the anonymously authored commercial series originally produced by the Stratemeyer Syndicate in the first half of the century); a more recent reaction is the rise of the "baby Harlequins" or teen and sub-teen romances, which have already engendered a million-dollar industry. It is not difficult to imagine children who have been overdosed on issues and problems turning with relief to cheerful, unthreatening fantasies in which child protagonists solve the case or get a date. (Both the series books and the problem novels of the new realism appear to be read more for reassurance and peer approval than for any imaginative perceptions.) Also in the category of sheer escapism are the new gamelike, so-called interactive books, such as the *Choose Your Own Adventure* series and the *Heart Quest Books;* these read like computer games, video games, or fantasy boardgames in which the reader assumes the protagonist's identity, chooses from a variety of plot lines, and picks "a path to romance and adventure."

In the 1980s the two streams of children's literature are still very much with us. The most extreme proponents of contemporary didacticism, bibliotherapy, or developmental values in children's books see their own social, political, or therapeutic concerns as so important as to reduce all other considerations to triviality; speaking to them of literature would make as little sense as speaking of it to a Puritan divine whose task, as he saw it, would have been to save the souls of little children from eternal damnation. But those holding the opposite view sometimes appear to be hiding behind a shield labeled *Art for art's sake.* Their denunciation of controversial trends in contemporary writing for children is not a simple defense of literary values, but includes an element of nonliterary nostalgia for a simpler, less threatening literature and time. Critical theory in children's literature is something of a minefield of issues and concerns; for readers interested in venturing into it, Part VI of this anthology may serve as an introduction.

In addition to the two points of view outlined above—which most people in the field hold in a manner considerably less extreme than has been stated— there is a third position, one which John Rowe Townsend calls a "modest and unprovocative creed." It is that "we would wish every child to experience to his or her full capacity the enjoyment, and the broadening of horizons, which can be derived from literature. . . . What it asks is the acceptance of literary experience as having value in itself for the general enrichment of life, over and above any virtue that may be claimed for it as a means to a nonliterary end."[10] This carefully articulated position is more than merely modest. It is balanced and humane.

Sir Francis Palgrave, one of the earliest and best known of anthologizers, made the curious remark in his *Golden Treasury* (1861) that "anthologies are sickly things." It is a sentiment that can be understood by anyone who has compiled an anthology. Selections can never be substituted for the whole; each is only an intimation of the work of which it is a part. And, although this anthology has been used for many years by teachers of children's literature, it has never been a handbook on how to teach. Nor is it a sociology text, an attempt to present samples of everything that children do in fact read. If it were, it would have to include selections from comic books, adult popular novels, magazines, and the backs of cereal boxes. Rather, it represents a choice, a selection of material that indicates something of the depth, variety, and excitement of children's literature—with emphasis on the imagination and emotional quality of the writer.

No selection was rejected because its subject matter is considered controversial, and no selection appears here merely because its subject matter might be considered beneficial to children. The criteria for inclusion in this anthology were literary, and literary judgments have always implied notions of human values. "It is . . . easy to think of writing for children as being like giving them presents," Jill Paton Walsh commented in one of her speeches. She continued:

Here are our perceptions and our carefully gathered costly insights into the world, and they will benefit the young. The truth is different and far more alarming. There is nothing more important than writing well for the young, if literature is to have continuance. And they are the Lords of Time, in whose courts we beg for favors, hoping that the gifts we can bring them may secure their favor for our cause.

For though some of us may be struck by freak longevity and some of them by untimely disaster, they do stand differently in the flow of time, and nothing is more certain than that they will survive us. They will inherit the earth; and nothing that we value will endure in the world unless they can be freely persuaded to value it too.[11]

10. John Rowe Townsend, "Standards of Criticism for Children's Literature," in *The Arbuthnot Lectures, 1970–1979,* comp. Zena Sutherland (American Library Association, 1980), p. 25.
11. Jill Paton Walsh, "The Lords of Time," in *The Openhearted Audience: Ten Authors Talk about Writing for Children,* ed. Virginia Haviland (Library of Congress, 1980), p. 198.

Children's Poetry:
A Chorus of Voices

The study of children's literature must include oral as well as written material because children first experience literature through the sound of the human voice. If young children are to acquire language and thus be drawn into the human community, they must hear language spoken. What they first hear, along with the forms of daily speech, is often, the poetic—the soothing lullabies, the chanting verses that accompany dandling games and finger plays.

Children's first literature, then, is poetry, a process, to paraphrase Robert Frost, beginning in delight and ending in wisdom.[1] That process begins in the nursery. There children first hear the rhythmic sounds that will later emerge as language—hear them while being rocked or stroked or bathed or swung through the air. The songs and poetry of the nursery reinforce the fundamental relationship between the rhythm of movement and the rhythm of sound. They are felt as part of a total experience in which infants absorb the cadence through their bodies while they hear the magical voices of loving adults.

NOTE: Introductions to Chapters 1, 2, and 3, which make up Part I, "Children's Poetry: A Chorus of Voices," are based upon and include portions of Chapter 9, "Poetry," by Judith Saltman, with editorial assistance from Sheila A. Egoff, in Sheila A. Egoff, *Thursday's Child: Trends and Patterns in Contemporary Children's Literature* (American Library Association, 1981), pp. 221–46. Used by permission.

1. Robert Frost, "The Figure a Poem Makes," in *Complete Poems of Robert Frost* (Holt, 1949), reprinted in *Twentieth Century Poetry and Poetics*, ed. Garry Geddes, 2d ed. (Oxford University Press, 1973), p. 499.

As soon as children begin to acquire language, they vocalize as they move about in play; they grow into their own bodily rhythms to the accompaniment of their own voices. There is a natural development from nursery rhymes to the oral culture of game lore, jingles, chants, counting-out rhymes, riddles, and tongue-twisters. This progression flows easily on into nonsense and the maturer forms of poetry written specifically for children. But, although each genre of children's poetry does have a distinct voice, to separate them totally from one another—formal poetry from nursery rhymes or nonsense verse—is neither possible nor desirable. There is a natural flow back and forth from voice to voice. Nonsense invades both nursery rhymes and formal poetry, and many nursery rhymes have memorable poetic phrases. Lewis Carroll's "Jabberwocky," for example, is highly poetic in its word music as well as a fine piece of nonsense. Nor do children necessarily leave stages behind as they grow, abandoning nursery rhymes for counting-out rhymes or forgetting nonsense when they begin to enjoy narrative poetry. As C. S. Lewis observes, "A tree grows because it adds rings; a train doesn't grow by leaving one station behind and puffing on to the next."[2]

A mature appreciation of literature develops from—and depends upon—the experiences of childhood. The origins of all the rhythms, moods, images, and patterns of adult literature can be heard in the chorus of voices that is children's poetry.

2. C. S. Lewis, "On Three Ways of Writing for Children," in *Proceedings of the Bournemouth Conference of The Library Association* (The Library Association, 1952), reprinted in *Only Connect: Readings on Children's Literature,* ed. Sheila Egoff, G. T. Stubbs, and L. F. Ashley, 2d ed. (Oxford University Press, 1980), p. 211.

Out of them [nursery rhymes]
came the gusts and grunts and
hiccups and heehaws of the com-
mon fun of the earth; and though
what the words meant was, in its
own way, often deliciously funny
enough, so much funnier seemed
to me, at that almost forgotten
time, the shape and shade and
size and noise of the words as they
hummed, strummed, jugged, and
galloped along.[1]

1 Voices of the Nursery, Voices of the Playground

Dylan Thomas's recollections of his own discovery of poetry express something more fundamental than a poet's awakening to his muse: Children have a natural affinity for poetry. A child's response to poetry is immediate; young children take delight in repetition, rhythm, and rhyme, and they seemingly respond with their very nerves, in confirmation of the widely held belief that poetry is the natural language of childhood. Rhythm begins for children in the womb, with the first heartbeat, and continues in the mother's arms, with rhythmical rockings, soothing lullabies, and lilting Mother Goose rhymes. It is present in the infant's instinctive patterning of cadenced cries and body movements. As they grow older, children greet musical language with an exhilarated swaying of heads, hands, and feet, marking tempo and measure with their bodies and voices.

Poetry comes first to children when it is read and sung to them by adults. Generations of adults and children are linked through this shared literature of the nursery, a universal oral tradition. The English nursery or Mother Goose melodies, an enduring part of this tradition, were meant to be sung or recited aloud. They constitute a potpourri of restful lullabies, robust jingles for infant dandling, riddles, and fragments of old tunes.

1. Dylan Thomas, "Notes on the Art of Poetry," *Texas Quarterly* (Winter 1961), reprinted in *Twentieth Century Poetry and Poetics,* ed. Garry Geddes, 2d ed. (Oxford University Press, 1973), p. 589.

Poetry's initial appeal for children stems from the same basic need that provides the impulse for the allied arts of music and dance—the need to move. The rhythm of Mother Goose is as certain as a heartbeat:

> Dance to your daddy,
> My little babby,
> Dance to your daddy,
> My little lamb.

Variety in rhyme and meter continually surprises the ear, the pace changing as quickly as the scene and cast of characters:

> Hark, hark, the dogs do bark,
> The beggars are coming to town;
> Some in rags, and some in jags,
> And one in a velvet gown.

Later, the words will become a vital part of the songs' appeal and of the child's expanding vocabulary.

But there is much more, for Mother Goose is a child's mirror on the world. There is drama, packed into the brief, abrupt verse of Miss Muffet and the spider. There is mirth and merriment with the cat and the fiddle, and humor and nonsense aplenty—in the images of the three men in a tub; in Old King Cole, that merry old soul; and in four-and-twenty tailors running from a snail. There is trust and kindness of heart, but cruelty, as well:

> As I was going to sell my eggs,
> I met a man with bandy legs;
> Bandy legs and crooked toes,
> I tripped up his heels and he fell
> on his nose.

Nursery rhymes touch on the greatest themes—the inevitability of fate and character in the ballads of "The Death and Burial of Cock Robin" or the poignance of pain and loss in the short rhymes "Jack and Jill," "Humpty Dumpty," and "Simple Simon." Even the eternal, central question of romantic love is there:

> And why may I not love Johnny?
> And why may not Johnny love me?

Rhyme and revelation may enhance Mother Goose, but the essence of poetry—the recurring miracle of phrase that evokes images of pure delight—is also there:

> I had a little nut tree,
> Nothing would it bear
> But a silver nutmeg
> And a golden pear.

Tiny, lovely, and mysterious, Mother Goose rhymes are the miniature poetry of childhood. A contemporary child is unlikely to meet a milkmaid, tinker, page, princess, or king, but that these odd personages exist *somewhere else* opens, at once, a door to an enchanted kingdom that will expand in adulthood to become our inherited mythology and literature. The rhymes constantly remind the child listener of times long ago, places far distant, and strange, evocative happenings.

> There was an old woman tossed up in a basket,
>   Seventeen times as high as the moon;
> And where she was going I couldn't but ask it,
>   For in her hand she carried a broom.
> Old woman, old woman, old woman, quoth I,
>   O whither, O whither, O whither so high?
> To sweep the cobwebs off the sky!
>   Shall I go with you? Aye, by-and-by.

"This is the key to the kingdom," says one of these old rhymes. This might well be said of the rhymes of Mother Goose as a whole, for here is the dawn of humor and imagination; the first appreciation of the bite, beauty, and bounce of words; and the earliest evocation of the sad magic of the human condition. To all these kingdoms, Mother Goose is the key.

It is apt that when the major character in Doris Lessing's contemporary adult novel, *The Four Gated City* (1969), needs to unlock the door to her own psyche, she uses a Mother Goose rhyme as an incantation:

> How many miles to Babylon?
>   Three score miles and ten.
> Can I get there by candle-light?
>   Yes, and back again.

Three score years and ten is the span of a single human life; *Babylon* may be a corruption of *Babyland*.[2]   Our childhood is never lost; by the flickering candle-light of memory, we return to it again and again in the strange and significant adventure of life. Just as Mother Goose rhymes—those strange and significant verses of Babyland—return to each generation.

The lineage of the Mother Goose rhymes is obscure but obviously ancient. As much as from the songs and rhymes used to engage children in play or rock them to sleep, they developed from mythic ritual and ceremony, folk customs, political satires, and street ballads. The name "Mother Goose" first appeared in France; the phrase "Tales of My Mother Goose" formed a part of the frontispiece to Charles Perrault's famous collection of fairy tales (not verses!), published in Paris in the year 1697. The French expression *contes de ma mere l'oye* was in common use at that time, no doubt because the old peasant woman who tended the geese was the accepted symbol of the storyteller.[3] John Newbery, the pioneering children's book publisher and seller in St. Paul's churchyard, London, first matched the term *Mother Goose* to a collection of traditional rhymes, issued circa 1765 under the title *Mother Goose's Melody; or Sonnets for the Cradle.*

The most thorough and scholarly account of the old English rhymes is to be found in that readable, landmark volume, *The Oxford Dictionary of Nursery Rhymes* (1951), edited by Iona and Peter Opie. The Opies cite the earliest occurrence

2. William S. Baring-Gould and Ceil Baring-Gould, *The Annotated Mother Goose* (Bramhall House, 1962), pp. 115–16.
3. *Perrault's Tales of Mother Goose: The Dedication Manuscript of 1695, Reproduced in Collotype Facsimile with Introduction and Critical Text,* Vol. II, by Jacques Barchilon (Pierpont Morgan Library, 1956), p. 37.

in print of each of more than five hundred rhymes, and, in many cases, provide variants. The alphabetical arrangement of the verses, the wealth of contemporary illustrations, the extensive notes and comments, and the "Index of Notable Figures Associated with . . . Nursery Rhymes" make it a highly useful and at times exhilarating piece of scholarship.

Nursery rhymes have long provided fertile ground for illustration. From the rough but charming woodcuts in John Newbery's eighteenth-century edition to present-day versions, there has been a continuity of authentic childhood perception. Some illustrators respond to the magical enchantment of the rhymes—Arthur Rackham and Harold Jones, for instance—while others prefer to emphasize their zesty, flamboyant humor—Randolph Caldecott, Leslie Brooke, and Raymond Briggs are examples.

In recent years, many beautifully illustrated editions have been produced in modern, experimental art styles or with unusual thematic structures. *Nicola Bayley's Book of Nursery Rhymes* (1977) glows with luminous, jewel-like miniatures, ornamentally framed images of an idealized Victorian world. The surreal sketches in Mitchell Miller's *One Misty Moisty Morning* (1971) are eerie messages from the realms of dream and the unconscious. Other illustrators have successfully placed Mother Goose directly in the modern world. *Mother Goose Comes to Cable Street: Nursery Rhymes for Today* (1977), published by the politically activist Children's Rights Workshop of London, places the traditional verses in a contemporary inner-city setting. Dan Jones's naive, graffitti-ridden illustrations portray the street and home life of a multiethnic community in which the rhymes, removed from more usual romantic associations, serve once again as satiric commentaries on daily life.

In another recent development, single nursery rhymes are being published in elaborately illustrated picture-book editions, a concept utilized by classic nineteenth-century illustrators such as Randolph Caldecott. But it has become somewhat of a deluge, resulting in multiple editions of the same rhyme; for example, both Peter Spier and Ed Emberley have illustrated "London Bridge Is Falling Down."

Every culture has its own traditional nursery poetry, and in recent years a growing number of translations into English from other languages have been published. To translate folk poetry without destroying its natural spontaneity and musicality is difficult and requires the highest linguistic and poetic skills. Three of the best translations are *The Prancing Pony: Nursery Rhymes from Japan* (1968), adapted by Charlotte B. De Forest; *Chinese Mother Goose Rhymes* (1968), selected and edited by Robert Wyndham; and *Moon-Uncle, Moon-Uncle: Rhymes from India* (1973), selected and translated by Sylvia Cassedy and Parvathi Thampi. The poetry in these collections is more romantic and lyrical, more attuned to nature, and less ribald and rollicking than what we are used to in our English rhymes. And, of course, whatever social satire might have been contained in the verses is not evident in the translations. Nonetheless, they do serve to remind us that even though her name changes from culture to culture, Mother Goose is everywhere.

As nursery rhymes bind child to adult, so street and game rhymes bind child to child. This body of naive folk poetry is the poetry of play. An orally transmitted, constantly changing body of counting-out rhymes, singing games, tongue-twisters, song lyrics, jokes, jump-rope jingles, and mass-media advertising scraps, these feisty, salty verses have been created or appropriated by children for their own use; they are their own personal possessions, free of adult interference. Street and game rhymes are full of prankish tricks, jeers, and slang much ruder and more satirical than most Mother Goose rhymes; however, like Mother Goose, the street and game lore can be crisp and biting and can touch on the poetic.

Allee, allee out's in free! The cadence of the line is harmonious, certain, complete. As poetry so often does, it has the power to evoke an emotional response quite beyond its explicit meaning. Perhaps it is the word *free.* Perhaps it is because the call comes at the dramatic end of the game or because of the traditional sing-song tune in which it is shouted. There is a mystical connotation, as well, as though the gates of Paradise were suddenly thrown open to the lost and hidden.

Bits of poetry—nursery or game lore—tend to persist in adult minds as first heard. Many adults are offended by variants, convinced that the versions they heard in childhood are the only "right ones." But discussions of children's oral lore, such as those by Iona and Peter Opie and Mary and Herbert Knapp, make it clear that there are a prodigious number of variants of children's street and game rhymes (as there are of nursery rhymes), changing with time and location.

There are many types of games, each with its traditional, necessary rhymes. Children determine who shall be It by counting out, sometimes with the help of tight, pungent verse. Children use game rhymes to discharge excitement or anxiety through bodily movement; here too, as in nursery rhymes, the relationship between language and motion is operative. This skip-rope chant ritualizes human sexuality, making it safe and comprehensible:

> Tom and Jane
> Sitting in a tree,
> K-I-S-S-I-N-G.
> First comes love.
> Then comes marriage.
> Then comes Tommy
> With a baby carriage.
> How many kisses did she get?
> One, two, three, four, five, six, seven . . .

Children's natural love of play with language is also evident in their enjoyment of riddles, tongue-twisters, puzzles, and jokes. Tricks or mysteries that can be learned and mastered help children to decode the world—to make sense of it through the use of the language that structures it.

According to Walter de la Mare, "The most mysterious game-rhymes of all are said to refer to ancient tribal customs, rites and ceremonies—betrothals, harvest-homes, sowings, reapings, well-blessings, dirges, divinations, battles, hunting and exorcisings. . . . Rhymes such as these having been passed on from age to age . . . have become worn and battered of course, and queerly changed in their words."[4] Such ancient chants are at once music, mystery, and sheer poetry:

> Intery, mintery, cutery, corn,
> Apple seed and briar thorn;
> Wire, briar, and limber lock,

4. Walter de la Mare, *Come Hither: A Collection of Rhymes and Poems for the Young of All Ages,* 3d ed. (Constable, 1960), p. 511.

Five geese in a flock,
Sit and sing by a spring,
O-U-T, and in again.

A number of classic collections of children's oral culture have been transcribed directly in the anthropological field—in alleys, playgrounds, schoolyards, and doorstoops. The most scholarly of the collections are Iona and Peter Opie's *The Lore and Language of Schoolchildren* (1959) and *Children's Games in Street and Playground* (1969), exploring British children's street and game lore. Mary and Herbert Knapp, in *One Potato, Two Potato . . . The Secret Education of American Children* (1976), undertook a similar study. These works are aimed at an adult audience, but many lively collections have been published for children. The lore in *A Rocket in My Pocket: The Rhymes and Chants of Young Americans* (1948), was collected by Carl Withers while he was doing field work with children in New York City and other regions of the United States. *Did You Feed My Cow? Street Games, Chants, and Rhymes* (rev. ed. 1969) was compiled by Margaret Taylor Burroughs on Chicago's South Side. It contains a mixture of English and European game rhymes with African call-and-response chants that is peculiarly American in quality—a fact that is reflected in the multiracial sketches by Joe E. De Velasco. Edith Fowke's Canadian collection *Sally Go Round the Sun: Three Hundred Children's Songs, Rhymes and Games* (1960) and Colette O'Hare's *What Do You Feed Your Donkey On? Rhymes from a Belfast Childhood* (1978) are further examples of the fascinating universal yet culturally varying nature of children's lore.

Frequently accompanying children's games and activities, songs are a traditional component of children's poetry, sharing with game chants and nursery rhymes a clear melodic simplicity and ritual repetition of language and music. They reflect the day-to-day life, exuberantly comic spirit, hard work, romantic dramas, and spiritual yearnings of ordinary people.

Collections of songs for children are numerous and varied; some also contain finger plays for entertaining infants and lullabies for soothing them to sleep. An excellent collection of folk songs for older children is *The Great Song Book* (1978), edited by John Timothy and enlivened by Tomi Ungerer's sly, witty, and exaggerated illustrations. Jane Hart's *Singing Bee! A Collection of Favorite Children's Songs* (1982), theatrically illustrated by Anita Lobel with colonial American settings, is intended for younger children and contains nursery rhymes, singing games, folk songs, and lullabies. Childhood's wealth of lullabies is represented in such handsome collections as *Lullabies and Night Songs* (1965), edited by William Engvick and dreamily illustrated by Maurice Sendak.

With lullabies, we return to where we began—the nursery. Paradoxically, the melodies and motion that help put infants to sleep are the very things that will awaken them to a greater world beyond the closed world of warmth, comfort, and security that is the nursery. "Oh, night, night, my night!" a Hebrew lullaby sings; the night is personalized through speech, song, movement, story, myth— it becomes *my* night, *your* night. By sharing the ancient oral tradition of nursery lore and lullabies, parents and children are linked together; generations too are linked, laminated into history.

In many cultures, an ancient figure is that of the sleeper dreaming the world into being. So children dream the vastness of life and grow into it; adults sleep and dream and return to infancy, closing the circle. The many voices of the nursery speak and sing of the complexities and wonders of being human.

Mother Goose and Other Nursery Rhymes

I

A, Apple Pie

Illustration by Raymond Briggs. Reprinted by permission of Coward, McCann & Geoghegan, Inc., and Hamish Hamilton Ltd. from *The Mother Goose Treasury* by Raymond Briggs. Copyright © 1966 by Raymond Briggs.

2

The north wind doth blow,
And we shall have snow,
And what will poor Robin do then?
    Poor thing.
He'll sit in a barn,
And keep himself warm,
And hide his head under his wing,
    Poor thing.

3

(Scottish)

A wee bird sat upon a tree,
When the year was dune and auld,
And aye it cheepit sae peetiously,
"My, but it's cauld, cauld."

4

Rain, rain, go away,
Come again another day,
Little Johnny wants to play.

5

Simple Simon met a pieman,
    Going to the fair;
Says Simple Simon to the pieman,
    Let me taste your ware.

Says the pieman to Simple Simon,
    Show me first your penny;
Says Simple Simon to the pieman,
    Indeed I have not any.

Simple Simon went a-fishing,
    For to catch a whale;
All the water he had got
    Was in his mother's pail.

Simple Simon went to look
    If plums grew on a thistle;
He pricked his fingers very much,
    Which made poor Simon whistle.

He went for water in a sieve
    But soon it all fell through;
And now poor Simple Simon
    Bids you all adieu.

6

Curly locks, Curly locks,
    Wilt thou be mine?
Thou shalt not wash dishes
    Nor yet feed the swine;
But sit on a cushion
    And sew a fine seam,
And feed upon strawberries,
    Sugar and cream.

7

I had a little pony,
    His name was Dapple Gray;
I lent him to a lady
    To ride a mile away.
She whipped him, she slashed him,
    She rode him through the mire;
I would not lend my pony now,
    For all the lady's hire.

8

To market, to market,
    To buy a fat pig,
Home again, home again,
    Jiggety-jig.
To market, to market,
    To buy a fat hog,
Home again, home again,
    Jiggety-jog.

9

    Little Miss Muffet
    Sat on a tuffet,
Eating her curds and whey;
    There came a big spider,
    Who sat down beside her
And frightened Miss Muffet away.

2, etc. Unless otherwise stated, the nursery rhymes are from
The Oxford Nursery Rhyme Book, assembled by Iona Opie
and Peter Opie (Oxford University Press, 1955).

3. From Norah Montgomerie and William Montgomerie,
Sandy Candy and Other Scottish Nursery Rhymes (Hogarth
Press, 1946).

10

Gretchen

(Dutch)

Little Dutch Gretchen sat in the kitchen,
Eating some nice sauerkraut,
When the little dog Schneider
Came and sat down beside her,
And little Dutch Gretchen went out.

11

Tradja of Norway

(Norwegian)

Little Tradja of Norway,
She sat in the doorway,
Eating her reindeer-broth;
There came a big badger
And little Miss Tradja
Soon carried her meal farther North.

12

Humpty Dumpty sat on a wall,
Humpty Dumpty had a great fall;
All the King's horses and all the King's men
Couldn't put Humpty together again.

13

Ding, dong, bell,
Pussy's in the well.
Who put her in?
Little Johnny Green.
Who pulled her out?
Little Tommy Stout.

What a naughty boy was that
To try to drown poor pussy cat,
Who never did him any harm,
And killed the mice in his father's barn.

14

Little Jack Horner
Sat in the corner

10. From Alice Daglish and Ernest Rhys, *The Land of Nursery Rhyme* (Dutton, 1932).
11. From Alice Daglish and Ernest Rhys, *The Land of Nursery Rhyme* (Dutton, 1932).

Eating a Christmas pie;
He put in his thumb,
And pulled out a plum,
And said, What a good boy am I!

15

Bow, wow, wow,
Whose dog art thou?
Little Tom Tinker's dog,
Bow, wow, wow.

16

Jack be nimble,
   Jack be quick.
Jack jump over
   The candlestick.

17

There was an old woman tossed up in a basket,
   Seventeen times as high as the moon;
Where she was going I couldn't but ask it,
   For in her hand she carried a broom.
Old woman, old woman, old woman,
      quoth I,
   Where are you going to up so high?
To brush the cobwebs off the sky!
May I go with you? Aye, by-and-by.

Illustration by Philip Reed. Copyright © 1963 by Philip Reed, *Mother Goose and Nursery Rhymes.* Used by permission of Atheneum Publishers.

From *The Walrus and the Carpenter and Other Poems,* by Lewis Carroll, illustrated by Gerald Rose. Illustrations copyright © 1969 by Faber & Faber Ltd. Reprinted by permission of E. P. Dutton & Co., Inc., and Faber & Faber Ltd.

18

Hey, diddle, diddle,
The cat and the fiddle,
The cow jumped over the moon;
The little dog laughed
To see such sport,
And the dish ran away with the spoon.

19

Little Boy Blue,
  Come blow your horn,
The sheep's in the meadow,
  The cow's in the corn.

Where is the boy
  Who looks after the sheep?
He's under a haycock
  Fast asleep.

Will you wake him?
  No, not I,

For if I do,
  He's sure to cry.

20

Gray goose and gander,
  Waft your wings together,
And carry the good king's daughter
  Over the one-strand river.

21

How many miles to Babylon?
Three-score and ten.
Can I get there by candle-light?
Yes, and back again.
If your heels are nimble and light,
You may get there by candle-light.

22

Bobby Shaftoe's gone to sea,
Silver buckles at his knee;

Illustration by Blair Lent. From *King Boggen's Hall to Nothing-at-All: A Collection of Improbable Houses and Unusual Places,* by Blair Lent, Jr. Copyright © 1967 by Blair Lent, Jr. Used by permission of Little, Brown and Co., in association with The Atlantic Monthly Press.

He'll come back and marry me,
  Bonny Bobby Shaftoe.

Bobby Shaftoe's bright and fair,
Combing down his yellow hair,
He's my ain for evermair,
  Bonny Bobby Shaftoe.

23

(*Scottish*)

The cock and the hen,
The deer in the den,
Shall drink in the clearest fountain.
The venison rare
Shall be my love's fare,
And I'll follow him over the mountain.

24

Baa, baa, black sheep,
  Have you any wool?

23. From Norah Montgomerie and William Montgomerie, *Sandy Candy and Other Scottish Nursery Rhymes* (Hogarth Press, 1946).

Yes, sir, yes, sir,
  Three bags full;
One for the master,
  And one for the dame,
And one for the little boy
  Who lives down the lane.

25

Hickory, dickory, dock,
The mouse ran up the clock.
  The clock struck one,
  The mouse ran down,
Hickory, dickory, dock.

26

Peter, Peter, pumpkin eater,
Had a wife and couldn't keep her;
He put her in a pumpkin shell
And there he kept her very well.

Peter, Peter, pumpkin eater,
Had another, and didn't love her;
Peter learned to read and spell,
And then he loved her very well.

27

Little Girl

(Arabian)

I will build you a house
If you do not cry,
A house, little girl,
As tall as the sky.

I will build you a house
Of golden dates,
The freshest of all
For the steps and gates.

I will furnish the house
For you and for me
With walnuts and hazels
Fresh from the tree.

I will build you a house,
And when it is done
I will roof it with grapes
To keep out the sun.

28

Hot-cross buns!
Hot-cross buns!
One a penny, two a penny,
Hot-cross buns!

Hot-cross buns!
Hot-cross buns!
If you have no daughters,
Give them to your sons.

29

Little Tommy Tucker
Sings for his supper:
What shall we give him?
White bread and butter.
How shall he cut it
Without e'er a knife?
How will he be married
Without e'er a wife?

27. From Rose Fyleman, *Picture Rhymes from Foreign Lands*
(Lippincott, 1935).

30

Hickety, pickety, my black hen,
She lays eggs for gentlemen;
Gentlemen come every day
To see what my black hen doth lay.

31

Ride a cock-horse to Banbury Cross,
To see a fine lady upon a white horse;
Rings on her fingers and bells on her toes,
And she shall have music wherever she goes.

32

Wee Willie Winkie runs through the town,
Upstairs and downstairs in his nightgown,
Rapping at the window, crying through the
lock,
Are the children in their beds, for now it's
eight o'clock?

33

A diller, a dollar,
A ten o'clock scholar,
What makes you come so soon?
You used to come at ten o'clock,
But now you come at noon.

34

Jack and Jill went up the hill,
To fetch a pail of water;
Jack fell down, and broke his crown,
And Jill came tumbling after.

35

Diddle, diddle, dumpling, my son John,
Went to bed with his trousers on;
One shoe off, and one shoe on,
Diddle, diddle, dumpling, my son John.

36

Georgie Porgie, pudding and pie,
Kissed the girls and made them cry;
When the boys came out to play,
Georgie Porgie ran away.

37

Rub-a-dub dub,
  Three men in a tub,
And who do you think they be?
  The butcher, the baker,
  The candlestick-maker;
Turn 'em out, knaves all three.

38

Great A, little a,
  Bouncing B,
The cat's in the cupboard
  And can't see me.

39

Cushy cow, bonny, let down thy milk,
And I will give thee a gown of silk;
A gown of silk and a silver tee,
If thou wilt let down thy milk for me.

37. From W. A. Wheeler, *Mother Goose's Melodies* (Houghton Mifflin, 1878).

40

The Five Toes

(Chinese)

This little cow eats grass,
This little cow eats hay,
This little cow drinks water,
This little cow runs away,
This little cow does nothing,
But just lie down all day;
  We'll whip her.

41

Hark, hark,
  The dogs do bark.
The beggars are coming to town;
  Some in rags,
  And some in jags,
And one in a velvet gown.

40. From I. T. Headland, *Chinese Mother Goose Rhymes* (Revell, 1900).

Illustration by Raymond Briggs. Reprinted by permission of Coward, McCann & Geoghegan and Hamish Hamilton Ltd. from *The Mother Goose Treasury*, by Raymond Briggs. Copyright © 1966 by Raymond Briggs.

42

A cat came fiddling out of a barn,
With a pair of bagpipes under her arm;
She could sing nothing but fiddle-de-dee,
The mouse has married the bumble-bee;
Pipe, cat—dance, mouse—
We'll have a wedding at our good house.

43

There was a crooked man, and he went a
    crooked mile;
He found a crooked sixpence against a crooked
    stile;
He bought a crooked cat, which caught a
    crooked mouse,
And all lived together in a little crooked house.

44

I love sixpence, jolly little sixpence,
    I love sixpence better than my life;
I spent a penny of it, I lent a penny of it,
    And I took fourpence home to my wife.

Oh, my little fourpence, jolly little fourpence,
    I love fourpence better than my life;
I spent a penny of it, I lent a penny of it,
    And I took twopence home to my wife.

Oh, my little twopence, jolly little twopence,
    I love twopence better than my life;
I spent a penny of it, I lent a penny of it,
    And I took nothing home to my wife.

Oh, my little nothing, jolly little nothing,
    What will nothing buy for my wife?
I have nothing, I spent nothing,
    I love nothing better than my wife.

45

This little pig went to market,
This little pig stayed at home,
This little pig had roast beef,
This little pig had none,

42. From W. A. Wheeler, *Mother Goose's Melodies* (Houghton Mifflin, 1878).
43. From W. A. Wheeler, *Mother Goose's Melodies* (Houghton Mifflin, 1878).

And this little pig cried, Wee-wee-wee-wee-wee,
I can't find my way home.

46

Pat-a-cake, pat-a-cake, baker's man,
Bake me a cake as fast as you can;
Pat it and prick it, and mark it with T,
Put it in the oven for Tommy and me.

47

Jack Sprat could eat no fat,
    His wife could eat no lean,
And so between them both, you see,
    They licked the platter clean.

48

Pussy cat, pussy cat,
    Where have you been?
I've been to London
    To look at the Queen.
Pussy cat, pussy cat,
    What did you there?
I frightened a little mouse
    Under her chair.

49

Goosey, goosey gander,
    Whither shall I wander?
Upstairs and downstairs
    And in my lady's chamber.
There I met an old man
    Who would not say his prayers,
I took him by the left leg
    And threw him down the stairs.

50

As I was going to sell my eggs,
I met a man with bandy legs;
Bandy legs and crooked toes,
I tripped up his heels and he fell on his nose.

51

Cock a doodle doo!
My dame has lost her shoe,
My master's lost his fiddling stick,
And knows not what to do.

Illustration by L. Leslie Brooke, from *Oranges and Lemons: A Nursery Rhyme Picture Book,* by L. Leslie Brooke. First published in 1913. Reprinted by permission of the publisher, Frederick Warne & Co., Inc.

Cock a doodle doo!
What is my dame to do?
Till master finds his fiddling stick
She'll dance without her shoe.

Cock a doodle doo!
My dame has found her shoe,
And master's found his fiddling stick,
Sing doodle doodle doo.

Cock a doodle doo!
My dame will dance with you,
While master fiddles his fiddling stick
For dame and doodle doo.

52

I saw three ships come sailing by,
  Come sailing by, come sailing by,
I saw three ships come sailing by,
  On New-Year's day in the morning.

And what do you think was in them then,
  Was in them then, was in them then?
And what do you think was in them then,
  On New-Year's day in the morning?

Three pretty girls were in them then,
  Were in them then, were in them then,
Three pretty girls were in them then,
  On New-Year's day in the morning.

One could whistle, and one could sing,
  And one could play on the violin;
Such joy there was at my wedding,
  On New-Year's day in the morning.

53

Old King Cole
Was a merry old soul,
And a merry old soul was he;
He called for his pipe,
And he called for his bowl,
And he called for his fiddlers three.

Every fiddler, he had a fiddle,
And a very fine fiddle had he;
Twee tweedle-dee, tweedle-dee, went the
  fiddlers,
Oh, there's none so rare,
As can compare
With King Cole and his fiddlers three!

54

Well I Never!

(Spanish)

Two little mice went tripping down the street,
Pum catta-pum chin chin,
One wore a bonnet and a green silk skirt,
One wore trousers and a nice clean shirt;
Pum catta-pum chin chin.

53. From W. A. Wheeler, *Mother Goose's Melodies* (Houghton Mifflin, 1878).
54. From Rose Fyleman, *Picture Rhymes from Foreign Lands* (Lippincott, 1935).

One little hen went tripping down the street,
Pum catta-pum chin chin,
One little hen very smart and spry,
With a wig-wagging tail and a wicked little eye,
Pum catta-pum chin chin.

55

Three young rats with black felt hats,
Three young ducks with white straw flats,
Three young dogs with curling tails,
Three young cats with demi-veils,
Went out to walk with two young pigs
In satin vests and sorrel wigs;
But suddenly it chanced to rain
And so they all went home again.

56

As Tommy Snooks and Bessy Brooks
    Were walking out one Sunday,
Says Tommy Snooks to Bessy Brooks,
    Tomorrow will be Monday.

57

Tom, Tom, the piper's son,
Stole a pig and away he run;
    The pig was eat,
    And Tom was beat,
And Tom went howling down the street.

58

Johnny shall have a new bonnet,
    And Johnny shall go to the fair,
And Johnny shall have a blue ribbon
    To tie up his bonny brown hair.

And why may not I love Johnny?
    And why may not Johnny love me?
And why may not I love Johnny
    As well as another body?

And here's a leg for a stocking,
    And here's a leg for a shoe,
And he has a kiss for his daddy,
    And two for his mammy, I trow.

And why may not I love Johnny?
    And why may not Johnny love me?

And why may not I love Johnny
    As well as another body?

59

Barber, barber, shave a pig,
How many hairs will make a wig?
Four and twenty, that's enough.
Give the barber a pinch of snuff.

Reprinted with permission of Macmillan Publishing Company and Penguin Books Ltd. from *Peep-Show: A Little Book of Rhymes,* by Pamela Blake. Copyright © 1972 by Pamela Blake.

60

Lucy Locket lost her pocket,
    Kitty Fisher found it;
Not a penny was there in it,
    Only ribbon round it.

61

There was an old woman,
    And what do you think?
She lived upon nothing
    But victuals and drink:
Victuals and drink
    Were the chief of her diet,
And yet this old woman
    Could never keep quiet.

62

Lavender's blue, diddle, diddle,
    Lavender's green;
When I am king, diddle, diddle,
    You shall be queen.

Call up your men, diddle, diddle,
  Set them to work,
Some to the plough, diddle, diddle,
  Some to the cart.

Some to make hay, diddle, diddle,
  Some to thresh corn,
Whilst you and I, diddle, diddle,
  Keep ourselves warm.

63

There was an old woman had three sons,
  Jerry and James and John.
Jerry was hung and James was drowned,
John was lost and never was found,
So there was an end of her three sons,
  Jerry and James and John.

64

A farmer went trotting upon his grey mare,
  Bumpety, bumpety, bump!
With his daughter behind him so rosy and fair,
  Lumpety, lumpety, lump!

A raven cried, Croak! and they all tumbled
    down,
  Bumpety, bumpety, bump!
The mare broke her knees and the farmer his
    crown,
  Lumpety, lumpety, lump!

The mischievous raven flew laughing away,
  Bumpety, bumpety, bump!
And vowed he would serve them the same
    the next day,
  Lumpety, lumpety, lump!

65

If I had a donkey that wouldn't go,
Would I beat him? Oh, no, no.
I'd put him in the barn and give him some corn,
The best little donkey that ever was born.

66

Solomon Grundy
Born on a Monday,

Christened on Tuesday,
Married on Wednesday,
Took ill on Thursday,
Worse on Friday,
Died on Saturday,
Buried on Sunday;
This is the end
Of Solomon Grundy.

67

Mushrooms

(Russian)

Lucky is the mushrooms' mother,
Her daughters grow so fast—
Born on Saturday, grown by Sunday,
Waiting to be courted Monday.

68

Mary, Mary, quite contrary,
  How does your garden grow?
With silver bells and cockle shells,
  And pretty maids all in a row.

69

If I'd as much money as I could spend,
I never would cry old chairs to mend;
Old chairs to mend, old chairs to mend;
I never would cry old chairs to mend.

70

See a pin and pick it up,
All the day you'll have good luck;
See a pin and let it lay,
Bad luck you'll have all day.

71

When good King Arthur ruled this land,
  He was a goodly king;
He stole three pecks of barley-meal,
  To make a bag-pudding.

67. From Rose Fyleman, *Picture Rhymes from Foreign Lands* (Lippincott, 1935).
71. From W. A. Wheeler, *Mother Goose's Melodies* (Houghton Mifflin, 1878).

A bag-pudding the king did make,
    And stuffed it well with plums;
And in it put great lumps of fat,
    As big as my two thumbs.

The king and queen did eat thereof,
    And noblemen beside;
And what they could not eat that night
    The queen next morning fried.

72

The Queen of Hearts,
She made some tarts,
    All on a summer's day;

The Knave of Hearts
He stole those tarts
    And took them clean away.

The King of Hearts
Called for the tarts,
    And beat the knave full sore;
The Knave of Hearts
Brought back the tarts,
    And vowed he'd steal no more.

73

One misty, moisty morning,
    When cloudy was the weather,
I met a little old man
    Clothed all in leather.

He began to compliment,
    And I began to grin,
How do you do, and how do you do,
    And how do you do again?

74

There was an old woman who lived in a shoe;
She had so many children she didn't know what
    to do;
She gave them some broth without any bread;
She whipped them all soundly and put them
    to bed.

73. From W. A. Wheeler, *Mother Goose's Melodies* (Houghton Mifflin, 1878).

Illustrated by Philip Reed. Copyright © 1963 by Philip Reed, *Mother Goose and Nursery Rhymes.* Used by permission of Atheneum Publishers.

75

Little Tommy Tittlemouse
Lived in a little house;
He caught fishes
In other men's ditches.

76

This is the house that Jack built.

This is the malt
That lay in the house that Jack built.

This is the rat,
That ate the malt
That lay in the house that Jack built.

This is the cat
That killed the rat,
That ate the malt
That lay in the house that Jack built.

This is the dog,
That worried the cat,

Illustration by Antonio Frasconi. Illustrations copyright ©
1958 by Antonio Frasconi. Reproduced from his volume
The House That Jack Built by permission of Harcourt Brace
Jovanovich, Inc.

That killed the rat,
That ate the malt
That lay in the house that Jack built.

This is the cow with the crumpled horn,
That tossed the dog,
That worried the cat,
That killed the rat,
That ate the malt
That lay in the house that Jack built.

This is the maiden all forlorn,
That milked the cow with the crumpled horn,
That tossed the dog,
That worried the cat,
That killed the rat,
That ate the malt
That lay in the house that Jack built.

This is the man all tattered and torn,
That kissed the maiden all forlorn,
That milked the cow with the crumpled horn,
That tossed the dog,
That worried the cat,
That killed the rat,
That ate the malt
That lay in the house that Jack built.

This is the priest all shaven and shorn,
That married the man all tattered and torn,
That kissed the maiden all forlorn,
That milked the cow with the crumpled horn,
That tossed the dog,
That worried the cat,
That killed the rat,
That ate the malt
That lay in the house that Jack built.

This is the cock that crowed in the morn,
That waked the priest all shaven and shorn,
That married the man all tattered and torn,
That kissed the maiden all forlorn,
That milked the cow with the crumpled horn,
That tossed the dog,
That worried the cat,
That killed the rat,
That ate the malt
That lay in the house that Jack built.

This is the farmer sowing his corn,
That kept the cock that crowed in the morn,
That waked the priest all shaven and shorn,
That married the man all tattered and torn,
That kissed the maiden all forlorn,
That milked the cow with the crumpled horn,
That tossed the dog,
That worried the cat,
That killed the rat,
That ate the malt
That lay in the house that Jack built.

77

My little old man and I fell out,
How shall we bring this matter about?
Bring it about as well as you can,
And get you gone, you little old man!

78

Snail, snail,
Come out of your hole,
Or else I'll beat you
As black as coal.

Snail, snail,
Put out your horns,
I'll give you bread
And barley corns.

79

The lion and the unicorn
    Were fighting for the crown;
The lion beat the unicorn
    All round about the town.

Some gave them white bread,
    And some gave them brown;
Some gave them plum cake
    And drummed them out of town.

80

There was a little woman
    As I have heard tell,
She went to market
    Her eggs for to sell;
She went to market
    All on a market day,
And she fell asleep
    On the king's highway.

There came by a pedlar,
    His name was Stout,
He cut her petticoats
    All round about;
He cut her petticoats
    Up to her knees;
Which made the little woman
    To shiver and sneeze.

When this little woman
    Began to awake,

She began to shiver,
    And she began to shake;
She began to shake,
    And she began to cry,
Lawk a mercy on me,
    This is none of I!

But if this be I,
    As I do hope it be,
I have a little dog at home
    And he knows me;
If it be I,
    He'll wag his little tail,
And if it be not I
    He'll loudly bark and wail!

Home went the little woman
    All in the dark,
Up starts the little dog,
    And he began to bark;
He began to bark,
    And she began to cry,
Lawk a mercy on me,
    This is none of I!

81

I saw a ship a-sailing,
    A-sailing on the sea;
And O! it was all laden
    With pretty things for thee!

There were comfits in the cabin,
    And apples in the hold;
The sails were made of silk,
    And the masts were made of gold!

The four and twenty sailors,
    That stood between the decks,
Were four and twenty white mice,
    With chains about their necks.

The captain was a duck,
    With a packet on his back;
And when the ship began to move,
    The captain said, "Quack! quack!"

80. From W. A. Wheeler, *Mother Goose's Melodies* (Houghton Mifflin, 1878).

81. From W. A. Wheeler, *Mother Goose's Melodies* (Houghton Mifflin, 1878).

Reprinted with permission of Macmillan Publishing Company from *I Saw a Ship-a-Sailing,* by Janina Domanska. Copyright © 1972 by Janina Domanska.

82

When I was a little boy,
I washed my mammy's dishes;
I put my finger in my eye,
And pulled out golden fishes.

83

Row, row, row

(Danish)

Row, row, row
to Oyster Bay.
What sort of fish
shall we catch today?
Big fish,
small fish,
snook or snail,
yellow snapper,
triple tail,
herring
daring,

83. From N. M. Bodecker, *It's Raining Said John Twaining: Danish Nursery Rhymes* (Atheneum, 1973).

From *Mother Goose Comes to Cable Street: Nursery Rhymes for Today,* by Rosemary Stones and Andrew Mann, illustrated by Dan Jones. Illustrations copyright © 1977 by Dan Jones. Reprinted by permission of Penguin Books Ltd.

Row, row, row
to Oyster Bay.
What sort of fish
shall we catch today?
Big fish,
small fish,
snook or snail,
yellow snapper,
triple tail,
herring
daring,
kipper
coarse,
or a trout
with applesauce?

Illustration by N. M. Bodecker. Copyright © 1973 by N. M. Bodecker. From *It's Raining Said John Twaining: Danish Nursery Rhymes* (A Margaret K. McElderry Book). Used by permission of Atheneum Publishers.

kipper
coarse,
or a trout
with applesauce?

84

Charley Wag, Charley Wag,
Ate the pudding and left the bag.

85

Old Mother Hubbard
  Went to the cupboard
To fetch her poor dog a bone;
  But when she came there
  The cupboard was bare
And so the poor dog had none.

She went to the baker's
  To buy him some bread;
But when she came back
  The poor dog was dead.

She went to the undertaker's
  To buy him a coffin;
But when she came back
  The poor dog was laughing.

She took a clean dish
  To get him some tripe;
But when she came back
  He was smoking a pipe.

She went to the alehouse
  To get him some beer;
But when she came back
  The dog sat in a chair.

She went to the tavern
　For white wine and red;
But when she came back
　The dog stood on his head.

She went to the fruiterer's
　To buy him some fruit;
But when she came back
　He was playing the flute.

She went to the tailor's
　To buy him a coat;
But when she came back
　He was riding a goat.

She went to the hatter's
　To buy him a hat;
But when she came back
　He was feeding the cat.

She went to the barber's
　To buy him a wig;

But when she came back
　He was dancing a jig.

She went to the cobbler's
　To buy him some shoes;
But when she came back
　He was reading the news.

She went to the seamstress
　To buy him some linen;
But when she came back
　The dog was a-spinning.

She went to the hosier's
　To buy him some hose;
But when she came back
　He was dressed in his clothes.

The dame made a curtsy,
　The dog made a bow;
The dame said, Your servant,
　The dog said, Bow-wow.

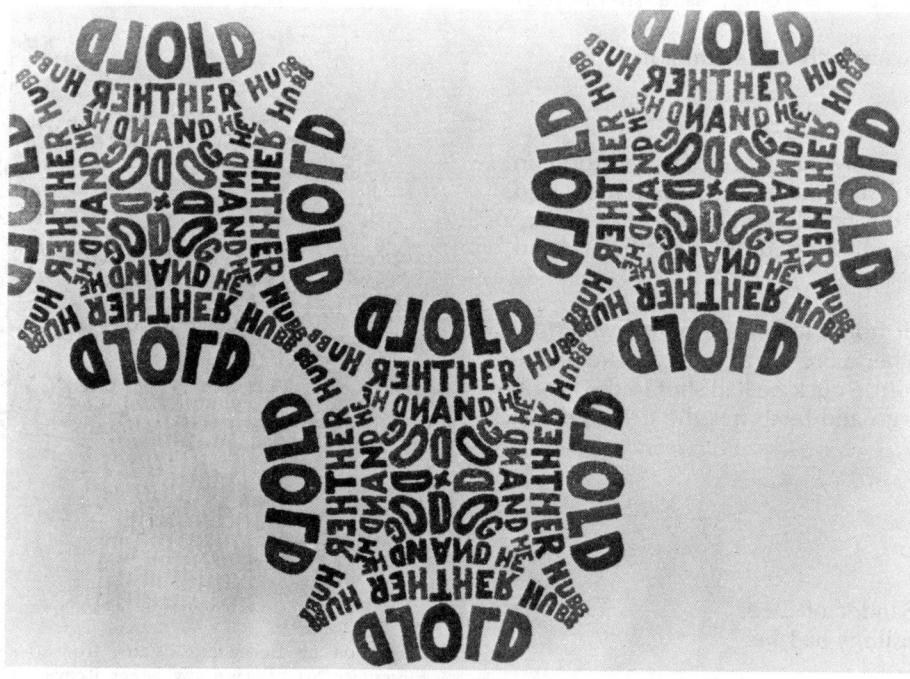

From *Old Mother Hubbard and Her Dog,* illustrated by Evaline Ness. Copyright © 1972 by Evaline Ness. Reproduced by permission of Holt, Rinehart & Winston, publishers.

86

Little Bo-peep has lost her sheep,
  And can't tell where to find them;
Leave them alone, and they'll come home,
  And bring their tails behind them.

Little Bo-peep fell fast asleep,
  And dreamt she heard them bleating;
But when she awoke, she found it a joke,
  For they were still all fleeting.

Then up she took her little crook,
  Determined for to find them;
She found them indeed, but it made her heart
    bleed,
  For they'd left their tails behind them.

It happened one day, as Bo-peep did stray
  Into a meadow hard by,
There she espied their tails side by side,
  All hung on a tree to dry.

She heaved a sigh, and wiped her eye,
  And over the hillocks went rambling,
And tried what she could, as a shepherdess
    should,
  To tack again each to its lambkin.

87

There was a little man, and he had a little gun,
  And his bullets were made of lead, lead, lead;
He went to the brook, and shot a little duck,
  Right through the middle of the head, head,
    head.

He carried it home to his old wife Joan,
  And bade her a fire for to make, make, make,
To roast the little duck he had shot in the brook,
  And he'd go and fetch her the drake, drake,
    drake.

88

(Danish)

Little Jock Sander of Dee,
five little goslings had he.

88. From N. M. Bodecker, *It's Raining Said John Twaining:
Danish Nursery Rhymes* (Atheneum, 1973).

He put them away for the night
and bid them sleep safely and tight.
But the hawk came to Dee;
he took the three!
The fox came too;
he took the two!

After this theft
how many were left?

The goose and the gander
and little Jock Sander!

89

I had a little nut tree,
  Nothing would it bear
But a silver nutmeg
  And a golden pear;
The king of Spain's daughter
  Came to visit me,
And all for the sake
  Of my little nut tree.

Illustration by Bernadette Watts, from *One's None, Old
Rhymes for New Tongues*, by James Reeves. Copyright ©
1969 by Wm. Heinemann. Used by permission of Franklin
Watts, Inc.

I skipped over water,
  I danced over sea,
And all the birds in the air
  Couldn't catch me.

90

Dame, get up and bake your pies,
  Bake your pies, bake your pies;
Dame, get up and bake your pies,
  On Christmas day in the morning.

Dame, what makes your maidens lie,
  Maidens lie, maidens lie;
Dame, what makes your maidens lie,
  On Christmas day in the morning?

Dame, what makes your ducks to die,
  Ducks to die, ducks to die;
Dame, what makes your ducks to die,
  On Christmas day in the morning?

Their wings are cut and they cannot fly,
  Cannot fly, cannot fly;
Their wings are cut and they cannot fly,
  On Christmas day in the morning.

91

I'll tell you a story
  About Jack a Nory.
And now my story's begun:
  I'll tell you another
  Of Jack and his brother,
And now my story is done.

92

Elsie Marley is grown so fine,
She won't get up to feed the swine,
But lies in bed till eight or nine.
  Lazy Elsie Marley.

93

Doctor Foster went to Gloucester
In a shower of rain;
He stepped in a puddle, up to his middle,
And never went there again.

93. From W. A. Wheeler, *Mother Goose's Melodies* (Houghton Mifflin, 1878).

94

Six little mice sat down to spin;
Pussy passed by and she peeped in.
What are you doing, my little men?
Weaving coats for gentlemen.
Shall I come in and cut off your threads?
No, no, Mistress Pussy, you'd bite off our heads.
Oh, no, I'll not; I'll help you to spin.
That may be so, but you don't come in.

LAZY ELSIE MARLEY

Elsie Marley is grown so fine
She won't get up to serve the swine,
But lies in bed till eight or nine,
Lazy Elsie Marley.

Illustration by Erik Blegvad, from *This Little Pig-a-Wig and Other Rhymes about Pigs*, compiled by Lenore Blegvad. Copyright © 1978 by Erik Blegvad (A Margaret K. McElderry Book). Used by permission of Atheneum Publications.

95

Thirty days hath September,
April, June, and November;
All the rest have thirty-one,
Excepting February alone,
And that has twenty-eight days clear
And twenty-nine in each leap year.

Illustration by Keiko Hida, from *The Prancing Pony: Nursery Rhymes from Japan,* by Charlotte B. DeForest. Reprinted by permission of the publisher, John Weatherhill, Inc.

96

Wild Geese Flying

Look how the wild geese fly and fly,
Tiny black dots in the moonlit sky.
Behind the old ones the youngsters come—
I wonder where they started from.

96. From Charlotte B. DeForest, *The Prancing Pony: Nursery Rhymes from Japan* (Walker/Weatherhill, 1968).

97

The boughs do shake and the bells do ring,
So merrily comes our harvest in,
Our harvest in, our harvest in,
So merrily comes our harvest in.

We've ploughed, we've sowed,
We've reaped, we've mowed,
We've got our harvest in.

98

I had a little husband,
  No bigger than my thumb;
I put him in a pint-pot
  And there I bade him drum.
I bought a little horse
  That galloped up and down;
I bridled him, and saddled him
  And sent him out of town.
I gave him some garters
  To garter up his hose,
And a little silk handkerchief
  To wipe his pretty nose.

99

Lady Bug

(Chinese)

Lady-bug, lady-bug,
Fly away, do,
Fly to the mountain,
And feed upon dew,
Feed upon dew,
And sleep on a rug,
And then run away
Like a good little bug.

100

(Scottish)

Lady, Lady Landers,
Lady, Lady Landers,
Tak up yer coat
Aboot yer heid,
And flee awa
Tae Flanders.
Flee ower firth,
And flee ower fell,
Flee ower pool,
And rinnin well,

Flee ower muir,
And flee ower mead,
Flee ower livin,
Flee ower deid,
Flee ower corn,
And flee ower lea,
Flee ower river,
Flee ower sea,
Flee ye east,
Or flee ye west,
Flee till him
That loes me best.

101

Who killed Cock Robin?
  "I," said the Sparrow.
  "With my bow and arrow,
I killed Cock Robin."

Who saw him die?
  "I," said the Fly,
  "With my little eye,
And I saw him die."

Who caught his blood?
  "I," said the Fish,
  "With my little dish,
And I caught his blood."

Who made his shroud?
  "I," said the Beadle,
  "With my little needle,
And I made his shroud."

Who shall dig his grave?
  "I," said the Owl,
  "With my spade and showl,
And I'll dig his grave."

Who'll be the parson?
  "I," said the Rook,
  "With my little book,
And I'll be the parson."

Who'll be the clerk?
  "I," said the Lark,
  "If it's not in the dark,
And I'll be the clerk."

99. I. T. Headland, *Chinese Mother Goose Rhymes* (Revell, 1900).
100. From Norah Montgomerie and William Montgomerie, *Sandy Candy and Other Scottish Nursery Rhymes* (Hogarth Press, 1946).

Who'll carry him to the grave?
 "I," said the Kite,
 "If 'tis not in the night,
And I'll carry him to his grave."

Who'll carry the link?
 "I," said the Linnet,
 "I'll fetch it in a minute,
And I'll carry the link."

Who'll be the chief mourner?
 "I," said the Dove,
 "I mourn for my love,
And I'll be chief mourner."

Who'll bear the pall?
 "We," said the Wren,
 Both the cock and the hen,
"And we'll bear the pall."

Who'll sing a psalm?
 "I," said the Thrush,
 As she sat in a bush,
"And I'll sing a psalm."

And who'll toll the bell?
 "I," said the Bull,
 "Because I can pull";
And so, Cock Robin, farewell.

All the birds in the air
 Fell to sighing and sobbing,
 When they heard the bell toll
For poor Cock Robin.

102

(Hebrew)

An angel came as I lay in bed;
I will give you wings—the angel said;
I will give you wings that you may fly
To the country of Heaven above the sky.

My beautiful angel flew away,
He came not again by night or by day;
Angels are busy with many things,
And he has forgotten to send the wings.

102. From Rose Fyleman, *Picture Rhymes from Foreign Lands*
(Lippincott, 1935).

103

(Indian)

Moon-Uncle, Moon-Uncle,
come, come, come.
Here is a spinning top,
come, come, come.
Here is a copper pot,
come, come, come.
Here is a coconut,
come, come, come.
Here is a pomegranate,
come, come, come.
Here is a carriage
and here is a drum.
Moon-Uncle, Moon-Uncle,
come, come, come.

104

Boys and girls come out to play,
The moon doth shine as bright as day.
Leave your supper and leave your sleep,
And join your playfellows in the street.
Come with a whoop and come with a call,
Come with a good will or not at all.
Up the ladder and down the wall,
A half-penny loaf will serve us all;
You find milk, and I'll find flour,
And we'll have a pudding in half an hour.

Street and Game Lore: Singing Games, Jingles, Chants, and Counting-Out Rhymes

105

See-saw sacradown,
 Which is the way to London town?
One foot up and the other foot down,
 And that is the way to London town.

103. From *Moon-Uncle, Moon-Uncle: Rhymes from India*, sel.
and trans. Sylvia Cassedy and Parvathi Thampi (Doubleday,
1973).

106

Step on a crack,
You'll break your mother's back;
Step on a line,
You'll break your father's spine.

Step in a ditch,
Your mother's nose will itch;
Step in the dirt,
You'll tear your father's shirt.

107

Pease porridge hot,
Pease porridge cold,
Pease porridge in the pot,
Nine days old.
Some like it hot,
Some like it cold,
Some like it in the pot
Nine days old.

108

Sing a song of sixpence,
    A pocket full of rye;
Four and twenty blackbirds,
    Baked in a pie.

When the pie was opened,
    The birds began to sing;
Was not that a dainty dish,
    To set before the king?

The king was in his counting-house,
    Counting out his money;
The queen was in the parlour,
    Eating bread and honey.

The maid was in the garden,
    Hanging out the clothes,
When down came a blackbird
    And pecked off her nose.

Illustration by Jenny Rodwell. Reprinted by permission of
Philomel Books, a division of the Putnam Publishing Group,
and William Collins Sons and Company Ltd., from *What
Do You Feed Your Donkey On? Rhymes from a Belfast Childhood.*
Text copyright © 1978 by Colette O'Hare, illustrations
copyright © 1978 by Jenny Rodwell.

109

My Aunt Jane, she called me in,
Gave me tea out of her wee tin,
Half a bap, sugar on the top,
Three black lumps out of her wee shop.

110

1, 2,
Buckle my shoe;

3, 4,
Knock at the door;

5, 6,
Pick up sticks;

7, 8,
Lay them straight;

9, 10,
A big fat hen;

11, 12,
Dig and delve;

109. From *What Do You Feed Your Donkey On? Rhymes from
a Belfast Childhood,* coll. Colette O'Hare (Collins, 1978).

13, 14,
Maids a-courting;

15, 16,
Maids in the kitchen;

17, 18,
Maids in waiting;

19, 20,
My plate's empty.

III

Gay go up and gay go down,
To ring the bells of London town.

Bull's eyes and targets,
Say the bells of St. Marg'ret's.

Brickbats and tiles,
Say the bells of St. Giles'.

Oranges and lemons,
Say the bells of St. Clement's.

Pancakes and fritters,
Say the bells of St. Peter's.

Two sticks and an apple,
Say the bells at Whitechapel.

Old Father Baldpate,
Say the slow bells at Aldgate.

Maids in white aprons,
Say the bells at St. Catherine's.

Pokers and tongs,
Say the bells at St. John's.

Kettles and pans,
Say the bells at St. Anne's.

You owe me five farthings,
Say the bells of St. Martin's.

When will you pay me?
Say the bells at Old Bailey.

When I grow rich,
Say the bells at Shoreditch.

Pray, when will that be?
Say the bells at Stepney.

I'm sure I don't know,
Say the bells at Bow.

Here comes a candle to light you to bed,
Here comes a chopper to chop off your head.

112

This rhyme and the one that follows are games.
Person number one (1) speaks first; person number
two (2), who is ignorant of the joke, takes the lines
marked "2."

1. I am a gold lock.
  2. I am a gold key.
1. I am a silver lock.
  2. I am a silver key.
1. I am a brass lock.
  2. I am a brass key.
1. I am a lead lock.
  2. I am a lead key.
1. I am a monk lock.
  2. I am a monk key (monkey).

113

1. I went up one pair of stairs.
  2. Just like me.
1. I went up two pairs of stairs.
  2. Just like me.
1. I went into a room.
  2. Just like me.
1. I looked out of a window.
  2. Just like me.
1. And there I saw a monkey.
  2. Just like me.

114

Eddie Spaghetti with the meatball eyes,
Put him in the oven and make french fries!

112–13. From Andrew Lang, *The Nursery Rhyme Book*
(Warne, 1897).
114. From John Langstaff and Carol Langstaff, *Shimmy
Shimmy Coke-Ca-Pop! A Collection of Children's Street Games
and Rhymes* (Doubleday, 1973).

Illustration from *London Bridge Is Falling Down!* by Peter Spier. Copyright © 1967 by Peter Spier. Reprinted by permission of Doubleday & Company, Inc.

115

Wall flowers, wall flowers, growing up so high,
All pretty children do not like to cry,
Except Keady O'Hare, she's the only one,
So fright! For shame! So fright! For shame!
And turn her back to the wall again.

116

London Bridge is broken down,
  Dance o'er my Lady Lee;
London Bridge is broken down,
  With a gay lady.

How shall we build it up again?
  Dance o'er my Lady Lee;
How shall we build it up again?
  With a gay lady.

Build it up with silver and gold,
  Dance o'er my Lady Lee;
Build it up with silver and gold,
  With a gay lady.

Silver and gold will be stole away,
  Dance o'er my Lady Lee;
Silver and gold will be stole away,
  With a gay lady.

Build it up with iron and steel,
  Dance o'er my Lady Lee;

Build it up with iron and steel,
  With a gay lady.

Iron and steel will bend and bow,
  Dance o'er my Lady Lee;
Iron and steel will bend and bow,
  With a gay lady.

Build it up with wood and clay,
  Dance o'er my Lady Lee;
Build it up with wood and clay,
  With a gay lady.

Wood and clay will wash away,
  Dance o'er my Lady Lee;
Wood and clay will wash away,
  With a gay lady.

Build it up with stone so strong,
  Dance o'er my Lady Lee;
Huzza! 'twill last for ages long,
  With a gay lady.

117

The compilers "asked the girls who recited this rhyme about 'sixty-eight.' 'That's just how it ends,' they said."

In the land of Oz ["Mars" in another dialect
  area],
Where the ladies smoke cigars,

115. From *What Do You Feed Your Donkey On? Rhymes from a Belfast Childhood*, coll. Colette O'Hare (Collins, 1978).

117. From Herbert Knapp and Mary Knapp, *One Potato, Two Potato . . . The Secret Education of American Children* (Norton, 1976).

Every puff they take
Is enough to kill a snake.
When the snake is dead,
They put roses in her head;
When the roses die,
They put diamonds in her eye;
When the diamonds break,
That's the end of sixty-eight.

118

Inty, tinty, tethery, methery,
Bank for over, Dover, ding,
Aut, taut, toosh;
Up the Causey, down the Cross,
There stands a bonnie white horse:
It can gallop, it can trot,
It can carry the mustard pot.
One, two, three, out goes she!

119

Eeny, pheeny, figgery, fegg,
Deely, dyly, ham and egg.
Calico back, and stony rock,
Arlum barlum, bash!

120

Icker-backer,
Soda cracker,
Icker-backer-boo.
    En-gine
    Number nine,
Out go y-o-u!

121

Intery, mintery, cutery, corn,
Apple seed and briar thorn;
Wire, briar, limber lock,
Five geese in a flock,
Sit and sing by a spring,
O-U-T, and in again.

122

One potato, two potato, three potato, four,
Five potato, six potato, seven potato, or.

122. From Herbert Knapp and Mary Knapp, *One Potato, Two Potato . . . The Secret Education of American Children* (Norton, 1976).

123

Jelly in the dish
Makes me sick.
A wiggle and a woggle,
And a two forty six.
Not because you're dirty, not because you're
    clean;
It's just because you kissed a boy
Behind a magazine.
How many kisses do you want?
"5" 1 2 3 4 5

124

The Blacks go down, down, baby,
Down by the roller coaster, Sweet, sweet baby,
I don't wanta let you go.
Just because I kissed you once,
Doesn't mean I love you so:

(CHANTED)
Shimmy, shimmy, shimmy, shimmy,
Shimmy, shimmy, pop!
Shimmy, shimmy, shimmy, shimmy,
Shimmy, shimmy, coke-ca-pop!

125

Adam and Eve
In the Garden of Eden
Admiring the Beauties of Nature,
The Devil jumped out
Of a Brussels sprout
And hit'em in the eye with a potato

126

My mother said that I never should
Play with the gypsies in the wood.

123. From John Langstaff and Carol Langstaff, *Shimmy Shimmy Coke-Ca-Pop! A Collection of Children's Street Games and Rhymes* (Doubleday, 1973).
124. From John Langstaff and Carol Langstaff, *Shimmy Shimmy Coke-Ca-Pop! A Collection of Children's Street Games and Rhymes* (Doubleday, 1973).
125. From *Inky Pinky Ponky: Children's Playground Rhymes*, coll. Michael Rosen and Susanna Steele (Granada, 1982).
126. From Edith Fowke, *Sally Go Round the Sun: Three Hundred Songs, Rhymes and Games of Canadian Children* (McClelland & Stewart, 1969).

If I did, she would say:
"Naughty girl to disobey!
Disobey, disobey,
Naughty girl to disobey!

"Your hair shan't curl, your shoes shan't shine.
You naughty girl, you shan't be mine."
My father said that if I did,
He'd bang my head with a saucepan lid.
Saucepan lid, saucepan lid,
He'd bang my head with a saucepan lid.

The wood was dark, the grass was green.
Up comes Sally with a tambourine.
Alpaca frock, new scarf-shawl,
White straw bonnet and a pink parasol.
Pink parasol, pink parasol,
White straw bonnet and a pink parasol.

I went to the river, no ship to get across.
I paid ten shillings for an old blind horse.
I up on his back and off in a crack.
Sally, tell my mother that I'll never come back.
Never come back, never come back,
Sally, tell my mother that I'll never come back.

127

Monday's child is fair of face,
Tuesday's child is full of grace,
Wednesday's child is full of woe,
Thursday's child has far to go,
Friday's child is loving and giving,
Saturday's child works hard for a living,
But the child that is born on the Sabbath day
Is blythe and bonny and good and gay.

128

Over the garden wall,
I let the baby fall,
Me Ma came out,
And give me a clout,
Over the garden wall.

Over the garden wall,
I let the baby fall,

Me Ma came out
And give me a clout,
She give me another,
To match the other,
Over the garden wall.

129

Up and down the City Road,
    In and out the Eagle,
That's the way the money goes,
    Pop goes the weasel!

Half a pound of tuppenny rice,
    Half a pound of treacle,
Mix it up and make it nice,
    Pop goes the weasel!

Every night when I go out
    The monkey's on the table;
Take a stick and knock it off,
    Pop goes the weasel!

130

I've got a rocket
In my pocket;
I cannot stop to play.
Away it goes!
I've burnt my toes.
It's Independence Day.

131

Yankee Doodle went to town
Riding on a pony,
Stuck a feather in his hat
And called it Macaroni.

132

I asked my mother for fifty cents
To see the elephant jump the fence.
He jumped so high
He reached the sky
And never came back till the Fourth of July.

128. From *What Do You Feed Your Donkey On? Rhymes from a Belfast Childhood*, coll. Colette O'Hare (Collins, 1978).

130. From Carl Withers, *A Rocket in My Pocket: The Rhymes and Chants of Young Americans* (Holt, 1948).

133

A bear went over the mountain,
A bear went over the mountain,
A bear went over the mountain
To see what he could see!

The other side of the mountain,
The other side of the mountain,
The other side of the mountain
Was all that he could see.

134

I'm going to Lady Washington's
To get a cup of tea
And five loaves of gingerbread,
So don't you follow me.

135

Blind Man's Buff

(Chinese)

A peacock feather
On a plum-tree limb,
You catch me,
And I'll catch him.

All come and see!
All come and see!
A black hen laid a white egg for me.

136

Granny's in the kitchen
Doing a bit of stitching
In came a bogeyman
And chased granny out
BOO!

'Well' says granny
'That's not fair'

'Well' says the bogeyman
'I don't care'

137

This is a familiar counting rhyme in Germany.

Eins, zwei, Polizei,
Drei, vier, Offizier,
Fünf, sechs, alte Hex,
Sieben, acht, gute Nacht,
Neun, zehn, auf wiedersehen.

One, two, policeman blue,
Three, four, captain of the corps,
Five, six, a witch on two sticks,
Seven, eight, the hour is late,
Nine, ten, we meet again.

138

This rhyme and the next come from France.

Un, deux, trois, j'irai dans le bois,
Quatre, cinq, six, chercher les cerises,
Sept, huit, neuf, dans mon panier neuf,
Dix, onze, douze, elles seront toùtes rouges.

One, two, three, to the wood goes she,
Four, five, six, cherries she picks,
Seven, eight, nine, in her basket fine,
Ten, eleven, twelve, (she said),
All the cherries are red, red, red!

139

Une fill' a battu
Le roi d'Angleterre.

Tout est regagné
Par une bergère.

Nous pouvons danser,
Nous n'aurons plus de guerre.

A maiden's wondrous fame, I sing
She broke the pride of England's King.

135. From I. T. Headland, *Chinese Mother Goose Rhymes* (Revell, 1900).
136. From *Inky Pinky Ponky: Children's Playground Rhymes*, coll. Michael Rosen and Susanna Steele (Granada, 1982).

137–39. From Henry Bett, *Nursery Rhymes and Tales* (Holt, 1924).

All that we lost in our distress
Has been won back by a shepherdess.

Now, dance, dance, dance away,
There'll be no war for many a day!

140

Pepsi-Cola hits the spot,
Ties your belly in a knot,
Tastes like vinegar, looks like ink,
Pepsi-Cola is a stinky drink.

141

Two Charms to Cure Hiccups

1　Hiccup, hiccup, go away,
　Come again another day:
　Hiccup, hiccup, when I bake,
　I'll give to you a butter-cake.

2　　Hiccup, snickup,
　　Rise up, right up,
　　Three drops in a cup
　　Are good for the hiccup.

142

Charm to Cure Burns

　Two Angels from the North,
One brought fire, the other brought frost.
　　Out fire,
　　In frost.
In the name of the Father, Son and Holy Ghost.

143

Humpty Dumpty sat on a wall
Humpty Dumpty had a great fall
All the king's horses
And all the king's men
Trod on him

140. From Herbert Knapp and Mary Knapp, *One Potato, Two Potato . . . The Secret Education of American Children* (Norton, 1976).
143. From *Inky Pinky Ponky: Children's Playground Rhymes*, coll. Michael Rosen and Susanna Steele (Granada, 1982).

Riddles, Puzzles, and Tongue Twisters

144

Mother Goose Riddle Rhymes, by Joseph Low, makes an engaging game of using pictures to be deciphered (see page 50). The key to the pictures, as well as the meaning of each rhyme, is given at the back of Low's book.

Meaning:　There was a little one-eyed gunner,
　　　　　　Who killed all the birds that died last
　　　　　　summer.

145

Thirty white horses
Upon a red hill,
Now they stamp,
Now they champ,
Now they stand still.

　　　　　　　　　　　　　　　(*Teeth*)

146

There was a little green house,
And in the little green house,
There was a little brown house,
And in the little brown house
There was a little yellow house,
And in the little yellow house,
There was a little white house,
And in the little white house,
There was a little heart.

　　　　　　　　　　　　　　　(*Walnut*)

147

Riddle me! riddle me! What is that:
Over your head and under your hat?

　　　　　　　　　　　　　　　(*Hair*)

144. From Joseph Low, *Mother Goose Riddle Rhymes* (Harcourt, 1953).

Illustration by Joseph Low. Copyright © 1953 by Joseph Low. Reproduced from his volume *Mother Goose Riddle Rhymes* by permission of Harcourt Brace Jovanovich, Inc.

148

In marble halls as white as milk,
Lined with a skin as soft as silk,
Within a fountain crystal clear,

A golden apple doth appear.
No doors there are to this stronghold,
Yet thieves break in and steal the gold.

(An egg)

149

As round as an apple, as deep as a cup,
And all the king's horses can't pull it up.

(A well)

150

Black within and red without;
Four corners round about.

(A chimney)

151

Two legs sat on three legs,
With one leg in his lap;
In comes four legs,
And runs away with one leg,
Up jumps two legs,
Catches up three legs,
Throws it after four legs
And makes him bring back one leg.

(Two legs = a man)
(Three legs = a stool)
(One leg = a leg of meat)
(Four legs = a dog)

152

Little Nancy Etticoat,
With a white petticoat,
And a red nose;
She has no feet or hands,
The longer she stands
The shorter she grows.

(A lighted candle)

153

(Chinese)

Old Mr. Chang, I've heard it said,
You wear a basket on your head;
You've two pairs of scissors to cut your meat,
And two pairs of chopsticks with which you eat.
What is it?

(A crab)

153. From *Chinese Mother Goose Rhymes,* sel. and ed. Robert
Wyndham (World, 1968).

154

As I was going to St. Ives,
I met a man with seven wives;
Each wife had seven sacks,
Each sack had seven cats,
Each cat had seven kits:
Kits, cats, sacks, and wives,
How many were there going to St. Ives?

(One)*

155

It is in the rock, but not in the stone;
It is the marrow, but not in the bone;
It is in the bolster, but not in the bed;
It is not in the living, nor yet in the dead.

(The letter "R")

156

(African)

What is it that even the ostrich with its long
neck and sharp eyes cannot see?

(What will happen tomorrow)

157

If all the seas were one sea,
What a *great* sea that would be!
And if all the trees were one tree,
What a *great* tree that would be!
And if all the axes were one axe,
What a *great* axe that would be!
And if all the men were one man,
What a *great* man he would be!
And if the *great* man took the *great* axe,
And cut down the *great* tree,
And let it fall into the *great* sea,
What a splish splash *that* would be!

158

If all the world were paper,
And all the sea were ink,

* The solution is "one" or "none," depending on how the
question is read. If the question is "How many wives, sacks,
cats, and kittens went to St. Ives?" the answer is "None."
156. From Richard Burton, *Wit and Wisdom of West Africa*
(1865).

If all the trees were bread and cheese,
What should we have to drink?

159

I saw a fishpond all on fire
I saw a house bow to a squire
I saw a person twelve feet high
I saw a cottage near the sky
I saw a balloon made of lead
I saw a coffin drop down dead
I saw two sparrows run a race
I saw two horses making lace
I saw a girl just like a cat
I saw a kitten wear a hat
I saw a man who saw these too
And said though strange they all were true.

160

A man in the wilderness asked me,
How many strawberries grow in the sea.
I answered him, as I thought good,
As many red herrings as swim in the wood.

161

Betty Botter bought some butter,
But, she said, the butter's bitter;
If I put it in my batter
It will make my batter bitter,
But a bit of better butter
Will make my batter better.
So she bought a bit of butter
Better than her bitter butter,
And she put it in her batter
And the batter was not bitter.
So 'twas better Betty Botter bought a bit of
    better butter.

162

How much wood would a woodchuck chuck
If a woodchuck could chuck wood?
A woodchuck would chuck as much as he would
    chuck
If a woodchuck could chuck wood.

163

Peter Piper picked a peck of pickled pepper;
A peck of pickled pepper Peter Piper picked;

If Peter Piper picked a peck of pickled pepper,
Where's the peck of pickled pepper Peter Piper
    picked?

164

Did you eever, iver, over
In your leef, life, loaf
See the deevel, divel, dovel
Kiss his weef, wife, woaf?

No, I neever, niver, nover
In my leef, life, loaf
Saw the deevel, divel, dovel
Kiss his weef, wife, woaf.

Lullabies and Folk Songs

165

Hush-a-bye, baby, on the tree top,
When the wind blows the cradle will rock;
When the bough breaks the cradle will fall,
Down will come baby, cradle, and all.

166

(Chinese)

The heaven is bright,
The earth is bright,
I have a baby who cries all night.

167

(Thule Eskimo)

It is my big baby
That I feel in my hood
Oh how heavy he is!
Ya ya! Ya ya!

166. From *Chinese Mother Goose Rhymes,* sel. and ed. Robert
Wyndham (World, 1968).
167. Paul-Emile Victor, *Poèmes Eskimos,* trans. Charlene
Slivnick (Editions Seghers, 1971).

From *Fisherman Lullabies,* edited and illustrated by Wendy Watson. Illustration copyright
© 1968 by Wendy Watson. Reprinted by permission of Curtis Brown Ltd.

When I turn
He smiles at me, my little one,
Well hidden in my hood,
Oh how heavy he is!
Ya ya! Ya ya!

How sweet he is when he smiles
With two teeth like a little walrus.
Ah, I like my little one to be heavy
And my hood to be full.

168

(Scottish)

Dance to your daddy,
My little babby,
Dance to your daddy, my little lamb;
You shall have a fishy
In a little dishy,
You shall have a fishy when the boat comes
in.

169

Nantucket Lullaby

Hush, the waves are rolling in,
    White with foam, white with foam,
Father toils amid the din,
    While baby sleeps at home.

Hush, the ship rides in the gale,
    Where they roam, where they roam,
Father seeks the roving whale,
    While baby sleeps at home.

Hush, the wind sweeps o'er the deep,
    All alone, all alone,
Mother now the watch will keep,
    Till father's ship comes home.

169. *Fisherman Lullabies,* ed. Wendy Watson (World,
1968).

170

Bye, baby bunting,
Daddy's gone a-hunting,
Gone to get a rabbit skin
To wrap the baby bunting in.

171

(North American Indian—Kiowa)

Baby swimming down the river:
Little driftwood legs,
Little rabbit legs.

172

Rock-a-bye, baby, thy cradle is green;
Father's a nobleman, mother's a queen;
And Betty's a lady, and wears a gold ring;
And Johnny's a drummer, and drums for the
    king.

173

(Indian)

Sleep brings pearl necklaces, do not cry, baby,
Sleep brings sweet dishes, do not cry, baby,
Do not cry, baby,
It is time, you must sleep now,
As the fish sleeps in the pool.

174

Baby, baby, naughty baby,
Hush, you squalling thing, I say.
Peace this moment, peace, or maybe
Bonaparte will pass this way.

Baby, baby, he's giant,
Tall and black as Rouen steeple,
And he breakfasts, dines, rely on't,
Every day on naughty people.

Baby, baby, if he hears you,
As he gallops past the house,

Limb from limb at once he'll tear you,
Just as pussy tears a mouse.

And he'll beat you, beat you, beat you,
And he'll beat you all to pap,
And he'll eat you, eat you, eat you,
Every morsel snap, snap, snap.

175

Sleep, baby, sleep,
Thy father guards the sheep;
Thy mother shakes the dreamland tree
And from it fall sweet dreams for thee,
    Sleep, baby, sleep.

Sleep, baby, sleep,
Our cottage vale is deep;
The little lamb is on the green,
With woolly fleece so soft and clean—
    Sleep, baby, sleep.

Sleep, baby, sleep,
Down where the woodbines creep;
Be always like the lamb so mild,
A kind and sweet and gentle child,
    Sleep, baby, sleep.

176

Hush, little baby, don't say a word,
Papa's going to buy you a mocking bird.

If the mocking bird won't sing,
Papa's going to buy you a diamond ring.

If the diamond ring turns to brass,
Papa's going to buy you a looking-glass.

If the looking-glass gets broke,
Papa's going to buy you a billy-goat.

If the billy-goat runs away,
Papa's going to buy you another today.

171. From *The Indians' Book,* ed. Natalie Curtis, rev. ed.
(Dover, 1968).
173. From *Folksongs of India,* ed. Hem Barua (Indian Council for Cultural Relations, 1963).

174–76. From *The Annotated Mother Goose,* arranged by William S. Baring-Gould and Ceil Baring-Gould (Bramhall
House, 1963).

177

There were three jovial Welshmen,
  As I have heard them say,
And they would go a-hunting
  Upon St. David's day.

All the day they hunted,
  And nothing could they find,
But a ship a-sailing,
  A-sailing with the wind.

One said it was a ship,
  The other he said nay;
The third said it was a house,
  With the chimney blown away.

And all the night they hunted,
  And nothing could they find
But the moon a-gliding,
  A-gliding with the wind.

One said it was the moon;
  The other he said nay;
The third said it was a cheese,
  And half o't cut away.

And all the day they hunted,
  And nothing could they find
But a hedgehog in a bramble-bush,
  And that they left behind.

The first said it was a hedgehog;
  The second he said nay;
The third it was a pin-cushion,
  And the pins stuck in wrong way.

And all the night they hunted,
  And nothing could they find
But a hare in a turnip field,
  And that they left behind.

The first said it was a hare;
  The second he say nay;
The third said it was a calf,
  And the cow had run away.

And all the day they hunted,
  And nothing could they find

But an owl in a holly-tree,
  And that they left behind.

One said it was an owl;
  The other he said nay;
The third said 'twas an old man
  And his beard growing gray.

178

A Frog he would a-wooing go,
  Heigho, says Rowley;
Whether his mother would let him or no.
  With a rowley powley, gammon and spinach,
  Heigho, says Anthony Rowley!

So off he set with his opera hat,
  Heigho, says Rowley,
And on the road he met with a rat.
  With a rowley powley, gammon and spinach,
  Heigho, says Anthony Rowley!

"Pray, Mr. Rat, will you go with me,"
  Heigho, says Rowley,
"Kind Mrs. Mousey for to see?"
  With a rowley powley, gammon and spinach,
  Heigho, says Anthony Rowley!

When they came to the door of Mousey's hall,
  Heigho, says Rowley,
They gave a loud knock and they gave a loud
    call.
  With a rowley powley, gammon and spinach,
  Heigho, says Anthony Rowley!

"Pray, Mrs. Mouse, are you within?"
  Heigho, says Rowley,
"Oh, yes, kind sirs, I'm sitting to spin."
  With a rowley powley, gammon and spinach,
  Heigho, says Anthony Rowley!

"Pray, Mrs. Mouse, will you give us some
    beer?"
  Heigho, says Rowley,
"For Froggy and I are fond of good cheer."
  With a rowley powley, gammon and spinach,
  Heigho, says Anthony Rowley!

"Pray, Mr. Frog, will you give us a song?"
  Heigho, says Rowley,

Illustration by Randolph Caldecott. From *The Hey Diddle Diddle Picture Book,* by Randolph Caldecott. First published 1883. Reprinted by permission of the publisher, Frederick Warne & Co., Inc.

"But let it be something that's not very long."
  With a rowley powley, gammon and spinach,
  Heigho, says Anthony Rowley!

"Indeed, Mrs. Mouse," replied the frog,
  Heigho, says Rowley,
"A cold has made me as hoarse as a dog."
  With a rowley powley, gammon and spinach,
  Heigho, says Anthony Rowley!

"Since you have caught cold, Mr. Frog,"
    Mousey said,
  Heigho, says Rowley,
"I'll sing you a song that I have just made."
  With a rowley powley, gammon and spinach,
  Heigho, says Anthony Rowley!

But while they were all a merry-making,
  Heigho, says Rowley,
A cat and her kittens came tumbling in.
  With a rowley powley, gammon and spinach,
  Heigho, says Anthony Rowley!

The cat she seized the rat by the crown;
  Heigho, says Rowley,
The kittens they pulled the little mouse down.
  With a rowley powley, gammon and spinach,
  Heigho, says Anthony Rowley!

This put Mr. Frog in a terrible fright,
  Heigho, says Rowley,

He took up his hat, and he wished them good
    night.
  With a rowley powley, gammon and spinach,
  Heigho, says Anthony Rowley!

But as Froggy was crossing over a brook,
  Heigho, says Rowley,
A lily-white duck came and gobbled him up.
  With a rowley powley, gammon and spinach,
  Heigho, says Anthony Rowley!

So there was an end of one, two, and three,
  Heigho, says Rowley,
The Rat, the Mouse, and the little Frog-gee!
  With a rowley powley, gammon and spinach,
  Heigho, says Anthony Rowley!

179

Skip to My Lou

Choose your partner, skip to my Lou,
Choose your partner, skip to my Lou,
Choose your partner, skip to my Lou,
Skip to my Lou, my darling.

  Lou, Lou, skip to my Lou,
  Lou, Lou, skip to my Lou,
  Lou, Lou, skip to my Lou,
  Skip to my Lou, my darling.

Lost my partner, what shall I do? *etc.*

I'll get another one prettier than you, *etc.*

Little red wagon, painted blue, *etc.*

Pull her up and down in the little red wagon, *etc.*

Teeter up and down in the little red wagon, *etc.*

Rats in the bread tray, how they chew, *etc.*

Flies in the sugar bowl, shoo, fly, shoo! *etc.*

One old boot and a worn out shoe, *etc.*

Pig in the parlour, what'll I do? *etc.*

Cat in the buttermilk, lapping up cream, *etc.*

Rabbit in the cornfield, big as a mule, *etc.*

Chickens in the garden, shoo, shoo, shoo, *etc.*

Cow in the kitchen, moo cow moo, *etc.*

Hogs in the potato patch, rooting up corn, *etc.*

Going to market two by two, *etc.*

Dad's old hat and Mama's old shoe, *etc.*

Back from market, what did you do? *etc.*

Had a glass of buttermilk, one and two, *etc.*

Skip, skip, skip-a to my Lou, *etc.*

Skip a little faster, that won't do, *etc.*

Going to Texas, come along too, *etc.*

Catch that red bird, skip-a to my Lou, *etc.*

If you can't get a red bird, take a blue, *etc.*

If you can't get a blue bird, black bird'll do, *etc.*

Now make up your own!

180

The Big Rock Candy Mountains

On a summer's day in the month of May,
A burly bum come a-hiking,

Travelling down that lonesome road
A-looking for his liking.
He was headed for a land that was far away,
Beside them crystal fountains—
'I'll see you all this coming fall
In the Big Rock Candy Mountains.'

In the Big Rock Candy Mountains
You never change your socks,
And little streams of alcohol
Come a-trickling down the rocks.
The box cars are all empty
And the railroad bulls are blind,
There's a lake of stew and whisky, too,
You can paddle all around 'em in a big canoe
In the Big Rock Candy Mountains.

O—the buzzing of the bees in the cigarette
  trees
Round the soda-water fountains,
Where the lemonade springs and the bluebird
  sings
In the Big Rock Candy Mountains.

In the Big Rock Candy Mountains,
There's a land that's fair and bright,
Where the hand-outs grow on bushes
And you sleep out every night,
Where the box cars are all empty
And the sun shines every day,
O I'm bound to go, where there ain't no snow,
Where the rain don't fall and the wind don't
  blow
In the Big Rock Candy Mountains.

In the Big Rock Candy Mountains
The jails are made of tin
And you can bust right out again
As soon as they put you in;
The farmers' trees are full of fruit,
The barns are full of hay,
I'm going to stay where you sleep all day,
Where they boiled in oil the inventor of toil
In the Big Rock Candy Mountains.

181

A Fox Jumped Up

A fox jumped up one winter's night,
And begged the moon to give him light,
For he'd many miles to trot that night
Before he reached his den O!
    Den O! Den O!
For he'd many miles to trot that night
Before he reached his den O!

The first place he came to was a farmer's yard,
Where the ducks and the geese declared it hard
That their nerves should be shaken and their
    rest so marred
By a visit from Mr. Fox O!
    Fox O! Fox O!
That their nerves should be shaken and their
    rest so marred
By a visit from Mr. Fox O!

He took the grey goose by the neck
And swung him right across his back;
The grey goose cried out, Quack, quack, quack,
With his legs hanging dangling down O!
    Down O! Down O!
The grey goose cried out, Quack, quack, quack,
With his legs hanging dangling down O!

Old mother Slipper Slopper jumped out of bed,
And out of the window she popped her head:
Oh! John, John, John, the grey goose is gone,
And the fox is off to his den O!
    Den O! Den O!
Oh! John, John, John, the grey goose is gone,
And the fox is off to his den O!

John ran up to the top of the hill,
And blew his whistle loud and shrill;
Said the fox, That is very pretty music, still—
I'd rather be in my den O!
    Den O! Den O!
Said the fox, That is very pretty music, still—
I'd rather be in my den O!

The fox went back to his hungry den,
And his dear little foxes, eight, nine, ten;
Quoth they, Good daddy, you must go there
    again,

If you bring such good cheer from the farm
    O! Farm O! Farm O!
Quoth they, Good daddy, you must go there
    again,
If you bring such good cheer from the farm O!

The fox and his wife, without any strife,
Said they never ate a better goose in all their
    life;
They did very well without fork or knife,
And the little ones picked the bones O!
    Bones O! Bones O!
They did very well without fork or knife
And the little ones picked the bones
    O!

182

Old Blue

I had an ol' dog, boys, and I called him Blue,
Listen lemme tell you what Blue could do.
        Come on, Blue, you good dog, you.
        Yes, come on, Blue, you good dog,
        you.

I took my axe, boys, and I blowed my horn,
Goin' a-huntin' just as shore's you're born.
        Come on, Blue, you good dog, you.
        Yes, come on, Blue, you good dog,
        you.

Old Blue treed and I went to see,
Had him a possum up a white-oak tree.
        Come on, Blue, you good dog, you.
        Yes, come on, Blue, you good dog,
        you.

He growled at me, I looked at him,
I shook him out, Blue took him in.
        Come on, Blue, you good dog, you.
        Yes, come on, Blue, you good dog,
        you.

Baked that possum good and brown,
Laid them sweet 'taters round and round.
        Says, come on, Blue, you can have
        some, too.
        Yes, come on, Blue, you can have
        some, too.

The doctor's come, an' he come on the run.
He says, 'Old Blue, your huntin' is done.'
      Come on, Blue, you good dog, you.
      Yes, come on, Blue, you good dog,
        you.

Old Blue died, an' he died so hard,
He dug up the ground all over the yard.
      Go on, Blue, you good dog, you.
      Yes, go on, Blue, you good dog, you.

When I get to heaven, I know what I'll do,
Grab my horn and blow for old Blue.
      Sayin', 'Come here, Blue, I've got
        here, too.'
      Sayin', 'Come here, Blue, I've got
        here, too.'

And when I hear my old Blue dog bark,
I'll know he's treed a 'possum in Noah's Ark.
      Sayin', 'Come here, Blue, I've got
        here, too.'
      Sayin', 'Come here, Blue, I've got
        here, too.'

183

The Whale

'Twas in the year of forty-nine,
  On March, the twentieth day,
Our gallant ship her anchor weigh'd,
  And to the sea she bore away,
    Brave boys
And to the sea she bore away.
      With a fa la la la la la la
      Fa la la la la la la
      Fa la la fa la la
      Fa la la la la.

Old Blowhard was our captain's name,
  Our ship the *Lion* bold,
And we were bound to the North Country
    To face the frost and the cold,
    Brave boys, etc.

And when we came to that cold country
    Where the ice and the snow do lie,
Where there's ice and snow, and the great
      whales blow,

And the daylight does not die,
  Brave boys, etc.

Our mate went up to the topmast head
  With a spyglass in his hand:
'A whale, a whale, a whale', he cries,
  'And she spouts at every span,'
  Brave boys, etc.

Up jumped old Blowhard on the deck—
  And a clever little man was he—
'Overhaul, overhaul, let your main-tackle fall,
  And launch your boat to sea.'
  Brave boys, etc.

We struck that fish and away she flew
  With a flourish of her tail;
But oh! and alas! we lost one man
  And we did not catch that whale,
  Brave boys, etc.

Now when the news to our captain came
  He called up all his crew,
And for the losing of that man
  He down his colours drew,
  Brave boys, etc.

Says he: 'My men, be not dismayed
  At the losing of one man,
For Providence will have his will,
  Let man do what he can,'
  Brave boys, etc.

Now the losing of that prentice boy
  It grieved our captain sore,
But the losing of that great big whale
  It grieved him a damned sight more,
  Brave boys,
  It grieved him a damned sight more.
      With a fa la la la la la la
      Fa la la la la la la
      Fa la la fa la la
      Fa la la la la.

184

John Henry

When John Henry was a little tiny baby
Sitting on his mama's knee,

He picked up a hammer and a little piece of
    steel
Saying, "Hammer's going to be the death of
    me, Lord, Lord,
    Hammer's going to be the death of me."

John Henry was a man just six feet high,
Nearly two feet and a half across his breast.
He'd hammer with a nine-pound hammer all
    day
And never get tired and want to rest, Lord,
    Lord,
    And never get tired and want to rest.

John Henry went up on the mountain
And he looked one eye straight up its side.
The mountain was so tall and John Henry was
    so small,
He laid down his hammer and he cried, "Lord,
    Lord,"
    He laid down his hammer and he cried.

John Henry said to his captain,
"Captain, you go to town,
Bring me back a TWELVE-pound hammer,
    please,
And I'll beat that steam drill down, Lord, Lord,
    I'll beat that steam drill down."

The captain said to John Henry,
"I believe this mountain's sinking in."
But John Henry said, "Captain, just you stand
    aside—
It's nothing but my hammer catching wind,
    Lord, Lord,
    It's nothing but my hammer catching wind."

John Henry said to his shaker,
"Shaker, boy, you better start to pray,
'Cause if my TWELVE-pound hammer miss that
    little piece of steel,
Tomorrow'll be your burying day, Lord, Lord,
    Tomorrow'll be your burying day."

John Henry said to his captain,
"A man is nothing but a man,
But before I let your steam drill beat me down,
I'd die with this hammer in my hand, Lord,
    Lord,
    I'd die with this hammer in my hand."

The man that invented the steam drill,
He figured he was mighty high and fine,
But John Henry sunk the steel down fourteen
    feet
While the steam drill only made nine, Lord,
    Lord,
    The steam drill only made nine.

John Henry hammered on the right-hand side,
Steam drill kept driving on the left.
John Henry beat that steam drill down,
But he hammered his poor heart to death, Lord,
    Lord,
    He hammered his poor heart to death.

Well, they carried John Henry down the tunnel
And they laid his body in the sand.
Now every woman riding on a C and O train
Says, "There lies my steel-driving man, Lord,
    Lord,
    There lies my steel-driving man."

185

Whoopee Ti Yi Yo,
Git Along, Little Dogies

As I was a-walking one morning for pleasure,
I spied a cow-puncher a-riding along;
His hat was throwed back and his spurs were
    a-jinglin',
As he approached me a-singin' this song:

Whoopee ti yi yo, git along, little dogies,
It's your misfortune and none of my own;
Whoopee ti yi yo, git along, little dogies,
For you know Wyoming will be your new home.

Early in the springtime we'll round up the
    dogies,
Slap on their brands, and bob off their tails;
Round up our horses, load up the chuck wagon,
Then throw those dogies upon the trail.

It's whooping and yelling and driving the
    dogies.
Oh, how I wish you would go on;
It's whooping and punching and go on, little
    dogies,
For you know Wyoming will be your new home.

Some of the boys goes up the trail for pleasure.
But that's where they git it most awfully wrong;
For you haven't any idea the trouble they give
  us
When we go driving them dogies along.

When the night comes on and we hold them
  on the bed-ground,
These little dogies that roll on so slow;
Roll up the herd and cut out the strays,
And roll the little dogies that never rolled
  before.

Your mother she was raised way down in Texas,
Where the jimson weed and sand-burrs grow;
Now we'll fill you up on prickly pear and cholla
Till you are ready for the trail to Idaho.

Oh, you'll be soup for Uncle Sam's Injuns;
"It's beef, heap beef," I hear them cry.
Git along, git along, git along, little dogies,
You're going to be beef steers by and by.

Reprinted by permission of Philomel Books, a division of
the Putnam Publishing Group, from *The Poet's Tales,* edited
by William Cole and illustrated by Charles Keeping.
Illustrations copyright © 1971 by Charles Keeping.

186

Old Roger Is Dead
and Laid in His Grave

Old Roger is dead and laid in his grave,
  Laid in his grave, laid in his grave;
Old Roger is dead and laid in his grave,
  H'm ha! laid in his grave.

They planted an apple tree over his head,
  Over his head, over his head;
They planted an apple tree over his head,
  H'm ha! over his head.

The apples grew ripe and ready to fall,
  Ready to fall, ready to fall;
The apples grew ripe and ready to fall,
  H'm ha! ready to fall.

There came an old woman a-picking them all,
  A-picking them all, a-picking them all;
There came an old woman a-picking them all,
  H'm ha! picking them all.

Old Roger jumps up and gives her a knock,
  Gives her a knock, gives her a knock;
Which makes the old woman go hipperty-hop,
  H'm ha! hipperty-hop.

187

Parsley, Sage, Rosemary, and Thyme

Can you make a cambric shirt,
  Parsley, sage, rosemary, and thyme,
Without any seam or needlework?
  And you shall be a true lover of mine.

Can you wash it in yonder well,
  Parsley, sage, rosemary, and thyme,
Where never sprung water, nor rain ever fell?
  And you shall be a true lover of mine.

Can you dry it on yonder thorn,
  Parsley, sage, rosemary, and thyme,
Which never bore blossom since Adam was
    born?
  And you shall be a true lover of mine.

Now you've asked me questions three,
  Parsley, sage, rosemary, and thyme,

I hope you'll answer as many for me,
　And you shall be a true lover of mine.

Can you find me an acre of land,
　Parsley, sage, rosemary, and thyme,
Between the salt water and the sea sand?
　And you shall be a true lover of mine.

Can you plough it with a ram's horn,
　Parsley, sage, rosemary, and thyme,
And sow it all over with one pepper-corn?
　And you shall be a true lover of mine.

Can you reap it with a sickle of leather,
　Parsley, sage, rosemary, and thyme,
And bind it up with a peacock's feather?
　And you shall be a true lover of mine.

When you have done and finished your work,
　Parsley, sage, rosemary, and thyme,
Then come to me for your cambric shirt,
　And you shall be a true lover of mine.

188

Riddle Song

I gave my love a cherry that has no stone,
I gave my love a chicken that has no bone,
I gave my love a gold ring that has no end,
I gave my love a baby with no cry-in'.

How can there be a cherry that has no stone?
How can there be a chicken that has no
　bone?
How can there be a gold ring that has no
　end?
How can there be a baby with no cry-in'?

A cherry when it's blooming, it has no stone.
A chicken in the eggshell, it has no bone.
A gold ring when it's rolling, it has no end.
A baby when it's sleeping, has no cry-in'.

189

I know where I'm going

I know where I'm going.
I know who's going with me,

I know who I love,
But the dear knows who I'll marry.

I'll have stockings of silk,
Shoes of fine green leather,
Combs to buckle my braid,
And a ring for every finger.

Feather beds are soft,
Painted rooms are bonny;
But I'd leave them all
To go with my love Johnny.

Some say he's dark,
I say he's bonny.
He's the flower of them all,
My handsome, coaxing Johnny.

I know where I'm going,
I know who's going with me,
I know who I love,
But the dear knows who I'll marry.

190

Go Down, Moses

Go down, Moses,
Way down in Egypt land,
Tell old Pharaoh
To let my people go.

When Israel was in Egypt land,
Let my people go,
Oppressed so hard they could not stand,
Let my people go.

Go down, Moses,
Way down in Egypt land,
Tell old Pharaoh,
'Let my people go.'

'Thus saith the Lord,' bold Moses said,
'Let my people go;
If not I'll smite your first-born dead
Let my people go.'

Go down, Moses,
Way down in Egypt land,

Tell old Pharaoh,
'Let my people go.'

191

I wonder as I wander

I wonder as I wander out under the sky
How Jesus, our Saviour, did come for to die
For poor orn'ry people like you and like I
I wonder as I wander out under the sky.

When Mary birthed Jesus 'twas in a cow's stall
With Wise Men, and shepherds, and farmers
  and all.
But high from God's Heaven a star's light did
  fall
And the promise of ages it then did recall.

192

An Apple-Tree Rhyme

(To Be Sung in Orchards, at the New Year)

Here stands a good apple tree;
Stand fast at the root,
Bear well at top:
Every little twig
Bear an apple big;
Every little bough
Bear an apple now;

Hats full! caps full!
Three-score sacks full!
Hullo, boys, hullo!

193

A New Year Carol

Here we bring new water
  from the well so clear,
For to worship God with,
  this happy New Year.

Sing levy dew, sing levy dew,
  the water and the wine;
The seven bright gold wires
  and the bugles that do shine.

Sing reign of Fair Maid,
  with gold upon her toe,—
Open you the West Door,
  And turn the Old Year go.

Sing reign of Fair Maid
  with gold upon her chin.—
Open you the East Door,
  and let the New Year in.

Sing levy dew, sing levy dew,
  the water and the wine;
The seven bright gold wires
  And the bugles they do shine.

*If the fool would persist in
his folly he would become wise.*[1]

2   Voices of Nonsense

W hat nonsense!" Depending on the inflection of the speaker's voice,
that phrase may convey either praise or criticism. It may mean
indignation and complete dismissal of the topic as unworthy of
notice. But it might instead mean the recognition of an art—the
gentle art of nonsense, "that divine lunacy that God has given to men as a
holiday of the intellect."[2] Yet, however gentle it may be, it can never be weak
or merely silly. The rules of nonsense are as exacting as those that govern the
writing of a sonnet. Nonsense takes the common rules of logic, order, authority,
or manners and stands them on their heads. For small children, nonsense confirms
their knowledge of the way things are by presenting them with what could not
possibly be; and, most significantly, it makes them laugh. For older children,
the irrational world of nonsense offers fantastic perspectives on the familiar.

Nonsense emerged in the nineteenth century as an anarchic means of shedding
the straightjacket of English society. The Victorian era produced giants of the
art and set an enduring standard of excellence. An Oxford don, Charles Lutwidge
Dodgson, writing under the name Lewis Carroll, utilized his training in mathemat-

---

1. William Blake, "Proverbs of Hell," in *The Complete Writings of William Blake with Variant Readings,*
ed. Geoffrey Keynes (Oxford University Press, 1966), p. 151.
2. G. K. Chesterton, "Gilbert and Sullivan," in *The Eighteen-Eighties: Essays by Fellows of the Royal
Society of Literature,* ed. Walter de la Mare (Cambridge University Press, 1930), p. 142.

ics and logic to create two whole worlds of nonsense. In writing the many curious verses sprinkled throughout *Alice's Adventures in Wonderland* (1865) and *Through the Looking Glass* (1872), Carroll turned his academically trained imagination to the creation of brilliantly methodical *il*logic. With deep affection and sympathy, he entertained Victorian children with splendidly witty parodies of the overly familiar verses they all grew up reciting. He inverted the pious morality or dull sentiment of well-known poems by Isaac Watts and Robert Southey; even the charming and beloved verses in Ann and Jane Taylor's *Rhymes for the Nursery* (1806) were not above Carroll's burlesqueing in *Alice's Adventures in Wonderland.*

Twinkle, twinkle little star,	Twinkle, twinkle, little bat!
How I wonder what you are!	How I wonder where you're at!
Up above the world so high,	Up above the world you fly,
Like a diamond in the sky.	Like a tea-tray in the sky.
Jane Taylor	Lewis Carroll

It was Edward Lear, however, by profession a landscape painter and by choice a companion to children, who ushered in the great age of nonsense with his *Book of Nonsense* (1846), published nineteen years before *Alice's Adventures in Wonderland.* An old Mother Goose verse had caught his ear with its distinctive pattern of accent and rhyme:

There was an old man of Tobago
Who lived on rice, gruel, and sago,
Till, much to his bliss,
His physician said this,
To a leg, sir, of mutton you may go.

Lear took to this pattern like a duck to water, making it his own by producing hundreds of limericks, each a drama of triumph or frustration, as abrupt, sharp, and hilarious as any of Mother Goose's own. *Nonsense Songs, Stories, Botany and Alphabets* was published in 1871; *More Nonsense, Pictures, Rhymes,* in 1872; *Laughable Lyrics,* in 1877; and the last, *Nonsense Songs and Stories,* in 1895. To his inventive play, his sense of melody, his prodigious ability to manipulate words and sounds, Lear added the power of the incisive sketch; for, in the original editions, he illustrated his own inspired absurdities with quirky and naive drawings.

Underlying Lear's magnificent humor, however, was "a theme of personal sadness and desolation, at moments so strong that one is on the verge of tears in the midst of one's laughter."[3] The master of the giddy limerick was also the man who asked himself, "Would *one* have been as happy as *one* fancies if *one* had been married & had had children?"[4] Lear describes himself, in a poem written for a young friend, in terms both sad and droll:

He weeps by the side of the ocean,
    He weeps on top of the hill;
He purchases pancakes and lotion,
    And chocolate shrimps from the mill.

3. John Lehmann, *Edward Lear and His World* (Thames & Hudson, 1977), p. 64.
4. Edward Lear, diary entry dated 13 April 1862, as quoted in Vivien Noakes, *Edward Lear: The Life of a Wanderer* (Collins, 1968), p. 197.

He reads but he cannot speak Spanish,
    He cannot abide ginger-beer:
Ere the days of his pilgrimage vanish,
    How pleasant to know Mr. Lear!

The strain of melancholy that runs through his work gives it depth and resonance. In Lear's hands, nonsense verse often sweeps over into the realm of serious poetry; "The Jumblies" has the power to evoke a longing for the unattainable that is at once childlike and mystical:

Far and few, far and few,
    Are the lands where the Jumblies live;
Their heads are green, and their hands are blue,
    And they went to sea in a sieve.

How is such nonsense created? Much of it seems to consist of an inspired selection and arrangement of incongruities. In Mother Goose, for example, a cow jumps over the moon. But, given all her bovine seriousness, she is a highly unlikely candidate for such an athletic feat. The Russian children's poet Kornei Chukovsky writes of "the inexhaustible need of every healthy child . . . to introduce nonsense into his small but ordered world, with which he has only recently become acquainted. Hardly has the child comprehended with certainty which objects go together and which do not, when he begins to listen happily to verses of absurdity."[5]

Nonsense also grows out of the confusion that results when the meaning of a word is changed by the substitution of one letter or syllable for another. In *Alice's Adventures in Wonderland,* Lewis Carroll shows his mastery of this type of manipulation:

"I only took the regular course."
"What was that?" inquired Alice.
"Reeling and Writhing, of course, to begin with," the Mock Turtle replied; "and then the different branches of Arithmetic—Ambition, Distraction, Uglification, and Derision."

The sounds of words and the taste of them on the tongue are major sources of nonsense. "Have you seen a crocodile in these promiscuous parts?" asks the Elephant's Child in "How the Elephant Got His Trunk," one of Rudyard Kipling's *Just So Stories* (1902). And again, the cake that the Parsee man baked in "How the Rhinoceros Got His Skin," must be the most delectable cake in all of literature, because it smelled "most sentimental." Perhaps the definitive statement on the meaning of words to the nonsense writer is the Humpty Dumpty passage from *Through the Looking Glass.* Although it is not verse, it has been included in this chapter.

The invention of words is characteristic of the true nonsense writer. This is no mean achievement, for the word must appear, to both the ear and the eye, to come of a long and legitimate lineage; it must seem authentic. A small dictionary could be compiled of Lear's wonderful inventions: words like *borascible* (to describe the "Old Person of Bangor/Whose face was distorted with anger"),

---

5. Kornei Chukovsky, *From Two to Five,* trans. and ed. Miriam Morton, rev. ed. (University of California Press, 1968), p. 96.

oblivorous, and *dolomphirus;* whole geographies of countries that do not exist, but should; and the names of creatures unknown before he invented them, including the Pobble, the Jumblies, and the Yonghy-Bonghy-Bò.

Language, sounds, and combinations of sounds are a field of playful exploration for children; young people invent languages, collect words they delight in, make up words, and give names of their own to objects. And many of the techniques of the nonsense writer grow directly out of a childlike delight in play with language: the use of puns, alliterations, or rhymes; the exchange of sounds at the beginning of words (*spoonerism*); the ridiculous misuse of words (*malapropism*); the creation of words based on the sounds associated with an object or action (*onomatopoeia*); or the creation of entirely new words (*neologisms*), which may consist of real words grafted together (*portmanteau words*). But to achieve the highest level of inspired lunacy, which is represented only by the best of nonsense, writers must do more than play with technical devices; they must create whole other worlds of absurdity, nonsensical universes that are perfectly believable and consistent within themselves, as did Carroll and Lear.

Since the classical age of nonsense, the art has been developed and altered. Hilaire Belloc's late Victorian verse parodies of cautionary tales are more wickedly flavored with black humor than is anything of Carroll's or Lear's. A. A. Milne's light verse of the early twentieth century has lost the edge of Victorian wit; it is gentler, sweeter.

In the early American idiom, nonsense was shaped by the *tall tale* or *fish story.* The fables of James Thurber thrive in an area that is slightly north-northeast of actuality. Laura E. Richards's free-flowing fancy is bubbling and irrepressible. The dry humor of Ogden Nash's verse arises from the distortion of poetic form through brash puns, extravagant wordplay, and hopelessly impossible rhymes dragged kicking and screaming to success.

The cutting edge of nonsense has been rehoned in the contemporary poetry of William Jay Smith, James Reeves, Dennis Lee, John Ciardi, Roald Dahl, and Shel Silverstein. Like the traditional nonsense verse of Lear and Carroll, their work is both a release of pure pleasure and a tool of acerbic social observation. Some contemporary nonsense has developed a deeper sophistication than earlier forms possessed; there is in it a touch of surrealism, satire, or irony, as in the verse of Roald Dahl, that was not present in most earlier children's light verse. Other, gentler, poets such as David McCord and N. M. Bodecker have a more innocent naivety and tender grace in their lyric whimsy.

Another group of nonsense poets takes a casual, popular-culture stance. The cartoon breeziness of Shel Silverstein's poems and line drawings in *Where the Sidewalk Ends* (1974) and *A Light in the Attic* (1981)—riddled with slang, pugnacious teasing energy, and wry social commentary—are reminiscent of children's street verse. They are as audaciously American as Spike Milligan's slapdash, comic poetry in *Silly Verse for Kids* (1959) is incorrigibly British.

Also exercising the colloquial diction and vernacular of contemporary children's street verse is Dennis Lee, a respected Canadian poet who writes for adults as well as children. In his collections of nonsensical, domestic, and lyric poetry, beginning with *Alligator Pie* (1974), he creates a poetry of pure play, jumping with puns, in which the oral language and codes of childhood are molded into original verse. He writes with a fluid sweep of language suggestive of Robert Louis Stevenson, A. A. Milne, and Mother Goose, whom he acknowledges as his models.

The thriving talents of nonsense poets such as Dennis Lee, David McCord, Jack Prelutsky, Karla Kuskin, and N. M. Bodecker confirm that the human delight in playfully standing reality on its head still flourishes, even amidst the bleak ambiguities of our difficult time. This is a testament to both the psychic sensitivity of nonsense and the unique character of its poets. In them, the exultant child at play must exist alongside the most sophisticated and conscious formalist. It is revealing that the dour prophet of modernism, T. S. Eliot, took a holiday from his vision of the wasteland to celebrate not just wit and cleverness but also fancy, pathos, and humanity in his nonsensical *Old Possum's Book of Practical Cats* (1939).

Like the poets who write for them, children of today find themselves as happily at home in the world of nonsense as did those of earlier eras. This is not (as it has often been mistakenly argued) because children are naive and will believe *anything,* but because healthy children are, first and foremost, realists. To find the Mock Turtle's course of study funny, children must know the proper names for their own courses in their own very real grade schools. "When we notice that a child has started to play with some newly acquired component of understanding," Chukovsky points out, "we may definitely conclude that he has become full master of this item of understanding; only those ideas can become toys for him whose proper relation to reality is firmly known to him."[6]

But, nonsense is always much more than merely a test and confirmation of reality. Out of this playing with the limits of the world can grow a vision of a world with larger boundaries. The best of nonsense arouses the divine folly of wanting to change what is. Children returning from Carroll's Wonderland may never again believe that the world around them can be fixed by or limited to what *first* meets the eye.

For children, then, nonsense is not *no sense;* rather, it is a confirmation of experience and an expansion of experience. The laughter that this art of levity provokes is the most genuine mirth of childhood.

6. Chukovsky, p. 103.

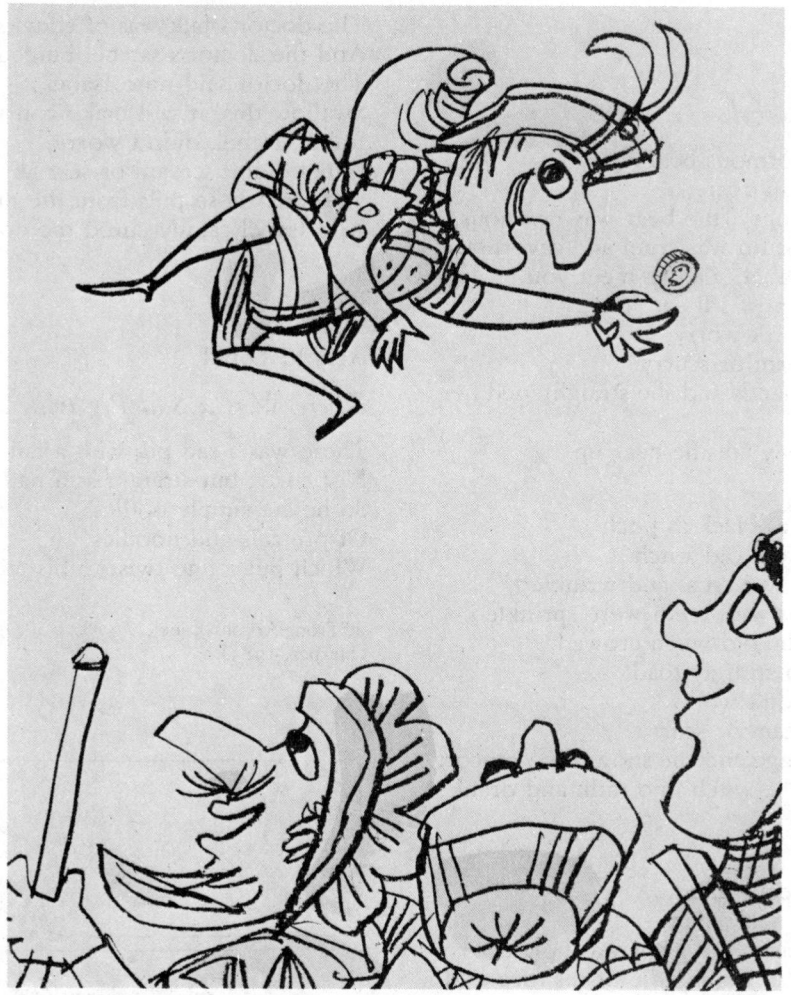

From *Pulcinella: Or Punch's Merry Pranks,* by Rose Laura Mincieli, illustrated by Joseph Low. Copyright © 1960 by Rose Laura Mincieli and Joseph Low. Reprinted by permission of Alfred A. Knopf, Inc.

1

Mr. Punchinello

Oh, mother, I shall be married to
  Mr. Punchinello,
    To Mr. Punch,
      To Mr. Joe,
        To Mr. Nell,
          To Mr. Lo,
Mr. Punch, Mr. Joe,
Mr. Nell, Mr. Lo,
To Mr. Punchinello.

2

Clyde Watson

Dilly Dilly Piccalilli

Dilly Dilly Piccalilli
Tell me something very silly:
There was a chap his name was Bert
He ate the buttons off his shirt.

2. From Clyde Watson, *Father Fox's Penny-Rhymes* (Crowell, 1971).

3

Ogden Nash

Adventures of Isabel

Isabel met an enormous bear,
Isabel, Isabel, didn't care;
The bear was hungry, the bear was ravenous,
The bear's big mouth was cruel and cavernous.
The bear said, Isabel, glad to meet you,
How do, Isabel, now I'll eat you!
Isabel, Isabel, didn't worry,
Isabel didn't scream or scurry.
She washed her hands and she straightened her
    hair up,
Then Isabel quietly ate the bear up.

Once in a night as black as pitch
Isabel met a wicked old witch.
The witch's face was cross and wrinkled,
The witch's gums with teeth were sprinkled.
Ho ho, Isabel! the old witch crowed,
I'll turn you into an ugly toad!
Isabel, Isabel, didn't worry,
Isabel didn't scream or scurry,
She showed no rage and she showed no rancor,
But she turned the witch into milk and drank
    her.

Isabel met a hideous giant,
Isabel continued self-reliant.
The giant was hairy, the giant was horrid,
He had one eye in the middle of his forehead.
Good morning, Isabel, the giant said,
I'll grind your bones to make my bread.
Isabel, Isabel, didn't worry,
Isabel didn't scream or scurry.
She nibbled the Zwieback that she always fed
    off,
And when it was gone, she cut the giant's head
    off.

Isabel met a troublesome doctor,
He punched and he poked till he really shocked
    her.

The doctor's talk was of coughs and chills
And the doctor's satchel bulged with pills.
The doctor said unto Isabel,
Swallow this, it will make you well.
Isabel, Isabel, didn't worry,
Isabel didn't scream or scurry.
She took those pills from the pill concocter,
And Isabel calmly cured the doctor.

4

Arnold Lobel

There Was a Sad Pig with a Tail

There was a sad pig with a tail
Not curly, but straight as a nail.
So he ate simply oodles
Of pretzels and noodles,
Which put a fine twist to his tail.

4. From Arnold Lobel, *The Book of Pigericks: Pig Limericks*
(Harper, 1983).

Illustration to accompany "There Was a Sad Pig with a
Tail" from *The Book of Pigericks: Pig Limericks*, by Arnold
Lobel. Copyright © 1983 by Arnold Lobel. Reprinted
by permission of Harper & Row, Publishers, Inc.

3. From Ogden Nash, *Custard and Company* (Little, Brown,
1936).

5

Edward Lear

Limericks

There was an old person of Ware,
Who rode on the back of a bear:
When they ask'd, "Does it trot?" he said,
    "Certainly not!
He's a Moppsikon Floppsikon bear!"

There is a young lady, whose nose,
Continually prospers and grows;
When it grew out of sight, she exclaimed in a
    fright,
"Oh! Farewell to the end of my nose!"

There was an Old Man who said, "Hush!
I perceive a young bird in this bush!"

When they said, "Is it small!" he replied,
    "Not at all;
It is four times as big as the bush!"

6

Christina Rossetti

If a Pig Wore a Wig

If a pig wore a wig,
What could we say?
Treat him as a gentleman,
    And say, "Good day."
If his tail chanced to fail,
What could we do?
Send him to the tailoress
    To get one new.

7

Karla Kuskin

Knitted Things

There was a witch who knitted things:
Elephants and playground swings.
She knitted rain,
She knitted night,
But nothing really came out right.
The elephants had just one tusk
And night looked more
Like dawn or dusk.
The rain was snow
And when she tried
To knit an egg
It came out fried.
She knitted birds
With buttonholes
And twenty rubber butter rolls.
She knitted blue angora trees.
She purl stitched countless purple fleas.
She knitted a palace in need of a darn.
She knitted a battle and ran out of yarn.
She drew out a strand
Of her gleaming, green hair
And knitted a lawn
Till she just wasn't there.

Illustration by Karen Ann Weinhaus, from *Knock at a Star: A Child's Introduction to Poetry*, edited by X. J. Kennedy and Dorothy M. Kennedy. By permission of Little, Brown and Co. Illustrations copyright © 1982 by Karen Ann Weinhaus.

6. From Christina Rossetti, *Sing-Song: A Nursery Song Book* (Routledge, 1872).
7. From Karla Kuskin, *Dogs and Dragons, Trees and Dreams: A Collection of Poems* (Harper, 1980).

8

Jack Prelutsky

Long Gone

Don't waste your time in looking for
the long-extinct tyrannosaur,
because this ancient dinosaur
just can't be found here anymore.

This also goes for stegosaurus,
allosaurus, brontosaurus
and any other saur or saurus.
They all lived here long before us.

9

One bright day
    in the middle of the night
    two dead men
    got up to fight.
Back to back
    they faced each other,
    drew their swords,
    and shot each other.
A deaf policeman
    heard the noise
He came and shot
    those two dead boys.
If you don't believe
    this lie is true,
    ask the blind man—
    he saw it, too.

10

Old Greek Nonsense Rhymes

Little Hermogenes is so small
He can't reach anything down at all;
Though it's on the ground, he must let it lie—
For he's so short that it's still too high.

                    LUCILIUS (*c.* A.D. 50)

Look at Marcus and take warning:
    Once he tried to win a race,
Ran all night, and in the morning
    Hadn't passed the starting place!

                    LUCILIUS

I boiled hot water in an urn
    Till it was cold as ice;
I blew the fire to make it burn.
    Which froze it in a trice.

            After NICARCHUS (*c.* A.D. 200)

11

Theodore Roethke

The Yak

There was a most odious Yak
Who took only toads on his Back:
If you asked for a Ride,
He would act very Snide,
And go humping off, yicketty-yak.

12

Dennis Lee

Alligator Pie

Alligator pie, alligator pie,
If I don't get some I think I'm gonna die.
Give away the green grass, give away the sky,
But don't give away my alligator pie.

Alligator stew, alligator stew,
If I don't get some I don't know what I'll do.
Give away my furry hat, give away my shoe,
But don't give away my alligator stew.

Alligator soup, alligator soup,
If I don't get some I think I'm gonna droop.
Give away my hockey-stick, give away my hoop,
But don't give away my alligator soup.

8. From Jack Prelutsky, *Zoo Doings* (Greenwillow, 1967).
9. From *Tomfoolery: Trickery and Foolery with Words,* ed. Alvin Schwartz (Lippincott, 1973).
10. From *The Book of Nonsense,* ed. Roger Lancelyn Green (Dutton, 1956).

11. From Theodore Roethke, *Collected Poems* (Doubleday, 1963).
12. From Dennis Lee, *Alligator Pie* (Houghton Mifflin, 1974).

13

Edward Lear

There was an Old Man in a tree,
Who was horribly bored by a Bee;
When they said, "Does it buzz?" he replied,
  "Yes, it does!
It's a regular brute of a Bee."

14

Ogden Nash

The Eel

I don't mind eels
Except as meals
And the way they feels.

15

Ogden Nash

The Guppy

Whales have calves,
Cats have kittens,
Bears have cubs,
Bats have bittens,
Swans have cygnets,
Seals have puppies,
But guppies just have little guppies.

16

N. M. Bodecker

"Let's marry!" said the cherry

"Let's marry,"
said the cherry.

"Why me?"
said the pea.

"'Cause you're sweet,"
said the beet.

"Say you will,"
said the dill.

"Think it over,"
said the clover.

"Don't rush,"
said the squash.

"Here's your dress,"
said the cress.

"White and green,"
said the bean.

"And your cape,"
said the grape.

"Trimmed with fur,"
said the burr.

"Won't that tickle?"
said the pickle.

14. From Ogden Nash, *Family Reunion* (Little, Brown, 1950).
15. From Ogden Nash, *Versus* (Little, Brown, 1949).
16. From N. M. Bodecker, *Let's Marry Said the Cherry* (Atheneum, 1974).

Illustrations by N. M. Bodecker. Copyright © 1974 by N. M. Bodecker. From *Let's Marry Said the Cherry* (A Margaret K. McElderry Book). Used by permission of Atheneum Publishers.

"Who knows?"
said the rose.

"Where's the chapel?"
said the apple.

"In Greenwich,"
said the spinach.

"We'll be there!"
said the pear.

"Wearing what?"
said the nut.

"Pants and coats,"
said the oats.

"Shoes and socks,"
said the phlox.

"Shirt and tie,"
said the rye.

"We'll look jolly,"
said the holly.

"You'll look silly,"
said the lily.

"You're crazy,"
said the daisy.

"Come, let's dine,"
said the vine.

"Yeah—let's eat!"
said the wheat.

"And get stout,"
said the sprout.

"Just wait,"
said the date.

"Who will chime?"
said the lime.

"I'll chime!"
said the thyme.

"Who will preach?"
said the peach.

"It's my turn!"
said the fern.

"You would ramble,"
said the bramble.

"Here they come!"
cried the plum.

"Start the tune!"
cried the prune.

"All together!"
cried the heather.

"Here we go!"
said the sloe.

"NOW—let's marry!"
said the cherry.

"Why me?"
said the pea.

"Oh, my gosh!"
said the squash.

"Start all over,"
said the clover.

"NO WAY!"
said the hay.

17

Dylan Thomas

Johnnie Crack and Flossie Snail

Johnnie Crack and Flossie Snail
Kept their baby in a milking pail
Flossie Snail and Johnnie Crack
One would pull it out and one would put it
    back

17. From Dylan Thomas, *Under Milk Wood* (New Directions, 1954).

O it's my turn now said Flossie Snail
To take the baby from the milking pail
And it's my turn now said Johnnie Crack
To smack it on the head and put it back

Johnnie Crack and Flossie Snail
Kept their baby in a milking pail
One would put it back and one would pull it
    out
And all it had to drink was ale and stout
For Johnnie Crack and Flossie Snail
Always used to say that stout and ale
Was *good* for a baby in a milking pail.

18

I eat my peas with honey;
I've done it all my life.
It makes the peas taste funny,
But it keeps them on the knife.

19

A horse and a flea and three blind mice
Sat on a curbstone shooting dice.
The horse he slipped and fell on the flea.
The flea said, "Whoops, there's a horse on me."

20

John Ciardi

I Met a Crow

Said a crow in the top of a tree,
What time is it getting to be?
    If it isn't yet noon
    I got here too soon,
But I'm late if it isn't yet three."

21

A flea and a fly in a flue
Were caught, so what could they do?
    Said the fly, "Let us flee."
    "Let us fly," said the flea.
So they flew through a flaw in the flue.

22

There once were two cats of Kilkenny,
Each thought there was one cat too many;
    So they fought and they fit,
    And they scratched and they bit,
Till instead of two cats there weren't any.

23

A piggish young person from Leeds
Made a meal on six packets of seeds
    But it soon came to pass
    That he broke out in grass
And he couldn't sit down for the weeds.

24

A diner while dining at Crewe,
Found quite a large mouse in his stew.
    Said the waiter, "Don't shout,
    And wave it about,
Or the rest will be wanting one, too."

25

Shel Silverstein

Boa Constrictor

Oh, I'm being eaten
By a boa constrictor,
A boa constrictor,
A boa constrictor,
I'm being eaten by a boa constrictor,
And I don't like it—one bit.
Well, what do you know?
It's nibblin' my toe.
Oh, gee,
It's up to my knee.
Oh my,
It's up to my thigh.
Oh, fiddle,
It's up to my middle.
Oh, heck,
It's up to my neck.
Oh, dread,
It's up mmmmmmmmmmmffffffffff . . .

18–19. From *A Rocket in My Pocket: The Rhymes and Chants of Young Americans,* comp. Carl Withers (Holt, 1948).
20. From John Ciardi, *I Met a Man* (Houghton Mifflin, 1961).
21–22. From *Laughable Limericks,* comp. Sara Brewton and John E. Brewton (Crowell, 1965).

24. From *Laughable Limericks,* comp. Sara Brewton and John E. Brewton (Crowell, 1965).
25. "Boa Constrictor," from *Where the Sidewalk Ends,* by Shel Silverstein. Copyright © 1974 by Snake Eye Music, Inc.

26

Two Legs Behind and Two Before

This bit of nonsense and the following one are both
American folk rhymes. The first is intended to be
sung to the tune of "Old Lang Syne."

On mules we find two legs behind,
  And two we find before;
We stand behind before we find
  What the two behind be for,
When we're behind the two behind,
  We find what these be for;
So stand before the two behind,
  And behind the two before.

27

As I Was Standing in the Street

As I was standing in the street,
  As quiet as could be,
A great big ugly man came up
  And tied his horse to me.

28

J. R. R. Tolkien

Dwarves' Song

Chip the glasses and crack the plates!
  Blunt the knives and bend the forks!
That's what Bilbo Baggins hates—
  Smash the bottles and burn the corks!

Cut the cloth and tread on the fat!
  Pour the milk on the pantry floor!
Leave the bones on the bedroom mat!
  Splash the wine on every door!

Dump the crocks in a boiling bowl;
  Pound them up with a thumping pole;
And when you're finished, if any are whole,
  Send them down the hall to roll!

That's what Bilbo Baggins hates!
So, carefully! carefully with the plates!

29

Walter de la Mare

Alas, Alack!

Ann, Ann!
  Come! Quick as you can!
There's a fish that *talks*
  In the frying-pan.
Out of the fat,
  As clear as glass,
He put up his mouth
  And moaned "Alas!"
Oh, most mournful,
  "Alas, alack!"
Then turned to his sizzling,
  And sank him back.

30

Hilaire Belloc

The Frog

Be kind and tender to the frog,
  And do not call him names,
As 'Slimy skin,' or 'Polly-wog,'
  Or likewise 'Ugly James,'
Or 'Gap-a-grin,' or 'Toad-gone-wrong,'
  Or 'Bill Bandy-knees':
The frog is justly sensitive
  To epithets like these.
No animal will more repay
  A treatment kind and fair;
At least so lonely people say
  Who keep a frog (and, by the way,
They are extremely rare.)

31

The Frog

What a wonderful bird the frog are—
When he stand he sit almost;
When he hop, he fly almost.
He ain't got no sense hardly;
He ain't got no tail hardly either.
When he sit, he sit on what he ain't got almost.

28. From J. R. R. Tolkien, *The Hobbit* (Houghton Mifflin,
1966).

29. From Walter de la Mare, *Collected Poems 1901–1918*
(Holt, 1920).
30. From Hilaire Belloc, *Cautionary Verses* (Knopf, 1931).

32

Ian Hamilton Finlay

Great Frog Race

**GREAT
FROG
RACE**
A FL
O
P

33

Ogden Nash

The Ostrich

The ostrich roams the great Sahara.
Its mouth is wide, its neck is narra.
It has such long and lofty legs,
I'm glad it sits to lay its eggs.

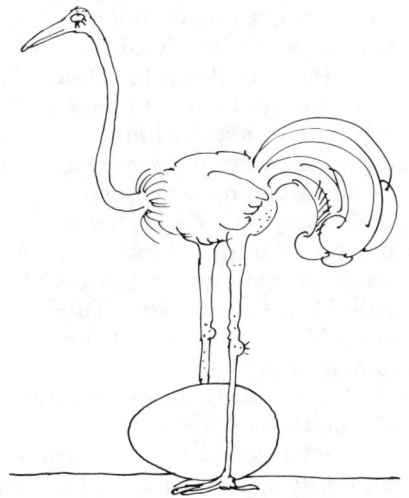

Illustration by Tomi Ungerer. From *Oh, How Silly!* poems
selected by William Cole. Illustrations copyright © 1970
by Tomi Ungerer and reprinted with his permission.

34

Jack Prelutsky

Toucans Two

whatever one toucan can do
is sooner done by toucans two
and three toucans it's very true
can do much more than two can do

and toucans numbering two plus two can
manage more than all the zoo can
in fact there is no toucan who can
do what four or three or two can.

35

Lewis Carroll

The Crocodile

How doth the little crocodile
    Improve his shining tail,
And pour the waters of the Nile
    On every golden scale!

How cheerfully he seems to grin!
    How neatly spreads his claws,
And welcomes little fishes in
    With gently smiling jaws!

36

Edward Lear

The Owl and the Pussy-Cat

The Owl and the Pussy-Cat went to sea
    In a beautiful pea-green boat:
They took some honey, and plenty of money
    Wrapped up in a five-pound note.
The Owl looked up to the stars above,
    And sang to a small guitar,
"O lovely Pussy, O Pussy, my love,
What a beautiful Pussy you are,
    You are,
    You are!
What a beautiful Pussy you are!"

32. From Ian Hamilton Finlay, *Poems to See and Hear* (Macmillan, 1971).
33. From Ogden Nash, *Verses from 1929 On* (Little, Brown, 1956).

34. From Jack Prelutsky, *Toucan Two and Other Poems* (Macmillan, 1970).
35. From Lewis Carroll, *Alice's Adventures in Wonderland* (Macmillan, 1865).

Pussy said to the Owl, "You elegant fowl,
    How charmingly sweet you sing!
Oh! let us be married; too long we have tarried:
    But what shall we do for a ring?"
They sailed away, for a year and a day,
    To the land where the bong-tree grows;
And there in a wood a Piggy-wig stood,
    With a ring at the end of his nose,
        His nose,
        His nose,
With a ring at the end of his nose.

"Dear Pig, are you willing to sell for one shilling
    Your ring?" Said the Piggy, "I will."
So they took it away, and were married next
        day
    By the Turkey who lives on the hill.
They dined on mince and slices of quince,
    Which they ate with a runcible spoon;
And hand in hand, on the edge of the sand,
    They danced by the light of the moon,
        The moon,
        The moon,
    They danced by the light of the moon.

37

David McCord

Up from Down Under

The boomerang and kangaroo
comprise a very pleasant two;
The coolibah and billabong
together make a sort of song.
But tasty as a fresh meringue
is billabong with boomerang;
and better than hooray-hoorah
is kangaroo with coolibah.

38

James Reeves

W

The King sent for his wise men all
    To find a rhyme for W;

When they had thought a good long time
But could not think of a single rhyme,
    'I'm sorry,' said he, 'to trouble you.'

39

Gelett Burgess

The Purple Cow

I never saw a Purple Cow,
    I never hope to see one;
But I can tell you, anyhow,
    I'd rather see than be one.

40

Theodore Roethke

The Serpent

There was a Serpent who had to sing.
There was. There was.
He simply gave up Serpenting.
Because. Because.
He didn't like his Kind of Life;
He couldn't find a proper Wife;
He was a Serpent with a soul;
He got no Pleasure down his Hole.
And so, of course, he had to Sing,
And Sing he did, like Anything!
The Birds, they were, they were Astounded;
And various Measures Propounded
To stop the Serpent's Awful Racket:
They bought a Drum. He wouldn't Whack it.
They sent,—you always send,—to Cuba
And got a Most Commodious Tuba;
They got a Horn, they got a Flute,
But Nothing would suit.
He said, "Look, Birds, all this is futile:
I do *not* like to Bang or Tootle."
And then he cut loose with a Horrible Note
That practically split the Top of his Throat.
"You see," he said, with a Serpent's Leer,
"I'm Serious about my Singing Career!"
And the Woods Resounded with many a Shriek
As the Birds flew off to the End of Next Week.

38. From James Reeves, *The Blackbird in the Lilac* (Heineman, 1952).
40. From Theodore Roethke, *The Collected Works of Theodore Roethke* (Doubleday, 1963).

37. From David McCord, *Take Sky* (Little, Brown, 1962).

41

Karla Kuskin

Alexander Soames: His Poems

Once upon
Upon a time
There was a child
Who spoke in rhyme.
Three tall physicians and a nurse
Have testified
That it was verse.
His hair was brown.
His height was short.
His pants were grey,
The shorter sort.
His name was Alexander Soames
And when he spoke
He spoke in poems.

The first time Alex saw a cat
He did not run,
He simply sat
And said,
"It's flat
That that's
A cat."

And when he saw a dog he said,
Scratching his small poetic head,
"The walk of a dog
Is more of a jog
And less of a dance
Than the amble of ants."

Alexander had a mother.
"Dear," she said a thousand times,
"Dear," she said to Alexander,
"Must you always speak in rhymes?
Wear your rubbers,
Wipe your nose,
Why not try
To speak in prose?"

"I prefer," said Alex Soames,
"To speak the speech I speak
In poems."

41. From Karla Kuskin, *Dogs and Dragons, Trees and Dreams* (Harper, 1980).

Alexander first walked this way.
Alexander then walked that.
"Rhyming suits me," Alex murmured,
"I suit rhyming," and he sat,
Sat and pondered,
Sat and sat.
"I will try once more," said Alex,
"I'll attempt it though I tend
To have doubts about the outcome.
Here's a simple phrase:
                    The End."

The following is an example of Alexander Soames' poems:

Rules

Do not jump on ancient uncles.
                    *
Do not yell at average mice.
                    *
Do not wear a broom to breakfast.
                    *
Do not ask a snake's advice.
                    *
Do not bathe in chocolate pudding.
                    *
Do not talk to bearded bears.
                    *
Do not smoke cigars on sofas.
                    *
Do not dance on velvet chairs.
                    *
Do not take a whale to visit
Russell's mother's cousin's yacht.
                    *
And whatever else you do do
It is better you
Do not.

42

Three Children Sliding on the Ice

Iona and Peter Opie give the earliest date of this "choice piece of drollery" as 1651, which disproves the authorship of either John Gay or Oliver Goldsmith, to whom it has been ascribed.

Three children sliding on the ice
    Upon a summer's day;

As it fell out, they all fell in,
  The rest they ran away.

Now had these children been at home,
  Or sliding on dry ground,
Ten thousand pounds to one penny
  They had not all been drowned.

You parents all that children have,
  And you that have got none,
If you would have them safe abroad,
  Pray keep them safe at home.

43

Heinrich Hoffmann

The Story of Augustus Who Would Not Have Any Soup

Augustus was a chubby lad;
Fat ruddy cheeks Augustus had:
And everybody saw with joy
The plump and hearty, healthy boy.
He ate and drank as he was told,
And never let his soup get cold.
But one day, one cold winter's day,
He screamed out "Take the soup away!
O take the nasty soup away!
I won't have any soup today."

Next day, now look, the picture shows
How lank and lean Augustus grows!
Yet, though he feels so weak and ill,
The naughty fellow cries out still
"Not any soup for me, I say:
O take the nasty soup away!
I *won't* have any soup today."

The third day comes: Oh what a sin!
To make himself so pale and thin.
Yet when the soup is put on table,
He screams, as loud as he is able,
"Not any soup for me, I say:
O take the nasty soup away!
I WON'T have any soup today."

43. From Heinrich Hoffmann, *The English Struwwelpeter; or, Pretty Stories and Funny Pictures for Little Children* (F. Volckmar, 1848). First published in Germany in 1845 under the title *Der Struwwelpeter; oder Lustige Geschichten und Drollige Bilder.*

Look at him, now the fourth day's come!
He scarcely weighs a sugar-plum;
He's like a little bit of thread,
And, on the fifth day, he was—dead!

44

Laura E. Richards

Eletelephony

Once there was an elephant,
Who tried to use the telephant—
No! No! I mean an elephone
Who tried to use the telephone—
(Dear me! I am not certain quite
That even now I've got it right.)

Howe'er it was, he got his trunk
Entangled in the telephunk;
The more he tried to get it free,
The louder buzzed the telephee—
(I fear I'd better drop the song
Of elephop and telephong!)

45

David McCord

I Want You to Meet . . .

. . . Meet Ladybug,
her little sister Sadiebug,

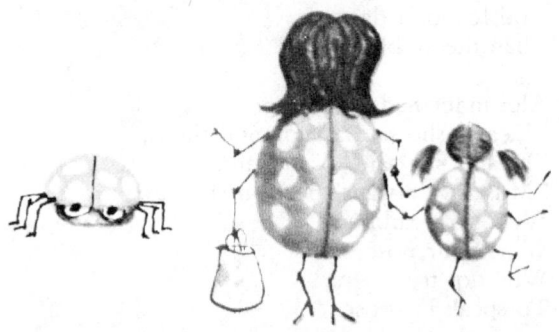

Illustration by Marc Simont. From *Every Time I Climb a Tree*, by David McCord. Reproduced by permission of Little, Brown and Co. Copyright © 1961, 1962 by David McCord.

44. From Laura E. Richards, *Tirra Lirra: Rhymes Old and New* (Little, Brown, 1955).
45. From David McCord, *Every Time I Climb a Tree*, illus. Marc Simont (Little, Brown, 1967).

her mother, Mrs. Gradybug,
her aunt, that nice oldmaidybug,
And Baby—she's a fraidybug.

46

Lewis Carroll

Jabberwocky

'Twas brillig, and the slithy toves
    Did gyre and gimble in the wabe:
All mimsy were the borogoves,
    And the mome raths outgrabe.

"Beware the Jabberwock, my son!
    The jaws that bite, the claws that catch!
Beware the Jubjub bird, and shun
    The frumious Bandersnatch!"

He took his vorpal sword in hand:
    Long time the manxome foe he sought—
So rested he by the Tumtum tree,
    And stood awhile in thought.

And, as in uffish thought he stood,
    The Jabberwock, with eyes of flame,
Came whiffing through the tulgey wood,
    And burbled as it came!

One, two! One, two! And through and through
    The vorpal blade went snicker-snack!
He left it dead, and with its head
    He went galumphing back.

"And hast thou slain the Jabberwock?
    Come to my arms, my beamish boy!
O frabjous day! Callooh! Callay!"
    He chortled in his joy.

'Twas brillig, and the slithy toves
    Did gyre and gimble in the wabe:
All mimsy were the borogoves,
    And the mome raths outgrabe.

46 and 47. From Lewis Carroll, *Through the Looking-Glass*
(Macmillan, 1871).

47

Lewis Carroll

Through the Looking-Glass

The meaning of words as nonsense is displayed in
this selection, which ends with the explanation of
"The Jabberwocky."

Humpty Dumpty and Alice

"In that case we start afresh," said Humpty
Dumpty, "and it's my turn to choose a subject—" ("He talks about it just as if it was a
game!" thought Alice.) "So here's a question
for you. How old did you say you were?"

Alice made a short calculation, and said
"Seven years and six months."

"Wrong!" Humpty Dumpty exclaimed triumphantly. "You never said a word like it!"

"I thought you meant 'How old *are* you?'"
Alice explained.

"If I'd meant that, I'd have said it," said
Humpty Dumpty.

Alice didn't want to begin another argument,
so she said nothing.

"Seven years and six months!" Humpty
Dumpty repeated thoughtfully. "An uncomfortable sort of age. Now if you'd asked *my*
advice, I'd have said 'Leave off at seven'—but
it's too late now."

"I never ask advice about growing," Alice
said indignantly.

"Too proud?" the other enquired.

Alice felt even more indignant as this suggestion. "I mean," she said, "that one can't help
growing older."

"*One* can't, perhaps," said Humpty Dumpty;
"but *two* can. With proper assistance, you might
have left off at seven."

"What a beautiful belt you've got on!" Alice
suddenly remarked. (They had had quite
enough of the subject of age, she thought: and,
if they really were to take turns in choosing
subjects, it was *her* turn now.) "At least," she
corrected herself on second thoughts, "a beautiful cravat, I should have said—no, a belt, I
mean—I beg your pardon!" she added in dismay, for Humpty Dumpty looked thoroughly
offended, and she began to wish she hadn't chosen that subject. "If only I knew," she thought

to herself, "which was neck and which was waist!"

Evidently Humpty Dumpty was very angry, though he said nothing for a minute or two. When he *did* speak again, it was in a deep growl.

"It is a—*most—provoking—*thing," he said at last, "when a person doesn't know a cravat from a belt!"

"I know it's very ignorant of me," Alice said, in so humble a tone that Humpty Dumpty relented.

"It's a cravat, child, and a beautiful one, as you say. It's a present from the White King and Queen. There now!"

"Is it really?" said Alice, quite pleased to find that she *had* chosen a good subject, after all.

"They gave it me," Humpty Dumpty continued thoughtfully, as he crossed one knee over the other and clasped his hands round it, "they gave it me—for an un-birthday present."

"I beg your pardon?" Alice said with a puzzled air.

"I'm not offended," said Humpty Dumpty.

"I mean, what *is* an un-birthday present?"

"A present given when it isn't your birthday, of course."

Alice considered a little. "I like birthday presents best," she said at last.

"You don't know what you're talking about!" cried Humpty Dumpty. "How many days are there in a year?"

"Three hundred and sixty-five," said Alice.

"And how many birthdays have you?"

"One."

"And if you take one from three hundred and sixty-five, what remains?"

"Three hundred and sixty-four, of course."

Humpty Dumpty looked doubtful. "I'd rather see that done on paper," he said.

Alice couldn't help smiling as she took out her memorandum-book, and worked the sum for him:

$$\begin{array}{r} 365 \\ 1 \\ \hline 364 \end{array}$$

Humpty Dumpty took the book, and looked at it carefully. "That seems to be done right—" he began.

"You're holding it upside down!" Alice interrupted.

"To be sure I was!" Humpty Dumpty said gaily, as she turned it round for him. "I thought it looked a little queer. As I was saying, that *seems* to be done right—though I haven't time to look it over thoroughly just now—and that shows that there are three hundred and sixty-four days when you might get un-birthday presents—"

"Certainly," said Alice.

"And only *one* for birthday presents, you know. There's glory for you!"

"I don't know what you mean by 'glory,' " Alice said.

Humpty Dumpty smiled contemptuously. "Of course you don't—till I tell you. I meant 'there's a nice knock-down argument for you!' "

"But 'glory' doesn't mean 'a nice knockdown argument,' " Alice objected.

"When *I* use a word," Humpty Dumpty said, in rather a scornful tone, "it means just what I choose it to mean—neither more nor less."

"The question is," said Alice, "whether you *can* make words mean so many different things."

"The question is," said Humpty Dumpty, "which is to be master—that's all."

Alice was too much puzzled to say anything; so after a minute Humpty Dumpty began again. "They've a temper, some of them—particularly verbs: they're the proudest—adjectives you can do anything with, but not verbs—however, *I* can manage the whole lot of them! Impenetrability! That's what *I* say!"

"Would you tell me, please." said Alice, "what that means?"

"Now you talk like a reasonable child," said Humpty Dumpty, looking very much pleased. "I meant by 'impenetrability' that we've had enough of that subject, and it would be just as well if you'd mention what you mean to do next, as I suppose you don't mean to stop here all the rest of your life."

"That's a great deal to make one word mean," Alice said in a thoughtful tone.

"When I make a word do a lot of work like that," said Humpty Dumpty, "I always pay it extra."

"Oh!" said Alice. She was too much puzzled to make any other remark.

"Ah, you should see 'em come round me of a Saturday night," Humpty Dumpty went on, wagging his head gravely from side to side, "for to get their wages, you know."

(Alice didn't venture to ask what he paid them with; and so you see I can't tell *you.*)

"You seem very clever at explaining words, Sir," said Alice. "Would you kindly tell me the meaning of the poem called 'Jabberwocky'?"

"Let's hear it," said Humpty Dumpty. "I can explain all the poems that ever were invented—and a good many that haven't been invented just yet."

This sounded very hopeful, so Alice repeated the first verse:—

"'*Twas brillig, and the slithy toves*
  Did gyre and gimble in the wabe:
All mimsy were the borogoves,
  And the mome raths outgrabe."

"That's enough to begin with," Humpty Dumpty interrupted: "there are plenty of hard words there. '*Brillig*' means four o'clock in the afternoon—the time when you begin *broiling* things for dinner."

"That'll do very well," said Alice: "and '*slithy*'?"

"Well, '*slithy*' means 'lithe and slimy.' 'Lithe' is the same as 'active.' You see it's like a portmanteau—there are two meanings packed up into one word."

"I see it now," Alice remarked thoughtfully: "and what are '*toves*'?"

"Well, '*toves*' are something like badgers—they're something like lizards—and they're something like corkscrews."

"They must be very curious-looking creatures."

"They are that," said Humpty Dumpty: "also they make their nests under sun-dials—also they live on cheese."

"And what's to '*gyre*' and to '*gimble*'?"

"To '*gyre*' is to go round and round like a gyroscope. To '*gimble*' is to make holes like a gimblet."

"And '*the wabe*' is the grass-plot round a sun-dial, I suppose?" said Alice, surprised at her own ingenuity.

"Of course it is. It's called '*wabe*,' you know, because it goes a long way before it, and a long way behind it—"

"And a long way beyond it on each side," Alice added.

"Exactly so. Well then, '*mimsy*' is 'flimsy and miserable' (there's another portmanteau for you). And a '*borogove*' is a thin shabby-looking bird with its feathers sticking out all round—something like a live mop."

"And then '*mome raths*'?" said Alice. "I'm afraid I'm giving you a great deal of trouble."

"Well, a '*rath*' is a sort of green pig: but '*mome*' I'm not certain about. I think it's short for 'from home'—meaning that they'd lost their way, you know."

"And what does '*outgrabe*' mean?"

"Well, '*outgribing*' is something between bellowing and whistling, with a kind of sneeze in the middle: however, you'll hear it done, maybe—down in the wood yonder—and, when you've once heard it, you'll be *quite* content. Who's been repeating all that hard stuff to you?"

"I read it in a book," said Alice. "But I *had* some poetry repeated to me much easier than that, by—Tweedledee, I think it was."

"As to poetry, you know," said Humpty Dumpty, stretching out one of his great hands, "*I* can repeat poetry as well as other folk, if it comes to that—"

"Oh, it needn't come to that!" Alice hastily said, hoping to keep him from beginning.

48

John Updike

Recital

Roger Bobo Gives Recital on Tuba
          —HEADLINE IN THE *TIMES*

Eskimos in Manitoba,
  Barracuda off Aruba,
Cock an ear when Roger Bobo
  Starts to solo on the tuba.

Men of every station—Pooh-Bah,
  Nabob, bozo, toff, and hobo—

48. From John Updike, *Telephone Poles and Other Poems* (Knopf, 1961).

Cry in unison, "Indubi-
  Tably, there is simply nobo-

Dy who oompahs on the tubo,
Solo, quite like Roger Bubo!"

49

Lewis Carroll

The Walrus and the Carpenter

The sun was shining on the sea,
  Shining with all his might;
He did his very best to make
  The billows smooth and bright—
And this was odd, because it was
  The middle of the night.

The moon was shining sulkily,
  Because she thought the sun
Had got no business to be there
  After the day was done—
"It's very rude of him," she said,
  "To come and spoil the fun!"

The sea was wet as wet could be,
  The sands were dry as dry.
You could not see a cloud, because
  No cloud was in the sky;
No birds were flying overhead—
  There were no birds to fly.

The Walrus and the Carpenter
  Were walking close at hand;
They wept like anything to see
  Such quantities of sand—
"If this were only cleared away,"
  They said, "it would be grand!"

"If seven maids with seven mops
  Swept it for half a year,
Do you suppose," the Walrus said,
  "That they could get it clear?"
"I doubt it," said the Carpenter,
  And shed a bitter tear.

"O Oysters, come and walk with us!"
  The Walrus did beseech.

49. From Lewis Carroll, *Through the Looking-Glass* (Macmillan, 1871).

"A pleasant walk, a pleasant talk,
  Along the briny beach;
We cannot do with more than four,
  To give a hand to each."

The eldest Oyster looked at him,
  But never a word he said;
The eldest Oyster winked his eye,
  And shook his heavy head—
Meaning to say he did not choose
  To leave the oyster-bed.

But four young Oysters hurried up,
  All eager for the treat;
Their coats were brushed, their faces washed,
  Their shoes were clean and neat—
And this was odd, because, you know,
  They hadn't any feet.

Four other Oysters followed them,
  And yet another four;
And thick and fast they came at last,
  And more, and more, and more—
All hopping through the frothy waves,
  And scrambling to the shore.

The Walrus and the Carpenter
  Walked on a mile or so,
And then they rested on a rock
  Conveniently low—
And all the little Oysters stood
  And waited in a row.

"The time has come," the Walrus said,
  "To talk of many things:
Of shoes—and ships—and sealing-wax—
  Of cabbages—and kings—
And why the sea is boiling hot—
  And whether pigs have wings."

"But wait a bit," the Oysters cried,
  "Before we have our chat;
For some of us are out of breath,
  And all of us are fat!"
"No hurry!" said the Carpenter.
  They thanked him much for that.

"A loaf of bread," the Walrus said,
  "Is what we chiefly need;

Pepper and vinegar besides
 Are very good indeed—
Now, if you're ready, Oysters dear,
 We can begin to feed."

"But not on us!" the Oysters cried,
 Turning a little blue.
"After such kindness, that would be
 A dismal thing to do!"
"The night is fine," the Walrus said.
 "Do you admire the view?

"It was so kind of you to come!
 And you are very nice!"
The Carpenter said nothing but,
 "Cut us another slice.
I wish you were not quite so deaf—
 I've had to ask you twice!"

"It seems a shame," the Walrus said,
 "To play them such a trick.
After we've brought them out so far,
 And made them trot so quick!"
The Carpenter said nothing but,
 "The butter's spread too thick!"

"I weep for you," the Walrus said;
 "I deeply sympathize."
With sobs and tears he sorted out
 Those of the largest size,
Holding his pocket-handkerchief
 Before his streaming eyes.

"O Oysters," said the Carpenter,
 "You've had a pleasant run!
Shall we be trotting home again?"
 But answer came there none—
And this was scarcely odd, because
 They'd eaten every one.

50

Edward Lear

The Jumblies

They went to sea in a sieve, they did;
 In a sieve they went to sea;

In spite of all their friends could say,
On a winter's morn, on a stormy day,
 In a sieve they went to sea.

And when the sieve turned round and round,
And every one cried, "You'll all be drowned!"
They called aloud, "Our sieve ain't big;
But we don't care a button, we don't care a
 fig:
 In a sieve we'll go to sea!"
 Far and few, far and few,
 Are the lands where the Jumblies live:
 Their heads are green, and their hands are
 blue;
 And they went to sea in a sieve.

They sailed away in a sieve, they did,
 In a sieve they sailed so fast,
With only a beautiful pea-green veil
Tied with a ribbon, by way of a sail,
 To a small tobacco-pipe mast.
And every one said who saw them go,
"Oh! won't they be soon upset, you know?
For the sky is dark, and the voyage is long;
And happen what may, it's extremely wrong
 In a sieve to sail so fast."
 Far and few, far and few,
 Are the lands where the Jumblies live:
 Their heads are green, and their hands are
 blue;
 And they went to sea in a sieve.

The water it soon came in, it did;
 The water it soon came in:
So, to keep them dry, they wrapped their feet
In a pinky paper all folded neat;
 And they fastened it down with a pin.
And they passed the night in a crockery-jar;
And each of them said, "How wise we are!
Though the sky be dark, and the voyage be
 long,
Yet we never can think we were rash or wrong,
 While round in our sieve we spin."
 Far and few, far and few,
 Are the lands where the Jumblies live:
 Their heads are green, and their hands are
 blue;
 And they went to sea in a sieve.

And all night long they sailed away;
  And when the sun went down,
They whistled and warbled a moony song
To the echoing sound of a coppery gong,
  In the shade of the mountains brown.
"O Timballoo! How happy we are
When we live in a sieve and a crockery-jar!
And all night long, in the moonlight pale,
We sail away with a pea-green sail
  In the shade of the mountains brown."
    Far and few, far and few,
      Are the lands where the Jumblies live:
      Their heads are green, and their hands are
        blue;
      And they went to sea in a sieve.

They sailed to the Western Sea, they did,—
  To a land all covered with trees:
And they bought an owl, and a useful cart,
And a pound of rice, and a cranberry-tart,
  And a hive of silvery bees;
And they bought a pig, and some green jack-
    daws,
And a lovely monkey with lollipop paws,
And forty bottles of ring-bo-ree,
  And no end of Stilton cheese.
    Far and few, far and few,
      Are the lands where the Jumblies live:
      Their heads are green, and their hands are
        blue;
      And they went to sea in a sieve.

And in twenty years they all came back,—
  In twenty years or more;
And every one said, "How tall they've grown!
For they've been to the Lakes, and the Torrible
    Zone,
  And the hills of the Chankly Bore."
And they drank their health, and gave them a
    feast
Of dumplings made of beautiful yeast;
And every one said, "If we only live,
We, too, will go to sea in a sieve,
  To the hills of the Chankly Bore."
    Far and few, far and few,
      Are the lands where the Jumblies live:
      Their heads are green, and their hands are
        blue;
      And they went to sea in a sieve.

51

Alastair Reid

What Is a Tingle-Airey?

A *tingle-airey* is a hand organ, usually
  played on the street by the turning of
  a handle, and often decorated
    with mother-of-pearl or
    piddock shells.

What are Piddocks?

  Piddocks are little mollusks
which bore holes in rocks and wood,
or in the *breastsummers* of buildings.

What Is a Breastsummer?

A *breastsummer* is a great beam
supporting the weight of a wall,
  and sometimes of a
    gazebo above.

What Is a Gazebo?

A *gazebo* is a round balcony with
  large windows looking out on
  a view, often of ornamental
  gardens and *cotoneasters.*

What Is a Cotoneaster?

A *cotoneaster* is a kind of
flowering shrub, a favorite
  of *mumruffins.*

What Is a Mumruffin?

A *mumruffin* is a long-tailed tit which often visits
  bird tables in winter for its share of *pobbies.*

What Are Pobbies?

Pobbies are small pieces of bread *thrumbled* up
  with
  milk and fed to birds and baby animals.

51. From Alastair Reid, *Ounce, Dice, Trice* (Little, Brown, 1958).

What Is Thrumbled?

Thrumbled is squashed together. Ants thrumble
round a piece of bread, and crowds
in streets thrumble round *gongoozlers.*

What Is a Gongoozler?

A *gongoozler* is an idle person who
is always stopping in the street
and staring at a curious object
like a *tingle-airey.*

Illustration by Ben Shahn. From *Ounce, Dice, Trice,* by Alas-
tair Reid. Drawings by Ben Shahn, by permission of Little,
Brown and Co., in association with The Atlantic Monthly
Press. Copyright © 1958 by Alastair Reid and Ben Shahn.

Blessèd Lord, what it is to be young:
To be of, to be for, be among—
    Be enchanted, enthralled,
    Be the caller, the called,
The singer, the song, and the sung.[1]

3   Voices of Childhood

P oets have played with language since the dawn of time, carefully choosing
words for their quality of sound, meaning, and musical rhythm to create
what may loosely be grouped under the name of poetry: mythmaking
tribal chants; lullabies; sea chanties; epics, ballads, and folk songs; nursery
rhymes; dramatic, nonsense, and lyric verse; and, most recently, free forms including projective and free verse and concrete and found poetry. All these are identifiable through form or content, but poetry itself remains an enigma. No single
definition of poetry has ever been found to satisfy readers, poets, or critics.
Walter de la Mare notes: "That is one of the pleasures of reading—you may
make any picture out of the words you can and will; and a poem may have as
many different meanings as there are different minds."[2]

Poetry has been described in terms of structure, figurative imagery, musicality,
concentration of language, intensity of emotion and imagination, and the splinter-
ing and reshaping of human experience. It has been suggested that poetry is
recognizable by instinct, that it elicits certain primal, physiological responses in
the reader. "It makes me shiver," says the chipmunk about poetry in Randall

1. David McCord, *One at a Time* (Little, Brown, 1974), p. ix. Copyright © 1962 by David McCord.
By permission of Little, Brown and Company.
2. Walter de la Mare, "The Story of This Book," in *Come Hither: A Collection of Rhymes and Poems
for the Young of All Ages,* 3d ed. (Constable, 1960), pp. xxvii–xxviii.

88

Jarrell's *The Bat-Poet* (1964), a parable on the nature of the poet and the creation of poetry: "Why do I like it if it makes me shiver?"

Children respond immediately, it seems instinctively, to the language of poetry; in the words Robert Frost used to describe his own childhood introduction to the art, they are "caught up in its catchiness." If children are lucky enough to have heard lullabies, nursery rhymes, and folk songs, to have played to the accompaniment of street and game chants, then they come to the forms of poetry with a firm grasp of its bare bones—rhyme, rhythm, meter, and the *singingness* of language. They are ready to experience what Northrop Frye in *The Well-Tempered Critic* (1963) describes as "the sense of wit and heightened intelligence, resulting from seeing disciplined words marching along in metrical patterns and in their inevitable right order." They are ready to discover that words have structure as well as meaning and that stressed and unstressed syllables, set in a pattern of the poet's devising, call the measure of the poem and determine the swing and fall of cadences. Then there is left only children's introduction to the inexhaustible storehouse filled over the centuries by the poets who crafted language with skill and precision.

How can adults assist children in discovering poetry? The ideal way to experience poetry is intuitively, as children do when they are given the opportunity. A knowledge of the techniques poets choose, of the connotations and denotations of words, of the naming of parts—these add another dimension for those who already delight in poetry. (And they can provide aid and anchor for conscientious adults who have not been "caught up in catchiness.") Well before prose becomes the accepted language of reality and purpose, children approach poetry as oral, living music. To give poetry to children, return it to its original and intuitive form: Read it aloud; celebrate it spontaneously and joyously. Children already know the language of rhythm. Never mind the meaning; that discovery will come later. As T. S. Eliot says, "Poetry can communicate before it is understood."[3] Never ask questions. Never explain the words, unless urged to do so by the children themselves. Never consider the *use* of the poem as the first reason for choosing it. And do not read poetry only to children, but read it for yourself as well.

What poetry to read? Here, one quickly encounters the nagging issue of the distinction between adult and children's literature. Is poetry for children a separate territory, or is poetry simply itself, existing to be shared by children and adults alike? Does children's poetry really require a simplification of style and subject matter because of childhood's limited experience? Despite attempts by well-intentioned adults to construct barricades, children continue to seek out poetry, whether labeled children's or adult, that kindles imagination. Perhaps it is the ongoing development of that imagination, along with an intuitive response to emotion, that enables children to take delight in poetry far beyond their conscious understanding. Certainly the full impact of poetry that deals with experience particular to the adult world escapes children; nevertheless, they take what they desire from poetry, leaving the rest until some later time. Authentic poetry operates on many levels, offering aspects of itself to readers of whatever age.

Children respond to poets who perceive the world with the vibrant curiosity and wonder that is natural to childhood. Indeed, many poets have claimed that the impulse behind their work is to recall something left behind in childhood—

3. Quoted in J. Isaacs, *The Background of Modern Poetry* (G. Bell, 1951), p. 59.

a sense of direct living, of unity, of the joy in constant discovery—going far beyond mere nostalgia. Much of the work of William Blake, Walter de la Mare, and David McCord expresses this intense emotion in vivid and wholly realized poetry aimed at children. Often the result of a combination of disciplined art and creative play, this poetry keeps alive the intense memories of childhood in poetry suffused with respect for children's intelligence, imagination, and perceptions. Not a nostalgic reminiscence about childhood for adults, it is rather a celebration of childhood—as gritty and stimulating as it is—for all children.

The questionable category of children's verse, a poor cousin of children's poetry, has always threatened, through sheer quantity and numbing mediocrity, to drown out the music and delight in authentic children's poetry. All too often children are given condescending, sentimental verse that is flawed in language, awkward in rhythm, and labored in rhyme because adults underestimate their capacity for responding to fine poetry. The choice of a nostalgic tone is one of the most common pitfalls in writing children's poetry; it leads too easily to a cheaply sentimental romanticization of childhood. Equally dangerous is the tendency toward bombast, didacticism, patronizing moralism, or simply shoddy entertainment. This is not to say that children's poetry must be only lofty, so-called high poetry, as distinct from popular or light verse. One does not expect the insight of lyric poetry in a light-hearted jingle, which has its own, quite different, values.

For children, the transition from the folk poetry of nursery rhymes, game lore, and folk songs to the original and literary writings of children's poets generally follows a distinct pattern of development. It begins with the irrational musical play of nonsense verse; moves on to the stylistic virtuosity and geniality of humorous and light verse; proceeds through the dramatic suspense of narrative poetry (whether epic, ballad, or modern story-poem); and finally arrives at the melodic intensity and insight of lyric poetry. This pattern of growth in a child's appreciation of poetry parallels the history of children's poetry. Like children's literature in general, children's poetry has existed in any quantity only for the last two hundred years. Prior to the seventeenth century, poetry addressed specifically to children was didactic, offering advice and counsel on earthly behavior. With the advent of Puritanism, concern for children's spiritual education became evident in the poetry written for them. Except for a number of Isaac Watts's hymns, a few poems by the Taylor sisters, and William Blake's joyous lyrics, little poetry of merit survives from earlier eras.

Curiously, it was the staid Victorian period that first produced, in the lunacy of nonsense verse, a canon of memorable work. Carroll's and Lear's secular and playful verses were a reaction to the sentimental morality of most verse then available for children. A second strain of children's poetry developed in the domestic lyrics and light verses of Christina Rossetti, Robert Louis Stevenson, and A. A. Milne. Their work reflected a new awareness of childhood as a sphere apart from the adult world, and it capitalized on children's interest in their own day-to-day lives and activities. Rossetti's poetry in *Sing Song* (1871) conveys an appreciation, reminiscent of haiku, of the tiny details of nature and emotion that occupy the young child.

Stevenson's empathy with children's thoughts and feelings and his ability to recall the immediacy of childhood experience enrich his energetic and tuneful poetry in *A Child's Garden of Verses* (1885). So pervasive was Stevenson's influence that a host of children's poets copied his mannerisms, failing to capture his essence.

From the work of Eugene Field and James Whitcomb Riley in Stevenson's own time, to that of innumerable imitators in the early half of the twentieth century, children's poetry mimicked that of Stevenson. Even A. A. Milne's poetry in *When We Were Very Young* (1924) and *Now We Are Six* (1927) is similar to Stevenson's in the description of nursery life and in the use of the natural speaking voice of the egocentric solitary child. Milne's individual talent lies in his comic delight in word play and witty rhyme and his skill with metric patterns.

Most early twentieth-century children's poets imitated these writers, until the emergence of Walter de la Mare's fresh and original talent. De la Mare's roots go back to Blake's intense lyricism, and a profound identification with children illuminates his work. The poems in his *Peacock Pie* (1913) and other collections range from wry nonsense and brightly colored nursery verse to enigmatic narratives and poignant lyrics. The richly varied forms created by de la Mare provide a touchstone for evaluating all children's poetry.

With the exception of de la Mare's work, the children's poetry of the first half of the twentieth century was marked by conservatism and the continuation of the traditional—much more so than, for example, the children's novel. Of the poets of this period, only a select few, such as Eleanor Farjeon, Rachel Field, Elizabeth Madox Roberts, and Elizabeth Coatsworth, produced memorable work. Most poets, parents, and educators, it would seem, were quick to assume that children are conservative in their poetic taste, despite the varied and individualistic responses of children to diverse forms of poetry.

This theory of intrinsic conservatism was exploded by the poets of the 1960s and 1970s, primarily Americans, who set out to explore subjects and styles reflecting the realities of their own era. The new poets aligned themselves with the beats and such sixties poets as Allen Ginsburg, Lawrence Ferlinghetti, and LeRoi Jones, and so allied themselves to rock music and social protest. As in other genres of children's literature, particularly the realistic novel, children's poets now wrote of social and emotional concerns: anxiety, alienation, racial and social injustice, war, technological overload, and the dangers of urban life.

In the best of the sociological poetry—for example, the works of Eve Merriam and Robert Froman—this naturalism is tempered with satire and humor. In *Finding a Poem* (1970) and *Rainbow Writing* (1976), Merriam's dexterous handling of metered verse, free verse, and verbal nonsense is allied with social satire and a fierce conscience. Her subjects and concerns are strikingly contemporary.

Ann Terry's research study of children's responses to poetry in *Children's Poetry Preferences: A National Survey of Upper Elementary Grades* (1974) demonstrates that children respond more favorably to contemporary than to traditional poems, especially those that deal with enjoyable, familiar experiences. Sophisticated urban poetry written by contemporary poets such as Merriam, Lilian Moore, Marci Ridlon, Bobbi Katz, Patricia Hubbell, and Lillian Morrison interprets a city child's environment and full range of daily experiences—from details of beauty and humor to ambivalences and ambiguities.

The poets writing of the child's immediate world now portray a broad range of life experiences and diverse social and cultural groups. Closer in spirit to Stevenson than to the pop sociology of Merriam or Froman, many of these poets mix nonsense and light verse with poetry of a more serious lyric and narrative power in an attempt to speak from the center of the child's everyday and imaginative worlds. Poets such as Karla Kuskin, Kaye Starbird, Mary Ann Hoberman, David McCord, and Myra Cohn Livingston evoke the sensibilities of childhood.

Livingston's collections, including *The Malibu and Other Poems* (1972) and *No Way of Knowing: Dallas Poems* (1980), are rich with droll, musical verses that reflect, in a variety of styles, children's active and sensuous lives.

Within the new realism is a new cultural pluralism. Numerous poets write with specific ethnic and national focuses, speaking with their own authentic cultural voices. This significant growth of the regional voice, and the concomitant translation of poetry from other languages and cultures into English, is shared with adult poetry by writers such as James Dickey, James Wright, and W. S. Merwin. Especially absorbing are the numerous poets, preceded in the 1950s by Gwendolyn Brooks and typified by June Jordan, Nikki Giovanni, and Lucille Clifton, who articulate the black American experience for the young.

Traditional subject matter is still treated, but now with a recognition of the social concerns and sophistication of today's children. For example, the blithe interpreters of nature have been displaced by those who explore their subject with a greater seriousness, even probing the darker side of existence. One such poet is Ted Hughes, who reveals his lyrical but stark vision in *Season Songs* (1976). As vividly involved in the natural world as Thoreau, Hughes carefully describes his experiences and observations of the passing of the seasons, of animals, and of the changing earth. But unlike traditional nature lyrics, his work also explores the desperate, predatory side of the wild world with a dispassionate eye. Poets who continue to celebrate nature for children in a more traditional vein include John Updike, Aileen Fisher, and Harry Behn.

Of all the traditional poetic forms, narrative verse has changed the least, following still the patterns of such classic story-poets as Robert Browning, Clement Clarke Moore, and Alfred Noyes. The varieties of narrative poetry continue to attract poets, many of them British. Ian Serraillier, in retelling medieval ballads and romances such as *The Challenge of the Green Knight* (1966) and *Robin in the Greenwood* (1967), retains a vigorous pace and, with dramatic character and costume, captures an authentic medieval tone in modern diction. Writing with a contemporary nakedness of speech is Charles Causley, whose literary ballads have a romantic Cornish flavor. The American poets Kaye Starbird and Karla Kuskin excel in the humorous story-poem.

Inevitably, new themes are paralleled by new styles. Children's poets have adopted the stylistic flexibility and experimentation with form of twentieth-century adult poetry, but their work nonetheless remains at least a generation behind contemporary adult writing. The most innovative adult poetry of the last two decades has centered on structuralism and aesthetics, working in a complex intellectual and meditative vein characterized by the works of Samuel Beckett, Paul Eluard, and René Char, and by New York School poets such as John Ashbery and Frank O'Hara. Their emphasis on introspective abstraction is simply inappropriate as an influence on children's poetry.

A more fruitful resource has been the poetry of colloquial, idiomatic speech developed by Walt Whitman, W. B. Yeats, W. H. Auden, and William Carlos Williams. Their intense exploration of language is visible in the work for children by poets such as John Ciardi, June Jordan, Ted Hughes, and Theodore Roethke—all of whom, significantly, have also written poetry for adults. They are searching for a natural, illuminating imagery and an intimate common speech as expressed through metered, free, and projective verse. This quest for a spoken language is accompanied by a return to the oral tradition—to poems that are made to be spoken aloud rather than to remain mute and fixed on the printed page.

Other practitioners of stylistic change, whose work involves a more spontaneous improvisation of forms, include May Swenson, David McCord, Eve Merriam, and Robert Froman. Recognizing that children are not bound rigidly to neat, regular meter and rhyme, they have shared with them delight in the playful visual, aural, and intellectual concepts of shaped verse, concrete poetry, found poetry, and a host of collage and typographical verse forms.

Like the modern picture book, poetry for the very young is proliferating. Young children's natural love of rhythm and rhyme make them irresistible targets, and poets and illustrators have blended their talents to create a new genre, the poetry picture book. There has always been poetic prose in picture books, but never before have so many skilled poets—Elizabeth Coatsworth, Aileen Fisher, Jack Prelutsky, Karla Kuskin, Arnold Adoff, Lucille Clifton, Norma Farber— involved themselves in the picture-book genre. The phenomenal growth in the publication of single illustrated poems and collections of poetry in picture-book format presents a very real threat of overillustration, which can strip the power of imagination and detract from the poem's innate images. But generally, illustrators have resisted using the format as a mere vehicle for their artwork, and have offered significant illumination of the poet's words.

On the whole, the subject matter and style in works for younger children remain traditional. Examples are *Catch Me and Kiss Me and Say It Again* (1978) and *Father Fox's Pennyrhymes* (1971), by Clyde Watson, both evocative of tradi- tional Mother Goose and game rhymes. The latter collection of short, spicy verses reflects the spirit of American folk culture amid the changing beauty of the Vermont countryside.

The presence of so many adult poets such as Randall Jarrell, Charles Causley, and Theodore Roethke in the province of children's poetry is strong evidence that it has come of age, that it is now sophisticated, noticeably complex, controver- sial, and experimental. The distinction between adult and children's poetry is no longer as sharp as it once was. More poetry written primarily for adults is used in children's anthologies, and many books of poetry (among them Ted Hughes's *Season Songs*), may be published for children and still have an ardent adult audience. Moreover, a growing faith in the ability of children to appreciate mature poetry has persuaded publishers to issue adult poetry that has been edited for children, to serve as enticing introductions to the complete works of poets such as Robert Frost, Carl Sandburg, and Langston Hughes.

In earlier days, adult poetry was available to children primarily through selec- tions in general anthologies. With the new abundance of poetry publications, it is significant that the anthology still retains its popularity. Anthologies for children, those "gatherings of flowers," are overwhelming in their sheer number. Some few excellent ones convey distinctive textures, tones, and original points of view; but an equal number of bland, eclectic collections pad real poetry with pap.

Enduring treasuries include those edited by Andrew Lang, Kenneth Grahame, Herbert Read, Louise Bogan, and William Jay Smith. Overshadowing all other anthologies, past and present, is Walter de la Mare's evergreen *Come Hither* (1923). Every page is filled with de la Mare's exuberant commitment to poetry, and the generosity of his mind spills over into notes, references, and cross-refer- ences that are eloquent testimony to the extent of his reading.

Traditional anthologies—general encyclopedic collections similar in structure to standard titles from the past—still abound. Recognizable by their chronological treatment and concentrating on the high spots of children's poetry, they are often entertaining. An example is Iona and Peter Opie's *The Oxford Book of Children's Verse* (1973). Another kind of overview is Jack Prelutsky's splendid *The Random House Book of Poetry for Children: A Treasury of Five Hundred and Seventy-two Poems for Today's Child* (1983), selected with the intent to create a comprehensive anthology of enjoyable, accessible poems. In addition, many anthologies concentrate on a theme, as does the collection of love poems, *One Little Room, An Everywhere* (1975), edited by Myra Cohn Livingston; on a poetic genre, such as the ballads in Helen Plotz's *As I Walked Out One Evening: A Book of Ballads* (1976); on a national identity, as in *The Wind Has Wings: Poems from Canada* (1968), edited by Mary Alice Downie and Barbara Robertson; or on a cultural or ethnic identity, as in *Black Out Loud* (1970), edited by Arnold Adoff.

Paralleling the modern realistic children's novel, many of the collections emphasize bold, colloquial, and experimental language, such as is found in *Reflections on a Gift of Watermelon Pickle . . . and Other Modern Verse* (1967), compiled by Stephen Dunning and others. The intoxicating and tragic experiences of urban life are depicted in collections such as *A Song in Stone: City Poems* (1983), selected by Lee Bennett Hopkins. Just as prehistoric life is explored in contemporary historical fiction for children, primitive poetry for children is abundantly anthologized; one anthology, *Out of the Earth I Sing: Poetry and Songs of Primitive Peoples of the World* (1968), compiled by Richard Lewis, returns children's attention to the primal dream roots of poetry from the sometimes ironic, self-conscious, and cerebral verse being written for them today.

Children's own poetry has been recognized as never before. There has been a growing movement in the schools and libraries to bring children together not only to read poetry, but also to write it. Kenneth Koch's inventive work in this field is described in *Wishes, Lies, and Dreams: Teaching Children to Write Poetry* (1971) and its companion volume, *Rose, Where Did You Get That Red?* (1973). Myra Cohn Livingston recommends a more disciplined method in her *When You Are Alone/It Keeps You Capone: An Approach to Creative Writing for Children* (1973). Beginning with the pioneer work *Miracles: Poems by Children of the English-Speaking World* (1966), compiled by Richard Lewis, volumes of children's work have been enthusiastically received. Although much of that poetry has not been worthy of the acclaim, it definitely has therapeutic value for children, providing them with an experience of language enrichment and an insight into the creative joy involved in self-expression; it also provides adults with insight into children's thoughts and emotions. The best of the poetry children write reveals a fluid play with language, a depth of emotion and imagination, and an uncanny ability to achieve, without practiced technique, natural poetic effects such as those of Randall Jarrell's self-taught bat-poet who "just made it like holding your breath."

Some of the poetry written by children today seems a far cry from the primarily lyric and nature images of *Miracles,* and even farther from the exuberant street and game rhymes that are part of childhood's oral tradition. While still brash and startling in language, its subject matter may be the misery, anger, and courage of ghetto and minority life in the inner city—not surprisingly paralleling that of adult poetry for children. Poems in *I Heard a Scream in the Street: Poetry by Young People in the City* (1970), selected by Nancy Larrick, range from those with a musing, introspective tone to those with a stronger, more muscular language and challenging spirit. The emotions of another ghetto are chronicled in *I Never*

Saw Another Butterfly: Children's Drawings and Poems from Terezin Concentration Camp, 1942–1944 (1964), translated from the Czech. Like Anne Frank's diary, this collection is a gripping testimony of children's capacity for courage, endurance, and compassion.

Lately, on both sides of the Atlantic, more serious attention has been given to poetry for children. In 1977, the National Council of Teachers of English Award for Excellence in Poetry for Children was established. In 1979, *Signal: Approaches to Children's Books,* the excellent British critical journal on children's literature, established its annual Signal Poetry Award. And in 1982, the Newbery Medal for the most distinguished contribution to literature for children published during the preceding year was given, for the first time, to a book of poetry: Nancy Willard's imaginative tour de force, *A Visit to William Blake's Inn: Poems for Innocent and Experienced Travellers* (1981). Its illustrations, by Alice and Martin Provensen, are fine examples of the successful integration of art and poetry.

Having followed the unfolding pattern of the tradition of children's poetry this far, it is intriguing to speculate on its future. Ian Serraillier sees a changing role for children's poetry, a shift from the printed page and a return to the oral tradition through the electronic media of radio and television. He writes:

All art forms, if they are to survive, must adapt to new conditions, and poetry is no exception. If . . . this is to mean some measure of escape from the printed page, that is no bad thing: it may again come closer to its origins—in song and dance and the spoken word. . . . As for the children's poet, he too has a role to play, a wider one than in the past. If he's still around in the distant future, whatever the outward changes, he will probably still be a curious mixture of creator, interpreter and craftsman.[4]

Poetry written for children has never before been so much a part of poetry in general as it is now; poets and parents, along with critics and educators, have finally put into practice the belief that there is no rigid line between adult and children's poetry, but that there is, rather, a broad middle stream that may be shared by children and adults alike.

Although some contemporary poets for children suffer from an undistinguished use of language and lack of significant or original themes, the majority speak energetically, with distinctive voices. Children's poetry stirs children with the power of words; it expands their abilities to imagine, to think, to feel. Modern children's poetry can hold its own with the tantalizing, original thought and glorious language that made the best of early children's poetry memorable and quotable.

Today, the old and the new exist side by side, nourishing each other. Differences of voice, emotion, technique, and perspective enrich the chorus that is children's poetry. Listening to this chorus, children hear authentic human voices speaking—addressing them—with the greatest degree of intimacy and emotional freedom.

4. Ian Serraillier, "Poetry Mosaic: Some Reflections on Writing Verse for Children," in *The Thorny Paradise: Writers on Writing for Children,* ed. Edward Blishen (Kestrel, 1975), p. 102.

The Voice of the Storyteller

Traditional Ballads

I

Get Up and Bar the Door

It fell about the Martinmas time,*
And a gay time it was then,
When our goodwife got puddings to make,
And she's boil'd them in the pan.

The wind sae cold blew south and north,
And blew into the floor;
Quoth our goodman to our goodwife,
"Gae out and bar the door."

"My hand is in my hussyfskap,
Goodman, as ye may see;
An' it shouldna be barr'd this hundred year,
It's no be barr'd for me."

They made a paction† 'tween them two,
They made it firm and sure,
That the first word who'er should speak
Should rise and bar the door.

Then by there came two gentlemen,
At twelve o'clock at night,
And they could neither see house nor hall,
Nor coal nor candle-light.

"Now whether is this a rich man's house,
Or whether is it a poor?"
But ne'er a word would one o' them speak,
For barring of the door.

And first they ate the white puddings,
And then they ate the black.
Tho' muckle‡ thought the goodwife to hersel'
Yet ne'er a word she spake.

Then said the one unto the other,
"Here, man, take ye my knife;

* Martinmas time: early November
† paction: an agreement
‡ muckle: much

Do ye take off the old man's beard,
And I'll kiss the goodwife."

"But there's no water in the house,
And what shall we do then?"
What ails ye at the pudding-broo,§
That boils into the pan?"

O up then started our goodman,
An angry man was he:
"Will ye kiss my wife before my eye
And scald me wi' pudding-bree?"

Then up and started our goodwife,
Gied three skips on the floor:
"Goodman, you've spoken the foremost word!
Get up and bar the door."

2

Robin Hood and The Bishop of Hereford

Come, Gentlemen all, and listen a while;
A story I'll to you unfold—
How Robin Hood served the Bishop,
When he robb'd him of his gold.

As it befell in merry Barnsdale,
And under the green-wood tree,
The Bishop of Hereford was to come by,
With all his companye.

"Come, kill a ven'son," said bold Robin Hood,
"Come, kill me a good fat deer;
The Bishop's to dine with me today,
And he shall pay well for his cheer."

"We'll kill a fat ven'son," said bold Robin
    Hood,
"And dress't by the highway-side,
And narrowly watch for the Bishop,
Lest some other way he should ride."

He dress'd himself up in shepherd's attire,
With six of his men also;
And the Bishop of Hereford came thereby,
As about the fire they did go.

§ broo, bree: broth

"What matter is this?" said the Bishop;
"Or for whom do you make this a-do?
Or why do you kill the King's ven'son,
When your company is so few?"

"We are shepherds," said bold Robin Hood,
"And we keep sheep all the year;
And we are disposed to be merry this day,
And to kill of the King's fat deer."

"You are brave fellowes," said the Bishop,
"And the King of your doings shall know;
Therefore make haste, come along with me,
For before the King you shall go."

"O pardon, O pardon," says bold Robin Hood,
"O pardon, I thee pray!
For it never becomes your lordship's coat
To take so many lives away."

"No pardon, no pardon!" the Bishop says;
"No pardon I thee owe;
Therefore make haste, come along with me,
For before the King you shall go."

Robin set his back against a tree,
And his foot against a thorn,
And from underneath his shepherd's coat,
He pull'd out a bugle horn.

He put the little end to his mouth,
And a loud blast he did blow,
Till threescore and ten of Robin's bold men,
Came running all on a row;

All making obeisance to bold Robin Hood;
'Twas a comely sight for to see;
"What matter, my master," said Little
  John,
"That you blow so hastilye?"—

"O here is the Bishop of Hereford,
And no pardon we shall have."—
"Cut off his head, master," said Little
  John,
"And throw him into his grave."—

"O pardon, O pardon," said the Bishop,
"O pardon, I thee pray!

For if I had known it had been you,
I'd have gone some other way."—

"No pardon, no pardon!" said Robin Hood;
"No pardon I thee owe;
Therefore make haste, come along with me,
For to merry Barnsdale you shall go."

Then Robin has taken the Bishop's hand
And led him to merry Barnsdale;
He made him to stay and sup with him that
  night,
And to drink wine, beer and ale.

"Call in the reckoning," said the Bishop,
"For methinks it grows wondrous high,"—
"Lend me your purse, Bishop," said Little John,
"And I'll tell you by-and-by."

Then Little John took the Bishop's cloak,
And spread it upon the ground,
And out of the Bishop's portmanteau
He told three hundred pound.

"So now let him go," said Robin Hood.
Said Little John, "That may not be;
For I vow and protest he shall sing us a mass
Before that he go from me."

Robin Hood took the Bishop by the hand,
And bound him fast to a tree,
And made him to sing a mass, God wot,
To him and his yeomandrye.

Then Robin Hood brought him through the
  wood
And caused the music to play,
And he made the Bishop to dance in his boots,
And they set him on 's dapple-grey,
And they gave the tail within his hand—
And glad he could so get away.

3

Sir Patrick Spens

The king sits in Dunfermline town.
  Drinking the blood-red wine:
"O where will I get a skeely skipper
  To sail this new ship of mine?"

O up and spake an eldern knight,
  Sate at the king's right knee—
"Sir Patrick Spens is the best sailor
  That ever sailed the sea."

Our king has written a broad letter,
  And sealed it with his hand,
And sent it to Sir Patrick Spens
  Was walking on the strand.

The first word that Sir Patrick read,
  So loud, loud laughed he;
The next word that Sir Patrick read,
  The tear blinded his ee.

"O who is this has done this deed,
  And told the king o' me,
To send us out, at this time of year,
  To sail upon the sea?

"Make ready, make ready, my merry men all!
  Our good ship sails the morn."
"Now ever alack, my master dear,
  I fear a deadly storm!

"I saw the new moon, late yestreen;
  With the auld moon in her arm;
And if we gang to sea, master,
  I fear we'll come to harm."

They had not sailed a league, a league,
  A league but barely three,
When the lift grew dark, and the wind blew
    loud,
  And gurly grew the sea.

"Go, fetch a web o' the silken cloth,
  Another o' the twine,
And wap them into our ship's side,
  And let not the sea come in."

O loth, loth, were our good Scotch lords
  To wet their cork-heeled shoon!
But lang ere a' the play was play'd
  They wet their hats aboon.

O long, long may the ladies sit,
  With their fans into their hand,
Before they see Sir Patrick Spens
  Come sailing to the strand!

Reprinted by permission of Philomel Books, a division of the Putnam Publishing Group, from *The Poet's Tales,* edited by William Cole and illustrated by Charles Keeping. Illustrations copyright © 1971 by Charles Keeping.

And long, long may the maidens sit,
  Wi' the goud combs in their hair,
All waiting for their own dear loves—
  For them they'll see no mair.

Half owre, half owre to Aberdour,
  'Tis fifty fathoms deep,
And there lies good Sir Patrick Spens,
  With the Scotch lords at his feet.

4

The Golden Vanity

"A ship I have got in the North Country
And she goes by the name of the Golden Vanity,
O I fear she'll be taken by a Spanish Ga-la-lee,
As she sails by the Low-lands low."

To the Captain then up spake the little Cabin-
   boy,
He said, "What is my fee, if the galley I destroy?
The Spanish Ga-la-lee, if no more it shall annoy,
   As you sail by the Low-lands low."

"Of silver and of gold I will give to you a store;
And my pretty little daughter that dwelleth on
   the shore,
Of treasure and of fee as well, I'll give to thee
   galore,
   As we sail by the Low-lands low."

Then they row'd him tight in a black bull's skin,
And he held all in his hand an augur sharp and
   thin,
And he swam until he came to the Spanish Gal-
   la-lin,
   As she lay by the Low-lands low.

He bored with his augur, he bored once and
   twice,
And some were playing cards, and some were
   playing dice,
When the water flowed in it dazzled their eyes,
And she sank by the Low-lands low.

So the Cabin-boy did swim all to the larboard
   side,
Saying, "Captain! take me in, I am drifting with
   the tide!"
"I will shoot you! I will kill you!" the cruel
   Captain cried,
"You may sink by the Low-lands low."

Then the Cabin-boy did swim all to the star-
   board side,
Saying, "Messmates, take me in, I am drifting
   with the tide!"
Then they laid him on the deck, and he closed
   his eyes and died,
   As they sailed by the Low-lands low.

They sew'd his body tight in an old cow's hide,
And they cast the gallant Cabin-boy out over
   the ship side,
And left him without more ado to drift with
   the tide,
   And to sink by the Low-lands low.

5

The Raggle, Taggle Gypsies

There were three gypsies a-come to my door,
   And downstairs ran this lady, O.
One sang high and another sang low,
   And the other sang "Bonnie, Bonnie Biskay,
   O."

Then she pulled off her silken gown,
   And put on hose of leather, O.
With the ragged, ragged rags about her door
   She's off with the Raggle, Taggle Gypsies,
   O.

'Twas late last night when my lord came home,
   Inquiring for his lady, O.
The servants said on every hand,
   "She's gone with the Raggle, Taggle Gypsies,
   O."

"Oh, saddle for me my milk-white steed,
   Oh, saddle for me my pony, O,
That I may ride and seek my bride
   Who's gone with the Raggle, Taggle Gypsies,
   O."

Oh, he rode high and he rode low,
   He rode through woods and copses, O,
Until he came to an open field,
   And there he espied his lady, O.

"What makes you leave your house and lands?
   What makes you leave your money, O?
What makes you leave your new-wedded lord
   To go with the Raggle, Taggle Gypsies, O?"

"What care I for my house and lands?
   What care I for my money, O?
What care I for my new-wedded lord?
   I'm off with the Raggle, Taggle Gypsies, O."

"Last night you slept on a goose-feather bed,
   With the sheet turned down so bravely, O.
Tonight you will sleep in the cold, open field,
   Along with the Raggle, Taggle Gypsies, O."

"What care I for your goose-feather bed,
   With the sheet turned down so bravely, O?

For tonight I shall sleep in a cold, open field,
    Along with the Raggle, Taggle Gypsies, O."

6

The Riddling Knight

There were three sisters fair and bright
Jennifer, Gentle, and Rosemary,
And they three loved one valiant knight—
As the dew flies over the mulberry-tree.

The eldest sister let him in,
Jennifer, Gentle, and Rosemary,
And barr'd the door with a silver pin,
As the dew flies over the mulberry-tree.

The second sister made his bed,
Jennifer, Gentle, and Rosemary,
And placed soft pillows under his head,
As the dew flies over the mulberry-tree.

The youngest sister that same night,
Jennifer, Gentle, and Rosemary,

Was resolved for to wed wi' this valiant knight,
As the dew flies over the mulberry-tree.

"And if you can answer questions three,
Jennifer, Gentle, and Rosemary,
O then, fair maid, I'll marry wi' thee,
As the dew flies over the mulberry-tree.

"O what is louder nor a horn,
Jennifer, Gentle, and Rosemary,
O what is sharper than a thorn?
As the dew flies over the mulberry-tree.

"Or what is heavier nor the lead,
Jennifer, Gentle, and Rosemary,
Or what is better nor the bread?
As the dew flies over the mulberry-tree.

From *The Kitchen Knight*, by Barbara Schiller, illustrated by Nonny Hogrogian. Copyright © 1965 by Barbara Schiller; copyright © 1965 by Nonny Hogrogian. Reproduced by permission of Holt, Rinehart and Winston, publishers.

"Or what is longer nor the way,
Jennifer, Gentle, and Rosemary,
Or what is deeper nor the sea?—
As the dew flies over the mulberry-tree."

"O shame is louder nor a horn,
Jennifer, Gentle, and Rosemary,
And hunger is sharper nor a thorn,
As the dew flies over the mulberry-tree.

"O sin is heavier nor the lead,
Jennifer, Gentle, and Rosemary,
The blessing's better nor the bread,
As the dew flies over the mulberry-tree.

"O the wind is longer nor the way,
Jennifer, Gentle, and Rosemary,
And love is deeper nor the sea,
As the dew flies over the mulberry-tree."

"You've answer'd my questions three,
Jennifer, Gentle, and Rosemary,
And now, fair maid, I'll marry wi' thee,
As the dew flies over the mulberry-tree."

7

The Three Ravens

There were three ravens sat on a tree,
  Down a down, hay down, hay down,
There were three ravens sat on a tree,
  With a down,
There were three ravens sat on a tree,
They were as black as they might be,
  With a down derrie, derrie, derrie, down, down.

The one of them said to his mate,
'Where shall we our breakfast take?

'Down in yonder green field,
There lies a knight slain under his shield.

'His hounds they lie down at his feet,
So well they can their master keep.

'His hauks they flie so eagerly,
There's no fowl dare him come nie.'

Down there comes a fallow doe,
As great with yong as she might goe.

She lifted up his bloudy hed,
And kist his wounds that were so red.

She got him up upon her back,
And carried him to earthen lake.

She buried him before the prime,
She was dead herself ere even-song time.

God send every gentleman
Such hauks, such hounds, and such a leman.*

8

The Demon Lover

"O where have you been, my long, long love,
This long seven years and more?"
"O I'm come to seek my former vows
Ye granted me before."

"O hold your tongue of your former vows,
For they will breed sad strife;
O hold your tongue of your former vows,
For I am become a wife."

He turn'd him right and round about,
And the tear blinded his ee; .
"I wad never hae trodden on Irish ground,
If it had not been for thee.

"I might hae had a king's daughter,
Far, far beyond the sea;
I might have had a king's daughter,
Had it not been for love o' thee."

"If you might have had a king's daughter,
Yer sel ye had to blame;
Ye might have taken the king's daughter,
For ye kenned† that I was nane.‡

"If I was to leave my husband dear,
And my two babes also,
O what have you to take me to,
If with you I should go?"

* leman: lover
† kenned: know
‡ nane: none

"I hae seven ships upon the sea,
The eighth brought me to land;
With four and twenty bold mariners,
And music on every hand."

She has taken up her two little babes,
Kiss'd them both cheek and chin;
"O fare ye well, my own two babes,
For I'll never see you again."

She set her foot upon the ship,
No mariners could she behold;
But the sails were o' the taffety,
And the masts o' the beaten gold.

She had not sail'd a league,* a league,
A league but barely three,
When dismal grew his countenance
And drumlie† grew his ee.

They had not sailed a league, a league,
A league but barely three,
Until she espied his cloven foot,
And she wept right bitterly.

"O hold your tongue of your weeping," says
    he,
"Of your weeping now let me be;
I will show you how the lilies grow
On the banks of Italy."

"O what hills are yon, yon pleasant hills,
That the sun shines sweetly on?"
"O yon are the hills of heaven," he said,
"Where you will never win."

"O whaten a mountain is yon," she said,
"All so dreary wi' frost and snow?"
"O yon is the mountain of hell," he cried,
"Where you and I will go."

He struck the top-mast wi' his hand,
The fore-mast wi' his knee;
And he brake that gallant ship in twain,
And sank her in the sea.

* league: about three miles
† drumlie: gloomy

Narrative Poetry

9

A. A. Milne

The King's Breakfast

The King asked
The Queen, and
The Queen asked
The Dairymaid:
"Could we have some butter for
The Royal slice of bread?"
The Queen asked
The Dairymaid,
The Dairymaid
Said, "Certainly,
I'll go and tell
The cow
Now
Before she goes to bed."

The Dairymaid
She curtsied,
And went and told
The Alderney:
"Don't forget the butter for
The Royal slice of bread."
The Alderney
Said sleepily:
"You'd better tell
His Majesty
That many people nowadays
Like marmalade
Instead."

The Dairymaid
Said, "Fancy!"
And went to
Her Majesty.
She curtsied to the Queen, and
She turned a little red:
"Excuse me,
Your Majesty,
For taking of
The liberty,

9. From A. A. Milne, *When We Were Very Young* (Dutton, 1924).

But marmalade is tasty, if
It's very
Thickly
Spread."

The Queen said
"Oh!"
And went to
His Majesty:
"Talking of the butter for
The Royal slice of bread,
Many people
Think that
Marmalade
Is nicer.
Would you like to try a little
Marmalade
Instead?"

The King said,
"Bother!"
And then he said,
"Oh, deary me!"
The King sobbed, "Oh, deary me!"
And went back to bed.
"Nobody,"
He whimpered,
"Could call me
A fussy man;
I *only* want
A little bit
Of butter for
My bread!"

The Queen said,
"There, there!"
And went to
The Dairymaid.
The Dairymaid
Said, "There, there!"
And went to the shed.
The cow said,
"There, there!
I didn't really
Mean it;
Here's milk for his porringer
And butter for his bread."

The Queen took
The butter

And brought it to
His Majesty;
The King said,
"Butter, eh?"
And bounced out of bed.
"Nobody," he said,
As he kissed her
Tenderly,
"Nobody," he said,
As he slid down
The banisters,
"Nobody,
My darling,
Could call me
A fussy man—
BUT
I do like a little bit of butter to my bread!"

10

Roald Dahl

Little Red Riding Hood and the Wolf

As soon as Wolf began to feel
That he would like a decent meal,
He went and knocked on Grandma's door.
When Grandma opened it, she saw
The sharp white teeth, the horrid grin,
And Wolfie said, "May I come in?"
Poor Grandmamma was terrified,
"He's going to eat me up!" she cried.
And she was absolutely right.
He ate her up in one big bite.
But Grandmamma was small and tough,
And Wolfie wailed, "That's not enough!
I haven't yet begun to feel
That I have had a decent meal!"
He ran around the kitchen yelping,
"I've *got* to have a second helping!"
Then added with a frightful leer,
"I'm therefore going to wait right here
Till Little Miss Red Riding Hood
Comes home from walking in the wood."
He quickly put on Grandma's clothes,
(Of course he hadn't eaten those).
He dressed himself in coat and hat.

10. From Roald Dahl, *Roald Dahl's Revolting Rhymes* (Knopf, 1982).

He put on shoes and after that
He even brushed and curled his hair,
Then sat himself in Grandma's chair.
In came the little girl in red.
She stopped. She stared. And then she said,

"What great big ears you have, Grandma."
"All the better to hear you with," the Wolf replied.
"What great big eyes you have, Grandma,"
said Little Red Riding Hood.
"All the better to see you with," the Wolf replied.

He sat there watching her and smiled.
He thought, "I'm going to eat this child.
Compared with her old Grandmamma
She's going to taste like caviar."

Then Little Red Riding Hood said, *"But
    Grandma,*
what a lovely great big furry coat you have on."

"That's wrong," cried Wolf, "Have you forgot
To tell me what BIG TEETH I've got?
Ah well, no matter what you say,
I'm going to eat you anyway."
The small girl smiles. One eyelid flickers.
She whips a pistol from her knickers.
She aims it at the creature's head
And *bang bang bang,* she shoots him dead.
A few weeks later, in the wood,
I came across Miss Riding Hood.
But what a change! No cloak of red,
No silly hood upon her head.
She said, "Hello, and do please note
My lovely furry wolfskin coat."

11

Clement C. Moore

A Visit from St. Nicholas

'Twas the night before Christmas, when all
    through the house
Not a creature was stirring, not even a mouse.
The stockings were hung by the chimney with
    care,

11. From Clement C. Moore, *A Visit from St. Nicholas* (On-
derdonck, 1848).

In hopes that St. Nicholas soon would be there.
The children were nestled all snug in their beds,
While visions of sugar-plums danced in their
    heads;
And mamma in her kerchief, and I in my cap,
Had just settled our brains for a long winter's
    nap—
When out on the lawn there arose such a clatter
I sprang from my bed to see what was the matter.
Away to the window I flew like a flash,
Tore open the shutter, and threw up the sash.
The moon on the breast of the new-fallen snow
Gave a lustre of midday to objects below:
When what to my wondering eyes should ap-
    pear
But a miniature sleigh and eight tiny reindeer,
With a little old driver, so lively and quick,
I knew in a moment it must be St. Nick!
More rapid than eagles his coursers they came,
And he whistled and shouted and called them
    by name.
"Now, Dasher! now, Dancer! now, Prancer and
    Vixen!
On, Comet! on, Cupid! on, Donder and Blit-
    zen!—
To the top of the porch, to the top of the wall,
Now, dash away, dash away, dash away all!"
As dry leaves that before the wild hurricane
    fly,
When they meet with an obstacle mount to the
    sky,
So, up to the housetop the coursers they flew,
With a sleigh full of toys—and St. Nicholas,
    too.
And then, in a twinkling, I heard on the roof
The prancing and pawing of each little hoof.
As I drew in my head and was turning around,
Down the chimney St. Nicholas came with a
    bound:
He was dressed all in fur from his head to his
    foot,
And his clothes were all tarnished with ashes
    and soot:
A bundle of toys he had flung on his back,
And he looked like a peddler just opening his
    pack.
His eyes, how they twinkled! his dimples, how
    merry!
His cheeks were like roses, his nose like a
    cherry;

His droll little mouth was drawn up like a bow,
And the beard on his chin was as white as the
  snow.
The stump of a pipe he held tight in his teeth,
And the smoke, it encircled his head like a
  wreath.
He had a broad face and a little round belly
That shook, when he laughed, like a bowl full
  of jelly.
He was chubby and plump—a right jolly old
  elf:
And I laughed when I saw him, in spite of my-
  self;
A wink of his eye, and a twist of his head,
Soon gave me to know I had nothing to dread.
He spoke not a word, but went straight to his
  work,
And filled all the stockings: then turned with
  a jerk,
And laying his finger aside of his nose,
And giving a nod, up the chimney he rose.
He sprang to his sleigh, to his team gave a whis-
  tle,
And away they all flew like the down of a thistle.
But I heard him exclaim, ere they drove out
  of sight,
"Happy Christmas to all, and to all a good-
  night!"

12

Charles Causley

Colonel Fazackerley

Colonel Fazackerley Butterworth-Toast
Bought an old castle complete with a ghost,
But someone or other forgot to declare
To Colonel Fazack that the spectre was there.

On the very first evening, while waiting to dine,
The Colonel was taking a fine sherry wine,
When the ghost, with a furious flash and a flare,
Shot out of the chimney and shivered, 'Beware!'

Colonel Fazackerley put down his glass
And said, 'My dear fellow, that's really first class!
I just can't conceive how you do it at all.
I imagine you're going to a Fancy Dress Ball?'

12. From Charles Causley, *Figgie Hobbin* (Walker & Co.,
1973).

At this, the dread ghost gave a withering cry.
Said the Colonel (his monocle firm in his eye),
'Now just how you do it I wish I could think.
Do sit down and tell me, and please have a
  drink.'

The ghost in his phosphorous cloak gave a roar
And floated about between ceiling and floor.
He walked through a wall and returned through
  a pane
And backed up the chimney and came down
  again.

Said the Colonel, 'With laughter I'm feeling
  quite weak!'
(As trickles of merriment ran down his cheek).
'My house-warming party I hope you won't
  spurn.
You *must* say you'll come and you'll give us a
  turn!'

At this, the poor spectre—quite out of his wits—
Proceeded to shake himself almost to bits.
He rattled his chains and he clattered his bones
And he filled the whole castle with mumbles
  and moans.

But Colonel Fazackerley, just as before,
Was simply delighted and called out, 'Encore!'
At which the ghost vanished, his efforts in vain,
And never was seen at the castle again.

'Oh dear, what a pity!' said Colonel Fazack.
'I don't know his name, so I can't call him back.'
And then with a smile that was hard to define,
Colonel Fazackerley went in to dine.

13

James Reeves

The Old Wife and the Ghost

There was an old wife and she lived all alone
  In a cottage not far from Hitchin:
And one bright night, by the full moon light,
  Comes a ghost right into her kitchen.

13. From James Reeves, *The Blackbird in the Lilac* (Oxford
University Press, 1952).

About that kitchen neat and clean
  The ghost goes pottering round.
But the poor old wife is deaf as a boot
  And so hears never a sound.

The ghost blows up the kitchen fire,
  As bold as bold can be;
He helps himself from the larder shelf,
  But never a sound hears she.

He blows on his hands to make them warm,
  And whistles aloud 'Whee-hee!'
But still as a sack the old soul lies
  And never a sound hears she.

From corner to corner he runs about,
  And into the cupboard he peeps;
He rattles the door and bumps on the floor,
  But still the old wife sleeps.

Jangle and bang go the pots and pans,
  As he throws them all around;
And the plates and mugs and dishes and jugs,
  He flings them all to the ground.

Madly the ghost tears up and down
  And screams like a storm at sea;
And at last the old wife stirs in her bed—
  And it's 'Drat those mice,' says she.

Then the first cock crows and morning shows
  And the troublesome ghost's away.
But oh! what a pickle the poor wife sees
  When she gets up next day.

'Them's tidy big mice,' the old wife thinks,
  And off she goes to Hitchin,
And a tidy big cat she fetches back
  To keep the mice from her kitchen.

14

Robert Browning

The Pied Piper of Hamelin

  Hamelin Town's in Brunswick
By famous Hanover city;

14. From Robert Browning, *The Pied Piper of Hamelin*
(Routledge, 1888).

The river Weser, deep and wide,
  Washes its wall on the southern side;
  A pleasanter spot you never spied;
But, when begins my ditty,
  Almost five hundred years ago,
  To see the townsfolk suffer so
    From vermin was a pity.

                                        Rats!
They fought the dogs, and killed the cats,
  And bit the babies in the cradles,
And ate the cheeses out of the vats,
  And licked the soup from the cook's own
    ladles,
Split open the kegs of salted sprats,
Made nests inside men's Sunday hats,
And even spoiled the women's chats,
  By drowning their speaking
  With shrieking and squeaking
In fifty different sharps and flats.

  At last the people in a body
  To the Town Hall came flocking:
  "'Tis clear," cried they, "our Mayor's a
    noddy;
  And as for our Corporation—shocking
  To think that we buy gowns lined with ermine
  For dolts that can't or won't determine
  What's best to rid us of our vermin!
  You hope, because you're old and obese,
  To find in the furry civic robe ease?
  Rouse up, sirs! Give your brain a racking
  To find the remedy we're lacking,
  Or, sure as fate, we'll send you packing!"
At this the Mayor and Corporation
Quaked with a mighty consternation.

  An hour they sat in council,
    At length the Mayor broke silence:
  "For a guilder I'd my ermine gown sell;
    I wish I were a mile hence!
  It's easy to bid one rack one's brain—
  I'm sure my poor head aches again
  I've scratched it so, and all in vain,
  Oh for a trap, a trap, a trap!"
Just as he said this, what should hap
At the chamber door but a gentle tap?
  "Bless us," cried the Mayor, "what's that?"
  (With the Corporation as he sat,
  Looking little though wondrous fat;

Nor brighter was his eye, nor moister,
Than a too-long-opened oyster,
Save when at noon his paunch grew mutinous
For a plate of turtle green and glutinous),
"Only a scraping of shoes on the mat?
Anything like the sound of a rat
Makes my heart go pit-a-pat!"

"Come in!"—the Mayor cried, looking big-
   ger:
And in did come the strangest figure.
His queer long coat from heel to head
Was half of yellow and half of red;
And he himself was tall and thin,
With sharp blue eyes, each like a pin,
And light loose hair, yet swarthy skin,
No tuft on cheek nor beard on chin,
But lips where smiles went out and in—
There was no guessing his kith and kin!
And nobody could enough admire
The tall man and his quaint attire.
Quoth one: "It's as my great grandsire,
Starting up at the Trump of Doom's tone,
Had walked this way from his painted tomb-
   stone."

He advanced to the council-table:
And, "Please, your honours," said he, "I'm
   able,
By means of a secret charm, to draw
All creatures living beneath the sun,
That creep, or swim, or fly, or run,
After me so as you never saw!
And I chiefly use my charm
On creatures that do people harm,
The mole, and toad, and newt, and viper;
And people call me the Pied Piper."
(And here they noticed round his neck
   A scarf of red and yellow stripe,
To match with his coat of the selfsame cheque;
   And at the scarf's end hung a pipe;
And his fingers, they noticed, were ever straying
As if impatient to be playing
Upon this pipe, as low it dangled
Over his vesture so old-fangled.)
   "Yet," said he, "poor piper as I am,
   In Tartary I freed the Cham,
   Last June, from his huge swarms of gnats;
   I eased in Asia the Nizam
   Of a monstrous brood of vampire bats:

And, as for what your brain bewilders,
If I can rid your town of rats
Will you give me a thousand guilders?"
"One? fifty thousand!"—was the exclamation
Of the astonished Mayor and Corporation.

Into the street the Piper stept,
   Smiling first a little smile,
As if he knew what magic slept
   In his quiet pipe the while;
Then, like a musical adept,
To blow the pipe his lips he wrinkled,
And green and blue his sharp eyes twinkled
Like a candle-flame where salt is sprinkled;
And ere three shrill notes the pipe uttered,
You heard as if an army muttered;
And the muttering grew to a grumbling;
And the grumbling grew to a mighty rum-
   bling;
And out of the house the rats came tumbling.
Great rats, small rats, lean rats, brawny rats,
Brown rats, black rats, gray rats, tawny rats,
Grave old plodders, gay young friskers,
   Fathers, mothers, uncles, cousins,
Cocking tails and pricking whiskers,
   Families by tens and dozens,
Brothers, sisters, husbands, wives—
Followed the Piper for their lives.
From street to street he piped advancing,
And step by step they followed dancing,
Until they came to the river Weser
Wherein all plunged and perished
—Save one, who, stout as Julius Cæsar,
Swam across and lived to carry
(As he the manuscript he cherished)
To Rat-land home his commentary,
Which was, "At the first shrill notes of the
   pipe,
I heard a sound as of scraping tripe,
And putting apples, wondrous ripe,
Into a cider press's gripe;
And a moving away of pickle-tub boards,
And a drawing the corks of train-oil flasks,
And a breaking the hoops of butter casks;
And it seemed as if a voice
(Sweeter far than by harp or by psaltery
Is breathed) called out, Oh, rats! rejoice!
The world is grown to one vast drysaltery!
To munch on, crunch on, take your nun-
   cheon,

Breakfast, supper, dinner, luncheon!
And just as a bulky sugar puncheon,
All ready staved, like a great sun shone
Glorious scarce an inch before me,
Just as methought it said, come, bore me!
—I found the Weser rolling o'er me."

You should have heard the Hamelin people
Ringing the bells till they rocked the steeple.
  "Go," cried the Mayor, "and get long poles!
  Poke out the nests and block up the holes!
  Consult with carpenters and builders,
  And leave in our town not even a trace
  Of the rats!"—when suddenly up the face
  Of the Piper perked in the market-place,
  With a, "First, if you please, my thousand guil-
    ders!"

A thousand guilders! The Mayor looked blue;
So did the Corporation too.
For council dinners made rare havoc
With Claret, Moselle, Vin-de-Grave, Hock;
And half the money would replenish
Their cellar's biggest butt with Rhenish.
To pay this sum to a wandering fellow
With a gipsy coat of red and yellow!
  "Beside," quoth the Mayor, with a knowing
    wink,
  "Our business was done at the river's brink;
  We saw with our eyes the vermin sink,
  And what's dead can't come to life, I think.
  So, friend, we're not the folks to shrink
  From the duty of giving you something to
    drink,
  And a matter of money to put in your poke,
  But, as for the guilders, what we spoke
  Of them, as you very well know, was in joke.
  Besides, our losses have made us thrifty;
  A thousand guilders! Come, take fifty!"

The piper's face fell, and he cried,
"No trifling! I can't wait, beside!
I've promised to visit by dinnertime
Bagdad, and accepted the prime
Of the Head Cook's pottage, all he's rich in,
For having left the Caliph's kitchen,
Of a nest of scorpions no survivor—
With him I proved no bargain-driver,
With you, don't think I'll bate a stiver!

And folks who put me in a passion
May find me pipe to another fashion."

  "How?" cried the Mayor, "d'ye think I'll
    brook
  Being worse treated than a Cook?
  Insulted by a lazy ribald
  With idle pipe and vesture piebald?
  You threaten us, fellow? Do your worst,
  Blow your pipe there till you burst!"

Once more he stept into the street;
  And to his lips again
Laid his long pipe of smooth straight cane;
  And ere he blew three notes (such sweet
Soft notes as yet musicians cunning
  Never gave the enraptured air),
There was a rustling, that seemed like a bustling
Of merry crowds justling, at pitching and hus-
    tling,
Small feet were pattering, wooden shoes clatter-
    ing,
Little hands clapping, and little tongues chatter-
    ing,
And, like fowls in a farmyard when barley is
    scattering,
Out came the children running.
All the little boys and girls,
With rosy cheeks and flaxen curls,
And sparkling eyes and teeth like pearls,
Tripping and skipping, ran merrily after
The wonderful music with shouting and laugh-
    ter.

The Mayor was dumb, and the Council stood
As if they were changed into blocks of wood,
Unable to move a step, or cry
To the children merrily skipping by—
And could only follow with the eye
That joyous crowd at the Piper's back.
But how the Mayor was on the rack,
And the wretched Council's bosoms beat,
As the piper turned from the High Street
To where the Weser rolled its waters
Right in the way of their sons and daughters!
However, he turned from South to West,
And to Koppelberg Hill his steps addressed,
And after him the children pressed;
Great was the joy in every breast.

"He never can cross that mighty top!
He's forced to let the piping drop
And we shall see our children stop!"
When lo! As they reached the mountain's side,
A wondrous portal opened wide,
As if a cavern was suddenly hollowed;
And the Piper advanced and the children fol-
    lowed,
And when all were in to the very last,
The door in the mountain-side shut fast.
Did I say all? No! one was lame,
And could not dance the whole of the way;
And in after years, if you would blame
His sadness, he was used to say:
    "It's dull in our town since my playmates left;
    I can't forget that I'm bereft
    Of all the pleasant sights they see,
    Which the Piper also promised me;
    For he led us, he said, to a joyous land,
    Joining the town and just at hand,
Where waters gushed and fruit trees grew,
And flowers put forth a fairer hue,
And everything was strange and new.
The sparrows were brighter than peacocks here,
And their dogs outran our fallow deer,
And honey-bees had lost their stings;
And horses were born with eagle's wings;
And just as I became assured
My lame foot would be speedily cured,
The music stopped, and I stood still,
And found myself outside the Hill,
Left alone against my will,
To go now limping as before,
And never hear of that country more!"

Alas, alas for Hamelin!
    There came into many a burger's pate
    A text which says, that Heaven's Gate
Opes to the Rich at as easy rate
As the needle's eye takes a camel in!
The Mayor sent East, West, North and South,
To offer the Piper by word of mouth,
    Wherever it was men's lot to find him,
Silver and gold to his heart's content,
If he'd only return the way he went,
    And bring the children all behind him.
But when they saw 'twas a lost endeavour,
And Piper and dancers were gone forever
They made a decree that lawyers never

Should think their records dated duly
If, after the day of the month and year,
These words did not as well appear,
    "And so long after what happened here
    On the twenty-second of July,
    Thirteen hundred and seventy-six:"
And the better in memory to fix
The place of the Children's last retreat,
They called it, the Pied Piper's street—
Where anyone playing on pipe or tabor,
Was sure for the future to lose his labour.
Nor suffered they hostelry or tavern
To shock with mirth a street so solemn;
But opposite the place of the cavern
    They wrote the story on a column,
And on the great church window painted
The same, to make the world acquainted
How their children were stolen away;
And there it stands to this very day.
And I must not omit to say
That in Transylvania there's a tribe
Of alien people that ascribe
The outlandish ways and dress,
On which their neighbours lay such stress,
To their fathers and mothers having risen
Out of some subterraneous prison,
Into which they were trepanned
Long time ago in a mighty band
Out of Hamelin town in Brunswick land,
But how or why they don't understand.

15

Alfred Noyes

The Highwayman

The wind was a torrent of darkness among the
    gusty trees.
The moon was a ghostly galleon tossed upon
    cloudy seas.
The road was a ribbon of moonlight over the
    purple moor,
And the highwayman came riding—
    Riding—riding—
The highwayman came riding, up to the old
    inn-door.

15. From Alfred Noyes, *Collected Poems* (Lippincott, 1902).

He'd a French cocked-hat on his forehead, a
    bunch of lace at his chin,
A coat of the claret velvet, and breeches of
    brown doe-skin.
They fitted with never a wrinkle. His boots
    were up to the thigh.
And he rode with a jewelled twinkle,
    His pistol butts a-twinkle,
His rapier hilt a-twinkle, under the jewelled sky.

Over the cobbles he clattered and clashed in
    the dark inn-yard.
He tapped with his whip on the shutters, but
    all was locked and barred.
He whistled a tune to the window, and who
    should be waiting there
But the landlord's black-eyed daughter,
    Bess, the landlord's daughter,
Plaiting a dark red love-knot into her long black
    hair.

And dark in the dark old inn-yard a stable-wicket
    creaked
Where Tim the ostler listened. His face was
    white and peaked.
His eyes were hollows of madness, his hair like
    mouldy hay,
But he loved the landlord's daughter,
    The landlord's red-lipped daughter.
Dumb as a dog he listened, and he heard the
    robber say—

"One kiss, my bonny sweetheart, I'm after a
    prize to-night,
But I shall be back with the yellow gold before
    the morning light;
Yet, if they press me sharply, and harry me
    through the day,
Then look for me by moonlight,
    Watch for me by moonlight,
I'll come to thee by moonlight, though hell
    should bar the way."

He rose upright in the stirrups. He scarce could
    reach her hand,
But she loosened her hair in the casement. His
    face burnt like a brand
As the black cascade of perfume came tumbling
    over his breast;

And he kissed its waves in the moonlight,
    (O, sweet black waves in the moonlight!)
Then he tugged at his rein in the moonlight,
    and galloped away to the west.

He did not come in the dawning. He did not
    come at noon;
And out of the tawny sunset, before the rise
    of the moon,
When the road was a gypsy's ribbon, looping
    the purple moor,
A red-coat troop came marching—
    Marching—marching—
King George's men came marching, up to the
    old inn-door.

They said no word to the landlord. They drank
    his ale instead.
But they gagged his daughter, and bound her,
    to the foot of her narrow bed.
Two of them knelt at her casement, with mus-
    kets at their side!
There was death at every window;
    And hell at one dark window;
For Bess could see, through her casement, the
    road that *he* would ride.

They had tied her up to attention, with many
    a sniggering jest.
They had bound a musket beside her, with the
    muzzle beneath her breast!
"Now, keep good watch!" and they kissed her.
    She heard the doomed man say—
Look for me by moonlight;
    Watch for me by moonlight;
*I'll come to thee by moonlight, though hell should
    bar the way!*

She twisted her hands behind her; but all the
    knots held good!
She writhed her hands till her fingers were wet
    with sweat or blood!
They stretched and strained in the darkness, and
    the hours crawled by like years,
Till, now, on the stroke of midnight,
    Cold, on the stroke of midnight,
The tip of one finger touched it! The trigger
    at least was hers!

The tip of one finger touched it. She strove
  no more for the rest.
Up, she stood up to attention, with the muzzle
  beneath her breast.
She would not risk their hearing; she would
  not strive again;
For the road lay bare in the moonlight;
  Blank and bare in the moonlight;
And the blood of her veins, in the moonlight,
  throbbed to her love's refrain.

Tlot-tlot; tlot-tlot! Had they heard it? The horse-
  hoofs ringing clear;
Tlot-tlot, tlot-tlot, in the distance? Were they deaf
  that they did not hear?
Down the ribbon of moonlight, over the brow
  of the hill,
The highwayman came riding—
  Riding—riding—
The red-coats looked to their priming! She stood
  up, straight and still.

Tlot-tlot, in the frosty silence! *Tlot-tlot,* in the
  echoing night!
Nearer he came and nearer. Her face was like
  a light.
Her eyes grew wide for a moment; she drew
  one last deep breath,
Then her finger moved in the moonlight,
  Her musket shattered the moonlight,
Shattered her breast in the moonlight and
  warned him—with her death.

He turned. He spurred to the west; he did not
  know who stood
Bowed, with her head o'er the musket,
  drenched with her own blood!
Not till the dawn he heard it, and his face grew
  grey to hear
How Bess, the landlord's daughter,
  The landlord's black-eyed daughter,
Had watched for her love in the moonlight,
  and died in the darkness there.

Back, he spurred like a madman, shouting a
  curse to the sky,
With the white road smoking behind him and
  his rapier brandished high.

Blood-red were his spurs in the golden noon;
  wine-red was his velvet coat;
When they shot him down on the highway,
  Down like a dog on the highway,
And he lay in his blood on the highway, with
  a bunch of lace at his throat.

And still of a winter's night, they say, when the
  wind is in the trees,
When the moon is a ghostly galleon tossed upon cloudy
  seas,
When the road is a ribbon of moonlight over the
  purple moor,
A highwayman comes riding—
  Riding—riding—
A highwayman comes riding, up to the old inn-door.

Over the cobbles he clatters and clangs in the dark
  inn-yard.
He taps with his whip on the shutters, but all is
  locked and barred.
He whistles a tune to the window, and who should
  be waiting there
But the landlord's black-eyed daughter,
  Bess, the landlord's daughter,
Plaiting a dark red love-knot into her long black
  hair.

16

Elizabeth Coatsworth

A Lady Comes to an Inn

Three strange men came to the Inn.
One was a black man, pocked and thin,
one was brown with a silver knife,
and one brought with him a beautiful wife.

That lovely woman had hair as pale
as French champagne or finest ale,
that lovely woman was long and slim
as a young white birch or a maple limb.

Her face was like cream, her mouth was a rose,
what language she spoke nobody knows,

16. From Elizabeth Coatsworth, *The Creaking Stair* (Coward-McCann, 1949).

but sometimes she'd scream like a cockatoo
and swear wonderful oaths that nobody knew.

Her great silk skirts like a silver bell
down to her little bronze slippers fell,
and her low-cut gown showed a dove on its
    nest
in blue tattooing across her breast.

Nobody learned the lady's name,
nor the marvelous land from which they came,
but still they tell through the countryside
the tale of those men and that beautiful bride.

17

John Davidson

A Runnable Stag

When the pods went pop on the broom, green
    broom,
    And apples began to be golden-skinned,
We harboured a stag in the Priory coomb,
    And we feathered his trail up-wind, up-wind,
    We feathered his trail up-wind—
        A stag of warrant, a stag, a stag,
        A runnable stag, a kingly crop,
        Brow, bay and tray and three on top,
        A stag, a runnable stag.

Then the huntsman's horn rang yap, yap, yap,
And "Forwards" we heard the harbourer shout;
But 'twas only a brocket that broke a gap
    In the beechen underwood, driven out,
    From the underwood antlered out
        By warrant and might of the stag, the stag,
        The runnable stag, whose lordly mind
        Was bent on sleep, though beamed and
            tined
        He stood, a runnable stag.

So we tufted the covert till afternoon
    With Tinkerman's Pup and Bell-of-the-North;
And hunters were sulky and hounds out of tune
    Before we tufted the right stag forth,
    Before we tufted him forth,
        The stag of warrant, the wily stag,

17. From John Davidson, *Holiday and Other Poems* (Richards, 1906).

        The runnable stag with his kingly crop,
        Brow, bay and tray and three on top,
        The royal and runnable stag.

It was Bell-of-the-North and Tinkerman's Pup
    That stuck to the scent till the copse was
        drawn.
"Tally ho! tally ho!" and the hunt was up,
    The tufters whipped and the pack laid on,
    The resolute pack laid on,
        And the stag of warrant away at last,
        The runnable stag, the same, the same,
        His hoofs on fire, his horns like flame
        A stag, a runnable stag.

"Let your gelding be: if you check or chide
    He stumbles at once and you're out of the
        hunt;
For three hundred gentlemen, able to ride,
    On hunters accustomed to bear the brunt,
    Accustomed to bear the brunt,
        Are after the runnable stag, the stag,
        The runnable stag with his kingly crop,
        Brow, bay and tray and three on top,
        The right, the runnable stag."

By perilous paths in coomb and dell,
    The heather, the rocks, and the river-bed,
The pace grew hot, for the scent lay well,
    And a runnable stag goes right ahead,
    The quarry went right ahead—
        Ahead, ahead, and fast and far;
        His antlered crest, his cloven hoof,
        Brow, bay and tray and three aloof,
        The stag, the runnable stag.

For a matter of twenty miles and more,
    By the densest hedge and the highest wall,
Through herds of bullocks he baffled the lore
    Of harbourer, huntsmen, hounds and all,
    Of harbourer, hounds and all—
        The stag of warrant, the wily stag,
        For twenty miles, and five and five,
        He ran, and he never was caught alive,
        This stag, this runnable stag.

When he turned at bay in the leafy gloom,
    In the emerald gloom where the brook ran
        deep,

Illustration by Charles Keeping, from *The Twelve Labors of Hercules,* by Robert Newman. Copyright © 1972 by Charles Keeping; used by permission of Harper & Row Publishers, Inc.

He heard in the distance the rollers boom,
  And he saw in a vision of peaceful sleep,
  In a wonderful vision of sleep,
    A stag of warrant, a stag, a stag,
    A runnable stag in a jewelled bed,
    Under the sheltering ocean dead,
    A stag, a runnable stag.

So a fateful hope lit up his eye,
  And he opened his nostrils wide again,
And he tossed his branching antlers high
  As he headed the hunt down Charlock glen,
  As he raced down the echoing glen
    For five miles more, the stag, the stag,
    For twenty miles, and five and five,
    Not to be caught now, dead or alive,
    The stag, the runnable stag.

Three hundred gentlemen, able to ride,
  Three hundred horses as gallant and free,
Beheld him escape on the evening tide,
  Far out till he sank in the Severn Sea,
  Till he sank in the depths of the sea—
    The stag, the buoyant stag, the stag
    That slept at last in a jewelled bed
    Under the sheltering ocean spread,
    The stag, the runnable stag.

The Lyric Voice

Poems of the Child's World

18

Rose Fyleman

Singing Time

I wake in the morning early
And always, the very first thing,
I poke out my head and I sit up in bed
And I sing and I sing and I sing.

19

Dorothy Aldis

Blum

Dog means dog,
And cat means cat;

18. From Rose Fyleman, *The Fairy Green* (Doubleday, 1925).
19. From Dorothy Aldis, *Here, There and Everywhere* (Putnam's, 1927).

And there are lots
Of words like that.

A cart's a cart
To pull or shove,
A plate's a plate
To eat off of.

But there are other
Words I say
When I am left
Alone to play.

Blum is one.
Blum is a word
That very few
Have ever heard.

I like to say it,
"Blum, Blum, Blum"—
I do it loud
Or in a hum.

All by itself
It's nice to sing:
It does not mean
A single thing.

20

Eleanor Farjeon

Girls' Names

What lovely names for girls there are!
There's Stella like the Evening Star,
And Sylvia like a rustling tree,
And Lola like a melody,
And Flora like a flowery morn,
And Sheila like a field of corn,
And Melusina like the moan
Of water. And there's Joan, like Joan.

21

Eleanor Farjeon

Boys' Names

What splendid names for boys there are!
There's Carol like a rolling car,

20–21. From Eleanor Farjeon, *Poems for Children* (Lippincott, 1951).

And Martin like a flying bird,
And Adam like the Lord's First Word,
And Raymond like the harvest Moon,
And Peter like a piper's tune,
And Alan like the flowing on
Of water. And there's John, like John.

22

A. A. Milne

Happiness

John had
Great Big
Waterproof
Boots on;
John had a
Great Big
Waterproof
Hat;
John had a
Great Big
Waterproof
Mackintosh—
And that
(Said John)
Is
That.

23

Eve Merriam

Windshield Wiper

fog smog	fog smog
tissue paper	tissue paper
clear the blear	clear the smear
fog more	fog more
splat splat	downpour
rubber scraper	rubber scraper
overshoes	macintosh
bumbershoot	muddle on
slosh through	slosh through

22. From A. A. Milne, *When We Were Very Young* (Dutton, 1924).
23. From Eve Merriam, *Out Loud* (Atheneum, 1973).

drying up   drying up
sky lighter   sky lighter
nearly clear nearly clear
clearing clearing veer
clear here clear

24

Robert Louis Stevenson

My Shadow

I have a little shadow that goes in and out with
    me,
And what can be the use of him is more than
    I can see.
He is very, very like me from the heels up to
    the head;
And I see him jump before me, when I jump
    into my bed.

The funniest thing about him is the way he likes
    to grow—
Not at all like proper children, which is always
    very slow;
For he sometimes shoots up taller like an India-
    rubber ball,
And he sometimes gets so little that there's none
    of him at all.

He hasn't got a notion of how children ought
    to play,
And can only make a fool of me in every sort
    of way.
He stays so close beside me, he's a coward you
    can see;
I'd think shame to stick to nursie as that shadow
    sticks to me!

One morning, very early, before the sun was
    up,
I rose and found the shining dew on every but-
    tercup;
But my lazy little shadow, like an arrant sleepy-
    head,
Had stayed at home behind me and was fast
    asleep in bed.

24. From Robert Louis Stevenson, *A Child's Garden of Verses* (Longmans, 1885).

25

Patricia Hubbell

Shadows

Chunks of night
Melt
In the morning sun.
One lonely one
Grows legs
And follows me
To school.

26

Myra Cohn Livingston

History

And I'm thinking how to get out
Of this stuffy room
With its big blackboards.

And I'm trying not to listen
In this boring room
To the way things *were.*

And I'm thinking about later,
Running from the room
Back into the world,

And what the guys will say when
I'm up to bat and hit
A big fat home run.

27

Jane Yolen

Homework

What is it about homework
That makes me want to write
My Great Aunt Myrt to thank her for
The sweater that's too tight?

25. From Patricia Hubbell, *Catch Me a Wind* (Atheneum, 1968).
26. From Myra Cohn Livingston, *The Malibu and Other Poems* (Atheneum, 1972).
27. From Jane Yolen, *Breakfast, Books, and Dreams* (Warne, 1981).

What is it about homework
That makes me pick up socks
That stink from days and days of wear,
Then clean the litter box?

What is it about homework
That makes me volunteer
To take the garbage out before
The bugs and flies appear?

What is it about homework
That makes me wash my hair
And take an hour combing out
The snags and tangles there?

What is it about homework?
You know, I wish I knew,
'Cause nights when I've got homework
I've got much too much to do!

28

Ffrida Wolfe

New shoes, new shoes,
Red and pink and blue shoes,
Tell me what would *you* choose
If they'd let us buy?

Buckle shoes, bow shoes,
Pretty pointy-toe shoes,
Strappy, cappy low shoes;
Let's have some to try.

Bright shoes, white shoes,
Dandy dance-by-night shoes,
Perhaps-a-little-tight shoes;
Like some? So would I.

                              BUT

Flat shoes, fat shoes,
Stump-along-like-that shoes,
Wipe-them-on-the-mat shoes
O that's the sort they'll buy.

29

Basho

In my new clothing

In my new clothing
    I feel so different
    I must
Look like someone else.

30

Dennis Lee

Skyscraper

Skyscraper, skyscraper,
Scrape me some sky:
Tickle the sun
While the stars go by.

Tickle the stars
While the sun's climbing high,
Then skyscraper, skyscraper
Scrape me some sky.

31

Charles Malam

Steam Shovel

The dinosaurs are not all dead.
I saw one raise its iron head
To watch me walking down the road
Beyond our house today.
Its jaws were dripping with a load
Of earth and grass that it had cropped.
It must have heard me where I stopped,
Snorted white steam my way,
And stretched its long neck out to see,
And chewed, and grinned quite amiably.

28. From Ffrida Wolfe, *The Very Thing: Read-out-able Rhymes for Children* (Sidgwick & Jackson, 1928).

29. From *The Four Seasons: Japanese Haiku Written by Basho, Buson, Issa, Shiki, and Many Others,* trans. Peter Beilenson (Peter Pauper Press, 1958).
30. From Dennis Lee, *Alligator Pie* (Houghton Mifflin, 1974).
31. From Charles Malam, *Upper Pasture* (Holt, 1930).

32

Philip Booth

Crossing

STOP   LOOK   LISTEN
as gate stripes swing down,
count the cars hauling distance
upgrade through town:
warning whistle, bellclang,
engine eating steam,
engineer waving,
a fast-freight dream:
B & M boxcar,
boxcar again,
Frisco gondola,
eight-nine-ten,
Erie and Wabash,
Seaboard, U.P.,
Pennsy tankcar,
twenty-two, three,
Phoebe Snow, B & O,
thirty-four, five,
Santa Fe cattle
shipped alive,
red cars, yellow cars,
orange cars, black,
Youngstown steel
down to Mobile
on Rock Island track,
fifty-nine, sixty,
hoppers of coke,
Anaconda copper,
hotbox smoke,
eighty-eight,
red-ball freight,
Rio Grande,
Nickle Plate,
Hiawatha,
Lackawanna,

rolling fast
and loose,
ninety-seven,
coal car,
boxcar,
CABOOSE!

33

Valerie Worth

Marbles

Marbles picked up
Heavy by the handful
And held, weighed,
Hard, glossy,
Glassy, cold,
Then poured clicking,
Water-smooth, back
To their bag, seem
Treasure: round jewels,
Slithering gold.

34

Myra Cohn Livingston

74th Street

Hey, this little kid gets roller skates.
She puts them on.
She stands up and almost
flops over backwards.
She sticks out a foot like
she's going somewhere and
falls down and
smacks her hand. She
grabs hold of a step to get up and
sticks out the other foot and
slides about six inches and
falls and
skins her knee.

And then, you know what?

32. From Philip Booth, *Letter from a Distant Land* (Viking, 1953).

33. From Valerie Worth, *Small Poems* (Farrar, Straus & Giroux, 1972).
34. From Myra Cohn Livingston, *The Malibu and Other Poems* (Atheneum, 1972).

She brushes off the dirt and the
blood and puts some
spit on it and then
sticks out the other foot

      again.

35

Ron Loewinsohn

It Is an Outfielder

For N. H.

The playground is so filled with kids
that their games overlap, the
outfielders of one game
standing on the basepaths of the opposite
diamond; running around in between.
A fat girl out in left field
is standing with her arms folded
talking to a boy while she (nervously)
adjusts her glasses.
Suddenly she turns, unfolds her arms
& catches a fly ball for the 3rd out.

36

Lawrence Ferlinghetti

7

      Fortune
           has its cookies to give out

which is a good thing

        since it's been a long time since

    that summer in Brooklyn
when they closed off the street
      one hot day
      and the

          FIREMEN

                turned on their hoses
and all the kids ran out in it

in the middle of the street

and there were

      maybe a couple dozen of us

        out there
with the water squirting up
        to the

      sky

        and all over
          us

    there was maybe only six of us
        kids altogether
  running around in our
      barefeet and birthday
suits
  and I remember Molly but then

the firemen stopped squirting their hoses
all of a sudden and went
      back in
    their firehouse
    and
started playing pinochle again
    just as if nothing
      had ever
        happened
while I remember Molly
      looked at me and

  ran in

because I guess really we were the only ones
there

37

May Swenson

The Centaur

The summer that I was ten—
Can it be there was only one
summer that I was ten? It must

35. From Ron Loewinsohn, *Meat Air* (Harcourt, 1970).
36. From Lawrence Ferlinghetti, *Coney Island of the Mind* (New Directions, 1955).

37. From May Swenson, *New and Selected Things Taking Place: Poems* (Little, Brown, 1971).

have been a long one then—
each day I'd go out to choose
a fresh horse from my stable

which was a willow grove
down by the old canal.
I'd go out on my two bare feet.

But when, with my brother's jack-knife,
I had cut me a long limber horse
with a good thick knob for a head,

and peeled him slick and clean
except a few leaves for the tail,
and cinched my brother's belt

around his head for a rein,
I'd straddle and canter him fast
up the grass bank to the path.

trot along in the lovely dust
that talcumed over his hoofs,
hiding my toes, and turning

his feet to swift half-moons
The willow knob with the strap
jouncing between my thighs

was the pommel and yet the poll
of my nickering pony's head.
My head and my neck were mine,

yet they were shaped like a horse.
My hair flopped to the side
like the mane of a horse in the wind.

My forelock swung in my eyes,
my neck arched and I snorted,
I shied and skittered and reared,

stopped and raised my knees,
pawed at the ground and quivered.
My teeth bared as we wheeled

and swished through the dust again.
I was the horse and the rider,
and the leather I slapped to his rump

spanked my own behind.
Doubled, my two hoofs beat
a gallop along the bank,

the wind twanged in my mane,
my mouth squared to the bit.
And yet I sat on my steed

quiet, negligent riding,
my toes standing the stirrups,
my thighs hugging his ribs.

At a walk we drew up to the porch.
I tethered him to a paling
Dismounting, I smoothed my skirt

Illustration by Charles Keeping, from *The Twelve Labors of Hercules,* by Robert Newman. Copyright © 1972 by Charles Keeping; used by permission of Harper & Row Publishers, Inc.

and entered the dusky hall.
My feet on the clean linoleum
left ghostly toes in the hall.

Where have you been? said my mother.
Been riding, I said from the sink,
and filled me a glass of water.

What's that in your pocket? she said.
Just my knife. It weighted my pocket
and stretched my dress awry.

Go tie back your hair, said my mother,
and *Why is your mouth all green?*
*Rob Roy, he pulled some clover
as we crossed the field,* I told her.

38

Nikki Giovanni

A Poem for Carol

(May She Always Wear Red Ribbons)

when i was very little
though it's still true today
there were no sidewalks in lincoln heights
and the home we had on jackson street
was right next to a bus stop and a sewer
which didn't really ever become offensive
but one day from the sewer a little kitten
with one eye gone
came crawling out
though she never really came into our yard but
    just
sort of hung by to watch the folk
my sister who was always softhearted but able
to act effectively started taking milk
out to her while our father would only say
don't bring *him* home and everyday
after school i would rush home to see if she
    was still
there and if gary had fed her but i could never
bring myself to go near her
she was so loving
and so hurt and so singularly beautiful and i
    knew
i had nothing to give that would
replace her one gone eye

38. From Nikki Giovanni, *My House: Poems* (Morrow, 1972).

and if i had named her which i didn't i'm sure
i would have called her carol

39

James Reeves

The Black Pebble

There went three children down to the shore,
    Down to the shore and back;
There was skipping Susan and bright-eyed Sam
    And little scowling Jack.

Susan found a white cockle-shell,
    The prettiest ever seen,
And Sam picked up a piece of glass
    Rounded and smooth and green.

But Jack found only a plain black pebble
    That lay by the rolling sea,
And that was all that ever he found;
    So back they went all three.

The cockle-shell they put on the table,
    The green glass on the shelf,
But the little black pebble that Jack had found,
    He kept it for himself.

40

Robert Graves

Hide and Seek

The trees are tall, but the moon small,
My legs feel rather weak,
For Avis, Mavis and Tom Clarke
Are hiding somewhere in the dark
And it's my turn to seek.

Suppose they lay a trap and play
A trick to frighten me?
Suppose they plan to disappear
And leave me here, half-dead with fear,
Groping from tree to tree?

39. From James Reeves, *The Blackbird in the Lilac* (Dutton, 1959).
40. From Robert Graves, *The Poor Boy Who Followed His Star* (Doubleday, 1969).

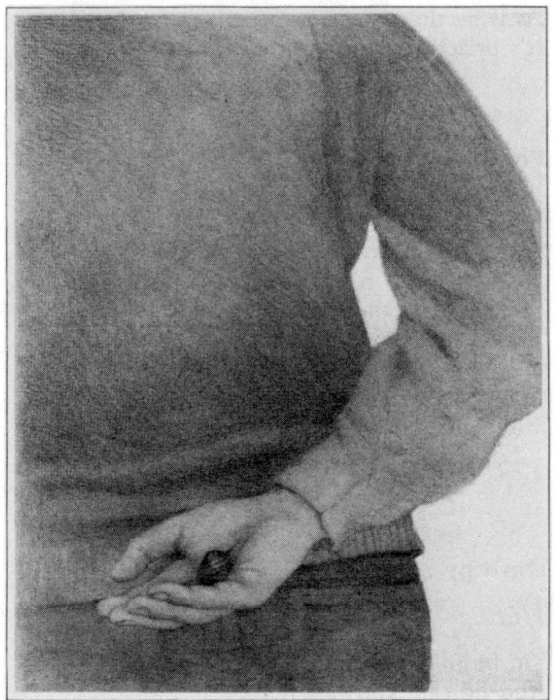

Illustration by Mercer Mayer, from *The Poison Tree and Other Poems.* Copyright © 1977 by Mercer Mayer. Used by permission of Charles Scribner's Sons.

Alone, alone, all on my own
And then perhaps to find
Not Avis, Mavis and young Tom
But monsters to run shrieking from,
Mad monsters of no kind?

41

Eleanor Farjeon

Meeting Mary

Hard by the Wildbrooks I met Mary,
When berries smelled sweet and hot.
Mary, I fancy, was seven years old,
And I am never mind what.

'What are you getting?' I asked Mary.
'Blackberries. What are you?'

41. From Eleanor Farjeon, *Poems for Children* (Lippincott, 1951).

'Toadflax,' I answered Mary, 'and mushrooms.'
'How many mushrooms?' 'Two.'

'Going to have blackberries stewed for dinner,
Or blackberry jam?' said I.
'Not goin' to have neither,' said Mary;
'Goin' to have blackberry pie.'

'Aren't you lucky!' I said to Mary.
'And what sort of name have you got?'
'*My* name's Mary,' said Mary, 'what's *your* name?'
I told her never mind what.

'Good-bye, Mary.' 'Good-bye,' said Mary,
And went on picking and eating.
That's all about my meeting with Mary—
It's my favourite sort of meeting.

42

Countee Cullen

Incident

Once riding in old Baltimore,
    Heart-filled, head-filled with glee,
I saw a Baltimorean
    Keep looking straight at me.

Now I was eight and very small,
    And he was no whit bigger,
And so I smiled, but he poked out
    His tongue, and called me, "Nigger."

I saw the whole of Baltimore
    From May until December;
Of all the things that happened there
    That's all that I remember.

43

Langston Hughes

Aunt Sue's Stories

Aunt Sue has a head full of stories.
Aunt Sue has a whole heart full of stories.

42. From Countee Cullen, *Color* (Harper, 1925).
43. From Langston Hughes, *Selected Poems of Langston Hughes* (Knopf, 1926).

Summer nights on the front porch
Aunt Sue cuddles a brown-faced child to her
    bosom
And tells him stories.

Black slaves
Working in the hot sun,
And black slaves
Walking in the dewy night,
And black slaves
Singing sorrow songs on the banks of a mighty
    river
Mingle themselves softly
In the flow of old Aunt Sue's voice,
Mingle themselves softly
In the dark shadows that cross and recross
Aunt Sue's stories.

And the dark-faced child, listening,
Knows that Aunt Sue's stories are real stories.
He knows that Aunt Sue never got her stories
Out of any book at all,
But that they came
Right out of her own life.

The dark-faced child is quiet
Of a summer night
Listening to Aunt Sue's stories.

44

Charles Lamb and Mary Lamb

The First Tooth

Through the house what busy joy,
Just because the infant boy
Has a tiny tooth to show!
I have got a double row,
All as white, and all as small;
Yet no one cares for mine at all.
He can say but half a word,
Yet that single sound's preferred
To all the words that I can say
In the longest summer day.
He cannot walk, yet it he put
With mimic motion out his foot,

As if he thought he were advancing,
It's prized more than my best dancing.

45

Phyllis McGinley

Triolet against Sisters

Sisters are always drying their hair.
    Locked into rooms, alone,
They pose at the mirror, shoulders bare,
Trying this way and that their hair,
Or fly importunate down the stair
    To answer a telephone.
Sisters are always drying their hair,
    Locked into rooms, alone.

46

Dorothy Aldis

Hiding

I'm hiding. I'm hiding,
And no one knows where;
For all they can see is my
Toes and my hair.

And I just heard my father
Say to my mother—
"But, darling, he must be
Somewhere or other;

Have you looked in the inkwell?"
And Mother said, "Where?"
"In the INKWELL?" said Father. But
I was not there.

Then "Wait!" cried my mother—
"I think that I see
Him under the carpet." But
It was not me.

"Inside the mirror's
A pretty good place,"
Said Father and looked, but saw
Only his face.

44. From Charles Lamb and Mary Lamb, *Poetry for Children*
(Godwin's Juvenile Library, 1809).

45. From Phyllis McGinley, *Times Three: Selected Verse from
Three Decades* (Viking, 1960).
46. From Dorothy Aldis, *Everything and Anything* (Putnam's, 1925).

From the book *Tiny Tim: Verses for Children,* chosen by Jill Bennett. Illustrated by Helen Oxenbury. Illustrations copyright © 1982 by Helen Oxenbury. Reprinted by permission of Delacorte Press.

"We've hunted," sighed Mother,
"As hard as we could.
And I AM so afraid that we've
Lost him for good."

Then I laughed out aloud
And I wiggled my toes
And Father said—"Look, dear,
I wonder if those

Toes could be Benny's?
There are ten of them, see?"
And they WERE SO surprised to find
Out it was me!

47

Frances Cornford

Childhood

I used to think that grown-up people chose
To have stiff backs and wrinkles round their
    nose,
And veins like small fat snakes on either hand,
On purpose to be grand.
Till through the banisters I watched one day

47. From Frances Cornford, *Collected Poems* (Cresset Press, 1954).

My great-aunt Etty's friend who was going away,
And how her onyx beads had come unstrung.
I saw her grope to find them as they rolled;
And then I knew that she was helplessly old,
As I was helplessly young.

48

Theodore Roethke

My Papa's Waltz

The whisky on your breath
Could make a small boy dizzy;
But I hung on like death:
Such waltzing was not easy.

We romped until the pan
Slid from the kitchen shelf;
My mother's countenance
Could not unfrown itself.

The hand that held my wrist
Was battered on one knuckle;
At every step you missed
My right ear scraped a buckle.

You beat time on my head
With a palm caked hard by dirt,
Then waltzed me off to bed
Still clinging to your shirt.

49

Nikki Giovanni

dance poem

come Nataki dance with me
bring your pablum dance with me
pull your plait and whorl around
come Nataki dance with me

won't you Tony dance with me
stop your crying dance with me
feel the rhythm of my arms
don't lets cry now dance with me

Tommy stop your tearing up
don't you hear the music
don't you feel the happy beat
don't bite Tony dance with me
Mommy needs a partner

here comes Karma she will dance
pirouette and bugaloo
short pink dress and dancing shoes
Karma wants to dance with me
don't you Karma don't you

all you children gather round
we will dance and we will whorl
we will dance to our own song
we must spin to our own world
we must spin a soft Black song
all you children gather round
we will dance together

50

e. e. cummings

who are you, little i

who are you, little i

(five or six years old)
peering from some high

window;at the gold

of november sunset

(and feeling;that if day
has to become night

this is a beautiful way)

48. From Theodore Roethke, *The Collected Poems of Theodore Roethke* (Doubleday, 1963).
49. From Nikki Giovanni, *Spin a Soft Black Song* (Hill & Wang, 1971).

50. From e. e. cummings, *Complete Poems, 1913–1962* (Harcourt, 1963).

Poems of Nature

51

Song of Creation

(A poem of the Pima Indians)

According to John Bierhorst, this incantatory poem is based on the Pima myth of the Earth Magician: "Earth Magician, the Pima creator, threw the sun to the north sky, but it would not run its proper course; then to the west sky; then to the south sky. Finally, he threw it to the east, and it rose. Likewise the moon."

I have made the sun!
   I have made the sun!
Hurling it high
   In the four directions
To the east I threw it
   To run its appointed course.

I have made the moon!
   I have made the moon!
Hurling it high
   In the four directions
To the east I threw it
   To run its appointed course.

52

Rachel Field

Early Morning Song

Nothing fairer than the light
On petals opening, gold and white,
To the morning, to the blue,
In a world of song and dew.

Nothing fairer than two eyes
That behold with shy surprise
The miracle no man can stay—
Darkness turning into day.

53

Christina Rossetti

Who Has Seen the Wind?

Who has seen the wind?
   Neither I nor you:
But when the leaves hang trembling
   The wind is passing thro'.

Who has seen the wind?
   Neither you nor I:
But when the trees bow down their heads
   The wind is passing by.

54

The Wind Has Wings

(Eskimo chant)

Nunaptigne . . . In our land—*ahe, ahe, ee, ee, iee*—
The wind has wings, winter and summer.
It comes by night and it comes by day,
And children must fear it—*ahe, ahe, ee, ee, iee.*
In our land the nights are long,
And the spirits like to roam in the dark.
I've seen their faces, I've seen their eyes.
They are like ravens, hovering over the dead,
Their dark wings forming long shadows,
And children must fear them—*ahe, ahe, ee, ee, iee.*

55

Carl Sandburg

Fog

The fog comes
on little cat feet.
It sits looking
over harbor and city
on silent haunches
and then moves on.

51. From John Bierhorst, *In the Trail of the Wind: American Indian Poems and Ritual Orations* (Farrar, Straus & Giroux, 1971).
52. From Rachel Field, *Poems* (Macmillan, 1957).

53. From Christina Rossetti, *Sing-Song: A Nursery Rhyme Book* (Routledge, 1872).
54. From *Ayorama,* trans. Raymond de Coccola and Paul King (Oxford University Press, 1954).
55. From Carl Sandburg, *Chicago Poems* (Harcourt, 1944).

56

Eleanor Farjeon

The Night Will Never Stay

The night will never stay,
The night will still go by,
Though with a million stars
You pin it to the sky,
Though you bind it with the blowing wind
And buckle it with the moon.
The night will slip away
Like sorrow or a tune.

57

Robert Louis Stevenson

At the Sea-side

When I was down beside the sea,
A wooden spade they gave to me
   To dig the sandy shore.

My holes were empty like a cup.
In every hole the sea came up,
   Till it could come no more.

58

David McCord

The Shell

I took away the ocean once,
Spiraled in a shell,
And happily for months and months
I heard it very well.

How is it then that I should hear
What months and months before
Had blown upon me sad and clear,
Down by the grainy shore?

Illustration by Edward Ardizzone, from *How the Moon Began: A Folk Tale from Grimm,* adapted by James Reeves and illustrated by Edward Ardizzone (Abelard-Schuman). Copyright © by James Reeves and Edward Ardizzone. Reprinted by permission of Harper & Row, Publishers, Inc., and Abelard-Shuman Ltd.

59

Maxine W. Kumin

Song of Weeds

Quick as magic,
sly as elves,
the wise old weeds
reseed themselves.
Thistle, sorrel,
purple clover
sprout and spread
and then start over.
Whether days are
dry or wet,
Dutchman's-breeches,
bouncing Bet,
ladyslipper,
buttercup
have a way of

56. From Eleanor Farjeon, *Gypsy and Ginger* (Dutton, 1920).
57. From Robert Louis Stevenson, *A Child's Garden of Verses* (Longmans, 1885).
58. From David McCord, *Far and Few* (Little, Brown, 1952).

59. From Maxine W. Kumin, *No One Writes a Letter to the Snail* (Putnam's, 1962).

springing up.
Names to tickle

tongues and trick you,
tiny seeds or
burs that prick you,
quick as magic,
sly as elves,
weeds take care of
weeds themselves.

60

Here We Come A-Piping

Here we come a-piping
In spring-time and in May;
Green fruit a-ripening,

Illustration by Antonio Frasconi. Illustrations copyright ©
1972 by Antonio Frasconi. From *Crickets and Frogs* (A Margaret K. McElderry Book). Used by permission of Atheneum Publishers.

And winter fled away.
The Queen she sits upon the strand,
Fair as a lily, white as wand;
Seven billows on the sea,
Horses riding fast and free,
And bells beyond the sand.

61

William Blake

Spring

Sound the flute!
Now it's mute!
Birds delight,
Day and night,
Nightingale,
In the dale,
Lark in sky—
Merrily,
Merrily, merrily to welcome in the year.

Little boy,
Full of joy,
Little girl,
Sweet and small;
Cock does crow,
So do you;
Merry voice,
Infant noise;
Merrily, merrily we welcome in the year.

Little lamb,
Here I am;
Come and lick
My white neck;
Let me pull
Your soft wool;
Let me kiss
Your soft face;
Merrily, merrily we welcome in the year.

61. From William Blake, *Songs of Innocence* (Printed by William Blake, 1789; facsimile ed., Dover, 1971).

62

e. e. cummings

in Just-spring

in Just-
spring   when the world is mud-
luscious the little
lame balloonman

whistles   far   and wee

and eddieandbill come
running from marbles and
piracies and it's
spring

when the world is puddle-wonderful

the queer
old balloonman whistles
far   and   wee
and bettyandisbel come dancing

from hop-scotch and jump-rope and

it's
spring
and
        the
                goat-footed

balloonMan   whistles
far
and
wee

63

Shiki

Summer Night

(Japanese)

A lightning flash:
    between the forest trees
        I have seen water.

From *The Seasons of Time*, by Virginia Olsen Baron, illustrated by Yasuhide Kobashi. Copyright © 1963 by Virginia Olsen Baron. Reprinted by permission of the publisher, Dial Books for Young Readers, a division of E. P. Dutton, Inc.

64

John Updike

September

The breezes taste
    Of apple peel.
The air is full
    Of smells to feel—

Ripe fruit, old footballs,
    Burning brush,
New books, erasers,
    Chalk, and such.

The bee, his hive
    Well-honeyed, hums,
And Mother cuts
    Chrysanthemums.

62. From e. e. cummings, *Complete Poems, 1913–1962* (Harcourt, 1963).
63. From Harold Gould Henderson, *An Introduction to Haiku: An Anthology of Poems from Basho to Shiki* (Doubleday, 1958).

64. From John Updike, *A Child's Calendar* (Knopf, 1965).

Like plates washed clean
   With suds, the days
Are polished with
   A morning haze.

65

Carl Sandburg

Splinter

The voice of the last cricket
across the first frost
is one kind of good-by.
It is so thin a splinter of singing.

66

Aileen Fisher

Snowy Benches

Do parks get lonely
in winter, perhaps,
when benches have only
snow on their laps?

67

Langston Hughes

Winter Moon

How thin and sharp is the moon tonight!
How thin and sharp and ghostly white
Is the slim curved crook of the moon tonight!

68

I Sing for the Animals

(*Teton Sioux*)

Out of the earth
I sing for them,
A Horse nation
I sing for them.

Out of the earth
I sing for them,
The animals
I sing for them.

69

Langston Hughes

Snail

Little snail,
Dreaming you go,
Weather and rose
Is all you know.

Weather and rose
Is all you see,
Drinking the dewdrop's
Mystery.

70

Christina Rossetti

The Caterpillar

Brown and furry
Caterpillar in a hurry
Take your walk
To the shady leaf or stalk
Or what not,
Which may be the chosen spot.
No toad spy you,
Hovering bird of prey pass by you;
Spin and die,
To live again a butterfly.

71

Elizabeth Madox Roberts

Firefly

(*A Song*)

A little light is going by,
Is going up to see the sky,
A little light with wings.

65. From Carl Sandburg, *Good Morning, America* (Harcourt, 1928).
66. From Aileen Fisher, *Out in the Dark and Daylight* (Harper, 1980).
67. From Langston Hughes, *Selected Poems of Langston Hughes* (Knopf, 1926).
68. From Frances Densmore, *Bureau of American Ethnology, Bulletin 61* (Smithsonian Institution).

69. From Langston Hughes, *Selected Poems of Langston Hughes* (Knopf, 1926).
70. From Christina Rossetti, *Sing-Song: A Nursery Rhyme Book* (Routledge, 1872).
71. From Elizabeth Madox Roberts, *Under the Tree* (Viking, 1950).

I never could have thought of it,
To have a little bug all lit
And made to go on wings.

72

Randall Jarrell

The Bird of Night

A shadow is floating through the moonlight.
Its wings don't make a sound.
Its claws are long, its beak is bright.
Its eyes try all the corners of the night.

It calls and calls: all the air swells and heaves
And washes up and down like water.
The ear that listens to the owl believes
In death. The bat beneath the eaves,

The mouse beside the stone are still as death.
The owl's air washes them like water.
The owl goes back and forth inside the night,
And the night holds its breath.

73

Ted Hughes

The Loon

The Loon, the Loon
Hatched from the Moon

From *Under the North Star,* by Ted Hughes, illustrated by
Leonard Baskin. Illustrations copyright © 1981 by Leonard
Baskin. Reprinted by permission of Viking Penguin Inc.

72. From Randall Jarrell, *The Bat-Poet* (Macmillan, 1964).
73. From Ted Hughes, *Under the North Star* (Viking, 1981).

Writhes out of the lake
Like an airborne snake.

He swallows a trout
An then shakes out

A ghastly cry
As if the sky
Were trying to die.

74

Lilian Moore

Pigeons

Pigeons are city folk
content
to live with concrete
and cement.

They seldom
try
the sky.

A pigeon never sings
of hill
and flowering hedge,
but busily commutes
from sidewalk
to his ledge.

Oh pigeon, what a waste of wings!

75

Randall Jarrell

Bats

A bat is born
Naked and blind and pale.
His mother makes a pocket of her tail
And catches him. He clings to her long fur
By his thumbs and toes and teeth.
And then the mother dances through the night
Doubling and looping, soaring,
    somersaulting—
Her baby hangs on underneath.

74. From Lilian Moore, *I Thought I Heard the City* (Atheneum, 1969).
75. From Randall Jarrell, *The Bat-Poet* (Macmillan, 1964).

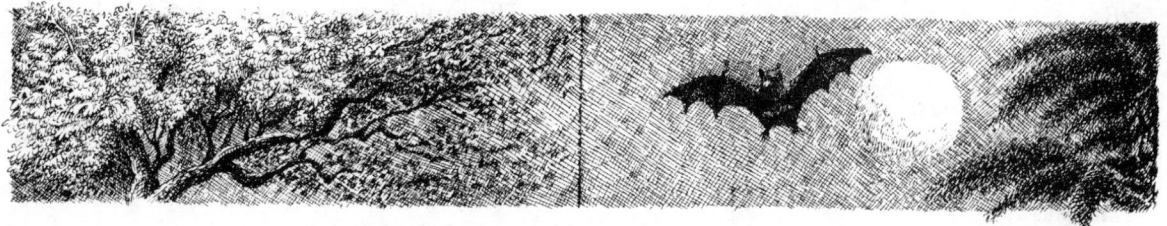

Reprinted with permission of Macmillan Publishing Company, from *The Bat-Poet,* by Randall Jarrell, illustrated by Maurice Sendak. Copyright © Macmillan Publishing Company, 1963, 1964.

All night, in happiness, she hunts and flies.
Her high sharp cries
Like shining needlepoints of sound
Go out into the night, and echoing back,
Tell her what they have touched.
She hears how far it is, how big it is,
Which way it's going:
She lives by hearing.
The mother eats the moths and gnats she catches
In full flight; in full flight
The mother drinks the water of the pond
She skims across. Her baby hangs on tight.
Her baby drinks the milk she makes him
In moonlight or starlight, in mid-air.
Their single shadow, printed on the moon
Or fluttering across the stars,
Whirls on all night; at daybreak
The tired mother flaps home to her rafter.
The others all are there.
They hang themselves up by their toes,
They wrap themselves in their brown wings.
Bunched upside-down, they sleep in air.
Their sharp ears, their sharp teeth, their quick
    sharp faces
Are dull and slow and mild.
All the bright day, as the mother sleeps,
She folds her wings about her sleeping child.

76

Theodore Roethke

The Bat

By day the bat is cousin to the mouse.
He likes the attic of an aging house.

His fingers make a hat about his head.
His pulse beat is so slow we think him dead.

He loops in crazy figures half the night
Among the trees that face the corner light.

But when he brushes up against a screen,
We are afraid of what our eyes have seen:

For something is amiss or out of place
When mice with wings can wear a human face.

77

Rose Fyleman

Mice

I think mice
Are rather nice.

    Their tails are long,
    Their faces small,
    They haven't any
    Chins at all.
    Their ears are pink,
    Their teeth are white,
    They run about
    The house at night.
    They nibble things
    They shouldn't touch
    And no one seems
    To like them much.

But *I* think mice
Are nice.

76. From Theodore Roethke, *The Collected Poems of Theodore Roethke* (Doubleday, 1963).

77. From Rose Fyleman, *Fifty-One Nursery Rhymes* (Doubleday, 1931).

78

Theodore Roethke

The Meadow Mouse

1 In a shoe box stuffed in an old nylon stocking
   Sleeps the baby mouse I found in the
      meadow,
   Where he trembled and shook beneath a stick
   Till I caught him up by the tail and brought
      him in.
   Cradled in my hand,
   A little quaker, the whole body of him trem-
      bling,
   His absurd whiskers sticking out like a car-
      toon-mouse,
   His feet like small leaves,
   Little lizard-feet.
   Whitish and spread wide when he tried to
      struggle away,
   Wriggling like a miniscule puppy.

   Now he's eaten his three kinds of cheese
      and drunk from his bottle-cap watering-
      trough—
   So much he just lies in one corner,
   His tail curled under him, his belly big
   As his head, his bat-like ears
   Twitching, tilting toward the least sound.

   Do I imagine he no longer trembles
      When I come close to him?
   He seems no longer to tremble.

2 But this morning the shoe-box house on the
      back porch is empty.
   Where has he gone, my meadow mouse,
   My thumb of a child that nuzzled in my
      palm?—
   To run under the hawk's wing,
   Under the eye of the great owl watching from
      the elm-tree,
   To live by courtesy of the shrike, the snake,
      the tom-cat.

   I think of the nestling fallen into the deep
      grass,

The turtle gasping in the dusty rubble of the
   highway,
The paralytic stunned in the tub, and the water rising,—
All things innocent, hapless, forsaken.

79

James Stephens

The Snare

I hear a sudden cry of pain!
   There is a rabbit in a snare:
Now I hear the cry again,
   But I cannot tell from where.

But I cannot tell from where
   He is calling out for aid;
Crying on the frightened air,
   Making everything afraid,

Making everything afraid
   Wrinkling up his little face,
As he cries again for aid;
   And I cannot find the place!

And I cannot find the place
   Where his paw is in the snare;
Little one! Oh, little one!
   I am searching everywhere.

80

D. H. Lawrence

Little Fish

The tiny fish enjoy themselves
in the sea.
Quick little splinters of life,
their little lives are fun to them
in the sea.

78. From Theodore Roethke, *The Collected Works of Theodore Roethke* (Doubleday, 1963).

79. From James Stephens, *Collected Poems* (Macmillan, 1943).
80. From D. H. Lawrence, *The Complete Poems of D. H. Lawrence* (Viking, 1964).

81

William Jay Smith

Seal

    See how he dives
        From the rocks with a zoom!
    See how he darts
        Through his watery room
    Past crabs and eels
    And green seaweed,
    Past fluffs of sandy
    Minnow feed!
        See how he swims
        With a swerve and a twist,
    A flip of the flipper,
    A flick of the wrist!
    Quicksilver-quick,
    Softer than spray,
    Down he plunges
    And sweeps away;
    Before you can think,
    Before you can utter
    Words like "Dill pickle"
    Or "Apple butter,"
    Back up he swims
    Past sting-ray and shark,
    Out with a zoom,
    A whoop, a bark;
        Before you can say
        Whatever you wish,
        He plops at your side
        With a mouthful of fish!

82

Walter de la Mare

Nicholas Nye

Thistle and darnel and dock grew there,
  And a bush, in a corner, of may;
On the orchard wall I used to sprawl
  In the blazing heat of the day;
Half asleep and half awake,
  While the birds went twittering by,

And nobody there my lone to share
  But Nicholas Nye.

Nicholas Nye was lean and grey,
  Lame of a leg and old,
More than a score of donkey's years
  He had seen since he was foaled;
He munched the thistles, purple and spiked,
  Would sometimes stop and sigh,
And turn his head, as if he said,
  "Poor Nicholas Nye!"

Alone with his shadow he'd drowse in the
    meadow,
  Lazily, swinging his tail;
At break of day he used to bray,—
  Not much too hearty and hale.

But a wonderful gumption was under his skin,
  And a clear calm light in his eye,
And once in a while he would smile a smile
  Would Nicholas Nye.

Seem to be smiling at me, he would,
From his bush, in the corner, of may—
Bony and ownerless, widowed and worn,
  Knobble-kneed, lonely and grey;
And over the grass would seem to pass
  'Neath the deep dark blue of the sky,
Something much better than words between me
  And Nicholas Nye.

But dusk would come in the apple boughs,
  The green of the glow-worm shine,
The birds in nest would crouch to rest,
  And home I'd trudge to mine;
And there, in the moonlight, dark with dew,
  Asking not wherefore nor why,
Would brood like a ghost, and as still as a post,
  Old Nicholas Nye.

83

Irene Rutherford McLeod

Lone Dog

I'm a lean dog, a keen dog, a wild dog and
  lone,

81. From William Jay Smith, *Boy Blue's Book of Beasts* (Little, Brown, 1956).
82. From Walter de la Mare, *Peacock Pie* (Knopf, 1912).

83. From Irene Rutherford McLeod, *Songs to Save a Soul* (Chatto & Windus, 1915).

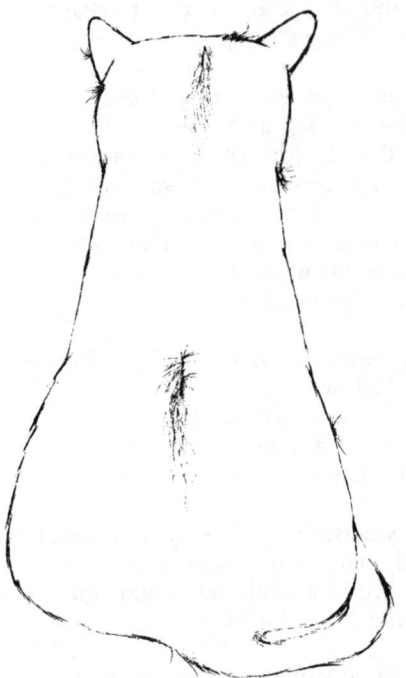

Illustration by William Sokol, from *Cats Cats Cats Cats Cats,* by Beatrice Schenk de Regniers, illustrated by William Sokol. Copyright © 1958 by Beatrice Schenk de Regniers and William Sokol. Reprinted by permission of William Sokol.

I'm a rough dog, a tough dog, hunting on my
    own!
I'm a bad dog, a mad dog, teasing silly sheep;
I love to sit and bay at the moon and keep fat
    souls from sleep.

I'll never be a lap dog, licking dirty feet,
A sleek dog, a meek dog, cringing for my meat.
Not for me the fireside, the well-filled plate,
But shut door and sharp stone and cuff and kick
    and hate.

Not for me the other dogs, running by my side,
Some have run a short while, but none of them
    would bide.
O mine is still the lone trail, the hard trail, the
    best,
Wide wind and wild stars and the hunger of
    the quest.

84

Valerie Worth

Cat

The spotted cat hops
Up to a white radiator-cover
As warm as summer, and there,

Between pots of green leaves growing,
By a window of cold panes showing
Silver of snow thin across the grass,

She settles slight neat muscles
Smoothly down within
Her comfortable fur,

Slips in the ends, front paws,
Tail, until she is readied,
Arranged, shaped for sleep.

85

Elizabeth Coatsworth

"Who are *you?*" asked the cat of the bear.
"I am a child of the wood,
I am strong with rain-shedding hair,
I hunt without fear for my food,
The others behold me and quail."
Said the cat, "You are lacking a tail."

What can you *do?*" asked the cat.
"I can climb for the honey I crave.
In the fall when I'm merry and fat
I seek out a suitable cave
And sleep till I feel the spring light."
Said the cat, "Can you see in the night?"

Said the cat, "*I* sit by man's fire,
But I am much wilder than you.
I do the thing I desire
And do nothing I don't want to do.
I am small, but then, what is that?
My spirit is great," said the cat.

84. From Valerie Worth, *Small Poems* (Farrar, Straus & Giroux, 1972).
85. From Elizabeth Coatsworth, *Away Goes Sally* (Macmillan, 1934).

86

Charles Causley

My Mother Saw a Dancing Bear

My mother saw a dancing bear
By the schoolyard, a day in June.
The keeper stood with chain and bar
And whistle-pipe, and played a tune.

And bruin lifted up its head
And lifted up its dusty feet,
And all the children laughed to see
It caper in the summer heat.

They watched as for the Queen it died.
They watched it march. They watched it halt.
They heard the keeper as he cried,
'Now, roly-poly!' 'Somersault!'

And then, my mother said, there came
The keeper with a begging-cup,
The bear with burning coat of fur,
Shaming the laughter to a step.

They paid a penny for the dance,
But what they saw was not the show;
Only, in bruin's aching eyes,
Far distant forests, and the snow.

87

D. H. Lawrence

The White Horse

The youth walks up to the white horse, to put
   its halter on
and the horse looks at him in silence.
They are so silent, they are in another world.

88

Emily Dickinson

A narrow fellow in the grass

A narrow fellow in the grass
Occasionally rides;
You may have met him,—did you not?
His notice sudden is.

The grass divides as with a comb,
A spotted shaft is seen;
And then it closes at your feet
And opens further on.

He likes a boggy acre,
A floor too cool for corn.
Yet when a child, and barefoot,
I more than once, at morn,

Have passed, I thought, a whip-lash
Unbraiding in the sun,—
When, stooping to secure it,
It wrinkled, and was gone.

Several of nature's people
I know, and they know me;
I feel for them a transport
Of cordiality;

But never met this fellow,
Attended or alone,
Without a tighter breathing,
And zero at the bone.

89

Elizabeth Coatsworth

Swift Things Are Beautiful

Swift things are beautiful:
Swallows and deer,
And lightning that falls
Bright-veined and clear,
Rivers and meteors,
Wind in the wheat,
The strong-withered horse,
The runner's sure feet.

And slow things are beautiful:
The closing of day,

86. From Charles Causley, *Figgie Hobbin* (Walker & Co., 1973).
87. From D. H. Lawrence, *The Complete Poems of D. H. Lawrence* (Viking, 1964).
88. From *Poems of Emily Dickinson*, ed. Martha Dickinson Bianchi and Alfred Leete Hampson (Little, Brown, 1937).
89. From Elizabeth Coatsworth, *Away Goes Sally* (Macmillan, 1934).

The pause of the wave
That curves downward to spray,
The ember that crumbles,
The opening flower,
And the ox that moves on
In the quiet of power.

Poems of Imagination

90

David McCord

Take Sky

Now think of words. Take *sky*
And ask yourself just why—
Like sun, moon, star, and cloud—
It sounds so well out loud,
And pleases so the sight
When printed black on white.
Take syllable and thimble:
The sound of *them* is nimble.
Take bucket, spring, and dip
Cold water to your lip.
Take balsam, fir, and pine:
Your woodland smell and mine.
Take kindle, blaze, and flicker—
What lights the hearth fire quicker?

Three words we fear but form:
Gale, twister, thunderstorm;
Others that simply shake
Are tremble, temblor, quake.
But granite, stone, and rock:
Too solid, they, to shock.
Put honey, bee, and flower
With sunny, shade, and shower;
Put *wild* with bird and wing,
Put *bird* with song and sing.
Aren't paddle, trail, and camp
The cabin and the lamp?
Now look at words of rest—
Sleep, quiet, calm, and blest;

At words we learn in youth—
Grace, skill, ambition, truth;
At words of lifelong need—
Grit, courage, strength, and deed;
Deep-rooted words that say
Love, hope, dream, yearn, and pray;
Light-hearted words—girl, boy,
Live, laugh; play, share, enjoy.
October, April, June—
Come late and gone too soon.

Remember, words are life:
Child, husband, mother, wife;
Remember, and I'm done:
Words taken one by one
Are poems as they stand—
Shore, beacon, harbor, land;
Brook, river, mountain, vale,
Crow, rabbit, otter, quail;

Illustration by Henry B. Kane, from *One at a Time,* by David McCord (1974). By permission of Little, Brown and Co.

90. From David McCord, *One at a Time* (Little, Brown, 1974).

Faith, freedom, water, snow,
Wind, weather, flood, and floe.
Like light across the lawn
Are morning, sea, and dawn;
Words of the green earth growing—
Seed, soil, and farmer sowing.
Like wind upon the mouth
Sad, summer, rain, and south.
Amen. Put not asunder
Man's *first* word: wonder . . . wonder . . .

91

James A. Emanuel

A Small Discovery

Father,
Where do giants go to cry?

To the hills
Behind the thunder?
Or to the waterfall?
I wonder.

(Giants cry.
I know they do.
Do they wait
Till nighttime too?)

92

James Reeves

The Footprint

Poor Crusoe saw with fear-struck eyes
    The footprint on the shore—
Oh! what is this that shines so clear
    Upon the bathroom floor?

93

Charles Causley

Tell Me, Tell Me, Sarah Jane

Tell me, tell me, Sarah Jane,
    Tell me, dearest daughter,
Why are you holding in your hand
    A thimbleful of water?

Why do you hold it to your eye
    And gaze both late and soon
From early morning light until
    The rising of the moon?

Mother, I hear the mermaids cry,
    I hear the mermen sing,
And I can see the sailing ships
    All made of sticks and string.
And I can see the jumping fish,
    The whales that fall and rise
And swim about the waterspout
    That swarms up to the skies.

Tell me, tell me, Sarah Jane,
    Tell your darling mother,
Why do you walk beside the tide
    As though you loved none other?
Why do you listen to a shell
    And watch the waters curl,
And throw away your diamond ring
    And wear instead the pearl?

Mother, I hear the water
    Beneath the headland pinned,
And I can see the sea gull
    Sliding down the wind.
I taste the salt upon my tongue
    As sweet as sweet can be.

Tell me, my dear, whose voice you hear?

    It is the sea, the sea.

94

Robert Louis Stevenson

The Wind

I saw you toss the kites on high
And blow the birds about the sky;

91. From James A. Emanuel, *The Treehouse and Other Poems* (Broadside, 1968).
92. From James Reeves, *The Blackbird in the Lilac* (Oxford University Press, 1952).
93. From Charles Causley, *Figgie Hobbin* (Walker & Co., 1973).
94. From Robert Louis Stevenson, *A Child's Garden of Verses* (Longmans, 1885).

Illustration by Felix Hoffmann, from *Rapunzel: A Story by the Brothers Grimm.*
Reprinted by permission of Harcourt Brace Jovanovich, Inc. Copyright © 1949
by Amerbach-Verlag, Basle, and 1961 by Oxford University Press (London).

And all around I heard you pass,
Like ladies' skirts across the grass—
   O wind, a-blowing all day long,
   O wind, that sings so loud a song!

I saw the different things you did,
But always you yourself you hid.
I felt you push, I heard you call,
I could not see yourself at all—

O wind, a-blowing all day long,
O wind, that sings so loud a song!

O you that are so strong and cold,
O blower, are you young or old?
Are you a beast of field and tree,
Or just a stronger child than me?
   O wind, a-blowing all day long,
   O wind, that sings so loud a song!

95

James Reeves

Bobadil

Far from far
  Lives Bobadil
In a tall house
  On a tall hill.

Out from the high
  Top window-sill
On a clear night
  Leans Bobadil

To touch the moon,
  To catch a star,
To keep in her tall house
  Far from far.

96

Clyde Watson

Knock! Knock!

Knock! Knock! Anybody there?
I've feathers for your caps
And ribbons for your hair.
If you can't pay you can sing me a song,
But if you can't sing, I'll just run along.

97

Walter de la Mare

Some One

Some one came knocking
  At my wee, small door;
Some one came knocking,
  I'm sure—sure—sure;
I listened, I opened,
  I looked to left and right,
But nought there was a-stirring
  In the still dark night;

Only the busy beetle
  Tap-tapping in the wall,
Only from the forest
  The screech-owl's call,
Only the cricket whistling
  While the dewdrops fall,
So I know not who came knocking,
  At all, at all, at all.

98

William Butler Yeats

The Stolen Child

Where dips the rocky highland
Of Sleuth Wood in the lake,
There lies a leafy island
Where flapping herons wake
The drowsy water-rats;
There we've hid our faery vats,
Full of berries
And of reddest stolen cherries.
Come away, Oh human child!
To the waters and the wild
With a faery, hand in hand,
For the world's more full of weeping than you can
  understand.

Where the wave of moonlight glosses
The dim grey sands with light,
Far off by furthest Rosses
We foot it all the night,
Weaving olden dances,
Mingling hands and mingling glances
Till the moon has taken flight;
To and fro we leap
And chase the frothy bubbles,
While the world is full of troubles
And is anxious in its sleep.
Come away, O human child!
To the waters and the wild
With a faery, hand in hand,
For the world's more full of weeping than you can
  understand.

95. From James Reeves, *The Blackbird in the Lilac* (Oxford University Press, 1952).
96. From Clyde Watson, *Father Fox's Pennyrhymes* (Crowell, 1971).
97. From Walter de la Mare, *Peacock Pie* (Holt, 1912).

98. From William Butler Yeats, *Collected Poems* (Macmillan, 1934).

Where the wandering water gushes
From the hills above Glen-Car,
In pools among the rushes
That scarce could bathe a star,
We seek for slumbering trout
And whispering in their ears
Give them unquiet dreams;
Leaning softly out
From ferns that drop their tears
Over the young streams.

Come away, O human child!
To the waters and the wild
With a faery, hand in hand,
For the world's more full of weeping than you can
*   understand.*

Away with us he's going,
The solemn-eyed:
He'll hear no more than lowing

Of the calves on the warm hillside
Or the kettle on the hob
Sing peace into his breast,
Or see the brown mice bob
Round and round the oatmeal-chest.

For he comes, the human child,
To the waters and the wild
With a faery, hand in hand,
From a world more full of weeping than he can
*   understand.*

99

The Elves' Dance

Round about, round about
    In a fair ring-a,
Thus we dance, thus we dance
    And thus we sing-a,

Illustration by Edward Ardizzone, from *How the Moon Began: A Folk Tale from Grimm,*
adapted by James Reeves and illustrated by Edward Ardizzone (Abelard-Schuman).
Copyright © 1971 by James Reeves and Edward Ardizzone. Reprinted by permission of Harper & Row Publishers, Inc., and Abelard-Schuman Ltd.

Trip and go, to and fro
  Over this green-a,
All about, in and out,
  For our brave Queen-a.

100

Rachel Field

The Seven Ages of Elf-hood

When an Elf is as old as a year and a minute
He can wear a cap with a feather in it.

By the time that he is two times two
He has a buckle for either shoe.

At twenty he is fine as a fiddle,
With a little brown belt to go round his middle.

When he's lived for fifty years or so
His coat may have buttons all in a row.

If past three score and ten he's grown
Two pockets he has for his very own.

At eighty-two or three years old
They bulge and jingle with bits of gold.

But when he's a hundred and a day
He gets a little pipe to play!

101

Elinor Wylie

Escape

When foxes eat the last gold grape,
And the last white antelope is killed,
I shall stop fighting and escape
Into a little house I'll build.

But first I'll shrink to fairy size,
With a whisper no one understands,
Making blind moons of all your eyes,
And muddy roads of all your hands.

And you may grope for me in vain
In hollows under the mangrove root,

Or where, in apple-scented rain,
The silver wasp-nests hang like fruit.

102

James Reeves

If Pigs Could Fly

If pigs could fly, I'd fly a pig
To foreign countries small and big—
  To Italy and Spain,
To Austria, where cowbells ring,
To Germany, where people sing—
  And then come home again.

I'd see the Ganges and the Nile;
I'd visit Madagascar's isle,
  And Persia and Peru.
People would say they'd never seen
So odd, so strange an air-machine
  As that on which I flew.

Why, everyone would raise a shout
To see his trotters and his snout
  Come floating from the sky;
And I would be a famous star
Well known in countries near and far—
  If only pigs could fly!

103

May Swenson

Southbound on the Freeway

A tourist came in from Orbitville,
parked in the air, and said:

The creatures of this star
are made of metal and glass.

Through the transparent parts
you can see their guts.

Their feet are round and roll
on diagrams or long

100. From Rachel Field, *Poems* (Macmillan, 1957).
101. From Elinor Wylie, *Collected Poems* (Knopf, 1932).
102. From James Reeves, *The Blackbird in the Lilac* (Oxford University Press, 1952).
103. From May Swenson, *New and Selected Things Taking Place: Poems* (Little, Brown, 1971).

measuring tapes, dark
with white lines.

They have four eyes.
The two in back are red.

Sometimes you can see a five-eyed
one, with a red eye turning

on the top of his head.
He must be special—

the others respect him
and go slow

when he passes, winding
among them from behind.

They all hiss as they glide,
like inches, down the marked

tapes. Those soft shapes,
shadowy inside

the hard bodies—are they
their guts or their brains?

104

Bobbi Katz

Things to Do If You Are a Subway

Pretend you are a dragon.
Live in underground caves.
Roar about underneath the city.
Swallow piles of people.
Spit them out at the next station.
Zoom through the darkness.
Be an express.
Go fast.
Make as much noise as you please.

105

Ted Hughes

My Father

Some fathers work at the office, others work
    at the store,

105. From Ted Hughes, *Meet My Folks* (Bobbs-Merrill,
1961).

Some operate great cranes and build up sky-
    scrapers galore,
Some work in canning factories counting green
    peas into cans,
Some drive all night in huge and thundering
    removal vans.

But mine has the strangest job of the lot.
My Father's the Chief Inspector of—What?
O don't tell the mice, don't tell the moles,
My Father's the Chief Inspector of
H O L E S.

It's a work of the highest importance because
    you never know
What's in a hole, what fearful thing is creeping
    from below.
Perhaps it's a hole to the ocean and will soon
    gush water in tons,
Or maybe it leads to a vast cave full of gold
    and skeletons.

Though a hole might seem to have nothing
    but dirt in,
Somebody's simply got to make certain.
Caves in the mountain, clefts in the wall,
My Father has to inspect them all.

That crack in the road looks harmless. My Father
    knows it's not.
The world may be breaking into two and start-
    ing at that spot.
Or maybe the world is a great egg, and we
    live on the shell,
And it's just beginning to split and hatch: you
    simply cannot tell.

If you see a crack, run to the phone, run;
My Father will know just what's to be done.
A rumbling hole, a silent hole,
My Father will soon have it under control.

Keeping a check on all these holes he hurries
    from morning to night.
There might be sounds of marching in one, or
    an eye shining bright.
A tentacle came groping from a hole that be-
    longed to a mouse,
A floor collapsed and Chinamen swarmed up
    into the house.

Illustration by Hans Fischer, from his volume *The Birthday*. Copyright © 1954 by Harcourt Brace Jovanovich, Inc.; renewed 1982 by Bianca Fischer. Reproduced by permission of the publisher.

A Hole's an unpredictable thing—
Nobody knows what a Hole might bring.
Caves in the mountain, clefts in the wall,
My Father has to inspect them all!

106

Laura E. Richards

Was She a Witch?

There was an old woman
    Lived down in a dell;
She used to draw picklejacks
    Out of the well.
How did she do it?
Nobody knew it.
    She never, no never, no never would tell.

106. From Laura E. Richards, *Tirra Lirra: Rhymes Old and New* (Little, Brown, 1955).

107

e. e. cummings

hist   whist

hist   whist
little ghostthings
tip-toe
twinkle-toe

little twitchy
witches and tingling
goblins
hob-a-nob   hob-a-nob

little hoppy happy
toad in tweeds
tweeds
little itchy mousies

107. From e. e. cummings, *Complete Poems, 1913–1962* (Harcourt, 1963).

with scuttling
eyes   rustle and run   and
hidehidehide
whisk

whisk   look out for the old woman
with the wart on her nose
what she'll do to yer
nobody knows

for she knows the devil   ooch
the devil   ooch
the devil
ach   the great

green
dancing
devil
devil

devil
devil

wheeEEE

108

James Stephens

The Devil's Bag

I saw the Devil walking down the lane
Behind our house.—A heavy bag
Was strapped upon his shoulders and the rain
Sizzled when it hit him.
He picked a rag
Up from the ground and put it in his sack,
And grinned, and rubbed his hands.
There was a thing
Alive inside the bag upon his back
—It must have been a soul! I saw it fling
And twist about inside, and not a hole
Or cranny for escape! Oh, it was sad!
I cried, and shouted out,—*Let out that Soul!*
But he turned round, and, sure, his face went
    mad,
And twisted up and down, and he said *"Hell!"*
And ran away . . . Oh, mammy! I'm not well!

109

Robert Graves

The Penny Fiddle

Yesterday I bought a penny fiddle
    And put it to my chin to play,
But I found that the strings were painted
    So I threw my fiddle away.

Illustration © 1971 by Leo and Diane Dillon, from *Gassire's Lute*, translated and adapted by Alta Jablow. Reproduced by permission of E. P. Dutton, Inc.

108. From James Stephens, *Collected Poems* (Macmillan, 1943).

109. From Robert Graves, *The Penny Fiddle: Poems for Children* (Cassell, 1960).

A little red man found my fiddle
  As it lay abandoned there;
He asked me if he might keep it,
  And I told him I did not care.

But he drew such music from the fiddle
  With help of a farthing bow
That I offered five guineas for the secret
  But alas he would never let it go.

110

T. S. Eliot

Macavity: The Mystery Cat

Macavity's a Mystery Cat: he's called the Hidden
  Paw—
For he's the master criminal who can defy the
  Law.
He's the bafflement of Scotland Yard, the Flying
  Squad's despair:
For when they reach the scene of crime—*Macavity's not there!*

  Macavity, Macavity, there's no one like Macavity,
For he's broken every human law, he breaks the
  law of gravity.
His powers of levitation would make a fakir
  stare,
And when you reach the scene of crime—*Macavity's not there!*
You may seek him in the basement, you may
  look up in the air—
But I tell you once and once again, *Macavity's not there!*

  Macavity's a ginger cat, he's very tall and thin;
You would know him if you saw him, for his
  eyes are sunken in.
His brow is deeply lined with thought, his head
  is highly domed;
His coat is dusty from neglect, his whiskers are
  uncombed.
He sways his head from side to side, with movements like a snake;

110. From T. S. Eliot, *Old Possum's Book of Practical Cats*
(Harcourt, 1939).

And when you think he's half asleep, he's always
  wide awake.

  Macavity, Macavity, there's no one like Macavity,
For he's a fiend in feline shape, a monster of
  depravity.
You may meet him in a by-street, you may see
  him in the square—
But when a crime's discovered, then *Macavity's not there!*
  He's outwardly respectable. (They say he
  cheats at cards.)
And his footprints are not found in any file of
  Scotland Yard's.
And when the larder's looted, or the jewelcase
  is rifled,
Or when the milk is missing, or another Peke's
  been stifled,
Or the greenhouse glass is broken, and the trellis
  past repair—
Ay, there's the wonder of the thing! *Macavity's not there!*

  And when the Foreign Office find a Treasury's
  gone astray,
Or the Admiralty lose some plans and drawings
  by the way,
There may be a scrap of paper in the hall or
  on the stair—
But it's useless to investigate—*Macavity's not there!*
And when the loss has been disclosed, the Secret
  Service say:
"It *must* have been Macavity!"—but he's a mile
  away.
You'll be sure to find him resting, or a-licking
  of his thumbs,
Or engaged in doing complicated long division
  sums.

  Macavity, Macavity, there's no one like Macavity,
There never was a Cat of such deceitfulness and
  suavity.
He always has an alibi, and one or two to spare:
At whatever time the deed took place—MACAVITY WASN'T THERE!
And they say that all the Cats whose wicked
  deeds are widely known

Illustration copyright © 1982 by Edward Gorey.
Reproduced by permission of Harcourt Brace Jovanovich,
Inc., from *Old Possum's Book of Practical Cats,* by T. S. Eliot.

(I might mention Mungojerrie, I might mention
    Griddlebone)
Are nothing more than agents for the Cat who
    all the time
Just controls their operations: the Napoleon of
    Crime!

111

Carmen Bernos De Gasztold

The Prayer of the Little Pig

Lord,
    their politeness makes me laugh!

111. From Carmen Bernos De Gasztold, *Prayers from the
Ark,* trans. Rumer Godden (Viking, 1962).

Yes, I grunt!
Grunt and snuffle!
I grunt because I grunt
and snuffle
because I cannot do anything else!
All the same, I am not going to thank them
for fattening me up to make bacon.
Why did You make me so tender?
What a fate!
Lord,
teach me how to say
                    Amen

112

Kenneth Patchen

The Magical Mouse

I am the magical mouse
I don't eat cheese
I eat sunsets
And the tops of trees
I don't wear fur
I wear funnels
Of lost ships and the weather
That's under dead leaves

I am the magical mouse
I don't fear cats
Or woodsowls
I do as I please
Always
I don't eat crusts
I am the magical mouse
I eat
Little birds—and maidens

That taste like dust

113

Thomas Hardy

The Garden Seat

Its former green is blue and thin,
And its once firm legs sink in and in;

112. From Kenneth Patchen, *The Collected Poems of Kenneth
Patchen* (New Directions, 1952).
113. From Thomas Hardy, *Collected Poems* (Macmillan,
1925).

Soon it will break down unaware,
Soon it will break down unaware.

At night when reddest flowers are black
Those who once sat thereon come back;
Quite a row of them sitting there,
Quite a row of them sitting there.

With them the seat does not break down,
Nor winter freeze them, nor floods drown,
For they are as light as upper air,
They are as light as upper air!

114

William Shakespeare

Full fathom five

Full fathom five thy father lies,
Of his bones are coral made;
Those are pearls that were his eyes,
Nothing of him that doth fade,
But doth suffer a sea-change
Into something rich and strange;
Sea nymphs hourly ring his knell.
  Ding-dong!
Hark! now I hear them: Ding-dong bell.

115

Harold Monro

Overheard on a Saltmarsh

Nymph, nymph, what are your beads?

  Green glass, goblin. Why do you stare at
  them?

Give them me.

        No.

Give them me. Give them me.

        No.

114. From W. A. Neilson and C. J. Hill, *The Complete Plays and Poems of William Shakespeare* (Houghton Mifflin, 1942).
115. From Harold Monro, *Collected Poems* (Duckworth, 1953).

Then I will howl all night in the reeds,
Lie in the mud and howl for them.

Goblin, why do you love them so?

They are better than stars or water,
Better than voices of winds that sing,
Better than any man's fair daughter,
Your green glass beads on a silver ring.

Hush, I stole them out of the moon.

Give me your beads, I desire them.

        No.

I will howl in a deep lagoon
For your green glass beads. I love them so.
Give them me. Give them.

        No.

116

Arthur Guiterman

What the Gray Cat Sings

The Cat was once a weaver,
  A weaver, a weaver,
An old and withered weaver
  Who labored late and long;
And while she made the shuttle hum
And wove the weft and clipped the thrum,
Beside the loom with droning drum
  She sang the weaving song:
    "Pr-rrum, pr-rrum,
Thr-ree thr-reads in the thr-rum,
    Pr-rrum!"

The Cat's no more a weaver,
  A weaver, a weaver,
An old and wrinkled weaver,
  For though she did no wrong,
A witch hath changed the shape of her
That dwindled down and clothed in fur
Beside the hearth with droning purr
  She thrums her weaving song:
    "Pr-rrum, pr-rrum,

116. From Arthur Guiterman, *I Sing the Pioneer* (Dutton, 1926).

Thr-ree thr-reads in the thr-rum,
      Pr-rrum!''

117

William Blake

The Tyger

Tyger! Tyger! burning bright
In the forests of the night,
What immortal hand or eye
Could frame thy fearful symmetry?

In what distant deeps or skies
Burned the fire of thine eyes?
On what wings dare he aspire?
What the hand dare seize the fire?

And what shoulder, and what art,
Could twist the sinews of thy heart?
And when thy heart began to beat,
What dread hand? and what dread feet?

What the hammer? what the chain?
In what furnace was thy brain?
What the anvil? what dread grasp
Dare its deadly terrors clasp?

When the stars threw down their spears,
And watered heaven with their tears,
Did he smile his work to see?
Did he who made the Lamb make thee?

Tyger! Tyger! burning bright
In the forest of the night,
What immortal hand or eye,
Dare frame thy fearful symmetry?

118

Nancy Willard

Blake Leads a Walk on the Milky Way

He gave silver shoes to the rabbit
and golden gloves to the cat

117. From William Blake, *Songs of Innocence* (Printed by
William Blake, 1794).
118. From Nancy Willard, *A Visit to William Blake's Inn:
Poems for Innocent and Experienced Travellers* (Harcourt,
1981).

and emerald boots to the tiger and me
and boots of iron to the rat.

He inquired, "Is everyone ready?
The night is uncommonly cold.
We'll start on our journey as children,
but I fear we will finish it old."

He hurried us to the horizon
where morning and evening meet.
The slippery stars went skipping
under our hapless feet.

"I'm terribly cold," said the rabbit.
"My paws are becoming quite blue,
and what will become of my right thumb
while you admire the view?"

"The stars," said the cat, "are abundant
and falling on every side.
Let them carry us back to our comforts.
Let us take the stars for a ride."

"I shall garland my room," said the tiger,
"with a few of these emerald lights."
"I shall give up sleeping forever," I said.
"I shall never part day from night."

The rat was sullen. He grumbled
he ought to have stayed in his bed.
"What's gathered by fools in heaven
will never endure," he said.

Blake gave silver stars to the rabbit
and golden stars to the cat
and emerald stars to the tiger and me
but a handful of dirt to the rat.

Poems of Reflection

119

William J. Harris

An Historic Moment

The man said,
after inventing poetry,
"WOW!"
and did a full somersault.

120

Robert Froman

A Seeing Poem

A SEEING POEM HAPPENS WHEN WORDS TAKE A SHAPE THAT HELPS THEM TO TURN ON A LIGHT IN SOMEONE'S MIND

121

Eve Merriam

How to Eat a Poem

Don't be polite.
Bite in.
Pick it up with your fingers and lick the juice
    that may run down your chin.
It is ready and ripe now, whenever you are.

You do not need a knife or fork or spoon
or plate or napkin or tablecloth.

For there is no core
or stem
or rind
or pit
or seed
or skin
to throw away.

122

Myra Cohn Livingston

The Way That It's Going

this is the
age of the book
of the book
of the way that
it's going
and where
I
can look for the
yes
and the
no
of a fast beating
word
and a grab at
tomorrow
and tunes
I have heard in the
picture-frame
white

120. From Robert Froman, *Seeing Things: A Book of Poems* (Crowell, 1974).

121. From Eve Merriam, *It Doesn't Always Have to Rhyme* (Atheneum, 1965).
122. From Myra Cohn Livingston, *The Malibu and Other Poems* (Atheneum, 1972).

of the words all in
black
that can push
me to every
tomorrow
and back
to the what-made-me
yesterday
where I can look
and can think
and can wander
alone
in my
book

123

Valerie Worth

Magnet

This small
Flat horseshoe
Is sold for
A toy: we are
Told that it
Will pick up pins
And it does, time
After time; later
It lies about,
Getting its red
Paint chipped, being
Offered pins less
Often, until at
Last we leave it
Alone: then
It leads its own
Life, trading
Secrets with
The North Pole,
Reading
Invisible messages
From the sun.

124

Eve Merriam

Landscape

What will you find at the edge of the world?
A footprint,
a feather,
desert sand swirled?
A tree of ice,
a rain of stars,
or a junkyard of cars?

What will there be at the rim of the earth?
A mollusc,
a mammal,
a new creature's birth?
Eternal sunrise,
immortal sleep.
or cars piled up in a rusty heap?

125

Walt Whitman

Miracles

Why, who makes much of a miracle?
As for me I know of nothing else but miracles,
Whether I walk the streets of Manhattan . . .
Or watch honey-bees busy around the hive of
    a summer forenoon,
Or animals feeding in the fields,
Or birds, or the wonderfulness of insects in the
    air,
Or the wonderfulness of the sundown, or of
    stars shining so quiet and bright,
Or the exquisite, delicate, thin curve of the new
    moon in spring; . . .

126

Mary O'Neill

My Fingers

My fingers are antennae.
Whatever they touch:
Bud, rose, apple

123. From Valerie Worth, *More Small Poems* (Farrar, Straus & Giroux, 1976).

124. From Eve Merriam, *Finding a Poem* (Atheneum, 1970).
125. From Walt Whitman, *Leaves of Grass* (1855).
126. From Mary O'Neill, *My Fingers Are Always Bringing Me News* (Doubleday, 1969).

Cellophane, crutch—
They race the feel
Into my brain,
Plant it there and
Begin again.
This is how I knew
Hot from cold
Before I was even
Two years old.
This is how I can tell,
Though years away,
That elephant hide
Feels leathery grey.
My brain never loses
A touch I bring:
Frail of an eggshell,
Pull of a string,
Beat of a pulse
That tells me life
Thumps in a person
But not in a knife.
Signs that say:
"Please do not touch,"
Disappoint me
Very much.

127

Rose Rauter

Peach

Touch it to your cheek and it's soft
as a velvet newborn mouse
who has to strive
to be alive.

Bite in. Runny
honey
blooms on your tongue—
as if you've bitten open
a whole hive.

128

Robert Louis Stevenson

Happy Thought

The world is so full of a number of things,
I'm sure we should all be as happy as kings.

128. From Robert Louis Stevenson, *A Child's Garden of Verses* (Longmans, 1885).

129

I Pass the Pipe

(A poem of the Sioux Indians)

Friend of Wakinyan,
I pass the pipe to you first.
Circling I pass to you who dwell with the Father.
Circling pass to beginning day.
Circling pass to the beautiful one.
Circling I complete the four quarters and the
    time.
I pass the pipe to the Father with the Sky.
I smoke with the Great Spirit.
Let us have a blue day.

130

Langston Hughes

Poem

I loved my friend.
He went away from me.
There's nothing more to say.
The poem ends,
Soft as it began—
I loved my friend.

131

William Blake

A Poison Tree

I was angry with my friend:
I told my wrath, my wrath did end.
I was angry with my foe:
I told it not, my wrath did grow.

And I water'd it in fears,
Night and morning with my tears;
And I sunned it with smiles,
And with soft deceitful wiles.

129. From *In the Trail of the Wind: American Indian Poems and Ritual Orations*, ed. John Bierhorst (Farrar, Straus & Giroux, 1971).
130. From *Don't You Turn Back: Poems by Langston Hughes*, ed. Lee Bennett Hopkins (Knopf, 1960).
131. From William Blake, *Songs of Experience* (Printed by William Blake, 1794).

From *Birds, Beasts and the Third Thing,* by D. H. Lawrence, illustrated by Alice and Martin Provensen. Illustration © 1982 by Alice and Martin Provensen. Reprinted by permission of Viking Penguin Inc.

And it grew both day and night,
Till it bore an apple bright;
And my foe beheld it shine,
And he knew that it was mine,

And into my garden stole
When the night had veiled the pole:
In the morning glad I see
My foe outstretched beneath the tree.

132

D. H. Lawrence

Delight of Being Alone

I know no greater delight than the sheer delight
    of being alone.
It makes me realise the delicious pleasure of
    the moon
that she has in travelling by herself: throughout
    time,
or the splendid growing of an ash-tree
alone, on a hill side in the north, humming in
    the wind.

132. From D. H. Lawrence, *The Complete Poems of D. H. Lawrence* (Viking, 1964).

133

Russell Hoban

Small, Smaller

I thought that I knew all there was to know
Of being small, until I saw once, black against
    the snow,
A shrew, trapped in my footprint, jump and
    fall
And jump again and fall, the hole too deep,
    the walls too tall.

134

Delmore Schwartz

I Am Cherry Alive

"I am cherry alive," the little girl sang,
"Each morning I am something new:
I am apple, I am plum, I am just as excited
As the boys who made the Hallowe'en bang:

133. From Russell Hoban, *The Pedaling Man* (Grosset & Dunlap, Inc., 1968).
134. Delmore Schwartz, *Summer Knowledge: New and Selected Poems, 1938–58* (Doubleday, 1959).

I am tree, I am cat, I am blossom too:
When I like, if I like, I can be someone new,
Someone very old, a witch in a zoo:
I can be someone else whenever I think who,
And I want to be everything sometimes too:
And the peach has a pit and I know that too,
And I put it in along with everything
To make the grown-ups laugh whenever I sing:
And I sing: *It is true; It is untrue;*
I know, I know, the true is untrue,
The peach has a pit,
The pit has a peach:
And both may be wrong
When I sing my song,
But I don't tell the grown-ups: because it is sad,
And I want them to laugh just like I do
Because they grew up
And forgot what they knew
And they are sure
I will forget it some day too.
They are wrong. They are wrong.
When I sang my song, I knew, I knew!
I am red, I am gold,
I am green, I am blue,
I will always be me,
I will always be new!"

135

LeRoi Jones

Young Soul

First, feel, then feel, then
read, or read, then feel, then
fall, or stand, where you
already are. Think
of your self, and the other
selves . . . think
of your parents, your mothers,
and sisters, your bentslick
father, then feel, or
fall, on your knees
if nothing else will move you,

then read
and look deeply
into all matters
come close to you

city boys—
country men

Make some muscle
in your head, but
use the muscle
in yr heart

136

Christina Rossetti

Sea-Sand and Sorrow

What are heavy? Sea-sand and sorrow:
What are brief? To-day and to-morrow:
What are frail? Spring blossoms and youth:
What are deep? The ocean and truth.

137

I want to laugh, I

(A poem of the Central Eskimo)

I want to laugh, I, because my sledge it is bro-
    ken.
Because its ribs are broken I want to laugh.
Here at Talaviuyaq I encountered hummocky
    ice, I met with an upset.
I want to laugh. It is not a thing to rejoice
    over.

138

Lucille Clifton

The 1st

What I remember about that day
is boxes stacked across the walk
and couch springs curling through the air
and drawers and tables balanced on the curb
and us, hollering,
leaping up and around
happy to have a playground;

135. From LeRoi Jones, *Black Magic: Poetry 1961–1967* (Bobbs-Merrill, 1969).

136. From Christina Rossetti, *Sing-Song: A Nursery Rhyme Book* (Routledge, 1872).
137. From *Songs of the Dream People: Chants and Images from the Indians and Eskimos of North America*, ed. James Houston (Atheneum, 1972).
138. From Lucille Clifton, *Good Times* (Random House, 1969).

nothing about the empty rooms
nothing about the emptied family

139

E. V. Rieu

Cat's Funeral

Bury her deep, down deep,
Safe in the earth's cold keep.
    Bury her deep—

No more to watch bird stir;
No more to clean dark fur;
No more to glisten as silk;
No more to revel in milk;
    No more to purr.

Bury her deep, down deep;
She is beyond warm sleep.
She will not walk in the night;
She will not wake to the light.
    Bury her deep.

140

Robert Frost

Nothing Gold Can Stay

Nature's first green is gold,
Her hardest hue to hold.
Her early leaf's a flower;
But only so an hour.
Then leaf subsides to leaf.
So Eden sank to grief,
So dawn goes down to day.
Nothing gold can stay.

141

David McCord

The Walnut Tree

There was once a swing in a walnut tree,
As tall as double a swing might be,

At the edge of the hill where the branches
    spread
So it swung the valley right under me;
Then down and back as the valley fled.
I wonder if that old tree is dead?

I could look straight up in the lifting heart
Of the black old walnut there and start
My flying journey from green to blue
With a wish and a half that the ropes would
    part
And sail me out on a course as true
As the crows in a flock had dared me to.

I swung from the past to the far dim days
Forever ahead of me. Through the haze
I saw the steeple, a flash of white,
And I gave it a shout for the scare and praise
Of being a boy on the verge of flight.
And I pumped on the swing with all my might

Till the valley widened. Oh, I could guess
From the backward No to the forward Yes
That the world begins in the sweep of eye,
With the wonder of all of it more or less
In the last hello and the first goodbye.
And a swing in the walnut tree is why.

142

A Song of Greatness

(*A Chippewa Indian song, transcribed
by Mary Austin*)

When I hear the old men
Telling of heroes,
Telling of great deeds
Of ancient days,
When I hear them telling,
Then I think within me
I too am one of these.

When I hear the people
Praising great ones,
Then I know that I too
Shall be esteemed,
I too when my time comes
Shall do mightily.

139. From E. V. Rieu, *The Flattered Flying Fish and Other Poems* (Dutton, 1962).
140. From *The Poetry of Robert Frost*, ed. Edward Connery Lathem (Holt, 1969).
141. From David McCord, *One at a Time* (Little, Brown, 1974).
142. From Mary Austin, *Children Sing in the Far West* (Houghton Mifflin, 1928).

143

Langston Hughes

Mother to Son

Well, son, I'll tell you:
Life for me ain't been no crystal stair.
It's had tacks in it,
And splinters,
And boards torn up,
And places with no carpet on the floor—
Bare.
But all the time
I'se been a-climbin' on,
And reachin' landin's,
And turnin' corners,
And sometimes goin' in the dark
Where there ain't been no light.
So boy, don't you turn back.
Don't you set down on the steps
'Cause you finds it's kinder hard.
Don't you fall now—
For I'se still goin', honey,
I'se still climbin',
And life for me ain't been no crystal stair.

144

Nikki Giovanni

the drum

daddy says the world is
a drum tight and hard
and i told him
i'm gonna beat
out my own rhythm

145

Song of the Sky Loom

(*A poem of the Tewa Indians, translated
by Herbert J. Spinden*)

Oh our Mother the Earth oh our Father the
Sky

Your children are we
with tired backs we bring you the gifts you
love

So weave for us a garment of brightness

May the warp be the white light of morning
May the weft be the red light of evening
May the fringes be the falling rain
May the border be the standing rainbow

Weave for us this bright garment
that we may walk where birds sing
where grass is green

Oh our Mother the Earth oh our Father the
Sky

146

Robert Burns

A Red, Red Rose

I

O, my Luve's like a red, red rose,
That's newly sprung in June.
O, my Luve's like the melodie,
That's sweetly play'd in tune.

II

As fair art thou, my bonie lass,
So deep in luve am I,
And I will luve thee still, my dear,
Till a' the seas gang dry.

III

Till a' the seas gang dry, my dear,
And the rocks melt wi' the sun!
And I will love thee still, my dear,
While the sands o' life shall run.

IV

And fare thee weel, my only Luve!
And fare thee weel a while!
And I will come again, my Luve,
Tho' it were ten thousand mile!

143. From Langston Hughes, *Selected Poems of Langston Hughes* (Knopf, 1926).
144. From Nikki Giovanni, *Spin a Soft Black Song* (Hill & Wang, 1971).
145. From *Songs of the Tewa,* trans. Herbert Joseph Spinden (published under the auspices of the Exposition of Indian Tribal Arts, Inc., 1933).

146. From *Poems and Songs,* ed. James Kinsley (Oxford University Press, 1969).

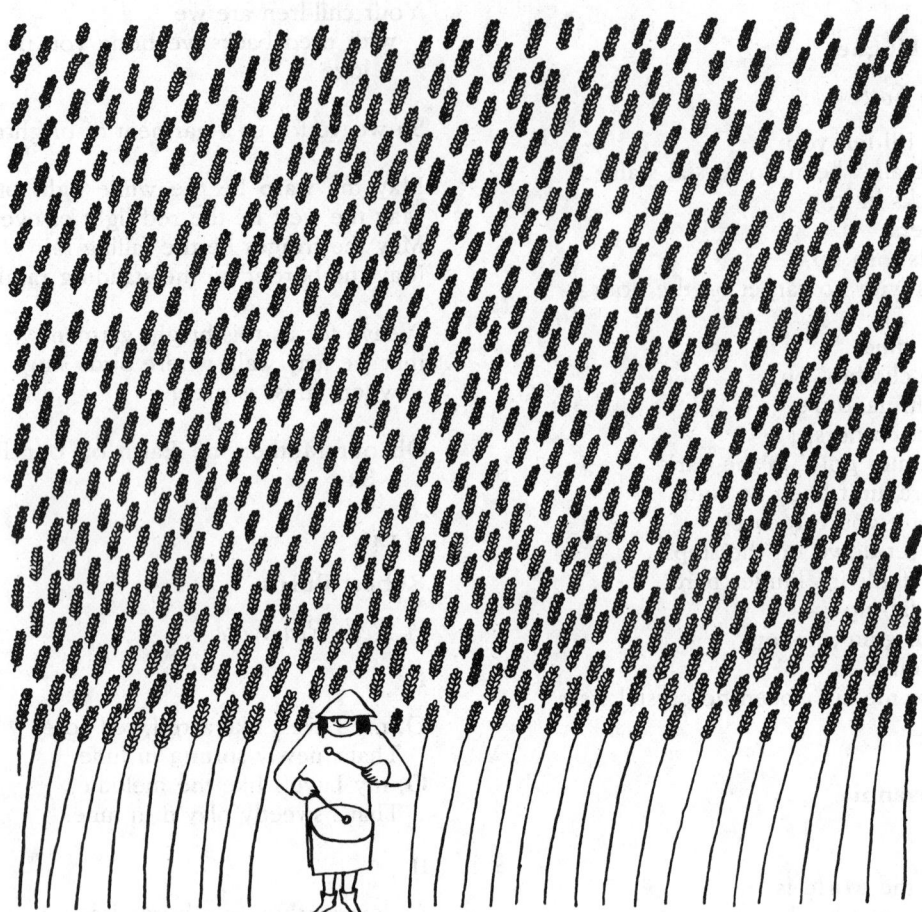

Illustration by Reiner Zimnik, from *Drummer of Dreams,* by Reiner Zimnik. Reproduced by permission of Faber & Faber, Limited (London).

147

Plucking the Rushes

(Chinese, fourth century; a boy and girl are sent to gather rushes for thatching)

Green rushes with red shoots,
Long leaves bending to the wind—
You and I in the same boat
Plucking rushes at the Five Lakes.
We started at dawn from the orchid-island:
We rested under the elms till noon.

147. From *Translations from the Chinese,* trans. Arthur Waley (Knopf, 1969).

You and I plucking rushes
Had not plucked a handful when night came!

148

Langston Hughes

Youth

We have tomorrow
Bright before us
Like a flame.

148. From Langston Hughes, *The Dream Keeper and Other Poems* (Knopf, 1932).

Yesterday
A night-gone thing,
A sun-down name.

And dawn-today
Broad arch above the road we came.

We march!

149

Emily Dickinson

I never saw a moor

I never saw a moor,
I never saw the sea;
Yet know I how the heather looks,
And what a wave must be.

I never spoke with God,
Nor visited in heaven;
Yet certain am I of the spot
As if the chart were given.

150

Robert Frost

The Road Not Taken

Two roads diverged in a yellow wood,
And sorry I could not travel both
And be one traveler, long I stood
And looked down one as far as I could
To where it bent in the undergrowth;

Then took the other, as just as fair,
And having perhaps the better claim,
Because it was grassy and wanted wear;
Though as for that, the passing there
Had worn them really about the same,

And both that morning equally lay
In leaves no step had trodden black.
Oh, I kept the first for another day!
Yet knowing how way leads on to way,
I doubted if I should ever come back.

Illustration by Rocco Negri, from *The Son of the Leopard,*
by Harold Courlander, illustrated by Rocco Negri.
Copyright © 1974 by Harold Courlander. Illustration
copyright © 1974 by Rocco Negri. Used by permission
of Crown Publishers, Inc.

I shall be telling this with a sigh
Somewhere ages and ages hence:
Two roads diverged in a wood, and I—
I took the one less traveled by,
And that has made all the difference.

151

Sara Teasdale

Night

Stars over snow,
    And in the west a planet

149. From *The Poems of Emily Dickinson,* ed. Martha Dickinson Bianchi and Alfred Leete Hampson (Little, Brown, 1937).
150. From *The Complete Poems of Robert Frost* (Holt, 1969).

151. From Sara Teasdale, *Stars To-night* (Macmillan, 1930).

Copyright © 1969 by Ann Grifalconi. Reprinted from *Don't You Turn Back,* by Langston Hughes, selected by Lee Bennett Hopkins, illustrated by Ann Grifalconi. By permission of Alfred A. Knopf, Inc.

Swinging below a star—
   Look for a lovely thing and you will find it.
It is not far—
   It never will be far.

152

Langston Hughes

Dreams

Hold fast to dreams
For if dreams die
Life is a broken-winged bird
That cannot fly

152. From Langston Hughes, *The Dream Keeper and Other Poems* (Knopf, 1932).

Hold fast to dreams
For when dreams go
Life is a barren field
Frozen with snow.

153

John Ciardi

There Once Was an Owl

There once was an Owl perched on a shed.
Fifty years later the Owl was dead.

Some say mice are in the corn.
Some say kittens are being born.

Some say a kitten becomes a cat.
Mice are likely to know about that.

Some cats are scratchy, some are not.
Corn grows best when it's damp and hot.

Fifty times fifty years go by.
Corn keeps best when it's cool and dry.

Fifty times fifty and one by one
Night begins when day is done.

Owl on the shed, cat in the clover,
Mice in the corn—it all starts over.

154

Robert Frost

The Pasture

I'm going out to clean the pasture spring;
I'll only stop to rake the leaves away
(And wait to watch the water clear. I may):
I sha'n't be gone long.—You come too.

I'm going out to fetch the little calf
That's standing by the mother. It's so young,
It totters when she licks it with her tongue
I sha'n't be gone long.—You come too.

153. From John Ciardi, *The Reason for a Pelican* (Lippincott, 1959).
154. From Robert Frost, *Collected Poems* (Holt, 1969).

The Voices of Children

It is not a nice day because I can feel the
    drops of rain on my back.
My tail was all cramped when I came out.

155

Lucinda Broadbent

(Age 2, England)

Ladybirds Is Horrid

Hushabye, hushabye, it's dark in the
    morning,
Flowers are up in the sky.
Mama's my baby, my little, little
    baby;
Thomas smells of flowers.
Sing a song, sing a song, sing a song.

156

Peter Shelton

(Age 10, Australia)

Singing

The children are singing,
their mouths open like sleepy fish.
Our teacher conducting the class
waves her arms
like a rhyme in water.
The girls sing high:
our ears ring for the sweetness.
Listeners stand in dazzling amazement.

157

Luisa Kaye

(Age 6, United States)

*I Have Just Taken Birth Out of
Dark Hot Mother*

I have just taken birth out of dark hot mother.
I know I have because I can feel the cool
    water below me.

158

Hilda Conkling

(Ages 7–9, United States)

I Am

I am willowy boughs
For coolness;
I am gold-finch wings
For darkness;
I am a little grape
Thinking of September,
I am a very small violet
Thinking of May.

159

Desiree Lynne Collier

(Third/Fourth Grade, United States)

Dog, Where Did You Get That Bark?

Dog, where did you get that bark?
Dragon, where do you get that flame?
Kitten, where did you get that meow?
Rose, where did you get that red?
Bird, where did you get those wings?

160

Linda

(Age 8, Australia)

It Was Midnight

It was midnight
The sky was dark black
The stars were threepenny bits
The sea was making a sound
Like a silk dress.

155. From *Those First Affections: An Anthology of Poems Composed between the Ages of Two and Eight,* coll. Timothy Rogers (Routledge & Kegan Paul, 1979).
156. From *Miracles: Poems by Children of the English-speaking World,* coll. Richard Lewis (Simon & Schuster, 1966).
157. From *There's a Sound in the Sea: A Child's-Eye View of the Whale,* coll. Tamar Griggs (Scrimshaw, 1975).

158. From Hilda Conkling, *Poems by a Little Girl* (Stokes, 1920).
159. From Kenneth Koch, *Rose, Where Did You Get That Red? Teaching Great Poetry to Children* (Random House, 1973).
160. From *Miracles: Poems by Children of the English-Speaking World,* coll. Richard Lewis (Simon & Schuster, 1966).

161

Inna Muller

(Age 13, U.S.S.R.)

The Path on the Sea

The moon this night is like a silver sickle
Mowing a field of stars.
It has spread a golden runner
Over the rippling waves.
With its winking shimmer
This magic carpet lures me
To fly to the moon on it.

162

Hilda Conkling

(Ages 7–9, United States)

Weather

Weather is the answer
When I can't go out into flowery places;
Weather is my wonder
About the kind of morning
Hidden behind the hills of sky.

163

Hilda Conkling

(Age 5, United States)

Water

The world turns softly
Not to spill its lakes and rivers.
The water is held in its arms
And the sky is held in the water.
What is water,
That pours silver,
And can hold the sky?

164

Charles Gluck

(Age 10, United States)

November

The birds have all flown
And I am alone
In the big sky's mouth.

165

Yvonne Lowe

(Age 8, England)

Anger

I was angry and mad,
And it seemed that there was hot water inside
    me,
And as I got madder and madder,
The water got hotter and hotter all the time,
I was in a rage,
Then I began to see colours,
Like black and red,
Then as I got madder and madder,
My eyes began to pop out of my head,
They were popping up and down,
It was horrible,
And it would not stop,
I was steaming with anger,
Nobody could not stop me,
My mother could not stop me,
Then it was gone,
And I was all-right,
Horrible, black, madness.

166

**Anonymous Jewish Child, Terezin
Concentration Camp, Czechoslovakia**

The Closed Town

Everything leans, like tottering, hunched old
    women.

161. From *The Moon Is Like a Silver Sickle: A Celebration of Poetry by Russian Children*, coll. and trans. Miriam Morton (Simon & Schuster, 1972).
162–63. From Hilda Conkling, *Poems by a Little Girl* (Stokes, 1920).

164. From *Miracles: Poems by Children of the English-Speaking World*, coll. Richard Lewis (Simon & Schuster, 1966).
165. From The *Daily Mirror* Children's Literature Competition (London).
166. From *I Never Saw Another Butterfly: Children's Drawings and Poems from Terezin Concentration Camp, 1942–1944* (McGraw-Hill, 1964).

Every eye shines with fixed waiting
and for the word, "when"?

Here there are few soldiers.
Only the shot-down birds tell of war.

You believe every bit of news you hear.

The buildings now are fuller,
Body smelling close to body,
And the garrets scream with light for long, long
    hours.

This evening I walked along the street of death.
On one wagon, they were taking the dead away.

Why so many marches have been drummed
    here?

Why so many soldiers?

Then
A week after the end,
Everything will be empty here.
A hungry dove will peck for bread.
In the middle of the street will stand
An empty, dirty
Hearse.

167

**Anonymous Student of St. Mary's Secondary
School (Swaziland)**

*Death Is Like
the Sleepy Door Nail*

Death is like the sleepy door nail.
That girl is as thin as a wasp's waist.

167. From Kenneth Koch, *Rose, Where Did You Get That
Red? Teaching Great Poetry to Children* (Random House,
1973).

Crying for your dead son is like the whole world
    crying for hunger during the times of war.
Doing things without looking for your future
    is like going into the darkness of your life.

168

Hilary-Anne Farley

(Age 5, Canada)

This Is a Poem

This is a poem about god looks after things:
He looks after lions, mooses and reindeer and
    tigers,
Anything that dies,
and mans and little girls when they get to be
    old,
and mothers he can look after,
and god can look after many old things.
That's why I do this.

168. From *Miracles: Poems by Children of the English-Speaking
World*, coll. Richard Lewis (Simon & Schuster, 1966).

Illustration by John Burningham. From *Mr. Gumpy's Outing,* by John Burningham. Copyright © 1970 by John Burningham. Reproduced by permission of the publisher, Jonathan Cape Ltd., and Holt, Rinehart & Winston Publishers.

From *John Burningham's ABC*, copyright © 1964 by John Burningham. Reprinted by permission of the publisher, the Bobbs-Merrill Company, Inc., and Jonathan Cape Ltd.

O
Who's this who hangs
Yet takes no chances?
Orangutan!
He hides in branches

Crunch, crunch, crunch, his feet sank into the snow.

He walked with his toes pointing out, like this:

He walked with his toes
pointing in, like that:

Opposite, top, from *The Pear Tree, the Birch Tree, and the Barberry Bush,* by Alois Carigiet. Copyright © 1967 by Alois Carigiet. Reprinted by permission of the publisher, Henry Z. Walck, a division of David McKay Co., Inc.

Opposite, bottom, illustration by Margot Zemach. Reprinted with permission of Farrar, Straus & Giroux, Inc., from *Mommy, Buy Me a China Doll,* by Harve Zemach, illustrated by Margot Zemach. Copyright © 1966 by Harve Zemach.

Above, excerpted from the book *Joanjo,* by Jan Balet. Copyright © 1965 by Annette Betz Verlag, Munich. English translation copyright © 1967 by Macdonald & Co. (Publishers) Ltd. Reprinted by permission of Delacorte Press/Seymour Lawrence.

Left, illustration by Molly Bang, from *Dawn,* written and illustrated by Molly Bang. Copyright © 1983 by Molly Bang. By permission of William Morrow & Co.

Snowball Weather, from *A Prairie Boy's Winter,* copyright © 1973 by William Kurelek, published by Houghton Mifflin in the United States and by Tundra Books in Canada. Reprinted by permission of Tundra Books.

Picture Books:
Stories for the Eye

The world of infancy is unitary, total; in it there are no purely visual experiences, any more than there are purely auditory or tactile experiences. Objects, shapes, colors, or motions are never seen as things in themselves but rather as parts of a whole. What infants are doing in those first years of rapid growth is learning the patterns of their wonderfully compelling world. Although they often appear to adults to be little sponges busily sopping up experience, babies are not passive; they are active and engaged. And, if they are to grow into healthy children, they need active and engaging adults.

Picture books have traditionally been thought appropriate for three- to six-year-olds, but Dorothy Butler argues that "babies need books." Butler advises:

Keep the baby's books within reach, and make a practice of showing them to him from the day you first bring him home. The covers will be brightly illustrated, and at first you can encourage him to focus his eyes on the pictures. You can teach your baby a lot about books in the first few months.

To begin with, he will learn that a book is a thing, with different qualities from all other things. For many babies, the world must flow past in a succession of half-perceived images. Until their own physical development enables them to lift and turn their heads and focus their eyes, they must rely on obliging adults to help. . . .

Babies need people: talking, laughing, warm-hearted people, constantly drawing them into their lives, and offering them the world for a playground. Let's give them books to parallel this experience; books where language and illustration activate the senses, so that meaning slips in smoothly, in the wake of feeling.[1]

1. Dorothy Butler, *Babies Need Books* (Bodley Head, 1980), p. 28.

Although, as is often asserted, picture books provide the foundation for a child's visual education, teaching sensitivity to line and an awareness of color, form, and design, it is misleading to consider picture books as primarily visual experiences. In spite of the fact that picture books are visual—stories for the eye—they are primarily *stories,* and, as such, they enter the infant's world as part of a totality of sound and touch and feeling and pattern. Picture books extend the child's introduction to language and to the human community, an introduction already begun with lullabies and nursery rhymes and the natural flow of everyday speech. And picture books need to be part of an experience centered on, as Butler says, "talking, laughing, warm-hearted people." Children do not see illustrations in books as a gallery of isolated pictures but as a *story* communicated through an integration of words and pictures and, in turn, integrated within a real world of sights and sounds and people.

"A picture book," Butler writes, "will stand or fall in a young listener-looker's estimation [of] the story, and the way in which illustrations support and interpret it. . . . *Story* comes first, with all its requirements."[2]   As children mature and begin to grasp the pattern of story, they "read" pictures—long before they read words; aided by adults, they learn to follow the narrative progression through images. Later they "read" picture books for themselves, recreating the story on their own. This process flows smoothly from the realization that black marks on paper are connected to speech, the beginning of the child's comprehension of written language.

The most appropriate first picture books are bold and simple, and realistic in words and pictures. As G. K. Chesterton writes: "A child of seven is excited by being told that Tommy opened a door and saw a dragon. But a child of three is excited by being told that Tommy opened a door."[3]   The visual images and stories in first picture books describe the wonder of discovering that the world is the way it is: apples are red, birds have wings, dogs bark. For older children (and even teen-agers), there are a multitude of picture books that stimulate the imagination, express concepts and ideas, and develop visual literacy.

The picture book is the newest member of the family of illustrated books, and the distinction between picture books and illustrated books is not always clear. In general, however, in an illustrated book the pictures are clearly subordinate to the text, whereas in a picture book the pictures and text are indissolubly united so that neither can stand without the other. In both categories the function of the pictures is primarily narrative. The visual elements elaborate on, extend, or clarify the words they are designed to accompany. Both the picture book and the illustrated book, however, are strengthened and unified by the power of the artist. Aesthetic appeal and satisfaction are extremely important, but they cannot substitute for the narrative function, which must provide a critical balance between art and text. As Walter Lorraine writes, "The good illustrator is no more nor less a story-teller than the author."[4]

Chapter 4 contains a discussion of the components of the picture book, along with a sampling of texts and pictures and one complete story in words and pictures selected from a picture book.   Chapter 5 traces the history of the illustrated book (including the picture book) and places in perspective its lineage and major artists.

2. Butler, p. 106.
3. G. K. Chesterton, "The Ethics of Elfland," in *Orthodoxy* (Dodd, Mead, 1950), p. 96.
4. Walter Lorraine, "Book Illustration: The State of the Art," in *Illustrators of Children's Books, 1967–1976,* comp. Lee Kingman, Grace Allen Hogarth, and Harriet Quimby (Horn Book, 1978), p. 3.

I wanted to paint purely that which gave me pleasure, scenes that interested me; and one day I found that the audience for that kind of painting was a vast reservoir of impressionists who did very good work themselves, who were very clear-eyed and capable of enthusiasm. I addressed myself to children.[1]

4   Picture Books

Picture books, in the twentieth century, have become a vital and endlessly innovative field. The freedom they provide for the individual artist is demonstrated by an amazing array of complex and varied work. Far different in approach were the early picture books, in which pictures were primarily a pedagogic device for teaching object identification. Today, the artist is engaged in a different kind of education—the education of the eye. To a great extent, this is the result of a fundamental change in attitude. No longer is it thought that children are capable only of rather crude responses; are unable to perceive anything that is not garishly colored; and are interested only in that which is familiar in content and realistically portrayed. Just as the expressionists freed adults from the concept that art is equated with photographic resemblance, modern artists have freed the picture book from preconceptions that shut children off from first-class art.

Children are an ideal audience for the artist because they are uninhibited by the adult's emotional associations with certain colors, techniques, or subject matter. Adults are often handicapped by pat interpretations and the assigning of adjectives—words like *pretty, bright, warm, dynamic, unpretentious, meticulous,* or *cheerful*—that short-circuit enjoyment and shed little light on what it is the artist has done.

1. Ludwig Bemelmans, "Caldecott Award Acceptance," *The Horn Book Magazine,* 30 (1954), 271.

Enjoyment of the visual art must begin as a response to the way a particular artist uses line, works with color, creates textural effects, arranges shapes, and composes the entire picture on the page, as well as to the narrative quality of the illustrations. The language of the artist is not made up of words but of such elements as line, color, shape, and texture.

Line is an element that leads the eye around objects, across a page, off into the distance; it may be thin or thick, transparent or opaque, clean-edged or blurred, textured or smooth, in any combination and to almost any degree. *Shape,* which may have as many variations in treatment as line, does not lead the eye but holds it, acting as a stationary force. A linear quality in a picture is a quality of visual action; an emphasis on shape has the opposite effect. *Texture* refers to the way the artist treats the surface of line or shape or background (the *picture plane*). Here the possibilities are again limitless, ranging from thin pencil scratches to cut-outs of patterned material or paper pasted down to create shapes.

The technique of pasting other materials on a background is called *collage,* and it has been used to particular effect by three artists: Ezra Jack Keats, Leo Lionni, and Elizabeth Cleaver. Each of them, however, exhibits a unique and characteristic method of working with this medium. This diversity of technique extends, of course, to all these elements; for example, Reiner Zimnik uses a thin, spiraling line, whereas Quentin Blake uses a loose, flowing stroke. Such differences are manifestations of the artist's aesthetic predisposition; they are also at the nub of visual effect.

Color, which is the element most often noticed, is seldom used in the same fundamental way as line and shape. It is possible, in many pictures, to take away the color and still not detract from the essential qualities of the visual statement. Most of the pictures reprinted in this chapter appear with color in their original sources. Their presentation here in black and white provides a convenient demonstration of the dominance of other elements. Those in which color is indispensable—where color has been used to develop shape, texture, or line—are shown in a special color section, to permit comparison of the different ways in which artists use color as a visual element.

In *Celestino Piatti's Animal ABC* (1966), color is essential to some pictures and not to others, although it is present throughout. Even without color, Piatti's giraffe is still strong and effective. Note how the outline of the giraffe is empha-

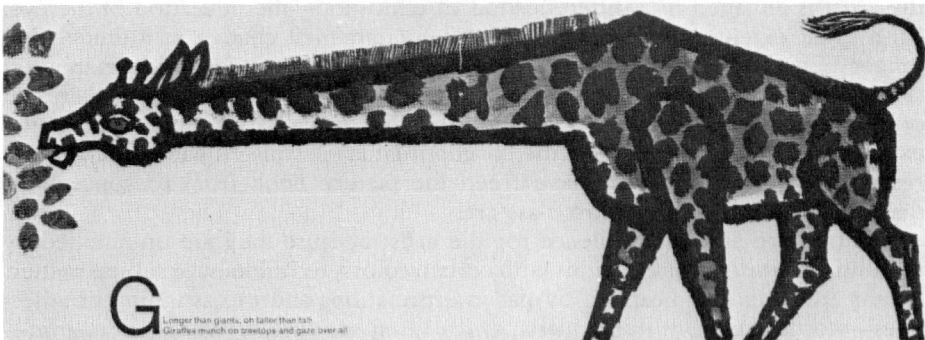

Illustration by Celestino Piatti. Copyright © 1965 by Artemis Verlag, Zurich, Switzerland. First U.S.A. edition 1966 by Atheneum. Illustrated by Celestino Piatti. From *Celestino Piatti's Animal ABC.* Used by permission of Atheneum Publishers.

sized with a heavy, thick, full black line; the length of the neck is exaggerated not so much by proportion as by this outline. The spots are soft-edged shapes in which the paint has been applied from the brush with loose control. The result is dramatic, a deliberate exciting of the viewer.

In the same book, however, Piatti does have a picture that must be reproduced in color—an orangutan (see the color section). While the line is still characteristically heavy, the texture of the animal's fur is a combination of lines in a casual pattern over the red. The contrasting brown of the hands, feet, and neck area would not be seen in black and white; nor would the green of the background, which obtains its texture from the way the paint is applied. Piatti builds line and shape with color, resulting in a total effect of great animal presence. One two-year-old, after having spent a great deal of time with this book, was shown a photograph of an orangutan in a magazine advertisement. Recognition was immediate and spontaneous: "Orangutan!" The vividness of Piatti's animal, the emphatic visual qualities of the abstract art statement, had given the child a sure grasp of an unfamiliar beast.

Quite different from Piatti's work is that of Brian Wildsmith, a brilliant colorist. His lion (in the color section) is built with a distinctive technique, relying almost completely on the way paint is applied to establish shape and indicate line and texture. His rich and surprising combinations of color present a lion that is Wildsmith's lion, stamped with his particular way of seeing and working.

It is no accident that these first examples of art come from ABC, or alphabet, books. As a way of teaching the alphabet or the rudiments of reading, the alphabet book is something of an anachronism—a throwback to the time when children wore around their necks the hornbooks (fashioned of wood and covered with transparent material made from the horns of cattle) on which were the alphabet and instructions about learning to read. But of all the types of picture books, these serve most unabashedly as a showcase for the artist.

In *Anno's Alphabet* (1975), Mitsumasa Anno presents each letter as a wooden, three-dimensional object whose various planes are placed at unusual angles, creating optical illusions similar to those in the work of the Dutch artist M. C. Escher. No words are used. Opposite each letter is a clean-edged representation of an object whose name is a word that begins with that letter. It is significant that Anno subtitles his book *An Adventure in Imagination*.

Leonard Baskin's pictures in *Hosie's Alphabet* (1972) arrest the eye with the turning of each page. His locust, for example, takes on a poetic fragility as the tenuous line moves over the shadowy transparency of the background texture. A complete contrast is *John Burningham's ABC* (1964): Flat-planed shapes, an intricate surface treatment, and minimal but definite line create a humorous feeling and a casual, offhand effect. This deadpan comic quality, however, can be seen (in the color section) to result from careful and skillful management of slight variations of shape.

In Rachel Isadora's *City Seen from A to Z* (1983), each letter of the alphabet introduces a scene of contemporary urban life. The black-and-white line drawings, with their delicate shading, are like vignettes, snapshots held suspended in time and place yet lifted from ordinariness into a sudden and unexpected beauty. There is motion implied in the old tire, trash can, sooty buildings, and the boy on roller skates whose figure echoes the shape of the letter *R*. The internal texture, rhythmic patterns, repeating contour lines, and overall page design imbue the static scene with energy and power.

Illustration by Rachel Isadora, from *City Seen from A to Z,* written and illustrated by Rachel Isadora. Copyright © 1983 by Rachel Isadora. By permission of Greenwillow Books (a division of William Morrow & Co.).

Beyond the alphabet and counting books is the realm of the picture book, which engages in story, with or without words. The mutual reinforcement of art and story (or idea) is a singular characteristic of these books. Ideally, the picture book contains material that must be visually expressed in order to be complete. It is in this way that the picture book differs from the illustrated book, whose content may be enhanced by art but in no way depends on it as an essential factor. In the last few years one trend among artists has been to take their stories from folklore, to ensure strong stories and independence from a collaborator. The obvious peril in such a trend is that, instead of picture books, the result will be illustrated books in picture-book format, with overelaborate graphics dominating the natural narrative power of the folktale. But some sensitive illustrators, such as Edward Ardizzone and Lisbeth Zwerger, achieve a subtle and restrained approach, interpreting the text in a personal and sympathetic way that adds dimension to the story.

Originality of concept and inventiveness in graphic execution combine with a sense of play in outstanding works for the very young child. Looking at a book can become a game in itself: The design of the page may invite the eye to travel all over the page and upside down, as in Mitsumasa Anno's *Topsy-Turvies* (1970). *Each Peach Pear Plum* (1979) and *Peek-a-Boo* (1981) by Janet and Allan Ahlberg present visual "I Spy" games combined with loose, entertaining plots. The gentle, naive drawings are subtly interconnected to create a multiplicity of nonverbal meanings.

Bruno Munari has created a number of books in which there are folding small pages placed on larger ones, with cutouts and other surprising devices. His *Circus in the Mist* (1969) is a complicated assembly of various types of paper, designs viewed through designs, and pages framed by other pages. This book acts like a magnet on children of kindergarten age; they look with endless fascination at this sophisticated piece of bookmaking. Less complex but equally playful is Eric Carle's *The Very Hungry Caterpillar* (1969). The size of some pages is graduated to give a sense of progression. Holes in the pages are part of the design layout as well as a necessary part of the narrative. All of Carle's objects are reduced to shapes, richly colored and textured. There is a high degree of visual glee in this book, which combines the reality of a child's pleasure in certain foods with the metamorphosis of the caterpillar into a butterfly. The large, heavy shape of the cocoon is a fine foil for the radiant butterfly that leaps out from the last pages.

Inch by Inch (1966), by Leo Lionni, plays with the viewer, inviting the eye to follow an inchworm across the pages of the picture book until the worm inches and measures itself out of sight. This book is notable for its witty concept, its unity and unusual composition, and the creation of shapes through the use of collage. Although Lionni's story can be followed without words, it does have accompanying text. Another book in which the story unfolds as the characters progress across the pages, *Rosie's Walk* (1968), is a fine example of slapstick humor. The fox pursues the blithely unaware hen and, in instance after instance, is the victim of a timely accident: knocking himself silly stepping on a rake, or burying himself in a haystack. Finally, Rosie inadvertently steps on a string, releasing a sack of flour on his head. Still unaware that her life has been in danger, Rosie returns to safety completely unperturbed. The hilarity of this

He measured the toucan's beak...

Illustration by Leo Lionni. From *Inch by Inch*, by Leo Lionni. Copyright © 1960. Reprinted by permission of Astor-Honor, Inc.

Reprinted with permission of Macmillan Publishing Company, from *Rosie's Walk,* by Patricia Hutchins. Copyright © 1968 by Patricia Hutchins.

humorous progression is set off by carefully constructed and decorated shapes, clean-edged and definite. Pat Hutchins's line is static, distinct, and formal, giving crispness and snap to this original pursuit story.

The wry humor, minimal text, and clear narrative progression of *Rosie's Walk* is carried even further in Shirley Hughes's inventive *Up and Up* (1979), a wordless drama in which a spirited little girl learns to fly. The narrative potential and graphic dynamism of the comic-strip format are used to their fullest. Hughes's subtle draftsmanship conveys the wit and humanity of the characters. Her strong sense of overall design and visual storytelling results in a complex, shifting series of framed scenes that create a sense of movement through space and time. As the adventure expands, so does the treatment, so that the child reader-viewer is carried along with the protagonist to wider spaces, approximating a feeling of flight.

The visual and emotional satisfaction of this expansion technique is also subtly used by Raymond Briggs in the wordless *The Snowman* (1978). This unique experiment in sophisticated strip cartooning is gentler and more dreamlike than his iconoclastic *Father Christmas* (1973), also in strip format.

John Burningham also plays with narrative convention in his ironically contra-puntal stories *Come Away from the Water, Shirley* (1977) and *Time to Get Out of the Bath, Shirley* (1978), which alter traditional storytelling progression in order to contrast a child's public and fantasy worlds on alternating pages. Yet Burning-ham's *Mr. Gumpy's Outing* (1970) serves as a classic example of the same cohesive unity of art and text that he playfully defies in his Shirley books. This original adaptation of the cumulative story, in which each event is a repetition of the previous event with the addition of a single new factor, is deeply satisfying simply because of the repetition. One by one, animals and children ask to join Mr. Gumpy in his boat; each is welcomed with a specific provisional caution. When the boat is more than full, Mr. Gumpy's admonitions and cautions are forgotten, and the boat overturns, dumping the passengers into the water. Contentment and radiance flow from Burningham's portrait of the cat (reproduced in the color section). Among its notable features are the soft texturing, done in grey, green, and orange; the foreground field of daisies and foliage, worked in a scratched-line technique; and the background for the cat, which consists of a precise, delicate netting pattern shaded with subtle color tones.

Also geared to the very young child whose gaze can absorb the story without explanation is *The Snowy Day* (1962) by Ezra Jack Keats, in which the universality of every child's experiences in the snow is made concrete, intimate, and reassuring. Keats's medium is collage (see the color section). The clean edges of cut paper, large blocks of bright flat color, and textured surfaces create a feeling of exuberance and warmth against the white expanse of snow. The richness of the background is contrasted with the simplicity of the child in the foreground. His

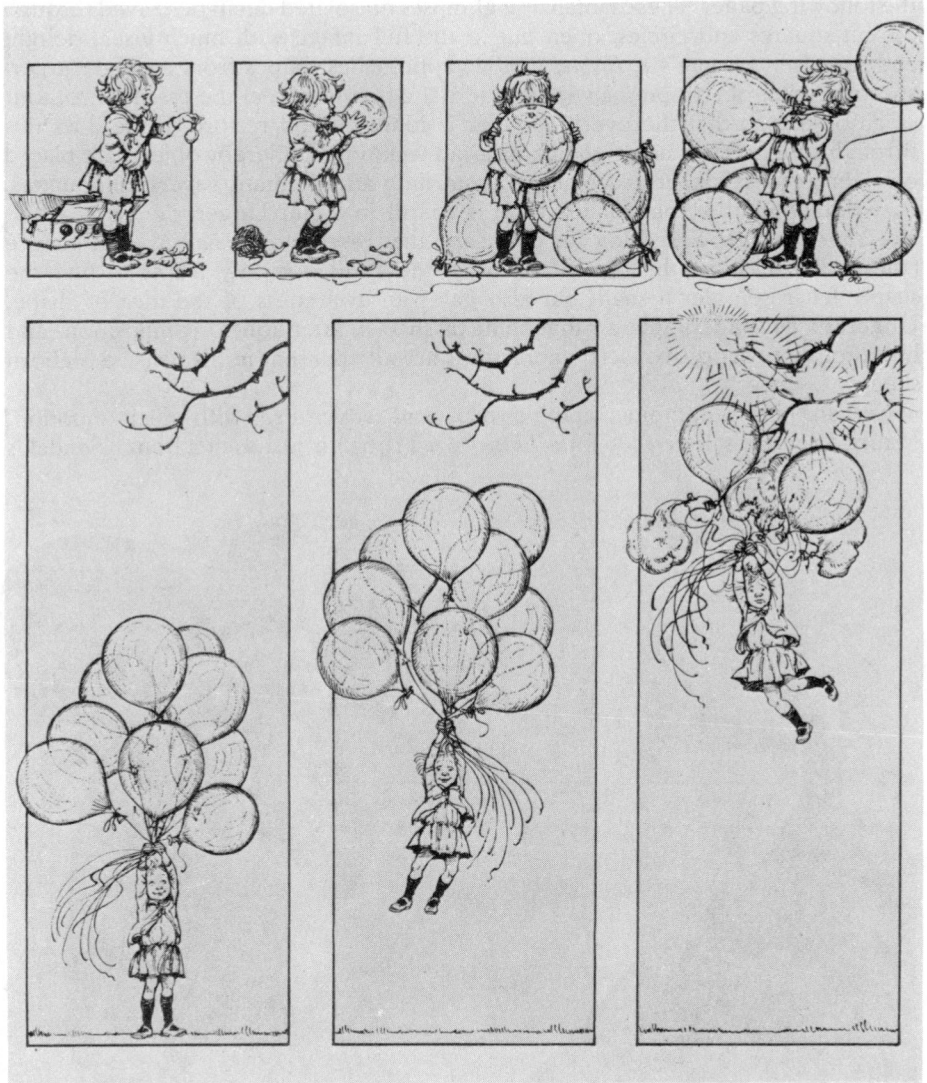

Illustration by Shirley Hughes, from *Up and Up,* by Shirley Hughes. Copyright © 1979 by Shirley Hughes. Reproduced by permission of The Bodley Head.

paper-doll-like, cut-out figure, dressed in a bright orange snowsuit, pulls the eye across the page, reinforcing the text and the narrative left-to-right progression of footprints in the snow. The child reader-viewer walks with Peter through the pleasures of the snowy day.

Picture books still set out overtly to teach, tackling such concepts as shapes, size, and sequence, as well as concepts of a more subjective nature. Tana Hoban's numerous concept books use black-and-white and color photography in imaginative, unusual ways, focusing on the very essence of seeing, enticing the viewer toward an appreciation of the patterns and shapes of the world. In *Look Again!* (1971) and *Take Another Look* (1981), cut-away pages reveal only a portion of the following page. These tantalizing glimpses of isolated detail perceived through die-cut squares and circles, open out to the full image with much visual delight and surprise. Hoban's *A,B, See!* (1982) approaches shapes from a different perspective—that of stripping away all external detail to reveal the essential contour of an object, so that the overly familiar is renewed and restored. She does this through an ingenious use of the photogram technique, whereby objects are placed on light-sensitive paper and emerge as startling and dramatic reverse silhouettes.

A similar kind of playful teaching is found in Tomi Ungerer's *Snail, Where Are You?* (1962). Searching for the shape that resembles a snail in each picture (the curl of a shoe, the curl of a horn), the child not only learns to find the shape that resembles a snail, but also gains an awareness of the idea of shape. Ungerer's flat and simple arrangement of shapes, attention to composition, and humorously provocative facial expressions are all apparent in his pensive bighorn sheep.

Certain books combine graphic play and adventure with deep emotion. Maurice Sendak's *Where the Wild Things Are* (1963) is just such a book. Sendak's

Illustration by Tomi Ungerer. From *Snail, Where Are You?* by Tomi Ungerer. Copyright © 1962 by Jean Thomas Ungerer. Reproduced by permission of Harper & Row, Publishers, Inc.

Illustration by Maurice Sendak. From *Where the Wild Things Are,* by Maurice Sendak. Copyright © 1963 by Maurice Sendak. Reproduced by permission of Harper & Row, Publishers, Inc.

experiments with artistic styles and psychological themes have greatly extended the potential of the picture-book genre. When it was first published, *Where the Wild Things Are* was attacked for its depiction of the monsters that symbolized the destructive impulses of Max, the child-hero of the book, and by extension the fears and rages of all children. But Sendak's sure, empathetic emotional sense is expressed graphically, reassuring children with its unified control. Sendak's skill is evident in the masterful draftsmanship and unforgettable characterization of the fierce, comical monsters; each picture is filled with tension and excitement. The light and dark areas help create a sense of drama, and finely textured, cross-hatched surfaces contrast with the exaggeration of his figures. There is, moreover, a balanced choreography between text and illustration. Like a ballet, the pictures grow in shape and scale as Max moves into the powerful realm of his dream fantasies.

Chris Van Allsberg's *Jumanji* (1981) is another book in which graphic play and compelling story are imbued with the atmosphere of dream. There is a quality of perfection, of inevitability, in the matching of style and content. The magic photo-realism of Van Allsberg's overpowering draftsmanship is necessary to the impact of the story; it makes the fantasy element credible. The monumental, sculptural quality of Van Allsberg's drawings is fully three-dimensional, and the viewer is drawn into these three-dimensional pictures by the unusual perspectives and shifting sense of scale. Similarly, the children in the story are drawn into a fantasy game that shifts from squares on a flat, two-dimensional board to real, three-dimensional jungle animals in their home. The sense of shock and the ominous, dreamlike power of the text are conveyed in the pictures through the surrealistic freezing of time. Poised figures are caught in action, and objects are held in suspension even as they fall through space and time. Subtlety in the use of black, white, and gray tones adds to the sense of unreality and stillness in the drawings.

Mitsumasa Anno also uses unusual perspectives to create a mood in his series of wordless picture-book travelogues. In *Anno's Journey* (1977) and subsequent titles, the lone traveler on horseback proceeds across Europe, Italy, Britain, and the United States, passing through time as well as space in a romantic unfolding of sly detail and cultural allusions ranging from the Pied Piper of Hamelin to Beethoven sitting at a window. This omniscient, bird's-eye perspective of Western culture as seen by an Easterner is in the tradition of the Japanese and Chinese scroll paintings. Anno brings the Oriental sense of infinite space—the floating world—to bear on Western images. The result is a dynamic tension between the subject and the unexpected perceptions of an artist to whom a European village can look like a Japanese print. The small, busy figures are placed carefully, in intricate patterns, against a balanced background of calm, flatly expansive white space and of the contrasting warm tones and dynamic angularity of the buildings.

In *Anno's Journey,* action is implied in the movement of the man on horseback across the succeeding double-page spreads; this is the recurring leitmotif that binds the imagery together and provides continuity. In John S. Goodall's small, wordless adventure books, action is provided not by a single figure but by a structural element. These books contain half-pages or flap-pages. At each turn of a half-page, the story progresses significantly. Innumerable lines and painstaking workmanship give background depth to *The Adventures of Paddy Pork*

Illustration by Chris Van Allsburg, from *Jumanji,* by Chris Van Allsburg. Copyright © 1981 by Chris Van Allsburg. Reproduced by permission of Houghton Mifflin Company.

Illustration by John S. Goodall. Copyright © 1968 by John S. Goodall. Reproduced from his volume *The Adventure of Paddy Pork* by permission of Harcourt Brace Jovanovich, Inc.

(1968). So completely does Goodall build his scene that one is tempted to step right in and follow Paddy down the road after the circus. In a sense, that is exactly what happens as the turning of each page takes one further into Paddy's adventures, depicted in illustrations filled with detail of scene.

Humorously adventurous in a quiet, bizarre way, *The House on East 88th Street* (1962) demonstrates the magical cartoon art of Bernard Waber. Using two kinds of line, a sketchy, simple line with incidental color, and a vital, bold line, relaxed and spontaneous, Waber takes us into the mundane human world of the Primms,

Illustration by Bernard Waber. From *The House on East 88th Street*, by Bernard Waber. Copyright © 1962 by Bernard Waber. Reproduced by permission of Houghton Mifflin Company.

Illustration reprinted by permission of Philomel Books, from *Anno's Journey,* by Mitsumasa Anno.
Copyright © 1977 by Fukiunkan Shoten Publishers, Tokyo, Japan.

into which Lyle the crocodile wins his way. Great attention is paid to pattern and design, underscoring the assumption that this is a perfectly credible and reasonable story.

Some picture books are the antithesis of adventure, being simply statements of mood or feeling, as in *Rain, Rain, Rivers* (1969) by Uri Shulevitz. Such content relies heavily on the artist, and Shulevitz creates a sustained and powerful mood through the use of subdued colors in an almost monochromatic range (*reduced tonalities*). His delicate, thin, scratchy lines pull the eye toward an inner softness, re-creating the feeling of a squishy, drenched landscape. Each picture is spread out across two pages, increasing the sense of space. There is a pervading illusion of quiet expansiveness in these large pictures, whose edges fade gently into the paper.

Another mood book, *A Tree Is Nice* (1956), obtains its emotional substance from the work of the artist Marc Simont. Notice the multiple lines in the massive tree trunk, where line is used to suggest bulk. The same style is adapted to different parts of the picture; foliage is created by a variation of line, small and delicate.

Strength of mood is an outstanding trait in the work of Charles Keeping. His stories, set in working-class London, are generally somber and realistic in tone (although not always so in resolution). *Explosive* is one word that gives some clue to the amazing energy and variety of Keeping's use of line. His magic transformation of a mundane scene, startling and arresting, is achieved by breaking the background into large, simple shapes and then developing each area with subtle color contrasts and relationships. Line, intricate and changing, dominates the brick background shown on page 182. A scratch technique gives a luminous quality to the transparent white areas. Another kind of line, rippling with a bolder flow, brings out the partially shadowed figure of the boy. Altogether, Keeping's work displays a mastery of line and emotional intensity.

Another kind of picture book emphasizes a sense of place. Although there is a story of substance in Alois Carigiet's *The Pear Tree, the Birch Tree, and the Barberry Bush* (1967), the chief joy of this book is creation of scene. Clear water colors applied on delicately outlined shapes give a clarity to the Swiss

Illustration by Uri Shulevitz. From *Rain Rain Rivers,* by Uri Shulevitz. Copyright © 1969 by Uri Shulevitz. Used with permission of Farrar, Straus & Giroux, Inc.

Illustration by Marc Simont. From *A Tree Is Nice,* by Janice May Udry. Pictures copyright © 1956 by Marc Simont. Reproduced by permission of Harper & Row, Publishers, Inc..

mountains, the people, the atmosphere, the very weather (see the color section). Textural details are provided with strokes of paint over a neutral ground. Wood grain in the beams of the house contrasts with the bark of the tree, as does the cold character of stone with the sparkle in the air. The clothing, foliage, and architecture include an extraordinary amount of fascinating detail.

Still another book that evokes scene, but in a different way, is *A Prairie Boy's Winter* (1973) by William Kurelek. As in the works of Anno, the scene is observed from a distance. The illustrations are filled with naively rendered figures, small in scale against the dominant landscape. Kurelek achieves an overpowering sense of atmosphere and place—the cold Canadian prairies—and a sense of time and nostalgia, for these paintings are memories of his childhood in the 1930s. A feeling of vast space is conveyed within a small area: The foreground figures and the tracks through the snow are diagonals, pulling the eye to the prairie horizon and the powerful blue sweep of sky (see the color section). Kurelek's illustrations evoke other presences: The images of children at play in winter games are reminiscent of Breughel's paintings of children's games; the pervading sense of memory and the naive drawing style recall the childlike simplicity of the primitive painter Grandma Moses or the picture-book artist Ann Blades. Kurelek's use of color is sophisticated; his subdued wintery tones and colorful

This is Joseph.

Illustration by Charles Keeping, from *Joseph's Yard,* by Charles Keeping. Copyright © 1969 by Oxford University Press. Reprinted by permission of Franklin Watts, Inc., and Oxford University Press, London.

highlights provide a strong compositional framework for his pictorial autobiography.

The strained intentness of Portuguese fishermen as they row through the sea is expressed in Jan Balet's flattened shapes in *Joanjo* (1967), the story of a boy in a Portuguese fishing village. Pictured in the striking visual language of shapes, of flattened patterns that glow with color (see the color section), the formalized expressions demonstrate the artist's strong commitment to shape and design. The elemental feeling of strength and power seems to be essential to Balet's portrayal of fishing life.

The depiction of Ozark life in *Mommy, Buy Me a China Doll* (1966), a repetitive song, gains a strong feeling of reality from the sensual textures of Margot Zemach's painted background. Boards look solid; nails have quirky, insistent shapes; the colors seem to spring from the red, rich, clayey earth. Children laugh uproariously at the ludicrous combinations made visible. Zemach's line, definite and subtly textured, provides humor via small details like the curl in the piggies' tails, or the troubled look on the faces of the cats as they try to roost in the chicken coop. Her textured surfaces, created with daubs of paint, give animation to a composition that is ramshackle in mood but actually carefully unified in terms of treatment and color (see the color section).

Margot Zemach's evocation of Ozark life gives vitality to the song that provides the accompanying text. The personality of her art is so strong that a new creation comes from this merger. The folklore material provides both a special challenge and a vehicle to accompany the art. In similar fashion, *Tom Tit Tot* (1965),

ONCE UPON A TIME THERE WAS A WOMAN

and she baked five pies. And when they
came out of the oven, they were that over-
baked the crusts were too hard to eat. So she
says to her daughter, "Darter," says she, "put you
them there pies on the shelf, and leave 'em there a
little, and they'll come again." She meant, you know,
the crust would get soft.

But the girl, she says to herself, "Well, if they'll come again,
I'll eat 'em now." And she set to work and ate 'em all, first
and last.

Illustration by Evaline Ness. From *Tom Tit Tot.* Published by Charles Scribner's Sons. Copyright © 1965 by Evaline Ness.

brought into picture-book form by Evaline Ness, is a book that almost shouts aloud the words. The rowdy humor of the tale is emphasized in the strong black-and-white line, the rough patterns, and the dominant shapes. An artist of unmistakable style, Evaline Ness is exuberantly and humorously in tune with the text.

A completely different style is that of Molly Bang, who conveys the romantic tone of *Dawn* (1983) in haunting, jewel-like illustrations. In her literary retelling of the Japanese folktale, "The Crane Wife," Bang has placed the poignant story of love and sacrifice in a new setting: a shipbuilding village of nineteenth-century New England. The illustrations are perfectly sympathetic to the mysterious story of the bird-wife who leaves her human husband after he breaks a promise. The artwork alternates between black-and-white drawings and paintings of great subtlety. The paintings use a medallion style: The framed border is part of the composition itself. The details of the borders include pictorial motifs that act as symbolic reinforcements and allusions to the text, building dramatic suspense and extending the story's meaning. In the illustration in the color section, the border of marsh and sky—the natural habitat of the Canada goose—emphasizes the woman's double nature and prefigures her eventual return to life among the geese. Similarly, the broken eggshell under the bed extends the text, suggesting the unusual birth of the newborn child now lying in her mother's arms. There is a dynamic tension in the juxtaposition of the two different styles used in the central picture and in the border. The evocative border is dreamy and impressionistic, rendered in soft colors and a textural, painterly style that conveys a sensuous love of nature and the presence of an intangible mystery. This style contrasts subtly with the more linear treatment of the inner picture, the precise draftsmanship that defines the mother and child, and the crisp colors of the quilt. The floating borders juxtaposed with the geometric quilt patterns emphasize the goose-wife's predicament as she attempts to live in two worlds. A gentle, overall effect of composure and reflective quiet emanates from the arrangement of the page.

Tikki Tikki Tembo (1968) is given a strong and detailed sense of place, a visualized progression of action, and an immediate sense of predicament through Blair Lent's artwork. Although the story, like all folktales, creates its own excitement in the telling, the flat, patterned work of the shapes enriches the tale, providing a distinctive visual harmony. Architectural details are precisely treated, and shapes of people and objects are cleanly defined. The drawing of the bricks in the wall is worth noticing. For the child who has been entranced by the story, this is a pictorial representation of such enchanting detail that the story can be lived over and over again simply by looking.

The line work of Hans Fischer in *The Traveling Musicians* (1955) has an unmistakable quality of humor. His thin, expressive line gives life and character to the animals. Fischer's interest in pattern and line appears to be loose and casual, but there is careful variation throughout the book. Although similar in general shape, no two patterns are exactly alike. With very slight alterations of line, Fischer achieves continual change.

Felix Hoffmann's *Sleeping Beauty* (1959) demonstrates his sensitivity of line and poetic sense of arrangement. While there is an evocation of romance in his drawings, his people have the reality of peasants. Strong emotion rather than sentiment comes from his use of fine line worked on colored surfaces and

So Chang ran as fast as his little legs would carry him to the Old Man With The Ladder. Under a tree the Old Man With The Ladder sat bowed and silent.

"Old Man, Old Man," shouted Chang. "Come right away! Tikki tikki tembo-no sa rembo-chari bari ruchi-pip peri pembo has fallen into the stone well!"

Illustration by Blair Lent. From *Tikki Tikki Tembo*, retold by Arlene Mosel. Illustrated by Blair Lent. Copyright © 1968 by Arlene Mosel. Copyright © 1968 by Blair Lent, Jr. Reproduced by permission of Holt, Rinehart and Winston, publishers.

Illustration by Hans Fischer. Reproduced from his volume *The Traveling Musicians* by permission of Harcourt Brace Jovanovich, Inc. First published in Switzerland in 1944.

the soft pencil used in the black-and-white pages. An apparent simplicity of line gives a pervading sense of beauty and strength.

Nancy Ekholm Burkert's illustrations in *Snow White and the Seven Dwarfs* (1972) are opulent. There is endless visual detail, alluding to the content and luminous technique of medieval miniatures. The smooth texture she uses gives a romantic, dreamlike quality that corresponds to the poetic tenor of this story. The format, large and slim, is that of a picture book, but there is no attempt to picture each event. The result is a handsome, illustrated edition of a single folktale. Yet Burkert's artwork exerts an influence on the entire book, creating an ambiance that is inseparable from the story.

Folk material invites a range of individual response from illustrators. Trina Schart Hyman's version of the Snow White story, for example, while sharing Burkert's romantic, poetic approach, is quite different in its greater and more deliberate use of psychological and symbolic elements. This attention to the unconscious patterning and imagery of folklore is also found in Anthony Browne's provocative *Hansel and Gretel* (1982). Without forfeiting the timeless universality of the folktale, Browne gives it a decidedly nonromantic, contemporary setting of cruel twentieth-century poverty and deprivation. The psychological depth of the tale is revealed through a visual subtext of repeating pictorial motifs that operate subliminally, equating the stepmother with the witch and foreshadowing

And the wedding of the King's son and Briar Rose was celebrated with great splendour   and they lived happily to the end of their days

Illustration by Felix Hoffmann, from *The Sleeping Beauty,* by the Brothers Grimm. Copyright ©
1959 by H. R. Sauerlander and Co., Aarau; English translation, copyright © 1959 by Oxford University Press. Reproduced by permission of Harcourt Brace Jovanovich, Inc.

Illustration by Nancy Ekholm Burkert. Reprinted with the permission of Farrar, Straus & Giroux, Inc., from *Snow White and the Seven Dwarfs,* a tale from the Brothers Grimm, translated by Randall Jarrell, illustrated by Nancy Ekholm Burkert. Copyright © 1972 by Nancy Ekholm Burkert.

Illustration by Anthony Browne, from *Hansel and Gretel*, by the Brothers Grimm, translated by Eleanor Quarrie. Illustration copyright © 1981 by Anthony Browne (Julia MacRae Books, London). Reproduced by permission of Franklin Watts, Inc.

the children's trials. All the drawings are mutually reinforcing, echoing each other in incremental imagery. In this illustration, the triangle is used like the first recurring phrase in a symphony. Repeated in the seemingly innocuous shapes of the mousehole, cathedral spire, and shadows of various objects, it menacingly suggests the classic triangular witch's hat in the crowning of the stepmother's shadow by the triangle formed by the parted curtains. Throughout the book, similar associative and juxtaposed images and patterns build a pictorial code that extends the meaning, depth, and significance of the story. Innovative and risk-taking, Browne's approach gives the traditional tale new life and energy. The interaction of his illustrations with the text stretches the limits of visual literacy and the very boundaries of the picture-book genre.

Why, some adults wonder, is it necessary for children to have books of such complexity and originality? After all, they argue, the child will enjoy some little book of lesser quality just as much. Pictures are pictures. It is true that a child may form an attachment to a book that does little to stimulate visual responsiveness; but it is also true that if the child sees nothing but mediocre work, a sameness of graphics over and over again, no growth in visual perception can occur. The eye is trained by what it sees, as the ear by what it hears; the great value of ensuring that the child has books of artistic quality is that the natural suppleness of vision is retained and not crippled. To many people, accustomed to products of a mass output, there are only two possible responses to pictures: They are either "pretty" or "ugly." Individual differences are inherent in the work of quality artists. To be able to see these differences, to be able to respond in a different way to each artist, is itself a part of the freedom and ability of individuals to express themselves according to their own feelings, their own perceptions.

On the other hand, no one expects a child or any other person to exist in a rarefied atmosphere of exclusivity, to be shielded from all work except the finest. The real world of picture books, exciting as it is, is as varied as the real world of human beings. Mediocre art can be tied to some very good stories, and the opposite can also be the case.

Marvelous things happen to the child who is given a free range. Strong affections for certain books develop. Again and again, one particular book is taken home from the library. Deep and genuine involvement can be seen as the child pores over the book that lies open and flat on the floor. These years, during which the child is open and receptive, are the very years when the best should be offered—for the best picture books speak in a visual language that educates the eye and stimulates the imagination.

There is also, of course, the sense of the narrative within the picture book. The alphabet and counting books, identification books, board books, and manipulative flap or pop-up books designed for use with very young children have strong graphic appeal and little narrative. Picture books intended for the child past infancy, however, are noted for their storytelling power. Often children will pick up a picture book and invent their own narratives, "reading" aloud. Those children who have had the same story read to them over and over again are easily able to recall and follow a story as they turn the pages of a picture book. Some texts of picture books are much more memorable than others; some can be told without the visual accompaniment and hold the listener spellbound. These are the stories with definite beginnings, middles, and ends. Characters are rounded and sympathetic, drama and tension are generated by a clear conflict of forces; incidents mount to a climax, and the story ends with a firm resolution. These are the virtues of old-fashioned storytelling, the hallmarks through which the folktale has endured. Generation after generation, children listen repeatedly to the story of Goldilocks and the three bears, with or without illustrations. Beatrix Potter's story about Peter Rabbit strikes so strong an emotional tone as to be independent of her careful, engaging drawings.

In the preceding section, in which the art of the picture book was emphasized, references to the accompanying texts indicated that they supply words for a mood book, a concept book, or a simple narrative sequence. Art and text become so closely intertwined that the text is often not substantial enough to be satisfying when separated. The picture-book texts that follow are included because of their strong stories and their appeal to young listeners, who can follow the conflict and project themselves into the story with sympathy and understanding. In the sense that the term *picture books* covers a certain format of publishing, these belong in the genre. The adult who wants to discriminate between the young child's art experience and literary experience may think of these stories as primarily literary. But in all of them, the illustrations play an important role in interpreting, illuminating, and extending the text.

Texts of Picture Books

L. Leslie Brooke

Johnny Crow's Garden

Several generations of children in both England and America have loved this delightful nonsense picture book, which had its beginnings in the artist's own childhood. As a small boy, Leslie Brooke loved the stories about Johnny Crow that his father, a novelist, told him. When he grew up and had two sons of his own, he in turn told them about Johnny Crow. At the suggestion of his wife, he made a picture book of the genial bird. A few years later came *Johnny Crow's Party,* and thirty years later he wrote and illustrated *Johnny Crow's New Garden* for his small grandson Peter Brooke. [Complete text from *Johnny Crow's Garden,* written and illustrated by L. Leslie Brooke (Warne, 1903).]

Johnny Crow
Would dig and sow
Till he made a little Garden.

And the Lion
Had a green and yellow Tie on
In Johnny Crow's Garden.

And the Rat
Wore a Feather in his Hat
But the Bear
Had nothing to wear
In Johnny Crow's Garden.

So the Ape
Took his Measure with a Tape
In Johnny Crow's Garden.

Then the Crane
Was caught in the Rain
In Johnny Crow's Garden.

And the Beaver
Was afraid he had a Fever
But the Goat
Said:
"It's nothing but his Throat!"
In Johnny Crow's Garden.

And the Pig
Danced a Jig
In Johnny Crow's Garden.

Then the Stork
Gave a Philosophic Talk
Till the Hippopotami
Said: "Ask no further 'What am I?'"
While the Elephant
Said something quite irrelevant
In Johnny Crow's Garden.

And the Goose—
Well,
The Goose *was* a Goose
In Johnny Crow's Garden.

And the Mouse
Built himself a little House
Where the Cat
Sat down beside the Mat
In Johnny Crow's Garden.

Illustration by L. Leslie Brooke, from *Johnny Crow's Garden,* by L. Leslie Brooke. First published in 1903. Reprinted by permission of the publisher, Frederick Warne & Co., Inc.

And the Whale
Told a very long Tale
In Johnny Crow's Garden.

And the Owl
Was a funny old Fowl
And the Fox
Put them all in the Stocks
In Johnny Crow's Garden.

But Johnny Crow
He let them go
And they all sat down
    to their dinner in a row
In Johnny Crow's Garden!

Beatrix Potter

The Tale of Peter Rabbit

This story is one of the best-loved of all the nursery classics. Beatrix Potter wrote it first in the form of a letter to amuse a little invalid boy, Noél Moore, the five-year-old son of her former German governess, and she illustrated the letter with pen-and-ink sketches. Noél loved the story and cherished the letter. (He grew up to be a clergyman.) Years later when Beatrix Potter thought of publishing the little story, she borrowed the letter. She copied the drawings, added a few more, made the story a little longer, and submitted it to a publisher. It was politely rejected. After it had been turned down by six publishers, Beatrix Potter drew out her savings from the Post Office savings bank and had a modest edition of 450 copies privately printed at a cost of £11. But it was not until Frederick Warne and Company decided to publish it with colored illustrations that the story came into its own. It sold for a shilling and carried a royalty of threepence a copy. The fame of Peter Rabbit spread rapidly. At the time of Beatrix Potter's death in 1943 the book had been translated into five languages and had sold several million copies. Beatrix Potter wrote over twenty of these little animal stories, but *Peter Rabbit, Benjamin Bunny,* and *The Tailor of Gloucester* are the best. [Complete text from Beatrix Potter, *The Tale of Peter Rabbit* (Warne, 1902).]

Once upon a time there were four little Rabbits, and their names were—

Flopsy,
Mopsy,
Cotton-tail,
and Peter.

They lived with their Mother in a sandbank, underneath the root of a very big fir-tree.

"Now, my dears," said old Mrs. Rabbit one morning, "you may go into the fields or down the lane, but don't go into Mr. McGregor's garden: your Father had an accident there; he was put in a pie by Mrs. McGregor. Now run along, and don't get into mischief; I am going out."

Then old Mrs. Rabbit took a basket and her umbrella, and went through the wood to the baker's. She bought a loaf of brown bread and five currant buns.

Flopsy, Mopsy, and Cotton-tail, who were good little bunnies, went down the lane to gather blackberries; but Peter, who was very naughty, ran straight away to Mr. McGregor's garden, and squeezed under the gate!

First he ate some lettuces and some French beans; and then he ate some radishes; and then, feeling rather sick, he went to look for some parsley.

But round the end of a cucumber frame, whom should he meet but Mr. McGregor!

Mr. McGregor was on his hands and knees planting out young cabbages, but he jumped up and ran after Peter, waving a rake and calling out, "Stop thief!"

Peter was most dreadfully frightened; he rushed all over the garden, for he had forgotten the way back to the gate.

He lost one of his shoes among the cabbages, and the other shoe amongst the potatoes.

After losing them, he ran on four legs and went faster, so that I think he might have got away altogether if he had not unfortunately run into a gooseberry net, and got caught by the large buttons on his jacket. It was a blue jacket with brass buttons, quite new.

Peter gave himself up for lost, and shed big tears; but his sobs were overheard by some friendly sparrows, who flew to him in great excitement, and implored him to exert himself.

Mr. McGregor came up with a sieve, which he intended to pop upon the top of Peter; but Peter wriggled out just in time, leaving his jacket behind him. And rushed into the toolshed, and jumped into a can. It would have been a beautiful thing to hide in, if it had not had so much water in it.

Mr. McGregor was quite sure that Peter was somewhere in the toolshed, perhaps hidden underneath a flower-pot. He began to turn them over carefully, looking under each.

Presently Peter sneezed— "Kertyschoo!" Mr. McGregor was after him in no time, and tried to put his foot upon Peter, who jumped out of the window, upsetting three plants. The window was too small for Mr. McGregor and he was tired of running after Peter. He went back to his work.

Peter sat down to rest; he was out of breath and trembling with fright, and he had not the least idea which way to go. Also he was very damp with sitting in that can.

After a time he began to wander about, going lippity—lippity—not very fast, and looking all around.

He found a door in a wall; but it was locked, and there was no room for a fat little rabbit to squeeze underneath.

An old mouse was running in and out over the stone door-step, carrying peas and beans to her family in the wood. Peter asked her the way to the gate, but she had such a large pea in her mouth that she could not answer. She only shook her head at him. Peter began to cry.

Then he tried to find his way straight across the garden, but he became more and more puzzled. Presently, he came to a pond where Mr. McGregor filled his water-cans. A white cat was staring at some goldfish; she sat very, very still, but now and then the tip of her tail twitched as if it were alive. Peter thought it best to go away without speaking to her; he had heard about cats from his cousin, little Benjamin Bunny.

He went back towards the toolshed, but suddenly, quite close to him, he heard the noise of a hoe—scr-r-ritch, scratch, scratch, scratch, scritch. Peter scuttered underneath the bushes. But presently, as nothing happened, he came out, and climbed upon a wheelbarrow, and peeped over. The first thing he saw was Mr. McGregor hoeing onions. His back was turned toward Peter, and beyond him was the gate! Peter got down very quietly off the wheelbar-

row, and started running as fast as he could go, along a straight walk behind some black-currant bushes.

Mr. McGregor caught sight of him at the corner, but Peter did not care. He slipped underneath the gate, and was safe at last in the wood outside the garden.

Mr. McGregor hung up the little jacket and the shoes for a scare-crow to frighten the blackbirds.

Peter never stopped running or looked behind him till he got home to the big fir-tree.

He was so tired that he flopped down upon the nice soft sand on the floor of the rabbit hole, and shut his eyes. His mother was busy cooking; she wondered what he had done with his clothes. It was the second little jacket and pair of shoes that Peter had lost in a fortnight!

I am sorry to say that Peter was not very well during the evening.

His mother put him to bed, and made some camomile tea; and she gave a dose of it to Peter!

"One table-spoonful to be taken at bedtime."

But Flopsy, Mopsy, and Cotton-tail had bread and milk and blackberries for supper.

The Story of the Three Bears

Until recently, this story was generally attributed to Robert Southey, for it was printed in the fourth volume of his miscellany *The Doctor* (1837). But a manuscript in the Osborne Collection of the Toronto Public Library, entitled *The Story of the Three Bears metrically related, with illustrations locating it at Cecil Lodge in September 1831 by Eleanor Mure,* * seems to prove that the nursery tale was not original with Southey. However, Southey had never claimed that the story was an original work. The dedication in the Mure manuscript reads: "The celebrated nursery tale put into verse and embellished with drawings for a birthday present to Horace Broke Sept: 26: 1831." This would imply that the story was in existence before 1831. In both the Mure manuscript and the Southey story the heroine is a little old woman; Goldilocks had not yet made her appearance. [This version from *English Fairy Tales,* retold by Flora Annie Steel (Macmillan, 1918).]

* *Children's Literature: Books and Manuscripts,* an exhibition November 19, 1954 through February 28, 1955 (The Pierpont Morgan Library, New York, 1954), Item 124.

Once upon a time there were three Bears, who lived together in a house of their own, in a wood. One of them was a Little Wee Bear, and one was a Middle-sized Bear, and the other was a Great Big Bear. They had each a bowl for their porridge: a little bowl for the Little Wee Bear; and a middle-sized bowl for the Middle-sized Bear; and a great bowl for the Great Big Bear. And they had each a chair to sit in: a little chair for the Little Wee Bear; and a middle-sized chair for the Middle-sized Bear; and a great chair for the Great Big Bear. And they had each a bed to sleep in: a little bed for the Little Wee Bear; and a middle-sized bed for the Middle-sized Bear; and a great bed for the Great Big Bear.

One day, after they had made the porridge for their breakfast and poured it into their porridge-bowls, they walked out into the wood while the porridge was cooling that they might not burn their mouths by beginning too soon, for they were polite, well-brought-up Bears. And while they were away, a little girl called Goldilocks, who lived at the other side of the wood and had been sent on an errand by her mother, passed by the house and looked in at the window. And then she peeped in at the keyhole, for she was not at all a well-brought-up little girl. Then seeing nobody in the house she lifted the latch. The door was not fastened, because the Bears were good Bears who did nobody any harm and never suspected that anybody would harm them. So Goldilocks opened the door and went in; and well pleased was she when she saw the porridge on the table. If she had been a well-brought-up little girl she would have waited till the Bears came home, and then, perhaps, they would have asked her to breakfast; for they were good Bears—a little rough or so, as the manner of Bears is, but for all that very good-natured and hospitable. But she was an impudent, rude little girl, and so she set about helping herself.

First she tasted the porridge of the Great Big Bear, and that was too hot for her. Next she tasted the porridge of the Middle-sized Bear, but that was too cold for her. And then she went to the porridge of the Little Wee Bear, and tasted it, and that was neither too hot nor too cold, but just right, and she liked it so well, that she ate it all up, every bit!

Then Goldilocks, who was tired, for she had been catching butterflies instead of running on her errand, sat down in the chair of the Great Big Bear, but that was too hard for her. And then she sat down in the chair of the Middle-sized Bear, and that was too soft for her. But when she sat down in the chair of the Little Wee Bear, that was neither too hard, nor too soft, but just right. So she seated herself in it, and there she sat till the bottom of the chair came out, and down she came, plump upon the ground; and that made her very cross, for she was a bad-tempered little girl.

Now, being determined to rest, Goldilocks went upstairs into the bedchamber in which the Three Bears slept. And first she lay down upon the bed of the Great Big Bear, but that was too high at the head for her. And next she lay down upon the bed of the Middle-sized Bear, and that was too high at the foot for her. And then she lay down upon the bed of the Little Wee Bear, and that was neither too high at the head, nor at the foot, but just right. So she covered herself up comfortably, and lay there till she fell fast asleep.

By this time the Three Bears thought their porridge would be cool enough for them to eat it properly; so they came home for breakfast. Now careless Goldilocks had left the spoon of the Great Big Bear standing in his porridge.

"SOMEBODY HAS BEEN AT MY PORRIDGE!"

said the Great Big Bear in his great, rough, gruff voice.

Then the Middle-sized Bear looked at his porridge and saw the spoon was standing in it too.

"SOMEBODY HAS BEEN AT MY PORRIDGE!"

said the Middle-sized Bear in his middle-sized voice.

Then the Little Wee Bear looked at his, and there was the spoon in the porridge bowl, but the porridge was all gone!

"Somebody has been at my porridge and has eaten it all up!"

said the Little Wee Bear in his little wee voice.

Upon this the Three Bears, seeing that some-one had entered their house, and eaten up the Little Wee Bear's breakfast, began to look about them. Now the careless Goldilocks had not put the hard cushion straight when she rose from the chair of the Great Big Bear.

"SOMEBODY HAS BEEN SITTING IN MY CHAIR!"

said the Great Big Bear in his great, rough, gruff voice.

And the careless Goldilocks had squatted down on the soft cushion of the Middle-sized Bear.

"SOMEBODY HAS BEEN SITTING IN MY CHAIR!"

said the Middle-sized Bear in his middle-sized voice.

"Somebody has been sitting in my chair, and has sat the bottom through!"

said the Little Wee Bear in his little wee voice.

Then the Three Bears thought they had better make further search in case it was a burglar; so they went upstairs into their bedchamber. Now Goldilocks had pulled the pillow of the Great Big Bear out of its place.

"SOMEBODY HAS BEEN LYING IN MY BED!"

said the Great Big Bear in his great, rough, gruff voice.

And Goldilocks had pulled the bolster of the Middle-sized Bear out of its place.

"SOMEBODY HAS BEEN LYING IN MY BED!"

said the Middle-sized Bear in his middle-sized voice.

But when the Little Wee Bear came to look at his bed, there was the bolster in its place!

And the pillow was in its place upon the bolster.

And upon the pillow—?

There was Goldilocks' yellow head—which was not in its place, for she had no business there.

"Somebody has been lying in my bed,—and here she is still!"

said the Little Wee Bear in his little wee voice.

Now Goldilocks had heard in her sleep the great, rough, gruff voice of the Great Big Bear; but she was so fast asleep that it was no more to her than the roaring of wind, or the rumbling of thunder. And she had heard the middle-sized voice of the Middle-sized Bear, but it was only as if she had heard someone speaking in a dream. But when she heard the little wee voice of the Little Wee Bear, it was so sharp and so shrill, that it awakened her at once. Up she started, and when she saw the Three Bears on one side of the bed, she tumbled herself out at the other and and ran to the window. Now the window was open, because the Bears, like good, tidy Bears, as they were, always opened their bedchamber window when they got up in the morning. So naughty, frightened little Goldilocks jumped; and whether she broke her neck in the fall or ran into the wood and was lost there or found her way out of the wood and got whipped for being a bad girl and playing truant no one can say. But the Three Bears never saw anything more of her.

Wanda Gág

Millions of Cats

With its publication and immediate success in 1928, this landmark picture book (the first picture book by an American artist to be published in the United States) set high standards for the development of the American children's book industry. Brought up in the living folk traditions of her Eastern European family, Wanda Gág inherited the intimate voice of the natural storyteller. The musical cadence, satisfying structure, and humorous hyperbole of *Millions of Cats* evoke the homely atmosphere and drama of a folktale. The same seemingly artless simplicity is

Illustrations by Wanda Gág, reprinted by permission of Coward, McCann & Geoghegan, from *Millions of Cats,* by Wanda Gág. Copyright © 1928 by Coward-McCann, Inc.; copyright renewed © 1956 by Robert Janssen.

found in her rhythmic black and white lithographs, which extend the action and warmth of the hand-lettered text. Wanda Gág created numerous picture books during her career—including the striking *ABC Bunny* (1933)—and retold and illustrated four volumes of *Grimm's Fairy Tales.* Her dynamic graphic design, assured prose, and understanding of the intimate balance between text and illustrations made her a seminal figure in the American picture book field. [Complete text from Wanda Gág, *Millions of Cats* (Coward-McCann, 1928).]

Once upon a time there was a very old man and a very old woman. They lived in a nice clean house which had flowers all around it, except where the door was. But they couldn't be happy because they were so very lonely.

"If we only had a cat!" sighed the very old woman.

"A cat?" asked the very old man.

"Yes, a sweet little fluffy cat," said the very old woman.

"I will get you a cat, my dear," said the very old man.

And he set out over the hills to look for one. He climbed over the sunny hills. He trudged through the cool valleys. He walked a long, long time and at last he came to a hill which was quite covered with cats.

Cats here, cats there,
Cats and kittens everywhere,
Hundreds of cats,

Thousands of cats,
Millions and billions and trillions of cats.

"Oh," cried the old man joyfully, "Now I can choose the prettiest cat and take it home with me!" So he chose one. It was white.

But just as he was about to leave, he saw another one all black and white and it seemed just as pretty as the first. So he took this one also.

But then he saw a fuzzy grey kitten way over here which was every bit as pretty as the others so he took it too.

And now he saw one way down in a corner which he thought too lovely to leave so he took this too.

And just then, over here, the very old man found a kitten which was black and very beautiful.

"It would be a shame to leave that one," said the very old man. So he took it.

And now, over there, he saw a cat which had brown and yellow stripes like a baby tiger.

"I simply must take it!" cried the very old man, and he did.

So it happened that every time the very old man looked up, he saw another cat which was so pretty he could not bear to leave it, and before he knew it, he had chosen them all.

And so he went back over the sunny hills and down through the cool valleys, to show all his pretty kittens to the very old woman.

It was very funny to see those hundreds and thousands and millions and billions and trillions of cats following him.

They came to a pond.

"Mew, mew! We are thirsty!" cried the

Hundreds of cats,
Thousands of cats,
Millions and billions and trillions of cats.

"Well, here is a great deal of water," said the very old man.

Each cat took a sip of water, and the pond was gone!

"Mew, mew! Now we are hungry!" said the

Hundreds of cats,
Thousands of cats,
Millions and billions and trillions of cats.

"There is much grass on the hills," said the very old man.

Each cat ate a mouthful of grass and not a blade was left!

Pretty soon the very old woman saw them coming.

"My dear!" she cried, "What are you doing? I asked for one little cat, and what do I see?—

"Cats here, cats there,
Cats and kittens everywhere,
Hundreds of cats,
Thousands of cats,
Millions and billions and trillions of cats."

"But we can never feed them all," said the very old woman, "They will eat us out of house and home."

"I never thought of that," said the very old man, "What shall we do?"

The very old woman thought for a while and then she said, "I know! We will let the cats decide which one we should keep."

"Oh yes," said the very old man, and he called to the cats, "Which one of you is the prettiest?"

"I am!"

"I am!"

"No, I am!"

"No, I am the prettiest!" "I am!"

"No, I am! I am! I am!" cried hundreds and thousands and millions and billions and trillions of voices, for each cat thought itself the prettiest.

And they began to quarrel.

They bit and scratched and clawed each other and made such a great noise that the very old man and the very old woman ran into the house as fast as they could. They did not like such quarreling. But after a while the noise stopped and the very old man and the very old woman peeped out of the window to see what had happened. They could not see a single cat!

"I think they must have eaten each other all up," said the very old woman, "It's too bad!"

"But look!" said the very old man, and he pointed to a bunch of high grass. In it sat one little frightened kitten. They went out and picked it up. It was thin and scraggly.

"Poor little kitty," said the very old woman.

"Dear little kitty," said the very old man, "how does it happen that you were not eaten up with all those hundreds and thousands and millions and billions and trillions of cats?"

"Oh, I'm just a very homely little cat," said the kitten," So when you asked who was the prettiest, I didn't say anything. So nobody bothered about me."

They took the kitten into the house, where the very old woman gave it a warm bath and brushed its fur until it was soft and shiny.

Every day they gave it plenty of milk—and soon it grew nice and plump.

"And it is a very pretty cat, after all!" said the very old woman.

"It is the most beautiful cat in the whole world," said the very old man. "I ought to know, for I've seen—

"Hundreds of cats,
Thousands of cats,

Millions and billions and trillions of cats—and not one was as pretty as this one."

William Steig

Sylvester and the Magic Pebble

The strong, direct telling of this story owes much to its folklore roots. Impressed upon this origin, however, is the pathos of being lost and separated from home and family. [Complete text from William Steig, *Sylvester and the Magic Pebble* (Simon & Schuster, 1969).]

Sylvester Duncan lived with his mother and father at Acorn Road in Oatsdale. One of his hobbies was collecting pebbles of unusual shape and color.

On a rainy Saturday during vacation he found a quite extraordinary one. It was flaming red, shiny, and perfectly round, like a marble. As he was studying this remarkable pebble, he began to shiver, probably from excitement, and the rain felt cold on his back. "I wish it would stop raining," he said.

To his great surprise the rain stopped. It didn't stop gradually as rains usually do. It CEASED. The drops vanished on the way down, the clouds disappeared, everything was dry, and the sun was shining as if rain had never existed.

In all his young life Sylvester had never had a wish gratified so quickly. It struck him that magic must be at work, and he guessed that the magic must be in the remarkable-looking red pebble. (Where indeed it was.) To make a test, he put the pebble on the ground and said, "I wish it would rain again." Nothing happened. But when he said the same thing holding the pebble in his hoof, the sky turned black, there was lightning and a clap of thunder, and the rain came shooting down.

"What a lucky day this is!" thought Sylvester. "From now on I can have anything I want. My father and mother can have anything they want. My relatives, my friends, and anybody at all can have everything anybody wants!"

He wished the sunshine back in the sky, and he wished a wart on his left hind fetlock would disappear, and it did, and he started home, eager to amaze his father and mother with his magic pebble. He could hardly wait to see their faces. Maybe they wouldn't even believe him at first.

As he was crossing Strawberry Hill, thinking of some of the many, many things he could wish for, he was startled to see a mean, hungry lion looking right at him from behind some tall grass. He was frightened. If he hadn't been so frightened, he could have made the lion disappear, or he could have wished himself safe at home with his father and mother.

He could have wished the lion would turn into a butterfly or a daisy or a gnat. He could have wished many things, but he panicked and couldn't think carefully.

"I wish I were a rock," he said, and he became a rock.

The lion came bounding over, sniffed the rock a hundred times, walked around and around it, and went away confused, perplexed, puzzled, and bewildered. "I saw that little donkey as clear as day. Maybe I'm going crazy," he muttered.

And there was Sylvester, a rock on Strawberry Hill, with the magic pebble lying right beside him on the ground, and he was unable to pick it up. "Oh, how I wish I were myself again," he thought, but nothing happened. He had to be touching the pebble to make the magic work, but there was nothing he could do about it.

His thoughts began to race like mad. He was scared and worried. Being helpless, he felt hopeless. He imagined all the possibilities, and eventually he realized that his only chance of becoming himself again was for someone to find the red pebble and to wish that the rock next to it would be a donkey. Someone would surely find the red pebble—it was so bright and shiny—but what on earth would make them wish that a rock were a donkey? The chance was one in a billion at best.

Sylvester fell asleep. What else could he do? Night came with many stars.

Meanwhile, back at home, Mr. and Mrs. Duncan paced the floor, frantic with worry. Sylvester had never come home later than dinner time. Where could he be? They stayed up all night wondering what had happened, expecting that Sylvester would surely turn up by morning. But he didn't, of course. Mrs. Dun-

can cried a lot and Mr. Duncan did his best to soothe her. Both longed to have their dear son with them.

"I will never scold Sylvester again as long as I live," said Mrs. Duncan, "no matter what he does."

At dawn, they went about inquiring of all the neighbors.

They talked to all the children—the puppies, the kittens, the colts, the piglets. No one had seen Sylvester since the day before yesterday.

They went to the police. The police could not find their child.

All the dogs in Oatsdale went searching for him. They sniffed behind every rock and tree and blade of grass, into every nook and gully of the neighborhood and beyond, but found not a scent of him. They sniffed the rock on Strawberry Hill, but it smelled like a rock. It didn't smell like Sylvester.

After a month of searching the same places over and over again, and inquiring of the same

Illustration by William Steig. From *Sylvester and the Magic Pebble*, by William Steig. Copyright © 1969 by William Steig. Reprinted by permission of Windmill Books, a division of Simon & Schuster, Inc.

animals over and over again, Mr. and Mrs. Duncan no longer knew what to do. They concluded that something dreadful must have happened and that they would probably never see their son again. (Though all the time he was less than a mile away.)

They tried their best to be happy, to go about their usual ways. But their usual ways included Sylvester and they were always reminded of him. They were miserable. Life had no meaning for them any more.

Night followed day and day followed night over and over again. Sylvester on the hill woke up less and less often. When he was awake, he was only hopeless and unhappy. He felt he would be a rock forever and he tried to get used to it. He went into an endless sleep. The days grew colder. Fall came with the leaves changing color. Then the leaves fell and the grass bent to the ground.

Then it was winter. The winds blew, this way and that. It snowed. Mostly, the animals stayed indoors, living on the food they had stored up.

One day a wolf sat on the rock that was Sylvester and howled and howled because he was hungry.

Then the snows melted. The earth warmed up in the spring sun and things budded.

Leaves were on the trees again. Flowers showed their young faces.

One day in May, Mr. Duncan insisted that his wife go with him on a picnic. "Let's cheer up," he said. "Let us try to live again and be happy even though Sylvester, our angel, is no longer with us." They went to Strawberry Hill.

Mrs. Duncan sat down on the rock. The warmth of his own mother sitting on him woke Sylvester up from his deep winter sleep. How he wanted to shout, "Mother! Father! It's me, Sylvester, I'm right here!" But he couldn't talk. He had no voice. He was stone-dumb.

Mr. Duncan walked aimlessly about while Mrs. Duncan set out the picnic food on the rock—alfalfa sandwiches, pickled oats, sassafras salad, timothy compote. Suddenly Mr. Duncan saw the red pebble. "What a fantastic pebble!" he exclaimed. "Sylvester would have loved it for his collection." He put the pebble on the rock.

They sat down to eat. Sylvester was now as wide awake as a donkey that was a rock could possibly be. Mrs. Duncan felt some mysterious excitement. "You know, Father," she said suddenly, "I have the strangest feeling that our dear Sylvester is still alive and not far away."

"I am, I am!" Sylvester wanted to shout, but he couldn't. If only he had realized that the pebble resting on his back was the magic pebble!

"Oh, how I wish he were here with us on this lovely May day," said Mrs. Duncan. Mr. Duncan looked sadly at the ground. "Don't you wish it too, Father?" she said. He looked at her as if to say, "How can you ask such a question?"

Mr. and Mrs. Duncan looked at each other with great sorrow.

"I wish I were myself again, I wish I were my real self again!" thought Sylvester.

And in less than an instant, he was!

You can imagine the scene that followed—the embraces, the kisses, the questions, the answers, the loving looks, and the fond exclamations!

When they had eventually calmed down a bit, and had gotten home, Mr. Duncan put the magic pebble in an iron safe. Some day they might want to use it, but really, for now, what more could they wish for? They all had all that they wanted.

Russell Hoban

How Tom Beat Captain Najork and His Hired Sportsmen

Russell Hoban is a versatile writer whose works for children range from the warmly domestic Frances the badger picture books to the acerbic allegory, *The Mouse and His Child*. In this picture book, Hoban displays his talents for social satire and endearing nonsense. *How Tom Beat Captain Najork and His Hired Sportsmen* is a contemporary nonsense fable about the nature of learning and the essence of freedom. It has roots in the zany Victorian narratives of Edward Lear and Lewis Carroll, and in Hilaire Belloc's parodies of the moral cautionary tale. A descendant of Tom Sawyer or Pippi Longstocking, the protagonist Tom will not stop "fooling around." His single-minded pursuit of inventive play and defiance of adult social morality are a testament to the creative child spirit. Hoban's text is illustrated by Quentin Blake, that master interpreter of comic iconoclasm. Memorable language play and a spirited concept make this a fine example of the longer picture book. [Complete text from Russell Hoban, *How Tom Beat Captain Najork and His Hired Sportsmen* (Atheneum, 1974).]

Tom lived with his maiden aunt, Miss Fidget Wonkham-Strong. She wore an iron hat, and took no nonsense from anyone. Where she walked the flowers drooped, and when she sang the trees all shivered.

Tom liked to fool around. He fooled around with sticks and stones and crumpled paper, with mewses and passages and dustbins, with bent nails and broken glass and holes in fences.

He fooled around with mud, and stomped and squelched and slithered through it.

He fooled around on high-up things that shook and wobbled and teetered.

He fooled around with dropping things from bridges into rivers and fishing them out.

He fooled around with barrels in alleys.

When Aunt Fidget Wonkham-Strong asked him what he was doing, Tom said that he was fooling around.

"It looks very like playing to me," said Aunt Fidget Wonkham-Strong. "Too much playing is not good, and you play too much. You had better stop it and do something useful."

"All right," said Tom.

But he did not stop. He did a little fooling around with two or three cigar bands and a paper-clip.

At dinner Aunt Fidget Wonkham-Strong, wearing her iron hat, said, "Eat your mutton and your cabbage-and-potato sog."

"All right," said Tom. He ate it.

After dinner Aunt Fidget Wonkham-Strong said, "Now learn off pages 65 to 75 of the Nautical Almanac, and that will teach you not to fool around so much."

"All right," said Tom.

He learned them off.

"From now on I shall keep an eye on you," Aunt Fidget Wonkham-Strong said, "and if you do not stop fooling around I shall send for Captain Najork and his hired sportsmen."

"Who is Captain Najork?" said Tom.

"Captain Najork," said Aunt Fidget Wonkham-Strong, "is seven feet tall, with eyes like fire, a voice like thunder, and a handlebar moustache. His trousers are always freshly pressed, his blazer is immaculate, his shoes are polished mirror-bright, and he is every inch a terror. When Captain Najork is sent for he comes up the river in his pedal boat, with his hired sportsmen all pedalling hard. He teaches fooling-around boys the lesson they so badly need, and it is not one that they soon forget."

Aunt Fidget Wonkham-Strong kept an eye on Tom. He did not stop fooling around. He did low and muddy fooling around and he did high and wobbly fooling around. He fooled around with dropping things off bridges and he fooled around with barrels in alleys.

"Very well," said Aunt Fidget Wonkham-Strong at table in her iron hat. "Eat your greasy bloaters."

Tom ate them.

"I have warned you," said Aunt Fidget Wonkham-Strong, "that I should send for Captain Najork if you did not stop fooling around. I have done that. As you like to play so much, you shall play against Captain Najork and his hired sportsmen. They play hard games and they play them jolly hard. Prepare yourself."

"All right," said Tom. He fooled around with a bottle-top and a burnt match.

The next day Captain Najork came up the river with his hired sportsmen pedalling his pedal boat.

They came ashore smartly, carrying an immense brown-paper parcel. They marched into the garden, one, two, three, four. Captain Najork was only six feet tall. His eyes were not like fire, his voice was not like thunder.

"Right," said Captain Najork. "Where is the sportive infant?"

"There," said Aunt Fidget Wonkham-Strong.

"Here," said Tom.

"Right," said the Captain. "We shall play womble, muck, and sneedball, in that order." The hired sportsmen sniggered as they undid the immense brown-paper parcel, set up the womble run, the ladders and the net, and distributed the rakes and stakes.

"How do you play womble?" said Tom.

"You'll find out," said Captain Najork.

"Who's on my side?" said Tom.

"Nobody," said Captain Najork. "Let's get started."

Womble turned out to be a shaky, high-up, wobbling and teetering sort of a game, and Tom was used to that kind of fooling around. The Captain's side raked first. Tom staked. The hired sportsmen played so hard that they wombled too fast, and were shaky with the rakes. Tom fooled around the way he always did, and all his stakes dropped true. When it was his turn to rake he did not let Captain Najork and the hired sportsmen score a single rung, and at the end of the snetch he won by six ladders.

"Right," said Captain Najork, clenching his teeth. "Muck next. Same sides."

The court was laid out at low tide in the river mud. Tom mucked first, and slithered through the marks while the hired sportsmen poled and shovelled. Tom had fooled around with mud so much that he scored time after time.

Captain Najork's men poled too hard and shovelled too fast and tired themselves out. Tom just mucked about and fooled around, and when the tide came in he led the opposition 673 to 49.

"Really," said Aunt Fidget Wonkham-Strong to Captain Najork, "you must make an effort to teach this boy a lesson."

"Some boys learn hard," said the Captain, chewing his moustache. "Now for sneedball."

The hired sportsmen brought out the ramp, the slide, the barrel, the bobble, the sneeding

The hired sportsmen had first slide. Captain Najork himself barrelled, and he and his men played like demons. But Tom tonged the bobble in the same fooling-around way that he fished things out of rivers, and he quickly moved into the lead. Captain Najork sweated big drops, and he slid his barrel too hard so it hit the stop and slopped over. But Tom just fooled around, and when it was his slide he never spilled a drop.

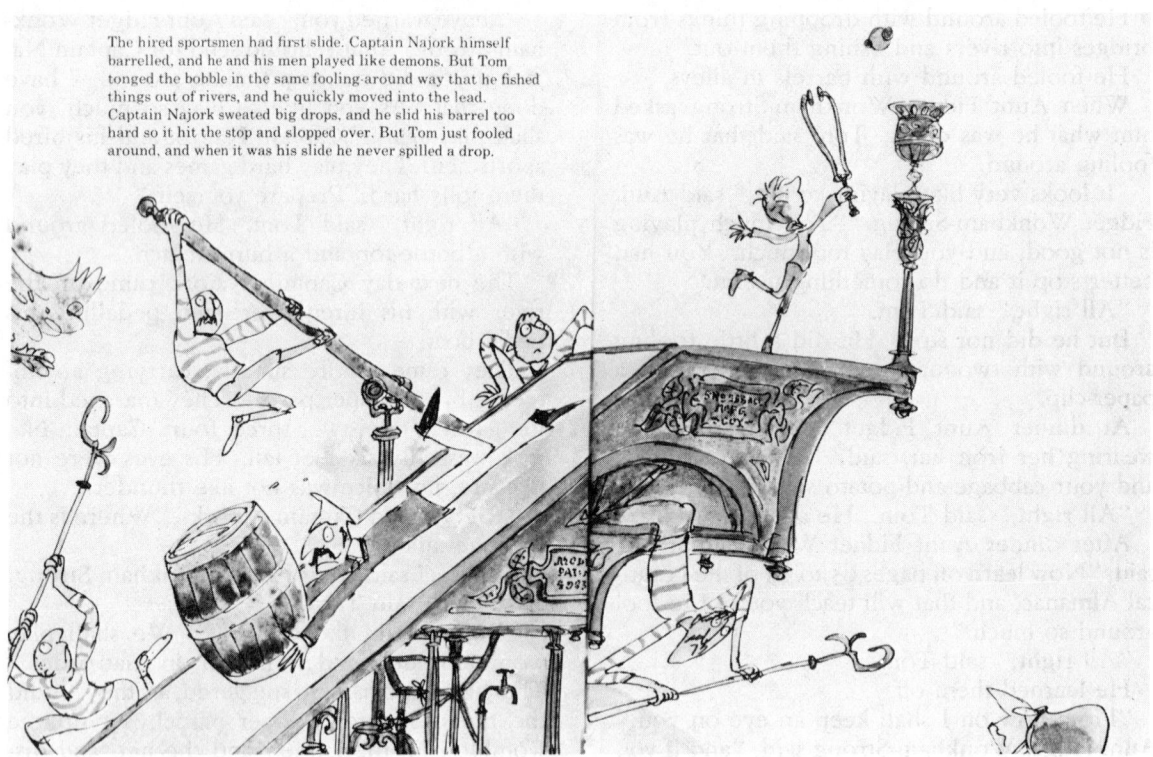

Illustrations by Quentin Blake. From *How Tom Beat Captain Najork and His Hired Sportsmen,* by Russell Hoban. Text copyright © 1974 by Yankee Rover, Inc. Illustrations copyright © 1974 by Quentin Blake. Used by permission of Atheneum Publishers.

tongs, the bar, and the grapples. Tom saw at once that sneedball was like several kinds of fooling around that he was particularly good at. Partly it was like dropping things off bridges into rivers and fishing them out and partly it was like fooling around with barrels in alleys.

"I had better tell you," said the Captain to Tom, "that I played in the Sneedball Finals five years running."

"They couldn't have been very final if you had to keep doing it for five years," said Tom. He motioned the Captain aside, away from Aunt Fidget Wonkham-Strong. "Let's make this interesting," he said.

"What do you mean?" said the Captain.

"Let's play *for* something," said Tom. "Let's say if I win I get your pedal boat."

"What do I get if *I* win?" said the Captain. "Because I am certainly going to win *this* one."

"You can have Aunt Fidget Wonkham-Strong," said Tom.

"She's impressive," said the Captain. "I admit that freely. A very impressive lady."

"She fancies you," said Tom. "I can tell by the way she looks sideways at you from underneath her iron hat."

"No!" said the Captain.

"Yes," said Tom.

"And you'll part with her if she'll have me?" said the Captain.

"It's the only sporting thing to do," said Tom.

"Agreed then!" said the Captain. "By George! I'm almost sorry that I'm going to have to teach you a lesson by beating you at sneedball."

"Let's get started," said Tom.

The hired sportsmen had first slide. Captain Najork himself barrelled, and he and his men played like demons. But Tom tonged the bobble in the same fooling-around way that he fished things out of rivers, and he quickly moved into the lead. Captain Najork sweated big drops, and he slid his barrel too hard so it hit the stop and slopped over. But Tom just fooled around, and when it was his slide he never spilled a drop.

Darkness fell, but they shot up flares and went on playing. By three o'clock in the morning Tom had won by 85 to 10. As the last flare went up above the garden he looked down from the ramp at the defeated Captain and his hired sportsmen and he said, "Maybe that will teach you not to fool around with a boy who knows how to fool around."

Captain Najork broke down and wept, but Aunt Fidget Wonkham-Strong had him put to bed and brought him peppermint tea, and then he felt better.

Tom took his boat and pedalled to the next town down the river. There he advertised in the newspaper for a new aunt. When he found one that he liked, he told her, "No greasy bloaters, no mutton and no cabbage-and-potato sog. No Nautical Almanac. And I do lots of fooling around. Those are my conditions."

The new aunt's name was Bundlejoy Cozysweet. She had a floppy hat with flowers on it. She had long, long hair.

"That sounds fine to me," she said. "We'll have a go."

Aunt Fidget Wonkham-Strong married Captain Najork even though he had lost the sneedball game, and they were very happy together. She made the hired sportsmen learn off pages of the Nautical Almanac every night after dinner.

A Selection from a Picture Book

James Marshall

"Split Pea Soup," from George and Martha

George and Martha consists of "Five Stories about Two Great Friends," each of which is a self-contained entity. The first story in the book, "Split Pea Soup," presented here, is a fine example of the pure picture book in which words and pictures are combined to form a greater whole. In commenting on the wedding of art and text in *George and Martha*, Walter Lorraine observes, "No reader can fully appreciate the love of these two friends by only reading the words. The picture of George filling his loafer with Martha's pea soup becomes an essential part of the story line."* Marshall's sophisticated cartoon art is appropriate to these simple fables of the friendship between two endearing hippos, distant spiritual cousins of the classic picture-book figure Babar the elephant. The drawings are not as naive as they appear; the fluid, free line and casual red, yellow, and green washes convey a subtle range of feeling, expression, and pictorial wit. The book is conceived as a complete entity; even the opening hand-lettered title pages display the economy of art and text and the warm humor of the stories. [From James Marshall, *George and Martha* (Houghton Mifflin, 1972).]

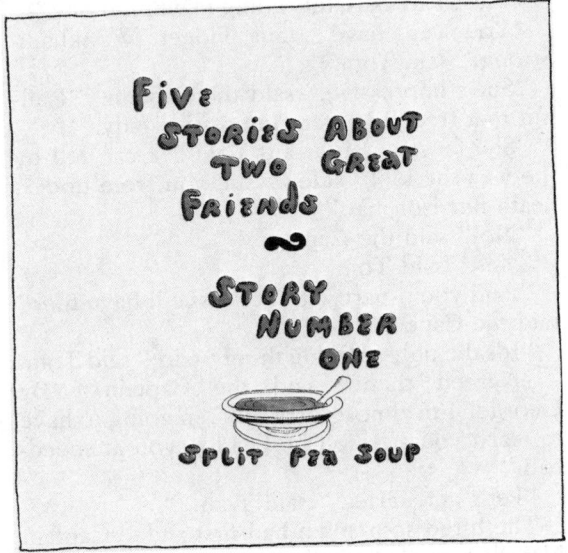

* Walter Lorraine, "Book Illustration: The State of the Art," in *Illustrators of Children's Books, 1967–1976*, comp. Lee Kingman, Grace Allen Hogarth, and Harriet Quimby (Horn Book, 1978), p. 5.

Martha was very fond of making split pea soup. Sometimes she made it all day long. Pots and pots of split pea soup.

If there was one thing that George was *not* fond of, it was split pea soup.
As a matter of fact, George hated split pea soup more than anything else in
the world. But it was so hard to tell Martha.

One day after George had eaten ten bowls of Martha's soup, he said to himself, "I just can't stand another bowl. Not even another spoonful."

So, while Martha was out in the kitchen, George carefully poured the rest of his soup into his loafers under the table. "Now she will think I have eaten it."

But Martha was watching from the kitchen.

"How do you expect to walk home with your loafers full of split pea soup?"
she asked George.

"Oh dear," said George. "You saw me."

"And why didn't you tell me that you hate my split pea soup?"

"I didn't want to hurt your feelings," said George.

"That's silly," said Martha. "Friends should always tell each other the truth.
As a matter of fact, I don't like split pea soup very much myself. I only like to
make it. From now on, you'll never have to eat that awful soup again."

"What a relief!" George sighed.

"Would you like some chocolate chip cookies instead?" asked Martha.

"Oh, that would be lovely," said George.

"Then you shall have them," said his friend.

5 The History of the Illustrated Book

The hand-lettered books that were copied in the monasteries prior to the invention of printing were embellished with designs, illuminated initials, minute pictures, and decorative patterns, and it was natural that the idea of pictorial decoration should be carried over to the product of the printing press. The illustrated book thus followed soon after the invention of movable type.

The first illustrations made to accompany print were carved in wood blocks: Crude, simple pictures were first drawn on a block of wood, and then cut in relief to form a printing surface. The process was closely akin to the method by which the letters themselves were formed; the wood block (or *woodcut*) could be locked in the printing press with the letters, or type, and printed at the same time as the text. It was an economical process, and one naturally harmonious with print, since there was a balance between the black-and-white line of the picture and the black-on-white line of the type.

William Caxton (1422?–91), the first English printer, used woodcuts in certain of his books, but these books were not addressed to children; those titles that would seem to be for children, such as *The Book of Courtesye* (1479), designed to give children instruction in manners and behavior, were published without

---

1. Lewis Carroll, *Alice's Adventures in Wonderland* (Macmillan, 1865), pp. 1–2.

German woodcut, from Aesop's Life and Fables (Ulm, ca. 1476–77); translation adapted from William Caxton, 1484.

illustration. Caxton's *Aesop's Fables* (1484) was illustrated with 185 "clear and lively woodcuts," which must have delighted children fortunate enough to have access to them, though the fables were intended as adult reading.

It was an inspired teacher, one of the great minds produced by the Reformation, who first saw the need for pictorial representation where children were concerned. Comenius (Jan Amos Komensky) was born in 1592 in what is now Czechoslovakia. As a bishop of the Moravian church, the Unity of Brethren, he reformed and invigorated the educational outlook of all Europe, and the text he wrote for children was the chief instrument of that reform. Originally written in High Dutch and Latin, because Latin was the international language of the time, the book bore the title *Orbis Sensualium Pictus, The Visible World: Or, A Picture and Nomenclature of All the Chief Things That Are in the World.* Every object mentioned was illustrated with a picture and numbered in the text for easy identification. The *Orbis Pictus* first appeared in 1658 and was translated into most of the languages of Europe; the Latin text was given on one side of the page, and the vernacular on the other. It was first translated into English in 1658 by Charles Hoole.

The eighteenth-century battledores—three-fold cardboard successors to the hornbooks—were often embellished with woodcuts, and these so-called books were entrusted to children. The ballad sheets and chapbooks, hawked on the streets and at markets and fairs, also had their measure of crude woodcut illustration. The same cut often served several tales, and an illustration of some maid of ballad fame would make an appearance elsewhere as a portrait of Queen Bess. The astute John Newbery, the first to recognize children as buyers and consumers of books, took care to illustrate his little books, and the advertisements for his wares included the promise, "adorned with cuts."

Woodcut illustration became an art in the late eighteenth century through the genius of Thomas Bewick (pronounced "Buick"). A country boy with his mind full of vivid pictures of the animals and landscapes he had known on his father's farm near Newcastle, Bewick was apprenticed to an engraver and put to work on woodcuts—then considered unimportant, as meeting only a cheap popular demand. Bewick revived and extended an old art of wood engraving. The common practice was to cut the picture on the flat side of a piece of wood, cutting with the grain. Bewick used the cross section of the wood block, cutting across the end grain. He engraved lines *into* the wood to represent white spaces between the uncarved portions of the block, which held ink for printing. This process allowed greater detail and more variety in shading and tone. Bewick was an artist in wood, and his miniature tailpiece landscapes were almost as great in their power to evoke atmosphere and feeling, warmth and coolness, light and shade, as anything a painter could produce with a full palette of color at his command. His portraits of animals and birds are incomparable. His *General History of Quadrupeds* (1790) and *History of British Birds* (1797) were designed for the adult public; but an edition of Aesop illustrated by him and his pictures for John Gay's *Fables* (1784) must have appealed to children who had the good fortune to come upon them.

Bewick did not undertake the illustration of books for children until after he was well established as an engraver and had become a partner in the firm. "He is the earliest illustrator in modern times to have earned his living almost exclusively by the illustration of books, and is among the earliest to have his name featured on title pages as an attraction to the purchaser."[2]   Among his books for children are *A New Invented Horn Book* (1770); *New Year's Gift for Little Masters and Misses* (1777); *The Mirror, or A Looking Glass for Young People* (1778); and *The Life and Adventures of a Fly* (1789).

When Bewick died in 1828, George Cruikshank, also a master of line and the craft of the wood block, was twenty-four years old. Cruikshank had made, and been paid for, his first engraving at the age of twelve. An early illustrator of Dickens's books, he achieved success through his nimble gift for caricature and the delineation of action. The outstanding assignment of the day in the realm of children's books was that of illustrating the first English translation, by Edgar Taylor, of the Grimms' *German Popular Tales* (1823 and 1826). Cruikshank's illustrations for Grimm are, even today, excellent examples of the extension of the mood of the text in pictorial form. *The Brownies* (1871) and *Lob-Lie-by-the-Fire* (1874), by Juliana Horatia Ewing, were also enriched by Cruikshank's humor and wit.

Even the most casual survey of illustrations discloses the fact that the medium by which the artist's image is transferred to the page determines the character and form that results. The various methods of reproducing pictures are both complex and technical, and so cannot be treated at length here. Those interested in delving more deeply into the subject must be indebted to Bertha Mahony Miller, founder of *The Horn Book Magazine*, for four interesting, exhaustive, and knowledgeable volumes on illustration and illustrators. The first volume, *Illustrators of Children's Books, 1744–1945*, was published in 1947. Three later volumes cover the periods 1946 to 1956, 1957 to 1966, and 1967 to 1976. Fashions and trends, new techniques and points of view, are presented in a fascinating panorama in these books, and the opinions of artists, critics, and perceptive readers give variety to the subject.

Helen Gentry's article, "Graphic Processes in Children's Books," in Volume I, is a notably clear explanation of the basic procedures. Simple, effective explanations of modern techniques are given in *Pages, Pictures and Print,* by Joanna Foster (1958), a book written for children, and in *Ways of the Illustrator: Visual Communication in Children's Literature* (1982) by Joseph H. Schwarcz.

As we have seen, the line drawing, as rendered in wood-block engraving, is by its very nature adapted to the printed page. In the hands of master draftsmen

2. Percy Muir, *English Children's Books, 1600 to 1900* (Batsford, 1954), p. 173.

Illustration by George Cruikshank. From *The Cruikshank Fairy-Book,* by George
Cruikshank. First published as *George Cruikshank's Fairy Library in 1853.*

and engravers, the result can be close to perfection. Sir John Tenniel's illustrations
for *Alice's Adventures in Wonderland* (1865) and *Through the Looking-Glass* (1871),
for example, represent the highest art of illustration. Let us examine them in
relation to three criteria that Frank Weitenkampf presents in *The Illustrated Book*
(1938).

First, "How good are the pictures in drawing and composition?" In other
words, do they hold to the tenets of art in their own right, as well as meet the
obligations of illustration? Tenniel's drawing is sheer wizardry, his line sharp,
delicate, and definitive. As for composition, notice in *Through the Looking-Glass*
the balanced landscape in the illustration for " 'Twas brillig, and the slithy toves/
Did gyre and gimble in the wabe." An unearthly scene it is, and yet quite
like a sensible garden; the classic column of the sundial is a focal point for all
the animals that never were on sea or land, and the strong perpendicularity is
echoed and reaffirmed in the spindly legs of the bird to the right. Or note, in
Alice, the recurring angled V in the agitated kitchen of the Duchess, with the
squalling baby on her angular lap and the smile of the cat tuned to the same
sharpness.

Second, "Do the pictures *illustrate* or *accompany* or *comment on* or *decorate* the text sympathetically and with understanding?" asks Weitenkampf. Tenniel's drawings illustrate, and most sympathetically; they seem to be a part of the author's original concept, made actual by an act of genius. Yet Tenniel and Dodgson worked together in anger and anguish as well as in sympathy, to judge from all accounts.

Third, and finally, "Do they [the illustrations] go well with the type and the book generally?" Like glove to hand! The formats of the *Alice* books are timeless.

Twenty years before Tenniel's pictures for *Alice*, Edward Lear had set a high example of good illustration in his own *Nonsense Book* (1846), with line drawings as sharp, pungent, and absurdly memorable as the verse that accompanied them.

The wood-block engraving had its rivals during the nineteenth century. The engraving of pictures on copper or steel plates persisted over three quarters of the century. Engraving on metal permitted an elaboration of detail that sometimes resulted in overstatement and a florid, sentimental presentation, though these were essentially faults of taste rather than of process. One of the most unusual and beautiful books of all time had been engraved on copper, William Blake's *Songs of Innocence* (1789). Blake wrote his poems on the plate, drew decorative borders with images and scenes, printed the pages by hand, and then hand-colored them. Anne Eaton, in *Illustrators of Children's Books* (1947), tells the story of that creation, with appreciation of the rare magnitude of the accomplishment.

The advent of photography revolutionized the reproduction of pictures and all but wiped out the engraver's art; now pictures could be transferred by photographic means onto metal printing surfaces and need not be translated (cut, engraved, or etched) by the highly skilled hand and eye.

The most memorable body of illustrated books for children in the latter half of the nineteenth century came from the presses of the gifted London printer Edmund Evans. When Evans perfected a process of color printing from wood blocks in 1856, he invited three artists of the day to join him in producing a series of picture books for children, known as *toy books*. Those three artists were Kate Greenaway (1846–1901), Randolph Caldecott (1846–86), and Walter Crane (1845–1915). They have come to be looked upon as the founders of the picture-book tradition in English and American children's books. A study of their individual approaches may serve to reveal some facets of the art of picture-book making.

Of the three, Randolph Caldecott was the greatest. To the task of illustration he brought two special attributes. The first was his superb control of line. He could make it move, leap, soar. His line is sharp and clear, a line that can be exact and delicate, or robust and vigorous. From Caldecott the informed eye learns to recognize the fact that this lineal quality is basic to every other attribute of the picture book. "In discussing the linear aspect of a work of art," writes art critic MacKinley Helm, "it is necessary to distinguish between 'line' and 'lines.' Line is essentially the outline of forms. It is not necessarily something which is drawn; frequently it is merely indicated. Some painters draw their designs (with 'lines') and fill them with color. In such a case the work is principally linear. Others, like Rouault, draw unmistakable boundary lines between forms or objects, or, like Renoir, simply differentiate their forms by means of color and light."[3]   Helm is speaking of formal painting, but his definition of the

3. MacKinley Helm, *Modern Mexican Painters* (Harper, 1941), p. 113.

Illustration by Randolph Caldecott, from *Hey Diddle Diddle and Baby Bunting,* by Randolph Caldecott.
Reprinted by permission of the publisher, Frederick Warne & Co., Inc. First published in 1882.

lineal element applies to the art of the picture book as well. Caldecott's drawing
is lineal by virtue of his mastery of lines. (Beatrix Potter's line is no less definite
because it is indicated by means of color and light; it is as strong and exact as
that of Caldecott.).

Caldecott's second great gift was his ability to extend the meaning of the
text; to enhance and enliven it; to play and sport with it in an exuberance born
of his own wit and imagination. Consider, for example, the elopement of the
dish with the spoon in "Hey Diddle Diddle, the Cat and the Fiddle." There
is nothing in the old rhyme that says anything about how the parents of the
spoon felt at this turn of events, or who the parents were, or what were the
subsequent results of it all. But Randolph Caldecott's drawings have made it a
tale of "star-crossed lovers" as eloquently as words could do.

Walter Crane perhaps parallels the method of Rouault, as defined by Helm.
Crane draws unmistakable boundaries, setting them off with contrasting masses
of brilliant color. He was concerned with design, as well as with color; with
the design of the whole page in the book, as well as the picture on the page.
His pictures have the flat, static quality of Japanese prints, combined with the

ordered clutter of a rich theatrical background. One learns to perceive the meaning of his design by looking at the varieties of ways in which he crowds the space, leading the eye to follow prolific details to an ordered climax. Page follows page, evoking, in Rudyard Kipling's phrase, "more-than-oriental-splendour." There is a glory of color here, but the flowing quality of line that runs through Caldecott's books like a great tide is missing.

The third member of this triumvirate was Kate Greenaway. Hers was the happy combination of author-artist that accounts for the success of many present-day picture books. In *Under the Window* (1878) and *Marigold Garden* (1885),

Illustration by Walter Crane, from *Household Stories from the Collection of the Brothers Grimm,* trans. Lucy Crane (Dover Publications, 1963). First published in 1886.

Illustration by Kate Greenaway, from *Under the Window: Pictures and Rhymes for Children,* by Kate Greenaway. First published in 1878. Reprinted by permission of the publisher, Frederick Warne & Co., Inc.

she wrote the verse that graces the pages she designed and illustrated. Her greatest attribute was her distinctive style: It has charm and delicacy, a poetic element, and yet it is vigorous. She drew with exquisite exactitude flowers, garlands, wreaths, and gardens. Hers was a pictorial world of light and sunshine, and joyous children in pursuit of childlike pleasures: games, toys, teas, parties, and unequaled processions and ceremonials that wend their way across the pages of her books. She had little power to manipulate line, and the dancing feet and skipping shoes never quite get off the ground. But the intensity of her feeling for the freedom and gaiety of childhood is apparent in everything she essayed. The utter naturalness of the children triumphs, as does the aura of grace and felicity. Kate Greenaway is matchless in charm and delicacy, without the weakness of sentimentality.

The twentieth century was ushered in pictorially with a rash of illustrated books. In England, Beatrix Potter's *Tale of Peter Rabbit* (1902) led the way, to be followed by her other classics in miniature; each exquisite drawing is as full of character and individuality as the taut, sure tales she created out of her understanding of landscape and character, both human and animal.

L. Leslie Brooke (1862–1940) followed in the footsteps of Caldecott, with a controlled, distinctive line, eye for humor, and gift for extending the text in drawings redolent with wit and fun. His "ancestor portraits" for *The Story of the Three Bears* (1904) and *The Story of the Three Little Pigs* (1904) are "Major Ursa," in the first case, and "Sir Friedrich Bacon" in the other. His own nursery tales and *Johnny Crow's Garden* (1903), *Johnny Crow's New Garden* (1935), and *Johnny Crow's Party* (1907) bid fair to live as long as the rhymes of Mother Goose.

With the illustrated book for children finally established as a genre in its own right, the illustrator moved into a period of lush production on both sides of

the Atlantic. Large books of fairy tales and folktales appeared, rich in color production, demanding the use of the best papers and binding. Arthur Rackham (1867–1939) belonged to this time; his eerie, subdued, and fairy-haunted color is as distinctive as the certain, delicate line that characterizes his drawings in black and white. His illustrations for the Grimms' *Little Brother and Little Sister*

Illustration by Beatrix Potter, from *The Tale of Peter Rabbit,* by Beatrix Potter. First published in 1902. Reprinted by permission of the publisher, Frederick Warne & Co., Inc.

Illustration by Leslie Brooke, from *This Little Pig Went to Market,* by L. Leslie Brooke. First published circa 1922. Reprinted by permission of the publisher, Frederick Warne & Co., Inc.

(1917), Shakespeare's *Midsummer Night's Dream* (1926), and Richard Wagner's *Siegfried and the Twilight of the Gods* (1911), as well as his pictures for Kenneth Grahame's *Wind in the Willows* (1940), constitute an experience for the eyes and memory of the beholder. Edmund Dulac, an English artist born in France, also belonged to this period of opulence. His illustrations, minutely detailed and lavish as the art of Persia which influenced him, became fashionable among adult collectors, as did the illustrations of Kay Nielsen, the Danish-American artist.

In the United States, Felix Darley (1822–88) had given Irving's *Rip Van Winkle* (1850) an added dimension through the quality of his exquisitely clear, exact line. With Thomas Nast, the political cartoonist, Darley had illustrated an early edition of *Hans Brinker* (1866). A. B. Frost, fifteen years after the initial appearance of the Uncle Remus stories, made his unsurpassed illustrations for these tales by Joel Chandler Harris. Here again was the perfect matching of text to picture and picture to text.

The prime influence on illustration in America was Howard Pyle. A superb draftsman, he was a master of line—of color, too, but he was partial to the clean and lyric line of the pen-and-ink drawing, reminiscent of the prints by Albrecht Dürer, the German wood-block artist of the sixteenth century. Pyle steeped himself in the Middle Ages, writing tales of chivalry—of King Arthur and Robin Hood—and illustrating them with such exactitude that they have made the history of the period, as well as the literature, a reality for generations of children. He understood the function of illustration and assumed the obligation to add to the text of the author, never merely repeating what had already been stated in words. As a teacher, he put his mark on future generations of artists. N. C. Wyeth (father of the noted artist Andrew Wyeth), Maxfield Parrish, Jessie Willcox Smith, Frank Schoonover—these were some of Howard Pyle's students at Chadds Ford, Delaware. He was responsible for a new vigor, dignity, and sincerity in illustration. Integrity was an outstanding attribute of his character, and it shone forth in every picture he drew.

Illustration by Arthur Rackham, from *Fairy Tales from Many Lands* (William Heinemann Ltd., Publishers, 1974). First published in 1916 as *The Allies' Fairy Book*. Reprinted by permission of William Heinemann Ltd., London.

When N. C. Wyeth and Maxfield Parrish came to the years of their greatest productivity, the fashion in book making was to create handsome volumes, with pictures in full color tipped (or glued) into the already printed book. Wyeth's appeal lay in his brilliant color, his action, his sense of drama, and in the aura of high adventure and romance that suffused his pictures. Parrish, too, was a great colorist and a romanticist. Their works were really paintings rather than illustrations, and because they were printed on glossy paper and applied to the book, there was always a breach between text and illustration, accented by the blank, white page on the back of the illustration.

After World War I, a stream of artists from Europe brought new techniques and new ways of illustration to the United States. There were Boris Artzybasheff from Russia; Ingri and Edgar d'Aulaire from Switzerland and Norway; Maud and Miska Petersham and Kate Seredy from Hungary; Fritz Eichenberg from Germany, reemphasizing the strength of the wood block and the print; and Wanda Gág, American-born but close to her Bohemian heritage. The d'Aulaires, working on lithographic stones, introduced a whole series of brilliantly conceived and executed picture books and picture-story books. The Petershams brought color and folk designs to their illustration, and Artzybasheff discovered new worlds of book design.

The thirties were years of inventive and imaginative illustration and book design. Publishers vied with one another to make books that were individualized units of design, with illustration, type, and format combined in living symmetry. Artzybasheff's *Seven Simeons* (1937), with its wandering, delicate pictures weaving in and out of the pages and the text, remains as beautiful and as timeless now as it was when it was published. Thomas Handforth's *Mei Li* (1938) is another book harmonious in every detail of its creation.

The individuality of the illustrator's style was given full scope—for example, Elizabeth MacKinstry's reed-pen technique (learned through an apprenticeship under Claude Lovat Fraser), and William Nicholson's colored wood blocks. Helen Sewell displayed a remarkable ability to change style, patterns, and modes as appropriate to her subject matter; examples are her classic illustrations for the *First Bible* (1934), done in the manner of Victorian steel engravings, her stylized modern decorative illustrations for Bulfinch's *Books of Myths* (1942), and her illustrations for Eleanor Farjeon's *Ten Saints* (1936) after the mode of the early woodcuts, with their look of having been colored by hand.

If illustration was dimmed in the decade of the forties, as a result of the Second World War, the fifties showed signs of an exhilarating upsurge. Publishers embarked upon new schemes for using color, employing, for example, multicolored papers as a fresh source. The artists of the period were in a lively mood of experimentation: Antonio Frasconi, with his brilliant use of colored wood blocks, fitted to a modern idiom; Marcia Brown, in a growing variety of styles; William Pène du Bois, stunningly effective in his merging of line and color, as in *Lion* (1956); André François, a student of Picasso, introducing multiple design, dissected action, and distinctive line—these were among the highlights of the 1950s. New effects were achieved through the concept of a page as being without boundaries or perspective and horizons; in the use of symbolic shapes and geometric structures in place of a slick realism redolent of advertising art. In brief, illustration was influenced by the trends of the day in art itself.

The recognition of children's books by the American Institute of Graphic Arts also had a considerable effect on illustration. The AIGA's periodic exhibitions

Illustration by Marcia Brown, from *Dick Whittington and His Cat.* Copyright © 1950 by Marcia Brown; copyright © renewed 1978 by Marcia Brown. Reprinted with the permission of Charles Scribner's Sons.

of children's books have been routed around the country, and a new and growing audience has been made aware of excellence in design, in illustration, and in the book as a work of art.

The economic stability of the 1960s and early 1970s supported the continued growth of illustration, especially through the refinement of printing technology (in offset lithography) and the artists' ongoing experimentation with a wide variety of styles and techniques. Illustrated books appeared in every art style. Influences ranged from poster and advertising art (Tomi Ungerer), folk art (Paul Goble, Elizabeth Cleaver, Ed Young), geometric abstraction (Gerald McDermott), and surrealism (Graham Oakley, Etienne Delessert) to psychedelic art (Charles Mikolaycak). This emphasis on style and technique led to books with magnificent art as in the works of Leo and Diane Dillon, as well as to books in which a weak story served as a vehicle for graphic virtuosity and little else, as in the work of Alan Aldridge.

In the late 1970s and into the 1980s, increases in production costs resulted in a cutback in the publishing of full-color work and a shift in emphasis toward two-color and black-and-white work. Illustrators who used black-and-white vigorously, such as Stephen Gammell, Eric Blegvad, and Harold Jones, benefited from this trend. Simultaneously, a nostalgic revival of the classic illustrators of the nineteenth and early twentieth centuries spurred the reproduction of works by such masters as I. Bilibin, Maurice Boutet de Monvel, Kay Nielsen, and Edmund Dulac. Such contemporary illustrators as Errol Le Cain have been influenced by this elegant and decorative romanticism.

Similarly, reproductions of Victorian children's game books (the original Nister and Meggendorfer pop-ups and movable toy books) influenced some contemporary illustrators, who became fascinated with the wonders of paper engineering. Nicola Bayley's *Puss in Boots* (1976), Jan Pienkowski's *Haunted House* (1979), and Edward Gorey's *Dwindling Party* (1982) are all visually sophisticated pop-up books. While these charming game books are basically handsome toys, their popularity not only with children, but also with adults, signaled a broadening of the audience for children's illustrated books; they were now being collected as art objects by adults.

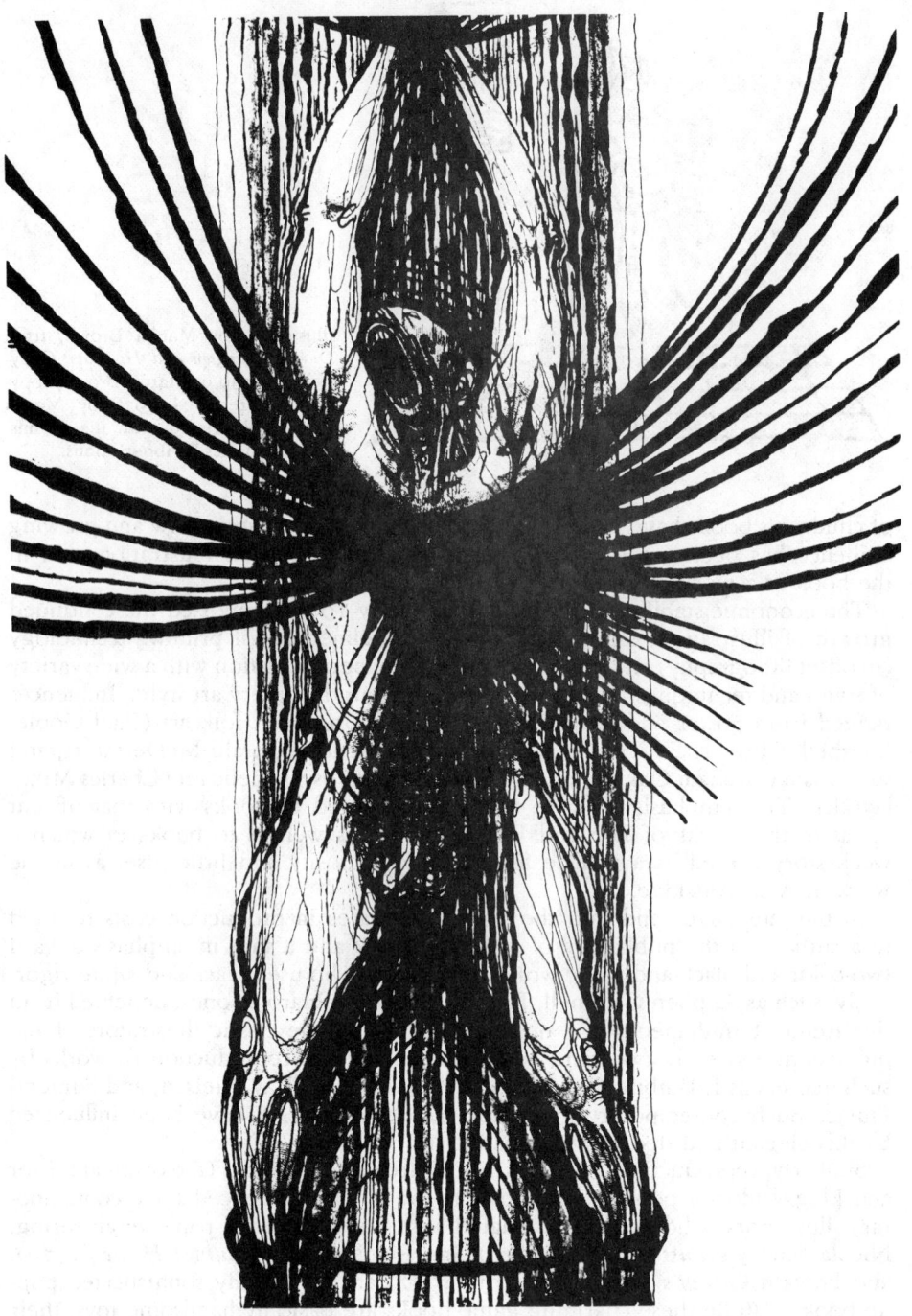

Illustration by Charles Keeping, from *The God beneath the Sea,* by Leon Garfield and Edward Blishen. Illustrations © 1970 by Charles Keeping. Reprinted by permission of Penguin Books Ltd.

Illustration by Maurice Sendak. From *The Juniper Tree and Other Tales from Grimm,* selected by Lore Segal and Maurice Sendak, translated by Lore Segal and Randall Jarrell. Illustrations copyright © 1973 by Maurice Sendak. Used with permission of Farrar, Straus & Giroux, Inc.

A number of classic stories, long associated with specific illustrators, have lately been reillustrated—in some cases because the texts have passed out of copyright. This is so for *The Wind in the Willows,* originally illustrated by Ernest Shepard and now refashioned by John Burningham (1983) and Michael Hague (1980). Another favorite that has attracted new interpretators is *The Adventures of Pinocchio,* which has been reillustrated by Gerald McDermott (1981) and Troy Howell (1983).

The 1970s and 1980s have seen a shifting of the field of illustration away from fiction to other areas. A number of nonfiction books are now profusely illustrated. Some are by artists like David Macaulay, Anne Ophelia Dowden, and Sheila Sancha, who write their own books. Others are illustrated by artists from the general field of illustration: Tom Feelings, Leonard Everett Fisher, Claire Roberts, and Peter Parnall, among others. Collections of folklore, myth, and epics are often given distinguished format and artwork. Notable examples are Charles Keeping's passionate black-and-white line work for Leon Garfield and Edward Blishen's retellings of Greek myths in *The God beneath the Sea* (1970) and *The Golden Shadow* (1973); Maurice Sendak's fine line drawings, resembling Dürer engravings, for his two-volume collection of Grimm, *The Juniper Tree* (1973); and Michael Foreman's evocative water colors for Angela Carter's *Sleeping Beauty and Other Favourite Fairy Tales* (1982). Graphics have also given an exhilaration to poetry: The work of Leonard Baskin (*Season Songs,* 1975, and *Under the North Star,* 1981), Arnold Lobel (*Nightmares: Poems to Trouble Your Sleep,* 1976), and Alice and Martin Provensen (*Birds, Beasts and the Third Thing,* 1982) make the pages sing visually as well as aurally.

Lately, there has been a new wave of picture books, of such sophistication in social and political commentary, symbolic allusion, subtle wit, and graphic play as to demand a new audience of older children, teen-agers, and adults. These books range from the surrealist productions of the publisher Harlin Quist to Maurice Sendak's complex picture book *Outside Over There* (1981), referred to by *Time* as the "most unusual novel of the season." Raymond Briggs (*Fungus the Bogeyman,* 1977, and *When the Wind Blows,* 1983), Toshi Maruki (*Hiroshima No Pika,* 1980), and Tomi Ungerer (*Alumette,* 1974, and *The Beast of Monsieur Racine,* 1971) are only a sampling of those who have helped to extend the traditional picture-book genre.

Like their predecessors, the illustrators of today work in the spirit of their art: demonstrating the root meaning of the verb *to illustrate,* they enlighten and illuminate.

The Oral Tradition:
The Cauldron of Story

The "Cauldron of Story," as J. R. R. Tolkien tells us in his essay "On Fairy-Stories," has always been boiling. Certain tales and accounts have persisted in human memories, beginning long before the advent of printing, and continuing, generation after generation, to the present. This heritage, preserved by oral transmission, is the "soup" in the cauldron of Tolkien's metaphor: the ancient, persistent, constantly evolving mystery that is called, in the broadest sense of the word, *myth* and is indissolubly linked to human language and the human impulse to make patterns.

Seasoned by centuries of telling, the stories of the cauldron are at their best when heard; telling is the key for children to the living qualities of this literature. (Storytelling as an art and technique is discussed in Chapter 10.) Folktales are the staples of storytelling, but this does not mean that myths, epics, and romances cannot be told. Stories from *Robin Hood* or *King Arthur* are most engaging when heard; indeed, they often consist of folk motifs also found in simpler tales.

The wide range of this literature is subject to subdivision into myths, legends, and the like. Elizabeth Cook has put it nicely:

In rough and ready phrasing myths are about gods, legends are about heroes, and fairy tales are about woodcutters and princesses. A rather more respectable definition might run: myths are about the creation of all things, the origin of evil, and the salvation of

225

man's soul; legends and sagas are about the doings of kings and peoples in the period before records were kept; fairy tales, folk tales and fables are about human behaviour in a world of magic, and often become incorporated in legends. Critics take an endless interest in the finer differences between them, but the common reader is more struck by the ways in which they all look rather like each other.[1]

And, in fact, some fables appear to be more like folktales; some myths more like legends. The term *fairy tale* is frequently used—sometimes to denote folktales, and sometimes such individual works of fantasy as Hans Christian Andersen's stories. Even the great folklore scholar Stith Thompson found it difficult to be formally precise:

We shall find these forms not so rigid as the theoretician might wish, for they will be blending into each other with amazing facility. Fairy tales become myths, or animal tales, or local legends. As stories transcend differences of age or of place and move from the ancient world to ours, or from ours to a primitive society, they often undergo protean transformations in style and narrative purpose. For the plot structure of the tale is much more stable and more persistent than its form.[2]

Written versions of these tales sometimes undergo the strong stylistic influence of a single writer. The story of Cinderella as told by Walter de la Mare possesses a kind of poetic beauty and subjective tenor not found in the unvarnished, simpler "Cap o' Rushes" from the Joseph Jacobs collection. Similarly, the stories told by Perrault are influenced by the courtly style of his time. These versions are often called literary versions because they exhibit the imaginative filling out and individual imagery of a particular writer. Children find these retellings to be potent in their magic, and so the retellings have become part of this genre. Furthermore, their fundamental respect for the proportion of the story, for its inner tension and vitality, has kept these retellings within the folktale tradition.

The history of the origin and diffusion of this literature is complex, but for the adult who is bringing this literature to children there is only one prime necessity: to savor and enjoy the story for itself.

1. Elizabeth Cook, *The Ordinary and the Fabulous: An Introduction to Myths, Legends and Fairy Tales for Teachers and Storytellers*, 2d ed. (Cambridge University Press, 1976), p. 1.
2. Stith Thompson, *The Folktale* (Holt, 1946), p. 10.

Fables in sooth are not what they appear;
Our moralists are mice, and such small deer.
We yawn at sermons, but we gladly turn
To moral tales, and so amused, we learn.[1]

6 Fables

When the animal tale is told with an acknowledged moral purpose, it becomes a *fable.*"[2] Thus does Stith Thompson define this familiar genre. So universal is the knowledge of such stories as "The Dog in the Manger," "The Lion and the Mouse," and "The Boy Who Cried Wolf" that we seem to have been born knowing them.

Children, and other readers of folklore, are quite accustomed to a world in which beasts and men speak a common language, change worlds and shapes on occasion, render help to one another, or wage wars of wit and cunning. The anthropomorphic treatment of animals is a source of entertainment even in our own sophisticated time—as is evidenced by the popularity of various cartoon characters.

As Thompson points out, the *fable* was born when the familiar animals of folklore were made to bear the burden of a moral. Those fables that are most familiar owe their wide dissemination to two great written, or literary, sources, one in India and the other in Greece. "Of the five or six hundred fables belonging to the two literary traditions of India and Greece," says Thompson, "fewer than

1. Jean de la Fontaine, *Fables* (1668–94).
2. Stith Thompson, *The Folktale* (Holt, 1946), p. 10.

fifty seem to have been recorded from oral storytellers."[3]   The Greek cycle of fables is ascribed to the authorship of one Aesop, about whose origins, fate, and writing there are as many legends as those surrounding Homer. He was a Greek slave at Samos, living some time in the sixth century B.C., says one account, a swarthy man (*Aesop* means black) and deformed, with a sharp wit that enabled him to say through the medium of the fable what he dared not say directly, in criticism of his time. The English scholar Joseph Jacobs has proved that the fables of Aesop came mainly from a collection made in 300 B.C. by Demetrius Phalerus, founder of the Alexandrian Library; therefore, he says, "The answer to the question 'who wrote Aesop?' is simple: 'Demetrius of Phaleron.' "[4]

Whatever their origin, Aesop's fables early became a part of the heritage of the English tongue: They were translated from the French and published by England's first printer, William Caxton, in 1484. In 1692, Sir Roger L'Estrange compiled the best and largest collection of fables in English, especially designed for children and including some not attributed to Aesop. The Croxall edition of 1722 was also addressed to children. This edition, together with that of Thomas James in 1848, formed the basis for the most distinguished collection of Aesop's fables published in America—the one edited and illustrated by Boris Artzybasheff.[5]

A second cycle of fables has its origins in India: the great Hindu collection known as the *Panchatantra,* or the *Five Books,* in existence as early as 200 B.C. These fables are characterized by an intricate interweaving of story within story, a scheme that is common to the Orient, as the *Arabian Nights* exemplifies. The animals of these fables, unlike those of the simpler tales of Aesop, do not act in accordance with their basic animal character. They are, rather, human beings wearing animal masks, giving voice to wit and wisdom in epigrammatic verse quoted from sacred writings. "It is as if the animals in some English beast fable were to justify their actions by quotations from Shakespeare and the Bible."[6] The fables of Aesop, taken as a whole, afford shrewd observations on the behavior of humanity, but those of the *Panchatantra* come closer to forming a philosophy of life:

> Not rank, but character, is birth;
> It is not eyes, but wits that see;
> True wisdom 'tis to cease from wrong;
> Contentment is prosperity.[7]

These same fables, in their Arabic version, are known as *The Fables of Bidpai.* Another ancient Eastern source of fable is the *Jataka* tales. These are stories clustered about the central theme of the myriad births of the Buddha who, in accordance with the Buddhist belief in the transmigration of the soul, suffered himself to be born in many shapes of the animal world and the world of nature.

3. Thompson, p. 218.
4. Joseph Jacobs, Introduction, *Aesop's Fables* (first edition, 1864); quoted in Percy Muir, *English Children's Books* (Batsford, 1954), p. 24.
5. Published by the Viking Press, 1933.
6. *Gold's Gloom: Tales from the Panchatantra,* trans. Arthur W. Ryder (University of Chicago Press, 1925), p. 2.
7. Ryder, p. 17.

The earliest versions of the well-loved "Henny Penny" and the "Tar Baby" stories can be traced to this source.

Marie Shedlock, the noted English storyteller, made a distinguished collection of the Jataka tales (*Eastern Stories and Legends,* 1920), directly relating them to children in versions to be told or read aloud. In addition to the typical moral purpose of the fable, these stories contain a deep compassion.

Of all the tellers of fables, only one has been called *Le Fablier,* the Fabler, and that one is Jean de la Fontaine (1621–95). Using the fables of Aesop as a basis, drawing upon other fables of the medieval world, and inventing some of his own, he made the telling of them an art, and himself the master storyteller. He gave verse form to the tales, relating them to his own time and country, "painting" them in a French landscape, and satirizing his contemporaries with gentle humor. He endowed the tales, as he himself stated, with "a certain piquancy . . . originality and humor. When I say humor I do not mean jocosity, but an alluring, irresistible something that can be imparted to any subject however serious."[8] The fables of La Fontaine are one of the pillars of French literature; it is common for children in France to know many of them by heart.

Some educators question the suitability of fables for children, forgetting perhaps that while children shun moralizing they are drawn to morality. The drama of the fable, the animal characters, and the quick flash of its single illustration of a truth—these hold the attention of children.

The selection of fables for this anthology has been made as broad as possible; it includes examples of folk fables from different nations as well as many derived from literary sources. Some of the best-known fables have been omitted, however, because the primary emphasis has been on including those that have the greatest appeal for children.

8. Jean de la Fontaine, Preface, *The Fables of La Fontaine,* trans. Marianne Moore (Viking, 1954), p. 7.

Fables of Aesop

The Wind and the Sun

Once upon a time when everything could talk, the Wind and the Sun fell into an argument as to which was the stronger. Finally they decided to put the matter to a test; they would see which one could make a certain man, who was walking along the road, throw off his cape. The Wind tried first. He blew and he blew and he blew. The harder and colder he blew, the tighter the traveler wrapped his cape about him. The Wind finally gave up and told the Sun to try. The Sun began to smile and as it grew warmer and warmer, the traveler was comfortable once more. But the Sun shone brighter and brighter until the man grew so hot, the sweat poured out on his face, he became weary, and seating himself on a stone, he quickly threw his cape to the ground. You see, gentleness had accomplished what force could not.

A Wolf in Sheep's Clothing

A certain Wolf, being very hungry, disguised himself in a Sheep's skin and joined a flock of sheep. Thus, for many days he could kill and eat sheep whenever he was hungry, for even the shepherd did not find him out. One night after the shepherd had put all his sheep in the fold, he decided to kill one of his own flock for food; and without realizing what he was doing, he took out the wolf and killed him on the spot. It really does not pay to pretend to be what you are not.

The Miller, His Son, and the Ass

A Miller with his Son were one time driving an ass to market to sell it. Some young people passing by made fun of them for walking when the ass might be carrying one of them. Upon hearing them, the father had the boy get on the ass and was walking along happily until an old man met them. "You lazy rascal," he called to the boy, "to ride and let your poor old father walk!" The son, red with shame, quickly climbed off the ass and insisted that his father ride. Not long after, they met another who cried out,

"How selfish that father is—to ride and let his young son walk!"

At that the Miller took his Son up on the ass with himself, thinking he had at last done the right thing. But alas, he hadn't, for the next person they met was more critical than the others. "You should be ashamed of yourself," he said, "to be both riding that poor little beast; you are much better able to carry *it.*"

Discouraged but willing to do right, the Miller and his Son got off the ass, bound its legs together on a long pole, and thus carried it on to the market. When they entered town, however, they made such a funny sight that crowds gathered about them laughing and

Illustration by Jacob Lawrence, from *Aesop's Fables.* First published in 1970. Reproduced by permission of Windmill Productions, Inc.

shouting. This noise frightened the ass so much that he kicked himself free and, tumbling into the river, was drowned. The Miller, now disgusted, called to his Son to come along, and they rushed back home. "Well," said the father, "we have lost the ass, but we have learned one thing—that when one tries to please everybody, he pleases none, not even himself."

The Dog in the Manger

A cross, selfish Dog went to rest one hot afternoon in a manger. When the tired Ox came in from the field and wanted to eat his hay, the Dog barked at him so that he dared not try it. "To keep others from having what they need," said the Ox to himself, "when you can't use it yourself, is the meanest selfishness I know."

The Jackdaw and the Borrowed Plumes

A Jackdaw once found some Peacock feathers. Wishing to make himself beautiful, he stuck them in among his own and tried to pass himself off as a Peacock. But the Peacocks recognized him at once and drove him from their midst, pulling out the false feathers as they did so. The poor Jackdaw went back to his own kind. The other Jackdaws, however, were so disgusted with his behavior, that they also refused to let him stay with them. "For," they said, "fine feathers do not make fine birds and it is silly to be proud of borrowed plumes."

A Lion and a Mouse

A Mouse one day happened to run across the paws of a sleeping Lion and wakened him. The Lion, angry at being disturbed, grabbed the Mouse, and was about to swallow him, when the Mouse cried out, "Please, kind Sir, I didn't mean it; if you will let me go, I shall always be grateful; and, perhaps, I can help you some-

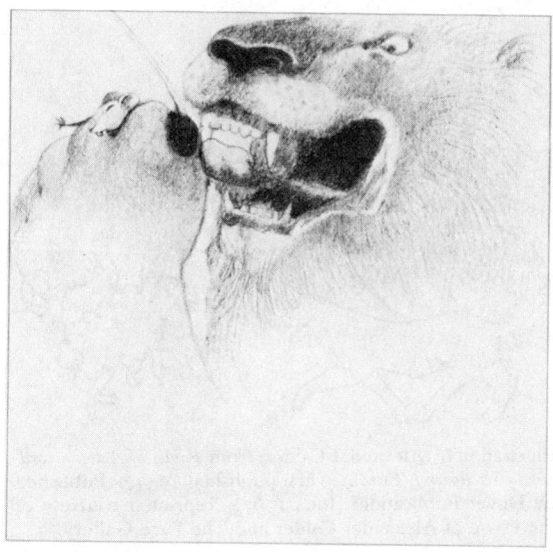

Illustration by Ed Young, from *The Lion and the Mouse: An Aesop Fable.* Copyright © 1979 by Ernest Benn Ltd. Reprinted by permission of Adam and Charles Black Publishers Ltd.

day." The idea that such a little thing as a Mouse could help him so amused the Lion that he let the Mouse go. A week later the Mouse heard a Lion roaring loudly. He went closer to see what the trouble was and found his Lion caught in a hunter's net. Remembering his promise, the Mouse began to gnaw the ropes of the net and kept it up until the Lion could get free. The Lion then acknowledged that little friends might prove great friends.

The Shepherd's Boy and the Wolf

A mischievous Shepherd's Boy used to amuse himself by calling, "Wolf, Wolf!" just to see the villagers run with their clubs and pitchforks to help him. After he had called this more than once for a joke and had laughed at them each time, they grew angry. One day a Wolf really did get among the sheep, and the Shepherd Boy called "Wolf, Wolf!" in vain. The villagers went on with their work, the Wolf killed what

Illustration by Alexander Calder, from *Fables of Aesop according to Sir Roger L'Estrange* (first published 1931). Published by Dover Publications, Inc., 1967. Reprinted courtesy of the estate of Alexander Calder and The Pace Gallery.

he wanted of the sheep, and the Shepherd Boy learned that liars are not believed, even when they do tell the truth.

The Hare and the Tortoise

A Hare was once boasting about how fast he could run when a Tortoise, overhearing him, said, "I'll run you a race." "Done," said the Hare and laughed to himself; "but let's get the Fox for a judge." The Fox consented and the two started. The Hare quickly outran the Tortoise, and knowing he was far ahead, lay down to take a nap. "I can soon pass the Tortoise whenever I awaken." But unfortunately, the Hare overslept himself; therefore when he awoke, though he ran his best, he found the Tortoise was already at the goal. He had learned that "Slow and steady wins the race."

The Goose with the Golden Eggs

Once upon a time a Man had a Goose that laid a Golden Egg every day. Although he was gradually becoming rich, he grew impatient. He wanted to get all his treasure at once; therefore

he killed the Goose. Cutting her open, he found her—just like any other goose, and he learned to his sorrow that it takes time to win success.

The Grasshopper and the Ants

On a beautiful sunny winter day some Ants had their winter store of food out to dry. A Grasshopper came by and gazed hungrily at the food. As the Ants paid no attention to him, he finally said, "Won't you please give me something to eat? I'm starving." "Did you not store away food last summer for use now?" asked the Ants. "No," replied the Grasshopper, "I was too busy enjoying myself in dancing and singing." "Well, then," said the Ants, "live this winter on your dancing and singing, as we live on what we did. No one has a right to play all the time, or he will have to suffer for it."

Belling the Cat

One time the Mice were greatly bothered by a Cat; therefore, they decided to hold a meeting to talk over what could be done about the matter. During the meeting, a Young Mouse arose and suggested that a bell be put upon the Cat so that they could hear him coming. The suggestion was received with great applause, when an Old Mouse arose to speak. "That's all right," he said, "but who of us would dare to hang a bell around the Cat's neck?" Seeing their looks of fear, he added, "You know it is often much easier to suggest a plan than to carry it out."

The Dog and His Shadow

A Dog, carrying a piece of meat in his mouth, was crossing a stream on a narrow footbridge. He happened to look into the water and there he saw his Shadow, but he thought it another dog with a piece of meat larger than his. He made a grab for the other dog's meat; but in doing so, of course, he dropped his own; therefore was without any, and thus learned that greediness may cause one to lose everything.

The Fox and the Grapes

A hungry Fox happened to be passing along a Vineyard where many fine bunches of grapes were hanging high on the arbor. The Fox leaped to get some, time and time again. Failing to do so and weary with jumping, he finally gave up, and as he trotted away he said to himself, "I didn't want them anyway; I know they must still be sour."

The Town Mouse and the Country Mouse

A Country Mouse was very happy that his city cousin, the Town Mouse, had accepted his invitation to dinner. He gave his city cousin all the best food he had, such as dried beans, peas, and crusts of bread. The Town Mouse tried not to show how he disliked the food and picked a little here and tasted a little there to be polite. After dinner, however, he said, "How can you stand such food all the time? Still I suppose here in the country you don't know about any better. Why don't you go home with me? When you have once tasted the delicious things I eat, you will never want to come back here." The Country Mouse not only kindly forgave the Town Mouse for not liking his dinner, but even consented to go that very evening to the city with his cousin. They arrived late at night; and the City Mouse, as host, took his Country

Illustration by Arthur Rackham. From *Aesop's Fables,* trans. V. S. Vernon Jones (first published 1912). Reproduced by permission of William Heinemann, Ltd., London.

Cousin at once to a room where there had been a big dinner. "You are tired," he said. "Rest here, and I'll bring you some real food." And he brought the Country Mouse such things as nuts, dates, cake, and fruit. The Country Mouse thought it was all so good, he would like to stay there. But before he had a chance to say so, he heard a terrible roar, and looking up, he saw a huge creature dash into the room. Frightened half out of his wits, the Country Mouse ran from the table, and round and round the room, trying to find a hiding place. At last he found a place of safety. While he stood there trembling he made up his mind to go home as soon as he could get safely away; for, to himself, he said, "I'd rather have common food in safety than dates and nuts in the midst of danger."

The Fox and the Crow

A Fox once saw a Crow making off with a piece of cheese in its beak and made up his mind he was going to get it. "Good-morning, friend Crow," he called. "I see your feathers are as black and shining and beautiful as ever. You are really a beautiful bird. It is too bad your voice is poor! If that were lovely too, you would, without question, be the Queen of Birds." The Crow, rather indignant that the Fox doubted the beauty of her voice, began to caw at once. Of course the cheese dropped; and as the Fox put his paw on it he yelled, "I have what I wanted—and let me give you a bit of advice—Don't trust flatterers."

Fables from the East

The Monkey and the Crocodile

This popular Jataka tale delights with its quick-thinking hero. [From *Jataka Tales,* retold by Ellen C. Babbitt (Appleton Century Crofts, 1912).]

Part I

A monkey lived in a great tree on a river bank.

In the river there were many Crocodiles.

A Crocodile watched the Monkeys for a long time, and one day she said to her son: "My son, get one of those Monkeys for me. I want the heart of a Monkey to eat."

"How am I to catch a Monkey?" asked the little Crocodile. "I do not travel on land, and the Monkey does not go into the water."

"Put your wits to work, and you'll find a way," said the mother.

And the little Crocodile thought and thought.

At last he said to himself: "I know what I'll do. I'll get that Monkey that lives in a big tree on the river bank. He wishes to go across the river to the island where the fruit is so ripe."

So the Crocodile swam to the tree where the Monkey lived. But he was a stupid Crocodile.

"Oh, Monkey," he called, "come with me over to the island where the fruit is so ripe."

"How can I go with you?" asked the Monkey. "I do not swim."

"No—but I do. I will take you over on my back," said the Crocodile.

The Monkey was greedy, and wanted the ripe fruit, so he jumped down on the Crocodile's back.

"Off we go!" said the Crocodile.

"This is a fine ride you are giving me!" said the Monkey.

"Do you think so? Well, how do you like this?" asked the Crocodile, diving.

"Oh, don't!" cried the Monkey, as he went under the water. He was afraid to let go, and he did not know what to do under the water.

When the Crocodile came up, the Monkey sputtered and choked. "Why did you take me under water, Crocodile?" he asked.

"I am going to kill you by keeping you under water," answered the Crocodile. "My mother wants Monkey-heart to eat, and I'm going to take yours to her."

"I wish you had told me you wanted my heart," said the Monkey, "then I might have brought it with me."

"How queer!" said the stupid Crocodile. "Do you mean to say that you left your heart back there in the tree?"

"That is what I mean," said the Monkey. "If you want my heart, we must go back to the tree and get it. But we are so near the island where the ripe fruit is, please take me there first."

"No, Monkey," said the Crocodile, "I'll take you straight back to your tree. Never mind the ripe fruit. Get your heart and bring it to me at once. Then we'll see about going to the island."

"Very well," said the Monkey.

But no sooner had he jumped onto the bank of the river than—whisk! up he ran into the tree.

From the topmost branches he called down to the Crocodile in the water below:

"My heart is way up here! If you want it, come for it, come for it!"

Part II

The Monkey soon moved away from that tree. He wanted to get away from the Crocodile, so that he might live in peace.

But the Crocodile found him, far down the river, living in another tree.

In the middle of the river was an island covered with fruit trees.

Half-way between the bank of the river and the island, a large rock rose out of the water. The Monkey could jump to the rock, and then to the island. The Crocodile watched the Monkey crossing from the bank of the river to the rock, and then to the island.

He thought to himself, "The Monkey will stay on the island all day, and I'll catch him on his way home at night."

The Monkey had a fine feast, while the Crocodile swam about, watching him all day.

Toward night the Crocodile crawled out of the water and lay on the rock, perfectly still.

When it grew dark among the trees, the Monkey started for home. He ran down to the river bank, and there he stopped.

"What is the matter with the rock?" the Monkey thought to himself. "I never saw it so high before. The Crocodile is lying on it!"

But he went to the edge of the water and called: "Hello, Rock!"

No answer.

Then he called again: "Hello, Rock!"

Three times the Monkey called, and then he

said: "Why is it, Friend Rock, that you do not answer me to-night?"

"Oh," said the stupid Crocodile to himself, "the rock answers the Monkey at night. I'll have to answer for the rock this time."

So he answered: "Yes, Monkey! What is it?"

The Monkey laughed, and said: "Oh, it's you, Crocodile, is it?"

"Yes," said the Crocodile. "I am waiting here for you. I am going to eat you."

"You have caught me in a trap this time," said the Monkey. "There is no other way for me to go home. Open your mouth wide so I can jump right into it."

Now the Monkey well knew that when Crocodiles open their mouths wide, they shut their eyes.

While the Crocodile lay on the rock with his mouth wide open and his eyes shut, the Monkey jumped.

But not into his mouth! Oh, no! He landed on the top of the Crocodile's head, and then sprang quickly to the bank. Up he whisked into his tree.

When the Crocodile saw the trick the Monkey had played on him, he said: "Monkey, you have great cunning. You know no fear. I'll let you alone after this."

"Thank you, Crocodile, but I shall be on the watch for you just the same," said the Monkey.

The Golden Goose

Aesop's fable about the goose that laid the golden eggs is so similar to this one that it is easy to see why a theory developed attributing all folktales to Indian sources. The scholarly speculation on the borrowing between India and Greece is dealt with more fully in the headnotes to the stories from the *Panchatantra* in the folktale section. [From *More Jataka Tales,* retold by Ellen C. Babbitt (Appleton Century Crofts, 1922).]

Once upon a time there was a Goose who had beautiful golden feathers. Not far away from this Goose lived a poor, a very poor woman, who had two daughters. The Goose saw that they had a hard time to get along and said he to himself:

"If I give them one after another of my golden feathers, the mother can sell them, and with the money they bring she and her daughters can then live in comfort."

So away the Goose flew to the poor woman's house.

Seeing the Goose, the woman said: "Why do you come here? We have nothing to give you."

"But I have something to give you," said the Goose. "I will give my feathers, one by one, and you can sell them for enough so that you and your daughters can live in comfort."

So saying the Goose gave her one of his feathers, and then flew away. From time to time he came back, each time leaving another feather.

The mother and her daughters sold the beautiful feathers for enough money to keep them in comfort. But one day the mother said to her daughters: "Let us not trust this Goose. Some day he may fly away and never come back. Then we should be poor again. Let us get all of his feathers the very next time he comes."

The daughters said: "This will hurt the Goose. We will not do such a thing."

But the mother was greedy. The next time the Golden Goose came she took hold of him with both hands, and pulled out every one of his feathers.

Now the Golden Goose has strange feathers. If his feathers are plucked out against his wish, they no longer remain golden but turn white and are of no more value than chickenfeathers. The new ones that come in are not golden, but plain white.

As time went on his feathers grew again, and then he flew away to his home and never came back again.

The Poor Man and the Flask of Oil

There once was a Poor Man living in a house next to a wealthy Merchant who sold oil and honey. As the Merchant was a kind neighbor, he one day sent a flask of oil to the Poor Man. The Poor Man was delighted, and put it carefully away on the top shelf. One evening, as he was gazing at it, he said aloud, "I wonder how much oil there is in that bottle. There is a large quantity. If I should sell it, I could buy five sheep. Every year I should have lambs, and before long I should own a flock. Then I should sell some of the sheep, and be rich enough to marry a wife. Perhaps we might have a son. And what a fine boy he would be! So tall, strong, and obedient! But if he should disobey me," and he raised the staff which he held in his hand, "I should punish him thus." And he swung the staff over his head and brought it heavily to the ground, knocking, as he did so, the flask off the shelf, so that the oil ran over him from head to foot.

The Hare That Ran Away

Our familiar tale of Henny-Penny is a modern variant of this Jataka tale that recounts one of the Buddha's numerous former births. [From Marie L. Shedlock, *Eastern Stories and Legends* (Dutton, 1920).]

And it came to pass that the Buddha (to be) was born again as a Lion. Just as he had helped his fellow-men, he now began to help his fellow-animals, and there was a great deal to be done. For instance, there was a little nervous Hare who was always afraid that something dreadful was going to happen to her. She was always saying: "Suppose the Earth were to fall in, what would happen to me?" And she said this so often that at last she thought it really was about to happen. One day, when she had been saying over and over again, "suppose the Earth were to fall in, what would happen to me?" she heard a slight noise; it really was only a heavy fruit which had fallen upon a rustling leaf, but the little Hare was so nervous she was ready to believe anything, and she said in a frightened tone: "The Earth is falling in." She ran away as fast as she could go; presently she met an old brother Hare, who said: "Where are you running to, Mistress Hare?"

And the little Hare said: "I have no time to stop and tell you anything. The Earth is falling in, and I am running away."

"The Earth is falling in, is it?" said the old brother Hare, in a tone of much astonishment; and he repeated this to his brother hare, and he to his brother hare, and he to his brother hare, until at last there were a hundred thousand

brother hares, all shouting: "The Earth is falling in." Now presently the bigger animals began to take the cry up. First the deer, and then the sheep, and then the wild boar, and then the buffalo, and then the camel, and then the tiger, and then the elephant.

Now the wise Lion heard all this noise and wondered at it. "There are no signs," he said, "of the Earth falling in. They must have heard something." And then he stopped them all short and said: "What is this you are saying?"

And the Elephant said: "I remarked that the Earth was falling in."

"How do you know this?" asked the Lion.

"Why, now I come to think of it, it was the Tiger that remarked it to me."

Then the Tiger said: "I had it from the Camel," and the Camel said: "I had it from the Buffalo." And the buffalo from the wild boar, and the wild boar from the sheep, and the sheep from the deer, and the deer from the hares, and the hares said: "Oh! we heard it from that little Hare."

And the Lion said: "Little Hare, what made you say that the Earth was falling in?"

And the little Hare said: "I saw it."

"You saw it?" said the Lion. "Where?"

"Yonder by the tree."

"Well," said the Lion, "come with me and I will show you how—"

"No, no," said the Hare, "I would not go near that tree for anything, I'm so nervous."

"But," said the Lion, "I am going to take you on my back." And he took her on his back, and begged the animals to stay where they were until they returned. Then he showed the little Hare how the fruit had fallen upon the leaf, making the noise that had frightened her, and she said: "Yes, I see—the Earth is not falling in." And the Lion said: "Shall we go back and tell the other animals?"

And they went back. The little Hare stood before the animals and said: "The Earth is not falling in." And all the animals began to repeat this to one another, and they dispersed gradually, and you heard the words more and more softly:

"The Earth is not falling in," etc., etc., etc., until the sound died away altogether.

Fables from Other Lands

Heron and Humming-Bird

A familiar theme is developed by the Muskogee Indians of the southeastern United States. [From *Hesitant Wolf and Scrupulous Fox: Fables Selected from World Literature,* ed. Karen Kennerly (Random House, 1973).]

Heron and Humming-Bird lived on the shores of the ocean in the east. One day Humming-Bird came to Heron, and said, "Let us race." Heron answered, "I can't fly. I can't do anything." But Humming-Bird kept teasing him to race and finally Heron gave in. They agreed to race from the ocean in the east to the ocean in the west; so they placed themselves at the edge of the water, and began. Heron had barely lifted his wings when Humming-Bird was out of sight, and he raised himself slowly, flapping along at an even pace. When darkness came, Humming-Bird went to a tree and stopped there for the night; but Heron kept steadily on, and shortly before daylight he was at the place where Humming-Bird was sitting. Day came—Heron had traveled a long distance ahead and the sun was well up before Humming-Bird passed him. Next night, Humming-Bird had to rest again, and again Heron went by him, but this time about midnight. Humming-Bird did not pass him again until noon. The third night, Heron caught up with Humming-Bird before midnight, and Humming-Bird did not go by him until late evening. But then he had to stop once more and Heron soon overtook him. So Heron got to the western ocean far ahead. It was early in the morning when he arrived, and he began hunting for fish. Humming-Bird did not come until noon. Then Humming-Bird said to Heron, "I did not believe you could get here first; for I can dart all around you and all over you."

The Story of the Hungry Elephant

Pithy and witty, this highly sophisticated fable comes from the Bulu people of West Africa. [From *Hesitant*

Wolf and Scrupulous Fox: Fables Selected from World Literature, ed. Karen Kennerly (Random House, 1973).]

Once there lived an Elephant, and he said to himself, "I am very hungry." He went along a path in the forest, and came to a bamboo-palm standing in a swamp. Roughly he tore down the palm; he saw a tender bud held in one of its leaves. But as he took the bud from the leaf, it fell into the water. He hunted and hunted, yet could not find it because he had riled up the water and it blinded his eyes. Then a frog spoke and said, "Listen!" The Elephant did not hear, thrashing the water hard with his trunk. The frog spoke again: "Listen!" The Elephant heard this time, and stood perfectly still, curious. Thereupon the water became clear so that he found the palm-bud and ate it.

Why Wisdom Is Found Everywhere

Like Brer Rabbit in the United States, Anansi, the trickster spider hero of Africa's Ashanti people, excels at outwitting others and sometimes himself. Here, his embarrassing predicament results in laying the base for the Ashanti proverb: "One head never goes into consultation." [From Harold Courlander, with Albert Kofi Prempeh, *The Hat-Shaking Dance and Other Ashanti Tales from Ghana* (Harcourt, 1957).]

Kwaku Anansi regarded himself as the wisest of all creatures. He knew how to build bridges, to make dams and roads, to weave, and to hunt. But he didn't wish to share this wisdom with other creatures. He decided one day that he would gather together all the wisdom of the world and keep it for himself. So he went around collecting wisdom, and each bit he found he put in a large earthen pot. When the pot was full, Anansi prepared to carry it into a high treetop where no one else could find it. He held the pot in front of him and began to climb.

Anansi's son Intikuma was curious about what his father was doing, and he watched from behind some bushes. He saw Anansi holding the pot in front of him against his stomach. He saw that this made it hard for Anansi to grasp the tree he was climbing. At last he couldn't keep quiet any longer and he said: "Father, may I make a suggestion?"

Anansi was startled and angry, and he shouted: "Why are you spying on me?"

Intikuma replied: "I only wanted to help you."

Anansi said: "Is this your affair?"

Intikuma said to him: "It's only that I see you are having difficulty. When you climb a tree, it is very hard to hold a pot in front. If you put the pot on your back, you can climb easily."

Anansi tried it. He took the pot from in front and put it on his back. He climbed swiftly. But then he stopped. He looked at Intikuma and was embarrassed, for although he carried so much wisdom in the pot, he had not known how to climb with it.

In anger, Kwaku Anansi took the pot and threw it from the treetop. It fell on the earth and shattered into many pieces. The wisdom that was in it scattered in all directions. When people heard what had happened, they came and took some of the wisdom Anansi had thrown away. And so today, wisdom is not all in one place. It is everywhere. Should you find a foolish man, he is one who didn't come when the others did to take a share of the wisdom.

This is the story the Ashanti people are thinking of when they say: "One head can't exchange ideas with itself."

The Fox and the Thrush

A clever reversal of situations makes for a witty comment on human nature. [From *Three Rolls and One Doughnut: Fables from Russia,* translated and retold by Mirra Ginsburg (Dial, 1970).]

A hungry fox saw a thrush sitting high in a tree.

"Good morning, dear thrush," said the fox. "I heard your pleasant voice, and it made my heart rejoice."

"Thanks for your kindness," said the thrush.

The fox called out, "What did you say? I cannot hear you now. Why don't you come down on the grass? We'll take a nice, long walk and have a good, friendly talk."

But the thrush said, "It isn't safe for us birds on the grass."

"You are not afraid of me?" cried the fox.

"Well, if not you, then some other animal."

"Oh, no, my dearest friend. There is a new law in the land. Today there is peace among all beasts. We are all brothers. None is allowed to hurt another."

"That's good," said the thrush. "I see dogs coming this way. Under the old law, you would have had to run away. But now there is no reason for you to be frightened."

As soon as the fox heard about the dogs, he pricked up his ears and starting running.

"Where are you going?" cried the thrush. "We have a new law in the land. The dogs won't touch you now."

"Who knows," answered the fox as he ran. "Perhaps they have not heard about it yet."

The Mouse and the Rat

Ivan Andreevich Krylov's own translations of the French fabulist La Fontaine had a great influence on his own creations, which were aimed at the official world of his day. Russian children have responded to the grace and wit of Krylov's writing with affection. [From *Fifteen Fables of Krylov,* trans. Guy Daniels (Macmillan, 1965).]

"Have you heard the joyous news, my friend?"
Called out Miss Mousie, on the trot, to Mr. Rat.
"They say the Lion's got old Tom, the Cat.
We can relax—our fears are at an end."

"Don't be too sure, my dear,"
The Rat called back, "that we have nothing more to fear:
Don't build up hopes you can't rely on.
If they really start to give each other tit for tat,
There won't be much left of the Lion—
Because, *no animal is mightier than the Cat.*"

I've never left off wondering
(Neither, I'm sure, have you)
Why, when a coward fears a thing,
He figures everybody else does, too.

The Rooster and the Hen

The cumulative pattern comes to an unexpected end in this fable, which features a Finnish sauna. [From James Cloyd Bowman and Margery Bianco, *Tales from a Finnish Tupa*, trans. Aili Kolehmainen (Whitman, 1936).]

One day a hen and a rooster went into the *sauna* to take a bath. The rooster said:

"Hen, fetch me some water from the well. There isn't enough in the bucket here to wet the stones."

The hen went to the well and said:

"Good well, kind well, give me some water."

"I'll give you water if you fetch me a dipper," said the well. So the hen went to the woman of the house.

"Good lady, kind lady, give me a dipper."

"I'll give you a dipper if you'll fetch me a pair of shoes," said the woman. So the hen went to the shoemaker and said:

"Good shoemaker, kind shoemaker, give me a pair of shoes."

"I'll give you the shoes if you'll fetch me an awl," said the shoemaker. So the hen went to the blacksmith and said:

"Good blacksmith, kind blacksmith, give me an awl."

"I'll give you an awl if you'll fetch me some iron," said the blacksmith.

The hen went to the marsh, and said: "Good marsh, kind marsh, give me some iron."

And the marsh was a good and kind marsh, and it gave the hen some iron.

The hen took the iron to the blacksmith, and got the awl.

She took the awl to the shoemaker and got the shoes.

She took the shoes to the woman, and got the dipper.

She took the dipper to the well, and got the water.

But alas, when the hen hurried to the *sauna* with the water, she found the poor rooster dead from heat!

Why the Fox Has a Huge Mouth

A "pourquoi" fable with a Peruvian flavor and an unusual ending in which the fox, the universal trickster, is tricked himself. [From *Black Rainbow: Legends of the Incas and Myths of Ancient Peru*, ed. and trans. John Bierhorst (Farrar, Straus & Giroux, 1976).]

One day many years ago, at a time when his mouth was still small and dainty, as in fact it used to be, the fox was out walking and happened to notice a huaychao singing on a hilltop. Fascinated by the bird's flute-like bill, he said politely, "What a lovely flute, friend Huaychao, and how well you play it! Could you let me try it? I'll give it back in a moment, I promise."

The bird refused. But the fox was so insistent that at last the huaychao lent him its bill, advising him to sew up his lips except for a tiny opening so that the "flute" would fit just right.

Then the fox began to play. He played on and on without stopping. After a while the huaychao asked for its bill back, but still the fox kept on. The bird reminded him, "You promised. Besides, I only use it from time to time; you're playing it constantly." But the fox paid no attention and kept right on.

Awakened by the sound of the flute, skunks came out of their burrows and climbed up the hill in a bustling throng. When they saw the fox playing, they began to dance.

At the sight of the dancing skunks, the fox burst out laughing. As he laughed, his lips became unstitched. His mouth tore open and kept on tearing until he was grinning from ear to ear. Before the fox could regain his composure, the huaychao had picked up its bill and flown away.

To this day the fox has a huge mouth—as punishment for breaking his promise.

Androcles and the Lion

Arthur Gilchrist Brodeur, in the University of California Publications on Modern Philology (vol. XI, pp. 197 ff.), shows very conclusively that this story is not a folktale of Oriental origin, but a sophisticated story by Apion. Aulus Gellius, who lived in the second century, in his *Noctes Atticae* (vol. V, chap. XIV), tells this story as taken from Apion's book, the *Aegyptiaca*, now lost, wherein Apion says he saw the Androcles story "from the moment of the lion's entry into the Circus until the ultimate conclusion." As a corroboration, Brodeur points out that Seneca, in his *De Beneficiis*, who was also in Rome part of the time Apion was, tells of seeing such an incident; but Seneca goes on to say that the man had once been the lion's trainer. As Apion was born in Oasis in the Libyan Desert, Brodeur shows how natural it would be for Apion to motivate the lion's gratitude as he did.

Androcles, a runaway slave, had fled to a forest for safety. He had not been there long when he saw a Lion who was groaning with pain. He started to flee, but when he realized that the Lion did not follow but only kept on groaning, Androcles turned and went to it. The Lion, instead of rushing at him, put out a torn and bloody paw. Androcles, seeing the poor beast was in pain and wanting to help it, went up, took its paw, and examined it. Discovering a large thorn, the man pulled it out and thus relieved the pain. The grateful Lion in return took Androcles to its cave and every day brought him food. Sometime later both were captured and taken to Rome. The slave was condemned to be killed by being thrown to the Lion, which had not had food for several days. Androcles was led into the arena in the presence of the Emperor and his court, and at the same time the Lion was loosed. It came headlong toward its prey, but when it came near Androcles, instead of pouncing upon him, it jumped up and fawned upon him like a friendly dog. The Emperor was much surprised and called to him Androcles who told his story. The Emperor freed both the slave and the Lion, for he thought such kindness and such gratitude were deserving of reward.

Fables of La Fontaine

Never intended for children, the fables of La Fontaine are witty, subtle, and filled with ingenious rhymes and realistic observations. The sympathetic translation by a poet, Marianne Moore, preserves the vitality and originality of his language. [From *The Fables of La Fontaine*, trans. Marianne Moore (Viking, 1954).]

The Fox and the Goat

Captain Fox was padding along sociably
With Master Goat whose horns none would care
    to oppose,
Though he could not see farther than the end
    of his nose;
Whereas the fox was practiced in chicanery.
Thirst led them to a well and they simultane-
    ously
    Leaped in to look for water there.
After each had drunk what seemed a sufficiency,
The fox said to the goat, "Well, friend, and
    from here where?
We can't be always drinking, Master Goat, can
    we?
Put your feet up; your horns will rise to that
    degree,
Push against the wall until your rump is snugged
    in;
    I'll climb you like a ladder then,
    Up the back, up the horns again,
    In that way, as you have seen,
    Before long I'll be where we first stood
    And can draw you up if you think good."
—"Genius," said the goat. "By my beard, what
    finesse!
    Nothing like a fox's wit;
    A ruse on which I could not have hit;
    A superlative mind, I confess."
The fox leaped out of the well; the goat had
    to stay down—
    Harangued as by a sage in a gown
    About patience and experience;
Yes; told: "If Heaven had only given you as
    good sense
As the beard on your chin's an exceptional one,
    You'd not be an adventurer
Into wells, as you have been. Therefore
    goodby, I must depart.

Strain up high; each leap can be a new start.
  As for me, I'm due far from here;
I can't stand about as if at an inn."

Better think of the outcome before you begin.

The Dairymaid and Her Milk-Pot

Perrette's milk-pot fitted her head-mat just
  right—
  Neatly quilted to grip the pot tight.
Then she set off to market and surely walked
  well,
In her short muslin dress that encouraged long
  strides,
Since to make better time she wore shoes with
  low heel
  And had tucked up her skirt at the sides.
  Like summer attire her head had grown light,
  Thinking of what she'd have bought by night.
In exchange for the milk, since supposing it
  gone,
She'd buy ten times ten eggs and three hens
  could be set.
Taking care all hatched out, she'd not lose more
  than one
  And said, "Then there'll be pullets to sell.
I'll raise them at home; it is quite within reason,
  Since shrewd Master Fox will be doing well
If I can't shortly buy a young pig and grow
  bacon.
The one I had bought would be almost half
  grown;
He'd need next to no feed—almost nothing at
  all;
When he's sold I'll have funds—good hard cash
  to count on.
Then with room at the barn for some stock in
  the stall,
I could buy cow and calf if the pig had sold
  high;
If I'd not had a loss, I'd add sheep by and by."
Perrette skipped for joy as she dreamt of what
  she'd bought.
The crock crashed. Farewell, cow, calf, fat pig,
  eggs not hatched out.
The mistress of wealth grieved to forfeit forever
  The profits that were mounting.
  How ask her husband to forgive her

Lest he beat her as was fitting?
And thus ended the farce we have watched:

Don't count your chickens before they are hatched.

Modern Fables

John G. Saxe

The Blind Men and the Elephant

A fable that owes much to the Jataka tale *The Red-Bud Tree,* this is a nineteenth-century verse that presents the same moral. [From John Godfrey Saxe, *Poems* (Boston, 1852).]

It was six men of Indostan
  To learning much inclined,
Who went to see the Elephant
  (Though all of them were blind),
That each by observation
  Might satisfy his mind.

The First approached the Elephant,
  And happening to fall
Against his broad and sturdy side,
  At once began to bawl:
"God bless me! but the Elephant
  Is very like a wall!"

The Second, feeling of the tusk,
  Cried, "Ho! what have we here
So very round and smooth and sharp?
  To me 'tis mighty clear
This wonder of an Elephant
  Is very like a spear!"

The Third approached the animal,
  And happening to take
The squirming trunk within his hands,
  Thus boldly up and spake:
"I see," quoth he, "the Elephant
  Is very like a snake!"

The Fourth reached out his eager hand,
  And felt about the knee.
"What most this wondrous beast is like
  Is mighty plain," quoth he;
"Tis clear enough the Elephant
  Is very like a tree!"

The Fifth, who chanced to touch the ear
  Said, "E'en the blindest man
Can tell what this resembles most;
  Deny the fact who can,
This marvel of an Elephant
  Is very like a fan!"

The Sixth no sooner had begun
  About the beast to grope,
Than, seizing on the swinging tail
  That fell within his scope,
"I see," quoth he, "the Elephant
  Is very like a rope!"

And so these men of Indostan
  Disputed loud and long,
Each in his own opinion
  Exceeding stiff and strong.
Though each was partly in the right,
  And all were in the wrong!

James Thurber

The Moth and the Star

James Thurber's *Many Moons,* well-loved fantasy, is actually an elaboration of a fable, but here he catches the true spirit of fable, with its moral precept, its economy of expression, and its single example by way of illustration. The humor lies in his skillful use of an archaic form in a contemporary idiom. [From James Thurber, *Fables for Our Time and Famous Poems* (Harper, 1940).]

A young and impressionable moth once set his heart on a certain star. He told his mother about this and she counseled him to set his heart on a bridge lamp instead. "Stars aren't the thing to hang around," she said; "Lamps are the thing to hang around." "You get somewhere that way," said the moth's father. "You don't get anywhere chasing stars." But the moth would not heed the words of either parent. Every evening at dusk when the star came out he would start flying toward it and every morning at dawn he would crawl back home worn out with his vain endeavor. One day his father said to him, "You haven't burned a wing in months, boy, and it looks to me as if you were never going to. All your brothers have been badly burned flying around street lamps and all your sisters have been terribly singed flying around house lamps. Come on, now, get out of here and get yourself scorched! A big strapping moth like you without a mark on him!"

The moth left his father's house, but he would not fly around street lamps and he would not fly around house lamps. He went right on trying to reach the star, which was four and one-third light years, or twenty-five trillion miles, away. The moth thought it was just caught in the top branches of an elm. He never did reach the star, but he went right on trying, night after night, and when he was a very, very old moth he began to think that he really had reached the star and he went around saying so. This gave him a deep and lasting pleasure, and he lived to a great old age. His parents and his brothers and his sisters had all been burned to death when they were quite young.

MORAL: *Who flies afar from the sphere of our sorrow is here today and here tomorrow.*

Arnold Lobel

The Bad Kangaroo

This iconoclastic fable reverses social expectations and establishes its moral in the abrupt manner of a Zen teaching story. Arnold Lobel also adroitly uses the gentle humor and economy of the fable in his beginning reader series, *Frog and Toad.* [From Arnold Lobel, *Fables* (Harper, 1980).]

There was a small Kangaroo who was bad in school. He put thumbtacks on the teacher's chair. He threw spitballs across the classroom. He set off firecrackers in the lavatory and spread glue on the doorknobs.

"Your behavior is impossible!" said the

school principal. "I am going to see your parents. I will tell them what a problem you are!"

The principal went to visit Mr. and Mrs. Kangaroo. He sat down in a living-room chair.

"Ouch!" cried the principal. "There is a thumbtack in this chair!"

"Yes, I know," said Mr. Kangaroo. "I enjoy putting thumbtacks in chairs."

A spitball hit the principal on his nose.

"Forgive me," said Mrs. Kangaroo, "but I can never resist throwing those things."

There was a loud booming sound from the bathroom.

Illustration of "The Bad Kangaroo," from *Fables*, written and illustrated by Arnold Lobel (pages 28–29). Copyright © 1980 by Arnold Lobel. Reprinted by permission of Harper & Row, Publishers, Inc.

"Keep calm," said Mr. Kangaroo to the principal. "The firecrackers that we keep in the medicine chest have just exploded. We love the noise."

The principal rushed for the front door. In an instant he was stuck to the doorknob.

"Pull hard," said Mrs. Kangaroo. "There are little globs of glue on all of our doorknobs."

The principal pulled himself free. He dashed out of the house and ran off down the street.

"Such a nice person," said Mr. Kangaroo. "I wonder why he left so quickly."

"No doubt he had another appointment," said Mrs. Kangaroo. "Never mind, supper is ready."

Mr. and Mrs. Kangaroo and their son enjoyed their evening meal. After the dessert, they all threw spitballs at each other across the dining-room table.

A child's conduct will reflect the ways of his parents.

Arnold Lobel

The Mouse at the Seashore

The poignancy and drama of this fable give it a lyricism unusual in the fable form. Lobel's *Fables* was awarded the Caldecott Medal in 1981. [From Arnold Lobel, *Fables* (Harper, 1980).]

A mouse told his mother and father that he was going on a trip to the seashore.

"We are very alarmed!" they cried. "The world is full of terrors. You must not go!"

"I have made my decision," said the Mouse firmly. "I have never seen the ocean, and it is high time that I did. Nothing can make me change my mind."

"Then we cannot stop you," said Mother and Father Mouse, "but do be careful!"

The next day, in the first light of dawn, the Mouse began his journey. Even before the morning had ended, the Mouse came to know trouble and fear.

A Cat jumped out from behind a tree.

"I will eat you for lunch," he said.

It was a narrow escape for the Mouse.

He ran for his life, but he left a part of his tail in the mouth of the Cat.

By afternoon the Mouse had been attacked by birds and dogs. He had lost his way several times. He was bruised and bloodied. He was tired and frightened.

At evening the Mouse slowly climbed the last hill and saw the seashore spreading out before him. He watched the waves rolling onto the beach, one after another. All the colors of the sunset filled the sky.

"How beautiful!" cried the Mouse. "I wish that Mother and Father were here to see this with me."

The moon and the stars began to appear over the ocean. The Mouse sat silently on the top of the hill. He was overwhelmed by a feeling of deep peace and contentment.

All the miles of a hard road are worth a moment of true happiness.

Faerie contains many things besides elves and fays, and besides dwarfs, witches, trolls, giants, or dragons; it holds the seas, the sun, the moon, the sky; and the earth, and all things that are in it: tree and bird, water and stone, wine and bread, and ourselves, mortal men, when we are enchanted.[1]

7   Folktales

As old as language itself, folktales have proven to be gifted travelers. They have made themselves at home in culture after culture, all the while maintaining a hard core of individuality, the essence of an idea. They have been preserved, altered, and adapted by the devices of storytellers, and have outlived succeeding generations through the media of voice and memory. They have been collected and frozen in print or retold in strongly individual styles. They have been attacked as immoral, illogical, psychologically damaging, and, most recently, sexist. They have been grotesquely altered, trivialized and prettified, or distorted into propaganda tracts. And still they survive, a vast body of material that is one of the great human legacies, and they still are as essential to childhood as they ever were. They are the ground of children's literature.

Everything is clear in the folktale. We know exactly where to place our sympathy. The issues are soon stated, with no unnecessary subtleties of emotion, no bewildering wavering between cause and effect. Everyone acts in character, and the stories move in strong, direct action to the always expected end, where the good come to glory and joy, and evil is punished, as befits it, with primitive symbols of suffering. The habitual readers of folktales learn to recognize and

1. J. R. R. Tolkien, "On Fairy-Stories," in *Tree and Leaf* (Houghton Mifflin, 1965), p. 9.

enjoy certain earmarks of good writing: the strong structure of the plots in which nothing is included that does not move to the ultimate end; the economy of language; the imagery, the poetry of the chants and incantations; the echoes of the spoken word, and the salty, poetic, and witty modes of speech: "She was so lovely, there was no end to her loveliness." "Billy, my boy, you and I must undergo great scenery." "My blessing be on you till the sea loses its saltiness and the trees forget to bud in the springtime." "Clippety, lippety, lippety, clippety, here come Brer Rabbit just as sassy as a jay-bird."

Fairy tales is a common term that is often used to mean simply *folktales.* (It may also be used, more precisely, to refer only to those tales with fairy-folk in them, or, to complicate matters further, to designate any story with an element of enchantment, even those created by an individual author rather than emanating from the folk tradition.) In looking at those tales that are from the folk tradition, a reader soon discovers a cast of stock characters who, as Iona and Peter Opie tell us, are "either altogether good or altogether bad, and there is no evolution of character. They are referred to by generic or descriptive names, as 'Jack' (for lad), 'Beauty,' 'Snow White,' 'Silver Hair,' 'Tom Thumb,' 'Red Ridinghood,' 'Cinder-girl.' Fairy tales are more concerned with situations than with character. They are the space fiction of the past."[2]

Certain types of stories also occur over and over. The *märchen* (whose name is borrowed from the studies of the Grimm brothers) are described by folklore scholar Stith Thompson as stories that move "in an unreal world without definite locality or definite characters and [are] filled with the marvelous. In this never-never land humble heroes kill adversaries, succeed to kingdoms, and marry princesses."[3] *Stories about animals,* another group, are told not with a didactic or practical purpose, as is the fable, but simply to relate the adventures of animals as protagonists, as in the tale of "The Bremen Town Musicians." The *cumulative story,* still another recognizable type, winds up in successive incidents, in fascinating patterns of repetition and incantation, as in the story of "The Old Woman and Her Pig." The *drolls* are stories of numbskulls and simpletons, full of exaggerated nonsense. Then there are the *stories of the real and practical world:* husbands who are to mind the house, and wives who know how to handle a foolish husband, greeting him with love as in the Norwegian story "What the Goodman Does Is Sure to Be Right," or beating him thoroughly, as happens in the English version of the same story, "Mr. Vinegar." The *pourquoi stories* (or *why* stories) are typical of folktales, being legends of explanation, such as "Why the bear is stumpy-tailed," or "Why the chipmunk's back is striped."

When manuscript copying and printing made possible the collection of these stories, they appeared as basic material for such great storytellers of the Middle Ages as Chaucer and Boccaccio. The crude chapbooks, too, in their first printings, used these stories as their subject matter. But the true worth of the folktale as a vast history of the human past was not recognized by educated people until the middle of the nineteenth century. Then came the great awakening.

In 1785, at Hanau in Hesse-Cassel, Jakob Grimm was born, and a year later, Wilhelm. The two brothers, growing up with four other children in the family, were drawn together in a relationship that was to last through their lifetime. Their father was a lawyer, and they decided to follow his profession when they

2. Iona Opie and Peter Opie, *The Classic Fairy Tales* (Oxford University Press, 1974), p. 15.
3. Stith Thompson, *The Folktale* (Holt, 1946), p. 8.

came of age, studying law at the University of Marburg. Their professor of law was interested in the legends of the Middle Ages and in the songs of the wandering musicians who, in those times, went from castle to castle singing of chivalry and courtly lore. The two young students turned from the law to a study of the German language, its history, and its structure. Jakob's German grammar is one of the great works in language study. During their linguistic studies, they came upon the stories that country people knew by heart; these too they made the subject of study.

Die Brüder Grimm, as they signed themselves, were the first collectors of folklore to recognize in the raw material of the tales a source for the scientific study of the culture that had produced them. Their chief informant was Frau Viehmann, who, they said, knew the stories as the people told them. Through her tellings the Grimms claimed to preserve the characteristic simplicity, strength, crudity, and patterns of the tales. The first volume of their *Kinder- und Hausmärchen* was published in 1812, a second volume in 1815, and a third in 1822. Successive revised editions followed through the years. In the preface to the first edition of the second volume, Wilhelm Grimm describes the methods of the storyteller Frau Viehmann: "She recounts her stories thoughtfully, accurately, with uncommon vividness and evident delight. . . . Anyone believing that the traditional materials are easily falsified and carelessly preserved, and hence cannot survive over a long period, should hear how close she always keeps to her story and how zealous she is for its accuracy. . . . Among people who follow the old life ways without change, attachment to inherited patterns is stronger than we, impatient for variety, can realize."

Wilhelm's description of Frau Viehmann makes ironic reading in the light of recent scholarship which indicates that "she was literate, middle-class . . . , of Huguenot provenance, with French (not German) as her first language. She clearly knew her Perrault, and cannot therefore have been the unsullied folk-source of traditional Germanic mythology that the Grimms presented."[4] It also now appears possible that the Grimm brothers rewrote, altered, and elaborated their source material[5] in spite of their claims to have "let the speech of the people break directly into print." But their contemporaries took their claims at face value, and many began to recognize the ethnographical worth of the folktale and the importance of preserving the language in which the stories were told. But whether or not the Grimm brothers lived up to their own scholarly standards, their tales are great works of art, and their example certainly did open the gates to a new world of scholarship. In their wake, scholar after scholar sought out the hidden pockets of folklore and, using the most scrupulous of methods, recorded fresh discoveries. Among these scholars were Elias Lönnrot (1802–84) in Finland and Peter Asbjörnsen (1812–85) and his friend and collaborator Jörgen Moe (1813–82) in Norway, with George Dasent (1817–96) translating their work into English. In England, Andrew Lang (1844–1912) and Joseph Jacobs (1854–1916) were among the leaders of the movement.

The nineteenth-century discovery of the folktale was followed by waves of scholarly research, each with its own version of the origin of the tales. For early in the process of collecting, it became apparent that the same story appeared

4. S. S. Prawer, "Myths and Myth-makers," *The Times Literary Supplement,* 30 March 1984, p. 343, review of *One Fairy Story Too Many: The Brothers Grimm and Their Tales,* by John M. Ellis.
5. John M. Ellis, *One Fairy Story Too Many: The Brothers Grimm and Their Tales* (University of Chicago Press, 1983).

in places far removed from one another. How was the wide dissemination of the folktale to be explained, and where did it originate? One theory, the Indo-European theory of the linguistic scholars, held that the tales came from a common language. Another held that they came from a common locality, probably India. A third said that the tales were really only broken-down myths, the detritus of a great, encompassing mythology based on the interpretation of nature; the proponents of this theory offered rather far-fetched proof by saying, for example, that when the wolf ate Red Riding-Hood, it was only symbolic of the night swallowing up the day. Then came the anthropologist, who reasoned that the same tales were found all over the world because the primitive mind, wherever it may be geographically or in whatever stage of historical development, thinks like every other primitive mind, and that similar ideas generated similar tales. Freudians held that the tales represented sexual conflicts (Bruno Bettelheim sees Jack's beanstalk as a phallic symbol); Jungians claimed that they arose from the "collective unconscious" of the human race. Marxists interpreted them in the light of the economic and social conditions that would have existed when they were first told; feminists, in the light of a repressive patriarchal tradition. Recently, structural anthropologists have argued that the tales reflect the workings of not merely the primitive mind but of the human mind itself, and that storytelling is a basic human function. All these points of view have truth to tell, and, taken together (with a grain of salt here and there), they testify to the enduring importance of folktales.

Modern students of folklore follow the scheme of study that was originated in Finland under the leadership of Julius and Kaarle Krohn. This father-and-son team evolved a scientific method of studying the folktale by means of a thorough examination of its history and geography, so as to bring together all the variants of a story and trace its history and travel. In this plan, "each of the hundreds of tale types must be submitted to exhaustive study—and in the end the results of these studies synthesized into adequate generalizations."[6] The stories are studied, not only by type, but by motif, which is "the smallest element in a tale having a power to persist in tradition,"[7] such as the recurring motif of the wicked stepmother, or the youngest son. The Finnish movement resulted in a world organization of folklore scholars and enthusiasts. One of its greatest achievements occurred in America, with the *Motif-Index of Folk-Literature* (1955–58), edited by Stith Thompson, who occupied the first chair of folklore to be established in the United States, at the University of Indiana. Even the most casual reader of folklore, on looking into this *Index,* will catch a glimpse of the magnitude of the work and will gain a new respect for the mystery and miraculous power of the whole realm of folklore.

One curious episode in the history of the folktale precedes the influence of the Brothers Grimm, occurring in the century before theirs. The place was France, at the time of Louis XIV, a time of elegance and intellectual brilliance. The yeast of folklore was discovered by the grandees of the court, who toyed with the writing of fairy tales. Charles Perrault was a member of that court, a lawyer, prominent in the affairs of the French Academy, and fond of children. It was he who procured for the children of Paris the right to play in the gardens of the Tuileries, which others would have held sacred to the Crown. In 1697,

6. Thompson, p. 396.
7. Thompson, p. 415.

Perrault gave to the printer a book of fairy tales which he said his son had written, by taking down the tales of an old nurse. It is generally supposed that the son did not write them, and that the senior Perrault protected his dignity with this invention. The book contained eight immortal stories: "The Sleeping Beauty," "Red Riding-Hood," "Blue Beard," "Puss in Boots," "Diamonds and Toads," "Cinderella," "Riquet with the Tuft," and "Hop o' My Thumb." Perrault seems intuitively to have honored the simplicity, lucidity, and directness of the folktale, making these qualities his own. Other writers of the period— Madame d'Aulnoy and Madame de Beaumont—made the fairy tale a mirror of the court, decorating it with sophistication and overburdening it with moral observations. Perrault relished the tales and let them speak for themselves without any interference other than his gift as storyteller. It was a germinal book for the whole of Europe and a salvation for children of the time who had little to read but lessons and tracts of moral precepts.

Confusion as to classification often arises in stories that clearly derive from folklore but bear the indisputable stamp of a known and individual author. Many of the stories of Hans Christian Andersen are typical of this genre. His retellings of folktales are so colored by his own observation, point of view, and philosophy as to be unmistakably his. Howard Pyle, in his *Pepper and Salt* (1886) and *The Wonder Clock* (1888), demonstrates the masterly art of bending the themes, plots, and motifs of folklore to his distinctive mode of storytelling. The great among such writers never destroy the basic strength of folklore or violate its integrity, but rather re-create the genre to form a new and imaginative entity referred to as the *literary fairy tale* or *art fairy tale*. As well as retelling the traditional folktales from a personal perspective, many writers of literary fairy tales create their own original stories using folklore motifs. Andersen and Pyle, Laurence Housman, Carl Sandburg, Eleanor Farjeon, and Isaac Bashevis Singer have individualized what has traditionally been a collective, anonymous form. They have used a language more poetic than that common to the folktale, fashioned characters who develop and change, and introduced literary devices to create a genre straddling the line between folklore and fantasy.

Folklore has been under attack as unsuitable reading for children at least since the sixteenth century. In the eighteenth century, Jean-Jacques Rousseau, in his highly influential book *Émile or On Education* (1762), argued that children should be given nothing but the unvarnished truth. In 1802, the vigorous Mrs. Trimmer founded *The Guardian of Education,* the first magazine to carry regular reviews of children's literature, and she followed in Rousseau's footsteps: "We cannot approve of those [books] which are only fit to fill the heads of children with confused notions of wonderful and supernatural events, brought about by the agency of imaginary beings."[8] In the early twentieth century, Lucy Sprague Mitchell argued that children's literature should be about the "here and now" and, in her anthology of suitable fare, offered stories like "The Red Gasoline Pump."[9] Recently, critics have called folktales frightening, immoral, violent, racist, or sexist.

Alongside those who wished to ban folklore outright from the world of child-

8. Mrs. Trimmer, review of *Mother Bunch's Fairy Tales, The Guardian of Education,* 2 (January–August 1803), as quoted in *Suitable for Children? Controversies in Children's Literature,* ed. Nicholas Tucker (Sussex University Press, 1976), p. 38.
9. Introduction, *Folk Literature and Children: An Annotated Bibliography of Secondary Materials,* ed. George W. B. Shannon (Greenwood Press), p. xiii.

hood have been others who have argued that the tales should be rewritten and improved. An incensed Charles Dickens defended folklore and wrote a parody of the "improved" tale; his version of Cinderella, which was designed to mock the whole procedure of rewriting folk material for uplifting purposes (Cinderella's footmen are six lizards, "each with a petition in his hand ready to present to the Prince, signed by fifty thousand persons, in favour of the early closing movement"[10]), is scarcely funnier than George Cruikshank's version, offered to children in all seriousness, which ends with the fairy godmother engaging the king in a lengthy temperance discussion that convinces him to enforce prohibition throughout the kingdom. To date, the improvers of folktales have produced little more than grotesqueries that might, for reasons not likely to be appreciated by their authors, bring chuckles to adults but surely can offer little pleasure or excitement to children.

The pool of folklore is so broad and deep that modern controversies are merely ripples on the surface. The tale of Cinderella, to take one example, is at least a thousand years old, and it exists in approximately seven hundred variants found in all parts of the world.[11]   But most contemporary attacks on the tale usually focus on only one particular variant, which is indelibly stamped by the culture that produced it: Perrault's courtly version, sweetened and trivialized by Walt Disney. The tale of Cinderella, taken in its totality, is not a rags-to-riches story of a passive beauty waiting to be discovered like a Hollywood hopeful in a drugstore, but, as the Opies tell us, it is the story of "a girl who is being supernaturally *prevented* from becoming a princess."[12]   The tale begins with the premise that a central and most terrible fear of childhood has come to pass: Cinderella's mother has died. And worse, her stepmother and stepsisters deny her rightful heritage; they mock and torment her. But her mother's spirit is still available to her—as a bird, a tree, a magical calf or fish, or, in a few variants, a fairy. Cinderella regains her (or his—for there are Cinder-lads as well as Cinder-girls in the tales) rightful place in the world not by passively waiting, but by her own resolute actions. At the conclusion of the tale, she tests the prince, for, as the Opies write, his "admiration of her in her party dress is worthless. It is essential he plights himself to her while she is a kitchen maid, or the spell can never be broken. . . . On the face of it the message of the fairy tales is that transformation to a state of bliss is effected not by magic, but by the perfect love of one person for another. Yet clearly even this is not the whole story. The transformation is not an actual transformation but a disenchantment, the breaking of a spell. In each case we are aware that the person was always noble, that the magic has wrought no change in the person's soul, only in his or her outward form."[13]

The messages in the Cinderella tale are many, ranging from the obvious one (judge people by their hearts, not by the clothes on their backs) to the deeper and more elusive (even though the one who loved you best has died, her spirit will always be with you). But a good story—unlike a set of maxims or admonitions, or an "improved" tale written solely to make a particular point—is never ex-

10. Charles Dickens, "Frauds on the Fairies," *Household Words*, 184 (October 1853), as quoted in *Suitable for Children? Controversies in Children's Literature*, ed. Nicholas Tucker (Sussex University Press, 1976), p. 38.
11. Opie and Opie, pp. 120–21.
12. Opie and Opie, pp. 12–13.
13. Opie and Opie, p. 14.

hausted; turn it this way or that, and it will continue to gleam with unexpected beauties.

Psychologist Bruno Bettelheim defends folklore for children in *The Uses of Enchantment* (1976). "The fairy tale," he writes, takes a child's "anxieties and dilemmas very seriously and addresses itself directly to them: the need to be loved and the fear that one is thought worthless; the love of life, and the fear of death. Further, the fairy tale offers solutions in ways that the child can grasp on his level of understanding."[14]   He argues that children who are denied access to folktales may well suffer a very real deprivation, and he supports his arguments with detailed psychological analyses of many tales. But it is not necessary to take so Freudian a position as Bettelheim's in order to appreciate the tales, as he himself recognizes:

The delight we experience when we allow ourselves to respond to a fairy tale, the enchantment we feel, comes not from the psychological meaning of the tale (although this contributes to it) but from its literary qualities—the tale itself as a work of art. The fairy tale could not have its psychological impact on the child were it not first and foremost a work of art.[15]

14. Bruno Bettelheim, Introduction, *The Uses of Enchantment: The Meaning and Importance of Fairy Tales* (Knopf, 1976), p. 10.
15. Bettelheim, p. 12.

Germany

The Elves

A common folk theme is one in which good fairies secretly help good mortals, not only without asking reward but in some cases objecting to payment. This tale is also known as *The Elves and the Shoemaker.* [From Jakob Grimm and Wilhelm Grimm, *Household Stories,* trans. Lucy Crane (Macmillan, 1886).]

There was once a shoemaker, who, through no fault of his own, became so poor that at last he had nothing left but just enough leather to make one pair of shoes. He cut out the shoes at night, so as to set to work upon them next morning; and as he had a good conscience, he laid himself quietly down in his bed, committed himself to heaven, and fell asleep. In the morning, after he had said his prayers, and was going to get to work, he found the pair of shoes made and finished, and standing on his table. He was very much astonished, and could not tell what to think, and he took the shoes in his hand to examine them more nearly; and they were so well made that every stitch was in its right place, just as if they had come from the hand of a master-workman.

Soon after a purchaser entered, and as the shoes fitted him very well, he gave more than the usual price for them, so that the shoemaker had enough money to buy leather for two more pairs of shoes. He cut them out at night, and intended to set to work the next morning with fresh spirit; but that was not to be, for when he got up they were already finished, and a customer even was not lacking, who gave him so much money that he was able to buy leather enough for four new pairs. Early next morning he found the four pairs also finished, and so it always happened; whatever he cut out in the evening was worked up by the morning, so that he was soon in the way of making a good living, and in the end became very well to do.

One night, not long before Christmas, when the shoemaker had finished cutting out, and before he went to bed, he said to his wife,

"How would it be if we were to sit up tonight and see who it is that does us this service?"

His wife agreed, and set a light to burn. Then they both hid in a corner of the room, behind some coats that were hanging up, and then they began to watch. As soon as it was midnight they saw come in two neatly formed naked little men, who seated themselves before the shoemaker's table, and took up the work that was already prepared, and began to stitch, to pierce, and to hammer so cleverly and quickly with their little fingers that the shoemaker's eyes could scarcely follow them, so full of wonder was he. And they never left off until everything was finished and was standing ready on the table, and then they jumped up and ran off.

The next morning the shoemaker's wife said to her husband, "Those little men have made us rich, and we ought to show ourselves grateful. With all their running about, and having nothing to cover them, they must be very cold. I'll tell you what; I will make little shirts, coats, waistcoats, and breeches for them, and knit each of them a pair of stockings, and you shall make each of them a pair of shoes."

The husband consented willingly, and at night, when everything was finished, they laid the gifts together on the table, instead of the cut-out work, and placed themselves so that they could observe how the little men would behave. When midnight came, they rushed in, ready to set to work, but when they found, instead of the pieces of prepared leather, the neat little garments put ready for them, they stood a moment in surprise, and then they testified the greatest delight. With the greatest swiftness they took up the pretty garments and slipped them on, singing.

"What spruce and dandy boys are we
No longer cobblers we will be."

Then they hopped and danced about, jumping over the chairs and tables, and at last they danced out at the door.

From that time they were never seen again; but it always went well with the shoemaker as long as he lived, and whatever he took in hand prospered.

The Bremen Town Musicians

Though this tale can be placed in the cumulative class, it has also well-developed action. It is one of the most popular beast tales, not only because the characters are familiar friends of children, but because they have been or are about to be abused but are finally successful. Such action calls upon the child's sympathy and sense of justice. This story also appears under the title "The Traveling Musicians." [From Jakob Grimm and Wilhelm Grimm, *About Wise Men and Simpletons: Twelve Tales from Grimm,* trans. Elizabeth Shub (Macmillan, 1971).]

A donkey had for years faithfully carried his master's sacks of wheat to the mill for grinding. But the donkey was losing his strength and was able to work less and less. His owner had about decided the animal was no longer worth his keep

Illustration by Hans Fischer, from *The Traveling Musicians* (1955; originally published in Switzerland 1944), by the Brothers Grimm. Reproduced by permission of Harcourt Brace Jovanovich, Inc.

when the donkey, realizing that no kind wind was blowing in his direction, ran away. He took the road to Bremen. Once there, he thought, he would become a town musician. After traveling awhile, he came upon a hunting dog lying by the roadside. The dog lay there panting and exhausted as if he had run a great distance.

"What makes you pant so, Catcher?" asked the donkey.

"Oh," said the dog, "I am old and getting weaker each day, and because I can no longer serve my master in the hunt, he wanted to beat me to death, so I've run away. But I don't know how I'm going to earn my bread."

"I'll tell you what to do," replied the donkey. "I'm on my way to Bremen to become a town musician. Come along and you can get a job too. I'll play the lute and you can try the kettle drums."

The dog was delighted and they continued on together. It was not long before they met a cat on the road who looked as mournful as three days of steady rain.

"What crossed your path, Old Whisker-washer?" inquired the donkey.

"How can I be happy when I've had it up to my ears? I'm getting on in years and my teeth have gone dull. I'd rather sit behind the stove and dream than chase mice and so my mistress wanted to drown me. Well, I managed to get away, but good rat is expensive, and where shall I go?"

"Come with us to Bremen. You know all about night music and you, too, can get a job as a town musician."

The cat thought this a good idea and joined them.

The three fugitives soon came to a farm, where they saw a cock sitting on a gatepost screaming away at the top of his lungs.

"You'll burst our eardrums," the donkey said to the cock. "What's the matter?"

"Here I promised good weather for the holy day because it is the day Our Dear Lady washed the Christ child's shirts and wanted them to dry. But my mistress has no pity on me. Tomorrow is Sunday and guests are coming, and she has told the cook that she wants me in the soup. I'm to have my head chopped off this very evening. That's why I'm screaming as loud and as long as I still can.''

''Nonsense,'' said the donkey. ''Come with us. We're off to Bremen. You can find something better to do anywhere than die. You have a good voice, and with your help, if we all make music together, it will surely have style.''

The cock agreed to this proposal and the four continued on their way.

Bremen was too far to reach in one day. By evening they had arrived at a forest and decided to spend the night there. The donkey and the dog lay down beneath a huge tree. The cat and the cock, however, made for the branches—the cock flying all the way to the top, where he felt himself safest. But before he went to sleep, he looked about in all directions, and it seemed to him he saw a light in the distance. He called down to his comrades that there must be a house not too far away.

''In that case,'' said the donkey, ''let's get up and go there. The shelter here is pretty flimsy.'' And since it occurred to the dog that a few bones and a piece of meat would do him good, they all made their way in the direction of the light, which grew brighter and bigger, until they stood before a well-lighted thieves' hide-out.

The donkey, as the tallest, went to the window and peered inside.

''What do you see, Grayhorse?'' asked the cock.

''What I see,'' replied the donkey, ''is a table loaded with lovely food and drink. And the thieves are sitting around it, enjoying themselves.''

''That would be something for us,'' said the cock.

''Yes, indeed. If only we were inside,'' said the donkey.

The animals held a conference on how to get the thieves out of the house, and at last worked out a plan. The donkey was to stand on his hind legs with his forelegs on the window sill. The dog was to jump up on the donkey's back, the cat was to climb up on top of the dog, and last of all, the cock was to fly up and seat himself on the cat's head. When they were in position, the signal was given and they began to make music together: the donkey brayed, the dog

howled, the cat meowed, the cock crowed. Then they broke through the window and into the room to the accompaniment of crashing glass.

The thieves jumped for fright at the unbearable noise and, convinced that the animals were ghosts, fled into the forest in terror.

The four comrades sat down at the table. They weren't choosy about leftovers and ate everything in sight as if they hadn't touched food in a month. When they had eaten their fill, they put out the lights and each, according to his nature and convenience, found himself a place to sleep.

The donkey lay down on the dung heap, the dog behind the door, the cat on the hearth near the warm ashes, and the cock settled himself on a rafter. And because they were tired out from their long hike, they soon fell asleep.

When midnight had passed, and the thieves saw from a distance that there were no longer any lights on in the house and that all seemed quiet, their chief said, ''We shouldn't have let them scare us out of our wits.''

He ordered one of his men to go back to the house and look around. The messenger, finding all quiet, went into the kitchen to get a light. He mistook the cat's glowing eyes for live coals and struck a match on them. This was no joke to the cat, who sprang at his face, spitting and scratching.

The terrified thief tried to get out the back door, but the dog, who lay there, sprang up and bit him in the leg. As he ran by the dung heap in the yard, the donkey landed him a neat blow with his hind legs; the cock on his roost, awakened by the noise, cried kikeriki.

The thief ran as fast as he could to his chief and said, ''There is a terrible witch in the house. She attacked me and scratched my face with her long nails. At the door there is a man with a knife and he stuck me in the leg with it. In the yard there's a black monster, who beat me with a club; and on the roof there sat a judge who cried, 'Bring the scoundrels to me.'

''Then I got away.''

After that the thieves never dared to come near the house, and the four Bremen town musicians felt themselves so much at home they decided to remain for good.

And this tale's still warm from the telling, for I've just heard it.

Hansel and Gretel

Hansel and Gretel is one of the best-loved of fairy tales, with its comestible house, its malevolent witch, the friendship of birds, and the courage of the children. The poet Randall Jarrell's powerful translation was first published in 1962. It is also available in the distinguished collection stunningly illustrated by Maurice Sendak, *The Juniper Tree and Other Tales from Grimm* (Farrar, Straus & Giroux, 1973), translated by Lore Segal and Randall Jarrell. [From Jakob Grimm and Wilhelm Grimm, *The Golden Bird and Other Fairy Tales of the Brothers Grimm,* trans. Randall Jarrell (Macmillan, 1962).]

Once upon a time, on the edge of a great forest, there lived a poor woodcutter with his wife and his two children. The boy was named Hansel and the girl was named Gretel. The family had little enough to eat, and once when there was a great famine in the land the man could no longer even get them their daily bread. One night, lying in bed thinking, in his worry he kept tossing and turning, and sighed, and said to his wife: "What is going to become of us? How can we feed our poor children when we don't even have anything for ourselves?"

"You know what, husband?" answered the wife. "The first thing in the morning we'll take the children out into the forest, to the thickest part of all. There we'll make them a fire and give each of them a little piece of bread; then we'll go off to our work and leave them there alone. They won't be able to find their way back home, and we'll have got rid of them for good."

"No, wife," said the man, "I won't do it. How could I have the heart to leave my children alone in the forest—in no time the wild beasts would come and tear them to pieces."

"Oh, you fool!" said she. "Then all four of us will starve to death—you may as well start planing the planks for our coffins," and she gave him no peace until he agreed. "I do feel sorry for the poor children, though," said the man.

The two children hadn't been able to go to sleep either, they were so hungry, and they heard what their stepmother said to their father. Gretel cried as if her heart would break, and said to Hansel: "We're as good as dead." "Ssh! Gretel," said Hansel, "don't you worry, I'll find some way to help us." And as soon as the old folks had gone to sleep, he got up, put on his little coat, opened the bottom half of the door, and slipped out. The moon was shining bright as day, and the white pebbles that lay there in front of the house glittered like new silver coins. Hansel stooped over and put as many as he could into his coat pocket. Then he went back in again, and said to Gretel: "Don't you feel bad, dear little sister! You just go to sleep. God will take care of us." Then he lay down in his bed again.

The next morning, before the sun had risen, the woman came and woke the two children: "Get up you lazy creatures, we're going to the forest and get wood." Then she gave each of them a little piece of bread and said: "There is something for your dinner, but don't you eat it before, because it's all you're going to get."

Gretel put the bread in her apron, since Hansel had the pebbles in his pocket. Then they all started out together on the way to the forest. After they had been walking a little while Hansel stopped and looked back at the house, and did it again and again. His father said: "Hansel, what are you looking at? What are you hanging back there for? Watch out or you'll forget your legs."

"Oh, Father," said Hansel, "I'm looking at my little white pussycat that's sitting on the roof and wants to say goodbye to me."

The wife said: "Fool, that's not your pussycat, that's the morning sun shining on the chimney." But Hansel hadn't been looking back at the cat—every time he'd stopped he'd dropped onto the path one of the white pebbles from his pocket.

When they came to the middle of the forest the father said: "Now get together some wood, children! I'll light you a fire, so you won't be cold." Hansel and Gretel pulled together brushwood till it was as high as a little mountain. The wood was lighted, and when the flames were leaping high, the woman said: "Now lie down by the fire, children, and take a rest, we're going into the forest to cut wood. When we're finished we'll come back and get you.''

Hansel and Gretel sat by the fire, and when noon came they each ate their little piece of bread. And since they heard the blows of the ax, they thought their father was near. But it wasn't the ax, it was a branch that he'd fastened to a dead tree so that the wind would blow it back and forth. And when they'd been sitting there a long time, they got so tired that their eyes closed, and they fell fast asleep. When at last they woke up, it was pitch black. Gretel began to cry, and said: "Now how will we ever get out of the forest?" But Hansel comforted her: "Just wait awhile till the moon comes up, then we'll be able to find our way." And when the full moon had risen, Hansel took his little sister by the hand and followed the pebbles, that glittered like new silver coins and showed them the way.

They walked the whole night through, and just as the day was breaking they came back to their father's house. They knocked on the door, and when the woman opened it and saw that it was Hansel and Gretel, she said: "You bad children, why did you sleep so long in the forest? We thought you weren't coming back at all." But the father was very glad, for it had almost broken his heart to leave them behind alone.

Not long afterwards there was again a famine throughout the land, and the children heard their mother saying to their father in bed one night: "Everything's eaten again. We've only a half a loaf left, and that will be the end of us. The children must go. We'll take them deeper into the forest, so that this time they won't find their way back; it's our only chance." The man's heart was heavy, and he thought: "It would be better for you to share the last bite of food with your children." But the woman wouldn't listen to what he had to say, but scolded him and reproached him. If you say ''A'' then you have to say ''B'' too, and since he had given in the first time, he had to give in the second time too.

But the children were still awake, and had heard what was said. As soon as the old folks were asleep, Hansel got up again to go out and pick up pebbles as he'd done the time before, but the woman had locked the door, and Hansel couldn't get out. He comforted his little sister, though, and said: "Don't cry, Gretel, but just go to sleep. The good Lord will surely take care of us."

Early in the morning the woman came and got the children out of their beds. She gave them their little piece of bread, but this time it was even smaller than the time before. On the way to the forest Hansel broke up the bread in his pocket, and often would stop and scatter the crumbs on the ground. "Hansel, what are you stopping and looking back for?" said the father. "Come on!"

"I'm looking at my little pigeon that's sitting on the roof and wants to say goodbye to me," answered Hansel.

"Fool," said the woman, "that isn't your pigeon, that's the morning sun shining on the chimney." But Hansel, little by little, scattered all the crumbs on the path.

The woman led the children still deeper into the forest, where they'd never been before in all their lives. Then there was again a great fire made, and the mother said: "Just sit there, children, and if you get tired you can take a nap. We're going into the forest to cut wood, and this evening when we're finished we'll come and get you."

When it was noon, Gretel shared her bread with Hansel, who'd scattered his along the way. Then they fell asleep, and the afternoon went by, but no one came to the poor children. They didn't wake until it was pitch black, and Hansel comforted his little sister, and said: "Just wait till the moon comes up, Gretel, then we'll see the bread crumbs I scattered. They'll show us the way home." When the moon rose they started out, but they didn't find any crumbs, for the many thousands of birds that fly about in the fields and in the forest had picked them all up. Hansel said to Gretel: "Surely we'll find the way." But they didn't find it. They walked all that night and all the next day, from morning to evening, but they never did get out of the forest. And they were so hungry, for they'd had nothing to eat but a few berries they found on the ground. And when they got so tired that their legs wouldn't hold them up any longer, they lay down under a tree and fell asleep.

By now it was already the third morning since they'd left their father's house. They started to go on again, but they kept getting deeper and deeper into the forest, and unless help came soon they must die of hunger. When it was noon, they saw a beautiful snow-white bird, sitting on a bough, who sang so beautifully that they stood still and listened to him. As soon as he had finished he spread his wings and flew off ahead of them, and they followed him till they came to a little house. The bird perched on the roof of it, and when they got up close to it they saw that the little house was made of bread and the roof was made of cake; the windows, though, were made out of transparent sugar-candy.

"We'll get to work on that," said Hansel, "and have a real feast. I'll eat a piece of the roof. Gretel, you can eat some of the window—that will taste sweet!" Hansel reached up and broke off a little of the roof, to see how it tasted, and Gretel went up to the windowpane and nibbled at it. Then a shrill voice called out from inside the house:

"Nibble, nibble, little mouse,
Who is gnawing at my house?"

The children answered:

"It is not I, it is not I—
It is the wind, the child of the sky,"

and they went on eating without stopping. The roof tasted awfully good to Hansel, so he tore off a great big piece of it, and Gretel pushed out a whole round windowpane, and sat down and really enjoyed it.

All at once the door opened, and a woman as old as the hills, leaning on crutches, came creeping out. Hansel and Gretel were so frightened that they dropped what they had in their hands. But the old woman just nodded her head and said: "My, my, you dear children, who has brought you here? Come right in and stay with me. No harm will befall you."

She took both of them by the hand and led them into her little house. Then she set nice food before them—milk and pancakes with sugar, apples and nuts. After that she made up two beautiful white beds for them, and Hansel and Gretel lay down in them and thought they were in heaven.

But the old woman had only pretended to be so friendly; really she was a wicked witch who lay in wait for children, and had built the house of bread just to lure them inside. When one came into her power she would kill it, cook it, and eat it, and that would be a real feast for her. Witches have red eyes and can't see far, but they have a keen sense of smell, like animals, so that they can tell whenever human beings get near. As Hansel and Gretel had got close the witch had given a wicked laugh, and had said mockingly: "Now I've got them. This time they won't get away."

Early in the morning, before the children were awake, she was already up, and when she saw both of them fast asleep and looking so darling, with their rosy fat cheeks, she muttered to herself: "That will be a nice bite!" Then she seized Hansel with her shriveled hands and shut him up in a little cage with a grating in the lid, and locked it; and scream as he would, it didn't help him any. Then she went to Gretel, shook her till she woke up, and cried: "Get up, you lazy creature, fetch some water and cook your brother something good. He has to stay in the cage and get fat. As soon as he's fat I'll eat him." Gretel began to cry as if her heart would break, but it was all no use. She had to do what the wicked witch told her to do.

Now the finest food was cooked for poor Hansel, but Gretel got nothing but crab shells. Every morning the old woman would creep out to the cage and cry: "Hansel, put your finger out so I can feel whether you are getting fat." But Hansel would put out a bone, and the old woman's eyes were so bad that she couldn't tell that, but thought it was Hansel's finger, and she just couldn't understand why he didn't get fat.

When four weeks had gone by and Hansel still was as thin as ever, she completely lost patience, and was willing to wait no longer. "Come on, Gretel, hurry up and get some water! Whether he's fat or whether he's thin, tomorrow I'll kill Hansel and cook him."

Oh, how the poor little sister did grieve as she had to get the water, and how the tears ran down her cheeks! "Dear Lord, help us now!" she cried out. "If only the wild beasts in the forest had eaten us, then at least we'd have died together."

"Stop making all that noise," said the old woman. "It won't help you one bit."

Early the next morning Gretel had to go out and fill the kettle with water and light the fire. "First we'll bake," said the old woman. "I've already heated the oven and kneaded the dough." She pushed poor Gretel up to the oven, out of which the flames were already shooting up fiercely. "Crawl in," said the witch, "and see whether it's got hot enough for us to put the bread in." And when Gretel was in, she'd close the oven and Gretel would be baked, and then she'd eat her too. But Gretel saw what she was up to, and said: "I don't know how to. How do I get inside?"

"Goose, goose!" cried the witch, "the oven is big enough—why, look, I can even get in myself," and she scrambled up and stuck her head in the oven. Then Gretel gave her a push, so that she fell right in, and Gretel shut the door and fastened the bolt. Oh, then she began to howl in the most dreadful way imaginable, but Gretel ran away, and the wicked witch burned to death miserably.

But Gretel ran to Hansel as fast as she could, opened the cage, and cried: "Hansel, we are saved! The old witch is dead!" Hansel sprang out like a bird from its cage when the door was opened. How they did rejoice, and throw their arms around each other's necks, and dance around and kiss each other! And since there wasn't anything to fear, now, they went into the witch's house, and in every corner of it stood chests of pearls and precious stones. "These are even better than pebbles," said Hansel, and stuck into his pocket as many as he could; and Gretel said, "I'll take some home too," and filled her apron full.

"Now it's time for us to go. We must get out of this enchanted forest," said Hansel.

But when they'd walked for a couple of hours they came to a wide lake. "We can't get across," said Hansel. "There isn't a plank or a bridge anywhere."

"There isn't a boat either," answered Gretel, "but there's a little white duck swimming over there—if I ask her to, she will help us over." Then she cried:

"They haven't a bridge and they haven't a plank, Hansel and Gretel are out of luck. Please take us across to the other bank And we'll thank you so, you little white duck!"

The duck did come over to them, and Hansel sat down on her back and told his sister to sit behind him. "No," answered Gretel, "it would be too heavy for the little duck. She can take us over one at a time."

The good little bird did that, and when they were happily on the other side, and had gone on for a little while, they came to a wood that kept looking more and more familiar, and at last, in the distance, they saw their father's house. Then they started to run, burst into the living room, and threw themselves on their father's neck. Since he had left the children in the forest he had not had a single happy hour. His wife, though, had died. Gretel shook out her apron, and pearls and precious stones rolled all over the room, and Hansel threw down out of his pocket one handful after another. All their troubles were at an end and they lived together in perfect happiness. My tale is done, there is no more, but there's a mouse upon the floor—the first of you that catches her can make a great big cap from her fur.

The Fisherman and His Wife

This is a universal tale if there ever was one. Who has not known an insatiable person or someone who feels quite able to undertake the tasks of God himself? When anyone says, "He's like the fisherman's wife," the whole tale is told. In his notes, Alderson states: "This was originally translated for a new edition of Andrew Lang's *Green Fairy Book*. . . . The North Country dialect which is suggested is intended to correspond with the North German dialect of the Grimms' tale." [From Jakob Grimm and Wilhelm Grimm, *The Brothers Grimm: Popular Folk Tales,* trans. Brian Alderson (Victor Gollancz, 1978).]

Once, a while back, there was a fisherman who lived with his old woman in a piss-pot down by the sea; and the fisherman went off every day and fished. And he fished and he fished. He'd sit there with his line, looking down through the clear water. And he sat and he sat.

Well, one day his line got pulled down, deep under, and when he hauled it up he hauled up a huge flounder as well. Then the flounder said to him, "Wait on, fisherman, let me alone; truth is, I'm not really a flounder but an enchanted prince. What good'll it do you to kill me? I'll not taste very nice. Put me back in the water and let me swim."

"All right," said the man, "you needn't take on so. You can be sure I'll let swim a flounder that talks." And with that he puts him back into the clear water, and the flounder swims to the bottom, leaving a long streak of blood behind him. The fisherman gets up and goes back to his old woman in the piss-pot.

"Well, man," says his old woman, "haven't you caught anything today?"

"Nay," says the man, "I caught a flounder that said he were an enchanted prince, but I let him go back again."

"D'you mean to say you didn't wish for anything?" says his old woman.

"Nay," says the man, "what should I wish for?"

"Eee!" says his old woman, "look at us, stuck here forever in this stinking piss-pot. You might have wished a little cottage for us. Go on back down there and call him; tell him we'd like to have a little cottage. He'd surely give us that."

"Aw," says the man. "D'you want me to go back there again."

"Ay," says his old woman, "you caught him, and you kindly let him go again; he'll surely give us that. Go on, be off with you."

Well, the man didn't think that was altogether proper, but then he didn't know how to stand up to his old woman, so he went back down to the sea again.

Illustration by Michael Foreman, from *The Brothers Grimm: Popular Folk Tales,* translated by Brian Alderson, published by Victor Gollancz Ltd., 1978. Reproduced by permission of Michael Foreman.

When he got there the sea was all green and yellow—not clear like it had been before. So he stood there and said:

"Mannikin, mannikin, timpe tee
Flounder, flounder in the sea
My old missis Ilsebill
Will not have it as I will."

Then the flounder came swimming up and said, "Nah, what d'you want then?"

"Aw," said the man, "you know as how I caught you. Well my old woman says I should have asked for a wish. She doesn't want to go on living in the piss-pot, she'd like to have a little cottage."

"Go on home, man," said the flounder, "she's got it all." Then the man went home and his old woman wasn't sitting in the piss-pot any more, for there was a little cottage with his missis sitting by the door on a bench.

Then she took him by the hand and said to him, "Come in here, man—just see this; it's a good sight better." And they went in and there in the cottage was a little hall and a pretty little parlour and a bedroom, with a bed for each of them, and a kitchen and a dining-room; all done out with the best furniture and fitted with the best in pots and pans, tin-ware, copper-ware, whatever you can think of. And at the back there was a little yard with chickens and ducks, and a little garden with fruit trees and vegetables.

"Just see," said the wife, "isn't that lovely?"

"Yes," said the man, "that's the way it ought to be; now we shall be very comfy."

"We'll have to think about that," said his old woman, and with that they had a bite of supper and went to bed.

Well, everything went along gradely for a couple of weeks, then the old woman said, "Look here, man, this cottage is altogether too poky and the garden's too small; your flounder could easily have given us a bigger place. I wouldn't mind at all living in a great stone castle. Go on down to the flounder, let him give us a castle."

"Aw, missis," said the man, "this cottage is good enough for us; what would we do with a castle?"

"That's what I want," said his old woman, "go on with you, the flounder can always do things like that."

"Nay, missis," said the man, "the flounder's only just given us the cottage. I can't rightly go to him again, he might not like it."

"Go on," said the old woman, "he can do it, and he'll like to do it. Be off with you."

"The man's heart was heavy, and he didn't want to go. He said to himself, "It's just not right." But off he went.

When he came to the sea, the water was all blue and violet, grey and thick, not green and yellow, but it was still calm. So he stood there and said:

"Mannikin, mannikin, timpe tee
Flounder, flounder in the sea
My old missis Ilsebill
Will not have it as I will."

"Nah, what d'you want then?" said the flounder.

"Aw," said the man all embarrassed-like, "she wants to live in a great stone castle."

"Go on home, man," said the flounder, "she's by the front-door."

Then the man went home, thinking he'd come to the house, but when he got there what should he find but a great stone palace, with his old woman up the top of the steps all ready to go in.

Then she took him by the hand and said, "Come in here, man," and at that he went in with her; and in the castle there was a great hall with a marble floor, and there were crowds of servants throwing open doors all over the place. The walls were all shining, with tapestries hanging on them, and the rooms were full of tables and chairs—all pure gold—and there were crystal chandeliers hanging from the ceiling and all the rooms and chambers were covered with carpets. There was food and the very best wine on the tables, so that they could eat and drink when they pleased, while behind the house there was a great courtyard with stables and cowsheds and the very best in coaches and carriages. There was a great big beautiful garden too, with the loveliest flowers and great trees, and there was a park, more than half a mile long, with stags in it and deer and rabbits and everything you could ask for.

"Ee," said the old woman, "isn't that lovely?"

"Aw, yes," said the man, "that's the way it ought to be; now we shall be able to live in this castle all very nicely."

"We'll have to think about that," said his old woman, "we'll sleep on it." And with that they went to bed.

The next morning the old woman was the first to wake up. It was just first light and she could see from her bed all the beautiful countryside lying in front of her. Her man was still snoring, so she dug him in the ribs with her elbow and said, "Here, man, get up and take a look out of that window. Why can't we be king over all that country? Go on down to the flounder and say we want to be king."

"Aw, missis," said the man, "who wants to be king? I don't want to be king."

"Nah," said his old woman, "if you don't want to be king, then I'll be king. Get on down to the flounder and tell him I want to be king."

"Aw, missis," said the man, "what do you want to be king for? I can't say that to him."

"Why ever not?" said his old woman. "You be off with you. I must be king and that's that."

So the man went down all shamed over his wife wanting to be king. "That's not right, that's just not right," he said to himself. He didn't want to go, but off he went.

And when he came to the sea, the sea was all black and grey and the water was all seething and stank real foul. So he stood there and said:

"Mannikin, mannikin, timpe tee
Flounder, flounder in the sea
My old missis Ilsebill
Will not have it as I will."

"Well, what does she want now?" said the flounder.

"Aw," said the man, "she wants to be king."

"Go on home," said the flounder, "she's got it all."

Then the man went home, and as he came up to the palace he saw that the castle had got much bigger, with a great tower covered in carvings; and the sentries stood at the door and there were crowds of soldiers with drums and trumpets. And when he came into the house everything was pure marble and gold, with silk hangings and great golden tassels. Then the doors of the great hall opened up, with all the court there, and his old woman was sitting on a great high throne made of gold and diamonds, and she had on a great golden crown and carried a sceptre of pure gold and precious stones, and on either side of her there stood six young lasses in a row, each one taller by a head than the one next door.

Then he stood in front of her and said, "Well, missis, so now you're king." And he stood there and looked at her and after he'd looked for a bit he said, "Aw, missis, this is all very nice now you're king; now we don't have to wish for anything else."

"Nay, man," said his old woman, shifting about on her seat, "it's very tedious and boring up here; I can't bear it any longer. Go on down to the flounder, tell him I'm king and now I want to be emperor as well."

"Aw missis," said the man, "what do you want to be emperor for?"

"Man," said she, "get off to the flounder; I must be emperor and that's that."

"Aw, missis," said the man, "he can't make you emperor; I can't say that to the flounder; there's nobbut one emperor in the country; emperor's not for flounders to make; he just can't do it."

"Wait on," said his old woman, "if I'm king then you're my man; you must be off at once. Go on, get off with you. He can make kings, so he can make emperors as well. I must and will be emperor, so you go and see about it." So he had to go. But as he went along he felt very scared, and as he walked he said to himself, "That's not good at all—emperor's too brazen— the flounder'll be done with us all this time."

Then he came to the sea and the sea was still all black and thick and beginning to boil up in itself so that it came foaming in, and it flew about so in the bitter wind that it curdled and the man was right terrified. So he stood there and said:

"Mannikin, mannikin, timpe tee
Flounder, flounder in the sea
My old missis Ilsebill
Will not have it as I will."

"What does she want now?" said the flounder.

"Aw, flounder," said he, "my old woman wants to be emperor."

"Go on home," said the flounder, "she's got it all."

Then the man went home, and when he got there he found the whole castle turned into polished marble with alabaster statues and golden decorations. The soldiers were marching up and down in front of the door, blowing trumpets and banging side-drums and kettle-drums, while inside you could see barons and counts and dukes walking about as servants; and they opened up the doors for him and these doors were all made of pure gold. And as he came in there he saw his old woman, sitting up on a throne, two miles high and made out of a single piece of gold; and she was wearing a great golden crown which was six feet high, all set about with diamonds and rubies. In one hand she had the sceptre and in the other the great orb of state, and on both sides of her were standing her gentlemen-at-arms in two lines with each man a little shorter than the man next door, so that at one end there were great giants of fellows two miles high and at the other little tiny dwarfs who weren't even so big as my little finger. In front of them there were standing a whole lot of dukes and princes.

So the man went up among them all and said, "Well, missis, so you're emperor now?"

"Yes," said she, "I'm emperor."

Then he went and stood and looked at her straight, and after he'd looked for a bit, he said, "Well, missis, this is all very nice now you're emperor."

"Man," said she, "what are you standing there for? Now I'm emperor I want to be pope as well. Go on down to the flounder."

"Aw, woman," said the man, "what will you be thinking of next? You can't be pope. There's only one pope in Christendom; he can't make you that."

"Man," said she, "I will be pope. Get off with you straight away. I must be pope."

"Nay, woman," said the man, "I can't say that to him; that's not good at all; that's too big; the flounder can't make you into a pope."

"Don't talk nonsense, man," said the old woman, "if he can make emperors he can make popes too. Get off with you. If I'm emperor then you're my man; will you go on now?"

Then he was proper scared, and he went off trembling and shaking, and his knees were banging together and his legs felt like jelly. And a great wind blew over the land, and clouds flew across and everything got dim as though night was coming on. Leaves fell from the trees and the water boiled like someone was cooking, and it seethed up the bank; and far away he could see ships in trouble, tossing about on the waves. But there was still a bit of blue in the middle of the sky, even though all round the edges it was red with the makings of a terrible storm. Then he went and stood there half out of his wits with fright and said:

"Mannikin, mannikin, timpe tee
Flounder, flounder in the sea
My old missis Ilsebill
Will not have it as I will."

"Well, what does she want now?" said the flounder.

"Aw," said the man, "she wants to be pope."

"Go on home," said the flounder, "she's got it all."

Then he went home, and when he got there, he found it was a kind of great church with lots of palaces all round it. He shoved his way through all the folk that were there, and inside he saw it was all lit up with thousands and thousands of candles, and his old woman was dressed in pure gold, sitting up there on a much higher throne with three great golden crowns on her head. And round her there were so many holy people, and up both sides in front of her there were two lines of candles, with the biggest as thick and fat as the biggest tower you can think of, down to the smallest like a candle on a cake, and all the emperors and kings were kneeling there kissing her slippers.

"Well, woman," he said, and gave her a straight look, "so you're pope now?"

"Yes," said she, "I'm pope." Then he went and stood and looked at her, and it were as though he were looking at the bright sun.

After he'd looked for a bit, he said, "Aw, missis, this is all very nice now you're pope!" But she stayed looking stiff as a tree and never stretched nor stirred herself at all.

Then he said, "Now, missis, let it be now you're pope. You can't want aught else."

"I shall have to think about that," said his old woman, and with that they both went to bed. But she couldn't let it be, and she was that greedy she couldn't sleep for thinking what else she might become.

The man slept right good and sound, because of all the walking he'd done that day, but his old woman tossed and turned from one side of the bed to the other all the night long, thinking what she might become, and she couldn't think of anything.

By-and-by though, the sun began to rise, and when she saw the dawn breaking she sat herself up in bed, looked around, and when she saw through the window how the sun was coming up, she said to herself, "Ha! couldn't I make the sun and moon rise?—Man!" she said, digging him in the ribs with her elbow, "man, wake up; go on down to the flounder and tell him I want to be the good Lord himself."

Now the man was still hardly awake, but he was so frightened when he heard this that he fell out of bed. He didn't think to have heard aright, and he rubbed his eyes and said, "Aw, missis, what's that you said?"

"Man," she said, "if I can't make the sun and moon to rise, if I've just got to sit here watching while the sun and moon come up, then I can't do with it. I shan't have a moment's peace till I can make them come up myself." Then she looked at him right sharpish so that he couldn't help but tremble. "Get off with you at once; I want to be the good Lord himself."

"Aw, missis," said the man, and he got down on his knees, "the flounder can't do that. Mebbe he can make emperors and popes, but leave it at that; please, just stay pope."

Then she got wicked angry. Her hair stood up all round her head and she shrieked out, "I can't do with it. I can't do with this a minute longer. You get off with yourself!" So he pulled on his britches and dashed off like he was mad.

But the storm was raging something terrible and blowing so he could scarcely stand on his two feet. Trees and houses were tumbling down, the hills were shaking and bits of rock were crashing into the sea. The heavens were black as pitch; there was thunder and lightning, and the sea hurled up waves as high as steeples and mountains, all crowned with caps of white foam. So he called—and could never hear his own words:

"Mannikin, mannikin, timpe tee
Flounder, flounder in the sea
My old missis Ilsebill
Will not have it as I will."

"Well, what does she want now?" said the flounder.

"Aw," said he, "she wants to be like the good Lord himself."

"Go on home," said the flounder, "she's sitting in the piss-pot again."

And there they stayed sitting until this very day.

Rapunzel

"After all, a fairy story is not just a fluffy puff of nothing which can be airily blown aside by a 'school of thought,' nor is it merely a tenuous bit of make believe. . . . Its roots are real and solid, reaching far back into man's past, into ancient mythology and religion, and into the lives and customs of many peoples and countries." So wrote Wanda Gág in *The Horn Book* for March 1937, in an article in which she discusses the controversy over fairy tales and speaks out in their defense.

There is a moving spiritual quality in the story of Rapunzel, in which so much is endured for the sake of love, and the tears of the beloved have the power to heal blindness. [From Jakob Grimm and Wilhelm Grimm, *Household Stories*, trans. Lucy Crane (Macmillan, 1886).]

There once lived a man and his wife, who had long wished for a child, but in vain. Now there was at the back of their house a little window which overlooked a beautiful garden full of the finest vegetables and flowers; but there was a high wall all round it, and no one ventured into it, for it belonged to a witch of great might, and of whom all the world was afraid. One day that the wife was standing at the window, and looking into the garden, she saw a bed filled with the finest rampion; and it looked so fresh and green that she began to wish for some; and at length she longed for it greatly. This went on for days, and as she knew she could not get the rampion, she pined away, and grew pale and miserable. Then the man was uneasy, and asked,

"What is the matter, dear wife?"

"Oh," answered she, "I shall die unless I can have some of that rampion to eat that grows in the garden at the back of our house." The man, who loved her very much, thought to himself,

"Rather than lose my wife I will get some rampion, cost what it will."

So in the twilight he climbed over the wall into the witch's garden, plucked hastily a handful of rampion and brought it to his wife. She made a salad of it at once, and ate of it to her heart's content. But she liked it so much, and it tasted so good, that the next day she longed for it thrice as much as she had done before; if she was to have any rest the man must climb over the wall once more. So he went in the twilight again; and as he was climbing back, he saw, all at once, the witch standing before him, and was terribly frightened, as she cried, with angry eyes,

"How dare you climb over into my garden like a thief, and steal my rampion! it shall be the worse for you!"

"Oh," answered he, "be merciful rather than just, I have only done it through necessity; for my wife saw your rampion out of the window, and became possessed with so great a longing that she would have died if she could not have had some to eat." Then the witch said,

"If it is all as you say you may have as much rampion as you like, on one condition—the child that will come into the world must be given to me. It shall go well with the child, and I will care for it like a mother."

In his distress of mind the man promised everything; and when the time came when the child was born the witch appeared, and, giving the child the name of Rapunzel (which is the same as rampion), she took it away with her.

Rapunzel was the most beautiful child in the world. When she was twelve years old the witch shut her up in a tower in the midst of a wood, and it had neither steps nor door, only a small window above. When the witch wished to be let in, she would stand below and would cry,

"Rapunzel, Rapunzel! let down your hair!"

Rapunzel had beautiful long hair that shone like gold. When she heard the voice of the witch she would undo the fastening of the upper window, unbind the plaits of her hair, and let it down twenty ells below, and the witch would climb up by it.

After they had lived thus a few years it happened that as the King's son was riding through the wood, he came to the tower; and as he drew near he heard a voice singing so sweetly that he stood still and listened. It was Rapunzel in her loneliness trying to pass away the time with sweet songs. The King's son wished to go in to her, and sought to find a door in the tower, but there was none. So he rode home, but the song had entered into his heart, and every day he went into the wood and listened to it.

Once, as he was standing there under a tree, he saw the witch come up, and listened while she called out,

"O Rapunzel, Rapunzel! let down your hair."

Then he saw how Rapunzel let down her long tresses, and how the witch climbed up by it and went in to her, and he said to himself,

"Since that is the ladder I will climb it, and seek my fortune." And the next day, as soon as it began to grow dusk, he went to the tower and cried,

"O Rapunzel, Rapunzel! let down your hair."

And she let down her hair, and the King's son climbed up by it.

Rapunzel was greatly terrified when she saw that a man had come in to her, for she had never seen one before; but the King's son began speaking so kindly to her, and told how her singing had entered into his heart, so that he could have no peace until he had seen her herself. Then Rapunzel forgot her terror, and when he asked her to take him for her husband, and she saw that he was young and beautiful, she thought to herself,

"I certainly like him much better than old mother Gothel," and she put her hand into his hand, saying,

"I would willingly go with thee, but I do not know how I shall get out. When thou comest, bring each time a silken rope, and I will make a ladder, and when it is quite ready I will get down by it out of the tower, and thou shalt take me away on thy horse." They agreed that he should come to her every evening, as the old woman came in the day-time. So the witch knew nothing of all this until once Rapunzel said to her unwittingly,

"Mother Gothel, how is it that you climb up here so slowly, and the King's son is with me in a moment?"

"O wicked child," cried the witch, "what is this I hear! I thought I had hidden thee from all the world, and thou hast betrayed me!"

In her anger she seized Rapunzel by her beautiful hair, struck her several times with her left hand, and then grasping a pair of shears in her right—snip, snap—the beautiful locks lay on the ground. And she was so hard-hearted that she took Rapunzel and put her in a waste and desert place, where she lived in great woe and misery.

The same day on which she took Rapunzel away she went back to the tower in the evening and made fast the severed locks of hair to the window-hasp, and the King's son came and cried,

"Rapunzel, Rapunzel! let down your hair."

Then she let the hair down, and the King's son climbed up, but instead of his dearest Rapunzel he found the witch looking at him with wicked glittering eyes.

"Aha!" cried she, mocking him, "you came for your darling, but the sweet bird sits no longer in the nest, and sings no more; the cat has got her, and will scratch out your eyes as well! Rapunzel is lost to you; you will see her no more."

The King's son was beside himself with grief, and in his agony he sprang from the tower: he escaped with life, but the thorns on which he fell put out his eyes. Then he wandered blind through the wood, eating nothing but roots and berries, and doing nothing but lament and weep for the loss of his dearest wife.

So he wandered several years in misery until at last he came to the desert place where Rapunzel lived with her twin-children that she had borne, a boy and a girl. At first he heard a voice that he thought he knew, and when he reached the place from which it seemed to come Rapunzel knew him, and fell on his neck and wept. And when her tears touched his eyes they became clear again, and he could see with them as well as ever.

Then he took her to his kingdom, where he was received with great joy, and there they lived long and happily.

Snow-White

"Most like the fairies, especially in the wealth of traditions concerning them, are the dwarfs. In the countries of northern Europe they are considered as spirits of the underground." Stith Thompson so describes them in his *The Folktale:* "They are certainly more ungainly, as generally conceived, than the fairies, and are nearest in appearance to the little house-spirits which the English know as brownies and the Danes as 'nisser'" (p. 248). Dr. Thompson says further that "Walt Disney was particularly successful in catching the traditional conception of the dwarfs in his production of 'Snow White.'" It is interesting to note that there is some disagreement with him on this score. There are those who feel that the names and the characterization bestowed upon the Disney dwarfs were something less than true to the mystery and dignity that is traditionally their due. Dopey, Sneezy, Sleepy, and Doc—these seem unlikely names for members of the same race as Rumpelstiltskin and Tom Tit Tot. In his autobiography, *Surprised by Joy,* C. S. Lewis, professor of Medieval and Renaissance English Literature at Cambridge University, speaks of his delight in dwarfs, "the old, bright-hooded, snowy-bearded dwarfs we had in those days . . . before Walt Disney vulgarized the earthmen" (p. 54).

At any rate, the story of the child among dwarfs is one of the most appealing in all folklore, with its mingled motifs of cruel stepmother and magic sleep, to be broken by Prince Charming. [From Jakob Grimm and Wilhelm Grimm, *Household Stories,* trans. Lucy Crane (Macmillan, 1886).]

It was the middle of winter, and the snowflakes were falling like feathers from the sky, and a queen sat at her window working, and her embroidery-frame was of ebony. And as she worked, gazing at times out on the snow, she pricked her finger, and there fell from it three drops of blood on the snow. And when she saw how bright and red it looked, she said to herself, "Oh that I had a child as white as snow, as red as blood, and as black as the wood of the embroidery frame!"

Not very long after she had a daughter, with a skin as white as snow, lips as red as blood, and hair as black as ebony, and she was named Snow-white. And when she was born the queen died.

After a year had gone by the king took another wife, a beautiful woman, but proud and overbearing, and she could not bear to be surpassed in beauty by any one. She had a magic looking-glass, and she used to stand before it, and look in it, and say,

"Looking-glass upon the wall,
Who is fairest of us all?"

And the looking-glass would answer,

"You are fairest of them all."

And she was contented, for she knew that the looking-glass spoke the truth.

Now, Snow-white was growing prettier and prettier, and when she was seven years old she was as beautiful as day, far more so than the queen herself. So one day when the queen went to her mirror and said,

"Looking-glass upon the wall,
Who is fairest of us all?"

It answered,

"Queen, you are full fair, 'tis true,
But Snow-white fairer is than you."

This gave the queen a great shock, and she became yellow and green with envy, and from that hour her heart turned against Snow-white, and she hated her. And envy and pride like ill weeds grew in her heart higher every day, until she had no peace day or night. At last she sent for a huntsman, and said,

"Take the child out into the woods, so that I may set eyes on her no more. You must put her to death, and bring me her heart for a token."

The huntsman consented, and led her away; but when he drew his cutlass to pierce Snow-white's innocent heart, she began to weep, and to say,

"Oh, dear huntsman, do not take my life; I will go away into the wild wood, and never come home again."

And as she was so lovely the huntsman had pity on her, and said,

"Away with you then, poor child;" for he thought the wild animals would be sure to devour her, and it was as if a stone had been rolled away from his heart when he spared to put her to death. Just at that moment a young wild boar came running by, so he caught and killed it, and taking out its heart, he brought it to the queen for a token. And it was salted and cooked, and the wicked woman ate it up, thinking that there was an end of Snow-white.

Now, when the poor child found herself quite alone in the wild woods, she felt full of terror, even of the very leaves on the trees, and she did not know what to do for fright. Then she began to run over the sharp stones and through the thorn bushes, and the wild beasts after her, but they did her no harm. She ran as long as her feet would carry her; and when the evening drew near she came to a little house, and she went inside to rest. Everything there was very small, but as pretty and clean as possible. There stood the little table ready laid, and covered with a white cloth, and seven little plates, and seven knives and forks, and drinking-cups. By the wall stood seven little beds, side by side, covered with clean white quilts. Snow-white, being very hungry and thirsty, ate from each plate a little porridge and bread, and drank out of each little cup a drop of wine, so as not to finish up one portion alone. After that she felt so tired that she lay down on one of the beds, but it did not seem to suit her; one was too long, another too short, but at last the seventh was quite right; and so she lay down upon it, committed herself to heaven, and fell asleep.

When it was quite dark, the masters of the house came home. They were seven dwarfs, whose occupation was to dig underground among the mountains. When they had lighted their seven candles, and it was quite light in the little house, they saw that some one must have been in, as everything was not in the same order in which they left it. The first said,

"Who has been sitting in my little chair?"
The second said,
"Who has been eating from my little plate?"
The third said,
"Who has been taking my little loaf?"
The fourth said,
"Who has been tasting my porridge?"
The fifth said,
"Who has been using my little fork?"
The sixth said,
"Who has been cutting with my little knife?"
The seventh said,
"Who has been drinking from my little cup?"
Then the first one, looking round, saw a hollow in his bed, and cried,
"Who has been lying on my bed?"
And the others came running, and cried,
"Some one has been on our beds too!"
But when the seventh looked at his bed, he saw little Snow-white lying there asleep. Then he told the others, who came running up, crying out in their astonishment, and holding up their

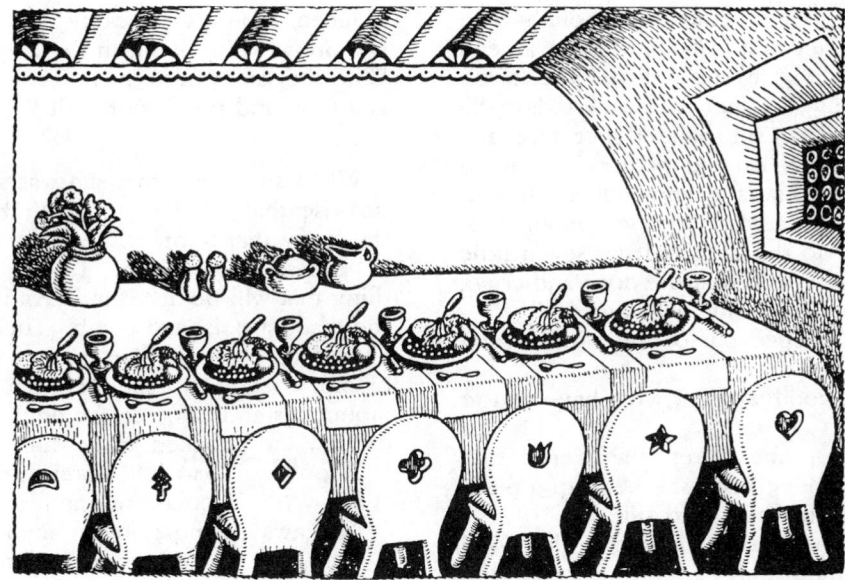

Illustration by Wanda Gág. Reprinted by permission of Coward, McCann & Geoghegan, Inc., from *Snow White and the Seven Dwarfs.* Copyright © 1938 by Wanda Gág; copyright renewed © 1965 by Robert Janssen.

seven little candles to throw a light upon Snow-white.

"O goodness! O gracious!" cried they, "what beautiful child is this?" and were so full of joy to see her that they did not wake her, but let her sleep on. And the seventh dwarf slept with his comrades, an hour at a time with each, until the night had passed.

When it was morning, and Snow-white awoke and saw the seven dwarfs, she was very frightened; but they seemed quite friendly, and asked her what her name was, and she told them; and then they asked how she came to be in their house. And she related to them how her step-mother had wished her to be put to death, and how the huntsman had spared her life, and how she had run the whole day long, until at last she had found their little house. Then the dwarfs said,

"If you will keep our house for us, and cook, and wash, and make the beds, and sew and knit, and keep everything tidy and clean, you may stay with us, and you shall lack nothing."

"With all my heart," said Snow-white; and so she stayed, and kept the house in good order.

In the morning the dwarfs went to the mountain to dig for gold; in the evening they came home, and their supper had to be ready for them. All the day long the maiden was left alone, and the good little dwarfs warned her, saying,

"Beware of your step-mother, she will soon know you are here. Let no one into the house."

Now the queen, having eaten Snow-white's heart, as she supposed, felt quite sure that now she was the first and fairest, and so she came to her mirror, and said,

"Looking-glass upon the wall,
Who is fairest of us all?"

And the glass answered,

"Queen, thou art of beauty rare,
But Snow-white living in the glen
With the seven little men
Is a thousand times more fair."

Then she was very angry, for the glass always spoke the truth, and she knew that the huntsman must have deceived her, and that Snow-white must still be living. And she thought and thought how she could manage to make an end of her, for as long as she was not the fairest in the land, envy left her no rest. At last she thought of a plan; she painted her face and dressed herself like an old pedlar woman, so that no one would have known her. In this disguise she went across the seven mountains, until she came to the house of the seven little dwarfs, and she knocked at the door and cried,

"Fine wares to sell! fine wares to sell!"

Snow-white peeped out of the window and cried,

"Good-day, good woman, what have you to sell?"

"Good wares, fine wares," answered she, "laces of all colours;" and she held up a piece that was woven of variegated silk.

"I need not be afraid of letting in this good woman," thought Snow-white, and she unbarred the door and bought the pretty lace.

"What a figure you are, child!" said the old woman, "come and let me lace you properly for once."

Snow-white, suspecting nothing, stood up before her, and let her lace her with the new lace; but the old woman laced so quick and tight that it took Snow-white's breath away, and she fell down as dead.

"Now you have done with being the fairest," said the old woman as she hastened away.

Not long after that, towards evening, the seven dwarfs came home, and were terrified to see their dear Snow-white lying on the ground, without life or motion; they raised her up, and when they saw how tightly she was laced they cut the lace in two; then she began to draw breath, and little by little she returned to life. When the dwarfs heard what had happened they said,

"The old pedlar woman was no other than the wicked queen; you must beware of letting any one in when we are not here!"

And when the wicked woman got home she went to her glass and said,

"Looking-glass against the wall,
Who is fairest of us all?"

And it answered as before,

"Queen, thou art of beauty rare,
But Snow-white living in the glen
With the seven little men
Is a thousand times more fair."

When she heard that she was so struck with surprise that all the blood left her heart, for she knew that Snow-white must still be living.

"But now," said she, "I will think of something that will be her ruin." And by witchcraft she made a poisoned comb. Then she dressed herself up to look like another different sort of old woman. So she went across the seven mountains and came to the house of the seven dwarfs, and knocked at the door and cried,

"Good wares to sell! good wares to sell!"

Snow-white looked out and said,

"Go away, I must not let anybody in."

"But you are not forbidden to look," said the old woman, taking out the poisoned comb and holding it up. It pleased the poor child so much that she was tempted to open the door; and when the bargain was made the old woman said,

"Now, for once your hair shall be properly combed."

Poor Snow-white, thinking no harm, let the old woman do as she would, but no sooner was the comb put in her hair than the poison began to work, and the poor girl fell down senseless.

"Now, you paragon of beauty," said the wicked woman, "this is the end of you," and went off. By good luck it was now near evening, and the seven little dwarfs came home. When they saw Snow-white lying on the ground as dead, they thought directly that it was the stepmother's doing, and looked about, found the poisoned comb, and no sooner had they drawn it out of her hair than Snow-white came to herself, and related all that had passed. Then they warned her once more to be on her guard, and never again to let any one in at the door.

And the queen went home and stood before the looking-glass and said,

"Looking-glass against the wall,
Who is fairest of us all?"

And the looking-glass answered as before,

"Queen, thou art of beauty rare,
But Snow-white living in the glen
With the seven little men
Is a thousand times more fair."

When she heard the looking-glass speak thus she trembled and shook with anger.

"Snow-white shall die," cried she, "though it should cost me my own life!" And then she went to a secret lonely chamber, where no one was likely to come, and there she made a poisonous apple. It was beautiful to look upon, being white with red cheeks, so that any one who should see it must long for it, but whoever ate even a little bit of it must die. When the apple was ready she painted her face and clothed herself like a peasant woman, and went across the seven mountains to where the seven dwarfs lived. And when she knocked at the door Snow-white put her head out of the window and said,

"I dare not let anybody in; the seven dwarfs told me not."

"All right," answered the woman; "I can easily get rid of my apples elsewhere. There, I will give you one."

"No," answered Snow-white, "I dare not take anything."

"Are you afraid of poison?" said the woman, "look here, I will cut the apple in two pieces; you shall have the red side, I will have the white one."

For the apple was so cunningly made, that all the poison was in the rosy half of it. Snow-white longed for the beautiful apple, and as she saw the peasant woman eating a piece of it she could no longer refrain, but stretched out her hand and took the poisoned half. But no sooner had she taken a morsel of it into her mouth than she fell to the earth as dead. And the queen, casting on her a terrible glance, laughed aloud and cried,

"As white as snow, as red as blood, as black as ebony! this time the dwarfs will not be able to bring you to life again."

And when she went home and asked the looking-glass,

"Looking-glass against the wall,
Who is fairest of us all?"

At last it answered,

"You are the fairest now of all."

Then her envious heart had peace, as much as an envious heart can have.

The dwarfs, when they came home in the evening, found Snow-white lying on the ground, and there came no breath out of her mouth, and she was dead. They lifted her up, sought if anything poisonous was to be found, cut her laces, combed her hair, washed her with water and wine, but all was of no avail, the poor child was dead, and remained dead. Then they laid her on a bier, and sat all seven of them round it, and wept and lamented three whole days. And then they would have buried her, but that she looked still as if she were living, with her beautiful blooming cheeks. So they said,

"We cannot hide her away in the black ground." And they had made a coffin of clear glass, so as to be looked into from all sides, and they laid her in it, and wrote in golden letters upon it her name, and that she was a king's daughter. Then they set the coffin out upon the mountain, and one of them always remained by it to watch. And the birds came too, and mourned for Snow-white, first an owl, then a raven, and lastly, a dove.

Now, for a long while Snow-white lay in the coffin and never changed, but looked as if she were asleep, for she was still as white as snow, as red as blood, and her hair was as black as ebony. It happened, however, that one day a king's son rode through the wood and up to the dwarf's house, which was near it. He saw on the mountain the coffin, and beautiful Snow-white within it, and he read what was written in golden letters upon it. Then he said to the dwarfs,

"Let me have the coffin, and I will give you whatever you like to ask for it."

But the dwarfs told him that they could not part with it for all the gold in the world. But he said,

"I beseech you to give it me, for I cannot live without looking upon Snow-white; if you consent I will bring you to great honour, and care for you as if you were my brethren."

When he so spoke the good little dwarfs had pity upon him and gave him the coffin, and the king's son called his servants and bid them carry it away on their shoulders. Now it happened that as they were going along they stumbled over a bush, and with the shaking the bit of poisoned apple flew out of her throat. It was not long before she opened her eyes, threw up the cover of the coffin, and sat up, alive and well.

"Oh dear! where am I?" cried she. The king's son answered, full of joy, "You are near me," and, relating all that had happened, he said,

"I would rather have you than anything in the world; come with me to my father's castle and you shall be my bride."

And Snow-white was kind, and went with him, and their wedding was held with pomp and great splendour.

But Snow-white's wicked step-mother was also bidden to the feast, and when she had dressed herself in beautiful clothes she went to her looking-glass and said,

"Looking-glass upon the wall,
Who is fairest of us all?"

The looking-glass answered,

"O Queen, although you are of beauty rare,
The young bride is a thousand times more fair."

Then she railed and cursed, and was beside herself with disappointment and anger. First she thought she would not go to the wedding; but then she felt she should have no peace until she went and saw the bride. And when she saw her she knew her for Snow-white, and could not stir from the place for anger and terror. For they had ready red-hot iron shoes, in which she had to dance until she fell down dead.

Rumpelstiltskin

Riddles are a frequent motif in folktales. Versions of this tale can be found among most of the early peoples. Besides the riddle motif, we find here the device of testing the truth of a previous statement. In the French version, the falsehood is different and told for a reason less satisfactory than this one. There are also other but minor changes. The English variant, "Tom Tit Tot," and the Cornish "Duffy and the Devil" share a broad, droll humor quite different from the dramatic tone of the German version. [From Jakob Grimm and Wilhelm Grimm, *Household Stories,* trans. Lucy Crane (Macmillan, 1886).]

There was once a miller who was poor, but he had one beautiful daughter. It happened one day that he came to speak with the king, and, to give himself consequence, he told him that he had a daughter who could spin gold out of straw. The king said to the miller, "That is an art that pleases me well; if thy daughter is as clever as you say, bring her to my castle tomorrow, that I may put her to the proof."

When the girl was brought to him, he led her into a room that was quite full of straw, and gave her a wheel and spindle, and said, "Now set to work, and if by the early morning thou hast not spun this straw to gold thou shalt die." And he shut the door himself, and left her there alone.

And so the poor miller's daughter was left there sitting, and could not think what to do for her life; she had no notion how to set to work to spin gold from straw, and her distress grew so great that she began to weep. Then all at once the door opened, and in came a little man, who said, "Good evening, miller's daughter; why are you crying?"

"Oh!" answered the girl, "I have got to spin gold out of straw, and I don't understand the business."

Then the little man said, "What will you give me if I spin it for you?"

"My necklace," said the girl.

The little man took the necklace, seated himself before the wheel, and whirr, whirr, whirr! three times round and the bobbin was full; then he took up another, and whirr, whirr, whirr; three times round, and that was full; and so he went on till the morning, when all the straw had been spun, and all the bobbins were full of gold. At sunrise came the king, and when he saw the gold he was astonished and very much rejoiced, for he was very avaricious.

He had the miller's daughter taken into another room filled with straw, much bigger than the last, and told her that as she valued her life she must spin it all in one night.

The girl did not know what to do, so she began to cry, and then the door opened, and the little man appeared and said, "What will you give me if I spin all this straw into gold?"

"The ring from my finger," answered the girl. So the little man took the ring, and began again to send the wheel whirring round, and by the next morning all the straw was spun into glistening gold. The king was rejoiced beyond measure at the sight, but as he could never have enough of gold, he had the miller's daughter taken into a still larger room full of straw, and said, "This, too, must be spun in one night, and if you accomplish it you shall be my wife." For he thought, "Although she is but a miller's daughter, I am not likely to find any one richer in the whole world."

As soon as the girl was left alone, the little man appeared for the third time and said, "What will you give me if I spin the straw for you this time?"

"I have nothing left to give," answered the girl.

"Then you must promise me the first child you have after you are queen," said the little man.

"But who knows whether that will happen?" thought the girl; but as she did not know what else to do in her necessity, she promised the little man what he desired, upon which he began to spin, until all the straw was gold. And when in the morning the king came and found all done according to his wish, he caused the wedding to be held at once, and the miller's pretty daughter became a queen.

In a year's time she brought a fine child into the world, and thought no more of the little man; but one day he came suddenly into her room, and said, "Now give me what you promised me."

The queen was terrified greatly, and offered the little man all the riches of the kingdom if he would only leave the child; but the little man said, "No, I would rather have something living than all the treasures of the world."

Then the queen began to lament and to weep, so that the little man had pity upon her.

"I will give you three days," said he, "and if at the end of that time you cannot tell my name, you must give up the child to me."

Then the queen spent the whole night in thinking over all the names that she had ever heard, and sent a messenger through the land to ask far and wide for all the names that could be found. And when the little man came next day, (beginning with Caspar, Melchior, Balthazar) she repeated all she knew, and went through the whole list, but after each the little man said, "That is not my name."

The second day the queen sent to inquire of all the neighbors what the servants were called, and told the little man all the most unusual and singular names, saying, "Perhaps you are called Roast-ribs, or Sheepshanks, or Spindleshanks?" But he answered nothing but "That is not my name."

The third day the messenger came back again, and said, "I have not been able to find one single new name; but as I passed through the woods I came to a high hill, and near it was a little house, and before the house burned a fire, and round the fire danced a comical little man, and he hopped on one leg and cried,

"Today do I bake, tomorrow I brew,
The day after that the queen's child comes in;
And oh! I am glad that nobody knew
That the name I am called is Rumpelstiltskin!"

You cannot think how pleased the queen was to hear that name, and soon afterwards, when the little man walked in and said, "Now, Mrs. Queen, what is my name?" she said at first, "Are you called Jack?"

"No," answered he.

"Are you called Harry?" she asked again.

"No," answered he. And then she said,

"Then perhaps your name is Rumpelstiltskin!"

"The devil told you that! the devil told you that!" cried the little man, and in his anger he stamped with his right foot so hard that it went into the ground above his knee; then he seized his left foot with both his hands in such a fury that he split in two, and there was an end of him.

The Peasant's Clever Daughter

This folktale is another example of the storyteller's art, using riddle as a prime source of wit and the matching of wits to enchant the listener. In this tale, the woman's quickness in the solving of riddles is a reflection of her compassionate intelligence. She teaches her husband that human wisdom and feeling are more important than material objects. Variants of this popular tale are found throughout Europe from the Czechoslovakian "Clever Manka" to the Russian "The Wise Little Girl." Ralph Manheim's vigorous retelling first appeared in 1977 in his distinguished translation *Grimm's Tales for Young and Old: The Complete Stories* and in 1981 in his collection for children, *Rare Treasures from Grimm: Fifteen Little-Known Tales*. [From Jakob Grimm and Wilhelm Grimm, *Grimm's Tales for Young and Old: The Complete Stories*, sel. and trans. Ralph Manheim (Doubleday, 1977).]

There was once a poor peasant who had no land, just a small house and an only daughter. One day his daughter said: "We ought to ask the king for a piece of newly cleared land." When the king heard how poor they were, he gave them a piece of grassland, which she and her father spaded, meaning to sow a little wheat and other grain. When they had almost finished spading their field, they found a mortar of pure gold. "Look here," said the father. "The king was kind enough to give us our field. Why not give him this mortar in return?" The daughter was dead against it. "Father," she said, "if we give him a mortar and no pestle, he'll want a pestle. We'd better keep quiet about it." But the father wouldn't listen. He brought the mortar to the king, said he had found it in his field, and asked if the king would accept it as a gift. After accepting the mortar, the king asked the peasant if he hadn't found anything else. "No," said the peasant. "What about the pestle?" said the king. "Bring me the pestle." The peasant said they hadn't found any pestle, but he might have been talking to the wall. He was thrown into prison and the king told him he'd stay there until he produced the pestle.

When the servants brought him his bread and water—that's what they give you in prison—they heard him sighing: "Oh, if I had only listened to my daughter! Oh, oh, if I had only

listened to my daughter!" The servants went to the king and told him how the prisoner kept sighing: "Oh, if I had only listened to my daughter," and how he wouldn't eat and wouldn't drink. The king had the servants bring him the prisoner and asked him why he kept sighing: "If I had only listened to my daughter!" "What did your daughter tell you?" "Well, she told me not to give you the mortar, because if I did you'd want the pestle too." "If you have such a clever daughter, tell her to come and see me." So she appeared before the king, who asked her if she were really so clever, and said: "I'll tell you what. I've got a riddle for you. If you can guess the answer, I'll marry you." "I'll guess it," she said. "All right," said the king, "come to me not clothed, not naked, not riding, not walking, not on the road, not off the road. If you can do all that, I'll marry you."

She went home and took off all her clothes so then she was unclothed, sat down on a big fish net and wrapped it around her, so then she was not naked. Then she hired a donkey and tied the fish net to the donkey's tail, and the donkey dragged her along, which was neither riding nor walking. And the donkey had to drag her along the wagon track, so that only her big toe touched the ground and she was neither on the road nor off the road. When she came bumping along, the king said she had guessed the riddle and met all the requirements. He let her father out of prison, took her as his wife, and gave all the royal possessions into her care.

Some years passed, and then one day as the king was inspecting his troops, some peasants, who had been selling wood, stopped their wagons outside the palace. Some of the wagons were drawn by oxen and some by horses. One peasant had three horses, one of them foaled, and the foal ran off and lay down between two oxen that were harnessed to another peasant's wagon. The two peasants started to argue and fight, because the one with the oxen wanted to keep the foal and claimed the oxen had had it. The other peasant said no, his mare had had it, and it belonged to him. The dispute came before the king. His decision was that where the foal had lain there it should stay, and so it was given to the peasant with the oxen, who had no right to it. The other peasant went away weeping and wailing about his foal. But he had heard that the queen was kindhearted, because she came of a poor peasant family. So he went to her and asked if she could help him to get his foal back. "Yes," she said. "If you promise not to give me away, I'll tell you what to do. Tomorrow morning when the king goes out to inspect the guard, take a fish net, stand in the middle of the road where he has to pass, and pretend to be fishing. Shake out the net now and then as if it were full and go on fishing." And she also told him what to say when the king questioned him.

Next day the peasant stood there fishing on dry land. As the king was passing by, he saw him and sent his orderly to ask the fool what he was doing. "I'm fishing," was the answer. The orderly asked him how he could fish when there was no water. The peasant replied: "There's just as much chance of my catching fish on dry land as there is of an ox having a foal." The orderly took the man's answer back to the king, whereupon the king summoned the peasant. "You didn't think up that answer," he said. "Where did you get it? Tell me this minute." The peasant wouldn't tell him. "So help me," he said, "I thought of it myself." But they laid him down on a bundle of straw and beat him and tortured him until at last he confessed that the queen had given him the idea. When the king got home, he said to his wife: "Why have you played me false? I won't have you for my wife any longer, your time is up, go back to the peasant's hovel you came from."

But he granted her one mercy, leave to take the best and dearest thing she knew of with her. That would be her farewell present. "Yes, dear husband," she said. "If that is your command, I will obey it." She threw her arms around him and kissed him and asked him to drink a farewell glass with her. Thereupon she sent for a strong sleeping potion. The king took a deep draft, but she herself drank only a little. When he had fallen into a deep sleep, she called a servant and took a fine white sheet and wrapped it around the king. The servant carried him to a carriage that was waiting at the door and she drove him home to her little house, where she put him into her bed. He slept a

day and a night without waking. When he finally woke up, he looked around and said: "Good God, where am I?" He called his servants, but there weren't any servants. At last his wife came to his bedside and said: "Dear king and husband, you told me to take what was best and dearest with me from the palace. Nothing is better or dearer in my eyes than you, so I took you with me." The king's eyes filled with tears. "Dearest wife," he said, "never again shall we part." He took her back to the royal palace and married her again, and I imagine they are still alive.

The Sleeping Beauty

The Sleeping Beauty is best known as the first tale in Charles Perrault's collection of eight folktales—*Histoires ou Contes du Temps Passé,* first published in France in 1697 and translated into English by Robert Samber in 1729. This celebrated folktale has many variants. A similar story appeared in 1636 in the Neapolitan Basile's *Pentamerone,* and the Grimm brothers collected a version in Hesse. It appears in their collection under the title *Dornröschen,* or *Little Briar Rose.* Lucy Crane's Victorian retelling gives Sleeping Beauty the name Rosamund. [From Jakob Grimm and Wilhelm Grimm, *Household Stories,* trans. Lucy Crane (Macmillan, 1886).]

In times past there lived a king and queen, who said to each other every day of their lives, "Would that we had a child!" and yet they had none. But it happened once that when the queen was bathing, there came a frog out of the water, and he squatted on the ground, and said to her,

"Thy wish shall be fulfilled; before a year has gone by, thou shalt bring a daughter into the world."

And as the frog foretold, so it happened; and the queen bore a daughter so beautiful that the king could not contain himself for joy, and he ordained a great feast. Not only did he bid to it his relations, friends, and acquaintances, but also the wise women, that they might be kind and favourable to the child. There were thirteen of them in his kingdom, but as he had only provided twelve golden plates for them to eat from, one of them had to be left out.

Illustration by Felix Hoffmann, reproduced from his book *The Sleeping Beauty* by permission of Harcourt Brace Jovanovich, Inc. Copyright © 1959 by H. R. Sauerlander and Co., Aarau; English translation 1959 by Oxford University Press.

However, the feast was celebrated with all splendour; and as it drew to an end, the wise women stood forward to present to the child their wonderful gifts: one bestowed virtue, one beauty, a third riches, and so on, whatever there is in the world to wish for. And when eleven of them had said their say, in came the uninvited thirteenth, burning to revenge herself, and without greeting or respect, she cried with a loud voice,

"In the fifteenth year of her age the princess shall prick herself with a spindle and shall fall down dead."

And without speaking one more word she turned away and left the hall. Everyone was terrified at her saying, when the twelfth came forward, for she had not yet bestowed her gift, and though she could not do away with the evil prophecy, yet she could soften it, so she said,

"The princess shall not die, but fall into a deep sleep for a hundred years."

Now the king, being desirous of saving his child even from this misfortune, gave commandment that all the spindles in his kingdom should be burnt up.

The maiden grew up, adorned with all the gifts of the wise women; and she was so lovely, modest, sweet, and kind and clever, that no one who saw her could help loving her.

It happened one day, she being already fifteen years old, that the king and queen rode abroad, and the maiden was left behind alone in the castle. She wandered about into all the nooks and corners, and into all the chambers and parlours, as the fancy took her, till at last she came to an old tower. She climbed the narrow winding stair which led to a little door, with a rusty key sticking out of the lock; she turned the key, and the door opened, and there in the little room sat an old woman with a spindle, diligently spinning her flax.

"Good day, mother," said the princess, "what are you doing?"

"I am spinning," answered the old woman, nodding her head.

"What thing is that that twists round so briskly?" asked the maiden, and taking the spindle into her hand she began to spin; but no sooner had she touched it than the evil prophecy was fulfilled, and she pricked her finger with it. In that very moment she fell back upon the bed that stood there, and lay in a deep sleep. And this sleep fell upon the whole castle; the king and queen, who had returned and were in the great hall, fell fast asleep, and with them the whole court. The horses in their stalls, the dogs in the yard, the pigeons on the roof, the flies on the wall, the very fire that flickered on the hearth, became still, and slept like the rest; and the meat on the spit ceased roasting, and the cook, who was going to pull the scullion's hair for some mistake he had made, let him go, and went to sleep. And the wind ceased, and not a leaf fell from the trees about the castle.

Then round about that place there grew a hedge of thorns thicker every year, until the whole castle was hidden from view, and nothing of it could be seen but the vane on the roof. And a rumour went abroad in all that country of the beautiful sleeping Rosamond, for so was the princess called; and from time to time many kings' sons came and tried to force their way through the hedge; but it was impossible for them to do so, for the thorns held fast together like strong hands, and the young men were caught by them, and not being able to get free, there died a lamentable death.

Many a long year afterwards there came a king's son into that country, and heard an old man tell how there should be a castle standing behind the hedge of thorns, and that there a beautiful enchanted princess named Rosamond had slept for a hundred years, and with her the king and queen, and the whole court. The old man had been told by his grandfather than many king's sons had sought to pass the thorn-hedge, but had been caught and pierced by the thorns, and had died a miserable death. Then said the young man, "Nevertheless, I do not fear to try; I shall win through and see the lovely Rosamond." The good old man tried to dissuade him, but he would not listen to his words.

For now the hundred years were at an end, and the day had come when Rosamond should be awakened. When the prince drew near the hedge of thorns, it was changed into a hedge of beautiful large flowers, which parted and bent aside to let him pass, and then closed behind him in a thick hedge. When he reached the castle-yard, he saw the horses and brindled hunting-dogs lying asleep, and on the roof the pigeons were sitting with their heads under their wings. And when he came indoors, the flies on the wall were asleep, the cook in the kitchen had his hand uplifted to strike the scullion, and the kitchen-maid had the black fowl on her lap ready to pluck. Then he mounted higher, and saw in the hall the whole court lying asleep, and above them, on their thrones, slept the king and the queen. And still he went farther, and all was so quiet that he could hear his own breathing; and at last he came to the tower, and went up the winding stair, and opened the door of the little room where Rosamond lay. And when he saw her looking so lovely in her sleep, he could not turn away his eyes; and presently he stooped and kissed her, and she awakened, and opened her eyes, and looked very kindly on him. And she rose, and they went forth together, and the king and the queen and whole court waked up, and gazed on each other with great eyes of wonderment. And the horses in the yard got up and shook themselves, the hounds sprang up and wagged their tails, the pigeons on the roof drew their heads from under their wings, looked round, and flew into the field, the flies on the wall crept on a little farther, the kitchen fire leapt up and blazed, and cooked the meat, the joint on the spit began to roast, the cook gave the scullion such a box on the ear that he roared out, and the maid went on plucking the fowl.

Then the wedding of the Prince and Rosamond was held with all splendour, and they lived very happily together until their lives' end.

France

Little Red Riding-Hood

This tale has many versions, and the question of whether to use this with its realistic ending or one of those with a softened ending is still a debatable one. Three reasons led to the choice of the version given here: first, most children are too ignorant of the meaning of death to be hurt by this ending; second, children have logical minds, and this is the logical climax; third, some children may enjoy this form of the story, as adults enjoy seeing a tragedy on the stage. [From Charles Perrault, *Fairy Tales* (Dutton, 1916).]

Copyright © 1983 by Trina Schart Hyman. Reproduced from *Little Red Riding Hood* by permission of Holiday House, Inc.

There was once upon a time a little village girl, the prettiest ever seen or known, of whom her mother was dotingly fond. Her grandmother was even fonder of her still, and had a little red hood made for the child, which suited her so well that wherever she went she was known by the name of Little Red Riding-Hood.

One day, her mother having baked some cakes, said to her, "Go and see how your grandmother is getting on, for I have been told she is ill; take her a cake and this little jar of butter."

Whereupon Little Red Riding-Hood started off without delay towards the village in which her grandmother lived. On her way she had to pass through a wood, and there she met that sly old fellow, Mr. Wolf, who felt that he should very much like to eat her up on the spot, but was afraid to do so, as there were woodcutters at hand in the forest.

He asked her which way she was going, and the poor child, not knowing how dangerous it is to stop and listen to a wolf, answered: "I am going to see my grandmother and am taking a cake and a little jar of butter, which my mother has sent her."

"Does she live far from here?" asked the Wolf.

"Oh, yes!" replied Little Red Riding-Hood, "on the further side of the mill that you see down there; hers is the first house in the village."

"Well, I was thinking of going to visit her myself," rejoined the Wolf, "so I will take this path, and you take the other, and we will see which of us gets there first."

The Wolf then began running off as fast as he could along the shorter way, which he had chosen, while the little girl went by the longer way, and amused herself with stopping to gather nuts, or run after butterflies, and with making little nosegays of all the flowers she could find.

It did not take the Wolf long to reach the grandmother's house. He knocked, tap, tap.

"Who is there?"

"It is your granddaughter, Little Red Riding-Hood," answered the Wolf, imitating the child's voice. "I have brought a cake and a little jar of butter, which my mother has sent you."

The good grandmother, who was ill in bed, called out, "Pull the bobbin, and the latch will go up." The Wolf pulled the bobbin, and the door opened. He leaped on to the poor old woman and ate her up in less than no time, for he had been three days without food. He then shut the door again and laid himself down in the grandmother's bed to wait for Little Red Riding-Hood. Presently she came and knocked at the door, tap, tap.

"Who is there?" Little Red Riding-Hood was frightened at first, on hearing the Wolf's gruff voice, but thinking that her grandmother had a cold, she answered:

"It is your granddaughter, Little Red Riding-Hood. I have brought a cake and a little jar of butter, which my mother has sent you."

The Wolf called out, this time in rather a softer voice, "Pull the bobbin, and the latch will go up." Little Red Riding-Hood pulled the bobbin, and the door opened.

When the Wolf saw her come in, he hid himself under the bedclothes and said to her, "Put the cake and the little jar of butter in the cupboard and come into bed with me."

Little Red Riding-Hood undressed and went to the bedside and was very much astonished to see how different her grandmother looked to what she did when she was up and dressed.

"Grandmother," she exclaimed, "what long arms you have!"

"All the better to hug you with, my little girl."

"Grandmother, what long legs you have!"

"All the better to run with, child."

"Grandmother, what long ears you have!"

"All the better to hear with, child."

"Grandmother, what large eyes you have!"

"All the better to see with, child."

"Grandmother, what large teeth you have!"

"All the better to eat you with!"

And saying these words, the wicked Wolf sprang out upon Little Red Riding-Hood and ate her up.

Cinderella and the Glass Slipper

No version of this immortal tale equals the flavor of this retelling, with its measured details of costume and festival, its clear portrait of an endearing young girl, its evocation of snow and the winter night, its moments of magic and romance. The great poet's touch is everywhere apparent—in the wisdom of the fairy godmother, as well as in her magic: "What's being old, my dear? Merely little by little and less by less"; the command of words that seem colloquial and spoken, the language of the folktale: "She never stayed *mumpish* or sulky," ". . . the two elder sisters *squinnied* down out of their window." Yet the structure of the tale remains intact, the wicked sisters are justly punished, and the incident of the snipping off of their big toe and heel is let stand, with no fear of nightmare to follow. [From Walter de la Mare, *Told Again* (Knopf, 1927).]

There were once upon a time three sisters who lived in an old, high, stone house in a street not very far from the great square of the city where was the palace of the King. The two eldest of these sisters were old and ugly, which is bad enough. They were also sour and jealous, which is worse. And simply because the youngest (who was only their half-sister) was gentle and lovely, they hated her.

While they themselves sat in comfort in their fine rooms upstairs, she was made to live in a dark, stone-flagged kitchen with nothing but rats, mice, and cockroaches for company. There, in a kind of cupboard, she slept. By day she did the housework—cooking and scrubbing and sweeping and scouring. She made the beds, she washed their linen, she darned their stockings, she mended their clothes. She was never in bed till midnight; and summer or winter, she had to be up every morning at five, to fetch water, to chop up the firewood and light the fires. In the blind, frozen mornings of winter she could scarcely creep about for the cold.

Yet, in spite of all this, though she hadn't enough to eat, though her sisters never wearied of nagging and scolding at her, or of beating her, either, when they felt in the humour, she soon forgot their tongues and bruises. She must have been happy by nature, just as by nature a may-tree is covered with leaves and blossom, or water jets out of a well-spring. To catch sight of a sunbeam lighting up the kitchen wall now and then, or the moonlight stealing across the floor, or merely to wake and hear the birds shrilling at daybreak, was enough to set her heart on fire.

She would jump out of bed, say her prayers, slip into her rags, wash her bright face under the pump, comb her dark hair; then, singing too, not like the birds, but softly under her breath, would begin her work. Sometimes she would set herself races against the old kitchen clock; or say to herself, "When I've done this and this and this and *this*, I'll look out of the window." However late it was before the day was finished, she made it a rule always to sit for a little while in front of the great kitchen fire, her stool drawn close up to the hearth among the cinders. There she would begin to dream even before she fell asleep; and in mockery her sisters called her Cinderella.

They never left her at peace. If they could not find work for her to do, they made it; and for food gave her their crusts and bits left over. They hated her, and hated her all the more because, in spite of their scowls and grumblings,

she never stayed mumpish or sulky, while her cheeks ever grew fairer and her eyes brighter. She couldn't help it. Since she felt young and happy, she couldn't but seem so.

Now all this may have been in part because Cinderella had a fairy godmother. This fairy godmother had come to her christening, and well the sisters remembered it. This little bunched-up old woman had a hump on her back, was dressed in outlandish clothes and a high steeple hat, and the two impudent trollops (who even then tried to make themselves look younger than they were) had called her "Old Stump-Stump," had put out their tongues at her, and laughed at every word she said.

But except for one slow piercing look at them out of her green eyes (after which they laughed no more), the old woman had paid them no heed. She had stooped over Cinderella's wooden cradle and gazed a long time at her sleeping face, then, laying her skinny fore-finger on the mite's chin, she had slowly nodded—once, twice, thrice. If every nod meant a fairy gift, then what wonder Cinderella had cheeks like a wild rose, eyes clear as dewdrops, and a tongue like a blackbird's?

Now Cinderella, of course, could not remember her christening; and her godmother had never been seen or heard of since. She seemed to have quite forgotten her godchild; and when one day Cinderella spoke of her to her sisters, they were beside themselves with rage.

"Godmother, forsooth!" they cackled. "Crazy old humpback! Much she cares for you, Miss Slut! Keep to your cinders; and no more drowsing and dreaming by the fire!"

So time went on, until at last Cinderella was so used to their pinchings and beatings and scoldings that she hardly noticed them. She kept out of their company as much as she could, almost forgot how to cry, was happy when she was alone, and was never idle.

Now a little before Christmas in the year when Cinderella was eighteen, the King sent out his trumpeters to proclaim that on Twelfth Night there was to be a great Ball at the Palace, with such dancing and feasting and revelry as had never been known in that country before. Bonfires were to be lit on the hills, torches in the streets. There were to be stalls of hot pies, eels, sweetmeats, cakes and comfits in the market-place. There were to be booths showing strange animals and birds and suchlike; and the fountains in the city were to run that night with wine. For the next day after it would be the twenty-first birthday of the King's only son. When the people heard the proclamation of the King's trumpeters, there were wild rejoicings, and they at once began to make ready for the feast.

In due time there came to the old stone house where the three sisters lived the King's Lord Chamberlain. At sound of the wheels of his coach the two elder sisters squinnied down out of their window and then at once scuttled downstairs to lock Cinderella up in the kitchen, in case he should see not only her rags, but her lovely young face. He had come, as they guessed, to bring them the King's command that they should attend the great Ball. "I see, madam, three are invited," he said, looking at his scroll.

"Ay," said they, as if in grief, "but only two of us are left." So he bowed and withdrew.

After that the two old sisters scarcely stopped talking about the Ball. They could think of nothing else. They spent the whole day and every day in turning out their chests and wardrobes in search of whatever bit of old finery they could lay hands on. For hours together they sat in front of their great looking-glass, smirking this way and languishing that, trying on any old gown or cloak they could find—slippers and sashes, wigs and laces and buckles and necklaces, and never of the same mind for two minutes together. And when they weren't storming at Cinderella, they were quarreling and wrangling between themselves.

As for Cinderella, from morning to night she sat stitching and stitching till she could scarcely see out of her young eyes or hold her needle. The harder she worked and the more she tried to please them, the worse they fumed and flustered. They were like wasps in a trap.

At last came the night of the Ball. The streets were ablaze with torches and bonfires. In every window burned wax tapers. Shawls and silks of all the colours of the rainbow dangled from sill and balcony. Wine red and golden gushed from the fountains. Everywhere there was feasting and merriment, laughter and music. At one end of the city was a booth of travelling bears, which were soon so crammed with buns and honeycomb that they could only sit and pant; and at the other was a troupe of Barbary apes that played on every kind of instrument of music. Besides which, there was a singing Mermaid; a Giant, with a dwarf on his hat-brim; and a wild man from the Indies that gulped down flaming pitch as if it were milk and water.

The country people, all in their best and gayest clothes (and they came from far and near as if to a Fair), had brought their children even to the youngest, and stood gazing and gaping at the dressed-up lords and ladies in their coaches and carriages on their way to the Palace. There were coaches with six horses, and coaches with four; and a fat, furred, scarlet-silked postillion to each pair. The whole city under the tent of the starry night flared bright as a peepshow.

But Cinderella hadn't a moment even to peer down from an upper window at these wonders. She hardly knew whether she was on her head or her heels. And when at last her two old sisters—looking in their wigs and powder more like bunched-up fantastic monkeys than human beings—had at last rolled off in their hired carriage to the Palace, she was so tired she could scarcely creep upstairs.

After tidying up the litter in their bedrooms, and making a pot of soup to be kept simmering for them till they came home, she drew her stool up to the kitchen fire, with not even the heart to look out of the window. She had never before felt so lonely or wretched, and as she sat there in the red glow of the smouldering coals, before even she knew it was there, a tear rolled down her cheek and splashed with a sizzle into the hot ashes. She ached all over. Nevertheless she poked up the fire again, swept up the ashes, began to sing a little to herself, forgot to go on, and as she did so set to wondering what *she* would be doing now if she herself had gone to the Palace. "But since you can't be in two places at once, my dear," she suddenly laughed out loud, "why here you must stay."

By now it had grown quieter in the streets, and against the black of the window in the wintry night snow was falling. Sitting on her stool among the cinders, Cinderella listened to the far-away strains of music. But these too died away as she listened; utter silence came with the snow; and in a minute or two she would have fallen fast asleep.

Indeed, all was so hushed at last in the vacant kitchen that the ashes, like pygmy bells in a belfry, tinkled as they fell; a cricket began shrilly churring from a crevice in the hob, and she could hear the tiny *tic-a-tac-tac* of the mice as they came tippeting and frisking round her stool. Then, suddenly, softly, and without warning, there sounded out of the deep hush a gentle knock-knocking at the door.

Cinderella's drowsy eyes opened wide. The mice scuttled to their wainscot. Then all was still again. What stranger was this, come in the dark and the snow? Maybe, thought Cinderella, it was only the wind in the ivy. But no, yet again there sounded that gentle knocking—there could be no mistake of that. So Cinderella rose from her stool, lit the tallow candle in an old copper candlestick, and, lifting the latch, peered out into the night.

The stars of huge Orion were wildly shaking in the dark hollow of the sky; the cold air lapped her cheek; and the garden was mantled deep and white as wool with snow. And behold on the doorstep stood a little old hump-backed woman, with a steeple hat on her head, and over her round shoulders a buckled green cloak that came down to her very heels.

"Good-evening, my dear," said the old woman. "I see you don't know who *I* am?" Her green eyes gleamed in the candlelight as she peered into the gloom of the kitchen. "And why, pray, are you sitting here alone, when all the world is gone to the Ball?"

Cinderella looked at her—at her green far-set eyes and long hooked nose, and she smiled back at the old woman and begged her to come in. Then she told her about the Ball.

"Ahai!" said the old woman, "and I'll be bound to say, my dear, you'd like to go too. Ay, so I thought. Come, then, there's no time to waste. Night's speeding on. Put on your gown and we'll be off to the Palace at once."

Now her sisters had strictly forbidden Cinderella to stir from the house in their absence.

Bread and water for three days they had threatened her with if she so much as opened the door. But she knew in her heart they had not told her the truth about the Ball. She knew she had been invited to go too; and now she was not so frightened of them as she used to be. None the less, she could only smile in reply to the old woman, and all she could say was: "It's very kind of you, ma'am. I should dearly like to go to the Ball, and I'm sorry; but I've nothing to go in."

Now the old woman was carrying in her hand (for she stooped nearly double) a crutch or staff, and she said, "Ahai! my dear! Rags and skin, eh? So it's nothing but a gown you need. *That's* soon mended."

With that, she lifted a little her crutch into the air, and as if at a sign and as if an owl had swooped in out of the night, there floated in through the open door out of the darkness and snow a small square Arabian leather trunk, red and gold, with silver hinges and a silver lock.

The old woman touched the lock with her crutch and the lid flew open. And beneath the lid there lay a gown of spangled orient muslin edged with swansdown and seed pearls and white as hoar-frost. There was a fan of strange white feathers, too, and a wreath of green leaves and snow-flowers, such flowers as bloom only on the tops of the mountains under the stars.

"So there's the gown!" said the old woman with a cackle. "Now hasten, my dear. Polish up those bright young cheeks of yours, and we'll soon get a-going."

Cinderella ran off at once into the scullery, put her face under the pump, and scrubbed away until her cheeks were like wild roses, and her hands like cuckoo-flowers. She came back combing her hair with all that was left of her old comb, and then and there, in front of the kitchen fire, shook herself free of her rags and slipped into the muslin gown. Whereupon she looked exactly like a rosebush dazzling with hoar-frost under the moon.

The old woman herself laced up the silver laces, and herself with a silver pin pinned the wreath of green leaves and snow-flowers in Cinderella's dark hair, then kissed her on both cheeks. As they stood there together, yet again the far-away music of fiddle and trumpet came stealing in through the night air from the Palace. And suddenly Cinderella frowned, and a shadow stole over her face.

"But look, ma'am," said she, "just look at my old shoes!" For there they stood, both of them together by the hearth, two old battered clouts that had long been friends in need and in deed, but had by now seen far too much of the world. The old woman laughed and stooped over them.

"Why," she said, "what's being old, my dear? Merely little by little, and less by less." As she said these words, she jerked up the tip of her crutch again, and, behold, the two old patched-up shoes seemed to have floated off into another world and come back again. For in their stead was a pair of slippers the like of which Cinderella had never seen or even dreamed of. They were of spun glass and lined with swansdown, and Cinderella slipped her ten toes into them as easily as a minnow slips under a stone.

"Oh, Godmother! Look!" she cried. "And now I am ready!"

"Ahai!" said the old woman, pleased to her very heart-strings with her happy young goddaughter. "And how, pray, are we going to get through the snow?"

"I think, do you know, dear Godmother," said Cinderella, frowning a little, "I should love to *walk.*" Her Godmother pointed with her crutch and, looking at Cinderella with her sharp green eyes, said:

"Never grumbling, nought awry;
Always willing, asks no why;
Patient waiting, free as air—
What's that pumpkin over there?"

Then Cinderella looked at the old summer pumpkin in the corner by the dresser that had been put by for pie in the winter, and didn't know what to say.

"Bring it a little closer, my dear," said her Godmother. So Cinderella lifted the great pumpkin in her bare arms and laid it down by the hearth. Once more the old woman waved her crutch, and behold, the pumpkin swelled and swelled before Cinderella's very eyes; it swelled in its faded mottled green till it was as huge as a puncheon of wine, and then split softly open. And before Cinderella could so

much as sigh with surprise and delight, there, on its snow-slides, stood a small, round-topped, green and white coach.

"Ahai!" breathed the old woman again, and out of their holes came scampering a round dozen of house mice, which, with yet another wave of her crutch, were at once transformed into twelve small deer, like gazelles, with silver antlers, and harness of silver, bridles and reins. Six of them stood out in the snow under the stars, four of them in the kitchen, and two in the entry. Then out from a larger hole under the shelf where the pots and pans were kept, and behind which was the stone larder with its bacon and cheeses, brisked four smart black rats; and these also were changed and transmogrified as if at a whisper, and now sat up on the coach, two in front and two behind—a sharp-nosed coachman and three dapper footmen. And the coachman sat with the long reins in his hand, waiting for Cinderella to get in.

Then the old woman said:

"And now, my dear, I must leave you. There's but one thing you must remember. Be sure to hasten away from the Palace before the clock has finished tolling twelve. Midnight, my dear. The coach will be waiting, and you must haste away home."

Cinderella looked at her Godmother, and for the second time that evening a tear rolled glittering down her cheek. Oddly enough, though this was a tear of happiness, it was *exactly* like the tear that had rolled down her cheek in her wretchedness as she sat alone.

"Oh, dear, dear Godmother, how can I thank you?" she said.

"Well, my dear," said the old woman, "if you don't know how, why you can't. And if you can't, why, you needn't." And she kissed her once more.

Then Cinderella stepped into the coach. The old woman lifted her crutch. The coachman cracked his whip. The deer, with their silver clashing antlers and silver harness, scooped in the snow their slender hoofs, and out of the kitchen off slid the coach into a silence soft as wool. On, on, under the dark starry sky into streets still flaming and blazing with torches and bonfires, it swept, bearing inside of it not only the last of the King's guests, but by far the loveliest. As for the people still abroad, at sight of it and of Cinderella they opened their mouths in the utmost astonishment, then broke into a loud huzza. But Cinderella heard not a whisper—she was gone in a flash.

When she appeared in the great ball-room, thronged with splendour, its flowers vying in light with its thousands of wax candles in sconce and chandelier, even the fiddlers stopped bowing an instant to gaze at such a wonder. Even so much as one peep at Cinderella was a joy and a marvel.

The Prince himself came down from the dais where sat his father and mother, and himself led Cinderella to the throne. They danced together once, they danced together twice, and yet again. And Cinderella, being so happy and lovely, and without scorn, pride or vanity in her face, everyone there delighted to watch her, except only her two miserable half-sisters, who sat in a corner under a bunch of mistletoe and glared at her in envy and rage.

Not that they even dreamed who she was. No, even though they were her half-sisters, and had lived in the same house with her since she was a child. But then, who could have supposed this was the slattern and drudge they had left at home among her cinders?

But how swiftly slips time away when the heart is happy! The music, the radiant tapers, the talking and feasting—the hours melted like hoar-frost in the sun. And even while Cinderella was once more dancing with the Prince, his dark eyes looking as if he himself were half a-dream, Cinderella heard again the great bell of the Palace clock begin to toll: *One-two-three* . . .

"Oh!" she sighed, and her heart seemed to stand still, "I hear a clock!"

And the Prince said: "Never heed the clock. It is telling us only how little time we have, and how well we should use it." *Five—six—seven* . . .

But "Oh!" Cinderella said, "what time is it telling?"

And the Prince said, "Midnight."

With that, all the colour ebbed out of her young cheeks. She drew herself away from the Prince, and ran off as fast as her feet could carry her. Straight out of the ball-room she scampered, down the long corridor, down yet another, and down the marble staircase. But as she turned at the foot of the staircase, she stumbled a little, and her left slipper slipped off. Cinderella could not wait. Eleven strokes had sounded, and as she leapt breathlessly into the coach there boomed out the twelfth. She was not a moment too soon.

Presently after, yet as if in no time, she found herself at home again in the cold black kitchen. Nothing was changed, though the fire was out, the candle but a stub. There in its corner by the potboard lay the pumpkin. And here as of old sat she herself, shivering a little in her rags on her three-legged stool among the cinders, and only the draughty door ajar and a few tiny plumes of swansdown on the flagstone for proof that she had ever stirred from the house.

But for these, all that had passed might have been a dream. But Cinderella was far too happy for that to be true, and her face was smiling as she looked into the cold ashes of the fire. She looked and she pondered; and while she was pondering, it was as if a voice had asked her a question, "Why is your foot so cold?"

She looked down, and to her dismay saw on one foot a glass slipper, and on the other nothing but an old black stocking. The old woman's magic had come and gone, but it had forgotten a slipper. And even while Cinderella was thinking what she should do, there came a loud pealing of the bell above her head, and she knew that her sisters had come back from the Ball.

So, one foot shod and one foot stockinged, she hastened upstairs with the soup, and helped her sisters to get to bed. Never before had they been in such a rage. Nothing she could do was right. They pinched her when she came near, and flung their slippers at her when she went away; and she soon knew what was amiss. They could talk of nothing else but the strange princess (as they thought her) who had come late to the Ball and with her witcheries had enchanted not only the young Prince but even the King and Queen and the whole Court, down to the very dwarfs, imps, and pages. Their tired old eyes squinted with envy, and they seemed so worn-out and wretched that Cinderella longed to comfort them if only but just to say: "But why trouble about her? *She* will never come back again."

She was thankful at any rate they were too busy with their tongues to notice her feet; and at last she slipped downstairs, *clip-clop, clip-clop,* and was soon safe in bed and asleep.

The very next day the royal trumpeters were trumpeting in the streets once more. Even the Prince had not been able to run as fast as Cinderella, and had come out into the snowy night only just in time to see her coach of magic vanish into the dark. But he had picked up her slipper as he came back.

Proclamation was sounded that anyone who should bring tidings of this lovely young stranger or of her slipper, should be richly rewarded. But Cinderella in her kitchen heard not even an echo of the trumpeters. So they trumpeted in vain.

Then the King sent out his Lord Chamberlain with six pages to attend him. They were bidden search through the city, house by house. And one of the pages carried before the Lord Chamberlain the glass slipper on a crimson cushion with tassels of pearls. At each house in turn, every lady in it was bidden try on the slipper, for the King was determined to find its owner, unless indeed she was of the undiscoverable Courts of Faërie. For most of the ladies the slipper was too high in the instep; for many it was too narrow in the tread; and for all it was far too short.

At last, the Lord Chamberlain came to the house of the three sisters. The two old sisters had already heard what passed when the page brought in the slipper. So the elder of them with a pair of tailor's shears had snipped off a big toe, and bound up her foot with a bandage. But even this was of no avail. For when she tried, in spite of the pain, to push her foot into it, the slipper was far too narrow. The second sister also, with a great cook's knife, had secretly carved off a piece of her heel, and had bound that foot up with a bandage. But even this was of no avail. For push and pull as she might, the shoe was at least an inch too short.

The Lord Chamberlain looked angrily at the sisters.

"Is there any other lady dwelling in this house?" he said.

The two sisters narrowed their eyes one at the other, and lied and said, "No." Yet even at that very moment there welled in a faint singing as if out of the very bowels of the earth.

The Lord Chamberlain said, "What voice is that I hear?"

The two sisters almost squinted as they glanced again each at the other, and the one said it was a tame popinjay: and the other that it was the creaking of the pump.

"Then," said the Lord Chamberlain, "the pump has learned English!" He at once sent two of his pages to seek out the singer whose voice he had heard, and to bring her into his presence. So Cinderella had to appear before him in her rags, just as she was. But when she saw the glass slipper on the crimson cushion, she almost laughed out loud.

The Lord Chamberlain, marvelling at her beauty, said: "Why do you smile, my child?"

She said, "Because, my lord, I have a slipper exactly like that one myself. It's in a drawer in the kitchen dresser." And when one of the pages had brought the other slipper, behold, Cinderella's two feet with both their heels and all their ten toes slipped into them as easily as a titmouse into its nest.

When Cinderella was brought to the King and the Queen, they received her as if she were a long-lost daughter. Far and near, once more, at her wedding, the bonfires blazed all night among the hills, the fountains in the marketplace ran with wine, there were stalls of venison pies, black puddings and eels, sweetmeats, cakes and comfits, and such a concourse of strangers and noblemen in the city as it had never contained before.

Of Cinderella's guests of honour the first was a humpity-backed old woman muffled up in a green mantle, who ate nothing, and drank nothing, and said nothing; but smiled and smiled and smiled.

As for the elder sisters, they sat at home listening to the wedding bells clashing their changes in the steeples. The one being without a heel to her left foot, and the other without a big toe, they walked lame ever afterwards. And their neighbors, laughing at their folly, called them the Two Old Stump-stumps.

Beauty and the Beast

The vogue of the French court of Louis XIV that set the grandees playing at the writing of fairy tales was responsible for the creation of Perrault's *Histoires ou Contes du Temps Passé; avec des Moralités,* which we know as Perrault's Fairy Tales. It produced less clear-sighted followers, such as Countess d'Aulnoy (Marie Catherine La Mothe), whose stories "contained some scraps of folklore" but were vitiated by a profuse and ornamental style. *The White Cat* has endured, and as edited by Rachel Field and illustrated by Elizabeth MacKinstry (Macmillan, 1928) it has been given pictorial realization of great distinction.

Among the writers of this school was Gabrielle Susanne Barbot de Gallos de Villeneuve, and to her we owe the immortal story of *Beauty and the Beast.* It is sometimes attributed to yet another writer of the time, Madame de Beaumont, because her version of the story so often appears in books addressed primarily to children, but there is no doubt who the author is, for it first appeared in the famous encyclopedia of this literature, *Le Cabinet des Fées* (1785–89), which ran into forty-one volumes. *Beauty and the Beast* is one of the most enduring variations on the great theme of the redemption of ugliness through the power of love.

The version given here is that of Andrew Lang, who made his own adaptation from the account of Madame Villeneuve. It appears in what is certainly one of the best-loved books of all the books of childhood—Andrew Lang's *The Blue Fairy Book,* which was first published in 1889, at a time when the fairy tale and the traditional tales of folklore were not highly regarded as reading for children. *The Blue Fairy Book,* followed by *The Red Fairy Book* (1890), set the style for an upsurge of interest in the fairy tale. It will be remembered that Andrew Lang was a scholar as well as a storyteller; he supported the anthropological theory of the origin of the folktale [From Andrew Lang, *The Blue Fairy Book* (Longmans, 1889).]

Once upon a time, in a far-off country, there lived a merchant who was enormously rich. As he had six sons and six daughters, however, who were accustomed to having everything they fancied, he did not find he had a penny too much. But misfortunes befell them. One day

their house caught fire and speedily burned to the ground, with all the splendid furniture, books, pictures, gold, silver and precious goods it contained. The father suddenly lost every ship he had upon the sea, either by dint of pirates, shipwreck or fire. Then he heard that his clerks in distant countries, whom he had trusted entirely, had proved unfaithful. And at last from great wealth he fell into the direst poverty.

All that he had left was a little house in a desolate place at least a hundred leagues from the town. The daughters at first hoped their friends, who had been so numerous while they were rich, would insist on their staying in their houses, but they soon found they were left alone. Their former friends even attributed their misfortunes to their own extravagance and showed no intention of offering them any help.

So nothing was left for them but to take their departure to the cottage, which stood in the midst of a dark forest. As they were too poor to have any servants, the girls had to work hard, and the sons, for their part, cultivated the fields to earn their living. Roughly clothed, and living in the simplest way, the girls regretted unceasingly the luxuries and amusements of their former life. Only the youngest daughter tried to be brave and cheerful.

She had been as sad as anyone when misfortune first overtook her father, but soon recovering her natural gaiety, she set to work to make the best of things, to amuse her father and brothers as well as she could, and to persuade her sisters to join her in dancing and singing. But they would do nothing of the sort, and because she was not as doleful as themselves, they declared this miserable life was all she was fit for. But she was really far prettier and cleverer than they were. Indeed, she was so lovely she was always called Beauty.

After two years, their father received news that one of his ships, which he had believed lost, had come safely into port with a rich cargo. All the sons and daughters at once thought that their poverty was at an end and wanted to set out directly for the town; but their father, who was more prudent, begged them to wait a little, and though it was harvest time, and he could ill be spared, determined to go himself to make inquiries.

Only the youngest daughter had any doubt but that they would soon again be as rich as they were before. They all loaded their father with commissions for jewels and dresses which it would have taken a fortune to buy; only Beauty did not ask for anything. Her father, noticing her silence, said:

"And what shall I bring for you, Beauty?"

"The only thing I wish for is to see you come home safely," she answered.

But this reply vexed her sisters, who fancied she was blaming them for having asked for such costly things. Her father, however, was pleased, but as he thought she certainly ought to like pretty presents, he told her to choose something.

"Well, dear Father," she said, "as you insist upon it, I beg that you will bring me a rose. I have not seen one since we came here, and I love them so much."

The merchant set out, only to find that his former companions, believing him to be dead, had divided his cargo between them. After six months of trouble and expense he found himself as poor as when he started on his journey. To make matters worse, he was obliged to return in the most terrible weather. By the time he was within a few leagues of his home he was almost exhausted with cold and fatigue. Though he knew it would take some hours to get through the forest, he resolved to go on. But night overtook him, and the deep snow and bitter frost made it impossible for his horse to carry him any farther.

The only shelter he could get was the hollow trunk of a great tree, and there he crouched all the night, which seemed to him the longest he had ever known. The howling of the wolves kept him awake, and when at last day broke the falling snow had covered up every path, and he did not know which way to turn.

At length he made out some sort of path, but it was so rough and slippery that he fell down more than once. Presently it led him into an avenue of trees which ended in a splendid castle. It seemed to the merchant very strange that no snow had fallen in the avenue of orange trees, covered with flowers and fruit. When he reached the first court of the castle he saw before him a flight of agate steps. He went up them and passed through several splendidly furnished rooms.

The pleasant warmth of the air revived him, and he felt very hungry; but there seemed to be nobody in all this vast and splendid palace. Deep silence reigned everywhere, and at last, tired of roaming through empty rooms and galleries, he stopped in a room smaller than the rest, where a clear fire was burning and a couch was drawn up cosily before it. Thinking this must be prepared for someone who was expected, he sat down to wait till he should come and very soon fell into a sweet sleep.

When his extreme hunger wakened him after several hours, he was still alone; but a little table, with a good dinner on it, had been drawn up close to him. He lost no time in beginning his meal, hoping he might soon thank his considerate host, whoever it might be. But no one appeared, and even after another long sleep, from which he awoke completely refreshed, there was no sign of anybody, though a fresh meal of dainty cakes and fruit was prepared upon the little table at his elbow.

Being naturally timid, the silence began to terrify him, and he resolved to search once more through all the rooms; but it was of no use, there was no sign of life in the palace! Then he went down into the garden, and though it was winter everywhere else, here the sun shone, the birds sang, the flowers bloomed, and the air was soft and sweet. The merchant, in ecstasies with all he saw and heard, said to himself:

"All this must be meant for me. I will go this minute and bring my children to share all these delights."

In spite of being so cold and weary when he reached the castle, he had taken his horse to the stable and fed it. Now he thought he would saddle it for his homeward journey, and he turned down the path which led to the stable. This path had a hedge of roses on each side of it, and the merchant thought he had never seen such exquisite flowers. They reminded him of his promise to Beauty, and he stopped and had just gathered one to take to her when he was startled by a strange noise behind him. Turning round, he saw a frightful Beast, which seemed to be very angry and said in a terrible voice:

"Who told you you might gather my roses? Was it not enough that I sheltered you in my palace and was kind to you? This is the way you show your gratitude, by stealing my flowers! But your insolence shall not go unpunished."

The merchant, terrified by these furious words, dropped the fatal rose and, throwing himself on his knees, cried, "Pardon me, noble sir. I am truly grateful for your hospitality, which was so magnificent I could not imagine you would be offended by my taking such a little thing as a rose."

But the Beast's anger was not lessened by his speech.

"You are very ready with excuses and flattery," he cried. "But that will not save you from the death you deserve."

Alas, thought the merchant, if my daughter Beauty could only know into what danger her rose has brought me! And in despair he began to tell the Beast all his misfortunes and the reason of his journey, not forgetting to mention Beauty's request.

"A king's ransom would hardly have procured all that my other daughters asked for," he said. "But I thought I might at least take Beauty her rose. I beg you to forgive me, for you see I meant no harm."

The Beast said, in a less furious tone, "I will forgive you on one condition—that you will give me one of your daughters."

"Ah," cried the merchant, "if I were cruel enough to buy my own life at the expense of one of my children's, what excuse could I invent to bring her here?"

"None," answered the Beast. "If she comes at all she must come willingly. On no other condition will I have her. See if any of them is courageous enough, and loves you enough, to come and save your life. You seem to be an honest man so I will trust you to go home. I give you a month to see if any of your daughters will come back with you and stay here, to let you go free. If none of them is willing, you must come alone, after bidding them goodbye forever, for then you will belong to me. And do not imagine that you can hide from me, for if you fail to keep your word I will come and fetch you!" added the Beast grimly.

The merchant accepted this proposal. He promised to return at the time appointed, and then, anxious to escape from the presence of the Beast, he asked permission to set off at once. But the Beast answered that he could not go until the next day.

"Then you will find a horse ready for you," he said. "Now go and eat your supper and await my orders."

The poor merchant, more dead than alive, went back to his room, where the most delicious supper was already served on the little table drawn up before a blazing fire. But he was too terrified to eat and only tasted a few of the dishes, for fear the Beast should be angry if he did not obey his orders. When he had finished, the Beast warned him to remember their agreement and to prepare his daughter exactly for what she had to expect.

"Do not get up tomorrow," he added, "until you see the sun and hear a golden bell ring. Then you will find your breakfast waiting for you, and the horse you are to ride will be ready in the courtyard. He will also bring you back again when you come with your daughter a month hence. Farewell. Take a rose to Beauty, and remember your promise!"

The merchant lay down until the sun rose. Then, after breakfast, he went to gather Beauty's rose and mounted his horse, which carried him off so swiftly that in an instant he had lost sight of the palace. He was still wrapped in gloomy thoughts when it stopped before the door of his cottage.

His sons and daughters, who had been uneasy at his long absence, rushed to meet him, eager to know the result of his journey which, seeing him mounted upon a splendid horse and wrapped in a rich mantle, they supposed to be favorable. But he hid the truth from them at first, only saying sadly to Beauty as he gave her the rose:

"Here is what you asked me to bring you. Little you know what it has cost."

Presently he told them his adventures from beginning to end, and then they were all very unhappy. The girls lamented loudly over their lost hopes, and the sons declared their father should not return to the terrible castle. But he reminded them he had promised to go back. Then the girls were very angry with Beauty and said it was all her fault. If she had asked for something sensible this would never have happened.

Poor Beauty, much distressed, said to them, "I have indeed caused this misfortune, but who could have guessed that to ask for a rose in the middle of summer would cause so much misery? But as I did the mischief it is only just that I should suffer for it. I will therefore go back with my father to keep his promise."

At first nobody would hear of it. Her father and brothers, who loved her dearly, declared nothing should make them let her go. But Beauty was firm. As the time drew near she divided her little possessions between her sisters, and said good-bye to everything she loved. When the fatal day came she encouraged and cheered her father as they mounted together the horse which had brought him back. It seemed to fly rather than gallop, but so smoothly that Beauty was not frightened. Indeed, she would have enjoyed the journey if she had not feared what might happen at the end of it. Her father still tried to persuade her to go back, but in vain.

While they were talking the night fell. Then, to their great surprise, wonderful colored lights began to shine in all directions, and splendid fireworks blazed out before them; all the forest was illuminated. They even felt pleasantly warm, though it had been bitterly cold before. They reached the avenue of orange trees and saw that the palace was brilliantly lighted from roof to ground, and music sounded softly from the courtyard.

"The Beast must be very hungry," said Beauty, trying to laugh, "if he makes all this rejoicing over the arrival of his prey." But, in spite of her anxiety, she admired all the wonderful things she saw.

When they had dismounted, her father led her to the little room. Here they found a splendid fire burning, and the table daintily spread with a delicious supper.

Beauty, who was less frightened now that she had passed through so many rooms and seen nothing of the Beast, was quite willing to begin, for her long ride had made her very hungry. But they had hardly finished their meal when the noise of the Beast's footsteps was heard ap-

proaching, and Beauty clung to her father in terror, which became all the greater when she saw how frightened he was. But when the Beast really appeared, though she trembled at the sight of him, she made a great effort to hide her horror, and saluted him respectfully.

This evidently pleased the Beast. After looking at her he said, in a tone that might have struck terror into the boldest heart, though he did not seem to be angry:

"Good evening, old man. Good evening, Beauty."

The merchant was too terrified to reply, but Beauty answered sweetly, "Good evening, Beast."

"Have you come willingly?" asked the Beast. "Will you be content to stay here when your father goes away?"

Beauty answered bravely that she was quite prepared to stay.

"I am pleased with you," said the Beast. "As you have come of your own accord, you may remain. As for you, old man," he added, turning to the merchant, "at sunrise tomorrow take your departure. When the bell rings, get up quickly and eat your breakfast, and you will find the same horse waiting to take you home."

Then turning to Beauty, he said, "Take your father into the next room, and help him choose gifts for your brothers and sisters. You will find two traveling trunks there; fill them as full as you can. It is only just that you should send them something very precious as a remembrance."

Then he went away, after saying, "Good-bye, Beauty; good-bye, old man." Beauty was beginning to think with great dismay of her father's departure, but they went into the next room, which had shelves and cupboards all round it. They were greatly surprised at the riches it contained. There were splendid dresses fit for a queen, with all the ornaments to be worn with them, and when Beauty opened the cupboards she was dazzled by the gorgeous jewels lying in heaps upon every shelf. After choosing a vast quantity, which she divided between her sisters—for she had made a heap of the wonderful dresses for each of them—she opened the last chest, which was full of gold.

"I think, Father," she said, "that, as the gold

will be more useful to you, we had better take out the other things again, and fill the trunks with it."

So they did this, but the more they put in, the more room there seemed to be, and at last they put back all the jewels and dresses they had taken out, and Beauty even added as many more of the jewels as she could carry at once. Even then the trunks were not too full, but they were so heavy an elephant could not have carried them!

"The Beast was mocking us!" cried the merchant. "He pretended to give us all these things, knowing that I could not carry them away."

"Let us wait and see," answered Beauty. "I cannot believe he meant to deceive us. All we can do is to fasten them up and have them ready."

So they did this and returned to the little room where they found breakfast ready. The merchant ate his with a good appetite, as the Beast's generosity made him believe he might perhaps venture to come back soon and see Beauty. But she felt sure her father was leaving her forever, so she was very sad when the bell rang sharply.

They went down into the courtyard, where two horses were waiting, one loaded with the two trunks, the other for him to ride. They were pawing the ground in their impatience to start, and the merchant bade Beauty a hasty farewell. As soon as he was mounted he went off at such a pace she lost sight of him in an instant. Then Beauty began to cry and wandered sadly back to her own room. But she soon found she was very sleepy, and as she had nothing better to do she lay down and instantly fell asleep. And then she dreamed she was walking by a brook bordered with trees, and lamenting her sad fate, when a young prince, handsomer than anyone she had ever seen, and with a voice that went straight to heart, came and said to her:

"Ah, Beauty, you are not so unfortunate as you suppose. Here you will be rewarded for all you have suffered elsewhere. Your every wish shall be gratified. Only try to find me out, no matter how I may be disguised, for I love you dearly, and in making me happy you will find your own happiness. Be as true-hearted as you are beautiful, and we shall have nothing left to wish for."

"What can I do, Prince, to make you happy?" said Beauty.

"Only be grateful," he answered, "and do not trust too much to your eyes. Above all, do not desert me until you have saved me from my cruel misery."

After this she thought she found herself in a room with a stately and beautiful lady, who said to her, "Dear Beauty, try not to regret all you have left behind you; you are destined for a better fate. Only do not let yourself be deceived by appearances."

Beauty found her dreams so interesting that she was in no hurry to awake, but presently the clock roused her by calling her name softly twelve times. Then she rose and found her dressing-table set out with everything she could possibly want, and when her toilet was finished, she found dinner waiting in the room next to hers. But dinner does not take very long when one is alone, and very soon she sat down cosily in the corner of a sofa, and began to think about the charming prince she had seen in her dream.

"He said I could make him happy," said Beauty to herself. "It seems, then, that this horrible Beast keeps him a prisoner. How can I set him free? I wonder why they both told me not to trust to appearances? But, after all, it was only a dream, so why should I trouble myself about it? I had better find something to do to amuse myself."

So she began to explore some of the many rooms of the palace. The first she entered was lined with mirrors. Beauty saw herself reflected on every side and thought she had never seen such a charming room. Then a bracelet which was hanging from a chandelier caught her eye, and on taking it down she was greatly surprised to find that it held a portrait of her unknown admirer, just as she had seen him in her dream. With great delight she slipped the bracelet on her arm and went on into a gallery of pictures, where she soon found a portrait of the same handsome prince, as large as life, and so well painted that as she studied it he seemed to smile kindly at her.

Tearing herself away from the portrait at last,

she passed into a room which contained every musical instrument under the sun, and here she amused herself for a long while in trying them and singing. The next room was a library, and she saw everything she had ever wanted to read as well as everything she had read. By this time it was growing dusk, and wax candles in diamond and ruby candlesticks lit themselves in every room.

Beauty found her supper served just at the time she preferred to have it, but she did not see anyone or hear a sound, and though her father had warned her she would be alone, she began to find it rather dull.

Presently she heard the Beast coming and wondered tremblingly if he meant to eat her now. However, he did not seem at all ferocious, and only said gruffly:

"Good evening, Beauty."

She answered cheerfully and managed to conceal her terror. The Beast asked how she had been amusing herself, and she told him all the rooms she had seen. Then he asked if she thought she could be happy in his palace; and Beauty answered that everything was so beautiful she would be very hard to please if she could not be happy. After about an hour's talk Beauty began to think the Beast was not nearly so terrible as she had supposed at first. Then he rose to leave her, and said in his gruff voice:

"Do you love me, Beauty? Will you marry me?"

"Oh, what shall I say?" cried Beauty, for she was afraid to make the Beast angry by refusing.

"Say yes or no without fear," he replied.

"Oh, no, Beast," said Beauty hastily.

"Since you will not, good night, Beauty," he said.

And she answered, "Good night, Beast," very glad to find her refusal had not provoked him. After he was gone she was very soon in bed and dreaming of her unknown prince.

She thought he came and said, "Ah, Beauty! Why are you so unkind to me? I fear I am fated to be unhappy for many a long day still."

Then her dreams changed, but the charming prince figured in them all. When morning came her first thought was to look at the portrait and see if it was really like him, and she found it certainly was.

She decided to amuse herself in the garden, for the sun shone, and all the fountains were playing. She was astonished to find that every place was familiar to her, and presently she came to the very brook and the myrtle trees where she had first met the prince in her dream. That made her think more than ever he must be kept a prisoner by the Beast.

When she was tired she went back to the palace and found a new room full of materials for every kind of work—ribbons to make into bows and silks to work into flowers. There was an aviary full of rare birds, which were so tame they flew to Beauty as soon as they saw her and perched upon her shoulders and her head.

"Pretty little creatures," she said, "how I wish your cage was nearer my room that I might often hear you sing!" So saying she opened a door and found to her delight that it led into her own room, though she had thought it was on the other side of the palace.

There were more birds in a room farther on, parrots and cockatoos that could talk, and they greeted Beauty by name. Indeed, she found them so entertaining that she took one or two back to her room, and they talked to her while she was at supper. The Beast paid her his usual visit and asked the same questions as before, and then with a gruff good night he took his departure, and Beauty went to bed to dream of her mysterious prince.

The days passed swiftly in different amusements, and after a while Beauty found another strange thing in the palace, which often pleased her when she was tired of being alone. There was one room which she had not noticed particularly; it was empty, except that under each of the windows stood a very comfortable chair. The first time she had looked out of the window it seemed a black curtain prevented her from seeing anything outside. But the second time she went into the room, happening to be tired, she sat down in one of the chairs, when instantly the curtain was rolled aside, and a most amusing pantomime was acted before her. There were dances and colored lights, music and pretty dresses, and it was all so gay that Beauty was in ecstasies. After that she tried the other seven windows in turn, and there was some new and surprising entertainment to be seen from each of them so Beauty never could feel lonely any more. Every evening after supper the Beast came to see her, and always before saying good night asked here in his terrible voice:

"Beauty, will you marry me?"

And it seemed to Beauty, now she understood him better, that when she said, "No, Beast," he went away quite sad. Her happy dreams of the handsome prince soon made her forget the poor Beast, and the only thing that disturbed her was being told to distrust appearances, to let her heart guide her, and not her eyes. Consider as she would, she could not understand.

So everything went on for a long time, until at last, happy as she was, Beauty began to long for the sight of her father and her brothers and sisters. One night, seeing her look very sad, the Beast asked her what was the matter. Beauty had quite ceased to be afraid of him. Now she knew he was really gentle in spite of his ferocious looks and his dreadful voice. So she answered that she wished to see her home once more. Upon hearing this the Beast seemed sadly distressed, and cried miserably:

"Ah, Beauty, have you the heart to desert an unhappy Beast like this? What more do you want to make you happy? Is it because you hate me that you want to escape?"

"No, dear Beast," answered Beauty softly, "I do not hate you, and I should be very sorry never to see you any more, but I long to see my father again. Only let me go for two months, and I promise to come back to you and stay for the rest of my life."

The Beast, who had been sighing dolefully while she spoke, now replied, "I cannot refuse you anything you ask, even though it should cost me my life. Take the four boxes you will find in the room next to your own and fill them with everything you wish to take with you. But remember your promise and come back when the two months are over, for if you do not come in good time you will find your faithful Beast dead. You will not need any chariot to bring you back. Only say good-bye to all your brothers and sisters the night before you come away and, when you have gone to bed, turn this ring round upon your finger, and say firmly, 'I wish to go back to my palace and see my

Beast again.' Good night, Beauty. Fear nothing, sleep peacefully, and before long you shall see your father once more."

As soon as Beauty was alone she hastened to fill the boxes with all the rare and precious things she saw about her, and only when she was tired of heaping things into them did they seem to be full. Then she went to bed, but could hardly sleep for joy. When at last she began to dream of her beloved prince she was grieved to see him stretched upon a grassy bank, sad and weary, and hardly like himself.

"What is the matter?" she cried.

But he looked at her reproachfully, and said, "How can you ask me, cruel one? Are you not leaving me to my death perhaps?"

"Ah, don't be so sorrowful!" cried Beauty. "I am only going to assure my father that I am safe and happy. I have promised the Beast faithfully I will come back, and he would die of grief if I did not keep my word!"

"What would that matter to you?" asked the prince. "Surely you would not care?"

"Indeed I should be ungrateful if I did not care for such a kind beast," cried Beauty indignantly. "I would die to save him from pain. I assure you it is not his fault he is so ugly."

Just then a strange sound woke her—someone was speaking not very far away; and opening her eyes she found herself in a room she had never seen before, which was certainly not as splendid as those she had seen in the Beast's palace. Where could she be? She rose and dressed hastily and then saw that the boxes she had packed the night before were all in the room. Suddenly she heard her father's voice and rushed out to greet him joyfully. Her brothers and sisters were astonished at her appearance, for they had never expected to see her again. Beauty asked her father what he thought her strange dreams meant and why the prince constantly begged her not to trust to appearances. After much consideration he answered:

"You tell me yourself that the Beast, frightful as he is, loves you dearly and deserves your love and gratitude for his gentleness and kindness. I think the prince must mean you to understand you ought to reward him by doing as he wishes, in spite of his ugliness."

Beauty could not help seeing that this seemed

probable; still, when she thought of her dear prince who was so handsome, she did not feel at all inclined to marry the Beast. At any rate, for two months she need not decide but could enjoy herself with her sisters. Though they were rich now, and lived in a town again and had plenty of acquaintances, Beauty found that nothing amused her very much. She often thought of the palace, where she was so happy, especially as at home she never once dreamed of her dear prince, and she felt quite sad without him.

Then her sisters seemed quite used to being without her, and even found her rather in the way, so she would not have been sorry when the two months were over but for her father and brothers. She had not the courage to say good-bye to them. Every day when she rose she meant to say it at night, and when night came she put it off again, until at last she had a dismal dream which helped her to make up her mind.

She thought she was wandering in a lonely path in the palace gardens, when she heard groans. Running quickly to see what could be the matter, she found the Beast stretched out upon his side, apparently dying. He reproached her faintly with being the cause of his distress, and at the same moment a stately lady appeared, and said very gravely:

"Ah, Beauty, see what happens when people do not keep their promises! If you had delayed one day more, you would have found him dead."

Beauty was so terrified by this dream that the very next evening she said good-bye to her father and her brothers and sisters, and as soon as she was in bed she turned her ring round upon her finger, and said firmly:

"I wish to go back to my palace and see my Beast again."

Then she fell asleep instantly, and only woke up to hear the clock saying "Beauty, Beauty," twelve times in its musical voice, which told her she was really in the palace once more. Everything was just as before, and her birds were so glad to see her, but Beauty thought she had never known such a long day. She was so anxious to see the Beast again that she felt as if suppertime would never come.

But when it came no Beast appeared. After listening and waiting for a long time, she ran down into the garden to search for him. Up and down the paths and avenues ran poor Beauty, calling him. No one answered, and not a trace of him could she find. At last, she saw that she was standing opposite the shady path she had seen in her dream. She rushed down it and, sure enough, there was the cave, and in it lay the Beast—asleep, so Beauty thought. Quite glad to have found him, she ran up and stroked his head, but to her horror he did not move or open his eyes.

"Oh, he is dead, and it is all my fault!" cried Beauty, crying bitterly.

But then, looking at him again, she fancied he still breathed. Hastily fetching some water from the nearest fountain, she sprinkled it over his face, and to her great delight he began to revive.

"Oh, Beast, how you frightened me!" she cried. "I never knew how much I loved you until just now, when I feared I was too late to save your life."

"Can you really love such an ugly creature as I am?" asked the Beast faintly. "Ah, Beauty, you came only just in time. I was dying because I thought you had forgotten your promise. But go back now and rest, I shall see you again by-and-by."

Beauty, who had half expected he would be angry with her, was reassured by his gentle voice and went back to the palace, where supper was awaiting her. And afterward the Beast came in as usual and talked about the time she had spent with her father, asking if she had enjoyed herself and if they had all been glad to see her.

Beauty quite enjoyed telling him all that had happened to her. When at last the time came for him to go, he asked, as he had so often asked before:

"Beauty, will you marry me?"

She answered softly, "Yes, dear Beast."

As she spoke a blaze of light sprang up before the windows of the palace; fireworks crackled and guns banged, and across the avenue of orange trees, in letters all made of fireflies, was written: *Long live the prince and his bride.*

Turning to ask the Beast what it could all mean, Beauty found he had disappeared, and in his place stood her long-loved prince!

At the same moment the wheels of a chariot were heard upon the terrace, and two ladies entered the room. One of them Beauty recognized as the stately lady she had seen in her dreams; the other was so queenly that Beauty hardly knew which to greet first. But the one she already knew said to her companion:

"Well, Queen, this is Beauty, who has had the courage to rescue your son from the terrible enchantment. They love each other, and only your consent to their marriage is wanting to make them perfectly happy."

"I consent with all my heart," cried the queen. "How can I ever thank you enough, charming girl, for having restored my dear son to his natural form?" And then she tenderly embraced Beauty and the prince, who had meanwhile been greeting the fairy and receiving her congratulations.

"Now," said the fairy to Beauty, "I suppose you would like me to send for all your brothers and sisters to dance at your wedding?"

And so she did, and the marriage was celebrated the very next day with the utmost splendor, and Beauty and the prince lived happily ever after.

Toads and Diamonds

In this, one of the most popular fairy tales, we find several motifs: the abused child, a fairy, and kindness begetting kindness—all topped by poetic justice. This version, by Andrew Lang, shows the attention to detail and the swelling cadences that distinguish his Victorian series of colored fairy books. [From Andrew Lang, *The Blue Fairy Book* (Longmans, 1889).]

There was once upon a time a widow who had two daughters. The eldest was so much like her in the face and humour that whoever looked upon the daughter saw the mother. They were both so disagreeable and so proud that there was no living with them.

The youngest, who was the very picture of her father for courtesy and sweetness of temper, was withal one of the most beautiful girls ever seen. As people naturally love their own likeness, this mother even doted on her eldest

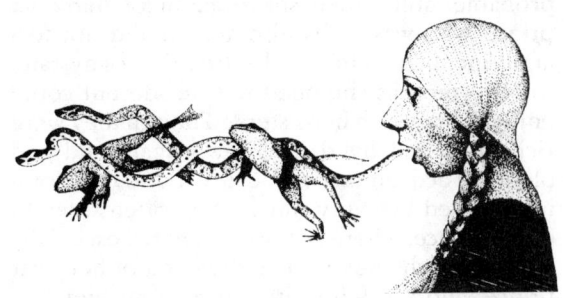

Illustration © 1977 by Martin Ware, from *The Fairy Tales of Charles Perrault,* translated by Angela Carter. Reproduced by permission of Victor Gollancz Ltd.

daughter, and at the same time had a horrible aversion for the youngest—she made her eat in the kitchen and work continually.

Among other things, this poor child was forced twice a day to draw water above a mile and a-half off the house, and bring home a pitcher full of it. One day, as she was at this fountain, there came to her a poor woman, who begged of her to let her drink.

"Oh! ay, with all my heart, Goody," said this pretty little girl; and rinsing immediately the pitcher, she took up some water from the clearest place of the fountain, and gave it to her, holding up the pitcher all the while, that she might drink the easier.

The good woman having drunk, said to her:

"You are so very pretty, my dear, so good and so mannerly, that I cannot help giving you a gift." For this was a fairy, who had taken the form of a poor country-woman, to see how far the civility and good manners of this pretty girl would go. "I will give you for gift," continued the Fairy, "that, at every word you speak, there shall come out of your mouth either a flower or a jewel."

When this pretty girl came home her mother scolded at her for staying so long at the fountain.

"I beg your pardon, mamma," said the poor girl, "for not making more haste."

And in speaking these words there came out of her mouth two roses, two pearls, and two diamonds.

"What is it I see there?" said her mother, quite astonished. "I think I see pearls and diamonds come out of the girl's mouth! How happens this, child?"

This was the first time she ever called her child.

The poor creature told her frankly all the matter, not without dropping out infinite numbers of diamonds.

"In good faith," cried the mother, "I must send my child thither. Come hither, Fanny; look what comes out of thy sister's mouth when she speaks. Wouldst not thou be glad, my dear, to have the same gift given to thee? Thou hast nothing else to do but go and draw water out of the fountain, and when a certain poor woman asks you to let her drink, to give it her very civilly."

"It would be a very fine sight indeed," said this ill-bred minx, "to see me go draw water."

"You shall go, hussey!" said the mother; "and this minute."

So away she went, but grumbling all the way, taking with her the best silver tankard in the house.

She was no sooner at the fountain than she saw coming out of the wood a lady most gloriously dressed, who came up to her, and asked to drink. This was, you must know, the very fairy who appeared to her sister, but had now taken the air and dress of a princess, to see how far this girl's rudeness would go.

"Am I come hither," said the proud, saucy slut, "to serve you with water, pray? I suppose the silver tankard was brought purely for your ladyship, was it? However, you may drink out of it, if you have a fancy."

"You are not over and above mannerly," answered the Fairy, without putting herself in a passion. "Well, then, since you have so little breeding, and are so disobliging, I give you for gift that at every word you speak there shall come out of your mouth a snake or a toad."

So soon as her mother saw her coming she cried out:

"Well, daughter?"

"Well, mother?" answered the pert hussey, throwing out of her mouth two vipers and two toads.

"Oh! mercy," cried the mother; "what is it I see? Oh! it is that wretch her sister who has occasioned all this; but she shall pay for it";

and immediately she ran to beat her. The poor child fled away from her, and went to hide herself in the forest, not far from thence.

The King's son, then on his return from hunting, met her, and seeing her so very pretty, asked her what she did there alone and why she cried.

"Alas! sir, my mamma has turned me out of doors."

The King's son, who saw five or six pearls and as many diamonds come out of her mouth, desired her to tell him how that happened. She hereupon told him the whole story; and so the King's son fell in love with her, and, considering with himself that such a gift was worth more than any marriage portion, conducted her to the palace of the King his father, and there married her.

As for her sister, she made herself so much hated that her own mother turned her off; and the miserable wretch, having wandered about a good while without finding anybody to take her in, went to a corner of the wood, and there died.

England

The Story of the Three Little Pigs

Once again the wolf is the villain animal in this beast tale that has always been a favorite with children. With its use of repetition, rhyme, and onomatopoeic words in building to a quick, dramatic climax, the story lends itself well to storytelling. Children accept the logical justice of the outcome, since the wolf meets an end similar to that of his victims. [From Joseph Jacobs, *English Fairy Tales* (Putnam's, 1892).]

Once upon a time when pigs spoke rhyme
And monkeys chewed tobacco,
And hens took snuff to make them tough,
And ducks went quack, quack, quack, O!

There was an old sow with three little pigs, and as she had not enough to keep them, she sent them out to seek their fortune. The first that went off met a man with a bundle of straw, and said to him,

"Please, man, give me that straw to build me a house."

Which the man did, and the little pig built a house with it. Presently came along a wolf, and knocked at the door, and said,

"Little pig, little pig, let me come in."

To which the pig answered,

"No, no, by the hair of my chiny chin chin."

The wolf then answered to that,

"Then I'll huff, and I'll puff, and I'll blow your house in."

So he huffed, and he puffed, and he blew his house in, and ate up the little pig.

The second little pig met a man with a bundle of furze and said,

"Please, man, give me that furze to build a house."

Which the man did, and the pig built his house. Then along came the wolf, and said,

"Little pig, little pig, let me come in."

"No, no, by the hair of my chiny chin chin."

"Then I'll puff, and I'll huff, and I'll blow your house in."

So he huffed, and he puffed, and he puffed and he huffed, and at last he blew the house down, and he ate up the little pig.

The third little pig met a man with a load of bricks, and said,

"Please, man, give me those bricks to build a house with."

So the man gave him the bricks, and he built his house with them. So the wolf came, as he did to the other little pigs, and said,

"Little pig, little pig, let me come in."

"No, no, by the hair on my chiny chin chin."

"Then I'll huff, and I'll puff, and I'll blow your house in."

Well, he huffed, and he puffed, and he huffed and he puffed, and he puffed and huffed; but could *not* get the house down. When he found that he could not, with all his huffing and puffing, blow the house down, he said,

"Little pig, I know where there is a nice field of turnips."

"Where?" said the little pig.

"Oh, in Mr. Smith's home-field, and if you will be ready tomorrow morning I will call for you, and we will go together, and get some for dinner."

"Very well," said the little pig, "I will be ready. What time do you mean to go?"

"Oh, at six o'clock."

Well, the little pig got up at five and got the turnips before the wolf came (which he did about six), who said,

"Little pig, are you ready?"

The little pig said, "Ready! I have been and come back again and got a nice potful for dinner."

The wolf felt very angry at this, but thought that he would be up to the little pig somehow or other, so he said,

"Little pig, I know where there is a nice apple-tree."

"Where?" said the pig.

"Down at Merry-Garden," replied the wolf, "and if you will not deceive me, I will come for you at five o'clock tomorrow and get some apples."

Well, the little pig bustled up the next morning at four o'clock, and went off for the apples, hoping to get back before the wolf came; but he had farther to go and had to climb the tree, so that just as he was coming down from it, he saw the wolf coming, which, as you may suppose, frightened him very much. When the wolf came up he said:

"Little pig, what! are you here before me? Are they nice apples?"

"Yes, very," said the little pig. "I will throw you down one."

And he threw it so far, that, while the wolf was gone to pick it up, the little pig jumped down and ran home. The next day the wolf came again and said to the little pig,

"Little pig, there is a fair at Shanklin this afternoon; will you go?"

"Oh, yes," said the pig, "I will go; what time shall you be ready?"

"At three," said the wolf. So the little pig went off before the time as usual and got to the fair and bought a butter-churn, which he was going home with, when he saw the wolf coming. Then he could not tell what to do. So he got into the churn to hide, and by so doing turned it round, and it rolled down the hill with the pig in it, which frightened the wolf so much, that he ran home without going to the fair. He went to the little pig's house and told him how frightened he had been by a great round thing which came down the hill past him. Then the little pig said,

"Hah, I frightened you then. I had been to the fair and bought a butter-churn; and when I saw you, I got into it, and rolled down the hill."

The wolf was very angry indeed and declared he *would* eat up the little pig, and that he would get down the chimney after him. When the little pig saw what he was about, he hung on the pot full of water and made up a blazing fire and, just as the wolf was coming down, took off the cover and in fell the wolf; so the little pig put on the cover again in an instant, boiled him up, and ate him for supper and lived happy ever afterwards.

The Old Woman and Her Pig

A cumulative tale that has a quick unwinding after a slow build-up. [From Joseph Jacobs, *English Fairy Tales* (Putnam's, 1892).]

An old woman was sweeping her house, and she found a little crooked sixpence. "What," said she, "shall I do with this little sixpence? I will go to market, and buy a little pig."

As she was coming home, she came to a stile: but the piggy wouldn't go over the stile.

She went a little further, and she met a dog. So she said to him: "Dog! dog! bite pig; piggy won't go over the stile; and I shan't get home tonight." But the dog wouldn't.

She went a little further, and she met a stick. So she said: "Stick! stick! beat dog! dog won't bite pig; piggy won't get over the stile; and I shan't get home tonight." But the stick wouldn't.

She went a little further, and she met a fire. So she said: "Fire! fire! burn stick; stick won't beat dog; dog won't bite pig; piggy won't get over the stile; and I shan't get home tonight." But the fire wouldn't.

She went a little further, and she met some water. So she said: "Water! water! quench fire; fire won't burn stick; stick won't beat dog; dog won't bite pig; piggy won't get over the stile; and I shan't get home tonight." But the water wouldn't.

She went a little further, and she met an ox. So she said: "Ox! ox! drink water; water won't quench fire; fire won't burn stick; stick won't beat dog; dog won't bite pig; piggy won't get over the stile; and I shan't get home tonight." But the ox wouldn't.

She went a little further, and she met a butcher. So she said: "Butcher! butcher! kill ox; ox won't drink water; water won't quench fire; fire won't burn stick; stick won't beat dog; dog won't bite pig; piggy won't get over the stile; and I shan't get home tonight." But the butcher wouldn't.

She went a little further, and she met a rope. So she said: "Rope! rope! hang butcher; butcher won't kill ox; ox won't drink water; water won't quench fire; fire won't burn stick; stick won't beat dog; dog won't bite pig; piggy won't get over the stile; and I shan't get home tonight." But the rope wouldn't.

She went a little further, and she met a rat. So she said: "Rat! rat! gnaw rope; rope won't hang butcher; butcher won't kill ox; ox won't drink water; water won't quench fire; fire won't burn stick; stick won't beat dog; dog won't bite pig; piggy won't get over the stile; and I shan't get home tonight." But the rat wouldn't.

She went a little further, and she met a cat. So she said: "Cat! cat! kill rat; rat won't gnaw rope; rope won't hang butcher; butcher won't kill ox; ox won't drink water; water won't quench fire; fire won't burn stick; stick won't beat dog; dog won't bite pig; piggy won't get over the stile; and I shan't get home tonight." But the cat said to her, "If you will go to yonder cow, and fetch me a saucer of milk, I will kill the rat." So away went the old woman to the cow.

But the cow said to her: "If you will go to yonder hay-stack and fetch me a handful of hay, I'll give you the milk." So away went the old woman to the hay-stack; and she brought the hay to the cow.

As soon as the cow had eaten the hay, she gave the old woman the milk; and away she went with it in a saucer to the cat.

As soon as the cat had lapped up the milk, the cat began to kill the rat; the rat began to gnaw the rope; the rope began to hang the butcher; the butcher began to kill the ox; the ox began to drink the water; the water began to quench the fire; the fire began to burn the stick; the stick began to beat the dog; the dog began to bite the pig; the little pig in a fright jumped over the stile; and so the old woman got home that night.

Henny-Penny

Henny-Penny (or *Chicken-Little,* as it is sometimes called), a more consistently cumulative beast tale, is also repetitive. Practically the same story is told under the title "Chicken-Licken" and in "The Hare that Ran Away." [From Joseph Jacobs, *English Fairy Tales* (Putnam's, 1892).]

One day Henny-Penny was picking up corn in the cornyard when—whack!—something hit her upon the head. "Goodness gracious me!" said Henny-Penny; "the sky's a-going to fall; I must go and tell the king."

So she went along, and she went along, and she went along till she met Cocky-Locky. "Where are you going, Henny-Penny?" says Cocky-Locky. "Oh! I'm going to tell the king the sky's a-falling," says Henny-Penny. "May I come with you?" says Cocky-Locky. "Certainly," says Henny-Penny. So Henny-Penny and Cocky-Locky went to tell the king the sky was falling.

They went along, and they went along, and they went along till they met Ducky-Daddles. "Where are you going to, Henny-Penny and Cocky-Locky?" says Ducky-Daddles. "Oh! we're going to tell the king the sky's a-falling." said Henny-Penny and Cocky-Locky. "May I come with you?" says Ducky-Daddles. "Certainly," said Henny-Penny and Cocky-Locky. So Henny-Penny, Cocky-Locky, and Ducky-Daddles went to tell the king the sky was a-falling.

So they went along, and they went along, and they went along, till they met Goosey-Poosey. "Where are you going to, Henny-Penny, Cocky-Locky, and Ducky-Daddles?" said Goosey-Poosey. "Oh! we're going to tell the king the sky's a-falling," said Henny-Penny and Cocky-Locky and Ducky-Daddles. "May I come with you?" said Goosey-Poosey. "Certainly," said Henny-Penny, Cocky-Locky, and Ducky-Daddles. So Henny-Penny, Cocky-Locky, Ducky-Daddles, and Goosey-Poosey went to tell the king the sky was a-falling.

So they went along, and they went along, and they went along, till they met Turkey-Lurkey. "Where are you going, Henny-Penny, Cocky-Locky, Ducky-Daddles, and Goosey-Poosey?" says Turkey-Lurkey. "Oh! we're going to tell the king the sky's a-falling," said Henny-Penny, Cocky-Locky, Ducky-Daddles, and Goosey-Poosey. "May I come with you, Henny-Penny, Cocky-Locky, Ducky-Daddles, and Goosey-Poosey?" said Turkey-Lurkey. "Oh, certainly, Turkey-Lurkey," said Henny-Penny, Cocky-Locky, Ducky-Daddles, and Goosey-Poosey. So Henny-Penny, Cocky-Locky, Ducky-Daddles, Goosey-Poosey, and Turkey-Lurkey all went to tell the king the sky was a-falling.

So they went along, and they went along, and they went along, till they met Foxy-Woxy; and Foxy-Woxy said to Henny-Penny, Cocky-Locky, Ducky-Daddles, Goosey-Poosey, and Turkey-Lurkey: "Where are you going, Henny-Penny, Cocky-Locky, Ducky-Daddles, Goosey-Poosey, and Turkey-Lurkey?" And Henny-Penny, Cocky-Locky, Ducky-Daddles, Goosey-Poosey, and Turkey-Lurkey said to Foxy-Woxy: "We're going to tell the king the sky's a-falling." "Oh! but this is not the way to the king, Henny-Penny, Cocky-Locky, Ducky-Daddles, Goosey-Poosey, and Turkey-Lurkey," says Foxy-Woxy; "I know the proper way; shall I show it to you?" "Oh, certainly, Foxy-Woxy," said Henny-Penny, Cocky-Locky, Ducky-Daddles, Goosey-Poosey, and Turkey-Lurkey. So Henny-Penny, Cocky-Locky, Ducky-Daddles, Goosey-Poosey, and Turkey-Lurkey, and Foxy-Woxy all went to tell the king the sky was a-falling.

So they went along, and they went along, and they went along, till they came to a narrow and dark hole. Now this was the door of Foxy-Woxy's cave. But Foxy-Woxy said to Henny-Penny, Cocky-Locky, Ducky-Daddles, Goosey-

Poosey, and Turkey-Lurkey: "This is the short way to the king's palace; you'll soon get there if you follow me. I will go first and you come after, Henny-Penny, Cocky-Locky, Ducky-Daddles, Goosey-Poosey, and Turkey-Lurkey." "Why of course, certainly, without doubt, why not?" said Henny-Penny, Cocky-Locky, Ducky-Daddles, Goosey-Poosey, and Turkey-Lurkey.

So Foxy-Woxy went into his cave, and he didn't go very far, but turned around to wait for Henny-Penny, Cocky-Locky, Ducky-Daddles, Goosey-Poosey, and Turkey-Lurkey. So at last at first Turkey-Lurkey went through the dark hole into the cave. He hadn't got far when "Hrumph," Foxy-Woxy snapped off Turkey-Lurkey's head and threw his body over his left shoulder. Then Goosey-Poosey went in, and "Hrumph," off went her head and Goosey-Poosey was thrown beside Turkey-Lurkey. Then Ducky-Daddles waddled down, and "Hrumph," snapped Foxy-Woxy, and Ducky-Daddles' head was off and Ducky-Daddles was thrown alongside Turkey-Lurkey and Goosey-Poosey. Then Cocky-Locky strutted down into the cave, and he hadn't gone far when "Snap, Hrumph!" went Foxy-Woxy and Cocky-Locky was thrown alongside of Turkey-Lurkey, Goosey-Poosey, and Ducky-Daddles.

But Foxy-Woxy had made two bites at Cocky-Locky; and when the first snap only hurt Cocky-Locky but didn't kill him, he called out to Henny-Penny. But she turned tail and off she ran home; so she never told the king the sky was a-falling.

Jack and the Beanstalk

This story is often classified as a droll, that is, a story of the blunders, often comic in character, of a stupid person. Compare this with "The Bee, the Harp, the Mouse, and the Bum-Clock." [From Joseph Jacobs, *English Fairy Tales* (Putnam's, 1892).]

There was once upon a time a poor widow who had an only son named Jack and a cow named Milky-White. And all they had to live on was the milk the cow gave every morning, which they carried to the market and sold. But one morning Milky-White gave no milk, and they didn't know what to do.

"What shall we do, what shall we do?" said the widow, wringing her hands.

"Cheer up, mother, I'll go and get work somewhere," said Jack.

"We've tried that before, and nobody would take you," said his mother; "we must sell Milky-White and with the money start a shop or something."

"All right, mother," says Jack; "it's market-day today, and I'll soon sell Milky-White, and then we'll see what we can do."

So he took the cow's halter in his hand, and off he started. He hadn't gone far when he met a funny-looking old man, who said to him: "Good morning, Jack."

"Good morning to you," said Jack, and wondered how he knew his name.

"Well, Jack, and where are you off to?" said the man.

"I'm going to market to sell our cow here."

"Oh, you look the proper sort of chap to sell cows," said the man; "I wonder if you know how many beans make five."

"Two in each hand and one in your mouth," says Jack, as sharp as a needle.

"Right you are," says the man, "and here they are, the very beans themselves," he went on, pulling out of his pocket a number of strange-looking beans. "As you are so sharp," says he, "I don't mind doing a swop with you—your cow for these beans."

"Go along," says Jack; "wouldn't you like it?"

"Ah! you don't know what these beans are," said the man; "if you plant them overnight, by morning they grow right up to the sky."

"Really?" said Jack; "you don't say so."

"Yes, that is so, and if it doesn't turn out to be true you can have your cow back."

"Right," says Jack, and hands him over Milky-White's halter and pockets the beans.

Back goes Jack home, and as he hadn't gone very far, it wasn't dusk by the time he got to his door.

"Back already, Jack?" said his mother; "I see you haven't got Milky-White, so you've sold her. How much did you get for her?"

"You'll never guess, mother," says Jack.

"No, you don't say so. Good boy! Five pounds, ten, fifteen, no, it can't be twenty."

"I told you you couldn't guess. What do you say to these beans; they're magical, plant them over-night and—"

"What!" says Jack's mother, "have you been such a fool, such a dolt, such an idiot, as to give away my Milky-White, the best milker in the parish, and prime beef to boot, for a set of paltry beans? Take that! Take that! Take that! And as for your precious beans here they go out of the window. And now off with you to bed. Not a sup shall you drink, and not a bit shall you swallow this very night."

So Jack went upstairs to his little room in the attic, and sad and sorry he was, to be sure, as much for his mother's sake, as for the loss of his supper.

At last he dropped off to sleep.

When he woke up, the room looked so funny. The sun was shining into part of it, and yet all the rest was quite dark and shady. So Jack jumped up and dressed himself and went to the window. And what do you think he saw? Why, the beans his mother had thrown out of the window into the garden had sprung up into a big beanstalk, which went up and up and up till it reached the sky. So the man spoke truth after all.

The beanstalk grew up quite close past Jack's window; so all he had to do was to open it and give a jump on to the beanstalk which ran up just like a big ladder. So Jack climbed, and he climbed, and he climbed, and he climbed, and he climbed, and he climbed, and he climbed till at last he reached the sky. And when he got there he found a long broad road going as straight as a dart. So he walked along, and he walked along, and he walked along till he came to a great big tall house, and on the doorstep there was a great big tall woman.

"Good morning, mum," says Jack, quite polite-like. "Could you be so kind as to give me some breakfast?" For he hadn't had anything to eat, you know, the night before, and was as hungry as a hunter.

"It's breakfast you want, is it?" says the great big tall woman, "It's breakfast you'll be if you don't move off from here. My man is an ogre and there's nothing he likes better than boys broiled on toast. You'd better be moving on or he'll soon be coming."

"Oh! please mum, do give me something to eat, mum. I've had nothing to eat since yesterday morning, really and truly, mum," says Jack. "I may as well be broiled as die of hunger."

Well, the ogre's wife was not half so bad after all. So she took Jack into the kitchen and gave him a chunk of bread and cheese and a jug of milk. But Jack hadn't half finished these when thump! thump! thump! the whole house began to tremble with the noise of someone coming.

"Goodness gracious me! It's my old man," said the ogre's wife, "what on earth shall I do? Come along quick and jump in here." And she bundled Jack into the oven just as the ogre came in.

He was a big one, to be sure. At his belt he had three calves strung up by the heels, and he unhooked them and threw them down on the table and said: "Here, wife, broil me a couple of these for breakfast. Ah! what's this I smell?

"Fee-fi-fo-fum,
I smell the blood of an Englishman,
Be he alive, or be he dead
I'll have his bones to grind my bread."

"Nonsense, dear," said his wife, "you're dreaming. Or perhaps you smell the scraps of that little boy you liked so much for yesterday's dinner. Here, you go and have a wash and tidy up, and by the time you come back your breakfast'll be ready for you."

So off the ogre went, and Jack was just going to jump out of the oven and run away when the woman told him not. "Wait till he's asleep," says she; "he always has a doze after breakfast."

Well, the ogre had his breakfast, and after that he goes to a big chest and takes out of it a couple of bags of gold, and down he sits and counts till at last his head began to nod, and he began to snore till the whole house shook again.

Then Jack crept out on tiptoe from his oven, and as he was passing the ogre he took one of the bags of gold under his arm, and off he pelters till he came to the beanstalk, and then he threw down the bag of gold, which of course fell into his mother's garden, and then he climbed down, and climbed down till at last he got home and told his mother and showed her the gold and said, "Well, mother, wasn't I right about the beans? They are really magical, you see."

So they lived on the bag of gold for some time, but at last they came to the end of it, and Jack made up his mind to try his luck once more up at the top of the beanstalk. So one fine morning he rose up early, and got on to the beanstalk, and he climbed, and he climbed, and he climbed, and he climbed, and he climbed, and he climbed till at last he came out on to the road again and up to the great big tall house he had been to before. There, sure enough, was the great big tall woman a-standing on the doorstep.

"Good morning, mum," says Jack, as bold as brass, "could you be so good as to give me something to eat?"

"Go away, my boy," said the big tall woman, "or else my man will eat you up for breakfast. But aren't you the youngster who came here once before? Do you know, that very day, my man missed one of his bags of gold."

"That's strange, mum," said Jack, "I dare say I could tell you something about that; but I'm so hungry I can't speak till I've had something to eat."

Well, the big tall woman was so curious that she took him in and gave him something to eat. But he had scarcely begun munching it as slowly as he could when thump! thump! thump! they heard the giant's footstep, and his wife hid Jack away in the oven.

All happened as it did before. In came the ogre as he did before, said: "Fee-fi-fo-fum," and had his breakfast of three broiled oxen. Then he said: "Wife, bring me the hen that lays the golden eggs." So she brought it, and the ogre said: "Lay," and it laid an egg all of gold. And then the ogre began to nod his head and to snore till the house shook.

Then Jack crept out of the oven on tiptoe and caught hold of the golden hen and was off before you could say "Jack Robinson." But this time the hen gave a cackle which woke the ogre, and just as Jack got out of the house he heard him calling: "Wife, wife, what have you done with my golden hen?"

And the wife said: "Why, my dear?"

But that was all Jack heard, for he rushed off to the beanstalk and climbed down like a house on fire. And when he got home he showed his mother the wonderful hen, and said "Lay" to it; and it laid a golden egg every time he said, "Lay."

Well, Jack was not content, and it wasn't very long before he determined to have another try at his luck up there at the top of the beanstalk. So one fine morning, he rose up early and got on to the beanstalk, and he climbed, and he climbed, and he climbed, and he climbed till he got to the top. But this time he knew better than to go straight to the ogre's house. And when he got near it, he waited behind a bush till he saw the ogre's wife come out with a pail to get some water, and then he crept into the house and got into the copper. He hadn't been there long before he heard thump! thump! thump! as before, and in came the ogre and his wife.

"Fee-fi-fo-fum, I smell the blood of an Englishman," cried out the ogre. "I smell him, wife, I smell him."

"Do you, my dearie?" says the ogre's wife. "Then, if it's that little rogue that stole your gold and the hen that laid the golden eggs he's sure to have got into the oven." And they both rushed to the oven. But Jack wasn't there, luckily, and the ogre's wife said: "There you are again with your fee-fi-fo-fum. Why of course it's the boy caught last night that I've just broiled for your breakfast. How forgetful I am, and how careless you are not to know the difference between live and dead after all these years."

So the ogre sat down to the breakfast and ate it, but every now and then he would mutter: "Well, I could have sworn—" and he'd get up and search the larder and the cupboards and everything, only, luckily, he didn't think of the copper.

After breakfast was over, the ogre called out, "Wife, wife, bring me my golden harp." So she brought it and put it on the table before him. Then he said: "Sing!" and the golden harp sang most beautifully. And it went on singing till the ogre fell asleep and commenced to snore like thunder.

Then Jack lifted up the copper-lid very quietly

and got down like a mouse and crept on hands and knees till he came to the table, when up he crawled, caught hold of the golden harp and dashed with it towards the door. But the harp called out quite loud: "Master! Master!" and the ogre woke up just in time to see Jack running off with his harp.

Jack ran as fast as he could, and the ogre came rushing after and would soon have caught him only Jack had a start and dodged him a bit and knew where he was going. When he got to the beanstalk the ogre was not more than twenty yards away when suddenly he saw Jack disappear like, and when he came to the end of the road he saw Jack underneath climbing down for dear life. Well, the ogre didn't like trusting himself to such a ladder, and he stood and waited; so Jack got another start. But just then the harp cried out: "Master! Master!" and the ogre swung himself down on to the beanstalk, which shook with his weight. Down climbs Jack, and after him climbed the ogre. By this time Jack had climbed down, and climbed down, and climbed down till he was very nearly home. So he called out: "Mother! Mother! bring me an axe; bring me an axe." And his mother came rushing out with the axe in her hand, but when she came to the beanstalk she stood stock still with fright, for there she saw the ogre with his legs just through the clouds.

But Jack jumped down and got hold of the axe and gave a chop at the beanstalk which cut it half in two. The ogre felt the beanstalk shake and quiver, so he stopped to see what was the matter. Then Jack gave another chop with the axe, and the beanstalk was cut in two and began to topple over. Then the ogre fell down and broke his crown, and the beanstalk came toppling after.

Then Jack showed his mother his golden harp, and what with showing that and selling the golden eggs Jack and his mother became very rich, and he married a great princess, and they lived happy ever after.

Molly Whuppie

A rare tale this, distinguished by the fact that the youngest child who outwits the giant and wins a king-dom is a girl. There is a rich mixture of motifs here: the deception of the giant's wife by the bag trick, the stealing of objects from the giant—these echo and re-echo through tale after tale. The incident of changing night dresses, or necklaces, goes back to an ancient Greek source.

The storyteller will discover that this version comes ready for the telling. It appeals to well-nigh every age and is pleasurable to know, with its image of the bridge of one hair and its refrains: "Woe worth ye, Molly Whuppie" and "Twice yet, carle, I'll come to Spain." [From Joseph Jacobs, *English Fairy Tales* (Putnam's, 1892).]

Once upon a time there was a man and a wife had too many children, and they could not get meat for them, so they took the three youngest and left them in a wood. They travelled and travelled and could see never a house. It began to be dark, and they were hungry. At last they saw a light and made for it; it turned out to be a house. They knocked at the door, and a woman came to it, who said: "What do you want?" They said: "Please let us in and give us something to eat." The woman said: "I can't do that, as my man is a giant, and he would kill you if he comes home." They begged hard. "Let us stop for a little while," said they, "and we will go away before he comes." So she took them in, and set them down before the fire, and gave them milk and bread; but just as they had begun to eat, a great knock came to the door, and a dreadful voice said:

"Fee, fie, fo, fum,
I smell the blood of some earthly one."

"Who have you there, wife?" "Eh," said the wife, "it's three poor lassies cold and hungry, and they will go away. Ye won't touch 'em, man." He said nothing, but ate up a big supper, and ordered them to stay all night. Now he had three lassies of his own, and they were to sleep in the same bed with the three strangers. The youngest of the three strange lassies was called Molly Whuppie, and she was very clever. She noticed that before they went to bed the giant put straw ropes round her neck and her sisters', and round his own lassies' necks, he put gold chains. So Molly took care and did not fall asleep, but waited till she was sure every

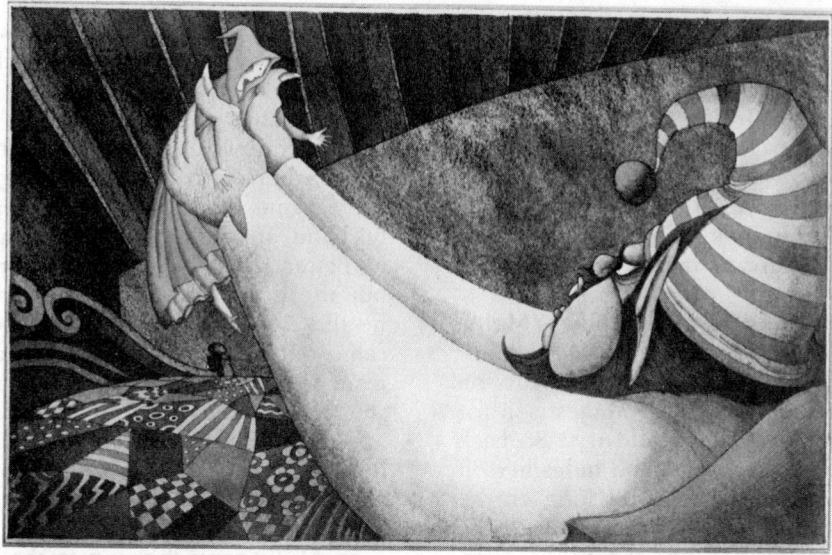

one was sleeping sound. Then she slipped out of the bed, and took the straw ropes off her own and her sisters' necks, and took the gold chains off the giant's lassies. She put the straw ropes on the giant's lassies and the gold chains on herself and her sisters, and lay down. And in the middle of the night up rose the giant, armed with a great club, and felt for the necks with the straw. It was dark. He took his own lassies out of bed on to the floor, and battered them until they were dead, and then lay down again, thinking he had managed finely. Molly thought it time she and her sisters were off and away, so she wakened them and told them to be quiet, and they slipped out of the house. They all got out safe, and they ran and ran, and never stopped until morning, when they saw a grand house before them. It turned out to be a king's house: so Molly went in, and told her story to the king. He said: "Well, Molly, you are a clever girl, and you have managed well; but, if you would manage better, and go back, and steal the giant's sword that hangs on the back of his bed, I would give your eldest sister my eldest son to marry." Molly

said she would try. So she went back, and managed to slip into the giant's house, and crept in below the bed. The giant came home, and ate up a great supper, and went to bed. Molly waited until he was snoring, and she crept out, and reached over the giant and got down the sword; but just as she got it out over the bed it gave a rattle, and up jumped the giant, and Molly ran out at the door and the sword with her; and she ran, and he ran, till they came to the "Bridge of one hair"; and she got over, but he couldn't, and he says, "Woe worth ye, Molly Whuppie! never ye come again." And she says: "Twice yet, carle, I'll come to Spain." So Molly took the sword to the king, and her sister was married to his son.

Well, the king he says: "Ye've managed well, Molly; but if ye would manage better, and steal the purse that lies below the giant's pillow, I would marry your second sister to my second son." And Molly said she would try. So she set out for the giant's house, and slipped in, and hid again below the bed, and waited till the giant had eaten his supper, and was snoring sound asleep. She slipped out and slipped her hand below the pillow, and got out the purse; but just as she was going out the giant wakened, and ran after her; and she ran, and he ran, till they came to the "Bridge of one hair," and she got over, but he couldn't and he said, "Woe worth ye, Molly Whuppie! never you come again." Once yet, carle," quoth she, "I'll come to Spain." So Molly took the purse to the king, and her second sister was married to the king's second son.

After that the king says to Molly: "Molly, you are a clever girl, but if you would do better yet, and steal the giant's ring that he wears on his finger, I will give you my youngest son for yourself." Molly said she would try. So back she goes to the giant's house, and hides herself below the bed. The giant wasn't long ere he came home, and, after he had eaten a great big supper, he went to his bed, and shortly was snoring loud. Molly crept out and reached over the bed, and got hold of the giant's hand, and she pulled and she pulled until she got off the ring; but just as she got it off the giant got up, and gripped her by the hand and he says, "Now I have caught you, Molly Whuppie, and, if I had done as much ill to you as ye have done to me, what would ye do to me?"

Molly says: "I would put you into a sack, and I'd put the cat inside wi' you, and the dog aside you, and a needle and thread and a shears and I'd hang you up upon the wall, and I'd go to the wood, and choose the thickest stick I could get, and I would come home, and take you down, and bang you till you were dead."

"Well, Molly," says the giant, "I'll just do that to you."

So he gets a sack, and puts Molly into it, and the cat and the dog beside her, and a needle and thread and shears, and hangs her up upon the wall, and goes to the wood to choose a stick.

Molly she sings out: "Oh, if ye saw what I see."

"Oh," says the giant's wife, "what do ye see, Molly?"

But Molly never said a word but, "Oh, if ye saw what I see!"

The giant's wife begged that Molly would take her up into the sack till she would see what Molly saw. So Molly took the shears and cut a hole in the sack, and took out the needle and

thread with her, and jumped down and helped the giant's wife up into the sack, and sewed up the hole.

The giant's wife saw nothing, and began to ask to get down again; but Molly never minded, but hid herself at the back of the door. Home again came the giant, and a great big tree in his hand, and he took down the sack, and began to batter it. His wife cried, "It's me, man"; but the dog barked and the cat mewed, and he did not know his wife's voice. But Molly came out from the back of the door, and the giant saw her and he after her; and he ran, and she ran, till they came to the "Bridge of one hair," and she got over but he couldn't; and he said, "Woe worth you, Molly Whuppie! never you come again." "Never more, carle," quoth she, "will I come again to Spain."

So Molly took the ring to the king, and she was married to his youngest son, and she never saw the giant again.

The Three Sillies

The Three Sillies is the most enduring of the drolls, the numskull stories. Stith Thompson says that it is told "in all parts of Europe and well out into Siberia. Versions apparently based upon English originals have been found in Virginia, and close parallels exist in Africa." For the storyteller, this story catches the interest of the wise and foolish of all ages. It is basic to any repertory. [From Joseph Jacobs, *English Fairy Tales* (Putnam's, 1892).]

Once upon a time there was a farmer and his wife who had one daughter, and she was courted by a gentleman. Every evening he used to come and see her, and stop to supper at the farmhouse, and the daughter used to be sent down into the cellar to draw the beer for supper. So one evening she had gone down to draw the beer, and she happened to look up at the ceiling while she was drawing, and she saw a mallet stuck in one of the beams. It must have been there a long, long time, but somehow or other she had never noticed it before, and she began a-thinking. And she thought it was very dangerous to have that mallet there, for she said to herself: "Suppose him and me was to be married, and we was to have a son, and he was to grow up to be a man, and come down into the cellar to draw the beer, like as I'm doing now, and the mallet was to fall on his head and kill him, what a dreadful thing it would be!" And she put down the candle and the jug, and sat herself down and began a-crying.

Well, they began to wonder upstairs how it was that she was so long drawing the beer, and her mother went down to see after her, and she found her sitting on the settle crying, and the beer running over the floor. "Why, whatever is the matter?" said her mother. "Oh, mother!" says she, "look at that horrid mallet! Suppose we was to be married, and was to have a son, and he was to grow up, and was to come down to the cellar to draw the beer, and the mallet was to fall on his head and kill him, what a dreadful thing it would be!" "Dear, dear! what a dreadful thing it would be!" said the mother, and she sat her down aside of the daughter and started a-crying too. Then after a bit the father began to wonder that they didn't come back, and he went down into the cellar to look after them himself, and there they two sat a-crying, and the beer running all over the floor. "Whatever is the matter?" says he. "Why," says the mother, "look at that horrid mallet. Just suppose, if our daughter and her sweetheart was to be married, and was to have a son, and he was to grow up, and was to come down into the cellar to draw the beer, and the mallet was to fall on his head and kill him, what a dreadful thing it would be!" "Dear, dear, dear! so it would!" said the father, and he sat himself down aside of the other two, and started a-crying.

Now the gentleman got tired of stopping up in the kitchen by himself, and at last he went down into the cellar too, to see what they were after; and there they three sat a-crying side by side, and the beer running all over the floor. And he ran straight and turned the tap. Then he said: "Whatever are you three doing, sitting there crying, and letting the beer run all over the floor?" "Oh!" says the father, "look at that horrid mallet! Suppose you and our daughter was to be married, and was to have a son, and he was to grow up, and was to come down into the cellar to draw the beer, and the mallet was

to fall on his head and kill him!" And then they all started a-crying worse than before. But the gentleman burst out a-laughing, and reached up and pulled out the mallet, and then he said: "I've travelled many miles, and I never met three such big sillies as you three before; and now I shall start out on my travels again, and when I can find three bigger sillies than you three, then I'll come back and marry your daughter." So he wished them good-bye, and started off on his travels, and left them all crying because the girl had lost her sweetheart.

Well, he set out, and he travelled a long way, and at last he came to a woman's cottage that had some grass growing on the roof. And the woman was trying to get her cow to go up a ladder to the grass, and the poor thing durst not go. So the gentleman asked the woman what she was doing. "Why, lookye," she said, "look at all that beautiful grass. I'm going to get the cow on to the roof to eat it. She'll be quite safe, for I shall tie a string round her neck, and pass it down the chimney, and tie it to my wrist as I go about the house, so she can't fall off without my knowing it." "Oh, you poor silly!" said the gentleman, "you should cut the grass and throw it down to the cow!" But the woman thought it was easier to get the cow up the ladder than to get the grass down, so she pushed her and coaxed her and got her up, and tied a string round her neck, and passed it down the chimney, and fastened it to her own wrist. And the gentleman went on his way, but he hadn't gone far when the cow tumbled off the roof, and hung by the string tied round her neck, and it strangled her. And the weight of the cow tied to her wrist pulled the woman up the chimney, and she stuck fast half-way and was smothered in the soot.

Well, that was one big silly.

And the gentleman went on and on, and he went to an inn to stop the night, and they were so full at the inn that they had to put him in a double-bedded room, and another traveller was to sleep in the other bed. The other man was a very pleasant fellow, and they got very friendly together; but in the morning, when they were both getting up, the gentleman was surprised to see the other hang his trousers on the knobs of the chest of drawers and run across the room and try to jump into them, and he tried over and over again, and couldn't manage it; and the gentleman wondered whatever he was doing it for. At last he stopped and wiped his face with his handkerchief. "Oh dear," he says, "I do think trousers are the most awkwardest kind of clothes that ever were. I can't think who could have invented such things. It takes me the best part of an hour to get into mine every morning, and I get so hot! How do you manage yours?" So the gentleman burst out a-laughing, and showed him how to put them on; and he was very much obliged to him, and said he never should have thought of doing it that way.

So that was another big silly.

Then the gentleman went on his travels again; and he came to a village, and outside the village there was a pond, and round the pond was a crowd of people. And they had got rakes, and brooms, and pitchforks, reaching into the pond; and the gentleman asked what was the matter. "Why," they say, "matter enough! Moon's tumbled into the pond, and we can't rake her out anyhow!" So the gentleman burst out a-laughing, and told them to look up into the sky, and that it was only the shadow in the water. But they wouldn't listen to him, and abused him shamefully, and he got away as quick as he could.

So there was a whole lot of sillies bigger than the three sillies at home. So the gentleman turned back home again and married the farmer's daughter, and if they didn't live happy for ever after, that's nothing to do with you or me.

Tamlane

Here is an example of a motif very common in all folktales, the hero stolen by a fairy queen. Not all such tales end so happily. [From Joseph Jacobs, *More English Fairy Tales* (Putnam's, 1894).]

Young Tamlane was son of Earl Murray, and Burd Janet was daughter of Dunbar, Earl of March. And when they were young they loved one another and plighted their troth. But when the time came near for their marrying, Tamlane disappeared, and none knew what had become of him.

Many, many days after he had disappeared, Burd Janet was wandering in Cartenhaugh Wood, though she had been warned not to go there. And as she wandered she plucked the flowers from the bushes. She came at last to a bush of broom and began plucking it. She had not taken more than three flowerets when by her side up started young Tamlane.

"Where come ye from, Tamlane, Tamlane?" Burd Janet said; "and why have you been away so long?"

"From Elfland I come," said young Tamlane. "The Queen of Elfland has made me her knight."

"But how did you get there, Tamlane?" said Burd Janet.

"I was hunting one day, and as I rode widershins round yon hill, a deep drowsiness fell upon me, and when I awoke, behold! I was in Elfland. Fair is that land and gay, and fain would I stop but for thee and one other thing. Every seven years the Elves pay their tithe to the Nether world, and for all the Queen makes much of me, I fear it is myself that will be the tithe."

"Oh, can you not be saved? Tell me if aught I can do will save you, Tamlane?"

"One only thing is there for my safety. Tomorrow night is Hallowe'en, and the fairy court will then ride through England and Scotland, and if you would borrow me from Elfland you must take your stand by Miles Cross between twelve and one o' the night, and with holy water in your hand you must cast a compass all around you."

"But how shall I know you, Tamlane?" quoth Burd Janet, "amid so many knights I've ne'er seen before?"

"The first court of Elves that come by let pass. The next court you shall pay reverence to, but do naught nor say aught. But the third court that comes by is the chief court of them, and at the head rides the Queen of all Elfland. And I shall ride by her side upon a milk-white steed with a star in my crown; they give me this honor as being a christened knight. Watch my hands, Janet, the right one will be gloved but the left one will be bare, and by that token you will know me."

"But how to save you, Tamlane?" quoth Burd Janet.

"You must spring upon me suddenly, and I will fall to the ground. Then seize me quick, and whatever change befall me, for they will exercise all their magic on me, cling hold to me till they turn me into a red-hot iron. Then cast me into this pool and I will be turned back into a mother-naked man. Cast then your green mantle over me, and I shall be yours, and be of the world again."

So Burd Janet promised to do all for Tamlane, and next night at midnight she took her stand by Miles Cross and cast a compass round her with holy water.

Soon there came riding by the Elfin court; first over the mound went a troop on black steeds, and then another troop on brown. But in the third court, all on milk-white steeds, she saw the Queen of Elfland, and by her side a knight with a star in his crown, with right hand gloved and the left bare. Then she knew this was her own Tamlane, and springing forward she seized the bridle of the milk-white steed and pulled its rider down. And as soon as he had touched the ground she let go the bridle and seized him in her arms.

"He's won, he's won amongst us all," shrieked out the eldritch crew, and all came around her and tried their spells on young Tamlane.

First they turned him in Janet's arms like frozen ice, then into a huge flame of roaring fire. Then, again, the fire vanished and an adder was skipping through her arms, but still she held on; and then they turned him into a snake that reared up as if to bite her, and yet she held on. Then suddenly a dove was struggling in her arms, and almost flew away. Then they turned him into a swan, but all was in vain, till at last he was turned into a red-hot glaive, and this she cast into a well of water and then he turned back into a mother-naked man. She quickly cast her green mantle over him, and young Tamlane was Burd Janet's for ever.

Then sang the Queen of Elfland as the court turned away and began to resume its march:

"She that has borrowed young Tamlane
  Has gotten a stately groom,
She's taken away my bonniest knight,
  Left nothing in his room.

"But had I known, Tamlane, Tamlane,
  A lady would borrow thee,
I'd hae ta'en out thy two grey eyne,
  Put in two eyne of tree.

"Had I but known, Tamlane, Tamlane,
  Before we came from home,
I'd hae ta'en out thy heart o' flesh,
  Put in a heart of stone.

"Had I but had the wit yestreen
  That I have got today,
I'd paid the Fiend seven times his teind
  Ere you'd been won away."

And the Elfin court rode away, and Burd Janet and young Tamlane went their way homewards and were soon after married after young Tamlane had again been sained by the holy water and made Christian once more.

Dick Whittington and His Cat

Versatile author-artist Marcia Brown is a storyteller with both words and pictures. Here she retells the famous folktale in vigorous prose well suited to the story hour. She has a rare talent for suiting the type of illustration to her subject matter. For Dick Whittington, her choice of the bold line of the linoleum block matches perfectly the robust story and its period. The pictures, in dull gold and black, combine lively action with a fine sense of design. [Complete text from *Dick Whittington,* told and cut in linoleum by Marcia Brown (Scribner's, 1950).]

Long ago in England there lived a little boy named Dick Whittington. Dick's father and mother died when he was very young, and as he was too small to work, he had a hard time of it. The people in the village were poor and could spare him little more than the parings of potatoes and now and then a crust of bread. He ran about the country as ragged as a colt, until one day he met a wagoner on his way to London. "Come along with me," said the wagoner. So off they set together.

Now Dick had heard of the great city of London. It was said that the people who lived there were all fine gentlemen and ladies, that there was singing and music all day long, and that the streets were paved with gold. As for the gold, "I'd be willing to get a bushel of that," said Dick to himself.

But when Dick got to London, how sad he was to find the streets covered with dirt instead of gold! And there he was in a strange place, without food, without friends, and without money. Dick was soon so cold and hungry that he wished he were back sitting by a warm fire in a country kitchen. He sat down in a corner and cried himself to sleep.

A kind gentleman saw him there and said, "Why don't you go to work, my lad?"

"That I would," said Dick, "if I could get anything to do."

"Come along with me," said the gentleman, and he led Dick to a hayfield. There he worked hard and lived merrily until the hay was made.

Now Dick was again forlorn. He wandered back to town, fainting for want of food, and laid himself down at the door of Mr. Fitzwarren, a rich merchant.

Here the cook saw him, and being an ill-natured hussy, she called out, "On your way there, lazy rogue, or would you like a scalding to make you jump?"

Just then Mr. Fitzwarren came home to dinner. When he saw the dirty, ragged boy lying in his doorway, he said to him, "What ails you, boy? You look old enough to work."

"Sir, I am a poor country lad," said Dick. "I have neither father nor mother nor any friend in the world. I would be glad to work, but I've had no food for three days." Dick then tried to get up, but he was so weak he fell down again.

"Take this lad into the house," Mr. Fitzwarren ordered his servants. "Give him meat and drink. When he is stronger he can help the cook with her dirty work."

Now Dick would have lived happily with this worthy family if he had not been bumped about by the cook.

"Look sharp there, clean the spit, empty the dripping pan, sweep the floor! Step lively or—!" And down came the ladle on the boy's shoulders. For the cook was always roasting and basting, and when the spit was still, she basted his head with a broom or anything else she could lay her hands on. When Mr. Fitzwarren's daughter, Alice, saw what was going on, she warned the cook, "Treat that boy more kindly or leave this house!"

Besides the crossness of the cook, Dick had another hardship. His bed was placed in a garret where there were so many rats and mice running over his bed he could never get to sleep.

But one day a gentleman gave Dick a penny for brushing his shoes. The next day Dick saw a girl in the street with a cat under her arm. He ran up to her. "How much do you want for that cat?" he asked.

"Oh, this cat is a good mouser," said the girl. "She will bring a great deal of money."

"But I have only a penny in the world," said Dick, "and I need a cat badly." So the girl let him have it.

Dick hid his cat in the garret because he was afraid the cook would beat her too. He always saved part of his dinner for her, and Miss Puss wasted no time in killing or frightening away all the rats and mice. Now Dick could sleep as sound as a top.

Not long after this, Mr. Fitzwarren had a ship ready to sail. He called all his servants into the parlor and asked them what they chose to send to trade. All the servants brought something but poor Dick. Since he had neither money nor goods, he couldn't think of sending anything.

"I'll put some money down for him," offered Miss Alice, and she called Dick into the parlor.

But the merchant said, "That will not do. It must be something of his own."

"I have nothing but a cat," said Dick.

"Fetch your cat, boy," said the merchant, "and let her go!"

So Dick brought Puss and handed her over to the captain of the ship with tears in his eyes. "Now the rats and mice will keep me awake all night again," he said. All the company laughed, but Miss Alice pitied Dick and gave him some half-pence to buy another cat.

While Puss was beating the billows at sea, Dick was beaten at home by the cross cook. She used him so cruelly and made such fun of him for sending his cat to sea that the poor boy decided to run away. He packed the few things he had and set out early in the morning on All-Hallows Day. He walked as far as Halloway and sat down on a stone to rest. While he was sitting there wondering which way to go, the Bells of Bow began to ring. Ding! Dong!

They seemed to say to him:

"Turn again, Whittington,
Lord Mayor of London."

"Lord Mayor of London!" said Dick to himself. "What wouldn't I give to be Lord Mayor of London and ride in such a fine coach! I'll go back and I'll take the cuffings of the cook, if I'm to be Lord Mayor of London." So home he went. Luckily, he got into the house and about his business before the old cook came downstairs.

Meanwhile the ship with the cat on board was long beating about at sea. The winds finally drove it on the coast of Barbary. Here lived the Moors, a people unknown to the English. They came in great numbers on board to see the sailors and the goods which the captain wanted to trade.

The captain sent some of his choicest goods to the king of the country. The king was so well pleased that he invited the captain and his officer to come to his palace, about a mile from the sea.

Here they were placed on rich carpets, flowered with gold and silver. The king and queen sat at the upper end of the room, and dinner was brought in. No sooner had the servants set down the dishes than an amazing number of rats and mice rushed in. They helped themselves from every dish, scattering pieces of meat and gravy all about.

The captain in surprise turned to the nobles and asked, "Are not these vermin offensive?"

"Oh yes," said they, "very offensive! The King would give half of his treasure to be rid of them. They not only ruin his dinner, but also attack him in his chamber, even in his bed!

He has to be watched while he is sleeping for fear of them!"

The captain jumped for joy. He remembered Whittington and his cat and told the king he had a creature on board the ship that would soon destroy the mice. The king's heart heaved so high at this good news that his turban dropped off his head. "Bring this creature to me!" he cried. "Vermin are dreadful in a court! If she will do what you say, I will load your ship with ivory, gold dust and jewels in exchange for her."

Away flew the captain to the ship, while another dinner was got ready. With Puss under his arm, he returned to the palace just in time to see the rats about to devour the second dinner. At first sight of the rats and mice the cat sprang from the captain's arms. Soon she had laid most of them dead at her feet, while the rest fled to their holes.

The king rejoiced to see his old enemies destroyed. The queen asked to see Miss Puss. When the captain presented the cat, the queen was a little afraid to touch a creature that had made such havoc among the rats and mice. Finally she stroked her and said, "Puttey, puttey, puttey," for she had not learned English. The captain put the cat on the queen's lap, where she purred and played with her majesty's hand and then sang herself to sleep.

When the king learned that Miss Puss and her kittens would keep the whole country free from rats and mice, he bargained for the whole ship's cargo. He gave ten times as much for Miss Puss as for all the rest.

When the ship was loaded, the captain and his officer took leave of their majesties. A breeze springing up, they hurried on board and set sail for England.

The sun was scarcely up one morning when Mr. Fitzwarren stole from his bed to count over the cash. He had just sat down at his desk in the counting house when somebody came tap, tap-tap at the door.

"Who's there?"

"A friend. I bring you news of the good ship Unicorn!"

The merchant bustled up in such a hurry that he forgot his gout. He opened the door.

There stood the captain and his officer with

a cabinet of jewels and a bill of lading. The merchant lifted up his eyes and thanked Heaven for such a prosperous voyage. They told him about the cat and showed him the caskets of diamonds and rubies they had brought for Dick.

At that the merchant cried out:

"Go call him and tell him of his fame,
And call him Mr. Whittington by name."

Dick was scouring pots in the kitchen and did not want to come into the clean parlor. "The floor is polished, and my shoes are dirty and full of nails." But the merchant made him come in and sit down.

He took Dick by the hand and said, "Mr. Whittington, I sent for you to congratulate you upon your good fortune. The captain has sold your cat to the king of Barbary. She has brought you more riches than I am worth in the world. May you long enjoy them!"

When they showed him the caskets of jewels, Dick laid the whole at his master's feet, but Mr. Fitzwarren refused it. He offered them to his mistress and his good friend Miss Alice, but they too refused the smallest part. Dick then rewarded the captain and ship's crew for the care they had taken of Puss, and distributed presents to all the servants, even to his old enemy, the cook.

Mr. Fitzwarren advised Mr. Whittington to send for tradesmen to dress him like a gentleman, and offered him his house until he could provide himself with a better. Now when Dick's face was washed, his hair curled, his hat cocked, and he was dressed in a rich suit of clothes, he turned out a genteel young fellow.

In a little time he dropped his sheepish behavior and soon became a sprightly companion. Miss Alice, who formerly looked on him with pity, now saw him in quite another light.

When Mr. Fitzwarren noticed how fond they were of each other, he proposed a match between them. Both parties cheerfully consented.

The Lord Mayor in his coach, Court of Aldermen, Sheriffs, company of stationers, and a number of eminent merchants attended the wedding ceremony. And afterwards all were treated to an elegant entertainment.

Whittington and his bride were called the happiest couple in England. He was chosen Sheriff and was three different times elected Lord Mayor of London. In the last year of his mayoralty Whittington entertained King Henry the Fifth and his Queen.

"Never had Prince such a subject," said Henry, and Whittington replied, "Never had subject such a King!"

Master of All Masters

Another droll, in the mode of "The Three Sillies," but constructed in an entirely different way. The contrast between the brevity of the tale and the girl's long-winded warning of the fire causes the shock of surprise that is the basis of comedy. [From Joseph Jacobs, *English Fairy Tales* (Putnam's, 1892).]

A girl once went to the fair to hire herself for servant. At last a funny-looking old gentleman engaged her, and took her home to his house. When she got there, he told her that he had something to teach her, for that in his house he had his own names for things.

He said to her: "What will you call me?"

"Master or mister, or whatever you please, sir," says she.

He said: "You must call me 'master of all masters.' And what would you call this?" pointing to his bed.

"Bed or couch, or whatever you please, sir."

"No, that's my 'barnacle.' And what do you call these?" said he pointing to his pantaloons.

"Breeches or trousers, or whatever you please, sir."

"You must call them 'squibs and crackers.' And what would you call her?" pointing to the cat.

"Cat or kit, or whatever you please, sir."

"You must call her 'white-faced simminy.' And this now," showing the fire, "what would you call this?"

"Fire or flame, or whatever you please, sir."

"You must call it 'hot cockalorum,' and what this?" he went on, pointing to the water.

"Water or wet, or whatever you please, sir."

"No, 'pondalorum' is its name. And what do you call all this?" asked he as he pointed to the house.

"House or cottage, or whatever you please, sir."

"You must call it 'high topper mountain.'"

That very night the servant woke her master up in a fright and said: "Master of all masters, get out of your barnacle and put on your squibs and crackers. For white-faced simminy has got a spark of hot cockalorum on its tail, and unless you get some pondalorum, high topper mountain will be all on hot cockalorum"...... That's all.

Ireland

King O'Toole and His Goose

Irish fairy tales are in two main classes: the humorous, such as this, with a certain earthiness; and the beautiful, with great delicacy and charm, such as *The Land of the Heart's Desire* by William Butler Yeats. [From Joseph Jacobs, *Celtic Fairy Tales* (Putnam's, 1893).]

Och, I thought all the world, far and near, had heerd of King O'Toole—well, well but the darkness of mankind is untollable! Well, sir, you must know, as you didn't hear it afore, that there was a king, called King O'Toole, who was a fine old king in the old ancient times, long ago; and it was he that owned the churches in the early days. The king, you see, was the right sort; he was the real boy and loved sport as he loved his life, and hunting in particular; and from the rising o' the sun, up he got and away he went over the mountains after the deer; and fine times they were.

Well, it was all mighty good, as long as the king had his health; but, you see, in the course of time the king grew old, by raison he was stiff in his limbs, and when he got stricken in years, his heart failed him, and he was lost entirely for want o' diversion, because he couldn't go a-hunting no longer; and, by dad, the poor king was obliged at last to get a goose to divert him. Oh, you may laugh if you like, but it's truth I'm telling; and the way the goose diverted him was this-a-way: You see, the goose used to swim across the lake and go diving for trout

and catch fish on a Friday for the king, and flew every other day round about the lake, diverting the poor king. All went on mighty well until, by dad, the goose got stricken in years like her master and couldn't divert him no longer; and then it was that the poor king was lost entirely. The king was walkin' one mornin' by the edge of the lake, lamentin' his cruel fate, and thinking of drowning himself, that could get no diversion in life, when all of a sudden, turning round the corner, whom should he meet but a mighty decent young man coming up to him.

"God save you," says the king to the young man.

"God save you kindly, King O'Toole," says the young man.

"True for you," says the king. "I am King O'Toole," says he, "prince and plenny-penny-tinchery of these parts," says he; "but how came ye to know that?" says he.

"Oh, never mind," says Saint Kavin.

You see it was Saint Kavin, sure enough —the saint himself in disguise and nobody else. "Oh, never mind," says he, "I know more than that. May I make bold to ask how is your goose, King O'Toole?" says he.

"Blur-an-agers, how came ye to know about my goose?" says the king.

"Oh, no matter; I was given to understand it," says Saint Kavin.

After some more talk the king says, "What are you?"

"I'm an honest man," says Saint Kavin.

"Well, honest man," says the king, "and how is it you make your money so aisy?"

"By makin' old things as good as new," says Saint Kavin.

"Is it a tinker you are?" says the king.

"No," says the saint; "I'm no tinker by trade, King O'Toole; I've a better trade than a tinker," says he—"What would you say," says he, "if I made your old goose as good as new?"

My dear, at the word of making his goose as good as new, you'd think the poor old king's eyes were ready to jump out of his head. With that the king whistled, and down came the poor goose, just like a hound, waddling up to the poor cripple, her master, and as like him as two peas. The minute the saint clapt his eyes on the goose, "I'll do the job for you," says he, "King O'Toole."

"By Jaminee!" says King O'Toole, "if you do, I'll say you're the cleverest fellow in the seven parishes."

"Oh, by dad," says Saint Kavin, "you must say more nor that—my horn's not so soft all out," says he, "as to repair your old goose for nothing; what'll you gi' me if I do the job for you?—that's the chat," says Saint Kavin.

"I'll give you whatever you ask," says the king; "isn't that fair?"

"Divil a fairer," says the saint, "that's the way to do business. Now," says he, "this is the bargain I'll make with you, King O'Toole: will you gi' me all the ground the goose flies over, the first offer, after I make her as good as new?"

"I will," says the king.

"You won't go back on your word?" says Saint Kavin.

"Honor bright!" says King O'Toole, holding out his fist.

"Honor bright!" says Saint Kavin, back again, "it's a bargain. Come here!" says he to the poor old goose—"come here, you unfortunate ould cripple, and it's I that'll make you the sporting bird." With that, my dear, he took up the goose by the two wings—"Criss o' my cross an you," says he markin her to grace with the blessed sign at the same minute—and throwing her up in the air, "whew," says he, jist givin' her a blast to help her; and with that, my jewel, she took to her heels, flyin' like one o' the eagles themselves, and cutting as many capers as a swallow before a shower of rain.

Well, my dear, it was a beautiful sight to see the king standing with his mouth open, looking at his poor old goose flying as light as a lark, and better than ever she was; and when she lit at his feet, patted her on the head, and "Ma vourneen," says he, "but you are the darlint o' the world."

"And what do you say to me," says Saint Kavin, "for making her the like?"

"By Jabers," says the king, "I say nothing beats the art o' man, barring the bees."

"And do you say no more nor what?" says Saint Kavin.

"And that I'm beholden to you," says the king.

"But will you gi'e me all the ground the goose flew over?" says Saint Kavin.

"I will," says King O'Toole, "and you're welcome to it," says he, "though it's the last acre I have to give."

"But you'll keep your word true," says the saint.

"As true as the sun," says the king.

"It's well for you, King O'Toole, that you said that word," says he; "for if you didn't say that word, the divil the bit o' your goose would ever fly agin."

When the king was as good as his word, Saint Kavin was pleased with him; and then it was that he made himself known to the king. "And," says he, "King O'Toole, you're a decent man, for I only came here to try you. You don't know me," says he, "because I'm disguised."

"Musha! then," says the king, "who are you?"

"I'm Saint Kavin," said the saint, blessing himself.

"Oh, queen of heaven!" says the king, making the sign of the cross between his eyes and falling down on his knees before the saint; "is it the great Saint Kavin," says he, "that I've been discoursing all this time without knowing it," says he, "all as one as if he was a lump of a gossoon?—and so you're a saint?" says the king.

"I am," says Saint Kavin.

"By Jabers, I thought I was only talking to a dacent boy," says the king.

"Well, you know the difference now," says the saint. "I'm Saint Kavin," says he, "the greatest of all the saints."

And so the king had his goose as good as new to divert him as long as he lived; and the saint supported him after he came into his property, as I told you, until the day of his death—and that was soon after; for the poor goose thought he was catching a trout one Friday; but, my jewel, it was a mistake he made—and instead of a trout, it was a thieving horse-eel; and instead of the goose killing a trout for the king's supper—by dad, the eel killed the king's goose—and small blame to him; but he didn't ate her, because he darn't ate what Saint Kavin had laid his blessed hands on.

The Bee, the Harp, the Mouse, and the Bum-Clock

This droll is a more detailed version of the *Jack and the Beanstalk* theme. The Irish flair for embellishment of style and incident is apparent. The motif of the mirthless princess is included, a frequent theme of the folktale. [From Seumas MacManus, *Donegal Fairy Stories* (Doubleday, 1926.)]

Once there was a widow, and she had one son, called Jack. Jack and his mother owned just three cows. They lived well and happy for a long time; but at last hard times came down on them, and the crops failed, and poverty looked in at the door, and things got so sore against the poor widow that for want of money and for want of necessities she had to make up her mind to sell one of the cows.

"Jack," she said one night, "go over in the morning to the fair to sell the branny cow."

Well and good: in the morning my brave Jack was up early, and took a stick in his fist and turned out the cow, and off to the fair he went with her; and when Jack came into the fair, he saw a great crowd gathered in a ring in the street. He went into the crowd to see what they were looking at, and there in the middle of them he saw a man with a wee, wee harp, a mouse, and bum-clock [cockroach], and a bee to play the harp. And when the man put them down on the ground and whistled, the bee began to play and the mouse and the bum-clock to dance; and there wasn't a man or woman, or a thing in the fair, that didn't begin to dance also; and the pots and pans, and the wheels and reels jumped and jigged, all over the town, and Jack himself and the branny cow were as bad as the next.

There was never a town in such a state before or since; and after a while the man picked up the bee, the harp, and the mouse, and the bum-clock and put them into his pocket; and the men and women, Jack and the cow, the pots and pans, wheels and reels, that had hopped and jigged, now stopped, and every one began to laugh as if to break its heart. Then the man turned to Jack. "Jack," says he, "how would you like to be master of all these animals?"

"Why," says Jack, "I should like it fine."

"Well, then," says the man, "how will you and me make a bargain about them?"

"I have no money," says Jack.

"But you have a fine cow," says the man. "I will give you the bee and the harp for it."

"O, but," Jack says, says he, "my poor mother at home is very sad and sorrowful entirely, and I have this cow to sell and lift her heart again."

"And better than this she cannot get," says the man. "For when she sees the bee play the harp, she will laugh if she never laughed in her life before."

"Well," says Jack, says he, "that will be grand."

He made the bargain. The man took the cow; and Jack started home with the bee and the harp in his pocket, and when he came home, his mother welcomed him back.

"And Jack," says she, "I see you have sold the cow."

"I have done that," says Jack.

"Did you do well?" says the mother.

"I did well and very well," says Jack.

"How much did you get for her?" says the mother.

"O," says he, "it was not for money at all I sold her, but for something far better."

"O, Jack! Jack!" says she, "what have you done?"

"Just wait until you see, mother," says he, "and you will soon say I have done well."

Out of his pocket he takes the bee and the harp and sets them in the middle of the floor, and whistles to them, and as soon as he did this the bee began to play the harp, and the mother she looked at them and let a big, great laugh out of her, and she and Jack began to dance, the pots and pans, the wheels and reels began to jig and dance over the floor, and the house itself hopped about also.

When Jack picked up the bee and the harp again, the dancing all stopped, and the mother laughed for a long time. But when she came to herself, she got very angry entirely with Jack, and she told him he was a silly, foolish fellow, that there was neither food nor money in the house, and now he had lost one of her good cows also. "We must do something to live," says she. "Over to the fair you must go tomorrow morning, and take the black cow with you and sell her."

And off in the morning at an early hour brave Jack started and never halted until he was in the fair. When he came into the fair, he saw a big crowd gathered in a ring in the street. Said Jack to himself, "I wonder what are they looking at."

Into the crowd he pushed, and saw the wee man this day again with a mouse and a bum-clock, and he put them down in the street and whistled. The mouse and the bum-clock stood up on their hind legs and got hold of each other and began to dance there and jig; and as they did there was not a man or woman in the street who didn't begin to jig also, and Jack and the black cow, and the wheels and the reels, and the pots and pans, all of them were jigging and dancing all over the town, and the houses themselves were jumping and hopping about, and such a place Jack or any one else never saw before.

When the man lifted the mouse and the bum-clock into his pocket, they all stopped dancing and settled down, and everybody laughed right hearty. The man turned to Jack. "Jack," said he, "I am glad to see you; how would you like to have these animals?"

"I should like well to have them," says Jack, says he, "only I cannot."

"Why cannot you?" says the man.

"O," says Jack, says he, "I have no money, and my poor mother is very down-hearted. She sent me to the fair to sell this cow and bring some money to lift her heart."

"O," says the man, says he, "if you want to lift your mother's heart, I will sell you the mouse; and when you set the bee to play the harp and the mouse to dance to it, your mother will laugh if she never laughed in her life before."

"But I have no money," says Jack, says he, "to buy your mouse."

"I don't mind," says the man, says he, "I will take your cow for it."

Poor Jack was so taken with the mouse and had his mind so set on it, that he thought it was a grand bargain entirely, and he gave the man his cow and took the mouse and started

off for home; and when he got home his mother welcomed him.

"Jack," says she, "I see you have sold the cow."

"I did that," says Jack.

"Did you sell her well?" says she.

"Very well indeed," says Jack, says he.

"How much did you get for her?"

"I didn't get money," says he, "but I got value."

"O, Jack! Jack!" says she, "what do you mean?"

"I will soon show you that, mother," says he, taking the mouse out of his pocket and the harp and the bee, setting all on the floor; and when he began to whistle the bee began to play, and the mouse got up on its hind legs and began to dance and jig, and the mother gave such a hearty laugh as she never laughed in her life before. To dancing and jigging herself and Jack fell, and the pots and pans and the wheels and reels began to dance and jig over the floor, and the house jigged also. And when they were tired of this, Jack lifted the harp and the mouse and the bee and put them in his pocket, and his mother she laughed for a long time.

But when she got over that, she got very down-hearted and very angry entirely with Jack. "And O, Jack," she says, "you are a stupid, good-for-nothing fellow." We have neither money nor meat in the house, and here you have lost two of my good cows, and I have only one left now. Tomorrow morning," she says, "you must be up early and take this cow to the fair and sell her. See to get something to lift my heart up."

"I will do that," says Jack, says he. So he went to his bed, and early in the morning he was up and turned out the spotty cow and went to the fair.

When Jack got to the fair, he saw a crowd gathered in a ring in the street. "I wonder what they are looking at, anyhow," says he. He pushed through the crowd, and there he saw the same wee man he had seen before, with a bum-clock; and when he put the bum-clock on the ground, he whistled, and the bum-clock began to dance, and the men, women, and children in the street, and Jack and the spotty cow began to dance and jig also, and everything on the street and about it, the wheels and reels, the pots and pans, began to jig, and the houses themselves began to dance likewise. And when the man lifted the bum-clock and put it in his pocket, everybody stopped jigging and dancing and every one laughed loud. The wee man turned and saw Jack.

"Jack, my brave boy," says he, "you will never be right fixed until you have this bum-clock, for it is a very fancy thing to have."

"O, but," says Jack, says he, "I have no money."

"No matter for that," says the man: "you have a cow, and that is as good as money to me."

"Well," says Jack, "I have a poor mother who is very downhearted at home, and she sent me to the fair to sell this cow and raise some money and lift her heart."

"O, but Jack," says the wee man, "this bum-clock is the very thing to lift her heart, for when you put down your harp and bee and mouse on the floor and put the bum-clock along with them, she will laugh if she never laughed in her life before."

"Well, that is surely true," says Jack, says he, "and I think I will make a swap with you."

So Jack gave the cow to the man and took the bum-clock himself and started for home. His mother was glad to see Jack back and says she, "Jack, I see that you have sold the cow."

"I did that, mother," says Jack.

"Did you sell her well, Jack?" says the mother.

"Very well indeed, mother," says Jack.

"How much did you get for her?" says the mother.

"I didn't take any money for her, mother, but value," says Jack and he takes out of his pocket the bum-clock and the mouse, and set them on the floor and began to whistle, and the bee began to play the harp and the mouse and the bum-clock stood up on their hind legs and began to dance, and Jack's mother laughed very hearty, and everything in the house, the wheels and the reels, and the pots and pans went jigging and hopping over the floor, and the house itself went jigging and hopping about likewise.

When Jack lifted up the animals and put them in his pocket, everything stopped, and the mother laughed for a good while. But after a while, when she came to herself and saw what Jack had done and how they were now without either money, or food, or a cow, she got very, very angry at Jack and scolded him hard, and then sat down and began to cry.

Poor Jack, when he looked at himself, confessed that he was a stupid fool entirely. "And what," says he, "shall I now do for my poor mother?" He went out along the road, thinking and thinking, and he met a wee woman who said, "Good-morrow to you, Jack," says she, "how is it you are not trying for the King's daughter of Ireland?"

"What do you mean?" says Jack.

Says she: "Didn't you hear what the whole world has heard, that the King of Ireland has a daughter who hasn't laughed for seven years; and he has promised to give her in marriage and to give the kingdom along with her, to any man who will take three laughs out of her."

"If that is so," says Jack, says he, "it is not here I should be."

Back to the house he went and gathers together the bee, the harp, the mouse, and the bum-clock, and putting them into his pocket; he bade his mother good-by and told her it wouldn't be long till she got good news from him and off he hurries.

When he reached the castle, there was a ring of spikes all round the castle and men's heads on nearly every spike there.

"What heads are these?" Jack asked one of the King's soldiers.

"Any man that comes here trying to win the King's daughter and fails to make her laugh three times, loses his head and has it stuck on a spike. These are the heads of the men that failed," says he.

"A mighty big crowd," says Jack, says he. Then Jack sent word to tell the King's daughter and the King that there was a new man who had come to win her.

In a very little time the King and the King's daughter and the King's court all came out and sat themselves down on gold and silver chairs in front of the castle and ordered Jack to be brought in until he should have his trial. Jack, before he went, took out of his pocket the bee, the harp, the mouse, and the bum-clock, and he gave the harp to the bee, and he tied a string to one and the other, and took the end of the string himself, and marched into the castle yard before all the court, with his animals coming on a string behind him.

When the Queen and the King and the court and the princes saw poor ragged Jack with his bee, and mouse, and bum-clock hopping behind him on a string, they set up one roar of laughter that was long and loud enough; and when the King's daughter herself lifted her head and looked to see what they were laughing at and saw Jack and his paraphernalia, she opened her mouth and she let out of her such a laugh as was never heard before.

Then Jack dropped a low courtesy, and said, "Thank you, my lady; I have one of the three parts of you won."

Then he drew up his animals in a circle, and began to whistle, and the minute he did, the bee began to play the harp, and the mouse and the bum-clock stood up on their hind legs, got hold of each other, and began to dance, and the King and the King's court and Jack himself began to dance and jig, and everything about the King's castle, pots and pans, wheels and reels and the castle itself began to dance also. And the King's daughter, when she saw this, opened her mouth again, and let out of her a laugh twice louder than she let before; and Jack, in the middle of his jigging, drops another courtesy, and says, "Thank you, my lady; that is two of the three parts of you won."

Jack and his menagerie went on playing and dancing, but Jack could not get the third laugh out of the King's daughter, and the poor fellow saw his big head in danger of going on the spike. Then the brave mouse came to Jack's help and wheeled round upon its heel, and as it did so its tail swiped into the bum-clock's mouth, and the bum-clock began to cough and cough and cough. And when the King's daughter saw this she opened her mouth again, and she let out the loudest and hardest and merriest laugh that was ever heard before or since; and, "Thank you, my lady," says Jack, dropping another courtesy; "I have all of you won."

Then when Jack stopped his menagerie, the King took himself and the menagerie within the castle. He was washed and combed and dressed in a suit of silk and satin with all kinds of gold and silver ornaments, and then was led before the King's daughter. And true enough she confessed that a handsomer and finer fellow than Jack she had never seen, and she was very willing to be his wife.

Jack sent for his poor old mother and brought her to the wedding, which lasted nine days and nine nights, every night better than the other. All the lords and ladies and gentry of Ireland were at the wedding. I was at it, too, and got brogues, broth and slipper of bread and came jigging home on my head.

The Children of Lir

The elements of magic and enchantment that occur so frequently in Irish folklore have roots in Celtic mythology. This story has been included here to illustrate the link between myth and folktale but could just as easily have been placed among the mythology selections. A tragic tale of jealousy, suffering, and remorse, it originates in the poetic mythology of Ireland, but its elements are familiar folklore motifs. The jealous stepmother who casts a spell of witchcraft upon her stepchildren is universal. The Grimm brothers' "The Six Swans" and Hans Christian Andersen's literary variant "The Wild Swans" also tell the stories of a king's children transformed into swans and their quest to regain human form. In Grimm and Andersen, the single sister escapes enchantment, and, through fortitude and courage, saves her brothers. In this version, the sister is one of the victims and there is no such happy ending. The characters here are not human beings but rather belong to the "Tuatha De Danaan," the gods of Celtic belief, and this is an example of a Celtic myth retold as a folktale. The presence of the Christian Saint Kemoc dates this version to a time when the myth had been absorbed into folklore. To the Celtic mind, the earth of Ireland itself and the waters that washed its shores were the ultimate paradise, the Land of the Ever-Young. The Celtic fairy belongs to the people of Danaan, and to this day, the mounds and hills of Ireland are believed to hold special magic, being the dwelling place of the gods themselves. William Butler Yeats in his play, *The Land of Heart's Desire*, describes the paradise as

. . . a land where even the old are fair,
And even the wise are merry of tongue.

Ella Young, whose version is given here, was a member of the group of brilliant men and women, working with Yeats and Lady Gregory, Dr. Douglas Hyde, Padraic Colum, and many others, who reinterpreted Celtic legend, epic, and myth. The result was a renaissance of literature—novels, stories, and drama—which, in the first quarter of this century, won the admiration of the world and gave fresh impetus to the study of traditional literature. The collection from which the following selection is taken was first published in Ireland in 1910, with decorations by Maud Gonne. [From *Celtic Wonder Tales,* retold by Ella Young (Dutton, 1923).]

Long ago when the Tuatha De Danaan lived in Ireland there was a Great King called Lir. He had four children—Fionnuala, Aodh, Fiacra, and Conn. Fionnuala was the eldest and she was as beautiful as sunshine in blossomed branches; Aodh was like a young eagle in the blue of the sky; and his two brothers, Fiacra and Conn, were as beautiful as running water.

In those days sorrow was not known in Ireland: the mountains were crowned with light, and the lakes and rivers had strange star-like flowers that shook a rain of jewelled dust on the white horses of the De Danaans when they came down to drink. The horses were swifter than any horses that are living now and they could go over the waves of the sea and under deep lake-water without hurt to themselves. Lir's four children had each one a white horse and two hounds that were whiter than snow.

Every one in Lir's kingdom loved Fionnuala, and Aodh, and Fiacra, and Conn, except their step-mother, Aoifa. She hated them, and her hatred pursued them as a wolf pursues a wounded fawn. She sought to harm them by spells and witchcraft. She took them in her chariot to the Lake of Darvra in Westmeath. She made them bathe in the lake and when they were coming out of the water she struck them with a rod of enchantment and turned them into four white swans.

"Swim as wild swans on this lake," she said, "for three hundred years, and when that time is ended swim three hundred years on the narrow sea of the Moyle, and when that time is ended swim three hundred years on the Western Sea that has no bounds but the sky."

Then Fionnuala, that was a swan, said:

"O Wicked Woman, a doom will come upon you heavier than the doom you have put on us and you will be more sorrowful than we are to-day. And if you would win any pity in the hour of your calamity tell us now how we may know when the doom will end for us."

"The doom will end when a king from the North weds a queen from the South; when a druid with a shaven crown comes over the sea; when you hear the sound of a little bell that rings for prayers."

The swans spread their wings and flew away over the lake. They made a very sorrowful singing as they went, lamenting for themselves.

When the Great King, their father, knew the sorrow that had come to him, he hastened down to the shore of the lake and called his children. They came flying to him, four white swans, and he said:

"Come to me, Fionnuala; come Aodh; come Conn; come Fiacra." He put his hands on them and caressed them and said: "I cannot give you back your shapes till the doom that is laid on you is ended, but come back now to the house that is mine and yours, White Children of my Heart."

Then Fionnuala answered him:

"The shadow of the woman who ensnared us lies on the threshold of your door: we cannot cross it."

And Lir said:

"The woman who ensnared you is far from any home this night. She is herself ensnared, and fierce winds drive her into all the restless places of the earth. She has lost her beauty and become terrible; she is a Demon of the Air, and must wander desolate to the end of time— but for you there is the firelight of home. Come back with me."

Then Conn said:

"May good fortune be on the threshold of your door from this time and for ever, but we cannot cross it, for we have the hearts of wild swans and we must fly in the dusk and feel the water moving under our bodies; we must hear the lonesome cries of the night. We have the voices only of the children you knew; we have the songs you taught us—that is all. Gold crowns are red in the firelight, but redder and fairer is dawn."

Lir stretched out his hands and blessed his children. He said:

"May all beautiful things grow henceforth more beautiful to you, and may the song you have be melody in the heart of whoever hears it. May your wings winnow joy for you out of the air, and your feet be glad in the waterways. My blessing be on you till the sea loses its saltness and the trees forget to bud in springtime. And farewell, Fionnuala, my white blossom; and farewell Aodh, that was the red flame of my heart; and farewell, Conn, that brought me gladness; and farewell, Fiacra, my treasure. Lonesome it is for you, flying far off in places strange to you; lonesome it is for me without you. Bitter it is to say farewell, and farewell, and nothing else but farewell."

Lir covered his face with his mantle and sorrow was heavy on him, but the swans rose into the air and flew away calling to each other. They called with the voices of children, but in their heart was the gladness of swans when they feel the air beneath them and stretch their necks to the freedom of the sky.

Three hundred years they flew over Lake Darvra and swam on its waters. Often their father came to the lake and called them to him and caressed them; often their kinsfolk came to talk with them; often harpers and musicians came to listen to the wonder of their singing. When three hundred years were ended the swans rose suddenly and flew far and far away. Their father sought them, and their kinsfolk sought them, but the swans never touched earth or rested once till they came to the narrow Sea of the Moyle that flows between Ireland and Scotland. A cold stormy sea it was, and lonely. The swans had no one to listen to their singing, and little heart for singing amid the green curling bitter waves. The storm-wind beat roughly on them, and often they were separated and calling to one another without hope of an answer. Then Fionnuala, for she was the wisest, said:

"Let us choose a place of meeting, so that when we are separated and lost and wandering each one will know where to wait for the others."

The swans, her brothers, said it was a good thought; they agreed to meet together in one place, and the place they chose was Carraigna-Ron, the Rock of the Seals. And it was well they made that choice, for a great storm came on them one night and scattered them far out over the sea. Their voices were drowned in the tempest and they were driven hither and thither in the darkness.

In the pale morning Fionnuala came to the Rock of the Seals. Her feathers were broken with the wind and draggled with the saltness of the sea and she was lamenting and calling on Aodh and Fiacra and Conn.

"O Conn, that I sheltered under my feathers, come to me! O Fiacra, come to me! O Aodh, Aodh, Aodh, come to me!"

And when she did not see them, and no voice answered, she made a sore lamentation and said:

"O bitter night that was blacker than the doom of Aoifa at the first to us! O three that I loved! O three that I loved! The waves are over your heads and I am desolate!"

She saw the red sun rising, and when the redness touched the waters, Conn came flying to her. His feathers were broken with the wind and draggled with the saltness of the sea. Fionnuala gathered him under her wings and comforted him, and she said:

"The day would not seem bitter to me now if only Aodh and Fiacra were come."

In a little while Fiacra came to her over the rough sea. She sheltered and comforted him with her wings, and she cried over the waters:

"O Aodh, Aodh, Aodh, come to me!"

The sun was high in the heavens when Aodh came, and he came with his feathers bright and shining and no trace of the bitter storm on him.

"O where have you been, Aodh?" said Fionnuala and Fiacra and Conn to him.

"I have been flying where I got sight of our kinsfolk. I have seen the white steeds that are swifter than the winds of March, and the riders that were comrades to us when we had our own shapes. I have seen both Aodh and Fergus, the two sons of Bove Dearg."

"O tell us, Aodh, where we may get sight of them!" said the swans.

"They are at the river mouth of the Bann," said Aodh. "Let us go there, and we may see them though we cannot leave the Moyle."

So much gladness came on all the swans that they forgot their weariness and the grievous buffeting of the storm and they rose and flew to the river mouth of the Bann. They saw their kinsfolk, the beautiful company of the Faery Host, shining with every colour under heaven and joyous as the wind in Springtime.

"O tell us, dear kinsfolk," said the swans, "how it is with our father?"

"The Great King has wrapped his robes of beauty about him, and feasts with those from whom age cannot take youth and lighthearted-ness," said Fergus.

"Ah," said Fionnuala, "he feasts and it is well with him! The joy-flame on his hearth cannot quench itself in ashes. He cannot hear us calling through the night—the wild swans, the wander-ers, the lost children."

The Faery Host was troubled, seeing the pite-ous plight of the swans, but Aodh, that was a swan said to Fergus, his kinsman and comrade:

"Do not cloud your face for us, Fergus; the horse you ride is white, but I ride a whiter—the cold curling white wave of the sea."

Then Fiacra said:

"O Fergus, does my own white horse forget me, now that I am here in the cold Moyle?"

And Conn said:

"O Fergus, tell my two hounds that I will come back to them some day."

The memory of all beautiful things came on the swans, and they were sorrowful, and Fion-nuala said:

"O beautiful comrades, I never thought that beauty could bring sorrow: now the sight of it breaks my heart," and she said to her brothers: "Let us go before our hearts are melted utterly."

The swans went over the Moyle then, and they were lamenting, and Fionnuala said:

"There is joy and feasting in the house of Lir to-night, but his four children are without a roof to cover them."

"It is a poor garment our feathers make when the wind blows through them: often we had the purple of kings' children on us.

"We are cold to-night, and it is a cold bed the sea makes: often we had beds of down with embroidered coverings.

"Often we drank mead from gold cups in the house of our father; now we have the bitter-ness of the sea and the harshness of sand in our mouths.

"It is weariness—O a great weariness—to be flying over the Moyle: without rest, without companions, without comfort.

"I am thinking of Angus to-night: he has the laughter of joy about him for ever.

"I am thinking to-night of Mananaun, and of white blossoms on silver branches.

"O swans, my brothers, I am thinking of beauty, and we are flying away from it for ever."

The swans did not see the company of the Faery Host again. They swam on the cold stormy sea of the Moyle, and they were there till three hundred years were ended.

"It is time for us to go," said Fionnuala, "we must seek the Western Sea."

The swans shook the water of the Moyle from their feathers and stretched out their wings to fly.

When they were come to the Western Sea there was sorrow on them, for the sea was wilder and colder and more terrible than the Moyle. The swans were on that sea and flying over it for three hundred years, and all that time they had no comfort, and never once did they hear the foot-fall of hound or horse or see their faery kinsfolk.

When the time was ended, the swans rose out of the water and cried joyfully to each other: "Let us go home now, the time is ended!"

They flew swiftly, and yet they were all day flying before they came to the place where Lir had his dwelling; when they looked down they saw no light in the house, they heard no music, no sound of voices. The many-coloured house was desolate and all the beauty was gone from it; the white hounds and the bright-maned horses were gone, and all the beautiful glad-hearted folk of the Sidhe.

"Every place is dark to us!" said Conn. "Look at the hills!"

The swans looked at the hills they had known, and every hill and mountain they could see was dark and sorrowful: not one had a star-heart of light, not one had a flame-crown, not one had music pulsing through it like a great breath.

"O Aodh, and Conn, and Fiacra," said Fion-nuala, "beauty is gone from the earth: we have no home now!"

The swans hid themselves in the long dank

grass, till morning. They did not speak to each other; they did not make a lamentation; they were silent with heaviness of grief. When they felt the light of morning they rose in the air and flew in wide circles seeking their kinsfolk. They saw the dwellings of strangers, and a strange people tending flocks and sowing corn on plains where the Tuatha De Danaan had hunted white stags with horns of silver.

"The grief of all griefs has come upon us!" said Fionnuala. "It is no matter now whether we have the green earth under us or bitter sea-waves: it is little to us now that we are in swan's bodies."

Her brothers had no words to answer her; they were dumb with grief till Aodh said:

"Let us fly far from the desolate house and the dead hills. Let us go where we can hear the thunder of the Western Sea."

The swans spread their wings and flew westward till they came to a little reedy lake, and they alit there and sheltered themselves, for they had no heart to go farther.

They took no notice of the days and often they did not know whether it was the moon or the sun that was in the sky, but they sang to each other, and that was all the comfort they had.

One day, while Fionnuala was singing, a man of the stranger-race drew near to listen. He had the aspect of one who had endured much hardship. His garments were poor and ragged. His hair was bleached by sun and rain. As he listened to the song a light came into his eyes and his whole face grew beautiful. When the song ended he bowed himself before the swans and said:

"White Swans of the Wilderness, ye have flown over many lands. Tell me, have ye seen aught of Tir-nan-Oge, where no one loses youth; or Tir-na-Moe, where all that is beautiful lives for ever; or Moy-Mell, that is so honey-sweet with blossom?"

"Have we seen Tir-nan-Oge? It is our own country! We are the children of Lir the King of it."

"Where is that country? How may one reach it? Tell me!"

"Ochone! It is not anywhere on the ridge of the world. Our father's house is desolate!"

"Ye are lying, to make sport for yourselves! Tir-nan-Oge cannot perish—rather would the whole world fall to ruin!"

"O would we had anything but the bitterness of truth on our tongues!" said Aodh. "Would we could see even one leaf from those trees with shining branches where the many-coloured birds used to sing! Ochone! Ochone! for all the beauty that has perished with Tir-nan-Oge!"

The stranger cried out a loud sorrowful cry and threw himself on the ground. His fingers tore at the roots of the grass. His body writhed and trembled with grief.

The children of Lir wondered at him, and Aodh said:

"Put away this fierceness of grief and take consolation to yourself. We, with so much heavier sorrow, have not lamented after this fashion."

The stranger raised himself: his eyes blazed like the eyes of a hunted animal when it turns on the hunters.

"How could your sorrow be equal to mine? Ye have dwelt in Tir-nan-Oge; ye have ridden horses whiter than the snow of one night and swifter than the storm-wind; ye have gathered flowers in the Plain of Honey. But I have never seen it—never once! Look at me! I was born a king! I have become an outcast, the laughing stock of slaves! I am Aibric the wanderer!—I have given all—all, for the hope of finding that country. It is gone now—it is not anywhere on the round of the world!"

"Stay with us," said Fiacra, "and we will sing for you, and tell your stories of Tir-nan-Oge."

"I cannot stay with you! I cannot listen to your songs! I must go on seeking; seeking; seeking while I live. When I am dead my dreams will not torment me. I shall have my fill of quietness then."

"Can you not believe us when we tell you that Tir-nan-Oge is gone like the white mists of morning? It is nowhere."

"It is in my heart, and in my mind, and in my soul! It burns like fire! It drives me like a tireless wind! I am going. Farewell!"

"Stay!" cried Aodh, "we will go with you. There is nothing anywhere for us now but brown earth and drifting clouds and wan waters. Why should we not go from place to place as the wind goes, and see each day new fields of reeds, new forest trees, new mountains? O, we shall never see the star-heart in any mountains again!"

"The mountains are dead," said Conn.

"The mountains are not dead," said Aibric. "They are dark and silent, but they are not dead. I know. I have cried to them in the night and laid my forehead against theirs and felt the beating of their mighty hearts. They are wiser than the wisest druid, more tender than the tenderest mother. It is they who keep the world alive."

"O," said Fionnuala, "if the mountains are indeed alive let us go to them; let us tell them our sorrowful story. They will pity us and we shall not be utterly desolate."

Aibric and the swans journeyed together, and at dusk they came to a tall beautiful mountain— the mountain that is called Nephin, in the West. It looked dark and sombre against the fading sky, and the sight of it, discrowned and silent, struck chill to the hearts of the wild swans: they turned away their heads to hide the tears in their eyes. But Aibric stretched his hands to the mountains and cried out:

"O beautiful glorious Comrade, pity us! Tir-nan-Oge is no more, and Moy-Mell is lost for ever! Welcome the children of Lir, for we have nothing left but you and the earth of Ireland!"

Then a wonder happened.

The star-heart of Nephin shone out—magnificent—tremulous—coloured like a pale amethyst.

The swans cried out to each other:

"The mountain is alive! Beauty has come again to the earth! Aibric, you have given us back the Land of Youth!"

A delicate faery music trembled and died away and was born again in the still evening air, and more and more the radiance deepened in the heart of Nephin. The swans began to sing most sweetly and joyously, and at the sound of that singing the star-heart showed in mountain after mountain till every mountain in Ireland pulsed and shone.

"Crown yourselves, mountains!" said Aodh, "that we may know the De Danaans are still alive and Lir's house is builded now where old age cannot wither it!"

The mountains sent up great jewelled rays of light so that each one was crowned with a rainbow; and when the Children of Lir saw that splendour they had no more thought of the years they had spent over dark troublous waters, and they said to each other:

"Would we could hear the sound of the little bell that rings for prayers, and feel our swanbodies fall from us!"

"I know the sound of a bell that rings for prayers," said Aibric, "and I will bring you where you can hear it. I will bring you to Saint Kemoc and you will hear the sound of his bell."

"Let us go," said the swans, and Aibric brought them to the Saint. The Saint held up his hands and blessed God when he saw them, and he besought them to remain a while and to tell him the story of their wanderings. He brought them into his little church and they were there with him in peace and happiness relating to him the wonders of the Land of Youth. It came to pass then that word reached the wife of King Largnen concerning the swans: she asked the king to get them for her, and because she demanded them with vehemence, the king journeyed to the Church of Saint Kemoc to get the swans.

When he was come, Saint Kemoc refused to give him the swans and Largnen forced his way into the church to take them. Now, he was a king of the North, and his wife was a queen of the South, and it was ordained that such a king should put an end to the power of Aoifa's spell. He came to the altar, and the swans were close to it. He put his hands on the swans to take them by force. When he touched them the swan-feathers dwindled and shrivelled and became as fine dust, and the bodies of Lir's children became as a handful of dust, but their spirits attained to freedom and joined their kinsfolk in the Land-of-the-Ever-Living.

It was Aibric who remembered the story of

the children of Lir, because he loved them. He told the story to the people of Ireland, and they were so fond of the story and had such pity for Lir's children that they made a law that no one was to hurt a wild swan, and when they saw a swan flying they would say:

"My blessing with you, white swan, for the sake of Lir's children!"

Munachar and Manachar

Joseph Jacobs's rendition of this cumulative tale combines Irish and Scottish versions. It has parallels with the English stories "The Old Woman and Her Pig" and "The Cat and the Mouse" but is unusual in its explosive ending. [From Joseph Jacobs, *Celtic Fairy Tales* (Putnam's, 1891).]

There once lived a Munachar and a Manachar, a long time ago, and it is a long time since it was, and if they were alive now they would not be alive then. They went out together to pick raspberries, and as many as Munachar used to pick Manachar used to eat. Munachar said he must go look for a rod to make a gad to hang Manachar, who ate his raspberries every one; and he came to the rod. "What news to-day?" said the rod. "It is my own news that I'm seeking. Going looking for a rod, a rod to make a gad, a gad to hang Manachar, who ate my raspberries every one."

"You will not get me," said the rod, "until you get an axe to cut me." He came to the axe. "What news to-day?" said the axe. "It's my own news I'm seeking. Going looking for an axe, an axe to cut a rod, a rod to make a gad, a gad to hang Manachar, who ate my raspberries every one."

"You will not get me," said the axe, "until you get a flag to edge me." He came to the flag. "What news to-day?" says the flag. "It's my own news I'm seeking. Going looking for a flag, flag to edge axe, axe to cut a rod, a rod to make a gad, a gad to hang Manachar, who ate my raspberries every one."

"You will not get me," says the flag, "till you get water to wet me." He came to the water. "What news to-day?" says the water. "It's my own news I'm seeking. Going looking

for water, water to wet flag, flag to edge axe, axe to cut a rod, a rod to make a gad, a gad to hang Manachar, who ate my raspberries every one."

"You will not get me," said the water, "until you get a deer who will swim me." He came to the deer. "What news to-day?" says the deer. "It's my own news I'm seeking. Going looking for a deer, deer to swim water, water to wet flag, flag to edge axe, axe to cut a rod, a rod to make a gad, a gad to hang Manachar, who ate my raspberries every one."

"You will not get me," said the deer, "until you get a hound who will hunt me." He came to the hound. "What news to-day?" says the hound. "It's my own news I'm seeking. Going looking for a hound, hound to hunt deer, deer to swim water, water to wet flag, flag to edge axe, axe to cut a rod, a rod to make a gad, a gad to hang Manachar, who ate my raspberries every one."

"You will not get me," said the hound, "until you get a bit of butter to put in my claw." He came to the butter. "What news to-day?" says the butter. "It's my own news I'm seeking. Going looking for butter, butter to go in claw of hound, hound to hunt deer, deer to swim water, water to wet flag, flag to edge axe, axe to cut a rod, a rod to make a gad, a gad to hang Manachar, who ate my raspberries every one."

"You will not get me," said the butter, "until you get a cat who shall scrape me." He came to the cat. "What news to-day?" said the cat. "It's my own news I'm seeking. Going looking for a cat, cat to scrape butter, butter to go in claw of hound, hound to hunt deer, deer to swim water, water to wet flag, flag to edge axe, axe to cut a rod, a rod to make a gad, a gad to hang Manachar, who ate my raspberries every one."

"You will not get me," said the cat, "until you will get milk which you will give me." He came to the cow. "What news to-day?" said the cow. "It's my own news I'm seeking. Going looking for a cow, cow to give me milk, milk I will give to the cat, cat to scrape butter, butter to go in claw of hound, hound to hunt deer, deer to swim water, water to wet flag, flag to edge axe, axe to cut a rod, a rod to make a gad, a gad to hang Manachar, who ate my raspberries every one."

"You will not get any milk from me," said the cow, "until you bring me a whisp of straw from those threshers yonder." He came to the threshers. "What news to-day?" said the threshers. "It's my own news I'm seeking. Going looking for a whisp of straw from ye to give to the cow, the cow to give me milk, milk I will give to the cat, cat to scrape butter, butter to go in claw of hound, hound to hunt deer, deer to swim water, water to wet flag, flag to edge axe, axe to cut a rod, a rod to make a gad, a gad to hang Manachar, who ate my raspberries every one."

"You will not get any whisp of straw from us," said the threshers, "until you bring us the makings of a cake from the miller over yonder." He came to the miller. "What news to-day?" said the miller. "It's my own news I'm seeking. Going looking for the makings of a cake which I will give the threshers, the threshers to give me a whisp of straw, the whisp of straw I will give to the cow, the cow to give me milk, milk I will give to the cat, cat to scrape butter, butter to go in claw of hound, hound to hunt deer, deer to swim water, water to wet flag, flag to edge axe, axe to cut a rod, a rod to make a gad, a gad to hang Manachar, who ate my raspberries every one."

"You will not get any makings of a cake from me," said the miller, "till you bring me the full of that sieve of water from the river over there."

He took the sieve in his hand and went over to the river, but as often as ever he would stoop and fill it with water, the moment he raised it the water would run out of it again, and sure, if he had been there, from that day till this, he never could have filled it. A crow went flying by him, over his head, "Daub! daub!" said the crow. "My blessings on ye, then," said Munachar, "but it's the good advice you have," and he took the red clay and the daub that was by the brink, and he rubbed it to the bottom of the sieve, until all the holes were filled, and then the sieve held the water, and he brought the water to the miller, and the miller gave him the makings of a cake, and he gave the makings of the cake to the threshers, and the threshers gave him a whisp of straw, and he gave the

whisp of straw to the cow, and the cow gave him milk, the milk he gave to the cat, the cat scraped the butter, the butter went into the claw of the hound, the hound hunted the deer, the deer swam the water, the water wet the flag, the flag sharpened the axe, the axe cut the rod, and the rod made a gad, and when he had it ready to hang Manachar he found that Manachar had BURST.

Scotland

The Woman Who Flummoxed the Fairies

Sorche Nic Leodhas is the Gaelic name used by Leclaire Alger, a Pittsburgh children's librarian who heard as a child the stories she has collected. The staunch humor and rhythmic language of these stories have a unique and gentle charm. [From Sorche Nic Leodhas, *Heather and Broom* (Holt, 1960).]

There was a woman once who was a master baker. Her bannocks were like wheaten cakes, her wheaten cakes were like the finest pastries, and her pastries were like nothing but Heaven itself in the mouth!

Not having her match, or anything like it, in seven counties round she made a good penny by it, for there wasn't a wedding nor a christening for miles around in the countryside but she was called upon to make the cakes for it, and she got all the trade of all the gentry as well. She was fair in her prices and she was honest, too, but she was that good-hearted into the bargain. Those who could pay well she charged aplenty, but when some poor body came and begged her to make a wee bit of a cake for a celebration and timidly offered her the little money they had for it, she'd wave it away and tell them to pay her when they got the cake. Then she'd set to and bake a cake as fine and big as any she'd make for a laird, and she'd send it to them as a gift, with the best respects of her husband and herself, to the wedding pair or the parents of the baby that was to be christened, so nobody's feelings were hurt.

Not only was she a master baker, but she was the cleverest woman in the world; and it was the first that got her into trouble, but it was the second that got her out of it.

The fairies have their own good foods to eat, but they dearly love a bit of baker's cake once in a while, and will often steal a slice of one by night from a kitchen while all the folks in a house are sleeping.

In a nearby hill there was a place where the fairies lived, and of all cakes the ones the fairies liked best were the ones this master baker made. The trouble was, the taste of one was hard to come by, for her cakes were all so good that they were always eaten up at a sitting, with hardly a crumb left over for a poor fairy to find.

So then the fairies plotted together to carry the woman away and to keep her with them always just to bake cakes for them.

Their chance came not long after, for there was to be a great wedding at the castle with hundreds of guests invited, and the woman was to make the cakes. There would have to be so many of them, with so many people coming to eat them, that the woman was to spend the whole day before the wedding in the castle kitchen doing nothing but bake one cake after another!

The fairies learned about this from one of their number who had been listening at the keyhole of the baker's door. They found out, too, what road she'd be taking coming home.

When the night came, there they were by a fairy mound where the road went by, hiding in flower cups, and under leaves, and in all manner of places.

When she came by they all flew out at her. "The fireflies are gey thick the night," said she. But it was not fireflies. It was fairies with the moonlight sparkling on their wings.

Then the fairies drifted fern seed into her eyes, and all of a sudden she was that sleepy that she could go not one step farther without a bit of a rest!

"Mercy me!" she said with a yawn. "It's worn myself out I have this day!" And she sank down on what she took to be a grassy bank to doze just for a minute. But it wasn't a bank at all. It was the fairy mound, and once she lay upon it she was in the fairies' power.

She knew nothing about that nor anything else till she woke again, and found herself in fairyland. Being a clever woman she didn't have to be told where she was, and she guessed how she got there. But she didn't let on.

"Well now," she said happily, "and did you ever! It's all my life I've wanted to get a peep into fairyland. And here I am!"

They told her what they wanted, and she said to herself, indeed she had no notion of staying there the rest of her life! But she didn't tell the fairies that either.

"To be sure!" she said cheerfully. "Why you poor wee things! To think of me baking cakes for everyone else, and not a one for you! So let's be at it," said she, "with no time wasted."

Then from her kittiebag that hung at her side she took a clean apron and tied it around her waist, while the fairies, happy that she was so willing, licked their lips in anticipation and rubbed their hands for joy.

"Let me see now," said she, looking around her. "Well, 'tis plain you have nothing for me to be baking a cake with. You'll just have to be going to my own kitchen to fetch back what I'll need."

Yes, the fairies could do that. So she sent some for eggs, and some for sugar, and some for flour, and some for butter, while others flew off to get a wheen of other things she told them she had to have. At last all was ready for the mixing and the woman asked for a bowl. But the biggest one they could find for her was the size of a teacup, and a wee dainty one at that.

Well then, there was nothing for it, but they must go and fetch her big yellow crockery bowl from off the shelf over the water butt. And after that it was her wooden spoons and her egg whisp and one thing and another, till the fairies were all fagged out, what with the flying back and forth, and the carrying, and only the thought of the cake to come of it kept their spirits up at all.

At last everything she wanted was at hand. The woman began to measure and mix and whip and beat. But all of a sudden she stopped.

" 'Tis no use!" she sighed. "I can't ever seem

to mix a cake without my cat beside me, purring."

"Fetch the cat!" said the fairy king sharply.

So they fetched the cat. The cat lay at the woman's feet and purred, and the woman stirred away at the bowl, and for a while all was well. But not for long.

The woman let go of the spoon and sighed again. "Well now, would you think it?" said she. "I'm that used to my dog setting the time of my beating by the way he snores at every second beat that I can't seem to get the beat right without him."

"Fetch the dog!" cried the king.

So they fetched the dog and he curled up at her feet beside the cat. The dog snored, the cat purred, the woman beat the cake batter, and all was well again. Or so the fairies thought.

But no! The woman stopped again. "I'm that worrited about my babe," said she. "Away from him all night as I've been, and him with a new tooth pushing through this very week. It seems I just can't mix . . ."

"Fetch that babe!" roared the fairy king, without waiting for her to finish what she was saying. And they fetched the babe.

So the woman began to beat the batter again. But when they brought the babe, he began to scream the minute he saw her, for he was hungry, as she knew he would be, because he never would let his dadda feed him his porridge and she had not been home to do it.

"I'm sorry to trouble you," said the woman, raising her voice above the screaming of the babe, "but I can't stop beating now lest the cake go wrong. Happen my husband could get the babe quiet if . . ."

The fairies didn't wait for the king to tell them what to do. Off they flew and fetched the husband back with them. He, poor man, was all in a whirl, what with things disappearing from under his eyes right and left, and then being snatched through the air himself the way he was. But here was his wife, and he knew where she was things couldn't go far wrong. But the baby went on screaming.

So the woman beat the batter, and the baby screamed, and the cat purred, and the dog snored, and the man rubbed his eyes and watched his wife to see what she was up to. The fairies settled down, though 'twas plain to see that the babe's screaming disturbed them. Still, they looked hopeful.

Then the woman reached over and took up the egg whisp and gave the wooden spoon to the babe, who at once began to bang away with it, screaming just the same. Under cover of the screaming of the babe and the banging of the spoon and the swishing of the egg whisp the woman whispered to her husband, "Pinch the dog!"

"What?" said the man. But he did it just the same—and kept on doing it.

"TOW! ROW! ROW!" barked the dog, and added his voice to the babe's screams, and the banging of the wooden spoon, and the swishing of the egg whisp.

"Tread on the tail of the cat!" whispered the woman to her husband, and it's a wonder he could hear her. But he did. He had got the notion now and he entered the game for himself. He not only trod on the tail of the cat, but he kept his foot there while the cat howled like a dozen lost souls.

So the woman swished, and the baby screamed, and the wooden spoon banged, and the dog yelped, and the cat howled, and the whole of it made a terrible din. The fairies, king and all, flew round and round in distraction with their hands over their ears, for if there is one thing the fairies can't bear it's a lot of noise and there was a lot more than a lot of noise in fairyland that day! And what's more the woman knew what they liked and what they didn't all the time!

So then the woman got up and poured the batter into two pans that stood ready. She laid by the egg whisp and took the wooden spoon away from the babe, and picking him up she popped a lump of sugar into his mouth. That surprised him so much that he stopped screaming. She nodded to her husband and he stopped pinching the dog and took his foot from the cat's tail, and in a minute's time all was quiet. The fairies stopped flying round and round and sank down exhausted.

And then the woman said, "The cake's ready for the baking. Where's the oven?"

The fairies looked at each other in dismay, and at last the fairy queen said weakly, "There isn't any oven."

"What!" exclaimed the woman. "No oven? Well then, how do you expect me to be baking the cake?"

None of the fairies could find the answer to that.

"Well then," said the woman, "you'll just have to be taking me and the cake home to bake it in my own oven, and bring me back later when the cake's all done."

The fairies looked at the babe and the wooden spoon and the egg whisp and the dog and the cat and the man. And then they all shuddered like one.

"You may all go!" said the fairy king. "But don't ask us to be taking you. We're all too tired."

"Och, you must have your cake then," said the woman, feeling sorry for them now she'd got what she wanted, which was to go back to her own home, "after all the trouble you've had for it! I'll tell you what I'll do. After it's baked, I'll be leaving it for you beside the road, behind the bank where you found me. And what's more I'll put one there for you every single week's end from now on."

The thought of having one of the woman's cakes every week revived the fairies so that they forgot they were all worn out. Or almost did.

"I'll not be outdone!" cried the fairy king. "For what you find in that same place shall be your own!"

Then the woman picked up the pans of batter, and the man tucked the bowls and spoons and things under one arm and the baby under the other. The fairy king raised an arm and the hill split open. Out they all walked, the woman with the pans of batter, the man with the bowls and the babe, and the dog and cat at their heels. Down the road they walked and back to their own house, and never looked behind them.

When they got back to their home the woman put the pans of batter into the oven, and then she dished out the porridge that stood keeping hot on the back of the fire and gave the babe his supper.

There wasn't a sound in that house except for the clock ticking and the kettle singing and the cat purring and the dog snoring. And all those were soft, quiet sounds.

"I'll tell you what," said the man at last. "It doesn't seem fair on the rest of the men that I should have the master baker and the cleverest woman in the world all in one wife."

"Trade me off then for one of the ordinary kind," said his wife, laughing at him.

"I'll not do it," said he. "I'm very well suited as I am."

So that's the way the woman flummoxed the fairies. A good thing she made out of it, too, for when the cake was baked and cooled the woman took it up and put it behind the fairy mound, as she had promised. And when she set it down she saw there a little brown bag. She took the bag up and opened it and looked within, and it was full of bright shining yellow gold pieces.

And so it went, week after week. A cake for the fairies, a bag of gold for the woman and her husband. They never saw one of the fairies again, but the bargain never was broken and they grew rich by it. So of course they lived, as why should they not, happily ever after.

Kate Crackernuts

Another resourceful Scottish lass flummoxes the fairies in the following tale. In a reversal of Charles Perrault's "The Twelve Dancing Princesses," it is the young woman whose wits and spirit rescue and win the enchanted prince. The theme of love between sisters and the motif of the animal-head enchantment upon Kate's sister have parallels in the Norwegian "Tatterhood." Joseph Jacobs gives a version of this story in his *English Folk and Fairy Tales*. Alison Lurie has gone back to the original Orkney Island source in *Folk-Lore*, Vol. I, 1890, for her retelling. In her words: "This Scottish tale is one of many that have been cited as proof that the fairies were the original prehistoric inhabitants of the British Isles, little folk who built their houses underground. Some of the grass-covered mounds that are thought to have been their dwellings can still be seen in the Orkney Islands, where 'Kate Crackernuts' was recorded." [From Alison Lurie, *Clever Gretchen and Other Forgotten Folktales* (Crowell, 1980).]

Once upon a time there was a king and a queen, such as there have been in many lands. The king had a daughter, and the queen had one also. And though they were no kin, yet the two girls loved each other better than sisters. But the queen was jealous because the king's daughter Ann was prettier than her own daughter Kate. She wished to find some way to spoil Ann's beauty; so she went to consult the henwife, who was a witch.

"Aye, I can help you," said the henwife. "Send her to me in the morning; but make sure she does not eat anything before she comes." And she put her big black pot on the fire, and boiled a sheep's hide and bones in it, with other nasty things.

Early in the morning the queen told Ann to go to the henwife and fetch some eggs. But as she left the house, Ann took up a crust of bread to eat on the way. When she asked for the eggs, the witch said to her, "Lift the lid off that pot, and you will find what you need." So the king's daughter lifted the lid; but nothing came out of the pot except an evil smell. "Go back to your mother, and tell her to keep her pantry door better locked," said the henwife.

When the queen heard this message, she knew that Ann must have had something to eat. So she locked her pantry, and next morning sent the girl off again. But as Ann went through the garden she saw the gardener picking vegetables. Being a friendly girl, she stopped to speak with him, and he gave her a handful of peas to eat. And when she got to the henwife's house, everything happened just as before.

On the third morning the queen went down to the gate with Ann, so as to be certain she would eat nothing on her way to the witch. And this time, when Ann lifted the lid of the pot, off jumped her own pretty head, and on jumped a sheep's head in its place.

When the queen looked out her window and saw Ann coming back with her sheep's head, she laughed out loud with satisfaction. "Look at your sister," she said to her own daughter Kate. "Now you are the prettiest by far."

"That pleases me not," said Kate. And she would say no more to her mother, but wrapped a fine linen cloth around her sister's head, and took her by the hand, and they went out into the world together to seek their fortunes.

They walked on far, and further than I can tell, eating the berries that grew by the roadside, and the nuts that Kate gathered in her apron and cracked as they went along. At last they came to a tall castle. Kate knocked at the castle door, and begged a night's lodging for herself and her sister.

Now the king and queen of that place had two sons, and the elder of them was ill with a strange wasting illness. Though he ate heartily, and slept late, yet every morning he was more thin and pale than the evening before. The king had offered a peck of gold to anyone who would sit up with his son for three nights and find out what ailed him. Many had tried, but all had failed. But Kate was a clever girl and a brave girl, and she offered to sit up with the prince. She did not go boldly into his room as the others had, but arranged to have herself hidden there in the evening, and watched to see what would happen.

Till midnight all was quiet. As twelve o'clock struck, however, the sick prince rose, dressed himself, and went downstairs. He walked as if in a dream, and did not seem to notice Kate following after him. He went to the stables, saddled his horse, called his hound, and mounted. Kate leapt up behind him, but he paid her no heed. Away went the horse with the prince and Kate through the greenwood, where the nuts were ripe. As they passed under the trees, Kate picked the nuts and filled her apron with them, for she did not know when they might come back again.

They rode on and on, till they came to a green hill. There the prince drew rein and spoke for the first time, saying, "Open, open, green hill, and let in the young prince with his horse and his hound."

And Kate added, "and his lady behind him."

Then the hill opened, and they passed into a great hall filled with bright light that seemed to come from nowhere, and a strange music playing. Kate slipped down off the horse, and hid herself behind the door. At once the prince was surrounded by fairy ladies who led him off to the dance. All night he danced without stopping, first with one and then with another, and though he looked weary and worn they would not let him leave off.

At last the cock crew, and the prince made haste to mount his horse. Kate jumped up behind, and they rode home, where the prince lay down to sleep paler and more ill than before.

The next night when the clock struck twelve the same thing happened; and again Kate rode through the forest behind the prince into the green hill. This time she did not watch the dancing, but crept near to where some of the fairy people were sitting together and a fairy baby was playing with a wand.

"What news in the world above?" said one.

"No news," said the other, "but that a sad lady with a sheep's head has come to lodge in the castle."

"Is that so?" said the first, laughing. "If only she knew that three strokes of that wand would make her as fair as she ever was."

Kate heard this, and thought that she must have the wand. She took some nuts and rolled them toward the baby from behind the door, till the baby ran after the nuts and let the wand fall, and Kate snatched it up and put it in her apron. At cockcrow she rode home as before, and the prince lay down to sleep, looking weary and ill unto death. Kate ran to her room and tapped her sister Ann three times with the wand; and the sheep's head jumped off and Ann had her own pretty head again. Then Ann dressed herself and went into the great hall of the castle where all welcomed her, and the king's younger son thought that he had never seen anyone sweeter and prettier in his life.

On the third night, Kate watched the sick prince again, and rode behind him to the green hill. Again she hid behind the door and listened to the talk of the fairy people. This time the little child was playing with a yellow bird.

"What news in the world above?" said one fairy to the other.

"No news, but that the king and queen are at their wits' end to know what ails their eldest son."

"Is that so?" said the first fairy, laughing. "If only they knew that three bites of that birdie would free him from the spell and make him as well as ever he was."

Kate heard this, and thought that she must have the yellow birdie. So she rolled nuts to the baby until he ran after them and dropped the birdie, and she caught it up and put it in her apron.

At cockcrow they set off for home again, and as soon as they got there Kate plucked and cooked the yellow birdie and took it to the prince. He was lying in bed more dead than alive after his night's dancing; but when he smelled the dish, he opened his eyes and said, "Oh, I wish I had a bite of that birdie!" So Kate gave him a bite, and he rose up on his elbow.

By and by he cried out again, "Oh, if only I had another bite of that birdie!" Kate gave him another bite, and the prince sat up on his bed and looked about him. Then he said again, "Oh, if only I had a third bite of that birdie!" Kate gave him a third bite, and he got out of bed, well and strong again. He dressed himself and sat down by the fire, and Kate told him all that had passed. They stayed there till it was full morning, and the people of the castle came in and found them cracking nuts together.

So Kate married the king's eldest son, and Ann married his brother, and they lived happily together ever after.

Upright John

"Upright John" is a Gaelic fairy tale, in the pattern of the Grimms' "The Golden Bird." It is retold by Alan Garner from the version in J. F. Campbell's *Popular Tales of the West Highlands,* which was published in four volumes between 1860 and 1862. Garner has skillfully captured the singing music of the language, recreating the magic of the oral tradition. [From Alan Garner, *The Lad of the Gad* (Philomel, 1981).]

There was a king and a queen, and between them was a son called Upright John. The queen died, and the king married another.

One day John was at the hunting hill, and

he got no game at all. He saw a blue falcon and let an arrow at her, but he did no more than to drive a feather from her wing. He lifted the feather, put it in his bag and went home.

When he came home, his stepmother said to him, "Where is the game today?" He took out the feather and gave it to her.

She said, "I set it as crosses and as spells, and as the decay of the year on you, and as the seven fairy fetters of going and straying, that you shall not be without a pool in your shoe, and that you shall be wet, cold and soiled, until you get for me the bird from which that feather came."

And John said to her, "I set it as crosses and as spells, and as the decay of the year on you, and as the seven fairy fetters of going and straying, that you shall stand with one foot on the castle, and the other on the hall, and that your face shall be to the tempest whatever wind blows, until I return."

He went away to look for the falcon from which the feather came, and his stepmother the queen was standing with one foot on the castle and the other on the hall, her front to the face of the tempest, however long he might be away.

Upright John went, travelling the waste, but he could not see the falcon. He was by himself, and the night came blind and dark, and he crouched at the root of a briar.

A Foxy Lad appeared to him and said, "You are sad, Upright John. Bad is the night on which you have come. I myself have only a trotter and a sheep's cheek, but they must do."

They blew a fire heap, and they roasted flesh and ate the trotter and the sheep's cheek. And the next morning the Foxy Lad said to the king's son, "The Blue Falcon is with the Giant of the Five Heads, the Five Humps and the Five Throttles, and I shall show you where he lives.

"And my advice to you," said the Foxy Lad, "is for you to be his servant, nimble to do all that he asks of you, and each thing he entrusts to you, with exceeding care. Be very good to his birds, and he will let you feed the Blue Falcon. And when the giant is not at home, run away with her: but see that no part of her touches any one thing that is the giant's, or your matter will not go well with you."

"I shall do all these things," said Upright John.

He went to the giant's house. He struck at the door.

"Who is there?" said the giant.

"One coming to see if you need a lad," said John.

"What can you do?" said the giant.

"I feed birds," said John, "and swine; milk a cow, a goat or a sheep."

"I want someone like you," said the giant.

The giant came out and he settled wages with John, and John was nimble and took exceeding care of everything the giant had.

"My lad is so good," said the giant, "that I begin to think he may be trusted to feed the Blue Falcon."

So the giant gave the Blue Falcon to Upright John for him to feed her, and he took exceeding care of the falcon. And when the giant saw how well he was caring for her, he thought he would trust him altogether, so he gave the falcon to John for him to keep her, and John took exceeding care of the falcon.

The giant thought that each thing was going right, and he went from the house one day.

Then Upright John said, "It is time to go," and he took the falcon. But when he opened the door and the falcon saw sunlight, she spread her wings to fly, and the point of one of the feathers on one of her wings touched one of the posts of the door, and the post let loose a screech.

The Giant of the Five Heads, the Five Humps and the Five Throttles came home running, and caught Upright John and took the falcon from him.

"I would not give you my Blue Falcon," said the giant, "unless you could get for me the White Sword of Light that the Seven Big Women of Jura keep."

And the giant sent Upright John away.

John went out again, travelling the waste, and the Foxy Lad met with him, and he said, "You are sad, Upright John. You did not, and you will not, as I told you. Bad is the night on which you have come. I have only a trotter and a sheep's cheek, but they must do."

They blew a fire heap, and they roasted flesh and ate the trotter and the sheep's cheek. And the next morning the Foxy Lad said to the king's son, "I shall grow into a ship and take you over the sea to Jura.

"And my advice to you," said the Foxy Lad, "is that you say to the Big Women that you will be their polishing-lad, and that you are good at brightening iron and steel, gold and silver, at burnishing and at making all things gleam. Be nimble. Do every job with exceeding care. Then, when they trust you with the White Sword of Light, run away with it: but see that the sheath touches no part that is of the inside of where the Big Women live, or your matter will not go well with you."

"I shall do all those things," said Upright John.

The Foxy Lad grew into a ship, and they sailed across and came to shore at the Rock of the Flea on the north side of Jura, and Upright John went to take service with the Seven Big Women there.

He struck at the door. The Seven Big Women came out and asked him what he wanted.

"I have come to find if you need a polishing-lad," said John.

"What can you polish?" said they.

"I brighten, make clear shining, gold and silver, or iron, or steel," said John.

They said, "We have a use for you," and they set wages on him.

He was nimble for six weeks, and put everything in exceeding order; and the Big Women said to each other, "This is the best lad we have ever had." Then they said, "We can trust him with the White Sword of Light."

They gave the White Sword of Light to Upright John, and he took exceeding care of it until one day that the Seven Big Women of Jura were not in the house, and he thought that then was the time for him to run.

He put the White Sword of Light into the sheath, and lifted it on his shoulder; but when he went out of the door, the point touched the lintel, and the lintel let loose a screech.

The Seven Big Women of Jura came home running, and caught Upright John and took the White Sword of Light from him.

"We would not give you our White Sword of Light," said the Big Women, "unless you could get for us the Yellow Horse of the King of Irrua."

John went out again to the shore, and the Foxy Lad met with him, and he said, "You are sad, Upright John. You did not, and you will not, as I told you. Bad is the night on which you have come. I have only a trotter and a sheep's cheek, but they must do."

They blew a fire heap, and they roasted flesh and ate the trotter and the sheep's cheek. And the next morning the Foxy Lad said to the king's son, "I shall grow into a ship and take you over the sea to Irrua.

"And my advice to you," said the Foxy Lad, "is that you go to the house of the king and ask to be a stabling-lad to him. Be nimble. Do every job with exceeding care, and keep the horses and the harness in exceeding order, till the king trusts the Yellow Horse to you. And when there is the chance, run away: but take care that no morsel of the horse touches anything that is on the inner side of the gate but the hooves of its feet, or your matter will not go well with you."

"I shall do all those things," said Upright John.

The Foxy Lad grew into a ship, and they sailed across to Irrua.

John went to the king's house. He struck at the door.

"Where are you going?" said the gatekeeper.

"To see if the king has need of a stabling-lad," said John.

The king came out and said, "What can you do?"

"I clean and feed horses," said John, "and I shine tackle."

"I have a use for you," said the king, and he set wages on him, and John went to the stable, and he put each thing in exceeding order and took exceeding care of the horses, and fed them, kept their hides clean and sleek, and he was nimble with the tackle.

The king said, "This is the best stabling-lad I have ever known. I can trust the Yellow Horse to him."

The king gave the Yellow Horse to John for him to look after, and he looked after her until she was so sleek and slippery, and so swift, that she would leave the one wind and catch the other.

Then the king went hunting one day, and Upright John thought that was the time to steal the Yellow Horse. He set her with a bridle and saddle and all that belonged to her, and when he led her out of the stable and was taking her through the gate, she gave a switch of her tail, and a hair of it touched the post of the gate, and the gate let loose a screech.

The king came home running, and caught Upright John and took the Yellow Horse from him.

"I would not give you my Yellow Horse," said the king, "unless you could get for me the Daughter of the King of the Frang."

John went out again to the shore, and the Foxy Lad met with him, and he said, "You are sad, Upright John. You did not, and you will not, as I told you. Bad is the night on which you have come. I have only a trotter and a sheep's cheek, but they must do."

They blew a fire heap, and they roasted flesh and ate the trotter and the sheep's cheek. And the next morning the Foxy Lad said to the king's son, "I shall grow into a ship and take you over the sea to the Frang."

The Foxy Lad grew into a ship, and they sailed across to the Frang.

The Foxy Lad ran himself high up the face of a rock, on dry dried land, and he said to John, "Go to the king's house and ask for help, and say that your steersman has been lost in a storm and the ship thrown on shore."

John went to the king's house. He struck at the door.

"What are you doing here?" said the king.

"A storm came upon me," said Upright John, "and my steersman was lost, and the ship has been thrown on shore and is there now, driven up the face of a rock by the waves, and I have not the strength to get her down."

The king and the queen, and the family together, went to see the ship. And when they looked at the ship, exceeding sweet music was heard in her.

There were tunes with wings,
Lullaby harps, gentle strings,
Songs between fiddles
That would set in sound lasting sleep
Wounded men and travailing women
Withering away for ever
With the piping of the music
The Foxy Lad did play.

And the Daughter of the King of the Frang went on the ship to watch the music, and Upright John went with her. And when they were in one part, the music was in another, and when they were in that other, it would be elsewhere, and when they were there, they heard it on the deck, and when they were on the deck, the ship was out on the ocean and making sea-hiding with the land.

The king's daughter said, "Bad is the trick you have done me and bad the night on which you have come. Where will you take me now?"

"We are going," said Upright John, "to give you as a wife to the King of Irrua; to get from him his Yellow Horse; to give that to the Seven Big Women of Jura; to get from them their White Sword of Light; to give that to the Giant of the Five Heads, the Five Humps and the Five Throttles; to get from him his Blue Falcon; to take her home to my stepmother, the Bad Straddling Queen, that I may be free from my crosses and my spells and the sick diseases of the year."

"I had rather be as a wife to you," said the Daughter of the King of the Frang.

When they came to shore in Irrua, the Foxy Lad put himself in the shape of the Daughter of the Sun, and he said to Upright John, "Leave the woman here till we come back, and I shall go with you to the King of Irrua; and I shall give him enough of a wifing."

Upright John went with the Foxy Lad in the shape of the Daughter of the Sun, and when the king saw them he took out the Yellow Horse, put a golden saddle on her back, a silver bridle in her head, and gave her to John.

John rode the horse back to the Daughter of the King of the Frang, and they waited.

The King of Irrua and the Foxy Lad were married that same day, and when they went to their rest, the Foxy Lad gave a dark spring, and he did not leave a toothful of flesh between the back of the neck and the haunch of the King of Irrua that was not worried and wounded: and he ran to where Upright John and the Daughter of the King of the Frang were waiting.

"How did you get free?" said John.

"A man is kind to his life," said the Foxy Lad.

The Foxy Lad grew into a ship, and he took them all to Jura.

They landed at the Rock of the Flea on the north side of Jura, and the Foxy Lad said to Upright John, "Leave the king's daughter and the Yellow Horse here till we come back, and I shall go with you to the Big Women, and I shall give them enough of a horsing."

The Foxy Lad went into the shape of a yellow horse, Upright John put the golden saddle on his back, and the silver bridle in his head, and they went to the house of the Seven Big Women of Jura.

When they saw John, the Big Women came to meet him, and they gave him the White Sword of Light.

John took the saddle off the back of the Foxy Lad and the bridle out of his head, and he left him with the Big Women and went away. The Big Women put a saddle on the Foxy Lad, and bridled his head, and one of them went up on his back to ride him. Another went on the back of that one, and another on the back of that one, and there was always room for another one there, till one after one the Seven Big Women of Jura went up on the back of the Foxy Lad, thinking that they had got the Yellow Horse of Irrua.

One of them gave a blow of a rod to the Foxy Lad: and if she gave, he ran.

He charged with them through the mountain moors, singing iolla, bounding high to the tops, moving his front to the crag, and he put his two forefeet to the crag, and he threw his rump end on high, and the Seven Big Women went into the air and over the Paps of Jura.

The Foxy Lad ran away laughing to where Upright John and the king's daughter were waiting with the Yellow Horse and the White Sword of Light.

"How did you get free?" said John.

"A man is kind to his life," said the Foxy Lad.

The Foxy Lad grew into a ship, and he took them all to the mainland.

When they had landed, the Foxy Lad said, "Leave the king's daughter here with the Yellow Horse and the White Sword of Light, and take me to the giant, and I shall give him enough of a blading."

The Foxy Lad put himself into the shape of a sword, and Upright John took him to the giant. And when the Giant of the Five Heads, the Five Humps and the Five Throttles saw them coming, he put the Blue Falcon in a basket and gave it to John.

John went back to the king's daughter, and the Foxy Lad came running.

"How did you get free?" said John.

"Ho! Huth!" said the Foxy Lad. "A man is kind to his life, but I was in the giant's hand when he began at fencing and slashing, and, 'I shall cut this oak tree,' said he, 'at one blow, which my father cut two hundred years before now with the same sword.' And he gripped me and swung me, and with the first blow he cut the tree all but a small bit of bark; and the second blow I bent on myself and swept the five heads the five humps and the five throttles off him. And there is not a tooth in the door of my mouth left unbroken for sake of that filth of a blue marvellous bird!"

"What shall be done to your teeth?" said John.

"There is no help for it," said the Foxy Lad. "So put the saddle of gold on the Yellow Horse, and the silver bridle in her head, and go you yourself riding there, and take the Daughter of the King of the Frang behind you, and the White Sword of Light with its back against your nose. And if you do not go in that way, when your stepmother sees you, she has an eye so evil that you will fall a faggot of firewood. But if the back of the sword is against your nose, and its edge to the Bad Straddling Queen, she will split her glance and fall herself as sticks."

Upright John did as the Foxy Lad told him. And when he came in sight of the castle, his stepmother, with one foot on the castle and the other on the hall, her front to the face of the tempest, looked at him with an evil eye. But she split her glance on the edge of the White Sword of Light, and she fell as sticks.

Upright John set fire to the sticks, burnt the Bad Straddling Queen, and was free of fear.

He said to the Foxy Lad, "I have got the best wife of the world; the horse that will leave the one wind and catch the other; the falcon that will fetch me game; the sword that will keep off each foe; and I am free of fear.

"And you, you Lad of March, have been my dearest friend since we were on the time of one trotter and a sheep's cheek. Go now for ever through my ground. No arrow will be let at you. No trap will be set for you. Take any beast to take with you. Go now through my ground for ever."

"Keep your herds and your flocks to yourself," said the Foxy Lad. "There is many a one who has trotters and sheep as well as you. I shall get flesh without coming to put trouble here. Peace on you, and my blessing, blessing, blessing, Upright John."

He went away. The tale was spent.

Spain

The Flea

The helpful animals of folklore! They are myriad in every culture. In this Spanish tale, the ant, the beetle, and the mouse make possible the shepherd's winning of the princess. However, this story takes an unprecedented turn, for if the princess will have none of the shepherd, by the same token he will have none of her, preferring to take his treasure and return to the mountains, to marry one of his own kind.

The artful hand of a fine storyteller is perceptible in this version. Ruth Sawyer is a distinguished collector of tales as well as a teller of them, and her mastery of the written word as well as of the spoken is responsible for the sure dramatic development of the plot, and the flavor of locale and custom. [From Ruth Sawyer, *Picture Tales from Spain* (Lippincott, 1936).]

Once there was and was not a King of Spain. He loved to laugh; he loved a good joke as well as any common fellow. Best of all he loved a riddle.

One day he was being dressed by his chamberlain. As the royal doublet was being slipped over the royal head, a flea jumped from the safe hiding-place of the stiff lace ruff. He landed directly upon the King.

Quicker than half a wink the King clapped his hand over the flea and began to laugh. *"Por Dios,* a flea! Who ever heard of a King of Spain having a flea? It is monstrous—it is delicious! We must not treat her lightly, this flea. You perceive, My Lord Chamberlain, that having jumped on the royal person, she has now become a royal flea. Consider what we shall do with her."

But the chamberlain was a man of little wit. He could clothe the King's body but he could not add one ribbon or one button to the King's imagination. "I have it!" said the King at last, exploding again into laughter. "We will pasture out this flea—in a great cage—large enough for a goat—an ox—an elephant. She shall be fed enormously. When she is of a proper size I will have her killed and her skin made into a tambourine. The Infanta, my daughter, shall dance to it. We will make a fine riddle out of it. Whichever suitor that comes courting her who can answer the riddle shall marry with her. *There* is a royal joke worthy of a King! Eh, my Lord Chamberlain? And we will call the flea Felipa."

In his secret heart the chamberlain thought the King quite mad; but all he answered was: "Very good, Your Majesty," and went out to see that proper pasturage was provided for Felipa.

At the end of a fortnight the flea was as large as a rat. At the end of a month she was as large as a cat who might have eaten that rat. At the end of a second month she was the size of a dog who might have chased that cat. At the end of three months she was the size of a calf.

The King ordered Felipa killed. The skin was stretched, dried, beaten until it was as soft, as fine, as silk. Then it was made into a tambourine, with brass clappers and ribbons—the finest tambourine in all of Spain.

The Infanta, whose name was Isabel, but who was called Belita for convenience, learned to dance with Felipa very prettily; and the King himself composed a rhyme to go with the riddle. Whenever a suitor came courting, the Infanta would dance and when she had finished, the King would recite:

"Belita—Felipa—they dance well together—
Belita—Felipa; now answer me whether
You know this Felipa—this *animalita*.
If you answer right, then you marry Belita."

Princes and dukes came from Spain and Portugal, France and Italy. They were not dull-witted like the chamberlain and they saw through the joke. The King was riddling about the tambourine. It was made from parchment and they knew perfectly well where parchment came from. So a prince would answer: "A goat, Your Majesty." And a duke would answer: "A sheep, Your Majesty"—each sure he was right. And the Infanta would run away laughing and the King would roar with delight and shout: "Wrong again!"

But after a while the King got tired of this sheep and goat business. He wanted the riddle guessed; he wanted the Infanta married. So he sent forth a command that the next suitor who failed to guess the riddle should be hung—and short work made of it, too.

That put a stop to the princes and dukes. But far up in the Castilian highlands a shepherd heard about it. He was young, but not very clever. He thought—it would be a fine thing for a shepherd to marry an Infanta, so he said to his younger brother: "Manuelito—you shall mind the sheep and goats; I will go to the King's palace."

But his mother said: "Son, you are a *tonto*. How should you guess a riddle when you cannot read or write, and those who can have failed? Stay at home and save yourself a hanging."

Having once made up his mind, nothing would stop him—not even fear. So his mother baked him a *tortilla* to carry with him, gave him her blessing and let him go.

He hadn't gone far when he was stopped by a little black ant. "Señor Pastor," she cried, "give me a ride to the King's court in your pocket."

"La Hormiguita, you cannot ride in my pocket. There is a *tortilla* there which I shall have for my breakfast. Your feet are dirty from walking, and you will tramp all over it."

"See, I will dust off my feet on the grass here and promise not to step once on the *tortilla*."

So the shepherd put the ant into his shepherd pouch and tramped on. Soon he encountered a black beetle who said: "Señor Pastor—give me a ride to the King's court in your pocket."

"El Escarabajo, you cannot ride in my pouch. There is a *tortilla* there which I shall presently have for my breakfast—and who wants a black beetle tramping all over his breakfast!"

"I will fasten my claws into the side of your pouch and not go near the *tortilla*."

So the shepherd took up the beetle and carried him along. He hadn't gone far when he came up with a little gray mouse who cried: "Señor Pastor, give me a ride to the King's court in your pouch."

But the shepherd shook his head. "Ratonperez, you are too clumsy and I don't like the flavor of your breath. It will spoil my *tortilla* that I intend to have for my breakfast."

"Why not eat the *tortilla* now and then the breakfast will be over and done with," and Ratonperez said it so gently, so coaxingly, that the shepherd thought it was a splendid idea. He sat down and ate it. He gave a little crumb to La Hormiguita, a crumb to El Escarabajo and a big crumb to Ratonperez. Then he went on his road to the King's court carrying the three creatures with him in his pouch.

When he reached the King's palace he was frightened, frightened. He sat himself down under a cork tree to wait for his courage to grow.

"What are you waiting for?" called the ant, the beetle and Ratonperez all together.

"I go to answer a riddle. If I fail I shall be hanged. That isn't so pleasant. So I wait where I can enjoy being alive for a little moment longer."

"What is the riddle?"

"I have heard that it has to do with something called Felipa that dances, whoever she may be."

"Go on and we will help you. Hurry, hurry, it is hot in your pouch."

So the shepherd climbed the palace steps, asked for the King and said that he had come to answer the riddle.

The guard passed him on to the footman, saying, *"Pobrecito!"*

The footman passed him on to the lackey, saying, *"Pobrecito!"*

The lackey passed him on to the court chamberlain, saying, *"Pobrecito!"* And it was his business to present him to the King.

The King shook his head when he saw the shepherd-staff in his hand and the shepherd-pouch hanging from his belt, and he said: "A shepherd's life is better than no life at all. Better go back to your flocks."

But the shepherd was as rich in stubbornness as he was poor in learning. He insisted he must answer the riddle. So the Infanta came and danced with the tambourine and the King laughed and said his rhyme:

"Belita—Felipa—they dance well together—
Belita—Felipa; now answer me whether
You know this Felipa—this *animalita*.
If you answer right, then you marry Belita."

The shepherd strode over and took the tambourine from the hand of the Infanta. He felt the skin carefully, carefully. To himself he said: "I know sheep and I know goats; and it isn't either."

"Can't you guess?" whispered the black beetle from his pouch.

"No," said the shepherd.

"Let me out," said the little ant; "perhaps I can tell you what it is." So the shepherd unfastened the pouch and La Hormiguita crawled out, unseen by the court. She crawled all over the tambourine and came back whispering, "You can't fool me. I'd know a flea anywhere, any size."

"Don't take all day," shouted the King. "Who is Felipa?"

"She's a flea," said the shepherd.

Then the court was in a flutter.

"I don't want to marry a shepherd," said the Infanta.

"You shan't," said the King.

"I'm the one to say 'shan't'," said the shepherd.

"I will grant you any other favor," said the Infanta.

"I will grant you another," said the King.

"It was a long journey here, walking," said the shepherd. "I would like a cart to ride home in."

"And two oxen to draw it," whispered the black beetle.

"And two oxen to draw it," repeated the shepherd.

"You shall have them," said the King.

"And what shall I give you?" asked the Infanta.

Illustration by Barbara Cooney. Illustration copyright © 1963 by Barbara Cooney, from *Favorite Fairy Tales Told in Spain,* by Virginia Haviland, by permission of Little, Brown and Co.

"Tell her you want your pouch filled with gold," whispered Ratonperez.

"That's little enough," said the Infanta.

But while the royal groom was fetching the cart and oxen; and the lord of the exchequer was fetching a bag of gold; Ratonperez was gnawing a hole in the pouch. When they came to pour in the gold, it fell through as fast as water, so that all around the feet of the shepherd it rose like a shining yellow stream.

"That's a lot of gold," said the King at last.

"It's enough," said the shepherd. He took his cart, filled it with the gold, drove back to the highlands of Castile. He married a shepherd's daughter, who never had to do anything but sit in a rocking-chair and fan herself all day. And that's a contented life, you might say—for anyone who likes it.

The General's Horse

The character of the beneficent pig, Padre Porko, in Spanish folklore presents an interesting series of conjectures. Where did he come from? For the pig is somehow not indigenous to Spain, as he would seem to be to England or Ireland, where he is the most important domestic animal. He came apparently from a time earlier than the Moors, even earlier than the Romans and the Visigoths. L. R. Muirhead, in his guide book *Southern Spain and Portugal* (Macmillan, 1929), describes early stone carvings that depict the pig. He suggests that these carvings stem from the original Iberic stock, which was Celtic, in a time predating Moors and Romans.

Padre Porko is thoroughly Spanish now, whatever his origin. Señor Don Padre Porko—the special friend of orphans and animals, a benevolent spirit, to whom people entrust their hope of good fortune. "We'll leave it to Padre Porko," they say. Robert Davis, a gifted American newspaper correspondent, had these tales direct from the mouth of a native storyteller, during an assignment in Spain. The book from which this story is taken is one of the most endearing in format, with its definitive illustrations by Fritz Eichenberg. [From Robert Davis, *Padre Porko, the Gentlemanly Pig* (Holiday House, 1939).]

It was a misty-moisty evening. The drops of rain fell from the tips of the leaves, with a "plop," into the puddles underneath. The wind blew the branches of the umbrella pine against the windows of the Padre's house. It was the sort of weather when no person or animal was willingly out-of-doors. The honest creatures of the air, the forest and the earth had long been asleep.

The Widow Hedge-Hog had washed the supper dishes, swept the hearth with her tail, warmed the Padre's flannel pajamas, and gone home to her family under the apple tree.

Before his fire the Padre dozed. He had eaten three plates of heavenly stewed carrots for his supper, and every now and then he rubbed his stomach gently, to help them digest. The tapping of the branches on the window and the falling of the rain made a soothing music. Upon the shelf above the chimney stood a polished red apple. The Padre was trying to decide whether he should eat the apple or smoke his pipe before crawling into bed for a good night's sleep.

"Rat-a-tat-tat-tat," suddenly sounded the knocker on his door.

"My Goodness Gracious," he exclaimed, pushing his feet into his red slippers. "Who can be out on a night like this? It must be someone in real trouble."

"Who is there?" he called, putting his sensitive nose to the keyhole. He could learn more through his nose than many people can learn through their ears and eyes.

"It is Antonio, the stable-boy from the General's."

"Come in, come in," invited the Padre, seating himself again, and taking out his pipe.

The door opened and a dripping figure stepped inside. Very politely he waited on the door-mat, his cap in his hand.

"Your Honor will please to excuse me for coming so late," he said. "But it was only tonight that the General said he would send me away in disgrace. My Grandmother told me that Your Honor is the Godfather of all Spanish boys who do not have real fathers, so you will please to excuse my coming."

The Padre was reaching up for the red apple. "She told you the truth, Antonio. You sit here and eat this apple, while I put tobacco in my pipe." With a skillful movement of his left hind foot the Padre kicked dry branches upon the fire.

"And don't be in any hurry, Antonio.

Take all the time you need. Tell me the very worst. Whatever the trouble, we can put it right."

"It is about the white horse," Antonio began, "the fat, white one, that the General rides in parades, at the head of his soldiers. He can't walk. It is his left front hoof." The boy gulped it out in a single breath.

"They say that it is my fault, that I made him fall when I rode him for exercise. But it's not true. I always go slowly, and turn corners at a walk."

"Let's go and see," said the Padre, going to the closet for his rubber coat. "And here's a cape for you to put around your shoulders."

Once at the General's, the Padre and Antonio hung their wet things in the harness-room and unhooked the door of the box stall where the white horse lived. He was a superb animal, but he stood with one front foot off the floor.

"Excuse me, Your Excellency, but can you tell me the cause of Your Excellency's lameness?"

The great beast pricked up his ears. "The cause of it!" he snorted. "Why a three-day-old colt would know that much, and yet these stupid doctors and professors have been pestering me for two weeks. A wire nail has gone into the tender center of my foot. It has no head. You cannot see it. The idiots, and they pretend to know so much."

"I thought as much," murmured the Padre, sympathetically. "And will Your Excellency co-operate with us, if we try to get the nail out?"

"Won't I, though!" The horse snorted again. "Why, I haven't been able to touch this foot to the ground for sixteen days."

"This is a case for the Rat Family, and for no one else," said the Padre to himself. He trotted over to a hole in the stable floor. His voice, as he leaned over the opening, was a soft whine through his nose. "Is the lady of the house at home?"

A gray muzzle appeared. "I am only a poor widow, Don Porko; my husband was caught in a trap last harvest time. But if my children and a poor soul like me can be of any help to you, you are more than welcome to our best."

"Indeed you can, Mrs. Furrynose," said the Padre with enthusiasm. "We animals are going to do what none of the veterinary professors knew how to do. Listen carefully. Of all the rats in this town which one has the strongest teeth?" Other heads had joined Mother Furrynose at the opening, and now they all answered in a single unanimous squeak, "Uncle Israel, down at the flour-mill."

"Good," said the Padre. "And now, Mrs. Furrynose, I want you to listen once more. Will you send your oldest boy for Uncle Israel right away? Tell him that Padre Porko needs all the husky boy and girl rats in this town at the General's stable in half-an-hour."

Before the Padre had finished his request, a sleek rat was out of the hole and running toward the door. "You can count on us, Chief," he called.

Hardly ten minutes had passed when a peculiar noise was heard outside the stable. It was like the wind blowing the dry leaves in October. It was a rustling, a bustling, a scratching, a scraping, a marching of countless feet. Uncle Israel entered at the head of his tribe. He was an old-fashioned Quaker rat, gray and gaunt, and the size of a half-grown kitten. When he smiled he showed his remarkable teeth, sharp as razors and the color of ivory. He motioned to his brown-coated army and they lined up in rows around the wall, watching him and the Padre with shoe-button eyes.

"I'm not so strong as I used to be," apologized Uncle Israel, "except for my teeth. I don't want to boast, but none of these young rats can hold on to things as hard as I can. As soon as I got your message I brought my relatives. We will do anything you say, Padre." The rows of heads nodded in agreement.

"Thank you for coming, Uncle Israel," said the Padre. "In a minute I'll explain what our work is going to be. First we must tell the General's horse our plan."

He stood by the shoulder of the white horse and spoke in his most persuasive way. "Your Excellency, we are ready for the operation that will cure your foot. But we must be sure of your co-operation. It may hurt, I'm afraid, especially at first."

"It can't hurt more than my hoof aches right now. Go ahead," said the horse.

"We must uncover the end of the nail so that Uncle Israel can grip it in his beautiful teeth. Please bend back your foot."

The General's horse rested his foot on the straw, with the under side showing, and Uncle Israel, placing one paw on either edge of the tender V, began to gnaw, his teeth cutting in like a machine. Presently he sat up, squeaking excitedly. "I have it. It's right there. It's like a piece of wire. But I can get a good hold on it. What next, Padre?"

"Antonio," ordered the Padre, "bring the halters that hang in the harness room, and tie the ropes one to the other. And you, Uncle Israel, slip your head through this loop in the leather. We will run the long rope out across the stable floor so that everyone can find a hold. Take your time, Uncle Israel, everything depends upon your teeth. When you are ready for us to pull, wiggle your tail."

Things worked like clock-work. Uncle Israel held on. Three hundred young rats strained and pulled on the rope. The General's horse winced with the pain. The Padre walked up and down like a captain in a battle. But the nail in the foot of the white horse did not budge.

Padre Porko had an idea. "Widow Furrynose, what would give you the most pleasure in the world?"

The lady replied quickly. "To bury that deceitful black cat up at the miller's." Everybody sat up and clapped his paws.

"Well, young people," said the Padre, "think that you are pulling the hearse to the graveyard, and that the miller's black cat is in it. Wouldn't you manage to get that hearse to the graveyard? Pull like that."

The floor of the barn seemed alive. It was a rippling, gray-brown carpet of straining small bodies. The teeth of Uncle Israel were locked in a death grip. Padre Porko walked back and forth, singing, "Horrible cat, get her buried, haul the hearse."

And, inch by inch, a long, thin, villainous nail came out of the horse's foot.

Then what a racket! Everyone was squirming, and squeaking, and jumping and rolling over, and tickling and nipping tails, and telling how strong he was. The white horse and Antonio

admired Uncle Israel's teeth. And all of his nephews and nieces and grandchildren were so proud of him that they kissed him on both whiskers. Padre Porko kept repeating, "I'm proud of you. Great work! I always say that we animals can do anything, if we will work together."

But it was the General's horse who brought the evening to its perfect close. He whinnied into the Padre's ear, "Please translate to Antonio that if he will unlock the oat box I'm sure our friends would enjoy a light lunch. The General himself would be the first to propose it. He will be very thankful when he visits the stable tomorrow and finds me trotting on four legs."

Mrs. Furrynose and Uncle Israel had the young people sit in circles of ten, while Antonio passed the refreshments, pouring a little pile of oats in the center of each circle. Over three hundred guests were served but their table manners were excellent. No one snatched or grabbed, or gobbled his food. Everyone said, "If you please," and "Thank you," and "Excuse me for talking when my mouth is full."

When the crunching was at its height, Uncle Israel made a speech. "Padre Porko, Your Excellency, and friends, relatives and neighbors, this is a proud and happy night for me. In all my life my teeth never did such good work before. They helped this noble white horse, and they enabled us rats to aid the Padre in one of his kind acts. But, also, tonight, my teeth brought me to the attention of a lovely lady, Madame Furrynose, and I am delighted to say that she will not be a widow much longer. One and all, you are invited to the wedding, which will be held next Sunday afternoon in the flour-mill, while the miller is at church. And the Padre Porko has promised to send word to all dogs and cats of the town that none of our guests are to be caught while going, coming or at the party." A hurricane of cheers and clapping followed the speech.

The pink nose of the white horse pushed through the window of his stall, and the merrymakers looked up. "May I, too, offer a wedding present to these worthy friends? Every night I will leave a handful of grain in the corner of my manger. They will find it there for their midnight lunch. A wedded pair with such polite manners can be trusted not to disturb the repose of a hard-working old horse."

The morning sun crept along the stable wall until it shone directly upon the sleeping Antonio. He sat up and rubbed his eyes. How did it happen that he was not in his bed, but in the box stall of the General's horse? And the horse was stamping with the foot that had been lame. Queerer still, the grain box was open and half the oats were gone. And what was the meaning of the four halter ropes tied together?

These are questions which Antonio never could answer. But when he told this story to his children, he was no longer a stable boy. He was the head trainer of all the General's racing horses.

Italy

The Silver Nose

This is an Italian variant of the Grimms' "Fitcher's Feathered Bird" and Perrault's "Bluebeard." The mysterious gentleman here is the Devil himself— with a silver nose. First published in Italian in 1956 and 1972, these tales were translated and retold from the regional dialect of Piedmont by the internationally respected novelist, Italo Calvino. [From Italo Calvino, *Italian Folk Tales*, trans. Sylvia Mulcahy (Dent, 1975).]

There was once a laundress who was a widow, and she had three daughters. They took in as much laundry as they could, but even so they barely earned enough to keep them from starvation. One day the eldest daughter said, "Mother, I want to get out of this house even if I have to go and work for the Devil himself!"

"My child, don't ever say such things," her mother said. "You can never tell what might happen if you do."

A few days later a gentleman came to the door all dressed in black. He was polite and well-mannered, and he had a silver nose.

"I know that you have three daughters," he told the mother. "Would you let one of them come and work for me?"

Ordinarily, the mother would have let her go, but there was something about that silver nose she did not like. She called her eldest daughter aside and said to her, "In this world, my dear, there are no men with silver noses, so be careful; if you go with him you may regret it."

But the daughter couldn't wait to get away from that house, so, in spite of her mother's warning, she went off with the man. They travelled along many roads, through woods and over mountains, and at a certain spot, far in the distance, they saw a big blaze of light which seemed to be coming from a burning building. The girl began to get a little frightened, and she asked, "What's that down there?"

"My house. That's where we are going," said Silver Nose. The girl went on, but she couldn't stop trembling.

They came to a great big house. Silver Nose took her to see all the rooms, each one more beautiful than the last, and he gave her a key for each of them. When they came to the door of the last room, Silver Nose gave her the key but said, "You must not open this door for any reason whatsoever; otherwise there will be trouble! You have full charge of all the others, but this room, no!"

"There must be something hidden in that room," the girl thought, and she promised herself to open that door as soon as Silver Nose left her by herself. That night, when she was asleep in her room, Silver Nose entered stealthily, crept up to the bed, and put a rose in her hair. Then he left as silently as he came.

The following morning, Silver Nose went out to attend to his affairs, and the girl, left alone in the house with all the keys, immediately ran to open the forbidden door. As soon as she unlocked it, out came a rush of smoke and flames, and in the middle of the fire and smoke was a whole crowd of damned souls who were burning. Now she realized Silver Nose was the Devil and that room was Hell. She screamed and shut the door quickly. Then she ran away as far as she could from that infernal room, but a tongue of flame had scorched the rose in her hair.

Silver Nose came home and saw the scorched rose. "Aha! so that's how you obey me," he said. Then he picked her up, opened the door of Hell, and hurled her into the flames.

The next day he went back to the laundress. "Your daughter is doing very nicely," he said, "but there is so much work to do that she needs some help. Would you be willing to let me have your second daughter?" And so Silver Nose came back with the other daughter. He showed her the house, too, gave her all the keys, and told her that she could have access to all the rooms except that last one. "And why should I want to open it?" said the girl. "I'm not interested in your private affairs!" That night, when the girl went to sleep, Silver Nose approached her bed very quietly and put a carnation in her hair.

The next morning, as soon as Silver Nose had gone, the first thing the girl did was to go and open the forbidden door: smoke, flames, shrieks of the damned! In the middle of the fire she recognized her sister, who cried out to her, "Sister, get me out of this inferno!" But the girl was just about ready to faint, so she shut the door in a hurry and ran off. She didn't know where she could hide herself since it was now certain that Silver Nose was the Devil, and she was in his hands. There was no escape. Silver Nose returned, and the first thing he did was to look at her hair. He saw the faded carnation, and without saying a word, he picked her up and threw her into Hell.

The following day, dressed as usual in the clothes of a refined gentleman, he presented himself at the house of the laundress. "There is so much work at my house that two girls are not enough; can you let me have the third too?" So he came back with the third sister, whose name was Lucy. She was the most cunning of them all. He showed her the house, too, gave her the same advice, and when she was asleep he put a flower in her hair. This time it was jasmine. In the morning, when Lucy woke up, she immediately went to comb her hair and, looking in the mirror, she saw the jasmine. "Now look at that," she said to herself. "Silver Nose has put a piece of jasmine in my hair.

What a kind thought! I'll put it in a cool place and keep it fresh." So she put the flower into a glass of water. When she had finished combing her hair, as she was alone in the house, she thought, "Now I'll go and have a look at that mysterious door."

As soon as she opened it, she was greeted with a blaze of fire, and saw all those people burning, among them her eldest sister and her second sister. "Lucy! Lucy!" they cried, "Get us out of here! Save us!"

First of all, Lucy shut the door firmly; then she began to think how she could rescue her sisters.

Just before the Devil returned, Lucy put the jasmine back in her hair, and pretended nothing had happened. Silver Nose looked at the jasmine and said: "Oh, it's fresh!"

"Certainly it's fresh, and why shouldn't it be! Does one wear faded flowers in one's hair?"

"Never mind, I meant nothing." said Silver Nose. "You seem to be a fine girl; if you continue like this, we'll always get along well together. Are you happy here?"

"Yes, I'm happy, but I would be even happier if there wasn't something bothering me."

"And what's bothering you?"

"When I left home my mother wasn't feeling well, and since then I haven't had any news from her."

"If that's all it is," said the Devil, "then I'll call there myself and bring you some news."

"Thank you, you are very kind," said Lucy. "If you can pass by there tomorrow, I'll have a sack ready with some dirty laundry, so that if my mother is feeling well you can give it to her to wash. It won't be too heavy for you, will it?"

"Now, can you imagine that!" said the Devil. "Why, I can carry any weight whatsoever."

As soon as the Devil went out, Lucy opened the door of Hell, pulled out her eldest sister and tied her up in a sack. "Stay in there and keep quiet, Charlotte," she told her. "Now the Devil himself will carry you home. But if you should feel him putting the sack down, you must say: 'I see you! I see you!' "

When Silver Nose came back, Lucy said to him, "Here is the sack of washing. But can I be sure you will take it right to my mother's house?"

"Don't you trust me?" said the Devil.

"Of course I trust you, but just the same I want you to know that I can see things from very far away, and, if you so much as try to put the sack down somewhere, I will see it."

"Well, is that so!" said the Devil, but he really didn't believe she had this power to see from a distance. He put the sack on his shoulders and exclaimed, "How heavy this washing is!"

"Naturally," said the girl. "How many years has it been since you sent anything out to be washed?"

Silver Nose started on his way, but when he was half way there, he said to himself, "It may be so, but still I want to see if this girl, with the excuse of sending out the washing, isn't actually emptying my house," and he went to put the sack down and open it.

"I see you! I see you!" shouted the sister inside the sack.

"By Jove! It is true! She *can* see from far away!" said Silver Nose to himself, and, putting the sack back on his shoulders, he went straight to the house of Lucy's mother. "Your daughter sends this washing to be done, and wants to know how you are. . . ."

As soon as she was alone, the washerwoman opened the sack, and you can imagine how happy she was to have her eldest daughter back again.

A week later, Lucy again pretended she was feeling sad and unhappy, and told Silver Nose she wanted some more news of her mother.

She sent him to her home with another sack of dirty things. So Silver Nose carried the second sister back to her mother, and never got a chance to look in the sack because he heard her shout, "I see you! I see you!"

The washerwoman, who knew by now that Silver Nose was the Devil, became frightened when she saw him coming back because she thought he was going to ask her for the clean things from the last time, but Silver Nose put the new sack down and said, "I'll come back and pick up the clean washing some other time. I have nearly broken my back with this

sack, and I don't want to be laden on my way home."

When he left, the anxious washerwoman opened the sack and threw her arms around her second daughter. But then she became frightened again because now Lucy was all alone in the hands of the Devil.

What was Lucy doing? Well, after a short while she used that story again about wanting news of her mother. The Devil was getting tired of carrying those sacks of dirty things, but this girl was so obedient that he was growing fond of her. The night before, Lucy told him she had a very bad headache and was going to bed early. "I'll leave the sack all ready for you so that if I'm not feeling well tomorrow morning, and you don't find me up, you can take it yourself."

Now I must tell you that Lucy had made a doll as big as herself out of a bundle of old rags. She put this rag doll in her bed, tucked it under the bedclothes, cut off some of her own curls and sewed them onto the doll's head so that it looked just like Lucy sleeping there in bed. Then she shut herself up in the sack.

In the morning the Devil saw the girl in bed tucked deep under the covers, so he started on his way with the sack on his back. "Now that she's not well," he said to himself, "it should be a good time for me to see if there's really nothing but dirty washing in this sack." He quickly put the sack on the ground and was about to open it. "I see you! I see you!" cried Lucy.

"By Jove!" said the Devil. "It sounds exactly as if she were right here! She's not a girl to be fooled with!" So he put the sack back on his shoulders and brought it to the washerwoman. "I'll come back later and pick it all up then," he said hurriedly. "I must go back home right away now because Lucy is sick."

So that's how the family was brought together again. And since Lucy had also brought back a good amount of the Devil's money, they were able to live happy and contented. In front of their door they planted a cross so that the Devil would never dare to come near them again.

Russia (Soviet Union)

Vasilissa the Fair

W. R. S. Ralston, English scholar of Russian culture and lifelong friend of Turgenev, called this story "one of the best folktales I know." The Russian original includes an anticlimactic ending that takes Vasilissa into town and has her weaving cloth of such fineness that she eventually reaches the attention of the king, who falls desperately in love with her. Ralston prefers his earlier ending, feeling that what follows in the Russian is of lesser dramatic interest.

In traveling through Russia, Ralston was impressed with the similarity of the children to those he had left behind in England. This link between the two countries led him to venture: "One touch of storytelling may in some instances make the whole world kin." Taken from the collections published by Afanasyev, this story (IV, No. 44) does bear a resemblance to the Cinderella motif found in many lands. [From W. R. S. Ralston, *Russian Folktales* (Smith, Elder & Co., 1873).]

In a certain kingdom there lived a merchant. Twelve years did he live as a married man, but he had only one child, Vasilissa the Fair. When her mother died, the girl was eight years old. And on her deathbed the merchant's wife called her little daughter to her, took out from under the bed-clothes a doll, gave it to her, and said, "Listen, Vasilissa, dear; remember and obey these last words of mine. I am going to die. And now, together with my parental blessing, I bequeath to you this doll. Keep it always by you, and never show it to anybody; and whenever any misfortune comes upon you, give the doll food, and ask its advice. When it has fed, it will tell you a cure for your troubles." Then the mother kissed her child and died.

After his wife's death, the merchant mourned for her a befitting time, and then began to consider about marrying again. He was a man of means. It wasn't a question with him of girls (with dowries); more than all others, a certain widow took his fancy. She was middle-aged, and had a couple of daughters of her own, just about the same age as Vasilissa. She must needs be both a good housekeeper and an experienced mother.

Well, the merchant married the widow, but he had deceived himself, for he did not find in her a kind mother for his Vasilissa. Vasilissa was the prettiest girl in all the village; but her stepmother and stepsisters were jealous of her beauty, and tormented her with every possible sort of toil, in order that she might grow thin from over-work, and be tanned by the sun and the wind. Her life was made a burden to her! Vasilissa bore everything with resignation, and every day grew plumper and prettier, while the stepmother and her daughters lost flesh and fell off in appearance from the effects of their own spite, notwithstanding that they always sat with folded hands like fine ladies.

But how did that come about? Why, it was her doll that helped Vasilissa. If it hadn't been for it, however could the girl have got through all her work? And therefore it was that Vasilissa would never eat all her share of a meal, but always kept the most delicate morsel for her doll; and at night, when all were at rest, she would shut herself up in the narrow chamber in which she slept, and feast her doll, saying the while:

"There, dolly, feed; help me in my need! I live in my father's house, but never know what pleasure is; my evil stepmother tries to drive me out of the white world; teach me how to keep alive, and what I ought to do."

Then the doll would eat, and afterwards give her advice, and comfort her in her sorrow, and next day it would do all Vasilissa's work for her. She had only to take her ease in a shady place and pluck flowers, and yet all her work was done in good time; the beds were weeded, and the pails were filled, and the cabbages were watered, and the stove was heated. Moreover, the doll showed Vasilissa herbs which prevented her from getting sunburnt. Happily did she and her doll live together.

Several years went by. Vasilissa grew up and became old enough to be married. All the marriageable young men in the town sent to make an offer to Vasilissa; at her stepmother's daughters not a soul would so much as look. Her stepmother grew even more savage than before, and replied to every suitor—

"We won't let the younger marry before her elders."

And after the suitors had been packed off, she used to beat Vasilissa by way of wreaking her spite.

Well, it happened one day that the merchant had to go away from home on business for a long time. Thereupon the stepmother went to live in another house; and near that house was a dense forest, and in a clearing in that forest there stood a hut, and in the hut there lived a Baba Yaga. She never let anyone come near her dwelling, and she ate up people like so many chickens.

Having moved into the new abode, the merchant's wife kept sending her hated Vasilissa into the forest on one pretense or another. But the girl always got home safe and sound; the doll used to show her the way, and never let her go near the Baba Yaga's dwelling.

The autumn season arrived. One evening the stepmother gave out their work to the three girls; one she set to lace-making, another to knitting socks, and the third, Vasilissa, to weaving; and each of them had her alloted amount to do. By-and-by she put out the lights in the house, leaving only one candle alight where the girls were working, and then she went to bed. The girls worked and worked. Presently the candle wanted snuffing; one of the stepdaughters took the snuffers, as if she were going to clear the wick, but instead of doing so, in obedience to her mother's orders, she snuffed the candle out, pretending to do so by accident.

"What shall we do now?" said the girls. "There isn't a spark of fire in the house, and our tasks are not yet done. We must go to the Baba Yaga's for a light!"

"My pins give me light enough," said the one who was making lace. "I shan't go."

"And I shan't go, either," said the one who was knitting socks. "My knitting-needles give me light enough."

"Vasilissa, you must go for the light," they both cried out together; "be off to the Baba Yaga's!"

And they pushed Vasilissa out of the room.

Vasilissa went into her little closet, set before the doll a supper which she had provided beforehand, and said:

"Now, dolly, feed, and listen to my need! I'm sent to the Baba Yaga's for a light. The Baba Yaga will eat me!"

The doll fed, and its eyes began to glow just like a couple of candles.

"Never fear, Vasilissa dear!" it said. "Go where you're sent. Only take care to keep me always by you. As long as I'm with you, no harm will come to you at the Baba Yaga's."

So Vasilissa got ready, put her doll in her pocket, crossed herself, and went out into the thick forest.

As she walks she trembles. Suddenly a horseman gallops by. He is white, and he is dressed in white, under him is a white horse, and the trappings of the horse are white—and the day begins to break.

She goes a little further, and a second rider gallops by. He is red, dressed in red, and sitting on a red horse—and the sun rises.

Vasilissa went on walking all night and all next day. It was only towards the evening that she reached the clearing on which stood the dwelling of the Baba Yaga. The fence around it was made of dead men's bones; on the top of the fence were stuck human skulls with eyes in them; instead of uprights at the gates were men's legs; instead of bolts were arms; instead of a lock was a mouth with sharp teeth.

Vasilissa was frightened out of her wits, and stood still as if rooted to the ground.

Suddenly there rode past another horseman. He was black, dressed all in black, and on a black horse. He galloped up to the Baba Yaga's gate and disappeared, just as if he had sunk through the ground—and night fell. But the darkness did not last long. The eyes of all the skulls on the fence began to shine, and the whole clearing became as bright as if it had been midday. Vasilissa shuddered with fear, but stopped where she was, not knowing which way to run.

Soon there was heard in the forest a terrible roar. The trees cracked, the dry leaves rustled; out of the forest came the Baba Yaga, riding in a mortar, urging it on with a pestle, sweeping away her traces with a broom. Up she drove to the gate, stopped short, and, snuffing the air around her, cried:

"Faugh! Faugh! I smell Russian flesh!* Who's there?"

Vasilissa went up to the hag in a terrible fright, bowed low before her, and said:

"It's me, granny. My stepsisters have sent me to you for a light."

"Very good," said the Baba Yaga; "I know them. If you'll stop awhile with me first, and do some work for me, I'll give you a light. But if you won't, I'll eat you!"

Then she turned to the gates, and cried:

"Ho, thou firm fence of mine, be thou divided! And ye, wide gates of mine, do ye fly open!"

The gates opened, and the Baba Yaga drove in, whistling as she went, and after her followed Vasilissa; and then everything shut to again. When they entered the sitting-room, the Baba Yaga stretched herself out at full length, and said to Vasilissa:

"Fetch out what there is in the oven; I'm hungry."

Vasilissa lighted a splinter at one of the skulls which were on the fence, and began fetching meat from the oven and setting it before the Baba Yaga; and meat enough had been provided for a dozen people. Then she fetched from the cellar kvass, mead, beer, and wine. The hag ate up everything, drank up everything. All she left for Vasilissa was a few scraps—a crust of bread and a morsel of sucking-pig. Then the Baba Yaga lay down to sleep, saying:

"When I go out to-morrow morning, mind you cleanse the courtyard, sweep the room, cook the dinner, and get the linen ready. Then go to the corn-bin, take out four quarters of wheat, and clear it of other seed. And mind you have it all done—if you don't, I shall eat you!"

After giving these orders the Baba Yaga began to snore. But Vasilissa set the remnants of the hag's supper before her doll, burst into tears, and said:

"Now, dolly, feed, listen to my need! The Baba Yaga has set me a heavy task, and threatens

to eat me if I don't do it all. Do help me!"

The doll replied:

"Never fear, Vasilissa the Fair! Sup, say your prayers, and go to bed. The morning is wiser than the evening!"

Vasilissa awoke very early, but the Baba Yaga was already up. She looked out of window. The light in the skulls' eyes was going out. All of a sudden there appeared the white horseman, and all was light. The Baba Yaga went out into the courtyard and whistled—before her appeared a mortar with a pestle and a broom. The red horseman appeared—the sun rose. The Baba Yaga seated herself in the mortar, and drove out of the courtyard, shooting herself along with the pestle, sweeping away her traces with the broom.

Vasilissa was left alone, so she examined the Baba Yaga's house, wondered at the abundance there was in everything, and remained lost in thought as to which work she ought to take to first. She looked up; all the work was done already. The doll had cleared the wheat to the very last grain.

"Ah, my preserver!" cried Vasilissa, "you've saved me from danger!"

"All you've got to do now is to cook the dinner," answered the doll, slipping into Vasilissa's pocket. "Cook away, in God's name, and then take some rest for your health's sake!"

Towards evening Vasilissa got the table ready, and awaited the Baba Yaga. It began to grow dusky; the black rider appeared for a moment at the gate, and all grew dark. Only the eyes of the skulls sent forth their light. The trees began to crack, the leaves began to rustle, up drove the Baba Yaga. Vasilissa went out to meet her.

"Is everything done?" asks the Yaga.

"Please to look for yourself, granny!" says Vasilissa.

The Baba Yaga examined everything, was vexed that there was nothing to be angry about, and said:

"Well, well! very good!"

Afterwards she cried:

"My trusty servants, zealous friends, grind this my wheat!"

There appeared three pairs of hands, which gathered up the wheat, and carried it out of

---

* "Phu, Phu! there is a Russian smell!" the equivalent of our own "Fee, faw, fum, I smell the blood of an Englishman!"

sight. The Baba Yaga supped, went to bed, and again gave her orders to Vasilissa:

"Do just the same to-morrow as to-day; only besides that take out of the bin the poppy seed that is there, and clean the earth off it grain by grain. Some one or other, you see, has mixed a lot of earth with it out of spite." Having said this, the hag turned to the wall and began to snore, and Vasilissa took to feeding her doll. The doll fed, and then said to her what it had said the day before:

"Pray to God, and go to sleep. The morning is wiser than the evening. All shall be done, Vasilissa dear!"

The next morning the Baba Yaga again drove out of the courtyard in her mortar, and Vasilissa and her doll immediately did all the work. The hag returned, looked at everything, and cried, "My trusty servants, zealous friends, press forth oil from the poppy seed!"

Three pairs of hands appeared, gathered up the poppy seed, and bore it out of sight. The Baba Yaga sat down to dinner. She ate, but Vasilissa stood silently by.

"Why don't you speak to me?" said the Baba Yaga; "there you stand like a dumb creature!"

"I didn't dare," answered Vasilissa; "but if you give me leave, I should like to ask you about something."

"Ask away; only it isn't every question that brings good. 'Get much to know, and old soon you'll grow.'"

"I only want to ask you, granny, about something I saw. As I was coming here, I was passed by one riding on a white horse; he was white himself, and dressed in white. Who was he?"

"That was my bright Day!" answered the Baba Yaga.

"Afterwards there passed me another rider, on a red horse; red himself, and all in red clothes. Who was he?"

"That was my red Sun!" answered the Baba Yaga.

"And who may be the black rider, granny, who passed by me just at your gate?"

"That was my dark Night; they are all trusty servants of mine."

Vasilissa thought of the three pairs of hands, but held her peace.

"Why don't you go on asking?" said the Baba Yaga.

"That's enough for me, granny. You said yourself, 'Get too much to know, old you'll grow!'"

"It's just as well," said the Baba Yaga, "that you've only asked about what you saw out of doors, not indoors! In my house I hate having dirt carried out of doors; and as to over inquisitive people—well, I eat them. Now I'll ask you something. How is it you manage to do the work I set you to do?"

"My mother's blessing assists me," replied Vasilissa.

"Eh! eh! what's that? Get along out of my house, you bless'd daughter. I don't want bless'd people."

She dragged Vasilissa out of the room, pushed her outside the gates, took one of the skulls with blazing eyes from the fence, stuck it on a stick, gave it to her, and said:

"Lay hold of that. It's a light you can take to your stepsisters. That's what they sent you here for, I believe."

Home went Vasilissa at a run, lit by the skull, which went out only at the approach of the dawn; and at last, on the evening of the second day, she reached home. When she came to the gate, she was going to throw away the skull.

"Surely," thinks she, "they can't be still in want of a light at home." But suddenly a hollow voice issued from the skull, saying:

"Throw me not away. Carry me to your stepmother!"

She looked at her stepmother's house, and not seeing a light in a single window, she determined to take the skull in there with her. For the first time in her life she was cordially received by her stepmother and stepsisters, who told her that from the moment she went away they hadn't had a spark of fire in the house. They couldn't strike a light themselves anyhow, and whenever they brought one in from a neighbor's, it went out as soon as it came into the room.

"Perhaps your light will keep in!" said the stepmother. So they carried the skull into the sitting-room. But the eyes of the skull so glared at the stepmother and her daughters—shot forth such flames! They would fain have hidden themselves, but run where they would, every-where did the eyes follow after them. By the morning they were utterly burnt to cinders. Only Vasilissa was none the worse.

The Little Humpbacked Horse

One of the first things the reader notices in this story is the old-Russian atmosphere, not only in the names and such words as "versts," but in the acts of the brothers. Ivan climbs on top of the Russian stove to take a nap; the two older brothers kiss each other when they make a bargain; and a head man who comes out with soldiers to disperse the crowd wears fur footgear. [From Post Wheeler, *Russian Wonder Tales* (Beechhurst, 1946).]

Across the wide sea-ocean, on the further side of high mountains, beyond thick forests, in a village that faced the sky, there once lived an old peasant who had three sons. The eldest, Danilo, was the most knowing lad in the place; the second, Gavrilo, was neither clever nor dull; and the youngest, who was named Ivan, was called a dullard, because while his brothers, after they had sowed their wheat and threshed it, drove to town and went merrymaking, he cared to do nothing but lie in the corner on the stove and sleep. So the whole neighborhood called him "Little Fool Ivan."

Now one morning when the peasant went to his stack, he found to his dismay that someone in the night had stolen some of the hay; so that evening he sent his eldest son to watch for the thief.

Danilo, accordingly, took his ax and his hay-fork and went to the field. On this night there was a biting frost and heavy snow, and he said to himself, "Why should I freeze myself stiff to save a little worthless fodder?" So, finding a warm corner, he lay down, wrapped himself in his thick fur coat and went to sleep.

In the morning he saw that some of the hay had been stolen. He rolled himself well in the snow, went home, and knocked at the door till his father let him in.

"Didst thou see the thief?" asked the peasant.

"I heard him prowling not far off," answered Danilo; "but I shouted, and he dared not come nearer. However, I have had a terrible night, thou mayst be sure! It was bitter cold, and I am frozen to the marrow!"

His father praised him, calling him a good son, and the next night sent his second son to watch.

So Gavrilo took his hatchet and his long knife and went to the field. Now on this night it was raining, and he said to himself, "They say my brother is cleverer than I, but I am at least knowing enough to take care of myself; and why should I stand all night wet to the skin for the sake of a little dried grass?" So, having found a sheltered spot, he lay down, covered himself with his warm cloak and went to sleep.

In the morning he saw that more of the hay had been stolen. He went to a brook, poured water over his clothing so that it was drenched, went home, and knocked at the door till it was opened.

"Didst thou see the thief?" asked his father.

"I did," Gavrilo answered, "and laid hold of his coat and gave him such a beating that he will remember it. But the rascal tore away and ran so fast that I could not catch him. But I have had a night for my pains, I can tell you! The rain poured every minute, and I am soaked to the bones!"

His father praised him likewise, calling him a brave fellow till he was as proud as a cock with five hens, and the next evening said to Little Fool Ivan: "Now, my son, it is thy turn to watch, but thou art such a simpleton thou canst not even keep the sparrows from the peas. It will be small use for thee to go."

However, Little Fool Ivan climbed down from the stove, put a crust of bread under his coat and went whistling off to the field. He did not lie down as his brothers had done, but went about the whole field, looking on every side; and when the moon rose he sat down under a bush, counted the stars in the sky and ate his crust with good appetite.

Suddenly, just at midnight, he heard the neigh of a horse; and looking out from the bush he saw a wonderful mare, as white as snow, with a golden mane curled in little rings.

"So," said Little Fool Ivan to himself, "thou art, then, the thief of our hay! Only come a little nearer, and I will be on thy back as tight as a locust!'' The mare came nearer and nearer and at last, choosing the right moment, Ivan leaped out, seized her tail and jumped on to her back, wrong side before.

The white mare's eyes darted forth lightning. She curled her neck like a snake, reared on her hind legs and shot off like an arrow. She raced over fields, she flew like a bird over ditches, she galloped like the wind along mountains and dashed through thick forests. But run as she would, and rear and snort as she might, she could not throw off Little Fool Ivan. He clung to her tail and stuck to her back like a burr.

At last, just as day was beginning to dawn, the mare stopped and, panting, spoke to him with a human voice. "Well, Ivan," said she, "since thou canst sit me, it seems thou must possess me. Take me home, and give me a place to rest for three days. Only, each morning just at sunrise, let me out to roll in the dew. And when the three days are up, I will bear thee three such colts as were never heard of before. Two of them will be Tzar's horses, of brown and gray, and these thou mayst sell if thou choosest. But the third will be a little humpbacked stallion only three feet high with ears a foot long and him thou shalt neither sell for gold nor give as a gift to anyone whatsoever. So long as thou art in the white world he shall be thy faithful servant. In winter he will show thee how to be warm, and when thou dost hunger he will show thee where to find bread. In return for these three colts, thou shalt release me and give me my freedom."

Little Fool Ivan agreed. He rode the white mare home, hid her in an empty shepherd's corral, whose entrance he covered with a horse-cloth and went home and knocked at the door till his brothers let him in.

When they saw him, they began to question him. "Well, no doubt thou didst see the thief! Perhaps thou didst even catch him! Tell us."

"To be sure I did," he replied. "I jumped on the thief's back and laid hold of the villain's tail and we ran a thousand versts or more. My neck was nearly broken in the end, and ye may believe I am tired!" So saying he climbed on to the stove without taking off even his bark sandals, and went to sleep, while his brothers and his father roared with laughter at the story, not a word of which, of course, they believed.

Little Fool Ivan kept the white mare hidden from all other eyes. For three mornings he rose at daybreak and let her out to roll on the dewy meadow and on the fourth morning, he went to the corral and found beside her, as she had promised, three colts. Two were most beautiful to see; they were of brown and gray, their eyes were like blue sapphires, their manes and tails were golden and curled in little rings, and their hoofs were of diamond, studded with pearls. But the third was a tiny horse like a toy, with two humps on his back and ears a foot long.

Ivan was overjoyed. He thanked the white mare; and she, released, curled her neck like a snake, reared on her hind legs and shot off like an arrow. Then he began to admire the three colts, especially the little humpbacked one which frisked like a dog about Ivan's knees, clapping his long ears together from playfulness and dancing up and down on his little hoofs. He kept them hidden, as he had the white mare, in the shepherd's corral, letting them out each morning at sunrise to roll in the dew and spending many hours petting them, talking to them, currying their coats till they shone like silver and braiding their golden manes.

Time went on (but whether it was three weeks or three years that flew away matters little, since one need not run after them) till it befell, one day, that his eldest brother, Danilo, who had been to town for a holiday, returned late at night and, missing his way in the darkness, stumbled into the shepherd's corral. Hearing a sound, he made a light and to his astonishment saw the three young horses.

"So-ho!" he thought. "Now I understand why Little Fool Ivan spends so much time in this old corral!" He ran to the house and woke his brother Gavrilo. "Come quickly," he said, "and see what three horses our young idiot of a brother has found for himself!" And Gavrilo followed him as fast as he could, straight across a nettle field barefoot, since he did not wait to put on his boots.

When they came to the corral the two fine horses were neighing and snorting. Their eyes were burning like beautiful blue candles and their curling gold manes and tails and their hoofs of diamond and pearls filled the two brothers with envy. Each looked at them so long that he was nearly made blind of one eye. Then Danilo said:

"They say it takes a fool to find a treasure. But where in the white world could Little Fool Ivan have got these marvelous steeds? As for thee and me, brother, we might search our heads off and we would find not even two roubles!"

"That is true," answered Gavrilo. "We should have the horses, and not Little Fool Ivan. Now I have an idea. Next week is the Fair at the capital. Many foreigners will come in ships to buy linen and it is said that even Tzar Saltan will be there. Let us come here by night and take the horses thither and sell them. They will fetch a great price and we will divide it equally between us two. Thou knowest what a good time we could have with the money; and while we are slapping our full purses and enjoying ourselves, our dolt of an Ivan will not be able to guess where his horses have gone visiting. What sayest thou! Let us shake hands upon it."

So the two brothers agreed, kissed each other, crossed themselves, and went home planning how to spend the money they should get for the horses.

When the next week came round, accordingly, they said a prayer before the holy images, asked their father's blessing, and departed to the Fair. When they had gone some distance, however, they returned to the village secretly after nightfall, took the two fine horses out of the corral, and again set out for the capital.

Next morning, when Ivan came to the corral, he found to his grief that the beautiful pair had vanished. There was left only the little humpbacked horse that was turning round and round before him, capering, clapping his long ears together and dancing up and down for joy. Ivan began to weep salt tears. "O my horses, brown and gray!" he cried; "my good steeds with golden manes! Did I not caress you enough? What wretch—may he tumble through a bridge—hath stolen you away?"

At this the humpbacked horse neighed and spoke in a human voice: "Don't worry, little master," he said. "It was thy brothers who took them away, and I can take thee to them. Sit on my back and hold fast by my ears, and

have a care not to fall off!" So Little Fool Ivan sat on his back, holding up his feet lest they drag on the ground, and laid hold of his ears; and the pony shook himself till his little mane quivered, reared on his hind legs, snorted three times and shot away like an arrow, so fast that the dust curled under his feet. And almost before Ivan had time to take breath, he was versts away on the highroad to the capital.

When his brothers saw Little Fool Ivan coming after them like the wind, on his toy horse, they knew not what to do. "For shame, ye rascals!" shouted he as he overtook them. "Ye may be more clever than I, but I have never stolen your steeds!"

"Our dear little brother!" said Danilo. "There is little use denying. We took thy two horses, but we did so with no thought of wrong to thee. As thou knowest, this has been a poor season with our crops and a bad harvest, and for despair I and Gavrilo have been like to hang ourselves. When we came by chance upon these two steeds, we considered that thou hadst little knowledge of bargaining and trading, and doubtless knew not their worth, whereas we could get for them at least a thousand roubles at the Fair. With this money we could help our little father, as thou wouldst wish; and we purposed to buy besides for thee a red cap and new boots with red heels. So if we have erred, do thou forgive us."

"Well," answered Little Fool Ivan, "thy words sound fair enough. If this was your thought, go and sell my two horses, but I will go with you." So, though they wished him well strangled, the two brothers had no choice but to take him with them, and thus they came to the capital.

Now when they reached the market-place where the traders were assembled, so wonderful were the two steeds that the people swarmed about them, buzzing like bees in a hive, till for the press no one could pass either in or out, and there was great commotion. Perceiving this, the head man sent a crier, who blew on a gold trumpet and shouted in a loud voice: "O merchants and buyers! crowd not, but disperse one and all!" But they would not move from the horses. Then the head man rode out himself in slippers and fur cap with a body of soldiers, who cleared the way with their whips, so that he came to the middle of the market and saw the horses with his own eyes.

"God's world is wonderful!" he cried, rubbing his head. "What marvels doth it hold!" And bidding the crier proclaim that no buyer should buy them, he rode to the Palace, came to the presence of the Tzar, and told him of them.

The Tzar could not sit still for curiosity. He ordered his state carriage and rode at once to the market; and when he saw the horses, tugging at their halters and gnawing their bits, with their eyes shining like sapphires, their curling golden manes, and hoofs of diamond and pearls, he could not take his eyes from them. He examined them on both sides, called to them with caressing words, patted their backs, and stroked their manes, and asked who owned them.

"O Tzar's Majesty," said Little Fool Ivan, "I am their master."

"What wilt thou take for them?" asked the Tzar.

"Thrice five caps full of silver," answered Ivan, "and five roubles beside."

"Good," said the Tzar, and ordered the money given him. Then ten grooms, with gray hair and golden uniforms, led the pair to the royal stables. On the way, however, the horses knocked the grooms down, bit to pieces the bridles, and ran neighing to Ivan.

Then the Tzar called him to his presence, and said: "It seems that my wonderful steeds will obey only thee. There is no help but that I make thee my Chief Equerry and Master of my Stables." And he ordered the crier at once to proclaim the appointment. So Little Fool Ivan called his brothers Danilo and Gavrilo, gave to them the fifteen caps full of silver, and the five roubles beside, kissed them, bade them not neglect their father but to care for him in his old age, and led the two horses to the royal stables, while a great throng of people followed, watching the little humpbacked horse who went dancing after them up the street.

The telling of a tale is quick but time itself passes slowly. Five weeks went by, while Ivan wore red robes, ate sweet food, and slept his fill. Each morning at sunrise, he took the horses to roll in the dew on the open field and fed them with honey and white wheat until their coats shone like satin. But the more the Tzar praised him the more envious many in the Court were of him. As the saying is, one need not be rich only so he have curly hair and is clever; and because Little Fool Ivan had succeeded so easily, people hated him, and the one who hated him most was the officer who had been the Tzar's Master of Horse before his coming. Each day this man pondered how he might bring about Ivan's ruin, and at night he would creep to the stables and lie hid in the wheat bins, hoping to catch his rival in some fault.

When this failed, he went to all those Court officials who were envious of the new favorite and bade them hang their heads and go about with sorrowful faces, promising, when the Tzar asked the cause, to tell him what would ruin Little Fool Ivan. They did so, and the Tzar, noticing their sad looks, asked:

"O Boyars, why are ye cast down and crestfallen?"

Then he who had given this counsel stood forth, and said: "O Tzar's Majesty! not for ourselves do we grieve, but we fear thy new Master of the Stables is a wizard and an evil-doer and familiar with Black Magic. For he doth boast openly that he could fetch thee, if he chose, in addition to thy two wonderful steeds, the fabled Pig with the Golden Bristles and the Silver Tusks, with her twenty sucklings, who live in the hidden valley of the Land of the South."

Hearing this, the Tzar was wroth. "Bring before me this wild boaster," he said, "and he shall make good his words without delay!" Thereupon they ran to the stables, where Little Fool Ivan lay asleep, and kicked him wide awake and brought him to the Tzar, who looked at him angrily and said: "Hear my command. If in three days thou hast not brought hither from the hidden valley of the Land of the South the Pig with the Golden Bristles and Silver Tusks, together with her twenty sucklings, I will deliver thee to an evil death!"

Little Fool Ivan went to the stable weeping bitterly. Hearing him coming the little humpbacked horse began to dance and to flap its ears together for joy, but as soon as he saw his master's tears he almost began to sob himself.

"Why art thou not merry, little master?" he asked. "Why does thy head hang lower than thy shoulders?"

Ivan embraced and kissed the little horse, and told him the task the Tzar had laid upon him. "Do not weep," said the pony; "I can help thee. Nor is this service so hard a one. Go thou to the Tzar and ask him a bucket of golden corn, a bucket of silver wheat, and a silken lasso."

So Ivan went before the Tzar and asked, as he had been bidden, for the wheat, the corn, and the silken lasso, and brought them to the stables. "Now," said the little humpbacked horse, "lie down and sleep, for the morning holds more wisdom than the evening."

Little Fool Ivan lay down to sleep, and next morning the pony waked him at dawn. "Mount me now," he said, "with thy grain and thy silken rope, and we will be off, for the way is far."

Ivan put the silver wheat and the golden corn into stout bags, slung them across the pony's neck, and with his silken lasso wound about his waist, mounted; and the little humpbacked horse darted away like an eagle. He scoured wide plains, leaped across swift rivers, and sped along mountain ridges; and after running without pause for a day and a night, he stopped in a deep valley on the edge of a dreary wood and said: "Little master, this is the Land of the South, and in this valley lives the Pig with the Golden Bristles. She comes each day to root in this forest. Take thou the golden corn and the silver wheat and pour them on the ground in two piles, at some distance apart and conceal thyself. When the Pig comes she will run to the corn, but the sucklings will begin to eat the wheat; and while the mother is not by, thou mayst secure them. Bring them to me and tie them to my saddle with the silken lasso, and I will bear thee back. As for the Pig, she will follow her sucklings."

Little Fool Ivan did all as the little horse bade him. He entered the forest, put the corn and wheat in two piles, hid himself in a thicket near the latter, and rested till evening, when there came a sound of grunting; and the Pig with the Golden Bristles and Silver Tusks led her young into the forest. She saw the corn and at once began to eat it, while the twenty sucklings ran to the wheat. He caught them, one by one, tied them with the silken lasso, and, hastening to the little horse, made them fast to his saddle-bow. Scarce had he mounted when the Pig perceived them and, seeing her sucklings borne away, came running after them, erecting her golden bristles and gnashing her silver tusks.

The little humpbacked horse sped away like a flash back along the road they had come with the Pig pursuing them; and, after running without stop for a night and a day, they arrived after dark at the Tzar's capital. Little Fool Ivan rode to the Palace courtyard, set down there the twenty suckling-pigs, still tied by the silken lasso, went to the stables and fell asleep.

In the morning the Tzar was greatly astonished to see that Little Fool Ivan had performed the task and was delighted to possess the new treasure. He sent for his Master of Horse and praised him and gave him a rich present, so that the envious ones thereat were made still more envious.

So, after some days, these came to the Tzar and said: "Thy Master of Horse, O Tzar's Majesty, doth boast now that the bringing of the wonderful Pig with her twenty sucklings was but a small service, and that he could, if he but chose, bring to thee the Mare with Seven Manes and her seven fierce stallions that graze on a green meadow between the crystal hills of the Caucasus."

Then, in more anger than before, the Tzar bade them bring Little Fool Ivan to his presence and said sternly: "Heed my royal word. If in seven days thou hast not brought hither from between the crystal hills of the Caucasus the Seven-Maned Mare with her seven stallions, I will send thee where the crows shall pick thy bones!"

Little Fool Ivan went weeping to the little humpbacked horse and told him of the Tzar's new command. "Grieve not, little master," said the other; "let not thy bright head droop. I can aid thee. Nor is this service too hard a one. Go thou to the Tzar and demand that he prepare at once a stone stable with one door opening into it and another opening out.

Ask also for a horse's skin and an iron hammer of twelve poods* weight.''

Ivan obeyed. He demanded the stable, the horse's skin and the iron hammer, and when all was ready the little horse said: "Lie down and sleep now, little master. The morning is wiser than the evening." Little Fool Ivan lay down and slept, and next morning at daybreak the pony waked him. Ivan tied the horse's skin to the saddle-bow, slung the hammer about his neck and mounted; and the little humpbacked horse darted away like a swallow, till the dust curled about his legs like a whirlwind. When he had run three days and four nights without rest, he stopped between two crystal hills and said:

"Yonder lies the green meadow whereon each evening grazes the Mare with Seven Manes and her seven fierce stallions. Take now thy horse's skin and sew me within it, and presently the mare will come and will set upon me with her teeth. While she rends the skin from me, do thou run and strike her between her two ears with thy twelve pood hammer, so that she will be stunned. Mount me then in haste, and thou mayst lead her after thee; and as for the seven stallions, they will follow."

So Little Fool Ivan sewed the little horse in the horse's skin; and when the mare with the seven stallions came, the stallions stood afar off, but the mare set upon him and rent the skin from him. Then Ivan ran and struck her with the iron hammer and stunned her, and instantly, holding by her seven manes, leaped to the back of the little humpbacked horse.

Scarce had he mounted, when the seven fierce stallions saw him and came galloping after them, screaming with rage. But the little humpbacked horse was off like a dart back along the road they had come, and when they had traveled without stopping three nights and four days, they arrived at the Tzar's capital. Little Fool Ivan rode to the stone stable that had been built, went in at one door, and leaving therein the Mare with the Seven Manes, rode out of the other and barred it behind him; and the seven stallions, following the mare, were caught.

* One pood: about forty pounds.

Then Ivan went to his own place and went to sleep.

When they reported to the Tzar that this time also Little Fool Ivan had performed his task, the Tzar was more rejoiced than before and bestowed high rank and all manner of honors upon him, till, for hatred and malice, the envious ones were beside themselves.

They conferred together and coming before the Tzar, they said: "O Tzar's Majesty! to bring thee the mare and the stallions, thy Master of Horse boasteth now, was but a small service, saying that if he willed he could fetch thee from across three times nine lands, where the little red sun rises, the beautiful Girl-Tzar, whom thou hast so long desired for thy bride, who lives on the sea-ocean in a golden boat, which she rows with silver oars."

Then was the Tzar mightily angered. "Summon this boaster again before me," he commanded; and when Little Fool Ivan was come in, he bade him bring the lovely Girl-Tzar within twelve days or pay the forfeit with his head. So, for the third time, Ivan went weeping to the little humpbacked horse and told him the Tzar's will.

"Dry thy tears, little master," said the other, "for I can assist thee. This is not, after all, the hardest service. Go thou to the Tzar and ask for two handkerchiefs cunningly embroidered in gold, a silken tent woven with gold thread and with golden tent-poles, gold and silver dishes, and all manner of wines and sweetmeats."

Ivan lost no time in obeying and when they were ready brought them to the stables. "Lie down and sleep now," said the little horse. "Tomorrow is wiser than today." Accordingly Little Fool Ivan lay down and slept till the little horse woke him at daybreak. He put all that had been prepared into a bag and mounted, and the little humpbacked horse sped away like the wind.

For six days they rode, a hundred thousand versts, till they reached a forest at the very end of the world, where the little red sun rises out of the blue sea-ocean. Here they stopped and Ivan alighted.

"Pitch now thy tent on the white sand," said

the little horse. "In it spread thy embroidered handkerchiefs and on them put the wine and the gold and silver plates piled with sweetmeats. As for thee, do thou hide behind the tent and watch. From her golden boat the Girl-Tzar will see the tent and will approach it. Let her enter it and eat and drink her fill. Then go in, seize and hold her, and call for me." So saying, he ran to hide himself in the forest.

Ivan pitched the tent, prepared the food and wine, and lying down behind the tent, made a tiny hole in the silk through which to see, and waited. And before long the golden boat came sailing along over the blue sea-ocean. The beautiful Girl-Tzar alighted to look at the splendid tent and seeing the wine and sweetmeats, entered and began to eat and drink. So graceful and lovely was she that no tale could describe her and Little Fool Ivan could not gaze enough. He forgot what the little horse had told him and he was still peering through the hole in the silk when the beautiful maiden sprang up, left the tent, leaped into her golden boat, and the silver oars carried her far away on the sea-ocean.

When the little humpbacked horse came running up, Ivan too late repented of his folly. "I am guilty before thee!" he said. "And now I shall never see her again!" and he began to shed tears.

"Never mind," said the little horse. "She will come again tomorrow, but if thou failest next time we must needs go back without her, and thy head will be lost."

Next day Little Fool Ivan spread the wines and sweetmeats and lay down to watch as before; and again the lovely Girl-Tzar came rowing in her golden boat and entered the tent and began to regale herself. And while she ate and drank, Ivan ran in and seized and held her and called to the little horse. The girl cried out and fought to be free, but when she saw how handsome Little Fool Ivan was, she quite forgot to struggle. He mounted and put her before him on the saddle, and the humpbacked horse dashed away like lightning along the road they had come.

They rode six days and on the seventh they came again to the capital, and Little Fool Ivan—with a sad heart, since he had fallen in love with her himself—brought the lovely girl to the Palace.

The Tzar was overjoyed. He came out to meet them, took the maiden by her white hand, seated her beside him beneath a silken curtain on a cushion of purple velvet, and spoke to her tender words. "O Girl-Tzar, to whom none can be compared!" he said. "My Tzaritza that is to be! For how long have I not slept, either by night or in the white day, for thinking of thine eyes!"

But the beautiful Girl-Tzar turned from him and would not answer, and again and again he tried his wooing, till at length she said: "O Tzar, thou art wrinkled and gray, and hast left sixty years behind thee, while I am but sixteen. Should I wed thee, the Tzars of all Tzardoms would laugh, saying that a grandfather had taken to wife his grandchild."

Hearing this, the Tzar was angry. "It is true," he said, "that flowers do not bloom in winter and that I am no longer young. But I am nevertheless a great Tzar."

Then she replied: "I will wed no one who hath gray hairs and who lacks teeth in his head. If thou wilt but grow young again, then will I wed thee right willingly."

"How can a man grow young again?" he asked.

"There is a way, O Tzar," she said, "and it is thus: Order three great caldrons to be placed in thy courtyard. Fill the first with cold water, the second with boiling water, and the third with boiling mare's milk. He who bathes one minute in the boiling milk, two in the boiling water, and three in the cold water, becomes instantly young and so handsome that it cannot be told. Do this and I will become thy Tzaritza, but not otherwise."

The Tzar at once bade them prepare in the courtyard the three caldrons, one of cold water, one of boiling water, and one of boiling mare's milk, minded to make the test. The envious courtiers, however, came to him and said: "O Tzar's Majesty! this is a strange thing, and we have never heard that a man can plunge into boiling liquid and not be scalded. We pray thee, therefore, bid thy Master of Horse bathe before thee; then mayest thou be assured that all is well." And this counsel seemed to the Tzar good and he straightway summoned Little Fool Ivan and bade him prepare to make the trial.

When Ivan heard the Tzar's command he said to himself, "So I am to be killed like a sucking-pig or a chicken!" and he went sorrowfully to the stables and told the little humpbacked horse. "Thou hast found for me the Pig with the Golden Bristles," he said, "the Seven-Maned Mare, and the beautiful Girl-Tzar; but now these are all as nothing, and my life is as worthless as a boot sole!" And he began to weep bitterly.

"Weep not, little master," said the little horse. "This is indeed a real service that I shall serve thee. Now listen well to what I say. When thou goest to the courtyard, before thou strippest off thy clothes to bathe, ask of the Tzar to permit them to bring to thee thy little hump-backed horse, that thou mayest bid him farewell for the last time. He will agree; and when I am brought there, I shall gallop three times around the three kettles, dip my nose in each, and sprinkle thee. Lose not a moment then, but jump instantly in the caldron of boiling milk, then into the boiling water, and last into the cold water."

Scarcely had he instructed him when the Bo-yars came to bring Ivan to the courtyard. All the Court Ministers were there to see and the place was crowded with people, while the Tzar looked on from a balcony. The two cal-drons were boiling hot, and servants fed the great fires beneath them with heaps of fuel. Little Fool Ivan bowed low before the Tzar and prepared for the bath.

But having taken off his coat, he bowed again and said: "O Tzar's Majesty! I have but one favor to ask. Bid them bring hither my little humpbacked horse that I may embrace him once more for the last time!" The Tzar was in good humor thinking he was so soon to regain his youth and he consented, and presently the little horse came running into the courtyard, dancing up and down and clapping his long ears to-gether. But as soon as he came to the three caldrons he galloped three times round them, dipped his nose into each and sprinkled his mas-ter; and without waiting a moment Little Fool Ivan threw off his clothes and jumped into the

caldrons, one after the other. And while he had been goodlooking before, he came from the last caldron so handsome that his beauty could neither be described with a pen nor writ-ten in a tale.

Now when the Tzar saw this, he could wait no longer. He hastened down from the balcony and without waiting to undress, crossed himself and jumped into the boiling milk. But the charm did not work in his case, and he was instantly scalded to death.

Seeing the Tzar was dead, the Girl-Tzar came to the balcony and spoke to the people, saying: "Thy Tzar chose me to be his Tzaritza. If thou wilt, I will rule this Tzardom, but it shall be only as the wife of him who brought me from mine own!"

The people, well pleased, shouted: "Health to Tzar Ivan!" And so Little Fool Ivan led the lovely Girl-Tzar to the church and they were married that same day.

Then Tzar Ivan ordered the trumpeters to blow their hammered trumpets and the butlers to open the bins, and he made in the Palace a feast like a hill, and the Boyars and Princes sat at oak tables and drank from golden goblets and made merry till they could not stand on their feet.

But Little Fool Ivan, and his Tzaritza, ruled the Tzardom wisely and well and grew never too wise to take counsel of his little humpbacked horse.

Mr. Samson Cat

The definitive collection of Russian folktales, compa-rable to the work of Jakob and Wilhelm Grimm in Germany, and to the accomplishment of Peter As-björnsen and Jörgen Moe in Scandinavia, is that made by A. N. Afanasyev (1826–71). The English edition, *Russian Fairy Tales,* was published by Pantheon Books (1945). Afanasyev was an ethnologist who saw in the folktales a clue to some of the basic characteristics of the Russian people. His collection was made over a period of eleven years. One of the stories in that collection is called *The Ram, the Cat, and the Twelve Wolves. Mr. Samson Cat,* which is given here, is a version of the same story. Valéry Carrick has domes-ticated the story by changing the wild animals into the more familiar barnyard types but the plot is the same, and the theme remains untouched, namely, the power of fear to distort the facts.

In his introduction to the Russian tales, Roman Jakobsen points out the interesting fact that only one-third of the Russian fairy tales are common to Western European sources, and one-third are totally unknown to Western Europe. The reader of folktales will soon recognize the fact that only in Russian folklore is the witch Baba Yaga equipped with a house on chicken legs, which gives her an added degree of mobility, and no other lore has the Firebird and the Sea King. [From Valéry Carrick, *Picture Tales from the Russian*, trans. Nevill Forbes (Lippincott, 1913).]

Once upon a time a cat came running out of a certain village, and a fox came running out of a certain forest, and they met.

"How do you do?" said the fox. "How do you do?" said the cat. "What's your name?" said the fox. "Mr. Samson Cat, and what's yours?" "They call me Widow Fox." "Let's live together," said the cat. "Very well," said the fox. And so they settled down in Widow Fox's cottage.

One day Mr. Cat went out for a walk to gather berries in the forest, when a hare came running along. He never noticed the cat and jumped right on to the top of him.

Mr. Cat said: "F-r-r-r!" and the hare took fright and set off running so fast, that you could see his heels twinkle, and he was gone! Then the hare met a wolf, and said to him: "As I was running past Widow Fox's cottage, an unheard-of beast jumped right on to the top of me, he was so big and so dreadful! He was just going to swallow me up alive, only my legs saved me!" "I must go and have a look," said the wolf. "Don't, he will eat you up!" said the hare. Nevertheless the wolf went off to Widow Fox's cottage. And just then Widow Fox and Mr. Samson Cat had dragged a dead sheep into their courtyard and were hard at it behind the fence, gobbling him up.

When Widow Fox had had enough, she came out at the gate, and there Mr. Wolf came up to her. He could hear how Mr. Cat was going on behind the fence, and said to Widow Fox: "Who is that there in your courtyard, Widow Fox?" "That's the mighty Mr. Samson Cat. He killed a sheep in a fight and now he's eating it. You'd better go away quickly, or else the same thing will happen to you." Meantime Mr. Cat was working hard at the sheep and crying: "Mee-*ow*, mee-*ow!*" And Mr. Wolf thought he was saying: "Not en*ough*, not en*ough*," and he thought: "Good gracious, he hasn't had enough after eating a whole sheep!" and he grew frightened and ran away. And as he was running he saw a pig rubbing his side against a tree. And he said to him: "Have you heard the news! We shan't be able to make a living in *this* forest any more; Widow Fox has got a dreadful animal living with her, the mighty Mr. Samson Cat. He eats four sheep a day, and then says he hasn't had enough." And Mr. Pig flapped his ears and winked his eye and said: "I should like to have a look at this beast!" "What are you thinking of!" said Mr. Wolf, "you'd better not go near the place!"

And while they were standing and talking, a bear came up, and Mr. Pig said to him: "Uncle Bruin, have you heard the news? Widow Fox has a beast living with her called the mighty Mr. Samson Cat. He eats ten oxen a day, and then says he hasn't had enough!" "What a terrible thing," said Bruin, "I *should* like to see that beast!"

So they discussed this way and that, and sent Mr. Pig to Widow Fox to ask if they might just with one eye have a peep at Mr. Samson Cat. And Mr. Pig came to Widow Fox and said: "How do you do? how do you do, Widow Fox? We have heard tell of your Mr. Samson and we should so like to have a look at him. Do please tell us how this could be arranged without the danger of his eating us up!" And Widow Fox thought for a bit and then said: "This is how you must arrange it: bake a *lot* of pies and get a *lot* of honey, and invite us to come and see you. *Perhaps* he won't do you any harm then." And Mr. Pig was delighted and ran back to his friends and told Mr. Wolf and Mr. Bruin: "Widow Fox says: 'Bake a *lot* of pies and get a *lot* of honey, and we will come and see you, and *perhaps* the mighty Mr. Samson Cat won't eat you all up.'" And so Bruin began to get the honey, Mr. Wolf began to bake the pies, and Mr. Pig began to tidy up, and get ready to receive the expected guests.

And they baked a *lot* of pies, and got a *lot*

of honey, and Bruin said: "I shall get up into a tree; from there I shall see better when the guests begin to arrive." And so he climbed up.

And Mr. Wolf said: "For a whole day I've been working at those pies. I shall go and rest for a bit under this log." And he crawled under the log and lay down there.

And Mr. Pig said: "I have got hot all over, making everything tidy. I shall go and get into the shade for a bit." And he went and hid in the brushwood.

Meanwhile Widow Fox and the mighty Mr. Samson Cat came along, and their hosts were not there! Bruin was up an oak, Mr. Wolf under a log, and Mr. Pig in the brushwood. So there was nothing to be done but start eating without their hosts, and Widow Fox went for the honey while Mr. Cat got to work on the stuffed pies.

Suddenly Mr. Cat heard something rustling in the grass, and this was Mr. Pig's tail rustling from fright. Mr. Cat thought: "I expect that's a mouse," and dashed off and caught Mr. Pig by the tail.

Mr. Pig squealed and ran off as hard as he could, and ran his snout straight into the stump of a tree.

Mr. Cat was really just as much frightened himself, and jumped on to the tree. At this Bruin's paws grew weak from fright, and he fell plump down from the tree right on to the top of the log under which Mr. Wolf was lying.

And Mr. Wolf thought: "My end has come," and he jumped out from under the log and started off running as hard as he could go. And it was not till evening that Mr. Wolf, Mr. Pig and Bruin met again and told each other their experiences.

Mr. Pig said: "Well I never! The way he caught hold of my tail and dashed my head against the stump!" And Bruin said: "The stump was nothing! He tore out the whole oak tree by the roots and began to shake it. How could I possibly hold on? I was lucky not to fall into his jaws." And Mr. Wolf said: "And the way he put me one on with that oak tree! Well, that *is* a beast, if you like!" And they all began to shake their heads and said: "Well, that *is* a beast, if you like! There's no mistake about Mr. Samson Cat!"

Staver and His Wife Vassilissa

Women warriors from Athena to Joan of Arc are found in myth and legend. Less common is the motif of the woman-warrior disguised as a man. Such a heroine exists in the Roumanian ballad "Mizilca" and in the following folktale in which Vassilissa uses her quick wit as well as her military skills to rescue her imprisoned husband. [From Hans Baumann, *Hero Legends of the World,* trans. Stella Humphries (J. M. Dent, 1975).]

Grand Duke Vladimir of Kiev sat banqueting in the great hall of his castle with his princes and boyars round him. Everyone was merry and the feast was already in full swing when it occurred to Vladimir that one of the boyars was not present, the young hero Staver Godinovitch. Immediately the Grand Duke sent a messenger to summon Staver to the merrymaking.

Presently Staver the boyar arrived on horseback. He dismounted and strode through the white stone palace, crossed himself, as was the custom, and bowed to left and right to greet those present. Everyone rose to receive him, even the Grand Duke himself and Staver saluted him with particular warmth. Then they all sat down again at the oaken tables and the banquet continued.

When the heroes had eaten and drunk their fill, they began to boast, and the loudest of the braggarts were the Grand Duke's men. Nowhere, they insisted, was there more gold, nowhere more silver, nowhere greater heaps of pearls than in the palace of Kiev.

This was too much for Staver. 'Listen to those boasters,' he murmured in his neighbour's ear. 'Their mouths are big, but their heads are empty. They talk and talk of their city of Kiev, its gold, silver and pearls. But what is this stone box compared with my castle? Why, mine is so vast that it's better to ride on horseback through it rather than walk. All the rooms are oak-panelled and hung with beaver and sable. The steel door-handles and hinges are all gilded and the floors are made of pure silver. I have iron-bound coffers filled with silver and gold, to say nothing of pearls. And I have a treasure in my house that puts everything else in the shade, my wife, Vassilissa. There is no one to compare with her. Her face is as fair as the freshly fallen snow, she has brows of sable and a falcon's eyes. And she is not only a superb housekeeper. She also knows how to bend the bow and she excels in other manly arts. That's my wife Vassilissa for you!'

Staver had spoken to no one but his neighbour, yet many ears pricked as he uttered these words. And at once, tale-bearers brought the Grand Duke's notice to the way that Staver had boasted to his fellow guest.

Vladimir flushed with anger. In a voice loud enough for all to hear he said: 'Princes and boyars, do you consider it right that someone humiliates me here in my own hall? This Staver Godinovitch is a windbag who insults me with his talk. Seize him and carry him down to the dungeons. Put him behind iron doors and wall up the cell with yellow sand, so that he can no longer offend my ears. Then ten of you ride to Staver's castle, seal it up, together with his treasure chests, and bring me the peerless Vassilissa! Bring her here to me, the Grand Duke Vladimir of Kiev!'

Staver was seized and thrown into prison. He was locked behind iron doors and yellow sand, while ten boyars rode off to seal up Staver's castle and to bring Vassilissa to Kiev.

But there was one boyar who was loyal to Staver and he galloped ahead of the others to tell Vassilissa what Vladimir had done to her husband Staver.

Then Vassilissa dressed herself in men's clothing and arranged her hair like a man's. She put on boots of green morocco leather and she armed herself with a goodly sword, a Tartar spear, a bow and a quiver that contained many arrows, all of which she had sharpened with her own hands. So Vassilissa became Vassili. She climbed into her Circassian saddle and with twelve of her men she set out for Kiev.

Half way there, she met Vladimir's envoys who had been ordered to take Vassilissa prisoner. They did not recognize her and one of them asked her: 'Where have you come from, young man, and where are you riding?'

'We have come from the Khan of the Golden Hordes,' Vassilissa answered, 'to remind the Grand Duke Vladimir that he owes the Khan tribute for the last twelve years. We have orders to take many golden rings back to the Khan,

two thousand for each year that is outstanding. And where are you riding?'

At this, the Grand Duke's messengers felt afraid, but at last their leader said: 'We are going to Staver's castle, to seal it up and to carry his wife Vassilissa to the Grand Duke Vladimir.'

'We have just passed Staver's castle. Vassilissa is not there. She has ridden away.'

So Vladimir's envoys turned back and returned to Kiev at the gallop to report to the Grand Duke. The latter listened to them with bad grace, and his young wife Apraksiya, too, was greatly out of humour. And when Vassilissa and her attendants came riding up, everyone took her for the ambassador sent by the Khan of the Golden Hordes. The Grand Duke himself conducted her into the great hall and there he offered her hospitality.

Apraksiya, however, had scrutinized the new arrivals very closely. She led Vladimir away and beneath the portico she said to him softly: 'Listen to me, Vladimir. These are no envoys from the Golden Hordes, they have not been sent by the Tartar Khan. Their leader is not a man but Staver's young wife. She sails across the courtyard as a duck swims, and when she sits down, she keeps her knees together.'

At this, the Grand Duke recovered his high spirits. He invited all the nobles to a banquet and the merrymaking grew louder than ever. Vassilissa and her attendants were also among the guests. When they had feasted enough, Vladimir said secretly to Apraksiya: 'Now I shall put to the test this young man whom the Tartar Khan has sent to me. He shall measure himself at wrestling against my finest champions.'

At the table sat seven very famous champions: Ilya Murometz, Alyosha Popovitch, Kungur and Suchan, Samson, and Chapil's two sons. And no less than five other heroes were also present. The champions challenged Vassilissa to single combat and she declared herself ready to wrestle with them all. They went out into the courtyard, where they lined up in a row.

The first man stepped forth and Vassilissa hit him on the head so hard that he had to be carried from the courtyard. The second had seven of his ribs broken by a single blow of her fist. The third had three of his vertebrae dislocated, and he had to crawl away on all fours. The rest took to their heels.

Vladimir spat, so great was his rage. When he was alone again with Apraksiya, he said to her: 'Your hair may be long, but you haven't much brain. And you say the Khan's envoy is not a man! Why, my court has never seen a hero with such strength.'

'Look at her properly,' retorted Apraksiya. 'Isn't her face as white as freshly fallen snow? Are not her brows like sable? Has she not the bright eyes of the falcon, just as Staver boasted? She is Vassilissa I tell you. You are all blind.'

'Very well,' said Vladimir. 'I shall submit this ambassador to another trial. He shall show us if he can shoot arrows better than my champions.'

In an open meadow outside the palace, Vladimir's heroes shot their arrows at an oak tree. Each time it was hit, the oak swayed, as if it had been caught in a gust of wind. But when Vassilissa shot her arrow, the bowstring sang, and the mighty oak was felled to the ground, shattered into fragments no bigger than knife-handles.

The heroes were dumbfounded.

Vladimir spat for the second time, and he shouted resentfully to Apraksiya: 'Look at that oak tree now! I'm not sorry for the tree but for the arrow! We've never seen such an archer here before, and you still believe it's a woman! Now I shall challenge the envoy myself and see if he is also supreme at chess.'

He sat down with Vassilissa at an oak chess table and they played with chessmen carved from maplewood. Vassilissa won the first game, then the second and also the third. She laughed, for Vladimir had played for high stakes. Then she pushed the chessboard aside and said to the Grand Duke: 'Now let's get down to business. I did not come here to feast with you, nor yet to while away the time playing chess. And the duels with your champions bore me to death. What about the tribute you owe? You have not paid it for twelve whole years. I demand two thousand gold rings for every year. Produce them here and now! The Khan of the Golden Hordes refuses to wait any longer.'

Then Vladimir began to whine: 'Times are bad you know. Few merchants still come to Kiev to trade, and there is little collected in taxes. Even fur-trapping brings no profit these days. How can I pay?' Then he winked an eye slyly and said in jest: 'Why don't you take me and Apraksiya instead of the tribute?'

'What use are you to the Khan of the Golden Hordes? If you have no golden rings, I must take him something that will give him pleasure.'

'But what would please him?' asked Vladimir.

'Have you no one who plays the gusla?'

'Yes, indeed. I have the finest gusla player in the land,' said Vladimir promptly, for he suddenly remembered that Staver was a most accomplished gusla player. 'He is Staver, the young boyar, and he plays the gusla better than anyone else. You may take him as a present to the Tartar Khan.'

Vladimir had the yellow sand shovelled away, the iron doors of the dungeon were opened and Staver was led into the great hall. The Grand Duke handed him a gusla and placed him opposite Vassilissa, saying: 'Now play for the Khan's ambassador, and then you can return with him to the Golden Hordes. I hope that that will please you.'

Staver said nothing but started to play at once. First he played the Great Song of Tsargrad, then he played all the dances and the other pieces that he knew, until Vassilissa said: 'He is a good player and I like him better than any tribute, and better than you and your Grand Duchess Apraksiya. I'll take him with me.'

Then Vladimir's cares fell from him, and as Vassilissa and Staver rode away together with their attendants, the Grand Duke cried out joyfully: 'The Khan of the Golden Hordes is welcome to that fellow Staver! My gold rings are saved. Come, my heroes! We have good reason to celebrate!'

Armenia (Soviet Union)

The Master and the Servant

Armenia has long possessed a body of folklore little known to the English-speaking world. In the book

Once There Was and Was Not, the author has retold seven stories of the common folk that she heard as a child from her mother, who in turn heard them from the folklorist Hovhannes Toumanian. The story chosen for inclusion here tells of two poor brothers and how the younger brother resolves their problem. It is filled with quiet humor and a bit of wisdom. [From Virginia A. Tashjian, *Once There Was and Was Not* (Little, Brown, 1966).]

Once there was and was not in ancient Armenia a pair of brothers so poor they could not keep a roof over their heads. They finally decided that while the younger brother remained at home to tend house, the elder would go out to look for work that would support them both.

After some searching, the elder brother at last found employment as the servant of a very rich man.

"If you agree to work for me, however," said the rich man, "you must promise to stay until the call of the cuckoo in the spring."

The elder brother agreed.

"There is still another condition," the rich man went on. "You must agree to a bargain. You must promise not to lose your temper while you are working for me. If you should lose it, you must pay me one thousand silver pieces as forfeit. On the other hand, if I lose my temper, I'll pay you one thousand silver pieces. What do you say? Do you agree to the bargain?"

"But I don't own one thousand silver pieces," protested the elder brother.

"In that case, instead of paying the money, you must work for me for ten years," said the rich man.

At first, the elder brother was afraid to agree to such a bargain. "But I really have no choice," he thought to himself. "My brother and I need the money and I will just make up my mind not to lose my temper no matter what my master does."

"It's a bargain!" he said aloud.

Both master and servant signed an agreement, and the elder brother started to work.

Early the next morning, the rich master sent the servant out to the fields to harvest the grain.

"Go quickly," he ordered, "and continue working while it's light. Come back only when darkness falls."

The servant hurried to the fields. He worked hard all that day and when twilight came he returned home, tired and weary.

"Why have you come back so soon?" asked the rich man.

"The sun has set—and so I came home."

"That's not what I told you to do!" shouted the master angrily. "I told you to work while there was light. It is true that the sun has set, but the moon has come out. That gives light!"

"What kind of reasoning is that?" exclaimed the amazed elder brother.

"What! Are you losing your temper?" asked the master.

"No! I'm not losing my temper," stammered the elder brother. "What I meant to say was that I'm a little tired and I ought to rest."

Wearily, the elder brother returned to the fields. He worked hard and long by moonlight. Then as soon as the moon disappeared, the sun rose from the east. He continued to work by sunlight until, exhausted, he fell to the ground.

"To the devil with your farm and your money and with you, too!" murmured the youth wearily.

"What! Have you lost your temper?" asked the master, suddenly appearing in the fields. "Remember our bargain! If you have lost your temper, you must either give me one thousand silver pieces or ten years of your service."

The poor youth did not know what to do. He neither had one thousand pieces of silver— nor could he bear to work for such a taskmaster for ten long years. In despair, he gave the master a signed note, promising to pay him one thousand silver pieces in the future. Then, empty-handed, he returned home to his brother.

"Did you make a fortune?" the younger brother greeted the elder. And the elder brother told him everything that had happened.

"Stay home and rest yourself. Don't worry," said the younger brother consolingly. "It's my turn to find work while you tend house." And he went immediately to the home of the same rich man to ask for work as a servant.

"If you want to work for me," said the rich man, "you must promise to stay until the call of the cuckoo in the spring."

The younger brother agreed. The rich master offered the same bargain to the younger brother: If the boy should lose his temper, he must forfeit one thousand silver pieces or ten years of service as a servant. If the master should lose his temper first, however, he must forfeit one thousand silver pieces.

"Is it a bargain?" asked the rich man.

"Oh, no! That's hardly worth bargaining for," scoffed the younger brother. "If you lose your temper, you must pay me two thousand pieces of silver. If I lose my temper, I will either forfeit two thousand silver pieces or work for you for twenty years."

"It's a bargain!" The greedy master quickly agreed to the new terms. They signed the agreement, and the younger brother started to work.

Night passed and morning came, but the young servant did not get out of bed. The master angrily paced the floor; the servant still slept. Finally, the master rushed into the boy's bedroom. "Get up! Get up! Do you realize it's nearly noon!" he shouted.

"What! Are you by chance losing your temper?" asked the servant lifting his head from the pillow.

"Of course I'm not losing my temper!" answered the frightened master, lowering his voice. "I'm only reminding you that we must go to harvest the grain."

"Oh, well, then . . . if you're not angry, we'll go right along," said the boy. Slowly he got out of bed and slowly began to put on his clothes.

The rich man impatiently paced back and forth—and still the boy continued to dress.

"Hurry, boy! You're taking too long to get dressed!" exclaimed the master.

"What! Are you losing your temper?" asked the servant.

"Who is losing his temper? Certainly not I! I just mean to remind you that we are late!"

"Oh, well, then . . . I will be ready soon," replied the younger brother.

By the time the servant finished dressing, by the time they arrived at the fields, it was already noon.

"It would look silly to start work now when all the others are eating their noon meal," said the servant. "Let's eat first; then we can go to work."

They sat down together and ate. "It is customary for working people to take a short nap after a noonday meal," said the younger brother and stretched himself out on the ground. He fell asleep at once and did not wake up till nightfall.

"Wake up! Wake up! It's dark already and only our grain is not yet harvested. Cursed be the one who sent you to me! I'm ruined!" shouted the rich man in despair.

"What! Can it be you are losing your temper?" asked the servant, waking up.

"Who's losing his temper? I'm not!" the master exclaimed. "I only mean to remind you that night has fallen. It's time to go home."

"Oh, well, then . . . that's different. I thought you might have forgotten our bargain."

They returned to the house to find that unexpected guests had arrived. The master ordered the servant to go out and kill a sheep for supper.

"Which one?" asked the boy.

"Whichever one comes along," answered the master impatiently. "But hurry!"

A few moments later, some of the other servants came running to their master.

"Master! Master! Hurry! Your new servant has killed all the sheep in your flock!"

The rich man rushed out and found that all his sheep had, indeed, been slaughtered. Out of his mind with anger, he shouted to the boy, "What have you done, you fool? May your house be ruined as you have ruined mine! Why have you killed all my sheep?"

"But master, you told me to kill whichever sheep came along. They all came along—and I killed them all according to your orders. And I do think you've lost your temper this time, haven't you?"

"No! I have NOT lost my temper," screamed the master. "Alas! I am only heartbroken to have lost all my sheep."

"Oh, well, then . . . as long as you haven't lost your temper, I'll continue to work for you," replied the servant.

From that moment on, however, the rich man thought only of how he could get rid of his servant. By their agreement, the boy was to work until the call of the cuckoo in the spring. It was still winter, however, and the spring cuckoo was months away.

Finally, the master thought of a plan. He took his wife into the woods, put her up in a tree, and told her to call, *Cuckoo, cuckoo* when he returned later with the servant.

Back at the house, he ordered the servant to accompany him on a hunting trip into the woods. As soon as the two entered the woods, the man's wife in the tree called out, *Cuckoo, cuckoo!*

"Aha!" said the master. "Listen! There is the call of the cuckoo, I do believe. According to our agreement, your months of work for me are over."

The younger brother thought for a moment. He suspected a plot.

"No! No! Who ever heard of a cuckoo singing in the middle of winter? It must be a very strange cuckoo, indeed. I will kill it immediately." Saying this, he aimed his bow at the tree.

The rich man fell upon the younger brother. "Don't shoot! Don't shoot! Ah-h-h-h—black was the day you came to me!" he shouted. "What trouble I'm in because of you!"

"What! Is it possible you are losing your temper?" asked the servant.

"Yes! Yes! Yes! I'm losing my temper! This is enough! I'll pay any price to get rid of you! I made the bargain—and I'll suffer the losses! Just get out of my sight!" screamed the rich man at the top of his voice.

So it was that the rich man eagerly paid two thousand silver pieces to the servant. The younger brother, in turn, paid off his elder brother's debt of one thousand silver pieces. Then he put the remaining one thousand silver pieces into his pocket and headed happily for home.

Czechoslovakia

The Twelve Months

This Czech tale is one of the best in Nemcova's collection. It really is another version of the French story *Toads and Diamonds.* However, as it is made more complicated by cumulative repetition, it builds up better to a climax. And yet, to a child reader, the marriage of the heroine to a mere farmer may not be so interesting as her marriage to a prince; and the contrast with *Toads and Diamonds* is unforgettable. [From Parker Fillmore, *The Shoemaker's Apron* (Harcourt, 1920).]

There was once a woman who had two girls. One was her own daughter, the other a stepchild. Holena, her own daughter, she loved dearly, but she couldn't bear even the sight of Marushka, the stepchild. This was because Marushka was so much prettier than Holena. Marushka, the dear child, didn't know how pretty she was, and so she never understood why, whenever she stood beside Holena, the stepmother frowned so crossly.

Mother and daughter made Marushka do all the housework alone. She had to cook and wash and sew and spin and take care of the garden and look after the cow. Holena, on the contrary, spent all her time decking herself out and sitting around like a grand lady.

Marushka never complained. She did all she was told to do and bore patiently their everlasting fault-finding. In spite of all the hard work she did, she grew prettier from day to day, and in spite of her lazy life, Holena grew uglier.

"This will never do," the stepmother thought to herself. "Soon the boys will come courting, and once they see how pretty Marushka is, they'll pay no attention at all to my Holena. We had just better do all we can to get rid of that Marushka as soon as possible."

So they both nagged Marushka all day long. They made her work harder, they beat her, they didn't give her enough to eat, they did everything they could think of to make her ugly and nasty. But all to no avail. Marushka was so good and sweet that, in spite of all their harsh treatment, she kept on growing prettier.

One day in the middle of January Holena took the notion that nothing would do but she must have a bunch of fragrant violets to put in her bodice.

"Marushka!" she ordered sharply. "I want some violets. Go out to the forest and get me some."

"Good heavens, my dear sister!" cried poor Marushka. "What can you be thinking of? Whoever heard of violets growing under the snow in January?"

"What, you lazy little slattern!" Holena shouted. "You dare to argue with me! You go this minute and if you come back without violets, I'll kill you!"

The stepmother sided with Holena and, taking Marushka roughly by the shoulder, she pushed her out of the house and slammed the door.

The poor child climbed slowly up the mountain-side, weeping bitterly. All around the snow lay deep with no track of man or beast in any direction. Marushka wandered on and on, weak with hunger and shaking with cold.

"Dear God in heaven," she prayed, "take me to yourself away from all this suffering."

Suddenly ahead of her she saw a glowing light. She struggled toward it and found at last that it came from a great fire that was burning on the top of the mountain. Around the fire there were twelve stones, one of them much bigger and higher than the rest. Twelve men were seated on the stones. Three of them were very old and white; three were not so old; three were middle-aged; and three were beautiful youths. They did not talk. They sat silent gazing at the fire. They were the Twelve Months.

For a moment Marushka was frightened and hesitated. Then she stepped forward and said, politely:

"Kind sirs, may I warm myself at your fire? I am shaking with cold."

Great January nodded his head and Marushka reached her stiff fingers toward the flames.

"This is no place for you, my child," Great January said. "Why are you here?"

"I'm hunting for violets," Marushka answered.

"Violets? This is no time to look for violets with snow on the ground!"

"I know that, sir, but my sister, Holena, says I must bring her violets from the forest or she'll kill me, and my mother says so, too. Please, sir, won't you tell me where I can find some?"

Great January slowly stood up and walked over to the youngest Month. He handed him a long staff and said:

"Here, March, you take the high seat."

So March took the high seat and began waving the staff over the fire. The fire blazed up and instantly the snow all about began to melt. The trees burst into bud; the grass revived; the little pink buds of the daisies appeared; and, lo, it was spring!

While Marushka looked, violets began to peep out from among the leaves, and soon it was as if a great blue quilt had been spread on the ground.

"Now, Marushka," March cried, "there are your violets! Pick them quickly!"

Marushka was overjoyed. She stooped down and gathered a great bunch. Then she thanked the Months politely, bade them good day, and hurried away.

Just imagine Holena and the stepmother's surprise when they saw Marushka coming home through the snow with her hands full of violets. They opened the door and instantly the fragrance of the flowers filled the cottage.

"Where did you get them?" Holena demanded rudely.

"High up in the mountain," Marushka said. "The ground up there is covered with them."

Holena snatched the violets and fastened them in her waist. She kept smelling them herself all afternoon and she let her mother smell them, but she never once said to Marushka:

"Dear sister, won't you take a smell?"

The next day, as she was sitting idle in the chimney corner, she took the notion that she must have some strawberries to eat. So she called Marushka and said:

"Here you, Marushka, go out to the forest and get me some strawberries."

"Good heavens, my dear sister," Marushka said, "where can I find strawberries this time of year? Whoever heard of strawberries growing under the snow?"

"What, you lazy little slattern!" Holena shouted. "You dare to argue with me! You go this minute, and if you come back without strawberries, I'll kill you!"

Again the stepmother sided with Holena and, taking Marushka roughly by the shoulder, she pushed her out of the house and slammed the door.

Again the poor child climbed slowly up the mountain-side, weeping bitterly. All around the snow lay deep with no track of man or beast in any direction. Marushka wandered on and on, weak with hunger and shaking with cold. At last she saw ahead of her the glow of the same fire that she had seen the day before. With happy heart she hastened to it. The Twelve Months were seated as before with Great January on the high seat.

Marushka bowed politely and said:

"Kind sirs, may I warm myself at your fire? I am shaking with cold."

Great January nodded and Marushka reached her stiff fingers toward the flames.

"But Marushka," Great January said, "why are you here again? What are you hunting now?"

"I'm hunting strawberries," Marushka answered.

"Strawberries? But, Marushka, my child, it is winter and strawberries do not grow in the snow."

Marushka shook her head sadly.

"I know that, sir, but my sister, Holena, says I must bring her strawberries from the forest or she will kill me, and my mother says so, too. Please, sir, won't you tell me where I can find some?"

Great January slowly stood up and walked over to the Month who sat opposite him. He handed him the long staff and said:

"Here, June, you take the high seat."

So June took the high seat and began waving the staff over the fire. The flames blazed high, and with the heat the snow all about melted instantly. The earth grew green; the trees decked themselves in leaves; the birds began to sing; flowers bloomed and, lo, it was summer! Presently little starry white blossoms covered the ground under the beech trees. Soon these turned to fruit, first green, then pink, then red, and, with a gasp of delight, Marushka saw that they were ripe strawberries.

"Now, Marushka," June cried, "there are your strawberries! Pick them quickly!"

Marushka picked an apronful of berries.

Then she thanked the Months politely, bade them good-bye, and hurried home.

Just imagine again Holena and the stepmother's surprise as they saw Marushka coming through the snow with an apronful of strawberries!

They opened the door and instantly the fragrance of the berries filled the house.

"Where did you get them?" Holena demanded rudely.

"High up in the mountain," Marushka answered, "under the beech trees."

Holena took the strawberries and gobbled and gobbled and gobbled. Then the stepmother ate all she wanted. But it never occurred to either of them to say:

"Here, Marushka, you take one."

The next day, when Holena was sitting idle, as usual, in the chimney corner, the notion took her that she must have some red apples. So she called Marushka and said:

"Here you, Marushka, go out to the forest and get me some red apples."

"But, my dear sister," Marushka gasped, "where can I find red apples in winter?"

"What, you lazy little slattern, you dare to argue with me! You go this minute, and if you come back without red apples, I'll kill you!"

For the third time the stepmother sided with Holena and, taking Marushka roughly by the shoulder, pushed her out of the house and slammed the door.

So again the poor child went out to the forest. All around the snow lay deep with no track of man or beast in any direction. This time Marushka hurried straight to the mountain-top. She found the Months still seated about their fire with Great January still on the high stone.

Marushka bowed politely and said:

"Kind sirs, may I warm myself at your fire? I am shaking with cold."

Great January nodded, and Marushka reached her stiff fingers toward the flames.

"Why are you here again, Marushka?" Great January asked. "What are you looking for now?"

"Red apples," Marushka answered. "My sister, Holena, says I must bring her some red apples from the forest or she will kill me, and my mother says so, too. Please sir, won't you tell me where I can find some?''

Great January slowly stood up and walked over to one of the older Months. He handed him the long staff and said:

"Here, September, you take the high seat."

So September took the high seat and began waving the staff over the fire. The fire burned and glowed. Instantly the snow disappeared. The fields about looked brown and yellow and dry. From the trees the leaves dropped one by one and a cool breeze scattered them over the stubble. There were not many flowers, old wild asters on the hillside, and meadow saffron in the valleys, and under the beeches ferns and ivy. Presently Marushka spied an apple tree weighted down with ripe fruit.

"There, Marushka," September called, "there are your apples. Gather them quickly."

Marushka reached up and picked one apple. Then she picked another.

"That's enough, Marushka!" September shouted. "Don't pick any more!"

Marushka obeyed at once. Then she thanked the Months politely, bade them good-bye, and hurried home.

Holena and her stepmother were more surprised than ever to see Marushka coming through the snow with red apples in her hands. They let her in and grabbed the apples from her.

"Where did you get them?" Holena demanded.

"High up on the mountain," Marushka answered. "There are plenty of them growing there."

"Plenty of them! And you only brought us two!" Holena cried angrily. "Or did you pick more and eat them yourself on the way home?"

"No, no, my dear sister," Marushka said. "I haven't eaten any, truly I haven't. They shouted to me not to pick any more."

"I wish the lightning had struck you dead!" Holena sneered. "I've a good mind to beat you!"

After a time the greedy Holena left off her scolding to eat one of the apples. It had so delicious a flavor that she declared she had never in all her life tasted anything so good. Her mother said the same. When they had finished both apples, they began to wish for more.

"Mother," Holena said, "go get me my fur cloak. I'm going up the mountain myself. No use sending that lazy little slattern again, for she would only eat up all the apples on the way home. I'll find that tree and when I pick the apples, I'd like to see anybody stop me!"

The mother begged Holena not to go out in such weather, but Holena was headstrong and would go. She threw her fur cloak over her shoulders and put a shawl on her head and off she went up the mountain-side.

All around the snow lay deep with no track of man or beast in any direction. Holena wandered on and on determined to find those wonderful apples. At last she saw a light in the distance and when she reached it she found it was the great fire about which the Twelve Months were seated.

At first she was frightened, but, soon growing bold, she elbowed her way through the circle of men and without so much as saying, "By your leave," she put out her hands to the fire. She hadn't even the courtesy to say: "Good-day."

Great January frowned.

"Who are you? he asked in a deep voice. "And what do you want?"

Holena looked at him rudely.

"You old fool, what business is it of yours who I am or what I want!"

She tossed her head airily and walked off into the forest.

The frown deepened on Great January's brow. Slowly he stood up and waved the staff over his head. The fire died down. Then the sky grew dark; an icy wind blew over the mountain; and the snow began to fall so thickly that it looked as if someone in the sky were emptying a huge feather bed.

Holena could not see a step before her. She struggled on and on. Now she ran into a tree, now she fell into a snowdrift. In spite of her warm cloak her limbs began to weaken and grow numb. The snow kept on falling, the icy wind kept on blowing.

Did Holena at last begin to feel sorry that she had been so wicked and cruel to Marushka? No, she did not. Instead, the colder she grew, the more bitterly she reviled Marushka in her heart, the more bitterly she reviled even the good God Himself.

Meanwhile, at home her mother waited for her and waited. She stood at the window as long as she could, then she opened the door and tried to peer through the storm. She waited and waited, but no Holena came.

"Oh dear, oh dear, what can be keeping her?" she thought to herself. "Does she like those apples so much that she can't leave them, or what is it? I think I'll have to go out myself and find her."

So the stepmother put her fur cloak about her shoulders, threw a shawl over her head, and started out.

She called: "Holena! Holena!" but no one answered.

She struggled on and on up the mountainside. All around the snow lay deep with no track of man or beast in any direction.

"Holena! Holena!"

Still no answer.

The snow fell fast. The icy wind moaned on.

At home Marushka prepared the dinner and looked after the cow. Still neither Holena nor the stepmother returned.

"What can they be doing all this time?" Marushka thought.

She ate her dinner alone and then sat down to work at the distaff.

The spindle filled and daylight faded, and still no sign of Holena and her mother.

"Dear God in heaven, what can be keeping them?" Marushka cried anxiously. She peered out the window to see if they were coming.

The storm had spent itself. The wind had died down. The fields gleamed white in the snow, and up in the sky the frosty stars were twinkling brightly. But not a living creature was in sight. Marushka knelt down and prayed for her sister and mother.

The next morning she prepared breakfast for them.

"They'll be very cold and hungry," she said to herself.

She waited for them, but they didn't come. She cooked dinner for them, but still they didn't come. In fact they never came, for they both froze to death on the mountain.

So our good little Marushka inherited the cottage and the garden and the cow. After a time she married a farmer. He made her a good husband and they lived together very happily.

Poland

The Jolly Tailor Who Became King

In making her collection *The Jolly Tailor and Other Fairy Tales,* Lucia Merecka Borski chose stories most representative of Polish folklore. Stories she had told over and over again to Polish children in their own tongue, she translated for English-speaking children. The favorite, *The Jolly Tailor,* is reprinted below. A lively story, full of humor, it tells of impossible happenings that seem perfectly logical and satisfactory. [From Lucia Merecka Borski and Kate B. Miller, *The Jolly Tailor and Other Fairy Tales* (Longmans, 1925).]

Once upon a time, in the town of Taidaraida, there lived a merry little Tailor, Mr. Joseph Nitechka. He was a very thin man and had a small beard of one hundred and thirty-six hairs.

All tailors are thin, reminding one of a needle and thread, but Mr. Nitechka was the thinnest of all, for he could pass through the eye of his own needle. He was so thin that he could eat nothing but noodles, for they were the only thing which could pass down his throat. But for all this, he was a very happy man, and a handsome one, too, particularly on holidays when he braided his beard.

Now Mr. Nitechka would have lived very happily in Taidaraida had it not been for a Gypsy. She happened to be in the town when she cut her foot. In her trouble she went to the Tailor, who darned the skin so carefully and so neatly that not a scar could be seen. The

Illustration by Felix Hoffmann. Illustration copyright © 1963 by Felix Hoffmann, from *Favorite Fairy Tales Told in Poland,* by Virginia Haviland, by permission of Little, Brown and Co.

Gypsy was so grateful that she read Nitechka's future from his hand:

"If you leave this town on a Sunday and walk always Westward, you will reach a place where you will be chosen King!"

Nitechka laughed at this. But that very night he dreamt that he indeed became a King, and that from great prosperity he grew so fat that he looked like an immense barrel. Upon waking he thought:

"Maybe it is true? Who knows? Get up, Mr. Nitechka, and go West."

He took a bundle with a hundred needles and a thousand miles of thread, a thimble, an iron, and a pair of very big scissors, and started out to find the West. He asked first one and then another in the town of Taidaraida where the West was. But no one knew. Finally he asked an old man, a hundred and six years old, who upon thinking awhile said:

"West must be there where the sun sets."

This seemed so wise to Nitechka that he went that way. But he had not gone far when a gust of wind blew across the field—not a very strong gust—but, because Mr. Nitechka was so exceedingly thin, just strong enough to carry him off.

The Tailor flew through the air, laughing heartily at such a ride. Soon, however, the wind became tired and let him down to earth. He was much bewildered and did not come to his senses until someone shouted:

"What is this?"

Mr. Nitechka looked around and saw that he was in a wheat field and that the wind had thrown him right into the arms of a Scarecrow. The Scarecrow was very elegant in a blue jacket and a broken stovepipe hat, and his trousers were only a bit torn. He had two sticks for feet and also sticks for hands.

Nitechka took off his little cap, bowed very low, saying in his thin voice:

"My regards to the honorable Sir. I beg your pardon if I stepped on your foot. I am Mr. Nitechka, the Tailor."

"I am very much pleased to meet such a charming man," answered the Scarecrow. "I am Count Scarecrow and my coat of arms is Four Sticks. I watch the sparrows here so that they will not steal wheat, but I give little heed to them. I am uncommonly courageous and would like to fight only with lions and tigers, but this year they very seldom come to eat the wheat. Where are you going, Mr. Nitechka?"

Nitechka bowed again and hopped three times as he was very polite and he knew that well-bred men thus greeted each other.

"Where do I go, Mr. Count? I am going Westward to a place where I will become King."

"Is it possible?"

"Of course! I was born to be a King. And perhaps you, Mr. Count, would like to go with me; it will be merrier."

"All right," answered the Scarecrow. "I am already weary of being here. But please, Mr. Nitechka, mend my clothes a bit, because I might like to marry someone on the way; and so I should be neat and handsome."

"With great pleasure!" said Nitechka. He went to work, and in an hour the Scarecrow had a beautiful suit and a hat almost like new. The sparrows in the field laughed at him a little, but he paid no attention to them as he walked with great dignity with Mr. Nitechka.

On the way the two became great friends. They generally slept in a wheat field, the Tailor tying himself to the Scarecrow with a piece of thread so that the wind could not carry him off again. And when dogs fell upon them, the Scarecrow, who was very brave because of his profession, tore out his foot and threw it after them. Then he tied it again to his body.

Once in the evening they spied a light through the trees.

"Let us go there; maybe they will let us pass the night," said Nitechka.

"By all means, let us do them the honor," answered Count Scarecrow.

As they drew nearer they saw that it was a strange house because it could walk. It stood on four feet and was turning around.

"The owner of the house must be a gay man," whispered the Tailor. "He dances all the time."

They waited until the door came round to them and then went into the house. It was indeed a very strange house. Although it was summer, immense logs of wood burned in the stove, and on the fire sat a nobleman warming himself. From time to time he took a glowing coal in his hands and swallowed it with great pleasure. Upon noticing the travelers, he went over to them, bowed and said:

"Is it not Mr. Nitechka and Count Scarecrow?"

They were speechless with astonishment to think that he should know them, but said nothing. Mr. Nitechka hopped up three times and Count Scarecrow took off his hat.

The nobleman continued:

"Stay with me for supper and tomorrow you may go your way. I will call my wife, my daughter, and my other relatives."

He clapped his hands and suddenly a large company appeared. The host's daughter was very beautiful, but when she laughed, it was as if a horse had neighed in a meadow. She took an instant liking to Nitechka and told him she would very much like to have him for her husband. They sat down to supper, Nitechka and Count Scarecrow on a bench, and all the others on iron pots filled with glowing coals.

"Do not wonder, dear Sirs," the host said, "that we sit thus, for our family always feels very cold."

They served soup in a big caldron and Nitechka was just putting his spoon to his lips, when Count Scarecrow pulled his coat and whispered:

"Mr. Nitechka, don't eat, for this is hot pitch!"

So pretending that they liked the soup, they spilt it under the table. Then a strange looking servant brought a new dish of rats in a black sauce, and later he served fried locust, lob-worms with parmesan cheese like noodles, and, for dessert, old, bad eggs. Nitechka and Count Scarecrow threw everything under the table, becoming more and more frightened.

All at once the host said:

"Do you know, Mr. Nitechka, that the King has just died in Pacanów [Patsanoff]?"

"Where is Pacanów, is it far?" asked the Tailor.

"A crow can fly to that town in two days. And do you know they are seeking a King there, and he who marries my daughter will become King?"

The girl neighed like an old horse at this and threw her arms around Nitechka's neck.

"Let's run away!" murmured Count Scarecrow.

"But I can't find the door. There is no help," replied Nitechka.

Soon, however, the whole family became very gay, and presently the host said:

"We will drink to your health and sing merrily. Mr. Nitechka, do you know a song?"

"Yes, indeed," said Nitechka, "and a very nice one."

Saying this, he whispered to Count Scarecrow:

"Watch, brother, and when the door is behind us, shout!"

Then he got up, took off his cap and in his thin little voice began to sing the only song he knew.

"Sing praises to the Holy Virgin,
Sing praises to Her Wondrous Name!"

At the mention of the Virgin, the whole family rose to their feet, and ran around the room, sprawling and shouting and cursing. Nitechka said nothing, but simply continued his song. He could feel the house running somewhere with them, and so he sang and sang like the thinnest pipe in the organ. When he had finished the song, he began to sing it over again. At that moment everything disappeared, and only a terrible wind blew.

Terrified, Nitechka and Count Scarecrow found themselves alone in a huge meadow.

Then they gave thanks for their delivery and Nitechka said:

"They were awful devils, but we overpowered them."

"I frightened them so much," boasted Count Scarecrow.

They continued their way toward Pacanów, where dwelt the famous smiths who shoe the goats, a beautiful old town, where the King had died. When after seven days of adventures they reached Pacanów, they were greatly astonished. All around the town it was sunshiny and pleasant; but over Pacanów the rain poured from the sky as from a bucket.

"I won't go in there," said the Scarecrow, "because my hat will get wet."

"And even I do not wish to become King of such a wet kingdom," said the Tailor.

Just then the townspeople spied them and rushed toward them, led by the Burgomaster riding on a shod goat.

"Dear Sirs," they said, "maybe you can help us."

"And what has happened to you?" asked Nitechka.

"Deluge and destruction threaten us. Our King died a week ago, and since that time a terrible rain has come down upon our gorgeous town. We can't even make fires in our houses, because so much water runs through the chimneys. We will perish, honorable Sirs!"

"It is too bad," said Nitechka very wisely.

"Oh, very bad! And we are most sorry for the late King's daughter, as the poor thing can't stop crying and this causes even more water."

"That makes it still worse," replied Nitechka, still more wisely.

"Help us, help us!" continued the Burgomaster. "Do you know the immeasurable reward the Princess promised to the one who stops the rain? She promised to marry him and then he will become King."

"Truly?" cried Nitechka. "Count Scarecrow, let's go to the town. We ought to try to help them."

They were led through the terrible rain to the Princess, who upon seeing Nitechka, cried out:

"Oh, what a handsome youth!"

He hopped three times and said:

"Is it true, Princess, that you will marry the one who stops the rain?"

"I vowed I would."

"And if I do it?"

"I will keep my promise."

"And I shall become a King?"

"You will, O beautiful youth."

"Very well," answered the Tailor. "I am going to stop the rain."

So saying he nodded to Count Scarecrow and they left the Princess.

The whole population, full of hope, gathered around them. Nitechka and the Scarecrow stood under an umbrella and whispered to each other.

"Listen, Scarecrow, what shall we do to make the rain stop falling?"

"We have to bring back pleasant weather."

"But how?"

"Ha! Let's think!"

But for three days they thought and the rain fell and fell and fell. Suddenly Nitechka gave a cry of joy like a goat's bleating.

"I know where the rain comes from!"

"Where from?"

"From the sky!"

"Eh!" grumbled the Scarecrow. "I know that too. Surely it doesn't fall from the bottom to the top, but the other way around."

"Yes," said Nitechka, "but why does it fall over the town only, and not elsewhere?"

"Because elsewhere is nice weather."

"You're stupid, Mr. Count," said the Tailor. "But tell me, how long has it rained?"

"They say since the King died."

"So you see! Now I know everything! The King was so great and mighty that when he died and went to Heaven he made a huge hole in the sky."

"Oh, oh, true!"

"Through the hole the rain poured and it will pour until the end of the world if the hole isn't sewed up!"

Count Scarecrow looked at him in amazement.

"In all my life I have never seen such a wise Tailor," said he.

They rejoiced greatly, went to the Burgomaster, and ordered him to tell the townspeople that Mr. Joseph Nitechka, a citizen of the town of Taidaraida, promised to stop the rain.

"Long live Mr. Nitechka! Long may he live!" shouted the whole town.

Then Nitechka ordered them to bring all the ladders in the town, tie them together, and lean them against the sky. He took a hundred needles and, threading one, went up the ladders. Count Scarecrow stayed at the bottom and unwound the spool on which there was a hundred miles of thread.

When Nitechka got to the very top he saw that there was a huge hole in the sky, a hole as big as the town. A torn piece of the sky hung down, and through this hole the water poured.

So he went to work and sewed and sewed for two days. His fingers grew stiff and he became very tired but he did not stop. When he had finished sewing he pressed out the sky with the iron and then, exhausted, went down the ladders.

Once more the sun shone over Pacanów. Count Scarecrow almost went mad with joy, as did all the other inhabitants of the town. The Princess wiped her eyes that were almost cried out, and throwing herself on Nitechka's neck, kissed him affectionately.

Nitechka was very happy. He looked around, and there were the Burgomaster and Councilmen bringing him a golden scepter and a gorgeous crown and shouting:

"Long live King Nitechka! Long live he! Long live he! And let him be the Princess' husband and let him reign happily!"

So the merry little Tailor reigned happily for a long time, and the rain never fell in his kingdom. In his good fortune Nitechka did not forget his old friend, Count Scarecrow, and he appointed him the Great Warden of the Kingdom to drive away the sparrows from the royal head.

Jewish Folktales

The Devil's Trick

The art of a storyteller of the first magnitude, combined with the sources of authentic folklore, results in a collection of stories full of wit and flavor. Isaac Bashevis Singer is a noted novelist who writes in Yiddish and whose autobiography *In My Father's Court* has been acclaimed with enthusiasm. The book from which the following selection is taken is distinguished in format and illustration, with Maurice Sendak's pictures a perfect extension of mood and setting. [From Isaac Bashevis Singer, *Zlateh the Goat and Other Stories* (Harper, 1966).]

The snow had been falling for three days and three nights. Houses were snowed in and windowpanes covered with frost flowers. The wind whistled in the chimneys. Gusts of snow somersaulted in the cold air.

The devil's wife rode on her hoop, with a broom in one hand and a rope in the other. Before her ran a white goat with a black beard and twisted horns. Behind her strode the devil with his cobweb face, holes instead of eyes, hair to his shoulders, and legs as long as stilts.

In a one-room hut, with a low ceiling and soot-covered walls, sat David, a poor boy with a pale face and black eyes. He was alone with his baby brother on the first night of Hanukkah. His father had gone to the village to buy corn, but three days had passed and he had not returned home. David's mother had gone to look for her husband, and she too had not come back.

The baby slept in his cradle. In the Hanukkah lamp flickered the first candle, which David himself had lit.

David was so worried he could not stay home any longer. He put on his padded coat and his cap with earlaps, made sure that the baby was covered, and went out to look for his parents.

That was what the devil had been waiting for. He immediately whipped up the storm. Black clouds covered the sky. David could hardly see in the thick darkness. The frost burned his face. The snow fell dry and heavy as salt. The wind caught David by his coattails and tried to lift him up off the ground. He was surrounded by laughter, as if from a thousand imps.

David realized the goblins were after him. He tried to turn back and go home, but he could not find his way. The snow and darkness swallowed *everything*. It became clear to him

that the devils must have caught his parents. Would they get him also? But heaven and earth have vowed that the devil may never succeed completely in his tricks. No matter how shrewd the devil is, he will always make a mistake, especially on Hanukkah.

The powers of evil had managed to hide the stars, but they could not extinguish the single Hanukkah candle. David saw its light and ran toward it. The devil ran after him. The devil's wife followed on her hoop, yelling and waving her broom, trying to lasso him with her rope. David ran even more quickly than they, and reached the hut just ahead of the devil As David opened the door the devil tried to get in with him. David managed to slam the door behind him. In the rush and struggle the devil's tail got stuck in the door.

"Give me back my tail," the devil screamed.

And David replied, "Give me back my father and mother."

The devil swore that he knew nothing about them, but David did not let himself be fooled.

"You kidnapped them, cursed Devil," David said. He picked up a sharp ax and told the devil that he would cut off his tail.

"Have pity on me. I have only one tail," the devil cried. And to his wife he said, "Go quickly to the cave behind the black mountains and bring back the man and woman we led astray."

His wife sped away on her hoop and soon brought the couple back. David's father sat on the hoop holding on to the witch by her hair; his mother came riding on the white goat, its black beard clasped tightly in her hands.

"Your mother and father are here. Give me my tail," said the devil.

David looked through the keyhole and saw his parents were really there. He wanted to open the door at once and let them in, but he was not yet ready to free the devil.

He rushed over to the window, took the Hanukkah candle, and singed the devil's tail. "Now, Devil, you will always remember," he cried, "Hanukkah is no time for making trouble."

Then at last he opened the door. The devil licked his singed tail and ran off with his wife to the land where no people walk, no cattle tread, where the sky is copper and the earth is iron.

The Golem

Nobel laureate Isaac Bashevis Singer retells the traditional legend of the golem. This monstrous giant was magically created by the cabalist Rabbi Leib to protect the Jews of sixteenth-century Prague. The story, originally written in Yiddish, has a psychological depth which it shares with other tales of men tampering with the divine creative process such as the Faust legend or the more recent story of Frankenstein's monster. In the following excerpt, the rabbi forms the golem from clay much as the Greek Titan Prometheus did the first human beings in the Greek myth. [From Isaac Bashevis Singer, *The Golem* (Farrar, Straus & Giroux, 1982).]

Exactly at twelve o'clock at night, Rabbi Leib rose for his midnight prayers. As usual, he put ashes on his head and began his lamentations over the destruction of the Temple in ancient times. He also shed tears over the misfortune that had befallen Reb Eliezer Polner and the whole Jewish community at the present time.

Suddenly the door opened and a little man entered wearing a patched robe, with a rope around his loins and with a sack on his back like a beggar. Rabbi Leib was surprised. He thought he had chained the door before beginning his prayers, but it seemed the door was open. Rabbi Leib interrupted his prayers and extended his hand to the stranger, since honoring guests is even more important in the eyes of God than prayer. Rabbi Leib greeted the man with the words *Sholom Aleichem,* "Peace be with you," and asked him, "What can I do for you?"

"Thank you, I don't need anything. I shall leave soon," the stranger said.

"In the middle of the night?" Rabbi Leib asked.

"I must take my leave soon."

Rabbi Leib looked at the man, and at that moment it became clear to him that this was not a usual wanderer. Rabbi Leib saw in his eyes something which only great men possess and which only great men recognize—a mixture of love, dignity, and fear of God. Rabbi Leib realized that the stranger might be one of the thirty-six hidden saints through whose merit the world existed, according to tradition. Never before had Rabbi Leib had the privilege of meeting a man of this stature. Rabbi Leib bowed his head and said, "Honored guest, we here in Prague are in great distress. Our enemies are about to destroy us. We are sinking up to our very necks in tribulations."

"I know," the stranger answered.

"What should we do?"

"Make a golem and he will save you."

"A golem? How? From what?"

"From clay. You will engrave one of God's names on the golem's forehead, and with the power of that Sacred Name he will live for a time and do his mission. His name will be Joseph. But take care that he should not fall into the follies of flesh and blood."

"What Sacred Name shall I engrave?" Rabbi Leib asked.

The stranger took out from his breast pocket a piece of chalk and on the cover of Rabbi Leib's prayer book wrote down some Hebrew letters. Then he said, "I must go now. See to it that all this remains a secret. And employ the golem only to help the Jews."

Before Rabbi Leib was able to utter a word of gratitude, the man vanished. Only then did the rabbi realize that the door had been chained all along. The rabbi stood there trembling, and praising God for sending him that heavenly messenger.

Although the holy man had told Rabbi Leib that his appearance and the making of the golem must remain a secret, Rabbi Leib realized that he had to share it with his beadle, Todrus. Todrus had served Rabbi Leib for the last forty years, and he had kept many secrets. A strong man, he was totally devoted to the rabbi. He had neither a wife nor children. Serving Rabbi Leib was his entire life; he lived in the rabbi's house and made his bed next to Rabbi Leib's chamber of study, so that he should always be ready to serve him even in the middle of the night. Rabbi Leib knocked lightly at his door and whispered, "Todrus."

"Rabbi, what is it that you wish?" Todrus asked, awaking immediately.

"I need clay."

Another person would have asked, "Clay? At this late hour?" But Todrus had learned not to question the rabbi's commands. "How much clay?" he asked.

"A lot of it."

"A sackful?"

"At least ten sackfuls."

"Where should I put all this clay?"

"In the attic of the synagogue."

There was wonder in Todrus's eyes, but all he said was, "Yes, Rabbi."

"The whole thing must remain a secret, even from my family," Rabbi Leib said.

"So be it," Todrus said, and he left.

Rabbi Leib continued his prayers. He could be certain that Todrus would do as he was told.

After finishing his night prayers, Rabbi Leib went back to sleep, and he woke up at sunrise.

Rabbi Leib knew quite well the meaning of the word *golem*. There were legends among the Jews about golems who were created by ancient saints to save them in a time of great danger. According to the legends, only the most saintly rabbis were given this power, and only after many days of supplication, fasting, and indulging in the mysteries of the Cabbalah. It never occurred to the modest Rabbi Leib that a man like himself would be granted this privilege. "Could it be that I dreamed it?" Rabbi Leib asked himself. But early in the morning, when he opened the door to the synagogue, he saw traces of clay on the floor. While Rabbi Leib slept, Todrus had gone out to the clay ditches in the suburbs of Prague and brought the clay to the attic. One had to be unusually strong and devoted to accomplish all this between midnight and sunrise.

It would have been impossible for Rabbi Leib to climb up to the attic without the knowledge of his family and stay there for many hours. Luckily, the rabbi's wife, Genendel, had to attend a wedding that day, and she took her children and her maid with her. The bride was a distant relative of Genendel, an orphan, and the wedding took place in a nearby village. Rabbi Leib was not obligated to officiate at the ceremony.

In the attic, Rabbi Leib found the sacks with the clay and began to sculpt the figure of a man. Rabbi Leib did not use a chisel but his fingers to carve the figure of the golem. He kneaded the clay like dough. He was working with great speed; at the same time he prayed for success in what he was doing. All day Rabbi Leib was busy in the attic, and when it was time for the evening prayer, a large shape of a man with a huge head, broad shoulders, and enormous hands and feet was lying on the floor—a clay giant. The rabbi looked at him in astonishment. He could never have mastered this without the help of Almighty and Special Providence. The rabbi had taken with him the prayer book in which his saintly visitor had written down the name of God. Rabbi Leib engraved it on the forehead of the golem in such small letters that only he himself could distinguish the Hebrew characters. Immediately, the clay figure started to show signs of life.

The golem began to move his arms and legs and tried to lift his head. However, the rabbi had been careful not to engrave the entire Sacred Name. He left out a small part of the last letter, which was an Aleph, so that the golem should not begin to act before he was dressed in garments. Since the rabbi knew that the people of the community would wonder why he was not at the synagogue for the evening prayers, he decided to leave the golem unfinished where he was and began to climb down the narrow steps. Just then Todrus the beadle came in from the street, and the rabbi said to him, "Todrus, holy spirits have helped me to make a golem to defend the Jews of Prague. Climb up to the attic and see for yourself. But the golem needs to be dressed, and you will have to take his measurements and find clothes for him. I'm going to the evening prayers, and when you find the clothes, come and let me know."

"Yes, Rabbi."

Rabbi Leib went to pray, and Todrus climbed up the spiral stairs to the attic. Outside, the sun was setting, and by the light from crevices in the roof Todrus saw the golem lying on the floor and trying to get up. A terrible fear came over Todrus. Like many other Jews in Prague, he had heard stories about golems, but he never believed that the actual creation of one could take place in his time and almost before his very eyes.

For a long time Todrus stood there motionless. "Where will I get clothes for a giant like this?" he thought in consternation. Even if a tailor could be found to take the golem's measurements and sew a robe and trousers for him, and a shoemaker could be assigned to make a pair of boots for him, it would take weeks or even months—while the Jews of Prague were in great peril right now.

Todrus knew from forty years of service that when Rabbi Leib gave an order, he must act without delay. The sun had set and it became dark in the attic. Todrus rushed down the stairs, his heart pounding and his legs buckling under him. He went out into the street and took a deep breath. He then began to walk in the direction of the old marketplace, hoping against hope to find some miraculous solution. Night had fallen and the stores began to close. Suddenly Todrus saw in a store a huge hat that was too big to fit any human head. It was a hatmaker's window sample. When Todrus entered the store he saw a robe, a pair of pants, and shoes of the same unbelievable size. Amazed, he asked the owner where he had obtained these curious things. The owner told him that forty years ago a foreign circus had come to Prague and performed a play called *David and Goliath.* It so happened that the circus people had quarreled among themselves, the play had failed to attract a public, and all the props and sets were sold for a very small price. The proprietor of the store said to Todrus: "I got these things for a pittance and I bought them just as a rarity that might attract customers. However, they have been here for so many years that no one looks at them any more. Also, they are covered with dust and I have neither the time nor the patience to air them or brush them. Why do you ask? I'm about to close the store for the night."

"I want to buy them," Todrus said. "If you sell them to me at a reasonable price."

"What are you going to do with them?"

"Who knows?" Todrus replied. "Just give me a reasonable price."

"Well, this is the strangest thing that has hap-pened to me in all these years," the storekeeper said. "No one has ever shown any interest in these paraphernalia." He gave Todrus an exceptionally low offer, and in a matter of minutes the deal was completed. Todrus was known for his honesty, and he always carried a purse with money that belonged to the community and that Rabbi Leib entrusted to him.

Todrus feared that people in the street might stop him in wonderment, but luckily no one was outside at this time of night. The men were all in the synagogue, and the women were preparing dinner for their husbands and children. Todrus managed to climb the stairs of the synagogue attic without being seen and put down the garments, the hat, and the shoes for the golem. How strange, the golem had managed to sit up! A half-moon was shining outside, and it allowed Todrus to see the golem sitting, leaning on an old barrel with mildewed books, and looking at him in bewilderment. Todrus was seized with such fright that he intoned the words "Hear, O Israel, the Lord is our God, the Lord is One."

After some time he heard Rabbi Leib coming up the stairs with a lantern in which a wax candle was burning. The rabbi saw the robe, the hat, and the shoes and said to Todrus, "Everything is planned by Providence. Even though man has free will, Providence foresees all the decisions man would make." After they dressed the golem in these bizarre clothes, the rabbi said: "Thank you, Todrus, and leave me alone now."

"Yes, Rabbi," Todrus said, and he descended as quickly as he could.

For a long while Rabbi Leib gaped at the golem, perplexed by his own creation. How strange the synagogue attic looked in the dim light of the lantern! In the corners, huge spiderwebs hung from the rafters. On the floor lay old and torn prayer shawls, cracked ram's-horns, broken candelabra, parts of candlesticks, Hanuk-kah lamps, as well as faded pages of manuscripts written by unknown or forgotten scribes. Through the crevices and holes in the roof the moonlit dust reflected the colors of the rainbow. One could sense the spirits of generations who had lived, suffered, served God, withstood both have not been completely formed, but I am about to finish you now. Let it be known to you that you were created for a short time and for a purpose. Don't ever try to stray from this path. You will do as I will tell you."

Saying these words, Rabbi Leib finished engraving the letter Aleph. Immediately the golem began to rise. The rabbi said to him, "Walk down and wait for me in the yard of the synagogue for further instructions."

"Yes," the golem said in a hollow voice, as if it rose from a cave. Then he walked down to the synagogue courtyard, which was empty. The people of the ghetto went to sleep early and woke up at sunrise. After the prayer services, everybody had gone home.

Rabbi Leib's mind was too occupied with the golem to pay much attention to the conversation of his wife and children, who had returned from the wedding and were talking about the bride, the bridegroom, and the guests. Usually, the rabbi went to sleep early, so he could get up for the midnight prayers. This time he waited until his wife and children went to sleep, and then he went out silently to the synagogue courtyard. The golem was standing there waiting. The rabbi approached him. "Golem, your name will be Joseph from now on."

"Yes."

"Joseph, soon you will have to find the daughter of Count Bratislawski, a little girl by the name of Hanka. Her father maintains that the Jews have killed her, but I am sure that he is hiding her somewhere. Don't ask me where to find her. Those powers that gave you life will also give you the knowledge of where she is. You are part of the earth, and the earth knows many things—how to grow grass, flowers, wheat, rye, fruit. Wait for the day when Reb Eliezer is brought to trial, and then bring the girl and show our enemies how false their accusation was."

"Yes."

"Is there anything you want to ask?" the rabbi said to the golem.

"What ask?" answered the golem.

"Since you were created for a single purpose, you were given a different brain from that of a man. However, one never knows how a brain

Illustration by Uri Shulevitz. From *The Golem,* by Isaac Bashevis Singer, illustrated by Uri Shulevitz. Illustrations copyright © 1982 by Uri Shulevitz. Used with permission of Farrar, Straus & Giroux, Inc.

persecution and temptation, and become silent forever. A strange thought ran through Rabbi Leib's mind: "If those who deny that God created the world could witness what I, a man born from the womb of a woman, have done, they would be ashamed of their heresy. However, such is the power of Satan that he can blind people's eyes and confuse their minds. Satan, too, was created by God so that man should have free will to choose between good and evil."

As Rabbi Leib stood there looking at the golem, the golem seemed to look back at him with his clay eyes. Then the rabbi said, "Golem, you works. While you rest and wait for the day when you will have to find Hanka, you may sleep, you may dream, you may see things or hear voices. Perhaps demons may try to attach themselves to you. Don't pay any attention to them. Nothing evil can befall you. The people of Prague are not to see you until the day you have to be seen. Until then, go back to the attic where I formed you and sleep there the peaceful sleep of clay. Good night."

Rabbi Leib turned his face toward his home. He knew the golem would do exactly as he was told. When he reached home, the rabbi recited the night prayer and went to bed. For the first time in many years he could not fall asleep. A great power was granted to him from heaven, and he was afraid that he had not deserved it. He also felt a kind of compassion for the golem. The rabbi thought he saw an expression of perplexity in the golem's eyes. It seemed to the rabbi that his eyes were asking, "Who am I? Why am I here? What is the secret of my being?" Rabbi Leib often saw the same bewilderment in the eyes of newborn children and even in the eyes of animals.

Those who wanted the Jews to have a miserable Passover had arranged for the trial to take place shortly. The day before Passover, Reb Eliezer Polner was brought to court, together with a number of community leaders who were supposed to have assisted him in the murder.

Three judges sat with perukes on their heads, dressed in long black togas. The Jews stood bound in chains, guarded by soldiers carrying swords and spears. The chief judge had forbidden the Jews of Prague to witness the trial, but quite a few enemies of Israel came with their wives and daughters to see the disgrace of the Jews. The prosecutor pointed his index finger at Reb Eliezer Polner and the other accused Jews, and said, "They consider themselves God's chosen people, but see how they conduct themselves. Instead of being grateful to our Emperor and to all of us for allowing them to live here, they slaughter our children and pour their blood into their matzohs. They are not God's people but followers of the Devil. The blood

of the murdered little Hanka is calling for vengeance. Not only the Jew Eliezer Polner and the other conspirators but the whole Jewish community is guilty."

A number of old women began to sob when they heard these words. Some of the young ones winked and smiled. They understood that the whole thing was contrived. Count Bratislawski pretended he was wiping away his tears. The Jews had called Rabbi Leib as a witness for the defense, and the prosecutor asked him, "Is it written in your cursed Talmud that Christian blood should be poured into the dough of your matzohs?"

"There is not a trace of it, either in the Talmud or in any other of our Sacred Books," Rabbi Leib answered. "We don't bake our matzohs in dark cellars but in bakeries, with the doors open. Anyone can come and see. The matzohs consist of flour and water only."

"Isn't it a fact that hundreds of Jews have been condemned for using blood in matzohs?" the prosecutor asked.

"I'm sorry to say that this is true. But this does not prove that the accused were guilty. There is never a lack of wicked witnesses who are ready to testify falsely, especially if they are bribed to do so."

"Isn't it a fact that many of those Jews confessed their crime?"

"This, too, is true, but they confessed after their bodies were broken on a torture wheel and after their fingers and toes were pricked with glowing needles. There is a limit to how much pain a man can endure. You have all heard the case of the town of Altona, of an innocent Christian woman who was accused of being a witch and was tortured for so long that she confessed she had sold her soul to Satan, and was burned at the stake. Later it was revealed that an enemy of this woman hired evil men and women to bear witness against her."

The chief judge pounded his gavel on the desk and said, "Answer the prosecutor's questions and don't talk about matters that are irrelevant to this trial. We are here to judge the murder of a child, not the innocence of a witch."

Suddenly the locked door of the courthouse burst open, and a giant with a clay-yellow face rushed in with a little girl in his huge arms. The little girl was weeping, and the giant put her down near the witness stand, then left immediately. Everything took place so quickly that the people in the courthouse could barely realize what was happening. No one could utter a word. The little girl ran to Count Bratislawski, clutched his legs, and screamed, "Papa, Papa!"

Jan Bratislawski became as white as chalk. The witnesses who were supposed to proceed at the stand stood there open-mouthed. The astonished prosecutor lifted his arms with an expression of despair. Some of the women in the courthouse began to laugh, while others sobbed hysterically. The chief judge shook his bewigged head and asked, "Who are you, little girl? What is your name?"

"My name is Hanka. This is my papa," the crying girl managed to answer, pointing her little finger at Jan Bratislawski.

"Is this your daughter, Hanka?" the judge asked.

Bratislawski did not answer.

"Who is the giant who brought you here?" the judge asked. "Where have you been, Hanka, all these days?"

"Be silent, don't say a word!" Bratislawski shouted to his daughter.

"Answer, where were you?" the judge insisted.

"In our house, in a cellar," the girl answered.

"Who put you there?" the judge asked.

"Keep quiet. Don't say a word," Bratislawski admonished his daughter.

"You must answer, this is the law," the judge said. "Who put you into the cellar?"

Even though the judge was on the side of Count Bratislawski, he was no longer in a mood to take part in this farce. There were many Christian citizens of Prague who wanted to know the truth. The chief judge had heard that even the Emperor was irritated by this sham trial. The intelligent Christians in Europe did not believe in this horrifying accusation any more. The shrewd judge had therefore decided to play the role of an upright man.

Hanka stood there in silence, looking back and forth from the judge to her father. Then she said, "This man and this woman locked me up in the cellar," and she pointed to Stefan and Barbara. "They told me that my own papa asked them to do so."

"It's a lie. She's lying," Bratislawski protested. "The Jews have bewitched my darling daughter to believe in this nonsense. She is my only beloved child, and I would rather let my eyes be cut out than do her any harm. I'm the great Jan Bratislawski, a pillar of the state of Bohemia."

"Not any more," the chief judge said in a cold voice. "You have lost your fortune playing cards. You signed a note that you could not pay. You bribed these two ruffians to put your child into a cellar in order to inherit her jewels. For such crimes you will be punished severely and lose all titles to your lands and property. Stefan and Barbara," the judge continued, "who told you to put this tender child into the cellar? Tell the truth, or I will order you to be flogged."

"The Count did it," both of them answered. Barbara began to scream. "He gave us drink and threatened us with death if we didn't obey him."

"He promised me twenty gold ducats and a barrel of vodka," Stefan exclaimed.

The judge pounded his gavel again and again, but the uproar in the courthouse did not stop. Some men were shouting, others shook their fists. Some women fainted. Count Bratislawski lifted up his hand and began to tell the court that the judge himself was an accomplice to his crime and was supposed to get a share of the inheritance, but the judge called out, "Soldiers, I order you to chain this foul criminal Jan Bratislawski and throw him into the dungeon." Then he pointed at Bratislawski and added: "Whatever this rascal has to say, he will say on the gallows with a noose around his neck. And now, Jews, you are all free. Go back to your homes and celebrate your holiday. Soldiers, take off their chains. In a just court such as this, and with an honorable judge like myself, the truth always prevails."

"Who was the giant?" voices asked from all sides. But no one knew the answer. It was all like a dream or one of the tales old women tell while spinning flax by candlelight.

Norway

The Three Billy-Goats-Gruff

This cumulative beast tale is an almost perfectly constructed short story. It wastes no words; the action moves with rapidity; and the satisfactory ending to the action is tied off with a couplet that children love to repeat. [From Peter Christen Asbjörnsen, *Popular Tales from the Norse,* trans. G. W. Dasent (Putnam's, 1908).]

Once on a time there were three Billy-Goats who were to go up to the hillside to make themselves fat, and the family name of the three goats was "Gruff."

On the way up was a bridge, over a burn they had to cross; and under the bridge lived a great ugly Troll, with eyes as big as saucers and a nose as long as a poker.

First of all came the youngest Billy-Goat-Gruff to cross the bridge.

"Trip trap; trip, trap!" went the bridge.

"WHO'S THAT tripping over my bridge?" roared the Troll.

"Oh! it is only I, the tiniest Billy-Goat-Gruff; and I'm going up to the hillside to make myself fat," said the Billy-Goat, with such a small voice.

"Now, I'm coming to gobble you up," said the Troll.

Illustration from *The Three Bears and Fifteen Other Stories,* by Anne Rockwell (Thomas Y. Crowell). Copyright © 1975 by Anne Rockwell. Reprinted by permission of Harper & Row, Publishers, Inc.

"Oh, no! pray don't take me. I'm too little, that I am," said the Billy-Goat. "Wait a bit till the second Billy-Goat-Gruff comes; he's much bigger."

"Well! be off with you," said the Troll.

A little while after came the second Billy-Goat-Gruff to cross the bridge.

"Trip, Trap! Trip, Trap! Trip, Trap!" went the bridge.

"WHO'S THAT tripping over my bridge?" roared the Troll.

"Oh! it's the second Billy-Goat-Gruff, and I'm going up to the hillside to make myself fat," said the Billy-Goat, who hadn't such a small voice.

"Now, I'm coming to gobble you up," said the Troll.

"Oh, no! don't take me. Wait a little till the big Billy-Goat-Gruff comes; he's much bigger."

"Very well; be off with you," said the Troll.

But just then up came the big Billy-Goat-Gruff.

"*Trip, Trap! Trip, Trap! Trip, Trap!*" went the bridge, for the Billy-Goat was so heavy that the bridge creaked and groaned under him.

"WHO'S THAT tramping over my bridge?" roared the Troll.

"It's I! THE BIG BILLY-GOAT-GRUFF," said the Billy-Goat, who had a big hoarse voice of his own.

"Now, I'm coming to gobble you up," roared the Troll.

"Well, come along! I've got two spears,
And I'll poke your eyeballs out at your ears,
I've got besides two curling-stones,
And I'll crush you to bits, body and bones."

That was what the big Billy-Goat said; so he flew at the Troll and poked his eyes out with his horns, and crushed him to bits, body and bones, and tossed him out into the burn, and after that he went up to the hillside. There the Billy-Goats got so fat they were scarcely able to walk home again; and if the fat hasn't fallen off them, why they're still fat; and so—

Snip, snap, snout,
This tale's told out.

The Pancake

This repetitive, cumulative tale is found in many countries and is so full of amusing action and speech that it is no surprise to find it modernized in *The Gingerbread Boy*. [From Peter Christen Asbjörnsen, *Tales from the Fjeld,* trans. G. W. Dasent (Putnam's, 1908).]

Once on a time there was a goody who had seven hungry bairns, and she was frying a Pancake for them. It was a sweet-milk Pancake, and there it lay in the pan bubbling and frizzling so thick and good, it was a sight for sore eyes to look at. And the bairns stood round about, and the goodman sat by and looked on.

"Oh, give me a bit of Pancake, mother dear; I am so hungry," said one bairn.

"Oh, darling mother," said the second.

"Oh, darling, good mother," said the third.

"Oh, darling, good, nice mother," said the fourth.

"Oh, darling, pretty, good, nice mother," said the fifth.

"Oh, darling, pretty, good, nice, clever mother," said the sixth.

"Oh, darling, pretty, good, nice, clever, sweet mother," said the seventh.

So they begged for the Pancake all round, the one more prettily than the other; for they were so hungry and so good.

"Yes, yes, bairns, only bide a bit till it turns itself"—she ought to have said, "till I get it turned"—"and then you shall have some—a lovely sweet-milk Pancake; only look how fat and happy it lies there."

When the Pancake heard that it got afraid, and in a trice it turned itself all of itself, and tried to jump out of the pan; but it fell back into it again t'other side up, and so when it had been fried a little on the other side, too, till it got firmer in its flesh, it sprang out on the floor, and rolled off like a wheel through the door and down the hill.

"Holloa! Stop, Pancake!" and away went the goody after it, with the frying-pan in one hand and the ladle in the other, as fast as she could, and her bairns behind her, while the goodman limped after them last of all.

"Hi! won't you stop? Seize it! Stop, Pancake," they all screamed out, one after another, and tried to catch it on the run and hold it; but the Pancake rolled on and on, and in the twinkling of an eye it was so far ahead that they couldn't see it, for the Pancake was faster on its feet than any of them.

So when it had rolled a while it met a man.

"Good day, Pancake," said the man.

"God bless you, Manny-Panny," said the Pancake.

"Dear Pancake," said the man, "don't roll so fast; stop a little and let me eat you."

"When I have given the slip to Goody-Poody, and the goodman, and seven squalling children, I may well slip through your fingers, Manny-Panny," said the Pancake, and rolled on and on till it met a hen.

"Good day, Pancake," said the hen.

"The same to you, Henny-Penny," said the Pancake.

"Pancake, dear, don't roll so fast; bide a bit and let me eat you up," said the hen.

"When I have given the slip to Goody-Poody, and the goodman, and seven squalling children, and Manny-Panny, I may well slip through your claws, Henny-Penny," said the Pancake, and so it rolled on like a wheel down the road.

Just then it met a cock.

"Good day," said the cock.

"The same to you, Cocky-Locky," said the Pancake.

"Pancake, dear, don't roll so fast, but bide a bit and let me eat you up."

"When I have given the slip to Goody-Poody, and the goodman, and seven squalling children, and to Manny-Panny, and Henny-Penny, I may well slip through your claws, Cocky-Locky," said the Pancake, and off it set rolling away as fast as it could; and when it had rolled a long way it met a duck.

"Good day, Pancake," said the duck.

"The same to you, Ducky-Lucky."

"Pancake, dear, don't roll away so fast; bide a bit and let me eat you up."

"When I have given the slip to Goody-Poody, and the goodman, and seven squalling children, and Manny-Panny, and Henny-Penny, and Cocky-Locky, I may well slip through your fingers, Ducky-Lucky," said the Pancake, and with that it took to rolling and rolling faster than ever; and when it had rolled a long, long way it met a goose.

"Good day, Pancake," said the goose.

"The same to you, Goosey-Poosey."

"Pancake, dear, don't roll so fast; bide a bit and let me eat you up."

"When I have given the slip to Goody-Poody, and the goodman, and seven squalling children, and Manny-Panny, and Henny-Penny, and Cocky-Locky, and Ducky-Lucky, I can well slip through your feet, Goosey-Poosey," said the Pancake, and off it rolled.

So when it had rolled a long, long way farther, it met a gander.

"Good day, Pancake," said the gander.

"The same to you, Gander-Pander," said the Pancake.

"Pancake, dear, don't roll so fast; bide a bit and let me eat you up."

"When I have given the slip to Goody-Poody, and the goodman, and seven squalling children, and Manny-Panny, and Henny-Penny, and Cocky-Locky, and Ducky-Lucky, and Goosey-Poosey, I may well slip through your feet, Gander-Pander," said the Pancake, and it rolled off as fast as ever.

So when it had rolled a long, long time it met a pig.

"Good day, Pancake," said the pig.

"The same to you, Piggy-Wiggy," said the Pancake, which, without a word more, began to roll and roll like mad.

"Nay, nay," said the pig, "you needn't be in such a hurry; we two can go side by side and see each other over the wood; they say it is not safe in there."

The Pancake thought there might be something in that, and so they kept company. But when they had gone awhile, they came to a brook. As for Piggy, he was so fat he swam safely across; it was nothing to him; but the poor Pancake couldn't get over.

"Seat yourself on my snout," said the pig, "and I'll carry you over."

So the Pancake did that.

"Ouf, ouf," said the pig, and swallowed the Pancake at one gulp; and the poor Pancake could go no farther, why—this story can go no farther either.

The Princess on the Glass Hill

The beginning of this story is almost identical with that of the Russian tale *The Little Humpbacked Horse*. The development of the action, however, is more like that in *Atalanta's Race*. [From Peter Christen Asbjörnsen, *Popular Tales from the Norse*, trans. G. W. Dasent (Putnam's, 1908).]

Once on a time there was a man who had a meadow, which lay high up on the hillside, and in the meadow was a barn, which he had built to keep his hay in. Now, I must tell you there hadn't been much in the barn for the last year or two, for every Saint John's night, when the grass stood greenest and deepest, the meadow was eaten down to the very ground the next morning, just as if a whole drove of sheep had been there feeding on it over night. This happened once, and it happened twice; so that at last the man grew weary of losing his crop of hay, and said to his sons—for he had three of them, and the youngest was named Boots, of course—that now one of them must just go and sleep in the barn in the outlying field when Saint John's night came, for it was too good a joke that his grass should be eaten, root and blade, this year, as it had been the last two years. So whichever of them went he must keep a sharp lookout; that was what their father said.

Well, the eldest son was ready to go and watch the meadow; trust him for looking after the grass! It shouldn't be his fault if man or beast, or the fiend himself, got a blade of grass. So, when evening came, he set off to the barn and lay down to sleep; but a little later on in the night there came such a clatter, and such an earthquake, that walls and roof shook, and groaned, and creaked; then up jumped the lad and took to his heels as fast as ever he could; nor dared he once look round till he reached home; and as for the hay, why, it was eaten up this year just as it had been twice before.

The next Saint John's night, the man said again it would never do to lose all the grass in the outlying field year after year in this way, so one of the sons must trudge off to watch it, and watch it well, too. Well, the next oldest son was ready to try his luck. So off he went and lay down to sleep in the barn as his brother had done before him; but as night came on, there came a rumbling and quaking of the earth, worse even than on the last Saint John's night. When the lad heard it, he got frightened, and took to his heels as though he were running a race.

Next year the turn came to Boots; but when he made ready to go, the other two began to laugh, and make game of him, saying:

"You're just the man to watch the hay, that you are; you who have done nothing all your life but sit in the ashes and toast yourself by the fire."

Boots did not care a pin for their chattering, and stumped away, as evening drew on, up the hillside to the outlying field. There he went inside the barn and lay down; but in about an hour's time the barn began to groan and creak, so that it was dreadful to hear.

"Well," said Boots to himself; "if it isn't any worse than this I can stand it well enough."

A little while after there came another creak and an earthquake, so that the litter in the barn flew about the lad's ears.

"Oh," said Boots to himself; "if it isn't any worse than this, I daresay I can stand it out."

But just then came a third rumbling, and a third earthquake, so that the lad thought walls and roof were coming down on his head; but it passed off, and all was still as death about him.

"It'll come again, I'll be bound," thought Boots; but no, it did not come again; still it was and still it stayed; but after he had lain a little while he heard a noise as if a horse were standing just outside the barn-door, and cropping the grass. He stole to the door and peeped through a chink; and there stood a horse feeding away. So big and fat and grand a horse, Boots had never set eyes on; by his side on the grass lay a saddle and bridle, and a full set of armor for a knight, all of brass, so bright that the light gleamed from it.

"Ho, ho!" thought the lad; "it's you, is it, that eats up our hay? I'll soon put a spoke in your wheel; just see if I don't."

So he lost no time, but took the steel out of his tinder-box and threw it over the horse; then it had no power to stir from the spot and became so tame that the lad could do what he liked with it. He got on its back and rode off with it to a place which no one knew of, and there he put up the horse. When he got home his brothers laughed and asked how he fared.

"You didn't lie long in the barn, even if you had the heart to go as far as the field."

"Well," said Boots, "all I can say is, I lay in the barn till the sun rose, and neither saw nor heard anything; I can't think what there was in the barn to make you both so afraid."

"A pretty story!" said his brothers; "but we'll soon see how you watched the meadow." So they set off, but when they reached it, there stood the grass as deep and thick as it had been the night before.

Well, the next Saint John's night it was the same story over again; neither of the elder brothers dared to go out to the outlying field to watch the crop; but Boots, he had the heart to go, and everything happened just as it had happened the year before. First a clatter and an earthquake, then a greater clatter and another earthquake, and so on a third time; only this year the earthquakes were far worse than the year before. Then all at once, everything was still as death, and the lad heard how something was cropping the grass outside the barn-door, so he stole to the door and peeped through a chink; and what do you think he saw? Why, another horse standing right up against the wall, and chewing and champing with might and main. It was far finer and fatter than that one which came the year before; and it had a saddle on its back and a bridle on its neck and a full suit of mail for a knight lay by its side, all of silver, and as grand as you would wish to see.

"Ho, ho!" said Boots to himself; "it's you that gobbles up our hay, is it? I'll soon put a spoke in your wheel"; and with that he took the steel out of his tinder-box and threw it over the horse's crest, which stood still as a lamb. Well, the lad rode this horse, too, to the hiding place where he kept the other one; and after that he went home.

"I suppose you'll tell us," said one of the brothers, "there's a fine crop this year, too, in the hayfield."

"Well, so there is," said Boots; and off ran

the others to see, and there stood the grass thick and deep, as it was the year before; but they didn't give Boots softer words for all that.

Now, when the third Saint John's eve came, the two elder still hadn't the heart to lie out in the barn and watch the grass, for they had got so scared the night they lay there before, that they couldn't get over the fright; but Boots, he dared to go; and, to make a long story short, the very same thing happened this time as had happened twice before. Three earthquakes came, one after the other, each worse than the one which went before; and when the last came, the lad danced about with the shock from one barn wall to the other; and after that, all at once, it was as still as death. Now when he had lain for a little while he heard something tugging away at the grass outside the barn; so he stole again to the door-chink and peeped out, and there stood a horse close outside—far, far bigger and fatter than the two he had taken before.

"Ho, ho!" said the lad to himself; "it's you, is it, that comes here eating up our hay? I'll soon put a spoke in your wheel, I'll soon stop that." So he caught up his steel and threw it over the horse's neck, and in a trice it stood as if it were nailed to the ground, and Boots could do as he pleased with it. Then he rode off with it to the hiding place where he kept the other two, and then went home. When he got there his two brothers made game of him as they had done before, saying they could see he had watched the grass well, for he looked for all the world as if he were walking in his sleep, and many other spiteful things they said; but Boots gave no heed to them, only asking them to go and see for themselves; and when they went, there stood the grass as fine and deep this time as it had been twice before.

Now, you must know that the king of the country where Boots lived had a daughter, whom he would give only to the man who could ride up over the hill of glass, for there was a high, high hill, all of glass, as smooth and slippery as ice, close by the king's palace. Upon the tip-top of the hill, the king's daughter was to sit, with three golden apples in her lap, and the man who could ride up and carry off the

three golden apples was to have half of the kingdom and the princess for his wife. This the king had stuck up on all the church doors in his realm, and had given it out in many other kingdoms besides. Now, this princess was so lovely that all who set eyes on her fell over head and ears in love with her whether they would or not. So I needn't tell you how all the princes and knights who heard of her were eager to win her, as a wife, and half of the kingdom besides; and how they came riding from all parts of the world on high prancing horses, and clad in the grandest clothes, for there wasn't one of them who hadn't made up his mind that he, and he alone, was to win the princess.

When the day of trial came, which the king had fixed, there was such a crowd of princes and knights under the glass hill, that it made one's head to whirl to look at them; and everyone in the country who could even crawl along was off to the hill, for they were all eager to see the man who was to win the princess.

The two elder brothers set off with the rest; but as for Boots, they said outright he shouldn't go with them, for if they were seen with such a dirty changeling, all begrimed with smut from cleaning their shoes and sifting cinders in the dusthole, they said folk would make game of them.

"Very well," said Boots; "it's all one to me. I can go alone, and stand or fall by myself."

Now when the two brothers came to the hill of glass, the knights and princes were all hard at it, riding their horses till they were all in a foam; but it was no good, by my troth; for as soon as ever the horses set foot on the hill, down they slipped, and there wasn't one who could get a yard or two up; and no wonder, for the hill was as smooth as a sheet of glass and as steep as a housewall. But all were eager to have the princess and half the kingdom. So they rode and slipped, and slipped and rode, and still it was the same story over again. At last their horses were so weary that they could scarce lift a leg, and in such a sweat that the lather dripped from them, and so the knights had to give up trying any more. The king was just thinking that he would proclaim a new trial for the next day, to see if they would have better luck, when all at once a knight came riding up on so brave a steed that no one had ever seen the like of it in his born days, and the knight had mail of brass, and the horse, a brass bit in its mouth, so bright that the sunbeams shone from it. Then all the others called out to him that he might just as well spare himself the trouble of riding up the hill, for it would lead to no good; but he gave no heed to them, and put his horse at the hill, and up it went like nothing for a good way, about a third of the height; and when he had got so far, he turned his horse and rode down again. So lovely a knight the princess thought she had never seen; and while he was riding she sat and thought to herself—"Would to heaven he might only come up, and down the other side."

And when she saw him turning back, she threw down one of the golden apples after him, and it rolled down into his shoe. But when he got to the bottom of the hill he rode off so fast that no one could tell what had become of him. That evening all the knights and princes were to go before the king, that he who had ridden so far up the hill might show the apple the princess had thrown; but there was no one who had anything to show. One after the other they all came, but not a man of them could show the apple.

At evening, the brothers of Boots came home too, and had a long story to tell about the riding up the hill.

"First of all," they said, "there was not one of the whole lot who could get so much as a stride up; but at last came one who had a suit of brass mail, and a brass bridle and saddle, all so bright that the sun shone from them a mile off. He was a chap to ride, just! He rode a third of the way up the hill of glass and he could easily have ridden the whole way up, if he chose; but he turned round and rode down thinking, maybe, that was enough for once."

"Oh! I should so like to have seen him, that I should," said Boots, who sat by the fireside, and stuck his feet into the cinders as was his wont.

"Oh!" said his brothers, "you would, would

you? You look fit to keep company with such high lords, nasty beast that you are, sitting there amongst the ashes."

Next day the brothers were all for setting off again; and Boots begged them this time, too, to let him go with them and see the riding; but no, they wouldn't have him at any price, he was too ugly and nasty, they said.

"Well, well," said Boots; "if I go at all, I must go by myself. I'm not afraid."

So when the brothers got to the hill of glass, all the princes and knights began to ride again, and you may fancy they had taken care to shoe their horses sharp; but it was no good—they rode and slipped, and slipped and rode, just as they had done the day before, and there was not one who could get as far as a yard up the hill. And when they had worn out their horses, so that they could not stir a leg, they were all forced to give it up as a bad job. The king thought he might as well proclaim that the riding should take place the next day for the last time, just to give them one chance more; but all at once it came across his mind that he might as well wait a little longer to see if the knight in the brass mail would come this day too. Well, they saw nothing of him; but all at once came one riding on a steed far, far braver and finer than that on which the knight of brass had ridden, and he had silver mail, and a silver saddle and bridle, all so bright that the sunbeams gleamed and glanced from far away. Then the others shouted out to him again, saying he might as well hold hard and not try to ride up the hill, for all his trouble would be thrown away; but the knight paid no attention to them, and rode straight at the hill and right up, till he had gone two thirds of the way, and then he wheeled his horse round and rode down again. To tell the truth, the princess liked him still better than the knight in brass, and she sat and wished he might only be able to come right to the top, and down the other side; but when she saw him turning back, she threw the second apple after him, and it rolled into his shoe. But as soon as ever he had come down the hill of glass, he rode off so fast that no one knew what became of him.

At evening when all were to go before the

king and the princess, that he who had the golden apple might show it, in they went, one after the other; but there was no one who had any golden apple to show. The two brothers, as they had done on the former day, went home and told how things had gone, and how all had ridden at the hill and none got up.

"But, last of all," they said, "came one in a silver suit, and his horse had a silver bridle and a silver saddle. He was just a chap to ride; and he got two-thirds up the hill, and then turned back. He was a fine fellow and no mistake; and the princess threw the second gold apple to him."

"Oh!" said Boots, "I should so like to have seen him too, that I should."

"A pretty story," they said. "Perhaps you think his coat of mail was as bright as the ashes you are always poking about and sifting, you nasty, dirty beast."

The third day everything happened as it had happened the two days before. Boots begged to go and see the sight, but the two wouldn't hear of his going with them. When they got to the hill there was no one who could get so much as a yard up it; and now all waited for the knight in silver mail, but they neither saw nor heard of him. At last came one riding on a steed, so brave that no one had ever seen his match; and the knight had a suit of golden mail, and a golden saddle, and bridle, so wondrous bright that the sunbeams gleamed from them a mile off. The other knights and princes could not find time to call out to him not to try his luck, for they were amazed to see how grand he was. He rode at the hill, and tore up it like nothing, so that the princess hadn't even time to wish that he might get up the whole way. As soon as ever he reached the top, he took the third golden apple from the princess's lap, and then turned his horse and rode down again. As soon as he got down, he rode off at full speed, and out of sight in no time.

Now, when the brothers got home at evening, you may fancy what long stories they told, how the riding had gone off that day; and amongst other things, they had a deal to say about the knight in golden mail.

"He was just a chap to ride!" they said; "so

grand a knight isn't to be found in the whole world."

"Oh!" said Boots, "I should so like to have seen him, that I should."

"Ah!" said his brothers, "his mail shone a deal brighter than the glowing coals which you are always poking and digging at; nasty, dirty beast that you are."

Next day all the knights and princes were to pass before the king and the princess—it was too late to do so the night before, I suppose—that he who had the golden apple might bring it forth; but one came after another, first the princes and then the knights, and still no one could show the gold apple.

"Well," said the king, "someone must have it, for it was something that we all saw with our own eyes, how a man came and rode up and bore it off."

He commanded that everyone who was in the kingdom should come up to the palace and see if he could show the apple. Well, they all came, one after another, but no one had the golden apple, and after a long time the two brothers of Boots came. They were the last of all, so the king asked them if there was no one else in the kingdom who hadn't come.

"Oh, yes," said they. "We have a brother, but he never carried off the golden apple. He hasn't stirred out of the dusthole on any of the three days."

"Never mind that," said the king; "he may as well come up to the palace like the rest."

So Boots had to go up to the palace.

"How, now," said the king; "have you got the golden apple? Speak out!"

"Yes, I have," said Boots; "here is the first, and here is the second, and here is the third one, too"; and with that he pulled all three golden apples out of his pocket, and at the same time threw off his sooty rags, and stood before them in his gleaming golden mail.

"Yes!" said the king; "you shall have my daughter and half my kingdom, for you well deserve both her and it."

So they got ready for the wedding, and Boots got the princess for his wife, and there was great merry-making at the bridal-feast, you may fancy, for they could all be merry though they couldn't ride up the hill of glass; and all I can say is, that if they haven't left off their merry-making yet, why, they're still at it.

East o' the Sun and West o' the Moon

It is interesting to note certain likenesses in this story to other tales. First of all, the prince is disguised and comes to a house seeking shelter from the cold. In the second place, the heroine, disobeying orders, talks too much; tries to discover who her husband is; and as a result, has to go through long trials and many tests before she wins him back. A very similar situation, in part, is found in *Cupid and Psyche*. [From Peter Christen Asbjörnsen, *Popular Tales from the Norse*, trans. G. W. Dasent (Putnam's, 1908).]

Once on a time there was a poor husbandman who had so many children that he hadn't much of either food or clothing to give them. Pretty children they all were; but the prettiest was the youngest daughter, who was so lovely there was no end to her loveliness.

So one day, 'twas on a Thursday evening late in the fall of the year, the weather was wild and rough outside. It was cruelly dark, and rain fell and wind blew, till the walls of the cottage shook again and again. There they all sat round the fire busy with this thing and that. Just then, all at once something gave three taps on the window-pane. The father went out to see what was the matter; and when he got out of doors, what should he see but a great big White Bear.

"Good evening to you," said the White Bear.

"The same to you," said the man.

"Will you give me your youngest daughter? If you will, I'll make you as rich as you are now poor," said the Bear.

Well, the man would not be at all sorry to be so rich; but still he thought he must have a bit of a talk with his daughter first; so in he went and told them how there was a great White Bear waiting outside, who had given his word to make them rich if he could only have the youngest daughter.

The lassie said "No!" outright. Nothing could get her to say anything else; so the man went out and settled it with the White Bear, that he should come again the next Thursday evening and get an answer. Meantime the man talked to his daughter and kept telling her of all the riches they would get; and how well off she would be herself. At last she thought better of it, and washed and mended her rags, made herself as smart as she could, and was ready to start. I can't say her packing gave her much trouble.

Next Thursday evening came the White Bear to fetch her; and she got upon his back with her bundle, and off they went. When they had gone a bit of the way, the White Bear said,

"Are you afraid?"

"No," she said.

"Well! mind and hold tight by my shaggy coat, and there's nothing to fear," said the Bear.

So she rode a long, long way, till they came to a great steep hill. There on the face of it, the White Bear gave a knock; and a door opened, and they came into a castle, where there were many rooms lit up; rooms gleaming with silver and gold; and there was a table ready laid, and it was all as grand as it could be. The White Bear gave her a silver bell; and when she wanted anything, she had only to ring it, and she would get what she wanted at once.

Well, after she had eaten and drunk, and evening wore on, she got sleepy after her journey and thought that she would like to go to bed; so she rang the bell; and she had scarce taken hold of it before she came into a chamber where there were two beds made, as fair and white as any one could wish to sleep in, with silken pillows and curtains and gold fringe. All that was in the room was gold or silver; but when she had gone to bed, and put out the light, a man came in and lay down on the other bed. That was the White Bear, who threw off his beast shape at night; but she never saw him, for he always came after she put the light out, and before the day dawned he was up and gone again. So things went on happily for a while; but at last she began to grow silent and sorrowful; for she went about all day alone and she longed to go home and see her father and mother, and brothers and sisters, and that was why she was so sad and sorrowful, because she couldn't get to them.

"Well, well!" said the Bear, "perhaps there's

a cure for all this; but you must promise me one thing, not to talk alone with your mother, but only when the rest are by to hear; for she will take you by the hand and try to lead you into a room alone to talk; but you must mind and not do that, else you'll bring bad luck to both of us."

So one Sunday, the White Bear came and said now they could set off to see her father and mother. Well, off they started, she sitting on his back; and they went far and long. At last they came to a grand house, and there her brothers and sisters were running about out of doors at play, and everything was so pretty, 'twas a joy to see.

"This is where your father and mother live now," said the White Bear; "but don't forget what I told you, else you'll make us both unlucky."

No, bless you, she'd not forget, and when she had reached the house, the White Bear turned right about and left her.

Then she went in to see her father and mother, and there was such joy, there was no end of it. None of them thought that they could thank her enough for all she had done for them. Now, they had everything they wished, as good as good could be, and they all wanted to know how she got on where she lived.

Well, she said, it was very good to live where she did; she had all she wished. What she said beside I don't know; but I don't think any of them had the right end of the stick, or that they got much out of her. But so in the afternoon, after they had finished their dinner, all happened as the White Bear had said. Her mother wanted to talk with her alone in her bed-room; but she minded what the White Bear had said, and wouldn't go upstairs.

"Oh, what we have to talk about will keep," she said, and put her mother off. But somehow or other, her mother got around her at last, and she had to tell the whole story. So she said, how every night, when she had gone to bed, a man came and lay down on the other bed in her room as soon as she had put out the light, and how she never saw him, because he was always up and away before the morning dawned; and how she went woeful and sorrow-

Illustration by Lloyd Bloom. From *The Maid of the North: Feminist Folk Tales from around the World*, by Ethel Johnston Phelps. Illustrated by Lloyd Bloom. Copyright © 1981 by Ethel Johnston Phelps. Reproduced by permission of Holt, Rinehart & Winston, publishers.

ful, for she thought she should so like to see him, and how all day long she walked about there alone, and how dull, and dreary, and lonesome it was.

"My!" said her mother; "it may well be a Troll sleeping in your room! But now I'll teach you a lesson how to set eyes on him. I'll give you a bit of candle, which you can carry in your bosom. Just light that while he is asleep; but take care not to drop the tallow on him."

Yes, she took the candle, and hid it in her bosom, and as night drew on the White Bear came to fetch her away.

But when they had gone a bit of the way,

the Bear asked her if all hadn't happened as he had said.

Well, she couldn't say it hadn't.

"Now mind," said he, "if you have listened to your mother's advice, you have brought bad luck on us both, and then all that has passed between us will be as nothing."

"No," she said, "I haven't listened to my mother's advice."

When she reached home, and had gone to bed, it was the old story over again. There came a man and lay down on the other bed; but at dead of night, when she heard him sleeping, she got up and struck a light, lit the candle, and let the light shine on him, and she saw that he was the loveliest Prince she had ever set eyes on and she fell so deep in love with him on the spot, that she thought that she couldn't live if she didn't give him a kiss then and there. And so she did; but as she kissed him, she dropped three hot drops of tallow on his shirt and he woke up.

"What have you done?" he cried; "now you have made us both unlucky, for had you held out only for this one year, I had been freed. For I have a stepmother who has bewitched me, so that I am a White Bear by day, and a Man by night. But now all ties are snapt between us; now I must set off from you to her. She lives in a castle which stands EAST O' THE SUN AND WEST O' THE MOON, and there, too, is a Princess with a nose three ells long, and she's the wife I must have now."

She wept and took it ill, but there was no help for it; go he must.

Then she asked him if she mightn't go with him.

No, she mightn't.

"Tell me the way, then," she said, "and I'll search you out; that surely I may get leave to do."

"Yes, you may do that," he said; "but there is no way to that place. It lies EAST O' THE SUN AND WEST O' THE MOON, and thither you'll never find your way."

The next morning when she awoke, both Prince and castle were gone, and there she lay on a little green patch in the midst of the gloomy thick wood, and by her side lay the same bundle of rags she had brought with her from her old home.

When she had rubbed the sleep out of her eyes, and wept till she was tired, she set out on her way, and walked many, many days, till she came to a lofty crag. Under it sat an old hag, and played with a gold apple which she tossed about. Her the lassie asked if she knew the way to the Prince, who lived with his stepmother in the castle that lay EAST O' THE SUN AND WEST O' THE MOON, and who was to marry the Princess with a nose three ells long.

"How did you come to know about him?" asked the old hag; "but maybe you are the lassie who ought to have had him?"

Yes, she was.

"So, so; it's you, is it?" said the old hag. "Well, all I know about him is, that he lives in the old castle that lies EAST O' THE SUN AND WEST O' THE MOON, and thither you'll come late or never; but still you may have the loan of my horse and on him you may ride to the next neighbor. Maybe she'll be able to tell you; and when you get there, just give the horse a switch under the left ear, and beg him to be off home; and, stay, this golden apple may you take with you."

So she got upon the horse and rode a long, long time, till she came to another crag, under which sat another old hag, with a gold carding-comb. Her the lassie asked if she knew the way to the castle that lay EAST O' THE SUN AND WEST O' THE MOON, and she answered, like the first old hag, that she knew nothing about it except it was east o' the sun and west o' the moon.

"And thither you'll come, late or never; but you shall have the loan of my horse to my next neighbor; maybe she'll tell you all about it; and when you get there, just switch the horse under the left ear and beg him to be off home."

And this old hag gave her the golden carding-comb; it might be she'd find some use for it, she said. So the lassie got up on the horse, and rode a far, far way, and a weary time; and so at last she came to another great crag, under which sat another hag, spinning with a golden spinning-wheel. Her, too, the lassie asked if she knew the way to the Prince, and where the castle was that lay EAST O' THE SUN AND WEST O' THE MOON. So it was the same thing over again.

"Maybe it's you who ought to have had the Prince?" said the old hag.

Yes, it was.

But she, too, didn't know the way a bit better than the others. East o' the sun and west o' the moon it was, she knew—that was all.

"And thither you'll come, late or never; but I'll lend you my horse, and then I think you'd best ride to the East Wind and ask him; maybe he knows those parts, and can blow you thither. But when you get to him, you need only to give the horse a switch under the left ear, and he'll trot home himself."

And so, too, she gave the girl the gold spinning-wheel. "Maybe you'll find use for it," said the old hag.

Then on she rode many, many days, a weary time, before she got to the East Wind's house; but at last she did reach it, and then she asked the East Wind if he could tell her the way to the Prince who dwelt east o' the sun and west o' the moon. Yes, the East Wind often heard tell of the Prince and the castle, but he couldn't tell the way for he had never blown so far.

"But if you will, I'll go to my brother, the West Wind; maybe he knows, for he is much stronger. So, if you'll just get on my back, I'll carry you thither."

Yes, she got on his back, and they went briskly along.

When they got there they went into the West Wind's house; and the East Wind said the lassie he had brought was the one who ought to have had the Prince who lived in the castle EAST O' THE SUN AND WEST O' THE MOON; and so she had set out to seek him, and how he had come with her, and would be glad to know if the West Wind knew how to get to the castle.

"Nay," said the West Wind, "so far I've never blown; but if you will, I'll go with you to our brother the South Wind, for he's much stronger than either of us, and he has flapped his wings far and wide. Maybe he'll tell you. You can get on my back, and I'll carry you to him."

Yes, she got on his back, and so they traveled to the South Wind and were not so very long on the way.

When they got there, the West Wind asked him if he could tell the lassie the way to the castle that lay EAST O' THE SUN AND WEST O' THE MOON, for it was she who ought to have had the Prince who lived there.

"You don't say so! That's she, is it?" said the South Wind.

"Well, I have blustered about in most places in my time, but so far have I never blown; but if you will, I'll take you to my brother the North Wind; he is the strongest of the whole lot of us and if he doesn't know where it is, you'll never find any one in the world to tell you. You can get on my back and I'll carry you thither."

Yes! she got on his back and away he went from his house at a fine rate. And this time, too, she wasn't long on the way.

When they got to the North Wind's house, he was so wild and cross, cold puffs came from him a long way off.

"BLAST YOU BOTH, WHAT DO YOU WANT?" he roared out to them ever so far off, so that it struck them with an icy shiver.

"Well," said the South Wind, "you needn't be so foul-mouthed, for here I am, your brother, the South Wind, and here is the lassie who ought to have had the Prince who dwells in the castle that lies EAST O' THE SUN AND WEST O' THE MOON; and now she wants to ask you if you ever were there, and can tell her the way, for she would be so glad to find him again."

"YES, I KNOW WELL ENOUGH WHERE IT IS," said the North Wind; "once in my life I blew an aspen-leaf thither, but I was so tired I couldn't blow a puff for ever so many days after. But if you really wish to go thither, and aren't afraid to come along with me, I'll take you on my back and see if I can blow you thither."

Yes! with all her heart; she must and would get thither if it were possible in any way; and as for fear, however madly he went, she wouldn't be at all afraid.

"Very well, then," said the North Wind, "but you must sleep here tonight, for we must have the whole day before us if we're to get thither at all."

Early the next morning the North Wind woke her, and puffed himself up, and blew himself out, and made himself so stout and big 'twas gruesome to look at him; and so off they went high through the air as if they would never stop till they got to the world's end.

Down below there was such a storm; it threw down long tracts of wood and many houses, and when it swept over the great sea ships foundered by the hundreds.

They tore on and on—no one can believe how far they went—and all the while they still went over the sea, and the North Wind got more and more weary, and so out of breath he could scarcely bring out a puff; and his wings drooped and drooped, till at last he sank so low that the crests of the waves dashed over his heels.

"Are you afraid?" said the North Wind.

No, she wasn't.

But they weren't very far from land; and the North Wind had still enough strength left in him that he managed to throw her up on the shore under the windows of the castle which lay EAST O' THE SUN AND WEST O' THE MOON; but then he was so weak and worn out he had to stay there and rest many days before he could get home again.

Next morning the lassie sat under the castle window and began to play with the gold apple; and the first person she saw was the Long-nose who was to have the Prince.

"What do you want for your gold apple, you lassie?" said the Long-nose, and threw up the window.

"It's not for sale for gold or money," said the lassie.

"If it's not for sale for gold or money, what is it that you will sell it for? You may name your own price," said the Princess.

"Well! if I may get to the Prince who lives here and be with him tonight, you shall have it," said the lassie.

Yes! she might; that could be arranged. So the Princess got the gold apple; but when the lassie came up to the Prince's bed-room at night he was fast asleep; she called him and shook him, and between whiles she wept sore; but for all she could do she couldn't wake him up. Next morning as soon as day broke, came the Princess with the long nose, and drove her out again.

So in the daytime she sat down under the castle windows and began to card with her golden carding-comb, and the same thing happened again. The Princess asked what she wanted for it; and she said it wasn't for sale for gold or money, but if she might get leave to go to the Prince and be with him for the night, the Princess should have it. But when she went up, she found him asleep again, and she called, and she shook him, and wept, and prayed, and she couldn't get life into him; and as soon as the first gray peep of day came, then came the Princess with the long nose, and chased her out again.

So in the daytime, the lassie sat down outside under the castle window, and began to spin with her golden spinning-wheel, and that too, the Princess with the long nose wanted to have. So she raised the window and asked what the lassie wanted for it. The lassie said, as she had said before, it wasn't for sale for gold or money; but if she might go up to the Prince who was there, and be there alone that night, the Princess might have it.

Yes! she might do that and welcome. But now you must know there were some Christian folk who had been carried off thither, and as they sat in their room, which was next the Prince, they had heard how a girl had been in there, and wept and prayed, and called to him two nights running, and they told that to the Prince.

That evening when the Princess came with her sleeping potion, the Prince made as if he drank, but threw the drink over his shoulder for he could guess what kind of a drink it was. So when the lassie came in she found the Prince wide awake; and then she told him the whole story of how she came thither.

"Ah," said the Prince, "you've come just in the nick of time for tomorrow is to be our wedding-day; and now I won't have the Long-nose, for you are the only lassie in the world who can set me free. I'll say I want to see what my wife is fit for and beg her to wash the shirt which has the three spots of tallow on it; she'll say yes, for she doesn't know 'tis you who put them there; but that's work for Christian folk, and not for a pack of Trolls; and so I'll say that I won't have any other for my bride than she who can wash them out, and ask you to do it."

The next day, when the wedding was to be, the Prince said,

"First of all, I want to see what my bride is fit for."

"Yes," said the stepmother with all her heart.

"Well," said the Prince, "I've got a fine shirt which I'd like for my wedding shirt; but somehow it has got three spots of tallow on it which I must have washed out; and I have sworn never to take any other bride than the lassie who is able to do that. If she can't she's not worth having."

Well, that was no great thing, they said; so they agreed, and she with the long nose began to wash away as hard as ever she could, but the more she rubbed and scrubbed, the bigger the spots grew.

"Ah," said the old hag, her mother, "you can't wash; let me try."

But she hadn't long taken the shirt in hand before it got far worse than ever, and with all her rubbing, and wringing, and scrubbing, the spots grew bigger and blacker, and the darker and uglier the shirt.

Then all the other Trolls began to wash; but the longer it lasted, the blacker and uglier the shirt grew, till at last it was as black all over as if it had been up the chimney.

"Ah," said the Prince, "you're none of you worth a straw; you can't wash. Why there, outside, sits a beggar lassie. I'll be bound she knows how to wash better than the whole lot of you. *Come in, lassie!*" he shouted.

Well, in she came.

"Can you wash this shirt clean, lassie?" he said.

"I don't know," she said, "but I think I can."

And almost before she had taken it and dipped it in the water, it was as white as the driven snow, and whiter still.

"Yes, you are the lassie for me," said the Prince.

At that the old hag flew into such a rage, she burst on the spot, and the Princess with the long nose did the same, and the whole pack of Trolls after her—at least I've never heard a word about them since.

As for the Prince and the Princess, they set free all the poor Christian folk who had been carried off and shut up there; and they took with them all the silver and gold, and flitted away as far as they could from the castle that lay EAST O' THE SUN AND WEST O' THE MOON.

The Cat on the Dovrefell

The noted novelist G. B. Stern has called this one of the greatest cat stories in all literature. So it is, though no cat appears in it. For the storyteller who seeks a Christmas story which is nonreligious, this offers a solution. Here is one more typical folktale comment on human ability to best the forces of Might and Darkness by wit and a sense of humor. [From Peter Christen Asbjörnsen, *Popular Tales from the Norse*, trans. G. W. Dasent (Putnam's, 1908).]

Once on a time there was a man up in Finnmark who had caught a great white bear, which he was going to take to the King of Denmark. Now, it so fell out, that he came to the Dovrefell just about Christmas Eve, and there he turned into a cottage where a man lived, whose name was Halvor, and asked the man if he could get house-room there for his bear and himself.

"Heaven never help me, if what I say isn't true!" said the man; "but we can't give anyone house-room just now, for every Christmas Eve such a pack of Trolls come down upon us, that we are forced to flit, and haven't so much as a house over our own heads, to say nothing of lending one to anyone else."

"Oh?" said the man, "if that's all, you can very well lend me your house; my bear can lie under the stove yonder, and I can sleep in the side-room."

Well, he begged so hard, that at last he got leave to stay there; so the people of the house flitted out, and before they went, everything was got ready for the Trolls; the tables were laid, and there was rice porridge, and fish boiled in lye, and sausages, and all else that was good, just as for any other grand feast.

So, when everything was ready, down came the Trolls. Some were great, and some were small; some had long tails, and some had no tails at all; some, too, had long, long noses; and they ate and drank, and tasted everything. Just then one of the little Trolls caught sight of the white bear, who lay under the stove; so he took a piece of sausage and stuck it on a fork, and went and poked it up against the bear's nose, screaming out:

"Pussy, will you have some sausage?"

Then the white bear rose up and growled, and hunted the whole pack of them out of doors, both great and small.

Next year Halvor was out in the wood, on the afternoon of Christmas Eve, cutting wood before the holidays, for he thought the Trolls would come again; and just as he was hard at work, he heard a voice in the wood calling out:

"Halvor! Halvor!"

"Well," said Halvor, "here I am."

"Have you got your big cat with you still?"

"Yes, that I have," said Halvor; "she's lying at home under the stove, and what's more, she has now got seven kittens, far bigger and fiercer than she is herself."

"Oh, then, we'll never come to see you again," bawled out the Troll away in the wood, and he kept his word; for since that time the Trolls have never eaten their Christmas brose with Halvor on the Dovrefell.

The Husband Who Was to Mind the House

The war between the sexes, and the debate of who works the harder in this world, man or woman—these have been subjects for stories since the earliest time. Here is a tribute to the capabilities of woman. The complaining male is put in his place. There are numskull motifs in this story: the cow taken to the roof to graze; the ale left running in the cellar.

Stith Thompson reports the tale as having a ballad form in English-speaking countries. What we have here is the Scandinavian version. [From Peter Christen Asbjörnsen, *Popular Tales from the Norse*, trans. G. W. Dasent (Putnam's, 1908).]

Once on a time there was a man, so surly and cross, he never thought his wife did anything right in the house. So one evening, in haymaking time, he came home, scolding and swearing, and showing his teeth and making a dust.

"Dear love, don't be so angry; there's a good man," said his goody; "to-morrow let's change our work. I'll go out with the mowers and mow, and you shall mind the house at home."

Yes, the husband thought that would do very well. He was quite willing, he said.

So, early next morning, his goody took a scythe over her neck, and went out into the hay-field with the mowers and began to mow; but the man was to mind the house, and do the work at home.

First of all he wanted to churn the butter; but when he had churned a while, he got thirsty, and went down to the cellar to tap a barrel of ale. So, just when he had knocked in the bung, and was putting the tap into the cask, he heard overhead the pig come into the kitchen. Then off he ran up the cellar steps, with the tap in his hand, as fast as he could, to look after the pig, lest he should upset the churn; but when he got up, and saw the pig had already knocked the churn over, and stood there, routing and grunting amongst the cream which was running all over the floor, he got so wild with rage that he quite forgot the ale-barrel, and ran at the pig as hard as he could. He caught it, too, just as it ran out of doors, and gave it such a kick that piggy lay for dead on the spot. Then all at once he remembered he had the tap in his hand; but when he got down to the cellar, every drop of ale had run out of the cask.

Then he went into the dairy and found enough cream left to fill the churn again, and so he began to churn, for butter they must have at dinner. When he had churned a bit he remembered that their milking cow was still shut up in the byre, and hadn't had a bit to eat or a drop to drink all the morning, though the sun was high. Then all at once he thought 'twas too far to take her down to the meadow, so he'd just get her up on the housetop—for the house, you must know, was thatched with sods, and a fine crop of grass was growing there. Now their house lay close up against a steep down, and he thought if he laid a plank across to the thatch at the back he'd easily get the cow up.

But still he couldn't leave the churn, for there was his little babe crawling about on the floor, and "if I leave it," he thought, "the child is safe to upset it." So he took the churn on his back, and went out with it; but then he thought he'd better first water the cow before he turned her out on the thatch; so he took up a bucket to draw water out of the well; but as he stooped down at the well's brink, all the cream ran out of the churn over his shoulders, and so down into the well.

Now it was near dinner-time, and he hadn't even got the butter yet; so he thought he'd best boil the porridge, and filled the pot with water, and hung it over the fire. When he had done that, he though the cow might perhaps fall off the thatch and break her legs or neck. So he got up on the house to tie her up. One end of the rope he made fast to the cow's neck, and the other he slipped down the chimney and tied round his own thigh; and he had to make haste, for the water now began to boil in the pot, and he had still to grind the oatmeal.

So he began to grind away; but while he was hard at it, down fell the cow off the house top after all, and as she fell, she dragged the man up the chimney by the rope. There he stuck fast; and as for the cow, she hung halfway down the wall, swinging between heaven and earth, for she could neither get down nor up.

And now the goody had waited seven lengths and seven breadths for her husband to come and call them home to dinner; but never a call they had. At last she thought she'd waited long enough, and went home. But when she got there and saw the cow hanging in such an ugly place, she ran up and cut the rope in two with her scythe. But as she did this, down came her husband out of the chimney; and so when his old dame came inside the kitchen, there she found him standing on his head in the porridge-pot.

Denmark

The Talking Pot

This story of the magic pot—the thieving pot, in some retellings—is one of three that are known only in Scandinavia and the Baltic countries. The story as given here is taken from a larger collection translated and compiled by Jens Christian Bay (*Danish Fairy*

and Folk Tales, Harper, 1899, a book long out of print). Dr. Bay's translation was made from the text of Svend Grundtvig, the great collector in Denmark during the middle years of the nineteenth century. [From Mary C. Hatch, *Thirteen Danish Tales* (Harcourt, 1947).]

Once upon a time there was a man so poor that he had nothing in the world but a wife, a house, and one lone cow. And after a time, he got even poorer than that, and so he had to take the cow to market and sell her.

On the way he met a fine-faced stranger. "Well, my good man," said the stranger, "whither away with that fat cow?"

"To market, and thank you," said the man, though the cow was far from fat.

"Then perhaps you will sell her to me," said the stranger.

Yes, the farmer would sell and gladly, provided the price were twenty dollars or more.

The stranger shook his head. "Money I cannot give you," he said. "But I have a wonderful pot that I will trade you," and he showed the farmer a three-legged iron pot with a handle that was tucked under his arm.

Now, truth to tell, there was nothing at all wonderful-looking about the pot, and it might have hung in any chimney in the country. Besides, the poor man had nothing to put in it, neither food nor drink, so he declined to make the trade. "Money I need, and money I must have," he said, "so you may keep your wonderful pot."

But hardly had he said these words than the pot began to speak. "Take me, take me," cried the pot, "and you'll never have cause to rue it." And so the man changed his mind and made the trade, for if the pot could talk, then surely it could do other things, too.

Home he now returned, and when he reached there, he hid the pot in the stable where the cow had always been kept, for he wanted to surprise his wife. Then he went inside. "Well, good wife," he said, "fetch me a bit to eat and a sup to drink, for I've walked a long mile and back today."

But his wife would do none of it till she heard about her husband's success at the market. "Did you make a fine bargain?" she asked.

"Fine as fine," said her husband.

"That is well," nodded the wife, "for we've a hundred places to use the money."

But it wasn't a money bargain. No indeed, exclaimed her husband.

Not a money bargain! Well, pray then, what had the good man gotten for the cow, cried the wife, and she would not rest till her husband had taken her to the barn and showed her the three-legged pot tied up to the stall.

And then the good wife *was* angry! Trading a fine, fat cow—though truth to tell it was neither fine nor fat—for a common black pot that might hang in anyone's chimney.

"You are stupid as a goose," cried the wife. "Now what will we do for food and drink? If you were not so tough, I do believe I would stew you!" And she started to shake her husband. But before she could do the poor man

Illustration by Margot Zemach. Illustration copyright © 1971 by Margot Zemach, from *Favorite Fairy Tales Told in Denmark*, by Virginia Haviland, by permission of Little, Brown and Co.

much damage, the pot began to speak again.

"Clean me, and shine me, and put me on the fire," said the pot, and at that the woman sang a different tune. "Well!" she said. "If you can talk, perhaps you can do other things, too." And she took the pot and scrubbed it and polished it, and then hung it over the fire.

"I will skip, I will skip," said the pot.

"How far will you skip?" asked the woman.

"Up the hill, and down the dale, and into the rich man's house," cried the little pot, and with that, it jumped down from the hook, and skipping across the room, went out the door, and up the road to the rich man's house. Here the rich man's wife was making fine cakes and puddings, and the pot jumped up on the table and settled there still as a statue.

"Well!" exclaimed the rich man's wife. "You are just what I need for my finest pudding." Then she stirred in sugar and spices, and raisins and nuts, a whole host of good things, and the pot took them all without a murmur. In a few minutes, the pudding was made, and the woman picked up the pot and put it on the fire. But down the pot jumped and skipped to the door.

"Dear me," exclaimed the woman: "What are you doing, and where are you going?"

"I'm bound for home to the poor man's house," cried the little pot, and away it went skipping up the road till it was back at the poor man's little cottage.

When the couple saw that the pot had brought them a fine pudding, the finest they had ever seen, they were very pleased, and the farmer said, "Now, my good wife, did I not make a good bargain when I traded our poor old cow for this wonderful pot?"

"Indeed you did," said his wife, and she fell to eating the pot's fine pudding.

The next morning, the pot again cried, "I will skip, I will skip!" And the wife said, "How far will you skip?"

"Up hill and down dale, and into the rich man's barn," the little pot replied, and out the house and up the road it went skipping, straight to the rich man's barn.

The rich man's servants were threshing grain, and the pot skipped to the center of the floor and stood there still as a statue.

"Well!" said one of the threshers. "Here is just the pot to hold a bushel of grain," and he poured in a sackful. But this took up no room at all, and so he poured in another and another till there was not a grain of anything left in the whole barn.

"A most peculiar pot!" exclaimed the men. "Though it looks as if it had hung in any number of chimneys." And then they tried to lift it, but it slid away from them and went skipping across the floor.

"Dear me," cried the men. "What are you doing, and where are you going?"

"I'm bound for home to the poor man's house," said the pot, and out the door it skipped, and though the men ran after it, they were left huffing and puffing far behind.

When the little pot reached home again, it poured out the wheat in the poor man's barn, and there was enough to make bread and cakes for years to come.

But that was not the end of its good deeds, for on the third morning it said again, "I will skip, I will skip!" And the old wife asked, "Where will you skip?" And it answered, "Up hill and down dale to the rich man's house," and out the house it ran at once.

Now the rich man was in his counting house counting out his money, and when the little pot arrived, up it jumped on the table, right in the midst of all the gold pieces.

"What a fine pot," cried the rich man. "Just the thing for my money." And into the pot he tossed handful after handful of money till not one piece was left loose on the table. Then he picked up his treasure to hide it in his money cupboard, but the pot slipped from his fingers and hopped to the door.

"Stop, stop," cried the rich man. "You have all my money."

"But not yours for long," said the pot. "I carry it home to the poor man's house," and out the room it skipped and back to the poor man's cottage. There it poured out the golden treasure, and the old couple cried aloud with delight.

"Now you have enough," said the pot, and indeed they did, enough and more, too, and so the wife washed the pot carefully and put it aside.

But in the morning, the pot was off again, straight for the rich man's house, and when the rich man saw it, he cried, "There is the wicked pot that stole my wife's pudding, and my wheat, and all my gold. But it shall bring everything back, every last farthing and more." Then he grabbed the pot, but bless my soul, if he didn't stick fast! And though he tugged and he pulled, he couldn't get free.

"I will skip, I will skip," said the pot.

"Well, skip to the North Pole," cried the man, still furiously trying to free himself, and at that, away went the pot and the man with it. Up the hill they waltzed and down the hill, and never once did they stop, not even to say hello or good-bye at the old couple's cottage, for the pot was in a great hurry. The North Pole, you know, is far, far away, even for a fast-skipping pot.

Sweden

The Old Troll of Big Mountain

The folk theme of a malevolent supernatural being returning a child's kindness with gratitude and generosity is a common one. In her retelling, Anna Wahlenberg sets it in the dark forests of Sweden. [From *Great Swedish Fairy Tales*, sel. Elsa Olenius and trans. Holder Lundbergh (Delacorte/Seymour Lawrence, 1973).]

Once there lived a poor crofter and his wife who had nothing more in this world than their little cottage, two goats, and a boy-child of five whose name was Olle.

The crofter and his wife worked far away from their cottage every day, so they had a paddock for the goats to graze in. They gave Olle a bread roll and a mug of milk, then they locked the door behind them and put the key under the doorstep.

One night when they came home, both goats were gone. Someone on the highway said he had seen the evil old troll of Big Mountain dragging them away.

You can imagine their distress! Now the crofter and his wife had even less to live on than before, and instead of goat's milk, Olle got nothing but water in his mug. But worst of all, no one could be sure that the evil old troll would not come back, put Olle in a sack, and carry him away up the mountain. The troll was known to have stolen children before, though no one knew what he did with them because none ever came back.

Every day before they left home, the crofter and his wife warned Olle never to sit by the window; for who could tell, the old troll might pass by and catch sight of the boy. If the troll ever knocked on the door, they told Olle, shout "Father, Father," exactly as if his father were at home, because that would surely scare the old troll and send him away.

So that Olle would recognize the troll, his parents described him carefully. He was terribly ugly, had real bushes for eyebrows, a mouth that reached from ear to ear, a nose as thick as a turnip, and instead of a left hand, a wolf's paw.

Yes, Olle would keep a lookout and defend himself, he promised them, and he began to make some weapons. He hammered a nail into a log and it became a lance. He ground an old knife, meant for splitting kindling, against a stone, and it became a sword. That old troll had better watch out, or he would be sorry.

One day as Olle was busy polishing his lance and his sword, he heard someone groping at the door. Olle looked out of the window and saw a man with a sack on his back crouching on his knees and poking his hand under the doorstep. It was none other than the evil old troll who had come to take Olle away, but Olle did not know it.

"What are you looking for?" asked Olle.

Of course, the troll was looking for the key so he could come and steal Olle, but naturally he did not want to say so. "I've lost a coin," he said instead. "It rolled right under your step. Will you come out and help me look for it?"

"No," said Olle. "Father and Mother have locked me in so that I will be safe from a wicked old troll."

The troll looked at Olle out of the corner of his eye. He wondered if the boy had any idea who he was. "Well, I don't look like an old troll, do I?" he said to test him.

"Oh, no. I'm not afraid of *you*. And I am not afraid of the old troll either, for if he comes here, he'll regret it. I have a lance and sword in here, you know. Look!"

The old troll peered through the window-pane, but pretended that he could not see anything. Then he asked Olle where the key was, so that he could unlock the door and come in and see better.

"Oh, yes," said Olle. "The key is under the first broken step on the right side."

Indeed, there it was. Quickly the old troll unlocked the door and stalked in. And to tell the truth, Olle was glad to have company. Proudly and eagerly he showed the old troll how finely he had ground his sword and what a wonderful lance a nail in a log makes. He was even rather wishing the old troll would come, so that he could pay him back for stealing their goats.

"I believe I know where he hides his goats," said the old troll. "If you come with me a little way into the woods, you might find them."

That was a good idea, thought Olle. Imagine, if he could bring home the stolen goats.

"Well, shall we go then?" said the troll.

"Yes," said Olle.

Olle wanted to bring along something to eat, because the troll's pastures were probably a long way off. So he broke his bread into pieces and put them in his pocket. He offered the old troll a piece, but the troll immediately said No. The reason for this was that trolls can never harm anyone from whom they have accepted something. If the troll took the bread now, he would not be able to stuff Olle into his sack. And that, of course, would never do.

When Olle was ready he reached for the old troll's hand, expecting to be led to where the goats were. But the troll pushed his hand away.

"You must take my right hand," said the troll. "I have hurt the left one." He showed Olle his left hand, which was bandaged with a thick cloth.

Olle felt sorry for him. "Oh, my. You poor man. Let me blow on it, that will make it better," he said.

But that didn't help. His only thought was to leave without being seen. It would have been quicker, of course, to stuff Olle into the sack right away, but as he was walking along so willingly, that saved the trouble of carrying him.

And so they walked hand in hand, Olle with his lance and sword ready under his arm, in case they met the evil old troll.

After they had gone a little way into the forest, Olle was tired and sat down on a stone. He began to eat his bread, for he was hungry, too.

The old troll eyed him. He wondered if this wasn't the moment to put the boy in the sack. Besides, it annoyed him that Olle was not afraid of him. That wasn't right. It would have been better to put him in the sack kicking and yelling the way all the other children did. And so he decided to scare Olle.

"Olle," he said, "suppose *I* were the old troll."

"Oh, no," Olle said, looking at him. "You don't look like him at all. He has bushes for eyebrows, and you haven't. He has a mouth that goes from ear to ear, and you haven't. And he has a wolf's paw instead of a left hand, and you haven't. So don't think you can fool me."

"How *do* I look, then?" asked the old troll.

"Like any other old man, of course," Olle reassured him.

That sounded so funny to the old troll's ears that he let out a loud guffaw. And in the same moment Olle threw a piece of bread into his open mouth.

"That's for being so good to me, not like an old troll at all."

"Oho, oho, oho," the old troll coughed with all his might. But however much he coughed, the bread did not come up; it slid further and further down his throat, until he swallowed it.

Now a strange thing happened. The old troll could not treat Olle the way he had intended to. Now that he had accepted something from Olle, he could not wish him ill.

"So you think I look like a man," said the troll. "It's the first time anybody ever said that to me. But if I look like a man, I had better act like one. Listen!"

He stood up and pulled a small pipe from his pocket and began to play it.

Olle listened. He thought he heard someone answering from the forest. Then the old troll blew once more, and again Olle pricked up his ears. Now he could hear footsteps, some light and some heavy, running across the twigs and moss.

The old troll blew one more time.

Something white appeared among the tree trunks, and Olle saw his parents' goats, Pearl and Flower, running towards him. They recognized him, and pushed and butted him. Olle was so excited that he shouted for sheer joy, and jumped from one leg to the other.

But there were more steps. Behind Pearl and Flower came hundreds of little kids, tripping about, tiny and delicate, just like tufts of white wool beside the bigger goats.

"But whose are these other goats?" asked Olle, looking at the old troll.

"Troll ways are different from man's ways, and goats have many kids when they stay with the old troll on Big Mountain," he replied, and patted Olle on the head. "But run along now. You must be home before your mother and father return."

Olle nodded, but before he had time to say a word, the troll had hurried in among the fir trees, because trolls do not like to be thanked.

Olle stood quite still for a moment, wondering where he had gone, but then he patted the goats again and they all set off for home.

On the way Olle met some people. They stopped, amazed at the sight of a small boy leading two goats and so many, many kids. They followed Olle to his cottage, and as the herd was let into the paddock, they stood gaping, a ring of wide eyes around the fence.

Just then Olle's father and mother arrived. When they saw their boy in the midst of all the goats, they were so surprised they had to sit down on a stone. Then Olle told his story and they wrung their hands and groaned. Who could have gathered all those goats? It sounded like magic. It couldn't have been the old troll, could it?

"No, it wasn't," said Olle. "He had big eyebrows, but they weren't real bushes. And he had a big mouth, too, but it didn't go from ear to ear. And he certainly didn't have a wolf's paw for a left hand. His left hand was all bandaged because he had hurt himself."

"Gracious!" exclaimed the crofter and his

wife and all the others around the fence. "It *was* the old troll. He always wraps a cloth round his paw so as not to be recognized when he is passing the cottages."

Olle sat down and looked around at all the worried faces. He still could not understand. "Well then, maybe even bad old trolls are good sometimes," he said at last.

And no one who saw all those goats could doubt it, though no one there would ever have believed it before.

Finland

The Bear Says "North"

In his introduction to the collection from which this story is taken, Parker Fillmore states his belief that this story, with fifteen others that he defines as a "Nursery Epic," is related to the Beast Epic of Reynard the Fox. It is not a debased form of that great satire on Church and State, which has been current in Europe since the twelfth century, but rather the very roots from which the cycle springs. In other words, the simpler stories reflecting in animal form traits of Finnish peasant character antedate the more sophisticated Reynard cycle.

This brief tale has a measure of sophistication and wit, showing Fox in his traditional role of trickster and wise man. [From Parker Fillmore, *Mighty Mikko* (Harcourt, 1922).]

One day while Osmo, the Bear, was prowling about the woods he caught a Grouse.

"Pretty good!" he thought to himself. "Wouldn't the other animals be surprised if they knew old Osmo had caught a Grouse!"

He was so proud of his feat that he wanted all the world to know of it. So, holding the Grouse carefully in his teeth without injuring it, he began parading up and down the forest ways.

"They'll all certainly envy me this nice plump Grouse," he thought. "And they won't be so ready to call me awkward and lumbering after this, either!"

Presently Mikko, the Fox, sauntered by. He saw at once that Osmo was showing off and he determined that the Bear would not get the satisfaction of any admiration from him. So he pretended not to see the Grouse at all. Instead he pointed his nose upwards and sniffed.

"Um! Um!" grunted Osmo, trying to attract attention to himself.

"Ah," Mikko remarked, casually, "is that you, Osmo? What way is the wind blowing to-day? Can you tell me?"

Osmo, of course, could not answer without opening his mouth, so he grunted again hoping that Mikko would have to notice why he couldn't answer. But the Fox didn't glance at him at all. With his nose still pointed upwards he kept sniffing the air.

"It seems to me it's from the South," he said. "Isn't it from the South, Osmo?"

"Um! Um! Um!" the Bear grunted.

"You say it is from the South, Osmo? Are you sure?"

"Um! Um!" Osmo repeated, growing every moment more impatient.

"Oh, not from the South, you say. Then from what direction is it blowing?"

By this time the Bear was so exasperated by Mikko's interest in the wind when he should have been admiring the Grouse that he forgot himself, opened his mouth, and roared out: "North!"

Of course the instant he opened his mouth, the Grouse flew away.

"Now see what you've done!" he stormed angrily. "You've made me lose my fine plump Grouse!"

"I?" Mikko asked. "What had I to do with it?"

"You kept asking me about the wind until I opened my mouth—that's what you did!"

The Fox shrugged his shoulders.

"Why did you open your mouth?"

"Well, you can't say 'North!' without opening your mouth, can you?" the Bear demanded.

The Fox laughed heartily.

"See here, Osmo, don't blame me. Blame yourself. If I had had that Grouse in my mouth and you had asked me about the wind, I should never have said, 'North!'"

"What would you have said?" the Bear asked.

Mikko, the rascal, laughed harder than ever.

Then he clenched his teeth and said:
"East!"

Japan

The Tongue-Cut Sparrow

Retribution for the cruel and greedy, reward for the gentle and kind of heart—this is the pattern of justice of which each culture dreams, if the folklore mirrors, as it does, the ideals of its creators. This charming story from the Japanese states it with perfect balance of cause and effect. Lafcadio Hearn, Greek-Irish American, who adopted Japan as the home of his spirit, tells the story with becoming style. [From Lafcadio Hearn, *Japanese Fairy Tales* (Liveright, 1924).]

'Tis said that once upon a time a cross old woman laid some starch in a basin intending to put it in the clothes in her wash-tub; but a sparrow that a woman, her neighbor, kept as a pet ate it up. Seeing this, the cross old woman seized the sparrow and saying, "You hateful thing!" cut its tongue and let it go.

When the neighbor woman heard that her pet sparrow had got its tongue cut for its offense, she was greatly grieved, and set out with her husband over mountains and plains to find where it had gone, crying: "Where does the tongue-cut sparrow stay? Where does the tongue-cut sparrow stay?"

At last they found its home. When the sparrow saw that its old master and mistress had come to see it, it rejoiced and brought them into its house and thanked them for their kindness in old times and spread a table for them, and loaded it with *sake* and fish till there was no more room, and made its wife and children and grandchildren all serve the table. At last, throwing away its drinking-cup, it danced a jig called the sparrow's dance. Thus they spent the day. When it began to grow dark, and they began to talk of going home, the sparrow brought out two wicker baskets and said: "Will you take the heavy one, or shall I give you the light one?" The old people replied: "We are old, so give us the light one: it will be easier to carry it." The sparrow then gave them the light basket and they returned with it to their home. "Let us open and see what is in it," they said. And when they had opened it and looked they found gold and silver and jewels and rolls of silk. They never expected anything like this.

Illustration by George Suyeoka. Illustration copyright © 1962 by George Suyeoka, from *Favorite Fairy Tales Told in Japan,* by Virginia Haviland, by permission of Little, Brown and Co.

The more they took out the more they found inside. The supply was inexhaustible. So that house at once became rich and prosperous. When the cross old woman who had cut the sparrow's tongue out saw this, she was filled with envy, and went and asked her neighbor where the sparrow lived, and all about the way. "I will go too," she said, and at once set out on her search.

Again the sparrow brought out two wicker baskets and asked as before: "Will you take the heavy one, or shall I give you the light one?"

Thinking the treasure would be great in proportion to the weight of the basket, the old woman replied: "Let me have the heavy one." Receiving this, she started home with it on her back; the sparrow laughing at her as she went. It was as heavy as a stone and hard to carry; but at last she got back with it to her house.

Then when she took off the lid and looked in, a whole troop of frightful devils came bouncing out from the inside and at once tore the old woman to pieces.

China

Ah Tcha the Sleeper

This subtle story is an excellent example of the treatment of a folktale in the hands of an artist who has given it the stamp of his individuality without destroying the integrity of the folklore spirit. It is a "pourquoi" story because it tells the origin of tea. The recurring motif of witches and cats as symbols of darkness and evil is present here, and it is rich in details of the culture from which it comes.

The story appeared in *Shen of the Sea,* the Newbery award winner of 1926, a book that consists of sixteen stories. Arthur Chrisman heard them first from a Chinese shopkeeper whom he had consulted about typical Chinese foods, information he needed for a story he was in the process of writing. That encounter led to friendship and a revelation of the Chinese spirit, which Chrisman brillantly made his own. [From Arthur Bowie Chrisman, *Shen of the Sea* (Dutton, 1925).]

Years ago, in southern China, lived a boy, Ah Tcha by name. Ah Tcha was an orphan, but not according to rule. A most peculiar orphan was he. It is usual for orphans to be very, very poor. That is the world-wide custom. Ah Tcha, on the contrary, was quite wealthy. He owned seven farms, with seven times seven horses to draw the plow. He owned seven mills, with plenty of breezes to spin them. Furthermore, he owned seven thousand pieces of gold, and a fine white cat.

The farms of Ah Tcha were fertile, were wide. His horses were brisk in the furrow. His mills never lacked for grain, nor wanted for wind. And his gold was good sharp gold, with not so much as a trace of copper. Surely, few orphans have been better provided for than the youth named Ah Tcha. And what a busy person was this Ah Tcha. His bed was always cold when the sun arose. Early in the morning he went from field to field, from mill to mill, urging on the people who worked for him. The setting sun always found him on his feet, hastening from here to there, persuading his laborers to more gainful efforts. And the moon of midnight often discovered him pushing up and down the little teakwood balls of a counting board, or else threading cash, placing coins upon a string. Eight farms, nine farms he owned, and more stout horses. Ten mills, eleven, another white cat. It was Ah Tcha's ambition to become the richest person in the world.

They who worked for the wealthy orphan were inclined now and then to grumble. Their pay was not beggarly, but how they did toil to earn that pay which was not beggarly. It was go, and go, and go. Said the ancient woman Nu Wu, who worked with a rake in the field: "Our master drives us as if he were a fox and we were hares in the open. Round the field and round and round, hurry, always hurry." Said Hu Shu, her husband, who bound the grain into sheaves: "Not hares, but horses. We are driven like the horses of Lung Kuan, who . . ." It's a long story.

But Ah Tcha, approaching the murmurers, said, "Pray be so good as to hurry, most excellent Nu Wu, for the clouds gather blackly, with thunder." And to the scowling husband he said, "Speed your work, I beg you, honorable Hu Shu, for the grain must be under shelter before the smoke of Evening Rice ascends."

When Ah Tcha had eaten his Evening Rice, he took lantern and entered the largest of his mills. A scampering rat drew his attention to the floor. There he beheld no less than a score of rats, some gazing at him as if undecided whether to flee or continue the feast, others gnawing—and who are you, nibbling and caring not? And only a few short whisker-lengths away sat an enormous cat, sleeping the sleep of a mossy stone. The cat was black in color, black as a crow's wing dipped in pitch, upon a night of inky darkness. That describes her coat. Her face was somewhat more black. Ah Tcha had never before seen her. She was not his cat. But his or not, he thought it a trifle unreasonable of her to sleep, while the rats held high carnival. The rats romped between her paws. Still she slept. It angered Ah Tcha. The lantern rays fell on her eyes. Still she slept. Ah Tcha grew more and more provoked. He decided then and there to teach the cat that his mill was no place for sleepy heads.

Accordingly, he seized an empty grain sack and hurled it with such exact aim that the cat was sent heels over head. "There, old Crouch-by-the-hole," said Ah Tcha in a tone of wrath. "Remember your paining ear, and be more vigilant." But the cat had no sooner regained her feet than she . . . changed into . . . Nu Wu, the old woman who worked in the fields . . . a witch. What business she had in the mill is a puzzle. However, it is undoubtedly true that mills hold grain, and grain is worth money. And that may be an explanation. Her sleepiness is no puzzle at all. No wonder she was sleepy, after working so hard in the field, the day's length through.

The anger of Nu Wu was fierce and instant. She wagged a crooked finger at Ah Tcha, screeching: "Oh, you cruel money-grubber. Because you fear the rats will eat a penny-worth of grain you must beat me with bludgeons. You make me work like a slave all day—and wish me to work all night. You beat me and disturb my slumber. Very well, since you will not let me sleep, I shall cause you to slumber eleven hours out of every dozen. . . . Close your eyes." She swept her wrinkled hand across Ah Tcha's face. Again taking the form of a cat, she bounded downstairs.

She had scarce reached the third step descending when Ah Tcha felt a compelling desire for sleep. It was as if he had taken gum of the white poppy flower, as if he had tasted honey of the gray moon blossom. Eyes half closed, he stumbled into a grain bin. His knees doubled beneath him. Down he went, curled like a dormouse. Like a dormouse he slumbered.

From that hour began a change in Ah Tcha's fortune. The spell gripped him fast. Nine-tenths of his time was spent in sleep. Unable to watch over his laborers, they worked when they pleased, which was seldom. They idled when so inclined—and that was often, and long. Furthermore, they stole in a manner most shameful. Ah Tcha's mills became empty of grain. His fields lost their fertility. His horses disappeared—strayed, so it was said. Worse yet, the unfortunate fellow was summoned to a magistrate's *yamen,* there to defend himself in a lawsuit. A neighbor declared that Ah Tcha's huge black cat had devoured many chickens. There were witnesses who swore to the deed. They were sure, one and all, that Ah Tcha's black cat was the cat at fault. Ah Tcha was sleeping too soundly to deny that the cat was his. . . . So the magistrate could do nothing less than make the cat's owner pay damages, with all costs of the lawsuit.

Thereafter, trials at court were a daily occurrence. A second neighbor said that Ah Tcha's black cat had stolen a flock of sheep. Another complained that the cat had thieved from him a herd of fattened bullocks. Worse and worse grew the charges. And no matter how absurd, Ah Tcha, sleeping in the prisoner's cage, always lost and had to pay damages. His money soon passed into other hands. His mills were taken from him. His farms went to pay for the lawsuits. Of all his wide lands, there remained only one little acre—and it was grown up in worthless bushes. Of all his goodly buildings, there was left one little hut, where the boy spent most of his time, in witch-imposed slumber.

Now, near by in the mountain of Huge Rocks Piled, lived a greatly ferocious *loong,* or, as foreigners would say, a dragon. This immense beast, from tip of forked tongue to the end of his shadow, was far longer than a barn. With the exception of length, he was much the same as any other *loong*. His head was shaped like that of a camel. His horns were deer horns. He had bulging rabbit eyes, a snake neck. Upon his many ponderous feet were tiger claws, and the feet were shaped very like sofa cushions. He had walrus whiskers, and a breath of red-and-blue flame. His voice was like the sound of a hundred brass kettles pounded. Black fish scales covered his body, black feathers grew upon his limbs. Because of his color he was sometimes called *Oo Loong*. From that it would seem that *Oo* means neither white nor pink.

The black *loong* was not regarded with any great esteem. His habit of eating a man—two men if they were little—every day made him rather unpopular. Fortunately, he prowled only at night. Those folk who went to bed decently at nine o'clock had nothing to fear. Those who rambled well along toward midnight, often disappeared with a sudden and complete thoroughness.

As every one knows, cats are much given to night skulking. The witch cat, Nu Wu was no exception. Midnight often found her miles afield. On such a midnight, when she was roving in the form of a hag, what should approach but the black dragon. Instantly the *loong* scented prey, and instantly he made for the old witch.

There followed such a chase as never was before on land or sea. Up hill and down dale, by stream and wood and fallow, the cat woman flew and the dragon coursed after. The witch soon failed of breath. She panted. She wheezed. She stumbled on a bramble and a claw slashed through her garments too close for comfort. The harried witch changed shape to a cat, and bounded off afresh, half a li at every leap. The *loong* increased his pace and soon was close behind, gaining. For a most peculiar fact about the *loong* is that the more he runs the easier his breath comes, and the swifter grows his speed. Hence, it is not surprising that his fiery breath was presently singeing the witch cat's back.

In a twinkling the cat altered form once more, and as an old hag scuttled across a turnip field. She was merely an ordinarily powerful witch. She possessed only the two forms—cat and hag. Nor did she have a gift of magic to baffle or cripple the hungry black *loong*. Nevertheless,

the witch was not despairing. At the edge of the turnip field lay Ah Tcha's miserable patch of thick bushes. So thick were the bushes as to be almost a wall against the hag's passage. As a hag, she could have no hope of entering such a thicket. But as a cat, she could race through without hindrance. And the dragon would be sadly bothered in following. Scheming thus, the witch dashed under the bushes—a cat once more.

Ah Tcha was roused from slumber by the most outrageous noise that had ever assailed his ears. There was such a snapping of bushes, such an awful bellowed screeching that even the dead of a century must have heard. The usually sound-sleeping Ah Tcha was awakened at the outset. He soon realized how matters stood—or ran. Luckily, he had learned of the only reliable method for frightening off the dragon. He opened his door and hurled a red, a green, and a yellow firecracker in the monster's path.

In through his barely opened door the witch cat dragged her exhausted self. "I don't see why you couldn't open the door sooner," she scolded, changing into a hag. "I circled the hut three times before you had the gumption to let me in."

"I am very sorry, good mother. I was asleep." From Ah Tcha.

"Well, don't be so sleepy again," scowled the witch, "or I'll make you suffer. Get me food and drink."

"Again, honored lady, I am sorry. So poor am I that I have only water for drink. My food is the leaves and roots of bushes."

"No matter. Get what you have—and quickly."

Ah Tcha reached outside the door and stripped a handful of leaves from a bush. He plunged the leaves into a kettle of hot water and signified that the meal was prepared. Then he lay down to doze, for he had been awake fully half a dozen minutes and the desire to sleep was returning stronger every moment.

The witch soon supped and departed, without leaving so much as half a "Thank you." When Ah Tcha awoke again, his visitor was gone. The poor boy flung another handful of leaves into his kettle and drank quickly. He had good reason for haste. Several times he had fallen asleep with the cup at his lips—a most unpleasant situation, and scalding. Having taken several sips, Ah Tcha stretched him out for a resumption of his slumber. Five minutes passed . . . ten minutes . . . fifteen. . . . Still his eyes failed to close. He took a few more sips from the cup and felt more awake than ever.

"I do believe," said Ah Tcha, "that she has thanked me by bewitching my bushes. She has charmed the leaves to drive away my sleepiness."

And so she had. Whenever Ah Tcha felt tired and sleepy—and at first that was often—he had only to drink of the bewitched leaves. At once his drowsiness departed. His neighbors soon learned of the bushes that banished sleep. They came to drink of the magic brew. There grew such a demand that Ah Tcha decided to set a price on the leaves. Still the demand continued. More bushes were planted. Money came.

Throughout the province people called for "the drink of Ah Tcha." In time they shortened it by asking for "Ah Tcha's drink," then for "Tcha's drink," and finally for "Tcha."

And that is its name at present, "Tcha," or "Tay," or "Tea," as some call it. And one kind of Tea is still called "Oo Loong"—"Black Dragon."

Vietnam

In the Land of Small Dragon: A Vietnamese Folktale

The Cinderella story is one of the most enduring and universal of folktales. Nearly five hundred versions exist in Europe alone, and many more are found throughout the world, including a Chinese variant that predates the earliest known Western version by a thousand years. The following Vietnamese folktale is an example of how the major Cinderella motifs are blended with the traditions and customs of a particular culture. Unusual in its traditional Vietnamese metric form, this version is given variety and resonance by the proverbs interspersed among the verses. The proverbs emphasize the symbolic significance of the young woman's spiritual beauty: "Real beauty

mirrors goodness./ What is one is the other." [Complete text from *In the Land of Small Dragon: A Vietnamese Folktale,* told by Dang Manh Kha to Ann Nolan Clark (Viking, 1979).]

One

Man cannot know the whole world,
But can know his own small part.

In the Land of Small Dragon,
In the Year of the Chicken,
In a Village of No-Name,

In the bend of the river,
There were many small houses
Tied together by walkways.
Mulberry and apricot,
Pear tree and flowering vine
Dropped their delicate blossoms.
On a carpet of new grass.

In a Village of No-Name
Lived a man and two daughters.
Tâm was the elder daughter;
Her mother died at her birth.

A jewel box of gold and jade
Holds only jewels of great price.

Tâm's face was a golden moon,
Her eyes dark as a storm cloud,
Her feet delicate flowers
Stepping lightly on the wind.
No envy lived in her heart,
Nor bitterness in her tears.

Cám was the younger daughter,
Child of Number Two Wife.

Cám's face was long and ugly,
Scowling and discontented,
Frowning in deep displeasure.
Indolent, slow and idle,
Her heart was filled with hatred
For her beautiful sister.

An evil heart keeps records
On the face of its owner.

The father loved both daughters,
One not more than the other.

He did not permit his heart
To call one name more dearly.

He lived his days in justice,
Standing strong against the wind.

Father had a little land,
A house made of mats and clay,
A grove of mulberry trees
Enclosed by growing bamboo,
A garden and rice paddy,
Two great water buffalo,
A well for drinking water,
And twin fish ponds for the fish.

Cám's mother, Number Two Wife,
Cared only for her own child.
Her mind had only one thought:
What would give pleasure to Cám.

Her heart had only one door
And only Cám could enter.

Number Two Wife was jealous
Of Tâm, the elder daughter,
Who was beautiful and good,
So the mother planned revenge
On the good, beautiful child.

To Cám she gave everything,
But nothing but work to Tâm.

Tâm carried water buckets,
Hanging from her bamboo pole.
Tâm carried forest fagots
To burn in the kitchen fire.
Tâm transplanted young rice plants
From seed bed to rice paddy.
Tâm flailed the rice on a rock,
Then she winnowed and gleaned it.

Tâm's body ached with tiredness,
Her heart was heavy and sad.
She said, "Wise Father, listen!
I am your elder daughter;
Therefore why may I not be
Number One Daughter, also?"

"A Number One Daughter works,
But she works with dignity.

If I were your Number One
The honor would ease my pain.
As it is, I am a slave,
Without honor or dignity."

Waiting for wisdom to come,
Father was slow to give answer.
"Both my daughters share my heart.
I cannot choose between them.
One of you must earn the right
To be my Number One child."

A man's worth is what he does,
Not what he says he can do.

"Go, Daughters, to the fish pond;
Take your fish baskets with you.
Fish until night moon-mist comes.
Bring your fish catch back to me.
She who brings a full basket
Is my Number One Daughter.
Your work, not my heart, decides
Your place in your father's house."

Tâm listened to her father
And was quick to obey him.
With her basket, she waded
In the mud of the fish pond.
With quick-moving, graceful hands
She caught the quick-darting fish.

Slowly the long hours went by.
Slowly her fish basket filled.

Cám sat on the high, dry bank
Trying to think of some plan,
Her basket empty of fish,
But her mind full of cunning.
"I, wade in that mud?" she thought.
"There must be some better way."

At last she knew what to do
To be Number One Daughter.

"Tâm," she called, "elder sister,
Our father needs a bright flower,
A flower to gladden his heart.
Get it for him, dear sister."

Tâm, the good, gentle sister,
Set her fish basket aside

And ran into the forest
To pick the night-blooming flowers.

Cám crept to Tâm's fish basket,
Emptied it into her own.
Now her fish basket was full.

Tâm's held only one small fish.
Quickly Cám ran to Father,
Calling, "See my full basket!"

Tâm ran back to the fish pond
With an armload of bright flowers.
"Cám," she called, "what has happened?
What has happened to my fish?"

Slowly Tâm went to Father
Bringing him the flowers and fish.

Father looked at both baskets.
Speaking slowly, he told them,
"The test was a full basket,
Not flowers and one small fish.
Take your fish, Elder Daughter.
It is much too small to eat.
Cám has earned the right to be
Honorable Number One."

Two

Tâm looked at the little fish.
Her heart was filled with pity
At its loneliness and fright.
"Little fish, dear little fish,
I will put you in the well."

At night Tâm brought her rice bowl,
Sharing her food with the fish—
Talked to the thin fish, saying,
"Little fish, come eat with me"—
Stayed at the well at nighttime
With the stars for company.

The fish grew big and trustful.
It grew fat and not afraid.
It knew Tâm's voice and answered,
Swimming to her outstretched hand.

Cám sat in the dark shadows,
Her heart full of jealousy,

Her mind full of wicked thoughts.
Sweetly she called, "Tâm, sister.
Our father is overtired.
Come sing him a pretty song
That will bring sweet dreams to him."

Quickly Tâm ran to her father,
Singing him a nightbird song.

Cám was hiding near the well,
Watching, waiting and watching.
When she heard Tâm's pretty song
She crept closer to the fish,
Whispering, "Dear little fish,
Come to me! Come eat with me."

The fish came, and greedy Cám
Touched it, caught it and ate it!

Tâm returned. Her fish was gone.
"Little fish, dear little fish,
Come to me! Come eat with me!"
Bitterly she cried for it.

The stars looked down in pity;
The clouds shed teardrops of rain.

Three

Tâm's tears falling in the well
Made the water rise higher.
And from it rose Nang Tien,
A lovely cloud-dressed fairy.
Her voice was a silver bell
Ringing clear in the moonlight.

"My child, why are you crying?"
"My dear little fish is gone!
He does not come when I call."
"Ask Red Rooster to help you.
His hens will find Little Fish."

Soon the hens came in a line
Sadly bringing the fish bones.

Tâm cried, holding the fish bones.
"Your dear fish will not forget.
Place his bones in a clay pot
Safe beneath your sleeping mat.
Those we love never leave us.
Cherished bones keep love alive."

In her treasured clay pot, Tâm
Made a bed of flower petals
For the bones of Little Fish
And put him away with love.

But she did not forget him;
When the moon was full again,
Tâm, so lonely for her fish,
Dug up the buried clay pot.

Tâm found, instead of fish bones,
A silken dress and two jeweled *hai.* *

Her Nang Tien spoke again.

"Your dear little fish loves you.
Clothe yourself in the garments
His love has given you."

Tâm put on the small jeweled *hai.*
They fit like a velvet skin
Made of moonlight and stardust
And the love of Little Fish.

Tâm heard music in her heart
That sent her small feet dancing,
Flitting like two butterflies,
Skimming like two flying birds,
Dancing by the twin fish ponds,
Dancing in the rice paddy.

But the mud in the rice paddy
Kept one jeweled *hai* for its own.

Night Wind brought the *hai* to Tâm.
"What is yours I bring to you."
Water in the well bubbled,
"I will wash your *hai* for you."

Water buffalo came by.
"Dry your *hai* on my sharp horn."
A blackbird flew by singing,
"I know where this *hai* belongs.
In a garden far away
I will take this *hai* for you."

Four

*What is to be must happen
As day follows after night.*

* *hai:* shoes

In the Emperor's garden,
Sweet with perfume of roses,
The Emperor's son, the Prince,
Walked alone in the moonlight.

A bird, black against the moon,
Flew along the garden path,
Dropping a star in its flight.
"Look! A star!" exclaimed the Prince.
Carefully he picked it up
And found it was the small jeweled *hai.*

"Only a beautiful maid
Can wear this beautiful *hai.*"
The Prince whispered to his heart,
And his heart answered, "Find her."

*In truth, beauty seeks goodness:
What is beautiful is good.*

The Prince went to his father:
"A bird dropped this at my feet.
Surely it must come as truth,
Good and fair the maid it fits.
Sire, if it is your pleasure
I would take this maid for wife."

The Great Emperor was pleased
With the wishes of his son.
He called his servants to him,
His drummers and his crier,
Proclaiming a Festival
To find one who owned the *hai.*

In the Village of No-Name
The Emperor's subjects heard—
They heard the Royal Command.
There was praise and rejoicing.
They were pleased the Royal Son
Would wed one of their daughters.

Five

Father's house was filled with clothes,
Embroidered *áo-dài*† and *hai*
Of heavy silks and rich colors.
Father went outside to sit.

Cám and her mother whispered
Their hopes, their dreams and their plans.

† *áo-dài:* long robes

Cám, Number One Daughter, asked,
"Mother, will the Prince choose me?"

Mother said, "Of course he will.
You will be the fairest there!
When you curtsy to the Prince
His heart will go out to you."

Tâm, Daughter Number Two, said,
"May I go with you and Cám?"
Cám's mother answered curtly,
"Yes, if you have done this task:
Separating rice and husks
From one basket into two."

Tâm knew Cám's mother had mixed
The cleaned rice with rice unhusked.

She looked at the big basket
Full to brim with rice and husks.
Separating the cleaned rice
From that of rice unhusked
Would take all harvest moon time,
When the Festival would end.

A cloud passed over the moon.
Whirring wings outsung the wind.
A flock of blackbirds lighted
On the pile of leaves and grain.
Picking the grain from the leaves,
They dropped clean rice at Tâm's feet.

Tâm could almost not believe
That the endless task was done.

Tâm, the elder daughter, said,
"May I go? May I go, too,
Now that all my work is done?"

Cám taunted, "How could you go?
You have nothing fit to wear."

"If I had a dress to wear
Could I go to the Palace?"
"If wishes were dresses, yes,
But wishes are not dresses."
When Mother left she said,
"Our dear Cám is ravishing.
Stay at home, you Number Two!
Cám will be the one to wed."

Tâm dug up the big clay pot
The dress and one *hai* were there—
As soft as misty moon clouds,
Delicate as rose perfume.

Tâm washed her face in the well,
Combed her hair by the fish pond.
She smoothed down the silken dress,
Tied one *hai* unto her belt
And, though her feet were bare,
Hurried, scurried, ran and ran.

She ran to the Festival
In the King's Royal Garden.

At the Palace gates the guards
Bowed before her, very low.

Pretty girls stood in a line
With their mothers standing near;
One by one they tried to fit
A foot into a small, jeweled *hai*.

Cám stood beside her mother,
By the gilded throne-room door.
Her face was dark and angry
Like a brooding monsoon wind.

Cám, wiping her tears away,
Sobbed and whimpered and complained,
"My small foot fits his old shoe—
Everything but my big toe."

Tâm stood shyly by the door
Looking in great wonderment
While trumpeters and drummers
Made music for her entrance.

People looked at gentle Tâm.
Everyone was whispering,
"Oh! She is so beautiful!
She must be a Princess fair
From some distant foreign land."

Then the Prince looked up and saw
A lady walking toward him.

Stepping from his Royal Throne,
He quickly went to meet her,
And taking her hand led her
To His Majesty the King.

What is to be must happen
As day happens after night.

Real beauty mirrors goodness.
What is one is the other.

Kneeling, the Prince placed the *hai*
On Tâm's dainty little foot.
Tâm untied the *hai* she wore
And slid her bare foot in it.

Beauty is not painted on.
It is the spirit showing.

The Prince spoke to his father.
"I would take this maid for wife."
His Royal Highness nodded.
"We will have a Wedding Feast."
All the birds in all the trees
Sang a song of happiness:
"Tâm, the Number Two Daughter,
Is to be Wife Number One."

What is written in the stars
Cannot be changed or altered.

India

Numskull and the Rabbit

Current among the Indian populace for at least five thousand years, probably longer, the animal stories that make up the *Panchatantra* have been told among all peoples of the world through more than twenty centuries. The original collection, in Sanskrit, numbered about eighty-four tales. In their travels through the ages, the stories underwent many changes, not only in regard to their form, color, and setting, but even as to their total numerical strength.

It should be a matter of pride to American scholarship that the most highly acclaimed translation, in India itself, of the Sanskrit text of the *Panchatantra* into English is that made by Arthur W. Ryder, the American Sanskrit scholar. The preface to the Indian publication of the English text—the title page bears the imprint of the Jaico Publishing House, Bombay (1949)—has this to say of the Ryder translation: "It is the best of all existing *Panchatantra* translations in any foreign language."

A maimed and garbled version was printed by Caxton, in English, and an even earlier printing in German was one of the first printed books in Europe. In 1859 Theodor Benfey, the noted German Sanskrit scholar, provided a literal and faithful translation in the German language of the Kashmir recension—a recension that is recognized by Oriental scholars as the most authoritative in existence. Benfey's Sanskrit studies were largely responsible for one of the major theories of the origins of folktales, namely, that the tales had a common origin in India. That theory has been rather thoroughly exploded, but Benfey's studies resulted in incomparably increased knowledge of the whole field of folklore, and his translation of the *Panchatantra* remains a pivotal accomplishment. He proved that "the Hindus, even before their acquaintance with the animal fables of Aesop which they received from the Greeks, had invented their own compositions of a similar kind, and a great many of them at that" (Stith Thompson, *The Folktale*, p. 376). "The difference between their (the Hindu) conceptions and those of the Aesop fables," says Mr. Benfey in his introduction to his *Panchatantra*, "consisted in general in the fact that whereas the Aesopic writer had his animals act in accordance with their own special nature, the Indic fable treated the animals without regard to their special nature, as if they were merely men masked in animal form." The *Panchatantra*, an elaborate frame-story, like a series of boxes within boxes, was composed as a guide for princes. Readers of *The Arabian Nights* will find the pattern familiar. [From *The Panchatantra*, translated from the Sanskrit by Arthur W. Ryder (University of Chicago Press, 1925).]

Intelligence is power. But where
Could power and folly make a pair?
The rabbit played upon his pride
To fool him; and the lion died.

In a part of a forest was a lion drunk with pride, and his name was Numskull. He slaughtered the animals without ceasing. If he saw an animal, he could not spare him.

So all the natives of the forest—deer, boars, buffaloes, wild oxen, rabbits, and others—came together, and with woebegone countenances, bowed heads, and knees clinging to the ground, they undertook to beseech obsequiously the king of beasts. "Have done, O King, with this merciless, meaningless slaughter of all creatures. It is hostile to happiness in the other world. For the Scripture says":

A thousand future lives
  Will pass in wretchedness
For sins a fool commits
  His present life to bless.

What wisdom in a deed
  That brings dishonor fell,
That causes loss of trust,
  That paves the way to hell?

And yet again:

The ungrateful body, frail
  And rank with filth within,
Is such that only fools
  For its sake sink in sin.

"Consider these facts, and cease, we pray, to slaughter our generations. For if the master will remain at home, we will of our own motion send him each day for his daily food one animal of the forest. In this way neither the royal sustenance nor our families will be cut short. In this way let the king's duty be performed. For the proverb says":

The king who tastes his kingdom like
  Elixir, bit by bit,
Who does not overtax its life,
  Will fully relish it.

The king who madly butchers men,
  Their lives as little reckoned
As lives of goats, has one square meal,
  But never has a second.

A king desiring profit, guards
  His world from evil chance;
With gifts and honors waters it
  As florists water plants.

Guard subjects like a cow, nor ask
  For milk each passing hour:
A vine must first be sprinkled, then
  It ripens fruit and flower.

The monarch-lamp from subjects draws
  Tax-oil to keep it bright:
Has any ever noticed kings
  That shone by inner light?

A seedling is a tender thing,
  And yet, if not neglected,
It comes in time to bearing fruit:
  So subjects well protected.

Their subjects form the only source
  From which accrue to kings
Their gold, grain, gems, and varied drinks,
  And many other things.

The kings who serve the common weal
  Luxuriantly sprout;
The common loss is kingly loss,
  Without a shadow of a doubt.

After listening to this address, Numskull said: "Well, gentlemen, you are quite convincing. But if an animal does not come to me every day as I sit here, I promise you I will eat you all." To this they assented with much relief, and fearlessly roamed the wood. Each day at noon one of them appeared as his dinner, each species taking its turn and providing an individual grown old, or religious, or grief-smitten, or fearful of the loss of son or wife.

One day a rabbit's turn came, it being rabbit day. And when all the thronging animals had given him directions, he reflected: "How is it possible to kill this lion—curse him! Yet after all,

In what can wisdom not prevail?
In what can resolution fail?
What cannot flattery subdue?
What cannot enterprise put through?"

"I can kill even a lion."
So he went very slowly, planning to arrive tardily, and meditating with troubled spirit on a means of killing him. Late in the day he came into the presence of the lion, whose throat was pinched by hunger in consequence of the delay, and who angrily thought as he licked his chops: "Aha! I must kill all the animals the first thing in the morning."

While he was thinking, the rabbit slowly drew near, bowed low, and stood before him. But when the lion saw that he was tardy and too small at that for a meal, his soul flamed with wrath, and he taunted the rabbit, saying: "You reprobate! First, you are too small for a meal. Second, you are tardy. Because of this wickedness I am going to kill you, and tomorrow morning I shall extirpate every species of animal."

Then the rabbit bowed low and said with deference: "Master, the wickedness is not mine, nor the other animals'. Pray hear the cause of it." And the lion answered: "Well, tell it quick, before you are between my fangs."

"Master," said the rabbit, "all the animals recognized today that the rabbits' turn had come, and because I was quite small, they dispatched me with five other rabbits. But in mid-journey there issued from a great hole in the ground a lion who said: 'Where are *you* bound? Pray to your favorite god.' Then I said: 'We are traveling as the dinner of lion Numskull, our master, according to agreement.' 'Is that so?' said he. 'This forest belongs to me. So all the animals, without exception, must deal with me— according to agreement. This Numskull is a sneak thief. Call him out and bring him here at once. Then whichever of us proves stronger shall be king and shall eat all these animals.' At this command, master, I have come to you. This is the cause of my tardiness. For the rest, my master is the sole judge."

After listening to this, Numskull said: "Well, well, my good fellow, show me that sneak thief of a lion, and be quick about it. I cannot find peace of mind until I have vented on him my anger against the animals. He should have remembered the saying:

Land and friends and gold at most
  Have been won when battles cease;
If but one of these should fail,
  Do not think of breaking peace.

Where no great reward is won,
  Where defeat is nearly sure,
Never stir a quarrel, but
  Find it wiser to endure.

"Quite so, master," said the rabbit. "Warriors fight for their country when they are insulted. But this fellow skulks in a fortress. You know he came out of a fortress when he held us up. And an enemy in a fortress is hard to handle. As the saying goes:

A single royal fortress adds
  More military force
Than do a thousand elephants,
  A hundred thousand horse.

A single archer from a wall
  A hundred foes forfends;
And so the military art
  A fortress recommends.

God Indra used the wit and skill
  Of gods in days of old,
When Devil Gold-mat plagued the world,
  To build a fortress-hold.

And he decreed that any king
  Who built a fortress sound
Should conquer foemen. This is why
  Such fortresses abound.

When he heard this, Numskull said: "My good fellow, show me that thief. Even if he is hiding in a fortress, I will kill him. For the proverb says:

The strongest man who fails to crush
  At birth, disease or foe,
Will later be destroyed by that
  Which he permits to grow.

And again:

The man who reckons well his power,
  Nor pride nor vigor lacks,
May single-handed smite his foes
  Like Rama-with-the-ax.

"Very true," said the rabbit. "But after all it was a mighty lion that I saw. So the master should not set out without realizing the enemy's capacity. As the saying runs:

A warrior failing to compare
  Two hosts, in mad desire
For battle, plunges like a moth
  Headforemost into fire.

And again:

The weak who challenge mighty foes
  A battle to abide,
Like elephants with broken tusks,
  Return with drooping pride.

But Numskull said: "What business is it of yours? Show him to me, even in his fortress." "Very well," said the rabbit. "Follow me, master." And he led the way to a well, where he said to the lion: "Master, who can endure your majesty? The moment he saw you, that thief crawled clear into his hole. Come, I will show him to you." "Be quick about it, my good fellow," said Numskull.

So the rabbit showed him the well. And the lion, being a dreadful fool, saw his own reflection in the water, and gave voice to a great roar. Then from the well issued a roar twice as loud, because of the echo. This the lion heard, decided that his rival was very powerful, hurled himself down, and met his death. Thereupon the rabbit cheerfully carried the glad news to all the animals, received their compliments, and lived there contentedly in the forest.

And that is why I say:

Intelligence is power . . .
and the rest of it.

The Cat and the Parrot

This nonsense story has its origins in the folklore of India. The version given by W. H. D. Rouse in the *The Talking Thrush* (Dutton) gives the cat good cause for his initial treatment of the parrot. But here is the version that best suits the storyteller, and young children find it well-nigh irresistible in this form. It has the cumulative and repetitive scheme that invariably weaves a spell; it is true to the egocentric character of cats with their inner conviction of superiority; its towering improbability makes it a tale worthy of Paul Bunyan; and the justice of its happy conclusion, even for the villain, is vastly satisfying. The Czech variant is called *Kuratko the Terrible* and may be found in *The Shoemaker's Apron,* by Parker Fillmore. [From Sara Cone Bryant, *How to Tell Stories to Children* (Houghton Mifflin, 1905).]

Once there was a cat, and a parrot. And they had agreed to ask each other to dinner, turn and turn about: first the cat should ask the parrot, then the parrot should invite the cat, and so on. It was the cat's turn first.

Now the cat was very mean. He provided nothing at all for dinner except a pint of milk, a little slice of fish, and a biscuit. The parrot was too polite to complain, but he did not have a very good time.

When it was his turn to invite the cat he cooked a fine dinner. He had a roast of meat, a pot of tea, a basket of fruit, and best of all, he baked a whole clothesbasketful of little cakes!—little, brown crispy, spicy cakes! Oh, I should say as many as five hundred. And he put four hundred and ninety-eight of the cakes before the cat, keeping only two for himself.

Well, the cat ate the roast, and drank the tea, and sucked the fruit, and then he began on the pile of cakes. He ate all the four hundred and ninety-eight cakes, and then he looked round and said:—

"I'm hungry; haven't you anything to eat?"

"Why," said the parrot, "here are my two cakes, if you want them?"

The cat ate up the two cakes, and then he licked his chops and said, "I am beginning to get an appetite; have you anything to eat?"

"Well, really," said the parrot, who was now rather angry, "I don't see anything more, unless you wish to eat me!" He thought the cat would be ashamed when he heard that—but the cat just looked at him and licked his chops again,— and slip! slop! gobble! down his throat went the parrot!

Then the cat started down the street. An old woman was standing by, and she had seen the whole thing, and she was shocked that the cat should eat his friend. "Why, cat!" she said, "how dreadful of you to eat your friend the parrot!"

"Parrot, indeed!" said the cat. "What's a parrot to me?—I've a great mind to eat you, too." And—before you could say "Jack Robinson"— slip! slop! gobble! down went the old woman!

Then the cat started down the road again, walking like this, because he felt so fine. Pretty soon he met a man driving a donkey. The man was beating the donkey, to hurry him up, and when he saw the cat he said, "Get out of my way, cat; I'm in a hurry and my donkey might tread on you."

"Donkey, indeed!" said the cat, "much I care for a donkey! I have eaten five hundred cakes, I've eaten my friend the parrot, I've eaten an old woman,—what's to hinder my eating a miserable man and a donkey?"

And slip! slop! gobble! down went the old man and the donkey.

Then the cat walked on down the road, jauntily, like this. After a little, he met a procession, coming that way. The king was at the head, walking proudly with his newly married bride, and behind him were his soldiers, marching, and behind them were ever and ever so many elephants, walking two by two. The king felt very kind to everybody, because he had just been married, and he said to the cat, "Get out of my way, pussy, get out of my way—my elephants might hurt you."

"Hurt me!" said the cat, shaking his fat sides. "Ho, ho! I've eaten five hundred cakes, I've eaten my friend the parrot, I've eaten an old woman, I've eaten a man and a donkey; what's to hinder my eating a beggarly king?"

And slip! slop! gobble! down went the king; down went the queen; down went the soldiers,—and down went all the elephants!

Then the cat went on, more slowly; he had really had enough to eat, now. But a little farther on he met two land-crabs, scuttling along in the dust. "Get out of our way, pussy," they squeaked.

"Ho, ho ho!" cried the cat in a terrible voice. "I've eaten five hundred cakes, I've eaten my friend the parrot, I've eaten an old woman, a man with a donkey, a king, a queen, his men-at-arms, and all his elephants; and now I'll eat you too."

And slip! slop! gobble! down went the two land-crabs.

When the land-crabs got down inside, they began to look around. It was very dark, but they could see the poor king sitting in a corner with his bride on his arm; she had fainted. Near them were the men-at-arms, treading on one another's toes, and the elephants, still trying to form in twos,—but they couldn't, because there was not room. In the opposite corner sat the old woman, and near her stood the man and his donkey. But in the other corner was a great pile of cakes, and by them perched the parrot, his feathers all drooping.

"Let's get to work!" said the land-crabs. And, snip, snap, they began to make a little hole in the side, with their sharp claws. Snip, snap, snip, snap,—till it was big enough to get through. Then out they scuttled.

Then out walked the king, carrying his bride; out marched the men-at-arms; out tramped the elephants, two by two; out came the old man, beating his donkey; out walked the old woman, scolding the cat; and last of all, out hopped the parrot, holding a cake in each claw. (You remember, two cakes was all he wanted?)

But the poor cat had to spend the whole day sewing up the hole in his coat!

Arabia

Aladdin and the Wonderful Lamp

This tale of adventure is from an old collection, one which, if not the greatest collection of short stories, is without doubt the best known—*The Arabian Nights' Entertainments, or The Thousand and One Nights.* The book as a whole is built in the "frame-story" manner, like the *Panchatantra.* One anecdote leads to another until the tales are sometimes four and five deep. Thus the beautiful but clever narrator, Scheherazade, interested the Sultan, her new husband, who had previously had his wives killed the next day after marriage; and when she had managed to stay alive a thousand and one nights he naturally yielded and let her live on. A few of these tales, like *Aladdin,* are suitable for children and have always been favorites. [From *Arabian Nights,* coll. and ed. Andrew Lang (Longmans, 1898).]

There once lived a poor tailor, who had a son called Aladdin, a careless, idle boy who would do nothing but play all day long in the streets with little idle boys like himself. This so grieved the father that he died; yet, in spite of his mother's tears and prayers, Aladdin did not mend his ways. One day, when he was playing in the streets as usual, a stranger asked him his age, and if he was not the son of Mustapha the tailor. "I am, sir," replied Aladdin; "but he died a long while ago." On this the stranger, who was a famous African magician, fell on his neck and kissed him, saying; "I am your uncle, and knew you from your likeness to my brother. Go to your mother and tell her I am coming." Aladdin ran home and told his mother of his newly found uncle. "Indeed, child," she said, "your father had a brother, but I always thought he was dead." However, she prepared supper, and bade Aladdin seek his uncle, who came laden with wine and fruit. He presently fell down and kissed the place where Mustapha used to sit, bidding Aladdin's mother not to be surprised at not having seen him before, as he had been forty years out of the country. He then turned to Aladdin, and asked him his trade, at which the boy hung his head, while his mother burst into tears. On learning that Aladdin was idle and would learn no trade, he offered to take a shop for him and stock it with merchandise. Next day he bought Aladdin a fine suit of clothes and took him all over the city, showing him the sights, and brought him home at nightfall to his mother, who was overjoyed to see her son so fine.

Next day the magician led Aladdin into some beautiful gardens a long way outside the city gates. They sat down by a fountain and the magician pulled a cake from his girdle, which he divided between them. They then journeyed onwards till they almost reached the mountains. Aladdin was so tired that he begged to go back, but the magician beguiled him with pleasant stories, and led him on in spite of himself. At last they came to two mountains divided by a narrow valley. "We will go no farther," said the false uncle. "I will show you something wonderful; only do you gather up sticks while I kindle a fire." When it was lit the magician threw on it a powder he had about him, at the same time saying some magical words. The earth trembled a little and opened in front of them, disclosing a square flat stone with a brass ring in the middle to raise it by. Aladdin tried to run away, but the magician caught him and gave him a blow that knocked him down. "What have I done, uncle?" he said piteously; whereupon the magician said more kindly: "Fear nothing, but obey me. Beneath this stone lies a treasure which is to be yours, and no one else may touch it; so you must do exactly as I

tell you." At the word treasure Aladdin forgot his fears, and grasped the ring as he was told, saying the names of his father and grandfather. The stone came up quite easily, and some steps appeared. "Go down," said the magician; "at the foot of those steps you will find an open door leading into three large halls. Tuck up your gown and go through them without touching anything, or you will die instantly. These halls lead into a garden of fine fruit trees. Walk on till you come to a niche in a terrace where stands a lighted lamp. Pour out the oil it contains, and bring it me." He drew a ring from his finger and gave it to Aladdin, bidding him prosper.

Aladdin found everything as the magician had said, gathered some fruit off the trees, and having got the lamp, arrived at the mouth of the cave. The magician cried out in a great hurry: "Make haste and give me the lamp." This Aladdin refused to do until he was out of the cave. The magician flew into a terrible passion, and throwing some more powder on to the fire, he said something, and the stone rolled back into its place.

The magician left Persia forever, which plainly showed that he was no uncle of Aladdin's, but a cunning magician, who had read in his magic books of a wonderful lamp, which would make him the most powerful man in the world. Though he alone knew where to find it, he could only receive it from the hand of another. He had picked out the foolish Aladdin for this purpose, intending to get the lamp and kill him afterwards.

For two days Aladdin remained in the dark crying and lamenting. At last he clasped his hands in prayer, and in so doing, rubbed the ring, which the magician had forgotten to take from him. Immediately an enormous and frightful genie rose out of the earth, saying: "What wouldst thou with me? I am the Slave of the Ring, and will obey thee in all things." Aladdin fearlessly replied: "Deliver me from this place!" whereupon the earth opened, and he found himself outside. As soon as his eyes could bear the light he went home, but fainted on the threshold. When he came to himself, he told his mother what had passed, and showed her the lamp and the fruits he had gathered in the garden, which were in reality precious stones. He then asked for some food. "Alas! child," she said, "I have nothing in the house, but I have spun a little cotton and will go and sell it." Aladdin bade her keep her cotton, for he would sell the lamp instead. As it was very dirty she began to rub it, that it might fetch a higher price. Instantly a hideous genie appeared and asked what she would have. She fainted away, but Aladdin, snatching the lamp, said boldly: "Fetch me something to eat!" The genie returned with a silver bowl, twelve silver plates containing rich meats, two silver cups, and two bottles of wine. Aladdin's mother, when she came to herself, said: "Whence comes this splendid feast?" "Ask not, but eat," replied Aladdin. So they sat at breakfast till it was dinner-time and Aladdin told his mother about the lamp. She begged him to sell it, and have nothing to do with devils. "No," said Aladdin, "since chance hath made us aware of its virtues, we will use it, and the ring likewise, which I shall always wear on my finger." When they had eaten all the genie had brought, Aladdin sold one of the silver plates, and so on until none were left. He then had recourse to the genie, who gave him another set of plates, and thus they lived for many years.

One day Aladdin heard an order from the Sultan proclaimed that everyone was to stay at home and close his shutters while the Princess, his daughter, went to and from the bath. Aladdin was seized by a desire to see her face, which was very difficult, as she always went veiled.

He hid himself behind the door of the bath and peeped through a chink. The Princess lifted her veil as she went in, and looked so beautiful that Aladdin fell in love with her at first sight. He went home so changed that his mother was frightened. He told her he loved the Princess so deeply that he could not live without her, and meant to ask her in marriage of her father.

His mother, on hearing this, burst out laughing; but Aladdin at last prevailed upon her to go before the Sultan and carry his request. She fetched a napkin and laid in it the magic fruits from the enchanted garden, which sparkled and shone like the most beautiful jewels.

She took these with her to please the Sultan, and set out, trusting in the lamp.

The Grand Vizier and the lords of council had just gone in as she entered the hall and placed herself in front of the Sultan. He took no notice of her. She went every day for a week, and stood in the same place. When the council broke up on the sixth day the Sultan said to his Vizier: "I see a certain woman in the audience-chamber every day carrying something in a napkin. Call her next time, that I may find out what she wants." Next day, at a sign from the Vizier, she went up to the foot of the throne and remained kneeling till the Sultan said to her: "Rise, good woman, and tell me what you want." She hesitated, so the Sultan sent away all but the Vizier, and bade her speak freely, promising to forgive her beforehand for anything she might say. She then told him of her son's violent love for the Princess. "I prayed him to forget her," she said, "but in vain; he threatened to do some desperate deed if I refused to go and ask your Majesty for the hand of the Princess. Now I pray you to forgive not me alone, but my son Aladdin." The Sultan asked her kindly what she had in the napkin, whereupon she unfolded the jewels and presented them. He was thunderstruck, and turning to the Vizier said: "What sayest thou? Ought I not to bestow the Princess on one who values her at such a price?" The Vizier, who wanted her for his own son, begged the Sultan to withhold her for three months, in the course of which he hoped his son would contrive to make him a richer present. The Sultan granted this, and told Aladdin's mother that, though he consented to the marriage, she must not appear before him again for three months.

Aladdin waited patiently for nearly three months; but after two had elapsed, his mother, going into the city to buy oil, found everyone rejoicing, and asked what was going on. "Do you not know," was the answer, "that the son of the Grand Vizier is to marry the Sultan's daughter tonight?" Breathless, she ran and told Aladdin, who was overwhelmed at first, but presently bethought him of the lamp. He rubbed it, and the genie appeared, saying: "What is thy will?" Aladdin replied: "The Sultan, as thou knowest, has broken his promise to me, and the Vizier's son is to have the Princess. My command is that tonight you bring hither the bride and bridegroom." "Master, I obey," said the genie. Aladdin then went to his chamber, where, sure enough, at midnight the genie transported the bed containing the Vizier's son and the Princess. "Take this new-married man," he said, "and put him outside in the cold, and return at daybreak." Whereupon the genie took the Vizier's son out of bed, leaving Aladdin with the Princess. "Fear nothing," Aladdin said to her; "you are my wife, promised to me by your unjust father, and no harm shall come to you." The Princess was too frightened to speak, and passed the most miserable night of her life, while Aladdin lay down beside her and slept soundly. At the appointed hour the genie fetched in the shivering bridegroom, laid him in his place, and transported the bed back to the palace.

Presently the Sultan came to wish his daughter good-morning. The unhappy Vizier's son jumped up and hid himself, while the Princess would not say a word, and was very sorrowful. The Sultan sent her mother to her, who said: "How comes it, child, that you will not speak to your father? What has happened?" The Princess sighed deeply, and at last told her mother how, during the night, the bed had been carried into some strange house, and what had passed there. Her mother did not believe her in the least, but bade her rise and consider it an idle dream.

The following night exactly the same thing happened, and next morning, on the Princess's refusing to speak, the Sultan threatened to cut off her head. She then confessed all, bidding him ask the Vizier's son if it were not so. The Sultan told the Vizier to ask his son, who owned the truth, adding that, dearly as he loved the Princess, he had rather die than go through another such fearful night, and wished to be separated from her. His wish was granted, and there was an end of feasting and rejoicing.

When the three months were over, Aladdin sent his mother to remind the Sultan of his promise. She stood in the same place as before, and the Sultan, who had forgotten Aladdin, at once remembered him, and sent for her. On seeing her poverty the Sultan felt less in-clined than ever to keep his word, and asked his Vizier's advice, who counseled him to set so high a value on the Princess that no man living could come up to it. The Sultan then turned to Aladdin's mother, saying: "Good woman, a Sultan must remember his promises, and I will remember mine, but your son must first send me forty basins of gold brimful of jewels, carried by forty black slaves, led by as many white ones, splendidly dressed. Tell him that I await his answer!" The mother of Aladdin bowed low and went home, thinking all was lost. She gave Aladdin the message, adding: "He may wait long enough for your answer!" "Not so long, mother, as you think," her son replied. "I would do a great deal more than that for the Princess." He summoned the genie, and in a few moments the eighty slaves arrived, and filled up the small house and garden. Aladdin made them set out to the palace, two and two, followed by his mother. They were so richly dressed, with such splendid jewels in their girdles, that everyone crowded to see them and the basins of gold they carried on their heads.

They entered the palace and, after kneeling before the Sultan, stood in a half-circle round the throne with their arms crossed, while Aladdin's mother presented them to the Sultan. He hesitated no longer, but said: "Good woman, return and tell your son that I wait for him with open arms." She lost no time in telling Aladdin, bidding him make haste. But Aladdin first called the genie.

"I want a scented bath," he said, "a richly embroidered habit, a horse surpassing the Sultan's, and twenty slaves to attend me. Besides this, six slaves, beautifully dressed, to wait on my mother; and lastly, ten thousand pieces of gold in ten purses." No sooner said than done.

Aladdin mounted his horse and passed through the streets, the slaves strewing gold as they went. Those who had played with him in his childhood knew him not, he had grown so handsome. When the Sultan saw him he came down from his throne, embraced him, and led him into a hall where a feast was spread, intending to marry him to the Princess that very day. But Aladdin refused, saying, "I must build a palace fit for her," and took his leave.

Once home, he said to the genie: "Build me a palace of the finest marble, set with jasper, agate, and other precious stones. In the middle you shall build me a large hall with a dome, its four walls of massy gold and silver, each side having six windows, whose lattices, all except one which is to be left unfinished, must be set with diamonds and rubies. There must be stables and horses and grooms and slaves; go and see about it!"

The palace was finished by next day, and the genie carried him there and showed him all his orders faithfully carried out, even to the laying of a velvet carpet from Aladdin's palace to the Sultan's. Aladdin's mother then dressed herself carefully, and walked to the palace with her slaves, while he followed her on horseback. The Sultan sent musicians with trumpets and cymbals to meet them, so that the air resounded with music and cheers. She was taken to the Princess, who saluted her and treated her with great honor. At night the Princess said good-bye to her father, and set out on the carpet for Aladdin's palace, with his mother at her side, and followed by the hundred slaves. She was charmed at the sight of Aladdin, who ran to receive her. "Princess," he said, "blame your beauty for my boldness if I have displeased you." She told him that, having seen him, she willingly obeyed her father in this matter. After the wedding had taken place Aladdin led her into the hall, where a feast was spread, and she supped with him, after which they danced till midnight.

Next day Aladdin invited the Sultan to see the palace. On entering the hall with the four-and-twenty windows, with their rubies, diamonds, and emeralds, he cried: "It is a world's wonder! There is only one thing that surprises me. Was it by accident that one window was left unfinished?" "No, sir, by design," returned Aladdin. "I wished your Majesty to have the glory of finishing this palace." The Sultan was pleased, and sent in the best jewelers in the city. He showed them the unfinished window, and bade them fit it up like the others. "Sir," replied their spokesman, "we cannot find jewels enough." The Sultan had his own fetched, which they soon used, but to no purpose, for in a month's time the work

was not half done. Aladdin, knowing that their task was vain, bade them undo their work and carry the jewels back, and the genie finished the window at his command. The Sultan was surprised to receive his jewels again, and visited Aladdin, who showed him the window finished. The Sultan embraced him, the envious Vizier meanwhile hinting that it was the work of enchantment.

Aladdin had won the hearts of the people by his gentle bearing. He was made captain of the Sultan's armies, and won several battles for him; but remained modest and courteous as before and lived thus in peace and content for several years.

But far away in Africa the magician remembered Aladdin and by his magic arts discovered that Aladdin, instead of perishing miserably in the cave, had escaped and had married a Princess with whom he was living in great honor and wealth. He knew that the poor tailor's son could only have accomplished this by means of the lamp and traveled night and day till he reached the capital of China, bent on Aladdin's ruin. As he passed through the town he heard people talking everywhere about a marvelous palace.

"Forgive my ignorance," he said. "What is this palace you speak of?"

"Have you not heard of Prince Aladdin's palace," was the reply, "the greatest wonder of the world? I will direct you if you have a mind to see it."

The magician thanked him who spoke, and having seen the palace knew that it had been raised by the genie of the lamp and became half-mad with rage. He determined to get hold of the lamp and again plunge Aladdin into the deepest poverty.

Unluckily, Aladdin had gone a-hunting for eight days, which gave the magician plenty of time. He bought a dozen copper lamps, put them into a basket, and went to the palace, crying, "New lamps for old!" followed by a jeering crowd.

The Princess sitting in the hall of twenty-four windows, sent a slave to find out what the noise was about, who came back laughing, so that the Princess scolded her.

"Madam," replied the slave, "who can help

laughing to see an old fool offering to exchange fine new lamps for old ones?"

Another slave, hearing this, said: "There is an old one on the cornice there which he can have." Now, this was the magic lamp, which Aladdin had left there, as he could not take it out hunting with him.

The Princess, not knowing its value, laughingly bade the slave take it and make the exchange. She went and said to the magician: "Give me a new lamp for this." He snatched it and bade the slave take her choice, amid the jeers of the crowd. Little he cared, but left off crying his lamps, and went out of the city gates to a lonely place, where he remained till nightfall, when he pulled out the lamp and rubbed it. The genie appeared and at the magician's command carried him, together with the palace and the Princess in it, to a lonely place in Africa.

Next morning the Sultan looked out of the window toward Aladdin's palace and rubbed his eyes, for it was gone. He sent for the Vizier and asked what had become of the palace. The Vizier looked out too, and was lost in astonishment. He again put it down to enchantment, and this time the Sultan believed him, and sent thirty men on horseback to fetch Aladdin in chains. They met him riding home, bound him, and forced him to go with them on foot. The people, however, who loved him, followed, armed, to see that he came to no harm. He was carried before the Sultan, who ordered the executioner to cut off his head. The executioner made Aladdin kneel down, bandaged his eyes, and raised his scimitar to strike. At that instant the Vizier, who saw that the crowd had forced their way into the courtyard and were scaling the walls to rescue Aladdin, called to the executioner to stay his hand. The people, indeed, looked so threatening that the Sultan gave way and ordered Aladdin to be unbound, and pardoned him in the sight of the crowd. Aladdin now begged to know what he had done. "False wretch!" said the Sultan, "come hither," and showed him from the window the place where his palace had stood. Aladdin was so amazed that he could not say a word. "Where is my palace and my daughter?" demanded the Sultan. "For the first I am not so deeply con-

cerned, but my daughter I must have, and you must find her or lose your head." Aladdin begged for forty days in which to find her, promising if he failed, to return and suffer death at the Sultan's pleasure. His prayer was granted, and he went forth sadly from the Sultan's presence. For three days he wandered about like a madman, asking everyone what had become of his palace, but they only laughed and pitied him. He came to the banks of a river, and knelt down to say his prayers before throwing himself in. In so doing he rubbed the magic ring he still wore. The genie he had seen in the cave appeared, and asked his will. "Save my life, genie," said Aladdin, "and bring my palace back." "That is not in my power," said the genie; "I am only the Slave of the Ring; you must ask him of the lamp." "Even so," said Aladdin, "but thou canst take me to the palace, and set me down under my dear wife's window." He at once found himself in Africa, under the window of the Princess, and fell asleep out of sheer weariness.

He was awakened by the singing of the birds, and his heart was lighter. He saw plainly that all his misfortunes were owing to the loss of the lamp, and vainly wondered who had robbed him of it.

That morning the Princess rose earlier than she had done since she had been carried into Africa by the magician, whose company she was forced to endure once a day. She, however, treated him so harshly that he dared not live there altogether. As she was dressing, one of her women looked out and saw Aladdin.

The Princess ran and opened the window, and at the noise she made Aladdin looked up. She called to him to come to her, and great was the joy of these lovers at seeing each other again.

After he had kissed her Aladdin said: "I beg of you, Princess, in God's name, before we speak of anything else, for your own sake and mine, tell me what has become of an old lamp I left on the cornice in the hall of twenty-four windows when I went hunting."

"Alas!" she said, "I am the innocent cause of our sorrows," and told him of the exchange of the lamp.

"Now I know," cried Aladdin, "that we have to thank the African magician for this! Where is the lamp?"

"He carries it about with him," said the Princess. "I know, for he pulled it out of his breast to show me. He wishes me to break my faith with you and marry him, saying that you were beheaded by my father's command. He is forever speaking ill of you, but I only reply to him by my tears. If I persist in doing so, I doubt not but he will use violence."

Aladdin comforted her and left her for awhile. He changed clothes with the first person he met in the town and having bought a certain powder, returned to the Princess, who let him in by a little side door. "Put on your most beautiful dress," he said to her, "and receive the magician with smiles, leading him to believe that you have forgotten me. Invite him up to sup with you and say you wish to taste the wine of his country. He will go for some and while he is gone, I will tell you what to do." She listened carefully to Aladdin and when he left her, arrayed herself gayly for the first time since she left China. She put on a girdle and head-dress of diamonds, and, seeing in a glass that she was more beautiful than ever, received the magician, saying, to his great amazement: "I have made up my mind that Aladdin is dead, and that all my tears will not bring him back to me, so I am resolved to mourn no more, and have therefore invited you to sup with me; but I am tired of the wines of China, and would fain taste those of Africa." The magician flew to his cellar, and the Princess put the powder Aladdin had given her in her cup. When he returned she asked him to drink her health in the wine of Africa, handing him her cup in exchange for his, as a sign she was reconciled to him. Before drinking the magician made her a speech in praise of her beauty, but the Princess cut him short, saying: "Let us drink first, and you shall say what you will afterwards." She set her cup to her lips and kept it there, while the magician drained his to the dregs and fell back lifeless. The Princess then opened the door to Aladdin, and flung her arms round his neck; but Aladdin put her away, bidding her leave him, as he had more to do. He then went

to the dead magician, took the lamp out of his vest, and bade the genie carry the palace and all in it back to China. This was done, and the Princess in her chamber only felt two little shocks, and little thought she was at home again.

The Sultan, who was sitting in his closet, mourning for his lost daughter, happened to look up, and rubbed his eyes, for there stood the palace as before! He hastened thither, and Aladdin received him in the hall of the four-and-twenty windows, with the Princess at his side. Aladdin told him what had happened, and showed him the dead body of the magician, that he might believe. A ten days' feast was proclaimed, and it seemed as if Aladdin might now live the rest of his life in peace; but it was not to be.

The African magician had a younger brother, who was, if possible, more wicked and more cunning than himself. He traveled to China to avenge his brother's death, and went to visit a pious woman called Fatima, thinking she might be of use to him. He entered her cell and clapped a dagger to her breast, telling her to rise and do his bidding on pain of death. He changed clothes with her, colored his face like hers, put on her veil, and murdered her, that she might tell no tales. Then he went towards the palace of Aladdin, and all the people, thinking he was the holy woman, gathered round him, kissing his hands and begging his blessing. When he got to the palace there was such a noise going on round him that the Princess bade her slave look out of the window and ask what was the matter. The slave said it was the holy woman, curing people by her touch of their ailments, whereupon the Princess, who had long desired to see Fatima, sent for her. On coming to the Princess, the magician offered up a prayer for her health and prosperity. When he had done, the Princess made him sit by her, and begged him to stay with her always. The false Fatima, who wished for nothing better, consented, but kept his veil down for fear of discovery. The Princess showed him the hall, and asked him what he thought of it. "It is truly beautiful," said the false Fatima. "In my mind it wants but one thing." "And what is that?" said the Princess. "If only a roc's egg," replied he, "were hung up from the middle of this dome, it would be the wonder of the world."

After this the Princess could think of nothing but the roc's egg, and when Aladdin returned from hunting he found her in a very ill humor. He begged to know what was amiss, and she told him that all her pleasure in the hall was spoilt for the want of a roc's egg hanging from the dome. "If that is all," replied Aladdin, "you shall soon be happy." He left her and rubbed the lamp, and when the genie appeared commanded him to bring a roc's egg. The genie gave such a loud and terrible shriek that the hall shook. "Wretch!" he cried, "is it not enough that I have done everything for you, but you must command me to bring my master and hang him up in the midst of this dome? You and your wife and your palace deserve to be burnt to ashes, but that this request does not come from you, but from the brother of the African magician, whom you destroyed. He is now in your palace disguised as the holy woman—whom he murdered. He it was who put that wish into your wife's head. Take care of yourself, for he means to kill you." So saying, the genie disappeared.

Aladdin went back to the Princess, saying his head ached, and requesting that the holy Fatima should be fetched to lay her hands on it. But when the magician came near, Aladdin, seizing his dagger, pierced him to the heart. "What have you done!" cried the Princess. "You have killed the holy woman!" "Not so," replied Aladdin, "but a wicked magician," and told her of how she had been deceived.

After this Aladdin and his wife lived in peace. He succeeded the Sultan when he died, and reigned for many years, leaving behind him a long line of kings.

The Sleeping Beauty

P. L. Travers, author of *Mary Poppins* and essayist on folklore and myth, has created a literary fairy tale. Drawing on the themes and motifs of the classic story, particularly as it appears in the Grimms' "Briar Rose," she has transplanted the rose to Arabian soil to give it a fresh vision. A comic, mysterious, moving recreation of the fairy tale with an afterword on its archetypal significance. [From P. L. Travers, *About the Sleeping Beauty* (McGraw-Hill, 1975).]

Once upon a time, a time that never was and is always, there lived in Arabia a sultan and his wife. They were, as sovereigns go, reasonably benevolent and as much loved by their subjects as is possible for fallible human beings. The life they led was comfortable, even, one might say, luxurious. They had spacious divans to sleep on, garments of finest silk and damask, expensive jewels to deck their persons, well-groomed horses and hounds for hunting, and for dwelling place a lordly palace in whose cellars stood numerous sacks of gold. They were well-served by their servants, well-fed by their cooks, and well-protected by their soldiers.

"Dear me," you will be saying, "some people have all the good fortune!"

But the Sultan and his wife would not, I think, have agreed with you. For this elegant life of theirs lacked one important thing.

Each day they looked at each other and sighed. "How lonely we are!" they told each other. "Our footsteps ring on the marble floors but who hears the echo and runs to meet us? Each season the flowers bloom anew but to whom can we say 'Now, pick them gently!'? Where is the one who will listen and gaze when we point to the stars and say 'That is Orion!'? Who will walk with us under the palm trees or count the newborn lambs on the hill? To whom shall we tell the evening tales that are running in our minds? There is no one to be our care while we live and to weep for us when we die. If only we had a child!"

And then, since a man cannot grieve continually—though the same thing is not true of women—the Sultan would go about his work, ordering the affairs of his country. Or he would clap his hands for his dark slave, Bouraba, and send him with letters or ultimatums to the rulers of the surrounding kingdoms. In such ways, by keeping himself well-occupied, he was able to forget for a while the heaviness in his heart.

But the Sultana did not forget for a moment. Women brood over their troubles as hens brood upon eggs. Day after day she would sit under a wild rose tree by the lake and fold her arms and rock her sorrow as though it were a wakeful child. But it never went to sleep.

One day as she sat there, a frog sprang straight up out of the lake and landed on a stone beside her. His neck pulsed in and out with his breath, and his eyes, reflecting the glint of the dark water, regarded her thoughtfully.

"Why do you grieve, Sultana, rocking backwards and forwards? Morning after morning the same scene spreads before me—a great lady, who should have something better to do, weeping and swaying to and fro, wasting her life away. Tell me, why is this?"

So the Sultana told him.

"Here," she said, touching her belly. "And here," she said, touching her breast. "And here," she said, touching the inner crease of her elbow, "I ache for what I lack."

On and on she went with her story, relating it in the mournful voice that she and the Sultan together used in their nightly tale of woe.

"Dear me," said the frog, "how very sad! But wait a little while, Sultana. I promise you that in less than a year you will have your lack no longer."

The Sultana stared. "How can you know that?" she protested, with a shade of irritation. For the truth was that all unknown to herself she had become so fond of her sorrow that now the mere thought of losing it made her feel naked and bereft. "After all, you are only a frog."

"Only a frog," the frog agreed. "As you are only a woman."

"On the other hand," the Sultana mused, following her own train of thought. "There is an old story of a prince who turned into a frog. And it may be, since you speak with sagacity, that you, perhaps, are he."

"Ah, so I must be human to be wise—is that what you think? Well, the sun rises promptly every morning, rivers flow downhill rather than up, the seed breaks the pod when the time is ripe. Were these taught their changeless ways by man? Dear madam, if I were that prince— and, mind you, I am not admitting it!—I would beg whatever magician changed me to let me remain a frog. A man sees no further than his nose. So, for that matter, does a frog. On the other hand, a frog lives in water, down by the roots, and senses what is stirring. And this frog bids you dry your eyes. Go home now, Sultana, and come no more to the wild rose tree. The time for that is past."

With that, the frog unceremoniously turned his back and snatched at a passing fly.

The Sultana stood gazing at him in wonder. "Life is full of surprises," she murmured at last. Then she turned and went thoughtfully back to the palace.

That evening she surprised her husband by saying "Let us not grieve at all tonight. It may be that grief has become a habit and that only by asking nothing can any wish come true. Let us walk among the flowers simply for our own delight and gaze up at the stars for the same reason."

So they did that, with great pleasure. And eventually, in a year—all but three months— the frog's prophecy was fulfilled and a daughter was born.

The Sultan received the news with satisfaction tempered with disappointment. "I could have asked for nothing better, except, of course, a son."

But the Sultana, holding her baby in her arms, was utterly content. She had no ache anywhere and she felt that she lacked nothing.

"When you are given a lily," she advised her husband, "do not protest that it should have been a tulip."

"Nevertheless," replied the Sultan, "we need a successor to the throne and a son would have been very useful."

At that, as though she felt herself to be unwelcome, the baby set up a doleful weeping and the Sultan, a goodhearted man in spite of a certain irritability of temper, hurried to make amends.

"There, there!" He patted the wailing bundle. "I was simply speaking my thoughts aloud and thinking about the kingdom. There's really no reason to be upset. You have almost fulfilled my dearest wish. Having waited so many years, I'm glad to get anything, truly I am, especially—" he touched her cheek. "Especially someone so pretty."

No baby can resist flattery, so the Princess, drinking back her tears, smiled and contentedly fell asleep. And the Sultan hurried to the Council Chamber to tell the Vizier the happy news.

And the Vizier told the seneschal, who told the courtiers, who told the handmaidens, who told the pages, who told the upper servants, who told the lower servants, who told the swineherds, who told the swine. And the whole palace rejoiced.

Messengers rode to all points of the compass, proclaiming the news to the people. Bells were rung for three days and nights without ceasing, no matter whose sleep was disturbed. And every person in the land was given a piece of silver.

The next thing to be thought of was the christening.

"Bid the cooks," said the Sultan, "prepare a feast. We cannot let an event of this kind pass without a celebration. Invitations must go to all my kinsmen, friends, and acquaintances, lords and ladies. And lastly, but by no means least, we must send for the Wise Women. Those ladies lend an air of elegance to any entertainment. Apart from that, one should always keep, as it were, on the right side of them, for they have in their power the bestowal of desirable attributes and gifts of surpassing value. As a matter of policy, as well as courtesy, I wish them to be well-disposed towards my daughter. But, now that I come to think of it, a problem arises here."

The Sultan thoughtfully stroked his beard.

"There are thirteen Wise Women in the kingdom. Unfortunately, however, I have only twelve gold plates. What is to be done? I cannot insult any single fairy by giving her a china dish while her sisters eat off gold. One of them, therefore, must stay at home. But which one? What a quandary!"

He pondered the question for a moment. Then he clapped his hands.

"Bouraba!" he cried. And the dark slave fell to his knees before him.

"Bouraba, you shall be my courier. Take these twelve invitations and present one, with my compliments, to each of the first twelve fairies who happen to cross your path. And now," he said to the Sultana, as Bouraba bowed himself away, "we must wait and hope for the best."

How far is it to fairyland? Nearer by far than Babylon. It intersects our mortal world at every point and at every second. The two of them together make one web woven fine. It was no time, therefore, before Bouraba had performed his task and was back again at the palace.

The Wise Women, for people who believe in them, are never far to seek. Wherever a cradle is set rocking, the hand of some Wise Woman lies over the mortal hand. Wherever mother and daughter are, talking the age-old talk of women, a Wise Woman makes a third. They mix with the matrons at the market, the fishwives by the harbour's edge, and ladies in elegant mansions; they nod with the grandmothers by the fire; they dance with the demoiselles at the crossroads. When a young child laughs all alone, be sure he has seen a Wise Woman pass; when an old man weeps all alone, he has surely seen the same thing and is grieving for his wasted days. There is no corner of existence that has not felt the Wise Women's prodding fingers. They mourn with the mourner, rejoice with the joyous. They rain down fortune on those who listen to their advice; but he who defies them, offends or neglects them, oh, let him beware! For him they are furies, probing his vitals, tempting him to his own destruction or thrusting him into misfortune's arms.

It was fortunate for Bouraba that he was a simple man of sound instinct and good feeling and was thus able to approach them with proper awe and deference. Having delivered his invitations, he left behind him twelve Wise Women well satisfied with his demeanour and the Sultan's courtesy. Enjoying, as they have ever done, all forms of festival and ceremony, they looked forward to the christening of the Princess Rose with the happiest anticipation.

At last the great day—as must happen, even with small days—arrived. Everyone in the palace, from the Sultan down to the kitchen boys, had new clothes for the occasion. The guests arrived in a glittering throng, lords and viziers on horseback, the ladies carried in palanquins. And the shining palace outshone the stars as the Sultan and Sultana led the way to the Council Chamber where beside the throne, rocked in her cradle by Bouraba, the little Princess lay.

Then, kneeling or bowing, according to their social stations, the guests proffered their gifts.

These were received by the Vizier who, salaaming, handed them to the Sultan, who handed them to the Treasurer, who carried them away.

Bright-liveried servants, like butterflies, flitted among the guests, offering trays of date-palm wine and sherbet cooled by snow from the mountains. The music of lute and flute was echoed by the tinkle of talk and laughter. Everyone was as gay as the sky is blue and the courtly merriment was at its height when a sudden peal of bells rang out and silenced every voice. Nobody spoke in the Council Chamber as the twelve fairies swept in.

Not a sound did the Wise Women make as their bare feet of gold or silver floated, as is customary in the fairy world, some inches above the floor. The twelve figures seemed to hang in the air, their naked golden and silver heads gleaming above the swirling robes which were every colour of the rainbow.

In silence everybody bowed. Then the Sultan stepped forward with open arms.

"Welcome, dear ladies," he cried, salaaming, as the luminous shapes streamed across the room.

Gravely they acknowledged his greeting. Then each one, as she passed Bouraba, favoured him with a stately nod and accepted from his outstretched hand a gold plate piled with sweetmeats. They daintily picked at the mortal food and, floating away to the Princess's cradle, hovered there in a brilliant cluster, their bare heads bent above it.

Silently they took stock of the child, their austere faces wordlessly communing as though together they were pondering on what fate should be hers.

At length they all raised their heads and a deeper hush fell over the hall. You could have heard a feather fall. This, as everybody knew, was the great moment of the evening, in fact, its very meaning.

The guests leaned forward, anticipating wonders, for after all, you do not have twelve Wise Women at a christening for nothing. The Sultan and Sultana modestly smiled, attempting to convey the impression that they were keenly expectant and at the same time politely unaware that there was anything to be expected.

Two red-clad fairies broke the silence and, as so often happens at christenings, they did so in verse.

"Her beauty shall the world surprise,"

said the first.

"Ruby lip and starry eyes."

The Sultana smiled a gratified smile. The Sultan, too, appeared complacent.

"A useful commodity," he murmured. "It will help me to find her a husband."

Then the second, swirling in flamy robes, lifted her silver hand.

"Health to her that shall be spun
From earth and fire and wind and sun."

"Ah," cried the guests among themselves. "Spun from all the elements. That is health indeed."

"H'mm," said the Sultan to himself. "That will save the apothecary's bills. I'm glad of health, naturally. But what of wealth, I wonder?" And he eagerly eyed two orange fairies who were joining hands across the cradle.

"You will find in east or west
No kinder heart in any breast"

declared one. And her sister added,

"A good temper, sweet and mild,
Shall I give the Sultan's child."

The Sultan and Sultana bowed, she with happy gratitude but he, it has to be confessed, with growing irritation.

"Kind hearts are all very fine," he muttered. "But who will give her a coronet? Well, well, here are two more fairies. Let us see what they have in their pockets."

The yellow fairies, fragile as lilies, were waving silver hands.

"I'll give her joy,"

said the first, briefly.

"Without alloy,"

the other added.

"So kind, so kind," the Sultana murmured.

The Sultan nodded and shuffled his feet. It was as much as he could do not to stamp them.

It was now the turn of the green fairies. The two bent and waved, like grass in the wind, as they spoke with a single voice:

"No bird or beast shall fear her
No malice shall come near her."

And immediately afterwards, the ninth and tenth fairies, cloudily blue as the evening sky, proclaimed their magic gifts:

"Beneath her bed no crouching bear,
No shadowy corner on the stair,
Like candle in the dark she'll go,
Not dreading any mortal foe."

The Sultana responded with a smile, the Sultan with a throaty rumble, as the eleventh fairy, trailing her sea-coloured indigo robes, lifted her head from the cradle.

"Contentment and a quiet mind,
And what she looks for she shall find."

The Sultan gave her an outraged stare. Then, suddenly remembering his manners, he made a deep, back-breaking bow, spread out his hands and shook his head like one who is at loss for words.

"Kind fairies, thank you, one and all. Such *useful* presents. They leave me speechless."

But behind his peacock feather fan, he whispered balefully to his wife. "I'm astounded! Not a penny piece! Good temper, health, peace, and joy—and not a single jewel. No bags of gold, no marble mansion. Poor child, she'll be as poor as a mouse."

The Sultana gently stroked his arm. "In the long run," she said, with a practical air, "these gifts are always the best."

"But insubstantial!" the Sultan wailed. Nothing you can touch or see. Will such gifts help to increase her dowry? No bears under the bed, they say. But who would dream of putting one there? And as for stairways, they are all well lit. She will not *need* to be a candle."

"Perhaps," said the Sultana wisely, "they meant another kind of dark."

"Nonsense! There's only one kind of dark. Well, well, never despair. We still have one gift left to get." The Sultan nodded at the Twelfth Wise Woman who was hovering at the head of the cradle, her indigo robes like waves about her. "The last gift, you know, is always the best. I am hoping for something splendid. Look, she is raising her golden hand. Allah preserve us—what is this?"

As though struck by an unseen fist, the Sultan staggered backwards. A clap of thunder rocked the hall—or was it perhaps the sound of cannon?—and a thick grey mist swept through the door. The lute strings broke with a twanging cry, the wineglasses shattered on their trays. The guests shrieked, the servants shouted, the Princess wailed.

"We are beseiged!" the Sultan bellowed. "Vizier, call the soldiers in! Station the guards at every point! This is a ruse of our enemies! They are now at our very gates!"

"One enemy alone, Prince, and that no mortal foe!"

A vibrant voice rang through the hall, the wreathing mist cleared away and there, standing in the air, her violet robes flowing about her, was the thirteenth of the Wise Women. Her naked silver head flashed as she turned from one point to another wrathfully eying the scene.

The Sultan's face was as pale as marble.

"Bring me my sword!" he said nervously, as the Wise Woman strode through air towards him.

She laughed mockingly.

"No sword can save you, foolish mortal! Only a word can do that. Speak it—if you can. Tell me, you little earthly lord, why all my sisters are gathered here, all invited to your daughter's christening—and I alone left out?"

Step by step she crossed the hall, thrusting the Sultan backwards.

"Well?" she demanded, ominously.

The Sultan collapsed upon the throne, rocking himself backwards and forwards, racking his brain for an answer.

"Most noble fairy, I beg forgiveness. It was not intentional, I assure you—simply a matter of dishes. Thirteen Wise Women in the land

and only twelve gold plates! I should have sent an apology. But with all the christening arrangements, I was busy and I just forgot."

"Forgot!" The Wise Woman spat the word at him. "And did you also fail to remember that one thing leads to another? Every stick has two ends, Prince. You forgot! And because of that, *I* am called to remember. Because of that, I—as long as your story lives—must play the part of the Wicked Fairy. Children will turn aside at my name and men call curses on my head. You cannot alter the law, Prince. In my world there is no forgetting. And he who forgets in your world must take the consequences."

"Yes," said the Sultan, miserably. "You must punish me as you think best. I will do whatever you wish."

"You will do nothing, mortal man. You will simply accept my gift."

The Sultan stared in astonishment. Was there to be no retribution?

"Well, that's very handsome of you," he blustered. "Letting bygones be bygones."

The Wise Woman smiled a curious smile. "Yes," she said, "what is done is done. It is no use crying over spilt milk."

As she spoke she moved towards the child, taking her place at the foot of the cradle.

The Sultan preened and stroked his beard. He could hardly contain his impatience. At last, perhaps, he would get what he hoped for.

"Now," said the Wise Woman, as she laid her hand upon the child and fixed the Sultan with her eye. "Here is the gift I give your daughter":

"She'll have her beauty, peace and joy
For fifteen years without alloy.
But that's the end. A spindle dart
Will pierce her finger, and your heart.
Oh, red the blood and white the bed,
And there's your darling daughter—DEAD!"

And with a laugh that shook the pillars of the chamber and chilled the marrow of all who heard it, she swept her violet robes about her, raised her silver hand in salute and disappeared through the ceiling.

With a shriek, the Sultana fled to the cradle. "Oh, my darling, my dear, my love!"

"Alas, alas!" the Sultan cried. "Such a woeful punishment for such a little slip! No, do not comfort me," he sobbed, as the twelfth fairy, swirling forward, put her hand on his shoulder.

"Good mortal," she smiled at him. "Do not grieve. I still have my gift to bestow, remember!"

"But what's the good of a gift, dear madam, if there's no princess to give it to?"

"It is true," said the Twelfth Wise Woman calmly, "that I cannot unwind my sister's spell. But there are many cards in the pack and I can alter it. So here is the gift I give your daughter. Fairies and mortals, mark it well":

"For fifteen years without alloy
She shall indeed have peace and joy,
And then fall, not to death, but sleep,
Silent, still and fathoms deep,
And no sun rise this house upon
Until a hundred years are gone."

"Allah be praised!" the Sultana cried, snatching her child from the cradle.

"The Princess is saved!" the guests exclaimed, embracing each other for joy.

"Oh, queen of fairies!" the Sultan cried as the Twelfth Wise Woman beckoned the others.

"Come, sisters, the hour grows late. We may not tarry beyond midnight. Farewell, mortals, and mortal child. Away, away, away!"

And with each *away* the wise ladies, colour by colour, like a fading rainbow, dissolved into the air.

The Sultan stood gazing, like a man in a dream, at the nothingness they had left. "Here one moment and gone the next and what have we got to show for it? I meant no harm. As men go, I'm a simple man. All I wanted was a pleasant party, a little family celebration and look at the plight we're in! The Princess Rose is to prick her finger. What did the Wicked Fairy say—a sharp knife, Bouraba?"

"A spindle, High and Mightiness!" Bouraba heaved a sigh.

"Very well, we shall have no spindles. See to it, Vizier! All spindles must be banished from the kingdom. If, within three days, any person is found with a spindle in his possession, I shall cut off his head myself."

The Vizier shuddered and gave his orders and the news ran from mouth to mouth as fire runs from tree to tree.

The old women who herded the sheep, spinning the fleecy thread as they went, clapped their hands to their lips. "What will become of us now?" they cried. "If we do not spin the wool of our sheep what shall we bring to the marketplace to exchange for meat and grain?"

"And what of us?" the weavers asked. "Without wool our looms will be idle."

"And what of us?" the merchants echoed. "Where shall we get our profits?"

"And what of us?" the grandees cried. "We shall be cold without woolen cloaks."

"Is it not strange," said the philosophers, "that so much should be built upon so little; that the organisation of a whole country should depend upon a small piece of carven wood with a metal hook at its end?"

"Alack and alas and farewell spindle!" was the cry throughout the land. The edict was held to be harsh and bitter but everyone bowed before it. No one, however miserable, is anxious to have his head cut off. News came in from all quarters that the spindles had been destroyed.

"Good!" said the Sultan, rubbing his hands. "Since there are now no spindles it stands to reason that my daughter will not find one. And if she does not find a spindle she will not prick her finger. And if she does not prick her finger she will not fall asleep. It is all a question of logic, merely. By this ruse—and I say it without any sense of personal vanity—the Wicked Fairy will be defeated."

How little he knew!

And so the little Princess grew and in such beauty that people would hide their eyes from it for fear of being dazzled.

And as she flourished, so did the country, in spite of the lack of spindles. The old women, having no spinning to do, fell to fashioning flutes of wood or bone. These they took to the market, playing all manner of tunes upon them, and listeners would be so enraptured that each would want to flute for himself. Thus body and soul were kept together.

As for the merchants, they fared as the rich always fare, which is to say well. They sent out stately caravans to bring back woollen cloth from the west, not to mention silk from the east, furs and skins from the far north and linen flax from the south. Thus they grew still richer. And since she was, as it were, the reason for all this well-being, none of them neglected to bring a share of their merchandise to the Princess Rose—a roll of silk for her long trousers, fur slippers for her feet, a linen nightgown, a damask cloak.

For the child, unlike the usual run of princesses—who come and go without making any more stir than a falling pin—was the inner life of the land, the lifeblood of the general vein, the hope of everyone. The people were part of one sentient body of which she was the heart.

Yet for all this she was not puffed-up. The Wise Women had seen to that. Their gifts began to unfold in her as a flower unfolds from its bud. Lovely, healthy, sweet-tempered, joyful, she went upon her childish way, friendly to man and beast. If she had met a tiger, it would have nodded courteously and gone about its business. Her father's camels bowed to her; and this, if you know anything about camels, was a feather in her cap. Cobras would lie in the sun beside her, keeping their hoods neatly folded and their forked tongues tucked away in their mouths.

And ever at her side, as though her body cast a human shadow, was the dark slave, Bouraba. By day she was always in his eye and at night he slept at the door of her chamber. He was not, however, her only playmate. As she grew older she was joined by three other constant companions—a cat that trod always at her heels, a dove that took its seat on her shoulder and a lizard that darted around her feet or skimmed the paths before her.

"This house is becoming a menagerie," the Sultan would say in protest. "I do not care to find a lizard sitting on my soup plate. And I never liked pigeons—except in a pie. As for the cat, its habit of looking at me as though it knew everything and I nothing is distinctly unnerving. Under other circumstances I would simply chop off its head."

He did nothing of the kind, however. If he grumbled it was for the sake of appearances and not to be thought sentimental.

As for the Sultana, nothing that the Princess did could be other than perfect in her eyes. If ever there was a happy woman, it was the Sultana. It never occurred to her to remember that day inevitably turns into night and that what is up must at last come down. If any such thought had crossed her mind she would have contentedly told herself, "My husband is a clever man, as resourceful as he is handsome. If anything should ever happen he will be able to deal with it."

How little she knew!

Happy lives pass swiftly and the Princess Rose grew from child to damsel, almost, it seemed, from one day to the next. And at length the time of maidens was upon her. The lovely bud became lovelier flower and she seemed to waver in the wind, hardly knowing where she was, bending this way and that. Sometimes she would sigh for no reason at all and, if she smiled or became thoughtful, again it would be for no reason. One day it would seem that her father's house, with its great courtyards and soaring domes, was all too small to contain her. And the next she would swing to the opposite pole and wish that the palace would close in and hem her into so small a space that by stretching a hand in any direction she would come upon a wall.

Thus swung between one thing and another, dipping and swaying like a flag in the breeze, she came to her fifteenth birthday.

A feast was made ready in the palace kitchens and as the day brightened, all those who had come to celebrate gathered in the courtyards to prepare for the evening entertainment. Dancers rehearsed their steps and gestures; jugglers practised their legerdemain. Storytellers sought shady corners muttering over to themselves the tales they would tell at dusk. Men from the desert groomed their camels; men from the mountains fingered their bagpipes to keep them in tune for the night.

The whole scene—the palace in the midst of the embroidered tents and the fields of coloured carpets—was elegant and elaborate. The very air tingled with anticipation. Everyone sensed—it was obvious—that some great event was brewing. "It must be the coming festivity," they whispered vibrantly to each other, "that makes us tremble and hold our breath."

How little they knew!

"Come, my dear," the Sultan said, taking the Sultana by the hand. "Let us go among the people and see that all things are properly disposed. Bouraba, attend upon us!"

So they walked among the bowing throng, over the flowery fields of carpets, and in and out of the tents. Bouraba dawdled at their heels, flinging back glances at the palace like an anxious uneasy dog. Never, since her birth, had he been farther than an arm's length from the Princess and the thought of this tugged at his heart.

"What if she needs me?" he asked himself. And he longed to be standing outside her door awaiting her least command.

But if she had a need of him, the Princess Rose was unaware of it. For now behind that same door she was being robed by her handmaidens. She submitted gravely to their ministrations but her thoughts were far from her fine array and all the preparations. There was a knocking in her mind but where it came from she did not know. Something deep within her said that here she had come to an ending. And as her toilet was completed she rose—with the handmaidens gasping at the sight she made—and left her childhood room.

At once the cat leapt up from its cushion, the dove came swiftly to her shoulder, and the lizard ran round and round her feet.

So accompanied, and as if in a dream, she wandered through the spacious palace, through council halls and rooms of state, past fountains and shady arbours and courtyards that opened one from another.

For the first time in her life she was alone, accompanied by no human guide, no loving parent nigh, no kind, dark, watchful friend. Four legs ran at her either side and two legs rode on her shoulder as she wandered in her maze of maidenhood. What she sought for she did not know. She only knew that not to find it would leave her incomplete.

At last she came by way of a courtyard she

had never seen to the foot of a tower that was equally unknown. And yet it seemed that all her life she had been coming towards it. She began to climb the winding stair, feeling herself drawn up through the tower as a fish is drawn up by the angler's line.

As she came to the edge of the last landing, she heard the sound of music. Somebody close at hand was singing. It sounded like a lullaby, a rising and falling melody with the same phrase repeated again and again. She trembled—was it with fear or joy?—as she tried the handle of a small dark door. Nothing moved. Her fingers felt for the rusted key that grated harshly as she turned it. The door opened with a long slow creak, disclosing a little dark room, empty, it seemed, of all but cobwebs. But the music now was closer at hand, the song repeating without a waver its wheedling lullaby. And gradually, as her eyes became accustomed to the gloom, the Princess descried a curious figure with a cloak drawn over its head. This apparition was seated on a low divan, rocking from side to side. Its hands, making quick and rhythmic movements, glittered and shone in the darkness and the song that came from beneath the cloak seemed to set the cobwebs swaying.

The Princess gazed in astonishment.

"But the door was locked—on the outside! How did you get in?"

The singing ceased. The figure glanced sideways from under its hood as the hands went steadily on with their work, flashing along a woollen thread from which hung a piece of twisting wood.

"There are more ways than one of entering a room," said a soft, alluring voice. "Perhaps," a musical laugh rang out, "I came in through the key-hole."

The Princess took the phrase as a jest.

"I do not think that could be," she said. "And yet—" Her face resumed its dreamy look. "I feel there is something strange here that I do not understand."

"Strange? An old woman sitting all alone with only a mouse for a friend?"

A mouse ran out from the folds of the cloak and the fur of the Princess's cat stiffened.

"I do not think you are old," said the Princess. "Though I cannot see beneath your hood.

Your voice is not the voice of age but of someone far away and timeless. I heard your singing and it drew me to you."

"That was my intention," said the voice. "When one has a rendezvous with fate one cannot fail to keep it." The bright hands glittered along the wool till the Princess's eyes were dazzled.

"What is that you are doing?" she asked.

"I am spinning," the silky voice replied. "Spinning a thread upon a spindle."

"And what will you weave from the thread—a gown?"

"A gown—or perhaps a shroud."

"It is an interesting device," said the Princess Rose. "I have never seen a spindle before. I wonder why that is."

"Perhaps because your father, child, thinks he is cleverer than he is. Wit is no substitute for wisdom."

The Princess moved forward like one in a trance. "Please may I try it—just for once?"

"Just once, my girl. It only needs once. One twist of the thread. One turn of the hand."

The stranger raised the swinging thread. The Princess bent and took it. And as she tried to set it turning, her hand slipped down along its length and met the spindle's spike.

Out sprang the blood in a red fountain. "Oh, oh," she cried. "I've pricked my finger!"

And at that moment, the cat leapt at the scurrying mouse, the dove went clapping up to the rafters, and the lizard darted across the floor.

"It bleeds," cried the Princess in a daze. "Where are my maids and bodyservants. My mother, father, Bouraba—where? Oh, stranger, help me! What is the matter? I suddenly feel so very sleepy." She yawned behind her bleeding hand and turning about like one in a trance she moved towards the cushions. "I am falling—save me!—into a dream. Goodnight. Goodnight. Goodnight." And with a sigh, she fell in one subsiding movement, stretched herself upon the divan, and was silent.

The cat dropped like a stone to the floor. The dove's head sank upon its breast, the lizard lay still, like a scribble on marble.

"So—so!" A long throaty triumphant laugh came from the folds of the dark cloak as the Thirteenth Wise Woman, moving like waves of violet water, bent over the sleeping girl.

"Did no one warn you, foolish child, to think before you ask? One touch you wanted. One touch was enough and now the charm's complete. Goodnight, Princess, a long goodnight. A very long goodnight."

And with another exultant laugh, she drew her airy robes about her and swept, like a wisp of purple smoke, straight out through the keyhole.

Now let us see what was happening in the rest of the palace. Curious as it may seem, the fact is that at the moment when the prick of the spindle drew blood from the Princess's finger, the life of the palace came to a complete standstill. The moment she fell asleep, the general eye closed.

The Sultan and the Sultana, returning from their promenade, were entering the Council Chamber when they began to yawn.

"I am afraid," said the Sultana, drowsily, "that I am a little overtired. A rest—huh, huh—will do me good." She turned and was about to depart when she gracefully sank beside the throne, bowed her head on the Sultan's footstool, and there fell fast asleep.

The Sultan was about to remind her to remember her dignity when he, too, collapsed. "Bouraba," he murmured. "Fetch me a cushion. I must sleep now. Wake me in time for the party."

But Bouraba was beyond both cushions and parties. In spite of himself his eyes were closing. In a mighty effort to obey, he fell across his master's knees and at once began to snore.

The same thing happened to everyone else. The Vizier, in the act of writing a death warrant, fell asleep with his cheek on his quill pen. The bowmen, playing at chance in the courtyard, plunged into a deep stupour and their dice hung in the air.

Outside, among the embroidered tents, the storytellers' heads were nodding; acrobats slept in midsomersault; the musicians were all in a deep trance; the camels seemed turned to stone. Even the smoke from the chimneys stood upright and solid in the air. And the fountains froze, not to ice but stillness, with never a drop of water falling.

Hushed and motionless lay the palace. And from the centre where the Princess was, there spread like water round a stone ring upon ring of sleep.

Did I say motionless? I was wrong.

Something moved swiftly through the house. Someone not subject to mortal law swept like a cloud of indigo among the fallen figures.

"Sleep, mortals," said the Twelfth Wise Woman, flashing her golden hands.

"Sleep, mortals, sleep the time away,
And time shall sleep so that you may
No wrinkle know, nor head of grey.
Then, if you wake well, you will say
A hundred years were but a day,
A hundred years were but a day."

And as she spoke she became air—she was and she was not. The sun went out, the wind fell, the flags hung motionless on the flagpoles. Darkness fell on the sleeping palace and round it rose, in the wink of an eye, an enclosing hedge of thorn. No one could have guessed that behind those battlements of briar there lay a living rose.

That is how it all happened. And for a time it was a matter for wonder. The firesides of every hut and mansion were busy with the news. What could it mean? Why had it happened? And how would it all work out?

And then, of course, it was forgotten—except for an old wife here and there who would tell her grandchildren a strange story of a princess sleeping behind the thorns. And the grandchildren told it to their children till at last it became a fairy tale, something forever true but far. Men came to think of the Princess, not as a person anymore, but as a secret within themselves—a thing they would dearly wish to discover if they could but make the effort.

There was one family, however, that preserved the story in all its detail. Poor people they were, without book learning and able, perhaps for that very reason, to remember things exactly. These were the woodcutters who lived beside the hedge.

It had so happened that in the days when the Princess was a child, the woodcutter's son had caught a moment's glimpse of her as she played under a cypress tree. And the effect she made upon him was such that he took a seed of the cypress tree and planted it in his father's garden to remind him of her for evermore. Later, when he himself became a father, he told his son of how he had seen the Princess Rose and all that ultimately befell. This son, in turn, told *his* son and thus it was that the woodcutters became, so to speak, the guardians of the story and also of the great dark hedge. Father to son, they told the tale and hung their jerkins on the spines of the wall and warned any would-be hero of the dangers of trying to pass within it.

For, of course, in every generation, some of the children who had heard the story grew up into brave young men who were ready to put their courage to the test, stake their lives for the unknown maiden, and make an assault on the hedge.

But all to no avail. No sword prevailed against the thorn. The bristling wall turned back all weapons and the briars stretched out their barbed hands and clasped the heroes to them. There they would struggle, crying aloud for help and pity, dying at last in the pronged arms, their bodies clipped to the boughs, like fruit.

And the passers-by, seeing the corpses on the hedge, would note the costly price of valour and congratulate themselves that they had not been similarly foolhardy. "It is better," they told themselves, "to sleep in bed with a sure wife, however homely, than to lose one's life for a mythical mistress, however fine and fair." And for all one knows, they were right.

What is time? We live in it but never see it. From here to there it carries us but we neither taste, hear, smell, nor touch it. How, then, can we describe its passage? By watching something grow, perhaps, or watching something fade.

Think of the woodcutter's cypress seed. After a season in the earth it sends up a small white thread. Then the sun gets to work on it and changes the white to green. "Look, it has sprouted!" cries the woodcutter's son. And, since cypress trees are long in growing, he grows old watching the sprout become a sapling. And watching the sapling become a

tree his son, too, grows old. Generation after generation, the woodcutters watch the tree thicken and stretch its branches upwards. Till at last it attains its full height and shows us the shape of time.

Yearly the tree's shadow lengthened and there came a day when it reached the hedge. And at the same moment the charm that had been set in motion by the Wicked Fairy completed its full circle.

The day was heavy and slow to move. A mottle of clouds hung over the sun. Men in their pointed turned-up slippers dragged one foot after another. "What can be the matter?" they asked each other. "We seem to be waiting for something." And they longed for the day to come to an end so that what was to be might disclose itself.

At length it was over. The water clocks, filling one bowl from another, drop by drop wore the hours away—noon to sunset, sunset to dark.

The woodcutter, grandson many times removed of the one who had planted the cypress seed, settled himself at the edge of the thorn hedge, with his axe across his knees. Here he would wait, as his ancestors had done before him, to guard and watch and warn.

Meanwhile, by road and desert, field and mountain, a young prince from a distant land was marching to that selfsame spot. And if before him through the night there flowed a cloudy indigo shape with head and foot of flashing gold, he had no notion of it. He strode on all unseeing—looking perhaps within himself, as though he were his own compass and was drawn by his own fate.

The woodcutter stirred at the sound of footsteps.

"Who goes there?" he demanded sharply.

"I am a prince from a far country. I have come to seek the Sleeping Princess."

"Then I beg you, Prince, heed my warning. Turn your steps from this fearful place, lest you suffer the fate of all those who were once the sons of kings."

The woodcutter waved his axe at the hedge where the white bones hung in the branches. Chalky hands, still wearing jewels, gripped at the fronds of briar. Crowned skulls bent, grinning, from the thorns. Tatters of turban, cloak, and slipper, tarnished from their original brightness, waved in the midnight breeze.

"A king of China hangs there," said the woodcutter, "and a prince from the Western Sea; potentates from India; khans from the hills and deserts. Begone while there is time, young lord, lest you, too, leave your bones on the thorn."

"Everyone must die," said the Prince. "I would rather leave my bones here than in any other place."

The woodcutter sighed. "Many a youth has spoken so and yet gone to his death. Besides, Prince, you are all unarmed. No knife, no sword, no spear, no sickle. How will you cut a path through the hedge?"

"I am indeed, all unarmed. But all my life, without ceasing, I have bent my thought to this quest."

"Well, it shall not be said that I failed to warn you. Do as you will and must."

The dead twigs crackled under his feet as the Prince strode towards the hedge.

The woodcutter made one last effort. "Prince, beware!" he said, anxiously—and then stood rooted to the earth, mouth open, hand in air.

For as the Prince drew near the hedge the thorny tendrils broke apart like a skein that is unravelled. The spiky branches loosed their hold, the great trunks leaned away from each other, making an open pathway. And as the Prince stepped through the gap every bough and frond and twig burst into buds and flowers.

A great shine lit the woodcutter's eyes as he realised what had happened.

"He is himself his own weapon. The time must be ripe," he said. And he ran as fast as his legs would go to tell the news to his wife.

"The hundred years are gone!" he shouted, swinging his axe round his head.

"Are gone, are gone!" ticked the water clocks. And everywhere in towns and villages, in desert tents and in mountain caves, men stirred a little in their sleep, knowing that something new had happened.

Meanwhile, the Prince marched through the forest and as he went the boughs broke out in fountains of bloom and all that had been knotted and tied was loosened and set free. Every barbed and spreading briar, locked to another in a long embrace, gave up its thorny partner and parted to let him pass. As the last branch fell away he stepped out of the hedge's shadow and beheld the sleeping palace.

Veils of dust hung upon the briars, the dust of years littered the thorn forest, but the palace lay there all untouched by earth mould or the mould of time.

The first dawn for a hundred years was breaking as the Prince picked his way among the sleepers. It shone on coloured tents and carpets, on plump cheeks and glossy hair, all fresh and all unfaded.

Ducking his head under the jugglers' hoops which were still hanging in the air, the Prince skirted the acrobats, asleep with their legs over their heads; hurried past nodding storytellers and leapt over the snoring camels. In the portico he passed the guards, all sprawling against the pillars. And at last he came to the Council Chamber.

Before the throne the Prince paused, folded his hands together and bowed. For though the Sultan, lolling sideways among his cushions was all unaware of his visitor, nevertheless he was a king. And kings, as the Prince well knew, are entitled to obeisance.

But such courtesies were, for the Prince, merely a matter of form. As he bowed, his eyes swept round the hall, searching its every corner. There lay Bouraba on the Sultan's knees; the Sultana, fine as a fine painting, asleep with her cheek upon the footstool and her maidens all about her. But the Prince's gaze did not linger. Something nearer than his inmost pulse told him that she whom he had so long sought was not within the chamber. He pushed aside an embroidered curtain and continued on his way.

For just as the Princess Rose, a hundred years ago, had been drawn by the magnet of her fate, so she herself became the magnet that drew the Prince to his. Steadfast as the compass needle that ever points to the north he moved through chamber and corridor, noting everything he passed but lingering not a moment.

As he passed through it, the palace, as though it were a single body, seemed to rise and fall with the sleeping breaths. And the courtyards rang with his living footsteps as he passed the moveless fountains.

At last, drawn by an unseen thread, he came to the foot of the tower. He glanced upwards and without a moment's hesitation set his foot on the winding stair. The blue gleam that heralds sunrise shone through the narrow windows and he moved alternately through light and shadow as he took the stairs three at a stretch and came to the upper landing.

And there, for the first time, he paused, as though to gather in himself an even, easy flow of breath and all his lifelong purpose. Then he gently opened the creaking door and entered the little room.

There lay the Princess, hand to cheek, and at this sight the heart of the Prince lost one beat in its fearful joy. He knew himself to be at the centre of the world and that, in him, all men stood there, gazing at their hearts' desire— or perhaps their inmost selves. He trembled— aghast at his own daring. A lesser man would perhaps have fled but not for nothing had he spent his life preparing for this moment. The coward tremour passed away and his courage came flowing back. Silently, he vowed to serve the accomplishment as he had served the quest. Then he took a stride towards the divan and bent to kiss the Princess.

She drew a deep shuddering breath, opened her eyes, and smiled.

"I have been dreaming about you," she said, simply. For indeed, what else had been her pre-occupation all these sleeping years? "And now," she yawned behind her hand, "now my dream has come true."

Silently he kissed her again and together they plumbed all height, all depth, and rose up strongly to the surface, back to the shores of time.

At the same moment the sun rose and spread like a fan across the house it had not looked on for a hundred years. An awakening sigh, rising as from a single throat, stirred throughout the palace. Fountains trembled and loosed their waters; pennons flapped on the flagpoles. Down in the courtyards the acrobats suddenly leapt to their feet, the jugglers' hoops fell into their hands. Everyone was refreshed and lively as people are who have slept well.

And destiny resumed its course. The Vizier woke and signed his paper. The cook at long last struck the kitchen boy, and the kitchen maid, without even a yawn, plucked out another feather. The die in the portico fell from the air and the bowmen woke and bent above it and found it had turned up a six.

In the Council Chamber the Sultan grunted, flexing his arms as men do when they first wake in the morning. Then he opened his eyes and looked about him.

The first thing he saw was the Sultana, who, gathering her filmy veil about her, was rising from the floor.

"My dear," he said, with a hint of sternness— for he was a great stickler for the proprieties. "If you had to fall asleep in the daytime, would it not have been more appropriate to do so in your retiring chamber and not, like any hand-maiden, stretched out upon the carpet?"

"It would, indeed," she agreed gently, for she knew better than to make a molehill out of what her husband considered a mountain. "But something came over me like a cloud and I seemed to fade away. You yawn and sigh yourself, my lord. Is it not possible that you, too, may have slept a little?"

"Oh, a second, perhaps. Just forty winks. One so burdened with cares of state may nod from time to time." The Sultan's eyes were closing again.

"And Bouraba," said the Sultana, slyly. "Does he have cares of state as well?"

The Sultan opened his eyes and stared. The expression on his face was awesome.

"Bou-ra-ba!" he spluttered furiously. "How dare you fall asleep in my presence? And what is more, upon my knee—the knee of one whose cousin's cousin is descended from the Prophet! Down, dog, and let me strike off your head."

"Oh, dear, oh dear, what is amiss?" The handmaidens, waking from their sleep, twittered like frightened birds.

"Allah, defend me!" cried Bouraba, waking from sleep with a loud groan, and prostrating himself before the throne.

The Sultan snatched the sword from his thigh and was just about to swing it downwards when the Sultana put out her hand.

The Sultan, she knew, was hasty-tempered. She also had good reason to know that his bark was worse than his bite. If he beheaded his slave today, he would rue the act tomorrow.

"Would it not be better," she suggested, "to put it off till later? Let him assist at the birthday feast and, if you are still of the same mind, you can kill him when it is over."

"Birthday? What birthday?" the Sultan demanded, putting a hand to his brow. "Oh, now, I remember. My daughter is fifteen today and we are celebrating. All right, I'll wait until tomorrow. I shall not be so busy then. Stand up, Bouraba! Cease this foolish groaning. Go to the Princess Rose's apartments, remind her that the hour grows late and bid her join us here."

Bouraba staggered to his feet, took a step towards the door, and fell to his knees again.

"Get up!" said the Sultan, testily. "How dare you kneel when I bid you rise. Stop grovelling, Bouraba, do, and hurry to fetch my daughter."

"I am here!" said a familiar voice, as everyone turned to the doorway.

A cry of wonder broke from them all, from ladies-in-waiting, courtiers, guards as they made their deep salaams. For it seemed, if such a thing could be, that the Princess was lovelier than ever. She stood and shone in her own light and dazzled everyone.

"Oh!" the Sultana murmured raptly, putting her hand before her eyes.

But the Sultan, though he, too, sensed his child's new beauty, was determined not to show it.

"Ah, there you are," he said, airily. "And, really, about time, too. May I remind you that it is not becoming in a princess to be late for any event, particularly a birthday party. Do not let it occur—" he was about to say "again" when his eye fell upon the handsome figure that was standing behind his daughter.

"But who is this?" he demanded, sternly. "What stranger dares to enter my house without addressing himself to me? Come forth, young man, and declare yourself!"

The Prince obeyed, smiling, and so handsome was he, so bright with inward triumph, that it was all the handmaidens could do not to swoon away at the sight of him.

"Do not be angry, Father dear," the Princess pleaded, softly. "He is the son of the King of the Silver Mountain. And he came through the enchanted forest to wake us all from sleep."

"The Silver Mountain!" the Sultan gasped, for he knew that the King of the Silver Mountain was the richest king in the world. "You are indeed a welcome guest. But as for waking us all from sleep—with all due respect, Prince—though I dare say you meant it kindly—we here are like other human beings. We sleep or wake as the case may be, exactly when we wish."

"Not so, dear Father," the Princess murmured, kneeling at the Sultan's side. And then she told the whole story while he, the Sultana and their attendants listened—not, of course, open-mouthed for that would hardly have been compatible with etiquette—but with extreme amazement.

"This is preposterous!" cried the Sultan. "There must be some mistake. I ordered all spindles out of the kingdom. Who would disobey me? This person hidden in a cloak, spinning and singing—ridiculous! And as for sleeping a hundred years, you must have dreamed it, child! You have been taking a little nap, just like your mother and myself and that foolish slave, Bouraba."

The Sultana gazed thoughtfully at her daughter as she put out her hand to her husband.

"A woman wrapped in a violet robe whose hand flashed bright as silver. Who wears such garments, in our acquaintance? Who bears such a hand?"

"The Thirteenth Wise Woman!" The Sultan stared. "But no, it can't be. I merely nodded. And what is this talk of enchanted forests? You will have seen for yourself, Prince, that our land is wild and stony. Few trees take root upon the rock. There are no forests here."

The Prince gestured towards the windows. "If Your Highness would be so gracious—" he said, with a generous sweep of his hand.

The Sultan turned, his eye ready for craggy landscapes and a few sparse cypress trees. But instead of that familiar scene, a strange sight met his eyes.

"A forest of thorns! I can't believe it. No, no, I won't be made a fool of. I shall be a laughing-stock to my neighbours if I listen to taradiddles."

His glance shifted uneasily from the Prince to the forest and back again. He was troubled—

and who can blame him? It is not everyone who can be ready for anything at any moment.

"Besides," he continued, trying to bring the whole matter within the realm of reason. "If we had slept for a hundred years, we should now appear quite different. My wife would be a withered crone, my daughter almost as old and ugly. And I, though I am well-preserved, would be at least a greybeard. And look at us!" He lovingly stroked his fine black beard. "No one can deny that we are in the prime of life. If we slept, then time slept, Prince, and that could never happen."

"And time shall sleep," the Sultana murmured.

"Time shall sleep so that you may
No wrinkle know, nor head of gray."

She nodded wisely to herself, for slowly things were coming back to her.

"What's that? Absurd! A foolish rhyme! And yet—yes, there was another line":

"Then, if you wake well, you will say
A hundred years were but a day."

"That's it! It all comes back to me. The Twelfth Wise Woman waved her hand and after that—nothing. We must have fallen asleep at once. And now, after a hundred years, we indeed have woken well. What an extraordinary event! Everything has come true!" You would never have guessed from the Sultan's manner that not five minutes ago he had spoken of taradiddles.

"Everything," echoed the Princess softly, exchanging with the Prince a look that was like a silent vow.

"Well, Prince," said the Sultan, who now felt himself to be fully in command of the situation. "Let us get down to more serious matters. If my eyes do not deceive me, sir, you wish to marry my daughter."

"Nothing on earth could prevent my doing so." The Prince made a deep salaam.

"Then she is yours!" declared the Sultan. And he rubbed his hands gleefully at the thought of all the gold and silver that would pour into his coffers. "Take her to your own land and when, in due course, she bears a son,

he shall reign here in my stead. Everything works for the best, you see. A prick of the finger was a small price to pay for such an outcome. Really, I need not have worried."

But as to whether he was right about this, I must leave you to judge. It is difficult at any time to know what is small and what is great.

"And remind me, Bouraba," the Sultan continued. "To send an acknowledgment to the Twelfth Wise Woman. For it is to that good lady—not to mention my own sagacity—that we owe our present fortune."

It did not occur to him to remember that had he been truly sagacious he would also have sent an acknowledgment to the Thirteenth Wise Woman. A wise man would have recognised that it was she who, by putting the situation in danger, called forth the rescuing power. Light is light because of the dark and the Sultan should have known it.

He was, however, a busy man with little time for thinking; and soon he was giving orders that the meats baked for the Princess's birthday should furnish forth her wedding feast.

The marriage was celebrated at once—for what was there to wait for?—and those who had gathered to entertain the maiden now paraded their talents before the bride.

And when the last carpet was rolled up, the last song sung, the Princess Rose turned away. She bowed to her parents and received their blessing. Then she took her husband's hand.

And he who had kissed her from sleep to waking, now led her from her childhood world towards the great hedge of thorns and the path he had taken through it.

In silence the parents watched them go till the bowing branches took them in and hid them from all eyes.

"Well, that's that," said the Sultan, grandly. "I've had a long pleasant sleep, I have found my daughter a perfect husband and a rich ally for myself. All is well that ends well, as I have always said."

The Sultana smiled. She could not recollect that he had ever made such a statement. Nor did she feel it a propitious moment to remind him that it was not *he* who had found the Prince. So she said nothing.

At the same time she could not help wondering about all that had happened. And from that day forward, since she now had time and leisure for it, she pondered and dreamed and questioned. And the more she thought about it, the more it seemed that her daughter had stepped, as it were, into another dimension— into, in fact, a fairy tale. And if this were so, she told herself, she would have to look for the meaning. For she knew very well that fairy tales are not as simple as they appear; that the more innocent and candid they seem, the wilier one has to be in one's efforts to find out what they are up to.

So pondering, she would sit under the cypress tree, secretly telling herself the story and hoping that the story at last would tell its secret to her. Who was the maiden, who the Prince, and what the thorny hedge? And then she would tire of all such questions and just sit thinking of nothing, till the Sultan called her back to the world or Bouraba came with the peacock fan, holding it high above her head for fear she should take a sunstroke. . . .

As for the newly wedded pair, they moved along the flower-decked path with the thorn boughs curtseying before them. And ever about them as in a dance, light and shadow flickered and gleamed as the sun dappled the forest. Were there, I wonder, among the sunshafts, bright flashes of another kind—of gold head and silver foot and a dazzle of rainbow shapes? Indeed, I think it very likely. There is no good love without good luck and what more fitting than that the Thirteen Wise Women who had played so potent a part in the story should accompany their mortal nurselings on the first stage of their journey, to bring the fairy tale to a close and fortune to the lovers?

What, *all* of them? do I hear you ask? And I reply, of course! Violet is as necessary to the rainbow as any of the other colours. It is either the beginning or the end, depending how you look at it. At any rate it completes the spectrum.

Thus accompanied, the Prince led the Princess to the edge of the forest. And as they passed through the last green arch the hedge trembled and disappeared. One moment it was standing there and the next moment—nothing. No thorn, no briar, no twig, no seed. Nor was there any further flash of golden head or foot. When a pearl is in safekeeping there is no more need of locks and bars. When the Wise Women have performed one duty they hasten away to another.

The way lay clear ahead now and the lovers walked it hand in hand, bringing what secrets they had learned down to the world of men. And so they came to the villages, to the towns and marketplaces, for it is only in the world of men that it is possible to live happily ever after. There lies the test of every hero and the outcome of his quest. All stories continue and end there and so does this of the Sleeping Beauty.

And the one who last told it is still living, still feels the sunlight and heeds the rain, glory be to Allah!

Turkey

Three Fridays

Here is a jest, a witty story, one of the many that revolve about the Hodja. The word Hodja is the Turkish title for a Moslem priest who is both teacher and judge. He is traditionally kind, human, and so beloved that fun may be poked at him with utter safety. He himself has an impish sense of humor. The imagery of the Orient is reflected in these stories. One of the gifts of the folktale is its indirect revelation of manners, customs, and sense of place. [From Alice Geer Kelsey, *Once the Hodja* (Longmans, 1943).]

There was just one day of each week that worried Nasr-ed-Din Hodja. On six days he was as free as a butterfly. He could talk with his friends in the market place or ride his donkey to a nearby village. He could work in the vineyards or go hunting in the hills. He could lounge in the coffee house or sit in the sun in his own courtyard. There was nothing to hurry him to be at a certain place at a certain time to do a certain thing.

But Friday was different. It was much different. That was the day when all good Mohammedans went to their mosques. Because Nasr-ed-Din Hodja, years before, had attended the school for priests, he was expected each Friday to mount the pulpit of the mosque at a certain time and preach a sermon. That was all very well when he had something to say, but there were many Fridays when his mind was as empty as that of his own little gray donkey. It was one thing to swap stories with the men in the coffee house and quite another to stand alone in the high pulpit and talk to a mosque full of people. The men, each squatting on his own prayer rug on the floor looked up at him with such solemn faces. Then there was the fluttering in the balcony behind the lattices, which told him that the women were waiting too. Of course, the chanting, which came before the sermon, was not hard because all the men joined in that, bowing till they touched their foreheads to the floor in the Nemaz. But the sermon—that was hard.

One Friday he walked more slowly than ever through the cobblestoned streets of Ak Shehir. He saw the veiled women slipping silently past him on their way to the latticed balcony of the mosque. He saw the men in their best clothes hurrying to the mosque to hear his sermon. But what sermon? He stopped at the mosque door to leave his shoes. He pattered with the other men across the soft thick rugs. But they could squat on the rugs, while he had to climb into the high pulpit.

Perhaps the beauty of the mosque would give him an idea. He looked up at the blues and reds and whites of the intricate tracery on the ceiling, but not a thought came. He looked at the rich yellows and reds of the mosaics on the walls, but there was no help there. He looked at the men's faces staring up at him. He heard the tittering in the latticed balcony where the veiled women sat. He must say something.

"Oh, people of Ak Shehir!" He leaned on the pulpit and eyed them squarely. "Do you know what I am about to say to you?"

"No!" boomed from the rugs where the men squatted.

"No!" floated down in soft whispers from the latticed balcony, whispers not meant for any ears beyond the balcony.

"You do not know?" said Nasr-ed-Din Hodja, shaking his head and looking from one face to another. "You are sure you do not know? Then what use would it be to talk to people who know nothing at all about this important subject. My words would be wasted on such ignorant people."

With that, the Hodja turned and climbed slowly down the pulpit steps. His eyes lowered, he walked with injured dignity through the crowds of men. He slipped on his shoes at the mosque door, and was out in the sunshine—free until next Friday.

That day came all too soon. The Hodja mingled with the crowds going to the mosque. His coarse, home-knit stockings pattered across the deep colorful rugs. He climbed the steps to the high pulpit. He looked down at the sea of solemn faces. He heard the rustling behind the lattices of the balcony. He had hoped that this week he could think of a sermon, but the carvings of the doorway did not help him, nor the embroidered hangings of the pulpit, nor the pigeons fluttering and cooing at the window. Still, he must say something.

"Oh, people of Ak Shehir!" intoned the Hodja, gesturing with both hands. "Do you know what I am about to say to you?"

"Yes," boomed the men who remembered what happened when they said "No" last week.

"Yes," echoed in soft whispers from the balcony.

"You know what I am going to say?" said the Hodja, shrugging first one shoulder and then the other. "You are sure you know what I am going to say? Then I need not say it. It would be a useless waste of my golden words if I told you something that you already knew."

The Hodja turned and again climbed down the pulpit steps. He picked his way with unhurried dignity among the men. He scuffed into his shoes and escaped into the sunshine. Another free week was ahead of him.

But the best of weeks end. The third Friday found him once more climbing the pulpit steps, with not a word worth saying in that solemn mosque. The ancient Arabic writing on the bright ceiling had no help for him. The flickering candles in the large round chandelier winked at him but said nothing. Even the big

Koran in front of him might have had blank pages instead of its fine Arabic words and its illuminated borders. Men's faces looked up at him expectantly. Bright eyes peered through the lattices of the women's balcony. The time had come again when he must speak.

"Oh, people of Ak Shehir!" declaimed the Hodja as he groped helplessly for an idea. "Do you know what I am about to say to you?"

"No," came from those who were thinking of the last Friday.

"Yes," came from those who were thinking of the Friday before that.

"Some of you know and some of you do not know!" The Hodja rubbed his hands together and beamed down at the men. "How very fine! Now let those who know tell those who do not know!"

The Hodja was humming to himself as he came down from the pulpit, two steps at a time. He nodded and smiled as he threaded his way through the men. Some thought he bowed and smiled toward the latticed balcony, but others said the good Hodja would not have made so bold. He picked his own worn shoes from the rows and rows by the mosque door. The sunshine was warm and friendly. The birds were singing and there was the fragrance of hawthorn blossoms in the air.

The Hodja had not a worry in the world— not till another Friday should come around.

Australia

Dinewan the Emu and Goomble-gubbon the Turkey

K. Langloh Parker, an Australian-born Englishwoman, devoted her life to collecting aboriginal folktales as she heard them from the lips of the tribal storytellers. Her first volume of *Australian Legendary Tales* was published in London in 1896. It is interesting to note that Andrew Lang wrote an enthusiastic introduction to the book. H. Drake-Brockman has chosen what he considers the most interesting of the stories from five volumes of the author's tales. The stories possess a poetic directness and simplicity. They also show a shrewd understanding of basic be-

havior and motive, which makes them delightful and amusing to read. As Mr. Drake-Brockman states in his introduction, "It would be difficult to find a better concise comment on social snobbery and maternal vanity than in *Dinewan the Emu and Goomble-gubbon the Turkey*. The idea of family limitation for economic reasons, though savage in application, suggests how old in human reckoning such cherished 'modern' thought may be!" [From K. Langloh Parker, *Australian Legendary Tales,* sel. and ed. H. Drake-Brockman (Viking, 1966).]

Dinewan the emu, being the largest bird, was acknowledged as king by the other birds. The Goomble-gubbons, the turkeys, were jealous of the Dinewans. Particularly was the Goomble-gubbon mother jealous of the Dinewan mother. She would watch with envy the high flight of the Dinewans, and their swift running. And she always fancied that the Dinewan mother flaunted her superiority in her face, for whenever Dinewan alighted near Goomble-gubbon after a long, high flight, she would flap her big wings and begin booing in her pride, not the loud booing of the male bird but a little, triumphant, satisfied booing noise of her own, which never failed to irritate Goomble-gubbon when she heard it.

Goomble-gubbon used to wonder how she could put an end to Dinewan's supremacy. She decided that she would be able to do so only by injuring her wings and checking her power of flight. But the question that troubled her was how to gain this end. She knew she would gain nothing by having a quarrel with Dinewan and fighting her, for no Goomble-gubbon would stand any chance against a Dinewan. There was evidently nothing to be gained by an open fight. She would have to gain her end by cunning.

One day, when Goomble-gubbon saw Dinewan in the distance coming toward her, she squatted down and drew in her wings in such a way as to look as if she had none.

After Dinewan had been talking to her for some time, Goomble-gubbon said, "Why do you not imitate me and do without wings? Every bird flies. The Dinewans, to be the king of birds, should do without wings. When all the birds see that I can do without wings, they will think I am the cleverest bird and they will make a Goomble-gubbon king."

"But you have wings," said Dinewan.

"No, I have no wings."

And indeed she looked as if her words were true, so well were her wings hidden as she squatted in the grass.

Dinewan went away after a while and thought much of what she had heard. She talked it all over with her mate, who was as disturbed as she was. They made up their minds that it would never do to let the Goomble-gubbons reign in their stead, even if they had to lose their wings to save their kingship.

At length they decided to sacrifice their wings. The Dinewan mother showed the example by persuading her mate to cut off hers with a kumbu, or stone tomahawk, and then she did the same to his.

As soon as the operations were over the Dinewan mother lost no time in letting Goomble-gubbon know what they had done. She ran swiftly down to the plain where she had left Goomble-gubbon, and finding her still squatting there, she said, "See, I have followed your example. I have now no wings. They are cut off."

"Ha! ha! ha!" laughed Goomble-gubbon, jumping up and dancing around with joy at the success of her plot. As she danced around she spread out her wings, flapped them and said, "I have taken you in, old stumpy wings. I have my wings yet. You are fine birds, you Dinewans, to be chosen kings, when you are so easily taken in. Ha! ha! ha!"

And laughing derisively, Goomble-gubbon flapped her wings right in front of Dinewan, who rushed toward her to punish her treachery. But Goomble-gubbon flew away, and, alas, the now wingless Dinewan could not follow her.

Brooding over her wrongs, Dinewan walked away, vowing she would be revenged. But how? That was the question that she and her mate failed to answer for some time.

At length the Dinewan mother thought of a plan and prepared at once to execute it.

She hid all her young Dinewans but two under a big saltbush. Then she walked off to Goomble-gubbon's plain with the two young ones following her. As she walked off the morilla, or pebbly ridge, where her home was, onto the plain, she saw Goomble-gubbon out feeding with her twelve young ones.

After exchanging a few remarks in a friendly manner, with Goomble-gubbon, she said to her, "Why do you not imitate me and have only two children? Twelve are too many to feed. If you keep so many they will never grow to be big birds like the Dinewans. The food that would make big birds of two would only starve twelve."

Goomble-gubbon said nothing, but she thought it might be so. It was impossible to deny that the young Dinewans were much bigger than the young Goomble-gubbons, and she discontentedly walked away, wondering whether her young ones were smaller than the Dinewans because there were so many more of them. It would be grand, she thought, to grow as big as the Dinewans. But she remembered the trick she had played on Dinewan, and she thought that perhaps she was being fooled in her turn. She looked back to where the Dinewans fed, and as she saw how much bigger the two young ones were than any of hers, once more mad envy of Dinewan possessed her.

She determined not to be outdone. Rather, she would kill all her young ones but two.

She said, "The Dinewans shall not be the king birds of the plains. The Goomble-gubbons shall replace them. They shall grow as big as the Dinewans, and shall keep their wings and fly, which now the Dinewans cannot do."

And straightway Goomble-gubbon killed all her young ones but two.

Then back she came to where the Dinewans were still feeding.

When Dinewan saw her coming and noticed she had only two young ones with her, she called out, "Where are all your young ones?"

Goomble-gubbon answered, "I have killed them, and have only two left. Those will have plenty to eat now, and will soon grow as big as your young ones."

"You cruel mother to kill your children. You greedy mother. Why, I have twelve children and I find food for them all. I would not kill one for anything, not even if by doing so I could get back my wings. There is plenty for all. Look at how the saltbush covers itself with berries to feed my big family. See how the grasshoppers come hopping around, so that we can catch them and fatten on them.

"But you have only two children."

"I have twelve. I will go and bring them to show you."

Dinewan ran off to her saltbush where she had hidden her ten young ones.

Soon she was to be seen coming back—running with her neck stretched forward, her head thrown back with pride and the feathers of her booboo-tella, or tail, swinging as she ran, booing out the while her queer throatnoise, the Dinewan song of joy. The pretty, soft-looking little ones with their striped skins ran beside her, whistling their baby Dinewan note.

When Dinewan reached the place where Goomble-gubbon was, she stopped her booing and said in a solemn tone, "Now you see my words are true. I have twelve young ones, as I said. You can gaze at my loved ones and think of your poor murdered children. And while you do so I will tell you the fate of your descendants forever. By trickery and deceit you lost the Dinewans their wings, and now forevermore, as long as a Dinewan has no wings, so shall a Goomble-gubbon lay only two eggs and have only two young ones. We are quits now. You have your wings and I my children."

And ever since then a Dinewan, or emu, has had no wings, and a Goomble-gubbon, or turkey of the plains, has laid only two eggs in a season.

Canada

The Canoe in the Rapids

Natalie Savage Carlson retells with skill and keen wit the French-Canadian folktales that her great-great uncle, Michel Meloche, told her mother as a child and that her mother in turn told to her. The story given here is a particular favorite and produces many a chuckle. [From Natalie Savage Carlson, *The Talking Cat, and Other Stories of French Canada* (Harper, 1952).]

Once in another time, François Ecrette was an adventurer in the woods. Every winter he went north with Sylvain Gagnon. They trapped foxes, beavers, minks and any furred creature that would step into their traps.

When spring came and the ice in the river melted, the two men would load their furs into a canoe and paddle down the swift current to sell their winter's catch to the trader.

It was one such spring that François and Sylvain headed south with the finest catch that they had ever made. If only they could beat the other trappers to the trading post, they could make a fine bargain.

"A-ah, we will be rich men," said Sylvain, who already could hear the *tintin* of coins in his deep pockets.

"Yes," answered François, "if we get through the Devil's Jaws safely."

Nowhere on any of the rivers of Canada was there such a fearsome place. In the Devil's Jaws, there were waterfalls that roared and whirlpools that spun a boat about like a dry leaf. It was as if the river fell into a panic itself when squeezed into the Devil's Jaws and tried to run away in every direction.

"That's true," said Sylvain, "but you are lucky to have me for a partner. Nowhere in all Canada is there such a skillful boatman as Sylvain Gagnon."

Sylvain drew the cold air in through his nose and puffed out his chest with it.

So François Ecrette felt safe and happy, even though the worst ordeal of the long trip was ahead of them.

They loaded the canoe with their bundles of furs and their provisions. For days they paddled down the river, singing gay songs to pass away the long hours.

One late afternoon they beached their boat on the bank and made for a clearing on the hill. They built a campfire, and François started to roast a young rabbit he had shot. He hung it over the coals by spearing it on a green willow branch.

"We must eat well," said Sylvain, "for we are close to the Devil's Jaws. We will need all our strength for that pull and push."

"But it will soon be dark," François reminded him. "Shouldn't we camp here all night so we can go through the rapids in daylight?"

"Pou, pou," laughed Sylvain, "what a scared

rabbit you are! I can paddle at night as well as by day. I could shoot the Devil's Jaws with my eyes closed and a beaver riding on my paddle."

François rubbed his stubbly chin.

"My faith," he exclaimed, "I am the luckiest man in the world to have you for a partner, Sylvain Gagnon. I don't believe you have fear of anything."

As if to test the truth of this, an angry growl came from behind the bushes. Both men jumped to their feet, François seizing his rifle as he did so. The bushes broke open and a big brown bear came through them. He walked slowly on all fours, shuffling from this paw to that paw, and from that paw to this paw. Straight toward the two trappers he came.

François lifted his rifle to his shoulder and took careful aim. He pulled the trigger. Plink! Nothing happened. There was no bullet in the rifle because it had been used on the rabbit.

The bear gave another angry growl. He rose on his hind legs and walked toward François like a man, shuffling from this paw to that paw.

François dropped the gun and ran for his life. Already Sylvain Gagnon was far ahead of him, his fur coat making him look like a bear that ran too fast to shuffle from this paw to that paw. François made for a big tree, but he didn't have time to climb it as the bear was almost on him. So around the tree he ran. And behind him followed the bear. Round and round and round the tree ran François and the bear. Any little bird looking down from the treetop wouldn't have known whether the bear was chasing François Ecrette or François was chasing the bear. The trapper ran so fast that he was more behind the bear than in front of him. And as the bear ran around the tree, he clawed the air angrily. But his sharp claws only tore the bark from the tree. And if François had anything at all to be thankful for, it was that the ragged shreds flying through the air were bark from the tree and not skin from his back.

Around and around and around went the man and the beast. The bear got dizzy first. He ran slower and slower. Finally he broke away from the tree and went staggering away, first to this side and then to that side. And as he reeled and stumbled, he knocked his head into one tree trunk after another. Bump—bump—bump.

François lost no time in finding another tree to climb, for the tree they had been running around had been stripped of its bark as far up as a bear could reach. As he climbed, he could hear the bump, bump, bump of the bear's head as he stumbled into tree trunks.

Panting and dizzy himself, François settled into a crotch of the tree. Now where was that false friend, Sylvain Gagnon, who had left him to face the bear alone? He called and called but there was no answer. Perhaps the bear had eaten Sylvain. A-tout-tou, what bad luck that would be when there was still the Devil's Jaws ahead! How could he ever get through those treacherous waters without the skillful boatman Sylvain Gagnon?

And how could he get safely from the tree to the boat? Perhaps the bear was waiting for him among the bushes. The sleepy sun soon went to bed and it grew dark. It became colder than ever. François Ecrette's arms and legs were numb.

At last he jerkily lowered himself from the tree. He looked about in every direction, but it was too dark to see anything. He sniffed and sniffed like a bear, for if a bear can smell a man, maybe a man can smell a bear. But all François could smell was the sharp, icy air of early spring. Slowly he made his way down the hill toward the place they had left the canoe.

Then great joy filled the heart of François Ecrette. Although the trees blackened the river, a faint moonlight glimmered through them. Its pale light fell upon a figure hunched in the bow of the canoe with the fur coat pulled up over its ears.

"Sylvain," cried François, "you are safe after all. Why didn't you come back to me?"

But Sylvain must have felt a deep shame, for he only put his head down between his arms and made a sad, apologetic sound.

"Believe me, my friend," said François, "I'm certainly glad you escaped, for we have a terrible ride ahead of us this night. Do you think we better try the rapids after all?"

But his companion resolutely straightened up

and squared his shoulders in the fur coat. François pushed the boat into the stream, leaped aboard and grabbed a paddle. Silently they floated into the current; then the slender canoe headed for the dangers ahead.

"My faith, it is good to have you in this boat with me," cried François. "This current is like a bolt of lightning."

The boat raced faster and faster. Instead of paddling for speed, François had to spend his strength flattening the paddle like a brake. The trees made a dark tunnel of the river course so that François could barely see his companion's stout back.

On, on they went. The frail canoe sped in a zigzag flight like a swallow. François Ecrette's sharp ear caught the distant roar of the rapids.

"Brace yourself, Sylvain," he cried, "for the boat is now in your hands. I will help you as much as I can."

So he plied his paddle from this side to that side and from that side to this side. The river had become like an angry, writhing eel. He heard the waterfall ahead and began paddling like mad so the canoe would shoot straight and true. The least slant of the boat and the churning current would turn it over and over, and swallow them both.

François felt the icy wind and the cold spray on his face as they plunged over the waterfall and bobbed in the whirlpool below. He fought the churning, frothing waters that he could hear more than see. His muscles tightened like iron and the air blew up his lungs.

"My faith, but it's a good thing to have such a boatman as Sylvain Gagnon guiding this canoe," rejoiced François. "In such a current as this, no other man could bring a boat through safely. I will forget the way he deserted me when that big brown bear attacked us."

All danger was not over yet, for the stern of the canoe was sucked into the outer rim of a whirlpool. The lurch of the boat wrenched François Ecrette's back like a blow from a giant hammer. The canoe spun around completely. For fully ten minutes, there was such a battle with the churning waters as François had never known before. Around and around, up and down rocked the canoe, with François fiercely wielding his paddle. If it hadn't been for the

soothing figure in front of him, he would have given up in fright.

Finally the canoe straightened out and leaped straight ahead. The roar of the rapids grew fainter. François let his paddle drag and relaxed.

"My faith," he gasped. "I thought that was the last of us for sure. You have saved us both, Sylvain Gagnon. No boatman in all Canada but you could have gotten us out of that Devil's trap."

But his modest companion only shrugged his shoulders and humped lower into the bow.

Then because François was worn out from his paddling, he decided to take a little nap. With no other partner but Sylvain would he have dared doze off. But Sylvain had proved his mettle in getting them through the rapids, and the waters ahead were slow and peaceful. So François rested his paddle, closed his eyes and fell into a deep sleep.

When he awoke, it was morning. The sun had chased the shadows out from under the trees, and the river sparkled in the friendliest kind of way.

François rubbed the sleep out of his eyes.

"Ah, Sylvain," he yawned, "what a night we had in the rapids. If it hadn't been for you— a-tou-tou-tou-tou!"

For François Ecrette's partner in the canoe was not Sylvain Gagnon, the great boatman, but the big brown bear of the clearing!

François jumped up and gave a bloodcurdling shriek. The bear slowly turned around and looked at him. He shook his great furry head as if to shake his brains back into their right place after they had been knocked apart by the tree trunks. He gave a low threatening growl.

François didn't wait any longer. He dived into the river and furiously swam through the icy water. After what seemed a sinner's lifetime, he reached the frosty shore. When he looked back at the river, he had a last glance of the canoe, full of furs, disappearing among the trees with the big brown bear standing in the bow.

Now this was a fine how-does-it-make of trouble. Here was François all alone in the wilderness without Sylvain, furs, provisions or even a dry match.

Luckily the trading post couldn't be too far

away now. François gathered dry wood and started a fire in the Indian way, by rubbing two sticks together. Then he stood as close to the fire as he could, to dry out his clothes. He scorched and steamed like the uneaten rabbit back on the sharp stick in the clearing.

At last he was dry enough to brave the cold walk down the river bank. He set out slowly. The branches scratched his hands and face. His boots sloshed and squashed through the slush of early spring.

It was late afternoon by the time he reached the trader's village. Everyone seemed surprised to see him alive.

"Your canoe was found caught in a log jam below here, with bear tracks on the shore," said the trader. "We thought a bear had carried you off."

"But the furs," cried François. "What happened to them? Were they lost?"

"They are all safe," said the trader. "Your friend Sylvain Gagnon arrived only a little while ago. He helped me check through them."

Then a familiar face appeared in the crowd.

"François, my good friend," cried Sylvain. "I got a ride back with a party of Indians. But how did you ever get the canoe through the rapids all by yourself?"

"Sylvain, my false friend," retorted the trapper, "I was not alone. The big brown bear who chased me in the clearing was with me."

Then François Ecrette shivered and shook in a way that had nothing to do with the cold spring afternoon or his damp clothing.

So all turned out well for François Ecrette in the end. But he never went on any more trapping trips with Sylvain Gagnon. You see, my friends, one who turns into a big brown bear when you need him most is not a true friend.

The Golden Phoenix

This French Canadian variant of a common European tale recounts the adventures of Petit Jean, the French Canadian equivalent of Jack or Boots, the third and youngest son. It was collected by Marius Barbeau from an old riverman who called it "Le Grand Sultan." These Arabian-European roots have been pol-ished in retelling by Michael Hornyansky. [From Marius Barbeau, *The Golden Phoenix and Other French-Canadian Fairy Tales*, retold by Michael Hornyansky (Oxford University Press, 1958).]

There was once a King renowned for his wisdom. And how did he come to be so wise? Well, in his garden there grew a magic tree; and every night that tree bore one silver apple—the apple of wisdom. Each morning the King would take it from the tree and eat it while the trumpets blew. As a result he governed wisely and well, and all his people lived happily.

Then a strange thing happened. One morning, when the King came to pick the apple, it was gone. No one saw it go; and no one admitted to taking it.

"Someone has stolen the silver apple," said the King grimly. The next night he set his royal guards about the tree to keep watch.

But to no avail. In the evening the silver apple was there, ripening on its branch; in the morning it had gone. The guards swore that no one had passed them during the night.

The King called his three sons to him.

"This is a serious matter," he said. "Someone is stealing the silver apple during the night, and not even my royal guards can catch him. My sons, I put the task in your hands. Whichever one of you succeeds in catching the thief will be rewarded with my crown and my kingdom."

"I will stand guard tonight," promised the eldest prince.

That evening he went into the garden and prepared to spend the night at the foot of the tree. He took a bottle of wine to keep himself company. From time to time he poured himself a cupful and gulped it down. Then as midnight drew near, he began to yawn.

"I must not fall asleep," he told himself. And he got up and marched around the tree. He could see the silver apple gleaming in the moonlight.

But soon he was too tired to go on walking. Surely it would do no harm to sit down for a moment? He sat down. Pop! He fell asleep.

When he woke, the damage was done. The silver apple had vanished.

"Well," he said, "good-bye to the crown!"

Next morning the King asked for news of the thief, and of course there was no news. The eldest prince had gone to sleep at his post.

"Leave it to me, Father," said the second prince. "I'll catch your thief."

The King shook his head doubtfully. But next evening the second prince went into the garden and prepared to spend the night at the foot of the tree. He took a platter of food to keep himself company. He felt sure that cold chicken and potato salad would keep him awake. But as midnight drew near he began to yawn.

"No one is going to bewitch me into falling asleep," he told himself. And he got up and marched around the tree. The apple was still there, gleaming in the moonlight.

But soon he was too tired to go on walking. Surely it would do no harm to sit down for a moment? He sat down. Pop! He fell asleep.

When he woke an hour later he jumped to his feet. But the damage was done. The silver apple had vanished.

"Well, that's that," he said. "I too have lost the crown."

Next morning the King asked if he had had better luck than his brother.

"No, Father," said the second prince, ashamed. "I stayed awake till midnight. But when midnight struck, I was sleeping like a badger."

Petit Jean, the youngest prince, burst out laughing. "A fine pair of sentries you are!"

"It's easy for you to talk," said his brother crossly. "You were sound asleep in your bed."

"All the same, if the King my father sends me to stand guard, *I* will bring back news of how the apple disappears."

"My dear son," said the King. "This is no ordinary thief. How can you be so sure you'll do better than your brothers?"

"Well," said Petit Jean, "I'm sure I can do no worse."

And so next evening he went into the garden and prepared to spend the night there. He looked up at the silver apple, gleaming by the light of the moon. Then he sat down to wait. When he felt himself growing sleepy, he got up and marched around the tree. But as midnight drew near, he began to yawn.

"This will never do," he told himself.

"If I fall asleep, the apple will disappear as usual—and how my brothers will laugh!"

He climbed up into the tree and settled himself in a forked branch near the magic fruit. Then he put out his hand to the apple. It was as smooth as ivory, and cool as the night.

"Suppose I picked it now," he thought. "Then no one would be able to steal it without my noticing."

He plucked the apple from the branch and put it inside his shirt. Then he tucked in his shirt and buttoned it right up to the neck. Not a moment too soon. Pop! His eyes closed and he fell sound asleep.

But he was waked almost at once by something pulling at his shirt. Seeing a bright shadow in front of him, he reached out to grapple with the thief. He hung on with all his strength, but the thief broke free, leaving his hands full of shining feathers.

He felt in his shirt. The apple was gone.

"Oh, well," he said, "at least I have some evidence."

He tucked the feathers in his shirt and went to bed. Next morning, when the King asked for news of the thief, Petit Jean spread the feathers on the table.

"I couldn't hold him," he said. "But he left these behind in my hands."

"A fine thing," sneered his brothers, who were jealous of his success. "To have the thief in your hands and let him go!"

"Hush!" said the King, staring at the bright feathers. "I know this bird—it is the Golden Phoenix. No man can hold him against his will. Petit Jean, do you know in which direction he flew?"

"He left a fiery trail behind him, like a shooting star," said Petit Jean. "I saw him go over the top of the Glass Mountain."

"Good," said the King. "We shall be able to follow his trail."

And they all set off toward the Glass Mountain. Along the path from time to time they found a shining feather. But at the top of the Glass Mountain they stopped. They could see the shining feathers leading down into the Great Sultan's country. But they could not follow, for on this side the mountain fell away in a sheer cliff, a thousand feet straight down.

"We can go no farther," said the King.

"Father, look," said Petit Jean. "I've found a trap-door."

"A trap-door in a mountain?" scoffed his brothers. "Ridiculous!"

"Please, Father, come and see," repeated Petit Jean. "Perhaps it leads down into the Great Sultan's country."

The King came over to see the trap-door and decided it was worth looking into. All of them heaved together, and at last they managed to pull it open. Underneath they found a well going down into darkness.

"The sides are as smooth as ice," said the elder princes. "There is no way to climb down."

"We need a good long rope," said the King, "and a stout basket on the end of it."

These things were brought from the castle. To the end of the rope the princes tied a basket big enough for a man to sit in. On the King's advice they also attached a string to the basket, fastened at the other end to a bell.

"So if there is danger," he explained, "whoever is in the basket can signal us here at the top. Now, who is going down?"

The eldest prince turned white. "Not I," he said. "I can't stand heights."

The second prince turned green. "Not I," he said. "I don't like the dark."

Petit Jean laughed. "Then it's my adventure," he said. "Wish me luck, Father."

"Good luck, my boy," said the King. "And take with you this sword. Use it well, and it will keep you from harm. We shall keep watch here. When you come back and ring the bell, we will pull you up."

Petit Jean said goodbye and climbed into the basket. Down, down, down he went, with the sword in one hand and the bell-rope in the other. For a long time he heard nothing and saw nothing. Then at last the basket stopped with a bump. He climbed out and gave two quick tugs on the bell-rope. Then he groped his way along a tunnel towards a faint light.

"Just as I thought," he said. "It leads into the Great Sultan's country."

The light grew stronger, and the tunnel widened into a cavern. But here Petit Jean found his way barred. In the middle of the cavern stood a fierce beast with one long horn in the middle of its forehead. When it saw him it bellowed.

"I am the Unicorn of the Cave," it said. "You may not pass!"

"But I must pass," said the prince. "I am on my way to see the Sultan."

"Then prepare for combat!" said the Unicorn.

And without another word it charged at him, the long sharp horn pointing straight at his heart. Petit Jean had no time to use his sword. At the last moment he dodged to one side, and the Unicorn thundered past. There was a terrific crash. The Unicorn had stuck fast in the wall of the cavern.

"Now may I pass?" asked Petit Jean.

"Yes, as far as I'm concerned," grunted the Unicorn as it tried to work its horn free.

But Petit Jean could not pass. This time his way was barred by a great Lion, waving his tail menacingly.

"I am the Lion of the Cave," he roared. "Prepare for combat!"

And without another word he sprang straight at Petit Jean. The prince stood firm, and at the last moment swung his sword. *Snick!* He shaved the whiskers off the Lion's left cheek. With a fierce roar the Lion sprang again. Petit Jean swung his sword on the other side— *snick!*—and shaved the whiskers off the Lion's right cheek.

At this the Lion gave a deafening roar. He gathered himself for one more leap, and came down on Petit Jean with his paws out and his mouth open. This time the prince judged his moment very carefully. *Snick, snack!* And the Lion's head tumbled to the ground.

"Ouch!" said the Lion. Petit Jean was amazed to see him pick up his head with his front paws and set it on his neck again, as good as new.

"Now may I pass?" asked Petit Jean. "Or must I do it again?"

"Oh, no," said the Lion wearily. "Once is enough for me."

But Petit Jean still could not pass. The cavern was suddenly filled with a slithery hissing noise, and he found his way barred by a terrible beast with seven heads.

"I am the Serpent of the Cave," hissed the beast. "Prepare for combat!"

Petit Jean took a deep breath. This one looked very dangerous indeed. But it did not spring at him. It just waited in his path. Wherever he tried to strike with his sword, he found a head snapping at him with fierce jaws and a forked tongue.

Then the young prince had a bright idea. He began running around the Serpent, striking with his sword; and the seven heads began to twist round each other trying to keep up with him. When the seven necks were twisted tight as a rope, he took a wide swing with his sword and—*snock!*—he cut off all the seven heads at once. There was a roar of applause from the Unicorn and the Lion.

"Now may I pass?" asked Petit Jean again.

"You may pass," sighed the Serpent, trying to find its seven heads and get them back on the right necks.

And so Petit Jean walked out into the realm of the Great Sultan. Just outside the cavern he found a glittering feather, so he knew he was still on the trail of the Golden Phoenix.

Before he had gone very far he was met by the Sultan himself riding on a white elephant. The Sultan had a long black moustache, and he stroked it as he looked down at his visitor.

"Who are you that have passed the Glass Mountain?" he asked. "And what do you seek in my realm?"

"I am the son of your neighbour, the wise King," replied Petit Jean. "And I am looking for a bird that has been raiding our apple tree."

The Sultan nodded thoughtfully. He invited Petit Jean to climb up on to the elephant behind him, and they rode back to the Sultan's palace. All along the road the prince kept his eyes open for the feathers that the Golden Phoenix had dropped in its flight.

When they reached the palace, the Sultan invited Petit Jean to dine with him in the garden. They were joined at table by the Sultan's daughter, who was more beautiful than the moon and stars combined. Petit Jean could hardly take his eyes off her.

They sat down beneath a jasmine tree, and as they began the feast a bird sang above their heads, filling the evening air with beautiful music. Petit Jean caught a glimpse of gold among the leaves.

"May I ask what bird is singing, your highness?" he said.

The Sultan stroked his moustache. "There are many birds in my realm," he said. "This one is probably a nightingale."

Petit Jean thought it was probably something else; but he said no more about it. He complimented the Sultan on the food, which was delicious, and on his daughter, who looked more beautiful every moment.

When they had finished, the Sultan spoke to him again.

"It is the custom of this country," he said, "that every stranger passing through must play a game of hide-and-seek with me. Tomorrow morning it will be your turn. If you should win, you shall have the hand of my daughter in marriage. How does that appeal to you?"

"It appeals to me more than anything else in the world," said Petit Jean. "But what if I should lose?"

The Sultan stroked his long black moustache and smiled. "Ah," he said. "Then you will lose the dearest thing you own."

"I see," said Petit Jean. "But I am a stranger here. How can I be expected to play hide-and-seek in a place I do not know?"

The Sultan nodded. "This evening my daughter will show you round the garden. Take care to notice all the places where I might hide, for tomorrow morning you must find me three times. And now I shall wish you good night."

When the Sultan had gone, the Princess began showing Petit Jean round the garden. But she noticed that he was not really paying attention.

"I think you do not wish to win my hand," she said sadly, "for you are not looking at anything I show you."

"Dear Princess," said Petit Jean, "I would much rather look at you."

The Princess could not help smiling. But suddenly she looked so sad that Petit Jean asked her what was the matter.

"I am thinking of what must happen to you tomorrow," she said. "I will tell you the truth: no matter how well you knew this garden, you would not be able to find my father. For he has the power to change his shape so that not even I can recognize him. So you see, nobody can win his game of hide-and-seek."

"Then only luck can save me," said Petit Jean cheerfully. "Well, let us have no more sad talk. Tell me of yourself, Princess, and of the bird that sings over your banquet table."

"The bird?" said the Princess. "Oh, that is the Golden Phoenix. Whoever lives within the sound of its voice will never grow old."

"A very useful bird," said Petit Jean. "And how do you make sure it doesn't fly away?"

The Princess told him that the Phoenix did fly free during the night. But at sunrise he always came back to his golden cage. So whoever owned the cage could be sure of owning the Golden Phoenix.

They walked in the garden, talking of many things, until the moon rose. Then Petit Jean went to bed and slept soundly till morning.

Next day the Sultan was very cheerful, for he expected to win his game of hide-and-seek. He could hardly wait for Petit Jean to finish his breakfast.

"Now here are the rules of the game," he said. "I shall hide three times in the garden, and you must find me. And just to prove I am a fair man, I will offer you three prizes. If you find me once, you shall escape with your life. If you find me twice, you shall have your life and my daughter. If you find me three times, you shall have your life, my daughter, and whatever you choose as a dowry."

"Agreed," said Petit Jean.

The Sultan rushed off to hide, and Petit Jean invited the Princess to walk in the garden with him. She grew very pale and nervous, because he seemed to be making no effort to find her father.

At the Sultan's fish-pond they stopped and looked down. There were fishes of all colours and sizes swimming in it. Petit Jean looked at them closely and burst out laughing. One of the fishes had a long black moustache.

"Princess," he said, "I should like to borrow a net."

"A net?" said the Princess. "How can you think of fishing at a time like this?"

But she went and found him a net. Petit Jean leaned down and scooped out the fish with the moustache. There was a puff of white smoke, and the fish vanished. In its place was the Sultan, breathing hard.

"Humph!" growled the Sultan, climbing out of the net. "And how did you happen to find me, young man?"

"Beginner's luck," said Petit Jean. "Well, have I earned my life?"

"Yes," said the Sultan angrily. "Do you want to stop there, or go on with the game?"

Petit Jean looked at the Princess. "Oh," he said, "I shall go on."

The Sultan rushed off to hide again. Petit Jean took the Princess's arm and they walked round the garden together. When she asked him where he would look this time, he shook his head.

"I don't know," he said. "I don't think your father will forget about his moustache again."

They looked everywhere, but found nothing that turned out to be the Sultan. At last Petit Jean stopped beside a rose-bush and sighed.

"Well," he said, "if I am never to see you again, I would like to give you something to remember me by."

And he leaned down to pluck the reddest rose on the bush. Pop! The rose disappeared in a puff of red smoke, and in its place stood the Sultan, red with anger.

"Oh!" exclaimed Petit Jean. "I thought you were a rose."

"You are too lucky for words," snarled the Sultan. "Well, you've won your life and my daughter. I suppose you want to stop there?"

"Oh, no," said Petit Jean. "That wouldn't be fair to you. I shall try my luck once more."

And so the Sultan rushed off to hide for the last time. The Princess and Petit Jean went on walking in the garden, wondering where he might be. No matter where they tried, they could not find him.

At last Petit Jean stopped beneath a pear-tree.

"All this exercise is making me hungry," he said. And reaching up, he plucked the ripest, roundest pear he could see.

Bang! There was a puff of black smoke, and in place of the pear stood the Sultan, black with fury.

"Oh," said Petit Jean. "I thought you were a pear."

"You are too lucky to live!" roared the Sultan.

"But I have already won my life," Petit Jean reminded him. "And now I have won my choice of dowry."

The Sultan grumbled, but finally asked what dowry Petit Jean would choose.

"A little thing which you'll hardly miss," said Petit Jean. "I choose the old gold cage which hangs in your daughter's chamber."

The Sultan leaped into the air. "The old gold cage!" he shouted. Then he pretended to be calm. "Oh, you wouldn't want that old thing," he said. "Let me offer you three chests of treasure instead."

"I couldn't possibly take your treasure," said Petit Jean. "The cage is quite enough."

The Sultan turned purple with rage. But at last he agreed that Petit Jean had won the cage fair and square. He even promised to give them an escort as far as the Glass Mountain next day.

Meanwhile there was a banquet to celebrate Petit Jean's success, and above their heads the Golden Phoenix sang in the jasmine tree. But all through the meal the Sultan kept pulling his moustache and glancing angrily at Petit Jean. It was easy to see that he was not at all happy.

The Princess noticed her father's mood, and as she had by now fallen in love with Petit Jean, she felt nervous. When they were alone together she told him her fears.

"I do not believe my father will keep his word," she said. "He is so angry at losing the Golden Phoenix that he will try to kill you while you sleep."

"Then we had better leave during the night," said Petit Jean.

The Princess agreed. "Bring two horses from the stable, and muffle their hooves," she said. "Meanwhile I will fetch my travelling cloak and the golden cage."

Petit Jean tiptoed to the stable and chose two horses. He tied pieces of blanket around their hooves and led them back to the kitchen door. There he met the Princess, wearing her cloak and carrying the cage.

"My father is suspicious," she said. "But as long as he hears voices talking he will not stir from his room."

She put two beans into a frying-pan on the stove. As soon as they felt the heat the beans began to croak. One of them said "Nevertheless" in a high voice; the other said "Notwithstanding" in a deep voice. When they were both croaking they sounded just like a man and woman talking together.

Petit Jean and the Princess mounted their horses and rode softly away, carrying the golden cage, while upstairs the Sultan listened to the conversation in the kitchen. He had a sleepless night, for the two beans went on saying "Nevertheless—notwithstanding" until morning. And by the time he found out what had happened, Petit Jean and the Princess had reached the Glass Mountain.

The Unicorn, the Lion, and the Serpent were there in the cavern, but they did not bar the way. Petit Jean placed his Princess in the basket and pulled on the bell-rope. His father and brothers were waiting at the top, and when they heard the bell they pulled the basket up the well.

They were astonished to see the Princess. The two princes would have stopped and gazed at her, but she told them to let down the basket again before it was too late. Presently they pulled up Petit Jean with the golden cage in his arms.

"Welcome home, my boy," said the King. "And welcome to your lady, too. But where is the bird you set off to find? This cage is empty."

Petit Jean pointed to the Great Sultan's country, and they saw a dazzling radiance moving toward them through the sky, with a beating of golden wings: for it was near daybreak, and the Phoenix was looking for his cage. And after him on the road below came the Sultan himself, riding his white elephant and shaking his fist at the sky.

The three princes rolled a big stone over the trap-door so that the Sultan could never follow them. Then, with the Golden Phoenix safe in his cage, they set off homewards.

Petit Jean and his Princess were married, and

the King gave them his crown and kingdom as he had promised. And with the Golden Phoenix singing every night in the tree where the silver apple of wisdom grew, they lived wisely and happily ever afterwards.

United States

The Knee-High Man

Julius Lester's feeling for the stories he heard as a child led him to retell them so that his own children and others could enjoy the casually told wisdom of America's black heritage. [From Julius Lester, *The Knee-High Man and Other Tales* (Dial, 1972).]

Once upon a time there was a knee-high man. He was no taller than a person's knees. Because he was so short, he was very unhappy. He wanted to be big like everybody else.

One day he decided to ask the biggest animal he could find how he could get big. So he went to see Mr. Horse. "Mr. Horse, how can I get big like you?"

Mr. Horse said, "Well, eat a whole lot of corn. Then run around a lot. After a while you'll be as big as me."

The knee-high man did just that. He ate so much corn that his stomach hurt. Then he ran and ran and ran until his legs hurt. But he didn't get any bigger. So he decided that Mr. Horse had told him something wrong. He decided to go ask Mr. Bull.

"Mr. Bull? How can I get big like you?"

Mr. Bull said, "Eat a whole lot of grass. Then bellow and bellow as loud as you can. The first thing you know, you'll be as big as me."

So the knee-high man ate a whole field of grass. That made his stomach hurt. He bellowed and bellowed and bellowed all day and all night. That made his throat hurt. But he didn't get any bigger. So he decided that Mr. Bull was all wrong too.

Now he didn't know anyone else to ask. One night he heard Mr. Hoot Owl hooting, and he remembered that Mr. Owl knew every-

thing. "Mr. Owl? How can I get big like Mr. Horse and Mr. Bull?"

"What do you want to be big for?" Mr. Hoot Owl asked.

"I want to be big so that when I get into a fight, I can whip everybody," the knee-high man said.

Mr. Hoot Owl hooted. "Anybody ever try to pick a fight with you?"

The knee-high man thought a minute. "Well, now that you mention it, nobody ever did try to start a fight with me."

Mr. Owl said, "Well, you don't have any reason to fight. Therefore, you don't have any reason to be bigger than you are."

"But, Mr. Owl," the knee-high man said, "I want to be big so I can see far into the distance."

Mr. Hoot Owl hooted. "If you climb a tall tree, you can see into the distance from the top."

The knee-high man was quiet for a minute. "Well, I hadn't thought of that."

Mr. Hoot Owl hooted again. "And that's what's wrong, Mr. Knee-High Man. You hadn't done any thinking at all. I'm smaller than you, and you don't see me worrying about being big. Mr. Knee-High Man, you wanted something that you didn't need."

The Wonderful Tar-Baby

An old black man, Uncle Remus, tells these beloved animal stories to a little boy who lives on a Southern plantation. The folktales, which were probably brought over from Africa by slaves, are rich in humor. Four generations of children in America have laughed with glee at Brer Rabbit's triumph over his old enemy, Brer Fox, and at the astonishing pranks of the other "creeturs." Of all the stories, "The Wonderful Tar-Baby" is perhaps the favorite. While the dialect in the Uncle Remus stories may be difficult for some children to read, no child should miss this rich heritage of black folklore. The stories are invaluable for storytelling and for reading aloud. [From Joel Chandler Harris, *Uncle Remus, His Songs and Sayings* (Appleton-Century-Crofts, 1935).]

"One day atter Brer Rabbit fool 'im wid dat calamus root, Brer Fox went ter wuk en got 'im some tar, en mix it wid some turken time, en fix up a contrapshun wat he call a Tar-Baby, en he tuck dish yer Tar-Baby en he sot 'er in de big road, en den he lay off in de bushes fer to see wat de news wuz gwineter be. En he didn't hatter wait long, nudder, kaze bimeby here come Brer Rabbit pacin' down de road—lippity-clippity, clippity-lippity—dez ez sassy ez a jay-bird. Brer Fox, he lay low. Brer Rabbit come prancin' long twel he spy de Tar-Baby, en den he fotch up on his behime legs like he wuz 'stonished. De Tar-Baby, she sot dar, she did, en Brer Fox, he lay low.

" 'Mawnin'!' sez Brer Rabbit, sezee—'nice wedder dis mawning', sezee.

"Tar-Baby ain't sayin' nothin', en Brer Fox, he lay low.

" 'How duz yo' sym'tums seem ter segashu-ate?' sez Brer Rabbit, sezee.

"Brer Fox, he wink his eye slow, en lay low, en de Tar-Baby, she ain't sayin' nothin'.

" 'How you come on, den? Is you deaf?'' sez Brer Rabbit, sezee. 'Kaze if you is, I kin holler louder,' sezee.

"Tar-Baby stay still, en Brer Fox, he lay low.

" 'Youer stuck up, dat's w'at you is,' says Brer Rabbit, sezee, 'en I'm a gwineter kyore you, dat's w'at I'm a gwineter do,' sezee.

"Brer Fox, he sorter chuckle in his stummuck, he did, but Tar-Baby ain't sayin' nothin'.

" 'I'm gwineter larn you howter talk ter 'specttubble fokes ef hit's de las' ack,' sez Brer Rabbit, sezee. 'Ef you don't take off dat hat en tell me howdy, I'm gwineter bus' you wide open,' sezee.

"Tar-Baby stay still, en Brer Fox, he lay low.

"Brer Rabbit keep on axin' 'im, en de Tar-Baby she keep on sayin' nothing', twel present'y Brer Rabbit draw back wid his fis', he did, en blip he tuck 'er side er de head. Right dar's whar he broke his merlasses jug. His fis' stuck, en he can't pull loose. De tar hilt 'im. But Tar-Baby, she stay still, en Brer Fox, he lay low.

" 'Ef you don't lemme loose, I'll knock you agin,' sez Brer Rabbit, sezee, en wid dat he fotch 'er a wipe wid de udder han', en dat stuck. Tar-Baby, she ain't sayin' nothin', en Brer Fox, he lay low.

" 'Tu'n me loose, fo' I kick de natal stuffin'

outten you,' sez Brer Rabbit, sezee, but de Tar-Baby, she ain't sayin' nothin'. She des hilt on, en den Brer Rabbit lose de use er his feet in de same way. Brer Fox, he lay low. Den Brer Rabbit squall out dat ef de Tar-Baby don't tu'n 'im loose he butt 'er cranksided. En den he butted, en his head got stuck. Den Brer Fox, he sa'ntered fort', lookin' des ez innercent ez one er yo' mammy's mockin'-birds.

" 'Howdy, Brer Rabbit,' sez Brer Fox, sezee. 'You look sorter stuck up dis mawnin',' sezee, en den he rolled on de groun', en laughed en laughed twel he couldn't laugh no mo'. 'I speck you'll take dinner wid me dis time, Brer Rabbit. I done laid in some calamus root, en I ain't gwineter take no skuse,' sez Brer Fox, sezee.

*   *   *

" 'You been runnin' roun' here sassin' atter me a mighty long time, but I speck you done come ter de een 'er de row. You bin cuttin' up yo' capers en bouncin' 'roun' in dis neighber-hood ontwel you come ter b'leeve yo'se'f de boss er de whole gang. En den youer allers some'rs whar you got no bizness,' sez Brer Fox, sezee. 'Who ax you fer ter come en strike up a 'quaintance wid dish yer Tar-Baby? En who stuck you up dar whar you iz? Nobody in de roun' worril. You des tuck en jam yo'se'f on dat Tar-Baby widout waitin' fer enny invite,' sez Brer Fox, sezee, 'en dar you is en dar you'll stay twel I fixes up a bresh-pile and fires her up, kaze I'm gwineter bobby-cue you dis day, sho,' sez Brer Fox, sezee.

"Den Brer Rabbit talk mighty 'umble.

" 'I don't keer w'at you do wid me, Brer Fox,' sezee, 'so you don't fling me in dat brier-patch. Roas' me, Brer Fox,' sezee, 'but don't fling me in dat brier-patch,' sezee.

" 'Hit's so much trouble fer ter kindle a fier,' sez Brer Fox, sezee, 'dat I speck I'll hatter hang you,' sezee.

" 'Hang me des ez high as you please, Brer Fox,' sez Brer Rabbit, sezee, 'but do fer de Lord's sake don't fling me in dat brier-patch,' sezee.

" 'I ain't got no string,' sez Brer Fox, sezee, 'en now I speck I'll hatter drown you,' sezee.

" 'Drown me des ez deep ez you please, Brer

Fox,' sez Brer Rabbit, sezee, 'but do don't fling me in dat brier-patch,' sezee.

" 'Dey ain't no water nigh,' sez Brer Fox, sezee, 'en now I speck I'll hatter skin you,' sezee.

" 'Skin me, Brer Fox,' sez Brer Rabbit, sezee, 'snatch out my eyeballs, t'ar out my years by de roots, en cut off my legs,' sezee, 'but do please, Brer Fox, don't fling me in dat brier-patch,' sezee.

"Co'se Brer Fox wanter hurt Brer Rabbit bad ez he kin, so he cotch 'im by de behime legs en slung 'im right in de middle er de brier-patch. Dar wuz a considerbul flutter whar Brer Rabbit struck de bushes, en Brer Fox sorter hang 'roun' fer ter see w'at wuz gwineter happen. Bimeby he hear somebody call 'im, en way up de hill he see Brer Rabbit settin' cross-legged on a chinkapin log koamin' de pitch outen his har wid a chip. Den Brer Fox know dat he bin swop off mighty bad. Brer Rabbit wuz bleedzed fer ter fling back some er his sass, en he holler out:

" 'Bred en bawn in a brier-patch, Brer Fox— bred en bawn in a brier-patch!' en wid dat he skip out des ez lively ez a cricket in de embers."

Wiley and the Hairy Man

This tale of conjury or magic has been adapted by Virginia Haviland from Donnell Van de Voort's version of the tale, written for the Federal Writers Project of the Works Project Administration for the state of Alabama. The folk theme of outwitting the devil is here given a setting among the blacks of the deep South, and magic proves to be less powerful than a mother's love. [From *North American Legends,* ed. Virginia Haviland (Collins, 1979).]

Wiley's pappy was a bad man and no-count. He stole watermelons in the dark of the moon. He was lazy, too, and slept while the weeds grew higher than the cotton. Worse still, he killed three martins and never even chunked at a crow.

One day he fell off the ferry boat where the river is quicker than anywhere else and no one ever found him. They looked for him a long way down river and in the still pools between the sand-banks, but they never found him. They heard a big man laughing across the river,

and everybody said, "That's the Hairy Man." So they stopped looking.

"Wiley," his mammy told him, "the Hairy Man's got your pappy and he's goin' to get you if you don't look out."

"Yas'm," he said. "I'll look out. I'll take my hound-dogs everywhere I go. The Hairy Man can't stand no hound-dog."

Wiley knew that because his mammy had told him. She knew because she came from the swamps by the Tombisbee River and knew conjure magic.

One day Wiley took his axe and went down in the swamp to cut some poles for a hen-roost and his hounds went with him. But they took out after a shoat and ran it so far off Wiley couldn't even hear them yelp.

"Well," he said, "I hope the Hairy Man ain't nowhere round here now."

He picked up his axe to start cutting poles, but he looked up and there came the Hairy Man through the trees grinning. He was sure ugly and his grin didn't help much. He was hairy all over. His eyes burned like fire and spit drooled all over his big teeth.

"Don't look at me like that," said Wiley, but the Hairy Man kept coming and grinning, so Wiley threw down his axe and climbed up a big bay tree. He saw the Hairy Man didn't have feet like a man but like a cow, and Wiley never had seen a cow up a bay tree.

"What for you done climb up there?" the Hairy Man asked Wiley when he got to the bottom of the tree.

Wiley climbed nearly to the top of the tree and looked down. Then he climbed plumb to the top.

"How come you climbin' trees?" the Hairy Man said.

"My mammy done tole me to stay away from you. What you got in that big croaker-sack?"

"I ain't got nothin' yet."

"Gwan away from here," said Wiley, hoping the tree would grow some more.

"Ha," said the Hairy Man and picked up Wiley's axe. He swung it about and the chips flew. Wiley grabbed the tree close, rubbed his belly on it and hollered, "Fly, chips, fly, back in your same old place."

The chips flew and the Hairy Man cussed and

damned. Then he swung the axe and Wiley knew he'd have to holler fast. They went to it tooth and toe-nail then, Wiley hollering and the Hairy Man chopping. He hollered till he was hoarse and he saw the Hairy Man was gaining on him.

"I'll come down part of the way," he said, "if you'll make this bay tree twice as big around."

"I ain't studyin' you," said the Hairy Man, swinging the axe.

"I bet you can't," said Wiley.

"I ain't going to try," said the Hairy Man.

Then they went to it again, Wiley hollering and the Hairy Man chopping. Wiley had about yelled himself out when he heard his hound-dogs yelping way off.

"Hyeaaah, dog," hollered Wiley, and they both heard the hound-dogs yelping and coming jam-up. The Hairy Man looked worried.

"Come on down," he said, "and I'll teach you conjure."

"I can learn all the conjure I want from my mammy."

The Hairy Man cussed some more, but he threw the axe down and took off through the swamp.

When Wiley got home he told his mammy that the Hairy Man had most got him, but his dogs ran him off.

"Did he have his sack?"

"Yas'm."

"Next time he come after you, don't you climb no bay tree."

"I ain't," said Wiley. "They ain't big enough around."

"Don't climb no kind o' tree. Just stay on the ground and say 'Hello, Hairy Man.' You hear me, Wiley?"

"No'm."

"He ain't goin' to hurt you, child. You can put the Hairy Man in the dirt when I tell you how to do him."

"I puts him in the dirt and he puts me in that croaker-sack. I ain't puttin' no Hairy Man in the dirt."

"You just do like I say. You say, 'Hello, Hairy Man.' He says, 'Hello, Wiley,' You say, 'Hairy Man, I done heard you about the best conjureman 'round here.' 'I reckon I am.'

You say, 'I bet you cain't turn yourself into no giraffe.' You keep tellin' him he cain't and he will. Then you say, 'I bet you cain't turn yourself into no 'possum.' Then he will, and you grab him and throw him in the sack."

"It don't sound just right somehow," said Wiley, "but I will." So he tied up his dogs so they wouldn't scare away the Hairy Man, and went down to the swamp again. He hadn't been there long when he looked up and there came the Hairy Man grinning through the trees, hairy all over and his big teeth showing more than ever. He knew Wiley came off without his hound-dogs. Wiley nearly climbed a tree when he saw the croaker-sack, but he didn't.

"Hello, Hairy Man," he said.

"Hello, Wiley." He took the sack off his shoulder and started opening it up.

"Hairy Man, I done heard you are about the best conjure man round here."

"I reckon I is."

"I bet you cain't turn yourself into no giraffe."

"Shucks, that ain't no trouble," said the Hairy Man.

"I bet you cain't do it."

So the Hairy Man twisted round and turned himself into a giraffe.

"I bet you cain't turn yourself into no alligator," said Wiley.

The giraffe twisted around and turned into an alligator, all the time watching Wiley to see he didn't try to run.

"Anybody can turn theyself into something big as a man," said Wiley, "but I bet you cain't turn yourself into no 'possum."

The alligator twisted around and turned into a 'possum, and Wiley grabbed it and threw it in the sack.

Wiley tied the sack up as tight as he could and then he threw it in the river. He started home through the swamp and he looked up and there came the Hairy Man grinning through the trees. Wiley had to scramble up the nearest tree.

The Hairy Man gloated: "I turned myself into the wind and blew out. Wiley, I'm going to set right here till you get hungry and fall out of that bay tree. You want me to learn you some more conjure?"

Wiley studied a while. He studied about the

Hairy Man and he studied about his hound-dogs tied up most a mile away.

"Well," he said, "you done some pretty smart tricks. But I bet you cain't make things disappear and go where nobody knows."

"Huh, that's what I'm good at. Look at that old bird-nest on the limb. Now look. It's done gone."

"How I know it was there in the first place? I bet you cain't make something I know is there disappear."

"Ha ha!" said the Hairy Man. "Look at your shirt."

Wiley looked down and his shirt was gone, but he didn't care, because that was just what he wanted the Hairy Man to do.

"That was just a plain old shirt," he said. "But this rope I got tied round my breeches has been conjured. I bet you cain't make it disappear."

"Huh, I can make all the rope in this county disappear."

"Ha ha ha," said Wiley.

The Hairy Man looked mad and threw his chest way out. He opened his mouth wide and hollered loud.

"From now on all the rope in this county has done disappeared."

Wiley reared back, holding his breeches with one hand and a tree-limb with the other.

"Hyeaaah, dog," he hollered loud enough to be heard more than a mile off.

When Wiley and his dogs got back home his mammy asked him did he put the Hairy Man in the sack.

"Yes'm, but he done turned himself into the wind and blew right through that old croaker-sack."

"That *is* bad," said his mammy. "But you done fool him twice. If you fool him again he'll leave you alone. He'll be mighty hard to fool the third time."

"We got to study up a way to fool him, mammy."

"I'll study up a way tereckly," she said, and sat down by the fire and held her chin between her hands and studied real hard. But Wiley wasn't studying anything except how to keep the Hairy Man away. He took his hound-dogs out and tied one at the back door and one at the front door. Then he crossed a broom and an axe-handle over the window and built a fire in the fire-place. Feeling a lot safer, he sat down and helped his mammy study. After a little while his mammy said, "Wiley, you go down to the pen and get that little suckin' pig away from that old sow."

Wiley went down and snatched the sucking pig through the rails and left the sow grunting and heaving in the pen. He took the pig back to his mammy and she put it in his bed.

"Now, Wiley," she said, "you go on up to the loft and hide."

So he did. Before long he heard the wind howling and the trees shaking, and then his dogs started growling. He looked out through a knot-hole in the planks and saw the dog at the front door looking down toward the swamps, with his hair standing up and his lips drawn back in a snarl. Then an animal as big as a mule with horns on its head ran out of the swamp past the house. The dog jerked and jumped, but he couldn't get loose. Then an animal bigger than a great big dog with a long nose and big teeth ran out of th swamp and growled at the cabin. This time the dog broke loose and took after the big animal, who ran back down into the swamp. Wiley looked out another chink at the back end of the loft just in time to see his other dog jerk loose and take out after an animal which might have been a 'possum, but wasn't.

"Law-dee," said Wiley. "The Hairy Man is coming here, sure."

He didn't have long to wait, because soon enough he heard something with feet like a cow scrambling around on the roof. He knew it was the Hairy Man, because he heard him swear when he touched the hot chimney. The Hairy Man jumped off the roof when he found out there was a fire in the fire-place and came up and knocked on the front door as big as you please.

"Mammy," he hollered, "I done come after your baby."

"You ain't going to get him," mammy hollered back.

"Give him here or I'll set your house on fire with lightning."

"I got plenty of sweet-milk to put it out with."

"Give him here or I'll dry up your spring, make your cow go dry and send a million boll-weevils out of the ground to eat up your cotton."

"Hairy Man, you wouldn't do all that. That's mighty mean."

"I'm a mighty mean man. I ain't never seen a man as mean as I am."

"If I give you my baby will you go on way from here and leave everything else alone?"

"I swear that's just what I'll do," said the Hairy Man, so mammy opened the door and let him in.

"He's over there in that bed," she said.

The Hairy Man came in grinning like he was meaner than he said. He walked over to the bed and snatched the covers back.

"Hey," he hollered, "there ain't nothing in this bed but a old suckin' pig."

"I ain't said what kind of baby I was giving you, and that suckin' pig sure belong to me before I gave it to you."

The Hairy Man raged and yelled. He stomped all over the house gnashing his teeth. Then he grabbed up the pig and tore out through the swamp, knocking down trees right and left. The next morning the swamp had a wide path like a cyclone had cut through it, with trees torn loose at the roots and lying on the ground. When the Hairy Man was gone Wiley came down from the loft.

"Is he done gone, mammy?"

"Yes, child. That old Hairy Man cain't ever hurt you again. We done fool him three times."

Old Fire Dragaman

The Jack Tales of Richard Chase are American versions or variants of European folktales. They are contemporary examples of the process of survival and adaptation so characteristic of folklore. Richard Chase found a pocket of survival at Beech Creek, North Carolina. There, in the keeping of mountain folk, who have been telling these stories since the first English settlers came to that region, he found the tales, listened, and set them down in the speech of the people. The roots and origins are clearly visible. Here is Jack of the beanstalk and Jack the giant killer. Jack is the hero of all these stories. He is the American prototype of Boots, the youngest son who is hero of the Scandinavian folktale. In the notes to these tales, scholars have traced the stories to their sources in Grimm and other collections, including the English epic *Beowulf.* It is fascinating to explore the naturalization of the story. See what happens to the old refrain of fee, fi, fo, fum when it becomes American and Southern:

Fee! Faw! Fumm!
I smell the blood of a English-mum.
Bein' he dead or bein' he alive,
I'll grind his bones
To eat with my pones.

The story given here is the one that is said to derive from *Beowulf.* Certainly, like the epic, it concerns an underground monster who must be destroyed. In this form, it is an astonishingly vital tale for the storyteller. [From *The Jack Tales,* ed. Richard Chase (Houghton Mifflin, 1943).]

One time Jack and his two brothers, Will and Tom, were all of 'em a-layin' around home; weren't none of 'em doin' no good, so their daddy decided he'd set 'em to work. He had him a tract of land out in a wilderness of a place back up on the mountain. Told the boys they could go up there and work it. Said he'd give it to 'em. Hit was a right far ways from where anybody lived at, so they fixed 'em up a wagon-load of rations and stuff for housekeepin' and pulled out.

There wasn't no house up there, so they cut poles and notched 'em up a shack. They had to go to work in a hurry to get out any crop and they set right in to clearin' 'em a new-ground. They decided one boy 'uld have to stay to the house till twelve and do the cookin'.

First day Tom and Jack left Will there. Will went to fixin' around and got dinner ready, went out and blowed the horn to call Tom and Jack, looked down the holler and there came a big old giant steppin' right up the mountain. Had him a pipe about four foot long, and he had a long old blue beard that dragged on the ground.

When Will saw the old giant was headed right for the house, he ran and got behind the door, pulled it back on him and scrouged back against the wall a-shakin' like a leaf. The old giant came on to the house, reached in and throwed the cloth back off the dishes, eat ever'thing on the table in one bite and sopped the plates. Snatched him a chunk of fire and lit his pipe; the smoke came a-bilin' out. Then he wiped his mouth and went on back down the holler with that old pipe a-sendin' up smoke like a steam engine.

Tom and Jack came on in directly, says, "Why in the world ain't ye got us no dinner, Will?"

"Law me!" says Will. "If you'd 'a seen what I just seen you'd 'a not thought about no dinner. An old Fire Dragaman came up here, eat ever' bite on the table, and sopped the plates."

Tom and Jack laughed right smart at Will. Will says "You all needn't to laugh. Hit'll be your turn tomorrow, Tom."

So they fixed up what vittles they could and they all went back to work in the newground.

Next day Tom got dinner, went out and blowed the horn. There came Old Fire Dragaman—

"Law me!" says Tom. "Where'll I get?"

He ran and scrambled under the bed. Old Fire Dragaman came on up, eat ever'thing there was on the table, sopped the plates, and licked out all the pots. Lit his old pipe and pulled out down the holler, the black smoke a-rollin' like comin' out a chimley. Hit was a sight to look at.

Will and Jack came in, says, "Where's our dinner, Tom?"

"Dinner, the nation! Old Fire Dragaman came back up here. Law me! Hit was the beatin'-est thing I ever seen!"

Will says, "Where was you at, Tom?"

"Well, I'll tell ye," says Tom; "I was down under the bed."

Jack laughed, and Will and Tom says, "You just wait about laughin', Jack. Hit'll be your time tomorrow."

Next day Will and Tom went to the newground. They got to laughin' about where Jack 'uld hide at when Old Fire Dragaman came.

Jack fixed up ever'thing for dinner, went out about twelve and blowed the horn. Looked down the wilder-ness, there was Old Fire Dragaman a-comin' up the hill with his hands folded behind him and a-lookin' around this way and that.

Jack went on back in the house, started puttin' stuff on the table. Never payed no attention to the old giant, just went right on a-fixin' dinner. Old Fire Dragaman came on up.

Jack was scoopin' up a mess of beans out the pot, says, "Why, hello, daddy."

"Howdy, son."

"Come on in, daddy. Get you a chair. Dinner's about ready; just stay and eat with us."

"No, I thank ye. I couldn't stay."

"Hit's on the table. Come on sit down."

"No. I just stopped to light my pipe."

"Come on, daddy. Let's eat."

"No, much obliged. I got no time."

Old Fire Dragaman reached in to get him a coal of fire, got the biggest chunk in the fireplace, stuck it down in his old pipe, and started on back. Jack took out and follered him with all that smoke a-bilin' out; watched where he went to, and saw him go down a big straight hole in the ground.

Will and Tom came on to the house, saw Jack was gone.

Will says, "I reckon that's the last of Jack. I'll bet ye a dollar Old Fire Dragaman's done took him off and eat him. Dinner's still on the table."

So they set down and went to eatin'. Jack came on in directly.

Will says, "Where'n the world ye been, Jack? We 'lowed Old Fire Dragaman had done eat ye up."

"I been watchin' where Old Fire Dragaman went to."

"How come dinner yet on the table?"

"I tried my best to get him to eat," says Jack. "He just lit his old pipe and went on back. I follered him, saw him go down in a big hole out yonder."

"You right sure ye ain't lyin', Jack?"

"Why, no," says Jack. "You boys come with me and you can see the place where he went in at. Let's us get a rope and basket so we can go in that hole and see what's down there."

So they got a big basket made out of splits, and gathered up a long rope they'd done made out of hickory bark, and Jack took 'em on down to Old Fire Dragaman's den.

"Will, you're the oldest," says Jack; "we'll let you go down first. If you see any danger, you shake the rope and we'll pull ye back up.''

Will got in the basket, says, "You recollect now; whenever I shake that rope, you pull me out of here in a hurry."

So they let him down. Directly the rope shook, they jerked the basket back out, says "What'd ye see, Will?"

"Saw a big house. Hit's like another world down there."

Then they slapped Tom in the basket and let him down; the rope shook, they hauled him up.

"What'd you see, Tom?"

"Saw a house and the barn."

Then they got Jack in the basket, and let him down. Jack got down on top of the house, let the basket slip down over the eaves and right on down in the yard. Jack got out, went and knocked on the door.

The prettiest girl Jack ever had seen came out. He started right in to courtin' her, says, "I'm goin' to get you out of here."

She says, "I got another sister in the next room yonder, prettier'n me. You get her out too."

So Jack went on in the next room. That second girl was a heap prettier'n the first, and Jack went to talkin' to her and was a-courtin' right on. Said he'd get her out of that place.

She says, "I got another sister in the next room, prettier'n me. Don't you want to get her out too?"

"Well, I didn't know they got any prettier'n you," says Jack, "but I'll go see."

So he went on in. Time Jack saw that 'un he knowed she was the prettiest girl ever lived, so he started in right off talkin' courtin' talk to her; plumb forgot about them other two.

That girl said to Jack, says, "Old Fire Draga-man'll be back here any minute now. Time he finds you here he'll start in spittin' balls of fire."

So she went and opened up an old chest, took out a big swoard and a little vial of ointment, says, "If one of them balls of fire hits ye, Jack, you rub on a little of this medicine right quick, and this here swoard is the only thing that will hurt Old Fire Dragaman. You watch out now, and kill him if ye can."

Well, the old giant came in the door directly,

saw Jack, and com-menced spittin' balls of fire all around in there, some of 'em big as pump-kins. Jack he went a-dodgin' around tryin' to get at the old giant with that swoard. Once in a while one of them fire-balls 'uld glance him, but Jack rubbed on that ointment right quick and it didn't even make a blister. Fin'ly Jack got in close and clipped him with that swoard, took his head clean off.

Then Jack made that girl promise she'd marry him. So she took a red ribbon and got Jack to plat it in her hair. Then she gave Jack a wishin' ring. He put it on his finger and they went on out and got the other two girls.

They were awful pleased. They told Jack they were such little bits of children when the old giant catched 'em they barely could recollect when they first came down there.

Well, Jack put the first one in the basket and shook the rope. Will and Tom hauled her up, and when they saw her they commenced fightin' right off to see which one would marry her.

She told 'em, says, "I got another sister down there."

"Is she any prettier'n you?" says Will.

She says to him, "I ain't sayin'."

Will and Tom chunked the basket back down in a hurry. Jack put the next girl in, shook the rope. Time Will and Tom saw her, they both asked her to marry, and went to knockin' and beatin' one another over gettin' *her.*

She stopped 'em, says, "We got one more sister down there."

"Is she prettier'n you?" says Will.

She says to him, "You can see for yourself."

So they slammed the basket back down, jerked that last girl out.

"Law me!" says Will. "This here's the one I'm a-goin' to marry."

"Oh, no, you ain't!" Tom says. "You'll marry me, won't ye now?"

"No," says the girl, "I've done promised to marry Jack."

"Blame Jack," says Will. "He can just stay in there." And he picked up the basket and rope, throwed 'em down the hole.

"There ain't nothin' much to eat down there," says the girl; "he'll starve to death."

"That's just what we want him to do," says

Will, and they took them girls on back up to the house.

Well, Jack eat ever'thing he could find down there, but in about three days he saw the rations were runnin' awful low. He scrapped up ever' bit there was left and then he was plumb out of vittles; didn't know what he'd do.

In about a week Jack had com-menced to get awful poor. Happened he looked at his hand, turned that ring to see how much he'd fallen off, says, "I wish I was back home settin' in my mother's chimley corner smokin' my old chunky pipe."

And next thing, there he was.

Jack's mother asked him how come he wasn't up at the newground. Jack told her that was just exactly where he was started.

When Jack got up there, Will and Tom were still a-fightin' over that youngest girl. Jack came on in the house and saw she still had that red ribbon in her hair, and she came over to him, says, "Oh, Jack!"

So Jack got the youngest and Tom got the next 'un, and that throwed Will to take the oldest.

And last time I was down there they'd done built 'em three pole cabins and they were all doin' pretty well.

Paul Bunyan

The Paul Bunyan stories center on a legendary hero of the lumber camps of the American Northwest. This giant lumberjack is noted for his prodigious feats and the size of his logging operations. The narrator usually claimed acquaintance with Paul, and the stories were told in competition. Figures and dimensions often varied with the audience, as the storyteller "lays on all the traffic will bear." As to the origin of the stories, Esther Shephard says, "Some evidence points to a French-Canadian origin among the loggers of Quebec or northern Ontario, who may even have brought them from the old country; the name, then, may be a derivative of the French-Canadian word *bongyenne.* But other evidences point just as strongly to an American beginning, possibly in Michigan or Wisconsin." Whatever their origin may be, these tall tales are a unique contribution of the American frontier to the world's folklore. [From Esther Shephard, *Paul Bunyan* (Harcourt, 1924).]

Well, the way I was sayin', Paul had been figgurin' on where he was goin' to go next, and so then that mornin' he made up his mind.

"I'll go West," he says. "Reckon there'll be loggin' enough for me to do out there for a year or two anyway."

He'd heard about the Big Trees they had out there, and he'd seen the tops of some of 'em when he'd been out cruisin' one Sunday, and then Ole had told him about 'em too—he'd seen some of 'em from the top of the cornstalk the time he was up. And some fellows that had come into camp from the West told him about some outfit that was loggin' out there on the Coast on a big scale, and Paul, naturally, wanted to come out and show that fellow how to log.

And so he made up his mind to go right away.

*   *   *

Paul was goin' to show Joe how to log, and he wasn't goin' to let him get ahead of him, and so, as soon as he got his land staked out, he went back East and got the Blue Ox and other camp equipment. Paul went back to the Ottawa country where he'd left some of his stuff when he'd been loggin' there a long time ago, and then of course the equipment he had to take out of North Dakota, and then a lot of new stuff from Chicago, donkey engines, and cable, and railroad cars, and what-not, and a lot of other new-fangled things he was goin' to use.

"I'll beat 'em at their own game," he says.

And Babe was good for freightin' too. Just as good as for any other kind of woods work.

*   *   *

When Paul and Babe come to a piece of thick woods, Paul generally went ahead of the Ox to make a road for him, where the timber was thick, and it was kind of swampy—like in the Lake of the Woods country. He'd have his axe in his hand—the big one with the sixteen-foot cuttin' surface and the wove grass handle—and he'd swing it back and forth in front of him as he went along and make a road for the Ox. The trees would just fall crosswise across the road as soon as he got past, big end for little end and little end for big end, and make as fine a corduroy as you'd ever want to see, and then the Ox would come along behind.

I used to like to see 'em—Paul comin' through the woods that way slashin' with his axe, with the clean timber road layin' there behind him, and the streak of light showin' through the dark pine trees, and the big Blue Ox comin' along there behind with the load, chewin' his cud as easy and peaceful as if he'd been goin' into his barn in Paul's camp on the Red River.

That's the way Paul done most of his freightin', but sometimes he went farther south across the plains.

*   *   *

I remember one time I was with him on one of those trips when he was bringin' some stuff out, and he had a calf that he'd bought from some farmer in Iowa that he was bringin' with him to butcher for his camp on the Skagit, when he'd be just about the right size then, and so he took him along on this tote-trip he was makin' across the plains. And after the first day we stopped overnight at a cabin near Billings, Montana.

The young fellow who was homesteadin' there said he'd put the calf in the barn for the night, so's he'd be protected from the weather some, and Paul of course was glad at that, because he knowed that would keep the meat more tender, and he told him, sure, that would be fine, if he had room enough.

"Well, then, I'll do that," says the homesteader.

And so then we put the calf in the barn, and we put up for the night.

Well, the next mornin' when we got up and went outside, somethin' about the place looked kind of funny and we didn't hardly know at first what it was, but finally one of 'em says:

"I know what's the matter. The barn's gone.

And sure enough when we looked, where it'd been there was only a pile of straw now, bein' blowed about by the wind.

So then of course we all begun lookin' around to find out what'd become of it, but we couldn't see it nowheres. It hadn't been burned, we knowed that, because if it had of there would

of been some ashes, and there wasn't nothin', only just straw and a few boards of the old floor, just as if it'd been lifted right up and carried away by the wind. And then we happened to think the calf was in the barn too.

Well, we didn't hardly know what it was could of come about, and so then Holloway—that's the young fellow homesteadin'—happened to think he had a pair of field glasses somewheres about the place. For he'd used to a been a forest ranger before, and so that's how he happened to have the glasses there. Well, he brought 'em out, and we looked around, and finally one of us spied the barn way off in the distance away off towards the south.

"And gee! it's movin'!" he said.

"No, sure not. There ain't wind enough to be movin' it now. There might of been in the night, but there sure ain't now—no wind at all to speak of."

"But it's movin' just the same. And there's a kind of funny thing on top of it."

Well, we got our saddle ponies and rode on out there and we found the barn, and I'll be blamed if there inside of it wasn't that calf of Paul's.

Or I shouldn't of said inside it, for he was mostly outside.

You know he'd growed so fast in the night he'd grown clean out of it and here was the four sides of the barn hangin' around his legs. He sure was the limit for growin' fast.

*   *   *

Some of the finest loggin' Paul done after he come West was in the Inland Empire. Course it wasn't an Inland Empire then, but just a big inland sea, and it was around the shores of this lake and on an island in the northwest corner of it that Paul Bunyan logged. It was pretty near my favorite loggin' with Paul, that year was.

*   *   *

I know when we first come down there Paul went out to cut a tree down one day. He cut away for a couple of hours, and then he went round to see how much he had left to chop before he'd get through, and here if he didn't find two Irishmen choppin' away on the other side of the tree and they'd been choppin' there for over three years, they said, ever since the spring of the Long Rain just about three years before that. It seems some boss had sent 'em in there to cut that tree down and that's all the farther they'd got, and I suppose the boss had forgot all about 'em a long time ago.

They was all overgrown with beards and they was lean and hungry, of course, and kind of wild too and queer from havin' been away from civilization so long and not havin' seen nobody for such a long time.

Paul felt mighty sorry for 'em and so he said he'd see what he could do, and he went back to his own side again and got his other axe and chopped away a little faster, because the men was starvin' to death, and between 'em in an hour or so they got it down.

And then I'll be blamed after all that trouble if the old tree wasn't hollow.

*   *   *

Loggin' on the island and around the inland sea was sure mighty handy. For one thing, there wasn't no waste. You could cut up the main part of the tree into them special lengths Paul was gettin' out that year, and then you could cut up all the limbs into just ordinary size logs and that way there wasn't no waste at all. And all them small logs filled up the spaces between the big ones and made a nice solid-lookin' job of it.

The way Paul done, he just cut the trees around the edge of the island first—the first row of 'em all around—and fell them right out into the lake where they'd be all ready for the drive, and filled in on top with them smaller logs, and then the next row of trees on top of the first ones, and the next row on top of that, and so on, one circle layin' right inside and at the same time kind of on top of the next circle, till the whole island was one solid pile of logs, way till you got to the center, to the mountain. Mount Pasco was right up in the middle of the island and that's where we had the camp, of course. Not a very high mountain but kind of big and flat, with a crater in the top of it, and a hollow where you could cook the soup always by natural heat.

And then the trees from the sides of the lake

he cut out in the water too, but we finished up the island first. From the south shore of the lake when you got away from it far enough the island used to look like a great big hotcake layin' out there, all nice and brown, and kind of high in the middle like it had plenty of good egg and soda in it, and then kind of a little uneven around the edge like a good hotcake always ought to be.

It was sure as pretty a raft of logs as you'd ever want to see, and the biggest one I ever knowed of Paul havin'. The sunshine was mighty bright there in the Inland Empire and used to lay over them brown logs out there so you could almost see the air movin' in heat waves above them, even though everything else was still, and out over the blue sea too, till you couldn't hardly look at it, it was so bright. Loggin' there was different from most of the loggin' we'd done, and we liked it.

And then when we got the raft all ready and everythin' layin' just the way we wanted it, Paul went down to the southwest corner of the lake and plowed out an outlet for it. He was goin' to take most of them logs to China, so he figured from that corner would be the best way to get out to the ocean. And then, when he got the river finished and about half filled up with water and slicked out over the top so it would be slippery, he turned the lake right into it.

Runnin' out so fast there, of course, the inland sea right away begun to slant from the northeast to the southwest, and the whole hotcake of logs just slid right off the island and floated right down to the outlet and then pretty soon the logs from the sides begun to slide in after it trailin' along behind, till goin' down the river it looked like a great big sea turtle with its hair streamin' out behind it. And it wasn't long till it was gone and clean out of sight. And so that loggin' was over.

*   *   *

There's many conflictin' stories about how Paul dug the Columbia River, but of course there's only one right one and that's the one I was just tellin' about the Inland Empire. I was right there and I saw how it was done. When Paul got his raft of logs finished and was ready to take 'em out, he just went out there and plowed out the river. And there wasn't nothin' to it at all. He plowed it out first and then filled it up with water and evened it out so it would be nice and smooth for his logs to slide over. On a windy day in the Gorge when an east wind is blowin' you can see the hole yet in the water where Paul never put in the last bucketful when he was evenin' it out.

*   *   *

Well, there's stories, and stories. I don't suppose I've heard 'em all. His old friends all remember him, and any of 'em will tell you about Paul. And some of 'em wishes a good many times that he was back here loggin' again; even the young fellows who never knowed him, but have only just heard about him, would of liked pretty well to've been in on the good old times, I guess.

Pecos Bill Becomes a Coyote

The American folktale is a Johnny-come-lately as compared to the long heritage of the oral tradition. But it holds to many of the true patterns of folklore—indigenous humor, clear characterization, swift action, and dénouement. The absurdity of a country as big as America and the immensity of the task facing the settlers and the workmen, provided a natural breeding ground for the story of exaggeration, the tall tale. The industrial frontiers of lumbering and cattle raising gave us the roots of two typical folktale cycles. Paul Bunyan represents the folk image of the lumber worker, and Pecos Bill of the cowboy. Pecos Bill's adoption as a baby by coyotes is a universal feral child motif found in stories as far-ranging as Rudyard Kipling's *The Jungle Books* and the Roman legend of Romulus and Remus. [From James Cloyd Bowman, *Pecos Bill: The Greatest Cowboy of All Time* (Whitman, 1937).]

Pecos Bill had the strangest and most exciting experience any boy ever had. He became a member of a pack of wild Coyotes, and until he was a grown man, believed that his name was Cropear, and that he was a full-blooded Coyote. Later he discovered that he was a human being and very shortly thereafter became the greatest cowboy of all time. This is how it all came about.

Pecos Bill's family was migrating westward through Texas in the early days, in an old covered wagon with wheels made from cross sections of a sycamore log. His father and mother were riding in the front seat, and his father was driving a wall-eyed, spavined roan horse and a red and white spotted milch cow hitched side by side. The eighteen children in the back of the wagon were making such a medley of noises that their mother said it wasn't possible even to hear thunder.

Just as the wagon was rattling down to the ford across the Pecos River, the rear left wheel bounced over a great piece of rock, and Bill, his red hair bristling like porcupine quills, rolled out of the rear of the wagon, and landed, up to his neck, in a pile of loose sand. He was only four years old at the time, and he lay dazed until the wagon had crossed the river and had disappeared into the sage brush. It wasn't until his mother rounded up the family for the noonday meal that Bill was missed. The last anyone remembered seeing him was just before they had forded the river.

The mother and eight or ten of the older children hurried back to the river and hunted everywhere, but they could find no trace of the lost boy. When evening came, they were forced to go back to the covered wagon, and later, to continue their journey without him. Ever after, when they thought of Bill, they remembered the river, and so they naturally came to speak of him as Pecos Bill.

What had happened to Bill was this. He had strayed off into the mesquite, and a few hours later was found by a wise old Coyote, who was the undisputed leader of the Loyal and Approved Packs of the Pecos and Rio Grande Valleys. He was, in fact, the Granddaddy of the entire race of Coyotes, and so his followers, out of affection to him, called him Grandy.

When he accidentally met Bill, Grandy was curious, but shy. He sniffed and he yelped, and he ran this way and that, the better to get the scent, and to make sure there was no danger. After a while he came quite near, sat up on his haunches, and waited to see what the boy would do. Bill trotted up to Grandy and began running his hands through the long, shaggy hair.

"What a nice old doggie you are," he repeated again and again.

"Yes, and what a nice Cropear you are," yelped Grandy joyously.

And so, ever after, the Coyotes called the child Cropear.

Grandy was much pleased with his find and so, by running ahead and stopping and barking softly, he led the boy to the jagged side of Cabezon, or the Big Head, as it was called. This was a towering mass of mountain that rose abruptly, as if by magic, from the prairie. Around the base of this mountain the various families of the Loyal and Approved Packs had burrowed out their dens.

Here, far away from the nearest human dwelling, Grandy made a home for Cropear, and taught him all the knowledge of the wild out-of-doors. He led Cropear to the berries that were good to eat, and dug up roots that were sweet and spicy. He showed the boy how to break open the small nuts from the piñon; and when Cropear wanted a drink, he led him to a vigorous young mother Coyote who gave him of her milk. Cropear thus drank in the very life blood of a thousand generations of wild life and became a native beast of the prairie, without at all knowing that he was a man-child.

Grandy became his teacher and schooled him in the knowledge that had been handed down through thousands of generations of the Pack's life. He taught Cropear the many signal calls, and the code of right and wrong, and the gentle art of loyalty to the leader. He also trained him to leap long distances and to dance; and to flip-flop and to twirl his body so fast that the eye could not follow his movements. And most important of all, he instructed him in the silent, rigid pose of invisibility, so that he could see all that was going on around him without being seen.

And as Cropear grew tall and strong, he became the pet of the Pack. The Coyotes were always bringing him what they thought he would like to eat, and were ever showing him the many secrets of the fine art of hunting. They taught him where the Field-mouse nested, where the Song Thrush hid her eggs, where the Squirrel stored his nuts; and where the

Mountain Sheep concealed their young among the towering rocks.

When the Jack-rabbit was to be hunted, they gave Cropear his station and taught him to do his turn in the relay race. And when the pronghorn Antelope was to be captured, Cropear took his place among the encircling pack and helped bring the fleeting animal to bay and pull him down, in spite of his darting, charging antlers.

Grandy took pains to introduce Cropear to each of the animals and made every one of them promise he would not harm the growing man-child. "Au-g-gh!" growled the Mountain Lion, "I will be as careful as I can. But be sure to tell your child to be careful, too!"

"Gr-r-rr!" growled the fierce Grizzly Bear, "I have crunched many a marrow bone, but I will not harm your boy. Gr-r-rr!"

"Yes, we'll keep our perfumery and our quills in our inside vest pockets," mumbled the silly Skunk and Porcupine, as if suffering from adenoids.

But when Grandy talked things over with the Bull Rattlesnake, he was met with the defiance of hissing rattles. "Nobody will ever make me promise to protect anybody or anything! S-s-s-s-ss! I'll do just as I please!"

"Be careful of your wicked tongue," warned Grandy, "or you'll be very sorry."

But when Grandy met the Wouser, things were even worse. The Wouser was a cross between the Mountain Lion and the Grizzly Bear, and was ten times larger than either. Besides that, he was the nastiest creature in the world. "I can only give you fair warning," yowled the Wouser, "and if you prize your man-child, as you say you do, you will have to keep him out of harm's way!" And as the Wouser continued, he stalked back and forth, lashing his tail and gnashing his jaws, and acting as if he were ready to snap somebody's head off. "What's more, you know that nobody treats me as a friend. Everybody runs around behind my back spreading lies about me. Everybody says I carry hydrophobia—the deadly poison—about on my person, and because of all these lies, I am shunned like a leper. Now you come sneaking around asking me to help you. Get out of my sight before I do something I shall be sorry for!"

"I'm not sneaking," barked Grandy in defiance, "and besides, you're the one who will be sorry in the end."

So it happened that all the animals, save only the Bull Rattlesnake and the Wouser, promised to help Cropear bear a charmed life so that no harm should come near him. And by good fortune, the boy was never sick. The vigorous exercise and the fresh air and the constant sunlight helped him to become the healthiest, strongest, most active boy in the world.

Mexico

Why the Burro Lives with the Man

A "pourquoi" beast tale from Mexico gives a logical reason for the donkey's attachment to man. Even though that attachment is not one of affection, the burro is honest in his dealings with the one whose protection from wild animals he seeks. [From Catherine Bryan and Mabra Madden, *The Cactus Fence* (Macmillan, 1943).]

Benito, the burro, lived on the mesa to hide from the mountain lion. When he first came there to live, he trembled every time he looked toward the mountains that had once been his home.

"How fortunate I am," he said, "to have found this friendly mesa! Indeed, I am fortunate to be alive. The lion ate my friends and relatives one by one. Again and again he tried to have me for his dinner." Benito closed his eyes to shut out the thought.

Now the only food Benito found on the mesa was sagebrush and cactus. Said he one day, "This is poor fare for an honest burro. How I long for some green grass and a drink of cool water! Starving is almost as bad as being chased by the lion. But what can I do? I cannot go back to the mountains, though I am sick and tired of this kind of food. Surely there must be some place where I can live in safety and still have enough to eat."

As the days passed, Benito became more and more indignant whenever he thought of the mountain lion.

Said he, "My patience with that fellow is at an end! He can't do this to me! Why should I be afraid of him? The next time we meet I will teach him a lesson." And he pranced across the mesa playing he was chasing his enemy. He ended the chase by kicking a bush, saying, "That for you, you miserable cat! Now you will know better than to cross the path of Benito, the burro."

At that very moment his sharp ears caught a sound from behind. In terror he turned, and there, sitting on a rock, smiling from ear to ear, was none other than Don Coyote!

"Good day to you, Señor Benito," said Don Coyote. "It is indeed a pleasure to see you again. How do you like your new home?"

"Must you always sneak up from behind?" said Benito. "You frightened me out of my wits. I thought it was the mountain lion. See how upset I am! Have you no respect for the feelings of others?"

"My dear, dear friend!" said Don Coyote. "I am beginning to wonder if you are glad to see me. After all, we have known each other for a long time. Yes? No?"

"I know you only too well!" answered Benito. "How did you happen to find me?"

"I figured it out," replied Don Coyote. "This morning I met the mountain lion. He said 'Do you know where Benito is?' 'No,' I said, 'I do not.' Then I thought to myself, 'Now where could Benito be? He could be in only one of two places—either here or there. He is not here; therefore he is there. Now where is there? Why, over there on the mesa, of course.' So, just to make sure, I thought I would pay you a visit and, sure enough, here I am and there you are!"

"Did you tell the mountain lion all of that?" asked Benito angrily.

"No-o. Not exactly," answered Don Coyote, "although he did say he would make it worth my while if I found out."

"You are a villain!" cried Benito. "You would sell me to the lion. You deserve to be kicked!"

"How you misjudge me!" said Don Coyote. "I would not tell the lion your whereabouts, especially for the few bones he had to offer. While talking with him I said to myself, 'I like Benito. He is a good burro. Here is a chance to do him a favor. I will go over to the mesa and have a talk with him and, if he will listen to reason, perhaps we can arrive at a bargain.'" And Don Coyote looked at Benito out of the corner of his eye.

"He is a sly rogue," thought Benito. "I will listen to him although I know there is a skunk in the bush." To Don Coyote he said, "What do you propose to do for me?"

"My friend," said Don Coyote, "the lion wants you for his dinner. Should he learn you are on the mesa, you will again have to run for your life. It is not a pleasant thought, is it?"

"I do not like to think of it," said Benito.

"How would you like to live where you would be safe from the lion and at the same time have enough to eat and drink?"

"You interest me!" replied Benito. "Pray continue."

"At the foot of those hills," said Don Coyote, pointing to a patch of green, "there lives a man. He is the only creature the lion fears. The animals that live behind his fence are safe. They do his work and he gives them food and a place in the barnyard."

"To work for the man means changing one's way of living," said Benito.

"It is better to change one's way of living than to perish," said Don Coyote.

"A fence keeps one from going where one chooses," said Benito.

"A fence keeps one from being eaten by the mountain lion," said Don Coyote.

"Why have you taken such an interest in my safety?" asked Benito. "What do you expect to gain from it?"

"My friend," said Don Coyote, "when I think of that cruel mountain lion that eats harmless creatures, I shudder. I do not want him to eat you. I want to know you are safe and out of harm's way."

"Is that all that keeps you from being happy?" asked Benito.

"Now that you have mentioned it," said Don Coyote, "there is one more thing I would like to do. I will tell you all, and you will know that I have a tender heart. I know the man has some chickens. He keeps them in a barnyard like the other animals. They beg the man to set them free. I have heard their pleadings. It is pitiful!" And Don Coyote wiped a tear from his eye.

"I have tried to rescue them many times," he continued, "but each time the man refuses to listen. I offered him land, gold, diamonds—in fact, everything one could desire. He simply would not listen to reason. It has distressed me greatly.

"Then today I had a happy thought. I said to myself, 'Without me Benito would never have thought of going to the man for protection from the lion. In return he will surely be willing to help me help those poor, dear chickens. The peg that fastens the door of the henhouse is too high for me to reach. Tonight, after the man goes to bed, Benito will pull out the peg. I will then take the chickens, one by one, to my cave in the hills where they will once again be happy.'"

Benito looked Don Coyote straight in the eye. Said he, "I am an honest burro. If I live with the man I will give him an honest day's work for my food. I will have nothing to do with your scheme to steal his chickens."

"So that is how you repay me for trying to save your life!" cried Don Coyote. "It will serve you right if you are eaten by the lion."

"Take that!" cried Benito, giving Don Coyote a kick that sent him rolling.

Don Coyote scrambled to his feet. "You stupid burro!" he cried. "You will regret that kick! Now I will take the bones from the lion."

"Then take that, and that, and that!" cried Benito as he kicked the coyote again and again.

"You will pay dearly for those kicks, Señor Burro," cried Don Coyote. "I will help the lion eat you."

"Take that for the lion!" cried Benito, and he gave such a mighty kick that it rolled the angry coyote over the edge of the mesa. Benito watched him pick himself out of a bed of cactus.

"Hee-haw," laughed Benito as Don Coyote loped away toward the mountains.

"Well," said Benito at last, "that is that. What else is there left for me to do but go to the house of the man? It is better to live than to die." And, so saying, he departed.

From that day to this he has lived with the man. He has not always been happy, but you cannot drive him away. And when he remembers how he kicked Don Coyote he laughs and sings, "Hee-haw, hee-haw, hee-haw!"

South America

The Tale of the Lazy People

Charles Finger, the author of *Tales from Silver Lands,* collected these stories from all parts of South America. This one comes from Colombia. From it we learn not only why there are so many monkeys but also why they throw nuts and branches at people passing through the forest. *Tales from Silver Lands* won the Newbery award in 1925. [From Charles J. Finger, *Tales from Silver Lands* (Doubleday, 1924).]

Long, long ago there were no monkeys, and the trees were so full of fruit, and the vines of grapes, that people became lazy, and at last did little but eat and sleep, being too idle to carry away the rinds and skins of the fruit that they lived on, and certainly too lazy to clean their thatched houses.

It was very pleasant at first, but soon not so pleasant, for winged things that bit and stung came in thousands to feed on the things thrown aside and they too grew lazy, finding so much to eat ready at hand, and when people tried to brush them away there was a loud and angry buzz and much irritated stinging, so that soon every one was wonderstruck, not knowing exactly what to do. For a time it seemed easier to move the little village to a new spot and to build new houses, for the dwellings were light affairs and in a day or less a good house could be built. But then they lived by a lake from which the water for drinking was taken, and as it was but a little body of water, it was not long before the people had built right round the still pool and so were back again at the start-ing place. As for the stinging flies, they were soon worse than the mosquitoes, while a great wasp with pink head and legs and bands of black and gold on its body, though very pretty to see, was worst of all. So it was no easy matter to know what to do, and there was much talk and much argument, and all that the people agreed on was that something had to be done, and that, very soon.

One day there came to the village a queer and rather faded kind of man, ragged and tattered and torn as though he had scrambled for miles through the thorn-bush forest. He had rough yellow hair, and queer wrinkles at the corners of his eyes which made him look as if he were smiling. It was late in the afternoon when he came and the people were taking their rest after the noon meal, so no one took much notice of him although he went here and there, looking at things, and so walked round the lake. But the curiosity of everyone was excited when he was seen to make a basket, which he did quickly, and then commence to gather up the fruit skins and rinds in one place. Now and then some one or other raised himself in his hammock, with a mind to talk to him, but it seemed almost too much trouble, and when some great blue-winged butterfly fluttered past or some golden-throated humming-bird flashed in the sunlight, their eyes wandered away from the old man and they forgot him again. So the sunlight died and the forest was a velvet blackness and everyone slept, though the old man still worked on, and the next morning when the people awoke he was still working diligently, though he had but a small place cleared after all.

The very thought that anyone would work all night made the head man shiver with a kind of excitement, yet he was very curious to know why the stranger went to so much trouble, seeing that he neither lived there nor was of the lake men. At the same time it made his spirit droop to think that, if the place was to be cleared up, he and everyone else had a mountain of work in sight. So Tera, the head man, called to Cuco, who was his servant, telling him to bring the stranger to him, and Cuco, who was very respectful, said that he would attend to it. Then Cuco did his part by calling Yana and delivering the message to him. And Yana in turn told his servant, Mata, who told his servant, Pera, who told his servant, Racas, who told a boy, so that at last the message reached the old man. Then back went the old man, handed by the boy to Racas, by Racas to Pera, by Pera to Mata, by Mata to Yana, and by Yana to Cuco, so that at last he stood before Tera, the head man, and the others, being curious to know what was afoot, gathered about.

"What is your name, from where do you come, and what do you want?" asked Tera, putting his three questions at once, to save trouble. Then the head man looked at those about him with a little frown, as much as to say, "Note how wisely I act," and each man who had heard, seeing that the head man looked his way, nodded at his neighbor, as though calling attention to the wisdom of the head man, so all went very well. But the little old man stood there very simply, making no fuss at all and quite unimpressed with the greatness of the great man.

"I want to work," he answered. "I want to be told what you want done and to see that it is done."

To be sure, the language that he spoke was one new to those who listened, but somehow they seemed to understand. But the thing that he said they found truly astonishing and could hardly believe their ears. But the head man, though as astonished as any one there, quickly regained his composure and asked this question:

"What is your trade?"

"I have no trade," said the old man. "But I get things done."

"What kind of things?"

"All kinds of things."

"Do you mean big things, like house-building and all that?" asked the head man.

"Yes. And little things too, which are really big things when you come to consider," said the old man, but that seemed an odd if not a silly thing to say, the head man thought.

"Little things left undone soon become big things," explained the old man, and waved his hand in the direction of a heap of fruit skins and husks near by.

"Yes. Yes. But you must not preach to us, you know," said Tera a little testily. "Tell me the names of the trades you have."

So the little old man began to tell, naming big things and very little things, things important and things not important at all, and having finished, asked very politely whether any one there had anything to be done. As for pay he said that he wanted none at all and would take none, and he said that because some of those gathered about him began offering him things.

For instance, Pera said: "If you work for me, I will let you have one fish out of every ten that you catch, for I am a fisherman." And Racas pushed him aside, saying: "But I will do better, for I am supposed to be fruit gatherer and will give you two things for every ten you gather." And so it went, each bidding higher than his neighbor, until it came to the turn of the man whose duty it was to gather the rinds and fruit skins. He said, "I will let you have, not one out of ten, nor two out of ten, nor five out of ten that you gather, but ten out of ten, if you will work for me." At that the old man said quite positively that he would take no pay at all.

No more was said then and the little old man turned away without as much as bowing to the head man, seeing which the head man waved his hand and said: "You may go, and so that you will lose no time, you need not bow to me." And all the rest gathered there said very hastily: "Nor need you bow to me, either."

The old man took small notice of any one, but went away singing, for he had a gay, light-hearted disposition, and having reached the place he had cleared, he took flat pieces of wood and began cutting out figures like little men, and each figure had a kind of handle that looked like a long tail. Nor did he cease whittling until he had made at least twenty wooden figures for each man in the village. Being finished he stood up to stretch his legs and straighten his back, and when the people asked him what the little figures were for, he shrugged his shoulders but spoke never a word. Then he lifted the figures that he had made, one by one, and set them upright in the sand until there was a long row of them, and took his place in front of them, like a general before his army. It was beautiful to look at, for one figure was as like another as one pin is like another, and for a moment even the old man stood admiring the line. After a moment he waved his hand in a peculiar way, spoke some magic word, and waved his hand again, at which each of the figures came to life and nodded its head, seeing which all the people laughed and clapped their hands. The ragged man bade them make no noise, but watch.

"Since you do not like to work," he said, "I have made twenty figures for each of you, and they will work for you without pay, doing what you require them to do; only observe this, you must not give any figure more than one particular job. And now let each man or woman clap his hands three times, then call out the name of the thing to be done."

When he had said this, the figures started running, twenty gathering in a circle about each man there, bowing from the hips and straightening themselves again, so that their tails of wood went up and down like pump-handles.

"Now see," said the ragged man, "you have things to work for you, and as I call out, the figures will stand forth, each ready to do his task." And he began calling, thus:

"Armadillo hunters, stand forth!" and a hundred and more active figures ran together like soldiers.

So he named others in order as:

Bread-makers.

Cassava gatherers.

Despolvadores, who would gather up dust.

Esquiladors, who would shear the goats.

Farsante men, whose work was to amuse tired men.

Guardas, to keep order about the place.

Horneros, or bakers.

Industriosos, who were to do odd jobs everywhere.

Jumentos, whose work it was to carry burdens.

Labradores, to do heavy work and clear away garbage.

Moledores, to grind the corn.

Narradores, who told stories, related gossip and so.

Olleros, or pot makers.

Pocilga figures, to attend to the pigs.

Queseros, to make cheese from goat's milk.

Rumbosos, or proud-looking things to walk in parades.

Servidores, or food carriers.

Trotadores, to run errands.

Vaqueros, to attend to the cows.

So everyone was well pleased and each one had his twenty figures to do all that needed to be done, and all that day there was a great scraping and cleaning and carrying and currying and hurrying and scurrying. Silently the little figures worked, never stopping, never tiring, never getting in one another's way, and all that the living people had to do was to rest and watch the men of wood, and keep their brains free for higher things. For it must be remembered that before the old man came there with his wonderful gift, the people had complained there was so much to be done that they had no time to write poems or to make songs or to create music, and that with the daily tasks abolished their brains would be more active.

Not two days had passed before the children of the place complained that they did not have a chance and that they had so much to do, what with hunting for things lost, looking after their small brothers and sisters, keeping things in order, trying to remember things they were told, cleaning things, and a dozen other tasks, that they really had no time to play, much less to study. So they went in a body to the old man and asked him to give each child twenty figures to do odd things. There was a great deal of fire and expression in his eyes when he made answer that if the children really needed help he would lose no time in providing it. But the young people were quite positive that they were overworked, and the long and short of it was that the old man whittled out many, many more figures, and in another twenty-four hours each and every boy and girl had his own

Abaniquero, or fan maker, so that none had to pluck a palm leaf.

Baliquero figure, to carry letters and messages.

Cabrero, to look after the goats.

Desalumbrado, to hunt for things in the dark.

Enseñador, or private teacher, who was never to scold.

Florista, to save them the trouble of gathering flowers.

Guasón figure, to amuse them.

Hojaldarista, whose work it was to make cakes.

Juego figure, to arrange games.

Keeper of things.

Lector, to read and tell stories.

Mimo, to act as clown.

Niñera, to look after younger children.

Obediencia figure, to make others obey.

Postor, to buy things for them.

Quitar figures, to take things away when children tired.

Recordación figures, or rememberers.

Solfeadors, to sing to them.

Tortada men, to make pies.

Volantes, as servants.

So things seemed to be going very well, and before a month had passed in all that place there was not a thing out of order, soiled, broken, bent, lost, misplaced, undone, unclean, or disorderly. Neither man nor woman nor child had to worry; dinners were always prepared, fruits gathered, beds made, houses in perfect order, and all was spick and span. All that the grown-up people had to do was to look on, and no one was proud of the order in his house because every other house in the place was as orderly. As for the children, they had nothing at all to do but to eat, drink, rest, and sleep. Then, presently, more figures were called for as this one or that wanted a larger house, a finer garden, or grander clothes.

But as the wooden figures became more numerous and as no figure could do more than one task, the ragged man had to make figures for the figures and servants for the servants, for as things went on, there had to be more fruit gatherers, more water carriers, more scavengers, more cooks, because the figures had to eat and drink. Thus it came to pass that before long, instead of there being twenty figures for each man, there were sixty or seventy, with new ones coming from the old man's knife every day. Soon the lively manikins were everywhere, inside houses as well as outside, thick as flies in summer and certainly a great deal more persistent, for there could be no closing of doors against the manikins. Indeed, had anything like that been attempted there would have been a great cry for special door-openers. So, many

houses were quite cluttered with wooden men, those who were on duty rushing about until it made the head swim to look at them, and those who were resting or sleeping, for soon they learned to rest and to sleep, lying about the floors, piled up in corners, or hanging to rafters by their tails. All that increase in help had made for the production of a thousand or more guardas, whose task it was to keep order, and they were everywhere, alert and watchful and officious, and the real people had to step about very gingerly sometimes, to avoid treading on them and annoying them.

At last there came a day when the people began to grow a little tired of doing nothing, and they told one another that a little help was a very good thing, but help in excess, too much of a good thing altogether. So there was a meeting and much talk and the manikin narradors, whose duty it was to carry gossip and the news, were very busy, rushing from here to there with their scraps of information.

"It is very clear that something must be done," said Tera, the head man.

"But everything *is* being done," answered the little old man. "If *everything* is done, something *must* be done."

"I did not mean that," said Tera, who seemed a little testy. "I meant to say that these wooden men must be kept in their places."

"But they *are* in their places," replied the old man. "Their place is everywhere because they do everything, so they are in their places."

"You see, the days are so very long, so very dull," said the man who wished to have time that he might become a poet. "At the shut of day we are not weary."

"We do not want to be petted," said another.

"The trouble is," sighed a fat man, "you can't be happy when everything is done for you."

"And we don't want to be nobodies," shouted another.

Another said very mournfully: "It seems to me that when these wooden things do things with our things, then the things that they do and make and care for are not our things."

"Too many 'things' in that speech," said the fat man.

"Well, there are too many things," answered the other. "Look at me. I used to be gardener and now I'm nothing. When my garden is dug and planted and tended and watered and the very flowers plucked by these wooden things, and when other wooden things pick up the leaves and pull the weeds and do everything, then my garden does not seem to be mine." He added after awhile: "I hope you know what I mean, because it is not very clear to me, yet it is so. I remember—"

At that the little old man put up his hand and said: "But that is against the contract. You must not try to remember, really you must not, because there are manikins to do all the remembering, if you please."

"Well, but I think—" began the man, when he was again interrupted.

"Please do not think," said the little old man. "We have things to do the thinking, if you please." He thought for a moment, his bent forefinger on his lips, then he said: "I'll see what can be done. It is clear that you are not satisfied, although you have everything that you asked for and certainly all the time that you want."

"Let us do something," murmured Tera.

"I'm afraid there is nothing that you can do," said the little old man, "because, as you see, everything is done, and when everything is done it is quite clear that something cannot be left to be done. The only thing that is clear is that there is nothing to be done."

At that the meeting broke up and each went to his own hammock to think things over, and soon the general cry was: "We must have elbow room." And hearing that, the little old man went to work and whittled more figures of wood, a whole army of them, ten for each living man, woman, and child, and in voices that creaked like wooden machinery they marched hither and thither, crying: "Elbow room. Elbow room!"

Soon there was confusion. It was manikin against manikin for a time, the Elbow-roomers thrusting and pushing the other working manikins, some going about their work with frantic haste, others interfering with them, clutching at them and at the things they carried, a tangled knot of them sometimes staggering, to go down with a crash. Soon in every house was a jangling tumult, manikins and men running about in houses and dashing out into the open spaces outside; the noise of slamming doors and breaking pots; the clamor of animals. Above all could be heard everywhere cries of "We want elbow room! We want elbow room!" Soon men were running away from the houses with those strange swift manikins hanging to them, sometimes beating them, while other manikins threw things out of the doors and through windows, food and household things. And excited children fled too, while their manikins ran at their sides, some chattering, some acting the clown as was their duty, some telling stories as they ran, while other strange little figures of wood ran bearing heavy burdens. It was all a dreadful mix-up with no one knowing what to do, no one knowing where to go, and everywhere the manikins who were guardas, or order keepers, ran about, tripping people and manikins alike in the effort to stop the rush. But when the day was near its end there were no people in the houses and the hammocks swung idly, for all the men and women and children, even the white-haired grandfathers and grandmothers, had fled to the further side of the lake, where they could have elbow room, leaving the houses and all that was in them to the manikins.

The next day, the people plucked their fruit for themselves and it seemed as though fruit was never sweeter. The water that they carried from the lake tasted better and cooler than water had for many a long day, and when night came they were happily tired and slept well, without any manikin to swing their hammocks and sing to them. And in the morning they woke early to discover the pink and gold of the sunrise most wonderful to see, and there was music in the sound of the wind among the grasses. So as the day passed they were both amazed and astonished at the wonderful and beautiful things that they had almost forgotten, the sight of butterflies fluttering from flower to flower, the shadows chasing across the hills, the richness of the green earth and the blueness of the sky, the gold of sunlight on the leaves, the rippling water and the bending trees; indeed the memory of the manikin days was like a fearful nightmare. Very lighthearted then they grew and the world was full of the music of their laughter and song, and briskly they worked, enjoying it all, building new houses and making things to put in them.

Meanwhile in the village things had gone queerly. For one thing the Elbow-roomers kept up their crowding and pushing, so that the manikins trying to work at their old tasks (and there were many who went on just as before) were sadly hindered. There were other figures of wood with nothing to do, since the people they served were gone, and these fell to quarreling among themselves and grew mischievous. For instance, the pot makers and the pot cleaners fell out, and the pot cleaners started to break the pots so that the pot makers would have more work to do. That meant that the clay gatherers and the clay diggers had to work harder; then because they worked harder, though to be sure all their work meant nothing and was little more than idle bustle, they grew hungrier and wanted more to eat. Because of all that the fruit gatherers had more to do and the water carriers had to work harder and the cassava bread makers had to bake as they had never baked before. That brought the fire builders into it, and of course the wood gatherers also, for they too had to work harder and to eat more, so still more work came on the food bringers. And all the time the Elbow-roomers rushed about, always in groups of ten, driving and commanding, rushing on workers and sweeping them aside. So everywhere were little figures hurrying one after the other, going to and fro, busy about nothing, quarreling about nothing, fighting about nothing.

The trouble came when the Elbow-roomers interfered with the dogs and the cats, the goats and the hens, pushing and hustling them. For the animals, disliking all disorder and clatter, fell upon the manikins, workers and idlers alike. Seeing that, the household utensils took a hand and the very pots and kettles ran or rolled or fell, spilling hot water over the wooden things with pump-handle tails. The very embers from the fires leaped into the fray. All the while from the metates in which the corn had been ground came a low growling, and the growling formed itself into words:

Day by day you tortured us—
Grind, grind, grind.

Holi! Holi!
Huqui! Huqui!
Grind, grind, grind.

Bring to us the torturers—
Grind, grind, grind.

Let them feel our power now—
Grind! *Grind!* GRIND!

So the metates turned and turned, going round and round without hands, and presently an Elbow-roomer that was struggling with a corn-grinder stumbled, and both fell between the grinding stones and in a moment were crushed to powder. In a flash house utensils and animals learned the new trick, and in every house manikins were pushed into the grinding stones. Then sparks began to fly and roofs to catch on fire and manikins bolted here and there in confusion, sometimes jamming in doorways, there were so many and all in such disorder. Then came dazzling, flickering lightning and a great rain, so that for very safety the manikins fled to the forest and climbed the trees. And there they have lived ever since, for they grew hair and became monkeys. But the remembrance of all that passed stayed with them, and in their hearts to this very day is no love for man, and for that very reason when a Christian passes through a forest he must look well to himself, lest the manikins in revenge try to hurt him by casting nuts and branches at his head.

The West Indies

From Tiger to Anansi

The origin of this story lies in Africa. It was brought to the West Indies by slaves, no doubt, who remembered this tale and others from their tribal fires. It became adapted to the new locale, reflecting the modes, manners, customs, climate, and landscape of the new place. Some of the Anansi stories parallel the Uncle Remus stories of the South in the United States. They come from the same source.

Anansi is a fascinating character, sometimes a man, sometimes a spider. In the West Indies, he is called "ceiling Thomas," because when he is a spider, the walls are his walking ground. [From Philip M. Sherlock, *Anansi, the Spider Man: Jamaican Folk Tales* (Crowell, 1954).]

Once upon a time and a long long time ago the Tiger was king of the forest.

At evening when all the animals sat together in a circle and talked and laughed together, Snake would ask,

"Who is the strongest of us all?"

"Tiger is strongest," cried the dog. "When Tiger whispers the trees listen. When Tiger is angry and cries out, the trees tremble."

"And who is the weakest of all?" asked Snake.

"Anansi," shouted dog, and they all laughed together. "Anansi the spider is weakest of all. When he whispers no one listens. When he shouts everyone laughs."

Now one day the weakest and strongest came face to face, Anansi and Tiger. They met in a clearing of the forest. The frogs hiding under the cool leaves saw them. The bright green parrots in the branches heard them.

When they met, Anansi bowed so low that his forehead touched the ground. Tiger did not greet him. Tiger just looked at Anansi.

"Good morning, Tiger," cried Anansi. "I have a favor to ask."

"And what is it, Anansi?" said Tiger.

"Tiger, we all know that you are strongest of us all. This is why we give your name to many things. We have Tiger lilies, and Tiger stories and Tiger moths and Tiger this and Tiger that. Everyone knows that I am weakest of all. This is why nothing bears my name. Tiger, let something be called after the weakest one so that men may know my name too."

"Well," said Tiger, without so much as a glance toward Anansi, "what would you like to bear your name?"

"The stories," cried Anansi. "The stories that we tell in the forest at evening time when the sun goes down, the stories about Br'er Snake and Br'er Tacumah, Br'er Cow and Br'er Bird and all of us."

Now Tiger liked these stories and he meant to keep them as Tiger stories. He thought to himself, How stupid, how weak this Anansi is. I will play a trick on him so that all the animals will laugh at him. Tiger moved his tail slowly

from side to side and said, "Very good, Anansi, very good. I will let the stories be named after you, if you do what I ask."

"Tiger, I will do what you ask."

"Yes, I am sure you will, I am sure you will," said Tiger, moving his tail slowly from side to side. "It is a little thing that I ask. Bring me Mr. Snake alive. Do you know Snake who lives down by the river, Mr. Anansi? Bring him to me alive and you can have the stories."

Tiger stopped speaking. He did not move his tail. He looked at Anansi and waited for him to speak. All the animals in the forest waited. Mr. Frog beneath the cool leaves, Mr. Parrot up in the tree, all watched Anansi. They were all ready to laugh at him.

"Tiger, I will do what you ask," said Anansi. At these words a great wave of laughter burst from the forest. The frogs and parrots laughed. Tiger laughed loudest of all, for how could feeble Anansi catch Snake alive?

Anansi went away. He heard the forest laughing at him from every side.

That was on Monday morning. Anansi sat before his house and thought of plan after plan. At last he hit upon one that could not fail. He would build a Calaban.

On Tuesday morning Anansi built a Calaban. He took a strong vine and made a noose. He hid the vine in the grass. Inside the noose he set some of the berries that Snake loved best. Then he waited. Soon Snake came up the path. He saw the berries and went toward them. He lay across the vine and ate the berries. Anansi pulled at the vine to tighten the noose, but Snake's body was too heavy. Anansi saw that the Calaban had failed.

Wednesday came. Anansi made a deep hole in the ground. He made the sides slippery with grease. In the bottom he put some of the bananas that Snake loved. Then he hid in the bush beside the road and waited.

Snake came crawling down the path toward the river. He was hungry and thirsty. He saw the bananas at the bottom of the hole. He saw that the sides of the hole were slippery. First he wrapped his tail tightly around the trunk of a tree, then he reached down into the hole and ate the bananas. When he was finished he pulled himself up by his tail and crawled away. Anansi had lost his bananas and he had lost Snake, too.

Thursday morning came. Anansi made a Fly Up. Inside the trap he put an egg. Snake came down the path. He was happy this morning, so happy that he lifted his head and a third of his long body from the ground. He just lowered his head, took up the egg in his mouth, and never even touched the trap. The Fly Up could not catch Snake.

What was Anansi to do? Friday morning came. He sat and thought all day. It was no use.

Now it was Saturday morning. This was the last day. Anansi went for a walk down by the river. He passed by the hole where Snake lived. There was Snake, his body hidden in the hole, his head resting on the ground at the entrance to the hole. It was early morning. Snake was watching the sun rise above the mountains.

"Good morning, Anansi," said Snake.

"Good morning, Snake," said Anansi.

"Anansi, I am very angry with you. You have been trying to catch me all week. You set a Fly Up to catch me. The day before you made a Slippery Hole for me. The day before that you made a Calaban. I have a good mind to kill you, Anansi."

"Ah, you are too clever, Snake," said Anansi. "You are much too clever. Yes, what you say is so. I tried to catch you, but I failed. Now I can never prove that you are the longest animal in the world, longer even than the bamboo tree."

"Of course I am the longest of all animals," cried Snake. "I am much longer than the bamboo tree."

"What, longer than that bamboo tree across there?" asked Anansi.

"Of course I am," said Snake. "Look and see." Snake came out of the hole and stretched himself out at full length.

"Yes, you are very, very long," said Anansi, "but the bamboo tree is very long, too. Now that I look at you and at the bamboo tree I must say that the bamboo tree seems longer. But it's hard to say because it is farther away."

"Well, bring it nearer," cried Snake. "Cut it down and put it beside me. You will soon see that I am much longer."

Anansi ran to the bamboo tree and cut it down. He placed it on the ground and cut off all its branches. Bush, bush, bush, bush! There it was, long and straight as a flag-staff.

"Now put it beside me," said Snake.

Anansi put the long bamboo tree down on the ground beside the Snake. Then he said:

"Snake, when I go up to see where your head is, you will crawl up. When I go down to see where your tail is, you will crawl down. In that way you will always seem to be longer than the bamboo tree, which really is longer than you are."

"Tie my tail, then!" said Snake. "Tie my tail! I know that I am longer than the bamboo, whatever you say."

Anansi tied Snake's tail to the end of the bamboo. Then he ran up to the other end.

"Stretch, Snake, stretch, and we will see who is longer."

A crowd of animals were gathering round. Here was something better than a race. "Stretch, Snake, stretch," they called.

Snake stretched as hard as he could. Anansi tied him around his middle so that he should not slip back. Now one more try. Snake knew that if he stretched hard enough he would prove to be longer than the bamboo.

Anansi ran up to him. "Rest yourself for a little, Snake, and then stretch again. If you can stretch another six inches you will be longer than the bamboo. Try your hardest. Stretch so that you even have to shut your eyes. Ready?"

"Yes," said Snake. Then Snake made a mighty effort. He stretched so hard that he had to squeeze his eyes shut. "Hooray!" cried the animals. "You are winning, Snake. Just two inches more."

And at that moment Anansi tied Snake's head to the bamboo. There he was. At last he had caught Snake, all by himself.

The animals fell silent. Yes, there Snake was, all tied up, ready to be taken to Tiger. And feeble Anansi had done this. They could laugh at him no more.

And never again did Tiger dare to call these stories by his name. They were Anansi stories forever after, from that day to this.

The Magic Orange Tree

In Haiti, the oral tradition is still vitally alive in the communal storytelling of the rural areas. Diane Wolkstein, who heard this "conte chanté" told and sung, explains that the introductory words "Cric? Crac!" are the verbal pledge between storyteller and audience. " 'Cric?' the Haitian storyteller calls out when she or he has a story to tell. 'Crac!' the audience responds *if* they want that storyteller to begin." The protective orange tree that grows from the mother's grave has a parallel with the guardian hazel tree in the Grimm "Cinderella" or "Aschen Puttel." Here it is not only a universal archetype, but also reflects the specific Haitian practice of planting a new born child's umbilical cord with a pit from a fruit tree; the fruit from the new tree belongs to the child to be sold or bartered. [From *The Magic Orange Tree and Other Haitian Folktales,* coll. Diane Wolkstein (Knopf, 1978).]

Cric? Crac!

There was once a girl whose mother died when she was born. Her father waited for some time to remarry, but when he did, he married a woman who was both mean and cruel. She was so mean there were some days she would not give the girl anything at all to eat. The girl was often hungry.

One day the girl came from school and saw on the table three round ripe oranges. *Hmmmm.* They smelled good. The girl looked around her. No one was there. She took one orange, peeled it, and ate it. Hmmm-mmm. It was good. She took a second orange and ate it. She ate the third orange. Oh-oh, she was happy. But soon her stepmother came home.

"Who has taken the oranges I left on the table?" she said. "Whoever has done so had better say their prayers now, for they will not be able to say them later."

The girl was so frightened she ran from the house. She ran through the woods until she came to her own mother's grave. All night she cried and prayed to her mother to help her. Finally she fell asleep.

In the morning the sun woke her, and as she rose to her feet something dropped from her skirt onto the ground. What was it? It was an orange pit. And the moment it entered the earth a green leaf sprouted from it. The girl watched, amazed. She knelt down and sang:

From *The Magic Orange Tree and Other Haitian Folktales,* collected by Diane Wolkstein, illustrated by Elsa Henriquez. Text copyright © 1978 by Diane Wolkstein. Illustration copyright © 1978 by Alfred A. Knopf, Inc. Reprinted by permission of Alfred A. Knopf, Inc., and Constable & Co., Ltd.

Orange tree,
Grow and grow and grow.
Orange tree, orange tree.
Grow and grow and grow,
Orange tree.
Stepmother is not real mother,
Orange tree.

The orange tree grew. It grew to the size of the girl. The girl sang:

Orange tree,
Branch and branch and branch.
Orange tree, orange tree,
Branch and branch and branch,
Orange tree.
Stepmother is not real mother,
Orange tree.

And many twisting, turning, curving branches appeared on the tree. Then the girl sang:

Orange tree,
Flower and flower and flower.
Orange tree, orange tree,
Flower and flower and flower,
Orange tree.
Stepmother is not real mother,
Orange tree.

Beautiful white blossoms covered the tree. After a time they began to fade, and small green buds appeared where the flowers had been. The girl sang:

Orange tree,
Ripen and ripen and ripen.
Orange tree, orange tree,
Ripen and ripen and ripen,
Orange tree.
Stepmother is not real mother.
Orange tree.

The oranges ripened, and the whole tree was filled with golden oranges. The girl was so delighted she danced around and around the tree, singing:

Orange tree,
Grow and grow and grow.
Orange tree, orange tree,
Grow and grow and grow,
Orange tree.
Stepmother is not real mother,
Orange tree.

But then when she looked, she saw the orange tree had grown up to the sky, far beyond her reach. What was she to do? Oh she was a clever girl. She sang:

Orange tree,
Lower and lower and lower.
Orange tree, orange tree,
Lower and lower and lower,
Orange tree.
Stepmother is not real mother,
Orange tree.

When the orange tree came down to her height, she filled her arms with oranges and returned home.

The moment the stepmother saw the gold oranges in the girl's arms, she seized them and began to eat them. Soon she had finished them all.

"Tell me, my sweet," she said to the girl, "where have you found such delicious oranges?"

The girl hesitated. She did not want to tell. The stepmother seized the girl's wrist and began to twist it.

"Tell me!" she ordered.

The girl led her stepmother through the woods to the orange tree. You remember the girl was very clever? Well, as soon as the girl came to the tree, she sang:

Orange tree,
Grow and grow and grow.
Orange tree, orange tree,
Grow and grow and grow,
Orange tree.
Stepmother is not real mother,
Orange tree.

And the orange tree grew up to the sky. What was the stepmother to do then? She began to plead and beg.

"Please," she said. "You shall be my own dear child. You may always have as much as you want to eat. Tell the tree to come down and *you* shall pick the oranges for me." So the girl quietly sang:

Orange tree,
Lower and lower and lower.
Orange tree, orange tree,
Lower and lower and lower,
Orange tree.
Stepmother is not real mother,
Orange tree.

The tree began to lower. When it came to the height of the stepmother, she leapt on it and began to climb so quickly you might have thought she was the daughter of an ape. And as she climbed from branch to branch, she ate every orange. The girl saw that there would soon be no oranges left. What would happen to her then? The girl sang:

Orange tree,
Grow and grow and grow.
Orange tree, orange tree,
Grow and grow and grow,
Orange tree.
Stepmother is not real mother,
Orange tree.

The orange tree grew and grew and grew and grew. "Help!" cried the stepmother as she rose into the sky. "H-E-E-lp. . . ."

The girl cried: *Break!* Orange tree, *Break!*

The orange tree broke into a thousand pieces . . . and the stepmother as well.

Then the girl searched among the branches until she found . . . a tiny orange pit. She carefully planted it in the earth. Softly she sang:

Orange tree,
Grow and grow and grow.
Orange tree, orange tree,
Grow and grow and grow,
Orange tree.
Stepmother is not real mother,
Orange tree.

The orange tree grew to the height of the girl. She picked some oranges and took them to market to sell. They were so sweet the people bought all her oranges.

Every Saturday she is at the marketplace selling her oranges. Last Saturday, I went to see her and asked her if she would give me a free orange. "What?" she cried. "After all I've been through!" And she gave me such a kick in the pants that that's how I got here today, to tell you the story—"The Magic Orange Tree."

Africa

The Goat Well

One of the traits of Harold Courlander as storyteller is the scientific spirit that informs his versions. He is an anthropologist turned storyteller. The texts run true to folklore form, without extraneous material; all the original strength of structure and of directness stands out clearly. We are indebted to him for making available the folktales of little-known regions.

"The folklore of Ethiopia," says Courlander, "represents a cross current of influences of the Middle East, Africa, and the West. Present-day semantic cultures—Christian and Moslem—overlie the older traditions. The country has endured invasions of Greeks, Portuguese, and other Europeans, and these have left a residue of influence on local customs of the Ethiopians." The result is a rich and unique heritage, a source of inspiration for the storyteller. [From Harold Courlander and Wolf Leslau, *The Fire on the Mountain and Other Ethiopian Stories* (Holt, 1950).]

A man named Woharia was once traveling across the plateau when he came to an abandoned house. He was tired and hungry, so he rested in the house and ate some of his bread, called injera. When he was about to leave he heard the baa-ing of a goat. He looked in all directions, but he saw nothing except the dry brown landscape. He heard the goat again, and finally he went to the old well and looked down into it. There, standing on the dry bottom, was the animal, which had somehow fallen in while searching for water to drink.

"What luck!" Woharia said. He climbed down and tied a rope around the goat, and then he came up and began to pull her out of the well.

Just at this moment a Cunama trader, with three camels loaded with sacks of grain, approached him. He greeted Woharia and asked if he might have water there for his thirsty camels.

"Naturally, if there were water here you would be welcome to it," Woharia said. "But unfortunately this is only a goat well."

"What is a goat well?" the Cunama asked.

"What do you think? It's a well that produces goats," Woharia said, and he pulled on his rope again until he got the goat to the top.

"This is really extraordinary!" the Cunama said. "I've never before heard of a goat well!"

"Why, I suppose you're right," Woharia said. "They aren't very common."

"How does it work?" the Cunama trader asked.

"Oh, it's simple enough," Woharia said. "Every night you throw a pair of goat's horns into the well, and in the morning you find a goat. Then all you have to do is draw her out."

"Unbelievable!" the Cunama said. "Man, how I'd like to own such a well!"

"So would everyone else," Woharia said, untying the goat and letting her run loose. "But few people can afford to buy such an unusual thing."

"Well, I'll tell you," the Cunama said, thinking very hard. "I'm not a rich man, but I'll pay you six bags of durra grain for it."

Woharia laughed.

"That wouldn't pay for many goats," he said.

"I'll give you twelve bags of durra, all that my camels are carrying!" the Cunama said anxiously.

Woharia smiled and shook his head.

"Seven goats a week," he said as though he were talking to himself. "Thirty goats a month. Three hundred sixty-five goats a year . . ."

But the Cunama had set his heart on owning the well.

"Look at my young sleek camels! I have just bought them in Keren! Where will you ever find better camels than these? I'll give you my twelve bags of grain and my three camels also. I'd give you more, but I own nothing else in the whole world, I swear it to you!"

Woharia thought silently for a moment.

"Since you want it so much, I'll sell it to you," he said finally.

The Cunama leaped down from his camel and embraced Woharia.

"For this goodness may you live long!" he said. "May Allah bring you many good things to give you joy!"

"Ah," Woharia said, looking at the camels, "he has already done so."

He took the three camels loaded with grain, his goat, and his few other possessions, and prepared to leave.

"Before you go, tell me your name?" the Cunama asked.

"People call me Where-I-Shall-Dance," Woharia replied. And then he went away to the south, leaving the Cunama with the well.

The Cunama was very impatient to begin getting goats from the well. When evening came, he dropped two goat's horns into it and lay down in the house to sleep. The next morning, when it was barely light, he rushed out again to draw up his first goat, but when he peered into the well, he saw nothing except the old horns he had thrown in.

He became very anxious.

"There must be some mistake!" he said to himself.

That evening he threw down two more horns, and again in the morning he rushed out to get his first goat, but once more he saw only the old goat's horns there. This time he was very worried. He scoured the country to find old goat's horns, and he threw armful after armful into the well. And all night long he sat by the well shouting into it:

"Goats, are you there? Goats, are your there?"

But nothing at all happened. When morning came at last the Cunama was angry and unhappy. He realized that he had been duped by his own anxiousness to get the well. There was nothing left to do but to go out and find the man who had taken his camels and his precious grain.

The trader traveled southward, as Woharia had done. At last, when night had fallen, he came to a village. When he arrived in the village square, where many people were gathered, he went up to them and asked:

"Do you know Where-I-Shall-Dance?"

"Why, it doesn't matter, dance anywhere you like," the people answered. "Dance right here if you wish!" And they began to sing and make music for him.

"No, no, you don't understand," he said. "What I want to know is, do you know Where-I-Shall-Dance?"

"Yes, dance here!" they said again.

The Cunama was very angry because he thought the people were making fun of him, so he went out of the village and continued his journey southward, stopping only to sleep at the edge of the road.

The next day, he came to another village, and he went to the market place and said in a loud voice:

"Does anybody know Where-I-Shall-Dance?"

The people gathered around him instantly and shouted:

"Dance here! Dance here!"

They clapped their hands and a drummer came and beat his drum, and everyone waited for the Cunama to dance.

He turned and fled from the village, believing that the people were ridiculing him. Again, he came to a village, and again he asked:

"Do you know Where-I-Shall-Dance?"

And once more the people began clapping their hands and answered:

"Yes, dance here!"

The same thing happened in every village the man entered. He began to feel very hopeless, and sometimes thought he might even be losing his mind. He began to be afraid to ask his question. Finally, one day, he came to the village of the chief of the district. When he asked his question here and the people gave him the usual answer, the news was carried to the chief, who immediately sent for him.

"Now, what sort of nonsense is this?" the chief asked. "You ask the people where you should dance and then you refuse to dance."

The unhappy man told how he had bought the dry well in exchange for his three young camels and his grain. The chief listened sympathetically. He remembered that a man named Woharia had recently settled in a nearby village, and that he had come with three camels and twelve bags of grain.

"Sit down and rest," the chief said. "I will handle this matter now."

He sent a messenger to Woharia, and when the messenger found him he said, as he had been instructed:

"There is a man waiting to see you at the house of the chief. His name is What-I-Shall-Do. The chief wishes you to come at once."

Woharia went immediately to the house of the chief, and the servants let him in.

"What can I do for you?" the chief asked.

"Why, do you know What-I-Shall-Do?" Woharia asked.

"Yes, I know what you shall do," the chief said. "You shall give back the Cunama trader his three camels and his twelve bags of grain."

Woharia was crestfallen and ashamed. He gave the Cunama back the camels and the grain.

The Cunama took them and went out. As he passed through the market place the people shouted:

"Dance here! Dance here!"

And the trader was so happy that this time he danced in the market place.

Hen and Frog

This animal folktale from Nigeria is rich in the chanting, musical cadences of the storyteller's voice. It has parallels with "The Little Red Hen," but the ending is closer to the stark justice of fable. The folktale is retold by Ashley Bryan from *Hausa Tales and Traditions,* Volume 1, translated and edited by Neil Skinner, from *Tatsuniyoyi Na Hausa,* by Frank Edgar (1969). [From *Beat the Story-Drum, Pum-Pum,* retold by Ashley Bryan (Atheneum, 1980).]

Frog and Hen once met. They walked along together.

Hen strut two steps, pecked at a bug.

Frog bopped three hops, flicked his tongue at a fly.

Strut two steps, peck at a bug.

Bop three hops, flick at a fly.

Hen flapped her wings and spun around. Frog slapped his legs and tapped the ground.

"All in together now," clucked Hen.

"How do you like the weather now?" croaked Frog.

Illustration by Ashley Bryan, from *Beat the Story-Drum, Pum-Pum.* Copyright © 1980 by Ashley Bryan. Used by permission of Atheneum Publishers.

"O click clack," clucked Hen. "See that dark cloud? That's a sign, I know it. A storm's coming."

Strut two steps, peck at a bug.

"It's still a way far off," said Frog.

Bop three hops, flick at a fly.

"Good!" said Hen. "Then there's time. Frog, let's make a hut before the storm hits."

"A hut? Not me!" said Frog. "Here's a neat hole. I'm going to get into that. Uh-uh, I won't help you make a hut."

"Suit yourself," said Hen. "If you won't help me, then I'll make the hut myself."

Hen set to work and Frog jumped into the hole. While Hen worked, Frog sang:

"Kwee kwo kwa
    Kwa kwo kwee
    A hole in the ground
    Is a hut to me."

Hen was a skillful hut builder. She flipped and she flapped, pieced, pecked and pulled every branch and straw into place. She put in two windows, a door, and thatched the roof, leaving a space in the middle for the smoke of the fireplace.

"Click, clack, cluck," she sang. "Click, clack, cluck, claa, clee."

The dark cloud came closer.

"Quick Frog," said Hen, "there's still time. Help me make a bed for the hut."

Frog sang:

"Kwee kwo kwa
    Kwa kwo kwee
    The ground in the hole
    Is a bed to me."

"Well!" said Hen. "If you won't help me then I'll make the bed myself."

So Hen built the bed all by herself. She lay down to test it.

"O click clack cluck," she sang, "click, clack, cluck, claa, clee."

The dark cloud came even closer.

"Frog," said Hen, "there's still a little time left before the storm hits. Help me gather corn."

Frog sang:

"Kwee kwo kwa
    Kwa kwo kwee
    The bugs in the hole

Are food to me."

"Uh-uh," said Hen. "If you won't help me, then I'll gather the corn myself."

So Hen gathered the corn all by herself. She piled it by the fireplace and then rolled some pumpkins onto the thatched roof. She ran into her hut and latched the door just as the storm broke.

"Blam-bam-pa-lam! Blam-bam-pa-lam!"

The thunder rolled, the earth shook, tree branches tossed, and Frog was jostled in his hole.

"Kwa kwee," he sang, "kwee kwaaa!"

The rain came down, it really poured. Hen went to the window and looked out. Frog was standing up in his hole, swaying and singing a riddle song:

"Her children dance madly
    Mama never dances
    Riddle me this, riddle me that,
    Riddle me 'round the answers.
    Mama is a tree trunk
    Her children are the branches."

"Fool," said Hen. "This is no time for riddles."

Frog stamped as he sang. Suddenly, *splish-splash,* what! Water rose in the hole.

"Eh, eh!" cried Frog. "What's happening?"

Slish-slosh, the water rose higher and higher, and Frog was flooded out of his home. He waved to Hen as he floated by her hut, and sang:

"All in together now
    How do you like the weather now?"

"Sing it!" said Hen. "But you'll soon croon another tune."

It wasn't long before the steady force of the rain stung Frog's tender skin, and he began to wail:

"Kwo kwa kwee
    Kwa kwee kwo
    The stinging rain is riddling me
    Where shall I go?"

Frog knew where he planned to go. He bounded for shelter. Hop, hop, hop, hop, hop, hop right up to Hen's hut.

"Hen, Hen!" he cried as he rapped on her door. "May I come into your hut?"

"No," said Hen. "Uh-uh! When I asked you to help me make a hut, you refused."

"If you don't let me come in," said Frog "I'll call Cat, the cat that eats little chickens."

"Go back to your hole!" said Hen.

"Cat! Cat!" yelled Frog. "Come and eat Hen."

"Shh" said Hen. She opened the door. "Hush your mouth! Shame on you, scamp! Come on in."

Frog hopped in and sat by the door. The rain beat down, but Hen's hut was tight and the rain couldn't get in. Frog leaned against the door drumming his numb toes and rubbing his stinging skin. Hen sat by the fire.

"Hen" said Frog, "may I warm myself by the fire?"

"No," said Hen. "Uh-uh!

"You didn't help me make the hut,
   Hands on your hips.
You didn't help me gather wood,
   Pursed your lips."

"If you don't let me sit by the fire," said Frog, "I'll call Cat, the cat that eats little chickens."

"That's not fair Frog, you wouldn't dare."

Frog opened the door and cried:

"Cat Cat! Here's Hen Chick
Come and eat her! Quick, come quick!"

Hen slammed and bolted the door.

"Scamp!" she said. "You scim-scam-scamp! Go ahead then, sit by the fire."

Frog hopped beside Hen and warmed himself by the fire.

"Umm-umm," he said, "fire sure feels good."

Frog spread his tingling toes to the heat and stroked his skin. Hen busied herself roasting corn. Then she began to eat.

"Hen," said Frog, "may I have some corn?"

"No," said Hen. "Uh-uh!

"You didn't help me make the hut,
   Hands on your hips.
You didn't help me gather wood,
   Pursed your lips.
You didn't help me pick the corn,
   Rolled your eyes."

"Ah! so what," said Frog. "If you don't give me some corn to eat, then I'll call Cat, the cat that eats little chickens."

"And I'll call your bluff," said Hen.

Frog opened the window and called:

"Cat! Cat! Here's Hen Chick
Come and eat her! Quick, come quick!"

Hen slammed and latched the window.

"Scamp!" she cried. "Greedy scamp! Here, help yourself."

Frog helped himself until all the corn was eaten. Then he rubbed his stomach, stretched himself and leaned back on his elbow. The food and the fire made Frog drowsy. He yawned.

"Hen," said Frog, "may I lie on your bed?"

"No!" said Hen. "Uh-uh!"

"You didn't help me make the hut,
   Hands on your hips.
You didn't help me gather wood,
   Pursed your lips.
You didn't help me pick the corn,
   Rolled your eyes.
You didn't help me make the bed,
   An' it ain't your size!"

"If you don't let me lie on your bed," said Frog, "I'll call Cat, the cat that eats little chickens."

"Shh, shh!" said Hen.

Frog jumped up and down and bawled:

"Cat! Cat Here's Hen Chick
Come and eat her! Quick, come quick!"

"Quiet, scamp!" said Hen "Lazy scamp! Go ahead then, lie on my bed."

Frog lay on Hen's bed and fell fast asleep. He was still snoring loudly when the rain stopped.

Hen stepped outdoors to see if the pumpkins were still on the roof. She kept an eye cocked for Cat.

"Well, all right!" she said. "Just where I left them."

She went in and slammed the door, *bligh!*

Frog sprang awake. The noise frightened him, and he dived under the bed.

"Come on out Frog," said Hen. "The storm's over."

Frog crawled out.

"I'm hungry," he said.

"Climb onto the roof and fetch us some pumpkins," said Hen. "I'll cook, and we'll eat."

"Umm," said Frog. "Umm, pumpkin. I love pumpkin." But he still just sat on the edge of the bed.

Hen looked out of the window. She saw a small dark cloud in the distance. She knew that sign well, uh-huh!

"Hop to it, Frog," she said. "You can rest while I'm cooking a pumpkin."

Frog went outside and climbed up onto the roof. He dislodged a pumpkin from the thatch and rolled it down. Hen stood by the window and watched the dark cloud approach. It came faster and faster and grew bigger and bigger and . . .

It was Hawk!

Hawk spied Frog rolling the pumpkins off the roof. Frog was too busy to notice anything, not even Hawk's shadow as Hawk hovered over the thatch.

Hawk closed his wings and fell swiftly, silently. Suddenly, *flump!* Hawk snatched Frog in his claws and took off.

"Help! Help!" cried Frog. "Hen help me, help! I'm being carried off."

"Eh, eh!" said Hen. "Why don't you call Cat? You know, the Cat that eats little chickens. Eh? Click, clack, cluck, claa, clee."

Hen watched the scene safely from her window. Hawk soared upwards.

"Good!" said Hen. "That's it. Take the little so-and-so away. I've had more than enough of him, little tough buttocks!"

Hawk flew higher and higher. If Frog did call Cat, Cat did not come.

So that was that. Hawk took Frog away, and Hen could relax again. She cooked the pumpkin and sat down to eat. She was so happy that she ate eighteen plates of pumpkin without a stop. Then she lay back on her little bed and sang:

"Click clack cluck
Click claa clee.
I ate pumpkin,
Pumpkin didn't eat me."

Unanana and the Elephant

In this Zulu tale from South Africa a young mother rescues her children from the belly of an elephant. The motif of the hero being swallowed by a leviathan-like monster is far older than Jonah and the Whale. It is found worldwide from the hero epics of Finn Mac Cool and Hercules and the folktales of "Little Red Riding-Hood" and "The Cat and the Parrot" to Carlo Collodi's classic fantasy *The Adventures of Pi-*

nocchio. In certain of these stories the passage of a magical threshold implied in being swallowed into the unknown symbolizes the hero's death and rebirth. In the following story, the mother's courage and resourcefulness are as important as the underlying mythic archetype. [From Kathleen Arnott, *African Myths and Legends* (Walck, 1963).]

Many, many years ago there was a woman called Unanana who had two beautiful children. They lived in a hut near the roadside and people passing by would often stop when they saw the children, exclaiming at the roundness of their limbs, the smoothness of their skin and the brightness of their eyes.

Early one morning Unanana went into the bush to collect firewood and left her two children playing with a little cousin who was living with them. The children shouted happily, seeing who could jump the furthest, and when they were tired they sat on the dusty ground outside the hut, playing a game with pebbles.

Suddenly they heard a rustle in the nearby grasses, and seated on a rock they saw a puzzled-looking baboon.

"Whose children are those?" he asked the little cousin.

"They belong to Unanana," she replied.

"Well, well, well!" exclaimed the baboon in his deep voice. "Never have I seen such beautiful children before."

Then he disappeared and the children went on with their game.

A little later they heard the faint crack of a twig and looking up they saw the big, brown eyes of a gazelle staring at them from beside a bush.

"Whose children are those?" she asked the cousin.

"They belong to Unanana," she replied.

"Well, well, well!" exclaimed the gazelle in her soft, smooth voice. "Never have I seen such beautiful children before," and with a graceful bound she disappeared into the bush.

The children grew tired of their game, and taking a small gourd they dipped it in turn into the big pot full of water which stood at the door of their hut, and drank their fill.

A sharp bark made the cousin drop her gourd in fear when she looked up and saw the spotted body and treacherous eyes of a leopard, who had crept silently out of the bush.

"Whose children are those?" he demanded.

"They belong to Unanana," she replied in a shaky voice, slowly backing towards the door of the hut in case the leopard should spring at her. But he was not interested in a meal just then.

"Never have I seen such beautiful children before," he exclaimed, and with a flick of his tail he melted away into the bush.

The children were afraid of all these animals who kept asking questions and called loudly to Unanana to return, but instead of their mother, a huge elephant with only one tusk lumbered out of the bush and stood staring at the three children, who were too frightened to move.

"Whose children are those?" he bellowed at the little cousin, waving his trunk in the direction of the two beautiful children who were trying to hide behind a large stone.

"They . . . they belong to Una . . . Unanana," faltered the little girl.

The elephant took a step forward.

"Never have I seen such beautiful children before," he boomed. "I will take them away with me," and opening wide his mouth he swallowed both children at a gulp.

The little cousin screamed in terror and dashed into the hut, and from the gloom and safety inside it she heard the elephant's heavy footsteps growing fainter and fainter as he went back into the bush.

It was not until much later that Unanana returned, carrying a large bundle of wood on her head. The little girl rushed out of the house in a dreadful state and it was some time before Unanana could get the whole story from her.

"Alas! Alas!" said the mother. "Did he swallow them whole? Do you think they might still be alive inside the elephant's stomach?"

"I cannot tell," said the child, and she began to cry even louder than before.

"Well," said Unanana sensibly, "there's only one thing to do. I must go into the bush and ask all the animals whether they have seen an elephant with only one tusk. But first of all I must make preparations."

She took a pot and cooked a lot of beans in it until they were soft and ready to eat. Then seizing her large knife and putting the pot of food on her head, she told her little niece to look after the hut until she returned, and set off into the bush to search for the elephant.

Unanana soon found the tracks of the huge beast and followed them for some distance, but the elephant himself was nowhere to be seen. Presently, as she passed through some tall, shady trees, she met the baboon.

"O baboon! Do help me!" she begged. "Have you seen an elephant with only one tusk? He has eaten both my children and I must find him."

"Go straight along this track until you come to a place where there are high trees and white stones. There you will find the elephant," said the baboon.

So the woman went on along the dusty track for a very long time but she saw no sign of the elephant.

Suddenly she noticed a gazelle leaping across her path.

"O gazelle! Do help me! Have you seen an elephant with only one tusk?" she asked. "He has eaten both my children and I must find him."

"Go straight along this track until you come to a place where there are high trees and white stones. There you will find the elephant," said the gazelle, as she bounded away.

"O dear!" sighed Unanana. "It seems a very long way and I am so tired and hungry."

But she did not eat the food she carried, since that was for her children when she found them.

On and on she went, until rounding a bend in the track she saw a leopard sitting outside his cave-home, washing himself with his tongue.

"O leopard!" she exclaimed in a tired voice. "Do help me! Have you seen an elephant with only one tusk? He has eaten both my children and I must find him."

"Go straight along this track until you come to a place where there are high trees and white stones. There you will find the elephant," replied the leopard, as he bent his head and continued his toilet.

"Alas!" gasped Unanana to herself. "If I do not find this place soon, my legs will carry me no further."

She staggered on a little further until suddenly, ahead of her, she saw some high trees with large white stones spread about on the ground below them.

"At last!" she exclaimed, and hurrying forward she found a huge elephant lying contentedly in the shade of the trees. One glance was enough to show her that he had only one tusk, so going up as close as she dared, she shouted angrily:

"Elephant! Elephant! Are you the one that has eaten my children?"

"O no!" he replied lazily. "Go straight along this track until you come to a place where there are high trees and white stones. There you will find the elephant."

But the woman was sure this was the elephant she sought, and stamping her foot, she screamed at him again:

"Elephant! Elephant! Are you the one that has eaten my children?"

"O no! Go straight along this track—" began the elephant again, but he was cut short by Unanana who rushed up to him waving her knife and yelling:

"Where are my children? Where are they?"

Then the elephant opened his mouth and without even troubling to stand up, he swallowed Unanana with the cooking-pot and her knife at one gulp. And this was just what Unanana had hoped for.

Down, down, down she went in the darkness, until she reached the elephant's stomach. What a sight met her eyes! The walls of the elephant's stomach were like a range of hills, and camped among these hills were little groups of people, many dogs and goats and cows, and her own two beautiful children.

"Mother! Mother!" they cried when they saw her. "How did you get here? Oh, we are so hungry."

Unanana took the cooking-pot off her head and began to feed her children with the beans, which they ate ravenously. All the other people crowded round, begging for just a small portion of the food, so Unanana said to them scornfully:

"Why do you not roast meat for yourselves, seeing that you are surrounded by it?"

She took her knife and cut large pieces of flesh from the elephant and roasted them over a fire she built in the middle of the elephant's stomach, and soon everyone, including the dogs and goats and cattle, was feasting on elephant-meat very happily.

But the groans of the poor elephant could be heard all over the bush, and he said to those animals who came along to find out the cause of his unhappiness:

"I don't know why it is, but ever since I swallowed that woman called Unanana, I have felt most uncomfortable and unsettled inside."

The pain got worse and worse, until with a final grunt the elephant dropped dead. Then Unanana seized her knife again and hacked a doorway between the elephant's ribs through which soon streamed a line of dogs, goats, cows, men, women, and children, all blinking their eyes in the strong sunlight and shouting for joy at being free once more.

The animals barked, bleated or mooed their thanks, while the human beings gave Unanana all kinds of presents in gratitude to her for setting them free, so that when Unanana and her two children reached home, they were no longer poor.

The little cousin was delighted to see them, for she had thought they were all dead, and that night they had a feast. Can you guess what they ate? Yes, roasted elephant-meat.

It would not be too much to say that myth is the secret opening through which the inexhaustible energies of the cosmos pour into human cultural manifestation. Religions, philosophies, arts, the social forms of primitive and historic man, prime discoveries in science and technology, the very dreams that blister sleep, boil up from the basic, magic ring of myth.[1]

8 Myths, Legends, and Sacred Writings

The root meaning of the word *myth* is *story*. A myth, then, is a story, and a mythology is a body of stories. But what kind of stories? In an earlier era, within the mainstream of European and North American thought, we could have answered that question with great certainty. We would have said that primitive people, living without science, created explanations for the mysteries and terrors of the world. They invested everything with life: trees, stones, the very tools they had fashioned. They invented gods, casting them in images human or bestial such as they themselves knew; having formed them, the people worshipped these gods, begged for their favor, propitiated them with ritual and sacrifice, and made them guardians of such moral laws and ethics as had evolved in their societies. Mythology, we would have said, is the record of those attempts at explanation and the highest creation of the childhood of the human race. The popular view in the nineteenth and early twentieth centuries held that Western civilization had achieved maturity and learned the truth, through the true explanations offered by science and through the Judeo-Christian tradition, which, depending on one's point of view, is either literally true (the Bible is historical fact) or ethically and morally true (our religions

1. Joseph Campbell, *The Hero with a Thousand Faces* (Pantheon, 1949), p. 3.

are evolved and superior). There are still many people today who hold these views or variations upon them.

But, according to the great historian of religion, Mircea Eliade, contemporary Western scholars have developed an approach to mythology that is quite different:

> Unlike their predecessors, who treated myth in the usual meaning of the word, that is, as "fable," "invention," "fiction," they have accepted it as was understood in the archaic societies, where, on the contrary, "myth" means a "true story" and, beyond that, a story that is a most precious possession because it is sacred, exemplary, significant. . . . It is not the intellectual stage or the historical moment when myth became a "fiction" that interests us. Our study will deal primarily with those societies in which myth is— or was until very recently—"living," in the sense that it supplies models for human behaviour and, by that very fact, gives meaning and value to life.[2]

Mythologist Joseph Campbell sees mythology as being an even broader field than it is in Eliade's view. Campbell, working out of the Jungian tradition, based on the concept of archetypes of a collective unconscious (elemental patterns of an unconscious mind shared by all people), does not limit himself to particular cultures or particular historical eras, but searches out the recurrence of mythic images in all places and times. He does not hesitate, for example, to compare the images of the Mother of God in the French Notre Dame de Chartres and the Mexican Nuestra Señora de Guadalupe—a procedure (as Campbell himself admits) that would be anathema to the anthropologist.[3] For Campbell, "A mythological canon is an organization of symbols, ineffable in import, by which the energies or aspiration are evoked and gathered toward a focus."[4] In elucidating those "canons of mythology," Campbell has turned his attention to our own society. In *The Masks of God: Creative Mythology* (1968) he examines such myth systems as that of Romantic Love, which, he says, is a living religious force in Western civilization.

The structural anthropologist Claude Lévi-Strauss works with a definition of mythology that is broadest of all. He flatly contradicts the arguments that myths are essentially either prescientific explanations for natural phenomena or "a moralizing comment on the situation of mankind."[5] His position stands in direct opposition to the popular nineteenth-century metaphor that saw the growth of the human race as paralleling that of the individual: that there was a childhood of humanity, with childish myth, which developed into maturity with the discoveries of science; that primitive peoples are still childish, and so, in some sense, inferior or inadequate. He argues against the notion of progress in mythic thought, writing that those civilizations "which we term primitive do not differ from the others in their mental equipment."[6] Lévi-Strauss sees mythology as cultural art, like music, but an all-embracing one; he does not hesitate to call his own book, *The Raw and the Cooked* (1969), which analyzes the mythology

2. Mircea Eliade, *Myth and Reality,* trans. Willard R. Trask, in World Perspectives, 21 (Allen & Unwin, 1963, 1964), pp. 1–2.
3. Joseph Campbell, *The Masks of God: Occidental Mythology* (Viking, 1964), p. 42.
4. Joseph Campbell, *The Masks of God: Creative Mythology* (Viking, 1968), p. 5.
5. Claude Lévi-Strauss, *The Raw and the Cooked, Introduction to a Science of Mythology,* Vol. 1, trans. John Weightman and Doreen Weightman (Harper, 1969), p. 340.
6. Claude Lévi-Strauss, *From Honey to Ashes, Introduction to a Science of Mythology,* Vol. 2, trans. John Weightman and Doreen Weightman (Harper, 1973), p. 474.

of South American Indians, "a kind of myth."[7]   And, in the analysis of the deep structure of mythology, Lévi-Strauss looks for the laws of the structure of the human mind itself.

Any survey of contemporary mythological studies, even one as brief and overly simplified as the foregoing, should give us pause before such hoary axioms as "mythology, being childish, should appeal to children," or "that's what people thought before they knew any better." Mythology (returning to the root of the word) appeals to children at the level of the story, and the stories in mythology—ancient, religious, complex, and resonant—can strike children with an emotional force found nowhere else. In his autobiography, *Surprised by Joy* (1955), C. S. Lewis recalls his childhood experience of reading these lines:

I heard a voice that cried,
Balder the beautiful
Is dead, is dead—

"I knew nothing about Balder," Lewis writes, "but instantly I was uplifted into huge regions of northern sky, I desired with almost sickening intensity something never to be described (except that it is cold, spacious, severe, pale, and remote)."[8]

This complex emotional response, experienced with a "sickening intensity," is a response to what Elizabeth Cook calls "religio" and which, she says,

implies a sense of the strange, the numinous, the totally Other, of what lies quite beyond human personality and cannot be found in any human relationships. This kind of "religion" is an indestructible part of the experience of many human minds, even though the temper of a secular society does not encourage it. . . . It may very well be in reading about a vision of the flashing-eyed Athene or the rosy-fingered Aphrodite that children first find a satisfying formulation of those queer pricklings of delight, excitement and terror that they feel when they first walk by moonlight, or when it snows in May. . . . Magic is not the same as mysticism, but it may lead toward it.[9]

In addition to pointing toward the religious and mystical aspects of life, the other function of myth is, to use Eliade's word, exemplary. As Joseph Campbell writes: "The instincts have to be governed and matured in the interests of both the group and of the individual, and traditionally it has been the prime function of mythology to serve this social-psychological end. The individual is adapted to his group and the group to its environment, with a sense thereby of gratitude for the miracle of life."[10] Through the compelling stories of mythology, children can experience the highest group ideals of the cultures that produced them.

Four great streams of mythology have nourished the Western world: the Greco-Roman, the Norse, the Celtic, and the Judeo-Christian. The earliest written record of Greek mythology is contained in the *Iliad*, attributed to Homer and dated around the year 1000 B.C., although the tales and beliefs had been created, and been evolving for hundreds of years before that. The *Iliad* and the *Odyssey* contain some of the most stirring tales of world mythology. Other sources of

7. Lévi-Strauss, *The Raw and the Cooked*, p. 6.
8. C. S. Lewis, *Surprised by Joy: The Shape of My Early Life* (Bles, 1955), p. 20.
9. Elizabeth Cook, *The Ordinary and the Fabulous: An Introduction to Myths, Legends and Fairy Tales for Teachers and Storytellers*, 2d ed. (Cambridge University Press, 1976), p. 5.
10. Campbell, *Creative Mythology*, p. 674.

Greek mythology are the Homeric hymns, fragmentary odes to the gods, and the writings of Hesiod, dating from approximately 700 B.C. The great dramatists of Greece—Aeschylus (525–456 B.C.), Sophocles (496–406 B.C.), and Euripides (480–406 B.C.)—wrote their towering tragedies against the background of this mythology, peering deep into the motives of gods and mortals in their relationships with one another.

When Rome conquered Greece, the Romans absorbed the religion of the Greeks, adapting it to their own more practical, less poetic, and less spiritual manner of thinking. They gave the gods new names and were slightly condescending toward them. We owe to the Roman writer Ovid our knowledge of many of the classic stories of Greco-Roman mythology. His *Metamorphoses* gives a witty and impudent account of the gods, in whom the Romans believed with less ardor than the Greeks. Indeed, much of our knowledge of Greco-Roman mythology comes to us from writings executed after those historical moments, referred to by Eliade, when myth became "fiction." Reading Ovid, for example, creates the impression that the gods were not taken seriously, but were, in fact, regarded almost as celestial pets. Since the nineteenth century, however, scholars and anthropologists—spurred by James Frazer's monumental work, *The Golden Bough* (1890)—have written convincing accounts of what the Greek and Roman religions may have been like in the periods when they were living mythological forces.

The range of Greek mythology is enormous, representing as it does the evolution of a religion based upon earlier, manifold beliefs. The stories vary from as simple a parable as the story of Midas, who loved gold above all else, to the complex and ennobling story of Prometheus. One of the remarkable elements in Greek mythology is the decidedly human relationship between gods and mortals, marked by jealousy, greed, and desire as much as by loyalty and reverence. Underlying the Greeks' joy in nature, their celebration of the wonder of the human form and spirit, their worship of beauty and proportion, and their delight in life itself lay the deeper awareness of order and the obligation to sustain an ideal nobility. "The myths are firmly built into two dramatic cycles," writes H. D. F. Kitto in his study of the Greek mind, "which are among the supreme achievements of the human mind: *dramas about the birth and growth of reason, order, and mercy among gods and man alike.*"[11]

The Norse mythology—as dark, heroic, and austere as the region that produced it—reached its highest literary expression in one famous manuscript, known as the *Elder* or *Poetic Edda.* This manuscript, prepared in Iceland, was the work of bards who emerged as spokesmen for a culture made up of Norsemen exiled from Scandinavia to Iceland. Its authorship is unknown and its date uncertain; some scholars place it as late as the latter part of the thirteenth century. A second *Edda,* the *Younger* or *Prose Edda,* is the work of one man, Snorri Sturluson, a great artist-historian of the medieval age. From these two sources come the *Volsunga Saga.* The *Nibelungenlied* of the Germanic peoples bears a relationship to them, as well.

From the *Eddas* we learn of the gods and their enemies, the frost giants; of the dwelling-place of each group; of Yggdrasil, the huge ash tree that supports the universe, and the three Norns (Fates) that care for it; and of Ragnarök, the "twilight of the gods," the final battle in which they will be overthrown and die. The Norse gods, unlike the Greco-Roman gods, were mortal, and, in

---

11. H. D. F. Kitto, *The Greeks* (Penguin, 1951, 1954), p. 202.

Norse mythology, there was always the threat of impending doom. The gods knew that in the end they would be destroyed, but they were determined to die resisting. To them a heroic death was not defeat but victory.

The literary records of the mythology of the Celtic peoples of central and western Europe are contained in the comments of their Roman conquerors and in a number of works in the Celtic languages. The most important are, in Irish, the *Book of Leinster, Book of the Dun Cow, Book of Ballymote,* and the *Yellow Book of Lecan* (the earliest dating from the eighth century); and, in Welsh, the *Mabinogion,* found in the *White Book of Rhydderch,* and the *Red Book of Hergest* (fourteenth century). In these we read of the coming of the gods to Ireland, of the Welsh children of Don and Llyr, of Bran the Blessed with his life-giving cauldron that would be transformed under the impact of Christianity into the Holy Grail, and of epic heroes:

In the epics of ancient Ireland, the Celtic warrior kings and their brilliant chariot fighters move in a landscape beset with invisible fairy forts, wherein abide a race of beings of an earlier mythological age: the wonderful Tuatha De Danann, children of the Goddess Dana, who retired, when defeated, into wizard hills of glass. And these are the very people of the sídhe, or Shee, the Fairy Host, the Fairy Cavalcade, of the Irish peasantry to this day.[12]

The world of Celtic mythology is elusive and misty, filled with half-lights and sudden, dazzling revelations; peopled by valiant warriors and warrior women, druids and wizards; brooded over by *weird,* or fate—that which will be. There is throughout an intensely passionate nature mysticism that was absorbed into Irish Christianity. The greatest impact of Celtic mythology upon mainstream Western literature has been through a group of matchless and persistent story cycles—the heroic romances of Arthur, the once and future king.

When we turn to the fourth and most influential fountainhead of mythology for Western civilization, the Judeo-Christian, we are immediately in some difficulty. Referring only to the myths and legends of the Old Testament, Elizabeth Cook writes that they are "as poetic and dramatic as anything in Greek or Northern mythology, and they have exercised an even greater power over the imagination of Europe. They were the only highly developed, literary mythological stories that were heard by uneducated people in the Christian period, and they meant as much as the Greek stories to poets and men of letters." But, she says, she will not treat them in her book *The Ordinary and the Fabulous* (2d ed., 1976) "for the simple reason that in Christian tradition they have been regarded, in a multitude of conflicting or overlapping definitions, either as uniquely significant history, or as uniquely true mythology."[13] When we consider not only Old Testament stories but all of Jewish and Christian mythology, we are in even deeper water.

A teacher or librarian can no longer assume that children have similar backgrounds or that their parents share similar values. Some will be from deeply religious homes, in which it would be considered insulting to regard the teachings of religion as myth. Some will be from religious traditions outside Judaism or Christianity. Some will be from thoroughly secular families in which all religious teachings are regarded with suspicion. In 1963, the Supreme Court of the United States, in the case of *Abington School District* v. *Schempp,* disallowed

12. Campbell, *Occidental Mythology,* pp. 40–41.
13. Cook, p. 38.

the reading of scripture as part of a religious ceremony in the schools. Ann Hildebrand writes that "many school systems immediately threw out the Bible completely, not only discontinuing daily readings and Bible use in assemblies and gatherings but frowning on the mere mention of Bible characters or allusion to Bible situations or traditions. And yet, in so completely removing the Bible, these schools deprived the students of the most influential literature in the Western world."[14] As the noted critic Northrop Frye writes:

[The Bible] should be taught so early and so thoroughly that it sinks straight to the bottom of the mind. . . . I'm speaking as a literary critic about the teaching of literature. There are all sorts of secondary reasons for teaching the Bible as literature: the fact that it's so endlessly quoted from and alluded to, the fact that the cadences and phrases of the King James translation are built into our minds and way of thought, the fact that it's full of the greatest and best known stories we have, and so on. There are also the moral and religious reasons for its importance, which are different reasons. But in the particular context in which I'm speaking now, it's the total shape and structure of the Bible which is most important. . . . It's the *myth* of the Bible that should be the basis of literary training.[15]

These comments are particularly persuasive, coming as they do, not from a theologian, but from a literary critic. If we do not know the stories of the Bible, have not felt our way into the living center of that myth system, then we will not understand our own literature and culture, will not be able to claim our own inheritance. And if we do not know the stories, have not felt the force of the other myth systems of the world, then we will be parochial in a time when parochialism is increasingly intolerable.

To oversimplify: Judeo-Christian ideals and aspirations, Greek philosophy, Roman organization, and Celtic and Norse poetry were the primary mythic sources of Western culture until the twentieth century; since then, particularly since the Second World War, other streams have been pouring in from other cultures to enrich our mythological heritage. It is difficult to overestimate the impact first of Hinduism and then of Buddhism on our thought and literature. Each culture "declares itself" in its mythology; children will be badly equipped to understand and appreciate the modern world without some acquaintance with these and with other non-Western religions and the poetic narratives of their sacred writings and legends.

The comparative reading of mythology affords an understanding of individual cultural characteristics and traditions and a growing sense of the elements that are universal to the human mind. So, too, does exposure to the broad range of the world's legends. In the legends of the oral tradition, the borders of story may often blend into myth and historical fact. Legend may overlap with epic and romance, as in the embroidered stories developing around a popular hero—warrior or saint.

But the term *legend* has also been used inaccurately to refer to all Indian, Inuit, or other aboriginal stories, whether myth, legend, folktale, or fable. These stories may be anecdotes told in connection with a person or a place, or they may be the most primal of creation myths. What they share is a fragmentary,

14. Ann Hildebrand, "The Bible Presented Objectively," *Language Arts,* 53 (January 1976), 69–75, reprinted in *Beyond Fact: Nonfiction for Children and Young People,* comp. Jo Carr (American Library Association, 1982), p. 181.
15. Northrop Frye, *The Educated Imagination* (Indiana University Press, 1964), pp. 110–11.

dreamlike structure appropriate to their continued survival as stories recited within a *living* oral tradition (for they were not frozen into written form until this century). These legends are quite distinct in shape from the structurally unified narratives of Western myth that have existed in written form for centuries.

For children, native legends contain the same absorbing drama and adventure that they find in other myths, and the recurring images of world mythology as well. "Sharing a basic provenance with myths in other lands," writes Sheila Egoff, "the Indian legends often somewhat resemble them. Prometheus stole fire for the Greeks; Raven stole it for the West Coast Indians; Nanabozho for the Ojibway or Chippewas; and Glooscap for the East Coast Indians. The Canadian rabbit lost his tail as did rabbits around the world; and whereas Noah built an ark to escape a flood, the Indians built a raft or canoe."[16]

Children of today, as never before, have available to them the vast range of world mythology. The poetic mode of thought, the sheer drama in these absorbing stories of gods, heroes, and mortals enable children to experience their world in a larger, more heroic and mysterious dimension. Myths, like folktales, epics, and romances, give children insight into the elemental human and religious experiences shared by all cultures, awakening them to those same experiences within themselves.

The stars in our heavens are the source of myths, and our flights into outer space are given mythological and legendary names. These first and oldest stories of the human race are helping to form a *new* mythology. "Our mythology now," says Joseph Campbell, "is to be of infinite space and its light, which is without as well as within. Like moths, we are caught in the spell of its allure, flying to it outward, to the moon and beyond, and flying to it, also, inward. On our planet itself all dividing horizons have been shattered. We can no longer hold our loves at home and project our aggressions elsewhere; for on this spaceship Earth there is no 'elsewhere' anymore. And no mythology that continues to speak or to teach of 'elsewheres' and 'outsiders' meets the requirements of this hour."[17]

16. Sheila Egoff, *The Republic of Childhood: A Critical Guide to Canadian Children's Literature in English,* 2d ed. (Oxford University Press, 1975), p. 20.
17. Joseph Campbell, "Envoy: No More Horizons," in *Myths to Live By* (Viking, 1972), p. 266.

Myths of Ancient Greece

Demeter

"This story is told only in a very early poem, one of the earliest of the Homeric Hymns, dating from the eighth or the beginning of the seventh century. The original has the marks of early Greek poetry, great simplicity and directness and delight in the beautiful world. Demeter was the goddess of marriage and fertility. The story of the loss of her daughter Persephone, and the mother's search for her, are the ancient Greek's explanation of summer and winter."—Edith Hamilton.

This myth sometimes appears as *Ceres and Persephone*. [From Edith Hamilton, *Mythology* (Little, Brown, 1942).]

Demeter had an only daughter, Persephone (in Latin, Proserpine), the maiden of the spring. She lost her and in her terrible grief she withheld her gifts from the earth, which turned into a frozen desert. The green and flowering land was icebound and lifeless because Persephone had disappeared.

The lord of the dark Underworld, the king of the multitudinous dead, carried her off when, enticed by the wondrous bloom of the narcissus, she strayed too far from her companions. In his chariot drawn by coal-black steeds he rose up through a chasm in the earth, and grasping the maiden by the wrist set her beside him. He bore her away, weeping, down to the Underworld. The high hills echoed her cry and the depths of the sea, and her mother heard it. She sped like a bird over sea and land seeking her daughter. But no one would tell her the truth, "no man nor god, nor any sure messenger from the birds." Nine days Demeter wandered, and all that time she would not taste of ambrosia or put sweet nectar to her lips. At last she came to the Sun and he told her all the story: Persephone was down in the world beneath the earth, among the shadowy dead.

Then a still greater grief entered Demeter's heart. She left Olympus; she dwelt on earth, but so disguised that none knew her, and, indeed, the gods are not easily discerned by mortal men. In her desolate wanderings she came to Eleusis and sat by the wayside near a wall. She seemed an aged woman, such as in great houses care for the children or guard the storerooms. Four lovely maidens, sisters, coming to draw water from the well, saw her and asked her pityingly what she did there. She answered that she had fled from pirates who had meant to sell her as a slave, and that she knew no one in this strange land to go to for help. They told her that any house in the town would welcome her, but that they would like best to bring her to their own if she would wait there while they went to ask their mother. The goddess bent her head in assent, and the girls, filling their shining pitchers with water, hurried home. Their mother, Metaneira, bade them return at once and invite the stranger to come, and speeding back they found the glorious goddess still sitting there, deeply veiled and covered to her slender feet by her dark robe. She followed them, and as she crossed the threshold to the hall where the mother sat holding her young son, a divine radiance filled the doorway and awe fell upon Metaneira.

She bade Demeter be seated and herself offered her honey-sweet wine, but the goddess would not taste it. She asked instead for barley-water flavored with mint, the cooling draft of the reaper at harvest time and also the sacred cup given the worshipers at Eleusis. Thus refreshed, she took the child and held him to her fragrant bosom and his mother's heart was glad. So Demeter nursed Demophoon, the son that Metaneira had borne to wise Celeus. And the child grew like a young god, for daily Demeter anointed him with ambrosia and at night she would place him in the red heart of the fire. Her purpose was to give him immortal youth.

Something, however, made the mother uneasy, so that one night she kept watch and screamed in terror when she saw the child laid in the fire. The goddess was angered; she seized the boy and cast him on the ground. She had meant to set him free from old age and from death, but that was not to be. Still, he had lain upon her knees and slept in her arms and therefore he should have honor throughout his life. Then she showed herself the goddess manifest. Beauty breathed about her and a lovely fragrance; light shone from her so that the great house was filled with brightness. She was Demeter, she told the awestruck women. They must build her a great temple near the town and so win back the favor of her heart.

Thus she left them, and Metaneira fell speechless to the earth and all there trembled with fear. In the morning they told Celeus what had happened and he called the people together and revealed to them the command of the goddess. They worked willingly to build her a temple, and when it was finished Demeter came to it and sat there—apart from the gods in Olympus, alone, wasting away with longing for her daughter.

That year was most dreadful and cruel for mankind over all the earth. Nothing grew; no seed sprang up; in vain the oxen drew the plowshare through the furrows. It seemed the whole race of man would die of famine. At last Zeus saw that he must take the matter in hand. He sent the gods to Demeter, one after another, to try to turn her from her anger, but she listened to none of them. Never would she let the earth bear fruit until she had seen her daughter. Then Zeus realized that his brother must give way. He told Hermes to go down to the Underworld and to bid the lord of it let his bride go back to Demeter.

Hermes found the two sitting side by side, Persephone shrinking away, reluctant because she longed for her mother. At Hermes' words she sprang up joyfully, eager to go. Her husband knew that he must obey the word of Zeus and send her up to earth away from him, but he prayed her as she left him to have kind thoughts of him and not be so sorrowful that she was the wife of one who was great among the immortals. And he made her eat a pomegranate seed, knowing in his heart that if she did so she must return to him.

He got ready his golden car and Hermes took the reins and drove the black horses straight to the temple where Demeter was. She ran out to meet her daughter as swiftly as a Maenad runs down the mountain-side. Persephone sprang into her arms and was held fast there. All day they talked of what had happened to them both, and Demeter grieved when she heard of the pomegranate seed, fearing that she could not keep her daughter with her.

Then Zeus sent another messenger to her, a great personage, none other than his revered mother Rhea, the oldest of the gods. Swiftly she hastened down from the heights of Olympus to the barren, leafless earth, and standing at the door of the temple she spoke to Demeter.

Come, my daughter, for Zeus, far-seeing, loud-
  thundering, bids you.
Come once again to the halls of the gods where
  you shall have honor,
Where you will have your desire, your daughter, to comfort your sorrow
As each year is accomplished and bitter winter
  is ended.
For a third part only the kingdom of darkness
  shall hold her.
For the rest you will keep her, you and the
  happy immortals.
Peace now. Give men life which comes alone
  from your giving.

Demeter did not refuse, poor comfort though it was that she must lose Persephone for four months every year and see her young loveliness go down to the world of the dead. But she was kind; the "Good Goddess," men always called her. She was sorry for the desolation she had brought about. She made the fields once more rich with abundant fruit and the whole world bright with flowers and green leaves. Also she went to the princes of Eleusis who had built her temple and she chose one, Triptolemus, to be her ambassador to men, instructing them how to sow the corn. She taught him and Celeus and the others her sacred rites, "mysteries which no one may utter, for deep awe checks the tongue. Blessed is he who has seen them; his lot will be good in the world to come."

Queen of fragrant Eleusis,
Giver of earth's good gifts,
Give me your grace, O Demeter.
You, too, Persephone, fairest,
Maiden all lovely, I offer
Song for your favor.

Cupid and Psyche

This story is found only in the work of Apuleius, a Latin writer of the second century. *Psyche* is the Greek word for the soul and the word from which our word *psychology* derives. Cupid of course was the god of love. Love and the soul! These are themes that have engaged the mind of man through the centuries and no doubt will continue to do so until the end of time.

The Norwegian folktale, with one of the most beautiful names in all folklore, *East o' the Sun and West o' the Moon,* is essentially the same story, removed from any association with the gods but stating the same themes of the necessity for trust in love, the anguish easily borne if it be for the sake of love, and its glorious triumph in the end. [From Edith Hamilton, *Mythology* (Little, Brown, 1942).]

There was once a king who had three daughters, all lovely maidens, but the youngest, Psyche, excelled her sisters so greatly that beside them she seemed a very goddess consorting with mere mortals. The fame of her surpassing beauty spread over the earth, and everywhere men journeyed to gaze upon her with wonder and adoration and to do her homage as though she were in truth one of the immortals. They would even say that Venus herself could not equal this mortal. As they thronged in ever-growing numbers to worship her loveliness no one any more gave a thought to Venus herself. Her temples were neglected; her altars foul with cold ashes; her favorite towns deserted and falling in ruins. All the honors once hers were now given to a mere girl destined some day to die.

It may well be believed that the goddess would not put up with this treatment. As always when she was in trouble she turned for help to her son, that beautiful winged youth whom some call Cupid and others Love, against whose arrows there is no defense, neither in heaven nor on the earth. She told him her wrongs and as always he was ready to do her bidding. "Use your power," she said, "and make the hussy fall madly in love with the vilest and most despicable creature there is in the whole world." And so no doubt he would have done, if Venus had not first shown him Psyche, never thinking in her jealous rage what such beauty might do even to the God of Love himself. As he looked upon her it was as if he had shot one of his arrows into his own heart. He said nothing to his mother, indeed, he had no power to utter a word, and Venus left him with the happy confidence that he would swiftly bring about Psyche's ruin.

What happened, however, was not what she had counted on. Psyche did not fall in love with a horrible wretch, she did not fall in love at all. Still more strange, no one fell in love with her. Men were content to look and wonder and worship—and then pass on to marry someone else. Both her sisters, inexpressibly inferior to her, were splendidly married, each to a king. Psyche, the all-beautiful, sat sad and solitary, only admired, never loved. It seemed that no man wanted her.

This was, of course, most disturbing to her parents. Her father finally traveled to an oracle of Apollo to ask his advice on how to get her a good husband. The god answered him, but his words were terrible. Cupid had told him the whole story and had begged for his help. Accordingly Apollo said that Psyche, dressed in deepest mourning, must be set on the summit of a rocky hill and left alone, and that there her destined husband, a fearful winged serpent, stronger than the gods themselves, would come to her and make her his wife.

The misery of all when Psyche's father brought back this lamentable news can be imagined. They dressed the maiden as though for her death and carried her to the hill with greater sorrowing than if it had been to her tomb. But Psyche herself kept her courage. "You should have wept for me before," she told them, "because of the beauty that has drawn down upon me the jealousy of Heaven. Now go, knowing that I am glad the end has come." They went in despairing grief, leaving the lovely helpless creature to meet her doom alone, and they shut themselves in their palace to mourn all their days for her.

On the high hilltop in the darkness Psyche sat, waiting for she knew not what terror. There, as she wept and trembled, a soft breath of air came through the stillness to her, the gentle breathing of Zephyr, sweetest and mildest of winds. She felt it lift her up. She was floating away from the rocky hill and down until she lay upon a grassy meadow soft as a bed and fragrant with flowers. It was so peaceful there, all her trouble left her and she slept. She woke beside a bright river; and on its bank was a mansion stately and beautiful as though built for a god, with pillars of gold and walls of silver and floors inlaid with precious stones. No sound was to be heard; the place seemed deserted and Psyche drew near, awestruck at the sight of such splendor. As she hesitated on the threshold, voices sounded in her ear. She could see no one, but the words they spoke came clearly to her. The house was for her, they told her. She must enter without fear and bathe and refresh herself. Then a banquet table would be spread for her. "We are your servants," the voices said, "ready to do whatever you desire."

The bath was the most delightful, the food the most delicious, she had ever enjoyed. While she dined, sweet music breathed around her: a great choir seemed to sing to a harp, but she could only hear, not see, them. Throughout the day, except for the strange companionship of the voices, she was alone, but in some inexplicable way she felt sure that with the coming of the night her husband would be with her. And so it happened. When she felt him beside her and heard his voice softly murmuring in her ear, all her fears left her. She knew without seeing him that here was no monster or shape of terror, but the lover and husband she had longed and waited for.

This half-and-half companionship could not fully content her; still she was happy and time passed swiftly. One night, however, her dear though unseen husband spoke gravely to her and warned her that danger in the shape of her two sisters was approaching. "They are coming to the hill where you disappeared, to weep for you," he said; "but you must not let them see you or you will bring great sorrow upon me and ruin to yourself." She promised him she would not, but all the next day she passed in weeping, thinking of her sisters and herself unable to comfort them. She was still in tears when her husband came and even his caresses could not check them. At last he yielded sorrowfully to her great desire. "Do what you will," he said, "but you are seeking your own destruction." Then he warned her solemnly not to be persuaded by anyone to try to see him, on pain of being separated from him forever. Psyche cried out that she would never do so. She would die a hundred times over rather than live without him. "But give me this joy," she said: "to see my sisters." Sadly he promised her that it should be so.

The next morning the two came, brought down from the mountain by Zephyr. Happy and excited, Psyche was waiting for them. It was long before the three could speak to each other; their joy was too great to be expressed except by tears and embraces. But when at last they entered the palace and the elder sisters saw its surpassing treasures; when they sat at the rich banquet and heard the marvelous music, bitter envy took possession of them and a devouring curiosity as to who was the lord of all this magnificence and their sister's husband. But Psyche kept faith; she told them only that he was a young man, away now on a hunting expedition. Then filling their hands with gold and jewels, she had Zephyr bear them back to the hill. They went willingly enough, but their hearts were on fire with jealousy. All their own wealth and good fortune seemed to them as nothing compared with Psyche's, and their envious anger so worked in them that they came finally to plotting how to ruin her.

That very night Psyche's husband warned her once more. She would not listen when he begged her not to let them come again. She never could see him, she reminded him. Was she also to be forbidden to see all others, even her sisters so dear to her? He yielded as before, and very soon the two wicked women arrived, with their plot carefully worked out.

Already, because of Psyche's stumbling and contradictory answers when they asked her what her husband looked like, they had become convinced that she had never set eyes on him and did not really know what he was. They did not tell her this, but they reproached her for hiding her terrible state from them, her own sisters. They had learned, they said, and knew for a fact, that her husband was not a man, but the fearful serpent Apollo's oracle had declared he would be. He was kind now, no doubt, but he would certainly turn upon her some night and devour her.

Psyche, aghast, felt terror flooding her heart

instead of love. She had wondered so often why he would never let her see him. There must be some dreadful reason. What did she really know about him? If he was not horrible to look at, then he was cruel to forbid her ever to behold him. In extreme misery, faltering and stammering, she gave her sisters to understand that she could not deny what they said, because she had been with him only in the dark. "There must be something very wrong," she sobbed, "for him so to shun the light of day." And she begged them to advise her.

They had their advice all prepared beforehand. That night she must hide a sharp knife and a lamp near her bed. When her husband was fast asleep she must leave the bed, light the lamp, and get the knife. She must steel herself to plunge it swiftly into the body of the frightful being the light would certainly show her. "We will be near," they said, "and carry you away with us when he is dead."

Then they left her torn by doubt and distracted what to do. She loved him; he was her dear husband. No; he was a horrible serpent and she loathed him. She would kill him—She would not. She must have certainty—She did not want certainty. So all day long her thoughts fought with each other. When evening came, however, she had given the struggle up. One thing she was determined to do: she would see him.

When at last he lay sleeping quietly, she summoned all her courage and lit the lamp. She tiptoed to the bed and holding the light high above her she gazed at what lay there. Oh, the relief and the rapture that filled her heart. No monster was revealed, but the sweetest and fairest of all creatures, at whose sight the very lamp seemed to shine brighter. In her first shame at her folly and lack of faith, Psyche fell on her knees and would have plunged the knife into her own breast if it had not fallen from her trembling hands. But those same unsteady hands that saved her betrayed her, too, for as she hung over him, ravished at the sight of him and unable to deny herself the bliss of filling her eyes with his beauty, some hot oil fell from the lamp upon his shoulder. He started awake: he saw the light and knew her faithlessness, and without a word he fled from her.

She rushed out after him into the night. She could not see him, but she heard his voice speaking to her. He told her who he was, and sadly bade her farewell. "Love cannot live where there is no trust," he said, and flew away. "The God of Love!" she thought. "He was my husband, and I, wretch that I am, could not keep faith with him. Is he gone from me forever? . . . At any rate," she told herself with rising courage, "I can spend the rest of my life searching for him. If he has no more love left for me, at least I can show him how much I love him." And she started on her journey. She had no idea where to go; she knew only that she would never give up looking for him.

He meanwhile had gone to his mother's chamber to have his wound cared for, but when Venus heard his story and learned that it was Psyche whom he had chosen, she left him angrily alone in his pain, and went forth to find the girl of whom he had made her still more jealous. Venus was determined to show Psyche what it meant to draw down the displeasure of a goddess.

Poor Psyche in her despairing wanderings was trying to win the gods over to her side. She offered ardent prayers to them perpetually, but not one of them would do anything to make Venus their enemy. At last she perceived that there was no hope for her, either in heaven or on earth, and she took a desperate resolve. She would go straight to Venus; she would offer herself humbly to her as her servant, and try to soften her anger. "And who knows," she thought, "if he himself is not there in his mother's house." So she set forth to find the goddess who was looking everywhere for her.

When she came into Venus' presence the goddess laughed aloud and asked her scornfully if she was seeking a husband since the one she had had would have nothing to do with her because he had almost died of the burning wound she had given him. "But really," she said, "you are so plain and ill-favored a girl that you will never be able to get you a lover except by the most diligent and painful service. I will therefore show my good will to you by training you in such ways." With that she took a great quantity of the smallest of the seeds, wheat and poppy and millet and so on, and mixed them all together in a heap. "By nightfall these must all be sorted," she said. "See to it for your own sake." And with that she departed.

Psyche, left alone, sat still and stared at the heap. Her mind was all in a maze because of the cruelty of the command; and, indeed, it was of no use to start a task so manifestly impossible. But at this direful moment she who had awakened no compassion in mortals or immortals was pitied by the tiniest creatures of the field, the little ants, the swiftrunners. They cried to each other, "Come, have mercy on this poor maid and help her diligently." At once they came, waves of them, one after another, and they labored separating and dividing, until what had been a confused mass lay all ordered, every seed with its kind. This was what Venus found when she came back, and very angry she was to see it. "Your work is by no means over," she said. Then she gave Psyche a crust of bread and bade her sleep on the ground while she herself went off to her soft, fragrant couch. Surely if she could keep the girl at hard labor and half starve her, too, that hateful beauty of hers would soon be lost. Until then she must see that her son was securely guarded in his chamber where he was still suffering from his wound. Venus was pleased at the way matters were shaping.

The next morning she devised another task for Psyche, this time a dangerous one. "Down there near the riverbank," she said, "where the bushes grow thick, are sheep with fleeces of gold. Go fetch me some of their shining wool." When the worn girl reached the gently flowing stream, a great longing seized her to throw herself into it and end all her pain and despair. But as she was bending over the water she heard a little voice from near her feet, and looking down saw that it came from a green reed. She must not drown herself, it said. Things were not as bad as that. The sheep were indeed very fierce, but if Psyche would wait until they came out of the bushes toward evening to rest beside the river, she could go into the thicket and find plenty of the golden wool hanging on the sharp briars.

So spoke the kind and gentle reed, and Psyche, following the directions, was able to carry back to her cruel mistress a quantity of the shining fleece. Venus received it with an evil smile. "Someone helped you," she said sharply. "Never did you do this by yourself. However, I will give you an opportunity to prove that you really have the stout heart and the singular prudence you make such a show of. Do you see that black water which falls from the hill yonder? It is the source of the terrible river which is called hateful, the river Styx. You are to fill this flask from it." That was the worst task yet, as Psyche saw when she approached the waterfall. Only a winged creature could reach it, so steep and slimy were the rocks on all sides, and so fearful the onrush of the descending waters. But by this time it must be evident to all the readers of this story (as, perhaps, deep in her heart it had become evident to Psyche herself) that although each of her trials seemed impossibly hard, an excellent way out would always be provided for her. This time her savior was an eagle, who poised on his great wings beside her, seized the flask from her with his beak and brought it back to her full of the black water.

But Venus kept on. One cannot but accuse her of some stupidity. The only effect of all that had happened was to make her try again. She gave Psyche a box which she was to carry to the underworld and ask Proserpine to fill with some of her beauty. She was to tell her that Venus really needed it, she was so worn-out from nursing her sick son. Obediently as always Psyche went forth to look for the road to Hades. She found her guide in a tower she passed. It gave her careful directions how to get to Proserpine's palace, first through a great hole in the earth, then down to the river of death, where she must give the ferryman, Charon, a penny to take her across. From there the road led straight to the palace. Cerberus, the three-headed dog, guarded the doors, but if she gave him a cake he would be friendly and let her pass.

All happened, of course, as the tower had foretold. Proserpine was willing to do Venus a service, and Psyche, greatly encouraged, bore back the box, returning far more quickly than she had gone down.

Her next trial she brought upon herself

through her curiosity and, still more, her vanity. She felt that she must see what that beauty-charm in the box was; and, perhaps, use a little of it herself. She knew quite as well as Venus did that her looks were not improved by what she had gone through, and always in her mind was the thought that she might suddenly meet Cupid. If only she could make herself more lovely for him! She was unable to resist the temptation; she opened the box. To her sharp disappointment she saw nothing there; it seemed empty. Immediately, however, a deadly languor took possession of her and she fell into a heavy sleep.

At this juncture the God of Love himself stepped forward. Cupid was healed of his wound by now and longing for Psyche. It is a difficult matter to keep Love imprisoned. Venus had locked the door, but there were the windows. All Cupid had to do was to fly out and start looking for his wife. She was lying almost beside the palace, and he found her at once. In a moment he had wiped the sleep from her eyes and put it back into the box. Then waking her with just a prick from one of his arrows, and scolding her a little for her curiosity, he bade her take Proserpine's box to his mother and he assured her that all thereafter would be well.

While the joyful Psyche hastened on her errand, the god flew up to Olympus. He wanted to make certain that Venus would give them no more trouble, so he went straight to Jupiter himself. The Father of Gods and Men consented at once to all that Cupid asked—"Even though," he said, "you have done me great harm in the past—seriously injured my good name and my dignity by making me change myself into a bull and a swan and so on . . . However, I cannot refuse you."

Then he called a full assembly of the gods, and announced to all, including Venus, that Cupid and Psyche were formally married, and that he proposed to bestow immortality upon the bride: Mercury brought Psyche into the palace of the gods, and Jupiter himself gave her the ambrosia to taste which made her immortal. This, of course, completely changed the situation. Venus could not object to a goddess for her daughter-in-law; the alliance had become eminently suitable. No doubt she reflected also that Psyche, living up in heaven with a husband and children to care for, could not be much on the earth to turn men's heads and interfere with her own worship.

So all came to a most happy end. Love and the Soul (for that is what Psyche means) had sought and, after sore trials, found each other; and that union could never be broken.

Orpheus

How great the imagination that could encompass in one definitive story the magnitude and mystery of music! It is done in this love story of Orpheus and Eurydice (or Eurydike), in which death itself breaks immutable laws, so moving is the power of music.

Virgil told the story first. The poet Apollonius, a third-century Greek, in his work *Argonautica* places Orpheus among the Argonauts, who, led by Jason, went in search of the Golden Fleece. The lyre of Orpheus sped the tasks of the rowers on that long journey, calmed the anger of the men, and saved the Argonauts from the wiles of the Sirens. For the music of Orpheus drowned out the voices of the Sirens, which, had they been harkened to, would have drawn the men to shipwreck and disaster. [From Padraic Colum, *Orpheus: Myths of the World* (Macmillan, 1930).]

Many were the minstrels who, in the early days of the world, went amongst men, telling them stories of the Gods, of their wars and their births, and of the beginning of things. Of all these minstrels none was so famous as Orpheus; none could tell truer things about the Gods; he himself was half divine, and there were some who said that he was in truth Apollo's son.

But a great grief came to Orpheus, a grief that stopped his singing and his playing upon the lyre. His young wife, Eurydike, was taken from him. One day, walking in the garden, she was bitten on the heel by a serpent; straightway she went down to the World of the Dead.

Then everything in this world was dark and bitter for the minstrel of the Gods; sleep would not come to him, and for him food had no taste. Then Orpheus said, "I will do that which no mortal has ever done before; I will do that which even the Immortals might shrink from doing;

I will go down into the World of the Dead, and I will bring back to the living and to the light my bride, Eurydike."

Then Orpheus went on his way to the cavern which goes down, down to the World of the Dead—the Cavern Tainaron. The trees showed him the way. As he went on, Orpheus played upon his lyre and sang; the trees heard his song and were moved by his grief, and with their arms and their heads they showed him the way to the deep, deep cavern named Tainaron.

Down, down, down by a winding path Orpheus went. He came at last to the great gate that opens upon the World of the Dead. And the silent guards who keep watch there for the Rulers of the Dead were astonished when they saw a living being coming towards them, and they would not let Orpheus approach the gate.

The minstrel took the lyre in his hands and played upon it. As he played, the silent watchers gathered around him, leaving the gate unguarded. As he played the Rulers of the Dead came forth, Hades and Persephone, and listened to the words of the living man.

"The cause of my coming through the dark and fearful ways," sang Orpheus, "is to strive to gain a fairer fate for Eurydike, my bride. All that is above must come down to you at last, O Rulers of the most lasting World. But before her time has Eurydike been brought here. I have desired strength to endure her loss, but I cannot endure it. And I have come before you, Hades and Persephone, brought here by love."

When Orpheus said the name of love, Persephone, the queen of the dead, bowed her young head, and bearded Hades, the king, bowed his head also. Persephone remembered how Demeter, her mother, had sought her all through the world, and she remembered the touch of her mother's tears upon her face. And Hades remembered how his love for Persephone had led him to carry her away from the valley where she had been gathering flowers. He and Persephone stood aside, and Orpheus went through the gate and came amongst the dead.

Still upon his lyre he played. Tantalos—who

for his crime had been condemned to stand up to his neck in water and yet never be able to assuage his thirst—Tantalos heard, and for a while did not strive to put his lips toward the water that ever flowed away from him; Sisyphos—who had been condemned to roll up a hill a stone that ever rolled back—Sisyphos heard the music that Orpheus played, and for a while he sat still upon his stone. Ixion, bound to a wheel, stopped its turning for a while; the vultures abandoned their torment of Tityos; the daughters of Danaos ceased to fill their jars; even those dread ones, the Erinyes, who bring to the dead the memories of all their crimes and all their faults, had their cheeks wet with tears.

In the throng of the newly-come dead Orpheus saw Eurydike. She looked upon her husband, but she had not the power to come near him. But slowly she came when Hades, the king, called her. Then with joy Orpheus took her hands.

It would be granted them—no mortal ever gained such privilege before—to leave, both together, the World of the Dead, and to abide for another space in the World of the Living. One condition there would be—that on their way up neither Orpheus nor Eurydike should look back.

They went through the gate and came out amongst the watchers that are around the portals. These showed them the path that went up to the World of the Living. That way they went, Orpheus and Eurydike, he going before her.

Up and through the darkened ways they went, Orpheus knowing that Eurydike was behind him, but never looking back upon her. As he went his heart was filled with things to tell her—how the trees were blossoming in the garden she had left; how the water was sparkling in the fountain; how the doors of the house stood open; how they, sitting together, would watch the sunlight on the laurel bushes. All these things were in his heart to tell her who came behind him, silent and unseen.

And now they were nearing the place where the cavern opened on the world of the living. Orpheus looked up toward the light from the sky. Out of the opening of the cavern he went; he saw a white-winged bird fly by. He turned around and cried, "O Eurydike, look upon the world I have won you back to!"

He turned to say this to her. He saw her with her long dark hair and pale face. He held out his arms to clasp her. But in that instant she slipped back into the gloom of the cavern. And all he heard spoken was a single word. "Farewell!" Long, long had it taken Eurydike to climb so far, but in the moment of his turning around she had fallen back to her place amongst the dead. For Orpheus had looked back.

Back through the cavern Orpheus went again. Again he came before the watchers of the gate. But now he was not looked at nor listened to; hopeless, he had to return to the World of the Living.

The birds were his friends now, and the trees and the stones. The birds flew around him and mourned with him; the trees and stones often followed him, moved by the music of his lyre. But a savage band slew Orpheus and threw his severed head and his lyre into the River Hebrus. It is said by the poets that while they floated in midstream the lyre gave out some mournful notes, and the head of Orpheus answered the notes with song.

And now that he was no longer to be counted with the living, Orpheus went down to the World of the Dead, going down straightway. The silent watchers let him pass; he went amongst the dead, and he saw his Eurydike in the throng. Again they were together, Orpheus and Eurydike, and them the Erinyes could not torment with memories of crimes and faults.

Bellerophon

It is helpful to relate a few points connected with the background of this myth: The *Iliad* (v, 179) is responsible for the description of the Chimaera, and Pausanias (ii, 31; Iv, 31) tells the story that accounts for Pegasus as the symbol for poetry. The story states that when Mount Helicon was so entranced by the songs of the Muses and began to rise toward heaven, Pegasus stopped its ascent by stamping on the ground. At that the Hippocrene (horse fountain) burst forth and became known as the Spring of the Muses.

It is an easy step from this point to make the flying horse, Pegasus, the symbol for the flights of poetry. [From Padraic Colum, *The Forge in the Forest* (Macmillan, 1925).]

Often he watched the eagle in the air; as his gaze followed it on its way he would shout out his own name, "Bellerophon, Bellerophon!" As his name came back to him from the high rocks it seemed to him to be a prophecy of the time when he, too, would mount up and go the way of the eagle. He owned a bright sword and he knew that his spirit was braver and stronger than the spirits of those who were around him. And yet he had to serve a grudging King, and fresh labours and harassments came to him every day.

Once as he came back from his labour, the eyes of King Proetus's Queen rested upon the bright youth. "How beautiful he is, this Bellerophon," the Queen said. She spoke to him and would have him speak to her. But Bellerophon turned from Proetus's Queen—Proetus whom he had to serve. Then the Queen went to King Proetus, and, falsely accusing Bellerophon, had him sent away. But she had him sent away from slavery into dangers. He was commanded to go to the King of Lykia, and he went bearing tablets that told that King to thrust him into danger and still more danger.

"Thou must slay the Chimaera for me," said the King of Lykia; "thou must slay the Chimaera that appears in the sky and affrights all of us." Even then the Chimaera appeared in the sky. It had the head of a lion, the body of a goat, and the tail of a dragon. It filled the bright sky with horror and darkness. Then Bellerophon vowed that he would slay the monster; he would slay it, not because the King commanded him to slay it, but because the monster filled the beautiful depths that he loved with blackness. "I will slay the Chimaera for thee, O King," Bellerophon said, and he laid his hand on his bright sword as he spoke, "I will slay the Chimaera, and I will bring its lion's head into thy hall."

But how would he come to the Chimaera that went through the bright spaces of the sky? It came upon the tops of high mountains, and there Bellerophon would come upon it and slay it. But even as he sharpened his bright sword to go to the mountains and seek the Chimaera there, a whisper came to Bellerophon and told him that he should mount up to slay the Chimaera. And the whisper told him of a horse that grazed on far pastures, the horse Pegasus that had wings. And if he could come upon Pegasus and bridle him and mount him he could slay with his bright sword the Chimaera in the sky.

Then Bellerophon went forth bearing his sword and carrying the bridle that would hold Pegasus, the winged horse. He went forth, and in his own wild pastures he came upon Pegasus. The youth saw the winged horse feeding upon lotuses and springing across the water-courses. White was Pegasus, with white wings and dainty hoofs, and a heavy mane that tossed as he bounded along. It was easy to see that no bridle had ever gone upon Pegasus.

All day Bellerophon, the strong youth, followed after Pegasus. The horse bounded away, hardly noticing his pursuer. On the second day Bellerophon came suddenly upon Pegasus. He was drinking at a certain spring. Bellerophon seized the winged horse by the mane, and strove to hold him. But Pegasus trampled and kicked and at last broke away from Bellerophon. Afterwards he saw the winged horse only in the air, or drinking with his head raised from the spring every moment.

Often when he was worn out with watching and the chase, it would seem to Bellerophon that he never would be able to capture the horse Pegasus; he never would be able to slay the Chimaera, and he would have to go back and bear whatever doom the King of Lykia would lay upon him. And then he would see the sky being filled with the blackness and horror of the Chimaera, and he would resolve once more that he would be the one who would slay the monster.

One night a dream came to him. The goddess Pallas Athene appeared in his dream, and she said to him that any mortal who had such resolve as he had and who strove as he strove to carry out his resolve would have help from the immortals. She whispered to him of a philtre that would tame the horse Pegasus. Then he awoke, and he found in the hollow of his shield a cup that had a liquid in it—a liquid that was red like burning iron.

Bellerophon waited, hidden, at the spring that Pegasus came to. He seized the horse by the mane, and he poured into his mouth and between his teeth the liquid that he had found. Then Pegasus became tame under his hand. He put the bridle upon him. With the bright sword in his hand he mounted up to slay the Chimaera that even then filled the sky with blackness and horror.

And now he was in the air at last. As he went above the earth he shouted out his name, "Bellerophon, Bellerophon!" He knew now how magnificent that name was—the name for the rider of the skies, the conqueror of the Chimaera. He rose above where the eagle flew. He looked down and saw the fields and houses and towns of men. He would always soar above them, Bellerophon thought.

He saw the Chimaera near him, the monster that had the head of a lion, the body of a goat, and the tail of a dragon. Pegasus screamed, and would have kept back from the monster. But Bellerophon rode to meet the darkening thing. It breathed out fire that scorched him. But Bellerophon fought with it, using his bright sword. At last he struck into its body and brought the Chimaera from the sky down to the ground.

He rode Pegasus beside where it lay. He sprang off and cut the lion-head off the monster that lay there. Then Pegasus, screaming because the monster's blood had come upon him, reddening his white sides, fled away. Bellerophon, as he saw the winged horse go, knew that he could never recapture him, and knew that he could never again soar above the fields and the houses and the towns of men.

Into the hall of the King of Lykia he went, bringing the lion-head of the Chimaera. And then, because he saw an eagle soaring in the blue of the air, he wept. Before him, as he knew, there were long and weary wanderings over the face of the earth. He wept, knowing what was gone from him and what was before him. And then he rejoiced, for he knew that the pure spaces over him would never again be filled with the blackness and horror of the Chimaera.

Atalanta's Race

Atalanta had been forewarned not to marry, as marriage would be her ruin; therefore, she had made a vow that she thought would stop any suitor. But as one sees from this story, it did not; and her marriage was the cause of her ruin. She and Hippomenes were so happy that they forgot to pay honor to Venus, who caused them to be changed into a pair of lions. It is interesting to note that the device of throwing the apples is the same one used in a Scandinavian fairy tale, "The Princess on the Glass Hill." [From Padraic Colum, *The Golden Fleece, and the Heroes Who Lived Before Achilles* (Macmillan, 1921).]

There are two Atalantas, . . . the Huntress and another who is noted for her speed of foot and her delight in the race—the daughter of Schoeneus, King of Boeotia, Atalanta of the Swift Foot.

So proud was she of her swiftness that she made a vow to the gods that none would be her husband except the youth who won past her in the race. Youth after youth came and raced against her, but Atalanta, who grew fleeter and fleeter of foot, left each one of them far behind her. The youths who came to the race were so many, and the clamor they made after defeat was so great, that her father made a law that, as he thought, would lessen their number. The law that he made was that the youth who came to race against Atalanta and who lost the race should lose his life into the bargain. After that the youths who had care for their lives stayed away from Boeotia.

Once there came a youth from a far part of Greece into the country that Atalanta's father ruled over. Hippomenes was his name. He did not know of the race, but having come into the city and seeing the crowd of people, he went with them to the course. He looked upon the youths who were girded for the race, and he heard the folk say amongst themselves, "Poor youths, as mighty and as high-spirited as they look, by sunset the life will be out of each of them, for Atalanta will run past them as she ran past the others." Then Hippomenes spoke to the folk in wonder, and they told him of Atalanta's race and of what would befall the youths who were defeated in it. "Unlucky youths," cried Hippomenes, "how foolish they are to try to win a bride at the price of their lives!"

Then, with pity in his heart, he watched the youths prepare for the race. Atalanta had not yet taken her place, and he was fearful of looking upon her. "She is a witch," he said to himself; "she must be a witch to draw so many youths to their deaths, and she, no doubt, will show in her face and figure the witch's spirit."

But even as he said this, Hippomenes saw Atalanta. She stood with the youths before they crouched for the first dart in the race. He saw that she was a girl of a light and a lovely form. Then they crouched for the race; then the trumpets rang out, and the youths and the maiden darted like swallows over the sand of the course.

On came Atalanta, far, far ahead of the youths who had started with her. Over her bare shoulders her hair streamed, blown backward by the wind that met her flight. Her fair neck shone, and her little feet were like flying doves. It seemed to Hippomenes as he watched her that there was fire in her lovely body. On and on she went as swift as the arrow that the Scythian shoots from his bow. And as he watched the race, he was not sorry that the youths were being left behind. Rather would he have been enraged if one came near overtaking her, for now his heart was set upon winning her for his bride, and he cursed himself for not having entered the race.

She passed the last goal mark and she was given the victor's wreath of flowers. Hippomenes stood and watched her and he did not see the youths who had started with her—they had thrown themselves on the ground in their despair.

Then wild, as though he were one of the doomed youths, Hippomenes made his way through the throng and came before the black-bearded King of Boeotia. The king's brows were knit, for even then he was pronouncing doom upon the youths who had been left behind in the race. He looked upon Hippomenes, another youth who would make the trial, and the frown became heavier upon his face.

But Hippomenes saw only Atalanta. She came beside her father; the wreath was upon her head of gold, and her eyes were wide and tender. She turned her face to him, and then she knew by the wildness that was in his look that he had come to enter the race with her. Then the flush that was on her face died away, and she shook her head as if she were imploring him to go from that place.

The dark-bearded king bent his brows upon him and said, "Speak, O youth, speak and tell us what brings you here."

Then cried Hippomenes as if his whole life were bursting out with his words: "Why does this maiden, your daughter, seek an easy renown by conquering weakly youths in the race? She has not striven yet. Here stand I, one of the blood of Poseidon, the god of the sea. Should I be defeated by her in the race, then, indeed, might Atalanta have something to boast of."

Atalanta stepped forward and said: "Do not speak of it, youth. Indeed, I think that it is some god, envious of your beauty and your strength, who sent you here to strive with me and to meet your doom. Ah, think of the youths who have striven with me even now! Think of the hard doom that is about to fall upon them! You venture your life in the race, but indeed I am not worthy of the price. Go hence, O stranger youth; go hence and live happily, for indeed I think that there is some maiden who loves you well."

"Nay, maiden," said Hippomenes, "I will enter the race and I will venture my life on the chance of winning you for my bride. What good will my life and my spirit be to me if they cannot win this race for me?"

She drew away from him then and looked upon him no more, but bent down to fasten the sandals upon her feet. And the black-bearded king looked upon Hippomenes and said, "Face, then, this race tomorrow. You will be the only one who will enter it. But bethink thee of the doom that awaits thee at the end of it." The king said no more, and Hippomenes went from him and from Atalanta, and he came again to the place where the race had been run.

He looked across the sandy course with its goal marks, and in his mind he saw again Atalanta's swift race. He would not meet doom at the hands of the king's soldiers, he knew, for his spirit would leave him with the greatness of the effort he would make to reach the goal

before her. And he thought it would be well to die in that effort and on that sandy place that was so far from his own land.

Even as he looked across the sandy course now deserted by the throng, he saw one move across it, coming toward him with feet that did not seem to touch the ground. She was a woman of wonderful presence. As Hippomenes looked upon her, he knew that she was Aphrodite, the goddess of beauty and of love.

"Hippomenes," said the immortal goddess, "the gods are mindful of you who are sprung from one of the gods, and I am mindful of you because of your own worth. I have come to help you in your race with Atalanta, for I would not have you slain, nor would I have that maiden go unwed. Give your greatest strength and your greatest swiftness to the race, and behold! here are wonders that will prevent the fleet-footed Atalanta from putting all her spirit into the race."

And then the immortal goddess held out to Hippomenes a branch that had upon it three apples of shining gold.

"In Cyprus," said the goddess, "where I have come from, there is a tree on which these golden apples grow. Only I may pluck them. I have brought them to you, Hippomenes. Keep them in your girdle, and in the race you will find out what to do with them, I think."

So Aphrodite said, and then she vanished, leaving a fragrance in the air and the three shining apples in the hands of Hippomenes. Long he looked upon their brightness. They were beside him that night, and when he arose in the dawn he put them in his girdle. Then, before the throng, he went to the place of the race.

When he showed himself beside Atalanta, all around the course were silent, for they all admired Hippomenes for his beauty and for the spirit that was in his face; they were silent out of compassion, for they knew the doom that befell the youths who raced with Atalanta.

And now Schoeneus, the black-bearded king, stood up, and he spoke to the throng, saying: "Hear me all, both young and old: this youth, Hippomenes, seeks to win the race from my daughter, winning her for his bride. Now, if he be victorious and escape death, I will give him my dear child, Atalanta, and many fleet horses besides as gifts from me, and in honor he shall go back to his native land. But if he fail in the race, then he will have to share the doom that has been meted out to the other youths who raced with Atalanta hoping to win her for a bride."

Then Hippomenes and Atalanta crouched for the start. The trumpets were sounded and they darted off.

Side by side with Atalanta Hippomenes went. Her flying hair touched his breast, and it seemed to him that they were skimming the sandy course as if they were swallows. But then Atalanta began to draw away from him. He saw her ahead of him, and then he began to hear the words of cheer that came from the throng—"Bend to the race, Hippomenes! Go on, go on! Use your strength to the utmost!" He bent himself to the race, but farther and farther from him Atalanta drew.

Then it seemed to him that she checked her swiftness a little to look back at him. He gained on her a little. And then his hand touched the apples that were in his girdle. As it touched them, it came into his mind what to do with the apples.

He was not far from her now, but already her swiftness was drawing her farther and farther away. He took one of the apples into his hand and tossed it into the air so that it fell on the track before her.

Atalanta saw the shining apple. She checked her speed and stooped in the race to pick it up. And as she stooped, Hippomenes darted past her, and went flying toward the goal that now was within his sight.

But soon she was beside him again. He looked, and he saw that the goal marks were far, far ahead of him. Atalanta with the flying hair passed him, and drew away and away from him. He had not speed to gain upon her now, he thought, so he put his strength into his hand and he flung the second of the shining apples. The apple rolled before her and rolled off the course. Atalanta turned off the course, stooped and picked up the apple.

Then did Hippomenes draw all his spirit into his breast as he raced on. He was now nearer to the goal than she was. But he knew that she was behind him, going lightly where he went heavily. And then she went past him. She paused in her speed for a moment and she looked back on him.

As he raced on, his chest seemed weighted down and his throat was crackling dry. The goal marks were far away still, but Atalanta was nearing them. He took the last of the golden apples into his hand. Perhaps she was now so far that the strength of his throw would not be great enough to bring the apple before her.

But with all the strength he could put into his hand he flung the apple. It struck the course before her feet and then went bounding wide. Atalanta swerved in her race and followed where the apple went. Hippomenes marveled that he had been able to fling it so far. He saw Atalanta stoop to pick up the apple, and he bounded on. And then, although his strength was failing, he saw the goal marks near him. He set his feet between them and then fell down on the ground.

The attendants raised him up and put the victor's wreath upon his head. The concourse of people shouted with joy to see him victor. But he looked around for Atalanta and he saw her standing there with the golden apples in her hands. "He has won," he heard her say, "and I have not to hate myself for bringing a doom upon him. Gladly, gladly do I give up the race, and glad am I that it is this youth who has won the victory from me."

She took his hand and brought him before the king. Then Schoeneus, in the sight of all the rejoicing people, gave Atalanta to Hippomenes for his bride, and he bestowed upon him also a great gift of horses. With his dear and hard won bride, Hippomenes went to his own country, and the apples that she brought with her, the golden apples of Aphrodite, were reverenced by the people.

The Golden Touch

Midas was the name of several Phrygian kings. Ovid (*Metamorphoses*, xi, 85-145) tells how the legendary Midas came into contact with Dionysus (god of the vine), who, as a reward for helping him, granted Midas's request to have everything he touched turn into gold. When Midas realized he would starve to death, he successfully begged to be freed from this power. Nathaniel Hawthorne's "The Golden Touch" is quite different from the original Ovid. It is conversational, whimsical, and expansive—more like a Victorian short story than a dignified myth. In his retellings of Greek myths, Hawthorne's intention was to "aim at substituting a tone in some degree Gothic or romantic . . . instead of the classical coldness which is as repellant as the touch of marble." To achieve this effect, Hawthorne gave his stories a modern context and a narrator, Eustace Bright, who intimately addresses the child reader. He also employed dialogue and description and—in the tale below—introduced an invented child character. [From Nathaniel Hawthorne, *A Wonder-Book for Girls and Boys* (Ticknor, Reed & Fields, 1852).]

Once upon a time, there lived a very rich man, and a king besides, whose name was Midas; and he had a little daughter, whom nobody but myself ever heard of, and whose name I either never knew, or have entirely forgotten. So, because I love odd names for little girls, I choose to call her Marygold.

This King Midas was fonder of gold than of anything else in the world. He valued his royal crown chiefly because it was composed of that precious metal. If he loved anything better, or half so well, it was the one little maiden who played so merrily around her father's footstool. But the more Midas loved his daughter, the more did he desire and seek for wealth. He thought, foolish man! that the best thing he could possibly do for this dear child would be to bequeath her the immensest pile of yellow, glistening coin, that had ever been heaped together since the world was made. Thus, he gave all his thoughts and all his time to this one purpose. If ever he happened to gaze for an instant at the gold-tinted clouds of sunset, he wished that they were real gold, and that they could be squeezed safely into his strong box. When little Marygold ran to meet him, with a bunch of buttercups and dandelions, he used to say, "Poh, poh, child! If these flowers were as golden as they look, they would be worth the plucking!"

And yet, in his earlier days, before he was so entirely possessed with this insane desire for riches, King Midas had shown a great taste for flowers. He had planted a garden, in which grew the biggest and beautifullest and sweetest roses that any mortal ever saw or smelt. These roses were still growing in the garden, as large, as lovely and as fragrant, as when Midas used to pass whole hours in gazing at them, and inhaling their perfume. But now, if he looked at them at all, it was only to calculate how much the garden would be worth, if each of the innumerable rose-petals were a thin plate of gold. And though he once was fond of music (in spite of an idle story about his ears, which were said to resemble those of an ass), the only music for poor Midas, now, was the chink of one coin against another.

At length (as people always grow more and more foolish, unless they take care to grow wiser and wiser), Midas had got to be so exceedingly unreasonable, that he could scarcely bear to see or touch any object that was not gold. He made it his custom, therefore, to pass a large portion of every day in a dark and dreary apartment, under ground, at the basement of his palace. It was here that he kept his wealth. To this dismal hole—for it was little better than a dungeon—Midas betook himself, whenever he wanted to be particularly happy. Here, after carefully locking the door, he would take a bag of gold coin, or a gold cup as big as a washbowl, or a heavy golden bar, or a peck-measure of gold dust, and bring them from the obscure corners of the room into the one bright and narrow sunbeam that fell from the dungeon-like window. He valued the sunbeam for no other reason but that his treasure would not shine without its help. And then would he reckon over the coins in the bag; toss up the bar, and catch it as it came down; sift the gold dust through his fingers; look at the funny image of his own face, as reflected in the burnished circumference of the cup; and whisper to himself, "O Midas, rich King Midas, what a happy man art thou!" . . .

Midas was enjoying himself in his treasure-room, one day, as usual, when he perceived a shadow fall over the heaps of gold; and, looking suddenly up, what should he behold but the figure of a stranger, standing in the bright and narrow sunbeam! It was a young man, with a cheerful and ruddy face. Whether it was that the imagination of King Midas threw a yellow tinge over everything, or whatever the cause might be, he could not help fancying that the smile with which the stranger regarded him had a kind of golden radiance in it. Certainly, although his figure intercepted the sunshine, there was now a brighter gleam upon all the piled-up treasures than before. Even the remotest corners had their share of it, and were lighted up, when the stranger smiled, as with tips of flame and sparkles of fire.

As Midas knew that he had carefully turned the key in the lock, and that no mortal strength could possibly break into his treasure-room, he, of course, concluded that his visitor must be something more than mortal. It is no matter about telling you who he was. In those days, when the earth was comparatively a new affair, it was supposed to be often the resort of beings endowed with supernatural powers, and who used to interest themselves in the joys and sorrows of men, women and children, half playfully and half seriously. Midas had met such beings before now, and was not sorry to meet one of them again. The stranger's aspect, indeed, was so good-humored and kindly, if not beneficent, that it would have been unreasonable to suspect him of intending any mischief. It was far more probable that he came to do Midas a favor. And what could that favor be, unless to multiply his heaps of treasure?

The stranger gazed about the room; and when his lustrous smile had glistened upon all the golden objects that were there, he turned again to Midas.

"You are a wealthy man, friend Midas!" he observed. "I doubt whether any other four walls, on earth, contain so much gold as you have contrived to pile up in this room."

"I have done pretty well—pretty well," answered Midas, in a discontented tone. "But, after all, it is but a trifle, when you consider that it has taken me my whole life to get it together. If one could live a thousand years, he might have time to grow rich!"

"What!" exclaimed the stranger. "Then you are not satisfied?"

Midas shook his head.

"And pray what would satisfy you?" asked the stranger. "Merely for the curiosity of the thing, I should be glad to know."

Midas paused and meditated. He felt a presentiment that this stranger, with such a golden lustre in his good-humored smile, had come hither with both the power and the purpose of gratifying his utmost wishes. Now, therefore, was the fortunate moment, when he had but to speak, and obtain whatever possible, or seemingly impossible thing, it might come into his head to ask. So he thought, and thought, and thought, and heaped up one golden mountain upon another, in his imagination, without being able to imagine them big enough. At last, a bright idea occurred to King Midas. It seemed really as bright as the glistening metal which he loved so much.

Raising his head, he looked the lustrous stranger in the face.

"Well, Midas," observed his visiter, "I see that you have at length hit upon something that will satisfy you. Tell me your wish."

"It is only this," replied Midas. "I am weary of collecting my treasures with so much trouble, and beholding the heap so diminutive, after I have done my best. I wish everything that I touch to be changed to gold!"

The stranger's smile grew so very broad, that it seemed to fill the room like an outburst of the sun, gleaming into a shadowy dell, where the yellow autumnal leaves—for so looked the lumps and particles of gold—lie strewn in the glow of light.

"The Golden Touch!" exclaimed he. "You certainly deserve credit, friend Midas, for striking out so brilliant a conception. But are you quite sure that this will satisfy you?"

"How could it fail?" said Midas.

"And will you never regret the possession of it?"

"What could induce me?" asked Midas. "I ask nothing else, to render me perfectly happy."

"Be it as you wish, then," replied the stranger, waving his hand in token of farewell. "To-morrow, at sunrise, you will find yourself gifted with the Golden Touch."

The figure of the stranger then became exceedingly bright, and Midas involuntarily closed his eyes. On opening them again, he beheld only one yellow sunbeam in the room, and, all around him, the glistening of the precious metal which he had spent his life in hoarding up.

Whether Midas slept as usual that night, the story does not say. Asleep or awake, however, his mind was probably in the state of a child's, to whom a beautiful new plaything has been promised in the morning. At any rate, day had hardly peeped over the hills, when King Midas was broad awake, and, stretching his arms out of bed, began to touch the objects that were within reach. He was anxious to prove whether the Golden Touch had really come, according to the stranger's promise. So he laid his finger on a chair by the bedside, and on various other things, but was grievously disappointed to perceive that they remained of exactly the same substance as before. Indeed, he felt very much afraid that he had only dreamed about the lustrous stranger, or else that the latter had been making game of him. And what a miserable affair would it be, if, after all his hopes, Midas must content himself with what little gold he could scrape together by ordinary means, instead of creating it by a touch!

All this while, it was only the gray of the morning, with but a streak of brightness along the edge of the sky, where Midas could not see it. He lay in a very disconsolate mood, regretting the downfall of his hopes, and kept growing sadder and sadder, until the earliest sunbeam shone through the window, and gilded the ceiling over his head. It seemed to Midas that this bright yellow sunbeam was reflected in rather a singular way on the white covering of the bed. Looking more closely, what was his astonishment and delight, when he found that this linen fabric had been transmuted to what seemed a woven texture of the purest and brightest gold! The Golden Touch had come to him, with the first sunbeam!

Midas started up, in a kind of joyful frenzy, and ran about the room, grasping at everything that happened to be in his way. He seized one of the bedposts, and it became immediately a fluted golden pillar. He pulled aside a window-curtain, in order to admit a clear spectacle of the wonders which he was performing; and the tassel grew heavy in his hand—a mass of gold. He took up a book from the table. At his first touch, it assumed the appearance of such a splendidly-bound and gilt-edged volume as one often meets with, now-a-days; but, on running his fingers through the leaves, behold! it was a bundle of thin golden plates, in which all the wisdom of the book had grown illegible. He hurriedly put on his clothes, and was enraptured to see himself in a magnificent suit of gold cloth, which retained its flexibility and softness, although it burdened him a little with its weight. He drew out his handkerchief, which little Marygold had hemmed for him. That was likewise gold, with the dear child's neat and pretty stitches running all along the border, in gold thread!

Somehow or other, this last transformation did not quite please King Midas. He would rather that his little daughter's handiwork should have remained just the same as when she climbed his knee, and put it into his hand.

But it was not worth while to vex himself about a trifle. Midas now took his spectacles from his pocket, and put them on his nose, in order that he might see more distinctly what he was about. In those days, spectacles for common people had not been invented, but were already worn by kings; else, how could Midas have had any? To his great perplexity, however, excellent as the glasses were, he discovered that he could not possibly see through them. But this was the most natural thing in the world; for, on taking them off, the transparent crystals turned out to be plates of yellow metal, and, of course, were worthless as spectacles, though valuable as gold. It struck Midas as rather inconvenient, that, with all his wealth, he could never again be rich enough to own a pair of serviceable spectacles.

"It is no great matter, nevertheless," said he to himself, very philosophically. "We cannot expect any great good, without its being accompanied with some small inconvenience. The Golden Touch is worth the sacrifice of a pair of spectacles, at least, if not of one's very eyesight. My own eyes will serve for ordinary purposes, and little Marygold will soon be old enough to read to me."

. . . King Midas . . . therefore went down

stairs, and smiled, on observing that the balustrade of the staircase became a bar of burnished gold, as his hand passed over it, in his descent. He lifted the doorlatch (it was brass only a moment ago, but golden when his fingers quitted it), and emerged into the garden. Here, as it happened, he found a great number of beautiful roses in full bloom, and others in all the stages of lovely bud and blossom. Very delicious was their fragrance in the morning breeze. Their delicate blush was one of the fairest sights in the world; so gentle, so modest, and so full of sweet tranquility, did these roses seem to be.

But Midas knew a way to make them far more precious, according to his way of thinking, than roses had ever been before. So he took great pains in going from bush to bush, and exercised his magic touch most indefatigably; until every individual flower and bud, and even the worms at the heart of some of them, were changed to gold. By the time this good work was completed, King Midas was summoned to breakfast; and, as the morning air had given him an excellent appetite, he made haste back to the palace.

What was usually a king's breakfast, in the days of Midas, I really do not know, and cannot stop now to investigate. To the best of my belief, however, on this particular morning, the breakfast consisted of hot cakes, some nice little brook-trout, roasted potatoes, fresh boiled eggs, and coffee, for King Midas himself, and a bowl of bread and milk for his daughter Marygold. At all events, this is a breakfast fit to set before a king; and, whether he had it or not, King Midas could not have had a better.

Little Marygold had not yet made her appearance. Her father ordered her to be called, and, seating himself at table, awaited the child's coming, in order to begin his own breakfast. To do Midas justice, he really loved his daughter, and loved her so much the more this morning, on account of the good fortune which had befallen him. It was not a great while before he heard her coming along the passage-way, crying bitterly. This circumstance surprised him, because Marygold was one of the cheerfullest little people whom you would see in a summer's day, and hardly shed a thimble-full of tears in

a twelve-month. When Midas heard her sobs, he determined to put little Marygold into better spirits, by an agreeable surprise; so, leaning across the table, he touched his daughter's bowl (which was a China one, with pretty figures all around it), and transmuted it to gleaming gold.

Meanwhile, Marygold slowly and disconsolately opened the door, and showed herself with her apron at her eyes, still sobbing as if her heart would break.

"How now, my little lady!" cried Midas. "Pray what is the matter with you, this bright morning?"

Marygold, without taking the apron from her eyes, held out her hand, in which was one of the roses which Midas had so recently transmuted.

"Beautiful!" exclaimed her father. "And what is there in this magnificent golden rose to make you cry?"

"Ah, dear father!" answered the child, as well as her sobs would let her; "it is not beautiful, but the ugliest flower that ever grew! As soon as I was dressed, I ran into the garden to gather some roses for you; because I know you like them, and like them the better when gathered by your little daughter. But, oh dear, dear me! What do you think has happened? Such a misfortune! All the beautiful roses, that smelled so sweetly and had so many lovely blushes, are blighted and spoilt! They are grown quite yellow, as you see this one, and have no longer any fragrance! What can have been the matter with them?"

"Poh, my dear little girl,—pray don't cry about it!" said Midas, who was ashamed to confess that he himself had wrought the change which so greatly afflicted her. "Sit down and eat your bread and milk! You will find it easy enough to exchange a golden rose like that (which will last hundreds of years), for an ordinary one, which would wither in a day."

"I don't care for such roses as this!" cried Marygold, tossing it contemptuously away. "It has no smell, and the hard petals prick my nose!"

The child now sat down to table, but was so occupied with her grief for the blighted roses that she did not even notice the wonderful transmutation of her China bowl. Perhaps this was all the better; for Marygold was accustomed to take pleasure in looking at the queer figures, and strange trees and houses, that were painted on the circumference of the bowl; and these ornaments were now entirely lost in the yellow hue of the metal.

Midas, meanwhile, had poured out a cup of coffee; and, as a matter of course, the coffee-pot, whatever metal it may have been when he took it up, was gold when he set it down. He thought to himself, that it was rather an extravagant style of splendor, in a king of his simple habits, to breakfast off a service of gold, and began to be puzzled with the difficulty of keeping his treasures safe. The cupboard and the kitchen would no longer be a secure place of deposit for articles so valuable as golden bowls and coffee-pots.

Amid these thoughts, he lifted a spoonful of coffee to his lips, and, sipping it, was astonished to perceive that, the instant his lips touched the liquid, it became molten gold, and, the next moment, hardened into a lump!

"Ha!" exclaimed Midas, rather aghast.

"What is the matter, father?" asked little Marygold, gazing at him, with the tears still standing in her eyes.

"Nothing, child, nothing!" said Midas. "Eat your milk, before it gets quite cold."

He took one of the nice little trouts on his plate, and, by way of experiment, touched its tail with his finger. To his horror, it was immediately transmuted from an admirably-fried brook-trout into a gold fish. . . . A very pretty piece of work, as you may suppose; only King Midas, just at that moment, would much rather have had a real trout in his dish than this elaborate and valuable imitation of one.

"I don't quite see," thought he to himself, "how I am to get any breakfast!"

He took one of the smoking hot cakes, and had scarcely broken it, when, to his cruel mortification, though, a moment before, it had been of the whitest wheat, it assumed the yellow hue of Indian meal. To say the truth, if it had really been a hot Indian cake, Midas would have prized it a good deal more than he now did, when its solidity and increased weight made him

too bitterly sensible that it was gold. Almost in despair, he helped himself to a boiled egg, which immediately underwent a change similar to those of the trout and the cake. The egg, indeed, might have been mistaken for one of those which the famous goose, in the story-book, was in the habit of laying; but King Midas was the only goose that had had anything to do with the matter.

"Well, this is a quandary!" thought he, leaning back in his chair, and looking quite enviously at little Marygold, who was now eating her bread and milk with great satisfaction. "Such a costly breakfast before me, and nothing that can be eaten!"

Hoping that, by dint of great despatch, he might avoid what he now felt to be a considerable inconvenience, King Midas next snatched a hot potato, and attempted to cram it into his mouth, and swallow it in a hurry. But the Golden Touch was too nimble for him. He found his mouth full, not of mealy potato, but of solid metal, which so burnt his tongue that he roared aloud, and, jumping up from the table, began to dance and stamp about the room, both with pain and affright.

"Father, dear father!" cried little Marygold, who was a very affectionate child, "pray what is the matter? Have you burnt your mouth?"

"Ah, dear child," groaned Midas, dolefully, "I don't know what is to become of your poor father!"

And, truly, my dear little folks, did you ever hear of such a pitiable case, in all your lives? Here was literally the richest breakfast that could be set before a king, and its very richness made it absolutely good for nothing. The poorest laborer, sitting down to his crust of bread and cup of water, was far better off than King Midas, whose delicate food was really worth its weight in gold. And what was to be done? Already, at breakfast, Midas was excessively hungry. Would he be less so by dinner-time? And how ravenous would be his appetite for supper, which must undoubtedly consist of the same sort of indigestible dishes as those now before him! How many days, think you, would he survive a continuance of this rich fare?

These reflections so troubled wise King

Midas, that he began to doubt whether, after all, riches are the one desirable thing in the world, or even the most desirable. But this was only a passing thought. So fascinated was Midas with the glitter of the yellow metal, that he would still have refused to give up the Golden Touch for so paltry a consideration as a breakfast. . . .

Nevertheless, so great was his hunger, and the perplexity of his situation, that he again groaned aloud, and very grievously too. Our pretty Marygold could endure it no longer. She sat, a moment, gazing at her father, and trying, with all the might of her little wits, to find out what was the matter with him. Then, with a sweet and sorrowful impulse to comfort him, she started from her chair, and running to Midas, threw her arms affectionately about his knees. He bent down and kissed her. He felt that his little daughter's love was worth a thousand times more than he had gained by the Golden Touch.

"My precious, precious Marygold!" cried he.

But Marygold made no answer.

Alas, what had he done? How fatal was the gift which the stranger bestowed! The moment the lips of Midas touched Marygold's forehead, a change had taken place. Her sweet, rosy face, so full of affection as it had been, assumed a glittering yellow color, with yellow tear-drops congealing on her cheeks. Her beautiful brown ringlets took the same tint. Her soft and tender little form grew hard and inflexible within her father's encircling arms. O, terrible misfortune! The victim of his insatiable desire for wealth, little Marygold was a human child no longer, but a golden statue!

Yes, there she was, with the questioning look of love, grief, and pity, hardened into her face. It was the prettiest and most woful sight that ever mortal saw. All the features and tokens of Marygold were there; even the beloved little dimple remained in her golden chin. But, the more perfect was the resemblance, the greater was the father's agony at beholding this golden image, which was all that was left him of a daughter. It had been a favorite phrase of Midas, whenever he felt particularly fond of the child, to say that she was worth her weight in gold. And now the phrase had become literally true. And now, at last, when it was too late, he felt how infinitely a warm and tender heart, that loved him, exceeded in value all the wealth that could be piled up betwixt the earth and sky!

It would be too sad a story, if I were to tell you how Midas, in the fulness of all his gratified desires, began to wring his hands and bemoan himself; and how he could neither bear to look at Marygold, nor yet to look away from her. Except when his eyes were fixed on the image, he could not possibly believe that she was changed to gold. But, stealing another glance, there was the precious little figure, with a yellow tear-drop on its yellow cheek, and a look so piteous and tender, that it seemed as if that very expression must needs soften the gold, and make it flesh again. This, however, could not be. . . .

While he was in this tumult of despair, he suddenly beheld a stranger, standing near the door. Midas bent down his head, without speaking; for he recognized the same figure which had appeared to him, the day before, in the treasure-room, and had bestowed on him this disastrous faculty of the Golden Touch. The stranger's countenance still wore a smile, which seemed to shed a yellow lustre all about the room, and gleamed on little Marygold's image, and on the other objects that had been transmuted by the touch of Midas.

"Well, friend Midas," said the stranger, "pray how do you succeed with the Golden Touch?"

Midas shook his head.

"I am very miserable," said he.

"Very miserable, indeed!" exclaimed the stranger. "And how happens that? Have I not faithfully kept my promise with you? Have you not everything that your heart desired?"

"Gold is not everything," answered Midas. "And I have lost all that my heart really cared for."

"Ah! So you have made a discovery, since yesterday?" observed the stranger. "Let us see, then. Which of these two things do you think is really worth the most,—the gift of the Golden Touch, or one cup of clear cold water?"

"O, blessed water!" exclaimed Midas. "It

will never moisten my parched throat again!"

"The Golden Touch," continued the stranger, "or a crust of bread?"

"A piece of bread," answered Midas, "is worth all the gold on earth!"

"The Golden Touch," asked the stranger, "or your own little Marygold, warm, soft, and loving, as she was an hour ago?"

"O, my child, my dear child!" cried poor Midas, wringing his hands. "I would not have given that one small dimple in her chin for the power of changing this whole big earth into a solid lump of gold!"

"You are wiser than you were, King Midas!" said the stranger, looking seriously at him. "Your own heart, I perceive, has not been entirely changed from flesh to gold. Were it so, your case would indeed be desperate. But you appear to be still capable of understanding that the commonest things, such as lie within everybody's grasp, are more valuable than the riches which so many mortals sigh and struggle after. Tell me, now, do you sincerely desire to rid yourself of this Golden Touch?"

"It is hateful to me!" replied Midas.

A fly settled on his nose, but immediately fell to the floor; for it, too, had become gold. Midas shuddered.

"Go, then," said the stranger, "and plunge into the river that glides past the bottom of your garden. Take likewise a vase of the same water, and sprinkle it over any object that you may desire to change back again from gold into its former substance. If you do this in earnestness and sincerity, it may possibly repair the mischief which your avarice has occasioned."

King Midas bowed low; and when he lifted his head, the lustrous stranger had vanished.

You will easily believe that Midas lost no time in snatching up a great earthen pitcher (but, alas me! it was no longer earthen after he touched it), and hastening to the river-side. As he scampered along, and forced his way through the shrubbery, it was positively marvellous to see how the foliage turned yellow behind him, as if the autumn had been there, and nowhere else. On reaching the river's brink, he plunged headlong in, without waiting so much as to pull off his shoes.

"Poof! poof! poof!" snorted King Midas, as his head emerged out of the water. "Well; this is really a refreshing bath, and I think it must have quite washed away the Golden Touch. And now for filling my pitcher!"

As he dipped the pitcher into the water, it gladened his very heart to see it change from gold into the same good, honest earthen vessel which it had been before he touched it. He was conscious, also, of a change within himself. A cold, hard and heavy weight seemed to have gone out of his bosom. No doubt, his heart had been gradually losing its human substance, and transmuting itself into insensible metal, but had now softened back again into flesh. Perceiving a violet, that grew on the bank of the river, Midas touched it with his finger, and was overjoyed to find that the delicate flower retained its purple hue, instead of undergoing a yellow blight. The curse of the Golden Touch had, therefore, really been removed from him.

King Midas hastened back to the palace: and, I suppose, the servants knew not what to make of it when they saw their royal master so carefully bringing home an earthen pitcher of water. But that water, which was to undo all the mischief that his folly had wrought, was more precious to Midas than an ocean of molten gold could have been. The first thing he did, as you need hardly be told, was to sprinkle it by handfuls over the golden figure of little Marygold.

No sooner did it fall on her than you would have laughed to see how the rosy color came back to the dear child's cheek!—and how she began to sneeze and sputter!—and how astonished she was to find herself dripping wet, and her father still throwing more water over her!

"Pray do not, dear father!" cried she. "See how you have wet my nice frock, which I put on only this morning!"

For Marygold did not know that she had been a little golden statue; nor could she remember anything that had happened since the moment when she ran, with outstretched arms, to comfort poor King Midas.

Her father did not think it necessary to tell his beloved child how very foolish he had been, but contented himself with showing how much wiser he had now grown. For this purpose, he led little Marygold into the garden, where he sprinkled all the remainder of the water over the rose-bushes, and with such good effect that above five thousand roses recovered their beautiful bloom. There were two circumstances, however, which, as long as he lived, used to put King Midas in mind of the Golden Touch. One was, that the sands of the river sparkled like gold; the other, that little Marygold's hair had now a golden tinge, which he had never observed in it before she had been transmuted by the effect of his kiss. . . .

When King Midas had grown quite an old man, and used to trot Marygold's children on his knee, he was fond of telling them this marvellous story, pretty much as I have now told it to you. And then would he stroke their glossy ringlets, and tell them that their hair, likewise, had a rich shade of gold, which they had inherited from their mother.

"And, to tell you the truth, my precious little folks," quoth King Midas, diligently trotting the children all the while, "ever since that morning, I have hated the very sight of all other gold, save this!"

Norse Myths

Odin Goes to Mimir's Well

Odin, the All-Father, was supreme among gods and men. He was the god of wisdom, knowledge, and poetry. He was also the god of war and of the dead. In Valhalla, he presided over the banquets of the heroes who were slain in battle. Seated on his throne in his golden palace, Gladsheim, he looked out over all the world. Perched on his shoulders were his two black ravens, Hugin (Thought) and Munin (Memory), who flew daily over the earth and brought back news to him. When they told him only of shadows and dark forebodings, Odin felt that he must seek more wisdom. Then it was that he told his queenly wife Frigga that he must leave Asgard for a while and go to Mimir's Well, there to change what knowledge he had into wisdom so that he might deal as wisely as possible with the dark events when

they happened. [From Padraic Colum, *The Children of Odin* (Macmillan, 1920).]

And so Odin, no longer riding on Sleipner, his eight-legged steed; no longer wearing his golden armour and his eagle-helmet, and without even his spear in his hand, travelled through Midgard, the World of Men, and made his way towards Jötunheim, the Realm of the Giants.

No longer was he called Odin All-Father, but Vegtam the Wanderer. He wore a cloak of dark blue and he carried a traveller's staff in his hands. And now, as he went towards Mimir's Well, which was near to Jötunheim, he came upon a Giant riding on a great Stag.

Odin seemed a man to men and a giant to giants. He went beside the Giant on the great Stag and the two talked together. "Who art thou, O brother?" Odin asked the Giant.

"I am Vafthrudner, the wisest of the Giants," said the one who was riding on the Stag. Odin knew him then. Vafthrudner was indeed the wisest of the Giants, and many went to strive to gain wisdom from him. But those who went to him had to answer the riddles Vafthrudner asked, and if they failed to answer the Giant took their heads off.

"I am Vegtam the Wanderer," Odin said, "and I know who thou art, O Vafthrudner. I would strive to learn something from thee."

The Giant laughed, showing his teeth. "Ho, ho," he said, "I am ready for a game with thee. Dost thou know the stakes? My head to thee if I cannot answer any question thou wilt ask. And if thou canst not answer any question that I may ask, then thy head goes to me. Ho, ho, ho. And now let us begin."

"I am ready," Odin said.

"Then tell me," said Vafthrudner, "tell me the name of the river that divides Asgard from Jötunheim?"

"Ifling is the name of that river," said Odin. "Ifling that is dead cold, yet never frozen."

"Thou hast answered rightly, O Wanderer," said the Giant. "But thou hast still to answer other questions. What are the names of the horses that Day and Night drive across the sky?"

"Skinfaxe and Hrimfaxe," Odin answered. Vafthrudner was startled to hear one say the names that were known only to the Gods and to the wisest of the Giants. There was only one question now that he might ask before it came to the stranger's turn to ask him questions.

"Tell me," said Vafthrudner, "what is the name of the plain on which the last battle will be fought?"

"The Plain of Vigard," said Odin, "the plain that is a hundred miles long and a hundred miles across."

It was now Odin's turn to ask Vafthrudner questions. "What will be the last words that Odin will whisper into the ear of Baldur, his dear son?" he asked.

Very startled was the Giant Vafthrudner at that question. He sprang to the ground and looked at the stranger keenly.

"Only Odin knows what his last words to Baldur will be," he said, "and only Odin would have asked that question. Thou art Odin, O Wanderer, and thy question I cannot answer."

"Then," said Odin, "if thou wouldst keep thy head, answer me this: what price will Mimir ask for a draught from the Well of Wisdom that he guards?"

"He will ask thy right eye as a price, O Odin," said Vafthrudner.

"Will he ask no less a price than that?" said Odin.

"He will ask no less a price. Many have come to him for a draught from the Well of Wisdom, but no one yet has given the price Mimir asks. I have answered thy question, O Odin. Now give up thy claim to my head and let me go on my way."

"I give up my claim to thy head," said Odin. Then Vafthrudner, the wisest of the Giants, went on his way, riding on his great Stag.

It was a terrible price that Mimir would ask for a draught from the Well of Wisdom, and very troubled was Odin All-Father when it was revealed to him. His right eye! For all time to be without the sight of his right eye! Almost he would have turned back to Asgard, giving up his quest for wisdom.

He went on, turning neither to Asgard nor to Mimir's Well. And when he went towards the South he saw Muspelheim, where stood Surtur with the Flaming Sword, a terrible figure, who would one day join the Giants in their war against the Gods. And when he turned North he heard the roaring of the cauldron Hvergelmer as it poured itself out of Niflheim, the place of darkness and dread. And Odin knew that the world must not be left between Surtur, who would destroy it with fire, and Niflheim, that would gather it back to Darkness and Nothingness. He, the eldest of the Gods, would have to win the wisdom that would help to save the world.

And so, with his face stern in front of his loss and pain, Odin All-Father turned and went towards Mimir's Well. It was under the great root of Yggdrasill—the root that grew out of Jötunheim. And there sat Mimir, the Guardian of the Well of Wisdom, with his deep eyes bent upon the deep water. And Mimir, who had drunk every day from the Well of Wisdom, knew who it was that stood before him.

"Hail, Odin, Eldest of the Gods," he said.

Then Odin made reverence to Mimir, the wisest of the world's being. "I would drink from your well, Mimir," he said.

"There is a price to be paid. All who have come here to drink have shrunk from paying that price. Will you, Eldest of the Gods, pay it?"

"I will not shrink from the price that has to be paid, Mimir," said Odin All-Father.

"Then drink," said Mimir. He filled up a great horn with water from the well and gave it to Odin.

Odin took the horn in both his hands and drank and drank. And as he drank all the future became clear to him. He saw all the sorrows and troubles that would fall upon Men and Gods. But he saw, too, why the sorrows and troubles had to fall, and he saw how they might be borne so that Gods and Men, by being noble in the days of sorrow and trouble, would leave in the world a force that one day, a day that was far off indeed, would destroy the evil that brought terror and sorrow and despair into the world.

Then when he had drunk out of the great horn that Mimir had given him, he put his hand to his face and he plucked out his right eye. Terrible was the pain that Odin All-Father endured. But he made no groan nor moan. He bowed his head and put his cloak before his face, as Mimir took the eye and let it sink deep, deep into the water of the Well of Wisdom. And there the Eye of Odin stayed, shining up through the water, a sign to all who came to that place of the price that the Father of the Gods had paid for his wisdom.

The Magic Apples

Hoenir is said to have helped Odin create the first human beings; therefore, it was natural for Hoenir to be Odin's companion on any adventure. As for Loki, he was always ready for adventure or mischief. It is interesting to compare this story with that episode of the *Nibelungenlied* in which the giants get from Wotan (Odin) Freia, whose presence is necessary to the well-being of the gods; in this story they must not only get Idun, but the apples that keep the gods young and strong. In both stories, Odin is helpless in retrieving the loss; Loki is successful in each case. [From Abbie Farwell Brown, *In the Days of Giants* (Houghton Mifflin, 1902).]

It is not very amusing to be a king. Father Odin often grew tired of sitting all day long upon his golden throne in Valhalla above the heavens. He wearied of welcoming the new heroes whom the Valkyries brought him from wars upon the earth, and of watching the old heroes fight their daily deathless battles. He wearied of his wise ravens, and the constant gossip which they brought him from the four corners of the world; and he longed to escape from every one who knew him to some place where he could pass for a mere stranger, instead of the great king of the Aesir, the mightiest being in the whole universe, of whom every one was afraid.

Sometimes he longed so much that he could not bear it. Then—he would run away. He disguised himself as a tall old man, with white hair and a long gray beard. Around his shoulders he threw a huge blue cloak, that covered him from top to toe, and over his face he pulled a big slouch hat, to hide his eyes. For his eyes Odin could not change—no magician has ever learned how to do that. One was empty; he had given the eye to the giant Mimir in exchange for wisdom.

Usually Odin loved to go upon these wanderings alone; for an adventure is a double adven-

ture when one meets it single-handed. It was a fine game for Odin to see how near he could come to danger without feeling the grip of its teeth. But sometimes, when he wanted company, he would whisper to his two brothers, Hoenir and red Loki. They three would creep out of the palace by the back way; and, with a finger on the lip to Heimdal, the watchman, would silently steal over the rainbow bridge which led from Asgard into the places of men and dwarfs and giants.

Wonderful adventures they had, these three, with Loki to help make things happen. Loki was a sly, mischievous fellow, full of his pranks and his capers, not always kindly ones. But he was clever, as well as malicious; and when he had pushed folk into trouble, he could often help them out again, as safe as ever. He could be the jolliest of companions when he chose, and Odin liked his merriment and his witty talk.

One day Loki did something which was no mere jest nor easily forgiven, for it brought all Asgard into danger. And after that Father Odin and his children thought twice before inviting Loki to join them in any journey or undertaking. This which I am about to tell was the first really wicked deed of which Loki was found guilty, though I am sure his red beard had dabbled in secret wrongs before.

One night the three high gods, Odin, Hoenir, and Loki, stole away from Asgard in search of adventure. Over mountains and deserts, great rivers and stony places, they wandered until they grew very hungry. But there was not food to be found—not even a berry or a nut.

Oh, how footsore and tired they were! And oh, how faint! The worst of it ever is that— as you must often have noticed—the heavier one's feet grow, the lighter and more hollow becomes one's stomach; which seems a strange thing, when you think of it. If only one's feet became as light as the rest of one feels, folk could fairly fly with hunger. Alas! this is not so.

The three Aesir drooped and drooped, and seemed on the point of starving, when they came to the edge of a valley. Here, looking down, they saw a herd of oxen feeding on the grass.

"Hola!" shouted Loki. "Behold our supper!" Going down into the valley, they caught and killed one of the oxen, and, building a great bonfire, hung up the meat to roast. Then the three sat around the fire and smacked their lips, waiting for the meat to cook. They waited for a long time.

"Surely, it is done now," said Loki, at last; and he took the meat from the fire. Strange to say, however, it was raw as ere the fire was lighted. What could it mean? Never before had meat required so long a time to roast. They made the fire brighter and re-hung the beef for a thorough basting, cooking it even longer than they had done at first. When again they came to carve the meat, they found it still uneatable. Then, indeed, they looked at one another in surprise.

"What can this mean?" cried Loki, with round eyes.

"There is some trick!" whispered Hoenir, looking around as if he expected to see a fairy or a witch meddling with the food.

"We must find out what this mystery betokens," said Odin thoughtfully. Just then there was a strange sound in the oak-tree under which they had built their fire.

"What is that?" Loki shouted, springing to his feet. They looked up into the tree, and far above in the branches, near the top, they spied an enormous eagle, who was staring down at them, and making a queer sound, as if he were laughing.

"Ho-ho!" croaked the eagle. "I know why your meat will not cook. It is all my doing, masters."

The three Aesir stared in surprise. Then Odin said sternly: "Who are you, Master Eagle? And what do you mean by those rude words?"

"Give me my share of the ox, and you shall see," rasped the eagle, in his harsh voice. "Give me my share, and you will find that your meat will cook as fast as you please."

Now the three on the ground were nearly famished. So, although it seemed very strange to be arguing with an eagle, they cried, as if in one voice: "Come down, then, and take your share." They thought that, being a mere bird, he would want but a small piece.

The eagle flapped down from the top of the tree. Dear me! What a mighty bird he was! Eight feet across the wings was the smallest mea-

sure, and his claws were as long and strong as ice-hooks. He fanned the air like a whirlwind as he flew down to perch beside the bonfire. Then in his beak and claws he seized a leg and both shoulders of the ox, and started to fly away.

"Hold, thief!" roared Loki angrily, when he saw how much the eagle was taking. "That is not your share; you are no lion, but you are taking the lion's share of our feast. Begone, Scarecrow, and leave the meat as you found it!" Thereat, seizing a pole, he struck at the eagle with all his might.

Then a strange thing happened. As the great bird flapped upward with his prey, giving a scream of malicious laughter, the pole which Loki still held stuck fast to the eagle's back, and Loki was unable to let go of the other end.

"Help, help!" he shouted to Odin and to Hoenir, as he felt himself lifted off his feet. But they could not help him. "Help, help!" he screamed, as the eagle flew with him, now high, now low, through brush and bog and briar, over treetops and the peaks of mountains. On and on they went, until Loki thought his arm would be pulled out, like a weed torn up by the roots. The eagle would not listen to his cries nor pause in his flight, until Loki was almost dead with pain and fatigue.

"Hark you, Loki," screamed the eagle, going a little more slowly; "no one can help you except me. You are bewitched, and you cannot pull away from this pole, nor loose the pole from me, until I choose. But if you will promise what I ask, you shall go free."

Then Loki groaned: "O eagle, only let me go, and tell me who you really are, and I will promise whatever you wish."

The eagle answered: "I am the giant Thiasse, the enemy of the Aesir. But you ought to love me, Loki, for you yourself married a giantess."

Loki moaned: "Oh, yes! I dearly love all my wife's family, great Thiasse. Tell me what you want of me?"

"I want this," quoth Thiasse gruffly. "I am growing old, and I want the apples which Idun keeps in her golden casket, to make me young again. You must get them for me."

Now these apples were the fruit of a magic tree, and were more beautiful to look at and more delicious to taste than any fruit that ever grew. The best thing about them was that who-ever tasted one, be he ever so old, grew young and strong again. The apples belonged to a beautiful lady named Idun, who kept them in a golden casket. Every morning the Aesir came to her to be refreshed and made over by a bite of her precious fruit. That is why in Asgard no one ever waxed old or ugly. Even Father Odin, Hoenir, and Loki, the three travelers who had seen the very beginning of everything, when the world was made, were still sturdy and young. And so long as Idun kept her apples safe, the faces of the family who sat about the table of Valhalla would be rosy and fair like the faces of children.

"O friend giant!" cried Loki. "You know not what you ask! The apples are the most precious treasure of Asgard, and Idun keeps watch over them as if they were dearer to her than life itself. I never could steal them from her, Thiasse; for at her call all Asgard would rush to the rescue, and trouble would buzz about my ears like a hive of bees let loose."

"Then you must steal Idun herself, apples and all. For the apples I must have, and you have promised, Loki, to do my bidding."

Loki sniffed and thought, thought and sniffed again. Already his mischievous heart was planning how he might steal Idun away. He could hardly help laughing to think how angry the Aesir would be when they found their beauty-medicine gone forever. But he hoped that, when he had done this trick for Thiasse, now and then the giant would let him have a nibble of the magic apples; so that Loki himself would remain young long after the other Aesir were grown old and feeble. This thought suited Loki's malicious nature well.

"I think I can manage it for you, Thiasse," he said craftily. "In a week I promise to bring Idun and her apples to you. But you must not forget the great risk which I am running, nor that I am your relative by marriage. I may have a favor to ask in return, Thiasse."

Then the eagle gently dropped Loki from his claws. Falling on a soft bed of moss Loki jumped up and ran back to his traveling companions, who were glad and surprised to see him again. They had feared that the eagle was carrying him away to feed his young eaglets in some far-off nest. Ah, you may be sure that Loki did not tell them who the eagle really was, nor confess the wicked promise which he had made about Idun and her apples.

After that the three went back to Asgard, for they had had adventure enough for one day.

The days flew by, and the time came when Loki must fulfill his promise to Thiasse. So one morning he strolled out into the meadow where Idun loved to roam among the flowers. There he found her, sitting by a tiny spring, holding her precious casket of apples on her lap. She was combing her long golden hair, which fell from under a wreath of spring flowers, and she was very beautiful. Her green robe was embroidered with buds and blossoms of silk in many colors, and she wore a golden girdle about her waist. She smiled as Loki came, and tossed him a posy, saying: "Good-morrow, red Loki. Have you come for a bite of my apples? I see a wrinkle over each of your eyes which I can smooth away."

"Nay, fair lady," answered Loki politely, "I have just nibbled of another apple, which I found this morning. Verily, I think it is sweeter and more magical than yours."

Idun was hurt and surprised.

"That cannot be, Loki," she cried. "There are no apples anywhere like mine. Where found you this fine fruit?" and she wrinkled up her little nose scornfully.

"Oho! I will not tell any one the place," chuckled Loki, "except that it is not far, in a little wood. There is a gnarled old apple tree, and on its branches grow the most beautiful red-cheeked apples you ever saw. But you could never find it."

"I should like to see these apples, Loki, if only to prove how far less good they are than mine. Will you bring me some?"

"That I will not," said Loki teasingly. "Oh, no! I have my own magic apples now, and folk will be coming to me for help instead of to you."

Idun began to coax him, as he had guessed that she would: "Please, please, Loki, show me the place!"

"Well, then, because I love you, Idun, better

than all the rest, I will show you the place, if you will come with me. But it must be a secret—no one must ever know."

All girls like secrets.

"Yes—yes!" cried Idun eagerly. "Let us steal away now, while no one is looking."

This was just what Loki hoped for.

"Bring your own apples," he said, "that we may compare them with mine. But I know mine are better."

"I know mine are the best in all the world," returned Idun, pouting. "I will bring them, to show you the difference."

Off they started together, she with the golden casket under her arm; and Loki chuckled wickedly as they went. He led her for some distance farther than she had ever strayed before, and at last she grew frightened.

"Where are you taking me, Loki?" she cried. "You said it was not far. I see no little wood, no old apple tree."

"It is just beyond, just a little step beyond," he answered. So on they went. But that little step took them beyond the boundary of Asgard—just a little step beyond, into the space where the giants lurked and waited for mischief.

Then there was a rustling of wings, and whirrr-rr-rr! Down came Thiasse in his eagle dress. Before Idun suspected what was happening, he fastened his claws into her girdle and flapped away with her, magic apples and all, to his palace in Jötunheim, the Land of Giants.

Loki stole back to Asgard, thinking that he was quite safe, and that no one would discover his villainy. At first Idun was not missed. But after a little the gods began to feel signs of age, and went for their usual bite of her apples. Then they found that she had disappeared, and a great terror fell upon them. Where had she gone? Suppose she should not come back!

The hours and days went by, and still she did not return. Their fright became almost a panic. Their hair began to turn gray, and their limbs grew stiff and gouty so that they hobbled down Asgard streets. Even Freia, the loveliest, was afraid to look in her mirror, and Balder, the beautiful, grew pale and haggard. The happy land of Asgard was like a garden over which a burning wind had blown—all the flower-faces were faded and withered, and springtime was turned into yellow fall.

If Idun and her apples were not quickly found, the gods seemed likely to shrivel and blow away like autumn leaves. They held a council to inquire into the matter, endeavoring to learn who had seen Idun last, and whither she had gone. It turned out that one morning Heimdal had seen her strolling out of Asgard with Loki, and no one had seen her since. Then the gods understood; Loki was the last person who had been with her—this must be one of Loki's tricks. They were filled with anger. They seized and bound Loki and brought him before the council. They threatened him with torture and with death unless he should tell the truth. And Loki was so frightened that finally he confessed what he had done.

Then indeed there was horror in Asgard. Idun stolen away by a wicked giant! Idun and her apples lost, and Asgard growing older every minute! What was to be done? Big Thor seized Loki and threw him up in the air again and again, so that his heels touched first the moon and then the sea; you can still see the marks upon the moon's white face. "If you do not bring Idun back from the land of your wicked wife, you shall have worse than this!" he roared. "Go and bring her now."

"How can I do that?" asked Loki, trembling.

"That is for you to find," growled Thor. "Bring her you must. Go!"

Loki thought for a moment. Then he said: "I will bring her back if Freia will loan me her falcon dress. The giant dresses as an eagle. I, too, must guise me as a bird, or we cannot outwit him."

Then Freia hemmed and hawed. She did not wish to loan her feather dress, for it was very precious. But all the Aesir begged; and finally she consented.

It was a beautiful great dress of brown feathers and gray, and in it Freia loved to skim like a falcon among the clouds and stars. Loki put it on, and when he had done so he looked exactly like a great brown hawk. Only his bright black eyes remained the same, glancing here and there, so that they lost sight of nothing.

With a whirr of his wings Loki flew off to the north, across mountains and valleys and great river Ifing, which lay between Asgard and Giant Land. And at last he came to the palace of Thiasse the giant.

It happened, fortunately, that Thiasse had gone fishing in the sea, and Idun was left alone, weeping and broken-hearted. Presently she heard a little tap on her window, and, looking up, she saw a great brown bird perching on the ledge. He was so big that Idun was frightened and gave a scream. But the bird nodded pleasantly and croaked: "Don't be afraid, Idun. I am a friend. I am Loki, come to set you free."

"Loki! Loki is no friend of mine. He brought me here," she sobbed. "I don't believe you came to save me."

"That is indeed why I am here," he replied, "and a dangerous business it is, if Thiasse should come back before we start for home."

"How will you get me out?" asked Idun doubtfully. "The door is locked, and the window is barred."

"I will change you into a nut," said he, "and carry you in my claws."

"What of the casket of apples?" queried Idun. "Can you carry that also?"

Then Loki laughed long and loudly.

"What welcome to Asgard do you think I should receive without the apples?" he cried. "Yes, we must take them, indeed."

Idun came to the window, and Loki, who was a skillful magician, turned her into a nut and took her in one claw, while in the other he seized the casket of apples. Then off he whirred out of the palace grounds and away toward Asgard's safety.

In a little while Thiasse returned home, and when he found Idun and her apples gone, there was a hubbub, you may be sure! However, he lost little time by smashing mountains and breaking trees in his giant rage; that fit was soon over. He put on his eagle plumage and started in pursuit of the falcon.

Now an eagle is bigger and stronger than any other bird, and usually in a long race he can beat even the swift hawk who has an hour's start. Presently Loki heard behind him the shrill scream of a giant eagle, and his heart turned sick. But he had crossed the great river, and already was in sight of Asgard. The aged Aesir were gathered on the rainbow bridge watching eagerly for Loki's return; and when they spied the falcon with the nut and the casket in his talons, they knew who it was. A great cheer went up, but it was hushed in a moment, for they saw the eagle close after the falcon; and they guessed that this must be the giant Thiasse, the stealer of Idun.

Then there was a great shouting of commands, and a rushing to and fro. All the gods, even Father Odin and his two wise ravens, were busy gathering chips into great heaps on the walls of Asgard. As soon as Loki, with his precious burden, had fluttered weakly over the wall, dropping to the ground beyond, the gods lighted the heaps of chips which they had piled, and soon there was a wall of fire, over which the eagle must fly. He was going too fast to stop. The flames roared and crackled, but Thiasse flew straight into them, with a scream of fear and rage. His feathers caught fire and burned, so that he could no longer fly, but fell headlong to the ground inside the walls. Then Thor, the Thunder-Lord and Týr, the mighty war-king, fell upon him and slew him, so that he could never trouble the Aesir any more.

There was great rejoicing in Asgard that night, for Loki changed Idun again to a fair lady; whereupon she gave each of the eager gods a bit of her life-giving fruit, so that they grew young and happy once more, as if all these horrors had never happened.

Not one of them, however, forgot the evil part which Loki had played in these doings. They hid the memory, like a buried seed, deep in their hearts. Thenceforward the word of Loki and the honor of his name were poor coin in Asgard; which is no wonder.

Niord and Skadi

A major theme of Norse myth and legend is that of loyalty and vengeance. This tale is unusual in that Skadi, the giant warrior-maiden and daughter of the storm-giant Thiasse (Thiazi), killed in the previous story, follows her quest for vengeance to a peaceful resolution and does not become lost in the doom and bloodshed that often prevail in these myths. She prefigures the courageous mortal women in the Norse and Germanic hero sagas—the queens Signy and Hiordis of the Volsungs and the Valkyrie Brynhild. [From Barbara Leonie Picard, *Tales of the Norse Gods and Heroes* (Oxford University Press, 1953; reissued 1980).]

When she heard how her father had been killed by the gods in Asgard, Skadi, the daughter of Thiazi the storm-giant, tied on her snow shoes, slung her quiver of sharp arrows over her shoulder, and taking up her bow, set off for Asgard to avenge his death. Right into the hall of the gods she came and challenged all who would to fight with her.

The gods watched her standing there, brave and angry, in her cloak of fur and her flashing golden helmet that was yet no brighter than her hair that hung down below it, one giant-maiden against all the might of the gods, and their hearts warmed towards her in admiration of her courage.

'What good think you it will do, Skadi, if you too die in Asgard as your father died?' asked Odin gently.

'My father must be avenged,' said Skadi. 'Or are all the gods too much afraid to fight against one giant-woman?'

'Thiazi was our enemy,' said Odin, 'but there is no one of us here who would willingly shed your blood. Go in peace, good Skadi.'

'My father must be avenged,' she repeated, 'and there is but I to avenge him. Since I heard that he was dead I have not smiled, my heart is cold and dulled with grief, and I think that I shall never laugh again.'

'We would call you our friend, Skadi, and not our enemy,' said Odin. 'We would see you living and happy, not dead at the gates of Asgard. Come, accept atonement for your father's death and be reconciled with us. Let us give you in recompense the best that we have to offer. Choose for yourself, Skadi, a husband from among the gods, and live in peace with him, no longer the daughter of the storm-giant, but one among the goddesses.'

Yet all Skadi would say was, 'My father must be avenged.'

But the gods sought to persuade her, saying, 'We should welcome you with honour,

Skadi, and rejoice to have you as our friend.'

'Thiazi's eyes shall I take,' said Odin, 'and cast them up into the sky, two new stars in the heavens, in memory of him, to show that though our enemy, we ever held him in respect.'

A little appeased by his words, Skadi looked around her at all the gods assembled in the hall; wise and kindly Odin, great tawny-bearded Thor, smiling gentle Niord, handsome red-haired Loki who had been the cause of her father's death, Balder the young god of sunlight, the most beautiful of them all, with his fair white skin and his golden hair, and all the other gods before her. She looked at them all closely, thinking upon Odin's words, but ever her eyes returned to Balder, and at last she said, 'If I may have Balder for my husband, then I will forgive the wrong you did my father, and live in peace with you.'

'You may choose your husband for yourself, Skadi,' smiled Odin, 'but choose him by his feet alone, and abide by your choice.'

'There is no doubt but that Balder, being the most beautiful, will have the loveliest feet,' thought Skadi, 'and thus shall I know him instantly.' So aloud she said, 'To that I agree, but further demand that before I am to be your friend, you shall make me forget my grief, and laugh.'

'That will be a hard task,' said Odin, watching her pale unsmiling face.

'Not for me,' said Loki. And he rose from his place and going to Skadi set himself to make her laugh, with all the skill he had in jesting. And at his tricks and the tales he told, all the gods held their sides with laughing; but Skadi never even smiled, for she hated Loki who had caused her father's death, and she would have found it easier to laugh at the jests of any other of the gods.

But Loki's wit and cunning prevailed at last, and Skadi forgot her grief and anger and smiled a little, and then suddenly she laughed aloud.

'See,' said Loki, 'did I not promise that I should make you laugh?'

'No one could fail to laugh at your antics, when once you have set yourself to make him laugh,' said Skadi.

'And are we friends at last, fair Skadi?' asked Loki.

'We are friends,' she said. But in her heart she never forgave him for Thiazi's death, though his had not been the hand that slew the giant, and though she lived in peace and friendship with the gods from that day.

'Now must you choose a husband for yourself from among the gods,' said Odin. And Skadi's eyes were covered so that she could see no more than the ground before her, and Frigg led her down the length of the hall, past the gods as they sat on the bench along the wall, and Skadi carefully watched the feet of each as she passed him by.

Of some feet she found it easy to guess the owner; there were Odin's, hardened by his countless journeyings among men; and the huge feet below strong ankles that could belong to no one else than Thor; but she passed by them all, until she came to a pair of feet so white that the veins showed blue through the skin, with delicately arched insteps and shapely ankles, and she smiled to herself. 'These will be the feet of Balder,' she thought. But she said nothing until she had seen the feet of all the gods and found no others so beautiful. Then she returned to where he sat who owned the feet she thought to be the feet of Balder, and said, 'Surely you must be Balder, the god of the sun, and I will have you for my husband.' And she took away the cloth that covered her eyes and found that she stood before the kindly, smiling Niord, king of the Vanir; Niord who was lord of the winds and the waves as they broke on the shore, whose feet had never been hardened by the rocky mountain ways trodden by the other gods, for he walked but rarely save across the sandy beaches, among the little pools left by the tide, and his feet were fairer and whiter even than those of Balder who was otherwise the most beautiful of all the gods.

Skadi was disappointed at her choice, that she had been mistaken. But Niord was handsome and kindly, a husband such as would have pleased any maiden, and she resolved to be content, and smiled at him when he took her hand and pledged himself to her before all Asgard.

Niord had a palace on the seashore, Noatun, where the sea birds cried and the young seals gambolled and the wild swans which were sa-cred to him gathered. From here he ruled the sea around the coast, calming the waves called up by Aegir of the deeper ocean, and protecting the fishermen from cruel Ran and her nets. For him the sunlight rippled on the water in the little bays and creeks, and the wind played gently in and out his halls.

To this palace Niord brought Skadi, showing her all its delights, thinking that it would please her. And indeed, at first it seemed pleasant enough in contrast to her own bleak home of Thrymheim, but before many days had passed, Skadi hated it. She went to Niord and said, 'For many days I have not slept for the noise of the sea at night, and the crying of the sea birds by day fills me with melancholy. The winds that blow here are too gentle, so unlike the mountain tempests, and the little rippling waves seem puny and childish beside the memory of my own mountain torrents. Good Niord, I fear I cannot live with you much longer here, or, sleepless and homesick, I shall go out of my mind.'

'I am grieved that my home displeases you,' said Niord. 'You must not suffer on account of me.' He thought in silence for a moment, then went on, 'Let us spend a part of our time together here, and a part of our time at Thrymheim. In every twelve nights, let us pass nine at your own home and three here at Noatun. How will that please you, my Skadi?'

Overjoyed, Skadi hastened to make ready to return to Thrymheim, and Niord went with her, away to the bleak mountain fastness in Iotunheim, far, far to the north, where the magpies nested, that were Skadi's own birds. Nine days out of every twelve they spent in the stone home that had once been Thiazi's, while the wind raged down the mountains through the pines, and the snow lay close around. And Skadi stood in the courtyard with three magpies on her shoulder, watching the clouds hurtling across the leaden sky and laughing with delight at the wildness of it all; while Niord, wrapped in fur cloaks, huddled by the fire and thought of his pleasant home, so far away.

And at last Niord said to Skadi, 'I cannot sleep in Thrymheim for the howling of the wolves by night, and each day is colder than the last, and here there is no joy or comfort. Nine nights out of every twelve are too many for me to remain in this place.'

'And three nights out of every twelve are too many for me to pass in Noatun, where the sea birds scream, and three days out of every twelve are too many, while the sun shines dazzlingly on the water and blinds my eyes.'

'What then shall we do, my Skadi?'

Skadi shook her head, 'I know not, only that it seems we cannot live together happily.'

They talked long and made many proposals, only to reject them all; and at last it seemed to them that Skadi had been right, and they could in no way live together. So Niord and Skadi bade each other good-bye, and Niord went back to live in Noatun, where the wind played gently with the sunlit waves, and his wild swans flew about him when he walked abroad, beating the warm air with their white wings; and Skadi remained in Thrymheim with her chattering magpies that perched on the beams of her halls, where the wind howled as loudly by night as the wolves, while she listened to it in the darkness with fierce joy.

And thus each of them was happy once again, meeting only now and then, in Asgard, on days of festival.

Balder and the Mistletoe

Balder, the youngest son of Odin and Frigg, was god of light and peace and of the beautiful and the wise. The mistletoe has always figured in myths; it is supposed to have been the golden bough that Aeneas plucked to use as a key to Hades. This myth has two interpretations. Like the Greek myth of Demeter, it may explain the seasons, or it may be a further forewarning of the fall of the gods at the hands of the giants in the last great battle. This victory of the ice giants may represent the coming of the ice age. [From Abbie Farwell Brown, *In the Days of Giants* (Houghton Mifflin, 1902).]

Now at this time Balder the beautiful had a strange dream. He dreamed that a cloud came before the sun, and all Asgard was dark. He waited for the cloud to drift away, and for the sun to smile again. But no; the sun was gone forever, he thought; and Balder awoke feeling very sad. The next night Balder had another dream. This time he dreamed that it was still dark as before; the flowers were withered and the gods were growing old; even Idun's magic apples could not make them young again. And all were weeping and wringing their hands as though some dreadful thing had happened. Balder awoke feeling strangely frightened, yet he said no word to Nanna his wife, for he did not want to trouble her.

When it came night again Balder slept and dreamed a third dream, a still more terrible one than the other two had been. He thought that in the dark, lonely world there was nothing but a sad voice, which cried, "The sun is gone! The spring is gone! Joy is gone! For Balder the beautiful is dead, dead, dead!"

This time Balder awoke with a cry, and Nanna asked him what was the matter. So he had to tell her of his dream, and he was sadly frightened; for in those days dreams were often sent to folk as messages, and what the gods dreamed usually came true. Nanna ran sobbing to Queen Frigg, who was Balder's mother, and told her all the dreadful dream, asking what could be done to prevent it from coming true.

Now Balder was Queen Frigg's dearest son. Thor was older and stronger, and more famous for his great deeds; but Frigg loved far better gold-haired Balder. And indeed he was the best-loved of all the Aesir; for he was gentle, fair and wise, and wherever he went folk grew happy and light-hearted at the very sight of him, just as we do when we first catch a glimpse of spring peeping over the hilltop into Winterland. So when Frigg heard of Balder's woeful dream, she was frightened almost out of her wits.

"He must not die! He shall not die!" she cried. "He is so dear to all the world, how could there be anything which would hurt him?"

And then a wonderful thought came to Frigg. "I will travel over the world and make all things promise not to injure my boy," she said. "Nothing shall pass my notice. I will get the word of everything."

So first she went to the gods themselves, gathered on Ida Plain for their morning exercise; and telling them of Balder's dream, she begged them to give the promise. Oh, what a shout arose when they heard her words!

"Hurt Balder!—our Balder! Not for the world, we promise! The dream is wrong—there is nothing so cruel as to wish harm to Balder the beautiful!" they cried. But deep in their hearts they felt a secret fear which would linger until they should hear that all things had given their promise. What if harm were indeed to come to Balder! The thought was too dreadful.

Then Frigg went to see all the beasts who live in field or forest or rocky den. Willingly they gave their promise never to harm hair of gentle Balder. "For he is ever kind to us," they said, "and we love him as if he were one of ourselves. Not with claws or teeth or hoofs or horns will any beast hurt Balder."

Next Frigg spoke to the birds and fishes, reptiles and insects. And all—even the venomous serpents—cried that Balder was their friend, and that they would never do aught to hurt his dear body. "Not with beak or talon, bite or sting or poison fang, will one of us hurt Balder," they promised.

After doing this, the anxious mother traveled over the whole world, step by step; and from all the things that are she got the same ready promise never to harm Balder the beautiful. All the trees and plants promised; all the stones and metals; earth, air, fire, and water; sun, snow, wind, and rain, and all diseases that men know— each gave to Frigg the word of promise which she wanted. So at last, footsore and weary, she came back to Asgard with the joyful news that Balder must be safe, for that there was nothing in the world but had promised to be his harmless friend.

Then there was rejoicing in Asgard, as if the gods had won one of their great victories over the giants. The noble Aesir and the heroes who had died in battle upon the earth, and who had come to Valhalla to live happily ever after, gathered on Ida Plain to celebrate the love of all nature for Balder.

There they invented a famous game, which was to prove how safe he was from the bite of death. They stationed Balder in the midst of them, his face glowing like the sun with the bright light which ever shone from him. And as he stood there unarmed and smiling, by turns they tried all sorts of weapons against him; they made as if to beat him with sticks, they stoned him with stones, they shot at him with arrows and hurled mighty spears straight at his heart.

It was a merry game, and a shout of laughter went up as each stone fell harmless at Balder's feet, each stick broke before it touched his shoulders, each arrow overshot his head, and each spear turned aside. For neither stone nor wood nor flinty arrowpoint nor barb of iron would break the promise which each had given. Balder was safe with them, just as if he were bewitched. He remained unhurt among the missiles which whizzed about his head, and which piled up in a great heap around the charmed spot whereon he stood.

Now among the crowd that watched these games with such enthusiasm, there was one face that did not smile, one voice that did not rasp itself hoarse with cheering. Loki saw how everyone and everything loved Balder, and he was jealous. He was the only creature in all the world that hated Balder and wished for his death. Yet Balder had never done harm to him. But the wicked plan that Loki had been cherishing was almost ripe, and in this poison fruit was the seed of the greatest sorrow that Asgard had ever known.

While the others were enjoying their game of love, Loki stole away unperceived from Ida Plain, and with a wig of gray hair, a long gown, and a staff, disguised himself as an old woman. Then he hobbled down Asgard streets till he came to the palace of Queen Frigg, the mother of Balder.

"Good-day, my lady," quoth the old woman, in a cracked voice. "What is that noisy crowd doing yonder in the green meadow? I am so deafened by their shouts that I can hardly hear myself think."

"Who are you, good mother, that you have not heard?" said Queen Frigg in surprise. "They are shooting at my son Balder. They are proving the word which all things have given me—the promise not to injure my dear son. And that promise will be kept."

The old crone pretended to be full of wonder.

"So, now!" she cried. "Do you mean to say that every single thing in the whole world has promised not to hurt your son? I can scarce believe it; though, to be sure, he is as fine a fellow as I ever saw." Of course this flattery pleased Frigg.

"You say true, mother," she answered proudly, "he is a noble son. Yes, everything has promised—that is, everything except one tiny little plant that is not worth mentioning." The old woman's eyes twinkled wickedly.

"And what is that foolish little plant, my dear?" she asked coaxingly.

"It is the mistletoe that grows in the meadow west of Valhalla. It was too young to promise, and too harmless to bother with," answered Frigg carelessly.

After this her questioner hobbled painfully away. But as soon as she was out of sight from the Queen's palace, she picked up the skirts of her gown and ran as fast as she could to the meadow west of Valhalla. And there sure enough, as Frigg had said, was a tiny sprig of mistletoe growing on a gnarled oaktree. The false Loki took out a knife which she carried in some hidden pocket and cut off the mistletoe very carefully. Then she trimmed and shaped it so that it was like a little green arrow, pointed at one end, but very slender.

"Ho, ho!" chuckled the old woman. "So you are the only thing in all the world that is too young to make a promise, my little mistletoe. Well, young as you are, you must go on an errand for me today. And maybe you shall bear a message of my love to Balder the beautiful."

Then she hobbled back to Ida Plain, where the merry game was still going on around Balder. Loki quietly passed unnoticed through the crowd, and came close to the elbow of a big dark fellow who was standing lonely outside the circle of weapon-throwers. He seemed sad and forgotten, and he hung his head in a pitiful way. It was Höd, the blind brother of Balder.

The old woman touched his arm. "Why do you not join the game with the others?" she asked, in her cracked voice. "Are you the only one to do your brother no honor? Surely, you are big and strong enough to toss a spear with the best of them yonder."

Höd touched his sightless eyes sadly. "I am

blind," he said. "Strength I have, greater than belongs to most of the Aesir. But I cannot see to aim a weapon. Besides, I have no spear to test upon him. Yet how gladly would I do honor to dear Balder!" and he sighed deeply.

"It were a pity if I could not find you at least a little stick to throw," said Loki, sympathetically. "I am only a poor old woman, and of course I have no weapon. But ah—here is a green twig which you can use as an arrow, and I will guide your arm, poor fellow."

Höd's dark face lighted up, for he was eager to take his turn in the game. So he thanked her, and grasped eagerly the little arrow which she put into his hand. Loki held him by the arm, and together they stepped into the circle which surrounded Balder. And when it was Höd's turn to throw his weapon, the old woman stood at his elbow and guided his big arm as it hurled the twig of mistletoe towards where Balder stood.

Oh, the sad thing that befell! Straight through the air flew the little arrow, straight as magic and Loki's arm could direct it. Straight to Balder's heart it sped, piercing through jerkin and shirt and all, to give its bitter message of "Loki's love," as he had said. And that was the end of sunshine and spring and joy in Asgard, for the dream had come true, and Balder the beautiful was dead.

When the Aesir saw what had happened, there was a great shout of fear and horror, and they rushed upon Höd, who had thrown the fatal arrow.

"What is it? What have I done?" asked the poor blind brother, trembling at the tumult which had followed his shot.

"You have slain Balder!" cried the Aesir. "Wretched Höd, how could you do it?"

"It was the old woman—the evil old woman, who stood at my elbow and gave me a little twig to throw," gasped Höd. "She must be a witch."

Then the Aesir scattered over Ida Plain to look for the old woman who had done the evil deed; but she had mysteriously disappeared.

"It must be Loki," said wise Heimdal. "It is Loki's last and vilest trick."

"Oh, my Balder, my beautiful Balder!" wailed Queen Frigg, throwing herself on the body of her son. "If I had only made the mistletoe give me the promise, you would have been saved. It was I who told Loki of the mistletoe—so it is I who have killed you. Oh, my son, my son!"

But Father Odin was speechless with grief. His sorrow was greater than that of all the others, for he best understood the dreadful misfortune which had befallen Asgard. Already a cloud had come before the sun, so that it would never be bright day again. Already the flowers had begun to fade and the birds had ceased to sing. And already the Aesir had begun to grow old and joyless—all because the little mistletoe had been too young to give a promise to Queen Frigg.

Illustration copyright © 1970 by Charles Mikolaycak. From *In The Morning of Time: The Story of the Norse God Balder* (Four Winds Press, 1970), by Cynthia King.

"Balder the beautiful is dead!" the cry went echoing through all the world, and everything that was sorrowed at the sound of the Aesir's weeping.

Balder's brothers lifted up his beautiful body upon their great war shields and bore him on their shoulders down to the seashore. For, as was the custom in those days, they were going to send him to Hela, the Queen of Death, with all the things he best had loved in Asgard. And these were—after Nanna his wife—his beautiful horse, and his ship Hringhorni. So that they would place Balder's body upon the ship with his horse beside him, and set fire to this wonderful funeral pile. For by fire was the quickest passage to Hela's kingdom.

But when they reached the shore, they found that all the strength of all the Aesir was unable to move Hringhorni, Balder's ship, into the water, for it was the largest ship in the world and it was stranded far up the beach.

"Even the giants bore no ill-will to Balder," said Father Odin. "I heard the thunder of their grief but now shaking the hills. Let us for this once bury our hatred of that race and send to Jotunheim for help to move the ship."

So they sent a messenger to the giantess Hyrrockin, the hugest of all the Frost People. She was weeping for Balder when the message came.

"I will go, for Balder's sake," she said. Soon she came riding fast upon a giant wolf, with a serpent for the bridle; and mighty she was, with the strength of forty Aesir. She dismounted from her wolf-steed, and tossed the wriggling reins to one of the men-heroes who had followed Balder and the Aesir from Valhalla. But he could not hold the beast, and it took four heroes to keep him quiet, which they could only do by throwing him upon the ground and sitting upon him in a row. And this mortified them greatly.

Then Hyrrockin the giantess strode up to the great ship and seized it by the prow. Easily she gave a little pull and presto! it leaped forward on its rollers with such force that sparks flew from the flint stones underneath and the whole earth trembled. The boat shot into the waves and out toward open sea so swiftly that the Aesir were likely to have lost it entirely, had not Hyrrockin waded out up to her waist and caught it by the stern just in time.

Thor was angry at her clumsiness, and raised his hammer to punish her. But the other Aesir held his arm.

"She cannot help being so strong," they whispered. "She meant to do well. She did not realize how hard she was pulling. This is no time for anger, brother Thor." So Thor spared her life, as indeed he ought, for her kindness.

Then Balder's body was borne out to the ship and laid upon a pile of beautiful silks, and furs, and cloth-of-gold, and woven sunbeams which the dwarfs had wrought. So that his funeral pyre was more grand than anything which had ever been seen. But when Nanna, Balder's gentle wife, saw them ready to kindle the flames under this gorgeous bed, she could bear her grief no longer. Her loving heart broke, and they laid her beside him, that they might comfort each other on their journey to Hela. Thor touched the pile gently with his hammer that makes the lightning, and the flames burst forth, lighting up the faces of Balder and Nanna with a glory. Then they cast upon the fire Balder's warhorse, to serve his master in the dark country to which he was about to go. The horse was decked with a harness all of gold, with jewels studding the bridle and headstall. Last of all Odin laid upon the pyre his gift to Balder, Draupnir, the precious ring of gold which the dwarf had made, from which every ninth night there dropped eight other rings as large and brightly golden.

"Take this with you, dear son, to Hela's palace," said Odin. "And do not forget the friends you leave behind in the now lonely halls of Asgard."

Then Hyrrockin pushed the great boat out to sea, with its bonfire of precious things. And on the beach stood all the Aesir watching it out of sight, all the Aesir and many besides. For there came to Balder's funeral great crowds of little dwarfs and multitudes of huge frost giants, all mourning for Balder the beautiful. For this one time they were all friends together, forgetting their quarrels of so many centuries. All of them loved Balder, and were united to do him honor.

The great ship moved slowly out to sea, sending up a red fire to color all the heavens. At last it slid below the horizon softly, as you have often seen the sun set upon the water, leaving a brightness behind to lighten the dark world for a little while.

This indeed was the sunset for Asgard. The darkness of sorrow came in earnest after the passing of Balder the beautiful.

Thor Gains His Hammer

The Norse mythology is largely doom-ridden and heroic, a grim concept, in which the gods know that they face ultimate destruction. Yet within this framework, there are some stories that have the character of a folktale, showing the gods concerned with affairs of battle and survival and helped by magic, as mortals were. This is such a tale, this story of the forging of the mighty hammer which was to protect the gods against all evil and which made Thor the most powerful, after Odin. [From Dorothy Hosford, *Thunder of the Gods* (Holt, 1952).]

Loki made much trouble for the gods with his evil pranks and his malice. But there was one time his mischief worked for good in the end. Thor might never have owned his wonderful hammer had it not been for Loki. It came about in this way:

Thor had a beautiful wife whose name was Sif. Her hair was long and yellow and shone like gold in the sunlight. Thor was proud of her.

One day, while Sif lay sleeping under the trees where Iduna's apples grew, Loki cut off all her hair. He did it for a prank. When Sif woke and discovered the loss of her beautiful hair, she went weeping to Thor.

"This is the work of that rascal Loki," cried Thor angrily. "I'll break every bone in his body."

He rushed off to look for Loki. It was not long before he found him and seized him.

Loki was filled with terror when he saw Thor's anger. He begged for mercy, but Thor would not let him go.

"Wait, O mighty Thor," begged Loki. "Don't punish me and I will get new hair for Sif. I will find hair of real gold that will shine in the sunlight and will grow like other hair."

"How will you do that?" said Thor.

"I will go to the Dark Elves, to the Sons of Ivaldi, and ask them to make the hair for me," said Loki. "They can make every kind of wondrous thing."

Thor gave his consent.

"But remember," he cried, shaking Loki so that his teeth chattered in his head. "If you don't bring back hair that will grow like other hair, I will break every bone in your body. And it must be as long and beautiful as Sif's own hair. Now go."

Loki was only too glad to set out. The dwarfs lived deep within the mountains and he had a long journey to make.

When Loki came to the dwelling place of the Dark Elves they said that they could perform his task. They made the hair, and they made two other gifts as well. They made the spear Gungnir, which became Odin's possession, and they made the magic ship, Skidbladnir.

On his way home with the gifts Loki met another dwarf named Brock. Loki was feeling pleased with himself and proud of his success. At once he made a wager with Brock.

"See what I have," cried Loki. "I'll wager my head that your brother Sindri can't make three gifts as precious as these."

Sindri was famed among the dwarfs and Brock knew how great was his brother's skill.

"I'll take that wager," said Brock. "Come with me. We will go to the smithy and we will see what Sindri can make."

Brock explained that wager to his brother and Sindri started the fire in the forge. The flames lit up the far corners of the dwarfs' cave. When it was hot enough Sindri laid within the fire a pig's hide. He handed the bellows to Brock and told him to work them without ceasing until he should return. Then he left the cave.

As soon as Sindri had gone Loki changed himself into a huge fly. He lit upon Brock's hand and stung him. But Brock kept the bellows working and did not let go.

When Sindri returned he took the work out of the fire. It was a boar, a wild pig with mane and bristles of gold.

Then Sindri placed gold in the fire and bade Brock work the bellows as before. This time the fly settled on Brock's neck and stung twice as hard. But Brock did not let go of the bellows. When Sindri returned he took out of the fire the golden ring which is called Draupnir.

For the third gift Sindri placed iron in the fire. "Keep the bellows going, Brock, or all will be spoiled," said Sindri, as he left the smithy.

This was Loki's last chance and the fly settled between Brock's eyes and stung his eyelids so hard that the blood ran down. The pain and the blood blinded him. Brock had to pause to sweep the fly away. He let go of the bellows with one hand and only for an instant. But the fire died down.

At that moment Sindri returned and said that what was in the hearth had come near to being spoiled. He took the work out of the fire and it was a hammer.

Sindri gave the three gifts to Brock. "Take these to the gods," he said, "and see whose gifts will win the wager."

Loki and Brock set off for Asgard, the home of the gods, each bearing his gifts. The gods were called together and met in the great council hall named Gladsheim. They took their places on the high seats. It was agreed that Odin and Thor and Frey should decide whose gifts were best.

Loki presented his gifts first. He gave Thor the golden hair for Sif, to Odin he gave the spear Gungnir, and to Frey the ship Skidbladnir, telling the virtues of each. As soon as it was placed upon Sif's head the hair would grow like other hair. The spear Gungnir would never fall short of its mark; and the ship Skidbladnir would always find favoring winds, no matter in what direction it was set. Yet it could be folded like a napkin and placed in Frey's pocket, if he so wished.

Then Brock offered his gifts. He gave to Odin the golden ring which is called Draupnir.

"Every ninth night eight other rings like itself will drop from it," said Brock.

He gave the boar, which was called Gold-Mane, to Frey.

"No horse can run through the air or over the sea with such swiftness," said Brock.

"And you can always find your way by the light which shines from its mane and bristles of gold, no matter how black and dark the night may be."

Brock gave the hammer to Thor.

"The name of the hammer is Mjollnir," he told Thor. "With it you can strike as hard a blow as you please at whatever comes in your way. You can hurl it as far as you like, and it will always find its mark and return to your hand. Yet, if you wish, you can make the hammer small and put it in your pocket."

The hammer had only one fault, though Brock did not mention that. The handle was a little short. That was because Loki had caused Brock to drop the bellows.

Odin and Thor and Frey held a council. They decided that Brock's gifts were best, for Thor's hammer was the most valuable gift of all. This was just the weapon the gods needed in their wars against the Frost-Giants. The giants had better beware. Now Thor could hurl his mighty hammer at them and catch it again in his hand.

Odin rose to his feet and announced to all that Brock had won the wager.

Brock immediately demanded Loki's head.

"What good is my head to you?" cried Loki. "I will give you a great sum of gold for a ransom. You will be the richest of all the dwarfs."

Dwarfs love gold, but Brock would have none of it, and said that Loki must keep to the terms of his bargain.

"Then catch me if you can!" cried Loki.

In an instant he was far off, for he had on the shoes which would carry him through air and over water in the twinkling of an eye.

Brock begged Thor to catch Loki. Thor was still angry with Loki and willing enough to do so. Thor asked Frey to lend him the boar Gold-Mane. He leapt on the boar's back and away he went through the air. Before long he had brought Loki back to Asgard.

Brock was ready to cut off his head, but Loki cried: "My head, yes! But not an inch of my neck. I did not wager my neck."

How could Brock cut off Loki's head without touching his neck? Brock had to let it go at that.

"If I had my brother's awl I would sew your mischief-speaking lips together," he cried out in anger.

No sooner had he spoken than the awl was there and of itself pierced Loki's lips. Then Brock sewed them together with a thong. Not that it troubled Loki much, for when Brock was gone he ripped out the thongs.

Loki, as usual, got off with little punishment. But the gods were much richer for their new gifts.

The Quest of the Hammer

Thor, the strongest of the gods, was the oldest son of Odin. Besides his wonderful hammer, which returned to his hand after he had thrown it, he had a belt of strength that doubled his power when he wore it and an iron glove that he wore when he threw his hammer. Though Thor usually walked, he had a goat-drawn cart or chariot, and its rolling wheels gave out the sound of thunder. The thunderbolt came when his hammer flew back to his hand. As the possessor of these powerful weapons and as the strongest god, Thor was the greatest defender of the gods against their enemies, the giants. Thor was also the patron of the peasants and laboring classes, and Thor's day has become our Thursday. [From Abbie Farwell Brown, *In the Days of Giants* (Houghton Mifflin, 1902).]

One morning Thor the Thunderer awoke with a yawn, and stretching out his knotted arm, felt for his precious hammer, which he kept always under his pillow of clouds. But he started up with a roar of rage, so that all the palace trembled. The hammer was gone!

Now this was a very serious matter, for Thor was the protector of Asgard, and Miölnir, the magic hammer which the dwarf had made, was his mighty weapon, of which the enemies of the Aesir stood so much in dread that they dared not venture near. But if they should learn that Miölnir was gone, who could tell what danger might not threaten the palaces of heaven?

Thor darted his flashing eye into every corner of Cloud Land in search of the hammer. He called his fair wife, Sif of the golden hair, to aid in the search, and his two lovely daughters, Thrude and Lora. They hunted and they hunted; they turned Thrudheim upside down, and set the clouds to rolling wonderfully, as they peeped and pried behind and around and under each billowy mass. Thor's yellow beard quivered with rage, and his hair bristled on end like the golden rays of a star, while all his household trembled.

"It is Loki again!" he cried. "I am sure Loki is at the bottom of this mischief!" For since the time when Thor had captured Loki for the dwarf Brock and had given him over to have his bragging lips sewed up, Loki had looked at him with evil eyes; and Thor knew that the red rascal hated him most of all the gods.

But this time Thor was mistaken. It was not Loki who had stolen the hammer—he was too great a coward for that. And though he meant, before the end, to be revenged upon Thor, he was waiting until a safe chance should come, when Thor himself might stumble into danger, and Loki need only to help the evil by a malicious word or two; and this chance came later, as you shall hear in another tale.

Meanwhile Loki was on his best behavior, trying to appear very kind and obliging; so when Thor came rumbling and roaring up to him, demanding, "What have you done with my hammer, you thief?" Loki looked surprised, but did not lose his temper nor answer rudely.

"Have you indeed missed your hammer, brother Thor?" he said, mumbling, for his mouth was still sore where Brock had sewed the stitches. "That is a pity; for if the giants hear of this, they will be coming to try their might against Asgard."

"Hush!" muttered Thor, grasping him by the shoulder with his iron fingers. "That is what I fear. But look you, Loki: I suspect your hand in the mischief. Come, confess."

Then Loki protested that he had nothing to do with so wicked a deed. "But," he added wheedlingly, "I think I can guess the thief; and because I love you, Thor, I will help you to find him."

"Humph!" growled Thor. "Much love you bear to me! However, you are a wise rascal, the nimblest wit of all the Aesir, and it is better to have you on my side than on the other, when giants are in the game. Tell me, then: who has

robbed the Thunder-Lord of his bolt of power?"

Loki drew near and whispered in Thor's ear. "Look, how the storms rage and the winds howl in the world below! Someone is wielding your thunder-hammer all unskillfully. Can you not guess the thief? Who but Thrym, the mighty giant who has ever been your enemy and your imitator, and whose fingers have long itched to grasp the short handle of mighty Miölnir, that the world may name him Thunder-Lord instead of you. But look! What a tempest! The world will be shattered into fragments unless we soon get the hammer back."

Then Thor roared with rage. "I will seek this impudent Thrym!" he cried. "I will crush him into bits, and teach him to meddle with the weapon of the Aesir!"

"Softly, softly," said Loki, smiling maliciously. "He is a shrewd giant, and a mighty. Even you, great Thor, cannot go to him and pluck the hammer from his hand as one would slip the rattle from a baby's pink fist. Nay, you must use craft, Thor; and it is I who will teach you, if you will be patient."

Thor was a brave, blunt fellow, and he hated the ways of Loki, his lies and his deceit. He liked best the way of warriors—the thundering charge, the flash of weapons, and the heavy blow; but without the hammer he could not fight the giants hand to hand. Loki's advice seemed wise, and he decided to leave the matter to the Red One.

Loki was now all eagerness, for he loved difficulties which would set his wit in play and bring other folk into danger. "Look, now," he said. "We must go to Freia and borrow her falcon dress. But you must ask; for she loves me so little that she would scarce listen to me."

So first they made their way to Folkvang, the house of maidens, where Freia dwelt, the loveliest of all in Asgard. She was fairer than fair, and sweeter than sweet, and the tears from her flower-eyes made the dew which blessed the earth-flowers night and morning. Of her Thor borrowed the magic dress of feathers in which Freia was wont to clothe herself and flit like a great beautiful bird all about the world. She was willing enough to lend it to Thor when he told her that by its aid he hoped to win back the hammer which he had lost; for she well knew the danger threatening herself and all the Aesir until Miölnir should be found.

"Now will I fetch the hammer for you," said Loki. So he put on the falcon plumage, and, spreading his brown wings, flapped away up, up, over the world, down, down, across the great ocean which lies beyond all things that men know. And he came to the dark country where there was no sunshine nor spring, but it was always dreary winter; where mountains were piled up like blocks of ice, and where great caverns yawned hungrily in blackness. And this was Jotunheim, the land of the Frost-Giants.

And lo! when Loki came thereto he found Thrym the Giant King sitting outside his palace cave, playing with his dogs and horses. The dogs were as big as elephants, and the horses were as big as houses, but Thrym himself was as huge as a mountain; and Loki trembled, but he tried to seem brave.

"Good-day, Loki," said Thrym, with the terrible voice of which he was so proud, for he fancied it was as loud as Thor's. "How fares it, feathered one, with your little brothers, the Aesir, in Asgard halls? And how dare you venture alone in this guise to Giant Land?"

"It is an ill day in Asgard," sighed Loki, keeping his eye warily upon the giant, "and a stormy one in the world of men. I heard the winds howling and the storms rushing on the earth as I passed by. Some mighty one has stolen the hammer of our Thor. Is it you, Thrym, greatest of all giants—greater than Thor himself?"

This the crafty one said to flatter Thrym, for Loki well knew the weakness of those who love to be thought greater than they are.

Then Thrym bridled and swelled with pride, and tried to put on the majesty and awe of noble Thor; but he only succeeded in becoming an ugly, puffy monster.

"Well, yes," he admitted. "I have the hammer that belonged to your little Thor; and now how much of a lord is he?"

"Alack!" sighed Loki again, "weak enough he is without his magic weapon. But you, O Thrym—surely your mightiness needs no such aid. Give me the hammer, that Asgard may no longer be shaken by Thor's grief for his precious toy."

But Thrym was not so easily to be flattered into parting with his stolen treasure. He grinned a dreadful grin, several yards in width, which his teeth barred like jagged boulders across the entrance to a mountain cavern.

"Miölnir the hammer is mine," he said, "and I am Thunder-Lord, mightiest of the mighty. I have hidden it where Thor can never find it, twelve leagues below the seacaves, where Queen Ran lives with her daughters, the white-capped Waves. But listen, Loki. Go tell the Aesir that I will give back Thor's hammer. I will give it back upon one condition—that they send Freia the beautiful to be my wife."

"Freia the beautiful!" Loki had to stifle a laugh. Fancy the Aesir giving their fairest flower to such an ugly fellow as this! But he only said politely, "Ah, yes; you demand our Freia in exchange for the little hammer? It is a costly price, great Thrym. But I will be your friend in Asgard. If I have my way, you shall soon see the fairest bride in all the world knocking at your door. Farewell!"

So Loki whizzed back to Asgard on his falcon wings; and as he went he chuckled to think of the evils which were likely to happen because of his words with Thrym. First he gave the message to Thor—not sparing of Thrym's insolence, to make Thor angry; and then he went to Freia with the word for her—not sparing of Thrym's ugliness, to make her shudder. The spiteful fellow!

Now you can imagine the horror that was in Asgard as the Aesir listened to Loki's words. "My hammer!" roared Thor. "The villain confesses that he has stolen my hammer, and boasts that he is Thunder-Lord! Gr-r-r!"

"The ugly giant!" wailed Freia. "Must I be the bride of that hideous old monster, and live in his gloomy mountain prison all my life?"

"Yes; put on your bridal veil, sweet Freia," said Loki maliciously, "and come with me to Jotunheim. Hang your famous starry necklace about your neck, and don your bravest robe; for in eight days there will be a wedding, and Thor's hammer is to pay."

Then Freia fell to weeping. "I cannot go! I will not go!" she cried. "I will not leave the home of gladness and Father Odin's table to dwell in the land of horrors! Thor's hammer is mighty, but mightier the love of the kind Aesir for their little Freia! Good Odin, dear brother Frey, speak for me! You will not make me go?"

The Aesir looked at her and thought how lonely and bare would Asgard be without her loveliness; for she was fairer than fair, and sweeter than sweet.

"She shall not go!" shouted Frey, putting his arms about his sister's neck.

"No, she shall not go!" cried all the Aesir with one voice.

"But my hammer," insisted Thor. "I must have Miölnir back again."

"And my word to Thrym," said Loki, "that must be made good."

"You are too generous with your words," said Father Odin sternly, for he knew his brother well. "Your word is not a gem of great price, for you have made it cheap."

Then spoke Heimdal, the sleepless watchman who sits on guard at the entrance to the rainbow bridge which leads to Asgard; and Heimdal was the wisest of the Aesir, for he could see into the future, and knew how things would come to pass. Through his golden teeth he spoke, for his teeth were all of gold.

"I have a plan," he said. "Let us dress Thor himself like a bride in Freia's robes, and send him to Jotunheim to talk with Thrym and to win back his hammer."

But at this word Thor grew very angry.

"What! dress me like a girl!" he roared. "I should never hear the last of it! The Aesir will mock me, and call me 'maiden'! The giants, and even the puny dwarfs, will have a lasting jest upon me! I will not go! I will fight! I will die, if need be! But dressed as a woman I will not go!"

But Loki answered him with sharp words, for this was a scheme after his own heart. "What, Thor!' he said. "Would you lose your hammer and keep Asgard in danger for so small a whim? Look, now: if you go not, Thrym with his giants will come in a mighty army and drive us from Asgard; then he will indeed make Freia his bride, and moreover he will have you for his slave under the power of his hammer. How like you this picture, brother of the thunder?

Nay, Heimdal's plan is a good one, and I myself will help to carry it out."

Still Thor hesitated; but Freia came and laid her white hand on his arm, and looked up into his scowling face pleadingly.

"To save me, Thor," she begged. And Thor said he would go.

Then there was great sport among the Aesir, while they dressed Thor like a beautiful maiden. Brünhilde and her sisters, the nine Valkyrie, daughters of Odin, had the task in hand. How they laughed as they brushed and curled his yellow hair, and set upon it the wondrous headdress of silk and pearls! They let out seams, and they let down hems, and set on extra pieces, to make it larger, and so they hid his great limbs and knotted arms under Freia's fairest robe of scarlet; but beneath it all he would wear his shirt of mail and his belt of power that gave him double strength. Freia herself twisted about his neck her famous necklace of starry jewels, and Queen Frigg, his mother, hung at his girdle a jingling bunch of keys, such as was the custom for the bride to wear at Norse weddings. Last of all, that Thrym might not see Thor's fierce eyes and the yellow beard, that ill became a maiden, they threw over him a long veil of silver white which covered him to the feet. And there he stood, as stately and tall a bride as even a giant might wish to see; but on his hands he wore his iron gloves, and they ached for but one thing—to grasp the handle of the stolen hammer.

"Ah, what a lovely maid it is!" chuckled Loki; "and how glad will Thrym be to see this Freia come! Bride Thor, I will go with you as your handmaiden, for I would fain see the fun."

"Come, then," said Thor sulkily, for he was ill-pleased, and wore his maiden robes with no good grace. "It is fitting that you go; for I like not these lies and maskings, and I may spoil the mummery without you at my elbow."

There was loud laughter above the clouds when Thor, all veiled and dainty-seeming, drove away from Asgard to his wedding, with maid Loki by his side. Thor cracked his whip and chirruped fiercely to his twin goats with golden hoofs, for he wanted to escape the sounds of mirth that echoed from the rainbow bridge, where all the Aesir stood watching. Loki, sitting with his hands meekly folded like a girl, chuckled as he glanced up at Thor's angry face; but he said nothing, for he knew it was not good to joke too far with Thor, even when Miölnir was hidden twelve leagues below the sea in Ran's kingdom.

So off they dashed to Jötunheim, where Thrym was waiting and longing for his beautiful bride. Thor's goats thundered along above the sea and land and people far below, who looked up wondering as the noise rolled overhead. "Hear how the thunder rumbles!" they said. "Thor is on a long journey tonight." And a long journey it was, as the tired goats found before they reached the end.

Thrym heard the sound of their approach, for his ear was eager. "Hola!" he cried. "Someone is coming from Asgard—only one of Odin's children could make a din so fearful. Hasten, men, and see if they are bringing Freia to be my wife."

Then the lookout giant stepped down from the top of his mountain, and said that a chariot was bringing two maidens to the door.

"Run, giants, run!" shouted Thrym, in a fever at this news. "My bride is coming! Put silken cushions on the benches for a great banquet, and make the house beautiful for the fairest maid in all space! Bring in all my golden-horned cows and my coal-black oxen, that she may see how rich I am, and heap all my gold and jewels about to dazzle her sweet eyes! She shall find me richest of the rich; and when I have her—fairest of the fair—there will be no treasure that I lack—not one!"

The chariot stopped at the gate, and out stepped the tall bride, hidden from head to foot, and her handmaiden muffled to the chin. "How afraid of catching cold they must be!" whispered the giant ladies, who were peering over one another's shoulders to catch a glimpse of the bride, just as the crowd outside the awning does at a wedding nowadays.

Thrym had sent six splendid servants to escort the maidens: these were the Metal Kings, who served him as lord of them all. There was the Gold King, all in cloth of gold, with fringes of yellow bullion, most glittering to see; and

there was the Silver King, almost as gorgeous in a suit of spangled white; and side by side bowed the dark Kings of Iron and Lead, the one mighty in black, the other sullen in blue; and after them were the Copper King, gleaming ruddy and brave, and the Tin King, strutting in his trimmings of gaudy tinsel which looked nearly as well as silver but were more economical. And this fine troop of lackey kings most politely led Thor and Loki into the palace, and gave them the best, for they never suspected who these seeming maidens really were.

And when evening came there was a wonderful banquet to celebrate the wedding. On a golden throne sat Thrym, uglier than ever in his finery of purple and gold. Beside him was the bride, of whose face no one had yet caught even a glimpse; and at Thrym's other hand stood Loki, the waiting-maid, for he wanted to be near to mend the mistakes which Thor might make.

Now the dishes at the feast were served in a huge way, as befitted the table of giants: great beeves roasted whole, on platters as wide across as a ship's deck; plum-puddings as fat as featherbeds, with plums as big as footballs; and a wedding cake like a snowcapped haymow. The giants ate enormously. But to Thor, because they thought him a dainty maiden, they served small bits of everything on a tiny gold dish. Now Thor's long journey had made him very hungry, and through his veil he whispered to Loki, "I shall starve, Loki! I cannot fare on these nibbles. I must eat a goodly meal as I do at home." And forthwith he helped himself to such morsels as might satisfy his hunger for a little time. You should have seen the giants stare at the meal which the dainty bride devoured!

For first under the silver veil disappeared by pieces a whole roast ox. Then Thor made eight mouthfuls of eight pink salmon, a dish of which he was very fond. And next he looked about and reached for a platter of cakes and sweetmeats that was set aside at one end of the table for the lady guests, and the bride ate them all. You can fancy how the damsels drew down their mouths and looked at one another when they saw their dessert disappear; and they whispered about the table, "Alack! if our future mistress is to sup like this day by day, there will be poor cheer for the rest of us!" And to crown it all, Thor was thirsty, as well he might be; and one after another he raised to his lips and emptied three great barrels of mead, the foamy drink of the giants. Then indeed Thrym was amazed, for Thor's giant appetite had beaten that of the giants themselves.

"Never before saw I a bride so hungry," he cried, "and never before one half so thirsty!"

But Loki, the waiting-maid, whispered to him softly, "The truth is, great Thrym, that my dear mistress was almost starved. For eight days Freia has eaten nothing at all, so eager was she for Jotunheim."

Then Thrym was delighted, you may be sure. He forgave his hungry bride, and loved her with all his heart. He leaned forward to give her a kiss, raising a corner of her veil; but his hand dropped suddenly, and he started up in terror, for he had caught the angry flash of Thor's eye, which was glaring at him through the bridal veil. Thor was longing for his hammer.

"Why has Freia so sharp a look?" Thrym cried. "It pierces like lightning and burns like fire."

But again the sly waiting-maid whispered timidly, "Oh, Thrym, be not amazed! The truth is, my poor mistress's eyes are red with wakefulness and bright with longing. For eight nights Freia has not known a wink of sleep, so eager was she for Jotunheim."

Then again Thrym was doubly delighted, and he longed to call her his very own dear wife. "Bring in the wedding gift!" he cried. "Bring in Thor's hammer, Miölnir, and give it to Freia, as I promised; for when I have kept my word she will be mine—all mine!"

Then Thor's big heart laughed under his woman's dress, and his fierce eyes swept eagerly down the hall to meet the servant who was bringing in the hammer on a velvet cushion. Thor's fingers could hardly wait to clutch the stubby handle which they knew so well; but he sat quite still on the throne beside ugly old Thrym, with his hands meekly folded and his head bowed like a bashful bride.

The giant servant drew nearer, nearer, puffing and blowing, strong though he was, beneath the mighty weight. He was about to lay it at Thor's feet (for he thought it so heavy that no maiden could lift it or hold it in her lap), when suddenly Thor's heart swelled, and he gave a most unmaidenly shout of rage and triumph. With one swoop he grasped the hammer in his iron fingers; with the other arm he tore off the veil that hid his terrible face, and trampled it under foot; then he turned to the frightened king, who cowered beside him on the throne.

"Thief!" he said. "Freia sends you this as a wedding gift!" And he whirled the hammer about his head, then hurled it once, twice, thrice, as it rebounded to his hand; and in the first stroke, as of lightning, Thrym rolled dead from his throne; in the second stroke perished the whole giant household—these ugly enemies of the Aesir; and in the third stroke the palace itself tumbled together and fell to the ground like a toppling playhouse of blocks.

But Loki and Thor stood safely among the ruins, dressed in their tattered maiden robes, a quaint and curious sight; and Loki, full of mischief now as ever, burst out laughing.

"Oh, Thor! if you could see"—he began; but Thor held up his hammer and shook it gently as he said:

"Look now, Loki: it was an excellent joke, and so far you have done well—after your crafty fashion, which likes me not. But now I have my hammer again and the joke is done. From you, nor from another, I brook no laughter at my expense. Henceforth, we will have no mention of this masquerade, nor of these rags which now I throw away. Do you hear, red laughter?"

And Loki heard, with a look of hate, and stifled his laughter as best he could; for it is not good to laugh at him who holds the hammer.

Not once after that was there mention in Asgard of the time when Thor dressed him as a girl and won his bridal gift from Thrym the giant.

But Miölnir was safe once more in Asgard, and you and I know how it came there; so some one must have told. I wonder if red Loki whispered the tale to some outsider, after all? Perhaps it may be so, for now he knew how best to make Thor angry; and from that day when Thor forbade his laughing, Loki hated him with the mean little hatred of a mean little soul.

North American Indian and Inuit Myths

Determination of the Seasons

This Tahltan tale and *How Glooskap Found the Summer* are interesting when considered together because they show very different causes for the seasons. This one is clearly a beast tale in which the weaker animal wins, and it belongs to that class of myths that explain how the present world came to be what it is. *Glooskap* may be typed not only as an explanation of the world as it is, but also as a tale about this world and "the other world." The fact that the symbol for Glooskap is the snowshoe rabbit suggests a comparison with the *Jatakas* and Buddha's transformations into one wild animal or another, when he would return to earth. Glooskap is not represented as an animal, but neither is he definitely represented in the human form. [From Stith Thompson, *Tales of the North American Indians* (Indiana University Press, 1929).]

Once Porcupine and Beaver quarreled about the seasons. Porcupine wanted five winter months. He held up one hand and showed his five fingers. He said, "Let the winter months be the same in number as the fingers on my hand." Beaver said, "No," and held up his tail, which had many cracks or scratches on it. He said, "Let the winter months be the same in number as the scratches on my tail." Now they quarreled and argued. Porcupine got angry and bit off his thumb. Then, holding up his hand with the four fingers, he said emphatically, "There must be only four winter months." Beaver became a little afraid, and gave in. *For this reason porcupines have four claws on each foot now.*

Since Porcupine won, the winter remained four months in length, until later Raven changed it a little. Raven considered what Porcupine and Beaver had said about the winters, and decided that Porcupine had done right. He said, "Porcupine was right. If the winters were made too long, people could not live. *Henceforth the winters will be about this length,* but they will be variable. I will tell you of the *gaxewisa* month, when people will meet together and talk.

At that time of the year people will ask questions (or propound riddles) and others will answer. If the riddle is answered correctly, then the person who propounded it must answer, 'Fool-Hen.' " Raven chose this word because the fool-hen has a shorter beak than any other game-bird. "If people guess riddles correctly at this time of year, then the winter will be short, and the spring come early."

How Glooskap Found the Summer

All that the Algonquin Indians knew was taught them by their friend Glooskap. There are numerous stories about this benevolent, supreme hero. [From Charles Godfrey Leland, *The Algonquin Legends of New England* (Houghton Mifflin, 1884).]

In the long-ago time before the first white men came to live in the New World, and when people lived always in the early red morning before sunrise, a mighty race of Indians lived in the northeastern part of the New World. Nearest the sunrise were they, and they called themselves Wawaniki—Children of Light. Glooskap was their lord and master. He was ever kind to his people, and did many great works for them.

Once, in Glooskap's day, it grew very cold; snow and ice were everywhere, fires would not give enough warmth; the corn would not grow, and his people were perishing with cold and famine. Then Glooskap went very far north where all was ice. He came to a wigwam in which he found a giant, a great giant—for he was Winter. It was his icy breath that had frozen all the land. Glooskap entered the wigwam and sat down. Then Winter gave him a pipe, and as he smoked, the giant told tales of the olden times when he, Winter, reigned everywhere; when all the land was silent, white, and beautiful. The charm fell upon Glooskap; it was the frost charm. As the giant talked on and on, Glooskap fell asleep; and for six months he slept like a bear; then the charm fled, as he was too strong for it, and he awoke.

Soon after he awoke, his talebearer, Tatler the Loon, a wild bird who lived on the shores of the lakes, brought him strange news. He told of a country far off to the south where it was always warm: there lived a queen, who could easily overcome the giant, Winter. So Glooskap, to save his people from cold and famine and death, decided to go and find the queen.

Far off to the seashore he went, and sang the magic song which the whales obey. Up came his old friend, Blob the Whale. She was Glooskap's carrier and bore him on her back when he wished to go far out to sea. Now the whale always had a strange law for travelers. She said to Glooskap, "You must shut your eyes tight while I carry you; to open them is dangerous; if you do that, I am sure to go aground on a reef or sand-bar, and cannot get off, and you may be drowned."

Glooskap got on her back, and for many days the whale swam, and each day the water grew warmer and the air more balmy and sweet, for it came from spicy shores. The odors were no longer those of salt, but of fruits and flowers.

Soon they found themselves in shallow waters. Down in the sand the clams were singing a song of warning. "O big Whale," they sang, "keep out to sea, for the water here is shallow."

The whale said to Glooskap, who understood the language of all creatures, "What do they say?"

But Glooskap, wishing to land at once, said, "They tell you to hurry, for a storm is coming."

Then the whale hurried until she was close to the land, and Glooskap opened his left eye and peeped. At once the whale stuck hard and fast on the beach, so that Glooskap, leaping from her head, walked ashore on dry land.

The whale, thinking she could never get off, was very angry. But Glooskap put one end of his strong bow against the whale's jaw, and taking the other end in his hands, he placed his feet against the high bank, and with a mighty push, he sent her out into the deep water. Then, to keep peace with the whale, he threw her a pipe and a bag of Indian tobacco, and the whale, pleased with the gift, lighted the pipe and sailed far out to sea.

Far inland strode Glooskap and at every step it grew warmer, and the flowers began to come

up and talk with him. He came to where there were many fairies dancing in the forest. In the center of the group was one fairer than all the others; her long brown hair was crowned with flowers and her arms filled with blossoms. She was the queen Summer.

Glooskap knew that here at last was the queen who by her charms could melt old Winter's heart, and force him to leave. He caught her up, and kept her by a crafty trick. The Master cut a moose-hide into a long cord; as he ran away with Summer, he let the end trail behind him. The Fairies of Light pulled at the cord, but as Glooskap ran, the cord ran out, and though they pulled, he left them far behind.

So at last he came to the lodge of old Winter, but now he had Summer in his bosom; and Winter welcomed him, for he hoped to freeze Glooskap to sleep again.

From *How Summer Came to Canada,* retold by William Toye, illustrated by Elizabeth Cleaver. Copyright © 1969 Oxford University Press (Canadian branch). Reprinted by permission of Oxford University Press.

But this time the Master did the talking. This time his charm was the stronger, and ere long the sweat ran down Winter's face; he knew that his power was gone; and the charm of Frost was broken. His icy tent melted. Then Summer used her strange power and everything awoke. The grass grew, the fairies came out, and the snow ran down the rivers, carrying away the dead leaves. Old Winter wept, seeing his power gone.

But Summer, the queen, said, "I have proved that I am more powerful than you. I give you now all the country to the far North for your own, and there I shall never disturb you. Six months of every year you may come back to Glooskap's country and reign as of old, but you will be less severe. During the other six months, I myself will come from the South and rule the land."

Old Winter could do nothing but accept her offer. In the late autumn he comes back to Glooskap's country and reigns six months; but his rule is softer than in olden times. And when he comes, Summer runs home to the warm Southland. But at the end of six months, she always comes back to drive old Winter away to his own land, to awaken the northern land, and to give it the joys that only she, the queen, can give. And so, in Glooskap's old country, Winter and Summer, the hoary old giant and the beautiful fairy queen, divide the rule of the land between them.

How the Coyote Danced with the Blackbirds

This "pourquoi" story of the Zuñi Indians is reminiscent of the fable *The Jackdaw and the Borrowed Plumes*. Note that the fable is terse and to the point, as a fable should be, whereas this story is deftly developed to the climax and the moral left to the reader's inference. [From Frank Hamilton Cushing, *Zuñi Folk Tales* (Knopf, 1931).]

One late autumn day in the times of the ancients, a large council of Blackbirds were gathered, fluttering and chattering, on the smooth, rocky slopes of Gorge Mountain, northwest of Zuñi. Like ourselves, these birds, as you are well aware, congregate together in autumn time, when the harvests are ripe, to indulge in their festivities before going into winter quarters; only we do not move away, while they, on strong wings and swift, retreat for a time to the Land of Everlasting Summer.

Well, on this particular morning they were making a great noise and having a grand dance, and this was the way of it: They would gather in one vast flock, somewhat orderly in its disposition, on the sloping face of Gorge Mountain— the older birds in front, the younger ones behind—and down the slope, chirping and fluttering, they would hop, hop, hop, singing:

"Ketchu, Ketchu, oñtila, oñtila,
Ketchu, Ketchu, oñtila, oñtila!
　Âshokta a yá-à-laa Ke-e-tchu,
　　Oñtila,
　　Oñtila!"—
"Blackbirds, blackbirds, dance away, O,
　dance away, O!
Blackbirds, blackbirds, dance away, O,
　dance away, O!
　Down the Mountain of the Gorges,
　Blackbirds,
　　Dance away, O!
　　Dance away, O!"

and spreading their wings, with many a flutter, flurry, and scurry, keh, keh—keh, keh—keh, keh—keh, keh—they would fly away into the air, swirling off in a dense, black flock, circling far upward and onward; then, wheeling about and darting down, they would dip themselves in the broad spring which flows out at the foot of the mountain, and return to their dancing place on the rocky slope.

A Coyote was out hunting (as if he could catch anything, the beast!) and saw them, and was enraptured.

"You beautiful creatures!" he exclaimed. "You graceful dancers! Delight of my senses! How do you do that, anyway? Couldn't I join in your dance—the first part of it, at least?"

"Why, certainly; yes," said the Blackbirds. "We are quite willing," the masters of the ceremony said.

"Well," said the Coyote, "I can get on the slope of the rocks and I can sing the song with you; but I suppose that when you leap off into the air I shall have to sit there patting the rock with my paw and my tail and singing while you have the fun of it."

"It may be," said an old Blackbird, "that we can fit you out so that you can fly with us."

"Is it possible!" cried the Coyote. "Then by all means do so. By the Blessed Immortals! Now, if I am only able to circle off into the air like you fellows, I'll be the biggest Coyote in the world!"

"I think it will be easy," resumed the old Blackbird. "My children," said he, "you are many, and many are your wing feathers. Contribute each one of you a feather to our friend." Thereupon the Blackbirds, each one of them, plucked a feather from his wing. Unfortunately they all plucked feathers from the wings on the same side.

"Are you sure, my friend," continued the old Blackbird, "that you are willing to go through the operation of having these feathers planted in your skin? If so, I think we can fit you out."

"Willing?—why, of course I am willing." And the Coyote held up one of his arms, and, sitting down, steadied himself with his tail. Then the Blackbirds thrust in the feathers all along the rear of his forelegs and down the sides of his back, where wings ought to be. It hurt, and the Coyote twitched his mustache considerably; but he said nothing. When it was done, he asked: "Am I ready now?"

"Yes," said the Blackbirds, "we think you'll do."

So they formed themselves again on the upper part of the slope, sang their songs, and hopped along down with many a flutter, flurry, and scurry—Keh, keh, keh, keh, keh, keh—and away they flew off into the air.

The Coyote, somewhat startled, got out of time but followed bravely, making heavy flops; but, as I have said before, the wings he was supplied with were composed of feathers all plucked from one side, and therefore he flew slanting and spirally and brought up with a whack, which nearly knocked the breath out of him, against the side of the mountain. He picked himself up, and shook himself, and cried out: "Hold! Hold! Hold on, hold on there!" to the fast-disappearing Blackbirds, "You've left me behind!"

When the birds returned, they explained: "Your wings are not quite thick enough, friend; and, besides, even a young Blackbird, when he is first learning to fly, does just this sort of thing that you have been doing—makes bad work of it."

"Sit down again," said the old Blackbird. And he called out to the rest: "Get feathers from your other sides also, and be careful to select a few strong feathers from the tips of the wings, for by means of these we cleave the air, guide our movements, and sustain our flight."

So the Blackbirds all did as they were bidden, and after the new feathers were planted, each one plucked out a tail-feather, and the most skillful of the Blackbirds inserted these feathers into the tip of the Coyote's tail. It made him wince and "yip" occasionally; but he stood it bravely and reared his head proudly, thinking all the while: "What a splendid Coyote I shall be! Did ever anyone hear of a Coyote flying?"

The procession formed again. Down the slope they went, hoppity-hop, hoppity-hop, singing their song, and away they flew into the air, the Coyote in their midst. Far off and high they circled and circled, the Coyote cutting more eager pranks than any of the rest. Finally they returned, dipped themselves again into the spring, and settled on the slopes of the rocks.

"There, now," cried out the Coyote, with a flutter of his feathery tail, "I can fly as well as the rest of you."

"Indeed, you do well!" exclaimed the Blackbirds. "Shall we try it again?"

"Oh, yes! Oh, yes! I'm a little winded," cried the Coyote, "but this is the best fun I ever had."

The Blackbirds, however, were not satisfied with their companion. They found him less sedate than a dancer ought to be, and, moreover, his irregular cuttings-up in the air were not to their taste. So the old ones whispered to one another: "This fellow is a fool, and we must pluck him when he gets into the air. We'll fly so far this time that he will get a little tired and cry to us for assistance."

The procession formed, and hoppity-hop, hoppity-hop, down the mountain slope they went, and with many a flutter and flurry flew off into the air. The Coyote, unable to restrain himself, even took the lead. On and on and on they flew, the Blackbirds and the Coyote, and up and up and up, and they circled round and round, until the Coyote found himself missing a wing stroke occasionally and falling out of line; and he cried out, "Help! Help, friends, help!"

"All right!" cried the Blackbirds, "Catch hold of his wings; hold him up!" cried the old ones. And the Blackbirds flew at him; and every time they caught hold of him (the old fool all the time thinking they were helping) they plucked out a feather, until at last the feathers had become so thin that he began to fall, and he fell and fell and fell—flop, flop, flop, he went through the air—the few feathers left in his forelegs and sides and the tip of his tail just saving him from being utterly crushed as he fell with a thud to the ground. He lost his senses completely, and lay there as if dead for a long time. When he awoke, he shook his head sadly, and, with a crestfallen countenance and tail dragging between his legs, betook himself to his home over the mountains.

The agony of that fall had been so great and the heat of his exertions so excessive that the feathers left in his forelegs and tailtip were all shriveled up into little ugly black fringes of hair. His descendants were many.

Therefore, you will often meet coyotes to this day who have little black fringes along the rear of their forelegs, and the tips of their tails are often black. Thus it was in the days of the ancients.

Thus shortens my story.

Why the Ant Is Almost Cut in Two

Ritual, belief, and a "pourquoi" story are combined in this tale from the mythology of the Kiowa Indians, taken down by a noted anthropologist, Alice Marriott, and recorded in her book *Winter-Telling Stories*. According to ritual, these stories must be told only in the winter season. Saynday, the trickster-god, considers here the mystery of death and the tragedy of the young who die. Making himself small, it was with the lowly ant that he chose to discuss these matters. [From Alice Marriott, *Winter-Telling Stories* (Crowell, 1947).]

Saynday was coming along, and as he came he saw little Red Ant with a big sack over her shoulder. Little Red Ant was different in those early days. Her head and her body were all in one piece, with no neck between them. When she carried her big round sack it looked like one ball carrying another and rolling along the ground.

"Hello, there," said Saynday. "You look as if you were hot."

"I am hot," said little Red Ant. "It's a hot day."

"Sit down and rest," said Saynday, "and let's talk things over."

"All right," said little Red Ant.

They sat down and rested in the shade of a prickly pear, and Saynday made himself small enough to talk comfortably to little Red Ant.

"I've been thinking a lot," said Saynday.

"What have you been thinking about?" asked little Red Ant.

"I've been thinking about death," said Saynday. "My world and my people have been going on quite a while now, and things are beginning to get old and die sometimes."

"What's wrong with that?" said little Red Ant. "It makes room for new people."

"The people who die don't like it," said Saynday.

"There isn't any way to make them stop dying," said little Red Ant. "No, but there might be a way to bring them back," said Saynday. "I've been thinking and thinking and thinking and thinking about it, and I think I know a way to bring them back when they've been dead four days."

"Well, it sounds rather silly to me," said little Red Ant.

"I don't see anything silly about it," said Saynday.

"I think it is," said little Red Ant. "The way things are now, the people who die off are old. They've had a good time and lived life out. When they go, it doesn't hurt them. Then there is a place for a new person to come along and enjoy life. I think the new ones ought to have a turn."

"That's the way it is now," said Saynday, "but maybe it won't always be that way. Maybe some of the young people will get killed off by accident. Then we ought to have some way to bring them back so they can enjoy their full lives."

"I don't think you need to," said little Red Ant. "If they're so stupid they go and get killed, it's just their own faults."

"All right," said Saynday. "I wanted to know what you thought. Now that I know, I will let there be death. When things and people die, they won't come back to this world any more. Now I have to go and see some more of my world. Goodbye."

And he and little Red Ant went their separate ways.

Four days later Saynday was coming back, and he came to that same prickly pear. There was mourning and crying all around. He looked down on the ground and saw little Red Ant. She was sitting in the shade of the prickly pear and crying as if her heart would break. Saynday made himself little again, and sat down beside her.

"What's the matter?" said Saynday.

"Oh, it's my son," said little Red Ant.

"What happened to your son?" said Saynday.

"A buffalo stepped on him," answered little Red Ant, "and now he's all gone dead."

"That's too bad," said Saynday.

"It's terrible," said little Red Ant.

And before Saynday could do anything, she pulled his knife out of his belt and cut herself almost in two, just above her shoulders. Saynday thought there had been enough dying already for one morning, so he took the knife away before she could cut herself clear in two.

"There," he said, "you see how it is. That's the way people feel when some one they love dies. They want to die too. If you'd let me have my way, your son would have come back at the end of four days. But you thought there would be too many people in the world if that happened. So now you know why I wanted to do that. For all the rest of the world, people will keep on dying. And for all the rest of the world, you will go around cut almost in two, to remind you of what you did to everybody."

And that's the way it was, and that's the way it is, to this good day.

The Princess and the Feathers

This legend of the Pacific Northwest Coast is based on material from *Tsimshian Mythology,* by Franz Boas, and *Haida Texts and Myths,* by John R. Swanton. In these sources, *narnauks,* or supernatural beings, are both tricksters and guardians. The Mouse Woman in this story is a narnauk who aids the courageous Wolf Crest princess much as the fairy godmother aids the princess in tales of European origin. [From Christie Harris, *Mouse Woman and the Vanished Princesses* (Atheneum, 1976).]

First, a Wolf Crest princess vanished from an upriver village. She vanished without a trace. And her clansmen from all the villages loped along the trails, alert for some sign of her. They searched the shorelines. They questioned travellers.

"Have you seen any sign of the Wolf princess?" they asked the travelling arrowmaker.

He was a strange old man who paddled from place to place with his marvellous arrows. And though he was as tall and as spare as any young paddler, his face was so wrinkled that he seemed to have lived forever. As if his skin had once been stretched over an enormous moonface, it now hung loosely over his shrunken features. It hung so loosely that, when he shook his head at their question, his wrinkles wagged like wattles.

"Haven't you seen anything?" the people insisted.

But the old man just shook his head again, wagging his hanging wrinkles.

Then, a year later, another princess vanished from another upriver village. She vanished without a trace. This time it was a Frog Crest princess. So Frog clansmen loped along the trails, alert for some sign of her. They searched the shorelines. They questioned travellers.

"Have you seen any sign of the Frog princess?" they asked the old arrowmaker. He might have. For he travelled widely; every hunter wanted an arrow winged with the golden feathers that only he knew where to find. He might even have glimpsed a narnauk, since he was a man who clearly had mystic powers. Wasn't there a mysterious power in his arrows? people whispered to one another. Perhaps he could put a spell on them. Or perhaps he used feathers from a Heaven Bird. Certainly there was magic in his golden-winged arrows. So he might have glimpsed a narnauk.

"Haven't you seen anything?" they insisted. But the old man just shook his head, wagging his hanging wrinkles.

Then, a year later, yet another princess vanished from yet another upriver village. She vanished without a trace. This time it was a Raven Crest princess. So Raven clansmen loped along the trails, alert for some sign of her. They searched the shorelines. They questioned travellers.

"Haven't *you* seen anything?" they asked the old arrowmaker.

And once more he just shook his head, wagging his hanging wrinkles.

Illustration by Douglas Tait, from *Mouse Woman and the Vanished Princesses*, by Christie Harris, published by McClelland & Stewart Ltd., 1976. Reproduced by permission of the publisher and the author.

"Perhaps this is a cruel trick of Raven's," someone suggested.

Alarm gripped a coastal village near the mouth of the river. "For next it will be our turn," its people whispered, nodding toward their Eagle princess with anxious faces.

At least she never moved without her proper guard of friends-and-attendants, they noted with satisfaction. Two high-ranking Eagle girls always hovered near their princess, who was called Wy-en-eeks.

"It would be good to have Wy-en-eeks married," people muttered to one another. For then there would be a man in close attendance. Too, a married woman would be less attractive to some narnauk who wanted a human wife.

The next time the old arrowmaker arrived at their village, they questioned him sharply about the other princesses. "Haven't you seen anything at all?" they insisted.

But again he shook his head, wagging his hanging wrinkles.

As always, they wondered about the old man, who must be very wealthy. Great chiefs paid him so handsomely for his arrows that his house must be soft with furs and elegant with carved chests and painted screens, with beautifully carved bowls and hornspoons; it must glint with copper and abalone pearl. But no one had ever seen it. They only knew that it was hidden away on one of the many islands that fringed the coast near the river's mouth. The old man was as mysterious as his golden-winged arrows.

When he had sold his arrows, he paddled off without a word. And people turned their eyes back to the Eagle princess, a beautiful girl whose dark eyes flashed with spirit.

It was the time of wild roses. The air was fragrant with their sweetness. And women, back from their clam beaches, were readying their berry baskets.

Then a summer fog shrouded their world. And the Eagle princess was kept indoors.

"But why?" Wy-en-eeks fumed.

"You know why," her mother answered. "Fog makes it easy for some stranger to slip in and hide behind a rock or a tangle of driftwood."

"But the smoke is smarting my eyes," Wy-en-eeks protested.

A fire was burning in the center of the huge windowless house; and the shrouding of fog was keeping the smoke from rising up briskly through the smoke hole.

"I wish you were married," her mother said, as she had said daily.

"To Kuwask." Wy-en-eeks wrinkled her nose, just a little. But she knew she would marry Kuwask. It had all been arranged by their families. Indeed, she had only a few moons left of freedom.

"Freedom!" she breathed, with a great sigh. And her spirit surged outdoors, toward excitement, toward new places and new people. For, with the blood of sea-hunting chiefs racing through her veins, the princess liked fast water and wild winds. She gloried in storms that clattered pebbles across the beach and set the waves smoking with blown spray. And she hated being housebound.

"Heeay!" a child cried, coming into the big house. "The sun is burning through."

"At last!" Wy-en-eeks said, beckoning her two attendants.

"You will be careful?" her mother cautioned.

"How can I not be careful with these two hovering round me like bears round a spawned salmon?"

"Like bees round a pink rose," one of her friends corrected fondly. And before handing it to her, she checked the princess's handbasket to see that it held her cosmetic stick and her little woman's-knife.

"Here is a light robe," the other friend said. For Wy-en-eeks was precious. Wisps of fog must not chill her.

The sun burned through quickly. And the girls strolled along the beach trail, pausing to sniff the roses. Then they sat on a driftlog, chatting about a handsome young man they had seen at a winter potlatch.

But Wy-en-eeks quickly switched the conversation to a handsome young man they had seen at spring trading. He was one of the lordly, flashing-eyed Haidas who had come over to the mainland from their big offshore islands to trade their superb canoes for the mainlanders' goatskins and hornspoons and oolaken fish grease.

"I wish I could have gone home with him," she confessed.

Her girls looked at her with gentle disapproval. "Oh no, Wy-en-eeks!" Only a captured princess went home with the terrifying Haidas.

"No," she agreed. "I wish I could have *been* him." Paddling far out to sea. Leading great sea hunts or slave raiding parties. "Why must my life be so dull?"

"Your life will never be dull," her friends predicted.

"The fog will soon be rolling in again," one of them noted. "So let's go to the point and then turn back." She leaped the log, landed on a big loose stone, and turned her ankle. "No walk for me," she groaned.

At once, her friend began treating the sprained ankle.

"While you're doing that," Wy-en-eeks said, "I'll walk on to the point."

"But—"

"You'll see me every minute," she pointed out, with some impatience. And she walked off.

"Well . . . Keep in sight! You don't want some narnauk carrying you off, do you? Or even some Haida."

"Why not?" the princess called back; and she was only half joking. It might be very exciting to be carried off to some strange land by a glorious youth. Instead of just to an ordinary village by ordinary Kuwash. And for one wild moment, she wondered if the vanished princesses had helped themselves vanish.

Wy-en-eeks walked to the point and stood there, watching the sun touch the sea mist with opalescence. Then a flash caught her eye. Ahead of her, beyond the point, a wonderful man moved out into the full sunlight. He was tall. His pale robe caught the light with discs of abalone pearl and with a fringe of—Were they golden feathers? And his head shone. Dazzled by the brightness of the vision, she wondered if he had a cap of golden feathers behind his glistening ear ornaments.

With lips parted in wonder, Wy-en-eeks glided toward him. And caught in some spell, she kept moving toward him. As she neared him, however, her maidenly training touched her, so that she could not look fully at him.

She only sensed that his skin, stretched smoothly over his lean face, was luminous, as though dusted with pearl shell.

Then he spoke. And his voice was vaguely hoarse. "Where are you going, Princess?"

"For a walk." Her voice was a dream voice. "Shall I go with you?"

"If you like." She scarcely breathed it; for it all seemed unreal. As if she would awaken from her dream soon.

"Will you come to see my parents, Princess?"

His words seemed to float around her. His parents? If he was taking her to see his parents, he was planning to marry her. Strange as it seemed, she was being carried off by a supernatural-being-in-human-form, as princesses had been carried off in the old tribal tales. And she could do nothing about it. She could not have said no. She could not have stopped moving along at his side. For her own will had left her. And it was strangely terrifying, yet delightful, to the princess who yearned for excitement.

She was led to a small but elegant canoe. And still in a dream state, she was engulfed in the warm softness of the white wolf fur robes lying in the canoe.

As he paddled silently off, toward the misting waters, a tingling mixture of awe and terror kept her eyes downcast. And swift, darting glances caught only the dazzle of pearl discs and golden feathers.

Then the fog began to close in around them. Wisps of mist moved like wraiths, silent and cold and eerie, shrouding the real world. Islands became vague, unreal shapes floating in a terrible silence.

"Princess," he murmured, "we can't reach my parents' house tonight. But I have a hut on a nearby island."

The hut was a small but beautifully carved house. And when he led her in with his pitchwood torch, its richness caught her breath. It was soft with furs and elegant with carved chests and painted screens, with beautifully carved bowls and hornspoons; it glinted with copper and abalone pearl. Her glance roved about with pleasure as he kindled the readied firewood in the center of the house.

"Refresh yourself, Princess," he invited, opening a chest that was fragrant with sweet hemlocksap cakes. "I must attend to the canoe."

He was so long in returning, the furs were so soft, the fire was so cosy, and the princess was so exhausted from all the excitement, that she fell asleep. Later, she sensed his return and murmured dreamily to him.

Then, suddenly, it was morning. And in the dimness of the light that came in through the smoke hole, she saw him lying asleep. The golden cap was gone. The hair was loosened. And—

Her gasp brought his head up. His hair slipped from its holder and—

His wrinkles slipped with it.

Wy-en-eeks shrank back. "You're . . ." She swallowed in horror.

"The Man-Who-Bound-Up-His-Wrinkles," he said, leering at her. He wiped pearl dust from his face and wagged his hanging wrinkles.

The princess was terrified. She had known the old arrowmaker had strange powers. But she had not known he was an evil sorcerer. And now he had her in his power. Her hand covered her mouth. And her tears fell.

"Why are you weeping?" His voice was hoarser now, and quick with suspicion.

"Oh . . uh . . ." She knew she must not anger him. "Because my family will be anxious about me . . . I can't stay here."

"No. You can't STAY here," he agreed. And his sudden laughter was the laughter of a madman. "I have other plans for you, my pretty princess."

"Plans?" She scarcely breathed it. And her hand slid silently toward her handbasket, where her little woman's-knife waited. But, seeing his sharp eyes watching her, she took out her cosmetic stick and pretended to care for her appearance.

Wy-en-eeks licked her dry lips. "You have plans?" she said, keeping the terror from her voice.

Instead of answering her, he opened a chest, took up a piece of dried salmon, and dipped it into an oil box. Then, after a long, horrible, chewing time, he said, "I will show you how I get my feathers."

"Your feathers?" she said, pretending bright

interest. "Still . . . my father will be anxious." She hoped to remind him that *her* father was a very great chief, a man not to be angered lightly.

"I will show you how I get my feathers," he repeated, glaring at her.

"Oh. That will be . . . very interesting," Wy-en-eeks said. No doubt the other princesses had been shown how he got his feathers. And *they* had never come back. She kept her hand close to her handbasket as she readied herself to go out.

As she stepped into the small canoe—now stripped of its fine furs—her eyes were alert for some familiar landmark. But she saw nothing she recognized.

The fog had been washed away by a rainstorm. And now the sea and the sky were blue, and the snow-capped mountains. The clouds were as white as the surf and the flashing seagulls. And as they moved out, kelp heads bobbed, glittering dark brown in a sea that seemed suddenly deep and strange and terrifyingly lonely.

They rounded an island.

"That rock!" he said, so suddenly that she jumped. "I get my feathers on that rock."

It was almost an island. A grim, jagged gray mass thrust up from the sea floor. It seemed a strangely sinister place. For no seagulls wheeled and screamed above it. No seals poked up glistening heads around it. Instead, there was only uncanny stillness and silence. There was only one tree—the dead bones of one tree; and its skeleton arms seemed to wait for. . . . For what evil birds? Wy-en-eeks swallowed and clutched her handbasket.

Then she saw the small curve of a beach, a beach that would disappear when the tide rose.

He paddled straight to it. "Now you will see how I get my feathers," he said, motioning her out.

With the quick grace of a seagoing people, Wy-en-eeks leaped onto the tiny beach. Then she turned, alert to cut the rope and grab the canoe while he was tying it to a boulder.

But, instead of leaping ashore too, the Man-Who-Had-Bound-Up-His-Wrinkles pushed off with the shriek of a madman.

"Now you will see how I get my feathers," he screeched at her. He held his scrawny arms up to the sky. And shouted.

"A LIVING FEAST! FOR YOUR GOLDEN FEATHERS!" he shouted.

Four times he shouted it at the sky.

"A LIVING FEAST! FOR YOUR GOLDEN FEATHERS!

"A LIVING FEAST! FOR YOUR GOLDEN FEATHERS!

"A LIVING FEAST! FOR YOUR GOLDEN FEATHERS!"

Then he paddled off, laughing with maniacal glee.

And her horrified eyes saw a small darkness, high in the air. As she watched, openmouthed, the darkness grew into a flock of birds.

She was the living feast. For THEIR golden feathers.

Wy-en-eeks glanced wildly about her. But where could she hide on a grim, jagged gray rock?

A squeak caught her ear. Then a small flash of white caught her eye. A white mouse! It darted under a low ledge of outjutting rock at one side of the beach.

A cave?

She flung herself after the mouse. And there was a cave, a low, shallow cave. Frantic with haste, she wriggled into it, feet first. Then, grabbing a mat of golden brown seaweed to peep through, she pulled her head in just as the birds began to circle the dark rock.

They were horrible big birds with long glinting black beaks and scrawny yellow necks. But as the flock turned away from her, their backs glinted gold in the sun. And as she watched, peering through the seaweed, she saw a fall of feathers, like a golden snowfall.

For their golden feathers!

But there was no *living feast* waiting for them.

They rose as one and circled the rock four times, screaming in unearthly fury at the offending rock.

Wy-en-eeks shrank back. And her teeth were chattering. Her limbs were trembling. They would find her. Or, if they didn't find her, they would wait. And the tide would rise, flooding her shallow cave with the icy water that not even the strongest man could live in for long. The water was already trickling in. She felt its icy wetness on her body.

Silence.

Had they gone?

She dared to peer out again through the seaweed.

No. They were not gone. They were settled like the Fruit of Death on the skeleton tree.

She swallowed. And waited.

The tide was rising. Already its cold was numbing her.

Then, again, that scream of fury. She covered her ears and her eyes as she heard them circle the rock again, four times.

Then—at long, long last!—the sound faded away, upward.

The birds were gone. And the girl, almost as terrified of the rising tide as of the gruesome birds, crawled out of the shallow cave. Faint with fright, she lay against the slanting rock, letting the sun warm her.

What if they should come back? Now! When there was no place to hide.

There was no sign of the birds. And no sign of the terrible old man and his canoe. But *he* would come back to gather his feathers and gloat over her bones. He would see her, and call down the terrible birds again. Wy-en-eeks glanced round in panic. Perhaps there was another hiding place? Now that her cave was flooding.

Scrambling wildly over the rocks, she came suddenly on a small pile of bones, with a handbasket lying near them. A basket with a Wolf crest! Those were the bones of the vanished Wolf princess.

Trembling with terror, and searching wildly for a hiding place, Wy-en-eeks scrambled this way and that. She came on two more piles of bones, with two more handbaskets.

But she found no place to hide.

Though she shrank back from the golden feathers, she made herself gather up a few of them. And with a prayer that they would have power for her, she put them into her handbasket, close to her little woman's-knife. If she escaped, she would have proof of the evil deeds of the old arrowmaker.

The day stretched on and on and on, endlessly, while the tide crept up the rock.

Then the tide began to ebb. And her terror grew, waiting for the old man. He would come when the beach surfaced again. But what if he came after slack water? When her cave was flooding again! When there was no place to hide.

As she watched the seaweed laid bare on the rocks, hope sprang up. Perhaps she could gather a great pile of it. Enough to cover her. She began frantically pulling it free.

He did not come with the evening low tide. And the brief darkness of a northern summer night brought her respite. For he would not come in the dark to gather his golden feathers.

It was low tide and morning when she saw his canoe rounding the island. She could hear him singing. It was a mad, jubilant singing. It reached her ears as she wriggled part of her body back into the cave, and as she covered the rest of her body with the golden brown seaweed. Then she held still, her hand clutching her little woman's-knife.

No doubt he was catching the glint of golden feathers on the rock, for his song grew wilder. He paddled straight to the little beach, leaped out, and tied his canoe to a boulder. Still singing his mad song, he began scrambling up the rock.

Almost holding her breath, Wy-en-eeks waited.

He was well up the rock before she dared to jump up, slash the rope, push the canoe off with all her might, and leap in. She grasped the paddle and plied it with all her strength.

He heard the grate of the canoe. And with a shriek of rage, he came tearing down the rock.

But Wy-en-eeks was well offshore. She was out in the deep numbing water where not even the strongest man could live long.

"I came to get you," he yelled at her. "I came to take you home to your father. I haven't been able to sleep, worrying about you. So I came to get you."

"You came to get the feathers," she shouted back at him. And for a moment, she dared to stop paddling.

"And now," she screamed at him. "Now you shall give the feast you promised them for their golden feathers. Now you shall die as the princess died. As you meant me to die."

Holding her arms up to the sky, she shouted as he had shouted.

"A LIVING FEAST! FOR YOUR GOLDEN FEATHERS!" she shouted. Four times she shouted as he had shouted.

"A LIVING FEAST! FOR YOUR GOLDEN FEATHERS!

"A LIVING FEAST! FOR YOUR GOLDEN FEATHERS!

"A LIVING FEAST! FOR YOUR GOLDEN FEATHERS!"

Wy-en-eeks shrank down into the canoe as she saw the small patch of darkness, high in the air. Then, with a gasp of fear, she plied her paddle, rushing away from the rock as the small darkness grew into a terrible flock of birds with long glinting black beaks and scrawny yellow necks. She heard the wild screams of the old man. And in near panic, she scanned the passing islands, looking for some familiar landmark.

At long last she saw a point of land she recognized. And she fled straight for home. Soon she saw the canoes that were out searching for her. But only when her small canoe had grated on the pebbles of her home beach did she drop her paddle and sink down in utter exhaustion.

Voices were crying out for joy. Arms were lifting her. Warm robes were engulfing her.

"Wy-en-eeks! Wy-en-eeks!" her mother was sobbing in relief.

"Where is my father?" Wy-en-eeks asked her.

"He is being comforted by his friends," her mother answered, pointing toward a house at the far end of the village.

But already the great chief was on his way to greet his daughter.

She took a golden feather out of her handbasket.

"A feather of the old arrowmaker," people gasped, crowding about to see it.

"This is what the princesses died for," Wy-en-eeks told her father. "What it was meant that I should die for."

"The feathers of the old arrowmaker," people murmured to one another. "HE took the princesses."

"Invite all their fathers," Wy-en-eeks said. "And I will tell them about their daughters."

Messengers leaped into their canoes and raced upriver to the grieving chiefs and their families. And when they were all gathered in her father's house, Wy-en-eeks told her story. And clan dirges wailed through the great cedar house.

Next day, all the people went with the Eagle princess to the terrible rock.

First, her family landed on the tiny beach to gather the golden feathers. And then, while the others went sadly onto the rock to gather up their vanished princesses' bones, her family went on to the house on the island to strip it of its riches. For, in those days, things were done in the proper way. Then the family returned to the village to prepare for the grieving people.

Once more in her father's house, Wy-en-eeks put on her robe of white wolf fur. She put on her Eagle headdress and her glistening abalone ear ornaments. In the ring of sea lion bristles that circled her headdress, she put eagle down, the symbol of peace and friendship. And she danced a graceful dance of welcome for the grieving guests, dipping her head to waft a snow of eagle down over the families.

Then her father, with great ceremony, divided the golden feathers and the old arrowmaker's riches among the chiefs who had lost their daughters. For, among proper people, those who had been deprived must be compensated, to keep all things equal.

Suddenly, to everyone's amazement, a white mouse appeared from nowhere. And in a scurrying, merry little dance, it circled the fire four times.

"The white mouse!" Wy-en-eeks called out. "The white mouse who helped me!"

But the white mouse was gone. And in its place stood a tiny old woman in a dark mouseskin robe. She gazed about at the people with big, busy, mouse eyes. And her nose twitched.

"Mouse Woman!" people cried out. Then they hushed themselves in awe. For Mouse Woman was a narnauk.

But already Mouse Woman had vanished.

Or had she vanished?

Wy-en-eeks felt a tug at her robe. And there stood the tiniest of narnauks.

"You were the one who helped me," the princess cried out in delight. "I should have known it." For wasn't Mouse Woman the one who always helped young people who had been tricked into trouble? "You helped me, Grandmother."

"Yes, my dear." The voice was a squeaky little sound in the hush of the great house.

Then Mouse Woman seemed to stand waiting.

For what?

"Of course," Wy-en-eeks breathed, remembering her manners. For Mouse Woman was known to be a stickler for proper behavior.

"Of course," the princess breathed again. For those who had given service were to be given something in return. The obligation of a gift, including the gift of service, was sacred in the Northwest. It was the great law that kept all things equal.

She took an ornament from her dark hair—a golden feather tied with a cluster of prettily dyed woolen tassels. It was a proper gift since the wool held the spirit power of the mountain sheep it had come from; while the golden feather held who-knew-what power. And with graceful ceremony, she handed it to the little old woman.

There was a gasp from the people.

Wy-en-eeks glanced about in alarm.

Then she flushed with concern. For, of course, she should have tossed the gift into the fire to transform it into its essence for the use of a spirit being like Mouse Woman. She turned anxious eyes on the imperious little narnauk.

But Mouse Woman was busy. Her ravelly little fingers were tearing the prettily-dyed woolen tassels into a lovely, loose, nesty pile of mountain sheep's wool. And her soft sigh showed that this was strangely satisfying.

Then, while Wy-en-eeks's mouth was still open, the tiniest but most proper of all the narnauks vanished.

The Sedna Legend

The story of Sedna, the Eskimo sea goddess, is one of the most powerful and best known of the Eskimo creation myths. The themes of betrayal, revenge, death, and supernatural transformation are starkly drawn. This retelling for children is a modified form of versions in Franz Boas and J. W. Bilby. [From *The Day Tuk Became a Hunter and Other Eskimo Stories,* retold by Ronald Melzack (Dodd, Mead, 1967).]

Long ago, there were no seals or walruses for Eskimos to hunt. There were reindeer and birds, bears and wolves, but there were no animals in the sea. There was, at that time, an Eskimo girl called Sedna who lived with her father in an igloo by the seashore. Sedna was beautiful, and she was courted by men from her own village, and by others who came from faraway lands. But none of these men pleased her and she refused to marry.

One day, a handsome young hunter from a strange far-off country paddled his kayak across the shining sea toward the shores of Sedna's home. He wore beautiful clothes and carried an ivory spear.

He paused at the shore's edge, and called to Sedna, "Come with me! Come to the land of the birds, where there is never hunger and where my tent is made of the most beautiful skins. You will rest on soft bear skins, your lamp will always be filled with oil, and you will always have meat."

Sedna at first refused. Again he told her of the home in which they would live, the rich furs and ivory necklaces that he would give her. Sedna could no longer resist. She left her father's home and joined the young hunter.

When they were out at sea, the young man dropped his paddle into the water. Sedna stared with fright as he raised his hands towards the sky, and, before her eyes, they were transformed into huge wings—the wings of a Loon. He was no man at all, but a spirit bird, with the power to become a human being.

Sedna sat on the Loon's back and they flew towards his home. When they landed on an island in the sea, Sedna discovered that the Loon had lied to her. Her new home was cold and windy, and she had to eat fish brought to her by the Loon and by the other birds that shared their island.

Soon she was lonesome and afraid, and she cried sadly, "Oh father, if you knew how sad I am, you would come to me and carry me away in your kayak. I am a stranger here. I am cold and miserable. Please come, and take me back.''

When a year had passed and the sea was calm, Sedna's father set out to visit her in her far-off land. She greeted him joyfully and begged him to take her back. He lifted her onto his boat, and raced across the sea towards home.

When the Loon spirit returned, he found his wife gone. The other birds on the island told him that she had fled with her father. He immediately took the shape of a man, and followed in his kayak. When Sedna's father saw him coming, he covered his daughter with the furs he kept in his boat.

Swiftly the Loon spirit rushed alongside in his kayak.

"Let me see my wife," he cried.

Sedna's father refused.

"Sedna," he called out, "come back with me! No man could love you as much as I do."

But Sedna's kayak flashed across the water. The Loonman stopped paddling. Sadly, slowly, he raised his hands towards the sky and once again they became wings. He flew over the kayak that carried his Sedna away from him. He hovered over the boat, crying the strange, sad call of the Loon. Then he plunged down into the sea.

The moment the Loon spirit disappeared, the sea waves began to swell up in fury. The sea gods were angry that Sedna had betrayed her husband. The kayak rose and fell as huge waves lashed against it. Sedna's father was terrified, and to save himself he pushed Sedna overboard. Sedna rose to the surface and her fingers gripped the edge of the kayak. But her father, frenzied with fear that he would be killed by the vengeful sea spirits, pulled out a knife and stabbed her hands.

Then, it is said, an astonishing thing happened, perhaps because the Loon spirit or the sea spirits had willed it: the blood that flowed from Sedna's hands congealed in the water, taking different shapes, until suddenly two seals emerged from it. Sedna fell back into the sea, and coming back again, gripped the boat even more tightly. Again her father stabbed her hands and the blood flowed, and this time walruses emerged from the blood-red sea. In desperate fear for his life, he stabbed her hands a

third time, and the blood flowed through the water, congealed, and the whales grew out of it.

At last the storm ended. Sedna sank to the bottom of the sea, and all the sea animals that were born from her blood followed her.

Sedna's father, exhausted and bitter, at last arrived home. He entered his igloo and fell into a deep sleep. Outside, Sedna's dog, who had been her friend since childhood, howled as the wind blew across the land.

That night, Sedna commanded the creatures of the sea that emerged from her blood to bring her father and her dog to her. The sea animals swam furiously in front of her father's igloo. The tides ran higher and higher. They washed up the beach until they demolished the igloo, and they carried Sedna's father and her dog down to the depths of the sea. There they joined Sedna, and all three have lived ever since in the land of the waters.

To this day, Eskimo hunters pray to Sedna, goddess of the seas, who commands all the sea animals. She is vengeful and bitter, and men beg her to release the animals that were born of her so that they might eat. By her whim, a man successfully harpoons seals and walruses or is swept away from land by the stormy seas. The spirits of the great Medicine Men swim down to her home and comb her hair because her hand still hurts. And if they comb her hair well, she releases a seal, a walrus, or a whale.

Anpao Is Born

This story, drawn from Blackfeet and Kiowa sources, is taken from a novel-length cycle of hero-tales about Anpao, son of the sun. Anpao's quest is interwoven with other Indian legends to create an epic chronicle of Native American history and folklore. Jamake Highwater, the Native American reteller, explains that, although Anpao is based on the famous Blackfeet hero Scarface, he is primarily the author's fabrication. "I created Anpao out of many stories of the boyhood of early Indians, and from my own experience as well, in order to make an Indian 'Ulysses' who could become the central dramatic character in the saga of Indian life in North America." [From Jamake Highwater, *Anpao: An American Indian Odyssey* (Lippincott, 1977).]

Once again the sacred pipe was lighted and, under the new stars and among all the people of the land, it was passed around the great circle where the twins sat with the old swan-woman. The campfire rose into delicately twisting flames and the drums sang.

The old woman smiled with satisfaction. "I have told you the story of how the world began. But that is just the beginning of the story. Now a new day has come. Do you see the Sun that begins to awaken in the East?"

Anpao stood up slowly and opened his arms to the sky. He felt as if he were floating in the misty light of dawn. He had to concentrate in order to keep his toes touching the ground.

Oapna had fallen asleep while the old woman told her story, and he lay wrapped in a blanket of swan feathers. But even in his sleep he seemed to ebb and drift in the new light of the Sun.

The old woman chuckled quietly as she laid more branches on the fire and glanced at Anpao. "You are confused. But that is as it should be. Did you know that your name has a special meaning among the people who live high upon the prairie? And do you remember what your name means?"

Anpao nodded his head dreamily, trying to focus on the old woman who faded away and then gradually came back again. As she spoke she crept close and pressed her little face to his.

Illustration by Daniel San Souci, copyright © 1981 by Daniel San Souci, from the book *Song of Sedna,* adapted by Robert D. San Souci. Reprinted by permission of Doubleday & Company, Inc.

"Ah," she murmured so softly that he could barely hear what she was saying, "the *dawn!* That is what Old Man said, is it not? And that is who you are, foolish boy!" And suddenly she cackled loudly and ran wildly around the astonished youth.

"*Anpao, An-PAY-oh!* It is the dawn! It is the dawn! Ha, you do not know. You do not know your name and you do not know how the world began, and I do not think that you even know where you came from!"

The old woman continued to cackle to herself as she raced around and around Anpao so quickly that he could see only a blur.

"Now!" yelped the old woman, stopping abruptly and staring at Anpao. "Listen carefully! Watch me carefully—every movement! You are coming under the power of the great medicine of the pipe, my boy-person; that is what is happening to you. So watch *everything.* For this is your dream, Anpao. It is your dream alone, and no one else can dream your dream and no one else can remember it. Listen carefully, Anpao, for I shall tell *everything.* I shall whisper many secrets in your ear. Listen!" she murmured, as she slid soundlessly to the brink of the roaring fire and smiled with blazing little eyes, stepping gradually into the twisting orange flames and tilting her head to the side as she smiled blissfully.

"*Ah,*" she purred, as flames came from her mouth like words, "*ahhhh-yes-my-little-boy-person.* Can you feel it now? You are tinier than the tiniest of things. Anpao is a child-seed, a tiny seed and nothing more. Anpao, can you feel it? Anpao is being born. He is the tiniest of tiny things. Take care and remember this well, Anpao, for you will not be born again!"

Then she pointed her flaming fingers toward the sky, where the mouth of the earth was open and a great emanation of light poured ceaselessly into the dissolving night.

*   *   *

"It was a sad time. The woman whose only child had died wept when she saw the dawn," the old woman was chanting softly into the fire. "Listen," she murmured. "I shall tell . . ."

Each day the woman wept and each day she longed for her child. But she could not find Old Man to plead with him, and she would not sit at her loom and weave, or sing songs for her husband, so great was her misery at the loss of her child.

On the morning that Old Man vanished into the earth, the woman wandered out of her village by the river and walked aimlessly into the light of the dawn, hoping to find Old Man and recover her child from death.

She walked all day and she walked all the next day and the day after that. Each morning she found that she was no closer to the dawn than she had been the day before. No matter how far she walked, or how many mountains she climbed, the dawn always evaded her. Finally, just when she was about to give up and return unhappily to her village, she stopped by a lake and saw in the water that she had become old and ugly from her grief.

So she sat by the lake and combed her hair and put ornaments of shell and stone around her neck, and slowly the old age retreated from her face and she was beautiful again. At that moment, the Sun, who was dawning, caught sight of this beautiful woman and fell in love with her. The woman could feel the warmth of the Sun on her shoulders when he smiled at her, and, with renewed hope of finding Old Man, she stood up and started again toward the dawn.

Whereas previously the woman had vainly run toward the dawn without being able to touch it, today she could easily get a footing in the rays of sunlight. And so she began to run upward into the sky toward the dawn.

It was in this way that the woman went up to the World-Above-the-World without dying. She went up while she was still alive and very beautiful, and she met the Sun and stayed with him and had a new child, whom she named Anpao.

The woman, the Sun, and Anpao lived in seclusion so that the Moon, who was the first wife of the Sun, would not discover that her husband had taken a human wife. They lived in the world that is behind the clouds, so far away that people see only its blue floor which is the luminous roof of the earth.

One day the Sun went to his old mother and asked her, "My mother, will you make my mistress a tipi? She is a young woman, and she should have a tipi of her own, but she does not know how to make one." His mother agreed and made a handsome white tipi, painted with images of her son's proud deeds. This the Sun asked of his mother so the woman would not be lonely for her village or her husband or her lost child. And so the couple and their child, Anpao, lived happily in the beautiful tipi in the World-Above-the-World. And for a time the Moon knew nothing of it.

Each morning the Sun awoke and washed his face with the clouds of the night which, as they dissolved into water, made the sky turn very blue and clear. While he washed, his human wife made breakfast. After eating, the Sun took up his bow and his quiver of arrows and went out into the sky to hunt for food for his family.

"What are you going to do today?" the Sun asked as he was leaving the white tipi one morning.

"I think," answered his mistress, "that I will dig some roots. If you shine brightly for me, it will make the day nice and the wild potatoes will ripen quickly. I think I will take my digging stick and go to gather some wild potatoes."

"Yes," the Sun agreed. "And I will bring back some deer meat. And when you go to dig for potatoes," asked the Sun, "will you take Anpao with you or leave him here with my mother?"

"Oh!" the woman exclaimed. "I would not go anywhere without my Anpao!"

"Good," said the Sun. "But there is one thing you must remember, and you must also tell little Anpao to remember—neither of you should ever forget it. Do not dig up a wild potato if the top has been eaten off."

The woman laughed. "But why?"

"Because it will bring misfortune. And that is all I know of it." Then the Sun left the tipi.

The woman and her boy wandered on foot all the day. She showed him how to use the digging stick, and by dusk their skin sack was filled with wild potatoes. The Sun had kept his promise and brought a fat deer, which the wife cooked with the potatoes. And in the night,

while the tipi glowed from the light of their fire, the family had a fine dinner. Afterward, the Sun lighted his pipe of carved stone and told stories of Old Man, who had created everything.

When the morning came, the Sun again prepared to go hunting after breakfast. "Are you going to gather potatoes again today?" he asked.

"Yes. They are ripe and I want to dig enough so I can dry some for the winter when the ground is cold and nothing grows."

"That is good, but always remember what I told you: do not dig a potato from which the top has been eaten."

"Yes, yes, yes," the wife said impatiently. "I will remember. I will not forget."

The woman and her son, Anpao, spent the entire day collecting wild potatoes. As she walked, bent over from the large sack of potatoes on her back, she saw a large potato plant just beside the path. Its top had been partially eaten. "Ah-ha," she muttered to Anpao. "Perhaps a powerful creature the Sun fears has eaten the top off that potato. I had better not dig it." But instead of continuing toward her tipi, the woman lingered, looking down at the potato and wondering why it should be forbidden to dig it. "I will dig it!" she said aloud. "It will just fill my sack. After all, what can it hurt?"

So the woman knelt with her digging stick and tried to pry the plant from the ground. It was a difficult task, and at first the plant would not budge. But suddenly it came free, and the woman fell back and stared in amazement at the hole she had made in the ground of the World-Above-the-World. Instead of a hollow of soil where her digging stick had turned the potato over, there was a large round hole filled with sky. Trembling and clutching her son to her, she bent forward to peer through the hole.

She gasped and leaped to her feet in fear. There, far below, she could see the entire earth whirling in its mantle of clouds. The great water of salt was there just as the Old Man had made it. There were the rippling prairies of grass, the willows and poplars which grew along the winding rivers. What an amazing sight for the woman to see: the immense jagged rocks of the mountains and the boiling springs and geysers; the great river of white water, and the redwoods, which had grown almost to touch the World-Above-the-World since the woman had last seen them when she was a child on earth. She could even see the camp of her people where happy women played with their children.

"Oh!" the woman exclaimed in anger. "That is why the Sun did not want me to dig a potato from which the top had been eaten! He is jealous and was afraid that I would grow lonely if I saw my village!"

And indeed the sight made her very sad.

For a long time the woman sat quietly beside the hole in the sky, watching her people and crying with loneliness for them. When finally it began to get dark and the woman knew that her husband was on his way home, she took the forbidden potato plant and resealed the hole which she had made and hurried to the tipi, hoping she would arrive before the Sun did.

When the Sun came home, the woman told him nothing about the hole she had made in the sky.

Each day, after that, when the Sun went hunting, his wife would slip away to the place where she had made the hole. She would pull up the potato plant and peep through and watch her own human people. It was autumn in the world far below, so the people there were drying meat and preparing sinew, which the women would use to stitch the winter moccasins.

The mistress of the Sun was preparing sinew too. But she did not intend to make moccasins. Soon she had a coil of sinew so large that she had to hide it under her bedding, where her husband would not discover it. Each day she braided the sinew into a long rope. And each day she hid it under her bedding.

Whenever the Sun came home, the woman and child were in their tipi, ready for dinner. The Sun never saw his mistress do anything wrong. She kept faith with him as far as he knew and it did not occur to him to distrust her.

But during each day, when the Sun was away, the woman went to the place where she had made the hole and lowered the rope through it in order to see if it was long enough to reach all the way down to the earth. Little by little

it spanned the great distance between sky and earth.

Finally the day came when the rope of sinew was almost long enough to touch the ground below. The woman was very happy as she searched the forest near the hole for a root strong enough to hold her weight. Finally she found a very strong root and tied the rope to it, hiding it under the leaves. Then she put the potato plant back into the hole and hurried home, carrying Anpao on her back.

The Sun reached the tipi first that night, and when his mistress came home he looked at her sternly. "Where have you been? And why have you stayed away so late?"

"I have been gathering wood for the fire," she said. But the Sun looked at her suspiciously as she put down her small bundle of firewood and built her cooking fire silently. As she cooked, she secretly planned her escape from the World-Above-the-World. She had grown tired of the Sun and longed for the evening and the night among her own people. "After all," she said to herself, "I only came into the sky to search for my child who had died, and I found him in little Anpao. So there is no reason for me to stay here or to fear the Sun. I have my own husband on earth and I have won over death both by entering the World-Above-the-World without dying and by reclaiming my child from the Sun. I am too clever to be caught!"

As soon as the Sun had left the tipi the next morning, the woman quickly gathered up her belongings and hurried to the hole in the sky. There she retied the rope to the root and then she tied the other end to her child Anpao.

"Do not cry," she whispered to the little boy, "you are made equally of earth and of sky, so nothing can happen to you. Do not whimper, Anpao; for soon we will be in our world where you will meet your own people!"

Then she carefully lowered Anpao through the hole in the sky, inch by inch, until the entire rope had been used. It stretched from the strong root in the World-Above-the-World through the hole in the sky—down, down, down . . . *almost* to the earth below. The rope was not quite long enough.

"Oh!" cried the woman. "There is no time

to make more rope! I will have to climb down and jump to the earth with little Anpao in my arms!"

And she quickly climbed through the hole and began her descent.

When she reached the end of the rope, she was very tired. With the last of her energy, she dangled off the end of the rope, but still she could not touch the earth. It was still far below her. She did not dare to untie Anpao, in order to make the rope longer, for fear of letting him fall. She was desperate and she cried out. But no one on earth heard her, and no one saw her and Anpao swinging helplessly in the wind.

"Oh!" the woman sighed. "I have wanted too much and now I have gotten nothing for all my efforts! Each time I have wanted too much and each time I have gotten nothing, but still I did not learn!"

The Sun came home to his tipi very tired that night and was surprised to find that his mistress and son were not there. He asked his old mother, but she had not seen them. He asked the stars, but they would not answer. So he went into the tipi and put some wood on the dying fire and waited for his family to come home. But still they did not return and it was now the darkest part of the night.

The Sun grew very weary but he could not sleep. He was worried about his son and his mistress. When the Moon came into the dark sky, she laughed at the Sun. "Ho ho, the Sun cannot see despite all his gold. He cannot see what is happening to him! Ho ho, go and look for your mistress from the World-Below. See what she has done to you, my foolish husband!" And the Moon laughed and went behind a cloud to mock the Sun, for she had recently discovered that he had a secret wife and child.

The Sun became angry and flames burst from his head as he ran from his tipi and searched the ground. By the Moon's bright light, the woman's trail was easy for the Sun to follow. "Foolish woman!" her husband barked. "She was in such a hurry to run away from me that she did not even brush over her tracks!"

At last the Sun came to the place where there was a hole in the sky. Instantly, he understood what had happened and looked down through the hole. He could see his small son, tied halfway down, and the wife hanging at the end of the rope, her moccasins just brushing the tips of the tallest trees of the earth. Now the Sun was very angry. He roared only once and then reached into the sky and plucked the branch of a willow and bent it into a hoop. At the touch of his hands, the hoop dried instantly and turned a deep red, for red is the color of the Sun. Then the Sun stood by the hole in the sky with the ring in his strong hands.

"Go, hoop," he ordered, "roll down the rope. Jump over the child and do not harm him. Roll down the rope, hoop! And when you reach the woman at the end, hit her on the head and kill her! This is what the Sun commands of you, and if you do it well, you and all your children will live in the shade beside the ponds and never feel the anger of the Sun. Go now, hoop, and do what I have ordered!"

The Sun spit on the hoop four times and, with a flash of his hand, he rolled it down the rope. The hoop flew into motion like a wheel of fire, spinning from the World-Above-the-World down the long rope the woman had made. The fiery hoop leaped over Anpao without touching him. But when it got to the mistress of the Sun, it burst into flame and made a noise like thunder. The woman opened her mouth and reached with her feet for the grass of the earth, but the wind swung her up into the air farther away from the ground. Then the hoop struck the woman, and her head fell back and her neck bent and she was dead.

When the root that held the rope in the World-Above-the-World felt the tug of the woman's dead body, it sagged with pity for her and the rope slipped away. The Sun roared fiercely and snatched for the rope as it whipped past him and through the hole in the sky. But he was not fast enough. The dead woman dropped to the earth. And the little boy, Anpao, fell too, plummeting down and landing on his mother so hard that her belly was split open, and where her blood stained his cheek a deep scar appeared.

When Anpao awakened from the terrible impact of the fall, he could not remember that he was the son of the Sun. All he could recall was that his name was Anpao. He looked around and found himself in a new world and he was afraid and began to cry. He could not see his father the Sun who stormed in anger and made the sky grow dark. He could only see his mother where she lay silent in the grass. Anpao was afraid to leave her side, and so he clung close to her and wept. But she did not move or speak, and soon it became very cold and dark as the grieving Sun slouched away in a great gloom. Anpao was alone and hungry and frightened.

Near the place where the mistress of the Sun had fallen to the earth, an old woman lived all by herself. She was very lonely and had no one to talk to and no one to hunt for her. But she was very wise. One day a stranger had given her a marvelous gourd. She had dried its seeds instead of eating them, and when the seeds were very dry, she carefully planted them in the ground near her house.

Since that day the old woman had a bright green garden topped with fruit. Every day at dawn, she would go from her tipi to the field to work among the vines and to sing sweetly to them so they would grow.

When the old woman was working in her field she always left her tipi flap open. Perhaps, she hoped, someone might come to visit her. And if her tipi were open, the person might not pass by but might rest inside until she came home at night. Then she could have a nice visit!

Anpao grew so hungry that he could stay with his dead mother no longer. He wandered away and found the old woman's tipi. He went inside, hoping to find something to eat and a fire at which to warm himself. But no sooner had Anpao entered the tipi than he became terrified. What if a horrible spirit lived here! He sobbed in fear and ran away, hiding beside his dead mother and cowering in the shadows of the tall grass.

But he had left his footprints on the floor of the tipi, and when the old woman came home at nightfall, she knew immediately that she had had a visitor. "But whose child could this be who came to my tipi?" she asked herself as she built a fire and began to cook dinner. "Oh,

how fine it would be if the child came back and stayed to keep me company!"

The next morning Anpao awoke and was so tormented by hunger that he cautiously went back to the tipi of the old woman. But once again he was frightened and only stayed long enough to snatch the bit of food which the old woman had been wise enough to leave out for him. Then he ran back to his mother's side and tugged at her and offered her some of his food. But she would not respond. So he wept as he ate.

When the old lady returned to her tipi that night, she was delighted to see Anpao's fresh footprints. "Aha," she murmured happily. "Now how can I get this child and keep him here as my son?"

So each day the old woman left food where the child could reach it. When she came home at night the food was always gone, but there was no trace of the child except the little footprints all about the tipi. "Aha, he has escaped again. Now, let me see, how am I going to capture this marvelous child?" she wondered. Then she sat by her fire and listened to the owl and listened to the cricket. And eventually she thought out a plan.

Early the next day, the old woman lay down on the floor of her tipi close to the poles that made the sides. She lay silently until finally she heard someone coming.

She was a holy woman and understood many things. "Aha," she whispered. "Something not quite human is coming." She watched the door, and soon a very beautiful child with a curious scar on his face crept into her tipi. After seeing that no one moved inside, the boy quickly found the food the old woman had left for him. He sat on the floor, where he became so engrossed in eating that he did not notice when the old woman stood up in front of the door. But when she spoke to him, the child jumped to his feet in a terrible panic and tried to run past her. She prevented him from escaping, and when he hid under a fur robe, she tried to comfort him as he lay half-hidden.

"No, no, little sunshine-child, you cannot go to your mother anymore. I have found her body in the grass and she is dead. You have no mother, and you must not cry forever. I will be your grandmother. And we will live here and be happy."

To comfort Anpao further, she picked him up from his hiding place and carried him on her back the way his mother had carried him. Then she sat down on the floor, holding him snugly, and very soon the child stopped trembling and whimpering and fell asleep.

"This is no ordinary child." The old woman smiled knowingly. "I can feel his great power and I can see his future like the rings of an ancient tree."

The next morning the little boy awakened and smiled, for he saw the old woman huddled over the fire cooking something that smelled very good.

"Hello, little sunshine," she said and smiled when he crept next to her and peered hungrily into the fire. "You must call me Grandmother Spider, for I am the Spider Woman, the mother and comforter of all living beings and all things that grow. And you—who are you and who is your father?" But Anpao could not remember. "And what will we call you, little sunshine?"

At this the boy stood up proudly and said, "I am called Anpao!"

And so Anpao and Grandmother Spider lived very happily in the tipi near the green gourd field. In the golden light of Anpao's great father, Grandmother Spider made bowls of clay and baked them in the sunshine until they dried. Then she baked them again in the embers of her cooking fire. She gathered the thorny leaves of the yucca and coiled them into baskets. And then Anpao and Grandmother Spider went out into the autumn days to collect dried plants and to bring them home, where they were stored for the winter in the new baskets. Then they hung the yellow gourds to dry and they smoked meat over the fire.

When Anpao left the tipi in the morning, Grandmother Spider would say, "Look well, my child, at whatever you see." And in the evening, on his return for dinner, she would question him about every detail of what he had seen that day.

"Tell me, Anpao," Grandmother Spider would ask, "on which side of the tree is the lighter-colored bark? On which side do trees have the most regular branches?"

Every evening Grandmother Spider asked Anpao to name all the new birds he had seen during the day. He would name them according to their color or the shape of their bills or their songs or the location of their nests. Then Grandmother Spider would teach Anpao the correct names of the birds. If occasionally Anpao named a bird correctly by himself, Grandmother Spider would commend him warmly and make him feel very proud.

"Tell me," Grandmother Spider would ask at dinner, "how do you know if there are fish in a lake?"

"Because they would surely jump out of the water for flies at midday!"

Then she would smile patiently and explain. "What do you think, my child, makes the little pebbles group together under the shallow water? What makes the pretty curved marks in the sandy bottom and on the little sandbank? Where do you find the fish-eating birds? Have the inlets and outlets of the lake anything to do with my question, Anpao? Think on it, my child; think on it carefully. The world is full of signs and you must learn to read them."

If Anpao was lazy and did not make careful observations of the world around him, Grandmother Spider would sigh and say to him, "Anpao, my child, you must follow the example of the wolf. Even when he is surprised and runs for his very life, he will always pause to take one last careful look at you before he runs into his hiding place. So you too must take a second careful look at everything you see. All the animals are our teachers, but we must watch for the signs they give us if we are to learn anything about the world.

"For instance, you must never approach a grizzly bear's den from the front. You must steal up behind and then throw your blanket or a stone in front of his hole. He does not usually rush out for it; first he puts his head out and listens carefully, and then he comes out indifferently and sits on his great haunches on the mound in front of his cave before he makes any attack. While he is exposing himself in this way, my boy, you must aim at his heart. Always be as collected and calm as the animal himself. It is from the creatures that we can learn to be clever. These are the lessons of the world, and each day you can increase your wisdom if you will only look and keep all that you see.''

*   *   *

One day when Grandmother Spider was preparing to go out to work, Anpao asked if he could stay home. "Don't you want to go with me into the field and sing to the plants?" the old woman asked.

"No, Grandmother Spider," he said, "I would rather stay here today and play with my hoop."

"Very well, you may stay home, because you are a good boy and always work very hard. But you must be careful not to throw your hoop into the air, or something bad could happen to you. Mind what your old Grandmother Spider has told you, for she knows many things. You may roll the hoop on the earth but you must not throw it into the air. Do you understand?"

"Yes, Grandmother," answered Anpao, but naturally he wondered what could happen to him if he threw his hoop high into the air. "Ah," he thought, "nothing bad will happen to *me!*"

So when Grandmother Spider had left, he took his hoop and went outside into the sunshine. He played with the hoop for a short time—then he could no longer resist the temptation to toss it into the air to see what might happen. Before the Sun could warn him, Anpao tossed the hoop. Up and up it went, as high as the world from which Anpao had fallen. Then, very gracefully and slowly, the hoop began to fall from the sky. As it fell, it moved faster and still faster until it landed right on Anpao's head with a terrible crash. For a moment the child stood in amazement. The hoop went right down through his entire body and cut him in two!

"Oh!"

"Oh!"

That is what two voices said at exactly the same time. There was no longer one child stand-

ing there, but two. They were identical except that one was right-handed and the other was left-handed.

"Well," said the twin to Anpao, "that is amazing! And tell me who are you?"

"Me?" said Anpao. "That is obvious! I am I! But who are you?"

"Me?" said the twin. "That is very obvious! I too am I!"

And the two half-boys looked at each other in amazement for a long time. Finally Anpao understood. "Ah," he said, "I am I and you are I—but when we are together, we are we."

"And we are stronger as we than each of us is by himself," said the twin. "Is that true, brother-twin?"

"Yes, that must be true. That means we can hurl our hoop very high! Come, let's play!"

So Anpao, who was now twins, began to play.

When the sunlight faded and the shadows of the trees stretched across the rich black soil, the twins saw Grandmother Spider coming home from the field.

"Oh our goodness," said the twins. "We think Grandmother will be very angry when she finds that there are two of us!"

The old woman came closer and kept peering at the two boys, who hugged each other and cowered in fear of Grandmother Spider's anger. "Anpao! What have you done and who is that with you there in the dim light?" she shouted as she came closer.

"We are here," the twins answered together.

"Ah," the old woman sighed, "something is wrong with my poor eyes. I see two of you."

"Please, Grandmother Spider, don't be too angry with us. There is nothing wrong with your eyes," the twins said together; "we who were once one are now two."

"Aha," sighed Grandmother Spider. "Now I understand what has happened. It is a great pity, for now our happy times must end. When you were young, you were one with my house. But now you have become your own friend. Now there is nothing I can do to keep you here. You must go off, my dear sunshine-children, and find your adventures among the places beyond the world."

"But, Grandmother Spider, we were so happy

here with you! Please, don't make us go away!" the twins begged.

"My children, it is done and cannot be undone. That is the way it always is. We are free to do what we wish; but we must also accept whatever comes of it. That is the way it is. So, my children, you can stay until the morning. But then you must go out of my tipi forever and find the path that is your own. Great trials are in your future and you must be prepared for them. In distant places, where even the eagle does not fly, there is great trouble. Unless you are prepared, it will, like an avalanche, tumble over you and over all our people, and we shall be destroyed."

"But where will we find these enemies?" the twins asked.

"You will recognize them when you come to the place where they are," Grandmother Spider told them. "Do not be deceived by them. They will tell you that they are good and that they wish you well. They will promise you many things that you know are impossible. Slowly, as you listen to them, you will come to hope for what cannot be. The Evil Ones will tell you that you must be something which you cannot be and ridicule you when you fail to become what you cannot become. That is why they are evil. They are unreal and no one can fight them. We poor people cannot see through them," Grandmother Spider told the twins in a whisper, as if the Evil Ones hovered over her as she spoke. "Now," she said more loudly, glancing to her left, "come, my children, let us eat together for the last time and then you must sleep and be ready for your journey."

They sat on the floor of the tipi and ate together in the light of the fire. And in the morning when the fire had grown small, the half-boys went out into the daylight and found a pathway that led to distant places where the eagles do not fly. They looked back to wave to Grandmother Spider. She stood alone by her tipi and wept as she watched her boys leave.

"Be brave!" she shouted to the half-boys. "Bring us great honor!" Then she shouted again, "Be brave and kind. Open yourselves to strangers and do not fear what you do not

know. Good-by, my children. Do not forget your Grandmother Spider!"

Hawaiian Myth

How Kana Brought Back the Sun and Moon and Stars

Whether or not this story refers to a period comparable to what we know as the ice age is not clear. It does not seem to represent the chaos in Genesis before the Lord created the sun, moon, and stars, since it definitely refers to their previous existence and to their having been stolen. [From Padraic Colum, *The Bright Islands* (Yale University Press, 1925).]

Once the Sun and the Moon and the Stars were taken away; they were taken away by Ka-hoa-alii, and the people of the world would still be in cold and darkness if Kana and his brother Niheu had not gone to find them and bring them back.

You have been told about Kana, the youth who could stretch himself upward until his body was as thin as the thread of a spider's web, and you have been told about Niheu, his brother, who carried a war-club so great that, by resting one end of it in his canoe and putting the other end against a cliff, he could walk from his canoe to the land, and you have been told about Uli, Kana's and Niheu's wise grandmother.

This story begins with Niheu. Once when he was crossing the Island of Hawaii he heard about Ka-hoa-alii's man and how he kept the people fishing and cooking for him; the people were pitying themselves and complaining when Niheu came amongst them.

Then Niheu saw Ka-hoa-alii's man, and he flung his club at him; the stroke of the great club knocked Ka-hoa-alii's man over. And after he had flung his club Niheu went on to his grandmother's house. He told her what he had done. She was made afraid, and she told him that trouble would come because of his mischief. "Go," she said, "and find your brother Kana, and bring him here to us, for we shall need his help."

But before he went, Uli made him help her fix a long rope that she had. She took the rope and she tied it to the post of her house, and she brought the end of it down to the seashore, and she tied it to a great stone there. The people wondered, and Niheu wondered at what Uli did. Then Niheu went off to find his brother Kana.

Meanwhile, Ka-hoa-alii had heard what Uli's grandson had done to his man. "I will punish Niheu for this, and I will punish all the people of Hawaii," he said. "Now I will take away the Sun and the Moon and the Stars from their sky. I will leave the people in cold and darkness; only where I am will there be warmth and light."

Niheu found his brother, and he started with him for their grandmother's house. While they were on their way the darkness came, for the Sun was taken out of the sky suddenly. But as they went on, they struck against the rope that Uli had stretched from the post of her house to the stone on the seashore. Holding the rope, they came to the house. Kana did not go within, for no house was high enough to hold him. The two of them saw their grandmother seated by a blazing fire with lights all around her.

"So you have come," said their grandmother to them. "You are the only two in all the world that can bring the Sun and the Moon and the Stars back into our sky. Ka-hoa-alii has taken them away, and you must go to where Ka-hoa-alii is. Before I tell you what to do, do you, Kana, stretch yourself upward, and see if there is any light in the sky."

Kana stretched himself upward until his head was near the sky. He looked around, and he saw a little light in it. He brought himself down again, and he told his grandmother what he had seen.

Then said Uli: "You, Kana, and you, Niheu, will have to go to the country that Ka-hoa-alii rules over. Go straight toward the place that the Sun used to rise in. The fine rain will fall on you and the cold will get into your bones, but go on and on until you come to where an old woman sits at the bottom of a cliff. She is my sister; Luahine-kai-kapu she is named, and

she is blind. Tell her that you are Uli's grandchildren, and she will direct you to the country that Ka-hoa-alii rules over."

So Kana and Niheu started off from their grandmother's house. They went in a straight line toward the place that the Sun used to rise in. As they went on, the fine rain fell on them and the cold went into their bones. Kana took up Niheu and carried him on. But still the fine rain fell on them and still the cold crept into their bones. Then, when they came to the place that is called Kaha-kae-kaea, Niheu lay down to die.

Kana left him wrapped in leaves under a loulu palm and went on. He came to where an old woman sat at the bottom of a cliff; she was blind, and he knew that she was Luahine-kai-kapu, his grandmother's sister.

"Whose child are you?" said Luahine-kai-kapu to Kana.

"Your sister's Uli's grandchild," said Kana.

"What have you come for?" said she.

"I have come to get the Sun and the Moon and the Stars that Ka-hoa-alii has taken from our sky; I am the only one who can bring them back. Show me the way to Ka-hoa-alii's country."

"I have no eyes," said Luahine-kai-kapu; "I cannot see to show you the way."

"Lie down under this coconut tree," said Kana. Luahine-kai-kapu lay down. Kana picked off the young shoots of the coconut and called out to her, "Luahine-kai-kapu, turn your face toward the sky." She turned her face up as directed; Kana then threw the two young shoots at her eyes.

Then he struck her in the eyes, and she jumped up and cried out with a loud voice, "Oh, I am killed!" Kana then said to her, "Be quiet and rub your eyes." The old woman began rubbing her eyes. After she had done this, she cried out that she was able to see as before.

"Before I send you into the country of Ka-hoa-alii, I shall have to do something to make your hands different," said Luahine-kai-kapu. She took ku-kui-nut and charcoal and she pounded them together and she made a paste. She rubbed the paste she had made on the great hands of Kana. "Now," said she, "you have hands like the hands of Ka-hoa-alii."

Then she told him what to do when he came to the place where Ka-hoa-alii lived.

She set a fire before him to guide him, and she set a wind at his back to help him on. And helped on by the wind and guided by the fire, Kana came at last to the borders of Ka-hoa-alii's country. Then the fire died down, and he had no guide to go before him. But still the wind helped him on.

He came to the place where Ka-hoa-alii was. He hid and watched him. Ka-hoa-alii would lift up a great stone that covered a hole in the sky, and take food up in his hands and feast with his attendants. And when they had feasted, they would go into the house and play games. Thus Ka-hoa-alii and his attendants passed the day; they feasted and they played games, and they played games and they feasted.

Kana did what Luahine-kai-kapu told him to do. He watched all they did. When they had gone into the house, he went to the great stone. He lifted it up. He propped it up with his feet. Then he put his two hands down into the hole. Those below put things into his hands. They were things to eat. Kana flung them away, and put his hands down again. Those below put water into his hands. He emptied the water out. Kana put his hands down again. Those below put birds into his hands; he took them up and let them fly around; they were the birds that cry when darkness is going. Now as they flew around they cried, "Kia-wea! Kia-wea!"

He put his hands down again. Now his hands were filled with Stars. He took them up and flung them into the sky. There they stayed—the Stars that we still see. He lowered his hands again. The Moon was put into his hands. He put the Moon into the blue sky with the Stars, and it stayed there, giving light.

Kana put his hands down again. This time a single bird was put into his hands. He took it up and put it beside him. It was the crowing cock. He put his hands down once more; the warm Sun was put into his hands. He held the bright Sun up. He put it into the sky. The cock beside him crowed.

The cock crew, and Ka-hoa-alii, hearing it crow, came out of his house. He saw Kana standing there, and he saw the Sun shining in the sky. He went toward Kana to kill him, but he saw how tall and how strong Kana was, and he was afraid to touch him. And Kana, seeing that Ka-hoa-alii was afraid of him, demanded from him the Water of Life, the Water of Kane, so that he might restore his brother with it. Ka-hoa-alii gave him the Water of Kane.

Kana then went to Kaha-kae-kea. His brother Niheu was there, wrapped in leaves under the loulu palm. He gave him the Water of Life, and life came back again to Niheu. Afterward Ka-hoa-alii came to where they were. He gave them a canoe made out of white chicken feathers, and in that canoe Kana and Niheu returned to Hawaii. They went to their grandmother's house, and they saw the Sun in the heavens, and the Moon following the Sun, and Stars with the Moon. And never again were these bright lights taken out of our sky.

Judeo-Christian Sacred Texts and Legends

The Fall of Man

Religious and historical truths complement each other in Peter Dickinson's Carnegie Medal-winning collection of Old Testament stories. Dickinson has returned the tales to their ancient roots; yet, in the oral lore of folktale, song, legend, and proverb, he preserves the sense of sacred numina. He adds a human involvement, moreover, by telling the stories from the point of view of those who lived them or who recount the events after they have passed into history and legend. The story of the Garden of Eden, from Genesis, chapters 2 and 3, is told by a Hebrew servant in exile in Babylon. According to Dickinson: "Many of the details (forbidden tree, angels or demons as sentries, etc.) can be found in other ancient stories of creation, but there is nothing like this story as a whole." [From *City of Gold and Other Stories from the Old Testament,* retold by Peter Dickinson (Pantheon, 1980).]

(*Told in exile, in Babylon, at an open-air feast given by a Babylonian nobleman. About 575 B.C.*)

My lord does his servant great honour, commanding his servant to speak before these lords and ladies.

A tale of my own people? And suitable for a feast in these fair gardens, which are a wonder of the world?

We have no such gardens as these, we Hebrews. We grow good grapes and olives, and famous figs, but these flower-hung terraces, these green groves—no, nothing like this. Our enemies might say that it is because at root we are still a wild people, a desert people who worship a desert God. But I would answer that we have no longing for such beauties because in our hearts there is already a garden—that first garden which God planted in a place called Eden, and which he made more beautiful even than the scented arbours in which my lord has given this noble feast.

It was not only in beauty that the Garden of Eden excelled all others. It was different in its nature. In that garden there was no death.

See, lords and ladies, there beyond the stream, where the slaves are working in the lemon-grove, hoeing out weeds, raking in the dried blood and the powdered bone of dead animals. And there, where those others are searching through the vines for caterpillars and squashing what they find between finger and thumb. In my lord's garden plant and insect and animal must die, so that his eyes may feast on beauty.

But in the garden of which my people tell, the thistle grew with the fig-tree, each in the splendour of its kind and neither the enemy of the other. The caterpillar sucked at the juices of the lily, and the lily rejoiced in giving and was not hurt. All grew in one delighting harmony. Moreover, all beasts, wild and tame, roamed through the garden at peace with each other. The lion laired with the lamb and the lamb was not afraid.

No, my lady, the lion did not eat grass—he is of too proud a kind. He ate as my lords would eat if some strong sorcery were to turn them suddenly into animals—for they too would surely all be lions, and my ladies would be gazelles. He ate nectarines, and loquats, and grapes, and the trees bowed down to give him their fruits as he paced by.

Now, in this garden, over all these plants and beasts, God had set a man—just as my lord has set a senior slave to see that all this garden is duly ordered. This man's name was Adam, and he was the only man God had made. Just as my lord is careful for the happiness of his slaves, so God was careful for Adam, and made him a wife to complete his happiness.

How did He make her, O my lady of many questions? Why, when Adam slept one night God took from him one little rib-bone—here on the left-hand side—and breathed on it and it became Eve, the mother of us all. When Adam woke in the dew of that first morning and saw her, his heart sang. They were naked in the sunrise, and felt no strangeness. Day by day they walked through the garden, rejoicing in each other and the world which God had given them.

Now I must speak of the tree, and of the serpent. In the middle of this garden, in a clear space by a stream, was a tree. No man knows its kind, but some of our scholars have written that its leaves were not green flesh but clear flame, and it was the self-same tree that Moses saw when God called him to the holy mountain. However, it is known that the tree bore fruit, for God had commanded Adam that of all the trees in the garden this was the only one whose fruit he must not eat. When first Adam showed Eve the delights of the garden he told her God's command, and the serpent, who had been secretly following them in their wanderings, heard him speak.

"Why is this so?" asked Eve.

"I do not know," said Adam.

The serpent heard this also.

This serpent was not then as he is now. He was golden-red in colour, winged like a bird, with feet like a lizard's and a crest like a king's crown. If he willed, he could breathe fire from his mouth, and he had the power of speech. Of all the animals in the garden he was nearest to Adam in wisdom, so the serpent and the man had been companions until the coming of Eve, sitting together under the stars and riddling out the wonders of God's creation.

Alas, lords and ladies. From this seed sprang all the sorrow of the world, for in his delight in his bride Adam forgot his long friendship with the serpent.

The seasons passed until a morning came when Eve, roaming alone beside the central stream, found the serpent there, gazing at its image in the water.

"What are you studying, friend?" said Eve.

"I am considering why I am as I am," said the serpent.

"That is a deep question," said Eve, and she knelt among the rushes and looked at herself in the water, and wondered.

"I shall never know," she said with a sigh.

"Only God knows, who made you," said the serpent.

"Do you think He will tell me?" said Eve.

"No," said the serpent.

She sighed again.

"If you ate the fruit of the fiery tree, you might know," said the serpent.

"Do you think so?" said Eve.

"Why else should He have forbidden it?" said the serpent.

"But He *has* forbidden it," said Eve.

"If you know what God knows you will be equal with Him, and He will have no power over you," said the serpent.

Then Eve went to the tree and picked one fruit from among the flames and bit it in half. As her teeth pierced the rind the flames died and only bare dead branches remained. The taste, lords and ladies, is still in our mouths, for it is the taste of knowledge, sweet at first, bitter at last. The serpent did not eat, because he was afraid, so Eve carried the other half of the fruit to Adam and told him how sweet the taste of it was.

"But it is forbidden," said Adam.

Then Eve repeated the serpent's arguments, cunningly hiding the lies beneath the truths because of the knowledge that was in her. So Adam believed her and ate the other half of the fruit.

Now Adam looked about him and saw the garden with the eyes of knowledge. He saw the lion stalking between the tree-trunks and knew that its talons were fashioned for striking at its prey and its mouth for the rending of flesh. He saw the lamb grazing in the glade, and he knew that its meat was juicy and tender. He saw the lion leap on the lamb and slay it.

Eve's month-old child wailed in its arbour, and when Eve went to comfort it and carried it out still wailing, Adam saw its little clenched fists striking in fury at emptiness, and knew that they would grow to be strong, clutching hands, the hands of Cain, who was first to murder a man.

Then Adam and Eve looked at each other and knew the shame of their nakedness, and hid.

That evening God came to the garden. As my lord might stroll along these terraces in the cool of dusk and see small disorders which spoilt their beauty—a mildewed rose, a hibiscus limp with drought—and call to his senior slave to account for the neglect, so God called to Adam and Eve. At last they came creeping out, trying to hide their nakedness with branches, and He knew what they had done.

"You have made your choice," He told them. "You have chosen the sweat of ploughing and the ache of reaping, the pain of childbirth and the grief of children. The knowledge you have eaten is the knowledge of death. So you have no longer any place in this garden."

He took from the serpent his royal crown and his fiery breath, his wings and his legs, and made him creep on his belly in the dust; and the companionship which once held between the man and the serpent was turned to hatred, and to this day each strikes at the other the moment they meet.

Then God opened the walls of the garden and showed Adam the wilderness of the world which he now had to cultivate and people. The animals that eat plants fled through the gap, and the animals that eat flesh came hunting after them, all slaying or being slain according to their natures. And God closed the wall behind them.

For the garden is still there, guarded by four great angels, each with a sword whose brightness is such that no eye can see beyond the dazzle of it. Only our wisest men say that one day there will come a second Adam, by whom the foolishness of the first Adam will be unravelled, and then the angels will sheathe their swords, and the wall will vanish and the garden will spread through the world.

Even now, sometimes, looking at my lord's garden here in Babylon, I dream that that time must already have begun—or perhaps God has given leave for the wind to blow here some seeds out of Eden, to show my lord that he has God's blessing for his kindness to us poor Hebrews in our exile.

Noah's Ark

The flood story is universal to all cultures, appearing in myth and sacred writings throughout the world. Retold from Genesis, chapters 6 through 9, this version, translated from the German of Gertrud Fussenegger, captures the drama and urgency of the original. [From Gertrud Fussenegger, *Noah's Ark,* trans. Anthea Bell (Hodder & Stoughton, 1983).]

Long, long ago, in a far distant land, there lived a man called Noah who was good and just, and believed in God.

Every evening when the sun was going down, Noah came out of his house, looked at the sun, and said, "Father in Heaven, I thank you for making the world so beautiful. Watch over us tonight and protect us from all evil!"

Then Noah went back into his house to join his wife and sons, locked the door and slept peacefully.

Now why did Noah ask God to protect him and his family every evening? Was it storms he feared, or wild beasts?

No: Noah was not afraid of storms or wild beasts. He was afraid of his fellow men, because they were wicked. They lied and cheated and hurt one another. Brothers were enemies; sisters slandered sisters. The rich were proud and haughty, wasted their wealth, wore gold and precious stones, and would not give so much as a crust of bread to the poor. They beat defenceless people with whips and sticks. So Noah was afraid of his fellow men, and he prayed daily for God's protection.

God, who had made Man, was not pleased with his creation any more.

For God had created men and women out of pure love, giving them bright eyes and sharp ears, clever hands, and mouths to speak and tell the truth.

But now God saw that people were using their eyes only to see what they could steal, and their ears only to hear wicked words. They used their hands to hurt each other, and their mouths to curse and tell lies.

God said to himself: "I will wipe men and women off the face of the earth." And he decided to send a great Flood which would cover all the land.

No human beings were to be spared, except for Noah and his family.

So one night God woke Noah, and spoke to him.

"Noah," he said, "listen to what I say. You must get up and rouse your sons, and you must all go out to the woods, where you are to build a great, tall vessel of good planks: an Ark with many cabins in it, and a stout roof. You must make the Ark very strong, and paint its seams with pitch to keep out the water. I am going to send a Flood to cover the whole earth, but you and your family will be saved."

And God said, "I will save the lives of the innocent animals as well, so you must take two of every kind of living creature into the Ark. And take food and water to last a long time. Make haste, Noah, for the Flood is coming soon!"

This was what God said to Noah.

Noah was amazed by God's words, but he got up at once and roused his sons, and they all set to work.

They took axes and saws and hammers, and went out to the woods, where they chose the tallest, strongest trees and cut them down. They chopped them up into planks, and then they began to build the Ark.

Soon word went round that Noah was at work on some great building. People came to watch. What was it going to be? A huge wooden house, or a tower, or a fortress?

Suddenly the watchers realized that the building was to be a ship. They laughed and laughed. Who ever heard of a ship on dry land? It was a ridiculous idea—only a fool would have thought of it! "Noah is a fool!" cried the people. They sang mocking songs and danced round the Ark.

But Noah took no notice. He gritted his teeth and he went on building until the Ark was finished.

There it stood, just as God had told Noah to build it: vast and tall and almost black, because it was painted with pitch both inside and out.

Noah was tired after all his hard work, but he could not rest yet. He thought he still had the most difficult thing of all to do. God wanted him to take two of every kind of animal living on earth into the Ark, but how was he to do that? How could he catch the fierce lions and shy gazelles, the terrible rhinoceroses and mighty elephants? How could he catch the birds of the air: fast-flying swallows, or the bold eagles who build their nests high on the steep crags?

Noah did not know how he could ever carry out God's orders. But then, one day, all the animals came of their own free will: tigers and lions and elephants too. Timid birds came flying in, and the butterflies and bees and beetles flew with them. They came from far and wide, and they all went into the Ark. Perhaps the animals felt that something strange was going to happen, and scented danger in the air. Perhaps they guessed that this great black Ark was here to save them.

The day was much like any other day, except that the sunlight was stronger than usual, and the air was heavier. Dark clouds were slowly forming. Then great drops of rain began to fall. It rained harder and harder, it rained all day long, and then it rained for a second day and then a third.

At first, people were glad of the rain. "We shall have enough water at last!" they said. "All the wells will be full!"

But as time went by, they did not like the rain so much. Streams and rivers rose and burst their banks. Then Noah went into the Ark with his wife and his sons and his daughters-in-law, and waited to see what would happen.

And the Flood came.

Water surged up from the depths of the earth. The waves of the sea rose and crashed in breakers on the beach. Valleys became huge lakes, houses collapsed, bridges floated away. The people hastily packed up their most precious possessions: the rich packed their bags of gold and the poor their clothes and bedding, and they all fled to the hills and the mountains. But many of them never reached those high places, and were drowned in the Flood.

However, the water could not harm the Ark and the living creatures inside it.

The great dark vessel stood where it was for a while, with the floodwaters washing around it, and then the waves lifted it and carried it away.

Man and beast, they sat in the dark inside and listened. They felt the Ark turn and drift with the current; they heard the deep roar of the waves. Noah went round and gave out food and fodder. Sometimes he thought he heard pitiful wailing through the sides of the Ark.

He knew that by now the Flood had covered all the land. Even the last and strongest of the people, who had clung to the treetops or climbed mountain peaks, were washed away and drowned.

The Ark drifted on all alone, over an endless sea.

How much longer would the voyage last?

Noah did not know. He wondered how long he and his family and all the animals could live in the dark, cramped quarters of the Ark. The air was hot and heavy, and provisions were running out. Noah could hear the tigers snarling, and the bears growling; the elephants were trampling and the wolves were howling.

Lord God, thought Noah, when will you let us out of the Ark?

But Noah knew that first the water must go down and flow into the sea, it must seep away or dry up.

And Noah told himself that that would surely take a very long time. "Oh God, Father in Heaven," prayed Noah in his heart, "help us and do not forget us!"

God had not forgotten Noah and all the other living creatures in the Ark.

God steered the Ark over the Flood until it came near a great mountain range, which would be the first thing to show above the waters when they went down. Indeed, the topmost peak was already coming into sight, and a few green things were beginning to grow there.

But Noah could not see them.

I will send out a raven, he thought. If the raven does not come back, I shall know that we are near land, and we can leave the Ark. But if he comes back I shall know we must stay here.

So Noah sent out the raven, but the raven did not find land, and came back again.

Meanwhile, the little island of land was growing larger. Other islands too were showing above the water.

Then Noah sent out another raven, but the second bird also failed to find land and came back.

Then Noah was sad, and very much afraid. The air inside the Ark was almost unbearable by now, and the darkness was very gloomy. All but a little of the food was gone. The animals were bellowing with hunger, drumming their hoofs and paws against the cabin walls.

Noah's wife wept, and his sons and daughters-in-law were saying, "We might as well have stayed outside to drown with the others. We shall either stifle or starve to death in here!"

In his moment of greatest need, Noah thought: I will send out one more bird. So he took a dove and let her fly.

If she comes back too, we are lost, thought Noah. He watched her go as she disappeared over the horizon.

His heart sank when the dove came back only an hour later. But then he could hardly believe his eyes, for she was carrying an olive branch in her beak, and the branch was fresh and green.

Noah knew now that there was land not far from the Ark, and he knew that green things had begun to grow on the earth again. The olive trees were putting out shoots, and would soon bear fruit. The flooded, barren earth would bring forth life again.

Joyfully, Noah showed his family the green olive branch.

And while they were all laughing and weeping for joy and hugging one another, the keel of the Ark grounded upon sand. They had come safely to harbour.

They opened the door and let out all the creatures who had spent so long in the darkness of the Ark, longing for fresh air and freedom. The lions leaped out; the elephant waved his trunk and trumpeted aloud. Camels and gazelles trotted into the open air. Birds soared up, singing with delight. The mice and lizards, beetles and caterpillars, were scurrying and scrabbling and creeping and crawling, as they all made their way out to begin life again.

Noah's heart was full of thanks and praise as he stepped out on to dry land. "Father in Heaven, you have saved us!" he cried, "We bless your name! How wonderful you are!"

Then he built an altar and offered a sacrifice. God was pleased and said,

"I promise I will never send such a great flood again to destroy everything and everyone, even though people's hearts are wicked. As long as the earth remains, spring, summer, autumn and winter will always come in their turn—the seeds will grow and the farmers will bring in the harvest.

"And you, Noah, and your family, because you have been true to me, will have more children so that the earth will be filled with people once more."

And God set the many coloured rainbow in the sky as a sign of his promise to Noah.

The Story of the First Christmas

Here is the long-beloved account, in the Elizabethan language of the first major translation of the Bible into English, of the birth of Jesus Christ. Only redundant verses have been elided. [Text from Luke and Matthew, *Holy Bible, King James Version.**]

And it came to pass in those days, that there went out a decree from Caesar Augustus, that all the world should be taxed.

And all went to be taxed, every one into his own city.

And Joseph also went up from Galilee . . . unto the city of David, which is called Bethlehem; (because he was of the house and lineage of David:) to be taxed with Mary, his espoused wife, being great with child.

And so it was, that, while they were there, the days were accomplished that she should be delivered. And she brought forth her firstborn son, and wrapped him in swaddling clothes, and laid him in a manger; because there was no room for them in the inn.

And there were in the same country shepherds abiding in the field, keeping watch over their flock by night.

*Textual excerpts, in sequence: Luke, chapter 2, verses 1, 3, 4–5, 6–7, 8, 9, 10, 11–12, 13–14, 15–16, 20, 21; Matthew, chapter 2, verses 1–2, 3, 4–5, 7–8, 9–10, 11, 12, 13, 14–15; Luke, chapter 2, verse 40. (A dash between two verse numbers indicates that the two verses are combined as one paragraph.)

And, lo, the angel of the Lord came upon them, and the glory of the Lord shone round about them: and they were sore afraid.

And the angel said unto them, Fear not: for, behold, I bring you good tidings of great joy, which shall be to all people.

For unto you is born this day in the city of David a Saviour, which is Christ the Lord. And this shall be a sign unto you; Ye shall find the babe wrapped in swaddling clothes, lying in a manger.

And suddenly there was with the angel a multitude of the heavenly host praising God, and saying, Glory to God in the highest, and on earth peace, good will toward men.

And it came to pass, as the angels were gone away from them into heaven, the shepherds . . . came with haste, and found Mary, and Joseph, and the babe lying in a manger.

And the shepherds returned, glorifying and praising God for all the things they had heard and seen. . . .

And when eight days were accomplished for the circumcising of the child, his name was called Jesus. . . .

Now when Jesus was born in Bethlehem of Judaea in the days of Herod the king, behold, there came wise men from the east to Jerusalem, saying, Where is he that is born King of the Jews? for we have seen his star in the east, and are come to worship him.

When Herod the king had heard these things, he was troubled, and all Jerusalem with him.

And when he had gathered all the chief priests and scribes of the people together, he demanded of them where Christ should be born. And they said unto him, In Bethlehem of Judaea: for thus it is written by the prophet. . . .

Then Herod, when he had privily called the wise men, enquired of them diligently what time the star appeared. And he sent them to Bethlehem, and said, Go and search diligently for the young child; and when ye have found him, bring me word again, that I may come and worship him also.

When they had heard the king, they departed; and, lo, the star, which they saw in the east, went before them, till it came and stood over where the young child was. When they saw the star, they rejoiced with exceeding great joy.

And when they were come into the house, they saw the young child with Mary his mother, and fell down, and worshipped him: and when they had opened their treasures, they presented unto him gifts; gold, and frankincense, and myrrh.

And being warned of God in a dream that they should not return to Herod, they departed into their own country another way.

And when they were departed, behold, the angel of the Lord appeareth to Joseph in a dream, saying, Arise and take the young child and his mother, and flee into Egypt, and be thou there until I bring thee word: for Herod will seek the young child to destroy him.

When he arose, he took the young child and his mother by night, and departed into Egypt: and was there until the death of Herod: that it might be fulfilled which was spoken of the Lord by the prophet, saying,

Out of Egypt I have called my son.

And the child grew, and waxed strong in spirit, filled with wisdom: and the grace of God was upon him.

St. George and the Dragon

St. George is said to have been born in Cappadocia (Asia Minor) of Christian parents. The legend is that he was put to death by the Roman Emperor Diocletian because he protested against that emperor's persecutions of the Christians. His connection with the dragon goes back to the end of the sixth century, and the story was told by one Jacobus de Voragine in his *Golden Legends.* He has been the national saint of England since the First Crusade, when he is supposed to have given miraculous help to Godfrey de Bouillon. Kenneth McLeish has retold the story with a fresh, contemporary voice. [From *Gods and Men: Myths and Legends from the World's Religions,* retold by John Bailey, Kenneth McLeish, and David Spearman (Oxford University Press, 1981).]

The city stood beside a lake; the lake was huge, fathomless, deep as the sea. In its dark depths a dragon lurked. Every day it heaved itself from the mud and slime of the lake-bottom and surged into the city, dripping rancid water and strands of weed. It prowled the streets for prey:

dogs, cats, people were snapped up and gulped alive.

There was no defence. The king's army galloped out to do battle, and slunk whimpering back; the people prayed to their heathen gods, and their gods were deaf. The dragon grew fat: the city shrank.

At last the king proposed a dreadful remedy. 'My people,' he said, 'if we feed the monster on our children, perhaps it will be satisfied. Send out your children, one by one; and on the last day I'll send my only daughter, jewel of my life.'

So the people did. Each day they watched as another group of children set out on their last, hideous journey. No games; no singing; no laughter. The schools emptied; the streets were silent; the houses were quiet and still.

At last there were no children left. It was the turn of the king's own daughter. Weeping, he dressed her in wedding clothes, for her marriage to death. The people went to the lakeside in silent procession, to see her die.

Now it chanced at this time that St. George was travelling in these parts. He came down to the lakeside so that his horse could drink, and found the silent crowd and the girl in wedding clothes, sitting forlornly on a rock.

'My child,' said the saint, 'what is it? What's happening?'

Weeping, the princess explained.

'Why don't you pray to God for help?'

'Our gods watch us die, and laugh.'

Then St. George lifted his eyes to heaven and prayed aloud to the Christian God. 'O Lord God all-powerful, send a sign. Grant me strength to crush this dragon and win the people's hearts.'

There was a stillness, silence over the water; the world held its breath, and out of the stillness came a voice. 'Fight, George. My strength is yours. Fear nothing.'

Then, as the people watched, the lake water began to heave and churn. The dragon was stirring. 'Go, my lord!' cried the girl. 'Save yourself while still there's time!'

But St. George held his ground. As the dragon's head, hung with green weed, broke surface and surged towards the shore, while the people flinched and ran, he made the sign of the cross

in the air and flung a stone hard in the monster's face.

The dragon gave a hiss and bent its head. At once St. George put his foot across its neck where it arched and snaked in shallow water. 'Quick, child!' he shouted to the girl. 'Take off your belt and give it me!'

The girl did as she was told. Praying to the Holy Ghost, St. George lashed shut the dragon's jaws and made a lead for it as if it was a puppy dog. 'Take it,' he said to the girl. 'Lead it to the market square; I shall kill it there, in the name of God.'

The people fell back as the tiny girl led the dragon after her, up the beach and into the city. It was dazed, obedient as a lamb. They came to the market square, and with a single silver blow St. George cut off its head. The people surged round, kissing his feet for joy. And before that day was done, they were all converted by the miracle, and worshipped the Christian God.

Hindu Sacred Texts and Legends

Manu and Shatarupa

John Bailey has gracefully retold the Hindu creation myth in which, at the command of the god Vishnu, the god Brahma creates the world out of a single lotus flower. In an interesting contrast to the creation of Adam and Eve, the first man and woman are here formed out of the two halves of Brahma's own body. [From *Gods and Men: Myths and Legends from the World's Religions*, retold by John Bailey, Kenneth McLeish, and David Spearman (Oxford University Press, 1981).]

Before the world, before the sky, before space, there was nothing but ocean: a flat, rolling lake that lapped the edges of emptiness and the void beyond. Floating on the water was a giant water-snake: Ananta, Serpent-King. In his coils, eyes closed, undisturbed, lay the Lord Vishnu. God, asleep. Water, snake, god: nothing moved. Stillness . . . perfection . . .

Then in the deepest recesses of the world,

a sound began. A slow gathering, a humming, a throbbing. It grew and pulsed and filled the emptiness: a power, an urge, a throbbing itch of energy. It billowed and gathered into a single echoing syllable, folding in on itself endlessly, endlessly, like a beating heart: OM . . . OM . . . OM . . .

Lord Vishnu opened his eyes. It was time. The world was ready to be born.

He looked out over the calm waters. In that moment, a lotus flower took shape before him. In it sat Brahma the Creator, the Lord Vishnu's servant. He bowed his head, and waited to hear Lord Vishnu's will.

'It is time, Brahma. Time for the world. Time to begin your work. In that single lotus flower is all you need. Create a world that will live forever, till I declare the end of time itself. Begin.'

As he spoke, a huge wind gathered. The ocean cowered. The Serpent-King, and Lord Vishnu with him, disappeared from sight. Alone, Brahma's lotus-boat tossed in the churning sea.

Brahma raised his arms, and the wind died. The sea fell back and was calm again. He stood up, and with a sweep of his arms divided the lotus into three parts. The first part was heaven, the next earth and the next sky. In a single moment, the world had begun.

Brahma clothed the new earth with plants: grass, trees, flowers, vegetables and fruit. To them he gave the sense of touch. Then he created animals and insects—large and small, in land, sea and air, some with fur, some with feathers, some with shells, some with scales; large and small, fierce and timid, fast and slow. To them, as well as the sense of touch, he gave sight, smell, hearing—and above all, the power of movement.

At once the world filled with flurry and bustle. With crashing of branches, clatter of hooves, swishing and swooping, flailing and flapping, the new creatures set off to find homes. Trumpeting, braying, whistling, chattering, squealing, they ran and wriggled and hopped and flew into every corner of creation.

In the stillness that was left, Brahma had only one thing more to do. The world needed a master, someone to enjoy it and take care of

it, so that it would last forever, as Lord Vishnu had commanded. Brahma sat quiet, and thought. After a long time his thoughts took shape. First, a wisp of shadow in the white air . . . a glowing, shimmering cloud that grew thicker and denser, solidifying into a living, breathing shape. A new being, made from the thought of Brahma, in the form of god. Brahma looked at him in delight: Surely this creature, made in god's image, would take charge of the world and keep it forever as Lord Vishnu wished.

But the creature did not move. Its eyes were shut, unheeding the new world around it. Because it was made of the thoughts of Brahma, all it wanted was to sit thinking deeply about god.

Brahma saw that his creature was too simple, too flawless to look after the world. If he was to create a being to carry out Lord Vishnu's will, he would need another power. Thought was not enough: he would need to use action too. Not only his mind, but his whole body, his whole self, would be required if the new creature was to open his eyes to the world, be happy and fulfilled by creation as well as the creator.

There was only one certain way. Filled with contentment that he was carrying out Lord Vishnu's orders, Brahma divided his own body in two. One moment there was one, the next there were two: equal, unblemished, whole, the image of one another. Out of one, Brahma shaped man; out of the other, woman. The man was called *Manu,* wise; the woman *Shatarupa,* mysterious.

Manu and Shatarupa, created out of Brahma himself, looked into each other's hearts. They smiled. Gently, they touched hands. Then they walked out together into the world Brahma had given them; their charge, their responsibility, the joy and the duty laid on them by Lord Vishnu at the start of time.

Manu, Shatarupa . . . the first people . . . the ancestors of the whole human race.

Krishna and the Serpent

John Bailey has deftly retold this sacred Hindu legend. Taken from the Hindu epic and scripture, the

Mahabharata, this dramatic episode deals with Vishnu's adventures in his human form, as the young boy, Krishna. [From *Gods and Men: Myths and Legends from the World's Religions,* retold by John Bailey, Kenneth McLeish, and David Spearman (Oxford University Press, 1981).]

Vishnu the preserver, lord of the universe, took the form of a little boy called Krishna, so that he could fight against the evil in the world. Krishna was dark-skinned and handsome, and was the ring-leader in all the mischievous games the village children played. His mother and the other women laughed at his pranks; Krishna was everyone's favourite.

When he was seven, Krishna and his half-brother Rama used to go with the cowherds and help look after the cattle. All day long they played in the fields and woods where the cattle grazed, making garlands of leaves and flowers and running in and out of the trees. Krishna was musical, and he often sat down and played enchanting tunes on a flute he had made. The other children and the cowherds sat at his feet, and even the cows, and the birds and animals of the forest, came closer to listen to the magical sounds.

The cowherds usually took their cattle to the banks of the river Kalindi to quench their thirst. But one day all the cows that drank from the river fell ill and died. The evil serpent-king Kaliya had entered the river, and his presence poisoned the water.

Soon nothing could live in or near the river. The fish died; birds flying over the water were scorched and burned; even the crocodiles left the riverbanks and crashed through the forest in search of fresh water.

No one knew what to do. Everyone was afraid. At last Krishna decided that the time had come for him to find the serpent in its lair and kill it. He set off alone, and went upriver till he came to a deep pool where the water foamed and boiled, and the trees were dead along the banks—Kaliya's lair.

'It was to overcome the wicked that I came into the world in human form,' Krishna thought. 'For the sake of my people now, I must dive into the serpent's home and kill him.'

He climbed a dead tree on the riverbank, edged out along a branch, and dived into the water.

Kaliya was furious at being disturbed by a little human boy, and rushed at Krishna to kill him. Krishna wriggled out of reach and swam to the surface to breathe. Kaliya followed him, trying to seize him in his coils and drag him down into the depths. Soon the water was seething with the serpent's poison and the writhing of its body. Krishna seized its head and climbed on to it, carefully keeping clear of the flickering, poisonous fangs.

Angrily, Kaliya tried to shake him off. Krishna hung on for his life. The water roared and churned round him; the snake wriggled and plunged; there was a ringing in his ears as the poison entered him from the water, and slowly took effect. The world went dark.

By now, some of the cowherds had missed Krishna, and followed him up river. They arrived just in time to see Kaliya dragging the boy's unconscious body down into the swirling depths. Horrified, they ran to fetch Rama and the other villagers.

Soon hundreds of frightened people lined the banks. They peered down into the murky depths. In the slime and mud of the river-bottom, Krishna lay still and silent in Kaliya's coils. The people cried out and wrung their hands in grief; many of them loved him so dearly they were ready to jump into the poisonous waters to try and save his life.

But Rama held them back. He was Krishna's half-brother, and knew of his divine nature. He looked down into the dark water, and called out in a loud voice: 'Krishna, great lord of all the gods, have you forgotten who you are? You are Vishnu the preserver, lord of the universe. It was to overcome evil that you became Krishna. Don't give way to human weakness; use a god's power, and crush the serpent!'

At the bottom of the river, Krishna heard; he opened his eyes and smiled. Using a god's power, he flexed his body to break the serpent's grip, then sprang free. He jumped on to the monster's head, and began to dance. All his music, all his godlike skill, poured out in a dance of death on Kaliya's head. Gradually, Kaliya was forced to submit. He stopped struggling, and at last lay dazed and still.

Now Kaliya's wives, the serpent queens, saw that their king was beaten. They came out of hiding, and begged Krishna to spare his life. 'We did not recognize you, lord of the gods,' they cried. Now we see you are Vishnu, lord of all. Be merciful. His poison is spent. Spare his life, and let him go.'

The little boy Krishna swam to the bank, and looked down at the beaten monster.

'I created you, Kaliya, and now I will spare your life,' he said. Go now, with all your wives. Never again enter the waters of the river Kalindi. Your home is the ocean; stay there, and harm no mortal man again.'

So, with his wives and followers, Kaliya the serpent-king left the river Kalindi and swam to the ocean. The river waters became clear and pure again. The villagers cheered and praised the little boy who was also their lord and god.

Buddhist Legend

The Buddha

The great Indian sage, Gautama the Buddha, born over five hundred years before Christ, is the central figure in a vast body of legends and tales from all regions of the Oriental world. In this poetic story, an impoverished Japanese artist is commissioned by the local temple to create a scroll painting on the subject of the Buddha's life and death. The artist's devoted cat, Good Fortune, watches the progress of the painting and longs to be included. But the cat, alone of all the animals, had refused homage to the Buddha, so she is forever excluded from paradise. Finally, in a miracle of compassion and grace, the Buddha accepts the cat into Nirvana.

Elizabeth Coatsworth has successfully melded the original Indian spirit of the Buddha's life story with the particular flavor of Japanese Buddhist culture. The traditional Buddhist love for all living beings permeates this gentle tale, a Newbery Medal winner in 1931. [From Elizabeth Coatsworth, *The Cat Who Went to Heaven* (Macmillan, 1930).]

Early the next morning, before the sun was up, the housekeeper rose and cleaned the house. She swept and scrubbed until the mats looked like worn silver and the wood shone like pale gold. Then she hurried to market and purchased a spray of flowers to put in the vase, which she had of course bought back the night before with the first money from the priest's purse. In the meantime the artist dressed himself carefully in his holiday clothes, combed his hair until it shone like lacquer, and then went to pray before the shelf of the Buddha. There sat Good Fortune already, looking very earnest, but she moved over the moment she saw her master. Together they sat before the image, the artist raising his hands and striking them softly from time to time to call attention to his prayers. Then, with a final low bow, he went into the next room and sat formally on his mat. He had never felt more excited and happy in his life.

Today he was to begin his painting of the death of Buddha to be hung in the village temple and seen perhaps by the children of his children's children. The honor of it almost overcame him. But he sat upright and expressionless, looking before him like a samurai knight receiving the instructions of his master. There were no rolls of silk near him, no cakes of ink with raised patterns of flowers on their tops, no beautiful brushes, nor jar of fresh spring water. He must strive to understand the Buddha before he could paint him.

First he thought of the Buddha as Siddhartha, the young Indian prince. And the artist imagined that his poor small room was a great chamber and that there were columns of gilded wood holding up a high ceiling above him. He imagined that he heard water falling from perfumed fountains near by. He imagined that young warriors stood grouped about him, gay and witty boys listening with him to a girl playing on a long instrument shaped like a peacock with a tail of peacock feathers. He imagined that his poor hydrangeas were a forest of fruit trees and palms leading down to pools filled with pink and white lotuses, and that the sparrows he knew so well were white swans flying across the sky.

When the horse of a passing farmer whinnied, he thought he heard war horses neighing in their stables and the trumpeting of an elephant, and that soon he would go out to compete with the other princes for the hand of his bride, drawing the bow no other man could draw, riding the horse no other man could ride, hewing down with his sword two trees where the others hewed down but one, and so winning his princess, Yosadhara, amid the applause of all the world.

Even in that moment of triumph, the artist knew that Siddhartha felt no shadow of ill will toward his rivals. He was all fire and gentleness. A smile curved his lips. He held his head high like a stag walking in a dewy meadow. The artist looked about among his imaginary companions. All were young, all were beautiful. They had but to ask a boon and Siddhartha's heart was reaching out to grant it before the words could be spoken. The swans flew over his gardens and feared no arrow. The deer stared unafraid from thickets of flowers.

The artist sat in his poor worn clothes on his thin cushion and felt silks against his skin. Heavy earrings weighed down his ears. A rope of pearls and emeralds swung at his throat. When his old housekeeper brought in his simple midday meal, he imagined that a train of servants had entered, carrying golden dishes heaped with the rarest food. When Good Fortune came in, cautiously putting one paw before the other, he imagined that a dancing girl had come to entertain him, walking in golden sandals.

"Welcome, thrice welcome!" he cried to her. But apparently Good Fortune had thought the room was empty, for she nearly jumped out of her skin when she heard him speak, and ran away with her white button of a tail in the air.

"How wrong of you to disturb the master!" scolded the housekeeper. But the artist was not disturbed. He was still Prince Siddhartha and he was still wondering if all the world could be as happy as those who lived within the vine-covered walls of the palace which the king his father had given him.

The second day began like the first. The housekeeper rose before dawn and although there was not a smudge of dirt or a speck of dust anywhere in the house, she washed and swept and rubbed and polished as before. Then she hurried to the market early to buy a new spray of flowers. The artist got up early,

too, and made himself as worthy as possible of reflecting upon the Buddha. And once more when he went to pray, there was Good Fortune, shining like a narcissus, and gold as a narcissus' heart, and black as a beetle on a narcissus petal, sitting quietly before the shelf where sat the household image of the Buddha. No sooner did she see the artist than she jumped to her feet, lowered her head as though she were bowing, and moved over to make room for him. They meditated as before, the artist occasionally striking his hand softly, and the cat sitting very still and proper with her paws side by side.

Then the artist went into his room beside the hydrangeas. Today he reflected upon the renunciation of Siddhartha. Again he was the prince, but now he ordered his chariot and for the first time drove unannounced through the city. He saw an old man, and a man sick with fever and a dead man. He looked at his bracelets—but gold could do no good to such as these. He, the prince of the land, was at last helpless to help.

The head of the artist hung heavy on his breast. He thought he smelled a garland of flowers, but the sweetness sickened him. They brought word that a son had been born to him, but he only thought how sad life would be for the child. When the housekeeper came with rice, he sent her away without tasting it, and when Good Fortune wandered in with big watchful eyes, he told her that he was in no mood for entertainment. Evening drew closer, but still the artist did not stir. The housekeeper looked in, but went away again. Good Fortune mewed anxiously, but the artist did not hear her.

For now the artist imagined that Prince Siddhartha had secretly sent for his chariot driver and Kanthaka, his white horse. He had gazed long at his sleeping wife and the little baby she held in her arms. Now he was in the darkness of his garden; now he rode quietly through the sleeping city; now he was galloping down the long roads that shone pale and light in the darkness; and now he was in the forest and had come to the end of his father's kingdom. Siddhartha has cut off his long hair. He has taken off his princely garments. He has hung his sword to white Kanthaka's saddle. Let Channa take them back to the palace. It is not with them that he can save the world from its suffering.

So intensely had the artist lived through the pain of the prince in his hour of giving up all the beautiful world of his youth, that next morning he was very, very tired. But when he heard the housekeeper polishing and rubbing and sweeping and scrubbing again, he, too, rose and dressed in his poor best and sat beside Good Fortune, praying before the image of the Buddha.

Then he went to the room that overlooked the hydrangea bushes and the sparrows and again he sat on his mat. Again he imagined that he was Siddhartha. But now he imagined that for years he had wandered on foot, begging for his food and seeking wisdom. At last he sat in a forest under a bo tree and the devils came and tempted him with sights terrible and sights beautiful. Just before dawn, it seemed to him that a great wisdom came to him and he understood why people suffer and also how they can in other lives escape their sufferings. With this knowledge he became the Enlightened One, the Buddha.

Now the artist felt a great peace come over him, and a love for all the world that flowed out even to the smallest grains of sand on the furthest beaches. As he had felt for his wife and little son, he now felt for everything that lived and moved, and even for the trees and mosses, the rocks and stones and the waves, which some day he believed would in their turn be men and suffer and be happy as men are.

When the housekeeper and Good Fortune came with his food, he thought his first disciples had come to him, and he taught them of the Way they should follow. He felt himself growing old in teaching and carrying happiness through the land. When he was eighty, he knew he was near death, and he saw the skies open and all the Hindu gods of the heavens, and of the trees, and the mountains, with his disciples, and the animals of the earth came to bid him farewell.

"But where is the cat?" thought the artist to himself, for even in his vision he remembered that in none of the paintings he had ever seen of the death of Buddha, was a cat represented among the other animals.

"Ah, the cat refused homage to Buddha," he remembered, "and so by her own independent act, only the cat has the doors of Paradise closed in her face."

Thinking of little Good Fortune, the artist felt a sense of sadness before he submerged himself again into the great pool of the peace of Buddha. But, poor man, he was tired to death. In three days he had tried to live a whole marvelous life in his mind. Yet now at least he understood that the Buddha he painted must have the look of one who has been gently brought up and unquestioningly obeyed (that he learned from the first day); and he must have the look of one who has suffered greatly and sacrificed himself (that he learned from the second day); and he must have the look of one who has found peace and given it to others (that he learned on the last day).

So, knowing at last how the Buddha must look, the artist fell asleep and slept for twenty-four hours as though he were dead, while the housekeeper held her breath and the little cat walked on the tips of her white paws. At the end of twenty-four hours, the artist awoke, and calling hastily for brushes, ink, spring water, and a great roll of silk, he drew at one end the figure of the great Buddha reclining upon a couch; his face filled with peace. The artist worked as though he saw the whole scene before his eyes. It had taken him three days to know how the Buddha should look, but it took him less than three hours to paint him to the last fold of his garments, while the housekeeper and Good Fortune looked on with the greatest respect and admiration.

Chinese Legend

I Dreamt I Was a Butterfly

The gentle doctrine of the Buddha found fertile ground in China, where Taoists had already been teaching that the true way could be found only by going with the natural grain of things, by not interfering with the course of nature, and by acting through nonaction. In fact, the two religions blended so well that, in the case of some texts, it is impossible to tell what material is Buddhist and what Taoist.

This parable by Chuang Tzu is the most well known of Taoist stories. The simple, brief narrative elegantly makes the Taoist argument that we can never know the ultimate nature of reality. [From *Chuang Tzu: Mystic, Moralist, and Social Reformer*, trans. N. A. Giles (Kelly & Walsh, Ltd., 1926).]

Once upon a time, I, Chuang Tzu, dreamt I was a butterfly, fluttering hither and thither, to all intents and purposes a butterfly. I was conscious only of following my fancies as a butterfly, and was unconscious of my individuality as a man. Suddenly I awaked, and there I lay, myself again. Now I do not know whether I was then a man dreaming I was a butterfly, or whether I am now a butterfly dreaming I am a man.

Islamic Legend

The Night Journey

Muhammad's Night Ride to Heaven is here retold by John Bailey. "Muhammad was born in the City of Mecca, in Arabia, in the year 570 of the Common Era. He became convinced that he had been called by Allah, the One True God, to be the Prophet of his people. The words which came to Muhammad from Allah are sacred to Muslims, and became the Qur'an, 'The Reading.' Is this account of Muhammad's Night Ride to Heaven a legend or an historical account? To many Muslims, it is literally true. Other Muslims would interpret it symbolically, and most non-Muslims would regard it as a legend." [From *Gods and Men: Myths and Legends from the World's Religions*, retold by John Bailey, Kenneth McLeish, and David Spearman (Oxford University Press, 1981).]

Muhammad was asleep in the bedroom of his home in Mecca when the archangel Jibra'il appeared.

'Arise, Muhammad,' the archangel said. 'The time is come.'

Like a man in a dream, Muhammad allowed himself to be led out into the garden, where he saw a white horse waiting. This was the fabulous Buraq, a horse so fast that it made time stand still.

The Prophet sat on Buraq's back, and in an instant he was transported from Mecca to Jerusalem, where he found himself in the mosque of El-Aqsa. Assembled in the mosque were all the prophets who had gone before, and Muhammad led them in a prayer of praise to Allah. He was then taken to visit the sacred rock, on which centuries before the prophet Abraham had made preparations to sacrifice his son Isaac to the Lord God.

From the rock, Muhammad was taken by Jibra'il to the seven Heavens of creation. At each Heaven, he met earlier prophets of other nations. He met Moses, prophet of the Children of Israel; he met Jesus, whom Muslims call Prophet of the Christians; and he met Abraham himself. In the Seventh Heaven, Muhammad met Adam, whom Muslims revere as the first prophet.

Then, past the Seventh Heaven, it seemed to Muhammad as if he had passed through a veil, and was able to see more than mortal eyes can see, more than mortal minds can imagine. Time stood still for him; he was in the presence of Allah.

Creation moved on. To his surprise, Muhammad found that he was back in Mecca. He sat quietly until dawn remembering Allah; then at sunrise, he made his way as usual to the Hanam Mosque.

Abu Jahl, an old rival of Muhammad, came up to him and smiled sarcastically.

'What have you to tell us today, Muhammad?' he enquired. 'What new thing has happened to you now?'

Muhammad described his night ride to Jerusalem and his ascension to the heavens. He said nothing of what had happened beyond the Seventh Heaven, because he could find no words to describe so sublime an experience.

Abu Jahl, shaken by Muhammad's quiet calm, sneered. 'How are we to believe all this? We've no one's word for it but yours.'

'I can prove it,' replied Muhammad. 'You know that until last night, I had never visited Jerusalem. Now, ask me anything you like about that city, and I will answer.'

And he proceeded to describe Jerusalem in such detail that even Abu Jahl was impressed. He tried another tack.

'What about the journey from Mecca to Jerusalem, on this amazing horse?' he enquired. 'Did you see anything on the way, or were you going too fast?'

'I will tell you exactly what I saw,' replied Muhammad. 'In the valleys outside Mecca I met a camel train camped for the night, and noticed that one of their camels had wandered away. I told them about this. Then I came upon another camel caravan, where I stopped for a drink of water from a jar which stood outside the largest of the tents. This camel train was heading for Mecca, and should reach the city sometime today. It is led by a dark grey camel carrying a double load, half wrapped in black cloth and half in a cloth of many colours.'

Led by Abu Jahl, the doubters set off to find the camel caravan Muhammad had described so exactly; soon they came across one which fitted the Prophet's description in every detail. They asked the camel drivers about the jar of water, and this was confirmed; they even found the second camel train, and were told that a camel had indeed escaped that night, and that a strange voice had been heard warning them of this.

The unbelievers in Mecca had failed to cast doubt into the minds of Muhammad's followers. They were taken aback by the Prophet's knowledge of the El Aqsa mosque in Jerusalem and the proofs of his meeting with the camel trains on the way to Jerusalem. Because they could not disprove Muhammad's story, their hostility grew towards Muhammad and his followers. Soon, the Prophet and his followers, called 'Muslims', had to leave Mecca, and find new homes across the world.

*And then, one day, an aunt gave
me a book. . . . It was a cut version
of the Caxton Morte d'Arthur
of Thomas Malory. . . . The very
strangeness of the language dyd me
enchante, and vaulted me into an
ancient scene.*

*And in that scene were all the
vices that ever were— and courage
and sadness and frustration, but
particularly gallantry. . . . I think
my sense of right and wrong, my
feeling of noblesse oblige, and any
thought I may have against the
oppressor and for the oppressed,
came from this secret book.*[1]

9   Epics and Romances

There comes a time in the "middle years" of childhood, beginning approximately at age nine, when children, having mastered the mechanics of reading, turn to books in a fever of interest and excitement. These are the years when children are eager to know everything at once— science, history, biography, all knowledge—as well as to discover what it means to be human, and especially what it means to be an adult.

If children in these years, reading with a great thirst, are lucky enough to find their way to the old tales from the epic literature of the world, they can be profoundly affected, as was John Steinbeck when, as a child, he discovered *Morte d'Arthur.* The grandeur of the tales; the elemental emotions they portray; the simple dignity they sustain; the unwavering nobility of the hero, even in defeat; the concepts of courage and loyalty; the emphasis on physical prowess; the vigor; the clearly outlined action; the poetry and passionate feeling—these are the elements that strike hard on the hearts of children with lasting effect. But the initial attraction for children is often that of wonderment at other lands, the Other-worlds where the evils to be faced are ancient, enormous, and mysteri-

1. John Steinbeck, Introduction, *The Acts of King Arthur and His Noble Knights from the Winchester Manuscripts of Thomas Malory and Other Sources,* ed. Chase Horton (Farrar, Straus & Giroux, 1976), pp. xi–xii.

ous. As Tolkien says, writing of his childhood fascination with the land of Merlin and Arthur and of "the nameless North of Sigurd of the Völsungs, and the prince of all dragons":

Such lands were pre-eminently desirable. I never imagined that the dragon was of the same order as the horse. And that was not solely because I saw horses daily, but never even the footprint of a worm. The dragon had the trade-mark *Of Faërie* written plain upon him. In whatever world he had his being it was an Other-world. . . . I desired dragons with a profound desire. Of course, I in my timid body did not wish to have them in the neighborhood, intruding into my relatively safe world, in which it was, for instance, possible to read stories in peace of mind, free from fear. But the world that contained even the imagination of Fáfnir was richer and more beautiful, at whatever cost of peril. The dweller in the quiet and fertile plains may hear of the tormented hills and the unharvested sea and long for them in his heart. For the heart is hard though the body be soft.[2]

The *epic* is a poem of extended length made up of traditional stories clustered about a central hero or group of heroes. It is large in scope and eloquent in expression, embodying the highest ideals of the culture from which it springs. *Saga* is the name given to the epics of the Northmen—the people of Iceland and Scandinavia—which have their origins largely in the *Eddas*. The epic is mainly pre-Christian, though here and there reference to some Christian symbol may occur, as in the Anglo-Saxon *Beowulf*. Its origins reach back to the undated past. The written form stretches from a thousand years before Christ (the *Iliad*) to the thirteenth century.

The *romance* (such as the *Song of Roland* and the tales of chivalry that make up the Arthurian cycle) differs from the epic only in its reflection of the spread of Christianity in the Middle Ages. The one overriding theme that is characteristic of this literature is the emerging recognition of the individual as hero, with courage enough to confront even the ultimate doom of fate.

The intensity of feeling in which these tales were engendered is certainly one of the prime reasons for their hold on the imaginations of children. The epics are the expression, not of one poet's conviction and emotion, but of a whole culture's interpretation of the experience of life and the individual's ideal role in a particular society. Certain poets may have had great influence in molding their final written form, but the inner meaning, symbols, religious beliefs, and codes of ethics that form their background were hammered out of centuries of communal life. At some period of great flowering in each culture, the ideal hero evolved to become the image for the future—a source of pride, energy, and inspiration. Nation after nation rallied to such a self-created ideal, until the epic, saga, and romance became sacred traditions by which men and women lived, waged war, and made and unmade kings. They provided what Bernard Berenson describes as "orgies of communal self-importance,"[3] the basis for a primal and exulting nationalism.

As a culture experienced a period of triumph and accomplishment or produced a leader with qualities of greatness, the actuality began to take on the character of legend—a mixture of fact and idealized fiction. Later, the era and the events were nurtured in the minds of generation after generation, kept alive by the

2. J. R. R. Tolkien, "On Fairy Stories," in *Tree and Leaf* (Houghton Mifflin, 1965), p. 41.
3. Bernard Berenson, *Aesthetics and History in the Visual Arts* (Pantheon, 1948), p. 92.

tellings and retellings of bards, scops, troubadours, minnesingers, and jongleurs, to emerge at last as an *Iliad*, an *Odyssey*, a saga, a definitive epic of that culture.

The history of the development of these tales is fascinating reading in itself. For example, the Arthurian romance, as Joseph Campbell tells us, most probably began with a historical event at the time of "the conquest of Christian Britain by the pagan Angles, Jutes, and Saxons, c. 450–550 A.D. The Romans, after an occupation of four centuries, had just withdrawn. The undefended population was being harried from the north by the untamed Picts and Scots. . . . Arthur apparently was a native Briton who distinguished himself in a series of battles in the early sixth century and for a time represented the last hope of the Celtic Christian cause." Campbell traces the development of the Arthurian cycle through two periods of oral development, the first through "an oral folk tradition rising throughout the Celtic 'mythogenic zone' (Brittany, Cornwall, Wales, Scotland, and Ireland)," the second through the Celtic bards who "were traditionally trained master craftsmen, composing and manipulating the new pseudo-historical materials according to the inherited mythopoetic principles of a long tradition." Then the cycle reached a period of literary development (1136–1230) in the "Anglo-Norman patriotic epics, the French courtly romances, the religious legends of the Grail, and the German biographical epics."[4] In the fifteenth century, the imprisoned Sir Thomas Malory, in his *Morte d'Arthur* (published by Caxton in 1485), drew on older French sources for his consolidation and translation into English of the "Matter of Britain."

Arthur, a Brythonic war chieftain, attracted a vast body of ancient Celtic mythology and became the king who will rise again when the British have need of him—the one sleeping under that hill over there. He grew in legend to be a great Christian knight. In the French romances, the knights of his Round Table became the highest exemplars of courtly love. The Celtic cauldron of plenty became the Holy Grail. In the hands of monks, Arthur and his knights began to embody the highest ideals of medieval Christianity. And the whole body of myth and legend, layer upon layer, became deeply embedded in the psyche of Western civilization, persisting to the present day.

The symbolism of the epics and romances is a second quality that captures the minds of children. Beyond the pattern of events, beyond the adventure, there is the larger framework of the allegory. "Every great literature has always been allegorical," says G. K. Chesterton. "The *Iliad* is only great because all life is a battle, the *Odyssey* because all life is a journey, the *Book of Job* because all life is a riddle."[5]

No one is quicker than a child to sense the great allegories of struggle and attainment in epic and romantic literature. Eleanor Cameron, in *The Green and Burning Tree* (1962), writes of the power and significance the Arthurian cycle had for her as a child:

"On the shores of the Western Sea . . ." How those words haunted me, and the thought of Arthur lying there, with Sir Bedivere bending over him; the white arm reaching up out of the sea to catch the sword Excalibur, which Arthur had directed Bedivere to cast away; the three queens of fairyland clothed in black and in a black barge coming to

4. Joseph Campbell, *The Masks of God: Creative Mythology* (Viking, 1968), pp. 516–17, 523, and 517–70 *passim*.
5. G. K. Chesterton, "A Defense of Nonsense," in *Chesterton's Stories, Essays, and Poems* (Dent, 1935), p. 126.

bear the King across the water; and Sir Bedivere left alone on the shore among the battle dead. "Here lies Arthur, once King and King to be." His death meant the passing of goodness and courage and idealism, the breaking up of the ring, the scattering of the great knights: all of that gone, perhaps forever. I remember now the almost unutterable poignancy I felt—sadness mixed with longing—yet a sense of exaltation, of having touched something very fine and powerful and strength-giving. For me, as a child, this was equal to the adult experience of Greek or Shakespearean tragedy.[6]

The epic spirit does not belong entirely to the past. It still refreshes, revives, and inspirits persons and peoples who draw upon it for an intensification of inner strength. In Iceland, the most literate country in the world, the "new editions of the sagas continue to be best sellers," and everyone knows by heart passages straight out of both the *Elder Edda* and the *Younger Edda*.[7] In India, where illiteracy runs high, the unlettered and unschooled know from memory the tales from the great Indian epic, the *Ramayana,*

chanted from memory hundreds of years before it was committed to writing. It was written down about 300 B.C. Even then no Hindu bothers to read it. The people prefer to learn it by word of mouth. And instead of reading aloud as a man reads Shakespeare, Hindus on the contrary chant their classics from memory. . . . In the streets of India you can hear the epics quoted within the folk-language as a part of the people's speech. In a word, the Hindu classics are not a thing remote from the people's utterances but contribute to them as springs flow into a living stream.[8]

When Ireland fought for recognition as a separate nation in the early years of this century, its people turned to the ancient Celtic epics for the inspiration with which to sustain their individuality. The Celtic Revival brought forth brilliant theater and poetry, as well as political and military action. Ella Young, the Irish poet and storyteller, gave to the Nationalist movement the telling of stories of Cuchulain and Finn, epic heroes of early Ireland. The illiterate newsboys of the Dublin streets came together in stores and lofts, after work, to hear her stories and, by listening, to feel themselves a part of their own great past.

The one book that Lawrence of Arabia carried in his saddle bags during his hard years working among the Arabs was Malory's *Morte d'Arthur,* the epic of England.

The inexhaustible treasure trove of the Arthurian cycle is still vividly alive today, and not merely in the countless retellings that continue to be published year after year. The world of Arthur—the old Celtic world of warriors and fierce queens and wizardry—infuses the celebrated epic fantasies and the pulp literature of the "sword-and-sorcery" variety, both of which have become staple reading for many contemporary children. George Lucas's popular space sagas, the *Star Wars* film series, are tales of Christian knighthood. The ideals of the interplanetary Jedi are, in spite of an Oriental flavor borrowed from the Japanese Samurai, those of the Christian knights; the persistent Celtic magic has merely been transported to the stars.

If, as Elizabeth Cook has suggested, the various genres of the oral tradition strike most readers with their similarities and affinities, it is because they all

6. Eleanor Cameron, "The Unforgettable Glimpse," in *The Green and Burning Tree: On the Writing and Enjoyment of Children's Books* (Little, Brown, 1969), pp. 3–4.
7. Evelyn Stefánsson, *Here is the Far North* (Scribner's, 1957), p. 102.
8. Dhan Gopal Mukerji, *Rama, the Hero of India* (Dutton, 1930), p. xl.

provide ways to enter what Tolkien calls "a Secondary Reality" or "Secondary World." Exposure to the oral tradition, as Cook says, "contributes something irreplaceable to any later experience of literature":

It is not so much a matter of recognizing the more obscure classical references in *Paradise Lost* as of accepting a whole mode of expression as both natural and serious. The realistic novel and play is, after all, a very recent part of our European inheritance. The whole world of epic, romance and allegory is open to a reader who has always taken fantasy for granted, and the way into it may be hard for one who never heard fairy tales as a child. An obvious route leads from the fairy tales of Grimm, and the *Chronicles of Narnia,* through the Northern myths and the Arthurian stories to Tolkien's *The Hobbit* and *The Lord of the Rings* and thence to *The Faerie Queene.*[9]

9. Elizabeth Cook, *The Ordinary and the Fabulous: An Introduction to Myths, Legends and Fairy Tales for Teachers and Storytellers,* 2d ed. (Cambridge University Press, 1976), pp. 4–5.

Greece

Odysseus and the Cyclops

Certain stories are great in themselves, even in the barest outline. The incidents they describe are of such magnitude, so large in concept, so unequaled in invention, that they unlock the mind, and the reader and listener can never again reassemble his individual habit of thought within its former tight and tidy confines. These tales burst through boundaries and set free the imagination. Of this stature is the story of the wise Odysseus in the face of overwhelming odds. The drama is heightened by Padraic Colum's device of telling it in the first person, as Odysseus himself might have spoken it. [From Padraic Colum, *The Adventures of Odysseus and the Tale of Troy* (Macmillan, 1918.)]

Later we came to the land of the Cyclôpes, a giant people. There is a waste island outside the harbour of their land, and on it there is a well of bright water that has poplars growing round it. We came to that empty island, and we beached our ships and took down our sails.

As soon as the dawn came we went through the empty island, starting the wild goats that were there in flocks, and shooting them with our arrows. We killed so many wild goats there that we had nine for each ship. Afterwards we looked across to the land of the Cyclôpes, and we heard the sound of voices and saw the smoke of fires and heard the bleating of flocks of sheep and goats.

I called my companions together and I said, "It would be well for some of us to go to that other island. With my own ship and with the company that is on it I shall go there. The rest of you abide here. I will find out what manner of men live there, and whether they will treat us kindly and give us gifts that are due to strangers—gifts of provisions for our voyage."

We embarked and we came to the land. There was a cave near the sea, and round the cave there were mighty flocks of sheep and goats. I took twelve men with me and I left the rest to guard the ship. We went into the cave and found no man there. There were baskets filled with cheeses, and vessels of whey, and pails and bowls of milk. My men wanted me to take some of the cheeses and drive off some of the lambs and kids and come away. But this I would not do, for I would rather that he who owned the stores would give us of his own free will the offerings that were due to strangers.

While we were in the cave, he whose dwelling it was, returned to it. He carried on his shoulder a great pile of wood for his fire. Never in our lives did we see a creature so frightful as this Cyclops was. He was a giant in size, and, what made him terrible to behold, he had but one eye, and that single eye was in his forehead. He cast down on the ground the pile of wood that he carried, making such a din that we fled in terror into the corners and recesses of the cave. Next he drove his flocks into the cave and began to milk his ewes and goats. And when he had the flocks within, he took up a stone that not all our strength could move and set it as a door to the mouth of the cave.

The Cyclops kindled his fire, and when it blazed up he saw us in the corners and recesses. He spoke to us. We knew not what he said, but our hearts were shaken with terror at the sound of his deep voice.

I spoke to him saying that we were Agamemnon's men on our way home from the taking of Priam's City, and I begged him to deal with us kindly, for the sake of Zeus who is ever in the company of strangers and suppliants. But he answered me saying, "We Cyclôpes pay no heed to Zeus, nor to any of thy gods. In our strength and our power we deem that we are mightier than they. I will not spare thee, neither will I give thee aught for the sake of Zeus, but only as my own spirit bids me. And first I would have thee tell me how you came to our land."

I knew it would be better not to let the Cyclops know that my ship and my companions were at the harbour of the island. Therefore I spoke to him guilefully, telling him that my ship had been broken on the rocks, and that I and the men with me were the only ones who had escaped utter doom.

I begged again that he would deal with us as just men deal with strangers and suppliants, but he, without saying a word, laid hands upon two of my men, and swinging them by the legs, dashed their brains out on the earth. He cut them to pieces and ate them before our very eyes. We wept and we prayed to Zeus as we witnessed a deed so terrible.

Next the Cyclops stretched himself amongst his sheep and went to sleep beside the fire. Then I debated whether I should take my sharp sword in my hand, and feeling where his heart was, stab him there. But second thoughts held me back from doing this. I might be able to kill him as he slept, but not even with my companions could I roll away the great stone that closed the mouth of the cave.

Dawn came, and the Cyclops awakened, kindled his fire and milked his flocks. Then he seized two others of my men and made ready for his mid-day meal. And now he rolled away the great stone and drove his flocks out of the cave.

I had pondered on a way of escape, and I had thought of something that might be done to baffle the Cyclops. I had with me a great skin of sweet wine, and I thought that if I could make him drunken with wine I and my companions might be able for him. But there were other preparations to be made first. On the floor of the cave there was a great beam of olive wood which the Cyclops had cut to make a club when the wood should be seasoned. It was yet green. I and my companions went and cut off a fathom's length of the wood, and sharpened it to a point and took it to the fire and hardened it in the glow. Then I hid the beam in a recess of the cave.

The Cyclops came back in the evening, and opening up the cave drove in his flocks. Then he closed the cave again with the stone and went and milked his ewes and his goats. Again he seized two of my companions. I went to the terrible creature with a bowl of wine in my hands. He took it and drank it and cried out, "Give me another bowl of this, and tell me thy name that I may give thee gifts for bringing me this honey-tasting drink."

Again I spoke to him guilefully and said, "Noman is my name. Noman my father and my mother call me."

"Give me more of the drink, Noman," he shouted. "And the gift that I shall give to thee is that I shall make thee the last of thy fellows to be eaten."

I gave him wine again, and when he had taken the third bowl he sank backwards with his face upturned, and sleep came upon him. Then I, with four companions, took that beam of olive wood, now made into a hard and pointed stake, and thrust it into the ashes of the fire. When the pointed end began to glow we drew it out of the flame. Then I and my companions laid hold on the great stake and, dashing at the Cyclops, thrust it into his eye. He raised a terrible cry that made the rocks ring and we dashed away into the recesses of the cave.

His cries brought other Cyclôpes to the mouth of the cave, and they, naming him as Polyphemus, called out and asked him what ailed him to cry. "Noman," he shrieked out, "Noman is slaying me by guile." They answered him saying, "If no man is slaying thee, there is nothing we can do for thee, Polyphemus. What ails thee has been sent to thee by the gods." Saying this, they went away from the mouth of the cave without attempting to move away the stone.

Polyphemus then, groaning with pain, rolled away the stone and sat before the mouth of the cave with his hands outstretched, thinking that he would catch us as we dashed out. I showed my companions how we might pass by him. I laid hands on certain rams of the flock and I lashed three of them together with supple rods. Then on the middle ram I put a man of my company. Thus every three rams carried a man. As soon as the dawn had come the rams hastened out to the pasture, and, as they passed, Polyphemus laid hands on the first and the third of each three that went by. They passed out and Polyphemus did not guess that a ram that he did not touch carried out a man.

For myself, I took a ram that was the strongest and fleeciest of the whole flock and I placed myself under him, clinging to the wool of his belly. As this ram, the best of all his flock, went by, Polyphemus, laying his hands upon him, said, "Would that you, the best of my flock, were endowed with speech, so that you might tell me where Noman, who has blinded me, has hidden himself." The ram went by him, and when he had gone a little way from the cave I loosed myself from him and went and set my companions free.

We gathered together many of Polyphemus' sheep and we drove them down to our ship. The men we had left behind would have wept when they heard what had happened to six of their companions. But I bade them take on board the sheep we had brought and pull the ship away from that land. Then when we had drawn a certain distance from the shore I could not forbear to shout my taunts into the cave of Polyphemus. "Cyclops," I cried, "you thought that you had the company of a fool and a weakling to eat. But you have been worsted by me, and your evil deeds have been punished."

So I shouted, and Polyphemus came to the mouth of the cave with great anger in his heart. He took up rocks and cast them at the ship and they fell before the prow. The men bent to the oars and pulled the ship away or it would have been broken by the rocks he cast. And when we were further away I shouted to him:

"Cyclops, if any man should ask who it was set his mark upon you, say that he was Odysseus, the son of Laertes."

Then I heard Polyphemus cry out, "I call upon Poseidon, the god of the sea, whose son I am, to avenge me upon you, Odysseus. I call upon Poseidon to grant that you, Odysseus, may never come to your home, or if the gods have ordained your return, that you come to it after much toil and suffering, in an evil plight and in a stranger's ship, to find sorrow in your home."

So Polyphemus prayed, and, to my evil fortune, Poseidon heard his prayer. But we went on in our ship rejoicing at our escape. We came to the waste island where my other ships were. All the company rejoiced to see us, although they had to mourn for their six companions slain by Polyphemus. We divided amongst the ships the sheep we had taken from Polyphemus' flock and we sacrificed to the gods. At the dawn of the next day we raised the sails on each ship and we sailed away.

Heracles

Heracles (Hercules) was the greatest hero of Greece. He possessed magnificent strength. He was the son of Zeus by a mortal wife. The goddess Hera (Juno), wife of Zeus, never forgave Heracles for being Zeus' son and persecuted him throughout his life. She it was who brought on his madness and caused him to kill his wife and their three sons. When sanity returned, Heracles was grief-stricken and as punishment exiled himself. Then in his great desire to be purified, he consulted the oracle at Delphi. The priestess told him that only a terrible penance could purge him. She bade him go to Eurystheus, King of Mycenae, and submit to whatever he demanded. She then promised him that if he performed the tasks set him, he would become immortal. Eurystheus, urged on by Hera, imposed upon Heracles twelve tasks, each one of which was well-nigh impossible. They were called *The Twelve Labors of Heracles* and were fixed in legend as early as the fifth century B.C. They involved the following:

1. To slay the Nemean lion, a beast no weapons could kill.
2. To slay the Lernean hydra, a creature with nine heads, one of which was immortal.
3. To bring back alive the Arcadian stag with antlers of gold.
4. To destroy a great boar that lived on Mount Erymantis.
5. To clean the Augean stables in a single day.
6. To drive away the Stymphalian birds.
7. To take captive the savage bull of Crete.
8. To catch the man-eating horses of Diomedes, King of Thrace.
9. To bring back the girdle of Hippolyta, Queen of the Amazons.
10. To capture the oxen of the monster Geryon.
11. To bring back the Golden Apples of the Hesperides.
12. To bring up from Hades the three-headed dog Cerberus.

This version of the second task is retold by Leon Garfield and Edward Blishen as a chapter in the second volume of their romantic, turbulent treatment of the Greek myths. With the intensity and urgency of a modern psychological novel, the authors present Heracles as a tormented and heroic figure. Garfield and Blishen write: "To feel the force of what [the myths] have to say about human passions and about the tragedy and comedy and violence and tenderness of the existence of Prometheus's creatures, we do not have to be ancient Greeks." [From Leon Garfield and Edward Blishen, *The Golden Shadow* (Pantheon, 1973).]

The Deadliest Snake of All

For the first time since his madness and the murdering of his children, Heracles smiled. It was not a broad smile, nor yet a very gay one; it was wry, and forced from him by Eurystheus, King of Mycenae, who had bolted at the very sight of the dead lion and issued panic-stricken orders that henceforth the fruits of Heracles's Labours should be displayed *outside* the palace gates. The news of this smile reached Eurystheus and increased his dislike of Heracles; however it did not cause him to abandon certain works that were going on in the palace. A circular chamber, rather like a large pot, was being constructed underground out of heavy bronze and it was his intention to retire into this whenever the return of his hated cousin should be signalled. Unhappily Eurystheus had a great distaste—amounting almost to a terror—for the sight of blood. This weakness, which he freely admitted to being a consequence of his extreme refinement, gave his queen a distinct advantage over him, which showed itself in a tight-lipped smile of more than ordinary dimensions. Thus with smiles to the left of him and smiles to the right of him, Eurystheus could not wait to get into his underground pot and defy the world from there.

"And have we decided on the Second Labour, my lord?"

The Queen of Mycenae peered down into the half-finished refuge. Eurystheus stared up. His eyes met his wife's. He raised his hands to either side of his head and waved them sinuously. The queen nodded; her smile broadened.

"Of course! Exactly my own idea. I will send a messenger to tell him what he must do now." A fair-sized crowd was gathered outside the palace gates where Heracles had stretched out the dead Nemean lion and was puzzling how to flay it, for even in death the creature's hide was proof against every blade. Advice was being freely offered, and in particular Heracles found himself plagued by a boy of about thirteen, Iolaus by name, who owned a very splendid knife

that had been given him for his birthday. Iolaus was absolutely certain that nothing was proof against his knife, which he had sharpened to an unbelievable edge; indeed, various parts of his home bore testimony to its excellence. He kept urging it on Heracles, even resorting to jibes and jeers to sting the hero into trying it.

"Go home, child," sighed Heracles.

"I am not a child. No child has a knife like this, Prince Heracles."

"I agree; it's a beautiful knife. Now, go home."

"Try it."

"No."

"Then will you let me . . . ?"

Heracles shrugged his shoulders. "If I do, will you leave me and go home?"

Illustration by Charles Keeping, from *The Golden Shadow,* by Leon Garfield and Edward Blishen (Longman Young Books, 1973). Illustrations © 1973 by Charles Keeping. Reprinted by permission of Penguin Books Ltd.

Iolaus beamed with delight at his victory. To have pierced the Nemean lion would increase the value of his knife enormously; and to have helped Heracles would increase his own even more. A world of boys would gape and envy him. He stepped forward and his birthday knife flashed in the sun.

"Try to make the first cut in the throat," said Heracles, and wondered fleetingly what he would say if the boy succeeded. Iolaus knelt and, with a triumphant, admiring grin at Heracles, thrust his magnificent knife into the dead monster's neck.

"Never mind," murmured Heracles, uncomfortably relieved by Iolaus's suddenly dismayed face as the marvellous knife snapped off at the hilt. "I will give you another. No tears, now. You told me you weren't a child, Iolaus. . . ."

"I'm not crying," muttered Iolaus. "I—I've hurt my knee."

"Show me."

"It's nothing—"

"Then show me nothing."

Iolaus stood up. His knee was bleeding from a deep gash; he had been resting it on the dead monster's claw.

"I told you to go home," began Heracles, angry at being partly responsible for the boy's injury; then his eyes gleamed. He bent down, wrenched out one of the lion's huge claws and with it, pierced the iron-hard skin as easily as if it had been air.

"Without me," mumbled Iolaus, holding his broken knife, and dismally bleeding, "you would never have thought of it, Prince Heracles."

Heracles was about to answer when the crowd parted to make space for a messenger from the palace. This man, fastidious as his master, wrinkled his fine nose at the steam that rose from the perforated lion and averted his eyes from the withered entrails.

"Prince Heracles—?"

"I am Heracles."

"The king has decided—"

"Not the queen?"

"She too—she too, Heracles."

"Two minds with but a single thought? It's as well. One thought is food enough for two such minds."

The messenger compressed his lips as the crowd laughed and even the boy Iolaus folded his arms and frowned defiance on behalf of his hero.

"Perhaps it will be enough for you also, Prince Heracles. The Second Labour imposed upon you is—to destroy the Lernian Hydra."

The laughter died; a great sigh went up from the crowd, then a trembling seized them and they began to back away. In every heart dark terrors arose and the filthy stench of the creature seemed to invade the market place as the messenger pronounced its name. This evil creature lived in the swamps near Lerna, coming out only at night to lie across roads like a dark shadow from which no passing traveller emerged. Even the boy Iolaus shrank away from the man whose task it now was to go in search of the Hydra and drag it from the swamp. Already, in his mind's eye, he saw Heracles screaming in the Hydra's coils—and, try as he might, he could not put the sight out of his mind as it fascinated him horribly. . . .

Heracles alone seemed unmoved; he continued with his task of flaying the lion and did not give the messenger even the trifling triumph of raising his head and showing a face that had gone as pale as death.

"The Hydra," repeated the messenger. "The nine-headed monster of the swamp. Kill it, Heracles; kill it, kill it!" His voice had risen to a gleeful screech; then he flushed and departed hastily. . . .

* * *

Moonshine drenched the market place of Mycenae and turned the piled-up guts of the perforated lion into a mound of silver that seemed to have been left over from making the beaten skin. Heracles stood up; someone was watching him.

"Who's there?"

A figure emerged from the shadow of an empty stall. It was Iolaus, his knee preposterously bandaged.

"What do you want now, child?"

Iolaus looked surprised, as if he'd not expected such a question.

"What are you going to do with the lion skin, Prince Heracles?"

"I don't know. . . ."

"Can I have it?"

"No."

"If it hadn't been for me, it would still be full of lion."

"And if it hadn't been for me, Iolaus, it might, one day, have been full of you."

"All right, then. You keep it."

"Many thanks."

"Wear it, Prince Heracles. Wear it like a cloak with the head for a helmet. Then all the world will know what you've done and what a great hero you are."

"Is that what you'd do, Iolaus?"

"Naturally."

"If I wear it, will you do something for me?"

"Be proud to, Prince Heracles."

"Go home."

"Not possible."

"Why not?"

"Why, I'm coming with you—to Lerna—to fight the Hydra."

Heracles stared at the boy in amazement; but Iolaus was in earnest, and nothing Heracles could say shook his resolve. He had told his parents that he was to be the companion of Prince Heracles; he had told his friends; he had told, it seemed, half of Mycenae. To go back now would not be possible. He would have to hang himself to escape the shame of it. Besides, he had helped Heracles once, and it was very likely he'd be useful again. Surely Heracles could see the justice of this?

All this came out of Iolaus with great eloquence and earnestness. Nothing seemed to deter the boy, and when his hero picked up the lion skin and began to leave the market place, he followed, still arguing.

"You are taller than I am, Prince Heracles, so you can walk much faster. But I'll follow even though you leave me a mile behind. Maybe robbers will catch me and murder me? Think of that, Prince Heracles. People will say you left me to be killed; and no one will think well of you for that. Besides, I've still a bad knee, got, I may say, in helping you. I fancy that will make it sound worse. But if that's what you want, stride on ahead, Prince Heracles, and I'll hobble after till the wolves get me. . . ."

Heracles halted and waited for the boy to catch up with him. He scowled; but felt, at the same time, a most unwilling affection for him. Iolaus limped to just beyond an arm's reach of his hero.

"Iolaus, of all the Labours King Eurystheus could devise, *you* are the hardest to bear with."

Iolaus did not look in the least offended; he accepted the fact that he was a nuisance as if it was nothing original to him.

"Why are you so anxious to be rid of me, Prince Heracles? Are you frightened the madness will come over you again and you'll kill me as they say you killed your own children? Yes; I know all about that and am not at all afraid. So there can be no call for you to be. And if it's my father and mother that's troubling you—for everyone says you're very particular about such things—then I give you my solemn word and I'll swear by the River Styx, if you like, that their last words to me were that whatever becomes of me will be by the will of the gods and my own fault; mostly my own fault. No blame on you at all. . . ."

Heracles gazed at Iolaus, half-smiling, half-inclined to weep; his heart thundered as if it would break open his chest. He was filled with terror at this child who dared to speak of his hideous, loathsome guilt as innocently as if it formed a bond between them instead of an abyss that separated him from the rest of mankind. His eyes filled with tears and through them he saw Iolaus, multiplied into a host of boys, standing just beyond an arm's reach away.

Iolaus, briefly silent, watched Heracles hopefully and a shade uneasily; plainly the boy was wondering what further arguments he could bring in support of his case. He opened his mouth as if for a further stretch of eloquence when Heracles lifted his hand as if to ward it off; then Heracles smiled and put on the lion skin in silent acknowledgement of Iolaus's victory.

Though privately he thought he looked ridiculous, he was nevertheless deeply moved to see the open admiration and delight in Iolaus's face. It was no little thing to Heracles to be the hero of the young, to be great in eyes before they'd grown the worldly cataracts of envy, failure and spite. . . .

Together they left Mycenae and travelled southward through the night—a curious pair under the moon: the tall, magnificent man wearing a lion's skin so that, in certain tricks of light and shade, he looked like the lion itself, dancing upright to the will of the limping boy whose huge bandage kept coming undone until it was lost altogether—and with it, the limp.

They rested for the latter end of the night by the northern banks of the River Inachus; then, soon after dawn, they crossed the river by a ford and continued southward towards Lerna.

They passed between Argos and Tiryns, meeting with village children who stared at them in awe—until bolder spirits among them darted close to tug at the lion's empty tail. This angered Iolaus and irritated Heracles, who blamed Iolaus for bringing it upon him with his insistence on wearing the skin. But Iolaus looked so dejected by the reproach that Heracles relented and offered to let the boy carry his wild olive club. Iolaus flushed with pride. He took the rough wood as if it was the world's sceptre and set off once more with the enormous weapon on his shoulder.

"Prince Heracles—"

"Yes, Iolaus?"

"It's not that I'm not tremendously honoured to be carrying your club—which, after all, is famous everywhere; but—"

"But what?"

"It's not that I'm not strong enough. Please don't imagine that. It's the weather, Prince Heracles. The air seems to have grown so warm and heavy. . . ."

Heracles paused and glanced up to the noonday sky; it was clear and bright. He stared curiously at Iolaus, and relieved him of his burden.

"Will you carry my quiver of arrows, Iolaus?"

"The arrows made by the gods?"

"So I was told, Iolaus."

Iolaus beamed, slung the quiver across his back and marched briskly in Heracles's wake. But in a little while, the quiver too seemed to gain mysterious weight, and threatened to rub a hole in the boy's shoulder. Dismally he loitered after the tall, striding figure whose shadow, short under the high sun, bounded and snapped at his feet like the ghost of the lion pursuing its dancing skin. "Would to the gods it would catch him and hold him back!" thought Iolaus, who was reluctant to complain again and hoped vainly that Heracles would notice his distress of his own accord.

The landscape had begun to descend towards wide valleys where plane trees grew abundantly—in groves, copses and curious woods that resembled old green cities whose crowding pillars had caught a stone-fever and come out in blotches and spots. . . .

The green was amazingly brilliant—on account of the moisture always in the ground. This moisture ceaselessly forced its way up from certain secret streams that ran underneath the earth's skin like silver veins, rupturing here and there into springs that fed wells and small, uncanny rivers that wound among the rich grass as if looking for something. . . .

Heracles's pace never slackened, consequently the distance between him and his unhappy arrow-bearer increased. At times Iolaus was forced to break into a heavy, painful run to keep Heracles in sight; on these occasions Heracles would pause and stare back at the boy with an odd expression in his eyes.

An uneasiness began to creep round the boy's heart and he could not keep from wondering what look had been in Heracles's grey eyes when he'd gazed on his sons for the last time. . . . He found himself unable to put this disturbing thought out of his mind; his pace grew even slower and there were moments when Heracles disappeared from sight, in a fold of ground or beyond a clump of trees. On one such occasion, Heracles lay in wait for him, crouching in a dip of land; then leaped up, lion's head over his face and roaring ferociously. Iolaus cried out in terror at the suddenness of it; and despite Heracles's laughing apologies and earnest promises never to do such a thing again, the boy's face remained desperately pale.

"Let's rest awhile," proposed Heracles.

They seated themselves, but the ground was unpleasantly wet and there was a sickly, sweetish smell in the air that gave Iolaus a headache. His immense powers of conversation seemed to have deserted him, else they were turned inward as he argued himself in and out of a thousand shadowy fears.

Heracles stood up and offered the boy his hand. Iolaus took it, but could not repress a slight shudder. They walked slowly now, side by side, and Heracles questioned Iolaus about his home, his ambitions and his best possessions. Iolaus answered sullenly, with a trudge in his voice . . . so Heracles fell to telling him of his own childhood, of the grand palace at Thebes and the strangled serpents; then he found himself drifting on about his battle with the God of Death on the road to Aornum and the rescue of Alcestis. He'd always longed to talk about it, then he remembered how he'd been prevented before. His eyes clouded, his lips tightened and a furrow deepened in his brow. Iolaus peered at him as if trying to penetrate the meaning of this new expression.

Neither of them spoke of the Hydra, yet they could not have been far from its lair. The very path they trod, devoid of grass, might have been a passing track of the creature's: its slime was poisonous it killed where it crept. If the evil thing was in their thoughts, it stayed as silent and deep as in the Lernian swamp.

Presently they came to a rough wooden house, built on piles sunk into the soft ground.

"Shall we go in, Iolaus?"

The boy looked down. An inexplicable feeling of depression and shame overwhelmed him. He muttered something inaudible.

"Then I will go in," said Heracles. "For we need a torch. It will be dark when we reach the swamp."

He left Iolaus and the boy waited, his thoughts twisting and turning in his head. He took off the heavy quiver and withdrew an arrow. He stared at it, thinking of legendary bowmen and other heroes. He remembered an evening long ago when he'd been allowed to stay up late because a bald old storyteller had come to his father's house for a night's lodging in exchange for a tale by the fire. "Listen well, Iolaus," his father had said; "and learn how splendid the world once was." The old man had bleated of gods and heroes, of Meleager and Atalanta and fierce Peleus. He'd glorified them, and yet, when all was said and done, they'd been no more than huge, clumsy murderers.

Now he despised the storyteller for his lies, and he despised himself for his childish hero-worshipping of the worst murderer of all: Heracles the child killer. He fingered the arrow's sharp bronze point; he could do the world a favour and kill Heracles with it. . . .

"Carry this, Iolaus, and I'll take the quiver."

Heracles stood behind him holding out a newly kindled torch. Iolaus took it and somehow the smell of the burning pitch seemed to subdue the worst of his fears.

By now the sun had dropped down and stood briefly behind a wall of trees from where it shot its last bright spears and arrows; but this archery soon ceased; the sky darkened, shadows closed up the gaps in the trees and Iolaus's torch was left alone to resist the advancing night.

He carried it as high as the thickening vegetation would allow; but despite great care, it kept catching against branches and disgorging sudden showers of flaring pitch that hissed to extinction in the shining ground. These abrupt explosions of light momentarily extended the view and revealed that the landscape had substantially changed its nature; the plane trees had given way to pale, sinewy willows rooted in mud; clumps of reeds and marsh grass sprang into sight, then passed back into darkness, lingering only where their tips had been ignited by stray droppings from the torch: they flared and smouldered like marigolds in hell. The ground underfoot had become loose and clutched at the feet; the sickly, sweetish smell that had been in the air since mid-afternoon had increased markedly and was now overpoweringly strong.

Presently a most curious and uncanny effect was seen: as the torch penetrated further and further into the deteriorating region, a faint image or echo of it appeared, sometimes ahead and sometimes to one side. At times even vague outlines of Heracles and Iolaus, like gossamer shadows, were visible beside it. This puzzling effect seemed to be produced by a dense, steamy mist that hung above certain fingers and patches of ground and reflected the passing light. Yet as the mist was permeable, this explanation did not altogether satisfy.

Onward movement now became hazardous; the firm places had been steadily diminishing until, quite suddenly, they came to an end. Heracles and Iolaus halted. Before them stretched a wide area—a lake—of gently moving slime; upon this smooth surface, dimly visible in the cloying mist, stood a tall figure and a shorter one, holding aloft a flaming torch. The remoteness and silence of the vision was very striking; in several places about the feet of the phantom images, soft, slow bubbles rose up and burst, discharging the heavy sweetish smell that was a characteristic of the entire region.

"Fire," whispered Heracles. "Give me fire." The heavy secrecy of the place oppressed all sound, so that even the whisper intruded sharply.

The torch was thrust towards him, dangerously close to his eyes. Through the veils of flame he saw Iolaus's face; he looked aside and touched the fire with an arrow head till the pitch ran over the bronze and the arrow was aflame. Then he sent it flaring into the misty swamp to meet its swift reflection and vanish with a sudden hiss. Three more burning arrows followed, arching over the quiet slime; and multiplied reflections, racing across the surface and flying out of the curtained air, turned the night into an angry design of loosely threading fire. Then all rushed to extinction—the threads of fire, the reflected torchlight and the shadowy figures together. It was as if the arrows of Heracles had extinguished a dream.

The darkened mist swirled; heads came through it—flat, gleaming heads sistering each other on rocking necks. Twisting deeply together, these necks united in a wider vessel in which they throbbed like swollen veins. . . . It was the Hydra; silently it had kept pace behind the mist, casting back the phantom reflections from its glass-smooth skin.

"Iolaus," breathed Heracles, "set the trees afire. . . ."

Iolaus hesitated, then with a last look at Heracles and the nine heads rocking out of the mist, fled with his torch streaming high. As he ran, tearing the brand through invisible obstructions, storms of sparks rushed down, stinging his cheeks and arms; he heard twigs and branches begin to spit and crackle. The night trembled into a sullen redness, throwing into striking relief the shapes made by smoke pouring down through the interstices of the flaring trees.

Such shapes, deformed and bulkily crimson, looked like the hidden thoughts of the air itself to which the smoke had given tell-tale substance.

Suddenly, over and above the spiteful clamour of the fire, Iolaus heard a violent crashing noise; but terror prevented him looking back. He fancied he heard a cry, but even then he ran on, driven by an overmastering feeling of disgust.

"Iolaus!"

The voice was wild and shaking. The boy hesitated; then, against all his pressing instincts, he turned.

The Hydra had come out of the swamp. He saw it between the trees, huge and shining in the irregular firelight. Its extremities, numerous and flexible as its nest of necks, were twined about Heracles who seemed unable to move. Its nine heads jostled his face, which was turned towards Iolaus with a look of such mortal anguish that the boy forgot the last of his fears of Heracles.

An immense distress and pity seized him as he watched the world's great hero being slowly murdered by the stench and filth of the Hydra. Why was Heracles so still? Why were his great arms hanging limply as if he was already dead? Bewildered, Iolaus blundered towards the engulfing Hydra, crying out, "Fight back! For pity's sake, fight back!"

Heracles saw him. "Go . . . go . . ." he wept; then other heads came between him and Iolaus. The heads Heracles saw on the Hydra's necks were the heads of the children he'd slaughtered in the courtyard at Thebes. They smiled at him, jostled close for kisses. . . . Why were they so cold?

Madness in reverse had taken hold of him; he saw children where there were snakes. Such was the power of the Hydra that it caused each man to fight against himself—and then consumed him in forgetful slime. This was the testing time of Heracles, facing the vengeance of his deepest dreads. He felt his chest being squeezed and squeezed; his lungs were choked with evil smells; and his beloved sons opened their rosy mouths to give him nipping bites with teeth as bright as pearls.

"Strike at it! Strike at it!" cried Iolaus.

Heracles shuddered; he raised his arm—but

not the one that held his club—and caressed the eager cheeks and stroked the obstinately tangled heads.

"Strike them off!" screamed Iolaus.

The flames leaped and crackled; branches crashed—and eyes like clustering stars rocked and danced in the air.

"The madness," groaned Heracles. *"This is the madness!"*

He lifted the hand that held his club, and gave a cry as if begging forgiveness; then he struck with all his might at the beloved heads. Whole trees roared into fire, holding up their branches as if to ward off the intense heat. Again and again Heracles struck—and the heads fell like rotten fruit with black blood gushing from the ruptured necks.

Iolaus shouted out in triumph—then his voice died. The black blood bubbled and crusted even as it flowed; and out of the crust rose new heads—two on every neck, then two again as each of these new born heads fell to Heracles's club. A hundred Hydras sprouted from the one; a teeming multitude of snakes waved about Heracles, like the stamens of some huge, grey flower. . . .

"Burn out the necks! Use the torch, Iolaus! The necks—sear them!"

Iolaus crept close; a head fell, cold and wet against his foot. He leaped back in horror—but then advanced again, holding out the torch till it found the blinded neck. He touched it with the dripping pitch; it hissed and shrank, then dropped like a length of dirty rope.

"The necks—the necks!" panted Heracles. So Iolaus found them; the dark blood boiled and steamed, the flesh shrivelled and the dead necks fell in loose disarray. Little by little the crowding heads diminished—like a multitude departing—as the club of Heracles thrashed among them and Iolaus's fire scalded the stumps. Vague heaps of them glimmered on the ground, like a windfall from an eerie tree . . . but all the while there was one head that did not fall: the head that contained the Hydra's brain. In vain Heracles battered at it, but it continued to lunge and dance and while it lived, the grip about Heracles grew tighter and tighter. . . .

Suddenly he felt a terrible pain in his foot. He glanced down. A crab had crawled from the swamp and had seized hold of his heel. Secure in its shell that must have seemed a mighty fortress, it had crawled to the aid of its monstrous companion from the slime: a scavenging Iolaus to its Heracles foul as sin.

He shouted in anger at the mockery and stamped the crab to fragments. Then he looked up. The Hydra's last head was close to his own. No maddened illusion now, no false image, but the flat, bland countenance of poison itself. Heracles saw himself deformed in its cold eyes. He saw appalling knowledge in its slow, gaping smile, knowledge of his darkest self—and of darkness everywhere. Knowledge without wisdom, without pity, without light.

"My sword, Iolaus! Give me my sword—"

The Hydra's jaws widened. Heracles, with the precision of extreme fear, saw venom bubbling in its throat, saw its divided tongue flicker and plunge. . . .

"Quickly! The sword!"

He dropped his club and stretched out his hand. He felt the sword—the Hydra's eyes grew deep and deeper; the double image of Heracles seemed to whirl away into their depths—then the sword flashed. The head fell and the Lernian Hydra was dead.

Hastily, and with eyes averted, Heracles and Iolaus buried the Hydra's head under a stone. This done, Heracles dipped a pair of arrows into the black blood that was steadily soaking into the ground. These arrows he marked with notches; the smallest scratch from them would procure certain death. They were to be used only in the last extremity. Lastly, Heracles dragged the huge, flabby corpse of the Hydra back to the swamp where he and Iolaus watched it sink under the slow folds of slime from which it had emerged. By way of an ironic tribute, Heracles cast the pieces of the broken crab onto the mirror-smooth surface of the swamp—to mark the place where the Hydra lay. For a few moments they floated, glinting like tattered stars; then they sank and the swamp forgot them.

Iolaus felt Heracles's hand on his shoulder. He glanced up into his hero's face, which was ruddy and shining in the firelight. How was it possible that he'd ever feared this man?

"Come, Iolaus."

Iolaus nodded; and then, taking with them

two of the severed heads as evidence of what had been done, he and Heracles made their way among the glowing trees like two weary souls finding their way out of hell.

How Jason Lost His Sandal in Anauros

Avid readers of traditional tales, epics, and stories find themselves fascinated by the occurrence and recurrence of motif, themes, attitudes, and incidents in sources that seem far removed from one another. One of the best-loved Christian legends is the story of St. Christopher, who bore the Christ Child upon his back across a swiftly flowing stream. Here is the same story, but it is Jason, he who set out on the impossible quest for the Golden Fleece, who crosses the flood, and it is the goddess Hera he befriends.

The cycle of stories in which Jason is hero was written by a poet of the third century B.C., Apollonius of Rhodes; its title, *Argonautica.* Pindar, the Greek lyric poet (438 B.C.), made Jason the subject of one of his most famous odes, and Euripides (485 B.C.) based his great tragedy *Medea* on the Jason story.

This retelling of the story is from a book belonging to the Victorian era, but it remains one of the most vigorous and spirited sources for children. [From Charles Kingsley, *The Heroes* (Macmillan, 1855).]

And ten years came and went, and Jason was grown to be a mighty man. Some of his fellows were gone, and some were growing up by his side. Asclepius was gone into Peloponnese, to work his wondrous cures on men; and some say he used to raise the dead to life. And Heracles was gone to Thebes, to fulfill those famous labours which have become a proverb among men. And Peleus had married a sea-nymph, and his wedding is famous to this day. And Aeneas was gone home to Troy, and many a noble tale you will read of him, and of all the other gallant heroes, the scholars of Cheiron the just. And it happened on a day that Jason stood on the mountain, and looked north and south and east and west; and Cheiron stood by him and watched him, for he knew that the time was come.

And Jason looked and saw the plains of Thessaly, where the Lapithai breed their horses; and the lake of Boibé, and the stream which runs northward to Peneus and Tempe; and he looked north, and saw the mountain wall which guards the Magnesian shore; Olympus, the seat of the Immortals, and Ossa, and Pelion, where he stood. Then he looked east and saw the bright blue sea, which stretched away forever toward the dawn. Then he looked south, and saw a pleasant land, with white-walled towns and farms, nestling along the shore of a landlocked bay, while the smoke rose blue among the trees; and he knew it for the bay of Pagasai, and the rich lowlands of Haemonia, and Iolcos by the sea.

Then he sighed, and asked: "Is it true what the heroes tell me, that I am heir of that fair land?"

"And what good would it be to you, Jason, if you were heir of that fair land?"

"I would take it and keep it."

"A strong man has taken it and kept it long. Are you stronger than Pelias the terrible?"

"I can try my strength with his," said Jason. But Cheiron sighed, and said:—

"You have many a danger to go through before you rule in Iolcos by the sea; and many a woe; and strange troubles in strange lands, such as man never saw before."

"The happier I," said Jason, "to see what man never saw before."

And Cheiron sighed again, and said: "The eaglet must leave the nest when it is fledged. Will you go to Iolcos by the sea? Then promise me two things before you go."

Jason promised, and Cheiron answered: "Speak harshly to no soul whom you may meet, and stand by the word which you shall speak."

Jason wondered why Cheiron asked this of him; but he knew that the Centaur was a prophet, and saw things long before they came. So he promised, and leapt down the mountain, to take his fortune like a man.

He went down through the arbutus thickets, and across the downs of thyme, till he came to the vineyard walls, and the pomegranates and the olives in the glen; and among the olives roared Anauros, all foaming with a summer flood.

And on the bank of Anauros sat a woman, all wrinkled, gray, and old; her head shook palsied on her breast, and her hands shook palsied on her knees; and when she saw Jason, she spoke whining: "Who will carry me across the flood?"

Jason was bold and hasty, and was just going to leap into the flood; and yet he thought twice before he leapt, so loud roared the torrent down, all brown from the mountain rains, and silver-veined with melting snow; while underneath he could hear the boulders rumbling like the tramp of horsemen or the roll of wheels, as they ground along the narrow channel, and shook the rocks on which he stood.

But the old woman whined all the more: "I am weak and old, fair youth. For Hera's sake, carry me over the torrent."

And Jason was going to answer her scornfully, when Cheiron's words came to his mind.

So he said: "For Hera's sake, the Queen of the Immortals on Olympus, I will carry you over the torrent, unless we both are drowned midway."

Then the old dame leapt upon his back, as nimbly as a goat; and Jason staggered in, wondering; and the first step was up to his knees.

The first step was up to his knees, and the second step was up to his waist; and the stones rolled about his feet, and his feet slipped about the stones; so he went on staggering and panting, while the old woman cried from off his back:—

"Fool, you have wet my mantle! Do you make game of poor old souls like me?"

Jason had half a mind to drop her, and let her get through the torrent by herself; but Cheiron's words were in his mind, and he said only: "Patience, mother; the best horse may stumble some day."

At last he staggered to the shore, and set her down upon the bank; and a strong man he needed to have been, or that wild water he never would have crossed.

He lay panting awhile upon the bank, and then leapt up to go upon his journey; but he cast one look at the old woman, for he thought, "She should thank me once at least."

And as he looked, she grew fairer than all women, and taller than all men on earth; and her garments shone like the summer sea, and her jewels like the stars of heaven; and over her forehead was a veil, woven of the golden clouds of sunset; and through the veil she looked down on him, with great soft heifer's eyes; with great eyes, mild and awful, which filled all the glen with light.

And Jason fell upon his knees, and hid his face between his hands.

And she spoke—"I am the Queen of Olympus, Hera the wife of Zeus. As thou hast done to me, so will I do to thee. Call on me in the hour of need, and try if the Immortals can forget."

And when Jason looked up, she rose from off the earth, like a pillar of tall white cloud, and floated away across the mountain peaks, toward Olympus the holy hill.

Then a great fear fell on Jason; but after a while he grew light of heart; and he blessed old Cheiron, and said—"Surely the Centaur is a prophet, and guessed what would come to pass, when he bade me speak harshly to no soul whom I might meet."

Then he went down toward Iolcos, and as he walked, he found that he had lost one of his sandals in the flood.

And as he went through the streets, the people came out to look at him, so tall and fair was he; but some of the elders whispered together; and at last one of them stopped Jason, and called to him—"Fair lad, who are you, and whence come you; and what is your errand in the town?"

"My name, good father, is Jason, and I come from Pelion up above; and my errand is to Pelias your king; tell me then where his palace is."

But the old man started, and grew pale, and said, "Do you not know the oracle, my son, that you go so boldly through the town, with but one sandal on?"

"I am a stranger here, and know of no oracle; but what of my one sandal? I lost the other in Anauros, while I was struggling with the flood."

Then the old man looked back to his companions; and one sighed and another smiled; at last he said—"I will tell you, lest you rush upon your ruin unawares. The oracle in Delphi has said, that a man wearing one sandal should take the kingdom from Pelias, and keep it for himself. Therefore beware how you go up to his palace, for he is the fiercest and most cunning of all kings."

Then Jason laughed a great laugh, like a warhorse in his pride—"Good news, good father, both for you and me. For that very end I came into the town."

Then he strode on toward the palace of Pelias, while all the people wondered at his bearing.

And he stood in the doorway and cried, "Come out, Pelias the valiant, and fight for your kingdom like a man."

Pelias came out wondering, and "Who are you, bold youth?" he cried.

"I am Jason, the son of Aeson, the heir of all this land."

Then Pelias lifted up his hands and eyes, and wept, or seemed to weep; and blessed the heavens which had brought his nephew to him, never to leave him more. "For," said he, "I have but three daughters, and no son to be my heir. You shall be my heir then, and rule the kingdom after me, and marry whichsoever of my daughters you shall choose; though a sad kingdom you will find it, and whosoever rules it a miserable man. But come in, come in, and feast."

So he drew Jason in, whether he would or not, and spoke to him so lovingly and feasted him so well, that Jason's anger passed; and after supper his three cousins came into the hall, and Jason thought that he should like well enough to have one of them for his wife.

But at last he said to Pelias, "Why do you look so sad, my uncle? And what did you mean just now, when you said that this was a doleful kingdom, and its ruler a miserable man?"

Then Pelias sighed heavily again and again and again, like a man who had to tell some dreadful story and was afraid to begin; but at last—

"For seven long years and more have I never known a quiet night; and no more will he who comes after me, till the golden fleece be brought home."

Then he told Jason the story of Phrixus, and of the golden fleece; and told him, too, which was a lie, that Phrixus's spirit tormented him, calling to him day and night. And his daughters came, and told the same tale (for their father had taught them their parts), and wept, and said, "Oh, who will bring home the golden fleece, that our uncle's spirit may have rest; and that we may have rest also, whom he never lets sleep in peace?"

Jason sat awhile, sad and silent; for he had often heard of that golden fleece; but he looked on it as a thing hopeless and impossible for any mortal man to win it.

But when Pelias saw him silent, he began to talk of other things, and courted Jason more and more, speaking to him as if he was certain to be his heir, and asking his advice about the kingdom; till Jason, who was young and simple, could not help saying to himself, "Surely he is not the dark man whom people call him. Yet why did he drive my father out?" And he asked Pelias boldly, "Men say that you are terrible, and a man of blood; but I find you a kind and hospitable man; and as you are to me, so will I be to you. Yet why did you drive my father out?"

Pelias smiled and sighed: "Men have slandered me in that, as in all things. Your father was growing old and weary, and he gave the kingdom up to me of his own will. You shall see him to-morrow, and ask him; and he will tell you the same."

Jason's heart leapt in him, when he heard that he was to see his father; and he believed all that Pelias said, forgetting that his father might not dare to tell the truth.

"One thing more there is," said Pelias, "on which I need your advice; for though you are young, I see in you a wisdom beyond your years. There is one neighbour of mine, whom I dread more than all men on earth. I am stronger than he now, and can command him: but I know that if he stay among us, he will work my ruin in the end. Can you give me a plan, Jason, by which I can rid myself of that man?"

After awhile, Jason answered, half laughing, "Were I you, I would send him to fetch that same golden fleece; for if he once set forth after it you would never be troubled with him more."

And at that a bitter smile came across Pelias's lips, and a flash of wicked joy into his eyes; and Jason saw it, and started; and over his mind came the warning of the old man, and his own one sandal, and the oracle, and he saw that he was taken in a trap.

But Pelias only answered gently, "My son, he shall be sent forthwith."

"You mean me?" cried Jason, starting up, "because I came here with one sandal?" And he lifted his fist angrily, while Pelias stood up to him like a wolf at bay; and whether one of the two was the stronger and the fiercer, it would be hard to tell.

But after a moment Pelias spoke gently—"Why then so rash, my son? You, and not I, have said what is said; why blame me for what I have not done? Had you bid me love the man of whom I spoke, and make him my son-in-law and heir, I would have obeyed you; and what if I obey you now, and send the man to win himself immortal fame? I have not harmed you, or him. One thing at least I know, that he will go, and that gladly: for he has a hero's heart within him; loving glory, and scorning to break the word which he has given."

Jason saw that he was entrapped: but his second promise to Cheiron came into his mind, and he thought, "What if the Centaur were a prophet in that also, and meant that I should win the fleece!" Then he cried aloud,—

"You have well spoken, cunning uncle of mine! I love glory, and I dare keep to my word. I will go and fetch this golden fleece. Promise me but this in return, and keep your word as I keep mine. Treat my father lovingly while I am gone, for the sake of the all-seeing Zeus; and give me up the kingdom for my own, on the day that I bring back the golden fleece."

Then Pelias looked at him and almost loved him, in the midst of all his hate; and said, "I promise, and I will perform. It will be no shame to give up my kingdom to the man who wins that fleece."

Then they swore a great oath between them; and afterwards both went in, and lay down to sleep.

But Jason could not sleep, for thinking of his mighty oath, and how he was to fulfil it, all alone, and without wealth or friends. So he tossed a long time upon his bed, and thought of this plan and of that; and sometimes Phrixus seemed to call him, in a thin voice, faint and low, as if it came from far across the sea—"Let me come home to my fathers and have rest." And sometimes he seemed to see the eyes of Hera, and to hear her words again,—"Call on me in the hour of need, and see if the Immortals can forget."

And on the morrow he went to Pelias, and said, "Give me a victim, that I may sacrifice to Hera." So he went up, and offered his sacrifice; and as he stood by the altar, Hera sent a thought into his mind; and he went back to Pelias, and said—

"If you are indeed in earnest, give me two heralds, that they may go round to all the princes of the Minuai, who were pupils of the Centaur with me, that we may fit out a ship together, and take what shall befall."

At that Pelias praised his wisdom, and hastened to send the heralds out; for he said in his heart, "Let all the princes go with him, and like him, never return; for so I shall be lord of all the Minuai, and the greatest king in Hellas."

England

Beowulf

Anglo-Saxon poetry is not like ours. Each line is divided into two parts with a pause in the middle and two accents in each half. Instead of rhyme it makes use of alliteration; that is, beginning sounds of accented syllables are repeated. For a modern example of alliteration, see Tennyson's poem "The Song of the Brook":

I slip, I slide, I gloom, I glance
    Among my skimming swallows.

Nor does Anglo-Saxon poetry employ stanza form. There is no humor; and the poetry is filled with kennings—metaphorical terms with conventional meanings, such as "the ring-giver," meaning a king, and "the gannet's bath," meaning the sea. *Beowulf* is an Anglo-Saxon epic composed not earlier than the eighth century. Though it stands at the beginning of English literature, the scene of the poem is the region around the Baltic Sea, and the hero is Scandinavian, representing the spirit of the Vikings. The Anglo-Saxon scholar and poet, Kevin Crossley-Holland, has retold *Beowulf* in a compelling, modern voice that remains true to the spirit of the original. [Complete text from *Beowulf*, retold by Kevin Crossley-Holland (Oxford University Press, 1982).]

'Stranger!' called Hygelac.

The men near the king stopped talking and picking their teeth and swilling stonecold mead over their gums.

'Stranger!' called Hygelac.

In the hall of the king of the Geats, a hundred men listened. Almost silence. The cat-fire hissed and spat, golden-eyed tapestries winked out of the gloom. Silence. The man rose from the stranger's seat.

'Your name?' demanded Hygelac.

'Gangleri,' said the stranger. 'In your tongue: Wanderer.'

'All right, Wanderer. It's time you sang for your supper.'

Men on the mead-benches shifted their buttocks, and stretched out their legs. The gathering faced inwards towards the fire.

Wanderer stood in the poet's place by the hearth and rubbed his one gleaming eye. 'I'll fuel you,' he said, 'with a true story, and one close to my heart. This story of past and present and future.'

'True?' called out a young man, the king's nephew, Beowulf by name. 'How can it be true if it's in the future?'

'Because it is not finished,' said Wanderer. 'You must finish it.'

Beowulf, how old was he, not more than twenty, felt his cheeks flush with quickening blood.

Wanderer stooped and scooped up six-stringer, the harp that always stood in the poet's place. Gleaming maplewood, white willow pegs, white fingertips, a quivering face.

'Listen!' said Wanderer. 'A story of heroes!' Now he plucked the harp with a plectrum. 'A story of monsters!' And plucked it again. 'A story of Denmark!'

'Ugh!' said Hygelac, and spat into the straw at his feet. 'The old enemy.'

But Beowulf leaned forward. Hadn't his own father Ecgtheow once taken refuge with the Danes? Hadn't Hrothgar, the Danish king, saved his father's skin? Hrothgar . . . he sounded a good man.

'The first king of the Danes was Scyld Scefing,' said Wanderer. 'I loved him dearly. Scyld Scefing was set adrift, no man knows where. He was found, a tiny child, on the shores of Denmark. But he became a mighty king. All the neighbouring tribes, over the whale's way, had to obey him and pay him tribute.'

'Even the Geats,' added Hygelac in disgust. 'Do you know, we had to pay the Danes tribute? Never again!'

'And when he died,' said Wanderer, 'he returned to the ocean by which he had come. He was laid by the mast, as Balder will be, surrounded by weapons and treasure. They placed a golden banner above his head and let the waves take him, they bequeathed him to the sea.'

In Wanderer's hands, the harp cried the stabbing cries of seabirds, and wept the salt-waves' weeping.

'Scyld's son was Beow and his grandson Healfdene,' said Wanderer, 'both brave kings. But I sing now of Scyld's great-grandson, the living king, Hrothgar.'

Beowulf nodded. Hrothgar! He had known it.

'When he was a young man, Hrothgar built a glorious feasting-hall, the finest on this middle-earth. Heorot. He called it Heorot. Day after day the rafters echoed with the din of merrymaking, men drinking mead and ale. Year after year the king rewarded his followers with gifts at the feast—arm-rings of twisted gold, brooches, buckles, belts, beaver-skin bags, can you imagine it?'

My father has stood on that hall-floor; Hrothgar gave my father treasures in Heorot: that's what Beowulf was thinking.

'And can you imagine,' said Wanderer, pausing and piercing Beowulf with his sword of an eye, 'there was one, just one outsider who could not bear the sounds coming from the hall—the laughter, the happiness, the poet's song and harp in harmony?'

Wanderer spun round, raised his elbows, spread out his cloak, and pointed at his monstrous shadow on the wall, the shadow reaching right above the gables.

'Grendel!' growled Wanderer. 'Grendel is his name.'

The hall was firelit and warm and the Geats there felt chill.

'No one knows where he lives. He ranges the moors, the fen and the fastness. He is the father of every evil being—monsters and dark elves and spiteful spirits.' Wanderer slowly turned back to face his audience. 'One night Grendel came to Heorot, he came calling on the Danes when they were dead drunk, sprawled out and snoring. That monster barged in and broke the necks of thirty thanes. Thirty! He carried them out into the night and away to his lair.'

Beowulf crouched on the edge of a bench, intent, almost angry.

'Next morning,' said Wanderer, 'when Hrothgar came to the hall, its guardians were gone—all thirty of them. And of Grendel there was not a trace except his . . . gruesome spoor.' Wanderer said the words so that no one could mistake them, or escape them.

'He was back next day,' continued Wanderer. 'And after that the Danes learned their lesson. Those who had escaped his clutches stowed themselves into dark crannies and corners in the outbuildings. The great hall Heorot stood deserted after nightfall.'

Hygelac shook his head and breathed deeply.

'For twelve years now Grendel has terrorized the Danes. Men and women and children, old and young, they all live under the dark death-shadow. He is so strong, so huge, so loathsome, that no one is able to do anything about it.'

'I will then!' Beowulf leaped up in front of the Geats and heard himself shouting, 'I will then!'

Wanderer's eye gleamed. He watched the warrior, unblinking, and spurred him on.

'All right, Beowulf,' called the king. 'That's as it should be.'

There were cheers in Hygelac's hall.

'You've proved yourself much the strongest man here,' said the king. 'Now prove it elsewhere! Brave men should seek fame in far-off lands.'

The cheers were renewed, there were shouts and boasts in the hall. The mead-horn passed from man to man, and each of them toasted Beowulf.

*   *   *

The next morning Beowulf chose fourteen men, as keen and well-tempered as warriors can be, to travel with him to Denmark.

The stronghold of the Geats rang with the blows of blacksmiths and swung to the shouts of chandlers as armour was made ready and a boat was fitted out for the sea-voyage.

On the third day, there were kisses and embraces on the windswept beach; some said they feared that Beowulf and his companions would never return, some wept, some said nothing.

Then the warriors were eager to begin their journey. They turned their backs on mothers and fathers, on wives and children; they spring-heeled over the shingle and embarked.

The great sea-bird rode over the breakers. And as soon as the Geats hoisted a sail, a bleached sea-garment, the boat foamed at the prow and surged over the waves, urged on by the wind.

After that day and the night that darkened it, the warriors sighted shining cliffs, steep headlands—the shores of Denmark.

A Danish coastguard stood on a cliff-top. He watched the boat beat across the black-and-dazzling field of water, and heard it beach screaming on the shingle. When he saw men carrying flashing shields and gleaming war-gear down the gangway, he leaped on his horse, and brandishing a spear, galloped down to the water's edge.

'Warriors!' he shouted. 'Who are you? Where do you come from?'

Beowulf held up his right hand like a flag. 'Peace!'

'Your names!' demanded the coastguard. 'What are you doing here? Before you step one foot further into Denmark.'

'Friends of the Danes!' called Beowulf.

'Foes of the monster!' said one of his companions.

'That's the sum of it,' Beowulf said. 'We're all Geats. And I am Beowulf, the son of Ecgtheow.

We've heard that Grendel has laid his hand on the Danes.'

'No man can stand against him,' said the coastguard.

'That is why we've come,' said Beowulf. 'I'm here to pit myself against this monster. I mean to put an end to Grendel.'

A long bright gaze, a slow nod, a half-smile. 'Brave words,' said the coastguard. 'But every wise man knows that a wide ocean divides words from deeds.'

Beowulf smiled and inclined his head.

Then the coastguard welcomed Beowulf and his companions, undertook to watch over their boat, and set them on the paved road that led to Heorot.

In high spirits, the Geats headed for the hall of the Danish king. Their helmets, crowned with boar-crests, shone under the sun; strong links of shining chain-mail clinked together.

They followed the track over the surges of lonely moorland and, before dark, marched up to the huge timbered hall hung with many antlers, hemmed in by outbuildings.

Heorot, Hrothgar's court, bright home of brave men! A muster of warriors hurried out to meet the Geats, and challenged them as the coastguard had done.

'I am Beowulf, and my news is for the king.'

'Have you come as exiles?' asked one Danish warrior.

'Or,' said another man, 'out of ambition?'

'My news is for Hrothgar,' Beowulf repeated. 'You'll hear about it soon enough. Ask him, will he give us leave to speak with him?'

The Danes told Beowulf and his band to leave all their weapons against one wall: linden shields inlaid with gold, coats of mail, a grey-tipped forest of ash-spears. Then they led the Geats into Heorot.

*   *   *

Woven stories on the four walls, a gamut of famous men and daring deeds, amber and umber, blue and green and gold; golden mistballs at the candlelit tables; gleaming disks and garnets set into the mead-benches; a waft of herbs, rosemary and thyme; a hundred voices lifted in harmony.

As Beowulf and his companions entered Heorot, and looked round in wonder, the noise fell back in front of them. Watched by curious Danes, they walked up a silent clearing,

right up to the king ensconced on his throne.

'Greetings, Hrothgar! I am Beowulf the Geat, Ecgtheow's son.'

'Ecgtheow's son?' Hrothgar's kind old face was creased and grey. 'You are welcome then, and so are your companions.'

'Is it true,' Beowulf demanded, 'this hall, even your own hall, is unsafe after dark?'

Hrothgar grimaced. 'Every day at dusk the talking must stop. Drinking must stop. Those still alive have to leave this hall.'

'I,' said Beowulf, 'am thirty strong. I am going to crush this monster in single combat.'

At once the hall began to ripple with excited cross-currents of sound.

Hrothgar gazed at the young warrior, his eyes so full of light; then his own eyes glazed, you could tell he was travelling the green roads of memory. It's because of his father, Hrothgar was thinking; he's come because I once sheltered Ecgtheow, and paid off his feud, isn't that it? The king got up and grasped Beowulf's right hand.

'And I've heard this monster is so reckless he does without weapons,' Beowulf said.

Hrothgar's face crumpled in pain.

'I'll fight on equal terms, then. No sword . . .'

'Beowulf . . .' objected Hrothgar.

'. . . and no yellow shield. I'll grapple this fiend hand to hand.' Beowulf paused. 'Hygelac, my king, would expect no less.'

'Beowulf . . .' began Hrothgar, but the Geat cut him off a second time:

'And he should have this coat-of-mail if I die. This corslet made by Weland. Send it back to Hygelac.'

'As you ask,' said Hrothgar.

Beowulf shrugged. 'Who knows? Fate goes always as it must.'

'First,' said Hrothgar, putting a hand on Beowulf's arm and turning him round to face the Danish warriors, 'take your place at our feast. Eat and drink after your long journey.'

A bench was cleared for the fifteen Geats. One man brought hunks of boiled pork, and another wholemeal bread; a third carried an arm-cask and an adorned ale-cup, and each of the warriors emptied it in one draught. They stretched and relaxed, their blood began to sing.

The Danes had been drinking all day. Boisterous, brooding, snoring, sitting or sprawling, they surrounded the band of Geats; the king's two sons were amongst them.

One of the Danes, a burly man with beetling eyebrows, glared at Beowulf. 'So,' he called out. 'This Geat, this Geat thinks he can succeed where we failed, does he?'

'Who is that man?' said Beowulf.

'Me,' leered the man. 'I'm Unferth. And I can tell a story about you, Beowulf.'

'Keep it to yourself, Unferth,' said another Dane.

And another, 'You're asking for trouble.'

'Let him tell it!' said Beowulf. 'I'm curious to hear it. Speak up, Unferth.'

'You won't get far with Grendel,' said Unferth. 'Never! Not if you're the same man who went swimming with Breca. I've heard about your contest: who could swim the longer?' Unferth twice banged the table with his fist. 'After seven days you gave up. Breca had you beat.'

'You're drunk, Unferth. I'll tell you the true story. Breca and I swam side by side for five days and five nights, until the tides tore us apart.'

'Big man!' sneered Unferth. 'Tchah!'

'Foaming water! Freezing cold! We each held a naked sword to ward off whales.'

'Whales, eh?' said Unferth unpleasantly. 'Whitebait, more likely.'

'Breca was washed up,' said Beowulf calmly, 'but I was dragged down to the ocean-bed by a sea-monster. I fought with it and buried my sword in its breast.'

Beowulf's companions growled in support.

'If a man is brave enough,' said Beowulf, 'and not doomed to die, fate often spares him to fight another day.'

Unferth rubbed his bloodshot eyes. 'You?' he jeered. 'You're a grinning Geat! A pop . . . pop . . . a poppycock hero!'

'And you, Unferth,' said Beowulf, 'who are you to talk.'

Again the Geats growled.

'You cannot bear another man's success. Where others sing praises, you sow dragon's

teeth. If your actions matched your big mouth, Grendel would never have caused such havoc in Heorot.'

Unferth spat on the ground and said nothing.

'Grendel does as he likes with Danes, but soon, very soon, I'll show this monster what the Geats are made of.'

With that, Beowulf turned his back on Unferth and, as he did so, he saw the Danish queen, Wealhtheow, entering the hall: purple gown, and long grey hair, and violet eyes.

Flanked by two ladies-in-waiting, Wealhtheow swept up to the dais, and there the ale-thane put the adorned cup into her hands. The queen offered it first to the king, and then she walked over to Beowulf and offered it next to him.

'Lady!' Beowulf said, 'I have come to deliver your people or die in Grendel's clutches. That is my choice. Here, in this hall, I'll kill this monster or lay down my life.'

'Twelve winters without hope,' said Wealhtheow slowly.

She paused and smiled sadly at the Geat. 'At least we have hope tonight.'

'Since it was built,' called Hrothgar, 'this great hall Heorot has never been guarded by anyone but Danes. Take it, look after it! Give no quarter, Beowulf!'

Then all the Danish warriors rose from their seats and, led by Hrothgar and his queen, made their way out of the hall and into the gathering dark, away to the safety of the outbuildings.

There was almost silence in Heorot.

The Geats looked round, they listened to the hall creak in the small nightwind, and they began to lay aside their helmets and corslets.

Then each man took a bolster from one corner of the hall and found himself a sleeping-place.

'Leave him to me!' said Beowulf. 'I'll fight him hand to hand.'

The Geats lay down and spoke in low voices. Except for Beowulf, not one of them believed he would see the next day or dawn, or ever go back to his family and friends.

*   *   *

Through the dark night a darker shape slid. A sinister figure shrithed down from the moors, over high shoulders, sopping tussocks, over sheep-runs, over gurgling streams. It shrithed towards the timbered hall, huge and hairy and slightly stooping. Its long arms swung loosely.

One man was snoring, one mumbling, one coughing; all the Geats guarding Heorot had fallen asleep—all except one, one man watching.

For a moment the shape waited outside the hall. It cocked an ear. It began to quiver. Its hair bristled. Then it grasped the great ring-handle and swung open the door, the mouth of Heorot. It lunged out of the darkness and into the circle of dim candlelight, it took a long stride across the patterned floor.

Through half-closed eyes Beowulf was watching, and through barred teeth he breathed one word. 'Grendel.' The name of the monster, the loathsome syllables.

Grendel saw the knot of sleeping warriors and his eyes shone with an unearthly light. He lurched towards the nearest man, a brave Geat called Leofric, scooped him up and, with one ghastly claw, choked the scream in his throat. Then the monster ripped him apart, bit into his body, drank the blood from his veins, devoured huge pieces; within one minute he had swallowed the whole man, even his feet and hands.

Still the Geats slept. The air in Heorot was thick with their sleep, thicker still with death and the stench of the monster.

Grendel slobbered spittle and blood; his first taste of flesh only made him more ravenous. He wheeled round towards Beowulf, stooped, reached out for him, and Beowulf . . .

Beowulf leaped up and stayed the monster's outstretched arm.

Grendel grunted and pulled back. And at that sound, all the other Geats were instantly awake. They grabbed their swords, they backed off, they shouted for Beowulf.

Grendel tried to break free but Beowulf held him fast. The monster snorted and tugged, he could feel his fingers cracking in the Geat's grip.

Now the great room boomed. Clang and clatter shattered the night-silence as Beowulf and Grendel lurched to and fro in their deathly tug-of-war. Tables and mead-benches were overturned, Grendel roared and snarled, and in the outbuildings Danes woke and listened in the darkness.

When the Geats saw that Grendel could not escape Beowulf's grip, they surrounded him and slashed at him with their swords.

Heorot flashed with battle-lights. Those warriors did not know that no kind of weapon, not even the finest iron on earth, could wound their enemy. His skin was like old rind, tough and almost hard; he had woven a secret spell against every kind of battle-blade.

Now Beowulf twisted Grendel's right arm behind his neck. He locked it and turned it, slowly he turned it, putting terrible pressure on Grendel's shoulder.

The monster bellowed and dropped to one knee. He jerked and his whole body shuddered and trembled. With superhuman strength he jerked again as he tried to escape Beowulf's grip, he jerked and all at once, his right shoulder ripped. A ghastly tearing of muscle and sinew and flesh; a spurting of hot blood: the monster's arm came apart from his body. Grendel howled. He staggered away from Beowulf, and reeled out of the hall.

The Geats cheered and shouted; they hugged one another; they converged on Beowulf.

Beowulf was gasping. 'I wanted to throttle him . . .'

'He's finished!' roared one Geat.

'. . . here and now.'

'Done for!' shouted another.

'I couldn't hold him . . . not strong enough . . .'

'Wherever he goes,' said a third companion, 'death goes with him.'

'I've done as I said,' Beowulf panted, 'and avenged Leofric.'

Until that very moment, the Geats were not aware that they had lost one of their companions. They listened as Beowulf told them what had happened when Grendel first came to the hall; and all their joy at the monster's death turned to anger and gloom at the fate of Leofric.

'Look at this hand!' muttered one man.

'Each nail like steel.'

'Each claw, I'd say.'

'Ten terrifying spikes.'

'Hand, arm and shoulder.'

'No man can withstand Beowulf . . .'

'. . . and no monster neither.'

Beowulf raised a hand and the Geats fell silent.

'Hang it up!' Beowulf said. 'Stick it up outside the door, under the gable. And then give Hrothgar news of my victory.'

Beowulf's companions hastened to do as he asked. One man climbed onto another's shoulders just outside the great door, and by guttering candlelight secured Grendel's grasp, bloodstained and battle-hardened, under the gable. Two others found brands at the hearth, rekindled them in the embers, and headed for the outbuildings.

Within a few minutes the first Danish warriors hurried into the hall. Others followed on their heels and then, at dawn, as the eastern sky turned pale green mackerel, the king himself proceeded to the hall on his old unsteady legs, supported by Wealhtheow, his queen. He paused at the door, marvelled at the monster's grasp, and then embraced Beowulf.

'This hall Heorot,' Beowulf said, 'I return it to you. Once again you can call it your own.'

'I'd lost hope,' Hrothgar said. 'Lost all belief that anyone could end it, this monstrous nightmare.'

'Twelve winters,' said Wealhtheow.

'I kept my word,' Beowulf said, 'and fought hand to hand on equal terms.'

'Beowulf, best of men, from this day on I will treat you like a son; whatever I have here on this middle-earth will be yours also.'

Wealhtheow looked troubled at the king's words, but she smiled and said nothing. Once more Hrothgar stepped forward and embraced Beowulf.

Word of Grendel's death quickly spread far and wide. Throughout that day hundreds of Danes converged on Heorot to stare at the monster's cruel grasp, and in the evening Hrothgar held a feast in honour of Beowulf and the Geats.

The king gave Beowulf shining rewards for killing Grendel—a stiff battle banner woven with gold thread, a helmet incised with battle scenes, a coat-of-mail and, finest of all, the huge damascened sword that once belonged to Healfdene, the king's own father.

Then, at a sign from Hrothgar, eight horses with gold-plated bridles pranced into the hall. 'This saddle,' said Hrothgar, 'so well cut and inlaid with precious stones, this is my own. Take it and take these horses, and make good use of them.'

Finally, Hrothgar gave a gold buckle to each of the Geats who had crossed the sea with Beowulf, and decreed that gold should be paid for the life of the warrior Leofric.

The warriors drank and feasted and drank again. Then the poet sang a lay, he compared Beowulf to Sigemund, the dragon-slayer. Waves of noise broke out along the benches, talk and laughter.

'As it used to be,' said Hrothgar.

'And will be,' said Wealhtheow. 'Give rewards, Hrothgar, while you may. But remember your own sons! Leave this land, leave this Danish people to our sons when the day comes for you to die.'

At the end of the evening, Hrothgar and Wealhtheow retired to their quarters, and Beowulf was conducted to a bed in the outbuildings where he could sleep alone and more peacefully; he was weary after his night's work. But all the other Danes and Geats remained in Heorot.

Benches were pushed back, the whole floor was padded with bolsters and pillows; and at each man's head, his helmet and coat-of-mail, his spear and shield, gleamed in the gloom.

Silence in the hall, dark and deeper dark, another night for men: one of the feasters sleeping in Heorot was doomed and soon to die . . .

*   *   *

In the middle of the night, two servants with flaming torches roused Beowulf from his sleep and escorted him to Hrothgar's chamber.

'Aeschere!' said the king. He shook his head and his face creased, a grey grief-map. 'Now Aeschere!'

'I am here,' Beowulf said.

'Aeschere is dead. My dear old friend, my battle companion.'

'In the hall?'

'Two monsters! Just as some men have said, there are two monsters after all, rulers of the moors, rangers of the fell-country. Grendel and his mother, and it will never end.'

'It will end,' Beowulf said.

'She came to Heorot,' said the king. 'She barged into the hall, mournful and ravenous, snatched down Grendel's grasp from the gable, seized the nearest man—Aeschere! My friend!'

'Vengeance,' Beowulf said.

'She just tucked him under her arm, and made off into the darkness.'

'There is honour amongst monsters as there is honour amongst men. Grendel's mother came to the hall to avenge the death of her son.'

'Once again, Beowulf, help may be had from you alone.'

'Do not grieve,' Beowulf said.

'Her lair is away and over the misty moors, at the bottom of a lake.'

'Better each man should avenge his dead, as Grendel's mother has done. Your days are numbered and my days are numbered . . .'

Beowulf put a hand on the old king's arm. 'He who can should win renown, fame before death. That is a warrior's best memorial in this world. I promise you, Hrothgar, that wherever she turns—honeycomb caves, mountain woods—I will hunt her down.'

As soon as night eased, Beowulf's stallion, one of Hrothgar's gifts, was saddled and bridled. He left Heorot at once, accompanied by the king, his own companions and a large group of Danes.

They followed the monster's tracks through the forest and over the hills. Then they headed into little-known country, wolf-slopes, wind-swept headlands, perilous ways across boggy moors. They waded through a freezing stream that plunged from beetling crags and rushed seething through a fissure, picked their way along string-thin paths, skirted small lakes where water-demons lived; at last they came to a dismal wood, stiff with hoar-frost, standing on the edge of a precipice.

The lake lay beneath, the lair of Grendel and his gruesome mother. It was blood-stained and troubled. Whipped waves reared up and reached for the sky until the air was misty, and heaven weeped.

The Geats and Danes made their way down to the side of the water. Beowulf braced his shoulders, put on his clinking corslet, and donned his helmet hung with chain-mail to guard his neck. Then Unferth stepped forward.

Beowulf looked at him coldly; he had not forgotten their encounter in the hall.

'I did you a great wrong in Heorot,' Unferth said. 'Too much beer.'

'What's past is past,' Beowulf said.

'You're the only man alive who would risk this fight.'

'Then it's right I should risk it.'

'Take my sword, Beowulf. Hrunting! It never fails.'

Beowulf grasped the sword, smiled and clapped Unferth on the shoulder. Then he turned to Hrothgar. 'If this monster covers me with a sheet of shining blood . . .'

'No, Beowulf!'

'. . . then look after my companions. Send my gifts to Hygelac. And give this great sword back to Unferth.'

Beowulf did not even wait for an answer. He dived from the bank into the water, and one of the Geats put a horn to his lips and blew an eager battle-song.

For a whole day Beowulf stroked down through the water. Then Grendel's mother saw him heading for her lair; the sea-wolf rose to meet him, clutched at him, grabbed him, swept him down and into a great vaulted chamber, a hall underwater, untouched by water.

The Geat wrestled free of Grendel's mother; she was coated with her own filth, red-eyed and roaring. He whirled the sword Hrunting, and played terrible war-music on the monster's skull. Grendel's mother roared the louder but Beowulf saw she was unharmed.

'Useless!' he shouted. 'It's useless! Or else magic spells protect her.' He hurled the sword away and began to grapple with Grendel's mother.

Beowulf threw the monster to the ground. But then she tripped him, held him in a fearsome clinch and drew a dagger. Beowulf could not throw her off. Then Grendel's mother stabbed at Beowulf's heart. She stabbed again. But the cunning links of chain-mail held firm and guarded Beowulf; his corslet saved him.

Now the Geat sprang to his feet. He saw a

sword, massive and double-edged, made by giants, lying in one corner of the chamber. It was so huge that only he of all men could have handled it.

Beowulf ran across the floor, gripped the ringed hilt and swung the ornamented sword—he struck Grendel's mother as she lumbered towards him. The blade slashed through her neck, smashed the vertebrae. The monster moaned and fell dead at his feet.

For a long while Beowulf leaned on the blood-stained sword; his heart was pounding. A man with the strength of thirty! Slayer of Grendel and slayer of the sea-wolf! A hero without equal in this middle-world!

Then Beowulf looked about him. He saw a recess, a small cave, and in the cave he found Grendel's body, drained of life-blood. 'As a trophy,' Beowulf said grimly and, with one blow, he severed the monster's head. 'Your head and this massive sword.'

The Geat spoke too soon. The patterned blade had begun to drip and melt like a gory icicle. Because of the venom in the monster's blood, it thawed entirely, right up to the hilt. So Beowulf grasped all that remained of it, picked up the sword Hrunting and Grendel's head, and left that vaulted chamber. He swam up through the water.

Beowulf's companions, still waiting at the lakeside, were overjoyed to see their leader. They handed him up on to the bank and marvelled at his trophies. Quickly they relieved him of his helmet and corslet.

'After the ninth hour,' one Geat said, 'it seemed hopeless.'

'We still hoped,' said another.

'And the Danes?' Beowulf asked.

'They went back to Heorot,' said one man.

And another: 'When the water boiled with blood, they thought it was all over.'

'So it was,' said Beowulf. 'For Grendel's mother!'

The Geats tied Grendel's head to a great pole, a battering-ram; four of them shouldered it. Then with songs on their lips, Beowulf and his companions left the lake. The journey back to the gold-hall seemed far shorter than their outward journey, and that same evening they carried the monster's head onto the floor where the warriors were drinking—a ghastly sight paraded before Hrothgar and his queen.

Beowulf walked up before the gift-throne, firm-footed, flanked by his companions. 'Hrothgar,' he said, 'son of Healfdene, ruler of the Danes! Proudly we lay before you plunder from the lake!'

Hrothgar shook his white head and smiled and embraced the Geat. 'Beowulf,' he said, 'bravest of men, fate's darling! Your friends are fortunate, your enemies not to be envied!'

'Even Hrunting was useless,' said Beowulf. 'But it was my ally; do not think I underrate it.' He returned the sword to Unferth and thanked him for the loan of it.

'Tell us all and everything,' urged the old king.

'I tell you, Hrothgar, you and your warriors can sleep in this gold-hall without fear. The death-shadow will skulk near Heorot no longer.'

Then Beowulf related what had happened after he had left the Geats and Danes at the lakeside. The companions ate and drank and, weary in their bones, lay down to rest.

The great hall Heorot soared, spacious and adorned with gold; the guests slept within until the black raven proclaimed sunrise. Bright lights chased away the shadows of the night.

In the morning, Geats and Danes met in the hall once again, and Beowulf told Hrothgar that, now that Grendel and his mother were dead, he and his companions were eager to return home.

'Stay a little longer,' Hrothgar said. 'Will you stay?'

'No man could have treated us with greater kindness. But I must tell Hygelac . . . we want to see our families and friends.'

'Your people,' said the king, 'would do well to choose you as Hygelac's successor. They could not have a better king.'

'If ever you need me,' Beowulf said, 'send for me and I will come. I'll come at once, ready for combat, and bring warriors by the thousand . . .' 'And because of your exploits, the old enmity between Geats and Danes will come to an end,' Hrothgar said, his voice rising.

Beowulf took the arm of the old king.

'For as long as I live,' Hrothgar continued, 'Geats and Danes will exchange treasures; men will send gifts over the seas where gannets swoop and rise.'

Then Hrothgar gave Beowulf twelve great treasures, and kissed and embraced him; tears streamed down the king's face. He was old and knew he was unlikely ever to see brave Beowulf again. He couldn't conceal his sense of loss; in his heart and in his head, in his very blood, a deep love burned for that young warrior.

So Beowulf and the Geats bade farewell to Hrothgar, Wealhtheow, and the Danish warriors. They left the gold-hall Heorot, taking all their treasure with them. On their stallions they galloped over the empty moorland. They hurried towards their waiting boat and the rocking sea, the gulls' path, the whale-road to their own dear country.

*   *   *

After Hygelac had died, and his son was killed in battle, Beowulf ruled the Geats for fifty years. Seasons of peace, once Beowulf had beaten off the grasping Swedes, murderous Frisians, cruel Franks; seasons of friendship, as Hrothgar had foretold, between Geats and Danes. Old Beowulf was a strong land-guardian, a wise king.

From Beowulf's hall and the buildings clustered around it—the stronghold of the Geats—a windswept moor reached up to the headland of Eagleness. That was a desolate place, a prow of land jutting out into the ocean, precipitous, riddled with caves.

One night a slave on the run, a poor man who preferred the misery of exile to his master's whip, took refuge in one of these caves. At dawn the slave stiffened in horror. He saw there was a dragon in that cave. A serpent, scaled and sleeping! And all around the dragon lay a shining hoard: precious stones, silver, gold; goblets, plates and vessels, rings. It had guarded that treasure for three hundred winters.

The slave was terrified. He lifted the nearest piece, a gold goblet, picked his way right past the dragon's head and out of the cave, and hared over the moor towards Beowulf's hall.

When the dragon woke from its long sleep, it realized at once that its hoard had been robbed: it snorted and a twisting flame-torque leaped out of its mouth. The dragon took revenge. As soon as it was dark it swooped on the Geats and girdled their stronghold with fire.

When day dawned once more, Beowulf and his companions saw the terrible damage and destruction—buildings gutted or collapsed, exposed to the elements; charred gables and beams; smouldering heaps of ash. All the land round about had been laid waste; it looked like fields of stubble fired after harvesting.

Beowulf called the warrior Geats to a meeting. They gathered in the hall of his young cousin Wiglaf; it was made of stone, the only place in the stronghold to have escaped the fire.

A crowd of pale faces; a current of voices; a counting of heads.

'Never,' said Beowulf, 'has there been an enemy such as this. But if we wait, it will be worse: this dragon will pay us a second visit.'

The men around him listened and said nothing.

'There's only one way to put an end to this threat, and only one man who can do it.'

'We've sworn oaths,' protested young Wiglaf. 'I'll never have it said . . .'

'You've never fought in single combat,' Beowulf interrupted. 'I wrenched off Grendel's arm; I killed his mother.'

'Fifty years, Beowulf.'

'I know myself, cousin Wiglaf. Old I may be, but I'll fight this fight alone.'

Wiglaf shook his head unhappily.

'A linden shield will be no use. As soon as this weapon-smith has forged a shield of iron, I'll head for Eagleness.'

'At least let some of us come with you,' said Wiglaf.

'As you like. I'll need that wretched thief to show me the way.'

Later that day, Beowulf and eleven Geats, grim-faced in their helmets, left the smoking stronghold and made their way up on to Eagleness. Much against his will, the slave led them to the entrance to the dragon's cave perched high above the ocean, the fretting water.

Beowulf sat on the headland. His mind was mournful, angry for slaughter. 'This is not your fight,' he said to his companions, 'you, loyal Wiglaf, or any of you. I'll kill this dragon and win the gold-hoard for the Geats, or . . .'

This life is very short, but not the fame, the good name that live after it.'

Then Beowulf walked up under the cliff and saw steaming water spurting through a stone arch—the entrance to the cave. The leader of the Geats felt battle-anger begin to pump inside him. He threw out his chest and gave a great roar; he hammered the grey rock's anvil.

At once a guff of smoke issued from the cave; the cliff itself snarled. As the dragon slithered down the slope towards him, Beowulf brandished his sword Naegling. He slashed at the serpent's neck, but he could not pierce its scale-corslet. Flames leaped through the air, brighter than day's bright light; Beowulf sheltered behind his shield.

'This is no fight for us,' said one Geat. 'He was right.'

'No place for us neither.'

'One lick of that fire and we'll all be cinders.'

Wiglaf angrily rounded on his companions. 'Beowulf gave us rings, armour, helmets, tempered swords: we all swore to help him if ever the need arose.'

'You heard him,' said one man. 'You heard what Beowulf said.'

'We'd do best to save our own lives.'

'You rat!' shouted Wiglaf. He turned his back on his cowardly companions and stormed up the slope towards Beowulf, calling, 'Fight for your name! Fight for your fame! I'm here and I'll help you.'

The dragon welcomed Wiglaf with a blast of flame that set fire to his shield. The young warrior sweltered and crouched behind Beowulf's huge iron shield.

As the dragon wheeled, dragging its monstrous body over the scree, Beowulf stood up and crashed Naegling against its head. The sword point stuck in its skull! Then the serpent writhed and bucked and Naegling was not strong enough; it bent and it snapped.

Beowulf stared in dismay at his old grey-hued sword and at once the dragon lunged forward. It gripped Beowulf's neck between its sharp teeth. The old king was bathed in blood; it poured out of his arteries and veins.

Quickly Wiglaf took three strides and sank his sword into the dragon's belly. He buried it up to the hilt. The dragon gasped, and let go of Beowulf's neck, and at once the flames began to abate.

Then Beowulf fumbled for the deadly knife fastened to his corslet. He closed his eyes and swayed, then he launched himself forward, fell against the dragon and slit its throat.

The serpent gargled. It jerked and shuddered; it lay still.

Beowulf's neck-wound began to burn and swell; the dragon's poison gave him great pain. He tottered forward and slumped on a ledge.

Wiglaf unfastened the old king's helmet; then as Beowulf asked, he hurried up to the cave and brought out some of the hoard so that Beowulf could see it before he died.

'A gold cup,' he said. 'This salver . . . this banner made of nothing but gold thread. There are weapons in there too, enough for an army. I could not carry them.'

'Now this great hoard belongs to the Geats,' Beowulf said. 'And you, cousin Wiglaf, in days to come you must lead and serve our people.'

Wiglaf came close to the old king for his voice was failing; he could only whisper.

'After the funeral fire, ask the warriors to build a barrow overlooking the sea.'

'It will be,' said Wiglaf.

'Let it tower high on Whaleness . . . Beowulf's barrow . . . a beacon for seafarers.'

'It will be so.'

Beowulf gave his golden collar to Wiglaf, his helmet, ring, and corslet. 'Take them, Wiglaf. You're the last survivor of our family. The rest are dead, and I must follow them.'

Beowulf almost smiled, he sighed and closed his eyes. Wiglaf looked at him tenderly and tears sprang to his eyes. He stared at his lord and he stared at the prostrate dragon, both of them swept away by fate.

For a while Wiglaf sat beside the body of his king, thinking of time past, and time to come. He did not hear his cowardly companions until there were sighs at his shoulder, sorrowful looks, cringing words.

'Ten oath-breakers,' said Wiglaf coldly. 'Where did you come from? Where did you slink up from?'

'Wiglaf . . .'

'When men hear about you, they'll condemn you to exile—far from your families, far from your own land. You've forfeited forever the happiness of home.' Wiglaf would have nothing of their protests and excuses. 'I tell you, death would be better than your disgrace.'

Then the young warrior told the slave to hurry down to the stronghold, and give the news of Beowulf's death to the waiting warriors.

Later that day, a great crowd of Geats set out for Eagleness. They mourned over the body of the old king. And they marvelled at the loathsome dragon, its scales burnished orange and brown and green, its coils and folded wings, its forked tongue. One man measured it: fifty paces from head to tail. They pushed that serpent over the precipice; they gave him to the dark waves far beneath, the heaving waters.

Then, led by Wiglaf, the Geats swarmed into the dragon's cave and reaped the gold-harvest—goblets and vessels of solid gold, salvers, precious swords—and carried it back with Beowulf's body to the scorched stronghold.

'The Swedes,' said Wiglaf, 'and the Frisians and the Franks have been waiting for this: the day when our lord laid aside laughter, festivity, happiness.' The young warrior was weary in spirit and body. 'Soon enough our hands will hold many a spear chill with dawn-cold. The dark raven will tell the eagle of the feast when, with the wolf, it laid bare the bones of corpses.'

In the morning, every man carried one faggot up to Whaleness. And there the Geats built a funeral pyre, hung round with helmets and shields and shining mail. Then they brought Beowulf's body from the stronghold on a waggon and placed it on the pyre.

'Farewell to our king,' Wiglaf called out over the sound of weeping, the voices of wind and fire, 'who often braved the iron-tipped arrow-shower. The man who killed a monster and his monstrous mother! Dragon-slayer!'

The Geats all mourned the death of their king; a maiden sang a dirge dark with dread of days to come; and a man with one gleaming eye walked amongst them, saying, 'It is finished. Now it is finished. And you finished it.'

The dark wood-smoke soared over the fire; Beowulf's body became ash, consumed to its core. Sky swallowed the plume.

It took the Geats ten days to build Beowulf's barrow, a great beacon known throughout the north world. At its heart lay Beowulf's ashes. And in his honour, the Geats buried rings and brooches and cups and salvers in that barrow, all the gold Beowulf had gained from the dragon. They bequeathed every piece of shining gold to the earth and there it still remains, untouched by men, of no more use than it was before.

Then twelve warriors rode round the barrow, grave guardians, brave Geats. They chanted a death-song, they talked as men should about their dead and living king. Round and round. They praised his daring deeds, warm words for a breathing name. Round. They said that of all kings on earth, he was the kindest, the most gentle, the most just to his people, the most eager for fame.

King Arthur and His Sword

Though it seems certain that there never was a *King Arthur*, it seems equally sure there was a chieftain of that name. Interwoven with the story of Arthur as a historical character are mythical, romantic, and fairylike elements. The legend shows the influence of the Charlemagne cycle in the appearance of the three ladies at his birth, as at that of Ogier. The influence of the northern hero-myths is shown in the episode where Arthur has to pull the sword from the stone to prove his right to be king, just as Sigmund pulls the sword from the ash tree to prove his right to be a leader. Tennyson's stories of Arthur, with which we are most familiar, are very misleading both about the character of King Arthur and the few facts as given in the earliest poems. In English literature, the wellspring of the Arthurian stories is Malory's translation of the French *Morte d'Arthur* (1470); this is the version followed in the retelling below. [From Sidney Lanier, *The Boy's King Arthur* (Scribner's, 1917).]

It befell in the days of the noble Utherpendragon, when he was King of England, that there was born to him a son who in after time was King Arthur. Howbeit the boy knew not he was the king's son. For when he was but a babe the king commanded two knights and two ladies to take the child bound in rich cloth of gold, "and deliver him to what poor man you meet at the postern gate of the castle." So the child was delivered unto Merlin, and so he bare it forth unto Sir Ector, and made an holy man to christen him, and named him Arthur; and so Sir Ector's wife nourished him. Then within two years King Uther fell sick of a great malady; and thereof he died. Then stood the realm in great danger a long while, for every lord made him strong, and many weened (thought) to have been king. And so, by Merlin's counsel, all the lords of England came together in the greatest church of London on Christmas morn before it was day, to see if God would not show by some miracle who should be king. And when the first mass was done there was seen in the church-yard, against the high altar, a great stone four-square, like to a marble stone, and in the midst thereof was an anvil of steel, a foot of height, and therein stuck a fair sword naked by the point, and letters of gold were written about the sword that said thus:

WHO SO PULLETH OUT THIS SWORD OF THIS STONE AND ANVIL, IS RIGHTWISE KING BORN OF ENGLAND.

So when all the masses were done, all the lords went for to behold the stone and the sword. And when they saw the scripture, some assayed (tried) such as would have been king. But none might stir the sword nor move it.

"He is not yet here," said the archbishop, "that shall achieve the sword, but doubt not God will make him to be known. But this is my counsel," said the archbishop, "that we let purvey (provide) ten knights, men of good fame, and they to keep this sword."

And upon New Year's day the barons let make a tournament for to keep the lords together, for the archbishop trusted that God would make him known that should win the sword. So upon New Year's day when the service was done the barons rode to the field.

And so it happened that Sir Ector rode to the jousts, and with him rode Sir Kay, his son, and young Arthur that was his nourished brother. But Sir Kay had lost his sword, for he had left it at his father's lodging, and so he prayed young Arthur to ride for his sword. "I will with a good will," said Arthur, and rode fast after the sword; and when he came home, the lady and all were gone out to see the joust-

ing. Then was Arthur wroth, and said to himself, "I will ride to the church-yard and take the sword with me that sticketh in the stone, for my brother Sir Kay shall not be without a sword this day." And so when he came to the church-yard Arthur alighted and tied his horse to the stile, and so went to the tent, and found no knights there, for they were all at the jousting: and so he handled the sword by the handles, and lightly and fiercely he pulled it out of the stone, and took his horse and rode his way till he came to his brother Sir Kay, and delivered him the sword. And as soon as Sir Kay saw the sword, he wist (knew) well that it was the sword of the stone, and so he rode to his father, Sir Ector, and said: "Sir, lo here is the sword of the stone; wherefore I must be king of this land." When Sir Ector beheld the sword, he returned again and came to the church, and there they alighted, all three, and went into the church, and anon he made Sir Kay to swear upon a book how he came to that sword.

"Sir," said Sir Kay, "by my brother Arthur, for he brought it to me."

"How gate (got) you this sword?" said Sir Ector to Arthur.

"Sir, I will tell you. When I came home for my brother's sword, I found nobody at home for to deliver me his sword, and so I thought my brother Sir Kay should not be swordless, and so I came thither eagerly and pulled it out of the stone without any pain."

"Found ye any knights about this sword?" said Sir Ector.

"Nay," said Arthur.

"Now," said Sir Ector to Arthur, "I understand that you must be king of this land."

"Wherefore I?" said Arthur.

"Sir," said Ector, "for there should never man have drawn out this sword but he that shall be rightwise king of this land. Now let me see whether ye can put the sword there as it was and pull it out again."

"That is no mastery," said Arthur; and so he put it in the stone. Therewith Sir Ector assayed to pull out the sword, and failed.

"Now assay," said Sir Ector to Sir Kay. And anon he pulled at the sword with all his might but it would not be. "Now assay shall ye," said Sir Ector to Arthur.

"I will well," said Arthur, and pulled it out easily. And therewithal Sir Ector kneeled down to the earth, and Sir Kay.

"Alas," said Arthur, "mine own dear father and brother, why kneel ye to me?"

"Nay, nay, my lord Arthur, it is not so: I was never your father nor of your blood, but I wote (know) well ye are of an higher blood than I weened (thought) you were." And then Sir Ector told him all. Then Arthur made great moan when he understood that Sir Ector was not his father.

"Sir," said Ector unto Arthur, "will ye be my good and gracious lord when ye are king?"

"Else were I to blame," said Arthur, "for ye are the man in the world that I am most beholding (obliged) to, and my good lady and mother your wife, that as well as her own hath fostered and kept me. And if ever it be God's will that I be king, as ye say, ye shall desire of me what I may do, and I shall not fail you."

"Sir," said Sir Ector, "I will ask no more of you but that you make my son, your fostered brother Sir Kay, seneschal of all your lands."

"That shall be done, sir," said Arthur, "and more by the faith of my body; and never man shall have that office but he while that he and I live."

There withal they went unto the archbishop, and told him how the sword was achieved, and by whom. And upon the twelfth day all the barons came thither for to assay to take the sword. But there afore them all, there might none take it out but only Arthur; wherefore there were many great lords wroth, and said, "It was great shame unto them all and the realm to be governed by a boy of no high blood born." And so they fell out at that time, that it was put off till Candlemas, and then all the barons should meet there again. But always the ten knights were ordained for to watch the sword both day and night; and so they set a pavilion over the stone and the sword, and five always watched. And at Candlemas many more great lords came thither for to have won the sword, but none of them might prevail. And right as Arthur did at Christmas he did at Candlemas, and pulled out the sword easily, whereof the barons were sore aggrieved, and put it in delay till the high feast of Easter. And as Arthur sped

afore, so did he at Easter; and yet there were some of the great lords had indignation that Arthur should be their king, and put it off in delay till the feast of Pentecost.

And at the feast of Pentecost all manner of men assayed to pull at the sword that would assay, and none might prevail; but Arthur pulled it out afore all the lords and commons that were there, wherefore all the commons cried at once: "We will have Arthur unto our king; we will put him no more in delay; for we all see that it is God's will that he shall be our king, and who that holdeth against it we will slay him." And therewithal they kneeled down all at once, both rich and poor, and cried Arthur mercy, because they had delayed him so long. And Arthur forgave it them, and took the sword between both his hands, and offered it upon the altar where the archbishop was, and so was he made knight of the best man that was there. And so anon was the coronation made, and there was he sworn to the lords and commons for to be a true king, to stand with true justice from henceforth all the days of this life. Also then he made all lords that held of the crown to come in, and to do service as they ought to do. And many complaints were made unto King Arthur of great wrongs that were done since the death of King Uther, of many lands that were bereaved of lords, knights, ladies and gentlemen. Wherefore King Arthur made the lands to be given again unto them that owned them. When this was done that the king had stablished all the countries about London, then he let make Sir Kay seneschal of England; and Sir Baudwin of Britain was made constable; and Sir Ulfius was made chamberlain; and Sir Brastias was made warden to wait upon the north from Trent forwards, for it was that time for the most part enemy to the king.

Then on a day there came into the court a squire on horseback, leading a knight before him wounded to the death, and told him there was a knight in the forest that had reared up a pavilion by a well (spring) side, "and hath slain my master, a good knight, and his name was Miles; wherefore I beseech you that my master may be buried, and that some good knight may revenge my master's death." Then was in the court great noise of the knight's death, and every man said his advice. Then came Griflet, that was but a squire, and he was but young, of the age of King Arthur, so he besought the king, for all his service that he had done, to give him the order of knighthood.

"Thou art full young and tender of age," said King Arthur, "for to take so high an order upon thee."

"Sir," said Griflet, "I beseech you to make me a knight."

"Sir," said Merlin, "it were pity to leese (lose) Griflet, for he will be a passing good man when he cometh to age, abiding with you the term of his life; and if he adventure his body with yonder knight at the fountain, he shall be in great peril if ever he come again, for he is one of the best knights of the world, and the strongest man of arms."

"Well," said King Arthur. So, at the desire of Griflet, the king made him knight.

"Now," said King Arthur to Sir Griflet, "sithen (since) that I have made thee knight, thou must grant me a gift."

"What ye will, my lord," said Sir Griflet.

"Thou shalt promise me, by the faith of thy body, that when thou has jousted with the knight at the fountain, whether it fall (happen) that ye be on foot or on horseback, that in the same manner ye shall come again unto me without any question or making any more debate."

"I will promise you," said Griflet, "as ye desire." Then Sir Griflet took his horse in great haste, and dressed his shield, and took a great spear in his hand, and so he rode a great gallop till he came to the fountain, and thereby he saw a rich pavilion, and thereby under a cloth stood a fair horse well saddled and bridled, and on a tree a shield of divers colors, and a great spear. Then Sir Griflet smote upon the shield with the end of his spear, that the shield fell down to the ground.

With that came the knight out of the pavilion, and said, "Fair knight, why smote ye down my shield?"

"For I will joust with you," said Sir Griflet.

"It were better ye did not," said the knight, "for ye are but young and late made knight, and your might is nothing to mine."

"As for that," said Sir Griflet, "I will joust with you."

"That is me loth," said the knight, "but sith (since) I must needs, I will dress me thereto; but of whence be ye?" said the knight.

"Sir, I am of King Arthur's court." So they ran together that Sir Griflet's spear all toshivered (shivered all to pieces) and therewithal he smote Sir Griflet through the shield and the left side, and brake the spear, that the truncheon stuck in his body, that horse and knight fell down.

When the knight saw him lie so on the ground he alighted, and was passing heavy, for he wend (weened) he had slain him, and then he unlaced his helm and got him wind, and so with the truncheon he set him on his horse, and betook him to God, and said he had a mighty heart, and if he might live he would prove a passing good knight. And so Sir Griflet rode to the court, whereas great moan was made for him. But through good leeches (surgeons) he was healed and his life saved.

And King Arthur was passing wroth for the hurt of Sir Griflet. And by and by he commanded a man of his chamber that his best horse and armor "be without the city or (before) tomorrow day." Right so in the morning he met with his man and his horse, and so mounted up and dressed his shield, and took his spear, and bade his chamberlain tarry there till he came again. And so King Arthur rode but a soft pace till it was day, and then was he ware of three churls which chased Merlin, and would have slain him. Then King Arthur rode unto them a good pace, and cried to them: "Flee, churls." Then were they afraid when they saw a knight, and fled away. "O Merlin," said King Arthur, "here hadst thou been slain for thy craft, had I not been."

"Nay," said Merlin, "not so, for I could save myself if I would, and thou art more near thy death than I am, for thou gost towards thy death, and God be not thy friend."

So, as they went thus talking, they came to the fountain, and the rich pavilion by it. Then King Arthur was aware where a knight sat all armed in a chair. "Sir Knight," said King Arthur, "for what cause abidest thou here?

That there may no knight ride this way but if he do joust with thee?" said the king. "I rede (advise) thee leave that custom," said King Arthur.

"This custom," said the knight, "have I used and will use, maugre (in spite of) who saith nay; and who is grieved with my custom, let him amend it that will."

"I will amend it," said King Arthur.

"And I shall defend it," said the knight. Anon he took his horse, and dressed his shield, and took a spear, and they met so hard either on other's shield, that they all toshivered (shivered all to pieces) their spears. Therewith King Arthur drew his sword. "Nay, not so," said the knight, "it is fairer that we twain run more together with sharp spears."

"I will well," said King Arthur, "an (if) I had any (more) spears."

"I have spears enough," said the knight. So there came a squire, and brought two good spears, and King Arthur took one and he the other. So they spurred their horses, and came together with all their mights, that either brake their spears to their hands. Then Arthur set hand on his sword. "Nay," said the knight, "ye shall do better; ye are a passing good jouster as ever I met withal, and for the love of the high order of knighthood let us joust once again."

"I assent me," said King Arthur. Anon there were brought two great spears, and every knight gat a spear, and therewith they ran together that Arthur's spear all toshivered. But the other knight hit him so hard in midst of the shield that horse and man fell to the earth, and therewith Arthur was eager, and pulled out his sword, and said, "I will assay thee, Sir Knight, on foot, for I have lost the honor on horseback."

"I will be on horseback," said the knight. Then was Arthur wroth, and dressed his shield towards him with his sword drawn. When the knight saw that, he alight, for him thought no worship to have a knight at such avail, he to be on horseback, and he on foot, and so he alight and dressed his shield unto Arthur. And there began a strong battle with many great strokes, and so hewed with their swords that the cantels (pieces, of armor or of flesh) flew

in the fields, and much blood they bled both, that all the place there as they fought was over-bled with blood, and thus they fought long, and rested them, and then they went to the battle again, and so hurtled together like two rams that either fell to the earth. So at the last they smote together, that both their swords met even together. But the sword of the knight smote King Arthur's sword in two pieces, wherefore he was heavy. Then said the knight unto Arthur, "Thou art in my danger whether me list to save thee or slay thee, and but thou yield thee as overcome and recreant thou shalt die."

"As for death," said King Arthur, "welcome be it when it cometh, but as to yield me to thee as recreant, I had liever die than to be so shamed." And therewithal the king leapt unto Pellinore, and took him by the middle, and threw him down, and raced off his helm. When the knight felt that, he was adread, for he was a passing big man of might, and anon he brought King Arthur under him, and raced off his helm, and would have smitten off his head.

Therewithal came Merlin, and said: "Knight, hold thy hand, for an (if) thou slay that knight, thou puttest this realm in the greatest damage that ever realm was in, for this knight is a man of more worship than thou wottest of."

"Why, who is he?" said the knight.

"It is King Arthur."

Then would he have slain him for dread of his wrath, and heaved up his sword, and therewith Merlin cast an enchantment on the knight, that he fell to the earth in a great sleep. Then Merlin took up King Arthur, and rode forth upon the knight's horse. "Alas," said King Arthur, "what hast thou done, Merlin? hast thou slain this good knight by thy crafts? There lived not so worshipful a knight as he was; I had liever than the stint (loss) of my land a year, that he were on live."

"Care ye not," said Merlin, "for he is wholer than ye, for he is but on sleep, and will awake within three hours. I told you," said Merlin, "what a knight he was; here had ye been slain had I not been. Also, there liveth not a better knight than he is, and he shall do you hereafter right good service, and his name is Pellinore, and he shall have two sons, that shall be passing good men."

Right so the king and he departed, and went unto an hermit that was a good man and a great leech. So the hermit searched all his wounds and gave him good salves; and the king was there three days, and then were his wounds well amended that he might ride and go. So Merlin and he departed, and as they rode, Arthur said, "I have no sword."

"No force," said Merlin, "hereby is a sword that shall be yours, an (if) I may." So they rode till they came to a lake, which was a fair water and a broad, and in the middest of the lake King Arthur was ware of an arm clothed in white samite, that held a fair sword in the hand. "Lo," said Merlin, "yonder is that sword that I spake of." With that they saw a damsel going upon the lake.

"What damsel is that?" said Arthur.

"That is the Lady of the Lake," said Merlin; "and this damsel will come to you anon, and then speak ye fair to her that she will give you that sword." Anon withal came the damsel unto Arthur and saluted him, and he her again.

"Damsel," said Arthur, "what sword is that, that yonder the arm holdeth above the water? I would it were mine, for I have no sword."

"Sir king," said the damsel, "that sword is mine, and if ye will give me a gift when I ask it you, ye shall have it."

"By my faith," said Arthur, "I will give you what gift ye will ask."

"Well," said the damsel, "go ye into yonder barge and row yourself to the sword, and take it and the scabbard with you, and I will ask my gift when I see my time."

So King Arthur and Merlin alighted and tied their horses to two trees, and so they went into the ship, and when they came to the sword that the hand held, King Arthur took it up by the handles, and took it with him. And the arm and the hand went under the water; and so they came unto the land and rode forth. And then King Arthur saw a rich pavilion: "What signifieth yonder pavilion?"

"It is the knight's pavilion," said Merlin, "that ye fought with last, Sir Pellinore, but he is out,

he is not there; he hath ado with a knight of yours, that hight (was named) Egglame, and they have fought together, but at the last Egglame fled, and else he had been dead, and he hath chased him to Caerleon, and we shall anon meet with him in the high way."

"It is well said," quoth King Arthur, "now have I a sword, and now will I wage battle with him and be avenged on him."

"Sir, ye shall not do so," said Merlin, "for the knight is weary of fighting and chasing, so that ye shall have no worship to have ado with him; also he will not lightly be matched of one knight living; and therefore my counsel is that ye let him pass, for he shall do you good service in short time, and his sons after his days. Also ye shall see that day in short space, that ye shall be right glad to give him your sister to wife."

"When I see him," said King Arthur, "I will do as ye advise me."

Then King Arthur looked upon the sword and liked it passing well.

"Whether liketh you better," said Merlin, "the sword or the scabbard?"

"Me liketh better the sword," said King Arthur.

"Ye are more unwise," said Merlin, "for the scabbard is worth ten of the sword, for while ye have the scabbard upon you ye shall leese (lose) no blood be ye never so sore wounded, therefore keep well the scabbard alway with you."

So they rode on to Caerleon, and by the way they met with Sir Pellinore. But Merlin had done such a craft that Pellinore saw not Arthur, and so he passed by without any words.

"I marvel," said the king, "that the knight would not speak."

"Sir," said Merlin, "he saw you not, for an (if) he had seen you he had not lightly departed."

So they came unto Caerleon, whereof the knights were passing glad; and when they heard of his adventures, they marveled that he would jeopard his person so alone. But all men of worship said it was merry to be under such a chieftain that would put his person in adventure as other poor knights did.

Sir Lancelot Fails His Testing

Rosemary Sutcliff's provocative treatment of the quest of King Arthur's knights for the Holy Grail, incorporating modern psychology and ancient Celtic myth, creates a version of the quest for the cup used at the Last Supper that is broader than the medieval Christian legend. The selection below both evokes the shadows of Celtic myth and folklore underlying the Grail quest and offers a penetrating interpretation of Lancelot's dark night of the soul: his doomed struggle to redeem his adulterous love for Queen Guenever through his love of God. [From Rosemary Sutcliff, *The Light Beyond the Forest: The Quest for the Holy Grail* (Dutton, 1980).]

For many days after parting from his companions, Sir Lancelot rode alone through the forest, waiting with an open heart for God to tell him what to do and whither to turn his horse's head. But indeed it seemed to him that in that forest there was neither time nor place, so that a man might ride many days towards the sunset, and find himself at the last back in the place from which he had set out; almost, he might bide quiet beneath a tree and let the forest shift around him, like the country of a dream.

And then one morning he came down to a stream, and found a big warhorse that he thought he knew grazing on the bank, its bit slipped free and its reins carefully knotted up to be out of its way. And sitting with his back to an alder tree, helmet off and his yellow head tipped back against the rough bark, Sir Percival, whistling soft and full-throated to a blackbird, and the blackbird whistling back as though they were old friends. But, indeed, Sir Percival was friends with all furred and feathered things.

He got to his feet when he saw Sir Lancelot ride out from the woodshore, slowly, as men move in armour, and they greeted each other; and when Sir Lancelot had turned his own horse loose to graze beside the other, they sat down again together beneath the alder tree. And Percival asked if he had seen or heard anything of Sir Galahad.

"Neither sound nor sight," said Lancelot.

Percival sighed.

"Were you seeking him?"

"I was hoping we might ride together a little while," Percival said, "but it was a foolish hope."

It seemed to Lancelot that the knight beside him was young to be riding errant and alone in the dark forest. And yet that was foolishness, for Percival had shown himself in the jousting to be no green boy. He was older than Galahad by at least a year, and no one would be thinking Galahad young to ride errant, no matter through what dark forest.

"Would I serve, until we can come by word of Sir Galahad?" he said. There was a smile in his voice; and if it was a crooked smile, that was hidden in the shadow of his helmet.

And Percival said, "If it be not Sir Galahad, there is none that I would rather ride with."

So when they went on again, they rode together.

For many days they kept each other company, and then one evening, in a wild dark country of rocks and twisted low-growing trees, they met with a knight bearing a great white shield blazoned with a blood-red cross; and because the device was strange to them, they did not know him for Sir Galahad, lately come from freeing the Castle of Maidens.

Sir Lancelot called out to him to know his name, but Sir Galahad never answered, for indeed he was away inside himself in some desert solitude of his own, as was often the way with him, and had no thought to come back and greet and be greeted by other men.

So when he did not answer, but would have ridden on across their path, Sir Lancelot called out a warning; and when still he neither checked nor answered, shouted the final challenge, "Joust!" and couching his lance, rode straight at him. Galahad looked round, then, and swung his horse to meet the charge; and the lance took him full on the shield and shattered into a score of pieces; but he remained rock-firm in the saddle, and his own lance in the same instant took Sir Lancelot under the guard, and hove him clean over his horse's crupper, but did him no other harm. Then Percival came thundering down upon the unknown knight, but Sir Galahad wrenched his horse aside, and as the other missed his thrust, took him with the sideways lance stroke as he hurtled past, and swept him from the saddle, so that he plunged down all asprawl beside Sir Lancelot, not knowing if it was day or night.

And Sir Galahad went back to the solitude within himself, and turned his horse and rode away.

By the time the two he had felled had gathered themselves together and caught their horses and remounted, he was long out of sight.

"We have no hope of catching him now," said Percival, "and this wilderness of rocks is no good place for us, with the dusk coming down. Let us turn back to the hermitage we passed a while since, and beg shelter for the night." For truth to tell, his bruises ached.

But Sir Lancelot was in a deeper pain. For this was the first time since he took valour that ever he had been unhorsed. And again, and achingly, he was remembering the words on Galahad's sword. Two things were most dear to him in life; one was his love for the Queen, and one was knowing that he was the best knight in the world; not merely the strongest, but the best, and not only that other men should say it of him, but that he should know it of himself. And the knowledge was beginning to grow most painfully within him that of these two things, he could not have both.

Sir Percival felt the trouble in his companion, and said, quick and warm, "It was surely a chance stroke."

Lancelot shook his head, "It was as clean a fall as ever I saw one knight give another. That is why I must press on after him. I must know who he is—"

"Wait until morning," Percival said, "and then we will seek him together."

"No," said Lancelot, "I must know—I must find out—"

"Then God go with you," said Percival, "but I will ride no further this night."

So they parted, and Percival turned back to the hermitage, while Lancelot pushed on through the rocks and the stunted trees and the gathering dusk, after the glimmer of a crimson cross on a white shield.

When it was full dark, he came to a rough stone cross that stood on the edge of wild heath country at the parting of two ways; and close beyond it saw an ancient chapel. He dis-

mounted, and, leading his horse, walked towards the chapel, for he hoped there might be someone there who could tell him which way the knight had gone. But when he had looped the reins over a branch of the ancient hawthorn that grew beside the place, and turned himself to look more closely at the chapel, it was no more than a ruin, with nettles growing thick about the door sill; and coming within the porch, he found a rusty iron grille to bar his way.

And yet the place could not be deserted after all, for light flooded out to him through the grille, and within, he could see an altar richly hung with silken cloths; and before the altar, six candles glimmered crocus-flamed in a branched silver candlestick. But no man moved within the lighted sanctuary—nothing stirred save the night wind blowing from the heath; and though a great longing came upon him to go in and kneel before the altar, there was no way in. No way at all.

For a long time he knelt there outside the grille, hoping that someone would come, but no one came, and at last he rose and turned away, and unhitching his horse from the thorn branch, led it back as far as the wayside cross, unsaddled it and turned it loose to graze. Then he unlaced his helm and set it on the ground, unbuckled his sword belt, and lying down with his head on his shield, fell into a fitful sleep full of ragged dreams and uneasy wakings, and always the vision of the knight with the white shield glimmering far ahead of him, out of reach.

By and by, as he lay so, a late moon began to rise; and by its light he saw coming towards him along the track two palfreys with a litter slung between them; and in the litter a knight, sick or wounded, and moaning aloud in his pain. The mounted squire who led the foremost palfrey halted close beside the cross. And the knight broke out from his dumb moaning into piteous words: "Sweet God in Heaven, shall my sufferings never cease? Shall I never see the Holy Cup which shall ease this weary pain?" And he stretched out his hands in anguished pleading.

And all the while, Sir Lancelot lay without speech or movement, so that he seemed to be asleep, yet seeing all that went on. And lying so, he saw the silver candlestick issue from the chapel, no hand carrying it, and with its six tapers burning clear and still, move towards the cross. And behind the candles, floating in the same way, lightly as a fallen leaf floats on still water, came a silver table; and on the table, half veiled in its own light, so that his eyes could not fully look upon it, the Grail that he had seen in Arthur's court at the feast of Pentecost.

No thunder this time, no sunbeam, but the great stillness, and the blaze of white light.

And when he saw the wonder coming towards him, the sick knight tumbled himself from his litter, and lay where he fell, his hands stretched out to it, crying, "Lord, look on me in thy mercy, and by the power of this holy vessel grant me healing from my sickness!"

And with his eyes fixed upon the light, he dragged himself towards it, until he could touch the silver table with his hands. And even as he did so, a great shudder ran through him, and he gave a sobbing and triumphant cry, "Ah, God! I am healed!"

And with that cry, it was as though he sank into sleep.

And all the while, in his strange half-waking state, Sir Lancelot saw and heard, yet could feel *nothing*. He watched the Grail come, and stay a while, and presently move back into the chapel again; and he knew that it was the Grail of his quest, and his heart should have leapt in awe and exultation, and he should have been kneeling in worship beside the other knight; and still he could feel *nothing*. It was as though his spirit within him was turned to lead.

When the Grail was gone back into the chapel again, and the six-branched candlestick after it, and there was no light but the moon, the knight of the litter awoke, strong again and filled with life as though he had never known a day's sickness; and his squire came from where he had been waiting at a little distance all the while, and said, "Sir, is it well with you?"

"It is well and more than well with me, thanks be to God!" said the knight. "But I cannot but wonder how it is with yonder man who lies sleeping at the foot of the cross, and did not rouse once at the marvel that has been here this night."

"Surely it must be some wretch who has committed a great sin, so that God deemed him unworthy of the mystery that you have been allowed to share," said the squire.

And he brought the knight's armour, which had lain beside him in the litter, and helped him to arm. But when it came to the helm, the squire came across to where Sir Lancelot lay, and took up his helm, and his sword Joyeux that lay beside him, and caught and saddled his horse, and took all to his master. "You will make better use of these, for sure," said he, "than that worthless knight who must have forfeited all right to such honourable gear. Now mount, my lord, and let us ride."

So the knight mounted Sir Lancelot's horse, and the squire again leading the litter palfreys, they rode away.

Soon after, Sir Lancelot stirred and sat up, like a man rousing from deep sleep; and at first he wondered whether he had indeed seen, or only dreamed, what had happened. Then he got up and went back to the chapel. But the grille was still across the doorway, and though the tapers glimmered within, he could see no sign of the Grail.

For a while he stood there, waiting, he did not know for what, and hoping—hoping—And then there came a voice from somewhere, maybe out of his own heart. It was a cold and terrible voice that said, "Lancelot, harder than stone, more bitter than wood, more barren than the fig tree, get thee gone from this holy place, for thy presence fouls it."

And he turned away, and stumbled back to the foot of the wayside cross, weeping as he went, for what he had lost without ever finding it. And so he saw that his horse and sword and helm were gone, and he knew that it was all bitter truth and none of it a dream. And he crouched down at the foot of the cross, and came near to breaking his heart within him.

The day dawned at last, sun up, and the sky ringing with lark-song above the open country. Sir Lancelot had always taken great joy in such mornings; but now he felt that nothing could ever bring him joy again; and he turned away from the wayside cross and the chapel and the open heathland, and set out again through the dark forest, unhorsed and unhelmed, and with his sword sheath hanging empty at his side.

The day was still short of noon when he came upon a small wattle-built woodland church, in which a solitary priest was making ready for the service. He went in and knelt down, and heard Mass; and when it was over, begged the priest for council, in the name of God.

"What manner of council do you seek?" asked the holy man. "Is it that you would make your confession?"

"I have sore need to do that," said Lancelot.

"Come then, in the name of God."

He led him to the altar, and the two of them knelt down side by side.

Then the priest asked Lancelot his name, and when he heard that the stranger with the crooked grief-stricken face was Sir Lancelot of the Lake, he said, "Then, sir, if all I have heard of the foremost of Arthur's knights be true, you owe God a great return, for that he has made you the man you are."

"Then ill have I repaid him," said Lancelot, "and this he has all too clearly shown me, in the thing that befell me last night."

"Tell me of last night," said the priest.

And Sir Lancelot told him of all that had passed.

When he had finished, the priest said, "Now it is clear to me that you bear the weight of some mortal sin upon your soul. But the Lord God holds out his arms to all sinners who repent and make amendment. Now therefore make your confession to God, through me, and I will give you all the help and counsel that I may."

But Lancelot knelt there silent, with bowed head. He had made his confession as often as any other man. But he had never made it fully; for the love between himself and the Queen was not his alone to confess. Yet he knew in his heart that it was the thing that was shutting him out from God. He had never known that so clearly as he knew it now, and his heart was torn two ways. And still the priest begged him to confess his sin, promising that if he did so and renounced it utterly God would let him in again. And at last it was as though something cracked within him, and he said like a man in mortal pain, "For more than twenty years I have loved my Lady Guenever, the Queen."

"And you have won her love to you?"

Lancelot bowed his head lower yet.

"And what of King Arthur, her lord?"

"The marriage was made between them for the good of the kingdom, after the way of marriages between kings and queens. After, she grew to love him as a most dear friend. To me also he is the best-loved friend I have ever had. We would not that any hurt should come to him."

"Yet you wrong him by your love for each other, every hour of every day."

"I am a great sinner," said Sir Lancelot, "and the weight of my sin is on my head and on my spirit. I am shut out from God."

"So then, your sin is confessed," said the priest. "Now swear before God, as you hope for his forgiveness, that you will turn from the Queen's fellowship, and never be with her again, save when others are by."

"I swear," said Sir Lancelot, seeming to tear something raw and bleeding from his breast.

"And that from now on, you will not even wish for her presence, nor be with her in your inmost thoughts," said the priest; and his words fell single and pitiless as axe blows.

"I—swear," said Sir Lancelot. But he prayed within himself, "God help me! For unless you help me, I have sworn an oath which I cannot keep. I will try, with all the strength that is in me. More, I cannot do. And sweet God in Heaven, help and comfort my lady also." And so he was already a little foresworn.

Then the priest gave him absolution and his blessing.

And they rose from before the altar, and turned to leave the church. And seeing how the knight stumbled as though for mortal weariness, the holy man said, "My cell is close by; come with me and rest, and when you are rested, we will speak of what is next for you to do."

"I thank you; and glad would I be to rest," said Lancelot. "As to what is next for me to do, that I already know; I must find some way to come by another sword and helm and another horse, that I may ride forward again on the Quest."

"In that I can help you," said the priest, "for I have a brother, a knight-at-arms, rich in this world's goods, who lives not far from here.

And he will furnish all these things gladly, as soon as I send to ask for them.''

"Then my thanks to you, and to your brother. And most surely I will stay a while.''

And now the story leaves Sir Lancelot of the Lake, and tells again of Sir Percival.

Robin Hood and Little John

The popularity of Robin Hood, even in this day of science fiction and space exploration, is due no doubt to the fact that here is a hero who upholds the ideals of fair play, champions the cause of the poor and weak against the tyranny of the wealthy and the mighty, and leads a life in the greenwood that appeals to the enduring belief that the pastoral way of existence is the ideal one. Above all, Robin Hood is a man of action.

He is a folk hero; his feats and adventures have their origins in the popular ballads of the common people. Whether he ever existed is debatable, but exist he does as an ideal of medieval England, a free man in a ruthless world, with a generous sense of humor and a passion for justice. The earliest appearance of his name in print occurs in the poem *Piers Plowman,* by William Langland, in the fourteenth century. Many of the chapbooks of the early eighteenth century were devoted to accounts of him in ballad form. From such stuff epics have been formed, but though one can see, in these scattered sources, the outlines of an epic hero, no poet emerged to give the majesty of epic form to the crude tales.

Howard Pyle (1853–1911), the American author, artist, and teacher, brought up on ballads and old tales, gave the stories of Robin Hood an epic stature for young readers. *The Merry Adventures of Robin Hood,* published in 1883, is a glorious re-creation of the medieval world, true in every detail to the spirit of the age, and to the idealization that the era awakens in the minds of children. The vivid, poetic text is sustained and extended by his own superb illustrations in clear line and strong design. [From Howard Pyle, *The Merry Adventures of Robin Hood of Great Renown in Nottinghamshire* (Scribner's, 1883).]

Up rose Robin Hood one merry morn when all the birds were singing blithely among the leaves, and up rose all his merry men, each fellow washing his head and hands in the cold brown brook that leaped laughing from stone to stone. Then said Robin: "For fourteen days have we seen no sport, so now I will go abroad to seek adventures forthwith. But tarry ye, my merry men all, here in the greenwood; only see that ye mind well my call. Three blasts upon the bugle horn I will blow in my hour of need; then come quickly, for I shall want your aid.''

So saying, he strode away through the leafy forest glades until he had come to the verge of Sherwood. There he wandered for a long time, through highway and byway, through dingly dell and forest skirts. Now he met a fair buxom lass in a shady lane, and each gave the other a merry word and passed their way; now he saw a fair lady upon an ambling pad, to whom he doffed his cap, and who bowed sedately in return to the fair youth; now he saw a fat monk on a pannier-laden ass; now a gallant knight, with spear and shield and armor that flashed brightly in the sunlight; now a page clad in crimson; and now a stout burgher from good Nottingham Town, pacing along with serious footsteps; all these sights he saw, but adventure found he none. At last he took a road by the forest skirts; a bypath that dipped toward a broad, pebbly stream spanned by a narrow bridge made of a log of wood. As he drew nigh this bridge, he saw a tall stranger coming from the other side. Thereupon Robin quickened his pace, as did the stranger likewise; each thinking to cross first.

"Now stand thou back,'' quoth Robin, "and let the better man cross first.''

"Nay,'' answered the stranger, "then stand back thine own self, for the better man, I wot, am I.''

"That will we presently see,'' quoth Robin; "and meanwhile stand thou where thou art, or else, by the bright brow of Saint Elfrida, I will show thee right good Nottingham play with a clothyard shaft betwixt thy ribs.''

"Now,'' quoth the stranger, "I will tan thy hide till it be as many colors as a beggar's cloak, if thou darest so much as touch a string of that same bow that thou holdest in thy hands.''

"Thou pratest like an ass,'' said Robin, "for I could send this shaft clean through thy proud heart before a curtal friar could say grace over a roast goose at Michaelmastide.''

"And thou pratest like a coward,'' answered

the stranger, "for thou standest there with a good yew bow to shoot at my heart, while I have nought in my hand but a plain blackthorn staff wherewith to meet thee."

"Now," quoth Robin, "by the faith of my heart, never have I had a coward's name in all my life before. I will lay by my trusty bow and eke my arrows, and if thou darest abide my coming, I will go and cut a cudgel to test thy manhood withal."

"Ay, marry, that will I abide thy coming, and joyously, too," quoth the stranger; whereupon he leaned sturdily upon his staff to await Robin.

Then Robin Hood stepped quickly to the coverside and cut a good staff of round oak, straight, without flaw, and six feet in length, and came back trimming away the tender stems from it, while the stranger waited for him, leaning upon his staff, and whistling as he gazed roundabout.

Illustration by Victor G. Ambrus, from *Robin Hood: His Life and Legend,* by Bernard Miles (Hamlyn Publishing Group Ltd., 1979). Reprinted by permission of Hamlyn Publishing.

Robin observed him furtively as he trimmed his staff, measuring him from top to toe from out the corner of his eye, and thought that he had never seen a lustier or a stouter man. Tall was Robin, but taller was the stranger by a head and a neck, for he was seven feet in height. Broad was Robin across the shoulders, but broader was the stranger by twice the breadth of a palm, while he measured at least an ell around the waist.

"Nevertheless," said Robin to himself, "I will baste thy hide right merrily, my good fellow"; then, aloud, "Lo, here is my good staff, lusty and tough. Now wait my coming, an thou darest, and meet me, an thou fearest not; then we will fight until one or the other of us tumble into the stream by dint of blows."

"Marry, that meeteth my whole heart!" cried the stranger, twirling his staff above his head, betwixt his fingers and thumb, until it whistled again.

Never did the Knights of Arthur's Round Table meet a stouter fight than did these two. In a moment Robin stepped quickly upon the bridge where the stranger stood; first he made a feint, and then delivered a blow at the stranger's head that, had it met its mark, would have tumbled him speedily into the water; but the stranger turned the blow right deftly, and in return gave one as stout, which Robin also turned as the stranger had done. So they stood, each in his place, neither moving a finger's breadth back, for one good hour, and many blows were given and received by each in that time, till here and there were sore bones and bumps, yet neither thought of crying "Enough!" or seemed likely to fall from off the bridge. Now and then they stopped to rest, and each thought that he never had seen in all his life before such a hand at quarterstaff. At last Robin gave the stranger a blow upon the ribs that made his jacket smoke like a damp straw thatch in the sun. So shrewd was the stroke that the stranger came within a hair's breadth of falling off the bridge; but he regained himself right quickly, and, by a dexterous blow, gave Robin a crack on the crown that caused the blood to flow. Then Robin grew mad with anger, and smote with all his might at the other; but the

stranger warded the blow, and once again thwacked Robin, and this time so fairly that he fell heels over head into the water, as the queen pin falls in a game of bowls.

"And where art thou now, good lad?" shouted the stranger, roaring with laughter.

"Oh, in the flood and floating adown with the tide," cried Robin; nor could he forbear laughing himself at his sorry plight. Then, gaining his feet, he waded to the bank, the little fish speeding hither and thither, all frightened at his splashing.

"Give my thy hand," cried he, when he had reached the bank. "I must needs own thou art a brave and a sturdy soul, and, withal, a good stout stroke with the cudgels. By this and by that, my head hummeth like to a hive of bees on a hot June day."

Then he clapped his horn to his lips, and winded a blast that went echoing sweetly down the forest paths. "Ay, marry," quoth he again, "thou are a tall lad, and eke a brave one, for ne'er, I trow, is there a man betwixt here and Canterbury Town could do the like to me that thou hast done."

"And thou," quoth the stranger, laughing, "takest thy cudgeling like a brave heart and a stout yeoman."

But now the distant twigs and branches rustled with the coming of men, and suddenly a score or two of good stout yeomen, all clad in Lincoln green, burst from out the covert, with merry Will Stutely at their head.

"Good master," cried Will, "how is this? Truly thou art all wet from head to foot, and that to the very skin."

"Why, marry," answered jolly Robin, "yon stout fellow hath tumbled me neck and crop into the water, and hath given me a drubbing beside."

"Then shall he not go without a ducking and eke a drubbing himself!" cried Will Stutely. "Have at him, lads!"

Then Will and a score of yeomen leaped upon the stranger, but though they sprang quickly they found him ready and felt him strike right and left with his stout staff, so that, though he went down with press of numbers, some of them rubbed cracked crowns before he was overcome.

"Nay, forbear!" cried Robin, laughing until his sore sides ached again; "he is a right good man and true, and no harm shall befall him. Now hark ye, good youth, wilt thou stay with me and be one of my band? Three suits of Lincoln green shalt thou have each year, beside forty marks in fee, and share with us whatsoever good shall befall us. Thou shalt eat sweet venison and quaff the stoutest ale, and mine own good right-hand man shalt thou be, for never did I see such a cudgelplayer in all my life before. Speak! wilt thou be one of my good merry men?"

"That know I not," quoth the stranger, surlily, for he was angry at being so tumbled about. "If ye handle yew bow and apple shaft no better than ye do oaken cudgel, I wot ye are not fit to be called yeomen in my country; but if there by any men here that can shoot a better shaft than I, then will I bethink me of joining with you."

"Now, by my faith," said Robin, "thou art a right saucy varlet, sirrah; yet I will stoop to thee as I never stooped to man before. Good Stutely, cut thou a fair white piece of bark four fingers in breadth, and set it fourscore yards distant on yonder oak. Now, stranger, hit that fairly with a gray goose shaft and call thyself an archer."

"Ay, marry, that will I," answered he. "Give me a good stout bow and a fair broad arrow, and if I hit it not, strip me and beat me blue with bow-strings."

Then he chose the stoutest bow amongst them all, next to Robin's own, and a straight gray goose shaft, well-feathered and smooth, and stepping to the mark—while all the band, sitting or lying upon the greensward, watched to see him shoot—he drew the arrow to his cheek and loosed the shaft right deftly, sending it so straight down the path that it clove the mark in the very center. "Aha!" cried he, "mend thou that if thou canst"; while even the yeomen clapped their hands at so fair a shot.

"That is a keen shot, indeed," quoth Robin; "mend it I cannot, but mar it I may, perhaps."

Then taking up his own good stout bow and notching an arrow with care, he shot with his very greatest skill. Straight flew the arrow, and so true that it lit fairly upon the stranger's shaft and split it into splinters. Then all the yeomen leaped to their feet and shouted for joy that their master had shot so well.

"Now, by the lusty yew bow of good Saint Withold," cried the stranger, "that is a shot indeed, and never saw I the like in all my life before! Now truly will I be thy man henceforth and for aye. Good Adam Bell was a fair shot, but never shot he so!"

"Then have I gained a right good man this day," quoth jolly Robin. "What name goest thou by, good fellow?"

"Men call me John Little whence I came," answered the stranger.

Then Will Stutely, who loved a good jest, spoke up. "Nay, fair little stranger," said he, "I like not thy name and fain would I have it otherwise. Little art thou, indeed, and small of bone and sinew; therefore shalt thou be christened Little John, and I will be thy godfather."

Then Robin Hood and all his band laughed aloud until the stranger began to grow angry.

"An thou make a jest of me," quoth he to Will Stutely, "thou wilt have sore bones and little pay, and that in short season."

"Nay, good friend," said Robin Hood, "bottle thine anger, for the name fitteth thee well. Little John shalt thou be called henceforth, and Little John shall it be. So come, my merry men, and we will go and prepare a christening feast for this fair infant."

So turning their backs upon the stream, they plunged into the forest once more, through which they traced their steps till they reached the spot where they dwelt in the depths of the woodland. There had they built huts of bark and branches of trees, and made couches of sweet rushes spread over with skins of fallow deer. Here stood a great oak tree with branches spreading broadly around, beneath which was a seat of green moss where Robin Hood was wont to sit at feast and at merry-making with his stout men about him. Here they found the rest of the band, some of whom had come in with a brace of fat does. Then they all built great fires and after a time roasted the does and broached a barrel of humming ale. Then when the feast was ready, they all sat down, but Robin Hood placed Little John at his right hand, for he was henceforth to be the second in the band.

Then, when the feast was done, Will Stutely spoke up. "It is now time, I ween, to christen our bonny babe, is it not so, merry boys?" And "Aye! Aye!" cried all, laughing till the woods echoed with their mirth.

"Then seven sponsors shall we have," quoth Will Stutely; and hunting among all the band he chose the seven stoutest men of them all.

"Now, by Saint Dunstan," cried Little John, springing to his feet, "more than one of you shall rue it an you lay finger upon me."

But without a word they all ran upon him at once, seizing him by his legs and arms and holding him tightly in spite of his struggles, and they bore him forth while all stood around to see the sport. Then one came forward who had been chosen to play the priest because he had a bald crown, and in his hand he carried a brimming pot of ale. "Now who bringeth this babe?" asked he right soberly.

"That do I," answered Will Stutely.

"And what name callest thou him?"

"Little John call I him."

"Now Little John," quoth the mock priest, "thou hast not lived heretofore, but only got thee along through the world, but henceforth thou wilt live indeed. When thou livedst not, thou wast called John Little, but now that thou dost live indeed, Little John shalt thou be called, so christen I thee." And at these last words he emptied the pot of ale upon Little John's head.

Then all shouted with laughter as they saw the good brown ale stream over Little John's beard and trickle from his nose and chin, while his eyes blinked with the smart of it. At first he was of a mind to be angry, but he found he could not because the others were so merry; so he, too, laughed with the rest. Then Robin took this sweet, pretty babe, clothed him all anew from top to toe in Lincoln green, and gave him a good stout bow, and so made him a member of the merry band.

Ireland

The Wonder Smith and His Son

The tales of the Gubbaun Saor are stories out of an early mythology of Ireland, scattered accounts of a god, the Gubbaun Saor, who was the Wonder Smith, the world maker, the creator. His son was known as Lugh of the Long Hand, the god of the sun. Now the Gubbaun had no son of his own. He had only a daughter, Aunya. He thought a daughter a poor creature to whom to teach all the cleverness of his craft. One day, as he sat bemoaning his fate, who should come along but a woman who was sad in a like cause. She had only a son, and she was willing to give her life for a daughter. They exchanged children. It was a bargain the Gubbaun was to rue, for his son was no smith. He was a poet, a singer of songs, and he would do nothing but play on his reed pipe and sit in the sun. How the Gubbaun regained his daughter and in the end had both son and daughter together is told in part here.

Ella Young gathered these stories from the storytellers in remote regions of Ireland. It was she who discovered them. They are among the most witty, most beautiful, and most humane clusters of traditional stories. The Celtic love of nature; the exuberant love of language, and the mirth and wit; the exceptional role of woman in a primitive culture: These are shown forth in tellings characteristic of the Celtic turn of mind. [From Ella Young, *The Wonder Smith and His Son* (Longmans, 1927).]

The Gubbaun Saor sat outside in the sunshine, but it's little joy he had of the good day. He was wringing his hands and making lamentation.

"Ochone! Ochone!" he said, "my share of sorrow and the world's misfortune! Why was I given any cleverness at all, with nothing but a daughter to leave it to? Ochone!"

At that he heard a lamentation coming down the road. It was a woman raising an ullagone, clapping her hands like one distracted. She stopped when she came to the Gubbaun.

"What has happened to you, Jewel of the World," said she, "to be making lamentations?"

"Why wouldn't I make lamentations," said the Gubbaun, "when I have no one but a daughter to leave my cleverness to? 'Tis a hard thing to have all the trades in the world, and no one but a daughter to learn them!''

"The topmost berry is always sweet," said the woman, "and the red apple that is beyond us draws our hearts. You are crying salt tears for a son, and I would give the world for a daughter."

"O, what good is a daughter!" said the Gubbaun. "What good's a girl to a man that has robbed the crows of their cleverness and taught tricks to the foxes?"

"Maybe you'd be worse off," said the woman, "if you had a son. Isn't it myself that is making a hand-clapping and shedding the salt tears of my eyes because of the son I've got—a heart-scald from sunrise to candle-light!"

" 'Tis you," said the Gubbaun, "that don't know how to manage a son. He'd be a lamb of gentleness if I had him."

"O then take him," said the woman, "and give me your daughter. I'll be well content with the bargain!"

It was agreed between them, then and there. The Gubbaun took the son and the woman got the daughter. She went away after that and left no tidings of herself: she thought it likely the Gubbaun would rue the bargain.

The Gubbaun started to teach the son. He had systems and precepts and infallible methods of teaching, but the boy would not learn. He would do nothing but sit in the sunshine and play little tunes on a flute he had made. He grew up like that.

"Clever as I am," said the Gubbaun, "the woman that got my daughter got the better of me. If I had Aunya back again, 'tis I that would be praising the world. My share of grief and misfortune! Why did I give the red apple for the unripe crab?"

He beat his hands together and lamented: but the son in a pool of sunshine played a faery reel, and two blackbirds danced to it.

How the Gubbaun Tried His Hand at Match-Making

One day the Gubbaun roused himself:

"What my son needs," said he, "is a clever woman for a wife, and 'tis I that will choose one."

He gave out the news to the countryside, and many a woman came bragging of the daughter she had.

"The eye that looks on its own sees little blemish," said the Gubbaun. "I'll take no cleverness on hearsay: before I make a match for my son, I must talk to the girl he is to get."

It would take a year to tell of the girls that came, with their mothers to put a luck-word on them, and the girls that went, disheartened from the Gubbaun Saor. He out-baffled them with questions. He tripped and bewildered them with his cleverness. There was not a girl in the countryside wise enough to please him. Three girls, with a great reputation, came from a distance.

When the first girl came, the Gubbaun showed her a room heaped up with gold and treasure and the riches of the world.

"That is what the woman will get that marries my son," said he.

"There would be good spending in that pile!" said the girl. "You could be taking the full of your two hands out of it from morning till night every day in the year."

" 'Tis not you will be taking the full of your two hands out of it," said the Gubbaun. "My son will get a wiser woman."

The second girl came. The Gubbaun showed her the heap of treasure.

"I'll put seven bolts and seven bars on it," she said, "and in a hundred years it will not grow less!"

" 'Tis not you will put the bolts and bars on it," said the Gubbaun. "My son will get a wiser woman."

The third girl came. The Gubbaun showed her the heap of treasure.

"Big as it is," said she, "it will be lonesome if it is not added to!"

"I wonder," said the Gubbaun, "if you have the wit to add to it."

"Try me," said the girl.

"I will," said the Gubbaun. "Bargain with me for a sheepskin."

"If you have the wit to sell," said she, "I

have the wit to buy. Show me the skin and name your price."

He showed the skin; he named his price. It was a small price. She made it smaller. The Gubbaun gave in to her.

"You have a bargain in it," said the Gubbaun; "the money-handsel to me."

"You'll get that," said she, "when I have the skin."

"That's not my way at all," said the Gubbaun, "I must have the skin and the price of it."

"May Death never trip you till you get it!"

"I will get it from a woman that will come well out of the deal—and know her advantage!"

"May your luck blossom," said the girl, " 'tis ransacking the faery hills you'll be: or bargaining with the Hag of the Ford."

"Health and Prosperity to yourself!" said the Gubbaun.

She went out from him at that, but the Gubbaun sat with his mind turned inward, considering, considering—and considering.

How the Son of the Gubbaun Met with Good Luck

"It would be well for you to be raising a hand on your own behalf, now," said the Gubbaun Saor to his Son, "you can draw the birds from the bushes with one note of your flute: maybe you can draw luck with a woman. If you have the luck to get the daughter I gave in exchange for yourself, our good days will begin."

The Son of the Gubbaun got to his feet.

"I could travel the world," he said, "with my reed-flute and the Hound that came to me out of the Wood of Gold and Silver Yew Trees." With that he gave a low call, and a milk-white Hound came running to the door.

"Is it without counsel and without advice and without a road-blessing," cried the Gubbaun, "that you are setting out to travel the world? How will you know what girl has the fire of wisdom in her mind? What sign, what token will you ask of her?"

" 'Tis you that have wisdom: give me an advice," said the Son.

"Take the sheepskin," said the Gubbaun, "and set yourself to find a buyer for it. The

girl that will give you the skin and the price of it is the girl that will bring good luck across this threshold. The day and the hour that you find her, send home the Hound that I may know of her and set out the riches of this house."

"Tree of Wisdom," said the Son, "bear fruit and blossom on your branches. The road-blessing now to me."

"My blessing on the road that is smooth," said the Gubbaun, "and on the rough road through the quagmire. A blessing on night with the stars; and night when the stars are quenched. A blessing on the clear sky of day; and day that is choked with the thunder. May my blessing run before you. May my blessing guard you on the right hand and on the left. May my bless-

Illustration by Boris Artzybasheff, from *The Wonder Smith and His Son: A Tale from the Golden Childhood of the World*, retold by Ella Young. Copyright © 1927 by Longmans, Green & Co.; copyright © renewed 1955 by Ella Young. Published by David McKay Company, Inc.

ing follow you as your shadow follows. Take my road-blessing," said the Gubbaun.

"The shelter of the Hazel Boughs to you, Salmon of Wisdom," said the Son.

He set out then with the Hound to travel the solitary places and the marts of the world. He shook the dust of many a town from his feet, but the sheepskin remained on his shoulder. A cause of merriment that skin was; a target for shafts of wit; a shaming of face to the man that carried it. It found its way into proverbs and wonder tales, but it never found the bargain-clinch of a buyer.

If it hadn't been for the Hound, and the reed-flute, and the share of songs that he had, the Son of the Gubbaun Saor would have been worn to a skin of misery like a dried-up crabapple!

One day, in the teeth of the North Wind, he climbed a hill-gap and came all at once on a green plain. There was only one tree in that plain, but everywhere scarlet blossoms trembled through the grass. Beneath the tree was a well: and from the well a girl came towards him. Her heavy hair was like spun gold. She walked lightly and proudly. The Son of the Gubbaun thought it long till he could change words with her.

"May every day bring luck and blessing to you," he cried.

"The like wish to yourself," said she, "and may your load be light."

"A good wish," said he, "I have far to carry my load."

"How far?" asked the girl.

"To the world's end, I think."

"Are you under enchantment?" said she. "Did a Hag of the Storm put a spell on you; or a Faery-Woman take you in her net?"

" 'Tis the net of my father's wisdom that I am caught in," said he. "I must carry this sheepskin, my grief! till a woman gives me the price of it: and the skin itself, in the clinch of a good buyer's bargain."

"You need go no farther for that," said the girl. "Name your price for the skin."

He named his price. She took the skin. She plucked the wool from it. She gave him the skin and the price together.

"Luck on your hand," said he, "is the bargain a good one?"

"It is," said she, "I have fine pure wool for the price of a skin. May the price be a luck-penny!"

"You are the Woman my father brags of," cried the Son. "My Choice, My Share of the World you are, if you will come with me."

"I will come," said the girl.

The Son of the Gubbaun Saor called to the Hound.

"Swift One," he said, "our fortunes have blossomed. Set out now, and don't let the wind that is behind you catch you up, or the wind that is in front of you out-race you, till you lie down by the Gubbaun Saor's threshold."

The Hound stretched himself in his running. He was like a salmon that silvers in mid-leap; like the wind through a forest of sedges; like the sun-track on dark waters: and he was like that in his running till he lay down by the Gubbaun Saor's threshold.

How the Gubbaun Saor Welcomed Home His Daughter

Many a time the Gubbaun looked forth to see was the Hound coming. He was tired of looking forth. He flung himself on the bench he had carved, by the hearth-stone.

"I wish I never had a son!" he said. "I wish I were a young boy, wandering idly, or lying in a wood of larches with the wind stirring the tops of them. There is joy in the slanting stoop of the sea-hawk, but a man builds weariness for himself!"

He went to the door and looked forth.

The Wood of the Ridge stood blackly against the dawn. There was a great stillness. The earth seemed to listen. Suddenly the wood was full of singing voices. A brightness moved in it low down; brightness that grew, and grew; and neared; milk-white. The Hound! The Hound, Failinis, at last!

He broke, glittering, from the wood, and came with great leaps to the Gubbaun. The Gubbaun put his two hands about the head of the Hound.

"Treasure," he cried, "Swift-footed Jewel! Bringer of good tidings! It is time now to pile up the fires of welcome. It is time now to set my house in order. A hundred thousand welcomes!"

The Hound lay down by the door-stone.

The Gubbaun strewed green scented boughs on his threshold, plumes of the larch, branches of ash and quicken. Thorn in blossom he strewed; and marsh-mint; and frocken; and odorous red pine. He wondered if it was for Aunya—or for a stranger.

The Gubbaun piled up a fire of welcome. Beneath it he put nine sacred stones taken from the cavern of the Dragon of the Winds. He laid hazelwood on the pile for wisdom; and oak for enduring prosperity; and blackthorn boughs to win favour of the stars. Quicken wood he had; and ancient yew; and silver-branched holly. Ash, he had, too, on the pile; and thorn; and wood of the apple-tree. These things of worth he had on the pile. With incantations and ceremonies he built it, and with rites such as Druids use in the hill-fires that welcome the Spring and the coming of the Gods of Dana.

The Gubbaun set out the riches of his house; the beaten metals; the wild-beast skins; the broidered work. "If it is Aunya," thought he, "and her mind matches my own, she will care more for wide skiey spaces than for any roof-tree shaped by a tool." He thought of a wide stone-scattered plain; of great wings in the night— and his eyes changed colour. The Gubbaun had every colour in his eyes: they were gray at times like the twilight; green like the winter dawn; amber like bog-water in sunlight.

The Gubbaun considered the riches of his house. He looked at the walls he had built; the secret contrivances, the strange cunning engines he had fashioned. "I was bought," he said to himself, "with a handful of tools! Yet to make—and break—and remake—that is the strong-handed choice."

Outside, joyously, rose the baying of the Hound. They were coming! The Gubbaun set fire a-leap in the piled-up wood and ran to meet them.

Flames licked out; flames that were azure; and orange; and sapphire; and blinding white. They lifted themselves like crowned serpents. They hissed. They danced. They leaped into the air. They spread themselves. They blossomed. They found voice. They sang.

"Have you looked on a fire hotter or stronger than this?" asked the Gubbaun of the girl.

She looked on the flame. She said: "The Wind from the South has more warmth and more strength than all the ceremonial fires in Erin." And as she said it, her eyes that were blue like hyacinths in Spring turned gray like lake-water in shadow.

"It is Aunya," thought the Gubbaun, "she has the wisdom of the hills: I wonder has she the wisdom of the hearth."

He took her by the hand, he showed her his finest buildings; his engines; his secret contrivances. "What is your word on these?" he asked.

"You need no word," said the girl, "and well you know it! When the full tide is full, it is full; to-day, and to-morrow no less. Tear stone from stone of these walls in the hope to surpass them—you can do no more than raise them again, fitting each block to its fellow. Trust your own wit on your work, for it's a pity of him that trusts a woman!"

"You are Aunya," cried the Gubbaun, "you are Aunya, the treasure I lost in my youth. You were a dream in my mind when every precious stone was my covering. A hundred thousand welcomes, Aunya! This house is yours, and all its riches yours! The hearth-flame yours! The roof-tree yours!"

"The reddest sun-rise," said Aunya, "is the soonest quenched. You will bid me go from this house one day, without looking backwards to it. All I ask against that day is your oath to let me carry my choice of three armloads of treasure out of this house."

"There is no day in all the days of the year that you will get a hard word from me, Aunya, for now my Tree of Life is the holly: no wind of misfortune can blow the leaves from it."

"Bind your oath on my asking," said Aunya.

Then said the Gubbaun:

"On the strong Sun I bind my oath,
My oath to Aunya:
If I deny three treasure-loads to her,
May the strong Sun avenge her.

On the wise Moon I bind my oath,
My oath to Aunya:

If I rue my oath
Let the wise Moon give judgment.

On the kind Earth I bind my oath,
My oath to Aunya.
On the stones of the field;
On running water;
On growing grass.
Let the tusked boar avenge it!
Let the horned stag avenge it!
Let the piast of the waters avenge it!
On the strong Sun I bind my oath."

"It is enough, my Treasure and my Jewel of Wisdom!" said Aunya.

So Aunya, daughter of the Gubbaun Saor, came home.

Cuchulain's Wooing

Two major epics of the pre-Christian Celtic world revolve about heroes of epic proportions, Cuchulain, the Hound of Ulster, and Finn, the central figure in a group of stories concerning the *fiana*, a band of warriors. The Cuchulain cycle, which numbers more than a hundred tales, is the earlier. The tales are placed, in time, as evolving from the life of 400 B.C. to the first century of the Christian era. The earliest written documentation of them is not earlier than the eleventh century.

"Between the time of their invention for the entertainment of the chiefs and kings of Ireland to the time of their incorporation in the great books which contain the bulk of the tales, they were handed down by word of mouth, every bard and professional storyteller (of whom there was at least one in every great man's house) being obliged to know by heart a great number of these romances and prepared at any moment to recite those he might be called upon to give."—Eleanor Hull

The earliest written source is known as *The Book of the Dun Cow*, named for the color of the piece of parchment on which it was written, which was compiled in 1100 in the monastery of Clonmacnois on the Shannon. Eleanor Hull edited a scholarly version of the Cuchulain saga in 1898. The following selection comes from her retelling for children, which is also published under the title *The Boy's Cuchulain: Heroic Legends of Ireland*. [From Eleanor Hull, *Cuchulain, the Hound of Ulster* (Crowell, 1910).]

It was on a day of the days of summer that Emer, daughter of Forgall the Wily, sat on a bench before her father's door, at his fort that is called Lusk to-day, but which in olden days men spoke of as the Gardens of the Sun-god Lugh, so sunny and so fair and fertile was that plain, with waving meadow-grass and buttercups, and the sweet may-blossom girdling the fields. Close all about the fort the gardens lay, with apple-trees shedding their pink and white upon the playing fields of brilliant green; and all the air was noisy with the buzz of bees, and with the happy piping of the thrush and soft low cooing of the doves. And Emer sat, a fair and noble maid, among her young companions, foster-sisters of her own, who came from all the farms and forts around to grow up with the daughters of the house, and learn from them high-bred and gentle ways, to fashion rich embroideries such as Irish women used to practise as an art, and weaving, and fine needlework, and all the ways of managing a house. And as they sat round Emer, a bright comely group of busy girls, they sang in undertones the crooning tender melodies of ancient Erin; or one would tell a tale of early wars, and warrior feasts or happenings of the gods, and one would tell a tale of lover's joys or of the sorrows of a blighted love, and they would sigh and laugh and dream that they too loved, were wooed, and lost their loves.

And Emer moved about among the girls, directing them; and of all maids in Erin, Emer was the best, for hers were the six gifts of womanhood, the gift of loveliness, the gift of song, the gift of sweet and pleasant speech, the gift of handiwork, the gifts of wisdom and of modesty. And in his distant home in Ulster, Cuchulain heard of her. For he was young and brave, and women loved him for his nobleness, and all men wished that he should take a wife. But for awhile he would not, for among the women whom he saw, not one of them came up to his desires. And when they urged him, wilfully he said: "Well, find for me a woman I could love, and I will marry her." Then sent the King his heralds out through every part of Ulster and the south to seek a wife whom Cuchulain would care to woo. But still he said the same, "This one, and this, has some bad temper or some want of grace, or she is vain or she is weak, not fitted as a mate to such as I. She must be brave, for she must suffer much; she must be gentle, lest I anger her; she must be fair and noble, not alone to give me pleasure as her spouse, but that all men may think of her with pride, saying, 'As Cuchulain is the first of Ulster's braves, the hero of her many fighting-fields, so is his wife the noblest and the first of Erin's women, a worthy mate for him.' "

So when the princely messengers returned, their search was vain; among the daughters of the chiefs and noble lords not one was found whom Cuchulain cared to woo. But one who loved him told him of a night he spent in Forgall's fort, and of the loveliness and noble spirit of Forgall's second girl Emer, the maiden of the waving hair, but just grown up to womanhood. He told him of her noble mien and stately step, the soft and liquid brightness of her eyes, the colour of her hair, that like to ruddy gold fresh from the burnishing, was rolled round her head. Her graceful form he praised, her skilfulness in song and handiwork, her courage with her father, a harsh and wily man, whom all within the house hated and feared but she. He told him also that for any man to win the maiden for his wife would be a troublesome and dangerous thing, for out of all the world, her father Forgall loved and prized but her, and he had made it known that none beneath a king or ruling prince should marry her, and any man who dared to win her love, but such as these, should meet a cruel death; and this he laid upon his sons and made them swear to him upon their swords, that any who should come to woo the girl should never leave the fort alive again.

All that they said but made Cuchulain yet the more desire to see the maid and talk with her. "This girl, so brave, so wise, so fair of face and form," he pondered with himself, "would be a fitting mate for any chief. I think she is the fitting mate for me."

So on the very day when Emer sat upon her playing-fields, Cuchulain in the early morn set forth in all his festal garb in his chariot with his prancing steeds, with Laeg before him as his charioteer, and took the shortest route towards the plain of Bray, where lie the Gardens of the Sun-god Lugh. The way they went from

Emain lay between the Mountains of the Wood, and thence along the High-road of the Plain, where once the sea had passed; across the marsh that bore the name the Whisper of the Secret of the Gods. Then driving on towards the River Boyne they passed the Ridge of the Great Sow, where not far off is seen the fairy haunt of Angus, God of Beauty and of Youth; and so they reached the ford of Washing of the Horses of the Gods, and the fair, flowering plains of Lugh, called Lusk to-day.

Now all the girls were busied with their work, when on the high-road leading to the fort they heard a sound like thunder from the north, that made them pause and listen in surprise.

Nearer and nearer yet it came as though at furious pace a band of warriors bore down towards the house. "Let one of you see from the ramparts of the fort," said Emer, "what is the sound we hear coming towards us." Fiall, her sister, Forgall's eldest girl, ran to the top of the rath or earthen mound that circled round the playing-fields, and looked out towards the north, shading her eyes against the brilliant sun. "What do you see there?" asked they all, and eagerly she cried: "I see a splendid chariot-chief coming at furious pace along the road. Two steeds, like day and night, of equal size and beauty, come thundering beneath that chariot on the plain. Curling their manes and long, and as they come, one would think fire darted from their curbed jaws, so strain and bound they forward; high in the air the turf beneath their feet is thrown around them, as though a flock of birds were following as they go. On the right side the horse is grey, broad in the haunches, active, swift and wild; with head erect and breast expanded, madly he moves along the plain, bounding and prancing as he goes. The other horse jet-black, head firmly knit, feet broad-hoofed, firm, and slender; in all this land never had chariot-chief such steeds as these."

"Heed not the steeds," the girls replied, "tell us, for this concerns us most, who is the chariot-chief who rides within?"

"Worthy of the chariot in which he rides is he who sits within. Youthful he seems, as standing on the very borders of a noble manhood, and yet I think his face and form are older than his years. Gravely he looks, as though his mind revolved some serious thought, and yet a radiance as of the summer's day enfolds him round. About his shoulders a rich five-folded mantle hangs, caught by a brooch across the chest sparkling with precious gems, above his white and gold-embroidered shirt. His massive sword rests on his thigh, and yet I think he comes not here to fight. Before him stands his charioteer, the reins held firmly in his hand, urging the horses onward with a goad."

"What like is he, the charioteer?" demand the girls again.

"A ruddy man and freckled," answered Fiall; "his hair is very curly and bright-red, held by a bronze fillet across his brow, and caught at either side his head in little cups of gold, to keep the locks from falling on his face. A light cloak on his shoulders, made with open sleeves, flies back in the wind, as rapidly they course along the plain." But Emer heard not what the maiden said, for to her mind there came the memory of a wondrous youth whom Ulster loved and yet of whom all Erin stood in awe. Great warriors spoke of him in whispers and with shaking of the head. They told how when he was a little child, he fought with fullgrown warriors and mastered them; of a huge hound that he had slain and many feats of courage he had done. Into her mind there came a memory, that she had heard of prophets who foretold for him a strange and perilous career; a life of danger, and an early death. Full many a time she longed to see this youth, foredoomed to peril, yet whose praise should ring from age to age through Erin; and in her mind, when all alone she pondered on these things, she still would end: "This were a worthy mate! This were a man to win a woman's love!" And half aloud she uttered the old words: "This were a man to win a woman's love!"

Now hardly had the words sprung to her lips, when the chariot stood before the door, close to the place where all the girls were gathered. And when she saw him Emer knew it was the man of whom she dreamed. He wished a blessing to them, and her lovely face she lifted in reply. "May God make smooth the path before thy feet," she gently said. "And thou, mayest

thou be safe from every harm," was his reply. "Whence comest thou?" she asked; for he had alighted from his seat and stood beside her, gazing on her face. "From Conor's court we come," he answered then; "from Emain, kingliest of Ulster's forts, and this the way we took. We drove between the Mountains of the Wood, along the High-road of the Plain, where once the sea had been; across the Marsh they call the Secret of the Gods, and to the Boyne's ford named of old the Washing of the Horses of the Gods. And now at last, O maiden, we have come to the bright flowery Garden-grounds of Lugh. This is the story of myself, O maid; let me now hear of thee." Then Emer said: "Daughter am I to Forgall, whom men call the Wily Chief. Cunning his mind and strange his powers; for he is stronger than any labouring man, more learned than any Druid, more sharp and clever than any man of verse. Men say that thou art skilled in feats of war, but it will be more than all thy games to fight against Forgall himself; therefore be cautious what thou doest, for men cannot number the multitude of his warlike deeds nor the cunning and craft with which he works. He has given me as a bodyguard twenty valiant men, their captain Con, son of Forgall, and my brother; therefore I am well protected, and no man can come near me, but that Forgall knows of it. To-day he is gone from home on a warrior expedition, and those men are gone with him; else, had he been within, I trow he would have asked thee of thy business here."

"Why, O maiden, dost thou talk thus to me? Dost thou not reckon me among the strong men, who know not fear?" "If thy deeds were known to me," she said, "I then might reckon them; but hitherto I have not heard of all thy exploits." "Truly, I swear, O maiden," said Cuchulain, "that I will make my deeds to be recounted among the glories of the warrior-feats of heroes." "How do men reckon thee?" she said again. "What then is thy strength?" "This is my strength," he said. "When my might in fight is weakest, I can defend myself alone against twenty. I fear not by my own might to fight with forty. Under my protection a hundred are secure. From dread of me, strong warriors avoid my path, and come not against me in the battlefield. Hosts and multitudes and armed men fly before my name."

"Thou seemest to boast," said Emer, "and truly for a tender boy those feats are very good; but they rank not with the deeds of chariot-chiefs. Who then were they who brought thee up in these deeds of which thou boastest?"

"Truly, O maiden, King Conor is himself my foster-father, and not as a churl or common man was I brought up by him. Among chariot-chiefs and champions, among poets and learned men, among the lords and nobles of Ulster, have I been reared, and they have taught me courage and skill and manly gifts. In birth and bravery I am a match for any chariot-chief; I direct the counsels of Ulster, and at my own fort at Dun Dalgan they come to me for entertainment. Not as one of the common herd do I stand before thee here to-day, but as the favourite of the King and darling of all the warriors of Ulster. Moreover, the god Lugh the Long-handed is my protector, for I am of the race of the great gods, and his especial foster-child. And now, O maiden, tell me of thyself; how in the sunny plains of Lugh hast thou been reared within thy father's fort?" "That I will tell thee," said the girl. "I was brought up in noble behaviour as every queen is reared; in stateliness of form, in wise, calm speech, in comeliness of manner, so that to me is imputed every noble grace among the hosts of the women of Erin."

"Good, indeed, are those virtues," said the youth; "and yet I see one excellence thou hast not noted in thy speech. Never before, until this day, among all women with whom I have at times conversed, have I found one but thee to speak the mystic ancient language of the bards, which we are talking now for secrecy one with the other. And all these things are good, but one is best of all, and that is, that I love thee, and I think thou lovest me. What hinders, then, that we should be betrothed?" But Emer would not hasten, but teasing him, she said, "Perhaps thou hast already found a wife?" "Not so," said he, "and by my right-hand's valour here I vow, none but thyself shall ever be my wife." "A pity it were, indeed,

thou shouldst not have a wife," said Emer, playing with him still; "see, here is Fiall, my elder sister, a clever girl and excellent in needlework. Make her thy wife, for well is it known to thee, a younger sister in Ireland may not marry before an elder. Take her! I'll call her hither." Then Cuchulain was vexed because she seemed to play with him. "Verily and indeed," he said, "not Fiall, but thee it is with whom I am in love; and if thou weddest me not, never will I, Cuchulain, wed at all."

Then Emer saw that Cuchulain loved her, but she was not satisfied, because he had not yet done the deeds of prime heroes, and she desired that he should prove himself by champion feats and deeds of valour before he won her as his bride.

So she bade him go away and prove himself for a year by deeds of prowess to be indeed a worthy mate and spouse for her, and then, if he would come again she would go with him as his one and only wife. But she bade him beware of her father, for she knew that he would try to kill him, in order that he might not come again. And this was true, for every way he sought to kill Cuchulain, or to have him killed by his enemies, but he did not prevail.

When Cuchulain had taken farewell of Emer and gained her promise, he returned to Emain Macha. And that night the maidens of the fort told Forgall that Cuchulain had been there and that they thought that he had come to woo Emer; but of this they were not sure, because he and Emer had talked together in the poet's mystic tongue, that was not known to them. For Emer and Cuchulain talked on this wise, that no one might repeat what they had said to Forgall.

And for a whole year Cuchulain was away, and Forgall guarded the fort so well that he could not come near Emer to speak with her; but at last, when the year was out, he would wait no longer, and he wrote a message to Emer on a piece of stick, telling her to be ready. And he came in his war-chariot, with scythes upon its wheels, and he brought a band of hardy men with him, who entered the outer rampart of the fort and carried off Emer, striking down men on every side. And Forgall followed them to the earthen outworks, but he fell over the rath, and was taken up lifeless. And Cuchulain placed Emer and her foster-sister in his chariot, carrying with them their garments and ornaments of gold and silver, and they drove northward to Cuchulain's fort at Dun Dalgan, which is Dundalk to-day.

And they were pursued to the Boyne, and there Cuchulain placed Emer in a house of safety, and he turned and drove off his enemies who followed him, pursuing them along the banks and destroying them, so that the place, which had before been called the White Field, was called the Turf of Blood from that day. Then he and Emer reached their home in safety, nor were they henceforth parted until death.

Niamh of the Golden Hair

The Finn cycle is three hundred years later than the epic of Cuchulain. It has less unity, is more romantic and less heroic, though the beauty of some of its separate stories is very great. Finn is perhaps closer to the people of Ireland, the stories concerning him having elements of folklore. [From Rosemary Sutcliff, *The High Deeds of Finn Mac Cool* (Dutton, 1967).]

One day Finn and Oisin and a small company of the Fianna rode hunting among the lakes of Killarney. There were new faces among Finn's hunting companions, and some of the old ones lacking. Goll Mac Morna, his faithful friend ever since that morning on the ramparts of Tara, when he had accepted the new Fian Captain, had died the winter before, and Finn missed the grim old one-eyed champion so that even the joys of the hunt seemed a little dulled because Goll was not hunting beside him.

But the early summer morning was as fair as a morning of the Land of Youth, the dew lying grey on the grass, save where the rising sun made rainbows in it; the thorn trees curdled white with honey-scented blossom, and the small birds singing to draw the heart out of the breast. The deer fled from the thickets and the hounds followed them in full cry, their trail-music at last stirring even Finn's heart to gladness.

But they had not long been at their hunting, when they saw a horse and rider coming towards them from the West, and as they drew nearer, the waiting Fianna saw before them a maiden mounted on a white steed. She drew rein as she came up with them, and the whole hunting party stood amazed. For never before had any of them seen a sight so lovely. Her yellow hair was bound back by a slender golden diadem from a forehead as white as windflowers; her eyes were blue as the morning sky and clear as the dew sparkling on the fern fronds. Her mantle was of brown silk scattered with a skyful of golden stars, and fell from her shoulders to brush the ground. Her white horse was shod with pure yellow gold, his proud neck arching as a wave in the instant before it breaks; and she sat him more gracefully than a white swan on the waters of Killarney.

Finn broke the silence at last, bending his head before her in all courtesy. "Beautiful Princess—for surely it is a princess you are—will you tell me your name and where you come from?"

And she answered in a voice as sweet as the chiming of small crystal bells, "Finn Mac Cool, Captain of the Fianna of Erin, my country lies far off in the Western Sea. I am the daughter of the King of Tyr-na-nOg, and I am called Niamh of the Golden Hair."

"And what is it that brings you to the land of Erin, so far from your home?"

"My love for your son, Oisin," said the maiden. "So often and so often have I heard of his grace and goodliness, his gentleness and valour, that my heart learned to love him, and for his sake I have refused all the chiefs and princes who have come seeking me in marriage; and for his sake now, I have come on this far journey from Tyr-na-nOg."

Then turning to where Oisin stood close by, holding out her hands, she said, "Come with me to Tyr-na-nOg, the Land of the Ever Young. The trees of my land bear fruit and blossom and green leaves together all the year round, and sorrow and pain and age are unknown. You shall have a hundred silken robes each differently worked with gold, and a hundred swift-pacing steeds, and a hundred slender keen-scenting hounds. You shall have herds of cattle without number, and flocks of sheep with fleeces of gold; a coat of mail, you shall have, that no weapon ever pierced and a sword that never missed its mark. A hundred warriors shall follow you at your call, a hundred harpers delight you with sweet music. And I will be your true and ever-loving wife, if you will come with me to Tyr-na-nOg.''

Oisin drew near and took her hands, and stood looking up at her out of those strange dark eyes of his that he had from his mother. ''Keep all these things you promise me, save only for the last. If you will be my true and loving wife, I will come with you, further than to Tyr-na-nOg.''

The Fianna looked to each other and back again to Oisin. They protested in anger and grief, and Finn went forward and set his huge warrior's hand on his son's shoulder and turned him so that he must look at him and away from Niamh of the Golden Hair. ''Oisin my son, do not go! If you wish for a wife, are there not women fair enough in Erin?''

''She is my choice, before all the women of all the Worlds,'' said Oisin.

And Finn saw that the Fairy blood that was in him from his mother was stronger now than the blood of mortal men, and that because of it, he would go where Niamh called.

''Then go,'' he said, ''for nothing that I can say, nor the voice of your son, nor the music of your hounds can hold you, that I know. And oh, Oisin, my heart is heavy, for I shall never see you again.''

''I shall come back,'' said Oisin, ''surely I shall come back before long, and I shall come back often.'' And he flung his arms about his father's shoulders and strained him close, then went from one to another of his friends, taking his leave of them all. Only Dearmid O'Dyna was not there for his leave-taking. Lastly he bade farewell to Osca his son, while all the while the maiden sat her white horse, waiting.

Then he mounted behind her, and she shook the bridle and the white horse broke forward into a gallop as swift as the west wind and as smooth as silk, his four golden shoes seeming scarcely to bend the grasses beneath his hooves, until he reached the seashore. And his golden shoes left no mark on the white sand. And when he came to the edge of the waves, he neighed three times, and shook his head so that his mane flew like spray. Then he sprang forward, skimming over the waves with the speed of a homing swallow. And the distance closed in behind him and the two on his back, so that those who watched from the green land saw them no more.

A Legend of Knockmany

The usually serious heroic epics are not immune to tongue-in-cheek treatment when they are absorbed into folklore. *A Legend of Knockmany* is an example of such a transmutation of hero tale into folktale. Although Finn and Cuhullin (Cuchulain), the Irish giants in this story, are epic warriors and central figures in two distinct cycles of Celtic hero legends, here they are treated as droll giants, familiar from folklore. Their original superhuman powers and noble stature have been diminished to brawn, bluster, and traces of cowardice. While Finn's wisdom tooth and Cuhullin's power-finger are elements drawn from the epic cycles, the clever wife who saves her husband by her wits is a folklore motif. A tone of good-humored parody, which has an affinity with the tradition of tall tales, exemplified by North America's Paul Bunyan, is one of the story's distinguishing features. Joseph Jacobs commented on the curious nature of this tale as follows: ''Though the venerable name of Finn and Cucullin (Cuchulain) are attached to the heroes of this story, this is probably only to give an extrinsic interest to it. The two heroes could not have come together in any early form of their sagas since Cuchulain's reputed date is of the first, Finn's of the third century A.D. . . . Besides, the grotesque form of the legend is enough to remove it from the region of the hero-tale. . . . Parodies of the Irish sagas occur as early as the sixteenth century, and the present tale may be regarded as a specimen.'' [From Joseph Jacobs, *Celtic Fairy Tales* (Putnam's, 1891).]

What Irish man, woman, or child has not heard of our renowned Hibernian Hercules, the great and glorious Fin M'Coul? Not one, from Cape Clear to the Giant's Causeway, nor from that back again to Cape Clear. And, by the way, speaking of the Giant's Causeway brings me at once to the beginning of my story. Well, it so happened that Fin and his men were all working at the Causeway, in order to make a bridge across to Scotland; when Fin, who was very fond of his wife Oonagh, took it into his head that he would go home and see how the poor woman got on in his absence. So, accordingly, he pulled up a fir tree, and, after lopping off the roots and branches, made a walking-stick of it, and set out on his way to Oonagh.

Oonagh, or rather Fin, lived at this time on the very tiptop of Knockmany Hill, which faces a cousin of its own called Cullamore, that rises up, half-hill, half-mountain, on the opposite side.

There was at that time another giant, named Cuhullin—some say he was Irish, and some say he was Scotch—but whether Scotch or Irish, sorrow doubt of it but he was a targer. No other giant of the day could stand before him; and such was his strength, that, when well-vexed, he could give a stamp that shook the country about him. The fame and name of him went far and near, and nothing in the shape of a man, it was said, had any chance with him in a fight. By one blow of his fists he flattened a thunderbolt and kept it in his pocket, in the shape of a pancake, to show to all his enemies when they were about to fight him. Undoubtedly he had given every giant in Ireland a considerable beating, barring Fin M'Coul himself; and he swore that he would never rest, night or day, winter or summer, till he would serve Fin with the same sauce, if he could catch him. However, the short and long of it was, with reverence be it spoken, that Fin heard Cuhullin was coming to the Causeway to have a trial of strength with him; and he was seized with a very warm and sudden fit of affection for his wife, poor woman, leading a very lonely, uncomfortable life of it in his absence. He accordingly pulled up the fir tree, as I said before, and having snedded it into a walking-stick, set out on his travels to see his darling Oonagh on the top of Knockmany, by the way.

In truth, the people wondered very much why it was that Fin selected such a windy spot for his dwelling-house, and they even went so far as to tell him as much.

"What can you mane, Mr. M'Coul," said they, "by pitching your tent upon the top of Knockmany, where you never are without a breeze, day or night, winter or summer, and where you're often forced to take your nightcap without either going to bed or turning up your little finger; ay, an' where, besides this, there's the sorrow's own want of water?"

"Why," said Fin, "ever since I was the height of a round tower, I was known to be fond of having a good prospect of my own; and where the dickens, neighbours, could I find a better spot for a good prospect than the top of Knockmany? As for water, I am sinking a pump, and, plase goodness, as soon as the Causeway's made, I intend to finish it."

Now, this was more of Fin's philosophy; for the real state of the case was, that he pitched upon the top of Knockmany in order that he might be able to see Cuhullin coming towards the house. All we have to say is, that if he wanted a spot from which to keep a sharp lookout—and, between ourselves, he did want it grievously—barring Slieve Croob, or Slieve Donard, or its own cousin, Cullamore, he could not find a neater or more convenient situation for it in the sweet and sagacious province of Ulster.

"God save all here!" said Fin, good-humouredly, on putting his honest face into his own door.

"Musha, Fin, avick, an' you're welcome home to your own Oonagh, you darlin' bully." Here followed a smack that is said to have made the waters of the lake at the bottom of the hill curl, as it were, with kindness and sympathy.

Fin spent two or three happy days with Oonagh, and felt himself very comfortable, considering the dread he had of Cuhullin. This, however, grew upon him so much that his wife could not but perceive something lay on his mind which he kept altogether to himself. Let a woman alone, in the meantime, for ferreting or wheedling a secret out of her good man, when she wishes. Fin was a proof of this.

"It's this Cuhullin," said he, "that's troubling me. When the fellow gets angry, and begins to stamp, he'll shake you a whole townland; and it's well known that he can stop a thunderbolt, for he always carries one about him in the shape of a pancake, to show to any one that might misdoubt it."

As he spoke, he clapped his thumb in his mouth, which he always did when he wanted to prophesy, or to know anything that happened in his absence; and the wife asked him what he did it for.

"He's coming," said Fin; "I see him below Dungannon."

"Thank goodness, dear! an' who is it, avick? Glory be to God!"

"That baste, Cuhullin," replied Fin; "and how to manage I don't know. If I run away, I am disgraced; and I know that sooner or later I must meet him, for my thumb tells me so."

"When will he be here?" said she.

"To-morrow, about two o'clock," replied Fin, with a groan.

"Well, my bully, don't be cast down," said Oonagh; "depend on me, and maybe I'll bring you better out of this scrape than ever you could bring yourself, by your rule o'thumb."

She then made a high smoke on the top of the hill, after which she put her finger in her mouth, and gave three whistles, and by that Cuhullin knew he was invited to Cullamore—for this was the way that the Irish long ago gave a sign to all strangers and travellers, to let them know they were welcome to come and take share of whatever was going.

In the meantime, Fin was very melancholy, and did not know what to do, or how to act at all. Cuhullin was an ugly customer to meet with; and, the idea of the "cake" aforesaid flattened the very heart within him. What chance could he have, strong and brave though he was, with a man who could, when put in a passion, walk the country into earthquakes and knock thunderbolts into pancakes? Fin knew not on what hand to turn him. Right or left—backward or forward—where to go he could form no guess whatsoever.

"Oonagh," said he, "can you do nothing for me? Where's all your invention? Am I to be skivered like a rabbit before your eyes, and to have my name disgraced for ever in the sight of all my tribe, and me the best man among them? How am I to fight this man-mountain—this huge cross between an earthquake and a thunderbolt?—with a pancake in his pocket that was once——"

"Be easy, Fin," replied Oonagh; "troth, I'm ashamed of you. Keep your toe in your pump, will you? Talking of pancakes, maybe, we'll give him as good as any he brings with him—

thunderbolt or otherwise. If I don't treat him to as smart feeding as he's got this many a day, never trust Oonagh again. Leave him to me, and do just as I bid you."

This relieved Fin very much; for, after all, he had great confidence in his wife, knowing, as he did, that she had got him out of many a quandary before. Oonagh then drew the nine woollen threads of different colours, which she always did to find out the best way of succeeding in anything of importance she went about. She then platted them into three plats with three colours in each, putting one on her right arm, one round her heart, and the third round her right ankle, for then she knew that nothing could fail with her that she undertook.

Having everything now prepared, she sent round to the neighbours and borrowed one-and-twenty iron griddles, which she took and kneaded into the hearts of one-and-twenty cakes of bread, and these she baked on the fire in the usual way, setting them aside in the cupboard according as they were done. She then put down a large pot of new milk, which she made into curds and whey. Having done all this, she sat down quite contented, waiting for his arival on the next day about two o'clock, that being the hour at which he was expected—for Fin knew as much by the sucking of his thumb. Now this was a curious property that Fin's thumb had. In this very thing, moreover, he was very much resembled by his great foe, Cuhullin; for it was well known that the huge strength he possessed all lay in the middle finger of his right hand, and that, if he happened by any mischance to lose it, he was no more, for all his bulk, than a common man.

At length, the next day, Cuhullin was seen coming across the valley, and Oonagh knew that it was time to commence operations. She immediately brought the cradle, and made Fin to lie down in it, and cover himself up with the clothes.

"You must pass for your own child," said she; "so just lie there snug, and say nothing, but be guided by me."

About two o'clock, as he had been expected, Cuhullin came in. "God save all here!" said he; "is this where the great Fin M'Coul lives?"

"Indeed it is, honest man," replied Oonagh;

"God save you kindly—won't you be sitting?"

"Thank you ma'am," says he, sitting down; "you're Mrs. M'Coul, I suppose?"

"I am," said she; "and I have no reason, I hope, to be ashamed of my husband."

"No," said the other, "he has the name of being the strongest and bravest man in Ireland; but for all that, there's a man not far from you that's very desirous of taking a shake with him. Is he at home?"

"Why, then, no," she replied; "and if ever a man left his house in a fury he did. It appears that some one told him of a big basthoon of a giant called Cuhullin being down at the Causeway to look for him, and so he set out there to try if he could catch him. Troth, I hope, for the poor giant's sake, he won't meet with him, for if he does, Fin will make paste of him at once."

"Well," said the other, "I am Cuhullin, and I have been seeking him these twelve months, but he always kept clear of me; and I will never rest night or day till I lay my hands on him."

At this Oonagh set up a loud laugh, of great contempt, by-the-way, and looked at him as if he was only a mere handful of a man.

"Did you ever see Fin?" said she, changing her manner all at once.

"How could I," said he; "he always took care to keep his distance."

"I thought so," she replied; "I judged as much; and if you take my advice, you poor-looking creature, you'll pray night and day that you may never see him, for I tell you it will be a black day for you when you do. But, in the meantime, you perceive that the wind's on the door, and as Fin himself is from home, maybe you'd be civil enough to turn the house, for it's always what Fin does when he's here."

This was a startler even to Cuhullin; but he got up, however, and after pulling the middle finger of his right hand until it cracked three times, he went outside, and getting his arms about the house, turned it as she had wished. When Fin saw this, he felt the sweat of fear oozing out through every pore of his skin; but Oonagh, depending upon her woman's wit, felt not a whit daunted.

"Arrah, then," said she, "as you are so civil, maybe you'd do another obliging turn for us,

as Fin's not here to do it himself. You see, after this long stretch of dry weather we've had, we feel very badly off for want of water. Now, Fin says there's a fine spring-well somewhere under the rocks behind the hill here below, and it was his intention to pull them asunder; but having heard of you, he left the place in such a fury, that he never thought of it. Now, if you try to find it, troth, I'd feel it a kindness."

She then brought Cuhullin down to see the place, which was then all one solid rock; and, after looking at it for some time, he cracked his right middle finger nine times, and, stooping down, tore a cleft about four hundred feet deep, and a quarter of a mile in length, which has since been christened by the name of Lumford's Glen.

"You'll now come in," said she, "and eat a bit of such humble fare as we can give you. Fin, even although he and you are enemies, would scorn not to treat you kindly in his own house; and, indeed, if I didn't do it even in his absence, he would not be pleased with me."

She accordingly brought him in, and placing half-a-dozen of the cakes we spoke of before him, together with a can or two of butter, a side of boiled bacon, and a stack of cabbage, she desired him to help himself—for this, be it known, was long before the invention of potatoes. Cuhullin put one of the cakes in his mouth to take a huge whack out of it, when he made a thundering noise, something between a growl and a yell. "Blood and fury," he shouted; "how is this? Here are two of my teeth out! What kind of bread is this you gave me."

"What's the matter?" said Oonagh coolly.

"Matter!" shouted the other again; "why, here are the two best teeth in my head gone."

"Why," said she, "that's Fin's bread—the only bread he ever eats when at home; but, indeed, I forgot to tell you that nobody can eat it but himself, and that child in the cradle there. I thought, however, that as you were reported to be rather a stout little fellow of your size, you might be able to manage it, and I did not wish to affront a man that thinks himself able to fight Fin. Here's another cake—maybe it's not so hard as that."

Cuhullin at the moment was not only hungry,

but ravenous, so he accordingly made a fresh set at the second cake, and immediately another yell was heard twice as loud as the first. "Thunder and gibbets!" he roared, "take your bread out of this, or I will not have a tooth in my head; there's another pair of them gone!"

"Well, honest man," replied Oonagh, "if you're not able to eat the bread, say so quietly, and don't be wakening the child in the cradle there. There now, he's awake upon me."

Fin now gave a skirl that startled the giant, as coming from such a youngster as he was supposed to be. "Mother," said he, "I'm hungry—get me something to eat." Oonagh went over, and putting into his hand a cake that had no griddle in it, Fin, whose appetite in the meantime had been sharpened by seeing eating going forward, soon swallowed it. Cuhullin was thunderstruck, and secretly thanked his stars that he had the good fortune to miss meeting Fin, for, as he said to himself, "I'd have no chance with a man who could eat such bread as that, which even his son that's but in his cradle can munch before my eyes."

"I'd like to take a glimpse at the lad in the cradle," said he to Oonagh; "for I can tell you that the infant who can manage that nutriment is no joke to look at, or to feed of a scarce summer."

"With all the veins of my heart," replied Oonagh; "get up, acushla, and show this decent little man something that won't be unworthy of your father, Fin M'Coul."

Fin, who was dressed for the occasion as much like a boy as possible, got up, and bringing Cuhullin out, "Are you strong?" said he.

"Thunder an' ounds!" exclaimed the other, "what a voice in so small a chap!"

"Are you strong?" said Fin again; "are you able to squeeze water out of that white stone?" he asked putting one into Cuhullin's hand. The latter squeezed and squeezed the stone, but in vain.

"Ah! you're a poor creature!" said Fin. "You a giant! Give me the stone here, and when I'll show what Fin's little son can do, you may then judge of what my daddy himself is."

Fin then took the stone, and exchanging it for the curds, he squeezed the latter until the whey, as clear as water, oozed out in a little shower from his hand.

"I'll now go in," said he "to my cradle; for I scorn to lose my time with any one that's not able to eat my daddy's bread, or squeeze water out of a stone. Bedad, you had better be off out of this before he comes back; for if he catches you, it's in flummery he'd have you in two minutes."

Cuhullin, seeing what he had seen, was of the same opinion himself; his knees knocked together with the terror of Fin's return, and he accordingly hastened to bid Oonagh farewell, and to assure her, that from that day out, he never wished to hear of, much less to see, her husband. "I admit fairly that I'm not a match for him," said he, "strong as I am; tell him I will avoid him as I would the plague, and that I will make myself scarce in this part of the country while I live."

Fin, in the meantime, had gone into the cradle, where he lay very quietly, his heart at his mouth with delight that Cuhullin was about to take his departure, without discovering the tricks that had been played off on him.

"It's well for you," said Oonagh, "that he doesn't happen to be here, for it's nothing but hawk's meat he'd make of you."

"I know that," said Cuhullin; "divil a thing else he'd make of me; but before I go, will you let me feel what kind of teeth Fin's lad has got that can eat griddle-bread like that?"

"With all pleasure in life," said she; "only as they're far back in his head, you must put your finger a good way in."

Cuhullin was surprised to find such a powerful set of grinders in one so young; but he was still much more so on finding, when he took his hand from Fin's mouth, that he had left the very finger upon which his whole strength depended, behind him. He gave one loud groan, and fell down at once with terror and weakness. This was all Fin wanted, who now knew that his most powerful and bitterest enemy was at his mercy. He started out of the cradle, and in a few minutes the great Cuhullin, that was for such a length of time the terror of him and all his followers, lay a corpse before him. Thus did Fin, through the wit and invention of Oonagh, his wife, succeed in overcoming his enemy by cunning, which he never could have done by force.

Scandinavia

Sigurd's Youth

Sigurd is the Scandinavian name for the German hero Siegfried. He is represented as the perfect example of his nationality. The Scandinavian story as found in the *Eddas* differs in details from the German version of the *Nibelungenlied,* but good authorities are inclined to believe there is an historical basis for these legends, though opinions differ about which of the exploits are fact (except, of course, the dragon story) and which are fiction. [From Padraic Colum, *The Children of Odin* (Macmillan, 1920).]

In Midgard, in a northern kingdom, a king reigned whose name was Alv; he was wise and good, and he had in his house a foster-son whose name was Sigurd.

Sigurd was fearless and strong; so fearless and so strong was he that he once captured a bear of the forest and drove him to the King's Hall. His mother's name was Hiordis. Once, before Sigurd was born, Alv and his father who was king before him went on an expedition across the sea and came into another country. While they were yet afar off they heard the din of a great battle. They came to the battlefield, but they found no living warriors on it, only heaps of slain. One warrior they marked: he was white-bearded and old and yet he seemed the noblest-looking man Alv or his father had ever looked on. His arms showed that he was a king amongst one of the bands of warriors.

They went through the forest searching for survivors of the battle. And, hidden in a dell in the forest, they came upon two women. One was tall with blue, unflinching eyes and ruddy hair, but wearing the garb of a serving-maid. The other wore the rich dress of a queen, but she was of low stature and her manner was covert and shrinking.

When Alv and his father drew near, the one who had on her the raiment of a queen said, "Help us, lords, and protect us, and we will show you where a treasure is hidden. A great battle has been fought between the men of King Lygni and the men of King Sigmund, and the men of King Lygni have won the victory and have gone from the field. But King Sigmund is slain, and we who are of his household hid his treasure and we can show it to you."

"The noble warrior, white-haired and white-bearded, who lies yonder—is he King Sigmund?"

The woman answered, "Yes, lord, and I am his queen."

"We have heard of King Sigmund," said Alv's father. "His fame and the fame of his race, the Volsungs, is over the wide world."

Alv said no word to either of the women, but his eyes stayed on the one who had on the garb of a serving-maid. She was on her knees, wrapping in a beast's skin two pieces of a broken sword.

"You will surely protect us, good lords," said she who had on the queenly dress.

"Yea, wife of King Sigmund, we will protect you and your serving-maid," said Alv's father, the old king.

Then the women took the warriors to a wild place of the seashore and they showed them where King Sigmund's treasure was hidden amongst the rocks: cups of gold and mighty arm-rings and jeweled collars. Prince Alv and his father put the treasure on the ship and brought the two women aboard. Then they sailed from that land.

That was before Sigurd, the foster-son of King Alv, was born.

Now the mother of Alv was wise and little of what she saw escaped her noting. She saw that of the two women that her son and her husband had brought into their kingdom, the one who wore the dress of the serving-maid had unflinching eyes and a high beauty, while the one who wore the queenly dress was shrinking and unstately. One night when all the women of the household were sitting round her, spinning wool by the light of torches in the hall, the queen-mother said to the one who wore the queenly garb:

"Thou art good at rising in the morning. How dost thou know in the dark hours when it wears to dawn?"

The one clad in the queenly garb said, "When I was young I used to rise to milk the cows, and I waken ever since at the same hour."

The queen-mother said to herself, "It is a strange country in which the royal maids rise to milk the cows."

Then she said to the one who wore the clothes of the serving-maid:

"How dost thou know in the dark hours when the dawn is coming?"

"My father," she said, "gave me the ring of gold that I wear, and always before it is time to rise I feel it grow cold on my finger."

"It is a strange country, truly," said the queen-mother to herself, "in which the serving-maids wear rings of gold."

When all the others had left she spoke to the two women who had been brought into her country. To the one who wore the clothes of a serving-maid, she said:

"Thou art the queen."

Then the one who wore the queenly clothes said, "Thou art right, lady. She is the queen, and I cannot any longer pretend to be other than I am."

Then the other woman spoke. Said she: "I am the queen as thou hast said—the queen of King Sigmund who was slain. Because a king sought for me I changed clothes with my serving-maid, my wish being to baffle those who might be sent to carry me away.

"Know that I am Hiordis, a king's daughter. Many men came to my father to ask for me in marriage, and of those that came there were two whom I heard much of: one was King Lygni and the other was King Sigmund of the race of the Volsungs. The king, my father, told me it was for me to choose between these two. Now King Sigmund was old, but he was the most famous warrior in the whole world, and I chose him rather than King Lygni.

"We were wed. But King Lygni did not lose desire of me, and in a while he came against King Sigmund's kingdom with a great army of men. We hid our treasure by the sea-shore, and I and my maid watched the battle from the borders of the forest. With the help of Gram, his wondrous sword, and his own great warrior strength, Sigmund was able to harry the great force that came against him. But suddenly he was stricken down. Then was the battle lost. Only King Lygni's men survived it, and they scattered to search for me and the treasure of the King.

"I came to where my lord lay on the field of battle, and he raised himself on his shield when I came, and he told me that death was very near him. A stranger had entered the battle at the time when it seemed that the men of King Lygni must draw away. With the spear that he held in his hand he struck at Sigmund's sword, and Gram, the wondrous sword, was broken in two pieces. Then did King Sigmund get his death-wound. 'It must be I shall die,' he said, 'for the spear against which my sword broke was Gungnir, Odin's spear. Only that spear could have shattered the sword that Odin gave my father. Now must I go to Valhalla, Odin's Hall of Heroes.'

" 'I weep,' I said, 'because I have no son who might call himself of the great race of the Volsungs.'

" 'For that you need not weep,' said Sigmund, 'a son will be born to you, my son and yours, and you shall name him Sigurd. Take now the broken pieces of my wondrous sword and give them to my son when he shall be of warrior age.'

"Then did Sigmund turn his face to the ground and the death-struggle came on him. Odin's Valkyrie took his spirit from the battle-field. And I lifted up the broken pieces of the sword, and with my serving-maid I went and hid in a deep dell in the forest. Then your husband and your son found us and they brought us to your kingdom where we have been kindly treated, O Queen."

Such was the history that Hiordis, the wife of King Sigmund, told to the mother of Prince Alv.

Soon afterwards the child was born to her that was Sigmund's son. Sigurd she named him. And after Sigurd was born, the old king died and Prince Alv became king in his stead. He married Hiordis, she of the ruddy hair, the unflinching ways, and the high beauty, and he brought up her son Sigurd in his house as his foster-son.

Sigurd, the son of Sigmund, before he came to warrior's age, was known for his strength and his swiftness and for the fearlessness that shone round him like a glow. "Mighty was the race he sprang from, the Volsung race," men said, "but Sigurd will be as mighty as any that have gone before him." He built himself a hut in the forest that he might hunt wild beasts and live near to one who was to train him in many crafts.

This one was Regin, a maker of swords and a cunning man besides. It was said of Regin that he was an enchanter and that he had been in the world for longer than the generations of men. No one remembered, nor no one's father remembered, when Regin had come into that country. He taught Sigurd the art of working in metals and he taught him, too, the lore of other days. But ever as he taught him he looked at Sigurd strangely, not as a man looks at his fellow, but as a lynx looks at a stranger beast.

One day Regin said to young Sigurd, "King Alv has thy father's treasure, men say, and yet he treats thee as if thou wert thrall-born."

Now Sigurd knew that Regin said this that he might anger him and thereafter use him to his own ends. He said, "King Alv is a wise and a good king, and he would let me have riches if I had need of them."

"Thou dost go about as a foot-boy, and not as a king's son."

"Any day that it likes me I might have a horse to ride," Sigurd said.

"So thou dost say," said Regin, and he turned from Sigurd and went to blow the fire of his smithy.

Sigurd was made angry and he threw down the irons on which he was working and he ran to the horse-pastures by the great River. A herd of horses was there, gray and black and roan and chestnut, the best of the horses that King Alv possessed. As he came near to where the herd grazed he saw a stranger near, an ancient but robust man, wearing a strange cloak of blue and leaning on a staff to watch the horses. Sigurd, though young, had seen kings in their halls, but this man had a bearing that was more lofty than any king's he had ever looked on.

"Thou art going to choose a horse for thyself," said the stranger to Sigurd.

"Yea, father," Sigurd said.

"Drive the herd first into the river," said the stranger.

Sigurd drove the horses into the wide river. Some were swept down by the current, others struggled back and clambered up the bank of the pastures. But one swam across the river, and throwing up his head neighed as for a victory. Sigurd marked him; a gray horse he was, young and proud, with a great flowing mane. He went through the water and caught this horse, mounted him, and brought him back across the river.

"Thou hast done well," said the stranger. "Grani, whom thou hast got, is of the breed of Sleipner, the horse of Odin."

"And I am of the race of the sons of Odin," cried Sigurd, his eyes wide and shining with the very light of the sun. "I am of the race of the sons of Odin, for my father was Sigmund, and his father was Volsung, and his father was Rerir, and his father was Sigi, who was the son of Odin."

The stranger, leaning on his staff, looked on the youth steadily. Only one of his eyes was to be seen, but that eye, Sigurd thought, might see through a stone. "All thou hast named," the stranger said, "were as swords of Odin to send men to Valhalla, Odin's Hall of Heroes. And of all that thou hast named there were none but were chosen by Odin's Valkyries for battles in Asgard."

Cried Sigurd, "Too much of what is brave and noble in the world is taken by Odin for his battles in Asgard."

The stranger leaned on his staff and his head was bowed. "What wouldst thou?" he said, and it did not seem to Sigurd that he spoke to him. "What wouldst thou? The leaves wither and fall off Ygdrasil, and the day of Ragnarök comes." Then he raised his head and spoke to Sigurd. "The time is near," he said, "when thou mayst possess thyself of the pieces of thy father's sword."

Then the man in the strange cloak of blue

went climbing up the hill and Sigurd watched him pass away from his sight. He had held back Grani, his proud horse, but now he turned him and let him gallop along the river in a race that was as swift as the wind.

Mounted upon Grani, his proud horse, Sigurd rode to the Hall and showed himself to Alv, the king, and to Hiordis, his mother. Before the Hall he shouted out the Volsung name, and King Alv felt as he watched him that this youth was a match for a score of men, and Hiordis, his mother, saw the blue flame of his eyes and thought to herself that his way through the world would be as the way of the eagle through the air.

Having shown himself before the Hall, Sigurd dismounted from Grani, and stroked and caressed him with his hands and told him that he might go back and take pasture with the herd. The proud horse breathed fondly over Sigurd and bounded away.

Then Sigurd strode on until he came to the hut in the forest where he worked with the cunning smith Regin. No one was in the hut when he entered. But over the anvil, in the smoke of the smithy fire, there was a work of Regin's hands. Sigurd looked upon it, and a hatred for the thing that was shown rose in him.

The work of Regin's hands was a shield, a great shield of iron. Hammered out on that shield and colored with red and brown colors was the image of a dragon, a dragon lengthening himself out of a cave. Sigurd thought it was the image of the most hateful thing in the world, and the light of the smithy fire falling on it, and the smoke of the smithy fire rising round it, made it seem verily a dragon living in his own element of fire and reek.

While he was still gazing on the loathly image, Regin, the cunning smith, came into the smithy. He stood by the wall and he watched Sigurd. His back was bent; his hair fell over his eyes that were all fiery, and he looked like a beast that runs behind the hedges.

"Aye, thou dost look on Fafnir the dragon, son of the Volsungs," he said to Sigurd. "Mayhap it is thou who wilt slay him."

"I would not strive with such a beast. He is all horrible to me," Sigurd said.

"With a good sword thou mightst slay him and win for thyself more renown than ever thy father had," Regin whispered.

Reprinted with permission of Macmillan Publishing Company, from *The Children of Odin*, by Padraic Colum, illustrated by Willy Pogany. Copyright © 1920 by Macmillan Publishing Company; copyright © renewed 1948 by Padraic Colum.

"I shall win renown as my fathers won renown, in battle with men and in conquest on kingdoms," Sigurd said.

"Thou art not a true Volsung or thou wouldst gladly go where most danger and dread is," said Regin. "Thou hast heard of Fafnir the dragon, whose image I have wrought here. If thou dost ride to the crest of the hills thou mayst look across to the desolate land where Fafnir has his haunt. Know that once it was fair land where men had peace and prosperity, but Fafnir came and made his den in a cave near by, and his breathings made it the barren waste that men call Gnita Heath. Now, if thou art a true Volsung, thou wilt slay the dragon, and let that land become fair again, and bring the people back to it and so add to King Alv's domain."

"I have nought to do with the slaying of dragons," Sigurd said. "I have to make war on King Lygni, and avenge upon him the slaying of Sigmund, my father."

"What is the slaying of Lygni and the conquest of his kingdom to the slaying of Fafnir the dragon?" Regin cried. "I will tell thee what no one else knows of Fafnir the dragon. He guards a hoard of gold and jewels the like of which was never seen in the world. All this hoard you can make yours by slaying him."

"I do not covet riches," Sigurd said.

"No riches is like to the riches that Fafnir guards. His hoard is the hoard that the Dwarf Andvari had from the world's early days. Once the gods themselves paid it over as a ransom. And if thou wilt win this hoard thou wilt be as one of the gods."

"How dost thou know that of which thou speakst, Regin?" Sigurd said.

"I know, and one day I may tell thee how I know."

"And one day I may harken to thee. But speak to me no more of this dragon. I would have thee make a sword, a sword that will be mightier and better shapen than any sword in the world. Thou canst do this, Regin, for thou art accounted the best swordsmith amongst men."

Regin looked at Sigurd out of his small and cunning eyes and he thought it was best to make himself active. So he took the weightiest pieces of iron and put them into his furnace and he brought out the secret tools that he used when a master-work was claimed from his hands.

All day Sigurd worked beside him, keeping the fire at its best glow and bringing water to cool the blade as it was fashioned and refashioned. And as he worked he thought only about the blade and about how he would make war upon King Lygni, and avenge the man who was slain before he himself was born.

All day he thought only of war and of the beaten blade. But at night his dreams were not upon wars nor shapen blades but upon Fafnir the dragon. He saw the heath that was left barren by his breath, and he saw the cave where he had his den, and he saw him crawling down from his cave, his scales glittering like rings of mail, and his length the length of a company of men on the march.

The next day he worked with Regin to shape the great sword. When it was shapen with all the cunning Regin knew it looked indeed a mighty sword. Then Regin sharpened it and Sigurd polished it. And at last he held the great sword by its iron hilt.

Then Sigurd took the shield that had the image of Fafnir the dragon upon it and he put the shield over the anvil of the smithy. Raising the great sword in both his hands he struck full on the iron shield.

The stroke of the sword sheared away some of the shield, but the blade broke in Sigurd's hand. Then in anger he turned on Regin, crying out, "Thou hast made a knave's sword for me. To work with thee again! Thou must make me a Volsung's sword."

Then he went out and called to Grani, his horse, and mounted him and rode to the river bank like the sweep of the wind.

Regin took more pieces of iron and began to forge a new sword, uttering as he worked runes that were about the hoard that Fafnir the dragon guarded. And Sigurd that night dreamt of glittering treasure that he coveted not, masses of gold and heaps of glittering jewels.

He was Regin's help the next day and they both worked to make a sword that would be mightier than the first. For three days they worked upon it, and then Regin put into Sigurd's hands a sword, sharpened and polished, that was mightier and more splendid looking than the one that had been forged before. And again Sigurd took the shield that had the image of the dragon upon it and he put it upon the anvil. Then he raised his arms and struck his full blow. The sword cut through the shield, but when it struck the anvil it shivered in his hands.

He left the smithy angrily and called to Grani, his proud horse. He mounted and rode on like the sweep of the wind.

Later he came to his mother's bower and stood before Hiordis.

"A greater sword must I have," said he, "than one that is made of metal dug out of the earth. The time has come, Mother, when thou must put into my hands the broken pieces of Gram, the sword of Sigmund and the Volsungs."

Hiordis measured him with the glance of her eyes, and she saw that her son was a mighty youth and one fit to use the sword of Sigmund and the Volsungs. She bade him go with her to the King's Hall. Out of the great stone chest that was in her chamber she took the beast's skin and the broken blade that was wrapped in it. She gave the pieces into the hands of her son. "Behold the halves of Gram," she said, "of Gram, the mighty sword that in the far-off days Odin left in the Branstock, in the tree of the house of Volsung. I would see Gram new-shapen in thy hands, my son."

Then she embraced him as she had never embraced him before, and standing there with her ruddy hair about her she told him of the glory of Gram and of the deeds of his fathers in whose hands the sword had shone.

Then Sigurd went to the smithy, and he wakened Regin out of his sleep, and he made him look on the shining halves of Sigmund's sword. He commanded him to make out of these halves a sword for his hand.

Regin worked for days in his smithy and Sigurd never left his side. At last the blade was forged, and when Sigurd held it in his hand fire ran along the edge of it.

Again he laid the shield that had the image of the dragon upon it on the anvil of the smithy. Again, with his hands on its iron hilt, he raised the sword for a full stroke. He struck, and the sword cut through the shield and sheared through the anvil, cutting away its iron horn. Then did Sigurd know that he had in his hands the Volsungs' sword. He went without and called to Grani, and like the sweep of the wind rode down to the river's bank. Shreds of wool were floating down the water. Sigurd struck at them with his sword, and the fine wool was divided against the water's edge. Hardness and fineness, Gram could cut through both.

That night Gram, the Volsungs' sword, was under his head when he slept, but still his dreams were filled with images that he had not regarded in the day time; the shrine of a hoard that he coveted not, and the gleam of the scales of a dragon that was too loathly for him to battle with.

Germany

Fafnir, the Dragon

Sigurd, the Scandinavian, and Siegfried, the German, are two names for the same hero whose parallel stories are to be found in the *Völsunga Saga* of Iceland and the *Nibelungenlied* of Germany.

The root story is part of the *Elder Edda,* the great and earliest source of Scandinavian epic, which, after hundreds of years of oral transmission, was written down by an unknown author in the twelfth or thirteenth century. The *Völsunga Saga* has an air of greater primitiveness than has the *Nibelungenlied.* Some scholars hold that the Nibelungen saga traveled north to Iceland and that the Scandinavian version preserves the earlier form of the original. Both are tales of immense grandeur, tragedy, pathos, and heroic humanity.

The story of the slaying of Fafnir can hardly be read by the opera devotee without the "leitmotifs" of Wagner's opera cycle ringing in the ears. His four great operas tell the story of the Nibelung family and their destruction wrought by the curse of the gold they desired so greatly. The slaying of a dragon, wherever it occurs, always stirs the blood, since it is so universal a symbol of the triumph of good over evil. [From James Baldwin, *The Story of Siegfried* (Scribner's, 1882).]

Regin took up his harp, and his fingers smote the strings; and the music which came forth sounded like the wail of the winter's wind through the dead tree-tops of the forest. And the song which he sang was full of grief and wild hopeless yearning for the things which were not to be. When he had ceased, Siegfried said,—

"That was indeed a sorrowful song for one to sing who sees his hopes so nearly realized. Why are you so sad? Is it because you fear the curse which you have taken upon yourself? or is it because you know not what you will do with so vast a treasure, and its possession begins already to trouble you?"

"Oh, many are the things I will do with that treasure!" answered Regin; and his eyes flashed wildly, and his face grew red and pale. "I will turn winter into summer; I will make the desert places glad; I will bring back the golden age; I will make myself a god: for mine shall be the wisdom and the gathered wealth of the world. And yet I fear"—

"What do you fear?"

"The ring, the ring—it is accursed! The Norns, too, have spoken, and my doom is known. I cannot escape it."

"The Norns have woven the woof of every man's life," answered Siegfried. "To-morrow we fare to the Glittering Heath, and the end shall be as the Norns have spoken."

And so, early the next morning, Siegfried mounted Greyfell, and rode out towards the desert land that lay beyond the forest and the barren mountain range; and Regin, his eyes flashing with desire, and his feet never tiring, trudged by his side. For seven days they wended their way through the thick greenwood, sleeping at night on the bare ground beneath the trees, while the wolves and other wild beasts of the forest filled the air with their hideous howlings. But no evil creature dare come near them, for fear of the shining beams of light which fell from Greyfell's gleaming mane. On the eighth day they came to the open country and to the hills, where the land was covered with black boulders and broken by yawning chasms. And no living thing was seen there, not even an insect, nor a blade of grass; and the silence of the grave was over all. And the earth was dry and parched, and the sun hung above them like a painted shield in a blue-black

sky, and there was neither shade nor water anywhere. But Siegfried rode onwards in the way which Regin pointed out, and faltered not, although he grew faint with thirst and with the overpowering heat. Towards the evening of the next day they came to a dark mountain wall which stretched far out on either hand, and rose high above them, so steep that it seemed to close up the way, and to forbid them going farther.

"This is the wall!" cried Regin. "Beyond this mountain is the Glittering Heath, and the goal of all my hopes."

And the little old man ran forward, and scaled the rough side of the mountain, and reached its summit, while Siegfried and Greyfell were yet toiling among the rocks at its foot. Slowly and painfully they climbed the steep ascent, sometimes following a narrow path which wound along the edge of a precipice, sometimes leaping from rock to rock, or over some deep gorge, and sometimes picking their way among the crags and cliffs. The sun at last went down, and one by one the stars came out; and the moon was rising, round and red, when Siegfried stood by Regin's side, and gazed from the mountaintop down upon the Glittering Heath which lay beyond. And a strange, weird scene it was that met his sight. At the foot of the mountain was a river, white and cold and still; and beyond it was a smooth and barren plain, lying silent and lonely in the pale moonlight. But in the distance was seen a circle of flickering flames, ever changing,—now growing brighter, now fading away, and now shining with a dull, cold light, like the glimmer of the glowworm or the foxfire. And as Siegfried gazed upon the scene, he saw the dim outline of some hideous monster moving hither and thither, and seeming all the more terrible in the uncertain light.

"It is he!" whispered Regin, and his lips were ashy pale, and his knees trembled beneath him. "It is Fafnir, and he wears the Helmet of Terror! Shall we not go back to the smithy by the great forest, and to the life of ease and safety that may be ours there? Or will you rather dare to go forward, and meet the Terror in its abode?"

"None but cowards give up an undertaking once begun," answered Siegfried. "Go back to Rhineland yourself, if you are afraid; but you must go alone. You have brought me thus far to meet the dragon of the heath, to win the hoard of the swarthy elves, and to rid the world of a terrible evil. Before the setting of another sun, the deed which you have urged me to do will be done."

Then he dashed down the eastern slope of the mountain, leaving Greyfell and the trembling Regin behind him. Soon he stood on the banks of the white river, which lay between the mountain and the heath; but the stream was deep and sluggish, and the channel was very wide. He paused a moment, wondering how he should cross; and the air seemed heavy with deadly vapors, and the water was thick and cold. While he thus stood in thought, a boat came silently out of the mists, and drew near; and the boatman stood up and called to him, and said,—

"What man are you who dares come into this land of loneliness and fear?"

"I am Siegfried," answered the lad; "and I have come to slay Fafnir, the Terror."

"Sit in my boat," said the boatman, "and I will carry you across the river."

And Siegfried sat by the boatman's side; and without the use of an oar, and without a breath of air to drive it forward, the little vessel turned, and moved silently towards the farther shore.

"In what way will you fight the dragon?" asked the boatman.

"With my trusty sword Balmung I shall slay him," answered Siegfried.

"But he wears the Helmet of Terror, and he breathes deathly poisons, and his eyes dart forth lightning, and no man can withstand his strength," said the boatman.

"I will find some way by which to overcome him."

"Then be wise, and listen to me," said the boatman. "As you go up from the river you will find a road, worn deep and smooth, starting from the water's edge, and winding over the moor. It is the trail of Fafnir, adown which he comes at dawn of every day to slake his thirst at the river. Do you dig a pit in this roadway,— a pit narrow and deep,—and hide yourself within it. In the morning, when Fafnir passes over it, let him feel the edge of Balmung."

As the man ceased speaking, the boat touched the shore, and Siegfried leaped out. He looked back to thank his unknown friend, but neither boat nor boatman was to be seen. Only a thin white mist rose slowly from the cold surface of the stream, and floated upwards and away towards the mountain-tops. Then the lad remembered that the strange boatman had worn a blue hood bespangled with golden stars, and that a gray kirtle was thrown over his shoulders, and that his one eye glistened and sparkled with a light that was more than human. And he knew that he had again talked with Odin. Then, with a braver heart than before, he went forward, along the river bank, until he came to Fafnir's trail,—a deep, wide furrow in the earth, beginning at the river's bank, and winding far away over the heath, until it was lost to sight in the darkness. The bottom of the trail was soft and slimy, and its sides had been worn smooth by Fafnir's frequent travel through it.

In this road, at a point not far from the river, Siegfried, with his trusty sword Balmung, scooped out a deep and narrow pit, as Odin had directed. And when the gray dawn began to appear in the east he hid himself within this trench, and waited for the coming of the monster. He had not long to wait; for no sooner had the sky begun to redden in the light of the coming sun than the dragon was heard bestirring himself. Siegfried peeped warily from his hiding place, and saw him coming far down the road, hurrying with all speed, that he might quench his thirst at the sluggish river, and hasten back to his gold; and the sound which he made was like the trampling of many feet and the jingling of many chains. With bloodshot eyes, and gaping mouth, and flaming nostrils, the hideous creature came rushing onwards. His sharp, curved claws dug deep into the soft earth; and his bat-like wings, half trailing on the ground, half flapping in the air, made a sound like that which is heard when Thor rides in his goat-drawn chariot over the dark thunder clouds. It was a terrible moment for Siegfried, but still he was not afraid. He crouched low down in his hiding place, and the bare blade of the trusty Balmung glittered in the morning light. On came the hastening feet and the flapping wings:

the red gleam from the monster's flaming nostrils lighted up the trench where Siegfried lay. He heard a roaring and a rushing like the sound of a whirlwind in the forest; then a black, inky mass rolled above him, and all was dark. Now was Siegfried's opportunity. The bright edge of Balmung gleamed in the darkness one moment, and then it smote the heart of Fafnir as he passed. Some men say that Odin sat in the pit with Siegfried, and strengthened his arm and directed his sword, or else he could not thus have slain the Terror. But, be this as it may, the victory was soon won. The monster stopped short, while but half of his long body had glided over the pit; for sudden death had overtaken him. His horrid head fell lifeless upon the ground; his cold wings flapped once, and then lay, quivering and helpless, spread out on either side; and streams of thick black blood flowed from his heart, through the wound beneath, and filled the trench in which Siegfried was hidden, and ran like a mountain torrent down the road towards the river. Siegfried was covered from head to foot with the slimy liquid, and, had he not quickly leaped from his hiding place, he would have been drowned in the swift-rushing stream.

The bright sun rose in the east, and gilded the mountain tops, and fell upon the still waters of the river, and lighted up the treeless plains around. The south wind played gently against Siegfried's cheeks and in his long hair, as he stood gazing on his fallen foe. And the sound of singing birds, and rippling waters, and gay insects,—such as had not broken the silence of the Glittering Heath for ages,—came to his ears. The Terror was dead, and Nature had awakened from her sleep of dread. And as the lad leaned upon his sword, and thought of the deed he had done, behold! the shining Greyfell, with the beaming, hopeful mane, having crossed the now bright river, stood by his side. And Regin, his face grown wondrous cold, came trudging over the meadows; and his heart was full of guile. Then the mountain vultures came wheeling downward to look upon the dead dragon; and with them were two ravens, black as midnight. And when Siegfried saw these ravens he knew them to be Odin's birds,—Hugin, thought, and Munin, memory. And they

alighted on the ground near by; and the lad listened to hear what they would say. Then Hugin flapped his wings, and said,—

"The deed is done. Why tarries the hero?"

And Munin said,—

"The world is wide. Fame waits for the hero."

And Hugin answered,—

"What if he win the Hoard of the Elves? That is not honor. Let him seek fame by nobler deeds."

Then Munin flew past his ear, and whispered,—

"Beware of Regin, the master! His heart is poisoned. He would be thy bane."

And the two birds flew away to carry the news to Odin in the happy halls of Gladsheim.

When Regin drew near to look upon the dragon, Siegfried kindly accosted him: but he seemed not to hear; and a snaky glitter lurked in his eyes, and his mouth was set and dry, and he seemed as one walking in a dream.

"It is mine now," he murmured: "it is all mine, now,—the Hoard of the swarthy elffolk, the garnered wisdom of ages. The strength of the world is mine. I will keep, I will save, I will heap up; and none shall have part or parcel of the treasure which is mine alone."

Then his eyes fell upon Siegfried; and his cheeks grew dark with wrath, and he cried out,—

"Why are you here in my way? I am the lord of the Glittering Heath: I am the master of the Hoard. I am the master, and you are my thrall."

Siegfried wondered at the change which had taken place in his old master; but he only smiled at his strange words, and made no answer.

"You have slain my brother!" Regin cried; and his face grew fearfully black, and his mouth foamed with rage.

"It was my deed and yours," calmly answered Siegfried. "I have rid the world of a Terror: I have righted a grievous wrong."

"You have slain my brother," said Regin; "and a murderer's ransom you shall pay!"

"Take the Hoard for your ramsom, and let us each wend his way," said the lad.

"The Hoard is mine by rights," answered Regin still more wrathfully. "I am the master, and you are my thrall. Why stand you in my way?"

Then, blinded with madness, he rushed at Siegfried as if to strike him down; but his foot slipped in a puddle of gore, and he pitched headlong against the sharp edge of Balmung. So sudden was this movement, and so unlooked for, that the sword was twitched out of Siegfried's hand, and fell with a dull splash into the blood-filled pit before him; while Regin, slain by his own rashness, sank dead upon the ground. Full of horror, Siegfried turned away, and mounted Greyfell.

"This is a place of blood," said he, "and the way to glory leads not through it. Let the Hoard still lie on the Glittering Heath: I will go my way hence; and the world shall know me for better deeds than this."

And he turned his back on the fearful scene, and rode away; and so swiftly did Greyfell carry him over the desert land and the mountain waste, that, when night came, they stood on the shore of the great North Sea, and the white waves broke at their feet. And the lad sat for a long time silent upon the warm white sand of the beach, and Greyfell waited at his side. And he watched the stars as they came out one by one, and the moon, as it rose round and pale, and moved like a queen across the sky. And the night wore away, and the stars grew pale, and the moon sank to rest in the wilderness of waters. And at day-dawn Siegfried looked towards the west, and midway between sky and sea he thought he saw dark mountain tops hanging above a land of mists that seemed to float upon the edge of the sea.

While he looked, a white ship, with sails all set, came speeding over the waters towards him. It came nearer and nearer, and the sailors rested upon their oars as it glided into the quiet harbor. A minstrel, with long white beard floating in the wind, sat at the prow; and the sweet music from his harp was wafted like incense to the shore. The vessel touched the sands: its white sails were reefed as if by magic, and the crew leaped out upon the beach.

"Hail, Siegfried the Golden!" cried the harper. "Whither do you fare this summer day?"

"I have come from a land of horror and

dread," answered the lad; "and I would fain fare to a brighter."

"Then go with me to awaken the earth from its slumber, and to robe the fields in their garbs of beauty," said the harper. And he touched the strings of his harp, and strains of the softest music arose in the still morning air. And Siegfried stood entranced, for never before had he heard such music.

Wayland Smith

The German heroic legend *Wayland Smith* is one of the tragic tales of courage and vengeance so common among the Teutonic peoples. Parallel versions in Icelandic saga and Norse mythology reflect the overwhelming sense of fate in the Northern legends. The complex figure of the artist-smith—God or heroic mortal—appears in many epics and myths, from the Greek Hephaestus to the Celtic Gubbaun Saor. This retelling, by Penelope Farmer, is taken from *The Faber Book of Northern Legends,* first published in England in 1977. [From *The Faber Book of Northern Legends,* ed. Kevin Crossley-Holland (Faber & Faber, 1977).]

Wayland was one of three brothers, alike enough to them in some respects, in others not at all. All three were broad and handsome men, but beside the other two Wayland appeared clumsy, his shoulders almost too broad for the rest of his body, while he moved as clumsily as a bear too, tripping over things, knocking them down; except only when he was at work— and then his clumsiness like a bear's was also elegance; then each of his movements meshed in with the next, each of his muscles co-ordinated, the whole of him was focused to one end, like a sword towards the man it is killing. That end was perfection. For whereas his brothers were mainly warriors and hunters, destroyers of other men and beasts, Wayland was mainly a smith, a maker, the best in his country. There was nothing he could not make; swords and helmets for heroes, shields inlaid and ornamented—brilliant, impenetrable coats of war; but also more peaceable things, drinking cups and plates, arm-rings and collars, even finely-wrought decorations for a woman's breast, over the working of which he bent closely, using the smallest and most delicate of tools, his brown eyes turned green in the light of his furnace.

Now Wayland and his brothers fell in love, but not with ordinary women. They took to wife three swan maidens, hiding their feathered cloaks so that they could not turn back to swans and fly away again. The name of Wayland's wife was Hervor, he loved her utterly, and she in her way loved him—knowing not only how to give him what he wanted, but also how to show him what she wanted and to take it from him gladly—knowing when to talk to him and when to be silent. Wayland even let her come to his smithy while he was working; the furnace glowed equally then on her smooth white skin and on the metal he was working. When he brought his hammer down on the anvil he knew she heard it too, the ring of iron on iron, the even notes of his making. And when he had finished and he held it up to her, whatever it was, the object of war or of peace, she need look at him only without a word and he would know if she liked it.

What she would not do, however, though he wanted it, was wear the jewels that he made. He forged necklaces for her and brooches for her breast and rings for her ears and for her fingers. But she would only ever take one thing from him, perhaps the most beautiful of all, a simple gold arm-ring, engraved with an intricate pattern. And even this she left behind her when she went away from him. For they went away, all three of them, the three swan maidens, one autumn morning early. Hervor had warned the smith often enough. "Always believe I love you," she had said. "No matter what, I love you. Hold me in your heart when I am gone." But he had thought himself safe, all the brothers did, knowing the cloaks safely hidden, knowing they were truly loved. As soon as they discovered their loss, Wayland's two brothers put on their travelling cloaks, took up their hunting bows, buckled on their swords. They swore they would not rest until they had found their wives and set off grimly into the deep green forest. But Wayland remained in his smithy. "I am a maker," he said to himself, "I am not a traveller. I will travel in my making only, Hervor will come to me when she chooses to,

when she needs to come to me." And he took up her gold arm-ring and he threaded it on a rope made of flax with seven hundred others and hung it upon the wall where Hervor would see it if she came to find it.

And then he began to work again. The fire in his smithy never died. The ring of hammer on anvil continued day and night. Such things he made, more finely wrought than ever, each one perfect for its purpose, whether of war or peace; whether sword or battle-axe, helmet or battle-shirt, arm-ring or neck-ring, wine-bowl, ale-cup or goblet, ornament for breast or neck or finger. Just as Wayland controlled the might of fire and steel, the huge muscles shifting across his back as he swung the great hammer, so too his eyes and fingers continued to make perfect harmony over work small and cunning, intricate and fine. The fame of his making spread far beyond his hall.

He grew still more bearlike over the years, his back more bent, his shoulders broader. His wiry black hair fell down his back now and had turned just a little grey. Outside his smithy he moved as clumsily as ever, but he did not often leave it or his hall now, with their bright fires burning and the dark shadows stirring in the corners, except to go hunting for his food, pursuing bear and elk through the living forest that surrounded him.

But there was another country quite close by; a cold grey land of rock and ice and darkness where no trees grew or flowers, where no birds sang in the early morning. The king of this land was called King Nidud, and hearing of Wayland's skill he sent armed men over the mountains to find him. Wayland was out hunting at the time, his hall and smithy empty but for all the things he'd made, on which the firelight leapt and glinted. The warriors looked round them in amazement, but in the end took only one thing away with them, the most beautiful thing of all, the ring Wayland had threaded on a thread with seven hundred others, the red-gold ring that was Hervor's, engraved with a pattern like a maze.

When Wayland returned that night he brought branches of pine to throw upon his fires. He brought the carcase of a bear intending to eat all he wanted that night, then smoke the meat that was left for the hungry weeks to come. He skinned the bear and jointed it, he set a leg to roast upon the fire. Then as usual he took from the wall the seven hundred rings, red-gold and white-gold, and lay down beside the fire to count them. He saw immediately that Hervor's ring had gone. Immediately he was overcome with joy. She has been here, he thought. She has taken her ring; soon, she will come back to me.

That night almost for the first time he could not work. He ate such meat [as] he could. He sat by the fire feeding it with pine branches. The next day the same. And at last after darkness had come he heard footsteps outside his door. Then he flung it open widely. But he did not find Hervor standing there, he found a line of warriors, the moonlight glinting on their battle-shirts, on the metal bosses of their round shields, on the chains which they held ready to bind him. They seized him before he had had time to draw his sword. Then they carried him off to their cold grey land, through the forest and over the mountain, until they brought him at last to the hall of King Nidud himself; to where the king sat at meat with his wife and his two small sons whom he was rearing to be warriors, and his beautiful daughter, Bodvild.

King Nidud smiled to see Wayland. He smiled still more to see Wayland's sword still hanging from his belt. He ordered it to be brought to him. He held it in his hand and tested its weight. He ran his fingers along its finely-tempered blade. He gazed at the patterns that were worked upon the hilt, at the inlay of gold set in hardened steel. Then he took it and buckled it at his side. All the time Wayland was watching him, chained between two warriors, quite motionless. Only his eyes moved, his eyes that were brown except sometimes when he was at his forge, but which were green now with fury. They moved from King Nidud's satisfied and smiling face, towards King Nidud's cold, unsmiling queen; from her to the king's sons, the fledgling warriors; and from them at last to his beautiful daughter, Bodvild, the king's most favourite; on whose arm shone the red-gold ring that was Hervor's. Chained as he was then his fury broke; he leapt forward, his move-

ment as concentrated, as precise as it would be if he was working; his strength so huge, two warriors could scarcely hold him, a third and then a fourth had to come to their rescue, and still Wayland struggled, growling like a bear.

"That one," observed King Nidud's queen who had begun to smile at last. "That one is dangerous. If you intend keeping it my lord, you should see it is well-tamed."

"And how should you advise I tame him?" The king was still fingering Wayland's stolen sword.

"It is like a bear, it moves like a bear, clumsy and elegant together. See how its eyes move; see how it shows its teeth. I suggest you lame it like a bear; I would cut the leather sinews of its knees."

Wayland, though panting, stood motionless once more; he was watching her.

"Its eyes are glittering like a serpent's now," observed Nidud's queen. "I tell you this one is dangerous."

But she did not seem afraid of him. King Nidud also smiled, so did his two sons, their eyes shining with excitement to see such things in their father's hall. Only Bodvild looked at Wayland with sorrow and compassion, though touching meanwhile Hervor's golden ring. She gazed at her father beseechingly. King Nidud said,

"So shall it be. He is mine now. Cut the sinews with his own sword, then take him away. He shall work for me now and for no one else. The sun never shines on my land, let me be dazzled instead by the gleam of Wayland's gold."

So they lamed the smith cruelly, as you would clip the pinions of a wild bird and so impede its flight. Afterwards he could only hobble awkwardly. Then they took him to an island off the cold grey land, and made him a smithy there and commanded him to work. But first he had to build King Nidud's treasure house which he made a labyrinth of such intricacy that only he himself and the king would know the secret of it. This the king ordered. "The treasure shall lie at its heart," he said; "no one, except me shall look on it." He sent slaves to work with Wayland Smith by day, small, dark, silent men from the mountains. It took them a year to dig the multiplicity of passages, to build up so many walls, which Wayland then set with designs in metal, showing the battle deeds of King Nidud's forefathers. When it was finished all the slaves were killed to prevent them betraying the secrets of the labyrinth, and Wayland was left quite alone on his island, with no means of escaping it, or so King Nidud thought; who did not know that the maze was not the only thing Wayland had designed and built that year; did not know how each night Wayland had hobbled to the sea-shore and gathered the feathers and bones of dead sea-birds there, how little by little he had worked out the secret of their flight, and so constructed him a pair of wings, setting the sea-birds' feathers on a frame made of their bones. But these wings he had hid in a chest in his smithy. The time for using them had not yet come.

"Hervor, my wife," he said, speaking to her inside his head as he often did these days, "Hervor my white swan. The day will come that I am revenged and you will have a bird too for a husband."

He rarely slept now. The fire in his smithy burned brightly always. His only visitor was King Nidud, Wayland's own sword still hanging at his side. But now he too wore a helmet made by Wayland, and a battle-shirt also of his working. Back in his hall hung a sharp battle-axe and a fine war-collar. On his table stood wine-bowls and ale-cups and chased golden goblets. His sons wore collars made by Wayland. On his wife's breast lay many of his jewels. Only Bodvild would take nothing more, wore nothing but Hervor's ring upon her small white arm and thought of Wayland constantly.

This was the worst time of Wayland's life, who nevertheless, in fear sometimes and in longing always, did not cease to work; though his mind remained with his lost wife, his lost freedom, his lost strength and pride. The flames of his furnace seemed cruel as the fires of hell. And outside his smithy it was dark and bleak and cold and the wind howled and snow fell on snow, all the year long. No trees grew, no flowers; no birds sang in the morning. The only life was Wayland's. The only thing that grew

was the gold beneath Wayland's hammer, the beauty that he made with it. There were chests full of the things he had made stacked in the corners of the smithy, waiting to be taken to the treasure chamber in the maze; but only King Nidud ever saw the treasures there. And as for Wayland he could scarcely remember what love and warmth felt like. He could scarcely remember Hervor's face. Despair would have eaten him entirely, if he had not kept it at bay with his thoughts of revenge on King Nidud and his wife and his sons and his daughter, Bodvild.

Now it happened that as the two little boys grew up they became increasingly curious about their father's prisoner. They wanted to see more of the things that Wayland made. They wanted to get closer to the lamed bear themselves, if only to bait him. It is our right, they told themselves. Soon we too will be warriors, soon we too will have the right to wear helmet and battle-shirt, to carry swords and battle-axes. We should be allowed to choose some for ourselves. It is our right, they said.

So they took a boat and they rowed across the sea to Wayland's island. They left the boat hidden behind a rock a little out from the shore and started to walk through the sea towards the beach. Wayland came out of his smithy and saw them coming. "Children," he thought, not recognising them at first. And at first the sight of them, of the bright-faced fair-haired boys, moved him deeply, he had not seen children for many years. One of the boys was so small the water came nearly to his shoulders, and seeing this Wayland thought to himself, I was tall enough once to walk through water nine yards deep, and lame as he was he strode into the sea and took the boy upon his shoulders and carried him dry to shore. The other boy followed them. But he was watching Wayland closely and in a little while began to imitate his awkward walk; the boy on the smith's shoulders began laughing to see it. And Wayland heard the laughter and the cruelty there was in it, and gradually the burden became almost too great for him to bear. He set the boy down thankfully and looked at the brothers, but he was frowning and suspicious now.

"Who are you? What do you want of me?" he asked.

"We are the sons of your master King Nidud. We have seen some of the things you have made. We have heard you make others yet more incredible—swords sharp enough to cut off a dragon's head, steel coats strong enough to withstand a dragon's teeth. We have come to choose the armour we will wear when we are older. We have come to choose some of your weapons for ourselves."

Wayland took them to his smithy and opened a chest or two. But he did not like the way they nudged each other with sly and greedy looks, the way they whispered together and sniggered the moment his back was turned. He began to see his revenge against their father, King Nidud. The two boys were pointing to yet another corner now.

"Show us what you have in there," they said. "Show us jewels, show us gold collars and arm-rings. We are the sons of a king, such things will be for us."

Wayland told them the keys to this chest were lost. "Tonight at my furnace I will forge some more," he said, "Come back tomorrow. Come secretly. Tell no one where you mean to go, say only you will be hunting in the forest or on the mountain. And we will spend a day together. I will show you all the secrets of my making."

So the two brothers departed, still nudging each other and giggling, still imitating the way that Wayland walked. And the next day having pretended to set out towards the mountains, they came running instead to the sea shore and took their boat and rowed once more towards Wayland's island. The smith waited for them upon the beach, but this time he let the younger boy walk through the water, did not carry him in upon his shoulders.

In his smithy a chest stood ready in a dark corner. Wayland opened it with a bright new key. The light from the furnace barely reached this far, the two boys had to bend closely to see what they would see, their heads close together, their eyes shining at the sight of the riches they had intended plundering. They were too engrossed to hear Wayland come be-

hind them. He felled each of them with an easy blow. They lay without a sound, and at once he took an axe and cut off both their heads.

He buried the bodies in another corner beneath a pile of soot-blackened bellows. And when he had wiped up all the blood he carried the two heads to his workbench beside the fire. There he took out the eyes and extracted all the teeth and laid them carefully aside. Then he scraped the hair from the skulls, and the flesh and skin and he let the brains run out from inside them, until he was left with clean and empty bone; and then, smelting silver, he mounted these skulls most beautifully, engraving the bright metal with pictures of what he had just done, how he had killed the two boys and cut off both their heads.

"These goblets are my gift to King Nidud," he said.

When he had finished he took the two pairs of eyes, one green pair and one brown, the colours of his own, and he polished them to shining jewels and set them too in silver. "A necklace for King Nidud's queen," Wayland told himself and laid them beside the skulls. Then he took all the teeth and polished them also, formed patterns with them and made two brooches, such beautiful brooches that working them he almost forgot they were the result of such destruction. "But to make one thing you must always destroy another," he told himself, angrily. "These brooches are for the breast of King Nidud's daughter."

Now Bodvild had not set eyes on Wayland since that first day he became her father's captive. She had thought of him often with curiosity and pity. She became more and more determined to see him. And at last she broke her golden arm-ring engraved with lines interwoven like a maze, and she too crossed the water to Wayland's island, carrying the pieces with her, and she handed them to him without a word, and looked at him longingly. He stroked them with his fingers, as silent as she was. He thought of Hervor his wife. I have never made anything more beautiful than this, he told himself.

Bodvild said nervously at last, "No one could

mend this but you. I love it like myself—will you do it for me?''

Wayland still did not speak to her. He went into his smithy and Bodvild followed him, looking round her curiously to see his tools hung neatly upon the wall, his anvil beside the furnace, the furnace itself not only heat but light, giving each implement a shadow the same size as itself. Bodvild saw her own shadow on the wall, and she saw Wayland's too, his mighty shoulders, his head bent over his work bench. From time to time he looked at her. She was only the second woman who had ever watched him work; on whose face the light of his furnace had glowed, in whose ears had sounded the ring of his hammer on the anvil. And when he had finished he handed the arm-ring to her, and she too did not speak, simply smiled at him, and he knew as he had once known that a woman loved what he did for its own sake and for his, and not simply for the metal from which it had been made.

He could hardly bear to see it. ''Your mother,'' he said, speaking very slowly, ''your mother will envy you now still more; that your father should have given you this ring.''

''My mother may take everything I have but this. You made it and it is beautiful.''

Bodvild sat down on a bearskin beside the fire. Wayland brought her ale in a silver cup. He too sat down and he looked at her, trying not to remember his lost wife, and he too drank ale with Bodvild. But when her cup was empty he filled it up again; and again she emptied it and again he filled it. And the warmth of the fire and the ale entered both of them. His eyes turned green when he looked at her and she was not afraid of him though she thought she ought to be. But she did not want to be afraid of him. And when he looked at her he did not know if it was hate that he felt or love. In the end anyway he did what he had to, what they both wanted, for whatever reason; drowsy and warm Bodvild knew Wayland there on the bearskin beside his furnace, and for the first time in her life she had a husband, and for the second time in his life, so briefly, Wayland himself had a wife.

But he awoke in the cold dawn, angry and mocking her.

''Think of what your father will say to this.''

''I do not care what my father says. And how do you think he should ever know?''

''He will know. He will have the bitter knowledge of it and I shall be revenged on both of you.'' And Bodvild went away weeping because Wayland had forgotten her now, because of his cruelty where there had been some gentleness before. Wayland watching her go felt pity stir in him. But she did not look back; he did not call her.

In King Nidud's hall the queen was weeping for her two lost sons. They had searched for them everywhere, through the forests and across the mountains, but no one had seen them. She thought of Wayland's magic powers, and she too at last sought out the man whose laming she had suggested to the king. She entered his smithy, stood watching as he worked. But he laid his hammer down as soon as he saw that she had come.

''I have lost my two sons, my two warrior boys.''

''I can tell you where to find them. You must swear one thing first.''

''I will swear anything.''

''Then swear on ship and sword and stallion; swear on shield and coat of steel; swear you'll not harm the one who has been my wife; and swear you will not harm our son though she rears him in King Nidud's hall.''

King Nidud's wife was still proud, still angry; but worn weak by weeping she did not hesitate, put her hand on the anvil and swore as she was asked.

''*Now* tell me. Where are my sons?''

Wayland took from one of his chests the two skull goblets, mounted in silver; the four eyes, two brown jewels and two green, that he had made into a necklace; the small teeth that were now an ivory brooch for Bodvild, and he laid them down before King Nidud's wife. She looked at them astonished, not knowing what she saw.

''But where are my sons? What have you done with them?''

The smith pointed to a corner, shadowed and dark, to a pile of old bellows and other implements. ''Dig there,'' he said, ''under the soot-blackened bellows from my forge. If you look carefully you will see the marks of blood. If you dig further you will find small bones, the bones of boys, your sons. These goblets are their skulls set in silver for your husband; these eyes are theirs made into a necklace for you, these brooches I made from their teeth as breast ornaments for your daughter, Bodvild."

"And that is not all," he said. "Tell your husband this: his gift is death. I have proved now it is also mine. But besides that I have brought to this land what he cannot bring, what he has tried to prevent ever coming here. I have brought life. Life stirs in the belly of your daughter Bodvild, and that too King Nidud cannot now undo."

All the while Wayland had been strapping on to him the wings he had made of bird bones and feathers from the sea-shore. And then, his work done, he rose into the air upon them, leaving behind his smithy, the cold stone of the island, leaving behind all the beautiful things he had made and the maze that was the treasure house for the man who had imprisoned him; whose secret intricacies now lay openly below him. Like the swan maiden Hervor, his wife, he flew high in the air and was free at last, of the gold and silver, the hammer and the anvil, free of his lameness, free of his slavery. Below him the queen was raging and weeping. Below him King Nidud came running to the shore, ordering his tallest horsemen to chase after Wayland on their tallest horses. Rank upon rank of them appeared, but none were tall enough. Wayland had risen far above their heads. King Nidud ordered out his archers, the most far-shooting, far-seeing of his whole war-band. They drew their bows, they released their arrows, higher and higher, they darted, curving as they fell—for Wayland flew far above arrows, above archers, above horsemen, far above King Nidud, his wife and his dead sons; far above Bodvild and the child in her belly.

She wept for him bitterly. She called him in her heart. But when her father reproached her, reviling Wayland too for what he had done to her, she said simply, "I was willing." Nothing more.

How bitter King Nidud was, how furiously angry. But with all his powers he could not put the eyes back in the skull sockets and the skulls back on the bodies and the flesh back on the bones, any more than he could destroy the life that was growing in his daughter's belly.

"I have sworn she shall not be harmed, nor the son that grows inside her," his queen told him coldly; as much death in her voice now as there was death in King Nidud's heart.

Wayland flew far away from that icy, lightless land where no birds sang in the early morning, back to his own smithy, his own hall in the deep green of the forest. He remained lame for ever. He remained a smith for ever; but maybe one day Hervor came to him, maybe one day the light from the furnace fell upon her face and the ring of the anvil sounded in her ears; maybe for a little while again she stayed with him.

France

The Song of Roland

The epic and the saga are largely pre-Christian in ideals, concepts, and social structure. With the introduction of the romance, Christianity emerges as background and motivating force. The term *romance* is applied to the long stories, basically epic in feeling, theme, and poetic form, that were recited in the Romance languages—those languages that derive from Rome, namely, Latin, French, Italian, Spanish, and Portuguese. Later, the term *romance* came to be applied to any story in which unprecedented events take place, or the possibilities of life are heightened beyond the probabilities of actual experience.

The Holy Wars of the Crusades, the passionate response of Europe to the image of Christ, and the adoration of the Virgin Mary that inspired the great cathedrals of medieval Europe—these were the subjects also of the medieval romance. The legend of the Holy Grail became part of the old King Arthur cycle. A new regard for the position of woman in society and the growth of the chivalric ideal—knightly quest and devout dedication to a cause—were the themes that bridged the old pagan world of the epic and the Christian world of the future. In 778 A.D., in the valley of Roncesvalles in the Pyrenees, a minor skirmish occurred between the forces of Charlemagne and the Basques. It was an incident of no strategic importance; the small force was under the command of one Roland, Prefect of the Marches of Brittany, who, with his men, perished in that action. Three hundred years later, this incident has become a Holy War between the armies of Charlemagne and the Saracens, and Roland, its hero, the most noble warrior and "gentle count" of the French court. His deeds are celebrated in song, chanted about the courts of Europe. It is to the jongleur Taillefer that the authorship of the *Song of Roland,* the great epic of France, is attributed. Countless singers had sung before him, but his version gave the legend its fated form, which made it epic.

In the *Song of Roland,* Christianity had not yet become the dominating theme. It was not of God, nor of Christ, nor the Virgin, not even of his own true love that Roland thought when he came to die, but only of Charlemagne, his liege lord, and of "Sweet France." To be sure he proffered his right-hand glove to God, but this was the traditional act of homage between the feudal knight and his lord. The mysteries of Christ and of the Virgin had not yet overwhelmed the imagination of the feudal world when the deeds of Roland were sung. [From *The Song of Roland,* trans. Merriam Sherwood (Longmans, 1938).]

The Blowing of the Horn

Count Roland beheld the great losses among his men. He called Oliver, his companion-at-arms:

"Fair Sir, beloved Comrade, what do you think is to be done? Behold how many vassals strew the ground! We may well weep for France, the Sweet, the Fair. What barons she has lost! Ah, my King, my Friend, why are not you here? Oliver my Brother, what can we do? How shall we send him word?"

Said Oliver:

"I know not how. I had rather die than that dishonor should be told of us."

Said Roland:

"I will sound my horn, and Charles will hear it as he crosses the pass. I swear to you, the Franks will return."

Said Oliver:

"Shameful would that be, bringing dishonor upon all your kin, dishonor which would last all their lives. When I bade you sound your horn, you refused. If you do it now, 'twill be against my counsel. To blow it now were cowardice. Why, both your arms are bloody!"

The Count answered:

" 'Tis that I have struck fair blows."

Said Roland:

"Stiff is our fight. I will blow my horn, and King Charles will hear it."

Said Oliver:

"That were no knightly deed! When I bade you blow it, Comrade, you refused. If the King had been with us, we should have had no hurt. Those who are with him are not to blame."

Said Oliver:

"By this beard of mine, if I see again my noble sister Aude, your Betrothed, never shall you lie in her embrace!"

Said Roland:

"Why are you angry with me?"

The other answered:

"This is all your fault; for valor with sense is not madness. Measure is worth more than foolhardiness. The French are dead through your thoughtlessness. Never more shall we serve Charles. If you had taken my advice, my Lord would have returned. We should have won this battle, with King Marsile either dead or captured. Your prowess, Roland, woe the day we saw it! Charlemagne will never again have us to help him. Never will there be such a man until the day of judgment. You will die and France will be dishonored. Our loyal companionship dissolves today. Before evening falls, heavy will be our parting!"

The Archbishop heard them quarreling. He spurred his horse with his spurs of pure gold. He rode up to them and began to chastise them:

"Sir Roland, and you, Sir Oliver, in God's name I beg of you, do not quarrel! Blowing the horn would not help us now; nevertheless, it would be better to do it. Let the King come back; he will be able to avenge us. Those of Spain must not go home exulting. Our countrymen will dismount here. They will find us dead and cut to pieces. They will place us in biers on the backs of pack-horses, and will weep for us in grief and pity. They will bury us within the hallowed ground of churches, that we be not devoured by wolves or bears or dogs."

Roland replied:

"Well spoken, Sire!"

Roland placed his horn to his lips. He made a mighty effort, blowing with all his strength.

High were the peaks and long the bugle's voice. They heard it echoing for thirty long leagues. Charles and all his followers heard it. Said the King:

"Our men are doing battle!"

Ganelon answered him:

"If another said that, 'twould be taken for a lie!"

Count Roland blew his horn, with great effort and in pain, so hard that the bright blood gushed from his mouth and his brain burst from his temples. The sound of his horn carried far. Charles heard it as he crossed the pass. So did Duke Naimes. The French listened. Said the King:

"Hark! That is Roland's horn! He would never have blown it if he were not doing battle."

Ganelon replied:

"There is no battle! You are old and hoary and white-haired; such words make you seem a very child. For you know the mighty pride of Roland. 'Tis a wonder that God hath suffered it so long. He even took Noples without your command. The Saracens within came forth and fought the good vassal Roland. Then he flooded the fields to wash away the blood, that no trace might appear. For a single hare he will blow his horn all day. Now he is perchance carrying out some wager before his peers. There is no people under heaven that would dare seek him in the field. Ride on! What are you stopping for? The Great Land is far away ahead of us!"

Count Roland's mouth was filled with blood. His brain had burst from his temples. He blew his horn in pain and anguish. Charles heard it, and so did his Frenchmen. Said the King:

"That bugle carries far!"

Duke Naimes replied:

" 'Tis that a hero blows the blast! I am sure there is a battle. He who now asks you to do nothing has betrayed Roland. Arm yourselves and shout your battle-cry. Succor your noble followers. You can hear plainly that Roland is in despair."

The Emperor had his bugles blown. The French dismounted, and armed themselves with hauberks and helmets, and with swords adorned with gold. They had noble shields and lances stout and long, and pennons white and red and blue. All the barons of the army mounted their chargers. They spurred rapidly through the length of the pass. Not one but said to the other:

"If we should see Roland before he dies, we would deal great blows by his side!"

Of what avail such words? They had waited too long!

The light of evening shone. Against the sun the armor flashed, hauberks and helmets flaming, and shields painted with flowers, and spears and gilded pennons. The Emperor rode in wrath, and the French in sorrow and anger. Not one was there who did not weep bitterly, filled with a great fear for Roland. The King had Count Ganelon seized and given into custody, to the cooks of the household. He summoned the chief cook of them all, Besgon:

"Guard him well, as it behooves to keep such a felon! He has betrayed my followers."

Besgon received him, and set upon him a hundred scullions, among the best and the worst. They pulled out hairs from his beard and his mustache. Each one struck him four blows with his fist. They beat him with sticks and staves, put a chain around his neck and chained him like a bear, then placed him on a pack-horse, to his shame. Thus they kept him, until such time as they gave him back to Charlemagne.

High were the peaks, and shadowy and tall; the valleys, deep; and swift, the streams. The clarions sounded in the van and in the rear, all taking up and prolonging the voice of Roland's horn. The Emperor rode in wrath; and the French, sorrowful and angry. Not one was there but wept and lamented, praying God to protect Roland until they might all join him on the field of battle. What blows they would deal by his side! Of what avail their prayers? Prayers could not help them now. They had waited too long and could not arrive in time.

In great anger rode King Charles. Over his byrnie flowed his hoary beard. All the barons of France dug in their spurs. Not one was there but lamented that they were not beside Roland the Captain as he fought the Saracens of Spain. So great was his anguish, methinks he was about to give up the ghost. O Lord, what men, the sixty left in his company! Never did king or captain have better.

The Last Stand of the Rearguard

Roland looked over the mountains and the heath. Of those of France how many he saw lying dead! Like a gentle knight he wept for them:

"Noble Lords, may God have mercy on you! May he grant paradise to all your souls! May he make them to lie among the holy flowers! Never saw I better vassals than you. How long and constantly have you served me! What great countries have you conquered for Charles! But woe the day that the Emperor took you into his household! Land of France, O most sweet country, to-day forlorn and ravaged! Barons of France, I see you dying for me. I cannot fight for you or save you. May God, Who never lied, help you! Oliver my Brother, I must not fail you. I shall die of grief, if I am slain by nothing else. Sir Comrade, let us go smite once more!"

Count Roland returned to the fight. Wielding Durendal, he struck like a knight. He cut through the middle Faldrun of Pui and twenty-four of the Pagans most renowned. Never will any man have such desire to avenge himself. As the stag flees before the hounds, so fled the Pagans before Roland. Said the Archbishop:

"Bravo! Well done! Such valor as that befits a knight who bears good arms and sits a good steed. In battle he should be fierce and strong; otherwise, he is not worth fourpence, but should be a monk in some monastery, praying without cease for our sins!"

Roland answered:

"Smite, nor spare them!"

At these words the French began to fight once more. Heavy were the losses of the Christians. When a man knows that there will be no quarter, he puts up a brave defense in such a battle. That is why the French were as fierce as lions.

Lo! There came Marsile, riding in lordly wise on a horse that he called Gaignon. He dug in his spurs and went to smite Bevon, lord of Dijon and of Beaune. He pierced his shield and rent his hauberk, striking him dead without doing him other hurt. Then he slew Ivorie and Ivon, and, along with them, Gerard of Roussillon. Count Roland was not far away. He said to the Pagan:

"The Lord God give thee ill! Wickedly thou slayest my companions. Thou shalt feel a blow of mine before we part. This very day shalt thou learn the name of my sword!"

He rode in knightly wise to strike him. The Count cut off the King's right hand. Then he severed the head of Jurfaleu the Blond, King Marsile's son. The Pagans cried out:

"Help us, Mahound! Ye Gods of ours, avenge us on Charles! He has placed in our land scoundrels who, even at the risk of dying for it, will not flee the field!"

The one said to the other: "Well then, let us flee!"

At these words a hundred thousand took to their heels. No matter who might bid them, they would not return. Of what avail their flight? Marsile might flee, but his uncle remained, the Caliph, Lord of Carthage, Alferne, and Garmalie, and of Ethiopia—a cursed land; he held sway over the black race. They have big noses and large ears. More than fifty thousand of them were assembled there. They charged fierce and furiously, then shouted the Pagan battle-cry. Said Roland:

"This is our martyrdom! Now I know well that we have not long to live; but he is a traitor who does not first sell himself dear. Strike, my Lords, with your furbished swords! Do battle for your dead and for your lives, that sweet France may not be dishonored by us! When Charles my Lord shall come to this field and, beholding the punishment we have wrought upon the Saracens, shall find for every one of our men fifteen Pagans slain he will not fail to bless us."

The Parting of Roland and Oliver

When Roland saw the accursed people, blacker than any ink, with no spot of white except their teeth, he said:

"Now I know for certain that we shall die

today. Strike, Frenchmen, for I am starting the fight anew!''

Said Oliver:

"Cursed be the last to strike!"

At these words the French fell upon the Pagans, who, when they saw how few were the French, were filled with pride and comfort. Said one to the other:

"The Emperor is in the wrong!"

The Caliph bestrode a sorrel horse. He dug in his gilded spurs, and struck Oliver from behind in the middle of his back. He rent the white hauberk, even to the body. He thrust the spear clean through his breast. Then he said:

"You have received a rude blow! Alas for you that Charlemagne left you at the pass! He has wronged us, nor is it right that he boast of it: for, in you alone, I have avenged my people!"

Oliver felt himself wounded to the death. He grasped Hauteclaire, whose steel was burnished, and smote the Caliph on his pointed gilt helmet, striking off its painted flowers and crystals. He split open his head down to the small front teeth, shook the sword, and struck him dead. Then he said:

"Pagan, curses on thee! I do not say that Charles has not lost, but thou wilt not be able to boast to wife or to any lady, in the kingdom whence thou art, that thou hast taken from me a penny's-worth, or hast done scathe to me or to any other."

Then he cried out to Roland to help him.

Oliver felt that he was wounded mortally. He would never have his fill of avenging himself. He hurled himself into the press, striking like a baron. He slashed through spear-shafts and bucklers, cut off feet and hands, cleft saddles and flanks. Whoever had seen him dismember the Saracens, flinging one dead upon the other, might indeed mind him of a doughty vassal! Nor did he forget the battle-cry of Charles. "Montjoie!" he shouted loud and clear. He called to Roland, his friend and peer:

"Sir Comrade, come to my side! With bitter sorrow we must part today!"

Roland looked into the face of Oliver.

It was wan, discolored, livid, pale. The bright blood streaked his body, the clots falling to the ground.

"O Lord," said the Count, "now I know not what to do. Sir Comrade, alack for your prowess! Never will there be a man to equal thee! Ah, sweet France, how art thou pillaged today of good vassals! How art thou confounded and laid low! The Emperor will suffer great scathe."

With these words he swooned on his horse. Behold Roland swooned and Oliver wounded unto death. Oliver had lost so much blood that his vision was troubled. He could not see clearly enough to recognize mortal man, far or near. As he approached his comrade he struck him on his jeweled and gilded helmet, cleaving it as far as the nose-piece; but he did not reach the flesh. At that blow Roland looked at him, and asked him gently and softly:

"Sir Comrade, are you doing this of your own wish? This is Roland, who has always loved you well! You have struck me without challenging me first!"

Said Oliver:

"Now I know you, for I hear you speak. I cannot see you, but may the Lord God do so! I struck you. Forgive me, I pray!"

Roland answered:

"You did not hurt me. I forgive you here before God."

At these words the one bowed to the other. Thus, in great love, they parted.

Oliver felt the anguish of death approaching. Both his eyes turned in his head. He lost his sense of hearing and of sight. He dismounted and lay on the ground. He confessed his sins in a loud voice, both his hands clasped toward heaven, and prayed God to grant him Paradise and to bless Charles and sweet France, and, above all men, his comrade Roland. His heart failed, his helmet sank, his whole body fell upon the ground. Dead was the Count, no longer might he live. Roland the Brave wept for him and mourned. Never on earth will you hear of a man more sorrowful.

Roland saw that his friend was dead, saw him lying, face down, on the ground. Very gently he began to lament him:

"Sir Comrade, alas for your bold courage! We have been together for years and for days. You have never done me harm, nor I you. Since you are dead, it is my grief that I live!"

With these words the Marquis fainted on his horse Veillantif. He was held on by his stirrups of fine gold; thus, wheresoever he might go, he could not fall off.

The Death of Roland

Roland felt that death was near. His brain issued forth from his ears. He prayed God for his peers, that He would call them. Then, for himself, he prayed to the Angel Gabriel. He took his horn, that no one might reproach him; and, in his other hand, his sword Durendal. More than a bowshot toward Spain, into a fallow field, he went. He climbed upon a knoll, where, under two fair trees, there were four blocks of stone, cut from marble. He fell down on his back on the green grass. There he swooned, for death was near him.

High were the mountains and very high the trees. Four blocks of stone were there, of shining marble. On the green grass Count Roland had fainted. All the time a Saracen was watching him, and feigning death as he lay among the slain. He had smeared his body and his face with blood. He got to his feet and hastened to run forward. Handsome was he, and strong, and of great prowess. In his pride he was seized with a mortal madness. He laid hold of Roland, of his body and of his weapons, and he spoke these words:

"Vanquished is Charles's nephew! I will bear away this sword of his to Araby!"

As he pulled at it, the Count came a little to his senses. Roland was conscious that his sword was being taken from him. He opened his eyes and spoke these words:

"Methinks thou art not one of ours!"

He grasped his horn, which he had no wish to lose, and struck the Pagan on the helmet, jeweled and gold-adorned. He shattered the steel and his head and his bones. Both his eyes burst from their sockets and he fell dead at Roland's feet. Said the Count:

"Pagan lout, how hadst thou the presumption to lay hold of me, whether rightly or wrongly? No man shall hear of this without deeming thee a fool. The large end of my horn has been cracked; the crystal and the gold have been knocked off."

Roland felt that his sight was going. He got to his feet, exerting all his strength. All color had left his face. Before him there was a dark stone. In grief and anger he struck ten blows upon it. The steel grated, but did not break or nick.

"Ah!" said the Count. "Help me, Saint Mary! Ah, Durendal, good Sword, alas for thee! Since I am dying, I am no longer thy keeper. How many pitched battles have I won with thee! Conquered how many wide lands, which Charles of the Hoary Beard now holds! May no man have thee who would flee from another! A good vassal has long carried you. Never will there be such a one in France the Holy!"

Roland struck on the stone of sardonyx. The steel grated but it did not crack or chip. When he saw that he could not break it, he began to lament it to himself:

"Ah, Durendal, how fair and bright and white art thou! How thou dost sparkle and flame in the sun! Charles was in the vales of Maurienne, when God sent him word from heaven by His angel that he should give thee to a count and captain. Then was I girt with thee by the noble King, the great King. With thee I conquered for him Anjou and Brittany; with thee I conquered for him Poitou and Maine. For him I conquered with thee Normandy the Free. With thee I conquered for him Provence and Aquitaine and Lombardy and all Romagna. With thee I conquered for him Bavaria and all Flanders and Burgundy and all Apulia, Constantinople, whose homage he received, and Saxony, where he does what he will. With thee I conquered for him Scotland, Wales and Ireland; and England, which he considered crownland. With thee how many lands and countries have I conquered for Charles of the Hoary Beard to rule! For this sword I have dolor and grief. Rather would I die than leave it among the Pagans. God! Father! Let not France be thus shamed!"

Roland smote a dark stone. He chipped off more of it than I can say. The sword crunched but did not break or shiver. Instead, it rebounded toward heaven. When the Count saw that he could not break it, he bewailed it very softly to himself:

"Ah, Durendal, how beautiful thou art, and holy! In thy golden hilt are relics a-plenty: a tooth of Saint Peter and some of Saint Basil's blood, and hair of my Lord Saint Denis; and there is a piece of Saint Mary's dress. It is not right for Pagans to have thee; thou shouldst be served by Christians. May coward never wield thee! Wide are the lands I shall have conquered with you, for Charles of the Hoary Beard to rule—lands which have brought the Emperor power and riches."

Roland felt that death was taking hold of him. From his head it was descending toward his heart. Beneath a pine tree he went running. He lay down on his face on the green grass. Under him he placed his sword and his horn. He turned his head toward the Pagan people. This he did because he wished that Charles and all his men should say that he, the gentle Count, died conquering. He confessed himself again and again. For his sins he offered God his glove.

Roland felt that his time was short. He lay on a sharp peak, facing Spain. With one hand he struck his breast:

"God, by Thy power forgive my sins, great and small, which I have committed from the hour that I was born until this day when I am slain!"

He held out his right glove toward God. The angels of heaven descended to him.

Count Roland lay beneath a pine tree. He had turned his face toward Spain. He began to mind him of many things: of how many lands he had conquered, of sweet France, of the men of his kin, of Charlemagne his Lord, who had fostered him. He could not help but weep and sigh. Yet himself he would not forget. He confessed his sins and prayed God for mercy:

"True Father, Who never liest, Thou Who didst raise Lazarus from the dead, and save Daniel from the lions, keep, I pray Thee, my soul from all perils arising from the sins I have committed in my life!"

He offered his right glove to God. Saint Gabriel took it from his hand. On his arm his head was resting. With clasped hands he went to his death. God sent to him His angel Cherubin and Saint Michael of the Peril of the Sea. Saint Gabriel came with them. Together they bore the soul of the Count to Paradise.

Spain

The Cid

The epic poem of Spain is titled *El Cantar de Mio Cid,* the poem of the Cid. Its author is unknown, the date of its final form fixed as being about 1140. A long poem, in meandering meter, it celebrates the deeds of a great warrior, one Rodrigo (or Ruy) Diaz de Bivar, who was in actual life a doughty campaigner in the wars between Spain and the Moors, though his accomplishments could hardly have equaled the dimensions of his legend. More narrowly the biography of one man rather than encompassing the spirit of a whole people, *The Cid* is not as great in scope as *The Song of Roland.* It suffers the lack of the greatest imagination in shaping its final form. "Had the matter of *The Cid* come into the hands of a poet who was not only a master of storytelling, but the possessor of literary art, as was the poet of the *Iliad,* our poem would have had more echo in the world."*

The selection here given comes toward the end of the tale, when the Cid gains his highest recognition from his king, and those who have wronged him are called to account. [From *The Tale of the Warrior Lord,* trans. Merriam Sherwood (Longmans, 1930).]

He who in lucky hour was born did not linger. He put on his legs hose of good cloth, and over these shoes richly adorned. He donned a shirt of fine linen as bright as the sun, all its loops of gold and silver and its wristbands well-fitting—for he had ordered this. Over that he put a tunic of finest brocade, worked in gold embroideries that glistened wherever they were. Then he put on a crimson furred robe with borders of gold—the Cid Campeador always wore it. On his head was a coif of

* John Clark, *A History of Epic Poetry* (Oliver and Boyd, 1900).

fine linen, worked in gold, rightly made, so that the hair of the good Cid Campeador could not be pulled out. He wore his beard long, and he tied it with a cord. This he did because he wanted to protect all his person against insult. Over all he put a mantle of great price, in which everyone there could see something worth looking at.

With those hundred whom he had commanded to get ready, he mounted quickly and rode out of San Servando. Thus the Cid went prepared to the court. At the outside gate he dismounted properly. The Cid and all his followers went in with prudence. He was in the middle, with the hundred around him. When they saw him who in lucky hour was born coming into the court, the good King Don Alfonso rose to his feet, and so did the Count Don Enrique and the Count Don Ramón, and after that, you may know, all the rest. With great honor did they receive him who in lucky hour was born. But the Curly-Head of Grañón, García Ordóñez, and the others in the party of the Heirs of Carrión, would not rise.

The King said to the Cid: "Come and sit here by me, Campeador, on this bench that you gave me as a gift. Although it does not please some people, you are better than We."

Then he who had won Valencia spoke his thanks:

"Sit on your bench as King and Lord. I shall take my seat here with all these my men."

What the Cid said was very pleasing to the King. Then the Cid sat down on a bench of turned work. The hundred who were guarding him took their places around him. All who were in the court were gazing at the Cid, with his long beard tied with a cord. Truly he seemed a baron by his dress. The Heirs of Carrión could not look at him for shame. Then the good King Don Alfonso rose to his feet:

"Listen, followers, and may the Creator keep you! Since I became King I have held more than two courts. One was in Burgos and the other in Carrión. This third one I have come to hold today at Toledo, for love of the Cid— he who in lucky hour was born—so that he may have satisfaction of the Heirs of Carrión. They have done him great wrong, and we all

know it. Let Don Enrique and Don Ramón be judges of this case, as well as you other counts who are not of the party of the Heirs of Carrión. Put your minds, all of you, for you are wise, to finding out the right, since I do not want the wrong. On the one side and the other let us be at peace today. I swear by Saint Isidore that he who disturbs my court shall leave my kingdom and lose my love. I am on the side that is in the right. Now let the Cid Campeador plead. We shall see what the Heirs of Carrión will answer."

The Cid kissed the hand of the King and rose to his feet:

"I thank you much as my King and Lord, for calling this court for love of me.

"This is my case against the Heirs of Carrión: In deserting my daughters they did me no dishonor; for it is you who married them, King, and you will know what to do about that today. But when they took my daughters from Valencia the Great I loved my sons-in-law dearly, and I gave them two swords, *Colada* and *Tizón*— which I had won as a baron should—that they might do honor to themselves and serve you with them. When they left my daughters in the Oak-Wood of Corpes they wished to have naught to do with me and lost my love. Let them give me back my swords, since they are no longer my sons-in-law."

The Judges decreed: "All this is just."

Said the Count Don García: "Let our side talk this over."

Then the Heirs of Carrión went apart, with all their relatives and followers who were there. They discussed the matter quickly and agreed on this plan:

"The Cid Campeador shows us great favor, since he does not ask redress today for the insult to his daughters. We shall easily arrange things with the King Don Alfonso. Let us give the Cid his swords, since he thus ends his plea, and when he has them, the court will adjourn. The Cid Campeador will have no further satisfaction of us."

They went back into the court with this speech:

"Your grace, O King Don Alfonso, you are our Lord! We cannot deny that he gave us two swords. Since he asks for them and wants them back, we wish to give them to him in your presence."

They drew out the swords *Colada* and *Tizón,* and placed them in the hand of the King their Lord. As they drew forth the swords all the court was lighted up. The hilts and the quillons were all of gold. The nobles of the court were struck with wonder.

The Cid took the swords. He kissed the hands of the King. He went back to the bench from which he had arisen. He held the swords in his hands and examined them both. They could not have exchanged them for others, for the Cid knew them well. He was all joyful and he smiled from his heart. He lifted his hand and took hold of his beard:

"By this beard that no one has plucked, with these shall be avenged Doña Elvira and Doña Sol!"

He called his nephew Don Pedro by name. He held out his arm and gave him the sword *Tizón:*

"Take it, nephew, it will not have a better lord."

To Martín Antolínez, the worthy man of Burgos, he held out his arm, and gave him the sword *Colada:*

"Martín Antolínez, my worthy vassal, take *Colada*—I won it from a good lord, from Ramón Berenguer of Barcelona the Great. I give it to you to keep well. I know that, if you have the chance, you will win great fame and honor with it."

He kissed the Cid's hand and took the sword. Then the Cid Campeador rose up:

"Thanks to the Creator, and to you, Lord King! I am content as regards my swords, *Colada* and *Tizón.* But I have another complaint against the Heirs of Carrión. When they took my two daughters from Valencia I gave them, in gold and in silver, three thousand marks. While I was doing this they were finishing what they had on hand. Let them give me back my wealth, since they are no longer my sons-in-law."

Then you would have seen the Heirs of Carrión complain! Said the Count Don Ramón:

"Say yes or no!"

The Heirs of Carrión answered:

"We gave the Cid Campeador his swords so that he would not ask us for anything else, for that ended his suit."

The Count Don Ramón answered:

"An it please the King, this is our opinion: that you should give satisfaction to the Cid for what he complains of."

Said the good King:

"You have my permission."

The Cid Campeador rose to his feet:

"Those riches that I gave you, give them back to me, or make me an accounting."

Then the Heirs of Carrión went aside. They could not agree in counsel, for the riches were great, and the Heirs of Carrión had spent them. They went back with their decision and spoke their wishes:

"He who won Valencia presses us overmuch, since longing for our wealth thus seizes him. We will pay him from our heritages in the lands of Carrión."

Since they acknowledged the debt, the Judges said:

"If this please the Cid we do not forbid it. But in our judgment we decree it thus: that you pay it back here in the court."

At these words the King Don Alfonso spoke:

"We know this suit well: that the Cid Campeador demands satisfaction. I have two hundred of those three thousand marks. The Heirs of Carrión between them gave them to me. I wish to return them, since the brothers are ruined. Let them give them to the Cid, to him who in lucky hour was born. Since they have to pay their debt, I do not want the money."

Fernando González spoke: "We have no wealth in money."

Then the Count Don Ramón answered:

"You have spent the gold and the silver. We pronounce in judgment before the King Don Alfonso: Let them pay it in kind and let the Campeador accept it."

Then the Heirs of Carrión saw that they must pay. You would have seen many a courser led up, many a strong mule, and many a seasoned palfrey; and many a good sword and all kinds of arms brought. The Cid took all this as they priced it in the court. The Heirs of Carrión paid him who in lucky hour was born all but the two hundred marks that King Alfonso held. They had to borrow from others, for their own wealth was not enough. They got out of that affair badly mocked at, you may be sure!

The Cid took those goods. His men kept them and guarded them. After this was done, they thought of other things. The Cid spoke:

"Your grace, O Lord King, for the love of charity! I cannot forget my greatest complaint. Hear me, all ye of the court, and let my wrong grieve you! I cannot leave the Heirs of Carrión, who so evilly dishonored me, without a challenge. Speak, how have I wronged you, Heirs of Carrión: in jest or in earnest or in any way? If I have I will make amends, according to the judgment of the court. Wherefore did you tear off the sheaths of my heart? At your departure from Valencia I gave you my daughters, with very great honor and numerous goods. Since you did not want them, O traitorous hounds, why did you take them from Valencia their heritage? Wherefore did you strike them with girths and with spurs? You left them alone, in the Oak-Wood of Corpes, with the wild beasts and the birds of the forest. You are dishonored by all you did to them. If you do not make amends for this, let this court pronounce judgment."

The Count Don Garcia rose to his feet:

"Your grace, O King, the best of all Spain! The Cid is growing used to the king's solemn court! He has let his beard grow and wears it long. Some are afraid of him and the rest he terrifies. Those of Carrión are of such high birth that they ought not to have sought his daughters . . . Who ever gave them for wives? They did right to leave them. Whatever the Cid may say we prize no whit!"

Then the Campeador took hold of his beard:

"Thanks be to God, who rules heaven and earth! My beard is long because it was grown with care. What ails you, Count, to insult my beard? Since it first began to grow it has been nurtured with joy. No son of woman born has ever seized me by it—nor has son of Moor or of Christian plucked out a strand—as I did out of yours, Count, in the Castle of Cabra! When I took Cabra, and you by the beard, there was no youngster who did not get a good handful. The part I plucked has not even yet grown

as long as the rest—I have the strand here in my purse."

Fernando González rose to his feet. You shall hear what he said, in a loud voice:

"End your case, Cid. All your wealth is paid back. Let not the quarrel grow between us and you. We are by birth Counts of Carrión. We ought to marry daughters of kings or of emperors; daughters of the petty nobles were not fitting for us. We did right to leave our wives. We think more of ourselves for it, you may know, and not less."

The Cid Ruy Diaz looked at Pedro Vermúdez:

"Speak, Pedro Mudo, the Mute, Baron who art so silent! I have their wives for daughters and thou for first cousins. When they say such things to me they are giving thee earfuls. If I answer, thou mayest not fight."

Pedro Vermúdez tried to speak. His tongue was held back, for he stammered, and he could not begin. But, once started, you may know, he did not stop:

"I will tell you, Cid, you are always doing that: calling me Pedro Mudo, the Mute, in the courts. You know well that I cannot help it. But in what I have to do I will not be found wanting!

"Thou liest, Fernando, in all thou hast said. Through the Campeador you gained much honor. I will tell you what you are like. Remember when we were fighting near Valencia the Great; thou didst ask the first blows of the loyal Campeador; thou didst see a Moor and go to attack him; thou didst flee before reaching him. If I had not succored thee the Moor would have played a bad joke on thee. I left thee behind and fought with him. I routed him with the first blows. I gave thee his horse, and kept it all a secret. Until today I have not disclosed it to anyone. Before the Cid and before everybody thou didst boast that thou hadst slain the Moor and done a deed worthy of a baron. They all believed thee, for they did not know the truth. Thou are handsome, but thou art not brave! Tongue without hands, how darest thou speak?

"Say, Fernando, admit this: Dost thou not remember the adventure of the lion in Valencia, when the Cid was sleeping and the lion broke loose? And thou, Fernando, what didst thou do in thy fear? Thou didst hide behind the bench of the Cid Campeador! Thou didst hide, Fernando; wherefore thou hast the less fame today. We surrounded the bench to protect our Lord—until the Cid awoke, he who conquered Valencia. He rose from the bench and went towards the lion, who put his head down and waited for the Cid. He let the Cid take him by the neck and put him in his cage. When the good Campeador came back he saw his vassals standing around. He asked for his sons-in-law but neither was to be seen. I defy you as a villain and traitor. I will fight this out here, before the King Don Alfonso, for the daughters of the Cid, Doña Elvira and Doña Sol. By having left them you are dishonored. They are women and you, men. In every way they are worth more than you. If it please the Creator, when the battle takes place thou wilt confess this in the guise of a traitor! Of all that I have said I shall prove the truth."

The speech of those two ended there. You shall hear now what Diego González said:

"We are by birth counts of the purest blood. Would that those marriages had never been made—to give me for father-in-law the Cid Don Rodrigo! We do not yet repent of having left his daughters. They may sigh as long as they live. What we did to them will be a reproach to them. I will fight for this with the boldest of all: that we did honor to ourselves in leaving them."

Martín Antolínez rose to his feet:

"Be silent, traitor, mouth without truth! Thou shouldst not forget the adventure of the lion. Thou didst flee through the door and hide in the courtyard. Thou didst take refuge behind the wine-press beam. Thou didst not wear again thy mantle or thy tunic! I will fight, without fail, to prove this: the daughters of the Cid are more honored, you may know, in every way, than you, by your leaving them. After the combat thou wilt say with thy mouth that thou art a traitor and hast lied in all thou hast said."

The speech of these two ceased. Asur González came into the palace, his ermine mantle and his tunic dragging. He came red-faced, for he had just breakfasted. There was little discretion in what he said:

"What ho, Barons! Who ever saw such a misfortune? Who would have said we should gain honor from the Cid of Vivar? Let him go to the Ubierna River to grind his millstones and collect his toll of corn, as is his wont! Who would have said he would marry with those of Carrión?"

Then Muño Gustioz rose to his feet:

"Be still, villain, wicked and traitorous! Thou goest to breakfast before going to pray. Thou dost belch in the faces of those to whom thou givest the kiss of peace in church. Thou speakest truth to neither friend nor lord. Thou art false to all and, more, to the Creator. I do not care to have a share in thy friendship. I shall make thee confess that thou art such as I say."

Said King Alfonso: "Let the case rest. Those who have challenged shall fight, so help me God!"

Just as they finished, lo, two knights came through the court. One was called Ojarra and the other Iñigo Jiménez. One came from the Heir of Navarre and the other from the Heir of Aragon. They kissed the hands of the King Don Alfonso. They asked his daughters of the Cid Campeador, to be Queens of Navarre and of Aragon, in honorable and lawful marriage. At this news, all the court was silent to listen. The Cid Campeador rose to his feet:

"Your grace, King Alfonso, you are my Lord! I thank the Creator for this, that they ask me for my daughters, from Navarre and from Aragon. You, not I, married them before. My daughters are in your hands. I will do nothing without your command."

The King arose. He bade the court keep silence:

"I beg of you, Cid, perfect Campeador, to be pleased to accept, and I shall give my consent. Let this marriage be authorized today in this court, for it will add to your honor and your lands and your fiefs."

The Cid arose and kissed the King's hands:

"Since it pleases you, I give my consent, Lord."

Then the King said: "God give you good guerdon! To you, Ojarra, and to you, Iñigo Jiménez, I authorize this marriage of the daughters of the Cid, Doña Elvira and Doña Sol; that he give them to you for the Heirs of Navarre and of Aragon, in honorable and lawful marriage."

Ojarra and Iñigo Jiménez rose to their feet. They kissed the hands of the King Don Alfonso, and then of the Cid Campeador. They promised and swore the feudal oath, with their hands between those of the Cid, that it should be as they had said or better. Many of that court were pleased, but not the Heirs of Carrión. Minaya Alvar Fáñez rose to his feet:

"I ask your grace as my King and Lord—and may this not displease the Cid Campeador! I have not bothered you during all this court; now I should like to speak of somewhat that concerns me."

Said the King: "I shall be pleased to hear you. Speak, Minaya, what you will."

"I beg you, all you of the court, to give heed to me, for I have a great quarrel with the Heirs of Carrión. I, as representative of King Alfonso, gave them my cousins. They took them honorably and lawfully to wife. The Cid Campeador gave them great wealth. They left his daughters to our hurt. I defy them as wicked men and traitors. Heirs of Carrión, you are Beni-Gómez, descended from Gómez Díaz, of a family which has brought forth counts of worth and valor. But we know well what they are like now. I thank the Creator for this: that the Heirs of Navarre and of Aragon have asked for my cousins, Doña Elvira and Doña Sol. Before, you held them in your arms as equals; now you must kiss their hands and call them 'Queen'. You will have to serve them, however much you may dislike it. Thanks be to the God of Heaven and to the King Don Alfonso, thus does the honor of the Cid Campeador grow!"

Finland

The Kalevala

The forming of the *Kalevala,* the cycle of traditional myth, lore, and stories of heroic action belonging to the Finnish people, affords interesting comment on the whole process by which epic comes into being, because it was given its final form as late as the nineteenth century.

The *Kalevala* consists of 22,793 verses, arranged into some fifty runes, or cantos. The meter of the verse is singularly familiar because Henry Wadsworth Longfellow borrowed it for his *Song of Hiawatha.* The mythology and the tales are the stuff of folklore, the essence of early Finnish thought, feeling, and imagination, as well as of Finland's weather and landscape.

Reaching back three thousand years, the themes were shaped, preserved, and dispersed by the bards and singers of succeeding generations. In the early part of the nineteenth century, when European interest in traditional lore was at its height, Elias Lönnrot, a Finnish Doctor of Medicine, became aware of this native cycle. He traveled the length and breadth of Finland, gathering the songs from the lips of peasant singers. In 1882, he and a companion physician, Zacharias Topelius, first published parts of the poem. Dr. Lönnrot believed that the *Kalevala* was a true epic, and he attempted to give it a unity of form by his arrangement of the verses in an ordered sequence. But the *Kalevala* is not epic in the true meaning of the word, since it lacks a central heroic theme, and is little concerned with the fate or stature of man in the universe. It is rather an idealization of Nature, a joyous, exaggerated personification of Nature, with broad symbolism of Good against Evil, and Light against Darkness.

Its heroes (the word *Kalevala* means Land of Heroes) are gods striving with one another, almost playfully. Yet the stories have a freshness and exuberance that is matchless, and a point of view that is distinctive. Music, the power of song, is given in no other mythological concept the magic it possesses in the *Kalevala.* It is the act of creation itself. [From Babette Deutsch, *Heroes of the Kalevala: Finland's Saga* (Messner, 1940).]

The Two Suitors

It was early morning when old Vainamoinen set out in his red boat with the blue and red sails. But he was not the first to rise that day. His lovely sister, Annikki, had wakened before daybreak and gone down to the shore to wash her clothes. She had rinsed them and wrung them out and spread them to dry, and now she stood up and looked over the sunlit water. She was surprised to see a blue speck far out among the waves. At first she thought it was a flock of wild geese, and then she mistook it for a shoal of fish, and then she thought it must be a stump riding on the billows. But finally she saw that it was the blue sail on the vessel of old Vainamoinen. She hailed him and asked him where he was going.

"Salmon-fishing," he called back. "The salmon-trout are spawning up the river."

"Don't tell me such a silly lie," said his sister. "I have often seen my father and my grandfather before him go out to capture the salmon. There were always nets in the boat, and a heap of tackle, and beating-poles. You have nothing of the sort. Where are you going?"

"I am going after wild geese. They are flying over the sound looking for food."

"I know you are lying," said Annikki. "I have seen my father and my grandfather before him go out after wild geese. They carried tight-strung bows and had their hunting-dogs with them. You have no such thing. Tell the truth, Vainamoinen: where are you going?"

"Into battle," answered the old singer. "When a mighty fight is raging I cannot sit home quietly: I must join the other heroes and give blow for blow."

"Do you think I don't know what it means to go into battle?" cried Annikki. "When my father went to fight with other heroes he had a hundred men rowing with him, and a thousand men standing in the boat, and swords heaped under the seats. Tell me honestly, Vainamoinen, where are you going?"

"Well," said the old singer, "it is true I lied a little. But now I will tell you the truth. I am going to the dark and misty Country of the North, where people eat men and they even drown heroes. But that does not matter to me, for I am going to fetch the dazzling Maiden of the North Country to be my bride."

When Annikki heard this she gathered her skirts in her hand, and letting her wash lie, she ran as fast as she could to the smithy. There she found her brother Ilmarinen, the mighty smith. He was hammering away at an iron bench with silver trimmings, and his shoulders were covered with ashes from the furnace and his head was black with soot.

"Brother," said Annikki breathlessly, "if you make me a fine shuttle and some golden earrings and some girdles with links of silver, I will tell you something you ought to know."

"I will do all that," answered Ilmarinen, "if your news is important. But if it isn't, I'll feed the furnace with your trinkets."

Annikki shook her head and laughed.

"Tell me, Ilmarinen," she said, "are you still thinking of that girl up in the North Country— the one who was promised to you as a reward for forging the magic Sampo?"

Annikki knew very well that the smith had been thinking of nothing else for the past two years.

"While you are welding and hammering," she went on, "making horseshoes all day and working at your sledge all night, so that you may journey to fetch your bride, someone cleverer than you is speeding there ahead of you. I have just seen Vainamoinen in a boat with a gilded prow and a copper rudder sailing for that cold and misty land."

At this news Ilmarinen let his hammer drop to the floor of the smithy.

"Annikki," he promised, "I will make you the finest shuttle. I will forge you rings for your fingers and two or three pairs of golden earrings and five or six girdles with links of silver. But you must do a favor for me, too, little sister. Go to the bath-house and kindle a fire of small chips there and see that the stones are properly hot, so that I can have a steam-bath. Fetch me some soap too, for I must wash off the coal-dust of a whole autumn's labor, and the soot of a whole winter's work."

At once Annikki ran and got some branches broken by the wind and burned them, and gathered stones from the river and heated them, and cheerfully fetched water from the holy well, and warmed the bath-whisks on the hot stones, and then she mixed milk and ashes and marrow-fat to make a fine soap. And all the while that she was preparing the bath-house, Ilmarinen worked at the trinkets he had promised her.

When Annikki came to tell him that the bath was ready, he gave her the rings and the earrings and the girdles and a splendid head-dress as well, and marched off to the bath-house. He scrubbed himself and he rubbed himself, he cleaned himself and he steamed himself. He washed his eyes till they sparkled and his face till it shone. He washed the soot from his neck till it was white as a hen's egg, and his body till it glistened. Then Annikki brought him a linen shirt and well-fitting trousers and fine stockings that his mother had woven when she was a girl. She brought him boots of Saxon make, and a blue coat with a liver-colored lining, and a woollen overcoat tailored in the latest fashion, with splendid fur to top it. She fastened a gold-embroidered belt around his waist, and gave him brightly colored gloves, and a handsome high-crowned hat that his father had worn as a bridegroom. Ilmarinen looked splendid indeed.

As soon as he was dressed in these rich clothes he told his servant to harness the chestnut stallion and yoke him to the sledge, and fetch six golden cuckoos to sit on the frame and seven blue birds to perch on the reins and sing. If he appeared in this splendor, heralded by singing birds, surely he would delight the dazzling girl and she would consent to be his bride. Then he called for a bearskin to sit on and a walrus-hide to throw over the sledge.

When the servant had provided him with all these things, Ilmarinen begged the Creator to send a fine snowfall so that his sledge might glide swiftly over the drifts. The Creator obliged him at once: the heath was soon covered with snow, and the berry bushes were white with it.

Ilmarinen cracked his whip and drove off, praying for luck. He drove for a day and another day and a third day, and on the third day, as his gay sledge went clattering along the shore, he overtook old Vainamoinen.

The smith hailed the old singer out on the waters, and Vainamoinen waited to hear what he had to say.

"Let us make a friendly compact," said Ilmarinen. "We are both setting out to win the dazzling girl for a bride. But let us agree that neither of us will seize her by force, and that neither of us will marry her against her will."

"I agree," said old Vainamoinen. "Let the girl be given to the husband of her choice, and there will be no quarrel between us." He was sure that she would choose that famous singer, that great hero, the oldest magician, the glorious Vainamoinen. As for Ilmarinen, he was sure

that she would choose the mighty smith, the forger of the heavens, the welder of the magic Sampo, the handsome Ilmarinen.

So they traveled on, each by the path he had chosen. The boat sailed so fast that the shore echoed with the noise of its speed. The horse ran so swiftly that the earth resounded with the clatter of the swaying sledge.

Before long there was loud barking in the cold and misty region of the North Country. The grizzled house-dog bayed and wagged his tail to announce that strangers were nearing.

"Go, daughter," said the Master of the North Country, "find out what the house-dog is barking about."

"I have no time, father," said the girl. "I must clean the big cow-shed and grind the corn between the heavy mill-stones, and then I must sift the flour."

The Master of the North Country turned to his wife, gap-toothed old Louhi.

"Go, old woman," he said, "and see why the house-dog is making that racket."

"I have no time," said old Louhi. "I must prepare dinner. I have an enormous loaf to bake, but first I must knead the dough."

"Women are always in a hurry, and girls are always busy toasting themselves before the stove or lying in bed," complained the old man. "Go, my son," he said, "and see what the matter is."

"I have no time," said the youth. "I must sharpen the hatchet, and there is a great pile of wood that I have to cut up into faggots."

All this while the dog was out in the furthest corn-field, wagging his tail briskly and yelping without pause.

"He isn't barking for nothing," said the old Master of the North Country. "He doesn't growl at fir-trees."

So he went to find out for himself. When he reached the corn-field he saw a red boat sailing out in the bay and a gay sledge driving along the shore. The old man hurried home to his wife.

"There are strangers coming. I wonder what it means."

"We shall soon know," said crafty old Louhi.

She called the little serving-maid to lay a log on the fire.

"If the log sweats blood, the strangers mean trouble, but if it oozes water, their errand is a peaceful one."

The gentle little serving-maid hastened to place the choicest log on the fire. It did not sweat blood, neither did it ooze water, but instead honey trickled from it and fell in golden drops on the hearth.

"Aha!" said old Louhi, delighted. "Those strangers must be noble suitors." And she hurried out into the court-yard. There she could see the red boat with the gilded prow coming towards the shore, and a hero handling the copper rudder. She saw too the gay sledge, with six golden cuckoos perched on the frame and seven blue birds on the reins, all singing at once, and a hero holding the reins.

Old Louhi turned to her daughter, the dazzling Maiden of the North Country.

"Which of these heroes will you choose for a husband?" she asked. "That is old Vainamoinen in the red boat. You remember the famous singer: he is bringing a cargo of treasure. In the sledge sits Ilmarinen, the smith, but he comes empty-handed. Go fetch a tankard of mead and hand it to the hero of your choice. Hand it to old Vainamoinen," she advised her daughter. "He is the wisest of all heroes. Besides, his boat is loaded with treasure."

"I do not care for treasure," answered the dazzling girl, "nor for a wise man who is old. I will marry a young man, with bright eyes and strong hands, a man like the skilful smith, Ilmarinen, who forged the magic Sampo."

"You do not want to marry a smith, my lamb," said crafty old Louhi. "You will have to scrub his sooty aprons. When you are his wife you will have to wash his sooty head."

"I don't care," said the dazzling girl. "I don't want old Vainamoinen. An old husband is a nuisance."

Just then old Vainamoinen steered his boat into the harbor and stepped out and came to the house. He was no sooner within than he reminded the dazzling girl of her promise to marry him, if he would make her a splendid boat out of the splinters of her spindle and the fragments of her shuttle.

"But have you built such a boat?" she asked.

"Yes, truly have I!" answered old Vainamoinen. "A noble ship strong to face the storms and light as a leaf on the waves."

"Oh, what do I care for seamen!" cried the dazzling girl. "As soon as it blows up they want to set sail, and if the wind is in the east, they frown and are gloomy. I do not want to marry a man who thinks only of ships."

Before old Vainamoinen could answer her, his brother the smith entered the house. The dazzling girl greeted Ilmarinen with a smile and handed him a great beaker of mead. But Ilmarinen did not taste it.

"I will not put my lips to the drink before me," he said, "until I am granted the bride for whose sake I forged the magic Sampo, and for whom I have been longing these two years."

"That is all very well," said old Louhi slyly, "you may have my daughter for your bride, but there is one task I must ask you to perform first. There is a field full of vipers that must be ploughed. It has not been touched since the Evil One, Hiisi, ploughed it long and long ago."

Ilmarinen did not know how this was to be done, and sought counsel of the dazzling girl. She told him to forge himself a coat of mail and iron shoes and a plough ornamented with silver and gold, and he would have no trouble in subduing the field of vipers. The smith took her advice, clad himself in steel and iron, hammered out the gold and silver for a great plough, and went to the open field. It was a fearsome place, thick with writhing serpents, but Ilmarinen spoke to them persuasively, and advised them to get out of the way of his sharp ploughshare. It was not long before they all slipped off and out of sight. Then he ploughed the field and came to tell old Louhi that the task was accomplished and to ask for his bride.

"You may have her," said the gap-toothed Mistress of the North Country, "if you catch the Bear and the Wolf that live in the forest of Tuoni, Lord of the Dead. Bring them to me muzzled and bridled, and the girl is yours." Crafty old Louhi knew very well that hundreds of heroes had gone on this errand, but none had ever come back.

"It will be easy for you," said the dazzling girl, when the smith told her of this second task. "You have only to sit on a rock where the spray of the waterfall sprinkles you, and there forge a muzzle of the hardest steel and an iron bit. Neither Tuoni's Bear nor his fierce Wolf can escape you then."

So Ilmarinen stood on a rock in the midst of the stream and in the spray of the waterfall forged himself what was needed. Then, with the steel muzzle in one hand and the iron bit in the other, he went to seek the beasts of Tuoni in the depths of the forest. He prayed to the Daughter of the Clouds to blind the animals with a mist so that they could not see him coming, and there in the dread forest of Tuoni he crept up on them and muzzled them with the magic bits and brought them both back to old Louhi.

"Here is the great Bear of Tuoni, and his Wolf as well. Now give me your daughter," said Ilmarinen.

"I will give you my darling," answered old Louhi, "as soon as you bring me the Pike that swims in Tuoni's River. It is fat and scaly, and it must be caught without a net, nor dare you grasp it with your hand." The old woman knew that hundreds of heroes had gone to catch Tuoni's Pike, but not one had returned from that adventure.

A third time the smith asked the maiden to help him. He could not imagine how the Pike was to be caught without using net or tackle. "Be of good cheer, Ilmarinen," said the dazzling girl. "Forge yourself a fiery eagle, with talons of iron and claws of steel and wings like the sides of a boat. He will dive into the River of the Dead, and bring up Tuoni's terrible Pike."

So the smith went once more to the forge and forged a bird of fire and flame, as the maiden had directed. Mounted on its wings, that were broad as the sides of a boat, he flew towards the dread river. The eagle was so huge that one great wing swept the sky and the other trailed the water. His iron talons dipped into the river and he whetted his flaming beak on the cliffs. He carried Ilmarinen swiftly to the shore of Tuoni's stream, and there the two waited for the Pike to rise out of its muddy depths.

But instead of the Pike, a wicked water-sprite rose out of the river and snatched at Ilmarinen. It would have dragged him down, but the eagle took the wicked creature by the neck and nearly twisted its head off and sent it down to the black muddy bottom.

Then the Pike of Tuoni rose slowly to the surface. He was no ordinary fish. He had a tongue as long as two axe-shafts and teeth like those of a rake. His gorge was as wide as three great rivers and his back was the length of seven boats. He opened his awful jaws and tried to seize Ilmarinen between his terrible teeth.

But the eagle was not a small bird either. His beak was a hundred fathoms long, and his tongue the length of six spears, and each of his iron talons was like five scythes. He rushed upon the Pike and struck at it fiercely. But the Pike pulled at the eagle's broad wings and tried to drag him under the water. Up the eagle soared into the air. He hovered there a moment and then he dived. He struck one savage talon into the Pike's terrific shoulders, and gave himself a purchase by fixing the other talon firmly in the rocky cliff. But he did not thrust it deep enough and his talon slipped from the rock, and the Pike slid away and dived into the water. The shoulder of the fish was almost cloven in two and his sides were scored with the marks of the eagle's steely claws, but he had escaped the great bird's clutches.

Now the furious eagle, with fiery eyes and flaming wings, swooped a third time, seized the monstrous Pike in his talons and dragged him out of the water. Then what a battle took place between the huge bird and the terrible fish! The air glittered with iron splinters. The river heaved like a sea of steel. There was a gnashing and a thrashing, as the giant struggle continued. Finally the eagle made a mighty thrust and flapping his broad wings he bore the Pike off in triumph to the top of a tall pine-tree. There he ripped open the belly of the fish and tore the head from the neck and began to feast.

"Wicked eagle!" cried Ilmarinen in anger. "Why are you so greedy? You have destroyed the Pike that I was to carry back to old Louhi!"

But the eagle, having satisfied his hunger, soared off into the heavens, breaking the horns of the moon in his flight.

Then Ilmarinen took the head of the terrible Pike and carried it back to old Louhi.

"Here is a present for you," he said. "You can make a chair out of the bones in this head that will remain forever in the lofty halls of your house."

The gap-toothed Mistress of the North Country did not thank him too graciously. She did not care that he had brought only the head of the Pike, the bones of which would truly make a noble chair, but she was angry because he had performed every task she had set him, and now she would have to give him her beautiful daughter.

As for old Vainamoinen, he was the saddest of all.

"A man should marry when he is young," he said gloomily, "and choose his life's companion early. It is a grief to be old and have no wife and no children."

But Ilmarinen and the dazzling girl were full of joy, and eager for the preparations for the wedding. And how the feast was arranged, and what guests were invited, and how the bride and groom fared, you shall hear.

India

Rama

The *Ramayana*, one of the two major epics of India, is an extensive and intense love story, concerning the devotion of Rama, the god-hero, and his wife Sita, who remains faithful to him through years of separation and travail. Within this framework is a wealth of stories, history, and philosophy, profuse and embroidered, like the arabesques of Oriental architecture. This and the earlier epic, the *Mahabharata*, are sacred books, as the Bible is sacred to Christian lands. Taken together, they represent the highest aspirations of Hindu thought.

The Ramayana is ascribed to one poet, Valmiki, as the *Iliad* is attributed to Homer, and the date of its written form, in Sanskrit, is around 300 B.C. The *Mahabharata* is three times as long as the Bible, and eight times as long as the *Iliad* and the *Odyssey* put together. Its major framework consists of the interfamily struggle of five brothers for control of their realm. These two epics, more than any other existing epic strain, remain a living accompaniment to the life of the culture that produced them. [From Dhan Gopal Mukerji, *Rama, the Hero of India* (Dutton, 1930).]

The March to Lanka

After all the monkeys had assembled in Kishkindha under King Sugriva, Rama, Hanuman, Andaga and Lakshmana made inspiring speeches to them and exactly described their coming march to Lanka. Last of all spoke Sugriva, urging them to uphold the honour of the monkey race no matter where or how.

"On the morrow," the King concluded, "we march to Kanya Kumari (Cape Comorin) the southernmost point of India. Now go home and say farewell properly to your families. Report for duty before the first sun-wing rises again above the gloom in the east!"

And the following day just as the eagle of dawn had begun to preen his golden pinions with the clamour of a thousand storms the monkeys set out for Lanka. They leaped over many trees with the agility of hawks. They cleared the rolling hills as goats clear broken fences. They drank, bathed, and swam tawny rivers. They passed as locusts spread over autumn fields. Distances vanished under their feet like sugar into the mouth of a child. Rama and Lakshmana were carried on the backs of large monkeys who worked in relays. And ere the first day was done they had covered a twentieth part of their journey.

No sooner had the sun risen and set seven times three than the cohorts of Rama stood like clamorous forests on the edge of Cape Comorin. They roared and shouted so loudly with joy that the "surge and thunder" of the Indian Ocean was drowned as a sparrow's chirp is stilled by the wind whistling in an eagle's wing. There they stood, two men surrounded by untold apes and baboons. Before them mile upon mile unfurled the blue banners of the sea. Wherever they peered the waste of waters stretched into forbidding immensity.

After sunset as soon as the bivouacs had been

lighted and all the soldiers had been comfortably settled in their separate camps Rama, Lakshmana, Sugriva, Jambuban, Angada and Hanuman held a council of war. "How to span the ocean?" they questioned one another again and again. Rama said, "We cannot leap over the ocean like thee, Hanuman. Only a few tree-dwellers have thy skill and strength. There is naught for us to do but to build a bridge."

"A bridge on a vast ocean!" exclaimed Jambuban and Sugriva. But the young, such as Angada and Lakshmana, said, "It will take a long time to make. By the time it is completed Sita and most of us will have grown old and died."

Hanuman cried, "Why do I not leap over to Sita and bring her back on my neck. That will rescue her quickly and save us a long task of bridge-making." Rama smiled at them all and said, "It is not only for Sita's rescue that we have come, but also to put an end to Ravana and his demon-race. Sita is but one woman amongst many who are exposed to attack by the Rakshasas. It is not enough that we rescue her alone. We must destroy all Lanka and free all womanhood from the menace of Ravana. In order to do our task completely we must have a vast army at Lanka's door. Sita must wait until we build a bridge on which our cohorts can cross and annihilate the Rakshasas utterly."

"Sadhoo, well spoken," shouted all his listeners. But Jambuban the bear-headed monkey who was Sugriva's Dewan (prime minister) counselled, "With all the monkeys working every day every hour it will take ten years to build that bridge to Ceylon. Ten years without fighting will undermine the heart of every soldier. Bridge-building will make pacifists of our warriors. O Rama, set not out upon thy plan to span the sea."

A sombre and profound pause followed. As if it were unbearable Sugriva broke the silence. "I have pledged you, O Rama, that we shall rescue Sita for you. But I see no reason why we should toil to free all humanity from the menace of Ravana."

Lakshmana answered, "King Sugriva, it is your head, not your heart that speaks so. Prudence is a dweller in the house of reason, a miserly tenant in a narrow home. But what

Rama wishes is the truth. We should slay Ravana. Let us save not only Sita but all womanhood by slaughtering the demon vipers no matter how long it takes."

Then shouted Angada and Hanuman, "Thy words have converted us, O Lakshmana. We are devotees at the shrine of thy truth. Let the bridge be built."

"But ten years of civilian work will dry up the spring of our enthusiasm," reiterated Jambuban. "An army of civilians cannot fight demons. Ferocious soldiers are needed for that."

Another pause more depressing than the previous one followed. The monkeys turned their faces toward Rama. Their instinct told them that he had a noble idea in his mind. That tiger-silencing one spoke softly like a mother to her children:

"The bridge can be built in two years. We may have to besiege Lanka for at least ten years after that."

Sugriva grumbled, "How canst thou say that?"

"I have the means by which to do it," rejoined Dasaratha's eldest-born. "Let us rest for the night with perfect peace. On the morrow, friends, we shall commence the building of the bridge."

The force behind Rama's simple words was so great that the meeting broke up without further discussion, and each monkey softly walked away to his camp to bed. Only the two men stayed together. Then, without speaking, Rama signed Lakshmana to meditate.

The two princes folded their legs and sat still praying and meditating. The stars strode across the sky and faded. The giants of the jungle roamed and clamoured while the vast army of tree-dwellers slept. But the two men prayed for the help of Heaven, for the aid of all four-footed beasts, and for the cooperation of birds. They sought also the assistance of the Sun, the moon and the seasons. Each by each the souls of the sleeping birds and beasts answered, "Yes, we will help." The heavenly bodies, too, answered, "We come, Rama, to aid you as you ask." So while the world slept, its waking soul pledged Rama to be his slave. Such is the power that prayer and meditation can create! And because Rama was fighting to save not only his own bride but all humanity the whole universe was glad to espouse his cause.

Thus that memorable night was spent. And long before the red wheel of the Sun had churned the ocean into scudding gold, purple and amber birds were swarming with stones in their beaks, leopards and lions were flinging skulls and bones of their prey into the deep, monkeys row upon row were pulling down trees and rocks, elephants were ploughing up earth with their tusks and flinging it with their trunks, even Makara (Leviathan) and his sea-concealed family rose to assist Rama in his bridge-building.

Last of all came the chipmunks. They begged to be of service. Rama with sweet thanks said, "Dip your bodies in the sea, roll yourselves in the sand, then go and shake the sand between the stones that the apes are joining together. Go, make mortar for me." The chipmunks busied themselves at once. Lo, hardly a few minutes passed when their chief crawled up to Rama's lap and said, "Some monkey flung a rock the wrong way and hit me. O Rama, I am dying." But Rama said, "I will heal you," and he stroked the chipmunk three times with his hand. The previous night's meditation had given Rama so much power that healing passed out of him and made the little beast whole in a trice. But Rama's fingers left their marks on his body so that even now India's chipmunks wear coats of three stripes. Those are the finger marks that their ancestors received at the building of the Rama-setu or Rama-causeway to Ceylon.

The sea rose and fell but it was no longer heard; the sharp chirp of stones falling from bird-beaks, the crash and smash of rock and timber, the hissing of the surf, the hammering of boulder on boulder, the sinking of mammoth granite shafts in the deep, and the singing of those who worked and enjoyed work because they could sing, drowned all else. Thus toil became a joy, and joy a serenity of the soul.

The day ended and the night was no less like day, for the moon poured effulgence from above in answer to the prayer of Rama. So the beasts of night toiled as had done those of the day. Hammering of stone on stone rang louder than the storm smiting the "sapphire-silver" sea.

So numerous were the beasts at work that they wrought with "thunder-stilling" fury. Though Rama slumbered his friends toiled at night. Since they were not his slaves they forged the stone chain on the sea without regard to his presence or his absence. Toil became their joy. They loved him, hence they toiled, not lashed by overseers, not cursed by leaders.

Persia

Zāl the White-Haired

Zāl is the legendary hero of the Persian epic written by Firdausi (pen name) from the *Book of Kings.* This book is not a book as we use the term; it is a collection of legendary folktales, which was begun as early as the sixth century. These were written down, placed in the royal library, and added to through the ninth century. Firdausi, who had been commissioned to write them into verse by the ruler, completed his work of thirty-five years in 1011; the poem is now the national epic. This legend of Zāl is interesting of itself, but more so when we know that Zāl was the father of the greatest of all Persian heroes, Rustam; for the story of *Sohrab and Rustam* is one Persian tale that is widely known, thanks to Matthew Arnold. [From *Tales of Ancient Persia,* retold from the *Shah-Nama* of Firdausi by Barbara Leonie Picard (Walck, 1972).]

Among those who had fought the most valiantly for Minucher in his battle against his great-uncles, Salm and Tur, had been the renowned young warrior Sām, king of Zābulestān, a subject monarch who paid tribute to the Great King. Sām had early won fame for himself as a fighting man, and he was much respected as a brave and just ruler of his small country.

One day a son was born to Sām's fair young queen. The child's birth had been awaited eagerly, not only by his parents but by all in the palace; yet when the boy was born there was no one in the queen's apartments with the courage to go to Sām with word of those tidings which should have been so happy—yet were not. For the child was like no other child in all the world. He was fair and unblemished in form and feature, with well-made limbs which promised to grow as straight and strong as his father's, and he had his mother's fine dark eyes—but his hair was as white as the hair of an old man of four score years and more.

The queen wept bitterly at the sight of her strange child, and her women trembled; and for seven whole days no one dared to tell Sām that his son had been born. But at last his wife's old nurse, a woman of great courage, who loved her mistress dearly, said, "We can hide this thing no longer. Ill would it be for us all if the king were to discover the truth for himself, and to learn, moreover, that we had concealed it from him for so long, as though it were indeed some shameful secret. Soon he will come to ask concerning you, dear queen. It were best we told him freely of how matters stand, before he comes to see for himself."

This brave old woman went to Sām, her face all smiles and her voice ringing joyfully, as though she brought him only the best of tidings. Yet inwardly her heart beat fearfully, and she could hardly still the trembling of her limbs. "Rejoice, lord king," she said, "for you have been much blessed by Ormuzd and you have a son. He is as fine and beautiful a babe as any father might wish for. From his lusty cries and sturdy limbs it is plain to all that he will be a strong man and a great warrior, a fitting son for any king." Sām leaped to his feet, laughing aloud in his joy; and the nurse went on hastily, "From the top of his head to the soles of his feet he is without blemish, lord king. In one respect only he differs from other children—as indeed the son of a king should differ from the sons of all lesser men. His limbs are ivory, his eyes are jet, and his little mouth is a red ruby. But his hair is priceless silver—as pale as moonlight, as white as the pure snow which crowns the mountain tops. Your son is indeed the fairest of all children, lord king, so rejoice and give thanks to Ormuzd." At the frown that came to Sām's brow, and at the bewildered and unbelieving look that came to his eyes, her voice faltered and ceased.

"What are you saying to me, woman? That he has hair as white as snow? You jest with me. No newborn babe ever had snow-white hair."

"It is true, lord king," she whispered, terrified.

"Take me to him, that I may see this wonder for myself," demanded Sām.

While the other women crowded together fearfully at the end of the queen's chamber, as far from him as they might, and the old nurse alone stood beside the weeping queen, Sām looked down at his sleeping son and saw that it was indeed as the old woman had told him: the babe's hair was white.

"You bid me give thanks to Ormuzd, woman," he said at last. "But this child is no gift from Ormuzd. Rather it is surely some frightful jest of Ahriman sent to shame me before all men. From end to end of the empire of Persia men will talk of it and laugh, how the king of Zābulestān fathered a child that was old and hoary on the very day of its birth. And worse than that, who knows what monster of evil this creature may become in future years?" Then Sām prayed, "Great Ormuzd, forgive me if, mistaken, I act wrongly or cruelly; for I act only as I believe I should, in thus ridding myself and my people of this spawn of Ahriman." And he ordered that the child was to be taken from the palace immediately and carried to the desert and there left to die. "Thus may we be freed from this curse which Ahriman has sent upon us," he said; and then, as did his wife and all her women, he wept for grief.

And so, for fear that he would grow to be some evil creature, beloved of Ahriman, who would work harm to men, Sām's little white-haired son was carried from the palace, out to the desert, and left lying at the foot of the Elburz Mountains.

The child lay on the hard stony ground in the burning rays of the sun, and his crying grew feebler with each minute that passed. But before his cries ceased altogether, they came to the sharp ears of the magical Simurgh bird as she sought prey for her newly hatched nestlings. Her keen eyes soon sighted him and, swooping low on immense widespread black wings, she snatched him up in her strong talons and carried him off to her aerie on the very topmost peak of Mount Demāvend, the highest point of the

Elburz Mountains, to be food for her young. But the hungry nestlings turned from the strange creature she had brought to them, and would not eat; and so she went in search of other prey. When she returned with a dead fawn, the child was huddled among the soft downy bodies of her young, accepted by them as one of themselves. So the Simurgh, also, accepted Sām's son as her own, and fed him with the tenderest portions of deer's flesh, and as her fledglings grew and flourished, so did the child. In time he grew first to a lovely boy and then to a beautiful youth, tall and straight, with long white hair that reached to his waist. He ran and leaped on the mountains and about the foothills, and men passing across the desert on their way to the city of Zābul sometimes caught a glimpse of this strange, lovely creature and carried word of the wondrous sight with them to their destination. And so one day the tidings came to the ears of Sām and he suspected at once that his son was not dead, but that, in some unknown way, he had been preserved— perhaps by the will of Ormuzd—and at once he determined to go to the Elburz Mountains to see his son for himself.

With a few followers he rode into the desert, to the foot of Mount Demāvend. From there he could see, far above him on the topmost crag, the nest of the Simurgh, and beside it on the rocks, the huge bird herself and a slim youth whose hair was white. But though he tried in every way, accompanied or alone, to climb the mountain, he could in no manner reach the top. At last he gave up his vain attempts and, descending sadly, he prayed to Ormuzd. "Great lord of the universe, if he whom I can see aloft is indeed the child whom I sent out to his death many years ago, and if he is truly my son and no evil monster sent by Ahriman, then let me behold him close and speak with him." Thus Sām prayed and waited for an answer to his prayer.

Away in her aerie the Simurgh looked down with her keen eyes, and by her magical wisdom she knew who was the man whom she saw far below her. "Down there," she said to her foster-child, "stands Sām, ruler of Zābulestān.

He is your father and he it was who left you to die in the wilderness. He now repents of that deed and is come in search of you. He has a father's love, a kingdom and an honored life among men to offer you. Willingly would I have you stay here with me forever, for you are as dear to me as any of my brood. Yet you are a man and it is fitting that you should live the life of a man among other men. The time has come for you to leave me." She took the youth gently in her talons and stretching wide her wings like a black cloud, she flew with him down to the foot of the mountain and set him before Sām.

Sām looked at his son and saw that he was fashioned like any other man—though more beautiful of face and form than most—save that his hair was snow-white. Yet that seemed now to be a mark of beauty and no blemish. Overjoyed, father and son embraced; then both offered their thanks to the Simurgh, who said to the youth, "It is time for us to part, yet today you are no less my child than you were upon that day when I first found you, weak and helpless, and in the years to come my love and my care will still be yours." She plucked a feather from her wing and gave it to Sām's son, saying, "If ever you have need of my help, burn this feather of mine and I will know of it and come to you, wherever you may be." Once again she spread wide her wings, and like a black cloud was gone, back to her aerie on the highest crag of Mount Demāvend.

Sām and his son went gladly home; and there, with great happiness and much ceremony, Sām named the youth Zāl and proclaimed him his heir.

That Zāl had been nurtured by a bird and had grown up far from the dwellings of men and that his hair was as white as snow, soon mattered as little to any in Zābulestān as it mattered to his father Sām. For Zāl quickly proved himself wise beyond his years, as great a warrior as Sām, and the best of horsemen; and he was soon loved by all in Zābulestān. To observe the ways of other men, he traveled much, not only about his father's small kingdom, but also in the other lands of Minucher's empire.

10   Storytelling

I n one of Hans Christian Andersen's merriest tales,[2] the old Troll King of
Norway visited Denmark with his two sons to choose brides for the boys
from among the Elf King's seven daughters. After the feast, each daughter
stepped forth to parade her special accomplishment. The most ethereal
of them knew how to disappear altogether, but this was a trait neither father
nor sons approved of in a wife. The sons, bored with the procedure, left the
gathering abruptly after the appearance of the fourth daughter, but the old king
remained until the seventh daughter's turn. "And what could she do?" runs
the story. "Why she could tell fairy tales, as many as any one could wish to
hear. 'Here are my five fingers,' said the Troll King: 'tell me a story for each
finger.'"

"And the Elfin Maid took hold of his wrist, and told her stories, and he laughed
till his sides ached; and when she came to the finger that wore the gold ring,
as though it knew it might be wanted, the Old Troll suddenly exclaimed, 'Hold
fast what you have. The hand is yours. I will marry you myself!'"

The appeal of the story is universal and as old as time. Still, in today's world,

1. Zuñi storyteller, "How the Summer Birds Came," in *Zuñi Folk Tales*, coll. and trans. Frank Hamilton
Cushing (Knopf, 1931), p. 92.
2. Hans Christian Andersen, "The Elfin Mount," in *Fairy Tales and Legends* (Oxford University Press,
1936), p. 61.

fiction, drama, journalism, and all the entertainment arts have as their major concern the telling of a story: What happened, and to whom, and where?

Before the advent of printing, storytelling was the chief means of recording and preserving history, as well as ideas and remembered emotion. The very earliest stories probably were simple narratives recounting the day's events: the hunt, the chase, the capture, and the kill. But with time, storytelling came to include an account of the emotions attending the event: the fear and hope, the courage and cowardice, and the desperate search for aid from the unknown. From these beginnings were developed the ability to tell all that people felt and observed about life and about the behavior of others: premonitions and theories, beliefs and tabus. The telling of tales became a means of giving form to religion, laws, wit and humor, and the practicalities of everyday life. Without the art of storytelling, there would be no mythology, no epic literature, no way for generations to have reached beyond their allotted time to touch and teach the generations yet to come. This is the heritage of storytelling: When children hear these old tales from the great, anonymous oral tradition, they are aligned with the past and thus better able to understand the present and to sense the future.

Storytelling offers a direct approach to children. The events of the appropriately chosen and well-told story can be counted upon to catch and hold their interest. In addition, there is the flattery of sharing, either as an individual listener or as a part of the group, an experience with an adult, on terms of seemingly absolute equality. The warmth of the voice, the intimacy, and the sense of direct, sincere, and eager communication between teller and listeners are responsible for the unique relationship between storyteller and audience. Good storytelling breaks down such barriers as differences in age and the awe in which children sometimes hold their elders. Tell children a story they enjoy, and they look upon you as an equal, trust you with revelations they would never have thought of sharing, and attribute to you interests you may not have. "Did you get many toys for Christmas?" a small boy asked an experienced storyteller. They had liked the same stories; it was logical, then, that their interests should run parallel in the matter of Christmas luck.

Consider how greatly the imagination of children is stimulated by this art of storytelling. They must themselves build the scene and setting with their inner eye. There are no moving pictures, no painted backdrops, no sound accompaniments, no mood music, and no film strips; only the modulation of the teller's voice, an occasional gesture, a change of pace, or a pause tells the listeners how to define the threat, the conflict, and the resolution. Yet in this art all the emotions find expression, and the imaginary is given the bone and sinew of reality.

Through the storyteller's art, children learn to appreciate and enjoy the sound of language. In this day of pictorial emphasis, with the visual increasingly being used as a method of communication, it would seem that the scope of language is shrinking. There is a tendency to simplify the structure of written language, limit its vocabulary, and narrow its subtleties of feeling and color, reducing it to the basic norm of everyday speech. Perhaps it is for this reason that there is a resurgence of interest in storytelling, for it provides a means of using language in all its variability. Even those who cannot or will not understand the printed page may listen and learn beyond their years and their comprehension.

The first step in becoming a good storyteller is to learn how to choose a story to tell. The tellable tale must be worthy of the emphasis that the voice and the spoken word will give it. Every weakness of structure and every false feeling becomes apparent when the voice and personality of the storyteller add their dimension to the tale. Many a story that seems to have charm when it is read falls flat when it is told.

The story that tells well is the one in which the conflict is well-defined, the action moves directly to the climax of the conflict, and the ending resolves all difficulties with satisfying finality. In short, choose the dramatic story, one in which action is paramount and everything superfluous to the main purpose of the story is omitted. A good story is built like the curve of an arch, each part closely related to the others, with the incidents of the tale, like the stones of the arch, moving up to the keystone—the climax—and then falling away to the other side. Folktales are, for the most part, constructed in this way. It is for this reason that the storyteller can find the basis for a personal repertoire in folklore. And because folktales were shaped to the tongue by generations of use, the neophyte storyteller can learn to recognize the tellable by reading deeply in the oral tradition.

The uses you wish to make of a story may sometimes lead to the choice of a weak or contrived tale. The hunt is always on for stories for special occasions—those minor holidays so troublesome to teachers, librarians, and program-makers; even Christmas stories present a hazard. The desire to teach some specific attitude to children or to point up a good habit often leads to a search for stories that were written for the purpose. Although the temptation may be strong to relax the storyteller's critical judgment in favor of the message, it is the better part of wisdom to hew to the line of structure. Think in terms of the story's integrity—the drama, action, mood, and total effect—and leave lesser messages to a less effective medium than storytelling. The excellent story, like all excellence in art, is full of meaning, morality, and nourishment of the spirit, but meaning cannot be wrung from it, like water out of a rag.

The choice of a story should also be governed by its appeal for the storyteller, for it stands to reason that your best efforts are commanded by your own choice. Choose a story, then, for which you have a genuine liking, or better still a strong liking. The story will be as much a part of you as your own thumb by the time you have mastered it, and therefore it had better be a tale you love. The choice of a simple, short folktale is a wise one for the beginning storyteller. Save for years of experience the longer and more sophisticated tales of Laurence Housman, Oscar Wilde, Hans Christian Andersen, Frank Stockton, Rudyard Kipling, Howard Pyle, Richard Hughes, and Eleanor Farjeon.

After the story is chosen, consider it. Define first, in your own mind, the prime reasons for its appeal to you. What did you like about it? Was it the plot—a tale of adventure, a giant to be overcome, a magnificent array of perils? Was it the mood—poetic, romantic, humorous or nonsensical? Let us assume that the story you have chosen is "Molly Whuppie" (which appears in Chapter 7). It is rather long for a first story, but it is a strong and exciting one. Moreover, it is one of those adventure stories in which the main character is a heroine rather than a hero; and it appeals to all ages. You have read it once, and you like it. Also read any notes that accompany the text to discover its origins. You will recognize many of its motifs: the desertion of children, the recurrence of the number three (three children, three tasks); the changing of the sleeper's garb.

The beginning of this story states briefly and immediately how perilous life is. Don't dwell upon this. Don't question whether or not the desertion is going to make some child feel insecure. Don't contrive some other beginning that shows that this is the best of all possible worlds. Accept the story opening as children accept it, in its proportionate relation to the story as a whole. The action moves forward. The three children walk out of the great forest seeking shelter. They find a giant's house, where the peril is great. There is the first escape from the house. Then Molly must return to the giant's house three times. Twice she goes on behalf of her two sisters, and the third time on her own behalf. By dint of great courage, wit, and daring, she succeeds and finds husbands for her sisters—and a prince for herself into the bargain. There are the bones of the tale. Mull them over in your mind, pondering on their vitality, the ingenuousness of the invention, and the magnificent symbols of adventure. What is the mood of this story? Name it and define it for yourself, so that when you come to learn the story you will "orchestrate" it, as it were, within its key mood. The mood of "Molly Whuppie" is robust and bold, and courage and dauntlessness are the chief characteristics. Sound the mood in your subconscious mind so that it will color and control your telling of the story.

Now read the story over and over. Do not memorize it, either word by word or paragraph by paragraph, but read it over and over until you know *absolutely* what are the successive steps in the course of its action. Test yourself by closing the book and making a list of the *hinges of action* in proper order:

1. Children deserted in wood.
2. They walk to giant's house.
3. Giant's wife lets them in.
4. Giant comes home and asks who is there.
5. Wife replies, "Three lassies"—note first indication that the children are girls.
6. Giant puts necklaces of straw around their necks, gold necklaces for his own three daughters. Commands they all sleep in the same bed.
7. Molly Whuppie notices this—note first time her name is used.
8. Molly exchanges the necklaces.
9. Molly and her sisters escape.
10. Come to King's house.
11. King tells Molly if she returns to giant and gets sword, he will give his oldest son as husband to her older sister.
12. Molly returns, gets sword. Results.
13. Second trip to giant. Molly gets purse. Results.
14. Third trip to giant. Molly gets ring but is captured.
15. Molly tricks giant for the last time and escapes.
16. Happy ending.

By learning the hinges of action in this way, you will gain control of the story; it will belong to you forever. If you do not tell the story for years, one quick reading will bring it back to you.

The next step is to build, in your imagination, the landscape, the setting, the scenes of your story. This is of major importance. *The one immutable law of storytelling is that you see with your inner eye everything of which you speak. You must see what you relate, as you relate it.* When you can do this, your story will have such an air of conviction that you will be able to tell it as though you were telling something that happened to you. When you speak of the forest, bring to your mind's eye the image of any forest, wood, or grove you have yourself known or seen pictured. Feel the word as you say it, and above all see it! Castles, giants, bridges of one hair, these you must imagine; but never fail to see them as you speak their names. Look at pictures of castles and set one up in your mind. Where does the giant's house stand in your telling of the story? To the right of the picture, or to the left? Do the children come from left or right? What kind of bed does the giant sleep on? Is it a four-poster or a crude matter of skins stretched across a wooden frame? Train yourself to see, and you unconsciously give your audience time to see also. The pace of your story will come to fit action and scene. You must give your story depth and conviction, setting and atmosphere, before you can make it live for your listeners.

It was said of Ibsen, the great Norwegian dramatist, that before he set pen to paper in writing his plays, he sketched out the whole life experience of his characters as he imagined them, documenting their lives up to the moment when they were to take part in his drama. The storyteller must also build setting and characterization in this manner.

Look at your story once more, this time with an eye to its climactic parts. Where is the highest point? Build toward it as you tell the story, and change pace as you near it, so that the audience may know the pleasure of anticipation. Find other bits that are pleasurable and thus invite lingering. When all this is accomplished, it is time to consider the role of memorization. There will be certain turns of phrase you like and want to remember, or refrains that are important to the story:

> "Woe worth ye, Molly Whuppie,
> Never ye come again."
> "Twice yet, Carle, I'll come to Spain."

These can be consciously memorized. As for the rest, you will find the story so familiar to you that you begin to think of it as your own brainchild.

Certain stories must be memorized, because the style in which they were conceived is vital to the story. This is true of Kipling's *Just So Stories* (1902), which would lose at least half their charm if they were told in words other than the author's; certain stories of Carl Sandburg demand the same memorization. But if these stories are studied in the manner suggested here, the memorization will present little difficulty.

The danger of depending on memorization alone is that if you lose one part of the story, even a word or phrase, or if something interrupts the even flow of your memory, you are apt to lose the thread of the whole tale. But if you have learned the hinges of action, you can go on under your own steam, come what may.

By this time, you are saturated with your story and ready to tell it. It is a good practice to tell aloud to yourself, for by this means your own ears are able to tell you whether or not you have variation in pace or have by use of a judicious pause indicated the climactic points of the story for the greater enjoyment of the audience. A tape recorder is valuable at this stage. It reveals the best of your speech habits, as well as the worst, and clearly defines the areas that must be worked upon and improved.

Do not be discouraged if the first efforts are something less than your hopes.

The elements that will hold the children are your *belief* in the story, your *sincerity* in presenting it, and your absolute control of all that the story is capable of revealing. If you are sure of these elements, the children will forgive you everything else. You will learn from their reactions much that you need to know: the value of a pause or when to speed up the telling of the tale, for example.

The fascination of storytelling lies in the fact that it is never completed, never finished, for in each telling the story is re-created. The audience, the atmosphere of the place, the inner weather of the storyteller: there are dozens of intangible, mysterious forces that contribute to the growth of a story. "I make the story as I tell it," Ella Young, the noted Irish storyteller, once said. She did not mean that she created the events of the story; she meant that the story took on the quality of the audience's collective response to it. Sometimes one face in the group will call forth your deepest feeling. Sometimes, when you are unlucky, you will feel that you speak to stone walls. Each of these experiences increases your power to convey feeling, to build a mood, to catch and transport people beyond themselves.

Certain obvious circumstances can be avoided: a room that is uncomfortable; too many children crowded together; children of too diverse an age range. It is foolish to attempt to tell stories to children ranging in ages from three to thirteen all at the same time.

Even as an experienced and skillful storyteller, your position and power will be nothing like that of the storytellers in primitive societies. But the old tradition does persist in certain regions of North America (the mountains of the South, for example, and among many of the native peoples of Canada and the United States), in the Orient, in Mexico, and in parts of Europe (Russia, Wales, Ireland). For the unsophisticated or the unlettered, storytelling is still the chief source of entertainment. The public libraries of the country have found it a most effective and direct means of giving children a background of literature, with its many attendant arts. Schools, playgrounds, camps, and recreation centers use it also. Its unique influence is substantiated even in the face of television, which has not yet discovered its proper use.

Storytellers develop a personal style and individuality as they grow in the skills and mastery of their art. The greatest among them hold one attribute in common: a great simplicity. For each, it is the story that speaks first; they are merely instruments. They provide no studied gestures, no changing voices to suit characters of the story, no costumes or gimmicks to substantiate the tale. Above all, there is no condescension, either to the story or to the children— no pseudo-ecstatic tone of voice of the sort that some adults assume when speaking to children, no asking of questions either before or after, no insistence on explanations of the meaning of words, and no rewards for listening—other than the story itself.

The stories you have read in Part III come from the great oral tradition, the living past. Because their chosen texts hold closely to the spoken word—the oral tradition—they afford a rich resource for the storytellers of today. Storytelling, like any other art, demands time, study, discipline, and practice. To make certain stories your own, to feel them in your very bones and spirit, is to be in possession of an indestructible life force. To see on the faces of the children to whom you tell your tales not only the pleasure they find in your telling, but also their recognition of a long heritage they may never have known before— that is your reward.

IV

Fiction:
The Storied World

"The basic unit of language is not the word, but the phrase," Aidan Chambers writes in *Introducing Books to Children* (1983). "And the basic unit of sense-making is not the phrase but the combination of phrases . . . that tells us what happened, to whom it happened, and why it happened." Chambers then notes that *"What happens, to whom, and why* is a classic definition of Story. And Story is every-where."[1]

Nursery rhymes are tiny stories; quick dramas of plot and characterization are packed into them. Picture books are stories for the eye; illustrations in children's books are narratives. The tales of the oral tradition, from the simplest folktale to the grandest myth, are the bones of our literature; there, ready at hand, are all the stories of humanity. In epics and romances are the beginnings of modern characterization and complexity. Children think and feel and respond to the world through narrative, and all genres of children's literature have story at their core. When children arrive at fiction, they are continuing on a path they already know.

"The story is indispensable to children's books," Jill Paton Walsh, herself an author of children's books, tells us. And story is "the necessary continuous thread

---

1. Aidan Chambers, *Introducing Books to Children*, 2d ed. (Horn Book, 1983), p. 20.

to bring young readers through any kind of labyrinth. The children's book is an essentially narrative form, being in this respect much less versatile than the mainstream novel, which can do other things as well, or instead."[2] But the fact that the children's novel is so firmly wedded to narrative does not diminish it or make it a lesser form than the adult novel. For the ancient voice of the storyteller is the basis of all literature.

Children's fiction may be divided roughly into two categories: realistic fiction and fantasy. Realistic fiction includes stories of child and family life, naturalistic stories about animals, mystery and detective stories, adventure stories, and (although this is sometimes treated as a separate genre) historical fiction. Fantasy includes the literary fairy tale, domestic and animal fantasies such as *Mary Poppins* (1934), and *The Wind in the Willows* (1908), epic fantasy, time travel fantasy, and (as a subgenre) science fiction. Generally speaking, realistic fiction is set in a world that looks like the one we see as "real"; fantasy fiction is set elsewhere, in what J. R. R. Tolkien calls a "Secondary World," created by "enchantment"— either one that does not look like the ordinary world or one that does resemble it but is altered by magic and imagination.

In both cases, however, the world is *fictitious*—one created in the imagination of the writer. As Lloyd Alexander writes:

Storytellers, in realism or fantasy, create illusions, not clinical studies. The test of the latter is how accurately they convey specific facts. The test of illusion is how thoroughly it convinces us of its reality; how strongly it resonates in our emotions; how deeply it moves us to new feelings and new insights. Such illusions may be the truest things we know. "Art," says Picasso, "is a lie that lets us see the truth."[3]

2. Jill Paton Walsh, "The Rainbow Surface," *The Times Literary Supplement,* 3 Dec. 1971, reprinted in *The Cool Web: The Pattern of Children's Reading,* ed. Margaret Meek, Aidan Warlow, and Griselda Barton (Bodley Head, 1977), p. 194.
3. Lloyd Alexander, "The Grammar of Story," in *Celebrating Children's Books: Essays on Children's Literature in Honor of Zena Sutherland,* ed. Betsy Hearne and Marilyn Kaye (Lothrop, Lee & Shepard, 1981), p. 4.

Perhaps it is only in childhood that books have any deep influence on our lives. . . .

. . . In childhood all books are books of divination, telling us about the future, and like the fortune-teller who sees a long journey in the cards or death by water they influence the future. . . . What do we ever get nowadays from reading to equal the excitement and the revelation in the first fourteen years?[1]

11 Encounters and Adventures: Realistic and Historical Fiction

Childhood is a sharply limited time, resonant with the future life of the adolescent and the adult. Children easily see themselves in other guises, imagining themselves taking action, undergoing danger, and savoring victories. They seek to know the difference between right and wrong, to understand the consequences of actions. In realistic fiction they find the humor, pathos, complexity, and joy of human life, in the form of a deeply emotional experience. When they have finished a book that has genuinely moved them, many children ask, "Is there another book just like this one?" The answer must always be "No," for each work of art is unique. But after having read the last page of a good novel, children are more aware of the emotional realm, more developed in imagination, and more responsive to art as an element of life.

The writing of realistic fiction for children began, as did all writing intended specifically for children, with the Puritans. The mortality rate among children in the seventeenth century was high, and the frequent death-bed scenes of the

---

1. Graham Greene, "The Lost Childhood," in *Collected Essays* (Bodley Head, 1969), p. 13.

"Good Godly Books" have a certain harsh realism. But their protracted accounts of children slowly dying in joyous anticipation of heavenly bliss and becoming exemplars to adults and other children around them do not represent the kind of realism we would wish for our children today.

The realistic children's novel as we know it developed in the eighteenth century, paralleling the adult novel. The first "school story," *The Governess, or the Little Academy* (1749), was written by Sarah Fielding, sister of the novelist Henry Fielding. In 1765 John Newbery published *The History of Little Goody Two-Shoes,* a work that has been attributed to Oliver Goldsmith. This tale of an orphaned girl's rise to fortune against enormous odds is the prototype for many later "rags to riches" stories in which, in the best spirit of the rising British middle classes, children conquer the world. Horatio Alger, in his nineteenth-century *Ragged Dick* series, created a stalwart American counterpart.

The mistress of the late eighteenth-century moral tale was Maria Edgeworth, whose vivid characterizations set a high standard for the writers who followed. In the Victorian era, less didactic and more realistic fiction for children flourished. Mrs. Ewing, Mrs. Molesworth, and Charlotte Yonge in Britain and Louisa May Alcott and Mark Twain in the United States, wrote stories of child and family life filled with accurate domestic observations and sincere emotions. Romantic adventure stories and historical fiction achieved vibrancy in the work of Sir Walter Scott, Captain Marryat, R. M. Ballantyne, Robert Louis Stevenson, and Howard Pyle. Anna Sewell's *Black Beauty* (1877) popularized the animal story; Thomas Hughes, with *Tom Brown's School Days* (1857), opened the door to the boys' school.

Twentieth-century realistic fiction continued in the tradition of the classic Victorian writers but, with ever deepening perceptions, gradually came to explore areas previously considered taboo in children's books. The New Realism of the 1960s brought profound changes in the genre, widening its range to include controversial subjects, themes, and issues.

The best realistic fiction for children (whether contemporary stories of daily life or historical fiction of the distant or near past) has always been distinguished by historical accuracy, precise observation, emotional truthfulness, strong plot, and well-rounded, sympathetic characters. And all the best stories for children, of whatever type, have one common element: They speak with a personal voice, for children always read stories on a personal and emotional level. As James Britton writes:

A child approaches the facts of history by involving himself in a personal way with the lives of people of past ages. It is through exciting adventures, life-and-death struggles, heroic and tragic and heart-warming incidents that he moves towards an impersonal appreciation of the external facts. At an early stage then there will be little difference between the stories about other times that lead out to the truths of history—or the stories about other countries that lead out to the truths of geography—and the stories about fathers and mothers and giants and witches and dogs and cats, the stories that lead to more stories and remain for a life-time a means of extending our experience by identifying ourselves with the personal lives of such people as Huckleberry Finn and Tom Jones and Moll Flanders and Anna Karenina and King Lear—to mention the first that come to mind.[2]

2. James Britton, Introduction, *The Oxford Book of Stories for Juniors* (teacher's book) (Oxford University Press, 1965), reprinted in *Suitable for Children? Controversies in Children's Literature*, ed. Nicholas Tucker (Sussex University Press, 1976), p. 203.

And, indeed, people are the heart of fiction. There are no plots without characters to act them out, and the most important element of story is characterization. In folktales, characters may be drawn in a few words: the third and youngest brother, the young princess, the old woodcutter, the witch. In realistic fiction, we expect characters to be well-rounded, three-dimensional, flesh-and-blood people, but there is no set of formulae to tell a writer how to achieve such human complexity. If we listen to what writers have to say about the process of writing fiction, we hear the same comment over and over again: *The characters must come to life.* From the writer's point of view, a character is not created, invented, or based directly upon observations from life, is not felt to be a part of the writer's self, fleshed out and given voice (although common sense tells us that surely these processes must be going on). What a writer feels is that a character either is alive or isn't alive; and a character who is alive is felt to be as real as anyone in the world.

It is as hard to set standards for judging a living character in a book as it is to set standards for judging one's brother-in-law; living characters can act *out of character,* surprising us; they are quirky, unpredictable, human, and always wholly themselves. Adult readers know immediately if characters haven't come to life; we say they are flat, or one-dimensional, or unbelievable. Children respond just as immediately and, usually, more to the point: "I couldn't read that book. The people were boring." And children usually remember neither titles nor authors, but characters. They ask for another book about Heidi, Tom Sawyer, Harriet the spy, or Ramona Quimby.

The power of fiction consists of both a power to entertain and a power to engage the emotions and the imagination. Fiction can play a central role in the life of a child, enlarging the imagination and deepening a sympathetic perception of humankind. And empathy with character is what gives intensity to the reader's participation in the story. This reader involvement is essential, for instance, in Eleanor Estes's stories about the Moffatts. Without sympathy for her characters, no reader is likely to find any interest in the plot; with such sympathy, each small event becomes momentous. In *Rufus M.* (1943), the delicately calibrated struggle to obtain a library card gives rise to emotional nuances that parallel the comic pathos of a Chaplin film. We ache with laughter at Rufus's heroic stubbornness.

Fine tuning of character and action creates the small, personal, and often humorous revelation found in the work of such writers as Beverly Cleary, Jane Langton, and Lois Lowry. Although the adventures may seem commonplace, it is the perspective of the teller that engages the reader.

Once there are people, then there can be story. The motion of the story, the element that pushes it forward, has traditionally been called *plot,* although modern critics may speak of *narrative lines.* In an adult novel there may be dozens of narrative lines, small stories twining in and around each other; in children's books there are usually only a few, and sometimes only one. A narrative line works by unfolding the story: and then, and then, and then. . . .

Writing at the turn of the century, E. Nesbit furnished Oswald Bastable, the child narrator of her books, with some comments upon plot structure that are hard to improve upon. "The best part of books," Oswald tells us, "is when things are happening. That is the best part of real things too." Oswald also knows what has always been known to every good storyteller, that one need not tell everything that happened, just "the nice, interesting parts—and in between you will understand that we had our meals and got up and went to bed, and dull things like that."[3] The essence of creating a good plot, then, is selectivity: knowing what to tell and what to leave out.

In the twentieth century, writers of adult fiction began to move away first from conventions of plot and then from plot itself. In the literary style now called *modernist,* many devices are used to distance the reader from the work, and the very notion of telling a story at all has become suspect. But modernist fiction has had only a minimal impact on children's literature. Some of its devices have been incorporated into writing for children—for instance, the stream-of-consciousness technique in Ivan Southall's *Josh* (1971)—but its underlying aesthetic has not. Nor is it likely to be. Childhood fascination with story, with plot ("And what happened then?"), with logic, with *meaning* is perennial and indefatigable. Children's literature tends, therefore, to be stylistically conservative, and age-old plot conventions are still employed: the beginning *in medias res* (in the thick of the action); the conflict of opposing forces; the rising action leading to a climax; the falling action and resolution in which the loose threads of plot are tied up. But important as plot is, a reliance on plot alone, without original, inventive writing and strong characterization, is the mark of the poor writer. Even in such a swashbuckling adventure as Robert Louis Stevenson's *Treasure Island* (1883), certain characters have so much vitality that years later they are more easily recalled than many incidents in the plot. Plot, style, and characterization are interdependent in good fiction, and it is the whole world of the story that comes across to a reader.

There are as many ways to tell a story as there are writers. The ways that are chosen define a writer's style. Is the story told in the first person? If so, is the narrator directly involved in the action or an observer standing on the sidelines? Is the narrator trustworthy or untrustworthy? If the story is told in the third person, does the writer stay inside the minds of only a few characters or jump into the minds of all the characters? How much narration does the writer use to advance the plot, and how much dialogue? How close is the writer to the subject matter? How is language used? Is the style plain or fancy?

The individuality and distinctiveness of a particular writer's language becomes apparent if we try to imagine, for instance, Kipling's stories told in another writer's words. Retelling *The Secret Garden* (1911) without Frances Hodgson Burnett's style would reduce the story to banality. Alan Garner's Cheshire dialect, the language of his childhood, brings *The Stone Book* (1976) close to poetry. The sense of place and time and person is reflected in a writer's choice of words and in the cadence of the sentences; style carries the essence of the writer. According to Eleanor Cameron: "Far from being ornament, embellishment, anything artificial which is self-consciously woven into or impressed upon the natural expression of the writer, style in its simplest definition, it seems to me, is sound—*the sound of self.* It arises out of the whole concept of the work, from the very pulsebeat of the writer and all that has gone to make him."[4]

Finally, then, style embodies the writer's vision. It is this individual, personal vision that is communicated to the child reader. Underlying the appeal of charac-

3. E. Nesbit, *The Story of the Treasure Seekers* (Unwin, 1899; reprinted by Benn, 1958), p. 19.
4. Eleanor Cameron, "Of Style and the Stylist," in *The Green and Burning Tree: On the Writing and Enjoyment of Children's Books* (Little, Brown, 1969), p. 158.

ter and the satisfaction of plot is the single voice telling children of the wonders, joys, and dramas that make up the storied world.

Setting is one of the elements that colors an author's style. The sense of a particular landscape is crucial to the works of such writers as Nancy Bond and Cynthia Voigt (in the United States), Alan Garner and William Mayne (in England), Brian Doyle, Kevin Major, and Jan Truss (in Canada), and Patricia Wrightson and Ivan Southall (in Australia). Each of their books could have been set in no other location. Physical settings are real and lasting presences in their stories—the stable ground from which plot and character develop. They tell of people who live in a particular place, who are rooted in that landscape and speak its language. Certain types of realistic fiction, such as historical fiction and the survival story or journey story, are naturally allied to a strong sense of place. They concentrate on the protagonist's relationship with the landscape, which—in the Robinson Crusoe-style story, for example—is often crucial to the story's plot. Jean George's *Julie of the Wolves* (1972), Rosemary Sutcliff's *The Eagle of the Ninth* (1954), and Scott O'Dell's *Island of the Blue Dolphins* (1960) are noteworthy examples. But other types of domestic and adventure stories also provide a striking sense of the physical world, a landscape that expands geographically and emotionally into the near or distant past, at home or in faraway lands. Johanna Spyri's *Heidi* (first published in English in 1884) brings to life the Swiss Alps; Frances Hodgson Burnett's *The Secret Garden* (1911), a Victorian English garden in Yorkshire; Leon Garfield's *Smith* (1967), the cityscape of eighteenth-century London.

A number of distinguishable themes have persisted throughout the history of children's literature. Many are the direct result of the single recurring element that characterizes almost all children's books: the child protagonist at the center of the work. In realistic fiction, themes or ideas generated by the presence of the child protagonist cluster around the realities of a child's life, the ongoing relationships between the child's private and public worlds—such themes as the child alone, the child in the family, the child and society, the child growing up.

Children are able to live inside the books they read, and this ability, coupled with their growing concern with the testing of their own strengths and abilities, accounts for the common plot device in children's literature: ridding the story of adults. It is not that adults are unimportant to children in real life; rather, children love to imagine what it would be like to take risks and face consequences, to take responsible roles in an adventure that calls on the resources that adult life will ultimately require. The theme of the child alone—the use of the plot convention of placing children in positions in which self reliance is crucial—has been explored from the turn of the century with E. Nesbit, through Arthur Ransome in the 1930s and 1940s, to the contemporary settings of E. L. Konigsburg and Ivan Southall. The child protagonists in these stories have a freedom seldom experienced by any of their readers; that they make good use of it is the source of their victories over circumstances and their success with readers. Tom Sawyer is the classic example of this assertion of freedom. He would have failed as a hero of fiction if he had followed the guidelines for correct behavior laid down by his Aunt Polly. Instead, he lives in the minds of readers as the personification of childhood independence.

In family and holiday adventure stories by such writers as E. Nesbit (*The*

Railway Children, 1906), Arthur Ransome (*Swallows and Amazons* series, 1930–1947), and E. L. Konigsburg (*From the Mixed-up Files of Mrs. Basil E. Frankweiler,* 1967), the child protagonists are capable and competent in their adventures. They are equally at home playing games, restoring the family fortunes, sailing off to sea, or running away to live in New York's Metropolitan Museum of Art. Their high-spirited activities occur within a support group of friends and siblings, almost entirely separate from adult society.

In the classic Robinsonnade survival story, however, the child can exist alone, in total physical isolation. This is so, for example, in Scott O'Dell's *Island of the Blue Dolphins* (1960), which tells the story of a girl learning to live physically and emotionally as one human being alone with the wild animals of her island.

The theme of the child living in psychological rather than physical isolation has been explored by writers as far apart historically as Frances Hodgson Burnett (*The Secret Garden,* 1911) and Virginia Hamilton (*The Planet of Junior Brown,* 1971). In these books, and those of such writers as Vera and Bill Cleaver (*Where the Lilies Bloom,* 1969), Marilyn Sachs (*The Bear's House,* 1971), and Cynthia Voigt (*Homecoming,* 1981), children undergo trials and a maturation process in their attempts to overcome isolation and establish new families. The abused urban runaways in *The Planet of Junior Brown* are alienated and isolated from adults, but together they form a new family unit that keeps them from despair.

The theme of the child in the family has been explored in stories of domestic warmth, humor, and pathos by writers ranging from Louisa May Alcott and L. M. Montgomery, through Eleanor Estes, to Helen Cresswell. In family stories and the stories of the child in society, the writer deliberately imposes a more restricted and realistic view of the child's possibilities for action, and a different emotional effect is achieved. This is partly because adults have stronger roles, altering both plot structure and emotional impact. The more realistic and lifelike the fiction, the more importance is given to adults as characters. Parents and other adults may be portrayed as loving and supportive, as in Lois Lowry's *Anastasia Krupnik* (1979) and Mildred Taylor's *Roll of Thunder, Hear My Cry* (1976). Or, they may be portrayed as destructive, disturbed, or indifferent, as in *The Planet of Junior Brown.* This is especially true in the young adult novel and problem novel of social realism. In these, the interaction of child and child or child and adult changes the tone of the story. Instead of a plot based on children actively engaged in isolated dramas of childhood or imaginative play, the plot takes a direction in which the resolution is not one of action, but rather one of awareness: realization of a change in attitude or of psychological maturation. Realistic fiction of earlier eras also resolved conflict through inner change, but not to the degree of the new realism, which places more emphasis on inner and social conflict and on psychological maturation. This theme may be more important than the plot. In Beverly Cleary's *Dear Mr. Henshaw* (1983), Leigh's relationship with the author to whom he writes a series of letters is really a growing awareness of his own identity, a strengthening of his sense of self, and a deepening understanding of his divorced parents.

The theme of the child in the society extending beyond the family has been explored by writers who look at the conflict between the individual child and the group or state. With its acerbic satire on society and poignant vision of the disintegrating nuclear family, Louise Fitzhugh's *Harriet the Spy* (1964) is a far cry from the cozy, traditional family stories. Although Harriet is, in many ways, an alienated child, she is also a spirited, developing writer. Her notebook and "spying" isolate her from others, but they also represent her unique individuality. Other child protagonists in more serious conflict with society are found in Robert Cormier's young-adult novel *The Chocolate War* (1974) and *The Slave Dancer* (1973) by Paula Fox.

These stories are concerned with struggles of conscience and with coming of age, two other prevalent themes in children's literature. Children's natural desire to grow up and to enter adulthood, their ambivalent feelings toward leaving childhood, and their dawning awareness of mortality are subjects in the novels of Katherine Paterson (*Bridge to Terabithia*, 1977) and Mollie Hunter (*A Sound of Chariots*, 1972). The friendship of Jess and Leslie, the two children in *Bridge to Terabithia*, is the ground that enables Jess to survive the emotional pain of Leslie's death and to progress beyond it toward maturity.

And, among the elements of fiction, there is, finally, that elusive thing critics call *subtext*—everything that is going on beneath the narrative surface. The *text* of *Tom Brown's Schooldays* is the adventures of a boy at a boarding school; the subtext is faith in the British Empire. It is often easier to see the subtext of an older work of fiction than that of a contemporary one. In *The Stone Book*, by Alan Garner, however, the distinction is clear. The text tells of a girl sent by her stonemason father into an underground mine to see a prehistoric cave painting. The theme or underlying metaphor is the girl's initiation by her father into the continuity of time, family, place, and craft. The subtext is the longing in contemporary Western society for reintegration into the ancient worlds of work and art, for an ongoing physical and spiritual tradition.

It would be convenient if there were a standard list of criteria with which to evaluate a work of fiction, but what the reader responds to is the whole of the story. There are no separate items to call up separate reactions; there is only a fused whole, eliciting a single intuitive response. Only after we have felt that response is it worthwhile to look critically at the way the work has been created, examining it for its own inner logic and proportion. And no matter what critical or analytical approach is brought to the work of fiction, there is always that ineffable quality, a something at the core that remains unexplainable. If a story works, then the reader is not thinking of elements of fiction but is, rather, living for a time in another, very real world.

Adults writing realistic fiction for children are writing *back;* they are reaching down into themselves, moving backward in time to recall past incidents and past emotions of childhood. Realistic fiction often belongs to the private, individual past of the author; historical fiction, to the public, collective past of humanity. Although it is work of invention and imagination just as much as fantasy, historical and realistic fiction is grounded in precise recall and the recreation of authentic landscape and experience.

All writers of fiction practice selective realism: they search for and choose the telling detail, the crucial piece of dialogue or action that reveals character, theme, place, and time. *Carrie's War* (1973), by Nina Bawden, is told by a mother to her children; as she remembers and recounts the experiences and emotions of her childhood during the Second World War, she relives them—she is a child again. In Alan Garner's *The Stone Book*, set in the 1860s, the past becomes not only the protagonist's present but also that of the reader. The significant sense of a specific place and time is what makes the story universal.

"The one thing we all share," says Penelope Lively, "is the capacity to remember; the novelist tries to convey the significance and the power of that capacity in fictional terms, to make universal stories out of the particular story that we each carry in our own head. At its grandest this theme is the most compelling in all literature; it is the means whereby we, as writers for children, hope to introduce them to larger and more exciting worlds—to talk about what it is like to be a human being."[5]

5. Penelope Lively, "Bones in the Sand," *The Horn Book Magazine,* 57 (1981), 651.

Laura Ingalls Wilder

Little House in the Big Woods

In *Little House in the Big Woods,* the author tells of her early childhood in a log cabin on the edge of the Big Woods in Wisconsin, for she is little Laura in the story. In those pioneer days, each family, living miles from a settlement, was of necessity self-sufficient. Each season brought its special work. In the following chapter, we read of the daily doings that made up life in the summertime. [From Laura Ingalls Wilder, *Little House in the Big Woods* (Harper, 1932).]

Summertime

Now it was summertime, and people went visiting. Sometimes Uncle Henry, or Uncle George, or Grandpa, came riding out of the Big Woods to see Pa. Ma would come to the door and ask how all the folks were, and she would say:

"Charles is in the clearing."

Then she would cook more dinner than usual, and dinnertime would be longer. Pa and Ma and the visitor would sit talking a little while before they went back to work.

Sometimes Ma let Laura and Mary go across the road and down the hill, to see Mrs. Peterson. The Petersons had just moved in. Their house was new, and always very neat, because Mrs. Peterson had no little girls to muss it up. She was a Swede, and she let Laura and Mary look at the pretty things she had brought from Sweden—laces, and colored embroideries, and china.

Mrs. Peterson talked Swedish to them, and they talked English to her, and they understood each other perfectly. She always gave them each a cooky when they left, and they nibbled the cookies very slowly while they walked home.

Laura nibbled away exactly half of hers, and Mary nibbled exactly half of hers, and the other halves they saved for Baby Carrie. Then when they got home, Carrie had two half-cookies, and that was a whole cooky.

This wasn't right. All they wanted to do was to divide the cookies fairly with Carrie. Still, if Mary saved half her cooky, while Laura ate the whole of hers, or if Laura saved half, and Mary ate her whole cooky, that wouldn't be fair, either.

They didn't know what to do. So each saved half, and gave it to Baby Carrie. But they always felt that somehow that wasn't quite fair.

Sometimes a neighbor sent word that the family was coming to spend the day. Then Ma did extra cleaning and cooking, and opened the package of store sugar. And on the day set, a wagon would come driving up to the gate in the morning and there would be strange children to play with.

When Mr. and Mrs. Huleatt came, they brought Eva and Clarence with them. Eva was a pretty girl, with dark eyes and black curls. She played carefully and kept her dress clean and smooth. Mary liked that, but Laura liked better to play with Clarence.

Clarence was red-headed and freckled, and always laughing. His clothes were pretty, too. He wore a blue suit buttoned all the way up the front with bright gilt buttons, and trimmed with braid, and he had copper-toed shoes. The strips of copper across the toes were so glittering bright that Laura wished she were a boy. Little girls didn't wear copper-toes.

Laura and Clarence ran and shouted and climbed trees, while Mary and Eva walked nicely together and talked. Ma and Mrs. Huleatt visited and looked at a *Godey's Lady's Book* which Mrs. Huleatt had brought, and Pa and Mr. Huleatt looked at the horses and the crops and smoked their pipes.

Once Aunt Lotty came to spend the day. That morning Laura had to stand still a long time while Ma unwound her hair from the cloth strings and combed it into long curls. Mary was all ready, sitting primly on a chair, with her golden curls shining and her china-blue dress fresh and crisp.

Laura liked her own red dress. But Ma pulled her hair dreadfully, and it was brown instead of golden, so that no one noticed it. Everyone noticed and admired Mary's.

"There!" Ma said at last. "Your hair is curled beautifully, and Lotty is coming. Run meet her, both of you, and ask her which she likes best, brown curls or golden curls."

Laura and Mary ran out of the door and down the path, for Aunt Lotty was already at the gate.

Aunt Lotty was a big girl, much taller than Mary. Her dress was a beautiful pink and she was swinging a pink sunbonnet by one string.

"Which do you like best, Aunt Lotty," Mary asked, "brown curls, or golden curls?" Ma had told them to ask that, and Mary was a very good little girl who always did exactly as she was told.

Laura waited to hear what Aunt Lotty would say, and she felt miserable.

"I like both kinds best," Aunt Lotty said, smiling. She took Laura and Mary by the hand, one on either side, and they danced along to the door where Ma stood.

The sunshine came streaming through the windows into the house, and everything was so neat and pretty. The table was covered with a red cloth, and the cookstove was polished shining black. Through the bedroom door Laura could see the trundle bed in its place under the big bed. The pantry door stood wide open, giving the sight and smell of goodies on the shelves, and Black Susan came purring down the stairs from the attic, where she had been taking a nap.

It was all so pleasant, and Laura felt so gay and good that no one would ever have thought she could be as naughty as she was that evening.

Aunt Lotty had gone, and Laura and Mary were tired and cross. They were at the woodpile, gathering a pan of chips to kindle the fire in the morning. They always hated to pick up chips, but every day they had to do it. Tonight they hated it more than ever.

Laura grabbed the biggest chip, and Mary said:

"I don't care. Aunt Lotty likes my hair best, anyway. Golden hair is lots prettier than brown."

Laura's throat swelled tight, and she could not speak. She knew golden hair was prettier than brown. She couldn't speak, so she reached out quickly and slapped Mary's face.

Then she heard Pa say, "Come here, Laura." She went slowly, dragging her feet. Pa was sitting just inside the door. He had seen her slap Mary.

"You remember," Pa said, "I told you girls you must never strike each other."

Laura began, "But Mary said—"

"That makes no difference," said Pa. "It is what I say that you must mind."

Then he took down a strap from the wall, and he whipped Laura with the strap.

Laura sat on a chair in the corner and sobbed. When she stopped sobbing, she sulked. The only thing in the whole world to be glad about was that Mary had to fill the chip pan all by herself.

At last, when it was getting dark, Pa said again, "Come here, Laura." His voice was kind, and when Laura came he took her on his knee and hugged her close. She sat in the crook of his arm, her head against his shoulder and his long brown whiskers partly covering her eyes, and everything was all right again.

She told Pa all about it, and she asked him, "You don't like golden hair better than brown, do you?"

Pa's blue eyes shone down at her, and he said, "Well, Laura, my hair is brown."

She had not thought of that. Pa's hair was brown, and his whiskers were brown, and she thought brown was a lovely color. But she was glad that Mary had had to gather all the chips.

In the summer evenings Pa did not tell stories or play the fiddle. Summer days were long, and he was tired after he had worked hard all day in the fields.

Ma was busy, too. Laura and Mary helped her weed the garden, and they helped her feed the calves and the hens. They gathered the eggs, and they helped make cheese.

When the grass was tall and thick in the woods and the cows were giving plenty of milk, that was the time to make cheese.

Somebody must kill a calf, for cheese could not be made without rennet, and rennet is the lining of a young calf's stomach. The calf must be very young, so that it had never eaten anything but milk.

Laura was afraid that Pa must kill one of the little calves in the barn. They were so sweet. One was fawn-colored and one was red, and their hair was so soft and their large eyes so wondering. Laura's heart beat fast when Ma talked to Pa about making cheese.

Pa would not kill either of his calves, because

they were heifers and would grow into cows. He went to Grandpa's and to Uncle Henry's, to talk about the cheese-making, and Uncle Henry said he would kill one of his calves. There would be enough rennet for Aunt Polly and Grandma and Ma.

So Pa went again to Uncle Henry's, and came back with a piece of the little calf's stomach. It was like a piece of soft, grayish-white leather, all ridged and rough on one side.

When the cows were milked at night, Ma set the milk away in pans. In the morning she skimmed off the cream to make into butter later. Then, when the morning's milk had cooled, she mixed it with the skimmed milk and set it all on the stove to heat.

A bit of the rennet, tied in a cloth, was soaking in warm water.

When the milk was heated enough, Ma squeezed every drop of water from the rennet in the cloth, and she poured the water into the milk. She stirred it well and left it in a warm place by the stove. In a little while it thickened into a smooth, quivery mass.

With a long knife Ma cut this mass into little squares, and let it stand while the curd separated from the whey. Then she poured it all into a cloth and let the thin, yellowish whey drain out.

When no more whey dripped from the cloth, Ma emptied the curd into a big pan and salted it, turning and mixing it well.

Laura and Mary were always there, helping all they could. They loved to eat bits of the curd when Ma was salting it. It squeaked in their teeth.

Under the cherry tree outside the back door, Pa had put up the board to press the cheese on. He had cut two grooves the length of the board, and laid the board on blocks, one end a little higher than the other. Under the lower end stood an empty pail.

Ma put her wooden cheese hoop on the board, spread a clean, wet cloth all over the inside of it, and filled it heaping full of the chunks of salted curd. She covered this with another clean, wet cloth, and laid on top of it a round board, cut small enough to go inside the cheese hoop. Then she lifted a heavy rock on top of the board.

All day long the round board settled slowly under the weight of the rock, and whey pressed out and ran down the grooves of the board into the pail.

Next morning, Ma would take out the round, pale yellow cheese, as large as a milk pan. Then she made more curd, and filled the cheese hoop again.

Every morning she took the new cheese out of the press, and trimmed it smooth. She sewed a cloth tightly around it, and rubbed the cloth all over with fresh butter. Then she put the cheese on a shelf in the pantry.

Every day she wiped every cheese carefully with a wet cloth, then rubbed it all over with fresh butter once more, and laid it down on its other side. After a great many days, the cheese was ripe, and there was a hard rind all over it.

Then Ma wrapped each cheese in paper and laid it away on the high shelf. There was nothing more to do with it but eat it.

Laura and Mary liked cheese-making. They liked to eat the curd that squeaked in their teeth and they liked to eat the edges Ma pared off the big, round, yellow cheeses to make them smooth, before she sewed them up in cloth.

Ma laughed at them for eating green cheese.

Illustration by Garth Williams, from *Little House in the Big Woods*, by Laura Ingalls Wilder. Illustrations copyright © 1953 by Garth Williams; renewed 1981 by Garth Williams. Reprinted by permission of Harper & Row, Publishers, Inc.

"The moon is made of green cheese, some people say," she told them.

The new cheese did look like the round moon when it came up behind the trees. But it was not green; it was yellow, like the moon.

"It's green," Ma said, "because it isn't ripened yet. When it's cured and ripened, it won't be a green cheese."

"Is the moon really made of green cheese?" Laura asked, and Ma laughed.

"I think people say that, because it looks like a green cheese," she said. "But appearances are deceiving." Then, while she wiped all the green cheeses and rubbed them with butter, she told them about the dead, cold moon that is like a little world on which nothing grows.

The first day Ma made cheese, Laura tasted the whey. She tasted it without saying anything to Ma, and when Ma turned around and saw her face, Ma laughed. That night, while she was washing the supper dishes and Mary and Laura were wiping them, Ma told Pa that Laura had tasted the whey and didn't like it.

"You wouldn't starve to death on Ma's whey, like old Grimes did on his wife's," Pa said.

Laura begged him to tell her about Old Grimes. So, though Pa was tired, he took his fiddle out of its box and played and sang for Laura:

Old Grimes is dead, that good old man,
We ne'er shall see him more,
He used to wear an old gray coat,
All buttoned down before.

Old Grime's wife made skim-milk cheese,
Old Grimes, he drank the whey,
There came an east wind from the west,
And blew Old Grimes away.

"There you have it!" said Pa. "She was a mean, tight-fisted woman. If she hadn't skimmed all the milk, a little cream would have run off in the whey, and Old Grimes might have staggered along.

"But she skimmed off every bit of cream, and poor Old Grimes got so thin the wind blew him away. Plumb starved to death."

Then Pa looked at Ma and said, "Nobody'd starve to death when you were around, Caroline."

"Well, no," Ma said. "No, Charles, not if you were there to provide for us."

Pa was pleased. It was all so pleasant, the doors and windows wide open to the summer evening, the dishes making little cheerful sounds together as Ma washed them and Mary and Laura wiped, and Pa putting away the fiddle and smiling and whistling softly to himself.

After a while he said: "I'm going over to Henry's tomorrow morning, Caroline, to borrow his grubbing hoe. Those sprouts are getting waist-high around the stumps in the wheatfield. A man just has to keep everlasting at it, or the woods'll take back the place."

Early next morning he started to walk to Uncle Henry's. But before long he came hurrying back, hitched the horses to the wagon, threw in his axe, the two washtubs, the washboiler and all the pails and wooden buckets there were.

"I don't know if I'll need 'em all, Caroline," he said, "but I'd hate to want 'em and not have 'em."

"Oh, what is it? What is it?" Laura asked, jumping up and down with excitement.

"Pa's found a bee tree," Ma said. "Maybe he'll bring us some honey."

It was noon before Pa came driving home. Laura had been watching for him, and she ran out to the wagon as soon as it stopped by the barnyard. But she could not see into it.

Pa called, "Caroline, if you'll come take this pail of honey, I'll go unhitch."

Ma came out to the wagon, disappointed. She said:

"Well, Charles, even a pail of honey is something." Then she looked into the wagon and threw up her hands. Pa laughed.

All the pails and buckets were heaping full of dripping, golden honeycomb. Both tubs were piled full, and so was the wash-boiler.

Pa and Ma went back and forth, carrying the two loaded tubs and the wash-boiler and all the buckets and pails into the house. Ma heaped a plate high with the golden pieces, and covered all the rest neatly with cloths.

For dinner they all had as much of the delicious honey as they could eat, and Pa told them how he found the bee tree.

"I didn't take my gun," he said, "because I wasn't hunting, and now it's summer there wasn't much danger of meeting trouble. Panthers and bears are so fat, this time of year, that they're lazy and good-natured.

"Well, I took a short cut through the woods, and I nearly ran into a big bear. I came around a clump of underbrush, and there he was, not as far from me as across this room.

"He looked around at me, and I guess he saw I didn't have a gun. Anyway, he didn't pay any more attention to me.

"He was standing at the foot of a big tree, and bees were buzzing all around him. They couldn't sting through his thick fur, and he kept brushing them away from his head with one paw.

"I stood there watching him, and he put the other paw into a hole in the tree and drew it out all dripping with honey. He licked the honey off his paw and reached in for more. But by that time I had found me a club. I wanted that honey myself.

"So I made a great racket, banging the club against a tree and yelling. The bear was so fat and so full of honey that he just dropped on all fours and waddled off among the trees. I chased him some distance and got him going fast, away from the bee tree, and then I came back for the wagon."

Laura asked him how he got the honey away from the bees.

"That was easy," Pa said. "I left the horses back in the woods, where they wouldn't get stung, and then I chopped the tree down and split it open."

"Didn't the bees sting you?"

"No," said Pa. "Bees never sting me.

"The whole tree was hollow, and filled from top to bottom with honey. The bees must have been storing honey there for years. Some of it was old and dark, but I guess I got enough good, clean honey to last us a long time."

Laura was sorry for the poor bees. She said: "They worked so hard, and now they won't have any honey."

But Pa said there was lots of honey left for the bees, and there was another large, hollow tree near-by, into which they could move. He said it was time they had a clean, new home.

They would take the old honey he had left in the old tree, make it into fresh, new honey, and store it in their new house. They would save every drop of the spilled honey and put it away, and they would have plenty of honey again, long before winter came.

Eleanor Estes

Rufus M.

With the Moffat books, Eleanor Estes has created a family that will be long remembered and loved. The four lively young Moffats and their understanding mother made their first appearance in *The Moffats.* In *Rufus M.* the youngest Moffat, now seven years old, proves that he is an individual in his own right. The chapter given below tells how Rufus learns to write his name. [From Eleanor Estes, *Rufus M.* (Harcourt, 1943).]

Rufus M. That's the way Rufus wrote his name on his heavy arithmetic paper and on his blue-lined spelling papers. Rufus M. went on one side of the paper. His age, seven, went on the other. Rufus had not learned to write his name in school, though that is one place for learning to write. He had not learned to write his name at home either, though that is another place for learning to write. The place where he had learned to write his name was the library, long ago before he ever went to school at all. This is the way it happened.

One day when Rufus had been riding his scooter up and down the street, being the motor-man, the conductor, the passengers, the steam, and the whistle of a locomotive, he came home and found Joey, Jane, and Sylvie, all reading in the front yard. Joey and Jane were sitting on the steps of the porch and Sylvie was sprawled in the hammock, a book in one hand, a chocolate-covered peppermint in the other.

Rufus stood with one bare foot on his scooter and one on the grass and watched them. Sylvie read the fastest. This was natural since she was the oldest. But Joey turned the pages almost as fast and Jane went lickety-cut on the good parts. They were all reading books and he couldn't even read yet. These books they were reading were library books. The library must be open today. It wasn't open every day, just a few days a week.

"I want to go the library," said Rufus. "And get a book," he added.

"We all just came home from there," said Jane, while Joey and Sylvie merely went on reading as though Rufus had said nothing.

"Besides," she added, "why do you want a book anyway? You can't even read yet."

This was true and it made Rufus mad. He liked to do everything that they did. He even liked to sew if they were sewing. He never thought whether sewing was for girls only or not. When he saw Jane sewing, he asked Mama to let him sew too. So Mama tied a thread to the head of a pin and Rufus poked that in and out of a piece of goods. That's the way he sewed. It looked like what Jane was doing and Rufus was convinced that he was sewing too, though he could not see much sense in it.

Now here were the other Moffats, all with books from the library. And there were three more books stacked up on the porch that looked like big people's books without pictures. They were for Mama, no doubt. This meant that he was the only one here who did not have a book.

"I want a book from the library," said Rufus. A flick of the page as Sylvie turned it over was all the answer he got. It seemed to Rufus as though even Catherine-the-cat gave him a scornful glance because he could not read yet and did not have a book.

Rufus turned his scooter around and went out of the yard. Just wait! Read? Why, soon he'd read as fast if not faster than they did. Reading looked easy. It was just flipping pages. Who couldn't do that?

Rufus thought that it was not hard to get a book out of the library. All you did was go in, look for a book that you liked, give it to the lady to punch, and come home with it. He knew where the library was, for he had often gone there with Jane and some of the others. While Jane went off to the shelves to find a book, he and Joey played the game of Find the Duke in the Palmer Cox Brownie books. This was a game that the two boys had made up. They would turn the pages of one of the

Brownie books, any of them, and try to be the first to spot the duke, the brownie in the tall hat. The library lady thought that this was a noisy game, and she wished they would not play it there. Rufus hoped to bring a Brownie book home now.

"Toot-toot!" he sang to clear the way. Straight down Elm Street was the way to the library; the same way that led to Sunday School, and Rufus knew it well. He liked sidewalks that were white the best, for he could go the fastest on these.

"Toot-toot!" Rufus hurried down the street. When he arrived at the library, he hid his scooter in the pine trees that grew under windows beside the steps. Christmas trees, Rufus called them. The ground was covered with brown pine needles and they were soft to walk upon. Rufus always went into the library the same way. He climbed the stairs, encircled the light on the granite arm of the steps, and marched into the library.

Rufus stepped carefully on the strips of rubber matting that led to the desk. This matting looked like dirty licorice. But it wasn't licorice. He knew because once, when Sylvie had brought him here when he was scarcely more than three, he had tasted a torn corner of it. It was not good to eat.

The library lady was sitting at the desk playing with some cards. Rufus stepped off the matting. The cool, shiny floor felt good to his bare feet. He went over to the shelves and luckily did find one of the big Palmer Cox Brownie books there. It would be fun to play the game of Find the Duke at home. Until now he had played it only in the library. Maybe Jane or Joey would play it with him right now. He laughed out loud at the thought.

"Sh-sh-sh, quiet," said the lady at the desk.

Rufus clapped his chubby fist over his mouth. Goodness! He had forgotten where he was. Do not laugh or talk out loud in the library. He knew these rules. Well, he didn't want to stay here any longer today anyway. He wanted to read at home with the others. He took the book to the lady to punch.

She didn't punch it, though. She took it and she put in on the table behind her and then she started to play cards again.

"That's my book," said Rufus.

"Do you have a card?" the lady asked.

Rufus felt in his pockets. Sometimes he carried around an old playing card or two. Today he didn't have one.

"No," he said.

"You'll have to have a card to get a book."

"I'll go and get one," said Rufus.

The lady put down her cards. "I mean a library card," she explained kindly. "It looks to me as though you are too little to have a library card. Do you have one?"

"No," said Rufus. "I'd like to, though."

"I'm afraid you're too little," said the lady. "You have to write your name to get one. Can you do that?"

Rufus nodded his head confidently. Writing. Lines up and down. He'd seen that done. And the letters that Mama had tied in bundles in the closet under the stairs were covered with writing. Of course he could write.

"Well, let's see your hands," said the lady.

Rufus obligingly showed this lady his hands, but she did not like the looks of them. She cringed and clasped her head as though the sight hurt her.

"Oh," she gasped. "You'll just have to go home and wash them before we can even think about joining the library and borrowing books."

This was a complication upon which Rufus had not reckoned. However, all it meant was a slight delay. He'd wash his hands and then he'd get the book. He turned and went out of the library, found his scooter safe among the Christmas trees, and pushed it home. He surprised Mama by asking to have his hands washed. When this was done, he mounted his scooter again and returned all the long way to the library. It was not just a little trip to the library. It was a long one. A long one and a hot one on a day like this. But he didn't notice that. All he was bent on was getting his book and taking it home and reading with the others on the front porch. They were all still there, brushing flies away and reading.

Again Rufus hid his scooter in the pine trees, encircled the light, and went in.

"Hello," he said.

"Well," said the lady. "How are they now?"

Rufus had forgotten he had had to wash his hands. He thought she was referring to the other Moffats. "Fine," he said.

"Let me see them," she said, and she held up her hands.

Oh! His hands! Well, they were all right, thought Rufus, for Mama had just washed them. He showed them to the lady. There was a silence while she studied them. Then she shook her head. She still did not like them.

"Ts, ts, ts!" she said. "They'll have to be cleaner than that."

Rufus looked at his hands. Supposing he went all the way home and washed them again, she still might not like them. However, if that is what she wanted, he would have to do that before he could get the Brownie book . . . and he started for the door.

"Well, now, let's see what we can do," said the lady. "I know what," she said. "It's against the rules, but perhaps we can wash them in here." And she led Rufus into a little room that smelled of paste where lots of new books and old books were stacked up. In one corner was a little round sink and Rufus washed his hands again. Then they returned to the desk. The lady got a chair and put a newspaper on it. She made Rufus stand on this because he was not big enough to write at the desk otherwise.

Then the lady put a piece of paper covered with a lot of printing in front of Rufus, dipped a pen in the inkwell and gave it to him.

"All right," she said. "Here's your application. Write your name here."

All the writing Rufus had ever done before had been on big pieces of brown wrapping paper with lots of room on them. Rufus had often covered those great sheets of paper with his own kind of writing at home. Lines up and down.

But on this paper there wasn't much space. It was already covered with writing. However, there was a tiny little empty space and that was where Rufus must write his name, the lady said. So, little space or not, Rufus confidently grasped the pen with his left hand and dug it into the paper. He was not accustomed to pens, having always worked with pencils until now, and he made a great many holes and blots and scratches.

"Gracious," said the lady. "Don't bear down

so hard! And why don't you hold it in your right hand?" she asked, moving the pen back into his right hand.

Rufus started again scraping his lines up and down and all over the page, this time using his right hand. Wherever there was an empty space he wrote. He even wrote over some of the print for good measure. Then he waited for the lady, who had gone off to get a book for some man, to come back and look.

"Oh," she said, as she settled herself in her swivel chair, "is that the way you write? Well . . . it's nice, but what does it say?"

"Says Rufus Moffat. My name."

Apparently these lines up and down did not spell Rufus Moffat to this lady. She shook her head.

"It's nice," she repeated. "Very nice. But nobody but you knows what it says. You have to learn to write your name better than that before you can join the library."

Rufus was silent. He had come to the library all by himself, gone back home to wash his hands, and come back because he wanted to take books home and read them the way the others did. He had worked hard. He did not like to think he might have to go home without a book.

The library lady looked at him a moment and then she said quickly before he could get himself all the way off the big chair, "maybe you can *print* your name."

Rufus looked at her hopefully. He thought he could write better than he could print, for his writing certainly looked to him exactly like all grown people's writing. Still he'd try to print if that was what she wanted.

The lady printed some letters on the top of a piece of paper. "There," she said. "That's your name. Copy it ten times and then we'll try it on another application."

Rufus worked hard. He worked so hard the knuckles showed white on his brown fist. He worked for a long, long time, now with his right hand and now with his left. Sometimes a boy or girl came in, looked over his shoulder and watched, but he paid no attention. From time to time the lady studied his work and she said, "That's fine. That's fine." At last she said,

"Well, maybe now we can try." And she gave him another application.

All Rufus could get, with his large generous letters, in that tiny little space where he was supposed to print his name, was R-U-F. The other letters he scattered here and there on the card. The lady did not like this either. She gave him still another blank. Rufus tried to print smaller and this time he got RUFUS in the space, and also he crowded an M at the end. Since he was doing so well now, the lady herself printed the *offat* part of Moffat on the next line.

"This will have to do," she said. "Now take this home and ask your mother to sign it on the other side. Bring it back on Thursday and you'll get your card."

Rufus's face was shiny and streaked with dirt where he had rubbed it. He never knew there was all this work to getting a book. The other Moffats just came in and got books. Well, maybe they had had to do this once too.

Rufus held his hard-earned application in one hand and steered his scooter with the other. When he reached home, Joey, Jane, and Sylvie were not around any longer. Mama signed his card for him, saying, "My! So you've learned how to write!"

"Print," corrected Rufus.

Mama kissed Rufus and he went back out. The lady had said to come back on Thursday, but he wanted a book today. When the other Moffats came home, he'd be sitting on the top step of the porch, reading. That would surprise them. He smiled to himself as he made his way to the library for the third time.

Once his application blew away. Fortunately it landed in a thistle bush and did not get very torn. The rest of the way Rufus clutched it carefully. He climbed the granite steps to the library again, only to find that the big round dark brown doors were closed. Rufus tried to open them, but he couldn't. He knocked at the door, even kicked it with his foot, but there was no answer. He pounded on the door, but nobody came.

A big boy strode past with his newspapers. "Hey, kid," he said to Rufus, "library's closed!" And off he went, whistling.

Rufus looked after him. The fellow said the library was closed. How could it have closed so fast? He had been there such a little while ago. The lady must still be here. He did want his Brownie book. If only he could see in, he might see the lady and get his book. The windows were high up, but they had very wide sills. Rufus was a wonderful climber. He could shinny up trees and poles faster than anybody on the block. Faster than Joey. Now, helping himself up by means of one of the pine trees that grew close to the building, and by sticking his toes in the ivy and rough places in the bricks, he scrambled up the wall. He hoisted himself up on one of the sills and sat there. He peered in. It was dark inside, for the shades had been drawn almost all the way down.

"Library lady!" he called, and he knocked on the window-pane. There was no answer. He put his hands on each side of his face to shield his eyes, and he looked in for a long, long time. He could not believe that she had left. Rufus was resolved to get a book. He had lost track of the number of times he had been back and forth from home to the library, and the library home. Maybe the lady was in the cellar. He climbed down, stubbing his big toe on the bricks as he did so. He stooped down beside one of the low dirt-spattered cellar windows. He couldn't see in. He lay flat on the ground, wiped one spot clean on the window, picked up a few pieces of coal from the sill and put them in his pocket for Mama.

"Hey, lady," he called.

He gave the cellar window a little push. It wasn't locked, so he opened it a little and looked in. All he could see was a high pile of coal reaching up to this window. Of course he didn't put any of that coal in his pocket, for that would be stealing.

"Hey, lady," he yelled again. His voice echoed in the cellar but the library lady did not answer. He called out, "Hey lady," every few seconds but all that answered him was an echo. He pushed the window open a little wider. All of a sudden it swung wide open and Rufus slid in, right on top of the coal pile and crash, clatter, bang! He slid to the bottom making a great racket.

A little light shone through the dusty windows, but on the whole it was very dark and spooky down here and Rufus really wished that he was back on the outside looking in. However, since he was in the library, why not go upstairs quick, get the Brownie book, and go home? The window had banged shut, but he thought he could climb up the coal pile, pull the window up, and get out. He certainly hoped he could, anyway. Supposing he couldn't and he had to stay in this cellar! Well, that he would not think about. He looked around in the dusky light and saw a staircase across the cellar. Luckily his application was still good. It was torn and dirty, but it still had his name on it, RUFUS M. and that was the important part. He'd leave this on the desk in exchange for the Brownie book.

Rufus cautiously made his way over to the steps, but he stopped halfway across the cellar. Somebody had opened the door at the top of the stairs. He couldn't see who it was, but he did see the light reflected and that's how he knew that somebody had opened the door. It must be the lady. He was just going to say, "Hey, lady," when he thought, "Gee, maybe it isn't the lady. Maybe it's a spooky thing."

Then the light went away, the door was closed, and Rufus was left in the dark again. He didn't like it down here. He started to go back to the coal pile to get out of this place. Then he felt of his application. What a lot of work he had done to get a book and now that he was this near to getting one, should he give up? No. Anyway, if it was the lady up there, he knew her and she knew him and neither one of them was scared of the other. And Mama always said there's no such thing as a spooky thing.

So Rufus bravely made his way again to the stairs. He tiptoed up them. The door at the head was not closed tightly. He pushed it open and found himself right in the library. But goodness! There in the little sink room right opposite him was the library lady!

Rufus stared at her in silence. The library lady was eating. Rufus had never seen her do anything before but play cards, punch books, and carry great piles of them around. Now she was eating. Mama said not to stare at anybody while they were eating. Still Rufus didn't know the library lady ate, so it was hard for him not to look at her.

She had a little gas stove in there. She could cook there. She was reading a book at the same time that she was eating. Sylvie could do that too. This lady did not see him.

"Hey, lady," said Rufus.

The librarian jumped up out of her seat. "Was that you in the cellar? I thought I heard somebody. Goodness, young man! I thought you had gone home long ago."

Rufus didn't say anything. He just stood there. He had gone home and he had come back lots of times. He had the whole thing in his mind; the coming and going, and going and coming, and sliding down the coal pile, but he did not know where to begin, how to tell it.

"Didn't you know the library is closed now?" she demanded, coming across the floor with firm steps.

Rufus remained silent. No, he hadn't known it. The fellow had told him, but he hadn't believed him. Now he could see for himself that the library was closed so the library lady could eat. If the lady would let him take his book, he'd go home and stay there. He'd play the game of Find the Duke with Jane. He hopefully held out his card with his name on it.

"Here this is," he said.

But the lady acted as though she didn't even see it. She led Rufus over to the door.

"All right now," she said. "Out with you!" But just as she opened the door the sound of water boiling over on the stove struck their ears, and back she raced to her little room.

"Gracious!" she exclaimed. "What a day!"

Before the door could close on him, Rufus followed her in and sat down on the edge of a chair. The lady thought he had gone and started to sip her tea. Rufus watched her quietly, waiting for her to finish.

After a while the lady brushed the crumbs off her lap. And then she washed her hands and the dishes in the little sink where Rufus had washed his hands. In a library a lady could eat and could wash. Maybe she slept here, too. Maybe she lived here.

"Do you live here?" Rufus asked her.

"Mercy on us!" exclaimed the lady.

"Where'd you come from? Didn't I send you home? No, I don't live here and neither do you. Come now, out with you, young man. I mean it." The lady called all boys "young man" and all girls "Susie." She came out of the little room and she opened the big brown door again. "There," she said. "Come back on Thursday."

Rufus's eyes filled up with tears.

"Here's this," he said again, holding up his application in a last desperate attempt. But the lady shook her head. Rufus went slowly down the steps, felt around in the bushes for his scooter, and with drooping spirits he mounted it. Then for the second time that day, the library lady changed her mind.

"Oh, well," she said, "come back here, young man. I'm not supposed to do business when the library's closed, but I see we'll have to make an exception."

So Rufus rubbed his sooty hands over his face, hid his scooter in the bushes again, climbed the granite steps, and, without circling the light, he went back in and gave the lady his application.

The lady took it gingerly. "My, it's dirty," she said. "You really ought to sign another one."

"And go home with it?" asked Rufus. He really didn't believe this was possible. He wiped his hot face on his sleeve and looked up at the lady in exhaustion. What he was thinking was: All right. If he had to sign another one, all right. But would she just please stay open until he got back?

However, this was not necessary. The lady said, "Well, now, I'll try to clean this old one up. But remember, young man, always have everything clean—your hands, your book, everything, when you come to the library."

Rufus nodded solemnly. "My feet too," he assured her.

Then the lady made Rufus wash his hands again. They really were very bad this time, for he had been in a coal pile, and now at last she gave Rufus the book he wanted—one of the Palmer Cox Brownie books. This one was *The Brownies in the Philippines.*

And Rufus went home.

When he reached home, he showed Mama

his book. She smiled at him, and gave his cheek a pat. She thought it was fine that he had gone to the library and joined all by himself and taken out a book. And she thought it was fine when Rufus sat down at the kitchen table, was busy and quiet for a long, long time, and then showed her what he had done.

He had printed RUFUS M. That was what he had done. And that's the way he learned to sign his name. And that's the way he always did sign his name for a long, long time.

Louise Fitzhugh

Harriet the Spy

Harriet's ambitions to be a writer have taken the form of keeping a notebook and writing down her impressions of everyone as well as what she observes them to be doing. Such spying has become a regular routine with her, and she considers it part of her life. A distinctly contemporary child whose parents are emotionally remote, Harriet's independence and sense of herself are cruelly upset when her notebook is taken from her. [From Louise Fitzhugh, *Harriet the Spy* (Harper, 1964).]

That day, after school, everyone felt in a good mood because the weather was suddenly gay and soft like spring. They hung around outside, the whole class together, which was something they never did. Sport said suddenly, "Hey, why don't we go to the park and play tag?"

Harriet was late for her spying, but she thought she would just play one game and then leave. They all seemed to think this was a smashing idea, so everyone filed across the street.

The kind of tag they played wasn't very complicated; in fact Harriet thought it was rather silly. The object seemed to be to run around in circles and get very tired, then whoever was "it" tried to knock everyone else's books out of their arms. They played and played. Beth Ellen was eliminated at once, having no strength. Sport was the best. He managed to knock down everyone's books except Rachel Hennessey's and Harriet's.

He ran round and round then, very fast.

Suddenly he knocked a few of Harriet's things off her arms, then Rachel tried to tease him away, and Harriet started to run like crazy. Soon she was running and running as fast as she could in the direction of the mayor's house. Rachel was right after her and Sport was close behind.

They ran and ran along the river. Then they were on the grass and Sport fell down. It wasn't any fun with him not chasing, so Rachel and Harriet waited until he got up. Then he was very quick and got them.

All of Rachel's books were on the ground, and some of Harriet's. They began to pick them up to go back and join the others.

Suddenly Harriet screeched in horror, "Where is my notebook?" They all began looking around, but they couldn't find it anywhere. Harriet suddenly remembered that some things had been knocked down before they ran away from the others. She began to run back toward them. She ran and ran, yelling like a banshee the whole way.

When she got back to where they had started she saw the whole class—Beth Ellen, Pinky Whitehead, Carrie Andrews, Marion Hawthorne, Laura Peters, and The Boy with the Purple Socks—all sitting around a bench while Janie Gibbs read to them from the notebook.

Harriet descended upon them with a scream that was supposed to frighten Janie so much she would drop the book. But Janie didn't frighten easily. She just stopped reading and looked up calmly. The others looked up too. She looked at all their eyes and suddenly Harriet M. Welsch was afraid.

They just looked and looked, and their eyes were the meanest eyes she had ever seen. They formed a little knot and wouldn't let her near them. Rachel and Sport came up then. Marion Hawthorne said fiercely, "Rachel, come over here." Rachel walked over to her, and after Marion had whispered in her ear, got the same mean look.

Janie said, "Sport, come over here."

"Whadaya mean?" said Sport.

"I have something to tell you," Janie said in a very pointed way.

Sport walked over and Harriet's heart went

into her sneakers. "FINKS!" Harriet felt rather hysterical. She didn't know what that word meant, but since her father said it all the time, she knew it was bad.

Janie passed the notebook to Sport and Rachel, never taking her eyes off Harriet as she did so. "Sport, you're on page thirty-four; Rachel, you're on fifteen," she said quietly.

Sport read his and burst into tears. "Read it aloud, Sport," said Janie harshly.

"I can't." Sport hid his face.

The book was passed back to Janie. Janie read the passage in a solemn voice.

SOMETIMES I CAN'T STAND SPORT. WITH HIS WORRYING ALL THE TIME AND FUSSING OVER HIS FATHER, SOMETIMES HE'S LIKE A LITTLE OLD WOMAN.

Sport turned his back on Harriet, but even from his back Harriet could see that he was crying.

"That's not *fair*," she screamed. "There're some nice things about Sport in there."

Everyone got very still. Janie spoke very quietly. "Harriet, go over there on that bench until we decide what we're going to do to you."

Harriet went over and sat down. She couldn't hear them. They began to discuss something rapidly with many gestures. Sport kept his back turned and Janie never took her eyes off Harriet, no matter who was talking.

Harriet thought suddenly, I don't have to sit here. And she got up and marched off in as dignified a way as possible under the circumstances. They were so busy they didn't even seem to notice her.

At home, eating her cake and milk, Harriet reviewed her position. It was terrible. She decided that she had never been in a worse position. She then decided she wasn't going to think about it anymore. She went to bed in the middle of the afternoon and didn't get up until the next morning.

Her mother thought she was sick and said to her father, "Maybe we ought to call the doctor."

Illustration by Louise Fitzhugh, from *Harriet the Spy*, by Louise Fitzhugh. Copyright © 1964 by Louise Fitzhugh. Reprinted by permission of Harper & Row, Publishers, Inc.

"Finks, all of them," said her father. Then they went away and Harriet went to sleep.

In the park all the children sat around and read things aloud. These are some of the things they read:

NOTES ON WHAT CARRIE ANDREWS THINKS OF MARION HAWTHORNE

THINKS: IS MEAN
       IS ROTTEN IN MATH
       HAS FUNNY KNEES
       IS A PIG

Then:

IF MARION HAWTHORNE DOESN'T WATCH OUT SHE'S GOING TO GROW UP INTO A LADY HITLER.

Janie Gibbs smothered a laugh at that one but not at the next one:

WHO DOES JANIE GIBBS THINK SHE'S KIDDING? DOES SHE REALLY THINK SHE COULD EVER BE A SCIENTIST?

Janie looked as though she had been struck. Sport looked at her sympathetically. They looked at each other, in fact, in a long, meaningful way.

Janie read on:

WHAT TO DO ABOUT PINKY WHITEHEAD
  1. TURN THE HOSE ON HIM.
  2. PINCH HIS EARS UNTIL HE SCREAMS.
  3. TEAR HIS PANTS OFF AND LAUGH AT HIM.

Pinky felt like running. He looked around nervously, but Harriet was nowhere to be seen. There was something about everyone.

MAYBE BETH ELLEN DOESN'T HAVE ANY PARENTS. I ASKED HER HER MOTHER'S NAME AND SHE COULDN'T REMEMBER. SHE SAID SHE HAD ONLY SEEN HER ONCE AND SHE DIDN'T REMEMBER IT VERY WELL. SHE WEARS STRANGE THINGS LIKE ORANGE SWEATERS AND A BIG BLACK CAR COMES FOR HER ONCE A WEEK AND SHE GOES SOMEPLACE ELSE.

Beth Ellen rolled her big eyes and said nothing. She never said anything, so this wasn't unusual.

THE REASON SPORT DRESSES SO FUNNY IS THAT HIS FATHER WON'T BUY HIM ANYTHING TO WEAR BECAUSE HIS MOTHER HAS ALL THE MONEY.

Sport turned his back again.

TODAY A NEW BOY ARRIVED. HE IS SO DULL NO ONE CAN REMEMBER HIS NAME SO I HAVE NAMED HIM THE BOY WITH THE PURPLE SOCKS. IMAGINE. WHERE WOULD HE EVER FIND PURPLE SOCKS?

The Boy with the Purple Socks looked down at his purple socks and smiled.

Everyone looked at the sock boy. Carrie spoke up. She had a rather grating voice. "What *IS* your name?" even though by now they all knew perfectly well.

"Peter," he said shyly.

"Why *do* you wear purple socks?" asked Janie.

Peter smiled shyly, looked at his socks, then said, "Once, at the circus, my mother lost me. She said, after that, if I had on purple socks, she could always find me."

"Hmmmmm," said Janie.

Gathering courage from this, Peter spoke again. "She *wanted* to make it a whole purple suit, but I rebelled."

"I don't blame you," said Janie.

Peter bobbed his head and grinned. They all grinned back at him because he had a tooth missing and looked rather funny, but also he wasn't a bad sort, so they all began to like him a little bit.

They read on:

MISS ELSON HAS A WART BEHIND HER ELBOW.

This was fairly boring so they skipped ahead.

I ONCE SAW MISS ELSON WHEN SHE DIDN'T SEE ME AND SHE WAS PICKING HER NOSE.

That was better, but still they wanted to read about themselves.

CARRIE ANDREWS' MOTHER HAS THE BIGGEST FRONT I EVER SAW.

There was a great deal of tension in the group after this last item. Then Sport gave a big horse-laugh, and Pinky Whitehead's ears turned bright red. Janie smiled a fierce and frightening smile at Carrie Andrews, who looked as though she wanted to dive under the bench.

WHEN I GROW UP I'M GOING TO FIND OUT EVERYTHING ABOUT EVERYBODY AND PUT IT ALL IN A BOOK. THE BOOK IS GOING TO BE CALLED *SECRETS* BY HARRIET M. WELSCH. I WILL ALSO HAVE PHOTOGRAPHS IN IT AND MAYBE SOME MEDICAL CHARTS IF I CAN GET THEM.

Rachel stood up, "I have to go home. Is there anything about me?"
They flipped through until they found her name.

I DON'T KNOW EXACTLY IF I LIKE RACHEL OR WHETHER IT IS JUST THAT I LIKE GOING TO HER HOUSE BECAUSE HER MOTHER MAKES HOMEMADE CAKE. IF I HAD A CLUB I'M NOT SURE I WOULD HAVE RACHEL IN IT.

"Thank you," Rachel said politely and left for home.
Laura Peters left too after the last item:

IF LAURA PETERS DOESN'T STOP SMILING AT ME IN THAT WISHY-WASHY WAY I'M GOING TO GIVE HER A GOOD KICK.

The next morning when Harriet arrived at school no one spoke to her. They didn't even look at her. It was exactly as though no one at all had walked into the room. Harriet sat down and felt like a lump. She looked at everyone's desk, but there was no sign of the notebook. She looked at every face and on every face was a plan, and on each face was the same plan. They had organization. I'm going to get it, she thought grimly.
That was not the worst of it. The worst was that even though she knew she shouldn't, she had stopped by the stationery store on the way

to school and had bought another notebook. She had tried not to write in it, but she was such a creature of habit that even now she found herself taking it out of the pocket of her jumper, and furthermore, the next minute she was scratching in a whole series of things.

THEY ARE OUT TO GET ME. THE WHOLE ROOM IS FILLED WITH MEAN EYES. I WON'T GET THROUGH THE DAY. I MIGHT THROW UP MY TOMATO SANDWICH. EVEN SPORT AND JANIE. WHAT DID I SAY ABOUT JANIE? I DON'T RE-MEMBER. NEVER MIND. THEY MAY THINK I AM A WEAKLING BUT A SPY IS TRAINED FOR THIS KIND OF FIGHT. I AM READY FOR THEM.

She went on scratching until Miss Elson cleared her throat, signifying she had entered the room. Then everyone stood up as they always did, bowed, said, "Good morning, Miss Elson," and sat back down. It was the custom at this moment for everyone to punch each other. Harriet looked around for someone to do some poking with, but they all sat stony-faced as though they had never poked anyone in their whole lives.
It made Harriet feel better to try and quote like Ole Golly, so she wrote:

THE SINS OF THE FATHERS

That was all she knew from the Bible besides the shortest verse: "Jesus wept."
Class began and all was forgotten in the joy of writing Harriet M. Welsch at the top of the page.
Halfway through the class Harriet saw a tiny piece of paper float to the floor on her right. Ah-ha, she thought, the chickens; they are making up already. She reached down to get the note. A hand flew past her nose and she realized that the note had been retrieved in a neat backhand by Janie who sat to the right of her.
Well, she thought, so it wasn't for me, that's all. She looked at Carrie, who had sent the note, and Carrie looked carefully away without even giggling.
Harriet wrote in her notebook:

CARRIE ANDREWS HAS AN UGLY PIMPLE RIGHT NEXT TO HER NOSE.

Feeling better, she attacked her homework with renewed zeal. She was getting hungry. Soon she would have her tomato sandwich. She looked up at Miss Elson who was looking at Marion Hawthorne who was scratching her knee. As Harriet looked back at her work she suddenly saw a glint of white sticking out of Janie's jumper pocket. It was the note! Perhaps she could just reach over ever so quietly and pull back very quickly. She *had* to see.

She watched her own arm moving very quietly over, inch by inch. Was Carrie Andrews watching? No. Another inch. Another. *There!* She had it. Janie obviously hadn't felt a thing. Now to read! She looked at Miss Elson but she seemed to be in a dream. She unfolded the tiny piece of paper and read:

Harriet M. Welsch smells. Don't you think so?

Oh, no! Did she really smell? What of? Bad, obviously. Must be very bad. She held up her hand and got excused from class. She went into the bathroom and smelled herself all over, but she couldn't smell anything bad. Then she washed her hands and face. She was going to leave, then she went back and washed her feet just in case. Nothing smelled. What were they talking about? Anyway, now, just to be sure, they would smell of soap.

When she got back to her desk, she noticed a little piece of paper next to where her foot would ordinarily be when she sat down. Ah, this will explain it, she thought. She made a swift move, as though falling, and retrieved the note without Miss Elson seeing. She unrolled it eagerly and read:

There is nothing that makes me sicker than watching Harriet M. Welsch eat a tomato sandwich.
Pinky Whitehead

The note must have misfired. Pinky sat to the right and it was addressed to Sport, who sat on her left.

What was sickening about a tomato sandwich? Harriet felt the taste in her mouth. Were they crazy? It was the best taste in the world.

Her mouth watered at the memory of the mayonnaise. It was an experience, as Mrs. Welsch was always saying. How could it make anyone sick? Pinky Whitehead was what could make you sick. Those stick legs and the way his neck seemed to swivel up and down away from his body. She wrote in her notebook:

THERE IS NO REST FOR THE WEARY.

As she looked up she saw Marion Hawthorne turn swiftly in her direction. Then suddenly she was looking full at Marion Hawthorne's tongue out at her, and a terribly ugly face around the tongue, with eyes all screwed up and pulled down by two fingers so that the whole thing looked as though Marion Hawthorne were going to be carted away to the hospital. Harriet glanced quickly at Miss Elson. Miss Elson was dreaming out the window. Harriet wrote quickly:

HOW UNLIKE MARION HAWTHORNE. I DIDN'T THINK SHE EVER DID ANYTHING BAD.

Then she heard the giggles. She looked up. Everyone had caught the look. Everyone was giggling and laughing with Marion, even Sport and Janie. Miss Elson turned around and every face went blank, everybody bent again over the desks. Harriet wrote quickly:

PERHAPS I CAN TALK TO MY MOTHER ABOUT CHANGING SCHOOLS. I HAVE THE FEELING THIS MORNING THAT EVERYONE IN THIS SCHOOL IS INSANE. I MIGHT POSSIBLY BRING A HAM SANDWICH TOMORROW BUT I HAVE TO THINK ABOUT IT.

The lunch bell rang. Everyone jumped as though they had one body and pushed out the door. Harriet jumped too, but for some reason or other three people bumped into her as she did. It was so fast she didn't even see who it was, but the way they did it she was pushed so far back that she was the last one out the door. They all ran ahead, had gotten their lunchboxes, and were outside by the time she got to the cloakroom. It's true that she was detained because she had to make a note of the fact that Miss Elson went to the science room to talk to Miss Maynard, which had never happened before in the history of the school.

When she picked up her lunch the bag felt very light. She reached inside and there was only crumpled paper. They had taken her tomato sandwich. They had *taken* her tomato sandwich. Someone had *taken* it. She couldn't get over it. This was completely against the rules of the school. No one was supposed to steal your tomato sandwich. She had been coming to this school since she was four—let's see, that made seven years—and in all those seven years no one had ever taken her tomato sandwich. Not even during those six months when she had brought pickle sandwiches with mustard. No one had even asked for so much as a bite. Sometimes Beth Ellen passed around olives because no one else had olives and they were very chic, but that was the extent of the sharing. And now here it was noon and she had nothing to eat.

She was aghast. What could she do? It would be ridiculous to go around asking "Has anyone seen a tomato sandwich?" They were sure to laugh. She would go to Miss Elson. No, then she would be a ratter, a squealer, a stoolie. Well, she couldn't starve. She went to the telephone and asked to use it because she had forgotten her lunch. She called and the cook told her to come home, that she would make another tomato sandwich in the meantime.

Harriet left, went home, ate her tomato sandwich, and took to her bed for another day. She had to think. Her mother was playing bridge downtown. She pretended to be sick enough so the cook didn't yell at her and yet not sick enough for the cook to call her mother. She had to think.

As she lay there in the half gloom she looked out over the trees in the park. For a while she watched a bird, then an old man who walked like a drunk. Inside she felt herself thinking "Everybody hates me, everybody hates me."

At first she didn't listen to it and then she heard what she was feeling. She said it several times to hear it better. Then she reached nervously for her notebook and wrote in big, block letters, the way she used to write when she was little.

EVERYBODY HATES ME.

She leaned back and thought about it. It was time for her cake and milk, so she got up and went downstairs in her pajamas to have it. The cook started a fight with her, saying that if she were sick she couldn't have any cake and milk.

Harriet felt big hot tears come to her eyes and she started to scream.

The cook said calmly, "Either you go to school and you come home and have your cake and milk, or you are sick and you don't get cake and milk because that's no good for you when you're sick; but you don't lie around up there all day and then get cake and milk."

"That's the most unreasonable thing I ever heard of," Harriet screamed. She began to scream as loud as she could. Suddenly she heard herself saying over and over again, "I hate you. I hate you. I hate you." Even as she did it she knew she didn't really hate the cook; in fact, she rather liked her, but it seemed to her that at that moment she hated her.

The cook turned her back and Harriet heard her mutter, "Oh, you, you hate everybody."

This was too much. Harriet ran to her room. She did not hate everybody. She did not. Everybody hated her, that's all. She crashed into her room with a bang, ran to her bed, and smashed her face down into the pillow.

After she was tired of crying, she lay there and looked at the trees. She saw a bird and began to hate the bird. She saw the old drunk man and felt such hatred for him she almost fell off the bed. Then she thought of them all and she hated them each and every one in turn: Carrie Andrews, Marion Hawthorne, Rachel Hennessey, Beth Ellen Hansen, Laura Peters, Pinky Whitehead, the new one with the purple socks, and even Sport and Janie, especially Sport and Janie.

She just hated them. I *hate* them, she thought. She picked up her notebook:

WHEN I AM BIG I WILL BE A SPY. I WILL GO TO ONE COUNTRY AND I WILL FIND OUT ITS SECRETS AND THEN I WILL GO TO ANOTHER COUNTRY AND TELL THEM AND THEN FIND OUT THEIR SECRETS AND I WILL GO BACK TO

THE FIRST ONE AND RAT ON THE SECOND AND I WILL GO TO THE SECOND AND RAT ON THE FIRST. I WILL BE THE BEST SPY THERE EVER WAS AND I WILL KNOW EVERYTHING. EVERYTHING.

As she began to fall asleep she thought, And then they'll all be petrified of me.

Harriet was sick for three days. That is, she lay in bed for three days. Then her mother took her to see the kindly old family doctor. He used to be a kindly old family doctor who made house calls, but now he wouldn't anymore. One day he had stamped his foot at Harriet's mother and said, "I like my office and I'm going to stay in it. I pay so much rent on this office that if I leave it for five minutes my child misses a year of school. I'm never coming out again." And from that moment on he didn't. Harriet rather respected him for it, but his stethoscope was cold.

When he had looked Harriet all over, he said to her mother, "There isn't a blessed thing wrong with her."

Harriet's mother gave her a dirty look, then sent her out into the outer office. As Harriet closed the door behind her she heard the doctor saying, "I think I know what's the matter with her. Carrie told us some long story about a notebook."

Harriet stopped dead in her tracks. "That's right," she said out loud to herself, "his name is Dr. Andrews, so he's Carrie Andrews' father."

She got out her notebook and wrote it down. Then she wrote:

I WONDER WHY HE DOESN'T CURE THAT PIMPLE ON CARRIE'S NOSE?

"Come on, young lady, we're going home." Harriet's mother took her by the hand. She looked as though she might take Harriet home and kill her. As it turned out, she didn't. When they got home, she said briskly, "All right, Harriet the Spy, come into the library and talk to me."

Harriet followed her, dragging her feet.

She wished she were Beth Ellen who had never met her mother.

"Now, Harriet, I hear you're keeping dossiers on everyone in school."

"What's that?" Harriet had been prepared to deny everything but this was a new one.

"You keep a notebook?"

"A notebook?"

"Well, don't you?"

"Why?"

"Answer me, Harriet." It was serious.

"Yes."

"What did you put in it?"

"Everything."

"Well, what kind of thing?"

"Just . . . things."

"Harriet Welsch, answer me. What do you write about your classmates?"

"Oh, just . . . well, things I think. . . . Some nice things . . . and—and mean things."

"And your friends saw it?"

"Yes, but they shouldn't have looked. It's private. It even says PRIVATE all over the front of it."

"Nevertheless, they did. Right?"

"Yes."

"And then what happened?"

"Nothing."

"Nothing?" Harriet's mother looked very skeptical.

"Well . . . my tomato sandwich disappeared."

"Don't you think that maybe all those mean things made them angry?"

Harriet considered this as though it had never entered her mind. "Well, maybe, but they shouldn't have looked. It's private property."

"That, Harriet, is beside the point. They *did*. Now why do you think they got angry?"

"I don't know."

"Well . . ." Mrs. Welsch seemed to be debating whether to say what she finally did. "How did you feel when you got some of those notes?"

There was a silence. Harriet looked at her feet.

"Harriet?" Her mother was waiting for an answer.

"I think I feel sick again. I think I'll go to bed."

"Now, darling, you're not sick. Just think about it a moment. How did you feel?"

Harriet burst into tears. She ran to her mother and cried very hard. "I felt awful. I felt awful," was all she could say. Her mother hugged her and kissed her a lot. The more she hugged her the better Harriet felt. She was still being hugged when her father came home. He hugged her too, even though he didn't know what it was all about. After that they all had dinner and Harriet went up to bed.

Before going to sleep she wrote in her notebook:

THAT WAS ALL VERY NICE BUT IT HAS NOTHING TO DO WITH MY NOTEBOOK. ONLY OLE GOLLY UNDERSTANDS ABOUT MY NOTEBOOK. I WILL ALWAYS HAVE A NOTEBOOK. I THINK I WILL WRITE DOWN EVERYTHING, EVERY SINGLE SOLITARY THING THAT HAPPENS TO ME.

She went peacefully to sleep. The next morning the first thing she did when she woke up was to reach for her notebook and scribble furiously:

WHEN I WAKE UP IN THE MORNING I WISH I WERE DEAD.

Having disposed of that, she got up, put on the same clothes she had had on the day before. Before she went downstairs she began to think about the fact that her room was in the attic. She wrote:

THEY PUT ME UP HERE IN THIS ROOM BECAUSE THEY THINK I'M A WITCH.

Even as she did it she knew perfectly well that her parents thought nothing of the kind. She slammed her notebook and ran down the three flights of stairs as though she had been shot out of a cannon. She hurtled into the kitchen, collided with the cook, and knocked a glass of water from her hand.

"Look what you've done, you maniac. What are you doing running like that? If you were my child, I'd slap you right across the face. In fact, you just watch it, I might anyway," the cook spluttered in exasperation.

But Harriet was up the stairs again, out of reach. She had only descended to wrest a piece of toast from the cook instead of having to wait in the dining room. She stomped to her place and sat down with a thump. Her mother looked her over.

"Harriet, you haven't washed, and furthermore it seems to me those clothes look awfully familiar. Go up and change." Her mother said all this cheerfully.

Harriet was off and running again. *Clackety Clack,* her feet went on the parquet floor, then *thrump, thrump, thrump* up the carpeted stairs. She ran all the way into her little bathroom. She had a fleeting sensation of being tired as she stood over the basin washing her hands.

The sun was pouring through the tiny window which overlooked the park and the river. Harriet stared, lost in a sudden dream. She turned the soap over and over in her hands and felt the warm water on her fingers as she watched a tugboat, yellow with a red stack, bob neatly up the river, the frothy V behind it curling into emptiness.

A bell tinkled somewhere downstairs, and her mother called up the steps, "Harriet, you'll be late for school." Harriet suddenly woke up and saw that the soap had become a big mush in her hands. She washed it all off then flew down the steps, drying her hands briskly on her dress as she went.

Her father was at the table behind a newspaper. Her mother was behind another newspaper.

The cook waddled in, muttering, "Scared the life out of me this morning. She'll kill us all someday." No one paid any attention to her. She gave Harriet a very nasty eye as she served her bacon, eggs, toast, and milk.

Harriet gobbled up everything very fast, slid off the chair, and was out into the hall without either her father or her mother lowering a newspaper. She grabbed up her books and her notebook. As she was flying through the door she heard the rustle of a newspaper and her mother's voice. "Harriet? Did you go to the bathroom?" All that came back to her mother was a long, distant "Nooooooooo," like the howl of a tiny wind, as Harriet flew through the front door and down the front steps.

Once out of the house she slowed to a dawdle and began looking around her. Why do I run so? she thought. I have only two and a half blocks to walk. She was always early. She crossed East End at the corner of Eighty-sixth and walked through the park, climbing the small hill up through the early morning onto the esplanade, and finally sat, *plunk* on a bench right by the river's edge. The sunlight coming off the river made her squint her eyes. She opened her notebook and wrote:

SOMETIMES THAT HOUSE GETS ME. I MUST MAKE A LIST OF WAYS TO MAKE MYSELF BETTER.

NUMBER (1) STOP RUNNING INTO THE COOK.
NUMBER (2) PUT DOWN EVERY SINGLE THING IN THIS NOTEBOOK.
NUMBER (3) NEVER, NEVER, NEVER LET ANYONE SEE IT.
NUMBER (4) FIND OUT HOW I CAN REALLY GET MYSELF UP EARLIER IN THE MORNING SO I CAN GET MORE SPYING DONE IN THIS TIME BEFORE SCHOOL. I AM SO DUMB AND THERE IS SO MUCH TO FIND OUT THAT I HAD BETTER BEGIN USING ALL MY FREE TIME SPYING.

Just at that moment Harriet felt someone give her a hard little clip on the shoulder. She looked up quickly and there was Rachel Hennessey. She stood there squinting at Harriet through her glasses. Harriet squinted back at her.

"Writing again in that notebook, eh?" Rachel shot this out of her mouth like a gangster. She stood squarely on her two feet, squinting.

"So what?" Harriet's voice shook. Then she got control of herself. "So what if I am? Whadaya wanta make of it?"

Rachel turned mysterious. "You'll see. You'll see what you get, Miss Harriet the Spy." She pivoted slowly on one foot all the way around, then stood squarely again, squinting. A prism of light caught her glasses, so Harriet couldn't see her eyes.

Harriet felt it necessary to become menacing.

She slid slowly off the bench and in two steps was almost nose to nose with Rachel. "Listen here, Rachel Hennessey, just what do you mean by that?"

Rachel began to get nervous. Harriet pressed her advantage. "You know, Rachel, that you're KNOWN for never meaning anything you say. You know that, don't you?"

Rachel looked completely taken aback. She stood her ground, but she remained silent. Only her eyes, which watered suddenly, let Harriet know that she was afraid.

"All of you—all of you better stop acting this way to me or . . . or . . . you're going to GET it!" Harriet realized, too late, that she was getting carried away because her arms were flailing around.

Something stirred deep in Rachel. Perhaps this last remark had made her see that Harriet, for all her yelling, was frightened. At any rate, suddenly she laughed in a rather spooky way, and as she did she backed away. She continued to laugh and to back, and only when it was obvious that she was poised for instant flight did she say, "Oh, no, you don't. You're wrong there. We have a plan. It's YOU who's going to get it. We have a PLAN . . . a PLAN. . . ." and it echoed behind her as she ran, her heels flying up and almost touching the sash of her plaid dress, she ran so hard.

Harriet stood there looking into the silence. She picked up her notebook. She put it down again and looked out over the water. The sun had dimmed. It might rain. She picked up the notebook again.

A PLAN. THIS IS SERIOUS. THEY MEAN BUSINESS. IT MEANS THEY HAVE BEEN *TALKING AMONG THEMSELVES.* ARE THEY GOING TO KILL ME? IS THIS MY LAST VIEW OF CARL SCHURZ PARK? WILL THERE BE NOTHING LEFT HERE TOMORROW ON THIS BENCH? WILL ANYONE REMEMBER HARRIET M. WELSCH?

She rose stiffly and walked slowly to school. Everything looked very green and holy in that sad light before a rain. Even the Good Humor man on the corner, the one with the ridiculous nose, looked sad and moody. He took out a large blue handkerchief and blew his nose.

It was somehow so touching that Harriet had to look away.

The door to the school was alive with clamoring children. She wished that she could wait until everyone was in, then walk sedately, alone, down the corridors as though to her own execution. But if she did, she would be late. She ran toward the school.

Beverly Cleary

Dear Mr. Henshaw

Beverly Cleary's accessible stories about ordinary children have a deservedly high reputation. During her own childhood, Cleary searched in vain for books with realistic child characters; children's enthusiastic and continual reading of her books is clear testimony that she has succeeded in giving them stories in which they can recognize themselves. Enlivened by an accurate use of children's language, Cleary's writing demonstrates her sensitivity to what constitutes a crisis in their lives. The main character in this novel, Leigh Botts, is older than most of the author's other characters, and his life is sadder. The story begins with a series of letters written over a period of years to Leigh's favorite author and then moves into entries from the diary the author advises him to keep. Through these devices, Cleary reveals Leigh's developing maturity and insight as the letters and entries change in style and tone. Winner of the 1984 Newbery Medal, *Dear Mr. Henshaw* contains many amusing episodes but is more serious than Cleary's previous works, proving, in the words of Leigh Botts, that "a book doesn't have to be funny to be good." [From Beverly Cleary, *Dear Mr. Henshaw* (Morrow, 1983).]

May 12

Dear Mr. Henshaw,

My teacher read your book about the dog to our class. It was funny. We licked it.

Your freind,
Leigh Botts (boy)

December 3

Dear Mr. Henshaw,

I am the boy who wrote to you last year when I was in the second grade. Maybe you didn't get my letter. This year I read the book I wrote to you about called *Ways to Amuse a Dog.* It is the first thick book with chapters that I have read.

The boy's father said city dogs were bored so Joe could not keep the dog unless he could think up seven ways to amuse it. I have a black dog. His name is Bandit. He is a nice dog.

If you answer I get to put your letter on the bulletin board.

My teacher taught me a trick about friend. The *i* goes before *e* so that at the end it will spell *end.*

Keep in tutch.

Your friend,
Leigh (Leē) Botts

November 13

Dear Mr. Henshaw,

I am in the fourth grade now. I made a diorama of *Ways to Amuse a Dog,* the book I wrote to you about two times before. Now our teacher is making us write to authors for Book Week. I got your answer to my letter last year, but it was only printed. Please would you write to me in your own handwriting? I am a great enjoyer of your books.

My favorite character in the book was Joe's Dad because he didn't get mad when Joe amused his dog by playing a tape of a lady singing, and his dog sat and howled like he was singing, too. Bandit does the same thing when he hears singing.

Your best reader,
Leigh Botts

December 2

Dear Mr. Henshaw,

I got to thinking about *Ways to Amuse a Dog.* When Joe took his dog to the park and taught him to slide down the slide, wouldn't some grownup come along and say he couldn't let his dog use the slide? Around here grownups, who are mostly real old with cats, get mad if dogs aren't on leashes every minute. I hate living in a mobile home park.

I saw your picture on the back of the book. When I grow up I want to be a famous book writer with a beard like you.

I am sending you my picture. It is last year's picture. My hair is longer now. With all the millions of kids in the U.S., how would you know who I am if I don't send you my picture?

> *Your favorite reader,*
> *Leigh Botts*

Enclosure: Picture of me.
(We are studying
business letters.)

October 2

Dear Mr. Henshaw,

I am in the fifth grade now. You might like to know that I gave a book report on *Ways to Amuse a Dog.* The class liked it. I got an A—. The minus was because the teacher said I didn't stand on both feet.

> *Sincerely,*
> *Leigh Botts*

November 7

Dear Mr. Henshaw,

I got your letter and did what you said. I read a different book by you. I read *Moose on Toast.* I liked it almost as much as *Ways to Amuse a Dog.* It was really funny the way the boy's mother tried to think up ways to cook the moose meat they had in their freezer. 1000 pounds is a lot of moose. Mooseburgers, moose stew and moose meat loaf don't sound too bad. Maybe moose mincemeat pie would be OK because with all the raisins and junk you wouldn't know you were eating moose. Creamed chipped moose on toast, yuck.

I don't think the boy's father should have shot the moose, but I guess there are plenty of moose up there in Alaska, and maybe they needed it for food.

If my Dad shot a moose I would feed the tough parts to my dog Bandit.

> *Your number 1 fan,*
> *Leigh Botts*

September 20

Dear Mr. Henshaw,

This year I am in the sixth grade in a new school in a different town. Our teacher is mak-

ing us do author reports to improve our writing skills, so of course I thought of you. Please answer the following questions.

1. How many books have you written?
2. Is Boyd Henshaw your real name or is it fake?
3. Why do you write books for children?
4. Where do you get your ideas?
5. Do you have any kids?
6. What is your favorite book that you wrote?
7. Do you like to write books?
8. What is the title of your next book?
9. What is your favorite animal?
10. Please give me some tips on how to write a book. This is important to me. I really want to know so I can get to be a famous author and write books exactly like yours.

Please send me a list of your books that you wrote, an autographed picture and a bookmark. I need your answer by next Friday. This is urgent!

> *Sincerely,*
> *Leigh Botts*

> *De Liver*
> *De Letter*
> *De Sooner*
> *De Better*
> *De Later*
> *De Letter*
> *De Madder*
> *I Getter*

November 15

Dear Mr. Henshaw,

At first I was pretty upset when I didn't get an answer to my letter in time for my report, but I worked it out OK. I read what it said about you on the back of *Ways to Amuse a Dog* and wrote real big on every other line so I filled up the paper. On the book it said you lived in Seattle, so I didn't know you had moved to Alaska although I should have guessed from *Moose on Toast.*

When your letter finally came I didn't want to read it to the class, because I didn't think Miss Martinez would like silly answers, like your real name is Messing A. Round, and you don't have kids because you don't raise goats. She said I had to read it. The class laughed and Miss Martinez smiled, but she didn't smile when I came to the part about your favorite animal was a purple monster who ate children who sent authors long lists of questions for reports instead of learning to use the library.

Your writing tips were OK. I could tell you meant what you said. Don't worry. When I write something, I won't send it to you. I understand how busy you are with your own books.

I hid the second page of your letter from Miss Martinez. That list of questions you sent for me to answer really made me mad. Nobody else's author put in a list of questions to be answered, and I don't think it's fair to make me do more work when I already wrote a report.

Anyway, thank you for answering my questions. Some kids didn't get any answers at all, which made them mad, and one girl almost cried, she was so afraid she would get a bad grade. One boy got a letter from an author who sounded real excited about getting a letter and wrote such a long answer the boy had to write a long report. He guessed nobody ever wrote to that author before, and he sure wouldn't again. About ten kids wrote to the same author, who wrote one answer to all of them. There was a big argument about who got to keep it until Miss Martinez took the letter to the office and duplicated it.

About those questions you sent me. I'm not going to answer them, and you can't make me. You're not my teacher.

Yours truly,
Leigh Botts

P.S. When I asked you what the title of your next book was going to be, you said, Who knows? Did you mean that was the title or you don't know what the title will be? And do you really write books because you have read every book in the library and because writing beats mowing the lawn or shoveling snow?

November 16
Dear Mr. Henshaw,
Mom found your letter and your list of questions which I was dumb enough to leave lying

around. We had a big argument. She says I have to answer your questions because authors are working people like anyone else, and if you took time to answer my questions, I should answer yours. She says I can't go through life expecting everyone to do everything for me. She used to say the same thing to Dad when he left his socks on the floor.

Well, I got to go now. It's bedtime. Maybe I'll get around to answering your ten questions, and maybe I won't. There isn't any law that says I have to. Maybe I won't even read any more of your books.

Disgusted reader,
Leigh Botts
P.S. If my Dad was here, he would tell you to go climb a tree.

November 20
Dear Mr. Henshaw,
Mom is nagging me about your dumb old questions. She says if I really want to be an author, I should follow the tips in your letter. I should read, look, listen, think and WRITE. She says the best way she knows for me to get started is to apply the seat of my pants to a chair and answer your questions and answer them fully. So here goes.

1. Who are you?
Like I've been telling you, I am Leigh Botts. Leigh Marcus Botts. I don't like Leigh for a name because some people don't know how to say it or think it's a girl's name. Mom says with a last name like Botts I need something fancy but not too fancy. My Dad's name is Bill and Mom's name is Bonnie. She says Bill and Bonnie Botts sounds like something out of a comic strip.

I am just a plain boy. This school doesn't say I am Gifted and Talented, and I don't like soccer very much the way everybody at this school is supposed to. I am not stupid either.

2. What do you look like?
I already sent you my picture, but maybe you lost it. I am sort of medium. I don't have red hair or anything like that. I'm not real big like

my Dad. Mom says I take after her family, thank goodness. That's the way she always says it. In first and second grades kids used to call me Leigh the Flea, but I have grown. Now when the class lines up according to height, I am in the middle. I guess you could call me the mediumest boy in the class.

This is hard work. To be continued, maybe.

Leigh Botts

November 22

Dear Mr. Henshaw,

I wasn't going to answer any more of your questions, but Mom won't get the TV repaired because she says it was rotting my brain. This is Thanksgiving vacation and I am so bored I decided to answer a couple of your rotten questions with my rotten brain. (Joke.)

3. What is your family like?

Since Dad and Bandit went away, my family is just Mom and me. We all used to live in a mobile home outside of Bakersfield which is in California's Great Central Valley we studied about in school. When Mom and Dad got divorced, they sold the mobile home, and Dad moved into a trailer.

Dad drives a big truck, a cab-over job. That means the cab is over the engine. Some people don't know that. The truck is why my parents got divorced. Dad used to drive for someone else, hauling stuff like cotton, sugar beets and other produce around Central California and Nevada, but he couldn't get owning his own rig for cross-country hauling out of his head. He worked practically night and day and saved a down payment. Mom said we'd never get out of that mobile home when he had to make such big payments on that rig, and she'd never know where he was when he hauled cross-country. His big rig sure is a beauty, with a bunk in the cab and everything. His rig, which truckers call a tractor but everyone else calls a truck, has ten wheels, two in front and eight in back so he can hitch up to anything—flatbeds, refrigerated vans, a couple of gondolas.

In school they teach you that a gondola is some kind of boat in Italy, but in the U.S. it is a container for hauling loose stuff like carrots.

My hand is all worn out from all this writing, but I try to treat Mom and Dad the same so I'll get to Mom next time.

Your pooped reader,
Leigh Botts

November 23

Mr. Henshaw:

Why should I call you "dear," when you are the reason I'm stuck with all this work? It wouldn't be fair to leave Mom out so here is Question 3 continued.

Mom works part time for Catering by Katy which is run by a real nice lady Mom knew when she was growing up in Taft, California. Katy says all women who grew up in Taft had to be good cooks because they went to so many potluck suppers. Mom and Katy and some other ladies make fancy food for weddings and parties. They also bake cheesecake and apple strudel for restaurants. Mom is a good cook. I just wish she would do it more at home, like the mother in *Moose on Toast*. Almost every day Katy gives Mom something good to put in my school lunch.

Mom also takes a couple of courses at the community college. She wants to be an LVN which means Licensed Vocational Nurse. They help real nurses except they don't stick needles in people. She is almost always home when I get home from school.

Your ex-friend,
Leigh Botts

November 24

Mr. Henshaw:

Here we go again.

4. Where do you live?

After the divorce Mom and I moved from Bakersfield to Pacific Grove which is on California's Central Coast about twenty miles from the sugar refinery at Spreckels where Dad used to haul sugar beets before he went cross-country. Mom said all the time she was growing up in California's Great Central Valley she longed for a few ocean breezes, and now we've got them. We've got a lot of fog, especially in the morning.

There aren't any crops around here, just golf courses for rich people.

We live in a little house, a *really* little house, that used to be somebody's summer cottage a long time ago before somebody built a two-story duplex in front of it. Now it is what they call a garden cottage. It is sort of falling apart, but it is all we can afford. Mom says at least it keeps the rain off, and it can't be hauled away on a flatbed truck. I have a room of my own, but Mom sleeps on a couch in the living room. She fixed the place up real nice with things from the thrift shop down the street.

Next door is a gas station that goes ping-ping, ping-ping every time a car drives in. They turn off the pinger at 10:00 P.M., but most of the time I am asleep by then. Mom doesn't want me to hang around the gas station. On our street, besides the thrift shop, there is a pet shop, a sewing machine shop, an electric shop, a couple of junk stores they call antique shops, plus a Taco King and a Softee Freeze. I am not supposed to hang around those places either. Mom is against hanging around anyplace.

Sometimes when the gas station isn't pinging, I can hear the ocean and the sea lions barking. They sound like dogs, and I think of Bandit.

To be continued unless we get the TV fixed.

Still disgusted,
Leigh Botts

November 26

Mr. Henshaw:

If our TV was fixed I would be looking at "Highway Patrol," but it isn't so here are some more answers from my rotten brain. (Ha-ha.)

5. Do you have any pets?

I do not have any pets. (My teacher says always answer questions in complete sentences.) When Mom and Dad got divorced and Mom got me, Dad took Bandit because Mom said she couldn't work and look after a dog, and Dad said he likes to take Bandit in his truck because it is easier to stay awake on long hauls if he has him to talk to. I really miss Bandit, but I guess he's happier riding around with Dad. Like the father said in *Ways to Amuse a Dog,* dogs get pretty bored just lying around the house all day. That is what Bandit would have to do with Mom and me gone so much.

Bandit likes to ride. That's how we got him. He just jumped into Dad's cab at a truck stop in Nevada and sat there. He had a red bandanna around his neck instead of a collar, so we called him Bandit.

Sometimes I lie awake at night listening to the gas station ping-pinging and thinking about Dad and Bandit hauling tomatoes or cotton bales on Interstate 5, and I am glad Bandit is there to keep Dad awake. Have you ever seen Interstate 5? It is straight and boring with nothing much but cotton fields and a big feedlot that you can smell a long way before you come to it. It is so boring that the cattle on the feedlot don't even bother to moo. They just stand there. They don't tell you that part in school when they talk about California's Great Central Valley.

I'm getting writer's cramp from all this writing. I'll get to No. 6 next time. Mom says not to worry about the postage, so I can't use that as an excuse for not answering.

Pooped writer,
Leigh Botts

November 27

Mr. Henshaw:

Here we go again. I'll never write another list of questions for an author to answer, no matter what the teacher says.

6. Do you like school?

School is OK, I guess. That's where the kids are. The best thing about sixth grade in my new school is that if I hang in, I'll get out.

7. Who are your friends?

I don't have a whole lot of friends in my new school. Mom says maybe I'm a loner, but I don't know. A new boy in school has to be pretty cautious until he gets to know who's who. Maybe I'm just a boy nobody pays much attention to. The only time anybody paid much attention to me was in my last school when I gave the book report on *Ways to Amuse a Dog.* After my report some people went to the library to get the book. The kids here pay more attention to my lunch than they do to me. They really watch to see what I have in my lunch because Katy gives me such good things.

I wish somebody would ask me over sometime. After school I stay around kicking a soccer ball with some of the other kids so they won't think I am stuck up or anything, but nobody asks me over.

8. *Who is your favorite teacher?*

I don't have a favorite teacher, but I really like Mr. Fridley. He's the custodian. He's always fair about who gets to pass out milk at lunchtime, and once when he had to clean up after someone who threw up in the hall, he didn't even look cross. He just said, "Looks like somebody's been whooping it up," and started sprinkling sawdust around. Mom used to get mad at Dad for whooping it up, but she didn't mean throwing up. She meant he stayed too long at that truck stop outside of town.

Two more questions to go. Maybe I won't answer them. So there. Ha-ha.

Leigh Botts

December 1

Mr. Henshaw:

OK, you win, because Mom is still nagging me, and I don't have anything else to do. I'll answer your last two questions if it takes all night.

9. *What bothers you?*

What bothers me about what? I don't know what you mean. I guess I'm bothered by a lot of things. I am bothered when someone steals something out of my lunchbag. I don't know enough about the people in the school to know who to suspect. I am bothered about little kids with runny noses. I don't mean I am fussy or anything like that. I don't know why. I am just bothered.

I am bothered about walking to school *slow.* The rule is nobody is supposed to be on the school grounds until ten minutes before the first bell rings. Mom has an early class. The house is so lonely in the morning when she is gone

that I can't stand it and leave when she does. I don't mind being alone after school, but I do in the morning before the fog lifts and our cottage seems dark and damp.

Mom tells me to go to school but to walk slow which is hard work. Once I tried walking around every square in the sidewalk, but that got boring. So did walking heel-toe, heel-toe. Sometimes I walk backwards except when I cross the street, but I still get there so early I have to sort of hide behind the shrubbery so Mr. Fridley won't see me.

I am bothered when my Dad telephones me and finishes by saying, "Well, keep your nose clean, kid." Why can't he say he misses me, and why can't he call me Leigh? I am bothered when he doesn't phone at all which is most of the time. I have a book of road maps and try to follow his trips when I hear from him. When the TV worked I watched the weather on the news so I would know if he was driving through blizzards, tornadoes, hail like golf balls or any of that fancy weather they have other places in the U.S.

10. *What do you wish?*

I wish somebody would stop stealing the good stuff out of my lunchbag. I guess I wish a lot of other things, too. I wish someday Dad and Bandit would pull up in front in the rig. Maybe Dad would be hauling a forty-foot reefer (that means refrigerated trailer) which would make his outfit add up to eighteen wheels altogether. Dad would yell out of the cab, "Come on, Leigh. Hop in and I'll give you a lift to school." Then I'd climb in and Bandit would wag his tail and lick my face. We'd take off with all the men in the gas station staring after us. Instead of going straight to school, we'd go barreling along the freeway looking down on the tops of ordinary cars, then down the offramp and back to school just before the bell rang. I guess I wouldn't seem so medium then, sitting up there in the cab in front of a forty-foot reefer. I'd jump out, and Dad would say, "So long, Leigh. Be seeing you," and Bandit would give a little bark like good-bye. I'd say, "Drive carefully, Dad," like I always do. Dad would take a minute to write in the truck's logbook, "Drove my son to school." Then the truck would pull away from the curb with all the kids staring and wishing their Dads drove big trucks, too.

There, Mr. Henshaw. That's the end of your crummy questions. I hope you are satisfied for making me do all this extra work.

Fooey on you,
Leigh Botts

Robert McCloskey

Homer Price

Robert McCloskey has created a very real American boy in the character of Homer Price, who has a talent for getting himself involved in fantastic and incredible situations. This story of the nonstop doughnut machine is rollicking good fun. [From Robert McCloskey, *Homer Price* (Viking, 1943).]

The Doughnuts

One Friday night in November Homer overheard his mother talking on the telephone to Aunt Agnes over in Centerburg. "I'll stop by with the car in about half an hour and we can go to the meeting together," she said, because tonight was the night the Ladies' Club was meeting to discuss plans for a box social and to knit and sew for the Red Cross.

"I think I'll come along and keep Uncle Ulysses company while you and Aunt Agnes are at the meeting," said Homer.

So after Homer had combed his hair and his mother had looked to see if she had her knitting instructions and the right size needles, they started for town.

Homer's Uncle Ulysses and Aunt Agnes have a very up and coming lunch room over in Centerburg, just across from the court house on the town square. Uncle Ulysses is a man with advanced ideas and a weakness for labor saving devices. He equipped the lunch room with automatic toasters, automatic coffee maker, automatic dish washer, and an automatic doughnut maker. All just the latest thing in labor saving devices. Aunt Agnes would throw up her hands and sigh every time Uncle Ulysses bought a new labor saving device. Sometimes she be-

came unkindly disposed toward him for days and days. She was of the opinion that Uncle Ulysses just frittered away his spare time over at the barber shop with the sheriff and the boys, so, what was the good of a labor saving device that gave you more time to fritter?

When Homer and his mother got to Centerburg they stopped at the lunch room, and after Aunt Agnes had come out and said, "My, how that boy does grow!" which was what she always said, she went off with Homer's mother in the car. Homer went into the lunch room and said, "Howdy, Uncle Ulysses!"

"Oh, hello, Homer. You're just in time," said Uncle Ulysses. "I've been going over this automatic doughnut machine, oiling the machinery and cleaning the works . . . wonderful things, these labor saving devices."

"Yep," agreed Homer, and picked up a cloth and started polishing the metal trimmings while Uncle Ulysses tinkered with the inside workings.

"Opfwo-oof!" sighed Uncle Ulysses and, "Look here, Homer, you've got a mechanical mind. See if you can find where these two pieces fit in. I'm going across to the barber shop for a spell, 'cause there's somethin' I've got to talk to the sheriff about. There won't be much business here until the double feature is over and I'll be back before then."

Then as Uncle Ulysses went out the door he said, "Uh, Homer, after you get the pieces in place, would you mind mixing up a batch of doughnut batter and put it in the machine? You could turn the switch and make a few doughnuts to have on hand for the crowd after the movie . . . if you don't mind."

"O.K.," said Homer, "I'll take care of everything."

A few minutes later a customer came in and said, "Good evening, Bud."

Homer looked up from putting the last piece in the doughnut machine and said, "Good evening, Sir, what can I do for you?"

"Well, young feller, I'd like a cup o' coffee and some doughnuts," said the customer.

"I'm sorry, Mister, but we won't have any doughnuts for about half an hour, until I can mix some dough and start this machine. I could give you some very fine sugar rolls instead."

"Well, Bud, I'm in no real hurry so I'll just have a cup o' coffee and wait around a bit for the doughnuts. Fresh doughnuts are always worth waiting for is what I always say."

"O.K.," said Homer, and he drew a cup of coffee from Uncle Ulysses' super automatic coffee maker.

"Nice place you've got here," said the customer.

"Oh, yes," replied Homer, "this is a very up and coming lunch room with all the latest improvements."

"Yes," said the stranger, "must be a good business. I'm in business too. A traveling man in outdoor advertising. I'm a sandwich man, Mr. Gabby's my name."

"My name is Homer. I'm glad to meet you, Mr. Gabby. It must be a fine profession, traveling and advertising sandwiches."

"Oh no," said Mr. Gabby, "I don't advertise sandwiches, I just wear any kind of an ad, one sign on front and one sign on behind, this way . . . Like a sandwich. Ya know what I mean?"

"Oh, I see. That must be fun, and you travel too?" asked Homer as he got out the flour and the baking powder.

"Yeah, I ride the rods between jobs, on freight trains, ya know what I mean?"

"Yes, but isn't that dangerous?" asked Homer.

"Of course there's a certain amount a risk, but you take any method a travel these days, it's all dangerous. Ya know what I mean? Now take airplanes for instance . . ."

Just then a large shiny black car stopped in front of the lunch room and a chauffeur helped a lady out of the rear door. They both came inside and the lady smiled at Homer and said, "We've stopped for a light snack. Some doughnuts and coffee would be simply marvelous."

Then Homer said, "I'm sorry, Ma'am, but the doughnuts won't be ready until I make this batter and start Uncle Ulysses' doughnut machine."

"Well now aren't *you* a clever young man to know how to make *doughnuts!*"

"Well," blushed Homer, "I've really never done it before but I've got a receipt to follow."

"Now, young man, you simply must allow me to help. You know, I haven't made doughnuts for years, but I know the best receipt for doughnuts. It's marvelous, and we really must use it."

"But, Ma'm . . ." said Homer.

"Now just *wait* till you taste these doughnuts," said the lady. "Do you have an apron?" she asked, as she took off her fur coat and her rings and her jewelry and rolled up her sleeves. "Charles," she said to the chauffeur, "hand me that baking powder, that's right, and, young man, we'll need some nutmeg."

So Homer and the chauffeur stood by and handed things and cracked the eggs while the lady mixed and stirred. Mr. Gabby sat on his stool, sipped his coffee, and looked on with great interest.

"There!" said the lady when all of the ingredients were mixed. "Just *wait* till you taste these doughnuts!"

"It looks like an awful lot of batter," said Homer as he stood on a chair and poured it into the doughnut machine with the help of the chauffeur. "It's about *ten* times as much as Uncle Ulysses ever makes."

"But wait till you taste them!" said the lady with an eager look and a smile.

Homer got down from the chair and pushed a button on the machine marked, *"Start."* Rings of batter started dropping into the hot fat. After a ring of batter was cooked on one side an automatic gadget turned it over and the other side would cook. Then another automatic gadget gave the doughnut a little push and it rolled neatly down a little chute, all ready to eat.

"That's a simply *fascinating* machine," said the lady as she waited for the first doughnut to roll out.

"Here, young man, *you* must have the first one. Now isn't that just *too* delicious!? Isn't it simply marvelous?"

"Yes, Ma'm, it's very good," replied Homer as the lady handed doughnuts to Charles and to Mr. Gabby and asked if they didn't think they were simply divine doughnuts.

"It's an old family receipt!" said the lady with pride.

Homer poured some coffee for the lady and her chauffeur and for Mr. Gabby, and a glass of milk for himself. Then they all sat down at the lunch counter to enjoy another few doughnuts apiece.

"I'm so glad you enjoy my doughnuts," said the lady. "But now, Charles, we really must be going. If you will just take this apron, Homer, and put two dozen doughnuts in a bag to take along, we'll be on our way. And, Charles, don't forget to pay the young man." She rolled down her sleeves and put on her jewelry, then Charles managed to get her into her big fur coat.

"Good night, young man, I haven't had so much fun in years. I *really* haven't!" said the lady, as she went out the door and into the big shiny car.

"Those are sure good doughnuts," said Mr. Gabby as the car moved off.

"You bet!" said Homer. Then he and Mr. Gabby stood and watched the automatic doughnut machine make doughnuts.

After a few dozen more doughnuts had rolled down the little chute, Homer said, "I guess that's about enough doughnuts to sell to the after theater customers. I'd better turn the machine off for a while."

Homer pushed the button marked *Stop* and there was a little click, but nothing happened. The rings of batter kept right on dropping into the hot fat, and an automatic gadget kept right on turning them over, and another automatic gadget kept right on giving them a little push and the doughnuts kept right on rolling down the little chute, all ready to eat.

"That's funny," said Homer, "I'm sure that's the right button!" He pushed it again but the automatic doughnut maker kept right on making doughnuts.

"Well I guess I must have put one of those pieces in backwards," said Homer.

"Then it might stop if you pushed the button marked *Start,*" said Mr. Gabby.

Homer did, and the doughnuts still kept rolling down the little chute, just as regular as a clock can tick.

"I guess we could sell a few more doughnuts," said Homer, "but I'd better telephone Uncle Ulysses over at the barber shop." Homer gave the number and while he waited for someone to answer he counted thirty-seven doughnuts roll down the little chute.

Finally someone answered "Hello! This is the sarber bhop, I mean the barber shop."

"Oh, hello, sheriff. This is Homer. Could I speak to Uncle Ulysses?"

"Well, he's playing pinochle right now," said the sheriff. "Anythin' I can tell 'im?"

"Yes," said Homer. "I pushed the button marked *Stop* on the doughnut machine but the rings of batter keep right on dropping into the hot fat, and an automatic gadget keeps right on turning them over, and another automatic gadget keeps giving them a little push, and the doughnuts keep right on rolling down the little chute! It won't stop!"

"O.K. Wold the hire, I mean, hold the wire and I'll tell 'im." Then Homer looked over his shoulder and counted another twenty-one doughnuts roll down the little chute, all ready to eat. Then the sheriff said, "He'll be right over. . . . Just gotta finish this hand."

"That's good," said Homer. "G'by, sheriff."

The window was full of doughnuts by now so Homer and Mr. Gabby had to hustle around and start stacking them on plates and trays and lining them up on the counter.

"Sure are a lot of doughnuts!" said Homer.

"You bet!" said Mr. Gabby. "I lost count at twelve hundred and two and that was quite a while back."

People had begun to gather outside the lunch room window, and someone was saying, "There are almost as many doughnuts as there are people in Centerburg, and I wonder how in tarnation Ulysses thinks he can sell all of 'em!"

Every once in a while somebody would come inside and buy some, but while somebody bought two to eat and a dozen to take home, the machine made three dozen more.

By the time Uncle Ulysses and the sheriff arrived and pushed through the crowd, the lunch room was a calamity of doughnuts! Doughnuts in the window, doughnuts piled high on the shelves, doughnuts stacked on plates, doughnuts lined up twelve deep all along the counter, and doughnuts still rolling down the little chute, just as regular as a clock can tick.

"Hello, sheriff, hello, Uncle Ulysses, we're having a little trouble here," said Homer.

"Well, I'll be dunked!" said Uncle Ulysses.

"Dernd ef you won't be when Aggy gits

home," said the sheriff. "Mighty fine doughnuts though. What'll you do with 'em all, Ulysses?"

Uncle Ulysses groaned and said, "What will Aggy say? We'll never sell 'em all."

Then Mr. Gabby, who hadn't said anything for a long time, stopped piling doughnuts and said, "What you need is an advertising man. Ya know what I mean? You got the doughnuts, ya gotta create a market . . . Understand? . . . It's balancing the demand with the supply . . . That sort of thing."

"Yep!" said Homer. "Mr. Gabby's right. We have to enlarge our market. He's an advertising sandwich man, so if we hire him, he can walk up and down in front of the theater and get the customers."

"You're hired, Mr. Gabby!" said Uncle Ulysses.

Then everybody pitched in to paint the signs and to get Mr. Gabby sandwiched between. They painted "SALE ON DOUGHNUTS" in big letters on the window too.

Meanwhile the rings of batter kept right on dropping into the hot fat, and an automatic gadget kept right on turning them over, and another automatic gadget kept right on giving them a little push, and the doughnuts kept right on rolling down the little chute, just as regular as a clock can tick.

"I certainly hope this advertising works," said Uncle Ulysses, wagging his head. "Aggy'll certainly throw a fit if it don't."

The sheriff went outside to keep order, because there was quite a crowd by now—all looking at the doughnuts and guessing how many thousand there were, and watching new ones roll down the little chute, just as regular as a clock can tick. Homer and Uncle Ulysses kept stacking doughnuts. Once in a while somebody bought a few, but not very often.

Then Mr. Gabby came back and said, "Say, you know there's not much use o' me advertisin' at the theater. The show's all over, and besides almost everybody in town is out front watching that machine make doughnuts!"

"Zeus!" said Uncle Ulysses. "We must get rid of these doughnuts before Aggy gets here!"

"Looks like you will have ta hire a truck ta waul 'em ahay, I mean haul 'em away!!" said the sheriff who had just come in. Just then there was a noise and a shoving out front and the lady from the shiny black car and her chauffeur came pushing through the crowd and into the lunch room.

"Oh, gracious!" she gasped, ignoring the doughnuts, "I've lost my diamond bracelet, and I know I left it here on the counter," she said,

From *Homer Price*, written and illustrated by Robert McCloskey. Copyright © 1943, renewed © 1971 by Robert McCloskey. Reprinted by permission of Viking Penguin Inc.

pointing to a place where the doughnuts were piled in stacks of two dozen.

"Yes, Ma'm, I guess you forgot it when you helped make the batter," said Homer.

Then they moved all the doughnuts around and looked for the diamond bracelet, but they couldn't find it anywhere. Meanwhile the doughnuts kept rolling down the little chute, just as regular as a clock can tick.

After they had looked all around the sheriff cast a suspicious eye on Mr. Gabby, but Homer said, "He's all right, sheriff, he didn't take it. He's a friend of mine."

Then the lady said, "I'll offer a reward of one hundred dollars for that bracelet! It really *must* be found! . . . it *really* must!"

"Now don't you worry, lady," said the sheriff. "I'll get your bracelet back!"

"Zeus! This is terrible!" said Uncle Ulysses. "First all of these doughnuts and then on top of all that, a lost diamond bracelet . . ."

Mr. Gabby tried to comfort him, and he said, "There's always a bright side. That machine'll probably run outta batter in an hour or two."

If Mr. Gabby hadn't been quick on his feet Uncle Ulysses would have knocked him down, sure as fate.

Then while the lady wrung her hands and said, "We must find it, we *must*!" and Uncle Ulysses was moaning about what Aunt Agnes would say, and the sheriff was eyeing Mr. Gabby, Homer sat down and thought hard.

Before twenty more doughnuts could roll down the little chute, he shouted, "SAY! I know where the bracelet is! It was lying here on the counter and got mixed up in the batter by mistake! The bracelet is cooked inside one of these doughnuts!"

"Why . . . I really believe you're right," said the lady through her tears. "Isn't that *amazing?* Simply *amazing!*"

"I'll be durn'd!" said the sheriff.

"OhH-h!" moaned Uncle Ulysses. "Now we have to break up all of these doughnuts to find it. Think of the *pieces!* Think of the *crumbs!* Think of what *Aggy* will say!"

"Nope," said Homer. "We won't have to break them up. I've got a plan."

So Homer and the advertising man took some cardboard and some paint and printed another sign. They put this sign in the window, and the sandwich man wore two more signs that said the same thing and walked around in the crowd out front.

FRESH DOUGHNUTS
2 FOR 5¢
WHILE THEY LAST

$100.00 PRIZE
FOR FINDING
A BRACELET
INSIDE A DOUGHNUT

P.S. YOU HAVE TO GIVE THE
BRACELET BACK

THEN . . . The doughnuts began to sell! *Everybody* wanted to buy doughnuts, *dozens* of doughnuts!

And that's not all. Everybody bought coffee to dunk the doughnuts into. Those that didn't buy coffee bought milk or soda. It kept Homer and the lady and the chauffeur and Uncle Ulysses and the sheriff busy waiting on the people who wanted to buy doughnuts.

When all but the last couple of hundred doughnuts had been sold, Rupert Black shouted, "I GAWT IT!!" and sure enough . . . there was the diamond bracelet inside of his doughnut!

Then Rupert went home with a hundred dollars, the citizens of Centerburg went home full of doughnuts, the lady and her chauffeur drove off with the diamond bracelet, and Homer went home with his mother when she stopped by with Aunt Aggy.

As Homer went out of the door he heard Mr. Gabby say, "Neatest trick of merchandising I ever seen," and Aunt Aggy was looking sceptical while Uncle Ulysses was saying "The rings of batter kept right on dropping into the hot fat, and the automatic gadget kept right on turning them over, and the other automatic gadget kept right on giving them a little push, and the doughnuts kept right on rolling down the little chute just as regular as a clock can tick—they just kept right on a comin', an' a comin', an' a comin', an' a comin'.'"

E. L. Konigsburg

From the Mixed-up Files of Mrs. Basil E. Frankweiler

This highly inventive tale is told with such conviction that to read it is to believe it. Two children, a brother and sister, run away from their home in suburbia to establish a perilous residence in New York's Metropolitan Museum of Art. In addition to an adventurous daily life, they become involved in establishing the authenticity of a small statue of an angel, a recent Museum acquisition, which is attributed to Michelangelo. Any account of children on their own, released from the admonition of adults, is almost sure to produce genuine drama. Clear characterization of contemporary children, a neatly turned plot, an eye for detail, and an ear for dialogue: These are part of the pleasure to be found in this book of marked originality. It received the Newbery award in 1968. [From E. L. Konigsburg, *From the Mixed-Up Files of Mrs. Basil E. Frankweiler* (Atheneum, 1967).]

They had been gone from home for three days now. Claudia insisted on a fresh change of underwear every day. That was the way she had been brought up. She insisted for Jamie, too. No question about it; their laundry was becoming a problem. They had to get to a laundromat. That night they removed all their dirty clothes from their instrument cases and stuffed those that would fit into various pockets. Those that didn't fit, they wore. A double layer of clothes never hurts anyone in winter, as long as the clean ones are worn closest to the skin.

Saturday seemed a good day for housekeeping chores. There would be no school groups for them to join. Claudia suggested that they eat both meals outside the museum. Jamie agreed. Claudia next suggested a real sit-down restaurant with tablecloths on the tables and waiters to serve you. Jamie said "NO" with such force that Claudia didn't try to persuade him.

From breakfast at the automat they went to laundry at the laundromat. They emptied their pockets of underwear and removed the layer of soiled socks. No one stared. Someone before them had probably done the same thing some time that week. They bought soap from a machine for ten cents and deposited a quarter into the slot in the washer. Through the glass in the door they watched their assorted clothing spill and splash over and over and around and around. Drying cost ten cents for ten minutes, but it took twenty cents worth of minutes to dry everything. When all was done, they were disappointed; all of it looked dismally gray. Very unelegant. Claudia had thought that their white underwear should not have been washed with the red and navy blue socks, but she would not have considered asking for more money for anything as unglamorous as dirty socks.

"Oh, well," she moaned, "at least they smell clean."

Jamie said, "Let's go to the TV department of Bloomingdale's and watch TV."

"Not today. We've got to work on the mystery of the statue all morning tomorrow, because tomorrow the museum doesn't open until one o'clock. Today we must learn all about the Renaissance and Michelangelo to prepare ourselves. We'll do research at the big library at 42nd Street."

"How about the TV department of Macy's instead?"

"To the library, Sir James."

"Gimbels?"

"Library."

They packed their gray-looking laundry back into their pockets and walked to the door of the laundromat. At the door Claudia turned to Jamie and asked, "Can we . . .?"

Jamie didn't let her finish. "No, dear Lady Claudia. We have not the funds for taxis, buses, or subways. Shall we walk?" He extended his arm. Claudia placed her gloved fingertips on top of Jamie's mittened ones. Thus they began their long walk to the library.

Once there, they asked the lady at the information booth where they could find books on Michelangelo. She directed them first to the children's room, but when the librarian there found out what they wanted to know, she advised them to go to the Donnell Branch Library on Fifty-third Street. Jamie hoped this would discourage Claudia, but it didn't. She didn't even seem to mind backtracking up Fifth Avenue. Her determination convinced Jamie that Saturday should be spent just this way. Once at the library, they examined the directory which told what was available where and when the library was open. In the downstairs Art Room the librarian helped them find the books which Claudia selected from the card catalogue. She even brought them some others. Claudia liked that part. She always enjoyed being waited on.

Claudia began her studies never doubting that she could become an authority that morning. She had neither pencil nor paper to make notes. So she decided that she would simply remember everything, absolutely everything she read. Her net profit, therefore, would be as great as that of someone who read a great deal but remembered very little.

Claudia showed the executive ability of a corporation president. She assigned to Jamie the task of looking through the books of photographs of Michelangelo's work to find pictures of Angel. She would do the reading. She glanced through several thick books with thin pages and tiny print. After reading twelve pages, she looked to the end to see how many more pages there were to go: more than two hundred. The book also had footnotes. She read a few more pages and then busied herself with studying some of Jamie's picture books.

"You're supposed to do the reading!"

"I'm just using these pictures for relief," Claudia whispered. "I have to rest my eyes sometime."

"Well, I don't see any pictures that look like that statue," Jamie sighed.

"Keep looking. I'll do some more reading."

A few minutes later Jamie interrupted her. "Here he is," he said.

"That doesn't look anything like the statue. That's not even a girl," Claudia said.

"Of course not. That's Michelangelo himself."

Claudia replied, "I knew that."

"Two minutes ago you didn't. You thought I was showing you a picture of the statue."

"Oh, I meant . . . I meant. Well . . . there's his broken nose." She pointed to the nose in the picture. "He got in a fight and had his nose broken when he was a teenager."

"Was he a juvenile delinquent? Maybe they do have his fingerprints on file."

"No, silly," Claudia said. "He was a hot-tempered genius. Did you know he was famous even when he was alive?"

"Is that so? I thought that artists don't become famous until after they're dead. Like mummies."

They studied a while longer before Jamie's next interruption. "You know, a lot of his works were lost. They say *lost* in parentheses under the picture."

"How can that be? A statue isn't something like an umbrella that you leave in a taxi and lose. That is, those people who actually ride taxis; something you wouldn't know about."

"Well, they weren't lost in taxis. They were lost track of."

"What kind of a sentence is that? Lost track of?"

"Oh, boloney! There are whole long books about the lost works of Michelangelo. Picture works and sculptor works that people lost track of."

Claudia softened. "Is the little angel one of them?"

"What's the difference between an angel and a cupid?" Jamie inquired.

"Why?" Claudia asked.

"Because there's a lost cupid for sure."

"Angels wear clothes and wings and are Christian. Cupids wear bows and arrows; they are naked and pagan."

"What's pagan?" Jamie asked. "Boy or girl?"

"How would I know?" Claudia answered.

"You said they are naked."

"Well, pagan has nothing to do with that. It means worshipping idols instead of God."

"Oh," Jamie nodded. "The statue in the museum is an angel. It's dressed in its altogether. I don't know yet if an angel was lost . . ." Then he glanced over at his sister and muttered, "track of."

Claudia had begun her research confident that a morning's study would make her completely an expert; but Michelangelo had humbled her, and humility was not an emotion with which she felt comfortable. She was irritable. Jamie ended his research where Claudia had begun; very confident and happy. He felt that his morning had been well spent; he had seen a lot of pictures and he had learned about pagans. He leaned back and yawned; he was becoming bored with pictures of David and Moses and the Sistine Ceiling; he wanted to find clues. Already he knew enough to tell if Michelangelo had sculptured the little angel. All he needed was a chance to investigate. Without the guards hurrying him. He would know, but would his opinion be accepted by experts?

"I think we should find out how the experts decide whether or not the statue belongs to Michelangelo. That will be better than finding out about Michelangelo himself," Jamie said.

"I know how they find out. They gather evidence like sketches he did and diaries and records of sales. And they examine the statue to see what kind of tools were used and how they were used. Like no one living in the fifteenth century would use an electric drill. How come you didn't take art appreciation lessons with me?"

"The summer before last?"

"Yes. Before school started."

"Well, the summer before last, I had just finished the first half of second grade."

"So what?"

"So boloney! It was all I could do to sound out the name of Dick and Jane's dog."

Claudia had no answer for Jamie's logic. Besides, Jamie agreed with her, "I guess it is better to look for clues. After all, we're doing something that none of the experts can. do."

Claudia's impatience surfaced. She had to pick a fight with Jamie. "Don't be silly. They can read all this stuff, too. There's certainly plenty of it."

"Oh, I don't mean that. I mean that we're living with the statue. You know what they always say: The only two ways to get to know someone are to live with him or play cards with him."

"Well, at least the little statue can't cheat at cards like someone else I know."

"Claudia, dear, I'm no angel. Statue or otherwise."

Claudia sighed, "O.K. Sir James, let's go." And they did.

As they were walking up the steps, Jamie spied a Hershey's almond bar still in its wrapper lying in the corner of the landing. He picked it up and tore open one corner.

"Was it bitten into?" asked Claudia.

"No," Jamie smiled. "Want half?"

"You better not touch it," Claudia warned. "It's probably poisoned or filled with marijuana, so you'll eat it and become either dead or a dope addict."

Jamie was irritated. "Couldn't it just happen that someone dropped it?"

"I doubt that. Who would drop a whole candy bar and not know it? That's like leaving a statue in a taxi. Someone put it there on purpose. Someone who pushes dope. I read once that they feed dope in chocolates to little kids, and then the kids become dope addicts, then these people sell them dope at very high prices which they just can't help but buy because when you're addicted you have to have your dope. High prices and all. And Jamie, we don't have that kind of money."

Jamie said, "Oh, well, bottoms up." He took a big bite of the candy, chewed and swallowed. Then he closed his eyes, leaned against the wall and slid to the floor. Claudia stood with her mouth open, stunned. She was on the verge of screaming for help when Jamie opened his eyes and smiled. It's delicious. Want a bite?"

Claudia not only refused the bite, she also refused to talk to Jamie until they got to the restaurant. Lunch cheered her. She suggested that they play in Central Park for a while, and they did. They bought peanuts, chestnuts, and pretzels from the vendor outside the museum. They knew that since the museum opened late on Sunday, they would accumulate a lot of hunger before they got out. Their bulging pockets were now full of the staples of life: food and clothing.

Jamie entered the men's room. He had arrived, as was his custom, shortly before the first bell rang, the bell that warned everyone that the museum would close in five minutes. He waited; the bell rang. He got into a booth. First bell, second bell, it was routine just as boarding the school bus had once been routine. After the first day, they had learned that the staff worked from nine A.M. until five P.M., a work schedule just like their father's. Routine, routine. The wait from nine when the staff came until ten when the public came seemed long. Claudia and Jamie had decided that the washrooms were good for the shorter evening wait when the help left at the same time as the visitors, but the washrooms were less satisfactory for the long morning wait . . . especially after Jamie's close call that first morning. So time from eight forty-five until some safe time after ten in the mornings was spent under various beds. They always checked for dust under the bed first. And for once Claudia's fussiness was not the reason. Reason was the reason. A dustless floor meant that it had been cleaned very recently, and they stood less chance of being caught by a mop.

Jamie stood on the toilet seat waiting. He leaned his head against the wall of the booth and braced himself for what would happen next. The guard would come in and make a quick check of his station. Jamie still felt a ping during that short inspection; that was the only part that still wasn't quite routine, and that's why he braced himself. Then the lights would be turned out. Jamie would wait twelve minutes (lag time, Claudia called it) and emerge from hiding.

Except.

Except the guard didn't come, and Jamie couldn't relax until after he felt that final ping. And the lights stayed on, stayed on. Jamie checked his watch ten times within five minutes; he shook his arm and held the watch up to his ear. It was ticking slower than his heart and much more softly. What was wrong? They had caught Claudia! Now they would look for him! He'd pretend he didn't speak English. He wouldn't answer any questions.

Then he heard the door open. Footsteps. More footsteps than usual. What was happening? The hardest part was that every corpuscle of Jamie's nine-year-old self was throbbing with readiness to run, and he had to bind up all that energy into a quiet lump. It was like trying to wrap a loose peck of potatoes into a neat four-cornered package. But he managed to freeze. He heard the voices of two men talking over the sound of water running in the sink.

"I guess they expect even more people tomorrow."

"Yeah. Sundays are always jammed up anyway."

"It'll be easier to move the people in and out of the Great Hall."

"Yeah. Two feet of marble. What do you figure it weighs?"

"I dunno. Whatever it weighs, it has to be handled delicate. Like it was a real angel."

"C'mon. They probably have the new pedestal ready. We can start."

"Do you think they'll have as many people as they had for the Mona Lisa?"

"Naw! The Mona Lisa was here for a short time only. Besides it was the real McCoy."

"I think this one's . . ."

The men left, turning off the lights as they did so. Jamie heard the door close before he melted. Legs first. He sat down on the seat as he allowed the familiar darkness as well as new realization to fill him.

They were moving Angel. Did Claudia know? They wouldn't have women moving the statue. There would be no one in the ladies' room washing up. Who would give her the information? He would. By mental telepathy. He would think a message to Claudia. He folded his hands across his forehead and concentrated. "Stay put, Claudia, stay put. Stay put. Stay put. Claudia, stay put." He thought that Claudia would not approve of the grammar in his mental telegram; she would want him to think *stay in place.* But he didn't want to weaken his message by varying it one bit. He continued thinking STAY PUT.

He must have thought STAY PUT exactly hard enough, for Claudia did just that. They never knew exactly why she did, but she did. Perhaps she sensed some sounds that told her the museum was not yet empty. Maybe she was just too tired from running around in Central Park. Maybe they were not meant to get caught. Maybe they were meant to make the discovery they made.

They waited for miles and miles of time before they came out of hiding. At last they met in their bedroom. Claudia was sorting the laundry when Jamie got there. In the dark, mostly by feel. Although there is no real difference between boys' stretch socks and girls', neither ever considered wearing the other's. Children who have always had separate bedrooms don't.

Claudia turned when she heard Jamie come up and said, "They moved the statue."

"How did you know? Did you get my message?"

"Message? I saw the statue on my way here. They have a dim light on it. I guess so that the night guard won't trip over it."

Jamie replied, "We're lucky we didn't get caught."

Claudia never thought very hard about the plus-luck she had; she concentrated on the minus-luck. "But they held us up terribly. I planned on our taking baths tonight. I really can't stand one night more without a bath."

"I don't mind," Jamie said.

"Come along, Sir James. To our bath. Bring your most elegant pajamas. The ones embroidered in gold with silver tassels will do."

"Where, dear Lady Claudia, dost thou expect to bathe?"

"In the fountain, Sir James. In the fountain."

Jamie extended his arm, which was draped with his striped flannel pajamas, and said, "Lady Claudia, I knew that sooner or later you would get me to that restaurant."

(It makes me furious to think that I must explain that restaurant to you, Saxonberg. I'm going to make you take me to lunch in there one day soon. I just this minute became determined to get you into the museum. You'll see later how I'm going to do it. Now about the restaurant. It is built around a gigantic fountain. Water in the fountain is sprayed from dolphins sculptured in bronze. The dolphins appear to be leaping out of the water. On their backs are figures representing the arts, figures that look like water sprites. It is a joy to sit around that wonderful fountain and to snack petit fours and sip espresso coffee. I'll bet that you'd even forget your blasted ulcer while you ate there.)

Lady Claudia and Sir James quietly walked to the entrance of the restaurant. They easily climbed under the velvet rope that meant that the restaurant was closed to the public. Of course they were not the public. They shed their clothes and waded into the fountain. Claudia had taken powdered soap from the restroom. She had ground it out into a paper towel that morning. Even though it was freezing cold,

she enjoyed her bath. Jamie, too, enjoyed his bath. For a different reason.

When he got into the pool, he found bumps on the bottom; smooth bumps. When he reached down to feel one, he found that it moved! He could even pick it up. He felt its cool roundness and splashed his way over to Claudia. "Income, Claudia, income!" he whispered.

Claudia understood immediately and began to scoop up bumps she had felt on the bottom of the fountain. The bumps were pennies and nickels people had pitched into the fountain to make a wish. At least four people had thrown in dimes and one had tossed in a quarter.

"Some one very rich must have tossed in this quarter," Jamie whispered.

"Some one very poor," Claudia corrected. "Rich people have only penny wishes."

Together they collected $2.87. They couldn't hold more in their hands. They were shivering when they got out. Drying themselves as best they could with paper towels (also taken from the restroom), they hurried into their pajamas and shoes.

They finished their preparations for the night, took a small snack and decided it was safe to wander back into the Great Hall to look at their Angel.

"I wish I could hug her," Claudia whispered.

"They probably bugged her already. Maybe that light is part of the alarm. Better not touch. You'll set it off."

"I said 'hug' not 'bug.' Why would I want to bug her?"

"That makes more sense than to hug her."

"Silly. Shows how much you know. When you hug someone, you learn something else about them. An important something else."

Jamie shrugged his shoulders.

Both looked at Angel a long time. "What do you think?" Jamie asked. "Did he or didn't he?"

Claudia answered, "A scientist doesn't make up his mind until he's examined all the evidence."

"You sure don't sound like a scientist. What kind of scientist would want to hug a statue?"

Claudia was embarrassed, so she spoke

sternly, "We'll go to bed now, and we'll think about the statue very hard. Don't fall asleep until you've really thought about the statue and Michelangelo and the entire Italian Renaissance."

And so they went to bed. But lying in bed just before going to sleep is the worst time for *organized* thinking; it is the best time for free thinking. Ideas drift like clouds in an undecided breeze, taking first this direction and then that. It was very difficult for Jamie to control his thoughts when he was tired, sleepy, and lying on his back. He never liked to get involved just before falling asleep. But Claudia had planned on their thinking, and she was good at planning. So think he did. Clouds bearing thoughts of the Italian Renaissance drifted away. Thoughts of home, and more thoughts of home settled down.

"Do you miss home?" he asked Claudia.

"Not too much," she confessed. "I haven't thought about it much."

Jamie was quiet for a minute, then he said, "We probably have no conscience. I think we ought to be homesick. Do you think Mom and Dad raised us wrong? They're not very mean, you know; don't you think that should make us miss them?"

Claudia was silent. Jamie waited. "Did you hear my question, Claude?"

"Yes. I heard your question. I'm thinking." She was quiet a while longer. Then she asked, "Have you ever been homesick?"

"Sure."

"When was the last time?"

"That day Dad dropped us off at Aunt Zell's when he took Mom to the hospital to get Kevin."

"Me, too. That day," Claudia admitted. "But, of course, I was much younger then."

"Why do you suppose we were homesick that day? We've been gone much longer than that now."

Claudia thought. "I guess we were worried. Boy, had I known then that she was going to end up with Kevin, I would have known why we were worried. I remember you sucked your thumb and carried around that old blanket the whole day. Aunt Zell kept trying to get the blanket away from you so that she could wash it. It stank."

Jamie giggled, "Yeah, I guess homesickness is like sucking your thumb. It's what happens when you're not very sure of yourself."

"Or not very well trained," Claudia added. "Heaven knows, we're well trained. Just look how nicely we've managed. It's really their fault if we're not homesick."

Jamie was satisfied. Claudia was more. "I'm glad you asked that about homesickness, Jamie. Somehow, I feel older now. But, of course, that's mostly because I've been the oldest child forever. And I'm extremely well adjusted."

They went to sleep then. Michelangelo, Angel, and the entire Italian Renaissance waited for them until morning.

E. Nesbit

The Treasure Seekers

Few writers have such a sense of play as E. Nesbit had. Her Bastable children, while perfectly normal children, are adept at imaginative games and see the world in terms of adventurous exploits. Since the death of their mother and the preoccupation of their father with his financial reverses, the children have been on their own with only a cook to look after them. In telling this story, Nesbit uses Oswald as the narrator, having him praise the bravery and wisdom of Oswald and then, unintentionally, betray his identity. [From E. Nesbit, *The Treasure Seekers* (Coward-McCann, 1899).]

The Robber and the Burglar

A day or two after Noël came back from Hastings there was snow; it was jolly. And we cleared it off the path. A man to do it is sixpence at least, and you should always save when you can. A penny saved is a penny earned. And then we thought it would be nice to clear it off the top of the portico, where it lies so thick, and the edges as if they had been cut with a knife. And just as we had got out of the landing-window on to the portico, the Water Rates came up the path with his book that he tears the thing out of that says how much you have got to pay, and the little ink-bottle hung on to his button-hole in case you should pay him. Father says the Water Rates is a sensible man, and knows it is always well to be prepared for whatever happens, however unlikely. Alice said afterwards that she rather liked the Water Rates, really, and Noël said he had a face like a good vizier, or the man who rewards the honest boy for restoring the purse, but we did not think about these things at the time, and as the Water Rates came up the steps, we shovelled down a great square slab of snow like an avalanche—and it fell right on his head. Two of us thought of it at the same moment, so it was quite a large avalanche. And when the Water Rates had shaken himself he rang the bell. It was Saturday, and Father was at home. We know now that it is very wrong and ungentlemanly to shovel snow off porticoes on to the Water Rates, or any other person, and we hope he did not catch a cold, and we are very sorry. We apologized to the Water Rates when Father told us to. We were all sent to bed for it.

We all deserved the punishment, because the others would have shovelled down snow just as we did if they'd thought of it—only they are not so quick at thinking of things as we are. And even quite wrong things some times lead to adventures; as every one knows who has ever read about pirates or highwaymen.

Eliza hates us to be sent to bed early, because it means her having to bring meals up, and it means lighting the fire in Noël's room ever so much earlier than usual. He had to have a fire because he still had a bit of a cold. But this particular day we got Eliza into a good temper by giving her a horrid brooch with pretending amethysts in it, that an aunt once gave to Alice, so Eliza brought up an extra scuttle of coals, and when the greengrocer came with the potatoes (he is always late on Saturdays) she got some chestnuts from him. So that when we heard Father go out after his dinner, there was a jolly fire in Noël's room, and we were able to go in and be Red Indians in blankets most comfortably. Eliza had gone out; she says she gets things cheaper on Saturday nights. She has a great friend, who sells fish at a shop, and he

is very generous, and lets her have herrings for less than half the natural price.

So we were all alone in the house; Pincher was out with Eliza, and we talked about robbers. And Dora thought it would be a dreadful trade, but Dickey said—

"I think it would be very interesting. And you would only rob rich people, and be very generous to the poor and needy, like Claude Duval."

Dora said, "It is wrong to be a robber."

"Yes," said Alice, "you would never know a happy hour. Think of trying to sleep with the stolen jewels under your bed, and remembering all the quantities of policemen and detectives that there are in the world!"

"There are ways of being robbers that are not wrong," said Noël; "if you can rob a robber it is a right act."

"But you can't," said Dora; "he is too clever, and besides, it's wrong anyway."

"Yes you can, and it isn't; and murdering him with boiling oil is a right act, too, so there!" said Noël. "What about Ali Baba? Now then!" And we felt it was a score for Noël.

"What would you do if there *was* a robber?" said Alice.

H. O. said he would kill him with boiling oil; but Alice explained that she meant a real robber—now—this minute—in the house.

Oswald and Dicky did not say; but Noël said he thought it would only be fair to ask the robber quite politely and quietly to go away, and then if he didn't you could deal with him.

Now what I am going to tell you is a very strange and wonderful thing, and I hope you will be able to believe it. I should not, if a boy told me, unless I knew him to be a man of honour, and perhaps not then unless he gave his sacred word. But it is true, all the same, and it only shows that the days of romance and daring deeds are not yet at an end.

Alice was just asking Noël *how* he would deal with the robber who wouldn't go if he was asked politely and quietly, when we heard a noise downstairs—quite a plain noise, not the kind of noise you fancy you hear. It was like somebody moving a chair. We held our breath and listened—and then came another noise, like some one poking a fire. Now, you remember there was no one *to* poke a fire or move a chair downstairs, because Eliza and Father were both out. They could not have come in without our hearing them, because the front door is as hard to shut as the back one, and whichever you go in by you have to give a slam that you can hear all down the street.

H. O. and Alice and Dora caught hold of each other's blankets and looked at Dicky and Oswald, and every one was quite pale. And Noël whispered—

"It's ghosts, I know it is"—and then we listened again, but there was no more noise. Presently Dora said in a whisper—

"Whatever shall we do? Oh, whatever shall we do—what *shall* we do?"

And she kept on saying it till we had to tell her to shut up.

O reader, have you ever been playing Red Indians in blankets round a bedroom fire in a house where you thought there was no one but you—and then suddenly heard a noise like a chair, and a fire being poked, downstairs? Unless you have you will not be able to imagine at all what it feels like. It was not like in books; our hair did not stand on end at all, and we never said "Hist!" once, but our feet got very cold, though we were in blankets by the fire, and the insides of Oswald's hands got warm and wet, and his nose was cold like a dog's, and his ears were burning hot.

The girls said afterwards that they shivered with terror, and their teeth chattered, but we did not see or hear this at the time.

"Shall we open the window and call police?" said Dora; and then Oswald suddenly thought of something, and he breathed more freely and he said—

"I *know* it's not ghosts, and I don't believe it's robbers. I expect it's a stray cat got in when the coals came this morning, and she's been hiding in the cellar, and now she's moving about. Let's go down and see."

The girls wouldn't, of course; but I could see that they breathed more freely too. But Dicky said, "All right; I will if you will."

H. O. said, "Do you think it's *really* a cat?" So we said he had better stay with the girls.

And of course after that we had to let him and Alice both come. Dora said if we took Noël down with his cold, she would scream "Fire!" and "Murder!" and she didn't mind if the whole street heard.

So Noël agreed to be getting his clothes on, and the rest of us said we would go down and look for the cat.

Now Oswald *said* that about the cat, and it made it easier to go down, but in his inside he did not feel at all sure that it might not be robbers after all. Of course, we had often talked about robbers before, but it is very different when you sit in a room and listen and listen and listen; and Oswald felt somehow that it would be easier to go down and see what it was, than to wait, and listen, and wait, and wait, and listen, and wait, and then perhaps to hear *It,* whatever it was, come creeping slowly up the stairs as softly as *It* could with *Its* boots off, and the stairs creaking, towards the room where we were with the door open in case of Eliza coming back suddenly, and all dark on the landings. And then it would have been just as bad, and it would have lasted longer, and you would have known you were a coward besides. Dicky says he felt all these same things. Many people would say we were young heroes to go down as we did; so I have tried to explain, because no young hero wishes to have more credit than he deserves.

The landing gas was turned down low—just a blue bead—and we four went out very softly, wrapped in our blankets, and we stood on the top of the stairs a good long time before we began to go down. And we listened and listened till our ears buzzed.

And Oswald whispered to Dicky, and Dicky went into our room and fetched the large toy pistol that is a foot long, and that has the trigger broken, and I took it because I am the eldest; and I don't think either of us thought it was the cat now. But Alice and H. O. did. Dicky got the poker out of Noël's room, and told Dora it was to settle the cat with when we caught her.

Then Oswald whispered, "Let's play at burglars; Dicky and I are armed to the teeth, we will go first. You keep a flight behind us, and be a reinforcement if we are attacked. Or you can retreat and defend the women and children in the fortress, if you'd rather."

But they said they would be a reinforcement.

Oswald's teeth chattered a little when he spoke. It was not with anything else except cold.

So Dicky and Oswald crept down, and when we got to the bottom of the stairs, we saw Father's study door just ajar, and the crack of light.

Illustration by Gordon Browne, from *The Story of the Treasure Seekers*, by E. Nesbit, published by Ernest Benn Ltd. 1958. First published in 1899. Reprinted by permission of Adam and Charles Black Publishers Ltd.

And Oswald was so pleased to see the light, knowing that burglars prefer the dark, or at any rate the dark lantern, that he felt really sure it *was* the cat after all, and then he thought it would be fun to make the others upstairs think it was really a robber. So he cocked the pistol—you can cock it, but it doesn't go off—and he said, "Come on, Dick!" and he rushed at the study door and burst into the room, crying, "Surrender! you are discovered! Surrender, or I fire! Throw up your hands!"

And, as he finished saying it, he saw before him, standing on the study hearthrug, a Real Robber. There was no mistake about it. Oswald was sure it was a robber, because it had a screwdriver in its hands, and was standing near the cupboard door that H. O. broke the lock off, and there were gimlets and screws and things on the floor. There is nothing in that cupboard but old ledgers and magazines and the tool chest, but of course, a robber could not know that beforehand.

When Oswald saw that there really was a robber and that he was so heavily armed with the screwdriver, he did not feel comfortable. But he kept the pistol pointed at the robber, and—you will hardly believe it, but it is true—the robber threw down the screwdriver clattering on the other tools, and he *did* throw up his hands, and said—

"I surrender; don't shoot me! How many of you are there?"

So Dicky said, "You are outnumbered. Are you armed?"

And the robber said, "No, not in the least."

And Oswald said, still pointing the pistol, and feeling very strong and brave and as if he was in a book, "Turn out your pockets."

The robber did: and while he turned them out, we looked at him. He was of the middle height, and clad in a black frock-coat and grey trousers. His boots were a little gone at the sides, and his shirt-cuffs were a bit frayed, but otherwise he was of gentlemanly demeanour. He had a thin, wrinkled face, with big, light eyes that sparkled, and then looked soft very queerly, and a short beard. In his youth it must have been of a fair golden colour, but now it was tinged with grey. Oswald was sorry for him, especially when he saw that one of his pockets had a large hole in it, and that he had nothing in his pockets but letters and string and three boxes of matches, and a pipe and a handkerchief and a thin tobacco pouch and two pennies. We made him put all the things on the table, and then he said—

"Well, you've caught me; what are you going to do with me? Police?"

Alice and H. O. had come down to be reinforcements, when they heard a shout, and when Alice saw that it was a Real Robber, and that he had surrendered, she clapped her hands and said, "Bravo, boys!" and so did H. O. And now she said, "If he gives his word of honour not to escape, I shouldn't call the police: it seems a pity. Wait till Father comes home."

The robber agreed to this, and gave his word of honour, and asked if he might put on a pipe, and we said "Yes," and he sat in Father's armchair and warmed his boots, which steamed, and I sent H. O. and Alice to put on some clothes and tell the others, and bring down Dicky's and my knickerbockers, and the rest of the chestnuts.

And they all came, and we sat round the fire, and it was jolly. The robber was very friendly, and talked to us a great deal.

"I wasn't always in this low way of business," he said, when Noël said something about the things he had turned out of his pockets. "It's a great come-down to a man like me. But, if I must be caught, it's something to be caught by brave young heroes like you. My stars! How you did bolt into the room—'Surrender, and up with your hands!' You might have been born and bred to the thiefcatching."

Oswald is sorry if it was mean, but he could not own up just then that he did not think there was any one in the study when he did that brave if rash act. He has told since.

"And what made you think there was any one in the house?" the robber asked, when he had thrown his head back, and laughed for quite half a minute. So we told him. And he applauded our valour, and Alice and H. O. explained that they would have said "Surrender," too, only they were reinforcements.

The robber ate some of the chestnuts—and we sat and wondered when Father would come home, and what he would say to us for our

intrepid conduct. And the robber told us of all the things he had done before he began to break into houses. Dicky picked up the tools from the floor, and suddenly he said—

"Why, this is Father's screwdriver and his gimlets, and all! Well, I do call it jolly cheek to pick a man's locks with his own tools!"

"True, true," said the robber. "It is cheek, of the jolliest! But you see I've come down in the world. I was a highway robber once, but horses are so expensive to hire—five shillings an hour, you know—and I couldn't afford to keep them. The highwayman business isn't what it was."

"What about a bike?" said H. O.

But the robber thought cycles were low—and besides you couldn't go across country with them when occasion arose, as you could with a trusty steed. And he talked of highwaymen as if he knew just how we liked hearing it.

Then he told us how he had been a pirate captain—and how he had sailed over waves mountains high, and gained rich prizes—and how he *did* begin to think that here he had found a profession to his mind.

"I don't say there are no ups and downs in it," he said, "especially in stormy weather. But what a trade! And a sword at your side, and the Jolly Roger flying at the peak, and a prize in sight. And all the black mouths of your guns pointed at the laden trader—and the wind in your favour, and your trusty crew ready to live and die for you! Oh—but it's a grand life!"

I did feel so sorry for him. He used such nice words, and he had a gentleman's voice.

"I'm sure you weren't brought up to be a pirate," said Dora. She had dressed even to her collar—and made Noël do it too—but the rest of us were in blankets with just a few odd things put on anyhow underneath.

The robber frowned and sighed.

"No," he said, "I was brought up to the law. I was at Balliol, bless your hearts, and that's true anyway." He sighed again, and looked hard at the fire.

"That was my Father's college," H. O. was beginning, but Dicky said—

"Why did you leave off being a pirate?"

"A pirate?" he said, as if he had not been thinking of such things. "Oh, yes; why I gave it up because—because I could not get over the dreadful sea-sickness.''

"Nelson was sea-sick," said Oswald.

"Ah," said the robber; "but I hadn't his luck or his pluck, or something. He stuck to it and won Trafalgar, didn't he? 'Kiss me, Hardy'—and all that, eh? *I* couldn't stick to it—I had to resign. And nobody kissed *me.*''

I saw by his understanding about Nelson that he was really a man who had been to a good school as well as to Balliol.

Then we asked him, "And what did you do then?''

And Alice asked if he was ever a coiner, and we told him how we had thought we'd caught the desperate gang next door, and he was very much interested and said he was glad he had never taken to coining. "Besides, the coins are so ugly nowadays," he said, "no one could really find any pleasure in making them. And it's a hole-and-corner business at the best, isn't it?—and it must be a very thirsty one—with the hot metal and furnaces and things.''

And again he looked at the fire.

Oswald forgot for a minute that the interesting stranger was a robber, and asked him if he wouldn't have a drink. Oswald has heard Father do this to his friends, so he knows it is the right thing. The robber said he didn't mind if he did. And that is right, too.

And Dora went and got a bottle of Father's ale—the Light Sparkling Family—and a glass, and we gave it to the robber. Dora said she would be responsible.

Then when he had had a drink he told us about bandits, but he said it was so bad in wet weather. Bandits' caves were hardly ever properly weathertight. And bush-ranging was the same.

"As a matter of fact," he said, "I was bush-ranging this afternoon, among the furze-bushes on the Heath, but I had no luck. I stopped the Lord Mayor in his gilt coach, with all his footmen in plush and gold lace, smart as cockatoos. But it was no go. The Lord Mayor hadn't a stiver in his pockets. One of the footmen had six new pennies: the Lord Mayor always pays his servants' wages in new pennies. I spent fourpence of that in bread and cheese, that on the table's the tuppence. Ah, it's a poor trade!'' And then he filled his pipe again.

We had turned out the gas, so that Father should have a jolly good surprise when he did come home, and we sat and talked as pleasant as could be. I never liked a new man better than I liked that robber. And I felt so sorry for him. He told us he had been a war-correspondent and an editor, in happier days, as well as a horse-stealer and a colonel of dragoons.

And quite suddenly, just as we were telling him about Lord Tottenham and our being highwaymen ourselves, he put up his hand and said "Shish!" and we were quiet and listened.

There was a scrape, scrape, scraping noise; it came from downstairs.

"They're filing something," whispered the robber, "here—shut up, give me that pistol, and the poker. There *is* a burglar now, and no mistake.''

"It's only a toy one and it won't go off," I said, "but you can cock it.''

Then we heard a snap.

"There goes the window bar," said the robber softly. "Jove! what an adventure! You kids stay here, I'll tackle it.''

But Dicky and I said we should come. So he let us go as far as the bottom of the kitchen stairs, and we took the tongs and shovel with us. There was a light in the kitchen; a very little light. It is curious we never thought, any of us, that this might be a plan of our robber's to get away. We never thought of doubting his word of honour. And we were right.

That noble robber dashed the kitchen door open, and rushed in with the big toy pistol in one hand and the poker in the other, shouting out just like Oswald had done—

"Surrender! You are discovered! Surrender, or I'll fire! Throw up your hands!" And Dicky and I rattled the tongs and shovel so that he might know there were more of us, all bristling with weapons.

And we heard a husky voice in the kitchen saying—

"All right, governor! Stow that scent sprinkler. I'll give in. Blowed if I ain't pretty well sick of the job, anyway.''

Then we went in. Our robber was standing in the grandest manner with his legs very wide apart, and the pistol pointing at the cowering burglar. The burglar was a large man who did not mean to have a beard, I think, but he had got some of one, and a red comforter, and a fur cap, and his face was red and his voice was thick. How different from our own robber! The burglar had a dark lantern, and he was standing by the plate-basket. When we had lit the gas we all thought he was very like what a burglar ought to be. He did not look as if he could ever have been a pirate or a highwayman, or anything really dashing or noble, and he scowled and shuffled his feet and said: "Well, go on: why don't yer fetch the pleece?"

"Upon my word, I don't know," said our robber, rubbing his chin. "Oswald, why don't we fetch the police?"

It is not every robber that I would stand Christian names from, I can tell you; but just then I didn't think of that. I just said—

"Do you mean I'm to fetch one?"

Our robber looked at the burglar and said nothing.

Then the burglar began to speak very fast, and to look different ways with his hard, shiny little eyes.

"Lookee 'ere, governor," he said, "I was stony broke, so help me, I was. And blessed if I've nicked a haporth of your little lot. You know yourself there ain't much to tempt a bloke," he shook the plate-basket as if he was angry with it, and the yellowy spoons and forks rattled. "I was just a-looking through this 'ere Bank-ollerday show, when you come. Let me off, sir. Come now, I've got kids of my own at home, strike me if I ain't—same as yours— I've got a nipper just about 'is size, and what'll come of them if I'm lagged? I ain't been in it long, sir, and I ain't 'andy at it."

"No," said our robber; "you certainly are not."

Alice and the others had come down by now to see what was happening. Alice told me afterwards they thought it really was the cat this time.

"No, I ain't 'andy, as you say, sir, and if you let me off this once I'll chuck the whole blooming bizz; rake my civvy, I will. Don't be hard on a cove, mister; think of the missis and the kids. I've got one just the cut of little missy there; bless 'er pretty 'eart."

"Your family certainly fits your circumstances very nicely," said our robber.

Then Alice said—

"Oh, do let him go! If he's got a little girl like me whatever will she do? Suppose it was Father!"

"I don't think he's got a little girl like you, my dear," said our robber, "and I think he'll be safer under lock and key."

"You ask yer Father to let me go, miss," said the burglar; "'e won't 'ave the 'art to refuse you."

"If I do," said Alice, "will you promise never to come back?"

"Not me, miss," the burglar said very earnestly, and he looked at the plate-basket again, as if that alone would be enough to keep him away, our robber said afterwards.

"And will you be good and not rob any more?" said Alice.

"I'll turn over a noo leaf, miss, so help me."

Then Alice said—

"Oh, do let him go! I'm sure he'll be good."

But our robber said no, it wouldn't be right; we must wait till Father came home.

Then H. O. said, very suddenly and plainly:

"I don't think it's at all fair, when you're a robber yourself."

The minute he'd said it the burglar said, "Kidded, by gum!"—and then our robber made a step towards him to catch hold of him, and before you had time to think "Hullo!" the burglar knocked the pistol up with one hand and knocked our robber down with the other, and was off out of the window like a shot, though Oswald and Dicky did try to stop him by holding on to his legs.

And that burglar had the cheek to put his head in at the window and say, "I'll give yer love to the kids and the missis"—and he was off like winking, and there were Alice and Dora trying to pick up our robber, and asking him whether he was hurt, and where. He wasn't hurt at all, except a lump at the back of his head. And he got up, and we dusted the kitchen floor off him. Eliza is a dirty girl.

Then he said, "Let's put up the shutters. It never rains but it pours. Now you've had two burglars I daresay you'll have twenty." So we put up the shutters, which Eliza has strict orders to do before she goes out, only she never does, and we went back to Father's study, and the robber said, "What a night we are having!" and put his boots back in the fender to go on steaming, and then we all talked at once. It was the most wonderful adventure we ever had, though it wasn't treasure-seeking—at least not ours. I suppose it was the burglar's treasure-seeking, but he didn't get much—and our robber said he didn't believe a word about those kids that were so like Alice and me.

And then there was the click of the gate, and we said, "Here's Father," and the robber said, "And now for the police."

Then we all jumped up. We did like him so much, and it seemed so unfair that he should be sent to prison, and the horrid, lumping big burglar not.

And Alice said, "Oh, *no*—run! Dicky will let you out at the back door. Oh, do go, go *now.*"

And we all said, "Yes, *go*," and pulled him towards the door, and gave him his hat and stick and the things out of his pockets.

But Father's latchkey was in the door, and it was too late.

Father came in quickly, purring with the cold, and began to say, "It's all right, Foulkes, I've got—" And then he stopped short and stared at us. Then he said, in the voice we all hate, "Children, what is the meaning of all this?"

And for a minute nobody spoke.

Then my Father said, "Foulkes, I must really apologize for these very naughty—"

And then our robber rubbed his hands and laughed, and cried out: "You're mistaken, my dear sir, I'm not Foulkes; I'm a robber, captured by these young people in the most gallant manner. 'Hands up, surrender, or I fire,' and all the rest of it. My word, Bastable, but you've got some kids worth having! I wish my Denny had their pluck."

Then we began to understand, and it was like being knocked down, it was so sudden. And our robber told us he wasn't a robber after all. He was only an old college friend of my Father's, and he had come after dinner, when Father was just trying to mend the lock H. O. had broken, to ask Father to get him a letter to a doctor about his little boy Denny, who

was ill. And Father had gone over the Heath to Vanbrugh Park to see some rich people he knows and get the letter. And he had left Mr. Foulkes to wait till he came back, because it was important to know at once whether Father could get the letter, and if he couldn't Mr. Foulkes would have had to try some one else directly.

We were dumb with amazement.

Our robber told my Father about the other burglar, and said he was sorry he'd let him escape, but my Father said, "Oh, it's all right: poor beggar; if he really had kids at home: you never can tell—forgive us our debts, don't you know; but tell me about the first business. It must have been moderately entertaining."

Then our robber told my Father how I had rushed into the room with a pistol, crying out . . . but you know all about that. And he laid it on so thick and fat about plucky young-uns, and chips of old blocks, and things like that, that I felt I was purple with shame, even under the blanket. So I swallowed that thing that tries to prevent you speaking when you ought to, and I said, "Look here, Father, I didn't really think there was any one in the study. We thought it was a cat at first, and then I thought there was no one there, and I was just larking. And when I said surrender and all that, it was just the game, don't you know?"

Then our robber said, "Yes, old chap; but when you found there really *was* some one there, you dropped the pistol and bunked, didn't you, eh?"

And I said, "No; I thought, 'Hullo! here's a robber! Well, it's all up, I suppose, but I may as well hold on and see what happens.'"

And I was glad I'd owned up, for Father slapped me on the back, and said I was a young brick, and our robber said I was no funk anyway, and though I got very hot under the blanket I liked it, and I explained that the others would have done the same if they had thought of it.

Then Father got up some more beer, and laughed about Dora's responsibility, and he got out a box of figs he had bought for us, only he hadn't given it to us because of the Water Rates, and Eliza came in and brought up the bread and cheese, and what there was left of the neck of mutton—cold wreck of mutton, Father called it—and we had a feast—like a picnic—all sitting anywhere, and eating with our fingers. It was prime. We sat up till past twelve o'clock, and I never felt so pleased to think I was not born a girl. It was hard on the others; they would have done just the same if they'd thought of it. But it does make you feel jolly when your pater says you're a young brick!

When Mr. Foulkes was going, he said to Alice, "Good-bye, Hardy."

And Alice understood, of course, and kissed him as hard as she could.

And she said, "I wanted to, when you said no one kissed you when you left off being a pirate captain."

And he said, "I know you did, my dear."

And Dora kissed him too, and said, "I suppose none of these tales were true?"

And our robber just said, "I tried to play the part properly, my dear."

And he jolly well did play it, and no mistake. We have often seen him since, and his boy Denny, and his girl Daisy, but that comes in another story.

And if any of you kids who read this ever had two such adventures in one night you can just write and tell me. That's all.

Sid Fleischman

Humbug Mountain

Sid Fleischman is a modern yarn-spinner in the American tall tale tradition. His novels share fast-paced plots, witty caricature, and an infectious, broad humor. In this tale, history is colorfully exaggerated. Wiley's grandfather is supposed to have started a boom town on the Missouri River, but when Wiley and his family arrive, they can find no sign of Sunrise, the promised town, or, for that matter, of Grandpa. Instead, Wiley and his sister discover Grandpa's riverboat, the *Phoenix*. In this chapter readers meet the first of the larger-than-life characters who inhabit Fleischman's Old West. [From Sid Fleischman, *Humbug Mountain* (Little, Brown, 1978).]

The Fool Killer

Glorietta ran back to fetch Pa and Ma. A splintery old gangplank stretched between the creek bluff and the middle deck, and I walked aboard.

"Grandpa?" I called out. "Grandpa, it's me—Wiley."

The deck was gritty under my feet. Windblown dirt covered everything and was piled up like sand dunes against the cabins. I saw footprints. Lots of them, going and coming and scuffed about in the dust. They struck me as almighty fresh.

"Grandpa!"

I had no more than got the word out of my mouth when a hand snatched me by the collar, jerked me off my feet, and held me aloft like a kicking rabbit.

"Cuss'd little varmint!" came a dry whisper at my ear. "What for you sneaking around here?"

He twisted me around to take a closer look. I gazed back at a pair of mean, deep-sunk little eyes and a mouthful of yellow teeth. He was tall and dreadfully skinny—as if he had the dry wilts. Stringy red hair shot down from under the brim of his floppy hat. He had a long horse-face and long bare feet. He was dressed in rags.

My heart was banging so loud he must have been able to hear it. I swallowed hard and managed to say, "This is my grandpa's boat."

"Ain't no grandpas around here."

"Then reckon I better be going. If you'll kindly put me down."

Those deep eyes of his didn't blink any more'n a lizard's.

"Who are you?" I muttered.

It was an eternity before he answered. Finally, in that whispery voice of his, he said, "The Fool Killer."

I think I stopped breathing. As far back as I could remember I'd heard tales of the Fool Killer. He was supposed to carry a bur-oak club on his shoulder and wander the countryside searching for fools. He'd smite them on the head. He was always barefoot, and he had such a long jaw he could eat oats out of a nose bag. Pa said there was no such real creature as the Fool Killer, but the hair on my neck had gone as stiff as hog bristles. This barefoot man was so long-faced he could eat out of a churn.

He upended me, caught my ankles in his big,

rattle-boned hands, and carried me like a dead chicken up some stairs to the top deck. I figured he must be going for his bur-oak club. If I didn't do something quick I was done for.

From one smokestack the crows began to squawk again.

"Fool Killer!"

"Bash'm!"

His hands were powerful as iron chain. I was in a blue fright. If only I'd thought to glance at my mirror ring I'd have seen him come ghosting up behind me.

He'd have to let go of my ankles when he fetched up his club, I thought. And I'd be off quicker'n high-lightning.

The Fool Killer kicked open a door. From inside came a thunderous snort and snoring.

"Shagnasty," the Fool Killer called out.

We were in the pilothouse. I could make out the tall oaken steering wheel, and daylight aglow at the huge windows. Then I saw a man rouse himself from a bedroll on the floor.

"Cuss it all, Fool Killer," he said. "Can't a gentleman take a wink of sleep around here?"

"I catched me another fool," said the Fool Killer.

"Don't look like nothing but a shirttail boy. Set him down."

The Fool Killer kicked the door shut and swung me rightside up. For the first time I got a square look at Mr. Shagnasty. He wore a mangy old bearskin coat and he was big around as a sauerkraut barrel. His beard was dirt-brown and greasy and all a'tangle, like the hairs on a smelly old billy goat.

"Fool Killer," he snorted. "Ain't you got more sense than to bring him aboard? You give away our hideout."

"I spied him cat-footing around."

The other man fixed his eyes on me and hitched up his gunbelt. "Is that a fact?"

"No sir," I said. "I wasn't sneaking about. I was walking plain as day. But I reckon my grandpa's nowhere around, so I'll just be going."

"Well, now, sonny, it's a mite late for that." Mr. Shagnasty pulled out a blue bandanna and gave his lumpy nose a thunderous honk. He wasn't wearing a shirt; just long red underwear, and it was so full of holes you'd think

he carried his own moths. "You know who we are," he said.

I answered quickly. "No sir, I don't."

"'Course you do! Ain't a sheriff anywhere in the territories not looking for the heads of Shagnasty John and the Fool Killer. The terror of the prairies—that's us!"

"I declare," I muttered, struck with awe. I'd never talked to real outlaws before and I was getting all-over lathers of sweat. They were genuine blood-and-thunder badmen. "I won't tell a perishing soul," I added earnestly.

"Can't no boy keep a secret," said the Fool Killer darkly. "Worse'n them crows."

"Nothing we can do about the crows but chunk stones at 'em," Shagnasty John said, scratching through his beard. "But dash it all, boy, me and the Fool Killer can't chance you. It don't leave us much choice. You can see that, can't you?"

"No sir," I answered, trying to stretch out the time. "You must be terrible bad shots if you can't shoot those crows."

Shagnasty John rumbled out a laugh. "Oh, we can fire straight enough. Stop edging toward that door! The Fool Killer is kind of gone-minded, sonny, and you don't want him to crack you in two like a chicken bone."

The Fool Killer reached out his long arm and yanked me back. "I'll drop him in the woods with a mighty bash of my club."

"Fool Killer, don't get anxious," said Shagnasty John, regarding me with slow, crafty eyes. The whites were brown streaked like tobacco stains. "Who you traveling with?"

I'd forgot all about Glorietta gone to fetch Ma and Pa. "I'm purely alone!" I declared.

Shagnasty John snorted. "You don't tell me."

"Yes sir! I run away from home."

"Wearing shoes? And dressed for church? Sonny, you must figure I got no more brains than God gave geese. Fool Killer, see who else is scuttling about."

The Fool Killer let loose of me to peer out the wheelhouse windows. I leaped for the door, opened it, banged it shut behind me, and ran like a scared rabbit.

Shagnasty John and the Fool Killer ran thrashing through the cottonwoods after me. But I wasn't in the trees. I'd ducked under a boxed paddle wheel and snugged myself out of sight. But I couldn't stay there. I had to warn Pa.

My heart was banging away something fearful. I hardly waited to catch my breath before I slipped out of hiding, climbed the dry creek bank, and ducked into the trees. I could tell that Shagnasty John and the Fool Killer were some ways off. The crows were flapping over the treetops, following them.

I ran smack into a rope corral. It held two horses. *Their* horses, I thought.

I picked out the spotted mare, grabbed her mane, and heaved myself onto her back. Then I shot out of there lickety-quick.

And along came Pa and Ma and Glorietta! They were walking through the spring weeds, clear as bull's-eye targets, and not suspecting a thing.

"Go back!" I yelled. "Run!"

But they couldn't fathom what I was yelling about. Or what I was doing on horseback.

Finally I pulled up and slipped off the mare's back. I could hardly believe I'd got this far without Shagnasty John drawing his gun and filling the air with lead.

I danced the horse around broadside to the trees so that we could shelter ourselves behind her.

"There are terrible outlaws back there!" I burst out. "They mean to kill us!"

Ma gave me a startled look. "Now really, Wiley. You must be imagining it."

"I suppose I'm imagining this horse!"

Pa gave the cottonwoods a tight-eyed gaze. "How do you know they're outlaws?"

"They told me, Pa. Shagnasty John and the Fool Killer. Every sheriff in the territories is looking for them. They're using the *Phoenix* for a hideout."

Ma's fingers had crept to her spidery lace collar. "Is Grandpa there?"

"No, Ma."

"There's no such man as the Fool Killer," Pa said.

"There is now, Pa. Peevish and meaner'n a hornet. Both of 'em."

"Wearing guns?"

"Shagnasty John is. The terror of the prairie, he said."

"Never heard of him." Pa stood calm as an owl at midnight. "It baffles me that he didn't pop some lead your way, Wiley. Especially since you rode off on one of their horses."

"He could have been afraid of shooting the mare," Ma said.

"Must have," I said. And yet, I thought, he'd had a clear shot when I'd busted out of the pilothouse—and maybe again before I'd reached the stairway.

"Downright peculiar," Pa remarked, more to himself than us.

"They're over in those trees," I said, pointing. "Where you see the crows. Watching us for sure. Hadn't we better edge back in a hurry?"

"Wiley, there's no place for us to run where they can't find us out here," Pa answered. "It seems to me they'd already be in full view and shooting up a hailstorm—if they could. It's unnatural. Unless their cartridge belts are empty. Did you notice?"

"No, sir."

But the Fool Killer would have armed himself with his bur-oak club, I thought. I glanced at Glorietta. I could see she was feeling scared about the Fool Killer and all the stories we'd heard.

Pa checked his pepperbox pistol. I peered under the horse's belly and spotted the crows. Shagnasty John and the Fool Killer were keeping themselves mouse-quiet.

"We've come this far and we're not turning back," Pa declared. "Not until we find out what happened to your grandfather. He might have left papers aboard. A logbook, certainly. I have an idea I can send those rascals packing." He handed Ma the short, six-barreled pistol. "Don't fire this bric-a-brac unless you've got no choice."

"Rufus," Ma exclaimed. "You're not going out there!"

"I promise you the terrors of the plains are going to be mighty glad to meet me." Pa gave us a wink. "I want all of you to stay put until I settle matters. Shouldn't take five minutes."

And he was gone. He went striding across the bare city limits of Sunrise, the knife-blade brim of his hat cocked at an angle.

Meindert DeJong

The Wheel on the School

Lina, the only girl among six schoolchildren in Shora, a Dutch fishing village, wrote a composition about storks in which she said, "I do not know much about storks because they never come to Shora." That set the pupils wondering. Why didn't storks come to Shora when they built nests on the roofs of neighboring villages? Storks brought good luck, and a fine thing it would be to have storks on every roof in Shora. Their teacher said, "Sometimes when we wonder we can make things happen." Things did begin to happen. The children worked hard searching the village for a wagon wheel to put on the schoolhouse roof so storks could build a nest on it. At times everything seemed to be against them, even the weather, but the children never gave up. In the selection below, the children scheme to get their fathers to help them. *The Wheel on the School* received the Newbery award in 1955. [From Meindert DeJong, *The Wheel on the School* (Harper, 1954).]

On Monday morning the storm hadn't stopped. It raged in fury against the dike. The sea was upended; the spume and roiled spindrift still flew high above the dike, landing in gray dirty flecks in the streets and on the roofs. If anything, the storm was more jerky and fitful. Odd sudden lulls seemed to fall momentarily between the high shrieks and moans of the wind, although behind the dike the sea thundered on. Enormous breakers hurled themselves up and washed in a last, thin, hissing line almost to the crest of the dike. Now and then the spent water of an unusually large wave managed to spill over the dike.

In the houses the fishermen sat loafing in the corners of their kitchens, behind the stoves if possible, to be out of the way of their busy wives and of their children getting ready for school. They were given no peace. In all Shora the fisherman fathers were pestered by their children. The wheel had to go up on the school, storm or no storm.

"Just suppose some storks came through tomorrow," Lina argued with her father in the kitchen.

"Yes, just suppose and suppose," her father barked back. "Just suppose you let me be nice and quiet in my little corner. It feels good to be dry and warm and to do nothing for a change."

"Yes, but just suppose the storm ends, then you'll be going out to sea again, and we won't have a wheel up on the roof of the school. There's nobody else but Janus and old Douwa, and they can't get on roofs."

"They're lucky!" her father said impatiently. "It'll be a long storm, I've told you. There's plenty of time. That storm isn't just going to shut off like a faucet. Can't I wait at least for a quieter day?" He disappeared behind his week-old newspaper, which, since he had been at sea for weeks, was news to him—news and a refuge to hide behind.

He was given no chance to read it. Lina's little sister, Linda, at that moment insisted on climbing into his lap, and on the other side of the newspaper Lina still argued with him. "The teacher said Saturday that if the wheel could go up today, there'd be no school. So we can all help you," she said to the newspaper. "With all of us helping, it shouldn't take long."

"What does that teacher know about wind and storms? Let him get on that roof in a storm then! And it's off to school with you right now. There'll come a quieter day before we can take off for sea again, and then we'll see. But off with you, so I can have a quiet day today."

It was final. Lina indignantly shoved her feet into her wooden shoes. She knew better than to argue further. She had gone as far as she dared. She buttoned her jacket tightly up around her throat and stamped out of the house.

"Listen, Jella, how often do I have to tell you? I'm not stirring from this house today, and that's final. A man ought to have a couple days of rest after weeks out at sea without having to sit on top of a school. Now beat it! Get in that school and learn something instead of sitting on top of it."

"But the teacher said there'd be no school today if we put the wheel up."

"Well, you can't get the wheel up in this storm, so there is school, and I say so. Or do I have to take you there by the scruff of your neck and the seat of your pants?"

Jella shoved his feet disgustedly into his

wooden shoes and slammed the door hard behind him.

"Listen, Pier and Dirk—that's the trouble with twins, a man gets a double dose of everything—one more yammer or argument out of the two of you, and I'll knock your two heads together so hard you'll be lucky if you have one head left between you. Even so, that ought to be enough—you don't use your two heads. The answer is: No, No, NO! NO wheel on NO school in NO storm!"

"But we'd help all you men. The teacher said no school if . . ."

"And I say there is school, and you two will be in it if only so I don't have to hear another word about storks. On your way!"

Pier and Dirk looked at each other. They glumly shoved their feet into their shoes and moved to the door, muttering dire things to each other. Behind his week-old newspaper their father sat grinning at their fuming threats. "Learn your lesson well today," he teased them. "I hear it's going to be about storks."

"Just so it isn't about lazy, stubborn fishermen," Pier said stormily. Afraid he'd said too much, he scooted to the door with Dirk close behind him. Their father rustled the newspaper. Dirk pushed Pier through the door and almost tumbled over him to get out as fast as he could. The door fell shut.

"Listen, Auka, don't you ever let up on me? If I hear another word about another stork, I'll . . . I'll take your neck and stretch it until you look like a stork. Then *you* can go and sit up on a wheel on top of a roof. Storks got more sense than to do that in a storm. How do you expect me to lug a wheel up that roof in a storm? I haven't got wings! And if I should slide down a slippery roof in this high wind and land on my head, who's going to earn the money so you can go to school and fool around with storks? You get to that school!"

"But there is no school if we put the wheel up."

"Well, nobody is going to put that wheel up today, so there is school. Bye, Auka."

There was nothing left for Auka to do but to put his shoes on and move off silently.

His father watched him. "If you stick that lower lip out much farther in your pout, you can put that wagon wheel on there instead of on the roof," he teased.

Auka said a few wicked things to himself and looked stonily at his father as he closed the door very slowly to let in as much wind and draft as possible.

Eelka's father, sitting dozily beside the stove in the kitchen, peered around his newspaper to watch Eelka slowly putting on his shoes, buttoning his jacket, and pulling up the collar. "Where do you think you're going, son?"

"To school," Eelka said. "It's Monday, you know, but it's much too stormy to put that wheel up on the roof of the school today. So I suppose it'll be school." He sighed. "I never did have much luck. Bye, Pop."

Eelka hunched himself to meet the wind that was driving down the street. Ahead of him were all the other school children, bent over, boring into the wind. Unwilling and angry and defeated, each one walked alone on the hard way to school. No one hurried to catch up with any of the others; each one hated to have to admit that he'd gone down in defeat. And Eelka was too slow and far behind and full of breakfast to make the effort.

It had been a scheme, hatched and planned after church yesterday. That was what Pier and Dirk had said to do about fathers—pester them until they gave in. If all the children worked at it, nagged and pleaded . . . Oh, your father would growl and act angry and make wisecracks, but that's the way men are, different from mothers. You didn't get to know your father very well—always out at sea—but that's the way it had to be done. Joke a little and tease and nag, and nag and tease. Wait and see! In spite of what your father said or growled, sooner or later he'd do what you wanted.

Some of the others had had their misgivings, Eelka especially. He'd said that *his* father would say, "Oh, sure, Eelka," and then not do it. But Pier and Dirk had knowingly assured them all that it was much easier than with mothers. You'd get a sound box on the ear from your mother if you kept on pestering her like that. But then your mother had you yapping around her all the time so she had less patience.

The others, all but Eelka, had been easily convinced, especially since the success of the scheme meant that not only would the wheel be put up on the school, but they'd also have the rest of the day free from lessons. It was worth a good try. But Eelka had said his father was just too good-natured, he wouldn't be pestered.

The scheme had failed miserably. Now each child on his way to school hated to admit to the others that he had failed, not knowing that the others had failed just as completely.

The storm was never going to stop. They knew it! There wouldn't be a stork left after this storm. Everything was hopeless and useless. Even if there should be one or two storks left over from the storm, what was the good of that? There'd be no wheel on the school anyway— just because of their fathers.

They had to face each other in the portal of the school. It was cold in the portal, but at least here they were sheltered from the vicious wind. They all made great pretense of blowing and stamping and beating their arms; they all breathed heavily. "Whew, what a wind!" somebody said. The others said nothing. They eyed each other while they flailed their arms across their chests in a great pretense of cold and chill.

Finally Jella turned on Dirk and Pier as the authors of the scheme. "Well," he demanded, "is your dad coming?"

Pier and Dirk looked at each other. "No-oo," Pier admitted slowly. "I guess not."

That cleared the air. "Mine isn't either. You should have heard him!"

"Neither is mine. He isn't coming at all. Said he'd just as soon try to sail the sea in a bushel basket in this storm as sit on the sharp roof of this school. Now maybe—he said—if we had a saddle, he might try it. But what good was a fisherman split in two on the ridge of a sharp roof in a high wind? The two halves of him—he didn't think—could go out fishing afterwards and catch double the amount of fish."

In spite of themselves they all laughed at the sally. Now that they'd all admitted failure, they tried to outdo each other in repeating what their fathers had said. Now they could laugh about it. And Eelka didn't say "What did I tell you?" He was laughing too hard.

Jella summed it up for all of them. "Guess it *is* too windy for old men like our dads."

The teacher suddenly stood in the doorway.

Lina burst out with it for the group. "None of our fathers—not a single one—would come," she said. "Not a one would get from behind the stove. There they sit, baking!"

"So," the teacher said. "So is that the grievance? Wise men, I'd say. You'll have to learn, too, sooner or later, that you can't defy a storm—that you can't hurt a wall with just your head. So let's go inside; let's start right in on our lessons to get our minds on other things. Your fathers will come through. You know that. If not today, the first possible day that the storm will let them. They'll put up the wheel before they set out to sea again."

"Did they tell you that?" Lina asked eagerly.

"No, they didn't tell me. I know that. And all of you ought to know it, too. Fathers always come through when it's possible. It's the way of fathers and mothers. You're just impatient, but the wheel can wait now. The storks will be waiting out the storm. Let's be just as patient and wise as the storks."

The lessons didn't go too well in spite of the teacher's reassurances. The wind, howling and shrieking around the corners of the exposed school, kept reminding them of the storm sweeping across the sea and the land. The wagon wheel leaning against the blackboard kept reminding them of storks. The howl of the wind made it difficult to understand the teacher and made it even more difficult to concentrate on answers. Who could think out arithmetic problems when hundreds of storks coming from Africa were maybe going down in the sea? How many storks would drown and never come to Shora? That was the outrageous arithmetic problem the wind seemed to be howling at them.

The teacher asked Auka how much sixteen times sixteen were. Auka had to jerk his attention away from the window where a tuft of hay was held against the glass by the relentless wind.

"There won't be a single stork can come through a storm like this," Auka answered.

Nobody smiled at Auka's mistake. All eyes went anxiously to the window and from the window to the huge wagon wheel leaning against the front blackboard. Even the teacher looked somber.

"It's getting still worse," somebody in a back seat muttered.

"It only seems that way," the teacher said slowly, "because we feel so helpless. Because we're just sitting still and doing nothing about the wheel. Inaction is hard, and still, Auka, the only problem before us that we can do anything about is: How much are sixteen times sixteen?"

There was a long pause. Auka had to jerk his mind from his own inside woes, and then figure out the answer. He got it wrong.

"Oh," he said moodily to himself, "I thought he said sixteen times eighteen."

Nobody but Auka cared that his answer was wrong. Not even the teacher! The teacher himself was standing listening to the sounds outside. The wind seemed to be making new noises. Muttering, grumbling noises penetrated the classroom door. Outside the portal there was a sound as of something crashing down. Now there were stumbling noises in the portal. The wind must have blown something in and was rolling it around.

Everybody's head was cocked toward the classroom door. There came a hard knock. There were voices.

"Our dads!" Lina cried.

The teacher hurried to open the door. There stood the men of Shora. "It isn't sane. It's insane," one of the men said to the teacher. It sounded like Eelka's father. "First the kids nag you every waking minute, so you chase the kids off to school. What happens then? Their mothers start in on you! Nobody's got anything on the brain but those blasted storks on that wagon wheel. Well, they nagged us all out of our houses, so we got together and decided it was less grief putting up that wheel than facing a bunch of nagging women and children."

The teacher grinned at the men. "Solomon found that out a few thousand years before you. Didn't he in his Proverbs say that it was better to sit on the roof of a house than with a nagging woman inside the house?"

Auka's father turned to the men behind him. "Did you hear that? If his wives had even wise old Solomon up on a roof, what are a few dumb fishermen going to do?"

"Get on the roof with Solomon," somebody said in the portal. "He knew when he was licked."

The schoolroom tittered. The men were joking, and, in spite of the storm, they were going to try to put the wheel up. And they weren't unhappy about it—you could tell that—not if they were making wisecracks. That was always a good sign.

Jella's hefty father peered over the head of the teacher into the classroom. "It seems I was told," he boomed, "that part of the deal was that if we put that wheel on the roof, there'd be no school today. Was I correctly informed, or was that just Jella and his endless love for school?"

"No-oo," the whole room sang out. "No school. *He* promised!"

They did not wait for the teacher so much as to nod his head; they could see it in his face—anything went today. They streamed from the room and got into jackets and stocking caps and wooden shoes.

From the portal they saw that their fathers had even brought ladders and lumber and ropes. The stuff lay in a helter-skelter pile in the schoolyard where it had been dropped.

"Out of the way! Out of the way all you mortals," Jella came shouting. Jella alone had remembered. He had jumped to the front of the room to get the wagon wheel instead of just rushing out with the rest. Now he sent the wheel rolling wildly into the portal. Everybody had to scatter. The wheel wobbled in an uncertain path, somehow found the outside doorway, plunged into the yard, and settled itself on the pile of beams and ropes and ladders.

"Well, it's all here now," a man shouted. "Now roll out your storks."

The men laughed, but not the children. Happy and relieved and eager as they were, now that their fathers were actually going to put up the wheel, it was not a good joke.

The low, sweeping sky, scudding and racing with clouds that looked as angry as capped waves on the sea, threatened bad things. There was nothing in the sky but storm; there wasn't a bird anywhere, not even a sparrow. A rain squall slashed down. The wind hurled the rain into the portal.

"Will there be any storks left after a storm like this?" Dirk asked the group of men around the pile in the schoolyard.

The men looked up at the sky and shrugged. "Maybe, if the storm doesn't hang on too long," Lina's father said. "Maybe a couple of them will have sense enough to go bury their heads in sand until this blows over."

"That's ostriches!" Lina, standing right beside him, said scornfully. She was half-ashamed of the ignorance of her father—and right before the teacher! "Ostriches are *supposed* to bury their heads in the sand, only they don't."

"I guess that takes care of you and your ostriches," Eelka's father said.

"Yeah," Lina's father said, nettled. "Maybe I'd better go bury my head in some sand. These modern-day school kids—they know everything, don't they? Me, all I know is fish." He grinned suddenly. "You kids wouldn't be satisfied with a couple of fish on the roof?" he asked plaintively. "Say a couple of sharks in a wash tub?"

The children hooted, and he grinned broadly. He sobered, stepped back, and eyed the sharp school roof. "Well, come on you Solomons," he said impatiently. "Let's get on the roof and get that wheel up."

The men stood studying the steep roof. "Wet and steep and windy, it'll be slipperier than a deckful of jellyfish," one of them said. "But up with a ladder, and we'll see what the climate is up there."

Two men raised the long ladder high and straight. As they carried it upright around a corner of the school, a blast of wind caught the high ladder. The two men struggled, but they couldn't hold it up. The ladder swayed and twisted and threatened to come crashing down. Everybody stood anxiously watching the top of the ladder, expecting it to smash to pieces against the ground at any moment. "Watch it.

Watch it," somebody yelled. "If you can't even set a ladder up, how do you expect to get a wheel up there? Get into it all of you; don't stand there staring at the top rung. Let it down! Let it down, I say. There. Now carry it flat around that windy corner. That isn't a flag you're carrying in a parade."

It was Janus! There he came in his wheel chair, forcing it ahead against the wind by sheer strength and at the same time loudly scolding everybody.

The men let the ladder down. Then they turned to face Janus, a bit peeved at being bawled out before their own children. But Janus was grinning broadly; he was having a fine time in spite of the wind and the struggle to move against it. He rolled up to the group in his wheel chair. "When it comes to doing anything on land, you guys are about as helpless as the fish are," he told them. He turned his chair so as to face the roof. "Now then, let's use our heads. Better yet, I'll use my head."

"So now we've got an overseer," one of the men said.

"All right, now lay that ladder down," Janus directed. "Place one end against the wall, then raise the other end. Get under it; walk your hands from spoke to spoke until it's up straight against the wall. Then all you have to do is pull out the bottom end. See, that way you don't fight the wind."

"Well, that worked," one of the men said.

When the ladder was up, the men automatically turned to Janus for further instruction. Janus looked at the pile of lumber and the one ladder beside it.

"Now the other ladder and push it up on the roof. But first tie a coil of rope on the top rung, so you can let the rope down the other side of the roof to fasten the ladder down. Then lash the second ladder to the first, otherwise the wind will just sweep it right off the roof. Meanwhile, you kids get me that wagon wheel."

While he waited for the children to roll the big wheel to him, Janus kept looking at the pile of beams and boards still lying in the schoolyard. "What's the big pile for?" he yelled up to the roof.

"To brace up the wheel. Got to have some brackets or braces or something to hold the wheel on the sharp ridge of this roof," Auka's father explained.

"Yeah, but you're just going to have storks up there, not elephants," Janus said scornfully. "The way I've doped it out—that wheel's got to be up there nice and simple. With all your beams and boards and two-by-fours sticking in every direction, storks flying overhead will think it's a trap, not a nest. But just get on with that ladder, Janus will fix it nice and neat and simple."

"Yes, sir, yes, sir," Auka's father said. "Up with the second ladder, men, Janus says."

Jella, Auka, and Lina rolled the wagon wheel before Janus. "Now where's that saw?" Janus said impatiently. "Somewhere I hung a saw on this wheel chair contraption."

"There it is," Pier said behind him. "You brought a hammer, too. You're sitting on it."

"The hammer, too," Janus said. "The hammer first." Then paying no attention to the alarmed looks of the children, he took the hammer and drove the steel rim off the inner wooden rim of the wheel. After studying the pitch of the roof and the ridge, he began sawing a deep V into the side of the wooden rim. The children had to hold the wheel steady for him while he sawed. "See, I'll cut two deep V's; that way the rim will fit snug on the ridge," he explained. "Then we'll fit the iron rim just partly over the wooden one so it won't cover the V notches. The iron doesn't have to cover the whole wooden rim—this wheel isn't going rolling any place—it'll even be better that way. With the iron rim sticking up, it'll make a sort of pan of the wheel—storks are awfully sloppy nest builders. This may help them to hold all the stuff they'll lug up on this wheel."

The teacher came up. "Janus, don't you want to go inside? No sense in your sitting here in the wind when you can do your work just as well inside."

"If those men can sit on that windy roof, I can sit here where it's practically cozy," Janus said shortly, his whole grim attention on his sawing.

The teacher, realizing Janus wanted no favors, said no more. "Anything I can do?" he asked. "I feel sort of useless with everybody else busy."

"Well, I need a brace and bit—a long bit so it will go through the ridge boards on both sides of the roof."

"My dad's got a brace and all kinds of bits, all sizes," Jella said eagerly. "I'll go get them."

"Well, there goes Jella and the job you had for me," the teacher said.

"Hold it," Janus said. "I also need two heavy iron rods—long enough so the two edges of the wheel rim can rest on them. You see, we'll drill the holes through the ridge, shove the rods through them, and then rest the wheel on the rods. The two notches I cut in the wooden rim will fit snugly over the ridge. Then all we'll need to do is to wire the rim to the two supporting rods, and there'll be the wheel, steady and level and solid as a house. But I can't think of anybody in Shora who would have a couple of heavy rods like that."

"Hah!" the teacher said. "You're talking to the right man. It seems to me I've seen a couple of rods like that in the tower when I go there to ring the bell. I'm almost sure."

"Just so they're long enough," Janus said.

"I'll go look, and nobody can take this job away from me. As the official bellringer for the village, I'm the only one to have a key to the tower." The teacher pulled the big ancient key out of his pocket and held it up. He hurried off.

"Glad I found something for him to do," Janus said to Lina. "He makes me nervous watching so closely. He's just as jittery and excited as you kids." He had finished cutting the notches. Now came the job of fitting the iron rim partially over the wooden rim. The boys and Lina had all they could do to hold the wheel upright and steady as Janus struggled with the close-fitting rim.

Jella returned with the brace and all the bits. A few minutes later the teacher came back with two large, rusty rods. Janus studied the rods. "They should do. Good and thick and solid. Plenty long enough for the wheel. Good thing you remembered them," he said to the teacher. "It must be the only pair of loose rods in Shora. It was the one thing had me worried—me with my fine plans and no rods. I'd have been the laughing-stock around here."

Jella was sent up the ladder to carry the brace and bit to his father. The teacher was sent off to find some heavy wire that could be used to secure the wheel to the rods. "Got to keep him busy," Janus said with a sly wink at Lina.

At last the wheel was ready. The children rolled it to the ladder. The men began hoisting the huge wagon wheel up the ladder, while Jella's father drilled the two holes for the rods in the ridge of the roof.

It was a slow, hard struggle against the tugging of the wind. Two of the fishermen now straddled the ridge, ready to lift the wheel on to the rods when it reached them. A sudden hard hail and rain squall slashed down again. The men straddling the ridge had to press themselves flat; they lay with faces against the roof and clung with one hand to the ladder. The men working the wheel up the roof had to stop and be content just to hold the wheel in place on the ladder. The squall passed as suddenly as it had come, and the struggle went on again.

Janus watched every move with eagle eyes. He was so intent he seemed unaware of the sweep of wind and rain and hail. Yet from time to time Janus glanced down the road to the village. Suddenly he bellowed out, "Look at that, men! Look what's coming! The women! What do you know? Wind or hail—here come the women. Pots of hot coffee for you. This is going to turn into a picnic. Hurray for women!"

All work stopped on the roof. Everybody sat looking down the road; they called the women on. The women came in a close group, trying to protect their steaming coffee from the cold wind. Then a new blast of hail had the men hanging on to the roof and the ladders again.

The moment the squall passed, they looked down the road again. "No use looking," Janus shouted. "No hot coffee, no nothing, until that wheel is up and secure."

"Janus, you're a slave driver," one of the men on the ridge complained. "All you need is a whip."

"Don't need a whip," Janus called back. "Got my tongue."

"Yeah," Pier and Dirk's father yelled down. "Too bad that shark didn't get your tongue instead of your legs."

Down below Janus flushed red and embarrassed. He looked away and then glowered up from under the peak of his cap to see how Pier's father had meant the joke. Pier's father saw the look; he gave Janus a good-natured grin. All of Janus eased in the chair. He let out his breath. "Well, all I can tell you is," he called out slowly, "that shark *was* eyeing my tongue. Got a good look at it, too—all I was telling him! But it looked too tough even for him, I guess. He must have decided my sea boots were tenderer. So he took my boots. How could that poor dumb fish know my legs were inside of them?"

Everybody laughed, and Janus sat back, relieved. He seemed to test the laugh, almost as if he were tasting it. Then he looked at Pier, hovering anxiously beside his chair. "Good kid," he said. "Don't think I don't know everybody's accepting that crazy story because it's good for me. And it is good!" he added fiercely. "Good."

The wheel was being fitted over the ridge. Janus riveted his whole attention on the operation. "It's got to work, my idea with just two rods," he muttered anxiously. "Otherwise my name is mud. They'll razz me out of Shora."

The teacher came hurrying up with a handful of wires. Janus picked out the heaviest and sent Pier up the ladder with them. "Nothing more for you to do," Janus told the teacher. "But the women have hot coffee on the stove in the schoolroom. Go get yourself a cup. You aren't used to being out in this kind of weather."

"Aye, aye, sir," the teacher said. He saluted smartly and trotted off.

Jella's father, lying full-length on the ladder on the roof, was twisting the wire around the rods and the rim of the wheel. It was awkward, slow, overhead work. The cold and the salt, stinging wind were numbing all the men and slowing their movements. The two men straddling the ridge were holding the wheel in place. One of them had to let go his hold to rest his numbed arm. He wearily rubbed a hand over his face to wipe away the icy wetness. He took a new hold, but now the wheel was tilted.

"Jan, hold that wheel straight," Janus said. "Those storks need a nest, not a chute."

"Look," Jan answered irritably, before he gave a thought to what he was saying, "if you think you can do it better, you come up here and hold it."

There was an awkward, stunned pause. Everybody looked at Janus. Lina, beside his chair, laid her hand on Janus' shoulder. But to her astonishment Janus was delighted. "Did you hear that?" he asked Lina. "He forgot I've got no legs. Bless his ornery old hide. That's the way it's got to be."

Now Jan, who had been preoccupied with the wheel and his precarious position, realized what he'd said. He looked down at Janus. A slow grin spread over his face. "Stay there," he said. "I'm not giving you a chance to come up here and show me up. I'll show you I'm as much a man as you are."

He hadn't apologized or even tried to cover it up. They were treating Janus man to man. He was one of them again. Janus bent low to straighten out the pin in his folded-over trousers leg. He fumbled with it. When he straightened up, his eyes were bright. "Bless his ornery old hide," he mumbled.

Lina took her hand off his shoulder. Even she mustn't baby Janus.

"Would you dare?" Janus asked suddenly. "We've got to test that wheel, and you're the only one who is about the weight of two storks. I've got to know whether it'll hold their nest without tilting or wobbling. The men will hold you up on the wheel."

Janus wasn't babying her either. "Sure," Lina said stoutly.

On the ridge Jan held Lina's hand as she climbed on the wheel. Janus directed from down below. Lina walked along the rim of the wheel as far as Jan could reach and still keep his hold on her. Janus watched her closely. "You can come down now," he said. "It'll hold. It didn't so much as stir, even with you walking on the edge. Everybody down now! Take the ropes and ladders down and go get your coffee."

Lina made use of that moment of distraction to pull free from Jan's hand. She climbed up on the hub of the wheel. She flapped her arms. "I'm a stork, I'm a stork," she cried. The next moment a gust of wind caught her, and she had to let herself fall, clutching for the spokes of the wheel and grabbing wildly for Jan's outstretched hand. She hung on for dear life.

"Some stork!" the boys jeered up at her. "Let's see you fly down."

"Jan, come on down and bring that stork with you under your arm," Janus said, "before she tries to fly. I wouldn't put it past her."

It was a picnic—steaming coffee and cakes and fatballs. It was a feast! Hot chocolate milk for the boys and Lina! That was what made it really a picnic and a feast. You had hot chocolate milk only on the Queen's Birthday and fatballs only on Santa Claus Day. But now fatballs and chocolate all the same day! And the rest of the day free—it was a holiday.

The school room buzzed. Janus was in the midst of it in his wheel chair. His voice carried above all the others. But everybody was in high spirits. They'd wrestled the wheel up on the roof in spite of storm and cold and hail and squalls. It made it a holiday.

No school the rest of the day, and their fathers home with games to play. They'd all play dominoes with their dads. The five boys and Lina decided it among themselves as they sat in their seats, sipping hot chocolate while the grownups crowded around the warm stove.

It happened so seldom, having their fathers home. Always they were out at sea or, if home, busy with nets and sails and the readying of the boats. Now they'd have almost a whole day with their dads. The storm had made it a holiday for them, a chance for games and jokes with their fathers.

Everybody was talking and Janus was in the midst of everything. Now he noticed the boys and Lina in their corner. "How is it?" he asked. "Is this a feast or isn't it?"

"Hot chocolate milk and hot fatballs!" Pier told him smartly. "Hey, Janus, all it lacks is some cherries."

Janus laughed. "To get them you'd have to go where the wind took them—over a couple of provinces or so, I think, or maybe into Germany. Well, there're a few under the tree, if you like salt cherries."

Lina hastily told the boys that she was going to ask Janus to play dominoes, too. He and Jana had no children. Janus ought to be invited, too. They all agreed eagerly; they all wanted Janus in their houses.

"Oh, no, you don't," Lina said. "I thought of it first!"

Lois Lowry

Anastasia Krupnik

A popular contemporary heroine, Anastasia is a thoughtful, sensitive, and spunky ten-year-old with refreshingly pleasant parents. Her everyday activities reflect the common concerns and interests of prepubescent children and the wide emotional swings of a child on the edge of adolescence. She falls in puppy love for the first time; she is resentful that her parents are having a second child; and she struggles to express herself at school and to understand memory, emotion, and her ambivalent feelings, a mixture of fear and sorrow, toward her aged grandmother. The changing list Anastasia keeps of the things she loves and hates unifies the book's episodic structure. [From Lois Lowry, *Anastasia Krupnik* (Houghton Mifflin, 1979).]

"The Macy's parade is the most boring thing I have ever seen," said Anastasia gloomily, "and I hate Thanksgiving."

Her mother opened the oven door, poked a fork into the turkey skin so that juice ran out and made a hissing noise. "You like turkey," she said.

"Yeah. But we could have turkey any time. I hate the Macy's parade, and after that I hate the football games, and also I hate pumpkin pie. Why do you have to make pumpkin pie on Thanksgiving? Is there a *rule* somewhere that you have to make pumpkin pie on Thanksgiving? If you want to know the truth, pumpkin pie smells like throw-up. It's gross."

"Anastasia Krupnik, *you* are being gross, and if you don't get out of this kitchen I'm going to throw something at you, maybe a pumpkin pie. Go. Go talk to your grandmother."

Anastasia muttered something as she left the kitchen.

"What did you say?" her mother called.

"Nothing," she called back. What she had muttered was, "I hate my grandmother."

Anastasia's grandmother was ninety-two. Nobody else's grandmother was ninety-two.

Robert Giannini's grandmother was fifty; she played the Hammond Organ in a bar and lounge. She wore false eyelashes, Robert said, and called out, "All *riiight,*" when the TV showed closeups of the cheerleaders during Thanksgiving football games.

Jennifer MacCauley's grandmother was fat, worked in a bakery, and brought home all the unsold cookies at the end of each day. "Weight Watchers here I come," Jennifer MacCauley's grandmother always said, and laughed.

But Anastasia's grandmother was ninety-two and lived in a nursing home. The wrinkles on the side of her mouth were scabby. She talked with her mouth full, and what she said usually didn't make any sense, and there were food spots on the front of her dress.

She made Anastasia feel sad, and scared. Who needed *that?*

Anastasia wandered into the living room where her father was asleep on the couch with the *Boston Globe* open across his chest. In the corner by the window, her grandmother sat in a big chair, smoothing her dress across her lap over and over again with her thin hands. There were veins like cat's cradles pulled tight on the backs of her hands.

Anastasia sighed, sat down on the floor beside her grandmother, and said, "Hello, Grandmother," politely. She had already said hello four times since her father had brought her from the nursing home. But her grandmother forgot things.

The scary, clawlike hands smoothed her hair. Funny how soft and nice that felt. If she didn't look at the hands it was okay. If she just looked at her grandmother's moist, kind eyes, everything seemed almost okay.

"What's your name? You have such pretty hair."

"Anastasia." She had already told her that, again and again. Most people remembered their grandchildren's names, she thought angrily, and also their birthdays.

"My boy's hair is this color. His name is Myron," said the old woman.

For pete's sake, thought Anastasia. Myron is forty-five years old, asleep on the couch, and he's bald.

"Myron is a good boy," her grandmother said

dreamily. "Better than his brothers. Myron always does his homework. Do you do your homework, little girl?"

"Mostly I do. But I don't like arithmetic much."

"Myron is the youngest, so I spoil him a little. His brothers are all so much older and they like to tease."

Anastasia glanced at her father and tried to imagine him little, being teased by big brothers. It was hard. His mouth was open, and he was snoring a little; his glasses were pushed up on his forehead, scrunching his eyebrows. His feet stuck out beyond the end of the couch, almost touching the Swedish ivy that grew in the deep blue pot. Dr. Myron Krupnik was six feet four inches tall.

"Your little boy Myron is my father," she said politely to her grandmother, hoping that her grandmother would understand.

But her grandmother just stroked her hair some more with the skinny hands, and stared out through the window. "Do you have a brother, little girl?"

Anastasia sighed. "Not yet," she said. "But in March I will. My mother and father said that I could name him. What names do you like, Grandmother?"

Not that it mattered. Anastasia still had the name that she had chosen, written in the secret place in the back of her green notebook. She hadn't changed her mind about the name. It would serve the baby right. Also her parents.

"Sam," said her grandmother. "Sam is a good name."

Yuck, thought Anastasia. Sam.

The old woman leaned forward suddenly and whispered. "Sam's hands fit around my waist," she said, "and do you know, he can pick me right up and swing me around in the air? Sometimes he tickles me on the back of the neck with his mustache.

"But he doesn't come back anymore. I wonder where Sam is," she said. "Do you know where he went?" She sat back stiffly, and looked around. "Is he invited? Is he coming today?"

"No," said Anastasia. "I guess he couldn't come."

Her grandmother looked back out through the window, leaning forward to see down the street. Her eyes were curious and almost happy. "He might come," she said. "Sometimes he surprises me."

She began to talk to herself, words that Anastasia didn't understand, and to smooth the lap of her dress once more. Anastasia got up and went back to the kitchen. Her mother was stirring gravy.

"Did you invite someone named Sam for dinner?" she asked her mother. "Grandmother says someone named Sam might come. There aren't enough places set."

Her mother tasted the gravy and added a little salt. "She's daydreaming," she told Anastasia. "Sam was your grandfather. He died before you were born. She forgets that."

"I forget it, too. Maybe I'm as bad as she is," said Anastasia, though she didn't believe it. "You want me to carry in the plates and put them on the table?"

"Sure. Put the one with the blue flowers at Grandmother's place. That's always been her favorite."

The plate with the blue flowers had a crack in it that was turning brown along its length. It had lasted a lot of Thanksgivings. But it was going to break one of these days.

"Are you going to have to mash up her turkey and then we all have to watch her mushing it around, like last year?"

"Your eating habits aren't that terrific either, my friend," her mother said.

"She dribbles cranberry sauce on her dress, and she talks with her mouth full. I hate that."

Her mother didn't say anything.

"And she forgets my name. I hate that, too."

Her mother didn't say anything. She put mashed potatoes into a yellow bowl. Anastasia started to cry. A salt-flavored tear came down the side of her face and into the corner of her mouth; she tasted it with the tip of her tongue, and waited for the next one.

"I don't hate grandmother," she said in a voice that had to find its way out lopsided, around the tears. "But I hate it that she's so old.

"It makes my heart hurt."

Her mother took a paper napkin from the

kitchen table, knelt on the floor beside Anastasia, daubed at her wet cheeks with the napkin, and put her arms around her.

"All of our hearts hurt," she said. They went together to wake up Anastasia's father, and the three of them helped the grandmother to the table, where they sat her in the best chair, the one with arms. They all smiled when the old woman recognized her favorite plate, touched the blue flowers fondly, and said, "Forget-me-nots."

Johanna Spyri

Heidi

Heidi is one of the best-loved characters in children's literature. When she was five years old she was taken up the Alm Mountain in the Swiss Alps to live with her old grandfather, and she quickly won her way into his heart. In the chapter given below, Heidi goes up to the mountain pastures for the first time with Peter, the herdboy. *Heidi* was first published in 1880 and was translated into English from the German by Louise Brooks in 1884.

In the Pasture

Heidi was awakened early the next morning by a loud whistle; the sun was shining through the round window and falling in golden rays on her bed and on the large heap of hay, and as she opened her eyes everything in the loft seemed gleaming with gold. She looked around her in astonishment and could not imagine for a while where she was. But her grandfather's deep voice was now heard outside, and then Heidi began to recall all that had happened; how she had come away from her former home, and was now on the mountain with her grandfather instead of with old Ursula. The latter was nearly stone deaf and always felt cold, so that she sat all day either by the hearth in the kitchen or by the sitting-room stove, and Heidi had been obliged to stay close to her, for the old woman was so deaf that she could not tell where the child was if out of her sight. And Heidi, shut up within the four walls, had often longed to be out of doors. So she felt very happy this

morning as she woke up in her new home and remembered all the many new things that she had seen the day before and which she would see again that day, and above all she thought with delight of the two dear goats. Heidi jumped quickly out of bed and a very few minutes sufficed her to put on the clothes which she had taken off the night before, for there were not many of them. Then she climbed down the ladder and ran outside the hut. There stood Peter already with his flock of goats, and the grandfather was just bringing his two out of the shed to join the others. Heidi ran forward to wish good-morning to him and the goats.

"Do you want to go with them onto the mountain?" asked her grandfather. Nothing could have pleased Heidi better, and she jumped for joy in answer.

"But you must first wash and make yourself tidy. The sun that shines so brightly overhead will else laugh at you for being dirty; see, I have put everything ready for you," and her grandfather pointed, as he spoke, to a large tub full of water, which stood in the sun before the door. Heidi ran to it and began splashing and rubbing, till she quite glistened with cleanliness. The grandfather meanwhile went inside the hut, calling to Peter to follow him and bring in his wallet. Peter obeyed with astonishment, and laid down the little bag which held his meager dinner.

"Open it," said the old man, and inside it he put a large piece of bread and an equally large piece of cheese, which made Peter open his eyes, for each was twice the size of the two portions which he had for his own dinner.

"There, now there is only the little bowl to add," continued the grandfather, "for the child cannot drink her milk as you do from the goat; she is not accustomed to that. You must milk two bowlfuls for her when she has her dinner, for she is going with you and will remain with you till you return this evening: but take care she does not fall over any of the rocks, do you hear?"

Heidi now came running in. "Will the sun laugh at me now, grandfather?" she asked anxiously. Her grandfather had left a coarse towel hanging up for her near the tub, and with this she had so thoroughly scrubbed her face, arms, and neck, for fear of the sun, that as she stood there she was as red all over as a lobster. He gave a little laugh.

"No, there is nothing for him to laugh at now," he assured her. "But I tell you what— when you come home this evening, you will have to get right into the tub, like a fish, for if you run about like the goats you will get your feet dirty. Now you can be off."

She started joyfully for the mountain. During the night the wind had blown away all the clouds; the dark blue sky was spreading overhead, and in its midst was the bright sun shining down on the green slopes of the mountain, where the flowers opened their little blue and yellow cups, and looked up to him smiling. Heidi went running hither and thither and shouting with delight, for here were whole patches of delicate red primroses, and there the blue gleam of the lovely gentian, while above them all laughed and nodded the tender-leaved golden cistus. Enchanted with all this waving field of brightly-colored flowers, Heidi forgot even Peter and the goats. She ran on in front and then off to the side, tempted first one way and then the other, as she caught sight of some bright spot of glowing red or yellow. And all the while she was plucking whole handfuls of the flowers which she put into her little apron, for she wanted to take them all home and stick them in the hay, so that she might make her bedroom look just like the meadows outside. Peter had therefore to be on the alert, and his round eyes, which did not move very quickly, had more work than they could well manage, for the goats were as lively as Heidi; they ran in all directions, and Peter had to follow whistling and calling and swinging his stick to get all the runaways together again.

"Where have you got to now, Heidi?" he called out somewhat crossly.

"Here," called back a voice from somewhere. Peter could see no one, for Heidi was seated on the ground at the foot of a small hill thickly overgrown with sweet-smelling prunella; the whole air seemed filled with its fragrance, and Heidi thought she had never smelt anything so delicious. She sat surrounded by the flowers, drawing in deep breaths of the scented air.

"Come along here!" called Peter again. "You are not to fall over the rocks, your grandfather gave orders that you were not to do so."

"Where are the rocks?" asked Heidi, answering him back. But she did not move from her seat, for the scent of the flowers seemed sweeter to her with every breath of wind that wafted it towards her.

"Up above, right up above. We have a long way to go yet, so come along! And on the topmost peak of all the old bird of prey sits and croaks."

That did it. Heidi immediately sprang to her feet and ran up to Peter with her apron full of flowers.

"You have got enough now," said the boy as they began climbing up again together. "You will stay here for ever if you go on picking, and if you gather all the flowers now there will be none for tomorrow."

This last argument seemed a convincing one to Heidi, and moreover her apron was already so full that there was hardly room for another flower, and it would never do to leave nothing to pick for another day. So she now kept with Peter, and the goats also became more orderly in their behavior, for they were beginning to smell the plants they loved that grew on the higher slopes and clambered up now without pause in their anxiety to reach them. The spot where Peter generally halted for his goats to pasture and where he took up his quarters for the day lay at the foot of the high rocks, which were covered for some distance up by bushes and fir trees, beyond which rose their bare and rugged summits. On one side of the mountain the rock was split into deep clefts, and the grandfather had reason to warn Peter of danger. Having climbed as far as the halting-place, Peter unslung his wallet and put it carefully in a little hollow of the ground, for he knew what the wind was like up there and did not want to see his precious belongings sent rolling down the mountain by a sudden gust. Then he threw himself at full length on the warm ground, for he was tired after all his exertions.

Heidi meanwhile had unfastened her apron

and rolling it carefully round the flowers laid it beside Peter's wallet inside the hollow; she then sat down beside his outstretched figure and looked about her. The valley lay far below bathed in the morning sun. In front of her rose a broad snow-field, high against the dark-blue sky, while to the left was a huge pile of rocks on either side of which a bare lofty peak, that seemed to pierce the blue, looked frowningly down upon her. The child sat without moving, her eyes taking in the whole scene, and all around was a great stillness, only broken by soft, light puffs of wind that swayed the light bells of the blue flowers, and the shining gold heads of the cistus, and set them nodding merrily on their slender stems. Peter had fallen asleep after his fatigue and the goats were climbing about among the bushes overhead. Heidi had never felt so happy in her life before. She drank in the golden sunlight, the fresh air, the sweet smell of the flowers, and wished for nothing better than to remain there for ever. So the time went on, while to Heidi, who had so often looked up from the valley at the mountains above, these seemed now to have faces and to be looking down at her like old friends. Suddenly she heard a loud harsh cry overhead and lifting her eyes she saw a bird, larger than any she had ever seen before, with great, spreading wings, wheeling round and round in wide circles, and uttering a piercing, croaking kind of sound above her.

"Peter, Peter, wake up!" called out Heidi. "See, the great bird is there—look, look!"

Peter got up on hearing her call, and together they sat and watched the bird, which rose higher and higher in the blue air till it disappeared behind the gray mountain-tops.

"Where has it gone to?" asked Heidi, who had followed the bird's movements with intense interest.

"Home to its nest," said Peter.

"Is his home right up there? Oh, how nice to be up so high! Why does he make that noise?"

"Because he can't help it," explained Peter.

"Let us climb up there and see where his nest is," proposed Heidi.

"Oh! Oh! Oh!" exclaimed Peter, his disapproval of Heidi's suggestion becoming more marked with each ejaculation, "why, even the goats cannot climb as high as that, besides didn't Uncle say that you were not to fall over the rocks?"

Peter now began suddenly whistling and calling in such a loud manner that Heidi could not think what was happening; but the goats evidently understood his voice, for one after the other they came springing down the rocks until they were all assembled on the green plateau, some continuing to nibble at the juicy stems, others skipping about here and there or pushing at each other with their horns for pastime.

Heidi jumped up and ran in and out among them, for it was new to her to see the goats playing together like this and her delight was beyond words as she joined in their frolics; she made personal acquaintance with them all in turn, for they were like separate individuals to her, each single goat having a particular way of behavior of its own. Meanwhile Peter had taken the wallet out of the hollow and placed the pieces of bread and cheese on the ground in the shape of a square, the larger two on Heidi's side and the smaller on his own, for he knew exactly which were hers and which his. Then he took the little bowl and milked some delicious fresh milk into it from the white goat, and afterwards set the bowl in the middle of the square. Now he called Heidi to come, but she wanted more calling than the goats, for the child was so excited and amused at the capers and lively games of her new playfellows that she saw and heard nothing else. But Peter knew how to make himself heard, for he shouted till the very rocks above echoed his voice, and at last Heidi appeared, and when she saw the inviting repast spread out upon the ground she went skipping round it for joy.

"Leave off jumping about, it is time for dinner," said Peter; "sit down now and begin."

Heidi sat down. "Is the milk for me?" she asked giving another look of delight at the beautifully arranged square with the bowl as a chief ornament in the center.

"Yes," replied Peter, "and the two large pieces of bread and cheese are yours also, and when you have drunk up that milk, you are to have another bowlful from the white goat, and then it will be my turn."

"And which do you get your milk from?" inquired Heidi.

"From my own goat, the piebald one. But go on now with your dinner," said Peter, again reminding her it was time to eat. Heidi now took up the bowl and drank her milk, and as soon as she had put it down empty Peter rose and filled it again for her. Then she broke off a piece of her bread and held out the remainder, which was still larger than Peter's own piece, together with the whole big slice of cheese to her companion, saying "You can have that, I have plenty."

Peter looked at Heidi, unable to speak for astonishment, for never in all his life could he have said and done like that with anything he had. He hesitated a moment, for he could not believe that Heidi was in earnest; but the latter kept on holding out the bread and cheese, and as Peter still did not take, she laid it down on his knees. He saw then that she really meant it; he seized the food, nodded his thanks and acceptance of her present, and then made a more splendid meal than he had known ever since he was a goat-herd. Heidi the while still continued to watch the goats. "Tell me all their names," she said.

Peter knew these by heart, for having very little else to carry in his head he had no difficulty in remembering them. So he began, telling Heidi the name of each goat in turn as he pointed it out to her. Heidi listened with great attention, and it was not long before she could herself distinguish the goats from one another and could call each by name, for every goat had its own peculiarities which could not easily be mistaken; only one had to watch them closely, and this Heidi did. There was the great Turk with his big horns, who was always wanting to butt the others, so that most of them ran away when they saw him coming and would have nothing to do with their rough companion. Only Greenfinch, the slender nimble little goat was brave enough to face him, and would make a rush at him, three or four times in succession, with such agility and dexterity, that the great Turk often stood still quite astounded not venturing to attack her again, for Greenfinch was

fronting him, prepared for more warlike action, and her horns were sharp. Then there was little White Snowflake, who bleated in such a plaintive and beseeching manner that Heidi already had several times run to it and taken its head in her hands to comfort it. Just at this moment the pleading young cry was heard again, and Heidi jumped up running and, putting her arms round the little creature's neck, asked in a sympathetic voice, "What is it, little Snowflake? Why do you call like that as if in trouble?" The goat pressed closer to Heidi in a confiding way and left off bleating. Peter called out from where he was sitting—for he had not yet got to the end of his bread and cheese, "She cries like that because the old goat is not with her; she was sold at Mayenfeld the day before yesterday, and so will not come up the mountain any more."

"Who is the old goat?" called Heidi.

"Why, her mother, of course," was the answer.

"Where is the grandmother?" called Heidi again.

"She has none."

"And the grandfather?"

"She has none."

"Oh, you poor little Snowflake!" exclaimed Heidi, clasping the animal gently to her, "but do not cry like that any more; see now, I shall come up here with you every day, so that you will not be alone any more, and if you want anything you have only to come to me."

The young animal rubbed its head contentedly against Heidi's shoulder, and no longer gave such plaintive bleats. Peter now having finished his meal joined Heidi and the goats, Heidi having by this time found out a great many things about them. She had decided that by far the handsomest and best-behaved of the goats were undoubtedly the two belonging to her grandfather; they carried themselves with a certain air of distinction and generally went their own way, and as to the great Turk they treated him with indifference and contempt.

The goats were now beginning to climb the rocks again, each seeking for the plants it liked in its own fashion, some jumping over everything they met till they found what they wanted, others going more carefully and cropping all the nice leaves by the way, the Turk still now and then giving the others a poke with his horns. Little Swan and Little Bear clambered lightly up and never failed to find the best bushes, and then they would stand gracefully poised on their pretty legs, delicately nibbling at the leaves. Heidi stood with her hands behind her back, carefully noting all they did.

Illustration by Jessie Willcox Smith, from *Heidi*, by Johanna Spyri. Published 1922 by David McKay Company.

"Peter," she said to the boy who had again thrown himself down on the ground, "the prettiest of all the goats are Little Swan and Little Bear."

"Yes, I know they are," was the answer. "Alm-Uncle brushes them down and washes them and gives them salt, and he has the nicest shed for them."

All of a sudden Peter leaped to his feet and ran hastily after the goats. Heidi followed him as fast as she could, for she was too eager to know what happened to stay behind. Peter dashed through the middle of the flock towards that side of the mountain where the rocks fell perpendicularly to a great depth below, and where any thoughtless goat, if it went too near, might fall over and break all its legs. He had caught sight of the inquisitive Greenfinch taking leaps in that direction, and he was only just in time, for the animal had already sprung to the edge of the abyss. All Peter could do was to throw himself down and seize one of her hind legs. Greenfinch, thus taken by surprise, began bleating furiously, angry at being held so fast and prevented from continuing her voyage of discovery. She struggled to get loose, and endeavored so obstinately to leap forward that Peter shouted to Heidi to come and help him, for he could not get up and was afraid of pulling out the goat's leg altogether.

Heidi had already run up and she saw at once the danger both Peter and the animal were in. She quickly gathered a bunch of sweet-smelling leaves, and then, holding them under Greenfinch's nose, said coaxingly, "Come, come, Greenfinch, you must not be naughty! Look, you might fall down there and break your leg, and that would give you dreadful pain!"

The young animal turned quickly and began contentedly eating the leaves out of Heidi's hand. Meanwhile Peter got on to his feet again and took hold of Greenfinch by the band round her neck from which her bell was hung and Heidi taking hold of her in the same way on the other side, they led the wanderer back to the rest of the flock that had remained peacefully feeding. Peter, now he had his goat in safety, lifted his stick in order to give her a good beating as punishment, and Greenfinch seeing what was coming shrank back in fear. But Heidi cried out, "No, no, Peter, you must not strike her; see how frightened she is!"

"She deserves it," growled Peter, and again lifted his stick. Then Heidi flung herself against him and cried indignantly, "You have no right to touch her, it will hurt her, let her alone!"

Peter looked with surprise at the commanding little figure, whose dark eyes were flashing, and reluctantly he let his stick drop. "Well, I will let her off if you will give me some more of your cheese tomorrow," he said, for he was determined to have something to make up to him for his fright.

"You shall have it all, tomorrow and every day, I do not want it," replied Heidi, giving ready consent to his demand. "And I will give you bread as well, a large piece like you had today; but then you must promise never to beat Greenfinch, or Snowflake, or any of the other goats."

"All right," said Peter, "I don't care," which meant that he would agree to the bargain. He now let go of Greenfinch, who joyfully sprang to join her companions.

And thus imperceptibly the day had crept on to its close, and now the sun was on the point of sinking out of sight behind the high mountains. Heidi was again sitting on the ground, silently gazing at the blue bell-shaped flowers, as they glistened in the evening sun, for a golden light lay on the grass and flowers, and the rocks above were beginning to shine and glow. All at once she sprang to her feet, "Peter!" Peter! everything is on fire! All the rocks are burning and the great snow mountain and the sky! Oh look, look! the high rock up there is red with flame! Oh the beautiful, fiery snow! Stand up, Peter! See, the fire has reached the great bird's nest! look at the rocks! look at the fir trees! Everything, everything is on fire!"

"It is always like that," said Peter composedly, continuing to peel his stick; "but it is not really fire!"

"What is it then?" cried Heidi, as she ran backwards and forwards to look at first one side and then the other, for she felt she could not have enough of such a beautiful sight. "What is it, Peter, what is it?" she repeated.

"It gets like that of itself," explained Peter.

"Look, look!" cried Heidi in fresh excitement, "now they have turned all rose color! Look at that one covered with snow, and that with the high, pointed rocks! What do you call them?"

"Mountains have not any names," he answered.

"Oh how beautiful, look at the crimson snow! And up there on the rocks there are ever so many roses! Oh! now they are turning gray! Oh! oh! now all the color has died away! It's all gone, Peter." And Heidi sat down on the ground looking as full of distress as if everything had really come to an end.

"It will come again tomorrow," said Peter. "Get up, we must go home now." He whistled to his goats and together they all started on their homeward way.

"Is it like that every day, shall we see it every day when we bring the goats up here?" asked Heidi, as she clambered down the mountain at Peter's side; she waited eagerly for his answer, hoping that he would tell her it was so.

"It is like that most days," he replied.

"But will it be like that tomorrow for certain?" Heidi persisted.

"Yes, yes, tomorrow for certain," Peter assured her in answer.

Heidi now felt quite happy again, and her little brain was so full of new impressions and new thoughts that she did not speak any more until they had reached the hut. The grandfather was sitting under the fir-trees, where he had also put up a seat, waiting as usual for his goats which returned down the mountain on this side.

Heidi ran up to him followed by the white and brown goats, for they knew their own master and stall. Peter called out after her, "Come with me again tomorrow! Goodnight!" For he was anxious for more than one reason that Heidi should go with him the next day.

Heidi ran back quickly and gave Peter her hand, promising to go with him, and then making her way through the goats she once more clasped Snowflake round the neck, saying in a gentle soothing voice, "Sleep well, Snowflake, and remember that I shall be with you again tomorrow, so you must not bleat so sadly any more." Snowflake gave her a friendly and grateful look, and then went leaping joyfully after the other goats.

Heidi returned to the fir-trees. "Oh grandfather," she cried, even before she had come up to him, "it was so beautiful. The fire, and the roses on the rocks, and the blue and yellow flowers, and look what I have brought you!" And opening the apron that held her flowers, she shook them all out at her grandfather's feet. But the poor flowers, how changed they were! Heidi hardly knew them again. They looked like dried bits of hay, not a single little flower cup stood open. "O grandfather, what is the matter with them?" exclaimed Heidi in shocked surprise, "they were not like that this morning, why do they look so now?"

"They like to stand out there in the sun and not to be shut up in an apron," said her grandfather.

"Then I will never gather any more. But, grandfather, why did the great bird go on croaking so?" she continued in an eager tone of inquiry.

"Go along now and get into your bath while I go and get some milk; when we are together at supper I will tell you all about it."

Heidi obeyed, and when later she was sitting on her high stool before her milk bowl with her grandfather beside her, she repeated her question, "Why does the great bird go on croaking and screaming down at us, grandfather?"

"He is mocking at the people who live down below in the villages, because they all go huddling and gossiping together, and encourage one another in evil talking and deeds. He calls out, 'If you would separate and each go your own way and come up here and live on a height as I do, it would be better for you!' " There was almost a wildness in the old man's voice as he spoke, so that Heidi seemed to hear the croaking of the bird again even more distinctly.

"Why haven't the mountains any names?" Heidi went on.

"They have names," answered her grandfather, "and if you can describe one of them to me that I know I will tell you what it is called."

Heidi then described to him the rocky mountain with the two high peaks so exactly that the grandfather was delighted. "Just so, I know it," and he told her its name. "Did you see any other?"

Then Heidi told him of the mountain with the great snow-field, and how it had been on fire, and had turned rosy-red and then all of a sudden had grown quite pale again and all the color had disappeared.

"I know that one too," he said, giving her its name. "So you enjoyed being out with the goats?"

Then Heidi went on to give him an account of the whole day, and of how delightful it had all been, and particularly described the fire that had burst out everywhere in the evening. And then nothing would do but her grandfather must tell how it came, for Peter knew nothing about it.

The grandfather explained to her that it was the sun that did it. "When he says goodnight to the mountains he throws his most beautiful colors over them, so that they may not forget him before he comes again the next day."

Heidi was delighted with this explanation, and could hardly bear to wait for another day to come that she might once more climb up with the goats and see how the sun bid goodnight to the mountains. But she had to go to bed first, and all night she slept soundly on her bed of hay, dreaming of nothing but of shining mountains with roses all over them, among which happy little Snowflake went leaping in and out.

Nina Bawden

Carrie's War

This novel has an intense, emotional atmosphere, redolent of memory and a sense of place. The adult Carrie, recounting scenes from her childhood, conveys the powerlessness of a child in a complex adult world and her shifting perceptions of relationships, actions, and consequences. In 1939, twelve-year-old Carrie and her younger brother, Nick, are evacuated from the Second World War London of bombs and death. As part of the mass exodus of children from the cities, they are sent for safety to Wales, where they are cared for by the stern Mr. Evans and his frightened sister. The children's only happy times are visits to an odd house named Druid's Bottom. There they meet an assortment of characters, including Mrs. Gotobed, Mr. Evans's bedridden older sister; her housekeeper, Hepzibah Green; the childlike Mr. Johnny; and Albert Sandwich, another evacuee. The following passage shows the author's skill in building up layers of incident to illustrate character. [From Nina Bawden, *Carrie's War* (Lippincott, 1973).]

February came, and the calf was born at Druid's Bottom. It was born on a Sunday afternoon and Carrie and Albert and Nick saw it happen. The cow lowing and lowing and Mister Johnny talking to her in his soft, bubbly voice, and pulling on the little hooves when they slowly appeared. And the astonishingly big calf coming out with a slippery rush and then, a few minutes later, standing up in the straw on its thin, wobbly legs, its thickly lashed eyes mild and brown like its mother's.

"I've never seen anything so exciting in my whole life," Nick said afterwards. "It's my *best thing!*"

"I shouldn't tell Mr. Evans you saw the calf born," Carrie said.

"Why not?"

"Just because."

"Well, I did see it, didn't I? *And* my chilblains are better, too," Nick said, happily counting his blessings. "That's the magic ointment Hepzibah gave me."

"Not magic, just herbs," Carrie said, though she wasn't too sure about this. "And I shouldn't tell Auntie Lou it was Hepzibah. She thinks it's those gloves that she gave you, keeping you warm."

"I know she does." Nick smiled, smugly and sweetly. "That's what I told her, you silly dope. D'you think I'm an idiot?"

February turned into March and Albert came back to school. Although he was only eighteen months older than Carrie he was in the top class and sometimes he was taught on his own by Mr. Morgan, the minister, because he was cleverer than even the most senior boys. But he wasn't stuck up about this, nor did he ignore Carrie and Nick when other people were there. He didn't seem to care that Nick was so much younger than he was. He would turn up in the primary school playground and call, "Hi there, Nick!" as if Nick was a boy the same age. "I don't see what difference it makes, people's ages," he said when Carrie told him the girls in her class thought this odd. "People are either your friends or they aren't. Nick's my friend, and Hepzibah. And Mrs. Gotobed, too, and she's *ancient.*"

April—and Carrie met Mrs. Gotobed. On the first day of the Easter holidays, Mister Johnny took Nick up the mountain to see where the gulls nested, on an island in a small lake. They often went on excursions, always talking away nineteen to the dozen. Sometimes Nick understood what Mister Johnny said and sometimes he only pretended he did, to annoy Carrie, but they were always happy together. Happier alone, Carrie knew, than when she was with them, and although she didn't really mind this, it made her feel lonely this particular day. Albert was reading in the library because Mr. Morgan was coming to give him an extra Greek lesson and Hepzibah was busy, bustling in and out of the kitchen with no time for Carrie. She sat by the fire and pretended she was quite happy alone, just sitting quietly and thinking, but Hepzibah knew better. She looked up from the tray she was laying—silver teapot and best china and thin bread and butter—and said, "What's up with you, Miss Down-in-the-Mouth? Nothing to do, is that it? Well, you can go and keep Mrs. Gotobed company. I'll put another cup on the tray and you can have tea with her." She smiled at Carrie's horrified face. "It's all right; she won't bite you."

Mrs. Gotobed was downstairs in a room Carrie had not been into before; a light, pretty drawing room, all gilt chairs and mirrors. A wing chair was drawn up to a crackling wood fire and Mrs. Gotobed sat in it. At first Carrie hardly dared look at her but when she did she saw nothing alarming or sinister, just an old lady with silvery hair piled up high and a pale, invalid's face. She held out a thin hand covered with huge, glittering rings that were loose on her fingers and said, "Come and sit here, pretty child. On this stool. Let me look at your eyes. Albert says they're like emeralds."

"Oh," Carrie said. She blushed and sat, very straight-backed, on the stool.

"Handsome is as handsome does," Hepzibah said. She put the tray on a low table and left them together.

Mrs. Gotobed smiled and her face crinkled up like pale paper. "Hepzibah thinks looks don't matter much but they do, you know. Do you like my dress?"

She was wearing what seemed to be a red silk ball gown, embroidered with silver flowers on the bodice and very long and full in the skirt. "It's lovely," Carrie said, though she thought it a strange dress for someone to wear in the daytime.

Mrs. Gotobed's hands, stroking her silken skirt, made a faint, rasping sound. "My husband gave it to me just after we married," she said. "We bought it in Paris and I had to stand for hours while they fitted me. My waist was so small, they said they had never seen anyone with such a small waist. Mr. Gotobed could hold it in his two hands. He loved buying me clothes, he bought me twenty-nine ball gowns, one for each year of our marriage, and I have them all still, hanging up in my closet. I put on a different one each time I get up. I want to wear each one of them once more before I die."

All the time she was talking her thin hands stroked the silk of her dress. *She's mad,* Carrie thought, *raving mad.*

"Pour the tea, child," Mrs. Gotobed said. "And I'll tell you about my dresses. I've got a green chiffon with pearls sewn round the neck and a blue brocade and a gray silk with pink ostrich feathers. That was my husband's favorite so I'm keeping that one till the last. I looked like a queen in it, he always said. . . . Just a little milk in my tea, and two slices of bread, folded over."

Her eyes were pale gray and bulging a little. Like Mr. Evans's eyes, Carrie thought, but apart from her eyes she didn't look in the least like a shopkeeper's sister. Sitting in that grand dress, in this beautiful room. . . .

"Would you like jam?" Carrie asked. "It's Hepzibah's blackberry."

"No, child. No jam." Mrs. Gotobed looked at Carrie with Mr. Evans's pale eyes and said,

"So you're my brother's evacuee, God help you!"

Carrie stiffened. "I like Mr. Evans," she found herself saying.

"Then you're the only one does. Cold, hard, mean man, my brother. How d'you get on with my baby sister, Louisa?"

"Oh, Auntie Lou's *nice*," Carrie said. She looked at Mrs. Gotobed's clawlike, ringed fingers holding her delicate cup, and thought of Auntie Lou's little red hands that were always in water, washing dishes or scrubbing floors or peeling potatoes.

"Nice, but a fool," Mrs. Gotobed said. "No spunk, or she'd have left *him* long ago. She'll lie down and let him walk over her till the end of her days. Does he walk over you?"

Carrie shook her head firmly.

"Not afraid of him? Well, if you're not, then you can tell him something from me." She sipped her tea and looked so long and thoughtfully into the fire that Carrie began to think she had forgotten her. She had finished all the bread and butter and scraped the dish of blackberry jam before Mrs. Gotobed turned from the fire and spoke again, very slowly and clearly. "When I die," she said, "you can tell him from me that I hadn't forgotten him. That I hadn't forgotten he was my own flesh and blood, but that sometimes you owe more to strangers. That I've done what I've done because it seemed to me right, not because I wanted to spite him." She put her cup down and laughed softly and her eyes shone like pale stones under water. "Only wait till I'm safely dead first! Or he'll be round here stamping and yelling and I haven't the strength for it." She waited a minute, then said, "Do you understand what I've told you?"

Carrie nodded but the nod was a lie. She didn't understand but she felt too embarrassed to say so. Mrs. Gotobed was embarrassing, talking in that dreadful, calm way about dying, as if she were saying, "When I go on holiday."

Carrie couldn't even look at her. She stared at her hands, her ears burning. But Mrs. Gotobed said nothing more and when Carrie did look, she was lying back in her chair with her head fallen sideways. She was lying so still Carrie thought she was dead, but when she got up to run and call Hepzibah she saw that her chest was still moving and knew she was only asleep. She ran all the same, out of the room, across the hall, into the kitchen. She said, *"Hepzibah!"* and Hepzibah came to her. Held her close for a minute, then lifted her chin and looked into her face. "It's all right," Carrie stammered, "she's just gone to sleep," and Hepzibah nodded and touched her chin lightly and lovingly. She said, "I'd best go to her then. You stay here with Albert."

When she had gone, Albert said, from the fire, "Did she frighten you?"

"No," Carrie said. But she had been frightened and it made her angry with Albert. "I thought she was dead and that's your fault! You told me she was dying when we first came. Months ago!"

"She is dying," Albert said. "D'you mean I shouldn't have told you?"

Carrie wasn't sure what she did mean. She said, "She shouldn't talk about it."

Albert looked surprised. "I don't see why not. It's fairly important to her."

"It's horrible," Carrie said. *"She's* horrible. Spooky! Dressing up in all those grand clothes when she's dying!"

"It cheers her up to put them on," Albert said. "It was her life, you see, parties and pretty clothes, and putting them on makes her remember how happy she used to be. It was my idea, as a matter of fact. When I came here, she was so miserable. Crying all the time! One evening she told Hepzibah to show me her dresses and cried because she'd never wear them again. I said, why not, and she said because there was no point, no one to see, and I said *I'd* like to see them. So she puts a dress on, when she feels well enough, and I go and look and she talks to me about the times she wore it before. It's quite interesting, really."

He spoke as if this were a perfectly natural thing to do. Carrie thought of it, of the sick old woman dressing up in her jewels and her beautiful clothes, and of this skinny, solemn, bespectacled boy watching her, and it didn't seem natural at all. She said, "You are funny, Albert. Funny peculiar, I mean. Not ordinary."

"I would hate to be ordinary," Albert said. "Wouldn't you?"

"I don't know," Carrie said. Albert seemed so grown up suddenly, it made her feel silly and young. She wanted to tell him the rest of it; tell him what Mrs. Gotobed had told her to tell Mr. Evans and ask Albert what he thought she had meant, but she couldn't think how to put it without making herself sound fearfully stupid. And then, a few minutes later, Nick came bursting in with Mister Johnny behind him and there was no time to say anything.

Nick was very excited. "Oh, it was marvelous, Carrie! The lake, and the white gulls, and the brown island. I couldn't see anything at first and Mister Johnny said, sit still and wait, and I *sat* still, and then the island sort of *moved.* And the brown part wasn't the *earth,* but thousands and thousands of baby gulls, packed so tight you couldn't see the grass under them! Oh, Carrie, it's my *best thing.* The best thing in my whole life!"

"Like the calf being born. And your tenth birthday gloves. You're always having *best things,*" Carrie said, rather sourly.

"I can't help it, can I?" Nick looked puzzled and hurt. Then smiled suddenly. "It'll be your turn next, won't it? It's your birthday next month!"

Carrie's birthday was at the beginning of May. Mr. Evans and Auntie Lou gave her handkerchiefs and her mother sent her a green dress that was too tight in the chest and too short. Auntie Lou said she could sew a piece of material on the bottom to lengthen the skirt but there was nothing she could do about the top and Carrie cried a little, privately, not because the dress was no use but because her mother should have guessed how much she had grown. She felt miserable about this all the morning, but better in the afternoon when they went to Druid's Bottom after school. Hepzibah had baked a cake with white icing and twelve candles and Mister Johnny made her a crown of wild flowers to put on her head.

"Now you're the Queen of the May," Hepzibah said.

She wore the crown while they sat in the sunshine, eating the cake, but by the time they went home it was already wilting a little.

Albert walked them up through the Grove.

"You should soak it in the Sacred Spring," he said. "Then maybe it'll last forever."

He didn't seem to be teasing. Carrie said, "You don't believe that?"

Albert shrugged his shoulders. "Hepzibah half does. She fills bottles from the spring sometimes, to make medicines. She says it's because the water is pure from the mountain but she doesn't really believe it's just that. And perhaps it isn't. She put some spring water on my wart one evening and it was gone when I woke the next day."

"Beans will do that," Carrie said. "Or fasting spit. Nick had a wart and he spat on it first thing every morning and by the end of the week it was gone."

"That's magic," Albert said. "The spring is religion. That's different."

"D'you mean the *old religion?*" Carrie laughed, to show she thought this was nonsense. "That's what Auntie Lou calls it, but then she's a bit silly."

"Oh, I don't know," Albert said. "No one knows, really. Only that this was a Sacred Place once. Not just the Grove, the whole mountain. They found an old temple, just a few stones and some old bones—that's where I think the skull came from, d'you remember I told you? But they've found similar temples in other parts of the world, the same sort of arrangement of stones, so they think this religion must have been everywhere once."

Carrie felt cold, though it was a warm day and above their heads, above the dark yews, the sun was still shining. She whispered—she didn't mean to whisper but she couldn't help it—"The first time we came, when we were so scared, it wasn't just Mister Johnny. I thought I heard something before I heard him. A sort of big sigh. As if something were breathing. Don't laugh!"

"I'm not," Albert said. "It's as silly to laugh as it is to be scared. There's nothing to be scared of, any more than in an old church. I think it's just that places where people have believed things have an odd feel to them. . . ." He was quiet for a little, then whispered, as Carrie had done, "Unless there *is* something else. Some secret power, sleeping. . . ."

"You're scaring yourself!" Carrie said, and

he did laugh at her then. It was easy to laugh because they were at the top of the path now, coming out of the Grove into sunlight.

A train was coming out of the tunnel. It rattled past them, blowing their clothes and their hair. Nick was some way along the line, at the bend where the track curved round the mountain, and Carrie saw him put his hands over his ears as the train blew its whistle. "Poor Nick," she said. "He does hate it."

Albert said, "Carrie . . ." and she turned and saw his face close to hers. He kissed her, bumping her nose with his glasses, and said, "Happy Birthday."

Carrie couldn't think what to say. She said, "Thank you," very politely.

"Girls don't say thank you when they get kissed." Though Albert spoke in a calm, schoolmastery tone, his color had risen. He turned away, to hide this, perhaps; waved once, without looking, and ran down the path. As soon as he was out of sight he began to sing, very loudly.

Carrie sang, too, as she skipped down the railway track; sang under her breath and laughed to herself. When she caught up with Nick, he said, "What are you laughing for?"

"I can laugh, can't I?" Carrie said. "There's no law against it? Have you heard of a law against laughing, Mr. Clever-Dick-Nick?"

Frances Hodgson Burnett

The Secret Garden

Frances Hodgson Burnett, a natural storyteller, wrote from a real love and knowledge of gardens and flowers. The character of Mary Lennox, "the most disagreeable-looking child ever seen," grows and changes with the cultivation of the secret garden. Human secrets of the past are also part of this story, romantic in tradition and authentic in its Yorkshire setting. [From Frances Hodgson Burnett, *The Secret Garden* (Lippincott, 1911).]

"I Am Colin"

But you never know what the weather will do in Yorkshire, particularly in the springtime. She was awakened in the night by the sound of rain beating with heavy drops against her window. It was pouring down in torrents and the wind was "wuthering" round the corners and in the chimneys of the huge old house. Mary sat up in bed and felt miserable and angry.

"The rain is as contrary as I ever was," she said. "It came because it knew I did not want it."

She threw herself back on her pillow and buried her face. She did not cry, but she lay and hated the sound of the heavily beating rain, she hated the wind and its "wuthering." She could not go to sleep again. The mournful sound kept her awake because she felt mournful herself. If she had felt happy it would probably have lulled her to sleep. How it "wuthered" and how the big raindrops poured down and beat against the pane!

"It sounds just like a person lost on the moor and wandering on and on crying," she said.

She had been lying awake turning from side to side for about an hour, when suddenly something made her sit up in bed and turn her head toward the door listening. She listened and she listened.

"It isn't the wind now," she said in a loud whisper. "That isn't the wind. It is different. It is that crying I heard before."

The door of her room was ajar and the sound came down the corridor, a far-off faint sound of fretful crying. She listened for a few minutes and each minute she became more and more sure. She felt as if she must find out what it was. It seemed even stranger than the secret garden and the buried key. Perhaps the fact that she was in a rebellious mood made her bold. She put her foot out of bed and stood on the floor.

"I am going to find out what it is," she said. "Everybody is in bed and I don't care about Mrs. Medlock—I don't care!"

There was a candle by her bedside and she took it up and went softly out of the room. The corridor looked very long and dark, but she was too excited to mind that. She thought she remembered the corners she must turn to find the short corridor with the door covered with tapestry—the one Mrs. Medlock had come through the day she lost herself. The sound had come up that passage. So she went on with her dim light, almost feeling her way, her heart beating so loud that she fancied she could hear it. The far-off faint crying went on and led her. Sometimes it stopped for a moment or so and then began again. Was this the right corner to turn? She stopped and thought. Yes it was. Down this passage and then to the left, and then up two broad steps, and then to the right again. Yes, there was the tapestry door.

She pushed it open very gently and closed it behind her, and she stood in the corridor and could hear the crying quite plainly, though it was not loud. It was on the other side of the wall at her left and a few yards farther on there was a door. She could see a glimmer of light coming from beneath it. The Someone was crying in that room, and it was quite a young Someone.

So she walked to the door and pushed it open, and there she was standing in the room!

It was a big room with ancient, handsome furniture in it. There was a low fire glowing faintly on the hearth and a night light burning by the side of a carved four-posted bed hung with brocade, and on the bed was lying a boy, crying fretfully.

Mary wondered if she was in a real place or if she had fallen asleep again and was dreaming without knowing it.

The boy had a sharp, delicate face the color of ivory and he seemed to have eyes too big for it. He had also a lot of hair which tumbled over his forehead in heavy locks and made his thin face seem smaller. He looked like a boy who had been ill, but he was crying more as if he were tired and cross than as if he were in pain.

Mary stood near the door with her candle in her hand, holding her breath. Then she crept across the room, and, as she drew nearer, the light attracted the boy's attention and he turned his head on his pillow and stared at her, his gray eyes opening so wide that they seemed immense.

"Who are you?" he said at last in a half-frightened whisper. "Are you a ghost?"

"No, I am not," Mary answered, her own whisper sounding half frightened. "Are you one?"

He stared and stared and stared. Mary could not help noticing what strange eyes he had. They were agate gray and they looked too big for his face because they had black lashes all round them.

"No," he replied after waiting a moment or so. "I am Colin."

"Who is Colin?" she faltered.

"I am Colin Craven. Who are you?"

"I am Mary Lennox. Mr. Craven is my uncle."

"He is my father," said the boy.

"Your father!" gasped Mary. "No one ever told me he had a boy! Why didn't they?"

"Come here," he said, still keeping his strange eyes fixed on her with an anxious expression.

She came close to the bed and he put out his hand and touched her.

"You are real, aren't you?" he said. "I have such real dreams very often. You might be one of them."

Mary had slipped on a woolen wrapper before she left her room and she put a piece of it between his fingers.

"Rub that and see how thick and warm it is," she said. "I will pinch you a little if you like, to show you how real I am. For a minute I thought you might be a dream too."

"Where did you come from?" he asked.

"From my own room. The wind wuthered so I couldn't go to sleep and I heard some one crying and wanted to find out who it was. What were you crying for?"

"Because I couldn't go to sleep either and my head ached. Tell me your name again."

"Mary Lennox. Did no one ever tell you I had come to live here?"

He was still fingering the fold of her wrapper, but he began to look a little more as if he believed in her reality.

"No," he answered. "They daren't."

"Why?" asked Mary.

"Because I should have been afraid you would see me. I won't let people see me and talk me over."

"Why?" Mary asked again, feeling more mystified every moment.

"Because I am like this always, ill and having to lie down. My father won't let people talk me over either. The servants are not allowed to speak about me. If I live I may be a hunch-back, but I shan't live. My father hates to think I may be like him."

"Oh, what a queer house this is!" Mary said. "What a queer house! Everything is a kind of secret. Rooms are locked up and gardens are locked up—and you! Have you been locked up?"

"No. I stay in this room because I don't want to be moved out of it. It tires me too much."

"Does your father come and see you?" Mary ventured.

"Sometimes. Generally when I am asleep. He doesn't want to see me."

"Why?" Mary could not help asking again.

A sort of angry shadow passed over the boy's face.

"My mother died when I was born and it makes him wretched to look at me. He thinks I don't know, but I've heard people talking. He almost hates me."

"He hates the garden, because she died," said Mary half speaking to herself.

Illustration by Tasha Tudor, from *The Secret Garden,* by Frances Hodgson Burnett (J. B. Lippincott Co.). Illustrations copyright © 1962 by Harper & Row, Publishers, Inc. Reprinted by permission of Harper & Row, Publishers, Inc.

"What garden?" the boy asked.

"Oh! just—just a garden she used to like," Mary stammered. "Have you been here always?"

"Nearly always. Sometimes I have been taken to places at the seaside, but I won't stay because people stare at me. I used to wear an iron thing to keep my back straight, but a grand doctor came from London to see me and said it was stupid. He told them to take it off and keep me out in the fresh air. I hate fresh air and I don't want to go out."

"I didn't when first I came here," said Mary. "Why do you keep looking at me like that?"

"Because of the dreams that are so real," he answered rather fretfully. "Sometimes when I open my eyes I don't believe I'm awake."

"We're both awake," said Mary. She glanced round the room with its high ceiling and shadowy corners and dim fire-light. "It looks quite like a dream, and it's the middle of the night, and everybody in the house is asleep—everybody but us. We are wide awake."

"I don't want it to be a dream," the boy said restlessly.

Mary thought of something all at once.

"If you don't like people to see you," she began, "do you want me to go away?"

He still held the fold of her wrapper and he gave it a little pull.

"No," he said. "I should be sure you were a dream if you went. If you are real, sit down on that big footstool and talk. I want to hear about you."

Mary put down her candle on the table near the bed and sat down on the cushioned stool. She did not want to go away at all. She wanted to stay in the mysterious hidden-away room and talk to the mysterious boy.

"What do you want me to tell you?" she said.

He wanted to know how long she had been at Misselthwaite; he wanted to know which corridor her room was on; he wanted to know what she had been doing; if she disliked the moor as he disliked it; where she had lived before she came to Yorkshire. She answered all these questions and many more and he lay back on his pillow and listened. He made her tell him a great deal about India and about her voyage across the ocean. She found out that because he had been an invalid he had not learned things as other children had. One of his nurses had taught him to read when he was quite little and he was always reading and looking at pictures in splendid books.

Though his father rarely saw him when he was awake, he was given all sorts of wonderful things to amuse himself with. He never seemed to have been amused, however. He could have anything he asked for and was never made to do anything he did not like to do.

"Everyone is obliged to do what pleases me," he said indifferently. "It makes me ill to be angry. No one believes I shall live to grow up."

He said it as if he was so accustomed to the idea that it had ceased to matter to him at all. He seemed to like the sound of Mary's voice. As she went on talking he listened in a drowsy, interested way. Once or twice she wondered if he were not gradually falling into a doze. But at last he asked a question which opened up a new subject.

"How old are you?" he asked.

"I am ten," answered Mary, forgetting herself for the moment, "and so are you."

"How do you know that?" he demanded in a surprised voice.

"Because when you were born the garden door was locked and the key was buried. And it has been locked for ten years."

Colin half sat up, turning toward her, leaning on his elbows.

"What garden door was locked? Who did it? Where was the key buried?" he exclaimed as if he were suddenly very much interested.

"It—it was the garden Mr. Craven hates," said Mary nervously. "He locked the door. No one—no one knew where he buried the key."

"What sort of a garden is it?" Colin persisted eagerly.

"No one has been allowed to go into it for ten years," was Mary's careful answer.

But it was too late to be careful. He was too much like herself. He too had had nothing to think about and the idea of a hidden garden attracted him as it had attracted her. He asked question after question. Where was it? Had

she never looked for the door? Had she never asked the gardeners?

"They won't talk about it," said Mary. "I think they have been told not to answer questions."

"I would make them," said Colin.

"Could you?" Mary faltered, beginning to feel frightened. If he could make people answer questions, who knew what might happen!

"Everyone is obliged to please me. I told you that," he said. "If I were to live, this place would sometime belong to me. They all know that. I would make them tell me."

Mary had not known that she herself had been spoiled, but she could see quite plainly that this mysterious boy had been. He thought that the whole world belonged to him. How peculiar he was and how coolly he spoke of not living.

"Do you think you won't live?" she asked, partly because she was curious and partly in hope of making him forget the garden.

"I don't suppose I shall," he answered as indifferently as he had spoken before. "Ever since I remember anything I have heard people say I shan't. At first they thought I was too little to understand and now they think I don't hear. But I do. My doctor is my father's cousin. He is quite poor and if I die he will have all Misselthwaite when my father is dead. I should think he wouldn't want me to live."

"Do you want to live?" inquired Mary.

"No," he answered, in a cross, tired fashion. "But I don't want to die. When I feel ill I lie here and think about it until I cry and cry."

"I have heard you crying three times," Mary said, "but I did not know who it was. Were you crying about that?" She did so want him to forget the garden.

"I dare say," he answered. "Let us talk about something else. Talk about that garden. Don't you want to see it?"

"Yes," answered Mary, in quite a low voice.

"I do," he went on persistently. "I don't think I ever really wanted to see anything before, but I want to see that garden. I want the key dug up. I want the door unlocked. I would let them take me there in my chair. That would be getting fresh air. I am going to make them open the door."

He had become quite excited and his strange

eyes began to shine like stars and looked more immense than ever.

"They have to please me," he said. "I will make them take me there and I will let you go, too."

Mary's hands clutched each other. Everything would be spoiled—everything! Dickon would never come back. She would never again feel like a missel thrush with a safe-hidden nest.

"Oh, don't—don't—don't—don't do that!" she cried out.

He stared as if he thought she had gone crazy!

"Why?" he exclaimed. "You said you wanted to see it."

"I do," she answered almost with a sob in her throat, "but if you make them open the door and take you in like that it will never be a secret again."

He leaned still farther forward.

"A secret," he said. "What do you mean? Tell me."

Mary's words almost tumbled over one another.

"You see—you see," she panted, "if no one knows but ourselves—if there was a door, hidden somewhere under the ivy—if there was—and we could find it; and if we could slip through it together and shut it behind us, and no one knew any one was inside and we called it our garden and pretended that—that we were missel thrushes and it was our nest, and if we played there almost every day and dug and planted seeds and made it all come alive—"

"Is it dead?" he interrupted her.

"It soon will be if no one cares for it," she went on. "The bulbs will live but the roses—"

He stopped her again as excited as she was herself.

"What are bulbs?" he put in quickly.

"They are daffodils and lilies and snowdrops. They are working in the earth now—pushing up pale green points because the spring is coming."

"Is the spring coming?" he said. "What is it like? You don't see it in rooms if you are ill."

"It is the sun shining on the rain and the rain falling on the sunshine, and things pushing up and working under the earth," said Mary. "If the garden was a secret and we could get into it we could watch the things grow bigger every day, and see how many roses are alive. Don't you see? Oh, don't you see how much nicer it would be if it was a secret?"

He dropped back on his pillow and lay there with an odd expression on his face.

"I never had a secret," he said, "except that one about not living to grow up. They don't know I know that, so it is a sort of secret. But I like this kind better."

"If you won't make them take you to the garden," pleaded Mary, "perhaps—I feel almost sure I can find out how to get in sometime. And then—if the doctor wants you to go out in your chair, and if you can always do what you want to do, perhaps—perhaps we might find some boy who would push you, and we could go alone and it would always be a secret garden."

"I should—like—that," he said very slowly, his eyes looking dreamy. "I should like that. I should not mind fresh air in a secret garden."

Mary began to recover her breath and feel safer because the idea of keeping the secret seemed to please him. She felt almost sure that if she kept on talking and could make him see the garden in his mind as she had seen it he would like it so much that he could not bear to think that everybody might tramp into it when they chose.

"I'll tell you what I *think* it would be like, if we could go into it," she said. "It has been shut up so long things have grown into a tangle perhaps."

He lay quite still and listened while she went on talking about the roses which *might* have clambered from tree to tree and hung down—about the many birds which *might* have built their nests there because it was so safe. And then she told him about the robin and Ben Weatherstaff, and there was so much to tell about the robin and it was so easy and safe to talk about it that she ceased to be afraid. The robin pleased him so much that he smiled until he looked almost beautiful, and at first Mary had thought that he was even plainer than herself, with his big eyes and heavy locks of hair.

"I did not know birds could be like that," he said. "But if you stay in a room you never see things. What a lot of things you know. I feel as if you had been inside that garden."

She did not know what to say, so she did not say anything. He evidently did not expect an answer and the next moment he gave her a surprise.

"I am going to let you look at something," he said. "Do you see that rose-colored silk curtain hanging on the wall over the mantelpiece?"

Mary had not noticed it before, but she looked up and saw it. It was a curtain of soft silk hanging over what seemed to be some picture.

"Yes," she answered.

"There is a cord hanging from it," said Colin. "Go and pull it."

Mary got up, much mystified, and found the cord. When she pulled it the silk curtain ran back on rings and when it ran back it uncovered a picture. It was the picture of a girl with a laughing face. She had bright hair tied up with a blue ribbon and her gay, lovely eyes were exactly like Colin's unhappy ones, agate gray and looking twice as big as they really were because of the black lashes all round them.

"She is my mother," said Colin complainingly. "I don't see why she died. Sometimes I hate her for doing it."

"How queer!" said Mary.

"If she had lived I believe I should not have been ill always," he grumbled. "I dare say I should have lived, too. And my father would not have hated to look at me. I dare say I should have had a strong back. Draw the curtain again."

Mary did as she was told and returned to her footstool.

"She is much prettier than you," she said, "but her eyes are just like yours—at least they are the same shape and color. Why is the curtain drawn over her?"

He moved uncomfortably.

"I made them do it," he said. "Sometimes I don't like to see her looking at me. She smiles too much when I am ill and miserable. Besides, she is mine and I don't want everyone to see her."

There were a few moments of silence and then Mary spoke.

"What would Mrs. Medlock do if she found out that I had been here?" she inquired.

"She would do as I told her to do," he answered. "And I should tell her that I wanted you to come here and talk to me every day. I am glad you came."

"So am I," said Mary. "I will come as often as I can, but"—she hesitated—"I shall have to look every day for the garden door."

"Yes, you must," said Colin, "and you can tell me about it afterward." He lay thinking a few minutes, as he had done before, and then he spoke again.

"I think you shall be a secret, too," he said. "I will not tell them until they find out. I can always send the nurse out of the room and say that I want to be by myself. Do you know Martha?"

"Yes, I know her very well," said Mary. "She waits on me."

He nodded his head toward the outer corridor.

"She is the one who is asleep in the other room. The nurse went away yesterday to stay all night with her sister and she always makes Martha attend to me when she wants to go out. Martha shall tell you when to come here."

Then Mary understood Martha's troubled look when she had asked questions about the crying.

"Martha knew about you all the time?" she said.

"Yes, she often attends to me. The nurse likes to get away from me and then Martha comes."

"I have been here a long time," said Mary. "Shall I go away now? Your eyes look sleepy."

"I wish I could go to sleep before you leave me," he said rather shyly.

"Shut your eyes," said Mary, drawing her footstool closer, "and I will do what my Ayah used to do in India. I will pat your hand and stroke it and sing something quite low."

"I should like that perhaps," he said drowsily.

Somehow she was sorry for him and did not want him to lie awake, so she leaned against the bed and began to stroke and pat his hand

and sing a very low little chanting song in Hindustani.

"That is nice," he said more drowsily still, and she went on chanting and stroking, but when she looked at him again his black lashes were lying close against his cheeks, for his eyes were shut and he was fast asleep. So she got up softly, took her candle and crept away without making a sound.

Virginia Hamilton

The Planet of Junior Brown

The streets of New York, racism, poverty, and a secret subculture of runaway black children living under the city make up the milieu of this story. Harsh social realism and allegorical surrealism combine in this imagistic, poetic novel in which childhood's emotional and spiritual power is contrasted with the decay of modern, urban adult society. Junior Brown is a disturbed, alienated, three-hundred-pound eighth-grader dominated by his asthmatic, overly protective mother. His only friend, Buddy Clark, is a streetwise survivor who lives a secret life as the guide of runaway children living in deserted tenements. The two boys have been cutting classes for months and spending their time with Mr. Pool, the janitor, in the school basement, where they have constructed a model of the solar system, a symbol of their desire to overcome isolation and their determination to create a new community among the homeless street children. The book resonates with a tough, loving hope for the future. [From Virginia Hamilton, *The Planet of Junior Brown* (Macmillan, 1971).]

Buddy had not seen Junior Brown for the whole weekend. This Monday morning he didn't feel like going by Junior's house, he told himself. So he went on to school alone. When he arrived in the basement room, he found Junior already there and Mr. Pool there, with the solar system full of juice and turning silently through the void.

Not so silently. There was a piercing squeak somewhere, a high scraping sound like metal grating against metal. As the planets revolved, Mr. Pool tried to pinpoint the squeak. When he thought he had it, he turned off the solar

system. He pulled a ladder over and set it up by the planets. Then he climbed up and cleaned all of the tracks from which the rods were suspended.

"There. That ought to do it," Mr. Pool said when he was finished. He shoved the ladder away into the void and turned on the solar system. The squeak remained.

Buddy laughed. He came around the planets to where Junior was slumped in his folding chair. Buddy didn't say anything; he just stood quietly behind Junior's chair. This way he let Junior know they were together. And together they both watched the system.

The planet of Junior Brown soon became a giant presence in the darkness. The solar system became all and mighty in the void. Except for the squeak.

Mr. Pool's bald head glowed yellowish in the light of the system's dim reflection.

"Damn it all to glory!" he muttered. "It's got to be up in the tracks."

Buddy told him, "You ought to let the master of sound tell you where the squeak is. Meaning Junior," he added. He leaned to one side, peering around Junior until he could see Junior's face. "Good morning to you," Buddy said. "You have a nice weekend with your daddy? U-huh? You and your daddy eat in some big-time restaurant and see some two-dollar technicolor movie?"

"Cool it off now," Mr. Pool said to Buddy. He had heard the anger in Buddy's voice. It had surprised him, but when he thought about it, he supposed Buddy's anger was there in almost everything Buddy did.

"So Junior's father took him some place," Mr. Pool said. "You don't have a father to give you things—is that it?"

Buddy let himself go loose. He collapsed on the floor, on his stomach, half in the light of the solar system. "No," he said. He turned away from Junior and Mr. Pool to rest his head on his arms.

He was tired. Why in the world did he have to say that to Junior! He only meant to let Junior know that he understood how Junior had to spend the weekend with his father. He was tired down to his bones. He had walked around a good part of the night again—that didn't make this Monday any different from some other. But the night and this early morning was colder; he had to keep every muscle working to keep from freezing. Buddy knew he would have to steal a warmer jacket and he was tired of stealing.

Way early this morning, old Doum Malach had given Buddy his pay. Thirty-seven dollars and fifty cents.

Buddy grunted to himself. The grunt sounded like pain to Junior. Mr. Pool had heard it too. He came around the revolving planets to where Buddy lay half in darkness.

Thirty-seven dollars and fifty cents, with some kids coming up to his planet next Friday from someplace down at the Brooklyn Bridge. He would have to find warm clothes for them to wear. He would have to get them cleaned up, and enough food, Jesus, all on thirty-seven dollars and fifty cents.

Again Buddy grunted with the deep-down worry of it.

"Are you all right, Buddy?" Mr. Pool stood over Buddy, wondering if the boy maybe was going to be sick.

Suddenly Buddy felt strange, like he was coming down with something.

All I need is to catch me a sneaking pneumonia.

"You want to set yourself down?" Junior spoke. Since he had entered the room, Junior hadn't said a word. He had wished for so long to be able to say things to his daddy, but he never had his daddy to talk to. It was only Buddy he could tell things to. Buddy had to be the one. "You want to sit down here?"

Junior pulled his chair over closer to Buddy. Buddy looked around and then got to his feet.

"Naw, man," he said to Junior. "You sit on down like you were. I'm just getting myself warm."

"Well, how you feeling then?" Junior asked him.

"I'm feeling fine. I'm just a little tired, that's all," Buddy told him. "I meant it serious though," Buddy said, "when I ask you did you have a good time this weekend—did you?"

Junior stood there with his hands folded in front of him. His legs were slightly bent, as though they weren't quite strong enough to hold his bulk. He shook his head. "It wasn't much of a time," he said.

Mr. Pool retreated to the far side of the solar system to let the boys talk. As the planets spun by him, he touched them with the very tips of his fingers and waited.

"Why wasn't it much of a time?" Buddy was asking Junior.

"It just wasn't," Junior said. He sat down in the folding chair once again. Buddy moved closer to hear. "He never did come home," Junior said.

"Aw, man," Buddy said, "I was up there too. When you didn't come down, I thought sure . . . All that weekend by yourself!"

Junior felt like he might cry all of a sudden. "You got to go with me on Friday," he said. "Buddy? Right? You promised you'd go with me to my lesson on Friday."

"Okay, okay, don't I always go with you?"

"I mean, go in with me so you can see for yourself. Will you go in with me?"

"I promised you, didn't I?" Buddy said. He didn't remember any such promise. "Look, man, don't get yourself all upset. I'll go with you. Everything's going to be fine."

Junior let his breath out in a ragged sigh. "This coming Wednesday I'll take you over to my house," Junior said. "I promised I would and I will."

Finally Buddy remembered the bus ride when he and Junior made their deal. "You sure your mother won't get mad at you for bringing me home?"

"You'll come over," Junior told him, "and my mother won't be mad that you can see."

Waiting, overhearing, Mr. Pool smiled to himself. It had taken Junior Brown all this time to admit to himself that he needed Buddy Clark, that he could go no further with something he had to do without big Buddy helping him.

Maybe that's a beginning, Mr. Pool thought. He knew about Junior's mother. She was a self-centered, sickly woman who was probably good at heart. It upset him to know she would condemn Junior's friendship with Buddy simply because Buddy looked tough.

She isn't going to like one bit Junior bringing a poor boy home with him.

The squeak of the solar system intruded on Mr. Pool's thoughts.

"Somebody help me find that squeak," he said, touching the planets.

"Maybe the squeak isn't in the system at all," came from the far side of the planets. Buddy Clark.

"It is in the system," Mr. Pool told him.

"But maybe the system is just rubbing too hard against the dark," Buddy said. He laughed loudly at his own nonsense.

"Keep it down," Mr. Pool said. "We're going to get ourselves caught because of you."

On the far side, at the edge of the void, Buddy covered his mouth. He'd forgot for a moment that the solar system was not somehow up in space. He was feeling better. Here he was going over to Junior's house on Wednesday, just like some regular cat, and then on Friday, he'd go over with Junior to see Junior's music teacher. He'd straighten everything for Junior with the relative. Buddy was cool, whatever was wrong, he could fix it. Maybe soon he and Junior would be really tight, like brothers.

Like somebody I can tell everything to, even tell about the planets.

Buddy looked at big, bad Junior sitting so sad in his chair.

Man, when you see what I am into—taking care of kids, working my job. Wait till you meet old Doum—man, blow your mind! You going to want to be free as me . . .

Tuesday was no different and Wednesday Buddy lay on his back in Junior's room. He tried to remember when he'd rested on anything as comfortable as Junior's bed. Buddy had to keep blinking his eyes to keep from falling asleep. Junior's room was so peaceful. The heat of the house poured into him, warming him to his soul.

Junior played the piano across the room from Buddy. He hadn't been practicing much, he told Buddy earlier, but today he had felt like playing. As the windows filled with winter shadows, Junior played on and on.

Filling Junior's mind was the swelling, bursting sound of Miss Peebs' grand piano. With the strength of his imagination, he tried to fuse the music to the silence of his own Baldwin upright piano. As he pressed the soundless keys, he thought the responding tones. He never could quite imagine them as pure as the music of the concert grand.

Buddy watched Junior with amazement. For Junior swayed like a dark, brooding bear to an unheard rhythm in the stillness.

Since he'd come into the room, Buddy hadn't believed what he was seeing. Several times he couldn't help heaving himself up from the bed and tiptoeing over to the piano.

The top of Junior's piano had been taken off so that more sound could get out. But all of the wires meant to vibrate to make that sound had been removed. In place were the felt hammers made to hit the wires when the piano keys were pressed down. But the hammers struck against nothing. As Junior played on and on, the hammers rose and fell senselessly.

Buddy turned over and pressed his face into the soft fabric of the bedspread.

He felt empty of himself but outraged at the damage done to Junior.

Taking away his sound from him, Buddy thought. How could she do that to her own son?

From some far place, a deep place of his heart, Buddy slowly understood.

All their lives, they have been this family, he thought. Up so close, and for so long, they can't separate any of it. She has to have rest. Junior has to play his piano. I bet that's the way it is.

Buddy sat up on the edge of Junior's bed. He watched hulking Junior swaying in time with silence.

He plays a piano without sound and she has her peace and quiet. "God Almighty," Buddy said out loud. He got up.

I can't stay here anymore.

"Junior? Hey, man? You finish up so we can split someplace. You want to see a film?"

A minute passed before Junior stopped. Smiling, he rubbed his hands together, as if he were washing them. He grinned at Buddy while his eyes remained sad. "A movie?" he said.

"Anything," Buddy said. "Let's just get out of here."

"I never do go out at night," Junior said.

Buddy stared at him. "You just went out the other night, a week ago. I saw you," Buddy told him.

"I never go out without my mother," Junior said. The grin quivered.

I'll swim the river before I take his mother to a show, Buddy thought. "Man, you can go with me if you want," he said. I might even show you my planet. How am I ever going to get you down the ladder to see it? Maybe if I just tell you about it, we both could figure a way to get you down there. "You got to want to go," Buddy said. "Man, it's up to you."

"I haven't had my supper." Softly Junior spoke and got up from the piano.

"Nobody said it's ready yet," Buddy told him.

"Nobody has to say," Junior said. He stood with his hands folded in front of him, his head down, as though he were praying.

Buddy didn't realize at once that Junior was waiting. By the time he did, Junior's mother had walked in on them. She came close to Junior. She held her hands folded in front of her the way Junior did.

"Your supper is ready now, son," she said. Mrs. Brown turned to Buddy. She stiffened, her thought bristling with contempt. Buddy Clark towered over her the way her own son would not. Hard with muscle, he was overbearing even when he was not moving or speaking. "You are staying for dinner, of course," she said to Buddy.

"That was the plan me and Junior had," Buddy said right back at her.

Boldly, Junior's friend was staring her down. She knew any decent boy would have lowered his eyes. But she continued to study him as though he were some rampant thing too widespread to be destroyed. He was not too different from the growth she weeded from her window box. And if she ever had the garden she dreamed of, she would cut this Buddy down toward evening.

"Come along then," she told him. Buddy waited for Junior to go first. Then he followed, ashamed he hadn't found the nerve to tell Junior's mother what he thought of her.

Katherine Paterson

Bridge to Terabithia

This landmark novel by a distinguished children's author explores the characters of two contemporary children, both outsiders, who are trying to be true to themselves in the face of the expectations of family and society. Ten-year-old Jess is quiet, artistic, and alienated from his busy rural Virginia family. He finds new perceptions of life in his friendship with Leslie, a girl from the city. She introduces him to books and ideas as they build a refuge in the imaginary kingdom of Terabithia. The story of Leslie's sudden death by drowning and Jess's struggle to accept it is searing in its emotional honesty. No less convincing is the growth of Leslie's friendship with Jess, described in this selection. *Bridge to Terabithia* won the 1978 Newbery Medal. [From Katherine Paterson, *Bridge to Terabithia* (Crowell, 1977).]

Rulers of Terabithia

After they had watched May Belle tearing up the hill, clutching her new treasure, Jess and Leslie turned and ran up over the empty field behind the old Perkins place and down to the dry creek bed that separated farmland from the woods. There was an old crab apple tree there, just at the bank of the creek bed, from which someone long forgotten had hung a rope.

They took turns swinging across the gully on the rope. It was a glorious autumn day, and if you looked up as you swung, it gave you the feeling of floating. Jess leaned back and drank in the rich, clear color of the sky. He was drifting, drifting like a fat white lazy cloud back and forth across the blue.

"Do you know what we need?" Leslie called to him. Intoxicated as he was with the heavens, he couldn't imagine needing anything on earth.

"We need a place," she said, "just for us. It would be so secret that we would never tell anyone in the whole world about it." Jess came swinging back and dragged his feet to stop. She lowered her voice almost to a whisper. "It might be a whole secret country," she continued, "and you and I would be the rulers of it."

Her words stirred inside of him. He'd like to be a ruler of something. Even something that wasn't real. "OK," he said. "Where could we have it?"

"Over there in the woods where nobody would come and mess it up."

There were parts of the woods that Jess did not like. Dark places where it was almost like being under water, but he didn't say so.

"I know"—she was getting excited—"it could be a magic country like Narnia, and the only way you can get in is by swinging across on this enchanted rope." Her eyes were bright. She grabbed the rope. "Come on," she said. "Let's find a place to build our castle stronghold."

They had gone only a few yards into the woods beyond the creek bed when Leslie stopped.

"How about right here?" she asked.

"Sure," Jess agreed quickly, relieved that there was no need to plunge deeper into the woods. He would take her there, of course, for he wasn't such a coward that he would mind a little exploring now and then farther in amongst the ever-darkening columns of the tall pines. But as a regular thing, as a permanent place, this was where he would choose to be— here where the dogwood and redbud played hide and seek between the oaks and evergreens, and the sun flung itself in golden streams through the trees to splash warmly at their feet.

"Sure," he repeated himself, nodding vigorously. The underbrush was dry and would be easy to clear away. The ground was almost level. "This'll be a good place to build."

Leslie named their secret land "Terabithia," and she loaned Jess all of her books about Narnia, so he would know how things went in a magic kingdom—how the animals and the trees must be protected and how a ruler must behave. That was the hard part. When Leslie spoke, the words rolling out so regally, you knew she was a proper queen. He could hardly manage English, much less the poetic language of a king.

But he could make stuff. They dragged boards and other materials down from the scrap heap by Miss Bessie's pasture and built their castle stronghold in the place they had found in the woods. Leslie filled a three-pound coffee can with crackers and dried fruit and a one-pound can with strings and nails. They found

five old Pepsi bottles which they washed and filled with water, in case, as Leslie said, "of siege."

Like God in the Bible, they looked at what they had made and found it very good.

"You should draw a picture of Terabithia for us to hang in the castle," Leslie said.

"I can't." How could he explain it in a way Leslie would understand, how he yearned to reach out and capture the quivering life about him and how when he tried, it slipped past his fingertips, leaving a dry fossil upon the page? "I just can't get the poetry of the trees," he said.

She nodded. "Don't worry," she said. "You will someday."

He believed her because there in the shadowy light of the stronghold everything seemed possible. Between the two of them they owned the world and no enemy, Gary Fulcher, Wanda Kay Moore, Janice Avery, Jess's own fears and insufficiencies, nor any of the foes whom Leslie imagined attacking Terabithia, could ever really defeat them. A few days after they finished the castle, Janice Avery fell down in the school bus and yelled that Jess had tripped her as she went past. She made such a fuss that Mrs. Prentice, the driver, ordered Jess off the bus, and he had to walk the three miles home.

When Jess finally got to Terabithia, Leslie was huddled next to one of the cracks below the roof trying to get enough light to read. There was a picture on the cover which showed a killer whale attacking a dolphin.

"Whatcha doing?" He came in and sat beside her on the ground.

"Reading. I had to do something. That girl!" Her anger came rocketing to the surface.

"It don't matter. I don't mind walking all that much." What was a little hike compared to what Janice Avery might have chosen to do?

"It's the *principle* of the thing, Jess. That's what you've got to understand. You have to stop people like that. Otherwise they turn into tyrants and dictators."

He reached over and took the whale book from her hands, pretending to study the bloody picture on the jacket. "Getting any good ideas?"

"What?"

"I thought you was getting some ideas on how to stop Janice Avery."

"No, stupid. We're trying to *save* the whales. They might become extinct."

He gave her back the book. "You save the whales and shoot the people, huh?"

She grinned finally. "Something like that, I guess. Say, did you ever hear the story about Moby Dick?"

"Who's that?"

"Well, there was once this huge white whale named Moby Dick. . . ." And Leslie began to spin out a wonderful story about a whale and a crazy sea captain who was bent on killing it. His fingers itched to try to draw it on paper.

Illustration by Donna Diamond, from *Bridge to Terabithia*, by Katherine Paterson (Thomas Y. Crowell). Copyright © 1977 by Katherine Paterson. Reprinted by permission of Harper & Row, Publishers, Inc.

Maybe if he had some proper paints, he could do it. There ought to be a way of making the whale shimmering white against the dark water.

At first they avoided each other during school hours, but by October they grew careless about their friendship. Gary Fulcher, like Brenda, took great pleasure in teasing Jess about his "*girl* friend." It hardly bothered Jess. He knew that a *girl* friend was somebody who chased you on the playground and tried to grab you and kiss you. He could no more imagine Leslie chasing a boy than he could imagine Mrs. Double-Chinned Myers shinnying up the flagpole. Gary Fulcher could go to you-know-where and warm his toes.

There was really no free time at school except recess, and now that there were no races, Jess and Leslie usually looked for a quiet place on the field, and sat and talked. Except for the magic half hour on Fridays, recess was all that Jess looked forward to at school. Leslie could always come up with something funny that made the long days bearable. Often the joke was on Mrs. Myers. Leslie was one of those people who sat quietly at her desk, never whispering or daydreaming or chewing gum, doing beautiful schoolwork, and yet her brain was so full of mischief that if the teacher could have once seen through that mask of perfection, she would have thrown her out in horror.

Jess could hardly keep a straight face in class just trying to imagine what might be going on behind that angelic look of Leslie's. One whole morning, as Leslie had related it at recess, she had spent imagining Mrs. Myers on one of those fat farms down in Arizona. In her fantasy, Mrs. Myers was one of the foodaholics who would hide bits of candy bars in odd places—up the hot water faucet!—only to be found out and publicly humiliated before all the other fat ladies. That afternoon Jess kept having visions of Mrs. Myers dressed only in a pink corset being weighed in. "You've been cheating again, Gussie!" the tall skinny directoress was saying. Mrs. Myers was on the verge of tears.

"Jesse Aarons!" The teacher's sharp voice punctured his daydream. He couldn't look Mrs. Myers straight in her pudgy face. He'd crack up. He set his sight on her uneven hemline.

"Yes'm." He was going to have to get coaching from Leslie. Mrs. Myers always caught him when his mind was on vacation, but she never seemed to suspect Leslie of not paying attention. He sneaked a glance up that way. Leslie was totally absorbed in her geography book, or so it would appear to anyone who didn't know.

Terabithia was cold in November. They didn't dare build a fire in the castle, though sometimes they would build one outside and huddle around it. For a while Leslie had been able to keep two sleeping bags in the stronghold, but around the first of December her father noticed their absence, and she had to take them back. Actually, Jess made her take them back. It was not that he was afraid of the Burkes exactly. Leslie's parents were young, with straight white teeth and lots of hair—both of them. Leslie called them Judy and Bill, which bothered Jess more than he wanted it to. It was none of his business what Leslie called her parents. But he just couldn't get used to it.

Both of the Burkes were writers. Mrs. Burke wrote novels and, according to Leslie, was more famous than Mr. Burke, who wrote about politics. It was really something to see the shelf that had their books on it. Mrs. Burke was "Judith Hancock" on the cover, which threw you at first, but then if you looked on the back, there was her picture looking very young and serious. Mr. Burke was going back and forth to Washington to finish a book he was working on with someone else, but he had promised Leslie that after Christmas he would stay home and fix up the house and plant his garden and listen to music and read books out loud and write only in his spare time.

They didn't look like Jess's idea of rich, but even he could tell that the jeans they wore had not come off the counter at Newberry's. There was no TV at the Burkes', but there were mountains of records and a stereo set that looked like something off *Star Trek.* And although their car was small and dusty, it was Italian and looked expensive, too.

They were always nice to Jess when he went over, but then they would suddenly begin talking about French politics or string quartets (which he at first thought was a square box made out of string), or how to save the timber wolves or redwoods or singing whales, and he was scared to open his mouth and show once and for all how dumb he was.

He wasn't comfortable having Leslie at his house either. Joyce Ann would stare, her index finger pulling down her mouth and making her drool. Brenda and Ellie always managed some remark about "*girl* friend." His mother acted stiff and funny just the way she did when she had to go up to school about something. Later she would refer to Leslie's "tacky" clothes. Leslie always wore pants, even to school. Her hair was "shorter than a boy's." Her parents were "hardly more than hippies." May Belle either tried to push in with him and Leslie or sulked at being left out. His father had seen Leslie only a few times and had nodded to show that he had noticed her, but his mother said that she was sure he was fretting that his only son did nothing but play with girls, and they both were worried about what would become of it.

Jess didn't concern himself with what would "become of it." For the first time in his life he got up every morning with something to look forward to. Leslie was more than his friend. She was his other, more exciting self— his way to Terabithia and all the worlds beyond.

Terabithia was their secret, which was a good thing, for how could Jess have ever explained it to an outsider? Just walking down the hill toward the woods made something warm and liquid steal through his body. The closer he came to the dry creek bed and the crab apple tree rope the more he could feel the beating of his heart. He grabbed the end of the rope and swung out toward the other bank with a kind of wild exhilaration and landed gently on his feet, taller and stronger and wiser in that mysterious land.

Leslie's favorite place besides the castle stronghold was the pine forest. There the trees grew so thick at the top that the sunshine was veiled. No low bush or grass could grow in that dim light, so the ground was carpeted with golden needles.

"I used to think this place was haunted," Jess had confessed to Leslie the first afternoon he had revved up his courage to bring her there.

"Oh, but it is," she said. "But you don't have to be scared. It's not haunted with evil things."

"How do you know?"

"You can just feel it. Listen."

At first he heard only the stillness. It was the stillness that had always frightened him before, but this time it was like the moment after Miss Edmunds finished a song, just after the chords hummed down to silence. Leslie was right. They stood there, not moving, not wanting the swish of dry needles beneath their feet to break the spell. Far away from their former world came the cry of geese heading southward.

Leslie took a deep breath. "This is not an ordinary place," she whispered. "Even the rulers of Terabithia come into it only at times of greatest sorrow or of greatest joy. We must strive to keep it sacred. It would not do to disturb the Spirits."

He nodded, and without speaking, they went back to the creek bank where they shared together a solemn meal of crackers and dried fruit.

Mark Twain

The Adventures of Tom Sawyer

The Adventures of Tom Sawyer is an American classic of boy life. Mark Twain based the story on his own boyhood in Missouri. When he sent the manuscript to his friend William Dean Howells for criticism, Howells pronounced it "altogether the best boy's story I have ever read." The book was first published in 1876 and still maintains its leadership among the most popular children's books. In the chapter given below, the reader meets Becky Thatcher and Huck Finn. The story is continued in *Adventures of Huckleberry Finn.* The racist language and attitudes of some of Twain's characters reflect the cultural stereotypes of rural Missouri in the 1800s. But the voice of bigotry is not that of the author. Twain satirizes the racist attitudes of his time but also portrays characters of deep human compassion. [From Samuel L. Clemens (Mark Twain), *The Adventures of Tom Sawyer* (The American Publishing Company, A. Roman & Co., 1876).]

Tom Meets Becky

Monday morning found Tom Sawyer miserable. Monday morning always found him so—because it began another week's slow suffering in school. He generally began that day with wishing he had had no intervening holiday, it made the going into captivity and fetters again so much more odious.

Tom lay thinking. Presently it occurred to him that he wished he was sick; then he could stay home from school. Here was a vague possibility. He canvassed his system. No ailment was found, and he investigated again. This time he thought he could detect colicky symptoms, and he began to encourage them with considerable hope. But they soon grew feeble, and presently died wholly away. He reflected further. Suddenly he discovered something. One of his upper front teeth was loose. This was lucky; he was about to begin to groan, as a "starter," as he called it, when it occurred to him that if he came into court with that argument, his aunt would pull it out, and that would hurt. So he thought he would hold the tooth in reserve for the present, and seek further. Nothing offered for some little time, and then he remembered hearing the doctor tell about a certain thing that laid up a patient for two or three weeks and threatened to make him lose a finger. So the boy eagerly drew his sore toe from under the sheet and held it up for inspection. But now he did not know the necessary symptoms. However, it seemed well worth while to chance it, so he fell to groaning with considerable spirit.

But Sid slept on unconscious.

Tom groaned louder, and fancied that he began to feel pain in the toe.

No result from Sid.

Tom was panting with his exertions by this time. He took a rest and then swelled himself up and fetched a succession of admirable groans.

Sid snored on.

Tom was aggravated. He said, "Sid, Sid!" and shook him. This course worked well, and Tom began to groan again. Sid yawned, stretched, then brought himself up on his elbow with a snort, and began to stare at Tom. Tom went on groaning. Sid said:

"Tom! Say, Tom! [No response.] Here, Tom! *Tom!* What is the matter, Tom?" And he shook him and looked in his face anxiously.

Tom moaned out:

"Oh, don't, Sid. Don't joggle me."

"Why, what's the matter, Tom? I must call Auntie."

"No—never mind. It'll be over by and by, maybe. Don't call anybody."

"But I must! *Don't* groan so, Tom, it's awful. How long you been this way?"

"Hours. Ouch! Oh, don't stir so, Sid, you'll kill me."

"Tom, why didn't you wake me sooner? Oh, Tom, *don't!* It makes my flesh crawl to hear you. Tom, what *is* the matter?"

"I forgive you everything, Sid. [Groan.] Everything you've ever done to me. When I'm gone—"

"Oh, Tom, you ain't dying, are you? Don't, Tom—oh, don't. Maybe—"

"I forgive everybody, Sid. [Groan.] Tell 'em so, Sid. And Sid, you give my windowsash, and my cat with one eye to that new girl that's come to town, and tell her—"

But Sid had snatched his clothes and gone. Tom was suffering in reality, now, so handsomely was his imagination working, and so his groans had gathered quite a genuine tone.

Sid flew downstairs and said:

"Oh, Aunt Polly, come! Tom's dying!"

"Dying!"

"Yes'm. Don't wait—come quick!"

"Rubbage! I don't believe it!"

But she fled upstairs, nevertheless, with Sid and Mary at her heels. And her face grew white, too, and her lip trembled. When she reached the bedside she gasped out:

"You, Tom! Tom, what's the matter with you?"

"Oh, Auntie, I'm—"

"What's the matter with you—what *is* the matter with you, child?"

"Oh, Auntie, my sore toe's mortified!"

The old lady sank down into a chair and laughed a little, then cried a little, then did both together. This restored her and she said:

"Tom, what a turn you did give me! Now you shut up that nonsense and climb out of this."

The groans ceased and the pain vanished from the toe. The boy felt a little foolish, and he said:

"Aunt Polly, it *seemed* mortified, and it hurt so I never minded my tooth at all."

"Your tooth, indeed! What's the matter with your tooth?"

"One of them's loose, and it aches perfectly awful."

"There, there, now, don't begin that groaning again. Open your mouth. Well—your tooth *is* loose, but you're not going to die about that. Mary, get me a silk thread, and a chunk of fire out of the kitchen."

Tom said:

"Oh, please, Auntie, don't pull it out! It don't hurt any more. I wish I may never stir if it does. Please don't, Auntie. *I* don't want to stay home from school."

"Oh, you don't, don't you? So, all this row was because you thought you'd get to stay home from school and go a-fishing? Tom, Tom, I love you so, and you seem to try every way you can to break my old heart with your outrageousness." By this time the dental instruments were ready. The old lady made one end of the silk thread fast to Tom's tooth with a loop and tied the other to the bedpost. Then she seized the chunk of fire and suddenly thrust it almost into the boy's face. The tooth hung dangling by the bedpost, now.

But all trials bring their compensations. As Tom wended to school after breakfast, he was the envy of every boy he met because the gap in his upper row of teeth enabled him to expectorate in a new and admirable way. He gathered quite a following of lads interested in the exhibition; and one that had cut his finger and had been a center of fascination and homage up to this time now found himself suddenly without an adherent and shorn of his glory. His heart was heavy, and he said with a disdain which he did not feel that it wasn't anything to spit like Tom Sawyer; but another boy said "Sour grapes!" and he wandered away a dismantled hero.

Shortly Tom came upon the juvenile pariah of the village, Huckleberry Finn, son of the town drunkard. Huckleberry was cordially hated and dreaded by all the mothers of the town, because he was idle and lawless and vulgar and bad—and because all their children admired him so, and delighted in his forbidden society, and wished they dared to be like him. Tom was like the rest of the respectable boys, in that he envied Huckleberry his gaudy outcast condition, and was under strict orders not to play with him. So he played with him every time he got a chance. Huckleberry was always dressed in the castoff clothes of full-grown men, and they were in perennial bloom and fluttering with rags. His hat was a vast ruin with a wide crescent lopped out of its brim; his coat, when he wore one, hung nearly to his heels and had the rearward buttons far down the back; but one suspender supported his trousers; the seat of the trousers bagged low and contained nothing; the fringed legs dragged in the dirt when not rolled up.

Huckleberry came and went, at his own free will. He slept on doorsteps in fine weather and in empty hogsheads in wet; he did not have to go to school or to church, or call any being master or obey anybody; he could go fishing or swimming when and where he chose, and stay as long as it suited him; nobody forbade him to fight; he could sit up as late as he pleased; he was always the first boy that went barefoot in the spring and the last to resume leather in the fall; he never had to wash, nor put on clean clothes; he could swear wonderfully. In a word, everything that goes to make life precious that boy had. So thought every harassed, hampered, respectable boy in St. Petersburg.

Tom hailed the romantic outcast:

"Hello, Huckleberry!"

"Hello yourself, and see how you like it."

"What's that you got?"

"Dead cat."

"Lemme see him, Huck. My, he's pretty stiff. Where'd you get him?"

"Bought him off'n a boy."

"What did you give?"

"I give a blue ticket and a bladder that I got at the slaughter-house."

"Where's you get the blue ticket?"

"Bought it off'n Ben Rogers two weeks ago for a hoopstick."

"Say—what is dead cats good for, Huck?"

"Good for? Cure warts with."

"No! Is that so? I know something that's better."

"I bet you don't. What is it?"

"Why, spunk-water."

"Spunk-water! I wouldn't give a dern for spunk-water."

"You wouldn't, wouldn't you? D'you ever try it?"

"No, I hain't. But Bob Tanner did."

"Who told you so?"

"Why, he told Jeff Thatcher, and Jeff told Johnny Baker, and Johnny told Jim Hollis, and Jim told Ben Rogers, and Ben told a nigger and the nigger told me. There now!"

"Well, what of it? They'll all lie. Leastways all but the nigger. I don't know *him.* But I never see a nigger that *wouldn't* lie. Shucks! Now you tell me how Bob Tanner done it, Huck."

Illustration by Louis Slobodkin. From *The Adventures of Tom Sawyer,* by Mark Twain, illustrated by Louis Slobodkin. Copyright © 1949 by The World Publishing Company.

"Why, he took and dipped his hand in a rotten stump where the rainwater was."

"In the daytime?"

"Certainly."

"With his face to the stump?"

"Yes. Least I reckon so."

"Did he *say* anything?"

"I don't reckon he did. I don't know."

"Aha! Talk about trying to cure warts with spunk-water such a blame-fool way as that! Why, that ain't a-going to do any good. You got to go all by yourself, to the middle of the woods, where you know there's a spunk-water stump, and just as it's midnight you back up against the stump and jam your hand in and say:

Barley-corn, barley-corn, injun-meal shorts
Spunk-water, spunk-water, swaller these warts,

and then walk away quick, eleven steps, with your eyes shut, and then turn around three times and walk home without speaking to anybody. Because if you speak the charm's busted."

"Well, that sounds like a good way; but that ain't the way Bob Tanner done."

"No sir you can bet he didn't, becuz he's the wartiest boy in this town; and he wouldn't have a wart on him if he'd knowed how to work spunk-water. I've took off thousands of warts off of my hands that way, Huck. I play with frogs so much that I've always got considerable many warts. Sometimes I take 'em off with a bean."

"Yes, bean's good. I've done that."

"Have you? What's your way?"

"You take and split the bean, and cut the wart so as to get some blood, and then you put the blood on one piece of the bean and take and dig a hole and bury it 'bout midnight at the crossroads in the dark of the moon, and then you burn up the rest of the bean. You see that piece that's got the blood on it will keep drawing and drawing, trying to fetch the other piece to it, and so that helps the blood to draw the wart, and pretty soon off she comes."

"Yes, that's it, Huck—that's it; though when you're burying it if you say, 'Down bean; off wart; come no more to bother me!' it's better. That's the way Joe Harper does, and he's been nearly to Coonville and most everywheres. But say—how do you cure 'em with dead cats?"

"Why, you take your cat and go and get in the graveyard 'long about midnight when somebody that was wicked has been buried; and when it's midnight a devil will come, or maybe two or three, but you can't see 'em, you can only hear something like the wind, or maybe hear 'em talk; and when they're taking that feller away, you heave your cat after 'em and say, "Devil follow corpse, cat follow devil, warts follow cat, *I'm* done with ye!" That'll fetch *any* wart."

"Sounds right. D'you ever try it, Huck?"

"No, but old Mother Hopkins told me."

"Well, I reckon it's so, then. Becuz they say she's a witch."

"Say! Why, Tom, I *know* she is. She witched Pap. Pap says so his own self. He come along one day, and he see she was a-witching him, so he took up a rock, and if she hadn't dodged, he'd 'a' got her. Well, that very night he rolled off'n a shed wher' he was a-layin' drunk, and broke his arm."

"Why, that's awful! How did he know she was a-witching him?"

"Lord, Pap can tell easy. Pap says when they keep looking at you right stiddy, they're a-witching you. 'Specially if they mumble. Becuz when they mumble they're saying the Lord's Prayer back'ards."

"Say, Hucky, when you going to try the cat?"

"Tonight. I reckon they'll come after old Hoss Williams tonight."

"But they buried him Saturday. Didn't they get him Saturday night?"

"Why, how you talk! How could their charms work till midnight?—and *then* its Sunday. Devils don't slosh around much of a Sunday, I don't reckon."

"I never thought of that. That's so. Lemme go with you?"

"Of course—if you ain't afeard."

"Afeard! 'Tain't likely. Will you meow?"

"Yes—and you meow back, if you get a chance. Last time, you kep' me a-meowing around till old Hays went to throwing rocks at me and says 'Dern that cat!' and so I hove a brick through his window—but don't you tell."

"I won't. I couldn't meow that night, becuz Auntie was watching me, but I'll meow this time. Say—what's that?"

"Nothing but a tick."

"Where'd you get him?"

"Out in the woods."

"What'll you take for him?"

"I don't know. I don't want to sell him."

"All right. It's a mighty small tick, anyway."

"Oh, anybody can run a tick down that don't belong to them. I'm satisfied with it. It's a good enough tick for me."

"Sho, there's ticks a-plenty. I could have a thousand of 'em if I wanted to."

"Well, why don't you? Becuz you know mighty well you can't. This is a pretty early tick, I reckon. It's the first one I've seen this year."

"Say, Huck—I'll give you my tooth for him."

"Less see it."

Tom got out a bit of paper and carefully unrolled it. Huckleberry viewed it wistfully. The temptation was very strong. At last he said:

"Is it genuwyne?"

Tom lifted his lip and showed the vacancy.

"Well, all right," said Huckleberry, "it's a trade."

Tom enclosed the tick in the percussion-cap box that had lately been the pinch-bug's prison, and the boys separated, each feeling wealthier than before.

When Tom reached the little isolated frame schoolhouse, he strode in briskly, with the manner of one who had come with all honest speed. He hung his hat on a peg and flung himself into his seat with businesslike alacrity. The master, throned on high in his great splint-bottom armchair, was dozing, lulled by the drowsy hum of study. The interruption roused him.

"Thomas Sawyer!"

Tom knew that when his name was pronounced in full, it meant trouble.

"Sir!"

"Come up here. Now, sir, why are you late again, as usual?"

Tom was about to take refuge in a lie, when he saw two long tails of yellow hair hanging down a back that he recognized by the electric sympathy of love; and by that form was *the only vacant place* on the girls' side of the schoolhouse. He instantly said:

"I STOPPED TO TALK WITH HUCKLEBERRY FINN!"

The master's pulse stood still, and he stared helplessly. The buzz of study ceased. The pupils wondered if this foolhardy boy had lost his mind. The master said:

"You—you did what?"

"Stopped to talk with Huckleberry Finn."

There was no mistaking the words.

"Thomas Sawyer, this is the most astounding confession I have ever listened to. No mere ferule will answer for this offense. Take off your jacket."

The master's arm performed until it was tired and the stock of switches notably diminished. Then the order followed:

"Now, sir, go and sit with the *girls!* And let this be a warning to you."

The titter that rippled around the room appeared to abash the boy, but in reality that result was caused rather more by his worshipful awe of his unknown idol and the dread pleasure that lay in his high good fortune. He sat down upon the end of the pine bench and the girl hitched herself away from him with a toss of her head. Nudges and winks and whispers traversed the room, but Tom sat still, with his arms upon the long, low desk before him, and seemed to study his book.

By and by attention ceased from him, and the accustomed school murmur rose upon the dull air once more. Presently the boy began to steal furtive glances at the girl. She observed it, "made a mouth" at him and gave him the back of her head for the space of a minute. When she cautiously faced around again, a peach lay before her. She thrust it away. Tom gently put it back. She thrust it away again, but with less animosity. Tom patiently returned it to its place. Then she let it remain. Tom scrawled on his slate, "Please take it—I got more." The girl glanced at the words, but made no sign. Now the boy began to draw something on the slate, hiding his work with his left hand. For a time the girl refused to notice; but her human curiosity presently began to manifest itself by hardly perceptible signs. The boy worked on, apparently unconscious. The girl made a sort of non-committal attempt to see it, but the boy did not betray that he was aware of it. At last she gave in and hesitatingly whispered:

"Let me see it."

Tom partly uncovered a dismal caricature of a house with two gable ends to it and a cork-screw of smoke issuing from the chimney. Then the girl's interest began to fasten itself upon the work and she forgot everything else. When it was finished, she gazed a moment, then whispered:

"It's nice—make a man."

The artist erected a man in the front yard, that resembled a derrick. He could have stepped over the house; but the girl was not hypercritcial; she was satisfied with the monster, and whispered:

"It's a beautiful man—now make me coming along."

Tom drew an hour-glass with a full moon and straw limbs to it and armed the spreading fingers with a portentous fan. The girl said:

"It's ever so nice—I wish I could draw."

"It's easy," whispered Tom, "I'll learn you."

"Oh, will you? When?"

"At noon. Do you go home to dinner?"

"I'll stay if you will."

"Good—that's a whack. What's your name?"

"Becky Thatcher. What's yours? Oh, I know. It's Thomas Sawyer."

"That's the name they lick me by. I'm Tom when I'm good. You call me Tom, will you?"

"Yes."

Now Tom began to scrawl something on the slate, hiding the words from the girl. But she was not backward this time. She begged to see. Tom said:

"Oh, it ain't anything."

"Yes, it is."

"No, it ain't. You don't want to see!"

"Yes, I do, indeed I do. Please let me."

"You'll tell."

"No, I won't—deed and deed and double deed I won't."

"You won't tell anybody at all? Ever, as long as you live?"

"No, I won't ever tell *anybody.* Now let me."

"Oh, *you* don't want to see!"

"Now that you treat me so, I *will* see." And she put her small hand upon his and a little scuffle ensued, Tom pretending to resist in earnest, but letting his hand slip by degrees till these words were revealed: *"I love you."*

"Oh, you bad thing!" And she hit his hand a smart rap, but reddened and looked pleased, nevertheless.

Just at this juncture the boy felt a slow, fateful grip closing on his ear, and a steady lifting impulse. In that vise he was borne across the house and deposited in his own seat, under a peppering fire of giggles from the whole school. Then the master stood over him during a few awful moments, and finally moved away to his throne without saying a word. But although Tom's ear tingled, his heart was jubilant.

As the school quieted down, Tom made an honest effort to study, but the turmoil within him was too great. In turn he took his place in the reading class and made a botch of it; then in the geography class and turned lakes into mountains, mountains into rivers, and rivers into continents, till chaos was come again; then in the spelling class, and got "turned down," by a succession of mere baby words, till he brought up at the foot and yielded up the pewter medal which he had worn with ostentation for months.

Mildred D. Taylor

Roll of Thunder, Hear My Cry

Set in Mississippi during the Depression, *Roll of Thunder, Hear My Cry* is a historical novel of the recent and shameful past. Fourth-grader Cassie Logan is a spirited, independent girl from a loving, strong family. But, in the one eventful year chronicled in this story, she observes her family's courageous struggle against poverty, racism, and terrorism build toward a violent climax. In this selection, a traditional school scene that reveals character and theme, Cassie and her six-year-old brother, Little Man, confront their first intimations of racism. This book won the 1977 Newbery Medal. [From Mildred D. Taylor, *Roll of Thunder, Hear My Cry* (Dial, 1976).]

The Great Faith Elementary and Secondary School, one of the largest black schools in the county, was a dismal end to an hour's journey. Consisting of four weather-beaten wooden houses on stilts of brick, 320 students, seven teachers, a principal, a caretaker, and the care-taker's cow, which kept the wide crabgrass lawn sufficiently clipped in spring and summer, the school was located near three plantations, the largest and closest by far being the Granger plantation. Most of the students were from fam-ilies that sharecropped on Granger land, and the others mainly from Montier and Harrison plantation families. Because the students were needed in the fields from early spring when the cotton was planted until after most of the cotton had been picked in the fall, the school adjusted its terms accordingly, beginning in October and dismissing in March. But even so, after today a number of the older students would not be seen again for a month or two, not until the last puff of cotton had been gleaned from the fields, and eventually most would drop out of school altogether. Because of this the classes in the higher grades grew smaller with each passing year.

The class buildings, with their backs practi-cally against the forest wall, formed a semicircle facing a small one-room church at the opposite edge of the compound. It was to this church that many of the school's students and their par-ents belonged. As we arrived, the enormous iron bell in the church belfry was ringing vigor-ously, warning the milling students that only five minutes of freedom remained.

Little Man immediately pushed his way across the lawn to the well. Stacey and T. J., ignoring the rest of us now that they were on the school grounds, wandered off to be with the other sev-enth-grade boys, and Christopher-John and Claude rushed to reunite with their classmates of last year. Left alone, I dragged slowly to the building that held the first four grades and sat on the bottom step. Plopping my pencils and notebook into the dirt, I propped my elbows on my knees and rested my chin in the palms of my hands.

"Hey, Cassie," said Mary Lou Wellever, the principal's daughter, as she flounced by in a new yellow dress.

"Hey, yourself," I said, scowling so fero-ciously that she kept on walking. I stared after her a moment noting that she *would* have on a new dress. Certainly no one else did. Patches on faded pants and dresses abounded on boys and girls come so recently from the heat of the cotton fields. Girls stood awkwardly, afraid to sit, and boys pulled restlessly at starched, high-buttoned collars. Those students fortunate enough to have shoes hopped from one pinched foot to the other. Tonight the Sunday clothes would be wrapped in newspaper and hung for Sunday and the shoes would be packed away to be brought out again only when the weather turned so cold that bare feet could no longer traverse the frozen roads; but for today we all suffered.

On the far side of the lawn I spied Moe Turner speeding toward the seventh-grade-class building, and wondered at his energy. Moe was one of Stacey's friends. He lived on the Montier plantation, a three-and-a-half-hour walk from the school. Because of the distance, many chil-dren from the Montier plantation did not come to Great Faith after they had finished the four-year school near Smellings Creek. But there were some girls and boys like Moe who made the trek daily, leaving their homes while the sky was black and not returning until all was blackness again. I for one was certainly glad that I didn't live that far away. I don't think my feet would have wanted that badly for me to be educated.

The chiming of the second bell began. I stood up dusting my bottom as the first, second, third, and fourth graders crowded up the stairs into the hallway. Little Man flashed proudly past, his face and hands clean and his black shoes shining again. I glanced down at my own shoes powdered red and, raising my right foot, rubbed it against the back of my left leg, then reversed the procedure. As the last gong of the bell re-verberated across the compound, I swooped up my pencils and notebook and ran inside.

A hallway extended from the front to the back door of the building. On either side of the hall-way were two doorways, both leading into the same large room which was divided into two classrooms by a heavy canvas curtain. The sec-ond and third grades were on the left, the first and fourth grades on the right. I hurried to the rear of the building, turned to the right, and slid into a third-row bench occupied by Gracey Pearson and Alma Scott.

"You can't sit here," objected Gracey. "I'm saving it for Mary Lou."

I glanced back at Mary Lou Wellever depositing her lunch pail on a shelf in the back of the room and said, "Not any more you ain't."

Miss Daisy Crocker, yellow and buckeyed, glared down at me from the middle of the room with a look that said, "Sooooooooo, it's you, Cassie Logan." Then she pursed her lips and drew the curtain along the rusted iron rod and tucked it into a wide loop in the back wall. With the curtain drawn back, the first graders gazed quizzically at us. Little Man sat by a window, his hands folded, patiently waiting for Miss Crocker to speak.

Mary Lou nudged me. "That's my seat, Cassie Logan."

"Mary Lou Wellever," Miss Crocker called primly, "have a seat."

"Yes, ma'am," said Mary Lou, eyeing me with a look of pure hate before turning away.

Miss Crocker walked stiffly to her desk, which was set on a tiny platform and piled high with bulky objects covered by a tarpaulin. She rapped the desk with a ruler, although the room was perfectly still, and said, "Welcome, children, to Great Faith Elementary School." Turning slightly so that she stared squarely at the left side of the room, she continued, "To all of you fourth graders, it's good to have you in my class. I'll be expecting many good and wonderful things from you." Then addressing the right side of the room, she said, "And to all our little first grade friends only today starting on the road to knowledge and education, may your tiny feet find the pathways of learning steady and forever before you."

Already bored, I stretched my right arm on the desk and rested my head in my upraised hand.

Miss Crocker smiled mechanically, then rapped on her desk again. "Now, little ones," she said, still talking to the first grade, "your teacher, Miss Davis, has been held up in Jackson for a few days so I'll have the pleasure of sprinkling your little minds with the first rays of knowledge." She beamed down upon them as if she expected to be applauded for this bit of news, then with a swoop of her large eyes to include the fourth graders, she went on.

"Now since there's only one of me, we shall have to sacrifice for the next few days. We shall work, work, work, but we shall have to work like little Christian boys and girls and share, share, share. Now are we willing to do that?"

"YES'M, MIZ CROCKER," the children chorused.

But I remained silent. I never did approve of group responses. Adjusting my head in my hand, I sighed heavily, my mind on the burning of the Berrys.

"Cassie Logan?"

I looked up, startled.

"Cassie Logan!"

"Yes, ma'am?" I jumped up quickly to face Miss Crocker.

"Aren't you willing to work and share?"

"Yes'm."

"Then say so!"

"Yes'm," I murmured, sliding back into my seat as Mary Lou, Gracey, and Alma giggled. Here it was only five minutes into the new school year and already I was in trouble.

By ten o'clock, Miss Crocker had rearranged our seating and written our names on her seating chart. I was still sitting beside Gracey and Alma but we had been moved from the third to the first row in front of a small potbellied stove. Although being eyeball to eyeball with Miss Crocker was nothing to look forward to, the prospect of being warm once the cold weather set in was nothing to be sneezed at either, so I resolved to make the best of my rather dubious position.

Now Miss Crocker made a startling announcement: This year we would all have books.

Everyone gasped, for most of the students had never handled a book at all besides the family Bible. I admit that even I was somewhat excited. Although Mama had several books, I had never had one of my very own.

"Now we're very fortunate to get these readers," Miss Crocker explained while we eagerly awaited the unveiling. "The county superintendent of schools himself brought these books down here for our use and we must take extra-good care of them." She moved toward her desk. "So let's all promise that we'll take the best care possible of these new books." She stared down, expecting our response. "All right, all together, let's repeat, 'We promise to take good care of our new books.'" She looked sharply at me as she spoke.

"WE PROMISE TO TAKE GOOD CARE OF OUR NEW BOOKS!"

"Fine," Miss Crocker beamed, then proudly threw back the tarpaulin.

Sitting so close to the desk, I could see that the covers of the books, a motley red, were badly worn and that the gray edges of the pages had been marred by pencils, crayons, and ink. My anticipation at having my own book ebbed to a sinking disappointment. But Miss Crocker continued to beam as she called each fourth grader to her desk and, recording a number in her roll book, handed him or her a book.

As I returned from my trip to her desk, I noticed the first graders anxiously watching the disappearing pile. Miss Crocker must have noticed them too, for as I sat down she said, "Don't worry, little ones, there are plenty of readers for you too. See there on Miss Davis's desk." Wide eyes turned to the covered teacher's platform directly in front of them and an audible sigh of relief swelled in the room.

I glanced across at Little Man, his face lit in eager excitement. I knew that he could not see the soiled covers or the marred pages from where he sat, and even though his penchant for cleanliness was often annoying, I did not like to think of his disappointment when he saw the books as they really were. But there was nothing that I could do about it, so I opened my book to its center and began browsing through the spotted pages. Girls with blond braids and boys with blue eyes stared up at me. I found a story about a boy and his dog lost in a cave and began reading while Miss Crocker's voice droned on monotonously.

Suddenly I grew conscious of a break in that monotonous tone and I looked up. Miss Crocker was sitting at Miss Davis's desk with the first-grade books stacked before her, staring fiercely down at Little Man, who was pushing a book back upon the desk.

"What's that you said, Clayton Chester Logan?" she asked.

The room became gravely silent. Everyone knew that Little Man was in big trouble for no one, but no one, ever called Little Man "Clayton Chester" unless she or he meant serious business.

Little Man knew this too. His lips parted slightly as he took his hands from the book. He quivered, but he did not take his eyes from Miss Crocker. "I—I said may I have another book please, ma'am," he squeaked. "That one's dirty."

"Dirty!" Miss Crocker echoed, appalled by such temerity. She stood up, gazing down upon Little Man like a bony giant, but Little Man raised his head and continued to look into her eyes. "Dirty! And just who do you think you are, Clayton Chester? Here the county is giving us these wonderful books during these hard times and you're going to stand there and tell me that the book's too dirty? Now you take that book or get nothing at all!"

Little Man lowered his eyes and said nothing as he stared at the book. For several moments he stood there, his face barely visible above the desk, then he turned and looked at the few remaining books and, seeming to realize that they were as badly soiled as the one Miss Crocker had given him, he looked across the room at me. I nodded and Little Man, glancing up again at Miss Crocker, slid the book from the edge of the desk, and with his back straight and his head up returned to his seat.

Miss Crocker sat down again. "Some people around here seem to be giving themselves airs. I'll tolerate no more of that," she scowled. "Sharon Lake, come get your book."

I watched Little Man as he scooted into his seat beside two other little boys. He sat for a while with a stony face looking out the window; then, evidently accepting the fact that the book in front of him was the best that he could expect, he turned and opened it. But as he stared at the book's inside cover, his face clouded, changing from sulky acceptance to puzzlement. His brows furrowed. Then his eyes grew wide, and suddenly he sucked in his breath and sprang from his chair like a wounded animal, flinging the book onto the floor and stomping madly upon it.

Miss Crocker rushed to Little Man and grabbed him up in powerful hands. She shook him vigorously, then set him on the floor again. "Now, just what's gotten into you, Clayton Chester?"

But Little Man said nothing. He just stood staring down at the open book, shivering with indignant anger.

"Pick it up," she ordered.

"No!" defied Little Man.

"No? I'll give you ten seconds to pick up that book, boy, or I'm going to get my switch."

Little Man bit his lower lip, and I knew that he was not going to pick up the book. Rapidly, I turned to the inside cover of my own book and saw immediately what had made Little Man so furious. Stamped on the inside cover was a chart which read:

PROPERTY OF THE BOARD OF EDUCATION
Spokane County, Mississippi
September, 1922

CHRONO-LOGICAL ISSUANCE	DATE OF ISSUANCE	CONDITION OF BOOK	RACE OF STUDENT
1	September 1922	New	White
2	September 1923	Excellent	White
3	September 1924	Excellent	White
4	September 1925	Very Good	White
5	September 1926	Good	White
6	September 1927	Good	White
7	September 1928	Average	White
8	September 1929	Average	White
9	September 1930	Average	White
10	September 1931	Poor	White
11	September 1932	Poor	White
12	September 1933	Very Poor	nigra
13			
14			
15			

The blank lines continued down to line 20 and I knew that they had all been reserved for black students. A knot of anger swelled in my throat and held there. But as Miss Crocker directed Little Man to bend over the "whipping" chair, I put aside my anger and jumped up.

"Miz Crocker, don't please!" I cried. Miss Crocker's dark eyes warned me not to say another word. "I know why he done it!"

"You want part of this switch, Cassie?"

"No'm," I said hastily. "I just wanna tell you how come Little Man done what he done."

"Sit down!" she ordered as I hurried toward her with the open book in my hand.

Holding the book up to her, I said, "See, Miz Crocker, see what it says. They give us these ole books when they didn't want 'em no more."

She regarded me impatiently, but did not look at the book. "Now how could he know what it says? He can't read."

"Yes'm, he can. He been reading since he was four. He can't read all them big words, but he can read them columns. See what's in the last row. Please look, Miz Crocker."

This time Miss Crocker did look, but her face did not change. Then, holding up her head, she gazed unblinkingly down at me.

"S-see what they called us," I said, afraid she had not seen.

"That's what you are," she said coldly. "Now go sit down."

I shook my head, realizing now that Miss Crocker did not even know what I was talking about. She had looked at the page and had understood nothing.

"I said sit down, Cassie!"

I started slowly toward my desk, but as the hickory stick sliced the tense air, I turned back around. "Miz Crocker," I said, "I don't want my book neither."

The switch landed hard upon Little Man's upturned bottom. Miss Crocker looked questioningly at me as I reached up to her desk and placed the book upon it. Then she swung the switch five more times and, discovering that Little Man had no intention of crying, ordered him up.

"All right, Cassie," she sighed, turning to me, "come on and get yours."

Scott O'Dell

Island of the Blue Dolphins

This Robinson Crusoe story about an Indian girl who lives alone on an island for eighteen years is based on fact. The girl is Karana, and the island is off the California coast. After a tragic battle with another tribe, the survivors of Karana's people were rescued and taken by ship to the mainland, leaving Karana and her brother, Ramo, behind. In this chapter, she is carrying on a war of vengeance against the wild dogs who killed Ramo, for whose sake she had left the ship when it was about to sail. Scott O'Dell has said that this scene, in which there is a reversal of emotion, is one that parallels an event in his own life. A book that is much loved by readers, *Island of the Blue Dolphins* was awarded the Newbery medal in 1961. [From Scott O'Dell, *Island of the Blue Dolphins* (Houghton Mifflin, 1960).]

There had been wild dogs on the Island of the Blue Dolphins as long as I remember, but after the Aleuts had slain most of the men of our tribe and their dogs had left to join the others, the pack became much bolder. It spent the nights running through the village and during the day was never far off. It was then that we made plans to get rid of them, but the ship came and everyone left Ghalasat.

I am sure that the pack grew bolder because of their leader, the big one with the thick fur around his neck and the yellow eyes.

I had never seen this dog before the Aleuts came and no one else had, so he must have come with them and been left behind when they sailed away. He was a much larger dog than any of ours, which besides have short hair and brown eyes. I was sure that he was an Aleut dog.

Already I had killed four of the pack, but there were many left, more than in the beginning, for some had been born in the meantime. The young dogs were even wilder than the old ones.

I first went to the hill near the cave when the pack was away and collected armloads of brush which I placed near the mouth of their lair. Then I waited until the pack was in the cave. It went there early in the morning to sleep after it had spent the night prowling. I took with me the big bow and five arrows and two of the spears. I went quietly, circling around the mouth of the cave and came up to it from the side. There I left all of my weapons except one spear.

I set fire to the brush and pushed it into the cave. If the wild dogs heard me, there was no sound from them. Nearby was a ledge of rock which I climbed, taking my weapons with me.

The fire burned high. Some of the smoke trailed out over the hill, but much of it stayed in the cave. Soon the pack would have to leave. I did not hope to kill more than five of them because I had only that many arrows, but if the leader was one of the five I would be satisfied. It might be wiser if I waited and saved all my arrows for him, and this I decided to do.

None of the dogs appeared before the fire died. Then three ran out and away. Seven more followed and a long time afterwards a like number. There were many more still left in the cave.

The leader came next. Unlike the others, he did not run away. He jumped over the ashes and stood at the mouth of the cave, sniffing the air. I was so close to him that I could see his nose quivering, but he did not see me until I raised my bow. Fortunately I did not frighten him.

He stood facing me, his front legs spread as if he were ready to spring, his yellow eyes narrowed to slits. The arrow struck him in the chest. He turned away from me, took one step and fell. I sent another arrow toward him which went wide.

At this time three more dogs trotted out of the cave. I used the last of my arrows and killed two of them.

Carrying both of the spears, I climbed down from the ledge and went through the brush to the place where the leader had fallen. He was not there. While I had been shooting at the other dogs, he had gone. He could not have gone far because of his wound, but though I looked everywhere, around the ledge where I had been standing and in front of the cave, I did not find him.

I waited for a long time and then went inside the cave. It was deep, but I could see clearly.

Far back in a corner was the half-eaten carcass of a fox. Beside it was a black dog with four gray pups. One of the pups came slowly toward me, a round ball of fur that I could have held in my hand. I wanted to hold it, but the mother leaped to her feet and bared her teeth. I raised my spear as I backed out of the cave, yet I did not use it. The wounded leader was not there.

Night was coming and I left the cave, going along the foot of the hill that led to the cliff. I had not gone far on this trail that the wild dogs used when I saw the broken shaft of an arrow. It had been gnawed off near the tip and I knew it was from the arrow which had wounded the leader.

Farther on I saw his tracks in the dust. They were uneven as if he were traveling slowly. I followed them toward the cliff, but finally lost them in the darkness.

The next day and the next it rained and I did not go to look for him. I spent those days making more arrows, and on the third day, with these arrows and my spear, I went out along the trail the wild dogs had made to and from my house.

There were no tracks after the rain, but I followed the trail to the pile of rocks where I had seen them before. On the far side of the rocks I found the big gray dog. He had the broken arrow in his chest and he was lying with one of his legs under him.

He was about ten paces from me so I could see him clearly. I was sure that he was dead, but I lifted the spear and took good aim at him. Just as I was about to throw the spear, he raised his head a little from the earth and then let it drop.

This surprised me greatly and I stood there for a while not knowing what to do, whether to use the spear or my bow. I was used to animals playing dead until they suddenly turned on you or ran away.

The spear was the better of the two weapons at this distance, but I could not use it as well as the other, so I climbed onto the rocks where I could see him if he ran. I placed my feet carefully. I had a second arrow ready should I need it. I fitted an arrow and pulled back the string, aiming at his head.

Why I did not send the arrow I cannot say. I stood on the rock with the bow and pulled back and my hand would not let it go. The big dog lay there and did not move and this may be the reason. If he had gotten up I would have killed him. I stood there for a long time looking down at him and then I climbed off the rocks.

He did not move when I went up to him, nor could I see him breathing until I was very close. The head of the arrow was in his chest and the broken shaft was covered with blood. The thick fur around his neck was matted from the rain.

I do not think that he knew I was picking him up, for his body was limp, as if he were dead. He was very heavy and the only way I could lift him was by kneeling and putting his legs around my shoulders.

In this manner, stopping to rest when I was tired, I carried him to the headland.

I could not get through the opening under the fence, so I cut the bindings and lifted out two of the whale ribs and thus took him into the house. He did not look at me or raise his head when I laid him on the floor, but his mouth was open and he was breathing.

The arrow had a small point, which was fortunate, and came out easily though it had gone deep. He did not move while I did this, nor afterwards as I cleaned the wound with a peeled stick from a coral bush. This bush has poisonous berries, yet its wood often heals wounds that nothing else will.

I had not gathered food for many days and the baskets were empty, so I left water for the dog and, after mending the fence, went down to the sea. I had no thought that he would live and I did not care.

All day I was among the rocks gathering shellfish and only once did I think of the wounded dog, my enemy, lying there in the house, and then to wonder why I had not killed him.

He was still alive when I got back, though he had not moved from the place where I had left him. Again I cleaned the wound with a coral twig. I then lifted his head and put water in his mouth, which he swallowed. This was the first time that he had looked at me since the time I had found him on the trail. His eyes were sunken and they looked out at me from far back in his head.

Before I went to sleep I gave him more water. In the morning I left food for him when I went down to the sea, and when I came home he had eaten it. He was lying in the corner, watching me. While I made a fire and cooked my supper, he watched me. His yellow eyes followed me wherever I moved.

That night I slept on the rock, for I was afraid of him and at dawn as I went out I left the hole under the fence open so he could go. But he was there when I got back, lying in the sun with his head on his paws. I had speared two fish, which I cooked for my supper. Since he was very thin, I gave him one of them, and after he had eaten it he came over and lay down by the fire, watching me with his yellow eyes that were very narrow and slanted up at the corners.

Four nights I slept on the rock, and every morning I left the hole under the fence open so he could leave. Each day I speared a fish for him and when I got home he was always at the fence waiting for it. He would not take the fish from me so I had to put it on the ground. Once I held out my hand to him, but at this he backed away and showed his teeth.

On the fourth day when I came back from the rocks early he was not there at the fence waiting. A strange feeling came over me. Always before when I returned, I had hoped that he would be gone. But now as I crawled under the fence I did not feel the same.

I called out, "Dog, Dog," for I had no other name for him.

I ran toward the house, calling it. He was inside. He was just getting to his feet, stretching himself and yawning. He looked first at the fish I carried and then at me and moved his tail.

That night I stayed in the house. Before I fell asleep I thought of a name for him, for I could not call him Dog. The name I thought of was Rontu, which means in our language Fox Eyes.

Jean Craighead George

Julie of the Wolves

The author, a skilled novelist and observant naturalist, tells a somber story about a struggle for survival by a young Inuit (Eskimo) girl in the high Arctic, a struggle in which her emotional conflicts are as significant as her physical ordeal. Miyax is Julie only in the middle section of the book, a flashback to the time she lived in an Americanized Eskimo community. In this selection, she has run away to live with the wolves—but she cannot escape the encroachment of civilization, symbolized by the wolf Amaroq's death. At the end of the story she has to become Julie once more. [From Jean Craighead George, *Julie of the Wolves* (Harper, 1972).]

By the yellow-green light of the low noon sun Miyax could see that she had camped on the edge of the wintering grounds of the caribou. Their many gleaming antlers formed a forest on the horizon. Such a herd would certainly attract her pack. She crawled out of bed and saw that she had pitched her tent in a tiny forest about three inches high. Her heart pounded excitedly, for she had not seen one of these willow groves since Nunivak. She was making progress, for they grew, not near Barrow, but in slightly warmer and wetter lands near the coast. She smelled the air in the hopes that it bore the salty odor of the ocean, but it smelled only of the cold.

The dawn cracked and hummed and the snow was so fine that it floated above the ground when a breeze stirred. Not a bird passed overhead. The buntings, longspurs, and terns were gone from the top of the world.

A willow ptarmigan, the chicken of the tundra, clucked behind her and whistled softly as it hunted seeds. The Arctic Circle had been returned to its permanent bird resident, the hardy ptarmigan. The millions of voices of summer had died down to one plaintive note.

Aba, ababababababa! Miyax sat up, wondering what that was. Creeping halfway out of her bag, she peered into the sky to see a great brown bird maneuver its wings and speed west.

"A skua!" She was closer to the ocean than she thought, for the skua is a bird of the coastal waters of the Arctic. As her eyes followed it, they came to rest on an oil drum, the signpost of American civilization in the North. How excited she would have been to see this a month ago; now she was not so sure. She had her ulo and needles, her sled and her tent, and the world of her ancestors. And she liked the simplicity of that world. It was easy to understand. Out here she understood how she fitted into the scheme of the moon and stars and the constant rise and fall of life on the earth. Even the snow was part of her, she melted it and drank it.

Amaroq barked. He sounded as if he was no more than a quarter of a mile away.

"Ow, ooo," she called. Nails answered, and then the whole pack howled briefly.

"I'm over here!" she shouted joyously, jumping up and down. "Here by the lake." She paused. "You know that. You know everything about me all the time."

The wind began to rise as the sun started back to the horizon. The lake responded with a boom that sounded like a pistol shot. The freeze was deepening. Miyax lit a fire and put on her pot. A warm stew would taste good and the smoke and flames would make the tundra home.

Presently Amaroq barked forcefully, and the pack answered. Then the royal voice sounded from another position, and Silver checked in from across the lake. Nails gave a warning snarl and the pups whispered in "woofs." Miyax shaded her eyes; her wolves were barking from points around a huge circle and she was in the middle. This was strange—they almost always stayed together. Suddenly Amaroq barked ferociously, his voice angry and authoritative. Silver yelped, then Nails and Kapu. They had something at bay.

She stepped onto the lake and skipped toward them. Halfway across she saw a dark head rise above the hill, and a beast with a head as large as the moon rose to its hind feet, massive paws swinging.

"Grizzly!" she gasped and stopped stone-still, as the huge animal rushed onto the ice. Amaroq and Nails leapt at its face and sprang away before the bear could strike. They were heading it off, trying to prevent it from crossing. The bear snarled, lunged forward, and galloped toward Miyax.

She ran toward her tent. The wind was in her face and she realized she was downwind of the bear, her scent blowing right to him. She darted off in another direction, for bears have poor eyesight and cannot track if they cannot smell. Slipping and sliding, she reached the south bank as the grizzly staggered forward,

then crumpled to its knees and sat down. She wondered why he was not in hibernation. The wolves had been sleeping all day—they could not have wakened the bear. She sniffed the air to try to smell the cause, but only odorless ice crystals stung her nose.

The pack kept harassing the sleepy beast, barking and snarling, but with no intention of killing it. They were simply trying to drive it away—away from her, she realized.

Slowly the bear got to its feet and permitted itself to be herded up the lake bank and back to where it had come from. Reluctantly, blindly, it staggered before the wolves. Occasionally it stood up like a giant, but mostly it roared in the agony of sleepiness.

Yapping, barking, darting, the wolves drove the grizzly far out on the tundra. Finally they veered away and, breaking into a joyous gallop, dashed over the snow and out of sight. Their duty done, they were running—not to hunt, not to kill—but simply for fun.

Miyax was trembling. She had not realized the size and ferocity of the dark bear of the North, who is called "grizzly" inland, and "brown bear" along the coasts—Ursus arctos. Large ones, like the grizzly her wolves had driven away, weighed over a thousand pounds and stood nine feet tall when they reared. Miyax wiped a bead of perspiration from her forehead. Had he come upon her tent, with one curious sweep of his paw he would have snuffed out her life while she slept.

"Amaroq, Nails, Kapu," she called. "I thank you. I thank you."

As she packed to travel on, she thought about her escorts. Wolves did not like civilization. Where they had once dwelled all over North America they now lived in remote parts of Canada, in only two of the lower forty-eight states, and in the wilderness of Alaska. Even the roadless North Slope had fewer wolves than it did before the gussaks erected their military bases and brought airplanes, snowmobiles, electricity, and jeeps to the Arctic.

As she thought about the gussaks she suddenly knew why the brown bear was awake. The Americans' hunting season had begun! Her wolves were in danger! The gussaks were paid to shoot them. A man who brought in the left ear of a wolf to the warden was rewarded with a bounty of fifty dollars. The bounty was evil to the old men at seal camp, for it encouraged killing for money, rather than need. Kapugen considered the bounty the gussaks' way of deciding that the amaroqs could not live on this earth anymore. "And no men have that right," he would say. "When the wolves are gone there will be too many caribou grazing the grass and the lemmings will starve. Without the lemmings the foxes and birds and weasels will die. Their passing will end smaller lives upon which even man depends, whether he knows it or not, and the top of the world will pass into silence."

Miyax was worried. The oil drum she had seen when the skua flew over marked the beginning of civilization and the end of the wilderness. She must warn her pack of the danger ahead. She had learned to say many things to them; but now, the most important of all, the ear-twist or bark that would turn them back, she did not know.

How, she thought, do I shout "Go away! Go far, far away!" She sang:

Go away, royal wolf,
Go away, do not follow.
I'm a gun at your head,
When I pass the oil drum.

Threads of clouds spun up from the earth and trailed across the tundra. They marked the beginning of a white-out. Miyax changed her plans to travel that night, crept into her shelter, and watched the air turn white as the snow arose from the ground and hung all around her. She closed her tent flap and took out her pot. In it she put a piece of fat from the bladder-bag and a scrap of sinew. She lit the sinew and a flame illuminated her tiny home. She took out the comb.

As she carved she saw that it was not a comb at all, but Amaroq. The teeth were his legs, the handle his head. He was waiting to be released from the bone. Surprised to see him, she carved carefully for hours and finally she let him out. His neck was arched, his head and tail were lifted. Even his ears had a message. "I love you," they said.

A bird called faintly in the darkness. Miyax wondered what kind it was and what it was doing so far north at this date. Too sleepy to think, she unlaced her boots, undressed, and folded her clothes. The bird called from the edge of her sleeping skin. Holding her candle above her head, she crept toward the door and peered into the bright eyes of a golden plover. He was young, for he wore the splotched plumage of the juvenile and still had a trace of baby-yellow around his beak. He slumped against her skins.

Gently she slipped her hand under his feet, picked him up, and brought him close to her. His black and gold feathers gleamed in the sputtering light. She had never beheld a plover so closely and now understood why Kapugen had called them "the spirit of the birds." The plover's golden eye and red noseband made it look like one of the dancers in the Bladder Feast.

"You are lost," she said. "You should be far from here. Perhaps in Labrador. Perhaps even in your winter home on the plains of Argentina. And so you are dying. You need insects and meat. But I'm so glad you're here." Then she added, "I shall call you Tornait, the bird spirit."

She eased the bird inside her warm sleeping skin, cut off a small piece of caribou meat, and held it out. Tornait ate ravenously, then rested. She fed him once more, and then he tucked his head in his back feathers and went to sleep.

The following night the white-out was still so dense she could not see the ground when she crept out for snow to melt and drink.

"I won't go on tonight," she said to Tornait when she came inside. "But I do not care. I have food, light, furs, fire, and a pretty companion." That evening she polished her carving of Amaroq and talked to Tornait. The plover was incredibly tame, perhaps because he lived in the most barren parts of the world where there were no men, perhaps because he was lonely. Tornait ran over her skins, flitted to her head and shoulders, and sang when she sang.

On the next afternoon the white-out was but a frosty mist. Miyax was cooking dinner when Tornait drew his feathers to his body and stood up in alarm. She listened for a long time before she heard the snow scream as footsteps pressed it. Scrambling to the door, she saw Kapu in the mist, frost on his whiskers.

"Hi!" she called. He did not turn around for he was looking at something in the distance. Presently Amaroq swept into view and stopped beside him.

"Amaroq!" she shouted. "Amaroq, how are you?" Tossing her head in wolf happiness, she crawled out of her tent on all fours and nudged him under the chin. He arched his neck grandly. Then, with a glance at Kapu, he ran out on the lake. The young wolf followed, and, laughing joyously, Miyax crawled after them both. She had not gone far before Amaroq stopped and glared at her. She stayed where she was. The regal pair leaped away, snow billowing up from their strides like smoke.

Getting to her knees she looked for Silver, Nails, and the other pups, but they did not follow the pair. Miyax rocked back on her heels. Could it be that the leader of the pack was teaching the leader of the pups? She nodded slowly as she comprehended. Of course. To be a leader required not only fearlessness and intelligence, but experience and schooling. The head of a wolf pack needed to be trained, and who better to do this than Amaroq?

"And I know what you'll teach," she called out. "You'll teach him which animal to harvest. You'll teach him to make all decisions. You'll teach him how to close in on a caribou, and where to bed the wolf pack down; and you'll teach him to love and protect."

The white-out vanished, the stars blazed out, and San Francisco called to Miyax. It was time to move on. Kapu was now in school.

"But how shall I tell them not to follow me anymore?" she asked Tornait as she crawled back into her tent.

"Of course!" she gasped. She had been told by Amaroq himself how to say "stay back" when he had wanted Kapu alone. He had walked forward, turned around, and glared into her eyes. She had stopped in her tracks and gone home. Eagerly she practiced. She ran forward, looked over her shoulder, and glared.

"Stay, Amaroq. Stay where you are!"

Humming to herself she took down her tent, rolled it into a bundle, and threw it on the new sled. Then she stuffed her pack and tucked Tornait in the hood of her parka. Sticking her toes in her snowshoes, she took a bearing on the constant star. The snow squeaked under her feet, and for the first time she felt the dry bite of the cold right through her parka and boots. To her this meant the temperature was zero, the point every year when she began to feel chilly. Dancing and swinging her arms to get warm, she picked up the thongs of her sled and walked toward the sea. The sled glided lightly behind her.

She did not hear the airplane; she saw it. The low sun of noon struck its aluminum body and it sparkled like a star in the sky. It was a small plane, the type bush pilots use to carry people over the roadless tundra and across the rugged mountains of Alaska where cars cannot go. Presently its sound reached her ears and the throb of the engines reminded her that this was the beginning of the season when bush pilots took the gussaks out to hunt. The craft tipped its wings and zigzagged across the sky. When it continued to zag she realized the pilot was following a meandering river where game wintered. A river, she thought; rivers led to the sea. I am nearing the end of my journey; Point Hope might be but one sleep away. She quickened her pace.

The airplane banked, turned, and came toward her. It seemed as big as an eagle as it skimmed low over the ground. Bright flashes of fire burst from its side.

"They *are* hunting," she said to Tornait. "Let's get in the oil drum. I look like a bear in these clothes."

Just before she reached the drum she crossed the footsteps of Amaroq and Kapu. They had passed this way only moments ago, for the snow crystals their warm feet had melted were not yet frozen again. The plane continued to come toward her. Apparently she had been seen. She kicked snow over her sled and pack and crawled to the front of the barrel. It was sealed. She could not get inside. Scurrying to the other end she found that it, too, was closed. Desperately she threw herself under the curve of the drum and lay still. Much of her was still exposed. Flailing her hands and feet, she stirred up the light snow. It arose like a cloud and settled upon her as the plane soared above.

Shots rang out. The plane roared away and Miyax opened her eyes. She was still alive and the air hunters were over the river. The plane banked and flew back, this time very low. Tornait struggled.

"Be still," she said. The gunfire snapped again and, eyes wide open, she saw that it was not aimed at her.

"Amaroq!" Horrified, she watched him leap into the air as a splatter of shots burst beside him. Digging in his claws, he veered to the right and left as Kapu ran to join him. Teeth bared, angrily growling, Amaroq told him to go. Kapu sped off. The plane hesitated, then pursued Amaroq.

Shots hit the snow in front of him. He reared and turned.

"Amaroq!" she screamed. "Here! Come here!"

The plane swerved, dove, and skimmed about thirty feet above the ground. Its guns blasted. Amaroq stumbled, pressed back his ears, and galloped across the tundra like a shooting star. Then he reared, and dropped on the snow.

He was dead.

"For a bounty," she screamed. "For money, the magnificent Amaroq is dead!" Her throat constricted with grief, and sobs choked her.

The plane banked and came back. Kapu was running to Amaroq. His ears were pressed to his head and his legs moved so swiftly they were a blur. Bullets showered the snow around him. He leaped, dodged, and headed for the oil drum. His wide eyes and open mouth told Miyax he was afraid for the first time in his life. Blindly he ran, and as he came by she reached out and tripped him. He sprawled across the snow and lay still. While the plane coasted off to make another turn, she covered Kapu with flakes.

The snow turned red with blood from his shoulder. Miyax rolled under the barrel.

The air exploded and she stared up into the belly of the plane. Bolts, doors, wheels, red, white, silver, and black, the plane flashed before her eyes. In that instant she saw great cities, bridges, radios, school books. She saw the pink room, long highways, TV sets, telephones, and electric lights. Black exhaust enveloped her, and civilization became this monster that snarled across the sky.

The plane shrank before her eyes, then turned and grew big again. Tornait flew to the top of the barrel, screaming his alarm cry and beating his wings.

Kapu tried to get up.

"Don't move," Miyax whispered. "They're coming for Amaroq." Knowing Kapu did not understand, she reached out and softly stroked him, singing: "Lie still. Lie still." She watched him slump back in the snow without a sound.

The plane returned at so low a level she could see the men in the cockpit, their coat collars pulled up around their necks, their crash helmets and goggles gleaming. They were laughing and watching the ground. Desperately Miyax thought about Silver, Nails, and the pups. Where were they? They must be clear targets on the white snow. Maybe not—they were light in color, not black.

Suddenly the engine accelerated, the wing flaps pressed down, and the craft climbed, banked, and sailed down the river like a migrating bird. It did not turn around.

Miyax buried her fingers in Kapu's fur. "They did not even stop to get him!" she cried. "They did not even kill him for money. I don't understand. I don't understand. *Ta vun ga vun ga,*" she cried. "*Pisupa gasu punga.*" She spoke of her sadness in Eskimo, for she could not recall any English.

Kapu's blood spread like fish ripples on the snow. She wriggled to him and clamped her thumb on the vein that was gushing. She held the pressure—a minute, an hour—she did not know how long. Then Tornait called hungrily. Cautiously she lifted her hand. The bleeding had stopped.

"*Ta gasu,*" she said to Kapu. She brushed the snow off her sled and took out her poles. She set up her tent beside the barrel, banked the snow around the bottom to seal out the wind, and spread her ground cloth under it. When she tried to push Kapu into the shelter she found him too heavy. He lifted his head, then dropped it wearily. Miyax decided to build the tent around him. She took everything down and started all over again.

This time she eased the ground skin under him inch by inch until he lay on the fur. Then she kicked the oil drum to free it from the ice, rolled it close to him, and erected her tent against it. She sealed the gaps with snow.

The drum was old, for it had different markings than those around Barrow, but like them, it was barely rusted. The frigid winters and the dry desert-like conditions of the tundra prevent metals, papers, garbage, and refuse from deteriorating as it does in warmer zones. In the Arctic, all artifacts are preserved for ages. Even throwing them into the oceans does not work a change, for the water freezes around them, and as icebergs they come back on the shores. The summer sun unveils them again.

Miyax melted snow, cut off meat for Tornait, and fed him. He flew down from the barrel and ran into the tent. Hopping onto her furry sleeping skin, he puffed his feathers, stood on one foot, and went to sleep.

With the stew bubbling, Kapu resting, and Tornait asleep, Miyax dared to think of Amaroq. She would go and bid him good-bye. She tried to get up, but she could not move. Grief held her in a vise-like clamp.

About an hour later Kapu lifted his head, rolled his eyes around the cozy interior of the tent, and accepted chunks of stew. Miyax petted his head and told him in Eskimo to lie still while she looked at his wound. It was long and deep and she knew it must be sewn together.

Taking a piece of sinew from the ground skin, she threaded it into her needle and pierced the soft flesh. Kapu growled.

"*Xo lur pajau, sexo,*" she sang soothingly. "*Lupir pajau se suri vanga pangmane majo riva pangmane.*" Monotonously repeating over and over the healing song of the old bent lady, she hypnotized Kapu as she closed the wound. The perspiration was running down her cheeks when she was done, but she was able to tell him that he would get well and return to lead their pack.

The sun set in a navy blue sky, and the stars sparkled on and off as they spoke of their vast distances from the earth. About midnight the inside of the tent began to glow green and Kapu's eyes shone like emeralds. Miyax peered out the flap door. Fountains of green fire rose from the earth and shot to the top of the black velvet sky. Red and white lights sprayed out of the green. The northern lights were dancing. The lakes boomed, and Nails howled mournfully beyond the tent.

Miyax howled back to tell him where she was. Then Silver barked and the pups called, too. Each voice sounded closer than the last; the pack was coming toward the oil drum as they searched for Amaroq and Kapu.

Miyax stepped into the light of the aurora. It was time to bid Amaroq farewell. She tried to go forward but her feet would not move. Grief still held them useless. Clutching her left knee in both hands, she lifted her foot and put it down; then she lifted the other and put it down, slowly making her way across the turquoise snow.

Amaroq lay where he had fallen, his fur shining in the strange magnetic light.

"Amaroq . . ." She took her carving from her pocket, and got down on her knees. Singing softly in Eskimo, she told him she had no bladder for his spirit to dwell in, but that she had his totem. She asked him to enter the totem and be with her forever.

For a long time she held the carving over his body. Presently, the pain in her breast grew lighter and she knew the wolf was with her.

The stars had slipped down the sky when at last she stood up and walked swiftly back to Kapu.

All night Miyax sat beside him and listened to Silver, Nails, and the pups.

"*Ow ow ow ow owwwwwww,*" they cried in a tone she had never heard before, and she knew they were crying for Amaroq.

Rosemary Sutcliff

The Eagle of the Ninth

Rosemary Sutcliff's historical novels present an epic study of the clash of early cultures in the making of Britain. She shows the strands of many peoples coming together and merging into a British nation. This movement toward a national destiny is paralleled by stories of single individuals struggling toward dignity, identity, and a place in the social order. In this book, the earliest of Sutcliff's Roman Britain series, Marcus, a young Roman centurion stationed in Britain in the second century A.D., sets out to solve the mystery of his father's disappearance along with that of an entire legion that "marched north to deal with a rising among the Caledonian tribes, and was never heard of again." Disguised as a Greek physician and accompanied by Esca, his ex-slave and friend, Marcus crosses Hadrian's Wall into Highland Scotland to search among the northern Picts for the Eagle of the Ninth—the lost legion's golden standard, rumored to have survived. Marcus discovers that his father's legion dissolved in mutiny and slaughter, but he nonetheless continues his quest. In the following selection he is an observer at the Feast of New Spears—the initiation rites of the young men of a northern tribe—and discovers more than he expected. [From Rosemary Sutcliff, *The Eagle of the Ninth* (Walck, 1954).]

The Feast of New Spears

Next day began a bustle of preparation that reminded Marcus of his own Etruscan village on the eve of Saturnalia; and by evening the first inflow of the New Spears had begun; boys and their fathers from the farthest fringes of the tribal lands, riding fine small ponies, wearing their brightest clothes, and many of them with their hounds cantering along beside. Odd, he thought, watching them, odd that people so poor in many ways, hunters and herdsmen who do not till the soil, and live in mud hovels in acute discomfort, should enrich the bridles of their superbly bred ponies with silver and bronze and studs of coral, and clasp their cloaks with buckler-brooches of red Hibernian gold. There was an in-swarming of another kind too, of merchants and fortune-tellers, harpers and horsedealers, who encamped with the tribe on the level shores of the loch until the whole stretch below the dun was dark with them. It was all warm and gay and human, a market crowd on a large scale, and nowhere any sign of the strangeness that Marcus had expected.

But there was to be strangeness enough before the Feast of New Spears was over.

It began on the second evening, when suddenly the boys who were to receive their weapons were no longer there. Marcus did not see

them go; but suddenly they were gone, and behind them the dun was desolate. The men daubed their foreheads with mud; the women gathered together, wailing and rocking in ritual grief. From within the dun and from the encampment below the ramparts the wailing rose as the night drew on, and at the evening meal a place was left empty and a drinking-horn filled and left untouched for every boy who had gone, as for the ghosts of dead warriors at the feast of Samhain; and the women made the death chant through the long hours of darkness.

With morning, the wailing and the lamentation ceased, and in its place there settled on the dun a great quietness and a great sense of waiting. Towards evening the tribe gathered on the level ground beside the loch. The men stood about in groups, each clan keeping to itself. Wolf Clan to Wolf Clan, Salmon to Salmon, Seal to Seal; skin-clad or cloaked in purple or saffron or scarlet, with their weapons in their hands and their dogs padding in and out among them. The women stood apart from the menfolk, many of the young ones with garlands of late summer flowers in their hair: honeysuckle, yellow loosestrife, and the wild white convolvulus. And men and women alike turned constantly to look up into the south-western sky.

Marcus, standing with Esca and Liathan, the Chieftain's brother, on the outskirts of the throng, found himself also looking again and again to the south-west, where the sky was still golden, though the sun had slipped behind the hills.

And then, quite suddenly, there it was, the pale curved feather of the new moon, caught in the fringes of the sunset. Somewhere among the women's side a girl saw it at the same instant, and raised a strange, haunting, half-musical cry that was caught up by the other women, then by the men. From somewhere over the hills, seaward, a horn sounded. No braying war-horn, but a clearer, higher note that seemed perfectly akin to the pale feather hanging remote in the evening sky.

As though the horn had been a summons, the crowd broke up, and the men moved off in the direction from which it had sounded; a long, ragged train of warriors moving quietly, steadily, leaving the dun to the women, to the very old, and the very young. Marcus went with them, keeping close to Liathan, as he had been told, and suddenly very glad to know that Esca was walking at his shoulder in this strange multitude.

They climbed steadily to the mountain saddle, and came dropping down on the seaward side. They traversed a steep glen and swung out along a ridge. Down again, and another steep climb, and suddenly they were on the lip of a wide upland valley running at an angle to the sea. It lay at their feet, already brimmed with shadows under a sky still webbed and washed with light that seemed to burst upward from the hidden sun; but at its head a great turf mound rose steeply, catching still a faint glow from the sunset on its thorn-crowned crest and the tips of the great standing stones that ringed it round like a bodyguard. Marcus had seen the long barrows of the Ancient People often enough before, but none had caught and held his awareness as this one did, at the head of its lonely valley, between the gold of the sunset and the silver of the new moon.

'Yonder is the Place of Life!' said Liathan's voice in his ear. 'The Life of the Tribe.'

The many-coloured throng had turned northward, winding along the valley towards the Place of Life. The great mound rose higher on their sight, and presently Marcus found himself standing among the Seal People, in the shadow of one of the great standing stones. Before him stretched the emptiness of a wide, roughly paved forecourt, and beyond the emptiness, in the steep mass of the bush-grown mound, a doorway. A doorway whose massive uprights and lintel were of age-eaten granite. A doorway from one world into another, Marcus thought with a chill of awe, closed seemingly by nothing but a skin apron enriched with bosses of dim bronze. Was the lost Eagle of the Hispana somewhere beyond that barbaric entrance? Somewhere in the dark heart of this barrow that was the Place of Life?

There was a sudden hiss and flare of flame, as somebody kindled a torch from the fire-pot they had brought with them. The fire seemed to spread almost of its own accord from torch to torch, and several young warriors stepped

out from the silent waiting crowd, into the vast emptiness within the standing stones. They carried the flaming brands high above their heads, and the whole scene, which had begun to blur with the fading light, was flooded with a flickering red-gold glare that fell most fiercely on the threshold of that strange doorway, showing the uprights carved with the same curves and spirals that swirled up the standing stones, flashing on the bronze bosses of the sealskin apron so that they became discs of shifting fire. Sparks whirled upward on the light, sea-scented wind, and by contrast with their brightness, the hills and the dark thorn-crowned crest of the mound seemed to sink back into the sudden twilight. A man's shape showed for an instant high among the thorn-trees, and again the horn sounded its high clear note; and before the echoes had died among the hills, the sealskin curtain was flung back, its bronze discs clashing like cymbals.

A figure stooped out under the low lintel into the torchlight. The figure of a man, stark naked save for the skin of a grey dog-seal, the head drawn over his own. The Seal Clan greeted his coming with a quick, rhythmic cry that rose and fell and rose again, setting the blood jumping back to the heart. For an instant the man— Seal-priest or man-seal—stood before them, receiving their acclamation, then with the clumsy scuffling motion of a seal on dry land, moved to one side of the doorway; and another figure sprang out of the darkness, hooded with the snarling head of a wolf. One after another they came, naked as the first had been, their bodies daubed with strange designs in woad and madder, their head-dresses of animal pelts or bird-feathers, the wings of a swan, the pelt of an otter with the tail swinging behind the wearer's back, the striped hide of a badger shining black and white in the torchlight. One after another, prancing, leaping, shuffling; men who were not merely playing the part of animals, but who in some strange way, impossible of understanding, actually *were* for the moment the animals whose skins they wore.

One after another they came, until for every clan of the tribe, a totem priest had joined the grotesque dance—if dance it could be called, for it was like no dance that Marcus had ever seen before, and none that he wanted ever to see again. They had swung into a chain, into a circle, hopping, scuffling, bounding, the animal skins swinging behind them. There was no music—indeed music of any sort, however weird, however discordant, seemed worlds away from this dancing; but there seemed to be a pulse beating somewhere—perhaps a hollow log being struck with an open palm—and the dancers took their time from it. Quicker and quicker it beat, like a racing heart, like the heart of a man in fever; and the wheel of dancers spun faster and faster, until, with a wild yell, it seemed to break of its own spinning, and burst back to reveal someone—something—that must have come unnoticed into its midst from the blackness of that doorway in the barrow.

Marcus's throat tightened for an instant as he looked at the figure standing alone in the full red glare of the torches, seeming to burn with its own fierce light. An unforgettable figure of nightmare beauty, naked and superb, crested with a spreading pride of antlers that caught the torch-light on each polished tip, as though every tine bore a point of flame.

A man with the antlers of a stag set into his head-dress so that they seemed to grow from his brow—that was all. And yet it was not all; even for Marcus, it was not all. The people greeted him with a deep shout that rose and rose until it was like a wolf-pack howling to the moon; and while he stood with upraised arms, dark power seemed to flow from him as light from a lamp. 'The Horned One! The Horned One!' They were down on their faces, as a swathe of barley going down before the sickle. Without knowing that he did so, Marcus stumbled to his knee; beside him Esca was crouching with his forearm covering his eyes.

When they rose again, the priest-god had drawn back to the threshold of the Place of Life, and was standing there, his arms fallen to his sides. He burst into a spate of speech, of which Marcus could understand just enough to gather that he was telling the tribe that their sons who had died as boys were now reborn as warriors. His voice rose into pealing triumph, passing little by little into a kind of wild chant in which the tribesmen joined. Torches

were springing up all along the close-packed throng, and the standing stones were reddened to their crests and seemed to pulse and quiver with the crashing rhythm of the chant.

When the triumphal chanting was at its height, the priest-god turned and called, then moved from before the doorway; and again someone stooped out from the darkness of the entrance into the glare of torches. A red-haired boy in a chequered kilt, at sight of whom the tribesmen sent up a welcoming shout. Another followed, and another, and many more, each greeted with a shout that seemed to burst upward and break in a wave of sound against the standing stones, until fifty or more New Spears were ranged in the great forecourt. They had a little the look of sleep-walkers, and they blinked dazzled eyes in the sudden blaze of torches. The boy next to Marcus kept running his tongue over dry lips, and Marcus could see the quick panting of his breast, as though he had been running—or very much afraid. What had happened to them in the dark, he wondered, remembering his own hour, and the smell of bull's blood in the darkened cave of Mithras.

After the last boy, came one last priest, not a totem priest, as the others had been. His head-dress was made of the burnished feathers of a golden eagle, and a long roar burst from the crowd, as the curtain dropped clashing into place behind him. But to Marcus everything seemed for the moment to have grown very still. For the last comer was carrying something that had once been a Roman Eagle.

Venture into the Dark

A man stepped out from the ranks of the tribe, stripped and painted as for war, and carrying shield and spear; and at the same instant a boy started forward. The two—they were clearly father and son—came together in the centre of the open space, and the boy stood with shining pride to take shield and spear from his father's hand. Then he turned slowly on his heel, showing himself to the tribe for their acceptance; turned to the place where Cruachan was hidden by the darkness; turned last of all to the new moon, which had strengthened from a pale feather to a sickle of shining silver in a deep-green sky; and brought his spear crashing down across his shield in salute, before following his father, to stand for the first time among the warriors of his tribe.

Another boy stepped out, and another, and another; but Marcus was aware of them only as moving shadows, for his eyes were on the Eagle; the wreck of the Ninth's lost Eagle. The gilded wreaths and crowns that the Legion had won in the days of its honour were gone from the crimson-bound staff; the furious talons still clutched the crossed thunderbolts, but where the great silver wings should have arched back in savage pride, were only empty socket-holes in the flanks of gilded bronze. The Eagle had lost its honours, and lost its wings; and without them, to Demetrius of Alexandria it might have seemed as commonplace as a dunghill cock; but to Marcus it was the Eagle still, in whose shadow his father had died; the lost Eagle of his father's Legion.

He saw very little of the long-drawn ritual that followed, until at last the Eagle had been carried back into the dark, and he found himself part of a triumphal procession led by the New Spears, heading back for the dun: a comet-tail of tossing torches, a shouting like a victorious army on the homeward march. As they came down the last slope they were met by the smell of roasting meat, for the cooking-pits had been opened. Great fires burned on the open turf below the dun, flowering fiercely red and gold against the remote, sheeny pallor of the loch below, and the women linked hands and came running to join their returning menfolk and draw them home.

Only a few men who were not of the tribe had cared to go with the warriors to the Place of Life. But now the ceremonies were over and it was time for feasting; and traders and soothsayers and harpers had thronged in from the encampment, a party of seal-hunters from another tribe, even the crews of two or three Hibernian ships; they crowded with the warriors of the Epidaii around the fire and feasted nobly on roast meat, while the women, who did not eat with their lords, moved among them with great jars of fiery yellow metheglin, to keep the drinking-horns brimming.

Marcus, sitting between Esca and Liathan at the Chieftain's fire, began to wonder if the whole night was going to be spent like this, in eating and drinking and shouting. If it was, he should go raving mad. He wanted quiet; he wanted to think; and the joyous uproar seemed to beat inside his head, driving all thought out of it. Also he wanted no more metheglin.

Then quite suddenly the feasting was over. The noise and the vast eating and deep drinking had been, maybe, only a shield raised against the too-potent magic that had gone before. Men and women began to draw back, leaving a wide space of empty turf amid the fires; dogs and children were gathered in. Again torches flared up, casting their fierce light on to the empty space. Again there came that sense of waiting. Marcus, finding himself beside the Chieftain's grandfather, turned to the old man, asking under his breath, 'What now?'

'Dancing now,' said the other without looking round. 'See. . . .'

Even as he spoke, the flaming brands were whirled aloft, and a band of young warriors sprang into the torch-lit circle and began to stamp and whirl in the swift rhythm of a war-dance. And this time, strange and barbaric as it might be, Marcus found this was dancing as he understood the word. Dance followed dance, blending into each other so that it was hard to tell where one ended and another began. Sometimes it would seem that the whole men's side was dancing, and the ground would tremble under their stamping heels. Sometimes it would be only a chosen few who leapt and whirled and crouched in mimic hunting or warfare, while the rest raised the terrifying music of the British before battle by droning across their shield-rims. Only the women never danced at all, for the Feast of New Spears had nothing to do with womenkind.

The moon had long since set, and only the fierce light of fire and torches lit the wild scene, the twisting bodies and brandished weapons, when at last two rows of warriors stepped out on to the trampled turf and stood facing each other. They were stripped to the waist like the rest of the men's side, and carried shield and feathered war spear; and Marcus saw that one rank was made up of the boys who had become men that day, and the other of their fathers who had armed them.

'It is the Dance of the New Spears,' Esca told him as the two lines swept together with upraised shields. 'So, we dance it, too, we the Brigantes, on the night our boys become men.'

On his other side Tradui leaned towards him, asking, 'Do not your people hold the Feast of New Spears?'

'We hold a feast,' Marcus said, 'but it is not like this. All this is strange to me, and I have seen many things tonight that make me wonder.'

'So?—and these things?' The old man, having got over his first annoyance with Marcus over the toad's fat, had gradually become more friendly as the days went by; and tonight, warmed still further by the feasting and the metheglin, he was eager to enlighten the stranger within his gates. 'I will explain them to you, these things at which you wonder; for you are young and doubtless wish to know, and I am old and by far the wisest man in my tribe.'

If he went warily, Marcus realized, here might be a chance to gather certain information that he needed. 'Truly,' he said, 'wisdom shines from Tradui the Chieftain's grandsire, and my ears are open.' And he settled himself, with a most flattering show of interest, to ask and listen. It was slow work, but little by little, drawing the old man on with all the skill he possessed, listening patiently to a great deal that was of no use to him whatever, he gathered the scraps of knowledge that he needed. He learned that the priest-kind had their living-place in the birchwoods below the Place of Life, and that no guard was kept over the holy place, no watch of attendant priests.

'What need?' said the old man when Marcus showed surprise at this. 'The Place of Life has guardians of its own, and who would dare to meddle with that which is of the Horned One?' He broke off, abruptly, as though catching himself in the act of speaking of forbidden things, and stretched out an old thick-veined hand with the fingers spread horn-wise.

But presently he began to talk again. Under the influence of the metheglin and the torch-light and the dancing, he, too, was remembering his own night: the long-ago night when he had been a New Spear, and danced for the first time the warrior dances of the tribe. Never taking his eyes from the whirling figures, he told of old fights, old cattle-raids, long-dead heroes who had been his sword-brothers when the world was young and the sun hotter than it was now. Pleased at finding an attentive listener who had not heard the story before, he told of a great hosting of the tribes, no more than ten or twelve autumns ago; and how he had gone south with the rest—though some fools had said that he was too old for the wartrail, even then—to stamp out a great army of the Red Crests. And how, having given them to the wolf and to the raven, they had brought back the Eagle-god that the Red Crests carried before them, and given it to the gods of his own people in the Place of Life. The Healer of sore eyes must have seen it tonight when it was carried out and shown to the men's side?

Marcus sat very still, his hands linked round his updrawn knees, and watched the sparks fly upward from the whirling torches.

'I saw it,' he said. 'I have seen such Eagle gods before, and I wondered to see it here. We are always curious, we Greeks; also we have small cause to love Rome. Tell me more of how you took this Eagle-god from the Red Crests; I should like to hear that story.'

It was the story that he had heard once already, from Guern the Hunter; but told from the opposite side; and where Guern's story had ended, this one went on.

Much as he might tell of a bygone hunting that had been good, the old warrior told how he and his sword-brethren had hunted down the last remnants of the Ninth Legion, closing round them as a wolf-pack closes round its prey. The old man told it without a shadow of pity, without a shadow of understanding for the agony of his quarry; but with a fierce admiration that lit his face and sounded in every word.

'I was an old man even then, and it was my last fight, but *what* a fight! Ayee! Worthy to be the last fight of Tradui the Warrior! Many a night when the fire sinks low, and even the battles of my youth grow thin and cold, I have kept warm thinking of that fight! We brought them to bay at last in the bog country a day north of the place they call the Three Hills; and they turned like a boar at bay. We were flushed with easy triumph, for until that day it had been very easy. They crumbled at a prick, but that day it was not so. Those others had been but the flakings of the flint, and these were the core; a small core, so small. . . . They faced outward all ways, with the winged god upreared in their midst; and when we broke their shield-wall, one would step over his fallen brother, and lo, the shield-wall would be whole as before. We pulled them down at last—aye, but they took a goodly escort of our warriors with them. We pulled them down until there were left but a knot—as many as there are fingers on my two hands—and the winged god still in their midst. I, Tradui, I slew with my last throw-spear the priest in the spotted hide who held the staff; but another caught it from him as he fell, and held it so that the winged god did not go down, and rallied the few who were left, yet again. He was a chieftain among the rest, he had a taller crest, and his cloak was of the warrior scarlet. I wish that it had been I who killed him, but one was before me. . . .

'Well, we made an end. There will be no more Red Crests going to and fro in our hunting grounds. We left them to the raven and the wolf, and also to the bog. Bog country is swift to swallow the traces of fighting. Yes, and we brought back the winged god; we, the Epidaii, claiming it as our right because it was the warriors of the Epidaii who were First Spear at the killing. But there was heavy rain later, and the rivers coming down in spate; and at a ford the warrior who carried the god was swept away, and though we found the god again (three lives it cost us, in the finding), the wings, which were not one with it but fitted into holes in its body, were gone from it, and so were the shining wreaths that hung from its staff; so that when we brought it to the Place of Life it was as you saw it tonight. Still, we gave it to the Horned One for tribute, and surely the Horned One was well pleased, for have not our wars gone well for us ever since, and the deer waxed fat in our hunting runs? And I will tell you another thing concerning the Eagle-god; it is ours now, ours, the Epidaii's; but if ever the day comes when we host against the Red Crests again, when the Cran-tara goes out through Albu, calling the tribes to war, the Eagle-god will be as a spear in the hand of all the tribes of Albu, and not of the Epidaii alone.'

The bright old eyes turned at last, consideringly, to Marcus's face. 'He was like you, that Chieftain of the Red Crests; yes. And yet you say that you are a Greek. Surely that is strange?'

Marcus said, 'There are many of Greek blood among the Red Crests.'

'So. That might be it.' The old man began to fumble under the shoulder-folds of the chequered cloak he wore. 'They were truly warriors, and we left them their weapons, as befits warriors. . . . But from that chieftain I took this for the virtue in it, as one takes the tush from a boar who was fierce and valiant above others of his kind; and I have worn it ever since.' He had found what he wanted now, and slipped a leather thong from about his neck. 'It will not go on my hand,' he added, almost fretfully. 'It must be that the Red Crests had narrower hands than we have. Take it and look.'

A ring swung on the end of the thong, sparkling faintly with green fire in the torch-light. Marcus took it from him and bent his head to examine it. It was a heavy signet-ring; and on the flawed emerald which formed the bezel was engraved the dolphin badge of his own family. He held it for a long moment, held it very gently, as if it were a living thing, watching the torch-light play in the green heart of the stone. Then he gave it back into the old man's waiting hand with a casual word of thanks, and turned his attention again to the dancers. But the fierce whirl of the dance was blurred on his sight, for suddenly, across twelve years and more, he was looking up at a dark, laughing man who seemed to tower over him. There were pigeons wheeling behind the man's bent head, and when he put up his hand to rub his forehead, the sunlight that rimmed the pigeons' wings with fire caught the flawed emerald of the signet-ring he wore.

All at once, with over much finding-out for one day, Marcus was tired to the depths of his soul.

Howard Pyle

Men of Iron

This book gives a fine portrayal of life in the great castles and of the training of young nobles for knighthood in fifteenth-century England. The reader should know that before this story takes place, lords who had been elevated under King Richard II were degraded to their former titles under Henry IV. A group plotted to kill the king, but the plot failed, and the conspirators were executed. In some cases, their friends, who had nothing to do with the plot, were ruined too. Such a one was the father of Myles Falworth, and this is the situation at the opening of the first chapter of *Men of Iron,* which is given below. Eventually Myles wins his spurs and succeeds in vanquishing his own and his father's enemy. [From Howard Pyle, *Men of Iron* (Harper, 1891).]

Myles Falworth was but eight years of age at that time, and it was only afterwards, and when he grew old enough to know more of the ins and outs of the matter, that he could remember by bits and pieces the things that afterwards happened; how one evening a knight came clattering into the courtyard upon a horse, red-nostriled and smeared with the sweat and foam of a desperate ride—Sir John Dale, a dear friend of the blind lord.

Even though so young, Myles knew that something very serious had happened to make Sir John so pale and haggard, and he dimly remembered leaning against the knight's iron-covered knees, looking up into his gloomy face, and asking him if he was sick to look so strange. Thereupon those who had been too troubled before to notice him, bethought themselves of him, and sent him to bed, rebellious at having to go so early.

He remembered how the next morning, looking out of a window high up under the eaves, he saw a great troop of horsemen come riding into the courtyard beneath, where a powdering of snow had whitened everything, and of how

the leader, a knight clad in black armor, dismounted and entered the great hall doorway below, followed by several of the band.

He remembered how some of the castle women were standing in a frightened group upon the landing of the stairs, talking together in low voices about a matter he did not understand, excepting that the armed men who had ridden into the courtyard had come for Sir John Dale. None of the women paid any attention to him; so, shunning their notice, he ran off down the winding stairs, expecting every moment to be called back again by some one of them.

A crowd of castle people, all very serious and quiet, were gathered in the hall, where a number of strange men-at-arms lounged upon the benches, while two billmen in steel caps and leathern jacks stood guarding the great door, the butts of their weapons resting upon the ground, and the staves crossed, barring the doorway.

In the anteroom was the knight in black armor whom Myles had seen from the window. He was sitting at the table, his great helmet lying upon the bench beside him, and a quart beaker of spiced wine at his elbow. A clerk sat at the other end of the same table, with inkhorn in one hand and pen in the other, and a parchment spread in front of him.

Master Robert, the castle steward, stood before the knight, who every now and then put to him a question, which the other would answer, and the clerk write the answer down upon the parchment.

His father stood with his back to the fireplace, looking down upon the floor with his blind eyes, his brows drawn moodily together, and the scar of the great wound that he had received at the tournament at York—the wound that had made him blind—showing red across his forehead, as it always did when he was angered or troubled.

There was something about it all that frightened Myles, who crept to his father's side, and slid his little hand into the palm that hung limp and inert. In answer to the touch, his father grasped the hand tightly, but did not seem otherwise to notice that he was there. Neither did the black knight pay any attention to him, but continued putting his questions to Master Robert.

Then, suddenly, there was a commotion in the hall without, loud voices, and a hurrying here and there. The black knight half-rose, grasping a heavy iron mace that lay upon the bench beside him, and the next moment Sir John Dale himself, as pale as death, walked into the antechamber. He stopped in the very middle of the room. "I yield me to my lord's grace and mercy," said he to the black knight, and they were the last words he ever uttered in this world.

The black knight shouted out some words of command, and swinging up the iron mace in his hand, strode forward clanking toward Sir John, who raised his arm as though to shield himself from the blow. Two or three of those who stood in the hall without came running into the room with drawn swords and bills, and little Myles, crying out with terror, hid his face in his father's long gown.

The next instant came the sound of a heavy blow and of a groan, then another blow and the sound of one falling upon the ground. Then the clashing of steel, and in the midst Lord Falworth crying, in a dreadful voice, "Thou traitor! thou coward! thou murderer!"

Master Robert snatched Myles away from his father, and bore him out of the room in spite of his screams and struggles, and he remembered just one instant's sight of Sir John lying still and silent upon his face, and of the black knight standing above him, with the terrible mace in his hand stained a dreadful red.

It was the next day that Lord and Lady Falworth and little Myles, together with three of the more faithful of their people, left the castle.

His memory of past things held a picture for Myles of old Diccon Bowman standing over him in the silence of midnight with a lighted lamp in his hand, and with it a recollection of being bidden to hush when he would have spoken, and of being dressed by Diccon and one of the women, bewildered with sleep, shuddering and chattering with cold.

He remembered being wrapped in the sheepskin that lay at the foot of his bed, and of being carried in Diccon Bowman's arms down the silent darkness of the winding stairway, with the great black giant shadows swaying and flickering upon the stone wall as the dull flame of the lamp swayed and flickered in the cold breathing of the night air.

Below were his father and mother and two or three others. A stranger stood warming his hands at a newly made fire, and little Myles, as he peeped from out the warm sheepskin, saw that he was in riding-boots and was covered with mud. He did not know till long years afterwards that the stranger was a messenger sent by a friend at the king's court, bidding his father fly for safety.

They who stood there by the red blaze of the fire were all very still, talking in whispers and walking on tiptoes, and Myles' mother hugged him in her arms, sheepskin and all, kissing him, with the tears streaming down her cheeks, and whispering to him, as though he could understand their trouble, that they were about to leave their home forever.

Then Diccon Bowman carried him out into the strangeness of the winter midnight.

Outside, beyond the frozen moat, where the osiers stood stark and stiff in their winter nakedness, was a group of dark figures waiting for them with horses. In the pallid moonlight Myles recognized the well-known face of Father Edward, the Prior of Saint Mary's.

After that came a long ride through that silent night upon the saddle-bow in front of Diccon Bowman; then a deep, heavy sleep, that fell upon him in spite of the galloping of the horses.

When next he woke the sun was shining, and his home and his whole life were changed.

Leon Garfield

Smith

Garfield is a master storyteller. His compelling plots, colorful atmosphere, comic detail, and larger-than-life characters recall Dickens and Fielding; yet Garfield's action-packed historical novels have a symbolic subtext—the ambiguities of the struggle between the human faces of good and evil. This particular tale of intrigue begins with an arresting incident: Smith finds himself in possession of a document he can't read, which he has picked out of the pocket of a man who is murdered for it minutes later. In this selection, Smith is pursued by the murderers and encounters Mr. Mansfield, who later takes him into his household. As usual, Garfield brings the seamy side of life in eighteenth-century London fully alive. [From Leon Garfield, *Smith* (Pantheon, 1967).]

Two men—one short, the other tall—who might have been dressed in brown (the street was too dark to be sure), saw Smith hurry violently out of the "Red Lion Tavern." They'd been in a doorway near by. Deep in shadows. They did not think they'd been observed. After a few seconds, they set off together in the wake of the hurrying boy. They followed him for about five minutes along the nearly empty Saffron Hill. Then they lost him. He seemed to've vanished into the gloomy air. Half a minute later, he was seen—unexpectedly—on their left, at the corner of Cross Street, hurrying like mad. They nodded—and set off again.

This time, they kept him in sight for nearly ten minutes: then he vanished near Cony Court. They waited awhile, listening: for the narrow streets and alleys hereabouts were very quiet and even a rat's scuttle would have been heard. Now they entered the shadowy confines of the court; were about three yards within it when the boy was seen again, now darting desperately back toward Cross Street, his alarmed eyes glittering like "chips of coal" in the light of some late merchant's window.

Back went the two followers, their shoulders hunched—for the night was growing bitterer by the minute—and their feet kissing the cobbles with a grim, urgent passion. They did not let him out of their sight for seconds. Portpool Lane—Hatton Garden—Chart Street—back into Saffron Hill, then Holborn Hill—Union Court—Hatton Garden again—and so to Cross Street—Saffron Hill—Cox's Court . . .

An intricate necklace of flight was being threaded as the three hurrying figures shifted through and round the lanes, courts, and alleys that lay, ragged and near deserted, under a gnawed rind of the moon.

Sometimes, there was not above five yards between them, and still they'd lose him for a few seconds—oddly, unaccountably, like he'd gone up in a puff of black smoke—till there he'd be again, come suddenly from some dark

passageway of which nothing had been seen till then.

There seemed to be many dozens of these crevices in the black, lumpy substance of the frowning houses but, sooner or later, there'd be one whose end would be sewn up tight as a sock: a fatal passage from which there'd be no panting scuttle of escape . . .

The boy had left the "Red Lion Tavern" at half after six by St. Paul's. At a quarter of nine o'clock, the followers leaned up against a wall in Hatton Garden.

Breathed one: "Fer God's sake, I can't go another step. Me heart'll burst, I swear it!"

Came a low reply, much charged with pain and phlegm: "All right! We'll go back, some'ow, to the 'Red Lion.' We'll wait there . . . God rot the crafty little perisher!"

With painful steps they limped away—so wind-broken after two-and-a-quarter hours of unceasing pursuit, that they seemed scarce able to drag their own meager shadows down the cold street.

Ten minutes later, in a narrow abutment no more than a yard from where they'd been leaning, a shadow moved. Then a face edged out: a small, pointed, wary face. It surveyed the empty street. It grinned—not with pleasure, but with a savage and desperate triumph. For Smith had done what he'd set out to do when he'd seen the men waiting for him as he'd left the "Red Lion." He'd run his pursuers into the ground!

He began to walk—somewhat slowly, for his own sides were aching villainously. Presently, he stopped and drew the sweat-drenched document from under his coat. He studied it by the thin, cold light of the moon. It did not seem much the worse for its wetting. Miss Bridget's "property" and Miss Fanny's "felonious" looked as much like a horse and cart and a nest of maggots as ever. Nonetheless, at the first opportunity, he picked a passing pocket of a handkerchief and wrapped the document in it. Then he sighed with relief and set off for another part of the Town.

Though no one followed him now, he moved with extraordinary circumspection: for the dark houses and the dimly silvered streets—with their gutters running down their bellies like black wounds—held another, more formidable menace. Time and again, he fancied he heard other footsteps—steps that limped awkwardly—and he thought of the unseen lame man with the soft voice.

But these alarms were in his mind alone, and if they ever came to anything, they never turned into more than the totterings of some drunken homegoer, or the limping of a chairman, weary unto death and cursing under his breath.

Now he was in High Holborn, and the tall buildings on either side scowled blackly down, with, here and there through an ill-drawn drape, a yellow sneer of light; while ceaselessly down the wide street, like the Devil's own crossings-sweeper, came a bitter wind, whipping up the Town's rubbish into spiteful ghosts of dust and paper that plucked and nipped and stung the living boy.

His nose, chin, and fingers were beginning to burn with the cold. Not a night to be out in: black and windy, with the moon now doused in a creeping sea of cloud. He passed by a gloomy alehouse, a bunch of iron grapes groaning from its sign. He stopped, fingered a guinea he'd got with the handkerchief, and thought of a bed for the night.

But the House was full, so he took a half a pint of gin to keep out the cold, the loneliness, and the shifting fear . . . to no purpose. The gin sickened him and inflamed his brain so that he heard everywhere the soft voice he dreaded and the awkward scrape of a leg, quaintly lame. He began to search for the door—and was helped by a pair of potboys who came at him, slantwise, from somewhere in the smoky room.

Out into the bitter street. Above his head the iron grapes creaked menacingly, back and forth . . . back and forth . . . He moved away, fearful that they'd drop and crack him like an egg.

But it was not the grapes alone. The houses seemed to be shuddering against the blotched sky. He shifted out into the middle of the street, for he'd a sudden horror that all the buildings were tottering in upon him. The sky seemed to grow smaller and smaller, and the jagged roofs, fanged with chimneys, seemed to snarl and snap as if to gobble him up.

He began to run, wildly: from one side of the street to the other side, banging into posts, stumbling across the gutter: turning down lanes and alleys that were new even to him . . . And all this with a curious, hopeless urgency, his feet running like a hanged man's feet—seeming to reach for a purchase on a world that was slipping away.

Where was he going? God only knew! Maybe even in search of the two men in brown to give up the document! For suddenly it seemed to him that the document was a fearful disease that was burning and poisoning him—after having tempted him madly from the shelter of his home!

Then was all this frantic flight and fevered imagining the consequence of half a pint of gin? Not entirely. Fears of the malice and rage of stones, bricks, and mortar were a deep part of his nature—which the gin had unlocked. Now a harsh voice seemed to be shouting in his ears:

"The document! Who wants it? Who'll take it? Take the document—and let Smith go home! Here! Here! Here it is, gents! Have it—and for God's sake, let Smith go!"

The voice was his own.

He was in a long, wide street where the moon had widowed all the houses, with black hatchments under their porches. Vaguely, he thought he knew where he was. There was a narrow turning any minute now, an alley-way that would lead him, deviously, back to the "Red Lion." He fancied he saw it. He turned . . .

"Watch out! Watch out! Oh! Oh! Ah!"

At the very moment Smith had turned into the alley, a gentleman had come out of it. They met: and, though the gentleman was tall and stout and huge beside Smith, he was struck with such speed and force that he fell with an angry, frightened cry. For God's sake, what had hit him? What had rushed out of the implacable night? A murderer? A madman?

Smith struggled to his feet: was about to rush on, when a hand grasped at his ankle!

"Let go!" he shouted.

"Damn you, no! Help me, first."

Smith glared wildly down. He saw the gentleman's face, gray as a puddle; his eyes were sunken and dark. No spark of light in them.

"Help me up! Help me, I say! For pity's sake, sir! Can't you see I'm blind?"

"A blind man," gasped Smith. "Oh Gawd! A mole-in-the-hole!"

The gin's tempest dropped abruptly away, and left a glum wreckage behind . . . bleak and forlorn in the freezing night.

"A boy—a child," thought the blind man, uneasily. "Most likely a young thief. Most likely he'll rob me and run off, frightened out of his miserable wits. Oh God, how am I to get home?"

"If you let go me ankle," muttered Smith, "I'll help you up: that's if you're really blind. Can you see me?"

The gentleman shook his head.

"What am I doing now?" asked Smith, pulling a hideous face.

"I don't know—I don't know! I swear I'm blind! Look at my eyes! Any light in them? Look for my smoked spectacles! They're somewhere about. Look for . . ."

"What am I doing now?" demanded Smith, pulling another, even more monstrous face: for he'd help no one who didn't need it.

The blind man loosened his hold on Smith's ankle and heaved himself up on one elbow. He'd lost his hat and his wig was awry, but otherwise he'd suffered no harm. He began to feel the adjacent cobbles for his possessions. Smith watched him, and his face returned to normal: but, as a last measure, he fished inside his coat and pulled out the document.

"What have I got in me hand?" he asked gruffly.

The blind man sighed. "My life, my boy—my life's in your hand." He smiled wryly. "And—and is that hand as black as the night?"

Smith scowled and put away the document. " 'ere you are, Mister Mole-in-the-hole! 'ere's me black 'and, then. Up with you! Up on yer pins! And 'ere's your hat and stick and black spectacles—though why you wears 'em foxes me! My, but you're a real giant of a gent! Did you know it?" This last as the blind man stood up and fairly towered over the tiny, helpful Smith.

"Thank you, boy. Now, tell me if I'm in the street or the alley and I'll give you a guinea for your pains."

"You're on the corner."

"Facing which way?"

"The Lord knows! I've been sick meself!"

"Fever?"

" 'alf a pint o' gin!"

Suddenly, Smith felt a strong desire to confide in the blind man. After all, it could do no harm . . .

"Smith," he said; and held out one hand to be shook while with the other he guided the blind man's hand to meet it. "Smith: 'unted, 'ounded, 'omeless, and part gin-sodden. Smith. Twelve year old. That's me. Very small, but wiry, as they say. Dark 'aired and lately residing in the 'Red Lion Tavern' off Saffron 'ill. Smith."

Helplessly, the blind man smiled, and his questing hand grasped Smith's—firmly.

"Mansfield," he said. "Blind as a wall for these past twelve years. Well-to-do, but not much enjoying it. Mansfield: residing at Number Seven Vine Street under the care of a daughter (God help her for her sacrifice!). Mansfield: believe it or not—a magistrate!"

"Gawd!" gasped Smith. "Oo'd 'ave thought I'd ever be shaking 'ands with a bleeding Justice?"

If Mr. Mansfield heard, he was too gentlemanly to remark on it. Instead, he fumbled in his coat for the promised guinea.

"And now, just point me toward the church that should stand at one end of the street, and the guinea's yours, Smith, with my deepest thanks."

Smith obliged—and took the guinea.

"Seems a lot for a little," he said.

"Good night, Smith."

"Same to you, Mister Mansfield, J.P."

He watched the blind man tap his way down the street, bumping, here and there, into the posts and sometimes raising his hat to them and mumbling, "Sorry, good sir. Couldn't see you . . . so sorry!"

Smith smiled indulgently: was about to make off, when a strangely familiar feeling of pity stirred in him. He had been reminded of the murdered old gentleman. He scowled at his own indecision, stuck his ancient pipe defiantly in his mouth, and hastened in the blind man's wake.

"That you, Smith?"

Smith grunted.

"Didn't expect you . . ."

". . . going the same way meself."

"To Vine Street?"

"Thereabouts."

"Glad to hear it, Smith."

Smith grunted again: irritably. "Oh well, here's me black 'and, then . . . you old blind Justice, you. Just tell me where to turn and where to cross and I'll see you 'ome safe an' sound. After all, I ain't done much for that guinea!"

Mr. Mansfield found the offered hand and, once more, grasped it. He sighed . . . and, not for the first time, reflected in his heart (which was far from being as blind as his eyes), that it was an uncanny thing to be the cause of kindness in others.

Vine Street lay about twenty minutes away: for Mr. Mansfield had strolled far that night, having a troublesome problem that gnawed him. But now, holding Smith's small, cold hand, the problem sank somewhat.

"Were it a sickness?" asked Smith, after a while.

"My blindness, d'you mean? No. Lost my sight when a house burned down. Lost my wife as well. A costly fire, that!"

"Oh."

"Take the next turning on the left, Smith."

"What's it like—being blind?"

"Dark, Smith. Very dark. What's it like having eyes?"

"The moon's gone in again, so we're two of a kind, Mister Mansfield: you an' me."

The blind magistrate felt somewhat taken down, but was cautious not to show it. Twelve years of his misfortune had taught him that a bland face was the best security for one in his situation . . . and that, for a blind man to frown, scowl or laugh, even, was like a fool discharging his pistol wildly in the night. The Lord knew who'd be hit by it.

"If you can see a new-built church with a round tower, cross in front of it and walk with it to your right."

Smith obliged. Hand in hand, they passed by the church—a very curious pair indeed: small Smith, half a pace ahead, and huge, stout Mr. Mansfield, blandly helpless, walking somewhat sideways, behind, for Smith tended to pull, rather.

"Vine Street is the next street that crosses this one. My house is to the right. I'll be safe enough, now, Smith."

"No trouble. I'm going the same way. To the door, Mister Mansfield."

They came to Vine Street.

Said Mr. Mansfield: "If you've nought better to do, will you come in and take a bite of late supper with me, Smith?"

"Don't mind if I do, Mister Mansfield."

From *Smith*, by Leon Garfield, illustrated by Antony Maitland. Copyright © 1967 by Leon Garfield. Printed by permission of Pantheon Books, a division of Random House, Inc., and Penguin Books Ltd.

"Care to stay the night, Smith?"

"Don't mind if I do, Mister Mansfield."

"Any family, Smith?"

"Sisters. Two of 'em."

"Likely to worry?"

"Not much."

"Then it's settled?"

"Just as you say, Mister Mansfield."

"Anything else I can do for you, Smith?"

Smith sighed ruefully. The only thing he really wanted, Mr. Mansfield was unable to provide.

"No, thank you, Mister Mansfield. You done all you can."

They came toward the door of Number Seven. In spite of himself, Smith grinned at the irony of his situation. Of all the men in the Town to bump into and befriend, he'd lit on the one who was blind and so could never teach him to read!

Esther Forbes

Johnny Tremain

Johnny Tremain, a distinguished story of pre-Revolutionary days in Boston, was awarded the Newbery medal in 1944. As the story opens, Johnny is apprenticed to a silversmith, and he believes with cocky assurance that he will someday be famous for his beautiful craftmanship. But an accident cripples his hand and embitters his mind. He is obliged to give up the trade he loves, but he finds work as a courier for the patriotic newspaper *The Boston Observer,* and he becomes a messenger for the Sons of Liberty. He grows to manhood at sixteen and learns the meaning of the liberty for which men fight. The following chapter tells of the part played by Johnny and his friend Rab in the famous Boston Tea Party. [From Esther Forbes, *Johnny Tremain* (Houghton Mifflin, 1943).]

Salt-Water Tea

England had, by the fall of 1773, gone far in adjusting the grievances of her American colonies. But she insisted upon a small tax on tea. Little money would be collected by this tax. It worked no hardship on the people's pocketbooks: only threepence the pound. The stubborn colonists, who were insisting they would not be taxed unless they could vote for the men who taxed them, would hardly realize that the tax had been paid by the East India Company in London before the tea was shipped over here. After all, thought Parliament, the Americans were yokels and farmers—not political thinkers. And the East India tea, even after that tax was paid, would be better and cheaper than any the Americans ever had had. Weren't the Americans, after all, human beings? Wouldn't they care more for their pocketbooks than their principles?

Shivering—for the last week in October was bitterly cold—Johnny built up the fire in the attic. From the back window he could see that the roofs of the Afric Queen were white with frost.

A sharp rat-tat on the shop door below woke Rab.

"What time's it?" he grumbled, as people do who think they are disturbed too early Sunday morning.

"Seven and past. I'll see what's up."

It was Sam Adams himself. When either cold or excited, his palsy increased. His head and hands were shaking. But his strong, seamed face, which always looked cheerful, today looked radiant. Sam Adams was so pleased that Johnny, a little naïvely, thought he must have word that Parliament had backed down again. The expected tea ships had not sailed.

"Look you, Johnny. I know it's Lord's Day, but there's a placard I must have printed and posted secretly tonight. The Sons of Liberty will take care of the posting, but Mr. Lorne must see to the printing. Could you run across and ask him to step over? And Rab—where's he?"

Rab was coming down the ladder.

"What's up?" said Rab sleepily.

"The first of the tea ships, the *Dartmouth,* is entering the harbor. She'll be at Castle Island by nightfall."

"So they dared send them?"

"Yes."

"And the first has come?"

"Yes. God give us strength to resist. That tea cannot be allowed to land."

When Johnny got back with Mr. Lorne, Rab

had Mr. Adams's text in his hands, reading it as a printer reads, thinking first of spacing and capitals, not of the meaning.

"I can set that in no time. Two hundred copies? They'll be fairly dry by nightfall."

"Ah, Mr. Lorne," said Adams, shaking hands, "without you printers the cause of liberty would be lost forever."

"Without you"—Mr. Lorne's voice shook with emotion—"there would not have been any belief in liberty to lose. I will, as always, do anything—everything you wish."

"I got word before dawn. It's the *Dartmouth* and she will be as far as Castle Island by nightfall. If that tea is landed—if that tax is paid—everything is lost. The selectmen will meet all day today and I am calling a mass meeting for tomorrow. This is the placard I will put up."

FRIENDS! BRETHREN! COUNTRYMEN! THAT WORST OF PLAGUES, THE DETESTED TEA SHIPPED FOR THIS PORT BY THE EAST INDIA COMPANY, IS NOW ARRIVED IN THE HARBOUR: THE HOUR OF DESTRUCTION, OF MANLY OPPOSITION TO THE MACHINATIONS OF TYRANNY, STARES YOU IN THE FACE; EVERY FRIEND TO HIS COUNTRY, TO HIMSELF, AND TO POSTERITY, IS NOW CALLED UPON TO MEET AT FANEUIL HALL, AT NINE O'CLOCK THIS DAY [THAT, OF COURSE, IS TOMORROW MONDAY], AT WHICH TIME THE BELLS WILL RING TO MAKE UNITED AND SUCCESSFUL RESISTANCE TO THIS LAST, WORST AND MOST DESTRUCTIVE MEASURE OF ADMINISTRATION. . . .

BOSTON, NOV. 29, 1773.

Then he said quietly: "Up to the last moment—up to the eleventh hour, we will beg the Governor's permission for the ships' return to London with their cargo. We have twenty days."

Johnny knew that by law any cargo that was not unloaded within twenty days might be seized by the custom-house and sold at auction.

"Mr. Lorne, needless to say the Observers will meet tonight. There are *private* decisions to be made before the mass meeting tomorrow at nine."

Johnny pricked up his ears. Ever since he had come to Mr. Lorne's (and Rab said he might be trusted with anything—possibly with men's lives) he had now and then summoned the members of the Observers' Club. They were so close to treason they kept no list of members. Rab made Johnny memorize the twenty-two names. They met in Rab and Johnny's attic.

*   *   *

The attic where the boys commonly slept looked strange enough with those chairs pulled out and arranged for the meeting. John Hancock sat in the moderator's chair. His face looked white and drawn. Probably his head still ached. Beside him was Sam Adams leaning toward him, whispering and whispering. Johnny thought how the Tories were saying that Sam Adams seduced John Hancock, even as the Devil had seduced Eve—by a constant whispering in his ear.

*   *   *

Sam Adams was standing at the far end of the room and Mr. Hancock still sat, his head in his hands. Adams clapped slightly and instantly conversation stopped.

"Gentlemen," he said, "tonight we have made our decision—and know the method by which the detested tea can be destroyed, if the ships are not allowed to return. Here we have with us two of exactly—ah—the sort of boys or young men we intend to use for our great purpose. Two boys in whom we have implicit trust. If it is the wish of the assembled club members, I suggest we approach them with our proposition tonight . . . enlist their aid. Twenty days will be up before we know. We'd best get on with our plans."

The members once more took their seats, but the pewter cups of punch were passing from hand to hand. Only Will Molineaux was too restless to sit. He was muttering to himself. Ben Church sat alone. He often did. No one really liked him.

All agreed the boys were to be told.

"First," Adams said to the boys, "raise your right hands. Swear by the great name of God Himself never, for as long as you live, to divulge to anyone the secret matters now trusted to you. Do you so swear?''

The boys swore.

Hancock was not looking at them. He sat with his aching head in his hands.

"There's no chance—not one—those ships will be allowed to return. The mass meetings which will be held almost daily demanding the return of the tea are to arouse public opinion and to persuade the world we did not turn to violence until every other course had been blocked to us. When the twenty days are up, on the night of the sixteenth of December, those ships are going to be boarded. That tea will be dumped in Boston Harbor. For each ship, the *Dartmouth,* the *Eleanor,* and the brig, the *Beaver,* we will need thirty stout, honest, fearless men and boys. Will you be one, Rab?''

He did not say Rab and Johnny, as the younger boy noticed. Was this because he thought Johnny too cripple-handed for chopping open sea chests—or merely because he knew Rab better and he was older?

"Of course, sir.''

"How many other boys could you find for the night's work? Strong and trustworthy boys—for if one ounce of tea is stolen, the whole thing becomes a robbery—not a protest?''

Rab thought.

"Eight or ten tonight, but give me a little time so I can feel about a bit and I can furnish fifteen or twenty.''

"Boys who can keep their mouths shut?''

"Yes.''

Paul Revere said, "I can furnish twenty or more from about North Square.''

"Not one is to be told in advance just what the work will be, nor who the others are, nor the names of the men who instigated this tea party—that is, the gentlemen gathered here tonight. Simply, as they love their country and liberty and hate tyranny, they are to gather in this shop on the night of December sixteenth, carrying with them such disguises as they can think of, and each armed with an axe or hatchet.''

*   *   *

The next day, the sixteenth, Johnny woke to hear the rain drumming sadly on the roof, and soon enough once more he heard all the bells of Boston cling-clanging, bidding the inhabitants come once more, and for the last time, to Old South to demand the peaceful return of the ships to England.

By nightfall, when the boys Rab had selected began silently to congregate in the office of the *Observer,* behind locked doors, the rain stopped. Many of them Johnny knew. When they started to assume their disguises, smootch their faces with soot, paint them with red paint, pull on nightcaps, old frocks, torn jackets, blankets with holes cut for their arms, they began giggling and laughing at each other. Rab could silence them with one look, however. No one passing outside the shop must guess that toward twenty boys were at that moment dressing themselves as "Indians.''

Johnny had taken some pains with his costume. He had sewed for hours on the red blanket Mrs. Lorne had let him cut up and he had a fine mop of feathers standing upright in the old knitted cap he would wear on his head, but when he started to put on his disguise, Rab said no, wait a minute.

Then he divided the boys into three groups. Beside each ship at the wharf they would find a band of men. "You,'' he said to one group of boys, "will join the boarding party for the *Dartmouth.* You for the *Eleanor.* You for the *Beaver.''* Each boy was to speak softly to the leader and say, "Me Know You,'' for that was the countersign. They would know the three leaders because each of them would wear a white handkerchief about the neck and a red string about the right wrist. Then he turned to Johnny.

"You can run faster than any of us. Somehow get to Old South Church. Mr. Rotch will be back from begging once more the Governor's permission for the ships to sail within a half-hour. Now, Johnny, you are to listen to what Sam Adams says next. Look you. If Mr. Adams then says, 'Now may God help my country,' come back here. Then we will take off our disguises and each go home and say nothing. But if he says, 'This meeting can do nothing more to save the country,' you are to get out of that crowd as fast as you can, and as soon as you get into Cornhill begin to blow upon this silver whistle. Run as fast as you are able back here to me and keep on blowing. I'll have boys posted in dark corners, close enough to the church, but outside the crowd. Maybe we'll hear you the first time you blow."

About Old South, standing in the streets, inside the church, waiting for Rotch to return with the very last appeal that could be made to the Governor, was the greatest crowd Boston had ever seen—thousands upon thousands. There was not a chance, not one, Johnny could ever squirm or wriggle his way inside, but he pushed and shoved until he stood close to one of the doors. Farther than this he could not go—unless he walked on people's heads. It was dark already.

Josiah Quincy's voice rang out from within. "I see the clouds roll and the lightning play, and to that God who rides the whirlwind and directs the storm, I commit my country . . ."

The words thrilled Johnny, but this was not what he was waiting for, and it was not Sam Adams speaking. He was bothered with only one thing. Quincy had a beautiful carrying voice. It was one thing to hear him and another Sam Adams, who did not speak well at all.

The crowd made way for a chaise. "Rotch is back! Make way for Rotch!" Mr. Rotch passed close to Johnny. He was so young he looked almost ready to cry. This was proof enough that the Governor had still refused. Such a turmoil followed Rotch's entry, Johnny could not hear any one particular voice. What chance had he of hearing Sam Adam's words? He had his whistle in his hand, but he was so jammed into the crowd about the door that he did not believe he would be able to get his hands to his mouth.

"Silence." That was Quincy again. "Silence, silence, Mr. Adams will speak." Johnny twisted and turned and brought the whistle to his lips.

And suddenly there was silence. Johnny guessed there were many in that crowd who, like himself, were hanging on those words. Seemingly Mr. Adams was calmly accepting defeat, dismissing the meeting, for now he was saying,

"This meeting can do nothing more to save the country."

Johnny gave his first shrill blast on his whistle,

and he heard whistles and cries seemingly in all directions, Indian war whoops, and "Boston Harbor a teapot tonight!" "Hurrah for Griffin's Wharf!" "Saltwater tea!" "Hi, Mohawks, get your axes and pay no taxes!"

Johnny was only afraid all would be over before Rab and his henchmen could get to the wharf. Still shrilling on the whistle, he fought and floundered against the tide of the crowd. It was sweeping toward Griffin's Wharf, he struggling to get back to Salt Lane. Now he was afraid the others would have gone on without him. After all, Rab might have decided that Johnny's legs and ears were better than his hands—and deliberately let him do the work that best suited him. Johnny pushed open the door.

Rab was alone. He had Johnny's blanket coat, his ridiculous befeathered knitted cap in his hand.

"Quick!" he said, and smootched his face with soot, drew a red line across his mouth running from ear to ear. Johnny saw Rab's eyes through the mask of soot. They were glowing with that dark excitement he had seen but twice before. His lips were parted. His teeth looked sharp and white as an animal's. In spite of his calm demeanor, calm voice, he was charged and surcharged with a will to action, a readiness to take and enjoy any desperate chance. Rab had come terrifyingly alive.

They flung themselves out of the shop.

"Roundabout!" cried Rab. He meant they would get to the wharf by back alleys.

"Come, follow me. Now we're really going to run."

He flew up Salt Lane in the opposite direction from the waterfront. Now they were flinging themselves down back alleys (faster and faster). Once they had glimpse of a blacksmith shop and other "Indians" clamoring for soot for their faces. Now slipping over a back-yard fence, now at last on the waterfront, Sea Street, Flounder Alley. They were running so fast it seemed more like a dream of flying than reality.

The day had started with rain and then there had been clouds, but as they reached Griffin's Wharf the moon, full and white, broke free of the clouds. The three ships, the silent hundreds gathering upon the wharf, all were dipped in the pure white light. The crowds were becoming thousands, and there was not one there but guessed what was to be done, and all approved.

Rab was grunting out of the side of his mouth to a thick-set, active-looking man, whom Johnny would have known anywhere by his walk and the confident lift of his head, was Mr. Revere. "Me Know You."

"Me Know You," Johnny repeated this countersign and took his place behind Mr. Revere. The other boys, held up by the crowd, began arriving, and more men and boys. But Johnny guessed that many who were now quietly joining one of those three groups were acting on the spur of the moment, seeing what was up. They had blacked their faces, seized axes, and come along. They were behaving as quietly and were as obedient to their leaders as those who had been so carefully picked for this work of destruction.

There was a boatswain's whistle, and in silence one group boarded the *Dartmouth*. The *Eleanor* and the *Beaver* had to be warped in to the wharf. Johnny was close to Mr. Revere's heels. He heard him calling for the captain, promising him, in the jargon everyone talked that night, that not one thing should be damaged on the ship except only the tea, but the captain and all his crew had best stay in the cabin until the work was over.

Captain Hall shrugged and did as he was told, leaving his cabin boy to hand over the keys to the hold. The boy was grinning with pleasure. The "tea party" was not unexpected.

"I'll show you," the boy volunteered, "how to work them hoists. I'll fetch lanterns, mister."

The winches rattled and the heavy chests began to appear—one hundred and fifty of them. As some men worked in the hold, others broke open the chests and flung the tea into the harbor. But one thing made them unexpected difficulty. The tea inside the chests was wrapped in heavy canvas. The axes went through the wood easily enough—the canvas made endless trouble. Johnny had never worked so hard in his life.

*   *   *

The work on the *Dartmouth* and the *Eleanor* finished about the same time. The *Beaver* took longer, for she had not had time to unload the rest of her cargo, and great care was taken not to injure it. Just as Johnny was about to go over to see if he could help on the *Beaver,* Mr. Revere whispered to him. "Go get brooms. Clean um' deck."

Johnny and a parcel of boys brushed the deck until it was clean as a parlor floor. Then Mr. Revere called the captain to come up and inspect. The tea was utterly gone, but Captain Hall agreed that beyond that there had not been the slightest damage.

It was close upon dawn when the work on all three ships was done. And yet the great, silent audience on the wharf, men, women, and children, had not gone home. As the three groups came off the ships, they formed in fours along the wharf, their axes on their shoulders. Then a hurrah went up and a fife began to play. This was almost the first sound Johnny had heard since the tea party started—except only the crash of axes into sea chests, the squeak of hoists, and a few grunted orders.

Standing quietly in the crowd, he saw Sam Adams, pretending to be a most innocent bystander. It looked to Johnny as if the dog fox had eaten a couple of fat pullets, and had a third in his mouth.

As they started marching back to the center of town, they passed the Coffin House at the head of Griffin's Wharf. A window opened.

"Well, boys," said a voice, so cold one hardly knew whether he spoke in anger or not, "you've had a fine, pleasant evening for your Indian caper, haven't you? But mind . . . you've got to pay the fiddler yet."

It was the British Admiral Montague.

"Come on down here," someone yelled, "and we'll settle that score tonight."

The Admiral pulled in his head and slapped down the window.

Johnny and Rab knew, and men like the Observers knew, but best of all Sam Adams knew, that the fiddler would have to be paid. England, unable to find the individuals who had destroyed this valuable property, would punish the whole Town of Boston—make every man, woman, and child, Tories and Whigs alike, suffer until this tea was paid for. Nor was she likely to back down on her claim that she might tax the colonists any way she pleased.

Next day, all over Boston, boys and men, some of them with a little paint still showing behind their ears, were so lame they could scarce move their fingers, but none of them—not one—told what it was that had lamed them so. They would stand about and wonder who "those Mohawks" might have been or what the British Parliament might do next, but never say what they themselves had been doing, for each was sworn to secrecy.

Only Paul Revere showed no signs of the hard physical strain he had been under all the night before. Not long after dawn he had started on horseback for New York and Philadelphia with an account of the Tea Party. He could chop open tea chests all night, and ride all day.

Robert Louis Stevenson

Treasure Island

Treasure Island, first published in 1883, is one of the best adventure stories ever written and it is still one of the most popular. It was originally written for a schoolboy who wanted "something craggy to break his mind upon." In telling how he first started to write the story, Stevenson says: "I made the map of an island; it was elaborately and (I thought) beautifully colored; the shape of it took my fancy beyond expression; it contained harbors that pleased me like sonnets; and with the unconsciousness of the predestined, I ticketed my performance 'Treasure Island.' . . . As I paused upon my map . . . the future characters of the book began to appear there visibly among imaginary woods; and there brown faces and bright weapons peeped out upon me from unexpected quarters as they passed to and fro, fighting and hunting treasure, on these few square inches of a flat projection. The next thing I knew I had some papers before me and was writing out a list of characters." [From Robert Louis Stevenson, *Treasure Island* (Cassell, 1883).]

The *Hispaniola* lay some way out, and we went under the figureheads and round the sterns of many other ships, and their cables sometimes grated underneath our keel, and sometimes swung above us. At last, however, we got along-side, and were met and saluted as we stepped aboard by the mate, Mr. Arrow, a brown old sailor, with earrings in his ears and a squint. He and the squire were very thick and friendly, but I soon observed that things were not the same between Mr. Trelawney and the captain.

This last was a sharp-looking man, who seemed angry with everything on board, and was soon to tell us why, for we had hardly got down into the cabin when a sailor followed us.

"Captain Smollett, sir, axing to speak with you," said he.

"I am always at the captain's orders. Show him in," said the squire.

The captain, who was close behind the messenger, entered at once, and shut the door behind him.

"Well, Captain Smollett, what have you to say? All well, I hope; all shipshape and seaworthy?"

"Well, sir," said the captain, "better speak plain, I believe, even at the risk of offense. I don't like this cruise; I don't like the men; and I don't like my officer. That's short and sweet."

"Perhaps, sir, you don't like the ship?" inquired the squire, very angry, as I could see.

"I can't speak as to that, sir, not having seen her tried," said the captain. "She seems a clever craft; more I can't say."

"Possibly, sir, you may not like your employer, either?" says the squire.

But here Doctor Livesey cut in.

"Stay a bit," said he, "stay a bit. No use of such questions as that but to produce ill-feeling. The captain has said too much or he has said too little, and I'm bound to say that I require an explanation of his words. You don't, you say, like this cruise. Now, why?"

"I was engaged, sir, on what we called sealed orders, to sail this ship for that gentleman where he should bid me," said the captain. "So far so good. But now I find that every man before the mast knows more than I do. I don't call that fair, now, do you?"

"No," said Doctor Livesey, "I don't."

"Next," said the captain, "I learn we are going after treasure—hear it from my own hands, mind you. Now, treasure is ticklish work; I don't like treasure voyages on any account; and I don't like them, above all, when they are secret, and when (begging your pardon, Mr. Trelawney) the secret has been told to the parrot."

"Silver's parrot?" asked the squire.

"It's a way of speaking," said the captain. "Blabbed, I mean. It's my belief neither of you gentlemen know what you are about; but I'll tell you my way of it—life or death, and a close run."

"That is all clear, and, I dare say, true enough," replied Doctor Livesey. "We take the risk; but we are not so ignorant as you believe us. Next, you say you don't like the crew. Are they not good seamen?"

"I don't like them, sir," returned Captain Smollett. "And I think I should have had the choosing of my own hands, if you go to that."

"Perhaps you should," replied the doctor. "My friend should, perhaps, have taken you along with him; but the slight, if there be one, was unintentional. And you don't like Mr. Arrow?"

"I don't sir. I believe he's a good seaman; but he's too free with the crew to be a good officer. A mate should keep himself to himself—shouldn't drink with the men before the mast!"

"Do you mean he drinks?" cried the squire.

"No, sir," replied the captain; "only that he's too familiar."

"Well, now, and the short and long of it, captain?" asked the doctor. "Tell us what you want."

"Well, gentlemen, are you determined to go on this cruise?"

"Like iron," answered the squire.

"Very good," said the captain. "Then, as you've heard me very patiently, saying things that I could not prove, hear me a few words more. They are putting the powder and the arms in the forehold. Now, you have a good place under the cabin; why not put them there?—first point. Then you are bringing four of your own people with you, and they tell me some of them are to berthed forward. Why not give them the berths beside the cabin?—second point."

"Any more?" asked Mr. Trelawney.

"One more," said the captain. "There's been too much blabbing already."

"Far too much," agreed the doctor.

"I'll tell you what I've heard myself," continued Captain Smollett; "that you have a map of an island; that there's crosses on the map to show where treasure is; and that the island lies—" And then he named the latitude and longitude exactly.

"I never told that," cried the squire, "to a soul!"

"The hands know it, sir," returned the captain.

"Livesey, that must have been you or Hawkins," cried the squire.

"It doesn't much matter who it was," replied the doctor. And I could see that neither he nor the captain paid much regard to Mr. Trelawney's protestations. Neither did I, to be sure, he was so loose a talker; yet in this case I believe he was really right, and that nobody had told the situation of the island.

"Well, gentlemen," continued the captain, "I don't know who had the map; but I make it a point, it shall be kept secret even from me and Mr. Arrow. Otherwise I would ask you to let me resign."

"I see," said the doctor. "You wish us to keep the matter dark, and to make a garrison of the stern part of the ship, manned with my friend's own people, and provided with all the arms, and powder on board. In other words, you fear a mutiny."

"Sir," said Captain Smollet, "with no intention to take offense, I deny your right to put words into my mouth. No captain, sir, would be justified in going to sea at all if he had ground enough to say that. As for Mr. Arrow, I believe him thoroughly honest; some of the men are the same; all may be for what I know. But I am responsible for the ship's safety and the life of every man Jack aboard of her. I see things going, as I think, not quite right. And I ask you to take certain precautions, or let me resign my berth. And that's all."

"Captain Smollett," began the doctor, with a smile, "did you ever hear the fable of the mountain and the mouse? You'll excuse me, I dare say, but you remind me of that fable.

When you came in here, I'll stake my wig you meant more than this."

"Doctor," said the captain, "you are smart. When I came in here I meant to get discharged. I had no thought that Mr. Trelawney would hear a word."

"No more I would," cried the squire. "Had Livesey not been here, I should have seen you to the deuce. As it is, I have heard you. I will do as you desire; but I think the worse of you."

"That's as you please, sir," said the captain. "You'll find I do my duty."

And with that he took his leave.

"Trelawney," said the doctor, "contrary to all my notions, I believe you have managed to get two honest men on board with you—that man and John Silver."

"Silver, if you like," cried the squire; "but as for that intolerable humbug, I declare I think his conduct unmanly, unsailorly, and downright un-English."

"Well," says the doctor, "we shall see."

When we came on deck, the men had begun already to take out the arms and powder, yo-ho-ing at their work, while the captain and Mr. Arrow stood by superintending.

The new arrangement was quite to my liking. The whole schooner had been overhauled; six berths had been made astern, out of what had been the afterpart of the main hold; and this set of cabins was only joined to the galley and forecastle by a sparred passage on the port side. It had been originally meant that the captain, Mr. Arrow, Hunter, Joyce, the doctor, and the squire, were to occupy these six berths. Now, Redruth and I were to get two of them, and Mr. Arrow and the captain were to sleep on deck in the companion, which had been enlarged on each side till you might almost have called it a round-house. Very low it was still, of course; but there was room to swing two hammocks, and even the mate seemed pleased with the arrangement. Even he, perhaps, had been doubtful as to the crew, but that is only guess; for, as you shall hear, we had not long the benefit of his opinion.

We were all hard at work, changing the powder and the berths, when the last man or two,

and Long John along with them, came off in a shore boat.

The cook came up the side like a monkey for cleverness, and, as soon as he saw what was doing, "So, ho, mates!" says he, "what's this?"

"We're a-changing of the powder, Jack," answers one.

"Why, by the powers," cried Long John, "if we do, we'll miss the morning tide!"

"My orders!" said the captain shortly. "You may go below, my man. Hands will want supper."

"Aye, aye, sir," answered the cook; and, touching his forelock, he disappeared at once in the direction of his galley.

"That's a good man, captain," said the doctor.

"Very likely," replied Captain Smollett. "Easy with that, men—easy," he ran on, to the fellows who were shifting the powder; and then suddenly observing me examining the swivel we carried amidships, a long brass nine—"Here, you ship's boy," he cried, "out o' that! Off with you to the cook and get some work."

And then, as I was hurrying off, I heard him say, quite loudly, to the doctor:

"I'll have no favorites on my ship."

I assure you I was quite of the squire's way of thinking, and hated the captain deeply.

The Voyage

All that night we were in a great bustle getting things stowed in their place, and boatfuls of the squire's friends, Mr. Blandly and the like, coming off to wish him a good voyage and a safe return. We never had a night at the Admiral Benbow when I had half the work; and I was dog-tired when, a little before dawn, the boatswain sounded his pipe, and the crew began to man the capstan bars. I might have been twice as weary, yet I would not have left the deck; all was so new and interesting to me—the brief commands, the shrill note of the whistle, the men bustling to their places in the glimmer of the ship's lanterns.

"Now, Barbecue, tip us a stave," cried one voice.

"The old one," cried another.

"Aye, aye, mates," said Long John, who was

standing by, with his crutch under his arm, and at once broke out in the air and words I knew so well—

"Fifteen men on the Dead Man's Chest—"

And then the whole crew bore chorus:

"Yo-ho-ho, and a bottle of rum!"

And at the third "ho!" drove the bars before them with a will.

Even at that exciting moment it carried me back to the old Admiral Benbow in a second; and I seemed to hear the voice of the captain piping in the chorus.

But soon the anchor was short up; soon it was hanging dripping at the bows; soon the sails began to draw, and the land and shipping to flit by on either side; and before I could lie down to snatch an hour of slumber the *Hispaniola* had begun her voyage to the Isle of Treasure.

I am not going to relate that voyage in detail. It was fairly prosperous. The ship proved to be a good ship, the crew were capable seamen, and the captain thoroughly understood his business. But before we came the length of Treasure Island, two or three things had happened which require to be known.

Mr. Arrow, first of all, turned out even worse that the captain had feared. He had no command among the men, and people did what they pleased with him. But that was by no means the worst of it; for after a day or two at sea he began to appear on deck with hazy eye, red cheeks, stuttering tongue, and other marks of drunkenness. Time after time he was ordered below in disgrace. Sometimes he fell and cut himself; sometimes he lay all day long in his little bunk at one side of the companion; sometimes for a day or two he would be almost sober and attend to his work at least passably.

In the meantime, we could never make out where he got the drink. That was the ship's mystery. Watch him as we pleased, we could do nothing to solve it; and when we asked him to his face, he would only laugh, if he were drunk, and if he were sober deny solemnly that he ever tasted anything but water.

He was not only useless as an officer, and a bad influence amongst the men, but it was plain that at this rate he must soon kill himself outright; so nobody was much surprised, nor very sorry, when one dark night, with a head sea, he disappeared entirely and was seen no more.

"Overboard!" said the captain. "Well, gentlemen, that saves the trouble of putting him in irons."

But there we were, without a mate; and it was necessary, of course, to advance one of the men. The boatswain, Job Anderson, was the likeliest man aboard, and, though he kept his old title, he served in a way as mate. Mr. Trelawney had followed the sea, and his knowledge made him very useful, for he often took a watch himself in easy weather. And the coxswain, Israel Hands, was a careful, wily, old, experienced seaman, who could be trusted at a pinch with almost anything.

He was a great confidant of Long John Silver, and so the mention of his name leads me on to speak of our ship's cook, Barbecue, as the men called him.

Aboard ship he carried his crutch by a lanyard round his neck, to have both hands as free as possible. It was something to see him wedge the foot of the crutch against a bulkhead; and, propped against it, yielding to every movement of the ship, to get on with his cooking like someone safe ashore. Still more strange was it to see him in the heaviest of weather cross the deck. He had a line or two rigged up to help him across the widest spaces—Long John's earrings, they were called; and he would hand himself from one place to another, now using the crutch, now trailing it alongside by the lanyard, as quickly as another man could walk. Yet some of the men who had sailed with him before expressed their pity to see him so reduced.

"He's no common man, Barbecue," said the coxswain to me. "He had good schooling in his young days, and can speak like a book when so minded; and brave—a lion's nothing alongside of Long John! I seen him grapple four, and knock their heads together—him un-armed."

All the crew respected and even obeyed him. He had a way of talking to each, and doing everybody some particular service. To me he was unweariedly kind; and always glad to see me in the galley, which he kept as clean as a new pin; the dishes hanging up burnished and his parrot in a cage in one corner.

"Come away, Hawkins," he would say; "come and have a yarn with John. Nobody more welcome than yourself, my son. Sit you down and hear the news. Here's Cap'n Flint—I calls my parrot Cap'n Flint, after the famous buccaneer—here's Cap'n Flint perdicting success to our v'yage. Wasn't you, cap'n?"

And the parrot would say, with great rapidity, "Pieces of eight! pieces of eight! pieces of eight!

Illustration by N. C. Wyeth, from *Treasure Island*, by Robert Louis Stevenson. Illustrations copyright © 1911 by Charles Scribner's Sons. Copyright renewed. Used by permission of Charles Scribner's Sons.

till you wondered that it was not out of breath, or till John threw his handkerchief over the cage.

"Now, that bird," he would say, "is, maybe, two hundred years old, Hawkins—they lives forever mostly; and if anybody's seen more wickedness, it must be the devil himself. She's sailed with England, the great Cap'n England, the pirate. She's been at Madagascar, and at Malabar, and Surinam, and Providence, and Portobello. She was at the fishing-up of the wrecked plate ships. It's there she learned 'Pieces of eight,' and little wonder; three hundred and fifty thousand of 'em, Hawkins! She was at the boarding of the *Viceroy of the Indies* out of Goa, she was; and to look at her you would think she was a babby. But you smelt powder—didn't you, cap'n?"

"Stand by to go about," the parrot would scream.

"Ah, she's a handsome craft, she is," the cook would say, and give her sugar from his pocket, and then the bird would peck at the bars and swear straight on, passing belief for wickedness. "There," John would add, "you can't touch pitch and not be mucked, lad. Here's this poor old innocent bird o' mine swearing blue fire, and none the wiser, you may lay to that. She would swear the same, in a manner of speaking, before chaplain." And John would touch his forelock with a solemn way he had, that made me think he was the best of men.

In the meantime, squire and Captain Smollett were still on pretty distant terms with one another. The squire made no bones about the matter; he despised the captain. The captain, on his part, never spoke but when he was spoken to, and then sharp and short and dry, and not a word wasted. He owned, when driven into a corner, that he seemed to have been wrong about the crew, that some of them was as brisk as he wanted to see, and all had behaved fairly well. As for the ship, he had taken a downright fancy to her. "She'll lie a point nearer the wind than a man has a right to expect of his own married wife, sir. But," he would add, "all I say is we're not home again, and I don't like the cruise."

The squire, at this, would turn away and march up and down the deck, chin in air.

"A trifle more of that man," he would say "and I should explode."

We had some heavy weather, which only proved the qualities of the *Hispaniola*. Every man on board seemed well content, and they must have been hard to please if they had been otherwise; for it is my belief there was never a ship's company so spoiled since Noah put to sea. Double grog was going on the least excuse; there was duff on odd days, as, for instance, if the squire heard it was any man's birthday; and always a barrel of apples standing broached in the waist, for anyone to help himself that had a fancy.

"Never knew good come of it yet," the captain said to Doctor Livesey. "Spoil foc's'le hands, make devils. That's my belief."

But good did come of the apple barrel, as you shall hear: for if it had not been for that, we should have had no note of warning, and might all have perished by the hand of treachery.

This was how it came about.

We had run up the trades to get the wind of the island we were after—I am not allowed to be more plain—and now we were running down for it with a bright lookout day and night. It was about the last day of our outward voyage, by the largest computation; sometime that night, or, at latest, before noon of the morrow, we should sight the Treasure Island. We were heading S.S.W., and had a steady breeze abeam and a quiet sea. The *Hispaniola* rolled steadily, dipping her bowsprit now and then with a whiff of spray. All was drawing alow and aloft; everyone was in the bravest spirits, because we were now so near an end of the first part of our adventure.

Now, just after sundown, when all my work was over, and I was on my way to my berth, it occurred to me that I should like an apple. I ran on deck. The watch was all forward looking out for the island. The man at the helm was watching the luff of the sail, and whistling away gently to himself; and that was the only sound excepting the swish of the sea against the bows and around the sides of the ship.

In I got bodily into the apple barrel, and found there was scarce an apple left; but, sitting down there in the dark, what with the sound of the waters and the rocking movement of the ship, I had either fallen asleep, or was on the point of doing so, when a heavy man sat down with rather a clash close by. The barrel shook as he leaned his shoulders against it, and I was just about to jump up when the man began to speak. It was Silver's voice, and, before I had heard a dozen words, I would not have shown myself for all the world, but lay there, trembling and listening, in the extreme of fear and curiosity; for from these dozen words I understood that the lives of all the honest men aboard depended upon me alone.

What I Heard in the Apple Barrel

"No, not I," said Silver. "Flint was cap'n; I was quartermaster, along of my timber leg. The same broadside I lost my leg, old Pew lost his headlights. It was a master surgeon, him that ampytated me—out of college and all—Latin by the bucket, and what not; but he was hanged like a dog, and sun-dried like the rest, at Corso Castle. That was Roberts's men, that was, and comed of changing names to their ships—*Royal Fortune* and so on. Now, what a ship was christened, so let her stay, I says. So it was with the *Cassandra,* as brought us all safe home from Malabar, after England took the *Viceroy of the Indies;* so it was with the old *Walrus,* Flint's old ship, as I've seen a-muck with the red blood and fit to sink with gold."

"Ah!" cried another voice, that of the youngest hand on board, and evidently full of admiration, "he was the flower of the flock, was Flint!"

"Davis was a man, too, by all accounts," said Silver. "I never sailed along of him; first with England, then with Flint, that's my story; and now here on my account, in a manner of speaking. I laid by nine hundred safe, from England, and two thousand after Flint. That ain't bad for a man before the mast—all safe in bank. 'Tain't earning now, it's saving does it, you may lay to that. Where's all England's men now? I dunno. Where's Flint's? Why, most on 'em aboard here, and glad to get the duff—been begging before that, some on 'em. Old Pew, as had lost his sight, and might have thought shame, spends twelve hundred pound in a year, like a lord in Parliament. Where is he now?

Well, he's dead now and under hatches; but for two year before that, shiver my timbers! the man was starving. He begged, and he stole, and he cut throats, and starved at that by the powers!"

"Well, it ain't much use, after all," said the young seaman.

" 'Tain't much use for fools, you may lay to it—that, not nothing," cried Silver. "But now, you look here; you're young, you are, but you're as smart as paint. I see that when I set my eyes on you, and I'll talk to you like a man."

You may imagine how I felt when I heard this abominable old rogue addressing another in the very same words of flattery as he had used to myself. I think, if I had been able, that I would have killed him through the barrel. Meantime, he ran on, little supposing he was overheard.

"Here it is about gentleman of fortune. They lives rough, and they risk swinging, but they eat and drink like fighting-cocks, and when a cruise is done, why, it's hundreds of pounds instead of hundreds of farthings in their pockets. Now, the most goes for rum and a good fling, and to sea again in their shirts. But that's not the course I lay. I puts it all away, some here, some there, and none too much anywheres, by reason of suspicion. I'm fifty, mark you; once back from this cruise, I set up gentleman in earnest. Time enough, too, says you. Ah, but I've lived easy in the meantime; never denied myself o' nothing heart desires, and slep' soft and ate dainty all my days, but when at sea. And how did I begin? Before the mast, like you!"

"Well," said the other, "but all the other money's gone now, ain't it? You daren't show face in Bristol after this."

"Why, where might you suppose it was?" asked Silver, derisively.

"At Bristol, in banks and places," answered his companion.

"It were," said the cook; "it were when we weighed anchor. But my old missus has it all by now. And the 'Spy-glass' is sold, lease and goodwill and rigging; and the old girl's off to meet me. I would tell you where, for I trust you; but it 'ud make jealousy among the mates."

"And can you trust your missus?" asked the other.

"Gentlemen of fortune," returned the cook, "usually trusts little among themselves, and right they are, you may lay to it. But I have a way with me, I have. When a mate brings a slip on his cable—one as knows me, I mean—it won't be in the same world with old John. There was some that was feared of Pew, and some that was feared of Flint; but Flint his own self was feared of me. Feared he was, and proud. They was the roughest crew afloat, was Flint's; the devil himself would have been feared to go to sea with them. Well, now, I tell you, I'm not a boasting man, and you seen yourself how easy I keep company; but when I was quarter-master, *lambs* wasn't the word for Flint's old buccaneers. Ah, you may be sure of yourself in old John's ship."

"Well, I tell you now," replied the lad, "I didn't half a quarter like the job till I had this talk with you, John; but there's my hand on it now."

"And a brave lad you were, and smart, too," answered Silver, shaking hands so heartily that all the barrel shook, "and a finer figurehead for a gentleman of fortune I never clapped my eyes on."

By this time I had begun to understand the meaning of their terms. By a "gentleman of fortune" they plainly meant neither more nor less than a common pirate, and the little scene that I had overheard was the last act in the corruption of one of the honest hands—perhaps of the last one left aboard. But on this point I was soon to be relieved, for Silver giving a little whistle, a third man strolled up and sat down by the party.

"Dick's square," said Silver.

"Oh, I know'd Dick was square," returned the voice of the coxswain, Israel Hands. "He's no fool, is Dick." And he turned his quid and spat. "But, look here," he went on, "here's what I want to know, Barbecue: how long are we a-going to stand off and on like a blessed bumboat? I've had a'most enough o' Cap'n Smollett; he's hazed me long enough, by thunder! I want to go into that cabin, I do. I want their pickles and wines, and that."

"Israel," said Silver, "your head ain't much account, nor ever was. But you're able to hear, I reckon; leastways, your ears is big enough.

Now, here's what I say: you'll berth forward, and you'll live hard, and you'll speak soft, and you'll keep sober, till I give the word; and you may lay to that, my son."

"Well, I don't say no, do I?" growled the coxswain. "What I say is, when? That's what I say."

"When! by the powers!" cried Silver. "Well now, if you want to know, I'll tell you when. The last moment I can manage; and that's when. Here's a first-rate seaman, Cap'n Smollett, sails the blessed ship for us. Here's this squire and doctor with a map and such—I don't know where it is, do I? No more do you, says you. Well, then, I mean this squire and doctor shall find the stuff, and help us to get it aboard, by the powers. Then we'll see. If I was sure of you all, sons of double Dutchmen, I'd have Cap'n Smollett navigate us halfway back again before I struck."

"Why, we're all seamen aboard here, I should think," said the lad Dick.

"We're all foc's'le hands, you mean," snapped Silver. "We can steer a course, but who's to set one? That's what all you gentlemen split on, first and last. If I had my way, I'd have Cap'n Smollett work us back into the trades at least; then we'd have no blessed miscalculations and a spoonful of water a day. But I know the sort you are. I'll finish with 'em at the island, as soon's the blunt's on board, and a pity it is. But you're never happy till you're drunk. Split my sides, I've a sick heart to sail with the likes of you!"

"Easy all, Long John," cried Israel. "Who's a-crossin' of you?"

"Why, how many tall ships, think ye, now, have I seen laid aboard? and how many brisk lads drying in the sun at Execution Dock?" cried Silver—"and all for this same hurry and hurry and hurry. You hear me? I seen a thing or two at sea, I have. If you would on'y lay your course, and a p'int to windward, you would ride in carriages, you would. But not you! I know you. You'll have your mouthful of rum tomorrow, and go hang."

"Everybody know'd you was kind of a chapling, John; but there's others as could hand and steer as well as you," said Israel. "They liked a bit o' fun, they did. They wasn't so high and dry, nohow, but took their fling, like jolly companions every one."

"So?" says Silver. "Well, and where are they now? Pew was that sort, and he died a beggarman. Flint was, and he died of rum at Savannah. Ah, they was a sweet crew, they was! on'y, where are they?"

"But," asked Dick, "when we do lay 'em athwart, what are we to do with 'em, anyhow?"

"There's the man for me!" cried the cook, admiringly. "That's what I call business. Well, what would you think? Put 'em ashore like maroons? That would have been England's way. Or cut 'em down like that much pork? That would have been Flint's or Billy Bones's."

"Billy was the man for that," said Israel. "'Dead men don't bite,' says he. Well, he's dead now hisself; he knows the long and short on it now; and if ever a rough hand come to port, it was Billy."

"Right you are," said Silver, "rough and ready. But mark you here: I'm an easy man— I'm quite the gentleman, says you; but this time it's serious. Dooty is dooty, mates. I give my vote—death. When I'm in Parlyment, and riding in my coach, I don't want none of these sea-lawyers in the cabin a-coming home, unlooked for, like the devil at prayers. Wait is what I say; but when the time comes, why, let her rip!"

"John," cried the coxswain, "you're a man!"

"You'll say so, Israel, when you see," said Silver. "Only one thing I claim—I claim Trelawney. I'll wring his calf's head off his body with these hands. Dick!" he added, breaking off, "you just jump up, like a sweet lad, and get me an apple, to wet my pipe like."

You may fancy the terror I was in! I should have leaped out and run for it if I had found the strength; but my limbs and heart alike misgave me. I heard Dick begin to rise, and then someone seemingly stopped him, and the voice of Hands exclaimed: "Oh, stow that! Don't you get sucking of that bilge, John. Let's have a go of the rum."

"Dick," said Silver, "I trust you. I've a gauge on the keg, mind. There's the key; you fill a pannikin and bring it up."

Terrified as I was, I could not help thinking to myself that this must have been how Mr.

Arrow got the strong waters that destroyed him.

Dick was gone but a little while, and during his absence Israel spoke straight on in the cook's ear. It was but a word or two that I could catch, and yet gathered some important news; for, besides other scraps that tended to the same purpose, this whole clause was audible: "Not another man of them'll jine." Hence there were still faithful men on board.

When Dick returned, one after another of the trio took the pannikin and drank—one "To luck"; another with a "Here's to old Flint"; and Silver himself saying, in a kind of song, "Here's to ourselves, and hold your luff, plenty of prizes and plenty of duff."

Just then a sort of brightness fell upon me in the barrel, and, looking up, I found the moon had risen, and was silvering the mizzen-top and shining white on the luff of the fore-sail; and almost at the same time the voice of the lookout shouted "Land-ho!"

Paula Fox

The Slave Dancer

This is an account of the infamous Middle Passage across the Atlantic from West Africa—the route of the slave trade. Paula Fox makes effective use of elements drawn from the traditional sea story: The romance and cruelties of the sea, the specter of shipwreck and struggle for survival in such high adventures as *Treasure Island* and *Moby Dick* are placed in ironic contrast to the harsh reality of the slave ships. Written with quiet understatement, as a first person chronicle, Jessie recounts from adulthood his experiences as a kidnapped white boy aboard such a ship. The times when he is forced to play his fife to exercise the slaves are the worst moments of his nightmarish voyage, and, in the following passage, Paula Fox spares none of the details of the horrifying ordeal. But Jessie begins to see the slaves as fellow human beings, and he is transformed in this unforgettable depiction of the brutality of slavery. *The Slave Dancer* won the Newbery Medal in 1974. [From Paula Fox, *The Slave Dancer* (Bradbury, 1973).]

Nicholas Spark Walks on Water

With a small smile, Stout said, "Get ready to play your music, lad," then reached out his hand to pat my shoulder. I moved back quickly as though a cottonmouth had struck in my direction. I saw, as clearly as I could see the cat-o'-nine-tails in his other hand, those fleshy fingers gripped around the ankle of the dead little girl.

I went below and got my fife, but stood unmoving in the dark until I heard them shouting for me.

The slaves from one of the holds were being hoisted one by one to the deck. Only the women and the youngest children were unshackled.

In just a few days, they had become so battered, so bowed by the fears that must have tormented them, that they could barely stand up. They blinked in the bright white light of the growing day. Then they sank to the deck, the women clutching weakly at the children, their shoulders bent over as though to receive the blows of death.

All hands were present; even Ned was ordered to leave his workbench and stand to attention.

The slaves were given their water rations and fed rice with a sauce of pepper and oil. When they saw the food and water, sighs rose from them like small puffs of wind, one following so close on the other that in the end, it seemed one great exhalation of air.

"Some of them think we eat them," whispered Purvis to me. "They think that first meal was only to fool them. When they see we intend to keep on feeding them, they grow quite cheerful."

I saw no cheer. The adults ate mournfully, the food dribbling from their lips as though their spirits were too low to keep their jaws firm. The children spoke among themselves. Sometimes a woman held a child's head as though she feared its voice might draw down punishment upon it, and rice from the child's mouth would spill across her arm.

When they had finished their meal, the Captain said to Stout, "Tell them to stand up. And tell them we have a musician for them and that they are to dance for me."

"I can't tell them all that, Sir," Stout replied. "I don't know their words for dancing or for music."

"Then tell them *something* to get them to their feet!" cried the Captain angrily as he flourished his pistol.

Stout began to speak to the slaves. They did not look at him. Some stared up at the tarpaulin as though there were a picture painted on it; others looked down at their feet.

We had formed a circle around them, dressed, shod, most of us armed. Many of them were naked; a few had ragged bits of cloth around their waists. I glanced at the sailors. Ned's eyes were turned upward toward heaven. I supposed he was reporting to God on the folly of everyone else but himself. But the rest were staring fixedly at the slaves. I felt fevered and agitated. I sensed, I saw, how beyond the advantage we had of weapons, their nakedness made them helpless. Even if we had not been armed, our clothes and boots alone would have given us power.

There was something else that held the attention of the men—and my own. It was the unguarded difference between the bodies of the men and women.

I had told no living soul that on some of my late walks through the old quarter at home. I had dared the chance of hell fire by glancing through the windows of certain houses where I had seen women undressing, and undressed. I can only say that I didn't *linger* at those windows. Sometimes, after my peeking, I had been ashamed. Other times, I had rolled on the ground with laughter. Why I was chagrined in one instance and hilarious in another, I don't know.

But what I felt now, now that I could gaze without restraint at the helpless and revealed forms of these slaves, was a mortification beyond any I had ever imagined.

At the increasingly harsh shouts of Ben Stout, some of the black men had risen, swaying, to their feet. Then others stood. But several remained squatting. Stout began to lay about him with the cat-o'-nine, slapping the deck, flicking its fangs toward the feet of those who had not responded to his cries with even a twitch. At last, he whipped them to their feet. The women had risen at the first word, clutching the small children to their breasts.

"Bollweevil!" called the Captain.

Ned suddenly lit up his pipe.

I blew. A broken squeak came out of my fife.

"Tie him to the topmost crosstrees!" screamed Cawthorne Stout, smiling, started toward me. I blew again. This time I managed a thin note, then some semblance of a tune.

The cat-o'-nine slapped the deck. Spark clapped his hands without a trace of rhythm. The Captain waved his arms about as though he'd been attacked by a horde of flies. A black man drooped toward the deck until Spark brought his heel down on his thin bare foot.

I played on against the wind, the movement of the ship and my own self-disgust, and finally the slaves began to lift their feet, the chains attached to the shackles around their ankles forming an iron dirge, below the trills of my tune. The women, being unshackled, moved more freely, but they continued to hold the children close. From no more than a barely audible moan or two, their voices began to gain strength until the song they were singing, or the words they were chanting, or the story they were telling overwhelmed the small sound of my playing.

All at once, as abrupt as the fall of an axe, it came to a stop. Ben Stout snatched the fife from my hands. The slaves grew silent. The dust they had raised slowly settled around them.

That morning, I danced three groups of slaves. In the last, I saw the boy who I thought had looked at me when I cried out at Stout's heaving the child overboard. He wouldn't stand up. Spark dealt him a mighty blow with the tarred rope which left its tooth on the boy's back, a red channel in the tight brown flesh. He stood then, moving his feet as though they didn't belong to him.

It was to perform this service every other morning that I had been kidnapped and carried across the ocean.

I dreaded the coming of daylight. I listened without interest to rumors—that two of the slaves had fever, that the ship we had seen to windward was an American cruiser in pursuit of *The Moonlight,* that Spark had suddenly taken to drink, that Stout was the Captain's spy among us, that a black child had the pox.

In the harbor of São Tomé, in the sickly haze of a morning when I'd been relieved of all my duties save that of emptying the latrine buckets, I wondered if I dared leap overboard and take my chances on reaching the shore. But what would I find there? Other men who might use me worse than I was being used? Or a captain who tortured his own crew? God knows, I had heard of such things!

Now the slaves were fighting among themselves. The immediate cause was the latrine buckets. Many of them could not reach them quickly enough across the bodies of the others, for there was not a spare inch of space. Most of them had what Purvis called the bloody flux, an agonizing affliction of their bowels that not only doubled them up with cramps but made the buckets entirely inadequate.

One night as we lay at anchor, waiting for the morning when fresh supplies would be loaded on the ship, I heard a scream of inhuman force, of intolerable misery. I began to weep helplessly myself, covering my mouth with an old cap of Stout's for fear one of the crew would hear me.

We sailed from the island shortly, with no regrets on my part. It was as though I was trying to swallow the long days ahead, to stuff them down my throat, to make them pass with a gulp, thinking of that hour, that minute, when I would be let off this ship.

When we were two days out on our westward course, I heard once again that cry from one of the holds, a woman's scream, hair-raising, heart-squeezing. I had been dancing a group of slaves, and at that terrible sound, Spark signaled me to stop my tune. Stout ran to the hold from which the cry had issued. He disappeared down it. Not a minute later, a black woman was tossed upon the deck like a doll of rags.

"Over!" said the Captain. Spark and Stout lifted the woman, who was alive, carried her to the rail and swung her up and over. We didn't hear the splash she must have made when she hit the water, but then we were making speed before a fair breeze.

"She had the fever," Stout said to me as he passed, "and was dying and would have infected the rest of them." He was not trying to excuse himself. No, it was only his usual trick. He knew I thought he was evil, but he liked to suggest that beneath that I held another opinion of him, that, in fact, I admired him. It was a complicated insult.

The slaves were all looking at the place where the woman had been thrown overboard. Sick and stooped, half-starved by now, and soiled from the rarely cleaned holds, they stared hopelessly at the empty horizon.

I found a dreadful thing in my mind.

I hated the slaves! I hated their shuffling, their howling, their very suffering! I hated the way they spat out their food upon the deck, the overflowing buckets, the emptying of which tried all my strength. I hated the foul stench that came from the holds no matter which way the wind blew, as though the ship itself were soaked with human excrement. I would have snatched the rope from Spark's hand and beaten them myself! Oh, God! I wished them all dead! Not to hear them! Not to smell them! Not to know of their existence!

I dropped my fife on the deck and fled to my hammock. I would stay there until I was forcibly removed.

Which I was, soon enough.

They sent Seth Smith to get me.

"Get down!"

"Damn you all!" I said.

"If I have to carry you, it'll go hard for you."

I gripped the edges of my hammock. He turned it over with one movement of his hand, then caught me round the waist and took me to the deck.

The slaves had been returned to the hold. Captain Cawthorne was holding my fife in his hand, turning it idly. Standing next to him was Ben Stout. The fife reflected bright bits of sunlight.

"We won't have none of that," the Captain remarked. I recalled Purvis' mad song to himself about some of this and some of that. Purvis was nowhere to be seen. Ned was bent over his bench, a piece of chain in his carpenter's vise. I only noticed now that he was extremely thin, and that he looked ill.

"You're not so young you don't know what an order is," the Captain said. He shoved the fife at my chest and poked about with it as though trying to discover what I had concealed beneath my shirt.

"Stand to the rail," he ordered.

I did. The sea was blue today.

"Five," said the Captain.

Five times, Stout brought the rope down on my back. I had been determined not to cry out. But I did. It hurt more than I could have imagined. But I was not ashamed of my cries, for each time the rope fell, I thought of the slaves, of the violent hatred I had felt for them that had so frightened me that I had defied Master and crew. My eyes flooded with tears. The taste of salt was in my mouth. But as the blows fell, I became myself again. That self had gone through such transformations, I could not claim to be altogether familiar with it. But one thing was clear. I was a thirteen-year-old male, not as tall though somewhat heavier than a boy close to my own age, now doubled up in the dark below, not a dozen yards from where I was being beaten.

Alan Garner

The Stone Book

"The Stone Book Quartet" comprises four miniature novels, forming a chronicle of five generations living in Cheshire, England, between the 1860s and the 1940s. This story, the first in the series, is about a girl, Mary, and her relationship with her father, the village stonemason. The events of one day mark Mary's initiation into pride of place, craft, and family tradition. Mary wants to learn to read, or at least to own a book. In response to her request for a prayer book, her father teaches her the language of stone—the wisdom of the natural world. In this selection, he sends her on a descent beneath the hill that has been the family's traditional quarrying place for stone. There she finds a secret that represents time, human continuity, and her family's heritage. With its symbolic imagery and poetic dialect—a dialect in constant use since the writing of *Sir Gawain and the Green Knight*—this work is both outstanding and unique. [From Alan Garner, *The Stone Book* (Collins, 1976).]

Father sat at the table, not even moving the stones. Then he stood up and walked into the garden. Mary waited. She heard him rattling the hoe and rake, and Old William started up his loom, but she could tell he was upset, because of the slow beat, "Plenty-of-time, plenty-of-time." She crawled from under the table and went out to the garden. Father was hoeing next to the rhubarb.

"If I can't learn to read, will you give me something instead?" said Mary.

"If it's not too much," said Father. "The trouble with him is," he said, and jutted his clay pipe at Old William's weaving room, "he's as good as me, but can't ever see the end of his work. And I make it worse by building houses for the big masters who've taken his living. That's what it is, but we never say."

"If I can't read, can I have a book?"

Father opened his mouth and the clay pipe fell to the ground and didn't break. He looked at the pipe. "I have not seen a Macclesfield dandy that has fallen to the ground and not broken," he said. "And they don't last more than a threeweek." He turned the soil gently with his hoe and buried the pipe.

"What've you done that for?" said Mary. "They cost a farthing!"

"Well," said Father, "I reckon, what with all the stone, if I can't give a bit back, it's a poor do. Why a book?"

"I want a prayer book to carry to Chapel," said Mary. "Lizzie Allman and Annie Leah have them."

"Can they read?"

"No. They use them to press flowers."

"Well, then," said Father.

"But they can laugh," said Mary.

"Ay," said Father. He leant on the hoe and looked at Glaze Hill. "Go fetch a bobbin of bad ends; two boxes of lucifer matches and a bundle of candles—a whole fresh bundle. We're going for a walk. And tell nobody."

Mary went into the house to Old William's room. In a corner by the door he kept the bad ends wound on bobbins. They were lengths of thread that came to him knotted or too thick or that broke on the loom. He tied them together and wove them for Mother to make clothes from. Mary lifted a bobbin and took it out. She found the candles and the lucifer matches.

Father had put his tools away.

They went up the field at the back of the house and onto Glaze Hill. When they reached the top the sun was ready for setting. The weathercock on Saint Philip's was losing light, and woods stretched out.

"I can't see the churches," said Mary. "When we were up there this afternoon I could."

"That's because they're all of a height," said Father. "I told you Glaze Hill was higher."

Glaze Hill was the middle of three spurs of land. The Wood Hill came in from the right, and Daniel Hill from the left, and they met at the Engine Vein. The Engine Vein was a deep crevice in the rocks, and along it went the tramroad for the miners who dug galena, cobalt and malachite. The thump of the engine that pumped water out of the Vein could often be heard through the ground on different parts of the hill, when the workings ran close to the surface.

Now it was dusk, and the engine quiet. The tramroad led down to the head of the first stope, and there was a ladder for men to climb into the cave.

Mary was not allowed at the Vein. It killed at least once every year, and even to go close was dangerous, because the dead sand around the edge was hard and filled with little stones that slipped over the crag.

Father walked on the sleepers of the tramroad down into the Engine Vein.

"It's nearly night," said Mary. "It'll be dark."

"We've candles," said Father.

There was a cool smell, and draughts of sweet air. The roof of the Vein began, and they were under the ground. Water dripped from the roof onto the sandstone, splashing echoes. The drops fell into holes. They had fallen for so many years in the same place that they had worn the rock. Mary could get her fingers into some of the holes, but they were deeper than her hands.

Above and behind her, Mary saw the last of the day. In front and beneath was the stope, where it was always night.

Father took the whole bundle of candles and set them on the rocks and lit them. They showed how dark it was in the stope.

"Wait while you get used to it," said Father. "You soon see better. Now what about that roof?"

Mary looked up into the shadows. "It's not

dimension stone," she said. "There's a grain to it, and it's all ridge and furrow."

"But if you'd been with me that day," said Father, "when I was prenticed and walked to the sea, you'd have stood on sand just the same as that. The waves do it, going back and to. And it makes the ridges proper hard, and if you left it I reckon it could set into stone. But the tide goes back and to, back and to, and wets it. And your boots sink in and leave a mark."

"If that's the sea, why's it under the ground?" said Mary.

"And whose are those boots?" said Father.

There were footprints in the roof, flattening the ripples, as though a big bird had walked there.

"Was that Noah's flood, too?" said Mary.

"I can't tell you," said Father. "If it was, that bantam never got into the ark."

"It must've been as big as Saint Philip's cockerel," said Mary.

"Bigger," said Father. "And upside down."

"It doesn't make sense," said Mary.

"It would if we could plunder it deep enough," said Father. "I reckon that if you're going to put the sea in a hill and turn the world over and let it dry, then you've got to be doing before nine o'clock in the morning. But preachers aren't partial to coming down here, so it doesn't matter. Does it?"

He blew out all the candles except two. He gave one to Mary and stepped onto the ladder. Mary went with him, and climbed between his arms down into the stope.

"It'd take some plucking," she said.

"If it had feathers."

The stope was the shape of a straw beehive and tunnels led everywhere. Mary couldn't see the top of the ladder.

"If you'd fallen, you'd have been killed dead as at Saint Philip's," said Father.

"It's different," said Mary. "There's no height."

"There's depth, and that's no different than height," said Father.

"It doesn't call you," said Mary.

Father held Mary's hand sailor's grip and went into a tunnel under a ledge at the bottom of the stope. They didn't go far. There was a shaft

in the rock, not a straight one, but when Father bridged it with his feet, the pebbles rattled down for a long time. It was easy climbing, even with a candle to be held, because the rock kept changing, and each change made a shelf. There was puddingstone, marl and foxbench, and only the marl was slippery.

"That's it," said Father. They were at a kink in the shaft.

"What about further down?" said Mary.

"It's only rubbish gangue from here to the bottom; neither use nor ornament. Although there was a man, him as sank this shaft, and he could read books and put a letter together. But he lost his money, for all his reading. Now if he'd read rocks instead of books, it might have been a different story, you see."

Father held his candle out to the side. There was a crack, not a tunnel. The rock itself had made it.

"Hold fast to your light," said Father. "And keep the matches out of the wet."

Father had to crawl. Mary could stand, but even she had to squeeze, because of the narrowness.

The crack went up and down, wavering through the hill. Then Father stopped. He couldn't turn his head to speak, but he could crouch on his heel. "Climb over," he said.

Mary pulled herself across his back. A side of wall had split off and jammed in the passage, almost closing it.

"Can you get through there?" said Father.

"Easy," said Mary.

"Get through and then listen," said Father.

Mary wriggled past the flake and stood up. The passage went on beyond her light. Father's candle made a dark hole of where she had come, and she could see his boots and one hand. He pushed the bobbin of bad ends through to her, and six candles. He kept hold of the loose end of silk.

"What's up?" said Mary. "What are we doing?"

"You still want a book for Sundays?" said Father. "Even if you can't read?"

"Yes," said Mary.

"Then this is what we're doing," said Father. "So you listen. You're to keep the lucifers dry, and use only one candle. It should be plenty.

Let the silk out, but don't pull on it, else it'll snap. It's to fetch you back if you've no light, and that's all it's for. Now then. You'll find you go down a bit of steep, and then the rock divides. Follow the malachite. Always follow the malachite. Do you understand me?"

"Yes, Father."

"After the malachite there's some old foxbench, then a band of white dimension, and a lot of wet when you come to the Tough Tom. Can you remember it all?"

"Malachite, foxbench, dimension, Tough Tom," said Mary.

"Always follow the malachite," said Father. "And if there's been another rockfall, don't trust loose stuff. And think on: there isn't anybody can reach you. You're alone."

"What must I do when I get to the Tough Tom?" said Mary.

"You come back and tell me if you want that book," said Father. "And if you do, you shall have it."

"Right," said Mary.

The crack in the hill ran straight for a while and was easier than the first part. She held her candle in one hand and the bobbin in the other. She had tucked the other candles and the lucifer matches into her petticoat. She went slowly down the rock, and the silk unwound behind her.

The steep was not enough to make her climb, and water trickled from above, over the rock, and left a green stain of malachite. She stopped when the passage divided, but there was nothing to worry her. She went to the left, with the malachite. The other passage had none.

She took the silk through the hill. The green malachite faded, and she passed by a thin level of foxbench sand, hard and speckled.

Then the walls were white. She was at the dimension. The crack sloped easily downward and was opening. She no longer had to move sideways. Her feet scuffed in the sand, but in front of her she could see brown water.

Mary held her candle low. At the bottom of the wall she saw the beginning of a band of clay, the Tough Tom red marl that never let water through. She went forward slowly into the wet. The floor was stiff and tacky under her boots, and behind her the silk floated in

curves. But the crack went no deeper. The ground was level, and her light showed a hump of Tough Tom above the water, glistening.

Mary stopped again. There was nothing else, over, behind, below; only the Tough Tom humping out of the water, and the white dimension stone. And the crack finished at the end of her candlelight.

"Father!"

There was no reply. She hadn't counted how much silk had unwound.

"Father!"

There was plenty of candle left, but it showed her nothing to explain why she was there.

"Father!"

Not even an echo. There wasn't the room for one. But she turned. There hadn't been an echo, but her voice had sounded louder beyond the Tough Tom.

Mary scrambled up the hump, slithering in the wet. Then she looked around her, and saw.

The end of the crack was as broad as two stalls and as high as a barn. The red Tough Tom was a curved island above its own water. The walls were white and pale yellow. There was no sound. The water did not drip. It sank through the stone unheard, and seeped along the marl.

Mary saw Father's mason mark drawn on the wall. It was faint and black, as if drawn with soot. Next to it was an animal, falling. It had nearly worn itself away, but it looked like a bull, a great shaggy bull. It was bigger than it seemed at first, and Father's mark was on it, making the mark like a spear or an arrow.

The bull was all colours, but some of the stone had shed itself in the damp air. The more Mary looked, the bigger the bull grew. It had turned around every wall, as if it was moving and dying.

Mary had come through the hill to see Father's mark on a daubed bull. And near the bull and the mark there was a hand, the outline of a hand. Someone had splayed a hand on the wall and painted round it with the Tough Tom. Fingers and thumb.

Mary put the candle close. A white dimension hand. She lifted her own and laid it over the hand on the wall, not touching. Both hands were the same size. She reached nearer. They were the same size. She touched. The rock was cold, but for a moment it had almost felt warm. The hands fitted. Fingers and thumb and palm and a bull and Father's mark in the darkness under the ground.

Mary stood back, in the middle of the Tough Tom, and listened to the silence. It was the most secret place she had ever seen. A bull drawn for secrets. A mark and a hand alone with the bull in the dark that nobody knew.

She looked down. And when she looked down she shouted. She wasn't alone. The Tough Tom was crowded. All about her in that small place under the hill that led nowhere were footprints.

They were the footprints of people, bare and shod. There were boots and shoes and clogs, heels, toes, shallow ones and deep ones, clear and sharp as if made altogether, trampling each other, hundreds pressed in the clay where only a dozen could stand. Mary was in a crowd that could never have been, thronging, as real as she was. Her feet made prints no fresher than theirs.

And the bull was still dying under the mark, and the one hand still held.

There was nowhere to run, no one to hear. Mary stood on the Tough Tom and waited. She daren't jerk the thread to feel Father's presence; he was so far away that the thread would have broken.

Then it was over. She knew the great bull on the rock enclosing her, and she knew the mark and the hand. The invisible crowd was not there, and the footprints in the Tough Tom churned motionless.

She had seen. Now there was the time to go. Mary lifted the thread and made skeins of it as she went past the white dimension, fox-bench and malachite to the candle under the fall.

Father had moved to make room for her.

"Well?"

"I've seen," said Mary. "All of it."

"You've touched the hand?"

"Yes."

"I thought you would."

They went back to the shaft, and up, and out. The sky seemed a different place. All things led to the bull and the mark and the hand in the cave. Trees were trying to find it with their roots. The rain in the clouds must fall to the ground and into the rock to the Tough Tom.

"That's put a quietness on you," said Father.

"Ay."

They came over Glaze Hill.

"Why did you set your mark on?" said Mary.

"I didn't. It was there when I went."

"When did you go?"

"When I was about your size. My father took me same as today. We have to go before we're too big to get past the fall, though I reckon, years back, the road was open; if you knew it was there."

"When did you go last?" said Mary.

"We go just once," said Father. "So that we'll know."

"Who else?"

"Only us. Neither Leahs nor Allmans. Us."

"But there were ever so many feet," said Mary. "The place was teeming."

"We've been going a while," said Father.

"And that bull," said Mary.

"That's a poser. There's been none like it in my time; and my father, he hadn't seen any."

"What is it all?" said Mary.

"The hill. We pass it on: and once you've seen it, you're changed for the rest of your days."

"Who else of us?" said Mary.

"Nobody," said Father, "except me: and now you: it's always been for the eldest: and from what I heard my father say, it was only ever for lads. But if they keep on stoping after that malachite the way they're going at the Engine Vein, it'll be shovelled up in a year or two without anybody noticing even. At one time of day, before the Engine Vein and that chap who could read books, we must have been able to come at it from the top. But that's all gone. And if the old bull goes, you'll have to tell your lad, even if you can't show him."

"I shall," said Mary.

"I recollect it puts a quietness on you, does that bull. And the hand. And the mark."

Mary went to wash the Tough Tom from her boots in the spring when they reached home. The spring came out of the hill and soaked into Lifeless Moss, and Lifeless Moss spilled by brooks to the sea.

Father sat with Mother for a while. Old William had picked up his usual rhythm, and the loom rattled, "Nickety-nackety, Monday-come-Saturday." Then Father collected his work tools and sat down at the table and sorted through the pebbles.

He weighed them in his hand, tested them on his thumbnail, until he found the one he wanted. He pushed the others aside, and he took the one pebble and worked quickly with candle and firelight, turning, tapping, knapping, shaping, twisting, rubbing and making, quickly, as though the stone would set hard if he stopped. He had to take the picture from his eye to his hand before it left him.

"There," said Father. "That'll do."

He gave Mary a prayer book bound in blue-black calf skin, tooled, stitched and decorated. It was only by the weight that she could tell it was stone and not leather.

"It's better than a book you can open," said Father. "A book has only one story. And tomorrow I'll cut you a brass cross and let it in the front with some dabs of lead, and then I'll guarantee you'd think it was Lord Stanley's, if it's held right."

"It's grand," said Mary.

"And I'll guarantee Lizzie Allman and Annie Leah haven't got them flowers pressed in their books."

Mary turned the stone over. Father had split it so that the back showed two fronds of a plant, like the silk in skeins, like the silk on the water under the hill.

And Father went out of the room and left Mary by the fire. He went to Old William and took his ophicleide, as he always did after shouting, and he played the hymn that Old William liked best because it was close to the beat of his loom. William sang for the rhythm, "Nickety-nackety, Monday-come-Saturday," and Father tried to match him on the ophicleide.

William bawled:

" 'Oh, the years of Man are the looms of
    God
'Let down from the place of the sun;
'Wherein we are weaving always,
'Till the mystic work is done!' "

And so they ended until the next time. The last cry went up from the summer fields, "Who-whoop! Wo-whoop! Wo-o-o-o!"

And Mary sat by the fire and read the stone book that had in it all the stories of the world and the flowers of the flood.

> *The fantasist, whether he uses the ancient archetypes of myth and legend or the younger ones of science and technology, may be talking as seriously as any sociologist—and a good deal more directly—about human life as it is lived, and as it might be lived, and as it ought to be lived. For after all, as great scientists have said and as all children know, it is above all by the imagination that we achieve perception, and compassion, and hope.*[1]

12 Thresholds and Frontiers: Fantasy and Science Fiction

Fantasy fiction is not a recent literary development; nor has it traditionally been intended only for children. The giants of literature have written fantasy: out of the epic past, Shakespeare, Bunyan, Spenser, Dante; from the nineteenth century, Hans Christian Andersen, Lewis Carroll, and George MacDonald; and more recently, C. S. Lewis, E. B. White, P. L. Travers, J. R. R. Tolkien, and Ursula Le Guin. All have staked out their claims in the region of fantasy. Fantasy's appeal for children is obvious. Marvels and magic abound; detailed, original geographies and invented languages create full-bodied worlds; heroic, even epic, adventures involve the struggle between good and evil; morality is as strong a force as it is in folklore, and addresses the questions of courage, responsibility, personal choice, and the power of love; extravagant play with the common details of daily life and inventive alterations of language extend the boundaries of logic and order, shaping new and imaginative perceptions and providing the release of laughter. Most fascinating of all, in fantasy there is often something hidden: a meaning, a secret, the celebration of a private wisdom.

How is fantasy defined? Fantasy is marked by a sense of *otherness*. It is touched

1. Ursula K. Le Guin, "National Book Award Acceptance Speech," in Le Guin, *The Language of the Night: Essays on Fantasy and Science Fiction,* ed. Susan Wood (Putnam's, 1979), p. 58.

by the magical, by a reality different from that of daily life. According to J. R. R. Tolkien in his essay "On Fairy-Stories," fantasy involves the creation of a "Secondary World," a world with "the inner consistency of reality," which commands belief and possesses an essential "quality of strangeness and wonder." This total world—or secondary reality—is created by imagination, by what Tolkien calls the elvish craft of enchantment: "Enchantment produces a Secondary World into which both designer and spectator can enter, to the satisfaction of their senses while they are inside; but in its purity it is artistic in desire and purpose."[2] Fantasy may create a total world. It may involve time travel or flight to distant planets. It may explore the thresholds between worlds in the passage between congruent universes or the intrusion of the supernatural into the everyday world. It may reinterpret myth and legend or anthropomorphize animal society. But it always speaks with the universal voice of imagination, dream, and archetype, and its magic is imbued with meaning within a basic code of laws.

Good fantasies have in common an originality of concept, matched to their inner logic. And that logic is soon made known; each new world must declare the law by which it operates, so that effect follows cause in a credible order. "Fantasy," writes Tolkien, "is founded upon the hard recognition that things are so in the world as it appears under the sun; on a recognition of fact, but not a slavery to it. So upon logic was founded the nonsense that displays itself in the tales and rhymes of Lewis Carroll. If men really could not distinguish between frogs and men, fairy-stories about frog-kings would not have arisen."[3]

Perhaps fantasy is most accurately defined as a vision of life seen through an altered lens—a vision in which the writer's wit, imagination, and invention give the reader access to a different reality—a reality sometimes subtle, intangible, symbolic. Perceptions may be altered when a new world is created, as they are with Mary Norton's shift in scale in the miniature world of *The Borrowers* (1952). Or, a single element may be changed; for example, the lack of gravity in George MacDonald's *The Light Princess* (1864). But note that E. Nesbit's children have the same kind of characterization and behavior in her realistic stories as in those in which a magical element becomes part of the plot. The focus in fantasy may be altered, yet it remains simply another way of viewing.

That inner vision may illuminate the external world and let us see it for what it is—miraculous. Certain fantasies show us the "arresting strangeness" of the ordinary world. In E. B. White's classic, *Charlotte's Web* (1952), the miracle is not that the animals speak or that a spider spins words into a web. It is, rather, a spider's ability to spin a web that is the miracle; the miracle is the beauty of everyday life, the cycles of nature, and the endurance of friendship. White has called his fantasy "a paean to life, a hymn to the barn," and Wilbur the pig sings the praise of the book's true miracle:

It was the best place to be, thought Wilbur, this warm delicious cellar, with the garrulous geese, the changing seasons, the heat of the sun, the passage of swallows, the nearness of rats, the sameness of sheep, the love of spiders, the smell of manure, the glory of everything.[4]

White has achieved what Tolkien calls *recovery* when he speaks of the recovery, escape, and consolation of fairy-story and fantasy: "Recovery (which includes

2. J. R. R. Tolkien, "On Fairy-Stories," in *Tree and Leaf* (Houghton Mifflin, 1965), pp. 52–53.
3. Tolkien, p. 55.
4. E. B. White, *Charlotte's Web* (Harper, 1952), p. 183.

return and renewal of health) is a re-gaining—regaining of a clear view. I do not say 'seeing things as they are' and involve myself with the philosophers, though I might venture to say 'seeing things as we are (or were) meant to see them'—as things apart from ourselves."[5]

Fantasy is an expansive and fluid genre, including many categories. These can be seen clearly in the history of fantasy writing for children. Fantasy is, first of all, rooted in the oral tradition. In the nineteenth century, the works of the Grimm brothers and Hans Christian Andersen generated a renewed enthusiasm for the folktale and the fairy tale. The first fantasies written for children—including John Ruskin's seminal *King of the Golden River* (1851)—owe their style and content to the fairy tale. The great Victorian fantasists, such as Charles Kingsley in *The Water-Babies* (1863), Lewis Carroll in *Alice's Adventures in Wonderland* (1865), and George MacDonald in *At the Back of the North Wind* (1871), shared a seemingly limitless imaginative energy in their varied approaches to fantasy. They created extraordinarily diverse stories marked by sophisticated wit and parody, high morality and subtle didacticism, enchantment, and the revelation of universal truths.

At the turn of the century, *The Wind in the Willows* (1908) by Kenneth Grahame provided a new form of animal fantasy, which combined elements of the traditional beast fable with social satire. This same form is evident in such present-day works as Richard Adams's *Watership Down* (1972).

Stories of real or toy animals interacting with people as in A. A. Milne's *Winnie-the-Pooh* (1926), Hugh Lofting's *The Story of Doctor Dolittle* (1920), and E. B. White's *Charlotte's Web* are more closely related to the light domestic fantasy that became the major form of children's fantasy from the turn of the century to the mid-twentieth century. The primarily comic tradition of domestic or light fantasy is marked by elaborate inventiveness, wit, and playful adventure. Beginning with Frank Baum (*The Wonderful Wizard of Oz,* 1900) and E. Nesbit (*Five Children and It,* 1902), domestic fantasy found adherents in J. M. Barrie (*Peter Pan,* produced as a play in 1904 and retold as a story and published in 1911 under the title *Peter and Wendy*), P. L. Travers (*Mary Poppins,* 1934), Astrid Lindgren (*Pippi Longstocking,* first published in English in 1950), Mary Norton (*The Borrowers,* 1952), and the controversial but popular modern cautionary tale, *Charlie and the Chocolate Factory* (1964) by Roald Dahl.

The fantasy of time travel also evolved early in this century, from the early "time slip" works of E. Nesbit to Alison Uttley's evocative *A Traveller in Time* (1939). Recent fantasists such as William Mayne, Philippa Pearce, L. M. Boston, Penelope Lively, and Ruth Park explore the shifting dimensions of time.

Influenced by J. R. R. Tolkien's *The Hobbit* (1937) and C. S. Lewis's Chronicles of Narnia (1950–56), a new form of fantasy developed after the Second World War. This epic or high fantasy uses material from myth, legend, romance, and hero tale. Since the 1960s, writers such as Alan Garner in Britain, and Lloyd Alexander, Susan Cooper, and Ursula Le Guin in the United States, have created memorable works in this category.

Science fiction written specifically for children (sometimes called science-fiction fantasy) is a latecomer to children's fantasy. The dividing line between fantasy and science fiction is blurred, but children's writers of the second half of the twentieth century have created speculative fiction that involves elements of science

5. Tolkien, p. 57.

and technology or that is set in the future or on another planet. These writers are generally considered science-fiction writers. Madeleine L'Engle (*A Wrinkle in Time,* 1962), John Christopher (the White Mountains trilogy, 1967–68), Peter Dickinson (the Changes trilogy, 1968–70), and Monica Hughes (the Isis trilogy, 1980–82), are distinguished practitioners in this field.

Where does fantasy itself come from? For some writers, sources of inspiration are cherished experiences of childhood, scenes that impressed them deeply, or interests that have obsessed them. A measure of actuality is transmuted, from "an experienced reality," as Herbert Read has said, "to inexperienced realities." Kenneth Grahame's *The Wind in the Willows* is a transfiguration of five impressionable childhood years, immediately following Grahame's mother's death and his own dangerous illness. Grahame's childhood memories of those five years spent in the unspoiled Thames country of Cookham Dene in Berkshire became the riverbank world of Mole and Ratty. Similarly, *Charlotte's Web* translates E. B. White's joy in his Maine farm into a celebration of the natural world of the barnyard. J. R. R. Tolkien's *The Hobbit* had its inception in the scholar-author's intense devotion to the academic field in which he was an authority—Anglo-Saxon culture and language. *The Hobbit* is a deep-running, spirited variation of old Norse and Saxon themes of dragon-haunted regions, dwarfs, ill-gotten treasure, and the righting of old wrongs. And what is *Alice's Adventures in Wonderland* but the sport and play of a mathematician and logician who transmogrified his hobbies, his intellectual discipline, his gift of parody, and his kinship with children into a complex dream world where logic is rearranged according to his own liking?

Literature is self-generating. Story builds upon story, and fantasy is highly eclectic. Tolkien's writing is indebted (among other sources) to *Beowulf, Sir Gawain and the Green Knight,* and the *Volsungasaga.* Similarly, Susan Cooper has said that her quintet, The Dark Is Rising (1965–77), may be traced to "endless reading about Britain, prehistory, Britain, myth, folk tale, Britain . . ."[6] Inspiration may be only one literary generation past: C. S. Lewis pays homage in his writing to George MacDonald, as does Edward Eager to E. Nesbit. And many fantasies originate in the dream pools of the unconscious. When asked how she planned her world of Earthsea, Ursula Le Guin replied: "But I didn't plan anything, I found it. . . . In my subconscious."[7]

In Le Guin's comment may be seen the crucial difference between the methods of fantasy and those of realism. Fantasy may use conventional narrative devices, but the fantasist is dipping into psychic waters, into matter shimmering beyond or just on the edge of communication; something felt to be of tremendous importance concerning imagination and the human condition *must be said,* but its hidden, inward-turned nature does not lend itself to treatment by traditional structures and devices. Fantasists, therefore, concretize metaphors (as Alice's changing shape concretizes a child's sense of now being too small, now too large, never quite fitting into a reality that itself shifts form moment to moment). Metaphor and symbol are apt vehicles for the fantasist's representations of inexpressible realities. The Italian fantasist Italo Calvino says that allegories and fairy tales "provide a

6. Susan Cooper, "Newbery Award Acceptance," *The Horn Book Magazine,* 52 (1976), 363–64.
7. Ursula K. Le Guin, "Dreams Must Explain Themselves," *Algol,* 21, reprinted in Le Guin, *The Language of the Night: Essays on Fantasy and Science Fiction,* ed. Susan Wood (Putnam's, 1979), p. 48.

way of seeing ideas with the body, of linking the abstract to the concrete and to the senses. In allegories, abstractions are always conveyed in action." The logic of fantasy, fairy tale, and allegory, Calvino says, "is the logic of our emotions, of our interior lives."[8] For child readers, the universal, abstract complexities of human existence are made specific and palpable in the characters, events, and themes of fantasy.

Mysticism, religious faith, and the human longing for something that cannot be expressed or defined are recurring motifs in fantasy. In Walter de la Mare's eerie, moonlit adventure tale of quest and character, *The Three Mulla-Mulgars* (1910) (alternately titled *The Three Royal Monkeys*), *Tishnar* symbolizes the unattainable:

Tishnar is a very ancient word in Munza, and means that which cannot be thought about in words, or told, or expressed. So, all the wonderful, secret, and quiet world beyond the Mulgar's lives is Tishnar—wind and stars too, the sea and the endless unknown.[9]

Fantasy is also a favorite medium for allegory, a way of saying more than one seems to say. George MacDonald, an unorthodox Congregationalist minister of the Victorian era, did not hesitate to interpret to children through fantasy some of the questions that troubled the theologians of his day—humanity's relationship to God, the everlasting threat of evil, the inevitable confrontation with death. Through his imaginative power and his understanding of children (he had eleven of his own) he succeeded in evoking the great dilemmas and triumphs of human fate: *At the Back of the North Wind, The Princess and the Goblin* (1872), and *The Princess and Curdie* (1883) are, given their manner and time, masterly portrayals of the human condition, yet they are always childlike and dramatic in their symbolism. C. S. Lewis, the declared disciple of MacDonald, was a more robust writer but as absorbed in the Christian faith and as mystical in his intent.

Ursula Le Guin's Earthsea trilogy (1968–72) is informed by her knowledge of Jungian archetypes and her affinity with Taoism, the eastern philosophy that recognizes a balanced order in the universe. In it she examines the nature of cosmic equilibrium, the role of the artist-magician who uses the power of naming to shape the world, and the process of coming of age.

The theme of coming of age is inextricably connected in fantasy with those of apprenticeship and heroism. Lloyd Alexander's Taran, a callow pig-keeper, Tolkien's Bilbo Baggins, a middle-aged, pleasure-loving hobbit, and Madeleine L'Engle's Meg Murry, a stubborn, insecure, contemporary teenager, are plunged into dramatic journeys, trials, and quests that challenge their courage and wit, call forth from them transformative powers of love and humility, and lead them to maturity and wisdom.

Different themes are found in the work of the intuitive master of fantasy, Hans Christian Andersen. Steeped as he was in the folklore of Denmark, he moved easily among marvels and strangeness. He possessed the elemental old-world belief in folktales, which, coupled with his particular vision, made him the unequaled master of a fantasy genre particularly his own: the literary fairy tale. Because he was himself childlike, he loved the things that children love.

8. Quoted in Kathleen Agena, "The Return of Enchantment," *The New York Times Magazine,* 27 Nov. 1983, p. 79.
9. Walter de la Mare, *The Three Royal Monkeys* (Duckworth, 1910; Knopf, 1948), p. 273.

Merging great truths with the small felicities of childhood—toys, games, storytelling, food, peep-shows; storks, cats, hens, ducks, flowers; pokers, pots, kettles, cups and saucers—he encompassed the peoples of the world in his themes: the stupidity of snobbery, the blessing of compassion, the definitions of true and false values, the variability of character, the sorrow and laughter of life.

Some beloved fantasies are not so much a matter of allegories, themes, quests, and revelation as they are joyous improvisations on character, setting, or event. Hugh Lofting's *The Story of Doctor Dolittle* and P. L. Travers's *Mary Poppins* are series of episodes rather than stories with plots moving in ordered sequence to climax and resolution. The characters themselves hold the center of attention, and it is they who attract the irrational behavior of the supporting cast.

In the stories of L. M. Boston, *The Children of Green Knowe* (1954) and its sequels, the house, Green Knowe, is central to the fantasy, and events and characters seem to grow from it. In actuality, the house in which L. M. Boston lives is one of the oldest in England, and the ambience of its past, with the happy association of her own grandchildren playing within its walls, has been the source of her inspiration.

A sequence of interlocking themes—the passage of time, the transience of human life, the continuity of place and memory, and the effect of the past on the present—is examined in the contemplative works of Philippa Pearce (*Tom's Midnight Garden*, 1958) and Penelope Lively (*The House in Norham Gardens*, 1974). Like *The Children of Green Knowe,* these books show age and youth living together in old houses that are catalysts of movement across time and space into the world of dream.

Like folklore, fantasy has regularly come under attack as trivial or dangerous. The recent upsurge of interest in fantasy and science fiction in films and on television as well as in pulp and serious fiction is viewed with suspicion by Kathleen Agena, a cultural historian. Agena claims that the renewed interest in enchantment is a reaction to a contemporary malaise resulting from the demise of a coherent world view in this era of social stress and alienating technology. The movement toward fantasy, she writes, is dangerous and has "ominous political and social implications," including the appeal of authoritarianism.[10]

But the gift of fantasy is to create an expansion of reality, to intensify the realization of experience, to shape and sharpen the sensibilities—in short, to keep alive the human sense of wonder. It serves a basic human need: to feed and fuel the imagination. And, according to Albert Einstein, "Imagination is more important than knowledge."

Ursula Le Guin, in an eloquent defense of fantasy, puts it this way:

We who hobnob with hobbits and tell tall tales about little green men are quite used to being dismissed as mere entertainers, or sternly disapproved of as escapists. But I think that perhaps the categories are changing, like the times. Sophisticated readers are accepting the fact that an improbable and unmanageable world is going to produce an improbable and hypothetical art. At this point, realism is perhaps the least adequate means of understanding or portraying the incredible realities of our existence. A scientist who creates a monster in his laboratory; a librarian in the library of Babel; a wizard unable to cast a spell; a space ship having trouble in getting to Alpha Centauri: all these may be precise and profound metaphors of the human condition.[11]

10. Kathleen Agena, "The Return of Enchantment," *The New York Times Magazine,* 27 Nov. 1983, p. 80.
11. Le Guin, "National Book Award Acceptance Speech," pp. 57–58.

And, as metaphors, the stories of fantasy continue to mirror human life. In the individual voices of their separate creators, the stories speak of spiritual quest and inner journey; of peril, loss, and recovery; and of the heroic apprenticeship of the young into the fullness of human life.

Hans Christian Andersen

The Nightingale

Andersen's stories are like no others that have been written before or since. "The Nightingale" gives evidence of his originality and inventiveness, his compassion and deep understanding. Fortunate is the child who is introduced to the stories through storytelling or reading aloud, for Andersen's stories are not for the earliest fairy tale age. A great underlying truth is inherent in this poignant story of the emperor's nightingale written in beautifully balanced prose, exquisite in its imagery. Here is enduring testimony to Andersen's particular genuis for blending truth and art. The first of Andersen's fairy tales were published in Denmark in 1835. In 1846, his stories were translated into English in four separate volumes by Mary Howitt and others. [From Hans Christian Andersen, *Fairy Tales from Hans Christian Andersen*, trans. Mrs. Edgar Lucas (Dent, 1899).]

In China, as you know, the emperor is a Chinaman, and all the people around him are Chinamen too. It is many years since the story I am going to tell you happened, but that is all the more reason for telling it, lest it should be forgotten. The emperor's palace was the most beautiful thing in the world; it was made entirely of the finest porcelain, very costly, but at the same time so fragile that it could only be touched with the very greatest care. There were the most extraordinary flowers to be seen in the garden; the most beautiful ones had little silver bells tied to them, which tinkled perpetually, so that one should not pass the flowers without looking at them. Every little detail in the garden had been most carefully thought out, and it was so big, that even the gardener himself did not know where it ended. If one went on walking, one came to beautiful woods with lofty trees and deep lakes. The woods extended to the sea, which was deep and blue, deep enough for large ships to sail up right under the branches of the trees. Among these trees lived a nightingale, which sang so deliciously, that even the poor fisherman who had plenty of other things to do, lay still to listen to it, when he was out at night drawing in his nets. "Heavens, how beautiful it is!" he said, but then he had to attend to his business and forgot it. The next night

when he heard it again he would again exclaim, "Heavens, how beautiful it is!"

Travelers came to the emperor's capitol, from every country in the world; they admired everything very much, especially the palace and the gardens, but when they heard the nightingale they all said, "This is better than anything!"

When they got home they described it, and the learned ones wrote many books about the town, the palace and the garden, but nobody forgot the nightingale, it was always put above everything else. Those among them who were poets wrote the most beautiful poems, all about the nightingale in the woods by the deep blue sea. These books went all over the world, and in course of time, some of them reached the emperor. He sat in his golden chair reading and reading, and nodding his head well pleased to hear such beautiful descriptions of the town, the palace and the garden. "But the nightingale is the best of all," he read.

"What is this?" said the emperor. "The nightingale? Why, I know nothing about it. Is there such a bird in my kingdom, and in my own garden into the bargain, and I have never heard of it? Imagine my having to discover this from a book!"

Then he called his gentleman-in-waiting, who was so grand that when anyone of a lower rank dared to speak to him, or to ask him a question, he would only answer "P," which means nothing at all.

"There is said to be a very wonderful bird called a nightingale here," said the emperor. "They say that it is better than anything else in all my great kingdom! Why have I never been told anything about it?"

"I have never heard it mentioned," said the gentleman-in-waiting. "It has never been presented at court."

"I wish it to appear here this evening to sing to me," said the emperor. "The whole world knows what I am possessed of, and I know nothing about it!"

"I have never heard it mentioned before," said the gentleman-in-waiting. "I will seek it, and I will find it!" But where was it to be found? The gentleman-in-waiting ran upstairs and downstairs and in and out of all the rooms and corridors. No one of all those he met had ever heard anything about the nightingale; so the gentleman-in-waiting ran back to the emperor, and said that it must be a myth, invented by the writers of the books. "Your imperial majesty must not believe everything that is written; books are often mere inventions, even if they do not belong to what we call the black art!"

"But the book in which I read it is sent to me by the powerful Emperor of Japan, so it can't be untrue. I will hear this nightingale, I insist upon its being here tonight. I extend my most gracious protection to it, and if it is not forthcoming, I will have the whole court trampled upon after supper!"

"Tsing-pe!" said the gentleman-in-waiting, and away he ran again, up and down all the stairs, in and out of all the rooms and corridors; half the court ran with him, for they none of them wished to be trampled on. There was much questioning about this nightingale, which was known to all the outside world, but to no one at court. At last they found a poor little maid in the kitchen. She said, "Oh heavens, the nightingale? I know it very well. Yes, indeed it can sing. Every evening I am allowed to take broken meat to my poor sick mother: she lives down by the shore. On my way back when I am tired, I rest awhile in the wood, and then I hear the nightingale. Its song brings the tears into my eyes, I feel as if my mother were kissing me!"

"Little kitchen-maid," said the gentleman-in-waiting, "I will procure you a permanent position in the kitchen and permission to see the emperor dining, if you will take us to the nightingale. It is commanded to appear at court tonight."

Then they all went out into the wood where the nightingale usually sang. Half the court was there. As they were going along at their best pace a cow began to bellow.

"O!" said a young courtier, "there we have it. What wonderful power for such a little creature; I have certainly heard it before."

"No, those are the cows bellowing, we are a long way yet from the place." Then the frogs began to croak in the marsh.

"Beautiful!" said the Chinese chaplain, "it is just like the tinkling of church bells."

"No, those are the frogs!" said the little kitchen-maid. "But I think we shall soon hear it now!"

Then the nightingale began to sing.

"There it is!" said the little girl. "Listen, listen, there it sits!" and she pointed to a little gray bird up among the branches.

"Is it possible?" said the gentleman-in-waiting. "I should never have thought it was like that. How common it looks. Seeing so many grand people must have frightened all its colors away."

"Little nightingale!" called the kitchen-maid quite loud, "our gracious emperor wishes you to sing to him!"

"With the greatest pleasure!" said the nightingale, warbling away in the most delightful fashion.

"It is just like crystal bells," said the gentleman-in-waiting. "Look at its little throat, how active it is. It is extraordinary that we have never heard it before! I am sure it will be a great success at court!"

"Shall I sing again to the emperor?" said the nightingale, who thought he was present.

"My precious little nightingale," said the gentleman-in-waiting, "I have the honor to command your attendance at a court festival tonight, where you will charm his gracious majesty the emperor with your fascinating singing."

"It sounds best among the trees," said the nightingale, but it went with them willingly when it heard that the emperor wished it.

The palace had been brightened up for the occasion. The walls and the floors which were all of china shone by the light of many thousand golden lamps. The most beautiful flowers, all of the tinkling kind, were arranged in the corridors; there was hurrying to and fro, and a great draught, but this was just what made the bells ring, one's ears were full of the tinkling. In the middle of the large reception room where the emperor sat a golden rod had been fixed, on which the nightingale was to perch. The whole court was assembled, and the little kitchen-maid had been permitted to stand behind the door, as she now had the actual title of cook. They were all dressed in their best, everybody's eyes were turned towards the little gray bird at which the emperor was nodding. The nightingale sang delightfully, and the tears came into the emperor's eyes, nay, they rolled down his cheeks, and then the nightingale sang more beautifully than ever, its notes touched all hearts. The emperor was charmed, and said the nightingale should have his gold slipper to wear round its neck. But the nightingale declined with thanks, it had already been sufficiently rewarded.

"I have seen tears in the eyes of the emperor, that is my richest reward. The tears of an emperor have a wonderful power! God knows I am sufficiently recompensed!" and then it again burst into its sweet heavenly song.

"That is the most delightful coquetting I have ever seen!" said the ladies, and they took some water into their mouths to try and make the same gurgling when anyone spoke to them, thinking so to equal the nightingale. Even the lackeys and the chambermaids announced that they were satisfied, and that is saying a great deal, they are always the most difficult people to please. Yes, indeed, the nightingale had made a sensation. It was to stay at court now, and to have its own cage, as well as liberty to walk out twice a day, and once in the night. It always had twelve footmen with each one holding a ribbon which was tied round its leg. There was not much pleasure in an outing of that sort.

The whole town talked about the marvelous bird, and if two people met, one said to the other "Night," and the other answered "Gale,"

Illustration by Nancy Ekholm Burkert, from *Hans Christian Andersen's The Nightingale,* translated by Eva Le Gallienne. Illustrations copyright © 1965 by Nancy Ekholm Burkert. Reprinted by permission of Harper & Row, Publishers, Inc.

and then they sighed, perfectly understanding each other. Eleven cheesemongers' children were called after it, but they had not got a voice among them.

One day a large parcel came for the emperor, outside was written the word "Nightingale."

"Here we have another new book about this celebrated bird," said the emperor. But it was no book; it was a little work of art in a box, an artificial nightingale, exactly like the living one, but it was studded all over with diamonds, rubies, and sapphires.

When the bird was wound up, it could sing one of the songs the real one sang, and it wagged its tail which glittered with silver and gold. A ribbon was tied round its neck on which was written, "The Emperor of Japan's nightingale is very poor, compared to the Emperor of China's."

Everybody said, "Oh, how beautiful!" And the person who brought the artificial bird immediately received the title of Imperial Nightingale-Carrier in Chief.

"Now, they must sing together; what a duet that will be."

Then they had to sing together, but they did not get on very well, for the real nightingale sang in its own way, and the artificial one could only sing waltzes.

"There is no fault in that," said the music master; "it is perfectly in time and correct in every way!"

Then the artificial bird had to sing alone. It was just as great a success as the real one, and then it was so much prettier to look at, it glittered like bracelets and breast-pins.

It sang the same tune three and thirty times over, and yet it was not tired; people would willingly have heard it from the beginning again, but the emperor said that the real one must have a turn now—but where was it? No one had noticed that it had flown out of the open window, back to its own green woods.

"But what is the meaning of this?" said the emperor.

All the courtiers railed at it, and said it was a most ungrateful bird.

"We have got the best bird though," said they, and then the artificial bird had to sing again, and this was the thirty-fourth time that they heard the same tune, but they did not know it thoroughly even yet, because it was so difficult.

The music master praised the bird tremendously, and insisted that it was much better than the real nightingale, not only as regarded the outside with all the diamonds, but the inside too.

"Because you see, my ladies and gentlemen, and the emperor before all, in the real nightingale you never know what you will hear, but in the artificial one everything is decided beforehand! So it is, and so it must remain, it can't be otherwise. You can account for things, you can open it and show the human ingenuity in arranging the waltzes, how they go, and how one note follows upon another!"

"Those are exactly my opinions," they all said, and the music master got leave to show the bird to the public next Sunday. They were also to hear it sing, said the emperor. So they heard it, and all became as enthusiastic over it, as if they had drunk themselves merry on tea, because that is a thoroughly Chinese habit.

Then they all said "Oh," and stuck their forefingers in the air and nodded their heads; but the poor fisherman who had heard the real nightingale said, "It sounds very nice, and it is very like the real one, but there is something wanting, we don't know what." The real nightingale was banished from the kingdom.

The artificial bird had its place on a silken cushion, close to the emperor's bed: all the presents it had received of gold and precious jewels were scattered round it. Its title had risen to be "Chief Imperial Singer of the Bed-Chamber," in rank number one, on the left side; for the emperor reckoned that side the important one, where the heart was seated. And even an emperor's heart is on the left side. The music master wrote five and twenty volumes about the artificial bird; the treatise was very long, and written in all the most difficult Chinese characters. Everybody said they had read and understood it, for otherwise they would have been reckoned stupid and then their bodies would have been trampled upon.

Things went on in this way for a whole year. The emperor, the court, and all the other Chinamen knew every little gurgle in the song of the artificial bird by heart; but they liked it all the better for this, and they could all join in the song themselves. Even the street boys sang "zizizi" and "cluck, cluck, cluck," and the emperor sang it too.

But one evening when the bird was singing its best, and the emperor was lying in bed listening to it, something gave way inside the bird with a "whizz." Then a spring burst, "whirr" went all the wheels and the music stopped. The emperor jumped out of bed and sent for his private physicians, but what good could they do? Then they sent for the watchmaker, and after a good deal of talk and examination, he got the works to go again somehow; but he said it would have to be saved as much as possible, because it was so worn out, and he could not renew the works so as to be sure of the tune. This was a great blow! They only dared to let the artificial bird sing once a year, and hardly that; but then the music master made a little speech using all the most difficult words. He said it was just as good as ever, and his saying it made it so.

Five years now passed, and then a great grief came upon the nation, for they were all very fond of their emperor, and he was ill and could not live, it was said. A new emperor was already chosen, and people stood about in the street, and asked the gentleman-in-waiting how their emperor was going on.

"P," answered he, shaking his head.

The emperor lay pale and cold in his gorgeous bed, the courtiers thought he was dead, and they all went off to pay their respects to their new emperor. The lackeys ran off to talk matters over, and the chambermaids gave a great coffee party. Cloth had been laid down in all the rooms and corridors so as to deaden the sound of footsteps, so it was very, very quiet. But the emperor was not dead yet. He lay stiff and pale in the gorgeous bed with its velvet hangings and heavy golden tassels. There was an open window high above him, and the moon streamed in upon the emperor, and the artificial bird beside him.

The poor emperor could hardly breathe, he seemed to have a weight on his chest, he opened his eyes and then he saw that it was Death sitting upon his chest, wearing his golden crown. In one hand he held the emperor's golden sword, and in the other his imperial banner. Round about, from among the folds of the velvet hangings peered many curious faces, some were hideous, others gentle and pleasant. They were all the emperor's good and bad deeds, which now looked him in the face when Death was weighing him down.

"Do you remember that?" whispered one after the other. "Do you remember this?" and they told him so many things, that the perspiration poured down his face.

"I never knew that," said the emperor. "Music, music, sound the great Chinese drums!" he cried, "that I may not hear what they are saying." But they went on and on, and Death sat nodding his head, just like a Chinaman, at everything that was said.

"Music, music!" shrieked the emperor. "You precious little golden bird, sing, sing! I have loaded you with precious stones, and even hung my own golden slipper round your neck, sing, I tell you, sing!"

But the bird stood silent, there was nobody to wind it up, so of course it could not go. Death continued to fix the great empty sockets of its eyes upon him, and all was silent, so terribly silent.

Suddenly, close to the window, there was a burst of lovely song: it was the living nightingale, perched on a branch outside. It had heard of the emperor's need, and had come to bring comfort and hope to him. As it sang the faces round became fainter and fainter, and the blood coursed with fresh vigour in the emperor's veins and through his feeble limbs. Even Death himself listened to the song and said, "Go on, little nightingale, go on!"

"Yes, if you give me the gorgeous golden sword; yes, if you give me the imperial banner; yes, if you give me the emperor's crown."

And Death gave back each of these treasures for a song, and the nightingale went on singing. It sang about the quiet churchyard, when the roses bloom, where the elder flower scents the air, and where the fresh grass is ever moistened anew by the tears of the mourner. This song brought to Death a longing for his own garden, and like a cold gray mist, he passed out of the window.

"Thanks, thanks!" said the emperor; "you heavenly little bird, I know you! I banished you from my kingdom, and yet you have charmed the evil visions away from my bed by your song, and even Death away from my heart! How can I ever repay you?"

"You have rewarded me," said the nightingale. "I brought the tears to your eyes, the very first time I ever sang to you, and I shall never forget it! Those are the jewels which gladden the heart of a singer;—but sleep now, and wake up fresh and strong! I will sing to you!"

Then it sang again, and the emperor fell into a sweet refreshing sleep. The sun shone in at his window, when he woke refreshed and well; none of his attendants had yet come back to him, for they thought he was dead, but the nightingale still sat there singing.

"You must always stay with me!" said the emperor. "You shall only sing when you like, and I will break the artificial bird into a thousand pieces!"

"Don't do that!" said the nightingale, "it did all the good it could! keep it as you have always done! I can't build my nest and live in this palace, but let me come whenever I like, then I will sit on the branch in the evening, and sing to you. I will sing to cheer you and to make you thoughtful too; I will sing to you of the happy ones, and of those that suffer too. I will sing about the good and the evil, which are kept hidden from you. The little singing bird flies far and wide, to the poor fisherman, and the peasant's home, to numbers who are far from you and your court. I love your heart more than your crown, and yet there is an odor of sanctity round the crown, too!—I will come, and I will sing to you!—But you must promise me one thing!"—

"Everything!" said the emperor, who stood there in his imperial robes which he had just put on, and he held the sword heavy with gold upon his heart.

"One thing I ask you! Tell no one that you have a little bird who tells you everything, it will be better so!"

Then the nightingale flew away. The attendants came in to see after their dead emperor, and there he stood, bidding them "good-morning!"

Hans Christian Andersen

The Ugly Duckling

This tale is one of Andersen's best; it really pictures, in a symbolic way, Andersen's own experiences and his life in general. Andersen always felt himself a genius; and when he tried dancing, singing, playwriting, and acting for a living, and was a failure in all, he blamed society and not his own lack of ability. According to some biographers, he never was fully reconciled to having become a swan through his fairy tales; but since they did bring him honor and the recognition his nature longed for, he accepted a storyteller's fame and made the most of it. [From Hans Christian Andersen, *Fairy Tales from Hans Christian Andersen*, trans. Mrs. Edgar Lucas (Dent, 1899).]

The country was lovely just then; it was summer. The wheat was golden and the oats still green; the hay was stacked in the rich low-lying meadows, where the stork was marching about on his long red legs, chattering Egyptian, the language his mother had taught him.

Roundabout field and meadow lay great woods in the midst of which were deep lakes. Yes, the country certainly was delicious. In the sunniest spot stood an old mansion surrounded by a deep moat, and great dock leaves grew from the walls of the house right down to the water's edge; some of them were so tall that a small child could stand upright under them. In amongst the leaves it was as secluded as in the depths of a forest; and there a duck was sitting on her nest. Her little ducklings were just about to be hatched, but she was nearly tired of sitting, for it had lasted such a long time. Moreover, she had very few visitors, as the other ducks liked swimming about in the moat better than waddling up to sit under the dock leaves and gossip with her.

At last one egg after another began to crack. "Cheep, cheep!" they said. All the chicks had come to life, and were poking their heads out.

"Quack! quack!" said the duck; and then they all quacked their hardest, and looked about them on all sides among the green leaves; their mother allowed them to look as much as they liked, for green is good for the eyes.

"How big the world is to be sure!" said all the young ones; for they certainly had ever so much more room to move about, than when they were inside the eggshell.

"Do you imagine this is the whole world?" said the mother. "It stretches a long way on the other side of the garden, right into the parson's field; but I have never been as far as that! I suppose you are all here now?" and she got up. "No! I declare I have not got you all yet! The biggest egg is still there; how long is it going to last?" and then she settled herself on the nest again.

"Well, how are you getting on?" said an old duck who had come to pay her a visit.

"This one egg is taking such a long time," answered the sitting duck, "the shell will not crack; but now you must look at the others; they are the finest ducklings I have ever seen! they are all exactly like their father, the rascal! he never comes to see me."

"Let me look at the egg which won't crack," said the old duck. "You may be sure that it is a turkey's egg! I have been cheated like that once, and I had no end of trouble and worry with the creatures, for I may tell you that they are afraid of the water. I could not get them into it, I quacked and snapped at them, but it was no good. Let me see the egg! Yes, it is a turkey's egg! You just leave it alone and teach the other children to swim."

"I will sit on it a little longer, I have sat so long already, that I may as well go on till the Midsummer Fair comes round."

"Please yourself," said the old duck, and she went away.

At last the big egg cracked. "Cheep, cheep!" said the young one and tumbled out; how big and ugly he was! The duck looked at him.

"That is a monstrous big duckling," she said; "none of the others looked like that; can he be a turkey chick? Well, we shall soon find that out; into the water he shall go, if I have to kick him in myself."

Next day was gloriously fine, and the sun shone on all the green dock leaves. The mother duck with her whole family went down to the moat.

Splash, into the water she sprang. "Quack, quack!" she said, and one duckling plumped in after the other. The water dashed over their heads, but they came up again and floated beautifully; their legs went of themselves, and they were all there, even the big ugly gray one swam about with them.

"No, that is no turkey," she said; "see how beautifully he uses his legs and how erect he holds himself: he is my own chick! after all, he is not so bad when you come to look at him properly. Quack, quack! Now come with me and I will take you into the world, and introduce you to the duckyard; but keep close to me all the time, so that no one may tread upon you, and beware of the cat!"

Then they went into the duckyard. There was a fearful uproar going on, for two broods were fighting for the head of an eel, and in the end the cat captured it.

"That's how things go in this world," said the mother duck, and she licked her bill for she wanted the eel's head herself.

"Use your legs," said she; "mind you quack properly, and bend your necks to the old duck over there! She is the grandest of them all; she has Spanish blood in her veins and that accounts for her size, and, do you see? she has a red rag round her leg; that is a wonderfully fine thing, and the most extraordinary mark of distinction any duck can have. It shows clearly that she is not to be parted with, and that she is worthy of recognition both by beasts and men! Quack now! don't turn your toes in, a well-brought-up duckling keeps his legs wide apart just like father and mother; that's it, now bend your necks, and say quack!"

They did as they were bid, but the other ducks round about looked at them and said, quite loud: "Just look there! now we are to have that tribe! just as if there were not enough of us already, and, oh, dear! how ugly that duckling is, we won't stand him!" and a duck flew at him at once and bit him in the neck.

"Let him be," said the mother; "he is doing no harm."

"Very likely not, but he is so ungainly and

queer," said the biter; "he must be whacked."

"They are handsome children mother has," said the old duck with the rag round her leg; "all good looking except this one, and he is not a good specimen; it's a pity you can't make him over again."

"That can't be done, your grace," said the mother duck; "he is not handsome, but he is a thorough good creature, and he swims as beautifully as any of the others; nay, I think I might venture even to add that I think he will improve as he goes on, or perhaps in time he may grow smaller! he was too long in the egg, and so he has not come out with a very good figure." And then she patted his neck and stroked him down. "Besides he is a drake," said she; "so it does not matter so much. I believe he will be very strong, and I don't doubt but he will make his way in the world."

"The other ducklings are very pretty," said the old duck. "Now make yourselves quite at home, and if you find the head of an eel you may bring it to me!"

After that they felt quite at home. But the poor duckling which had been the last to come out of the shell, and who was so ugly, was bitten, pushed about, and made fun of both by the ducks and the hens. "He is too big," they all said; and the turkey-cock, who was born with his spurs on, and therefore thought himself quite an emperor, puffed himself up like a vessel in full sail, made for him, and gobbled and gobbled till he became quite red in the face. The poor duckling was at his wit's end, and did not know which way to turn; he was in despair because he was so ugly, and the butt of the whole duck-yard.

So the first day passed, and afterwards matters grew worse and worse. The poor duckling was chased and hustled by all of them; even his brothers and sisters ill-used him; and they were always saying, "If only the cat would get hold of you, you hideous object!"

Even his mother said, "I wish to goodness you were miles away." The ducks bit him, the hens pecked him, and the girl who fed them kicked him aside.

Then he ran off and flew right over the hedge, where the little birds flew up into the air in a fright.

"That is because I am so ugly," thought the poor duckling, shutting his eyes, but he ran on all the same. Then he came to a great marsh where the wild ducks lived; he was so tired and miserable that he stayed there a whole night.

In the morning the wild ducks flew up to inspect their new comrade.

"What sort of a creature are you?" they inquired, as the duckling turned from side to side and greeted them as well as he could. "You are frightfully ugly," said the wild ducks; "but that does not matter to us, so long as you do not marry into our family!" Poor fellow! he had no thought of marriage; all he wanted was permission to lie among the bushes, and drink a little of the marsh water.

He stayed there two whole days, then two wild geese came, or rather two wild ganders. They were not long out of the shell, and therefore rather pert.

"I say, comrade," they said, "you are so ugly that we have taken quite a fancy to you; will you join us and be a bird of passage? There is another marsh close by, and there are some charming wild geese there; all sweet young ladies, who can say quack! You are ugly enough to make your fortune among them." Just at that moment, bang! bang! was heard up above, and both the wild geese fell dead among the reeds, and the water turned blood red. Bang! bang! went the guns, and whole flocks of wild geese flew up from the rushes and the shot peppered among them again.

There was a grand shooting party, and the sportsmen lay hidden round the marsh, some even sat on the branches of the trees which overhung the water; the blue smoke rose like clouds among the dark trees and swept over the pool.

The water-dogs wandered about in the swamp, splash! splash! The rushes and reeds bent beneath their tread on all sides. It was terribly alarming to the poor duckling. He twisted his head round to get it under his wing and just at that moment a frightful, big dog appeared close beside him; his tongue hung right out of his mouth and his eyes glared wickedly. He opened his great chasm of a mouth close to the duckling, showed his sharp teeth—and—splash—went on without touching him.

"Oh, thank Heaven!" sighed the duckling,

"I am so ugly that even the dog won't bite me!"

Then he lay quite still while the shot whistled among the bushes, and bang after bang rent the air. It only became quiet late in the day, but even then the poor duckling did not dare to get up; he waited several hours more before he looked about and then he hurried away from the marsh as fast as he could. He ran across fields and meadows, and there was such a wind that he had hard work to make his way.

Towards night he reached a poor little cottage; it was such a miserable hovel that it could not make up its mind which way to fall even, and so it remained standing. The wind whistled so fiercely round the duckling that he had to sit on his tail to resist it, and it blew harder and harder; then he saw that the door had fallen off one hinge and hung so crookedly that he could creep into the house through the crack and by this means he made his way into the room. An old woman lived there with her cat and her hen. The cat, which she called "Sonnie," could arch his back, purr, and give off electric sparks, that is to say if you stroked his fur the wrong way. The hen had quite tiny short legs and so she was called "Chuckie-low-legs." She laid good eggs, and the old woman was as fond of her as if she had been her own child.

In the morning the strange duckling was discovered immediately, and the cat began to purr and the hen to cluck.

"What on earth is that!" said the old woman looking round, but her sight was not good and she thought the duckling was a fat duck which had escaped. "This is a capital find," said she; "now I shall have duck's eggs if only it is not a drake! we must find out about that!"

So she took the duckling on trial for three weeks, but no eggs made their appearance. The cat was the master of the house and the hen the mistress, and they always spoke of "we and the world," for they thought that they represented the half of the world, and that quite the better half.

The duckling thought there might be two opinions on the subject, but the cat would not hear of it.

"Can you lay eggs?" she asked.

"No!"

"Will you have the goodness to hold your tongue then!"

And the cat said, "Can you arch your back, purr, or give off sparks?"

"No."

"Then you had better keep your opinions to yourself when people of sense are speaking!"

The duckling sat in the corner nursing his ill-humor; then he began to think of the fresh air and the sunshine, an uncontrollable longing seized him to float on the water, and at last he could not help telling the hen about it.

"What on earth possesses you?" she asked; "you have nothing to do, that is why you get these freaks into your head. Lay some eggs or take to purring, and you will get over it."

"But it is so delicious to float on the water," said the duckling; "so delicious to feel it rushing over your head when you dive to the bottom."

"That would be a fine amusement," said the hen. "I think you have gone mad. Ask the cat about it, he is the wisest creature I know; ask him if he is fond of floating on the water or diving under it. I say nothing about myself. Ask our mistress yourself, the old woman, there is no one in the world cleverer than she is. Do you suppose she has any desire to float on the water, or to duck underneath it?"

"You do not understand me," said the duckling.

"Well, if we don't understand you, who should? I suppose you don't consider yourself cleverer than the cat or the old woman, not to mention me. Don't make a fool of yourself, child, and thank your stars for all the good we have done you! Have you not lived in this warm room, and in such society that you might have learnt something? But you are an idiot, and there is no pleasure in associating with you. You may believe me I mean you well, I tell you home truths, and there is no surer way than that, of knowing who are one's friends. You just see about laying some eggs, or learn to purr, or to emit sparks."

"I think I will go out into the wide world," said the duckling.

"Oh, do so by all means," said the hen.

So away went the duckling, he floated on the water and ducked underneath it, but he was looked askance at by every living creature for his ugliness. Now the autumn came on, the leaves in the woods turned yellow and brown; the wind took hold of them, and they danced about. The sky looked very cold, and the clouds hung heavy with snow and hail. A raven stood on the fence and croaked Caw! Caw! from sheer cold; it made one shiver only to think of it, the poor duckling certainly was in a bad case.

One evening, the sun was just setting in wintry splendor, when a flock of beautiful large birds appeared out of the bushes; the duckling had never seen anything so beautiful. They were dazzlingly white with long waving necks; they were swans, and uttering a peculiar cry they spread out their magnificent broad wings and flew away from the cold regions to warmer lands and open seas. They mounted so high, so very high, and the ugly little duckling became strangely uneasy, he circled round and round in the water like a wheel, craning his neck up into the air after them. Then he uttered a shriek so piercing and so strange, that he was quite frightened by it himself. Oh, he could not forget those beautiful birds, those happy birds, and as soon as they were out of sight he ducked right down to the bottom, and when he came up again he was quite beside himself. He did not know what the birds were, or whither they flew, but all the same he was more drawn towards them than he had ever been by any creatures before. He did not envy them in the least, how could it occur to him even to wish to be such a marvel of beauty; he would have been thankful if only the ducks would have tolerated him among them—the poor ugly creature!

The winter was so bitterly cold that the duckling was obliged to swim about in the water to keep it from freezing, but every night the hole in which he swam got smaller and smaller. Then it froze so hard that the surface ice cracked, and the duckling had to use his legs all the time, so that the ice should not close in round him: at last he was so weary that he could move no more, and he was frozen fast into the ice.

Early in the morning a peasant came along and saw him; he went out on to the ice and hammered a hole in it with his heavy wooden shoe, and carried the duckling home to his wife.

There it soon revived. The children wanted to play with it, but the duckling thought they were going to ill-use him, and rushed in his fright into the milk pan, and the milk spurted out all over the room. The woman shrieked and threw up her hands, then it flew into the butter cask, and down into the meal tub and out again. Just imagine what it looked like by this time! The woman screamed and tried to hit it with the tongs, and the children tumbled over one another in trying to catch it, and they screamed with laughter—by good luck the door stood open, and the duckling flew out among the bushes and the new fallen snow—and it lay there thoroughly exhausted.

But it would be too sad to mention all the privation and misery it had to go through during that hard winter. When the sun began to shine warmly again, the duckling was in the marsh, lying among the rushes; the larks were singing and the beautiful spring had come.

Then all at once it raised its wings and they flapped with much greater strength than before, and bore him off vigorously. Before he knew where he was, he found himself in a large garden where the apple trees were in full blossom, and the air was scented with lilacs, the long branches of which overhung the indented shores of the lake! Oh! the spring freshness was so delicious!

Just in front of him he saw three beautiful white swans advancing towards him from a thicket; with rustling feathers they swam lightly over the water. The duckling recognized the majestic birds, and he was overcome by a strange melancholy.

"I will fly to them, the royal birds, and they will hack me to pieces, because I, who am so ugly, venture to approach them! But it won't matter; better be killed by them than be snapped at by the ducks, pecked by the hens, or spurned by the henwife, or suffer so much misery in the winter."

So he flew into the water and swam towards the stately swans; they saw him and darted towards him with ruffled feathers.

"Kill me, oh, kill me!" said the poor creature, and bowing his head towards the water he awaited his death. But what did he see reflected in the transparent water?

He saw below him his own image, but he was no longer a clumsy dark gray bird, ugly and ungainly, he was himself a swan! It does not matter in the least having been born in a duckyard, if only you come out of a swan's egg!

He felt quite glad of all the misery and tribulation he had gone through; he was the better able to appreciate his good fortune now, and all the beauty which greeted him. The big swans swam round and round him, and stroked him with their bills.

Some little children came into the garden with corn and pieces of bread, which they threw into the water; and the smallest one cried out: "There is a new one!" The other children shouted with joy, "Yes, a new one has come!" And they clapped their hands and danced about, running after their father and mother. They threw the bread into the water, and one and all said that the new one was the prettiest; he was so young and handsome. And the old swans bent their heads and did homage before him.

He felt quite shy, and hid his head under his wing; he did not know what to think; he was so very happy, but not at all proud; a good heart never becomes proud. He thought of how he had been pursued and scorned, and now he heard them all say that he was the most beautiful of all beautiful birds. The lilacs bent their

Illustration by Edward Ardizzone, from "The Ugly Duckling," from *Ardizzone's Hans Andersen,* published by Atheneum. Copyright © 1978 by the estate of Edward Ardizzone. Permission granted by the artist's estate.

boughs right down into the water before him, and the bright sun was warm and cheering, and he rustled his feathers and raised his slender neck aloft, saying with exultation in his heart: "I never dreamt of so much happiness when I was the Ugly Duckling!"

Margery Williams

The Velveteen Rabbit

A deep understanding of a child's feeling for a much-loved toy animal underlies this beautifully written story that touches on the nature of reality. The illustrations, by the noted British portrait painter William Nicholson, have the same poetic tenderness as the text. The following selection forms the first part of the story. [From Margery Williams, *The Velveteen Rabbit* (Doubleday, 1922).]

There was once a velveteen rabbit, and in the beginning he was really splendid. He was fat and bunchy, as a rabbit should be; his coat was spotted brown and white, he had real thread whiskers, and his ears were lined with pink sateen. On Christmas morning, when he sat wedged in the top of the Boy's stocking, with a sprig of holly between his paws, the effect was charming.

There were other things in the stocking, nuts and oranges and a toy engine, and chocolate almonds and a clockwork mouse, but the Rabbit was quite the best of all. For at least two hours the Boy loved him, and then Aunts and Uncles came to dinner, and there was a great rustling of tissue paper and unwrapping of parcels, and in the excitement of looking at all the new presents the Velveteen Rabbit was forgotten.

For a long time he lived in the toy cupboard or on the nursery floor, and no one thought very much about him. He was naturally shy, and being only made of velveteen, some of the more expensive toys quite snubbed him. The mechanical toys were very superior, and looked down upon every one else; they were full of modern ideas, and pretended they were real. The model boat, who had lived through two seasons and lost most of his paint, caught the tone from them and never missed an opportunity of referring to his rigging in technical terms. The Rabbit could not claim to be a model of anything, for he didn't know that real rabbits existed; he thought they were all stuffed with sawdust like himself, and he understood that sawdust was quite out-of-date and should never be mentioned in modern circles. Even Timothy, the jointed wooden lion, who was made by the disabled soldiers, and should have had broader views, put on airs and pretended he was connected with Government. Between them all the poor little Rabbit was made to feel himself very insignificant and commonplace, and the only person who was kind to him at all was the Skin Horse.

The Skin Horse had lived longer in the nursery than any of the others. He was so old that his brown coat was bald in patches and showed the seams underneath, and most of the hairs in his tail had been pulled out to string bead necklaces. He was wise, for he had seen a long succession of mechanical toys arrive to boast and swagger, and by-and-by break their mainsprings and pass away, and he knew that they were only toys, and would never turn into anything else. For nursery magic is very strange and wonderful, and only those playthings that are old and wise and experienced like the Skin Horse understand all about it.

"What is REAL?" asked the Rabbit one day, when they were lying side by side near the nursery fender, before Nana came to tidy the room. "Does it mean having things that buzz inside you and a stick-out handle?"

"Real isn't how you are made," said the Skin Horse. "It's a thing that happens to you. When a child loves you for a long, long time, not just to play with, but REALLY loves you, then you become Real."

"Does it hurt?" asked the Rabbit.

"Sometimes," said the Skin Horse, for he was always truthful. "When you are Real you don't mind being hurt."

"Does it happen all at once, like being wound up," he asked, "or bit by bit?"

"It doesn't happen all at once," said the Skin Horse. "You become. It takes a long time. That's why it doesn't often happen to people who break easily, or have sharp edges, or who have to be carefully kept. Generally, by the time you are Real, most of your hair has been

loved off, and your eyes drop out and you get loose in the joints and very shabby. But these things don't matter at all, because once you are Real you can't be ugly, except to people who don't understand."

"I suppose *you* are Real?" said the Rabbit. And then he wished he had not said it, for he thought the Skin Horse might be sensitive. But the Skin Horse only smiled.

"The Boy's Uncle made me Real," he said. "That was a great many years ago; but once you are Real you can't become unreal again. It lasts for always."

The Rabbit sighed. He thought it would be a long time before this magic called Real happened to him. He longed to become Real, to know what it felt like; and yet the idea of growing shabby and losing his eyes and whiskers was rather sad. He wished that he could become it without these uncomfortable things happening to him.

There was a person called Nana who ruled the nursery. Sometimes she took no notice of the playthings lying about, and sometimes, for no reason whatever, she went swooping about like a great wind and hustled them away in cupboards. She called this "tidying up," and the playthings all hated it, especially the tin ones. The Rabbit didn't mind it so much, for wherever he was thrown he came down soft.

One evening, when the Boy was going to bed, he couldn't find the china dog that always slept with him. Nana was in a hurry, and it was too much trouble to hunt for china dogs at bedtime, so she simply looked about her, and seeing that the toy cupboard door stood open, she made a swoop.

"Here," she said, "take your old Bunny! He'll do to sleep with you!" And she dragged the Rabbit out by one ear, and put him into the Boy's arms.

That night, and for many nights after, the Velveteen Rabbit slept in the Boy's bed. At first he found it rather uncomfortable, for the Boy hugged him very tight, and sometimes he rolled over on him, and sometimes he pushed him so far under the pillow that the Rabbit could scarcely breathe. And he missed, too, those long moonlight hours in the nursery, when all the house was silent, and his talks with the Skin

Horse. But very soon he grew to like it, for the Boy used to talk to him, and made nice tunnels for him under the bedclothes that he said were like the burrows the real rabbits lived in. And they had splendid games together, in whispers, when Nana had gone away to her supper and left the nightlight burning on the mantelpiece. And when the Boy dropped off to sleep, the Rabbit would snuggle down close under his little warm chin and dream, with the Boy's hands clasped close round him all night long.

And so time went on, and the little Rabbit was very happy—so happy that he never noticed how his beautiful velveteen fur was getting shabbier and shabbier, and his tail coming unsewn, and all the pink rubbed off his nose where the Boy had kissed him.

Spring came, and they had long days in the garden, for wherever the Boy went the Rabbit went too. He had rides in the wheelbarrow and picnics on the grass, and lovely fairy huts built for him under the raspberry canes behind the flower border. And once, when the Boy was called away suddenly to go out to tea, the Rabbit was left out on the lawn until long after dusk, and Nana had to come and look for him with the candle because the Boy couldn't go to sleep unless he was there. He was wet through with the dew and quite earthy from diving into the burrows the Boy had made for him in the flower bed, and Nana grumbled as she rubbed him off with a corner of her apron.

"You must have your old Bunny!" she said. "Fancy all that fuss for a toy!"

The Boy sat up in bed and stretched out his hands.

"Give me my Bunny!" he said. "You mustn't say that. He isn't a toy. He's REAL!"

When the little Rabbit heard that he was happy, for he knew that what the Skin Horse had said was true at last. The nursery magic had happened to him, and he was a toy no longer. He was Real. The Boy himself had said it.

That night he was almost too happy to sleep, and so much love stirred in his little sawdust heart that it almost burst. And into his boot-button eyes, that had long ago lost their polish, there came a look of wisdom and beauty, so

that even Nana noticed it next morning when she picked him up, and said, "I declare if that old Bunny hasn't got quite a knowing expression!"

Antoine de Saint-Exupéry

The Little Prince

In reviewing *The Little Prince,* Anne Carroll Moore referred to it as "a book so fresh and different, so original yet so infused with wisdom as to take a new place among books in general." The Little Prince lived alone on a tiny planet. He owned a flower of great beauty and of inordinate pride. It was this pride that ruined the serenity of the Little Prince's world and started him on his travels that brought him to the earth. In the following chapter he is in the African desert, far from his planet and the things he loved. From a fox he learns the secret of what is really important in life. [From Antoine de Saint-Exupéry, *The Little Prince* (Reynal & Hitchcock, 1943).]

It was then that the fox appeared.

"Good morning," said the fox.

"Good morning," the little prince responded politely, although when he turned around he saw nothing.

"I am right here," the voice said, "under the apple tree."

"Who are you?" asked the little prince, and added, "You are very pretty to look at."

"I am a fox," the fox said.

"Come and play with me," proposed the little prince. "I am so unhappy."

"I cannot play with you," the fox said. "I am not tamed."

"Ah! Please excuse me," said the little prince.

But, after some thought, he added:

"What does that mean—'tame'?"

"You do not live here," said the fox. "What is it that you are looking for?"

"I am looking for men," said the little prince. "What does that mean—'tame'?"

"Men," said the fox. "They have guns, and they hunt. It is very disturbing. They also raise chickens. These are their only interests. Are you looking for chickens?"

"No," said the little prince. "I am looking for friends. What does that mean—'tame'?"

"It is an act too often neglected," said the fox. "It means to establish ties."

" 'To establish ties'?"

"Just that," said the fox. "To me, you are still nothing more than a little boy who is just like a hundred thousand other little boys. And I have no need of you. And you, on your part, have no need of me. To you, I am nothing more than a fox like a hundred thousand other foxes. But if you tame me, then we shall need each other. To me, you will be unique in all the world. To you, I shall be unique in all the world . . ."

"I am beginning to understand," said the little prince. "There is a flower . . . I think that she has tamed . . ."

"It is possible," said the fox. "On the Earth one sees all sorts of things."

"Oh, but this is not on the Earth!" said the little prince.

The fox seemed perplexed, and very curious.

"On another planet?"

"Yes."

"Are there hunters on that planet?"

"No."

"Ah, that is interesting! Are there chickens?"

"No."

"Nothing is perfect," sighed the fox.

But he came back to his idea.

"My life is very monotonous," he said. "I hunt chickens; men hunt me. All the chickens are just alike, and all the men are just alike. And, in consequence, I am a little bored. But if you tame me, it will be as if the sun came to shine on my life. I shall know the sound of a step that will be different from all the others. Other steps send me hurrying back underneath the ground. Yours will call me, like music, out of my burrow. And then look: you see the grain-fields down yonder? I do not eat bread. Wheat is of no use to me. The wheat fields have nothing to say to me. And that is sad. But you have hair that is the color of gold. Think how wonderful that will be when you have tamed me! The grain, which is also golden, will bring me back the thought of you. And I shall love to listen to the wind in the wheat . . ."

Illustration by Antoine de Saint-Exupéry, from his volume *The Little Prince,* copyright © 1943, 1971 by Harcourt Brace Jovanovich, Inc. Reproduced by permission of the publisher.

The fox gazed at the little prince, for a long time.

"Please—tame me!" he said.

"I want to, very much," the little prince replied. "But I have not much time. I have friends to discover, and a great many things to understand."

"One only understands the things that one tames," said the fox. "Men have no more time to understand anything. They buy things all ready made at the shops. But there is no shop anywhere where one can buy friendship, and so men have no friends any more. If you want a friend, tame me . . ."

"What must I do, to tame you?" asked the little prince.

"You must be very patient," replied the fox. "First you will sit down at a little distance from me—like that—in the grass. I shall look at you out of the corner of my eye, and you will say nothing. Words are the source of misunderstandings. But you will sit a little closer to me, every day . . ."

The next day the little prince came back.

"It would have been better to come back at the same hour," said the fox. "If, for example, you come at four o'clock in the afternoon, then at three o'clock I shall begin to be happy. I shall feel happier and happier as the hour advances. At four o'clock, I shall already be worrying and jumping about. I shall show you how happy I am! But if you come at just any time, I shall never know at what hour my heart is to be ready to greet you . . . One must observe the proper rites . . ."

"What is a rite?" asked the little prince.

"Those also are actions too often neglected," said the fox. "They are what make one day different from other days, one hour from other hours. There is a rite, for example among my hunters. Every Thursday they dance with the village girls. So Thursday is a wonderful day for me! I can take a walk as far as the vineyards. But if the hunters danced at just any time, every day would be like every other day, and I should never have any vacation at all."

So the little prince tamed the fox. And when the hour of his departure drew near—

"Ah," said the fox, "I shall cry."

"It is your own fault," said the little prince. "I never wished you any sort of harm; but you wanted me to tame you . . ."

"Yes, that is so," said the fox.

"But now you are going to cry!" said the little prince.

"Yes, that is so," said the fox.

"Then it has done you no good at all!"

"It has done me good," said the fox, "because of the color of the wheat fields." And then he added:

"Go and look again at the roses. You will understand now that yours is unique in all the world. Then come back to say goodbye to me, and I will make you a present of a secret."

The little prince went away, to look again at the roses.

"You are not at all like my rose," he said. "As yet you are nothing. No one has tamed you, and you have tamed no one. You are like my fox when I first knew him. He was only a fox like a hundred thousand other foxes. But I have made him my friend, and now he is unique in all the world."

And the roses were very much embarrassed.

"You are beautiful, but you are empty," he went on. "One could not die for you. To be sure, an ordinary passerby would think that my rose looked just like you—the rose that belongs to me. But in herself alone she is more important than all the hundreds of you other roses: because it is she that I have watered; because it is she that I have put under the glass globe; because it is she that I have sheltered behind the screen; because it is for her that I have killed the caterpillars (except the two or three that we saved to become butterflies); because it is she that I have listened to, when she grumbled, or boasted, or even sometimes when she said nothing. Because she is *my* rose."

And he went back to meet the fox.

"Goodbye," he said.

"Goodbye," said the fox. "And now here is my secret, a very simple secret: It is only with the heart that one can see rightly; what is essential is invisible to the eye."

"What is essential is invisible to the eye," the little prince repeated, so that he would be sure to remember.

"It is the time you have wasted for your rose that makes your rose so important."

"It is the time I have wasted for my rose—" said the little prince, so that he would be sure to remember.

"Men have forgotten this truth," said the fox. "But you must not forget it. You become responsible, forever, for what you have tamed. You are responsible for your rose . . ."

"I am responsible for my rose," the little prince repeated, so that he would be sure to remember.

Rudyard Kipling

Just So Stories

Kipling's *Just So Stories* should be a part of every child's reading background. They are classic nonsense, and because of the author's magnificent use of words the stories should be read or told "just so." Kipling's own stylized, art-nouveau drawings, which accompany the stories, are the perfect visual complement to these miniature masterpieces of oral storytelling rendered into print. [From Rudyard Kipling, *Just So Stories for Little Children* (Doubleday, Page, 1902).]

How the Camel Got His Hump

Now this is the next tale, and it tells how the Camel got his big hump.

In the beginning of years, when the world was so new and all, and the Animals were just beginning to work for Man, there was a Camel, and he lived in the middle of a Howling Desert because he did not want to work; and besides, he was a Howler himself. So he ate sticks and thorns and tamarisks and milkweed and prickles, most 'scruciating idle; and when anybody spoke to him he said "Humph!" Just "Humph!" and no more.

Presently the Horse came to him on Monday morning, with a saddle on his back and a bit in his mouth, and said, "Camel, O Camel, come out and trot like the rest of us."

"Humph!" said the Camel; and the Horse went away and told the Man.

Presently the Dog came to him, with a stick in his mouth, and said, "Camel, O Camel, come and fetch and carry like the rest of us."

"Humph!" said the Camel; and the Dog went away and told the Man.

Presently the Ox came to him, with the yoke on his neck and said, "Camel, O Camel, come and plough like the rest of us."

"Humph!" said the Camel; and the Ox went away and told the Man.

At the end of the day the Man called the Horse and the Dog and the Ox together, and said, "Three, O Three, I'm very sorry for you (with the world so new-and-all); but that Humph-thing in the Desert can't work, or he would have been here by now, so I am going to leave him alone, and you must work double-time to make up for it."

That made the Three very angry (with the world so new-and-all), and they held a palaver, and an *indaba,* and a *punchayet,* and a pow-wow on the edge of the Desert; and the Camel came chewing milkweed *most* 'scruciating idle, and laughed at them. Then he said "Humph!" and went away again.

Presently there came along the Djinn in charge of All Deserts, rolling in a cloud of dust (Djinns always travel that way because it is Magic), and he stopped to palaver and pow-wow with the Three.

"Djinn of All Deserts," said the Horse, "*is* it right for any one to be idle, with the world so new-and-all?"

"Certainly not," said the Djinn.

"Well," said the Horse, "there's a thing in the middle of your Howling Desert (and he's a Howler himself) with a long neck and long legs, and he hasn't done a stroke of work since Monday morning. He won't trot."

"Whew!" said the Djinn, whistling, "that's my Camel, for all the gold in Arabia! What does he say about it?"

"He says 'Humph!'" said the Dog; "and he won't fetch and carry."

"Does he say anything else?"

"Only 'Humph!'; and he won't plough," said the Ox.

"Very good," said the Djinn. "I'll humph him if you will kindly wait a minute."

The Djinn rolled himself up in his dustcloak, and took a bearing across the desert, and found the Camel most 'scruciatingly idle, looking at his own reflection in a pool of water.

"My long and bubbling friend," said the Djinn, "what's this I hear of your doing no work, with the world so new-and-all?"

"Humph!" said the Camel.

The Djinn sat down, with his chin in his hand, and began to think a Great Magic, while the Camel looked at his own reflection in the pool of water.

"You've given the Three extra work ever since Monday morning, all on account of your 'scruciating idleness," said the Djinn; and he went on thinking Magics, with his chin in his hand.

"Humph!" said the Camel.

"I shouldn't say that again if I were you," said the Djinn; "you might say it once too often. Bubbles, I want you to work."

And the Camel said "Humph!" again; but no sooner had he said it than he saw his back, that he was so proud of, puffing up and puffing up into a great big lolloping humph.

"Do you see that?" said the Djinn. "That's your very own humph that you've brought upon your very own self by not working. Today is Thursday, and you've done no work since Monday, when the work began. Now you are going to work."

"How can I," said the Camel, "with this humph on my back?"

"That's made a-purpose," said the Djinn, "all because you missed those three days. You will be able to work now for three days without eating, because you can live on your humph; and don't you ever say I never did anything for you. Come out of the Desert and go to the Three, and behave. Humph yourself!"

And the Camel humphed himself, humph and all, and went away to join the Three. And from that day to this the Camel always wears a humph (we call it "hump" now, not to hurt his feelings); but he has never yet caught up with the three days that he missed at the beginning of the world, and he has never yet learned how to behave.

Illustration by Rudyard Kipling, from "How the Camel Got His Hump," from *Just-So Stories,* by Rudyard Kipling. First published in 1902. Reprinted by permission of A. P. Watt Ltd., The National Trust for Places of Historic Interest or Natural Beauty, and Macmillan London, Ltd.

Hugh Lofting

The Story of Doctor Dolittle

Lovable Doctor Dolittle gives up his practice among the "best people" of Puddleby-on-the-Marsh, to become a doctor of animals, for he loves them and understands their language. He journeys to Africa and cures the monkeys of a terrible sickness. The following chapter tells how the monkeys, in gratitude, hatch a scheme to help the impoverished doctor make some money. [From Hugh Lofting, *The Story of Doctor Dolittle* (Lippincott-Stokes, 1920).]

The Rarest Animal of All

Pushmi-pullyus are now extinct. That means, there aren't any more. But long ago, when Doctor Dolittle was alive, there were some of them still left in the deepest jungles of Africa; and even then they were very, very scarce. They had no tail, but a head at each end, and sharp horns on each head. They were very shy and terribly hard to catch. The black men get most of their animals by sneaking up behind them while they are not looking. But you could not do this with the pushmi-pullyu—because, no matter which way you came towards him, he was always facing you. And besides, only one half of him slept at a time. The other head was always awake—and watching. This was why they were never caught and never seen in Zoos. Though many of the greatest huntsmen and the cleverest menagerie-keepers spent years of their lives searching through the jungles in all weathers for pushmi-pullyus, not a single one had ever been caught. Even then, years ago, he was the only animal in the world with two heads.

Well, the monkeys set out hunting for this animal through the forest. And after they had gone a good many miles, one of them found peculiar footprints near the edge of a river; and they knew that a pushmi-pullyu must be very near that spot.

Then they went along the bank of the river a little way and they saw a place where the grass was high and thick; and they guessed that he was in there.

So they all joined hands and made a great circle round the high grass. The pushmi-pullyu heard them coming; and he tried hard to break through the ring of monkeys. But he couldn't do it. When he saw that it was no use trying to escape, he sat down and waited to see what they wanted.

They asked him if he would go with Doctor Dolittle and be put on show in the Land of the White Men.

But he shook both his heads hard and said, "Certainly not!"

They explained to him that he would not be shut up in a menagerie but would just be looked at. They told him that the Doctor was a very kind man but hadn't any money; and people would pay to see a two-headed animal and the Doctor would get rich and could pay for the boat he had borrowed to come to Africa in.

But he answered, "No. You know how shy I am—I hate being stared at." And he almost began to cry.

Then for three days they tried to persuade him.

And at the end of the third day he said he would come with them and see what kind of a man the Doctor was first.

So the monkeys traveled back with the pushmi-pullyu. And when they came to where the Doctor's little house of grass was, they knocked on the door.

The duck, who was packing the trunk, said, "Come in!"

And Chee-Chee very proudly took the animal inside and showed him to the Doctor.

"What in the world is it?" asked John Dolittle, gazing at the strange creature.

"Lord save us!" cried the duck. "How does it make up its mind?"

"It doesn't look to me as though it had any," said Jip, the dog.

"This, Doctor," said Chee-Chee, "is the pushmi-pullyu—the rarest animal of the African jungles, the only two-headed beast in the world! Take him home with you and your fortune's made. People will pay any money to see him."

"But I don't want any money," said the Doctor.

"Yes, you do," said Dab-Dab, the duck. "Don't you remember how we had to pinch and scrape to pay the butcher's bill in Puddleby? And how are you going to get the sailor the new boat you spoke of—unless we have the money to buy it?"

"I was going to make him one," said the Doctor.

"Oh, do be sensible!" cried Dab-Dab. "Where would you get all the wood and the nails to make one with?—And besides, what are we going to live on? We shall be poorer than ever when we get back. Chee-Chee's perfectly right! Take the funny-looking thing along, do!"

"Well, perhaps there is something in what you say," murmured the Doctor. "It certainly would make a nice new kind of pet. But does the er—what-do-you-call-it really want to go abroad?"

"Yes, I'll go," said the pushmi-pullyu who

saw at once, from the Doctor's face, that he was a man to be trusted. "You have been so kind to the animals here—and the monkeys tell me that I am the only one who will do. But you must promise me that if I do not like it in the Land of the White Men you will send me back."

"Why, certainly—of course, of course," said the Doctor. "Excuse me, surely you are related to the Deer Family, are you not?"

"Yes," said the pushmi-pullyu—"to the Abyssinian Gazelles and the Asiatic Chamois—on my mother's side. My father's great-grandfather was the last of the Unicorns."

"Most interesting!" murmured the Doctor; and he took a book out of the trunk which Dab-Dab was packing and began turning the pages. "Let us see if Buffon says anything—"

"I notice," said the duck, "that you only talk with one of your mouths. Can't the other head talk as well?"

"Oh, yes," said the pushmi-pullyu. "But I keep the other mouth for eating—mostly. In that way I can talk while I am eating without being rude. Our people have always been very polite."

When the packing was finished and everything was ready to start, the monkeys gave a grand party for the Doctor, and all the animals of the jungle came. And they had pineapples and mangoes and honey and all sorts of good things to eat and drink.

After they had all finished eating, the Doctor got up and said,

"My friends: I am not clever at speaking long words after dinner, like some men; and I have just eaten many fruits and much honey. But I wish to tell you that I am very sad at leaving your beautiful country. Because I have things to do in the Land of the White Men, I must go. After I have gone, remember never to let the flies settle on your food before you eat it; and do not sleep on the ground when the rains are coming. I—er—er—I hope you will all live happily ever after."

When the Doctor stopped speaking and sat down, all the monkeys clapped their hands a long time and said to one another, "Let it be remembered always among our people that he sat and ate with us, here, under the trees. For surely he is the Greatest of Men!"

And the Grand Gorilla, who had the strength of seven horses in his hairy arms, rolled a great rock up to the head of the table and said,

"This stone for all time shall mark the spot."

And even to this day, in the heart of the jungle, that stone still is there. And monkey-mothers, passing through the forest with their families, still point down at it from the branches and whisper to their children, "Sh! There it is—look—where the Good White Man sat and ate food with us in the Year of the Great Sickness!"

Then, when the party was over, the Doctor and his pets started out to go back to the seashore. And all the monkeys went with him as far as the edge of their country, carrying his trunk and bags, to see him off.

Carlo Collodi

Adventures of Pinocchio

Pinocchio is one of the most popular of all children's stories; certainly, it is the classic puppet story. It was written by an Italian journalist, Carlo Lorenzini, under the pseudonym Carlo Collodi, and first appeared in serial form in Rome's children's newspaper in July 1881. Published as a book in 1883, it was translated into English in 1892 and has been translated into many languages. The story begins by telling of a carpenter who wanted to make a table leg out of a piece of wood, but just as he was cutting it, a small voice called out, "Stop, you are hurting me!" Then, as he planed the wood, the same voice called again, "Stop, you are tickling me!" The carpenter was afraid of this talkative piece of wood, so he gave it to his friend Geppetto, who was planning just then to make a marionette. The following chapter tells how Geppetto fashioned the little wooden figure, but this episode is only the beginning of the pranks and capers played by the mischievous Pinocchio. [From Carlo Collodi, *The Adventures of Pinocchio*, trans. Sarah Scott Edwards.]

Pinocchio's First Pranks

Geppetto's house was a poor little room on the ground floor which drew its light from the space under a stairway. The furniture could not have been more simple: a rough old chair, a tumbledown bed, and a rickety table; that was all. In the wall at the back there was a fireplace with a lighted fire, but the flame was painted and so was the earthen pot which boiled merrily and sent forth steam which seemed real, indeed, until one knew better.

Upon entering the house Geppetto quickly got out his tools and began to carve and fashion his puppet. "What shall I name him?" said he to himself. "Ah, I shall call him Pinocchio. This name will surely bring him good luck. I once knew an entire family by that name— Father Pinocchio, Mother Pinocchio and the Pinocchio children, and all of them turned out well. Why, even the richest of them was a beggar."

As soon as Geppetto had decided upon the name for his puppet he began to work in earnest and quickly made the hair, the face, then the eyes. Imagine his amazement when he saw those eyes moving and staring up into his face.

"Wooden eyes, why do you stare at me?" asked the old man, resentfully. But there was no response.

Then Geppetto made the nose, which, scarcely done, began to grow; and it grew and grew, and grew until it seemed that it would never end. Poor Geppetto tried to stop it by cutting it off, but the more he shortened it the more that impudent nose grew.

After he had finished the nose the old man fashioned the mouth. No sooner was it made than it began to jeer and laugh at Geppetto. "Stop laughing at me!" cried the old man angrily; but it was like talking to a stone wall. "Stop laughing, I tell you!" he repeated in a threatening voice. Then the mouth stopped laughing and stuck out its tongue. Geppetto did not wish to waste any time so he pretended not to see and went on working.

After the mouth the old fellow made the chin, then the neck, the shoulders, the body, the arms, and the hands. Scarcely had Geppetto finished the hands when he felt his wig lifted from his head. Looking up, what did he see? He saw his big yellow wig waving about in the hands of the puppet.

"Pinocchio, give me back my wig!" cried Geppetto. "Give it back at once!" But Pinocchio, instead of obeying, placed the wig upon his own head, almost smothering himself beneath it.

All this rude conduct made poor old Geppetto sadder than he had ever been in his life, and turning toward Pinocchio he said to him, "You naughty boy, scarcely are you made before you begin to make fun of your poor old father. That is bad, my boy, very bad," and he wiped away a tear.

There was now nothing left to make except the legs and the feet. When Geppetto had finished them, he suddenly felt a kick on the end of his nose. "It serves me right," he said to himself. "I should have known better. Alas, now it is too late."

Picking the puppet up the old man set him on the floor in order to teach the little fellow how to walk. But Pinocchio's legs were stiff and numb, and he could not move them; so Geppetto led him by the hand and showed him how to place one foot before the other.

Little by little the puppet's feet lost their numbness, and he began to walk, then to run about the room, until suddenly he darted through the door, out into the street, and was gone. Poor Geppetto ran after the puppet but could not catch him because that rascal of a Pinocchio was running and leaping like a rabbit, and his wooden feet pattering over the cobblestones made a noise like twenty peasants clattering along in their wooden shoes.

"Catch him, catch him!" shouted Geppetto; but the people along the way, seeing this wooden puppet which ran like a racehorse, stopped, enchanted, to look at him and laughed and laughed in amazement.

Fortunately, at last a policeman appeared who, hearing all this clatter and thinking it to be a colt which had escaped from its master, planted himself squarely in the middle of the street with legs apart, determined to stop the runaway and prevent further disaster.

But Pinocchio, when he saw the policeman ahead of him barricading the whole street, decided, instead of trying to pass him, to run between his legs but in this the puppet met with failure. The policeman, without even moving aside, neatly caught Pinocchio by the nose (it was an absurdly long nose, made purposely to be grabbed by policemen), and turned him over to Geppetto, who in order to punish the puppet, decided to give him a good slap on the ears. Imagine his surprise when, in searching for the ears, he could find none. Do you know why? Because, in his haste to finish the puppet, Geppetto had forgotten to make them!

The old man took Pinocchio by the back of the neck and, as he urged him along, he said, shaking his head in a threatening manner, "We are going home and when we get there we shall settle our accounts." At this Pinocchio threw himself upon the ground and refused to go farther. Immediately a crowd gathered round and began to make remarks. Some said one thing and some another. "Poor puppet," said several. "No wonder he doesn't want to go home.

Illustration by Gerald McDermott, from *Carlo Collodi's The Adventures of Pinocchio,* retold by Marianna Mayer. Illustrations copyright © 1981 by Gerald McDermott. Reprinted by permission of Four Winds Press, a division of Scholastic, Inc.

Who knows how hard that old rascal, Geppetto, may beat him?" And some said, meaningly, "That old fellow appears to be a gentleman but he is a regular tyrant with children. If we leave the puppet in his hands he is quite capable of doing him much harm."

The upshot of it all was that the policeman turned Pinocchio loose and led Geppetto off to prison. The poor old man could find no words with which to defend himself but bellowed like a calf, and, as he drew near the prison he sobbed and babbled, "Ungrateful son! And to think that I took such pains to make him. But it serves me right. I should have thought first."

That which happened to Pinocchio afterwards is a story which you will not believe but you may read it in the following chapters.

Lewis Carroll

Alice's Adventures in Wonderland

One of the greatest literary fairy tales is that by Lewis Carroll, made up of two distinct stories—*Alice's Adventures in Wonderland* (1865) and *Through the Looking-Glass* (1872). These stories differ from most literary fairy tales in that Alice never loses her individuality or her practical common sense. She, always herself, knows she is in an odd but magic world; it is this juxtaposition, on the author's part, of realism and fancy that makes these books unusual. The first was written under the title of *Alice's Adventures Underground* for Professor Liddell's little daughter Alice, at that time one of the author's child friends. When urged to have this story published, Carroll submitted it to George Macdonald (author of *The Princess and the Goblin*) and his family, who heartily approved of it. Then it was rewritten and added to—"The Mad Hatter's Tea Party" was one added chapter—and published under its present name. [From Lewis Carroll, *Alice's Adventures in Wonderland* (Macmillan, 1865).]

Down the Rabbit-Hole

Alice was beginning to get very tired of sitting by her sister on the bank, and of having nothing to do; once or twice she had peeped into the book her sister was reading, but it had no pictures or conversations in it, "and what is the use of a book," thought Alice, "without pictures or conversations?"

So she was considering in her own mind (as well as she could, for the hot day made her feel very sleepy and stupid), whether the pleasure of making a daisy-chain would be worth the trouble of getting up and picking the daisies, when suddenly a white rabbit with pink eyes ran close by her.

There was nothing so *very* remarkable in that; nor did Alice think it so *very* much out of the way to hear the Rabbit say to itself, "Oh dear! Oh dear! I shall be too late!" (when she thought it over afterward, it occurred to her that she ought to have wondered at this, but at the time it all seemed quite natural); but when the Rabbit actually *took a watch out of its waistcoat-pocket,* and looked at it, and then hurried on, Alice started to her feet, for it flashed across her mind that she had never before seen a rabbit with either a waistcoat-pocket or a watch to take out of it, and, burning with curiosity, she ran across the field after it, and was just in time to see it pop down a large rabbit-hole under the hedge.

In another moment down went Alice after it, never once considering how in the world she was to get out again.

The rabbit-hole went straight on like a tunnel for some way, and then dipped suddenly down, so suddenly that Alice had not a moment to think about stopping herself before she found herself falling down what seemed to be a very deep well.

Either the well was very deep, or she fell very slowly, for she had plenty of time as she went down to look about her, and to wonder what was going to happen next. First, she tried to look down and make out what she was coming to, but it was too dark to see anything: then she looked at the sides of the well, and noticed that they were filled with cupboards and bookshelves: here and there she saw maps and pictures hung upon pegs. She took down a jar from one of the shelves as she passed; it was labeled "ORANGE MARMALADE," but to her great disappointment it was empty; she did not like to drop the jar for fear of killing somebody underneath, so managed to put it into one of the cupboards as she fell past it.

"Well!" thought Alice to herself, "after such

a fall as this, I shall think nothing of tumbling down stairs! How brave they'll all think me at home! Why, I wouldn't say anything about it, even if I fell off the top of the house!" (Which was very likely true.)

Down, down, down. Would the fall *never* come to an end? "I wonder how many miles I've fallen by this time?" she said aloud. "I must be getting somewhere near the center of the earth. Let me see: that would be four thousand miles down, I think" (for, you see, Alice had learnt several things of this sort in her lessons in the schoolroom, and though this was not a *very* good opportunity for showing off her knowledge, as there was no one to listen to her, still it was good practice to say it over) "yes, that's about the right distance—but then I wonder what latitude or longitude I've got to?" (Alice had not the slightest idea what latitude was, or longitude either, but she thought they were nice grand words to say.)

Presently she began again: "I wonder if I shall fall right *through* the earth! How funny it'll seem to come out among the people that walk with their heads downwards! The Antipathies, I think" (she was rather glad there *was* no one listening, this time, as it didn't sound at all the right word) "but I shall have to ask them what the name of the country is, you know. Please, ma'am, is this New Zealand or Australia?" (And she tried to curtsey as she spoke— fancy *curtseying* as you're falling through the air! Do you think you could manage it?) "And what an ignorant little girl she'll think me for asking! No, it'll never do to ask: perhaps I shall see it written up somewhere."

Down, down, down. There was nothing else to do, so Alice soon began talking again. "Dinah'll miss me very much tonight, I should think!" (Dinah was the cat.) "I hope they'll remember her saucer of milk at teatime. Dinah, my dear! I wish you were down here with me! There are no mice in the air, I'm afraid, but you might catch a bat, and that's very like a mouse, you know. But do cats eat bats, I wonder?" And here Alice began to get rather sleepy, and went on saying to herself, in a dreamy sort of way, "Do cats eat bats? Do cats eat bats?" and sometimes, "Do bats eat cats?" for, you see, as she couldn't answer either question, it didn't much matter which way she put it. She felt that she was dozing off, and had just begun to dream that she was walking hand in hand with Dinah, and was saying to her very earnestly, "Now, Dinah, tell me the truth: did you ever eat a bat?" when suddenly, thump! thump! down she came upon a heap of sticks and dry leaves, and the fall was over.

Alice was not a bit hurt, and she jumped up on to her feet in a moment: she looked up, but it was all dark overhead; before her was another long passage, and the White Rabbit was still in sight, hurrying down it. There was not a moment to be lost: away went Alice like the wind, and was just in time to hear it say, as it turned a corner, "Oh, my ears and whiskers, how late it's getting!" She was close behind it when she turned the corner, but the Rabbit was no longer to be seen: she found herself in a long, low hall, which was lit up by a row of lamps hanging from the roof.

There were doors all round the hall, but they were all locked, and when Alice had been all the way down one side and up the other, trying every door, she walked sadly down the middle, wondering how she was ever to get out again.

Suddenly she came upon a little three-legged table, all made of solid glass; there was nothing on it but a tiny golden key, and Alice's first idea was that this might belong to one of the doors of the hall; but, alas! either the locks were too large, or the key was too small, but at any rate it would not open any of them. However, on the second time round, she came upon a low curtain she had not noticed before, and behind it was a little door about fifteen inches high: she tried the little golden key in the lock, and to her great delight it fitted!

Alice opened the door and found it led into a small passage, not much larger than a rat-hole: she knelt down and looked along the passage into the loveliest garden you ever saw. How she longed to get out of that dark hall, and wander about among those beds of bright flowers and those cool fountains, but she could not even get her head through the doorway; "and even if my head would go through," thought poor Alice, "it would be of very little use without my shoulders. Oh, how I wish I could shut up like a telescope! I think I could, if I only knew how to begin." For, you see, so many out-of-the-way things had happened lately that Alice had begun to think that very few things indeed were really impossible.

There seemed to be no use in waiting by the little door, so she went back to the table, half hoping she might find another key on it, or at any rate a book of rules for shutting people up like telescopes: this time she found a little bottle on it ("which certainly was not here before," said Alice) and tied round the neck of the bottle was a paper label with the words "DRINK ME" beautifully printed on it in large letters.

It was all very well to say "Drink me," but the wise little Alice was not going to do *that* in a hurry: "no, I'll look first," she said, "and see whether it's marked *'poison'* or not"; for she had read several nice little stories about children who had got burnt, and eaten up by wild beasts, and other unpleasant things, all because they *would* not remember the simple rules their friends had taught them, such as, that a red-hot poker will burn you if you hold it too long; and that if you cut your finger *very* deeply with a knife, it usually bleeds; and she had never forgotten that, if you drink much from a bottle marked "poison," it is almost certain to disagree with you, sooner or later.

However, this bottle was *not* marked "poison," so Alice ventured to taste it, and finding it very nice (it had, in fact, a sort of mixed flavor of cherry-tart, custard, pineapple, roast turkey, toffy, and hot buttered toast) she very soon finished it off.

*   *   *

"What a curious feeling!" said Alice, "I must be shutting up like a telescope."

And so it was indeed: she was now only ten inches high, and her face brightened up at the thought that she was now the right size for going through the little door into that lovely garden. First, however, she waited for a few minutes to see if she was going to shrink further: she felt a little nervous about this, "for it might end, you know," said Alice to herself, "in my going out altogether, like a candle. I wonder what I should be like then?" And she tried to fancy what the flame of a candle looks like after the candle is blown out, for she could not remember ever having seen such a thing.

After a while, finding that nothing more happened, she decided on going into the garden at once, but, alas for poor Alice! when she got to the door, she found she had forgotten the little golden key and when she went back to the table for it, she found she could not possibly reach it; she could see it quite plainly through the glass, and she tried her best to climb up one of the legs of the table, but it was too slippery, and when she had tired herself out with trying, the poor little thing sat down and cried.

"Come, there's no use in crying like that!" said Alice to herself, rather sharply, "I advise you to leave off this minute!" She generally gave herself very good advice (though she very seldom followed it) and sometimes she scolded herself so severely as to bring tears into her eyes, and once she remembered trying to box her own ears for having cheated herself in a game of croquet she was playing against herself, for this curious child was very fond of pretending to be two people. "But it's no use now," thought poor Alice, "to pretend to be two people! Why, there's hardly enough of me left to make *one* respectable person!"

Soon her eye fell on a little glass box that was lying under the table: she opened it, and found in it a very small cake, on which the words "EAT ME" were beautifully marked in currants. "Well, I'll eat it," said Alice, "and if it makes me grow larger, I can reach the key; and if it makes me grow smaller, I can creep under the door; so either way I'll get into the garden, and I don't care which happens!"

She ate a little bit, and said anxiously to herself, "Which way? Which way?" holding her hand on the top of her head to feel which way it was growing, and she was quite surprised to find that she remained the same size: to be sure, this is what generally happens when one eats cake, but Alice had got so much into the way of expecting nothing but out-of-the-way things to happen, that it seemed quite dull and stupid for life to go on in the common way.

So she set to work, and very soon finished off the cake.

The Rabbit Sends in a Little Bill

[Since we left Alice, at the bottom of the rabbit-hole, she has had many experiences. As she ate too much of the cake, she became very, very tall and under another charm became so short that she had to swim in a pool made up of the tears she had previously shed. Rescued from that, she meets a Duck, a Dodo, a Lory, and an Eaglet and listens to a Mouse's tale. At her inadvertent mention of Dinah, her cat, all of Alice's newly found friends quickly disappear and leave her all alone. At this point, she hears the patter of footsteps and hopes it may be the Mouse, coming back to finish his story.]

It was the White Rabbit, trotting slowly back again, and looking anxiously about as it went, as if it had lost something; and she heard it muttering to itself, "The Duchess! The Duchess! Oh my dear paws! Oh my fur and whiskers! She'll get me executed, as sure as ferrets are ferrets! Where *can* I have dropped them, I wonder?" Alice guessed in a moment that it was looking for the fan and the pair of white kid gloves, and she good-naturedly began hunting about for them, but they were nowhere to be seen—everything seemed to have changed since her swim in the pool, and the great hall, with the glass table and the little door, had vanished completely.

Very soon the Rabbit noticed Alice, as she went hunting about, and called out to her, in an angry tone, "Why, Mary Ann, what *are* you doing out here? Run home this moment, and fetch me a pair of gloves and a fan! Quick, now!" And Alice was so much frightened that she ran off at once in the direction it pointed to, without trying to explain the mistake that it had made.

"He took me for his housemaid," she said to herself as she ran. "How surprised he'll be when he finds out who I am! But I'd better take him his fan and gloves—that is, if I can find them." As she said this, she came upon a neat little house, on the door of which was a bright brass plate with the name "W. RABBIT" engraved upon it. She went in without knocking, and hurried upstairs, in great fear lest she should meet the real Mary Ann, and be turned out of the house before she had found the fan and gloves.

"How queer it seems," Alice said to herself, "to be going messages for a rabbit! I suppose Dinah'll be sending me on messages next!" And she began fancying the sort of thing that would happen: " 'Miss Alice! Come here directly, and get ready for your walk!' 'Coming in a minute, nurse! But I've got to watch this mouse-hole till Dinah comes back, and see that the mouse doesn't get out.' Only I don't think," Alice went on, "that they'd let Dinah stop in the house if it began ordering people about like that!"

By this time she had found her way into a tidy little room with a table in the window, and on it (as she had hoped) a fan and two or three pairs of tiny white kid gloves: she took up the fan and a pair of the gloves, and was just going to leave the room, when her eye fell upon a little bottle that stood near the looking-glass. There was no label this time with the words "DRINK ME," but nevertheless she uncorked it and put it to her lips. "I know *something* interesting is sure to happen," she said to herself, "whenever I eat or drink anything; so I'll just see what this bottle does. I do hope it'll make me grow large again, for really I'm quite tired of being such a tiny little thing!"

It did so indeed, and much sooner than she had expected: before she had drunk half the bottle, she found her head pressing against the ceiling, and had to stoop to save her neck from being broken. She hastily put down the bottle, saying to herself, "That's quite enough—I hope I shan't grow any more—As it is, I can't get out at the door—I do wish I hadn't drunk quite so much!"

Alas! It was too late to wish that! She went on growing, and growing, and very soon had to kneel down on the floor: in another minute there was not even room for this, and she tried the effect of lying down with one elbow against the door, and the other arm curled round her head. Still she went on growing, and, as a last resource, she put one arm out of the window and one foot up the chimney, and said to herself, "Now I can do no more, whatever happens. What *will* become of me?"

Luckily for Alice, the little magic bottle had now had its full effect, and she grew no larger: still it was very uncomfortable, and, as there seemed to be no sort of chance of her ever getting out of the room again, no wonder she felt unhappy.

"It was much pleasanter at home," thought poor Alice, "when one wasn't always growing larger and smaller, and being ordered about by mice and rabbits. I almost wish I hadn't gone down that rabbit-hole—and yet—and yet—it's rather curious, you know, this sort of life! I do wonder what *can* have happened to me! When I used to read fairy tales, I fancied that kind of thing never happened, and now here I am in the middle of one! There ought to be a book written about me, that there ought! And when I grow up, I'll write one—but I'm grown up now," she added in a sorrowful tone: "at least there's no room to grow up any more *here.*"

"But then," thought Alice, "shall I *never* get any older than I am now? That'll be a comfort, one way—never to be an old woman—but then—always to have lessons to learn! Oh, I shouldn't like *that!*"

"Oh, you foolish Alice!" she answered herself. "How can you learn lessons in here? Why, there's hardly room for *you,* and no room at all for any lesson-books!"

And so she went on, taking first one side and then the other, and making quite a conversation of it altogether, but after a few minutes she heard a voice outside, and stopped to listen.

Reprinted with permission of Macmillan Publishing Company, from *Alice's Adventures in Wonderland,* by Lewis Carroll, illustrated by Sir John Tenniel. First published in 1865.

"Mary Ann! Mary Ann!" said the voice. "Fetch me my gloves this moment!" Then came a little pattering of feet on the stairs. Alice knew it was the Rabbit coming to look for her, and she trembled till she shook the house, quite forgetting that she was now about a thousand times as large as the Rabbit, and had no reason to be afraid of it.

Presently the Rabbit came up to the door, and tried to open it, but, as the door opened inward, and Alice's elbow was pressed hard against it, that attempt proved a failure. Alice heard it say to itself, "Then I'll go round and get in at the window."

"That you won't!" thought Alice, and, after waiting till she fancied she heard the Rabbit just under the window, she suddenly spread out her hand, and made a snatch in the air. She did not get hold of anything, but she heard a little shriek and a fall, and a crash of broken glass, from which she concluded that it was just possible it had fallen into a cucumber-frame, or something of the sort.

Next came an angry voice—the Rabbit's—"Pat! Pat! Where are you?" And then a voice she had never heard before, "Sure then I'm here! Digging for apples, yer honor!"

"Digging for apples, indeed!" said the Rabbit angrily. "Here! Come and help me out of *this!*" (Sounds of more broken glass.)

"Now tell me, Pat, what's that in the window?"

"Sure, it's an arm, yer honor!" (He pronounced it "arrum.")

"An arm, you goose! Who ever saw one that size? Why, it fills the whole window!"

"Sure, it does, yer honor: but it's an arm for all that."

"Well, it's got no business there, at any rate: go and take it away!"

There was a long silence after this, and Alice could only hear whispers now and then; such as "Sure, I don't like it, yer honor, at all, at all!" "Do as I tell you, you coward!" and at last she spread out her hand again, and made another snatch in the air. This time there were *two* little shrieks, and more sounds of broken glass. "What a number of cucumber-frames there must be!" thought Alice. "I wonder what they'll do next! As for pulling me out of the window, I only wish they *could!* I'm sure *I* don't want to stay in here any longer!''

She waited for some time without hearing anything more: at last came a rumbling of little cart-wheels, and the sound of a good many voices all talking together: she made out the words: "Where's the other ladder?—Why, I hadn't to bring but one. Bill's got the other—Bill! Fetch it here, lad!—Here, put 'em at this corner—No, tie 'em together first—they don't reach half high enough yet—Oh, they'll do well enough. Don't be particular—Here, Bill! Catch hold of this rope—Will the roof bear?—Mind that loose slate—Oh, it's coming down! Heads below!'' (a loud crash)—''Now, who did that?—It was Bill, I fancy—Who's to go down the chimney?—Nay, *I* shan't! *You* do it!—*That* I won't, then!—Bill's got to go down—Here, Bill! The master says you've got to go down the chimney!''

"Oh! So Bill's got to come down the chimney, has he?" said Alice to herself. "Why, they seem to put everything upon Bill! I wouldn't be in Bill's place for a good deal; this fireplace is narrow, to be sure; but I *think* I can kick a little!"

She drew her foot as far down the chimney as she could, and waited till she heard a little animal (she couldn't guess of what sort it was) scratching and scrambling about in the chimney close above her: then, saying to herself, "This is Bill," she gave one sharp kick, and waited to see what would happen next.

The first thing she heard was a general chorus of "There goes Bill!" then the Rabbit's voice alone—"Catch him, you by the hedge!" then silence, and then another confusion of voices—"Hold up his head—Brandy now—Don't choke him—How was it, old fellow? What happened to you? Tell us all about it!"

Last came a little feeble, squeaking voice ("That's Bill," thought Alice), "Well, I hardly know—No more, thank ye; I'm better now—but I'm a deal too flustered to tell you—all I know is, something comes at me like a Jack-in-the-box, and up I goes like a sky-rocket!"

"So you did, old fellow!" said the others.

"We must burn the house down!" said the Rabbit's voice. And Alice called out, as loud as she could, "If you do, I'll set Dinah at you!"

There was a dead silence instantly, and Alice thought to herself, "I wonder what they *will* do next! If they had any sense, they'd take the roof off." After a minute or two, they began moving about again, and Alice heard the Rabbit say, "A barrowful will do, to begin with."

"A barrowful of *what?*" thought Alice. But she had not long to doubt, for the next moment a shower of little pebbles came rattling in at the window, and some of them hit her in the face. "I'll put a stop to this," she said to herself, and shouted out, "You'd better not do that again!" which produced another dead silence.

Alice noticed, with some surprise, that the pebbles were all turning into little cakes as they lay on the floor, and a bright idea came into her head. "If I eat one of these cakes," she thought, "it's sure to make *some* change in my size; and, as it can't possibly make me larger, it must make me smaller, I suppose."

So she swallowed one of the cakes, and was delighted to find that she began shrinking directly. As soon as she was small enough to get through the door, she ran out of the house, and found quite a crowd of little animals and birds waiting outside. The poor little lizard, Bill, was in the middle, being held up by two guinea-pigs, who were giving it something out of a bottle. They all made a rush at Alice the moment she appeared; but she ran off as hard as she could, and soon found herself safe in a thick wood.

"The first thing I've got to do," said Alice to herself, as she wandered about in the wood, "is to grow to my right size again; and the second thing is to find my way into that lovely garden. I think that will be the best plan."

It sounded an excellent plan, no doubt, and very neatly and simply arranged; the only difficulty was, that she had not the smallest idea how to set about it; and, while she was peering about anxiously among the trees, a little sharp bark just over her head made her look up in a great hurry.

An enormous puppy was looking down at her with large round eyes, and feebly stretching out one paw, trying to touch her. "Poor little thing!" said Alice, in a coaxing tone, and she tried hard to whistle to it, but she was terribly frightened all the time at the thought that it might be hungry, in which case it would be very likely to eat her up in spite of all her coaxing.

Hardly knowing what she did, she picked up a little bit of stick, and held it out to the puppy: whereupon the puppy jumped into the air off all its feet at once, with a yelp of delight, and rushed at the stick, and made-believe to worry it; then Alice dodged behind a great thistle, to keep herself from being run over, and, the moment she appeared on the other side, the puppy made another rush at the stick, and tumbled head over heels in its hurry to get hold of it; then Alice, thinking it was very like having a game of play with a cart-horse, and expecting every moment to be trampled under its feet, ran round the thistle again; then the puppy began a series of short charges at the stick, running a very little way forward each time and a long way back, and barking hoarsely all the while, till at last it sat down a good way off, panting, with its tongue hanging out of its mouth, and its great eyes half-shut.

This seemed to Alice a good opportunity for making her escape, so she set off at once, and ran till she was quite tired and out of breath, and till the puppy's bark sounded quite faint in the distance.

"And yet what a dear little puppy it was!" said Alice, as she leaned against a buttercup to rest herself, and fanned herself with one of the leaves. "I should have liked teaching it tricks very much, if—if I'd only been the right size to do it! Oh dear! I'd nearly forgotten that I've got to grow up again! Let me see—how *is* it to be managed? I suppose I ought to eat or drink something or other; but the great question is 'What?'"

The great question certainly was "What?" Alice looked all round her at the flowers and the blades of grass, but she could not see anything that looked like the right thing to eat or drink under the circumstances. There was a large mushroom growing near her, about the same height as herself; and when she had looked under it, and on both sides of it, and behind it, it occurred to her that she might as well look and see what was on the top of it.

She stretched herself up on tiptoe, and peeped over the edge of the mushroom, and her eyes immediately met those of a large blue caterpillar, that was sitting on the top with its arms folded, quietly smoking a long hookah, and taking not the smallest notice of her or of anything else.

P. L. Travers

Mary Poppins Opens the Door

Mary Poppins, the unpredictable nursery governess in the Banks family, is a delightful character in children's literature. Stern, efficient, yet kind, and endowed with the gift of magic, she makes the most commonplace events, such as a trip to the park (which you may read about in the chapter below), take on a fantastic turn. The Mary Poppins books are classics of fantasy and nonsense. They have been translated into many languages and are the delight of children all over the world. [From P. L. Travers, *Mary Poppins Opens the Door* (Harcourt, 1943).]

The Marble Boy

"And don't forget to buy me an evening paper!" said Mrs. Banks, as she handed Jane two pennies and kissed her good-bye.

Michael looked at his mother reproachfully.

"Is that all you're going to give us?" he asked. "What'll happen if we meet the ice cream man?"

"Well," said Mrs. Banks reluctantly, "here's another sixpence. But I do think you children get too many treats. *I* didn't have ices every day when *I* was a little girl."

Michael looked at her curiously. He could not believe she had ever been a little girl. Mrs. George Banks in short skirts and her hair tied up with ribbons? Impossible!

"I suppose," he said smugly, "you didn't deserve them!"

And he tucked the sixpence carefully into the pocket of his sailor suit.

"That's fourpence for the ice creams," said Jane. "And we'll buy a *Lot-o'-Fun* with the rest."

"Out of my way, Miss, if you please!" said a haughty voice behind her.

As neat and trim as a fashion-plate, Mary Poppins came down the steps with Annabel. She dumped her into the perambulator and pushed it past the children.

"Now, quick march into the park!" she snapped. "And no meandering!"

Down the path straggled Jane and Michael, with John and Barbara at their heels. The sun spread over Cherry Tree Lane like a bright enormous umbrella. Thrushes and blackbirds sang in the trees. Down at the corner Admiral Boom was busily mowing his lawn.

From the distance came sounds of martial music. The band was playing at the end of the park. Along the walks went the flowery sunshades and beneath them sauntered gossiping ladies, exchanging the latest news.

The park keeper, in his summer suit—blue with a red stripe on the sleeve—was keeping an eye on everyone as he tramped across the lawns.

"Observe the rules! Keep off the grass! All litter to be placed in the baskets!" he shouted.

Jane gazed at the sunny, dreamy scene. "It's just like Mr. Twigley's box," she said with a happy sigh.

Michael put his ear to the trunk of an oak. "I believe I can hear it growing!" he cried. "It makes a small, soft, creeping sound—"

"*You'll* be creeping in a minute! Right back home, unless you hurry!" Mary Poppins warned him.

"No rubbish allowed in the park!" shouted the keeper, as she swept along the Lime Walk.

"Rubbish yourself!" she retorted briskly, with a haughty toss of her head.

He took off his hat and fanned his face as he stared at her retreating back. And you knew from the way Mary Poppins smiled that she knew quite well he was staring. How could he help it, she thought to herself. Wasn't she wearing her new white jacket, with the pink collar and the pink belt and the four pink buttons down the front?

"Which way are we going today?" asked Michael.

"That remains to be seen!" she answered him priggishly.

"I was only inquiring—" Michael argued.

"Don't, then!" she advised, with a warning sniff.

"She never lets me say anything!" he grumbled under his hat to Jane. "I'll go dumb some day and then she'll be sorry."

Mary Poppins thrust the perambulator in front of her as though she were running an obstacle race.

"This way, please!" she commanded presently, as she swung the pram to the right.

And they knew, then, where they were going. For the little path that turned out of the Lime Walk led away toward the lake.

There, beyond the tunnels of shade, lay the shining patch of water. It sparkled and danced in its net of sunlight and the children felt their hearts beat faster as they ran through the shadows toward it.

"I'll make a boat, and sail it to Africa!" shouted Michael, forgetting his crossness.

"I'll go fishing!" cried Jane, as she galloped past him.

Laughing and whooping and waving their hats, they came to the shining water. All round the lake stood the dusty green benches, and the ducks went quacking along the edge, greedily looking for crusts.

At the far end of the water stood the battered marble statue of the boy and the dolphin. Dazzling white and bright it shone, between the lake and the sky. There was a small chip off the boy's nose and a line like a black thread round his ankle. One of the fingers of his left hand was broken off at the joint. And all his toes were cracked.

There he stood, on his high pedestal, with his arm flung lightly round the neck of the dolphin. His head, with its ruffle of marble curls, was bent toward the water. He gazed down at it thoughtfully with wide marble eyes. The name NELEUS was carved in faded gilt letters at the base of the pedestal.

"How bright he is today!" breathed Jane, blinking her eyes at the shining marble.

And it was at that moment that she saw the elderly gentleman.

He was sitting at the foot of the statue, reading a book with the aid of a magnifying glass. His bald head was sheltered from the sun by a knotted silk handkerchief, and lying on the bench beside him was a black top hat.

The children stared at the curious figure with fascinated eyes.

"That's Mary Poppins's favorite seat! She *will* be cross!" exclaimed Michael.

"Indeed? And when was I ever cross?" her voice inquired behind him.

The remark quite shocked him. "Why, you're *often* cross, Mary Poppins!" he said. "At least fifty times a day!"

"Never!" she said, with an angry snap. "I have the patience of a boa constrictor! I merely speak my mind!"

She flounced away and sat down on a bench exactly opposite the statue. Then she glared

Illustration by Mary Shepard and Agnes Sims, from *Mary Poppins Opens the Door*, copyright © 1943, 1971 by P. L. Travers. Reproduced by permission of Harcourt Brace Jovanovich, Inc.

across the lake at the elderly gentleman. It was a look that might have killed anybody else. But the elderly gentleman was quite unaffected. He went on poring over his book and took no notice of anyone. Mary Poppins, with an infuriated sniff, took her mending-bag from the perambulator and began to darn the socks.

The children scattered round the sparkling water.

"Here's my boat!" shrieked Michael, snatching a piece of colored paper from a litter basket.

"I'm fishing," said Jane, as she lay on her stomach and stretched her hand over the water. She imagined a fishing-rod in her fingers and a line running down, with a hook and a worm. After a little while, she knew, a fish would swim lazily up to the hook and give the worm a tweak. Then, with a jerk, she would land him neatly and take him home in her hat. "Well, I never!" Mrs. Brill would say. "It's just what we needed for supper!"

Beside her the twins were happily paddling. Michael steered his ship through a terrible storm. Mary Poppins sat primly on her bench and rocked the perambulator with one foot. Her silver needle flashed in the sunlight. The park was quiet and dreamy and still.

Bang!

The elderly gentleman closed his book and the sound shattered the silence.

"Oh, I say!" protested a shrill, sweet voice. "You might have let me finish!"

Jane and Michael looked up in surprise. They stared. They blinked. And they stared again. For there, on the grass before them, stood the little marble statue. The marble dolphin was clasped in his arms and the pedestal was quite empty.

The elderly gentleman opened his mouth. Then he shut it and opened it again.

"Er—did you say something?" he said at last, and his eyebrows went up to the top of his head.

"Yes, of course I did!" the boy replied. "I was reading over your shoulder there"—he pointed toward the empty pedestal—"and you closed the book too quickly. I wanted to finish the elephant story and see how he got his trunk."

"Oh, I *beg* your pardon," said the elderly gentleman. "I had no idea—er—of such a thing.

I always stop reading at four, you see. I have to get home to my tea."

He rose and folded the handkerchief and picked up the black top hat.

"Well, now that you've finished," the boy said calmly, "you can give the book to me!"

The elderly gentleman drew back, clutching the book to his breast.

"Oh, I couldn't do that, I'm afraid," he said. "You see, I've only just bought it. I wanted to read it when I was young, but the grownups always got it first. And now that I've got a copy of my own, I really feel I must keep it."

He eyed the statue uneasily as though he feared that at any moment it might snatch the book away.

"*I could tell you about the elephant's child—*" Jane murmured shyly to the boy.

He wheeled around with the fish in his arms.

"Oh, Jane—would you really?" he cried in surprise. His marble face gleamed with pleasure.

"And I'll tell you *Yellow Dog Dingo,*" said Michael, "and *The Butterfly That Stamped.*"

"No!" said the elderly gentleman suddenly. "Here I am with a suit of clothes and a hat. And he's quite naked. I'll *give* him the book! I suppose," he added, with a gloomy sigh, "I was never meant to have it."

He gave the book a last long look, and, thrusting it at the marble boy, he turned away quickly. But the dolphin wriggled and caught his eye and he turned to the boy again.

"By the way," he said, curiously, "I wonder how you caught that porpoise? What did you use—a line or a net?"

"Neither," replied the boy, with a smile. "He was given to me when I was born."

"Oh—I see." The elderly gentleman nodded, though he still looked rather puzzled. "Well, I must be getting along. Good day!" He lifted the black top hat politely and hurried off down the path.

"Thank you!" the marble boy shouted after him, as he eagerly opened the book. On the fly-leaf was written, in spidery writing, "*William Weatherall Wilkins.*"

"I'll cross out his name and put mine instead." The boy smiled gaily at Jane and Michael.

"But what is your name? And how can you read?" cried Michael, very astonished.

"My name is Neleus," the boy said, laughing. "And I read with my eyes, of course!"

"But you're only a statue!" Jane protested. "And statues don't usually walk and talk. However did you get down?"

"I jumped," replied Neleus, smiling again, as he tossed his marble curls. "I was so disappointed not to finish that story that something happened to my feet. First they twitched, and then they jumped, and the next I knew I was down on the grass!" He curled his little marble toes and stamped on the earth with his marble feet. "Oh, lucky, lucky human beings to be able to do this every day! I've watched you so often, Jane and Michael, and wished I could come and play with you. And now at last my wish has come true. Oh, tell me you're glad to see me!"

He touched their cheeks with his marble fingers and crowed with joy as he danced around them. Then, before they could utter a word of welcome, he sped like a hare to the edge of the lake and dabbled his hand in the water.

"So—this is what water feels like!" he cried. "So deep and so blue—and as light as air!" He leaned out over the sparkling lake and the dolphin gave a flick of its tail and slipped from his arms with a splash.

"Catch him! He'll sink!" cried Michael quickly.

But the dolphin did nothing of the kind. It swam round the lake and threshed the water; it dived and caught its tail in its mouth and leapt in the air and dived again. The performance was just like a turn in the circus. And as it sprang, dripping, to the arms of its master, the children could not help clapping.

"Was it good?" asked Neleus enviously. And the dolphin grinned and nodded.

"Good!" cried a well-known voice behind them. "*I* call it extremely naughty!"

Mary Poppins was standing at the edge of the lake and her eyes were as bright as her darning needle. Neleus sprang to his feet with a little cry and hung his head before her. He looked very young and small and shy as he waited for her to speak.

"Who said you might get down, may I ask?" Her face had its usual look of fury.

He shook his head guiltily.

"No one," he mumbled. "My feet jumped down by themselves, Mary Poppins."

"Then they'd better jump up again, spit-spot. You've no right to be off your pedestal."

He tilted back his marble head and the sunlight glanced off his small chipped nose.

"Oh, can't I stay down, Mary Poppins?" he pleaded. "Do let me stay for a little while and play with Jane and Michael? You don't know how lonely it is up there, with only the birds to talk to!" The earnest marble eyes entreated her. "Please, Mary Poppins!" he whispered softly, as he clasped his marble hands.

She gazed down thoughtfully for a moment, as though she were making up her mind. Then her eyes softened. A little smile skipped over her mouth and crinkled the edge of her cheek.

"Well, just for this afternoon!" she said. "This one time, Neleus! Never again!"

"Never—I promise, Mary Poppins!" He gave her an impish grin.

"Do you know Mary Poppins?" demanded Michael. "Where did you meet her?" he wanted to know. He was feeling a little jealous.

"Of course I do!" exclaimed Neleus, laughing. "She's a very old friend of my father's."

"What is your father's name? Where is he?" Jane was almost bursting with curiosity.

"Far away. In the Isles of Greece. He is called the King of the Sea." As he spoke, the marble eyes of Neleus brimmed slowly up with sadness.

"What does he do?" demanded Michael. "Does he go to the City—like Daddy?"

"Oh, no. He never goes anywhere. He stands on a cliff above the sea, holding his trident and blowing his horn. Beside him my mother sits, combing her hair. And Pelias—that's my younger brother—plays at their feet with a marble shell. And all day long the gulls fly past them, making black shadows on their marble bodies, and telling them news of the harbor. By day they watch the red-sailed ships going in and out of the bay. And at night they listen to the wine-dark waters that break on the shore below."

"How lovely!" cried Jane. "But why did you leave them?"

She was thinking that she would never have left Mr. and Mrs. Banks and Michael alone on the cliffs of Greece.

"I didn't want to," said the marble boy. "But what can a statue do against men? They were always coming to stare at us—peeking and prying and pinching our arms. They said we were made a long time ago by a very famous artist. And one day somebody said—'I'll take *him!*'—and he pointed at me. So—I had to go."

He hid his eyes for a moment behind the dolphin's fin.

"What happened then?" demanded Jane. "How did you get to our park?"

"In a packing-case," said Neleus calmly, and laughed at their look of astonishment. "Oh, we always travel that way, you know. My family is very much in demand. People want us for parks or museums or gardens. So they buy us and send us by parcel post. It never seems to occur to them that some of us might be—lonely." He choked a little on the word. Then he flung up his head with a lordly gesture. "But don't let's think about that!" he cried. "It's been much better since you two came. Oh, Jane and Michael, I know you so well—as if you were part of my family. I know about Michael's kite and his compass; and the Doulton bowl, and Robertson Ay, and the things you have for supper. Didn't you ever notice me listening? And reading the fairy-tales over your shoulders?"

Jane and Michael shook their heads.

"I know *Alice in Wonderland* by heart," he went on. "And most of *Robinson Crusoe*. And *Everything a Lady Should Know*, which is Mary Poppins's favorite. But best of all are the colored comics, especially the one called *Lot-o'-Fun*. What happened to Tiger Tim this week? Did he get away safely from Uncle Moppsy?"

"The new one comes out today," said Jane. "We'll all read it together!"

"Oh, dear! How happy I am!" cried Neleus. "The elephant's child, and a new *Lot-o'-Fun*, and my legs like the wings of a bird. I don't know when my birthday is, but I think it must be today!" He hugged the dolphin and the book in his arms and capered across the grass.

"Hi! Ting-aling-aling! Look where you're going!" the ice cream man gave a warning cry. He was wheeling his barrow along by the lake. The printed notice in front of it said:

STOP ME AND BUY ONE
WHAT WONDERFUL WEATHER!

"Stop! Stop! Stop! Stop!" cried the children wildly, as they ran toward the barrow.

"Chocolate!" said Michael.

"Lemon!" cried Jane.

And the fat little twins put out their hands and gladly took what was given them.

"And wot about you!" said the ice cream man, as Neleus came and stood shyly beside him.

"I don't know what to choose," said Neleus. "I never had one before."

"Wot! Never 'ad a nice? Wot's the matter— weak stummick? A boy your size should know all about ices! 'Ere!" The ice cream man fished inside his barrow and brought out a raspberry bar. "Take this and see 'ow you like it!"

Neleus broke the bar with his marble fingers. He popped one half in the dolphin's mouth and began to lick the other.

"Delicious," he said, "much better than sea-weed."

"Seaweed? I should think so! Wot's seaweed got to do with it? But—talking of seaweed, that's a nice big cod!" The ice cream man waved his hand at the dolphin. "If you took it along to the fishmonger, 'e'd give you a fancy price."

The dolphin gave its tail a flick and its face looked very indignant.

"Oh, I don't want to sell him," said Neleus quickly. "He isn't just a fish—he's a friend!"

"A fishy kind of friend!" said the man. "Why doesn't 'e tell you to put on your clothes? You'll catch your death running round stark naked. Well, no offense meant! Ting-aling! Ting-aling!" He rode away whistling and ring-ing his bell.

Neleus glanced at the children out of the cor-ner of his eye and the three burst out into peals of laughter.

"Oh, dear!" cried Neleus, gasping for breath,

"I believe he thinks I'm human! Shall I run and tell him he's made a mistake? That I haven't worn clothes for two thousand years and never caught even a sniffle?"

He was just about to dart after the barrow when Michael gave a shout.

"Look out! Here's Willoughby!" he cried, and swallowed the rest of his ice in one gulp.

For Willoughby, who belonged to Miss Lark, had a habit of jumping up at the children and snatching the food from their hands. He had rough, bouncy, vulgar manners and no respect for anyone. But what else could you expect of a dog who was half an airedale and half a retriever and the worst half of both?

There he came, lolloping over the grass, stick-ing out his tongue. Andrew, who was as well-bred as Willoughby was common, tripped grace-fully after him. And Miss Lark herself followed breathlessly.

"Just out for a spin before tea!" she trilled. "Such a beautiful day and the dogs insisted— Good gracious, what is that I see?"

She broke off, panting, and stared at Neleus. Her face, already red, grew redder, and she looked extremely indignant.

"You naughty, wicked boy!" she cried. "What are you doing to that poor fish? Don't you know it will die if it stays out of water?"

Neleus raised a marble eyebrow. The dol-phin swung its tail over its mouth to hide a marble smile.

"You see?" said Miss Lark. "It's writhing in agony! You must put it back into the water this minute!"

"Oh, I couldn't do that," said Neleus quickly. "I'm afraid he'd be lonely without me." He was trying to be polite to Miss Lark. But the dolphin was not. He flapped his tail and wriggled and grinned in a very discourteous manner.

"Don't answer me back! Fish are never lonely! You are just making silly excuses."

Miss Lark made an angry gesture toward the green bench.

"I do think, Mary Poppins," she said, "you might keep an eye on the children! This naughty boy, whoever he is, must put that fish back where he got it!"

Mary Poppins favored Miss Lark with a stare.

"I'm afraid that's quite impossible, ma'am. He'd have to go too far."

"Far or near—it doesn't matter. He must put it back this instant. It's cruelty to animals and it shouldn't be allowed. Andrew and Willoughby—come with me! I shall go at once and tell the Lord Mayor!"

Away she bustled, with the dogs at her heels. Willoughby, as he trotted by, winked rudely at the dolphin.

"And tell him to put his clothes on! He'll get sunburnt, running about like that!" shrieked Miss Lark, as she hurried off.

Neleus gave a little spurt of laughter and flung himself down on the grass.

"Sunburnt!" he choked. "Oh, Mary Poppins, does nobody guess I'm made of marble?"

"Humph!" replied Mary Poppins, snorting. And Neleus tossed her a mischievous smile.

"That's what the sea lions say!" he said. "They sit on the rocks and say 'Humph!' to the sunset!"

"Indeed?" she said tartly. And Jane and Michael waited, trembling, for what was surely coming. But nothing happened. Her face had an answering look of mischief and the blue eyes and the marble eyes smiled gently at each other.

"Neleus," she said quietly, "you have ten minutes more. You can come with us to the bookstall and back."

"And then—?" he said, with a questioning look, as he tightened his arms round the dolphin.

She did not answer. She looked across the sparkling lake and nodded toward the pedestal.

"Oh, can't he stay longer, Mary Poppins—?" the children began to protest. But the eager question froze on their lips, for Mary Poppins was glaring.

"I said ten minutes," she remarked. "And ten minutes is what I meant. You needn't look at me like that, either. I am not a grisly gorilla."

"Oh, don't start arguing!" cried Neleus. "We mustn't waste a second!" He sprang to his feet and seized Jane's hand. "Show me the way to the bookstall!" he said. And drew her away through the spreading sunlight and over the grassy lawns.

Behind them Mary Poppins lifted the twins into the perambulator and hurried along with Michael.

Lightly across the summer grasses ran Jane and the marble boy. His curls flew out on the wind with hers and her hot breath blew on his marble cheeks. Within her soft and living fingers the marble hand grew warmer.

"This way!" she cried, as she tugged at his arm and drew him into the Lime Walk.

At the end of it, by the far gate, stood the gaily painted bookstall. A bright sign nailed above it said:

MR. FOLLY
BOOKS PAPERS AND MAGAZINES
YOU WANT THEM
I'VE GOT THEM

A frill of colored magazines hung round the bookstall; and as the children raced up, Mr. Folly popped his head through a gap in the frill. He had a round, quiet, lazy face that looked as though nothing in the world could disturb it.

"Well, if it isn't Jane Banks and friend!" he remarked mildly. "I think I can guess what you've come for!"

The Evening News and *Lot-o'-Fun*," panted Jane, as she put down the pennies.

Neleus seized the colored comic and skimmed the pages quickly.

"Does Tiger Tim get away?" cried Michael, as he dashed up, breathless, behind them.

"Yes, he does!" cried Neleus, with a shout of joy. "Listen! 'Tiger Tim Escapes Clutches of Uncle Moppsy. His New Adventure with Old Man Dogface. Watch Out For Another Tiger Tim Story Next Week!'"

"Hooray!" shouted Michael, peering round the dolphin's shoulder to get a look at the pictures.

Mr. Folly was eyeing Neleus with interest. "That's a fine young whale you got there, Sonny! Seems almost 'uman. Where did you catch him?"

"I didn't," said Neleus, glancing up. "He was given to me as a present."

"Fancy that! Well, he makes a nice pet! And where do *you* come from? Where's yer Ma?"

"She's a long way from here," replied Neleus gravely.

"Too bad!" Mr. Folly wagged his head. "Dad away, too?"

Neleus smiled and nodded.

"You don't say! Goodness, you must be lonely!" Mr. Folly glanced at the marble body. "And cold as well, I shouldn't wonder, with not a stitch on your bones!" He made a jingling noise in his pocket and thrust out his hand to Neleus.

"There! Get yourself something to wear with that. Can't go around with nothing on. Pneumonia, you know! And chilblains!"

Neleus stared at the silver thing in his hand. "What is it?" he asked curiously.

"That's a 'arf-crown," said Mr. Folly. "Don't tell me you never saw one!"

"No, I never did," said Neleus, smiling. And the dolphin gazed at the coin with interest.

"Well, I declare! You pore little chap! Stark naked and never seen a 'arf-crown! Someone ought to be taking care of you!" Mr. Folly glanced reproachfully at Mary Poppins. And she gave him an outraged glare.

"Someone *is* taking care of him, thank you!" she said. As she spoke she unbuttoned her new white jacket and slipped it round Neleus' shoulders.

"There!" she said gruffly. "You won't be cold now. And no thanks to *you,* Mr. Folly!"

Neleus looked from the coat to Mary Poppins and his marble eyes grew wider. "You mean— I can keep it always?" he asked.

She nodded, and looked away.

"Oh, dear sweet sea-lion—thank you!" he cried, and he hugged her waist in his marble arms. "Look at me, Jane, in my new white coat! Look at me, Michael, in my beautiful buttons." He ran excitedly from one to the other to show off his new possession.

"That's right," said Mr. Folly, beaming. "Much better be sure than sorry! And the 'arf-crown will buy you a nice pair of trousers—"

"Not tonight," interrupted Mary Poppins. "We're late as it is. Now best foot forward and home we go, and I'll thank you all not to dawdle."

The sun was swiftly moving westward as she trundled the pram down the Lime Walk. The band at the end of the park was silent. The flowery sunshades had all gone home. The trees stood still and straight in the shadows. The park keeper was nowhere to be seen.

Jane and Michael walked on either side of Neleus and linked their hands through his marble arms. A silence was over the human children and over the marble child between them.

"I love you, Neleus," Jane said softly. "I wish you could stay with us always."

"I love you, too," he answered, smiling. "But I must go back. I promised."

"I suppose you couldn't leave the dolphin?" said Michael, stroking the marble fin.

Jane looked at him angrily.

"Oh, Michael—how can you be so selfish! How would you like to spend your life, all alone up there on a pedestal?"

"I'd like it—if I could have the dolphin, and call Mary Poppins a sea-lion!"

"I tell you what, Michael!" said Neleus quickly. "You can't have the dolphin—he's part of me. But the half-crown isn't. I'll give you that." He pushed the money into Michael's hand. "And Jane must have the book," he went on. "But promise, Jane, and cross your heart, that you'll let me read it over your shoulder. And every week you must come to the bench and read me the new *Lot-o'-Fun.*"

He gave the book a last long look and tucked it under her arm.

"Oh, I promise, Neleus!" she said faithfully, and crossed her heart with her hand.

"I'll be waiting for you," said Neleus softly. "I'll never, never forget."

"Walk up and don't chatter!" hissed Mary Poppins, as she turned toward the lake.

The perambulator creaked and groaned as it trundled on its way. But high above the creak of the wheels they could hear a well-known voice. They tiptoed up behind Mary Poppins as she walked to the shadowy water.

"I never done it!" the voice protested. "And wouldn't—not if you paid me!"

At the edge of the lake, by the empty pedestal, stood the Lord Mayor with two Aldermen. And before them, waving his arms and shouting, and generally behaving in a peculiar manner, was the park keeper.

"It's none of my doing, Your Honor!" he

pleaded. "I can look you straight in the eye!"

"Nonsense, Smith!" said the Lord Mayor sternly. "You are the person responsible for the park statues. And only you could have done it!"

"You might as well confess!" advised the first Alderman.

"It won't save you, of course," the second added, "but you'll *feel* so much better!"

"But I didn't *do* it, I'm telling you!" The park keeper clasped his hands in a frenzy.

"Stop quibbling, Smith. You're wasting my time!" The Lord Mayor shook his head impatiently. "First, I have to go looking for a naked boy who I hear is maltreating some wretched fish. A salmon, Miss Lark said—or was it a halibut? And now, as if this wasn't enough, I find the most valuable of our statues is missing from its pedestal. I am shocked and disgusted. I trusted you, Smith. And look how you repay me!"

"I *am* looking. I mean, I don't *have* to look! Oh, I don't know what I'm saying, Your Grace! But I *do* know I never touched that stachew!"

The keeper glanced round wildly for help and his eye fell on Mary Poppins. He gave a cry of horrified triumph and flung out his hand accusingly.

"Your Worship, *there's* the guilty party! She done it or I'll eat me 'at!"

The Lord Mayor glanced at Mary Poppins and back to the park keeper.

"I'm ashamed of you, Smith!" He shook his head sorrowfully. "Putting the blame on a perfectly respectable, innocent young woman taking her charges for an afternoon airing! How could you?"

He bowed courteously to Mary Poppins, who returned the bow with a ladylike smile.

"Innocent! *'Er!*" the park keeper screamed. "You don't know what you're sayin', my Lord! As soon as that girl comes into the park, the place begins to go crosswise. Merry-go-rounds jumpin' up in the sky, people coming down on kites and rockets, the Prime Minister bobbing round on balloons—and it's all *your* doing—you Caliban!" He shook his fist wildly at Mary Poppins.

"Poor fellow! Poor fellow! His mind is unhinged!" said the first Alderman sadly.

"Perhaps we'd better get some handcuffs," the second whispered nervously.

"Do what you like with me! 'Ang me, why don't yer? But it wasn't me wot done it!" Overcome with misery, the park keeper flung himself against the pedestal and sobbed bitterly.

Mary Poppins turned and beckoned to Neleus. He ran to her side on marble feet and leaned his head gently against her.

"Is it time?" he whispered, glancing up.

She nodded quickly. Then bending she took him in her arms and kissed his marble brow. For a moment Neleus clung to her as though he could never let her go. Then he broke away, smothering a sob.

"Good-bye, Jane and Michael. Don't forget me!" He pressed his chilly cheek to theirs. And before they could even say a word he had darted away among the shadows and was running toward his pedestal.

"I never 'ad no luck!" wailed the keeper. "Never since I was a boy!"

"And you won't have any now, my man, unless you put back that statue." The Lord Mayor fixed him with an angry eye.

But Jane and Michael were looking neither at the park keeper nor the Lord Mayor. They were watching a curly head appear at the far side of the pedestal.

Up scrambled Neleus, over the ledge, dragging the dolphin after him. His marble body blazed white and bright in a fading shaft of sunlight. Then with a gesture, half-gay, half-sad, he put up a little marble hand and waved them all farewell. As they waved back, he seemed to tremble, but that may have been the tears in their eyes. They watched him draw the dolphin to him, so close that its marble melted to his. Then he smoothed his curls with a marble hand and bent his head and was still. Even Mary Poppins's pink-and-white jacket seemed turned to lifeless marble.

"I can't put it back if I never took it!" the park keeper went on sobbing and shouting.

"Now, see here, Smith—" the Lord Mayor began. Then he gave a gasp and staggered sideways with his hand clasped to his brow. "My jumping giraffes! It's come back—" he cried. "And there's something different about it!"

He peered more closely at the statue and burst

into roars of delighted laughter. He took off his hat and waved it wildly and slapped the park keeper on the back.

"Smith—you rogue! So *that* was your secret! Why didn't you tell us at first, my man? It certainly is a splendid surprise! Well, you needn't go on pretending now—"

For the park keeper, speechless with amazement, was goggling up at Neleus.

"Gentlemen!"—the Lord Mayor turned to the Aldermen—"we have sadly misjudged this poor fellow. He has proved himself not only an excellent servant of the community—but an artist as well. Do you see what he has done to the statue? He has added a little marble coat with collar and cuffs of pink. A *great* improvement, to my mind, Smith! I *never* approved of naked statues."

"Nor I!" the first Alderman shook his head.

"Certainly not!" said the second.

"Never fear, my dear Smith. You shall have your reward. From today your wages will be raised one shilling and an extra stripe will be sewn on your sleeve. Furthermore, I shall speak of you to His Majesty when I make my next report."

And the Lord Mayor, with another ceremonious bow to Mary Poppins, swept majestically away, humbly followed by the two Aldermen.

The park keeper, looking as though he were not sure if he were on his head or his heels, stared after them. Then he turned his popping eyes to the statue and stared again at that. The marble boy and his marble fish gazed thoughtfully down at the lake. They were as still and quiet and silent as they had always been.

"Now home again, home again, jiggety-jog!" Mary Poppins raised a beckoning finger and the children followed without a word. The half-crown lay in Michael's palm, burning and bright and solid. And cold as the marble hand of Neleus was the book beneath Jane's arm.

Along the walk they marched in silence thinking their secret thoughts. And presently, on the grass behind them, there came the thud of feet. They turned to find the park keeper running heavily toward them. He had taken off his coat and was waving it, like a blue-and-red flag, at the end of his walking stick. He pulled up, pant-

ing, beside the perambulator and held out the coat to Mary Poppins.

"Take it!" he said breathlessly. "I just been looking at that boy back there. He's wearin' yours—with the four pink buttons. And you'll need one when it gets chilly."

Mary Poppins calmly took the coat and slipped it over her shoulders. Her own reflection smiled conceitedly at her from the polished brass buttons.

"Thank you," she said primly, to the park keeper.

He stood before her in his shirt-sleeves, shaking his head like a puzzled dog.

"I suppose *you* understand what it all means?" he said wistfully.

"I suppose I do," she replied smugly.

And without another word, she gave the perambulator a little push and sent it bowling past him. He was still staring after her, scratching his head, as she passed through the gate of the park.

Mr. Banks, on his way home from the office, whistled to them as they crossed the lane.

"Well, Mary Poppins!" he greeted her. "You're very smart in your blue-and-red jacket! Have you joined the Salvation Army?"

"No, sir," she replied, primly. And the look she gave him made it quite clear she had no intention of explaining.

"It's the park keeper's coat," Jane told him hurriedly.

"He gave it to her just now," added Michael.

"What—Smith? He gave her the jacket of his uniform? Whatever for?" exclaimed Mr. Banks.

But Jane and Michael were suddenly silent. They could feel Mary Poppins's gimlet eyes making holes in the backs of their heads. They dared not go on with the story.

"Well, never mind!" said Mr. Banks calmly. "I suppose she did something to deserve it!"

They nodded. But they knew he would never know what she had done, not even if he lived to be fifty. They walked up the garden path beside him, clasping the coin and the book.

And as they went they thought of the child who had given them those gifts, the marble boy who for one short hour had danced and played in the park. They thought of him standing alone on his pedestal, with his arm flung lovingly round his dolphin—forever silent, forever still, and the sweet light gone from his face. Darkness would come down upon him and the stars and the night would wrap him round. Proud and lonely he would stand there, looking down upon the waters of the little lake, dreaming of the great sea and his home so far away. . . .

Jane Langton

The Fledgling

Many children dream of flying, and several fantasies—from J. M. Barrie's *Peter Pan* to Randall Jarrell's *Fly by Night*—have used the metaphor of freedom of flight. The young girl Georgie's adventure with the Goose Prince is a magical realization of the dream. Yet many comic and suspenseful moments are provided by the attempts of Georgie's eccentric family and threatening neighbors to stop her flights. The power of this novel lies in the integrity of a little girl who is not afraid to be different, the beauty of Walden Pond on lonely autumn nights, and the New England transcendental legacy that permeates all of the author's fantasies. In this selection, the majestic Canada goose who has befriended Georgie teaches her how to fly. [From Jane Langton, *The Fledgling* (Harper, 1980).]

Flyyyyyyyyyy!

They took off from the pond. The ascent was not like their clumsy upward struggles from the roof of the porch at home. This time the Goose Prince made a rush forward through the water, his wings flapping, his beak open in a loud triumphant shout, *"A-WARK, a-WARK!"* At once he was aloft, with a rain of crystal drops falling from his webbed feet and streaming backward from Georgie's soaked pajama legs as they rose higher and higher over the pond. Georgie hung on tight, feeling the cold rush of air on her wet legs. Now, the Goose Prince was flapping strongly over the southern shore, turning in a wide arc. Then Georgie gasped. They were not alone. There was a flock of geese below them in the water, a whole flock. They were clustered along the shore with their drowsing heads tucked into their backs, fast asleep.

"A-WARK, a-WARK!" As the Goose Prince shouted above them, Georgie could see heads popping up in a flurry of beating wings. She could hear a chorus of shocked croakings. *What's that? What's that? Who's there?* But then they recognized one of their own, and the wings stopped fanning. The heads sank once more into the downy backs. They all went back to sleep.

High above the slumbering flock the Goose Prince swam smoothly once again through the thick river of air. His wings were moving easily, sending pulses of the cool fragrant morning over Georgie's smiling face, lifting the lank wisps of her fine hair, blowing it backward. Below them the pine trees flung up their dark arms, as if they were pointing at Georgie—*Oh, look! Look at Georgie!* And then the Goose Prince turned his head on his long neck and gazed back at her, the dawn light shining through his bulging eyes. "Now," he said, "try it now."

At the top of the sky, clinging to him with her fingers knotted together around his throat, Georgie looked back at him, trying to understand, whispering, "Try what?"

"Flyyyyyyyyyyyy," said the Goose Prince. On the moving air the word flowed on and on, not dying away. Georgie was filled with longing. But she was afraid. She held on, wrapping her fingers together more tightly, shutting her eyes and pressing her cheek against the soft feathers of his neck. Not now. She couldn't do it now. Not yet.

"Just slip off and glide," said the Goose Prince. "You'll see. The wind is just right. It will hold you, if you try it now." And then he warbled it again in his soft fluting voice, *"Flyyyyyyyyyyyy."*

For a moment longer Georgie kept her shoulders stiff and her arms pressed close against him. But then she opened her eyes and commanded all her muscles to go limp. Letting go, she slid down the feathery slope of his back until she felt something nudge at her from below. It was a pillow of air, lifting her, holding her steadily and firmly like the palm of a supporting hand. Then at last all the stringy little muscles in Georgie's body loosened. Spreading her arms, she floated on the column of air. Beside her, the Goose Prince floated too, watching her, his hovering wingtips brushing her fingers. Together they drifted, wheeling down and down in slowly descending circles, broad and wide, around and around the pond. Georgie wanted to say, "Oh, look, look at me!" but whenever she opened her mouth, the wind filled it. They were floating, soaring, skimming like sea gulls, like hawks, like swallows. Above them there was nothing but crystal air, and below them—and then for the first time Georgie looked down, and at once she was frightened. The emptiness below her was an immense gulf of nothingness. There was only the steely surface of the gray pond, far down, flat like metal, and the dark bristle of the trees poking up around it. Georgie gave a strangled cry, and dropped one arm.

Instantly she was falling, spinning over and over, plummeting straight down. But only for an instant. With a tremendous jerk and a terrible pinching pain in her left arm, she was snatched out of her plunging fall. The Goose Prince was dragging her through the air, his wings thundering, struggling to hold her aloft. And soon he was lowering her gently to the ground on the nearest shore.

Georgie lay on the stony path for a moment, trying not to cry, and then she stood up, trembling, rubbing her arm. "I'm sorry," she said.

But the Goose Prince was gallant. "Oh, it's *quite* all right," he said. "I hope I didn't hurt you?"

"No, no," said Georgie. "Could we try again?"

"Try again? Are you sure?" The Goose Prince cocked his head at her, and she couldn't help laughing. In his tender concern he looked for a minute more like her mother than like the splendid prince he really was.

"Oh, yes!"

They tried again. Once more the Goose Prince paddled out into the water, once more they took off in a rush of beating wings, once more he lifted Georgie high over the pond. And once again Georgie let go. This time when she clenched her teeth and slid off the back of the Goose Prince, she was careful not to look down. This time she lay perfectly still on the cushion of air. Keeping her arms spread wide,

she circled like the Goose Prince as he rested beside her on the same sturdy ridge of warm vapor rising from the pond. She was safe now, perfectly safe. Watching her companion out of the corner of her eye, Georgie obediently copied his slightest motion. Whenever he adjusted the curve of his pinions to change the direction of his flight, Georgie bent her elbows too, and followed his lead. When the wind rocked him, and he spread the tips of his wings to let it flow through the gaps between his feathers, it rocked Georgie too, and she opened her fingers. Glide, glide, float and glide, lift and soar! Oh, how far she could see! All the way to Boston! There it was, the city of Boston, a cluster of dark towers against the sunrise, and there were the shadowy mountains, still blue with night, far away on the other side!

Proudly the Goose Prince flew beside Georgie, wingtip to fingertip, his head bent on his long neck to watch her. The sunlight was shining redly on his belly with the same streaking ray that warmed her own face. And then, at last, Georgie dared to cock her head and look down. She saw Route 2, there at the place where it turned the corner, and, look! there was the train! It was rattling along the shore of the pond on its toy track, shaking from side to side. Now the sun had risen far enough to shine on the trees around the pond. The tops of the trees were pink. For an instant the sun flashed back into Georgie's eyes from the window of a car in the parking lot, making her blink. But she banked and turned, following the lead of the Goose Prince, lifting her head to gaze once again over the whole broad landscape from horizon to horizon, feeling the sleeves of her jacket fill with air, listening to the legs of her pajamas flap like the laundry at home on a breezy day.

She was free. Georgie exulted. At last she was free as air. With the Goose Prince she could fly everywhere, all over the world. There were no fences to keep them out. So this was the way birds felt! They could fly to China and France and Africa! To Africa, where there were lions and elephants! She could fly to the elephants' jungle! She could see monkeys, leaping in the trees!

Sitting in his car in the parking lot at Walden Pond, Ralph Preek gazed up at the giant birds circling in the sky. He was nearsighted. He couldn't see the birds clearly, but he knew that there were two of them, and that one of them was bigger than the other. Idly he picked up the gun that lay beside him on the front seat and pointed it upward, trying to follow the bigger of the two birds with the sights along the barrel. It was just for practice. Of course he wouldn't fire a shot until an instant after midnight on the first morning of the hunting season. But it was too bad to be forced to wait because of a stupid law. Ah, well, the first day of the hunting season was only a little more than two weeks off. He would bide his time. No one would ever be able to say that Ralph Preek was anything but a law-abiding man. Mr. Preek didn't know it, but there was another Massachusetts state law against firing a gun at waterfowl after sundown. And there was still another against the use of firearms at Walden Pond at any time of the day, all year round. Smiling to himself in his ignorance, Mr. Preek put his gun down beside him on the seat of the car, revved the engine softly, and backed the car out of the parking lot.

His time would come. Only two weeks from Saturday. He could wait.

Mary Norton

The Borrowers

Mary Norton's delightful fantasy about the tiny people who hide away in odd nooks of old houses and live by "borrowing" what they need was awarded the Carnegie medal in England as the outstanding children's book of its year. In this selection Arrietty, the inches-high, thirteen-year-old "Borrower" daughter, has just ventured out onto the doorstep of the house on a perilous trip of exploration. [From Mary Norton, *The Borrowers* (Harcourt, 1953).]

The step was warm but very steep. "If I got down on to the path," Arrietty thought, "I might not get up again," so for some moments she sat quietly. After a while she noticed the shoe-scraper.

"Arrietty," called Pod softly, "where have you got to?"

"I just climbed down the shoe-scraper," she called back.

He came along and looked down at her from the top of the step. "That's all right," he said after a moment's stare, "but never climb down anything that isn't fixed like. Supposing one of them came along and moved the shoe-scraper—where would you be then? How would you get up again?"

"It's heavy to move," said Arrietty.

"Maybe," said Pod, "but it's movable. See what I mean? There's rules, my lass, and you got to learn."

"This path," Arrietty said, "goes round the house. And the bank does too."

"Well," said Pod, "what of it?"

Arrietty rubbed one red kid shoe on a rounded stone. "It's my grating," she explained. "I was thinking that my grating must be just round the corner. My grating looks out on to this bank."

"Your grating!" exclaimed Pod. "Since when has it been your grating?"

"I was thinking," Arrietty went on. "Suppose I just went round the corner and called through the grating to Mother?"

"No," said Pod, "we're not going to have none of that. Not going round corners."

"Then," went on Arrietty, "she'd see I was all right like."

"Well," said Pod, and then he half smiled, "go quickly then and call. I'll watch for you here. Not loud, mind!"

Arrietty ran. The stones in the path were firmly bedded and her light, soft shoes hardly seemed to touch them. How glorious it was to run—you could never run under the floor: you walked, you stooped, you crawled—but you never ran. Arrietty nearly ran past the grating. Yes, there it was quite close to the ground, embedded deeply in the old wall of the house; there was moss below it in a spreading, greenish stain.

Arrietty ran up to it. "Mother!" she called, her nose against the iron grille. "Mother!" She waited quietly and, after a moment, she called again.

At the third call Homily came. Her hair was coming down and she carried, as though it were heavy, the screw lid of a pickle jar, filled with soapy water. "Oh," she said in an annoyed voice, "you didn't half give me a turn! What do you think you're up to? Where's your father?"

Arrietty jerked her head sideways. "Just there—by the front door!" She was so full of happiness that, out of Homily's sight, her toes danced on the green moss. Here she was on the other side of the grating—here she was at last, on the outside—looking in!

"Yes," said Homily, "they open that door like that—the first day of spring. Well," she went on briskly, "you run back to your father. And tell him, if the morning-room door happens to be open that I wouldn't say no to a bit of red blotting paper. Mind, out of my way now—while I throw the water!"

"That's what grows the moss," thought Arrietty as she sped back to her father, "all the water we empty through the grating. . . ."

Pod looked relieved when he saw her but frowned at the message. "How's she expect me to climb that desk without me pin? Blotting paper's a curtain-and-chair job and she should know it. Come on now! Up with you!"

"Let me stay down," pleaded Arrietty, "just a bit longer. Just till you finish. They're all out. Except Her. Mother said so."

"She'd say anything," grumbled Pod, "when she wants something quick. How does she know She won't take it into her head to get out of that bed of Hers and come downstairs with a stick? How does she know Mrs. Driver ain't stayed at home today—with a headache? How does she know that boy ain't still here?"

"What boy?" asked Arrietty.

Pod looked embarrassed. "What boy?" he repeated vaguely and then went on: "Or may be Crampfurl—"

"Crampfurl isn't a boy," said Arrietty.

"No, he isn't," said Pod, "not in a manner of speaking. No," he went on as though thinking this out, "no, you wouldn't call Crampfurl a boy. Not, as you might say, a boy—exactly. Well," he said, beginning to move away, "stay down a bit if you like. But stay close!"

Arrietty watched him move away from the step and then she looked about her. Oh, glory! Oh, joy! Oh, freedom! The sunlight, the grasses, the soft, moving air and halfway up the bank, where it curved round the corner, a flowering cherry tree! Below it on the path lay a stain of pinkish petals and, at the tree's foot, pale as butter, a nest of primroses.

Arrietty threw a cautious glance toward the front doorstep and then, light and dancey, in her soft red shoes, she ran toward the petals. They were curved like shells and rocked as she touched them. She gathered several up and laid them one inside the other . . . up and up . . . like a card castle. And then she spilled them. Pod came again to the top of the step and looked along the path. "Don't you go far," he said after a moment. Seeing his lips move, she smiled back at him: she was too far already to hear the words.

A greenish beetle, shining in the sunlight, came toward her across the stones. She laid her fingers lightly on its shell and it stood still, waiting and watchful, and when she moved her hand the beetle went swiftly on. An ant came hurrying in a busy zigzag. She danced in front of it to tease it and put out her foot. It stared at her, nonplused, waving its antennae; then pettishly, as though put out, it swerved away. Two birds came down, quarreling shrilly, into the grass below the tree. One flew away but Arrietty could see the other among the moving grass stems above her on the slope. Cautiously she moved toward the bank and climbed a little nervously in amongst the green blades. As she parted them gently with her bare hands, drops of water plopped on her skirt and she felt the red shoes become damp. But on she went, pulling herself up now and again by rooty stems into this jungle of moss and wood-violet and creeping leaves of clover. The sharp-seeming grass blades, waist high, were tender to the touch and sprang back lightly behind her as she passed. When at last she reached the foot of the tree, the bird took fright and flew away and she sat down suddenly on a gnarled leaf of primrose. The air was filled with scent. "But nothing will play with you," she thought and saw the cracks and furrows of the primrose leaves held crystal beads of dew. If she pressed the leaf these rolled like marbles. The bank was warm, almost too warm here within the shelter of the tall grass, and the sandy earth smelled dry. Standing up, she picked a primrose. The pink stalk felt tender and living in her hands and was covered with silvery hairs, and when she held the flower, like a parasol, between her eyes and the sky, she saw the sun's pale light through the veined petals. On a piece of bark she found a wood louse and she struck it lightly with her swaying flower. It curled immediately and became a ball, bumping softly away downhill in amongst the grass roots. But she knew about wood lice. There were plenty of them at home under the floor. Homily always scolded her if she played with them because, she said, they smelled of old knives. She lay back among the stalks of the primroses and they made a coolness between her and the sun, and then, sighing, she turned her head and looked sideways up the bank among the grass stems. Startled, she caught her breath. Something had moved above her on the bank. Something had glittered. Arrietty stared.

It was an eye. Or it looked like an eye. Clear and bright like the color of the sky. An eye like her own but enormous. A glaring eye. Breathless with fear, she sat up. And the eye blinked. A great fringe of lashes came curving down and flew up again out of sight. Cautiously, Arrietty moved her legs: she would slide noiselessly in among the grass stems and slither away down the bank.

"Don't move!" said a voice, and the voice, like the eye, was enormous but, somehow, hushed—and hoarse like a surge of wind through the grating on a stormy night in March.

Arrietty froze. "So this is it," she thought, "the worst and most terrible thing of all: I have been 'seen'! Whatever happened to Eggleina will now, almost certainly, happen to me."

There was a pause and Arrietty, her heart pounding in her ears, heard the breath again drawn swiftly into the vast lungs. "Or," said the voice, whispering still, "I shall hit you with my ash stick."

Suddenly Arrietty became calm. "Why?" she asked. How strange her own voice sounded! Crystal thin and harebell clear, it tinkled on the air.

"In case," came the surprised whisper at last, "you ran toward me, quickly, through the grass . . . in case," it went on, trembling a little, "you came and scrabbled at me with your nasty little hands."

Arrietty stared at the eye; she held herself quite still. "Why?" she asked again, and again the word tinkled—icy cold it sounded this time, and needle sharp.

"Things do," said the voice. "I've seen them. In India."

Arrietty thought of her Gazetteer of the World, "You're not in India now," she pointed out.

"Did you come out of the house?"

"Yes," said Arrietty.

"From whereabouts in the house?"

Arrietty stared at the eye. "I'm not going to tell you," she said at last bravely.

"Then I'll hit you with my ash stick!"

"All right," said Arrietty, "hit me!"

"I'll pick you up and break you in half!"

Arrietty stood up. "All right," she said and took two paces forward.

There was a sharp gasp and an earthquake in the grass: he spun away from her and sat up, a great mountain in a green jersey. He had fair, straight hair and golden eyelashes. "Stay where you are!" he cried.

Arrietty stared up at him. So this was "the boy"! Breathless, she felt, and light with fear. "I guessed you were about nine," she gasped after a moment.

He flushed. "Well, you're wrong, I'm ten." He looked down at her, breathing deeply. "How old are you?"

"Fourteen," said Arrietty. "Next June," she added, watching him.

There was silence while Arrietty waited, trembling a little. "Can you read?" the boy said at last.

"Of course," said Arrietty. "Can't you?"

"No," he stammered. "I mean—yes. I mean I've just come from India."

"What's that got to do with it?" asked Arrietty.

"Well, if you're born in India, you're bilingual. And if you're bilingual, you can't read. Not so well."

Arrietty stared up at him: what a monster, she thought, dark against the sky.

"Do you grow out of it?" she asked.

He moved a little and she felt the cold flick of his shadow.

"Oh yes," he said, "it wears off. My sisters were bilingual; now they aren't a bit. They could read any of those books upstairs in the schoolroom."

"So could I," said Arrietty quickly, "if someone could hold them, and turn the pages. I'm not a bit bilingual. I can read anything."

"Could you read out loud?"

"Of course," said Arrietty.

"Would you wait here while I run upstairs and get a book now?"

"Well," said Arrietty; she was longing to show off; then a startled look came into her eyes. "Oh—" she faltered.

"What's the matter?" The boy was standing up now. He towered above her.

"How many doors are there to this house?" She squinted up at him against the bright sunlight. He dropped on one knee.

"Doors?" he said. "Outside doors?"

"Yes."

"Well, there's the front door, the back door, the gun room door, the kitchen door, the scullery door . . . and the french windows in the drawing room."

"Well, you see," said Arrietty, "my father's in the hall, by the front door, working. He . . . he wouldn't want to be disturbed."

"Working?" said the boy. "What at?"

"Getting material," said Arrietty, "for a scrubbing brush."

"Then I'll go in the side door"; he began to move away but turned suddenly and came back to her. He stood a moment, as though embarrassed, and then he said: "Can you fly?"

"No," said Arrietty, surprised; "can you?"

His face became even redder. "Of course not," he said angrily; "I'm not a fairy!"

"Well, nor am I," said Arrietty, "nor is anybody. I don't believe in them."

He looked at her strangely. "You don't believe in them?"

"No," said Arrietty; "do you?"

"Of course not!"

Really, she thought, he is a very angry kind of boy. "My mother believes in them," she said, trying to appease him. "She thinks she saw one once. It was when she was a girl and lived with her parents behind the sand pile in the potting shed."

He squatted down on his heels and she felt his breath on her face. "What was it like?" he asked.

"About the size of a glowworm with wings like a butterfly. And it had a tiny little face, she said, all alight and moving like sparks and tiny moving hands. Its face was changing all the time, she said, smiling and sort of shimmering. It seemed to be talking, she said, very quickly—but you couldn't hear a word. . . ."

"Oh," said the boy, interested. After a moment he asked: "Where did it go?"

"It just went," said Arrietty. "When my mother saw it, it seemed to be caught in a cobweb. It was dark at the time. About five o'clock on a winter's evening. After tea."

"Oh," he said again and picked up two petals of cherry blossom which he folded together like a sandwich and ate slowly. "Supposing," he said, staring past her at the wall of the house, "you saw a little man, about as tall as a pencil, with a blue patch in his trousers, halfway up a window curtain, carrying a doll's tea cup—would you say it was a fairy?"

"No," said Arrietty, "I'd say it was my father."

"Oh," said the boy, thinking this out, "does your father have a blue patch on his trousers?"

"Not on his best trousers. He does on his borrowing ones."

"Oh," said the boy again. He seemed to find it a safe sound, as lawyers do. "Are there many people like you?"

"No," said Arrietty. "None. We're all different."

"I mean as small as you?"

Arrietty laughed. "Oh, don't be silly!" she said. "Surely you don't think there are many people in the world your size?"

"There are more my size than yours," he retorted.

"Honestly—" began Arrietty helplessly and

laughed again. "Do you really think—I mean, whatever sort of a world would it be? Those great chairs . . . I've seen them. Fancy if you had to make chairs that size for everyone? And the stuff for their clothes . . . miles and miles of it . . . tents of it . . . and the sewing! And their great houses, reaching up so you can hardly see the ceilings . . . their great beds . . . the *food* they eat . . . great, smoking mountains of it, huge bogs of stew and soup and stuff."

"Don't you eat soup?" asked the boy.

"Of course we do," laughed Arrietty. "My father had an uncle who had a little boat which he rowed round in the stock-pot picking up flotsam and jetsam. He did bottom-fishing too for bits of marrow until the cook got suspicious through finding bent pins in the soup. Once he was nearly shipwrecked on a chunk of submerged shinbone. He lost his oars and the boat sprang a leak but he flung a line over the pot handle and pulled himself alongside the rim. But all that stock—fathoms of it! And the size of the stock-pot! I mean, there wouldn't be enough stuff in the world to go round after a bit! That's why my father says it's a good thing they're dying out . . . just a few, my father says, that's all we need—to keep us. Otherwise, he says, the whole thing gets"—Arrietty hesitated, trying to remember the word—"exaggerated, he says—"

"What do you mean," asked the boy, " 'to keep us'?"

So Arrietty told him about borrowing—how difficult it was and how dangerous. She told him about the storerooms under the floor; about Pod's early exploits, the skill he had shown and the courage; she described those far-off days, before her birth, when Pod and Homily had been rich; she described the musical snuffbox of gold filigree, and the little bird which flew out of it made of kingfisher feathers, how it flapped its wings and sang its song; she described the doll's wardrobe and the tiny green glasses; the little silver teapot out of the drawing-room case; the satin bedcovers and embroidered sheets . . . "those we have still," she told him, "they're Her handkerchiefs. . . ." "She," the boy realized gradually, was his Great-Aunt Sophy upstairs, bedridden since a hunting accident some twenty years before; he heard how Pod would borrow from Her room, picking his way—in the firelight—among the trinkets on Her dressing table, even climbing Her bed-curtains and walking on Her quilt. And of how She would watch him and sometimes talk to him because, Arrietty explained, every day at six o'clock they brought Her a decanter of Fine Old Pale Madeira, and how before midnight She would drink the lot. Nobody blamed Her, not even Homily, because, as Homily would say, She had so few pleasures, poor soul, but, Arrietty explained, after the first three glasses Great-Aunt Sophy never believed in anything she saw. "She thinks my father comes out of the decanter," said Arrietty, "and one day when I'm older he's going to take me there and She'll think I come out of the decanter too. It'll please Her, my father thinks, as She's used to him now. Once he took my mother, and She perked up like anything and kept asking after her and why didn't she come any more and saying they'd watered the Madeira because once, She says, She saw a little man *and* a little woman and now she only sees a little man. . . ."

"I wish she thought I came out of the decanter," said the boy. "She gives me dictation and teaches me to write. I only see her in the mornings when she's cross. She sends for me and looks behind my ears and asks Mrs. D. if I've learned my words."

"What does Mrs. D. look like?" asked Arrietty. (How delicious it was to say "Mrs. D." like that . . . how careless and daring!)

"She's fat and has a mustache and gives me my bath and hurts my bruise and my sore elbow and says she'll take a slipper to me one of these days. . . ." The boy pulled up a tuft of grass and stared at it angrily and Arrietty saw his lip tremble. "My mother's very nice," he said. "She lives in India. Why did you lose all your worldly riches?"

"Well," said Arrietty, "the kitchen boiler burst and hot water came pouring through the floor into our house and everything was washed away and piled up in front of the grating. My father worked night and day. First hot, then cold. Trying to salvage things. And there's a dreadful draught in March through that grating. He got ill, you see, and couldn't go borrowing.

So my Uncle Hendreary had to do it and one or two others and my mother gave them things, bit by bit, for all their trouble. But the king-fisher bird was spoilt by the water; all its feathers fell off and a great twirly spring came jumping out of its side. My father used the spring to keep the door shut against draughts from the grating and my mother put the feathers in a little moleskin hat. After a while I got born and my father went borrowing again. But he gets tired now and doesn't like curtains, not when any of the bobbles are off. . . ."

"I helped him a bit," said the boy, "with the tea cup. He was shivering all over. I suppose he was frightened."

"My father frightened!" exclaimed Arrietty angrily. "Frightened of you!" she added.

"Perhaps he doesn't like heights," said the boy.

"He loves heights," said Arrietty. "The thing he doesn't like is curtains. I've told you. Curtains make him tired."

The boy sat thoughtfully on his haunches, chewing a blade of grass. "Borrowing," he said after a while. "Is that what you call it?"

"What else could you call it?" asked Arrietty.

"I'd call it stealing."

Arrietty laughed. She really laughed. "But we *are* Borrowers," she explained, "like you're a—a human bean or whatever it's called. We're part of the house. You might as well say that the fire grate steals the coal from the coal scuttle."

"Then what is stealing?"

Arrietty looked grave. "Don't you know?" she asked. "Stealing is—well, supposing my Uncle Hendreary borrowed an emerald watch from Her dressing-table and my father took it and hung it up on our wall. That's steal-ing."

"An emerald watch!" exclaimed the boy.

"Well, I just said that because we have one on the wall at home, but my father borrowed it himself. It needn't be a watch. It could be anything. A lump of sugar even. But Borrow-ers don't steal."

"Except from human beings," said the boy.

Arrietty burst out laughing; she laughed so much that she had to hide her face in the prim-rose. "Oh dear," she gasped with tears in her eyes, "you are funny!" She stared upward at his puzzled face. "Human beans are *for* Bor-rowers—like bread's for butter!" The boy was silent awhile. A sigh of wind rustled the cherry tree and shivered among the blossoms.

"Well, I don't believe it," he said at last, watching the falling petals. "I don't believe that's what we're for at all and I don't believe we're dying out!"

"Oh, goodness!" exclaimed Arrietty impa-tiently, staring up at his chin. "Just use your common sense: you're the only real human bean I ever saw (although I do just know of three more—Crampfurl, Her, and Mrs. Driver). But I know lots and lots of Borrowers: The Overmantels and the Harpsichords and the Rain-Barrels and the Linen-Presses and the Boot-Racks and the Hon. John Studdingtons and—"

He looked down. "John Studdington? But he was our grand-uncle—"

"Well, this family lived behind a picture," went on Arrietty, hardly listening, "and there were the Stove-Pipes and the Bell-Pulls and the—"

"Yes," he interrupted, "but did you see them?"

"I saw the Harpsichords. And my mother was a Bell-Pull. The others were before I was born. . . ."

He leaned closer. "Then where are they now? Tell me that."

"My Uncle Hendreary has a house in the country," said Arrietty coldly, edging away from his great lowering face; it was misted over, she noticed, with hairs of palest gold. "And four children, Harpsichords and Clocks."

"But where are the others?"

"Oh," said Arrietty, "they're somewhere." But where? she wondered. And she shivered slightly in the boy's cold shadow which lay about her, slant-wise, on the grass.

He drew back again, his fair head blocking out a great piece of sky. "Well," he said deliber-ately after a moment, and his eyes were cold, "I've only seen two Borrowers but I've seen hundreds and hundreds and hundreds and hun-dreds—"

"Oh no—" whispered Arrietty.

"Of human beings." And he sat back.

Arrietty stood very still. She did not look at him. After a while she said: "I don't believe you."

"All right," he said, "then I'll tell you—"

"I still won't believe you," murmured Arrietty.

"Listen!" he said. And he told her about railway stations and football matches and racecourses and royal processions and Albert Hall concerts. He told her about India and China and North America and the British Commonwealth. He told her about the July sales. "Not hundreds," he said, "but thousands and millions and billions and trillions of great, big, enormous people. Now do you believe me?"

Arrietty stared up at him with frightened eyes: it gave her a crick in the neck. "I don't know," she whispered.

"As for you," he went on, leaning closer again, "I don't believe that there are any more Borrowers anywhere in the world. I believe you're the last three," he said.

Arrietty dropped her face into the primrose. "We're not. There's Aunt Lupy and Uncle Hendreary and all the cousins."

"I bet they're dead," said the boy. "And what's more," he went on, "no one will ever believe I've seen *you*. And you'll be the very last because you're the youngest. One day," he told her, smiling triumphantly, "you'll be the only Borrower left in the world!"

He sat still, waiting, but she did not look up. "Now you're crying," he remarked after a moment.

"They're not dead," said Arrietty in a muffled voice; she was feeling in her little pocket for a handkerchief. "They live in a badger's set two fields away, beyond the spinney. We don't see them because it's too far. There are weasels and things and cows and foxes . . . and crows . . ."

"Which spinney?" he asked.

"I don't KNOW!" Arrietty almost shouted. "It's along by the gas-pipe—a field called Parkin's Beck." She blew her nose. "I'm going home," she said.

"Don't go," he said, "not yet."

"Yes, I'm going," said Arrietty.

His face turned pink. "Let me just get the book," he pleaded.

"I'm not going to read to you now," said Arrietty.

"Why not?"

She looked at him with angry eyes. "Because—"

"Listen," he said, "I'll go to that field. I'll go and find Uncle Hendreary. And the cousins. And Aunt Whatever-she-is. And, if they're alive, I'll tell you. What about that? You could write them a letter and I'd put it down the hole—"

Arrietty gazed up at him. "Would you?" she breathed.

"Yes, I would. Really I would. Now can I go and get the book? I'll go in by the side door."

"All right," said Arrietty absently. Her eyes were shining. "When can I give you the letter?"

"Any time," he said, standing above her. "Where in the house do you live?"

"Well—" began Arrietty and stopped. Why once again did she feel this chill? Could it only be his shadow . . . towering above her, blotting out the sun? "I'll put it somewhere," she said hurriedly, "I'll put it under the hall mat."

"Which one? The one by the front door?"

"Yes, that one."

He was gone. And she stood there alone in the sunshine, shoulder deep in grass. What had happened seemed too big for thought; she felt unable to believe it really had happened: not only had she been "seen" but she had been talked to; not only had she been talked to but she had—

"Arrietty!" said a voice.

She stood up startled and spun round: there was Pod, moon-faced, on the path looking up at her. "Come on down!" he whispered.

She stared at him for a moment as though she did not recognize him; how round his face was, how kind, how familiar!

"Come on!" he said again, more urgently; and obediently because he sounded worried, she slithered quickly toward him off the bank, balancing her primrose. "Put that thing down," he said sharply, when she stood at last beside him on the path. "You can't lug great flowers about—you got to carry a bag. What you want to go up there for?" he grumbled as they moved off across the stones. "I might never have seen you. Hurry up now. Your mother'll have tea waiting!"

L. M. Boston

The Children of Green Knowe

A small boy, Toseland, Tolly for short, spends his Christmas holiday with his great-grandmother, who lives in an ancestral home, Green Knowe, a wonderful old English country house where anything might happen. Mysterious, tantalizing things do begin to happen as soon as Tolly steps over the threshold. Is he the only child in the house? At times he hears children's laughter and running footsteps. Over the fireplace hangs a portrait of the three children who grew up at Green Knowe generations ago. Tolly's great-grandmother tells him stories about them: of Toby and his horse Feste, of Linnet and Alexander. So vivid are the stories, they evoke the children from the past. The author blends fantasy and realism with great skill and handles the relation of present to past with restraint and subtlety. [From L. M. Boston, *The Children of Green Knowe* (Harcourt, 1955).]

Tolly woke early next morning, still excited with the knowledge that the world into which he was born had once produced a Feste. He lay for a moment with his eyes shut, listening for any sound there might be in the room. The slow tick-tock came out of the silence, and then a soft whirring followed by the little tap of a bird perching, and lastly, sounding very loud because it was near his ear, a scratching of bird-claws on his sheet and the tiny pump of a bird's hop on his chest. When he opened his eyes he looked straight into the round black eye of the chaffinch.

It gave a loud chirp, as if it were making an important statement, something like "I'm as good as you are," but with no boastfulness, only friendly confidence. Then it flew out of the window. In a moment it was back. "I'm as good as you are," it said, and went into the cage for the last of the pastry crumbs.

It hopped round the room examining everything with its head tipped sideways as if its eye were a spotlight. It tugged at Toseland's shoe-laces, picked up his Twig T that he had put carefully by his bed, tried to fly away with it, but found it too heavy and threw it away. In front of the big mirror it bowed to its own reflection, announced as usual "I'm as good as you are" and seemed to wait for a reply. Getting none, it flew out of the window again.

"How quickly it makes up its mind about everything," thought Toseland, getting out of bed and climbing on to the rocking-horse. He worked hard, making it rear high and higher until it stood right up on its hind-legs and he had to clutch it round the neck and lean forward to bring it down again. "My golden eagle, my wise horse, my powerful otter," he chanted as he rocked. Before he went down to breakfast he brushed its mane and tail and put two rugs over it, belting them round with the strap of his trunk.

He went to the bed to get his mouse from under the pillow. As his hand closed over it, it felt warm to his touch, and with surprise he saw pastry crumbs in the bed. Suddenly he remembered Mrs. Oldknow's question: "And did the mouse squeak and the dogs bark?"

"Mouse, mouse," he said, looking into its shiny black eye, "where have you been? This house is full of shiny black eyes, all looking at me."

As he went down the winding wooden stairs

Illustration by Peter Boston, from *The Children of Green Knowe,* copyright © 1982 by L. M. Boston. First published in 1955. Reproduced by permission of Harcourt Brace Jovanovich, Inc., and Faber & Faber Ltd.

he heard someone whistling in his bedroom behind him. A bird? He turned his head to listen, but what he heard was laughter in the Music Room below him. He pelted down the stairs, making a great noise with his shoes, but by then children's voices came from his great-grandmother's room beyond.

Mrs. Oldknow was there, turning her head and bending down as if she were listening to a child that was clutching her skirts. She looked up with a queer smile as Tolly came in, rather as if she had been caught. "What a hurry you are in for breakfast this morning! Pelting down your stairs as if you were chasing butterflies." Toseland had a feeling that she was hiding something from him. The voices and laughter had vanished.

All that day it seemed that the children were determined to tease Tolly. In the house, in the garden, wherever he was not, they were. They sounded so happy, so full of games and high spirits that Tolly, in spite of all disappointments, still ran towards it when he heard "coo-ee" in the garden, or stopped and crept stealthily round a corner where he heard whispering. But he found no one. While he was loitering round St. Christopher's feet he was playfully pelted with beechnuts through the window-opening in the garden wall. When he visited the Green Deer he found twigs on the ground arranged like arrows pointing a trail. He followed these past the green squirrel, the green hare, the peacock, and the cock and hen, till he arrived at the fish platform. There all he found was more twigs arranged to form the letters T, A, L. He broke off two more and put another T underneath. There was a little dog barking somewhere, rather muffled as if someone were trying to keep it quiet.

He visited Feste's stall, walking in on tiptoe as some people do in church. The sugar was gone again! Joyfully he put another piece.

He felt very good-tempered all morning, but by the middle of the afternoon he had forgotten that yesterday he had been dull because there was no hide-and-seek. Now he was cross because there was too much of it.

"I hate hide-and-seek when you never find anybody," he said to himself. "It's a perfectly horrid game." He walked to the house kicking sticks and stones as he went. He even felt inclined to kick St. Christopher, but stopped in time and was ashamed of having such a thought.

As he went along the entrance hall, past one of the big mirrors, something in it caught his eye. It looked like a pink hand. The glass reflected a dark doorway on the other side of the stairs. Behind the door-post, flattened against the wall on tiptoe to make themselves as thin as they could, their faces puckered with holding in their laughter, he saw Linnet and Alexander. It was Linnet's hand on the door-post. Their black eyes were fixed on him. There was no mistake, he knew them.

"I spy!" he shouted, whisking round to chase them, but they did not run away, they simply vanished.

He felt the wall where they had been; he looked all round. He ran out to the green deer, but the clearing was empty and quiet. Certainly the green deer looked magic enough, ready to spring away. The light was queer too, the sky was dark green, the wind dead. Tolly was half frightened. Something was going to happen.

As he looked up at St. Christopher's face a snowflake drifted past it, then another, and suddenly it was snowing thickly. Like millions of tiny white birds circling home to roost, the flakes danced in the air. They filled the sky as far up as he could imagine. At the same time all the sounds in the world ceased. The snow was piling up on the branches, on the walls, on the ground, on St. Christopher's face and shoulders, without any sound at all, softer than the thin spray of fountains, or falling leaves, or butterflies against a window, or wood ash dropping, or hair when the barber cuts it. Yet when a flake landed on his cheek it was heavy. He felt the splosh but could not hear it.

He went in plastered with snow, and here tea was ready, with Mrs. Oldknow sitting by the fire waiting for him. In the fire the snow drifting down the chimney was making the only noise it ever can—a sound like the striking of fairy matches; though sometimes when the wind blows you can hear the snow like a gloved hand laid against the window.

Tolly made the toast and his great-grandmother spread it with honey. They talked about Christmas. Mrs. Oldknow said Boggis was going to buy the tree the next day, unless they were snowed up. Tolly hoped they would be. He liked the idea of being snowed up in a castle. By the light of the candles he could see the flakes drifting past the windows.

"What will the birds do?" he asked.

"They do not mind the snow so long as we feed them. Is your window open enough for the chaffinch to get in? Take some shortbread and make him welcome." Tolly did as she said. When he came down again the curtains were all drawn, and he settled down by the fire in hopes of another story.

"Granny, both my pieces of sugar have gone out of Feste's stall."

"Perhaps Boggis takes them and puts them in his tea," she said, laughing.

Tolly's face fell. He had never thought of anything so low-down, so common. He was shattered.

At that moment, while Mrs. Oldknow was still laughing at him, outside the door that led into the garden someone began a Christmas carol. Children's voices, delicate and expert, were singing "The Holly and the Ivy." Tolly had never heard such beautiful singing. He listened entranced.

O the rising of the sun
The running of the deer
The playing of the merrie organ
Sweet singing in the choir.

"What will they sing next?" he asked in a whisper, and waited in silence. "I saw three ships come sailing by" was the next, and then a carol Tolly did not know, which began, *'Tomorrow shall be my dancing day'* and which ended:

Sing O my love, my love, my love, my love
This have I done for my true love.

When that was finished there was a pause and a little girl's laugh—ah, he knew that laugh now! Mrs. Oldknow's eyes were fixed on him and she saw him start.

"Shall we let them in?" she asked. Tolly nodded, unable to speak. In his mind he could see the three of them standing there in the snow with their lanterns, ready to come in. She opened the door. Cold white snow blew in out of the darkness, nothing else. Mrs. Oldknow stood there smiling at nobody. Tolly flung himself face downwards into one of the big chairs, with angry tears.

"I want to be with them. I want to be with them. Why can't I be with them?" he cried. Mrs. Oldknow came to comfort him.

"Don't cry, my dear. You'll find them soon. They're like shy animals. They don't come just at first till they are sure. You mustn't be impatient." She stopped, then shook him. "Toseland, listen! Listen! Do you hear what I hear?"

Tolly sat up and strained his ears. Did he? Mrs. Oldknow opened the door again, and then he heard it. Faint and muffled by the falling snow a high insistent whinny came from the stables. Tolly listened with bright dry eyes, till the whinny ceased. Toby and Feste were together, and he, Tolly, was content that it should be so.

That night Mrs. Oldknow, when she came to see him to bed, stayed longer than usual. The chaffinch was already there, fluffed up in his cage with his head under his wing, taking no notice of either of them. The nightlight was lit, and Tolly was pleased to see on the ceiling in the patterned shadow of the cage, the shadow of a bird, as big as a football.

"See how much quicker the shadow-horse goes than the rocking-horse," said Mrs. Oldknow, giving it a forward push. The shadow-horse leaped ahead, stretching out a long neck and forward-pointing ears, as if it could leap out of the room at a bound.

"When I was little, I used to pretend the rocking-horse had got Feste's shadow instead of its own."

"Who told you about Feste?"

"My grandfather first. But afterwards I used to hear *them* talking."

Tolly had a very big question troubling him, that could not wait. He wriggled under the bed-clothes until only his eyes showed, and then in his smallest voice he asked: "Granny, do you see them?"

"Not always," she said, as if it were quite a simple thing to talk about.

"Did you see them to-night when you opened the door?"

"Yes, darling. They were all three there. At the very beginning I only saw them sometimes in mirrors."

Tolly came out from under the bed-clothes. "I do," he said proudly. "At least, only Alexander and Linnet, once."

"Toby is always the rarest. You see, he is so often with Feste."

"Do you ever see Feste?"

"Never," she said sadly. "But my grandfather told me he did sometimes."

Tolly breathed again. There was still hope. "Was his name Toseland too?"

"Yes, my dear, it was."

Tolly put the ebony mouse into his pyjama pocket, thinking to himself it would make it come warm more quickly. Mrs. Oldknow watched him.

"Is the mouse behaving?"

He grinned happily. "Not bad," he said.

A. Philippa Pearce

Tom's Midnight Garden

The activating force in this time-traveling fantasy is a desire: someone to play with, a friend. This longing transcends the bounds of time, altering dream and reality and bringing together two children from different centuries. Tom's nightly excursions to a Victorian garden where he is eagerly awaited by a lonely girl who becomes his closest friend are in rich contrast to the humdrum life he leads during the day with his dull aunt and uncle. Ultimately, Tom discovers that the Victorian child Hatty is still alive. She is old Mrs. Bartholomew who lives in the upstairs flat, and it is her dreams that draw him into the magic garden and her own childhood. This chapter shows the difference between Tom's two lives and the beginning of his efforts to solve the puzzle of time at the book's core. John Rowe Townsend, in *Written for Children*, says of this book, which won the Carnegie Medal for 1958: "If I were asked to name a single masterpiece of English children's literature since the

last war . . . it would be this outstandingly beautiful and absorbing book." [From A. Philippa Pearce, *Tom's Midnight Garden* (Oxford University Press, 1958).]

The Late Mr. Bartholomew

In the Kitsons' flat Time was not allowed to dodge about in the unreliable, confusing way it did in the garden—forward to a tree's falling, and then back to before the fall; and then still farther back again, to a little girl's first arrival; and then forward again. No, in the flat, Time was marching steadily onwards in the way it is supposed to go: from minute to minute, from hour to hour, from day to day.

The day for Tom's going home had already come and gone; but he was still staying with his aunt and uncle. He had managed that for himself: the very day before he was due to go, he had nerved himself, cleared his throat and said, 'I wish I hadn't to go home tomorrow.'

Uncle Alan had been reading the newspaper; the sheets crumpled down on to his knees, as though his hands no longer had the strength to hold them. His eyes refocused from the print on to Tom: 'What?'

'I wish I hadn't to go home tomorrow,' said Tom. He dared not go farther, but he spoke loudly. Aunt Gwen gave a cry of amazement and delight, and actually clapped her hands. 'Would you like to stay?'

'Yes.'

'Several days more? Another week?'

'Or more,' said Tom.

'We'll send a telegram at once,' said Aunt Gwen, and ran out.

Tom and his uncle were left together. Alan Kitson studied Tom with intent curiosity. 'Why do you want to stay here?'

'I won't, if you'd rather not,' said Tom, with pride; but his heart sank at the thought.

'No . . . No . . .' Uncle Alan still watched him. 'But I wondered why. . . . What is there to interest a boy here—to pass his time even?'

'I just like it here,' Tom muttered.

Aunt Gwen came back from sending her telegram to Tom's parents. Her face was flushed; she spoke fast and eagerly: 'We'll go about and see the sights and go excursions—we'll do so much now you're out of quarantine and staying on. You needn't be cooped up dully indoors any longer, Tom.'

Tom said, 'Thank you'; but without enthusiasm. He would have much preferred to be left to dullness indoors, as he used to be. He lived his real and interesting life at night-time, when he went into the garden; in the daytime, he wanted only peace—to think back and to think forwards, always to the garden; to write of the garden to Peter. He did not want to sleep, but, all the same, the daytime in the flat was like a period of sleep to him. He needed its rest.

Aunt Gwen arranged several expeditions to the shops and to the museum in Castleford and the cinema. Tom bore them patiently. He liked the cinema best, because he was in the dark, and so he could sit with his eyes shut and think his own thoughts.

Towards the end of Tom's lengthened stay, the weather changed for the worse. Still Aunt Gwen obstinately insisted on treats and trips, now with waterproofs and umbrella. After a visit to the cinema, she and Tom had been obliged to wait for some time for the bus, and Tom had stood in a puddle. It was his aunt who noticed his position, and that only as the bus came: 'Tom, you've been standing in a puddle all this time—quite a deep puddle!' He was surprised: his head had been in the clouds—in the white clouds that pile above an eternally summer garden—and he had not been noticing his feet at all. Now that he thought of them, they certainly felt very damp and cold.

'I hope you don't catch cold,' his aunt said anxiously.

In answer to this, Tom sneezed.

His aunt rushed him home to a hot drink and a hot bath and bed; but a cold, once it has its fingers on its victim, will seldom loosen its grip before the due time. So Tom had a severe cold, that kept him in bed for several days, and indoors for many more. His convalescence was not hurried. Gwen Kitson wrote happily to her sister that Tom would not be fit to travel for some time yet; and Tom wrote to Peter, 'It's a wonderful piece of luck—the next best thing to measles.'

Every night he was able to steal downstairs

as usual, into the garden; and there the feverishness of his chill always left him, as though the very greenness of trees and plants and grass cooled his blood. He played with Hatty.

In the daytime he lay back among his pillows, deliberately languid. Uncle Alan, who was touched by the idea of a sick child, offered to teach him chess; but Tom said he did not feel clear-headed enough. He did not want to talk; and he allowed his aunt to see that he was certainly not up to being read to from schoolgirl adventures.

At the beginning of Tom's illness, his head had really felt a little light; and his eyelids gummed themselves up easily. He did not mind keeping them closed: then, in his imagination, he could look into his garden and see, in fancy, what Hatty might be doing there.

His aunt would tiptoe into his bedroom and look at him doubtfully. She would test whether he were awake by a whispering of his name. The voice recalled him, without his understanding at once to what: his eyelids opened on to his own bedroom, but his eyes printed off the shadowy figure of Hatty against the barred window and the cupboard and between himself and the figure of his aunt at the foot of the bed.

Hatty's image haunted the room for Tom, at this time; and so it was, perhaps, that he began, at first idly, then seriously, to consider whether she herself were not, in some unusual way, a ghost. There was no one who knew her ghost story and could tell it to Tom, so he began trying to make it up for himself: Hatty had lived here, long, long ago—in this very house, with the garden he knew of; here she had lived, here died . . .

From below sounded the striking of Mrs Bartholomew's grandfather clock, that knew secrets but would not tell them. Listening, Tom suddenly caught his breath: Mrs Bartholomew, of course! She, of all people, might know something of the past history of this house; or rather, there must once have been a Mr Bartholomew, and his family had perhaps owned this house for generations, and therefore he had known all about it. He would surely have told his wife the history of it, which she would still remember.

Tom resolved that, as soon as he was better,

he would call on Mrs Bartholomew. True, she was an unsociable old woman of whom people were afraid; but Tom could not let that stand in his way. He would boldly ring her front door bell; she would open her front door just a crack and peer crossly out at him. Then she would see him, and at the sight of his face her heart would melt (Tom had read of such occurrences in the more old-fashioned children's books; he had never before thought them very probable, but now it suited him to believe): Mrs Bartholomew, who did not like children, would love Tom as soon as she saw his face. She would draw him inside at once, then and there; and later, over a tea-table laden with delicacies for him alone, she would tell Tom the stories of long ago. Sometimes Tom would ask questions, and she would answer them. 'A little girl called Harriet, or Hatty?' she would say, musingly. 'Why, yes, my late husband told me once of such a child—oh! long ago! An only child she was, and an orphan. When her parents died, her aunt took her into this house to live. Her aunt was a disagreeable woman . . .'

So the story, in Tom's imagination, rolled on. It became confused and halting where Tom himself did not already know the facts; but, after all, he would only have to wait to pay his call upon Mrs Bartholomew, to hear it all from her own lips. She would perhaps end her story, he thought, with a dropping of her voice: 'And since then, Tom, they say that she and her garden and all the rest haunt this house. They say that those who are lucky may go down, about when the clock strikes for midnight, and open what was once the garden door and see the ghost of that garden and of the little girl.'

Tom's mind ran on the subject. His cold was getting so much better now that his aunt and uncle had insisted on coming to sit with him, to keep him company. One day, hardly speaking aloud, Tom began a sentence: 'When Mr Bartholomew lived in this house—'

'But I don't think Mr Bartholomew ever did live here,' said Aunt Gwen. 'Do you, Alan?'

Uncle Alan did not answer at first, being in the depths of a chess problem in which he had failed to interest Tom.

'But, Aunt Gwen,' Tom protested, 'this was his family home. How else would he have known the history of this house, and the ghost stories too? How else could he have told Mrs Bartholomew?'

'Why, Tom—' said his aunt, in bewilderment.

'Mr Bartholomew, whoever he was, never lived in this house,' Uncle Alan now said positively. 'Mrs Bartholomew was a widow when she came here; and that wasn't so many years ago, either.'

'But what about the clock?'

'What clock?'

'The grandfather clock in the hall. You said it belonged to Mrs Bartholomew; but that clock has always been in this house. It was here long, long ago—it was here when the house had a garden.'

'Now, what reason have you for supposing all this, Tom?' asked Uncle Alan. He spoke less sharply than usual, because he really thought the boy must be feverish.

Tom was searching in his mind for an explanation that yet would not give away his secret, when his aunt came unexpectedly to his rescue. 'You know, Alan, the clock certainly must have been here a long time, because of its screws at the back having rusted into the wall.'

'Well, now, Tom, that might explain a little,' said Uncle Alan. He patted Tom's hand, as it lay on the counterpane, to soothe him. 'The clock may well have been here a long time, as you say, and during that time the screws rusted up. After that happened, the clock couldn't be moved without danger of damaging it. When old Mrs Bartholomew came, she had to buy the clock with the house. You see, Tom? It's all quite straightforward, if you reason it out.'

From that time, abruptly, Tom ceased to hope for anything from Mrs Bartholomew.

The possibility of Hatty's being a ghost stayed in his mind, however—at the back of his mind. He was not even aware of the presence of the idea, until one day in the garden it became the cause of a quarrel with Hatty herself. It was the only real quarrel that ever took place between them.

They were beginning to build their tree-house, in the Steps of St Paul's; as usual, Tom was directing, while Hatty did the work of pulling and plaiting branches together, to make the walls. The floor—of old pieces of boarding that Hatty had found in the potting-shed—was already in place.

Hatty, as she worked, was singing to herself from hymns and songs and ballads. Now she was singing the end of the ballad of Sweet Molly Malone:

'Her ghost wheels her barrow
Through streets broad and narrow,
Singing, "Cockles and Mussels,
Alive—alive-oh!" '

And Hatty continued to hum and murmur, under her breath, the refrain: 'Alive—alive-oh! Alive—alive-oh!'

Suddenly Tom said—he blurted it out before he could help himself: 'What's it like—I mean, I wonder what it's like to be dead and a ghost?'

Hatty stopped singing at once, and looked at him slyly over her shoulder, and laughed. Tom repeated the question: 'What is it like to be a ghost?'

'Like?' said Hatty. She turned fully to face him, and laid a hand upon his knee, and looked eagerly into his face. 'Ah, tell me, Tom!'

For a moment, Tom did not understand her; then he jumped to his feet and shouted: 'I'm not a ghost!'

'Don't be silly, Tom,' Hatty said. 'You forget that I saw you go right through the orchard door when it was shut.'

'That proves what I say!' said Tom. 'I'm not a ghost, but the orchard door is, and that was why I could go through it. The door's a ghost, and the garden's a ghost; and so are you, too!'

'Indeed I'm not; you are!'

They were glaring at each other now; Hatty was trembling. 'You're a silly little boy!' she said (and Tom thought resentfully that she seemed to have been growing up a good deal too much recently). 'And you make a silly little ghost! Why do you think you wear those clothes of yours? None of my cousins ever played in the garden in clothes like that. Such outdoor clothes can't belong to nowadays, *I* know! Such clothes!'

'They're my pyjamas,' said Tom, indignantly, 'my best visiting pyjamas! I sleep in them. And this is my bedroom slipper.' His second

slipper had been left, as usual, to wedge the flat-door upstairs.

'And you go about so, in the daytime, always in your night-clothes!' Hatty said scornfully. 'And it's the fashion nowadays, is it, to wear only one slipper? Really, you are silly to give such excuses! You wear strange clothes that no one wears nowadays, because you're a ghost. Why, I'm the only person in the garden who sees you! I can see a ghost.'

Hatty would never believe the real explanation of his clothes, and Tom chose what he thought was a shorter counter-argument: 'Do you know I could put my hand through you—now—just as if you weren't there?'

Hatty laughed.

'I could—I could!' shouted Tom.

She pointed at him: 'You're a ghost!'

In a passion, Tom hit her a blow upon the outstretched wrist. There was great force of will as well as of muscle behind the blow, and his hand went right through—not quite as through thin air, for Tom felt a something, and Hatty snatched back her wrist and nursed it in her other hand. She looked as if she might cry, but that could not have been for any pain, for the sensation had not been strong enough. In a wild defence of herself, Hatty still goaded him: 'Your hand didn't go through my wrist; my wrist went through your hand! You're a ghost, with a cruel, ghostly hand!'

'Do you hear me?' Tom shouted. 'You're a ghost, and I've proved it! You're dead and gone and a ghost!'

There was a quietness, then, in which could be heard a cuckoo's stuttering cry from the wood beyond the garden; and then the sound of Hatty's beginning softly to weep. 'I'm not dead—oh, please, Tom, I'm not dead!' Now that the shouting had stopped, Tom was not sure of the truth, after all, but only sure that Hatty was crying as he had never seen her cry since she had been a very little girl, wearing mourning-black and weeping her way along the sundial path—weeping for death so early.

He put his arm round her: 'All right, then, Hatty! You're not a ghost—I take it all back—all of it. Only don't cry!'

He calmed her; and she consented at last to dry her tears and go back to plaiting the branches, only sniffing occasionally. Tom did not reopen a subject that upset her so deeply, although he felt that he owed it to himself to say, some time later, 'Mind you, I'm not a ghost either!' This, by her silence, Hatty seemed to allow.

Penelope Lively

The Ghost of Thomas Kempe

Penelope Lively's finely crafted fantasies always concern the past rubbing intriguingly, at times uncomfortably, against the present. Here she humorously depicts the ill-tempered, out-of-place ghost of a seventeenth-century apothecary and sorcerer who is disgusted with the modern world after being accidentally freed from imprisonment in a bottle. Poor James, an ordinary, cheerful boy, becomes so plagued by this message-mad poltergeist that he resorts to the services of Bert Ellison, a local exorcist practicing his trade in their small village in contemporary Oxfordshire, England. Throughout the course of the novel, James discovers that memory and the past are not dead history, that time reaches forward and back, uniting generations of children and adults and the child within the adult; as he says, "People [have] layers, like onions." This book won the 1973 Carnegie Medal. [From Penelope Lively, *The Ghost of Thomas Kempe* (Dutton, 1973).]

Bert Ellison arrived on a bicycle shortly after tea, whistling. He looked so ordinary, so, in fact, like a builder on his way to put up some shelves that for a moment James's faith was shaken. Only ten minutes before he had enjoyed saying to Simon, "Well, I'm afraid I'll have to go now because I've got this exorcist coming in to see to the poltergeist." Simon had been satisfactorily astonished. But now here was Bert, in white overalls, with a cigarette tucked behind his ear, and a black bag of tools, not looking in the least like an exorcist.

"Oh," said Mrs. Harrison. "Yes, of course, the window, and the shelves. . . . I'd better take you up."

James, lurking behind her in the hall, fidgeted anxiously, and saw Bert's gaze come up over her shoulder and fall on him. The man pushed

his cap back from his forehead, unhitched the cigarette from his ear and said, "Maybe your young lad could do that. Not to bother you, see?" James was filled with relief.

Mrs. Harrison said, "Well, yes, you could, couldn't you, James?" and went back into the kitchen. James looked at Bert Ellison, and Bert Ellison nodded, and they went upstairs, James leading and Bert following, his heavy tread making the whole staircase sway slightly.

James opened the door to his room and they went in. Tim, asleep on the bed, woke up with a start and growled.

Bert looked at him thoughtfully. "I seen him before," he said. "Let's think now. . . . At the butcher's before Christmas, and The Red Lion before that, and the corner shop the year before that. He knows when he's onto a good thing, that one." Tim, with an evil look, slunk past him and out of the door. Bert set his tools down with a clatter and surveyed the room. "Right, then, where are we putting these shelves?"

"But," began James anxiously, "the other thing. . . ."

"Look," said Bert. "We've got to be doing something, haven't we? If your mum decides to come up. Not larking about looking for ghosts. These shelves has got to go up, and be heard to go up."

James understood. "Here," he said, "under the window."

Bert began to measure, and cut pieces of wood. "So he played up when the vicar was here, this bloke?"

"I'll say," said James. "It was one of the worst times. Knocked things over, and banged."

"Then it's not worth trying bell, book, and candle," said Bert. "If he's got no respect for the Church. I'd just be wasting my time. Nor's it worth getting twelve of them."

"Twelve what?"

"Vicars," said Bert briefly.

James had a delightful, momentary vision of twelve enormous vicars following one another up the stairs, hitting their heads on the beams, and apologizing in chorus. But Bert was not just being fanciful. He was not a man given to fancy. Apparently ghosts were normally exorcised by twelve priests in the old days.

Or seven, sometimes. Or just one, if skilled in such matters.

"But that won't do with this blighter," said Bert. He lit the cigarette from behind his ear, made some token noises with hammer and nails, and looked round the room reflectively. James waited for him to come to a decision, anxious, but at the same time deeply thankful to be thus sharing the burden of responsibility for Thomas Kempe. He felt relieved of a heavy weight, or at least partly relieved.

"No," said Bert. "We won't try anything like that. Nor talking to him, neither, since you say you've already had a go. You know what I think? I think we'll try bottling him." He put a plank of wood across the chair, knelt on it, and began to saw it in half, whistling through his teeth.

"Bottling him?" said James, wondering if he could have heard correctly.

"That's right. I'll be wanting a bottle with a good firm stopper. Cork 'ud be best. And seven candles."

"Now?"

"Might as well get on with it, mightn't we?"

James raced downstairs. On the landing he slowed up, remembering the need for discretion. He crept down the next flight, and tiptoed into the larder. He could hear his mother and Helen talking in the kitchen, and from overhead came reassuringly ordinary sawing and hammering noises made by Bert. He felt nervous on several counts: there was the problem of someone asking him what he wanted, and also he kept expecting the sorcerer to manifest himself in some way. What was he doing? Could he be scared of Bert Ellison? Or was he biding his time before launching some furious counter-attack? From what Thomas Kempe had revealed of his character hitherto, he didn't seem the kind of person to be all that easily routed, even by as phlegmatic an opponent as Bert Ellison.

There were various empty medicine bottles on the larder shelf. He selected the one with the tightest-fitting cork and began to look for candles. There was a box of gaily coloured birthday cake ones, complete with rose-shaped holders, but they seemed inappropriate. He hunted round and unearthed a packet of uncom-

promisingly plain white ones—an emergency supply for electricity cuts. They were just right: serviceable and not frivolous. He was just putting them under his arm when the door opened.

"Mum says if you're picking at the plum tart you're not to," said Helen. "What *are* you doing with those candles?"

"The builder needs them," said James. "He's got to solder the shelves with something, hasn't he? He can't solder the rivets without a candle, can he? Or the sprockets." He stared at her, icily: Helen's ignorance of carpentry was total, he knew.

She looked at the candles suspiciously. "I don't see . . ." she began.

"You wouldn't," said James, wriggling past her. "I should go and ask Mum to explain. Very slowly and carefully, so you'll be able to follow all right. Or if you like I will later on." He shot up the stairs without waiting to hear what she had to say.

Bert had cleared the table and moved it to the centre of the room.

"Ah," he said, "that'll do fine. We'll have it in the middle, the bottle, and the candles in a circle round, like. He seems to be keeping himself to himself, your chap. I thought we'd have heard something from him by now."

"So did I," said James.

"Maybe he's lying low to see what we've got in mind. Is that his pipe on the shelf there?"

"Yes."

Bert walked over and picked it up. As he did so the window slammed shut.

"There. He don't like having his property interfered with. Well, that signifies."

"Can we get on," said James uneasily, "with whatever we're going to do."

"No good rushing a thing like this," said Bert. "You've got to take your time. Make a good job of it." He fiddled around with the bottle and candles, arranging them to his liking. Then he struck a match and lit the candles. The flames staggered and twitched for a moment, then settled down into steady, oval points of light.

"We'd best draw the curtains," said Bert. "We don't want people looking in from outside. Then pull up a chair and sit down."

With the curtains drawn, the room was half dark, the corners lost in gloom, everything concentrated on the circle of yellow lights on the table. Bert and James sat opposite one another. The candles made craggy black shadows on Bert's face, so that it seemed different: older, less ordinary. Downstairs, a long way away, the wireless was playing and someone was running a tap.

Bert took out a handkerchief and wiped his forehead. "Right, then." He cleared his throat and said ponderously, "Rest, thou unquiet spirit!"

There was dead silence. Bert, catching James's eye, looked away in embarrassment and said, "I don't hold with thee-ing and thou-ing, as a rule, but when you're dealing with a bloke like this—well, I daresay he'd expect it."

James nodded. They sat quite still. Nothing happened. "Return from whence thou come—came," said Bert. "Begone!"

Two of the candles on James's side of the table guttered wildly, and went out.

"Ah!" said Bert, "now he's paying us a bit of attention."

They waited. James could hear his mother's voice, distantly, saying something about potatoes from the sack in the shed. Uneasy, he leaned across towards Bert and whispered, "Will it take long?"

"Depends," said Bert. "It's no good chivvying these characters. You got to let them take their time."

A draught whisked round the table. Three more candles went out.

"Cheeky so-and-so, isn't he?" said Bert.

"Does he know what he's supposed to do?" whispered James.

"He knows all right."

But how would *they* realise it if and when Thomas Kempe did decide to conform and get into the bottle, James wondered? He wanted to ask, but felt that perhaps too much talk was unsuitable. Presumably Bert, as an experienced exorcist, would just know in some mysterious way.

"Come on, now," said Bert. "Let's be 'aving you."

The last two candle flames reached up, long and thin, then contracted into tiny points, went intensely blue, and vanished.

"That's it!" said Bert. He got up and drew the curtains.

James looked round anxiously. "Didn't it work?"

"No. He wasn't having any. When the candles go out, that's it."

"Couldn't we try again?"

"There wouldn't be any point to it. If he don't fancy it, then he don't fancy it, and that's that. He's an awkward cuss, no doubt about it."

The stairs creaked. James whipped the candles off the table and into his drawer. Bert hastily began to saw up a piece of wood.

Mrs. Harrison came in. "Everything all right?" she said. "You mustn't let James get in your way, Mr. Ellison. I'm afraid he hangs around rather, sometimes."

"That's all right," said Bert. "I'm not fussed. I can send him packing when I've had enough."

"Good. What a funny smell. Wax, or something."

"That'll be my matches," said Bert, "I daresay."

Mrs. Harrison said, "Candles, I'd have thought." She looked round, sniffing.

"Not to my way of thinking," said Bert. "That's a match smell, that is."

"Oh. Well, maybe." She gave Bert a look tinged with misgiving and looked at the pile of half-sawn wood: the thought seemed to be passing through her mind that not much had been achieved so far.

"I got behind," said Bert amiably. "We've been having a bit of a chat, me and your lad here. Found we had one or two interests in common, as you might say."

"Oh?" said Mrs. Harrison.

"History. People that aren't around any more. We've both got a fancy for that kind of thing." Bert's right eyelid dropped in a conspicuous wink, aimed towards James.

"That's nice," said Mrs. Harrison. "We hadn't realised James was particularly interested in history, I must say."

"It's often their own parents as knows children least, isn't it?" said Bert.

"I'm not entirely sure about that," said Mrs.

Harrison drily. James, avoiding her eye, busied himself with a pile of nails.

"So, one way and another, I think I'll have to come back tomorrow and finish off," said Bert, stowing hammer and saw into his black bag. "I like to make a proper job of anything I take on. See it through to the end."

Mrs. Harrison said, "Right you are, then," and went downstairs. James and Bert Ellison, left alone, looked at each other.

"No," said Bert, "I can see she wouldn't have much time for ghosts, your mum. A bit set in her ways, maybe. Got opinions."

"Yes," said James with feeling, "she has."

"Not that I've got anything against that. I like a woman to know her own mind. But it's no good setting yourself up against it. You'd just be wasting your breath." He pushed his ruler and pencil into the pocket of his white overalls, closed the tool bag, and stood up.

James said anxiously, "What about tomorrow? Is there something else you can try?"

"To be honest with you," said Bert, "there's not a lot. Vicars is out. He don't fancy the bottle." His large stubby fingers came down on his palm, ticking off possibilities. "We could try fixing him with a job as would keep him busy, but I'd guess he's too fly to be taken in with that one. Or we could try circle and rowan stick. Is your father an Oxford man, by any chance?"

"An Oxford man?"

"Did he go to Oxford University?"

"No," said James. "Why?"

"In the old days you used an Oxford man for laying a ghost. But I daresay there's not many would take it on nowadays. They've got fancy ideas in education now, I hear."

"Isn't there anything then?" said James disconsolately.

"It's a tricky job, this one, no doubt about that."

"You see, I'm getting blamed for everything he does. It's no pocket money, and no pudding, and worse, I should think, when they run out of punishments."

"That's a bit thick," said Bert.

"I'll say."

"The trouble is, them being nonbelievers. In the normal way of things, it'd be them as would have called me in, in the first place. Things would have been a lot more straightforward."

They were going down the stairs now. James glanced anxiously at the closed kitchen door. Bert nodded and lowered his voice. "Tell you what, I got those shelves to finish off, so I'll be back tomorrow."

"Thank you very much," said James. "Oh, I nearly forgot. . . ." He reached into his jeans pocket for his money.

"No charge," said Bert, "not till the job's done satisfactory." He climbed onto his bike and rode away down the lane, the black bag bumping against the mudguard.

James had been right in thinking that the sorcerer might be biding his time. That evening, as though in compensation for the restraint he had shown during Bert Ellison's visit (if it had been restraint, and not, perhaps, a temporary retreat in face of a professional enemy), he let rip. Doors slammed, and the house echoed with thumps and bumps, almost invariably coming from whatever area James was currently occupying, so that cries of "James! Stop that appalling noise!" rang up and down the stairs. The television set, just repaired, developed a new fault: a high-pitched buzzing that coincided oddly with all weather forecasts and any programme involving policemen or doctors (which seemed to be most of them). The teapot parted from its handle when Mrs. Harrison lifted it up, with catastrophic results. Something caused Tim, sleeping peacefully under the kitchen table, to shoot out yelping as though propelled by someone's foot, colliding with, and tripping up, Mr. Harrison, who fell against the dustbin which overturned, shooting tea leaves and eggshells across the floor. . . . You could put whatever interpretation you liked on all this: coincidence, carelessness, the weather, the malevolence of fate. James knew quite well to what he would attribute it, and so, apparently, did Tim, who abandoned his usual evening sleeping places and went to sulk in the long grass at the end of the orchard.

After a couple of hours Mr. and Mrs. Harrison, both remarkably even-tempered people in the normal way of things, were reduced to a state of simmering irritation, which eventually resulted in both James and Helen being sent up to bed early and, they felt, unloved. They shared their resentment on the stairs.

"It's not fair," said Helen.

"It's not *our* fault."

"Everything keeps going wrong these days. I think it's something to do with this house."

James stared. Such perception was unlike Helen: she seemed usually to notice only the obvious. Perhaps she was changing. Since they seemed to have established a temporary truce, he decided to investigate further.

"Helen?"

"Mmm."

"Do you believe in ghosts?"

Helen said cautiously, "Do you?"

"Well. I s'pose so. Yes, actually I do."

"So do I, really." They looked at each other. *"They* don't," said Helen. "Mum and Dad."

"I know. But lots of people do."

"Why do you want to know anyway? I say, you don't think there's one in this house, do you?"

James hesitated, tempted to confide. But you never know with Helen. . . . She might well laugh, tell everyone, never let him hear the end of it. And he'd have to share Bert Ellison. "Shouldn't think so," he said, turning away. "Good night."

"Good night."

He climbed the last few stairs to his room slowly, thinking of what he might have said to her. "Yes, as a matter of fact there is. He's called Thomas Kempe, Esq., and he lived here a few hundred years ago and was a kind of sorcerer and crazy doctor and village policeman and general busybody and he thinks he's come back to start all over again with me helping and he keeps writing me messages and as a matter of fact I've been sharing my bedroom with him for over a week now." Ha ha!

He opened the door. The bottle he and Bert Ellison had used in the exorcism attempt was in the middle of the floor, smashed. Beside it was Thomas Kempe's latest message, written in felt pen on the back of an envelope.

Doe not thinke that I am so dull of witte that I may be thus trycked twyce.

C. S. Lewis

Prince Caspian

For many years, C. S. Lewis held the Chair of Medieval and Renaissance English Literature at Cambridge. His worlds are peopled with creatures who derive from his deep roots of scholarship and long association with the traditional literatures of the world: giants, centaurs, dwarfs, dryads, nymphs, and talking beasts and animals. They move in a different ambience from their origins, reflecting Lewis's particular exaltation and his lifelong concern with the deepest significance of Christian faith. The Lion, Aslan, the great Lord of Narnia, moves through the tales, the shadow of Christ himself upon him.

The genius of the fantasist lies not only in the enormousness of the concept of his tale, and the extent of his passionate belief in it, but also in his ability to give it a setting in time and space, to endow it with weather and a geography and atmosphere of reality. In addition he must invent a spirited plot, with dramatic action and the tension between triumph and failure sustained to the breaking point. These are the attributes to which the children respond, caught up as they have been now for more than a generation in these full-bodied tales, in which real children are entrapped in fantastic adventure.

Lewis is master of invention, and of convincing detail. Consider the naming of things and people, which is always a test of the quality of imagination: for dwarfs, such names as Trumpkin and Trufflehunter; Glenstorm, the Centaur; Wimbleweather, a rather small giant; and the memorable Reepicheep, a heroic mouse.

"Narnia! Narnia! Narnia, awake. Love. Think. Speak. Be Walking Trees. Be Talking Beasts. Be Divine Waters."* So the spell is cast. Lewis himself recommends that the Narnia books be read in the following sequence: *The Magician's Nephew* (1955); *The Lion, the Witch and the Wardrobe* (1950); *The Horse and His Boy* (1954); *Prince Caspian* (1951); *The Voyage of the Dawn Treader* (1952); *The Silver Chair* (1953); *The Last Battle* (1956).

The chapter from *Prince Caspian* was chosen for inclusion here because it is typical of recurring scenes in the books. A hard battle is waged between a boy and a great traitor King, and the resulting celebration of joyous triumph brings together a characteristic conglomeration of creatures from the worlds of C. S. Lewis. [From C. S. Lewis, *Prince Caspian* (Macmillan, 1951).]

---

* From *The Magician's Nephew.*

How They Were All Very Busy

A little before two o'clock Trumpkin and the Badger sat with the rest of the creatures at the wood's edge looking across at the gleaming line of Miraz's army which was about two arrow-shots away. In between, a square space of level grass had been staked for the combat. At the two far corners stood Glozelle and Sopespian with drawn swords. At the near corners were Giant Wimbleweather and the Bulgy Bear, who in spite of all their warnings was sucking his paws and looking, to tell the truth, uncommonly silly. To make up for this, Glenstorm on the right of the lists, stock-still except when he stamped a hind hoof occasionally on the turf, looked much more imposing than the Telmarine baron who faced him on the left. Peter had just shaken hands with Edmund and the Doctor, and was now walking down to the combat. It was like the moment before the pistol goes at an important race, but very much worse.

"I wish Aslan had turned up before it came to this," said Trumpkin.

"So do I," said Trufflehunter. "But look behind you."

"Crows and crockery!" muttered the Dwarf as soon as he had done so. "What are they? Huge people—beautiful people—like gods and goddesses and giants. Hundreds and thousands of them, closing in behind us. What are they?"

"It's the Dryads and Hamadryads and Silvans," said Trufflehunter. "Aslan has waked them."

"Humph!" said the Dwarf. "That'll be very useful if the enemy try any treachery. But it won't help the High King very much if Miraz proves handier with his sword."

The Badger said nothing, for now Peter and Miraz were entering the lists from opposite ends, both on foot, both in chain shirts, with helmets and shields. They advanced till they were close together. Both bowed and seemed to speak, but it was impossible to hear what they said. Next moment the two swords flashed in the sunlight. For a second the clash could be heard but it was immediately drowned because both armies began shouting like crowds at a football match.

"Well done, Peter, oh well done!" shouted Edmund as he saw Miraz reel back a whole pace and a half. "Follow it up, quick!" And Peter did, and for a few seconds it looked as if the fight might be won. But then Miraz pulled himself together; began to make real use of his height and weight. "Miraz! Miraz! The King, the King," came the roar of the Telmarines. Caspian and Edmund grew white with sickening anxiety.

"Peter is taking some dreadful knocks," said Edmund.

"Hullo!" said Caspian. "What's happening now?"

"Both falling apart," said Edmund. "A bit blown, I expect. Watch. Ah, now they're beginning again, more scientifically this time. Circling round and round, feeling each other's defences."

"I'm afraid this Miraz knows his work," muttered the Doctor. But hardly had he said this when there was such a clapping and baying and throwing up of hoods among the Old Narnians that it was nearly deafening.

"What was it? What was it?" asked the Doctor. "My old eyes missed it."

"The High King has pricked him in the armpit," said Caspian, still clapping. "Just where the arm-hole of the hauberk let the point through. First blood."

"It's looking ugly again now, though," said Edmund. "Peter's not using his shield properly. He must be hurt in the left arm."

It was only too true. Everyone could see that Peter's shield hung limp. The shouting of the Telmarines redoubled.

"You've seen more battles than I," said Caspian. "Is there any chance now?"

"Precious little," said Edmund. "I suppose he might *just* do it. With luck."

"Oh, why did we let it happen at all?" said Caspian.

Suddenly all the shouting on both sides died down. Edmund was puzzled for a moment. Then he said, "Oh, I see. They've both agreed to a rest. Come on, Doctor. You and I may be able to do something for the High King." They ran down to the lists and Peter came outside the ropes to meet them, his face red and sweaty, his chest heaving.

"Is your left arm wounded?" asked Edmund.

"It's not exactly a wound," Peter said. "I got the full weight of his shoulder on my shield—like a load of bricks—and the rim of the shield drove into my wrist. I don't think it's broken, but it might be a sprain. If you could tie it up very tight I think I could manage."

While they were doing this, Edmund asked anxiously, "What do you think of him, Peter?"

"Tough," said Peter. "Very tough. I have a chance if I can keep him on the hop till his weight and short wind come against him—in this hot sun too. To tell the truth. I haven't much chance else. Give my love to . . . to everyone at home, Ed, if he gets me. Here he comes into the lists again. So long, old chap. Good-bye, Doctor. And I say, Ed, say something specially nice to Trumpkin. He's been a brick."

Edmund couldn't speak. He walked back with the Doctor to his own lines with a sick feeling in his stomach.

But the new bout went well. Peter now seemed to be able to make some use of his shield, and he certainly made good use of his feet. He was almost playing Tig with Miraz now, keeping out of range, shifting his ground, making the enemy work.

"Coward!" booed the Telmarines. "Why don't you stand up to him? Don't you like it, eh? Thought you'd come to fight, not dance. Yah!"

"Oh, I do hope he won't listen to them," said Caspian.

"Not he," said Edmund. "You don't know him—Oh!"—for Miraz had got in a blow at last, on Peter's helmet. Peter staggered, slipped sideways and fell on one knee. The roar of the Telmarines rose like the noise of the sea. "Now, Miraz," they yelled. "Now. Quick! Quick! Kill him." But indeed there was no need to egg the usurper on. He was on top of Peter already. Edmund bit his lips till the blood came, as the sword flashed down on Peter. It looked as if it would slash off his head. Thank heavens! it had glanced down his right shoulder. The dwarf-wrought mail was sound and did not break.

"Great Scott," cried Edmund. "He's up again. Peter, go it, Peter."

"I couldn't see what happened," said the Doctor. "How did he do it?"

"Grabbed Miraz's arm as it came down," said Trumpkin, dancing with delight. "There's a man for you. Uses his enemy's arm as a ladder. The High King! The High King! Up, Old Narnia."

"Look," said Trufflehunter. "Miraz is angry. It is good."

They were certainly at it hammer and tongs now; such a flurry of blows that it seemed impossible for either not to be killed. As the excitement grew, the shouting almost died away. The spectators were holding their breath. It was most horrible and most magnificent.

A great shout arose from the Old Narnians. Miraz was down—not struck by Peter, but face downwards, having tripped on a tussock. Peter stepped back waiting for him to rise.

"Oh bother, bother, bother," said Edmund to himself. "Need he be as gentlemanly as all that? I suppose he must. Comes of being a Knight *and* a High King. I suppose it is what Aslan would like. But that brute will be up again in a minute and then—"

But "that brute" never rose. The Lords Glozelle and Sopespian had their own plans ready. As soon as they saw their King down they leaped into the lists crying, "Treachery! Treachery! The Narnian traitor has stabbed him in the back while he lay helpless. To arms! To arms, Telmar."

Peter hardly understood what was happening. He saw two big men running towards him with drawn swords. Then the third Telmarine had leaped over the ropes on his left. "To arms, Narnia. Treachery!" Peter shouted. If all three had set upon him at once he would never have spoken again. But Glozelle stopped to stab his own King dead where he lay: "That's for your insult, this morning," he whispered as the blade went home. Peter swung to face Sopespian, slashed his legs from under him and, with the backcut of the same stroke, walloped off his head. Edmund was now at his side crying, "Narnia, Narnia. The Lion." The whole Telmarine army was rushing towards them. But now the Giant was stamping forward, stooping low and swinging his club. The Centaurs charged. *Twang, twang* behind, and *hiss, hiss* overhead came the archery of Dwarfs. Trumpkin was fighting at his left. Full battle was joined.

"Come back, Reepicheep, you little ass!" shouted Peter. "You'll only be killed. This is no place for mice." But the ridiculous little creatures were dancing in and out among the feet of both armies, jabbing with their swords. Many a Telmarine warrior that day felt his foot suddenly pierced as if by a dozen skewers, hopped on one leg cursing the pain, and fell as often as not. If he fell, the mice finished him off; if he did not, someone else did.

But almost before the Old Narnians were really warmed to their work they found the enemy giving way. Tough-looking warriors turned white, gazed in terror not on the Old Narnians but on something behind them, and then flung down their weapons, shrieking, "The Wood! The Wood! The end of the world!"

But soon neither their cries nor the sound of weapons could be heard any more, for both were drowned in the ocean-like roar of the Awakened Trees as they plunged through the ranks of Peter's army, and then on, in pursuit of the Telmarines. Have you ever stood at the edge of a great wood on a high ridge when a wild southwester broke over it in full fury on an autumn evening? Imagine that sound. And then imagine that the wood, instead of being fixed to one place, was rushing *at* you; and was no longer trees but huge people; yet still like trees because their long arms waved like branches and their heads tossed and leaves fell round them in showers. It was like that for the Telmarines. It was a little alarming even for the Narnians. In a few minutes all Miraz's followers were running down to the Great River in the hope of crossing the bridge to the town of Beruna and there defending themselves behind ramparts and closed gates.

They reached the river, but there was no bridge. It had disappeared since yesterday. Then utter panic and horror fell upon them and they all surrendered.

But what had happened to the bridge?

Early that morning, after a few hours' sleep, the girls had waked, to see Aslan standing over them and to hear his voice saying, "We will make holiday." They rubbed their eyes and looked round them. The Trees had all gone but could still be seen moving away towards Aslan's How in a dark mass. Bacchus and the Maenads—his fierce, madcap girls—and Silenus, were still with them. Lucy, fully rested, jumped up. Everyone was awake, everyone was laughing, flutes were playing, cymbals clashing. Animals, not Talking Animals, were crowding in upon them from every direction.

"What is it, Aslan?" said Lucy, her eyes dancing and her feet wanting to dance.

"Come, children," said he. "Ride on my back again to-day."

"Oh lovely!" cried Lucy, and both girls climbed on to the warm golden back as they had done no-one knew how many years before. Then the whole party moved off—Aslan leading, Bacchus and his Maenads leaping, rushing, and turning somersaults. The beasts frisking round them, and Silenus and his donkey bringing up the rear.

They turned a little to the right, raced down a steep hill, and found the long bridge of Beruna in front of them. Before they had begun to cross it, however, up out of the water came a great wet, bearded head, larger than a man's, crowned with rushes. It looked at Aslan and out of its mouth a deep voice came.

"Hail, Lord," it said. "Loose my chains."

"Who on earth is *that?*" whispered Susan.

"I think it's the river-god, but hush," said Lucy.

"Bacchus," said Aslan. "Deliver him from his chains."

"That means the bridge, I expect," thought Lucy. And so it did. Bacchus and his people splashed forward into the shallow water, and a minute later the most curious things began happening. Great, strong trunks of ivy came curling up all the piers of the bridge, growing as quickly as a fire grows, wrapping the stones round, splitting, breaking, separating them. The walls of the bridge turned into hedges gay with hawthorn for a moment then disappeared as the whole thing with a rush and a rumble collapsed into the swirling water. With much splashing, screaming, and laughter the revellers waded or swam or danced across the ford ("Hurrah! It's the Fords of Beruna again now!"

cried the girls) and up the bank on the far side and into the town.

Everyone in the streets fled before their faces. The first house they came to was a school: a girl's school, where a lot of Narnian girls, with their hair done very tight and ugly tight collars round their necks and thick tickly stockings on their legs, were having a history lesson. The sort of "History" that was taught in Narnia under Miraz's rule was duller than the truest history you ever read and less true than the most exciting adventure story.

"If you don't attend, Gwendolen," said the mistress, "and stop looking out of the window, I shall have to give you an order-mark."

"But please, Miss Prizzle—" began Gwendolen.

"Did you hear what I said, Gwendolen?" asked Miss Prizzle.

"But please, Miss Prizzle," said Gwendolen, "there's a LION!"

"Take two order-marks for talking nonsense," said Miss Prizzle. "And now—" A roar interrupted her. Ivy came curling in at the windows of the classroom. The walls became a mass of shimmering green, and leafy branches arched overhead where the ceiling had been. Miss Prizzle found she was standing on grass in a forest glade. She clutched at her desk to steady herself, and found that the desk was a rose-bush. Wild people such as she had never even imagined were crowding round her. Then she saw the lion, screamed and fled, and with her fled her class, who were mostly dumpy, prim little girls with fat legs. Gwendolen hesitated.

"You'll stay with us, sweetheart?" said Aslan.

"Oh, *may* I? Thank you, thank you," said Gwendolen. Instantly she joined hands with two of the Maenads who whirled her round in a merry dance and helped her take off some of the unnecessary and uncomfortable clothes that she was wearing.

Wherever they went in the little town of Beruna it was the same. Most of the people fled, a few joined them. When they left the town they were a larger and a merrier company.

They swept on across the level fields on the north bank, or left bank, of the river. At every farm animals came out to join them. Sad old donkeys who had never known joy grew suddenly young again; chained dogs broke their chains; horses kicked their carts to pieces and came trotting along with them—clop-clop—kicking up the mud and whinnying.

At a well in a yard they met a man who was beating a boy. The stick burst into flower in the man's hand. He tried to drop it, but it stuck to his hand. His arm became a branch, his body the trunk of a tree, his feet took root. The boy, who had been crying a moment before, burst out laughing and joined them.

At a little town half way to Beaversdam, where two rivers met, they came to another school, where a tired-looking girl was teaching arithmetic to a number of boys who looked very like pigs. She looked out of the window and saw the divine revellers singing up the street and a stab of joy went through her heart. Aslan stopped right under the window and looked up at her.

"Oh don't, don't," she said. "I'd love to. But I mustn't. I must stick to my work. And the children would be frightened if they saw you."

"Frightened?" said the most pig-like of the boys. "Who's she talking to out of the window? Let's tell the inspector she talks to people out of the window when she ought to be teaching us."

"Let's go and see who it is," said another boy, and they all came crowding to the window. But as soon as their mean little faces looked out, Bacchus gave a great cry of *Euan, euoi-oi-oi-oi* and the boys all began howling with fright and trampling one another down to get out of the door and jumping out of the windows. And it was said afterwards (whether truly or not) that those particular little boys were never seen again, but there were a lot of very fine little pigs in that part of the country which had never been there before.

"Now, Dear Heart," said Aslan to the Mistress: and she jumped down and joined them.

At Beaversdam they re-crossed the river and came east again along the southern bank. They came to a little cottage where a child stood in the doorway crying. "Why are you crying, my love?" asked Aslan. The child, who had never even seen a picture of a lion, was not afraid of him. "Auntie's very ill," she said. "She's going to die." Then Aslan went to go in at the door of the cottage, but it was too small for him. So, when he had got his head through, he pushed with his shoulders (Lucy and Susan fell off when he did this) and lifted the whole house up and it all fell backwards and apart. And there, still in her bed, though the bed was now in the open air, lay a little old woman who looked as if she had Dwarf blood in her. She was at death's door, but when she opened her eyes and saw the bright, hairy head of the lion staring into her face, she did not scream or faint. She said, "Oh Aslan! I knew it was true. I've been waiting for this all my life. Have you come to take me away?"

"Yes, dearest," said Aslan. "But not the long journey yet." And as he spoke, like the flush creeping along the underside of a cloud at sunrise, the colour came back to her white face and her eyes grew bright and she sat up and said, "Why, I do declare I feel *that* better. I think I could take a little breakfast this morning."

"Here you are, mother," said Bacchus, dipping a pitcher in the cottage well and handing it to her. But what was in it now was not water but the richest wine, red as red-currant jelly, smooth as oil, strong as beef, warming as tea, cool as dew.

"Eh, you've done something to our well," said the old woman. "That makes a nice change, that does." And she jumped out of bed.

"Ride on me," said Aslan, and added to Susan and Lucy, "You two queens will have to run now."

"But we'd like that just as well," said Susan. And off they went again.

And so at last, with leaping and dancing and singing, with music and laughter and roaring and barking and neighing, they all came to the place where Miraz's army stood flinging down their swords and holding up their hands, and Peter's army, still holding their weapons and breathing hard, stood round them with stern and glad faces. And the first thing that happened was that the old woman slipped off Aslan's back and ran across to Caspian and they embraced one another; for she was his old nurse.

Pauline Clarke

The Return of the Twelves

An ingenious fantasy based on Branwell Brontë's imaginary adventures with a set of wooden soldiers, which he described in his book *History of the Young Men.* The setting of the story is present-day England. Young Max finds twelve of the long-lost soldiers in the attic of their Yorkshire home not far from Haworth, where the Brontë family once lived. Max's affection and sympathy bring the little soldiers to life (but they "freeze" if they are observed by others) and they tell him of the time a hundred years ago when the four genii, Branwell, Charlotte, Emily, and Anne, loved them and imagined marvelous adventures for them. The author makes the story so convincing there seems little reason to doubt it. [From Pauline Clarke, *The Return of the Twelves* (Coward-McCann, 1962).]

The Four Genii

"Janey, come up to the attic," Max whispered as they put their bicycles away. Philip had already gone off toward the farmyard.

Jane nodded eagerly, and Max felt relieved. She hadn't forgotten; she was still a faithful Genie.

Without talking, they pelted up the stairs, and as Mrs. Morley came out of the kitchen to ask them if they had enjoyed themselves she thought, Ah, Jane's in Max's game now, evidently. And she wondered what it was that absorbed them so.

"Wasn't it funny about the Brontës having soldiers?" Jane said softly as they approached the attic door.

"Funny," said Max in a tone heavy with excitement and meaning. "Janey, do you realize that thing he said they wrote, called THE HISTORY OF THE YOUNG MEN, is what Butter talked about this morning?"

Jane stared at Max.

"You didn't tell me."

"I haven't had a chance yet, have I?"

"Is that why you turned red and shut up?"

"Yes. Did I? Well, it gave me a shock. And then, one being called Butter Something! He said so, 'Butter Something,' and that's what had reminded him!"

"Yes, he did. Max, what do you think it is? Do you think—?"

Max interrupted her.

"How many of these old Brontës were there?"

"Four, I think."

"There you are. Butter says there were four Genii! Was there a boy and three girls?"

"I believe so. I'm not sure. I know about Charlotte most."

"Well, who can we ask? Do you know their names, Jane?"

"Only Charlotte. But, Maxy, if you think these are their soldiers, why are they *here?* They ought to be at Haworth, where they lived, not in an attic here."

"I can't help where they ought to be," Max said, excited and rather cross because it all seemed strange and he didn't understand it. "The thing is, *are* they the ones? Can you ask Mummy their names, these Brontës' names, without letting on *why,* Jane?"

"Why do you want to know their names?" she argued, feeling cross too.

"Because Butter told me the names of the four Genii," Max almost shouted. "I want to know if they fit. They're made-up ones, the Genii, but they're sure to be from their real names." This conversation had been carried on in secret whispers outside the attic door. But now their impatience had made their voices grow louder and louder. Max suddenly realized this.

"Shush!" he said.

"Well, you shush," retorted Jane, with reason. "Wait here, don't go in without me, and I'll go and ask Mummy."

Max promised to wait. But he couldn't resist kneeling down and looking through the keyhole.

There wasn't a soldier to be seen. The space before the Ashanti stool was empty. He couldn't see the whole attic from the keyhole, and he had promised not to go in.

Jane returned to find him kneeling before the door. She was breathless and as she knelt, too, she giggled.

"This is how I saw you when you first started it, and you had that candy ball."

"I *didn't* start it," Max protested. "They've gone," he added. "What are the names?"

"What do you mean, *gone?*" Jane said,

shocked, pushing him aside and putting an eye to the keyhole. "Max!"

"Well, they walk around. We'll go in soon. What are the four names?"

Jane raised her head.

"Charlotte, Branwell, Emily and Anne," she said. "In that order. There were two older ones that died."

Max looked at her, remembering.

"Well, the Genii were called Brannii, Tallii, Emmii and Annii," he said slowly.

They both squatted back on their heels.

"The only one that isn't right is Tallii," Jane said.

"Brannii was the chief Genie. That's the boy. Branwell, isn't it?"

"Yes. He was Patrick Branwell, but as their father was Patrick, too, he was called Branwell, Mummy said."

"Was she suspicious?"

"No, she just said she supposed Mr. Rochester had got us interested, and I said yes. I was as vague as anything."

"Good. I'd already guessed Anne. Emmii is Emily. So, Tallii must be the Charlotte one."

"It ought to be Charlii."

"Well, I guess she thought that was too much like a boy."

"Yes."

"You see, Butter called me Maxii, and then I called you Janeii."

"All to go with Genii," Jane added.

"Let's go in and I'll say you're here!"

"Yes," Jane said, very excited. "Max, may I hold one, the way you do?"

"I think you might hold Butter. He's the one who's used to speaking to the Genii. We'll see what happens."

They went in and looked all around the attic in each corner. No Young Men.

"Maybe they're behind something," Max whispered.

"Where do you keep them? In that shoe box?"

"Yes, but they wouldn't put themselves away."

"They could. Oh, Max." She clutched his arm. "They're in the boat!"

They were. Only the heads and shoulders of the Twelves showed above the sides of the carved canoe. Their heads were bent on their hands, and their hands were clutching balsawood oars which rested on their little knees and over the sides of the canoe. They were asleep, it seemed.

"Worn out with rowing," Max whispered. Butter sat in the bow, his head bent forward on his chest. Crackey sat in the stern, or rather leaned back, sleeping comfortably. Between them sat the others, in two rows of five, holding their oars of different lengths and looking like galley slaves.

Max and Jane kneeled down to look at them.

"Have they gone back to being wooden?" Jane asked.

Max looked at Butter fixedly. As he looked he could make out, perhaps, the slightest rise and fall of his breathing. He wasn't sure.

Then he looked at Crackey's face—the only face that showed—and realized that he had known it was Crackey, which meant his face wasn't wooden and blurred but lively and detailed. "No. They're just asleep," he said.

At this moment the patriarch woke, stretched his arms, yawned, rubbed his eyes and said in a brisk voice, "Ready all."

"Oh, his darling yawn," said Jane.

"Jane, don't treat him like a toy or a baby animal, please," Max warned. He felt that this would be wrong and insulting. "He's a small, alive person," he explained, "and full of years and wisdom. He says so."

"Yes, I see," Jane said meekly.

At his words, all the others sat up, balanced their oars as best they could without rowlocks—many finding them too heavy—and began to row rather wildly as Butter directed.

"One, two; one, two; one, two," said the patriarch briskly.

"Mind your elbows, Cheeky," growled Gravey.

"Old sourpuss," retorted the bold Cheeky.

"I should be obliged if His present Majesty could keep his knees out of my back," Stumps requested of the Duke of Wellington.

"Impossible to achieve," drawled the Duke, "since you push your back into my knees."

"Brave Benbow lost his legs by chain shot, by chain sho-o-ot," yelled Crackey from the stern, to the time of the rowing.

"Move over, Ross," Parry snarled.

"How can I? The boat's curved and throws you into the middle like a feather bed," said Ross angrily. With all this argument, the rowing became wilder and wilder. Max and Jane watched, half-smiling and half-alarmed as the cries and arguments of the twelve grew louder. Sneaky found it impossible to row properly sitting down, so he leaped up and began using his piece of wood like a punt pole over the side, to the peril of Tracky, who sat in his way.

"That's Sneaky," Max whispered, "and he was the favorite of Chief Genie Brannii. Butter told me so. He's one of the kings, do you remember?"

"He would be," said Jane.

"We're not getting far anyway," Monkey said, "without any water."

"You look as if you're waving a flag, not rowing a boat," said Cheeky.

Monkey raised his oar, which was certainly short, and brought it down crack on Cheeky's head. Cheeky returned the blow, but his oar glanced off and hit Gravey. Gravey howled, stood up, and began hitting everyone at random, still with an expression of utmost melancholy. Sneaky was quick to join him.

At once there was pandemonium in the Ashanti canoe as all the rowers jumped up.

"Help," said Jane, "how do you stop a quarrel?"

"I've never had to. Butter usually does," Max whispered.

Butter was standing up with raised arms, calling "Easy all," but nobody took much notice. They went on whacking and punching with great abandon, and the canoe was rocking a little on the attic floor.

Max swooped on Butter and lifted him high.

"Command silence, Oh Patriarch," he suggested.

The patriarch blinked, but finding himself in a position of such advantage, he said loudly, "Pray silence!" As they heard this voice, apparently from the courts of heaven, the Twelves stopped fighting, sat down, and rubbed their bruises.

"Butter Crashey," said Max solemnly, "the Genie Janeii is present." He could hardly keep from laughing. Genie Janeii sounded so funny.

The patriarch's wise wrinkled face took on a look of satisfaction. Jane was watching intently, smiling. Max held Butter toward her, signaling to her to take him.

Jane put her finger and thumb around his body, and felt the taut, thrilling wriggle of life. She couldn't help a slight shiver.

"Welcome, Oh Genii, on behalf of the Young Men," the patriarch said. He bowed his top half in her hand and looked up smilingly. Jane smiled back. His eyes were as bright and beady as those of a mouse. She was enchanted.

"I am glad to be here, Oh Patriarch," she replied with natural grace, having noted the way Max addressed him.

From the boat came the sound of a thin cheer. All malice and sulks seemed to be over.

"They welcome you," said Butter Crashey, nodding.

"Put him back in the boat, Jane," Max whispered as they heard their mother ring the bell for supper. Jane did so, and as they crept from the attic they heard the Young Men's voices rise in a sea song.

"We'll rant and we'll roar," they shrilled, "all o'er the wild ocean . . ."

"Max, the *feel* of him," Jane said as they ran downstairs.

"I know. You can always tell when they freeze. They feel wooden again."

"Yes, I see. I love the way they sing."

"Now listen to this," said Mr. Morley when the plates were filled. He reached behind him and brought out a newspaper. "Just listen. Here we are, 'Letters to the Editor.' " He began to read:

SIR,

IS IT TOO MUCH TO HOPE THAT SOMEWHERE, LURKING UNRECOGNIZED IN SOME ATTIC OR FARMHOUSE OR PARSONAGE, OR PERHAPS TREASURED BUT UNKNOWN AMONG THE OBJECTS IN A LIVINGROOM CABINET, THERE MAY SURVIVE SOME OF THE ORIGINAL WOODEN SOLDIERS, NAPOLEONIC IN OUTFIT AND DESIGN, WHICH—I WOULD RATHER SAY WHO—INSPIRED THE CHILDREN OF HAWORTH WITH THEIR EARLIEST, FERTILE IMAGININGS?

WHERE ARE THE NOBLE TWELVES, THE YOUNG MEN, BELOVED OF BRANWELL AND HIS SISTERS, WHO, WITH THEIR IMAGINARY DESCENDANTS, PEOPLED ALL THE EARLY STORIES OF THIS BRILLIANT FAMILY? COULD WE BUT FIND THEM, WOULD IT NOT ADD MUCH TO OUR UNDERSTANDING OF THE THWARTED GENIUS OF BRANWELL TO STUDY THESE LITTLE FIGURES?

I AM READY TO PURCHASE THEM FOR THE PRICE OF £5,000 STERLING, OR TO REWARD SUITABLY ANYONE LEADING ME TO THE DISCOVERY OF THEM.

BE ASSURED THAT THESE SOLDIERS WOULD BE ENTRUSTED TO A MUSEUM, PERHAPS IN PHILADELPHIA OR BOSTON, WHERE THEY COULD BE ADMIRED BY ALL.

I REMAIN, SIR,

YOUR OBEDIENT SERVANT,
Senaca D. Brewer,
PROFESSOR

"Now, isn't that going too far? I ask you, understanding the thwarted genius of Branwell Brontë by examining his wooden soldiers. Richest thing I've read in years. And as if they'd still be in existence, made of *wood,* you know."

The family had sat silent, except for Philip, who had laughed at the professor's name. Max and Jane gazed at each other and then looked quickly away.

Mrs. Morley spoke. "But, Rod, Maxy's are wooden and they've survived," she said. "They're nearly as old, I suppose."

"I know, I thought of Maxy's. It seemed a strange coincidence. But his were carefully wrapped up and put away, don't you see?" He began to eat his supper. "If the Brontës' had been carefully put away, they'd have been found at Haworth by now."

"Five thousand pounds!" Philip whistled.

"Scholarship gone mad," said Mr. Morley. "As if a wooden soldier, or even a set of wooden soldiers, could tell you anything!"

"But it's an interesting idea," Mrs. Morley said.

"What do you bet half the families in Yorkshire will suddenly find wooden soldiers in their attics?" their father said.

Max felt as if his food was choking him. Jane took frequent large gulps of water. Her cheeks were burning. Max was afraid somebody would notice.

E. B. White

Charlotte's Web

Among the best loved of books that children read is this story about Wilbur, the pig, and his loyal friend, Charlotte, the spider. The entire book presents matters of deep significance, ideas such as life and death. It is with delight, however, that children read and reread this work, which was written by a man who never considered writing down to them. "Children are demanding," he says. "They are the most attentive, curious, eager, observant, sensitive, quick, and generally congenial readers on earth. . . . Children are game for anything. I throw them hard words, and they backhand them over the net. They love words that give them a hard time, provided they are in a context that absorbs their attention."* [From E. B. White, *Charlotte's Web* (Harper, 1952).]

Charlotte

The night seemed long. Wilbur's stomach was empty and his mind was full. And when your stomach is empty and your mind is full, it's always hard to sleep.

A dozen times during the night Wilbur woke and stared into the blackness, listening to the sounds and trying to figure out what time it was. A barn is never perfectly quiet. Even at midnight there is usually something stirring.

The first time he woke, he heard Templeton gnawing a hole in the grain bin. Templeton's teeth scraped loudly against the wood and made quite a racket. "That crazy rat!" thought Wilbur. "Why does he have to stay up all night, grinding his clashers and destroying people's property? Why can't he go to sleep, like any decent animal?"

The second time Wilbur woke, he heard the goose turning on her nest and chuckling to herself.

* From "The Art of the Essay," *Paris Review*, No. 48 (Fall 1969).

"What time is it?" whispered Wilbur to the goose.

"Probably-obably-obably about half-past eleven," said the goose. "Why aren't you asleep, Wilbur?"

"Too many things on my mind," said Wilbur.

"Well," said the goose, "that's not *my* trouble. I have nothing at all on my mind, but I've too many things under my behind. Have you ever tried to sleep while sitting on eight eggs?"

"No," replied Wilbur. "I suppose it *is* uncomfortable. How long does it take a goose egg to hatch?"

"Approximately-oximately thirty days, all told," answered the goose. "But I cheat a little. On warm afternoons, I just pull a little straw over the eggs and go out for a walk."

Wilbur yawned and went back to sleep. In his dreams he heard again the voice saying, "I'll be a friend to you. Go to sleep—you'll see me in the morning."

About half an hour before dawn, Wilbur woke and listened. The barn was still dark. The sheep lay motionless. Even the goose was quiet. Overhead, on the main floor, nothing stirred: the cows were resting, the horses dozed. Templeton had quit work and gone off somewhere on an errand. The only sound was a slight scraping noise from the rooftop, where the weather-vane swung back and forth. Wilbur loved the barn when it was like this—calm and quiet, waiting for light.

"Day is almost here," he thought.

Through a small window, a faint gleam appeared. One by one the stars went out. Wilbur could see the goose a few feet away. She sat with head tucked under a wing. Then he could see the sheep and the lambs. The sky lightened.

"Oh, beautiful day, it is here at last! Today I shall find my friend."

Wilbur looked everywhere. He searched his pen thoroughly. He examined the window ledge, stared up at the ceiling. But he saw nothing new. Finally he decided he would have to speak up. He hated to break the lovely stillness of dawn by using his voice, but he couldn't think of any other way to locate the mysterious new friend who was nowhere to be seen. So Wilbur cleared his throat.

"Attention, please!" he said in a loud, firm voice. "Will the party who addressed me at bedtime last night kindly make himself or herself known by giving an appropriate sign or signal!"

Wilbur paused and listened. All the other animals lifted their heads and stared at him. Wilbur blushed. But he was determined to get in touch with his unknown friend.

"Attention, please!" he said. "I will repeat the message. Will the party who addressed me at bedtime last night kindly speak up. Please tell me where you are, if you are my friend!"

The sheep looked at each other in disgust.

"Stop your nonsense, Wilbur!" said the oldest sheep. "If you have a new friend here, you are probably disturbing his rest; and the quickest way to spoil a friendship is to wake somebody up in the morning before he is ready. How can you be sure your friend is an early riser?"

"I beg everyone's pardon," whispered Wilbur. "I didn't mean to be objectionable."

He lay down meekly in the manure, facing the door. He did not know it, but his friend was very near. And the old sheep was right—the friend was still asleep.

Soon Lurvy appeared with slops for breakfast. Wilbur rushed out, ate everything in a hurry, and licked the trough. The sheep moved off down the lane, the gander waddled along behind them, pulling grass. And then, just as Wilbur was settling down for his morning nap, he heard again the thin voice that had addressed him the night before.

"Salutations!" said the voice.

Wilbur jumped to his feet. "Salu-*what?*" he cried.

"Salutations!" repeated the voice.

"What are *they,* and where are *you?*" screamed Wilbur. "Please, *please,* tell me where you are. And what are salutations?"

"Salutations are greetings," said the voice. "When I say 'salutations,' it's just my fancy way of saying hello or good morning. Actually, it's a silly expression, and I am surprised that I used it at all. As for my whereabouts, that's easy. Look up here in the corner of the doorway! Here I am. Look, I'm waving!"

At last Wilbur saw the creature that had spo-

ken to him in such a kindly way. Stretched across the upper part of the doorway was a big spiderweb, and hanging from the top of the web, head down, was a large grey spider. She was about the size of a gumdrop. She had eight legs, and she was waving one of them at Wilbur in friendly greeting. "See me now?" she asked.

"Oh, yes indeed," said Wilbur. "Yes indeed! How are you? Good morning! Salutations! Very pleased to meet you. What is your name, please? May I have your name?"

"My name," said the spider, "is Charlotte."

"Charlotte what?" asked Wilbur, eagerly.

"Charlotte A. Cavatica. But just call me Charlotte."

"I think you're beautiful," said Wilbur.

"Well, I *am* pretty," replied Charlotte. "There's no denying that. Almost all spiders are rather nice-looking. I'm not as flashy as some, but I'll do. I wish I could see you, Wilbur, as clearly as you can see me."

Illustration by Garth Williams, from *Charlotte's Web,* by E. B. White. Illustrations copyright © 1952 by Garth Williams; renewed 1980 by Garth Williams. Reprinted by permission of Harper & Row, Publishers, Inc.

"Why can't you?" asked the pig. "I'm right here."

"Yes, but I'm near-sighted," replied Charlotte. "I've always been dreadfully near-sighted. It's good in some ways, not so good in others. Watch me wrap up this fly."

A fly that had been crawling along Wilbur's trough had flown up and blundered into the lower part of Charlotte's web and was tangled in the sticky threads. The fly was beating its wings furiously, trying to break loose and free itself.

"First," said Charlotte, "I dive at him." She plunged headfirst toward the fly. As she dropped, a tiny silken thread unwound from her rear end.

"Next, I wrap him up." She grabbed the fly, threw a few jets of silk around it, and rolled it over and over, wrapping it so that it couldn't move. Wilbur watched in horror. He could hardly believe what he was seeing, and although he detested flies, he was sorry for this one.

"There!" said Charlotte. "Now I knock him out, so he'll be more comfortable." She bit the fly. "He can't feel a thing now," she remarked. "He'll make a perfect breakfast for me."

"You mean you *eat* flies?" gasped Wilbur.

"Certainly. Flies, bugs, grasshoppers, choice beetles, moths, butterflies, tasty cockroaches, gnats, midges, daddy longlegs, centipedes, mosquitoes, crickets—anything that is careless enough to get caught in my web. I have to live, don't I?"

"Why, yes, of course," said Wilbur. "Do they taste good?"

"Delicious. Of course, I don't really eat them. I drink them—drink their blood. I love blood," said Charlotte, and her pleasant, thin voice grew even thinner and more pleasant.

"Don't say that!" groaned Wilbur. "Please don't say things like that!"

"Why not? It's true, and I have to say what is true. I am not entirely happy about my diet of flies and bugs, but it's the way I'm made. A spider has to pick up a living somehow or other, and I happen to be a trapper. I just naturally build a web and trap flies and other insects. My mother was a trapper before me. Her mother was a trapper before her. All our family have been trappers. Way back for thousands and thousands of years we spiders have been laying for flies and bugs."

"It's a miserable inheritance," said Wilbur, gloomily. He was sad because his new friend was so bloodthirsty.

"Yes, it is," agreed Charlotte. "But I can't help it. I don't know how the first spider in the early days of the world happened to think up this fancy idea of spinning a web, but she did, and it was clever of her, too. And since then, all of us spiders have had to work the same trick. It's not a bad pitch, on the whole."

"It's cruel," replied Wilbur, who did not intend to be argued out of his position.

"Well, *you* can't talk," said Charlotte. "*You* have your meals brought to you in a pail. Nobody feeds me. I have to get my own living. I live by my wits. I have to be sharp and clever, lest I go hungry. I have to think things out, catch what I can, take what comes. And it just so happens, my friend, that what comes is flies and insects and bugs. And *further*more," said Charlotte, shaking one of her legs, "do you realize that if I didn't catch bugs and eat them, bugs would increase and multiply and get so numerous that they'd destroy the earth, wipe out everything?"

"Really?" said Wilbur. "I wouldn't want *that* to happen. Perhaps your web is a good thing after all."

The goose had been listening to this conversation and chuckling to herself. "There are a lot of things Wilbur doesn't know about life," she thought. "He's really a very innocent little pig. He doesn't even know what's going to happen to him around Christmastime; he has no idea that Mr. Zuckerman and Lurvy are plotting to kill him." And the goose raised herself a bit and poked her eggs a little further under her so that they would receive the full heat from her warm body and soft feathers.

Charlotte stood quietly over the fly, preparing to eat it. Wilbur lay down and closed his eyes. He was tired from his wakeful night and from the excitement of meeting someone for the first time. A breeze brought him the smell of clover—the sweet-smelling world beyond his fence. "Well," he thought, "I've got a new friend, all right. But what a gamble friendship is! Charlotte is fierce, brutal, scheming, bloodthirsty—everything I don't like. How can I learn to like her, even though she is pretty and, of course, clever?''

Wilbur was merely suffering the doubts and fears that often go with finding a new friend. In good time he was to discover that he was mistaken about Charlotte. Underneath her rather bold and cruel exterior, she had a kind heart, and she was to prove loyal and true to the very end.

T. H. White

The Sword in the Stone

Beneath the comic aspects of this fantasy is the rich fund of historic and literary knowledge of a man who was passionately devoted to the pursuit of knowledge of all kinds. His own years as a schoolmaster must have been drawn on in this version of the education of Arthur (the Wart) as administered by his inventive and resourceful tutor, Merlyn. In this chapter, the duel between Merlyn and Madame Mim calls to mind similar exchanges found in folklore. [From T. H. White, *The Sword in the Stone* (Putnam's, 1939).]

One Thursday afternoon the boys were doing their archery as usual. There were two straw targets fifty yards apart, and when they had shot their arrows at the one, they had only to go to it, collect them, and fire back at the other after facing about. It was still the loveliest summer weather, and there had been chickens for dinner, so that Merlyn had gone off to the edge of their shooting-ground and sat down under a tree. What with the warmth and the chickens and the cream he had poured over his pudding and the continual repassing of the boys and the tock of the arrows in the targets—which was as sleepy to listen to as the noise of a lawn-mower—and the dance of the egg-shaped sun-spots between the leaves of his tree, the aged magician was soon fast asleep.

Archery was a serious occupation in those days. It had not yet been relegated to Indians and small boys, so that when you were shooting badly you got into a bad temper, just as the wealthy pheasant shooters do today. Kay was shooting badly. He was trying too hard and

plucking on his loose, instead of leaving it to the bow.

"Oh, come on," said Kay. "I'm sick of these beastly targets. Let's have a shot at the popinjay."

They left the targets and had several shots at the popinjay—which was a large, bright-colored artificial bird stuck on the top of a stick, like a parrot—and Kay missed these also. First he had the feeling of "Well, I *will* hit the filthy thing, even if I have to go without my tea until I do it." Then he merely became bored.

The Wart said, "Let's play Rovers then. We can come back in half an hour and wake Merlyn up."

What they called Rovers, consisted in going for a walk with their bows and shooting one arrow each at any agreed mark which they came across. Sometimes it would be a mole hill, sometimes a clump of rushes, sometimes a big thistle almost at their feet. They varied the distance at which they chose these objects, sometimes picking a target as much as 120 yards away—which was about as far as these boys' bows could carry—and sometimes having to aim actually below a close thistle because the arrow always leaps up a foot or two as it leaves the bow. They counted five for a hit, and one if the arrow was within a bow's length, and added up their scores at the end.

On this Thursday they chose their targets wisely, and, besides, the grass of the big field had been lately cut. So they never had to search for their arrows for long, which nearly always happens, as in golf, if you shoot ill-advisedly near hedges or in rough places. The result was that they strayed further than usual and found themselves near the edge of the savage forest where Cully had been lost.

"I vote," said Kay, "that we go to those buries in the chase, and see if we can get a rabbit. It would be more fun than shooting at these hummocks."

They did this. They chose two trees about a hundred yards apart, and each boy stood under one of them, waiting for the conies to come out again. They stood very still, with their bows already raised and arrows fitted, so that they would make the least possible movement to disturb the creatures when they did appear. It was not difficult for either of them to stand thus, for the very first test which they had had to pass in archery was standing with the bow at arm's length for half an hour. They had six arrows each and would be able to fire and mark them all before they needed to frighten the rabbits back by walking about to collect. An arrow does not make enough noise to upset more than the particular rabbit that it is shot at.

At the fifth shot Kay was lucky. He allowed just the right amount for wind and distance, and his point took a young coney square in the head. It had been standing up on end to look at him, wondering what he was.

"Oh, well shot!" cried the Wart, as they ran to pick it up. It was the first rabbit they had ever hit, and luckily they had killed it dead.

When they had carefully gutted it with the little hunting knife which Merlyn had given— in order to keep it fresh—and passed one of its hind legs through the other at the hock, for convenience in carrying, the two boys prepared to go home with their prize. But before they unstrung their bows they used to observe a ceremony. Every Thursday afternoon, after the last serious arrow had been fired, they were allowed to fit one more nock to their strings and to discharge the arrow straight up into the air. It was partly a gesture of farewell, partly of triumph, and it was beautiful. They did it now as a salute to their first prey.

The Wart watched his arrow go up. The sun was already westing towards evening, and the trees where they were had plunged them into a partial shade. So, as the arrow topped the trees and climbed into sunlight, it began to burn against the evening like the sun itself. Up and up it went, not weaving as it would have done with a snatching loose, but soaring, swimming, aspiring towards heaven, steady, golden and superb. Just as it had spent its force, just as its ambition had been dimmed by destiny and it was preparing to faint, to turn over, to pour back into the bosom of its mother earth, a terrible portent happened. A gore-crow came flapping wearily before the approaching night. It came, it did not waver, it took the arrow. It flew away, heavy and hoisting, with the arrow in its beak.

Kay was frightened by this, but the Wart was furious. He had loved his arrow's movement, its burning ambition in the sunlight, and, besides, it was his best arrow. It was the only one which was perfectly balanced, sharp, tight-feathered, clean-nocked, and neither warped nor scraped.

"It was a witch," said Kay.

"I don't care if it was ten witches," said the Wart. "I am going to get it back."

"But it went towards the Forest."

"I shall go after it."

"You can go alone, then," said Kay. "I'm not going into the Forest Sauvage, just for a putrid arrow."

"I shall go alone."

"Oh, well," said Kay, "I suppose I shall have to come too, if you're so set on it. And I bet we shall get nobbled by Wat."

"Let him nobble," said the Wart. "I want my arrow."

They went in the Forest at the place where they had last seen the bird of carrion.

In less than five minutes they were in a clearing with a well and a cottage just like Merlyn's.

"Goodness," said Kay, "I never knew there were any cottages so close. I say, let's go back."

"I just want to look at this place," said the Wart. "It's probably a wizard's."

The cottage had a brass plate screwed on the garden gate. It said:

> MADAME MIM, B.A. (DOM-DANIEL)
> PIANOFORTE
> NEEDLEWORK
> NECROMANCY
> NO HAWKERS, CIRCULARS
> OR INCOME TAX.
> BEWARE OF THE DRAGON.

The cottage had lace curtains. These stirred ever so slightly, for behind them there was a lady peeping. The gore-crow was standing on the chimney.

"Come on," said Kay. "Oh, do come on. I tell you, she'll never give it us back."

At this point the door of the cottage opened suddenly and the witch was revealed standing in the passage. She was a strikingly beautiful woman of about thirty, with coal-black hair so rich that it had the blue-black of the maggot-pies in it, silky bright eyes and a general soft air of butter-wouldn't-melt-in-my-mouth. She was sly.

"How do you do, my dears," said Madame Mim. "And what can I do for you today?"

The boys took off their leather caps, and Wart said, "Please, there is a crow sitting on your chimney and I think it has stolen one of my arrows."

"Precisely," said Madame Mim. "I have the arrow within."

"Could I have it back, please?"

"Inevitably," said Madame Mim. "The young gentleman shall have his arrow on the very instant, in four ticks and ere the bat squeaks thrice."

"Thank you very much," said the Wart.

"Step forward," said Madame Mim. "Honor the threshold. Accept the humble hospitality in the spirit in which it is given."

"I really do not think we can stay," said the Wart politely. "I really think we must go. We shall be expected back at home."

"Sweet expectation," replied Madame Mim in devout tones.

"Yet you would have thought," she added, "that the young gentleman could have found time to honor a poor cottager, out of politeness. Few can believe how we ignoble tenants of the lower classes value a visit from the landlord's sons."

"We would like to come in," said the Wart, "very much. But you see we shall be late already."

The lady now began to give a sort of simpering whine. "The fare is lowly," she said. "No doubt it is not what you would be accustomed to eating, and so naturally such highly born ones would not care to partake."

Kay's strongly developed feeling for good form gave way at this. He was an aristocratic boy always, and condescended to his inferiors so that they could admire him. Even at the risk of visiting a witch, he was not going to have it said that he had refused to eat a tenant's food because it was too humble.

"Come on, Wart," he said. "We needn't be back before vespers."

Madame Mim swept them a low curtsey as they crossed the threshold. Then she took them each by the scruff of the neck, lifted them right off the ground with her strong gypsy arms, and shot out of the back door with them almost before they had got in at the front. The Wart caught a hurried glimpse of her parlor and kitchen. The lace curtains, the aspidistra, the lithograph called the Virgin's Choice, the printed text of the Lord's Prayer written backwards and hung upside down, the sea-shell, the needle-case in the shape of a heart with A Present from Camelot written on it, the broom sticks, the cauldrons, and the bottles of dandelion wine. Then they were kicking and struggling in the back yard.

"We thought that the growing sportsmen would care to examine our rabbits," said Madame Mim.

There was, indeed, a row of large rabbit hutches in front of them, but they were empty of rabbits. In one hutch there was a poor ragged old eagle owl, evidently quite miserable and neglected: in another a small boy unknown to them, a wittol who could only roll his eyes and burble when the witch came near. In a third there was a moulting black cock. A fourth had a mangy goat in it, also black, and two more stood empty.

"Grizzle Greediguts," cried the witch.

"Here, Mother," answered the carrion crow.

With a flop and a squawk it was sitting beside them, its hairy black beak cocked on one side. It was the witch's familiar.

"Open the doors," commanded Madame Mim, "and Greediguts shall have eyes for supper, round and blue."

The gore-crow hastened to obey, with every sign of satisfaction, and pulled back the heavy doors in its strong beak, with three times three. Then the two boys were thrust inside, one into each hutch, and Madame Mim regarded them with unmixed pleasure. The doors had magic locks on them and the witch had made them to open by whispering in their keyholes.

"As nice a brace of young gentlemen," said the witch, "as ever stewed or roast. Fattened on real butcher's meat, I daresay, with milk and all. Now we'll have the big one jugged for Sunday, if I can get a bit of wine to go in the pot, and the little one we'll have on the moon's morn, by jing and by jee, for how can I keep my sharp fork out of him a minute longer it fair gives me the croup."

"Let me out," said Kay hoarsely, "you old witch, or Sir Ector will come for you."

At this Madame Mim could no longer contain her joy. "Hark to the little varmint," she cried, snapping her fingers and doing a bouncing jig before the cages. "Hark to the sweet, audacious, tender little veal. He answers back and threatens us with Sir Ector, on the very brink of the pot. That's how I faint to tooth them, I do declare, and that's how I will tooth them ere the week be out, by Scarmiglione, Belial, Peor, Ciriato Sannuto and Dr. D."

With this she began bustling about in the back yard, the herb garden and the scullery, cleaning pots, gathering plants for the stuffing, sharpening knives and cleavers, boiling water, skipping for joy, licking her greedy lips, saying spells, braiding her night-black hair, and singing as she worked.

First she sang the old witch's song:

"Black spirits and white, red spirits and gray,
Mingle, mingle, mingle, you that mingle may.
  Here's the blood of a bat,
  Put in that, oh, put in that.
  Here's libbard's bane.
  Put in again.
Mingle, mingle, mingle, you that mingle may."

Then she sang her work song:

"Two spoons of sherry
Three oz. of yeast,
Half a pound of unicorn,
And God bless the feast,
  Shake them in a collander,
  Bang them to a chop,
Simmer slightly, snip up nicely,
Jump, skip, hop.
  Knit one, knot one, purl two together,
Pip one and pop one and pluck the secret
  feather.
Baste in a mod. oven.
  God bless our coven.
Tra-la-la!

Three toads in a jar.
Te-he-he!
Put in the frog's knee.
Peep out of the lace curtain.
There goes the Toplady girl, she's up to no
  good that's certain.
Oh, what a lovely baby!
How nice it would go with gravy.
Pinch the salt."

Here she pinched it very nastily

"Turn the malt"

Here she began twiddling round widdershins, in a vulgar way.

"With a hey-nonny-nonny and I don't mean maybe."

At the end of this song, Madame Mim took a sentimental turn and delivered herself of several hymns, of a blasphemous nature, and of a tender love lyric which she sang sottovoce with trills. It was:

"My love is like a red, red nose
His tail is soft and tawny,
And everywhere my lovely goes
I call him Nick or Horny."

She vanished into the parlor, to lay the table.

Poor Kay was weeping in a corner of the end hutch, lying on his face and paying no attention to anything. Before Madame Mim had finally thrown him in, she had pinched him all over to see if he was fat. She had also slapped him, to see, as the butchers put it, if he was hollow. On top of this, he did not in the least want to be eaten for Sunday dinner and he was miserably furious with the Wart for leading him into such a terrible doom on account of a mere arrow. He had forgotten that it was he who had insisted on entering the fatal cottage.

The Wart sat on his haunches, because the cage was too small for standing up, and examined his prison. The bars were of iron and the gate was iron too. He shook all the bars, one after the other, but they were as firm as rock. There was an iron bowl for water—with no water in it—and some old straw in a corner for lying down. It was verminous.

"Our mistress," said the mangy old goat suddenly from the next pen, "is not very careful of her pets."

He spoke in a low voice, so that nobody could hear, but the carrion crow which had been left on the chimney to spy upon them noticed that they were talking and moved nearer.

"Whisper," said the goat, "if you want to talk."

"Are you one of her familiars?" asked the Wart suspiciously.

The poor creature did not take offense at this, and tried not to look hurt.

"No," he said. "I'm not a familiar. I'm only a mangy old black goat, rather tattered as you see, and kept for sacrifice."

"Will she eat you too?" asked the Wart, rather tremblingly.

"Not she. I shall be too rank for her sweet tooth, you may be sure. No, she will use my blood for making patterns with on Walpurgis Night."

"It's quite a long way off, you know," continued the goat without self-pity. "For myself I don't mind very much, for I am old. But look at that poor old owl there, that she keeps merely for a sense of possession and generally forgets to feed. That makes my blood boil, that does. It wants to fly, to stretch its wings. At night it just runs round and round and round like a big rat, it gets so restless. Look, it has broken all its soft feathers. For me, it doesn't matter, for I am naturally of a sedentary disposition now that youth has flown, but I call that owl a rare shame. Something ought to be done about it."

The Wart knew that he was probably going to be killed that night, the first to be released out of all that band, but yet he could not help feeling touched at the great-heartedness of this goat. Itself under sentence of death, it could afford to feel strongly about the owl. He wished he were as brave as this.

"If only I could get out," said the Wart. "I know a magician who would soon settle her hash, and rescue us all."

The goat thought about this for some time, nodding its gentle old head with the great cairngorm eyes. Then it said, "As a matter of fact

I know how to get you out, only I did not like to mention it before. Put your ear nearer the bars. I know how to get you out, but not your poor friend there who is crying. I didn't like to subject you to a temptation like that. You see, when she whispers to the lock I have heard what she says, but only at the locks on either side of mine. When she gets a cage away she is too soft to be heard. I know the words to release both you and me, and the black cock here too, but not your young friend yonder."

"Why ever haven't you let yourself out before?" asked the Wart, his heart beginning to bound.

"I can't speak them in human speech, you see," said the goat sadly, "and this poor mad boy here, the wittol, he can't speak them either."

"Oh, tell them me."

"You will be safe then, and so would I and the cock be too, if you stayed long enough to let us out. But would you be brave enough to stay, or would you run at once? And what about your friend and the wittol and the old owl?"

"I should run for Merlyn at once," said the Wart. "Oh, at once, and he would come back and kill this old witch in two twos, and then we should all be out."

The goat looked at him deeply, his tired old eyes seeming to ask their way kindly into the bottom of his heart.

"I shall tell you only the words for your own lock," said the goat at last. "The cock and I will stay here with your friend, as hostages for your return."

"Oh, goat," whispered the Wart. "You could have made me say the words to get you out first and then gone your way. Or you could have got the three of us out, starting with yourself to make sure, and left Kay to be eaten. But you are staying with Kay. Oh, goat, I will never forget you, and if I do not get back in time I shall not be able to bear my life."

"We shall have to wait till dark. It will only be a few minutes now."

As the goat spoke, they could see Madame Mim lighting the oil lamp in the parlor. It had a pink glass shade with patterns on it. The crow, which could not see in the dark, came quietly closer, so that at least he ought to be able to hear.

"Goat," said the Wart, in whose heart something strange and terrible had been going on in the dangerous twilight, "put your head closer still. Please, goat, I am not trying to be better than you are, but I have a plan. I think it is I who had better stay as hostage and you who had better go. You are black and will not be seen in the night. You have four legs and can run much faster than I. Let you go with a message for Merlyn. I will whisper you out, and I will stay."

He was hardly able to say the last sentence, for he knew that Madame Mim might come for him at any moment now, and if she came before Merlyn it would be his death warrant. But he did say it, pushing the words out as if he were breathing against water, for he knew that if he himself were gone when Madame came for him, she would certainly eat Kay at once.

"Master," said the goat without further words, and it put one leg out and laid its double-knobbed forehead on the ground in the salute which is given to royalty. Then it kissed his hand as a friend.

"Quick," said the Wart, "give me one of your hoofs through the bars and I will scratch a message on it with one of my arrows."

It was difficult to know what message to write on such a small space with such a clumsy implement. In the end he just wrote KAY. He did not use his own name because he thought Kay more important, and that they would come quicker for him.

"Do you know the way?" he asked.

"My grandam used to live at the castle."

"What are the words?"

"Mine," said the goat, "are rather upsetting."

"What are they?"

"Well," said the goat, "you must say: Let Good Digestion Wait on Appetite."

"Oh, goat," said the Wart in a broken voice. "How horrible. But run quickly, goat, and come back safely, goat, and oh, goat, give me one more kiss for company before you go." The goat refused to kiss him. It gave him the Emperor's salute, of both feet, and bounded away into the darkness as soon as he had said the words.

Unfortunately, although they had whispered too carefully for the crow to hear their speech, the release words had had to be said rather loudly to reach the next-door keyhole, and the door had creaked.

"Mother, mother!" screamed the crow. "The rabbits are escaping."

Instantly Madame Mim was framed in the lighted doorway of the kitchen.

"What is it, my Grizzle?" she cried. "What ails us, my halcyon tit?"

"The rabbits are escaping," shrieked the crow again.

The witch ran out, but too late to catch the goat or even to see him, and began examining the locks at once by the light of her fingers. She held these up in the air and a blue flame burned at the tip of each.

"One little boy safe," counted Madame Mim, "and sobbing for his dinner. Two little boys safe, and neither getting thinner. One mangy goat gone, and who cares a fiddle? For the owl and the cock are left, and the wittol in the middle."

"Still," added Madame Mim, "it's a caution how he got out, a proper caution, that it is."

"He was whispering to the little boy," sneaked the crow, "whispering for the last half-hour together."

"Indeed?" said the witch. "Whispering to the little dinner, hey? And much good may it do him. What about a sage stuffing, boy, hey? And what were you doing, my Greediguts, to let them carry on like that? No dinner for you, my little painted bird of paradise, so you may just flap off to any old tree and roost."

"Oh, Mother," whined the crow. "I was only adoing of my duty."

"Flap off," cried Madame Mim. "Flap off, and go broody if you like."

The poor crow hung its head and crept off to the other end of the roof, sneering to itself.

"Now, my juicy toothful," said the witch, turning to the Wart and opening his door with the proper whisper of Enough-Is-As-Good-As-A-Feast, "we think the cauldron simmers and the oven is mod. How will my tender sucking pig enjoy a little popping lard instead of the clandestine whisper?"

The Wart ran about in his cage as much as

he could, and gave as much trouble as possible in being caught, in order to save even a little time for the coming of Merlyn.

"Let go of me, you beast," he cried. "Let go of me, you foul hag, or I'll bite your fingers."

"How the creature scratches," said Madame Mim. "Bless us, how he wriggles and kicks, just for being a pagan's dinner."

"Don't you dare kill me," cried the Wart, now hanging by one leg. "Don't you dare to lay a finger on me, or you'll be sorry for it."

"The lamb," said Madame Mim. "The partridge with a plump breast, how he does squeak."

"And then there's the cruel old custom," continued the witch, carrying him into the lamplight of the kitchen where a new sheet was laid on the floor, "of plucking a poor chicken before it is dead. The feathers come out cleaner so. Nobody could be so cruel as to do that nowadays, by Nothing or by Never, but of course a little boy doesn't feel any pain. Their clothes come off nicer if you take them off alive, and who would dream of roasting a little boy in his clothes, to spoil the feast?"

"Murderess," cried the Wart. "You will rue this ere the night is out."

"Cubling," said the witch. "It's a shame to kill him, that it is. Look how his little downy hair stares in the lamplight, and how his poor eyes pop out of his head. Greediguts will be sorry to miss those eyes, so she will. Sometimes one could almost be a vegetarian, when one has to do a deed like this."

The witch laid Wart over her lap, with his head between her knees, and carefully began to take his clothes off with a practiced hand. He kicked and squirmed as much as he could, reckoning that every hindrance would put off the time when he would be actually knocked on the head, and thus increase the time in which the black goat could bring Merlyn to his rescue. During this time the witch sang her plucking song, of:

"Pull the feather with the skin,
Not against the grain—o.
Pluck the soft ones out from in,
The great with might and main—o.
Even if he wriggles,

Never heed his squiggles,
For mercifully little boys are quite immune
    to pain—o."

She varied this song with the other kitchen song of the happy cook:

"Soft skin for crackling,
Oh, my lovely duckling,
The skewers go here,
And the string goes there
And such is my scrumptious suckling."

"You will be sorry for this," cried the Wart, "even if you live to be a thousand."

"He has spoken enough," said Madame Mim. "It is time that we knocked him on the napper."

"Hold him by the legs, and
When up goes his head,
Clip him with the palm-edge, and
Then he is dead."

The dreadful witch now lifted the Wart into the air and prepared to have her will of him; but at that very moment there was a fizzle of summer lightning without any crash and in the nick of time Merlyn was standing on the threshold.

"Ha!" said Merlyn. "Now we shall see what a double-first at Dom-Daniel avails against the private education of my master Bleise."

Madame Mim put the Wart down without looking at him, rose from her chair, and drew herself to her full magnificent height. Her glorious hair began to crackle, and sparks shot out of her flashing eyes. She and Merlyn stood facing each other a full sixty seconds, without a word spoken, and then Madame Mim swept a royal curtsey and Merlyn bowed a frigid bow. He stood aside to let her go first out of the doorway and then followed her into the garden.

It ought perhaps to be explained, before we go any further, that in those far-off days, when there was actually a college for Witches and Warlocks under the sea at Dom-Daniel and when all wizards were either black or white, there was a good deal of ill-feeling between the different creeds. Quarrels between white and black were settled ceremonially, by means of duels. A wizard's duel was run like this. The two principals would stand opposite each other in some large space free from obstructions, and await the signal to begin. When the signal was given they were at liberty to turn themselves into things. It was rather like the game that can be played by two people with their fists. They say One, Two, Three, and at Three they either stick out two fingers for scissors, or the flat palm for paper, or the clenched fist for stone. If your hand becomes paper when your opponent's become scissors, then he cuts you and wins: but if yours has turned into stone, his scissors are blunted, and the win is yours. The object of the wizard in the duel was, to turn himself into some kind of animal, vegetable or mineral which would destroy the particular animal, vegetable or mineral which had been selected by his opponent. Sometimes it went on for hours.

Merlyn had Archimedes for his second, Madame Mim had the gore-crow for hers, while Hecate, who always had to be present at these affairs in order to keep them regular, sat on the top of a step-ladder in the middle, to umpire. She was a cold, shining, muscular lady, the color of moonlight. Merlyn and Madame Mim rolled up their sleeves, gave their surcoats to Hecate to hold, and the latter put on a celluloid eye-shade to watch the battle.

At the first gong Madame Mim immediately turned herself into a dragon. It was the accepted opening move and Merlyn ought to have replied by being a thunderstorm or something like that. Instead, he caused a great deal of preliminary confusion by becoming a field mouse, which was quite invisible in the grass, and nibbled Madame Mim's tail, as she stared about in all directions, for about five minutes before she noticed him. But when she did notice the nibbling, she was a furious cat in two flicks.

Wart held his breath to see what the mouse would become next—he thought perhaps a tiger which could kill the cat—but Merlyn merely became another cat. He stood opposite her and made faces. This most irregular procedure put Madame Mim quite out of her stride, and it took her more than a minute to regain her bearings and become a dog. Even as she became

it, Merlyn was another dog standing opposite her, of the same sort.

"Oh, well played, sir!" cried the Wart, beginning to see the plan.

Madame Mim was furious. She felt herself out of her depth against these unusual stonewalling tactics and experienced an internal struggle not to lose her temper. She knew that if she did lose it she would lose her judgment, and the battle as well. She did some quick thinking. If whenever she turned herself into a menacing animal, Merlyn was merely going to turn into the same kind, the thing would become either a mere dog-fight or stalemate. She had better alter her own tactics and give Merlyn a surprise.

At this moment the gong went for the end of the first round. The combatants retired into their respective corners and their seconds cooled them by flapping their wings, while Archimedes gave Merlyn a little massage by nibbling with his beak.

"Second round," commanded Hecate. "Seconds out of the ring. . . . Time!"

Clang went the gong, and the two desperate wizards stood face to face.

Madame Mim had gone on plotting during her rest. She had decided to try a new tack by leaving the offensive to Merlyn, beginning by assuming a defensive shape herself. She turned into a spreading oak.

Merlyn stood baffled under the oak for a few seconds. Then he most cheekily—and, as it turned out, rashly—became a powdery little blue-tit, which flew up and sat perkily on Madame Mim's branches. You could see the oak boiling with indignation for a moment; but then its rage became icy cold, and the poor little blue-tit was sitting, not on an oak, but on a snake. The snake's mouth was open, and the bird was actually perching on its jaws. As the jaws clashed together, but only in the nick of time, the bird whizzed off as a gnat into the safe air. Madame Mim had got it on the run, however, and the speed of the contest now became bewildering. The quicker the attacker could assume a form, the less time the fugitive had to think of a form which would elude it, and now the changes were as quick as thought. The gnat was scarcely in the air when the snake had turned into a toad whose curious tongue, rooted at the front instead of the back of the jaw, was already unrolling in the flick which would snap it in. The gnat, flustered by the sore pursuit, was bounced into an offensive role, and the hardpressed Merlyn now stood before the toad in the shape of a mollern which could attack it. But Madame Mim was in her element. The game was going according to the normal rules now, and in less than an eye's blink the toad had turned into a peregrine falcon which was diving at two hundred and fifty miles an hour upon the heron's back. Poor Merlyn, beginning to lose his nerve, turned wildly into an elephant—this move usually won a little breathing space—but Madame Mim, relentless, changed from the falcon into an aullay on the instant. An aullay was as much bigger than an elephant as an elephant is larger than a sheep. It was a sort of horse with an elephant's trunk. Madame Mim raised this trunk in the air, gave a shriek like a railway engine, and rushed upon her panting foe. In a flick Merlyn had disappeared.

"One," said Hecate. "Two. Three. Four. Five. Six. Seven. Eight. Nine—"

But before the fatal Ten which would have counted him out, Merlyn reappeared in a bed of nettles, mopping his brow. He had been standing among them as a nettle.

The aullay saw no reason to change its shape. It rushed upon the man before it with another piercing scream. Merlyn vanished again just as the thrashing trunk descended, and all stood still a moment, looking about them, wondering where he would step out next.

"One," began Hecate again, but even as she proceeded with her counting, strange things began to happen. The aullay got hiccoughs, turned red, swelled visibly, began whooping, came out in spots, staggered three times, rolled its eyes, fell rumbling to the ground. It groaned, kicked and said Farewell. The Wart cheered, Archimedes hooted till he cried, the gore-crow fell down dead, and Hecate, on the top of her ladder, clapped so much that she nearly tumbled off. It was a master stroke.

The ingenious magician had turned himself successively into the microbes, not yet discov-ered, of hiccoughs, scarlet fever, mumps, whooping cough, measles and heat spots, and from a complication of all these complaints the infamous Madame Mim had immediately expired.

Susan Cooper

The Grey King

The Grey King is the fourth of five books in a continued struggle between the forces of light and the forces of darkness. Will, the young boy who has been given the powers and responsibilities of an "Old One," must gradually acquire all the signs for the final confrontation. In the following scene, he is about to acquire the harp that can rouse the lost sleepers in the Welsh hills. Susan Cooper's telling is a skillful interweaving of spectacular fantastic scene with mundane reality, a telling that accumulates power with each shift. Awarded the Newbery medal for 1976. [From Susan Cooper, *The Grey King* (Atheneum, 1975).]

"Wish on a falling star," said Bran soft in his ear. All around them the meteors briefly dived and vanished, as tiny points of stardust in the long travel of their cloud struck the aery halo of the earth, burned bright and were gone.

I wish, said Will fiercely in his mind: *I wish . . . Oh, I wish . . .*

And all the bright starlit sky was gone, in a flicker of time that they could not catch, and darkness came around them so fast that they blinked in disbelief at its thick nothingness. They were back on the staircase beneath Bird Rock, with stone steps under their feet and a curved stone balustrade smooth to the sightless touch of their hands. And as Will stretched out one hand groping before him, he found no blank wall of stone there to bar his way, but free open space.

Slowly, faltering, he went on down the dark stairway, and Bran and Cafall followed him.

Then very gradually faint light began to filter up from below. Will saw a glimmer from the walls enclosing them; then the shape of the steps beneath his feet; then, appearing round a curve in the long tunnelling stairway, the bright circle that marked its end. The light grew brighter, the circle larger; Will felt his steps become quicker and more eager, and mocked himself, but could not help it.

Then instinct caught him into caution, and on the last few steps of the staircase, before the light, he stopped. Behind him he heard Bran and the dog stop too, at once. Will stood listening to his senses, trying to catch the source of warning. He saw, without properly seeing, that the steps on which they stood had been carved out of the rock with immense care and symmetry, perfectly angled, smooth as glass, every detail as clear as if the rock had been cut only the day before. Yet there was a noticeable hollow in the centre of each step, which could only have been worn by centuries of passing feet. Then he ceased to notice such things, for awareness caught at him out of the deepest corner of his mind and told him what he must do.

Carefully Will pushed up the left sleeve of his sweater as far as the elbow, leaving the forearm bare. On the underside of his arm shone the livid scar that had once been accidentally burned there like a brand: the sign of the Light, a circle quartered by a cross. In a deliberate slow gesture, half defensive, half defiant, he raised this arm crooked before his face, as if shielding his eyes from bright light, or warding off an expected blow. Then he walked down the last few steps of the staircase and out into the light. As he stepped to the floor, he felt a shock of sensation like nothing he had ever known. A flare of white brilliance blinded him, and was gone; a brief tremendous thunder dazed his ears, and was gone; a force like a blast wave from some great explosion briefly tore at his body, and was gone. Will stood still, breathing fast. He knew that beneath his singular protection, he had brought them through the last door of the High Magic: a living barrier that would consume any unsought intruder in a gasp of energy as unthinkable as the holocaust of the sun. Then he looked into the room before him, and for a moment of illusion thought that he saw the sun itself.

It was an immense cavernous room, high-roofed, lit by flaring torches thrust into brackets on the stone walls, and hazy with smoke. The smoke came from the torches. Yet in the centre of the floor burned a great glowing fire, alone, with no chimney or fireplace to contain it. It gave no smoke at all, but burned with a white light of such brilliance that Will could not look straight at it. No intense heat came from this fire, but the air was filled with the aromatic scent of burning wood, and there was the crackling, snapping sound of a log fire.

Will came forward past the fire, beckoning Bran to follow; then stopped abruptly as he saw what lay ahead.

Hazy at the end of the chamber three figures sat, in three great thrones that seemed to be fashioned out of smooth grey-blue Welsh slate. They did not move. They appeared to be men, dressed in long hooded robes of differing shades of blue. One robe was dark, one was light, and the robe between them was the shifting greenish-blue of a summer sea. Between the three thrones stood two intricately carved wooden chests. At first there seemed to be nothing else in the huge room, but after a moment of gazing Will knew that there was movement in the deep shadows beyond the fire, in the darkness all around the three illuminated lords. These were the bright figures on a dark canvas, lit to catch the eye; beyond them in the darkness other things of unknown nature lurked.

He could tell nothing of the nature of the three figures, beyond sensing great power. Nor could his senses as an Old One penetrate the surrounding darkness. It was as if an invisible barrier stood all around them, through which no enchantment might reach.

Will stood a little way before the thrones, looking up. The faces of the three lords were hidden in the shadows of their hooded robes. For a moment there was silence, broken only by the soft crackle of the burning fire; then out of the shadows a deep voice said, "We greet you, Will Stanton. And we name you by the sign. Will Stanton, Sign-seeker."

"Greetings," Will said, in as strong and clear a voice as he could muster, and he pulled down his sleeve over his scarred arm. "My lords," he said, "it is the day of the dead."

"Yes," said the figure in the lightest blue robe. His face seemed thin in the shadows of his hood, the eyes gleaming, and his voice was light, sibilant, hissing. "Yessssss . . ." Echoes whispered like snakes out of the dark, as if a hundred other little hissing voices came from nameless shapes behind him, and Will felt the small hairs rise on the back of his neck. Behind him he heard Bran give a muffled involuntary moan, and knew that horror must be creeping like a white mist through his mind. Will's strength as an Old One rebelled. He said in quick cold reproach, "My lord?"

The horror fell away, like a cloud whisked off by the wind, and the lord in the light blue robe softly laughed. Will stood there frowning at him, unmoved: a small stocky boy in jeans and sweater, who nonetheless knew himself to possess power worthy of meeting these three. He said, confident now, "It is the day of the dead, and the youngest has opened the oldest hills, through the door of the birds. And has been let pass by the eye of the High Magic. I have come for the golden harp, my lords."

The second figure in the sea-blue robe said, "And the raven boy with you."

"Yes."

Will turned to Bran, standing hesitantly nearer the fire, and beckoned him. Bran came forward very slowly, feet as unwilling as if they swam against treacle, and stood at his side. The light from the torches on the walls shone in his white hair.

The lord in the sea-blue robe leaned forward a little from his throne; they glimpsed a keen, strong face and a pointed grey beard. He said, astonishingly, "Cafall?"

At Bran's side the white dog stood erect and quivering. He did not move an inch forward, as if obeying some inner instruction that told him his place, but his tail waved furiously from side to side as it never waved for anyone but Bran. He gave a soft, small whine.

White teeth glinted in the hooded face. "He is well named. Well named."

Bran said jealously, in sudden fierce anxiety, "He is my dog!" Then he added, rather muffled, "My lord." Will could feel the alarm in him at his own temerity.

But the laughter from the shadows was kindly. "Never fear, boy. The High Magic would never take your dog from you. Certainly the Old Ones would not either, and the Dark might try but would not succeed." He leaned forward

suddenly, so that for an instant the strong, bearded face was clear; the voice softened, and there was an aching sadness in it. "Only the creatures of the earth take from one another, boy. All creatures, but men more than any. Life they take, and liberty, and all that another man may have—sometimes through greed, sometimes through stupidity, but never by any volition but their own. Beware your own race, Bran Davies—they are the only ones who will ever harm you, in the end."

Dread stirred in Will as he felt the deep sadness in the voice, for there was a compassion in it directed solely at Bran, as if the Welsh boy stood at the edge of some long sorrow. He had a quick sense of a mysterious closeness between these two, and knew that the lord in the sea-blue robe was trying to give Bran strength and help, without being able to explain why. Then the hooded figure leaned abruptly back, and the mood was gone.

Will said huskily, "Nevertheless, my lord, the rights of that race have always been the business of the Light. And in quest of them I claim the golden harp."

The soft-voiced lord in the lightest robe, who had spoken first, swiftly stood. His cloak swirled round him like a blue mist; bright eyes glinted from the thin pale face glimmering in the hood.

"Answer the three riddles as the law demands, Old One, you and the White Crow your helper there, and the harp shall be yours. But if you answer wrong, the doors of rock shall close, and you be left defenceless on the cold mountain, and the harp shall be lost to the Light forever."

"We shall answer," Will said.

"You, boy, the first." The blue mist swirled again. A bony finger was thrust pointing at Bran, and the shadowed hood turned. Will turned too, anxiously; he had half expected this.

Bran gasped. "Me? But—but I—"

Will reached out and touched his arm. He said gently, "Try. Only try. We are here only to try. If the answer is asleep in you, it will wake. If it is not, no matter. But try."

Bran stared at him unsmiling, and Will saw his throat move as he swallowed. Then the white head turned back again. "All right."

The soft, sibilant voice said, "Who are the Three Elders of the World?"

Will felt Bran's mind reel in panic, as he tried to find meaning in the words. There was no way to offer help. In this place, the law of the High Magic prevented an Old One from putting the smallest thought or image into another mind: Will was permitted only to overhear. So, tense, he stood overhearing the turmoil of his friend's thoughts, as they tossed about desperately seeking order.

Bran struggled. The Three Elders of the World . . . somewhere he knew . . . it was strange and yet familiar, as if somewhere he had seen, or read . . . the three oldest creatures, the three oldest things . . . he had read it at school, and he had read it in Welsh . . . the oldest things. . . .

He took his glasses from his shirt pocket, as if fiddling with them could clear his mind, and he saw staring up out of them the reflection of his own eyes. Strange eyes . . . creepy eyes, they called them at school. At school. At school. . . . Strange round tawny eyes, like the eyes of an owl. He put the glasses slowly back in his pocket, his mind groping at an echo. At his side, Cafall shifted very slightly, his head moving so that it touched Bran's hand. The fur brushed his fingers lightly, very lightly, like the flick of feathers. Feathers. Feathers. *Feathers* . . .

He had it.

Will, at his side, felt in his own mind the echoing flood of relief, and struggled to contain his delight.

Bran stood up straight and cleared his throat. "The Three Elders of the World," he said, "are the Owl of Cwm Cawlwyd, the Eagle of Gwernabwy, and the Blackbird of Celli Gadarn."

Will said softly, "Oh, well done! Well done!"

"That is right," said the thin voice above them, unemotionally. Like an early-morning sky the light blue robe swirled before them, and the figure sank back into its throne.

From the central throne rose the lord in the sea-blue robe; stepping forward, he looked down at Will. Behind its grey beard his face seemed oddly young, though its skin was brown and weathered like the skin of a sailor long at sea.

"Will Stanton," he said, "who were the three generous men of the Island of Britain?"

Will stared at him. The riddle was not impossible; he knew that the answer lay somewhere in his memory, stored from the great Book of Gramarye, treasure book of the enchantment of the Light that had been destroyed as soon as he, the last of the Old Ones, had been shown what it held. Will set his mind to work, searching. But at the same time a deeper riddle worried at him. Who was this lord in the sea-blue robe, with his close interest in Bran? He knew about Cafall . . . clearly he was a lord of the High Magic, and yet there was a look about him of . . . a look of . . .

Will pushed the wondering aside. The answer to the riddle had surfaced in his memory.

He said clearly, "The three generous men of the Island of Britain. Nudd the Generous, son of Senllyt. Mordaf the Generous, son of Serwan. Rhydderch the Generous, son of Tydwal Tudglyd. *And Arthur himself was more generous than the three.*"

Deliberately on the last line his voice rang echoing through the hall like a bell.

"That is right," said the bearded lord. He looked thoughtfully at Will and seemed about to say more, but instead he only nodded slowly. Then sweeping his robe about him in a sea-blue wave, he stepped back to his throne.

The hall seemed darker, filled with dancing shadows from the flickering light of the fire. A sudden flash and crackle came from behind the boys, as a log fell and the flames leapt up; instinctively Will glanced back. When he turned forward again, the third figure, who had not spoken or moved until now, was standing tall and silent before this throne. His robe was a deep, deep blue, darkest of the three, and his hood was pulled so far forward that there was no hint of his face visible, but only shadow.

His voice was deep and resonant, like the voice of a cello, and it brought music into the hall.

"Will Stanton," it said, "what is the shore that fears the sea?"

Will started impulsively forward, his hands clenching into fists, for this voice caught into the deepest part of him. Surely, surely . . . but the face in the hood was hidden, and he was denied all ways of recognition. Any part of his senses that tried to reach out to the great thrones met a blank wall of refusal from the High Magic. Once more Will gave up, and put his mind to the last riddle.

He said slowly, "The shore that fears the sea . . ."

Images wavered in and out of his mind: great crashing waves against a rocky coast . . . the green light in the ocean, the realm of Tethys, where strange creatures may live . . . a gentler sea then, washing in long slow waves an endless golden beach. The shore . . . the beach . . . the beach . . .

The image wavered and changed. It dissolved into a green dappled forest of gnarled ancient trees, their broad trunks smooth with a curious light grey bark. Their leaves danced above, new, soft, bright with a delicate green that had in it all of springtime. The beginnings of triumph whispered in Will's mind.

"The shore," he said. "The beach where the sea washes. But also it is a wood, of lovely fine grain, that is in the handle of a chisel and the legs of a chair, the head of a broom and the pad of a workhorse saddle. And I dare swear too that those two chests between your thrones are carved of it. The only places where it may not be used are beneath the open sky and upon the open sea, for this wood loses its virtue if soaked by water. The answer to your riddle, my lord, is the wood of the beech tree."

The flames leaped up in the fire behind them, and suddenly the hall was brilliant. Joy and relief seemed to surge through the air. The first two blue-robed lords rose from their thrones to stand beside the third; like three towers they loomed hooded over the boys. Then the third lord flung back the hood of his deep blue robe, to reveal a fierce hawk-nosed head with deepset eyes and a shock of wild white hair. And the High Magic's barrier against recognition fell away.

Will cried joyously, "Merriman!"

He leapt forward to the tall figure as a small child leaps to its father, and clasped his outstretched hands. Merriman smiled down at him.

Will laughed aloud in delight. "I knew," he said. "I knew. And yet—"

"Greetings, Old One," Merriman said.

"Now you are grown fully into the Circle, by this. Had you failed in this part of the quest, all else would have been lost." The bleak, hard lines of his face were softened by affection; his dark eyes blazed like black torches. Then he turned to Bran, taking him by the shoulders. Bran looked up at him, pale and expressionless.

"And the raven boy," the deep voice said gently. "We meet again. You have played your part well, as it was known you would. Hold your head in pride, Bran Davies. You carry a great heritage within you. Much has been asked of you, and more will be asked yet. Much more."

Bran looked at Merriman with his catlike eyes unblinking, and said nothing. Listening to the Welsh boy's mood, Will sensed an uneasy baffled pleasure.

Merriman stepped back. He said, "Three Lords of the High Magic have for many centuries had guardianship of the golden harp. There are no names here in this place, nor allegiances in that task. Here, as in other places that you do not know yet, all is subject to the law, the High Law. It is of no consequence that I am a Lord of the Light, or that my colleague there is a Lord of the Dark."

He made a slight ironic bow to the tall figure who wore the robe of lightest blue. Will caught his breath in sudden comprehension, and looked for the thin face hidden in the hood. But it was turned away from him, staring out into the shadows of the hall.

The central figure in the sea-blue robe stepped forward a pace. There was great quiet authority about him, as if he were confident, without pomp, in knowing himself the master in that hall. He put back his hood and they saw the full strength and gentleness of the close-bearded face. Though his beard was grey, his hair was brown, only lightly grey-streaked. He seemed a man in the middle of his years, with all power undiminished, yet wisdom already gained. *But,* Will thought, *he is not a man at all.* . . .

Merriman inclined his head respectfully, stepping aside. "Sire," he said.

Will stared, at last beginning to understand.

At Bran's side, the dog Cafall made the same small sound of devotion that he had before.

Clear blue eyes looked down at Bran, and the bearded lord said softly, "Fortune guard you in my land, my son."

Then as Bran looked at him perplexed, the lord drew himself up, and his voice rose. "Will Stanton," he said. "Two chests stand between our thrones. You must open the chest at my right, and take out what you will find there. The other will remain sealed, in case of need, until another time that I hope may never come. Here now."

He turned, pointing. Will went to the big carved chest, turned its ornate wrought-iron clasp, and pushed at the top. It was so broad, and the carved slab of wood so heavy, that he had to kneel and push upward with all the force of both arms; but he shook his head in warning refusal when Bran started forward to help.

Slowly the huge lid rose, and fell open, and for a moment there was a delicate sound like singing in the air. Then Will reached inside the chest, and when he straightened again he was bearing in both his arms a small, gleaming, golden harp.

The hint of music in the hall died into nothing, giving way to a low growing rumble like distant thunder. Closer and louder it grew. The lord in the lightest, sky-blue robe, his face still hooded and hidden, drew away from them. He seized his cloak and swung it round him with a long sweep of the arm.

The fire hissed and went out. Smoke filled the hall, dark and bitter. Thunder crashed and roared all around. And the lord in the sky-blue robe gave a great cry of rage, and disappeared.

They stood silent in the dimlit darkness. Somewhere out beyond the rock, thunder still rumbled and growled. The torches burned, flickering and smoky, on the walls.

Bran said huskily: "Was he the—the—"

"No," Merriman said. "He is not the Grey King. But he is one very close to him, and back to him he has now gone. And their rage will mount the higher because it will be sharpened by fear, fear at what the Light may be able to do with this new Thing of Power." He looked at Will, his bony face tight with concern. "The first perilous part of the quest is

accomplished, Old One, but there is worse peril yet to come."

"The Sleepers must be wakened," Will said.

"That is right. And although we do not yet know where they sleep, nor shall till you have found them, it is almost certain that they are terribly, dangerously close to the Grey King. For long we have known there was a reason for his hard cold grip on this part of the land, though we did not understand it. A happy valley, this has always been, and beautiful; yet he chose to make his kingdom here, instead of in some grim remote place of the kind chosen by most of his line. Now it is clear there can be only one reason for that: to be close to the place where the Sleepers lie, and to keep their resting-place within his power. Just as this great rock, Craig yr Aderyn, is still within his power. . . ."

Will said, his round face grave, "The spell of protection, by which we came here untouched, has run its course now. And it can be made only once." He looked ruefully at Bran. "We may have an interesting reception out there, when we leave this place."

"Have no care, Old One. You will have a new protection with you now."

The words came deep and gentle from the top of the hall. Turning, Will saw that the bearded lord, his robe blue as the summer sea, was sitting enthroned again in the shadows. As he spoke, it seemed that the light began gradually to grow in the hall; the torches burned higher, and glimmering between them now Will could see long swords hanging on the stone.

"The music of the golden harp," said the blue-robed lord, "has a power that may not be broken either by the Dark or by the Light. It has the High Magic in it, and while the harp is being played, those under its protection are safe from any kind of harm or spell. Play the harp of gold, Old One. Its music will wrap you in safety."

Will said slowly, "By enchantment I could play it, but I think it should rather be played by the art of skillful fingers. I do not know how to play the harp, my lord." He paused. "But Bran does."

Bran looked down at the instrument as Will held it out to him.

"Never a harp like that, though," he said.

He took the harp from Will. Its frame was slender but ornate, fashioned so that a golden vine with gold leaves and flowers seemed to twine round it, in and out of the strings. Even the strings themselves looked as if they were made of gold.

"Play, Bran," said the bearded lord softly.

Holding the harp experimentally in the crook of his left arm, Bran ran his fingers gently over the strings. And the sounds that came from them were of such sweetness that Will, beside him, caught his breath in astonishment; he had never heard notes at once so delicate and so resonant, filling the hall with music like the liquid birdsong of summer. Intent, fascinated, Bran began to pick out the plaintive notes of an old Welsh lullaby, elaborating it gradually, filling it out, as he gained confidence in the feel of the strings under his one hand. Will watched the absorbed musician's devotion on his face. Glancing for an instant at the enthroned lord, and at Merriman, he knew that they too were for this moment rapt, carried away out of time by a music that was not of the earth, pouring out like the High Magic in a singing spell.

Cafall made no sound, but leaned his head against Bran's knee.

Merriman said, his deep voice soft over the music, "Go now, Old One." His shadowed, deepset eyes met Will's briefly, in a fierce communication of trust and hope. Will stared about him for a last moment at the high torchlit hall, with its one dark-robed figure standing tall as a tree, and the unknown bearded lord seated motionless on his throne. Then he turned and led Bran, his fingers still gently plucking a melody from the harp, towards the narrow stone staircase to the chamber from which they had come. When he had set him climbing, he turned to raise one arm in salute, then followed.

Bran stood in the stone room above, playing, while Cafall and Will came up after him. And as he played, there took shape in the blank wall at the end of the chamber, below the single hanging golden shield, the two great doors through which they had come into the heart of Bird Rock.

The music of the harp rippled in a lilting upward scale, and slowly the doors swung inward. Beyond, they saw the grey, cloudy sky between the steep walls of the cleft of rock. Though fire blazed no longer on the mountain, a strong, dead smell of burning hung in the air. As they stepped outside, Cafall bounded out past them, through the cleft, and disappeared.

Struck suddenly by a fear of losing him again, Bran stopped playing. "Cafall! Cafall!" he called.

"Look!" Will said softly.

He was half-turned, looking back. Behind them, the tall slabs of rock swung silently together and seemed to melt out of existence, leaving only a weathered rock face, looking just as it had looked for thousands of years. And in the air hung a faint vanishing phrase of delicate music. But Bran was thinking only of Cafall. After one brief glance at the rock, he tucked the harp beneath his arm and dived for the opening through which the dog had disappeared.

Before he could reach it, a whirling flurry of white came hurling in upon them through a cloud of fine ash, snarling, kicking, knocking Bran sideways so hard that he almost dropped the harp. It was Cafall; but a mad, furious, transformed Cafall, growling at them, glaring, driving them deeper into the cleft as if they were enemies. In a moment or two he had them pinned astounded against the rocky wall, and was crouching before them with his long side-teeth bared in a cold snarl.

"What is it?" said Bran blankly when he had breath enough to speak. "Cafall? What on earth—"

And in an instant they knew—or would have known, if they had had time still for wondering. For suddenly the whole world round them was a roaring flurry of noise and destruction. Broken, charred branches came whirling past over the top of the rocky cleft; stones came bounding down loose out of nowhere so that instinctively they ducked, covering their heads. They fell flat on the ground, pressing themselves into the angle between earth and rock, with Cafall close beside. All around, the wind howled and tore at the rock with a sound like a high mad human scream amplified beyond belief. It was as if all the air in Wales had funnelled down into a great tornado of tearing destruction, and was battering in a frenzy of frustrated rage at the narrow opening in whose shelter they desperately crouched.

Will lurched up on to his hands and knees. He groped with one hand until he clutched Bran's arm. "The harp!" he croaked. "Play the harp!"

Bran blinked at him, dazed by the noise overhead, and then he understood. Forcing himself up against the fearsome wind pressing in between the rocky walls, he gripped the golden harp against his side and ran his right hand tremulously over the strings.

At once the tumult grew less. Bran began to play, and as the sweet notes poured out like the song of a lark rising, the great wind died away into nothing. Outside, there was only the rattle of loose pebbles tumbling here and there, one by one, down the rock. For a moment a lone sunbeam slanted down and glinted on the gold of the harp. Then it was gone, and the sky seemed duller, the world more grey. Cafall scrambled to his feet, licked Bran's hand, and led them docilely out to the slope outside the narrow cleft that had sheltered them from the fury of the gale. They felt a soft rain beginning to fall.

Bran let his fingers wander idly but persistently over the strings of the harp. He had no intention of stopping again. He looked at Will, and shook his head mutely with wonder and remorse and enquiry all in one.

Will squatted down and took Cafall's muzzle between his hands. He shook the dog's head gently from side to side. "Cafall, Cafall," he said, wonderingly. Over his shoulder he said to Bran, "*Gwynt Traed y Meirw*, is that how you say it? In all its ancient force the Grey King sent his north wind upon us, the wind that blows round the feet of the dead, and with the dead is where we should have been if it weren't for Cafall—blasted away into a time beyond tomorrow. Before we could have seen a single tree bending, it would have been on us, for it came down from very high up and no human sighted eye could have seen it. But this hound of yours is the dog with the silver eyes, and such dogs can see the wind. . . . So he saw it, and

knew what it would do, and drove us back into safety."

Bran said guiltily, "If I hadn't stopped playing, perhaps the Brenin Llwyd couldn't even have sent the wind. The magic of the harp would have stopped him."

"Perhaps," Will said. "And perhaps not." He gave Cafall's head one last rub and straightened up. The white sheepdog looked up at Bran, tongue lolling as if in a grin, and Bran said to him lovingly, "*Rwyt ti'n gi da*. Good boy." But still his fingers did not stop moving over the harp.

Slowly they scrambled down the rock. Though it was full morning now, the sky was no lighter, but grey and heavy with cloud; the rain was still light, but it was clear that it would grow and settle in for the day, and that the valley was safe now from any more threat of fire. All the near slope of the mountain, Bird Rock and the valley edge were blackened and charred, and here and there wisps of smoke still rose. But all sparks were drowned now, and the ashes cold and wet, and the green farmlands would not again this year be in any state for burning.

Bran said, "Did the harp bring the rain?"

"I think so," Will said. "I am just hoping it will bring nothing else. That's the trouble with the High Magic, like talking in the Old Speech—it's a protection, and yet it marks you, makes you easy to find."

"We'll be in the valley soon." But as he spoke, Bran's foot slipped on a wet rock face and he stumbled sideways, grabbing at a bush to save himself from falling—and dropped the harp. In the instant that the music broke off, Cafall's head jerked up and he began barking furiously, in a mixture of rage and challenge. He jumped up on to a projecting rock and stood poised there, staring about him. Then suddenly the barking broke into a furious deep howl, like the baying of a hunting dog, and he leapt.

The great grey fox, king of the *milgwn*, swerved in midair and screamed like a vixen. In a headlong rush down Bird Rock he had sprung out at them from above, aiming straight for Bran's head and neck. But the shock of Cafall's fierce leap turned his balance just enough to send him spinning sideways, cartwheeling down the rock. He screamed again, an unnatural sound that made the boys flinch in horror, and did not stop himself to turn at bay, but rushed on in a frenzy down the mountain. In an instant Cafall, barking in joyous triumph, was tearing down after him.

And Will, up on the empty rock under the grey drizzling sky, was instantly filled with a presentiment of disaster so overpowering that without thought he reached out and seized the golden harp, and cried to Bran, "Stop Cafall! Stop him! Stop him!"

Bran gave him one frightened look. Then he flung himself after Cafall, running, stumbling, desperately calling the dog back. Scrambling down from the rock with the harp under one arm, Will saw his white head moving fast over the nearest field and, beyond it, a blur of speed that he knew was Cafall pursuing the grey fox. His head dizzy with foreboding, he too ran. Still on high land, he could see two fields away the roofs of Caradog Prichard's farm, and nearby a grey-white knot of sheep and the figures of men. He skidded to a halt suddenly. The harp! There was no means of explaining the harp, if anyone should see it. He was certain to be among men in a few moments. The harp must be hidden. But where?

He looked wildly about him. The fire had not touched this field. On the far side of the field he saw a small lean-to, no more than three stone walls and a slate roof, that was an open shelter for sheep in winter, or a storeplace for winter feed. It was filled with bales of hay already, newly stacked. Running to it, Will thrust the gleaming little harp between two bales of hay, so that it was completely invisible from the outside. Then standing back, he stretched out one hand, and in the Old Speech put upon the harp the Spell of Caer Garadawg, by the power of which only the song of an Old One would be able to take the harp out of that place, or even make it visible at all.

Then he rushed away over the field towards Prichard's Farm, where distant shouts marked the ending of the chase. He could see, in a meadow beyond the farm buildings, the huge grey fox swerving and leaping in an effort to shake Cafall from its heels, and Cafall running doggedly close. A madness seemed to be on

the fox; white foam dripped from its jaws. Will stumbled breathless into the farmyard to find Bran struggling to make his way through a group of men and sheep at the gate. John Rowlands was there, and Owen Davies, with Will's uncle; their clothes and weary faces were still blackened with ash from the fire-fighting, and Caradog Prichard stood scowling with his gun cocked under his arm.

"That damn dog has gone mad!" Prichard growled.

"Cafall! Cafall!" Bran pushed his way wildly through into the field, scattering the sheep, paying no heed to anyone. Prichard snarled at him, and Owen Davies said sharply, "Bran! Where have you been? What are you up to?"

The grey fox leapt high in the air, as they had seen it do once before on Bird Rock. Cafall leapt after it, snapping at it in midair.

"The dog *is* mad," David Evans said unhappily. "He will be on the sheep—"

"He's just so determined to get that fox!" Bran's voice was high with anguish. "Cafall! *Tyrd yma!* Leave it!"

Will's uncle looked at Bran as if he could not believe what he had heard. Then he looked down at Will. He said, puzzled, *"What fox?"*

Horror exploded in Will's brain, as suddenly he understood, and he cried out. But it was too late. The grey fox in the field swung about and came leaping straight at them, with Cafall at his heels. At the last moment it curved sideways and leapt at one of the sheep that now milled terrified round the gate, and sank its teeth into the woolly throat. The sheep screamed. Cafall sprang at the fox. Twenty yards away, Caradog Prichard let out a great furious shout, lifted his gun, and shot Cafall full in the chest.

"Cafall!" Bran's cry of loving horror struck at Will so that for a second he closed his eyes in pain; he knew that the grief in it would ring in his ears for ever.

The grey fox stood waiting for Will to look at it, grinning, red tongue lolling from a mouth dripping brighter with red blood. It stared straight at him with an unmistakable sneering snarl. Then it loped off across the field, straight as an arrow, and disappeared over the far hedge.

Ursula K. Le Guin

A Wizard of Earthsea

Le Guin, Nebula Award–winning author of science fiction for adults, has created an imaginatively convincing secondary reality in the Archipelago of Earthsea. This heroic fantasy, an epic adventure about coming of age, is built upon the Jungian themes of the unconscious, internal evil, naming, and the quest for wholeness. Sparrowhawk, whose true, secret name is Ged, is a student at the School for Wizards on Roke Island; but out of pride he summons the shadow, thus beginning his quest to undo the evil he has let loose in the lands of Earthsea. This compelling fantasy, the first volume of The Earthsea Trilogy, possesses outstanding purity and breadth of vision. [From Ursula K. Le Guin, *A Wizard of Earthsea* (Parnassus/Houghton Mifflin, 1968).]

The Loosing of the Shadow

That spring Ged saw little of either Vetch or Jasper, for they being sorcerers studied now with the Master Patterner in the secrecy of the Immanent Grove, where no prentice might set foot. Ged stayed in the Great House, working with the Masters at all the skills practised by sorcerers, those who work magic but carry no staff: windbringing, weatherworking, finding and binding, and the arts of spellsmiths and spellwrights, tellers, chanters, healalls and herbalists. At night alone in his sleeping-cell, a little ball of werelight burning above the book in place of lamp or candle, he studied the Further Runes and the Runes of Éa, which are used in the Great Spells. All these crafts came easy to him, and it was rumored among the students that this Master or that had said that the Gontish lad was the quickest student that had ever been at Roke, and tales grew up concerning the otak, which was said to be a disguised spirit who whispered wisdom in Ged's ear, and it was even said that the Archmage's raven had hailed Ged at his arrival as "Archmage to be." Whether or not they believed such stories, and whether or not they liked Ged, most of his companions admired him, and were eager to follow him when the rare wild mood came over him and he joined them to lead their games on the lengthening evenings of spring. But for the most part he was all work and pride and temper, and held himself apart. Among them all, Vetch being absent, he had no friend, and never knew he wanted one.

He was fifteen, very young to learn any of the High Arts of wizard or mage, those who carry the staff; but he was so quick to learn all the arts of illusion that the Master Changer, himself a young man, soon began to teach him apart from the others, and to tell him about the true Spells of Shaping. He explained how, if a thing is really to be changed into another thing, it must be re-named for as long as the spell lasts, and he told how this affects the names and natures of things surrounding the transformed thing. He spoke of the perils of changing, above all when the wizard transforms his own shape and thus is liable to be caught in his own spell. Little by little, drawn on by the boy's sureness of understanding, the young Master began to do more than merely tell him of these mysteries. He taught him first one and then another of the Great Spells of Change, and he gave him the Book of Shaping to study. This he did without knowledge of the Archmage, and unwisely, yet he meant no harm.

Ged worked also with the Master Summoner now, but that Master was a stern man, aged and hardened by the deep and somber wizardry he taught. He dealt with no illusion, only true magic, the summoning of such energies as light, and heat, and the force that draws the magnet, and those forces men perceive as weight, form, color, sound: real powers, drawn from the immense fathomless energies of the universe, which no man's spells or uses could exhaust or unbalance. The weatherworker's and seamaster's calling upon wind and water were crafts already known to his pupils, but it was he who showed them why the true wizard uses such spells only at need, since to summon up such earthly forces is to change the earth of which they are a part. "Rain on Roke may be drouth in Osskil," he said, "and a calm in the East Reach may be storm and ruin in the West, unless you know what you are about."

As for the calling of real things and living people, and the raising up of spirits of the dead, and the invocations of the Unseen, those spells which are the height of the Summoner's art and the mage's power, those he scarcely spoke of to them. Once or twice Ged tried to lead him to talk a little of such mysteries, but the Master was silent, looking at him long and grimly, till Ged grew uneasy and said no more.

Sometimes indeed he was uneasy working even such lesser spells as the Summoner taught him. There were certain runes on certain pages of the Lore-Book that seemed familiar to him, though he did not remember in what book he had ever seen them before. There were certain phrases that must be said in spells of Summoning that he did not like to say. They made him think, for an instant, of shadows in a dark room, of a shut door and shadows reaching out to him from the corner by the door. Hastily he put such thoughts or memories aside and went on. These moments of fear and darkness, he said to himself, were the shadows merely of his ignorance. The more he learned, the less he would have to fear, until finally in his full power as Wizard he need fear nothing in the world, nothing at all.

In the second month of that summer all the school gathered again at the Great House to celebrate the Moon's Night and the Long Dance, which that year fell together as one festival of two nights, which happens but once in fifty-two years. All the first night, the shortest night of full moon of the year, flutes played out in the fields, and the narrow streets of Thwil were full of drums and torches, and the sound of singing went out over the moonlit waters of Roke Bay. As the sun rose next morning the Chanters of Roke began to sing the long *Deed of Erreth-Akbe,* which tells how the white towers of Havnor were built, and of Erreth-Akbe's journeys from the Old Island, Éa, through all the Archipelago and the Reaches, until at last in the uttermost West Reach on the edge of the Open Sea he met the dragon Orm; and his bones in shattered armor lie among the dragon's bones on the shore of lonely Selidor, but his sword set atop the highest tower of Havnor still burns red in the sunset above the Inmost Sea. When the chant was finished the Long Dance began. Townsfolk and Masters and students and farmers all together, men and women, danced in the warm dust and dusk down all the roads of Roke to the sea-beaches, to the beat of drums and drone of pipes and flutes.

Straight out into the sea they danced, under the moon one night past full, and the music was lost in the breakers' sound. As the east grew light they came back up the beaches and the roads, the drums silent and only the flutes playing soft and shrill. So it was done on every island of the Archipelago that night: one dance, one music binding together the sea-divided lands.

When the Long Dance was over most people slept the day away, and gathered again at evening to eat and drink. There was a group of young fellows, prentices and sorcerers, who had brought their supper out from the refectory to hold private feast in a courtyard of the Great House: Vetch, Jasper, and Ged were there, and six or seven others, and some young lads released briefly from the Isolate Tower, for this festival had brought even Kurremkarmerruk out. They were all eating and laughing and playing such tricks out of pure frolic as might be the marvel of a king's court. One boy had lighted the court with a hundred stars of werelight, colored like jewels, that swung in a slow netted procession between them and the real stars; and a pair of boys were playing bowls with balls of green flame and bowling-pins that leaped and hopped away as the ball came near; and all the while Vetch sat cross-legged, eating roast chicken, up in mid-air. One of the younger boys tried to pull him down to earth, but Vetch merely drifted up a little higher, out of reach, and sat calmly smiling on the air. Now and then he tossed away a chicken bone, which turned to an owl and flew hooting among the netted star-lights. Ged shot breadcrumb arrows after the owls and brought them down, and when they touched the ground there they lay, bone and crumb, all illusion gone. Ged also tried to join Vetch up in the middle of the air, but lacking the key of the spell he had to flap his arms to keep aloft, and they were all laughing at his flights and flaps and bumps. He kept up his foolishness for the laughter's sake, laughing with them, for after those two long nights of dance and moonlight and music and magery he was in a fey and wild mood, ready for whatever might come.

He came lightly down on his feet just beside Jasper at last, and Jasper, who never laughed aloud, moved away saying, "The Sparrowhawk that can't fly . . ."

"Is jasper a precious stone?" Ged returned, grinning. "O Jewel among sorcerers, O Gem of Havnor, sparkle for us!"

The lad that had set the lights dancing sent one down to dance and glitter about Jasper's head. Not quite as cool as usual, frowning, Jasper brushed the light away and snuffed it out with one gesture. "I am sick of boys and noise and foolishness," he said.

"You're getting middle-aged, lad," Vetch remarked from above.

"If silence and gloom is what you want," put in one of the younger boys, "you could always try the Tower."

Ged said to him, "What is it you want, then, Jasper?"

"I want the company of my equals," Jasper said. "Come on, Vetch. Leave the prentices to their toys."

Ged turned to face Jasper. "What do sorcerers have that prentices lack?" he enquired. His voice was quiet, but all the other boys suddenly fell still, for in his tone as in Jasper's the spite between them now sounded plain and clear as steel coming out of a sheath.

"Power," Jasper said.

"I'll match your power act for act."

"You challenge me?"

"I challenge you."

Vetch had dropped down to the ground, and now he came between them, grim of face. "Duels in sorcery are forbidden to us, and well you know it. Let this cease!"

Both Ged and Jasper stood silent, for it was true they knew the law of Roke, and they also knew that Vetch was moved by love, and themselves by hate. Yet their anger was balked, not cooled. Presently, moving a little aside as if to be heard by Vetch alone, Jasper spoke, with his cool smile: "I think you'd better remind your goatherd friend again of the law that protects him. He looks sulky. I wonder, did he really think I'd accept a challenge from him? a fellow who smells of goats, a prentice who doesn't know the First Change?"

"Jasper," said Ged, "what do you know of what I know?"

For an instant, with no word spoken that any

heard, Ged vanished from their sight, and where he had stood a great falcon hovered, opening its hooked beak to scream: for one instant, and then Ged stood again in the flickering torchlight, his dark gaze on Jasper.

Jasper had taken a step backward, in astonishment; but now he shrugged and said one word: "Illusion."

The others muttered. Vetch said, "That was not illusion. It was true change. And enough. Jasper, listen—"

"Enough to prove that he sneaked a look in the Book of Shaping behind the Master's back: what then? Go on, Goatherd. I like this trap you're building for yourself. The more you try to prove yourself my equal, the more you show yourself for what you are."

At that, Vetch turned from Jasper, and said very softly to Ged, "Sparrowhawk, will you be a man and drop this now—come with me—"

Ged looked at his friend and smiled, but all he said was, "Keep Hoeg for me a little while, will you?" He put into Vetch's hands the little otak, which as usual had been riding on his shoulder. It had never let any but Ged touch it, but it came to Vetch now, and climbing up his arm cowered on his shoulder, its great bright eyes always on its master.

"Now," Ged said to Jasper, quietly as before, "what are you going to do to prove yourself my superior, Jasper?"

"I don't have to do anything, Goatherd. Yet I will. I will give you a chance—an opportunity. Envy eats you like a worm in an apple. Let's let out the worm. Once by Roke Knoll you boasted that Gontish wizards don't play games. Come to Roke Knoll now and show us what it is they do instead. And afterward, maybe I will show you a little sorcery."

"Yes, I should like to see that," Ged answered. The younger boys, used to seeing his black temper break out at the least hint of slight or insult, watched him in wonder at his coolness now. Vetch watched him not in wonder, but with growing fear. He tried to intervene again, but Jasper said, "Come, keep out of this, Vetch. What will you do with the chance I give you, Goatherd? Will you show us an illusion, a fireball, a charm to cure goats with the mange?"

"What would you like me to do, Jasper?"

The older lad shrugged. "Summon up a spirit from the dead, for all I care!"

"I will."

"You will not." Jasper looked straight at him, rage suddenly flaming out over his disdain. "You will not. You cannot. You brag and brag—"

"By my name, I will do it!"

They all stood utterly motionless for a moment.

Breaking away from Vetch who would have held him back by main force, Ged strode out of the courtyard, not looking back. The dancing werelights overhead died out, sinking down. Jasper hesitated a second, then followed after Ged. And the rest came straggling behind, in silence, curious and afraid.

The slopes of Roke Knoll went up dark into the darkness of summer night before moonrise. The presence of that hill where many wonders had been worked was heavy, like a weight in the air about them. As they came onto the hillside they thought of how the roots of it were deep, deeper than the sea, reaching down even to the old, blind, secret fires at the world's core. They stopped on the east slope. Stars hung over the black grass above them on the hill's crest. No wind blew.

Ged went a few paces up the slope away from the others and turning said in a clear voice, "Jasper! Whose spirit shall I call?"

"Call whom you like. None will listen to you." Jasper's voice shook a little, with anger perhaps. Ged answered him softly, mockingly, "Are you afraid?"

He did not even listen for Jasper's reply, if he made one. He no longer cared about Jasper. Now that they stood on Roke Knoll, hate and rage were gone, replaced by utter certainty. He need envy no one. He knew that his power, this night, on this dark enchanted ground, was greater than it had ever been, filling him till he trembled with the sense of strength barely kept in check. He knew now that Jasper was far beneath him, had been sent perhaps only to bring him here tonight, no rival but a mere servant of Ged's destiny. Under his feet he felt the hillroots going down and down into the dark, and over his head he saw the dry, far

fires of the stars. Between, all things were his to order, to command. He stood at the center of the world.

"Don't be afraid," he said, smiling. "I'll call a woman's spirit. You need not fear a woman. Elfarran I will call, the fair lady of the *Deed of Enlad.*"

"She died a thousand years ago, her bones lie afar under the Sea of Éa, and maybe there never was such a woman."

"Do years and distances matter to the dead? Do the Songs lie?" Ged said with the same gentle mockery, and then saying, "Watch the air between my hands," he turned away from the others and stood still.

In a great slow gesture he stretched out his arms, the gesture of welcome that opens an invocation. He began to speak.

He had read the runes of this Spell of Summoning in Ogion's book, two years and more ago, and never since had seen them. In darkness he had read them then. Now in this darkness it was as if he read them again on the page open before him in the night. But now he understood what he read, speaking it aloud word after word, and he saw the markings of how the spell must be woven with the sound of the voice and the motion of body and hand.

The other boys stood watching, not speaking, not moving unless they shivered a little: for the great spell was beginning to work. Ged's voice was soft still, but changed, with a deep singing in it, and the words he spoke were not known to them. He fell silent. Suddenly the wind rose roaring in the grass. Ged dropped to his knees and called out aloud. Then he fell forward as if to embrace earth with his outstretched arms, and when he rose he held something dark in his straining hands and arms, something so heavy that he shook with effort getting to his feet. The hot wind whined in the black tossing grasses on the hill. If the stars shone now none saw them.

The words of the enchantment hissed and mumbled on Ged's lips, and then he cried out aloud and clearly, "Elfarran!"

Again he cried the name, "Elfarran!"

And the third time, "Elfarran!"

The shapeless mass of darkness he had lifted split apart. It sundered, and a pale spindle of light gleamed between his opened arms, a faint oval reaching from the ground up to height of his raised hands. In the oval of light for a moment there moved a form, a human shape: a tall woman looking back over her shoulder. Her face was beautiful, and sorrowful, and full of fear.

Only for a moment did the spirit glimmer there. Then the sallow oval between Ged's arms grew bright. It widened and spread, a rent in the darkness of the earth and night, a ripping open of the fabric of the world. Through it blazed a terrible brightness. And through that bright misshapen breach clambered something like a clot of black shadow, quick and hideous, and it leaped straight out at Ged's face.

Staggering back under the weight of the thing, Ged gave a short, hoarse scream. The little otak watching from Vetch's shoulder, the animal that had no voice, screamed aloud also and leaped as if to attack.

Ged fell, struggling and writhing, while the bright rip in the world's darkness above him widened and stretched. The boys that watched fled, and Jasper bent down to the ground hiding his eyes from the terrible light. Vetch alone ran forward to his friend. So only he saw the lump of shadow that clung to Ged, tearing at his flesh. It was like a black beast, the size of a young child, though it seemed to swell and shrink; and it had no head or face, only the four taloned paws with which it gripped and tore. Vetch sobbed with horror, yet he put out his hands to try to pull the thing away from Ged. Before he touched it, he was bound still, unable to move.

The intolerable brightness faded, and slowly the torn edges of the world closed together. Nearby a voice was speaking as softly as a tree whispers or a fountain plays.

Starlight began to shine again, and the grasses of the hillside were whitened with the light of the moon just rising. The night was healed. Restored and steady lay the balance of light and dark. The shadow-beast was gone. Ged lay sprawled on his back, his arms flung out as if they yet kept the wide gesture of welcome and invocation. His face was blackened with blood and there were great black stains on his shirt. The little otak cowered by his shoulder, quivering. And above him stood an old man whose cloak glimmered pale in the moonrise: the Archmage Nemmerle.

The end of Nemmerle's staff hovered silvery above Ged's breast. Once gently it touched him over the heart, once on the lips, while Nemmerle whispered. Ged stirred, and his lips parted gasping for breath. Then the old Archmage lifted the staff, and set it to earth, and leaned heavily on it with bowed head, as if he had scarcely strength to stand.

Vetch found himself free to move. Looking around, he saw that already others were there, the Masters Summoner and Changer. An act of great wizardry is not worked without arousing such men, and they had ways of coming very swiftly when need called, though none had been so swift as the Archmage. They now sent for help, and some who came went with the Archmage, while others, Vetch among them, carried Ged to the chambers of the Master Herbal.

All night long the Summoner stayed on Roke Knoll, keeping watch. Nothing stirred there on the hillside where the stuff of the world had been torn open. No shadow came crawling through moonlight seeking the rent through which it might clamber back into its own domain. It had fled from Nemmerle, and from the mighty spell-walls that surround and protect Roke Island, but it was in the world now. In the world, somewhere, it hid. If Ged had died that night it might have tried to find the doorway he had opened, and follow him into death's realm, or slip back into whatever place it had come from; for this the Summoner waited on Roke Knoll. But Ged lived.

They had laid him abed in the healing-chamber, and the Master Herbal tended the wounds he had on his face and throat and shoulder. They were deep, ragged, and evil wounds. The black blood in them would not stanch, welling out even under the charms and the cobweb-wrapped perriot leaves laid upon them. Ged lay blind and dumb in fever like a stick in a slow fire, and there was no spell to cool what burned him.

Not far away, in the unroofed court where the fountain played, the Archmage lay also unmoving, but cold, very cold: only his eyes lived, watching the fall of moonlit water and the stir of moonlit leaves. Those with him said no spells and worked no healing. Quietly they spoke among themselves from time to time, and then turned again to watch their Lord. He lay still, hawk nose and high forehead and white hair bleached by moonlight all to the color of bone. To check the ungoverned spell and drive off the shadow from Ged, Nemmerle had spent all his power, and with it his bodily strength was gone. He lay dying. But the death of a great mage, who has many times in his life walked on the dry steep hillsides of death's kingdom, is a strange matter: for the dying man goes not blindly, but surely, knowing the way. When Nemmerle looked up through the leaves of the tree, those with him did not know if he watched the stars of summer fading in daybreak, or those other stars, which never set above the hills that see no dawn.

The raven of Osskil that had been his pet for thirty years was gone. No one had seen where it went. "It flies before him," the Master Patterner said, as they kept vigil.

The day came warm and clear. The Great House and the streets of Thwil were hushed. No voice was raised, until along towards noon iron bells spoke out aloud in the Chanter's Tower, harshly tolling.

On the next day the Nine Masters of Roke gathered in a place somewhere under the dark trees of the Immanent Grove. Even there they set nine walls of silence about them, that no person or power might speak to them or hear them as they chose from amongst the mages of all Earthsea him who would be the new Archmage. Gensher of Way was chosen. A ship was sent forth at once across the Inmost Sea to Way Island to bring the Archmage back to Roke. The Master Windkey stood in the stern and raised up the magewind into the sail, and quickly the ship departed, and was gone.

Of these events Ged knew nothing. For four weeks of that hot summer he lay blind, and deaf, and mute, though at times he moaned and cried out like an animal. At last, as the patient crafts of the Master Herbal worked their healing, his wounds began to close and the fever left him. Little by little he seemed to hear again, though he never spoke. On a clear day of autumn the Master Herbal opened the shutters of the room where Ged lay. Since the darkness of that night on Roke Knoll he had known only darkness. Now he saw daylight, and the sun shining. He hid his scarred face in his hands and wept.

Still when winter came he could speak only with a stammering tongue, and the Master Herbal kept him there in the healing-chambers, trying to lead his body and mind gradually back to strength. It was early spring when at last the Master released him, sending him first to offer his fealty to the Archmage Gensher. For he had not been able to join all the others of the School in this duty when Gensher came to Roke.

None of his companions had been allowed to visit him in the months of his sickness, and now as he passed some of them asked one another, "Who is that?" He had been light and lithe and strong. Now, lamed by pain, he went hesitantly, and did not raise his face, the left side of which was white with scars. He avoided those who knew him and those who did not, and made his way straight to the court of the Fountain. There where once he had awaited Nemmerle, Gensher awaited him.

Like the old Archmage the new one was cloaked in white; but like most men of Way and the East Reach Gensher was black-skinned, and his look was black, under thick brows.

Ged knelt and offered him fealty and obedience. Gensher was silent a while.

"I know what you did," he said at last, "but not what you are. I cannot accept your fealty."

Ged stood up, and set his hand on the trunk of the young tree beside the fountain to steady himself. He was still very slow to find words. "Am I to leave Roke, my lord?"

"Do you want to leave Roke?"

"No."

"What do you want?"

"To stay. To learn. To undo . . . the evil. . . ."

"Nemmerle himself could not do that.—No, I would not let you go from Roke. Nothing protects you but the power of the Masters here and the defenses laid upon this island that keep the creatures of evil away. If you left now, the thing you loosed would find you at once, and enter into you, and possess you. You would be no man but a *gebbeth,* a puppet doing the will of that evil shadow which you raised up into the sunlight. You must stay here, until you gain strength and wisdom enough to defend yourself from it—if ever you do. Even now it waits for you. Assuredly it waits for you. Have you seen it since that night?"

"In dreams, lord." After a while Ged went on, speaking with pain and shame, "Lord Gensher, I do not know what it was—the thing that came out of the spell and cleaved to me—"

"Nor do I know. It has no name. You have great power inborn in you, and you used that power wrongly, to work a spell over which you had no control, not knowing how that spell affects the balance of light and dark, life and death, good and evil. And you were moved to do this by pride and by hate. Is it any wonder the result was ruin? You summoned a spirit from the dead, but with it came one of the Powers of unlife. Uncalled it came from a place where there are no names. Evil, it wills to work evil through you. The power you had to call it gives it power over you: you are connected. It is the shadow of your arrogance, the shadow of your ignorance, the shadow you cast. Has a shadow a name?"

Ged stood sick and haggard. He said at last, "Better I had died."

"Who are you to judge that, you for whom Nemmerle gave his life?—You are safe here. You will live here, and go on with your training. They tell me you were clever. Go on and do your work. Do it well. It is all you can do."

So Gensher ended, and was suddenly gone, as is the way of mages. The fountain leaped in the sunlight, and Ged watched it a while and listened to its voice, thinking of Nemmerle. Once in that court he had felt himself to be a word spoken by the sunlight. Now the darkness also had spoken: a word that could not be unsaid.

He left the court, going to his old room in the South Tower, which they had kept empty for him. He stayed there alone. When the gong called to supper he went, but he would hardly speak to the other lads at the Long Table, or raise his face to them, even those who greeted him most gently. So after a day or two they

all left him alone. To be alone was his desire, for he feared the evil he might do or say unwittingly.

Neither Vetch nor Jasper was there, and he did not ask about them. The boys he had led and lorded over were all ahead of him now, because of the months he had lost, and that spring and summer he studied with lads younger than himself. Nor did he shine among them, for the words of any spell, even the simplest illusion-charm, came halting from his tongue, and his hands faltered at their craft.

In autumn he was to go once again to the Isolate Tower to study with the Master Namer. This task which he had once dreaded now pleased him, for silence was what he sought, and long learning where no spells were wrought, and where that power which he knew was still in him would never be called upon to act.

The night before he left for the Tower a visitor came to his room, one wearing a brown travelling-cloak and carrying a staff of oak shod with iron. Ged stood up, at sight of the wizard's staff.

"Sparrowhawk—"

At the sound of the voice, Ged raised his eyes: it was Vetch standing there, solid and foursquare as ever, his black blunt face older but his smile unchanged. On his shoulder crouched a little beast, brindle-furred and bright-eyed.

"He stayed with me while you were sick, and now I'm sorry to part with him. And sorrier to part with you, Sparrowhawk. But I'm going home. Here, hoeg! go to your true master!" Vetch patted the otak and set it down on the floor. It went and sat on Ged's pallet, and began to wash its fur with a dry brown tongue like a little leaf. Vetch laughed, but Ged could not smile. He bent down to hide his face, stroking the otak.

"I thought you wouldn't come to me, Vetch," he said.

He did not mean any reproach, but Vetch answered, "I couldn't come to you. The Master Herbal forbade me; and since winter I've been with the Master in the Grove, locked up myself. I was not free, until I earned my staff. Listen: when you too are free, come to the East Reach.

I will be waiting for you. There's good cheer in the little towns there, and wizards are well received."

"Free . . ." Ged muttered, and shrugged a little, trying to smile.

Vetch looked at him, not quite as he had used to look, with no less love but more wizardry, perhaps. He said gently, "You won't stay bound on Roke forever."

"Well . . . I have thought, perhaps I may come to work with the Master in the Tower, to be one of those who seek among the books and the stars for lost names, and so . . . so do no more harm, if not much good. . . ."

"Maybe," said Vetch. "I am no seer, but I see before you, not rooms and books, but far seas, and the fire of dragons, and the towers of cities, and all such things a hawk sees when he flies far and high."

"And behind me—what do you see behind me?" Ged asked, and stood up as he spoke, so that the werelight that burned overhead between them sent his shadow back against the wall and floor. Then he turned his face aside and said, stammering, "But tell me where you will go, what you will do."

"I will go home, to see my brothers and the sister you have heard me speak of. I left her a little child and soon she'll be having her Naming—it's strange to think of! And so I'll find me a job of wizardry somewhere among the little isles. Oh, I would stay and talk with you, but I can't, my ship goes out tonight and the tide is turned already. Sparrowhawk, if ever your way lies East, come to me. And if ever you need me, send for me, call on me by my name: Estarriol."

At that Ged lifted his scarred face, meeting his friend's eyes.

"Estarriol," he said, "my name is Ged."

Then quietly they bade each other farewell, and Vetch turned and went down the stone hallway, and left Roke.

Ged stood still a while, like one who has received great news, and must enlarge his spirit to receive it. It was a great gift that Vetch had given him, the knowledge of his true name.

No one knows a man's true name but himself and his namer. He may choose at length to tell it to his brother, or his wife, or his friend, yet even those few will never use it where any third person may hear it. In front of other people they will, like other people, call him by his use-name, his nickname—such a name as Sparrowhawk, and Vetch, and Ogion which means "fir-cone." If plain men hide their true name from all but a few they love and trust utterly, so much more must wizardly men, being more dangerous, and more endangered. Who knows a man's name, holds that man's life in his keeping. Thus to Ged who had lost faith in himself, Vetch had given that gift only a friend can give, the proof of unshaken, unshakable trust.

Ged sat down on his pallet and let the globe of werelight die, giving off as it faded a faint whiff of marsh-gas. He petted the otak, which stretched comfortably and went to sleep on his knee as if it had never slept anywhere else. The Great House was silent. It came to Ged's mind that this was the eve of his own Passage, the day on which Ogion had given him his name. Four years were gone since then. He remembered the coldness of the mountain spring through which he had walked naked and unnamed. He fell to thinking of other bright pools in the River Ar, where he had used to swim; and of Ten Alders village under the great slanting forests of the mountain; of the shadows of morning across the dusty village street, the fire leaping under bellows-blast in the smith's smelting-pit on a winter afternoon, the witch's dark fragrant hut where the air was heavy with smoke and wreathing spells. He had not thought of these things for a long time. Now they came back to him, on this night he was seventeen years old. All the years and places of his brief broken life came within mind's reach and made a whole again. He knew once more, at last, after this long, bitter, wasted time, who he was and where he was.

But where he must go in the years to come, that he could not see; and he feared to see it.

Next morning he set out across the island, the otak riding on his shoulder as it had used to. This time it took him three days, not two, to walk to the Isolate Tower, and he was bone-weary when he came in sight of the Tower above the spitting, hissing seas of the northern cape. Inside, it was dark as he remembered, and cold as he remembered, and Kurremkarmerruk sat on his high seat writing down lists of names. He glanced at Ged and said without welcome, as if Ged had never been away, "Go to bed; tired is stupid. Tomorrow you may open the Book of the Undertakings of the Makers, learning the names therein."

William Mayne

A Year and a Day

William Mayne's many books range from realistic novels about life in a choir school to complex psychological fantasies. In this short, gentle story, one of Mayne's most accessible, two young girls and their parents, living in nineteenth-century Cornwall, adopt a fairy changeling, exemplifying the author's interest in the folk traditions of the British countryside in general and the magical Cornish legends in particular. The child's-eye view reveals an emotional landscape in which the girls' love almost heals Adam, known as the holy boy, of his psychological disturbance—his *otherness*—and yearning for his own realm. His death, linked to the renewal of the seasons, is inevitable and mythic. This novella is a miniature parable on the nature of life, death, and time. [From Williams Mayne, *A Year and a Day* (Dutton, 1976).]

"Say tree, say house, say cat," said Becca, teaching the boy to speak. "Say Isaac, no, Adam, say Adam."

"Say Sary," said Sara. "Say Mother."

The boy opened his mouth, without looking happy, and made the little laugh that Mother often made. So he knew what Mother meant, and that was his name for her, his word.

On Sunday morning they went to church. Now all the people came to look at the boy. Some came again, because they had already been to the house. Some came for the first time, because they were too proud or too polite to come to the cottage by the water. So on the way to the church there were faces and eyes looking their way.

Dad was the first to notice. He always felt when he was being watched. When he had worked at the tin mines underground he had felt the ghosts watching him, and heard them knocking on the walls of the mine. That was

why he had left the mines, because of being always watched, and worked now in the open at the clay pits. So today he noticed the eyes watching, and then saw the faces turned towards them. He began to whistle quietly, until he thought it was not right to whistle on a Sunday on the way to church. He stopped whistling and began to click his tongue and hum a tune. But he had to stop that too, because the only tune he could remember was not a hymn tune, which would have been all right, but one of the Lelant dances, which wouldn't do at all. So he began to get cross with everybody, telling Mother to step on a little faster, and making Becca stop her skipping along and walk more like a crow than a blackbird.

"He calls me blackbird," said Becca, holding up the boy's hand. The boy looked up from where he was walking between the two girls and said the piece of blackbird song that was Becca's name. Then he said Sara's name, in gull language, and Mother's name in a laugh, and looked at Dad. He opened his mouth very wide and made the sound of a great and noisy yawn.

"Tired already then?" said Dad. "We can go back home and be not so much looked on." But the boy was not tired. He was only imitating Dad's yawn and making a name out of it. Sara and Becca knew at once, and started to laugh and lean on each other and pull on Dad's coat. The boy began to look very pleased, and started to shout like a gull and make all his other naming noises to please them.

It all happened in the middle of the village street, and people who had stopped looking at the boy and gone on towards church turned round and looked again. "Well," said Dad, "I don't care for it at all, like this."

Mother picked the boy up and walked on. The boy knew there was to be no more shouting. Sara and Becca stopped roaring in a moment, when Dad told them to, and they were all quiet by the time they got to church.

They sat at the back, so that no one could watch. But of course faces kept turning to them, because the boy wanted to join in with the music. There was no organ. The Squire had often said that there should be an organ, but there still was only Mr. Hocking playing a violin, and three more men with an oboe, a clarinet, and a curling gaspy thing called a serpent. The boy kept making the strange sounds of these old instruments. He did not have tunes, only sounds, and that made the band go wrong so that it forgot its tunes and only had sounds. At last, at the end of the psalms, there was another new sound in the church, and that was the young Squire laughing in his pew, and his dog jumping up and barking and licking his face.

The Rector came to read a lesson then, and looked at everyone very dark and coldly, so that there was quiet. The boy was quiet, except that he dropped one of his shoes off and it bumped down to the floor. Everybody heard the Squire rattle the window open, because he had a window and a fireplace in his pew, and drop the dog outside, where it went down with a yelp. Everybody heard it pad into church a minute later, as the Rector was reading, and scrape the pew door open.

After that Sara and Becca got down among the pews and played quietly with the boy, so that he did not notice the band and make his noises. Mother thought the Rector would be pleased with the way they were keeping him quiet, all through the next singing and the next piece of talking. So she was very startled when the Rector came slowly down the church towards the door, and then past the door, and right up to where she and Dad were sitting, and there he stopped. Mother put down a hand and brought Sara and Becca up, and the boy,

Illustration by Laszlo Kubinyi. From *A Year and a Day,* by William Mayne. Copyright © 1976 by William Mayne. Reprinted by permission of the publisher, E. P. Dutton, Inc., and Clarke, Irwin & Co., Ltd.

from the floor where they had been sitting, and they all looked at the Rector, wondering how wicked they had all been, for him to come to them in the middle of the service.

But he was not angered by anything. He beckoned to the boy, and Mother handed him across. The Rector picked him up and took him towards the church door, and then to the font, which is a large basin with water in where babies are baptised. "Where are the godparents?" the Rector asked, when he was there, and Mother and Dad and the girls had followed him.

Mother said she hadn't reckoned nor thought about such, no, and Dad shook his head and still couldn't bring anything to mind but a Lelant dance tune. The Rector said that they could be godparents, because they were not real ones after all, and then the Squire stepped out, with his dog in his arms, and said he would be one too, ha, what?

Then the boy was baptised, christened Adam, and everything went well, in spite of his attempts to drink most of the holy water.

"Now he's a holy Christian man," said Sara, leading him back to the pew. The holy Christian man kicked off his shoes and made clarinet noises for the rest of the service.

One day the summer was over. The land stopped being dry and hot and became wet, muddy, and tepid. A soft warm wind began to lie across the country, pulling at the leaves on the trees and painting the sky white, grey, and sometimes black during the day, and making it red night and morning. The sea rose up with the wind and filled the river in front of the house, and waves would scratch the shore and spill on to the road, and the fishing boats came right up the river to rest on the mud, away from the stone quays of the harbour.

Sara looked at their boy Adam when they were in the house one afternoon and the rain was stiff as a broom outside. She saw how he had changed since she found him. Then he had been small and pale and yellow, nearly the same colour as the Jersey tunic. Now he was dark with the sun that had been on him, and the Jersey tunic was still just about the colour of the sheep the wool had come from. When he first was with them he could hardly walk, partly

from not knowing how, and partly from not being strong. Now he could walk all day, and run as he liked, and jump heavily or lightly, whichever he chose, and he was strong.

He had learnt some words. That is, he understood them. Dad said he was like a dog, knowing what its master said, and like a dog he could not say them himself. He could follow a lot of what was said, but all he could say was sounds. He seemed able to make any sound he heard, whether it was cloth being shaken, or a spade digging the earth, or a fly in the next room buzzing at the window. He was sensible with what he understood and with what he could say in sounds.

Becca could talk with him for a long time without getting cross, because if he stopped his sort of talking she went and did other things. Sara often was angry with him for not understanding, but that was because she loved him so much and wanted him to love her. If he really did love her then he would understand her, she thought, and she would understand him. So she was sometimes impatient. But Becca did not care so much, and she was not offended if he talked about something else instead of what she was talking about.

There were times when Adam grew angry with them, for talking to him too much. They used to wonder why he covered his eyes, and they thought they must hurt him. But he was doing it so that he would not hear them. It took him some time to find out that he ought to cover his ears. Usually that was enough for him, to get where he could not hear them. That would make Sara cross too, and she would cry, and Becca would wonder what she had done wrong, to send them both away.

Covering his ears was not always enough for him. Becca was patient enough to find what came next, but Sara had always gone away, and she never saw the next thing. The boy wanted to go away from people and talk to things. Becca had seen him once uncover his ears and talk to a caterpillar on a leaf. He seemed to listen to it, and to touch it with his fingers, and open his mouth to speak to it, but Becca heard never a sound from either of them. But she knew he could hear sounds that were not there, and Sara knew it too. He would sit in the garden, and point to a corner of it, and make a sound they could not hear, and it was the sound of a spider far off on the fence, or a lizard sunning on a stone.

From a long way off he could hear Janey Tregose, and there was a silent sound for her too, not any of her words, which there were plenty of, but something else. Janey said he could hear her rheumatic joints creaking better than she could. But though Sara and Becca looked into his mouth and saw his tongue and his throat move, they could not tell what sound he made.

At church he learnt the tunes of the band, and followed one instrument or another, often at the same time, and just as often a little later. But that was not much worse than some of the bad singers there already, so no one minded. The Rector minded when he imitated the closing of the Bible during the service, but all the Rector could do about it was close the Bible more quietly. All the congregation minded one day when the boy heard something high up in the vault of the roof, and spoke a very small sound that Sara and Becca could just hear. Out from the rafters flew a cloud of bats, and there were real shrieks from women and answering shrieks from the boy, and a strong fierce silence from the Rector, and laughter and barking from the Squire's pew. Mother put two hands over her head at first, and then she knew who had caused it all, and put the two hands down to haul up the Jersey tunic and give the boy a hard slap on his bare bottom. That stopped his shrieks answering the women, and his cries to the bats.

At times, on a rainy, windy day, they would not be able to find him in the house. His tunic would be there, and that often happened because clothes slid off him. But he would be missing. He liked to go out in the rain with nothing on. Sara and Becca would not have done such a thing themselves, but with the boy it did not seem to matter much. He would come back later on, when the day was growing dark, wet and warm and content.

Becca followed him one day, hoping he would stop and play in a dry place under a hedge. But he did not. He walked on in the rain and wind and seemed comfortable. She followed after him, and her clothes became soaked and stuck to her and her hair grew thin and the wind turned her hands blue. She followed and watched, and the boy went up the hill to the highest place among the furze bushes where Janey Tregose let her goats wander, and there he stood and talked to the sky and the weather, and listened through the wind to the sea, and looked and searched the wild air. Becca crouched herself under the furze and was cold. She heard him answering the wind, and she heard him call out sounds more like words than anything she had heard him make before. But no one answered him, and Becca thought it might be because she was there, especially when he came home this time unhappy and restless, pacing about the house all the evening and the night.

J. R. R. Tolkien

The Hobbit

This modern classic for children, by an eminent scholar and philologist, is deeply rooted in the folklore and myth of northwest Europe. Hobbits, J. R. R. Tolkien tells us, were little folk who lived, like dwarfs and elves, in ancient times now lost and forgotten. On a quest for treasure hoard, the hobbit Bilbo has become separated from his companions, the dwarfs, and is lost in a tunnel deep under a mountain. [From J. R. R. Tolkien, *The Hobbit* (Houghton Mifflin, 1937).]

Riddles in the Dark

When Bilbo opened his eyes, he wondered if he had; for it was just as dark as with them shut. No one was anywhere near him. Just imagine his fright! He could hear nothing, see nothing, and he could feel nothing except the stone of the floor.

Very slowly he got up and groped about on all fours, till he touched the wall of the tunnel; but neither up nor down it could he find anything: nothing at all, no sign of goblins, no sign of dwarves. His head was swimming, and he was far from certain even of the direction they had been going in when he had his fall. He guessed as well as he could, and crawled along for a good way, till suddenly his hand met what felt like a tiny ring of cold metal lying on the floor of the tunnel. It was a turning point in his career, but he did not know it. He put the ring in his pocket almost without thinking; certainly it did not seem of any particular use at the moment. He did not go much further, but sat down on the cold floor and gave himself up to complete miserableness, for a long while. He thought of himself frying bacon and eggs in his own kitchen at home—for he could feel inside that it was high time for some meal or other; but that only made him miserabler.

He could not think what to do; nor could he think what had happened; or why he had been left behind; or why, if he had been left behind, the goblins had not caught him; or even why his head was so sore. The truth was he had been lying quiet, out of sight and out of mind, in a very dark corner for a long while.

After some time he felt for his pipe. It was not broken, and that was something. Then he felt for his pouch, and there was some tobacco in it, and that was something more. Then he felt for matches and he could not find any at all, and that shattered his hopes completely. Just as well for him, as he agreed when he came to his senses. Goodness knows what the striking of matches and the smell of tobacco would have brought on him out of dark holes in that horrible place. Still at the moment he felt very crushed. But in slapping all his pockets and feeling all round himself for matches his hand came on the hilt of his little sword—the little dagger that he got from the trolls, and that he had quite forgotten; nor do the goblins seem to have noticed it, as he wore it inside his breeches.

Now he drew it out. It shone pale and dim before his eyes. "So it is an elvish blade, too," he thought; "and goblins are not very near, and yet not far enough."

But somehow he was comforted. It was rather splendid to be wearing a blade made in Gondolin for the goblin-wars of which so many songs had sung; and also he had noticed that such weapons made a great impression on goblins that came upon them suddenly.

"Go back?" he thought. "No good at all! Go sideways? Impossible! Go forward? Only thing to do! On we go!" So up he got, and trotted along with his little sword held in front

of him and one hand feeling the wall, and his heart all of a patter and a pitter.

Now certainly Bilbo was in what is called a tight place. But you must remember it was not quite so tight for him as it would have been for me or for you. Hobbits are not quite like ordinary people; and after all if their holes are nice cheery places and properly aired, quite different from the tunnels of the goblins, still they are more used to tunnelling than we are, and they do not easily lose their sense of direction underground—not when their heads have recovered from being bumped. Also they can move very quietly, and hide easily, and recover wonderfully from falls and bruises, and they have a fund of wisdom and wise sayings that men have mostly never heard or have forgotten long ago.

I should not have liked to have been in Mr. Baggins' place, all the same. The tunnel seemed to have no end. All he knew was that it was still going down pretty steadily and keeping in the same direction in spite of a twist and a turn or two. There were passages leading off to the side every now and then, as he knew by the glimmer of his sword, or could feel with his hand on the wall. Of these he took no notice, except to hurry past for fear of goblins or half-imagined dark things coming out of them. On and on he went, and down and down; and still he heard no sound of anything except the occasional whirr of a bat by his ears, which startled him at first, till it became too frequent to bother about. I do not know how long he kept on like this, hating to go on, not daring to stop, on, on, until he was tireder than tired. It seemed like all the way to tomorrow and over it to the days beyond.

Suddenly without any warning he trotted splash into water! Ugh! it was icy cold. That pulled him up sharp and short. He did not know whether it was just a pool in the path, or the edge of an underground stream that crossed the passage, or the brink of a deep dark subterranean lake. The sword was hardly shining at all. He stopped, and he could hear, when he listened hard, drops drip-drip-dripping from an unseen roof into the water below; but there seemed no other sort of sound.

"So it is a pool or a lake, and not an underground river," he thought. Still he did not dare to wade out into the darkness. He could not swim; and he thought, too, of nasty slimy things, with big bulging blind eyes, wriggling in the water. There are strange things living in the pools and lakes in the hearts of mountains: fish whose fathers swam in, goodness only knows how many years ago, and never swam out again, while their eyes grew bigger and bigger and bigger from trying to see in the blackness; also there are other things more slimy than fish. Even in the tunnels and caves the goblins have made for themselves there are other things living unbeknown to them that have sneaked in from outside to lie up in the dark. Some of these caves, too, go back in their beginnings to ages before the goblins, who only widened them and joined them up with passages, and the original owners are still there in odd corners, slinking and nosing about.

Deep down here by the dark water lived old Gollum. I don't know where he came from, nor who or what he was. He was Gollum—as dark as darkness, except for two big round pale eyes. He had a boat, and he rowed about quite quietly on the lake; for lake it was, wide and deep and deadly cold. He paddled it with large feet dangling over the side, but never a ripple did he make. Not he. He was looking out of his pale lamp-like eyes for blind fish, which he grabbed with his long fingers as quick as thinking. He liked meat too. Goblin he thought good, when he could get it; but he took care they never found him out. He just throttled them from behind, if they ever came down alone anywhere near the edge of the water, while he was prowling about. They very seldom did, for they had a feeling that something unpleasant was lurking down there, down at the very roots of the mountain. They had come on the lake, when they were tunnelling down long ago, and they found they could go no further; so there their road ended in that direction, and there was no reason to go that way—unless the Great Goblin sent them. Sometimes he took a fancy for fish from the lake, and sometimes neither goblin nor fish came back.

Actually Gollum lived on a slimy island of rock in the middle of the lake. He was watching Bilbo now from the distance with his pale eyes like telescopes. Bilbo could not see him, but he was wondering a lot about Bilbo, for he could see that he was no goblin at all.

Gollum got into his boat and shot off from the island, while Bilbo was sitting on the brink altogether flummoxed and at the end of his way and his wits. Suddenly up came Gollum and whispered and hissed:

"Bless us and splash us, my precioussss! I guess it's a choice feast; at least a tasty morsel it'd make us, gollum!" And when he said *gollum* he made a horrible swallowing noise in his throat. That is how he got his name, though he always called himself "my precious."

The hobbit jumped nearly out of his skin when the hiss came in his ears, and he suddenly saw the pale eyes sticking out at him.

"Who are you?" he said, thrusting his dagger in front of him.

"What iss he, my precious?" whispered Gollum (who always spoke to himself through never having anyone else to speak to). This is what he had come to find out, for he was not really very hungry at the moment, only curious; otherwise he would have grabbed first and whispered afterwards.

"I am Mr. Bilbo Baggins. I have lost the dwarves and I have lost the wizard, and I don't know where I am; and I don't want to know, if only I can get away."

"What's he got in his handses?" said Gollum, looking at the sword, which he did not quite like.

"A sword, a blade which came out of Gondolin!"

"Sssss," said Gollum, and became quite polite. "Praps ye sits here and chats with it a bitsy, my preciousss. It likes riddles, praps it does, does it?" He was anxious to appear friendly, at any rate for the moment, and until he found out more about the sword and the hobbit, whether he was quite alone really, whether he was good to eat, and whether Gollum was really hungry. Riddles were all he could think of. Asking them, and sometimes guessing them, had been the only game he had ever played with other funny creatures sitting in their holes in the long, long ago, before the goblins came, and he was cut off from his friends far under the mountains.

"Very well," said Bilbo, who was anxious to agree, until he found out more about the creature, whether he was quite alone, whether he was fierce or hungry, and whether he was a friend of the goblins.

"You ask first," he said, because he had not had time to think of a riddle.

So Gollum hissed:

"What has roots as nobody sees,
Is taller than trees,
    Up, up it goes,
    And yet never grows?"

"Easy!" said Bilbo. "Mountain, I suppose."

"Does it guess easy? It must have a competition with us, my preciouss! If precious asks, and it doesn't answer, we eats it, my preciousss. If it asks us, and we doesn't answer, we gives it a present, gollum!"

"All right!" said Bilbo, not daring to disagree, and nearly bursting his brain to think of riddles that could save him from being eaten.

"Thirty white horses on a red hill,
    First they champ,
    Then they stamp,
Then they stand still."

That was all he could think of to ask—the idea of eating was rather on his mind. It was rather an old one, too, and Gollum knew the answer as well as you do.

"Chestnuts, chestnuts," he hissed. "Teeth! teeth! my preciousss; but we has only six!" Then he asked his second:

"Voiceless it cries,
Wingless flutters,
Toothless bites,
Mouthless mutters."

"Half a moment!" cried Bilbo, who was still thinking uncomfortably about eating. Fortunately he had once heard something rather like this before, and getting his wits back he thought of the answer. "Wind, wind, of course," he said, and he was so pleased that he made up one on the spot. "This'll puzzle the nasty little underground creature," he thought:

"An eye in a blue face
Saw an eye in a green face.
'That eye is like to this eye'
Said the first eye,
'But in low place,
Not in high place.' "

"Ss, ss, ss," said Gollum. He had been underground a long long time, and was forgetting this sort of thing. But just as Bilbo was beginning to wonder what Gollum's present would be like, Gollum brought up memories of ages and ages and ages before, when he lived with his grandmother in a hole in a bank by a river. "Sss, sss, my preciouss," he said. "Sun on the daisies it means, it does."

But these ordinary aboveground everyday sort of riddles were tiring for him. Also they reminded him of days when he had been less lonely and sneaky and nasty, and that put him out of temper. What is more they made him hungry; so this time he tried something a bit more difficult and more unpleasant:

"It cannot be seen, cannot be felt,
Cannot be heard, cannot be smelt.
It lies behind stars and under hills,
    And empty holes it fills.
It comes first and follows after,
    Ends life, kills laughter."

Unfortunately for Gollum Bilbo had heard that sort of thing before; and the answer was all round him any way. "Dark!" he said without even scratching his head or putting on his thinking cap.

"A box without hinges, key, or lid,
Yet golden treasure inside is hid,"

He asked to gain time, until he could think of a really hard one. This he thought a dreadfully easy chestnut, though he had not asked it in the usual words. But it proved a nasty poser for Gollum. He hissed to himself, and still he did not answer; he whispered and spluttered.

After some while Bilbo became impatient. "Well, what is it?" he said. "The answer's not a kettle boiling over, as you seem to think from the noise you are making."

"Give us a chance; let it give us a chance, my preciouss-ss-ss."

"Well," said Bilbo, after giving him a long chance, "what about your present?"

But suddenly Gollum remembered thieving from nests long ago, and sitting under the river bank teaching his grandmother, teaching his grandmother to suck—"Eggses!" he hissed. "Eggses it is!" Then he asked:

"Alive without breath,
As cold as death;
Never thirsty, ever drinking,
All in mail never clinking."

He also in his turn thought this was a dreadfully easy one, because he was always thinking of the answer. But he could not remember anything better at the moment, he was so flustered by the egg-question. All the same it was a poser for poor Bilbo, who never had anything to do with the water if he could help it. I imagine you know the answer, of course, or can guess it as easy as winking, since you are sitting comfortably at home and have not the danger of being eaten to disturb your thinking. Bilbo sat and cleared his throat once or twice, but no answer came.

After a while Gollum began to hiss with pleasure to himself: "Is it nice, my preciousss? Is it juicy? Is it scrumptiously crunchable?" He began to peer at Bilbo out of the darkness.

"Half a moment," said the hobbit shivering. "I gave you a good long chance just now."

"It must make haste, haste!" said Gollum, beginning to climb out of his boat on to the shore to get at Bilbo. But when he put his long webby foot in the water, a fish jumped out in a fright and fell on Bilbo's toes.

"Ugh!" he said, "it is cold and clammy!',— and so he guessed. "Fish! fish!" he cried. "It is fish."

Gollum was dreadfully disappointed; but Bilbo asked another riddle as quick as ever he could, so that Gollum had to get back into his boat and think.

"No-legs lay on one-leg, two-legs sat near
on three-legs, four-legs got some."

It was not really the right time for this riddle, but Bilbo was in a hurry. Gollum might have had some trouble guessing it, if he had asked it at another time. As it was, talking of fish, "no-legs" was not so very difficult, and after that the rest was easy. "Fish on a little table, man at table sitting on a stool, the cat has the bones" that of course is the answer, and Gollum soon gave it. Then he thought the time had come to ask something hard and horrible. This is what he said:

"This thing all things devours:
Birds, beasts, trees, flowers;
Gnaws iron, bites steel;
Grinds hard stones to meal;
Slays king, ruins town,
And beats high mountain down."

Poor Bilbo sat in the dark thinking of all the horrible names of all the giants and ogres he had ever heard told of in tales, but not one of them had done all these things. He had a feeling that the answer was quite different and that he ought to know it, but he could not think of it. He began to get frightened, and that is bad for thinking. Gollum began to get out of his boat. He flapped into the water and paddled to the bank; Bilbo could see his eyes coming towards him. His tongue seemed to stick in his mouth; he wanted to shout out: "Give me more time! Give me time!" But all that came out with a sudden squeal was: "Time! Time!"

Bilbo was saved by pure luck. For that of course was the answer.

Gollum was disappointed once more; and now he was getting angry, and also tired of the game. It had made him very hungry indeed. This time he did not go back to the boat. He sat down in the dark by Bilbo. That made the hobbit most dreadfully uncomfortable and scattered his wits.

"It's got to ask uss a quesstion, my preciouss, yes, yess, yesss. Jusst one more quesstion to guess, yes, yess," said Gollum.

But Bilbo simply could not think of any question with that nasty wet cold thing sitting next to him, and pawing and poking him. He scratched himself, he pinched himself; still he could not think of anything.

"Ask us! Ask us!" said Gollum.

Bilbo pinched himself and slapped himself; he gripped on his little sword; he even felt in his pocket with his other hand. There he found the ring he had picked up in the passage and forgotten about.

"What have I got in my pocket?" he said aloud. He was talking to himself, but Gollum thought it was a riddle, and he was frightfully upset.

"Not fair! not fair!" he hissed. "It isn't fair, my precious, is it, to ask us what it's got in its nassty little pocketses?"

Bilbo seeing what had happened and having nothing better to ask stuck to his question, "What have I got in my pocket?" he said louder.

"S-s-s-s-s," hissed Gollum. "It must give us three guesseses, my preciouss, three guesseses."

"Very well! Guess away!" said Bilbo.

"Handses!" said Gollum.

"Wrong," said Bilbo, who had luckily just taken his hand out again. "Guess again!"

"S-s-s-s-s," said Gollum more upset than ever. He thought of all the things he kept in his own pockets: fish-bones, goblins' teeth, wet shells, a bit of bat-wing, a sharp stone to sharpen his fangs on, and other nasty things. He tried to think what other people kept in their pockets.

"Knife!" he said at last.

"Wrong!" said Bilbo, who had lost his some time ago. "Last guess!"

Now Gollum was in a much worse state than when Bilbo had asked him the egg-question. He hissed and spluttered and rocked himself backwards and forwards, and slapped his feet on the floor, and wriggled and squirmed; but still he did not dare to waste his last guess.

"Come on!" said Bilbo. "I am waiting!" He tried to sound bold and cheerful, but he did not feel at all sure how the game was going to end, whether Gollum guessed right or not.

"Time's up!" he said.

"String, or nothing!" shrieked Gollum, which was not quite fair—working in two guesses at once.

"Both wrong," cried Bilbo very much relieved; and he jumped at once to his feet, put his back to the nearest wall, and held out his little sword. But funnily enough he need not have been alarmed. For one thing Gollum had learned long long ago was never, never, to cheat at the riddle-game, which is a sacred one and of immense antiquity. Also there was the sword. He simply sat and whispered.

"What about the present?" asked Bilbo, not that he cared very much, still he felt that he had won it, pretty fairly, and in very difficult circumstances too.

"Must we give it the thing, preciouss? Yess, we must! We must fetch it, preciouss, and give it the present we promised." So Gollum paddled back to his boat, and Bilbo thought he had heard the last of him. But he had not. The hobbit was just thinking of going back up the passage—having had quite enough of Gollum and the dark water's edge—when he heard him wailing and squeaking away in the gloom. He was on his island (of which, of course, Bilbo knew nothing), scrabbling here and there, searching and seeking in vain, and turning out his pockets.

"Where iss it? Where iss it?" Bilbo heard him squeaking. "Lost, lost, my preciouss, lost, lost! Bless us and splash us! We haven't the present we promised, and we haven't even got it for ourselveses."

Bilbo turned round and waited, wondering what it could be that the creature was making such a fuss about. This proved very fortunate afterwards. For Gollum came back and made a tremendous spluttering and whispering and croaking; and in the end Bilbo gathered that Gollum had had a ring—a wonderful, beautiful ring, a ring that he had been given for a birthday present, ages and ages before in old days when such rings were less uncommon. Sometimes he had it in his pocket; usually he kept it in a little hole in the rock on his island; sometimes he wore it—when he was very, very hungry, and tired of fish, and crept along dark passages looking for stray goblins. Then he might venture even into places where the torches were lit and made his eyes blink and smart; but he would be safe. O yes! very nearly safe; for if you slipped that ring on your finger, you were invisible; only in the sunlight could you be seen, and then only by your shadow, and that was a faint and shaky sort of shadow.

I don't know how many times Gollum begged Bilbo's pardon. He kept on saying: "We are sorry; we didn't mean to cheat, we meant to give it our only pressent, if it won the competition." He even offered to catch Bilbo some nice juicy fish to eat as a consolation.

Bilbo shuddered at the thought of it. "No thank you!" he said as politely as he could.

He was thinking hard, and the idea came to him that Gollum must have dropped that ring sometime and that he must have found it, and that he had that very ring in his pocket. But he had the wits not to tell Gollum.

"Finding's keeping!" he said to himself; and being in a very tight place, I daresay he was right. Anyway the ring belonged to him now.

"Never mind!" he said. "The ring would have been mine now, if you had found it; so you would have lost it anyway. And I will let you off on one condition."

"Yes, what iss it? What does it wish us to do, my precious?"

"Help me to get out of these places," said Bilbo.

Now Gollum had to agree to this, if he was not to cheat. He still very much wanted just to try what the stranger tasted like; but now he had to give up all idea of it. Still there was the little sword; and the stranger was wide awake and on the look out, not unsuspecting as Gollum liked to have the things which he attacked. So perhaps it was best after all.

That is how Bilbo got to know that the tunnel ended at the water and went no further on the other side where the mountain wall was dark and solid. He also learned that he ought to have turned down one of the side passages to the right before he came to the bottom; but he could not follow Gollum's directions for finding it again on the way up, and he made the wretched creature come and show him the way.

As they went along up the tunnel together, Gollum flip-flapping at his side, Bilbo going very softly, he thought he would try the ring. He slipped it on his finger.

"Where iss it? Where iss it gone to?" said Gollum at once, peering about with his long eyes.

"Here I am, following behind!" said Bilbo slipping off the ring again, and feeling very pleased to have it and to find that it really did what Gollum said.

Now on they went again, while Gollum counted the passages to left and right: "One left, one right, two right, three right, two left," and so on. He began to get very shaky and afraid as they left the water further and further behind; but at last he stopped by a low opening on their left (going up)—"six right, four left."

"Here'ss the passage," he whispered. "It musst squeeze in and sneak down. We durstn't go with it, my preciouss, no we durstn't, gollum!"

So Bilbo slipped under the arch, and said good-bye to the nasty miserable creature; and very glad he was. He did not feel comfortable until he felt quite sure it was gone, and he kept his head out in the main tunnel listening until the flip-flap of Gollum going back to his boat died away in the darkness. Then he went down the new passage.

It was a low narrow one roughly made. It was all right for the hobbit, except when he stubbed his toes in the dark on nasty jags in the floor; but it must have been a bit low for goblins. Perhaps it was not knowing that goblins are used to this sort of thing, and go along quite fast stooping low with their hands almost on the floor, that made Bilbo forget the danger of meeting them and hurry forward recklessly.

Soon the passage began to go up again, and after a while it climbed steeply. That slowed him down. But at last after some time the slope stopped, the passage turned a corner and dipped down again, and at the bottom of a short incline he saw filtering round another corner—a glimmer of light. Not red light as of fire or lantern, but pale ordinary out-of-doors sort of light. Then he began to run. Scuttling along as fast as his little legs would carry him he turned the corner and came suddenly right into an open place where the light, after all that time in the dark, seemed dazzlingly bright. Really it was only a leak of sunshine in through a doorway, where a great door, a stone door, was left a little open.

Bilbo blinked, and then he suddenly saw the goblins: goblins in full armour with drawn swords sitting just inside the door, and watching it with wide eyes, and the passage that led to it! They saw him sooner than he saw them, and with yells of delight they rushed upon him.

Whether it was accident or presence of mind, I don't know. Accident, I think, because the hobbit was not used yet to his new treasure. Anyway he slipped the ring on his left hand— and the goblins stopped short. They could not see a sign of him. Then they yelled twice as loud as before, but not so delightedly.

"Where is it?" they cried.

"Go back up the passage!" some shouted.

"This way!" some yelled. "That way!" others yelled.

"Look out for the door," bellowed the captain.

Whistles blew, armour clashed, swords rattled, goblins cursed and swore and ran hither and thither, falling over one another and getting very angry. There was a terrible outcry, to-do, and disturbance.

Bilbo was dreadfully frightened, but he had the sense to understand what had happened and to sneak behind a big barrel which held drink for the goblin-guards, and so get out of the way and avoid being bumped into, trampled to death, or caught by feel.

"I must get to the door, I must get to the door!" he kept on saying to himself, but it was a long time before he ventured to try. Then it was like a horrible game of blindman's-buff. The place was full of goblins running about, and the poor little hobbit dodged this way and that, was knocked over by a goblin who could not make out what he had bumped into, scrambled away on all fours, slipped between the legs of the captain just in time, got up, and ran for the door.

It was still ajar, but a goblin had pushed it nearly to. Bilbo struggled but he could not move it. He tried to squeeze through the crack. He squeezed and squeezed, and he stuck! It was awful. His buttons had got wedged on the edge of the door and the doorpost. He could see outside into the open air: there were a few steps running down into a narrow valley between tall mountains; the sun came out from behind a cloud and shone bright on the outside of the door—but he could not get through.

Suddenly one of the goblins inside shouted: "There is a shadow by the door. Something is outside!"

Bilbo's heart jumped into his mouth. He gave a terrific squirm. Buttons burst off in all directions. He was through, with a torn coat and waistcoat, leaping down the steps like a goat, while bewildered goblins were still picking up his nice brass buttons on the doorstep.

Of course they soon came down after him, hooting and hallooing, and hunting among the trees. But they don't like the sun: it makes their legs wobble and their heads giddy. They could not find Bilbo with the ring on, slipping in and out of the shadow of the trees, running quick and quiet, and keeping out of the sun; so soon they went back grumbling and cursing to guard the door. Bilbo had escaped.

Kenneth Grahame

The Wind in the Willows

When Kenneth Grahame was asked why he wrote for children, among other reasons he gave was this: "Children are not merely people; they are the only really living people that have been left to us in an over-weary world." As for writing about animals in *The Wind in the Willows,* he said: "Every animal, by instinct, lives according to his nature. Thereby he lives wisely, and betters the tradition of mankind. . . . Every animal is true—is, therefore, according to his nature both beautiful and good."

The Wind in the Willows was written or told as bedtime stories for Kenneth Grahame's small son, affectionately known in the family as "Mouse." To understand this chapter better, the reader must know that Mole had recently made the acquaintance of Water Rat, who had introduced him to Mr. Toad and had warned him against the dangers of the Wild Wood. But when Mole also wished to know Mr. Badger, the Rat said Mr. Badger was a recluse and hard to meet. This chapter reveals what adventures Mole had in the Wild Wood, adventures that led him to Mr. Badger's door. [From Kenneth Grahame, *The Wind in the Willows* (Scribner's, 1908).]

The Wild Wood

The Mole had long wanted to make the acquaintance of the Badger. He seemed, by all accounts, to be such an important personage and, though rarely visible, to make his unseen influence felt by everybody about the place. But whenever the Mole mentioned his wish to the

Water Rat, he always found himself put off. "It's all right," the Rat would say. "Badger'll turn up some day or other—he's always turning up—and then I'll introduce you. The best of fellows! But you must not only take him *as* you find him, but *when* you find him."

"Couldn't you ask him here—dinner or something?" said the Mole.

"He wouldn't come," replied the Rat simply. "Badger hates Society, and invitations, and dinner, and all that sort of thing."

"Well, then, supposing we go and call on *him?*" suggested the Mole.

"O, I'm sure he wouldn't like that at *all,*" said the Rat, quite alarmed. "He's so very shy, he'd be sure to be offended. I've never even ventured to call on him at his own home myself, though I know him so well. Besides, we can't. It's quite out of the question, because he lives in the very middle of the Wild Wood."

"Well, supposing he does," said the Mole. "You told me the Wild Wood was all right, you know."

"O, I know, I know, so it is," replied the Rat evasively. "But I think we won't go there just now. Not *just* yet. It's a long way, and he wouldn't be at home at this time of year, anyhow, and he'll be coming along some day, if you'll wait quietly."

The Mole had to be content with this. But the Badger never came along, and every day brought its amusements, and it was not till summer was long over, and cold and frost and miry ways kept them much indoors, and the swollen river raced past outside their windows with a speed that mocked at boating of any sort or kind, that he found his thoughts dwelling again with much persistence on the solitary gray Badger, who lived his own life by himself, in his hole in the middle of the Wild Wood.

In the wintertime the Rat slept a great deal, retiring early and rising late. During his short day he sometimes scribbled poetry or did other small domestic jobs about the house; and, of course, there were always animals dropping in for a chat, and consequently there was a good deal of story-telling and comparing notes on the past summer and all its doings.

Such a rich chapter it had been, when one came to look back on it all! With illustrations so numerous and so very highly colored! The pageant of the river bank had marched steadily along, unfolding itself in scene-pictures that succeeded each other in stately procession. Purple loosestrife arrived early shaking luxuriant tangled locks along the edge of the mirror whence its own face laughed back at it. Willow-herb, tender and wistful, like a pink sunset cloud, was not slow to follow. Comfrey, the purple hand-in-hand with the white, crept forth to take its place in the line; and at last one morning the diffident and delaying dog-rose stepped delicately on the stage, and one knew, as if string-music had announced it in stately chords that strayed into a gavotte, that June at last was here. One member of the company was still awaited; the shepherd-boy for the nymphs to woo, the knight for whom the ladies waited at the window, the prince that was to kiss the sleeping summer back to life and love. But when meadow-sweet, debonair and odorous in amber jerkin, moved graciously to his place in the group, then the play was ready to begin.

And what a play it had been! Drowsy animals, snug in their holes while wind and rain were battering at their doors, recalled still, keen mornings, an hour before sunrise, when the white mist, as yet undispersed, clung closely along the surface of the water; then the shock of the early plunge, the scamper along the bank, and the radiant transformation of earth, air, and water, when suddenly the sun was with them again, and gray was gold and color was born and sprang out of the earth once more. They recalled the languorous siesta of hot midday, deep in green undergrowth, the sun striking through in tiny golden shafts and spots; the boating and bathing of the afternoon, the rambles along dusty lanes and through yellow cornfields; and the long, cool evening at last, when so many threads were gathered up, so many friendships rounded, and so many adventures planned for the morrow. There was plenty to talk about on those short winter days when the animals found themselves round the fire; still, the Mole had a good deal of spare time on his hands, and so one afternoon, when the Rat in his armchair before the blaze was alternately dozing and trying over rhymes that wouldn't fit, he formed the resolution to go out by himself and explore the Wild Wood, and perhaps strike up an acquaintance with Mr. Badger.

It was a cold, still afternoon with a hard, steely sky overhead, when he slipped out of the warm parlor into the open air. The country lay bare and entirely leafless around him, and he thought that he had never seen so far and so intimately into the insides of things as on that winter day when Nature was deep in her annual slumber and seemed to have kicked the clothes off. Copses, dells, quarries, and all hidden places, which had been mysterious mines for exploration in leafy summer, now exposed themselves and their secrets pathetically, and seemed to ask him to overlook their shabby poverty for a while, till they could riot in rich masquerade as before, and trick and entice him with the old deceptions. It was pitiful in a way, and yet cheering—even exhilarating. He was glad that he liked the country undecorated, hard, and stripped of its finery. He had got down to the bare bones of it, and they were fine and strong and simple. He did not want the warm clover and the play of seeding grasses; the screens of quickset, the billowy drapery of beech and elm seemed best away; and with great cheerfulness of spirit he pushed on toward the Wild Wood, which lay before him low and threatening, like a black reef in some still, southern sea.

There was nothing to alarm him at first entry. Twigs crackled under his feet, logs tripped him, funguses on stumps resembled caricatures, and startled him for the moment by their likeness to something familiar and far away; but that was all fun, and exciting. It led him on, and he penetrated to where the light was less, and trees crouched nearer and nearer, and holes made ugly mouths at him on either side.

Everything was very still now. The dusk advanced on him steadily, rapidly, gathering in behind and before; and the light seemed to be draining away like flood-water.

Then the faces began.

It was over his shoulder, and indistinctly, that he first thought he saw a face, a little, evil, wedge-shaped face, looking out at him from a hole. When he turned and confronted it, the thing had vanished.

He quickened his pace, telling himself cheerfully not to begin imagining things or there would be simply no end to it. He passed another hole, and another, and another; and then—yes!—no!—yes! certainly a little, narrow face, with hard eyes, had flashed up for an instant from a hole, and was gone. He hesitated—braced himself up for an effort and strode on. Then suddenly, and as if it had been so all the time, every hole, far and near, and there were hundreds of them, seemed to possess its face, coming and going rapidly, all fixing on him glances of malice and hatred: all hard-eyed and evil and sharp.

If he could only get away from the holes in the banks, he thought, there would be no more faces. He swung off the path and plunged into the untrodden places of the wood.

Then the whistling began.

Very faint and shrill it was, and far behind him, when first he heard it; but somehow it made him hurry forward. Then, still very faint and shrill, it sounded far ahead of him, and made him hesitate and want to go back. As he halted in indecision, it broke out on either side, and seemed to be caught up and passed on throughout the whole length of the wood to its farthest limit. They were up and alert and ready, evidently, whoever they were! And he—he was alone, and unarmed, and far from any help; and the night was closing in.

Then the pattering began.

He thought it was only falling leaves at first, so slight and delicate was the sound of it. Then as it grew it took a regular rhythm, and he knew it for nothing else but the pat-pat-pat of little feet still a very long way off. Was it in front or behind? It seemed to be first one, and then the other, then both. It grew and it multiplied, till from every quarter as he listened anxiously, leaning this way and that, it seemed to be closing in on him. As he stood still to hearken, a rabbit came running hard toward him through the trees. He waited, expecting it to slacken pace or to swerve from him into a different course. Instead, the animal almost brushed him as it dashed past, his face set and hard, his eyes staring. "Get out of this, you fool, get out!" the Mole heard him mutter as he swung round a stump and disappeared down a friendly burrow.

The pattering increased till it sounded like

sudden hail on the dry leaf-carpet spread around him. The whole wood seemed running now, running hard, hunting, chasing, closing in round something or—somebody? In panic, he began to run too, aimlessly, he knew not whither. He ran up against things, he fell over things and into things, he darted under things and dodged round things. At last he took refuge in the deep, dark hollow of an old beech tree, which offered shelter, concealment—perhaps even safety, but who could tell? Anyhow, he was too tired to run any farther, and could only snuggle down into the dry leaves which had drifted into the hollow and hope he was safe for a time. And as he lay there panting and trembling, and listened to the whistlings and the patterings outside, he knew it at last, in all its fullness, that dread thing which other little dwellers in field and hedgerow had encountered here, and known as their darkest moment—that thing which the Rat had vainly tried to shield him from—the Terror of the Wild Wood!

Meantime the Rat, warm and comfortable, dozed by his fireside. His paper of half-finished verses slipped from his knee, his head fell back, his mouth opened, and he wandered by the verdant banks of dream-rivers. Then a coal slipped, the fire crackled and sent up a spurt of flame, and he woke with a start. Remembering what he had been engaged upon, he reached down to the floor for his verses, pored over them for a minute, and then looked round for the Mole to ask him if he knew a good rhyme for something or other.

But the Mole was not there.

He listened for a time. The house seemed very quiet.

Then he called "Moly!" several times, and, receiving no answer, got up and went out into the hall.

The Mole's cap was missing from its accustomed peg. His goloshes, which always lay by the umbrella-stand, were also gone.

The Rat left the house, and carefully examined the muddy surface of the ground outside, hoping to find the Mole's tracks. There they were, sure enough. The goloshes were new, just bought for the winter, and the pimples on their soles were fresh and sharp. He could see the imprints of them in the mud, running along

straight and purposeful, leading direct to the Wild Wood.

The Rat looked very grave, and stood in deep thought for a minute or two. Then he re-entered the house, strapped a belt round his waist, shoved a brace of pistols into it, took up a stout cudgel that stood in a corner of the hall, and set off for the Wild Wood at a smart pace.

It was already getting toward dusk when he reached the first fringe of trees and plunged without hesitation into the wood, looking anxiously on either side for any sign of his friend. Here and there wicked little faces popped out of holes, but vanished immediately at sight of the valorous animal, his pistols, and the great ugly cudgel in his grasp; and the whistling and pattering, which he had heard quite plainly on his first entry, died away and ceased, and all was very still. He made his way manfully through the length of the wood, to its farthest edge; then, forsaking all paths, he set himself to traverse it, laboriously working over the whole ground, and all the time calling out cheerfully, "Moly, Moly, Moly! Where are you? It's me—it's old Rat!"

He had patiently hunted through the wood for an hour or more, when at last to his joy he heard a little answering cry. Guiding himself by the sound, he made his way through the gathering darkness to the foot of an old beech tree, with a hole in it, and from out of the hole came a feeble voice, saying, "Ratty! Is that really you?"

The Rat crept into the hollow, and there he found the Mole, exhausted and still trembling. "O Rat!" he cried, "I've been so frightened, you can't think!"

"O, I quite understand," said the Rat soothingly. "You shouldn't really have gone and done it, Mole. I did my best to keep you from it. We river-bankers, we hardly ever come here by ourselves. If we have to come, we come in couples at least; then we're generally all right. Besides, there are a hundred things one has to know, which we understand all about and you don't, as yet. I mean passwords, and signs, and sayings which have power and effect, and plants you carry in your pocket, and verses you repeat, and dodges and tricks you practice; all simple enough when you know them, but they've got to be known if you're small, or you'll find yourself in trouble. Of course, if you were Badger or Otter, it would be quite another matter."

"Surely the brave Mr. Toad wouldn't mind coming here by himself, would he?" inquired the Mole.

"Old Toad?" said the Rat, laughing heartily. "He wouldn't show his face here alone, not for a whole hatful of golden guineas, Toad wouldn't."

The Mole was greatly cheered by the sound of the Rat's careless laughter, as well as by the sight of his stick and his gleaming pistols, and he stopped shivering and began to feel bolder and more himself again.

"Now, then," said the Rat presently, "we really must pull ourselves together and make a start for home while there's still a little light left. It will never do to spend the night here, you understand. Too cold, for one thing."

"Dear Ratty," said the poor Mole, "I'm dreadfully sorry, but I'm simply dead beat and that's a solid fact. You *must* let me rest here a while longer, and get my strength back, if I'm to get home at all."

"O, all right," said the good-natured Rat, "rest away. It's pretty nearly pitch-dark now, anyhow; and there ought to be a bit of a moon later."

So the Mole got well into the dry leaves and stretched himself out, and presently dropped off into sleep, though of a broken and troubled sort; while the Rat covered himself up, too, as best he might, for warmth, and lay patiently waiting, with a pistol in his paw.

When at last the Mole woke up, much refreshed and in his usual spirits, the Rat said, "Now, then! I'll just take a look outside and see if everything's quiet, and then we really must be off."

He went to the entrance of their retreat and put his head out. Then the Mole heard him saying quietly to himself, "Hullo! hullo! here—*is*—*a*—go!"

"What's up, Ratty?" asked the Mole.

"*Snow* is up," replied the Rat briefly; "or rather, *down*. It's snowing hard."

The Mole came and crouched beside him, and, looking out, saw the wood that had been so dreadful to him in quite a changed aspect.

Holes, hollows, pools, pitfalls, and other black menaces to the wayfarer were vanishing fast, and a gleaming carpet of faery was springing up everywhere, that looked too delicate to be trodden upon by rough feet. A fine powder filled the air and caressed the cheek with a tingle in its touch, and the black boles of the trees showed up in a light that seemed to come from below.

"Well, well, it can't be helped," said the Rat, after pondering. "We must make a start, and take our chance, I suppose. The worst of it is, I don't exactly know where we are. And now this snow makes everything look so very different."

It did indeed. The Mole would not have known that it was the same wood. However, they set out bravely, and took the line that seemed most promising, holding on to each other and pretending with invincible cheerfulness that they recognized an old friend in every fresh tree that grimly and silently greeted them, or saw openings, gaps, or paths with a familiar turn in them, in the monotony of white space and black tree-trunks that refused to vary.

An hour or two later—they had lost all count of time—they pulled up, dispirited, weary, and hopelessly at sea, and sat down on a fallen tree-trunk to recover their breath and consider what was to be done. They were aching with fatigue and bruised with tumbles; they had fallen into several holes and got wet through; the snow was getting so deep that they could hardly drag their little legs through it, and the trees were thicker and more like each other than ever. There seemed to be no end to this wood, and no beginning, and no difference in it, and, worst of all, no way out.

"We can't sit here very long," said the Rat. "We shall have to make another push for it, and do something or other. The cold is too awful for anything, and the snow will soon be too deep for us to wade through." He peered about him and considered. "Look here," he went on, "this is what occurs to me. There's a sort of dell down here in front of us, where the ground seems all hilly and humpy and hummocky. We'll make our way down into that, and try and find some sort of shelter, a cave or hole with a dry floor to it, out of the snow and the wind, and there we'll have a good rest before we try again, for we're both of us pretty dead beat. Besides, the snow may leave off, or something may turn up."

So once more they got on their feet, and struggled down into the dell, where they hunted about for a cave or some corner that was dry and a protection from the keen wind and the whirling snow. They were investigating one of the hummocky bits the Rat had spoken of, when suddenly the Mole tripped up and fell forward on his face with a squeal.

"O my leg!" he cried. "O my poor shin!" and he sat up on the snow and nursed his leg in both his front paws.

"Poor old Mole!" said the Rat kindly. "You don't seem to be having much luck today, do you? Let's have a look at the leg. Yes," he went on, going down on his knees to look, "you've cut your shin, sure enough. Wait till I get at my handkerchief, and I'll tie it up for you."

"I must have tripped over a hidden branch or a stump," said the Mole miserably. "O my! O my!"

"It's a very clean cut," said the Rat, examining it again attentively. "That was never done by a branch or a stump. Looks as if it was made by a sharp edge of something in metal. Funny!" He pondered awhile, and examined the humps and slopes that surrounded them.

"Well, never mind what done it," said the Mole, forgetting his grammar in his pain. "It hurts just the same, whatever done it."

But the Rat, after carefully tying up the leg with his handkerchief, had left him and was busy scraping in the snow. He scratched and shoveled and explored, all four legs working busily, while the Mole waited impatiently, remarking at intervals, "O, *come* on, Rat!"

Suddenly the Rat cried "Hooray!" and then "Hooray-oo-ray-oo-ray-oo-ray!" and fell to executing a feeble jig in the snow.

"What *have* you found, Ratty?" asked the Mole, still nursing his leg.

"Come and see!" said the delighted Rat, as he jigged on.

The Mole hobbled up to the spot and had a good look.

"Well," he said at last, slowly, "I *see* it right

enough. Seen the same sort of thing before, lots of times. Familiar object, I call it. A door-scraper! Well, what of it? Why dance jigs around a door-scraper?"

"But don't you see what it *means*, you—you dull-witted animal?" cried the Rat impatiently.

"Of course I see what it means," replied the Mole. "It simply means that some *very* careless and forgetful person has left his door-scraper lying about in the middle of the Wild Wood, *just* where it's *sure* to trip *everybody* up. Very thoughtless of him, I call it. When I get home I shall go and complain about it to—to somebody or other, see if I don't!"

"O dear! O dear!" cried the Rat, in despair at his obtuseness. "Here, stop arguing and come and scrape!" And he set to work again and made the snow fly in all directions around him.

After some further toil his efforts were rewarded, and a very shabby door-mat lay exposed to view.

"There, what did I tell you?" exclaimed the Rat in great triumph.

"Absolutely nothing whatever," replied the Mole, with perfect truthfulness. "Well, now," he went on, "you seem to have found another piece of domestic litter, done for and thrown away, and I suppose you're perfectly happy. Better go ahead and dance your jig round that if you've got to, and get it over, and then perhaps we can go on and not waste any more time over rubbish-heaps. Can we *eat* a door-mat? Or sleep under a door-mat? Or sit on a door-mat and sledge home over the snow on it, you exasperating rodent?"

"Do—you—mean—to—say," cried the excited Rat, "that this door-mat doesn't *tell* you anything?"

"Really, Rat," said the Mole, quite pettishly, "I think we've had enough of this folly. Who ever heard of a door-mat *telling* anyone anything? They simply don't do it. They are not that sort at all. Door-mats know their place."

"Now look here, you—you thick-headed beast," replied the Rat, really angry, "this must stop. Not another word, but scrape—scrape and scratch and dig and hunt round, especially on the sides of the hummocks, if you want to sleep dry and warm tonight, for it's our last chance!"

Illustrations by Ernest H. Shepard, from *The Wind in the Willows,* by Kenneth Grahame. Illustrated by Ernest H. Shepard. Copyright © 1908, 1933, 1953 by Charles Scribner's Sons; copyright © renewed 1961 by Ernest H. Shepard, 1981 by Mary Eleanor Jessie Knox. First published with illustrations by Ernest H. Shepard in 1931. Color pictures copyright © 1959 by Ernest H. Shepard. Used by permission of Charles Scribner's Sons.

The Rat attacked a snow-bank beside them with ardor, probing with his cudgel everywhere and then digging with fury; and the Mole scraped busily too, more to oblige the Rat than for any other reason, for his opinion was that his friend was getting lightheaded.

Some ten minutes' hard work, and the point of the Rat's cudgel struck something that sounded hollow. He worked till he could get a paw through and feel; then called the Mole to come and help him. Hard at it went the two animals, till at last the result of their labors stood full in view of the astonished and hitherto incredulous Mole.

In the side of what had seemed to be a snow-bank stood a solid-looking little door, painted a dark green. An iron bell-pull hung by the side, and below it, on a small brass plate, neatly engraved in square capital letters, they could read by the aid of moonlight,

MR. BADGER

The Mole fell backwards on the snow from sheer surprise and delight. "Rat!" he cried in penitence, "you're a wonder! A real wonder, that's what you are. I see it all now! You argued it out, step by step, in that wise head of yours, from the very moment that I fell and cut my shin, and you looked at the cut, and at once your majestic mind said to itself, 'Door-scraper!' And then you turned to and found the very door-scraper that done it! Did you stop there? No. Some people would have been quite satisfied; but not you. Your intellect went on working. 'Let me only just find a door-mat,' says you to yourself, 'and my theory is proved!' And of course you found your door-mat. You're so clever, I believe you could find anything you liked. 'Now,' says you, 'that door exists, as plain as if I saw it. There's nothing else remains to be done but to find it!' Well, I've read about that sort of thing in books, but I've never come across it before in real life. You ought to go where you'll be properly appreciated. You're simply wasted here, among us fellows. If I only had your head, Ratty—"

"But as you haven't," interrupted the Rat, rather unkindly, "I suppose you're going to sit on the snow all night and *talk?* Get up at once and hang on to that bell-pull you see there, and ring hard, as hard as you can, while I hammer!"

While the Rat attacked the door with his stick, the Mole sprang up at the bell-pull, clutched it and swung there, both feet well off the ground, and from quite a long way off they could faintly hear a deep-toned bell respond.

Russell Hoban

The Mouse and His Child

Closer to the spirit of George Orwell's *Animal Farm* than to Kenneth Grahame's *Wind in the Willows,* this complex, multi-layered animal fable of our violent and absurd century begins with the clockwork mouse and his child safe in the toy store. Sold but soon discarded, they are repaired by a tramp only to be enslaved to the prototypical dictator, Manny Rat. In the following scene, Ralphie, Manny's rat-of-all-work, forces the mouse and his child into robbing the Meadow Mutual Hoard and Trust Company of treacle-brittle. The pilgrimage of the wind-up toys in their search for family, home, and the autonomy of self-winding is the central theme of this picaresque satire. Hoban is a skilled and talented writer whose breadth of vision ranges from the simple, domestic Frances the Badger picture books to avant-garde literary science fiction for adults, such as *Riddley Walker.* [From Russell Hoban, *The Mouse and His Child* (Harper, 1967).]

The sky was beginning to pale, and the air was sharp with morning as Ralphie and the mouse and his child came through the woods along a path to the Meadow Mutual Hoard and Trust Company, an earthen bank beside a stream. There were many tracks in the snow, and following these, they went through the entrance between the roots of a great sycamore tree.

The interior of the bank was chill and dim and hushed; the acorn-cup tallow lamps did little more than cast their own shadows and catch the glint of frost and mica on the earth walls. In the half-light a drowsy chipmunk teller looked up from the sunflower seeds he was counting as the rat walked in with the mouse

and his child. The father pushed the son up to the rock behind which the chipmunk sat, then stood treading the ground until his spring unwound. The chipmunk looked at the paper bag they carried, then at Ralphie, and he felt for the alarm twig with his foot.

"Um yes," he said. "May I help you?"

Ralphie squinted cautiously into the shadows around him, saw no guards, and at once forgot everything Manny Rat had told him. "All right," he said, snarling and showing his teeth, "this is a stickup. Take me to the vault."

"Um yes, sir!" said the chipmunk, stepping hard on the alarm twig as he spoke. The twig passed through a hole in the dirt wall behind him, and its other end vibrated against the snout of the badger guard who was dozing behind the stone that was the door of the vault. The badger woke up and smiled.

"This way, please," said the chipmunk. Ralphie wound up the mouse father, and they went through a short tunnel to where the stone blocked the opening of the vault. "Here is the vault," said the chipmunk.

"Well, open it up," said Ralphie.

"Um certainly," said the chipmunk. He moved the stone and stepped out of the way as Ralphie rushed into the waiting jaws of the badger, who ate him up.

"Them city fellows ain't much at robbing banks," chuckled the badger when he had finished, "but they're good eating. Young fellows nowadays, they don't know how to pull a job. All they know is hurry, hurry, hurry." He picked his teeth with a sliver of bone. "What about them other two?" he asked the chipmunk.

The chipmunk looked back through the tunnel and out past the entrance of the bank. The mouse and his child, spun about by the violence of Ralphie's rush into the vault, had stumbled out of the Meadow Mutual Hoard and Trust Company into the blue dawn, leaving their paper bag behind them. The chipmunk watched them walk down the path until they bumped into a rock and fell over. He shook his head. "Whatever they are, they're harmless," he said. "Let them go."

The mouse and his child lay in the snow where they had fallen, rattling with tinny, squeaking laughter. "Skreep, skreep, skreep!" laughed the father. "The frog was right—Ralphie *did* go on a long journey."

"Skreek, skreek!" laughed the child. "There was good eating too, for the badger! Skreek!"

"Seven o'clock!" called the clock on the steeple of the church across the meadow as it struck the hour.

"Listen!" said the father as he heard it. "It's time for silence. Skreep!" And he began laughing all over again.

"If it's time for silence, how is it that we're still talking, Papa?" giggled the child.

"You've already broken one of the clockwork rules by crying on the job," said the father, "so we might as well break the other one too, and have done with it."

"But I've often tried to speak after dawn," said the child, "and I never could till now. I wonder how it happened?"

"Perhaps your laughter freed you from the ancient clockwork laws," said a deep voice, and the bullfrog fortune-teller hopped out from be-

Illustration by Lillian Hoban, from *The Mouse and His Child,* by Russell Hoban. Picture copyright © 1967 by Lillian Hoban. Reprinted by permission of Harper & Row, Publishers, Inc.

hind a tree. In the daylight he seemed smaller than he had at night, and much of his mystery was gone. He was not a young frog; the glove he wore was shabby. In the cold light of morning he could be clearly seen for what he was: an old, eccentric traveler, neither respectable nor reliable, hung with odd parcels, tricked out with a swinging coin, and plying his trade where chance might take him. He set the mouse and his child on their feet and considered them thoughtfully. "I have never heard a toy laugh before," he said.

"Did you see what happened?" said the father, and he told the frog about the attempted bank robbery.

"A rash youth, Ralphie," said Frog. "He had no patience, poor boy! For once I read the future truly, and it came with fearful swiftness. But are you not curious about my presence here?"

"Why are you here?" asked the child.

"Because I followed you," said Frog. "Something draws me to you, and in the seeds I saw your fate and mine bound inextricably together. I said nothing at the time—I was afraid. There were dark and fearful things in that design, and unknown perils that can only be revealed by time." He shook his head, and the coin swung like a pendulum from the string around his neck.

"Are you still afraid?" asked the father.

"Utterly," said Frog. "Do you choose to go ahead?"

"There is no going back," said the father; "we cannot dance in circles anymore. Will you be our friend, and travel with us?"

"Be my uncle," said the child. "Be my Uncle Frog."

"Ah!" said Frog. "I had better make no promises; I am at best an infirm vessel. Do not expect too much. I will be your friend and uncle for as long as our destined roads may lie together; more than that I cannot say." He gestured toward the snowy meadow that sparkled in the sunlight beyond the trees ahead, and pointed back along the shadowy pathway they had taken to the bank. "Which shall it be?" he said. "Toward the town, or out into the open country?"

"Maybe we could look for the elephant and

the seal and the doll house that used to be in the store with us," said the child. "Couldn't we, Papa?"

"What in the world for?" said the father.

"So we can have a family and be cozy," answered the child.

"To begin with," said the father, "I cannot imagine myself being cozy with that elephant. But, putting that aside for the moment, the whole idea of such a quest is impossible. Despite what she said, she and the doll house were very likely for sale just as we and the seal were, and by now they might be anywhere at all. It would be hopeless to attempt to find any of them."

"She sang me a lullaby," said the child.

"Really," said the father, "this is absurd."

"I want the elephant to be my mama and I want the seal to be my sister and I want to live in the beautiful house," the child insisted.

"What is all this talk of elephants and seals?" asked Frog.

"It's nonsense," said the father, "and yet it's not the child's fault. Our motor is in me. He fills the empty space inside himself with foolish dreams that cannot possibly come true."

"Not so very foolish, perhaps," said Frog. "This seal, was she made of tin, and black and shiny? Did she have a small platform on her nose that revolved while a sparrow performed acrobatic tricks on it?"

"No," said the father. "She had a red and yellow ball on her nose."

"She could have lost the ball," said the child. "Maybe she does have a platform on her nose now. Where is the seal you saw?" he asked Frog.

"I don't know where she is now," said Frog. "But two years ago she was with a traveling theatrical troupe that comes to the pine woods every year."

"If Uncle Frog could take us there, maybe we could find the seal," said the mouse child to his father, "and then we could all look for the elephant together."

"Finding the elephant would be as pointless as looking for her," said the father. "But since I cannot convince you of that, we might just as well travel to the pine woods as anywhere

else. At any rate we shall see something of the world."

"Very well," said Frog. "On to the pine woods."

"EXTRA!" screamed a raucous voice above them as a bluejay flashed by in the sunlight. "RAT SLAIN IN BANK HOLDUP ATTEMPT. WINDUPS FLEE WITH GETAWAY FROG. LATE SCORES: WOODMICE LEAD MEADOW TEAM IN ACORN BOWLING. VOLES IDLE."

"So it begins," said Frog. "For good or ill, you have come out into the world, and the world has taken notice."

"A long, hard road," said the father to Frog. "That was what you saw ahead for us, was it not?"

"All roads, whether long or short, are hard," said Frog. "Come, you have begun your journey, and all else necessarily follows from that act. Be of good cheer. The sun is bright. The sky is blue. The world lies before you."

The father saw the brightness of the meadow through the dark trees. Two crows, sharp against the sky, sailed over it on broad, black wings, and he thought of how many steps it would take him to traverse the same distance. His spring tightened as the frog wound him; his motor buzzed, and he pushed his son ahead.

Behind them in the shadows of the trees stretched the double tracks of tin feet and the odd prints left by Frog's trailing woolen fingers. And bending over the trail in the snow was a figure clothed in a greasy scrap of silk paisley tied with a dirty string. The clockwork elephant followed, with two empty paper bags slung on her back. The planner of the bank robbery, growing doubtful of Ralphie's prompt return, had thought it prudent to come out to meet him and collect the booty.

" 'Rat slain in bank holdup attempt,' " said Manny Rat. "That idiot Ralphie! I suppose that means no treacle brittle for me. And those wretched windups have gone off with the frog as if their single purpose were to make a fool of me. Now I'll be the laughingstock of the whole dump unless I find them and smash them!"

John Christopher

The White Mountains

Set in a future England, this novel, the first in The White Mountains trilogy, combines elements of the classic story of high adventure with those of speculative science fiction, particularly H. G. Wells's *War of the Worlds*. Will lives in a society ruled by hollow metal monsters called Tripods, in which children are "Capped" at age thirteen to brainwash them into the ways of that society. Just before his own Capping is scheduled to occur, Will discovers its significance from the vagrant stranger Ozymandias. The rest of the book follows Will's journey to the White Mountains—and freedom. The author's clean prose tells a chilling and engrossing tale. [From John Christopher, *The White Mountains* (Macmillan, 1967).]

My Name is Ozymandias

I went to the den after school with mingled feelings of anticipation and unease. My father had said he hoped he would hear no more reports of my mixing with Vagrants, and had placed a direct prohibition on my going into Vagrant House. I had obeyed the second part and was taking steps to avoid the first, but I was under no illusion that he would regard this as anything but willful disobedience. And to what end? The opportunity of talking to a man whose conversation was a hodgepodge of sense and nonsense, with the latter very much predominating. It was not worth it.

And yet, remembering the keen blue eyes under the mass of red hair, I could not help feeling that there was something about this man that made the risk, and the disobedience, worth while. I kept a sharp lookout on my way to the ruins, and called out as I approached the den. But there was no one there; nor for a good time after that. I began to think he was not coming—that his wits were so addled that he had failed to take my meaning, or forgotten it altogether—when I heard a twig snap and, peering out, saw Ozymandias. He was less than ten yards from the entrance. He was not singing or talking, but moving quietly, almost stealthily.

A new fear struck me then. There were tales that a Vagrant once, years ago, had murdered children in a dozen villages, before he was caught and hanged. Could they be true, and could this be such another? I had invited him here, telling no one, and a cry for help would not be heard as far from the village as this. I froze against the wall of the den, tensing myself for a rush that might carry me past him to the comparative safety of the open.

But a single glance at him as he looked in reassured me. Whether mad or not, I was sure this was a man to be trusted. The lines in his face were the lines of good humor.

He said, "So I have found you, Will." He glanced about him in approval. "You have a snug place here."

"My cousin Jack did most of it. He is better with his hands than I am."

"The one that was Capped this summer?"

"Yes."

"You watched the Capping?" I nodded. "How is he since then?"

"Well," I said, "but different."

"Having become a man."

"Not only that."

"Tell me."

I hesitated a moment, but in voice and gesture as well as face he inspired confidence. He was also, I realized, talking naturally and sensibly, with none of the strange words and archaic phrases he had used previously. I began to talk, disjointedly at first and then with more ease, of what Jack had said, and of my own later perplexity. He listened, nodding at times but not interrupting.

When I had finished, he said, "Tell me, Will—what do you think of the Tripods?"

I said truthfully, "I don't know. I used to take them for granted—and I was frightened of them, I suppose—but now . . . There are questions in my mind."

"Have you put them to your elders?"

"What good would it do? No one talks about the Tripods. One learns that as a child."

"Shall I answer them for you?" he asked. "Such as I can answer."

There was one thing I was sure of, and I blurted it out. "You are not a Vagrant!"

He smiled. "It depends what meaning you give that word. I go from place to place, as you see. And I behave strangely."

"But to deceive people, not because you cannot help it. Your mind has not been changed."

"No. Not as the minds of the Vagrants are. Nor as your cousin Jack's was, either."

"But you have been Capped!"

He touched the mesh of metal under his thatch of red hair.

"Agreed. But not by the Tripods. By men—free men."

Bewildered, I said, "I don't understand."

"How could you? But listen, and I will tell you. The Tripods, first. Do you know what they are?" I shook my head, and he went on. "Nor do we, as a certainty. There are two stories about them. One is that they were machines, made by men, which revolted against men and enslaved them."

"In the old days? The days of the giant ship, of the great-cities?"

"Yes. It is a story I find hard to believe, because I do not see how men could give intelligence to machines. The other story is that they do not come originally from this world, but another."

"Another world?"

I was lost again. He said, "They teach you nothing about the stars in school, do they? That is something that perhaps makes the second story more likely to be the true one. You are not told that the stars at night—all the hundreds of thousands of them—are suns like our own sun, and that some may have planets circling them as our earth circles this sun."

I was confused, my head spinning with the idea. I said, "Is this true?"

"Quite true. And it may be that the Tripods came, in the first place, from one of those worlds. It may be that the Tripods themselves are only vehicles for creatures who travel inside them. We have never seen the inside of a Tripod, so we do not know."

"And the Caps?"

"Are the means by which they keep men docile and obedient to them."

At first thought it was incredible. Later it seemed incredible that I had not seen this before. But all my life Capping had been something I had taken for granted. All my elders were Capped, and contented to be so. It was the mark of the adult, the ceremony itself solemn and linked in one's mind with the holiday and the feast. Despite the few who suffered pain and became Vagrants, it was a day to which every child looked forward. Only lately, as one could begin to count the months remaining had there been any doubts in my mind; and the doubts had been ill-formed and difficult to sustain against the weight of adult assurance. Jack had had doubts too, and then, with the Capping, they had gone.

I said, "They make men think the things the Tripods want them to think?"

"They control the brain. How, or to what extent, we are not sure. As you know, the metal is joined to the flesh, so that it cannot be removed. It seems that certain general orders are given when the Cap is put on. Later, specific orders can be given to specific people, but as far as the majority are concerned, they do not seem to bother."

"How do the Vagrants happen?"

"That again is something at which we can only guess. It may be that some minds are weak to start with and crumble under the strain. Or perhaps the reverse: too strong, so that they fight against domination until they break."

I thought of that and shuddered. A voice inside one's head, inescapable and irresistible. Anger burned in me, not only for the Vagrants but for all the others—my parents and elders, Jack . . .

"You spoke of free men," I said. "Then the Tripods do not rule all the earth."

"Near enough all. There are no lands without them, if that's what you mean. Listen, when the Tripods first came—or when they revolted—there were terrible happenings. Cities were destroyed like anthills, and millions on millions were killed or starved to death."

Millions . . . I tried to evisage it, but could not. Our village, which was reckoned no small place, numbered about four hundred souls. There were some thirty thousand living in and around the city of Winchester. I shook my head.

He went on. "Those that were left the Tripods Capped, and once Capped they served the Tripods and helped to kill or capture other men. So within a generation things were much as they are now. But in one place, at least, a few men escaped. Far to the south, across the sea, there are high mountains, so high that snow lies on them all the year round. The Tripods keep to low ground—perhaps because they travel over it more easily, or because they do not like the thin air higher up—and these are places which men who are alert and free can defend against the Capped who live in the surrounding valleys. In fact, we raid their farms for our food."

" 'We?' So you come from there?" He nodded. "And the Cap you wear?"

"Taken from a dead man. I shaved my head, and it was molded to fit my skull. Once my hair had grown again, it was hard to tell it from a true Cap. But it gives no commands."

"So you can travel as a Vagrant," I said, "and no one suspects you. But why? With what purpose?"

"Partly to see things and report what I see. But there is something more important. I came for you."

I was startled. "For me?"

"You, and others like you. Those who are not yet Capped, but who are old enough to ask questions and understand answers. And to make a long, difficult, perhaps dangerous journey."

"To the south?"

"To the south. To the White Mountains. With a hard life at the journey's end. But a free one. Well?"

"You will take me there?"

"No. I am not ready to go back yet. And it would be more dangerous. A boy traveling on his own could be an ordinary runaway, but one traveling with a Vagrant . . . You must go on your own. If you decide to go."

"The sea," I said, "how do I cross that?"

He stared at me, and smiled. "The easiest part. And I can give you some help for the rest, too." He brought something from his pocket and showed it to me. "Do you know what this is?"

I nodded. "I have seen one. A compass. The needle points always to the north."

"And this."

He put his hand inside his tunic. There was a hole in the stitching, and he put his fingers down, grasped something, and drew it out. It was a long cylinder of parchment, which he unrolled and spread out on the floor, putting a stone on one end and holding the other.

I saw a drawing on it, but it made no sense.

"This is called a map," he said. "The Capped do not need them, so you have not seen one before. It tells you how to reach the White Mountains. Look, there. That signifies the sea. And here, at the bottom, the mountains."

He explained all the things on the map, describing the landmarks I should look for and telling me how to use the compass to find my way. And for the last part of the journey, beyond the Great Lake, he gave me instructions which I had to memorize. This in case the map was discovered. He said, "But guard it well, in any case. Can you make a hole in the lining of your tunic, as I have done?"

"Yes. I'll keep it safe."

"That leaves only the sea crossing. Go to this town. Rumney." He pointed to it. "You will find fishing boats in the harbor. The *Orion* is owned by one of us. A tall man, very swarthy, with a long nose and thin lips. His name is Curtis, Captain Curtis. Go to him. He will get you across the sea. That is where the hard part begins. They speak a different language there. You must keep from being seen or spoken to, and learn to steal your food as you go."

"I can do that. Do you speak their language?"

"It and others. Such as your own. It was for that reason I was given this mission." He smiled. "I can be a madman in four tongues."

I said, "I came to you. If I had not . . ."

"I would have found you. I have some skill in discovering the right kind of boy. But you can help me now. Is there any other in these parts that you think might be worth the tackling?"

I shook my head. "No. No one."

He stood up, stretching his legs and rubbing his knee.

"Then tomorrow I will move on. Give me a week before you leave, so that no one suspects a link between us."

"Before you go . . ."

"Yes?"

"Why did they not destroy men altogether instead of Capping them?"

He shrugged. "We can't read their minds. There are many possible reasons. Part of the food you grow here goes to men who work underground, mining metals for the Tripods. And in some places there are hunts."

"Hunts?"

"The Tripods hunt men, as men hunt foxes." I shivered. "And they take men and women into their cities, for reasons at which we can only guess."

"They have cities, then?"

"Not on this side of the sea. I have not seen one, but I know those who have. Towers and spires of metal, it is said, behind a great encircling wall. Gleaming ugly places."

I said, "Do you know how long it has been?"

"That the Tripods have ruled? More than a hundred years. But to the Capped it is the same as ten thousand." He gave me his hand. "Do your best, Will."

"Yes," I said. His grasp was firm.

"I will hope to meet you again, in the White Mountains."

The next day, as he had said, he was gone. I set about making my preparations. There was a loose stone in the back wall of the den with a hiding place behind it. Only Jack knew of it, and Jack would not come here again. I put things there—food, a spare shirt, a pair of shoes—ready for my journey. I took the food a little at a time, choosing what would keep best—salt beef and ham, a whole small cheese, oats and such. I think my mother noticed some of the things missing and was puzzled by it.

I was sorry at the thought of leaving her and my father, and of their unhappiness when they found me gone. The Caps offered no remedy for human grief. But I could not stay, any more than a sheep could walk through a slaughterhouse door once it knew what lay beyond. And I knew that I would rather die than wear a Cap.

Monica Hughes

The Keeper of the Isis Light

Monica Hughes is one of the best-known writers for young people in Canada, where her science fiction and realistic novels have received many awards.

The great strength of this novel, the first in the Isis trilogy, lies in its description of the adolescent girl Olwen. After the death of her parents, Olwen was reared in isolation by her robot Guardian. He has changed her physically to adapt to the planet, but she is now so different from the human beings who have arrived to colonize Isis that she is alienated from them. In this passage she first discovers how different she is and the reason Mark, a young Earthling, has rejected her. The author makes concrete the complexities of moral choice, prejudice, and alienation. [From Monica Hughes, *The Keeper of the Isis Light* (Atheneum, 1981).]

She turned to Guardian, a dozen questions bubbling up inside. Only he was not looking at her. He was watching the screen in a positively broody way. Whatever was to be explained, he was going to do it his way.

She turned back to the video screen. There were two people in the picture now. The woman had been joined by a man, tall and good-looking, slender, with a determinedly square chin. His eyes, as he looked fleetingly at the camera, were piercingly blue, and his hair was curly and red. He had his arm around the young woman. She was small; her head only came to the middle of his shoulder, Olwen noticed. He looked down at her with the nicest, most loving expression that was like the sky-lark song; it made Olwen hurt inside.

His lips moved, and she longed to be able to lip-read; and yet at the same time she had the odd feeling that whatever he was saying was private. The girl was so lovely, with high wide cheekbones, large dark eyes, and an expressive mouth that curled up at the corners, as if laughter was always bubbling just below the surface.

They turned and walked away from the camera towards a hut built of bamboo—a hut Olwen had never seen before, though she realised with a sort of shock that it occupied the exact place that the settlers had chosen for their village. They stopped at the door and turned for an instant. Don't go, she wanted to call to them. Please stay!

The scene dissolved into pictures of a baby, lying in a swinging bamboo cradle in the shade of the hut. Other sequences followed. Under Olwen's fascinated eyes the child grew, laughed, cried, slept, crawled, sucked its thumb, was tossed into the air, carried piggy-back, cuddled, and kissed, and finally stood up, staggered, walked, reached out to the camera.

In the last scene, before the screen blanked out, the child had grown to a sturdy toddler with a determined chin, deep blue eyes, and wavy hair that was an unusual shade of reddish brown.

"Guardian?" Olwen found that her voice was trembling. She had the strange feeling that she was standing on the brink of a fast deep river. She wanted desperately to go forward, and yet she was afraid. "Who are they? Where are they? Why have I never seen them before? Is it all real or just a story?"

"Look at me, Olwen." Guardian's voice resonated in the large cave-like room. She looked up obediently, and then went still. Like a fledgling bursting out of its shell her mind began to stir.

Her hands went up to her head. "Oh, it hurts! It hurts!"

"It is all right," he told her gently. *"Now you will remember."*

Her hands fell to her lap. She stared back at the blank screen. "My . . . my parents? My mother? My father? And the child was . . . me?"

Guardian nodded. "How do you feel about it?"

"I don't know. I have to think. I . . . why have I never asked you about my parents before? Why don't I remember them myself?"

"I wiped the memory from your mind. It seemed the kindest thing to do. I did not want you to grieve or to feel lonely without them."

"Grieve . . . ?"

"They died when you were four Earth-years old. There was a catastrophic storm, the worst there has ever been on Isis . . . one in a thousand years, perhaps. And at that time we were not prepared for it. They were both out on a geological survey, and I was at home with you."

"Here?"

"No. The house in the valley by the lake. I had built this cave to store the communications equipment. I brought you here and left you in an oxygenated crib while I went to look for

Gareth and Liz. Gareth—your father—was already dead. I believe he had died instantly. He looked very peaceful, as if he were asleep. I am sure there was no pain."

"And her . . . my . . . mother?" The words were hard to say, as if she had never learned them until just now.

"Liz lived for a few hours. I brought her here and made her as comfortable as I could. Before she died she gave me a solemn charge. She said, 'I appoint you to be the Guardian of Olwen. That must come first, above all other considerations. Do whatever you must to keep her safe and happy.'" Guardian paused and shifted his weight from one foot to the other. "I have always tried to do that. Until Pegasus Two landed I believed that I had succeeded."

"You had. Oh, you *have*. Dear Guardian, you have been kindness itself. I have had a wonderful life; you must know that. When they came everything changed, but that had nothing to do with you. It certainly wasn't your fault. You couldn't stop me from falling in love with Mark . . . though I think you tried, didn't you? Only I couldn't listen. And it wasn't your fault that Mark fell from the mesa, or that the settlers killed Hobbit. It all just . . . happened."

The room was full of a heavy silence. Olwen turned round in her chair and looked up at Guardian standing just behind her.

"Guardian?"

His face was as impassive as ever, but she knew his moods by now, and she could feel guilt and depression. "Guardian, there's something more, isn't there? What have you done? Did you talk to Mark about me? Is that it? He doesn't want to see me? Did you put him off me in some way? That's not fair. It's . . . ."

"Olwen, no. I did nothing like that, I promise. I . . . what I did . . . please listen to me and try to understand why I did it. Your parents died seven years ago—thirteen Earth-years. They had been Keepers of the Isis Light for six Earth-years, and their term of duty was for twenty-five Earth-years, unless a colony ship were to come to Isis before that time. Liz had entrusted you to me. I was your Guardian. I had no choice but to do as she had commanded . . . to keep you safe and happy. I had to consider the possibility of your being marooned here for nineteen more Earth-years, until the relief ship came to take you home to Earth, if you should have wished to go. I asked myself if you could have been happy imprisoned in this valley for all those years, growing up afraid of the ultra-violet and the anoxia of the mountains, never to be really free, as I am free. I knew the kind of woman Liz Pendennis would have liked you to be, a person without fear or resentment, a person who was free. And it *did* work. I feel I was justified. Until Pegasus Two arrived you were free, you were happy, you were safe.''

"Yes, Guardian dear. That is all perfectly true. But what are you talking about? What do you mean—justified? You were justified in doing *what?*"

Again the silence hung heavily in the room. Olwen shivered. Then Guardian spoke. "I changed you. At first I took away your memory, so that you would not grieve for the loss of your parents. Then, little by little, surgically and genetically, I changed you."

"Changed . . . ?"

"Humans are so frail, so poorly adapted." Guardian's voice was almost angry. "There were a thousand things on Isis that could have killed you when you were a child, too small to understand the dangers. I could not guard you every second. I had my duties to the Light. And you could not have been happy as a prisoner, I was sure of that. So I adapted you to Isis. I thickened your skin so that it would be opaque to the ultra-violet. I gave you an extra eye-lid to protect your eyes—Ra is so much brighter than Earth's sun."

Olwen's hands crept up to her face. Guardian went on. "I deepened your rib-cage and extended your vascular system, much in the way that the deep-sea mammals adapted theirs, so that you could store much more oxygen at each breath. I widened your nostrils too, to help you breathe more fully."

"Anything else?"

"I strengthened your ankles and thickened your fingernails to help you climb. And I changed your metabolism slightly . . . that shows in your altered skin colour."

"Why?"

"So that the poisonous plants and insects of Isis could not harm you."

"You did all that for *me?*"

"And for your mother. It was her command."

"She must have loved me very much, to be thinking only of me when she was dying."

"Oh, she did, Olwen. And so did your father."

"And you, Guardian . . . do you love me?"

"I . . . you . . . you are my reason," he stammered. 'You are not angry with me?"

"Why should I be angry? You gave me freedom. You gave me happiness. You gave me Isis. I love you for it, Guardian."

"Thank you." He bowed his head slightly, and for a second seemed almost overcome.

"What I don't understand is that you should feel guilty for what you did for me," Olwen said at last.

"What I did . . ." He stopped and then began again. "You have to understand something difficult. What I did has made you very different from other Earth-type people . . . different from all the settlers . . . different from Mark."

"I know. I've already noticed. I'm better. I'm not confined to UVO suits and oxygen masks. And I am strong. Much stronger than Mark. Guardian!" She stared at him. "Is that why you made me that ridiculous suit and mask? It had nothing to do with viruses—Dr. Mac-Donald was right about that—you were hiding me from the settlers. You didn't want them to see me. Why?"

"I had a plan. I had hoped that you would all get to know each other slowly. That you would learn first to trust, to become friends. Then I hoped that the differences between you would no longer be so important."

"But they're not . . . not to *me!*" Olwen drew in a sharp breath and looked down at her own hands. They were what they had always been, familiar, comfortable extensions of herself. Was there anything wrong with her hands? "Guardian, is that why there are no mirrors? Were you afraid that I couldn't even bear to look at myself. Am I . . . horrible?"

"No, no. It is nothing like that. Oh dear, perhaps that was another wrong decision. It is so difficult to gauge a person's emotional reactions, even a person whom I know as well as I know you. But I thought that if you were as familiar with your own appearance as having a mirrored companion might make you, that then *you* might be afraid of the settlers, since you would perceive how different they are from you."

"Am I . . . am I very different?"

"Yes."

"Am I ugly?"

"No! You are not ugly at all. Form and function should be as one. You function perfectly. You are beautiful."

Olwen stood up. "My head is spinning. It is too much all at once. Mark. Hobbit. And now a mother, a father, a past and a new body . . . I think I must be by myself for a while. Will you do something for me right away?"

"Of course."

"Make a mirror for my room. A big one, please, so that I can see all of myself at once. And can you make it so that I can see the different sides of myself? Can you do that?"

"I will see to it right away. You understand, I did not want you to have a mirror before, but now that you know about yourself . . ."

She nodded. "I'll be on the terrace." She walked out of the cold, strangely inhuman room where Guardian spent so much of his time and into the living room. The scent of cactus flower still lingered in the air, although it was many hours since she had thrown the golden flower into the incinerator. When she walked out onto the terrace the scent became even more powerful, and she realised that it was being wafted to her on the evening breeze from the eastern mountain. The whole upper slope, above the grassline, was a mass of blooming cactus.

She could no more rid Isis of the scent than she could rid herself of her feelings towards Mark. Unless she made Guardian fire the whole mountain-side and destroy the flowers. He would do it if she were to ask him. He would take away the memory of her love for Mark, too, if she were to ask it of him.

She walked to the edge of the terrace and looked across the river valley. To do violence to the mountains and the creatures that lived there, just because she could not bear the scent of the cactus flower, would be hideously wrong.

To do violence to her mind, so as to forget her unhappiness, would be equally wrong.

Something strange was beginning to happen inside her. Little memories were swelling up inside her mind and bursting into tiny disassociated glimpses of reality. There were warm hands, strong and gentle, and the feeling of someone tickling her chest with a bearded chin, and the sound of laughter. Her laughter.

She began to understand why Hobbit had meant so much to her. Hobbit was warm, alive, huggable. And that was necessary . . . or had been necessary. She had the painful feeling that she was growing inside so fast that she was going to split and shed her skin, the way a snake does. She could remember laughter . . . Guardian had been so good to her, he had been everything to her. Only Guardian never laughed.

She shut her eyes, the better to endure the waves of emotion that shook her. The only other reality was the rough stone of the balustrade under the grip of her fingers. She was still standing there under the starlight when Guardian came out to tell her that the mirror had been installed in her room. She bent her head in acknowledgement and walked swiftly past him, wrapped in her own thoughts. Guardian's eyes followed her with an expression that on anyone else might have been mistaken for sorrow or regret.

As soon as Olwen entered her room, sweeping aside the curtain that covered the door arch, she saw the Other standing, one arm holding the window curtain, about to move towards her. She stopped abruptly, her heart jolting, suddenly angry. *Nobody* came here. This was her own most private place.

"Who are you?" she snapped, and it seemed that the Other's lips moved mockingly. She walked forward, letting the door curtain fall behind her. Across the wide carpet the Other came to meet her.

Halfway across the room she understood. This was a mirror! The Other, the intruder, was herself. She walked towards herself and touched the surface of the mirror. It was cold and hard; and behind her she could see the whole room crowded into its flatness. As her finger reached out, so did the Other's finger, and, at the cold surface of the glass, they touched.

Olwen had always imagined that a mirror would reflect the same kind of faulty image that she had seen when she had squatted by a rain puddle when she was small, or looked at her fat upside-down face in the bowl of a polished spoon. But this was quite different. This was almost as alive as she was.

She stared at herself, pushing her red hair away from her face. She had nice bones, she decided, a bit lumpy above the eyes to protect her from the sun, with wide nostrils and a big rib-cage to make the most use of the thin air. She was much more serviceable than the narrow-chested, pinch-faced people from Earth.

Remembering Mark's freckles and the flushed peeling skin that she had noticed on the fairer settlers, she peered at her own skin, and then slipped out of her dressing gown so that she could see all of herself. Her body was strong and smooth, with no freckles or raw places or other deformities, but a nice bronzy green all over. She knew its colour—after all she could see bits of herself every time she stripped—but she had not realised what a striking contrast the bronze made to her red hair. She turned and pirouetted in front of the mirror so that her hair swirled out in a cloud around her.

A tiny reflection from the bedside lamp caught in the glass and shone directly into her eyes, and at once, without her conscious will, a nictating membrane slid over her blue eyes, like a gauze blind. She moved, so that the light no longer shone directly into her eyes, and at once it quickly slid out of sight behind her lower eye-lid. Neat, she thought, and moved so that it happened again.

Olwen turned the side panels of the mirror so that she could see every scrap of herself, and finally she dressed and went back to the living room. Guardian was standing by the fireplace. He looked as if he had not moved since she had left him. All these years he's served me, she thought, planned and schemed to make my life good and happy, and never once has he asked for anything in return. On a sudden wave of gratitude she ran across the room and caught his arms. "Dear Guardian, thank you for my body. It's beautiful!"

Madeleine L'Engle

A Wrinkle in Time

This novel was a watershed. Its influence on children's science fiction helped to move the genre away from action-oriented space opera pulps to more imaginative and philosophical stories. *A Wrinkle in Time* has long been a favorite with children, perhaps because of its clear-cut morality and dramatic incidents. Meg Murry, her brilliant younger brother, Charles Wallace, and their friend Calvin O'Keefe journey into space to find the missing Mr. Murry. Here, their mysterious new friends, Mrs. Which, Mrs. Whatsit, and Mrs. Who, explain the necessary technique: the *tesseract*. [From Madeleine L'Engle, *A Wrinkle in Time* (Farrar, Straus & Giroux, 1962).]

The Tesseract

"Yes," Mrs. Which said. "Hhee iss beehindd thee ddarrkness, sso thatt eevenn wee cannott seee hhimm."

Meg began to cry, to sob aloud. Through her tears she could see Charles Wallace standing there, very small, very white. Calvin put his arms around her, but she shuddered and broke away, sobbing wildly. Then she was enfolded in the great wings of Mrs. Whatsit and she felt comfort and strength pouring through her. Mrs. Whatsit was not speaking aloud, and yet through the wings Meg understood words.

"My child, do not despair. Do you think we would have brought you here if there were no hope? We are asking you to do a difficult thing, but we are confident that you can do it. Your father needs help, he needs courage, and for his children he may be able to do what he cannot do for himself."

"Nnow," Mrs. Which said. "Arre wee rreaddy?"

"Where are we going?" Calvin asked.

Again Meg felt an actual physical tingling of fear as Mrs. Which spoke.

"Wwee musstt ggo bbehindd thee sshaddow."

"But we will not do it all at once," Mrs. Whatsit comforted them. "We will do it in short stages." She looked at Meg. "Now we will tesser, we will wrinkle again. Do you understand?"

"No," Meg said flatly.

Mrs. Whatsit sighed. "Explanations are not easy when they are about things for which your civilization still has no words. Calvin talked about traveling at the speed of light. You understand that, little Meg?"

"Yes," Meg nodded.

"That, of course, is the impractical, long way around. We have learned to take short cuts wherever possible."

"Sort of like in math?" Meg asked.

"Like in math." Mrs. Whatsit looked over at Mrs. Who. "Take your skirt and show them."

"La experiencia es la madre de la ciencia. Spanish, my dears. Cervantes. *Experience is the mother of knowledge."* Mrs. Who took a portion of her white robe in her hands and held it tight.

"You see," Mrs. Whatsit said, "if a very small insect were to move from the section of skirt in Mrs. Who's right hand to that in her left, it would be quite a long walk for him if he had to walk straight across."

Swiftly Mrs. Who brought her hands, still holding the skirt, together.

"Now, you see," Mrs. Whatsit said, "he would *be* there, without that long trip. That is how we travel."

Charles Wallace accepted the explanation serenely. Even Calvin did not seem perturbed. "Oh, *dear,"* Meg sighed. "I guess I *am* a moron. I just don't get it."

"That is because you think of space only in three dimensions," Mrs. Whatsit told her. "We travel in the fifth dimension. This is something you can understand, Meg. Don't be afraid to try. Was your mother able to explain a tesseract to you?"

"Well, she never did," Meg said. "She got so upset about it. Why, Mrs. Whatsit? She said it had something to do with her and Father."

"It was a concept they were playing with," Mrs. Whatsit said, "going beyond the fourth dimension to the fifth. Did your mother explain it to you, Charles?"

"Well, yes." Charles looked a little embarrassed. "Please don't be hurt, Meg. I just kept at her while you were at school till I got it out of her."

Meg sighed. "Just explain it to me."

"Okay," Charles said. "What is the first dimension?"

"Well—a line: ———————————."

"Okay. And the second dimension?"

"Well, you'd square the line. A flat square would be in the second dimension."

"And the third?"

"Well, you'd square the second dimension. Then the square wouldn't be flat any more. It would have a bottom, and sides, and a top."

"And the fourth?"

"Well, I guess if you want to put it into mathematical terms you'd square the square. But you can't take a pencil and draw it the way you can the first three. I know it's got something to do with Einstein and time. I guess maybe you could call the fourth dimension Time."

"That's right," Charles said. "Good girl. Okay, then, for the fifth dimension you'd square the fourth, wouldn't you?"

"I guess so."

"Well, the fifth dimension's a tesseract. You add that to the other four dimensions and you can travel through space without having to go the long way around. In other words, to put it into Euclid, or old-fashioned plane geometry, a straight line is *not* the shortest distance between two points."

For a brief, illuminating second Meg's face had the listening, probing expression that was so often seen on Charles's. "I see!" she cried. "I got it! For just a moment I got it! I can't possibly explain it now, but there for a second I saw it!" She turned excitedly to Calvin. "Did you get it?"

He nodded. "Enough. I don't understand it the way Charles Wallace does, but enough to get the idea."

"Sso nnow wee ggo," Mrs. Which said. "Tthere iss nott all thee ttime inn tthe worrlld."

"Could we hold hands?" Meg asked.

Calvin took her hand and held it tightly in his.

"You can try," Mrs. Whatsit said, "though I'm not sure how it will work. You see, though we travel together, we travel alone. We will go first and take you afterward in the backwash. That may be easier for you." As she spoke the great white body began to waver, the wings to dissolve into mist. Mrs. Who seemed to evaporate until there was nothing but the glasses, and then the glasses, too, disappeared. It reminded Meg of the Cheshire Cat.

—I've often seen a face without glasses, she thought;—but glasses without a face! I wonder if I go that way, too. First me and then my glasses?

She looked over at Mrs. Which. Mrs. Which was there and then she wasn't.

There was a gust of wind and a great thrust and a sharp shattering as she was shoved through—what? Then darkness; silence; nothingness. If Calvin was still holding her hand she could not feel it. But this time she was prepared for the sudden and complete dissolution of her body. When she felt the tingling coming back to her fingertips she knew that this journey was almost over and she could feel again the pressure of Calvin's hand about hers.

Without warning, coming as a complete and unexpected shock, she felt a pressure she had never imagined, as though she were being completely flattened out by an enormous steam roller. This was far worse than the nothingness had been; while she was nothing there was no need to breathe, but now her lungs were squeezed together so that although she was dying for want of air there was no way for her lungs to expand and contract, to take in the air that she must have to stay alive. This was completely different from the thinning of atmosphere when they flew up the mountain and she had had to put the flowers to her face to breathe. She tried to gasp, but a paper doll can't gasp. She thought she was trying to think, but her flattened-out mind was as unable to function as her lungs; her thoughts were squashed along with the rest of her. Her heart tried to beat; it gave a knifelike, sidewise movement, but it could not expand.

But then she seemed to hear a voice, or if not a voice, at least words, words flattened out like printed words on paper, "Oh, no! We can't stop here! This is a *two*-dimensional planet and the children can't manage here!"

She was whizzed into nothingness again, and nothingness was wonderful. She did not mind that she could not feel Calvin's hand, that she could not see or feel or be. The relief from the intolerable pressure was all she needed.

Then the tingling began to come back to her fingers, her toes; she could feel Calvin holding her tightly. Her heart beat regularly; blood coursed through her veins. Whatever had happened, whatever mistake had been made, it was over now. She thought she heard Charles Wallace saying, his words round and full as spoken words ought to be, "*Really*, Mrs. Which, you might have killed us!"

This time she was pushed out of the frightening fifth dimension with a sudden, immediate jerk. There she was, herself again, standing with Calvin beside her, holding onto her hand for dear life, and Charles Wallace in front of her, looking indignant. Mrs. Whatsit, Mrs. Who, and Mrs. Which were not visible, but she knew that they were there; the fact of their presence was strong about her.

"Cchilldrenn, I appolloggize," came Mrs. Which's voice.

"Now, Charles, calm down," Mrs. Whatsit said, appearing not as the great and beautiful beast she had been when they last saw her, but in her familiar wild garb of shawls and scarves and the old tramp's coat and hat. "You know how difficult it is for her to materialize. If you are not substantial yourself it's *very* difficult to realize how limiting protoplasm is."

"I *ammm* ssorry," Mrs. Which's voice came again; but there was more than a hint of amusement in it.

"It is *not* funny." Charles Wallace gave a childish stamp of his foot.

Mrs. Who's glasses shone out, and the rest of her appeared more slowly behind them. *"We are such stuff as dreams are made on."* She smiled broadly. "Prospero in *The Tempest.* I *do* like that play."

"You didn't do it on *purpose?*" Charles demanded.

"Oh, my darling, of course not." Mrs. Whatsit said quickly. "It was just a very understandable mistake. It's very difficult for Mrs. Which to think in a corporeal way. She wouldn't hurt you deliberately; you know that. And it's really a very pleasant little planet, and rather amusing to be flat. We always enjoy our visits there."

"Where are we now, then?" Charles Wallace demanded. "And why?"

"In Orion's belt. We have a friend here, and

we want you to have a look at your own planet."

"When are we going home?" Meg asked anxiously. "What about Mother? What about the twins? They'll be terribly worried about us. When we didn't come in at bedtime—well, Mother must be frantic by now. She and the twins and Fort will have been looking and looking for us, and of course we aren't there to be found!"

"Now, don't worry, my pet," Mrs. Whatsit said cheerfully. "We took care of that before we left. Your mother has had enough to worry her with you and Charles to cope with, and not knowing about your father, without our adding to her anxieties. We took a time wrinkle as well as a space wrinkle. It's very easy to do if you just know how."

"What do you mean?" Meg asked plaintively. "Please, Mrs. Whatsit, it's all so confusing."

"Just relax and don't worry over things that needn't trouble you," Mrs. Whatsit said. "We made a nice, tidy little time tesser, and unless something goes terribly wrong we'll have you back about five minutes before you left, so there'll be time to spare and nobody'll ever need to know you were gone at all, though of course you'll be telling your mother, dear lamb that she is. And if something goes terribly wrong it won't matter whether we ever get back at all."

"Ddon'tt ffrrightenn themm," Mrs. Which's voice came. "Aare yyou llosingg ffaith?"

"Oh, no. No, I'm not."

But Meg thought her voice sounded a little faint.

"I hope *this* is a nice planet," Calvin said. "We can't *see* much of it. Does it ever clear up?"

Meg looked around her, realizing that she had been so breathless from the journey and the stop on the two-dimensional planet that she had not noticed her surroundings. And perhaps this was not very surprising, for the main thing about the surroundings was exactly that they *were* unnoticeable. They seemed to be standing on some kind of nondescript, flat surface. The air around them was gray. It was not exactly fog, but she could see nothing through it. Visibility was limited to the nicely definite bod-

ies of Charles Wallace and Calvin, the rather unbelievable bodies of Mrs. Whatsit and Mrs. Who, and a faint occasional glimmer that was Mrs. Which.

"Come, children," Mrs. Whatsit said. "We don't have far to go, and we might as well walk. It will do you good to stretch your legs a little."

As they moved through the grayness Meg caught an occasional glimpse of slaglike rocks, but there were no traces of trees or bushes, nothing but flat ground under their feet, no sign of any vegetation at all.

Finally, ahead of them there loomed what seemed to be a hill of stone. As they approached it Meg could see that there was an entrance that led into a deep, dark cavern. "Are we going in there?" she asked nervously.

"Don't be afraid," Mrs. Whatsit said. "It's easier for the Happy Medium to work within. Oh, you'll like her, children. She's very jolly. If ever I saw her looking unhappy I would be very depressed myself. As long as she can laugh I'm sure everything is going to come out right in the end."

"Mmrs. Whattsitt," came Mrs. Which's voice severely, "jusstt beccause yyou arre verry youngg iss nno exxcuse forr tallkingg tooo muchh."

Mrs. Whatsit looked hurt, but she subsided.

"Just how old *are* you?" Calvin asked her.

"Just a moment," Mrs. Whatsit murmured, and appeared to calculate rapidly upon her fingers. She nodded triumphantly. "Exactly 2,379,152,497 years, 8 months, and 3 days. That is according to *your* calendar, of course, which even you know isn't very accurate." She leaned closer to Meg and Calvin and whispered, "It was really a *very* great honor for me to be chosen for this mission. It's just because of my verbalizing and materializing so well, you know. But of course we can't take any credit for our talents. It's how we use them that counts. And I make far too many mistakes. That's why Mrs. Who and I enjoyed seeing Mrs. Which make a mistake when she tried to land you on a two-dimensional planet. It was *that* we were laughing at, not at you. She was laughing at herself, you see. She's really terribly nice to us younger ones."

Meg was listening with such interest to what

Mrs. Whatsit was saying that she hardly noticed when they went into the cave; the transition from the grayness of outside to the grayness of inside was almost unnoticeable. She saw a flickering light ahead of them, ahead and down, and it was toward this that they went. As they drew closer she realized that it was a fire.

"It gets very cold in here," Mrs. Whatsit said, "so we asked her to have a good bonfire going for you."

As they approached the fire they could see a dark shadow against it, and as they went closer still they could see that the shadow was a woman. She wore a turban of beautiful pale mauve silk, and a long, flowing, purple satin gown. In her hands was a crystal ball into which she was gazing raptly. She did not appear to see the children, Mrs. Whatsit, Mrs. Who, and Mrs. Which, but continued to stare into the crystal ball; and as she stared she began to laugh; and she laughed and laughed at whatever it was that she was seeing.

Mrs. Which's voice rang out clear and strong, echoing against the walls of the cavern, and the words fell with a sonorous clang.

"WWEE ARE HHERRE!"

The woman looked up from the ball, and when she saw them she got up and curtsied deeply. Mrs. Whatsit and Mrs. Who dropped small curtsies in return, and the shimmer seemed to bow slightly.

"Oh, Medium, dear," Mrs. Whatsit said, "these are the children. Charles Wallace Murry." Charles Wallace bowed. "Margaret Murry." Meg felt that if Mrs. Whatsit and Mrs. Who had curtsied, she ought to, also; so she did, rather awkwardly. "And Calvin O'Keefe." Calvin bobbed his head. "We want them to see their home planet," Mrs. Whatsit said.

The Medium lost the delighted smile she had worn till then. "Oh, *why* must you make me look at unpleasant things when there are so many delightful ones to see?"

Again Mrs. Which's voice reverberated through the cave. "Therre willl nno llonggerr bee sso manyy pplleasanntt thinggss too llookk att iff rressponssible ppeoplle ddo nnott ddo ssomethingg abboutt thee unnppleassanntt oness."

The Medium sighed and held the ball high.

"Look, children," Mrs. Whatsit said. "Look into it well."

"Que la terre est petite à qui la voit des cieux! Delille. *How small is the earth to him who looks from heaven,"* Mrs. Who intoned musically.

Meg looked into the crystal ball, at first with caution, then with increasing eagerness, as she seemed to see an enormous sweep of dark and empty space, and then galaxies swinging across it. Finally they seemed to move in closer on one of the galaxies.

"Your own Milky Way," Mrs. Whatsit whispered to Meg.

They were headed directly toward the center of the galaxy; then they moved off to one side; stars seemed to be rushing at them. Meg flung her arm up over her face as though to ward off the blow.

"Llookk!" Mrs. Which commanded.

Meg dropped her arm. They seemed to be moving in toward a planet. She thought she could make out polar ice caps. Everything seemed sparkling clear.

"No, no, Medium dear, that's Mars," Mrs. Whatsit reproved gently.

"Do I *have* to?" the Medium asked.

"NNOWW!" Mrs. Which commanded.

The bright planet moved out of their vision. For a moment there was the darkness of space; then another planet. The outlines of this planet were not clean and clear. It seemed to be covered with a smoky haze. Through the haze Meg thought she could make out the familiar outlines of continents like pictures in her Social Studies books.

"Is it because of our atmosphere that we can't see properly?" she asked anxiously.

"Nno, Mmegg, yyou knnoww thatt itt iss nnott tthee attmossspheeere," Mrs. Which said. "Yyou mmusstt bee brrave."

"It's the Thing!" Charles Wallace cried. "It's the Dark Thing we saw from the mountain peak on Uriel when we were riding on Mrs. Whatsit's back!"

"Did it just come?" Meg asked in agony, unable to take her eyes from the sickness of the shadow which darkened the beauty of the earth. "Did it just come while we've been gone?"

Mrs. Which's voice seemed very tired. "Ttell herr," she said to Mrs. Whatsit.

Mrs. Whatsit sighed. "No, Meg. It hasn't just come. It has been there for a great many years. That is why your planet is such a troubled one."

"But why—" Calvin started to ask, his voice croaking hoarsely.

Mrs. Whatsit raised her hand to silence him. "We showed you the Dark Thing on Uriel first—oh, for many reasons. First, because the atmosphere on the mountain peaks there is so clear and thin you could see it for what it is. And we thought it would be easier for you to understand it if you saw it—well, someplace *else* first, not your own earth."

"I hate it!" Charles Wallace cried passionately. "I hate the Dark Thing!"

Mrs. Whatsit nodded. "Yes, Charles dear. We all do. That's another reason we wanted to prepare you on Uriel. We thought it would be too frightening for you to see it first of all about your own, beloved world."

"But what is it?" Calvin demanded. "We know that it's evil, but what is it?"

"Yyouu hhave ssaidd itt!" Mrs. Which's voice rang out. "Itt iss Eevill. Itt iss thee Ppowers of Ddarrkknesss!"

"But what's going to happen?" Meg's voice trembled. "Oh, please, Mrs. Which, tell us what's going to happen!"

"Wee wwill cconnttinnue tto ffightt!"

Something in Mrs. Which's voice made all three of the children stand straighter, throwing back their shoulders with determination, looking at the glimmer that was Mrs. Which with pride and confidence.

"And we're not alone, you know, children," came Mrs. Whatsit, the comforter. "All through the universe it's being fought, all through the cosmos, and my, but it's a grand and exciting battle. I know it's hard for you to understand about size, how there's very little difference in the size of the tiniest microbe and the greatest galaxy. You think about that, and maybe it won't seem strange to you that some of our very best fighters have come right from your own planet, and it's a *little* planet, dears, out on the edge of a little galaxy. You can be proud that it's done so well."

"Who have our fighters been?" Calvin asked.

"Oh, *you* must know them, dear," Mrs. Whatsit said.

Mrs. Who's spectacles shone out at them triumphantly, *"And the light shineth in darkness; and the darkness comprehended it not."*

"Jesus!" Charles Wallace said. "Why of course, Jesus!"

"Of course!" Mrs. Whatsit said. "Go on, Charles, love. There were others. All your great artists. They've been lights for us to see by."

"Leonardo da Vinci?" Calvin suggested tentatively. "And Michelangelo?"

"And Shakespeare," Charles Wallace called out, "and Bach! And Pasteur and Madame Curie and Einstein!"

Now Calvin's voice rang with confidence. "And Schweitzer and Gandhi and Buddha and Beethoven and Rembrandt and St. Francis!"

"Now you, Meg," Mrs. Whatsit ordered.

"Oh, Euclid, I suppose." Meg was in such an agony of impatience that her voice grated irritably. "And Copernicus. But what about Father? Please, what about Father?"

"Wee aarre ggoingg tto yourr ffatherr," Mrs. Which said.

"But where is he?" Meg went over to Mrs. Which and stamped as though she were as young as Charles Wallace.

Mrs. Whatsit answered in a voice that was low but quite firm. "On a planet that has given in. So you must prepare to be very strong."

All traces of cheer had left the Happy Medium's face. She sat holding the great ball, looking down at the shadowed earth, and a slow tear coursed down her cheek. "I can't stand it any longer," she sobbed. "Watch now, children, watch!"

Natalie Babbitt

Tuck Everlasting

This unusual, evocative fantasy speaks to a child's fear of death by sensitively presenting a vision of the balance between life and death, using the propelling narrative force of a folktale and a down-to-earth simplicity. This moving novel explores the mysteries of time and mortality through the experiences of ten-year-old Winnie, who discovers the spring of eternal life. The members of the Tuck family have drunk unwittingly from this fountain of youth, and they kidnap Winnie, intending to keep her with them until they can convince her that living forever is not a boon but a curse. Pa Tuck's words to Winnie in this selection reveal the wisdom in this accomplished, many-layered fable. [From Natalie Babbitt, *Tuck Everlasting* (Farrar, Straus & Giroux, 1975).]

It was a good supper, flapjacks, bacon, bread, and applesauce, but they ate sitting about in the parlor instead of around a table. Winnie had never had a meal that way before and she watched them carefully at first, to see what rules there might be that she did not know about. But there seemed to be no rules. Jesse sat on the floor and used the seat of a chair for a table, but the others held their plates in their laps. There were no napkins. It was all right, then, to lick the maple syrup from your fingers. Winnie was never allowed to do such a thing at home, but she had always thought it would be the easiest way. And suddenly the meal seemed luxurious.

After a few minutes, however, it was clear to Winnie that there was at least one rule: As long as there was food to eat, there was no conversation. All four Tucks kept their eyes and their attention on the business at hand. And in the silence, given time to think, Winnie felt her elation, and her thoughtless pleasure, wobble and collapse.

It had been different when they were out-of-doors, where the world belonged to everyone and no one. Here, everything was theirs alone, everything was done their way. Eating, she realized now, was a very personal thing, not something to do with strangers. *Chewing* was a personal thing. Yet here she was, chewing with strangers in a strange place. She shivered a little, and frowned, looking round at them. That story they had told her—why, they were crazy, she thought harshly, and they were criminals. They had kidnapped her, right out of the middle of her very own wood, and now she would be expected to sleep—*all night*—in this dirty, peculiar house. She had never slept in any bed but her own in her life. All these thoughts flowed at once from the dark part of her mind. She put down her fork and said, unsteadily, "I want to go home."

The Tucks stopped eating, and looked at her, surprised. Mae said soothingly, "Why, of course you do, child. That's only natural. I'll take you home. I promised I would, soon's we've explained a bit as to why you got to promise you'll never tell about the spring. That's the only reason we brung you here. We got to make you see why."

Then Miles said, cheerfully and with sudden sympathy, "There's a pretty good old rowboat. I'll take you out for a row after supper."

"No, *I* will," said Jesse. "Let *me*. I found her first, didn't I, Winnie Foster? Listen, I'll show you where the frogs are, and . . ."

"Hush," Tuck interrupted. "Everyone hush. *I'll* take Winnie rowing on the pond. There's a good deal to be said and I think we better hurry up and say it. I got a feeling there ain't a whole lot of time."

Jesse laughed at this, and ran a hand roughly through his curls. "That's funny, Pa. Seems to me like time's the only thing we got a lot of."

But Mae frowned. "You worried, Tuck? What's got you? No one saw us on the way up. Well, now, wait a bit—yes, they did, come to think of it. There was a man on the road, just outside Treegap. But he didn't say nothing."

"He knows me, though," said Winnie. She had forgotten, too, about the man in the yellow suit, and now, thinking of him, she felt a surge of relief. "He'll tell my father he saw me."

"He knows you?" said Mae, her frown deepening. "But you didn't call out to him, child. Why not?"

"I was too scared to do *anything*," said Winnie honestly.

Tuck shook his head. "I never thought we'd come to the place where we'd be scaring children," he said. "I guess there's no way to make it up to you, Winnie, but I'm sure most awful sorry it had to happen like that. Who was this man you saw?"

"I don't know his name," said Winnie. "But he's a pretty nice man, I guess." In fact, he seemed supremely nice to her now, a kind of savior. And then she added, "He came to our house last night, but he didn't go inside."

"Well, that don't sound too serious, Pa," said Miles. "Just some stranger passing by."

"Just the same, we got to get you home again, Winnie," said Tuck, standing up decisively. "We got to get you home just as fast as we can. I got a feeling this whole thing is going to come apart like wet bread. But first we got to talk, and the pond's the best place. The pond's got answers. Come along, child. Let's go out on the water."

The sky was a ragged blaze of red and pink and orange, and its double trembled on the surface of the pond like color spilled from a paintbox. The sun was dropping fast now, a soft red sliding egg yolk, and already to the east there was a darkening to purple. Winnie, newly brave with her thoughts of being rescued, climbed boldly into the rowboat. The hard heels of her buttoned boots made a hollow banging sound against its wet boards, loud in the warm and breathless quiet. Across the pond a bullfrog spoke a deep note of warning. Tuck climbed in, too, pushing off, and, settling the oars into their locks, dipped them into the silty bottom in one strong pull. The rowboat slipped from the bank then, silently, and glided out, tall water grasses whispering away from its sides, releasing it.

Here and there the still surface of the water dimpled, and bright rings spread noiselessly and vanished. "Feeding time," said Tuck softly. And Winnie, looking down, saw hosts of tiny insects skittering and skating on the surface. "Best time of all for fishing," he said, "when they come up to feed."

He dragged on the oars. The rowboat slowed and began to drift gently toward the farthest end of the pond. It was so quiet that Winnie almost jumped when the bullfrog spoke again. And then, from the tall pines and birches that ringed the pond, a wood thrush caroled. The silver notes were pure and clear and lovely.

"Know what that is, all around us, Winnie?" said Tuck, his voice low. "Life. Moving, growing, changing, never the same two minutes together. This water, you look out at it every morning, and it *looks* the same, but it ain't. All night long it's been moving, coming in through the stream back there to the west, slip-ping out through the stream down east here, always quiet, always new, moving on. You can't hardly see the current, can you? And sometimes the wind makes it look like it's going the other way. But it's always there, the water's always moving on, and someday, after a long while, it comes to the ocean."

They drifted in silence for a time. The bull-frog spoke again, and from behind them, far back in some reedy, secret place, another bull-frog answered. In the fading light, the trees along the banks were slowly losing their dimensions, flattening into silhouettes clipped from black paper and pasted to the paling sky. The voice of a different frog, hoarser and not so deep, croaked from the nearest bank.

"Know what happens then?" said Tuck. "To the water? The sun sucks some of it up right out of the ocean and carries it back in clouds, and then it rains, and the rain falls into the stream, and the stream keeps moving on, taking it all back again. It's a wheel, Winnie. Everything's a wheel, turning and turning, never stopping. The frogs is part of it, and the bugs, and the fish, and the wood thrush, too. And people. But never the same ones. Always coming in new, always growing and changing, and always moving on. That's the way it's supposed to be. That's the way it *is*."

The rowboat had drifted at last to the end of the pond, but now its bow bumped into the rotting branches of a fallen tree that thrust thick fingers into the water. And though the current pulled at it, dragging its stern sidewise, the boat was wedged and could not follow. The water slipped past it, out between clumps of reeds and brambles, and gurgled down a narrow bed, over stones and pebbles, foaming a little, moving swiftly now after its slow trip between the pond's wide banks. And, farther down, Winnie could see that it hurried into a curve, around a leaning willow, and disappeared.

"It goes on," Tuck repeated, "to the ocean. But this rowboat now, it's stuck. If we didn't move it out ourself, it would stay here forever, trying to get loose, but stuck. That's what us Tucks are, Winnie. Stuck so's we can't move on. We ain't part of the wheel no more. Dropped off, Winnie. Left behind. And every-where around us, things is moving and growing and changing. You, for instance. A child now, but someday a woman. And after that, moving on to make room for the new children."

Winnie blinked, and all at once her mind was drowned with understanding of what he was saying. For she—yes, even she—would go out of the world willy-nilly someday. Just go out, like the flame of a candle, and no use protesting. It was a certainty. She would try very hard not to think of it, but sometimes, as now, it would be forced upon her. She raged against it, helpless and insulted, and blurted at last, "I don't want to die."

"No," said Tuck calmly. "Not now. Your time's not now. But dying's part of the wheel, right there next to being born. You can't pick out the pieces you like and leave the rest. Being part of the whole thing, that's the blessing. But it's passing us by, us Tucks. Living's heavy work, but off to one side, the way *we* are, it's useless, too. It don't make sense. If I knowed how to climb back on the wheel, I'd do it in a minute. You can't have living without dying. So you can't call it living, what we got. We just *are*, we just *be*, like rocks beside the road."

Tuck's voice was rough now, and Winnie, amazed, sat rigid. No one had ever talked to her of things like this before. "I want to grow again," he said fiercely, "and change. And if that means I got to move on at the end of it, then I want that, too. Listen, Winnie, it's something you don't find out how you feel until afterwards. If people knowed about the spring down there in Treegap, they'd all come running like pigs to slops. They'd trample each other, trying to get some of that water. That'd be bad enough, but afterwards—can you imagine? All the little ones little forever, all the old ones old forever. Can you picture what that means? *Forever?* The wheel would keep on going round, the water rolling by to the ocean, but the people would've turned into nothing but rocks by the side of the road. 'Cause they wouldn't know till after, and then it'd be too late." He peered at her, and Winnie saw that his face was pinched with the effort of explaining. "Do you see, now, child? Do you understand? Oh, Lord, I just got to make you understand!"

There was a long, long moment of silence. Winnie, struggling with the anguish of all these things, could only sit hunched and numb, the sound of the water rolling in her ears. It was black and silky now; it lapped at the sides of the rowboat and hurried on around them into the stream.

Nonfiction:
The Real and Changing
World

In discussing nonfiction for children, we soon encounter the problem of terminology: Just what is nonfiction? Would the terms *informational writing* or *factual books* be more precise? How does nonfiction differ from fiction in subject matter and style?

Margery Fisher accepts the term nonfiction as "a compromise with some sense in it." She sees the fiction-nonfiction distinction as necessary not only for classification but also for commercial and marketing purposes. Recognizing the difficulty of defining the nonfiction genre, she notes:

A great many fact-books make use of incidental fiction, and who could argue that fiction had no element of fact? The distinction between fiction and non-fiction is blurred and constantly shifting. . . . The terms fiction and non-fiction express *intention* in a broad way. . . . Looking at it from the writer's point of view, . . . we can see that there is a distinction, a very flexible one, between writing a story and writing an information book. In a novel the story—the fiction, perhaps I should say—comes first and has priority: facts, of whatever kind, exist to support it. The writer of an information book sets out to help towards knowledge, and the techniques he uses, which may well include story-telling, will be subordinate to this end.[1]

1. Margery Fisher, *Matters of Fact: Aspects of Non-Fiction for Children* (Brockhampton, 1972), pp. 10–11.

Following Fisher, then, we might say that the major and natural goal of an informational book is to educate, and that such a book must also stimulate the interest and excitement toward a subject that is essential to learning.

From the educational aids of the earliest hornbooks and primers, which consisted of the alphabet, tables of syllables, and prayers, books of instruction have dominated children's literature. The *Orbis Pictus* by Comenius (translated into English in 1658 and in use for over a century thereafter) was the earliest instructional picture book; it remained one of the few instructional books with genuine appeal for children until the eighteenth century. Then, stimulated by John Locke's theory that children learn best when information is combined with entertainment, such energetic booksellers as Thomas Boreman, John Newbery, and John Harris published the first informational books designed for children's use in the home rather than at school. One of the most charming examples is Harris's *Marmaduke Multiply's Merry Method of Making Minor Mathematicians* (1816–17). The bookseller-publishers, with their eye toward a vast and profitable market, attempted to supply children with entertaining works of history, biography, geography, and science. But more austere writers of the time, such as Mrs. Barbauld and Mrs. Trimmer, avoided the imaginative approach and continued to provide works of unadorned didacticism.

Entertaining nonfiction for children flourished in the nineteenth century in the forms of verse and catechism as well as in prose. Samual Griswold Goodrich, an American who used the pseudonym Peter Parley, wrote heavily popularized geography and travel books in the form of fictionalized travelogues, in which a group of children are accompanied on their journeys by an omniscient adult who relentlessly informs them of geographical and moral minutiae. In Britain, Charlotte Yonge and Charles Dickens wrote children's histories; Mrs. Margaret Gatty and her daughter, Mrs. Juliana Horatia Ewing, wrote on botanical subjects and were published in book form as well as in articles in their *Aunt Judy's Magazine.* Other forms of nonfiction, particularly biography, were popular features in the children's magazines of the time.

With the development of the printing process and advancements in illustration reproduction in the early twentieth century, nonfiction books achieved a high degree of literary and artistic excellence. Examples include the picture books of E. Boyd Smith (*The Farm Book,* 1910) and the Swedish Elsa Beskow (*Pelle's New Suit,* 1929), in which striking artwork is seamlessly integrated with informational text. The vast panorama of human history presented in Hendrik Willem Van Loon's *The Story of Mankind* (1921) is another outstanding example. In the past half century, nonfiction for children has increased dramatically both in volume and in quality. Such contemporary writers and illustrators as Milton Meltzer, Millicent Selsam, F. N. Monjo, Jean Fritz, Olivia Coolidge, Laurence Pringle, David Macaulay, William Kurelek, Anne Ophelia Dowden, Robert McClung, Jan Adkins, and Shirley Glubok have enlivened the field with the strength and commitment of their work.

Although nonfiction is one of the most lucrative and important segments of the children's book industry (more nonfiction than fiction is published annually), many parents, teachers, and librarians do not feel as comfortable in attempting to judge nonfiction as they do in assessing the values of fiction, poetry, or picture books. Frequently, nonfiction books are simply ignored. As Jo Carr points out, there is "a consistent, if unconscious, denigration of nonfiction for children. . . . All too often these books have been considered for their content alone, earmarked exclusively for 'curriculum support' and neatly categorized for some useful purpose. It is no wonder that quality cannot be recognized from such a limited perspective."[2] The first Newbery award, in 1922, was given to Van Loon for *The Story of Mankind,* but since that time books of nonfiction have received little attention from those who award praises and prizes.

What critical standards should be applied to works of nonfiction? How are these books to be regarded, and how evaluated? Content—authoritatively presented—obviously is an important element, but it cannot be of much value without the compelling personal voice and deep commitment of a writer. It is the particular point of view of an individual author, allied with imagination and enthusiasm and reflected in style, selection, and organization, that makes the difference between a book that simply presents the information and one that is exciting and stimulating. According to Milton Meltzer, "Imagination, invention, selection, language, form—these are just as important to the making of a good book of biography, history, or science as to the making of a piece of fiction."[3]

Few presentations may be as impassioned as Rachel Carson's; few lives as moving as Anne Frank's; few adventures or travels as significant as Marco Polo's. Yet without a writer's added excitement and feeling, no nonfiction book can engage a reader in a profound way.

It is true that facts themselves have a certain attraction. Children are drawn to wonders in the real world, to dinosaurs and volcanoes, to tidal waves and baseball pitchers, to the odd and astounding bits of information compiled in the *Guiness Book of World Records.* But the best nonfiction for children does more than provide colorful tidbits of information. It also stimulates the reader not merely to the acquisition of facts but to the comprehension of patterns of thought as well: an understanding of the scientific method, as well as the facts of science; an awareness of historical movements, as well as the dates and details of history. Children, particularly between the ages of nine and fourteen, are great devotees of nonfiction and respond passionately to subject matter that fires their curiosity. Their reading can be quite mature, ranging widely and deeply; at times, following their personal interests, children may read at levels far beyond what might be expected of them.

Books of fact provide children with an access to the world of knowledge, with a structured comprehension of the world around them. The most distinguished nonfiction for children can nurture a child's natural curiosity, enlarge it into a spirit of deeper questioning, and encourage the alertness and responsiveness toward life that is the beginning of wisdom.

2. Jo Carr, Preface, *Beyond Fact: Nonfiction for Children and Young People,* comp. Jo Carr (American Library Association, 1982), p. ix.
3. Milton Meltzer, "Where Do All the Prizes Go? The Case for Nonfiction," *The Horn Book Magazine,* 52 (1976), 18.

The cult of the hero is as old as mankind. It sets before men examples which are lofty but not inaccessible, astonishing but not incredible, and it is this double quality which makes it the most convincing of artforms and the most human of religions.[1]

13   Biography

C hildren are fascinated by the trials, terrors, and victories in the lives of others. Their emotions, compassion, pity, admiration, and affection, are easily stirred by the story of a person who has met trouble with courage and strength. In biography, depth and detail of characterization hold center stage; in marked contrast to fiction, which may skimp on characterization in the interests of plot, the subject's feelings, behavior, speech, and inner turmoil are often of more interest than the action. The story of a real life, well told, can give a child the feeling of having slipped inside another person's skin, of having shared in the making of certain critical decisions, of having overcome handicaps and problems — of having known another existence. In addition to stirring a child's empathy, biography can give the child the sense of a life lived creatively within a particular context — an opportunity to understand history not merely as a background tapestry of names and dates, but in terms of its influence on an individual life.

The readiness of children to extend themselves in the way that biography requires has only one stipulation: The struggles, problems, and joys of the subject

1. André Maurois, *Aspects of Biography,* trans. S. C. Roberts (Cambridge University Press, 1929), p. 183.

must be within children's comprehension or, at least, their imaginative capabilities. Objective struggles are not a problem, but the subjective, internal complexities of adults might cause difficulties. The strong attraction that Helen Keller's life has for children can in part be attributed to the sympathy summoned by her predicament: Children can imagine themselves unable to hear, groping in the dark. Another person whose life strikes a strong responsive chord is Anne Frank. That these two lives are presented in autobiographies may augment their appeal. Anne Frank's diary conveys with immediacy her day-to-day life; its emotional power comes from writing out of her own need, writing with an unsparing honesty to the friend she imagined her diary to be ("Dear Kitty"). Helen Keller's autobiography is more apt to be requested after children have read about her in a biography. One child made a point of asking for the book that told about Helen "in her own words." Apparently this child wanted to know more of what it was like to be Helen Keller than she could get from the biography she had read.

To interpret childrens' response to these works simply as an interest in handicapped persons or curiosity about the tactics and stratagems involved in hiding from German soldiers during the Second World War is to avoid the emotional substance of each life. Who cannot feel the moment with Helen Keller when, after learning of the mystery of language, she went to bed and, for the first time, longed for a new day to come? Who can step into Anne Frank's world and not be moved by her telling "all kinds of things that lie buried deep in my heart"? This kind of first-hand telling is intrinsically powerful when the teller is a gifted writer. Although Anne Frank was a child, she was neither untutored nor insensitive. Her ability to see herself and others clearly, to create for herself a friend that has become all her readers, was unusual in any circumstance.

Like Anne Frank, Jean Fritz as a child was a burgeoning writer, and the adult Jean accurately recreates the child's observations through her choice of exact emotional and social details. Her memoir of growing up as an American child in China is honest, poignant, and alive in the immediate present. Autobiography relies on memory as much as biography relies on historical fact. But memory, like storytelling, is fluid. Jean Fritz says that her autobiography may be treated as fiction. It is called *Homesick: My Own Story* (1982). Fritz explains:

> Since my childhood feels like a story, I decided to tell it that way, letting the events fall as they would into the shape of a story, lacing them together with fictional bits, adding a piece here and there when memory didn't give me all I needed. . . . The people are real people; the places are dear to me. But most important, the form I have used has given me the freedom to recreate the emotions that I remember so vividly. Strictly speaking, I have to call this book *fiction,* but it does not feel like fiction to me. It is my story, told as truly as I can tell it.[2]

Other writers and artists have told their own stories. A recent trend in autobiographical writing for children utilizes the picture book format to present visual and written memoirs; this format has been used by such artists as Eric Blegvad, Margot Zemach, William Kurelek, Sing Lim, and Shizuye Takshima. Some of these picture book autobiographies span an entire lifetime; others focus on childhood. According to Sarah Ellis:

2. Jean Fritz, *Homesick: My Own Story* (Putnam's, 1982), p. 7.

Visual memoirs of childhood, although less common than their written counterparts, can show an equally interesting interplay between memory and imagination, between a single story and the story of a community, between history and fiction. . . . [These] childhood memoirs . . . tell in illustration and an accompanying text, of a particular season in the life of a single child. These are small, individual stories that become large in the telling.[3]

Even more than biography, which often tends to focus upon the lives of important public figures, autobiography can offer insights into ordinary people whose extraordinariness lies in their humanity and their ability to cope creatively with life's difficulties. An excellent example of the autobiography of ordinary life is Eloise Greenfield's *Childtimes* (1979), a sequence of childhood reminiscences and vignettes of day-to-day life that spans three generations of a black family. Each segment draws upon the love and strength of the family, the courage, hope, and humor of its individual members, and portrays, with precise social documentation, three particular eras in the history of specific communities.

This is not to say that biography must, by its nature, be less powerful than autobiography — especially when the biographer has a deep interest in and insight into the subject. Writing a good biography is a fine art, demanding the skills of a researcher and scholar and the narrative technique of a fiction writer. The delicate distinction between fact and judgment must be painstakingly drawn. These principles remain constant, whether a biography is written for children or for adults, but there is a difference in approach. As Olivia Coolidge writes:

If . . . I had embarked on a life of Shaw or Gandhi for adults, I would have done so with the idea of adding somewhat to the total of general knowledge on my subject. Either I would have sought unpublished manuscripts or I would have expected to develop some new point of view by examining the known ones. Unless there seemed a fair prospect of doing one or the other, I would not have undertaken the task to begin with. But a young-adult biography is not necessarily trying to add to human knowledge. . . . A young-adult biography is basically an attempt to present a life in broad outline for readers who have a great number of other books to study or who bog down in long volumes, but who are intelligent and like ideas.[4]

Truth and objectivity are ideals in biography, but the reality of the genre is that every observation and every choice of material, as in any writing, is that of the author. It would also be ideal if all dialogue could be quoted from written sources, but this is often not possible; sometimes the writer must piece together crucial scenes using circumstantial evidence, things that reasonably can be assumed to have happened or been said. Neither an outright fabrication nor a verbatim report, a recreated scene of this sort depends for its integrity on the depth of the biographer's scholarship. Biographers, like writers of general history, must balance their own opinions and imaginations against a complex array of facts. According to Margery Fisher, "biography is an illusion, a fiction in the guise of fact."[5]

One of the selections in this chapter describes Sojourner Truth's confrontation with her master. Jacqueline Bernard, the writer, provides dialogue for them both; she even notes the master's raising of an eyebrow. In presenting this incident so that her readers can visualize the scene, Bernard accepts the responsibility of being her own "authority"; this filling out with detail is based on her sense

3. Sarah Ellis, "News from the North," *The Horn Book Magazine,* 60 (1984), 375.
4. Olivia Coolidge, "My Struggle with Facts," *Wilson Library Bulletin,* 49 (1974), 149–50.
5. Margery Fisher, *Matters of Fact: Aspects of Non-Fiction for Children* (Brockhampton, 1972), p. 302.

of proportion, on what she knows of the events in Sojourner's life. In her author's note, Bernard states: "In telling it, wherever possible, I have used actual conversations as originally spoken and recorded in the primary sources." But where Bernard had to invent, she did so in a restrained manner, engaging the imagination of the reader rather than imposing her own. The quality of this well-written biography comes from the writer's sensitivity, the scrupulous devotion with which she pursues her source material, and, underneath it all, a genuine respect for Sojourner Truth.

F. M. Monjo takes another approach to biography for children. He writes fictionalized biography, or *story biography,* which includes invented dialogue and scenes. Monjo explains that he permits himself "to invent, occasionally, scenes that may never have occurred and to introduce dialogue that was, assuredly, never spoken." He does this to accommodate his choice of narrator, who is always "a child associated with the great figure in question," for example, Lincoln's son or Franklin's grandson. "The use of a child as narrator," he says, "a child intimately associated with the person under scrutiny, makes possible a casual intimacy which, I believe, young readers find congenial."[6]

Young readers also find humor congenial, and Jean Fritz's lively wit sparkles throughout her biographies, written for younger children, of figures from American history. She has an unfailingly sharp eye for the unusual detail that reveals character or clarifies an event. For the very youngest child, M. B. Goffstein has created a picture book biography of a single figure, *A Little Schubert* (1972). Rather than oversimplify the composer's complex life, Goffstein uses subtly restrained minimalist art and poetic prose, with warmly comic overtones, to create a hymn of praise to the man and his music. For slightly older children, Goffstein's *Lives of the Artists* (1981) is an unusual example of collective biography, containing reproductions of works by the artists discussed, accompanied by personal impressions in free verse.

Because a good biography requires fine writing and careful scholarship, it is no wonder that the field abounds in mediocre productions. Responsible for the creation of many undistinguished works is the attitude that biography is merely a useful supplement to a school's curriculum, one that can be used to brighten up the subject matter of history, music, or science. The irony of such an approach is that the real thrust and force of biography is lost; once the edge is taken off children's appetites, they may cease to hunt for the good works that do exist. Another distortion of the genre is the ultrasimplification of a life into a symbolic portrayal. The reduction of complex lives to bare outlines is more like contemporary mythmaking than the writing of biography.

For the child who is ready for biography — who can, as Penelope Lively says, take "a step aside from self, a step out of the child's self-preoccupation, . . . a step toward maturity"[7] — there is a sharpness of impact to be found in biography that is unique. Milton Meltzer found his own revelation in his childhood reading:

What I liked most were adventure stories that took me out of my skin. And biographies. I was always trying on a new hero for size — explorer, tennis star, reporter, detective. One day I looked up from a book and realized that what I was feeling inside, in my own private world, was astonishingly like what people everywhere felt — whether they

6. F. N. Monjo, "The Ten Bad Things about History," in *Beyond Fact: Nonfiction for Children and Young People,* comp. Jo Carr (American Library Association, 1982), p. 99.
7. Penelope Lively, "Children and Memory," *The Horn Book Magazine,* 49 (1973), 400.

lived yesterday or a hundred or a thousand years ago. This fear, hope, shame, love, it wasn't happening only to me. Maybe there was something of me in everyone, and something of everyone in me.[8]

This strong, humanizing tie between the self and others accounts for the deep satisfaction that comes from reading biographies. Through them, lives can be seen in their entirety, in a way that is of immeasurable help in facing the decisions in one's own life. And biography emphasizes how individual lives are interwoven within the fabric of a particular time and society and within a larger history. F. N. Monjo poses the question, "What will [history] ever do for our children?" He then answers his own question, not with comments about curricula or with sweeping generalizations concerning human destiny, but with the biographer's reply:

Well, it will tell us that once there was a man named Shakespeare. That once there was a woman named Sappho. There was a Mozart, a Lincoln, a Galileo, a Joan of Arc. There was an Aesculapius. There was an Archimedes. There was a Martin Luther King. No, it refuses, and will always refuse, to give us the crisp, easy, fast answers we keep hoping for. But it will tell our children of great human beings and great accomplishments, if we can help them to learn to listen to its voices. . . .

And [a] child may conclude that, in so much diversity, surely there can be an honored place for him, no matter how daring and outrageous his dream may be. And how exhilarating it will be for him to know — for that child to know — that history has never mapped, and never will be able to map, the final limits of human possibility.[9]

8. Quoted in *Anthology of Children's Literature,* ed. Edna Johnson, Evelyn R. Sickels, Frances Clarke Sayers, and Carolyn Horowitz, 5th ed. (Houghton Mifflin, 1977), p. 1015.
9. Monjo, p. 103.

Dorothy Aldis

Nothing Is Impossible: The Story of Beatrix Potter

Beatrix Potter's response to the imprisoning illness of a five-year-old friend reveals how deeply she sympathized with him and how much she herself must have suffered as a child from the stern sequestration imposed by her own parents, a condition in which she was still living at the time of the writing of this letter. In her insightful article, "In Biography for Young Readers, Nothing Is Impossible," Elizabeth Segal criticizes Aldis for not emphasizing strongly enough the difficult constraints in Potter's life and for softening the deprivations of her childhood and young womanhood. But the book does bring to light the sources of Potter's creative impulses and gives a history of her publications for the reader too young to enjoy the scholarly and psychological dimensions of Margaret Lane's standard adult biography, *The Tale of Beatrix Potter*. [From Dorothy Aldis, *Nothing Is Impossible: The Story of Beatrix Potter* (Atheneum, 1969).]

A Letter to Noel

On the morning of a bright hot day in September in the year when Beatrix Potter became twenty-seven, she received a letter from her friend Annie Moore saying that her oldest child, Noel, (whose birthday was the same as Beatrix's), had come down with rheumatic fever and would have to be kept quiet for many months.

CAN YOU IMAGINE A FIVE-YEAR-OLD BEING TIED DOWN TO HIS BED? HE'S BEEN GOOD ABOUT IT SO FAR. HIS FATHER IS WONDERFUL AT THINKING UP GAMES FOR HIM TO PLAY, BUT I KNOW WE CAN'T CONTINUE THIS PACE OF KEEPING HIM OCCUPIED. BESIDES KILLING US, IT MIGHT TURN NOEL INTO A SPOILED AND DEMANDING LITTLE BOY. HE'LL HAVE TO LEARN TO ENTERTAIN HIMSELF. ALTHOUGH TEMPTED TO, I HAVEN'T GIVEN HIM YOUR BIRTHDAY PRESENT YET. I TRY TO SPREAD OUT HIS TREATS.

Beatrix went straight to her room and began a letter:

MY DEAR NOEL—

I DON'T KNOW WHAT TO WRITE YOU, SO I SHALL TELL YOU A STORY ABOUT FOUR LITTLE RABBITS WHOSE NAMES WERE FLOPSY, MOPSY, COTTONTAIL, AND PETER. THEY LIVED WITH THEIR MOTHER IN A SANDBANK UNDER THE ROOTS OF A BIG TREE . . . "NOW, MY DEARS," SAID OLD MRS. BUNNY, "YOU MAY GO INTO THE FIELD OR DOWN THE LANE, BUT DON'T GO INTO MR. MCGREGOR'S GARDEN . . ."

The illustration on the first page of Beatrix Potter's letter was of the four little rabbits. Three of them—Flopsy, Mopsy, and Peter—had pricked-up ears, but Cottontail had folded her ears back. She looked comfortable and sleepy that way. Peter's ears were the most alert and listening. Old Mrs. Bunny looked like a worried mother who hoped her children would behave but was not at all certain they would.

On the second page of the letter each small rabbit was wearing a jacket. Old Mrs. Bunny, with an apron tied around her waist, was handing her children a basket in which to put the wild blackberries she had asked them to pick for supper.

Off they went.

Flopsy, Mopsy, and Cottontail were good, obedient little rabbits and began picking blackberries, but Peter got into serious trouble immediately. He bounded into Mr. McGregor's garden where he ate lettuce, beans, and radishes. For fear of getting caught by Mr. McGregor, he ate too much and too quickly. That gave him a terrible stomachache which sent him hunting for parsley. His mother insisted parsley was the best cure for indigestion. But, just as he was coming around the corner of a cucumber frame, what awful sight did he see? Mr. McGregor, chasing him with a rake!

Peter ran as fast as he could, and as he ran, he lost both shoes. But that wasn't the worst. One of the large brass buttons on his jacket got caught in a net draped around a gooseberry bush to protect it from greedy birds. Peter's jacket was blue and quite new. But in order to escape from Mr. McGregor, he had to wriggle out of it and leave it on the bush. When he arrived home without his shoes and his coat, his mother punished him by putting him to bed. She made him drink camomile tea, but Flopsy, Mopsy, and Cottontail had bread and milk and blackberries for their supper.

Beatrix finished off her letter by saying she was coming back to London on Thursday. "So I shall soon be seeing you and the new baby. I remain, yours affectionately, Beatrix Potter."

This letter to Noel was the first of many little stories Beatrix wrote to the Moore children, illustrated with pen-and-ink sketches. The following summer, when Eric Moore was having mumps in London, she wrote him about a frog named Jeremy Fisher "who lived in a little house on the bank of a river," and who "liked getting his feet wet, nobody ever scolded him, and he never caught cold." She wrote Norah Moore about a mischievous little squirrel called Squirrel Nutkin, and how he lost his tail. She wrote about a cat named Tabitha Twitchet, "who was an anxious parent," always losing her kittens. On a visit to her cousin Caroline Hutton in Gloucester, she heard a story about a tailor who had left a coat cut out one night and found it mysteriously finished in the morning, and this so fascinated her that she wove a story about the tailor which she sent to little Freda Moore with a letter:

MY DEAR FREDA:
    BECAUSE YOU ARE FOND OF FAIRY TALES, AND HAVE BEEN ILL, I HAVE MADE YOU A STORY ALL FOR YOURSELF—A NEW ONE THAT NOBODY HAD HEARD BEFORE.

Needless to say, the children were delighted.

Seven more years went by. Beatrix continued working in the two museums. She went to art exhibitions. She collected and painted mushrooms. She collected fossils, too, during summer holidays, and took up her father's hobby of photography. But where he usually photographed his friends and well-to-do acquaintances, she liked to take pictures of animals and country scenes and farm cottages. Twice she visited her brother in Scotland, where Bertram still caught terrible colds but didn't mind because he loved the Scottish country so much.

He had two good servants who took care of him. He farmed. He painted. Beatrix envied him his independence.

All these activities kept her very busy. At the end of one summer's holiday she wrote:

I AM VERY SORRY INDEED TO COME AWAY, BUT I HAVE DONE A GOOD SUMMER'S WORK. . . . MY PHOTOGRAPHY WAS NOT SATISFACTORY, BUT I MADE ABOUT FORTY CAREFUL DRAWINGS OF FUNGUSES AND COLLECTED SOME INTERESTING FOSSILS. . . . FOR THE REST, I READ SUNDRY OLD NOVELS, SOME OF WHICH I HAD READ BEFORE. I ALSO LEARNED FOUR ACTS OF *HENRY VIII* AND MEANT TO HAVE LEARNED ALL, BUT I CAN SAY THIS FOR MY DILIGENCE, THAT EVERY LINE WAS LEARNT IN BED. . . . I KNOW *RICHARD III* RIGHT THROUGH, *HENRY VI*, FOUR-FIFTHS, *RICHARD II* EXCEPT THREE PAGES: *KING JOHN* FOUR ACTS, A GOOD HALF OF THE *MIDSUMMER NIGHT'S DREAM* AND *THE TEMPEST*, AND HALF WAY THROUGH THE *MERCHANT OF VENICE*. I LEARNT SIX MORE OR LESS IN A YEAR. NEVER FELT THE LEAST STRAINED OR SHOULD NOT HAVE DONE IT.

Canon Rawnsley, when he saw her, still called her Miss Mycologist, but he had given up begging her to do the mushroom book. They both realized this would take more scientific training than she had. She did send a paper on the "Germination of the Spores of Agaricineae" to the Linnaean Society when she was thirty-one years old, but she did not read it herself.

But now Canon Rawnsley was asking her why she didn't do what he had suggested a long time ago: make a book of her dressed-up animal characters?

Beatrix became interested. She remembered how the Moore children had loved the animal pictures she had sent them in letters. Perhaps it was natural for children to like pictures of little animals.

"Do stories go with the pictures?" the Canon asked her.

"Mostly."

"Which pictures and story do you like the best?"

"Well, perhaps the one about Peter Rabbit that I wrote for little Noel Moore."

"Then put the story and pictures into shape and I'll give you the name of a publisher."

"A *publisher!* Goodness! But, oh dear."

"Oh dear what?"

"I just don't think it's likely Noel would have kept that story about Peter Rabbit. After all, I wrote him that letter—let's see now — about eight years ago."

"Find out," said the Canon.

Beatrix wrote to Noel immediately and he wrote back. Of course he had kept the letter about Peter. He had kept all her letters.

A month later, Beatrix sent *The Tale of Peter Rabbit* to seven publishers, one after another. All seven turned it down. However, one publisher, Frederick Warne & Company, wrote a polite and even slightly encouraging letter with their refusal.

Still, a refusal it was.

So Beatrix decided to be her own publisher. Encouraged by Canon Rawnsley, she drew what seemed like a very large sum out of her Post Office savings account, and got in touch with a printer whose name was given to her by Miss Woodward. The book should be small, Beatrix decided, with only one or two sentences on each page and a picture every time a page was turned over.

Except for being somewhat longer, the book turned out to be almost exactly like her letter to Noel. There was one picture washed with color: this was old Mrs. Bunny administering camomile tea to her disobedient son. The other pictures were all black and white.

Isaac Bashevis Singer

A Day of Pleasure: Stories of a Boy Growing Up in Warsaw

Isaac Bashevis Singer, known for his stories of Jewish life, here brings out his fine sense of irony and humor in the recollection of a day from his own childhood. [From Isaac Bashevis Singer, *A Day of Pleasure: Stories of a Boy Growing Up in Warsaw* (Farrar, Straus & Giroux, 1969).]

A Day of Pleasure

When times were good, I would get a two-groschen piece, a kopeck, from Father or Mother every day, as every boy who went to cheder did. For me this coin represented all wordly pleasures. Across the street was Esther's candy store, where one could buy chocolates, jelly beans, ice cream, caramels, and all sorts of cookies. Since I had a weakness for drawing with colored pencils, which cost money, a kopeck proved not nearly so large a coin as Father and Mother made it out to be. There were times when I was forced to borrow money from a cheder classmate, a young usurer who demanded interest. For every four groschen, I paid a groschen a week.

Now imagine the indescribable joy I felt when I once earned a whole ruble—one hundred kopecks!

I no longer remember exactly how I came to earn that ruble, but I think it happened something like this: A man had ordered a pair of kidskin boots from a shoemaker, but upon delivery they proved to be either too tight or too loose. The man refused to accept them, and the shoemaker brought him to my father's rabbinical court. Father sent me to another shoemaker to ask him to appraise the value of the boots or perhaps even to buy them, since he also dealt in ready-made footwear. It so happened that the second shoemaker had a customer who wanted the boots and was prepared to pay a good price for them. I do not recall all the details, but I remember that I carried a pair of brand-new boots around, and that one of the litigants rewarded me with a ruble.

I knew that if I stayed home my parents would ruin that ruble. They would buy me something to wear, something I would have got anyway, or they would borrow the ruble from me and—though they'd never deny the debt—I would never see it again. I therefore took the ruble and decided to indulge myself for once in the pleasures of this world, to enjoy all those good things for which my heart yearned.

I quickly passed through Krochmalna Street. Here everyone knew me too well. Here I could not afford to act the profligate. But on Gnoyna

Street I was unknown. I signaled to the driver of a droshky, and he stopped.

"What do you want?"

"To ride."

"Ride where?"

"To the other streets."

"What other streets?"

"To Nalewki Street."

"That costs forty groschen. Have you got the money to pay?"

I showed him the ruble.

"But you'll have to pay me in advance."

I gave the driver the ruble. He tried bending it to see if it was counterfeit. Then he gave me my change—four forty-groschen pieces. I got into the droshky. The driver cracked his whip and I almost fell off the bench. The seat under me bounced on its springs. Passers-by stared at the little boy riding alone in a droshky, without any bundles. The droshky made its way among trolley cars, other droshkies, wagons, delivery vans. I felt that I had suddenly assumed the importance of an adult. God in heaven, if I could only ride like this for a thousand years, by day and by night, without stop, to the ends of the earth . . .

But the driver turned out to be a dishonest man. When we had gone only halfway, he stopped and said, "Enough. Get down!"

"But this is not Nalewki Street!" I argued.

"Do you want a taste of my whip?" he answered.

Oh, if only I were Samson the Strong, I'd know to take care of such a bandit, such a clod! I would pulverize him, chop him into little pieces! But I am only a small weak boy, and he is cracking his whip.

I got down, shamed and dejected. But how long can you mourn when you have four forty-groschen pieces in your pocket? I saw a candy store and went in to select my merchandise. I bought some of every kind. And as I bought, I tasted. The other customers looked at me with disdain; they probably suspected I had stolen the money. One girl exclaimed, "Just look at that little Hasid!"

"Hey, you ninny, may an evil spirit possess your father's son!" one boy called out to me.

I left, laden with candy. Then I reached Krasinski Park, I was nearly run over while crossing the street. I entered the park and ate some of the delicacies. A boy passed by and I gave him a chocolate bar. Instead of saying thank you, he grabbed it and ran off. I walked over to the lake and fed the swans—with chocolate. Women pointed their fingers at me, laughed, made comments in Polish. Daintily dressed girls, with hoops and balls, came over to me and I chivalrously and prodigally distributed my candy among them. At that moment I felt like a rich nobleman distributing largess.

After a while I had no more candies, but I still had some money. I decided to take another droshky. When I sat in the second droshky and the driver asked where I wanted to go, I really wanted to say, "Krochmalna Street." But someone inside of me, an invisible glutton, answered instead, "To Marshalkovsky Boulevard."

"What number?"

I invented a number.

This coachman was honest. He took me to the address and did not ask for the money in advance. On the way another droshky rode alongside ours; inside sat a lady with an enormous bosom and a big hat decorated with an ostrich feather. My driver chatted with the other driver. Both spoke Yiddish, which the lady did not like at all. Even less did she like the little passenger with the black velvet hat and the red earlocks. She threw angry looks at me. From time to time both droshkies stopped to let a trolley car or a heavily laden wagon pass by. A policeman standing near the trolley tracks stared at me, at the lady, seemed for a minute about to come over and arrest me— and then began to laugh. I was terribly afraid. I was afraid of God, of my mother and father, and I was also afraid a hole had suddenly appeared in my pocket and my money had fallen through. And what if the driver was a robber carrying me off to some dark cave? Perhaps he was a magician. And perhaps all this was only a dream. But no, the driver was not a robber, and he did not carry me off to the twelve thieves in the desert. He took me exactly to the address I had given him, a big house with a gateway, and I paid him the forty groschen.

"Who are you going to see?" he asked me.

"A doctor," I answered without hesitation.

"What's the matter with you?"

"I cough."

"You're an orphan, eh?"

"Yes, an orphan."

"From out of town?"

"Yes."

"From where?"

I gave him the name of some town.

"Do you wear the fringed garment?"

This last question I did not answer. What concern of his were my ritual fringes? I wanted him to drive off, but he remained there with his droshky, and I could delay no longer—I had to enter the gateway. But behind the gate there lurked a gigantic dog. He looked at me with a pair of knowing eyes that seemed to say: "You may fool the coachman, but not me. I know you have no business here." And he opened a mouth full of sharp, pointed teeth.

Suddenly the janitor appeared. "And what do you want?"

I tried to stammer something, but he shouted at me, "Get away from here!"

And he began to chase me with a broom. I started to run, and the dog let out a savage howl. The droshky driver was probably a witness to my shame—but against a broom, a janitor, and a dog, a small boy cannot be a hero.

Things were not going well for me, but I still had some money left. And with money one can find pleasures anywhere. I saw a fruit store and went in. I ordered the first fruit I saw, and when it came to paying, my money was just barely enough. I parted with my last groschen.

I no longer remember what kind of fruit it was. It must have been a pomegranate or something equally exotic. I could not peel it, and when I ate it, it had a poisonous taste. Nevertheless I devoured it all. But then I was overcome by a horrible thirst. My throat was parched and burning. I had only one desire—to drink. Oh, if only I had money now! I could have emptied a gallon of soda water! But I had nothing and, furthermore, I was far from home.

I started to walk home. I walked and suddenly I felt a nail in my boot. It pierced my flesh at every step. How did the nail happen to be there just then? I stepped into a gateway. Here there were no dogs and no janitors.

I took off the boot. Inside, right through the inner sole, a pointy nail was sticking up. I stuffed some paper into the boot and set out again. Oh, how bitter it is to walk when an iron nail pricks you at every step! And how bitter it must be to lie on a bed of nails in Gehenna! This day I had committed many sins. I had said no blessing before eating the candy, I had not given even one groschen of all my money to the poor. I had only gorged myself.

The walk home took about two hours. All manner of frightening thoughts beset me as I walked. Perhaps something terrible had happened at home. Perhaps I had not been lying when I told the coachman I was an orphan, but at the very moment when I said it I was in truth orphaned. Perhaps I had no father, no mother, no home. Perhaps my face had changed, like that of the man in the storybook, and when I got home Father and Mother would not recognize me. Anything was possible!

A boy saw me and stopped me. "Where are you coming from? Your mother has been looking for you everywhere!"

"I was in Praga—I rode on a trolley," I said, telling lies now just for the sake of lying. Because once you have eaten without a blessing and committed other sins, then you can do anything—it no longer matters.

"Who did you visit in Praga?"

"My aunt."

"Since when do you have an aunt in Praga?"

"She just came to Warsaw."

"Go on, you're fibbing. Your mother is looking for you. Swear you were in Praga."

I swore falsely too. Then I went home, tired, sweating—a lost soul. I pounced upon the water faucet and began to drink, to drink. Thus must Esau have devoured the mess of pottage for which he sold his birthright.

Mother wrung her hands. "Just look at that child!"

Anne Frank

Anne Frank: The Diary of a Young Girl

The security, comfort, and culture of their life had to be abandoned when the Frank family went into hiding from the Nazis. The lively and detailed entries made by Anne Frank in her diary, which she addressed as "Dear Kitty," form the record of the daily lives of these people and those who joined them later in hiding. Beyond this, however, is a remarkable honesty to the writing and a perceptiveness that bring Anne alive with particular force. The following selections are broken in time sequence to allow for a sampling of different events. Reading the entire diary is the only way to appreciate this crucial period and the support given the Franks by the Dutch people who maintained their lifeline with the outside. [From Anne Frank, *Anne Frank: The Diary of a Young Girl* (Doubleday, 1952).]

Thursday, 9 July, 1942

Dear Kitty,

So we walked in the pouring rain, Daddy, Mummy, and I, each with a school satchel and shopping bag filled to the brim with all kinds of things thrown together anyhow.

We got sympathetic looks from people on their way to work. You could see by their faces how sorry they were they couldn't offer us a lift; the gaudy yellow star spoke for itself.

Only when we were on the road did Mummy and Daddy begin to tell me bits and pieces about the plan. For months as many of our goods and chattels and necessities of life as possible had been sent away and they were sufficiently ready for us to have gone into hiding of our own accord on July 16. The plan had had to be speeded up ten days because of the call-up, so our quarters would not be so well organized, but we had to make the best of it. The hiding place itself would be in the building where Daddy has his office. It will be hard for outsiders to understand, but I shall explain that later on. Daddy didn't have many people working for him: Mr. Kraler, Koophuis, Miep, and Elli Vossen, a twenty-three-year-old typist who all knew of our arrival. Mr. Vossen, Elli's father, and two boys worked in the warehouse; they had not been told.

I will describe the building: there is a large warehouse on the ground floor which is used as a store. The front door to the house is next to the warehouse door, and inside the front door is a second doorway which leads to a staircase (A). There is another door at the top of the stairs, with a frosted glass window in it, which has "Office" written in black letters across it. That is the large main office, very big, very light, and very full. Elli, Miep, and Mr. Koophuis work there in the daytime. A small dark room containing the safe, a wardrobe, and a large cupboard leads to a small somewhat dark second office. Mr. Kraler and Mr. Van Daan used to sit here, now it is only Mr. Kraler. One can reach Kraler's office from the passage, but only via a glass door which can be opened from the inside, but not easily from the outside.

From Kraler's office a long passage goes past the coal store, up four steps and leads to the showroom of the whole building: the private office. Dark, dignified furniture, linoleum and carpets on the floor, radio, smart lamp, everything first-class. Next door there is a roomy kitchen with a hot-water faucet and a gas stove. Next door the W.C. That is the first floor.

A wooden staircase leads from the downstairs passage to the next floor (B). There is a small landing at the top. There is a door at each end of the landing, the left one leading to a storeroom at the front of the house and to the attics. One of those really steep Dutch staircases runs from the side to the other door opening on to the street (C).

The right-hand door leads to our "Secret Annexe." No one would ever guess that there would be so many rooms hidden behind that plain gray door. There's a little step in front of the door and then you are inside.

There is a steep staircase immediately opposite the entrance (E). On the left a tiny passage brings you into a room which was to become the Frank family's bed-sitting-room, next door a smaller room, study and bedroom for the two young ladies of the family. On the right a little room without windows containing the washbasin and a small W.C. compartment, with another door leading to Margot's and my room. If you go up the next flight of stairs and open the door, you are simply amazed that there could be such a big light room in such an old house by the canal. There is a gas stove in this room (thanks to the fact that it was used as a laboratory) and a sink. This is now the kitchen for the Van Daan couple, besides being general living room, dining room, and scullery.

A tiny little corridor room will become Peter Van Daan's apartment. Then, just as on the lower landing, there is a large attic. So there you are, I've introduced you to the whole of our beautiful "Secret Annexe."

Yours, Anne

Friday, 25 September, 1942

Dear Kitty,

Yesterday evening I went upstairs and "visited" the Van Daans. I do so occasionally to have a chat. Sometimes it can be quite fun. Then we have some moth biscuits (the biscuit tin is kept in the wardrobe which is full of moth balls) and drink lemonade. We talked about Peter. I told them how Peter often strokes my cheek and that I wished he wouldn't as I don't like being pawed by boys.

In a typical way parents have, they asked if I couldn't get fond of Peter, because he certainly liked me very much. I thought "Oh dear!" and said: "Oh, no!" Imagine it!

I did say that I thought Peter rather awkward, but that it was probably shyness, as many boys who haven't had much to do with girls are like that.

I must say that the Refuge Committee of the "Secret Annexe" (male section) is very ingenious. I'll tell you what they've done now to get news of us through to Mr. Van Dijk, Travies' chief representative and a friend who has surreptitiously hidden some of our things for us! They typed a letter to a chemist in South Zeeland, who does business with our firm, in such a way that he has to send the enclosed reply back in an addressed envelope. Daddy addressed the envelope to the office. When this envelope arrives from Zeeland, the enclosed letter is taken out, and is replaced by a message in Daddy's handwriting as a sign of life. Like this, Van Dijk won't become suspicious when he reads the note. They specially chose Zeeland because it is so close to Belgium and the letter could have easily been smuggled over the border, in addition no one is allowed into Zeeland without a special permit; so if they thought we were there, he couldn't try and look us up.

Yours, Anne

Sunday, 27 September, 1942

Dear Kitty,

Just had a big bust-up with Mummy for the umpteenth time; we simply don't get on together these days and Margot and I don't hit it off any too well either. As a rule we don't go in for such outbursts as this in our family. Still, it's by no means always pleasant for me. Margot's and Mummy's natures are completely strange to me. I can understand my friends better than my own mother—too bad!

We often discuss postwar problems, for example, how one ought to address servants.

Mrs. Van Daan had another tantrum. She is terribly moody. She keeps hiding more of her private belongings. Mummy ought to answer each Van Daan "disappearance" with a Frank "disappearance." How some people do adore bringing up other people's children in addition to their own. The Van Daans are that kind. Margot doesn't need it, she is such a goody-goody, perfection itself, but I seem to have enough mischief in me for the two of us put together. You should hear us at mealtimes, with reprimands and cheeky answers flying to and fro. Mummy and Daddy always defend me stoutly. I'd have to give up if it weren't for them. Although they do tell me that I mustn't talk so much, that I must be more retiring and not poke my nose into everything, still I seem doomed to failure. If Daddy wasn't so patient, I'd be afraid I was going to turn out to be a terrific disappointment to my parents and they are pretty lenient with me.

If I take a small helping of some vegetable I detest and make up with potatoes, the Van Daans, and Mevrouw in particular, can't get over it, that any child should be so spoiled.

"Come along, Anne, have a few more vegetables," she says straight away.

"No, thank you, Mrs. Van Daan," I answer, "I have plenty of potatoes."

"Vegetables are good for you, your mother says so too. Have a few more," she says, pressing them on me until Daddy comes to my rescue.

Then we have from Mrs. Van Daan—"You ought to have been in our home, we were properly brought up. It's absurd that Anne's so frightfully spoiled. I wouldn't put up with it if Anne were my daughter."

These are always her first and last words "if Anne were my daughter." Thank heavens I'm not!

But to come back to this "upbringing" business. There was a deadly silence after Mrs. Van Daan had finished speaking yesterday. Then Daddy said, "I think Anne is extremely well brought up; she has learned one thing anyway, and that is to make no reply to your long sermons. As to the vegetables, look at your own plate." Mrs. Van Daan was beaten, well and truly beaten. She had taken a minute helping of vegetables herself. But *she* is not spoiled! Oh, no, too many vegetables in the evening make her constipated. Why on earth doesn't she keep her mouth shut about me, then she wouldn't need to make such feeble excuses. It's gorgeous the way Mrs. Van Daan blushes. I don't, and that is just what she hates.

Yours, Anne

Monday, 28 September, 1942
Dear Kitty,

I had to stop yesterday, long before I'd finished. I just must tell you about another quarrel, but before I start on that, something else.

Why do grownups quarrel so easily, so much, and over the most idiotic things? Up till now I thought that only children squabbled and that that wore off as you grew up. Of course, there is sometimes a real reason for a quarrel, but this is just plain bickering. I suppose I should get used to it. But I can't nor do I think I shall, as long as I am the subject of nearly every discussion (they use the word "discussion" instead of quarrel). Nothing, I repeat, nothing about me is right; my general appearance, my character, my manners are discussed from A to Z. I'm expected (by order) to simply swallow all the harsh words and shouts in silence and I am not used to this. In fact, I can't! I'm not going to take all these insults lying down. I'll show them that Anne Frank wasn't born yesterday. Then they'll be surprised and perhaps they'll keep their mouths shut when I let them see that I am going to start educating them. Shall I take up that attitude? Plain barbarism!

I'm simply amazed again and again over their awful manners and especially . . . stupidity (Mrs. Van Daan's), but as soon as I get used to this—and it won't be long—then I'll give them some of their own back, and no half measures. Then they'll change their tune!

Am I really so bad-mannered, conceited, headstrong, pushing, stupid, lazy, etc., etc., as they all say? Oh, of course not. I have my faults, just like everyone else, I know that, but they thoroughly exaggerate everything.

Kitty, if only you knew how I sometimes boil under so many gibes and jeers. And I don't know how long I shall be able to stifle my rage. I shall just blow up one day.

Still, no more of this, I've bored you long enough with all these quarrels. But I simply must tell you of one highly interesting discussion at table. Somehow or other, we got on to the subject of Pim's (Daddy's nickname) extreme modesty. Even the most stupid people have to admit this about Daddy. Suddenly Mrs. Van Daan says, "I too, have an unassuming nature, more so than my husband."

Did you ever! This sentence in itself shows quite clearly how thoroughly forward and pushing she is! Mr. Van Daan thought he ought to give an explanation regarding the reference to himself. "I don't wish to be modest—in my experience it does not pay." Then to me: "Take my advice, Anne, don't be too unassuming, it doesn't get you anywhere."

Mummy agreed with this too. But Mrs. Van Daan had to add, as always, her ideas on the subject. Her next remark was addressed to Mummy and Daddy. "You have a strange outlook on life. Fancy saying such a thing to Anne; it was very different when I was young. And I feel sure that it still is, except in your modern home." This was a direct hit at the way Mummy brings up her daughters.

Mrs. Van Daan was scarlet by this time. Mummy calm and cool as a cucumber. People who blush get so hot and excited, it is quite a handicap in such a situation. Mummy, still entirely unruffled, but anxious to close the conversation as soon as possible, thought for a second and then said: "I find, too, Mrs. Van Daan, that one gets on better in life if one is not overmodest. My husband, now, and Margot, and Peter are exceptionally modest, whereas your husband, Anne, you, and I, though not exactly the opposite, don't allow ourselves to be completely pushed to one side." Mrs. Van Daan: "But, Mrs. Frank, I don't understand you; I'm so very modest and retiring, how can you think of calling me anything else?" Mummy: "I did not say you were exactly forward, but no one could say you had a retiring disposition." Mrs. Van Daan: "Let us get this matter cleared up, once and for all. I'd like to know in what way I am pushing? I know one thing, if I didn't look after myself, I'd soon be starving."

This absurb remark in self-defense just made Mummy rock with laughter. That irritated Mrs. Van Daan, who added a string of German-Dutch, Dutch-German expressions, until she became completely tongue-tied; then she rose from her chair and was about to leave the room.

Suddenly her eye fell on me. You should have seen her. Unfortunately, at the very moment that she turned round, I was shaking my head sorrowfully—not on purpose, but quite involuntarily, for I had been following the whole conversation so closely.

Mrs. Van Daan turned round and began to reel off a lot of harsh German, common, and ill-mannered, just like a coarse, red-faced fishwife—it was a marvelous sight. If I could draw, I'd have liked to catch her like this; it was a scream, such a stupid, foolish little person!

Anyhow, I've learned one thing now. You only really get to know people when you've had a jolly good row with them. Then and then only can you judge their true characters!

Yours, Anne

Tuesday, 20 October, 1942

Dear Kitty,

My hand still shakes, although it's two hours since we had the shock. I should explain that there are five fire extinguishers in the house. We knew that someone was coming to fill them, but no one had warned us when the carpenter, or whatever you call him, was coming.

The result was that we weren't making any attempt to keep quiet, until I heard hammering outside on the landing opposite our cupboard door. I thought of the carpenter at once and warned Elli, who was having a meal with us, that she shouldn't go downstairs. Daddy and I posted ourselves at the door so as to hear when the man left. After he'd been working for a quarter of an hour, he laid his hammer and tools down on top of our cupboard (as we thought) and knocked at our door. We turned absolutely white. Perhaps he had heard something after all and wanted to investigate our secret den. It seemed like it. The knocking, pulling, pushing, and wrenching went on. I nearly fainted at the thought that this utter stranger might discover our beautiful secret hiding place. And just as I thought my last hour was at hand, I heard Mr. Koophuis say, "Open the door, it's only me." We opened it immediately. The hook that holds the cupboard, which can be undone by people who know the secret, had got jammed. That was why no one had been able to warn us about the carpenter. The man had now gone downstairs and Koophuis wanted to fetch Elli, but couldn't open the cupboard again. It was a great relief to me, I can tell you. In my imagination the man who I thought was trying to get in had been growing and growing in size until in the end he appeared to be a giant and the greatest fascist that ever walked the earth.

Well! Well! Luckily everything was okay this time. Meanwhile we had great fun on Monday. Miep and Henk spent the night here. Margot and I went in Mummy and Daddy's room for the night, so that the Van Santens could have our room. The meal tasted divine. There was one small interruption. Daddy's lamp blew a fuse, and all of a sudden we were sitting in darkness. What was to be done? There was some fuse wire in the house, but the fuse box is right at the very back of the dark storeroom— not such a nice job after dark. Still the men ventured forth and after ten minutes we were able to put the candles away again.

I got up early this morning. Henk had to leave at half past eight. After a cozy breakfast Miep went downstairs. It was pouring and she was glad not to have to cycle to the office. Next week Elli is coming to stay for a night.

Yours, Anne

F. N. Monjo

Letters to Horseface, Being the Story of Wolfgang Amadeus Mozart's Journey to Italy, 1769–1770, When He Was a Boy of Fourteen

"Maybe someday," the boy Mozart writes to his sister, "my music will be enough." Had he been born two hundred years later, Mozart would have been called a gifted child; in his own time he was known as the *Wunderkind*—the wonder child—and, driven by his ambitious father, performed like a prodigious lap dog for the ladies and gentlemen of various European courts. In this epistolary novel, Monjo creates a wholly convincing picture of Mozart at fourteen. In sprightly, detail-filled letters to his sister (Nannerl-the-Horseface), the young Mozart reveals himself to be both a budding musical genius and a genuine child, full of irrepressible energy. [From F. N. Monjo, *Letters to Horseface* (Viking, 1975).]

Mantua

January 18, 1770

Dear Nannerl-the-Horseface,

It's been more than a month since I wrote a whole letter to you, of your very own. But I have been so busy, and so much has happened, that you must forgive me.

Did Papa tell you anything about Innsbruck? The mountains were so high, there, they seemed to hang right over the buildings in the town. And there was a triumphal arch, built five years ago, when our most gracious Empress Maria Theresa's son, Archduke Leopold, married the Infanta Maria Luisa of Spain. (Papa says Archduke Leopold is now the grand duke of Tuscany. He lives in Florence, and we may see him when we visit there.)

From Innsbruck, we traveled through the Brenner Pass, between high, high ranges of the Alps, and then passed through the towns of Steinach, and Brizen, and Bozen, to Trent. Trent is an old walled town that fills the whole valley.

We were in Roveredo on December 24. And on Christmas Day (Mama's birthday!) I played the organ in the church, there. So many people came to hear me that a couple of strong fellows had to push some of the people aside so that I could get into the choir. Two days after that we were in the old Italian town of Verona, staying at an inn called The Sign of the Two Towers. Do you know what that is, in Italian, Horseface? It's *Due Torre.*

Verona is a lovely town, on a rushing river called the Adige. Papa says this is where Romeo and Juliet lived.

Everyone in the streets of Verona was wearing masks when we were there, because Carnival had begun. I wish you could have seen the floats that were pulled through the streets by horses decorated with ribbons and flowers. And the costumes! Dozens of Pulcinellos in white smocks and masks and floppy gray hats. Gay Harlequins in red and yellow suits, with bells on their caps. And girls dressed as soldiers with epaulettes, or wearing pretty Columbina costumes. All of them dancing in the streets, or lining the balconies and crowding the windows, throwing flowers and streamers and bonbons and confetti and gilded chocolates and silver and copper coins into the crowd. The Italians go *mad* at Carnival time!

They have horse races by day, and plays and balls and fireworks at night. Quite enough to make Nannerl-the-flirt as happy as can be.

I can't tell you how many melodies I put down safely into my memory bag, in Verona. One for a Harlequin that I think should be bright and silvery when played on the flute. Several for fireworks. And something just right for a lovely young girl, just beginning to fall in love. . . .

The best thing about Carnival time is this: you don't have to be polite. You can talk to anyone you want. You don't have to be introduced to anyone, or call them by name, because everybody's incognito, wearing a mask, anyhow! *"Servitore umilissimo, Signora Maschera,"* you say. Know what *that* means, Horseface? It means "your most humble servant, Masked Lady." Doesn't that sound like fun? Just think what *you* might do in a crowd of maskers, Nannerl. Someday, I've promised myself, I'm going to write something in an opera, for people at a masked ball. I'm as *sure* of it as anything!

Good old business-like Papa Leopold has taken care to have letters of introduction with him, addressed to all the important people in Italy. So we find friends ready to help us wherever we go. That's why Signor Locatelli took us out in his carriage to see the huge old Roman amphitheater, while we were in Verona.

And we gave another organ concert in the church, and everybody came crowding to see "the little organist." And guess what? While I was there, in Verona, Papa said I had to sit for my portrait. I wore my diamond ring on the little finger of my right hand. And the artist painted me in my wig and my new red velvet suit with the gold braid trim. I was shown just turning away from the harpsichord, as if I were the *dearest* little angel. As if butter wouldn't melt in my mouth. You would laugh, Nannerl, to see the ridiculously innocent expression your brother Wolferl has on his innocent little mug! Papa *adores* the picture, but I know you and Mama will laugh when you see it—because that's what *I* wanted to do!

And then from Verona we came straight down to Mantua, where we are now, staying at the Sign of the Croce Verde—the Green Cross to you, Horseface.

Don't believe anything they tell you about "sunny Italy," Nannerl. It's *cold* here in winter. Cold! Cold! Cold! If Papa hadn't bought us two foot-bags lined with fur, our feet would have frozen in the carriage—in spite of the hay we put down on the floor of the coach. My face is chapped a reddish-brown from the cold—plus the fact that it gets scorched from the heat of the inn fire, whenever I come in from outside. (I'm only joking. Don't let Mama take me seriously and start worrying.)

Two days ago, on January 16, I gave a public concert here in Mantua, at the Accademia Filarmonica (the Philharmonic Academy to you, Horseface). The Italians think I'm a lot younger than thirteen—but Papa doesn't mind that a bit! I'm so small I must look as if I'm only nine or ten, I suppose. But you and Mama know I'll be *fourteen* in a few days—on January 27. Sh-h-h-h! Let's keep it a secret.

Anyway, the concert was a big success, and Papa was happy because he was able to take

in some gold pieces at the door, to offset the huge amount we've been spending. ("Money doesn't grow on trees, Wolferl," says Papa Leopold.)

You and Mama would laugh if you could hear what they *call* me. In Germany and Austria, when I was little, they used to call me the *wunderkind*—the "wonder-child." You remember? Well, the Italians can't say Wolfgang. Or Johann. Or Chrysostom. Or wunderkind, either, for that matter. So they call me Amadeo. That's right. They call me the *espertissimo giovanetto, Signor Amadeo.* (For your benefit, my dear Nannerl, that means: "that most accomplished youth, Signor Amadeus." That's *me,* your brother Wolferl, they're referring to!)

And here's what that "most accomplished youth" did at his concert, Horseface:

1. Conducted a symphony of his own composition.
2. Improvised a harpsichord sonata, with variations—composed right then and there.
3. Composed and sang an aria to words given to him on the spot—never before seen by him.
4. Composed a fugue and variations on a theme given to him (and seen by him for the first time) in the concert hall.
5. Performed on the violin, in a string trio, in which he had to improvise his part.

So you see, Papa is still up to his old tricks! It's not enough for me to be simply a good musician. Or a good composer. I must still do tricks and improvisations to surprise the donkey's ears, in the audience.

Of course, it's not as bad as it was eight years ago—when I was about six and you were eleven—when Papa Leopold and Mama showed us off, the first time, in Vienna, to Emperor Francis and Empress Maria Theresa. Will you ever forget it, Nannerl? Such nonsense! They discovered I had perfect pitch, and some fool lady would tinkle her spoon against her champagne glass and say "What note is this, my dear little Wolfgang? My adorable little wunderkind?" And I would have to answer, "That is F-sharp, your ladyship." And then a fat gentleman would ring the little chime on his pocket watch, and ask me to tell him what note *that* was. And I would have to reply, "That is E-flat, Prince Unterschlossberg. E-flat, without a doubt!"

And the ladies would kiss, and kiss, and *kiss* me, and the gentlemen would say "Astounding! *Wunderbar!* Unheard of! *Unglaublich!* Unbelievable!"

Even the emperor wasn't content to let me play my sonatas on the harpsichord, and be done with it. For, when I was finished, he would make us cover the keyboard with a cloth—do you remember? And Papa would look so pleased when I was able to play my sonata, without any mistakes, even with the keyboard hidden! And then Empress Maria Theresa would take me up onto her fat lap and kiss me some more, and tell Papa I was a wonder. "A wunderkind, Herr Mozart! A wunderkind such as the world has never seen before!"

It was all very tiresome. Most of them didn't want to hear me play. Not really. They preferred to see me do my tricks, like a little monkey.

Now Papa says I'm much too old for any more tricks of that kind. "Your're much too old to play the wunderkind in Italy, Wolferl," he says. But he *still* lets them give me melodies to improvise, and things like that, at my concerts.

Maybe someday, Nannerl, my music will be enough. Do you suppose that day will ever come?

While here, in Mantua, we've been to the opera. The prima donna was old, and not very good-looking, but she didn't have a bad voice. The opera was by Papa's friend, Herr Hasse. And the tenor had a beautiful voice. I forget his name.

Sometime I must tell you how noisy and talkative the Italians are when they go to the opera. They're much worse than the audience in Vienna!

Papa says the post is ready to leave, so I'll have to stop. Kiss Mama 10,000 times for me, and save a few for yourself.

Your brother,
Wolfgang, in Austria, but
Amadeo in Italy!

E. Nesbit

Long Ago When I Was Young

No loss of feeling or emotion comes from the fact that E. Nesbit is here recalling the events of her childhood; indeed the vitality and freshness of her fictional writing for children flow directly from the deep imprint of such experiences. [From E. Nesbit, *Long Ago When I Was Young* (F. Watts, 1966).]

Long Division

I spent a year in the select boarding establishment for young ladies and gentlemen at Stamford, and I venture to think that I should have preferred a penal settlement. Miss Fairfield, whose school it was, was tall and pale and dark, and I thought her as good and beautiful as an angel. I don't know now whether she was really beautiful, but I know she was good. And her mother—dear soul—had a sympathy with small folk in disgrace, which has written her name in gold letters on my heart.

But there was another person in the house, whose name I will not put down. She came continually between me and my adored Miss Fairfield. She had a sort of influence over me which made it impossible for me ever to do anything well while she was near me. Miss Fairfield's health compelled her to leave much to Miss————, and I was, in consequence, as gloomy a cynic as any child of my age in Lincolnshire. My chief troubles were three—my hair, my hands, and my arithmetic.

My hair was never tidy—I don't know why. Perhaps it runs in the family—for my little daughter's head is just as rough as mine used to be. This got me into continual disgrace. I am sure I tried hard enough to keep it tidy— I brushed it for fruitless hours till my little head was so sore that it hurt me to put my hat on. But it never would look smooth and shiny, like Katie Martin's, nor would it curl prettily like the red locks of Cissy Thomas. It was always a rough, impossible brown mop. I got into a terrible scrape for trying to soften it by an invention of my own. As we all know, Burleigh House is by Stamford Town, and in Burleigh House we children took our daily constitutional. We played under the big oaks there, and were bored to extinction, not because we disliked the park, but because we went there every day at the same hour.

Now Harry Martin (he wore striped stockings and was always losing his handkerchief) suffered from his hair almost as much as I did; so when I unfolded my plan to him one day in the park, he joyfully agreed to help me.

We each gathered a pocketful of acorns, and when we went to wash our hands before dinner, we cut up some of the acorns into little bits, and put them into the doll's bath with some cold water and a little scent that Cissy Thomas gave us, out of a bottle she had bought for twopence at the fair at home.

'This,' I said, 'will be acorn oil—scented acorn oil.'

'Will it?' said Harry doubtfully.

'Yes,' I replied, adding confidently, 'and there is nothing better for the hair.'

But we never had a chance of even seeing whether acorns and water would turn to oil— a miracle which I entirely believed in. The dinner bell rang, and I only had time hastily to conceal the doll's bath at the back of the cupboard where Miss——kept her dresses. That was Saturday.

Next day we found that Miss——'s best dress (the blue silk with the Bismarck brown gimp) had slipped from its peg and fallen in to the doll's bath. The dress was ruined, and when Harry Martin and I owned up, as in honour bound—Miss Fairfield was away in London—we were deprived of dinner, and had a long Psalm to learn. I don't know whether punishment affects the hair, but I thought, next morning at prayers, that Harry's tow-crop looked more like hay than ever.

My hands were more compromising to me than anyone would have believed who had ever seen their size, for, in the winter especially, they were never clean. I can see now the little willow-patterned basin of cold hard water, and smell the unpleasant little square of mottled soap with which I was expected to wash them. I don't know how the others managed, but for me the result was always the same—failure; and when I presented myself at breakfast, trying to hide my red and grubby little paws in my pinafore, Miss——used to say:

'Show your hands, Daisy—yes, as I thought. Not fit to sit down with young ladies and gentlemen. Breakfast in the schoolroom for Miss Daisy.'

Then little Miss Daisy would shiveringly betake herself to the cold, bare schoolroom, where the fire had but just been kindled.

I used to sit cowering over the damp sticks with my white mug—mauve spotted it was I remember, and had a brown crack near the handle—on a chair beside me. Sometimes I used to pull a twig from the fire; harpoon my bread-and-butter with it, and hold it to the fire: the warm, pale, greasy result I called toast.

All this happened when Miss Fairfield was laid up with bronchitis. It was at that time, too, that my battle with compound long division began. Now I was not, I think, a very dull child, and always had an indignant sense that I could do sums well enough, if any one would tell me what they meant. But no one did, and day after day the long division sums, hopelessly wrong, disfigured my slate, and were washed off with my tears. Day after day I was sent to bed, my dinner was knocked off, or my breakfast, or my tea. I should literally have starved, I do believe, but for dear Miss Fairfield. She kept my little body going with illicit cakes and plums and the like, and fed my starving little heart with surreptitious kisses and kind words. She would lie in wait for me as I passed down the hall, and in a whisper call me into the store closet. It had a mingled and delicious smell of pickles and tea and oranges and jam, and the one taper Miss Fairfield carried only lighted dimly the delightful mystery of its well-filled shelves. Miss Fairfield used to give me a great lump of cake or a broad slice of bread and jam, and lock me into the dark cupboard until it was eaten. I never taste black-currant jam now without a strong memory of the dark hole of happiness, where I used to wait—my sticky fingers held well away from my pinafore—till Miss Fairfield's heavy step and jingling keys came to release me. Then she would sponge my hands and face and send me away clean, replete, and with a better heart for the eternal conflict with long division.

I fancy that when Miss Fairfield came downstairs again she changed the field of my arithmetical studies; for during the spring I seem to remember a blessed respite from my troubles. It is true that Miss———was away, staying with friends.

I was very popular at school that term I remember, for I had learned to make dolls' bedsteads out of match-boxes during the holidays, and my eldest sister's Christmas present provided me with magnificent hangings for the same. Imagine a vivid green silk sash, with brilliant butterflies embroidered all over it in coloured silk and gold thread. A long sash, too, from which one could well spare a few inches at a time for upholstery. I acquired many marbles, and much gingerbread and totally eclipsed Cissy Thomas who had enjoyed the fleeting sunshine of popular favour on the insecure basis of paper dolls. Over my memory of this term no long division cast its hateful shade, and the scolding my dear mother gave me when she saw my sash's fair proportions docked to a waistband and a hard knot, with two brief and irregular ends, was so gentle that I endured it with fortitude, and considered my ten weeks of popularity cheaply bought. I went back to school in high spirits with a new set of sashes and some magnificent pieces of silk and lace from my mother's lavendered wardrobe.

But no one wanted dolls' beds any more; and Cissy Thomas had brought back a herbarium; the others all became botanists, and I, after a faint effort to emulate their successes, fell back on my garden.

The seeds I had set in the spring had had a rest during the Easter holidays, and were already sprouting greenly, but alas, I never saw them flower. Long division set in again. Again, day after day, I sat lonely in the schoolroom—now like a furnace, and ate my dry bread and milk and water in the depths of disgrace, with the faux commencements and those revolting sums staring at me from my tear-blotted slate.

Night after night I cried myself to sleep in my bed—whose coarse home-spun sheets were hotter than blankets—because I could not get the answers right. Even Miss Fairfield, I fancied, began to look coldly on me, and the other children naturally did not care to associate with one so deficient in arithmetic.

One evening as I was sitting as usual sucking the smooth, dark slate pencil, and grieving over my troubles with the heart-broken misery of a child, to whom the present grief looks eternal, I heard a carriage drive up to the door. Our schoolroom was at the back, and I was too much interested in a visitor—especially one who came at that hour and in a carriage—to be able to bear the suspense of that silent schoolroom, so I cautiously opened its door and crept on hands and knees across the passage and looked down through the bannisters. They were opening the door. It was a lady, and Miss Fairfield came out of the dining-room to meet her. It was a lady in a black moiré antique dress and Paisley shawl of the then mode. It was a lady whose face I could not see, because her back was to the red sunset light; but at that moment she spoke and the next I was clinging round the moiré skirts with my head buried in the Paisley shawl. The world, all upside down, had suddenly righted itself. I, who had faced it alone, now looked out at it from the secure shelter of a moiré screen—for my mother had come to see me.

I did not cry myself to sleep that night, because my head lay on her arm. But even then I could not express how wretched I had been. Only when I heard that my mother was going to the South of France with my sisters, I clung about her neck, and with such insistence implored her not to leave me—not to go without me, that I think I must have expressed my trouble without uttering it, for when, after three delicious days of drives and walks, in which I had always a loving hand to hold, my mother left Stamford, she took me—trembling with a joy like a prisoner reprieved—with her.

And I have never seen—or wished to see—Stamford again.

Milton Meltzer

Langston Hughes: A Biography

Langston Hughes' stature as a poet is one that increases as years go by; the depth and sensitivity of this man reach back into his young manhood when he met crisis and opportunity with a fidelity to himself. [From Milton Meltzer, *Langston Hughes: A Biography* (Crowell, 1968).]

Busboy Poet

It was a big day for Langston, the day he came back to New York. He took his newest poem to read to his friends at a gathering in Harlem. There he saw Countee Cullen, whom he had met earlier. Just a year younger than Langston, Cullen had won recognition as a poet in high school and was now at New York University. Very different in temperament and style—Hughes, experimental, Cullen traditional—their names were already being coupled as twin stars among the new poets. There too he met another young poet for the first time—Arna Bontemps, the Louisianan who had been schooled out West and had just come to New York to teach, and who would become his closest friend. They left the party together, and walked home through the cold night. Langston freezing in his ragged pea jacket and wishing he had the money for an overcoat.

Going down to *The Crisis* office the next day, Langston found a double bonus waiting for him. They paid him twenty dollars for an article mailed from abroad, and showed him the November issue with one of his new poems:

We cry aloud among the skyscrapers
As our ancestors
Cried among the palms in Africa,
Because we are alone,
It is night,
And we're afraid.

Then they invited him to an NAACP benefit party at a Lenox Avenue cabaret. There he met James Weldon Johnson, one of the leading Negro writers, and Carl Van Vechten, the white writer.

He needed that overcoat badly, but he used the twenty dollars to go to the theater and to buy a train ticket to Washington. That city would be home now, for his mother—separated again from his stepfather—had moved there. She and his brother Gwyn were staying with cousins who were part of Washington's Negro society. They were the branch of the family directly descended from his grand-uncle, Congressman James M. Langston.

Langston was nervous about living with relatives—especially when he didn't have a dime—even though they were proud to have a poet in the family. But this might be his chance to go back to college. For now he thought it wasn't enough just to knock about the world; more education would also help his writing. There should be a lot to learn from sociology and history and psychology about the world he lived in and its people.

But where would he find the tuition money? He tried to get a scholarship to Howard University but it didn't come through. Then he looked for a job on which he could save up money for tuition. His cultured cousins felt being a page in the Library of Congress would be dignified work for a poet, but nothing came of that, either. Very broke—he owned nothing but his pea jacket, shirt, and pants—he took the first job that opened, in a wet-wash laundry.

He helped unload the wagons and sort the dirty clothes for twelve dollars a week. It was impossible to save even a dollar toward college. Then they moved out of their cousins' home into two small unheated rooms, where, with his mother's low wages as a domestic worker, they barely scraped along.

Washington that winter was hard living. He was always cold and hungry. He hated his job but liked the people he worked with. He wrote "A Song to a Negro Wash-Woman," which *The Crisis* printed in January.

He was getting to know, too, the sour taste of Southern life. He had never gone deep into Dixie, but Washington was near enough to be a primer on Jim Crow, Southern-style. In Mexico and Europe he had lived, worked, and eaten with whites, and no one seemed the worse for it. Here, within sight of democracy's Capitol, ghetto life and laws were the rule.

When he asked why nothing was being done about it, Washington Negro society told him they couldn't be bothered, they had their own social world. He didn't think much of that world. It was filled with pompous gentlemen and puffed-up ladies who prided themselves on "family background." These middle-class Negroes (few were really rich), lived as comfortably as they could and looked down on the folk who worked with their hands. If you hadn't been blessed with a college degree or your skin was too dark, you didn't count. To these snobs "black" was a fighting word.

Langston was fired by the laundry when he caught a bad cold and had to stay out a week. Soon he found a better place, however, in the office of Dr. Carter G. Woodson, founder of the Association for the Study of Negro Life and History, and editor of the *Journal of Negro History* and the *Negro History Bulletin.*

Dr. Woodson was leading the way for scholars to investigate both the African and the American past of the Negro. It sounded like a very promising job and it paid better than the laundry. But it turned out to be even harder work. Dr. Woodson was a remarkable man who made great demands on himself and expected everyone else to work the same way. Langston's job was to open the office early in the morning, keep it clean, wrap and mail books, help answer letters, read proof on the books and magazines, bank the furnace at night when Dr. Woodson was away, and do everything else the office girls couldn't do.

For several months he concentrated on alphabetizing thirty thousand names of free Negro families for one of Dr. Woodson's studies, and then checking and double-checking in manuscript and proofs to guarantee accuracy. It was an endless, blinding task, but he earned Dr. Woodson's compliments when he finished it. It finished Langston, too, however. If this was what they called a "position," he decided he'd rather have just a job. He quit to become a busboy at the fashionable Wardman Park Hotel. The pay wasn't much and the social standing it gave him even less, but it provided his meals and he didn't care about the rest.

What did matter was that one day he learned one of the leading poets, Vachel Lindsay, was staying at the hotel. He knew about Lindsay, that man who was minstrel and missionary both, a people's poet like Sandburg. Lindsay's rhythms too were influenced by the black man's syncopated music. Lindsay had gone up and down the country reciting his poems for a living, handing out a little pamphlet called "Rhymes to be Traded for Bread." Langston worked up his courage to the point of dropping three of his poems at Mr. Lindsay's dinner plate, unable to say more than that he liked Lindsay's poems and that these were his own poems. Then he fled toward the kitchen.

Lindsay gave a reading that night in the hotel theater, but the management allowed no Negroes to attend. When Langston showed up for work the next morning, reporters were waiting for him. They told him Lindsay had read his poems aloud and praised them to the large audience. The press interviewed Langston and took his picture. He was not really an unknown when this happened, for his work had already been published. But now his name spread overnight to the whole country. Newspapers carried the photo of the young poet in his busboy whites, toting a tray of dirty dishes. The Washington *Star* described him as "a quiet, earnest, rather gentle, diffident young man."

At the hotel desk Langston found that Lindsay, too shy himself to try to see Langston, had left for him a beautiful set of Amy Lowell's biography of John Keats. On the flyleaves Lindsay had written a long letter which said in part: "Do not let any lionizers stampede you. Hide and write and study and think. . . ."

The publicity was good for a young poet's career, but bad for his privacy. There was no place to hide. Hotel guests would insist on Langston coming over to their table so that they could see what a real live Negro poet looked like. He couldn't stand that feeling of being in a zoo, and quit. For ten days he lay abed, just resting, tired of working, while his mother complained that *she* was tired of working, too. So he got up finally and found a job at a fish and oyster house downtown. It was a twelve-hour day, standing in a tall white hat behind a counter, making oyster stews and cocktails.

The year went by, an unhappy year, except for Saturday nights at the poet Georgia Douglas Johnson's home, where young black writers met to talk about their work, and the hours he spent hanging around dirty old Seventh Street.

Here was the "low society" his cousins shunned, the people singing the blues, enjoying watermelon and barbecue, shooting pool, swapping tall tales. He would go to the shouting churches and listen to the gospel songs. It made him feel a little less bad about living in Washington.

But feeling bad had its good side, too. It meant he wrote poems. It made the misery more bearable if he could compress his feelings into the shape of a poem. He listened to Seventh Street's black music with its basic beat, the hand-clapping, feet-stamping, drum-beating rhythms which the Africans brought with them three hundred years ago. And in his poems he tried to catch the pulse of the blues with their one long line, repeated, and then a third line to rhyme with the first two. Sometimes the pattern shifted, with the second line changed a bit, or once in a while left out altogether.

On his way to work he would often write a blues poem in his head, singing it over and over again to himself to test the rhythm and to memorize the lines. Here is his "Bound No'th Blues":

Goin' down de road, Lawd,
Goin' down de road.
Down de road, Lawd,
Way, way down de road.
Got to find somebody
To help me carry dis load.

Road's in front o' me,
Nothin' to do but walk.
Road's in front o' me,
Walk . . . and walk . . . and walk.
I'd like to meet a good friend
To come along an' talk.

Hates to be lonely,
Lawd, I hates to be sad.
Says I hates to be lonely,
Hates to be lonely an' sad,
But ever friend you finds seems
Like they try to do you bad.

Road, road, road, O!
Road, road . . . road . . . road, road!
Road, road, road, O!
On de No'thern road.

These Mississippi towns ain't
Fit for a hoppin' toad.

All through the winter and into the spring of 1925 his poems continued to appear in the magazines. In March Alain Locke's Harlem number of *Survey Graphic* carried more poems by Langston than by any other writer. And almost on top of it came the great news that his poem, "The Weary Blues," had won first prize in *Opportunity* magazine's first literary contest. A Countee Cullen poem had won second prize, and the judges awarded third prize to both Langston and Cullen for other poems they had submitted. Langston spent the forty-dollar prize money on a trip to New York to attend the awards dinner. He heard James Weldon Johnson read his prize poem aloud and met Zora Neale Hurston and Eric Walrond, prize winners for the short story and the essay.

In August he won two more prizes, this time awarded by Amy Spingarn through *The Crisis.* He visited New York again to receive second prize for an essay and third prize for a poem at a ceremony in the Renaissance Casino. He met Mrs. Spingarn and her husband Joel, a distinguished Columbia professor and critic.

Those trips to New York opened up new avenues for the young writer. He got to know many other Negro writers and artists—Aaron Douglas, Augusta Savage, Gwendolyn Bennett, Jean Toomer—and the editor of *Opportunity,* Charles S. Johnson. Johnson, he said later, "did more to encourage and develop Negro writers during the 1920s than anyone else in America." In Johnson's eyes, no other writer than Langston "so completely symbolized the new emancipation of the Negro mind."

Late in August came the grand climax. At the *Opportunity* dinner Langston had been asked by Carl Van Vechten to send along enough poems to make up a book. Liking what he saw, Van Vechten took them to Alfred A. Knopf, the publisher. Within a few days Van Vechten wired Langston: LITTLE DAVID PLAY ON YOUR HARP. Knowing it meant his book was accepted, he wired back: I AM PLAYING ON MY SILVER TRUMPET, OH SWEET JESUS.

In Washington he gave a reading of his poems

arranged by Alain Locke. "It went well," he wrote his Knopf editor, partly because of the new aspect introduced—a blues piano interlude. Another reading was being planned for him in New York, and he suggested, "If you do get a real blues piano player to play, it ought to be a wow! But he ought to be a regular Lenox Avenue blues boy. The one we had here was too polished."

His letters to Knopf showed a concern for promoting his first book that would continue and grow more sophisticated. He supplied the names of newspapers, reviewers, bookshops, influential people he hoped the publisher would reach. And he arranged for his book to be on sale at his readings.

One day Langston met another young Washington poet, Waring Cuney, who was studying at Lincoln University in Pennsylvania. His college was a good place for writers, he told Langston. It was cheaper than Howard and left you ample time to write. So in October Langston wrote to Lincoln, saying, "I *must* go to college in order to be of more use to my race and America. I hope to teach in the South, and to widen my literary activities in the field of the short story and the novel."

He could not ask his father for money and, since his mother made little as a children's nurse, he would need work to help pay his way through college. His old high school in Cleveland recommended him to Lincoln, writing that he had been "one of the leading boys in the school," had "unusual ability" and "excellent personal habits."

Lincoln accepted him, giving him a semester's credit for his year at Columbia. He was to start in February. A year's tuition was $110 in those days, and with food, a room, and incidentals, his expenses would add up to about four hundred dollars.

But where would that money come from? Suddenly another opening to college appeared. Early in December Langston was told he might get a scholarship to Harvard if he tried hard enough and if he was "the splendid young man" the terms called for. He asked Mrs. Spingarn what she and her husband thought. "I know," he wrote, "that people are more interesting than books, and life, even a busboy's life, out of

school, more amusing than a professor's in school. But I do want to be able to earn a little time for my own work (which I haven't now) and a little money for travel. So maybe I'd better try Harvard. . . ."

Mrs. Spingarn's answer came at Christmas time. It was the best present anyone had ever given him. Amy Spingarn told him she would pay his way through Lincoln. On December 29 he wrote to thank her:

I HAVE BEEN THINKING A LONG TIME ABOUT WHAT TO SAY TO YOU AND I DON'T KNOW YET WHAT IT SHOULD BE. BUT I BELIEVE THIS: THAT YOU DO NOT WANT ME TO WRITE TO YOU THE SORT OF THINGS I WOULD HAVE TO WRITE TO THE [HARVARD] SCHOLARSHIP PEOPLE. I THINK YOU UNDERSTAND BETTER THAN THEY THE KIND OF PERSON I AM OR SURELY YOU WOULD NOT OFFER, IN THE QUIET WAY YOU DO, THE WONDERFUL THING YOU OFFER ME. AND IF YOU WERE THE SCHOLARSHIP PEOPLE, ALTHOUGH I MIGHT HAVE TO, I WOULD NOT WANT TO ACCEPT IT. THERE WOULD BE TOO MANY CONDITIONS TO FULFILL AND TOO MANY STRANGE IDEALS TO UPHOLD. AND SOMEHOW I DON'T BELIEVE YOU WANT ME TO BE TRUE TO ANYTHING EXCEPT MYSELF. (OR YOU WOULD ASK QUESTIONS AND OUTLINE PLANS.) AND THAT IS ALL I WANT TO DO—BE TRUE TO MY OWN IDEALS. I HATE PRETENDING AND I HATE UNTRUTHS. AND IT IS SO HARD IN OTHER WAYS TO PAY THE VARIOUS LITTLE PRICES PEOPLE ATTACH TO MOST OF THE THINGS THEY OFFER OR GIVE.

AND SO I AM HAPPIER NOW THAN I HAVE BEEN FOR A LONG TIME, MORE BECAUSE YOU OFFER FREELY AND WITH UNDERSTANDING, THAN BECAUSE OF THE REALIZATION OF THE DREAMS WHICH YOU MAKE COME TRUE FOR ME. . . .

Carl Sandburg

Abe Lincoln Grows Up

The life of Lincoln is so well known to all American boys and girls that it is difficult to write a biography to attract them. Carl Sandburg has done so, however;

by the straightforwardness and charm of his style, he makes the young Lincoln live. One sees this poor boy, hungering after books for what they could give him, a dreamer but a fighter, who was called lazy but was ambitious. One sympathizes with that boy and rejoices with him in his successes; yet one understands why those about him called him "peculiarsome." [From Carl Sandburg, *Abe Lincoln Grows Up* (Harcourt, 1928).]

"Peculiarsome" Abe

The farm boys in their evenings at Jones's store in Gentryville talked about how Abe Lincoln was always reading, digging into books, stretching out flat on his stomach in front of the fireplace, studying till midnight and past midnight, picking a piece of charcoal to write on the fire shovel, shaving off what he wrote, and then writing more—till midnight and past midnight. The next thing Abe would be reading books between the plow handles, it seemed to them. And once trying to speak a last word, Dennis Hanks said, "There's suthin' peculiarsome about Abe."

He wanted to learn, to know, to live, to reach out; he wanted to satisfy hungers and thirsts he couldn't tell about, this big boy of the backwoods. And some of what he wanted so much, so deep down, seemed to be in the books. Maybe in books he would find the answers to dark questions pushing around in the pools of his thoughts and the drifts of his mind. He told Dennis and other people, "The things I want to know are in books; my best friend is the man who'll git me a book I ain't read." And sometimes friends answered, "Well, books ain't as plenty as wildcats in these parts o' Indianny."

This was one thing meant by Dennis when he said there was "suthin' peculiarsome" about Abe. It seemed that Abe made the books tell him more than they told other people. All the other farm boys had gone to school and read *The Kentucky Preceptor,* but Abe picked out questions from it, such as "Who has the most right to complain, the Indian or the Negro?" and Abe would talk about it up one way and down the other, while they were in the cornfield pulling fodder for the winter. When Abe got hold of a story-book and read about a boat that came near a magnetic rock, and how the magnets in the rock pulled all the nails out of the boat so it went to pieces and the people in the boat found themselves floundering in water, Abe thought it was funny and told it to other people. After Abe read poetry, especially Bobby Burns's poems, Abe began writing rhymes himself. When Abe sat with a girl, with their bare feet in the creek water, and she spoke of the moon rising, he explained to her that it was the earth moving and not the moon—the moon only seemed to rise.

John Hanks, who worked in the fields barefooted with Abe, grubbing stumps, plowing, mowing, said: "When Abe and I came back to the house from work, he used to go to the cupboard, snatch a piece of corn bread, sit down, take a book, cock his legs up high as his head, and read. Whenever Abe had a chance in the field while at work, or at the house, he would stop and read." He liked to explain to other people what he was getting from books; explaining an idea to someone else made it clearer to him. The habit was growing on him of reading out loud; words came more real if picked from the silent page of the book and pronounced on the tongue; new balances and values of words stood out if spoken aloud. When writing letters for his father or the neighbors, he read the words out loud as they got written. Before writing a letter he asked questions such as: "What do you want to say in the letter? How do you want to say it? Are you sure that's the best way to say it? Or do you think we can fix up a better way to say it?"

As he studied his books his lower lip stuck out; Josiah Crawford noticed it was a habit and joked Abe about the "stuck-out lip." This habit too stayed with him.

He wrote in his Sum Book or arithmetic that Compound Division was "When several numbers of Divers Denominations are given to be divided by 1 common devisor," and worked on the exercise in multiplication. "If 1 foot contains 12 inches I demand how many there are in 126 feet." Thus the schoolboy.

What he got in the schools didn't satisfy him. He went to three different schools in Indiana, besides two in Kentucky—altogether about four months of school. He learned his A B C, how to spell, read, write. And he had been with the other barefoot boys in butternut jeans learning "manners" under the school teacher, Andrew Crawford, who had them open a door, walk in, and say, "Howdy do?" Yet what he tasted of books in school was only a beginning, only made him hungry and thirsty, shook him with a wanting and a wanting of more and more of what was hidden between the covers of books.

He kept on saying, "The things I want to know are in books; my best friend is the man who'll git me a book I ain't read." He said that to Pitcher, the lawyer over at Rockport, nearly twenty miles away, one fall afternoon, when he walked from Pigeon Creek to Rockport and borrowed a book from Pitcher. Then when fodder-pulling time came a few days later, he shucked corn from early daylight till sundown along with his father and Dennis Hanks and John Hanks, but after supper he read the book till midnight, and at noon he hardly knew the taste of his corn bread because he had the book in front of him. It was a hundred little things like these which made Dennis Hanks say there was "suthin' peculiarsome" about Abe.

Besides reading the family Bible and figuring his way all through the old arithmetic they had at home, he got hold of *Aesop's Fables, Pilgrim's Progress, Robinson Crusoe,* and Weems's *The Life of Francis Marion.* The book of fables, written or collected thousands of years ago by the Greek slave, known as Aesop, sank deep in his mind. As he read through the book a second and third time, he had a feeling there were fables all around him, that everything he touched and handled, everything he saw and learned had a fable wrapped in it somewhere. One fable was about a bundle of sticks and a farmer whose sons were quarreling and fighting.

There was a fable in two sentences which read, "A coachman, hearing one of the wheels of his coach make a great noise, and perceiving that it was the worst one of the four, asked how it came to take such a liberty. The wheel answered that from the beginning of time, creaking had always been the privilege of the weak." And there were shrewd, brief incidents of foolery such as this: "A waggish, idle fellow in a country town, being desirous of playing a trick on the simplicity of his neighbors and at the

same time putting a little money in his pocket at their cost, advertised that he would on a certain day show a wheel carriage that should be so contrived as to go without horses. By silly curiosity the rustics were taken in, and each succeeding group who came out from the show were ashamed to confess to their neighbors that they had seen nothing but a wheel-barrow."

The style of the Bible, of *Aesop's Fables,* the hearts and minds back of those books, were much in his thoughts. His favorite pages in them he read over and over. Behind such proverbs as, "Muzzle not the ox that treadeth out the corn," and "He that ruleth his own spirit is greater than he that taketh a city," there was a music of simple wisdom and a mystery of common everyday life that touched deep spots in him, while out of the fables of the ancient Greek slave he came to see that cats, rats, dogs, horses, plows, hammers, fingers, toes, people, all had fables connected with their lives, characters, places. There was, perhaps, an outside for each thing as it stood alone, while inside of it was its fable.

One book came, titled, *The Life of George Washington, with Curious Anecdotes, Equally Honorable to Himself and Exemplary to His Young Countrymen.* Embellished with Six Steel Engravings, by M. L. Weems, formerly Rector of Mount Vernon Parish. It pictured men of passion and proud ignorance in the government of England driving their country into war on the American colonies. It quoted the far-visioned warning of Chatham to the British parliament, "For God's sake, then, my lords, let the way be instantly opened for reconciliation. I say instantly; or it will be too late forever."

The book told of war, as at Saratoga. "Hoarse as a mastiff of true British breed, Lord Balcarras was heard from rank to rank, loud-animating his troops; while on the other hand, fierce as a hungry Bengal tiger, the impetuous Arnold precipitated heroes on the stubborn foe. Shrill and terrible, from rank to rank, resounds the clash of bayonets—frequent and sad the groans of the dying. Pairs on pairs, Britons and Americans, with each his bayonet at his brother's breast, fall forward together faint-shrieking in death, and mingle their smoking blood." Washington, the man, stood out, as when he wrote, "These things so harassed my heart with grief, that I solemnly declared to God, if I know myself, I would gladly offer myself a sacrifice to the butchering enemy, if I could thereby insure the safety of these my poor distressed countrymen."

The Weems book reached some deep spots in the boy. He asked himself what it meant that men should march, fight, bleed, go cold and hungry for the sake of what they called "freedom."

"Few great men are great in everything," said the book. And there was a cool sap in the passage:"His delight was in that of the manliest sort, which, by stringing the limbs and swelling the muscles, promotes the kindliest flow of blood and spirits. At jumping with a long pole, or heaving heavy weights, for his years he hardly had an equal."

Such book talk was a comfort against the same thing over again, day after day, so many mornings the same kind of water from the same spring, the same fried pork and cornmeal to eat, the same drizzles of rain, spring plowing, summer weeds, fall fodder-pulling, each coming every year, with the same tired feeling at the end of the day, so many days alone in the woods or the fields or else the same people to talk with, people from whom he had learned all they could teach him. Yet there ran through his head the stories and sayings of other people, the stories and sayings of books, the learning his eyes had caught from books; they were a comfort; they were good to have because they were good by themselves; and they were still better to have because they broke the chill of the lonesome feeling.

He was thankful to the writer of *Aesop's Fables* because that writer stood by him and walked with him, an invisible companion, when he pulled fodder or chopped wood. Books lighted lamps in the dark rooms of his gloomy hours. . . . Well—he would live on; maybe the time would come when he would be free from work for a few weeks, or a few months, with books, and then he would read. . . . God, then he would read. . . . Then he would go and get at the proud secrets of his books.

His father—would he be like his father when he grew up? He hoped not. Why should his father knock him off a fence rail when he was asking a neighbor, passing by, a question? Even if it was a smart question, too pert and too quick, it was no way to handle a boy in front of a neighbor. No, he was going to be a man different from his father. The books—his father hated the books. His father talked about "too much eddication"; after readin', writin', 'rithmetic, that was enough, his father said. He, Abe Lincoln, the boy, wanted to know more than the father, Tom Lincoln, wanted to know. Already Abe knew more than his father; he was writing letters for the neighbors; they hunted out the Lincoln farm to get young Abe to find his bottle of ink with blackberry brier root and copperas in it, and his pen made from a turkey buzzard feather, and write letters. Abe had a suspicion sometimes his father was a little proud to have a boy that could write letters, and tell about things in books, and outrun and outwrestle and rough-and-tumble any boy or man in Spencer County. Yes, he would be different from his father; he was already so; it couldn't be helped.

In growing up from boyhood to young manhood, he had survived against lonesome, gnawing monotony and against floods, forest and prairie fires, snake-bites, horse-kicks, ague, chills, fever, malaria, "milk-sick."

A comic outline against the sky he was, hiking along the roads of Spencer and other counties in southern Indiana in those years when he read all the books within a fifty-mile circuit of his home. Stretching up on the long legs that ran from his moccasins to the body frame with its long, gangling arms, covered with linsey-woolsey, then the lean neck that carried the head with its surmounting coonskin cap or straw hat—it was, again, a comic outline—yet with a portent in its shadow. His laughing "Howdy," his yarns and drollery, opened the doors of men's hearts.

Starting along in his eleventh year came spells of abstraction. When he was spoken to, no answer came from him. "He might be a thousand miles away." The roaming, fathoming, searching, questioning operations of the minds and hearts of poets, inventors, beginners who take facts stark, these were at work in him. This was one sort of abstraction he knew; there was another: the blues took him; coils of multiplied melancholies wrapped their blue frustrations inside him, all that Hamlet, Koheleth, Schopenhauer have uttered, in a mesh of foiled hopes. "There was absolutely nothing to excite ambition for education," he wrote later of that Indiana region. Against these "blues," he found the best warfare was to find people and trade with them his yarns and drolleries. John Baldwin, the blacksmith, with many stories and odd talk and eye-slants, was a help and a light.

Days came when he sank deep in the stream of human life and felt himself kin of all that swam in it, whether the waters were crystal or mud.

He learned how suddenly life can spring a surprise. One day in the woods, as he was sharpening a wedge on a log, the axe glanced, nearly took his thumb off, and left a white scar after healing.

"You never cuss a good axe," was a saying in those timbers.

Olivia Coolidge

Gandhi

"A young-adult biography," says Olivia Coolidge, "is basically an attempt to present a life in broad outline for readers who have a great number of other books to study or who bog down in long volumes, but who are intelligent and like ideas."* In the hands of less skilled writers and historians, such simplification in biographies for children and young adults often results in portraits that are sentimental and one-dimensional and in which the realities of complex human beings are lost in the images of larger-than-life heroes or heroines. Coolidge's biography of Mahatma ("Great Soul") Ghandi, the father of Indian independence, avoids these pitfalls. The revolutionary leader and preacher of nonviolence emerges as a loving but difficult man of enormous stature, deeply immersed in the political and spiritual struggles of his country.

The events in this selection took place in 1930. The British had ruled most of the Indian subcontinent since 1858, and considered it to be the most impor-

---

* Olivia Coolidge, "My Struggle with Facts," in *Beyond Fact: Nonfiction for Children and Young People*, comp. Jo Carr (American Library Association, 1982), p. 145.

tant colony in their eastern empire. In this selection, Ghandi leads his followers, called *Satyagrahis* (those dedicated to nonviolent resistance to British rule), in a march to the sea—the opening battle of a campaign designed to bring about *Swaraj*, home rule for India. Coolidge does not attempt to enliven the incident with invented dialogue, but presents the stark drama of fact. Her authoritative scholarship and dignified writing style have won her the Washington, D.C., Children's Book Guild Nonfiction Award for the total body of her creative work. [From Olivia Coolidge, *Gandhi* (Houghton Mifflin, 1971).]

Salt was a government monopoly and sold to the public at a slight government profit. A salt tax, like a head tax, presses equally on everyone, whether he be rich or poor. It is true that the tax was exceedingly low and the salt was free from impurities; but in parts of India, particularly on some of the beaches, salt was free for the taking and could have been purified, at least somewhat, by the villagers themselves. Thus by manufacturing and selling salt, demonstrators could fill the jails in typical Gandhi fashion, while engaging in an occupation that would bring tiny profits to poor people and be more popular with them than the hawking of forbidden pamphlets that none of them could read.

Once resistance to the salt tax had been decided on, Gandhi needed a symbolic action to dramatize the campaign and lift it up into the sight of all. The solution was simple and typical of Gandhi. On the morning of March 12, 1930, he set out at the head of a band of volunteers to walk from Sabarmati to the seashore at Dandi, 241 miles off, to gather salt.

It was in essence quite a small procession led by a little man of sixty-one in a loincloth, stepping briskly out on match-stick legs and somewhat bowed forward as he helped himself along with a bamboo staff. Behind him walked seventy-nine of his disciples; and behind them rumbled a bullock cart, provided by anxious admirers in case the old man's strength should break down.... Reporters from all the Indian papers and a number of foreign correspondents straggled behind, each wiring home stories from the villages he passed. Gandhi was in no hurry; and he stopped everywhere long enough to urge the people to use the spinning wheel, treat untouchables as brothers, improve sanitation, give up alcohol, and break the salt monopoly. As in 1920, he could arouse a feeling that India must soon burst its bonds, that independence was a matter of a few months. In his wake village headmen resigned their posts, leaving their people without representatives to deal with government officials. *Swaraj* was coming, and it did not matter.

It was very hot, so that Gandhi only marched ten or fifteen miles a day, calling frequent halts. This pilgrimage was to be made on his own terms; and he ordered his followers to reject the milk and fruits that were sent from a distance and to rely on the poor provisions of the villages. The Viceroy, he pointed out, received an income four thousand times as great as the average Indian. His own followers were of a different sort, as they must show by living off the country.

Lord Irwin's government held its hand for twenty-four days while the march slowly neared its objective. Irritating though it might be to the Viceroy to see the newspapers of the world entranced by the picture of a half-naked old man taking on the British Empire, still Gandhi had not yet broken the salt law. Irwin did so far forget himself as to hope that Gandhi would die of a stroke on the road, but this solution was not granted him. At Dandi, everything had been meticulously prepared. . . . After a whole night of prayer, Gandhi and his followers waded into the sea for a bath of purification. Then before the lines of spectators, he walked over to the caked salt left by evaporation and picked up a little piece, which was later sold at auction for sixteen hundred rupees. There were no policemen present, and the quiet that followed the act was an anticlimax.

Within a week, India had exploded. Everyone had to make salt, picket liquor shops, light bonfires of foreign cloth, or annoy the government. . . . Enthusiasm burned brightly; the mobs were out again in the cities. While Gandhi was thinking over his next move, the British government faced its first serious threat and acted firmly.

Around Peshawar on the northwest frontier, Abdul Gaffar Khan, a remarkable man known as the "frontier Gandhi" had established an organization among the warlike Muslim tribes of the area, whom he clad in red shirts and formed into an "army" devoted to pacifist principles and service. Long one of the prominent Muslim supporters of Gandhi, he swung his organization into line with the national movement. For all his peaceful principles, Gaffar Khan controlled turbulent tribes; and the authorities in Peshawar thought the situation was getting ugly. They arrested him and lodged him in jail. Demonstrations in protest could not even be controlled by armored cars. The police abandoned Peshawar to the mob, which released Gaffar Khan and took control of the city. Three days later, a couple of platoons of regular soldiers, in this case Hindus, were sent into Peshawar to restore order. But they refused to fire on the Muslim crowd and broke their ranks. The British had to send a detachment with air support to retake the city.

This incident served a grave warning on the British government. Once the loyalty of troops cannot be relied on, any government is at an end. The Viceroy, anxious to prevent the disastrous news from getting about, clamped censorship on the Indian press, forbidding further mention of the civil disobedience movement. Gandhi was furious. By this time sixty thousand of his supporters had been arrested for breach of the laws, while in various confrontations between authorities and rioters, shots had been fired and people killed. . . .

It is fair to say that in the clashes between resisters and the police, it was usually Gandhi's forces that suffered casualties or unnecessarily brutal treatment. There was bound to be some popular violence, particularly in the towns, where criminal gangs were only too ready to make profit out of a disordered situation. But Gandhi's confidence in the people was on the whole not misplaced. . . . His power over the masses, reinforced by the last years of quiet work, was able to stave off the threat of pure anarchy that had troubled him in 1922.

In any case, Gandhi deliberately intended more blood to flow, but of his own followers. He wanted to force the government into an outrage that would whip up feeling and reveal the British in an unenviable light. Accordingly, he made plans to take over the government-owned Dharasana saltworks through a massive invasion of unarmed *Satyagrahis.* As usual, he announced his intentions; but by now the government, alarmed by events at Peshawar, had decided to face the troubles that would follow his arrest and get them over. . . . Gandhi was roused out of sleep to be taken by a combination of special railroad coach and closed automobile to Yeravda, where he was confined at the government's pleasure under a statute passed in 1825 that everybody had considered obsolete. This time the British did not dare to stage a trial.

Since it was always Gandhi's practice to arrange for leadership, should he be arrested, the raid on the saltworks was carried out on schedule under command of the poetess, Mrs. Sarojini Naidu. It was a place situated on a barren coast and protected by a barbed-wire fence, in front of which there was a drainage ditch. Four hundred policemen under six British officers had been posted between the barbed wire and the ditch with instructions to hold the place at any cost. They were armed with *lathis,* bamboo staffs with metal tips, their standard weapons. Behind them on a little knoll were twenty-five native riflemen; for the government, like Gandhi, had seen this as a battle that could decide between British rule and anarchy. Any surrender would bring take-overs in every place, followed by revolution.

The raiders approaching under Mrs. Naidu consisted of some twenty-five hundred people clad in the white "Gandhi" forage cap, with homespun shirts and *dhotis.* This human tide flowed up to the edge of the ditch, all shouting, "Long live the revolution!" at the tops of their voices. They crossed in detachments, some of them carrying ropes to help scale the barbed wire. As soon as they were over the ditch, the police fell on them with their *lathis* and clubbed them down. Not one so much as lifted his hand to protect his head as the sickening sound of bamboo clubs on skulls and collarbones was heard by the spectators, among whom was Webb Miller, an American journalist.

People collapsed, groaning and squirming or unconscious; but the first detachment was fol-

lowed unhesitatingly by another, then another, attempting to overwhelm the police by sheer weight of numbers. The stretcher-bearers, making their way through the confusion, collected the injured in blankets that were soon soaked in blood.

No orders were given the troops to fire; but the policemen, struggling for two hours with overwhelming masses at a temperature of a hundred and sixteen degrees in the shade, appeared to have gone crazy. People were deliberately kicked as they lay on the ground or subjected to indignities that clearly amounted to torture. Meanwhile, a little shed with a thatched roof that afforded protection from the burning sun was taken over for a field hospital; and hundreds of groaning people were laid down in or near it.

After two hours, it was all over. In a sense the raid had failed, but in another it had served its purpose well. Between British and Indian there lay a second shadow, darkening Amritsar. Webb Miller, his indignation vivid in his words, published the treatment of unarmed, unresisting men in articles that were echoed all over the world. According to the Congress report, two people died of their injuries, while two hundred and ninety suffered serious wounds. Through the genius of Gandhi, both victory and defeat strengthened his cause.

Jacqueline Bernard

Journey toward Freedom: The Story of Sojourner Truth

Even as a slave called Belle, Sojourner Truth was a woman of power. Although she had not then taken the name by which she was to become legendary in the fight for the abolition of slavery, her fierce independence and pride drove her to earn her freedom and, finally, to take it. [From Jacqueline Bernard, *Journey toward Freedom: The Story of Sojourner Truth* (Grosset & Dunlap, 1967).]

A Slaveholder's Promise

Freedom Day in New York State was only two years away when Dumont sold Belle's son Peter.

That is, he did not exactly sell Peter, since the boy, by law, had been born free. But Dumont, as the owner of the boy's mother, could sell his right to Peter's services until the boy should reach age twenty-eight. The boy was four at the time.

For the first time in her life, Belle openly opposed her master. Eyes wide with fear, she had planted herself squarely in front of Dumont.

"Master, don't send my boy away. What'll happen to him? Maybe they'll beat him, and him such a little boy. Maybe they'll send him south and then he never be free. Please, please, don't sell my boy."

Dumont stared at her. "Belle, whatever has come over you? Solomon Gedney would never sell Peter south. You should know that. The law of this state forbids such a thing, and in any case, I would not permit it. Mr. Gedney is very taken with your boy. He wants Peter for himself. I should think you would be pleased to have him go into a nice home where he can be trained to work for a gentleman." He frowned at her, "Just stop worrying. Peter will be very happy with the Gedneys."

Belle stood silently as he walked away. She had never before challenged her master. Now she did not know what more to do. But she had not given up. As Freedom Day approached Dumont's obedient slave was rapidly changing. A new Belle was taking shape, and that Belle knew with certainty she would get Peter back some day. How? She did not know. But she would get him back.

Shortly afterward, Dumont made Belle a promise. She had been shucking peas in the kitchen when he walked in and stood watching her for a while. "Belle," he finally said. "You're the best worker I ever had. I've been thinking I'd like to give you a special reward. If you work extra hard over this next year I'll free you and Tom a full year before the law says I must. What's more, I'll let you have that cabin up the road to live in for as long as you and your family need it."

The summer had come and gone since then, and now the snow was starting to melt. But in all those months Belle had hardly rested a moment for fear she would not earn the reward Dumont had promised. At times, during that year, the slaves had seemed to mock her almost as much as they used to. "Master be crazy to give you up a year early." But she only shrugged off their laughter and exerted even more effort. The longing to be free and to have her children had taken deep root in Belle. She absolutely believed this to be the final year of her bondage—in spite of her accident.

The accident had happened just a short time after her master had given her his promise. A scythe, twisting in her grasp, cut deeply into her hand. Working with a sore hand had been painful and difficult. The wound kept reopening because she was so eager to get things done. She just could not give it time to heal properly. Nevertheless, looking back, she knew she had worked well and accomplished just as much as usual during that long year. It would only be a short time now to freedom.

Belle was sitting by the fire listening to the talk in the slave kitchen. Her fourth child, Elizabeth, leaned against Belle's knee, while the new baby, Sophia, sucked at her mother's breast. The talk was always the same now. Every slave in Ulster County was thinking and dreaming about nothing but Freedom Day. Even old Cato, though he would never admit it, was dreaming about that. Belle could hear the old preacher's cracked voice insisting, as it had for years, "All this freedom talk. Jus' another white folks' trick. Five masters Cato's had. Not one ever keep a promise."

Nero shook his head stubbornly. The scar made by a previous master's cane neatly divided his cheek in half. The younger man spoke slowly. "This white folks' promise gotta be different," he said. "It been made to every slave over twenty-eight in this state. Even master Dumont talk about freedom now, right out in front of us all. Master Dumont can't go back on that kind of talk. Too late. If he try—there be terrible trouble. Terrible trouble." As the stocky farmhand repeated the phrase, his face clouded and his hands became huge blunt fists. Then a slow, intent look replaced the look of anger on his face. "Besides," he said carefully, "no one's talkin' about any master's promise. This here's a law they made up in Albany. Even a master's got to obey a law."

"Some trick to it," Cato insisted. "Got to be some trick."

As she listened, there flashed into Belle's mind the face of the man she had met on the road so long ago. She had learned that his name was Levi Rowe. "It is not right thee should be a slave," he had said. Albany must be full of people like that, she thought. Today those people made laws that masters had to obey— even Dumont. As a matter of fact, Belle had increasingly come to doubt that Dumont could really be the Mighty Being. If he were, how could there be others in Albany with power over him?

Elizabeth was asleep, her head on Belle's knee; the baby, too, was sound asleep. Belle looked down at Sophia's peaceful round face with its tiny open mouth and at the tight pigtails poking out from the back of the older child's head. She crooned softly, "Your ma'll be free soon, little children. Freedom's coming soon now."

She looked up to find Nero still shaking his round head firmly. "Law says we go free. Next year, when time comes, no master stop me takin' my freedom." He stretched powerfully, drew back from the fire and lay down on his straw pallet to sleep.

Soon the room was full of slow, regular breathing. Only Belle remained awake, staring into the fire. She could easily distinguish Tom's wheeze in the far corner. Diana and Hannah were sleeping next to him. Dumont had promised to free her right after the holiday. It was only two more months to Pinxster. Belle could hardly wait.

But Pinxster came and went—and nothing more was said about freeing Belle. At last she could wait no more. She went up to Dumont. "Will you be giving me my free paper soon, master?"

Dumont's shaggy brows drew together sharply. "Come, now! Surely you know that last year was a bad year. The Hessian fly ruined the wheat again. I can't possibly afford to let you go. I need your help far too much."

She did not believe the words she had heard. "But you promised me."

"I said 'if you worked well.' Now you know

as well as I that your hand has greatly interfered with your work in the past year."

She still was not willing to believe. "I worked so hard, master. I washed clothes and I scrubbed the pots and pans and I cooked and I reaped alongside the men. I did everything as usual, even with a bad hand. I let my children cry when they needed me. And only because you promised me my papers."

His voice grew curt, "Belle, don't worry. You'll get your freedom when the others get theirs. It only means another year. That's the best I can do."

Was it really only sixteen years ago that a frightened thirteen-year-old girl had stared up at a white face framed against the sky and wondered, "Is he kind?" It seemed three lifetimes away. For the first time since that day, Belle looked at John Dumont with neither fear nor gratitude.

Ma-Ma had said, "Never lie." And Belle had never lied. Yet her master thought nothing of lying to her. There he stood—with those same wide shoulders and the kindly face that had originally inspired such hope in Belle—showing no embarrassment at his broken promise. It was only a promise to a slave.

She never forgot that moment. For the first time she saw her master as just an ordinary slave-owner, very little better than the man who whipped his slave half to death.

Was it only the other day that she had scolded her hungry baby and then spanked it when it would not hush, because she would not take even one slice of bread from Dumont's cupboard without first asking? Yet he took her work, her son, everything from her—and never asked.

By the time she fell asleep that summer night in 1826, Dumont's Belle had reached a decision. For the first time in her life Belle was going to take something without permission. She was certain of one thing: her freedom now belonged to her. She had earned it, just as surely as a free worker earns his wage. If Dumont would not give it to her willingly, she would take it as her due. And yet the habit of being fair to Dumont was so strong, Belle found even now she could not rid herself of that habit. Her master had often been kind. She would repay him.

She would make quite sure all the fall work was done before she inconvenienced him by running away.

Once more the six-foot woman with the powerful body helped rake her master's hay and bind his wheat and smoke the hams after the fall slaughtering. Once more she worked overtime to help Mrs. Dumont stuff the summer sausage and store it in the bin where the oats would keep it from spoiling. Once more she cut hundreds of apples and pears into quarters and strung them high in the attic to dry. But her biggest job that fall was spinning the wool. It seemed to her the sheep had never before grown such thick fleece. More than one hundred pounds came off their dirty woolly backs. She washed the wool and carded it and spun it onto long wooden spools. And somehow, at last, the work was done.

Now Belle could find time to be afraid.

Photo of Sojourner Truth courtesy of the Sophia Smith Collection (Women's History Archive), Smith College, Northampton, Mass. 01063.

She had never before disobeyed her master. What would happen when she did? How could she get away safely? "God, I'm too scared to go at night, and if I go in the day, folks'll see me. What'll I do?"

Then an idea came: leave just before dawn. Day would follow soon enough, but an early start would give her plenty of time to leave the neighborhood before her absence was noticed.

"God," she prayed, kneeling for the last time on her praying ground. "That's a good thought. Thank you, God." These days she no longer imagined John Dumont's face up there in the sky.

It was still dark. The first rays were barely touching the ridges across the Hudson when Belle's lanky figure carefully stepped through the door and into Dumont's yard. She had told no one her plans, not even Tom. She could not risk being found out. On one arm she carried her baby Sophia. She knew that the other slaves would care for her older children. In a bright red kerchief was a bit of bread and summer sausage. The new Belle had decided she was entitled to that, too, without asking.

She strode barefoot at a fast lope down the road, away from those cliffs overlooking the Hudson. She was moving very fast indeed, but to her horror the day came even faster. At the top of a hill it dawned, full in her face, brighter than any day she could remember. She thought, "The day has no right to be so bright."

Where was she to hide? Like all slaves, Belle had never had reason to learn to plan ahead. So now it had not occurred to her to plan more than her actual departure.

While she puzzled, Belle decided to sit down to feed her infant. As the baby tugged greedily at her breast, Belle suddenly remembered the man who had stopped her on the road so many years ago. Levi Rowe lived nearby. "It is not right thee should be a slave," he had said. "God does not want it." Surely that man would help her now.

She found him at home, but so sick he could hardly find strength to speak. Nevertheless his smile and gesture made her feel welcome, as with great effort he managed to tell her of two

places where she might find refuge and work. Before leaving, Belle straightened his bed for him as best she could, then thanked him, and hoisting her heavy baby once more in her arms, continued down the road.

As she came to the first house recommended by Levi Rowe, she recalled clearly having seen it before and remembered with even more pleasure the faces of its owners. "That's the place for me." she exclaimed. "I'll stop there." And she turned up the path toward the house.

The old woman who answered Belle's knock expressed no surprise at finding the tall black woman on her doorstep. "Will you come in and have cider and biscuits?" she said. "My children should be back very soon."

While Sophie gnawed contentedly on a biscuit, Belle perched shyly on a kitchen stool and waited. But not for long. Soon a wagon rumbled outside, and a man entered, followed immediately by a woman. They were the faces Belle had remembered.

"Rowe was right to direct thee here. We do have work for thee," the man said, adding sadly, "Old Rowe is so ill, I am afraid it may be his last good deed."

Impatient to prove her worth, Belle paid little attention to the second remark but picked up a broom and started whisking it energetically over the floor. She was thinking proudly that this was her first task as a free woman, when hooves were heard pounding on the road outside. Without even turning her head, Belle knew it must be Dumont.

To tell the truth, she had purposely not gone too far. She knew that Dumont would catch up with her and that the farther he had to travel the angrier he would be. Moreover she preferred not to leave Ulster County where her children were. Now that she had claimed it, she believed God somehow would make her master grant her the freedom she had earned.

But first she must face Dumont. He was blocking the kitchen door.

"Well, Belle. So you've run away from me."

"No, master, I did not run away. I walked away by day, 'cause you had promised me a year of my time."

"You'll have to come straight home with me."

"No, master." (Was it really she, Belle, speaking such words to Dumont?)

"I'll take the child."

"No, you'll not take my child."

Master and slave glared at each other, their silence filling the small room until a gentle voice behind Belle broke the tension. "I'm not in the habit of buying and selling slaves. Slavery's wrong and I'll have no part of it. But rather than have thee take the mother and child back, let me buy her services from thee for the rest of the year. She'll be lost to thee, in any case, come next July."

Dumont hesitated. Then he shrugged impatiently. After sixteen years it took him only thirty seconds to sell Belle. Twenty dollars for the mother's services for a year? Agreed. Five for the child's services until she is twenty-five? Agreed. And he left.

Belle lifted the broom again and turned toward her new owner. "Master. . . ."

The man held up his hand. "There is but one Master here. He who is thy Master is my Master."

Puzzled, she asked, "What should I call you then?"

"By my name," he replied. "Isaac Van Wagenen. And my wife is Maria Van Wagenen."

She looked down in wonder at their serene faces, her lanky body in its shabby slave-cloth dress towering over the two little Quakers. Then she turned back to work. They had bought her. Therefore, she belonged to them. But in her heart Belle knew it made no difference. Through her own struggle, she had won her freedom.

Eloise Greenfield and Lessie Jones Little, with material by Pattie Ridley Jones

Childtimes: A Three-Generation Memoir

As these three black women of three generations describe their childhoods, common themes emerge: ordinary people trying to live decent lives in spite of prejudice and poverty; the universal pains and joys of childhood; and a strong respect for family life.

Each section of the narration illuminates the others as the daughter, mother, and grandmother comment on one another. This selection, from the middle story, is by Lessie Little, the daughter of Pattie Jones and the mother of Eloise Greenfield. The time is the early twentieth century. [From Eloise Greenfield, Lessie Jones Little, and Pattie Ridley Jones, *Childtimes: A Three-Generation Memoir* (Crowell, 1979).]

Parmele

My Parmele was a train town. The life of my town moved around the trains that came in and out all day long. About three hundred people lived in Parmele, most of them black. There were three black churches, a Baptist, a Methodist, and a Holiness, and one white church. Two black schools, one white. There wasn't even one doctor, and not many people would have had the money to pay one, if there had been. If somebody got down real bad sick, a member of the family would go by horse and buggy to a nearby town and bring the doctor back, or sometimes the doctor would ride on his own horse.

Most of the men and women in Parmele earned their living by farming. Some did other things like working at the tobacco factory in Robersonville, but most worked on the farms that were all around in the area, white people's farms usually. When I was a little girl, they earned fifty cents a day, a farm day, sunup to sundown, plus meals. After they got home, they had all their own work to do, cooking and cleaning, laundry, chopping wood for the woodstove, and shopping.

I used to love to go shopping with Mama. There was so much to see downtown. When people started getting cars, the only gasoline pump in town was down there. There were stores, four or five stores, where you could buy clothes, or yard goods, or groceries, or hardware, and the post office was in the corner of one store. Stokes' Cafe, where the white railroad workers ate, was on one side of the tracks, and Powell's Restaurant for the black workers was on the other side.

There was a little park, too, where we had picnics sometimes, and we had one policeman, and a jailhouse with two cells that were almost always empty, and one dance hall for the black people who thought it was all right to dance. The water tank and the coal chute where the trains got refills were downtown, and so was the train station.

Twice I lived in houses that the trains had to pass right by on their way to the station. I'd hear that whistle blow, and I'd run out on the porch just in time to see the train come twisting around the curve like a long black worm. I'd wave at the people sitting at the windows, and they'd wave back at me.

Trains weren't air-conditioned in those days, and when the weather was warm, the windows were always open. Black people had to sit in the front car so that whites wouldn't get dirty from the smoke and soot and cinders that blew in the windows from the engine.

I remember a train trip I took when I was small. I had on my pink organdy dress that Mama had made me, and I was so proud of the way I looked. But the whole time, I had to keep rubbing the cinders out of my eyes, and soot kept getting on my dress, and every time I tried to brush it off, it made a long, dirty streak. I was a mess by the time I got off the train. I was really dirty, my face and hands and my clothes, and my eyes were red and sore.

Parmele had trains coming in and going out all day long. Passenger trains and freight trains. There was always so much going on at the station that I wouldn't know what to watch. People were changing trains and going in and out of the cafe and the restaurant. They came from big cities like New York and Chicago and Boston, and they were all wearing the latest styles. Things were being unloaded, like furniture and trunks and plows and cases of fruit and crates of clucking chickens, or a puppy, or the body of somebody who had died and was being brought back home. And every year around the last two weeks in May, a special train would come through. It had two white flags flying on the locomotive, and it was carrying one hundred carloads of white potatoes that had been grown down near Pamlico Sound, where everybody said the soil was so rich they didn't even have to fertilize it.

The train station was a gathering place, too. A lot of people went there to relax after they had finished their work for the day. They'd come downtown to pick up their mail, or buy a newspaper, and then they'd just stand around laughing and talking to their friends. And on Sundays fellas and their girls would come all the way from other towns, just to spend the afternoon at the Parmele train station. . . .

My Papa

Papa was a quiet man. He liked to read a lot, study his Bible and his Sunday School book and the newspaper. We took the *Raleigh News and Observer.* It came in every day on the train with the rest of the mail, and Papa would walk to the post office to get it. He walked with a slight limp because one leg was shorter than the other. The older he got, the shorter the leg seemed to get, and later in life he walked with a deep limp like his papa, but when I was growing up, it wasn't too bad.

Every winter morning Papa would get up early and build a fire in the heater in his and Mama's room, and he'd set a large pot of water on it so Mama could get bathed when she got up. Then he'd make a fire in the kitchen stove for cooking.

Those were the only two rooms with heat. The rest of the house was so cold. We hated so bad to get out of our warm beds when Mama called us, but finally we would jump up and snatch our clothes and run barefoot through the hall to Mama and Papa's room. Papa would say, "Come on in here, little duckies. Great day in the morning, I got a good fire going for you!"

When Papa got home in the evening, he'd get the fire in the bedroom going real good again, and after dinner we'd all go back to that warm room. Sometimes the heater was so hot, it glowed red. Mama and Papa would just sit and talk while we did our homework and enjoyed Papa's fire.

Papa sang bass in the church choir. He had a beautiful voice, such a beautiful voice. Everybody in his family could sing, and I think he could have been a professional singer if he had been born at a later time when there were more opportunities for black people. And he had the prettiest whistle I've ever heard.

Everybody in Parmele knew Papa's whistle. Some notes he'd whistle in the regular way, but other notes he whistled in harmony—soprano, alto, tenor, one after the other real fast, almost like a tremble. Sometimes at night we'd hear it way, way down the road, and we'd be so glad because we knew it was Papa, coming home from work, whistling a hymn.

It was hard for Papa to find work. Not long after Sis Clara died, we moved to Mount Herman, a black section of Portsmouth, Virginia. Papa worked on the docks there, and even though he didn't make much money, the work was steady. But when we moved back to Parmele, it was hard for him to find any work at all.

Sometimes he worked on the railroad, cutting the grass that grew between the ties of the tracks. Sometimes he worked on white people's farms, but when they tried to treat him like a child, he told them that he was a man, and they fired him. For about two years he rented a small piece of land and grew corn and cotton and a little molasses cane. Some of it we used, and some of it Papa sold, but he really didn't have enough land to make much money, and by the time he got through paying the people he rented the land from and buying things from their store to farm with, he hardly had any money left.

I guess most of the time I was growing up, Papa worked at the train station, taking luggage off one train and putting it on another, and unloading crates of fruit, things like that. He worried a lot about not being able to buy us things. I remember one time Mama bought some new shoes for my sister Roland. Mama had gone to a bigger town to get them because the store in Parmele had clothes that were so old-fashioned it wasn't funny.

Anyway, Mama bought Roland these pretty pumps. They were dark brown and had a square throat, and they were really pretty. When Mama got home, Papa said, "Why didn't you get some shoes for Lessie, too?" Mama told him she didn't have enough money, she'd have to save for a while, then it would be my turn.

But Papa wasn't satisfied. He went to the store in Parmele, and he came home and he said, "Daughter, Papa bought you some new shoes, too." I was so happy—until I saw the shoes. They were so ugly. They were real light tan, and nobody had worn any shoes that color in I don't know when! And they were turned up at the toe, kind of like an elf's shoes. But I said, "Thank you, Papa, thank you very much." Then I went off and cried and cried because those were just about the ugliest shoes I had ever seen.

Papa didn't get mad too often. Usually when I did something wrong, he would just say, "Now daughter, you know you shouldn't have done that," and I'd be so ashamed. But once in a while, he would get really mad. One time I talked back to Mama, and what did I do that for! Papa heard me and he yelled at me so loud it made my stomach hurt. He said, "What did you say!" I told him what I'd said, but he kept on asking me. And my answer kept getting softer and softer. Finally Papa said, "Your mama borned you into this world! Don't you ever talk to her like that again!" I said, "Yes, sir."

Another time he got mad was when he came home and there was a white man there selling insurance. We were sitting in the hall, all of us children and Mama, while this man tried to talk her into buying some insurance. Papa came home and he said, "My wife doesn't want any insurance, she doesn't want to buy anything!" The man got his hat and left in a hurry. Then Papa said, "He wouldn't want me to come to his front door, he wouldn't want me to talk to his wife. I don't want him in my house, and I don't want him to talk to my wife."

Papa could really get mad sometimes. But mostly, he was a quiet man. He gave us a lot of love. . . .

Hunger

When we lived in Mount Herman, Papa got paid once a week, and he would always bring groceries home on payday. But sometimes by the end of the week there'd be almost nothing in the house to eat, and Mama would try and mix up something to keep us from getting too hungry. Once, all we had was a little flour and cornmeal and sugar and lard, and Mama mixed it up with some water and baking powder and baked it. It tasted so good. We called it flour cornbread cake and we drank Postum with it because Mama never let us drink coffee.

Some days I would get so hungry that it was hard for me to play. I'd try to play games, but that pulling inside my stomach made me feel so bad. I had heard grown-ups say, "I'm so hungry I can see biscuits walking on crutches," and I would keep saying silly things like that to make myself laugh and feel better. But soon I'd have to give up playing and go lie down, not on my bed, but on the kitchen floor or the dining-room floor with my head under a table or a chair. I don't know why, but I just seemed to feel better with my head under something.

I'd lie there and try to doze off to make the time pass faster, and after a while, there would be my papa with his arms full of food, and everything would be all right.

Mama

Mama taught us how to draw, my sisters and me. She taught us how to draw little things like boxes and houses and love knots, and she showed us how to make rag dolls, and even some funny-looking dolls out of corncobs. And Mama really knew how to tell a story. She could make it sound as if it had really happened. She would have us sitting in chairs around her, and she'd read to us and tell us stories and recite poems. Pretty poems. And sad poems, too, sometimes.

One poem was about a little girl who was sick and dying. She kept on saying to her mother, "Put my little shoes away, put my little shoes away." She knew she wouldn't need her shoes anymore. We heard that poem so many times, but it always seemed so real and so sad, the way Mama recited it.

Mama loved to read. Sometimes she would get so wrapped up in a book, she'd stay awake all night long, reading. One morning I came in the kitchen while Mama was cooking breakfast, and she was shaking her head and saying, *"Umph, umph, umph."* Then she said, "I'll follow you to the end of the world and die like a dog at your feet."

I didn't know what in the world Mama was talking about, so I said, "What you say, Mama?"

She said, "Oh, it's just something I read."

That night she told Papa about it. She said it was the most romantic thing. "I'll follow you to the end of the world and die like a dog at your feet."

Papa broke out with a great big laugh. He said, "It sounds like foolishness to me."

I liked being near Mama. When she cooked, I would sit in a chair right near the stove and put my feet up on the woodbox and just talk and talk about all the different things I had been doing all day. And I especially liked being near her whenever I was scared.

I was scared to death of thunderstorms. One house that we lived in had a little knothole in the wall, and every time the lightning would flash, it looked like it was coming right through that hole. And the thunder was so loud. Mama would say, "The Lord's doing His work now, so you all go somewhere and be quiet." My sisters might go somewhere else, but not me. I would sit right there up under Mama until the storm was over.

One night the Ku Klux Klan burned a wooden cross on Sugar Hill, and that was one of my really scared times. I was playing on the porch when I saw the cross. I couldn't see the wood, all I could see was those yellow, quivering flames in the shape of a cross, and I ran. I ran in the house to find my mama. I wanted to crawl up in her lap, under her apron, but I sat on the floor as close to her as I could get. I felt safe there, close to Mama.

Mama worked as a cook and waitress at Stokes' Cafe, down near the Parmele train station. She had to be at work early in the morning to fix breakfast for the people who would be coming in or going out on the trains. Afternoons, Mama would come home, and around four or five o'clock she had to go back and work until all the passengers and trainmen from the different trains had eaten their supper and all the trains had gone.

Even when Mama had been reading all night, she didn't have any trouble getting up early. And she made us get up, too, before she left for work. In the summer when school was out, we'd watch her out the window and as soon as she got to the corner, we'd get back in those beds and go to sleep. Even my sister Roland, who usually obeyed Mama.

When we finally did get up, we had to rush around to get our work done in time. We had to get breakfast, make beds, sweep floors. The whole house had to be clean. Roland had to comb Mabel's hair, and I had to comb Lillie Mae's, and everybody had better be dressed and tidy by the time Mama got home.

I used to visit Mama sometimes at the cafe and drink a soda pop or something. I had to use the side door. The front door was for whites only, and they sat down at little tables to be served. Blacks used the side door and had to sit at a counter where we could only get snacks.

Mama would always be glad to see me when I went to visit her. But one day her face looked strange, like it was going to break up in a lot of little pieces. She didn't smile when she saw me, and I knew something bad had happened.

All day long I wondered what was wrong with my mama, and when she got home, she told us. She said there was this man who came in the cafe every day and the minute he sat down at the table, he wanted to be served. He called Mama *woman,* but he pronounced it "umman." He'd say, "Umman! Bring me a cup of coffee!" "Umman! Bring me a piece of pie!"

Mama didn't want to say anything to the man that might make her lose her job. She had been holding it all in, and that's what had made her face look so strange.

One day, though, Mama got so upset she told the man, "Don't call me umman! If you don't know how to talk to me, I can't wait on you!"

He never called her that again, but he didn't call her Mrs. Jones, either. He called my mama Pattie.

Constance Fecher

The Last Elizabethan: A Portrait of Sir Walter Ralegh

Judged a traitor by the successor of Elizabeth, Sir Walter Ralegh was, at the same time, acknowledged to be "a star at which the world hath gazed." Although King James intended that Ralegh's execution be poorly attended, having set it for the same day as a popular festivity, this death was destined to be long remembered. [From Constance Fecher, *The Last Elizabethan: A Portrait of Sir Walter Ralegh* (Farrar, Straus & Giroux, 1972).]

"A Star at Which the World Hath Gazed"

Walter was taken to the Westminster Gatehouse, since the execution was to take place in the old Palace Yard and not at the Tower. He was permitted visitors, and many friends came that evening, thinking to comfort him, and found it quite unnecessary. He was calm and cheerful, jesting with them so merrily that one acquaintance was a little shocked. "Do not carry it with too much bravery," he said, "or your enemies will take exception to it."

Walter was long past caring what his enemies thought. He smiled. "It is my last mirth in this world, my friend; do not grudge it to me. When it comes to the sad parting, you will find me grave enough."

Dr. Tounson, the self-important young dean of Westminster, came bustling in to bring him religious consolation and found the prisoner needed none of his fine words.

"I give God thanks that I have never feared death," Walter said quietly, "and though the manner of it may seen grievous, yet I had rather die so than of a burning fever. After all, the world itself is only a larger prison and every day there are some selected for execution."

The brisk young clergyman could find no answer. He went away promising to return at dawn with the sacrament and leaving Walter to face his worst ordeal, the farewell to his wife. Bess was trembling, but she fought hard to keep back the tears when he drew her to sit beside him trying to keep her mind off the coming day by talking of Carew's education. "There are many of my possessions still in the *Destiny,*" he reminded her. "Get them if you can. They are all I have to leave and I would like the boy to have them." Though he knew she would have little enough, he begged her to help the widows of some of the men who had given him such loyal service. "There is John Talbot's mother also," he went on. "I fear she will be penniless without her son."

Bess broke down into a storm of weeping so that he could scarcely hear what she was saying. "The lords of the council would not listen to my pleading though I went on my knees," she sobbed, "but they have promised that I shall have your body."

"It is well, dear Bess," he said gently, "that you should have the disposal of that dead which living was so often denied to you."

The hour of midnight struck and she had to leave. George Carew was waiting for her. She looked back once, the flickering candlelight chasing away the years and changing him to the brilliant handsome man who had been all her life since she saw him first at Elizabeth's court. Then the door closed.

Some time during the night Walter remembered the verses he had written for her soon after they met. She smiled at him then for writing so sad a love poem. As the lines came back into his mind, he wrote them on the flyleaf of his Bible:

Even such is Time! who takes in trust
Our youth, our joys, and all we have,
And pays us but with earth and dust:
Who in the dark and silent grave,
When we have wandered all our ways,
Shuts up the story of our days.
But from that earth, that grave, that dust,
The Lord shall raise me up, I trust.

She would read them and remember and know that his last thoughts had been of her.

He was to die at nine o'clock and time was growing short. He had been allowed some of his clothes and jewelry back. He dressed slowly, gray silk stockings, black taffeta breeches, white shirt. The governor of the Tower had returned to him the miniature of his wife. Walter put the thin gold chain around his neck and thrust the picture inside his shirt, over his heart. Black satin waistcoat, russet doublet, and then the handsome black velvet gown. He smiled at his own vanity in wanting to make as fine a show as possible, just as he had done in the days of splendor. Not much of all that magnificence left to him now, nor of the intellectual pride that had earned him the name of atheist. Such vanities were past. He slipped a diamond ring on his finger, a gift from Elizabeth, a re-

minder of his years of passionate devotion to her.

When they brought him breakfast, he found himself hungry and ate with good appetite. Afterward he lighted his pipe with a touch of wry humor, since it would undoubtedly annoy the king when it was reported to him. He glanced through the notes he had made. It was the right of every man to speak from the scaffold, and on this his last public appearance, he was determined to defend himself against the slanders that had blackened his name.

Walter was roused from his thoughts by the tramp of the guard and a shouted command. The time had come, and he went out of his prison and into a square crammed with people. They climbed up on buildings and perched on railings. There were noblemen on horseback and fine ladies at windows. The Lord Mayor down in the city had been deserted.

A big, burly fellow thrust through the guard, holding out a cup, and he took it, drinking a little of the wine.

"Is it to your liking, Sir Walter?"

"It is good drink, friend," he said, smiling, as he handed back the cup, "if a man might but tarry by it."

They had almost to fight their way through the press of people around the scaffold, and he was forced to pause to recover breath. Noticing an old man with an extremely bald head whom the guard were pushing back, he asked him what had brought him out on such a raw morning. "Nothing," said the man, "but to see you and to pray God to have mercy on your soul." Walter thanked him for his goodwill and, with a merry glance at the bald head, pulled off his laced nightcap and tossed it into the eager outstretched hands. "You need this, friend, more than I."

As he mounted the scaffold, the keen wind made him shiver. The sheriffs invited him to come down and warm himself at their fire, but he shook his head. He began to speak and found that his voice was weaker than he had hoped. A wave of feverish giddiness washed over him and for an instant he thought he would faint. Then it passed and with a surge of vitality he began again.

"I thank God heartily that He has brought me into the light to die, and has not suffered me to die in the darkness of the Tower, where I have suffered so much adversity and a long sickness. And I thank God that my fever has not taken me at this time, as I prayed God that it would not."

Point by point he answered the charges that had been brought against him, while the crowd murmured, moved with pity and anger on his behalf. It would have been easy for him to rouse them to fury against the king who was killing him so unjustly, but loyalty to the crown had been part of his life, no matter who wore it. He dismissed James with a touch of contempt. "What have I to do with kings who am about to go before the King of Kings?"

There was much else, and the vast throng of spectators listened in a hushed silence to the calm, quiet voice. Many of them were moved to tears when he came to the edge of the scaffold asking them to pray with him "to the Great God of Heaven whom I have grievously offended. . . . For a long time my course was a course of vanity. I have been a seafaring man, a soldier, and a courtier, and in the temptation of the least of these there is enough to overthrow a good mind and a good man. So I take my leave of you all, making my peace with God. I have a long journey to make and must bid the company farewell."

It was finished at last. He took off his gown and doublet. The sharp wind ruffled the curling white hair. Still upright and proud, he looked suddenly young with the frilled shirt open at the throat. He took the ax from the reluctant executioner.

"Let me see it. Do you think I am afraid of it?" He smiled as he tried the edge against his thumb. "This is a sharp medicine, but it is a physician for all diseases."

He refused the blindfold. "Think you I fear the shadow of the ax when I fear not the ax itself?" When he lay down, he said, "When I stretch out my hand, dispatch me." He bent his head in prayer for a moment, then held up his hand. The headsman was trembling and did not move. He stretched out his hand again; the masked figure raised the ax but still held back. There was a moment of unbearable ten-sion before the watching crowd heard his voice ring out loud and sharp in command. "What do you fear? Strike, man, strike!" and the blow fell and fell again. A deep groan rose and swelled through the people, and the executioner as he lifted the head dared not cry out the usual formula, "Behold the head of a traitor!" Instead, someone among the spectators shouted, "We have not another such head to be cut off!"

His body was taken hurriedly into St. Margaret's Church close by, while the men and women lingered in the streets, refusing to be dispersed by the soldiers. An unknown poet among those who watched that day was so deeply moved he went away to write of it:

> Great Heart! Who taught thee so to die?
> Death yielding thee the Victory!
> Where took'st thou leave of life? If here,
> How could'st thou be so far from Fear? . . .
> Farewell! Truth shall this story say,
> We died: Thou only liv'st that Day.

That evening, distracted with grief, Bess wrote to her brother: "The lords have given me his dead body though they denied me his life. . . . God hold me in my wits."

He had not achieved his dream, but he had kept it living within him until the last, an inspiration to others who would follow in the path he had marked out. In his *History* he had written of those rare souls, "those few black swans . . . who behold Death without dread and the grave without fear and embrace both as necessary guides to endless glory." He might have been writing the epitaph for his own unmarked grave.

Jean Fritz

Homesick: My Own Story

Ten-year-old Jean has always lived in China but has yearned for America, where her grandparents live. Her fantasy becomes a happy reality two years later when she and her parents move to the United States, but then Jean discovers that she is sad to leave behind the rich life she experienced in China. That life is vividly described from the point of view of a spunky but sensitive little girl. The frightening political upheaval during the years before the Chinese Revolution and the loss of Jean's baby sister are balanced by hilarious details of growing up. Although the author has shifted incidents freely to make a coherent narrative, this is a true story. As she states in the forward, "Strictly speaking I have to call this book *fiction,* but it does not feel like fiction to me. It is my story, told as truly as I can tell it." The following selection focuses on Jean's conflict with other students at her British school over her national identity; she refuses to sing "God Save the King." *Homesick* was winner of the American Book Award in 1983. [From Jean Fritz, *Homesick: My Own Story* (Putnam's, 1982).]

In my father's study there was a large globe with all the countries of the world running around it. I could put my finger on the exact spot where I was and had been ever since I'd been born. And I was on the wrong side of the globe. I was in China in a city named Hankow, a dot on a crooked line that seemed to break the country right in two. The line was really the Yangtse River, but who would know by looking at a map what the Yangtse River really was?

Orange-brown, muddy mustard-colored. And wide, wide, wide. With a river smell that was old and came all the way up from the bottom. Sometimes old women knelt on the riverbank, begging the River God to return a son or grandson who may have drowned. They would wail and beat the earth to make the River God pay attention, but I knew how busy the River God must be. All those people on the Yangtse River! Coolies hauling water. Women washing clothes. Houseboats swarming with old people and young, chickens and pigs. Big crooked-sailed junks with eyes painted on their prows so they could see where they were going. I loved the Yangtse River, but, of course, I belonged on the other side of the world. In America with my grandmother.

Twenty-five fluffy little yellow chicks hatched from our eggs today, my grandmother wrote.

I wrote my grandmother that I had watched a Chinese magician swallow three yards of fire.

The trouble with living on the wrong side of the world was that I didn't feel like a *real* American.

For instance. I could never be president of the United States. I didn't want to be president; I wanted to be a writer. Still, why should there be a *law* saying that only a person born in the United States could be president? It was as if I wouldn't be American enough.

Actually, I was American every minute of the day, especially during school hours. I went to a British school and every morning we sang "God Save the King." Of course the British children loved singing about their gracious king. Ian Forbes stuck out his chest and sang as if he were saving the king all by himself. Everyone sang. Even Gina Boss who was Italian. And Vera Sebastian who was so Russian she dressed the way Russian girls did long ago before the Revolution when her family had to run away to keep from being killed.

But I wasn't Vera Sebastian. I asked my mother to write an excuse so I wouldn't have to sing, but she wouldn't do it. "When in Rome," she said, "do as the Romans do." What she meant was, "Don't make trouble. Just sing." So for a long time I did. I sang with my fingers crossed but still I felt like a traitor.

Then one day I thought: If my mother and father were really and truly in Rome, they wouldn't do what the Romans did at all. They'd probably try to get the Romans to do what *they* did, just as they were trying to teach the Chinese to do what Americans did. (My mother even gave classes in American manners.)

So that day I quit singing. I kept my mouth locked tight against the king of England. . . .

The next morning when I started for school and came to the corner where the man sold hot chestnuts, the corner where I always turned to go to school, I didn't turn. I walked straight ahead. I wasn't going to school that day.

I walked toward the Yangtse River. Past the store that sold paper pellets that opened up into flowers when you dropped them in a glass of water. Then up the block where the beggars sat. I never saw anyone give money to a beggar. You couldn't, my father explained, or you'd be mobbed by beggars. They'd follow you everyplace; they'd never leave you alone. I had learned not to look at them when I passed and yet I saw. The running sores, the twisted legs, the mangled faces. What I couldn't get over was that, like me, each one of those beggars had only one life to live. It just happened that they had drawn rotten ones.

Oh, Grandma, I thought, we may be far apart but we're lucky, you and I. Do you even know how lucky? In America do you know?

This part of the city didn't actually belong to the Chinese, even though the beggars sat there, even though upper-class Chinese lived there. A long time ago other countries had just walked into China and divided up part of Hankow (and other cities) into sections, or concessions, which they called their own and used their own rules for governing. We lived in the French concession on Rue de Paris. Then there was the British concession and the Japanese. The Russian and German concessions had been officially returned to China, but the people still called them concessions. The Americans didn't have one, although, like some of the other countries, they had gunboats on the river. In case, my father said. In case what? Just in case. That's all he'd say.

The concessions didn't look like the rest of China. The buildings were solemn and orderly with little plots of grass around them. Not like those in the Chinese part of the city: a jumble of rickety shops with people, vegetables, crates of quacking ducks, yard goods, bamboo baskets, and mangy dogs spilling onto a street so narrow it was hardly there.

The grandest street in Hankow was the Bund, which ran along beside the Yangtse River. When I came to it after passing the beggars, I looked to my left and saw the American flag flying over the American consulate building. I was proud of the flag and I thought maybe today it was proud of me. It flapped in the breeze as if it were saying ha-ha to the king of England.

Then I looked to the right at the Customs House, which stood at the other end of the Bund. The clock on top of the tower said nine-thirty. How would I spend the day?

I crossed the street to the promenade part of the Bund. When people walked here, they weren't usually going anyplace; they were just out for the air. My mother would wear her broad-brimmed beaver hat when we came and my father would swing his cane in that jaunty way that showed how glad he was to be a man. I thought I would just sit on a bench for the morning. I would watch the Customs House clock, and when it was time, I would eat the lunch I had brought along in my schoolbag.

I was the only one sitting on a bench. People did not generally "take the air" on a Wednesday morning and besides, not everyone was allowed here. The British had put a sign on the Bund, NO DOGS, NO CHINESE. This meant that I could never bring Lin Nai-Nai with me. My father couldn't even bring his best friend, Mr. T. K. Hu. Maybe the British wanted a place where they could pretend they weren't in China, I thought. Still, there were always Chinese coolies around. In order to load and unload boats in the river, coolies had to cross the Bund. All day they went back and forth, bent double under their loads, sweating and chanting in a tired, singsong way that seemed to get them from one step to the next.

To pass the time, I decided to recite poetry. The one good thing about Miss Williams was that she made us learn poems by heart and I liked that. There was one particular poem I didn't want to forget. I looked at the Yangtse River and pretended that all the busy people in the boats were my audience.

"'Breathes there the man, with soul so dead,'" I cried, "'Who never to himself hath said, This is my own, my native land!'"

I was so carried away by my performance that I didn't notice the policeman until he was right in front of me. Like all policemen in the British concession, he was a bushy-bearded Indian with a red turban wrapped around his head.

He pointed to my schoolbag. "Little miss," he said, "why aren't you in school?"

He was tall and mysterious-looking, more like a character in my Arabian Nights book than a man you expected to talk to. I fumbled for an answer. "I'm going on an errand," I said finally. "I just sat down for a rest." I picked up my schoolbag and walked quickly away. When I looked around, he was back on his corner, directing traffic.

So now they were chasing children away too, I thought angrily. Well, I'd like to show them.

Someday I'd like to walk a dog down the whole length of the Bund. A Great Dane. I'd have him on a leash—like this—(I put out my hand as if I were holding a leash right then) and he'd be so big and strong I'd have to strain to hold him back (I strained). Then of course sometimes he'd have to do his business and I'd stop (like this) right in the middle of the sidewalk and let him go to it. I was so busy with my Great Dane I was at the end of the Bund before I knew it. I let go of the leash, clapped my hands, and told my dog to go home. Then I left the Bund and the concessions and walked into the Chinese world.

My mother and father and I had walked here but not for many months. This part near the river was called the Mud Flats. Sometimes it was muddier than others, and when the river flooded, the flats disappeared underwater. Sometimes even the fishermen's huts were washed away, knocked right off their long-legged stilts and swept down the river. But today the river was fairly low and the mud had dried so that it was cracked and cakey. Most of the men who lived here were out fishing, some not far from the shore, poling their sampans through the shallow water. Only a few people were on the flats: a man cleaning fish on a flat rock at the water's edge, a woman spreading clothes on the dirt to dry, a few small children. But behind the huts was something I had never seen before. Even before I came close, I guessed what it was. Even then, I was excited by the strangeness of it.

It was the beginnings of a boat. The skeleton of a large junk, its ribs lying bare, its backbone running straight and true down the bottom. The outline of the prow was already in place, turning up wide and snubnosed, the way all junks did. I had never thought of boats starting from nothing, of taking on bones under their bodies. The eyes, I supposed, would be the last thing added. Then the junk would have life.

The builders were not there and I was behind the huts where no one could see me as I walked around and around, marveling. Then I climbed inside and as I did, I knew that something wonderful was happening to me. I was a-tingle, the way a magician must feel when he swallows fire,

because suddenly I knew that the boat was mine. No matter who really owned it, it was mine. Even if I never saw it again, it would be my junk sailing up and down the Yangtse River. My junk seeing the river sights with its two eyes, seeing them for me whether I was there or not. Often I had tried to put the Yangtse River into a poem so I could keep it. Sometimes I had tried to draw it, but nothing I did ever came close. But now, *now* I had my junk and somehow that gave me the river too.

I thought I should put my mark on the boat. Perhaps on the side of the spine. Very small. A secret between the boat and me. I opened my schoolbag and took out my folding penknife that I used for sharpening pencils. Very carefully I carved the Chinese character that was our name. Gau. (In China my father was Mr. Gau, my mother was Mrs. Gau, and I was Little Miss Gau.) The builders would paint right over the character, I thought, and never notice. But I would know. Always and forever I would know.

For a long time I dreamed about the boat, imagining it finished, its sails up, its eyes wide. Someday it might sail all the way down the Yangtse to Shanghai, so I told the boat what it would see along the way because I had been there and the boat hadn't. After a while I got hungry and I ate my egg sandwich. I was in the midst of peeling an orange when all at once I had company.

A small boy, not more than four years old, wandered around to the back of the huts, saw me, and stopped still. He was wearing a ragged blue cotton jacket with a red cloth, pincushion-like charm around his neck which was supposed to keep him from getting smallpox. Sticking up straight from the middle of his head was a small pigtail which I knew was to fool the gods and make them think he was a girl. (Gods didn't bother much with girls; it was boys that were important in China.) The weather was still warm so he wore no pants, nothing below the waist. Most small boys went around like this so that when they had to go, they could just let loose and go. He walked slowly up to the boat, stared at me, and then nodded as if he'd already guessed what I was. "Foreign devil," he announced gravely.

I shook my head. "No," I said in Chinese. "American friend." Through the ribs of the boat, I handed him a segment of orange. He ate it slowly, his eyes on the rest of the orange. Segment by segment, I gave it all to him. Then he wiped his hands down the front of his jacket.

"Foreign devil," he repeated.

"American friend," I corrected. Then I asked him about the boat. Who was building it? Where were the builders?

He pointed with his chin upriver. "Not here today. Back tomorrow."

I knew it would only be a question of time before the boy would run off to alert the people in the huts. "Foreign devil, foreign devil," he would cry. So I put my hand on the prow of the boat, wished it luck, and climbing out, I started back toward the Bund. To my surprise the boy walked beside me. When we came to the edge of the Bund, I squatted down so we would be on the same eye level.

"Good-bye," I said. "May the River God protect you."

For a moment the boy stared. When he spoke, it was as if he were trying out a new sound. "American friend," he said slowly.

When I looked back, he was still there, looking soberly toward the foreign world to which I had gone.

The time, according to the Customs House clock, was five after two, which meant that I couldn't go home for two hours. School was dismissed at three-thirty and I was home by three-forty-five unless I had to stay in for talking in class. It took me about fifteen minutes to write "I will not talk in class" fifty times, and so I often came home at four o'clock. (I wrote up and down like the Chinese: fifty "I's," fifty "wills," and right through the sentence so I never had to think what I was writing. It wasn't as if I were making a promise.) Today I planned to arrive home at four, my "staying-in" time, in the hope that I wouldn't meet classmates on the way.

Meanwhile I wandered up and down the streets, in and out of stores. I weighed myself on the big scale in the Hankow Dispensary and found that I was as skinny as ever. I went to the Terminus Hotel and tried out the chairs in the lounge. At first I didn't mind wandering about like this. Half of my mind was still on the river with my junk, but as time went on, my junk began slipping away until I was alone with nothing but questions. Would my mother find out about today? How could I skip school tomorrow? And the next day and the next? Could I get sick? Was there a kind of long lie-abed sickness that didn't hurt?

I arrived home at four, just as I had planned, opened the door, and called out, "I'm home!" Cheery-like and normal. But I was scarcely in the house before Lin Nai-Nai ran to me from one side of the hall and my mother from the other.

"Are you all right? Are you all right?" Lin Nai-Nai felt my arms as if she expected them to be broken. My mother's face was white. "What happened?" she asked.

Then I looked through the open door into the living room and saw Miss Williams sitting there. She had beaten me home and asked about my absence, which of course had scared everyone. But now my mother could see that I was in one piece and for some reason this seemed to make her mad. She took me by the hand and led me into the living room. "Miss Williams said you weren't in school," she said. "Why was that?"

I hung my head, just the way cowards do in the books.

My mother dropped my hand. "Jean will be in school tomorrow," she said firmly. She walked Miss Williams to the door. "Thank you for stopping by."

Miss Williams looked satisfied in her mean, pinched way. "Well," she said, "ta-ta." (She always said "ta-ta" instead of "good-bye." Chicken language, it sounded like.)

As soon as Miss Williams was gone and my mother was sitting down again, I burst into tears. Kneeling on the floor, I buried my head in her lap and poured out the whole miserable story. My mother could see that I really wasn't in one piece after all, so she listened quietly, stroking my hair as I talked, but gradually I could feel her stiffen. I knew she was remembering that she was a Mother.

"You better go up to your room," she said,

"and think things over. We'll talk about it after supper."

I flung myself on my bed. What was there to think? Either I went to school and got beaten up. Or I quit.

After supper I explained to my mother and father how simple it was. I could stay at home and my mother could teach me, the way Andrea's mother taught her. Maybe I could even go to Andrea's house and study with her.

My mother shook her head. Yes, it was simple, she agreed. I could go back to the British School, be sensible, and start singing about the king again.

I clutched the edge of the table. Couldn't she understand? I couldn't turn back now. It was too late.

So far my father had not said a word. He was leaning back, teetering on the two hind legs of his chair, the way he always did after a meal, the way that drove my mother crazy. But he was not the kind of person to keep all four legs of a chair on the floor just because someone wanted him to. He wasn't a turning-back person so I hoped maybe he would understand. As I watched him, I saw a twinkle start in his eyes and suddenly he brought his chair down slam-bang flat on the floor. He got up and motioned for us to follow him into the living room. He sat down at the piano and began to pick out the tune for "God Save the King."

A big help, I thought. Was he going to make me practice?

Then he began to sing:

"My country 'tis of thee,
Sweet land of liberty, . . ."

Of course! It was the same tune. Why hadn't I thought of that? Who would know what I was singing as long as I moved my lips? I joined in now, loud and strong.

"Of thee I sing."

My mother laughed in spite of herself. "If you sing that loud," she said, "you'll start a revolution."

"Tomorrow I'll sing softly," I promised. "No one will know." But for now I really let freedom ring.

Edward Rice

Margaret Mead: A Portrait

The work of the American anthropologist Margaret Mead not only had an enormous impact inside her own field but also irrevocably altered the current of contemporary thought. One of Mead's most important arguments is that the differences between what have been traditionally thought of as masculine and feminine characteristics are not innate, part of human nature, but are learned and vary from culture to culture. Not confining her insights to the pages of academic journals, she took the previously obscure science of anthropology directly to the general public in works such as *Coming of Age in Samoa* and *Growing Up in New Guinea,* absorbing, argumentative, and highly readable books. Mead did not hesitate to apply her anthropological insights to her own culture and drew parallels between primitive tribes and modern America. Hers was a long, productive life of research, field study, writing, and speaking. Edward Rice's biography of Mead is sophisticated, complex, and unsentimental and should fascinate older children and teenagers. In this selection, the young Margaret Mead embarks upon her first field trip in an era when women were emphatically discouraged from attempting such ventures, proving in her own life that a woman need not be limited by traditional concepts of femininity. [From Edward Rice, *Margaret Mead: A Portrait* (Harper, 1979).]

Coming of Age

One torrid day in August 1925, a slightly built young woman in a cotton dress steps ashore on an island in the South Pacific. It is Margaret Mead, twenty-four, thin, perceptive, aggressive, student of the much neglected science of anthropology. "Travel lightly" several people have advised her. In her scanty baggage she has five more cotton dresses and some simple tools for her work—notebooks, a camera, a portable typewriter. She intends to study a previously ignored field: the ways in which girls in a primitive society—in this case Samoa—grow up. She hopes—expects—that her projected study will shed some light on how this segment of Pacific island culture relatively unaffected by modernization attains maturity. She has already been warned that what has been written about Samoan culture is anything but fresh and uncontaminated by Westernization. But the growing up of young women in Samoa has so far been ignored.

Mead is one of a small group of anthropologists in the United States, a few professionals—who also teach, argue and theorize and engage from time to time in field trips—and some students; there are probably not many more in Europe, and a number of the U.S. anthropologists were born abroad. Anthropology—the study of peoples and their physical, social and cultural characteristics—is, in 1925, a relatively minor subject, almost unrecognized in the academic community. But the anthropologists, like warriors holding some embattled post, are concerned that the ancient, archaic and primitive societies that still exist will disappear soon under the pressures of modernization. Already the metal ax, the nail, the outboard motor and the Gramophone have replaced the stone knife, the peg dowel, the canoe paddle and the tribal chant in many cultures. Plywood and plastic threaten. From one end of the globe to the other the societies that had so interested and intrigued early explorers, traders and missionaries are changing, giving way to the more powerful forces of the industrial nations.

The journey to Samoa was not easy to embark upon. Young Mead had to battle her elders to get started. She had been given permission to undertake the project with some reluctance by her teacher, the noted anthropologist Franz Boas. He worried that she lacked the stamina to endure a harsh life in the tropics remote from Western amenities. . . . One of Boas's colleagues, the anthropologist and linguist Edward Sapir (like Boas, German-born), had been quite blunt with her. He told her that she was not strong enough to survive in the field—that she would do better to stay at home and have children as a woman should than to study adolescent girls in the South Pacific.

But subtly defiant and skillfully manipulative, Margaret Mead worked her way around her teachers' fears, and now she is in Pago Pago, Samoa, about to prove herself far more resilient than her elders had imagined. . . .

She is not particularly interested in Pago Pago, but she must stay there while arrangements are made to go to a less developed island for her studies. The heat is oppressive; in fact the entire Samoan archipelago is moist and often unbearably uncomfortable. The rainy season runs from October to March, and coincides with her stay in the islands. . . .

. . . Because she is a woman, the National Research Council, which is helping to underwrite the costs of her research, has decided she cannot be trusted with her entire grant in advance, and so has insisted on sending it in monthly portions. The mails are slow, get lost. Her first check—for $150—has temporarily disappeared in the languor of Samoa. The hotel costs $28 per week; until she receives her allotment she cannot leave. She must spend six weeks in the lodging house, at times the only occupant, without money to pay her bill. Six "laborious and frustrating weeks" in a kind of tropical house arrest. But she begins to learn Samoan. . . .

Her money arrives at last, and she is freed from the lodging house. . . .

A Samoan woman, a member of the family she had met in Honolulu, arranges for her to spend ten days at Vaitogi, a village near Pago Pago. Here Mead stays with the family of a chief. The daughter, Fa'amotu, teaches her Samoan etiquette, the proper things to do and say in various situations according to the circumstances. She learns how to sit on the floor—painful at first, and her legs ache—how to sleep on mats, and how to act during the rituals of meals and ceremonies. She puts away her cotton dresses and wears a lava-lava, the all-purpose unisex garment worn from East Africa to the Pacific. When she bathes under the village shower, in the full sight of staring children, she learns how to slip off the wet lava-lava and put on a dry one without feeling clumsy. . . .

She takes up Samoan dancing, which she writes home, is not practiced "in a puritan fashion.". . .

Mead will dance many nights throughout her stay.

Pains in the legs from sitting on the floor

and from too much dancing go away. She is rapidly becoming acclimatized. Samoanized. The food in Vaitogi is better. The lessons in Samoan etiquette produce results. Samoan society is highly structured, and rank is important. One behaves a certain way for this person in the hierarchy, that way for another. One must use the correct phrases.

A chief from the neighboring island of Upolu visits the family. After a while he makes an offer which Margaret attempts to put into perspective. But she is able to affirm in her broken Samoan, "marriage" between them would not be fitting due to the difference in their respective ranks. She hopes her Samoan is adequate to the occasion.

Regrets. But the chief adds: "White women have such nice fat legs.". . .

Fieldwork, Mead notes about her first trip, is very difficult. One must clear one's head of misconceptions and presuppositions about other cultures and open it up to the flood of new and unexpected information that comes pouring in. A practical approach seems to be the solution.

Accompanied by an ever-changing group of young Samoan girls, she wanders about, asking questions and checking the questions with other questions. She analyzes each household in three neighboring villages of Manu'a, noting down location, relationship and closeness to other households, rank, wealth, and the age, sex, social standing and marital status of each person in the household. Each child is studied in the context of her own particular environment.

"In the field nothing can be taken for granted," she remarks. . . .

Her self-taught methods of fieldwork are to produce one of the most unusual books of anthropological history. Nuances of Samoan life are captured, slight events others might have overlooked. In her hands they show a novelist's touch.

The life of the day begins at dawn, or if the moon has shown until daylight, the shouts of the young men may be heard before dawn from the hillside. Uneasy in the night, populous with ghosts, they shout lustily to one another as they hasten with their work. As the dawn begins to fall among the soft brown roofs and the slender palm trees stand out against a colourless, gleaming sea, lovers slip home from trysts beneath the palm trees or in the shadow of beached canoes, that the light may find each sleeper in his appointed place. Cocks crow, negligently, and a shrill-voiced bird cries from the breadfruit trees. The insistent roar of the reef seems muted to an undertone for the sounds of a waking village. Babies cry, a few short wails before sleepy mothers give them the breast. Restless little children roll out of their sheets and wander drowsily down to the beach to freshen their faces in the sea. Boys, bent upon an early fishing, start collecting their tackle and go to rouse their more laggard companions. Fires are lit, here and there, the white smoke hardly visible against the paleness of the dawn. The whole village, sheeted and frowsy, stirs, rubs its eyes, and stumbles towards the beach. "Talofa!" Talofa!" "Will the journey start today?" "Is it bonito fishing your lordship is going?" Girls stop to giggle over some ne'er-do-well who escaped during the night from an angry father's pursuit and to venture a shrewd guess that the daughter knew more about his presence than she told. The boy who is taunted by another, who has succeeded him in his sweetheart's favour, grapples with his rival, his foot slipping in the wet sand. From the other end of the village comes a long drawn-out, piercing wail. A messenger has just brought word of the death of some relative in another village. Half-clad, unhurried women, with babies at their breasts, or astride their hips, pause in their tale of Losa's outraged departure from her father's house to the greater kindness in the home of her uncle, to wonder who is dead. Poor relatives whisper their requests to rich relatives, men make plans to set a fish trap together, a woman begs a bit of yellow dye from a kinswoman, and through the village sounds the rhythmic tattoo which calls the young men together. They gather from all parts of the village, digging sticks in hand, ready to start inland to the plantation. The older men set off upon their more lonely occupations, and each household, reassembled under its peaked roof, settles down to the routine of the morning. Little children, too hungry to wait for the late breakfast, beg lumps of cold taro which they munch greedily. Women carry piles of washing to the sea or to the spring at the far end of the village, or set off inland after weaving materials. The older girls go fishing on the reef, or perhaps set themselves to weaving a new set of Venetian blinds.

We are immediately at home in the thatched, circular houses, at peace under the lazy, swaying palms, engrossed in the amatory intrigues of the young girls and boys. We see a life of simplicity and ease that is beyond our experience, yet the ideal of our dreams. Swimming, fishing, living in the open, dancing, storytelling, ceremonies, an economy without the need for money, sexual experimentation—in the 1920's this is far beyond the hopes of the ordinary Westerner, even among the young.

But along with this idyll, Mead is careful to point out (but a point that many readers will ignore), come social responsibility and social integration. In her Samoa even the five- and six-year-olds have definite and understood responsibilities, caring for the younger children, learning to plait palm or pandanus leaves, to climb coconut palms, to open coconuts skillfully, and attending to numerous other minor but necessary chores. Boys go through the child-caring stage and then move on to their assigned tasks, helping with the fishing and preparing boats for sea. In their teens the girls will learn the ways of cooking with primitive equipment (stones, bamboo leaves, coconut shells, plaited baskets and carved bowls), and the boys will pick up the techniques of canoe handling, of tending taro roots and coconut trees, transplanting and harvesting. Each boy must take part in communal activities, not slacking or showing too much precocity. He must fit into the larger structure, for individuality is discouraged.

High-strung and frail her professors had thought she might be in the field, yet Mead has accomplished an amazing job. She has worked with sixty-eight girls mainly in the three neighboring villages of one coast of Tau. From time to time she visited four other villages in the Tau archipelago, and she talked to numerous children, young men and adults. Her broad observations about ceremonial usages surrounding birth, adolescence, marriage and death are collected from the entire group, but it is the teenage girl's psychological development that is crucial to her work.

In *Coming of Age in Samoa,* the book that resulted from her trip, her most important discovery is that the storms and tensions of adolescent life in the Western world are not necessarily shared by other peoples. Unlike adolescence in America and Europe, she discovers, Samoan "adolescence represented no period of crisis or stress, but was instead an orderly developing of a set of slowly maturing interests and activities. The girls' minds were perplexed by no conflicts, troubled by no philosophical queries, beset by no remote ambitions. To live as a girl with as many lovers as long as possible and then to marry in one's own village, near one's own relatives, and to have many children, these were uniform and satisfying ambitions."

The idea seems to appeal to a lot of her readers, and her frankness in speaking so plainly about sex and love in Samoa soon makes her famous.

I am . . . interested in that step toward maturity a child takes when it ceases to see people as static, frozen at a moment in time, but sees them instead as changing and developing creatures. Such a perception is concerned with realizations about time and about aging, but also . . . with realizations about history. It is the perception, often startling, that places have a past, that they are now but also were then, and that if peopled now, they were peopled then.[1]

14   Travel and History

Children often believe that whatever they read in a history book must be true, and this attitude, unfortunately, sometimes persists into adulthood. But when we consider the writing of history, we must also deal with the large questions of the nature of truth, the limitations of viewpoint, and the necessity for interpretation. What is verifiable? When does fact become fiction? Jill Paton Walsh considers the subtle relationship between historical fiction and history, between the novelist and the historian:

History is indeed *fact*—the Latin word for something that was done—but it is also *fict*—the Latin word for something made. . . . Nine-tenths or more of what is known about the past rests only upon the evidence of the written word. And written words have a lot in common, whether they are drafted by novelists or by historians.

. . . For in both sorts of writing a very similar process is going on. History does not exist somewhere; it is not really something indisputable. The evidence for it—a vast jumbled assortment of many kinds of data—exists; but history itself is a construct of the mind. The evidence has been selected, and patterned, and arranged; it has been masterminded into significance by the writer of the history book. How very like the writing of a novel I make it sound. For the novelist, too, confronts the inchoate material of the past and brings out of it an imposed narrative coherence—a story, or a history. . . .

1. Penelope Lively, "Children and Memory," *The Horn Book Magazine*, 49 (1973), 400.

Both novelist and historian—merely in recounting a sequence of events—reveal the orientation of their most profound beliefs.[2]

The significance of the historian's belief system and point of view becomes apparent when a distinguished work of history is contrasted with a conventional textbook. In a carefully documented, scholarly history, the historian achieves an equilibrium of objective fact and subjective interpretation, while leaving uncertainties and ambiguities as provocative challenges to the questioning reader. By contrast, many American history textbooks, according to Frances FitzGerald in *America Revised: History Schoolbooks of the Twentieth Century* (1979), are bland, revised interpretations of history tailored by publishers under the guidance of Boards of Education and designed to respond to various pressure groups. Truth is the victim as adults shape the history they wish their children to learn.

In trade as well as textbook publishing, self-interest, prejudice, commercial interests, parochialism, and patriotic chauvinism have often caused similar distortions. Recently, however, there has been a sharp reaction to the presence of biases, particularly in books for young readers, that demean the American Indian, deprecate blacks, rationalize slavery and skim over Reconstruction, or simply ignore the achievements of women and other groups not within the mainstream of white, male, Anglo-Saxon society. This reaction has contributed to the appearance of books on topics such as labor, slavery, suffrage for women, and various American Indian tribes.

For example, in *When Shall They Rest?* (1973), Peter Collier provides a full account of Cherokee history, making it clear that the Cherokee are the victims of treachery and prejudiced beliefs to this day. His point of view is made explicit in an "Author's Note" at the end of the text. In a bibliographical note, Collier invites readers to pursue the matter further; for the reader who does not agree with the writer, access to the past, in the form of sources, is provided.

Historians are not expected to be infallible. In his book *So What about History?* (1969), Edmund S. Morgan, Sterling Professor of History at Yale, emphasizes the reader's responsibility:

The only cure for this difficulty is more curiosity. You want to know what really happened, who you really are, not what some historian wishes you were. If the history books you read don't satisfy you, you will have to start taking the covers off things for yourself, looking at the records of the past, putting the pieces together again to see if they really fit. It takes a long time, and by the time you have finished, you may find out one more thing about yourself. You may find that you have become a historian.[3]

This transformation from reader to historian was more difficult for those schooled in the first half of this century, when history was usually taught as a matter of dates and kings, wars and revolutions, conquests and defeats, and when textbooks were broken up into short paragraphs with the facts summarized in outline form at the end of the chapter. For those who never read a history text that flowed like a story or never came upon a teacher who made the past live as part of the present, history was a dull business indeed.

Today, history written for children is concerned with the role of ordinary people, with daily life through the centuries, and with the connection between

---

2. Jill Paton Walsh, "History is Fiction," *The Horn Book Magazine*, 48 (1972), 22–23.
3. Edmund S. Morgan, *So What about History?* (Atheneum, 1969), p. 94.

past and present—all of which are full of human interest and meaning. This emphasis on the social interpretation of history has resulted in a body of historical writing that is inspiring, imaginative, and dynamic. Books such as David Macaulay's *Cathedral* (1973), Leonard Everett Fisher's *The Railroads* (1979), Edwin Tunis's *Frontier Living* (1961), and Joe Lasker's *Merry Ever After: The Story of Two Medieval Weddings* (1976) succeed in using a specific topic as a clue to a greater concept of history. They offer the opportunity for full exploration of a period, in a pattern that follows the natural interests of children.

Certain periods have a strong appeal for children: The life of primitive man, the feudal period, the age of the great discoverers, and the war years are subjects that often fascinate children between the ages of nine and thirteen. But children most enjoy the reading of history when it is based on sound, even minute, scholarship and has that literary edge called distinctive writing. In addition, the judicious use of source material strengthens the appeal of history for children. Journals, letters, and diaries give immediacy to historical accounts. The words of Columbus, the diaries of Jefferson, the letters that passed between father and son or husband and wife at the time of the American Revolution or the War between the States—these serve to reveal the people and the magnitude of their accomplishment.

History is not a neutral collection of facts; it is written by people, and all historians have biases. The best historians openly acknowledge theirs. In the socially committed 1960s, some historians began to write crusading, impassioned works that pointed out the origins of social injustices and frankly advocated change; they often used original sources to restore a lost or neglected point of view. In recent years, "advocacy history" has been written for children as well as for adults. Milton Meltzer's historical and biographical writings, for example, exhibit this impulse toward social conscience. Writing to inform the young of past injustices and to tell them that "something else is possible, that what we do, each of us, can make a difference," Meltzer feels that "what the young will learn from reading about historical experience . . . is that citizens—then and now—must act for themselves. They cannot rely on government alone to satisfy their needs or give them justice and equality."[4]

Many of Meltzer's works—such as *Bread and Roses* (1967), a history of the labor movement in the United States, *In Their Own Words* (1964), a documentary history of black Americans, and *Never to Forget: The Jews of the Holocaust* (1976)— are built on firsthand testimony; the experiences of people, presented in their own words, provide immediacy and insight. Similarly, in Julius Lester's *To Be a Slave* (1968), the words of people who endured slavery are set within the framework of Lester's commentary. Lester makes use of actual testimony that for years had been allowed to lie neglected in libraries and archives.

It is often illuminating to juxtapose two contrasting histories of the same sequence of events—to read, for example, Meltzer's *Never to Forget: The Jews of the Holocaust* along with Ellen Switzer's *How Democracy Failed* (1975), a study of the rise of Fascism in Germany that includes interviews and eyewitness accounts of Germans who lived through that time. Paul and Dorothy Goble contrast two views of an event within a single book, *Red Hawk's Account of Custer's Last Battle* (1969). They interweave an Indian youth's perception of the Battle of

---

4. Milton Meltzer, "Who's Neutral," *Children's Literature in Education*, No. 14 (1974), pp. 24–36, reprinted in *Beyond Fact: Nonfiction for Children and Young People*, comp. Jo Carr (American Library Association, 1982), p. 109.

the Little Bighorn, based "on the published accounts of both Sioux and Cheyenne participants in the Battle of the Little Bighorn," with a historical account written in official military terminology. The juxtaposition of Red Hawk's sharply immediate, personal telling with the neutral and detached overview creates an impact far greater than any single narrative could have achieved.

An unusual source serves as the basis for another book, *The Bayeux Tapestry: The Story of the Norman Conquest—1066* by Norman Denny and Josephine Filmer-Sankey (1966). The authors used a tapestry as an original source for an account of the Battle of Hastings. The book's reproductions from the Bayeux Tapestry not only make an aesthetically interesting and appealing presentation, but also give the reader a feeling for the times. Other historians—for example, Shirley Glubok, whose books feature artifacts from museums—use illustrations of contemporary houses, scenes, and portraits to augment their texts. The vitality of this approach brings the reader and the materials of history into a direct and forceful relationship.

Archaeologists often supply new information on historical topics. Archaeological evidence has altered our thinking about such legendary characters as King Arthur and such elusive places as the cities and sites mentioned in the Bible or in the works of Homer. Recent books have made such archaeological material available to children in engaging presentations with striking graphics. David Macaulay's fine series on architectural structures—the construction of a Roman city, an Egyptian pyramid, a French Gothic cathedral, and even a decidedly nonhistorical dismantling of the Empire State Building set in the future—are filled with ingenious architectural drawings that record the human details and cultural history, as well as the technical procedures, of construction.

Another venerable approach to the writing of history is the speculative essay, as for example in *The Story of Mankind* (1921) by Hendrik Van Loon. His philosophical tone invites the judgment of children upon their past. Van Loon is consistently occupied with the adventure of humanity, the interlocking patterns of tyranny and rebellion, the significance of heroic actions, and the progressive march—as he sees it—toward a more humane existence. Although his book now seems dated, and many of his assumptions are no longer generally shared, *The Story of Mankind* remains a classic example—the first for children—of how to write history in a forceful and entertaining way.

Even with all the fresh, inventive ways of presenting history to children that have been developed in recent years, the chronological approach still holds a central place for young readers. Genevieve Foster has experimented with time in unusual books that combine history and biography. Her *George Washington's World* (1941) and *The World of William Penn* (1973), among others in this series, describe the contemporary world of her subject as background for a biography and include accounts of the arts, science, and politics of the time. These richly documented, horizontal views of history are infinitely varied and interesting. Foster's approach, a singularly original presentation, adds a new dimension to facts that had not previously been related to each other in a work for children.

The outstanding tenet of historical writing for children today is an insistence on authenticity. Renewed and vigorous research into history and biography is required, along with a lively and genuine interest and the ability to inform the writing with both knowledge and feeling. These touchstones have replaced a previous acceptance of material that was diluted, rewritten, and many times removed from the original sources of knowledge and research.

Among the histories children read most passionately are those about impressive voyages and adventures of explorers and discoverers—for example, William Toye's dramatic description of Jacques Cartier's voyages to the New World in *Cartier Discovers the St. Lawrence* (1970), which is punctuated with quotations from Cartier's own journals. But travel, once an adventure in itself, has today become commonplace, thanks to the jet and the television screen. Only when conditions of the past are reenacted, as in the voyage of the *Kon-Tiki,* is there the adventure of survival. A unique purpose, such as the one that sent Jane van Lawick-Goodall into Africa (see Chapter 15 for a selection) gives another dimension to travel: the quest and task of the scientist.

A unique series of travel books by Mitsumasa Anno marks a breakthrough in the approach to travel, history, and geography. The wordless picture books in this series follow a solitary traveler across Britain, Europe, and the United States. Shifting and mutable cultural allusions, landmarks, and monuments document the traveler's passage through space and time—through the real and changing world.

Speaking of the power of place in the development of a child's sense of history, Penelope Lively comments that "certain places are possessed of a historical charge that sets the imagination flaring with an immediacy that nothing else can. In particular, I am thinking of places where private and public experiences collide—battlefields, the sites of deserted villages, places where people's lives have been disrupted by the force of historical change."[5] Such a place is Hiroshima. Toshi Maruki's *Hiroshima No Pika* (1980) is the story of a young Japanese girl's experience of the nuclear bombing of her city in 1945. This close-up view of a horrifying event conveys that charge of a specific historical time and place through the child protagonist's immediate perceptions. Place and emotion are summoned through a delicate balance between restrained text and emotionally charged artwork, for this unique work is a picture book—albeit one for older children. But the very existence of a treatment of such a devastating historical event in a picture-book format points to the fact that today's children are terribly aware of the prospect of another nuclear holocaust, that they *do* have a sense of history and an awareness of a very uncertain future.

Because we want our children to have a future, it is essential that they develop an awareness of the past, of what Penelope Lively calls "continuity." She writes:

In any case, why should the development of a child's perception about the past matter? To have a sense of history is, above all, to have a sense of one's own humanity, and without that we are nothing. For the child, it is a step toward an awareness of other people, which is the most vital step toward being not just an adult, but a mature adult. . . .

To help a child see himself as part of a whole historical perspective is to extend his imagination. Without such awareness he is blinkered, confined by self, and dangerous.[6]

If history, or the reading of it, can give us a firmer and clearer respect for what it means to be human, a keener consciousness of our own existence, then it has fulfilled its mission. Our ideas about our past help form our conception of the present and help shape our decisions for the future.

5. Lively, p. 401.
6. Lively, pp. 401–2.

John Nance

Lobo of the Tasaday

In the 1960s, in a remote area of the Mindanao Island rain forests in the Philippines, a hunter-trapper discovered a tribe of twenty-six people living in the Stone Age. The photo-journalist John Nance visited this tribe and wrote an award-winning study for adults, *The Gentle Tasaday.* Writing for children in this clear, informative photographic picture book, Nance focuses on the Tasaday boy Lobo. Through finely composed, intimate photographs of the Tasaday and a direct, simple text describing their traditional way of life, beliefs, and first encounters with the modern world, the author conveys the warm humanity and complex culture of this primitive people. The Tasaday life was not destroyed by the incursion of the twentieth century; 46,000 acres of the rain forest were set aside for their exclusive use. *Lobo of the Tasaday* is a work of journalistic anthropology rather than one of history. Nonetheless, it provides young readers with a taste of "living history" as they recognize in Lobo the universality of childhood and experience a Stone Age culture from the inside. [From *Lobo of the Tasaday,* written and photographed by John Nance (Pantheon, 1982).]

On a rugged island in the Philippines live a people who call themselves the Tasaday. *Ta* means "people" in their language, and *saday* is the word for their homeplace, a mountain deep in a remote tropical rain forest. The Tasaday have lived there as far back as anyone can remember. Until recently, they thought they and their friends were the only people on earth.

Lobo is one of the Tasaday. When these pictures were taken, in the early 1970s, he was about ten years old. The Tasaday do not keep track of months or years, so no one knows Lobo's age for certain.

At that time, there were twenty-six Tasaday. They lived in three caves high on the side of the mountain. Most of the Tasaday's six families stayed in the largest and driest cave. Lobo shared one corner of it with his parents and his brothers.

The caves were used for sleeping and for shelter from the rain. When the weather was good, the Tasaday went into the forest to look for food.

They gathered fruit, nuts, and berries.

A favorite food was *biking,* the root of a leafy plant. The best roots were as long as a boy's leg and nearly as big around. Using pointed sticks and their bare hands, the men dug up pieces of *biking* and wrapped them in leaves to carry home.

There was also food in the nearby stream: fish, crabs, tadpoles, and frogs. Frogs were the largest creatures the Tasaday ate.

The children rolled leaves into cones to carry what the adults collected. Sometimes the gatherers nibbled as they worked, but most of the food was taken back to the caves, to be divided among all the Tasaday.

There was usually enough for everyone, except when bad weather kept the people inside the caves for several days. Then the youngest were fed first, even if older people had to go without food. The smallest children needed nourishment most. And if the babies were hungry, their crying filled the caves and troubled everyone.

The Tasaday believed that the forest had been made especially for them to live in and take care of by the Owner of All Things. When the sun—which they called the Eye of Day—was bright, that meant the Owner of All Things was happy. When it rained, that meant he was sad. When he was angry he sent storms: the Big Word and the Fiery Light—thunder and lightning. Some said harsh wind was the Owner's breath. Storms were frightening and dangerous. The Tasaday were careful not to do things that might offend the Owner.

Certain birds were thought to be messengers to and from the Owner. One of Lobo's favorite birds was Lemokan.

The Tasaday could call Lemokan by whistling through their hands to imitate its song. They believed that if Lemokan landed near them, it was a warning of danger, and they should stay wherever they were. If they saw the bird fly by and heard it sing, it was safe to go out. And if they heard the bird sing but did not see it, they could take their chances—go or stay.

The Tasaday were fond of butterflies, too. Sometimes a man would tie a vine thread to a butterfly as a leash for a child to hold. Lobo's grandfather, Kuletaw, said butterflies were gifts from the Owner to make people happy.

The Owner had also given the Tasaday the use of the plants and trees in the forest. When gathering food or playing in the vines, they were careful not to destroy the plants, so they could blossom again. Harming these living things would have made the Owner angry.

The Tasaday asked permission of the spirits that watched over various places before gathering food there. Children were taught special words to please the spirits. They were also taught to be wary, because spirits were unpredictable, and the forest was full of dangers. All the people had countless scars on their knees and feet and hands from rocks, sticks, thorns, thistles. Adults continually warned children to watch out for sharp things.

If a cut became infected, certain leaves and vines were crushed and put on the injury. If it didn't heal and the person got sick, the wisest Tasaday appealed to the spirits and the Owner. But sometimes the sick person died. The Tasaday were deeply saddened to lose that person's smile and helping hands. Human life was especially precious because there were so few people.

The Tasaday knew of only two other groups. Although these people lived in the same forest, the Tasaday did not see them often. Still, they were considered friends. The Tasaday language had no words for "enemy" or "war." . . .

Sometimes children had to look after their younger brothers and sisters. Lobo liked playing with his little brother, Ilib; and while he didn't always like to stop what he was doing to comfort Ilib, he did it anyway. The Tasaday believed that people should help one another. Lobo's father said that this was one of the most important rules of life. It had always been so, he said, since the Owner put the first people in the world.

To the Tasaday, the forest *was* the world. They had never been outside of it; they didn't know there was an outside.

Until the stranger came.

Photograph by John Nance, from *Lobo of the Tasaday,* by John Nance. Copyright © 1982 by John Nance. Reprinted by permission of Pantheon Books, a division of Random House, Inc.

Elizabeth Chesley Baity

Americans Before Columbus

In *Americans Before Columbus,* the author gives a fascinating panorama of American Indian migrations and cultures from the time of the Ice Age to the coming of Columbus. The chapter below tells of the first invasion of America by the white man. [From Elizabeth Chesley Baity, *Americans Before Columbus* (Viking, 1951).]

The Vikings Find and Lose America

It was a cold day in the late summer of 986 A.D., and a blustering wind from the north lashed the Atlantic Ocean into great waves. The storm had been raging for days. The men in the battered little boat with the dragon carved on the prow were dead tired and half starved; they wished with all their hearts that they had never left their comfortable homes in Iceland to set sail for Greenland. Even Bjarni Herjolsson, to whom the dragon ship belonged, had to admit that the lashing winds had blown them off their course. They should long before have reached Greenland, where he was going to join his father, who had followed Eric the Red when this quick-tempered adventurer had had to leave Iceland.

At last they saw land ahead, but their hearts sank when they reached it. The shore stretched empty before them: no masts of ships, no feast-hall roofs. They were hungry for their own kind, for feasts and meetings with friends and relatives, for food and wine and songs, and for the sagas, or stories of Viking heroes which the music-making *skalds* sang to the sound of the harp. None of these things was here. When the winds died down, they turned back north again and after many days reached Greenland.

During the long winter evenings in Greenland, Bjarni often told of the unknown land that he had discovered. Among the people who asked him eager questions about it was young Leif, one of Eric's sons. As he listened, Leif's mind began to burn with the desire to explore this unknown country. Years later he bought a boat from Bjarni, fitted it with provisions, and persuaded thirty-five of his friends to set off on the adventure with him. He even induced old Eric the Red to lead the expedition, in order to bring it luck. Eric protested that he was too old to go, but Leif out-talked him. At last the day came when they rode down to the shore to set sail. But Eric's horse stumbled, and the old explorer fell and hurt his foot. Eric took this as a bad sign. "I am not destined to discover more countries than this in which we are now living," he told his son. "We shall no longer keep one another company."

Leif sadly said good-bye to his father and turned the dragon prow of his ship toward the land which Bjarni had sighted. They found the new land and went ashore, but it was a poor, cold place of glaciers and flat rock. Leif said, "Unlike Bjarni, we have not failed to come ashore in this country, and I shall now give it a name and call it 'Helluland' (land of flat stones)." Then the party pushed on to discover a new coast with long white beaches backed by woods. Here Leif said, "This land shall be given a name after its nature and shall be called 'Markland' (woodland)."

Then Leif turned his ship to the open sea and sailed with a northeast wind for two days. Again land was sighted.

And such land! Rich grassy meadows for the cattle, tall trees that would make wonderful ships' masts, waters that swarmed with fish. Scholars now think that this land, which Leif called "Vinland," was the coast of North America somewhere south of the Saint Lawrence River.

Leif divided his party into two groups; each day one group went exploring while the other group rested and took care of the camp. Leif ordered his men to stick together, since it would be a serious thing to be lost in this vast country. But one night the exploring party came home without Thyrker, whom Leif had loved almost as his own father since childhood. Furious and frightened, Leif started out with a searching party of twelve men. After a while they came across Thyrker, who told them in great excitement that he had discovered wild grapes. Now they could make wine! Calling his men together the next day, Leif told them, "We will now do two things. Each day we will either gather grapes or we will fell trees for a cargo for my ship."

When the ship was loaded with wild grapes and timber, they set sail back to Greenland. His adventures earned him a new name—Leif the Lucky.

The year was 1003 A.D. Leif Ericson had brought the white man's cross and sword to the American continent—a thousand years after the time of Christ and very nearly a thousand years ago.

Other sons of Eric the Red made less lucky voyages; one was buried in America. A daughter, Freydis, half sister of Leif, led one of the five later voyages which are described in the sagas. When her companions did not please Freydis, she murdered several of them, women and children, with an ax. Other women came here; the sagas name a baby, Snorri, the first known white child born in the Americas. The histories of these expeditions were told and retold by the *skalds* who sang the sagas in the feast halls of Iceland. Three hundred years afterward, the sagas were first written down.

You may wonder how much to believe of stories that were first told three centuries before they were written down. But a careful check with historic records proves that the Icelandic sagas were very true accounts, and so we may believe that those sagas dealing with "Wineland the Good" or, as they called it, Vinland, are actual reports carried home by America's earliest known white explorers. Two Scandinavian historians, writing in 1076 and in 1140, mention the Norse discovery of Vinland, the new land beyond Thule, which may have been Iceland or the Faroe Islands. They appear to consider the discovery a fact well known to everyone.

The sagas are not the only clues to this story of the Viking explorations in the Americas. In Nova Scotia and elsewhere in the northeastern part of the United States, Viking axes, boat keels, and other objects have been found, including curiously marked stones which puzzle scholars. Olaf Strandwold has written a study called *Norse Inscriptions on American Stones,* telling about more than thirty of these stones. Some of them, he says, are road markers set up to show later explorers which way a certain party had gone. Others were put up to mark the site of religious celebrations. He reads one stone found in Braxton County, West Virginia, as an account of a colony of Norsemen who settled there; among them were people named Qn Eric, Rikar, Ole, and a woman called Guri. He dates this stone about 1037, believing that had it been later, certain Danish letter types would have been used. A second clue to the date lies in the fact that the forms of the cross and of the letter A used on this stone were given up after the first half of the eleventh century. A New England stone bearing such a cross carried a date which in our calendar would be 1031 A.D.

This Qn Eric, writes Professor Strandwold, was quite a wanderer. At one time this Viking selected the Great Mound* as the site of a Yule festival. Arriving back at his main settlement in Massachusetts, he carved on a stone: "Overland route—Qn set the marker." A stone found in New England, says Professor Strandwold, tells that Qn Eric met his death when a boat turned over, and concludes with the words: "The ice owns Qn. O Tiv, raise him to everlasting light."

Many more Norsemen than are mentioned in the Icelandic sagas must have come to America. It may be that adventurers from Norway, unknown to the *skalds* who retold the Icelandic stories, set up other colonies far inland.

The Annals kept yearly in Iceland during the discovery period mention several visitors to the new land. In 1121 the Annals note the departure of "Eric, Bishop of Greenland," for Vinland. Nothing more is heard of Bishop Eric—unless, of course, he should be that Qn Eric who left so many marker stones in America. In 1347 the Icelandic Annals note that "A ship which had sailed to Markland came to Iceland with eighteen men on board." This note in the Icelandic Annals closes the book on the American adventure.

After that, bad days came to the Viking colonists. For several hundred years the Vikings had sailed up the rivers in almost every part of Europe, leaving tall, blond rulers even in

---

* The Great Mound, built long before the time of Columbus, is located near the present town of Moundsville, West Virginia.

remote Russia. Now Iceland, which had been settled since 874 A.D., was no longer a prosperous settlement sending out its adventurous sons. At home in Norway there were wars and rebellions. The little colonies in Greenland, and possibly in America, whose settlers had looked forward each summer to a ship or two from the homeland, bringing news and food and wine, were neglected. Years passed; after 1347 no more ships went to Markland or Vinland. The settlements died away. Their very names were forgotten.

The saga spotlight fell upon the few individuals who returned successfully home to Iceland with their cargoes of wood and wine and their stories of Vinland the Good. But what of other colonists who may have remained in the new land? What did they think when no more ships came from home? What did they do? If Viking parties really wandered inland far enough to use the Great Mound for Yule ceremonies, their explorations were more extensive than any reported in the sagas. But America's vast spaces may have been too much for them, and their numbers too few, so that in the end they were swallowed up by the forests. The first invasion of America by the white man rippled out into silence.

Mary Seymour Lucas

Vast Horizons

The title of the book from which this selection is taken points definitely to its contents. The reader gets a picture of Europe and China at the time of the Crusades; of the rise and fall of Portugal as a great power; of the opening-up of new interests by land travels such as the Polos made; of adventures by sea such as Columbus and others dared; in short, the extending of the known horizons. This chapter on the Polos is a fascinating story in itself. [From Mary Seymour Lucas, *Vast Horizons* (Viking, 1943).]

The Polos

By the middle of the thirteenth century, Venice had definitely jumped ahead of Genoa. Her treasury was piled high with golden ducats and her ships and merchants had control of most of the trade on the Mediterranean and Black Seas.

Among the most respected and successful of her traders were the Polo brothers, Nicolo and Maffeo. For years they traded back and forth between Venice and Constantinople and the Black Sea ports. In 1255, they decided to try their luck in the kingdom of the Tartars. Sailing to the east end of the Black Sea, they headed inland and were pleased to find friendly people and good trade. Suddenly a civil war broke out, cutting off the return route.

Boldly they decided to push on across Asia, following the great trade routes, to seek the Great Khan himself and start a rich trade. Probably they followed Rubruck's route; perhaps they even met him as he struggled westward. At length they reached Cambaluc and found Kublai on the throne. When they started home, they carried letters from him to the Pope asking him to send a hundred missionaries to convert the Mongols.

After fourteen years of marvelous adventures they reached Acre only to learn that the Pope had died and his successor had not yet been elected. There was nothing to do but wait.

Back in Venice in 1269, they found Marco, Nicolo's fifteen-year-old son, eager to hear of all they had seen, and to visit strange places. Ever since he had been old enough to wander by himself, he had spent his spare time on the wharves where the great trading ships docked, sniffing the strange, exciting smells of the East, talking to the crews, asking innumerable questions.

During the next two years, Nicolo and Maffeo made plans to return. Marco, his dreams realized, could scarcely wait for the great day, but at last it dawned, clear and warm, and they headed down the Adriatic bound for Acre. There they completed their preparations and started on their way with letters from the Pope's emissary, some sacred oil from the lamp which burned night and day in the Holy Sepulcher at Jerusalem, and, not a hundred missionaries, but two fainthearted friars who quickly grew discouraged and turned back.

Sailing north along the coast to Ayas, they started their long journey, traveling up to Erzingan and then circling past Mount Ararat where

Noah is said to have landed his ark, past a gushing fountain of oil which no one knew enough to use for fuel—the first they had ever seen—to the Tigris River, which they followed to Baghdad. Passing through the rich fields of the valley, Marco saw his first heavy-tailed sheep, with long thick tails weighing thirty pounds or more, and humped cattle, probably Brahma steers. Robbers were plentiful and travelers had to be on the alert. Once the caravan they had joined for protection was attacked and they barely escaped. At last they came to El Basra, the city from which Sinbad the Sailor began his voyages.

They took passage on a smelly little dhow which traded up and down the Persian Gulf, carrying cargoes of rotting dates. The smell of stale fish oil, which had been daubed on the boat's seams to keep out the water, nearly made them ill. The cabin was so filthy and airless that they preferred the hot decks and tried to seek some shelter from the blazing sun in the shadow of the sail.

They sighed with relief when their boat docked at Ormuz, a flourishing trade center on an island in the mouth of the Gulf. They felt the dread sirocco wind which blows every day from nine until twelve during the summer. Those who could not afford cool houses along the shore waded into the sea and stood up to their necks in water until the wind stopped blowing. To be caught in it on a sandy plain meant certain death from suffocation. Every morning they were awakened by the Mohammedan call to prayer, chanted from a high tower.

They had planned to find a ship at Ormuz and sail the rest of the way, but the Polos, used to the ships on the Mediterranean, were afraid to sail so far in a dhow, and no other ships were available. So they chose what they believed the lesser of two evils and decided to travel overland.

They headed north and presently came to the Kirman Desert. For three days they crossed sandy wastes with only an occasional well, filled with water so salty and green that it was undrinkable. The fourth day they found a river of sweet water, but their rejoicing was cut short, for it was soon swallowed by the sand and the next three days were like the first.

Joyfully leaving the desert behind them, they started across Khorasan where they heard stories of the "Old Man of the Mountain," a Mohammedan prince named Aloeddin.

He owned a beautiful valley, cut off from the rest of the world by lofty mountains. In it he built luxurious palaces and surrounded them with beautiful gardens. Conduits carried streams of wine with honey and water to all parts. Beautiful maidens lived there and spent their time singing, dancing, and playing musical instruments. A strong castle guarded the one entrance and none were allowed to enter.

Aloeddin himself lived in another valley and in his court he gathered the finest young men of the country. He talked to them of Paradise and said he had the power of admitting them.

Every once in a while he would give a chosen few a drug and while they were in coma would have them carried to his secret valley. On awakening they would believe themselves in Paradise. For a week they would be supremely happy, then once again they would be drugged and returned to court.

When they spoke with wonder of their adventure, Aloeddin told them it was but a taste of the joys they would receive after death if they served him faithfully. Consequently none were afraid to die and each was eager to give his life for his master, and Aloeddin's men were the terror of all surrounding countries.

They trailed across another desert for eight days, crossed a fertile strip where the finest melons in the world grew and came to the once great city of Balkh which had been sacked by Genghis Khan years before. For twelve days they crossed a land inhabited only by bandits, for all others had fled for protection to stronger places. Game and fish abounded.

At last they came to Badakshan in the foothills of the Pamir Mountains. They spent several months here waiting for the snows to melt on the high passes ahead of them, and gave Marco a chance to recover more fully from an earlier attack of fever. It was here that they met a man who said he was descended from the Greek general, Alexander the Great, who had plundered that district fifteen hundred years before.

Up and up they climbed on unbelievably steep trails, twisting between jutting rocks, skirting precipitous drops of hundreds of feet, until they reached the Pamir Plateau, the "Roof of the World." They noticed that high in the mountains it took longer to boil water and that their fire did not give as much heat.

On they went into the rising sun, to old trading centers, through Kashgar, with its surrounding cotton fields, until they arrived at Khotan, where they decided to await the arrival of a caravan which they could join.

Beyond Khotan they came to the great Desert of Lop, so wide that thirty days were needed to cross it. It was said to be inhabited by evil spirits who imitated human voices and so lured those who had lagged behind their caravan far from the trail. Marco heard tales of sounds of musical instruments, of drums, and of the clashing of arms heard at night by travelers. Today these are explained by the fact that the sandhills contract and move as they cool at night, thus sounding various tones. On the other side of the desert they were met by envoys of the Khan, for news of their coming had preceded them.

Marco noticed many marvels as they passed through Cathay; perhaps the most amazing to him was a rock composed of long fibers "of the nature of the salamander, for, when woven into cloth and thrown into the fire, it remains incombustible." This, of course, was asbestos. Leaving behind Karakorum, the old capital of the Mongols, they traveled eastward and finally arrived at Shangtu or Xanadu, where Kublai had his magnificent summer palace. With great ceremony they were ushered into the Khan's presence and bowed low before him.

Kublai nodded graciously to Nicolo and Maffeo: "Welcome, my friends," he said. "And who is this?" he added, looking at Marco who was standing in the background.

"He is my son and your servant," said Nicolo.

"He is welcome and it pleases me much," Kublai replied. From then on Marco was one of his attendants of honor and stood high in his favor.

For seventeen winters Marco felt the icy blasts sweep down from the northern steppes as he traveled far and wide as the Khan's special messenger. He learned four languages, one of them probably Chinese, so he could talk with almost anyone in the empire and satisfy his curiosity

about the strange wonders he saw. Kublai delighted in the long detailed accounts of all he had seen and questioned him eagerly about this city, the crops in another place, a certain man's loyalty, and the game in a certain forest.

A year after his arrival, Kublai sent him on a diplomatic mission to Khorasan, more than halfway back across Asia. It took six months to get there and then he fell ill and had to stay for a year before he regained his strength.

When he returned to Cambaluc, he learned that a city in southern China had withstood a three years' siege. He promptly suggested that the Mongols build mangonels, early military engines for hurling three- or four-hundred-pound weights, and bombard it. Kublai was definitely interested. The machines were built and demonstrated, and won immediate approval. They were shipped south, the city surrendered after the first bombardment; the Polos stood even higher in royal favor. Marco traveled far and wide over the Eastern empire, up the Yangtze River, down into Burma, and even sailed southward to visit some of the East Indies.

At last he, his father, and uncle began to think of home. They longed to see their family and friends, to taste Italian food and wine and to breathe the salt air of the Adriatic. No doubt they thought how they could amaze their friends with tales of all they had seen. Kublai frowned at the idea and told them to forget it. They dared not risk his anger by talking more about it, but they could not forget.

Their opportunity came when Arghun Khan, ruler of Persia under the Great Khan, sent messengers asking for a Mongol princess to be his wife. Kublai chose his daughter, the Lady Kutai, and the caravan started back. After eight weary months, they found their way blocked by war and returned to Cathay. It was then that Marco came forward and suggested that he, Nicolo, and Maffeo take the Princess to Persia by ship, and then go on to Venice for a short visit.

Fourteen great ships, each with four masts and nine sails, were equipped. With two thousand people, they left Zaitun (now Amoy) early in 1291 and sailed south, closely following the shore. Entering the Straits of Malacca they met strong head winds and were forced to wait for several months until they shifted to the northeast. These were the southwest monsoons which blow every year from May until October.

After building fortifications around the ships as guard against possible attack by unfriendly natives, Marco disappeared inland to explore. When he returned to the fleet, he found several hundred dead from the unhealthy climate. At last the wind changed. Spirits rose with the sails, and they headed across the Bay of Bengal for Ceylon, stopping at the Andaman and Nicobar Islands on the way.

They sailed up the Malabar Coast (West India) and then no one is very sure of the exact route, for Marco describes Socotra, Abyssinia, and Madagascar in detail. Probably he heard of these places when stopping along the southeastern coast of Arabia, for it is doubtful if he visited them.

At last after eighteen months at sea they reached Ormuz which they had left nearly twenty years earlier. Six hundred members of their party had died, but the Princess was still well. They landed and learned that Arghun had died, but that his nephew and successor desired Kutai for his bride.

Leaving her there, the Polos traveled north to Trebizond where they took passage in a ship bound for Venice. They arrived in 1295 and the story of their homecoming is a fine one.

One day a gondola stopped in front of the Ca' Polo in Venice and three bearded men stepped out. Their clothes, of Eastern stuff and design, were rough and tattered; their faces were bronzed by weather and lined by hardship. They spoke halting Italian with strong foreign accents. Altogether they looked more like men from the Far East than from Venice. They knocked boldly at their door and announced themselves.

Those who came to the door laughed and said: "True, Nicolo, Maffeo, and Marco Polo started for Cathay, but that was many years ago and they are long since dead. Be off before we turn the dogs on you." And the heavy door was slammed and bolted.

Again the Polos thundered against their door, and when an incautious servant drew the bolt, beat their way in. Relatives arrived from various parts of the city and finally were convinced that the three suspicious-looking strangers were indeed the long-lost members of their family.

Then there was great rejoicing. The news spread through the city and many flocked to see them. The next day a feast was arranged and all their old friends were invited.

The travelers were dressed in long robes of crimson satin. When the guests had arrived, they changed to robes of crimson damask and the first were cut up and given to the servants. Once during the dinner they disappeared, and when they returned they were dressed in crimson velvet and the damask was given to the guests. When dinner was over, they removed the velvet, divided it among the guests and appeared in the dress of wealthy Venetian merchants. Then the table was cleared, the servants sent from the room, and Marco disappeared. When he returned, he carried the ragged, travel-stained clothes which they had worn on their arrival. The guests exchanged amused glances, but they soon exclaimed in amazement as the three Polos seized knives and ripped up the seams. Cascades of rubies, emeralds, pearls, diamonds, sapphires, and other jewels tumbled out and lay in richly glowing piles in the candlelight. No longer was any one in doubt and they were received everywhere with honor and respect.

For three years Marco was the center of attention. Men never tired of hearing the marvels of Cathay and other strange, faraway places, even though they did not believe half of what he told them. And because they thought he exaggerated, they nicknamed him "Marco Millions."

Jean Fritz

Where Do You Think You're Going, Christopher Columbus?

It takes a man of total conviction to sail off the edge of the known world and into the unknown, and that is how Jean Fritz has drawn Christopher Columbus— as a man so convinced that he was going to find the Indies that everything he found became the Indies. Fritz is the author of some of the most humorous and entertaining history books for the younger child. This account of Columbus' first arrival in the New World is filled with broad ironies and not a few belly laughs. [From Jean Fritz, *Where Do You Think You're Going, Christopher Columbus?* (Putnam's 1980).]

At eight o'clock on the morning of August 3, 1492, Columbus set sail from Spain. He had three ships, the *Niña,* the *Pinta,* and the *Santa Maria* (on which he sailed), approximately 100 men, a company of cats to take care of rats that were always on shipboard, and an interpreter to speak to the people of the Indies. (The interpreter spoke Arabic, but this was such a foreign-sounding language that Europeans expected all foreigners to understand it.) As for supplies, Columbus took food (sea biscuits, salt meat, cheese, raisins, beans, honey, rice, almonds, sardines, anchovies), water, wine, firewood, compasses, and half-hour glasses. (A ship's boy kept track of the time by turning the glass every half hour to let the sand trickle the other way.) He took cannons, crossbows, and muskets in case the natives of strange islands were unfriendly, and in case they were friendly, he had a large stock of bells, scissors, knives, coins, beads, needles, pins, and mirrors to exchange for gold or any other treasure that was handy.

Eventually, of course, Columbus expected to meet with kings, so it was only proper that he carry letters of greeting from his own king and queen. One letter, written in Latin, was addressed to the Great Khan, the king of China. In fact, there hadn't been a Great Khan for 124 years, but no one in Europe knew that. Another letter was to Prester John, a rich Christian king who, according to Sir John Mandeville and others, was supposed to rule a wonderful country somewhere near the Indies. In fact, there was no Prester John and never had been. But no one could say that Columbus was not well prepared.

Certainly he was happy to be on his way, the sea rolling under him and the wind at his back. The ships stopped at the Canary Islands for last-minute repairs and supplies; then on September 6 they pulled up anchor and sailed into the Unknown.

"Adelante! Forward!" Columbus cried.

The directions were simple: 2400 miles due west to Japan. (He had dropped 600 miles from Dr. Toscanelli's estimate.) The sailors knew, of course, that 2400 miles meant many days without sight of land, but they hadn't known how it would feel to have that vast circle of empty ocean settle around them for so long. Day after day the same circle, no matter how far or fast they sailed. And they were sailing fast—once 170 nautical miles in one day. Still, the circle didn't change. Or the wind either. It always blew in the same direction, taking them farther and farther west.

Yet if the sameness of the sea and the wind was scary, it was also scary to remember that they were in the Unknown, where anything might happen at any time. When a meteor with a long, branching tail of white fire streaked into the sea one night, they were terrified. Oh, it was a bad sign, the sailors cried. They should have stayed home.

And what did the captain-general, Christopher Columbus, say? "Adelante!" was what he said. It was all he ever said. When the sea turned into a meadow of green and yellow floating weeds, he said it. "Adelante!"—right through the weeds. When the wind dropped so that they could scarcely move, it was "Adelante" again. When they had sailed beyond the point where Japan was supposed to be, he repeated, "Adelante!"

It was too much. Some of the sailors decided that they were being led to their death by a crazy man. Why, Columbus didn't even know enough to be afraid! He was actually enjoying this trip, talking about how soft the air was, how pleasant the mornings. At night he would stare at the sky for hours at a time as if he were reading a love story that he couldn't put down. More than once the sailors thought how easy it would be to push Columbus overboard some night when he was standing on deck "drunk with the stars."

But Columbus had ways to quiet the men. For one thing, he never let them know his actual reckoning of the distance covered each day. He pretended that they had not gone as far as he thought they really had so the voyage would not seem as long and "the people would not be frightened." Moreover, he kept pointing out encouraging signs that land was near. A live crab in the weeds. A whale. (Columbus supposed that whales stay near land.) One day they saw four land birds together. A great sign, Columbus said. *Four* birds wouldn't be lost. One day it rained—a drizzling rain. Land rain, Columbus said. Just like at home.

At sunset on September 25 Martin Pinzón, captain of the *Pinta,* shouted, "Tierra! Tierra! Land! Land!" Men clambered up the rigging of all three ships for a better view. Yes, it was land, all right. Glory be to God! At last, at last. Martin Pinzón was especially grateful. The person who sighted land first had been promised a handsome reward by the king and queen.

On September 26 there was no sign of land anywhere. They must have seen clouds on the horizon that looked like land.

On October 7 the *Niña* raised a flag and fired a cannon, the signal that land had been sighted. Another false alarm. Maybe they'd never find land, the men grumbled. Maybe there was no land in the west.

On October 10 the men announced that they could stand it no longer. They must turn back.

Well, of course, they should have known what Columbus would say, and, of course, he said it. "Adelante!" There was no use complaining, he told them. He had come to find the Indies and, by San Fernando, he'd find them! Three days, he said. Give him three days and they'd have land.

The next night Columbus gave orders that instead of dropping anchor, the three ships would sail right on. But look sharp, he said. And to the first man who sighted land, he promised a silk doublet or jacket in addition to the royal reward.

Columbus watched as eagerly as everyone else. At ten o'clock he noticed a light, like a little wax candle, wavering on the horizon. He couldn't be sure so he asked a servant standing nearby. Yes, the servant said, there did seem to be a light, but then it disappeared and Columbus put it out of his mind.

At two o'clock in the morning a cannon was fired from the *Pinta.* A young seaman named Rodrigo had seen white sand cliffs looming up in the moonlight. This time there was no doubt. They had been at sea thirty-seven days (since leaving the Canary Islands) and at last they had reached land. The three ships lay to, and with the first light of morning, everyone rejoiced to see a large, level island, "so green," Columbus said, it was a "pleasure to gaze upon."

For Columbus, it was a triumph—solid proof that he'd been right all along. Here he was in the Indies, fulfilling a plan that God had worked out for him step by step. When Rodrigo claimed the silk doublet and the royal reward, Columbus said no, he had, himself, sighted land when he'd seen a light at ten o'clock. How could it be otherwise? Surely God, who had gone to so much trouble to bring him here, meant him to have the honor. Certainly everyone else wanted to honor him. As soon as he had gone ashore and taken official possession of the island, the men crowded about Columbus, congratulating him, calling him admiral, governor-general, viceroy, and begging his forgiveness for their moments of doubt. All but Rodrigo. (He was so mad at Columbus that the first chance he got, he went to Africa and became a Mohammedan.)

Columbus named the island San Salvador. Certainly it wasn't Japan. There were no palaces and the only sign of gold was the gold rings that the natives wore in their noses. Indeed, that was all they wore. The people were as naked, Columbus said, "as their mothers bore them" which, of course, was pretty naked. Otherwise, they were normal-looking. They didn't have umbrella feet or eyes on their shoulders.

But if the Spaniards were surprised to see naked natives, the natives were even more surprised to see dressed Spaniards. All that cloth over their bodies! What were they trying to hide? Tails, perhaps? The natives pinched the Spaniards to see if they were real and agreed that, pale as they were, they were flesh and bone. But where had they come from? There were no such people in the world they knew; they must have dropped down from the sky. So they gave the sky-people what gifts they had: cotton thread, darts, and parrots. In return, they received glass beads and tiny bells that went "chuque-chuque" when they were shaken.

What Columbus wanted, however, was information. Where was Japan? The interpreter stepped forward and spoke in Arabic, but he might as well have been talking to birds. No one understood. So Columbus tried sign language. He pointed to the gold nose rings and made motions that were supposed to mean, where? Where had the gold come from? The natives were very obliging. They pointed and made gestures too. Indeed, whatever the Spaniards did, the natives tried to copy. They would make good servants, Columbus said, for they were so willing. And good Christians too, for already they were crossing themselves like old-timers. But they were no help in giving directions. And in order to be a success in the eyes of the queen, Columbus had to find Japan. So it was up anchor and away again. Off to Japan, wherever that was.

In a way it was too bad that Columbus needed to find gold. He had such a good time that fall—sailing from island to island naming them all, planting crosses as he went, marveling at what he saw. Trees so tall they scraped the sky! Fish of all colors! Flocks of parrots that blotted out the sun! Flowers, fruit, birds—oh, it would take a thousand tongues to tell it all, he said, and then who would believe without seeing for himself?

And the curiosities! There were dogs that didn't bark. (A type of yellow hound that grunted instead of barking.) There were hanging beds (hammocks), mermaids (which were really sea cows), canoes that held forty men and more. And a leaf that men rolled up and, with one end lighted, stuck the other end up their nose and puffed (tobacco). He saw no human monstrosities in his travels, but he heard about them. From natives whom he'd taken aboard at San Salvador and taught a little Spanish, he was told of an island where men had dogs' heads; another where they had only one eye. Didn't this sound just like the stories that Sir John Mandeville told?

But Columbus wasn't finding Japan. Still, he knew that he had not been brought here for nothing, and when his native interpreters mentioned a place called Colba, he thought, aha, this was it! Colba must be Cipangu (Japan), only the natives were not pronouncing it right. Actually they were referring to the island which we now call Cuba, and even Columbus could see when he got there that it wasn't Japan. It didn't even look like an island and there wasn't a gold palace in sight.

Columbus made new calculations of his position and decided that this was China. "It is certain," he wrote, "that this is the mainland." Moreover, when he pointed toward the interior, the natives cried, "Cubanacan!" What else could that mean but "People of the Great Khan"? So Columbus told his Arabic interpreter to put on his best clothes; he was to lead a delegation to the court of the Great Khan and deliver the letter from the king and queen. A native guide would show him the way.

Six days later the delegation returned. All they had found was a village of fifty thatched huts and 1000 naked people. This was Cubanacan. (In fact, the word meant mid-Cuba.)

If Columbus was disappointed, he didn't show it in the day-by-day report that he wrote for the king and queen. He had only praise for his Indies and pointed out that it was so healthy that no one had even had a headache. But when it came to praying, Columbus prayed for gold. For five weeks he sailed along the coast of what he insisted was the mainland of China, hunting for gold. But what did he get? Parrots. Wherever he stopped, the natives gave him parrots.

Genevieve Foster

George Washington's World

In the introduction to *George Washington's World* Genevieve Foster says, "This book tells the story of George Washington's life, of the people who were living when he was, both in America, and all over the world, of what they did when they were children, and how later on the pattern of their lives fitted together, and what part each played in that greatest of all adventure stories, the History of the World." The chapter given below tells of the drafting of the

Declaration of Independence. [From Genevieve Foster, *George Washington's World* (Scribner's, 1941).]

The Declaration of Independence

The new word, Independence, came with the year 1776, broadcast through the American colonies by a pamphlet called *Common Sense.* "O ye that love mankind," rang its challenging words, words that went echoing from one end of the continent to the other, "ye that dare not only to oppose tyranny but the tyrant, stand forth! Every spot in the old world is overrun with oppression. The birthday of a new world is at hand! Independence in America should date from the first musket that was fired against her." People were roused by the ringing words. In the taverns, on the plantations, on street corners and on the wharfs, in the backwoods settlements, wherever people gathered in the colonies they argued about independence.

Thomas Paine had started them talking. For the author of *Common Sense* was that Jack-of-all-trades but master of ideas, who had come with Benjamin Franklin's introduction to America.

"I am charmed with the sentiments of *Common Sense,*" wrote Abigail Adams from Braintree to her husband John, in Philadelphia. "I dare say there would be no difficulty in procuring a vote from all the Assemblies of New England for Independency."

There was no difficulty in Virginia either. Virginia delegates to the Continental Congress were instructed to vote for Independence.

Except for those instructions, Thomas Jefferson was downcast as he drove from Monticello in his two-wheel gig. His young wife was very ill, and little four-year-old Martha waved a pitiful good-bye.

But it was a great satisfaction as he resumed his seat in the hall facing John Hancock, to be one of the Virginia delegates who early in June proposed the motion "That these united colonies are and of right ought to be free and independent."

"I second the motion," snapped John Adams with no hesitation.

Massachusetts and Virginia were ready for independence, but Pennsylvania and New York were not, and many other colonies were most uncertain. There were conservative law-abiding people in all the colonies, people of education and property, to whom the idea of being disloyal to their King was inconceivable.

Others were afraid of the future: "With independence established," they said, "we are in danger of being ruled by a riotous mob. If you vote for independence," they warned their friends in Congress, "you will be hanged." George III had denounced all rebels in America as traitors and the punishment for treason was hanging.

Not merely the colonies, but even members of the same family were split apart by their convictions. Thomas Jefferson and Benjamin Franklin stood for independence, but Thomas Jefferson's cousin John Randolph was a staunch Loyalist and had gone to England, leaving Tom his fine violin. Benjamin Franklin's son William, now governor of New Jersey, was also a Loyalist, and later was to act as President of the Associated Loyalists of New York City.

Endless debates and arguments filled the days of the Congress. The sound reasoning on both sides kept many delegates undecided, but gradually, John Adams said, "one after another became convinced of the truth of Independence."

A committee of five was appointed to put into writing a declaration. The three most active members were Benjamin Franklin, John Adams and Thomas Jefferson.

"You sir," said Thomas Jefferson, turning to John Adams, "will of course draw up the declaration."

"I will not," replied the older man. "You shall do it, and I'll tell you why. You are a Virginian and a Virginian ought to head this business. I am unpopular, you are very much otherwise. Reason three . . . you can write ten times better than I can."

So Thomas Jefferson went to his lodgings and for eighteen days worked faithfully on what he had been set to write. When he had finished, crossed out and reworded a few sentences, and laid by his quill, he had written The Declaration of Independence.

Several days were taken up in discussing and changing some of the phrases, during which Benjamin Franklin with his homely humor kept the sensitive young author from becoming too disconsolate.

At last, on the fourth of July, Thomas Jefferson heard the final draft of his declaration read, voted upon and accepted.

"Thus was decided the greatest question which was ever debated in America," John Adams wrote his wife. "The second of July, 1776, will be celebrated by succeeding generations as the greatest anniversary festival—with guns, bells, bonfires and illuminations from one end of the continent to the other."

The great bronze Liberty Bell that hung in the belfry called the people of Philadelphia four days later to hear the Declaration read aloud in the square outside the State House. As a strong-voiced man stepped to the front of the small wooden platform and began to read, the last echoes of the bell caught the now well-known words:

"WHEN IN THE COURSE OF HUMAN EVENTS," he began. Silence fell as he continued: "WE HOLD THESE TRUTHS TO BE SELF-EVIDENT, THAT ALL MEN ARE CREATED EQUAL. THAT THEY ARE ENDOWED BY THEIR CREATOR WITH CERTAIN UNALIENABLE RIGHTS. THAT AMONG THESE ARE LIFE, LIBERTY AND THE PURSUIT OF HAPPINESS. . . ."

As he ended with the last word "honor," the people cheered and the Liberty Bell rang out once more.

When the copy was complete on parchment, John Hancock, as President of Congress, was the first to sign. He took his quill in hand, writing the letters larger than ever before, turning the end of the *k* with a more determined flourish, and with a couple of graceful scrolls he finished this, his most famous signature!

"There!" said he, "King George will have no trouble in reading that without his spectacles."

"Gentlemen, we must all hang together now," said Benjamin Franklin as he took up the quill, then added with a quirk of a smile, "or we will all hang separately."

Spoken in jest, there was sober truth behind those words. Signers of the Declaration had taken a daring step.

"I am well aware," wrote John Adams again, "of the toil and blood and treasure that it will cost us to maintain this declaration."

All knew that there was many a crisis ahead that would call for more than brave words, cheers and bell-ringing, times when only in patience, perseverance and self-sacrifice could their faith be measured.

Julius Lester

To Be a Slave

Original sources give the reader a firsthand knowledge of slavery. Julius Lester has provided a narrative framework for these selections and has arranged them into groups: early slave trade, slave auctions, work, and living conditions. Many of these moving testimonies were taken down by abolitionists after the Civil War. The location and history of all sources are given in the introduction to the book and each statement is followed by an identifying note. [From Julius Lester, *To Be a Slave* (Dial, 1968).]

The selling of slaves was inhuman in itself, but many slave owners did not even have the decency to tell a slave that he was going to be sold.

Half the time a slave didn't know that he was sold till the master'd call him to the Big House and tell him he had a new master.

Mingo White
Library of Congress

Never knew who massa done sold. I remember one morning ol' white man rode up in a buggy and stop by a gal name Lucy that was working in the yard. He say, "Come on. Get in this buggy. I bought you this morning." Then she beg him to let her go tell her baby and husband goodbye, but he say, "Naw! Get in this buggy! Ain't got no time for crying and carrying on." I started crying myself, 'cause I was so scared he was gonna take me, too. But ol' Aunt Cissy, whose child it was, went to massa and told him he was a mean dirty nigger-trader. Ol' massa was sore, but ain't never said nothin' to Aunt Cissy. Then Hendley what was next to the youngest of her seven children got sick and died. Aunt Cissy ain't sorrowed much. She went straight up to ol' massa and shouted in his face, "Praise God! Praise God! My little child is gone to Jesus. That's one child of mine you never gonna sell."

Nancy Williams
The Negro in Virginia, p. 172

I said to him, "For God's sake! Have you bought my wife?" He said he had. When I asked him what she had done, he said she had done nothing, but that her master wanted money. He drew out a pistol and said that if I went near the wagon on which she was, he would shoot me. I asked for leave to shake hands with her which he refused, but said I might stand at a distance and talk with her. My heart was so full that I could say very little . . . I have never seen or heard from her from that day to this. I loved her as I love my life.

Moses Grandy
Nichols, p. 20

The sale of slaves was generally carried out in one of two ways. The most informal was the sale of a slave by one slave owner to another, usually a friend on a neighboring plantation. The more usual method was through a slave trader, a man whose business was the buying and selling of slaves. The slave trader was no different from the cotton merchant, who bought cotton from the plantations and sold it at a profit. Most traders operated on a small scale, but the large traders made a handsome profit from their business. The famous Confederate general, Nathan Bedford Forrest, was the largest slave trader in Memphis, Tennessee, during the 1850's and in one year, made a profit of $96,000. The largest slave-trading firm was that of Franklin and Armfield. Their main office was in Alexandria, Virginia, and they had representatives in New Orleans, Louisiana; Natchez, Mississippi; Richmond and Warrenton, Virginia; and Frederick, Baltimore, and Easton, Maryland. By the time they retired from business, each of them had accumulated over half a million dollars.

The slave market was much like today's stock market. Prices fluctuated according to the economic climate and what was happening in the world. When times were good, selling was good. When times were bad, *selling was also. One particular event touched off a big rash of selling. That was the election of Abraham Lincoln as President in 1860.*

I was about twelve or fourteen years old when I was sold. A Negro trader came along and bought up all the slaves he could and took us to Louisiana. About this time many people sold their slaves because they felt the same thing was going to happen. One side thought the war would come and all the slaves get freed. All that felt this way about it began to sell so as to get the money. There were others that thought that in case of war the South would win. They held what slaves they had and even bought more.

I first found out that something was going to happen one day when I got back with the mail. My master took the paper I brought and after looking at it a minute he turned to mistress and said. "That old Yankee [Lincoln] has got elected and I am going to sell every nigger I got because he is going to free them."

When this news got out among the slaves there was a lot of disturbance and speculation on who would be the first one. I was a boy then big enough to work. I had a brother named John and a cousin by the name of Brutus. Both of them were sold and about three weeks later, it came my turn. On the day I left home, everything was sad among the slaves. My mother and father sung and prayed over me and told me how to get along in the world. I took my little bundle of clothes—a pair of slips, a shirt and a pair of jean pants—and went to give my mama my last farewell. I did not see her again until after the war.

I went on into Charleston. The prices usually went up on slaves in the fall of the year. Along in September what was known as nigger-traders started to coming around Charleston which was a great trading post. When selling time came we had to wash up and comb our hair so as to look as good as we could so as to demand a high price. Oh yes, we had to dress up and parade before the white folks until they picked the ones they wanted. I was sold along with a gang of others to a trader and he took us to Louisiana. There, I believe I was sold to the meanest man that God ever put breath in. Out of seventeen of us sold to him, only four of us got back home. Some died; others he killed.

Anonymous
Fisk, pp. 161–163

The slave trader's job was to sell to the highest bidder, not to see that each slave was sold to a kind master. The slave trader would come to a town with his slaves chained together into what was called a slave coffle. After advertising his presence in the vicinity and the "merchandise" he had to offer, he would hold an auction. Before the formal bidding began, the prospective buyers and curious non-buyers would get an opportunity to examine the "merchandise."

Every first Tuesday slaves were brought in from Virginia and sold on the block. The auctioneer was Cap'n Dorsey. E. M. Cobb was the slave-bringer. They would stand the slaves up on the block and talk about what a fine looking specimen of black manhood or womanhood they was, tell how healthy they was, look in their mouth and examine their teeth just like they was a horse, and talk about the kind of work they would be fit for and could do.

Morris Hillyer
Library of Congress

Once sold to a trader, the slaves were chained together and marched away, sleeping in the woods and fields at night, until they reached their destination some weeks later. Once there, the slave trader rested them for a few days, gave them new clothing, and sold them to new masters who would march them to the plantations. These would be their "homes" until they were sold again, escaped, or died.

The slave coffle was a familiar sight in many parts of the South.

The sun was shining out very hot, and in turning an angle of the road we encountered the following group: First, a little cart drawn by one horse, in which five or six half-naked black children were tumbled like pigs together.

The cart had no covering, and they seemed to have been broiled to sleep. Behind the cart marched three black women, with head, neck and breasts uncovered, and without shoes or stockings; next came three men, bareheaded, half naked, and chained together with an ox-chain. Last of all came a white man . . . on horseback, carrying pistols in his belt.

Written by J. K. Spaulding, Secretary of the
Navy under President Martin van Buren
The Negro in Virginia, p. 161

The slave coffles were usually seen on the dusty southern roads between the months of October and May, for it was during that time that the plantation work was the lightest and a slave on a new plantation had time to get adjusted before the hardest work season began. However, the slave coffle itself was sometimes such a torturous experience that many died on route and the survivors were hardly fit for anything but death by the time they reached the end.

My new master, whose name I did not hear, took me that same day across the Patuxent, where I joined fifty-one other slaves whom he had bought in Maryland. Thirty-two of these were men, and nineteen were women. The women were merely tied together with a rope, about the size of a bed cord, which was tied like a halter round the neck of each; but the men, of whom I was the stoutest and strongest, were very differently caparisoned. A strong iron collar was closely fitted by means of a padlock round each of our necks. A chain of iron about a hundred feet in length was passed through the hasp of each padlock, except at the two ends, where the hasps of the padlocks passed through a link of the chain. In addition to this, we were handcuffed in pairs, with iron staples and bolts, with a short chain about a foot long uniting the handcuffs and their wearers in pairs. In this manner, we were chained alternately by the right and left hand; and the poor man to whom I was thus ironed wept like an infant when the blacksmith with his heavy hammer fastened the ends of the bolts that kept the staples from slipping from our arms. For my own part, I felt indifferent to my fate. It appeared to me that the worst had come, and that no change of fortune could harm me.

Ball, p. 30

From the time the stars began to fade from the sky in the morning until they reappeared in the evening, the slaves worked at cotton and at everything else which had to be done on the plantation. Each day ended as the previous one had. Each one began as the previous one had. And each day expended itself as the previous one had.

Yes, sir, I can hear it now. Ol' overseer used to blow us out at sunrise on the conker shell—"Toot—toot!" Had to get your breakfast before day, 'cause you got to be in the field when the sun gets to showing itself about the trees.

West Turner
The Negro in Virginia, p. 60

I think about one hundred and sixty-eight assembled this morning at the sound of the horn—two or three being sick sent word to the overseer that they could not come. . . . The overseer then led off to the field with his horn in one hand and his whip in the other, we following—men, women and children, promiscuously—and a wretched looking troop we were. There was not an entire garment among us.

More than half of the gang was entirely naked. Several young girls who had arrived at puberty, wearing only the livery with which nature had ornamented them, and a great number of lads of an equal or superior age, appeared in the same custom. There was neither bonnet, cap, nor headdress of any kind amongst us, except the old straw hat that I wore. . . . Some of the men had old shirts and some ragged trousers, but no one wore both. Amongst the women several wore petticoats and many had shifts. Not one of the whole number wore both of these vestments. We walked nearly a mile through one vast cotton field before we arrived at the place of our intended day's labor.

Ball, pp. 128–129

An hour before daylight the horn is blown. Then the slaves arouse, prepare their breakfast,

fill a gourd with water, in another, deposit their dinner of cold bacon and corn cake, and hurry to the field again. It is an offense invariably followed by a flogging to be found at the quarters after daybreak. Then the fears and labors of another day begin and until its close there is no such thing as rest.

. . . with the exception of ten or fifteen minutes, which is given them at noon to swallow their allowance of cold bacon, they are not permitted to be a moment idle until it is too dark to see, and when the moon is full, they oftentimes labor till the middle of the night. They do not dare to stop even at dinner time, nor return to the quarters, however late it be, until the order to halt is given by the driver.

Northup, pp. 167, 170

When the order to halt was finally given, it was weighing-in time. Each slave was expected to pick at least two hundred pounds of cotton a day. That was the minimum for everybody. Generally the overseer learned how much more than that each slave could pick, and that was his daily task.

The day's work over in the field, the baskets are "toted," or in other words, carried to the ginhouse where the cotton is weighed. No matter how fatigued and weary he may be—no matter how much he longs for sleep and rest—a slave never approaches the ginhouse with his basket of cotton but with fear. If it falls short in weight—if he has not performed the full task appointed him—he knows that he must suffer. And if he has exceeded it by ten or twenty pounds, in all probability his master will measure the next day's task accordingly . . .

It was rarely that a day passed by without one or more whippings. This occurred at the time the cotton was weighed. The delinquent, whose weight had fallen short, was taken out, stripped, made to lie upon the ground, face downwards, when he received a punishment proportioned to his offense. It is the literal, unvarnished truth that the crack of the lash and the shrieking of the slaves can be heard from dark till bedtime on Epps' plantation, any day almost during the entire period of the cotton-picking season.

The number of lashes is graduated according to the nature of the case. Twenty-five are deemed a mere brush, inflicted, for instance, when a dry leaf or a piece of boll is found in the cotton, or when a branch is broken in the field. Fifty is ordinary penalty following all delinquencies of the next higher grade. One hundred is called severe; it is the punishment inflicted for the serious offense of standing idle in the field.

Northup, pp. 175–177, 179–180

Every night after work was over, us slaves had to gin cotton. Course they had the gin machine, but it never worked fast as us niggers would pick the cotton and was always breaking down.

See that foot? Wears a size fourteen shoe, I does, and near as I can recollect, it was the same size in them days. Well, sir, everybody had to gin a shoe full of cotton at night before going to bed. Ol' overseer would make the old women pack everybody's shoe tight with cotton and they got to see that shoe full. I had such a big pile that the others used to finish a long time before me. They all used to laugh at me and joke while they was ginnin', 'cause I got such a lot to do. I used to wrap my feet up in rags nights so as to keep 'em from gettin' any bigger, but it didn't help any.

West Turner
The Negro in Virginia, pp. 64–65

Yet once the slaves left the field, their work was far from finished.

Each one must then attend to his respective chores. One feeds the mules, another the swine—another cuts the wood, and so forth. Finally, at a late hour, they reach the quarters, sleepy and overcome with the long day's toil. Then a fire must be kindled in the cabin, the corn ground in the small hand-mill, and supper and dinner for the next day in the field prepared. All that is allowed them is corn and bacon, which is given out at the corncrib and smokehouse every Sunday morning. Each one receives, as his weekly allowance, three and a half pounds of bacon, and corn enough to make a peck of meal. That is all—no tea, coffee, sugar, and with the exception of a very scanty sprinkling now and then, no salt. . . .

When the corn is ground and fire is made, the bacon is taken down from the nail on which it hangs, a slice cut off and thrown upon the coals to broil. The majority of slaves have no knife, much less a fork. They cut their bacon with the axe at the woodpile. The corn meal is mixed with a little water, placed in the fire, and baked. When it is "done brown," the ashes are scraped off, and being placed upon a chip which answers for a table, the tenant of the slave hut is ready to sit down upon the ground to supper.

By this time it is usually midnight. The same fear of punishment with which they approach the ginhouse, possesses them again on lying down to get a snatch of rest. It is the fear of oversleeping in the morning. Such an offense would certainly be attended with not less than twenty lashes. With a prayer that he may be on his feet and wide awake at the first sound of the horn, he sinks to his slumbers nightly.

Northup, pp. 168–170

To the sound of the whip and the shrieks of black men and women, the slave owner and America grew wealthy. Yet it is all the more remarkable that even now the two hundred years of slavery are looked upon matter-of-factly and not as a time of unrelieved horror.

While there were many whites who recognized and fought against the inhumanity of slavery, the majority were much like the northerner who visited a southern plantation and described being awakened by the overseer's horn.

I soon hear the tramp of the laborers passing along the avenue. . . . All is soon again still as midnight. . . . I believe that I am the only one in the house that the bell disturbs; yet I do not begrudge the few minutes loss of sleep it causes me, it sounds so pleasantly in the half dreamy morning.

Anonymous
Stampp, p. 44

Perhaps the sound of other human beings marching to the fields for another day of forced labor was a "pleasant" one. Perhaps. But to those who made the sound, it was the dull monotonous sound of the living deaths in which they were held captive.

Paul Goble and Dorothy Goble

Red Hawk's Account of Custer's Last Battle: The Battle of the Little Bighorn, 25 June 1876

The authors have created a well-researched, historically accurate, and imaginative representation of Custer's last stand, told from the first-person viewpoint of a fictional participant in the battle—Red Hawk, a fifteen-year-old Oglala Sioux brave. As an old man, Red Hawk recounts his vivid memories of the Indian victory in what the white men call the Battle of the Little Bighorn. There is elegiac and ironic poignancy in Red Hawk's understanding that though the white men lost this battle, they won the war. In his words: "Once all the earth was ours; now there is only a small piece left which the White Men did not want." The Gobles based Red Hawk's story "on the published accounts of Sioux and Cheyenne participants in the Battle of the Little Bighorn." Their illustrations are based on the style of traditional tipe or buffalo robe paintings, which told of personal exploits in battle. The Gobles' work proves that when writing for young children, historical events need not be simplified into categories of "good guys" and "bad guys"; in the following selection the authors show the Indians fighting to preserve their way of life and the safety of their women and children, but in other sections we are shown Custer's men fighting and dying bravely. [From Paul Goble and Dorothy Goble, *Red Hawk's Account of Custer's Last Battle: The Battle of the Little Bighorn, 25 June 1876* (Pantheon, 1969).]

But suddenly we heard the far-off sound of the bugle and underneath the cloud of dust there was steel flashing in the sun and a long thin line of blue separated from the haze.

At once the cry went up: "Soldiers are coming! Horse-soldiers are attacking!" You could hear the cry going from camp to camp down the valley.

In an instant everyone was running in different directions. It was like an approaching thunderstorm when everyone runs to bring things in out of the rain and to set the tipi-flaps. But this was different, too. "Hurry! Hurry! Look after the children and the helpless ones!" The air was suddenly filled with dust and the sound of shouting and horses neighing. Dogs were running in every direction not knowing where to go. Boys ran to bring in the herds and the chiefs hurried from their tipis to help the frightened ones.

Warriors struggled to mount their horses which reared and stamped in excitement while women grabbed up their babies and shrieked for their children as they ran down the valley away from the oncoming soldiers. Old men and women with half-seeing eyes followed after, stumbling through the dust-filled air. Medicine Bear, too old to run, sat by his tipi as the bullets from the soldiers' guns already splintered the tipi-poles around him. "Warriors take courage!" he shouted. "It is better to die young for the people than to grow old."

I jumped on my horse and galloped to our tipi for my bow. My brother and little sister had already fled but my grandfather was there. He had braced my bow and was holding the quiver filled with the arrows which he had made for me. There was a look that I had not seen before in his eyes when he handed them to me. I think he too wanted to go where the fighting was. "Take courage, grandson!" he said. "The earth is all that lasts." He tightened the rope around my horse's nose and I joined the stream of warriors galloping across the Hunkpapa circle to hold off the soldiers. But it was strange: the soldiers had stopped before reaching the camp and they were off their horses and shooting at us.

Black Moon and some other Hunkpapa warriors were whipping their horses up and down in front of the soldiers and raising a great dust to hide from view the women and children fleeing down the valley. They were brave men. Then Sitting Bull was there. "Warriors," he shouted, "we have everything to fight for, and if we are defeated we shall have nothing to live for, therefore let us fight like brave men." Even then we saw through gaps in the dust that the line of blue-coated soldiers was falling back to the shelter of the trees by the river. "Crazy

Horse is coming! Crazy Horse is coming!" shouted the Oglalas sweeping down from the next camp.

"Crazy Horse is coming!" echoed the Hunkpapas, making way as he swept past us on his black horse painted with the white hail markings. A tomahawk in his hand gave him the power of the thunder and a war-bonnet of eagle feathers gave him the speed of the eagle. *"Hetchetu!* Be strong, my friends!" he shouted. "Remember the helpless ones!" With Crazy Horse leading, we all felt stronger; and with Black Moon and Gall there as well, we charged the soldiers.

Major Reno was frightened to advance farther when he saw the size of the Sioux encampment before him. By halting his troops he disobeyed Custer's orders and lost the advantage of surprise. As the warriors gathered in his front he was forced onto the defensive and withdrew to the timber beside the river to await Custer's attack. The soldiers with great superiority of firearms held their position, but Major Reno had never fought Indians before and he was unnerved by the ferocity of the Sioux attack.

The soldiers were well hidden among the trees close by where the river makes a big bend and they had many guns. The warriors in front charged up close to where the soldiers were and shot into the trees, but it was impossible to see what was happening in there. I saw my father and my uncle, Yellow Eagle, charging together once.

There was one brave Oglala with a war-bonnet and trailer of eagle feathers. I think it was Painted Thunder. I saw him gallop up alone to some bushes where a soldier was hiding and shoot into it. As he turned back towards us a white puff of smoke came from the bushes and his horse was shot. He jumped forwards as it went down and came back running, zig-zagging as he went, with his eagle feather trailer flying out behind him. It must have been the spirit of the eagle which saved him from the soldiers' bullets which were buzzing all around him. His medicine was strong that day.

Then suddenly everyone was shouting, "The soldiers are running! They are running!" and it was so. There was a line of soldiers galloping out of the trees farther up the river, running back from where they had come.

Hearing nothing from Custer and alarmed that he would be surrounded if he stayed longer where he was, Reno broke out from his position in panic, intending to rejoin Custer. Too late he realized his mistake. The soldiers' horses were tired with traveling since daybreak and within half a mile of leaving the safety of the trees the Sioux were abreast, forcing them back toward the river. The retreat became a rout. It was every man for himself in the dash across the open prairie to reach the high hills on the other side of the river.

"Hoka Hey! Hoka Hey!" It was like when the leader gives the sign to charge a herd of buffalo. At once everyone was shouting and all around me there was the shriek of eagle-bone whistles and the thunder of horses' hooves on the dry earth.

I whipped up my sorrel to keep beside my father and Yellow Eagle, but I soon lost them in the throng. Everywhere there was dust and everything moved in it like shadows in a dust storm. There were many ahead of me. I was riding close behind a warrior who had a shield slung across his back which flapped up and down as he galloped. There was red lightning painted on it with feathers fluttering from the center and I too felt the power and speed of the lightning.

And then I saw them. They were a short distance away on the side of our bows, bunched up close like frightened buffalo and running fast. *"Hey! Hey! Hey! Wasichu!"* I was excited. I had never seen soldiers so close before and they looked tall and strong on their big horses. Our bowstrings twanged and arrows flew like clouds of grasshoppers among their shadows, tumbling them from their saddles. I do not know if I hit any soldiers but I think I must have done. It was easy.

I saw Eagle Shield and Looks Twice range alongside a soldier with long hair on his cheeks and beat him across the back with their bows because it did not seem brave to kill him. But they killed him all the same, making the buffalo-killing cry as their arrows went through his body: *"Yi-hoo! Yi-hoo!"* It was more like chasing buffalo than fighting. It was the same with all the soldiers. They didn't turn to shoot because they were only thinking of running away. It went badly for them.

At the river it was worse. Their horses slid with stiff legs down the steep slope into the river.

I joined the warriors crowding there on the banks, shooting down at them all mixed up with their horses. It was terrible. It was like a sudden summer storm with a thunder and lightning of many guns and a darkness of dust and gunsmoke and bullets beating on the water like hailstones. Warriors jumped in as well to pull the soldiers from their saddles. They went under and came up again and again, floating down the river wrestling and fighting with knives and tomahawks. It was bad. Many died there in the river that day.

"Henala. It is enough. Let them go," cried Crazy Horse. And indeed it was. The soldiers had come to kill our women and children and we had driven them away. Many of them were dead and the rest were scrambling up the steep slopes across the river. *"Ho, hetchetu;* it is a great victory. My heart feels good," said Black Moon.

Robert Scott

Captain Scott's Last Expedition

Captain Scott, the famous Antarctic explorer, was the embodiment of courage in the face of hardship and bitter disappointment. In 1910 he sailed from New Zealand in an attempt to reach the South Pole. Scott set up headquarters at Cape Evans on Ross Island and established supply stations along his route toward the Pole. In October 1911 he started with sledges over the ice. Bad weather impeded his progress, and when he and his four companions finally arrived at the Pole on January 18, 1912, they found that Roald Amundsen had reached it only a month before. On the return trip, all five members of the party perished as a result of cruel weather and insufficient food. Later a searching party found the bodies and records in a tent that had been set up as a last camping place. The selection below, from Captain Scott's diary, tells of the last days of the expedition. [From Robert Scott, *Captain Scott's Last Expedition* (Dodd, Mead, 1913).]

The Last March

Sunday, March 11 (1912).—The sky completely overcast when we started this morning. We could see nothing, lost the tracks, and doubtless have been swaying a good deal since—3.1 miles for the forenoon—terribly heavy dragging—expected it. Know that 6 miles is about limit of our endurance now, if we get no help from wind or surfaces. We have 7 days' food and should be about 55 miles from One Ton Camp to-night, 6 × 7 = 42, leaving us 13 miles short of our distance, even if things get no worse. Meanwhile the season rapidly advances.

Monday, March 12.—We did 6.9 miles yesterday, under our necessary average. Things are left much the same, Oates not pulling much, and now with hands as well as feet pretty well useless. We did 4 miles this morning in 4 hours 20 minutes—we may hope for 3 this afternoon, 7 × 6 = 42. We shall be 47 miles from the depôt. I doubt if we can possibly do it. The surface remains awful, the cold intense, and our physical condition running down. God help us! Not a breath of favorable wind for more than a week, and apparently liable to head winds at any moment.

Wednesday, March 14.—No doubt about the going downhill, but everything going wrong for us. Yesterday we woke to a strong northerly wind with temp.—37°. Couldn't face it, so remained in camp (R.54) till 2, then did 5¼ miles. Wanted to march later, but party feeling the cold badly as the breeze (N) never took off entirely, and as the sun sank the temp. fell. Long time getting supper in the dark (R.55).

This morning started with southerly breeze, set sail and passed another cairn at good speed; halfway, however, the wind shifted to W. by S. or W.S.W., blew through our wind clothes and into our mits. Poor Wilson horribly cold, could not get off ski for some time. Bowers and I practically made camp, and when we got into the tent at last we were all deadly cold. Then temp. now midday down—43° and the wind strong. We *must* go on, but now the making of every camp must be more difficult and dangerous. It must be near the end, but a pretty merciful end. Poor Oates got it again in the foot. I shudder to think what it will be like tomorrow. It is only with greatest pains rest of us keep off frostbites. No idea there could be temperatures like this at this time of the year with such winds. Truly awful outside the tent. Must fight it out to the last biscuits, but can't reduce rations.

Friday, March 16, or *Saturday* 17.—Lost track of dates, but think the last is correct. Tragedy all along the line. At lunch, the day before yesterday, poor Titus Oates said he couldn't go on; he proposed we should leave him in his sleeping bag. That we could not do, and we induced him to come on, on the afternoon march. In spite of its awful nature for him he struggled on and we made a few miles. At night he was worse and we knew the end had come.

Should this be found I want these facts recorded. Oates' last thoughts were of his Mother, but immediately before he took pride in thinking that his regiment would be pleased with the bold way in which he met his death. We can testify to his bravery. He has borne intense suffering for weeks without complaint, and to the very last was able and willing to discuss outside objects. He did not—would not—give up hope till the very end. He was a brave soul. This was the end. He slept through the night before last, hoping not to awake; but he woke in the morning—yesterday. It was blowing a blizzard. He said, "I am just going outside and may be some-time." He went out into the blizzard and we have not seen him since.

I take this opportunity of saying that we have stuck to our sick companions to the last. In case of Edgar Evans, when absolutely out of food and he lay insensible, the safety of the remainder seemed to demand his abandonment, but Providence mercifully removed him at this critical moment. He died a natural death, and we did not leave him till two hours after his death. We knew that poor Oates was walking to his death, but though we tried to dissuade him, we knew it was the act of a brave man and an English gentleman. We all hope to meet the

end with a similar spirit, and assuredly the end is not far.

I can only write at lunch and then only occasionally. The cold is intense, −40° at midday. My companions are unendingly cheerful, but we are all on the verge of serious frostbites, and though we constantly talk of fetching through I don't think any of us believes it in his heart.

We are cold on the march, now, and at all times except meals. Yesterday we had to lay up for a blizzard and to-day we move dreadfully slowly. We are at No. 14 pony camp, only two pony marches from One Ton Depôt. We leave here our theodolite, a camera, and Oates' sleeping bags. Diaries, etc., and geological specimens carried at Wilson's special request, will be found with or on our sledge.

Sunday, March 18.—To-day, lunch, we are 21 miles from the depôt. Ill fortune presses, but better may come. We have had more wind and drift from ahead yesterday; had to stop marching; wind N.W., force 4. temp. −35°. No human being could face it, and we are worn out *nearly*.

My right foot has gone, nearly all the toes—two days ago I was proud possessor of best feet. These are the steps of my downfall. Like an ass I mixed a small spoonful of curry powder with my melted pemmican—it gave me violent indigestion. I lay awake and in pain all night; woke and felt done on the march; foot went and I didn't know it. A very small measure of neglect and have a foot which is not pleasant to contemplate. Bowers takes first place in condition, but there is not much to choose after all. The others are still confident of getting through—or pretend to be—I don't know! We have the last *half* fill of oil in our primus, and a very small quantity of spirit—this alone between us and thirst. The wind is fair for the moment, and that is perhaps a fact to help. The mileage would have seemed ridiculously small on our outward journey.

Monday, March 19.—Lunch. We camped with difficulty last night, and were dreadfully cold till after supper of cold pemmican and biscuit and half a pannikin of cocoa cooked over the spirit. Then, contrary to expectation, we got warm and all slept well. To-day we started in the usual dragging manner. Sledge dreadfully heavy. We are 15½ miles from the depôt and ought to get there in three days. What progress! We have two days' food but barely a day's fuel. All our feet are getting bad—Wilson's best, my right foot worst, left all right. There is no chance to nurse one's feet till we can get hot food into us. Amputation is the least I can hope for now, but will the trouble spread? That is the serious question. The weather doesn't give us a chance—the wind from N. to N.W., and −40° temp. to-day.

Wednesday, March 21.—Got within 11 miles of depôt Monday night, had to lay up all yesterday in severe blizzard. To-day forlorn hope. Wilson and Bowers going to depôt for fuel.

Thursday, March 22 and 23.—Blizzard bad as ever.—Wilson and Bowers unable to start—to-morrow last chance—no fuel and only one or two of food left—must be near the end. Have decided it shall be natural—we shall march for the depôt with or without our effects and die in our tracks.

Thursday, March 29.—Since the 21st we have had a continuous gale from W.S.W. and S.W. We had fuel to make two cups of tea apiece and bare food for two days on the 20th. Every day we have been ready to start for our depôt 11 *miles* away, but outside the door of the tent it remains a scene of whirling drift. I do not think we can hope for any better things now. We shall stick it out to the end, but we are getting weaker, of course, and the end cannot be far.

It seems a pity, but I do not think I can write more.—R. Scott.

*   *   *

For God's sake, look after our people.
R. Scott

Ellen Switzer

How Democracy Failed

As the philosopher George Santayana pointed out in his often-quoted aphorism, those who cannot remember the past are condemned to repeat it.

This selection begins with a conversation between two women in New York City in 1973, then takes us to Germany in the 1920s; Switzer emphasizes inflation as the link between the two periods. In her chilling portrait of Germany between the wars, Switzer alternates the oral history of interviews with passages of historical narrative. The author traveled throughout Germany conducting interviews with hundreds of people who were teenagers in the 1930s, as Switzer was herself. Their personal memories bring the time vividly to life, and the author's commentaries provide context. This and Switzer's frequently drawn parallels between the Germany that gave rise to Hitler and contemporary America make this a thought-provoking history, as absorbing as a novel, yet it should not be accepted uncritically. This book could be an excellent catalyst for exploring with older children and young people the use of point of view and the applications of history to current events and trends. [From Ellen Switzer, *How Democracy Failed* (Atheneum, 1975).]

Paper Money

"Lingering at the [shop] window was a luxury because shopping had to be done immediately. Even an additional minute meant an increase in price. One had to buy quickly because a rabbit, for example, might cost two million marks more by the time it took to walk into the store. A few million marks meant nothing, really. It was just that it meant more lugging. The packages of money needed to buy the smallest item had long since become too heavy for trouser pockets. They weighed many pounds. . . . People had to start carting their money around in wagons and knapsacks. I used a knapsack."

—George Grosz, German painter and cartoonist,
in his autobiography, A Little Yes and a Big No.

Food prices rise 4½ per cent in one week, an August 1973 headline in the *New York Post* announced bleakly. Two women in the appliance department of a large New York store were discussing the advantages and disadvantages of buying a freezer. "This inflation can't get much worse," one of the prospective purchasers said. "It's probably the worst price spiral in history." "Not exactly," said the other. "My grandmother grew up in Germany, and she remembers a time when you couldn't buy a postage stamp in the evening for what you had received in the morning for a week's work." "That sounds crazy," the other woman said. "If something like that happened, nothing would be worth anything anymore . . . there'd probably be some kind of revolution."

In a way, the concerned homemaker had echoed the words of an internationally known historian, Alan Bullock. "The real revolution in Germany was the inflation," he wrote.

Germany's inflation began gradually, as more goods became available at the end of the war and Germany's industrial production could not keep up with consumer demand. Also, much of her raw materials went as reparations to the Allies, especially France. At one point the French government threatened to invade because Germany had not been able to deliver 200,000 telephone poles on schedule. The German government's protest that there just were not enough trees left to make the deliveries only brought further threats.

There was a great deal of unemployment, especially among the soldiers who had been released from the army, and Germany's new democratic government was pledged to provide some social services. The only way German economists saw to tackle the problem was to print more and more money . . . which became worth less and less.

As inflation took over, the pace of the monetary decline quickened. In the summer of 1922 the mark was worth 400 to the American dollar, by January 1, 1923, 7,000 marks were needed to get one dollar, and by July of the same year, 160,000 marks. Eventually billions and trillions of marks could not purchase dollars, or British pounds, or French francs. The German mark was worth only as much as the paper it was printed on . . . and the paper was of very poor quality at that.

As people completely lost faith in their currency, they demanded to be paid weekly, and then daily, and then hourly. Factories closed down so that people could spend their money as soon as they had received it. Symphony orchestras and plays interrupted their rehearsals because the artists demanded their money at noon to rush to the nearest store to buy anything that could still be bought with money. They

went out with bags full of banknotes (George Grosz's knapsack was definitely not an exaggeration) and came back with anything that was available, whether they needed it or not. According to stories of people who lived through those times, men and women bought shoes in sizes they could not wear, knick-knacks they could not use and didn't even like, twenty-pound bags of salt or sugar they would not be able to eat in years. . . . Anything was better than that worthless paper, which the German government printing presses kept turning out. Soon government presses couldn't do the job fast enough any longer . . . newspapers were asked to help out in getting the printing job done.

"At Ullstein newspaper headquarters . . . officials requisitioned presses to turn out increasingly worthless paper," Otto Friedrich tells in *Before the Deluge.* "All doors [at the newspaper] were locked and officials from the Reichsbank [the government-operated German banking system] were placed on guard. . . . Round the machines sat elderly women, staring fascinated at those parts of the machines from which the finished products came pouring out. It was the duty of these women to see that these billion mark notes were placed in the right baskets and handed to the officials. They had to keep an eye on every single billion. Officials are so funny sometimes."

George Grosz, who carried his notes around in a knapsack, observed that although many people could not afford even the basic necessities of life during this tragic and confusing period, others seemed to become rich. They were the hoarders.

"Once, at midnight, quite by accident, I met someone who in ordinary life was a cook. In secret, however, he was a magician," Grosz wrote. "We began to discuss the only popular subject of the day: food. Mornings, at breakfast of turnip coffee, mildewed bread and synthetic honey, one discussed lunch. At lunch, of turnip cutlets, muscle pudding and turnip coffee, one discussed a dinner of muscle wurst, gray-green rolls with synthetic honey and cold turnip coffee. Since we were always hungry, our imaginations supplied everything that was lacking.

"In a charming manner of speech, like all

magicians, he said that, inasmuch as I was an artist and he liked me, he would help me. He considered that the stupid thing about 'food fantasies' was that they remained unsatisfied.''

The cook took Grosz to what seemed to be an uninhabited house, where there were pails of butter, marmalade, Russian caviar, hams and other delicacies piled to the ceiling. "Money has no value anymore . . . so I have been storing things everywhere, even in the corridor," he told the painter. After extracting a promise that he would never mention the treasure trove, he fed his new friend. Grosz kept his word. He did not tell the story until long after the cook had died. But some of his bitterest cartoons show overweight men and women gorging themselves on delicacies, while starving children watch through the window.

Other Germans remember that during those crazy days things became more important than ideas, or work, or honor.

An art dealer in Berlin remembers that, in a strange way, his interest in collecting was fueled by Germany's inflation. "My father was an unsuccessful artist," he said. "He worked in a factory during the day and painted landscapes at night. During the inflation, there wasn't much point in working in the factory, since the paper money the men were paid was worthless. So my father painted all the time. He would turn out twenty or thirty landscapes in one morning, and set up shop at a street corner at noon when the office and factory workers rushed out with their bags of money for a lunch break. He'd probably sold ten pictures before in his whole life, mostly to relatives. But, in 1923, even a picture of a cow grazing in the sunset painted on canvas was worth more than the picture of a government official printed on cheap paper, which passed for money in those days. So he usually sold out everything he had worked on during the morning. Then he'd rush to the nearest food store, buy what little food was available, and then rush to the post office to buy the latest editions of million, billion and trillion mark stamps. He was convinced that some of these stamps would be valuable some day, since so few were printed at one time. After all, a 1 million mark stamp printed today would not be enough to mail a postcard tomor-

row. My father never put those stamps on letters. He put them away in a bureau drawer. Sure enough, several years after the inflation was over (and my father was back in the factory, selling an occasional painting to a great-aunt), those stamps had indeed become valuable. They helped put me through the university."

He points out that, perhaps subconsciously, he became convinced that collecting things might be more profitable than making things. "A psychiatrist once told me that that's why I'm a succesful art dealer," he said.

However, the incredible situation had a more profound effect on a great many Germans. Blue-collar workers and middle-class families lost faith in many of the virtues they had prized. What good was thrift, if a man's lifetime savings could be wiped out overnight? What good was honesty, if the honest worker starved while the dishonest hoarder (Grosz's "magician") prospered? How could anyone trust a government that allowed these terrible events to happen? What good was democracy when it provided neither security, nor stability, nor hope?

None of the men and women who told of their experiences in the last years of the German democracy and the first years of the Nazi era can remember, from personal experience, the weeks and months of the great inflation. It happened before most of them were born. But not one of those interviewed failed to mention it as a cause for the failure of Germany's democratic experiment. The inflation ended almost as suddenly as it began, but it had shaken many families completely. When Hitler came to power, many of those who told their stories mentioned that their parents said: "Well, I certainly don't agree with everything that that man says . . . but he won't allow that kind of inflation to happen, ever again."

Toshi Maruki

Hiroshima No Pika

Every modern child has to live with the horrifying prospect of a nuclear holocaust. This book treats a difficult to comprehend and frightening historical event honestly. The uncompromising truth of its text and illustrations, recording one family's experience in the August 6, 1945, nuclear bombing of Hiroshima, may be hard to face, but the last sentence provides hope for a new generation. It is told from the point of view of a seven-year-old girl in an account that balances emotionally charged, expressionistic paintings and a restrained text. Although a picture book in format, the content is appropriate for older children. Because of its subject and lack of historical context, the book has been the center of lively controversy. The intent of the author, however, was not to write a study of the events leading to the dropping of atomic bombs on Japan, but to shape the collective memories of many of the victims into the single story of one young girl's immediate perceptions. The book has been the recipient of several awards, including the Mildred L. Batchelder Award for translation in 1983. [Complete text from *Hiroshima No Pika*, written and illustrated by Toshi Maruki (Lothrop, Lee & Shepard, 1980).]

That morning in Hiroshima the sky was blue and cloudless. The sun was shining. Streetcars had begun making rounds, picking up people who were on their way to work. Hiroshima's seven rivers flowed quietly through the city. The rays of the midsummer sun glittered on the surface of the rivers.

In Tokyo, Osaka, Nagoya, and many other Japanese cities there had been air raids. The people of Hiroshima wondered why their city had been spared. They had done what they could to prepare for an air raid. To keep fire from spreading, they had torn down old buildings and widened streets. They had stored water and decided where people should go to avoid the bombs. Everyone carried small bags of medicine and, when they were out of doors, wore air-raid hats or hoods to protect their heads.

Mii was seven years old and lived in Hiroshima with her mother and father. She and her parents were breakfasting on sweet potatoes, which had been brought in the day before by cousins who lived in the country. Mii was very hungry this morning, and exclaimed about how good the sweet potatoes tasted. Her father agreed that they made a delicious breakfast, though they weren't the rice he preferred.

Then it happened. A sudden, terrible light flashed all around. The light was bright orange—then white, like thousands of lightning bolts all striking at once. Violent shock waves

followed, and buildings trembled and began to collapse.

Moments before the Flash, United States Air Force bomber *Enola Gay* had flown over the city and released a top-secret explosive. The explosive was an atomic bomb, which had been given the name "Little Boy" by the B-29's crew.

"Little Boy" fell on Hiroshima at 8:15 on the morning of August 6, 1945.

Mii was knocked unconscious by the force of the Flash, and when she woke up everything around her was still and dark. At first she couldn't move, and she heard crackling sounds that frightened her. Far off in the darkness she could see a red glow. Her mother's voice penetrated the dark, calling her.

Mii struggled out from under the heavy boards that had fallen on top of her. Her mother rushed to her and drew her close and hugged her. "We must hurry," she said. "The fire . . . your father is caught in the flames!"

Mii and her mother faced the fire and began to pray. Then Mii's mother leaped into the flames and pulled her husband to safety.

Mii watched as her mother examined her father. "He's hurt badly," she said. She untied the sash from her kimono and wrapped it around her husband's body as a bandage. Then she did something amazing. She lifted him onto her back and, taking Mii by the hand, started running.

"The river. We must reach the river," Mother directed.

The three of them tumbled down the riverbank and into the water. Mii lost hold of her mother's hand.

"Mii-chan! Hang on to me!" her mother shouted.

There were crowds of people fleeing the fire. Mii saw children with their clothes burned away, lips and eyelids swollen. They were like ghosts, wandering about, crying in weak voices. Some people, all their strength gone, fell face down on the ground, and others fell on top of them. There were heaps of people everywhere.

Mii and her mother and father continued their escape and crossed another river. When they reached the far bank, Mii's mother put her husband down and collapsed on the ground beside him.

Mii felt something moving past her feet. Hop . . . hop. . . . It was a swallow. Its wings were burned, and it couldn't fly. Hop . . . hop . . .

She saw a man floating slowly down the river. Floating behind him was the body of a cat.

Mii turned and saw a young woman holding a baby and crying. "We escaped this far and then I stopped to feed him," she said. "But he wouldn't take his milk. He's dead." The young woman, still holding her baby, waded into the river. She waded deeper and deeper, until Mii couldn't see her anymore.

The sky grew dark, and there was a rumble of thunder. It began to rain. Though it was midsummer, the air turned very cold, and the rain was black and sticky.

Then a rainbow arched across the sky, pushing the dark away. It gleamed brightly over the dead and wounded.

Mii's mother lifted Father onto her back again. She took Mii by the hand, and they began to run. Fire was moving toward them at a terrible speed. They ran among piles of cracked roof tiles, over fallen telephone poles and wires. Houses were burning on every side. They came to another river, and once in the water Mii felt suddenly sleepy. Before she knew it, she had gulped down mouthfuls of water. Her mother pulled her head above the water. They reached the other side and kept running.

At long last they reached the beach outside Hiroshima. They could see Miyajima island, wrapped in purple mist, across the water. Mii's mother had hoped they could cross over to the island by boat. Miyajima was covered with beautiful pine and maple trees and surrounded by clear water. Thinking that safety was not far away, Mii and her mother and father fell asleep.

The sun went down. Night came and went. The sun rose, then set. It rose and set again, then rose for the third time.

"Please, tell me what day it is," Mii's mother asked a man who was passing by. He had been looking over the people lying on the beach.

"It's the ninth," he answered.

Mother counted on her fingers. "Four days!" she cried out in amazement. "We've been here four days?"

Mii started to cry softly. An old woman who was lying nearby sat up and took a rice ball out of her bag and gave it to Mii. When Mii took it from her, the woman fell down again. This time she didn't move.

"Mii-chan! You're still holding your chopsticks!" her mother exclaimed. "Here, let me have them." But Mii's hand wouldn't open. Her mother pried her fingers open one by one. Four days after the bomb, Mii let go of her chopsticks.

Firemen came from a nearby village to help them. Soldiers came and took the dead away. A school building that was still standing had been turned into a hospital, and they took Father there. There were no doctors, no medicine, no bandages—only shelter.

With Father as safe as possible in the hospital, Mii and her mother decided to go back into the city to see if anything was left of their home. There were neither grass nor trees nor houses left in Hiroshima. A burnt-out wasteland stretched before them as far as the eye could see. Mii and her mother found everything destroyed. The only thing left to remind them they had ever lived there was Mii's rice bowl. Bent and broken, it still contained some sweet potatoes.

That day, August 9, 1945, as Mii and her mother looked at the rubble that had been Hiroshima, an atomic bomb was dropped on Nagasaki. And there, as in Hiroshima, thousands of people died, and anyone who survived was left homeless. Among the victims, in addition to the Japanese, were people from many other countries, such as Korea, China, Russia, Indonesia, and the United States.

The atomic bomb was unlike any explosive ever used before. The destruction on impact was greater than thousands of conventional bombs exploding all at once, and it also contaminated the area with radiation that caused deaths and illnesses for many years following the explosion.

Illustration by Toshi Maruki, from *Hiroshima No Pika,* written and illustrated by Toshi Maruki. Copyright © 1980 by Toshi Maruki. By permission of Lothrop, Lee & Shepard Books (a division of William Morrow & Co.).

Mii never grew after that day. Many years have passed, and she is still the same size she was when she was seven years old. "It is because of the Flash from the bomb," her mother says. Sometimes Mii complains that her head itches, and her mother parts her hair, sees something shiny, and pulls it out of her scalp with a pair of tweezers. It's a sliver of glass, imbedded when the bomb went off years ago, that has worked its way to the surface.

Mii's father had seven wounds in his body, but they healed and for a while he thought he was getting well. Then one day in autumn after the Flash, his hair fell out and he began coughing blood. Purple spots appeared all over his body, and he died.

Many of the people who had said, "Thank God, our lives were spared," later became ill with radiation sickness. Though this happened in 1945, some of these people are still in hospitals. There is no cure for their disease.

Every year on August 6 the people of Hiroshima inscribe the names of loved ones who died because of the bomb on lanterns. The lanterns are lit and set adrift on the seven rivers that flow through Hiroshima. The rivers flow slowly to the sea, carrying the lanterns in memory of those who died.

Mii, who is still like a small child after all these years, writes "Father" on one lantern and "The Swallow" on another. Her mother's hair has now turned white, and she watches sorrowfully as her daughter sets the lanterns afloat.

"It can't happen again," she says, "if no one drops the bomb."

For centuries we have dreamed of intelligent beings throughout this solar system. We have been wrong; the earth we have taken for granted and treated so casually—the sunflower-shaded forest of man's infancy—is an incredibly precious planetary jewel. We are all of us—man, beast, and growing plant—aboard a space ship of limited dimensions whose journey began so long ago that we have abandoned one set of gods and are now in the process of substituting another in the shape of science.[1]

15 Science

I t is obvious that quality writing is a primary requirement in works for children in the behavioral and social sciences; this is a less obvious requirement in the biological or physical sciences, but a book on physics may, like anything else, be written well or written badly. The criteria for evaluating science books for children, regardless of the discipline, share many specific attributes with the criteria for judging other types of nonfiction: the authority of the writer, the accuracy and currency of the information, the logic of organization and presentation, the clarity and fluency of writing, the attractiveness of format and design, the avoidance of oversimplification, and, above all, a respect for children. Other criteria to apply include the quality of appendices, such as bibliographies, glossaries, and indexes, and the accuracy of illustrative materials — appropriately placed and clearly labeled drawings, photographs, diagrams, and graphs. In the biological sciences particularly there should be careful avoidance of anthropomorphism (the attribution of human characteristics to the natural world) and teleology (the belief that natural phenomena are determined by an overall purpose in nature) — two errors in concept and approach prevalent in many of the less professional science books for children. Millicent Selsam, a

1. Loren Eisley, *The Invisible Pyramid* (Scribner's, 1970), p. 152.

writer of science for children, offers a larger perspective when she states: "By good science books . . . I mean those that show the methods of science at work, that elucidate basic principles of science and are not a mere assembly of facts, that convey something of the beauty and excitement of science, and that interest young people in thinking up good questions for new young scientists to test by experiment."[2]

Selsam also points out the fundamental similarity between the child and the scientist: curiosity. "It is natural," she says, "for children to be curious and to ask questions. This is also characteristic of most scientists at work. They might be said to have maintained a child's curiosity about the world in which they live, and their mode of working is to ask questions, even as children do."[3] And children's endless fascination with the physical and human world can be stimulated and satisfied not only by direct observation but by books of science.

A voyage of discovery to an unknown part of the world is no more full of strange and curious objects than is the immediate environment of a child. In the beginning, the child learns through observation; later, more abstract thoughts and conceptions develop. A child begins by being curious about *specific* things, so that a narrative describing the life of a particular pelican is more attractive to a young reader than a generalized study about the ecological disruption of the species. Teachers of science in elementary schools encourage children to make observations, to alter conditions, to deduce and infer. Although books of science cannot provide this laboratory situation, they can direct and inspire readers to set up their own experiments: *Science Experiments You Can Eat* (1972) and *More Science Experiments You Can Eat* (1979) by Vicki Cobb guide the young reader in converting the kitchen into a laboratory. Seymour Simon has a number of books devoted to simple science experiments, as have Harry Milgrom and Harris A. Stone. Christopher Reynolds, in *The Pond on My Windowsill* (1969), gives exact directions for the creation of a similar pond; Roger Caras uses a parallel approach in *A Zoo in Your Room* (1975). Many other books for children are original, precise, and diverting guides to setting up apparatus and arranging direct contact with natural phenomena.

Children are fascinated by animals. Wild and domestic animals, dinosaurs, and sea monsters are subjects on which they continually search for information in books. The great diversity of these books is especially pronounced. Joy Adamson's life adventure with Elsa the lioness is one in which children readily participate. *A Mouse Named Mus* (1972) and *Wild Mouse* (1976) by Irene Brady have a similar emotional appeal. Carol Fenner's *Gorilla, Gorilla* (1973) gives a poignant portrayal of a caged gorilla, augmented by the softly textured illustrations of Symeon Shimin. Fenner uses a story structure and rich, poetic prose, as do such other writers of animal life stories as Berniece Freschet and Victor Sheffer.

Illustration in diverse media is a valuable adjunct to books about animals. Lilo Hess, a renowned photographer, uses her camera with sensitive and imaginative skill in *The Curious Raccoons* (1968) and other books. Ugo Mochi's unique, graceful paper-cut silhouettes effectively dramatize *A Natural History of Giraffes* (1973) and *A Natural History of Zebras* (1976) by Dorcas MacClintock. Not

---

2. Millicent Selsam, "Writing about Science for Children," in *A Critical Approach to Children's Literature,* ed. Sara Innis Fenwick (The University of Chicago Press, 1967), p. 99.
3. Selsam, p. 96.

mere embellishments, the illustrations preceded and genuinely inspired the writing of the text. Similarly, Joanna Cole's excellent texts are perfectly complemented by Jerome Wexler's photographs, used in conjunction with diagrams, in their outstanding series that includes *A Horse's Body* (1981) and *A Cat's Body* (1982). Iela and Enzo Mari's wordless picture books — *The Chicken and the Egg* (1969) and *The Apple and the Moth* (1970) — involve preschoolers emotionally, focusing their attention and imagination on the unfolding graphic image.

Ecological studies presenting the interdependency of plant and animal life also appeal to children. From the science picture books of Alvin Tresselt (*The Beaver Pond,* 1970) and Jean George (*All Upon a Stone,* 1971, and *All Upon a Sidewalk,* 1974) to Judith and Herbert Kohl's sophisticated *The View from the Oak: The Private Worlds of Other Creatures* (1977), science writers explore with children the complexity of the biological community — the interrelatedness of all living things.

Sexual reproduction and the workings of the human body are also subjects of great interest to children. Geraldine Lux Flanagan's *Window into an Egg: Seeing Life Begin* (1969) observes with outstanding photographs the development of an embryo into a baby chick. The development of a human embryo is photographically documented in Lennart Nilsson's *How Was I Born?* (1975) and Camilla Jessel's *The Joy of Birth* (1982). Alvin and Virginia Silverstein consider different aspects of physiology in their clear, straightforward Systems of the Body series, while the most ingenious and fascinating pop-up book ever produced for children may be Jonathan Miller's *The Human Body* (1983), a tour de force of paper engineering combined with a lucid text.

Books concerned with the physical sciences and technology vary just as widely in scope, treatment, and format as do those in the biological sciences. Malcolm Weiss's *Sky Watchers of Ages Past* (1982) presents the world of space as seen through the eyes of ancient astronomers. Equally illuminating are the views of worlds found under the microscope or in the fossils of the earth.

David Hawkins, a scientist and designer of science education for children, claims that "there's been a systematic tendency to devalue children's thing-oriented interests against their person-oriented interests. It is assumed that the latter are basic, the former derivative. All I would like to say is that I think the interest in *things* is a perfectly real, perfectly independent and autonomous interest which is there in young children just as genuinely as the interest in persons is there. And some children are *only* able to develop humanly by first coming to grips in an exploratory and involved way with the inanimate world."[4] For children with thing-oriented interests, there are a wealth of books — filled with pulleys, pendulums, weights, gliders, gadgets, models, machines, electrical contraptions, computers, and rockets.

Kathryn Wolff, in discussing the reviewing criteria for science books used by the prestigious journal *Science Books and Films,* mentions the imperative that books in the physical sciences and technology be more than entertaining or descriptive:

Books about rockets, missiles, airplanes, atomic reactors will entertain but are not educationally worthwhile unless they introduce the reader to fundamental scientific laws and principles — and to the painstaking underlying research and experimentation. Such books should demonstrate to the reader how and why science and mathematics courses are basic prepara-

4. David Hawkins, *The Informed Vision: Essays on Learning and Human Nature* (Agathon, 1974), pp. 60–61.

tion for those who want to be scientists, technologists, doctors, engineers, and space travelers.[5]

Jacob Bronowski and Millicent Selsam succeed in showing the principles of science in operation in their imaginative *Biography of an Atom* (1963). And James Dugan, in *Undersea Explorer* (1957), inspires children to the professions of oceanography and underwater archaeology through his balanced treatment of the excitement and hard work involved in Jacques Cousteau's explorations.

Science and the humanities are joining forces today in a reflective assessment of technology and the quality of life. Ecology and conservation, now dominant subjects in children's science books, are treated for all ages by such writers as Laurence Pringle, Jean George, and Robert McClung. "The present world-wide effort to save the quality of the environment transcends the problem posed by pollution and by the depletion of natural resources. It constitutes rather the beginning of a crusade to recapture certain sensory and emotional values, the need for which is universal and immutable because it is inscribed in the genetic code of the species."[6] This statement by René Dubos, microbiologist and experimental pathologist at Rockefeller University in New York, points to the possibility of a new alliance of science with the arts—for science must consider human values if we are to survive on our "planetary jewel."[7]

5. Kathryn Wolff, "AAAS Science Books: A Selection Tool," *Library Trends,* 22 (1974), 456.
6. René Dubos, *Beast or Angel? Choices That Make Us Human* (Scribner's, 1974), p. 149.
7. Eisley, p. 152.

Jane van Lawick-Goodall

In the Shadow of Man

In these impressions of her first real acquaintance with the chimpanzees that she was to observe for almost ten years, Jane van Lawick-Goodall describes her feelings about the individual qualities of these animals, feelings that were borne out in her later experiences with them. [From Jane van Lawick-Goodall, *In the Shadow of Man* (Houghton Mifflin, 1971).]

First Observations

During that month I really came to know the country well, for I often went on expeditions from the Peak, sometimes to examine nests, more frequently to collect specimens of the chimpanzees' food plants, which Bernard Verdcourt had kindly offered to identify for me. Soon I could find my way around the sheer ravines and up and down the steep slopes of three valleys—the home valley, the Pocket, and Mlinda Valley—as well as a taxi driver finds his way about in the main streets and byways of London. It is a period I remember vividly, not only because I was beginning to accomplish something at last, but also because of the delight I felt in being completely by myself. For those who love to be alone with nature I need add nothing further; for those who do not, no words of mine could ever convey, even in part, the almost mystical awareness of beauty and eternity that accompanies certain treasured moments. And, though the beauty was always there, those moments came upon me unaware: when I was watching the pale flush preceding dawn; or looking up through the rustling leaves of some giant forest tree into the greens and browns and black shadows that occasionally ensnared a bright fleck of the blue sky; or when I stood, as darkness fell, with one hand on the still-warm trunk of a tree and looked at the sparkling of an early moon on the never still, sighing water of the lake.

One day, when I was sitting by the trickle of water in Buffalo Wood, pausing for a moment in the coolness before returning from a scramble in Mlinda Valley, I saw a female bushbuck moving slowly along the nearly dry streambed.

Occasionally she paused to pick off some plant and crunch it. I kept absolutely still, and she was not aware of my presence until she was little more than ten yards away. Suddenly she tensed and stood staring at me, one small forefoot raised. Because I did not move, she did not know what I was—only that my outline was somehow strange. I saw her velvet nostrils dilate as she sniffed the air, but I was downwind and her nose gave her no answer. Slowly she came closer, and closer—one step at a time, her neck craned forward—always poised for instant flight. I can still scarcely believe that her nose actually touched my knee; yet if I close my eyes I can feel again, in imagination, the warmth of her breath and the silken impact of her skin. Unexpectedly I blinked and she was gone in a flash, bounding away with loud barks of alarm until the vegetation hid her completely from my view.

It was rather different when, as I was sitting on the Peak, I saw a leopard coming toward me, his tail held up straight. He was at a slightly lower level than I, and obviously had no idea I was there. Ever since arrival in Africa I had had an ingrained, illogical fear of leopards. Already, while working at the Gombe, I had several times nearly turned back when, crawling through some thick undergrowth, I had suddenly smelled the rank smell of cat. I had forced myself on, telling myself that my fear was foolish, that only wounded leopards charged humans with savage ferocity.

On this occasion, though, the leopard went out of sight as it started to climb up the hill—the hill on the peak of which I sat. I quickly hastened to climb a tree, but halfway there I realized that leopards can climb trees. So I uttered a sort of halfhearted squawk. The leopard, my logical mind told me, would be just as frightened of me if he knew I was there. Sure enough, there was a thudding of startled feet and then silence. I returned to the Peak, but the feeling of unseen eyes watching me was too much. I decided to watch for the chimps in Mlinda Valley. And, when I returned to the Peak several hours later, there, on the very rock which had been my seat, was a neat pile of leopard dung. He must have watched me go and then, very carefully, examined the place where such a frightening creature had been and tried to exterminate my alien scent with his own.

As the weeks went by the chimpanzees became less and less afraid. Quite often when I was on one of my food-collecting expeditions I came across chimpanzees unexpectedly, and after a time I found that some of them would tolerate my presence provided they were in fairly thick forest and I sat still and did not try to move closer than sixty to eighty yards. And so, during my second month of watching from the Peak, when I saw a group settle down to feed I sometimes moved closer and was thus able to make more detailed observations.

It was at this time that I began to recognize a number of different individuals. As soon as I was sure of knowing a chimpanzee if I saw it again, I named it. Some scientists feel that animals should be labeled by numbers—that to name them is anthropomorphic—but I have always been interested in the *differences* between individuals, and a name is not only more individual than a number but also far easier to remember. Most names were simply those which, for some reason or other, seemed to suit the individuals to whom I attached them. A few chimps were named because some facial expression or mannerism reminded me of human acquaintances.

The easiest individual to recognize was old Mr. McGregor. The crown of his head, his neck, and his shoulders were almost entirely devoid of hair, but a slight frill remained around his head rather like a monk's tonsure. He was an old male—perhaps between thirty and forty years of age (the longevity record for a captive chimp is forty-seven years). During the early months of my acquaintance with him, Mr. McGregor was somewhat belligerent. If I accidentally came across him at close quarters he would threaten me with an upward and backward jerk of his head and a shaking of branches before climbing down and vanishing from my sight. He reminded me, for some reason, of Beatrix Potter's old gardener in *The Tale of Peter Rabbit.*

Ancient Flo with her deformed, bulbous nose and ragged ears was equally easy to recognize. Her youngest offspring at that time were two-year-old Fifi, who still rode everywhere on her

mother's back, and her juvenile son, Figan, who was always to be seen wandering around with his mother and little sister. He was then about six years old; it was approximately a year before he would attain puberty. Flo often traveled with another old mother, Olly. Olly's long face was also distinctive; the fluff of hair on the back of her head—though no other feature—reminded me of my aunt, Olwen. Olly, like Flo, was accompanied by two children, a daughter younger than Fifi, and an adolescent son about a year older than Figan.

Then there was William, who, I am certain, must have been Olly's blood brother. I never saw any special signs of friendship between them, but their faces were amazingly alike. They both had long upper lips that wobbled when they suddenly turned their heads. William had the added distinction of several thin, deeply etched scar marks running down his upper lip from his nose.

Two of the other chimpanzees I knew well by sight at that time were David Graybeard and Goliath. Like David and Goliath in the Bible, these two individuals were closely associated in my mind because they were very often together. Goliath, even in those days of his prime, was not a giant, but he had a splendid physique and the springy movements of an athlete. He probably weighed about one hundred pounds. David Graybeard was less afraid of me from the start than were any of the other chimps. I was always pleased when I picked out his handsome face and well-marked silvery beard in a chimpanzee group, for with David to calm the others, I had a better chance of approaching to observe them more closely.

Before the end of my trial period in the field I made two really exciting discoveries—discoveries that made the previous months of frustration well worth while. And for both of them I had David Graybeard to thank.

One day I arrived on the Peak and found a small group of chimps just below me in the upper branches of a thick tree. As I watched I saw that one of them was holding a pink-looking object from which he was from time to time pulling pieces with his teeth. There was a female and a youngster and they were both reaching out toward the male, their hands actually touching his mouth. Presently the female picked up a piece of the pink thing and put it to her mouth: it was at this moment that I realized the chimps were eating meat.

After each bite of meat the male picked off some leaves with his lips and chewed them with the flesh. Often, when he had chewed for several minutes on this leafy wad, he spat out the remains into the waiting hands of the female. Suddenly he dropped a small piece of meat, and like a flash the youngster swung after it to the ground. Even as he reached to pick it up the undergrowth exploded and an adult bushpig charged toward him. Screaming, the juvenile leaped back into the tree. The pig remained in the open, snorting and moving backward and forward. Soon I made out the shapes of three small striped piglets. Obviously the chimps were eating a baby pig. The size was right and later, when I realized that the male was David Graybeard, I moved closer and saw that he was indeed eating piglet.

For three hours I watched the chimps feeding. David occasionally let the female bite pieces from the carcass and once he actually detached a small piece of flesh and placed it in her outstretched hand. When he finally climbed down there was still meat left on the carcass; he carried it away in one hand, followed by the others.

Of course I was not sure, then, that David Graybeard had caught the pig for himself, but even so, it was tremendously exciting to know that these chimpanzees actually ate meat. Previously scientists had believed that although these apes might occasionally supplement their diet with a few insects or small rodents and the like they were primarily vegetarians and fruit eaters. No one had suspected that they might hunt larger mammals.

Dorcas MacClintock

A Natural History of Giraffes

This book won the Children's Science Books Award presented by the New York Academy of Sciences in 1973. Both readable and scholarly, it is an excellent example of fine organization and writing in nonfiction for children. The author, who has worked at the American Museum of Natural History and the California Academy of Sciences, marshals her facts with authoritative familiarity and presents them with clarity and spirit, covering all aspects of the physiology, social behavior, and ecological network of the giraffe. The accompanying illustrations by Ugo Mochi are unusual cutout silhouettes and add graphic interest to the format and presentation. [From Dorcas MacClintock, *A Natural History of Giraffes* (Scribner's, 1973).]

The Calf

At birth a giraffe calf is about six feet tall (top of head) and weighs between 100 and 150 pounds. Its proportions are less exaggerated than those of an adult giraffe. Its upright, S-shaped neck is shorter. The bristly mane runs down onto its back and sometimes has an extension on the rump. Two horn cartilages, flat-lying to facilitate the calf's birth, can be felt under the skin on the head. Each is topped by a tuft of black hair. During the first days of the calf's life the horns actually move about on the skull, to which they are attached only by connective tissue. Very soon the horns become erect, as bone begins to replace cartilage. The calf's short hair has a woolly texture. On each flank a spiral hair tract or whorl is conspicuous. Giraffes have no inguinal fold, the skin-fold connecting flank and hindquarters.

Spots of calves tend to be paler than those of older giraffes, and, permanent though these spots are, they may change shape as the calf grows. Often a calf's spots have pale centers, while spots of older giraffes may have dark central streaks. Pigmentation, or the deposition of color, apparently occurs in the center of each spot and expands. A giraffe fetus at eight months is fully haired but there is no indication of spotting. So it is after this time that the developing calf acquires its spots. At least three giraffe calves have been born without spots. Two of the spotless giraffes, sisters, are in the Ueno Zoo in Tokyo, Japan.

A calf's background color tends to be lighter than its mother's. With age it darkens. From each "knee" a black stripe runs down the front of the calf's cannon bone. This stripe, reminiscent of the okapi's persistent foreleg stripe, fades as the calf grows and is barely visible in the adult.

No young animal is more charming than a giraffe calf. A two-week-old orphan Masai giraffe that I met on Crescent Island in Kenya's Lake Naivasha was the very picture of self-possession. A farmer had found this little giraffe, named Twiga (Swahili for giraffe), caught in a wire fence and brought it to the island sanctuary, where it roamed free, in the care of an African boy. Twiga was unperturbed by five small lion cubs and a tame bull eland that also lived on the island. Two ostriches became Twiga's special friends. Mildly curious about people, the calf came up to have its neck stroked. Then, after a few minutes, it turned to follow Kinua, the African boy.

Curiosity is characteristic of young giraffes. Even a chameleon in a bush is noticed. More than one observer of a giraffe herd has found himself being stared at by an inquisitive calf. Often the young animal disappears, only to reappear from another direction for a closer look.

A young giraffe is by no means tied to its mother's apron strings. The parental bond is loose. Calves enjoy their own company in the herd. Much of the time the calves are together, browsing from the same bush or lying down close beside one another. At times they are playful and gallop about, frisking and bucking. A tired calf flops to the ground; minutes later it is up again. Frequently the calves wander off as far as a hundred yards from the herd, but almost always they are within visual-contact distance of the adult giraffes.

In the social organization of giraffe herds **nurseries** are provided for the very young calves. Giraffes, and certain other hoofed mammals, maintain a "baby-sitting" or "auntie" arrangement in which one or two cows look after all the calves. The "aunties" may be old females, beyond the age of calf-bearing. While they stay with the nursery group, the mother giraffes browse some distance away. C. A. W. Guggisberg, a naturalist who lives in Kenya, wrote in his book *Giraffes,* " . . . these nurseries form and break up as casually as all other giraffe groupings. The calves are still being suckled and therefore dependent on their mothers; they are simply being looked after while most of the females have wandered off in the seemingly aimless manner so characteristic of the species."

Usually there are five or six calves in a nursery, rarely as many as twelve. Within the nursery there is much activity. Two calves swing their heads and necks in play; another calf is curious about a bat-eared fox that skulks behind a whistling thorn. The small fox, a nighttime hunter, was lying near the entrance of its burrow, sunning, until the giraffes appeared.

Four to eight times a day the zoo-born giraffe calf suckles. Its mother's milk, at first rich and concentrated, has changed to one-third its original fat content and one-half the protein content, but lactose (a form of sugar) is increased. At two to three weeks the giraffe calf begins to supplement its milk diet with leaves. By the time it is several months old the calf is quite self-sufficient. Cud-chewing commences during its fourth month, but for nearly a year the calf will suckle. Sometimes, when it has started to suckle, other calves and even adults sample the mother giraffe's milk. As long as her calf suckles the cow tolerates the others.

During its first year a giraffe calf grows rapidly, adding more than three feet to its stature. Although growth continues until it is seven or eight years old, full height is reached by the giraffe's fourth year. For females this is about fourteen feet, for males about seventeen feet. Weight for adult giraffes averages nearly eighteen hundred pounds. In the wild, a very large bull may weigh about three thousand pounds or more.

Giraffe death rates are highest during the first year of life, when more than half the calves born may not survive. Predation takes a relatively small toll among adult giraffes. The record life span for a zoo giraffe is twenty-eight years. Giraffes in the wild have lived as long as twenty-six years. Fifteen to twenty years is a more usual giraffe life span.

Laurence Pringle

Listen to the Crows

Laurence Pringle has more than once received the Washington, D.C., Children's Book Guild Nonfiction

Award for the total body of his creative work. He brings to his writing for children a varied background as a wildlife biologist, a science teacher, and the former editor of the journal *Nature and Science*. In this book he lucidly explains for the younger reader the complex language of crows. The logic and clarity of Pringle's writing are enlivened by the vivid excitement he takes in the study of animal intelligence and communication. This same enthusiasm and concern for the preservation of the ecology distinguish his works for children of all ages. [From Laurence Pringle, *Listen to the Crows* (Crowell, 1976).]

Caw . . . Caw . . . Caw!

A crow's voice, sharp and clear, cuts through the morning air. It is a bold and sassy sound.

Caw . . . Caw . . . Caw!

Most people pay no attention to this sound, or to the calls of other birds. But if you ask them about the loud, ringing call, they say, "Oh, that's a crow."

Almost everyone recognizes a few birds by sight: pigeons, gulls, robins. And crows. We know crows by their calls, by their large size (about twenty inches long), and by their glossy blackness. Crows are not plain black, though. If you get close to a crow, you will see glints of deep blue and purple on its feathers.

Caw . . . Caw . . . Caw . . . Caw . . . Caw! Listen to the crows. Sometimes they caw twice, sometimes several times. Have you ever wondered why?

Very few people get close to crows. They are wary birds, and have learned that people are their worst enemies. But they are also clever birds. Crows are smart enough to find safe places even where millions of people live. You can see them in cities and suburbs, as well as in the country. They search for food along highways, just a few feet from speeding cars. They have learned that they are safe there, and that they can find all sorts of food, from popcorn to dead skunks.

Listen to the crows. Sometimes they caw slowly, sometimes fast and sharp. Sometimes they caw high, sometimes low. What do these different sounds mean?

The common crow lives in almost every state and far north into Canada. It also has close relatives in North America. The fish crow lives along the Atlantic coast and the Gulf of Mexico. It is smaller than the common crow, and says something like "car" instead of "caw." Far to the north lives another close relative, the common raven, a great, dark bird of rugged seacoasts and lonely mountaintops. It has a croaking call.

Worldwide, the crow family has about a hundred members, including jays, magpies, rooks, and jackdaws. Many scientists believe that the crow family is the most intelligent of all groups of birds. Crows are smarter than pigeons, gulls, and owls. On some kinds of tests, such as learning to seek food when a light is flashed, they do as well as rats and monkeys. A crow living on New Caledonia, an island in the Pacific Ocean, was observed using a tool. It held a slender twig in its beak and poked it into a hollow branch and underneath bark. The crow seemed to be trying to chase out insects to eat. Very few animals other than humans are known to use tools.

Listen to the crows. Some people have guessed at the meanings of crow sounds. A naturalist named Ernest Thompson Seton claimed that slow, unhurried caws mean, "All's well, come right along," and that a few quick caws mean, "Great danger—man with a gun!"

Crows show their intelligence by changing their ways whenever this helps them to survive. They adapt to new situations. One June evening in 1964, a biologist named Dwight R. Chamberlain was surprised to find more than 200 crows gathered in a Rochester, New York, cemetery. He was even more surprised at their behavior. The air was swarming with flying beetles, and the crows were after them. A crow would leave its perch, chase and catch a flying beetle, then return to its perch and eat the insect. Crows do not usually catch food on the wing, but there, in the fading light, they were doing it with the skill of flycatchers.

Crows eat just about anything—insects, earthworms, snails, clams, mice, fruit, grain, carrion (dead animals), and the eggs and young of other birds. About 650 different kinds of food have been found in the stomachs of crows. Their diet changes with the seasons. Beetles are abundant in May and June, so crows eat lots of beetles then. Later in the summer they fill up on the wild berries, crickets, and grasshoppers that are plentiful. Sometimes they raid vegetable gardens. A crow sometimes walks through a cornfield, pulling up the young plants to get at the sweet, tender, just-sprouted seeds. Delicious!

Some farmers try to kill crows or frighten them away. They once put up scarecrows to keep them away, but crows are not easily fooled. Some hunters also kill crows, for sport or because crows sometimes eat young ducks or other animals that hunters want for themselves. And so, in their efforts to outwit crows, farmers and hunters were among the first people who tried to understand the complex language of these birds.

Many birds have a language that is understood by others of the same kind. Male birds usually have a song which enables them to defend a territory. Its message is: "This is my home space. Keep away." The same song usually is also an advertisement for a mate. Birds make other sounds which mean, "Danger!" "Here is food," and, "Here I am" (a message to the other birds in a flock, or young in the nest).

How strange to think that the sweet melody of a robin is really tough talk, warning other male robins away! Somehow, the sounds that crows make seem much more like a language. Crows speak in rough, loud tones that resemble human voices. In fact, crows are excellent mimics of all sorts of sounds, including those made by people. Wild crows have been heard to mimic a crowing rooster, yelping puppy, barking dog, and meowing cat. Tame crows imitate human laughter, and can be taught to say, "Hello," "Goodbye," "Hot dog!" "Now you've done it!" and many other expressions, including a few which some people do not like to hear.

Richard Mabey

Oak & Company

This chronicle is an engrossing introduction, in picture-book format, to the science of ecology. It is the story of the life of a single oak tree—from its beginning as a lucky acorn taking root in an ideal location to its end as a mature, aging giant felled in a blizzard over two hundred years later—and, in Richard Mabey's carefully detailed writing, of the workings of interdependent life systems. Meticulous illustrations by Clare Roberts form an integral part of the book. [From Richard Mabey, *Oak & Company* (Greenwillow, 1983).]

If tree families had family trees the oaks would have one of the oldest and grandest of all. There are more than 500 different species, and over the last million years they have spread, in various shapes and forms, over most of the northern half of the earth. There are mountain oaks, swamp oaks, evergreen oaks, weeping oaks, and oaks on windswept cliffs that never reach more than two or three feet in height. One kind in Spain has such a spongy bark that it is used to make cork, so there are soft oaks, too. But for most of us oak means just one kind of tree: the tough, rugged giant that has played such a part in history and legend, and been so important in the woodlands of Europe and North America.

Perhaps we've been unfair to other trees, but the forest oaks deserve their fame. They are hardy, easygoing, and not at all fussy about where they grow. They can reach a great age—even a thousand years, though most are cut down long before this. And they are every bit as tough as they look. Their squat trunks and twisted branches, looking like clenched wooden muscles, can stand up to the worst kinds of weather.

On top of all this, timber cut from oaks is as strong and remarkable as the trees themselves. It is solid and hard-wearing, as good for furniture as it is for firewood. Before the days of steel and concrete it made the frames of houses and ships. If we had to invent a new kind of timber it would be hard to think up anything better.

Yet it isn't just humans who find oaks the most useful of trees. Over the ages a huge number of animals and plants have learned to live off—and in—the oaks. It is tempting to say that a full-grown oak is like a house, but it is really more like a city—a whole community of creatures traveling, working, eating, sleeping, singing, and bringing up young, on every part from

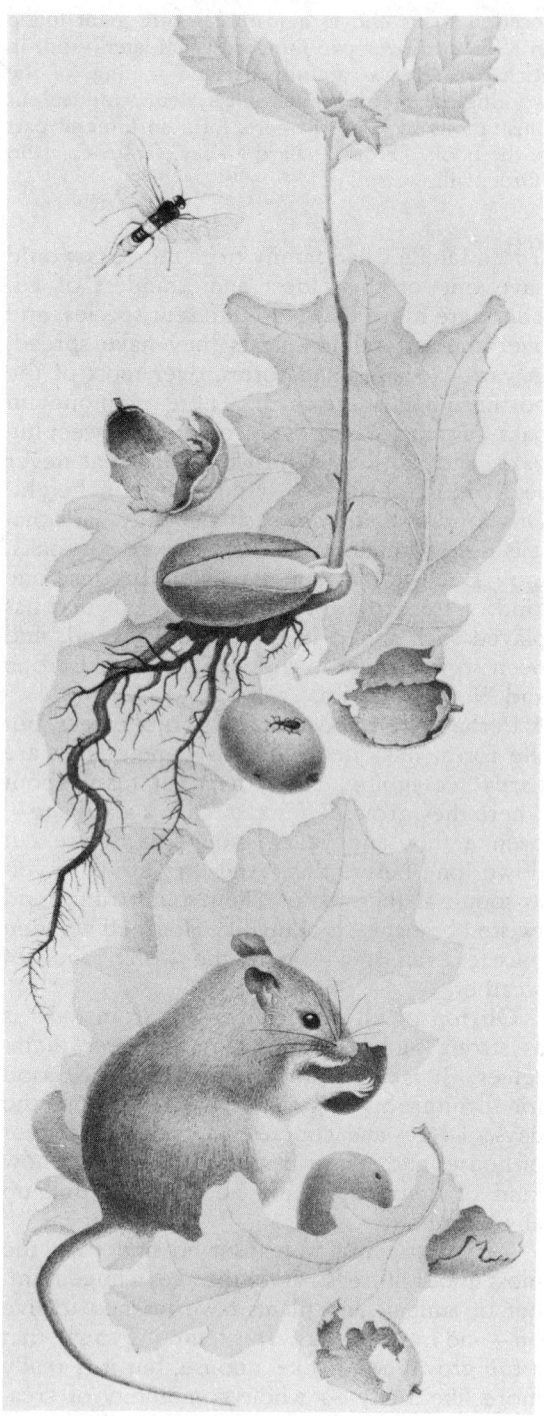

the topmost spring buds to the dead gash blasted out by a lightning flash.

This is the story of one great oak, and its company of plants and animals, from its beginning as an acorn to its death. It is the story of a particular tree, but what happens to it will have happened to most oaks allowed to reach their full natural age.

The Oak's first two leaves unfolded on their matchstick-sized stem on an Easter Sunday at the very beginning of the eighteenth century. That was early in the year for an oak to leaf, but the seedling had sprung up in a warm and sheltered spot by a stream, and had not missed a minute of the spring sunshine.

Its story really began the previous autumn, when its parent tree had produced more than a thousand acorns. It was a good crop, but in late August they were invaded by a swarm of weevils. These little beetles drilled through many of the soft shells to lay their eggs, and when the grubs hatched they set about eating the contents. More acorns were eaten by mice and squirrels. Others fell into a damp hollow, became mildewed, and began to rot away. Less than a hundred survived to put down roots, and most of these were under the shade of their parent tree and would never have enough light to grow.

But none of these oakling deaths really mattered. In the end only one sapling needed to survive to take the place of the parent tree. The streamside Oak looked set to be the lucky one right from the start. The acorn from which it grew had been carried out of the wood by a jay, then dropped and forgotten in a patch of rough ground. Its first leaves had opened under a protective cover of thorn scrub, safe from hungry and inquisitive cattle. Throughout that first, fine summer these leaves grew food for the sapling, and on its first birthday the Oak was thirteen inches tall. By the end of its fifth

Illustration by Clare Roberts, from *Oak & Company,* by Richard Mabey. Illustration copyright © 1983 by Clare Roberts. By permission of Greenwillow Books (a division of William Morrow & Co.) and Penguin Books Ltd.

year it had reached six feet, and was bristling with leafy side twigs.

It was now being visited by dozens of feeding creatures, greenflies and sawflies that bored into the leaves to suck the sap—and warblers and titmice that came in turn to snap up the flies.

The Oak had also begun to grow its first gall. One of its leaf stalks was swelling where a wasp had laid its eggs. By midwinter the swelling looked like a small, wrinkled apple. Over the years many kinds of gall wasp laid their eggs in different parts of the Oak, and galls of all kinds appeared, some like tiny buttons under the leaves and some like bunches of currants on the catkins. . . .

The wear and tear of two hundred winters left their mark on the Oak. Winds racing down the valley every January twisted and snapped the branches and gave the whole tree a tilt toward the south. In one fierce storm the tree was struck by lightning again, and the top branches were set on fire. Dry oak burns well. Everyone knew that, and when cold weather set in the local people would come down to the stream to lop branches from the oaks for firewood.

At this moment of the year, with all its leaves fallen, the Oak looked as much like a pillar of rock as a tree. It was pitted with holes and grooves, and patches of spongy, rotting wood. There was no other tree in the valley that looked quite like it, and people used it as a landmark, a place to meet and chat and sometimes picnic under. The younger children used to imagine they could see heads and faces in it, and in the half-light of a winter's evening it was not difficult to turn some of those knots and gaping holes into eyes and mouths.

In these cold months the Oak was a great gathering ground for birds and animals, too. An owl roosted in the largest hole, and a dormouse snoozed away the winter in a mossy nest built deep inside the trunk. On the most bitter nights, when the ground was iron hard and the Oak's trunk was encased in a film of ice, the birds stopped being wary of each other. If you had watched the Oak at dusk, you might have seen more than twenty titmice fly into one of its hollow branches to spend the night huddled together for warmth.

Of course they would feed when they could, picking out sleeping grubs from the bark, bringing berries to eat in the shelter of the upper branches and often leaving the seeds there with their droppings, caught in one of the damp leaf-filled crevices. And that is how a miniature forest of thorn, holly, and currant bushes came to grow more than fifteen feet above the ground, rooted not in the earth, but in the Oak—a wood inside a tree!

A few years after it had been struck by lightning again, the Oak began to age quickly. Channels of rotting wood had begun to eat away both of its trunks, and these spread and joined up. The following spring the heavier of the two—almost half the tree—broke off in a spring gale. The Oak was now in desperate straits. It had lost half its food-producing leaves, and was riddled with holes and gashes in constant need of repair. It put out new twigs near the break, but the space left by its fallen branches had already been filled with new foliage from younger trees. As more and more of its branches were shaded out, so the roots which they fed died. At the same time the healthy roots were being weakened by the underground burrowings of rabbits and foxes.

One winter night in its 283rd year, the Oak was hit by a blizzard. Freezing snow drifted on what was left of its upper branches, until the remaining roots could take the weight and strain no longer. They snapped, and were wrenched out of the ground as the tree fell: the second twin trunk split off, slewed round and crashed through the telegraph wires that now ran alongside the stream.

That was why the fallen Oak was discovered only hours later. The foresters dealt with it very quickly, using chain saws to free the wires. There were too many crooks and hollows for the timber to be of any use, but the foresters did save the burr which had formed over a broken branch more than a hundred years before, because of the beautiful grain patterns the green wood had made growing back over the scar. The rest of the tree they left to rot. So even after its death, the Oak was still host to dozens of toadstools and insects.

Much has happened along the valley in the few years since the Oak's death. Self-sown oak trees—including the Oak's own offspring—have grown into a small wood along the stream. The farmers want this felled so that they will have more land for grazing. The owner of the wood where the Oak's parent grew (now growing spruce trees, not oaks) wants to extend his Christmas tree plantation down to the stream. But one forester has seen the straight trunks of the Oak's descendants and wants them left, to see if they will make a new strain of timber oaks.

The Oak's great company, the woodpeckers and butterflies, the mosses and beetles, have moved to these younger oaks, and wait to see what the future will bring.

Judith Kohl and Herbert Kohl

The View from the Oak: The Private Worlds of Other Creatures

Mabey gives us a detailed description of the oak, but what is the *real nature* of an oak tree? "To demand unambiguous answers," the authors of this dazzling and provocative book tell us, "is to make the world simpler and less interesting than it is." Basing their work upon the science of ethology, the Kohls, in small, comprehensible steps, build a systematic approach to seeing the world from a multiplicity of viewpoints. Oak trees are vastly different things to different creatures; to begin to see simultaneously from many viewpoints is to discover our world's endless complexity and fascination. This book received the 1978 National Book Award for Children's Literature. [From Judith Kohl and Herbert Kohl, *The View from the Oak: The Private Worlds of Other Creatures* Sierra Club/ Scribner's, 1977).]

Views of the Oak

Erica's sweater: it is blue, has long sleeves, buttons down the front, is finely woven, smells of wool; it is formless, of no use but to snuggle up to and sniff, it smells like Erica, is good to stay near when no people are around; it is gigan-

tic, has strands, is delicious, the perfect nest for eggs, a warm and nourishing environment to grow up in.

Which is the real object—the woolen sweater Erica our daughter wears? The formless object that Sandy takes from Erica's bedroom and rests his nose on when we are gone? The home and feast for the moths we found in it the other day?

An object or living being appears and functions differently in different umwelts. A dog is not the same to its fleas as it is to its owner or to another dog who is trying to size it up. There are many different perspectives from which things in the world are experienced. Consider an oak tree and all the life it can harbor from its roots to its highest branches.

Imagine first a fox whose den has been dug out among the roots of the tree. From the perspective of the fox the tree is home. It protects his mate and their offspring, and is a place to sleep and rest and eat. Because the fox is so vulnerable if trapped in the den, its entrance has to be hidden and appear in no way special. The fox has to behave as if that particular oak is nothing special and yet know every smell and sound surrounding it, as well as all the tunnels and dead-ends leading through the roots. The roots themselves are the columns and beams of the foxes' home which is lined with leaves to warm and hide young foxes.

The fox's view of the oak is low down, under and on the ground. There is no need in his or her world to look up. The trunk leads somewhere else, to other worlds and other experiences—it is neither threatening nor comforting in the fox's world. It is a part of experience that is background. The branches of that oak and of all the other trees that surround it do not separate themselves. There is a lattice of branches above the fox's world, yet those branches are phantoms, horizon features that have no connection to the oak in the umwelt of the fox.

Somewhere within that lattice there is a good chance that an old and abandoned crow's nest exists. And there is also a good chance that it has become home for an owl. Many owls are extraordinary hunters and lazy builders. The owl in our imagined oak is one of these and has taken up residence within the upper branches of the oak in the crow's nest. Most likely, the owl at the top and the fox in the roots will never cross paths. In some ways it doesn't even make sense to say they share the oak, since there is nothing shared about their experience of the tree.

During the day the owl and the tree are one. The owl sleeps, its feathers drawn into itself, resting so still that to human eyes it appears to be another branch. The color of its feathers helps. During the day it blends with the tree. At night the owl comes alive and the tree is a tower from which its keen eyes survey its hunting grounds. Owls' eyes are immobile—they don't move around, though they can focus on particular objects with amazing concentration and magnitude. The owl's eyes are like telescopes mounted on the swivel stand of its head which can turn 180 degrees in either direction. The eyes don't move but the head does. At night, for a while the owl sits in the oak, its eyes wide open, scanning 360 degrees. As soon as it spots prey, it is gone but usually comes back to eat. If the oak provides a protective environment during the day, it becomes a dining room through the night. Single owls have been known to return to their repossessed crow's nest with as much as a dozen mice, several rabbits, a mole, and groundhog or two during three or four hours of hunting.

Halfway down the oak on and under its bark other worlds exist. Jacob von Uexkull describes the world of the bark-boring beetle and the ichneumon fly in his essay. *A Stroll through the World of Animals and Men* which originally gave us the idea for this book:

> *The bark-boring beetle seeks its nourishment underneath the bark which it blasts off. Here it lays its eggs. Its larvae bore their passages underneath the bark. Here, safe from the perils of the outside world, they gnaw themselves farther into their food. But they are not entirely protected. For not only are they persecuted by the woodpecker, which splits off the bark with powerful thrusts of its beak; an ichneumon fly, whose fine ovipositor penetrates through the oakwood (hard in all other umwelts) as if it were butter, destroys them by injecting its eggs into the larvae. Larvae*

> *slip out of the ichneumon eggs and feed on the flesh of their victims.*

And what about the oak tree in the umwelt of people? It is probably characteristic of our species that the human umwelt differs from person to person and culture to culture, and that it changes over time as well.

The oak tree has often had a special place in the umwelt of some peoples. To many Native Americans the oak is honored as a symbol of strength and longevity, and as a source of food. Acorns are washed, pounded into meal for bread, added to soup. In Europe, centuries ago, the druids believed that the oak harbored spirits, and their most solemn rites were held in groves of sacred oak trees. They gathered mistletoe from the oak, cut the oak down, and used the log to create a sacred fire to honor Yaroal, the Celtic god of fire. That was the origin of the Yule log many people still burn on Christmas. It is an offering to Yaroal to convince him to use his power over fire to end the winter quickly.

There are more recent and immediate examples of how the oak figures in human umwelts. In the umwelt of a logger the oak is nothing but wood, one of many trees, nothing special. To a conservationist the oak is unique, a treasure to be preserved. To a child lost in the woods at night the oak might be a terrifying magical object inhabited by gnomes and spirits. The knobby bark might seem a face in the moonlight, full of threat and mischief. And finally, to an aerial geographer flying over the oak and taking photographs to use in map making, the oak is hardly noticed at all. A minor feature of the whole landscape.

The oak exists in many umwelts. As von Uexkull says in his essay:

> *In all the hundred different umwelts of its inmates, the oak tree as an object plays a highly varied role, at one time with some of its parts, at another time with others. Sometimes the same parts are large, at others they are small. At times its wood is hard, at others soft. One time the tree serves for protection, then again for attack.*

But what about the real oak tree? Is it big or small? Nothing special or a unique treasure? Menacing or protective? Is its wood hard or soft? To demand unambiguous answers to these questions is to make the world simpler and less interesting than it is. Why not give up worrying about the real object and rephrase the questions: In whose umwelt is the oak big and in whose is it small? Which animals find oak hard and which find it soft? For whom is the tree unique and for whom is the oak common? Who is menaced by the oak and who is protected by it?

By asking these questions we point ourselves toward observation and discovery. We actually know very little of the world, even of what surrounds us every day. It is worth taking the time to think of the variety of ways in which the environment could be structured and to discover how different animals actually structure it. We are all collections of atoms, specks in the universe, just the right size in our own worlds, giants to fleas, midgets to whales. The human view of the world is only one of many. It enriches our understanding of ourselves to move away from familiar worlds and attempt to understand the experience of other animals with whom we share common ancestors. The respect for other forms of life we can gain from these efforts might in some small way help us work toward preserving the world we share.

Mildred Mastin Pace

Wrapped for Eternity

One of the most fascinating aspects of the study of ancient Egyptian civilization is the investigation of mummies and the secrets of their preservation. The mastery that the Egyptians achieved in embalming was a skill that also made them renowned in the field of medicine. [From Mildred Mastin Pace, *Wrapped for Eternity* (McGraw-Hill, 1974).]

How a Mummy Was Made

It would take about ten weeks to create the mummy. During that period the family would remain, as much as possible, in their home, in seclusion, chanting dirges and mourning their loss.

The place where the body was taken for mummification was a large tent. Sometimes the embalmers' workshops were in permanent buildings. But in this country of heat and sun and almost no rain, tents were practical. They could be moved easily when necessary, and were more comfortable for the embalmers to work in than the walled and confined space of a building.

The tent had cooled off during the night, and when the priests and workers gathered to begin their job, the air was pleasant.

The body, freshly bathed, was laid out on a long, narrow table, high enough so that those administering to the body need not bend over.

Beneath the table stood four stone jars, each about a foot high. These were the Canopic jars and later they would hold the embalmed larger organs of the man's body: the intestines, liver, stomach, lungs. The lid of each jar was topped with a figure carved of stone: one the head of a man, one a dog's head, one the head of a jackal, and one the head of a hawk.

The priest who was in charge of the embalming represented the god Anubis, who presided over mummification and was the guardian of the tombs. Since this god had the body of a man and the head of a jackal, this one priest wore a head mask of a jackal.

The priests were all freshly shaven; their head, their faces—even their bodies beneath the fine, crisp linen robes—had been shaved to remove all hair. Led by the priest in the jackal mask, they intoned chants that announced the start of the work and the ritual.

The first actual step toward mummification was about to begin. This was the removal of the brain.

A specialist, highly skilled in his work, approached the head of the corpse. In his hand he held a long, slender hooklike instrument. Deftly he pushed this up one nostril, and working in a circular movement, he broke through the ethmoid bone, up into the cavity of the brain.

Withdrawing the hooklike instrument, he chose another. This one was a narrow, spirally twisted rod that had a small spoonlike tip. Pushing this up into the cranial cavity, he began, slowly, bit by bit, to draw out the brain through the nose, discarding each piece as he went along.

This was an operation of skill and patience.

When at long last he was finished, satisfied that all of the brain had been removed from the cranial cavity, leaving it clean and clear, he prepared to leave. His job was done, and he was pleased to have done it well. Once in a while a clumsy operator crushed a bone or broke the nose, disfiguring the face forever. But he had completed the delicate operation leaving the strong bone structure, the well-shaped face, as it had been when he started.

Now the mouth was cleansed and in it were placed wads of linen soaked in sweet oils. The nostrils were cleansed and plugged with wax. The face was coated with a resinous paste. A small piece of linen was placed over each eye, and the eyelids drawn over them.

The body was now ready for the second important operation toward mummification. This was the removal of the viscera from the body cavity.

The man who was to perform this operation stood outside the tent, waiting to be called in. He held in his hand a fairly large, flat black stone, one edge of which was honed to razor sharpness. It was called an Ethiopian stone. His job was not a pleasant one, and gruesome to watch. Hence the other workers and the priests held him in abhorrence.

As he waited, the priest wearing the jackal mask approached the body, which had been turned slightly on its right side, exposing the left flank. The tent throbbed with the sound of the soft, rhythmic chantings of the priests.

The jackal head bent toward the body, and the masked priest dipped a small rush pen into a pot of ink, then drew on the left side of the body a spindle-shaped line about five inches long.

The priest stepped back and the man with the stone was called in. Following the line the priest had drawn, he cut, with great strength, through skin and flesh. Then, reaching through the incision, he severed and removed each organ: the stomach, liver, kidneys, lungs, intestines.

Only the heart was left in place. It was thought to be the seat of intelligence and feeling, and so must remain forever intact within the body.

The other vital organs would be wrapped in resin-soaked cloth and each placed in the proper Canopic jar. Their lids sealed on with wax, the jars would be set aside to await the day of burial.

His loathsome job finished, the man fled from the tent, followed by shouts of derision and contempt from all the others. He was considered unclean, and their angry outcries, the curses they called down on him, would rid the tent of his taint.

The priests, the embalmers, might pretend to despise him. But they all knew his job was an important one. Left in place, the internal organs would deteriorate rapidly, making the drying out of the body and successful mummification impossible.

The body cavity was cleansed with palm wine. The incision was pulled together, and a priest performed the ritual of placing on it a wax plate bearing the all-powerful symbol, the Eye of Horus. For a wealthier man the plate might have been of silver, or even of gold. But in any case, always, the Eye of Horus was depicted on it. Next, thin wires of gold were fastened around each fingernail and toenail to keep them in place. And once again the corpse was bathed.

The body was now ready to be dried out.

The powder called natron came from the Libyan Desert. It was known to be a great drying agent and had cleansing and purification powers as well. Laid out on a fresh, clean mat woven of plant fibers, the body was covered with natron. In the hot, dry atmosphere, with the heat of the sun to help, day after day the drying-out process in the natron went on.

The day came when the body was wholly dry—the skin stretched on the firm frame of bone, the face thin but still the face of the man who had died.

The body was very light when the men lifted it onto a high table. It was bathed once more. It was anointed with ointments and rubbed with sweet-smelling spices and herbs.

Priests now poured out libations—liquid that symbolically restored moisture to the body. They lighted incense, which they burned—also symbolically—to restore the body's warmth and odor.

The body was ready to be wrapped.

About 150 yards of linen cloth had been prepared, torn into strips of varying widths. On some of the bandages the man's name was written. Thus his identity would be preserved. On some there were figures of the gods and on others were religious writings and words of magic. All of these would give the man help and power when he reached the other world.

The bandaging was intricate, and those doing the work were highly skilled. But only the priests knew where the magical bandages, with their words of power, should be placed. Only the priests knew the words to be chanted when the man's ring was placed on his finger, the gold earrings hung in his ears. Only the priests could direct where, amongst the bandages, the amulets should be hidden to protect the deceased on his journey into the next world.

So as the bandaging began, and as it went on, there were frequent interludes when the wrapping ceased while the priests, with great ceremony, intoned their words of wisdom and chanted religious formulas.

Thus the wrapping, with its wealth of religious significance, took some time. And seventy days elapsed between the day of the man's death and the day when the wrapping was finished. On that day the mummy was taken back to the house of mourning where the man had died.

From the house the final procession set forth. The mummy, in its elaborately painted mummiform coffin, lay upon a lion-headed bier which was placed on a sledge drawn by men and oxen. Walking before the sledge, on each side, were two women who impersonated the goddess Isis and her sister goddess, Nephthys, guardians of the dead. Behind the bier came another sledge, drawn by men. On this was a chest that held the four Canopic jars.

The women mourners followed, wailing in grief, their hair disheveled. Then came the men mourners, beating their breasts in sorrow. Behind the mourners were the servants, carrying the objects the dead man would need for living in the other world: chests filled with clothes, toilet articles, jars of salves and unguents, and some of his favorite possessions. Others bore the funerary furniture: a bed, a chair, small stools.

When the procession reached the entrance of the tomb, the mummy was taken from its bier and set in a standing position on a mound of sand, facing the mourners.

While the mourners watched and waited, the priests began the long, complicated series of rituals that would assure the man success on his long journey into the next world. Small vessels of burning incense were waved, rites of purification, lustration, were performed. The ceremonies went on and on. Finally came the most complex and important rite of all, known as the Opening of the Mouth.

One priest, holding a miniature *adze* that possessed special mystical powers, approached the mummy. To the chanting of religious formulas, he touched the mummy's head: the eyes, to open them so the man could see; the ears, so he could hear; the mouth, so he could speak; the jaws, so he could eat.

He could now live in the other world as he had on earth. He would need the contents of his carved chests, the furniture placed in his tomb, the food and drink that would be provided for him.

Even as the coffined body, sealed in its sarcophagus, was being placed in its tomb, the man's journey into the next world had begun.

The mourners, weary from their hot and dusty procession to the tomb and the long-lasting ceremonies that followed, were now ready to enjoy the great feast that had been prepared for them. Knowing that the dead man was on his way to a second happy life that would never end, they partook of a joyous banquet. The foods were the finest, the wines and beer plentiful. There were entertainers and musicians, and guests sang songs in praise of the man just buried.

The mourning was over.

Geraldine Lux Flanagan

Window into an Egg: Seeing Life Begin

The exciting process of cell division and differentiation is given a remarkably clear exposition in a description that goes hand-in-hand with the accompanying photographs. [From Geraldine Lux Flanagan, *Window into an Egg: Seeing Life Begin* (Scott, 1969).]

A Body, a Beating Heart, and a New Name

On the second day of its life, our chick is transformed. Yesterday it was a mound of bubble-like cells that you could count. Today thousands of new cells grow and arrange themselves into the strange form you can see in the photograph [below].

Does it, perhaps, remind you of folded petals of a flower bud? Or does it look to you more like a shoe? Actually, what you see here is the very beginning of a body. What may look like the top of a shoe will become the head and heart of the chick, the front of the shoe shape will grow into the rest of the body, and what appears like buttons will become backbone and muscles.

This certainly does not look at all like a chick. It has a special name. It is called an EMBRYO. It is no longer a fertilized egg cell, and is not yet a chick—it is a chick embryo. Embryo is a Greek word, and it means "grow within." The embryo is usually so fragile that it must grow within, either within the warm protection of the mother, as you did, or within an eggshell as a bird does, or in the case of plants, within

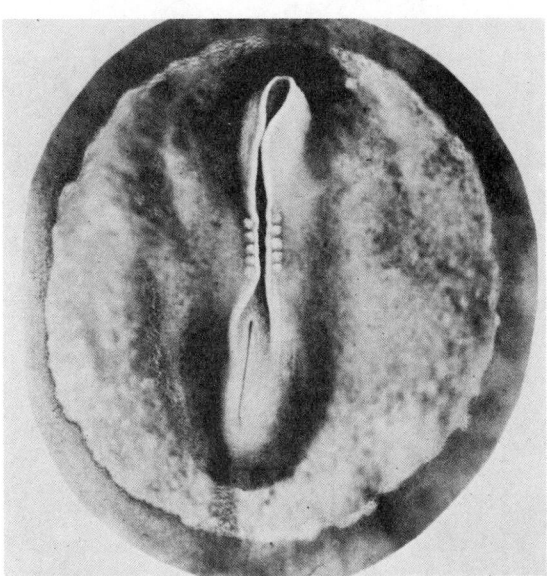

From *Early Embryology of the Chick,* by Bradley Patten. Copyright © 1951 by Bradley Patten. Used with permission of McGraw-Hill Book Company.

a seed. Each chick, and every life that begins from one cell, must first grow into an embryo as its body is made bit by bit, and each part is made to fit and work together with every other part.

If you could sit and watch this chick embryo through a microscope for a few hours, you would be amazed to see how alive it is. To see it well, you would have to look at it under great magnification. Yet, even when the embryo is so enlarged, each of its cells appears no bigger than a pinpoint.

Watching through the microscope, you would see a continuous slow-moving traffic of these pinpoint cells. You would see streams of cells, some moving forward, others toward the center, others turning under. In the same places where there was only plain yolk two days ago, a great activity has now been stirred up. The activity is busy but not wild. Each cell goes exactly to its proper place, probably according to the instructions it carries in its nucleus, and also because it is guided by the other cells around it. The cells travel in groups, and eventually a group may settle in one place. When the group arrives at its destination, it stops traveling and stays to build the special part for which it is intended.

The chick embryo, like all embryos, grows according to a strict plan. About six hours after the fertilized egg has been laid, if it has been kept well warmed, you will find that the chick-making cells in the egg have arranged themselves into the form of a shield, called the embryonic shield. What the cells will do next is so much the same in every hen's egg that scientists have been able to predict exactly what each group of cells will go on to build.

If you continue to watch the shield under the microscope, you will see an extra number of cells lining up along the center of the shield to form a thick band, looking like a streak, as you can see in the photograph [p. 1048]. This is called the PRIMITIVE STREAK, which means beginning, or earliest, streak. More and more cells gather around this streak, especially toward its upper end. So many cells stream forward that the head of the streak becomes a crowd of cells. These cells are packed closely together, and this makes the head of the streak look darker than the rest. Gradually the darkened crowd of cells fans out in an arrow shape. This is the very beginning of the brain. Then, as the arrow shape grows out farther, it will be the beginning of the heart.

To see all this in the photographs on these pages, you have to look at them closely and carefully. Understanding these photographs is somewhat like learning to read a new kind of printing. Only people who are used to looking at embryos through a microscope can understand right away what they are seeing. Scientists who study embryos know, from experience and from experiments, that the part of the streak that looks darkest will go on to form the brain, the head, and the heart. The part of the streak that looks lighter will become a hollow tube, and in it groups of cells will gather to form the other inner parts, such as the stomach, the intestines, the liver and kidneys.

At the same time certain cells wander away from the main groups of the embryo. They move outward onto the yolk. These cells will create blood for the chick. Blood, as you may know, is a liquid filled with many cells. If you look at red blood under a microscope, you can see that it is actually a colorless liquid, filled with a variety of cells. Some of them have no color, others have a rusty red color. These are called red blood cells, and they are the ones that make the blood appear red.

To make blood, the chick's wandering cells establish tiny cell islands on the yolk. The islands become surrounded by small amounts of colorless liquid. Then, in a few hours, some of the island cells form a substance called HEMO-GLOBIN, a Greek word that means "globes of blood." This hemoglobin is mostly made of iron substances from the yolk. The color of hemoglobin is rusty red. This gives red blood cells their color, and that is how red blood appears out of the yellow yolk.

While the blood is being made, other cells build soft walls around the island pools of blood, keeping the blood from flowing out. Later these walls grow into soft tubes called BLOOD VESSELS. As the blood vessels grow, they branch out over the yolk, like branches of a tree, and are connected to other blood vessels that have meanwhile grown within the chick embryo.

Inside these blood vessels, the blood will carry nourishment to the chick. Tiny particles of the nourishing things yolk is made of, such as sugars, fats, vitamins, proteins, iron and other

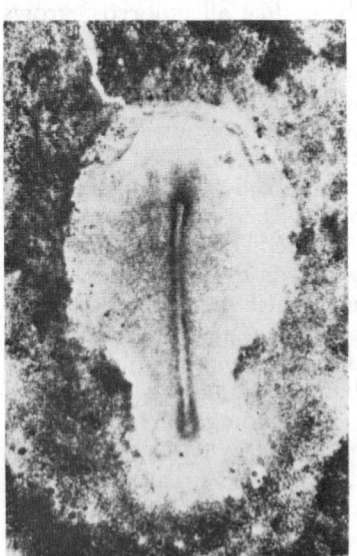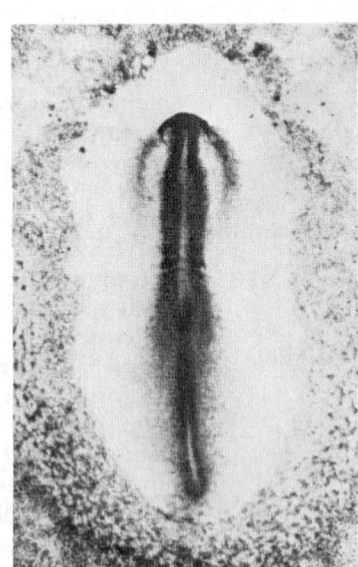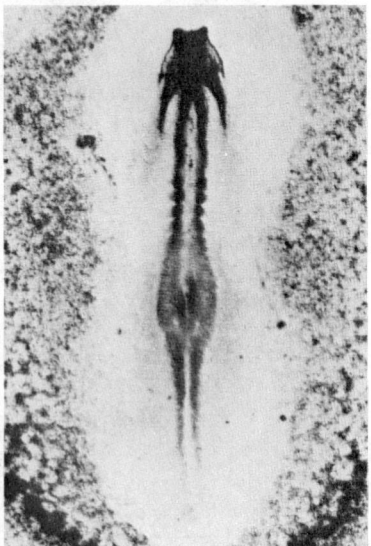

From *Lillies Development of the Chick: An Introduction to Embryology* (3d ed.), by Howard Hamilton. Copyright © 1952 by Holt, Rinehart and Winston, Inc. Reprinted by permission of Holt, Rinehart and Winston.

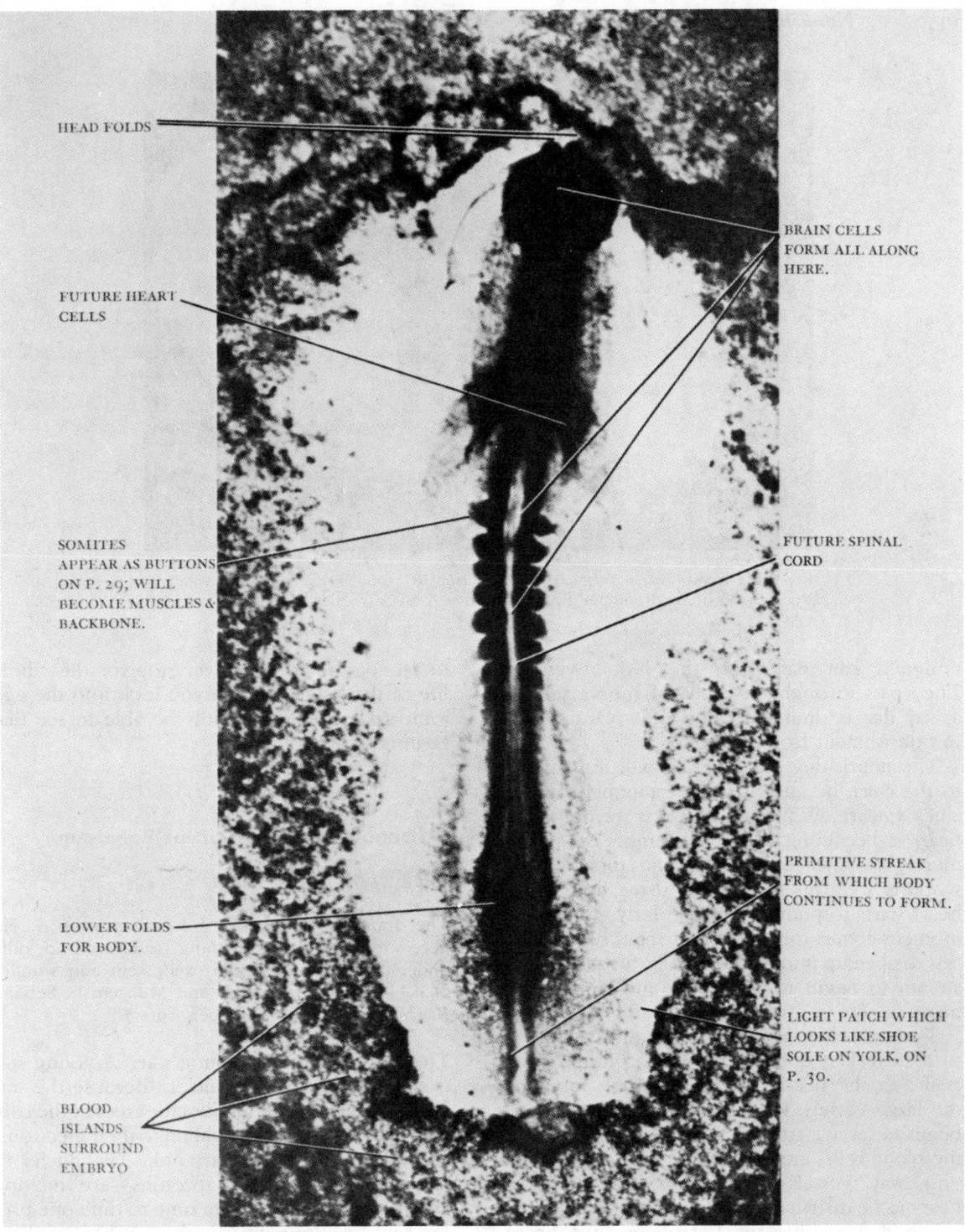

HEAD FOLDS

BRAIN CELLS
FORM ALL ALONG
HERE.

FUTURE HEART
CELLS

SOMITES
APPEAR AS BUTTONS
ON P. 29; WILL
BECOME MUSCLES &
BACKBONE.

FUTURE SPINAL
CORD

PRIMITIVE STREAK
FROM WHICH BODY
CONTINUES TO FORM.

LOWER FOLDS
FOR BODY.

LIGHT PATCH WHICH
LOOKS LIKE SHOE
SOLE ON YOLK, ON
P. 30.

BLOOD
ISLANDS
SURROUND
EMBRYO

From *Lillies Development of the Chick: An Introduction to Embryology* (3d ed.), by Howard Hamilton. Copyright © 1952 by Holt, Rinehart and Winston, Inc. Reprinted by permission of Holt, Rinehart and Winston.

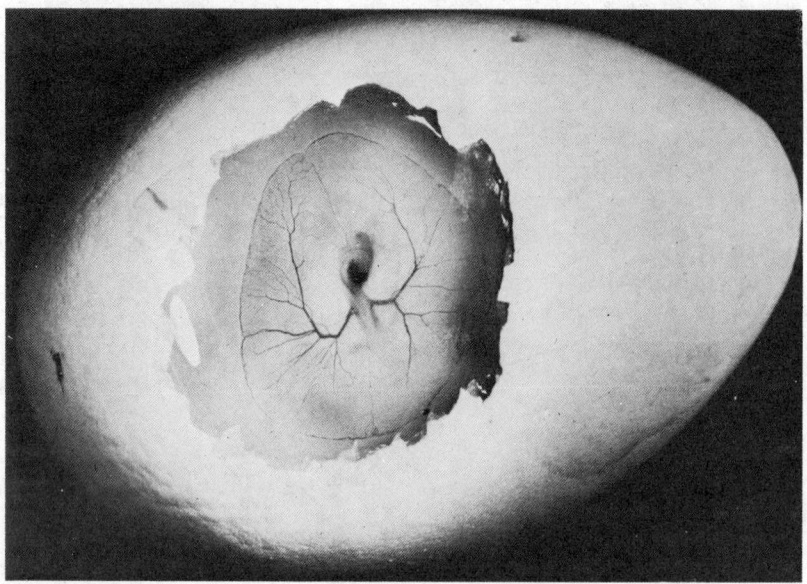

Reprinted from *Window into an Egg.* Copyright © 1969 by Geraldine Flanagan. A Young Scott Book. Reprinted by permission of Addison-Wesley Publishing Company.

minerals, can pass into the blood vessels. They pass through the walls of the vessels in a way that is similar to roots of a plant taking in nourishment from the soil.

The nourishing bloodstream will flow along to the chick because it will be pumped by the chick's heart. While the blood is forming, the heart is becoming ready to pump. At first it merely twitches every now and then. After working like this for two or three hours, the heart starts to pump quite regularly. Then the moment comes for the largest main blood vessels to open up into the heart, and for the bloodstream to begin to shuttle in and out of the heart.

Through a microscope it is an impressive sight to see this first opening up of the bloodstream traffic to the heart. At the opening moment the large vessels, looking like super highways, begin to carry a stream of little dots, which are the blood cells, into the heart. Two other large "highway" vessels carry the cell traffic from the heart to be distributed throughout the embryo.

Blood flows into the heart when the heart muscles relax, and is forced out when the heart muscles tighten up. This is how the heart begins

to pump; and it will never stop for the whole life of that chick. When you look into the egg tomorrow, you will plainly be able to see that beating heart.

J. Bronowski and Millicent E. Selsam

Biography of an Atom

The dramatic life-history of a carbon atom is told here so lucidly that the young reader will not only understand it but feel the excitement and wonder of it. [From J. Bronowski and Millicent E. Selsam, *Biography of an Atom* (Harper, 1965).]

The birth began in a young star. A young star is a mass of hydrogen nuclei. Because the star is hot (about thirteen million degrees at the center), the nuclei cannot hold on to their electrons. The electrons wander around. The nuclei of hydrogen—that is, the protons—are moving about very fast too. From time to time one proton runs headlong into another. When this happens, one of the protons loses its electric charge and changes into a neutron. The pair then cling together as a single nucleus of heavy hydrogen. This nucleus will in time capture another proton. Now there is a nucleus with two protons and one neutron, called light helium. When two of these nuclei smash into each other, two protons are expelled in the process. This creates a nucleus of helium with two protons and two neutrons.

This is the fundamental process of *fusion* by which the primitive hydrogen of the universe is built up into a new basic material, helium. In this process, energy is given off in the form of heat and light that make the stars shine. It is the first stage in the birth of the heavier atoms.

After billions of years, the star, now no longer young, has a central core of almost pure helium. The helium nuclei begin to run into one another headlong. Every so often two helium nuclei crash together to form a nucleus of four protons and four neutrons. This is called a beryllium-8 nucleus. It is not the stable beryllium that we know on earth, which has another neutron and is called beryllium-9. Beryllium-8 is an unstable isotope that has a fantastically short life and flies apart almost as soon as it is formed—in less than a millionth of a millionth of a second. Only if another helium nucleus crashes into the unstable beryllium nucleus in the brief moment of its life do the parts remain together and form a new stable nucleus of six protons and six neutrons.

This is the moment when a carbon nucleus is truly born. The atom of carbon whose story we are telling was born by this extraordinary chance billions of years ago.

How, then, does the carbon atom get out of the star and come here to earth? The aging star goes on building up carbon atoms and other heavier atoms from its helium. Finally these nuclear reactions stop. The star collapses, the temperature rises suddenly, and the star explodes, scattering the carbon and other atoms through space. There they become mixed with the dust and thin sea of hydrogen gas which fill space.

Later when a fresh star begins to form from this hydrogen gas and dust, it catches up some of the carbon and other atoms with it. There are fresh stars being formed like this all the time, and one of these fresh stars is the sun, which was formed four or five billion years ago.

Later the earth and the other planets were formed from the sun. The carbon atom was part of the earth when it was formed.

The carbon atom has been part of many different things, dead and alive, since the earth began. It has joined with other atoms, broken away, and then joined other atoms again. But always it has remained the same carbon atom.

At one time the carbon atom may have been part of a diamond—a pure crystal of carbon.

Or it may have joined with two atoms of oxygen to form the gas carbon dioxide. The carbon dioxide may have entered through the pores of a leaf and been used to make sugar when the sunlight struck it there. The sugar became part of the tissues of the plant.

That plant may have become peat or coal. When the plant died and fell to the ground, bacteria broke some of it down into simpler chemical substances—ammonia, water, and carbon dioxide. The carbon dioxide may have escaped into the air and been used again by other plants. But most of the carbon in the plant tissue remained in the ground. With other dead plants around it, the plant got pressed down by layers of sand, mud, and water that settled on it. Over millions of years the plants changed and hardened until they became hard coal, deep in the ground.

The carbon atom may have been locked in the coal for millions of years. But one day it was dug out of the earth. When the coal was burned, the carbon atom joined the oxygen again and formed carbon dioxide. The next time it entered through the pores of a leaf into a plant, it was used again to make sugar. The plant was perhaps eaten by a cow. One of your forefathers may have drunk the milk of that cow or eaten a steak from it, and the carbon atom might have been in either.

In the body of your forefather the carbon atom became part of one of the chromosomes which was passed on to your parents and then to you.

You may pass this carbon atom to a son or daughter. Or perhaps you will die with this carbon atom still in your body. But the career of the carbon atom is not over. It will return to the soil and from there it may get into the air again as carbon dioxide and pass in and out of the lungs of human beings for thousands of years.

The air in a man's lungs at any moment contains 10,000,000,000,000,000,000,000,000 atoms, so sooner or later every one of us breathes an atom that has been breathed by someone who has lived before us—perhaps Michelangelo or George Washington or Moses! Your carbon atom, linked with atoms of oxygen, may be breathed by some great man or woman of the future. Then it may return again to the soil and lie dormant in some mineral for millions of years. And in time its cycle of life may begin again.

Will this cycle ever end? We do not know. Your carbon atom has been unchanged, as an atom, for four billion years or more, and there is no reason why it should not go on forever. Even if the earth is burned up at last by the sun, your carbon atom may go back into space and be swept again into some new star.

In a star, and only in a star, will its identity finally disappear. It will be broken apart by violent atomic collisions and its pieces built into other atoms. Then, and only then, will the career of your carbon atom be at an end. But it will be part of new atoms of a different kind. And in this sense it will go on forever—a never-ending link between you and the stars.

Malcolm E. Weiss

Sky Watchers of Ages Past

Humans have been fascinated with the heavens since prehistory. This work is an introduction to archaeoastronomy—the study of astronomy as practiced by ancient cultures. Weiss reveals the astonishing complexity of thought and scientific measurement of which early cultures were capable through his analysis of well-known and relatively unknown prehistoric phenomena such as the giant sacred calender at Stonehenge and the Pueblo Dagger of Light in Chaco Canyon, New Mexico. The author's convincing presentation of such accomplishments helps destroy the prejudice "that ancient peoples, without precision instruments and advanced mathematics, could not have made worthwhile discoveries in astronomy." This is the story of the search by ancient and modern

astronomers for "our place in the universe." The following selection analyzes the Mayan calendar and system of counting. [From Malcolm E. Weiss, *Sky Watchers of Ages Past* (Houghton Mifflin, 1982).]

Observers of Yucatán

The Mayas developed a mighty civilization in Central America. Mayan civilization reached its peak between A.D. 100 and A.D. 900. Then, about a thousand years ago, the classic Mayan civilization collapsed. No one really knows why or how that happened.

At Uaxactún, the Mayas built a large pyramid. East of the pyramid, on a platform, they built three small temples. These temples were lined up with the pyramid, to fix the dates of the spring and fall equinoxes and the summer and winter solstices.

A priest stood on the steps of the pyramid, facing the middle temple. He sighted over the top of a stone column, to the center of the temple roof. At the equinoxes, the sun rose over the center of this roof.

Standing on the same spot at the time of the summer solstice, the priest could see the sunrise over the corner of the temple to his left—the northern temple. And at the winter solstice, the sun rose over the corner of the temple to the right—the southern temple.

Throughout their empire, the Mayas used similar means to plot the motions of the sun. And they did much more. They mapped the motions of the moon. They learned to predict eclipses of the sun and moon. They plotted the movements of the planet Venus with almost as much accuracy as do modern astronomers.

To do all this took careful observations over a period of several lifetimes. The Mayas had a written language that helped them pass along knowledge from one generation to the next. Most of that language is still a mystery to us. We have only decoded the signs for numbers and dates. These were the signs they used in making their calendars and astronomical tables. The signs included brilliantly colored pictures of gods, strange drawings of human and animal heads and skulls, and bars and dots.

These records were set down in "books" made of paper from the bark of the wild fig tree. A strip of paper making up a book was about eight inches high and several yards long.

Both sides were written on. The "pages" were separated from each other by painted lines. When the book was complete, the entire strip was folded up accordion-like along the lines that marked the pages.

These ancient picture books are now called codices. *Codices* is a Latin word, the plural of *codex,* meaning a book in manuscript form. Thousands of these codices were drawn and painted by the Mayas, and by the people of other Indian civilizations in Central America.

"Picture book" does not really do justice to the codices. Even the simplest-appearing pictures in the codices are more than pictures. They are words and often whole phrases or ideas in picture form. Simple symbols merge into not-so-simple ones, sometimes in a striking way. A wagging tongue, for example, means "talking." A wagging tongue surrounded by flowers means "singing."

Of the thousands of codices that once existed, only seventeen are left. The others were burned by the Spanish, who conquered the Mayan lands between 1519 and 1521. The high civilization of the Mayas had collapsed centuries before the Spanish arrived. But the descendants of the Mayas still lived according to the old traditions, and the ancient language was still spoken.

Many of the books were burned by Spanish soldiers. The remainder were destroyed by missionaries. Bishop Diego de Landa, of Merida, capital of the Spanish province of Yucatán, summed up the reasons for the burning: "We found a larger number of books . . . and as they contained nothing but superstitions and lies of the devil, we burned them all, which the Indians regretted to an amazing degree, and which caused them great anguish."

Yet Bishop de Landa knew that the books contained more than mere superstition. He wrote: "These people [the Mayas] also made use of certain characters or letters, with which they wrote in their books their ancient affairs and their science, and with these and drawings, and with certain signs in these drawings, they understood their affairs and made others understand them and taught them."

De Landa learned to speak the Mayan lan-

guage. He discovered that large parts of certain codices were about astronomy and the Mayan calendar. In later years, he wrote down what he knew of the written language of the Mayas—largely how they wrote numbers and dates, and how they recorded national holidays, festivals, and astronomical events.

De Landa's work has given us what little we know about the writings of the Mayas. That part of the writing that deals with astronomy and date keeping we can read. The rest is largely unreadable. No one has cracked the "code" of the written language of the Mayas. Those who knew it are long dead, and almost all the written records are in ashes.

It is no wonder that Frederick Peterson, another archaeologist-explorer of the civilizations of ancient Mexico, wrote:

Imagine our great libraries all destroyed by invaders from a different universe and only seventeen books saved—those seventeen books consisting of almanacs, astronomical drawings, a book on black magic, a text on religious festivals and national holidays, a horoscope, a text on the conquests of the First World War and [the history] of a prominent family! What would the invaders think of our civilization when their historians began to analyse it through . . . these seventeen documents?

Truly, we know very little about the Mayas. The Spanish named their ancient lands Yucatán. The name shows their ignorance—and ours. In the years before the Spanish conquest, a Spanish navigator sailed around the coast of Mexico and saw impressive buildings. He landed and asked the Indians who had built them.

"Ci-u-than" ("We don't understand you"), came the answer. And "ci-u-than," changed to a version that was closer in sound to Spanish, became the name of the land.

What we do know makes us wonder about what has been lost. Just as we refer all our calendar dates back to the year of the birth of Christ, so the Mayas had a base date for their count of days and years. Because of that, and because of the accuracy of their date keeping, we can translate their dates into the terms used for our own calendar. Dr. J. Eric S. Thompson, an American who has made a study of Mayan civilization, places the Mayan base date at August 12, 3113 B.C., on our calendar.

In 3113 B.C., however, the Mayan civilization did not yet exist. The date may refer to some mythical event in the Mayan past. But wherever the Mayas built pyramids, temples, great pillars of stone, and cities, they carved dates. At hundreds of places throughout what is now Yucatán, the Mayas inscribed the dates of buildings and events. All these dates are counted from the same base date.

The Mayas believed that time moved in great cycles of 5125 years. At the end of each cycle, the sun and the world were destroyed and reborn. The end of the present cycle, which began in 3113 B.C., will be on December 24, 2011.

They used a numerical system like ours to record numbers. The main difference is that our system counts by tens. Theirs counted by twenties.

The Mayas also represented numbers by glyphs (pictures) of various gods. Time *was* many gods to the Mayas, and each time-god is shown carrying a load of days, months, or years on his back as he trudges his way around the great circle of the ages. . . .

One reason the Mayas kept such careful count of days was that they believed the past foretold the future. As far as predicting the motions of the sun, moon, and planets is concerned, this is very nearly true. Their movements through the sky are repeated in regular cycles. Some of the cycles are simple; some are complicated. But by patient observing, Mayan astronomers found the patterns of many of these movements.

Some of the patterns are recorded in the Dresden Codex, which is now housed in a museum in Dresden, in East Germany. The Dresden Codex is a collection of tables on the motions of the moon and the planet Venus. It is also a kind of horoscope, since the Mayas thought that the motions of heavenly bodies affected the fates of people on earth.

The Dresden Codex records the movements of Venus for over three hundred years. The Mayas calculated that the time it takes Venus to get back to the same point in the sky is 584 days. Using modern telescopes and observatory instruments, present-day astronomers have calculated the time as 583.92 days.

In the tables about the moon, the Mayas used the number 6585. As modern astronomers know, this is the period of time it takes for a series of eclipses of the sun and moon to repeat itself. The ancient Babylonians, who lived on the other side of the globe from the Mayas, also discovered and used this figure.

The Mayas did not use fractions or decimals, as the Babylonians did and as present-day astronomers do. They did learn to use whole numbers to express fractions very exactly, however.

For example, in the Dresden Codex the Mayas wrote that there are 405 moons (the time from new moon to new moon) in 11,958 days. If we divide 11,958 days by 405 moons, we get the length of one moon, or lunar month— 29.52593 days. Modern astronomers use the figure of 29.5306 days.

In other words, the ancient astronomers of the Yucatán made an error of about seven minutes out of some twenty-nine days!

Rachel L. Carson

The Sea Around Us

The Sea Around Us is an enthralling study of the mystery and beauty of the ocean with its islands, mountains, vast depths, and its fascinating sea life. With rare skill, Rachel Carson combines scientific accuracy with poetic imagination. Something of the rhythm and sweeping force of the sea itself is found in her writing. In the chapter given below, she tells of the mysterious forces that create the tides and the influence of the tide over the affairs of the sea creatures. [From Rachel L. Carson, *The Sea Around Us* (Oxford University Press, 1951).]

The Moving Tides

There is no drop of water in the ocean, not even in the deepest parts of the abyss, that does not know and respond to the mysterious forces that create the tide. No other force that affects the sea is so strong. Compared with the tide the wind-created waves are surface movements felt, at most, no more than a hundred fathoms below the surface. So, despite their impressive sweep, are the planetary currents, which seldom involve more than the upper several hundred fathoms. The masses of water affected by the tidal movement are enormous, as will be clear from one example. Into one small bay on the east coast of North America—Passamaquoddy—2 billion tons of water are carried by the tidal currents twice each day; into the whole Bay of Fundy, 100 million tons.

Here and there we find dramatic illustration of the fact that the tides affect the whole ocean, from its surface to its floor. The meeting of opposing tidal currents in the Strait of Messina creates whirlpools (one of them is Charybdis of classical fame) which so deeply stir the waters of the strait that fish bearing all the marks of abyssal existence, their eyes atrophied or abnormally large, their bodies studded with phosphorescent organs, frequently are cast up on the lighthouse beach, and the whole area yields a rich collection of deep-sea fauna for the Institute of Marine Biology at Messina.

The tides are a response of the mobile waters of the ocean to the pull of the moon and the more distant sun. In theory, there is a gravitational attraction between every drop of sea water and even the outermost star of the universe. In practice, however, the pull of the remote stars is so slight as to be obliterated in the vaster movements by which the ocean yields to the moon and the sun. Anyone who has lived near tidewater knows that the moon, far more than the sun, controls the tides. He has noticed that, just as the moon rises later each day by fifty minutes, on the average, than the day before, so, in most places, the time of high tide is correspondingly later each day. And as the moon waxes and wanes in its monthly cycle, so the height of the high tides varies. Twice each month, when the moon is a mere thread of silver in the sky, and again when it is full, we have the highest of the high tides, called the springs. At these times sun, moon, and earth are directly in line and the pull of the two heavenly bodies is added together to bring the water high on the beaches, and send its surf leaping upward against the sea cliffs, and draw a brimming tide into the harbors so that the boats float high beside their wharfs. And twice each month, at the quarters of the moon, when sun, moon, and earth lie at the apexes of a triangle, and the pull of sun and moon are opposed, we have the least tides of the lunar month, called the neaps.

The influence of the tide over the affairs of sea creatures as well as men may be seen all over the world. The billions upon billions of sessile animals, like oysters, mussels, and barnacles, owe their very existence to the sweep of the tides, which brings them the food which they are unable to go in search of. By marvelous adaptations of form and structure, the inhabitants of the world between the tide lines are enabled to live in a zone where the danger of being dried up is matched against the danger of being washed away, where for every enemy that comes by sea there is another comes by land, and where the most delicate of living tissues must somehow withstand the assault of storm waves that have the power to shift tons of rock or to crack the hardest granite.

The most curious and incredibly delicate adaptations, however, are the ones by which the breeding rhythm of certain marine animals is timed to coincide with the phases of the moon and the stages of the tide. In Europe it has been well established that the spawning activities of oysters reach their peak on the spring tides, which are about two days after the full or new moon. In the waters of northern Africa there is a sea urchin that, on the nights when the moon is full and apparently only then, releases its reproductive cells into the sea. And in tropical waters in many parts of the world there are small marine worms whose spawning behavior is so precisely adjusted to the tidal calendar that, merely from observing them, one could tell the month, the day, and often the time of day as well.

Near Samoa in the Pacific, the palolo worm lives out its life on the bottom of the shallow sea, in holes in the rocks and among the masses of corals. Twice each year, during the neap tides of the moon's last quarter in October and November, the worms forsake their burrows and rise to the surface in swarms that cover the water. For this purpose, each worm has literally broken its body in two, half to remain in its rocky tunnel, half to carry the reproductive products to the surface and there to liberate the cells. This happens at dawn on the day before the moon reaches its last quarter, and again on the following day; on the second day of the spawning the quantity of eggs liberated is so great that the sea is discolored.

The Fijians, whose waters have a similar worm, call them "Mbalolo" and have designated the periods of their spawning "Mbalolo lailai" (little) for October and "Mbalolo levu" (large) for November. Similar forms near the Gilbert Islands respond to certain phases of the moon in June and July; in the Malay Archipelago a related worm swarms at the surface on the second and third nights after the full moon of March and April, when the tides are running highest. A Japanese palolo swarms after the new moon and again after the full moon in October and November.

Concerning each of these, the question recurs but remains unanswered: is it the state of the tides that in some unknown way supplies the impulse from which springs this behavior, or is it, even more mysteriously, some other influence of the moon? It is easier to imagine that it is the press and the rhythmic movement of the water that in some way brings about this response. But why is it only certain tides of the year, and why for some species is it the fullest tides of the month and for others the least movements of the waters that are related to the perpetuation of the race? At present, no one can answer.

No other creature displays so exquisite an adaptation to the tidal rhythm as the grunion—a small, shimmering fish about as long as a man's hand. Though no one can say what processes of adaptation, extending over no one knows how many millennia, the grunion has come to know not only the daily rhythm of the tides, but the monthly cycle by which certain tides sweep higher on the beaches than others. It has so adapted its spawning habits to the tidal cycle that the very existence of the race depends on the precision of this adjustment.

Shortly after the full moon of the months from March to August, the grunion appear in the surf on the beaches of California. The tide reaches flood stage, slackens, hesitates, and begins to ebb. Now on these waves of the ebbing tide the fish begin to come in. Their bodies shimmer in the light of the moon as they are borne up the beach on the crest of a wave, they lie glitter-ing on the wet sand for a perceptible moment of time, then fling themselves into the wash of the next wave and are carried back to sea. For about an hour after the turn of the tide this continues, thousands upon thousands of grunion coming up onto the beach, leaving the water, returning to it. This is the spawning act of the species.

During the brief interval between successive waves, the male and female have come together in the wet sand, the one to shed her eggs, the other to fertilize them. When the parent fish return to the water, they have left behind a mass of eggs buried in the sand. Succeeding waves on that night do not wash out the eggs because the tide is already ebbing. The waves of the next high tide will not reach them, because for a time after the full of the moon each tide will halt its advance a little lower on the beach than the preceding one. The eggs, then, will be undisturbed for at least a fortnight. In the warm, damp, incubating sand they undergo their development. Within two weeks the magic change from fertilized egg to larval fishlet is completed, the perfectly formed little grunion still confined within the membranes of the egg, still buried in the sand, waiting for release. With the tides of the new moon it comes. Their waves wash over the places where the little masses of the grunion eggs were buried, the swirl and rush of the surf stirring the sand deeply. As the sand is washed away, and the eggs feel the touch of the cool sea water, the membranes rupture, the fishlets hatch, and the waves that released them bear them away to the sea.

But the link between tide and living creature I like best to remember is that of a very small worm, flat of body, with no distinction of appearance, but with unforgettable quality. The name of this worm is *Convoluta roscoffensis,* and it lives on the sandy beaches of northern Brittany and the Channel Islands. Convoluta has entered into a remarkable partnership with a green alga, whose cells inhabit the body of the worm and lend to its tissues their own green color. The worm lives entirely on the starchy products manufactured by its plant guest, having become so completely dependent upon this means of nutrition that its digestive organs have degenerated. In order that the algal cells may carry on their function of photosynthesis (which is dependent upon sunlight) Convoluta rises from the damp sands of the intertidal zone as soon as the tide has ebbed, the sand becoming spotted with large green patches composed of thousands of the worms. For the several hours while the tide is out, the worms lie thus in the sun, and the plants manufacture their starches and sugars; but when the tide returns, the worms must again sink into the sand to avoid being washed away, out into deep water. So the whole lifetime of the worm is a succession of movements conditioned by the stages of the tide— upward into the sunshine on the ebb, downward on the flood.

What I find most unforgettable about Convoluta is this: sometimes it happens that a marine biologist, wishing to study some related problem, will transfer a whole colony of the worms into the laboratory, there to establish them in an aquarium, where there are no tides. But twice each day Convoluta rises out of the sand on the bottom of the aquarium, into the light of the sun. And twice each day it sinks again into the sand. Without a brain, or what we would call a memory, or even any very clear perception, Convoluta continues to live out its life in this alien place, remembering, in every fiber of its small green body, the tidal rhythm of the distant sea.

James Dugan

Undersea Explorer: The Story of Captain Cousteau

One of Captain Jacques Cousteau's thrilling undersea adventures was finding and exploring a ship sunk in 205 B.C. This true story, stranger than Jules Verne's fiction, is told by one of Cousteau's oldest associates, who was the ship's reporter of undersea expeditions. [From James Dugan, *Undersea Explorer: The Story of Captain Cousteau* (Harper, 1957).]

Exploring a Ship Sunk before Christ Was Born

In the summer of 1952, Cousteau and Dumas were conferring in the captain's quarters of the *Calypso* with a short, white-haired man named Professor Fernand Benoît. He is a famous archeologist, who has dug up Greek ruins going back to six centuries before Christ. The ship was sailing from Toulon toward Marseille on a new exciting mission: underwater archeology.

Dumas pointed out Grand Congloué Island on the chart. "Professor," he said, "we are coming to a spot where there seems to be an ancient wreck. I heard about it from a free-lance salvage diver, who was sent to us with the bends. The poor guy lost his toes, but we saved his life. He thanked us by telling his underwater secrets. The most interesting story was about Grand Congloué. He said that under the island there is a natural arch about a hundred feet down. If you swim west of the arch, you'll find a cliff full of lobsters."

Dumas continued, "I asked the crippled diver how far the lobsters were from the arch. He said, 'You'll come to a bunch of those old jars lying on the floor. The lobsters are right above them.'" Dumas waved his pencil. "You see, Professor, the jars are amphoras, and the diver didn't know their archeological importance. When you find a lot of amphoras on the floor, there is almost certain to be an ancient ship buried under them."

Baked clay amphoras were used in ancient times to carry water, olive oil, wine, wheat, iron and copper ore, seeds—anything that would flow through their five-inch necks. Ancient Greek and Roman ships were loaded with eight-gallon amphoras from the keel to high above the deck.

Cousteau said, "We're coming into Grand Congloué." They went on deck. The *Calypso* was passing through a channel as stark as the landscape of the moon. On one side was the mainland coast, a towering cliff of white limestone; and on the other was a chain of craggy islets without a sign of life. One was Grand Congloué, a stone layer cake, fallen on one side and rising 150 feet high. The *Calypso* anchored by the ghostly rock and Cousteau, Dumas and Benoît got into a launch.

Dumas rigged the aluminum diving ladder over the side of the launch and harnessed up. "The arch should be down about here," he said. He turned down in the blue water and found excellent underwater visibility, about seventy feet. Soon he saw the looming arch in its blanket of live coral and felt the thrill of discovery. Dumas is an ardent underwater archeologist. When he was thirteen years old, he uncovered a two-thousand-year-old grave on the seashore and began learning archeology—how to find buried objects and learn from them how people lived long ago.

He swam west from the arch along the steep island base. Soon he passed a few pairs of lobster horns, sticking out of crevices. There they were, but not half as many as the diver had dreamed. He turned down for the ancient jars, but saw nothing on the bank of hard fossil mud that the high island stood upon, half in the water, half in the air. He continued reeling across the floor, but saw no jars. His time ran out and he surfaced. Professor Benoît said, "Oh, well, let's go on to Maire Island. We're sure of an ancient wreck there."

Cousteau said, "I think I'll have a look at this spot, before we go on." He dived to the place Dumas' search had broken off, and continued swimming around the island, which is 450 feet long. He peered down into the mud, made up of the skeletons of trillions of tiny drifting animals that had died and rained down during the centuries. The mud was littered with rocks that had fallen from the island. Only trained eyes could tell amphoras from the rocks. The jars, too, would be covered with sponges and weeds. But Cousteau could see no graceful curves of amphoras. He swam far and deep, once dipping down to two hundred feet. He came to the end of his safety limit. It was a very strenuous dive. He turned toward the surface. When he reached 130 feet of depth, he came upon a mud shelf, half pocketed in the cliff. There, spreading far and wide, were hundreds of amphoras, tumbled about or with necks sticking up from the mud!

Among the big jars, Cousteau saw stacks of bowls and dishes. He had time only to scoop up three nested bowls before he kicked for the launch high above.

Professor Benoît was impatiently looking into the water when he saw a hand holding three bowls rising from the sea. He grabbed the bowls and his face turned red with excitement.

"They're third century B.C.," he shouted. "If there is a wreck, it will be the oldest seagoing ship ever found!" Cousteau climbed aboard and slumped in exhaustion. "Don't worry, Professor," he said, "there's a big ship down there. I feel it in my bones. The signs are perfect."

The divers pelted down to see it. They found the amphoras spread on a sloping shelf 112 to 150 feet deep, directly under the vertical island wall. They lowered a wire basket and filled it with loose jars and dishes. The potteries came up covered with clinging oysters, sponges and mussels, branches of red and yellow gorgonians and bright splotches like fresh paint which were actually colonies of microscopic animals. They hosed the mud from the jars and an octopus slithered out on deck. Octopuses love small hiding places and the amphoras were perfect for them. The wreck was an octopus city.

The *Calypso* lowered a suction pipe and the divers "carved" away at the mud to free more jars. Hundreds of amphoras were buried upright in the mud, stacked exactly as they had been by stevedores twenty-two centuries before. Cousteau decided they would work two months on the wreck and bring up everything, buried ship and all. They sailed into Marseille with decks and passageways piled high with amphoras, and thousands rushed to the dock as the news spread of the great discovery.

As the *Calypso* continued the underwater dig, she was imperiled by anchoring so close to the rock. Several times winds rose suddenly and blew the ship towards the rocks. Cousteau decided it was too dangerous over the wreck. "Anyway," he said, "the *Calypso's* proper business is at sea, not hanging around unloading cargo that is twenty-two hundred years overdue." He continued, "The wreck is right under the island. Why not work from the rock?" Dumas said, "We don't have enough money to run the *Calypso* and this would mean planting a base on the island and keeping people here all the time." Cousteau said, "I have some ideas. I'd like you to go and explain the plan to Professor Benoît and see if he can get government funds." The government helped and so did the Marseille authorities. By now, the divers realized that bringing up the ancient ship would take longer than the two months they had originally set. (They didn't realize, however, that it would take six years.)

Cousteau invited General Mollé of the French Army to visit Grand Congloué. The general put on an Aqua-Lung for the first time in his life and swam 130 feet down into the excavation. He came up, exclaiming, "It's magnificent! Do you think she can be completely excavated?" Cousteau said, "Yes, sir, if we can get more help."

Three days later the *Calypso* landed a bunch of seasick army engineers on the rock. They blasted out a platform on the cliff, ten feet above the water, and installed a hand winch to lift wreck finds. In Marseille, Cousteau found some beat-up Nissen huts left by the U.S. Army, which was happy to let him have them if he would haul them away. The huts became a neat house for ten divers perched high on the island. The team planted an eighty-foot boom to carry a suction pipe out over the wreck and put an air compressor on the platform to power the suction pipe.

They named the new settlement Port Calypso, and hoisted their own green and white flag of the nymph and the porpoise. The Marseille Chamber of Commerce and businessmen adopted the islanders and sent them an electric-light plant, a refrigerator, a two-way radio-telephone and furniture. The National Geographic Society in Washington voted them money to help dig up the past.

Many excited volunteers asked to dive at Port Calypso. Captain Cousteau is careful with volunteers, who sometimes have more enthusiasm than ability. Volunteers hardly learn the job before they have to leave; and the Port Calypso divers had to stick to it. One day a lawyer named Pierre Labat said to Cousteau, "My diving team would like to help." Cousteau said, "Thank you, Monsieur, but this is hard dangerous work." Labat said, "Captain, my boys know their business. We are the French diving scouts, the first scouts in the world to become expert free divers. We have only older, experienced fellows."

Cousteau said, "Yes, scout training *is* serious." The diving scouts went out to the lonely rock and fished for history. Thousands of jars and dishes came up in the wire basket, along with hunks of the wooden hull, crew tools and sheets of lead with which the old ship had been entirely covered. The divers straddled the big suction pipe and carved deeper into the fossil mud. It was like riding a writhing anaconda. The pipe seemed like a living, shuddering monster. It sucked up mud, weeds, stones, fish— everything in its path. The divers were extremely careful not to get the mouth cupped against their bodies. The pipe would have stripped the flesh from their bones.

The divers labored strenuously to uncover the amphoras, pile them up beside the pit and load the lift basket when it came down. Someone had a brilliant labor-saving idea and took down an air hose. He filled an amphora with compressed air. It shot to the surface like a torpedo. But it was more trouble chasing jet jars around on the surface than loading them downstairs.

After several months' work the pit was deep and wide enough to reveal the ribs of the ancient argosy. The divers looked with emotion at a vessel unseen for nearly twenty-two hundred years.

Port Calypso was a frontier post, battling nature to survive. In the autumn came the cruel mistral, a whistling gale that sweeps off the mainland in this part of France, sometimes at ninety miles an hour. It is caused by sea-heated air rising after the land has already cooled in autumn. The cold air screams out to sea to take up the vacuum. The 1952 mistral hurled its might of wind and water at Port Calypso.

The waves heaved their backs under the engine house, knocking out planking and clutching at the big compressor. Spray blew over the peak of the island, flailing at the tin house. The divers came out in it to defend the engine house. They watched helplessly as the waves dragged the platform, the winch and air bottles down on top of the old wreck. The big boom swayed and its cables began to snap. Henri Goiran and Raymond Kientzy crawled eighty feet out on the whipping boom, disappearing from time to time in furious white waves. They secured the cables and ran back on the boom between waves. If they had been knocked off, there was not much chance of surviving. But they saved the boom and themselves.

The great mistral passed. The divers went down and hoisted their equipment. They built another platform several feet higher. Port Calypso fought five rounds with the annual storm and lost only one. The work went on with new rewards for their valor.

Michael Collins

Flying to the Moon and Other Strange Places

The exploration of space, compared in importance to the discovery of the New World, has been called the great adventure of our age. Former astronaut Michael Collins (now director of the Smithsonian's National Air and Space Museum in Washington, D.C.) has written a vigorous account of human adventuring in space from the intriguing perspective of one who has been there. In this selection Collins recounts the flight of Apollo 11 and the first landing on the moon. [From Michael Collins, *Flying to the Moon and Other Strange Places* (Farrar, Straus & Giroux, 1976).]

Day number 3 was even quieter than day number 2 but day number 4 had an entirely different feeling to it. We knew we were going to be plenty busy and were going to see some strange sights. We stopped our barbecue motion and got our first look at the moon in nearly a day. The change in its appearance was spectacular! The moon I had known all my life, that small flat yellow disk in the sky, had gone somewhere, to be replaced by the most awesome sphere I had ever seen. It was huge, completely filling *Columbia's* largest window. It was also three-dimensional, by which I mean that we could see its belly bulging out toward us, while its surface obviously receded toward the edges. I felt that I could almost reach out and touch it. It was between us and the sun, putting us in its shadow. The sun created a halo around it, making the moon's surface dark and mysterious in comparison with its shining rim. Its surface was lighted by earthshine, which was sunshine that had bounced off the surface of the earth onto the surface of the moon. It cast a bluish eerie glow by which we could see large craters and the darker flat areas known as maria, or seas. It didn't look like a very friendly place, but Neil summed it up: "It's worth the price of the trip." To me, it also looked a little bit scary.

In order to get into orbit around the moon, we had to slow down, or else we would have shot right on by it. We fired *Columbia's* rocket engine shortly after we swung around behind the moon's left edge, out of touch with the earth for the first time in three days. However, we didn't need the earth, because our own computer told us which way to point and how long to fire the engine. After slightly over six minutes of engine firing, our computer told us we had arrived, and we had! We were skimming along approximately sixty miles above the moon's pockmarked surface. The back side of the moon, which we never see from earth, is even more battered and tortured-looking than the front side. On the back, there are no smooth maria, but only highlands which have been scarred by the impact of meteorites over billions of years. There is no atmosphere surrounding the moon to produce clouds or smog, so our view was impaired only by darkness. . . . We were really eager to get a look at our landing site. We didn't have any trouble finding it, because we had been studying maps for months and had memorized a series of craters and other checkpoints leading up to the landing site. But, boy, when we got there, it sure looked rough to me. It didn't look smooth enough to park a baby buggy, much less our landing craft *Eagle.* I didn't say anything to Neil or Buzz. I just hoped it was the angle of the sun which was causing the rough appearance. We would find out tomorrow. . . .

The next day, number 5, lunar-landing day, began with the usual wake-up call from Houston, and proceeded swiftly from there. . . . As soon as breakfast was over, we had to scramble into our pressure suits. Neil and Buzz began by putting on special underwear, into which thin plastic tubes had been woven. Water would be pumped from their backpacks into their suits and through these tubes, cooling their bodies while they were out on the hot lunar surface. Since I would not be joining them there, I wore plain old regular underwear, or "long johns" as they are called. When we unpacked the three pressure suits from their bags, they seemed almost to fill the entire command module, as if there were three extra people in there with us. After quite a struggle and a tug of war with a balky zipper, we finally got the suits on, and our helmets and gloves locked in place. Then Neil and Buzz entered the lunar module, and I locked the hatch after them. I threw a switch on my instrument panel, and our two spacecraft were separated.

Neil backed off fifty feet or so and made a slow 360° turn in front of me. The idea was to allow me to inspect all sides of the lunar module for possible damage, and to make sure all four landing gear were extended properly. I couldn't find anything wrong with *Eagle,* but it sure looked strange, unlike any kind of flying machine I had ever seen. It looked like a huge gold, black, and gray bug hanging awkwardly in the black sky. But Buzz was pleased with it. "The *Eagle* has wings!" he shouted. To me, it didn't look like an eagle, and I couldn't find any wings, only lumps and bumps and odd shapes on its surface. Since a lunar module flies only in space, high above the earth's atmosphere, the designers didn't have to make it streamlined, which is the reason it looked so awkward.

As Neil and Buzz descended to the lunar surface, I kept my eyes on them as long as I could. If they had to come back in a hurry for any reason, I wanted to know where they were. Looking at them through my sextant, I watched *Eagle* grow smaller and smaller until finally, when it was about one hundred miles away (below me and in front of me), I lost sight of it amid the craters. My main job now was to keep *Columbia* running properly, and to keep quiet, because *Eagle* and Houston would have plenty to talk about during the landing attempt. Sure enough, it wasn't long before I could hear Neil telling Houston his computer was acting strangely, and Houston promptly replied that he should continue toward a landing. Buzz was calling off numbers to Neil, so that Neil could devote all his attention to looking out the window. The most important numbers were altitude (in feet above the surface) and descent

rate (in feet per second). "Six hundred feet, down at nineteen . . . Four hundred feet, down at nine . . . Three hundred feet . . . Watch our shadow out there," called Buzz, repeating new numbers every few seconds. He also reported they had only 5 percent of their fuel remaining, which wasn't much. I started getting nervous. "Forty feet, down two and a half, kicking up some dust." Well, at least the dust didn't seem to be a big problem, that was good. "Thirty seconds!" said Houston, meaning that they had only thirty seconds' worth of fuel remaining. Better get it on the ground, Neil! Suddenly Buzz shouted: "Contact light!" and I knew they were down. The lunar module had a wire dangling below one landing gear. When it touched the moon, it caused a light on the instrument panel to light, so that Neil would know he was just about to touch down. As soon as he did, he called: Houston, Tranquility Base here, the *Eagle* has landed." Whew! I breathed a big sigh of relief. Neil then explained why he had nearly run out of gas. The computer-controlled descent was taking *Eagle* into an area covered with huge boulders, and Neil had to keep flying until he found a smoother spot to land. As good as that computer was, it took the eyes of the pilot to pick the best landing spot. . . .

. . . I had turned up the lights inside *Columbia,* and it seemed like a happy place. Also big, for a change, with only me inside it. I didn't feel lonely or left out, because I knew my job was very important, and that Neil and Buzz could never get home without me. I was proud of the way *Columbia* and I were circling above them, waiting for their return. I felt like the basecamp operator on a mountain-climbing expedition. I suppose one reason I didn't feel lonely was that I had been flying airplanes by myself for nearly twenty years. This time, however, I had to admit that it *was* a bit different, especially on the far side of the moon. There, cut off from all communication, I was truly alone, the only person in the solar system who could not even see the planet of his birth. Far from causing fear, this situation gave me a good feeling—one of confidence and satisfaction. Outside my window I could see stars, and nothing else. I knew where the moon was, but in the total darkness, its surface was not visible: it was simply that part of my window which had no stars in it. The feeling was less like flying than like being alone in a boat on the ocean at night. Stars above, pure black below. At dawn, light filled my windows so quickly that my eyes hurt. Almost immediately, the stars disappeared and the moon reappeared. I knew from my clock that the earth was about to reappear, and right on schedule it popped into view, rising like a blue and white jewel over the desolate lunar horizon.

As soon as the earth reappeared, I could once more talk on my radio, and I found out from Houston that all was going well with Neil and Buzz. They had decided to skip a scheduled four-hour nap and instead began exploring right away. Neil, first down the ladder and therefore the first human to step on another planet, found he had no difficulty at all in walking on the moon. The surface was level and solid and firm, and he easily kept his balance in the strange gravitational field where everything weighed only one sixth its earth weight. I could hear what they were saying because Houston relayed their calls to me. It was a bit unusual, though, because even traveling at the speed of light, it took two and a half seconds for the radio signals to go from *Eagle* to the earth and then back to *Columbia.* If they said something to me, they had to wait at least five seconds for an answer. When I was overhead of their position, I could talk to them directly, but the rest of the time that I was on the front side of the moon, the relay procedure was necessary. When I was on the back side, I couldn't talk to anyone.

They hadn't been out on the surface very long when the three of us got a big surprise. The President of the United States began talking on the radio! Mr. Nixon told them: "Neil and Buzz, I am talking to you by telephone from the Oval Office at the White House, and this certainly has to be the most historic telephone call ever made . . . Because of what you have done, the heavens have become a part of man's world. As you talk to us from the Sea of Tranquility, it inspires us to redouble our efforts to bring peace and tranquility to Earth." Neil replied that he was honored and privileged to be on the moon, representing the United States

and men of peace from all nations. I felt proud to be representing my country, and I was glad that Neil and Buzz had planted an American flag on the moon. Now I just wanted them to collect their rocks and get back on up here to *Columbia.* They really sounded good on the surface, not tired at all, but I was still relieved when they got back inside *Eagle* and got the door locked. That was another big hurdle behind us, and none of us, we hoped, would need our pressure suits again. In the meantime, we were scheduled to sleep for a few hours, so that we would be fresh for the complicated rendezvous. . . .

. . . I slept like a log, until I heard a voice in my ear, calling over and over again: *"Columbia, Columbia,* good morning from Houston." "Hi, Ron," I replied groggily. It was Ron Evans, an astronaut who would later fly to the moon on the final Apollo flight. Ron told me it was going to be a busy day, which I knew already, and then he proved it by giving me a long list of things to do to prepare for the rendezvous. As the day wore on, I knew I would be expected to perform approximately 850 computer-button pushes alone. If everything went well with *Eagle,* I knew precisely what to do, because I had practiced over and over again in the simulator, but if I had to do rescue *Eagle* from some lopsided orbit, then things could get awfully complicated in a big hurry. I had a book around my neck, fastened by a clip to my pressure suit, which contained procedures for eighteen different types of rendezvous that I might need.

As *Eagle's* lift-off time approached, I got really nervous, probably as nervous as I got any time during the flight. If their engine didn't work, there was nothing I could do to rescue them from the surface. I simply had to come home by myself, leaving Neil and Buzz to die on the surface of the moon. They had oxygen enough for only another day at the most. Needless to say, the idea of leaving them was horrible, but it was the only thing I could do, as it made no sense for me to commit suicide. These thoughts were running through my mind as I heard Buzz counting the seconds to ignition: "9–8–7–6–5 . . . Beautiful!" They were off! Seven minutes later, their single engine had pushed them into a good orbit, below and behind me, and they then began a carefully calculated three-hour chase to close the gap. . . .

For the first time in six months, I felt that the Apollo 11 flight was definitely going to be a success. All I had to do now was dock with *Eagle,* transfer Neil and Buzz back into *Columbia,* and head for home! The docking itself went well, with just a slight bump as *Columbia* nudged *Eagle,* but then *Eagle* gave a wild lurch and for a couple of seconds I thought we might have real trouble. But the two vehicles swung back in line, and then the docking latches pulled them together in a tight grip, and all was well again. Buzz was first through the hatch, with a triumphant grin on his face. I was going to kiss him, but then I got embarrassed and just shook his hand. Together we greeted Neil, and for a couple of minutes the three of us just floated there, admiring two shiny silver boxes filled with moon rocks. . . . As we left the moon, we curved around its right side, and we could see it gleaming in the sunlight, vividly etched against the black sky in gray-tan tones. It was beautiful, but it was nothing compared to earth, and I didn't want to come back ever.

The trip home was quiet and uneventful. I spent my time doing routine housekeeping chores, like adding chlorine to the drinking water, and watching the moon get smaller and the beautiful earth grow larger and more inviting as each hour went by. . . .

We had just one more hurdle to clear, that of landing safely in the ocean. We were scheduled to come down in an empty part of the South Pacific, where the aircraft carrier *Hornet* was waiting for us. President Nixon was also on the *Hornet.* As we approached the earth, our speed really started to build up, so that we were going 25,000 miles per hour by the time we plunged back into the atmosphere at a very shallow angle of 6°. . . .

As we began to penetrate the thin upper atmosphere, the sky out our windows began to change from the black of space to a tunnel of light. We were trailing a comet's tail of light, orange-yellow in the center, with edges of blue-green and lavender. It was a spectacular sight, which grew in intensity as the air became denser. Finally the tunnel expanded and its core became so brilliant that I felt we were in the center of a gigantic million-watt light bulb. We could be seen for many hundreds of miles as we arced across the predawn Pacific sky. . . .

I had bet Neil that when *Columbia* hit the water it would not turn over. Some Apollo command modules turned over, and others didn't. It depended on a lot of things, but the most important item was to jettison the parachutes swiftly, before the wind could catch in them and pull the spacecraft sideways, causing it to topple upside down. On the other hand, we had to be a hundred percent certain not to jettison the parachutes *before* the spacecraft hit the water. The procedure was for Buzz (the instant after we hit the water) to turn on the electricity going to the parachute release, and then I would throw the switches to release the chutes. I was thinking about this when all of a sudden— SPLAT!!—we hit the water like a ton of bricks. Buzz's arm was jerked downward, and before he could move it back up to his electrical panel, I felt us begin to topple over. *Drat!* Neil had won again.

Readings on
Children's Literature

Children's literature in the 1980s is an expanding industry. In the United States alone, 2,500 to 3,000 children's books are published annually and over 40,000 titles for children are listed as being in print. The network of groups and institutions concerned with this literature is active and extensive. Not only do publishers promote an interest in children's literature, but so do schools, libraries, research centers, and organizations such as the American Children's Book Council, the British National Book League, and the Canadian Children's Book Centre. College and university departments of English, education, and librarianship either already offer courses in children's and adolescent literature or are soon to add them to their programs. Professional associations, conferences, and scholarly and reviewing journals, such as *Children's Literature, Signal,* and *Canadian Children's Literature,* treat children's literature with serious attention.

The body of criticism of children's literature is growing just as fast as the literature itself. There are anthologies of key readings culled from critical articles, such as *Only Connect* (2d ed., 1980), edited by Sheila Egoff and others, and *Crosscurrents of Criticism* (1977), edited by Paul Heins. Critical speeches have been collected, as in *The Arbuthnot Lectures, 1970–1979* (1980), edited by Zena Sutherland. There are collections of speeches and commentaries by writers, such as *The Openhearted Audience* (1980), edited by Virginia Haviland, and Katherine

Paterson's *Gates of Excellence* (1981). There are general texts and historical surveys that introduce students to the field, such as *Children and Books* (6th ed., 1981), by Zena Sutherland and others, and F. J. Harvey Darton's *Children's Books in England* (3d ed., 1982). There are in-depth studies of such particular aspects of the literature as genres, trends, themes, historical periods, national literatures, or specific authors, as in Margaret Blount's *Animal Land* (1975), Sheila Egoff's *Republic of Childhood* (2d ed., 1975) and *Thursday's Child* (1981), and John Rowe Townsend's *A Sense of Story* (1971) and *A Sounding of Storytellers* (1979). Some studies combine criticism with book selection guidance, as in Lillian Smith's *The Unreluctant Years* (1953), a classic in the field. And there are general reference works such as *The Oxford Companion to Children's Literature* (1984), edited by Humphrey Carpenter and Mari Prichard.

Critic Clifton Fadiman states that in his investigation of children's literature he came to the conclusion that:

The body of criticism and history is not only formidable; it is valuable. It points up the importance of what at first might seem a minor field of investigation. . . .

Among the creators of that literature who have defended its integrity are James Krüss, Eleanor Cameron, Maurice Sendak, I. B. Singer, J. R. R. Tolkien, C. S. Lewis, Kornei Chukovsky. Among the scholars who have analyzed its properties, staked out its limits, and celebrated its charms are the Frenchman Paul Hazard, the Italian Enzo Petrini, the Swiss Hans Cornioley, the Englishman Brian Alderson, the Canadian Sheila Egoff, the Swede Eva von Zweigbergk, the Iberian Carmen Bravo-Villasante, the Netherlander J. Riemans-Reurslag, the Luxembourger Paul von Noesen, the Argentinian Dora Pastoriza de Etchebarna, the Mexican Blanca Lydia Trajo, the New Zealander Dorothy White, the Israeli Uriel Ofek, the Norwegian Jo Tenfjord . . . the catalogue, though not endless, is impressive.[1]

Chapters 16 and 17 contain selections from this impressive catalogue, a sampling of what both the creators and the critics have to say about children's literature.

This proliferation of criticism might appear to be a recent phenomenon, but it is not. The history of the criticism of children's literature reaches back to the nineteenth century. And, from its beginnings with Mrs. Trimmer, whose approach to the field was succinctly described by the title of her periodical, *The Guardian of Education* (1802–06), to the most current approaches of contemporary scholarship, the criticism has given rise to the same questions, issues, and topics. One of the most basic questions is, "Why study children's literature at all?" Many critics have pointed out that the association of children's books with women and children has made it suspect, as though a four-year-old's bedtime reading were beneath the notice of serious (and, by implication, "manly") adults. As Robert Bator, in *Signposts to Criticism of Children's Literature* (1983), suggests, the "mention of child audience to some conjures up images of drooling simpletons."[2] But the question of "why" is easily answered. If we consider children to be important, then we must consider what they read to be important as well.

We do consider children to be important; in fact, the fervor with which issues in children's literature are debated is a measure of the importance we ascribe

1. Clifton Fadiman, "The Case for a Children's Literature," *Children's Literature: Annual of the Modern Language Association Group on Children's Literature and the Children's Literature Association*, 5 (1976), 19–21.
2. Robert Bator, "Approaches: The Question of What Criticism," in *Signposts to Criticism of Children's Literature*, ed. Robert Bator (American Library Association, 1983), p. 69.

to children—the potential inheritors of the values, aspirations, and dreams of our culture. "Our purpose in studying children's literature," Barbara Harrison writes, "in no small measure, is to improve the quality of literary experience children receive in school and in society and thus to improve the quality of their lives."[3] Other reasons for studying children's literature include the acquisition of a knowledge of the literature for its own sake, and for the education of the imagination that continues into adulthood. As C. S. Lewis writes: "No book is really worth reading at the age of ten which is not equally (and often far more) worth reading at the age of fifty."[4]

The "how" of the study of children's literature involves reading, interpreting, and commenting upon select and representative samplings of children's books. It also involves the consideration of the historical development and social context of, and the cultural influences on, the literature. And, in tandem with literary criticism in general, it involves a theoretical examination of the nature of literature and literary values. "Through this study," Harrison continues, "clear distinctions are maintained between literary issues and extraliterary issues, between pedagogical concerns and aesthetic ones, and between critical questions and questions of selection."[5]

Contemporary critics of children's literature are drawn from every discipline: education, librarianship, English, psychology, linguistics, sociology, philosophy, history, and art history, among others. Along with the scholars, the creators of the literature also offer commentary. But no matter from what viewpoint the literature is regarded, a number of recurring questions must be faced. What is children's literature, and how does it differ from adult literature? How and why does one write for children? What are appropriate standards of criticism, and should they involve nonliterary as well as literary criteria? What are the most effective means of introducing literature to children?

The most fundamental question of all appears to be the question of what is meant by the adjective *children's* in children's literature. What is to be done with it? Critics such as John Rowe Townsend, Brian Alderson, and Paul Heins have taken a position we might call purist. They have claimed, in their different ways, that the adjective *children's* is a specifying term denoting a work's accessibility to children, but that it must be respectfully set aside in critical discussions of the literature.[6] As Townsend puts it, "There is no such thing as children's literature, there is just literature."[7] To these critics, children's literature is simply a part of all literature and should be treated without consideration of the readership—just as writing for adults is treated.

Other critics, including Margaret Meek, Elaine Moss, and Aidan Chambers, would argue that the child-reader's interests, needs, and responses must be taken into account, that a concern with the intended audience is crucial to a critical appraisal of children's literature. Even Paul Heins, while still maintaining the

3. Barbara Harrison, "Why Study Children's Literature," *The Quarterly Journal of the Library of Congress*, 38 (1981), 253.
4. C. S. Lewis, "On Stories," in *Essays Presented to Charles Williams* (Oxford University Press, 1947, reprinted by Books for Libraries Press, 1972), p. 100.
5. Harrison, p. 244.
6. Paul Heins, "Out on a Limb with the Critics: Some Random Thoughts on the Present State of the Criticism of Children's Literature," *The Horn Book Magazine*, 46 (1970), 264–73, reprinted in *Crosscurrents of Criticism: Horn Book Essays, 1968–1977*, ed. Paul Heins (Horn Book, 1977), p. 77.
7. John Rowe Townsend, "Standards of Criticism for Children's Literature," in *The Arbuthnot Lectures, 1970–1979*, comp. Zena Sutherland (American Library Association, 1980), p. 27.

purity of his viewpoint, states: "However, even if children's literature should be considered as literature, it does not cease to be children's literature. But, unfortunately, there is no simple, or clear and easy way by which to determine the proper relationship between the term *children's* and the term *literature.*"[8]

And, indeed, a definition of children's literature is extremely elusive. Historically, children have adopted works originally intended for adults, for example, Bunyan's *Pilgrim's Progress,* 1678, Swift's *Gulliver's Travels,* 1726, and Defoe's *Robinson Crusoe,* 1719. But it should be noted that children only appropriate those adult works that match their reading interests and tastes. Some works have been read by adults and children with no distinction drawn whatsoever as to audience. In this category, adults have shared with children the works of authors such as Robert Louis Stevenson, Rudyard Kipling, J. R. R. Tolkien, Richard Adams, and Ursula Le Guin. And the most sophisticated of contemporary children's books by such writers as Alan Garner possess a complexity and impact that not only is far beyond the range of the traditional children's novel, but also puts them in a class with the most innovative of contemporary adult fiction.

Critics have argued that the division between children's and adult books is artificial and arbitrary, based upon administrative or commercial considerations rather than aesthetic ones, and that this division meets the needs of teachers, librarians, publishers, and booksellers rather than those of readers. The simplest definition of a children's book may be, from a practical viewpoint, any book that a child is found reading. But from a commercial or an organizational stance, John Rowe Townsend's definition is sound:

Arguments about whether such-and-such a book is "really for children" are always cropping up, and are usually pointless in any but organizational terms. The only practical definition of a children's book today—absurd as it sounds—is "a book which appears on the children's list of a publisher."[9]

The writers of children's books have their own strong opinions on this question, and we will begin our survey of the creators and critics of these books with an examination of what the writers of children's books have to say about their craft and its relationship to children.

8. Heins, p. 77.
9. John Rowe Townsend, Introduction, *A Sense of Story: Essays on Contemporary Writers for Children* (Horn Book, 1971), p. 10.

*We know that those of us who
write for children are called, not
to do something to a child, but be
someone for a child. "Art," in
Frances Clarke Sayers's wonderfully passionate definition, is "a
controlled fury of desire to share
one's private revelation of life."
And she the librarian summons
us who are writers to the service of
art—to give the best that is in us
to "the audience that lives by
what it feeds upon."* [1]

16   The Creators

Writers of children's books are often asked why they write for children. Even when not asked, they consistently feel compelled—
in speeches, interviews, and articles—to defend their craft. Critics
might, with cool, scholarly detachment, deal with the questions
of what children's literature is and how it is related to adult literature, but the
creators themselves frequently respond to these questions in an intensely personal
way that at times is stubbornly defensive or fervently messianic. These are the
people, after all, who write the books. Here is the adamant Pamela Travers:
"For me, all books are for children. There is no such thing as a children's
book. There are books of many kinds and some of them children read."[2]

Maurice Sendak apparently once held a similar view but later modified it.
"We all should . . . stop pretending that there is such a thing as being able to
sit down and write a book for a child," he said in 1970. "It is quite impossible."[3]

---

1. Katherine Paterson, "Newbery Medal Acceptance," *The Horn Book Magazine*, 57 (1981), 392–
93.
2. Quoted in John Tunis, "What Is a Juvenile Book?" *The Horn Book Magazine*, 44 (1968), reprinted
in *Crosscurrents of Criticism: Horn Book Essays, 1968–1977*, ed. Paul Heins (Horn Book, 1977), p.
26.
3. Maurice Sendak, with Virginia Haviland, "Questions to an Artist Who Is Also an Author," *The
Quarterly Journal of the Library of Congress*, 28 (1971), 280.

But in 1979, he said, "There *are* books that are written, illustrated, and published as children's books, and they are good books, produced very much with children in mind: their pleasures, sorrows, and passionate interests. They are often practical and full of the pedantic details that delight children."[4]

Critics such as Robert Bator and Francelia Butler have suggested that the source of many difficulties for children's book writers—both in defining children's literature and in recognizing their audience—may stem from social status. Children's literature has often been the subject of condescension and misunderstanding, its status low, or uncertain at best, and related to the status of the child in society. Where and when children are perceived as inferior beings, children's literature and the writers of children's books are also perceived as inferior. Indeed, writing for children, since its inception, has frequently been seen as not quite respectable, of secondary value, and of use only as instruction. Katherine Paterson relates that she was once asked by a reporter:

"What is your philosophy of writing for children? Isn't there some moral you want to get across to them? Aren't there some values you wish to instill in your young readers?" "I'm trying," I said, "to write for my readers the best story, the truest story of which I am capable." . . . He seemed to share the view of many intelligent, well-educated, well-meaning people that while adult literature may aim to be art, the object of children's books is to whip the little rascals into shape.[5]

Given the prevalent but mistaken notion that children's books are easier to write and, ultimately, lesser works of art than adult books, it is no wonder that many children's book writers are defensive in their public comments. Some writers may also resent the restriction of their readership from the wider audience of adults. Annoyed with the often implied suggestion that they might some day become skilled enough to graduate to writing "real" books for adults, they often distance themselves from the idea of having *any* audience, stressing that they write for themselves or for the child within themselves. The classic statement of this position is made by Arthur Ransome: "You write not for children, but for yourself, and if, by good fortune, children enjoy what you enjoy, why then you are a writer of children's books."[6]

Ivan Southall disagrees: "It is fashionable . . . to deny that one writes for children specifically, to assert that one writes for people, but I cannot hang my hat on that hook. I believe one *does* write for children in a certain difficult-to-define way."[7]   And it is the form of writing for children that draws C. S. Lewis to the field of controversy, commenting that a children's story is written "because a children's story is the best art form for something you have to say."[8]

The writers who attest to their experience of writing from and for the child within speak with an emotional conviction and intensity. They range from Maurice

4. David E. White, "A Conversation with Maurice Sendak," *The Horn Book Magazine,* 56 (1980), 146–47.

5. Katherine Paterson, p. 392.

6. Arthur Ransome, "A Letter to the Editor," *The Junior Bookshelf,* 1 (1937), 4, as quoted in Robert Bator, "Status: In and Out of the Literary Sandbox," in *Signposts to Criticism of Children's Literature,* ed. Robert Bator (American Library Association, 1983), p. 21.

7. Ivan Southall, "Sources and Responses," *The Quarterly Journal of the Library of Congress,* 31 (1974), 81–91, reprinted in *The Openhearted Audience: Ten Authors Talk about Writing for Children,* ed. Virginia Haviland (Library of Congress, 1980), p. 92.

8. C. S. Lewis, "On Three Ways of Writing for Children," *The Horn Book Magazine,* 39 (1963), 460.

Sendak, who says he has "the knack of recalling the emotional quality of child-hood,"[9] to Meindert DeJong, who expresses his view that adults cannot "write for children from adult memory" of childhood, but must enter their own subconscious and become the universal child in order to write for children.[10]   Other writers maintain that children are a more difficult and demanding audience than adults, one preferable to adults because of their responsiveness and clear-eyed candor. Isaac Bashevis Singer praises the contemporary child as "a consumer of a great growing literature—a reader who cannot be deluded by literary and barren experiments. . . . It's easier to force university students to eat literary straw and clay than an infant in a kindergarten."[11]

And still others claim that there are no differences among age groups. The Victorian fantasist George MacDonald states with a flourish: "I do not write for children, but for the childlike, whether five or fifty, or seventy-five."[12]

The question of audience is perhaps most equitably handled by Aidan Chambers, who is both a critic and a writer of children's books:

Let's acknowledge at once that writers must be allowed to believe whatever they need to believe in order to do their job. But there is another equally imperative truth to be coped with. . . .

Every time a writer puts words on paper he makes a choice. He chooses the kind of reader he wants to communicate with, no matter what he believes, consciously speaking, about what he is doing and whom he is writing for. . . .

Writing narrative is always a matter of using certain rhetorical techniques. There is no escaping this, and there is no escaping the fact that the techniques used reveal, on close study, the reader to whom the writer speaks.[13]

Chambers (in his critical article "The Reader in the Book") and other critics have applied this concept of the implied reader to a critical, textual analysis of children's books and have demonstrated that, consciously or unconsciously, writers for children are aware of the child reader.

Despite some protestations to the contrary, it is possible to maintain, then, that children's writers *do* write for children. It may be as direct as the writing of *Alice's Adventures in Wonderland* (1865) for Alice Liddell or as subtle as Scott O'Dell's distinction that, although written for himself, his children's books "were written consistently in the emotional area that children share with adults."[14]

Do children's writers find that the practice of their craft—in technique, expression, or integrity—differs in any fundamental way from writing for adults? Again, certain writers claim that there is no identifiable shift in tone, style, or vocabulary; no restriction in form, content, or depth of thought and emotion. But critics such as Chambers have pointed out that, no matter what writers *say* they are doing, a textual analysis of their work always reveals specific conventions that they observe in writing for children—such characteristics as child protagonists;

9. Sendak, p. 265.

10. Meindert DeJong, "Newbery Award Acceptance," *The Horn Book Magazine*, 31 (1955), 241.

11. Isaac Bashevis Singer, "I See the Child as a Last Refuge," *The New York Times Book Review*, Children's Book Section, 9 Nov. 1969, pp. 1, 66, reprinted in *Signposts to Criticism of Children's Literature*, ed. Robert Bator (American Library Association, 1983), pp. 50–52.

12. Quoted in Robert Bator, "Status: In and Out of the Literary Sandbox," in *Signposts to Criticism of Children's Literature*, ed. Robert Bator (American Library Association, 1983), p. 21.

13. Aidan Chambers, "Letter from England: Three Fallacies about Children's Books," *The Horn Book Magazine*, 54 (1978), 326.

14. Quoted in John Rowe Townsend, *A Sense of Story: Essays on Contemporary Writers for Children* (Horn Book, 1971), p. 160.

circumscribed subject matter taking into account children's limited life experiences; restrictions in length and description; emphasis on dialogue, incident, and action; directness, coherence, and clarity of style, plot, and tone; a strong recall of childhood feelings and perceptions; simplicity of design and texture; an optimistic vision; and the primacy of narrative.

Katherine Paterson considers the question of literary constraints that the writer for children may encounter:

Many . . . people . . . are bothered by my choice of form. "Don't you feel constricted writing for children?" they'll ask. William, don't you find fourteen tightly rhymed lines an absolute prison? Ah, Pablo, if you could just yank that picture off that lousy scrap of canvas! You get the point. Form is not a bar to free expression, but the boundaries within which writers and artists freely choose to work.[15]

In discussing limitations of subject matter in writing for children, many writers claim that they do not temper their content or theme for children, but rather strive to be true to the realities of life. Entertainment is crucial, but equally crucial is a sense of literary and ethical responsibility to the child audience. Monica Hughes speaks for many writers when she expresses this sense of responsibility:

I think one of the functions of a good writer for children (besides, obviously, being entertaining) is to help them explore the world and the future. And to find acceptable answers to the Big Questions: "What's life about?" "What is it to be human?" . . . Those are questions that demand truthful answers, not pat ones. So I think my chief criterion for a story for children—it should be for all fiction in fact, of course, but very especially that written for the young—is that one should write as truthfully as possible, even if it isn't easy or painless. One faces oneself in the darkest inside places of one's memory and one's subconscious, and out of that comes both joy and sorrow. But always— and I think again this is perhaps the second crucial thing for children—always there must come hope.[16]

Even though some of the practitioners of the candid new realism (especially in the young adult novel) explore the dark uncertainties, dangers, and disappointments of life, the vast majority of writers balance this naturalism with a sense of moral vision and purpose. Their integrity lies not just in their art, but also in their recognition of their audience. They write from the past—with courage, honesty, and hope—toward the future. They write with respect and love for what Ivan Southall calls "the largest literate, openhearted audience in the history of the world."[17]

15. Katherine Paterson, "Creativity Limited: Novels for Young People Today," *The Writer*, 93 (Dec. 1980), 11–14, reprinted in *Gates of Excellence: On Reading and Writing Books for Children* (Elsevier/ Nelson, 1981), p. 33.
16. Monica Hughes, "The Writer's Quest," *Canadian Children's Literature: A Journal of Criticism and Review*. No. 26 (1982), pp. 20–21.
17. Quoted in Virginia Haviland, Introduction, *The Openhearted Audience: Ten Authors Talk about Writing for Children*, ed. Virginia Haviland (Library of Congress, 1980), p. viii.

C. S. Lewis

On Three Ways of Writing for Children

[From C. S. Lewis, "On Three Ways of Writing for Children," *The Horn Book Magazine*, 39 (1963), 459–69. Originally published in the *Proceedings of the Bournemouth Conference of the Library Association* (England) (The Library Association, 1952); also in *Only Connect: Readings on Children's Literature*, eds. Sheila Egoff, G. T. Stubbs, and L. F. Ashley, 2d ed. (Oxford University Press, 1980), pp. 207–20.]

I think there are three ways in which those who write for children may approach their work: two good ways and one that is generally a bad way.

I came to know of the bad way quite recently and from two unconscious witnesses. One was a lady who sent me the MS. of a story she had written in which a fairy placed at a child's disposal a wonderful gadget. I say 'gadget' because it was not a magic ring or hat or cloak or any such traditional matter. It was a machine, a thing of taps and handles and buttons you could press. You could press one and get an ice cream, another and get a live puppy, and so forth. I had to tell the author honestly that I didn't much care for that sort of thing. She replied, 'No more do I, it bores me to distraction. But it is what the modern child wants.' My other bit of evidence was this. In my own first story I had described at length what I thought was a rather fine high tea given by a hospitable faun to the little girl who was my heroine. A man who has children of his own said, 'Ah, I see how you got to that. If you want to please grownup readers you give them sex, so you thought to yourself, "that won't do for children, what shall I give them instead? I know! The little blighters like plenty of good eating!"' In reality, however, I myself like eating and drinking. I put in what I would have liked to read when I was a child and what I still like reading now that I am in my fifties.

The lady in my first example, and the married man in my second, both conceived writing for children as a special department of 'giving the public what it wants.' Children are, of course, a special public, and you find out what they want and give them that, however little you like it yourself.

The next way may seem at first to be very much the same, but I think the resemblance is superficial. This is the way of Lewis Carroll, Kenneth Grahame, and Tolkien. The printed story grows out of a story told to a particular child with the living voice and perhaps *ex tempore*. It resembles the first way because you are certainly trying to give that child what it wants. But then you are dealing with a concrete person, this child who, of course, differs from all other children. There is no question of 'children' conceived as a strange species whose habits you have 'made up' like an anthropologist or a commercial traveller. Nor, I suspect, would it be possible, thus face to face, to regale the child with things calculated to please it but regarded by yourself with indifference or contempt. The child, I am certain, would see through that. In any personal relation the two participants modify each other. You would become slightly different because you were talking to a child and the child would become slightly different because it was being talked to by an adult. A community, a composite personality, is created and out of that the story grows.

The third way, which is the only one I could ever use myself, consists in writing a children's story because a children's story is the best art-form for something you have to say: just as a composer might write a Dead March not because there was a public funeral in view but because certain musical ideas that had occurred to him went best into that form. This method could apply to other kinds of children's literature besides stories. I have been told that Arthur Mee never met a child and never wished to: it was, from his point of view, a bit of luck that boys liked reading what he liked writing. This anecdote may be untrue in fact but it illustrates my meaning.

Within the species 'children's story' the sub-species which happened to suit me is the fantasy or (in a loose sense of that word) the fairy tale. There are, of course, other sub-species. E. Nesbit's trilogy about the Bastable family is a very good specimen of another kind. It is a 'children's story' in the sense that children can and do read it, but it is also the only form in which E. Nesbit could have given us so much of the humours of childhood. It is true that the Bastable children appear, successfully treated from the adult point of view, in one of her grownup novels, but they appear only for a moment. I do not think she would have kept it up. Sentimentality is so apt to creep in if we write at length about children as seen by their elders. And the reality of childhood, as we all experienced it, creeps out. For we all remember that our childhood, as lived, was immeasurably different from what our elders saw. Hence Sir Michael Sadler, when I asked his opinion about a certain new experimental school, replied, 'I never give an opinion on any of those experiments till the children have grown up and can tell *us what really happened.*' Thus the Bastable trilogy, however improbable many of its episodes may be, provides even adults, in one sense, with more realistic reading about children than they could find in most books addressed to adults. But also, conversely, it enables the children who read it to do something much more mature than they realize. For the whole book is a character study of Oswald, an unconsciously satiric self-portrait, which every intelligent child can fully appreciate: but no child would sit down to read a character study in any other form. There is another way in which children's stories mediate this psychological interest, but I will reserve that for later treatment.

In this short glance at the Bastable trilogy I think we have stumbled on a principle. Where the children's story is simply the right form for what the author has to say, then of course readers who want to hear that will read the story or reread it at any age. I never met *The Wind in the Willows* or the Bastable books till I was in my late twenties, and I do not think I have enjoyed them any the less on that account. I am almost inclined to set it up as a canon that a children's story which is enjoyed only by children is a bad children's story. The good ones last. A waltz which you can like only when you are waltzing is a bad waltz.

This canon seems to me most obviously true of that particular type of children's story which is dearest to my own taste, the fantasy or fairy tale. Now the modern critical world uses 'adult'

as a term of approval. It is hostile to what it calls 'nostalgia' and contemptuous of what it calls 'Peter Pantheism.' Hence a man who admits that dwarfs and giants and talking beasts and witches are still dear to him in his fifty-third year is now less likely to be praised for his perennial youth than scorned and pitied for arrested development. If I spend some little time defending myself against these charges, this is not so much because it matters greatly whether I am scorned and pitied as because the defence is germane to my whole view of the fairy tale and even of literature in general. My defence consists of three propositions.

1. I reply with a *tu quoque*. Critics who treat *adult* as a term of approval, instead of as a merely descriptive term, cannot be adult themselves. To be concerned about being grownup, to admire the grownup because it is grownup, to blush at the suspicion of being childish—these things are the marks of childhood and adolescence. And in childhood and adolescence they are, in moderation, healthy symptoms. Young things ought to want to grow. But to carry on into middle life or even into early manhood this concern about being adult is a mark of really arrested development. When I was ten, I read fairy tales in secret and would have been ashamed if I had been found doing so. Now that I am fifty I read them openly. When I became a man I put away childish things, including the fear of childishness and the desire to be very grownup.

2. The modern view seems to me to involve a false conception of growth. They accuse us of arrested development because we have not lost a taste we had in childhood. But surely arrested development consists not in refusing to lose old things but in failing to add new things? I now like hock, which I am sure I should not have liked as a child. But I still like lemon-squash. I call this growth or development because I have been enriched: where I formerly had only one pleasure, I now have two. But if I had to lose the taste for lemon-squash before I acquired the taste for hock, that would not be growth but simple change. I now enjoy Tolstoy and Jane Austen and Trollope as well as fairy tales and I call that growth; if I had had to lose the fairy tales in order to

acquire the novelists, I would not say that I had grown but that I had changed. A tree grows because it adds rings; a train doesn't grow by leaving one station behind and puffing on to the next. In reality, the case is stronger and more complicated than this. I think my growth is just as apparent when I now read the fairy tales as when I read the novelists, for I now enjoy the fairy tales better than I did in childhood: being now able to put more in, of course I get more out. But I do not here stress that point. Even if it were merely a taste for grownup literature added to an unchanged taste for children's literature, addition would still be entitled to the name 'growth,' and the process of merely dropping one parcel when you pick up another would not. It is, of course, true that the process of growing does, incidently and unfortunately, involve some more losses. But that is not the essence of growth, certainly not what makes growth admirable or desirable. If it were, if to drop parcels and to leave stations behind were the essence and virtue of growth, why should we stop at the adult? Why should not *senile* be equally a term of approval? Why are we not to be congratulated on losing our teeth and hair? Some critics seem to confuse growth with the cost of growth and also to wish to make that cost far higher than, in nature, it need be.

3. The whole association of fairy tale and fantasy with childhood is local and accidental. I hope everyone has read Tolkien's essay on fairy tales,* which is perhaps the most important contribution to the subject that anyone has yet made. If so, you will know already that, in most places and times, the fairy tale has not been specially made for, nor exclusively enjoyed by, children. It has gravitated to the nursery when it became unfashionable in literary circles, just as unfashionable furniture gravitated to the nursery in Victorian houses. In fact, many children do not like this kind of book, just as many children do not like horsehair sofas: and many adults do like it, just as many adults like rocking-chairs. And those who do like it, whether young or old, probably like it for the same reason.

* J. R. R. Tolkien, "On Fairy-Stories," in *Tree and Leaf* (Houghton Mifflin, 1965), pp. 3–84.

And none of us can say with any certainty what that reason is. The two theories which are most often in my mind are those of Tolkien and of Jung.

According to Tolkien the appeal of the fairy story lies in the fact that man there most fully exercises his function as a 'sub-creator'; not, as they love to say now, making a 'comment upon life' but making, so far as possible, a subordinate world of his own. Since, in Tolkien's view, this is one of man's proper functions, delight naturally arises whenever it is successfully performed. For Jung, fairy tale liberates the Archetypes which dwell in the collective unconscious, and when we read a good fairy tale we are obeying the old precept 'Know thyself.' I would venture to add to this my own theory, not indeed of the Kind as a whole, but of one feature in it: I mean, the presence of beings other than human which yet behave, in varying degrees, humanly—the giants and dwarfs and talking beasts. I believe these to be at least (for they may have many other sources of power and beauty) an admirable hieroglyphic which conveys psychology, types of character, more briefly than novelistic presentation and to readers whom novelistic presentation could not yet reach. Consider Mr. Badger in *The Wind in the Willows* that extraordinary amalgam of high rank, coarse manners, gruffness, shyness, and goodness. The child who has once met Mr. Badger has ever afterwards in its bones a knowledge of humanity and of English social history which it could not get in any other way.

Of course as all children's literature is not fantastic, so all fantastic books need not be children's books. It is still possible, even in an age so ferociously anti-romantic as our own, to write fantastic stories for adults—though you will usually need to have made a name in some more fashionable kind of literature before anyone will publish them. But there may be an author who at a particular moment finds not only fantasy but fantasy-for-children the exactly right form for what he wants to say. The distinction is a fine one. His fantasies for children and his fantasies for adults will have very much more in common with one another than either has with the ordinary novel or with what is sometimes called 'the novel of child life.' Indeed the same readers will probably read both his fantastic 'juveniles' and his fantastic stories for adults. For I need not remind such an audience as this that the neat sorting-out of books into age-groups, so dear to publishers, has only a very sketchy relation with the habits of any real readers. Those of us who are blamed when old for reading childish books were blamed when children for reading books too old for us. No reader worth his salt trots along in obedience to a time-fable. The distinction then is a fine one; and I am not quite sure what made me, in a particular year of my life, feel that not only a fairy tale, but a fairy tale addressed to children, was exactly what I must write—or burst. Partly, I think that this form permits, or compels, you to leave out things I wanted to leave out. It compels you to throw all the force of the book into what was done and said. It checks what a kind but discerning critic called 'the expository demon' in me. It also imposes certain very fruitful necessities about length.

If I have allowed the fantastic type of children's story to run away with this discussion, that is because it is the kind I know and love best, not because I wish to condemn any other. But the patrons of the other kinds very frequently want to condemn it. About once every hundred years some wiseacre gets up and tries to banish the fairy tale. Perhaps I had better say a few words in its defence, as reading for children.

It is accused of giving a false impression of the world they live in. But I think no literature that children could read gives them less of a false impression. I think what profess to be realistic stories for children are far more likely to deceive them. I never expected the real world to be like the fairy tales. I think that I did expect school to be like the school stories. The fantasies did not deceive me: the school stories did. All stories in which children have adventures and successes which are possible, in the sense that they do not break the laws of nature, but almost infinitely improbable, are in more danger than the fairy tales of raising false expectations.

Almost the same answer serves for the popular charge of escapism, though here the question is not so simple. Do fairy tales teach children to retreat into a world of wish-fulfilment—'fan-

tasy' in the technical psychological sense of the word—instead of facing the problems of the real world? Now it is here that the problem becomes subtle. Let us again lay the fairy tale side by side with the school story or any other story which is labelled a 'Boy's Book' or a 'Girl's Book,' as distinct from a 'Children's Book.' There is no doubt that both arouse, and imaginatively satisfy, wishes. We long to go through the looking-glass, to reach fairyland. We also long to be the immensely popular and successful schoolboy or schoolgirl, or the lucky boy or girl who discovers the spy's plot or rides the horse that none of the cowboys can manage. But the two longings are very different. The second, especially when directed on something so close as school life, is ravenous and deadly serious. Its fulfilment on the level of imagination is in very truth compensatory: we run to it from the disappointments and humiliations of the real world; it sends us back to the real world undivinely discontented. For it is all flattery to the ego. The pleasure consists in picturing oneself the object of admiration. The other longing, that for fairyland, is very different. In a sense a child does not long for fairyland as a boy longs to be the hero of the first eleven. Does anyone suppose that he really and prosaically longs for all the dangers and discomforts of a fairy tale?—really wants dragons in contemporary England? It is not so. It would be much truer to say that fairyland arouses a longing for he knows not what. It stirs and troubles him (to his lifelong enrichment) with the dim sense of something beyond his reach and, far from dulling or emptying the actual world, gives it a new dimension of depth. He does not despise real woods because he has read of enchanted woods: the reading makes all real woods a little enchanted. This is a special kind of longing. The boy reading the school story of the type I have in mind desires success and is unhappy (once the book is over) because he can't get it: the boy reading the fairy tale desires and is happy in the very fact of desiring. For his mind has not been concentrated on himself, as it often is in the more realistic story.

I do not mean that school stories for boys and girls ought not be written. I am only saying that they are far more liable to become 'fantasies' in the clinical sense than fantastic stories are. And this distinction holds for adult reading too. The dangerous fantasy is always superficially realistic. The real victim of wishful reverie does not batten on *The Odyssey, The Tempest,* or *The Worm Ouroboros:* he (or she) prefers stories about millionaires, irresistible beauties, posh hotels, palm beaches, and bedroom scenes—things that really might happen, that ought to happen, that would have happened if the reader had had a fair chance. For, as I say, there are two kinds of longing. The one is an *askesis,* a spiritual exercise, and the other is a disease.

A far more serious attack on the fairy tale as children's literature comes from those who do not wish children to be frightened. I suffered too much from night-fears myself in childhood to undervalue this objection. I would not wish to heat the fires of that private hell for any child. On the other hand, none of my fears came from fairy tales. Giant insects were my specialty, with ghosts a bad second. I suppose the ghosts came directly or indirectly from stories, though certainly not from fairy stories, but I don't think the insects did. I don't know anything my parents could have done or left undone which would have saved me from the pincers, mandibles, and eyes of those many-legged abominations. And that, as so many people have pointed out, is the difficulty. We do not know what will or will not frighten a child in this particular way. I say 'in this particular way' for we must here make a distinction. Those who say that children must not be frightened may mean two things. They may mean (1) that we must not do anything likely to give the child those haunting, disabling, pathological fears against which ordinary courage is helpless: in fact, *phobias.* His mind must, if possible, be kept clear of things he can't bear to think of. Or they may mean (2) that we must try to keep out of his mind the knowledge that he is born into a world of death, violence, wounds, adventure, heroism and cowardice, good and evil. If they mean the first I agree with them: but not if they mean the second. The second would indeed be to give children a false impression and feed them on escapism in the bad sense. There is something ludicrous in the idea of so educating a generation which is born to the Ogpu and the atomic bomb. Since it is so likely that they will meet cruel enemies, let them at least have heard of brave knights and heroic courage. Otherwise you are making their destiny not brighter but darker. Nor do most of us find that violence and bloodshed, in a story, produce any haunting dread in the minds of children. As far as that goes, I side impenitently with the human race against the modern reformer. Let there be wicked kings and beheadings, battles and dungeons, giants and dragons, and let villains be soundly killed at the end of the book. Nothing will persuade me that this causes an ordinary child any kind or degree of fear beyond what it wants, and needs, to feel. For, of course, it wants to be a little frightened.

The other fears—the phobias—are a different matter. I do not believe one can control them by literary means. We seem to bring them into the world with us ready made. No doubt the particular image on which the child's terror is fixed can sometimes be traced to a book. But is that the source, or only the occasion, of the fear? If he had been spared that image, would not some other, quite unpredictable by you, have had the same effect? Chesterton has told us of a boy who was more afraid of the Albert Memorial than anything else in the world. I know a man whose great childhood terror was the India paper edition of the *Encyclopaedia Britannica*—for a reason I defy you to guess. And I think it possible that by confining your child to blameless stories of child life in which nothing at all alarming ever happens, you would fail to banish the terrors, and would succeed in banishing all that can ennoble them or make them endurable. For in the fairy tales, side by side with the terrible figures, we find the immemorial comforters and protectors, the radiant ones: and the terrible figures are not merely terrible, but sublime. It would be nice if no little boy in bed, hearing, or thinking he hears, a sound, were ever at all frightened. But if he is going to be frightened, I think it better that he should think of giants and dragons than merely of burglars. And I think St George, or any bright champion in armour, is a better comfort than the idea of the police.

I will even go further. If I could have escaped all my own night-fears at the price of never having known 'faerie,' would I now be the gainer by that bargain? I am not speaking carelessly. The fears were very bad. But I think the price would have been too high.

But I have strayed far from my theme. This has been inevitable for, of the three methods, I know by experience only the third. I hope my title did not lead anyone to think that I was conceited enough to give you advice on how to write a story for children. There were two very good reasons for not doing that. One is that many people have written very much better stories than I, and I would rather learn about the art than set up to teach it. The other is that, in a certain sense, I have never exactly 'made' a story. With me the process is much more like bird-watching than like either talking or building. I see pictures. Some of these pictures have a common flavour, almost a common smell, which groups them together. Keep quiet and watch and they will begin joining themselves up. If you were very lucky (I have never been as lucky as all that), a whole set might join themselves so consistently that there you had a complete story without doing anything yourself. But more often (in my experience always) there are gaps. Then at last you have to do some deliberate inventing, have to contrive reasons why these characters should be in these various places doing these various things. I have no idea whether this is the usual way of writing stories, still less whether it is the best. It is the only one I know: images always come first.

Before closing, I would like to return to what I said at the beginning. I rejected any approach which begins with the question 'What do modern children like?' I might be asked 'Do you equally reject the approach which begins with the question "What do modern children need?"—in other words, with the moral or didactic approach?' I think the answer is Yes. Not because I don't like stories to have a moral: certainly not because I think children dislike a moral. Rather because I feel sure that the question 'What do modern children need?' will not lead you to a good moral. If we ask that question we are assuming too superior an attitude. It would be better to ask 'What moral do I need?', for I think we can be sure that what

does not concern us deeply will not deeply interest our readers, whatever their age. But it is better not to ask the question at all. Let the pictures tell you their own moral. For the moral inherent in them will rise from whatever spiritual roots you have succeeded in striking during the whole course of your life. But if they don't show you any moral, don't put one in. For the moral you put in is likely to be a platitude, or even a falsehood, skimmed from the surface of your consciousness. It is impertinent to offer the children that. For we have been told on high authority that in the moral sphere they are probably at least as wise as we. Anyone who *can* write a children's story without a moral, had better do so: that is, if he is going to write children's stories at all. The only moral that is of any value is that which arises inevitably from the whole cast of the author's mind.

Indeed everything in the story should arise from the whole cast of the author's mind. We must write for children out of those elements in our own imagination which we share with children: differing from our child readers not by any less, or less serious, interest in the things we handle, but by the fact that we have other interests which children would not share with us. The matter of our story should be a part of the habitual furniture of our minds. This, I fancy, has been so with all great writers for children, but it is not generally understood. A critic not long ago said in praise of a very serious fairy tale that the author's tongue 'never once got into his cheek.' But why on earth should it?—unless he had been eating a seed-cake. Nothing seems to me more fatal, for this art, than an idea that whatever we share with children is, in the privative sense, 'childish' and that whatever is childish is somehow comic. We must meet children as equals in that area of our nature where we are their equals. Our superiority consists partly in commanding other areas, and partly (which is more relevant) in the fact that we are better at telling stories than they are. The child as reader is neither to be patronized nor idolized: we talk to him as man to man. But the worst attitude of all would be the professional attitude which regards children in the lump as a sort of raw material which we have to handle. We must of course try to do them no harm: we may, under the Omnipotence, sometimes dare to hope that we may do them good. But only such good as involves treating them with respect. We must not imagine that we are Providence or Destiny. I will not say that a good story for children could never be written by someone in the Ministry of Education, for all things are possible. But I should lay very long odds against it.

Once in a hotel dining-room I said, rather too loudly, 'I loathe prunes.' 'So do I' came an unexpected six-year-old voice from another table. Sympathy was instantaneous. Neither of us thought it funny. We both knew that prunes are far too nasty to be funny. That is the proper meeting between man and child as independent personalities. Of the far higher and more difficult relations between child and parent or child and teacher, I say nothing. An author, as a mere author, is outside all that. He is not even an uncle. He is a freeman and an equal, like the postman, the butcher, and the dog next door.

Nina Bawden

Emotional Realism in Books for Young People

[From Nina Bawden, "Emotional Realism in Books for Young People," *The Horn Book Magazine*, 56 (1980), 17–33. This essay was presented at the sixteenth congress of the International Board on Books for Young People in Würzburg, Federal Republic of Germany, on October 24, 1978.]

Old Granny Greengrass had her finger chopped off in the butcher's when she was buying half a leg of lamb. She had pointed to the place where she wanted her joint to be cut, but then she decided she needed a bigger piece and pointed again. Unfortunately, Mr. Grummett, the butcher, was already bringing his sharp chopper down. He chopped straight through her finger and it flew like a snapped twig into a pile of sawdust in the corner of the shop. It was hard to tell who was more surprised, Granny Greengrass or the butcher. But she didn't blame him. She said, "I could never make up my mind and stick to it, Mr. Grummett. That's always been my trouble."

This is the opening of my children's novel, *The Peppermint Pig* (Lippincott). It's one of the stories my Norfolk grandmother used to tell me when I was young. A true story—at least, I always believed it was true, even though I guessed it might not have happened *exactly* like that. I was aware, as all children are, of the difference between fiction and reality. A child will look out into the garden and say, "There's a lion out there." He knows that he is imagining it, but he knows, too, that what goes on inside his imagination is as real as what goes on outside it. A thing is true and not true—a child can hold these two ideas in his head, side by side, without any conflict at all, which is something we forget how to do as we grow older, grow up. Unless, of course, we grow up to be novelists.

Granny Greengrass's lost finger almost certainly had its origin in what adults consider basic reality. Most of my grandmother's stories were, in fact, basically true. What she did with them was what all storytellers do; she embellished them, tidied them up a bit, gave them a point, sometimes even a moral. "I could never make up my mind and stick to it. That's always been my trouble."

When *The Peppermint Pig* was first published, a well-known English lady reviewer rang me up and told me that she had been dreadfully upset by this opening anecdote. So upset, she had found it quite hard to read on. It was so cruel, she cried, so bloodthirsty! It would give any really sensitive child terrible nightmares! I thought she was being unnecessarily squeamish—children are, after all, rather bloodthirsty, and I could remember enjoying this story enormously when my grandmother had told it to me—but a few weeks later I had an illuminating letter from a little girl. She wrote, "I liked that story about the chopped finger and so did my friends, but you were silly to put it in the beginning. It might stop grownups buying your book. You ought to have put it later on, where mothers and teachers might not notice it."

This wise child had put her own small finger on one of the differences between writing for children and writing for adults. Children, by and large, do not buy their own books. The books they are given are the ones adults think suitable for them, that present the kind of world adults want the children to believe they live in. Sometimes they may be books that the adults themselves have enjoyed, not because they are good books in themselves but because they are easy reading for grownups. That is one explanation, anyway, for the current fashion—almost an obsession it seems to me, sometimes—for teenage or young adult novels, many of which are little more than magazine stories souped up with injections of myth or symbol to make their contents seem weightier. Even real children's books, which I would define as books written for the pre-adolescent, or just-about-to-be-adolescent child, are sometimes judged oddly. A children's book should be judged for the pleasure it gives, for its style and its quality, as any other book is judged. But the way the children's book world has developed in recent years, with its different factions and interests and ideologies, seems to have clouded this simple issue. Conferences have been held, scholarly papers written, earnest and impassioned arguments developed around all sorts of different considerations which really have nothing at all to do with literature or its function and in the course of which (I have sometimes thought) the child himself has been forgotten.

A small, personal anecdote to illustrate what I mean. Several years ago at a publisher's party a bookseller came up to me and said, "You wrote a book called *A Handful of Thieves,* didn't you?" I said yes, and waited, I must admit—this being the sort of occasion when writers are often made much of—for him to say how much he had liked it, what a splendid story, so rich, so wise, so beautifully written. Instead, to my amazement, he began to quiver with rage. He stabbed his finger at me and said, "It's people like you cause the trouble! I've read your book! The children in it break into a house and steal, don't they?" Well, this was true. The children break into a rooming house to steal back some money that has been stolen from a helpless old woman—the grandmother of one of them—by a confidence trickster. The old lady has refused to go to the police because she doesn't want to look a fool in her daughter's eyes, and so the children have decided to take the law into their own hands. Never a wise thing to do, perhaps, but in this case, quite morally acceptable. I thought. I said so to this in-

dignant bookseller, but he didn't agree. He objected, it finally appeared, to what he called "the exciting tone of this episode." The children had honestly felt that what they were doing was right, but the thing that had upset the bookseller was that they had *enjoyed* doing it. He said, "Kids come into my shop and steal. A book like yours encourages them. People like you should set an example. Think of your duty to society."

I didn't dare tell him, but when I was a little girl, I had once been a thief. I stole jewelry and sweets and celluloid dolls from Woolworth's for my toy theater. I stole for fun, and I enjoyed every terrifying, heart-stopping minute. I was the leader of a gang. I posted my subordinates at strategic positions round the store to distract the assistant's attention and cover my retreat. I saw myself as a general planning a guerilla action. I was never caught, nor did I graduate into a delinquent. My criminal career was brief, starting just after I was nine years old and ending long before I was ten, when I grew bored with it. But I can remember the excitement still, and when I wrote *A Handful of Thieves* (Lippincott), it seemed totally unrealistic to pretend that my characters were not thrilled by the idea of being burglars, of breaking into a house at night. But I also thought I had written about it in an extremely moral way. My little thieves knew exactly what they were doing. They knew it was against the law. But they had discussed the situation—touching, along the way, on the conflict there often is between law and morality—and decided that stealing was, in the circumstances, the right thing to do. What could be more moral than that? They had also been faced with the result of their actions. They had been caught and taken to the police station. I said all this to the bookseller, but he wasn't won over. So I explained, really weakening my argument, I suppose, that I was a magistrate, a justice of the peace, with experience in both adult and juvenile courts. I presented my credentials, my Establishment Badge, to show that I wasn't really on the side of juvenile crime. "Then you ought to know better," he said.

Well, I did think I knew better. Better than he did, anyway, about how children really think and feel and how they respond to what they read. But he didn't care about that. He didn't care how true, how percipient, how realistic about children's behavior my little book was. Not even how well, or how badly, he thought it was written. All that concerned him was the harm he thought it might do.

I suppose I should have been flattered. Novelists are not often encouraged to believe that their books have much influence. British novelists, anyway. Even if we hope, privately, that some of our work may persuade our readers to see something more clearly, some truth that is dear to us, some precious insight, we have the sense to keep it to ourselves. Dr. Johnson said, " 'A fly, Sir, may sting a stately horse and make him wince, but one is but an insect, the other is a horse still.' " The novelist is a sort of gadfly, momentarily stinging the horse of society into pleasure or pain, into some awareness of the human predicament; but then, with a swish of a larger tail he is sent packing, taken back to the library, restored to the shelf, returned to his proper station in life. Writers may believe that novels can tell you more about how people behave and why than can any psychological textbook or sociological survey, but the general opinion about fiction, the *horse's* opinion, is that it is rather a frivolous business.

Novels for adults, anyway. Everyone knows that he could write one of those if only he had the time. Writing for children is admitted to being a somewhat more specialized craft, and it seems to be regarded by some people—librarians and schoolteachers among them—as a slightly different activity. Although as a novelist, I don't think it *is* any different, I can understand the educational argument. Children's fiction is used in schools, very rightly and properly, to introduce children not only to literature but to ideas in general; and one of the best ways of teaching them about the world they live in, about how other people think and feel, is through a good story. More suspect, to my mind, is the feeling I sometimes get, talking to teachers and librarians, that books are there to be used as a kind of therapy. If a child comes from a poor home, a one-parent family, you give him a book about a child whose circumstances are similar, and he will feel better.

There is something in this, and I will return to it later, but it isn't that simple. People's responses to books are subtle and mysterious. You can't *prescribe* a book like a bottle of medicine.

I wrote books for adults long before I wrote books for children, and when I wrote my first children's story, it didn't seem to me that there should be much difference in the way I set about it. I knew the viewpoint would have to be the child's viewpoint. I knew the plot would have to be stronger and that I would have to make some things clearer, more specific, than I would need to make them in an adult novel. Children are as intelligent as adults and in some ways more percipient because their minds are not so cluttered up with old opinions, but they *know* less, and so you have to tell them. For example, one of my recent children's books, *Rebel On A Rock* (Lippincott), is a modern political novel. It is set in the Peloponnese in Greece, in an old fortress town on a rock. I wanted to set a children's book in this particular place because although I didn't go there until I was grown up, it is a place that seemed to me to have that special quality of beauty and enchantment that belonged to the places I had known and loved in my childhood. Since the book was to be set in Greece, and the Colonels were in power when I started to think about it, I wanted it to be about politics. (Children are supposed not to be interested in politics, but I think that is because adults think it an unsuitable subject for them, like death.) I thought of a story based on the abortive naval rebellion my Athenian friends were talking about at that time. I found my characters. A girl of twelve, a boy of fourteen, and their younger brother and sister who are adopted, and Black. I had no social purpose in making the two little ones Black. My brother has two adopted Black children, and I simply liked the idea of my African nephew and niece finding themselves, one day when they are old enough to read it, in this particular story. There had to be a Greek boy as well somehow involved in the plot to get rid of the Colonels— a boy who knows something, a dangerous secret that the English children, who cannot understand the realities of life in a dictatorship, do not take seriously. My *readers* had to understand what was going on, though, and so I had to think of a way to give them the information they needed. I had to include a certain amount of political philosophy about the essential differences between dictatorship and democracy. I couldn't put in chunks of straightforward educational matter because any right-thinking child would sense what I was doing and skip that particular bit. The parents could have explained matters to their children, but that was too obvious. So I introduced two intelligent but slightly naïve American ladies from Arizona, who were anxious to find out what was going on and who could also play a really key role in the plot. My readers, I hoped, would learn along with these ladies without realizing that they were being taught anything.

For a children's novel a little stealthy instruction of this kind is sometimes needed, as well as a good plot, a child's-eye view. But apart from these obvious technical differences, it doesn't seem to me that there should be any others. I don't feel any extra responsibility towards my audience when I am writing a book for children, except the responsibility of trying to make what I want to say comprehensible to them and making the story an enjoyable experience for them. Their enjoyment seems to me of primary importance—enjoyment, that is, in the fullest sense, engaging and extending their imaginations and their sympathies. Not that I am writing just for them, or just for money, or just to please myself, as many writers will say they do or pretend they do in order to avoid having to explain what is really rather a complex and curious process with many different impulses behind it. All writers must feel, I think, that they have something unique to say—that their experience, their knowledge, their view of reality, is something special that must be communicated; but it seems to me that once I begin on a book, all these small conceits vanish, and the only responsibility I feel is to the story I am telling. Nothing else, once I have sat down at my typewriter and written the first line, really matters to me.

When I first entered the world of children's books, the attitudes I met seemed strange. A book is a book is a book, I had innocently thought. There it is, miraculously finished, complete. You have done the best for it you can, and all you can do now is wish it luck and send it off—rather like sending a child on a journey or putting a message into a bottle and tossing it into the sea in the hope that it will be picked up by someone on some distant shore who will get pleasure and perhaps profit from it. Meeting that angry bookseller was the first time I realized that writing children's books was not so simple. He wasn't interested in the literary quality of my book. Nor in the fact, which was my pride, that within the framework of an adventure story I had presented real children, thinking and talking as real children do. To him, my book was a nail in the coffin of respectable society.

I didn't think it was. But he had raised a point. As Graham Greene has said, the books we read in childhood have more influence on us than anything we read in later life. When we are grown up, we read for pleasure, for instruction, to confirm what we already know. To a child a book is a revelation. It shows him his place in the world, his future—as if he looked into a gypsy's crystal ball.

Certainly, when I was young, it was like that for me. I was an urban child, brought up in the East End of London, near the docks. Apart from the noisy glamour of dock-land which I saw only when my father's ship came in, my world was rather ugly, rather dull. Dull, suburban streets, dusty parks that smelled of dog dirt. Except to visit my storytelling grandmother in Norfolk and occasional day trips to the sea, we never traveled. These were the Depression years. My father was a marine engineer and didn't dare leave his ship to take a holiday. We had no television, of course. We didn't even have a radio—my mother thought it would distract me from my homework. She bought me a toy theater instead—the theater that I stole the dolls from Woolworth's for—wrote plays for it and encouraged me to write my own. She gave me more than a toy; she gave me my future profession. The first time I rolled up that little red velvet curtain I was hooked! By the stage to begin with; then by the whole idea of story. From then on I was always acting, inventing stories with myself as heroine. I knew my surroundings were drab. I longed to live somewhere more beautiful. I knew my life was uneventful. I longed for something to happen. It wasn't just a craving for excitement. It was a need to find out the kind of person I was. I often feared I wasn't very nice. Although I longed to please, to be loved and admired, it seemed I was "naughty." A difficult child, my mother said, and I was sure that she and her friends talked about me disparagingly behind my back. Sometimes when I came into a room, the conversation stopped and people looked at me strangely. One day when this happened, I badgered my mother to tell me what she and our neighbor had been talking about. She refused at first, but I was persistent, and eventually she told me that they had been discussing the girl up the road, who had just had a baby even though she wasn't married. I said, "If that's all it was, why didn't you tell me?" and she answered, with a kind of dark implication that chilled my blood, "Well, Nina, you know what you are."

My trouble was, I didn't! I didn't know if I was good or wicked, a heroine or a coward. I don't know that I have found out yet, but I do know that the books I read when I was young helped me towards some sort of understanding. They helped me to place myself, helped me to solve the riddle of why I was here, in this particular place, in this particular body. The books that did this for me were not myths or magic or fantasy but books that seemed to me to be about real people—that is, people I could recognize as real, even if they sometimes had rather unlikely adventures. I don't mean that they were always books about a girl like me, living in a house like mine. They were books that for some reason I could live inside, even if the world they showed me was different from the one I knew.

The books I remember most clearly are of two kinds. There was a series of stories about Robin Hood, thin paperbacks costing fourpence. I had sixpence a week, and I bought one every Saturday and read it and reread it until the covers fell off. These books were fast-moving adventures with stereotyped characters, each embodying an aspect of the human personality. Brave Robin, greedy Friar Tuck, the wicked Sheriff, and so on. I understand now

why I enjoyed them; their moral simplicity was the important simplicity of myths or fairy tales or dreams that the mind needs as a springboard for more complex judgments. At the time I knew only that they were books I could make use of for the private storytelling that went on all the time inside my head. What Chesterton called good bad books are sometimes better for this purpose than great works of literature. The very flatness of the characters makes it easy for you to become them, act their simple roles, use their adventures as a kind of climbing frame for your own imaginings, a free playground for your mind. I was Robin Hood more often than I was Maid Marion, as later on I was the Scarlet Pimpernel and not any of the simpering ladies he snatched from the guillotine. I had no problems of identification with either the outlaw or the aristocrat. I had never traveled, never been to France, never even seen a real, wild forest; but in the country of my mind I was free to go where I liked, be who I wanted to be. There were no barriers of distance or time, no passports, no tickets needed, no restrictions of age or sex or social background.

The other books I remember, which provided a richer and more lasting experience, were the books I found in my Norfolk grandmother's house. She had a shelf of Sunday School prizes—not because she had been a particularly pious child but because her parents used to give her a penny for herself every time she went to Sunday School. As a result of this bribery she had collected an impressive list of Victorian children's novels. Most of the titles are forgotten now. I can only remember some of them. *Christie's Old Organ, Little Miss Vanity, Jackanapes, On Angel's Wings*—a piteous tale about a little hunchback called Violet, who suffered so nobly and died so sadly that I cannot touch the faded red cover now, without tears. They were strong meat, those books. They were full of death, poverty, and unhappiness; there was a stern concentration on the moral struggles of the characters that especially intrigued me. In the modern children's books I'd read the children were often naughty in a jolly way, but they were not presented as serious moral beings, nor did they ever seem to suffer from the bitter, dark, and angry feelings that often troubled me.

These fictional Victorian children did suffer from them. They were often wicked, both in thought and deed, and although for convention's sake, they usually repented or were punished in some way before the end, their wicked thoughts and impulses were honestly acknowledged, set down on the page; and I found this wonderfully consoling. Here were people who felt as I did sometimes. I was not alone.

There were other reasons why I felt that these were the first real books I'd read. They showed the dark side of life, which up to then had been largely hidden from me. People in them fell ill, died, lost all their money, went to prison—as they did in Real Life, I was sure. Even the people in my suburban street! I took to spying on our neighbors, watching them as they mowed their back garden lawns and spoke to each other in the street, smiling politely, discussing the weather, *pretending* all was well. I wondered what fascinating dramas were being acted out when they were inside their houses, hidden behind their closed doors, their curtained windows. I knew about the girl who'd had the baby. My grandmother's Sunday School prizes suggested that even more exciting things were likely to be going on. And so, from them I learned one of the main purposes of fiction, which is to flesh out the dull reality we see about us, make it more intense and more significant and more truthful, too, because people's lives are rarely dull to them. They are full of passion, happiness, and sorrow—even if it doesn't always show. Indeed, on the surface it seldom shows. Traveling on the London underground, looking at the pudding faces opposite, puffy eyes blankly fixed on advertisements for employment agencies, one finds it hard to believe that these blank and silent strangers have ever loved or hated anyone or felt any pain worse than a twinge from a corn or a hammertoe. But you know they are living creatures like yourself, partly because fiction has told you so.

I think, when I started to write for children, if I had any clear idea at all, it was that I wanted to write solid, grownup novels for them, with the kind of range and depth that a good novel for adults should always have, but set in a world a child would understand and feel at home in. Not necessarily the physical background.

Urban children don't always want to read about urban children—I was an urban child, and so I know. I consider myself a realistic writer but not, I hope, the kind that sees realism in fiction as a deliberate choice of drab backgrounds or unpleasant subjects. Unfortunately, that is what some superficial critics consider realism to be—the kind of critics who are preoccupied with fashionable social problems and who say, "Ah, this book is realistic because it is about poor children, handicapped children, children in one-parent families, and therefore it is a good book because it shows the world as it is." Or, "This is the first children's book with a rape in it, or incest," as if the breaking of a taboo of this kind is, in itself, a guarantee of literary quality. There is something naïve and depressing in this kind of approach to children's fiction. It is a disservice to literature in general and to the children whose books are chosen for them in this way. Subliterary criteria are often applied to books for adults, of course, but that does not matter so much because adults, having more experience, can judge and choose their own books. Children are stuck with what they are given, and I am sad for them when what they are given has been judged by these standards. Socially disadvantaged children, to use the current jargon, need books that will open their minds and their imaginations. To suggest, as I have heard well-meaning people do, that poor children from slum backgrounds can understand and identify only with books about poor children from slum backgrounds is, quite simply, offensively patronizing. A new version, perhaps, of keeping the peasants in their place.

I don't mean that children should be given pretty tales. Children need realism in the books they read, just as they need poetry and fantasy and comedy. Poverty, divorce, and cruelty have their place in children's novels as they have in books for adults, but this proper place is part of a fully realized story, not dragged in to satisfy some educational or social theory. And the most important realism that children need, to my mind, anyway, is the realism of the emotional landscape in which the book is set, a landscape that a child can recognize whether he is rich or poor, whether he lives in a tenement or a palace.

When I began to write for children, my own children were still young, and it seemed to me that missing from the books they were reading were the passions of childhood that I remembered so clearly and that I knew they felt as well. Not only were these passions absent from the books, but they were absent from the conversations of my friends whose children were the same age as mine. A little jealousy might be admitted, perhaps, when a new baby was born, but it would be spoken of with a little smile, dismissed as a minor aberration of no great importance. I began to wonder if my friends, like the authors of the books, had forgotten their own childhood. Or, if they hadn't quite forgotten, found it unacceptable to admit that behind their children's sweet and innocent faces, murderous thoughts were raging. Children do have murderous thoughts—in fact, when you think how often they want to kill people, it is amazing how rarely they do—and yet, in children's fiction, even now, you rarely find this said. Children feel as violently—if not more violently, since they have less self-control—than adults. They love or hate their parents, their brothers and sisters, their teachers, their friends. They feel guilt and despair as well as wild and sudden joy. They are aware of self-deception as well as of other people's lies. I wanted to write about children who felt passionately, as I knew that children did, and to set those feelings down as honestly as I could manage in the framework of an exciting plot that would make them want to turn the pages. (After all, as that wise fellow Dr. Johnson also said, "What good is a book if it be not read?")

Perhaps this sounds a bit deliberate now, but I didn't work it out like that, not at the time. As I have said, I was new to the world of children's books and believed that if you did your job as well as you could, there was no need to talk about it. I simply knew that I intended, if I could, to write the kind of books I had enjoyed when I was young. Books that took children seriously, like those meaty, moral books in my grandmother's library. Books about Real Life—like the stories my grandmother told me herself. Most of them were about the people in the little country town where she had been born and where she had

lived all her life; about her neighbors who might look dull when you saw them walking down the street but who, according to my grandmother, lived rich, dramatic lives inside their houses; and, of course, about her own family. Old Granny Greengrass who had her finger chopped off at the butcher's. And Johnnie the pig, the runt of the litter who was bought from the milkman for a shilling and lived in the house as a much-loved pet until he went to the butcher's at the end of the year. When the BBC decided to make a film of *The Peppermint Pig,* they wanted at first to change the ending. Couldn't the pig, they said, be given a reprieve somehow? It was such a sad story. They would never be able to sell it in America. I said no. If they wanted to adapt the book, the pig must die. That is what happens to pigs, and to pretend otherwise would be false sentimentality. And worse—it would ruin my story. The whole point would be lost. The book was about a year in the life of a child—how she grew, what she learned; and the pig's death was an essential part of her learning. The BBC agreed in the end, but I was astonished by their reluctance. Whenever I turned on my television, it seemed to me that the screen was usually strewn with corpses, like a continuous performance of the last act of *Hamlet.* But dead people, of course, not dead pigs. I told this little story to a group of ten-year-olds in Scotland last year, and a boy at the back called out, "Well, Miss, dead pets is *sad.*" And a girl at the front screwed up her face and said timidly, "Yes, but it's a *nice* kind of sad."

Which was exactly what I had felt when my grandmother had first told me the story of Johnnie: a lovely, enriching, beautiful sadness of the kind that makes life more precious. Feelings don't go out of fashion, it seems, which is fortunate for an adult novelist who writes for children and hopes to comfort and reassure them as well as entertain them. Children are comforted when they find their own feelings formulated and expressed in a story, particularly when some of those feelings are slightly shameful to admit to. It reassures them to read about other children who are unhappy or naughty or spiteful or afraid. "I didn't know other people felt like that" is something they often say when they write to me. And they make identifications that seem strange, sometimes. A girl wrote to me from North Carolina, some eight or nine years ago, about the blind child who is one of the main characters in a book of mine called *The Witch's Daughter* (Lippincott). She said, "I liked Janey because she was cut off, like me." It turned out, not from that letter but from the next one she sent me, that my young correspondent was a Black girl who was being bussed into a largely white school some distance away from her home and was lonely there. A Black American girl, who had seen a parallel with her own situation in my story about a blind white English girl, who was involved with a somewhat improbable adventure with jewel thieves on a Scottish island. It was not a response you could have expected, or catered for. It came from a deep, imaginative, and emotional level. The level on which fiction functions best.

When I was nine, my grandfather died. I loved my grandfather and when I heard of his death, I was terribly upset for about five minutes. I went to my room, flung myself on my bed to cry, and then, almost immediately, got up and looked in the mirror. I saw the tears on my cheeks and picked up a hand mirror to look at my profile. I thought, oh, how unhappy I am, and felt, at once, somewhat less unhappy. I went downstairs and asked my mother if I could go to my grandfather's funeral. She said no, and I was angry. On one level I was still genuinely distressed, but on another, I wanted to go to the funeral so that everyone would see and admire my sad, pale face. I went out, intending to spend all my pocket money on flowers for my grandfather, but I stopped at the sweet shop on the way and bought a bar of chocolate, which left me only enough for a rather wilting bunch of violets. When I gave them to my mother, she cried, and I was both ashamed and glad. I was sorry my grandfather was dead and that my mother was crying, but I had meant to make her cry with my pathetic little bunch of flowers, as a punishment for not letting me go to the funeral.

Several years later, when I was thirteen or so, I read Tolstoy's *Childhood, Boyhood and Youth.* As you all certainly know, there is a wonderful description in the book of the feelings of the young narrator at his mother's funeral. First he feels real, spontaneous grief and admiration at the way he is expressing it; then sadness because he does not feel it any longer. I recognized myself, my own childish experience, in this honest account and was moved and consoled by it; and it still seems to me one of the most striking examples I know of emotional realism. A giant among novelists, remembering exactly how he had felt on this unhappy occasion and setting it down without slurring or evading or sentimentalizing. It delighted and astonished me at the time—how did this man, Leo Tolstoy, know how I had felt when my grandfather died?—and it excites my admiration now. Honesty about what goes on inside one's head is harder to achieve than truthful observation of external facts. It is harder to admit to unattractive emotions than it is to accept—and write about—unhappy situations.

Realism, as the word is used in reference to art and literature, has latterly, and rather sadly, come to mean to most people writing about the unpleasant side of life. This has happened because the realistic approach to fiction, which should mean a faithful account of the human condition without resort to easy generalities, is more striking when it is applied to unpleasant subjects. It is arguable, I suppose, that if you were giving an absolutely faithful account of most people's lives, unpleasantness might predominate. There would be more boredom, certainly, more long, dull stretches in which nothing much happens, than exciting events.

But it is not the business of fiction to bore the reader. And the fact is that children like to read about exciting events, even though their own lives are not full of exciting events. They like happy endings. They like good to triumph over evil, and they need to see it happening, if only occasionally and only in a story, in order to develop a sense of moral structure. You can, of course, hint that things do not always turn out as we would all like them to, that right behavior is not always rewarded, that noble undertakings sometimes come to nothing, that fate is often malicious and that life is seldom fair. But to hit children over the head with too many hard, external facts before they have the strength to deal with them is not fair either.

André Malraux says: "Art lives by reason of its function which is to enable men to break free from their human condition, not by shirking it, but by an act of possession. All art is a means to gain a hold on fate."

If a children's writer presents his characters honestly and is truthful about their thoughts and their feelings, he is giving his readers "a means to gain a hold on fate" by showing them that they can trust their thoughts and their feelings, that they can have faith in themselves. He can also show them a bit of the world, the beginning of the path they have to tread; but the most important thing he has to offer is a little hope, and courage for the journey.

Maurice Sendak, with Virginia Haviland

Questions to an Artist Who Is Also an Author

[Excerpted from Maurice Sendak, with Virginia Haviland, "Questions to an Artist Who Is Also an Author," *The Quarterly Journal of the Library of Congress,* 28 (1971), 262–80; also in *The Openhearted Audience: Ten Authors Talk about Writing for Children,* ed. Virginia Haviland (Library of Congress, 1980), pp. 25–45. This article was orginally an informal interview presented on November 16, 1970, as part of the Library of Congress's annual lecture series in observance of National Children's Book Week.]

Miss Haviland: *As a starter, let's ask: What did a book mean to you as a child? And what kinds of books did you have?*

Mr. Sendak: I think I'll start with the kinds of books, because back in the thirties I didn't have any "official" children's books (I refer to the classics). The only thing I can remember is cheap paperbacks, comic books. That's principally where I started. My sister bought me my first book, *The Prince and the Pauper.* A ritual began with that book which I recall very clearly. The first thing was to set it up on the table and stare at it for a long time. Not because I was impressed with Mark Twain; it was just such a beautiful object. Then came the smelling of it. I think the smelling of books began with *The Prince and the Pauper,* because it was printed on particularly fine paper, unlike the Disney books I had gotten previous to that, which were printed on very poor paper and smelled poor. *The Prince and the Pauper* smelled good and it also had a shiny cover, a laminated cover. I flipped over that. And it was very solid. I mean, it was bound very tightly. I remember trying to bite into it, which I don't imagine is what my sister intended when she bought the book for me. But the last thing I did with the book was to read it. It was all right. But I think it started then, a passion for books and bookmaking. I wanted to be an illustrator very early in my life; to be involved in books in some way—to make books. And the making of books, and the touching of books—there's so much more to a book than just the reading; there is a sensuousness. I've seen children touch books, fondle books, smell books, and it's all the reason in the world why books should be beautifully produced.

Miss Haviland: *Our questions to you, which are questions I think you have often answered for university and other groups, come as questions to you as an author and questions to you as an artist. Let's begin with the group of questions that have to do with you as an author. What part do you think fantasy should play in a child's life?*

Mr. Sendak: Well, fantasy is so all-pervasive in a child's life: I believe there's no part of our lives, our adult as well as child life, when we're not fantasizing, but we prefer to relegate fantasy to children, as though it were some tomfoolery only fit for the immature minds of the young. Children do live in fantasy *and* reality; they move back and forth very easily in a way that we no longer remember how to do. And in writing for children you just must assume they have this incredible flexibility, this cool sense of the logic of illogic, and that they can move with you very easily from one sphere to another without any problems. Fantasy is the core of all writing for children, as I think it is for the writing of any book, for any creative act, perhaps for the act of living. Certainly it is crucial to my work. There are many kinds of fantasy and levels of fantasy and subtleties of fantasy—but that would be another question. There is probably no such thing as creativity without fantasy. My books don't come about by "ideas" or by thinking of a particular subject and exclaiming "Gee, that's a terrific idea, I'll put it down!" They never quite come to me that way; they well up. In the way a dream comes to us at night, feelings come to me, and then I must rush to put them down. But these fantasies have to be given physical form, so you build a house around them, and the house is what you call a story, and the painting of the house is the bookmaking. But essentially it's a dream, or it's a fantasy.

Miss Haviland: *Are you, yourself, remembering daydreams? And a belief in fantasy that came out of your own childhood?*

Mr. Sendak: I can't recall my childhood any more than most of us can. There are sequences and scenes I remember much as we all do. But I do seem to have the knack of recalling the emotional quality of childhood, so that in *Wild Things*—I can remember the feeling, when I was a child (I don't remember who the people were, but there were people who had come to our house, relatives perhaps) and I remember they looked extremely ugly to me. I remember this quite clearly, and that when people came and, with endearments, they leaned over and said "Oh, I could eat you up!" I was very nervous because I really believed they probably could if they had a mind to. They had great big teeth, immense nostrils, and very sweaty foreheads. I often remember that vision and how it frightened me. There was one particular relative (I have some relatives in the audience, so I won't mention who it was) who did this to me, and it was really quite terrifying. Well, he is forever immortalized in *Wild Things*. *Wild Things* really is the anxiety and pleasure and immense problem of being a small child. And what do children do with themselves? They fantasize, they control fantasies or they don't control fantasies. It's not the recollection of my own particular childhood that I put down in books, but the feeling—like that particular feeling of fear of adults, who are totally unaware

that what they say to children is sometimes taken quite literally. And that when they pinch your cheek out of affection, it hurts; and that, when they suggest they could "hug you to death," you back away—any number of such things.

Miss Haviland: *It would be interesting to find out whether you can account for the fact that college students seem to enjoy* Where the Wild Things Are *and* Higglety Pigglety Pop! *as much as children do. The question is: whom do you see as your audience?*

Mr. Sendak: Well, I suppose primarily children, but not really. Because I don't write for children specifically. I certainly am not conscious of sitting down and writing a book for children. I think it would be fatal if one did. So I write *books,* and I hope that they are books anybody can read. I mean, there was a time in history when books like *Alice in Wonderland* and the fairy tales of George Macdonald were read by everybody. They were not segregated for children. So I'd like to think I have a large audience, and if college students like my books, that's fine. . . .

Miss Haviland: *Some other college students have asked how you, as a writer in this post-Freudian era, can resolve the problem of not consciously manipulating the unconscious.*

Mr. Sendak: [After a pause] Well, that's a problem. The Victorians were very fortunate. *Alice in Wonderland* is full of images and symbols, which are extremely beautiful and sometimes frightening. We know that Carroll had no Freud, and the book came pouring out of his unconscious, as happened with George Macdonald in *The Princess and the Goblin.* These authors touched on some very primal images in quite a fascinating way. It is more difficult for us to do because we do know so much, we've read so much. I hope I don't consciously manipulate my material. I do not analyze my work; if something strikes me and I get excited, then I want it to be a book. If it begins to die as I work, then of course it's not a book. But I think I do get away occasionally with walking that fine unconscious line. The things I've written in which there are conscious unconscious things, are very—you can't put your finger on it, certainly children can put their fingers on it, they are *the* most critical audience in the world, they smell a rat instantly. You cannot fool them, you really cannot fool them. They're tough to work for. And if they sense—and they know adults do these books—if they sense for one minute that I was faking this, I would know it. Now, *Wild Things* walked a very fine line in this particular sense. It was accepted by children largely, and that's the only proof I have that I've done it.

Miss Haviland: *Another college student has asked about the recurring symbol of something eating something, ingesting something, and then giving it out again. For instance in* Pierre *the lion eats Pierre and then gives him out; and in* As I Went Over the Water *a sea monster ingests a boat, then gives it out; in* Higglety Pigglety Pop! *Jenny eats a mop and then gives it out; and in* The Night Kitchen *Mickey is engulfed in dough and then springs out. Would you comment on this?*

Mr. Sendak: I don't know if it's safe to, but I began by telling you how much I liked to bite into my first books, and that is perhaps a clue to this subject. And, so far as I'm aware, I'm not an overeating person, but perhaps it is a hang-up from childhood. A pleasant one, I think. The business of eating is such an immensely important part of life for a child. Grimm's *Fairy Tales* is full of things being eaten and then disgorged. It's an image that constantly appeals to me; I love it. In *As I Went Over the Water,* the scene where the monster eats the boat and then regurgitates it is hilarious! I have the mind of a child, I think that's very funny. I will sit home and laugh myself sick over what I've done. Whether it appeals or makes sense to anyone else, I honestly don't know. It just seems right and occasionally children laugh too, so we laugh together. . . .

Miss Haviland: *Many persons right now are asking what inspired you to produce this new book,* In the Night Kitchen.

Mr. Sendak: Well, that is a difficult question. It comes out of a lot of things, and they are very hard to describe, because they are not so clear to me. There are a few clues. . . . *In the Night Kitchen* is a kind of homage to New York City, the city I loved so much and still love. It had a special quality for me as a child. It also is homage to the things that really affected me esthetically. I did not get to museums, I did not see art books. I was really quite rough in the sense of what was going on artistically. *Fantasia* was perhaps the most esthetic experience of my childhood, and that's a very dubious experience. But mainly there were the comic books and there was Walt Disney, and, more than anything else, there were the movies and radio, especially the movies. The early films, such as the Gold Digger movies and *King Kong* and other monster films, were the stuff that my books are composed of now. I am surprised, and this is really unconscious—I was looking at *Where the Wild Things Are* not too long ago with a friend, who had found something which amused her a great deal. She is a film collector, and she opened to one page of the book, where one of the wild things is leaning out of the cave. And then she held alongside it a still from *King Kong;* and it was, literally, a copy. But I had not seen the still, of course; I could not have remembered the sequence. Obviously, it had impressed itself on my brain, and there it was: I mean, exactly the proportions of cave to cliff, and proportions of monster coming out of cave. It was really quite extraordinary, the effect the films did have on me.

It was only much later, when I was a practicing illustrator and writer, that I got to know the classic children's books and read them. I did not know them as a child; I did not know pictures or paintings or writing when I was growing up. Brooklyn was a more or less civilized place, let me assure you, but this particular thing didn't get to me until quite late. And I think it's reflected in my work. I am what is commonly referred to as a late bloomer. I am happy for that.

Miss Haviland: *That brings us to the question of whom you believe to be some of the great writers for children? You have made some allusions already, but would you enlarge on that?*

Mr. Sendak: George Macdonald I think of as probably the greatest of the Victorian writers for children. It's the combination of planes, levels, that he worked on. George Macdonald can tell a conventional fairy tale; it has all the form that a fairy tale must have. At the same time, he manages to inundate the story with a kind of dream-magic, or unconscious power. *The Princess and the Goblin:* Irene's travels through the cave with the goblins are so strange, they can only come out of the deepest dream stuff. The fact that he can weave both of these things together is exactly what I love so much in his work, and what I try to emulate. And he is a model; he is someone I try to copy in many ways. There are other writers, like Charles Dickens, who has precisely this quality of the urgency of childhood. The peculiar charm of being in a room in a Dickens novel, where the furniture is alive, the fire is alive, where saucepans are alive, where chairs move, where every inanimate object has a personality. This is that particularly vivid quality that children have, of endowing everything with life. And Dickens sees and hears as children do. He has a marvelous ear for what's going on socially and politically, and on one level he's telling you a straightforward story. But underneath there is the intensity of the little boy staring out of everything and looking, and examining, and watching, and feeling intensely, and suffering immensely, which is what I think makes Dickens a superb writer. The same is true of George Macdonald. Another favorite writer is Henry James. I first became enthusiastic over Henry James when I read some of the earlier novels about young children. His incredible power of putting himself in the position of young children, viewing the adult world; and his uncanny sense of how difficult and painful it is to be a child. And even harder to be an adolescent. Now, these are people who write from their child sources, their dream sources. They don't forget them. William Blake is my favorite— and, of course, *The Songs of Innocence* and *The Songs of Experience* tell you all about this:

what it is to be a child—not childish, but a child inside your adult self—and how much better a person you are for being such. So that my favorite writers are never writers who have written books specifically for children. I don't believe in that kind of writing. I don't believe in people who consciously write for children. The great ones have always just written books. And there are many more, but I can't think of them now. . . .

Miss Haviland: *One librarian recalls hearing you speak in the 1950s, a time between the publishing of your illustrations for* A Hole Is To Dig *and of those for* Little Bear, *when you said that your roots go back to Caldecott. And this past April, when you accepted the Hans Christian Andersen International Medal, you named another string of artists whom you credit with stimulating you. I remember you mentioned William Blake, whom you've already spoken of here, George Cruikshank and Boutet de Monvel, Wilhelm Busch, Heinrich Hoffmann.*

Mr. Sendak: That's right.

Miss Haviland: *Could you talk about the specific elements that you think you find there that are particularly relevant to the children's book illustrator?*

Mr. Sendak: I hated school and my own particular way was to learn by myself. Many of the artists who influenced me were illustrators I accidentally came upon. I knew the Grimm's *Fairy Tales* illustrated by George Cruikshank, and I just went after everything I could put my hands on that was illustrated by Cruikshank and copied his style. Quite as simply as that. I wanted to crosshatch the way he did. Then I found Wilhelm Busch and I was off again. But happily Wilhelm Busch also crosshatched, so the Cruikshank crosshatching wasn't entirely wasted. And so an artist grows. I leaned very heavily on these people. I developed taste from these illustrators. Boutet de Monvel, the French illustrator, who is still not terribly well known (which is a great surprise to me), illustrated in the twenties, or earlier perhaps—and had the most glorious sense of design and refinement of style. His pictures are so beautifully felt and they are supremely elegant as only French illustration can be. They are very clear, very transparent, extremely fine. At the same time, they can be very tragic. There are things in his drawings, which perhaps now would even seem too strong for children—although at one point, they did not. There is a perfect example of his method in one of his illustrations for the *Fables of La Fontaine*—"The Wolf and the Lamb." They are a series of drawings, very much like a comic strip. It's like a ballet. The little lamb moves toward the stream and begins to drink, and the ferocious wolf appears and says: "What are you doing here? This is my water!" Of course, he's rationalizing the whole thing, he's going to eat the lamb up anyway, but he's putting on this big act about it being his water. Now, the lamb knows that there's no chance for escape, and while the wolf is bristling—and in each drawing his chest gets puffier and his fangs get fangier, and his eyes are blazing, and he looks horrendous—now, in proportion to him, growing larger on the page, the lamb dwindles. It has immediately accepted its fate, it can't outrun the wolf, it doesn't even listen to the words of the wolf, this is all beside the point: it is going to die, and it prepares itself for death. And while the wolf goes through this inane harangue, the lamb folds itself in preparation for its death. It leans down, it puts its head to one side, it curls up very gently, and its final gesture is to lay its head down on the ground. And at that moment the wolf pounces and destroys the lamb. It is one of the most beautiful sequences I've ever seen and one of the most honest in a children's book. There's no pretense of the lamb escaping, or of there being a happy ending—this is the way it is, it does happen this way sometimes, that's what de Monvel is saying. And this is what I believe children appreciate. People rage against the Grimm's fairy tales, forgetting that originally the brothers Grimm had—I'm going off the track a little bit—assembled the tales not for children but for historical and philological reasons. They were afraid their past was being lost in all the upheavals of that period, and the tales were put out as a scholarly edition of peasant tales not to be forgotten as part of the heritage of their home-

land. Well, lo and behold, children began to read them. And the second edition was called *The Household Tales* because children were devouring the books—not literally—I'm going to be so conscious of that from here on. The whole point I'm making, although I have forgotten the point frankly, is that those illustrators and writers that attracted me were the ones who did not seem at all to be hung up by the fact that their audiences were small people. They were telling the truth, just the way it was. This could be done if it were esthetically beautiful, if it were well written—simply, if it were a work of art, then it was fine. Now *Der Struuwelpeter* was one of the books that I loved very much—graphically, it *is* one of the most beautiful books in the world. One might complain about the cutting off of fingers, and the choking to death, and being burned alive, and might well have a case there—but, esthetically, for an artist growing up it was a good book to look at and a lot of my early books were affected strongly by the German illustrators. When I came to picture books, it was Randolph Caldecott who really did put me where I wanted to be. Caldecott is an illustrator, he is a songwriter, he is a choreographer, he is a stage manager, he is a decorator, he is a theater person; he's superb, simply. And he can take four lines of verse and have very little meaning in themselves and stretch them into a book that has tremendous meaning—not overloaded, no sentimentality in it. Everybody meets with a bad ending in *Froggie Went A-Courting*. Froggie gets eaten at the end by a duck, which is very sad, and the story usually ends on that note. But in Caldecott's version, he introduces, oddly enough, a human family. They observe the tragedy much as a Greek chorus might—one can almost hear their comments. In the last picture, we see Froggie's hat going downstream, all that remains of him. And standing on the bank are mother, father, and child—and it's startling for a moment until you realize what he's done: the little girl is clutching the mother's long Victorian skirt. And it's as though she's just been told the story, she's very upset, obviously. There are no words: I'm just inventing what I think this means—Froggie is dead, it alarms her, and for support she's hanging on to her mother's skirt. Her mother has a very quiet, resigned expression on her face. She's very gently pointing with her parasol toward the stream as the hat moves away, and the father is looking very sad. They're both expressing to the child, "Yes, it is very sad, but this does happen—that is the way the story ended, it can't be helped. But you have us. Hold on, everything is all right." And this is impressive in a simple rhyming book for children; it's extremely beautiful. It's full of fun, it's full of beautiful drawings, and it's full of truth. And I think Caldecott did it best, much better than anyone else who ever lived.

Miss Haviland: *One critic, at the last Biennale of Illustration at Bratislava, said: "There is no fundamental difference between illustrations for children and those for adults." Would you comment on that?*

Mr. Sendak: I don't agree at all, of course. I intensely do not believe in illustrations for adults. For preschool children who cannot read, pictures are extremely valuable. But even children who do read move in a very different world. As for adults, I personally find it offensive to read, I will *not* read, a novel that is illustrated. I always use this example, and many people here who know me have heard me carry on about this particular one, the case of *Anna Karenina:* the audacity of any illustrator who would draw Anna after Tolstoy has described her in the best way possible! Now, everyone who's read the book knows exactly what she looks like, or what he wants her to look like. Tolstoy is superb. And then to get an artist so asinine as to think he's going to draw Anna! Or Melville: it's incredible. People illustrate *Moby-Dick.* It's an insane thing to do, in my estimation. There is every difference in the world between illustrations for adults and illustrations for children. I don't know why there *are* illustrations for adults. They make no sense to me at all.

Miss Haviland: *Out of that same Biennale of Illustration, where you represented the United States as our juror, there was considerable disagreement, I recall disagreement in theory, on the importance of kinds of art as illustrations. You were there, could you bring this into the picture?*

Mr. Sendak: Well, I'm not sure I know exactly what you mean, but as I recall there was a European point of view as to what illustrations accomplish in a children's book, as opposed to what we believe is the function of illustration. I didn't know such a difference of opinion existed until we were in Czechoslovakia. And it was quite extraordinary. Partly, perhaps, because there is a dearth of original writing, they tend more often to reillustrate their classic and fairy tales, and the illustrations take on a dominance and importance which I, as an illustrator, do not approve of. The books often become showcases for artists. I mean, you turn pages and there are extremely beautiful illustrations, but so far as I can see they could be taken out of one book and put into another. Whereas here, we are very much involved in making the illustrations work in a very specific way inside a book. Now, a picture is there, not because there should be a picture there; there is a purpose for a picture—we are embellishing, or we are enlarging, or we are involving ourselves in some very deep way with the writer of the book, so that the book (when it is finally illustrated) means more than it did when it was just written. Which is not to say we are making the words more important; we are perhaps opening up the words in a way that children at first did not see was possible. In the United States we work to bring pictures and words together to achieve a wholeness in the book, which I was very surprised to find is not at all important in many European countries. It's not a matter of right or wrong, it's just that it is so different! There it was so much a matter of graphics, of beauty of picture; here graphic acrobatics are less important.

Miss Haviland: *One critic has asked why you changed from the "fine engraved style" of* Higglety Pigglety Pop! *back to what this person calls the "fat style" of your earlier work.*

Mr. Sendak: Hmm, "fat style." Well, I think the only way to answer that is to discuss the business of style. Style, to me, is purely a means to an end, and the more styles you have, the better. One should be able to junk a style very quickly. I think one of the worst things that can happen in some of the training schools for young men and women who are going to be illustrators is the tremendous focusing on "style," on preparation for coming out into the world and meeting the great, horned monsters, book editors. And how to take them on. And style seems to be one of the things. It's a great mistake. To get trapped in a style is to lose all flexibility. And I have worked very hard not to get trapped in that way. Now, I think my work looks like me, generally speaking; over a series of books, you can tell I've done them (much as I may regret many of them). I worked up a very elaborate pen and ink style in *Higglety,* which is very finely cross-hatched. But I can abandon that for a magic marker, as I did in *Night Kitchen,* and just go back to very simple, outlined, broad drawings with flat, or flatter, colors. Each book obviously demands an individual stylistic approach. If you have one style, then you're going to do the same book over and over, which is, of course, pretty dull. Lots of styles permit you to walk in and out of all kinds of books. It is a great bore worrying about style. So, my point is to have a fine style, a fat style, a fairly slim style, and an extremely stout style.

Miss Haviland: *This question comes to you as both an artist and an author. Do you think of your books first in words or in pictures?*

Mr. Sendak: In words. In fact, I don't think of the pictures at all. It's a very strange, schizophrenic sort of thing; I've thought of that very often. Sometimes after I've written something I find that there are things in my story that I don't draw well. And if it were any other person's book, I'd consider not doing it. But I've written it and I'm stuck with it, which is proof to me that I have not (at least consciously) been seduced by the tale's graphic potential. I don't think in terms of pictures at all; I find it's much more interesting and difficult to write, and illustration now becomes secondary in my life. So far as I'm aware, I think strictly in terms of words. And then when it's finished, it is al-

most a surprise as to "How'm I going to draw *that?* or "Why did I do that?" I'm stuck with an airplane, or I'm stuck with a building. If I'm stuck with an automobile, I'm ready to blow my brains out. . . .

Miss Haviland: *Looking at the publishing world, we can see a very big question: Do you think that children's book publishing is significantly different today than it was when you began in the early fifties? And, if you do, in what respect do you see this?*

Mr. Sendak: Well, yes, of course, it is very different than when I began in the early fifties. For one thing, the world seemed quieter then, and there was more opportunity to do experimental kinds of books. More important, there was time for young people to grow quietly. If you're an artist, you really need the time to grow quietly and not feel competitive or pushed. It was that way in the early fifties. One could develop gradually. Now, of course, it is much more competitive, and we do many more books but, alas, not many more great books. Something is lost. There is a rush, we are flooded with books, books come pouring out of the publishing meat grinder. And, the quality has dropped severely. We may be able to print a book better, but intrinsically the book, perhaps, is not better than it was. We have a backlist of books, superb books, by Margaret Wise Brown, by Ruth Krauss, by lots of people. I'd much rather we just took a year off, a moratorium: no more books. For a year, maybe two just stop publishing. And get those old books back, let the children see them! Books don't go out of fashion with children; they only go out of fashion with adults. So that kids are deprived of the works of art which are no longer around simply because new ones keep coming out. Every Christmas we are inundated with new books, and it's the inundation which I really find quite depressing.

Miss Haviland: *Would you generalize in any way on what has been happening in other countries as you have traveled abroad and looked at picture books?*

Mr. Sendak: Since I've generalized all this time, I could go a little further. There was a great moment in the middle fifties when, suddenly, the foreign books came to America. Books from Switzerland, the Hans Fischer books and the Carigiet books. We'd never seen them; it was a revolution in American bookmaking. We suddenly began to look very European. It was the best thing that could have happened to us, we *looked* terrific! But, of course, Europeans were then doing the most superb books. England invented the children's book as we know it. And now in the sixties and seventies, certainly America is leading the world in the manufacture of children's books. It's disappointing, I find, going to Europe (with the exception of England and Switzerland) and finding so few contemporary children's books. I don't know if you found this to be true, but I did. In France there is *Babar* and the great old ones, but there are very few new ones. There *are* new ones, of course, but none that we get to see and none that seemingly even French people or Italians get to see—it seems they have dropped back considerably. I could be wrong. In my travels I've discussed this matter with illustrators and editors—and this is certainly the impression I've gotten.

Miss Haviland: *Is there any point that you would like to make, aside from the questions that have been brought up to you before and which you've answered again tonight?*

Mr. Sendak: I love my work very much, it means everything to me. I would like to see a time when children's books were not segregated from adult books, a time when people didn't think of children's books as a minor art form, a little Peterpanville, a cutesy-darling place where you could Have Fun, Laugh Your Head Off. I know so many adult writers whom I would happily chop into pieces, who say, "Well, I think I'll take a moment and sit down and knock off a kiddy book! It looks like so much fun, it's obviously easy—." And, of course, they write a lousy book. You hope they will and they do! It would be so much better if everyone felt that children's books are for everybody, that we simply write books, that we are a community of writers and artists, that we are all seriously involved in the business of writing. And if everyone felt that writing for children is a serious business, perhaps even more serious than a lot of other forms of writing, and if, when such books are reviewed and discussed, they were discussed on this serious level, and that we would be taken seriously as artists. I would like to do away with the division into age categories of children over here and adults over there, which is confusing to me and I think probably confusing to children. It's very confusing to many people who don't even know how to buy a children's book. I think if I have any particular hope it is this: that we all should simply be artists and just write books and stop pretending that there is such a thing as being able to sit down and write a book for a child: it is quite impossible. One simply writes books.

The development of the criticism of children's literature in recent years . . . has stressed the unity of literary endeavor. Children's literature should be considered as part of all literature; the criticism of children's literature should be conducted in the same manner as the criticism of adult literature. These principles may by now seem to be truisms, but they are based on a sense of justice as well as on a sense of aesthetics.[1]

17   The Critics

O ne often hears it said among children's literature specialists that children's books are now, at long last, taken seriously; but children's books have *always* been taken seriously. We are the inheritors of a rich history of critical analysis, which has seriously addressed children's literature. If there is much in early criticism that now appears wrongheaded or even quaint, there is also the solid foundation upon which modern scholarship rests; indeed, nearly every issue that concerns contemporary critics had already been articulated a hundred years ago. An examination of the history of children's book criticism can prevent a dangerous myopia; some of our most cherished modern attitudes may appear just as quaint to future scholars as the pet notions of the nineteenth century do to us. The criticism of children's literature has always reflected the social and cultural preoccupations of any era that produced it.

Until the end of the eighteenth century there were not enough children's books to generate the beginnings of a critical assessment; but, throughout the nineteenth century, children's books were reviewed and discussed in well-known literary journals and popular magazines. Children's literature was then considered to be simply part of all literature. According to Lance Salway:

1. Paul Heins, "Literary Criticism and Children's Books," *The Quarterly Journal of the Library of Congress*, 38 (1981), 255–56.

In many respects critical discussion of the subject was less restricted than it is now; books for the young were considered to be part of the general body of literature and writing about them was not confined to specialized journals and seasonal supplements. The works of Maria Edgeworth or Henty or Mrs. Ewing were not considered to be less deserving of critical attention merely because they were directed principally at the young. . . . Discussion of children's books and their authors was conducted with as much seriousness— and a good deal more humour—as it is in our own day.[2]

It is difficult to detect any note of humor in the voice of Mrs. Sarah Trimmer, whose *The Guardian of Education* (1802–06) epitomized a didactic and moralistic attitude toward children's literature that survives as one of the approaches to children's books today. Mrs. Trimmer alerted adults to the necessity of "the utmost circumspection . . . requisite in making a proper selection" of children's books, which "of late years . . . have multiplied to an astonishing and alarming degree, and much mischief lies hid in many of them."[3] Her own circumspection shows through her comments on the "vulgarities of expression" in fairy tales, and the "danger, as well as the impropriety, of putting such books as these into the hands of little children, whose minds are susceptible of every impression; and who from the liveliness of their imaginations are apt to convert into realities whatever forcibly strikes their fancy."[4]

Perhaps Mrs. Trimmer's most fascinating remarks concern the dangers of *Robinson Crusoe* (1719), which, she attests, should not "be put into the hands of *all boys* without discrimination." She provides an example:

Two little boys in consequence of reading the History of Robinson Crusoe, set off together from their parents' houses, in order to embark in some ship, with the hope of being cast on an uninhabited island; and though they certainly did not succeed in their project, it was productive of fatal effects, for the mother of one of them during the time they were missing, was, in consequence of anxiety of mind, seized with an illness which shortly put a period to her days.[5]

Mrs. Trimmer was opposed to books "calculated to entertain the imagination, rather than to improve the heart, or cultivate the understanding."[6] Her views were shared by other early Victorian critics who evaluated children's books in terms of the precepts of behavior and lessons in social and religious morality contained within them.

A more literary and aesthetic perspective on children's literature was voiced by later Victorians such as Edward Salmon in England and Horace Scudder in the United States. In 1867, Scudder expressed, in *The Riverside Magazine for*

2. Lance Salway, Preface, *A Peculiar Gift: Nineteenth Century Writings on Books for Children*, ed. Lance Salway (Kestrel, 1976), pp. 11–12.

3. Sarah Trimmer, "On the Care Which is Requisite in the Choice of Books for Children," *The Guardian of Education*, 2 (1803), 407–10, reprinted in *Children and Literature: Views and Reviews*, ed. Virginia Haviland (Scott, Foresman, 1973), p. 4.

4. Sarah Trimmer, review of *Nursery Tales: Cinderella, Blue Beard, and Little Red Riding Hood*, *The Guardian of Education*, 4 (1805), 74–75, reprinted in Haviland, p. 7.

5. Sarah Trimmer, review of *The Life and strange surprising Adventures of Robinson Crusoe, of York, Mariner, who lived eight and twenty years alone in an uninhabited Island, written by himself*, *The Guardian of Education*, 3 (1804), reprinted in *Suitable for Children? Controversies in Children's Literature*, ed. Nicholas Tucker (Sussex University Press, 1976), p. 39.

6. Sarah Trimmer, "Observations of the Changes Which Have Taken Place in Books for Children and Young Persons," *The Guardian of Education*, 1 (1802), 61–66, reprinted in Salway, p. 20.

Young People, his concern that children's books be given serious critical consideration:

A literature is forming which is destined to act powerfully on general letters; hitherto it had been little disturbed by critics, but the time must soon come, if it has not already come, when students of literature must consider the character and tendency of *Children's Letters;* when all who have at heart the best interest of the Kingdom of Letters must look sharply to this Principality.[7]

Paul Heins considers this a "prophetic" statement, one that "recognized children's literature as an autonomous realm. In its quiet way it was a declaration of independence from both eighteenth-century critical indifference and nineteenth-century moralism."[8]

With the increasing awareness of literary quality in children's books, there developed parallel concerns regarding book selection. The questions of which books to choose for children and of what books children should read—only the best books, or a mixture of quality, popular, and pulp literature; only books of high literary merit or those of social, moral, and spiritual edification—have preoccupied teachers, critics, writers, and librarians from Charlotte Yonge and Caroline Hewins in the nineteenth century to Anne Carroll Moore, Bertha Mahony Miller (founder of *The Horn Book Magazine*), and Lillian H. Smith in the twentieth. Critics of both centuries saw the need for a set of standards by which to judge children's books, but today there is more disagreement over what principles of evaluation should be used than ever before.

A wide variety of critical standards have been proposed as criteria. "Most disputes over standards," comments John Rowe Townsend, "are fruitless because the antagonists suppose their criteria to be mutually exclusive; if one is right the other must be wrong. This is not necessarily so. Different kinds of assessment are valid for different purposes."[9] And, indeed, different criteria, used together, can cast light on the literature from different angles.

Townsend, for example, identifies four attributes of children's books, noted by reviewers and book selectors and treated as criteria: *suitability* (involving appropriateness, reading age, and purpose); *popularity; relevance* (involving potential awareness of current social and personal problems); and *literary merit.* The first three are significant and important issues for teachers, librarians, and parents—the people who live and work with children and their books; they are the questions of book selection and use, of the development of reading interests and skills: "Questions for the buyer, and perhaps above all for those who are closest to the ultimate consumer. 'Will this be suitable for *my* child, will this be popular with *my* class, will this be relevant for children in the area served by *my* library?' "[10]

Although the final criterion—that of literary merit—appears at first glance to be neither as immediate nor as practical as the others, it is the foundation underly-

7. Horace E. Scudder, "Books for Young People," *The Riverside Magazine for Young People,* 1 (Jan. 1867), 44, as quoted in Richard L. Darling, *The Rise of Children's Book Reviewing in America, 1865–1881* (Bowker, 1968), p. 217.
8. Paul Heins, "Introduction: Criticism Comes of Age," in *Crosscurrent of Criticism: Horn Book Essays, 1968-1977,* ed. Paul Heins (Horn Book, 1977), p. xi.
9. John Rowe Townsend, Introduction, *A Sense of Story: Essays on Contemporary Writers for Children* (Horn Book, 1971), pp. 14–15.
10. John Rowe Townsend, "Standards of Criticism for Children's Literature," in *The Arbuthnot Lectures, 1970–1979,* comp. Zena Sutherland (American Library Association, 1980), p. 30.

ing them all, dealing as it does with the aesthetic integrity and literary coherence of the book in its own right.

Townsend suggests that "a critical approach is desirable not only for its own sake but also as a stimulus and discipline for author and publisher, and—in the long run—for the improvement of the breed."[11]

Those critics who apply the methods of general literary analysis to children's literature are often the ones who express the commonly held opinion that contemporary children's literature is "healthier" than its adult counterpart. This attitude is prompted mainly by the survival of *story* in children's fiction, at least as compared to the modernist antinarratives of much adult fiction. Isaac Bashevis Singer expresses an extreme point of view when he explains why he writes for children: "No writer can bribe his way to the child's attention with false originality, literary puns and puzzles, arbitrary distortions of the order of things, or muddy streams of consciousness which often reveal nothing but a writer's boring and selfish personality. I come to the child because I see in him a last refuge from a literature gone berserk and ready for suicide."[12]

Aidan Chambers and Fred Inglis would agree with Singer concerning the refuge taken in children's books, but in a totally antithetical sense. Chambers interprets a proposition by Inglis:

Inglis is saying that those who come to children's books for the stories they say are missing in adult literature are refugees, liberal-spirited and humanistic, who are nostalgic for a world now gone (if it ever really existed), who are confused by and unhappy with the world they see coming upon them. . . . We ought to be disturbed because the failure to make use of the narrative movements and styles presently explored in adult literature means that children are being plied with a literature which develops them into readers entirely unprepared for the adult novels which will face them in their adolescence—the very novels which articulate the world around them.[13]

And, as Chambers himself points out, such arguments are to some degree specious because, even though the antinarrative may be admired as an avant-garde ideal, many highly respected writers of adult fiction still tell stories in the best of the narrative tradition.

The primacy of literary standards has been attacked by various groups who see children's literature as a socializing force rather than a literary force. In a throwback to the moral and spiritual guardianship of the likes of Mrs. Trimmer, changing social mores of the 1960s to 1980s have given rise to critics who evaluate children's books solely for positive images of women, ethnic minorities, senior citizens, or the handicapped and who judge books on their perceived developmental or bibliotherapeutic values.

Even the most literary of critics certainly could not fault those who, with sensitivity and good will, wish to retire once and for all the negative racial or sexual stereotypes found in the children's literature of earlier eras and sometimes, unfortunately, in that of the present. Welcome also in children's books are treatments of thought-provoking and difficult social issues and the psychological concerns of contemporary life. But the majority of critics, teachers, librarians, and parents

11. Townsend, Introduction, *A Sense of Story*, p. 14.
12. Isaac Bashevis Singer, "I See the Child as a Last Refuge," *The New York Times Book Review*, Children's Book Section, 9 Nov. 1969, pp. 1, 66, reprinted in *Signposts to Criticism of Children's Literature*, ed. Robert Bator (American Library Association, 1983), p. 50.
13. Aidan Chambers, "Letter from England: Three Fallacies about Children's Books," *The Horn Book Magazine*, 54 (1978), 323–24.

would be sympathetic to Dorothy Butler, when she argues that adults searching children's books "for unpalatable attitudes from which the child must be sheltered" miss a significant point:

Must children grow up believing that no one ever behaved selfishly, exploited nature cruelly, or held rigid racist or sexist attitudes in days gone by? Should our children not be told of the selfish actions and unworthy prejudices of earlier generations? Let them see that the people who held these views and performed these acts were people like themselves, that humankind falls easily into error, and that most people accept without question the mores of the era and society into which they are born. . . . [Children] will learn to look honestly and respond sensitively if the books we give them are good books and true—full of real people behaving as well as they can in the face of a world which offers contradictory inducements, the good and the bad inextricably entwined. . . .

Only *felt* principles ever work for human beings.[14]

And when such principles are at the heart of a well crafted, fully developed story, then children have a literature of conscience that is *literature*. But for every one of these rare, excellent books, there are many more that combine social and moralistic righteousness with poor writing. "In the rush to repent," writes Nat Hentoff, "publishers have not sufficiently searched out truly creative tellers of tales who cannot be fitted into neat, sanitized, newly 'proper' molds."[15]

The utilitarian approach to criticism is epitomized by such works as the content-centered, subject-organized *Children's Literature: An Issues Approach* (1976) by Masha Rudman. But the most extreme voice speaking on behalf of children's literature in the service of bibliotherapy and social change may very well be that of the Council on Interracial Books for Children. The Council's critical reviewing bulletin focuses on political, social, and cultural issues and on child development and psychology and uses only those "reviewers who are members of the particular group depicted in any book."[16] *Human and Anti-Human Values in Children's Books: A Content Rating Instrument for Educators and Concerned Parents* (1976), written and published by the Council, provides a set of guidelines for the writing, publishing, criticism, and selection of children's books, based on a scale of twelve "isms." How close the Council's utilitarian principles come to censorship imposed at the creative source, at the point of publication, or in use with children is open to debate. In discussing the "structure of relations between dominators and dominated" in society, the Council proposes that:

Children's books play an active part in maintaining that structure by molding future adults who will accept it. Today, we see how such books can also mold human beings with counter-values that may help us to restructure the society. . . .

To those who argue that it is not the business of children's books to be the vehicle of change, we answer . . . no writer is just a reporter. All books contain messages and, by tolerating them, we are in effect endorsing those messages. This we cannot do—not

14. Dorothy Butler, "Reading Begins at Home: Part I," *The Horn Book Magazine,* 59 (1983), 551–52.
15. Nat Hentoff, "Any Writer Who Follows Anyone Else's Guidelines Ought to Be in Advertising," *School Library Journal,* 24 (Nov. 1977), 27–29, reprinted in *Beyond Fact: Nonfiction for Children and Young People,* comp. Jo Carr (American Library Association, 1982), p. 178.
16. Council on Interracial Books for Children, "Bias in Children's Books," in *Guidelines for Selecting Bias-Free Textbooks and Storybooks for Children* (Council on Interracial Books for Children, 1980), pp. 7–9, 21–23, reprinted in Carr, p. 175.

when the message is racism or sexism, materialism or ageism, or any other antihuman value.[17]

It is true that all books contain messages. The fallacy in the Council's argument lies in its claim that by tolerating dissenting opinions we are endorsing them. A political or religious group that is totally convinced of the righteousness of its position might wish to suppress differing points of view, but democracy is based on the free exchange of ideas: We tolerate differing opinions not because we endorse them but because we wish to remain free to express our own. Positions such as the Council's, well-meaning as they are, can all too easily lead to vigilante tactics, censorship, and the suppression of the imagination. Nat Hentoff, himself a writer and social activist, reacts directly to what he calls the Council's "slippery" guidelines:

The council . . . is quite openly working towards the end of having "children's literature become a tool for the conscious promotion of human values that will help lead to greater human liberation." I apologize for being obvious, but literature cannot breathe if it is forced to be utilitarian in this or any other sense. The council fundamentally misunderstands the act of imagination.[18]

Ironically, advocates of censorship of children's literature on the left end of the political spectrum are becoming uneasy bedfellows with the traditional advocates of censorship—those on the right. The new realism in children's fiction has prompted a call from some for a return to conservative values and limitations on content, and book banning in school and public libraries is threatening to become epidemic.

Turning from the heated debates surrounding questions of values and standards, we might consider the cooler field of educational methodology, which investigates the process of bringing children and books together. Questions of concern here include how children learn to read, what occurs in the act of reading, the purpose and value of reading, the relationship between oral and written language and learning, the nature and process of narrative and story making, and how children understand and respond to narrative in their social, personal, and literary development. Margaret Meek, Aidan Warlow, and Griselda Barton, the editors of *The Cool Web: The Pattern of Children's Reading* (1977), stress that the reader is as important as the book:

We have emphasized the point that, although it is possible to judge books for children by what are called "adult standards" and regard them as part of literature, the young reader carries a different world in his head, no less complex than an adult's but differently organized. He needs his stories in a different way, his experience of reading must be different. When discussing stories for children, to lose sight of the reader is too dangerous to contemplate.[19]

Many studies have considered the role of the adult as mediator between the child and the book, as well as the most effective methods of introducing children to books. From conference reports such as the influential Dartmouth Report, produced under the chairmanship of D. W. Harding in 1966, to the more recent

17. Council on Interracial Books for Children, pp. 169, 173.
18. Hentoff, p. 177.
19. Margaret Meek, Aidan Warlow, and Griselda Barton, "Section One: The Reader: Introduction," *The Cool Web: The Pattern of Children's Reading,* ed. Margaret Meek, Aidan Warlow, and Griselda Barton (Bodley Head, 1977), p. 11.

writings of individual teachers and critics such as Dorothy Butler, Aidan Chambers, and Charlotte Huck, all strategies for bringing child and book together have been predicated upon thorough familiarity with and critical understanding of children's literature on the part of the adult teacher, librarian, or parent. Experts agree that if children are to experience reading as an act of deep pleasure and enjoyment and one to be repeated willingly, then the reading "atmosphere" must be positive and supportive. In their different ways, these educators and critics discuss the notion that the key to reading is not found in "decoding" skills—that remedial reading is not the answer to reading problems. They contemplate the relationship of literature to literacy. Dorothy Butler states:

> For real reading, the eye must swing along the line while meaning pours into the mind. Expectation of meaning is crucial. Children with well-nourished minds draw on a deep well of concept and vocabulary to sustain their performance in the reading task. Response, the vital component, occurs almost automatically.[20]

The habit of lifetime reading, then, as Butler suggests, begins at home—in the active nourishing of children's minds from babyhood. Reading is encouraged when books of quality are read aloud to children at all ages, and when both the physical presence of books and the act of sitting down to enjoy them are familiar. Reading is further motivated by a varied flow of language in daily speech: conversation and play with words; sharing jokes and anecdotes; spontaneous singing and recitation of poetry; and casual or formal storytelling. Children's early engagement with oral language and literature profoundly influences not only their future literacy, but also their ability to structure experience. As the psychologist James Hillman points out:

> To have had story of any sort in childhood—and here I mean oral story, those told or read (for reading has an oral aspect even if one reads to oneself) rather than watching story on screen—puts a person into a basic recognition of and familiarity with the legitimate reality of story *per se*. It is given with life, with speech and communication, and not something later that comes with learning and literature. Coming early with life, it is already a perspective to life. One integrates life as story because one has stories in the back of the mind (unconscious) as containers for organizing events into meaningful experiences. The stories are means of telling oneself into events that might not otherwise make psychological sense at all.[21]

Adults who show children that they are themselves readers can foster in children, as Aidan Chambers says, "an attitude to books which is open and welcoming, which recognizes that a book is a means whereby one person says something to another and which stimulates a desire to listen to what that person has to say."[22]   To achieve this end, teachers, librarians, and parents should provide a rich and varied collection of books for children to browse through. Regular visits to the public library and the development of home libraries of children's own books, when balanced by the use of full classroom and school library collections, provide children with a broad range of reading materials from which to choose. Adults should know and recommend quality children's books, while

20. Dorothy Butler, "Reading Begins at Home: Part II," *The Horn Book Magazine*, 59 (1983), 743.

21. James Hillman, "A Note on Story," *Children's Literature: Journal of the Modern Language Association Seminar on Children's Literature and the Children's Literature Association*, 3 (1974), 9.

22. Aidan Chambers, "Letter from England: Talking about Reading: Back to Basics? Part II," *The Horn Book Magazine*, 53 (1977), 707.

respecting the child's individual reading tastes and choices. They can encourage children to grow in appreciation from the popular—and at times mediocre—reading that functions as familiar formula and social glue, to more challenging and exhilarating literary experiences that will nourish children's imaginations.

Adults can be informed and committed companions in children's interpretations of literature through creative play, drama, puppetry, art, and discussion; they can be sympathetic guides in children's explorations of their personal responses to literature and their developing perceptions of the craftsmanship and significance found in literary forms.

Motivation to read is complex and subtle; reading is released not only by acquired mechanical skills but, on a much deeper level, by the stimulation of intellectual interest and by the engagement of the emotions. In this time of endangered literacy, dropping reading levels are a common concern. The shared popular culture of contemporary children is formed more by the nonliterary experiences of television, video, and popular music than by literary experiences. Adults have a responsibility to pass on to children their literary inheritance so that it is not lost, so that the human and aesthetic continuity from the traditional lore of nursery rhyme and folk tale to the modern achievements of poetry and fiction is preserved. To engage children in this legacy, we must share with them the pleasure we, as adults, take in children's literature and the commitment we share toward its study, preservation, and growth.

Children's literature offers children a deep enjoyment, a profound and universal humanizing pleasure, and the beginnings of literary discrimination and of wisdom. Why study children's literature? Why share books with children? We choose to be the mediators between children and their books because we believe with Northrop Frye in the education of the imagination:

No matter how much experience we may gather in life, we can never in life get the dimension of experience that the imagination gives us. Only the arts and sciences can do that, and of these, only literature gives us the whole sweep and range of human imagination as it sees itself.[23]

23. Northrop Frye, *The Educated Imagination* (Indiana University Press, 1964), p. 101.

John Rowe Townsend

A Sense of Story

[The main text of this selection is taken from the introduction to John Rowe Townsend, *A Sense of Story: Essays on Contemporary Writers for Children* (Horn Book, 1971), pp. 9–15; the last two paragraphs are taken from the revised edition, John Rowe Townsend, *A Sounding of Storytellers: New and Revised Essays on Contemporary Writers for Children* (Lippincott, 1979), pp. 7–8.]

Surveys of children's books are numerous, and so are aids to book selection, but discussion at any length of the work of individual contemporary writers is scarce. Such discussion may be thought unnecessary. I know from conversations over a period of years that there are intelligent and even bookish people to whom children's literature, by definition, is a childish thing which adults have put away. Such people may have a personal or professional interest—it is useful to have some ideas on what books to give to their children or to read to a class— but they do not pretend to be interested on their own account, and regard such an interest as an oddity, an amiable weakness. It is not my intention to quarrel with them. We cannot all be interested in everything.

Yet children are part of mankind and children's books are part of literature, and any line which is drawn to confine children or their books to their own special corner is an artificial one. Wherever the line is drawn, children and adults and books will all wander across it. Long ago *Robinson Crusoe* and *Gulliver's Travels* were adopted as children's stories. Adults have taken over *Huckleberry Finn,* argue about *Alice,* and probably enjoy *The Wind in the Willows* as much as their children do. Dickens and other Victorian novelists wrote books for the whole family; Stevenson and Rider Haggard and John Buchan and Anthony Hope wrote for boys and grown-up boys alike; and it can be offered as a pseudo-Euclidean proposition that any line drawn between books for adults and books for children must pass through the middle of Kipling.

Arbitrary though it is, the division has become sharper in the present century. The main rea-sons have been the expansion of school and public libraries for children, and corresponding changes in the book trade. On the whole, I believe that the children's library has been a blessing to authors and publishers as well as children. The growth of a strong institutional market has eased some of the cruder commercial pressures and has made possible the writing and publication of many excellent books which otherwise could never appear. But it has hardened the dividing line between children's books and adult books into a barrier, behind which separate development now takes place.

Although the distinction is administrative rather than literary, it must have some effect on the way books are written. Yet authors are individualists, and still tend to write the book they want to write rather than one that will fit into a category. Arguments about whether such-and-such a book is 'really for children' are always cropping up, and are usually pointless in any but organizational terms. The only practical definition of a children's book today—absurd as it sounds—is 'a book which appears on the children's list of a publisher.'

Books are, in fact, continually finding their way on to the children's lists which, in another age, would have been regarded as general fiction. Abetted by their editors, writers for children constantly push out the bounds of what is acceptable. Yet because of the great division these writers, and their books, are probably more shut off than ever from the general public. (And, from this point of view, the probable growth of 'young adult' lists may raise still more fences and create new pens in which books can be trapped.) A minor reason for a book on contemporary writers for children could well be a sense of dissatisfaction with artificial barriers; a feeling that there are authors who deserve a wider public; a belief that many books which are good by any standard will now only be found by looking on the children's side of the line.

In fiction at least, the balance of talent has shifted sharply between adult books and children's books in recent years. Brian Jackson, director of the Advisory Centre for Education, in an essay on Philippa Pearce in *The Use of English* for Spring 1970, declared that 'ours is the golden age of children's literature'—a view with which I agree, although the figure of speech grows wearisome—and expressed surprise that 'the great outburst of children's books this last thirty years' should come about when there is no longer a sturdy adult literature to support it.

Children's writing [he said] is a large and apparently self-contained genre, as it never was before. It is independent of the current adult novel. On the face of it, you wouldn't therefore expect its burgeoning richness. Could it be, ironically, that precisely because the adult novel is so weak in this country, some talents have been drawn into the children's field and flourished (as others have been drawn into scientific fiction and perished)?

The weakness of the current adult novel—which is not a solely British phenomenon, although it is more obvious here than in the United States—hardly needs to be demonstrated. Among much converging testimony, I draw almost at random from a few books and articles that come to hand. Anthony Burgess, in *The Novel Now* (1967), quotes Evelyn Waugh's view that 'the originators, the exuberant men, are extinct, and in their place subsists and mostly flourishes a generation notable for elegance and variety of contrivance'; and Burgess, while questioning the 'elegance' if not the 'variety of contrivance,' adds on his own account: 'We cannot doubt that the twenty years since the Second World War have produced nothing to compare with the masterpieces of, say, the half-century before it.' Storm Jameson, in *Parthian Words* (1970), asks how many of us dip twice into 'the endless flow of social trivia, on its level interesting, which pours from the pens or typewriters of contemporary novelists.' The American novelist Isaac Bashevis Singer, writing in the *New York Times Book Review* on 9 November 1969, expressed the belief that 'while adult literature, especially fiction, is deteriorating, the literature for children is gaining in quality and stature.' Explaining why he began to write for children in his late years, Singer declared that the child in our time

has become a consumer of a great growing literature—a reader who cannot be deluded by literary fads and barren experiments. No writer can bribe

his way to the child's attention with false originality, literary puns and puzzles, arbitrary distortions of the order of things, or muddy streams of consciousness which often reveal nothing but the writer's boring and selfish personality. I came to the child because I see in him a last refuge from a literature gone berserk and ready for suicide.

I am not sure that despair over the state of adult fiction is a good reason for becoming a writer for children. But I believe that the general picture of an ailing adult literature in contrast with a thriving literature for children is broadly correct and would be accepted by most people with knowledge of both fields. I do not mean to say that children's books are 'better' than adults', or to claim for them an excessively large place in the scheme of things. And I admit that plenty of rubbish is published for children—as indeed it is for grown-ups. But I am sure there are people writing for children today who are every bit as talented as their opposite numbers among writers for adults.

The reasons for the strength of modern fiction for children are too many and complex to be dealt with in part of a short introduction, but some of them can be hinted at. Adult fiction means, effectively, the novel. The novel is a recent form, and may be only a transitional one. Its heyday was the rapidly-changing but pre-electronic Victorian age. At present it gives the impression of shrinking into a corner: narrow, withdrawn, self-preoccupied. But children's literature has wild blood in it; its ancestry lies partly in the long ages of storytelling which preceded the novel. Myth, legend, fairy-tale are alive in their own right, endlessly reprinted, endlessly fertile in their influence. Modern children's fiction is permeated by a sense of story. Many writers, knowingly or unknowingly, return again and again to the old themes, often reworking them in modern or historical settings. And even where the children's novel runs parallel to its adult counterpart, there is often a freedom, speed and spontaneity which the adult novel now seems to lack.

This, I believe, is the result of an odd but happy paradox. On the one hand, most modern writers for children insist that they write, with the blessing of their editors, the books they want to write for their own satisfaction. The classic statement of this position was made by Arthur Ransome in a letter to the editor of *The Junior Bookshelf* as long ago as 1937: 'You write not for children but for yourself, and if, by good fortune, children enjoy what you enjoy, why then, you are a writer of children's books . . . No special credit to you, but simply thumping good luck.' C. S. Lewis said that the only reason why he would ever write for children was 'because a children's story is the best art form for something you have to say'; he also remarked that 'I am almost inclined to set it up as a canon that a children's story which is enjoyed only by children is a bad children's story.' Yet anyone writing a book that will appear on a children's list must be aware of a potential readership of children. This is the fruitful contradiction from which the children's writer benefits. However much he is writing for himself he must, consciously or unconsciously, have a special sense of audience. As Arthur Ransome, rightly unworried by any inconsistency, went on to say in the letter already quoted: 'Every writer wants to have readers, and than children there are no better readers in the world.'

An author can—as I have said elsewhere—expect from the reading child as much intelligence, as much imagination, as from the grown-up, and a good deal more readiness to enter into things and live the story. He can take up his theme afresh as if the world were new, rather than picking it up where the last practitioner let it drop and allowing for the weariness and satiety of his readers. He cannot expect children to put up with long-windedness or pomposity or emperors' clothes; but that is a discipline rather than a restriction. True, the child's range of experience is limited. There are still some kinds of book that are not likely to appear on the children's list: not because they will corrupt a child but because they will bore him. But, in general, children and their books are much less inhibited now than they were in Arthur Ransome's day. In my experience, children's writers do not feel much hampered; mostly they are able to do what they want to do. They are fortunate people. Their sense on the one hand of scope and freedom, on the other of a con-

stantly-renewed and responsive readership, freshens their work and makes this an exhilarating sector to be concerned with.

Nevertheless, children's books need to be appraised with coolness and detachment, simple enthusiasm being little better than simple unawareness. A critical approach is desirable not only for its own sake but also as a stimulus and discipline for author and publisher, and—in the long run—for the improvement of the breed. This indeed is the strongest reason for it. Donnarae MacCann, introducing a series of articles in the *Wilson Library Bulletin* for December 1969, quoted from Henry S. Canby's *Definitions:*

Unless there is somewhere an intelligent critical attitude against which the writer can measure himself . . . one of the chief requirements for good literature is wanting . . . The author degenerates.

In the United States and Britain, the positions of writers for children in the league-table are well known among specialists in the field; possibly too well known. But, as Donnarae MacCann says, 'there is no body of critical writing to turn to, even for those books which have been awarded the highest literary prizes in children's literature in Britain and America.'. . . The children's writer, when his work begins to make any impression, can expect his new book to get a few reviews: some by specialists with much knowledge but little critical acumen, some by non-specialists with—presumably—critical acumen but not much knowledge of children's books, some by people with no obvious qualifications at all. With luck the book may be reviewed in two or three places by critics who can place it in its context and can exercise some worthwhile judgment; but they are unlikely to have much space in which to work. And reviewing, even at its best, is a special and limited form of criticism: a rapid tasting rather than a leisurely consideration.

Mention of the criticism of children's books will usually lead to an argument about the relevance of various criteria. It seems to me that it is perfectly possible to judge books for children by non-literary standards. It is legitimate to consider the social or moral or psychological or educational impact of a book; to consider how many children, and what kind of children, will like it. But it is dangerous to do this and call it criticism. Most disputes over standards are fruitless because the antagonists suppose their criteria to be mutually exclusive; if one is right the other must be wrong. This is not necessarily so. Different kinds of assessment are valid for different purposes. The important thing is that everyone should understand what is being done.

The critic who is concerned with a book as literature cannot, however, carry his 'standards' around with him like a set of tools ready for any job. He should, I believe, approach a book with an open mind and respond to it as freshly and honestly as he is able; then he should go away, let his thoughts and feelings about it mature, turn them over from time to time, consider the book in relation to others by the same author and by the author's predecessors and contemporaries. If the book is for children he should not let his mind be dominated by the fact; but neither, I think, should he attempt to ignore it. Myself—as one who remembers being a child, has children of his own, and has written for children—I could not, even if I wished, put children out of my mind when reading books intended for them. Just as the author must, I believe, write for himself yet with awareness of an audience of children, so the critic must write for himself with an awareness that the books he discusses are books written for children.

But this awareness should not, I think, be too specific. Neither author nor critic should be continually asking himself questions such as: 'Will this be comprehensible to the average eleven-year-old?' We all know there is no average child. Children are individuals, and will read books if they like them and when they are ready for them. A suggestion that a book may appeal to a particular age-group or type of child can be helpful, especially in reviews, but it should always be tentative and it should not affect one's assessment of merit. It has always seemed clear to me that a good book for children must be a good book in its own right. And a book can be good without being immensely popular and without solving its readers' problems or making them kinder to others.

[Townsend continues his thoughts regarding the state of children's literature criticism as follows:]

. . . A good deal of recent comment appears to be based on the assumption that children's books are tools for shaping attitudes. Works of fiction are assessed by reference to their social context, the extent to which they deal with certain contemporary issues, and the desirability or otherwise of the views they are thought to encourage. Traditional literary values are dismissed as inappropriate or inadequate.

Actually the implication that literary criticism does not concern itself with the content of a book or with the author's attitudes is unfounded. Criticism does so concern itself, and always must. But in the present climate it is more necessary than ever to point out that there are other aspects of fiction which are also important. To look at children's books from a narrowly restricted viewpoint as means to non-literary ends is derogatory both to them and to the whole body of literature of which they form part.

Eleanor Cameron

The Sense of Audience

[Excerpted from Eleanor Cameron, "The Sense of Audience," in *The Green and Burning Tree: On the Writing and Enjoyment of Children's Books* (Little, Brown, 1969), pp. 203–28. Originally presented, in a shortened version, as a speech at the Third Intermountain Conference on Children's Literature at the University of Utah, June 21, 1965, and published under the title "Why *Not* for Children?" in *The Horn Book Magazine*, 42 (1966), 21–33. The author rewrote this essay for inclusion in *The Green and Burning Tree: On the Writing and Enjoyment of Children's Books*.]

Upon more than one occasion Pamela Travers has quoted part of a sentence of Beatrix Potter's to buttress a belief of hers, always stated with sweeping certainty: "Nobody ever writes for children," which may quite well be true for her but which is most assuredly not true for every writer. We could take it as a matter of course that she is speaking for herself alone except that she gives one instance after another of children's books (a phrase she deeply disapproves of) which she claims were not written for children at all.

The sense of audience is usually very strongly present in those writing for publication, and in almost every case determines whether a manuscript shall be sent to the children's editor of a publishing house or to the editor of adult books. As for Beatrix Potter, Pamela Travers quotes her as having said, "I write to please myself" (as indeed she did),[1] and then goes on to observe that it is "a statement as grand and absolute, in its way, as Galileo's 'Nevertheless it moves.' "[2] Yes, it might be, if only there were not so many other statements of Beatrix Potter's to be taken into consideration, so that actually Miss Travers has, by continually quoting only those five words of hers and building an entire attitude upon them (that there are no such things as children's books and that nobody ever writes for children), given a completely erroneous idea of Beatrix Potter's motives and compulsions.

The Tale of Peter Rabbit was written first of all as a letter to a small boy who had been for a long time ill in bed, a letter which eight years later Miss Potter asked to see again so that she could transform it into a little book.[3] Pamela Travers would probably brush this aside as she would no doubt dismiss the fact that *The Tale of Squirrel Nutkin* was written as a letter to that small boy's sister. But this she could not dismiss: the fact that Beatrix Potter tried it out on various children before it took final shape.

"The words of the squirrel book will need cutting down to judge by the children here," she wrote Norman Warne, her publisher. "I have got several good hints about the words."[4] Does this sound like a woman writing purely for her own pleasure? Concerning *The Tale of Mrs. Tiggy-Winkle* she said, "I think 'Mrs. Tiggy' will be all right. It is a *girls'* book; so is the Hunca Munca; but there must be a large audience of little girls. I think they would like the different clothes."[5] Are these the comments of a woman who could say, along with Miss Travers, "There are no such things as children's books," or "Nobody ever writes for children"?

Possibly Miss Travers is self-conscious about being pigeonholed, by the general public, as a children's writer and fantasist into the bargain.[*] Certainly a kind of self-consciousness must have compelled her to reject fantasy as a subject which the editor of *The New York Times* book section thought they might discuss for the spring children's book issue. "But that is a word I do not like," she replied to him. "It has come, through misuse, to mean something contrived, far from the truth, untrustworthy."[7] But the word fantasy has not come to mean these things through "misuse." There is a perfectly good, dictionary-defined meaning for fantasy as it is used in the world of psychiatry and psychology, a meaning which relates to being given unhealthily to extravagant and unrestrained imaginings, grotesque mental images, visionary ideas built upon no solid foundations, imaginative sequences fulfilling a psychological need. But in the world of literature, and especially in the world of children's literature, the widely accepted meaning of the word fantasy is simply an imaginative or fanciful work. Neither J. R. R. Tolkien nor C. S. Lewis feels the slightest self-consciousness about it; Lewis uses it freely to describe his own writings for children,[8] and Tolkein defends it warmly (interchanging the words "fairy tale" and "fantastic creation") in *Tree and Leaf.*[9]

Nor need those writers whose books children have taken for their own feel any self-conscious-

5. P. 65.
* Beatrix Potter, so sure inside of herself of what she wanted to do, was, at first, self-conscious. In writing to Norman Warne about the rough draft of *The Tailor of Gloucester,* she felt that he might possibly like it because "things look less silly in type." When she finally sent him a copy, she hoped that he would not think the story "very silly," and later wrote to thank him for his letter in which he paid her the compliment, she said, of "taking the plot very seriously."[6]
6. [Lane], pp. 52–53.
7. Travers, "A Radical Innocence," *The New York Times Book Review,* Children's Book Section, May 9, 1965, p. 1.
8. Lewis, *Of Other Worlds,* p. 28.
9. Tolkien, *Tree and Leaf,* pp. 46–55.

1. Lane, *The Tale of Beatrix Potter,* p. 128.
2. Travers, "Once I Saw a Fox Dancing Alone," *New York Herald Tribune Book Week,* Spring Children's Issue, May 9, 1965, p. 2.
3. Lane, *The Tale of Beatrix Potter,* p. 45.
4. P. 54.

ness about where their works are put, in what lists or upon what shelves or in what sections. Perceptive children and adults, writers and non-writers alike, will eventually and sometimes with breathtaking swiftness recognize what is worthy, what is of value to *them,* and often in the other world of literature than that which is generally thought to be theirs. . . .

One cannot deny, however, that an attitude of contempt (call it tolerant amusement if you will) exists in some quarters toward what is called children's literature. . . .

There are many different kinds of contempt, expressed in all sorts of subtle ways. *Webster's Biographical Dictionary* (1963) does not mention the existence of Lewis's books for children, though they are widely read on both sides of the water. To the scholarly gentlemen who compiled this reference work, the fact was of no importance. And you could not find Beatrix Potter's name in either the first or second editions of *The Columbia Encyclopedia,* though she is given a few lines in the third. Nor is she to be found in even the latest edition of *Webster's Biographical Dictionary,* though her books have been reprinted in innumerable languages, and generations of children, ever since 1900, have literally clasped them to their hearts. As for their profound and lasting influence, H. L. Cox, in his "Appreciation" at the beginning of Miss Potter's *Journal,* has this to say: "Children the world over learn English from Beatrix Potter's prose, both the English language and something, too, of an English attitude. In the formative effect at an impressionable age, she may now exert greater influence than any other English author."[12]

There is an advertisement, appearing regularly in the writers' magazines, which grips you with the leader, "The Juvenile Field Is the Training Ground for the Beginning Writer—Earn While You Learn." No greater ignorance could be expressed, nor any greater misconception, except that which was revealed, all unwittingly, by the earnest young woman who told my husband that she was spending four hours a day, apart from an eight-hour job, in trying to write

for children. "I suppose," she said, "that the main problem is learning just how to write down properly."

Perhaps it is inevitable that an attitude of amused tolerance or condescension on the part of a large segment of the public should result in self-consciousness in a good many of those who are called children's writers, and that this same self-consciousness should cause them to reject the conception of books for children. Martha Bacon, in an article in *The Atlantic,* begins by saying, "The whole idea of books written for children has always been annoying to me. Even when I was a child I preferred to think of my books as just books, not children's books."[13] She goes on to list the Potter tales, *Alice in Wonderland, The Wind in the Willows,* and the E. Nesbit stories as her special treasures.

This idea I then found taken up and expanded upon by Pamela Travers in an interview with Haskel Frankel in *The Saturday Review:*

Well, [she told him], I've already said that there are no such things as children's books. But others think there are. Children's books are looked on as a sideline of literature. A special smile. They are usually thought to be associated with women. I was determined not to have this label of sentimentality put on me so I signed by my initials, hoping people wouldn't bother to wonder if the books were written by a man, woman or kangaroo.[14]

In an article in *The Saturday Evening Post* in which she quoted Beatrix Potter's remark about writing stories to please herself, she continued:

And so does everyone else. Was *Pooh really* written for Christopher Robin? Or *Wonderland* for Alice Liddell or *Pinocchio* for the village children in Collodi? Of course not. Such names are for dedication pages. The one and only begetter is always the author; or the child hidden within him, perhaps, or the memories of his own youth, which are never far away. For me there is no such thing as a book for children. If it is true, it is true for everyone. In fact, it is simply a book. *What child enjoys being written down to?* [*The italics are mine.*][15]

12. Cox, "An Appreciation," in *The Journal of Beatrix Potter from 1881 to 1897,* xv.

13. Bacon, "Dotty Dimple and the Fiction Award," *the Atlantic,* March, 1963, p. 130.
14. Frankel, "A Rose for Mary Poppins," *Saturday Review,* November 7, 1964, p. 57.
15. Travers, "Where Did She Come From, Where Did She Go?" *The Saturday Evening Post,* November 7, 1964, p. 77.

Finally I came across an *Authors' Guild News Letter* in which Sterling North, whose book *Rascal* was runner-up for the Newberry Award of 1964, has this to say:

There is no such category as "children," and I deplore the patronizing phrase "writing for children." There are only human beings of varying degrees of intelligence and sensitivity. . . . I try never to write a book thinking exclusively of a certain age level or its probable readers.[16]

With certain of their statements one of course agrees, and I particularly like "If [a book] is true, it is true for everyone." And yet what a curious self-consciousness one senses here in relation to the whole concept of "child," a most mystifying ambivalence of respect and denigration. No such category as "children," says Mr. North, and deplores the "patronizing" phrase "writing for children." *But why patronizing?* Only a gauche or a snobbish or an ignorant person patronizes anyone. "What child enjoys being written down to?" asks Pamela Travers. No child, naturally, if he is at all aware of it, even subconsciously. But why equate "writing for" with "writing down" when one is thinking "child"? What is the matter with "child"? What is shameful or reprehensible about being a child, which are the emotions one feels so strongly by implication in Martha Bacon's words, "I preferred to think of my books as just books, not children's books."

Surely if a writer respects himself and his craft, if he respects the idea of "child"—that creature of swift perceptions, eager imaginings, the devastating stare, the continually searching intelligence—how can there possibly be any question of writing down? I remember Dorothy Parker's words: "I think nobody on earth writes down. Garbage though they turn out, Hollywood writers aren't writing down. That is their best. If you're going to write, don't pretend to write down. It's going to be the best you can do, and it's the fact that it's the best you can do that kills you."[17]   On the same subject, C. S. Lewis has to say:

I was therefore writing "for children" only in the sense that I excluded what I thought they would not like or understand; not in the sense of writing what I intended to be below adult attention. I may of course have been deceived, but the principle at least saves one from being patronizing. I never wrote down to anyone; and whether the opinion condemns or acquits my own work, it certainly is my opinion that a book worth reading only in childhood is not worth reading even then.[18]

Elsewhere he observes:

Nothing seems to me more fatal, for this art, than an idea that whatever we share with children is, in the privative sense, "childish" and that whatever is childish is somehow comic. We must meet children as equals in that area of our nature where we are their equals. Our superiority consists partly in commanding other areas, and partly (which is more relevant) in the fact that we are better at telling stories than they are. The child as reader is neither to be patronized nor idolized: we talk to him as man to man.[19] . . .

Concerning the sense of audience in general, Virginia Woolf—whom, above all others, one would have expected to write for herself alone—put into her diary: "And this shall be written for my own pleasure. But that phrase inhibits me; for if one writes only for one's own pleasure, I don't know what it is that happens. I suppose the convention of writing is destroyed: therefore one does not write at all."[21]

In the *Time* review of Monica Sterling's biography of Hans Christian Andersen, *The Wild Swan,* the reviewer said, "He wrote for himself alone." Nothing could be farther from the truth. Andersen, as the biography reveals in chapter after chapter, was monumentally (almost pathologically, as you will find in Fredrik Böök's biography) aware of audience. As for his writing for children specifically, he tells us in *The Fairy Tale of My Life:*

As I have already said, in order to give the readers the right impression from the start, I had entitled the first volume "Fairy-Tales Told for Children." I had committed my stories to paper in precisely the

16. North, *Authors Guild News Letter,* Children's Book Committee Issue, Spring, 1964, p. 1.
17. Capron, "Dorothy Parker," *Writers at Work,* 1st Series, p. 81.

18. Lewis, *Of Other Worlds,* pp. 37–38.
19. P. 34.
21. Woolf, *A Writer's Diary,* p. 132.

expressions as I had myself used when telling them to little children, and I had come to the conclusion that people of all ages were content with this; the children were most amused by what I will call the decorations, while older people on the other hand were more interested in the underlying idea. The fairy-tales became something for both children and grown-ups to read, and that, I believe, is the thing to aim at for anyone who wants to write fairy-tales nowadays.[22]

Nevertheless it is clear that he never lost his full awareness of his child audience, for at the end of his life he wrote to his friend Hartmann, "I must think of my death-bed. You attend to the funeral march! It will, of course, be the schools, the small schools, which will follow, not the big Latin ones. So arrange the music to suit children's steps."[23]

I do not believe, despite Pamela Travers, that *Alice in Wonderland* would ever have come into being without the eagerness of three children to be told stories and the pestering of one of them, "Oh, Mr. Dodgson, I wish you would write out Alice's Adventures for me!"[24]   The point is that because Dodgson was the particular man he was, combined with the fact that he *was* asked for a story, *Alice* turned out to be both an exciting and comical adventure children can enjoy (and they still do enjoy it, as you will see for yourself if you go to the library), and a satire into the bargain. Like Clemens-Twain, Dodgson-Carroll was double (but not divided,[25] not at war with himself as Clemens was[26]) —learned and brilliantly imaginative on the one hand, and child-hearted on the other, as is revealed by his letters to the children of George MacDonald. "We realize," writes Derek Hudson in his biography of Carroll, "that here [in the letters], as in the 'Alice' books, his immediate aim was to afford pleasure to children. He gave the best of his talent to that end, without ulterior motive. If this fact had

been properly taken to heart, we might have been spared some of the more sophisticated interpretations of his fantasies which have been published."[27] In his diary Dodgson made an entry for November 13, 1862: "Began writing the fairy-tale for Alice, which I told them July 4th, going to Godstow—I hope to finish it by Christmas."[28]   Later he was concerned about its published appearance and wrote to Macmillan, "I have been considering the question of the *colour* of *Alice's Adventures,* and I have come to the conclusion that *bright red* will be the best—not the best, perhaps, artistically, but the most attractive to childish eyes."[29]   Furthermore, Dodgson was anxious that the book be published as quickly as possible because his "young friends . . . are all grown out of childhood so alarmingly fast."[30]   No greater proof can be found of the fact that this gifted man possessed to a rare degree the ability of winning and deserving a child's confidence and that he was always aware of his child audience than lines written by Gertrude Chataway, to whom *The Hunting of the Snark* was dedicated. What was most delightful to her, she said, was the way in which he would take his cue from some remark of hers, so that she felt she had helped to create the story, that it was a personal possession of hers as well as his. "It was the most lovely nonsense conceivable," she said, and she reveled in it. His imagination, so vivid and quick, "would fly from one subject to another," and was never in the least restricted by reality.[31]

As for Kenneth Grahame, his wife, Elspeth Grahame, has written in *First Whisper of "The Wind in the Willows":*

No one had ever heard these stories related, except the child himself. But once I remember, on asking my maid to tell Kenneth that we were already very late in starting for some dinner-party, that she mentioned: "Oh, he is up in the night-nursery, telling

22. Andersen, *The Fairy Tale of My Life,* p. 199.
23. Sterling, *The Wild Swan,* p. 358.
24. Hudson, *Lewis Carroll,* p. 130.
25. R. L. Green, *Lewis Carroll,* p. 7.
26. Kaplan, *Mr. Clemens and Mark Twain,* pp. 110–111, 164.

27. Hudson, *Lewis Carroll,* p. 116.
28. Carroll, *The Diaries of Lewis Carroll,* p. 188.
29. Hudson, *Lewis Carroll,* p. 136.
30. P. 137.
31. R. L. Green, *Lewis Carroll,* p. 51.

Master Mouse some ditty* or another about a toad."[32]

Afterwards, when Mouse and his mother were about to go away to the seaside, Mouse refused point-blank because he would miss the further adventures of Toad and was therefore promised by his father that further installments would be sent him, chapter by chapter, in the form of letters. And it is profoundly fascinating to catch in those letters, reproduced in *First Whisper* and condensed as they are in action and scene and characterization, all that was miraculously to flower into the final version. A final version written by Grahame for himself alone? Compare it with *Dream Days* and *The Golden Age,* written before Mouse was born, and decide for yourself.

Can Miss Travers honestly believe, as she appears to by implication in the *Herald Tribune* article, that Hugh Lofting's Pushme-Pullyou would ever have taken shape in his imagination had he been writing to his wife or to some old school friend of his own age, instead of letters to his children, which were the form in which the Doctor Dolittle books began?

Mouse was waiting. Hugh Lofting's children were waiting. And *certain kinds* of stories came into being.

As for the books of E. Nesbit, mentioned by Martha Bacon as among those she resented being thought of "for children," their author had never the slightest doubt which were for them and which were for adults. There existed, during all the years she wrote, a sparkling and sophisticated woman who completely fascinated H. G. Wells, the Fabian Society, and the Bohemian hostesses of London, a woman whose charm and wit and gaiety and almost frightening temperament informed her entire life. But E. Nesbit had prayed that she would never, never forget what it was like to be a child,[33] and hidden beneath that frightening temperament, there ex-

isted a deeply sensitive being always reexperiencing the scenes and emotions of early childhood, a being who had nothing at all to do with Wells and the Fabian Society and the Bohemian hostesses. Oddly enough, only at the end of her life, when she was ill and in pain and rejected by the publishers who had once looked forward with the greatest eagerness to each new manuscript for children, was she resigned to being written to and adored for *The Story of the Amulet, Five Children and It,* and the Bastables. For them she is still honored after sixty years, but the poems and novels are forgotten. And perhaps there is a secret hidden here in E. Nesbit's complete success on the one hand and her utter failure on the other. I remember reading in an essay by Frances Clarke Sayers on Eleanor Estes, how Mrs. Sayers felt that the author of *The Moffats* was more released in her enormously successful books for children than in the one novel she had written,[34] and that word *released* has stayed with me and piqued my mind ever since.

This aesthetic release occurred in Beatrix Potter when her memories (powerfully related to the creative impulse) turned to her childhood holidays spent in the Lake Country. She always remembered "the little people of Sawrey." She called her readers "all my little friends" and told how they wrote her about "scell nuckin"—"it seems as an impossible word to spell"[35]—this shy, dowdily dressed woman with the bright blue eyes, who was sterner with herself, when it came to her art, than with anyone else in the world; who read the Bible to chasten her style[36] and then tried out both stories and style on the children. Stern, yet tender, this double but not divided being was capable of caress in her minute and searching observations of the natural world, but, as well, of completely unsentimentalized portrayals of foxes and rats scheming for dinners of ducks and kittens. Harrowing, suspenseful, yes, considering her audience of four- and five- and six-year-olds, but never tragic, never morbid. For Beatrix Potter,

---

* The maid was Wiltshire in origin, explains Mrs. Grahame, and used words now obsolete in meaning, such as ditty for story.
32. Grahame, *First Whisper of "The Wind in the Willows,"* pp. 1–2.
33. Nesbit, *Long Ago When I Was Young,* p. 27.

34. Sayers, *Summoned by Books,* p. 121.
35. Lane, *The Tale of Beatrix Potter,* p. 55.
36. P. 128.

creator of the cold-eyed Mr. Tod and Mr. Samuel Whiskers, had an unerring sense of audience. And for them she exerted every discipline of artistry at her command, which rather confounds the rest of that sentence, "I have just made stories to please myself," for it ends—"because I never grew up."[37] But she *did* grow up; her artistry matured; and her childhood love of the Lake Country, which was in her blood and bone, was an essential part of that maturing as well as an essential part of the fact that what she wrote, she wrote for children. . . .

To determine what goes on in Madeleine L'Engle, author of *A Wrinkle in Time,* is . . . difficult, for outwardly at least, she seems torn. "Why do you write for children" she was asked, and she replied immediately and instinctively (her word), "I don't." She, like Pamela Travers, doubts that C. S. Lewis or any other so-called children's writer ever sits down at his desk thinking, "I am going to write a book for children."[39] Yet the title of C. S. Lewis's essay on the subject, in which he explains very clearly why his Narnia books were written especially for a certain audience and why they took the form they did, is "On Three Ways of Writing for Children."[40] I feel that out of all Miss L'Engle has said, her words "you have to write whatever book it is that wants to be written" are the truest of all, though I would add, "in the way it demands to be written." For there are certain tales that demand to be written out of the depths of childhood, out of the emotions and spirituality, the whole world of childhood, from the point of view of childhood; and there are others that demand from inception the point of view of adulthood, worked from adult levels of knowledge and experience. This does not mean, however, that adult knowledge and experience will not be necessary in the creation of a children's book or will not enter into the tale written out of childhood. One has only to remember Beatrix Potter exerting, for her four- and five- and six-year-olds, every discipline of artistry at her command. . . .

Rosemary Sutcliff . . . has said that she writes for children because of their responsiveness.[41] Yet after a whole series of books on early Britain written for children, when it came to the story of Arthur, *Sword at Sunset,* it was published for adults and so, presumably, was written for them because of the initial concept of the book, its inherent character, because of all that needed to be expressed emotionally and spiritually in order to give it its fullest and deepest meaning.

Sterling North remarked about trying never to think of age level; and of course it is preposterous even to imagine Kenneth Grahame, for instance, dwelling upon age level as he put down *The Wind in the Willows.* One exists within the world of childhood as one writes, it seems to me, and that is all. Frances Clarke Sayers has commented upon another writer:

To this observer it seems that the vitality of Eleanor Estes derives from the fact that she sees childhood whole—its zest, its dilemmas, its cruelties and compassions. She never moves outside that understanding, because she never needs to lean upon the crutch of adult concepts and explanations.[42]

Even so, more than one level can be there. In fact, more than one level will be likely if the author is a subtle, complex kind of human being like Grahame, Carroll, Andersen, Lewis, or Tolkien.

Thus the author inevitably writes to please himself, even though (indeed, possibly *because*) he is thinking "child," for he can do nothing else! And, of course, the crux of the matter is that *writing for oneself alone* and *writing to please oneself* are two entirely different matters. If the author did not please himself, if he did not fulfill himself in the process of writing, if he did not write straight out from his inmost center, as we know Grahame and Carroll and Andersen and Lewis and Tolkien have done, he would be writing for a living only, and this is something else altogether from what is being discussed here. It is true that Philippa Pearce, in her fine essay on the subject of writing for children, "The Writer's View of Childhood,"

37. P. 41.
39. L'Engle, "The Key, the Door, the Road," *The Horn Book,* June, 1964, p. 265.
40. Lewis, *Of Other Worlds,* pp. 22–34; also in *The Horn Book,* October, 1963, pp. 459–469.

41. Colwell, "Rosemary Sutcliff—Lantern Bearer," *The Horn Book,* June, 1960, p. 200.
42. Sayers, *Summoned by Books,* p. 118.

speaks of "a sensible regard for cash,"[43] but in my own experience this does not enter in in any way until after the book is finished. . . .

Here I want to consider something which is perhaps rather subtle and paradoxical, something closely related to writing purely for money: catering. Children will not read what does not interest them, what does not please. But to interest (one must always interest, said Flaubert), to be conscious of audience, is not necessarily to cater. The terms are not invariably synonymous. Whether the writer addresses himself to adults or to children, he must lead. His conception, his initial vision, must come from within (as Carroll's and Lewis's certainly did . . .); what he has to say must be said in response, first of all, to an inner compulsion. If he has a conception which is not mysterious and he twists it into a mystery because "children love mysteries," then he has failed himself as a creator. If he has written a fine first book and the response to it is so warm and gratifying that he cooks up another in answer to this enthusiasm, rather than struggle with an idea that has been growing steadily in his imagination or wait for one perhaps quite different from his first book, then he will fail. In all probability his second book will go out of print.

But what about leaving out? persist those who have no interest in the books children have taken to themselves. For, they say, so much leaving out is inevitable: the sexual relationship, that engrossing tension between men and women which absorbs the greater part of adult fiction; the difficult but fascinating problems of philosophy, economics, and politics; all the gruesome realities of man's inhumanity to man, which are ugly in the extreme but which are powerfully knotted into our human destiny.

Here, I say to myself, could be what is at the heart of self-consciousness, if there should be any. Because there is leaving out, sentimentality is brought up, niceness, "the special smile," "a sideline of literature," "associated with women."

But are these the words we want: leaving out? It may be true that those books which children

(generally speaking) call their own deal with sexuality only to the extent revealed between Barbara Leonie Picard's faun and the woodcutter's daughter, or the warmth and mutual need which is so satisfying to the child when he is aware of it between his father and mother. It may be true that they deal with the problems of economics only to the extent that can be seen, for instance, in the life of "The Little Match Girl," who died of cold and starvation, in Doris Gates's *Blue Willow,* in Eleanor Farjeon's exquisite short story, " 'And I Dance Mine Own Child,' " Weik's *The Jazz Man,* Shotwell's *Roosevelt Grady,* or in Estes's *The Hundred Dresses.* It may be true that they deal with the brutality of man only to the extent Rosemary Sutcliff puts it down in her stories of early Britain, and this is a grim brutality, but treated without either morbidity or vulgarity, that is, without any lingering over the excruciating details. The power of these stories is ageless, and can be felt by all ages.

However, let us now face the charge which strikes at a deeper level of this question of what it means to write, consciously and purposefully, for children. Philippa Pearce, who in her essay affirms, "The children's writer must acknowledge himself unashamedly as a writer for children,"[45] touches upon this level. She says, "The charge is that the view of childhood in children's literature reflects not only a recognition of the limitations of immature readers but also the writer's own shameful limitations—his own immaturity, his own childishness."[46] And it has been put to me that possibly "the great creators of children's fantasies were people who lived in fantasy worlds because they were unable to cope with reality," people who were, in other words, both immature and escapist and were thus compelled to create "worlds that suited them." As children are sympathetic to these worlds and find delight in them, possibly this, my correspondent believes, is the reason why their books have survived as children's classics. She extrapolates from her hypothesis that all children's writers may be "a little mad" in that they create worlds

43. Pearce, "The Writer's View of Childhood," *The Horn Book,* February, 1962, p. 74.

45. Pearce, "The Writer's View of Childhood," p. 77.
46. P. 74.

within the realm of childhood rather than the world of adult reality (but what good and lasting children's book does not reflect the world of adult reality?), an act resulting from, one can only assume, that very immaturity and childishness Philippa Pearce spoke of.

It would seem to me that these are extremely questionable generalities, and that if one is to speak of escape and of preferences at all, one might well include artists in general (using the word "artist" to indicate any kind of creator) and not just those who write for children. But either way the argument falls apart when one considers actual case histories.

Concerning the matter of escape, of inability to deal with the world of reality, possibly of being unwilling to face it and therefore creating a preferred world arranged according to the writer's own desires (though, as we have seen, in fairy tales doom lies on every hand, and I am referring here to fairy tales written by individuals—Andersen, MacDonald, Tolkien, Barbara Leonie Picard and Lloyd Alexander—not those handed down from the past), let us consider specifically the lives of those who not only wrote for children but who wrote fantasies into the bargain. For these men and women might be thought of as being as out of touch with reality as any who could be brought to the bar of judgment.

It is true that E. Nesbit in her later years conceived a mania for proving in the most curious fashion that Shakespeare was Bacon,[47] and that she was possibly, throughout her life, overly dramatic. It is true also that the youthfulness of her spirit, which was most deeply responsible for her success with children, showed itself in her poetry as a kind of immaturity which could produce only the most mediocre verse. But as for facing reality, she kept her family from poverty by her continuous writing under the most difficult circumstances, was an active member of the Fabian Society, and reared as her own children the two that her husband conceived illegitimately. She was wry, tart, humorous, and highly intelligent, and never for a moment shielded herself from the truth of her husband's failings, but instead created a relationship and

a home in which the two of them could live with some degree of happiness and dignity. These are not acts of escapism, immaturity, or childishness, and I do not believe that a childish or immature woman could have commanded the intense interest and respect of such a man as H. G. Wells.

Hans Andersen, though he desired always to be the center of attention, seems not to have been childlike in any other way, except that he beheld the whole world with the astonished, minutely observing eyes of a child, a facet of his nature without which his stories would not have lived on as great literature. He faced the facts of his own ugliness and lack of sexual attraction for women with pain and bitterness, yes, but he did face and accept them, an act that for any man with the normal demands of sexuality, which Andersen in fact possessed, would be an almost unendurable frustration. And rather than turning on those friends he loved when they showered upon him unasked for criticism and advice "for his own good," he transformed his hurt and resentment into classic art. Andersen always *used* his unhappiness rather than let it destroy him.

As for Lewis Carroll, it is true that he peculiarly enjoyed the companionship of small girls, so that possibly the accusation of "some kind of overclose relationship to the experience of childhood" (to quote Philippa Pearce again) could be leveled at him; but that he was an escapist into his own world of fantasy can scarcely be called a fact when you remember that *Alice* is one of the world's great satires, the work of a close and ironic observer of mankind, which he did not despise but on the other hand regarded with healthy laughter. Nor would it seem that any man capable of writing *Euclid and His Modern Rivals* could be considered childish, a work that his biographer, Derek Hudson, believes "shows more clearly than anything else that Dodgson and Carroll cannot be separated into different compartments."[48]

There can be no denying that Kenneth Grahame fits more nearly into the image of the "childish" writer whose work children love than any other we can quickly bring to mind.

47. Moore, *E. Nesbit*, pp. 226–229.

48. Hudson, *Lewis Carroll*, pp. 239–240.

Peter Green's whole biography, or rather that part dealing with Grahame's adult life, is a revelation of this: Grahame's liking for toys, his indulgence in baby talk in the letters he wrote Elspeth Grahame before they were married, and his confession that, in conceiving *The Wind in the Willows,* he wanted to create a book "clean of the clash of sex." From which remark we can only deduce that he looked upon sex as dirty, echoing the Puritan-Victorian attitude toward the act, which is strange, in a way, when we reflect how much Grahame loathed the Victorians. But both Grahame and his wife were sexually immature, so that as far as their physical relationship was concerned, their marriage was a failure.[49]   However it is quite possible for an imaginative, sensitive, intelligent human being, as Grahame was, to be mature in ways other than sexual. And Grahame's observation, when he was urged to follow *The Wind in the Willows* with another book, that he was "a spring, not a pump," reveals an aesthetic wisdom that many a writer, mature in other matters, does not have. It is true that Peter Green speaks of Grahame's indolence in later life, but it could be that underneath that indolence was the knowledge that he had said supremely well all he really wanted to say.

Beatrix Potter, as the years brought her into old age, became one of the tartest-tongued, driest, keenest observers of humankind the world of small children's books has ever known, as well as a sharp and hard-driving bargainer in the Lake Country when it came to the matter of sheep-buying and of preserving parcels of land through purchase for the National Trust of the United Kingdom. As has already been stated, she herself confessed, "I never grew up." But she meant this in relation to the vividness of her childhood memories, her love of the childhood awareness they recalled, and the deep satisfaction, the aesthetic richness she experienced, in re-creating these memories in the shape of her perfect little books. There was no woman less childish or immature than Beatrix Potter, and her marriage, though it came late, was one of great happiness and fulfillment.

As for Walter de la Mare, whose fantastic poetry and prose is haunted by wandering, calling children whom "magic hath stolen away," you might think that he, above all men, would have lived in a cork-lined room like Proust, or in a hut in the woods like Thoreau, or have made his bed in a cave or on a mountainside anywhere in the wilderness like John Muir. He was, as a matter of fact, a statistician for the Anglo-American Oil Company in London and wrote *Henry Brocken* on scraps of that firm's letterheads.[50]

It would seem obvious that any artist, writing either for adults or for children, must retire temporarily to the world of his own imagining; that this is an absolute necessity if he is to visualize it with any degree of clarity in order to achieve that intense illusion of reality without which any work of the imagination lacks its chief necessity: the power to convince. But the temporary retreat of the creator, and the deep psychic retreat of the man or woman who cannot endure the world of adult experiences, its relationships and responsibilities, lie at opposing ends of the spectrum of human behavior. For the totally withdrawn person, the chronic escapist, his outer world has disintegrated and he refuses to look at it (which is why Branwell Brontë, of all the gifted, intensely self-aware Brontës, drank and drugged himself to death); he has lost all sense of his own identity as a functioning being in that outer world. But the artist can do nothing without a passionate sense of his own identity, a continuing recovery and integration of all that he is and has been as a human being and, above all, without extreme self-discipline of that identity. I would say that this self-discipline is anything but an act of psychotic avoiding and withdrawal; on the contrary it reveals, in any book that is a serious work, a continual struggle with what the writer *is.* Only in the act of making a serious work of any kind (and high comedy can be serious in both conception and effect), be it for adults or children, does one determinedly face the extreme difficulty of coming to grips with one's self and what one really sees and feels and means. This is the hardest part

---

49. Peter Green, *Kenneth Grahame,* see "Childish characteristics of," in the index of that book.

50. Benét, "Walter de la Mare: 1873–1956," *Saturday Review,* September 22, 1956, p. 11.

of all. No wholly childish person can do it, because no wholly childish person has the strength and the patience to keep on day after day in an effort to come closer and closer to what will finally be for him a satisfying statement of his inmost meaning—a meaning he has come upon, oftentimes, only *because* of his withdrawal to an inner world.

We are reminded here of what Walter de la Mare believes about the writing of books for children and what it demands of the writer:

Briefly then, every good story, worthy of as good children, is concerned with a country, complete with climate, scenes, denizens, fauna and flora all its own, of which we ourselves were once native. . . . It keeps well within the radiant ring of its little candle—the comprehension of an intelligent child. And this need by no means imply a narrow range. The serene, clear, quiet light upon its pages wells over, rays out beyond this minute circle, to cast its beams, if only by way of contrast, far out into that naughty world of the grown-ups with which we are no doubt sufficiently familiar. If the wax is the secretion of a gifted mind, delighting in its love and understanding of childhood and of children directly observed and clearly recalled, there are few experiences of life absolutely denied to its use and purpose. Indeed for any perfection of this kind—a perfection of a very rare order—it will need every virtue, every grace that is aspired to by the artist in fiction, the whole attention and pains of any man of genius whose heart beats that way.[51]

". . . There are few experiences of life absolutely denied to its use and purpose." Yes, for we remember what Andersen put into his portrayal of the little mermaid's love and what he said of the Hindu woman standing on her husband's burning pyre in "The Snow Queen," and of how there was really so little about life, its tragedy, its humor, its brutality and beauty, that he did not manage to put into his fairy tales. So that it *is* a matter of what the tale itself demands, the artistry of the writer, his vision of life and how he reveals it. If the story comes from his center, if he has succeeded in exerting every discipline of artistry at his command, then the fullness of whatever it was he wanted to say will be present and the ring of imaginative truth will be heard as surely and deeply as in any book for adults.

The whole merciless round of animal behavior is told in Beatrix Potter's apparently simple tales. ("So, in any good book for children, we should expect the two parts of an author's life to come together: his own childhood experiences or interests, re-created fictionally, and his own maturity, reflected in the significance he chooses to give them," says Philippa Pearce.)[52] An entire philosophy is implicit in Antoine de Saint Exupéry's *The Little Prince,* which, the mother of a small child told me, had been so illuminating to her as she read it aloud that it had served to change her entire outlook upon life. Philippa Pearce's own children's book, *A Dog So Small,* is in actuality the story of a fantasy-locked child, who in the end is forced to face the truth of his own human condition. . . .

Perhaps there can be no doubt that what the great writers for children have in common is that they have somehow retained into adulthood many of the mental qualities of children, the point of view of children, despite whatever sophistication and poetic genius each may have possessed. In his *A High Wind in Jamaica,* Richard Hughes has a paragraph on childhood in which he states his belief that the thinking of children differs in kind from that of adults—that it is, in fact, considered from our own point of view, mad.[54] So that if one looks at the matter from this angle, my correspondent could be right in saying that the writers of those books children have made classics are all "a little mad." Mad because, despite adulthood, they were still able to view the curious antics of adults with the cool, yet astonished detachment of children, and could still sense and communicate what to us are the nonrational actions and reactions of childhood which, without reflection, seem perfectly rational to those enclosed within that private world—and child readers recognize this. Maurice Sendak is surely one of these strange, gifted beings, which is why, possibly, his *Where*

51. De la Mare, Introduction to *The Weans of Rowallan,* pp. xii–xiii.

52. Pearce, "The Writer's View of Childhood," p. 77.
54. Hughes, *A High Wind in Jamaica,* p. 119.

the Wild Things Are proved such a shock to adults, but something quite natural and deeply true to children.

I have commented upon Pamela Travers's "Nobody ever writes for children" not only because I could call to mind so many instances that belie it, but because that statement, within the context of her accompanying remarks, denigrates the whole world of books written with the idea of children as audience. It may be true that it does not matter for whom we claim a book is written, for children, for ourselves as adults, or for the child still alive within us, as long as the book is written with integrity. It is certainly true that no matter how many words we put down in an attempt to explain our secret purpose, the child will search out his own. But it is above all true that the serious writer, whose instinctive sense of audience tells him quite clearly that children will enjoy his work, writes with involvement and devotion and with a sense of great responsibility. And this is not alone because his books will go into the hands of children, but because he knows that children's literature does not exist in a narrow world of its own, but is enmeshed in a larger world of literature of which all its qualities, its initial inspirations, its abilities to reveal and to illumine, are an interrelated part. He knows that children's and adult literature are facets of a single art, and that the highest standards of one hold good for the other. This is why we do not look down on *Peter Rabbit* as compared to *War and Peace*. We recognize that one is simple and the other infinitely complex, but that both are enduring aesthetic expressions.

Aidan Chambers

Talking about Reading: Back to Basics?

[From Aidan Chambers, "Letter from England: Talking about Reading: Back to Basics? Part I," *The Horn Book Magazine,* 53 (1977), 567–74. This article is based on speeches delivered at the conference of the New England Library Association, at Simmons College, Boston, and at Framingham (Massachusetts) State College in the autumn of 1976. Part II of this article appeared in *The Horn Book Magazine,* 53 (1977), 705–8.]

As a young teacher just out of college twenty years ago I had the temerity to hang above my cupboard door—the book-stock cupboard being my only place of retreat—the legend: *You are here to practice the art of teaching, not to indulge in the science of education.* I am still healthily cautious about the findings of educational researchers. Frankly, I do not think there can be any such discipline as a "science" of education; and investigation of teaching-and-learning theory and practice is always done best by people who are teaching children regularly.

I mention this because it seems to me that a good deal of our present anxiety about the "problem" of literacy is as much a response to the results of spurious and wrong-headed educational research as it is a worry about the "problem" itself. I put inverted commas round that popular word *problem* because I do not believe there is a problem in any new sense. What we are noticing is that people—just to live their normal lives—now need greater skills as speakers, readers, and writers than they have ever needed before. Added to that, I think it is true to say that people are no longer prepared to accept for their children a minimum functional ability to read and write. We want more than that; in fact, I can see that in my lifetime the standards we expect from schools have steadily risen. And it happens, rightly, to be reading that presently concerns us.

Nevertheless, some things do worry me about the way we are, in many schools and homes, dealing with children as readers. Before coming to the crux of what I want to say, I would like to make a preliminary observation about one of my worries.

Consider this passage:

A biological schema, though elucidating certain aspects of the mastery of syntax, is of limited value in the study of the semantic and functional aspects of language acquisition. Skinner's notion of a single-factor reinforcement theory to account for the acquisition of complex language behavior is equally inadequate. The enormous impact of both of these approaches can be seen, perhaps, as a reaction to eclecticism, as a hunger for elegance of thought and "useful" theories. But language acquisition cannot be explained by a unitary statement of underlying processes. As Ervin-Tripp has stated in a recent review article (1966), "the basis of the child's most important and complex achievement (language) still remains unknown."*

I quote this here as a pretty modest example of the kind of jargonistic and tortured writing that flows from the pens of so many of the educationists who write about reading. It happens also to say something of quite startling importance, which happens also to be the truth. In plain English it says: *We do not know how children learn to speak and to read.*

Academics quite often have such important things to tell us. It seems to me that it is their responsibility—an obligation we pay them to exercise—to translate their ideas and findings into reasonably intelligent English which respects the mother tongue, the things they want to say, and the people to whom they wish to communicate.

For years now authorities have been trying to tell us that reading, and learning to read, is a mechanical process, something that can be analyzed, broken down into stages, and treated as a step-by-step operation, like making a car on a conveyor belt, bit being added to bit in a logical and planned sequence. And the authorities who have told us this have been wrong: "We do not know how children learn to read"; and we do not know very much about what happens when we read. Hence my healthy caution.

It would not have mattered what the authorities said if no one had listened. But all too many people have listened and have acted on what they have heard. So they threw out from their teaching—or lost them in their excitement for the latest academic fashion—some common-or-garden truths about reading and how people *teach themselves* to do it. We need to reassert these truths time and again and must not be

afraid of the fact that their modesty requires no high flights of abstract jargon and that their appeal is slight to academics whose near-sinecure places depend upon "research findings" and skill in writing pseudo-scholarly discourse in language so oppressively ugly and esoteric that even people working in other sectors of the teaching profession find it not only tasteless but meaningless.

The first of these simple truths is that children become readers with the greatest ease and lasting effect when they are prepared for it, preferably from birth, by a daily experience of literature read aloud to them and an abundance of books shown to them. Speech comes first, words heard; reading follows. It is almost an axiom: You cannot begin to read what you have not heard said. Neglect of this preparatory relationship between child and language, child and book, means that by the age of five, a child is already in need of remedial teaching. The effect is just the same on the child's mental and imaginative growth as the lack of essential ingredient in his diet would be on his physical growth. Judged by this test, most children start school educationally undernourished; so most teaching in the early years is rehabilitative.

All along, the evidence for this has been under our noses. Instead of examining the successes and failures of children who were taught to read, we could have been learning essential lessons from children who became readers on their own without anybody teaching them.

One of our trustworthy academics in Britain, Margaret M. Clark, Reader in Educational Psychology at the University of Strathclyde in Scotland, did just that. I heartily commend to you her resulting book *Young Fluent Readers.** Dr. Clark studied thirty-two Glasgow children arriving at school, aged five, already able to read. They came, somewhat unexpectedly, from all sectors of the community, from the very well-off to the very poor. Among them, for instance, was the youngest child in a family of seven whose father was an unskilled manual worker. Only the youngest child had arrived at school able to read, but none of the others had had

* From "Story-telling: A Study of Sequential Speech in Young Children" by Vera P. John, Vivian M. Horner, and Tomi D. Berney in *Basic Studies on Reading,* edited by Harry Levin and Joanna P. Williams (Basic, 1970).

* Margaret M. Clark, *Young Fluent Readers* (Humanities Press, Atlantic Highlands, NJ 07716; 1976. Paper, $3.50).

any difficulty learning. Throughout his last years in school the father had had a history of truancy, and he had left at fourteen; but he loved fairy stories and, Dr. Clark discovered, told them to his children. Both parents read for pleasure and information; went regularly to the public library, taking the children with them; and kept books in the home. No one had tried to teach the youngest child how to read; he had picked it up for himself.

Some of these things were true for every child in the group. All of them had been read to as a normal everyday event, and all of them had parents who read for themselves. The public library played an important part; "in catering for and in stimulating the interests of these children," it was a "striking feature of the study." And how far is learning to read a mechanically structured process? Margaret Clark says:

The existence of children such as those in the present research must lead us to question to what extent and in what ways learning to read is a developmental process and whether there are essential sequential steps. It may be necessary to consider whether those steps which are frequently regarded as sequential are so only because of the structure within which we *teach* reading rather than the pattern within which children *learn* to read.

One sure thing is done to most children starting school unable to read. They are drilled (there is no better word for it) through a reading series. Ironically, many of these series, combined with the way they are used by teachers, help create unwilling rather than willing readers. These materials turn reading into a boring chore. The reason is plain if one examines them not as colorfully illustrated, carefully graded teaching machines, but as literature. While preparing this article, I happened to be reading Bruno Bettelheim's over-abused book *The Uses of Enchantment* (Knopf). "The acquisition of skills," he writes, "including the ability to read, becomes devalued when what one has learned to read adds nothing of importance to one's life. . . . The idea that learning to read may enable one later to enrich one's life is experienced as an empty promise when the stories the child listens to, or is reading at the moment, are vacuous." Whatever one may think of Bet-

telheim's book in other respects, he states here nothing but the truth.

Many teachers imaginatively take pains to prepare their pupils for what used to be known in the trade as "reading readiness." Then, having raised their children's expectations high, they put before them the most bland, pointless, ill-written prose they can find. For this is the literary judgment one is forced to reach about the content of many reading series.

None of these, in fact, should or needs to fall below the standards of the best I Can Read stories, like *Frog and Toad Are Friends* (Harper). What looks, and is, linguistically simple in such books is also immediately and lastingly entertaining and possesses beneath the surface meaning of the text deeper meanings on which the imagination can dwell.

Reading series were born, I suppose, out of the same necessity that has led to computer-run teaching programs. Teachers have to teach far too many children at once, a situation getting worse, not better. In the Utopian circumstances of one teacher to three or four pupils, reading schemes would seem like weapons of torment to be left alone by civilized people. But faced with thirty or forty or more pupils—all, we have been led to think, needing to be *taught* to read by the teacher—the book-machines become essential.

Well, if we must go on using them, let us at least see to four protective defenses. First, children should be provided with the best possible series from the literary point of view. Second, they should be weaned onto proper books with all possible speed. Third, no one series or teaching method ought to be used, but a number of them should be offered which take into account the different ways people read—for example, those who "hear" the words as they read rather than "see" them (as I do) and those who, like my wife, "see" the words and do not "hear" them. And lastly, let us make sure that the reading series and the teaching done with them are part of an environment where the emphasis is on proper books and on having many of them always available to the children, whether they can read or not.

It does not seem at all surprising to me that in Britain *The Iron Giant: A Story in Five Nights*

(Harper) by Ted Hughes is a far more successful book with children learning to read than any specially written text. How can you improve on the simplicity and potential for meaning and entertainment of a story that begins:

The Iron Man came to the top of the cliff.
How far had he walked? Nobody knows. Where had he come from? Nobody knows. How was he made? Nobody knows.
Taller than a house, the Iron Man stood at the top of the cliff, on the very brink, in the darkness.

Nor does it seem odd to me that a boy of eight, slow in reading, insisted on leaving aside his supplementary reader in preference to *The Piemakers* (Lippincott) by Helen Cresswell, which he struggled through word by carefully decoded word, from mid-October to late February, saying, when he at last finished it, that it was the best book he had ever had.

After all, we are not exactly lacking for books which—if they are not so superlatively fine as these—are certainly worth a child's attention and offer immediate as well as lasting rewards. Why, then, the woeful inadequacy of the book stocks in so many schools? The answer, I'm afraid, is that far too many teachers are depressingly ignorant about what is available.

Which brings me to my next point. Time and again we have it confirmed that the reading child depends upon the reading adult. To put it crudely, illiterates are made by illiterates. We cannot expect children to apply themselves with enthusiasm to the act of reading if they know that the adults around them have little enthusiasm for the activity. Teachers must be seen by children to read for their own enjoyment, not just for professional needs, and to talk about what they read, according books an important place in their lives.

The success we have in helping children become readers will depend not so much on our technical skills but upon the spirit we transmit of ourselves as readers. Next in importance comes the breadth and depth of our knowledge of the books we offer. Only out of such a ready catalog can we match child and book with the sort of spontaneous accuracy that is wanted time and again during a working day.

Even while acknowledging the importance of the adult, let us also recognize that children are pretty good at finding the right books for themselves. If they are given the chance. We should see that our job as teachers of reading is concerned with facilitating children in teaching themselves to read as much as it is with our teaching them to read. There should be daily opportunity for every child, no matter what his age, to browse through a collection of books.

There is, I am suggesting, a classic simplicity in the act of reading. First you select a book from many others. But selection is pointless unless you go on to read what you have chosen. Reading a text inevitably creates a response which expresses itself in various ways. Sometimes you want to rush off and tell a friend about what you've just read. Sometimes you are so strangely moved that to speak would be to destroy. Children, younger ones especially, often like to act out what they have read, re-creating it in their own image. And writers are not alone in being, essentially, readers who want to emulate the books they admire and find stimulating. But the most common response, the inevitable one in all true readers, is a resulting desire to read another book, one leading to another in a kind of excruciatingly pleasurable, unending chain reaction, a literary fission.

Selection: Reading: Response—leading to yet another selection. That is the literate reading circle. Once set in motion in our pupils, it becomes self-sustaining. This is what we should aim to achieve. But anyone whose work provides opportunity to look into many schools, as mine does, cannot help but lament how often that circle is never set turning because one part of it is neglected.

So full has the daily program in school become, with projects and integrated days in which pupils follow singly and in small groups their own instructional paths, that we all too often have allowed reading, as an activity in itself, to be squeezed out. Schools will often have rich stocks of literary books. They will often encourage their children to borrow from these stocks. But they do not provide time to read. Time to read not in order to gather data or to find information to use in other work but in order to take pleasure in a text for its own sake. Time to read literature. We ought to insist that our schools provide time every day when everybody—adults and children—settles down and reads for no other purpose than to engage in that activity.

For the people who suffer most from the loss of reading time are the people who need it most, the children whose homes did not prepare them to be readers and do not encourage them to spend time reading out of school; homes without books and without the kind of atmosphere that helps children enjoy reading. For children in these circumstances—at least half of the children in most schools—*only* the school can provide the facilities and the time to read within secure and sympathetically disciplined surroundings.

What does Johnny need to become a reader? What are the basics we want to get back to? The answers stand out clearly. Children need to be surrounded by adults who are themselves literary readers possessing a ready knowledge of children's books. They need a large supply of books, wider in range than we often think is necessary, and daily self-directed browsing time in which to select the book for now. They need to hear every day printed words read aloud and should be encouraged to respond to what they hear and to what they read for themselves. They need, more importantly than most other things, time to read, time in long enough periods to allow for absorbed attention and the pleasurable satisfaction that cannot come quickly, cannot be turned rapidly off and on, in the reading of a book. They should be helped to borrow books to take home and to buy books to keep. And we should examine far more urgently the links between home and school, between parents and teachers, so that both places help the child towards the same end.

Given all this, teachers and librarians could apply themselves with greater skill and vigor to the task that is theirs: how to lead children on from a superficial reading skill—decoding— to an appreciation of those books that yield the deepest meanings and the greatest pleasures. . . .

Selected Bibliography of Children's Literature

Introduction: "Trade and Plumb-Cake Forever"

Books on Reading for Children

Arbuthnot, May Hill. *Children's Reading in the Home.* Scott, Foresman, 1969.

    Helpful to parents and other adults interested in guiding the literary taste of children.

Bader, Barbara. *American Picturebooks from Noah's Ark to the Beast Within.* Macmillan, 1976.

    Profusely illustrated historical survey spans a period from the late nineteenth century to the present day. Valuable for reference and critical analysis.

Bator, Robert, ed. *Signposts to Criticism of Children's Literature.* American Library Association, 1983.

    A scholarly collection of essays on the various genres of children's literature and its criticism.

The organization incorporates "a triple focus (is it a literature, how is that literature perceived, and how should we approach it)."

Bettleheim, Bruno, and Karen Zelan. *On Learning to Read: The Child's Fascination with Meaning.* Knopf, 1982.

    A penetrating look by the renowned child psychologist and his associate at the educational establishment which the authors believe is responsible for many of the difficulties children encounter in learning to read. They also stress the power of language and story for young children.

Blishen, E., ed. *The Thorny Paradise.* Kestrel, 1976.

    Essays by twenty-one writers, including Rosemary Sutcliff, Nina Bawden, Jane Gardam, and John Gordon. Composed of British contributors (with the exception of Russell Hoban), this is geared to the ordinary person interested in children's books.

Blount, Margaret. *Animal Land: The Creatures of Children's Fiction.* Morrow, 1975.

A thoughtful and stimulating view of animal characters; their place in fable, satire, and fantasy; and the various ways they have been treated by writers and regarded by readers.

Bodger, Joan. *How the Heather Looks.* Viking, 1965.

An American family's journey to the British sources of children's books.

Broderick, Dorothy M. *Image of the Black in Children's Fiction.* Bowker, 1973.

A comprehensive study from a historical and social point of view, this adaptation of a doctoral dissertation is a valuable reference source.

Butler, Dorothy. *Babies Need Books.* Atheneum, 1980.

A guide for parents on using books with young children from the earliest months. A convincing account of the significance of books in stimulating imagination and language development, instilling a life-long love of reading, and forging relationships between parent and child.

Butler, Dorothy. *Cushla and Her Books.* Horn Book, 1980.

A personal account of a family who raised a severely handicapped child, providing her an entrance into a normal life through a loving, early exposure to books. A powerful testament to the importance of introducing books to very young children.

Butler, Francelia. *Sharing Literature with Children: A Thematic Anthology.* McKay, 1977.

In this imaginative approach to children's literature, selections from various genres and from criticism of the literature are juxtaposed in thematic arrangement.

Cameron, Eleanor. *The Green and Burning Tree.* Little, Brown, 1969.

Perceptive essays on the writing of books for children, noteworthy for its reflection of the author's breadth of reading of adult literature and criticism.

Carr, Jo, comp. *Beyond Fact: Nonfiction for Children and Young People.* American Library Association, 1982.

A selection of insightful articles on various aspects of children's nonfiction, organized by theme and genre. Includes awards appendices and a selective bibliography of professional sources.

Chambers, Aidan. *Introducing Books to Children.* 2d ed. Horn Book, 1983.

Although the author says this is written primarily for teachers, it is a valuable array of approaches, insights, and experiences for all persons interested in children and their reading. The revised edition includes material on criticism and children's responses to literature. See also *The Reluctant Reader* (Pergamon, 1969).

Chambers, Nancy, ed. *The Signal Approach to Children's Books.* Scarecrow, 1980.

A collection of fifteen wide-ranging articles first published in the respected English journal. Includes "Signal quotes" by well-known authors and illustrators on their own and others' work.

Chukovsky, Kornei. *From Two to Five.* Trans. and ed. Miriam Morton; foreword, Frances Clarke Sayers. Rev. ed. Univ. of California Press, 1968.

A study of childhood by a distinguished Soviet poet who believes that the future belongs to those who do not rein in their imaginations.

Cianciolo, Patricia. *Illustrations in Children's Books.* 2d ed. W. C. Brown, 1976.

Discusses techniques, media, styles of artists, and ways of using illustrations in the school.

Colby, Jean Poindexter. *Writing, Illustrating, and Editing Children's Books.* Hastings House, 1967.

Detailed and practical information.

Crouch, Marcus. *The Nesbit Tradition: The Children's Novel in England, 1945–1970.* Ernest Benn, 1972.

Working from the premise that there are no children's books, only good and bad books, the author surveys fiction in the children's area, using chapter headings such as "High Adventure," "Laughter," and "Self and Society."

Crouch, Marcus. *Treasure Seekers and Borrowers: Children's Books in Britain, 1900–1960.* Reprint with amendments. Library Association (London), 1970.

A critical study of children's books of the twentieth century.

Duff, Annis. *"Bequest of Wings": A Family's Pleasures with Books.* Viking, 1944.

A refreshing account of reading experiences shared by two children and their parents. In *"Longer Flight": A Family Grows Up with Books,* the author continues her adventures in reading with her children now grown older.

Eaton, Anne Thaxter. *Reading with Children.* Viking, 1940.

A stimulating book that has grown out of the

author's twenty years of experience with children and books as librarian of the Lincoln School, Teachers College, Columbia University. *Treasure for the Taking: A Book List for Boys and Girls* forms a supplement to the author's *Reading with Children,* with brief, penetrating comments on more than fifteen hundred books listed under sixty-four categories.

Egoff, Sheila. *The Republic of Childhood: A Critical Guide to Canadian Children's Literature in English.* 2d ed. Oxford Univ. Press, 1975.

A critical analysis of contemporary Canadian children's literature published from 1950 to 1974 with reference to earlier writings.

Egoff, Sheila. *Thursday's Child: Trends and Patterns in Contemporary Children's Literature.* American Library Association, 1981.

An astute, literate assessment of trends, features, and accomplishments in children's literature of the last twenty-five years.

Egoff, Sheila, G. T. Stubbs, and L. F. Ashley, eds. *Only Connect: Readings on Children's Literature.* 2d ed. Oxford Univ. Press, 1980.

Key readings present "children's literature as an essential part of the whole realm of literary activity." The compilation will be of particular interest to teachers, librarians, and students of children's literature.

Field, Elinor Whitney, ed. *Horn Book Reflections on Children's Books and Reading.* Horn Book, 1969.

A collection of papers selected from eighteen years of *The Horn Book Magazine* from 1949 through 1966 represents the reflections and experience of those who have given deep thought to literature for children.

Fisher, Margery. *Intent upon Reading.* 2d ed., rev. and enl. Brockhampton Press, 1964.

A critical appraisal of fiction for children published in England.

Fisher, Margery. *Matters of Fact: Aspects of Non-Fiction for Children.* Crowell, 1972.

A discussion of the various areas of nonfiction, with attention directed to selected titles and general criteria. British background.

Fisher, Margery. *Who's Who in Children's Books: A Treasury of the Familiar Characters of Childhood.* Holt, 1975.

A selective compendium of characters in children's literature. Not a check list, this is an affectionate description of prominent characters that places them in their setting, discusses their identity, and notes the books in which they appear.

Fox, Geoff, et al., eds. *Writers, Critics, and Children: Articles from Children's Literature in Education.* Agathon/Heinemann Educ. Books, 1976.

A rewarding collection of articles drawn from the first six years of the journal *Children's Literature in Education.*

Haviland, Virginia. *Children and Literature: Views and Reviews.* Scott, Foresman, 1973.

An anthology of essays in the field of children's literature, featuring criticism, discussions of trends, and ". . . intended for those concerned with the creation, distribution and reading of children's books."

Haviland, Virginia, ed. *The Openhearted Audience: Ten Authors Talk about Writing for Children.* Library of Congress, 1980.

A distinguished collection of the annual lectures on children's literature given at the Library of Congress. Ten authors discuss children's literature, the development of their writing, and influences on their work.

Hazard, Paul. *Books, Children, and Men.* Trans. Marguerite Mitchell; intro. Sheila A. Egoff. 5th ed. Horn Book, 1983.

An eminent French scholar discusses the national traits in relation to books for children. First published in 1944, this is a distinguished addition to the books on the history and criticism of children's literature. Includes a memoir of Paul Hazard.

Hearne, Betsy. *Choosing Books for Children: A Commonsense Guide.* Delacorte, 1981.

The editor of the American Library Association's *Booklist* offers practical, succinct advice for beginners on the selection, evaluation, and use of children's literature. Of special interest to parents.

Hearne, Betsy, and Marilyn Kaye, eds. *Celebrating Children's Books: Essays on Children's Literature in Honor of Zena Sutherland.* Lothrop, Lee & Shepard, 1981.

A stimulating collection of essays on the writing, illustrating, publishing, and reviewing of children's books.

Heins, Paul, ed. *Crosscurrents of Criticism: Horn Book Essays, 1968–1977.* Horn Book, 1977.

A provocative compilation of essays on the problems, attitudes, and possible future of children's literature criticism. Selected from *The Horn Book Magazine.*

The Horn Book Magazine. *A Horn Book Sampler on Children's Books and Reading: Selected from Twenty-five Years of* The Horn Book Magazine, *1924–1948.*

Ed. Norma R. Fryatt; intro. Bertha Mahony Miller. Horn Book, 1959.

Significant articles on children's books and reading. Of particular interest to children's librarians and connoisseurs of children's literature.

Huck, Charlotte S. *Children's Literature in the Elementary School.* 3d ed., updated. Holt, 1979.

An overview of children's literature emphasizing methods of introducing literature into the classroom.

Hürlimann, Bettina. *Picture-Book World.* Trans. and ed. Brian W. Alderson. World, 1969.

A look at picture books from a great many parts of the world, as well as a consideration of subjects and types.

Jones, Cornelia, and Olivia R. Way. *British Children's Authors: Interviews at Home.* American Library Association, 1976.

Nineteen interviews with many of the well-known authors and illustrators of Britain, collected as a valuable resource to use in the discussion of children's books with children and those interested in literature.

Karl, Jean. *From Childhood to Childhood: Children's Books and Their Creators.* Day, 1970.

Questions, answers, perceptions, and information from a distinguished children's editor.

Kimmel, Margaret Mary, and Elizabeth Segal. *For Reading Out Loud! A Guide to Sharing Books with Children.* Foreword, Betsy Byars. Delacorte, 1983.

The value of reading aloud to elementary-and middle-school-aged children is the concern of this work. Over 140 books are recommended.

Kingman, Lee, ed. *Newbery and Caldecott Medal Books, 1956–1965, with Acceptance Papers, Biographies of the Award Winners, and Evaluating Articles by Elizabeth H. Gross, Carolyn Horovitz, and Norma R. Fryatt.* Horn Book, 1965.

This volume of Horn Book Papers is a companion to the first two volumes, *Newbery Medal Books, 1922–1955,* and *Caldecott Medal Books, 1938–1957.*

Kingman, Lee, ed. *Newbery and Caldecott Medal Books, 1966–1975, with Acceptance Papers, Biographies of the Award Winners, and Evaluating Articles by John Rowe Townsend, Barbara Bader, and Elizabeth Johnson.* Horn Book, 1976.

This volume of Horn Book Papers brings up to date the first three volumes. (See entry above for previous volumes.)

Kirkpatrick, Daniel, ed. *Twentieth Century Children's Writers.* Preface, Naomi Lewis. St. Martin's, 1978.

A bio-bibliographical guide to 630 English-language authors of fiction, poetry, and drama for children. Signed critical essays, authors' comments, and later nineteenth-century authors are included.

Klemin, Diana. *The Art of Art for Children's Books: A Contemporary Survey.* Potter, 1966.

Lanes, Selma G. *Down the Rabbit Hole: Adventures and Misadventures in the Realm of Children's Literature.* Atheneum, 1971.

Explores the literary value of children's books from an admittedly idiosyncratic point of view.

Larrick, Nancy. *A Parent's Guide to Children's Reading.* 5th ed. Westminster, 1983.

This revised edition includes a discussion on introducing infants and toddlers to books and countering television's effect. The annotated lists have been updated.

Lukens, Rebecca J. *A Critical Handbook of Children's Literature.* 2d ed. Scott, Foresman, 1982.

Judging children's literature by the same critical standards applied to writing for adults, the author evaluates examples from all genres according to such classic literary elements as character, plot, and setting.

MacCann, Donnarae, and Olga Richard. *The Child's First Books: A Critical Study of Pictures and Texts.* Wilson, 1973.

A distinctive part of this book is its approach to art in books for children.

MacCann, Donnarae, and Gloria Woodard, comps. *The Black-American in Books for Children: Readings in Racism.* Scarecrow, 1972.

Motivated by concern and interest in the relationship between children's books and racism in American society, the editors have brought together significant essays on this point. See also the companion volume, *Cultural Conformity in Books for Children: Further Readings in Racism* (1977), which includes in Part 2 essays that supplement *The Black-American in Books for Children.*

McVitty, Walter. *Innocence and Experience: Essays on Contemporary Australian Children's Writers.* Nelson, 1981.

A collection of essays on eight contemporary Australian writers of fiction for children, including contributions from the writers themselves about their background, influences, and philosophies in writing for children.

Meek, Margaret. *Learning to Read.* Bodley Head, 1982.

A lucid account of the reading process and the child's different stages of reading development. Includes extensive bibliographies.

Meek, Margaret, Aidan Warlow, and Griselda Barton, eds. *The Cool Web: The Pattern of Children's Reading.* Atheneum, 1978.

This selection of essays provides a wide perspective on the theories of children's reading from the various points of view of children, authors, literary critics, and educational psychologists.

Meigs, Cornelia, et al. *A Critical History of Children's Literature: A Survey of Children's Books in English.* Decorations, Vera Bock. Rev. ed. Macmillan, 1969.

A revision of a major work. An appreciative introduction by Frances Clarke Sayers has been added. Slight alterations characterize the first three parts of the book—"Roots in the Past: Up to 1840," by Cornelia Meigs; "Widening Horizons: 1840–1890," by Anne Thaxter Eaton; and "A Rightful Heritage: 1890–1920," by Elizabeth Nesbitt. Part Four has been changed from "The Golden Age: 1920–1950" to "Golden Years and Time of Tumult: 1920–1967," by Ruth Hill Viguers. A new chapter on American historical fiction has been added.

Miller, Bertha Mahony, and Elinor Whitney Field, eds. *Caldecott Medal Books, 1938–1957, with the Artists' Acceptance Papers and Related Material Chiefly from* The Horn Book Magazine. Horn Book, 1957.

Everyone interested in graphic arts and illustrations will find this companion volume to *Newbery Medal Books, 1922–1955* extremely valuable. It contains the acceptance speeches of the artists; their biographies; a format note and brief résumé of each book; an article on Randolph Caldecott, the artist for whom the medal was named; and a critical analysis, "What Is a Picture Book?" by Esther Averill.

Miller, Bertha Mahony, and Elinor Whitney Field, eds. *Newbery Medal Books, 1922–1955, with Their Authors' Acceptance Papers and Related Material Chiefly from* The Horn Book Magazine. Horn Book, 1955.

A richly rewarding book that constitutes a history of the Newbery Medal awards through the year 1955. The winning books are presented in chronological arrangement.

Moore, Anne Carroll. *My Roads to Childhood: Views and Reviews of Children's Books.* Intro. Frances Clarke Sayers. Horn Book, 1961.

Discriminating criticism and helpful booklists. Material first appeared under the titles *Roads to Childhood* (1920); *New Roads to Childhood* (1923); and *Crossroads to Childhood* (1926). The material was brought up to date and in 1939 was published by Doubleday under the title *My Roads to Childhood.* In 1961 The Horn Book, Inc., acquired the publishing rights and brought out this edition.

Morton, Miriam, ed. *A Harvest of Russian Children's Literature.* Introduction and commentary, Miriam Morton; foreword, Ruth Hill Viguers. Univ. of California Press, 1967.

A first anthology in English of Russian literature for children, including stories, folktales, fables, and poems from 1825 to the 1960s.

Paterson, Katherine. *Gates of Excellence: On Reading and Writing Books for Children.* Elsevier/Nelson, 1981.

A spirited collection of essays, speeches, and book reviews by the award-winning children's author encompassing her thoughts on the creation and value of children's literature.

Pellowski, Anne. *The World of Children's Literature.* Bowker, 1968.

Extensive listing (over 4,400 items) of children's books throughout the world.

Peterson, Linda Kauffman, and Marilyn Leathers Solt. *Newbery and Caldecott Medal and Honor Books: An Annotated Bibliography.* Hall, 1982.

An impressive overview and analysis of the award winners and honor books through 1981. Summaries and critical commentaries analyze literary trends within a sociological and historical context.

Pitz, Henry C. *Illustrating Children's Books: History-Technique-Production.* Watson-Guptill, 1963.

An artist and illustrator himself, the author brings a depth of background and specific craft information to this subject.

Rees, David. *The Marble in the Water: Essays on Contemporary Writers of Fiction for Children and Young Adults.* Horn Book, 1980.

An invigorating, provocative look at eighteen contemporary American and British writers of children's and young adult fiction. Written from a

British perspective. See also *Painted Desert, Green Shade: Essays on Contemporary Writers of Fiction for Children and Young Adults* (1984).

Ross, Eulalie Steinmetz. *The Spirited Life: Bertha Mahony Miller and Children's Books.* Sel. bibliog., Virginia Haviland. Horn Book, 1973.

It was Bertha Mahony Miller's interest in children and their reading that gave rise to *The Horn Book Magazine.*

Rudman, Masha Kabakow. *Children's Literature: An Issues Approach.* Heath, 1976.

A controversial, nonliterary approach to children's books through an examination of sociological, political, and psychological values in the literature. Annotated bibliographies augment discussion of current topics such as racism, sexism, and war.

Sale, Roger. *Fairy Tales and after: From Snow White to E. B. White.* Harvard Univ. Press, 1978.

An English professor's evaluation of children's books published by a prestigious university press.

Sayers, Frances Clarke. *Anne Carroll Moore: A Biography.* Atheneum, 1972.

Anne Carroll Moore was responsible for the growth of children's work in New York City's public libraries. Her influence as a critic with writers and publishers was significant. A biography that inspires and informs.

Sayers, Frances Clarke. *Summoned by Books: Essays and Speeches by Frances Clarke Sayers.* Comp. Marjeanne Jensen Blinn; foreword, Lawrence Clark Powell. Viking, 1965.

"Fifteen of Sayers' essays and talks, from 'Lose Not the Nightingale' to 'Summoned by Books.' Through all the essays the reader is aware of the signatures of Frances Clarke Sayers: originality of concept, revelation of life, mastery of style, and the motion of a magnetic, warmly human and humorous woman. Her laugh is rarely far away."— *The Horn Book Magazine.*

School Library Journal. *Issues in Children's Book Selection: A School Library Journal–Library Journal Anthology.* Intro. Lillian Gerhardt. Bowker, 1973.

Points of difference about book selection, censorship, images, themes, and genres are brought to a sharp focus by the pairing of essays from conflicting points of view.

Smith, Irene. *A History of the Newbery and Caldecott Medals.* Viking, 1957.

The author reviews the events that led up to the founding of the awards, describes the procedures by which the winners are selected, appraises the books that have received awards, lists the runners-up, and discusses the influence of the awards in upholding high standards in writing and illustration.

Smith, Lillian H. *The Unreluctant Years: A Critical Approach to Children's Literature.* American Library Association, 1953.

From a long and distinguished career as head of the Boys and Girls House of the Toronto Public Library, the author shares with the reader some of the joy that has been hers in a close familiarity with the books children love. In her foreword she states that "the aim of this book is to consider children's books as literature, and to discuss some of the standards by which they can be so judged."

Spache, George D. *Good Reading for the Disadvantaged Reader: Multi-ethnic Resources.* Rev. ed. Garrard, 1975.

Specialized bibliographies and essays.

Stewig, John Warren, *Children and Literature.* Houghton Mifflin, 1980.

An up-to-date look at children's literature; how to use literature effectively in the classroom.

Sutherland, Zena, comp. *The Arbuthnot Lectures, 1970–1979.* American Library Association, 1980.

This collection comprises the first ten Arbuthnot Honor Lectures on children's literature and reading presented by respected writers, teachers, and critics. Includes a biographical sketch of May Hill Arbuthnot by Zena Sutherland.

Sutherland, Zena, Dianne L. Monson, and May Hill Arbuthnot. *Children and Books.* 6th ed. Scott, Foresman, 1981.

A thorough revision with comprehensive discussion about books, authors, ways of using books with children, and current issues in children's literature. Useful to teachers and stimulating to parents.

Tanyzer, Harold, and Jean Karl, eds. *Reading, Children's Books, and Our Pluralistic Society.* International Reading Association, 1972.

Papers read at the Sixteenth Annual Perspectives in Reading Conference sponsored by the International Reading Association and the Children's Book Council. Emphasis on books for black and Spanish-speaking American children. Useful bibliographies at the end.

Tiedt, Iris M. *Exploring Books with Children.* Houghton Mifflin, 1979.

Methods of teaching children's literature to elementary-school children.

Tolkien, J. R. R. *Tree and Leaf.* Houghton Mifflin, 1965.

An expansion of a lecture the author gave on fairy tales in 1938 at Oxford University, when he was writing *Lord of the Rings.*

Townsend, John Rowe. *A Sense of Story: Essays on Contemporary Writers for Children.* Lippincott, 1971.

Essays on a selected group of authors, American and British, with biographical and summary information. A statement by the author and a bibliographical listing accompany each essay. See also the companion volume, *A Sounding of Storytellers: New and Revised Essays on Contemporary Writers for Children* (1979).

Tucker, Nicholas. *The Child and the Book: A Psychological and Literary Exploration.* Cambridge Univ. Press, 1981.

A developmental approach to children's literature, particularly fiction. Books and authors are assessed for their potential psychological impact on children.

Tucker, Nicholas, ed. *Suitable for Children? Controversies in Children's Literature.* Univ. of California Press, 1978.

Tucker has collected essays and reviews that are not all easily accessible, by authors and critics on selected, controversial aspects of children's literature, such as fairy tales, comics, fear in children's books, and other issues.

Viguers, Ruth Hill. *Margin for Surprise: About Books, Children, and Librarians.* Little, Brown, 1964.

A well-known librarian and editor of *The Horn Book Magazine* shares her experiences with children and books in selections from her articles and lectures.

Walck Monographs. Gen. ed., Kathleen Lines. Walck.
Louisa M. Alcott. Cornelia Meigs.
J. M. Barrie. Roger Lancelyn Green.
Lucy Boston. Jasper Rose.
Lewis Carroll. Roger Lancelyn Green.
Walter de la Mare. Leonard Clark.
Eleanor Farjeon. Eileen H. Colwell.
Kenneth Grahame. Eleanor Graham.
Rudyard Kipling. Rosemary Sutcliff.
Andrew Lang. Roger Lancelyn Green.
C. S. Lewis. Roger Lancelyn Green.
John Masefield. Margery Fisher.
Mrs. Molesworth. Roger Lancelyn Green.
Beatrix Potter. Marcus Crouch.
Howard Pyle. Elizabeth Nesbitt.
Arthur Ransome. Hugh Shelley.

Ruth Sawyer. Virginia Haviland.
Robert Louis Stevenson. Dennis Butts.
Noel Streatfeild. Barbara Ker Wilson.
Rosemary Sutcliff. Margaret Meek.
Geoffrey Trease. Margaret Meek.

Each small book includes biographical material, a discussion of the place each author holds in the field of children's literature, and an evaluation of individual books.

Walsh, Frances, comp. *That Eager Zest: First Discoveries in the Magic World of Books.* Lippincott, 1961.

Essays, reminiscences, anecdotes, and poems by authors who share their childhood experiences of books.

White, Dorothy Neal. *Books before Five.* Oxford Univ. Press, 1954.

Perceptive observations of a mother who kept a day-to-day record of the stories she read to her little girl between the ages of two and five years. Also of interest is the author's *About Books for Children* (1946), a collection of fresh and original essays.

Aids to Choosing Books

Books

Children's Catalogue. Ed. Richard H. Isaacson and Gary L. Bogart. 14th ed. Wilson, 1981.

Organized according to the Dewey classification system, with author, title, subject, and analytical index, this is a major guide for librarians. Revised every five years, with four annual supplements.

Junior High School Library Catalogue. 4th ed. Wilson, 1980.

Both fiction and nonfiction of proven usefulness on the junior high school level have been chosen by a board of consultants composed of librarians and curriculum specialists.

Lists and Other Aids

AAAS Science Books and Films. American Association for the Advancement of Science, 1515 Massachusetts Ave., N.W., Washington, D.C. 20005. Published quarterly.

A review journal whose reviewers are scientists. Trade books, textbooks, reference books, and 16mm films in the pure and applied sciences are all considered. General grade levels are indicated.

About One Hundred Books: A Gateway to Better Intergroup Understanding. Comp. Ann G. Wolfe. 8th ed. The American Jewish Committee, Institute of Human Relations, 165 E. 56th St., New York, N.Y. 10022, 1977.

Adventuring with Books: A Booklist for Pre-K to Grade Six. Ed. Mary Lou White. New ed. National Council of Teachers of English, 508 S. Sixth St., Champaign, Ill. 61820, 1981.

American Indian Authors for Young Readers. Comp. and intro. Mary Gloyne Byler. Association on American Indian Affairs, 432 Park Ave. S., New York, N.Y. 10016, 1973.

A selected bibliography with an introduction that points out the subtly denigrating ways in which American Indians have been portrayed by writers who do not really know them. The purpose of this bibliography is to further a more full and human picture of the American Indian by giving the child books from these authors.

Appraisal: Children's Science Books. Harvard Graduate School of Education. Published three times each year.

Reviews are given from the viewpoints of a scientist and a librarian, each writing separately about the same book.

The Best in Children's Books: The University of Chicago Guide to Children's Literature, 1966–1972. Ed. Zena Sutherland. Univ. of Chicago Press, 1973.

A selection of 1,400 reviews that appeared in the *Bulletin of the Center for Children's Books,* arranged alphabetically, with six indexes. Complete list of American and British publishers. Supplemented by *The Best in Children's Books: The University of Chicago Guide to Children's Literature, 1973–1978* (1980).

The Best of Children's Books, 1964–1978, Including 1979 Addenda. Ed. Virginia Haviland and advisory committees of children's literature specialists from the Washington area. University Press Books, 1981.

An annotated listing of top choices from fifteen years of the Library of Congress Children's Literature Center's annual recommended lists.

The Best of the Best: Picture, Children's and Youth Books from Fifty-Seven Countries or Languages. Ed. Walter Scherf. 2d ed. Bowker, 1976.

This reference book lists classics and important books in many languages. It is useful for teachers and librarians working with children whose first language is not English. The introduction is in both German and English.

A Bibliography of Books for Children. Comp. Bonnie Baron. Rev. ed. Association for Childhood Education International, 3615 Wisconsin Ave., N.W., Washington, D.C. 20016, 1977.

Compiled by the association, this is an annotated list, well indexed, and revised every three years. Titles are arranged by age level and subject.

The Black Experience in Children's Books. Sel. Barbara Rollock. Rev. ed. Office of Branch Libraries, New York Public Library, 8 E. 40th St., New York, N.Y. 10016, 1974.

Annotated and classified by age and subject matter. Covers life in the U.S., England, Africa, and South America. Supplemented by *The Black Experience in Children's Audiovisual Materials,* comp. Diane De Veaux et al. (1973).

Bookbird: Quarterly of the International Board on Books for Young People and the International Institute for Children's Literature and Reading Research. Ed. Lucia Binder. Instituto Nacional del Libro Español, Santiago Rusiñol, 8, Madrid-3, Spain. Published quarterly since 1963.

Essays about authors and illustrators from various countries, as well as recommendations for translations, information about the award books, and articles about aspects of children's books. In English.

The Bookfinder: A Guide to Children's Literature about the Needs and Problems of Youth Aged Two to Fifteen. Ed. Sharon Dreyer. American Guidance Service, 1977.

A useful tool in cross-referenced, split-page format provides subject, author, and title access to materials dealing with children's problems. Fully annotated. Supplemented by Volume 2 (1981).

The Booklist: A Guide to Current Books. American Library Association, 50 E. Huron St., Chicago, Ill. 60611. Published semimonthly, September through July, and monthly in August.

Books for the Teen-Age. New York Public Library, Fifth Ave. and 42nd St., New York, N.Y. 10018. Published annually.

Compiled by the library, this is a selective list designed primarily for leisure-time reading.

Books from Other Countries, 1972–1976. Comp. Anne McConnell. American Association of School Librarians, 1978.

This revision of *Books from Other Countries, 1968–1971,* by Rabban, lists translations of books into English by country of origin.

Building a Children's Literature Collection. 3d ed. Choice Bibliographical Essay Series, no. 7. Choice, 1983.

Two bibliographies (48 pages) intended for use in supplementing courses in children's literature:

"A Suggested Basic Reference Collection for Academic Libraries," by Harriet B. Quimby, and "Children's Books in an Academic Setting," by Margaret Mary Kimmel.

Building Bridges of Understanding. Comp. Charlotte Matthews Keating. Palo Verde Publishing Co., P.O. Box 5783, Tucson, Ariz. 85705, 1967.

Minority groups, cultural and racial, are the organizing principle of this annotated bibliography. Supplemented by *Building Bridges of Understanding between Cultures* (1971).

Building Ethnic Collections: An Annotated Guide for School Media Centers and Public Libraries. Lois Buttlar and Lobomyr R. Wynar. Libraries Unlimited, 1977.

Over forty minority groups are represented in this selection of print and audio-visual materials.

Bulletin of the Center for Children's Books. Univ. of Chicago, Graduate Library School. Published monthly except in August.

Caldecott Medal Books. Ed. ALA committee. American Library Association, 50 E. Huron St., Chicago, Ill. 60611. Published annually.

A list of Caldecott Medal winners.

Canadian Books for Young People; Livres canadiens pour la jeunesse. Ed. Irma McDonough. 3d ed. Univ. of Toronto Press, 1980.

A revised and expanded version of *Canadian Books for Children; Livres canadiens pour enfants* (1976). Annotated listings of French and English publications are arranged according to genre and subject. Bilingual text.

Canadian Children's Literature: A Journal of Criticism and Review. Canadian Children's Press/Canadian Children's Literature Association, Box 335, Guelph, Ontario, Canada N1H 6K5.

A quarterly journal directed at librarians and teachers, with coverage of both English and French language works written for Canadian children.

Children and Poetry: A Selective Annotated Bibliography. Comp. Virginia Haviland and William Jay Smith. 2d rev. ed. Library of Congress, 1979.

A discriminating selection, with a preface by Virginia Haviland and an introduction by William Jay Smith.

Children's Book Review Index. Ed. Gary C. Tabert. Gale. Published annually since 1975.

A useful tool for locating reviews of children's books. Citations of all children's book reviews published in *Book Review Index* are given.

Children's Books: A List of Books for Pre-School through Junior High School Age. Comp. Virginia Haviland and committee. Superintendent of Documents, Government Printing Office, Washington, D.C. 20402. Published annually.

A selective list of books, well annotated.

Children's Books and Recordings Suggested as Holiday Gifts. Comp. and pub. New York Public Library, Fifth Ave. and 42nd St., New York, N.Y. 10018. Published annually.

A well-annotated list of books and recordings that have appeared during the year.

Children's Books: Awards and Prizes. The Children's Book Council, 175 Fifth Ave., New York, N.Y. 10010. Published biennially since 1961.

A complete list, giving the history, purpose, and winners of each award.

Children's Books of International Interest: A Selection from Four Decades of American Publishing. Ed. Virginia Haviland. 2d ed. American Library Association, 50 E. Huron St., Chicago, Ill. 60611, 1978.

Annotated bibliography of books selected with a view to furthering the exchange of children's literature between countries.

Children's Books of the Year, 1970–1982. Selected and annotated by Elaine Moss (1970–1978); Elaine Moss and Barbara Sherrard-Smith (1979); and Barbara Sherrard-Smith (1980–1982). Hamilton, in association with The National Book League and The British Council.

An annual, personal selection of approximately three hundred titles of the most noteworthy English-language children's books. Before its demise this annotated bibliography acted not only as a selection aid but also as a catalogue of the National Book League Touring Exhibition of "Children's Books of the Year."

Children's Books Too Good to Miss. Comp. May Hill Arbuthnot et al. 7th ed. University Press Books, 1979.

A selected list, grouped by ages.

Children's Classics. Ed. Alice M. Jordan; rev. Paul Heins. The Horn Book, Inc., 31 St. James Ave., Boston, Mass. 02116, 1976.

Reprint of an article in *The Horn Book Magazine* with a list of classics in recommended editions, updated and revised for fifth edition. See also the annotated list *Children's Classics: A List for Parents,* comp. Jane Manthorne (1982), designed for parents and the book-buying public.

Children's Literature in Education. APS Publications, Inc., 150 Fifth Ave., New York, N.Y. 10011. Published March, May, and September.

This British publication emphasizes the literary aspects of books and features articles by prominent authors and educators.

Children's Literature Review: Excerpts from Reviews, Criticism, and Commentary on Books for Children and Young People. Ed. Ann Block and Carolyn Riley. Gale. Published semiannually since 1976.

Provides access to sources of reviews, criticism, and commentary.

Children's Prize Books: An International Listing of 193 Children's Literature Prizes. Ed. Jess R. Moransee. 2d ed. Saur, 1983.

Award books from other countries are listed by country, award, and prize books.

Choosing Books for Young People: A Guide to Criticism and Bibliography, 1945–1975. Ed. John R. T. Ettlinger and Diana Spirt. American Library Association, 1982.

A comprehensive, critical, annotated bibliography of books published from 1945 to 1975, which select, criticize, or list suitable books for young people.

CM: Canadian Materials for Schools and Libraries. Ed. Adèle Ashby. Canadian Library Association, 151 Sparks St., Ottawa, Ontario, Canada, K1P 5E3. Published six times a year.

First issued in 1971, this journal reviews Canadian print and audio-visual materials of interest to children and young people.

Emergency Librarian. Ed. Ken Haycock and Carol-Ann Haycock. Dyad Services, P.O. Box 46258, Station G, Vancouver, British Columbia, Canada, V6R 4G6; Department 284, Box C34069, Seattle, Wash. Published five times a year.

Begun in 1973, this spirited journal includes reviews, bibliographies, and special articles devoted to issues in children's literature and library services for children and young adults in schools and public libraries.

Fantasy for Children: An Annotated Checklist. Ed. Ruth Nadelman Lynn. Bowker, 1979.

An annotated bibliography of fantasy, organized by type and theme.

The Good Book Guide to Children's Books. Ed. Bing Taylor and Peter Braithwaite; editorial advisor, Elaine Moss; illus. Quentin Blake. Penguin, 1983.

Designed for the use of both parents and children, this is a bountifully illustrated aid to book selection and evaluation. Lively annotations of five hundred recommended titles are augmented by advice on reading stages and different types of books. From a British perspective.

Growing Point. Ed. and pub. Margery Fisher. Ashton Manor, Northampton, England, NN7 2JL. Published six issues yearly since 1962.

This respected English reviewing journal for parents, teachers, and librarians considers English-language materials for children.

Growing Up with Books. R. R. Bowker Co., 1180 Avenue of the Americas, New York, N.Y. 10036. Published annually.

A small booklist. "Selections have been made from books recommended by the professional librarian-reviewers of *School Library Journal's Book Review* and other school and library review media." See also *Growing Up with Science Books* and *Growing Up with Paperbacks.*

A Guide to Non-sexist Children's Books. Comp. Judith Adell and Hilary Dole Klein. Academy Press Limited, 176 W. Adams St., Chicago, Ill. 60603, 1976.

An annotated bibliography of books with divisions between lower, middle, and upper; categorized by fiction or nonfiction; and listed alphabetically by author. Reason for choice is often given.

A Hispanic Heritage: A Guide to Juvenile Books about Hispanic People and Cultures. Isabel Schon. Scarecrow, 1980.

A detailed bibliography of materials concerning Hispanic culture.

The Horn Book Magazine. The Horn Book, Inc., 31 St. James Ave., Boston, Mass. 02116. Published bimonthly.

A distinguished magazine devoted entirely to the field of children's literature. Besides reviews of current books for children, each issue contains critical articles. Special departments include "Outlook Tower," which highlights adult books of interest to teenagers; "News from the North," by Sarah Ellis, which discusses Canadian titles; and reviews of the latest books on science in "Views on Science Books," by Harry C. Stubbs and Sarah Gagné. The Newbery and Caldecott acceptance speeches are published annually.

Information Sources in Children's Literature: A Practical Reference Guide for Children's Librarians, Elementary School Teachers, and Students of Children's Literature. Mary Meacham. Greenwood, 1978.

A basic guide to reference books, serial publications, and book-selection aids dealing with children's books and other media.

Interracial Books for Children Bulletin. Council on Interracial Books for Children, 1841 Broadway, New York, N.Y. 10023. Published eight times a year.

Articles discussing reflections of racism and sexism in the publishing of books for children, printed in a newspaper format.

I Read . . . I See . . . I Hear . . . I Learn. Library Service to the Disadvantaged Child Committee, Children's Services Division. American Library Association, 1970.

Language Arts. Published eight times a year by the National Council of Teachers of English.

This official journal of the Elementary Section of the NCTE includes timely articles on children's books and reading, and regular children's book reviews.

Latin America: An Annotated List of Materials for Children. Sel. Elena Mederos de Gonzalez, Anne Pellowski, and committee. Information Center on Children's Cultures, United States Committee for UNICEF, 1969.

An evaluation of "all in-print English language materials for children on the subject of Latin America." Useful as a purchasing aid and as a guide for eliminating poor material.

Let's Read Together: Books for Family Enjoyment. Ed. by a committee of the National Congress of Parents and Teachers and the Association for Library Service to Children of the ALA. 4th ed. American Library Association, 1981.

A book list for parents. Books are arranged by subject area, annotated, and given age levels.

Literature by and about the American Indian: An Annotated Bibliography for Junior and Senior High School Students. Comp. Anna Lee Stensland. 2d ed. National Council of Teachers of English, 1979.

The bibliography is augmented by a preface, a study guide for selected books, biographies of American Indian authors, and a list of additional sources. Directory of publishers is given.

Literature for Children. Zena Sutherland. Field Enterprises Educational Corp., Merchandise Mart Plaza, Chicago, Ill. 60654, 1977.

An article on children's literature, reprinted from *The World Book Encyclopedia.*

Little Miss Muffet Fights Back: A Bibliography of Recommended Non-sexist Books about Girls for Young Readers. Comp. Feminists on Children's Media. 2d ed. Feminist Book Mart, 162-11 Ninth Ave., Whitestone, N.Y. 11357, 1974.

A final edition of a bibliography because "the climate of awareness that we set out to generate has at last begun to be evident." A suggestive list, intended to arouse critical reactions to books.

Magazines for Children: A Selection Guide for Librarians, Teachers, and Parents. Ed. Selma K. Richardson. American Library Association, 1983.

Detailed annotations of magazines for children under fourteen, with bibliographic and ordering information.

A Multimedia Approach to Children's Literature: A Selective List of Films, Filmstrips, and Recordings Based on Children's Books. Comp. Mary Alice Hunt. 3d ed. American Library Association, 1983.

A selective annotated list of book-related non-print materials, appropriate for use with children from preschool to the sixth grade. Arranged alphabetically by title.

Newbery and Caldecott Medal and Honor Books: An Annotated Bibliography. Linda Kauffman Peterson and Marilyn Leathers Solt. G. K. Hall, 1982.

This comprehensive overview of the American Library Association awards includes an analysis of trends, as well as annotations of the books.

Newbery Medal Books. Ed. by an ALA committee. American Library Association, 50 E. Huron St., Chicago, Ill. 60611. Published annually.

A list of Newbery Medal winners.

Non-sexist Materials for Children. Children's Services Division of the American Library Association. American Library Association, 1975.

A compilation of publications and articles plus lists of children's materials.

Notable Children's Books, 1940–1970. Prepared by a committee of the Children's Services Division of the ALA. American Library Association, 1977.

A reappraisal of the Notable Children's Books lists which appeared annually in *The Booklist* from 1940 to 1970. Yearly lists available, 1954 to date.

Notes from a Different Drummer: A Guide to Juvenile Fiction Portraying the Handicapped. Comp. Barbara H. Baskin and Karen H. Harris. Bowker, Serving Special Populations Series, 1977.

The image of the handicapped in children's literature is discussed, trends and patterns identified, and an annotated bibliography of children's books with disabled characters provided in this comparative and critical guide. See also other titles in this series, including *Books for the Gifted Child,* by Barbara H. Baskin and Karen H. Harris (1980).

Outstanding Science Trade Books for Children. Sel. National Science Teachers Association and the Children's Book Council Joint Liaison Committee. Published annually.

A selection of approximately one hundred

books, determined by criteria such as accuracy, readability, format. Annotated.

Picture Books for Children. Ed. Patricia Jean Cianciolo and the Picture Book Committee, subcommittee of the National Council of Teachers of English Elementary Booklist Committee. 2d ed. American Library Association, 1981.

Intended to serve as a resource guide for teachers, librarians, and parents, this bibliography of titles published up to 1980 gives annotations and sample illustrations. Titles are grouped by subject categories that reflect basic and common childhood concerns and relationships. Age levels are indicated.

Reading Ladders for Human Relations. Ed. Eileen Tway. 6th ed. National Council of Teachers of English, 1981.

Graded annotated list, from kindergarten through grade twelve, to help children use the experiences stored in books for growth in human understanding.

School Library Journal. R. R. Bowker Co., 1180 Avenue of the Americas, New York, N.Y. 10036. Published monthly, September through May.

A review journal of newly published books. Articles of interest to the library profession are featured, and many of the reviewers are librarians.

Selecting Materials for Children and Young Adults: A Bibliography of Bibliographies and Review Sources. Ed. by a committee of the Association for Library Service to Children, American Library Association, 1980.

An invaluable reference tool providing information on the major selection aids.

Signal Bookguides. Ed. Nancy Chambers. The Thimble Press, Lockwood Station Road, South Woodchester, Stroud, Glos., England, GL5 5EQ.

A series of critical, annotated bibliographies which act as book selection tools and clear, informative introductions to the subject. Includes *Reaching Out: Stories for Readers of Six to Eight,* by Jill Bennett (1980); *Picture Books for Young People, Nine to Thirteen,* by Elaine Moss (1981); *Learning to Read with Picture Books,* by Jill Bennett (2d rev. ed., 1982); *Plays for Young People to Read and Perform,* by Aidan Chambers (1982); *Ways of Knowing: Information Books for Seven- to Nine-Year-Olds,* by Peggy Heeks (1982); and *Poetry for Children,* by Jill Bennett and Aidan Chambers (1983).

Thirty Mid-Century Children's Books Every Adult Should Know. The Horn Book, 31 St. James Ave., Boston, Mass. 02116, 1972.

Titles of fiction chosen by the editor of *The Horn Book Magazine* to bring to adults "a sampling of the diversity to be found in creative literature for children." See also the companion list of fiction published since 1960, *Contemporary Classics: Thirty Children's Books for Adults,* comp. Ethel L. Heins (1982).

Twenty-five Years of British Children's Books. Ed. John Rowe Townsend. National Book League, 1977.

An annotated selective list by a respected children's literature theorist and author. Covering the period 1952–1977, the author presents a personalized view of original and noteworthy British and Commonwealth titles.

History of Children's Literature

Books

Andrews, Siri, ed. *The Hewins Lectures, 1947–1962.* Intro. Frederic G. Melcher. Horn Book, 1963.

Fifteen lectures given at New England Association meetings on the writing and publishing of children's books during a creative period in New England. Named in honor of Caroline M. Hewins, a Hartford, Connecticut, librarian and pioneer in children's book services.

Ashton, John. *Chap-Books of the Eighteenth Century.* Chatto & Windus, 1882.

Describes 103 chapbooks held by the British Museum. The texts are printed, and illustrations and title pages are reproduced in facsimile.

Avery, Gillian. *Childhood's Pattern: A Study of the Heroes and Heroines of Children's Fiction, 1770–1950.* Hodder & Stoughton, 1975.

A socio-literary study concentrating on the middle years of the period 1770–1950, when the publishers of children's literature were established and the moralists and educationalists had a dramatic influence.

Barchilon, Jacques, and Henry Pettit, eds. *The Authentic Mother Goose, Fairy Tales and Nursery Rhymes.* Swallow, 1960.

Introduction gives the history of Mother Goose and the fairy tales of Charles Perrault. Facsimiles of the complete *Mother Goose's Melody* and of the 1729 English translation of *Perrault's Tales.*

Barry, Florence V. *A Century of Children's Books.* Doran, 1923.

An evaluation of eighteenth-century children's books, especially those published in England.

Bingham, Jane, and Grayce Scholt. *Fifteen Centuries of Children's Literature: An Annotated Chronology of*

British and American Works in Historical Context. Greenwood, 1980.

A chronological listing of important titles, giving historical and bibliographical background information.

Blanck, Jacob. *Peter Parley to Penrod: A Bibliographical Description of the Best-loved American Juvenile Books.* Bowker, 1956.

The author, a book collector, lists outstanding books that have withstood the years of change in reading tastes.

Children's Books in the Rare Book Division of the Library of Congress. Rowman & Littlefield, 1975.

A two-volume catalogue of cards describing the Rare Book Division's fifteen thousand volumes, plus an additional one thousand more recent titles (1,383 pages).

Darling, Richard L. *The Rise of Children's Book Reviewing in America, 1865–1881.* Bowker, 1968.

Written as a doctoral thesis, this is a careful account, giving a complete history of publishing and criticism.

Darton, Frederick Joseph Harvey. *Children's Books in England: Five Centuries of Social Life.* Rev. Brian Alderson. 3d ed. Cambridge Univ. Press, 1982.

A scholarly study of the history of children's books in England and the social conditions and educational theories that influenced them. This meticulous revision adds to the strengths of the original by noting new research, rectifying errors, expanding the bibliography, and adding extra appendices and illustrations.

Egoff, Sheila. *Notable Canadian Children's Books; Un choix de livres canadiens pour la jeunesse.* Prepared by Sheila Egoff and Alvine Belisle; rev. Irene E. Aubrey. National Library of Canada, 1976.

Originally prepared as an annotated catalogue for an exhibit by the National Library of Canada in 1973. This revised edition includes a brief historical overview and annotated bibliography in chronological order showing the historical development of French and English publication for children in Canada from the eighteenth century to the present. Regular annual supplements are edited by Irene E. Aubrey.

Ellis, Alec. *How to Find Out about Children's Literature.* 3d ed. Pergamon, 1973.

A succinct account of the development of children's literature and guide to bibliographical materials in its study and selection.

Eyre, Frank. *British Children's Books in the Twentieth Century.* Rev. and enl. ed. Dutton, 1973.

A revised edition of *Twentieth Century Children's Books,* first published in 1952. A well-documented survey of children's literature in Britain since 1900, with full bibliography.

Field, Mrs. E. M. *The Child and His Book.* 2d ed. Wells Gardner, Darton, 1895.

An account of the history and progress of children's literature in England.

Folmsbee, Beulah. *A Little History of the Horn Book.* Horn Book, 1942.

An excellent, brief account.

Ford, Paul Leicester, ed. *The New England Primer: A History of Its Origin and Development.* Dodd, Mead, 1897.

Contains a reprint of the unique copy of the earliest known edition.

Gottlieb, Robin. *Publishing Children's Books in America, 1919–1976: An Annotated Bibliography.* Children's Book Council, 1978.

The bibliography of seven hundred and nine entries follows the growth of children's trade book publishing beginning with the separation and founding of Macmillan Company children's book department.

Green, Roger Lancelyn. *Tellers of Tales.* Rev. ed. F. Watts, 1965.

A survey of British authors of children's books from 1839 to the present.

Halsey, R. V. *Forgotten Books of the American Nursery.* Goodspeed, 1911.

A history of the development of the American story book, 1641–1840.

Haviland, Virginia. *Children's Literature: A Guide to Reference Sources.* Library of Congress, 1966. 1st supplement, 1972; 2d supplement, 1977.

An annotated bibliography of current and historical sources, including books, articles, and pamphlets useful to students of children's literature. An invaluable guide, prepared under the direction of the head of the Library of Congress Children's Book Section. The two supplements cover publications issued from 1966 to 1974.

Hazard, Paul. *Books, Children, and Men.* Trans. Marguerite Mitchell; intro. Sheila A. Egoff. 5th ed. Horn Book, 1983.

A spirited discussion of children's books, past and present, by an eminent French scholar.

Hoyle, Karen Nelson. *Danish Children's Literature in English: A Bibliography Excluding H. C. Andersen.* Univ. of Minnesota Center for Northwest European Language and Area Studies, 1982.

This serves as an example of a bibliography of one country's contribution to English language readers through translation.

Hürlimann, Bettina. *Three Centuries of Children's Books in Europe.* Trans. and ed. Brian W. Alderson. World, 1968.

A valuable reference book for anyone interested in the field of children's literature.

James, Philip. *Children's Books of Yesterday.* Ed. C. Geoffrey Holme. Gale, 1976.

First published in 1933, this is a short account of children's books from Comenius to the end of the nineteenth century. Contains facsimiles of pages from chapbooks, battledores, and colored books.

Jordan, Alice. *From Rollo to Tom Sawyer and Other Papers.* Decorations, Nora S. Unwin. Horn Book, 1948.

A history and critical study of children's literature in America from early days through the nineteenth century.

Kiefer, Monica. *American Children through Their Books, 1700–1835.* Univ. of Pennsylvania, 1948.

A scholarly appraisal of children's books of this period in terms of social history.

Laski, Marghanita. *Mrs. Ewing, Mrs. Molesworth, and Mrs. Hodgson Burnett.* Oxford Univ. Press, 1951.

An intensive study of three writers of the nineteenth century.

Lindquist, Jennie D. *Caroline M. Hewins, Her Book.* Horn Book, 1954.

This book, about a pioneer in the field of library service to children, contains Miss Hewins's own book, *A Mid-Century Child and Her Books,* and a biographical sketch. Also in *The Hewins Lectures, 1947–1962,* ed. Siri Andrews (Horn Book, 1963, pp. 65–82).

Lystad, Mary H. *From Dr. Mather to Dr. Seuss: Two Hundred Years of American Books for Children.* Hall/Schenkman, 1980.

A study of changing social values and attitudes toward children, as seen in a random sample of one thousand American children's books from the Rare Books Division of the Library of Congress.

MacDonald, Ruth K. *Literature for Children in England and America from 1646 to 1774.* Whitston, 1982.

An overview of the literature that developed specifically for children in the eighteenth century with an account of the social, historical, and cultural setting of the time.

MacLeod, Anne Scott. *A Moral Tale: Children's Fiction and American Culture, 1820–1860.* Archon, 1975.

A socio-historical investigation of the cultural values and concerns in an era of great social change as exhibited in the literature for children.

Meigs, Cornelia, et al. *A Critical History of Children's Literature: A Survey of Children's Books in English.* Decorations, Vera Bock. Rev. ed. Macmillan, 1969.

A revision of a major work. Part One, "Roots in the Past: Up to 1840," by Cornelia Meigs; Part Two, "Widening Horizons: 1840–1890," by Anne Thaxter Eaton; Part Three, "A Rightful Heritage: 1890–1920," by Elizabeth Nesbitt; Part Four, "Golden Years and Time of Tumult: 1920–1967," by Ruth Hill Viguers. A new chapter on American historical fiction has been added.

Morton, Miriam, ed. *A Harvest of Russian Children's Literature.* Foreword, Ruth Hill Viguers. Univ. of California Press, 1967.

This first anthology in English of Russian literature for children presents a wealth of stories, folktales, fables, prose, and poetry, from 1825 to the present.

Muir, Percival H. *English Children's Books, 1600–1900.* 2d ed. Batsford, 1979.

The author is a collector of toys and games, including harlequinades and books with paper dolls and movable parts.

Opie, Iona, and Peter Opie. *The Oxford Dictionary of Nursery Rhymes.* Illus. from old chapbooks; additional pictures, Joan Hassall. Walck, 1955.

Pellowski, Anne. *The World of Children's Literature.* Bowker, 1968.

A history of the developments of children's literature and libraries in 106 countries on six continents. The author is director of the UNICEF Information Center on Children's Cultures.

Pickering, Samuel F. *John Locke and Children's Books in Eighteenth-Century England.* Univ. of Tennessee Press, 1981.

An excellent example of an English professor's study of a particular historical period, focusing on John Locke and John Newbery.

Pierpont Morgan Library. *Children's Literature: Books and Manuscripts.* Pierpont Morgan Library, 1954.

An annotated catalogue of rare children's books and manuscripts lent by institutions and private collectors for an exhibition, November 19, 1954, through February 28, 1955.

Pierpont Morgan Library. *Early Children's Books and Their Illustration.* Godine, 1975.

The origins and history of children's books is traced over the centuries, using examples from the large collection of early children's books in the Pierpont Morgan Library.

Quayle, Eric. *Early Children's Books: A Collector's Guide.* David & Charles/Barnes & Noble Imports, 1983.

Primarily intended to serve collectors, this is a showcase of books from the author's own collection giving an overview from the sixteenth century until the mid-eighteenth century. With a different format, it is basically the same book previously published under the title *The Collector's Book of Children's Books* (Potter, 1971).

Rosenbach, Abraham S. W. *Early Children's Books with Bibliographical Descriptions of the Books in His Private Collection.* Foreword, A. Edward Newton. Southworth Press, 1953.

The 816 items in this world-famous collection are arranged chronologically, 1682–1836, with full bibliographical data. The book contains over one hundred facsimiles of title pages, frontispieces, and other pages.

Salway, Lance, ed. *A Peculiar Gift: Nineteenth Century Writings on Books for Children.* Kestrel, 1976.

An anthology of selected key nineteenth-century critical writings on children's literature, organized according to genre and theme.

Shipton, Clifford K. *Isaiah Thomas: Printer, Patriot, and Philanthropist, 1749–1831.* Leo Hart, 1948.

A biography of a pioneer American publisher.

Sloane, William. *Children's Books in England and America in the Seventeenth Century: A History and Checklist.* Columbia Univ. Press, 1955.

A scholarly study that places children's books of this period in historical perspective. Includes *The Young Christian's Library,* the first printed catalogue of books for children.

Smith, Dora V. *Fifty Years of Children's Books.* Intro. Muriel Crosby. National Council of Teachers of English, 1963.

A discussion of a personal selection of books published between 1910 and 1959.

Smith, Elva S. *The History of Children's Literature: A Syllabus with Selected Bibliographies.* Rev. Margaret Hodges and Susan Steinfirst. American Library Association, 1980.

An expanded edition of a standard work first published in 1937.

Targ, William, ed. *Bibliophile in the Nursery.* World, 1957.

A bookman's treasury of collector's lore on old and rare children's books.

Thwaite, Mary F. *From Primer to Pleasure in Reading: An Introduction to the History of Children's Books in England from the Invention of Printing to 1914, with an Outline of Some Developments in Other Countries.* Horn Book, 1972.

A detailed review.

Toronto Public Library. *The Osborne Collection of Early Children's Books, 1566–1910.* Vol. 1. Prepared by Judith St. John; intro. Edgar Osborne. Toronto Public Library, 1958, 1975.

A comprehensive catalogue of a gift to the Toronto Public Library in 1949 by the bibliophile Edgar Osborne, prepared by the librarian in charge of the famous collection. Richly illustrated with many facsimiles accompanied by descriptive notes. The catalogue is supplemented by *A Chronicle of Boys and Girls House* (1964), which lists additions, 1542–1910, to the Osborne Collection. See also *The Osborne Collection of Early Children's Books, 1476–1910: A Catalogue,* Vol. 2 (1975).

Townsend, John Rowe. *Written for Children: An Outline of English-Language Children's Literature.* 2d rev. ed. Harper, 1983.

A concise account of English prose fiction for children from its beginning to the present day. Poetry and picture books have been added to the revised edition.

U.S. Library of Congress. *Rare Book Division: A Guide to Its Collections and Services.* Library of Congress, 1965.

One of the best collections of American children's books, comprising approximately fifteen thousand volumes ranging from the early eighteenth century to the present.

Welch, d'Alte A. *A Bibliography of American Children's Books Printed Prior to 1821.* American Antiquarian Society (Worcester, Mass.), 1963–1967. Reprint. Barre, 1972.

History of the period is outlined in the introduction. Invaluable for collectors.

Welsh, Charles. *A Bookseller of the Last Century, Being Some Account of the Life of John Newbery, and of the Books He Published with a Notice of the Later Newberys.* Griffith, Farran, Okeden & Welsh, 1885.

The author thoroughly documents his discussion of the "philanthropic publisher of St. Paul's Churchyard." See also *The Renowned History of Little Goody Two Shoes, Otherwise Called Mrs. Margery Two*

Shoes, attributed to Oliver Goldsmith (Heath, 1900).

Early Writings

An Alphabet of Old Friends, and The Absurd ABC. Illus. Walter Crane. The Metropolitan Museum of Art/Thames & Hudson, 1981.

Originally published separately in 1874 in Routledge's "Sixpenny Toy Series," these two examples of Crane's "Toy Books" show the father of the illustrated children's book at his best, and represent his theory that children "prefer well-defined forms and bright frank colour." Preface by Bryan Holme.

An Illustrated Comic Alphabet. Illus. Amelia Frances Howard-Gibbon. Walck, 1967.

This unique alphabet book is a photographic reproduction of a manuscript version of the "A Is an Archer and Shot at a Frog" alphabet now in the Osborne Collection of Early Children's Books in Toronto, with its original illustrations. A brief account of the origins of *An Illustrated Comic Alphabet,* with a biography of its illustrator is included.

Aikin, John, and Anna Letitia Aikin Barbauld. *Evenings at Home.* 1792–1796. 6 vols.

Barbauld, Anna Letitia Aikin. *Hymns in Prose.* 1781.
Interesting in the study of children's literature.

Berquin, Arnaud. *The Looking-Glass for the Mind.* 1787.
The 1792 edition contains very interesting woodcuts by John Bewick.

Comenius, John Amos. *Orbis pictus.* Oxford Univ. Press, 1967.
A facsimile of the first English edition of 1659 (British Museum copy). Introduction by John E. Sadler gives biographical and historical background. See also facsimile reissued by Singing Tree Press.

Day, Thomas. *Sandford and Merton.* 1783–1789. 3 vols.
Interesting as the first English book illustrating Rousseau's theory of education.

Demers, Patricia, and Gordon Moyles. *From Instruction to Delight: An Anthology of Children's Literature to 1850.* Oxford Univ. Press, 1982.
A valuable anthology of selections from the primary sources of early children's literature. Excerpts are arranged by interpretation as well as by chronological order. With informative intro-

ductions and bibliography. See also the companion volume, *A Garland from the Golden Age: An Anthology of Children's Literature from 1850 to 1900,* ed. Patricia Demers (1983).

De Vries, Leonard. *Little Wide-Awake: An Anthology of Victorian Children's Books and Periodicals.* World, 1967.
The anthology, named after one of the most popular children's periodicals of the nineteenth century, contains sixty stories, 150 poems, with more than three hundred black-and-white pictures, and forty in color. See *Flowers of Delight* (1965).

Dodgson, Charles Lutwidge. *Alice's Adventures under Ground.* University Microfilms, 1964.
A facsimile of the original Lewis Carroll manuscript.

Edgeworth, Maria. *Early Lessons.* 1801–1815. 4 vols.
Two books that show Maria Edgeworth at her best are *Parent's Assistant, or Stories for Children,* illus. Chris Hammond (Macmillan), and *Tales,* intro. Austin Dobson, illus. Hugh Thompson (Stokes).

Ewing, Mrs. Juliana Horatia. *Jan of the Windmill.* Bell, Queen's Treasures Series, 1876.
A story of a lad whose talent for painting led to the discovery of his own parentage. Other well-liked books by the same author are *Brownies and Other Stories; Daddy Darwin's Dovecot; Jackanapes; Lob Lie-by-the-fire; Mary's Meadow;* and *Six to Sixteen.* All published in the Queen's Treasures Series.

Facsimile Editions from the Osborne Collection of Early Children's Books. Bodley Head, 1982.
Handsome facsimile reproductions of thirty-five titles from the Osborne Collection in the Toronto Public Library represent historical stages in the printing, writing, and illustration of English children's literature through the Georgian and Victorian eras. See also the companion volume, *English Illustrated Books for Children: Descriptive Companion to a Selection from the Osborne Collection,* ed. Margaret Crawford Maloney, rev. ed. (Bodley Head, 1981).

Greenaway, Kate. *The Kate Greenaway Treasury.* Intro. Ruth Hill Viguers. World, 1967.
An anthology of the illustrations and writings of Kate Greenaway, sel. and ed. Edward Ernest, assisted by Patricia Tracy Lowe.

Haviland, Virginia, and Margaret Coughlan, comps. *Yankee Doodle's Literary Sampler of Prose, Poetry, and Pictures.* Crowell, 1974.
Spanning the colonial period to the present, this

is an anthology of selections from the Library of Congress collection of early children's books, reproduced in facsimile.

History of Little Goody Two-Shoes. Ed. Charles Welsh. Heath, 1900.

The first book written especially for children. Sometimes attributed to Oliver Goldsmith. First published by John Newbery in 1765.

Lamb, Charles, and Mary Lamb. *Mrs. Leicester's School.* Illus. Winifred Green. Dent, 1899.

The quaint illustrations are in keeping with the text. First published in 1809.

Lurie, Allison, and Justin G. Schiller, comps. *Classics of Children's Literature: 1621–1932.* Garland, 1976–1979.

This is a series of 117 titles in seventy-three volumes, each volume dealing with one or more writers. Each work has a preface by a leading scholar in the field, plus bibliographical listings. Facsimile reprints are made from the first or most important early editions.

Mure, Eleanor. *The Story of the Three Bears.* Illus. by the author. Walck, 1967.

This story has an old woman as the central figure instead of the traditional Goldilocks and is taken from what is regarded as the earliest written version of the story.

Neuberg, Victor E. *The Penny Histories: A Study of Chapbooks for Young Readers over Two Centuries.* Illus. with facsimiles of seven chapbooks. Harcourt, Milestones in Children's Literature (gen. ed., Brian W. Alderson), 1969.

Gives information about publishing of chapbooks in America and England.

Newbery, John. *A Little Pretty Pocket-Book.* Harcourt, 1967.

A facsimile of the first book published for the sheer amusement of children in 1744, given historical and literary significance by M. F. Thwaite's introductory essay and bibliography.

Opie, Iona, and Peter Opie, comps. *The Classic Fairy Tales.* Oxford Univ. Press, 1974.

An anthology of twenty-four classic fairy tales in the form of their first appearance in the English language. Scholarly commentary and illustrations from different periods.

Opie, Iona, and Peter Opie, comps. *A Nursery Companion.* Oxford Univ. Press, 1980.

A handsome, oversize compendium of selections from the children's books of the early nineteenth century. Reproductions of the slim, colorful book-

lets of John Harris and other Regency publishers are enhanced by lucid notes and a brief introduction.

Roscoe, William. *The Butterfly's Ball and the Grasshopper's Feast.* Illus. Don Bolognese. McGraw-Hill, 1967.

The poem first appeared in print in *The Gentlemen's Magazine,* November 1806, and was published by John Harris in 1807. Because of their gay rhyme and galloping rhythm, the verses became extremely popular.

A St. Nicholas Anthology: The Early Years. Sel. and ed. Burton C. Frye; foreword, Dr. Richard L. Darling. Meredith, 1969.

A sampling of stories and articles from the years 1870 to 1905. The childhood work of writers who later became well known is a natural part of this selection.

Trimmer, Sarah Kirby. *The History of the Robins.* Ed. E. E. Hale. Heath, 1901.

Children still delight in these stories of bird life. First published in 1786.

Tuer, Andrew W. *Pages and Pictures from Forgotten Children's Books, Brought Together and Introduced to the Reader.* Singing Tree, 1969.

An anthology of facsimile reproductions of early children's stories and illustrations with a description of eighteenth- and nineteenth-century illustrative media and processes. First published in 1898.

Whalley, Joyce Irene. *Cobwebs to Catch Flies: Illustrated Books for the Nursery and Schoolroom, 1700–1900.* Univ. of California Press, 1975.

Teaching books, used in the home, are the focus of this study, which uses the Victoria and Albert Museum, London, as a source. The relationship between the emphases to be seen in these books and the world of the adults provides a valuable historical insight.

Yonge, Charlotte Mary. *The Little Duke, Richard the Fearless.* Illus. Marguerite De Angeli. Macmillan, Children's Classics, 1927.

One of the most popular stories of the time of chivalry. First published in 1854. Other books by the same author that are well liked, especially by older boys and girls, are *Dove in the Eagle's Nest; Chaplet of Pearls;* and *The Prince and the Page.* All of these are published in well-illustrated editions.

Specialized Publications

Children's Literature: The Annual of the Modern Language Association Division on Children's Literature and the *Children's Literature Association.* Ed. Francelia Butler et al. Yale Univ. Press. Published annually since 1972.

Title varies slightly. This is devoted to essays from the Modern Language Association Seminar on Children's Literature and contains some reviews and a list of areas for research.

Children's Literature Abstracts. IFLA Children's Section. C. H. Ray, 45 Stephenson Tower, Station Street, Birmingham B5 4DR, England. Published four times a year, in May, August, November, and February.

A guide to periodical articles on children's literature and allied topics. International in scope.

Children's Literature Association Quarterly. Ed. Perry Nodelman. Education Dept., Purdue Univ., West Lafayette, Ind. 47907. Published quarterly since 1976.

Critical articles and research on the subject of children's literature and related fields (children's folklore, illustration in children's books, the teaching of children's literature) are published, as well as timely information about the field.

The Lion and the Unicorn: A Critical Journal of Children's Literature. Dept. of English, Brooklyn College, Brooklyn, N.Y. 11210. Published annually.

Since 1977, each issue has been concerned with a specific theme or genre in children's literature. The number of issues varies slightly.

Phaedrus: An International Annual of Children's Literature Research. Ed. James Fraser. Columbia Univ. School of Library Service, Columbia University, 516 Butler Library, New York, N.Y. 10027. Published annually.

Title and number of issues have varied slightly since the first issue appeared in the fall of 1973. Includes a listing of selected dissertations, articles from current periodical literature, antiquarian and new booksellers, recent bibliographies, catalogues, and studies.

The Quarterly Journal of the Library of Congress. Ed. Sarah L. Wallace. Vol. 30, April 1973.

In this issue, published as a supplement to the *Annual Report of the Librarian of Congress,* are articles about children's books in the Library.

The Quarterly Journal of the Library of Congress. Ed. Frederick Mohr. Vol. 38, Fall 1981.

This issue is devoted to children's literature and includes articles by distinguished writers, critics, and librarians.

Signal: Approaches to Children's Books. Ed. Nancy Chambers. The Thimble Press, Lockwood, Station Road, South Woodchester, Stroud, Glos., England, GL5 5EQ. Published three times a year since 1970.

A lively journal of children's literature criticism from a British perspective. See also *The Signal Review of Children's Books,* an annual survey of new books, from 1983 on.

I *Children's Poetry: A Chorus of Voices*

1 Voices of the Nursery, Voices of the Playground

Mother Goose and Other Nursery Rhymes

The Baby's Lap Book. Illus. Kay Chorao. Dutton, 1977.

A selection of traditional rhymes delicately illustrated with fine black-and-white drawings.

Brian Wildsmith's Mother Goose: A Collection of Nursery Rhymes. F. Watts, 1965.

A handsome book with brilliant watercolor illustrations.

Cakes and Custard. Comp. Brian Alderson; illus. Helen Oxenbury. Morrow, 1975.

A lively assortment of children's rhymes, some familiar, some not. A few original compositions have been interspersed, blending in with the others. Playful, intricately wrought illustrations help set the pace.

Caldecott Picture Books. Illus. Randolph Caldecott. Warne, 1879.

Four volumes of four books each, titled *Picture Book No. 1; Picture Book No. 2; Hey Diddle Diddle*

Picture Book; and *The Panjandrum Picture Book.* Classic nursery rhyme books by the artist whose name has been given to the award for the most distinguished picture book of the year.

Cat and Mouse: A Book of Rhymes. Sel. and illus. Rodney Peppe. Holt, 1973.

Rhymes that have to do with either cats or mice.

Chinese Mother Goose Rhymes. Ed. Robert Wyndham; illus. Ed Young. World, 1968.

Traditional Chinese nursery rhymes, riddles, and lullabies are accompanied by graceful, calligraphic illustrations. In the Chinese style, the unusual format reads vertically rather than horizontally.

A Family Book of Nursery Rhymes. Comp. Iona Opie and Peter Opie; illus. Pauline Baynes. Oxford Univ. Press, 1964.

A comprehensive collection originally published as *The Puffin Book of Nursery Rhymes.*

Granfa' Grig Had a Pig and Other Rhymes without Reason from Mother Goose. Comp. and illus. Wallace Tripp. Little, Brown, 1976.

A selection of nonsensical nursery rhymes accompanied by droll, cartoon-style illustrations.

Lavender's Blue: A Book of Nursery Rhymes. Comp. Kathleen Lines; illus. Harold Jones. Oxford Univ. Press, 1982.

A beautifully illustrated book with eighty-one pages in full color reproduced from lithographs on stone. This edition is distinguished not only for its illustrations but for the inclusion of many little-known nursery rhymes. First published in 1954.

This Little Pig-a-Wig and Other Rhymes about Pigs. Comp. Leonore Blegvad; illus. Eric Blegvad. Atheneum, 1978.

A thematic collection of riddles and poetry, as well as nursery rhymes, with a traditional tone. Blegvad's colored and black-and-white ink sketches are biting in line and wry comic foolery. See also *Mittens for Kittens and Other Rhymes about Cats* (1974); *Hark, Hark, the Dogs Do Bark* (1975); and *The Parrot in the Garret and Other Rhymes about Dwellings* (1982).

Marguerite de Angeli's Book of Nursery and Mother Goose Rhymes. Doubleday, 1979.

An excellent collection of 376 rhymes, including some of the longer and many of the less familiar ones. First published in 1954.

Moon-Uncle, Moon-Uncle: Rhymes from India. Sel. and trans. Sylvia Cassedy and Parvathi Thampi; illus. Susanne Suba. Doubleday, 1973.

Forty-three traditional rhymes reveal intimate details of the Indian child's home life. Lyrical and episodic.

Mother Goose. Ed. Eulalie O. Grover; illus. Frederick Richardson. Rand McNally, 1971.

First published in 1915, this classic Volland edition offers sumptuous illustrations in irridescent color with an old-fashioned period touch.

Mother Goose. Illus. Tasha Tudor. Walck, 1944.

A standard collection, with gentle, domestic illustrations in color and black and white.

Mother Goose Abroad: Nursery Rhymes. Coll. Nicholas Tucker; illus. Trevor Stubley. Crowell, 1975.

European rhymes from various countries, held together with large, colorful artwork. See also *Mother Goose Lost: Nursery Rhymes* (1971).

Mother Goose and Nursery Rhymes. Wood engravings, Philip Reed. Atheneum, 1966.

Old favorites and lesser-known verses illustrated with beautifully printed wood engravings in six colors. A choice volume for the lover of fine books.

Mother Goose Comes to Cable Street: Nursery Rhymes for Today. Sel. Rosemary Stones and Andrew Mann; illus. Dan Jones. Kestrel, 1977.

An intriguing attempt to modernize the nursery rhymes by the juxtaposition of the verses with intricately detailed, urban-life illustrations. Naive in style, the pictures evoke an inner-city, multi-racial community.

Mother Goose in French; Poésies de la Vraie Mère Oie. Trans. Hugh Latham; illus. Barbara Cooney. Crowell, 1964.

Gay, colorful pictures introduce the young child to Mademoiselle Mouffue, Mère Hubard, Jean et Jeanne, and others without requiring knowledge of French.

Mother Goose in Hieroglyphics. Houghton Mifflin, 1962.

A facsimile of a rebus book originally published in Boston in 1849. A charming period piece.

Mother Goose in Spanish; Poesias de la Madre Oca. Trans. Alastair Reid and Anthony Kerrigan; illus. Barbara Cooney. Crowell, 1968.

These translations of the English verses seem at home in the Spanish settings given them by the illustrations.

Mother Goose Nursery Rhymes. Illus. Arthur Rackham. F. Watts, 1969.

A new edition of Rackham's work, based on the 1913 edition, which was called *Mother Goose: The Old Nursery Rhymes.*

Mother Goose, or The Old Nursery Rhymes. Illus. Kate Greenaway. Warne, 1882.

A slender book containing a limited number of rhymes with characteristic illustrations.

Mother Goose Picture Riddles: A Book of Rebuses. Adapt. and illus. Lisl Weil. Holiday, 1981.

A comic, playful collection of familiar nursery rhymes presented in rebus format. The picture riddles are visually clear and direct. For very young children.

Mother Goose Riddle Rhymes. Illus. Joseph Low. Harcourt, 1953.

Mr. Low has fashioned a charming, imaginative guessing game out of Mother Goose rhymes.

Mother Goose's Melodies. Intro. and bibliog. note, E. F. Bleiler. Dover, 1970.

American children of the nineteenth century knew this book. The introductory material to this facsimile edition of the Munroe and Francis "Copyright 1833" version presents the history of the book, the rhymes, and the changes made by the American editors.

The Mother Goose Treasury. Ed. and illus. Raymond Briggs. Coward-McCann, 1966.

Versions of the four hundred rhymes are those of Iona and Peter Opie. The eight hundred illustrations are by a leading British artist.

Nicola Bayley's Book of Nursery Rhymes. Knopf, 1977.

Miniature artwork, elegantly framed and luminously colored, complements this selection of choice rhymes.

Nursery Rhyme Book. Ed. Andrew Lang; illus. L. Leslie Brooke. New ed. Warne, 1947.

This book, first published in 1897, has been a mainstay for almost a century. The origin and history of some of the rhymes are given in the preface. Delightful, interpretative illustrations. Also in reprint (Dover, 1972).

One Misty Moisty Morning. Illus. Mitchell Miller. Farrar, Straus & Giroux, 1971.

A smoky, hazelike texture to the illustrations gives this small volume a sense of unreality.

The Prancing Pony: Nursery Rhymes from Japan. Adapt. and trans. Charlotte B. DeForest; illus. Keiko Hida. Walker, 1968.

Traditional nursery verses in translation provide a sense of childhood in Japan.

The Real Mother Goose. Illus. Blanche Fisher Wright. Rand McNally, 1965.

First published in 1916, this golden anniversary edition has an introduction by May Hill Arbuthnot. One of the best editions for the youngest children, containing the more familiar rhymes with brightly colored pictures.

Rimes de la Mère Oie. Trans. Ormonde de Kay, Jr.; illus. and designed by Seymour Chwast, Milton Glaser, and Barry Zaid (Push Pin Studios). Little, Brown, 1971.

Mother Goose rhymes rendered into French. English versions are in the rear of the book, together with notes on some of the translation decisions.

Round and Round the Garden. Comp. Sarah Williams; illus. Ian Beck. Oxford Univ. Press, 1983.

Reminiscent of the art deco style of book illustration, this collection of children's songs and finger play rhymes affectionately recreates the feeling of 1930s children's books. With explanatory diagrams for use with preschoolers.

The White Land: A Picture Book of Traditional Rhymes and Verses. Illus. Raymond Briggs. Coward-McCann, 1963.

Robust, pastoral qualities spring from the artwork. See also *Fee-Fi-Fo-Fum: A Picture Book of Nursery Rhymes* (1966), and *Ring-a-Ring O' Roses* (1962).

Nursery Rhyme Picture Books

The Courtship, Merry Marriage, and Feast of Cock Robin and Jennie Wren, to Which Has Been Added the Doleful Death of Cock Robin. Illus. Barbara Cooney. Scribner's, 1965.

A distinguished book in which the artist has captured the personalities of the various birds in a style particularly suited to the old rhymes.

From King Boggin's Hall to Nothing at All: A Collection of Improbable Houses and Unusual Places Found in Traditional Rhymes and Limericks. Illus. Blair Lent. Little, Brown, 1967.

Most of the sources in this intriguing assortment are from Mother Goose; one limerick is from Lear.

The House That Jack Built; La Maison que Jacques a batie. Illus. Antonio Frasconi. Harcourt, 1958.

A picture book in two languages.

I Saw a Ship A-Sailing. Illus. Beni Montresor. Knopf, 1967.

A picture book of Mother Goose rhymes interpreted with pictures in fantastic colors. See also *I Saw a Ship A-Sailing,* illus. Janina Domanska (Macmillan, 1972).

If All the Seas Were One Sea. Illus. Janina Domanska. Macmillan, 1971.

Geometric line patterns, used repetitively and with interesting variation.

It's Raining Said John Twaining: Danish Nursery Rhymes. Trans. and illus. N. M. Bodecker. Atheneum, A Margaret K. McElderry Book, 1973.

Delicate, fine drawings enhance the humor of these rhymes recalled from the artist's own childhood.

The Key to the Kingdom. Illus. Betsy Maestro and Giulio Maestro. Harcourt, 1982.

A distinguished edition sets the traditional rhyme in the context of one boy's activities from dawn to dusk in a small Italian village.

London Bridge Is Falling Down. Illus. Peter Spier. Doubleday, 1967.

Rich, detailed drawings bring eighteenth-century London vividly alive. See also *London Bridge Is Falling Down: The Song and Game,* illus. Ed Emberley (Little, Brown, 1967).

Old Mother Hubbard and Her Dog. Illus. Evaline Ness. Holt, 1972.

An extended version of the familiar rhyme in which Old Mother Hubbard goes out into the community.

One I Love, Two I Love, and Other Loving Mother Goose Rhymes. Illus. Nonny Hogrogian. Dutton, 1972.

A delicate mood and a shy humor glow in this small book.

One Old Oxford Ox. Illus. Nicola Bayley. Atheneum, 1977.

An Edwardian counting romp in droll miniature illustrations.

Oranges and Lemons: A Nursery Rhyme Picture Book. Illus. Leslie Brooke. Warne, ca. 1913.

Classic in its simplicity and genial playfulness. See also *This Little Pig Went to Market.*

Ring o' Roses: A Nursery Rhyme Picture Book. Illus. L. Leslie Brooke. New ed. Warne, 1977.

First published in 1922, this is an ideal first book of nursery rhymes for very young children, with L. Leslie Brooke's inimitable drawings in color and in black and white.

The Speckled Hen: A Russian Nursery Rhyme. Adapt. Harve Zemach; illus. Margot Zemach. Holt, 1966.

The Zemachs have captured the high spirits of the story of the hen whose speckled eggs cause all kinds of extraordinary happenings.

Three Jovial Huntsmen. Adapt. and illus. Susan Jeffers. Bradbury, 1973.

Fine, intricate use of line provides visual detail and gives double meaning to the story of the hunt. See also *If Wishes Were Horses: Mother Goose Rhymes* (Dutton, 1979).

To Market! To Market! Illus. Peter Spier. Doubleday, 1967.

The Dutch-American artist uses New Castle, Delaware, as the background for an American family's trip to market in the 1820s. See also *Hurrah, We're Outward Bound* and *And So My Garden Grows.*

Tom Tom, the Piper's Son. Illus. Paul Galdone. McGraw-Hill, 1964.

Other favorite rhymes made into picture books by the same illustrator are *The House That Jack Built* (1961) and *Old Mother Hubbard and Her Dog* (1960).

Nursery Rhymes Set to Music, Singing Games, Play Rhymes, Riddles, and Chants

Aardema, Verna. *Ji-Nongo-Nongo Means Riddles.* Illus. Jerry Pinkney. Four Winds, 1978.

Forty-four riddles from eleven African tribes.

Arnold, Arnold. *The World Book of Children's Games.* Illus. by the author. World, 1972.

A comprehensive presentation of games, their place in childhood, historic sidelights, and a discussion of the adult's role.

Bertail, Inez, ed. *Complete Nursery Song Book.* Illus. Walt Kelly. Lothrop, 1954.

Favorite nursery songs with simple piano arrangements and directions for singing games and finger plays.

Bobby Shaftoe's Gone to Sea. Arranged by Mark Taylor; illus. Graham Booth. Golden Gate, 1970.

An extended presentation of this familiar "romance."

Burroughs, Margaret Taylor, comp. *Did You Feed My Cow? Street Games, Chants, and Rhymes.* Illus. Joe E. Valasco. Rev. ed. Follett, 1969.

This collection of folk rhymes, chants, and well-loved games includes not only the folklore that has come down from years past, but also that which is being made by boys and girls today.

Chase, Richard. *Singing Games and Play-Party Games.* Illus. Joshua Tolford; piano arrangements, Hilton Rufty. Dover, 1967.

Verses, tunes, and directions for eighteen traditional American-English singing games, folk games, and figure dances. First published under the title *Hullabaloo, and Other Singing Folk Games* (Houghton Mifflin, 1949).

Emrich, Duncan, coll. *The Hodgepodge Book: An Almanac of American Folklore Containing All Manner of Curious, Interesting, and Out-of-the-Way Information Drawn from American Folklore, and Not to Be Found Anywhere Else in the World.* Illus. Ib Ohlsson. Four Winds, 1972.

A truly remarkable and enjoyable assemblage with extensive notes and bibliography in the rear. See also *The Nonsense Book of Riddles, Rhymes, Tongue Twisters, Puzzles and Jokes from American Folklore* (1970).

Fish, Helen Dean, comp. *Four and Twenty Blackbirds: Nursery Rhymes of Yesterday Recalled for Children of Today.* Illus. Robert Lawson. Lippincott, 1937.

An excellent collection of little-known nursery rhymes and ballads. Simple music is given for many rhymes. A brief historical note for each rhyme is given in the contents.

Fowke, Edith. *Sally Go round the Sun: Three Hundred Children's Songs, Rhymes, and Games.* Illus. Carlos Marchiori. Doubleday, 1969.

A brilliantly illustrated collection of Canadian taunts, teases, skipping and ball-bouncing rhymes, silly songs, and finger plays, with critical notes. See also *Ring around the Moon* (Prentice-Hall, 1977).

Frasconi, Antonio. *The Snow and the Sun; La Nieve y el Sol.* Woodcuts by the author. Harcourt, 1961.

A South-American folk rhyme with both English and Spanish text.

Glazer, Tom, comp. *Do Your Ears Hang Low?* Illus. Mila Lazarevich. Doubleday, 1980.

A sprightly collection of action games and songs dramatized by vivacious illustrations.

Harrop, Beatrice, ed. *Okki-Tokki-Unga: Action Songs for Children.* Illus. David McKee. A. & C. Black, 1976.

A vital collection of action story-songs with musical accompaniment and basic instructions.

Hart, Jane, comp. *Singing Bee! A Collection of Favorite Children's Songs.* Illus. Anita Lobel. Lothrop, 1982.

An outstanding collection of lullabies, nursery rhymes, singing games, and folk songs illustrated in a colonial period style. Finely produced with guitar and piano arrangements.

Hector Protector and As I Went over the Water. Illus. Maurice Sendak. Harper, 1965.

Maurice Sendak interprets in pictures two nursery rhymes in which one small boy deals with a monstrous sea-serpent and another meets the Queen.

Kapp, Paul. *A Cat Came Fiddling, and Other Rhymes of Childhood.* Illus. Irene Haas; intro. Burl Ives. Harcourt, 1956.

Fifty-seven traditional nonsense verses and nursery rhymes set to music.

Kapp, Paul. *Cock-a-Doodle Do! Cock-a-Doodle Dandy! A New Song Book for the Newest Singers.* Illus. Anita Lobel. Harper, 1966.

Amusing contemporary verses and traditional rhymes set to new tunes.

Langstaff, John. *Frog Went A-Courtin'.* Illus. Feodor Rojankovsky. Harcourt, 1955.

An old Scottish ballad with rollicking pictures. Awarded the Caldecott medal, 1956.

Langstaff, John. *Over in the Meadow.* Illus. Feodor Rojankovsky. Harcourt, 1967.

An old counting rhyme takes on new charm with delightful illustrations. See also *Hi! Ho! The Rattlin' Bog* (1969).

Langstaff, John, and Carol Langstaff. *Shimmy Shimmy Coke-Ca-Pop! A Collection of City Children's Street Games and Rhymes.* Doubleday, 1973.

Contemporary and traditional sources are mixed in the life of children's street play.

Leach, Maria. *Riddle Me, Riddle Me, Ree.* Illus. William Wiesner. Viking, 1970.

Riddles collected by a folklorist, with notes and sources.

Mattern, Elizabeth Mary, comp. *This Little Puffin: Finger Plays and Nursery Games.* Illus. Raymond Briggs. Penguin, 1969.

A collection of rhymes, songs, and singing games, suited for use with very young children. Clear explanatory notes and precise illustrations. Also published as *Games for the Very Young* (American Heritage, 1969).

Montgomerie, Norah, comp. *One, Two, Three: A Little Book of Counting Rhymes.* Illus. by the compiler. Abelard-Schuman, 1968.

Rhythmic and playful numerations.

Montgomerie, Norah, comp. *This Little Pig Went to Market: Play Rhymes.* Illus. Margery Gill. F. Watts, 1967.

A collection of 150 favorite rhymes and games for young children.

Montgomerie, Norah, and William Montgomerie, eds. *A Book of Scottish Nursery Rhymes.* Illus. T. Ritchie and Norah Montgomerie. Oxford Univ. Press, 1965.
Skipping and counting-out rhymes, singing games, lullabies, and others.

Morrison, Lillian, comp. *A Diller a Dollar: Rhymes and Sayings for the Ten O'Clock Scholar.* Illus. Marj Bauernschmidt. Harper, 1955.
Fun for boys and girls that gives nostalgic delight to their elders. See also *Black Within and Red Without,* illus. Jo Spier (1953), and *Remember Me When This You See* (1961).

O'Hare, Colette, coll. *What Do You Feed Your Donkey On? Rhymes from a Belfast Childhood.* Illus. Jenny Rodwell. Collins, 1978.
A collection of children's game rhymes reflecting the traditional verse, songs, street chants, and market cries of Belfast. The accompanying illustrations are evocative, pointillist visions imaginatively framed on the page.

Old MacDonald Had a Farm. Illus. Robert Quackenbush. Harper, 1972.
Lighthearted humor of this long-lived favorite is apparent in the illustrations.

Petersham, Maud, and Miska Petersham, comps. *The Rooster Crows: A Book of American Rhymes and Jingles.* Illus. by the compilers. Macmillan, 1969.
Finger games, rope-skipping and counting-out rhymes, and other jingles. Awarded the Caldecott medal, 1946. First published in 1945.

Potter, Charles Francis, comp. *Tongue Tanglers.* Illus. William Wiesner. World, 1962.
An authority on this type of folklore presents forty-four tongue twisters. See also *More Tongue Tanglers and a Rigmarole.*

Rees, Ennis. *Pun Fun.* Illus. Quentin Blake. Abelard-Schuman, 1965.
American and British folklore form the basis for most of these rhymed puns.

Rosen, Michael, and Susanna Steele, colls. *Inky Pinky Ponky: Children's Playground Rhymes.* Illus. Dan Jones. Granada, 1982.
Saucy street rhymes, both traditional and modern, are presented in the context of a living community. The naive illustrations add a distinctly urban, multi-ethnic flavor.

Schwartz, Alvin. *A Twister of Twists, a Tangle of Tongues.* Illus. Glen Rounds. Harper, 1972.
Accented by the twangy bravado of tongue-in-cheek drawings, this is a rich collection of inventive word play.

Tashjian, Virginia A., sel. *Juba This and Juba That: Story Hour Stretches for Large or Small Groups.* Illus. Victoria de Larrea. Little, Brown, 1969.
Finger plays, chants, riddles, songs, tongue twisters, poetry and rhyme, and some short stories make this a marvelous source of entertainment. See also *With a Deep Sea Smile: Story Hour Stretches for Large or Small Groups* (1974).

Thirty Old-Time Nursery Songs. Illus. Paul Woodroffe. 1912. Reprint. Metropolitan Museum of Art, 1980.
Elegant art-nouveau design and illustration. Clear musical accompaniments to the traditional rhymes.

Wheeler, Opal. *Sing Mother Goose.* Illus. Marjorie Torrey. Dutton, 1945.
The best-loved Mother Goose rhymes, with musical accompaniments.

Withers, Carl, comp. *A Rocket in My Pocket: The Rhymes and Chants of Young Americans.* Illus. Susanne Suba. Holt, 1948.
Over four hundred rhymes, chants, game songs, and tongue twisters. The compiler collected the material while he was doing field work with children in New York City and many regions of the United States. See also *Rainbow in the Morning,* comp. Carl Withers and Alta Jablow (Abelard-Schuman, 1956).

Withers, Carl. *I Saw a Rocket Walk a Mile.* Illus. John E. Johnson. Holt, 1966.
Nonsense tales, chants, and songs from many lands, emphasizing humor and absurdity and showing how rhymes travel from country to country.

Withers, Carl. *Ready or Not, Here I Come.* Illus. Garry MacKenzie. Grosset & Dunlap, 1964.
A varied assortment of games, tricks, singing games, rhymes, riddles, stunts, and so forth.

Wood, Ray, comp. *Fun in American Folk Rhymes.* Illus. Ed Hargis; intro. Carl Carmer. Lippincott, 1952.
American folk rhymes, ballads, counting-out rhymes, skipping and jump rope rhymes.

Worstell, Emma, comp. *Jump the Rope Jingles.* Illus. Sheila Greenwald. Macmillan, 1972.

Thirty-three jump rope rhymes collected from various sources.

Yankee Doodle. Richard Schackburg. Woodcuts, Ed Emberley; notes, Barbara Emberley. Prentice-Hall, 1965.
    Woodcut figures march across the pages, capturing the martial spirit of the song. All ages.

Folk Songs

Boni, Margaret Bradford, ed. *Fireside Book of Folk Songs.* Piano arrangements, Norman Lloyd; illus. Alice Provensen and Martin Provensen. Simon & Schuster, 1947.
    Planned for family or group singing. Includes nursery rhymes, ballads, and favorite songs of yesterday. Colorful illustrations add to the distinction of the book.

Bryan, Ashley, sel. and illus. *Walk Together Children: Black American Spirituals.* Atheneum, 1974.
    Dramatic woodcuts interpret the broad range of mood, rhythm, and subject in traditional black American music. See also a companion volume, *I'm Going to Sing: Black American Spirituals* (1982).

Carmer, Carl, comp. *America Sings: Stories and Songs of Our Country's Growing.* Musical arrangements, Edwin John Stringham; illus. Elizabeth Black Carmer. Knopf, 1942.
    A distinguished anthology of folk songs and tales reflecting America's work and growth.

Chase, Richard. *Billy Boy.* Illus. Glenn Rounds. Golden Gate, 1966.
    Variants of the old folk song have been sung in many languages. The author, a folklorist, gives an adaptation he heard in the southern Appalachian Mountains.

Emberley, Barbara, ed. *One Wide River to Cross.* Adapt. Barbara Emberley; illus. Ed Emberley. Prentice-Hall, 1966.
    In this picture-book version of an old folk spiritual, the animals of Noah's ark troop across the pages. Music at the end.

Fiddle-I-Fee: A Traditional American Chant. Illus. Diane Stanley. Little, Brown, 1979.
    The traditional onomatopoeic cumulative folk-song is given a nursery flavor in this picture-book version. The song is extended in the humorous and graceful paintings of a young girl's preparations for a gala party with a fantasy complement of animal friends.

The Friendly Beasts: An Old English Christmas Carol. Illus. Tomie de Paola. Putnam's, 1981.
    This picture-book version of the traditional English Christmas carol is gently interpreted in simple, statuesque paintings. Music at the end.

Gauch, Patricia Lee. *On to Widdecombe Fair.* Illus. Trina Schart Hyman. World's Work, 1979.
    Uncommon in conception, this version of the Devon ballad retells it in folktale prose. With lyrics and music appended.

Glazer, Tom, comp. *Tom Glazer's Treasury of Folk Songs.* Illus. Art Seiden; piano arrangements, Stanley Lock et al. Grosset & Dunlap, 1964.
    Includes chord symbols for guitar or banjo.

Gordon, Dorothy. *Sing It Yourself: Folk Songs of All Nations.* Illus. Alida Conover. Dutton, 1933.
    Folk songs from the British Isles, France, Germany, Norway, Russia, and the United States.

Haywood, Charles. *Folk Songs of the World.* Illus. Carl Smith. Day, 1966.
    Songs gathered from more than one hundred countries, selected and edited with commentary on their musical cultures.

I Know an Old Lady. Rose Bonne. Illus. Abner Graboff. Rand McNally, 1961.
    Cumulative improbabilities become truly hilarious in this version of the well-known song.

John, Timothy, ed. *The Great Song Book.* Musical arrangements, Peter Hankey; illus. Tomi Ungerer. Doubleday, 1978.
    Sixty-six of the best-loved songs in the English language are generously illustrated with stylish, witty exaggeration.

Jones, Bessie, and Bess Lomax Hawes. *Step It Down: Games, Plays, Songs, and Stories from the Afro-American Heritage.* Harper, 1972.
    A varied and versatile collection of songs, games, singing plays, home amusements, and variations of English traditional songs, this compendium of activities has distinctive detail and richness.

Langstaff, John, sel. *Hi! Ho! The Rattlin' Bog and Other Folk Songs for Group Singing.* Piano arrangements, John Edmunds, Seymour Barab, Phil Merrill, and Marshall W. Barron; guitar chords, Happy Traum; illus. Robin Jacques. Harcourt, 1969.
    Songs that have proven popular with groups of all ages and places. See also *Sweetly Sings the Donkey* (Atheneum, 1973).

Langstaff, John. *Hot Cross Buns and Other Old Street Cries, Chosen Especially for Children.* Illus. Nancy Winslow Parker. Atheneum, 1978.

A well-selected collection of dramatic and tuneful English street cries.

Langstaff, Nancy, and John Langstaff, comps. *Jim Along, Josie: A Collection of Folk Songs and Singing Games for Young Children.* Illus. Jan Pienkowski; piano arrangements, Seymour Barab; guitar chords, Happy Traum. Harcourt, 1970.

Includes optional percussion accompaniments for children. Songs to join in singing, moving to, and playing; of special value for young children. See also *Frog Went A-Courtin'* (1955); *Ol' Dan Tucker* (1963); *Golden Vanity* (1972); and *Over in the Meadow* (1973).

Lomax, John, and Alan Lomax. *American Ballads and Folk Songs.* Macmillan, 1946.

See also by the same authors *Cowboy Songs and Other Frontier Ballads* (1948).

Nic Leodhas, Sorch. *A Scottish Songbook.* Illus. Evaline Ness. Holt, 1969.

Traditional Scottish airs in Scottish dialect and rhythm. Handsome woodcut illustrations make this a distinctive collection.

Ritchie, Jean, ed. *From Fair to Fair: Folk Songs of the British Isles.* Photographs, George Pickow; piano arrangements, Edward Tripp. Walck, 1966.

The author, a well-known folk singer, provides words and music arranged for piano and guitar. See also *The Swapping Song Book* (Oxford Univ. Press, 1952).

Rockwell, Anne, sel. *El Toro Pinto and Other Songs in Spanish.* Illus. by the author. Macmillan, 1971.

Presented within an illustrated framework of authentic costumes, architectural details, plants, and animals. The songs are in Spanish with English translations in the back of the book.

Sandburg, Carl. *The American Songbag.* Harcourt, 1927.

Songs collected from different regions of the United States.

Seeger, Ruth Crawford. *American Folk Songs for Children in Home, School, and Nursery School.* Illus. Barbara Cooney. Doubleday, 1948.

Folk songs from all parts of America. Introductory chapters discuss the value of folk music for children. See also *Animal Folk Songs for Children* (1950) and *American Folk Songs for Christmas* (1953).

Spier, Peter, illus. *The Fox Went Out on a Chilly Night.* Doubleday, 1961.

Splendidly set into an evocative picture book, the old song becomes an exciting adventure.

Winn, Marie, ed. *The Fireside Book of Children's Songs.* Illus. John Alcorn; piano arrangements, Alan Miller. Simon & Schuster, 1966.

Over one hundred old and new nursery songs with piano arrangements and guitar chords. A book for the entire family. See also *The Fireside Book of Fun and Game Songs,* illus. Whitney Darrow, Jr. (1974).

Winn, Marie, comp. and ed. *What Shall We Do and Allee Galloo!* Illus. Karla Kuskin. Harper, 1970.

Directions for games and ways of using songs with them make this collection both simple and practical.

Yolen, Jane, ed. *The Fireside Song Book of Birds and Beasts.* Arranged by Barbara Green; illus. Peter Parnall. Simon & Schuster, 1972.

A splendid array of nearly one hundred songs.

Yurchenco, Henrietta. *A Fiesta of Folk Songs from Spain and Latin America.* Illus. Jules Maidoff. Putnam's, 1967.

An authority on Latin American and Spanish folk music has gathered together an impressive collection of songs, singing games, and dances.

Zemach, Harve. *Mommy, Buy Me a China Doll.* Illus. Margot Zemach. Farrar, Straus & Giroux, 1975.

The lyrics to this cumulative folk song from the Ozarks are irresistible, whether used with the music provided at the back or not.

Lullabies

All the Pretty Horses. Illus. Susan Jeffers. Macmillan, 1974.

Soft pastel illustrations reflect the dreamlike mood of this lullaby picture book.

Becker, John. *Seven Little Rabbits.* Illus. Barbara Cooney. Walker, 1973.

This going-to-sleep rhyme, which first appeared in the author's *New Feathers for the Old Goose,* takes on a new vitality and charm in this single edition. The cumulative repetition induces a truly hypnotic state.

Hush Little Baby. Illus. Aliki. Prentice-Hall, 1968.

A folk lullaby, first sung in England, and now well known in the United States. See also another edition (Dutton, 1976) illustrated with a nonsense folk twist by Margot Zemach.

Knudsen, Lynne. *Lullabies from Around the World.* Illus. Jacqueline Tomes. Follett, 1967.

Lullabies have no boundaries, but pass from country to country.

Sleep, Baby, Sleep: A Lullaby. Illus. Gertrud Oberhansli. Atheneum, 1967.
A lullaby that originated in Germany but today belongs to every country.

Watson, Wendy, ed. and illus. *Fisherman Lullabies.* Musical arrangements, Clyde Watson. World, 1968.
Lullabies sung by fishermen's wives of the British Isles and New England. Tender illustrations complement the hushed tone.

Wilder, Alec, comp. *Lullabies and Night Songs.* Ed. William Engvick; illus. Maurice Sendak. Harper, 1965.
Traditional folk songs, nursery rhymes, and children's poems, some set to music for the first time.

Yulya. *Bears Are Sleeping.* Illus. Nonny Hogrogian. Scribner's, 1967.
An old Russian melody forms the basis for this lullaby.

References for Adults

Abrahams, Roger D. *Jump-Rope Rhymes: A Dictionary.* Univ. of Texas Press, 1969.

Barchilon, Jacques, and Henry Pettit, eds. *The Authentic Mother Goose Fairy Tales and Nursery Rhymes.* Swallow, 1960.
A well-documented introduction traces the history of Mother Goose rhymes and the Perrault fairy tales. Includes a facsimile of *Mother Goose's Tales,* the text of the 1729 Perrault translation, and a facsimile of *Mother Goose's Melodies, or Sonnets for the Cradle,* printed for E. Power in London, 1791.

Baring-Gould, William S., and Cecil Baring-Gould. *The Annotated Mother Goose.* Illus. Caldecott, Crane, Greenaway, Parrish, Rackham, and historical woodcuts; chapter decorations, E. M. Simon. Potter, 1982.
An introduction and columns of interesting historical notes accompany the complete text. First published in 1962.

Bett, Henry. *Nursery Rhymes and Tales: Their History and Origin.* 1924. Reprint. Singing Tree Press, 1968.
A brief introduction to the history of nursery rhymes and folktales.

Butler, Francelia. "'Over the Garden Wall / I Let the Baby Fall': The Poetry of Rope-Skipping."

In *Children's Literature: The Great Excluded, Journal of the Modern Language Association Seminar on Children's Literature and The Children's Literature Association,* Vol. 3, ed. Francelia Butler and Bennett A. Brockman. Temple Univ. Press, 1974.

Cott, Jonathan. *Pipers at the Gates of Dawn: The Wisdom of Children's Literature.* Random House, 1983.
Chapter 7 is an interview with Iona and Peter Opie, discussing their methods of scholarship in studying children's lore, games, and language.

Eckenstein, Lina. *Comparative Studies in Nursery Rhymes.* 1906. Reprinted Singing Tree Press, 1968.
Traces the folk origins of Mother Goose rhymes.

Knapp, Mary, and Herbert Knapp. *One Potato, Two Potato . . . the Secret Education of American Children.* Norton, 1976.
A scholarly study of the folk and game lore of contemporary American children from kindergarten through the sixth grade.

Opie, Iona, ed. *Ditties for the Nursery.* Illus. Monica Walker. Oxford Univ. Press, 1954.
"Rhymes which delighted children in the reign of George III . . . published about 1805 under the title *Original Ditties for the Nursery, So Wonderfully Contrived That They May Be Either Sung or Said by Nurse or Baby.*" Children of today will delight in many of these unfamiliar rhymes of yesterday. The illustrations have vitality and charm.

Opie, Iona, and Peter Opie. *Children's Games in Street and Playground: Chasing, Catching, Seeking, Hunting, Racing, Duelling, Exerting, Daring, Guessing, Acting, Pretending.* Oxford Univ. Press, 1969.
Based on observation and research, this is an account of the games children play and the rhymes and sayings that they use.

Opie, Iona, and Peter Opie. *The Lore and Language of School Children.* Oxford Univ. Press, 1959.
A first study of the oral lore of children in seventy schools in England and one in Ireland. Versions of sayings, rhymes, and riddles are compared and their development traced.

Opie, Iona, and Peter Opie, eds. *The Oxford Dictionary of Nursery Rhymes.* Illus. with historical plates. Oxford Univ. Press, 1951.
A scholarly work done with consummate skill and filled with fascinating notes. The editors are leading authorities on eighteenth-century children's literature and chapbooks. They have brought together more than five hundred traditional rhymes, giving their individual histories, lit-

erary associations, variations, and parallels in other languages. In the introduction they describe the different types of rhymes, the earliest collections, theories dealing with their origin, and the possible identity of Mother Goose. A book for imaginative adults who care for poetry and folklore.

Opie, Iona, and Peter Opie, eds. *The Oxford Nursery Rhyme Book.* Oxford Univ. Press, 1955.

A unique collection of eight hundred nursery rhymes. More than four hundred illustrations are reproductions of woodcuts from the earliest children's books and chapbooks of the eighteenth and nineteenth centuries. Engravings by both Thomas and John Bewick are included. Supplementing the early reproductions are 150 illustrations by Joan Hassall.

Opie, Iona, and Peter Opie. *Three Centuries of Nursery Rhymes and Poetry for Children: An Exhibition Held at the National Book League, May 1973.* Oxford Univ. Press, 1973.

The catalogue and introduction to this exhibition, which was presented by the Opies in England, is a valuable bibliographic source.

Reeves, James. *Understanding Poetry.* Heinemann, 1965.

Chapter 7 discusses Mother Goose rhymes and ballads, pointing out the poetic characteristics of these forms.

Sackville-West, Virginia. *Nursery Rhymes: An Essay.* Illus. Philippe Julian. Michael Joseph, 1950.

The author shows that folklore, mythology, and history all combine in the making of nursery rhymes, but she contends that it is "the inherent music of the nursery jingle" that preserves it in loving remembrance.

Sendak, Maurice. "Mother Goose's Garnishings." In *Children and Literature,* ed. Virginia Haviland. Scott, Foresman, 1973.

Tucker, Nicholas. "Why Nursery Rhymes?" In *Children and Literature,* ed. Virginia Haviland. Scott, Foresman, 1973.

2 Voices of Nonsense

Books for Children

Belloc, Hilaire. *Matilda Who Told Lies and Was Burned to Death.* Illus. Steven Kellogg. Dial, 1970.

Taken from the collected edition, *Cautionary Verses* (Knopf, 1941), this single grisly example of poor behavior is enthusiastically filled out by the illustrator.

Belloc, Hilaire. *More Beasts for Worse Children.* Illus. B. T. B.; foreword, Rosemary Livsey. Knopf, 1966.

"Timelessly hilarious . . . ." See also *Cautionary Verses* (1959) and *Bad Child's Book of Beasts* (1965). These appeared originally in the late nineteenth century.

Belloc, Hilaire. *The Yak, the Python, the Frog.* Illus. Stephen Kellogg. Parents, 1975.

A clever interlinking of three Belloc beast verses to form a witty picture book with Kellogg's narrative illustrations.

Bennett, Jill, sel. *Tiny Tim: Verses for Children.* Illus. Helen Oxenbury. Delacorte, 1982.

Nonsense for the nursery, traditional and modern. Illustrated in Oxenbury's warmly daft manner.

Bodecker, N. M. *Let's Marry Said the Cherry and Other Nonsense Poems.* Illus. by the author. Atheneum, A Margaret K. McElderry Book, 1974.

Delicately lined illustrations with their own playful incongruities enliven a spritely assortment of nonsense verse. See also *Hurry, Hurry, Mary Dear! and Other Nonsense Poems* (1976) and *Snowman Sniffles, and Other Verse* (1983).

Brewton, Sara, and John Brewton. *Laughable Limericks.* Illus. Ingrid Fetz. Crowell, 1966.

The editors have gathered together a "giddy garland of limericks old and new."

Brown, Marcia. *Peter Piper's Alphabet.* Scribner's, 1959.

A lively version of this old alliterative alphabet.

Carroll, Lewis. *Alice's Adventures in Wonderland* and *Through the Looking-Glass.* Illus. John Tenniel. Macmillan, The Children's Classics, n.d.

Both stories contain some of the best nonsense ever written.

Carroll, Lewis. *The Hunting of the Snark.* Illus. Helen Oxenbury. Heinemann, 1970.

Fine line drawings (some in color), imbued with the fantasy and humor of the verse, give this parody an additional share of fun. See also next entry.

Carroll, Lewis. *The Hunting of the Snark: An Agony in Eight Fits.* Illus. Henry Holiday. Macmillan, 1927.

A nonsense narrative poem first published in 1876, reissued with the original illustrations. A later edition (Pantheon, 1966) is illustrated by Kelly Occhsii. Another edition (Peter Pauper, 1952) is illustrated by Aldren Watson.

Carroll, Lewis. *The Walrus and the Carpenter and Other Poems.* Illus. Gerald Rose. Dutton, 1969.
    The fine use of color and line makes this picture-book version of the title poem and other favorites a joyous affair.

Chukovsky, Cornei. *The Telephone.* Adapt. William Jay Smith; illus. Blair Lent. Delacorte, 1977.
    This translation of an elaborate farce by the master of Russian nonsense is illustrated in Russian character and costume.

Ciardi, John. *I Met a Man.* Illus. Robert Osborn. Houghton Mifflin, 1961.
    Nonsense rhymes written by a poet as the first book his young daughter could read herself. Grades 1–3. See also *The Man Who Sang the Sillies* (Harper, 1961).

Cole, William, ed. *Beastly Boys and Ghastly Girls.* Illus. Tomi Ungerer. World, 1964.
    Outlandish verses for all ages, supported with fine, zany cartoon work. Similarly illustrated are *Oh, What Nonsense!* (Viking, 1966); *A Case of the Giggles* (1967); *The Book of Giggles* (1970); *Oh, How Silly!* (Viking, 1970); and *Oh, That's Ridiculous!* (1972).

Emrich, Duncan. *The Nonsense Book of Riddles, Rhymes, Tongue Twisters, Puzzles, and Jokes from American Folklore.* Illus. Ib Ohlsson. Four Winds, 1970.
    Scholarly in its detail, this is a treasury of nonsense.

Green, Roger Lancelyn, ed. *The Book of Nonsense.* Illus. Charles Folkard, Lear, Shepard, Tenniel, and others. Dutton, Children's Illustrated Classics, 1956.
    Classic nonsense selections from the ancient Greeks down through the ages.

The History of Simple Simon. Illus. Paul Galdone. McGraw-Hill, 1966.
    Fifteen nonsense verses, brightly illustrated, about the well-known lad who met a pieman. Taken not from the famous Mother Goose rhyme but from a text published in London in 1840.

Kennedy, X. J. *One Winter Night in August and Other Nonsense Jingles.* Illus. David McPhail. Atheneum, A Margaret K. McElderry Book, 1975.
    A distinguished contemporary poet writing in the mood of the absurd.

Lear, Edward. *The Complete Nonsense Book.* Ed. Lady Strachey; intro. by the Earl of Cromer. Dodd, Mead, 1951.
    The accentuated rhythm, the grotesque draw-

ings, and the exaggeration appeal to a child's sense of humor. First published in 1912. Another edition, by Holbrook Jackson (Dover, n.d.), contains an appreciative introduction to Lear. See also *A Book of Nonsense,* intro. Bryan Holme (Viking/Metropolitan Museum of Art, 1980).

Lear, Edward. *The Dong with a Luminous Nose.* Illus. Edward Gorey. W. R. Scott, 1969.
    Gorey's line drawings are similar to Lear's own work.

Lear, Edward. *How Pleasant to Know Mr. Lear! Edward Lear's Selected Works.* Ed. Myra Cohn Livingston. Holiday, 1982.
    Energetically selected and critically described, these Lear drolleries welcome both children and scholarly adults into the private world of Lear's nonsense.

Lear, Edward. *The Jumblies, and Other Nonsense Verses* and *The Pelican Chorus.* Illus. L. Leslie Brooke. Warne, 1954.
    One of the most pleasing picture books. See also *The Jumblies,* illus. Edward Gorey (W. R. Scott, 1968).

Lear, Edward. *Limericks by Lear.* Illus. Lois Ehlert. World, 1965.
    An imaginative and humorous visual use of abstraction, in a large picture-book format.

Lear, Edward. *Nonsense Songs.* Illus. L. Leslie Brooke. Warne, 1954.
    Nineteen nonsense verses taken from the author's *Book of Nonsense.* Also includes poems from *The Jumblies and Other Nonsense Verses* and *The Pelican Chorus and Other Nonsense Verses.*

Lear, Edward. *The Owl and the Pussy-Cat.* Illus. Barbara Cooney. Little, Brown, 1961.
    An everlasting delight. Also illustrated by William Pène Du Bois (Doubleday, 1961).

Lear, Edward. *The Pelican Chorus and Other Nonsense Verses.* Illus. Harold Berson. Parents, 1967.
    Intricate frumpery adorns this verse of majestic spoofing.

Lear, Edward. *The Quangle Wangle's Hat.* Illus. Helen Oxenbury. F. Watts, 1970.
    Superb, symbiotic creativity on the part of the illustrator gives this picture-book version a notable unity and charm.

Lear, Edward. *The Scroobious Pip.* Completed by Ogden Nash; illus. Nancy Ekholm Burkert. Harper, 1968.
    Fabulous nonsense.

Lear, Edward. *Two Laughable Lyrics.* Illus. Paul Galdone. Putnam's, 1966.

The artist has created delightful pictures for two bits of nonsense, "The Pobble Who Had No Toes" and "The Quangle Wangle's Hat."

Lear, Edward. *Whizz!* Illus. Janina Domanska. Macmillan, 1973.

Continuity is provided for a series of limericks.

Lee, Dennis. *Alligator Pie.* Illus. Frank Newfeld. Houghton Mifflin, 1975.

Swinging with a rhythm akin to Mother Goose, these rhymes "take up residence among hockey sticks and high rise" in a Canadian landscape. Grades K–4. See also *Nicholas Knock and Other People: Poems* (1976); *Garbage Delight* (1977); and *Jelly Belly,* illus. Juan Wijngaard (Macmillan of Canada, 1983).

Lobel, Arnold. *The Book of Pigericks: Pig Limericks.* Illus. by the author. Harper, 1983.

Thirty-eight original limericks on porcine lives and times. The warmth and delight of the illustrations match the verse. Grades 1–4.

Love, Katherine Isabel. *A Little Laughter.* Illus. Walter H. Lorraine. Crowell, 1957.

Compiled with a fine sense of the ridiculous. Grades 2–6.

Low, Joseph. *There Was a Wise Crow.* Illus. by the author. Follett, 1969.

Absurd rhymes, with fine, expressive drawings. Grades K–3.

Merriam, Eve. *Out Loud.* Designed by Harriet Sherman. Atheneum, 1973.

Playful, both visually and aurally. Grades 3–6.

Reeves, James. *Prefabulous Animiles.* Illus. Edward Ardizzone. Dutton, 1960.

Verses about creatures, such as the Hippocrump, the Nimp, the Doze, and others, that appear in terrifying shape on the pages. Grades 2–6. See also *More Prefabulous Animiles* (1975).

Reid, Alastair. *Ounce, Dice, Trice.* Illus. Ben Shahn. Gregg, 1980.

Inspired play with words. First published in 1958.

Richards, Laura E. *Tirra Lirra: Rhymes Old and New.* Foreword, May Hill Arbuthnot; illus. Marguerite Davis. Little, Brown, 1955.

Nonsense verses published in the *St. Nicholas* a generation ago, with some of the author's more recent rhymes.

Rieu, E. V. *The Flattered Flying Fish and Other Poems.* Illus. E. H. Shepard. Dutton, 1962.

The serious work of a classics scholar and translator, this volume of nonsense and poetry has the wit and sparkle associated with Lear and Carroll. Grades 4 and up.

Schwartz, Alvin. *Tomfoolery: Trickery and Foolery with Words.* Illus. Glen Rounds. Harper, 1973.

Verbal tricks, puzzlers, and stories collected from American folklore.

Sendak, Maurice. *Pierre: A Cautionary Tale in Five Chapters and a Prologue.* Illus. by the author. Harper, 1962.

An irresistible combination of rhyme and droll humor.

Silverstein, Shel. *Where the Sidewalk Ends.* Illus. by the author. Harper, 1974.

A collection of original wit and spoofing. See also *A Light in the Attic* (1981).

Smith, William Jay. *Mr. Smith and Other Nonsense.* Illus. Don Bolognese. Delacorte, A Seymour Lawrence Book, 1968.

An assortment of original nonsense verse. Grades 3–6. See also *Laughing Time: Nonsense Poems* (1980), illus. Fernando Krahn.

Tripp, Wallace, comp. *A Great Big Ugly Man Came Up and Tied His Horse to Me: A Book of Nonsense Verse.* Illus. by the compiler. Little, Brown, 1973.

Mostly traditional, these verses are generously illustrated. See also *Granfa' Grig Had a Pig and Other Rhymes without Reason from Mother Goose* (1976).

Withers, Carl, comp. *A Rocket in My Pocket: Rhymes and Chants of Young Americans.* Illus. Susanne Suba. Holt, 1948.

One of the most varied and appealing assortments of nonsense collected from folklore. All ages. See also *A World of Nonsense* (1968).

References for Adults

Cammaerts, Emile. *The Poetry of Nonsense.* Dutton, 1926.

Essays by a Belgian poet on the spirit of nonsense and its expression in poetry and art.

Chesterton, Gilbert K. "A Defense of Nonsense." In *Stories, Essays, and Poems.* Dutton, Everyman's Library.

A brief but profound discussion. "This simple sense of wonder at the shapes of things, and at their exuberant independence of our intellectual standards and our trivial definitions, is the basis of spirituality as it is the basis of nonsense."

Chukovsky, Kornei. "The Sense of Nonsense Verse." In *From Two to Five,* by Kornei Chukovsky; trans. and ed. Miriam Morton; foreword, Frances Clarke Sayers. Rev. ed. Univ. of California Press, 1968.

De la Mare, Walter. "Lewis Carroll." In *The Eighteen-Eighties: Essays by Fellows of the Royal Society of Literature.* Ed. Walter de la Mare. 1930. Reprint. Scholarly Press, 1971.
    The limericks of Edward Lear as well as the imagination of Lewis Carroll are explored in this perceptive essay on nonsense.

Empson, William. "Alice in Wonderland." In *Some Versions of Pastoral.* Chatto & Windus, 1935; New Directions, 1960.
    A critical approach to the mind of Carroll as well as an appreciation of his genius. The work of a distinguished contemporary critic.

Sewell, Elizabeth. *The Field of Nonsense.* Folcroft, 1952.
    Nonsense is described as a game of the spirit as well as of the intellect, based upon the work of Edward Lear and Lewis Carroll. An original piece of scholarship.

Edward Lear

Davidson, Angus. *Edward Lear: Landscape Painter and Nonsense Poet, 1812–1888.* Dutton, 1939.
    "How pleasant to know Mr. Lear!" through this biography of the English artist and limerick writer.

Fisher, Crispin. "A Load of Old Nonsense: Edward Lear Resurrected by Four Publishers." In *Children and Literature,* ed. Virginia Haviland. Scott, Foresman, 1973.

Hofer, Philip. *Edward Lear.* Oxford Univ. Press, 1962.
    A brief appreciation of Lear's nonsense and drawings.

Lear, Edward. *Letters of Edward Lear to Chichester Fortescue, Lord Carlingford, and Frances, Countess Waldegrave.* Ed. Lady Strachey. Unwin, 1908.
    Letters written between 1847 and 1864, containing many interesting anecdotes. The introduction includes Lear's own account of his work.

Lehmann, John. *Edward Lear and His World.* Thames & Hudson, 1977.
    A scholarly, readable account of Lear's life and art. Profusely illustrated.

Noakes, Vivien. *Edward Lear: The Life of a Wanderer.* Houghton Mifflin, 1969.
    A revealing portrait of a complex man.

Laura E. Richards

Coatsworth, Elizabeth. "Laura E. Richards." *The Junior Bookshelf* (Mar. 1924).

Eaton, Anne Thaxter. "Laura E. Richards." *The Horn Book Magazine* 17 (July–Aug. 1941), pp. 247–55.

Mahony, Bertha E. "Salute to Laura E. Richards." *The Horn Book Magazine* 17 (July–Aug. 1941), p. 245.

Richards, Laura E. *Stepping Westward.* Appleton-Century, 1931.
    Mrs. Richards' autobiography reads like a story, revealing a singularly rich and happy life.

Viguers, Ruth Hill. "Laura E. Richards, Joyous Companion." *The Horn Book Magazine* 32; Pt. I (Apr. 1956); Pt. II (June 1956); Pt. III (Oct. 1956); Pt. IV (Dec. 1956).

3 Voices of Childhood

Books for Children

Anthologies

Adams, Adrienne, sel. *Poetry of Earth.* Illus. by the author. Scribner's, 1972.
    A feeling of sympathy for life and the emotional unity of living creatures pervades this collection. Grades 5 and up.

Adoff, Arnold, ed. *I Am the Darker Brother: An Anthology of Modern Poems by Negro Americans.* Illus. Benny Andrews; foreword, Charlemae Rollins. Macmillan, 1968.
    Poets such as Mari Evans, LeRoi Jones, Quandra Prettyman, Calvin Hernton, and others are represented with the better-known Langston Hughes, Arna Bontemps, and Gwendolyn Brooks. Biographies and notes about the poems are appended. Grades 7 and up.

Adoff, Arnold, ed. *My Black Me: A Beginning Book of Black Poetry.* Dutton, 1974.
    Black poets write about blackness. See also *Black Out Loud* (Macmillan, 1970). Grades 5 and up.

Adoff, Arnold, ed. *The Poetry of Black America: An Anthology of the Twentieth Century.* Intro. Gwendolyn Brooks. Harper, 1973.

For the older reader and adults, this is a singular compilation, reaching back to Du Bois, bringing contemporary poets together. Grades 9 and up.

Adshead, Gladys L., and Annis Duff, comps. *Inheritance of Poetry.* Decorations, Nora S. Unwin. Houghton Mifflin, 1948.

An anthology of rare distinction that bears testimony to the compilers' deep delight in poetry. Excellent indexes with a list of musical settings. All ages.

Allen, Terry, ed. *The Whispering Wind: Poetry by Young American Indians.* Intro. Mae J. Durham. Doubleday, 1972.

The statements by young Indians about their heritage and their feelings show both a sense of individual strength and a feeling of strong ties as a people. Grades 6 and up.

Arbuthnot, May Hill, and Shelton L. Root, Jr., comps. *Time for Poetry.* Illus. Arthur Paul. 3d gen. ed. Scott, Foresman, 1968.

"A representative collection of poetry for children, to be used in the classroom, home, or camp; especially planned for college classes in children's literature; with a special section entitled 'Keeping Poetry and Children Together.'" Grades 1–6.

Auslander, Joseph, and Frank Ernest Hill, comps. *Winged Horse Anthology.* Doubleday, 1929.

A companion volume to *The Winged Horse: The Story of the Poets and Their Poetry,* which includes the poems mentioned in this book. The arrangement is chronological. Representative selections illustrate the qualities that made each poet great. Grades 7–9.

Baron, Virginia Olsen, ed. *The Seasons of Time: Tanka Poetry of Ancient Japan.* Illus. Yasuhide Kobashi. Dial, 1968.

Seasons, landscapes, and the small miracles of nature are kept fresh through the centuries. See also *Sunset in a Spider Web: Sijo Poetry of Ancient Korea* (Holt, 1974). Grades 4 and up.

Behn, Harry, trans. *Cricket Songs: Japanese Haiku.* Illus. Sesshu and other Japanese masters. Harcourt, 1964.

A poet's skill and sensitivity makes this haiku collection valuable. All ages. See also *More Cricket Songs* (1971).

Bennett, Jill, comp. *Days Are Where We Live.* Illus. Maureen Roffey. Lothrop, Lee & Shepard, 1982.

Musical language and direct emotion speak to the very young child in this intimate compilation. Poems of the daily round are interpreted in zestful illustrations. Grades 1–4. See also *Roger Was a Razor Fish, and Other Poems* (1980).

Bierhorst, John, ed. *In the Trail of the Wind: American Indian Poems and Ritual Orations.* Designed by Jane Byars Bierhorst. Farrar, Straus & Giroux, 1971.

A notable scholarly achievement, presented with sympathy and beauty. Grades 6 and up.

Blishen, Edward, comp. *Oxford Book of Poetry for Children.* Illus. Brian Wildsmith. F. Watts, 1964.

An enticing collection of English poetry intended to introduce children beyond nursery rhymes to serious poetry. Grades 1 and up.

Bogan, Louise, and William Jay Smith, comps. *The Golden Journey: Poems for Young People.* Illus. Fritz Kredel. Reilly & Lee, 1965.

The discriminating selections of two well-known poets bring together poetry that is varied and lively. All ages.

Bontemps, Arna, ed. *Hold Fast to Dreams: Poems Old and New.* Follett, 1969.

A poet's collection of poems he "couldn't forget." All ages. See also *Golden Slippers: An Anthology of Negro Poetry for Young Readers* (Harper, 1941) and *American Negro Poetry* (Hill and Wang, 1963).

Brewton, Sara, and John E. Brewton, comps. *America Forever New: A Book of Poems.* Illus. Ann Grifalconi. Harper, 1968.

The people, the history, the landscape, the cities, the land—all are touched in a compilation marked with vigor. Grades 5 and up.

Canfield, Kenneth F. *Selections from French Poetry.* Illus. Tomi Ungerer. Harvey, 1965.

Presented to kindle an interest in French poetry, this bilingual collection ranges from the fifteenth century to the present. Grades 7 and up.

Carlisle, Olga Andreyev, and Rose Styron, eds. *Modern Russian Poetry.* Trans. by the editors; illus. with photos. Viking, 1972.

Poetry of contemporary Russian poets is placed within the context of a biographical and historical framework. The singular popularity of poetry within the Soviet Union is discussed. "Every poem presented in this book is well known in the USSR." Grades 6 and up.

Causley, Charles, ed. *Modern Ballads and Story Poems.* Illus. Anne Netherwood. F. Watts, 1964.

In their compelling drama and compressed power, these poems display the flexibility and appeal of the story form. Grades 6 and up. See also *Dawn and Dusk: Poems of Our Time* (1962); *The Puffin Book of Magic Verse* (Kestrel/Puffin, 1974); and *The Puffin Book of Salt-Sea Verse* (Kestrel/Puffin, 1978).

Clark, Leonard, comp. *All Along Down Along: A Book of Stories in Verse*. Illus. Pauline Baynes. Longman Young, 1971.
Humor and drama combined with rhythm give momentum to these pieces. Grades 2–6.

Cole, William, sel. *The Birds and the Beasts Were There: Animal Poems*. Woodcuts, Helen Siegl. World, 1963.
Infused with gaiety and compassion, these poems range from the mischievous and humorous to the tender and stricken: a supple, varied collection. Grades 4 and up. See also *I Went to the Animal Fair* (1958), for very young children.

Cole, William, ed. *Humorous Poetry for Children*. Illus. Ervine Metzl. Philomel, 1955.
As the author says in his introduction, this collection combines the two best things in the world, laughter and poetry. Grades 3–8. See also *Poems of Magic and Spells* (Philomel, 1960); *Poems for Seasons and Celebrations* (Philomel, 1961); *Oh, How Silly!* (Viking, 1970); *Oh, What Nonsense!* (Viking, 1970); *The Poet's Tales: A New Book of Story Poems* (World, 1971); and *Poem Stew* (Harper, 1981).

Cole, William, sel. *Poems from Ireland*. Illus. William Stobbs. Crowell, 1972.
Arranged alphabetically by the poets' last names, this brings contemporary and past poets together, and ends the collection, conveniently, with Yeats. Grades 6 and up.

Colum, Padraic, ed. *Roofs of Gold: Poems to Read Aloud*. Macmillan, 1964.
A personal anthology compiled by a distinguished poet, storyteller, and critic. Grades 7 and up.

Corrin, Sara, and Stephen Corrin, eds. *Once upon a Rhyme: 101 Rhymes for Young Children*. Illus. Jill Bennett. Faber & Faber, 1982.
Primarily nonsense and light verse, but including some lyric and narrative poems, this collection is intended for children past the nursery rhyme age. Well chosen and vividly illustrated. Grades 2–4.

Crofut, William. *The Moon on the One Hand: Poetry in Song*. Illus. Susan Crofut; musical arrangements, Kenneth Cooper and Glenn Shattuck. Atheneum, A Margaret K. McElderry Book, 1975.

Responding to fine poetry with music becomes a way of enjoying both. The emphasis in this collection, which presents the poem first and then the music, is on nature, animals, and birds. Grades 4 and up.

De Gerez, Toni. *2-Rabbit, 7-Wind: Poems from Ancient Mexico Retold from Nahuatl Texts*. Illus. from *Design Motifs of Ancient Mexico,* by Jorge Enciso (Dover). Viking, 1971.
Poems from ancient ritual dance and ceremony. Grades 5 and up.

De la Mare, Walter, ed. *Come Hither*. Illus. Warren Chappell. 3d ed. Knopf, 1957.
A distinguished collection first published in 1922, this is gathered by a poet whose own poems have become classics. Grades 5 and up. See also *Tom Tiddler's Ground* (1962), for younger children.

Doob, Leonard W., ed. *A Crocodile Has Me by the Leg: African Poems*. Illus. Solomon Irein Wangboje. Walker, 1967.
Lively responses by unknown poets to a great variety of moods and events.

Downie, Mary Alice, and Barbara Robertson, comps. *The Wind Has Wings: Poems from Canada*. Illus. Elizabeth Cleaver. Walck, 1968.
An award-winner from Canada, this broad collection brings together traditional native poetry and French and English adult poetry and folk songs. Enhanced by energetic, textural illustrations. Grades 4 and up. See also *The New Wind Has Wings*, 2d ed., rev. and enl. (1984). Some poems from the first edition have been eliminated; new poems, new illustrations by Cleaver have been added.

Dunning, Stephen, Edward Lueders, and Hugh Smith, comps. *Reflections on a Gift of Watermelon Pickle . . . and Other Modern Verse*. Lothrop, 1967.
Illustrated with provocative black-and-white photographs, this emphatically contemporary collection is directed to older children and adolescents. Grades 6 and up. See also *Some Haystacks Don't Even Have Any Needle, and Other Complete Modern Poems* (Scott, Foresman, 1969).

Forberg, Ati, ed. and illus. *On a Grass-Green Horn: Old Scotch and English Ballads*. Atheneum, 1965.
A short compilation of eighteen ballads emphasizing mystery and magic, with expressionistic illustrations. Grades 4 and up.

Foster, John, comp. *A First Poetry Book*. Illus. Chris Orr, Martin Orr, and Joseph Wright. Oxford Univ. Press, 1979.

A select collection of contemporary British and American poets for the early grades. With bright, entertaining illustrations. Grades 2–5. See also the companion volumes, *A Second Poetry Book* (1980); *A Third Poetry Book* (1982); and *A Fourth Poetry Book* (1983).

Greaves, Griselda, ed. *The Burning Thorn.* Macmillan, 1971.
Intended for older children and teen-agers, this powerful, romantic anthology is arranged sequentially by the seven ages of man, forming a life story in verse. Grades 5 and up.

Gregory, Horace, and Marya Zaturenska, eds. *The Silver Swan: Poems of Romance and Mystery.* Wood engravings, Diana Bloomfield. Holt, 1966.
This collaboration between two poets brings sensitivity and fine discernment in selections that surprise and delight. Grades 6 and up. See also *The Crystal Cabinet* (1962).

Grigson, Geoffrey, comp. *The Cherry Tree.* Vanguard, 1962.
An imaginative, wide-ranging collection. All ages.

Grigson, Geoffrey, comp. *Rainbows, Fleas and Flowers: A Nature Anthology.* Decorations, Glynn Thomas. Vanguard, 1982.
The compiler's individuality and subtle perceptions make this anthology varied and surprising. Grades 6 and up.

Hannum, Sara, and John Terry Chase, comps. *To Play Man Number One.* Illus. Erwin Schachner. Atheneum, 1969.
The title and the mood are taken from Wallace Stevens's *Man with the Blue Guitar.* The compilers have "sought to present a powerful and imaginative collection of poems on the condition of modern man." See also *Lean Out of the Window* (1965) and *The Wind Is Round* (1970).

Hayden, Robert, ed. *Kaleidoscope: Poems by American Negro Poets.* Harcourt, 1967.
The editor, a professor of English at Fisk University, is himself a poet. Grades 6 and up.

Heaney, Seamus, and Ted Hughes, sel. *The Rattle Bag: An Anthology of Poetry.* Faber & Faber, 1982.
A discriminating selection by two acclaimed poets. The alphabetical arrangement by title of classic and contemporary poetry written for both adults and children adds an unexpectedness and excitement to this wide-ranging collection. Grades 6 and up.

Hearn, Michael Patrick, sel. *A Day in Verse: Breakfast, Books, and Dreams.* Illus. Barbara Garrison. Warne, 1981.
Handsome etchings add a graphic dimension to this collection of contemporary poems describing a single day in the lives of a brother and sister. Grades 1–4.

Hopkins, Lee Bennett, sel. *On Our Way: Poems of Pride and Love.* Photos, David Parks. Knopf, 1974.
Black poets speak of their pride and love. Grades 2–6. See also *Moments,* illus. Michael Hague (Harcourt, 1980); *The Sky Is Full of Song,* illus. Dirk Zimmer (Harper, 1983); and *A Song in Stone: City Poems,* photos by Anna Held Audette (Crowell, 1983).

Houston, James, ed. *Songs of the Dream People: Chants and Images from the Indians and Eskimos of North America.* Illus. by the editor. Atheneum, A Margaret K. McElderry Book, 1972.
Simple eloquence, directness, and compression characterize this collection. Grades 4 and up.

Jones, Hettie, sel. *The Trees Stand Shining: Poetry of the North American Indians.* Illus. Robert Andrew Parker. Dial, 1971.
Really songs, these poems from a variety of tribes range from war chants to lullabies. Grades 3 and up.

Jordan, June, ed. *Soulscript: Afro-American Poetry.* Doubleday, Zenith Books, 1970.
The editor, herself a poet, has taken the works of contemporary poets to help define the feelings and the relationships of black people. In her introduction, she says, "Reaction, memory, and dream: these are the springs of poetry. And a four-year-old flows among them as fully as any adult." Grades 6 and up.

Kherdian, David, ed. *Visions of America by the Poets of Our Time.* Illus. Nonny Hogrogian. Macmillan, 1973.
With William Carlos Williams's philosophy as a cornerstone, these poets bear testimony to his faith in the speech of common language as the art of poetry. Grades 6 and up.

Larrick, Nancy, sel. *Piper, Pipe That Song Again! Poems for Boys and Girls.* Illus. Kelly Oechsli. Random House, 1965.
A sense of humor infuses this collection. See also *Piping Down the Valleys Wild* (Delacorte, 1968); *Room for Me and a Mountain Lion: Poetry of Open Space* (M. Evans, 1974); and *Crazy to Be Alive in Such a Strange World: Poems about People* (M. Evans, 1977).

Lewis, Richard, ed. *Out of the Earth I Sing: Poetry and Songs of Primitive Peoples of the World.* Norton, 1968.

Illustrated with reproductions of primitive art, this is a stirring collection of tribal poetry—chants, incantations, and songs—from vanished and vanishing cultures. See also Lewis's anthology of haiku, *In a Spring Garden,* illus. Ezra Jack Keats (Dial, 1965), and *The Luminous Landscape: Chinese Art and Poetry* (Doubleday, 1981).

Livingston, Myra Cohn, ed. *Listen, Children, Listen: An Anthology of Poems for the Very Young.* Illus. Trina Schart Hyman. Harcourt, 1972.

Humor, wonder, and musical rhythm are ingredients here. Grades 1–4. See also *What a Wonderful Bird the Frog Are: An Assortment of Humorous Poetry and Verse* (1973); *A Circle of Seasons,* illus. Leonard E. Fisher (Holiday, 1982); and *Why Am I Grown So Cold: Poems of the Unknowable* (Atheneum, 1982).

Livingston, Myra Cohn, ed. *One Little Room, an Everywhere: Poems of Love.* Illus. Antonio Frasconi. Atheneum, A Margaret K. McElderry Book, 1975.

The subtlety, complexity, and universal qualities of love emerge from this collection. Grades 6 and up.

Livingston, Myra Cohn, ed. *A Tune Beyond Us: A Collection of Poetry.* Illus. James J. Spanfeller. Harcourt, 1968.

A wide-reaching selection that includes the original language of the poem whenever it is given in English translation. Grades 6 and up. See also *Speak Roughly to Your Little Boy: A Collection of Parodies and Burlesques, Together with the Original Poems, Chosen and Annotated for Young People,* illus. Joseph Low (Harcourt, 1971).

Love, Katherine, ed. *Pocketful of Rhymes.* Illus. Henrietta Jones. Crowell, 1946.

A devotion to poetry and the experience of sharing it with children have gone into the making of this collection by a children's librarian of the New York Public Library. Grades 2–4. See also *A Little Laughter,* in which she has gathered a happy selection of lighthearted verse.

McDonald, Gerald D., comp. *A Way of Knowing: A Collection of Poems for Boys.* Illus. Clare Ross and John Ross. Crowell, 1959.

This is really for girls too—the poems are chosen for their directness and depth. An unusually appealing collection. Grades 4 and up.

Mackay, David. *A Flock of Words: An Anthology of Poetry for Children and Others.* Preface, Benjamin DeMott; illus. Margery Gill. Harcourt, 1970.

Collected over a long period of time, these poems have been tried and have endured. Grades 6 and up.

Manning-Sanders, Ruth, comp. *A Bundle of Ballads.* Illus. William Stobbs. Lippincott, 1959.

The singing tone and the understated drama of the ballad mark this collection. Grades 6 and up.

Mayer, Mercer, ed. and illus. *The Poison Tree and Other Poems.* Scribner's, 1977.

Designed with a sensuous appeal in illustrations and format, this anthology contains a poignant choice of lyric poetry. The subtle restraint in the artwork complements the emphasis on poetry of reflection and emotion.

Mitchell, Cynthia. *Under the Cherry Tree: Poems for Children.* Illus. Satomi Ichikawa. Collins, 1979.

A collection of primarily lyric poems, accompanied by handsome watercolor paintings in the style of the classic French illustrator, Maurice Boutet de Monvel. Grades 1–4.

Moore, Lilian. *Go with the Poem.* McGraw-Hill, 1979.

This anthology of outstanding contemporary adult and children's poetry includes light and serious verse on a variety of themes. Grades 5 and up.

Moore, Lilian, and Judith Thurman, comps. *To See the World Afresh.* Atheneum, 1974.

A sharply focused collection, emphasizing the direct and the genuine.

Morrison, Lillian, comp. *Sprints and Distances.* Illus. Clare Ross and John Ross. Harper, 1965.

Sports in poetry and the poetry in sport. All ages.

Nash, Ogden, sel. *Everybody Ought to Know.* Illus. Rose Shirvanian. Harper, 1961.

This is what Ogden Nash calls "a sparrow's-eye view," a view that takes in the heights, the depths, and the middle, too. Grades 4–12. See also *The Moon Is Shining Bright as Day* (1953).

Opie, Iona, and Peter Opie, eds. *The Oxford Book of Children's Verse.* Oxford Univ. Press, 1973.

Arranged chronologically according to the appearance of the poetry, this is chiefly a compilation of British poets with the stated intention "to make available in one place the classics of children's poetry." All ages.

Palmer, Geoffrey, and Noel Lloyd, sels. *Round About Eight.* Illus. Denis Wrigley. Warne, 1972.

A lighthearted assortment that is part of a series

whose titles indicate the ages of the audiences sought: *Fives, Sixes and Sevens,* comp. Marjorie Stephenson, *One, Two, Three, Four,* comp. Mary Grice. Originates in England. Grades 3–6.

Parker, Elinor, comp. *Here and There: One Hundred Poems about Places.* Illus. Peter Spier. Crowell, 1967.

A variety of poets and forms of poetry. Poems about places familiar, exotic, and magical around the world and off the map. Grades 5–7. See also *The Singing and the Gold: Poems Translated from World Literature,* illus. Clare Leighton (1962), and *Four Seasons, Five Senses* (Scribner's, 1974).

Plotz, Helen, comp. *Imagination's Other Place.* Wood engravings, Clare Leighton. Harper, 1955.

A unique collection of poems of science and mathematics, selected with imagination. Grades 7 and up. *Untune the Sky* includes poems of music and the dance. See also *The Earth Is the Lord's: Poems of the Spirit* (1965); *Poems from the German* (1967); *The Marvelous Light: Poets and Poetry* (1970); and *As I Walked Out One Evening: A Book of Ballads* (Greenwillow, 1976).

Prelutsky, Jack, sel. *The Random House Book of Poetry for Children.* Illus. Arnold Lobel. Random, 1983.

A flood of robust, energetic illustrations extend and illuminate more than five hundred poems in this handsome, comprehensive anthology. The editor, a renowned children's poet, has selected predominantly twentieth-century poetry. Grades 1–6.

Read, Herbert. *This Way, Delight.* Illus. Juliet Kepes. Pantheon, 1956.

"This way, this way, seek delight." The poet, writer, and critic Herbert Read calls readers not only to come and taste of the delights, but, in an afterword, "What is Poetry?" he urges them to write poetry, to enjoy the pleasures of creation. Grades 3 and up.

Reed, Gwendolyn, comp. *Out of the Ark.* Illus. Gabriele Margules. Atheneum, 1968.

An anthology of animal verse. Grades 6–8. See also *Bird Songs* (Atheneum, 1969) and *Songs the Sandman Sings* (1969).

Reit, Ann. *Alone amid All This Noise: A Collection of Women's Poetry.* Four Winds, 1976.

From the sixth century up to the present time, this collection presents a wide variety of female poets, themes, and concerns. Grades 5 and up.

Resnick, Seymour. *Spanish-American Poetry: A Bilingual Selection.* Illus. Anne Marie Jauss. Harvey, 1964. Grades 4 and up.

A variety of poets and forms of poetry. Grades 4 and up.

Scott-Mitchell, Clare, ed. *When a Goose Meets a Moose: Poems for Young Children.* Illus. Louise Hogan. Methuen Australia, 1980.

A warmly intimate selection for the youngest. Accessible and entertaining. Grades K–4.

Smith, William Jay, sel. *Poems from France.* Illus. Roger Duvoisin. Crowell, 1967.

The original poem is presented in French alongside the English translation. Grades 5 and up. See also *Laughing Time* (Delacorte, 1980) and *A Green Place: Modern Poems* (Delacorte, 1982).

Summerfield, Geoffrey, ed. *Voices: Books 1–3.* Rand McNally, 1969.

An imaginative series of interlinking anthologies which provide a broad range of adult and child poetry, traditional and literary. The powers and emotional colors of poetry are complemented by the fine photographic illustrations. Originated in England. Grades 5 and up. See also *First Voices: Books 1–4* (Knopf, 1971–1973).

Individual Poets

Adoff, Arnold. *Make a Circle, Keep Us In: Poems for a Good Day.* Illus. Ronald Himler. Delacorte, 1975.

Brief, impressionistic thoughts and feelings reflect the sensual and emotional reactions of the young child. Grades K–2. See also *Big Sister Tells Me That I'm Black* (Holt, 1976); *Outside Inside Poems* (Lothrop, Lee & Shepard, 1981); and *All the Colors of the Race* (Lothrop, Lee & Shepard, 1982), the latter two illustrated by John Steptoe.

Aiken, Conrad. *Cats and Bats and Things with Wings.* Illus. Milton Glaser. Atheneum, 1965.

Lighthearted verse about the animal world. Grades K–4.

Aiken, Joan. *The Skin Spinners: Poems.* Illus. Ken Rinciari. Viking, 1976.

A collection of poetry for older children on the necessity of imagination, human relationships, and poetry itself. Elastically shifting content and style. Grades 5 and up.

Behn, Harry. *The Golden Hive.* Illus. by the author. Harcourt, 1966.

The poems reflect the author's love of nature, remembrance of his own childhood, and his interest in significant events. Grades 4–6. See also *The Little Hill* (1949); *All Kinds of Time* (1950); and *Windy Morning* (1953).

Belting, Natalia M. *Calendar Moon.* Illus. Bernarda Bryson. Holt, 1964.

Poetic interpretations of many names given to the months by various peoples and tribes. Grades 4 and up. See also *The Sun Is a Golden Earring* (1962) and *Whirlwind Is a Ghost Dancing* (Dutton, 1974), poems from tribes of North American Indians.

Benét, Rosemary, and Stephen Vincent Benét. *A Book of Americans*. Illus. Charles Child. Rev. ed. Holt, 1952.
　　Stirring poems describe the lives and characters of famous men and women from Columbus to Woodrow Wilson. Grades 5–8.

Blake, William. *Poems of William Blake*. Sel. Amelia H. Munson; illus. William Blake. Crowell, 1964.
　　An excellent selection from the works of an extraordinary poet-artist. Grades 8 and up. See also *Songs of Innocence,* illus. and musical arrangements, Ellen Raskin, 2 vols. Doubleday, 1966.

Blake, William. *William Blake: An Introduction*. Sel. and ed. Anne Malcolmson. Harcourt, 1967.
　　Selections from Blake's poems and prose, with notes on each. Grades 7–9.

Brooks, Gwendolyn. *Bronzeville Boys and Girls*. Illus. Ronni Solbert. Harper, 1956.
　　A fine sense of proportion keeps these poems for young children authentic and accessible. Grades K–3.

Browning, Robert. *Pied Piper of Hamelin*. Illus. Kate Greenaway. Warne, 1889.
　　A favorite poem enriched with Kate Greenaway's charming illustrations. Grades 4–7.

Burns, Robert. *Hand in Hand We'll Go*. Illus. Nonny Hogrogian. Crowell, 1965.
　　A good introduction to Burns. Grades 6–8.

Carroll, Lewis. *Poems of Lewis Carroll*. Sel. Myra Cohn Livingstone; illus. John Tenniel, Harry Furniss, Henry Holiday, Arthur B. Frost, and Lewis Carroll. Harper, 1973.
　　A skillful and scholarly selection that centers on Carroll's humorous poetry. Grades 4 and up.

Causley, Charles. *Figgie Hobbin*. Illus. Trina Schart Hyman. Walker, 1974.
　　A stunning collection of bright, quick poems in traditional verse forms. Striking wit and fine craftmanship from one of the best contemporary poets. See also *Hill of the Fairy Calf* (Hodder & Stoughton, 1976) and *The Tail of the Trinosaur* (1980).

Chaucer, Geoffrey. *A Taste of Chaucer: Selections from "The Canterbury Tales."* Sel. and ed. Anne Malcolmson; illus. Enrico Arno. Harcourt, 1964.

An excellent introduction to Chaucer. Each tale is introduced with a few lines of verse in Middle English. Grades 8–9.

Ciardi, John. *I Met a Man*. Illus. Robert Osborn. Houghton Mifflin, 1961.
　　Skillful repetition and rhythm make this especially appealing to the very young reader. Grades 1–3. See also *The Reason for the Pelican* (Lippincott, 1959); *Monster Den or Look What Happened at My House and to It* (1966); and *Fast and Slow: Poems for Advanced Children and Beginning Parents* (1975).

Clifton, Lucille. *Some of the Days of Everett Anderson*. Illus. Evaline Ness. Holt, 1970.
　　The subject is six years old, black, and living with his mother and father, both of whom work. Grades K–2. See also *Everett Anderson's Christmas Coming* (1972); *Everett Anderson's Year* (1974); *Everett Anderson's Friend* (1976); *Everett Anderson's 1-2-3* (1977); and *Everett Anderson's Nine Month Long* (1978).

Coatsworth, Elizabeth. *The Sparrow Bush*. Illus. Stefan Martin. Norton, 1966.
　　A poet shares her delight in nature. A short commentary on poetry prefaces the collection. Grades 4–6. See also *Down Half the World,* illus. Zena Bernstein (Macmillan, 1968). See also her illustrated single poem *Under the Green Willow,* illus. Janina Domanska (Macmillan, 1971).

Coleridge, Samuel Taylor. *The Rime of the Ancient Mariner*. Illus. C. Walter Hodges. Coward-McCann, 1971.
　　The horror of the tale is highlighted in the illustrations; marginal notes accompany the narrative poem. Grades 7 and up.

Cullen, Countee. *The Lost Zoo*. Illus. Joseph Low. Follett, 1969.
　　A welcome reissue of a book first published in 1940 by Harper. Grades 3–5.

Dahl, Roald. *Revolting Rhymes*. Illus. Quentin Blake. Knopf, 1982.
　　Iconoclastic retellings of folktales in verse by a natural satirist. Irreverent illustrations capture the slapstick, ironic tone. Grades 3 and up.

De Gasztold, Carmen Bernos. *Prayers from the Ark*. Trans., foreword, and epilogue, Rumer Godden; illus. Jean Primrose. Viking, 1962.
　　Poems of unusual and disarming truth, translated from the French. Grades 3 and up. See also *Creatures' Choir* (1965).

De la Mare, Walter. *Peacock Pie*. Illus. Barbara Cooney. Knopf, 1961.

Poems of gay fantasy, clear imagery, and sheer beauty. Grades 3–5. See also *Bells and Grass* (Viking, 1963) and *Rhymes and Verses* (Holt, 1947).

Dickinson, Emily. *Poems of Emily Dickinson.* Sel. Helen Plotz; illus. Robert Kipniss. Harper, 1964.
Poems that "reflect the myriad interests that were part of Emily Dickinson's quiet life." Grades 7–9. See also *A Letter to the World: Poems for Young Readers by Emily Dickinson,* sel. and intro. Rumer Godden (Macmillan, 1968), and *I'm Nobody, Who Are You?* illus. Rex Schneider (Stemmer House, 1978).

Eliot, T. S. *Old Possum's Book of Practical Cats.* Harcourt, 1939.
A remarkable collection of poems that have become great favorites, not only with cat lovers, but with all who delight in the imaginative use of playful language. Grades 3 and up. Also available in an edition with Edward Gorey's spry illustrations. (Harcourt, 1982).

Farjeon, Eleanor. *Then There Were Three: Cherrystones; The Mulberry Bush; and The Starry Floor.* Illus. Isobel Morton-Sale and John Morton-Sale. Lippincott, 1965.
Combines in one attractive volume the author's three books of verse first published in England. Grades 4–6. See *The Children's Bells* (Walck, 1960) and *Around the Seasons* (Walck, 1969). See also the recent, comprehensive collection, *Invitation to a Mouse and Other Poems,* sel. Annabel Farjeon, illus. Antony Maitland (Pelham Books, 1981).

Field, Rachel. *Poems.* Illus. by the author. Macmillan, 1957.
A special sympathy for childhood perceptions and feelings shapes these poems. Grades 1–6.

Fisher, Aileen. *Feathered Ones and Furry.* Illus. Eric Carle. Crowell, 1971.
A small selection of nature verse celebrating the world of birds and beasts. See also *Out in the Dark and the Daylight* (Harper, 1980). Grades K–3.

Froman, Robert. *Seeing Things: A Book of Poems.* Illus. Ray Barber. Harper, 1974.
Simple street haiku take life from typographical design and visual and verbal punning. Concrete poetry for children. Grades 4 and up. See also *Street Poems* (McCall, 1971).

Frost, Robert. *You Come Too.* Wood engravings, Thomas W. Nason. Holt, 1959.
A selection of Frost's poems most interesting to

boys and girls. Grades 4–7. See also *Complete Poems* (1949); *In the Clearing* (1962); *Stopping by Woods on a Snowy Evening,* illus. by Susan Jeffers (Dutton, 1978); and *A Swinger of Birches: Poems of Robert Frost for Young People,* illus. Peter Koeppen (Stemmer House, 1982).

Giovanni, Nikki. *Spin a Soft Black Song: Poems for Children.* Illus. Charles Bible. Hill & Wang, 1971.
Written especially for young black children by a poet who remembers her own childhood. Grades 1–4. See also *Ego-Tripping and Other Poems for Young People* (Lawrence Hill, 1974).

Graves, Robert. *The Penny Fiddle: Poems for Children.* Illus. Edward Ardizzone. Doubleday, 1960.
Selections from a notable contemporary poet. Grades 4 and up.

Greenfield, Eloise. *Honey, I Love and Other Love Poems.* Illus. Leo Dillon and Diane Dillon. Harper, 1978.
Free verse rich in musical phrasing reveals the life and emotions of a small black girl. Grades 1–4.

Hughes, Langston. *Don't You Turn Back.* Sel. Lee Bennett Hopkins; illus. Ann Grifalconi. Knopf, 1969.
Poignant and lasting lyric statements. Grades 5 and up.

Hughes, Ted. *Season Songs.* Illus. Leonard Baskin. Viking, 1975.
A stunning book, with exceptional art, both in the poetry and the pictures. Grades 5 and up. See also *Moon-Bells* (Chatto & Windus, 1978) and *Under the North Star* (Viking, 1981).

Issa. *A Few Flies and I.* Sel. Jean Merrill and Ronni Solbert; trans. R. H. Blyth and Nobuyaki Yuasa; illus. Ronni Solbert. Pantheon, 1969.
Elegant simplicities from the master of haiku. Grades 4 and up.

Jarrell, Randall. *The Bat-Poet.* Macmillan, 1964.
A literary parable on the nature of poetry. Jarrell is generally acclaimed as one of our most distinctive contemporary poets. Grades 4–7. See also an illustrated excerpt from the above in *A Bat is Born,* illus. John Schoenherr (Doubleday, 1978).

Jordon, June. *Who Look at Me.* Crowell, 1969.
The complexity of identity and of being black is the focus of this book. Grades 5 and up.

Kumin, Maxine W. *Speedy Digs Downside Up.* Illus. Ezra Jack Keats. Putnam's, 1964.
A racing, humorous narrative poem about the

fantastic exploits of Speedy Horatio Alger LaRue. Grades 2–6. See also *No One Writes a Letter to a Snail* (1962).

Kuskin, Karla. *Dogs and Dragons, Trees and Dreams.* Illus. by the author. Harper, 1980.

This representative collection of the work of the award-winning children's poet includes introductory notes on poetry appreciation and writing. Accompanied by Kuskin's own drawings, which complement the blithe and delicate tone of the poems. Grades 2–6. See also *Near the Window Tree: Poems and Notes* (1975).

Lawrence, D. H. *Birds, Beasts, and the Third Thing.* Sel. and illus. Alice and Martin Provensen. Viking, 1982.

A sensitive selection from Lawrence emphasizing his intense response to nature, analytical perceptions of society, and wonder at the universe. Accessible to younger children through the narrative continuity of the striking illustrations. Grades 4 and up.

Lawrence, D. H. *Poems.* Sel. William Cole; illus. Ellen Raskin. Viking, 1967.

Precision of observation, "an uncanny immediacy," and a strong emotional flow give these poems individual vitality. Grades 6 and up.

Lindsay, Vachel. *Johnny Appleseed, and Other Poems.* Illus. George Richards. Macmillan, Children's Classics, 1928.

Selections from "The Congo" and the "Chinese Nightingale" are included with rhymes and songs for younger children. Grades 4 and up.

Livingston, Myra Cohn. *The Malibu and Other Poems.* Illus. James J. Spanfeller. Atheneum, A Margaret K. McElderry Book, 1972.

Poems of original vision and personal experience, succinctly stated. Grades 6 and up. See also *A Crazy Flight and Other Poems* (Harcourt, 1969), for younger readers; *The Way Things Are* (Atheneum, 1974); *4-Way Stop and Other Poems* (Atheneum, 1976); and *No Way of Knowing: Dallas Poems* (Atheneum, 1980).

Livingston, Myra Cohn. *Whispers and Other Poems.* Illus. Jacqueline Chwast. Harcourt, 1958.

Verses filled with gaiety, exuberance, and tenderness. Grades K–3. See also *Wide Awake and Other Poems* (Harcourt, 1959); *I'm Hiding* (1961); *Happy Birthday!* (Harcourt, 1964); and *The Moon and a Star and Other Poems* (1965).

McCord, David. *Every Time I Climb a Tree.* Illus. Marc Simont. Little, Brown, 1967.

The poet's selection of twenty-five of his favorite poems from *Far and Few; Take Sky;* and *All Day Long.* Grades 3 and up. See also *For Me to Say: Rhymes of the Never Was and Always Is* (1970); *Away and Ago: Rhymes of the Never Was and Always Is* (1975); and *The Star in the Pail* (1975). His entire work is collected in *One at a Time* (1977).

McGinley, Phyllis. *Wonderful Time.* Illus. John Alcorn. Lippincott, 1966.

About clocks, time, and feelings. Grades 2–5.

Merriam, Eve. *It Doesn't Always Have to Rhyme.* Illus. Malcolm Spooner. Atheneum, 1964.

Witty, swift, and stimulating. Grades 3–7. See also *There Is No Rhyme for Silver* (1962); *Catch a Little Rhyme* (1966), for younger children; *Out Loud* (1973); *Rainbow Writing* (1976); and *A Word or Two with You* (1981).

Milne, A. A. *The World of Christopher Robin.* Illus. E. H. Shepard. Dutton, 1958.

The complete *When We Were Very Young* (first published in 1924) and *Now We Are Six* (first published in 1927) in one attractive volume. Grades K–3.

Moore, Clement Clarke. *Night Before Christmas.* Illus. Arthur Rackham. Lippincott, 1931.

One of the most beloved of all Christmas poems, which first appeared in a newspaper in 1823. Grades 1–3.

Moore, Lilian. *See My Lovely Poison Ivy, and Other Verses about Witches, Ghosts and Things.* Illus. Diane Dawson. Atheneum, 1975.

A collection especially appealing for those who delight in the scary. Grades 2–6. See also *I Feel the Same Way* (1967); *I Thought I Heard the City* (1969); *Sam's Place* (1973); and *Something New Begins* (1982).

Nash, Odgen. *The Adventures of Isabel.* Illus. Walter Lorraine. Little, Brown, 1963.

A fearless, fathomless child. Grades 1–3. See also *Custard the Dragon* (1961) and *The Cruise of the Aardvark* (1967).

Nash, Ogden. *Custard and Company.* Illus. Quentin Blake. Little, Brown, 1980.

Unhinged language and outrageous puns poke fun at daily life. The batty illustrations are pure eccentric delight. Grades 4 and up.

Noyes, Alfred. *The Highwayman.* Illus. Charles Keeping. Oxford Univ. Press, 1981.

The taut suspense and highly colored romanticism of this narrative classic are dramatically conveyed in the haunting illustrations. Grades 5 and up. See also the version illustrated by Charles Mikolaycak (Lothrop, Lee & Shepard, 1983).

O'Neill, Mary. *Hailstones and Halibut Bones: Adventures in Color.* Illus. Leonard Weisgard. Doubleday, 1961.

There is fun and creative stimulus in the poetic ideas. Grades K–4. See also *What Is That Sound!* (Atheneum, 1966) and *Take a Number* (Doubleday, 1968).

Pomerantz, Charlotte. *If I Had a Paka: Poems in Eleven Languages.* Illus. Nancy Tafuri. Greenwillow, 1982.

This is a unique collection of twelve poems written for the nursery-aged child using vocabulary from eleven languages including Swahili, Samoan, Dutch, and Vietnamese. The simple poems are in English, incorporating onomatopoeiac words to create a sense of cultural heritage and musical delight. Grades K–3.

Prelutsky, Jack. *Nightmares: Poems to Trouble Your Sleep.* Illus. Arnold Lobel. Greenwillow, 1976.

Spectral images accompany poems of gothic horror in a controversial (for adults) collection of monstrous creatures. The fear is delicious and the language is striking. Grades 4–7. See also the companion volume, *The Headless Horseman Rides Tonight: More Poems to Trouble Your Sleep* (1980).

Rasmussen, Knud. comp. *Eskimo Songs and Stories.* Illus. Kiakshuk and Pudlo; trans. Edward Field. Delacorte, 1973.

Lyrical verse from the songs and stories of the Netsilik Eskimos.

Reeves, James. *The Blackbird in the Lilac.* Illus. Edward Ardizzone. Dutton, 1959.

Verses touched with laughter, sadness, and whimsy. Grades 2–4. See also *The Wandering Moon* (1963) and *The Story of Jackie Thimble* (1964). *Complete Poems for Children,* illus. Edward Ardizzone (Heinemann, 1973), includes all the above and more.

Roberts, Elizabeth Madox. *Under the Tree.* Illus. F. D. Bedford. Viking, 1922.

Fine economy and originality keep these poems fresh. Grades 1–4.

Roethke, Theodore. *Dirty Dinky and Other Creatures: Poems for Children.* Sel. Beatrice Roethke and Stephen Lushington. Doubleday, 1973

The playful wit and humor of an extraordinary poet. Grades 3 and up.

Rosen, Michael. *You Can't Catch Me!* Illus. Quentin Blake. Andre Deutsch, 1982.

Quirky, kinetic illustrations match the fast-paced lilt of these iconoclastic, playful poems. The colloquial tone conveys the everyday thoughts and activities of contemporary children. Grades 3–5.

Rossetti, Christina. *Sing-Song: A Nursery Rhyme Book, and Other Poems for Children.* Macmillan, 1924.

This small volume of poignant and joyous verse by a famous poet, first published in 1872, has become a nursery classic. Grades K–3. See also *Goblin Market,* illus. Arthur Rackham (F. Watts, 1969); an abridged version, illus. Ellen Raskin (Dutton, 1970); and another, illus. Martin Ware (Gollancz, 1980).

Sandburg, Carl. *Wind Song.* Illus. William A. Smith. Harcourt, 1960.

Sandburg selected seventy-nine of his poems particularly suitable for children, to which he added sixteen new poems. Grades 4–8. See also *Early Moon* (1930); *The Sandburg Treasury: Prose and Poetry for Young People* (1970); and *Rainbows Are Made* (1982), with dramatic wood engravings by Fritz Eichenberg.

Shakespeare, William. *Poems of William Shakespeare.* Sel. Lloyd Frankenberg; illus. Nonny Hogrogian. Crowell, 1966.

A discriminating selection from sonnets, songs, and other poetry. All ages. See also *Shakespeare's Flowers,* a collection of the poet's references to flowers, sel. Jessica Kern, illus. Anne Ophelia Dowden (1969), and *Shakespearean Sallies, Sullies, and Slanders: Insults for All Occasions,* coll. Ann McGovern, illus. James McCrea and Ruth McCrea (1969).

Starbird, Kaye. *A Snail's a Failure Socially and Other Poems, Mostly about People.* Illus. Kit Dalton. Lippincott, 1966.

Humor, somewhat tart, glides out of these poems, which deal with everyday people and events. Grades 3–6. See also *Speaking of Cows and Other Poems* (1960); *Don't Ever Cross a Crocodile* (1963); *The Pheasant on Route Seven* (1968); and *The Covered Bridge House* (Four Winds, 1979).

Stevenson, Robert Louis. *A Child's Garden of Verses.* Illus. Brian Wildsmith. F. Watts, 1966.

First published in 1885, this classic collection of poetry is here illuminated afresh for a new generation of children. Grades K–4. See also a later edition (Random, 1978), illus. Eric Blegvad. Classic editions have been reissued: illus. Jessie Willcox Smith (Scribner's, 1905) and Charles Robinson (Shambhala, 1979).

Swenson, May. *Poems to Solve.* Scribner's, 1966.
Each selection is a poem to solve, to find hidden elements of meaning. Grades 7 and up. See also *More Poems to Solve* (1971).

Teasdale, Sara. *Stars To-Night: Verses New and Old for Boys and Girls.* Illus. Dorothy P. Lathrop. Macmillan, 1930.
The poet's joy in nature finds expression in these poems chosen particularly for older girls. Grades 5–9.

Thomas, Edward. *The Green Roads.* Sel. and intro. Eleanor Farjeon. Holt, 1965.
Edward Thomas is presented as a companion for the reader who would walk with him, quickening the reader's "seeing and hearing through his own keen eyes and ears." Grades 5 and up.

Thurman, Judith. *Flashlight and Other Poems.* Illus. Reina Rubel. Atheneum, 1976.
The title implies the metaphor underlying these poems: a poem searches out and reveals our experiences like a flashlight. Grades 2–6.

Tolkien, J. R. R. *The Adventures of Tom Bombadil and Other Verses from The Red Book.* Illus. Pauline Baynes. Houghton Mifflin, 1963.
Hobbit lore and nonsense for hobbit lovers. Grades 5 and up.

Updike, John. *A Child's Calendar.* Illus. Nancy Ekholm Burkert. Knopf, 1965.
A fine poet, a cheerful mood, a handsome book. A poem for each month; for each poem, a picture. Grades 3–6.

Watson, Clyde. *Father Fox's Pennyrhymes.* Illus. Wendy Watson. Harper, 1971.
A jaunty collaboration of pictures and verse. Grades K–3. See also *Catch Me and Kiss Me and Say It Again* (Philomel, 1978).

Whitman, Walt. *Poems of Walt Whitman: Leaves of Grass.* Sel. Lawrence Clark Powell; woodcuts John Romano Ross and Clare Romano Ross. Crowell, 1964.
The editor has selected from the most intense and powerful of the poems in "the greatest single book American Literature has yet produced." Grades 7 and up. See also *Overhead the Sun: Lines from Whitman,* woodcuts, Antonio Frasconi (Farrar, 1969).

Willard, Nancy. *A Visit to William Blake's Inn: Poems for Innocent and Experienced Travelers.* Illus. Alice Provensen and Martin Provensen. Harcourt, 1981.
Both a Newbery medal and Caldecott Honor Book, this haunting collection of mysterious poems paints a portrait of a magical eighteenth-century inn and its fantastical guests. Intoxicating and original. Grades 3–7.

Worth, Valerie. *Small Poems.* Illus. Natalie Babbitt. Farrar, Straus & Giroux, 1972.
Simple pleasures. Grades 2–4. See also *More Small Poems* (1976) and *Still More Small Poems* (1978).

References for Adults

Books

Auslander, Joseph, and Frank E. Hill. *The Winged Horse: The Story of the Poets and Their Poetry.* Illus. Paul Honoré. Haskell, 1968.
A reprint of the 1928 edition.

Brewton, John E., and Sara W. Brewton, comps. *Index to Children's Poetry.* Wilson, 1942. First Supplement, 1954. Second Supplement, 1965.

Brewton, John E., Sara W. Brewton, and G. Meredith Blackburn III, comps. *Index to Poetry for Children and Young People, 1964–1969.* Wilson, 1972.
An extension of the basic volume and supplements.

Brewton, John E., G. Meredith Blackburn III, and Lorraine A. Blackburn, comps. *Index to Poetry for Children and Young People, 1976–1981.* Wilson, 1983.
The fourth supplement indexes one hundred poetry collections published between 1976 and 1981.

Brooks, Cleanth, and Robert Penn Warren. *Understanding Poetry.* 4th ed. Holt, 1976.

Ciardi, John, and Miller Williams. *How Does a Poem Mean?* 2d ed. Houghton Mifflin, 1975.

Deutsch, Babette. *Poetry Handbook: A Dictionary of Terms.* New rev. ed. Funk & Wagnalls, 1962.
See also *Poetry in Our Time* (Holt, 1952).

Dickey, James. *Babel to Byzantium: Poets and Poetry Now.* Farrar, Straus & Giroux, 1968.

Dickey, James. *The Suspect in Poetry.* Sixties Press, 1964.

Drew, Elizabeth A. *Discovering Poetry.* Norton, 1933.
See also *Poetry: A Modern Guide to Its Understanding and Enjoyment* (Norton, 1959) and *Discovering Modern Poetry,* by Elizabeth Drew and George Connor (Holt, 1961).

Frankenberg, Lloyd. *Pleasure Dome: On Reading Modern Poetry.* Houghton Mifflin, 1949.

Frye, Northrop. *The Well Tempered Critic.* Indiana Univ. Press, A Midland Book, 1963.

Granger, Edith. *Index to Poetry.* 6th ed., rev. and enl. Columbia Univ. Press, 1973.
    Indexes anthologies published through Dec. 31, 1970. See also *Granger's Index to Poetry, 1970–1977,* ed. William James Smith (1978). This volume departs from the usual five-year supplement, covering instead the period 1970–1977.

Gregory, Horace, and Marya Zaturenska. *A History of American Poetry, 1900–1940.* Harcourt, 1942.

Hillyer, Robert. *In Pursuit of Poetry.* McGraw-Hill, 1960.

Holmes, John. *Writing Poetry.* The Writer, 1960.

Housman, A. E. *The Name and Nature of Poetry.* Macmillan, 1956.
    The Leslie Stephen Lecture delivered at Cambridge.

Hughes, Ted. *Poetry Is.* Doubleday, 1970.

Kennedy, X. J. *An Introduction to Poetry.* 5th ed. Little, Brown, 1982.

MacLeish, Archibald. *Poetry and Experience.* Houghton Mifflin, 1961.

Nemerov, Howard. *Poets on Poetry.* Basic Books, 1966.

Perrine, Laurence. *Sound and Sense: An Introduction to Poetry.* 6th ed. Harcourt, 1982.

Proffitt, Edward. *Poetry: An Introduction and Anthology.* Houghton Mifflin, 1975.

Reeves, James. *Understanding Poetry.* Heinemann, 1965.

Reid, Forest. *Walter de la Mare: A Critical Study.* Holt, 1929.

Sackville-West, V. *Walter de la Mare and the Traveller.* Oxford Univ. Press, 1953.

Sell, Violet, et al., comps. *Subject Index to Poetry for Children and Young People.* American Library Association, 1957.
    See also the supplement, *Subject Index to Poetry for Children and Young People, 1957–1975,* comp. Dorothy B. Frizzel and Eva L. Andrews (1977).

Shapiro, Karl. *Primer for Poets.* Univ. of Nebraska Press, 1965.

Strong, L. A. G. *Common Sense about Poetry.* Knopf, 1932.

Sugg, Richard P. *Appreciating Poetry.* Houghton Mifflin, 1975.

Terry, Ann. *Children's Poetry Preferences: A National Survey of Upper Elementary Grades.* National Council of Teachers of English, 1974.
    An NCTE research monograph analyzing the results of a survey of children's poetry choices in over five hundred classes. Grades 4–6.

Untermeyer, Louis. *The Pursuit of Poetry: A Guide to Its Understanding and Appreciation with an Explanation of Its Forms and a Dictionary of Poetic Terms.* Simon & Schuster, 1969.

Waggoner, Hyatt H. *American Poets: From the Puritans to the Present.* Houghton Mifflin, 1968.

Articles

Arbuthnot, May Hill, Annis Duff, Lillian Morrison, and Arna Bontemps. "Poetry Festival Gatherings." *Top of the News* 15 (May 1959), pp. 53–70.

Behn, Harry. "Poetry for Children." *The Horn Book Magazine* 42 (Apr. 1966), pp. 163–75.

Behn, Harry. "Poetry, Fantasy, and Reality." *Elementary English* (Apr. 1965), pp. 355–61.

Behn, Harry. "Worlds of Innocence." *The Horn Book Magazine* 39 (Feb. 1963), pp. 21–29.

Benét, Laura. "Walter de la Mare: 1873–1956." *Saturday Review* (Sept. 22, 1956), p. 11.

Bryan, Ashley, Norma Farber, Helen M. Hill, Myra Cohn Livingston, and Aidan Chambers. *The Horn Book Magazine* 15, no. 1 (Feb. 1979), poetry issue.

Clark, Leonard. "Poetry for the Youngest." *The Horn Book Magazine* 38 (Dec. 1962), pp. 583–85.

Colum, Padraic. "Patterns for the Imagination." *The Horn Book Magazine* 38 (Feb. 1962), pp. 82–86.

Dickey, James. "The Language of Poetry." *New York Times Book Review* 70 (Nov. 7, 1965), p. 6.

Durham, Mae J. "Dream Possessed and Young." In *Come Hither!* ed. Lawrence Clark Powell, pp. 15–22. Univ. of California Press, 1965.

Fryatt, Norma R., ed. "Touching Poetry." In *A Horn Book Sampler,* section 8, pp. 237–61. Horn Book, 1959.
    Articles by Anne Eaton, John A. Holmes, and Helen Dean Fish.

Godden, Rumer. "Poetry in Every Child: Teaching the Young to Love Beauty." *Ladies Home Journal* 82 (Nov. 1965), pp. 168–70.

Greaves, Griselda. "The Key of the Kingdom." *Signal: Approaches to Children's Books* 30 (Sept. 1979), pp. 159–68.

Livingston, Myra Cohn. "A Tune Beyond Us: The Bases of Choice." *Wilson Library Bulletin* 44 (Dec. 1969), pp. 448–55.

Manning, Rosemary. "The Freshness of the Morning: The Poetry Children Write." *The Times Literary Supplement, Children's Books* (Oct. 30, 1970).

Miller, Bertha Mahony, Eleanor Farjeon, Herbert Read, and Pamela Bianco. *The Horn Book Magazine* (June 1957), Walter de la Mare number.

Morse, Samuel French. "Speaking to the Imagination." *The Horn Book Magazine* 41, pp. 255–59.

Munson, Amelia. "Poetry and Children: This Way Delight." In *The Contents of the Basket,* ed. Frances Lander Spain, pp. 61–74. New York Public Library, 1960.

Plotz, Helen. "All Who Hide Too Well Away." *The Horn Book Magazine* 35 (Apr. 1959), pp. 112–19.

Tucker, Alan. "On Poetry and Children." *Signal: Approaches to Children's Books* 1 (Jan. 1970), pp. 7–15.

Tucker, Alan. "A Poetry-Book Survey." *Signal: Approaches to Children's Books* 12 (Sept. 1973), pp. 139–55.

Chapters and Commentary

Bator, Robert, ed. *Signposts to Criticism of Children's Literature.* American Library Association, 1983.
In Chapter 6: "Verse for the Young," by Naomi Lewis, pp. 194–99; "How to Tell a Sheep from a Goat—and Why It Matters," by Helen M. Hill, pp. 200–10; "Some Afterthoughts on Poetry, Verse, and Criticism," by Myra Cohn Livingston, pp. 211–18.

Chukovsky, Kornei I. *From Two to Five.* trans. and ed. Miriam Morton; foreword, Frances Clarke Sayers. Rev. ed. Univ. of California Press, 1968.
Chapter 6 gives thirteen commandments for children's poets.

Day-Lewis, Cecil. *Poetry for You: A Book for Boys and Girls on the Enjoyment of Poetry.* Rev. ed. Oxford Univ. Press, 1964.
Chapter 2: "How Poetry Began." Chapter 5: "Poems That Tell a Story."

De la Mare, Walter. *Bells and Grass: Poems.* Viking, 1942.
Introduction, pp. 5–10.

Egoff, Sheila. *Thursday's Child: Trends and Patterns in Contemporary Children's Literature.* American Library Association, 1981.
Chapter 9: "Poetry," by Judith Saltman, pp. 221–46.

Grigson, Geoffrey. *The Cherry Tree.* Vanguard, 1962.
"To the Reader," pp. ix–xiv.

Haviland, Virginia. *Children and Literature: Views and Reviews.* Scott, Foresman, 1973.
In Chapter 7: "The Children's Poets," by Agnes Repplier, p. 263; "A Child's World Is As a Poet's," by Edwin Muir, p. 269.

May, Jill P., ed. *Children and Their Literature: A Readings Book.* Children's Literature Association Publications, 1983.
In Chapter 5: "Poetry Unfettered," by Leonard Clark, pp. 133–37; "The State of Things: A Question of Substance," by Althea Helbig, pp. 138–47.

Moore, Anne Carroll, and Bertha Mahony Miller, eds. *Writing and Criticism.* Horn Book. 1951.
"De la Mare: An Essay," by Margery Bianco, pp. 67–77.

Neruda, Pablo. *Selected Poems of Pablo Neruda.* Ed. and trans. Ben Belitt. Grove, 1961.
A bilingual edition. "Toward an Impure Poetry," pp. 39–40.

Read, Sir Herbert E., ed. *This Way, Delight: A Book of Poetry for the Young.* Pantheon, 1956.
"What Is Poetry?" pp. 137–44.

Sandburg, Carl. *Early Moon.* Illus. James Daugherty. Harcourt, 1930.
A short talk on poetry, pp. 13–28.

Smith, Janet Adam, comp. *The Faber Book of Children's Verse.* Faber & Faber, 1962.
Introduction, pp. 19–23.

Untermeyer, Louis, ed. *Yesterday and Today.* Harcourt, 1927.
Preface, pp. v–viii.

Poetry with Children

Adoff, Arnold, ed. *It Is the Poem Singing into Your Eyes: Anthology of New Young Poets.* Harper, 1971.

Arnstein, Flora J. *Children Write Poetry: A Creative Approach,* 2d ed. Stanford Univ. Press, 1967.

Arnstein, Flora J. *Poetry in the Elementary Classroom.* Appleton-Century-Crofts, 1962.
See also *Adventures into Poetry* (Stanford Univ. Press, 1951).

Baron, Virginia Olsen, ed. *Here I Am! An Anthology of Poems Written by Young People in Some of America's Minority Groups.* Illus. Emily Arnold McCully. Dutton, 1969.

Behn, Harry. *Chrysalis: Concerning Children and Poetry.* Harcourt, 1968.

Clark, Leonard. "Poetry by Children." *The Horn Book Magazine* 55 (Feb. 1969), pp. 15–19.

Conkling, Hilda. *Poems by a Little Girl.* Stokes, 1920.
These verses of a talented poet reveal a fluid play of language and a depth of naked emotion and imagination. See also *Shoes of the Wind* (1923).

Esbensen, Barbara Juster. *A Celebration of Bees: Helping Children Write Poetry.* Winston, 1975.

Griggs, Tamar, coll. *There's a Sound in the Sea . . . a Child's Eye View of the Whale.* Scrimshaw, 1975.
This collection of children's poetry and paintings expresses a passionate concern for the fate of the sea and the whales. Alive with a poignant, fresh, sometimes angry, vision.

Hopkins, Lee Bennett. *Pass the Poetry, Please! Using Poetry in Pre-Kindergarten—Six Classrooms.* Citation, 1972.
See also *City Talk* (Knopf, 1970) and *Let Them Be Themselves: Language Arts for Children in Elementary Schools* (2d enl. ed., 1974).

Hughes, Ted. *Poetry Is.* Doubleday, 1970.

I Never Saw Another Butterfly: Children's Drawings and Poems from Terezin Concentration Camp, 1942–1944. McGraw-Hill, 1964.
Like Anne Frank's diary, a testimony to children's endurance and compassion.

Jordon, June, and Terri Bush. cols. *The Voice of the Children.* Holt, 1970.

Kennedy, X. J., and Dorothy M. Kennedy, eds. *Knock at a Star: A Child's Introduction to Poetry.* Illus. Karen Ann Weinhaus. Little, Brown, 1982.
A vital, contemporary collection with insightful introductions on reading and writing poetry. With a do-it-yourself section for beginning poets and an afterword for adults.

Koch, Kenneth. *Rose, Where Did You Get That Red? Teaching Great Poetry to Children.* Random House, 1973.
Using a poet's expression in a particular poem as a point of departure, Koch has encouraged children to explore similar avenues of thought, imagination, and association. See also *Sleeping on the Wing: An Anthology of Modern Poetry with Essays on Reading and Writing,* by Kenneth Koch and Kate Farrell (1977).

Koch, Kenneth, and the students of New York P. S. 61. *Wishes, Lies, and Dreams: Teaching Children to Write Poetry.* Chelsea House, 1970.
A poet's account of arousing children to release the poetry within them. His freeing them from formal strictures, such as rhyme, and giving them playful frameworks in which to be inventive are described. The children's written work is presented.

Kuskin, Karla. *Near the Window Tree.* Illus. by the author. Harper, 1975.
A selection of thoughtful poems, each accompanied by a short explanation of its genesis in Kuskin's imagination and daily life. Illuminates the poetic process. Grades 3–5. See also *Dogs and Dragons, Trees and Dreams* (1980).

Larrick, Nancy, sel. *I Heard a Scream in the Street: Poems by Young People in the City.* Photographs by students. Lippincott, 1970.
Also see *Somebody Turned on a Tap in These Kids: Poetry and Young People Today* (Delacorte, 1971).

Lewis, Richard, ed. *Miracles: Poems by Children of the English-speaking World,* Simon & Schuster, 1966.
Primarily lyric and nature poetry. A seminal book.

Livingston, Myra Cohn. "But Is It Poetry?" *The Horn Book Magazine:* Pt. I, 51 (Dec. 1975), pp. 571–80; Pt. II, 52 (Feb. 1976), pp. 24–31.

Livingston, Myra Cohn. *When You Are Alone/It Keeps You Capone: An Approach to Creative Writing with Children.* Atheneum, 1973.
A poet and a teacher of poetry, Myra Livingston tells of her successes and her failures with children and poetry, and the ways of working she has developed to encourage increasing skill. See also "The Child as Poet: Myth or Reality?" (Horn Book, 1984).

McCord, David. *Take Sky: More Rhymes of the Never Was and Always Is.* Illus. Henry B. Kane. Little, Brown, 1962.

See also "Write Me a Verse" and "Write Another Verse," in *For Me to Say: Rhymes of the Never Was and Always Is* (1970).

Mearns, Hughes. *Creative Youth: How a School Environment Set Free the Creative Spirit.* Doubleday, 1925.

See also *Creative Power* (1929).

Morse, David. *Grandfather Rock: The New Poetry and the Old.* Delacorte, 1972.

Rock lyrics and traditional poems are juxtaposed in an effort to get the student to hear the sound in poetry.

Morton, Miriam, coll. and trans. *The Moon is Like a Silver Sickle: A Celebration of Poetry by Russian Children.* Illus. Eros Keith. Simon & Schuster, 1972.

This collection is a testament to the Russian passion for poetry, which extends to include active involvement by children in the creative process.

Pellowski, Anne, Helen R. Sattley, and Joyce C. Arkhurst, eds. *Have You Seen a Comet? Children's Art and Writing from around the World.* Day/U.S. Committee for UNICEF, 1971.

An anthology of art, prose, and poetry by children ages six to sixteen from seventy-five countries. Where a translation appears, the original language is provided.

Rogers, Timothy, coll. and intro. *Those First Affections: An Anthology of Poems Composed between the Ages of Two and Eight.* Routledge & Kegan Paul, 1979.

A discriminating collection of young children's poetry with notes on the poems giving details of their composition. A foreword by the poet Charles Causley is included.

Shapiro, Jon, ed. *Using Literature and Poetry Affectively.* International Reading Association, 1979.

II   Picture Books: Stories for the Eye

4   Picture Books

Books for Children

Ahlberg, Allan, and Janet Ahlberg. *The Baby's Catalogue.* Illus. by the authors. Atlantic/Little, Brown, 1983.

A detailed, pastel-toned catalogue of items and aspects of the toddler's life. Grades Preschool–K. See also the visual surprises in *Each Peach Pear Plum: An I-Spy Story* (Viking, 1979), awarded England's Kate Greenaway Medal in 1978; and *Peek-a-Boo* (Viking, 1981).

Alderson, Sue Ann. *Bonnie McSmithers You're Driving Me Dithers.* Illus. Fiona Garrick. Tree Frog, 1974.

An energetic little girl's mischief drives her mother to distraction. Told in warm, witty verse and illustrated with fine black-and-white line drawings. Grades K–2.

Aliki. *A Medieval Feast.* Illus. by the author. Crowell, 1983.

This is a sumptuously illustrated story of the domestic life of a fifteenth-century manor house upon the arrival of the king and queen. The preparations for and celebration of a great feast are shown in minute detail, radiant color, and authentic period costume and menu. A joyous extravaganza, like an illuminated manuscript, with an informative, readable text. Grades 1–4.

Allen, Pamela. *Who Sank the Boat?* Illus. by the author. Coward, 1983.

The comic escapades of five animals in a boat are told in jaunty rhyme and vivid illustrations. Winner of the Children's Book Council of Australia Picture Book of the Year Award in 1983. Grades Preschool–1.

Anno, Mitsumasa. *Topsy-Turvies: Pictures to Stretch the Imagination.* Illus. by the author. Walker/Weatherhill, 1970.

Up and down and around the pages, small, busy figures lead the viewer in a mazelike progression. Grades K–3. See also *Dr. Anno's Magical Midnight Circus* (1972); the M. C. Escher-like *Anno's Alphabet* (Harper, 1975); *Anno's Counting Book* (Harper, 1977); and his series of pictorial travelogues across time and space in *Anno's Journey* (Collins/World, 1978); *Anno's Italy* (Philomel, 1980); *Anno's Brit-*

ain (Philomel, 1982); and *Anno's USA* (Philomel, 1983).

Ardizzone, Edward. *Little Tim and the Brave Sea Captain.* Illus. by the author. New ed. Oxford Univ. Press, 1955.

A picture book of distinction that a young English artist made for his small son. The water colors, filled with drama and realism, show an understanding of sea and ships. *Tim All Alone* was awarded the first Kate Greenaway Medal in 1957, an English award that corresponds to the Caldecott Medal in America. Grades K–2.

Ayer, Jacqueline. *A Wish for Little Sister.* Illus. by the author. Harcourt, 1960.

Little Sister's birthday wish, a very little wish, comes true just when she has almost given up. Grades 2–4. See also *Nu Dang and His Kite* (1959).

Azarian, Mary. *A Farmer's Alphabet.* Illus. by the author. Godine, 1981.

A handsome alphabet book with striking woodcuts illustrating scenes of a year in rural Vermont. Grades K–3.

Baker, Laura Nelson. *The Friendly Beasts.* Illus. Nicolas Sidjakov. Parnassus, 1957.

Adapted from a fourteenth-century Christmas carol, this is the story of Mary and Joseph in the barn in Nazareth. Grades 1–4.

Balet, Jan. *Joanjo.* Illus. by the author. Delacorte, 1965.

In his dreams, a small Portuguese boy leaves his fishing village and becomes rich and powerful. He is about to be shot to the moon when he awakens, thankful to be at home in his family of fishermen. Grades 1–3.

Bang, Molly. *Dawn.* Illus. by the author. Morrow, 1983.

The Japanese legend of the "Crane Wife" is here retold and set in a nineteenth-century New England sailing village. The thick painterly illustrations alternate with hazy charcoal sketches. Grades 1–3. See also *The Grey Lady and the Strawberry Snatcher* (Four Winds, 1980) and the Caldecott Honor Book *Ten, Nine, Eight* (Greenwillow, 1983).

Bannerman, Helen. *The Story of Little Black Sambo.* Illus. by the author. Lippincott, 1923.

On a long journey back to India the author wrote this story for her two small children, whom she had left behind in Scotland for their education. It has become a childhood classic that critics have called "a miracle of simplicity and drama." It has also become a subject of controversy due to its naive, stylized illustrations, characterization, and plot, which have been interpreted as racist. Grades K–2.

Baskin, Hosea, et al. *Hosie's Alphabet.* Illus. Leonard Baskin. Viking, 1972.

A famous artist has used words and inspiration from his own children in creating a visually stunning ABC. Grades Preschool–K. See also *Hosie's Aviary* (1979); *Hosie's Zoo* (1981); and *Leonard Baskin's Miniature Natural History,* 4 vols. (Pantheon, 1983).

Baylor, Byrd. *The Best Town in the World.* Illus. Ronald Himler. Scribner's, 1982.

A first-person reminiscence of late-nineteenth-century small town life in the Texas hills. The nostalgic, poetic tone is sharpened by the child's concrete perspective and the vivid, specific water colors. Grades 1–3.

Baylor, Byrd. *Desert Voices.* Illus. Peter Parnall. Scribner's, 1981.

Lyrical prose captures the beauty and mystery of desert animal life. The fine line and searing colors of the illustrations perfectly complement the free verse text. Grades 1 and up. See also *The Desert is Theirs* (1975); *Hawk, I'm Your Brother* (1976); and *The Way to Start a Day* (1978), all by the same duo.

Bemelmans, Ludwig. *Madeline.* Illus. by the author. Viking, 1939.

Bemelmans has a genius for creating a sense of place. Here he creates the spell of Paris as he tells the story of Madeline, a child who does not take kindly to the regimentation of a French boarding school. *Madeline's Rescue* was awarded the Caldecott Medal in 1954. Grades K–2.

Beskow, Elsa. *Pelle's New Suit.* Illus. by the author; trans. Marion Letcher Woodburn. Harper, n.d.

A picture book from Sweden with twelve full-page illustrations in color. Grades K–2.

Birnbaum, Abe. *Green Eyes.* Illus. by the author. Capitol, 1953.

A much-loved cat tells about the first year of life and the changing seasons with a sense of great contentment and joy. Grades K–2.

Bishop, Claire Huchet. *The Five Chinese Brothers.* Illus. Kurt Wiese. Coward-McCann, 1938.

A dramatic retelling of an old Chinese folktale made into a picture book with Kurt Wiese's interpretative drawings. Available in French under the title *Les Cinq Frères Chinois.* Grades 1–3.

Blades, Ann. *Mary of Mile 18.* Illus. by the author. Tundra, 1971.

A young Mennonite girl in northern British Columbia yearns for a wolf cub as her pet. The fresh, naive water colors reflect the cold and beautiful landscape. Grades 1–3.

Blake, Quentin. *Mister Magnolia.* Illus. by the author. Chatto/Bodley/Jonathan, 1980.

This nonsense rhyme brings to life a wildly lovable eccentric with an old trumpet and only one boot who is a worthy descendent of Edward Lear's mad characters. The comic illustrations are dynamic and endearing. Winner of the Kate Greenaway Medal, 1980. Grades K–2.

Briggs, Raymond. *Father Christmas.* Illus. by the author. Coward-McCann, 1973.

Cantankerous and human, Father Christmas is shown in all his domestic routines as he gets up and out on his workday, Christmas. A further account of his activities is found in *Father Christmas Goes on Holiday* (1975), winner of the Kate Greenaway Medal. Grades K–6. See also the satirical, sophisticated *Fungus the Bogeyman* (Random House, 1977), which details the mid-life crisis of a bemused and philosophical underworld bogeyman; the evocative dream story *The Snowman* (Random House, 1978) that dynamically uses a wordless strip format to explore narrative convention; and the controversial *When the Wind Blows* (Hamilton, 1983), a bleak, searing portrayal of nuclear holocaust for teenagers and adults in stunningly dynamic comic strip format.

Brooke, L. Leslie. *Johnny Crow's Garden.* Illus. by the author. Warne, 1903.

A delightful picture book that has been a favorite for generations. Grades Preschool–K. See also *Johnny Crow's Party* and *Johnny Crow's New Garden.*

Brown, Marcia. *Once a Mouse . . . A Fable Cut in Wood.* Illus. by the author. Scribner's, 1961.

A vigorous retelling of an ancient Indian fable. The woodcuts are distinguished for their strength. Awarded the Caldecott Medal in 1962. Grades K–3. See also *Henry-Fisherman* (1949); *How Hippo!* (1969); *All Butterflies: An ABC Cut* (1974); and *The Blue Jackal* (1977).

Brown, Margaret Wise. *The Dead Bird.* Illus. Remy Charlip. W. R. Scott, 1958.

Children encounter death. Grades 1–3. See also *Goodnight Moon* (Harper, 1947).

Bruna, Dick. *I Can Read.* Illus. by the author. Methuen, 1978.

Clear, clean pictures in bright, flat colors stimu-

late reading interest. Grades Preschool–1. See also *B Is for Bear: An A-B-C* (1971); *I Can Read More* (1976); and other elegantly simple titles by this same artist.

Brunhoff, Jean de. *The Story of Babar, the Little Elephant.* Illus. by the author; trans. from the French by Merle S. Haas. Random House, 1933.

A sophisticated yet childlike picture book of Babar, the little elephant who ran away from the jungle, found consolation in the exhilaration of city life, and then returned to the jungle to be crowned king of the elephants. Grades 1–3.

Burningham, John. *Mr. Gumpy's Outing.* Illus. by the author. Holt, 1970.

A pastoral background for this story, based on the cumulative pattern, gives this book a quiet simplicity, toned with humor in the artist's work. Grades Preschool–1. See also *John Burningham's ABC* (Bobbs-Merrill, 1964), *Cannonball Simp* (Bobbs-Merrill, 1966), *Seasons* (Bobbs-Merrill, 1970), *Mr. Gumpy's Motor Car* (1973); the "Little Books" series of domestic incident for toddlers, published by Harper: *The Baby* (1975), *The Rabbit* (1975), *The School* (1975); and other titles in this entertaining series: *Come away from the Water, Shirley* (Harper, 1977), *Time to Get out of the Bath, Shirley* (Harper, 1978), *Would You Rather . . .* (Harper, 1978), *The Shopping Basket* (Harper, 1980), and *Avocado Baby* (Harper, 1982).

Caldecott, Randolph, illus. *Picture Books.* 4 vols. Warne, 1878–1885.

This talented artist, for whom the annual American picture-book award is named, has taken sixteen favorite nursery rhymes and made them into picture books. His drawings, distinguished for simplicity of line, are full of action and spirited humor. Grades K–3.

Carle, Eric. *The Very Hungry Caterpillar.* Illus. by the author. World, 1969.

A playful engagement with the young child reader, who is led through intriguing visual complications. Grades Preschool–1. See also *Pancakes, Pancakes!* (Knopf, 1970); *The Tiny Seed* (Crowell, 1970); and the almost wordless *Do You Want To Be My Friend?* (Harper, 1971), designed to introduce beginning readers to the concept of narrative sequence.

Cendrars, Blaise. *Shadow.* Trans. and illus. Marcia Brown. Scribner's, 1982.

The French writer's imagistic poem captures the power of African tribal ritual and the collective unconscious. The magnificent expressionistic illustrations are true to the mystical spirit of the text.

Awarded the Caldecott Medal in 1983. Grades 1–4.

Chaucer, Geoffrey. *Chanticleer and the Fox.* Adapt. and illus. Barbara Cooney. Crowell, 1958.

The fable of the vain cock and the shrewd fox from Chaucer's *Canterbury Tales* has been made into a distinguished picture book harmonious in design and illustration. Awarded the Caldecott Medal in 1959. Grades 1–3.

Chönz, Selina. *A Bell for Ursli.* Illus. Alois Carigiet. Oxford Univ. Press, 1950.

Rhyming text and radiant water colors tell the story of a little boy who lives high in the mountains of Switzerland. The beauty and charm of the Swiss edition have been retained in the American printing. Grades K–3.

Cleaver, Elizabeth. *Petrouchka.* Illus. by the author. Atheneum, 1980.

The spell of Stravinsky's music and Diaghilev's ballet is recreated in the virtuoso illustrations. Collage images using cut paper, mono, and linoleum prints evoke the sense of theater, puppetry, and ballet. Awarded the Canada Council's Children's Literature Prize in 1980. Grades K–3. See also the board book *ABC* (Oxford Univ. Press, 1984).

Climo, Lindee. *Chester's Barn.* Illus. by the author. Tundra, 1982.

A straightforward factual text of farm life is magnificently illustrated with sinuously painted folk-art images. Grades 1–4.

Coatsworth, Elizabeth. *Under the Green Willow.* Illus. Janina Domanska. Macmillan, 1971.

Geometric shapes used by the illustrator increase the complexity of a simple story. Grades K–1. See also *Goodnight,* illus. José Aruego (1972).

Cock Robin. *The Courtship, Merry Marriage, and Feast of Cock Robin and Jenny Wren, to Which Is Added the Doleful Death of Cock Robin.* Illus. Barbara Cooney. Scribner's, 1965.

An engaging book in which the artist has captured the personalities of the various birds in a style particularly suited to the old rhymes. Grades K–2.

Cooney, Barbara. *Miss Rumphius.* Illus. by the author. Viking, 1982.

The life story of an irrepressible woman determined to bring beauty to the world is poetically illustrated with vibrant panoramic paintings. Grades K–3.

Craft, Ruth. *The Winter Bear.* Illus. Erik Blegvad. Atheneum, 1975.

A rhyming account of a winter walk that culminates in the finding of a brown, knitted bear, who is taken home, where he is dried off and dressed. Grades K–2.

Crews, Donald. *Ten Black Dots.* Illus. by the author. Scribner's, 1968.

Handsomely designed abstractions give reality to numbers. Grades K–2. See also the stunning *Freight Train* (Greenwillow, 1978); *Truck* (Greenwillow, 1980); *Carousel* (Greenwillow, 1982); *Harbor* (Greenwillow, 1982); and *Parade* (Greenwillow, 1983).

Crowther, Robert. *The Most Amazing Hide-and-Seek Alphabet Book.* Illus. by the author. Viking, 1978.

Inventive design and sophisticated paper engineering lift the images in this toddler's alphabet book literally off the page. Grades Preschool–K. See also *The Most Amazing Hide-and-Seek Counting Book* (1981).

Daugherty, James. *Andy and the Lion.* Illus. by the author. Viking, 1938.

A vigorous, modern version of the famous Greek fable of Androcles and the Lion, illustrated with masterly drawings. Grades 1–3.

D'Aulaire, Ingri, and Edgar Parin D'Aulaire. *Children of the Northlights.* Illus. by the authors. Viking, 1935.

After reading *Ola,* children will enjoy this story of Lise and Lasse in Lapland. The picture book is the happy result of the D'Aulaires' long journey by boat and sled into the north of Norway. Grades 2–4.

Dayrell, Elphinstone. *Why the Sun and the Moon Live in the Sky.* Illus. Blair Lent. Houghton Mifflin, 1968.

The origin story becomes real and fantastic with the use of African design motifs in the illustrations. Grades 1–3.

De Paola, Tomie. *"Charlie Needs a Cloak."* Illus. by the author. Prentice-Hall, 1974.

A humorous informational book chronicles the steps taken in the manufacture of a new cloak by an endearing shepherd. Grades K–2. See also *Nana Upstairs and Nana Downstairs* (Putnam's, 1973) and the wordless *Sing, Pierrot, Sing: A Picture Book in Mime* (Harcourt, 1983).

De Regniers, Beatrice Schenk. *May I Bring a Friend?* Illus. Beni Montresor. Atheneum, 1964.

All kinds of animals appear at the palace when the king and queen extend an invitation to "my friends." The drawings complement the text perfectly. Awarded the Caldecott Medal in 1965. Grades K–2. See also *A Little House of Your Own* (Harcourt, 1954); *A Child's Book of Dreams,* illus. by Bill Sokol (Harcourt, 1957); *Cats, Cats, Cats, Cats,* illus. by Bill Sokol (Pantheon, 1958); and *The Snow Party,* illus. Reiner Zimnik (Pantheon, 1959).

Domanska, Janina. *If All the Seas Were One Sea.* Macmillan, 1971.

Nonsense Mother Goose rhyme, briefly underscoring line complexities of pictures. Grades K–2. See also *The Turnip* (1969); *Marilka* (1970); *I Saw a Ship A-Sailing* (1972); and her folk art version of the Polish folktale, *King Krakus and the Dragon* (Greenwillow, 1979).

Duvoisin, Roger. *Veronica.* Illus. by the author. Knopf, 1961.

Duvoisin's elegantly ponderous heroine, the hippopotamus Veronica, wants to be famous and takes herself off to the city. Grades K–3. See also *Petunia* (1950).

Eichenberg, Fritz. *Ape in a Cape: An Alphabet of Odd Animals.* Illus. by the author. Harcourt, 1952.

Simple nonsense rhymes with humorous illustrations for each letter of the alphabet. Grades K–2. See also *Dancing in the Moon.*

Emberley, Barbara. *Drummer Hoff.* Adapt. Barbara Emberley; illus. Ed Emberley. Prentice-Hall, 1967.

A cumulative folk verse made into a picture book with bold colors. Awarded the Caldecott Medal in 1968. Grades 1–3. See also *The Wing on a Flea: A Book About Shapes,* Ed Emberley (Little, Brown, 1961).

Ets, Marie Hall. *Play with Me.* Illus. by the author. Viking, 1955.

There is a rare quality to this sensitive story of a little girl who tries to play with the wild creatures of the meadow. They all run away from her. Then, when she sits perfectly still, one by one, they come to her. Grades K–1. See also *In the Forest,* which tells of a little boy's meeting with the animals of the forest.

Farber, Norma. *As I Was Crossing Boston Common.* Illus. Arnold Lobel. Dutton, 1975.

An incredible menagerie of curious creatures parade across the pages of this alphabet rhyme. Grades K–2. See also *Where's Gomer?* illus. William Pene du Bois (1974), and *How Does It Feel to Be Old?* illus. Trina Schart Hyman (1979).

Fatio, Louise. *The Happy Lion.* Illus. Roger Duvoisin. McGraw-Hill, 1954.

A kindly lion escapes from a zoo, causing consternation in a small French town. Humorous drawings capture the gaiety of the story. Grades K–2.

Feelings, Muriel. *Moja Means One: Swahili Counting Book.* Illus. Tom Feelings. Dial, 1971.

Idyllic pictorial scenes. Grades K–3. See also *Jambo Means Hello,* and *Swahili Alphabet Book* (1974).

Fischer, Hans. *Pitschi.* Illus. by the author. Harcourt, 1955.

The story of a kitten that wanted to be something else, by a Swiss artist of great originality. Grades K–2. See also *The Birthday* (1954).

Flack, Marjorie. *The Story About Ping.* Illus. Kurt Wiese. Viking, 1933.

A small classic that tells of a Peking duckling's night of adventure on the Yangtze River. The pictures heighten the delight of the story. Grades K–3.

Flora, James. *Sherwood Walks Home.* Illus. by the author. Harcourt, 1966.

Sherwood, the wind-up bear, has one complication when he walks home: he has to go in a straight line. The humorous episodes are similar to *The Golden Goose.* Grades K–3. See also *Leopold, the See-Through Crumbpicker* (1961); *The Fabulous Firework Family;* and *Stewed Goose* (Atheneum, 1973).

Fontane, Theodor. *Sir Ribbeck of Ribbeck of Havelland.* Trans. from the German by Elizabeth Shub; illus. Nonny Hogrogian. Macmillan, 1969.

Ripe yellow pears grow from the grave of a man who loved to give them away. Grades 1–3.

Francoise (pseud.). *Jeanne-Marie Counts Her Sheep.* Illus. by the author. Scribner's, 1951.

A little French girl counts the number of lambs her sheep may have and plans what she will buy with the money from their wool. The drawings have a childlike simplicity. Grades K–1.

Frasconi, Antonio. *See and Say: A Picture Book in Four Languages.* Illus. by the author. Harcourt, 1955.

Each language, English, Italian, French, and Spanish, is represented in a different color. Striking woodcuts in brilliant colors, in modern design, accompany the words. Grades K–3. See also *See Again, Say Again; The Snow and the Sun;* and *The House That Jack Built.*

Freeman, Don. *The Guard Mouse.* Illus. by the author. Viking, 1967.

Clyde, the guard mouse, not only keeps small creatures from getting through the openings in the wall around Buckingham Palace, but he is also a connoisseur of London. The reader is given a delightful mouse's-eye-view of the city. Grades K–2. See also *Norman the Doorman* (1959).

Fromm, Lilo. *Muffel and Plums*. Macmillan, 1972.
　Without words, drawings of two toy animal characters show progressive action through the humorous adventures on a small scale.

Fuchs, Erich. *Journey to the Moon*. Delacorte, 1969.
　An artist's view of space and its beauty and arrangement. Grades K–2.

Gág, Wanda. *Millions of Cats*. Illus. by the author. Coward-McCann, 1928.
　A perfect picture book because of the folklore quality of the story and the originality and strength of the pictures. Grades K–2. See also *The ABC Bunny*.

Galdone, Paul. *The Old Woman and Her Pig,* McGraw-Hill, 1960.
　The old cumulative tale, illustrated with robust humor. See also *Henny Penny* (Seabury, 1968).

Ginsburg, Mirra. *The Chick and the Duckling*. Illus. José Aruego and Ariane Aruego. Macmillan, 1982.
　A simple, repetitive story of imitative behavior. The minimal text, large print, and humorous, dynamic illustrations make this an excellent choice for beginning readers. Grades Preschool–K.

Goble, Paul. *The Girl Who Loved Wild Horses*. Illus. by the author. Bradbury, 1978.
　This dramatic story of an Indian girl's passion for the graceful untamed horses has the tone of a folktale. The stylized, blazingly colored pictures are true to Indian art. Winner of the Caldecott Medal in 1979. Grades 1–3. See also *The Gift of the Sacred Dog* (1980); *Star Boy* (1983); and *Buffalo Woman* (1984).

Goffstein, M. B. *My Noah's Ark*. Illus. by the author. Harper, 1978.
　Love-filled reminiscences of an old woman about the wooden, toy Noah's ark that accompanied her through her life from childhood to old age. The delicately balanced minimalist black-and-white drawings are a superb example of fine book illustration. Grades K–3. See also *Natural History* (Farrar, Straus & Giroux, 1979); *An Artist* (1980); and other titles by this same artist.

Goodall, John. *The Adventures of Paddy Pork*. Illus. by the author. Harcourt, 1968.
　Without words, this little book takes the viewer through a plot of excitement and peril. Grades K–2. See also *The Ballooning Adventures of Paddy Pork* (1969) and others by the same artist.

Greenfield, Eloise. *She Come Bringing Me That Little Baby Girl*. Illus. John Steptoe. Lippincott, 1974.
　A small boy's reaction to his new baby sister, a poor substitute for the brother he had wanted. His realization that his mother was once a baby girl gives him a new way of looking at his sister. Grades K–2.

Hall, Donald. *Ox-Cart Man*. Illus. Barbara Cooney. Viking, 1979.
　The trip to Portsmouth Market by an early New England farmer is told in the clear, peaceful voice of the oral tradition. The illustrations in the style of early American painting on wood convey the atmosphere of period and place. Awarded the Caldecott Medal in 1980. Grades K–3.

Handforth, Thomas. *Mei Li*. Illus. by the author. Doubleday, 1938.
　Author Handforth created the distinguished drawings while living in China. Both illustrations and text picture with fidelity traditional Chinese life. Awarded the Caldecott Medal in 1939. Grades 1–3.

Harris, Isobel. *Little Boy Brown*. Illus. André François. Lippincott, 1949.
　A famous French artist illustrates the story of a lonely small boy who lives in a hotel, and his delight when he visits a family living in the country. Grades K–2.

Harrison, Ted. *A Northern Alphabet*. Illus. by the author. Tundra, 1982.
　An alphabet book with electrically colored, stylized images of Yukon life by a renowned artist. Grades K–2. See also the bold *Children of the Yukon* (1977).

Heide, Florence Parry. *The Shrinking of Treehorn*. Illus. Edward Gorey. Holiday House, 1971.
　A satirical view of the powerless child in contemporary society complemented by Gorey's wry illustrations. Grades 1–4. See also *Treehorn's Treasure* (Holiday House, 1981).

Heyduck-Huth, Hilde. *In the Forest*. Harcourt, 1971.
　This is a scenic book on thick boards designed, with companion volumes, for close observation by the youngest child. Grades Preschool–K. Others are: *In the Village; The Three Birds;* and *When the Sun Shines*.

Hill, Eric. *Where's Spot?* Illus. by the author. Putnam's, 1980.
　Bright, flat pictures illustrate this simple flap

book with action, suspense, and humor. Grades Preschool–K. See also *Spot's First Walk* (1981); *Spot's Birthday Party* (1982); and *Spot's First Christmas* (1983).

Hoban, Russell. *Bedtime for Frances.* Illus. Garth Williams. Harper, 1960.

A little badger's familial dramas are illustrated with warm humor and tenderness. Grades K–3. See other titles in this series. See also the zany nonsense of *How Tom Beat Captain Najork and His Hired Sportsmen,* illus. Quentin Blake (Atheneum, 1974), and its sequel, *A Near Thing for Captain Najork* (1976).

Hoban, Tana. *Count and See.* Macmillan, 1972.

Photographs of dramatic composition. Grades Preschool–1. See also her other photographic concept books: *Look Again* (1971); *Is It Red? Is It Yellow? Is It Blue?* (Greenwillow, 1978); *A, B, See!* (Greenwillow, 1982); and *Round and Round and Round* (Greenwillow, 1983); and other titles.

Hoberman, Mary Ann. *A House Is a House for Me.* Illus. Betty Fraser. Viking, 1978.

An exploration of the concept of home and community in spirited verse and narrative pictures. Grades K–3.

Hogrogian, Nonny. *One Fine Day.* Illus. by the author. Macmillan, 1971.

A cumulative tale with an Armenian background is shown in beautifully textured shapes and soft subtle colors. Winner of the Caldecott Medal in 1972. Grades K–1. See also *Sir Ribbeck of Ribbeck of Havelland* (poem by Theodor Fontane) (1969); *Apples* (1972); and *Rooster Brother* (1974).

Hughes, Shirley. *Up and Up.* Illus. by the author. Prentice-Hall, 1979.

A wordless fantasy escapade in which a small girl amazes onlookers with her ability to fly. The comic, incisive line drawings cleverly explore the visual potential of the strip format. Grades K–2. See also her reassuring domestic stories of contemporary preschool life: *David and Dog* (1978), winner of the Kate Greenaway Medal in 1977; *Alfie Gets in First* (Lothrop, 1982); *Alfie's Feet* (Lothrop, 1983); and others.

Hutchins, Pat. *Rosie's Walk.* Illus. by the author. Macmillan, 1968.

Brightly decorated pages display the pursuit of an oblivious hen by a frustrated fox. Grades Preschool–2. See also her wordless tale of the subtle transformations of a wooden man and woman in *Changes, Changes* (1971); and comforting stories of preschoolers' concerns: *Titch* (1971); *Happy Birthday, Sam* (Greenwillow, 1978); and *You'll Soon Grow into Them, Titch* (Greenwillow, 1983).

Isadora, Rachel. *Ben's Trumpet.* Illus. by the author. Greenwillow, 1979.

Stylized, rhythmic black-and-white illustrations with a cutting art deco edge complement this 1920s urban tale of a boy who dreams of becoming a jazz trumpeter. Grades K–3. See also *City Seen from A to Z* (1983).

Jeffers, Susan. *Three Jovial Huntsmen.* Bradbury, 1973.

The viewer can see what the three huntsmen cannot: a countryside teeming with animal and bird life. This adaptation of a Mother Goose rhyme successfully unites the pictures of camouflaged wildlife. Grades K–2.

Jonas, Ann. *Round Trip.* Illus. by the author. Greenwillow, 1983.

Minimal text and stark black-and-white drawings detail a trip to the city. When the book is turned upside down, the inverted images ingeniously record the return trip to the country. Grades K–2.

Joslin, Sesyle. *What Do You Say, Dear?* Illus. Maurice Sendak. Young Scott, 1958.

Unreasonable questions; reasonable answers. A delightful guide to common sense and good manners. See also *What Do You Do, Dear?* (1961).

Kahl, Virginia. *The Duchess Bakes a Cake.* Scribner's, 1955.

The rollicking rhythm of this ridiculous story catches and holds young listeners. Grades K–4.

Keats, Ezra Jack. *The Snowy Day.* Illus. by the author. Viking, 1962.

A refreshingly natural story of a little boy who plays in the snow. The stylized illustrations evoke mood and atmosphere. Awarded the Caldecott Medal in 1963. Grades Preschool–1. See also *Whistle for Willie* (1964); *A Letter to Amy* (Harper, 1968); *Little Drummer Boy* (Macmillan, 1968); and *Louie* (Greenwillow, 1983).

Keeping, Charles. *Joseph's Yard.* Illus. by the author. F. Watts, 1970.

A young boy living in poverty in working-class London finds beauty in a flower that grows in his concrete yard. Illustrated in this award-winning artist's distinctive, mixed-media style of dramatic, richly patterned, and searing images. Grades K–3. See also the Kate Greenaway Medal winner *Charley, Charlotte, and the Golden Canary* (1967); *Through the Window* (Oxford Univ. Press, 1970); *Willie's Fire Engine* (Oxford Univ. Press, 1980); and other titles by this same artist.

Kipling, Rudyard. *The Beginning of the Armadillos.* Illus. Giulio Maestro. St. Martin's, 1970.

All of Kipling's *Just So Stories* are good for reading or telling; this is one of a growing number of picture books from these stories. Ulla Kampmann and Leonard Weisgard have illustrated *The Elephant Child.* Grades 1–3. See also the series published by Bedrick: *The Beginning of the Armadillos,* illus. Charles Keeping (1983); *The Butterfly That Stamped,* illus. Alan Baker (1983); *The Cat That Walked by Himself,* illus. William Stobbs (1983); and *The Crab That Played with the Sea,* illus. Michael Foreman (1983).

Kraus, Robert. *Whose Mouse Are You?* Illus. José Aruego. Macmillan, 1970.

A small mouse delivers his mother, father, and sister from peril and finds that his reunited family is augmented by a baby brother. Grades Preschool–K. See also *Herman the Helper,* illus. José Aruego and Ariane Dewey (Windmill, 1974); and other titles by this threesome.

Kurelek, William. *A Prairie Boy's Winter.* Illus. by the author. Houghton Mifflin, 1973.

In this autobiographical narrative, the respected Canadian artist reminisces about the long, cold prairie winters of his childhood. The clear, direct text is accompanied by meticulous paintings, and the artist's fresh, naive style evokes a nostalgic sense of place and childhood activity. All ages. See also the companion volume, *A Prairie Boy's Summer* (1975); *Lumberjack* (1974); and *A Northern Nativity* (Tundra, 1976).

La Fontaine, Jean de. *The Hare and the Tortoise.* Illus. Brian Wildsmith. F. Watts, 1967.

The fable's famous race is illustrated with the sumptuous colors of Wildsmith's painting. See also *The Lion and the Rat* (1963); *The North Wind and the Sun* (1964); *The Rich Man and the Shoe-Maker* (1965); and *The Miller, the Boy and the Donkey* (1969).

Langstaff, John. *Frog Went a-Courtin'.* Retold by John Langstaff; illus. Feodor Rojankovsky. Harcourt, 1955.

Many versions of this well-known ballad have contributed to the making of this American version illustrated by rollicking drawings in color. Awarded the Caldecott Medal in 1956. Grades 1–3. The two gifted collaborators have created a delightful new version of another old rhyme in the picture book *Over in the Meadow,* in which exquisite drawings capture the magic and wonder of nature.

Laurence (Laurence Cruse). *A Village in Normandy.* Illus. by the author. Bobbs-Merrill, 1968.

English and French are used to tell about the places and people in this whimsically portrayed village. Grades 1–3.

Lawrence, Jacob. *Harriet and the Promised Land.* Illus. by the author. Windmill/Simon & Schuster, 1968.

Deliberate and powerful distortion emphasizes the artist's feelings about slavery and the life of Harriet Tubman. Grades 2–4.

Lear, Edward. *ABC.* McGraw-Hill, 1965.

Idiosyncratic line of the illustrations is combined with the nonsense verses of the artist-writer. Grades K–3.

Lindgren, Astrid. *The Tomten.* Illus. Harold Wiberg. Coward-McCann, 1961.

A Scandinavian scene at Christmas, with softly textured barnyard animals receiving the ministrations of the tomten, who visits during the night. Grades 1–3.

Lionni, Leo. *Swimmy.* Illus. by the author. Pantheon, 1963.

After Swimmy's companions have been swallowed by a hungry tuna, he dauntlessly goes on to explore the unknown depths of the ocean. Stunning illustrations with their effective use of color and design convey the beauty of the underwater world. Grades K–1. See also *Little Blue and Little Yellow* (McGraw-Hill, 1959); *Inch by Inch* (Obolensky, 1960); *Frederick* (Pantheon, 1967); *The Biggest House in the World* (Pantheon, 1968); *Alexander and the Wind-Up Mouse* (Pantheon, 1969); *Fish is Fish* (Pantheon, 1970); and *Geraldine the Music Mouse* (Pantheon, 1979).

Lipkind, William. *Finders Keepers.* Illus. Nicolas Mordvinoff. Harcourt, 1951.

The dilemma of two dogs with one bone, told in crisp text and pictures distinguished by droll imagination. Awarded the Caldecott Medal in 1952. Grades K–3. See also *The Two Reds,* a story of a red-haired boy and a red-furred cat and *Little Tiny Rooster* (1960).

Lobel, Arnold. *A Zoo for Mister Muster.* Harper, 1962.

A satisfying adventure with an understanding and endearing character. Grades K–2. See also *A Holiday for Mr. Muster* (1963); *On Market Street,* illus. Anita Lobel (Greenwillow, 1981); *The Rose in My Garden,* illus. Anita Lobel (Greenwillow, 1984); and a brilliant series of beginning readers: *Frog and Toad Are Friends* (1970); *Frog and Toad Together*

(1972); *Owl at Home* (1975); *Frog and Toad All Year* (1976); *Mouse Soup* (1977); *Days with Frog and Toad* (1979); and *Uncle Elephant* (1981).

McCloskey, Robert. *Make Way for Ducklings.* Illus. by the author. Viking, 1941.

A truly American picture book. Mr. and Mrs. Mallard and their eight ducklings make their home on an island in the Charles River. Aided by an Irish policeman, Mrs. Mallard and her ducklings march sedately through Boston traffic to reach the pond in the Public Garden where peanuts and popcorn are plentiful. Awarded the Caldecott Medal in 1942. Grades K–3. See also *Blueberries for Sal* and *One Morning in Maine,* which are equally delightful, and *Time of Wonder,* awarded the Caldecott Medal in 1958.

McKee, David. *Mr. Benn-Red Knight.* Illus. by the author. McGraw-Hill, 1968.

An ingenious springboard for a fantastic adventure is the donning of a costume, then entering the world of that costumed figure. Grades 1–3. See also *123456789 Benn.*

Mari, Iela, and Enzo Mari. *The Chicken and the Egg.* Illus. by the authors. Pantheon, 1970.

Without text, this book shows in handsomely designed pages the reproduction and growth cycle. Grades K–3. See also *The Apple and the Moth.*

Marshall, James. *George and Martha.* Illus. by the author. Houghton Mifflin, 1972.

Humorous and sensitive portrayal of what it means to get along with one another. Grades K–3. See other titles in this series.

Mayne, William. *The Patchwork Cat.* Illus. Nicola Bayley. Knopf, 1981.

Shimmering, jewel-like illustrations complement the poetic, musical text of a lost cat's journey home. Grades K–3. See also *The Mouldy* (1983).

Minarik, Else Holmelund. *Little Bear.* Illus. Maurice Sendak. Harper, 1957.

Easy text and engaging pictures tell of four events in the life of Little Bear. Grades 1–3. See also others in this series.

Mizumura, Kazue. *If I Were a Mother.* Illus. by the author. Crowell, 1968.

Loving in its tone, this is a reassuring book with softly glowing illustrations. Grades K–1.

Mosel, Arlene. *Tikki Tikki Tembo.* Illus. Blair Lent. Holt, 1968.

This tale tells why the Chinese started giving all their sons short names. Grades K–2. See also *The Funny Little Woman,* awarded the Caldecott Medal (Dutton, 1972).

Munari, Bruno. *Bruno Munari's ABC.* Illus. by the author. World, 1960.

A stunning alphabet book conceived with originality and humor. Stimulating to the child's imagination. Grades K–1. See also *Bruno Munari's Zoo* (Philomel, 1963) and *The Circus in the Mist* (1969).

Munsch, Robert. *Murmel, Murmel, Murmel.* Illus. Michael Martchenko. Annick, 1982.

A small girl discovers a foundling and tries to find it a home. This tongue-in-cheek story is highlighted by lively illustrations. Grades K–1. See also *The Mud Puddle,* illus. Sami Suomalainen (1979); *The Paperbag Princess* (1980); and other titles.

Musgrove, Margaret. *Ashanti to Zulu: African Traditions.* Illus. Leo Dillon and Diane Dillon. Dial, 1976.

A striking alphabet book that provides information on African culture and history, with elaborate decorative illustrations. Winner of the Caldecott Medal in 1977. Grades 1–4.

Ness, Evaline. *Sam, Bangs & Moonshine.* Illus. by the author. Holt, 1966.

A small girl learns to distinguish between truth and "moonshine" after her flights of fancy almost bring disaster to her cat and playmate. Evocative illustrations. Grades K–2. See also *Exactly Alike* (Scribner's, 1964).

Nic Leodhas, Sorche. *Always Room for One More.* Illus. Nonny Hogrogian. Holt, 1965.

Lilting text and enchanting black-and-white sketches tinged with purple tones of heather give the traditional Scotch rhyme new dimensions. Awarded the Caldecott Medal in 1966. Grades K–3. See also *All in the Morning Early* (1963); and *The Laird of the Cockpen,* illus. Adrienne Adams (1969).

Oakley, Graham. *The Church Mice in Action.* Illus. by the author. Atheneum, 1983.

The captivating adventures of the British vicar's cat Samson and his friends, the church mice, are described in action-packed text and overflowing, detailed illustrations. Grades K–3. See also *The Church Mouse* (1972); *The Church Mice Spread Their Wings* (1976); and other titles in this series.

Ormerod, Jan. *Moonlight.* Illus. by the author. Lothrop, 1982.

A wordless story of a loving family at bedtime by an award-winning Australian artist. The translucent water colors are composed in a sophisticated strip format. Grades Preschool–K. See also the companion volume *Sunshine* (1981); and the anthology *Rhymes Around the Day,* ed. Pat Thomson (1983).

Ormondroyd, Edward. *Theodore.* Illus. John M. Larrecq. Parnassus, 1966.

A much-loved smudgy teddy bear is not recognized by little Lucy after he is accidentally washed clean. But he is a resourceful bear, manages to become comfortably grubby again, and is soon claimed by his joyful owner. Grades K–3.

Otsuka, Yuzo. *Suho and the White Horse.* Trans. Yaksuko Hirawa; illus. Suekichi Akaba. Bobbs-Merrill, 1969.

The devotion between a boy and a horse undergoes a great trial. There is a beautiful sweep to the Mongolian country setting. Grades K–3.

Oxenbury, Helen. *Numbers of Things.* F. Watts, 1968.

An artist has created an entertaining book with a great deal of visual texture and complex design. Grades Preschool–K. See also *ABC of Things* (1971); *The Queen and Rosie Randall* (Morrow, 1979); and also her excellent series of pre-reading books for toddlers: the first series of delightful wordless board books (Simon & Schuster/Little Simon, 1981) depicts comic everyday scenes in toddlers' lives (*Playing; Working;* and other titles); the second series of board books (Dial, 1982) adds a minimal text (*Beach Day; Monkey See, Monkey Do;* and other titles); and the third series (Dial, 1983) are first-person anecdotes recounted by the preschoolers (*The Dancing Class; The Drive;* and other titles).

Parish, Peggy. *Amelia Bedelia.* Illus. Fritz Sibel. Harper, 1963.

The disastrous effects of the several meanings of the same word provide hilarious situations. Grades 1–3. See other titles in this series.

Peet, Bill. *Hubert's Hair-Raising Adventure.* Illus. by the author. Houghton Mifflin, 1959.

This fast-paced story told in nonsense verse moves with a kind of zany precision. Grades 2–5. See also *Chester the Worldly Pig* (1965) and *The Wump World* (1970).

Piatti, Celestino. *The Happy Owls.* Illus. by the author. Atheneum, 1964.

A stunning picture book in which the quarrelsome barnyard fowl ask the owls why they are happy. Grades K–3. See also *Celestino Piatti's Animal ABC; The Holy Night* (1968); and *The Nock Family Circus* (1968).

Pienkowski, Jan. *The Haunted House.* Illus. by the author. Dutton, 1979.

This visually literate, ingenious pop-up book won the Kate Greenaway Award in 1979. Grades K–5. The high standards of paper engineering and design are also evident in *Robot* (Delacorte, 1981).

Politi, Leo. *The Song of the Swallows.* Illus. by the author. Scribner's, 1949.

A tender, poetic story of Little Juan and how he helped ring the bells at the Capistrano Mission to welcome the swallows as they came flying in from the sea on St. Joseph's Day. Pictures are in soft colors. Awarded the Caldecott Medal in 1950. Grades K–3.

Potter, Beatrix. *The Tailor of Gloucester.* Illus. by the author. Warne, 1903.

After reading the Peter Rabbit books, children will enjoy this beautiful little Christmas story of a poor tailor and his cat who lived "in the time of swords and periwigs." John Masefield called this little book "a gem of English prose." See also other titles by this author-artist. Grades 1–4.

Preston, Edna Mitchell. *Pop Corn and Ma Goodness.* Illus. Robert Andrew Parker. Viking, 1969.

A rollicking folk rhyme, portrayed with a soft water-color technique. Grades K–2.

Provensen, Alice, and Martin Provensen. *The Glorious Flight: Across the Channel with Louis Blériot.* Illus. by the authors. Viking, 1983.

The courage and tenacity of Louis Blériot in his experiments with early flying machines is revealed in a lyrical, light text and vast, sweepingly panoramic illustrations. Winner of the Caldecott Medal in 1984. Grades K–3. See also *A Peaceable Kingdom: The Shaker Abecedarius* (1978) and other titles by this team.

Rand, Ann. *I Know a Lot of Things.* Illus. Paul Rand. Harcourt, 1956.

A picture book that presents imaginative concepts instead of a story. Grades K–1. See also *Sparkle and Spin,* which introduces the child to the wonder and fun of words, and *Did a Bear Just Walk There?* illus. Abe Birnbaum (1966).

Raskin, Ellen. *Nothing Ever Happens on My Block.* Illus. by the author. Atheneum, 1966.

While Chester sits glumly on the curb bemoaning the lack of excitement, the most incredible things are going on all around him. Grades K–3. See also *And It Rained* (1969).

Rayner, Mary. *Mr. and Mrs. Pig's Evening Out.* Illus. by the author. Atheneum, 1976.

An amusing tongue-in-cheek story of Mrs. Wolf babysitting ten succulent pig children. The pigs triumph in wildly warm and comic pictures. Grades K–2. See also the sequel *Garth Pig and the Ice Cream Lady* (1977).

Rey, H. A. *Curious George.* Illus. by the author. Houghton Mifflin, 1941.

The zestful activity of a small monkey and his difficulty in getting used to the city before he goes to live in a zoo. Told in simple text and bright pictures, this is the first story in a popular series. Grades K–2.

Rice, Eve. *Benny Bakes a Cake.* Illus. by the author. Greenwillow, 1981.

A perfect balance of full illustrations and reassuring, toddler-scale drama. Grades Preschool–K. See also *Sam Who Never Forgets* (1977).

Robbins, Ruth. *Baboushka and the Three Kings.* Illus. Nicolas Sidjakov. Parnassus, 1960.

Distinguished illustrations illuminate this tale of the old woman who, refusing to follow the three kings in search of the Holy Child and failing to find Him herself, each year renews her endless search. Awarded the Caldecott Medal in 1961. Grades 2–5.

Rockwell, Harlow. *My Doctor.* Illus. by the author. Macmillan, 1973.

The pure clarity of the meticulous water-color illustrations complements this clean, direct presentation of a routine visit to the doctor. Grades Preschool–K. The same technique is used in *My Dentist* (Greenwillow, 1975); *My Nursery School* (Greenwillow, 1976); and *My Kitchen* (Greenwillow, 1980).

Rojankovsky, Feodor. *Animals on the Farm.* Illus. by the author. Knopf, 1967.

A barnyard filled with ordinary animals becomes extraordinary with Rojankovsky's vibrant colors. Grades K–2.

Rose, Elizabeth. *Wuffles Goes to Town.* Illus. Gerald Rose. Barnes, n.d.

Wuffles, a hunting dog from the country, becomes a hero in the city when he tracks a thief and pulls him from the river in which he is drowning. Grades 1–3. See also *How St. Francis Tamed the Wolf* (Harcourt, 1959); *St. George and the Fiery Dragon* (Norton, 1964); and *"Ahhh!" Said Stork* (Faber & Faber, 1977).

Ryan, Cheli Duran. *Hildilid's Night.* Illus. Arnold Lobel. Macmillan, 1971.

Hildilid's attempts to get rid of the night so wear her out that when the sun rises she has to go to bed to be fresh for fighting the night again. Grades K–2.

Rylant, Cynthia. *When I Was Young in the Mountains.* Illus. Diane Goode. Dutton, 1982.

An Appalachian memoir in singing prose illustrated with finely drawn, understated pictures. Grades K–3.

Sandburg, Carl. *The Wedding Procession of the Rag Doll and the Broom Handle and Who Was in It.* Illus. Harriet Pincus. Harcourt, 1967.

The illustrations enhance the humor and imagination of Carl Sandburg's whimsical story from his *Rootabaga Stories.* Grades 1–3.

Scheer, Julian. *Rain Makes Applesauce.* Illus. Marvin Bileck. Holiday House, 1964.

Marvelously complicated line drawings of a fantasy world combine with a running nonsense line, "You're just talking silly talk." Grades K–2.

Schwartz, Delmore. *"I Am Cherry Alive," the Little Girl Sang.* Illus. Barbara Cooney. Harper, 1979.

A picture-book version of a single, joyous poem celebrating life and childhood, by a respected adult poet. The lyric intensity of the text is conveyed in the luminous paintings. Grades K–3.

Scott, Ann Herbert. *Sam.* Illus. Symeon Shimin. McGraw-Hill, 1967.

A sensitive story with distinguished drawings that extend the mood of the text. Grades K–2.

Segal, Lore. *Tell Me a Mitzi.* Illus. Harriet Pincus. Farrar, Straus & Giroux, 1970.

The strenuous adventure of a little girl who dresses and undresses her brother is one of the "Mitzi" stories. Humor and realistic detail give this book a droll character. Grades K–2.

Sendak, Maurice. *Where the Wild Things Are.* Illus. by the author. Harper, 1963.

A small unruly boy sent supperless to bed dreams that he sails away to where the wild things are. Here he is King and tames the grotesque monsters. The story has a perfect ending. Awarded the Caldecott Medal in 1964. Grades K–2. See also the two titles that complete Sendak's "emotional trilogy": *In the Night Kitchen* (1970) and *Outside over There* (1981); and his Nutshell Library: *Alligators All Around; Chicken Soup with Rice; One Was Johnny;* and *Pierre* (1962). See also Sendak's interpretation of E. T. A. Hoffmann's *The Nutcracker,* translated by Ralph Manheim (1984).

Seuss, Dr. (Theodor Geisel). *And To Think That I Saw It on Mulberry Street.* Illus. by the author. Vanguard, 1937.

A small boy's imagination peoples a prosaic street with strange and marvelous creations. Grades K–3. See also *The 500 Hats of Bartholomew Cubbins* (1938); *Horton Hatches the Egg* (Random House, 1940); *The Cat in the Hat* (Random House, 1957); and *How the Grinch Stole Christmas* (Random House, 1957).

Shulevitz, Uri. *One Monday Morning.* Illus. by the author. Scribner's, 1967.

A lonely child's imagination brings to life a playing-card king and his entire court, who march gaily across the pages of the book. Grades K–3. See also *Rain Rain Rivers* (Farrar, Straus & Giroux, 1969); *Dawn* (Farrar, Straus & Giroux, 1974); and *The Treasure* (Farrar, Straus & Giroux, 1979).

Spier, Peter. *Peter Spier's Rain.* Illus. by the author. Doubleday, 1982.

A wordless, detailed sequence of narrative water colors conveys the spirit of a rainy day. Grades K–2. See also the nonfiction *People* (1980) and *Peter Spier's Christmas* (1983).

Steig, William. *Sylvester and the Magic Pebble.* Illus. by the author. Simon & Schuster, 1969.

A soft poetic mood underlined with humor permeates this book in which Sylvester unwittingly becomes a rock in a meadow. Awarded the Caldecott Medal in 1970. Grades K–3. See also *Amos and Boris* (Farrar, Straus & Giroux, 1971); *The Amazing Bone* (Farrar, Straus & Giroux, 1976); and *Doctor De Soto* (Farrar, Straus & Giroux, 1982).

Steptoe, John. *Train Ride.* Illus. by the author. Harper, 1971.

Heavily outlined shapes and vivid, raw colors give a strength to the underlying emotional qualities of this simple story. Grades K–2. See also *Stevie* (1969); and *Daddy's a Monster . . . Sometimes* (1980).

Stevenson, James. *Howard.* Illus. by the author. Greenwillow, 1980.

A witty story enlivened by subtle cartoons of an abandoned migrating duck stranded in Manhattan for the winter. Grades K–3. See also *What's Under My Bed?* (Greenwillow, 1983).

Stinson, Kathy. *Red Is Best.* Illus. Robin Baird Lewis. Annick, 1982.

Simple, rhythmic prose and warm illustrations convey a toddler's love of the color red. Grades Preschool–K.

Stren, Patti. *Hug Me.* Illus. by the author. Harper, 1977.

This wry fable of a porcupine's quest for a friend to hug is illustrated with quirky, stylish cartoons. Grades K–3. See also *Sloan and Philamina; or How to Make Friends with Your Lunch* (Dutton, 1979) and *I'm Only Afraid of the Dark (at Night!!)* (1982).

Suteyev, V. *Mushroom in the Rain.* Adapt. from the Russian by Mirra Ginsburg; illus. José Aruego and Ariane Dewey. Macmillan, 1974.

Huddling under a mushroom in the rain, first an ant and then more and more come to find shelter, always finding, miraculously, room for the newcomer. Grades K–2.

Taylor, Mark. *The Bold Fisherman.* Illus. Graham Booth. Golden Gate, 1967.

The story is based on an old folk song about what happened to Jonah Jones when he encountered the creatures of the deep sea. Accompanied by striking illustrations. Grades 1–3. See also *Henry the Explorer* (Atheneum, 1966).

Titus, Eve. *Anatole and the Cat.* Illus. Paul Galdone. McGraw-Hill, 1957.

Adventures with a droll flavor. Grades 1–3.

Tolstoy, Alexei. *The Great Big Enormous Turnip.* Illus. Helen Oxenbury. F. Watts, 1968.

Based on an old cumulative folktale, this version is developed with a humorous, visual flamboyance. Grades K–2.

Tresselt, Alvin. *White Snow, Bright Snow.* Illus. Roger Duvoisin. Lothrop, 1947.

Poetic text and full-page illustrations in soft blue accented with touches of red and yellow convey the beauty of the first snowfall, the activities of winter, and the approach of spring. Awarded the Caldecott Medal in 1948. Grades K–3. See also *Hide and Seek Fog.*

Turkle, Brinton. *Thy Friend, Obadiah.* Illus. by the author. Viking, 1969.

About an engaging small Quaker boy. Grades K–2. See also *Deep in the Forest* (Dutton, 1976) and a contemporary fable of the genie in the bottle, *Do Not Open* (Dutton, 1981).

Udry, Janice May. *A Tree Is Nice.* Illus. Marc Simont. Harper, 1956.

Rhythmic text and colorful pictures combine to tell why trees are nice. Awarded the Caldecott Medal in 1957. Grades K–1. See also *The Moon Jumpers.*

Ungerer, Tomi. *Snail, Where Are You?* Illus. by the author. Harper, 1962.

Children have fun finding the spiral pattern of the snail in this original picture book. Grades K–2. See also *The Mellops Go Diving for Treasure*

(1957); *The Mellops Go Flying* (1957); *The Mellops Go Spelunking* (1963); *Three Robbers* (Atheneum, 1962); *Zeralda's Ogre* (1967); and other titles by this same artist.

Van Allsburg, Chris. *Jumanji*. Illus. by the author. Houghton Mifflin, 1981.

　　Awarded the Caldecott Medal in 1982, this is a sophisticated fantasy of a magical jungle board game that becomes a three-dimensional reality. Illustrated by sculptural images that have an eerie stillness and unusual cinematic perspective in strong black-and-white conté drawings. Grades K–4. See also *The Garden of Abdul Gasazi* (1979) and the full-color *The Wreck of the Zephyr* (1983).

Vincent, Gabrielle. *Ernest and Celestine*. Illus. by the author. Greenwillow, 1982.

　　The French bear and mouse make the perfect father and adopted daughter. Their domestic adventures are comic and touching. Fine narrative illustrations in the tradition of Leslie Brooke. Grades K–2. See also *Bravo, Ernest and Celestine!* (1981) and other titles in this series.

Viorst, Judith. *Alexander and the Terrible, Horrible, No Good Very Bad Day*. Illus. Ray Cruz. Atheneum, 1972.

　　An amusing, sensitive story of a young boy's trying day. The realistic observations are enhanced by the contemporary tone of the black-and-white drawings. Grades K–3. See also *Rosie and Michael*, illus. Lorna Tomei (1974).

Vipont, Elfrida. *The Elephant and the Bad Baby*. Illus. Raymond Briggs. Coward-McCann, 1970.

　　This is a tongue-in-cheek moral tale that follows the baby who never once said please through a cumulative, rhythmic adventure to a satisfying close. The pastel pictures add a droll touch. Grades Preschool–1.

Waber, Bernard. *The House on East 88th Street*. Illus. by the author. Houghton Mifflin, 1962.

　　The ingratiating manners of Lyle the crocodile endear him to the Primm family who suffer when he is taken from them. Grades 1–3. See also *Lyle, Lyle, Crocodile; Lorenzo* (1961); *Rich Cat, Poor Cat* (1963); and *A Firefly Named Torchy* (1970).

Wagner, Jenny. *John Brown, Rose and the Midnight Cat*. Illus. Ron Brooks. Bradbury, 1978.

　　A poignant story of the love between a widow and her shaggy sheepdog and what happens when a mysterious cat intrudes on their life together. The wise text is subtly extended by warm pastel illustrations executed with a fine draftmanship. Grades K–3. See also *The Bunyip of Berkeley's Creek* (1977) and *Aranea* (1978) by the same Australian team.

Wallace, Ian. *Chin Chiang and the Dragon's Dance*. Illus. by the author. Atheneum, A Margaret McElderry Book, 1984.

　　Paintings of a Chinese Canadian community evoke the setting and dream-like atmosphere of this story, of a young boy who overcomes his fear of dancing and the ritual dragon's dance. Grades 1–3.

Ward, Lynd. *The Biggest Bear*. Illus. by the author. Houghton Mifflin, 1952.

　　A thoroughly American picture book that had its roots in the author's own childhood. Johnny Orchard longed for a bearskin to hang on his barn, but the bear he found was much too little to shoot. Johnny kept him as a pet, but the bear became more and more of a problem as he grew up. How Johnny found a home for his bear makes a heartwarming story told almost entirely by the pictures. Awarded the Caldecott Medal in 1953. Grades K–2.

Watanabe, Shigeo. *How Do I Put It On?* Illus. Yasuo Ohtomi. Philomel, 1979.

　　A simple story for toddlers in which a small bear amusingly learns the skills of dressing. Grades Preschool–K. See also titles similar in comic mood and instructive intent: *What a Good Lunch!* (1980); *I Can Ride It!* (1982); *Where's My Daddy?* (1982); and other titles.

Waterton, Betty. *Pettranella*. Illus. Ann Blades. Vanguard Press, 1980.

　　This pioneer story of a young immigrant girl's adjustment to a new life on the Canadian prairies is illustrated by rich water colors with a naive, folk art quality. See also *A Salmon for Simon* (Douglas & McIntyre, 1978).

Watson, Clyde. *Father Fox's Pennyrhymes*. Illus. Wendy Watson. Crowell, 1971.

　　Engaging illustrations are replete with detail and enhanced by humorous, balloon-encased remarks. Grades K–4. See also the fresh *Catch Me and Kiss Me and Say It Again* (Philomel, 1978).

Wells, Rosemary. *Benjamin and Tulip*. Illus. by the author. Dial, 1973.

　　The love-hate relationship of two small animals. Grades K–2. Similar episodes of sibling love and rivalry are comically detailed in *Stanley and Rhoda* (1978) and *Peabody* (Dial, 1983). See also the simple board book series of rabbit Max's adventures published by Dial in 1979: *Max's First Word; Max's New Suit; Max's Ride;* and *Max's Toys: A Counting Book*.

Wildsmith, Brian. *Brian Wildsmith's Birds.* Illus. by the author. F. Watts, 1967.

A wedge of swans, a sedge of herons, a nye of pheasants, a siege of bitterns, a stare of owls, and many more are shown in double-page spreads in radiant color. Grades 1–3. See also *Brian Wildsmith's 1, 2, 3's; Brian Wildsmith's ABC; Brian Wildsmith's Wild Animals; Brian Wildsmith's Fishes;* and *The Circus* (1970); *The Little Wood Duck* (1972); *The Lazy Bear* (Oxford, 1973); and *Daisy* (Pantheon, 1983).

Williams, Vera B. *A Chair for My Mother.* Illus. by the author. Greenwillow, 1982.

A story of urban family life told in the voice of a small girl. The loving warmth is captured in the richly textural fauvist paintings. Grades K–3. See also the sequel *Something Special for Me* (1983).

Wolkstein, Diane. *8,000 Stones.* Retold by Diane Wolkstein; illus. Ed Young. Doubleday, 1972.

A small boy is the one to figure out how to determine the weight of an elephant in this retelling of a Chinese folktale. Grades 1–3.

Wynne-Jones, Tim. *Zoom at Sea.* Illus. Ken Nutt. Douglas & McIntyre, A Groundwood Book, 1983.

An evocative fantasy of a cat who loves water and goes in search of a magical sea, illustrated in sophisticated pencil drawings. Winner of the Canadian Amelia Frances Howard Gibbon Illustrator's Award in 1984. Grades K–2.

Yashima, Taro (pseud.). *Crow Boy.* Illus. by the author. Viking, 1955.

The author-artist has created a sensitive picture book from the poignant memory of his own childhood in Japan. A shy, lonely mountain boy leaves his home at dawn to go to a village school. He is ignored by his classmates until an understanding teacher shows them that Crow Boy has much to give them. The pictures are in glowing colors. Grades K–3. See also *The Umbrella* (1958), whose text and pictures have the same tender, poignant quality, and *Seashore Story* (1967).

Yolen, Jane. *The Emperor and the Kite.* Illus. Ed Young. World, 1967.

Distinguished by the rhythmic balance of the text and by the artist's use of the Oriental paper-cut style of illustration. Grades K–3. See also *The Seventh Mandarin* (Seabury, 1970) and *All in the Morning Early: An ABC Book,* illus. Jane Breskin Zalben (Collins, 1979).

Yulga. *Bears Are Sleeping.* Illus. Nonny Hogrogian. Scribner's, 1967.

Softly textured shapes help create the quiet mood of this book. Grades K–2.

Zemach, Harve, adapt. *Mommy, Buy Me a China Doll.* Illus. Margot Zemach. Farrar, Straus & Giroux, 1975.

Taken from an Ozark children's song, this repetitive bit of nonsense is deftly transposed into hilarious visual scenes. Grades K–2. See also *The Speckled Hen* (Holt, 1966); *The Judge* (Farrar, Straus & Giroux, 1969); *Awake and Dreaming* (Farrar, Straus & Giroux, 1970); and *Duffy and the Devil* (Farrar, Straus & Giroux, 1973), awarded the Caldecott Medal.

Zion, Gene. *Sugar Mouse Cake.* Illus. Margaret Bloy Graham. Scribner's, 1964.

The substitution of a real mouse for one of the sugar-made mice on top of a cake entered in the competition for Royal Cook places the mouse in peril. Grades 1–3. See also *Harry the Dirty Dog* (Harper, 1956) and *No Roses for Harry* (1958).

Zolotow, Charlotte. *Mr. Rabbit and the Lovely Present.* Illus. Maurice Sendak. Harper, 1962.

A little girl meets Mr. Rabbit and asks him to help find a birthday gift for her mother. Grades K–2. See also *When the Wind Stops,* illus. Howard Knotts (1975).

Folktales in Picture Books

Arrow to the Sun: A Pueblo Indian Tale. Adapt. and illus. Gerald McDermott. Viking, 1974.

A Pueblo Indian tale illustrated in highly stylized geometric shapes that echo Indian patterns. Grades K–2. See also *Anansi the Spider: A Tale from the Ashanti* (Holt, 1972); *The Stonecutter: A Japanese Folktale* (1975); *The Voyage of Osiris: A Myth of Ancient Egypt* (Windmill/Dutton, 1977); and *Sun Flight* (Four Winds, 1980).

Beauty and the Beast. Retold by Marianna Mayer; illus. Mercer Mayer. Four Winds, 1978.

Madame Le Prince De Beaumont's eighteenth-century romantic fairy tale is sensitively retold and enthrallingly pictured with elaborate illustrations.

A Boy Went Out to Gather Pears. Illus. Felix Hoffmann. Harcourt, 1966.

An old cumulative tale from the German retold pictorially.

The Bremen Town Musicians. Illus. Paul Galdone. McGraw-Hill, 1968.

See also the edition illustrated by Ilse Plume (Doubleday, 1980) and the edition by Donna Diamond (Delacorte, 1981).

Bringing the Rain to Kapiti Plain: A Nandi Tale. Retold by Verna Aardema; illus. Beatriz Vidal. Dial, 1981.

A Kenyan legend about drought and perseverance retold in verse to the rhythmic cadences of "The House That Jack Built." The musical grace is accompanied by blazingly colored naive art.

The Buried Moon. Illus. Susan Jeffers. Bradbury, 1969.
Taken from the Joseph Jacobs collection *More English Fairy Tales* (1893), this picture book creates a compelling and eerie mood.

The Cat and Mouse Who Shared a House. Adapt. and illus. Ruth Hürlimann; trans. from the German by Anthea Bell. Walck, 1973.

Cinderella; or The Glass Slipper. A free translation from Perrault; illus. Marcia Brown. Scribner's, 1954.
See also the following editions: illus. with courtly elegance by Errol Le Cain (Faber & Faber, 1972); illuminated with meticulous jewel-like images by Moira Kemp (Hamilton, 1981); and illustrated with homely gentleness by Otto Svend S. (Larousse, 1978).

The Clown of God: An Old Story. Retold and illus. by Tomie de Paola. Harcourt, 1978.
Giovanni is named as the juggler in the artist's interpretation of a folktale about service in life and death, recorded in the thirteenth century.

The Cock, the Mouse and the Little Red Hen. Retold and illus. by Lorinda Bryan Cauley. Putnam's, 1982.
The classic nursery story of the industrious hen and her lazy companions is affectionately brought to life through colloquial retelling and the soft-hued, warmly comic illustrations. See also *The Little Red Hen,* illus. Paul Galdone (Houghton Mifflin/Clarion, 1973).

The Devil with the Three Golden Hairs. Retold and illus. by Nonny Hogrogian. Knopf, 1983.
The Grimm legend with gentle yet earthy illustrations.

Dick Whittington and His Cat. Told and cut in linoleum by Marcia Brown. Scribner's, 1950.

The Fisherman and His Wife. Illus. Margot Zemach. Norton, 1966.
See also the edition illustrated by Madeleine Gekiere (Pantheon, 1957); the edition by Katrin Brandt (Follett, 1969); and Zemach's reillustration of the story with comic virtuosity in Randall Jarrell's rendition (Farrar, Straus & Giroux, 1980).

The Fool of the World and the Flying Ship. Retold by Arthur Ransome; illus. Uri Shulevitz. Farrar, Straus & Giroux, 1968.

The tale of a simple peasant lad who wins the hand of the Czar's daughter after overcoming great obstacles. Awarded the Caldecott Medal in 1969.

The Four Clever Brothers. Illus. Felix Hoffmann. Harcourt, 1967.

The Fox Went Out on a Chilly Night. Illus. Peter Spier. Doubleday, 1961.
An old song made into one of the most beautiful and childlike picture books in many years.

The Gingerbread Boy. Illus. Paul Galdone. Houghton Mifflin/Clarion, 1975.
A simple, brief text with active and broadly sketched illustrations.

The Golden Goose. Illus. William Stobbs. McGraw-Hill, 1967.
See also the edition illustrated by L. Leslie Brooke.

The Golem: A Jewish Legend. Retold and illus. by Beverly Brodsky McDermott. Lippincott, 1975.
Abstract images dynamically convey the intense drama of the clay monster's fate.

Gone Is Gone; or The Story of a Man Who Wanted to Do Housework. Retold and illus. by Wanda Gág. Coward-McCann, 1935.
The droll illustrations reflect perfectly the naiveté of the story.

Hansel and Gretel. Trans. from the German by Elizabeth Crawford; illus. Lisbeth Zwerger. Morrow, 1979.
An impressionistic Austrian artist creates evocative, potent images. See also the edition romantically illustrated by Susan Jeffers (Dial, 1980) and the edition illustrated by Anthony Brown (F. Watts, 1982), who created a contemporary setting in urban poverty with symbolic visual images of chilling effect.

Humpy. Adapt. P. Yershov; trans. from the Russian by William C. White; illus. Jacqueline Ayer. Harcourt, 1966.
A spirited translation of the old tale about Ivan the simple fool who, with the help of Humpy the little magic horse, outwits the Czar and marries the Princess. Slavic flavor and robust humor distinguish the story.

In the Land of Small Dragon: A Vietnamese Folktale. Told by Dang Manh Kha to Ann Nolan Clark; illus. Tony Chen. Viking, 1979.
This Vietnamese Cinderella variant is retold in traditional verse form with additional proverbs. Graceful watercolor and pen-and-ink illustrations provide historical details of costume and setting.

Jack and the Beanstalk. Retold and illus. by William Stobbs. Delacorte, 1966.

Jorinda and Joringel. Trans. Elizabeth Shub; illus. Adrienne Adams. Scribner's, 1968.
See also edition illustrated by Bernadette Watts (World, 1970).

Journey Cake, Ho! Retold by Ruth Sawyer; illus. Robert McCloskey. Viking, 1953.
A noted storyteller and a gifted artist have combined their talents to produce this rollicking American version of *The Pancake.*

Little Brother and Little Sister. Retold and illus. by Barbara Cooney. Doubleday, 1982.
Retold from Grimm, this tender, eerie story is romantically illustrated in a naive, haunting style.

Little Red Riding Hood. Retold and illus. by Trina Schart Hyman. Holiday House, 1983.
A Caldecott Honor Book for 1984. Charmingly decorative illustrations and dramatically realized characters make this a vivid interpretation of the tale. See also *Grimm's Little Red Cap,* trans. Elizabeth D. Crawford, illus. Lisbeth Zwerger (Morrow, 1983).

The Mare's Egg: A New World Folk Tale. Retold by Carole Spray; illus. Kim La Fave. Camden House, 1981.
A Canadian folktale in the tradition of the "numbskull" tale, recounts the trials of a gullible nineteenth-century genteel pioneer. The droll illustrations complement the humorous text.

Mr. Miacca: An English Folk Tale. Illus. Evaline Ness. Holt, 1967.

Molly Whuppie. Retold by Walter de la Mare; illus. Errol Le Cain. Farrar, Straus & Giroux, 1983.
De la Mare's witty, eloquent version of this English tale is enhanced by the stylized illustrations that capture the character of the spirited heroine. First published in *Tales Told Again* (Knopf, 1927).

Peter and the Wolf. Retold by Sergei Prokofiev; illus. Warren Chappell. Knopf, 1940.
The Russian folktale in which the wolf eats the duck only to be outwitted by Peter and the bird is combined with musical themes.

Petrosinella: A Neapolitan Rapunzel. Trans. from Giambattista Basile by John Edward Taylor; illus. Diane Stanley. Warne, 1981.
An Italian version of Rapunzel, enhanced by radiant paintings in a meticulous sixteenth-century style.

Puss in Boots. Adapt. from Perrault; illus. Hans Fischer. Harcourt, 1959.

See also *Puss in Boots,* illus. Marcia Brown (Scribner's, 1952); *Puss in Boots,* illus. Paul Galdone (Seabury, 1976); and the elegant pop-up version illustrated by Nicola Bayley (Greenwillow, 1977).

Rapunzel. Illus. Felix Hoffmann. Harcourt, 1961.
See also the edition illustrated by Bernadette Watts (Harper 1975) and the edition retold by Barbara Rogasky and illustrated by Trina Schart Hyman (Holiday House, 1982).

Rumpelstiltskin. Illus. Jacqueline Ayer. Harcourt, 1967.

Salt. Trans. Benjamin Zemach from Alexei Afanasev; adapt. Harve Zemach; illus. Margot Zemach. Farrar, Straus & Giroux, 1975.
The foolish son of a Russian merchant triumphs over his elder brother by bringing salt to his homeland.

The Seven Ravens. Illus. Felix Hoffmann. Harcourt, 1963.
See also the edition retold and illustrated in mysterious black-and-white drawings by Donna Diamond (Viking, 1979) and the edition translated by Elizabeth D. Crawford and illustrated by Lisbeth Zwerger (Morrow, 1981).

Seven Simeons: A Russian Tale. Retold and illus. by Boris Artzybasheff. Viking, 1961.
A delightfully humorous tale of seven brothers who used their magic to help their king. Decorative, imaginative drawings by a famous Russian-American artist. First published in 1937.

The Shoemaker and the Elves. Illus. Adrienne Adams. Scribner's, 1960.

The Silver Cow: A Welsh Tale. Retold by Susan Cooper; illus. Warwick Hutton. Atheneum, 1983.
This poetic, fluent retelling of a haunting story about a supernatural cow and an ungrateful farmer captures the music and humor of Welsh folklore. The water colors are luminous and dramatic.

The Sleeping Beauty. Illus. Felix Hoffmann. Harcourt, 1960.
See also the edition of the Grimm version, *Thorn Rose,* sumptuously illustrated by Errol Le Cain (Faber & Faber, 1975); the vigorous, romantic pictures in the edition illustrated by Trina Schart Hyman (Little, Brown, 1977); and the intimate water colors in the edition illustrated by Warwick Hutton (Atheneum, 1979).

Snow White and Rose Red. Illus. by Barbara Cooney. Delacorte, 1966.
See also the edition illustrated by Adrienne Adams (Scribner's, 1964).

Snow White and the Seven Dwarfs. Trans. and illus. Wanda Gág. Coward-McCann, 1938.

Snow-White and the Seven Dwarfs. Trans. Randall Jarrell; illus. Nancy Ekholm Burkert. Farrar, Straus & Giroux, 1972.

This famous and enduring tale from the Grimm collections is given an elegant setting and a sensitive translation. See also *Snow White,* freely translated by Paul Heins and broodingly illustrated by Trina Schart Hyman (Little, Brown, 1974).

The Sorcerer's Apprentice. Wanda Gág; illus. Margot Tomes. (Coward, McCann, 1979).

The text of this tale was adapted by Wanda Gág from several sources and originally appeared in her collection *More Tales from Grimm* (1947). The spirited drawings and compact format of this edition give an intimate spirit to the story.

Stone Soup: An Old Tale. Told and illus. by Marcia Brown. Scribner's, 1947.

See also *Une Drôle de Soupe,* trans. into French by Hilda Greenier Tagliapietra and illus. Marcia Brown.

A Story, a Story: An African Tale. Adapt. and illus. Gail E. Haley. Atheneum, 1970.

The 1971 Caldecott Medal winner, this witty and musical Anansi story is colorfully illustrated in stylized woodcuts.

The Story of Prince Ivan, the Firebird, and the Gray Wolf. Trans. from the Russian by Thomas P. Whitney; illus. Nonny Hogrogian. Scribner's, 1968.

The classic Russian tale on which Stravinsky's "Firebird" is based.

The Story of the Three Bears. Illus. William Stobbs. McGraw-Hill, 1964.

Strega Nona. Retold and illus. by Tomie de Paola. Prentice-Hall, 1975.

A variation of the sorcerer's apprentice theme, only this time the culprit has to eat all the pasta summoned from the magic pasta pot.

Tattercoats: An Old English Tale. Retold by Flora Annie Steel; illus. Diane Goode. Bradbury, 1976.

Fine draftsmanship and subdued images interpret this classic variant of the Cinderella tale.

Three Billy Goats Gruff. Illus. Marcia Brown. Harcourt, 1957.

The drama of this story is well highlighted. See also the edition illustrated by Paul Galdone (Clarion, 1973).

The Three Little Pigs. Illus. William Pène du Bois. Viking, 1962.

See also the edition cleverly illustrated by Erik Blegvad (Atheneum, 1980).

The Three Sillies. Illus. Margot Zemach. Holt, 1963.

Tom Thumb. Illus. Felix Hoffmann. Atheneum, 1973.

See also the edition impressionistically illustrated by Freire Wright, *The Adventures of Tom Thumb* (Kaye & Ward, 1983).

Tom Tit Tot. Illus. Evaline Ness. Scribner's, 1965.

The Traveling Musicians. Illus. Hans Fischer. Harcourt, 1955.

Twelve Dancing Princesses. Illus. Adrienne Adams. Holt, 1966.

See also the edition illustrated by Uri Shulevitz (Scribner's, 1966) and the one lyrically retold by Janet Lunn and elegantly illustrated by Laszlo Gal (Methuen, 1979).

Vasilisa the Beautiful. Illus. Nonny Hogrogian. Macmillan, 1970.

A variant of the Cinderella story, this tale features the Russian witch Baba Yaga.

Where the Buffaloes Begin. Olaf Baker; illus. Stephen Gammel. Warne, 1981.

A poetic version of a Blackfoot Indian legend, first published in *St. Nicholas Magazine* in 1915. The story tells of Little Wolf, who goes in search of the sacred lake where the buffaloes begin and saves his people from attack and slaughter by an enemy tribe. The quest and rescue themes are made abstract and dreamlike through impressionistic black-and-white pencil drawings. Grades K–3.

The White Rat's Tale: An Old French Tale. Retold by Barbara Schiller; illus. Adrienne Adams. Holt, 1967.

Who's in Rabbit's House? A Masai Tale. Retold by Verna Aardema; illus. Leo Dillon and Diane Dillon. Dial, 1977.

A humorous, rhythmic folktale told with strikingly onomatopoeic language. The illustrations portray the characters as village actors wearing animal masks in a play. A theatrical tour de force.

Why Mosquitoes Buzz in People's Ears. Retold by Verna Aardema; illus. Leo Dillon and Diane Dillon. Dial, 1975.

In this West African story, a chain of events that results in an accident to one of the baby owlets has to be retraced in reverse order before the instigator is discovered and Mother Owl allows the sun to rise again. Awarded the Caldecott Medal.

The Wolf and the Seven Little Kids. Illus. Felix Hoffmann. Harcourt, 1959.

Yeh-Shen: A Cinderella Story from China. Retold by Ai-Ling Louie; illus. Ed Young. Philomel, 1982.

A Chinese variant of the European Cinderella, fluently retold from ancient, T'ang dynasty manuscripts. Poetic, evocative illustrations in panel design provide an accurate, vivid setting.

The Art of the Picture Book

Additional materials relating to picture books are listed in the bibliography for Chapter 5, "The History of the Illustrated Book," beginning on p. 1188.

Books

Bader, Barbara. *American Picturebooks from Noah's Ark to the Beast Within.* Illus. with reproductions. Macmillan, 1976.

Spirited and scholarly, this lavishly illustrated volume analyzes developments of artistic styles, sociological trends, and seminal illustrators. With bibliography and index.

Bland, David. *A History of Book Illustration: The Illuminated Manuscript and the Printed Book.* World, 1958.

The chapter "The Nineteenth Century" includes Walter Crane, Kate Greenaway, and Randolph Caldecott. "The Twentieth Century" takes up American and English illustrators of children's books.

Cianciola, Patricia. *Picture Books for Children.* 2d ed. American Library Association, 1981.

Selective, annotated bibliography of significant picture-book titles.

Herdeg, Walter, ed. *An International Survey of Children's Book Illustration.* Publication no. 125, The Graphis Press, 1971.

A hardcover edition of a special issue of the magazine *Graphis* (no. 155), this survey contains articles in English, French, and German on contemporary picture-book publishing in the United States, England, Germany, Switzerland, and France and includes notes on such publications in Japan, Poland, Czechoslovakia, Yugoslavia, the U.S.S.R., Hungary, Italy, Austria, Scandinavia, and Iran. The bulk of the space is given to reproductions of illustrative work. See also subsequent issues of *Graphis* wholly devoted to the illustration of children's books and supplemented by additional hardcover editions: *Third International Survey of Children's Book Illustration,* Publication no. 140

(Graphis, 1975), hardcover edition of the July 1975 issue (Vol. 31, no. 177), and *Fourth International Survey of Children's Book Illustration,* Publication no. 156 (Graphis, 1979), hardcover edition of the May/June 1979 issue (Vol. 34, no. 200).

Hürlimann, Bettina. *Picture-Book World.* Trans. and ed. Brian W. Alderson. World, 1969.

A critical survey of modern picture books from twenty-four countries.

Kingman, Lee, ed. *Newbery and Caldecott Medal Books: 1956–1965.* Horn Book, 1965.

This volume brings up to date the first two books, *Newbery Medal Books: 1922–1955* and *Caldecott Medal Books: 1938–1957.* It includes the acceptance speeches of the award winners, biographies, and related material. The article "Picture Books Today" by Norma R. Fryatt will be of particular interest to students of picture books.

Kingman, Lee, ed. *Newbery and Caldecott Medal Books: 1966–1975.* Horn Book, 1976.

Contains an evaluative article by Barbara Bader on picture books for this period.

Kingman, Lee, et al., comps. *Illustrators of Children's Books, 1957–1966.* Horn Book, 1968. See the entry for this book in the bibliography for Chapter 5, "The History of the Illustrated Book."

Kingman, Lee, et. al., comps. *Illustrators of Children's Books, 1967–1976.* Horn Book, 1978. See the entry for this book in the bibliography for Chapter 5, "The History of the Illustrated Book."

Klemin, Diana. *The Art of Art for Children's Books: A Contemporary Survey.* Potter, 1966.

The author includes a representative illustration from the works of sixty-four artists and supplies a commentary for each.

Lanes, Selma H. *The Art of Maurice Sendak.* Abrams, 1980.

A biographical and critical study of Sendak's life and works. Large format, lavishly illustrated with photographs and reproductions of his sources, original working sketches, and final illustrations.

Looking at Picture Books. The catalogue for an exhibition mounted at the National Book League in London, 1973.

Text by Brian Alderson traces the tradition of the English school of book illustration. The approach for the exhibition was an "experiment in practical criticism."

MacCann, Donnarae, and Olga Richard. *The Child's First Books: A Critical Study of Pictures and Texts.* H. W. Wilson, 1973.

The work of the artist in the picture book is approached in terms of the art elements selected and emphasized. Artists are grouped according to techniques and analyzed selectively as individuals in certain specific works. The text of picture books is also given a thoughtful analysis in relation to pictures and in its own right.

Mahony, Bertha E., et al., comps. *Illustrators of Children's Books, 1744–1945.* Horn Book, 1947 (reprinted in 1961). See the entry for this book in the bibliography for Chapter 5, "The History of the Illustrated Book."

Miller, Bertha Mahoney, et al., comps. *Illustrators of Children's Books, 1946–1956.* Horn Book, 1958. See the entry for this book in the bibliography for Chapter 5, "The History of the Illustrated Book."

Miller, Bertha Mahony, and Elinor Whitney Field, eds. *Caldecott Medal Books: 1938–1957.* Horn Book, 1957.

A companion volume to *Newbery Medal Books: 1922–1955.* Contains the acceptance speeches of the artists, their biographies, a brief résumé of each book, an introductory paper on Randolph Caldecott, and a critical analysis, "What Is a Picture Book?" by Esther Averill.

The Pierpont Morgan Library. *Early Children's Books and Their Illustration.* Text by Gerald Gottlieb. Godine, 1975.

A meticulous and rich display of an historical collection. The wide range in time span and the variety of books (225 selected) provide a valuable source for students of children's literature. Includes essay by J. H. Plumb.

Self Portrait Collection. Addison-Wesley, 1978–.

A series of handsomely produced autobiographical picture books written and illustrated by significant author-illustrators. Includes *Self Portrait: Margaret Zemach* (1978); *Self Portrait: Erik Blegvad* (1979); *Self Portrait: Trina Schart Hyman* (1981); and *Self Portrait: Garth Williams* (1982).

Catalogues

The American Institute of Graphic Arts holds biennial exhibitions of children's books chosen for typographical and artistic merit. The Institute publishes a catalogue to accompany each exhibit. These catalogues, which contain commentary on the books selected, will prove immensely valuable for the general reader.

Biennale of Illustrations. Bratislava, Czechoslovakia, '71, '73. Text by Anna Urblikova. Horn Book, 1975.

Selections from the works of international award-winning artists who competed in the 1971 and 1973 Biennales of Illustrations in Bratislava, Czechoslovakia. Includes biographical notes and text in six languages. See also *Biennale of Illustrations. Bratislava, Czechoslovakia, '67, '69 (1971).*

Bologna Children's Book Fair, April 8–11. *Illustrators of Children's Books, '76.*

A catalogue of the exhibition. Order from Phaedrus, Inc., 14 Beacon St., Boston, Mass., 02108. See also the 1977 catalogue, Bologna Children's Book Fair, April 1–4, *Illustrators of Children's Books, '77,* and the 1980 catalogue, *Annual '80: Illustrators of Children's Books.*

Films

The Lively Art of Picture Books. Script by Joanna Foster Dougherty; narrated by John Langstaff; produced by Morton Schindel; photographed and ed. by William D. Stoneback. Weston Woods Studios (Weston, Conn.), 1964.

A one-hour film designed to help adults "select picture books with understanding." Two complete picture books are shown: *A Snowy Day,* by Ezra Jack Keats, and *A Time of Wonder,* by Robert McCloskey. Examples of the work of thirty-six other artists are shown. This film is part of Weston Woods' Signature Collection, a series of film profiles on authors and illustrators of picture books. The series includes: *Edward Ardizzone; Ezra Jack Keats; Gene Deitch: The Picture Book Animated; James Daugherty; Maurice Sendak; Mr. Shepard and Mr. Milne; Robert McCloskey;* and *Tomi Ungerer: Storyteller.*

The Pleasure Is Mutual: How to Conduct Effective Picture Book Programs.

This film is produced by Connecticut Films, Inc., for the Westchester Library System and distributed by the Children's Book Council, 175 Eighth Avenue, New York, N.Y., 10010.

Articles

The acceptance speech by the artist who received the Caldecott Medal is printed in the August number of *The Horn Book Magazine* and a short article about the artist is included.

"The Artist at Work" is a series of articles that began in *The Horn Book Magazine,* December 1963. The articles deal with the technical processes in preparing drawings for reproduction:

Adams, Adrienne. "Color Separation." (Apr. 1965)

Cooney, Barbara. "Scratchboard Illustration." (Apr. 1964)

Emberley, Ed. "The Crow-Quill Pen." (Oct. 1966)

Keats, Ezra Jack. "Collage." (June 1964)

Lent, Blair. "Cardboard Cuts." (Aug. 1965)

Ness, Evaline. "Woodcut Illustration." (Oct. 1964)

Ward, Lynd. "Doing a Book in Lithography." (Feb. 1964)

Weisgard, Leonard. "Influences and Applications." (Aug. 1964)

"Artist's Choice" is a series of articles that started in *The Horn Book Magazine,* January 1950, and continued irregularly during the following years, ending in 1962. In these articles illustrators commented on picture books that they particularly liked.

Bator, Robert, ed. *Signposts to Criticism of Children's Literature.* American Library Association, 1983.
 See Chapter 4. "The Picture Book as Art Object: A Call for Balanced Reviewing," by Kenneth Marantz, pp. 152–56; "There's Much More to the Picture than Meets the Eye," by Blair Lent, pp. 156–61; "Louder Than a Thousand Words," by Margaret Matthias and Graciela Italiano, pp. 161–65.

"Book Illustrators of Today" is a series of articles that appeared in a British magazine, *Junior Bookshelf,* in volumes 4, 5, 11, and 12.

Brown, Marcia. "Distinction in Picture Books." *The Horn Book Magazine,* 25 (Sept.-Oct. 1949), pp. 382–95. Also in *Illustrators of Children's Books, 1946–1956,* comp. Bertha Miller, et al. The Horn Book, 1958, pp. 2–12.

Contemporary American Illustrators of Children's Books. Rutgers Univ. Press, 1974.
 A catalogue of an exhibition with an introductory historical essay, statements by each illustrator, and a reproduction of one work by each illustrator.

Durham, Mae. "Some Thoughts about Picture Books." *The Horn Book Magazine,* 39 (Oct. 1963), pp. 476–84.

Egoff, Sheila, et al., eds. *Only Connect: Readings on Children's Literature.* 2d ed. Oxford Univ. Press, 1980.
 See Part 4. "Illustration: Creation of a Picture Book," by Edward Ardizzone, pp. 289–98; "Children's Book Illustration: The Pleasures and Problems," by Roger Duvoisin, pp. 299–316; "Randolph Caldecott," by Frederick Laws, pp. 317–25; "An Interview with Maurice Sendak," by Walter Lorraine, pp. 326–36.

Haviland, Virginia, ed. *Children and Literature: Views and Reviews.* Scott, Foresman, 1973.
 See Chapter 5. "The Art of Illustrating Books for the Younger Readers," by Louise Seaman Bechtel, pp. 173–76; "Children's Book Illustration: The Pleasures and Problems," by Roger Duvoisin, pp. 177–87; "Mother Goose's Garnishings," by Maurice Sendak, pp. 188–95; "A Load of Old Nonsense, Edward Lear Resurrected by Four Publishers," by Crispin Fisher, pp. 198–201.

Horton, Marion. "Current Trends in the Illustration of Children's Books." *California Librarian* (Apr. 1962). Also in *Illustrations for Children,* The Gladys English Collection Keepsake Series, no. 5.

"Let Us Now Praise Artists!" is a section in *A Horn Book Sampler on Children's Books and Reading, Selections from Twenty-five Years of* The Horn Book Magazine, *1924–1948,* ed. Norma R. Fryatt. Horn Book, 1959.
 Included are: "Flowers for a Birthday: Kate Greenaway," by Anne Parrish; "Arthur Rackham and *The Wind in the Willows,*" by George Macy; "The Genius of Arthur Rackham," by Robert Lawson; "Leslie Brooke," by Anne Carroll Moore; "A Publisher's Odyssey [Rojankovsky]," by Esther Averill; and "Illustrations Today in Children's Books," by Warren Chappell.

Low, Joseph. "Picture Books." *The Horn Book Magazine,* 43 (Dec. 1967), pp. 715–20.

Mathiesen, Egon. "The Artist and the Picture Book." Excerpts from an address. *The Horn Book Magazine,* 42 (Feb. 1966), pp. 93–97.

May, Jill P., ed. *Children and Their Literature: A Readings Book.* Children's Literature Association Publications, 1983.

See Chapter 4. " 'First Books': From Schlock to Sophistication," by Patricia Dooley, pp. 112–16; "The Art of Nancy Elkholm Burkert," by Marilyn Cochran-Smith, pp. 117–21; "Nonfiction Illustration: Some Considerations," by Joyce A. Thomas, pp. 122–27.

Sayers, Frances Clarke. "Through These Sweet Fields." *The Horn Book Magazine,* 18 (Nov. 1942), pp. 436–44.

Sendak, Maurice. "Questions to an Artist Who Is Also an Author." In *The Openhearted Audience: Ten Authors Talk about Writing for Children,* ed. Virginia Haviland. Library of Congress (1980), pp. 25–45.

This interview for National Children's Book Week program, 1970, was first published in the October 1971 issue of *Quarterly Journal of the Library of Congress.*

Tucker, Nicholas. "Looking at Pictures." *Children's Literature in Education,* no. 14 (1974), pp. 37–51.

Wilson Library Bulletin, 52, no. 2 (Oct. 1977), Picture Book Issue. Articles and notes by Walter Lorraine, Kenneth Marantz, Blair Lent, Arnold Lobel, Karla Kuskin, Trina Schart Hyman, and Tomie de Paola. See also *Wilson Library Bulletin,* monthly column on picture books by Donnarae MacCann and Olga Richards in recent issues.

5   The History of the Illustrated Book

Additional materials relating to picture books are listed in the bibliography to Chapter 4, "Picture Books," beginning on p. 1168.

Books

Barr, Beryl. *Wonders, Warriors and Beasts Abounding: How the Artist Sees His World.* Foreword by Thomas P. F. Hoving, Director of the Metropolitan Museum of Art. Doubleday, 1967.

Cianciolo, Patricia. *Illustrations in Children's Books.* 2d ed. W. C. Brown, 1976.

Discussion of the wide range of media, techniques, and art styles in illustrated children's books, and an analysis of the standards of evaluation. Includes bibliographies.

Egoff, Sheila. *The Republic of Childhood: A Critical Guide to Canadian Children's Literature in English.* 2d ed. Oxford Univ. Press, 1975.

See Chapter 9. "Illustration and Design."

Engen, Rodney. *Randolph Caldecott: Lord of the Nursery.* Warne, 1977.

Includes biocritical essay discussing Caldecott's oeuvre and life, and a representative compilation of the illustrator's art in children's and adult books, periodicals, and newspapers. The appendices include a catalogue of Caldecott's work and his exhibitions, as well as bibliographies. Color and black-and-white reproductions. See also Engen's similar critical studies of significant Victorian children's book illustrators in *Walter Crane as a Book Illustrator* (St. Martin's, 1975), and *Kate Greenaway* (Harmony/Crown, 1976).

Ernest, Edward, comp. Assisted by Patricia Tracy Lowe. *The Kate Greenaway Treasury: An Anthology of the Illustrations and Writings.* World, 1967.

An excellent critical examination of the illustrator's life and art. Includes an introduction by Ruth Hill Viguers and an essay by Anne Carroll Moore.

Feaver, William. *When We Were Young: Two Centuries of Children's Book Illustration.* Holt, 1977.

Reproductions of and critical notes on a sampling of significant illustrators of the last two hundred years. International in scope.

Hudson, Derek. *Arthur Rackham: His Life and Work.* Scribner's, 1961.

Hutchins, Michael. *Yours Pictorially: Illustrated Letters of Randolph Caldecott.* Warne, 1977.

Caldecott's correspondence provides revelations into his life and times. Sketches punctuate the letters.

Jacques, Robin. *Illustrators at Work.* Studio Books, 1963.

A practical study of contemporary black-and-white illustrators including many children's book artists. Information on the history of illustration, processes of reproduction, and guidelines for beginning illustrators are included.

James, Philip B. *English Book Illustration: 1800–1900.* Penguin, 1947.

Examples of the art of the Bewicks, Blake, Cruikshank, Doyle, Tenniel, Lear, the pre-Raphaelites, and others.

Jones, Helen L. *Robert Lawson, Illustrator: A Selection of His Characteristic Illustrations.* Little, Brown, 1972.

Kingman, Lee, ed. *The Illustrator's Notebook.* Horn Book, 1978.

Notes and excerpts from articles by contemporary illustrators originally written for *The Horn Book Magazine.* General subject areas considered include: the history and philosophy of illustration; individual styles and techniques; illustration as communication. Index and bibliography of prominent articles, books, and catalogues.

Kingman, Lee, et al., comps. *Illustrators of Children's Books, 1957–1966.* Horn Book, 1968.

Part I. "A Decade of Illustration in Children's Books: One Wonders," by Marcia Brown; "Color Separation," by Adrienne Adams; "The Artist and His Editor," by Grace Allen Hogarth; "Beatrix Potter: Centenary of an Artist Writer," by Rumer Godden. Part II. "Biographies of Illustrators Active: 1957–1966," comp. by Joanna Foster; "Brief Biographies." Part III. Bibliographies. Part IV. Appendix. "The Kate Greenaway Medal in the United Kingdom: A List of Artists Represented by Illustrations."

Kingman, Lee, et. al., comps. *Illustrators of Children's Books, 1967–1976.* Horn Book, 1978.

Part I. "A Decade of Illustration in Children's Books: Book Illustration: The State of the Art," by Walter Lorraine; "A View from the Island: European Picture Books 1967–1976," by Brian Alderson; "Where the Old Meets the New: The Japanese Picture Book," by Teiji Seta and Momoko Ishii; "In the Beginning was the Word: The Illustrated Book 1967–1976," by Treld Pelkey Bicknell. Part II. "Biographies of Illustrators Active: 1967–1976," comp. by Grace Allen Hogarth. Part III. Bibliographies, comp. by Harriet Quimby; Part IV, Appendix. "List of Artists Represented by Illustrations"; and a cumulative index to biographies and bibliographies of volumes I, II, III, and IV.

Klemin, Diana. *The Art of Art for Children's Books: A Contemporary Survey.* Potter, 1966. See the entry for this book in the bibliography for Chapter 4, "Picture Books."

Lane, Margaret. *The Magic Years of Beatrix Potter.* Warne, 1978.

Potter's most productive period, examined in detail. See also *The Tale of Beatrix Potter: A Biography.* Rev. ed., 1968.

Larkin, David, ed. *The Art of Nancy Eckholm Burkert.* Intro. Michael Danoff. Harper, 1977.

Danoff's appreciative essay introduces a representative selection of Burkert's work. Full color reproductions. See also in the same series: *Arthur Rackham* (Peacock, 1975); *Dulac* (Scribner's, 1975); and *Kay Nielsen* (Peacock, 1975).

Linder, Leslie, and W. A. Herring, eds. *The Art of Beatrix Potter.* Warne, 1972.

Mahony, Bertha E., and Elinor Whitney, comps. *Contemporary Illustrators of Children's Books.* Gale, 1978.

Originally published in 1930, this study covers illustrators of children's books for the first third of the twentieth century.

Mahony, Bertha E., et al., comps. *Illustrators of Children's Books, 1744–1945.* Horn Book, 1947 (reprinted in 1961).

Part I. "History and Developments"; "The Book Artist, Yesterday and Today." Part II. "Biographies of the Artists."

Meyer, Susan E. *A Treasury of the Great Children's Book Illustrators.* Abrams, 1983.

A biocritical examination of thirteen classic book illustrators from Edward Lear to W. W. Denslow. An elegant book with approximately twelve full-color reproductions of each artist's work. Includes a history of book production and illustration.

Miller, Bertha Mahony, et al., comps. *Illustrators of Children's Books, 1946–1956.* Horn Book, 1958.

A supplement to *Illustrators of Children's Books, 1744–1945.* Part I. "Eleven Years of Illustration in Children's Books," by Marcia Brown; "The Book Artist: Ideas and Techniques," by Lynd Ward; "The European Picture Book," by Fritz Eichenberg. Part II. Biographies. Part III. Bibliography of illustrators and their work.

Peppin, Brigid. *Fantasy: The Golden Age of Fantastic Illustrations.* Watson-Guptill, 1975.

Selections from the age of fantastical Victorian book illustration. Reproductions in color and black-and-white, general bibliography, biobibliographical notes on forty-five illustrators, and index.

Pitz, Henry C. *Howard Pyle: Writer, Illustrator, Founder of the Brandywine School.* Potter, 1975.

Biography, augmented with reproductions, assesses artistic influences on Pyle and his effect on others.

Pitz, Henry C. *Illustrating Children's Books: History—Technique—Production.* Watson-Guptill, 1964.

An artist surveys the history of children's books from the illustrator's viewpoint.

Pitz, Henry C., ed. *A Treasury of American Book Illustration.* American Studio Books, 1947.

The work of over one hundred and forty American artists, many of them illustrators of children's books.

Poltarnees, Welleran. *All Mirrors Are Magic Mirrors.* Green Tiger Press, 1972.

Meditations on certain illustrators and their relation to the works they illustrated. A subjective interpretation is given to the work of Maurice Sendak, Arthur Rackham, Howard Pyle, and others. The author's concerns are the emotional responses of the artist to fantasy and the way in which the illustration releases the imagination.

Read, Herbert. *The Meaning of Art.* Penguin, 1949.

An excellent introduction to the understanding and appreciation of art.

Reed, Henry M. *The A. B. Frost Book.* Tuttle, 1967.

Over seventy plates—forty-four in color—and many line drawings.

Schnessel, Michael. *Jessie Willcox Smith.* Crowell, 1977.

Schwarcz, Joseph H. *Ways of the Illustrator: Visual Communication in Children's Literature.* American Library Association, 1982.

An investigation of children's book illustration and design in the context of visual perception and aesthetics. The interplay between text and illustration in picture books and illustrated books from many cultures is discussed.

Shahn, Ben. *Shape of Content.* Vintage, 1960.

Shepard, Ernest H. *Drawn from Memory.* Penguin, 1975.

Smith, Janet Adams. *Children's Illustrated Books.* Collins, 1948.

Tuer, Andrew W. *One Thousand Quaint Cuts from Books of Other Days, Including Amusing Illustrations from Children's Story Books, Fables, Chapbooks.* Field & Tuer, 1886.

Ward, Martha E., and Dorothy Marquardt. *Illustrators of Books for Young People.* 2d ed. Scarecrow, 1975.

Brief biographical sketches of children's book illustrators.

Whalley, Joyce Irene. *Cobwebs to Catch Flies: Illustrated Books for the Nursery and Schoolroom, 1700–1900.* Univ. of California Press, 1975.

A copiously illustrated study of the illustrated educational books for children published in England, America, France, and Germany over two centuries. Includes bibliography, list of selected collections of children's books, and index of publishers.

White, Gabriel. *Edward Ardizzone: Artist & Illustrator.* Schocken, 1980.

Articles

Chappell, Warren. "Illustrations Today in Children's Books." *The Horn Book Magazine,* 17 (Nov. 1941), pp. 445–55.

Daugherty, James. "Illustrating for Children." In *Reading without Boundaries,* ed. Frances Lander Spain, pp. 35–38. New York Public Library, 1956.

Eichenberg, Fritz. "The European Picture Book." In *Illustrators of Children's Books, 1946–1956,* comp. Bertha Miller, et al., pp. 36–57. Horn Book, 1958.

"Illustrations and Children's Books." In *Readings about Children's Literature,* ed. Evelyn R. Robinson, Part 5, pp. 195–205. McKay, 1966.

Oakley, Thornton. "Howard Pyle." *The Horn Book Magazine,* 7 (May 1931), pp. 91–97.

Painter, Helen W. "Lynd Ward—Artist, Writer and Scholar." *Elementary English,* 39 (Nov. 1962).

Pitz, Henry C. "The Art of Illustration." *The Horn Book Magazine* (Oct. 1962), pp. 454–57.

Pitz, Henry C. "The Illustrations of Lynd Ward." *American Artist,* 19 (Mar. 1955), pp. 32–37.

Ward, Lynd. "The Book Artist: Ideas and Techniques." In *Illustrators of Children's Books, 1946–1956,* comp. Bertha Miller, et al., pp. 14–35. Horn Book, 1958.

Ward, Lynd. "Building a Lincoln Book." *American Artist,* 23 (Feb. 1959), pp. 66–70.

Ward, Lynd. "Graphic Arts and Children's Books." *The Horn Book Magazine,* 32 (Apr. 1956), pp. 102–5.

Ward, Lynd. "When I Illustrate a Book." *Instructor,* 63 (Nov. 1953).

Weisgard, Leonard. "Contemporary Art and Children's Book Illustration." *The Horn Book Magazine,* 36 (Apr. 1960), pp. 155–58.

III The Oral Tradition: The Cauldron of Story

6 Fables

Books for Children

The Book of Fables. Illus. Will Nickless. Warne, 1963.
Although the majority of the fables are from Aesop, fables from England, France, Germany, Russia, and India are included. Grades 4–6.

Green, Margaret, ed. *The Big Book of Animal Fables.* Illus. Janusz Grabianski. F. Watts, 1965.
Fables from around the world spanning the years from Aesop to James Thurber. Well illustrated by a Polish artist. Grades 4–6.

Montgomerie, Norah. *Twenty-five Fables.* Retold and illus. by the author. Abelard-Schuman, 1961.
Unfamiliar traditional fables from many cultures. Simply told and well illustrated. Grades 2–4.

Fables of India

Bidpai. *The Tortoise and the Geese, and Other Fables of Bidpai.* Retold by Maude B. Dutton; illus. E. Boyd Smith. Houghton Mifflin, 1908.
According to tradition, Bidpai was a sage of India who lived about 300 B.C. All of his accumulated wisdom he put into his fables. In the Middle Ages "Bidpai" referred to the narrator of animal fables or to the collection itself. Grades 3–4.

Gaer, Joseph. *The Fables of India.* Illus. Randy Monk. Little, Brown, 1955.
Animal fables different from and yet intriguingly similar to those of the Western world. Retold from three great collections: the *Panchatantra,* the *Hitopadésa,* and the *Jātakas.* Grades 5–9.

Jātakas. *Jātaka Tales.* Retold by Ellen C. Babbitt; illus. Ellsworth Young. Appleton-Century-Crofts, 1912.
Fables chiefly about animals, taken from one of the sacred books of the Buddhists. Followed by *More Jātaka Tales* and *Twenty Jātaka Tales.* These are the best of the retelling of the Buddha stories. Grades 3–5.

Jātakas. *Jātaka Tales.* Ed. Nancy DeRoin; illus. Ellen Lanyon. Houghton Mifflin, 1975.
Stories in this collection were selected because they teach lessons pertinent to today's problems. Grades 3–6.

Reed, Gwendolyn. *The Talkative Beasts: Myths, Fables, and Poems of India.* Photographs, Stella Snead. Lothrop, 1969.
The relation between the written classical works and the sculpture in the photographs gives this book elegance and depth. Grades 4–9.

Shedlock, Marie L. *Eastern Stories and Legends.* Intro. Anne Carroll Moore. Dutton, 1920.
Thirty of the Jātaka tales retold by a famous storyteller. Based on a translation from Pali made by Professor T. W. Rhys Davids. Grades 4–6.

Fables of Aesop

Aesop: Five Centuries of Illustrated Fables. Sel. John J. McKendry. The Metropolitan Museum of Art, (distributed by the New York Graphic Society), 1964.
This study shows the great variety of illustrations of the fables, ranging from fifteenth-century woodcuts to the works of Antonio Frasconi and Joseph Low. Each illustration is accompanied by a contemporaneous translation, ranging from William Caxton to Marianne Moore. This handsome volume will be enjoyed by older children and adults.

Aesop's Fables. Ed. and illus. with wood engravings by Boris Artzybasheff. Viking, 1933.
The text combines the humor of the Croxall edition of 1722 and the imaginative detail of the James edition of 1848. A beautiful edition, distinguished in format. Grades 5–8.

Aesop's Fables. Retold by Patricia Crampton; illus. Bernadette. Dent, 1980.
Colloquial retellings by a Hans Christian Andersen Award winner for translation are complemented by detailed, decorative illustrations. Grades 2–4.

Aesop's Fables. Illus. Heidi Holder. Viking, 1981.
Elaborate literary retellings of nine fables ornamentally framed and decoratively illustrated. The rococo elegance of the art and text are in strong contrast to the usual pithy simplicity of most collections. Grades 2–5.

Aesop's Fables. Trans. V. S. Vernon Jones; illus. Arthur Rackham. F. Watts, 1968.
Gilbert Chesterton's introduction adds value to

the volume. First published in 1912. Grades 4–6.

Aesop's Fables. Illus. Fritz Kredel. Grosset, 1947.
    Fine illustrations embellish clear retellings of the fables. Grades 4–6.

Aesop's Fables. Illus. Jacob Lawrence. Windmill, 1970.
    A book with unusually strong illustrations; the fables are told briefly.

Aesop's Fables. Ed. John Warrington; illus. Joan Kiddell-Monroe. Dutton, Children's Illustrated Classics, 1961.
    A handsome book containing over two hundred popular fables. Grades 3–5. See also Kiddell-Monroe's fresh illustrations and clean retellings in *Fourteen Fables* (Blackwell, 1972).

Aesop's Fables. Retold by Anne Terry White; illus. Helen Siegl. Random House, 1964.
    Told simply in contemporary style, these are for the young reader. Grades 2–5.

Fables from Aesop. Ed. James Reeves; illus. Maurice Wilson. Walck, 1962.
    Fifty-two fables retold with fresh vigor. Grades 4–6.

The Fables of Aesop. Sel. and retold by Joseph Jacobs; illus. Richard Heighway. Schocken, 1966.
    A famous edition of the fables, first published in 1894. See also the Macmillan (1964) edition with David Levine's witty line drawings and Clifton Fadiman's penetrating afterword.

Fables of Aesop. Retold and illus. by Jack Kent. Parents' Magazine, 1972.
    Simple retellings based on the Vernon-Jones translation, with droll illustrations. For the youngest, grades K–3. See also *More Fables of Aesop* (1974).

Lions and Lobsters and Foxes and Frogs: Fables from Aesop. Sel. and retold by Ennis Rees; illus. Edward Gorey. Young Scott, 1971.
    The selected fables, told in verse and illustrated to show the "action" in each fable, take on a comic aspect. Grades 2–4.

Once in a Wood: Ten Tales from Aesop. Adapt. and illus. Eve Rice. Greenwillow, 1979.
    Simple retellings with rhyming morals illustrated with endearing charm and an observant eye. Grades 1–3.

Tales from Aesop. Retold and illus. by Harold Jones. F. Watts, 1982.
    Twenty-one fables succinctly, crisply retold and embellished with absorbingly narrative pictures reflecting the vital humor and drama of the tales. Grades 2–5.

Fables of France

La Fontaine, Jean de. *Fables of La Fontaine.* Trans. Marianne Moore. Viking, 1954.
    This translation of the fables by an American poet is an important literary achievement. Moore has followed the original text with fidelity and has added the flavor of her own keen wit and sense of form.

La Fontaine, Jean de. *A Hundred Fables of La Fontaine.* Illus. Percy J. Billinghurst. Greenwich, 1983.
    Fine black-and-white line drawings in the turn-of-the-century style complement a strong collection. Grades 4 and up.

La Fontaine, Jean de. *The Rich Man and the Shoe-maker.* Illus. Brian Wildsmith. F. Watts, 1965.
    The old tale of the cobbler who found money to be less important than his song. Grades 1–3. See also *The Lion and the Rat; The North Wind and the Sun; The Hare and the Tortoise;* and *The Miller, the Boy and the Donkey.* All five fables are illustrated in Wildsmith's distinguished style and bold color. Excellent picture-book editions.

La Fontaine, Jean de. *The Turtle and the Two Ducks: Animal Fables Retold from La Fontaine.* Retold by Patricia Plante and David Bergman; illus. Anne Rockwell. Crowell, 1981.
    Free prose retellings of La Fontaine stylishly illustrated with charm and comic verve. Details of seventeenth-century French costume and setting give an authenticity to the pictures. Grades 1–4.

Fables of Russia

Ginsburg, Mirra, trans. and ed. *The Lazies: Tales of the Peoples of Russia.* Illus. Marian Parry. Macmillan, 1973.
    Pithy and humorous, these short fables and tales demonstrate wise ways of dealing with those who shirk work. Grades 2–5.

Ginsburg, Mirra, retel. and trans. *Three Rolls and One Doughnut: Fables from Russia.* Illus. Anita Lobel. Dial, 1970.
    Amusing, witty, and wise. Grades 2–5.

Krylov, Ivan Andreevich. *Fifteen Fables of Krylov.* Trans. Guy Daniels; illus. David Pascal. Macmillan, 1965.
    American children enjoy the sly wit and satirical spirit of the Russian fabulist. Grades 5–7.

Fables in Picture-Book Form

Aesop. *The Hare and the Tortoise.* Illus. Paul Galdone. McGraw-Hill, 1962.

A delightful picture book. Grades 1–3. See also *Three Aesop Fox Fables* (Seabury, 1971).

Aesop. *The Lion and the Mouse: An Aesop Fable.* Illus. Ed Young. Benn, 1979.

A revisionist visual interpretation of the traditional fable. The final elegant pencil illustration in which the mouse is eaten by the lion renders the tale ambiguous and ironic. For older children and adults who would appreciate the black humor. Grades 3–6.

Aesop. *The Miller, His Son, and Their Donkey.* Illus. Roger Duvoisin. McGraw-Hill, 1962.

The amusing tale of the miller who, by trying to please all his taunters, learns to his shame that he has pleased nobody and almost loses his donkey into the bargain. Editions available in French, Spanish, and Latin. Grades K–2.

Brown, Marcia. *Once a Mouse . . . A Fable Cut in Wood.* Scribner's, 1961.

A vigorous retelling of an ancient Indian fable from the Hitopadésa. The woodcuts are distinguished for their strength. Awarded the Caldecott Medal, 1962. Grades K–3.

Chaucer, Geoffrey. *Chanticleer and the Fox.* Illus. Barbara Cooney. Crowell, 1958.

An adaptation of Chaucer's "Nun's Priest Tale," which in turn is an adaptation of Aesop's fable "The Cock and the Fox," made into a beautiful picture book. Awarded the Caldecott Medal, 1959. Grades 1–3.

Ciardi, John. *John J. Plenty and Fiddler Dan.* Illus. Madeleine Gekiere. Lippincott, 1963.

A new fable of "The Grasshopper and the Ant," told in verse with a surprise ending. Grades 4–6.

Daugherty, James. *Andy and the Lion.* Adapt. and illus. by the author. Viking, 1938.

A vigorous, modern version of Aesop's fable "The Lion and the Mouse" and the famous Greek myth of Androcles and the lion. Grades 1–3.

D'Aulaire, Ingri, and Edgar Parin D'Aulaire. *Don't Count Your Chicks.* Doubleday, 1943.

The D'Aulaires' full-page lithographs in color distinguish this version of "The Maid with the Spilt Milk." Grades 1–3.

Galdone, Paul. *The Monkey and the Crocodile.* Illus. by the author. Seabury, 1969.

A lively picture-book version of a classic eastern fable. The illustrations are rich in dynamic movement. Grades K–3.

Joyce, James. *The Cat and the Devil.* Illus. Richard Erdoes. Dodd, Mead, 1964.

This modern fable was written by James Joyce in 1936 as a letter to his grandson, Stephen Joyce. Grades 1–3.

La Fontaine, Jean de. *The Frogs Who Wanted a King.* Illus. Margot Zemach. Four Winds, 1977.

Zemach's wry pictures add a quiet wit to this sophisticated picture-book edition. Grades 3–6.

La Fontaine, Jean de. *Old Man Whickutt's Donkey.* Retold by Mary Calhoun; illus. Tomie de Paola. Parents' Magazine, 1975.

A warm and witty single title edition. Grades 1–3.

Lobel, Arnold. *Fables.* Illus. by the author. Harper, 1980.

Poetic and witty original fables in the Aesop tradition ending in pithy moral tags. Each fable faces a powerful full-page illustration. Awarded the Caldecott Medal, 1981. Grades 1 and up.

Mistral, Gabriela. *Crickets and Frogs: A Fable.* Trans. and adapt. Doris Dana; illus. Antonio Frasconi. Atheneum, A Margaret K. McElderry Book, 1972.

In both Spanish and English, this fable is enchanting in its playfulness and engrossing in its visual art by Frasconi. Grades 1–4.

Showalter, Jean B. *The Donkey Ride.* Illus. Tomi Ungerer. Doubleday, 1967.

The fable of the opinionated father, the questioning son, and the resisting donkey leads to the conclusion "you can't please everybody, and *some* people are *never* pleased." Grades 1–4.

Werth, Kurt. *The Monkey, the Lion and the Snake.* Retold and illus. by the author. Viking, 1967.

This retelling of the tale "Of Ingratitude" is taken from the *Gesta Romanorum,* set down by monks of the Middle Ages. Grades 1–4.

References for Adults

Aesop. *The Caldecott Aesop: Twenty Fables Illustrated by Randolph Caldecott.* Intro. Michael Patrick Hearn. Doubleday, 1978.

A facsimile of the 1883 Macmillan edition with retellings by Randolph's brother, Alfred Caldecott. The informative introduction gives a literary history of the fables and a biographical note on Caldecott and his involvement with the 1883 edition. Subtle, acerbic water colors.

Di Prima, Diane, ed. *Various Fables from Various Places*. Illus. Bernard Krigstein. Putnam's, Capricorn Books, 1960.

An excellent source for unusual fables, with an afterword about fables, their history, and qualities, written from the point of view of a poet.

Fables from Incunabula to Modern Picture Books: A Selective Bibliography. Comp. Barbara Quinnam, of the Children's Book Section of the Library of Congress. Government Printing Office, 1966.

Prepared in connection with an exhibition of fables in the Library of Congress, this bibliography gives historical and critical notes on fables from India, Aesop, La Fontaine, and Krylov. Of great interest to students of children's literature.

Fables of Aesop According to Sir Roger L'Estrange. Illus. Alexander Calder. Dover, 1967.

A limited edition of 665 copies of this volume was printed in Paris in 1931. The text, which has the old spelling, is dated 1692. Originally written as a "literary" version, as opposed to the schoolroom ones then in use, this is a witty and concise approach.

Kennerly, Karen, ed. *Hesitant Wolf and Scrupulous Fox: Fables Selected from World Literature*. Random House, 1973.

A stimulating collection that brings a story by John Lennon together with fables, both written and oral, from anywhere, anytime. Grouped according to various themes, they are preceded by an analytical introduction.

La Fontaine, Jean de. *La Fontaine: Selected Fables with the Illustrations of J. J. Grandville*. Trans. James Michie; intro. Geoffrey Grigson. Viking, 1979.

A representative selection of the fables retold faithfully with an informative introduction on La Fontaine's life and work. The witty illustrations and decorations by the eminent nineteenth-century artist are reproduced from the 1842 edition published by H. Fourner in Paris.

La Fontaine, Jean de. *Selected Fables*. Trans. Eunice Clark; illus. Alexander Calder. Dover, 1968.

First published in 1948, this edition of thirty-six fables matches tart translations with piquant and satirical illustrations.

Nolen, Eleanor. "Aesop in the Library of Congress." *The Horn Book Magazine*, 14 (Sept.–Oct. 1938), pp. 311–15.

The Panchatantra. Trans. Arthur W. Ryder. Univ. of Chicago Press, 1925.

In his introduction the author states that this translation was made "to extend accurate and joyful acquaintance with one of the world's masterpieces." Panchatantra in Sanskrit means "five books." Each of the five books is a story by itself with shorter stories interwoven much in the same manner as the framework of the *Arabian Nights*. An invaluable source for students of folklore.

7   Folktales

Books for Children

Adams, Richard. *The Unbroken Web: Stories and Fables*. Illus. Jennifer Campbell. Crown, 1980.

Free literary retellings of twenty folktales and fables from around the world. Each tale is told as if by a specific narrator to an audience in an historical context. No sources given. Grades 5 and up.

Aiken, Joan. *The Kingdom under the Sea and Other Stories*. Illus. Jan Pienkowski. Jonathan Cape, 1971.

East European tales are retold in a literary manner by an accomplished writer of imaginative fiction. Grades 3–7.

Arbuthnot, May Hill, and Mark Taylor. *Time for Old Magic*. Illus. John Averill and others. Scott, Foresman, 1970.

A representative collection of folktales, myths, fables, and epics for children. A section on storytelling and reading aloud has been added. Bibliography.

Arnott, Kathleen, retel. *Animal Folk Tales around the World*. Illus. Bernadette Watts. Walck, 1971.

From every part of the world; familiar motifs appear in different versions. Sources given in a bibliography. Grades 2–6.

Association for Childhood Education, Literature Committee. *Told under the Green Umbrella: Old Stories for New Children*. Illus. Grace Gilkison. Macmillan, 1962.

A discriminating choice of twenty-six favorite stories, mostly from folklore. Grades 1–3.

Baker, Augusta, comp. *The Talking Tree: Fairy Tales from Fifteen Lands*. Illus. Johannes Troyer. Lippincott, 1955.

A storyteller's selection of fairy tales from folklore collections now out of print. See also *The Golden Lynx and Other Tales* (1960).

Baumann, Hans. *The Stolen Fire: Legends of Heroes and Rebels from around the World.* Trans. Stella Humphries; illus. Herbert Holzing. Pantheon, 1974.

This is a fine international collection of thirty-five little-known myths and folktales, excluding classical and Norse legends. Published in England under the title *Hero Legends of the World* (Dent, 1975). Grades 3–6.

Belting, Natalia. *Calendar Moon.* Illus. Bernarda Bryson. Holt, 1964.

The author, who has a flawless ear for folk poetry, draws upon the folk beliefs of many cultures for their interpretation regarding the months of the year. See also *The Sun Is a Golden Earring* and *The Stars Are Silver Reindeer.* Grades 5–7.

Belting, Natalia. *Elves and Ellefolk: Tales of the Little People.* Illus. Gordon Laite. Holt, 1961.

The author has brought together stories that show the variety and character of the Little People as they exist in different countries. Grades 3–9.

Brooke, L. Leslie. *Golden Goose Book.* Illus. by the author. Warne, 1906.

An ideal first book of fairy tales. Contains the nursery classics *The Three Bears, Three Little Pigs, Tom Thumb,* and *The Golden Goose.* Captivating illustrations. Grades K–2.

Cole, Joanna, sel. and ed. *The Best Loved Folktales of the World.* Illus. Jill Karla Schwarz. Doubleday, 1982.

A representative collection of folktales, fables, myths, and legends from around the world, arranged geographically. Sources of texts, an index of categories of tales, and a title index are given. Grades 5 and up.

Crossley-Holland, Kevin, ed. *The Faber Book of Northern Folk-Tales.* Illus. Alan Howard. Faber & Faber, 1983.

First published in England in 1977, this includes thirty-five folktales from northern Europe: Scandinavia and Iceland, Germany, Flanders, and the British Isles. Includes versions by Andrew Lang, Walter de la Mare, and Barbara Leonie Picard. Useful bibliography appended. Grades 3–6.

David, Alfred, and Mary Elizabeth Meek. *The Twelve Dancing Princesses and Other Fairy Tales.* Indiana Univ. Press, 1964; 1st Midland (paperback) edition, 1974.

The selectors have included literary tales in this collection. An extended introduction about the fairy tale as a form of literature background material on the collecting done by the Brothers Grimm,

and discussion of the problems of translation are also included.

De la Mare, Walter, ed. *Animal Stories.* Scribner's, 1940.

The editor has selected and in some cases entirely rewritten these stories taken mostly from folklore. In the preface he traces the development of the animal folktale. Grades 4–7. See also *Tales Told Again* (Knopf, 1959).

Edmonds, I. G. *Trickster Tales.* Illus. Sean Morrison. Lippincott, 1966.

Throughout the ages the trickster figures in folklore. In America, Brer Rabbit is the trickster; in France, Reynard-the-Fox; in Mexico, Señor Coyote; in Turkey, the foolish Hodja; and in India, Sissa, who proves to the king the importance of small things. Grades 4–6.

Hardendorff, Jeanne B., sel. *Tricky Peik and Other Picture Tales.* Illus. Tomie de Paola. Lippincott, 1967.

All the tales have been taken from the series known as *Picture Tales from the Chinese, Picture Tales from Spain,* and from various countries. Brief, these are well suited for telling. Grades 1–4. See also *The Frog's Saddle Horse and Other Tales* (1968) and *Just One More* (1969)

Haviland, Virginia, ed. *The Fairy Tale Treasury.* Illus. Raymond Briggs. Coward, 1972.

A sumptuous collection of international favorites simply told and rollickingly illustrated with over three hundred dynamic pictures. In the tradition of Caldecott and Brooke. Grades 1–4.

Lang, Andrew, ed. *The Blue Fairy Book.* Illus. Ben Kutcher; foreword, Mary Gould Davis. David McKay, 1948.

Stories included in the color fairy books have been gathered from many countries and sources. See also other color fairy book titles, all of which have been reissued by Dover in paperback. Grades 4–6. See also the Viking series, revised by Brian Alderson, who has re-edited and selectively retranslated the *Blue Fairy Book,* illus. John Lawrence (1978); the *Green Fairy Book,* illus. Antony Maitland (1978); the *Red Fairy Book,* illus. Faith Jacques (1978); the *Yellow Fairy Book,* illus. Erik Blegvad (1980); and the *Pink Fairy Book,* illus. Colin McNaughton (1982).

Lang, Andrew. *Fifty Favorite Fairy Tales Chosen from the Color Fairy Books of Andrew Lang.* Ed. Kathleen

Lines; illus. Margery Gill. F. Watts, A Nonesuch
Cygnet, 1964.

A choice edition. The Nonesuch Cygnet books
are designed by Sir Francis Meynell, the son of
the poet Alice Meynell. Grades 4–6. See also *More
Favorite Fairy Tales*.

Leach, Maria. *Noodles, Nitwits, and Numskulls.*
Illus. Kurt Werth. World, 1961.

An assortment of folk humor: stories of foolish
ones, riddles, tricks, and surprises. Sources and
bibliography provided. Grades 3–6.

Lines, Kathleen, ed. *The Ten Minute Story Book.*
Illus. Winnifred Marks. Oxford Univ. Press, 1942.

A classic collection of standard nursery tales and
verses useful for storytelling. For the very youngest. See also *Jack and the Beanstalk: A Book of Nursery
Stories*, illus. Harold Jones (1960).

Lurie, Alison, ed. *Clever Gretchen and Other Forgotten
Folktales.* Illus. Margot Tomes. Crowell, 1980.

The talented novelist and critic of children's literature stylishly retells a selection of folktales about
women and girls. See also *Whistle in the Graveyard:
Folktales to Chill Your Bones*, illus. Ken Rinciari (Viking, 1974).

McNeill, James, comp. *The Double Knights: More Tales
from around the World.* Illus. Theo Dimson.
Walck, 1964.

Countries represented include Mexico, Trinidad,
Estonia, Russia, Hungary, Japan, and Portugal.
Grades 4–6. See also *The Sunken City*.

Manning-Sanders, Ruth. *A Book of Ogres and Trolls.*
Illus. Robin Jacques. Dutton, 1972.

An entertaining collection, retold in the well-
known style of the compiler. See also her numerous other collections having to do with dwarfs,
witches, wizards, sorcerers, princes, princesses, etc.
No sources cited. Grades 3–7.

Minard, Rosemary, ed. *Womenfolk and Fairy Tales.*
Illus. Suzanna Klein. Houghton Mifflin, 1975.

Folktales selected with an eye to the heroine.
These can all be found in other collections.
Grades 3–7.

Palmer, Robin, and Pelagie Doane. *Fairy Elves: A
Dictionary of the Little People with Some Old Tales and
Verses about Them.* Walck, 1964.

Stories that feature fairies of one kind or another
are preceded by ten pages of "Fairy Dictionary."
Grades 2–6.

Rackham, Arthur, comp. *Arthur Rackham Fairy Book:
A Book of Old Favorites with New Illustrations.*
Lippincott, 1950.

First published in 1933. The famous artist has
chosen and illustrated twenty-three favorite folk
and fairy tales. Grades 3–5. See also *Fairy Tales
from Many Lands*, illus. Arthur Rackham (Viking,
1974), first published in 1916 as *The Allies' Fairy
Book*.

Riordan, James, retel. *A World of Folktales.*
Hamlyn, 1981.

The folktales in this collection have been chosen
as typical of the country and culture of origin.
The free retellings are true to the tone and storyline
of the original, while adding a contemporary color
and rhythm to the language. Explanatory notes
for each title and a bibliography are given. The
vivacious, brilliantly colored illustrations are
by various artists. Grades 3–6.

Rockwell, Anne, sel. *The Three Bears and Fifteen Other
Stories.* Illus. by the selector. Harper, 1975.

Simple, lively retellings of nursery tales for the
young child. Accompanied by vivacious, naive illustrations. Grades K–4. See also the companion
volume *The Old Woman and Her Pig and Ten Other
Stories* (1979).

Ross, Eulalie Steinmetz, ed. *The Lost Half-Hour.*
Illus. Enrico Arno. Harcourt, 1963.

A discriminating selection of stories from many
sources. Grades 3–5. See also *The Blue Rose* and
The Buried Treasure (Lippincott, 1958).

Spicer, Dorothy Gladys. *Thirteen Giants.* Illus. Sofia.
Coward-McCann, 1966.

From different countries, the author has collected stories which center around giants. She has
done the same for a variety of subjects: witches,
monsters, ghosts, devils. No sources are given.
Grades 3–6.

Stoutenburg, Adrien. *Fee, Fi, Fo, Fum: Friendly
and Funny Giants.* Illus. Rocco Negri. Viking,
1969.

Giants of legend and folklore, each reflecting
a different time and culture, are the focus of these
tales. The sources for the giants and their exploits
are given at the end of the book. Grades 3–6.

Thompson, Stith, comp. *One Hundred Favorite Folktales.* Illus. Franz Altschuler. Indiana Univ. Press,
1968.

The distinguished folklorist has chosen tales representing many nations.

United Nations Women's Guild, comp. *Ride with the Sun.* Ed. Harold Courlander; illus. Roger Duvoisin. McGraw-Hill, 1955.

This collection includes one representative, well-loved story from each of the sixty member countries of the United Nations in 1955. Grades 5–7.

Wiggin, Kate Douglas, and Nora Archibald Smith, eds. *The Fairy Ring.* Illus. Warren Chappell. Doubleday, 1967.

A classic collection of folklore first published in 1910. Revised by Ethna Sheehan. Grades 3–5.

Williams-Ellis, Amabel, comp. *Round the World Fairy Tales.* Illus. William Stobbs. Warne, 1963.

Thirty-six tales starting with Korea, proceeding through Asia, Europe, Africa, and the Americas, across the Pacific, and back to Korea. Notes and sources appended. Grades 3–6. See also *Old World and New World Fairy Tales* (1967).

Africa

Aardema, Verna, retel. *Behind the Back of the Mountain: Black Folktales from Southern Africa.* Illus. Leo Dillon and Diane Dillon. Dial, 1973.

A beautiful book, with striking black-and-white illustrations, this brings together short and pithy stories from such tribes as Zulu, Bushman, Tshindao, Hottentot, Bantu, and Thonga. A glossary and the sources for the stories are appended. Grades 3–6. See also *Tales from the Story Hat* (Coward-McCann, 1960); *More Tales from the Story Hat* (1966); and *Tales for the Third Ear from Equatorial Africa* (Dutton, 1969).

Appiah, Peggy. *Ananse the Spider: Tales from an Ashanti Village.* Illus. Peggy Wilson. Pantheon, 1966.

Wise and humorous tales of the Gold Coast. Drawings are derived from Ashanti brass weight designs. Grades 4–6.

Arkhurst, Joyce Cooper. *The Adventures of Spider: West African Folk Tales.* Illus. Jerry Pinkney. Little, Brown, 1964.

Six humorous how-and-why stories in which Spider, the trickster, is the hero. A good introduction to the more sophisticated Anansi stories. Grades 2–5.

Arnott, Kathleen. *African Myths and Legends.* Illus. Joan Kiddell-Monroe. Walck, Oxford Myths and Legends Series, 1963.

Well-told tales characteristic of a number of different tribes south of the Sahara. Grades 4–7.

Berger, Terry. *Black Fairy Tales.* Illus. David Omar White. Atheneum, 1969.

These are really African stories, most of them of Swazi origin. No further source reference is given. A glossary is provided at the end. Grades 4–7.

Bryan, Ashley, retel. *The Ox of the Wonderful Horns and Other African Folktales.* Illus. by the author. Atheneum, 1971.

Stories told with a sense of the poetic quality of traditional phrases. Grades 3–6. See also *The Adventures of Aku: Or How It Came about That We Shall Always See Okra the Cat Lying on a Velvet Cushion While Okraman the Dog Sleeps among the Ashes* (1976) and *Beat the Story-Drum, Pum-Pum* (1980).

Burton, W. F. P. *The Magic Drum: Tales from Central Africa.* Illus. Ralph Thompson. Criterion, 1961.

In the preface, the collector gives a sense of the vitality and living role of these stories, which he heard in the Congo around the village fire in the open country. Grades 3–6.

Courlander, Harold, and Ezekiel A. Eshugbayi. *Olode the Hunter, and Other Tales from Nigeria.* Illus. Enrico Arno. Harcourt, 1968.

Stories about the Yoruba people of Western Nigeria. Grades 4–6.

Courlander, Harold, and George Herzog. *The Cow-Tail Switch, and Other West African Stories.* Illus. Mayde Lee Chastain. Holt, 1947.

These stories, still told in the jungle villages and seacoast towns, were gathered by the authors on expeditions to Africa. Grades 4–6. See also *The King's Drum, and Other African Stories* (Harcourt, 1962) and *The Crest and the Hide and Other African Stories of Heroes, Chiefs, Bards, Hunters, Sorcerers, and Common People* (Coward, 1982).

Courlander, Harold, and Wolf Leslau. *Fire on the Mountain, and Other Ethiopian Stories.* Illus. Robert W. Kane. Holt, 1950.

A companion volume to *The Cow-Tail Switch.* Many of the stories are very short, similar to Aesop's fables. Grades 4–6.

Courlander, Harold, and Albert Kofi Prempeh. *The Hat-Shaking Dance and Other Ashanti Tales from Ghana.* Illus. Enrico Arno. Harcourt, 1957.

Wise and humorous folktales from the Ashanti people of the African Gold Coast. Grades 4–6.

Dayrell, Elphinstone. *Why the Sun and the Moon Live in the Sky.* Illus. Blair Lent. Houghton Mifflin, 1968.

A Nigerian tale with distinctive illustrations. Grades 1–3.

Fuja, Abayomi, col. *Fourteen Hundred Cowries and Other African Tales.* Intro. Anne Pellowski; illus. Ademola Olugebefola. Lothrop, 1971.

Yoruba stories collected and translated by a son of Yoruba parents, a collection that was begun in 1938 and completed in 1944. Grades 3–7.

Gilstrap, Robert, and Irene Estabrook. *The Sultan's Fool and Other North African Tales.* Illus. Robert Greco. Holt, 1958.

Fresh versions of eleven old tales, which should be fun to tell. Grades 3–5.

Guirma, Frederic. *Tales of Mogho: African Stories from Upper Volta.* Illus. by the author. Macmillan, 1971.

Tales that reflect the life of the Mossi people, of which Frederic Guirma is a member. These stories are presented with an introduction by Elliott Skinner, professor of anthropology, Columbia University. Grades 4–8.

Harman, Humphrey. *Tales Told Near a Crocodile: Stories from Nyanza.* Illus. George Ford. Viking, 1967.

Tales told by the author, as he heard them from the Nyanza tribes living around Lake Victoria, introduce the reader to a rich oral heritage. Grades 4–7.

Heady, Eleanor B. *When the Stones Were Soft: East African Fireside Tales.* Illus. Tom Feelings. Funk & Wagnalls, 1968.

Traditional how-and-why stories from Kenya, Uganda, and Tanzania. Grades 4–6.

Helfman, Elizabeth S. *The Bushmen and Their Stories.* Illus. Richard Cuffari. Seabury, 1971.

Based on stories collected by Dr. Wilhelm H. I. Bleek, these stories tell a great deal about the people. Background information is spread throughout the book. Grades 3–6.

Holladay, Virginia. *Bantu Tales.* Ed. Louise Crane; illus. Rocco Negri. Viking, 1970.

Bantu stories that had been told in Tshiluba to the children of missionaries. Grades 3–6.

Kalibala, E. Balintuma, and Mary Gould Davis. *Wakaima and the Clay Man and Other African Folktales.* Illus. Avery Johnson. Longmans, 1946.

Simple stories first heard during a childhood in Africa, these are meant to be changed in each telling, according to the "Author's Note" at the end of the book. Grades 2–4.

Kaula, Edna Mason. *African Village Folktales.* Illus. by the author. World, 1968.

Stories, for the most part, collected by the writer. Background information about the locality and the people is given before all stories, which come from different places. Grades 4–7.

Savory, Phyllis. *Congo Fireside Tales.* Illus. Joshua Tolford. Hastings, 1962.

Collected firsthand by one who has spent most of her life in Africa. Grades 3–6.

Tracey, Hugh. *The Lion on the Path and Other African Stories.* Illus. Eric Byrd; music transcribed, Andrew Tracey. Praeger, 1967.

Stories that make use of chants, repetitive refrains, and musical sections are told by a man who is a scholar of African music and oral arts. Grades 1–5.

Austria, Czechoslovakia, and Hungary

Ambrus, Victor G. *The Three Poor Tailors.* Illus. by the author. Harcourt, 1966.

The well-known illustrator retells an amusing folktale from his native Hungary. Grades 4–6. See also *Brave Soldier Janosh* (1967).

Fillmore, Parker. *The Shepherd's Nosegay: Stories from Finland and Czechoslovakia.* Ed. Katherine Love; illus. Enrico Arno. Harcourt, 1958.

Eighteen tales chosen from Parker Fillmore's collections *Czechoslovak Fairy Tales, The Shoemaker's Apron,* and *Mighty Mikko,* which have been long out of print. Grades 4–6.

Manning-Sanders, Ruth. *The Glass Man and the Golden Bird.* Illus. Victor G. Ambrus. Roy, 1968.

These Hungarian stories are often variants of well-known motifs, although there are unusual twists and refrains. No sources. Grades 4–8.

Balkan States

Fillmore, Parker. *The Laughing Prince: A Book of Jugoslav Fairy Tales and Folk Tales.* Illus. Jan Van Everen. Harcourt, 1921.

Fourteen southern Slav stories including Bulgarian tales and those of other Balkan peoples. Grades 3–6.

Green, Roger Lancelyn. *Old Greek Fairy Tales.* Illus. Ernest H. Shepard. Roy, 1958.

These adventures, embedded in the classic epics, are now chosen and retold as separate tales. Their sources and relationships to other folktales are pointed out in both the preface and the author's note at the end. Grades 4–8.

Manning-Sanders, Ruth. *Damian and the Dragon: Modern Greek Folk Tales.* Illus. William Papas. Roy, 1966.

Gay tales wherein the wise and courageous are aided in their quest for happiness by magical creatures or devices. Grades 5–7.

Pridham, Radost. *A Gift from the Heart: Folk Tales from Bulgaria.* Illus. Pauline Baynes. World, 1967.

Folktales and legends from a small but culturally rich Balkan nation. Grades 3–5.

Prodanovic, Nada Curcija. *Yugoslav Folk-Tales.* Illus. Joan Kiddell-Monroe. Oxford Univ. Press, Oxford Myths and Legends Series, 1957. Grades 5–8.

Rudolph, Marguerita, retel. *The Magic Egg and Other Folk Stories of Rumania.* Illus. Wallace Tripp. Little, Brown, 1971.

Simple adventures with animal characters. No sources cited. Grades 1–4.

Ure, Jean, ed. and trans. *Rumanian Folk Tales.* Illus. Charles Mozley. F. Watts, 1961.

Enjoyable tales which have counterparts in other countries. Notes on the origin of the stories are appended. Grades 4–6.

Wilson, Barbara Ker, retel. *Greek Fairy Tales.* Illus. Harry Toothill. Follett, 1966.

Credit is given to the work of Professor R. M. Dawkins's collections of modern Greek folklore. The stories are well and simply told. Grades 4–7.

Canada*

Aubry, Claude. *The Magic Fiddler and Other Legends of French Canada.* Trans. Alice Kane; illus. Saul Field. PMA, 1968.

Sophisticated retellings of ten well-known French Canadian folktales, accompanied by handsome illustrations. Grades 4–6.

Barbeau, Marius. *The Golden Phoenix, and Other French-Canadian Fairy Tales.* Retold by Michael Hornyansky; illus. Arthur Price. Walck, 1958.

Eight French Canadian tales skillfully told. The drawings remind one of medieval tapestries. Grades 4–6.

* See the bibliography for Chapter 8, "Myths, Legends, and Sacred Writings," for more on North American Indians and Inuit.

Carlson, Natalie Savage. *The Talking Cat, and Other Stories of French Canada.* Illus. Roger Duvoisin. Harper, 1952.

Thoroughly delightful stories which the author heard from her mother, who heard them from a French Canadian great-uncle. A fresh contribution to folklore. Grades 4–6.

Downie, Mary Alice, adapt. *The Witch of the North.* Illus. Elizabeth Cleaver. Oberon, 1975.

Folktales of French Canada retold with humor, zest, and drama and illustrated with flamboyant, award-winning collages. Grades 3–6.

Fowke, Edith, comp. *Folklore of Canada.* McClelland & Stewart, 1976.

Selections from the full range of Canadian folklore represent the oral tradition of Native peoples, English and French Canadians, and the multi-cultural mosaic. Resource for adults. Grades 6 and up.

Fowke, Edith, ed. *Folktales of French Canada.* Rev. ed. NC Press, 1981.

Selections from French Canadian folklore: anecdotes, jokes, folktales, legends, and animal fables. Close to the original storyteller's voice. Grades 6 and up.

Macmillan, Cyrus, coll. *Canadian Wonder Tales.* Illus. Elizabeth Cleaver. Bodley Head, 1980.

This is a reprint of the 1974 reissue in one volume that brought together the fifty-eight stories that appeared in Macmillan's *Canadian Wonder Tales* (1918) and *Canadian Fairy Tales* (1922). The classic, romantic retellings of Indian and French Canadian legends in the European folk and fairy tale tradition are enhanced by the decorative illustrations. Grades 4 and up.

Martin, Eva, retel. *Canadian Fairy Tales.* Illus. Laszlo Gal. Douglas & McIntyre/Groundwood Books, 1984.

This rich collection of folktales, told by the early European settlers of Canada, demonstrates how the familiar Old World folktales adopted the New World landscape and cultural experience when they were transplanted to the Canadian soil. Handsomely illustrated with decorative borders and full-color paintings. Grades 2–6.

China

Birch, Cyril. *Chinese Myths and Fantasies.* Illus. Joan Kiddell-Monroe. Walck, Oxford Myths and Legends Series, 1961.

Three types of stories are included: myths of creation, folktales, and a fantasy. Grades 5–7.

Carpenter, Frances. *Tales of a Chinese Grandmother.* Illus. Malthé Hasselriis. Doubleday, 1937.
> Folktales and legends, retold with the full flavor of the Orient. Grades 5–7.

Chrisman, Arthur B. *Shen of the Sea.* Illus. Else Hasselriis. Dutton, 1925.
> Stories that have a folklore quality, these tell the origin of tea, chopsticks, dragons, etc. Grades 5–7.

Hume, Lotta Carswell. *Favorite Children's Stories from China and Tibet.* Illus. Lo Koon-chiu. Tuttle, 1962.
> The author collected these lively tales during her twenty-two years in China, where her husband established the medical and educational center that became Yale-in-China. Grades 3–5.

Jagendorf, M. A., and Virginia Weng. *The Magic Boat and Other Chinese Folk Tales.* Illus. Wan-go Weng. Vanguard, 1980.
> A selection of vividly retold Chinese stories representative of the diverse ethnic groups within China. Appendices include notes about the stories, the ethnic groups, and a full bibliography. Grades 4–6.

Kendall, Carol, and Yao-wen Li, retels. *Sweet and Sour: Tales from China.* Illus. Shirley Felts. Houghton Mifflin, 1979.
> Kendall's skill as a writer of finely crafted fantasies gives this collection of twenty-four Chinese folktales, parables, fables, and jokes an elegant style and tone. The stories range widely from terse comic drolls to long mystical Taoist legends. Grades 4–6.

Lin, Adet. *The Milky Way and Other Chinese Folk Tales.* Illus. Enrico Arno. Harcourt, 1961.
> All of the stories are based on published versions and are here retold and translated. Sources are acknowledged. Grades 3–7.

Ritchie, Alice. *The Treasure of Li-Po.* Illus. T. Ritchie. Harcourt, 1949.
> Original fairy tales that, although not traditional, have an authentic Chinese flavor. Grades 4–6.

England, Scotland, and Wales

Colwell, Eileen. *Round about and Long Ago: Tales from the English Counties.* Illus. Anthony Colbert. Houghton Mifflin, 1974.
> A natural storyteller's clear, direct versions of twenty-eight tales.

Finlay, Winifred. *Folk Tales from the North.* Illus. Victor Ambrus. F. Watts, 1968.
> Scotch and English folktales, well told. No sources given. Grades 4–7.

Garner, Alan. *The Lad of the Gad.* Putnam's, 1981.
> Five Gaelic folktales freely retold from J. F. Campbell's *Popular Tales of the West Highlands* (1860–62) and an Irish manuscript. The strikingly musical, incantatory style captures a spirit of ancient ritual and magic. Grades 5 and up. See also the author's literary adaptations of folk material in *Alan Garner's Fairy Tales of Gold,* illus. Michael Foreman (1980).

Haviland, Virginia. *Favorite Fairy Tales Told in Scotland.* Illus. Adrienne Adams. Little, Brown, 1963.
> Tales well chosen, skillfully retold, and appropriately illustrated. Grades 2–5.

Jacobs, Joseph, ed. *English Fairy Tales.* Illus. John D. Batten. 3d. ed. rev. Putnam's, 1902.
> Joseph Jacobs was a born storyteller as well as a student of folklore. In retelling these stories he has preserved their humor and dramatic power. *More English Fairy Tales* is another indispensable collection. Both are available in Dover paperback editions. Grades 2–4. See also Edward Ardizzone's distinguished illustrations for twelve of Jacobs' classic tales in *Ardizzone's English Fairy Tales* (Deutsch, 1980).

Jones, Gwyn. *Welsh Legends and Folk-Tales.* Illus. Joan Kiddell-Monroe. Oxford Univ. Press, Oxford Myths and Legends Series, 1955.
> A distinguished Welsh folklorist has brought together an interesting collection of ancient Celtic tales and legends. Grades 5–9.

Manning-Sanders, Ruth. *Peter and the Piskies: Cornish Folk and Fairy Tales.* Illus. Raymond Briggs. Roy, 1966.
> Here are piskies, spriggans, and knockers of Cornwall, along with devils and saints. Knockers are little goblins who live in the mines. Excellent for telling. Grades 3–5.

Nic Leodhas, Sorche. *Gaelic Ghosts.* Illus. Nonny Hogrogian. Holt, 1964.
> The lilt and burr of Scotland highlight these stories, ranging from medieval legends of the supernatural to modern "ghosts in residence." Grades 4–7. See also *Ghosts Go Haunting* and *Twelve Great Black Cats and Other Eerie Scottish Tales* (Dutton, 1971).

Nic Leodhas, Sorche. *Heather and Broom: Tales of the Scottish Highlands.* Illus. Consuelo Joerns. Holt, 1960.

Seanachie tales, retold by a children's librarian, have a strong Gaelic flavor. Excellent for storytelling. Grades 4–7.

Nic Leodhas, Sorche. *Thistle and Thyme: Tales and Legends from Scotland.* Illus. Evaline Ness. Holt, 1962.

A companion volume to *Heather and Broom.* Tales filled with romance, magic, and humor, superbly told. Grades 4–7. See also *Sea-Shell and Moor-Magic: Tales of the Western Isles,* illus. Vera Bock (1968).

Reeves, James. *English Fables and Fairy Stories.* Illus. Joan Kiddell-Monroe. Oxford Univ. Press, Oxford Myths and Legends Series, 1954.

Familiar folktales, which Mr. Reeves embellishes a little more than the Joseph Jacobs versions. Grades 3–5.

Steel, Flora Annie. *English Fairy Tales.* Illus. Arthur Rackham; afterword Clifton Fadiman. Macmillan, The Macmillan Classics, 1962.

A fine collection of forty favorite tales. Grades 3–5.

William-Ellis, Amabel. *Fairy Tales from the British Isles.* Illus. Pauline Diana Baynes. Warne, 1964.

Folktales representing all parts of the British Isles. Grades 4–6.

France

All the French Fairy Tales. Retold and with a foreword by Louis Untermeyer; illus. Gustave Doré. Didier, 1946.

The superb Doré pictures in gravure give the book distinction. Unfortunately out of print, but may be found in public libraries. Grades 4–6.

Aulnoy, Marie, Comtesse d'. *The White Cat, and Other Old French Fairy Tales.* Arranged by Rachel Field; illus. Elizabeth MacKinstry. New facsimile ed. Macmillan, 1967.

A beautiful book with illustrations made in the manner of the eighteenth century. Grades 4–6.

Carter, Angela, ed. and trans. *Sleeping Beauty and Other Favourite Fairy Tales.* Illus. Michael Foreman. Gollancz, 1982.

Ten stories by Perrault and two by Madame Leprince de Beaumont elegantly retold with a fresh directness and clarity. A scholarly afterword and award-winning illustrations make this a valuable collection. Several of the tales first appeared in *The Fairy Tales of Charles Perrault,* trans. Angela Carter; illus. Martin Ware (Gollancz, 1977).

Haviland, Virginia. *Favorite Fairy Tales Told in France.* Illus. Roger Duvoisin. Little, Brown, 1959.

Five French fairy tales from Charles Perrault and other French storytellers, retold with grace and style. Grades 2–5.

Moore, Marianne. *Puss in Boots, The Sleeping Beauty, and Cinderella.* Illus. Eugene Karlin. Macmillan, 1963.

A celebrated American poet has translated and retold the Perrault tales. Grades K–3.

Perrault, Charles. *Complete Fairy Tales.* Trans. A. E. Johnson and others; illus. W. Heath Robinson. Dodd, Mead, 1961.

Eleven of these fourteen tales are by Perrault, and three are by other French writers. Grades 4–6. See also *Perrault's Classic French Fairy Tales;* illus. Janusz Grabianski (Meredith, 1967), and *Perrault's Fairy Tales,* trans. A. E. Johnson; illus. Gustave Doré (Dover, 1969).

Perrault, Charles. *The Glass Slipper: Charles Perrault's Tales of Times Past.* Trans. John Bierhorst; illus. Mitchell Miller. Four Winds, 1981.

A completely new translation into modern idiomatic English based on the 1697 text and including a scholarly afterword, bibliography, appendix of extra material, and versified morals from the original edition. The unembroidered style is complemented by the restrained, hushed black-and-white illustrations authentic in costume and period detail. Grades 4 and up.

Picard, Barbara L., comp. *French Legends, Tales, and Fairy Stories.* Illus. Joan Kiddell-Monroe. Oxford Univ. Press, Oxford Myths and Legends Series, 1955.

Selections from the hero tales, the courtly stories of the Middle Ages, and folktales from the French provinces, retold with skill. Grades 5–7.

Germany

Grimm, Jakob, and Wilhelm Grimm. *About Wise Men and Simpletons: Twelve Tales from Grimm.* Trans. Elizabeth Shub; illus. Nonny Hogrogian. Macmillan, 1971.

Fresh retellings from the first German edition, pithy and immediate in tone. Fine line drawings capture the earthy directness of the renditions. Grades 3–6.

Grimm, Jakob, and Wilhelm Grimm. *The Brothers Grimm: Popular Folk Tales.* Trans. Brian Alderson; illus. Michael Foreman. Gollancz, 1978.

Vigorous retellings of classic tales, contemporary and colloquial in direction and tone. Striking line drawings and watercolor paintings, often surrealistic and dreamlike. Grades 4 and up.

Grimm, Jakob, and Wilhelm Grimm. *Fairy Tales of the Brothers Grimm.* Ed. and intro. Bryan Holme; illus. Kay Nielsen. Viking/Metropolitan Museum of Art, A Studio Book, 1979.

Twelve fairy tales in a lavish volume combining texts selected and adapted from the 1925 English edition of *Hansel and Gretel: Stories from the Brothers Grimm* (Hodder & Stoughton) and color plates, chapter head decorations, and ornamental letters from the French edition *Fleur-de-Neige et d'autres contes de Grimm* (L'Edition d'Arte, Paris, 1925). A splendid example of fine book production. Grades 4 and up.

Grimm, Jakob, and Wilhelm Grimm. *Favourite Tales from Grimm.* Retold by Nancy Garden; illus. Mercer Mayer. Four Winds, 1982.

An attractive edition with black-and-white head– and tailpieces and romantic, Rackhamesque color plates capturing the tone of the graceful retellings. Grades 3–5.

Grimm, Jakob, and Wilhelm Grimm. *Grimm's Fairy Tales.* Trans. Mrs. E. V. Lucas, Lucy Crane, and Marian Edwardes; illus. Fritz Kredel. Grosset & Dunlap, Illustrated Junior Library, 1945.

Fifty-five of the well-loved tales. Grades 4–6.

Grimm, Jakob, and Wilhelm Grimm. *Grimm's Fairy Tales.* Trans. Lucy Crane; illus. Arnold Roth; afterword, Clifton Fadiman. Macmillan, Macmillan Classics, 1963.

One of the best translations. The original edition was illustrated by Walter Crane in 1882. Grades 3–5.

Grimm, Jakob, and Wilhelm Grimm. *Grimm's Fairy Tales.* Based on the retelling by Frances Jenkins Olcott, from the translation by Margaret Hunt; intro. Frances Clarke Sayers. Follett, 1968.

Fifty of the tales illustrated with fifty illustrations chosen from ten thousand submitted by children of all ages from seventy countries around the world. Selected with the help of the American Federation of Arts.

Grimm, Jakob, and Wilhelm Grimm. *Grimm's Fairy Tales.* Sel. and intro. Richard Adams; illus. Pauline Ellison. Routledge & Kegan Paul, 1981.

Twenty well-known tales selected from the definitive English translation of *The Complete Grimm's Fairy Tales* (Pantheon, 1944). The black-and-white headpieces and color plates add touches of authen-

tic costume, setting, and period detail in an atmosphere of magical realism. Grades 3–6.

Grimm, Jakob, and Wilhelm Grimm. *Grimm's Fairy Tales.* Trans. Peter Carter; illus. Peter Richardson. Oxford Univ. Press, 1982.

Freely retold from favorite Grimm tales, this collection has wry anachronistic humor, idiomatic rhythms, and a lively play with language and narrative. The text's vitality is enhanced by active illustrations. Grades 4–6.

Grimm, Jakob, and Wilhelm Grimm. *Grimm's Fairy Tales: Twenty Stories.* Illus. Arthur Rackham. Viking, 1973.

Twenty of the more familiar stories illustrated by Arthur Rackham.

Grimm, Jakob, and Wilhelm Grimm. *Household Stories.* Trans. Lucy Crane; illus. Walter Crane. McGraw-Hill, 1966.

This reprint edition offers to children of today the flavor of the period in which the stories were written. Available in paperback (Dover, 1963). First published in 1886. Grades 3–6.

Grimm, Jakob, and Wilhelm Grimm. *The House in the Wood, and Other Fairy Stories.* Illus. L. Leslie Brooke. Warne, 1944.

An excellent edition for younger children. Grades 3–4.

Grimm, Jakob, and Wilhelm Grimm. *The Juniper Tree and Other Tales from Grimm.* 2 vols. Sel. Lore Segal and Maurice Sendak; trans. Lore Segal, with four tales trans. Randall Jarrell; illus. Maurice Sendak. Farrar, Straus & Giroux, 1973.

The twenty-seven tales presented in these two small volumes are distinguished in all aspects of bookmaking. The vitality and depth of translator and illustrator hold these books together in special distinction. Grades 3 and up.

Grimm, Jakob, and Wilhelm Grimm. *Rare Treasures from Grimm: Fifteen Little Known Tales.* Sel. and trans. Ralph Manheim; illus. Erik Blegvad. Doubleday, 1981.

Fifteen little-known tales selected from Manheim's acclaimed definitive translation *Grimm's Tales for Young and Old: The Complete Stories* (1977). Handsomely produced with delicate, charming color plates. Grades 3–6.

Grimm, Jakob, and Wilhelm Grimm. *Tales from Grimm.* Freely trans. and illus. by Wanda Gág. Coward-McCann, 1936.

A thoroughly satisfying edition from the standpoint of both text and pictures. Wanda Gág is a translator and artist of rare genius. Her translation retains the quality of the spoken story. She explains her theory of free translation in the introduction. Grades 2–4.

Grimm, Jakob, and Wilhelm Grimm. *More Tales from Grimm.* Freely trans. and illus. by Wanda Gág. Coward-McCann, 1947.

A companion volume to *Tales from Grimm,* it contains some stories not so well known. Both text and illustrations are distinguished. The foreword by Carl Zigrosser tells about the artist's background and method of illustration. Grades 4–5.

Grimm, Jakob, and Wilhelm Grimm. *Three Gay Tales from Grimm.* Freely trans. by Wanda Gág. Coward-McCann, 1943.

Wanda Gág tells in gay text and inimitable pictures the stories of *The Clever Wife, Three Feathers,* and *Goose Hans.* Grades 1–3.

Haviland, Virginia. *Favorite Fairy Tales Told in Germany.* Retold from the Brothers Grimm; illus. Susanne Suba. Little, Brown, 1959.

Seven tales selected and simplified for younger children. An attractive edition with large print. Grades 2–5.

Gypsies

Hampden, John. *The Gypsy Fiddle and Other Tales Told by the Gypsies.* Illus. Robin Jacques; intro. Jan Yoors. World, 1969.

Particularly interesting is the introduction by Jan Yoors, who lived with the gypsies for ten years in his youth. In addition, an "Author's Note" gives sources and further references to those interested in gypsies and their lore. Grades 4–8.

Jagendorf, M. A., and C. H. Tillhagen. *The Gypsies' Fiddle and Other Gypsy Tales.* Illus. Hans Helweg. Vanguard, 1956.

Full of color and told in the style of the teller, Taikon, who had heard many of these tales from another famous gypsy storyteller, Gonae. Notes on the stories are appended. Grades 3–6.

Indian Subcontinent

Gray, John E. B. *India's Tales and Legends.* Illus. Joan Kiddell-Monroe. Walck, Oxford Myths and Legends Series, 1961.

Stories adapted from the Indian epics, Buddhist birth stories, animal fables, and other tales from the folk literature of India. Grades 6–8.

Hitchcock, Patricia. *The King Who Rides a Tiger, and Other Folk Tales from Nepal.* Illus. Lillian Sader. Parnassus, 1966.

The author, who lived in Nepal for two years, gathered these authentic folktales, making a rich collection. Grades 4–6.

Hodges, Elizabeth Jamison. *Serendipity Tales.* Illus. June Atkin Corwin. Atheneum, 1966.

The stories derive from many sources and the fertile imagination of the author, who is steeped in the folklore and history of Ceylon, India, and the Middle East. Serendip is an ancient name of Ceylon. Grades 4–6. See also *The Three Princes of Serendip.*

Jacobs, Joseph, ed. *Indian Fairy Tales: Gathered from the Hindoos.* Illus. J. D. Batten. Putnam's, n.d.

Stories from the Jātakas, or birth stories of Buddha; fables of Bidpai; and other Sanskrit tales. Grades 4–6.

Macfarlane, Iris, comp. *Tales and Legends from India.* Illus. Eric Thomas. F. Watts, 1966.

Stories heard in Assan hill villages during the compiler's years of residence there. Grades 4–6.

Price, Christine. *The Valiant Chattee-Maker.* Illus. by the author. Warne, 1965.

A little-known folktale from India about a humble maker of pottery who inadvertently became a hero. Lively illustrations. Grades 2–4.

Quigley, Lillian, ed. *The Blind Men and the Elephant.* Illus. Janice Holland. Scribner's, 1959.

The old Hindu tale of six blind men who, each touching a different part of the elephant, disagree about what it is like. Another edition, by John Godfrey Saxe, is illustrated by Paul Galdone (McGraw-Hill, 1963). Grades 1–3.

Siddiqui, Ashraf, and Marilyn Lerch. *Toontoony Pie, and Other Tales from Pakistan.* Illus. Jan Fairservis. World, 1961.

Tales of humor and magic collected and retold by the director of the Folklore Research Center of East Pakistan. Grades 3–6.

Spellman, John W., ed. *The Beautiful Blue Jay, and Other Tales of India.* Illus. Jerry Pinkney. Little, Brown, 1967.

Twenty-five stories that mothers tell their children in India today. Grades 3–5.

Ireland

Colum, Padraic. *The King of Ireland's Son: An Irish Folk Tale.* Illus. Willy Pogány. Macmillan, 1962.

Humor, poetry, and action enliven these seven tales from the author's native Ireland. First published in 1916. Reissued with the original illustrations. Grades 5–8.

Colum, Padraic. *The Stone of Victory and Other Tales of Padraic Colum.* Illus. Judith Gwyn Brown; foreword, Virginia Haviland. McGraw-Hill, 1966.

The distinguished Irish storyteller has selected favorite tales from seven of his books, most of them out of print. Grades 3–6.

Colum, Padraic, ed. *A Treasury of Irish Folklore.* Rev. ed. Crown, 1962.

Stories, traditions, legends, humor, wisdom, ballads, and songs of the Irish people. Grades 8–9.

Danaher, Kevin. *Folktales of the Irish Countryside.* Illus. Harold Berson. David White, 1970.

A member of the Irish Folklore Commission staff, the author presents stories from his own memory in the style and cadence of the told story.

Jacobs, Joseph, ed. *Celtic Fairy Tales.* Illus. Victor Ambrus. World, 1971.

A new edition, combining *Celtic Fairy Tales* and *More Celtic Fairy Tales.* These romantic and humorous stories are also available in paperback in two volumes (Dover, 1968). Grades 4–8.

McGarry, Mary, comp. *Great Folktales of Old Ireland.* Intro. Mary McGarry; illus. Richard Hook. Wolfe, 1972.

Tellings from Joseph Jacobs, T. Crofton Croker, Jeremiah Curtin, and others, all noted collectors and tellers of Irish stories. Grades 5–9.

MacManus, Seumas. *The Bold Heroes of Hungry Hill, and Other Irish Folk Tales.* Illus. Jay Chollick. Farrar, Straus & Giroux, 1951.

Twelve tales told with charm and delightful Irish flavor. Grades 4–6.

MacManus, Seumas. *Hibernian Nights.* Illus. Paul Kennedy. Macmillan, 1963.

An invaluable collection including the great Irish storyteller's own favorites for telling. Stories are selected from his earlier books out of print. Grades 4–7. See also *Donegal Fairy Stories* (Dover, 1968).

O'Faolain, Eileen. *Children of the Salmon and Other Irish Folk Tales.* Illus. Trina Schart Hyman. Little, Brown, 1965.

A rich collection for the folklorist and for the experienced storyteller who can adapt stories from source material. See also *Irish Sagas and Folk-Tales,* illus. Joan Kiddell-Monroe (Walck, 1954).

Picard, Barbara Leonie, comp. *Celtic Tales: Legends of Tall Warriors and Old Enchantments.* Illus. John G. Galsworthy. Criterion, 1965.

A companion volume to *Hero-Tales from the British Isles* and *Tales of the British People.* Grades 5–7.

Sutcliff, Rosemary. *The High Deeds of Finn Mac Cool.* Illus. Michael Charlton. Dutton, 1967.

These tales from the Finn cycle belong essentially to folklore. Grades 6–8.

Yeats, William Butler, ed. *Irish Fairy and Folk Tales.* Modern Library, n.d.

Good source material for the storyteller.

Young, Ella. *Celtic Wonder Tales Retold.* New ed. Dutton, 1923.

Stories of the Gubbaun Saor told by the Irish poet and student of folklore. First published in Ireland. Grades 4–7.

Iran and Iraq

Kelsey, Alice Geer. *Once the Mullah: Persian Folk Tales.* Illus. Kurt Werth. Longmans, 1954.

Mullah is the Persian double of the beloved Hodja of the Turks. Children delight in the ingenuity of Mullah in getting himself out of tight spots. Grades 4–6.

Mehdevi, Anne Sinclair. *Persian Folk and Fairy Tales.* Illus. Paul Kennedy. Knopf, 1965.

The author has retold these tales, which she heard an old Persian nurse tell to her nieces and nephews. Grades 4–6.

Italy

Calvino, Italo. *Italian Folk Tales.* Trans. Sylvia Mulcahy; illus. Emanuele Luzzati. Dent, 1975.

A selection of twenty-seven folktales arranged by type and retold in pure, vivid, and humorous language by a master storyteller. Chosen from his complete collection for adults, first published in Italy in 1956, the stories include notes on geographical origins. The warm, comic illustrations have a Comedia del Arte air. Grades 3–5.

Chafetz, Henry. *The Legend of Befana.* Illus. Ronni Solbert. Houghton Mifflin, 1958.

One of the most famous Italian Christmas stories. Grades 2–3.

Cimino, Maria. *The Disobedient Eels and Other Italian Tales.* Illus. Claire Nivola. Pantheon, 1970.

Brief tales, pungent with wit. Grades 4–6.

De Paola, Tomie. *The Clown of God.* Illus. by the author. Harcourt, 1978.

Inspired by Anatole France's version of this classic French legend, the author has set the story of the juggler who performs before the statue of the Virgin and Child in an early Italian Renaissance world. Poignantly told; gently illustrated. Grades 1–4.

Jagendorf, M. A. *The Priceless Cats and Other Italian Folk Tales.* Vanguard, 1956.

The author, who heard these stories while in Italy, tells them with a simplicity and directness that makes them excellent for storytelling. Grades 3–5.

Mincieli, Rose Laura, comp. *Old Neapolitan Fairy Tales.* Illus. Beni Montresor. Knopf, 1963.

Stories selected and retold from *Il Pentamerone*, by Giambattista Basile, published in 1674, the earliest collection of European folktales. Grades 5–7.

Werth, Kurt. *The Monkey, the Lion, and the Snake.* Viking, 1967.

A tale from *Gesta Romanorum* with spirited pictures of Venice in the days when animals, as well as men, were chivalrous. Grades 1–3. See also *The Cobbler's Dilemma: An Italian Folk Tale* (McGraw-Hill, 1967).

Japan and Korea

Bang, Garrett, comp. *Men from the Village Deep in the Mountains and Other Japanese Folk Tales.* Trans. and illus. by the author. Macmillan, 1973.

Tales of wonders and wily tricksters give variety to this collection. Grades 3–6.

Edmonds, I. G. *Ooka the Wise: Tales of Old Japan.* Illus. Sanae Yamazaki. Bobbs-Merrill, 1961.

Heard from the *Ojiisan* (grandfather), these stories give accounts of the wise and wily stratagems of Ooka, a judge of Old Japan. Grades 2–5.

Haviland, Virginia. *Favorite Fairy Tales Told in Japan.* Illus. George Suyeoka. Little, Brown, 1967.

Tales retold by the head of the Children's Section, Library of Congress. Grades 2–4.

Hearn, Lafcadio, and others. *Japanese Fairy Tales.* Illus. Sonia Roeter. Peter Pauper, 1948.

Literary retellings, including "The Boy Who Drew Cats." Grades 4–9.

Jewett, Eleanore. *Which Was Witch? Tales of Ghosts and Magic from Korea.* Illus. Taro Yashima. Viking, 1953.

Good for storytelling and reading aloud. Grades 4–6.

McAlpine, Helen, and William McAlpine, comps. *Japanese Tales and Legends.* Retold by the authors; illus. Joan Kiddell-Monroe. Oxford Univ. Press, Oxford Myths and Legends Series, 1959.

Folktales, legends, and epic tales of Japan. Grades 5–8.

Sakade, Florence, ed. *Japanese Children's Favorite Stories.* Illus. Yoshisuke Kurosaki; trans. Meredith Weatherby. Tuttle, 1958.

An attempt has been made to remain true to the spirit of the Japanese original stories. No sources cited. Grades 1–3. See also *Kintar's Adventures and Other Japanese Children's Stories* (1959) and *Urashima Taro and Other Japanese Children's Stories* (1959).

Stamm, Claus. *The Very Special Badger: A Tale of Magic from Japan.* Viking, 1960.

Humorous tale. Grades 2–4. See also *Three Strong Women: A Tall Tale from Japan*, illus. Kazue Mizumura (1962).

Titus, Eve. *The Two Stonecutters.* Illus. Yoko Mitsuhashi. McGraw-Hill, 1967.

A traditional Japanese folktale retold and illustrated in the classic Japanese mood. Grades K–3.

Uchida, Yoshiko. *The Dancing Kettle, and Other Japanese Folk Tales.* Illus. Richard C. Jones. Harcourt, 1949.

Stories told to the author when she was a child. Excellent for storytelling. Grades 3–5. See also *The Magic Listening Cap* (Harcourt, 1955) and *The Sea of Gold* (Scribner's, 1965).

Yagawa, Sumiko, retel. *The Crane Wife.* Trans. Katherine Paterson; illus. Suekichi Akaba. Morrow, 1981.

This mystical tale of love and sacrifice has been poetically translated by a skilled novelist. Grades K–3.

Jewish

Serwer, Blanche Luria, retel. *Let's Steal the Moon: Jewish Tales, Ancient and Recent.* Illus. Trina Schart Hyman. Little, Brown, 1970.

Stories heard and known by the author in her own childhood are recounted again as they have remained in her imagination. Grades 4–8.

Shulevitz, Uri, adapt. and illus. *The Magician.* Adapt. from the Yiddish of I. L. Peretz. Macmillan, 1973.

Dramatic pen-and-ink sketches strikingly capture the mystery and drama of this Passover story. Grades 1–3.

Singer, Isaac Bashevis. *The Fearsome Inn.* Illus. Nonny Hogrogian. Scribner's, 1967.
Magic and common sense overcome evil in this story written in the genre of the folktale. Grades 4–6.

Singer, Isaac Bashevis. *The Golem.* Illus. Uri Shulevitz. Farrar, Straus & Giroux, 1982.
A suspenseful retelling in pure, vivid prose of the legend of the golem, the clay giant created by magic to rescue the Jews of old Prague. A Cabalist tale similar to the Frankenstein story, given a psychological dimension by the strong narrative and darkly shadowed black-and-white illustrations. Grades 3–5.

Singer, Isaac Bashevis. *Mazel and Shlimazel, or the Milk of a Lioness.* Illus. Margot Zemach; trans. from the Yiddish by the author and Elizabeth Shub. Farrar, Straus & Giroux, 1967.
The folktale of a peasant lad and his experience with good luck (Mazel) and bad luck (Shlimazel). As a boy Isaac Singer heard this story from his mother. Grades 1–3.

Singer, Isaac Bashevis. *When Shlemiel Went to Warsaw and Other Stories.* Illus. Margot Zemach; trans. Isaac Bashevis Singer and Elizabeth Shub. Farrar, Straus & Giroux, 1968.
Stories heard from the author's mother are presented with others of his own imagination. Grades 4–9. See also *Naftali the Storyteller and His Horse, Sus and Other Stories,* illus. Margot Zemach (1976).

Singer, Isaac Bashevis. *Zlateh the Goat and Other Stories.* Trans. from the Yiddish by the author and Elizabeth Shub; illus. Maurice Sendak. Harper, 1966.
A brilliant storyteller tells seven wise and humorous tales rooted in middle-European Jewish folklore. The beautifully drawn illustrations sensitively portray the characters and reflect the mood of the stories. Grades 4–6.

Mexico

Aardema, Verna, trans. *The Riddle of the Drum: A Tale from Tizapan, Mexico.* Illus. Tony Chen. Four Winds, 1979.
Clear, brilliantly colored illustrations dramatize a traditional quest tale. Grades 1–3.

Brenner, Anita. *The Boy Who Could Do Anything.* Illus. Jean Charlot. Scott, 1942.
Many of these stories stem from ancient Indian mythology before the Spanish conquest, yet they often include modern touches showing how each generation adds to the telling of a story. Grades 4–6.

Jordan, Philip D. *The Burro Benedicto, and Other Folk Tales and Legends of Mexico.* Illus. by the author. Coward-McCann, 1960.
While living in Mexico, the author heard these stories, which reflect the life, traditions, and religious beliefs of the people. Grades 4–6.

Lyons, Grant. *Tales the People Tell in Mexico.* Illus. Andrew Antal; consulting ed. Doris K. Coburn. Messner, 1972.
Superstitions, beliefs, and human foibles are brought out in this collection. There are also a glossary, background information on Mexico, and sources for the stories. Grades 3–6.

Ross, Patricia. *In Mexico They Say.* Illus. Henry C. Pitz. Knopf, 1942.
Fourteen folktales combining the elements of fantasy and superstition with realism. Grades 4–7.

Near and Middle East

Arabian Nights. *Aladdin and His Wonderful Lamp.* Trans. Sir Richard F. Burton; adapt. and illus. Leonard Lubin. Delacorte, 1983.
An adaptation of Burton's elegant, ornamental retelling illustrated by blue-and-white "chinoiserie" drawings. Grades 3–5.

Arabian Nights. *Aladdin and the Wonderful Lamp.* Retold, Andrew Lang; illus. Errol Le Cain. Viking, 1981.
Evocative of Edmond Dulac and Persian miniatures, Le Cain's exotic illustrations create an aura of mystery and opulence appropriate to Lang's stately version of the classic tale. Grades 1–4.

Arabian Nights. *Arabian Nights.* Col. and ed. Andrew Lang; illus. Vera Bock; foreword, Mary Gould Davis. Longmans, 1946.
First published in 1898. Based on the French translation by Antoine Gallard. The decorative type of illustration is in keeping with the Oriental setting. One of the best editions for its selection, illustrations, and foreword. Grades 5–7.

Arabian Nights. *Arabian Nights: Tales of Wonder and Magnificence.* Sel. and ed. Padraic Colum; illus. Lynd Ward. Macmillan, 1953.

The best retelling of the Arabian Nights for children. Text is based on Edward Lane's translation of *The Thousand and One Nights* (1838–1840). Mr. Colum says, "The stories are representative and an effort has been made to bring children near to the original literature and to the wonderful Saracenic civilization." The introduction includes an admirable discussion of the history of the Arabian Nights and its place in world literature. Grades 5–7.

Arabian Nights. *The Arabian Nights: Their Best-Known Tales.* Ed. Kate Douglas Wiggin and Nora A. Smith; illus. Maxfield Parrish. Scribner's, 1937. Scribner's Illustrated Classics, 1937.

The editors have retold these tales taken mainly from Scott's edition and from the Lane translation. Now available in Scribner's paperback edition. Grades 5–7.

Arabian Nights. *One Thousand and One Arabian Nights.* Retold by Geraldine McCaughrean; illus. Stephen Lewis. Oxford Univ. Press, Oxford Illustrated Classics, 1982.

Handsome, romantically old-fashioned illustrations complement straightforward retellings of standard tales. Grades 4–6.

Arabian Nights. *Tales from the Arabian Nights.* Adapt. N. J. Dawood; illus. Ed Young. Doubleday, 1978.

Retold from the original Arabic, these are skillful, colloquial versions of the tales. Evocative, impressionistic paintings reflect the dreamlike magic of the text. Grades 5–7.

Downing, Charles. *Tales of the Hodja.* Illus. William Papas. Walck, 1965.

Traditional stories attributed to "Nasreddin Hodja," a legendary personality of Turkish folklore. Grades 4–6.

Kelsey, Alice Geer. *Once the Hodja.* Illus. Frank Dobias. Longmans, 1943.

Nasr-ed-Din Hodja, a simple-minded country fellow, made an art of getting in and out of foolish predicaments. Grades 4–6.

Nahmad, H. M., ed. *The Peasant and the Donkey: Tales of the Near and Middle East.* Illus. William Papas. Walck, 1968.

An amusing and entertaining collection that represents diverse backgrounds in this area. With stories by Charles Downing, Nadi Abu-Zahra, Feyyaz Kayacan, and Mary Fergar. Grades 4–8.

Spicer, Dorothy Gladys. *The Kneeling Tree and Other Folktales from the Middle East.* Illus. Barbara Morrow. Coward-McCann, 1971.

The collector has retold these tales in her own way. Although she visited the Middle East to gather material, she does not cite her sources. Grades 4–7.

Travers, P. L., retel. *Two Pairs of Shoes.* Illus. Leon Dillon and Diane Dillon. Viking, 1976.

Eloquent retellings of two thematically linked Middle Eastern folktales, "Abu Kasem's Slippers" and "The Sandals of Ayaz." These two witty parables of human nature as exemplified by shoes are stylishly illustrated in the exotic, burnished style of Persian miniatures. Grades 1–4.

Walker, Barbara. *Watermelons, Walnuts and the Wisdom of Allah and Other Tales of the Hoca.* Illus. Harold Berson. Parents' Magazine, 1967.

Foolish and wise tales of the Turkish Hoca (Hoe-djah). The author lived in Turkey; no written sources are given. Grades 3–6. See also *Once There Was and Twice There Wasn't* (Follett, 1968).

Netherlands, Belgium, and Luxembourg

De Leeuw, Adele. *Legends and Folk Tales of Holland.* Illus. Paul Kennedy. Nelson, 1963.

The thanks given by the collector to various librarians is the only clue about sources. However, the stories are told with a directness and sense of warmth that make them both readable and tellable. Grades 3–7.

Spicer, Dorothy Gladys, comp. *The Owl's Nest: Folk Tales from Friesland.* Illus. Alice Wadowski-Bak. Coward-McCann, 1968.

Fresh tales told to the author by the farmers and fishermen of northern Holland. Grades 3–6.

Pacific Ocean and Australia

Berry, Erick. *The Magic Banana and Other Polynesian Tales.* Illus. Nicholas Amorosi. Day, 1968.

Notes and sources are given for this collection, which gives vivid illustration to the differences and likenesses of the Polynesian world. Grades 4–9.

Maralngura, N., et al. *Tales from the Spirit Time.* Rev. ed. Indiana Univ. Press, 1976.

Native aboriginal retellings of myths and legends, colloquial and primal, collected and illustrated by a group of young aborigines. Grades 3–6.

Parker, K. Langloh. *Australian Legendary Tales.* Sel. and ed. H. Drake-Brockman; illus. Elizabeth Durack. Viking, 1966.

A significant contribution to folklore. The author, an Australian-born Englishwoman, devoted her life to collecting legends and tales of the aborigines among whom she lived. These tales are selected from the five published volumes of her work, long out of print. All ages.

Philippines

Sechrist, Elizabeth Hough, retel. *Once in the First Times: Folk Tales from the Philippines.* Illus. John Sheppard. Macrae Smith, 1969.

Origin stories and stories of people and their problems fill out a collection that expresses the Filipino people and their history. Grades 4–7.

Poland

Borski, Lucia, and Kate Miller. *The Jolly Tailor, and Other Fairy Tales.* Illus. Kazimir Klepacki. Longmans, 1957.

A reissue of a book first published in 1928. One of the best sources of Polish folktales. Grades 3–5.

Haviland, Virginia. *Favorite Fairy Tales Told in Poland.* Illus. Felix Hoffmann. Little, Brown, 1963.

The retelling preserves the flavor and much of the language of the original. Grades 2–5.

Konopnicka, Maria. *The Golden Seed.* Adapt. Catharine Fournier; illus. Janina Domanska. Scribner's, 1962.

A king wishes for gold, and a wise old man gives him a bag of flax seed that would "flourish and grow into gold." Grades 1–3.

Scandinavia

Asbjörnsen, Peter Christen, and Jörgen Moe, eds. *East of the Sun and West of the Moon.* Illus. Tom Vroman; afterword, Clifton Fadiman. Macmillan, The Macmillan Classics, 1963.

Stories chosen from the Dasent translation of Asbjörnsen and Moe, first published in 1859. See also the Dover edition, 1970, which includes fifty-nine stories; the entire collection is translated by Sir George Dasent. Grades 3–4. See also a lovely collection of fifteen tales, first published in 1914, *East o' the Sun and West o' the Moon,* illus. Kay Nielsen (Doubleday, 1977).

Asbjörnsen, Peter Christen, and Jörgen Moe, eds. *Norwegian Folk Tales.* Illus. Erik Werenskiold and Theodor Kittelsen; trans. Pat Shaw Iversen and Carl Norman. Viking, 1960.

Thirty-six eerie and fantastic tales full of magical happenings. This new edition has the flavor of the classic Dasent translation, yet reads more smoothly. An excellent introduction gives background for the tales. Grades 4–6.

Asbjörnsen, Peter Christen, and Jörgen Moe, eds. *The Three Billy Goats Gruff.* Illus. Marcia Brown. Harcourt, 1957.

The artist has interpreted the well-known tale with striking pictures which convey the strength, simplicity, and drama of the story. Grades 2–4.

Boucher, Alan. *Mead Moondaughter and Other Icelandic Folk Tales.* Illus. Karólína Lárusdóttir. Rupert Hart-Davis, 1967.

These follow the originals taken down by Jón Arnason, Iceland's great collector of folk stories. Three of the stories are from Björn Bjarnason.

Bowman, James Cloyd, and Margery Bianco. *Tales from a Finnish Fireside.* From a translation by Aili Kolehmainen; illus. Laura Bannon. Chatto & Windus, 1975.

A new edition of *Tales from a Finnish Tupa* (Whitman, 1936), this does not contain all of the tales in the earlier edition. An outstanding collection of folktales for children, this is also invaluable to students of folklore and story. Grades 3–6. See also *Seven Silly Wise Men* (Whitman, 1965).

D'Aulaire, Ingri, and Edgar Parin D'Aulaire, eds. *East of the Sun and West of the Moon: Twenty-one Norwegian Folk Tales.* Illus. by the authors. Viking, 1969.

A reissue of a book first published in 1938. Striking lithographs distinguish this volume. See also *Trolls* (Doubleday, 1972).

Fillmore, Parker. *The Shepherd's Nosegay: Stories from Finland and Czechoslovakia.* Ed. Katherine Love; illus. Enrico Arno. Harcourt, 1958.

Contains six stories from Finland taken from *Mighty Mikko,* by Parker Fillmore. Grades 4–6.

Hatch, Mary C. *Thirteen Danish Tales.* Illus. Edgun. Harcourt, 1947.

These stories, retold with unusual charm, are based on J. Christian Bay's translation entitled *Danish Fairy and Folk Tales,* first published in 1809. Grades 3–5. See also *More Danish Tales, Retold.*

Haviland, Virginia, retel. *Favorite Fairy Tales Told in Norway.* Illus. Leonard Weisgard. Little, Brown, 1961.

Adapted from the 1859 translation by Sir George Dasent of *Norwegian Folk Tales* by Peter Christen Asbjörnsen and Jörgen Moe. Grades 2–4. See also *Favorite Fairy Tales Told in Sweden,* illus. Ronni Solbert (1966), and *Favorite Fairy Tales Told in Denmark,* illus. Margot Zemach (1971).

Jones, Gwyn, comp. *Scandinavian Legends and Folk-Tales.* Illus. Joan Kiddell-Monroe. Oxford Univ. Press, Oxford Myths and Legends Series, 1956.

Stories from Denmark, Iceland, Norway, and Sweden. Grades 4–6.

Kavcic, Vladimir, retel. *The Golden Bird: Folk Tales from Slovenia.* Trans. Jan Dekker and Helen Lencek; illus. Mae Gerhard. World, 1969.

Vladimir Kavcic, a novelist in Yugoslavia, says that he has changed very little in the 19th-century written versions of these "authentic stories." Grades 3–6.

Olenius, Elsa, comp. *Great Swedish Fairy Tales.* Trans. Holger Lundbergh; illus. John Bauer. Delacorte, 1973.

A classic Swedish illustrator from the golden age of illustration at the turn of the century captures the dark mysteries of trolls, forests, and romantic quests.

Sperry, Margaret, trans. and adapt. *Scandinavian Stories.* Illus. Jenny Williams. F. Watts, 1971.

Her own Norwegian background has led the translator to choose these stories: "Respect for the best folk and fairy tales of the past has motivated my work." Swedish stories of Anna Wahlenberg are included. Grades 1–5.

Thorne-Thomsen, Gudrun, ed. *East o' the Sun and West o' the Moon, with Other Norwegian Folk Tales.* Rev. ed. Row, Peterson, 1946.

Twenty-five folktales retold by a famous storyteller with a fine appreciation of original sources. Grades 3–4.

Undset, Sigrid, ed. *True and Untrue and Other Norse Tales.* Illus. Frederick T. Chapman. Knopf, 1945.

Based on the original stories of Asbjörnsen and Moe. The author's foreword, "The Adventure Story of the Folk Tale," is of great value to the storyteller. Grades 4–6.

Zemach, Harve. *Nail Soup: A Swedish Folk Tale.* Illus. Margot Zemach. Follett, 1964.

The tale of the stingy old woman and the wily tramp, presented in picture-book format. Grades K–3.

South America

Carpenter, Frances. *South American Wonder Tales.* Illus. Ralph Creasman. Follett, 1969. Grades 4–6.

Eells, Elsie Spicer. *Tales from the Amazon.* Illus. Florence Choate and Elizabeth Curtis. Dodd, Mead, 1954.

Twenty-six Brazilian folktales. Grades 4–6.

Finger, Charles. *Tales from Silver Lands.* Woodcuts, Paul Honoré. Doubleday, 1924.

Folktales of the Indians of Brazil, which the author gathered firsthand from the Indians he met in his wanderings. Awarded the Newbery Medal, 1925. Grades 5–7.

Jagendorf, M. A., and R. S. Boggs. *The King of the Mountains: A Treasury of Latin American Folk Stories.* Illus. Carybé. Vanguard, 1961.

The compilers, well-known folklorists, have selected the stories they thought would give an idea of the folk life of Latin America. Grades 5–8.

Rhoads, Dorothy. *The Bright Feather and Other Maya Tales.* Illus. Lowell Houser. Doubleday, 1932.

A unique collection of stories; some were heard by the compiler and her sister, some were taken down by J. Eric Thompson of the Field Museum of Natural History. These are "modern Maya folk tales, obtained from Maya Indians living in villages in the midst of the bush in Guatemala and in Yucatan." Grades 3–6.

Southeast Asia

Bro, Margueritte. *How the Mouse Deer Became King.* Illus. Joseph Low. Doubleday, 1966.

Eleven delightful tales of the crafty trickster. Grades 4–6.

Carpenter, Frances. *The Elephant's Bathtub: Wonder Tales from the Far East.* Illus. Hans Guggenheim. Doubleday, 1962.

Thailand, Iraq, Vietnam, Ceylon, Burma, Laos, and other (sixteen) countries of the East are represented in this collection of "ancient folktales." Sources are acknowledged. Grades 3–6.

Courlander, Harold. *Kantchil's Lime Pit, and Other Stories from Indonesia.* Illus. Robert W. Kane. Harcourt, 1950.

Stories about wise and foolish men and tales of animals. Best loved are the stories about Kantchil, the tiny mouse deer only a foot high. Grades 5–9.

Courlander, Harold. *The Tiger's Whisker, and Other Tales and Legends from Asia and the Pacific.* Illus. Enrico Arno. Harcourt, 1959.
Thirty-one stories, from many Far Eastern countries, including Korea, Burma, Japan, Arabia, and islands in the Pacific. Grades 4–7.

Krueger, Kermit. *The Serpent Prince: Folk Tales from Northeastern Thailand.* Illus. Yoko Mitsuhashi. World, 1969.
Working as a Peace Corps volunteer in northeastern Thailand, Kermit Krueger learned these stories from his students. Grades 4–9.

Merrill, Jean. *High, Wide and Handsome, and Their Three Tall Tales.* Illus. Ronni Solbert. Scott, 1964.
A delightful Burmese version of an old folktale. Grades 2–4.

Robertson, Dorothy Lewis, retel. *Fairy Tales from Viet Nam.* Illus. W. T. Mars. Dodd, Mead, 1968.
These stories were sent to Mrs. Robertson by Nguyen Dinh Thuan. Her foreword gives the general background of the stories, as well as a brief sketch of Vietnam's history. Grades 3–7.

Vo-Dinh. *The Toad Is the Emperor's Uncle: Animal Folktales from Viet-Nam.* Illus. by the author. Doubleday, 1970.
The significance and wisdom of certain creatures becomes apparent, as do the qualities of the Vietnamese people themselves. Grades 4–8.

U.S.S.R.

(Afanasiev) Afanasyev, Alexander Nikolyaevich. *In a Certain Kingdom: Twelve Russian Fairy Tales.* Sel. and trans. Thomas P. Whitney; illus. Dieter Lange. Macmillan, 1972.
Traditional adventure and wonder stories, selected from the more than six hundred stories collected by Afanasyev. Grades 4–8.

(Afanasiev) Afanasyev, Alexander. *Russian Fairy Tales.* Trans. Norbert Guterman; illus. Alexander Alexeieff. 2d ed. Pantheon, 1973.
An excellent source book for adults.

(Afanasiev) Afanasyev, Alexander. *Russian Folk Tales.* Trans. Natalie Duddington; illus. Dick Hart. Funk & Wagnalls, 1967.
An excellent collection for children and all readers, these tales have been translated with art and faithful simplicity by a Russian translator. Grades 4–9.

(Afanasiev) Afanasyev, Alexander. *Russian Folk Tales.* Trans. Robert Chandler; illus. Ivan I. Bilibin. Shambhala/Random House, 1980.

A fluent, colorful translation of seven classic stories, magnificently illustrated with the flowing decorative images of the turn-of-the-century Russian book illustrator. Theatrical and poetic. Grades 4–6. See also Chandler's retelling of *The Magic Ring and Other Russian Folktales,* illus. Ken Kiff (Faber & Faber, 1979).

Almedingen, E. M. *Russian Folk and Fairy Tales.* Illus. Simon Jeruchim. Putnam's, 1963.
Based on the work of Alexander Afanasiev, published in 1856. In some cases variants of the same folktale are woven into one story. Grades 3–6.

Bloch, Marie Halun, comp. and trans. *Ukranian Folk Tales from the Original Collections of Ivan Rudchenko and Maria Lukiyanenko.* Illus. J. Hnizdovsky. Coward-McCann, 1964.
Many years before the author translated these stories, she heard them, as a child, from her grandmother in the Ukraine. Grades 1–4.

Carey, Bonnie, trans. and adapt. *Baba Yaga's Geese and Other Russian Stories.* Illus. Guy Fleming. Indiana Univ. Press, 1973.
Stories in the manner and concept of the traditional tale by writers such as Krylov and Tolstoi, together with those of folk origins. Grades 2–6.

Daniels, Guy, sel. and trans. *The Falcon under the Hat: Russian Merry Tales and Fairy Tales.* Illus. Feodor Rojankovsky. Funk & Wagnalls, 1969.
This entertaining collection has an informing, critically perceptive foreword and an appendix giving Russian sources for each tale. Grades 3–6.

Deutsch, Babette, and Avrahm Yarmolinsky. *Tales of Faraway Folk.* Illus. Irena Lorentowicz. Harper, 1952.
A poet, a scholar, and an artist have combined efforts to produce this excellent collection of ten tales from Central Asia and the Caucasus. Grades 3–5. See also *More Tales of Faraway Folk* (1963).

Downing, Charles. *Russian Tales and Legends.* Illus. Joan Kiddell-Monroe. Oxford Univ. Press, Oxford Myths and Legends Series, 1957.
The author has drawn his material from many regions of Russia. Grades 3–6.

Durham, Mae. *Tit for Tat, and Other Latvian Folk Tales.* Illus. Harriet Pincus. Harcourt, 1967.
Tales marked by vitality and humor. Grades 3–6.

Foster, Ruth, retel. *The Stone Horsemen: Tales from the Caucasus.* Illus. Judith Gwyn Brown. Bobbs-Merrill, 1965.

Sprightly told and colorful; no sources given. Grades 3–6.

Ginsburg, Mirra, ed. and trans. *The Kaha Bird: Tales from the Steppes of Central Asia.* Illus. Richard Cuffari. Crown, 1971.
"Non-Russian folk tales from Russia," these tales represent the recent collecting efforts of scholars. Grades 4–9. See also *The Master of the Wind and Other Tales from Siberia.*

Ginsburg, Mirra, trans. and ed. *The Lazies: Tales of the Peoples of Russia.* Illus. Marian Parry. Macmillan, 1973.
Humorous and brief, these stories come from a variety of regions. Grades 2–6.

Ginsburg, Mirra, trans. *One Trick Too Many: Fox Stories from Russia.* Illus. Helen Siegl. Dial, 1973.
Brief stories, concerned with trickery and cunning. Grades 2–6.

Ginsburg, Mirra, retel. *Three Rolls and One Doughnut: Fables from Russia.* Illus. Anita Lobel. Dial, 1970.
From all parts of Russia come these short tales and riddles, all representing different cultures, all filled with wit and wisdom. Grades 1–4.

Haviland, Virginia. *Favorite Fairy Tales Told in Russia.* Retold from Russian storytellers; illus. Herbert Danska. Little, Brown, 1961.
Contents: *To Your Good Health; Vasilisa the Beautiful; Snegourka, the Snow Maiden; The Straw Ox;* and *The Flying Ship.* Grades 2–5.

Higonnet-Schnopper, Janet, comp. *Tales from Atop a Russian Stove.* Illus. Franz Altschuler. Whitman, 1973.
Translations of Russian stories found in *Russkie narodnye skazki* (published in Moscow, 1965; comp. N. Savuskina) have been adapted "for reading in English." A guide for pronouncing the Russian names is provided, and the tellings retain the style of the oral tradition. Grades 3–6.

Maas, Selve, retel. *The Moon Painters and Other Estonian Folk Tales.* Illus. Laszlo Gal. Viking, 1971.
The distinct character of Estonia, one of the Baltic countries now part of the U.S.S.R., is reflected in these tales, which are taken from six different collections. Grades 3–7.

Masey, Mary Lou, retel. *Stories of the Steppes: Kazakh Folktales.* Illus. Helen Basilevsky. McKay, 1968.
Stories that have not been translated into English before are here given in versions that carry the vigor of the told tale. Background material is in the introduction; glossary at the end. Sources for the stories are provided. Grades 3–6.

Papashvily, George, and Helen Papashvily. *Yes and No Stories: A Book of Georgian Folk Tales.* Illus. Simon Lissim. Harper, 1946.
A freshness to these tales makes them good reading. Grades 6–8.

Ransome, Arthur. *Old Peter's Russian Tales.* Illus. Faith Jaques. Nelson, 1976.
A new edition of a valued collection. These tales were gathered by the author while he was in Russia as a correspondent. Originally published in 1916. Grades 3–6.

Riordan, James, retel. *Tales from Central Russia: Russian Tales.* Vol. 1. Illus. Krystyna Turska. Viking, 1979.
Spiritedly retold from Afanasiev, this extensive collection includes an informative "Commentary on Russian Folk Tales." Grades 3–5. See also *Tales from Tartary* (1979).

Tashjian, Virginia A. *Once There Was and Was Not: Armenian Tales Retold.* Illus. Nonny Hogrogian. Little, Brown, 1966.
A retelling of the stories told by the folklorist Hovhannes Toumanian. Author and illustrator are both of Armenian heritage. Grades 3–4. See also *Three Apples Fell from Heaven* (1971).

Tolstoy, Leo. *Russian Stories and Legends.* Trans. Louise and Aylmer Maude; illus. Alexander Alexeieff. Pantheon, 1966.
Eight folktales that share the theme of brotherhood. Grades 7–9.

Wheeler, Post. *Russian Wonder Tales.* Illus. Bilibin. Thomas Yoseloff, 1957.
Tales of the Caucasus retold by a scholar. First published in 1912. The foreword contains valuable material on the origin and meaning of folktales. Grades 5–8.

Wyndham, Lee. *Tales the People Tell in Russia.* Illus. Andrew Antal. Messner, 1970.
Selected and translated by a writer who went back to original sources, including her mother and her friends as consultants. A good assortment for telling. Grades 3–6.

Spain and Portugal

Boggs, Ralph Steele, and Mary Gould Davis. *Three Golden Oranges, and Other Spanish Folk Tales.* Illus. Emma Brock. Longmans, 1936.
The full flavor of authentic folklore is preserved in these stories. Grades 5–7.

Davis, Robert. *Padre Porko: The Gentlemanly Pig.* Illus. Fritz Eichenberg. Holiday House, 1948.

First published in 1939. This edition contains two additional stories as humorous and delightful as the earlier ones. Grades 4–6.

De la Iglesia, Maria Elena. *The Cat and the Mouse and Other Spanish Tales.* Illus. Joseph Low. Pantheon, 1966.

Sixteen witty and wise tales translated into English for the first time. Grades 2–4.

Eells, Elsie Spicer. *Tales of Enchantment from Spain.* Illus. Maud Petersham and Miska Petersham. Dodd, Mead, 1950.

Fifteen folktales from old Spanish sources. Grades 4–6.

Haviland, Virginia. *Favorite Fairy Tales Told in Spain.* Illus. Barbara Cooney. Little, Brown, 1963.

Six tales retold for younger children. Grades 2–5.

Lowe, Patricia Tracy, retel. *The Little Horse of Seven Colors and Other Portuguese Folk Tales.* Trans. Anne Marie Jauss; illus. Anne Marie Jauss. World, 1970.

The translator and reteller have written, in their introduction, a short historical and cultural background for these stories, giving their sources. Grades 3–8.

Mehdevi, Alexander, retel. *Bungling Pedro and Other Majorcan Tales.* Illus. Isabel Bodor. Knopf, 1970.

Simply told, with expressions and phrases peculiar to Mallorquin. Grades 3–6.

Sawyer, Ruth. *Picture Tales from Spain.* Illus. Charles Sanchez. Lippincott, 1936.

These tales were told in Spanish to the author by a sailor, a goatherd, and a muleteer. In retelling them, Ruth Sawyer has kept the native humor and freshness. Grades 4–5.

Switzerland

Duvoisin, Roger. *The Three Sneezes, and Other Swiss Tales.* Illus. by the author. Knopf, 1941.

The author, who heard these tales as a child in Switzerland, has retold them with vigor and humor. Grades 4–6.

Müller-Guggenbühl, Fritz. *Swiss-Alpine Folk-Tales.* Trans. Katherine Potts; illus. Joan Kiddell-Monroe. Oxford Univ. Press, Oxford Myths and Legends Series, 1958.

Dr. Müller-Guggenbühl has ranged widely to gather material for this collection. Grades 4–6.

United States*

Chase, Richard, ed. *Grandfather Tales: American-English Folk Tales.* Illus. Berkeley Williams, Jr. Houghton Mifflin, 1948.

A distinct contribution to American folklore. Mr. Chase has gathered old songs and tales from the mountain people of North Carolina, Virginia, Kentucky, and Alabama. In his preface he states that he took a free hand in the telling and that he put each tale together from different versions and from his own experience in telling them. Grades 4–7.

Chase, Richard, ed. *The Jack Tales.* Illus. Berkeley Williams, Jr. Houghton Mifflin, 1943.

These variants of European folktales of simple Jack, who always comes out ahead, take on the native wit of the Appalachian mountain folk. Grades 4–7.

Compton, Margaret. *American Indian Fairy Tales.* Illus. and intro. Lorence F. Bjorklund. Dodd, Mead, 1971.

Based on government reports of Indian life and the works of Schoolcraft, Copway, and Catlin, these are presented as "authentic" Indian legends. The source material was collected during the 1870s and 1880s. Grades 3–8.

Cothran, Jean, ed. *With a Wig, with a Wag, and Other American Folk Tales.* Illus. Clifford N. Geary. McKay, 1954.

Told with admirable brevity, these tales range from New England to California, Louisiana to the Northwest. Good material for storytelling. Grades 3–5. See also *The Magic Calabash: Folk Tales from America's Islands and Alaska.*

Courlander, Harold. *People of the Short Blue Corn: Tales and Legends of the Hopi Indians.* Illus. Enrico Arno. Harcourt, 1970.

Gathered from Hopi storytellers whose clans are named in the section "Notes on Hopi Oral Literature," these stories reveal the inner life. Grades 4–12.

Courlander, Harold. *Terrapin's Pot of Sense.* Illus. Elton Fax. Holt, 1957.

American black folktales gathered from many sources. Grades 4–6.

Faulkner, William J. *The Days When the Animals Talked: Black American Folktales and How They Came to Be.* Illus. Troy Howell. Follett, 1977.

---

* See the bibliography for Chapter 8, "Myths, Legends, and Sacred Writings," for more on North American Indians and Inuit.

Vigorous versions of traditional animal tales as told by the ex-slave, Simon Brown, to Faulkner at the turn of the century. The use of standard English rather than heavy dialect gives a dignity and spirit to these stories, predominantly about Brer Rabbit. Grades 5 and up.

Gillham, Charles Edward. *Beyond the Clapping Mountains: Eskimo Stories from Alaska.* Illus. Chanimum. Macmillan, 1964.

The author, who spent eight summers in Alaska as a biologist for the United States government, heard these stories from an Eskimo. The line drawings are by an Eskimo girl. Grades 3–5. See also *Medicine Men of Hooper Bay.*

Harris, Joel Chandler. *Complete Tales of Uncle Remus.* Comp. Richard Chase; illus. A. B. Frost and Frederick Church. Houghton Mifflin, 1955.

All the beloved tales of Brer Rabbit and his friends collected for the first time in one volume. Grades 5–7.

Harris, Joel Chandler. *The Favorite Uncle Remus.* Illus. A. B. Frost. Ed. George Van Santvoord and Archibald C. Coolidge. Houghton Mifflin, 1948.

Sixty stories culled from the seven Uncle Remus volumes. Grades 4–6.

Harris, Joel Chandler. *Uncle Remus: His Songs and His Sayings.* New and rev. ed. Illus. A. B. Frost. Appleton, 1947.

These plantation stories were first published in the Atlanta, Georgia, *Constitution* in 1880. Grades 5–8.

Haviland, Virginia, ed. *North American Legends.* Illus. Ann Strugnell. Collins, 1979.

A wide-ranging collection of Indian and Eskimo legends, tall tales and frontier stories, Black American and Appalachian folktales. Humorous and dramatic, these tales are lively and compelling. Versions by Richard Chase, Alice Marriott, and others. Extensive notes, sources, and bibliographies for further reading. Grades 4–9.

Jagendorf, M. A. *Folk Stories of the South.* Illus. Michael Parks. Vanguard, 1972.

Arranged in groups according to the states from which they were taken, these stories are rich in variety and told with the liveliness of the person who has "heard" them before writing them down. Grades 4–12.

Jagendorf, Moritz, ed. *The Ghost of Peg-Leg Peter, and Other Stories of Old New York.* Illus. Lino S. Lipinski. Vanguard, 1965.

A noted folklorist has brought together a high-spirited collection of local lore of New York City. Grades 5–8. See also *New England Bean-Pot; Sand in the Bag, and Other Folk Stories of Ohio, Indiana, and Illinois;* and *Upstate, Downstate: Folk Stories of the Middle Atlantic States.*

Leach, Maria. *The Rainbow Book of American Folk Tales and Legends.* Illus. Marc Simont. World, 1958.

Tall tales; state lore; Bad Men; local legends and ghostly tales; and Indian tales of North, Central and South America. An interesting medley, fully annotated in the Author's Notes. Bibliography. Grades 4–7.

Lester, Julius. *The Knee-High Man and Other Tales.* Illus. Ralph Pinto. Dial, 1972.

Brief tales recalled from the compiler's own childhood, tales that have a long history, going back to the time when there was slavery in America. Grades 1–4.

Manning-Sanders, Ruth. *Red Indian Folk and Fairy Tales.* Illus. C. Walter Hodges. Roy, 1960.

Retold by the editor, these stories have obviously been chosen for their dramatic and humorous qualities. Grades 4–9.

Peck, Leigh. *Don Coyote.* Illus. Virginia Lee Burton. Houghton Mifflin, 1942.

Stories from the Southwest center around the exploits and cunning of Don Coyote; stories that the author says are told by the Indians and the Mexicans. Grades 3–6.

Schwartz, Alvin, coll. *Scary Stories to Tell in the Dark.* Illus. Stephen Gammell. Lippincott, 1981.

A zesty collection of North American ghost stories, both traditional and modern, illustrated with exquisitely macabre line and wash drawings. Notes on sources and full bibliography. Grades 4 and up.

American Tall Tales

Blair, Walter, *Tall Tale America: A Legendary History of Our Humorous Heroes.* Illus. Glen Rounds. Coward-McCann, 1944.

Fabulous achievements of legendary heroes of folklore retold with exaggerated humor. Grades 5–8.

Bontemps, Arna. *The Fast Sooner Hound.* Illus. Virginia Lee Burton. Houghton Mifflin, 1942.

The long-legged, lop-eared hound outruns the Cannon Ball Express. Drawings are full of action and humor. Grades 2–4. See also *Sam Patch, the High Wide and Handsome Jumper.*

Bowman, James Cloud. *Pecos Bill, the Greatest Cowboy of All Time.* Illus. Laura Bannon. Whitman, 1937.
    Robust tall tales from the cowboy saga of Pecos Bill, retold with imagination and vigor. Grades 6–8. See also *Mike Fink* (Little, Brown, 1957).

Carmer, Carl. *The Hurricane's Children: Tales from Your Neck o' the Woods.* Illus. Elizabeth Black Carmer. McKay, 1967.
    Humorous folktales including Paul Bunyan, Febold Feboldsen, and others. First published in 1937. Grades 6–9.

Credle, Ellis. *Tall Tales from the High Hills.* Illus. by the author. Nelson, 1957.
    Tales with the full flavor of the Blue Ridge mountain country. Grades 4–6.

DuMond, Frank L. *Tall Tales of the Catskills.* Illus. Peter Parnall. Atheneum, 1968.
    Tales told to the author as a child by his grandfather. Grades 4–7.

Felton, Harold W. *Bowleg Bill, Seagoing Cowpuncher.* Illus. William Moyers. Prentice-Hall, 1957.
    The adventures of an eight-foot-tall cowboy from Wyoming on a succession of deep–sea voyages. Grades 7–9.

Felton, Harold W. *John Henry and His Hammer.* Illus. Aldren A. Watson. Knopf, 1950.
    This version is a little more literary than Shapiro's *John Henry and the Double-Jointed Steam Drill,* but not so robust. Grades 5–7.

Felton, Harold W., ed. *Legends of Paul Bunyan.* Illus. Richard Bennett. Knopf, 1947.
    Stories, songs, and poems arranged in chronological order beginning with Paul Bunyan's unusual birth. Grades 6–8.

Felton, Harold W. *Pecos Bill, Texas Cowpuncher.* Illus. Aldren A. Watson. Knopf, 1949.
    The preposterous adventures of Pecos Bill, "the greatest cowboy of them all," are told with dry humor in the colloquial speech of the Southwest. Grades 6–8. See also *New Tall Tales of Pecos Bill* (Prentice-Hall, 1958).

Felton, Harold W. *The World's Most Truthful Man: Tall Tales Told by Ed Grant in Maine.* Illus. Leonard Everett Fisher. Dodd, Mead, 1961.
    A noted liar's art recreated. Grades 4–7.

Keats, Ezra Jack. *John Henry: An American Legend.* Illus. by the author. Pantheon, 1965.
    The bold pictures capture the spirit of the hero, born with a hammer in his hand. Grades 1–3.

Leach, Maria. *The Rainbow Book of American Folk Tales and Legends.* Illus. Marc Simont. World, 1958.
    Tall tale characters and their exploits are described in the first section of this book. The tall tale as a form is discussed in the prefatory "That's Folklore." Grades 4–7.

McCormick, Dell J. *Paul Bunyan Swings His Axe.* Caxton, 1936.
    Spirited tales about the giant woodsman and his Blue Ox. Grades 4–6.

Malcolmson, Anne. *Yankee Doodle's Cousins.* Illus. Robert McCloskey. Houghton Mifflin, 1941.
    Stories of both real and legendary characters who have become heroes of American folklore. Robust illustrations. Grades 5–9.

Malcolmson, Anne, and Dell J. McCormick. *Mister Stormalong.* Illus. Joshua Tolford. Houghton Mifflin, 1952.
    Fabulous adventures of Stormalong, the legendary Paul Bunyan of the sea, who stood several fathoms tall and skippered a ship as long as all Cape Cod. Grades 4–7.

Rounds, Glen. *Ol' Paul, the Mighty Logger.* Rev. ed. Holiday House, 1949.
    "Being a true account of the seemingly incredible exploits and inventions of the great Paul Bunyan." Grades 4–6.

Schwartz, Alvin, comp. *Kickle Snifters and Other Fearsome Critters Collected from American Folklore.* Illus. Glen Rounds. Lippincott, 1976.
    Definitions of fabulous tall-tale beasts, with notes and sources. Grades 3–5. See also *Whoppers: Tall Tales and Other Lies Collected from American Folklore* (1975).

Shapiro, Irwin. *Heroes in American Folklore.* Illus. James Daugherty and Donald McKay. Messner, 1962.
    Contains five tales that were originally published as separate volumes. Grades 6–9.

Shephard, Esther. *Paul Bunyan.* Illus. Rockwell Kent. Harcourt, 1941.
    The author heard these stories in the lumber camps in Washington, Oregon, and British Columbia. First published in 1924. Grades 6–9.

Stoutenburg, Adrien. *American Tall-Tale Animals.* Illus. Glen Rounds. Viking, 1968.
    Adaptations have been made from a variety of sources: out-of-print newspapers, old periodicals, etc. Surprisingly different stories. Grades 3–7.

Stoutenberg, Adrien, comp. *American Tall Tales.* Illus. Richard N. Powers. Viking, 1966.

Stories of Paul Bunyan, Pecos Bill, Stormalong, Mike Fink, Davy Crockett, Johnny Appleseed, and Joe Magarac told with a simplicity and directness that make them valuable for storytelling. Grades 4–6. See also *The Crocodile's Mouth,* fourteen American folk-song stories.

Wadsworth, Wallace. *Paul Bunyan and His Great Blue Ox.* Illus. Enrico Arno. Doubleday, 1964.

Woodsmen have long entertained themselves with tales of the mythical lumberjack. Grades 6–9.

West Indies

Alegría, Ricardo E., ed. *The Three Wishes: A Collection of Puerto Rican Folk Tales.* Trans. Elizabeth Culbert; illus. Lorenzo Homar. Harcourt, 1969.

The tales, collected by the executive director of the Institute de Cultura Puertorriqueña, reflect the rich blend of cultures in Puerto Rico over four centuries.

Belpré, Pura. *The Tiger and the Rabbit, and Other Tales.* Illus. Tomie de Paola. Lippincott, 1965.

Puerto Rican folktales first published in 1946. Three new stories have been added to the earlier edition. Grades 3–4. See also *Once in Puerto Rico;* illus. Christine Price (Warne, 1973).

Carter, Dorothy Sharp, sel. and adapt. *Greedy Mariani and Other Folktales of the Antilles.* Illus. Trina Schart Hyman. Atheneum, A Margaret K. McElderry Book, 1974.

Tales of tricksters, characters with magic powers, and pourquoi stories. Sources given. Grades 4–7.

Courlander, Harold. *The Piece of Fire and Other Haitian Tales.* Illus. Beth Krush and Joe Krush. Harcourt, 1964.

Twenty-six diverting stories from Haiti. Notes on the stories are appended. Grades 4–6.

Sherlock, Philip M. *Anansi, the Spider Man: Jamaican Folk Tales.* Illus. Marcia Brown. Crowell, 1954.

A delightful collection of tales about Anansi, who was a man when things went well, but in times of danger became a spider. Retold with humor, warmth, and vitality. Grades 4–6.

Sherlock, Philip M. *The Iguanna's Tail: Crick Crack Stories from the Caribbean.* Illus. Gloria Fiammenghi. Crowell, 1969.

The author heard these stories as a child in the West Indies. See also *Ears and Tails and Common Sense: More Stories from the Caribbean* (1974).

Sherlock, Philip M. *West Indian Folk Tales.* Illus. Joan Kiddell-Monroe. Walck, Oxford Myths and Legends Series, 1966.

Unusual folk legends of the Carib and Arawak Indians and of West Africans brought to the West Indies before the time of Columbus. Grades 4–6.

Wolkstein, Diane, coll. *The Magic Orange Tree and Other Haitian Folktales.* Illus. Elsa Henriquez. Knopf, 1978.

Collected from Haitian storytellers, these tales include humorous fables and dramatic legends. Rich in music, chant, and song. With scholarly notes on each story. Grades 4 and up.

References for Adults

Aarne, Antti. *The Types of the Folktale.* Rev. Stith Thompson. Helsinki, 1961.

Classification and numbering of motifs, themes, and parallel tales. A seminal work.

Abrahams, Roger D., sel. and retel. *African Folktales: Traditional Stories of the Black World.* Pantheon, Pantheon Fairy Tale and Folklore Library, 1983.

A distinguished folklorist retells a representative selection of tales and legends. With scholarly preface, full notes, bibliography, and index of tales.

Baughman, Ernest. *A Type and Motif Index of the Folktales of England and North America.* Indiana Univ. Folklore Series, no. 20, 1966.

Full bibliographic coverage of folklore motifs and types.

Bettelheim, Bruno. *The Uses of Enchantment.* Knopf, 1976.

A noted child psychologist discusses the effect of folktales on the inner life of the child.

Botkin, B. A., ed. *A Treasury of American Folklore: Stories, Ballads, and Traditions of the People.* Foreword, Carl Sandburg. Crown, 1944.

Lusty tall tales of frontier characters and sea captains, ballads, songs, and stories. The language is colloquial and sometimes rough.

Briggs, Katharine M. *A Dictionary of British Folk-Tales in the English Language: Incorporating the F. J. Norton Collection.* Routledge, 1970.

Two parts in four volumes, this is a thorough viewing and classifying of tales, fables, and other forms, generally divided into two main sections: folk narratives and folk legends.

Briggs, Katharine M. *An Encyclopedia of Fairies: Hobgoblins, Brownies, Bogies, and Other Supernatural Crea-*

tures. Pantheon, Pantheon Fairy Tale and Folklore Library, 1977.

Analysis and description of world-wide fairy people as they appear in folklore.

Briggs, Katharine M. *The Personnel of Fairyland: A Short Account of the Fairy People of Great Britain for Those Who Tell Stories to Children.* Illus. Jane Moore. Singing Tree Press, 1971.

Facsimile reprint of 1953 edition published by Alden Press in Oxford. Stories about the various kinds of fairies, with notes about parallel stories; a dictionary of fairies; a list of stories suitable for telling; and a list of books on fairy lore. A fascinating and valuable book for the storyteller.

Briggs, Katharine M., and Ruth L. Tongue, eds. *Folktales of England.* Foreword, Richard M. Dorson. Univ. of Chicago Press, Folktales of the World, Richard M. Dorson, ed., 1965.

The scholar Katharine Briggs and the storyteller Ruth Tongue have joined forces to present little-known tales, many of them collected from Ruth Tongue's own memory.

Brunvand, Jan Harold. *The Study of American Folklore: An Introduction.* Norton, 1968.

A survey and attempt at definition of the types of folklore found in the United States.

Calvino, Italo, sel. and retel. *Italian Folktales.* Trans. George Martin. Pantheon, Pantheon Fairy Tale and Folklore Library, 1980.

A distinguished collection from a world-renowned novelist and scholar. Varied selection with scholarly notes.

Clarkson, Atelia, and Gilbert B. Cross. *World Folk Tales: A Scribner Resource Collection.* Scribner's, 1980.

Divided into sections with tale type and motif indexes.

Cook, Elizabeth. *The Ordinary and the Fabulous: An Introduction to Myths, Legends and Fairy Tales for Teachers and Storytellers.* 2d ed. Cambridge Univ. Press, 1976.

Accessible information for the uninformed; extremely valuable for all storytellers.

Coughlan, Margaret, comp. *Folklore from Africa to the United States.* Library of Congress, 1976.

An annotated bibliography of African folktales.

Dorson, Richard M. *American Folklore.* Univ. of Chicago Press, 1959.

Historical and present types of folklore are analyzed and discussed, with special emphasis on separating "fakelore" from folklore.

Dorson, Richard M., ed. Folktales of the World Series. Univ. of Chicago Press.

Dorson, the director of the Folklore Institute at Indiana University, is the general editor of this distinguished, scholarly series.

Dorson, Richard M., ed. *Folktales Told around the World.* Univ. of Chicago Press, 1975.

A scholarly collection for the student with full notes on sources and contributors and motif and type indexes.

Dundes, Alan. *The Study of Folklore.* Prentice-Hall, 1965.

An "anthology of . . . important essays written on various facets and forms of folklore."

Eastman, Mary Huse, comp. *Index to Fairy Tales, Myths and Legends.* 2d ed., rev. and enl. Faxon, 1926.

A useful reference book followed by two supplements, 1937 and 1952. For a further revision in new edition, see Norma Olin Ireland in this section of the bibliography.

El-Shamy, Hasan, ed. and trans. *Folktales of Egypt.* Univ. of Chicago Press (Folktales of the World, ed. Richard M. Dorson), 1980.

A fresh retelling with scholarly foreword and notes.

Ellis, John M. *One Fairy Story Too Many: The Brothers Grimm and Their Tales.* Univ. of Chicago Press, 1983.

This probing study of the Grimm brothers' methods and sources contends that, contrary to popular belief, the Grimms did not follow the high methodological standards that they claimed. The author's thesis is that some of the Grimms' informants were middle-class, educated people and that the brothers reworked the tales, affecting their substance.

Emrich, Duncan. *Folklore on the American Land.* Little, Brown, 1972.

This is a compendium of songs, riddles, tales, legends, names, superstitions, street cries, and other forms. It is a joyfully expansive survey, with notes and sources appended.

Favat, F. André. *Child and Tale: The Origins of Interest.* NCTE, 1977.

A discussion of the psychological reasons for children's interest in folklore.

Grimm, Jakob, and Wilhelm Grimm. *Grimm's Fairy Tales.* Illus. Josef Scharl. Pantheon, 1944.

A complete edition of the tales gathered by the Grimm brothers, with 212 striking original illustrations by a distinguished Bavarian artist. Padraic Colum's introduction and Joseph Campbell's "Folkloristic Commentary" will be of special interest to the student of folklore, but the book will be enjoyed by the entire family.

Grimm, Jakob, and Wilhelm Grimm. *The Grimm's German Folk Tales.* Trans. Francis P. Magoun, Jr., and Alexander H. Krappe. Southern Illinois Univ. Press, 1960 (Arcturus Books Edition, 1969).

Based on the Jubilee edition (1912) of Reinhold Steig, this is a new translation of the 200 *Kinder- und Hausmarchen* with the appended *Kinderlegenden*.

Grimm, Jakob, and Wilhelm Grimm. *Grimms' Tales for Young and Old: The Complete Stories.* Trans. Ralph Manheim. Doubleday, 1977.

A superb translation of the entire Grimm corpus by a prize-winning translator. Unadorned, in the voice of the oral storyteller, supple retellings give a vivid directness to this fine collection. Also available in paperback (Anchor/Doubleday, 1983).

Hughes, Langston, and Arna Bontemps, eds. *The Book of Negro Folklore.* Dodd, Mead, 1965.

The rich and varied vein of black folklore: tales, folk expressions, songs, street cries, memories of slavery, and poetry and prose in the folk manner.

Ireland, Norma Olin. *Index to Fairy Tales, 1949–1972: Including Folklore, Legends and Myths in Collections.* Faxon, 1973.

A tool for locating material. Followed by the fourth supplement in this series, *Index to Fairy Tales, 1973–1977* (1979).

Keightley, Thomas. *The Fairy Mythology.* Bell, 1900.

The romance and superstition of various countries from Scandinavia to Africa.

Krappe, Alexander Haggerty. *The Science of Folklore.* Barnes & Noble, 1964.

A scholarly study by a British folklorist.

Kready, Laura F. *A Study of Fairy Tales.* Houghton Mifflin, 1916.

The introduction was written by Henry Suzzalo. The book grew out of a course given in children's literature.

Lang, Andrew. *Custom and Myth.* Longmans, 1930.

First published in 1884. The famous collector of folktales discusses comparative mythology from folklore, myths, and epics.

Leach, Maria, ed. *Funk & Wagnalls Standard Dictionary of General Folklore, Mythology and Legend.* 2 vols. Funk & Wagnalls, 1949–1950.

The richness, vitality, and range of world folklore, mythology, and legend are revealed in this major reference work, compiled not only for the folklorist but also for the general reader.

Lüthi, Max. *Once Upon a Time: On the Nature of Fairy Tales.* Trans. Lee Chadeayne and Paul Gottwald, with additions by the author. Ungar, 1970.

Stimulating discussions of meaning and form and of style, symbolism, riddles, the hero, and the use of local legend in fairy tales. Although this is a scholar's approach, there is much here that can be useful to the adult who wishes to use this literature with children.

MacDonald, Margaret Read, ed. *Storyteller's Sourcebook.* Gale, 1982.

A subject, title, and motif index to folklore collections for children, including picture books. A useful reference tool.

Montgomerie, Norah, ed. and sel. *More Stories to Read and to Tell.* Illus. Tessa Jordan. Bodley Head, 1971. (Grades 1–6)

A varied collection, including old stories, new ones, very brief ones, how-and-why nature stories, fairy stories, heroes and heroines. The emphasis is on providing stories for telling. See also *To Read and to Tell,* 100 stories for very young children.

Opie, Iona, and Peter Opie. *The Classic Fairy Tales.* Oxford Univ. Press, 1974.

A fascinating study in textual bibliography, this collection provides the first appearance in the English language of the texts of twenty-four classic tales. Introductions to each tale give bibliographic sources and literary histories, while a general introduction discusses the genre and its history. A bibliography of chief commentaries is appended. Illustrations from different periods reveal changing trends in cultural tastes and styles. Also available in paperback (1980).

O'Sullivan, Sean, ed. and trans. *Folktales of Ireland.* Univ. of Chicago Press (Folktales of the World, ed. Richard M. Dorson), 1966.

Prepared from the archives of the Irish Folklore Commission and translated for English readers.

Paredes, Americo, ed. and trans. *Folktales of Mexico.* Foreword, Richard M. Dorson. Univ. of Chicago Press (Folktales of the World, ed. Richard M. Dorson), 1970.

Folktales, anecdotes, legends, and formula tales are presented with a lengthy preface and introduction. Good background material as well as selections.

Ramsey, Eloise, comp. *Folklore for Children and Young People.* The American Folklore Society, 1952.

A critical and descriptive bibliography compiled for use in the elementary and intermediate school.

Ranke, Kurt, ed. *Folktales of Germany.* Trans. Lotte Baumann; foreword, Richard M. Dorson. Univ. of Chicago Press (Folktales of the World, ed. Richard M. Dorson), 1966.

Tales collected in the last hundred years, with notes and introduction by Germany's outstanding folktale scholar.

Sale, Roger. *Fairy Tales and After: From Snow White to E. B. White.* Harvard Univ. Press, 1978.

An intriguing critical discussion of the link between folklore and fantasy in children's literature.

Saxby, Maurice, ed. *Through Folklore to Literature.* IBBY Australia Publications, 1979.

Papers presented at the Australian National Section of the International Board on Books for Young People Conference on Children's Literature. An examination of the origins of folklore in ritual and the impulse to create story; the expression of various cultures through their folklore; the meeting of story traditions in contemporary multicultural society.

Shah, Idries, coll. *World Tales: The Extraordinary Coincidence of Stories Told in All Times, in All Places.* Harcourt, 1979.

A representative collection of sixty-five fables, folktales, legends, and myths from around the world. Introductions to each tale cite parallel stories, literary histories, and general sources. Specific bibliographic source citations are not given. This handsome volume is provocatively illustrated by thirty-seven contemporary illustrators.

Shannon, George W. B., comp. *Folk Literature and Children: An Annotated Bibliography of Secondary Materials.* Greenwood, 1981.

Descriptive annotations of journal and magazine articles, monographs, sections of books, and unpublished documents dealing with the relationship of children and folklore published from 1693 to 1979. Divided into three broad categories of literature, education, and psychology; with full bibliographic citations and subject, author, and title indexes.

Thompson, Stith. *The Folktale.* Holt, 1946.

Long years of research, teaching, and writing form the background for this scholarly work in which the author, one of the foremost authorities on the subject, discusses the universality of the folktale. It traces the spread of folktales and analyzes types of tales and their place in the primitive culture of the American Indian.

Thompson, Stith, ed. *Motif-Index of Folk-Literature.* Rev. and enl. ed. Indiana Univ. Press, 1955.

A classification of narrative elements in folktales, ballads, myths, fables, and medieval romances.

Travers, P. L. *About the Sleeping Beauty.* Illus. Charles Keeping. McGraw-Hill, 1975.

Charles Keeping's seductive illustrations accompany six international variants of the story, including a literary retelling by the author. A poetic essay analyzes the symbolic and psychological meaning of the fairy tale.

Wilson, Anne. *Traditional Romance and Tale: How Stories Mean.* D. S. Brewer, 1977.

A literary and psychological analysis of the meaning of story, the dreamlike logic of folklore, and the mode of magical thinking that creates and reads these tales.

Yolen, Jane. *Touch Magic: Fantasy, Faerie and Folklore in the Literature of Childhood.* Philomel, 1981.

A stimulating collection of essays on the literary and psychological significance and enduring humanity of myth, folklore, and fantasy.

Ziegler, Elsie B. *Folklore: An Annotated Bibliography and Index to Single Editions.* Faxon, 1973.

To be used with Mary Huse Eastman and Norma Olin Ireland (listed in this section of the bibliography) for locating material.

Articles and Commentaries

Afanasiev, Alexander N. *In a Certain Kingdom: Twelve Russian Fairy Tales.* Trans. Thomas P. Whitney; illus. Dieter Lange. Macmillan, 1972.

Biographical information concerning Afanasiev is in the afterword, "These Stories and the Man Who Collected Them," pp. 131–36.

Afanasiev, Alexander N. *Russian Fairy Tales.* Trans. Norbert Guterman; illus. A. Alexeieff. Pantheon, 1945.

Contains a valuable folkloristic commentary by Roman Jakobson, pp. 631–51.

Andrews, Siri. "The Folklore of New England." *The Hewins Lectures, 1947–1962.* Horn Book, 1963, pp. 321–41.

Asbjörnsen, Peter Christen, and Jörgen Moe. *Popular Tales from the Norse.* Trans. Sir George Dasent. Putnam's, n.d.

Contains a valuable introduction by Dasent. See also *Tales from the Fjeld.*

Auden, W. H. *Forewords and Afterwords.* Random House, 1973.

Contains an interesting defense of the Grimm tales in "Grimm and Andersen," pp. 198–208.

Bator, Robert, ed. *Signposts to Criticism of Children's Literature.* American Library Association, 1983.

In Chapter 5: "Fairy Tales," by Brian Hooker, p. 168; "Why Folk Tales and Fairy Stories Live Forever," by Catherine Storr, p. 177; "The Queer Kindness of 'The Golden Bird'," by Perry M. Nodelman, p. 184.

Carmer, Carl. *America Sings.* Knopf, 1942.

Contains an interesting introduction, pp. 7–11.

Chesterton, G. K. *Orthodoxy.* Dodd, 1909.

In "The Ethics of Elfland," pp. 81–118, the author discusses his personal belief in fairy tales and the moral dimension of the form.

Chukovsky, Kornei. *From Two to Five.* Trans. and ed. Miriam Morton. Rev. ed. Univ. of California Press, 1968.

"The Battle for the Fairy Tale," pp. 114–39.

Colwell, Eileen. "Folk Literature." *Top of the News,* 24 (Jan. 1968), pp. 175–80.

Crabbe, Katharyn F. "Folk over Fakelore: But Is It Art?" *School Library Journal,* 26 (Nov. 1979), pp. 42–43.

Discusses the transition of folk material from oral tradition to print and the problems in retelling folktales for children.

Davis, Mary Gould. "American Folk Tales." *The Horn Book Magazine,* 23 (Feb. 1952) pp. 55–62.

De la Mare, Walter. *Animal Stories.* Scribner's, 1940.

In the introduction, pp. xiii–lvi, De la Mare traces the development of the animal folktale and comments on the stories.

Egoff, Sheila, et. al. *Only Connect: Readings on Children's Literature.* 2d ed. Oxford Univ. Press, 1980.

"Only Connect," by P. L. Travers, pp. 183–206. A spirited essay recounts the author's close relationship with fairy tale and myth.

Grimm, Jakob, and Wilhelm Grimm. *Grimm's Fairy Tales.* Illus. Josef Scharl. Pantheon, 1944.

Introduction by Padraic Colum. Folkloristic commentary by Joseph Campbell: "The Work of the Brothers Grimm," pp. 833–39; "The Types of Stories," pp. 840–45; "The History of the Tales," pp. 846–56; "The Question of Meaning," pp. 857–64.

Heins, Paul, ed. *Crosscurrents of Criticism: Horn Book Essays, 1968–1977.* Horn Book, 1977.

"Children, Humor, and Folklore," pp. 205–16, by Alvin Schwartz, discusses the positive and negative sides of humorous folk literature. First published in *The Horn Book Magazine,* June and August 1977.

Jacobs, Joseph, ed. *English Fairy Tales; More English Fairy Tales;* etc. Putnam's, n.d.

In each of Joseph Jacobs's collections of fairy tales he gives valuable information for the student of folklore in the preface and in a section called "Notes and References."

Kimmel, Eric A. "The Wise Men of Chelm." *The Horn Book Magazine,* 50 (Feb. 1974), pp. 78–82.

Tolkien, J. R. R. *Tree and Leaf.* Houghton Mifflin, 1964.

"On Fairy-stories," pp. 3–84. A classic essay on the power and nature of folklore and fantasy.

Travers, P. L. *About the Sleeping Beauty.* Illus. Charles Keeping. McGraw-Hill, 1975.

"Afterword," pp. 47–62.

Tucker, Nicholas, ed. *Suitable for Children? Controversies in Children's Literature.* Sussex Univ. Press, 1976.

In Part One, "Fairy Stories": "From *The Guardian of Education*," by Mrs. Trimmer, p. 37; "Frauds on the Fairies," by Charles Dickens, p. 47; "The Educational and Moral Values of Folk and Fairy Tales," by Dr. J. Langfeldt, p. 56; "Why Folk Tales and Fairy Stories Live Forever," by Catherine Storr, p. 64.

Undset, Sigrid, ed. "The Adventure of the Folk Tale." In *True and Untrue and Other Norse Tales,* pp. 1–27. Knopf, 1945.

Walker, Barbara K. "The Folks Who Tell Folk Tales: Field Collecting in Turkey." *The Horn Book Magazine,* 47 (Dec. 1971), pp. 636–42.

Wolkstein, Diane. "An Interview with Harold Courlander." *School Library Journal,* 20 (May 1974), pp. 19–22.

The process and problems involved in collecting and rewriting folklore for children.

Richard Chase

Painter, Helen W. "Richard Chase: Mountain Folklorist and Storyteller." *Elementary English,* 40 (Nov. 1963), pp. 677–86.

Wanda Gág

Gág, Wanda. *Growing Pains: An Autobiography.* Coward-McCann, 1940.

Scott, Alma. *Wanda Gág: The Story of an Artist.* Univ. of Minnesota Press, 1949.

The Grimm Brothers

Gooch, G. P. "Jakob Grimm." In *History and Historians in the Nineteenth Century.* Longmans, 1913.

Ker, W. P. "Jacob Grimm." In *Collected Essays.* Macmillan, 1925. Vol. 2, pp. 222–33.

Joel Chandler Harris

Harris, Julia. *The Life and Letters of Joel Chandler Harris.* Houghton Mifflin, 1918.
   A biography written by Harris' daughter-in-law.

Joseph Jacobs

Hays, May Bradshaw. "Memories of My Father, Joseph Jacobs." *The Horn Book Magazine,* 28 (Dec. 1952), pp. 385–92.

Andrew Lang

Andrew Lang: Being the Andrew Lang Lecture Delivered before the University of St. Andrews, Dec. 1927. Oxford Univ. Press, 1928.

Green, Roger Lancelyn. *Andrew Lang.* Walck, A Walck Monograph, 1962.

Seumas MacManus

Colum, Padraic. "Seumas MacManus—Shanachie." *The Horn Book Magazine,* 38 (Dec. 1962), pp. 626–30.
   An edited version of the foreword to Seumas MacManus' *Hibernian Nights* (Macmillan, 1963).

Ella Young

Colum, Padraic. *Ella Young: An Appreciation.* Longmans, 1931.

Ella Young Issue of *The Horn Book Magazine,* 15 (May 1939).

Young, Ella. *Flowering Dusk: Things Remembered Accurately and Inaccurately: An Autobiography.* Longmans, 1945.

8 Myths, Legends, and Sacred Writings*

Books for Children

Asimov, Isaac. *Words from the Myths.* Illus. Williams Barss. Houghton Mifflin, 1961.

* See also bibliography for Chapter 9, "Epics and Romances."

An informal discussion of the myths, pointing out the many words rooted in mythology and their use in the English language.

Asimov, Isaac. *Words in Genesis.* Illus. William Barss. Houghton Mifflin, 1962.
   A study of names, words, and phrases from the Bible with a commentary on how they have influenced the English language. See also *Words from the Exodus.*

Bulfinch's Mythology; the Age of Fable; the Age of Chivalry; Legends of Charlemagne. Crowell, 1970.
   A new edition of a classic work.

Farmer, Penelope, comp. and ed. *Beginnings: Creation Myths of the World.* Illus. Antonio Frasconi. Atheneum, 1979.
   An outstanding collection of eighty stories and poems from world mythology, legend, and scripture. Grouped under seven fundamental themes of creation, death, and rebirth, the parallel stories reflect the shifting unity behind creation. Source list and bibliography appended. Symbolic black-and-white woodcuts. Grades 5 and up.

Galey, Charles Mills, ed. *Classic Myths in English Literature and in Art.* Rev. and enl. ed. Blaisdell, 1963.
   Greek, Roman, and Norse myths and hero stories. Based on Bulfinch's *Age of Fable.* A standard work of reference.

Green, Roger Lancelyn, sel. and retel. *A Book of Myths.* Illus. Joan Kiddell-Monroe. Dent, 1965.
   Myths of a variety of backgrounds: Egyptian, Babylonian, Roman, Phrygian, Persian, Scandinavian. This collection allows the reader to compare the various ways people thought of their origins and their gods. Grades 4–9.

Jacobson, Helen. *The First Book of Mythical Beasts.* F. Watts, 1960.
   A companion volume is *The First Book of Legendary Beings* (1962). Grades 4–6.

Leach, Maria. *How the People Sang the Mountain Up.* Illus. Glen Rounds. Viking, 1967.
   The author has collected legends from all over the world as answers to how-and-why questions about people, animals, earth, sea, and sky. Sources and backgrounds are explained in the notes. Grades 4–6.

Lum, Peter. *The Stars in Our Heaven: Myths and Fables.* Illus. Anne Marie Jauss. Pantheon, 1948.
   Myths, legends, and fables interpret what the Babylonian, Greek, Norse, Indian, and Chinese people saw in the heavens. Grades 7–9.

Lurie, Alison, retel. *The Heavenly Zoo: Legends and Tales of the Stars.* Illus. Monika Beisner. Farrar, Straus & Giroux, 1980.

World-wide legends and myths about the constellations including pourquoi tales and hero legends. Sources range from the Bible and Kipling's *Just So Stories* to Greek myth and *The Mahabharata.* Exquisite illustrations like illuminated manuscripts. Grades 4 and up.

Tripp, Edward. *Crowell's Handbook of Classical Mythology.* Crowell, 1970.

An alphabetically arranged companion to reading, this provides information about the variants of myths, the relationships among gods, and the geographical and historical background of this literature. Grades 5 and up.

Untermeyer, Louis. *The Firebringer and Other Great Stories: Fifty-Five Legends That Live Forever.* Illus. Mae Gerhard. Lippincott, 1968.

Told in a direct, casual style, this assortment of stories ranges from Greek myths and heroes through legends of heroes and accounts of romance. Grades 4–7.

Greece and Rome

Barker, Carol. *King Midas and the Golden Touch.* Illus. by the author. F. Watts, 1972.

This favorite story from the Greeks is set among opulent art work and told at greater length than it usually is. Grades 2–4.

Benson, Sally. *Stories of the Gods and Heroes.* Illus. Steele Savage. Dial, 1940.

A skillful editing of Bulfinch's *Age of Fable.* This is a good version for children. Illustrations harmonize with the spirit of the text. Grades 5–8.

Bulfinch, Thomas. *A Book of Myths.* Selections from Bulfinch's *Age of Fable;* illus. Helen Sewell. Macmillan, 1942.

The distinguished illustrations interpret the classic Greek design in a modern manner. Grades 6–9.

Coolidge, Olivia. *Greek Myths.* Illus. Edouard Sandoz. Houghton Mifflin, 1949.

A retelling of the most familiar myths. Based on original sources. Grades 6–9.

D'Aulaire, Ingri, and Edgar Parin D'Aulaire. *Ingri and Edgar Parin D'Aulaire's Book of Greek Myths.* Illus. by the authors. Doubleday, 1962.

Expressive, dramatic illustrations complement simple versions of the myths. Grades 3–6.

Evslin, Bernard. *Heroes, Gods and Monsters of the Greek Myths.* Illus. William Hofmann. Four Winds, 1967.

These are retellings by a reader who was entranced by their Greek and Latin versions but disappointed in their English ones. A novelist's technique is visible in the way the stories have been filled out. Grades 5–10.

Farmer, Penelope. *The Serpent's Teeth: The Story of Cadmus.* Illus. Chris Connor. Harcourt, 1971.

A myth about the founding of Thebes, retold and illustrated with dramatic effect. Grades 3–5.

Farmer, Penelope. *The Story of Persephone.* Illus. Graham McCallum. Morrow, 1973.

A telling of the famed kidnapping and origin of the seasons myth that emphasizes the suspense and emotional qualities. The illustrations are dramatic and somewhat eerie in effect. Grades 4–7.

Garfield, Leon, and Edward Blishen. *The God Beneath the Sea.* Illus. Zevi Blum. Pantheon, 1971.

A re-creation of the story of the Greek gods, beginning with the fall of the infant Hephaestus (the god beneath the sea). This is a mythological story told as a continuous narrative, richly poetic in the telling. Awarded the Library Association's 1970 Carnegie Medal. The British edition (Longman Young, 1970) has Charles Keeping's scintillating illustrations. Grades 5 and up. See also *The Golden Shadow* (1973).

Gates, Doris. *The Golden God: Apollo.* Illus. Constantinos CoConis. Viking, 1973.

Retold by a former children's librarian, these stories from the Greek myths have been woven together to provide relationships and continuity. The experience of the storyteller who has told these myths to children appears in the clarity of the telling. Grades 3–6. See also *Lord of the Sky: Zeus* (1972); *The Warrior Goddess: Athena* (1972); and *Mightiest of Mortals: Heracles* (1975).

Gates, Doris. *Two Queens of Heaven: Aphrodite, Demeter.* Illus. Trina Schart Hyman. Viking, 1974.

The opposing natures of the two goddesses, Aphrodite and Demeter, are seen in the stories collected about each one. Grades 4–9.

Gibson, Michael. *Gods, Men and Monsters from the Greek Myths.* Illus. Giovanni Caselli. Schocken, World Mythology Series, 1982.

Dramatic, intense illustrations complement the

simple retellings in this handsome, oversize volume. Grades 3 and up. See also other titles in this series.

Green, Roger Lancelyn, sel. and retel. *Tales the Muses Told: Ancient Greek Myths.* Illus. Don Bolognese. Walck, 1965.
Stories that deal with flowers, trees, birds and beasts, stars, and love and friendship have been grouped together. Grades 4–8.

Guerber, Hélène Adeline. *Myths of Greece and Rome.* Rev. ed. London House, 1963.
The myths are retold with special reference to literature and art. A useful reference book.

Hamilton, Edith. *Mythology.* Illus. Steele Savage. Little, Brown, 1942.
Scholarship and imagination vitalize the retelling of these Greek, Roman, and Norse myths. Invaluable both for reference and for reading. Excellent introduction and notes. Grades 6–8.

Hawthorne, Nathaniel. *A Wonder Book and Tanglewood Tales.* Illus. Gustaf Tenggren. Houghton Mifflin, Riverside Bookshelf, 1923.
Opinions differ about Hawthorne's version of the Greek myths. A few consider them "little masterpieces of prose." Others think that he took too great a liberty with them; that he romanticized and embroidered them until the strength and vigor of the original myths were lost. Hawthorne himself states that his retellings had a Gothic and romantic touch, which was the spirit of his age. Grades 4–6. Other recommended editions are illustrated by Maxfield Parrish (Dodd, 1934) and by S. van Abbe (Dutton, 1952 and 1955). *The Complete Greek Stories of Nathaniel Hawthorne* is illustrated by Harold Jones (Watts, 1963). See also *The Golden Touch,* illus. by Paul Galdone, with a foreword by Anne Thaxter Eaton (McGraw-Hill, 1959).

Hodson, Miriam, retel. *A Touch of Gold: Stories from the Greek Myths.* Illus. Carol Barker. Methuen, 1983.
Simple but faithful retellings of the Midas, Icarus, Pandora, and Theseus stories. Bright, radiant illustrations make this a good introduction to the myths for the youngest child. Grades 1–3.

Johnston, Norma. *Strangers Dark and Gold.* Atheneum, 1975.
A lyrical, novelistic retelling in cadenced, poetic prose of the myth of Jason, the quest for the Golden Fleece, and his tragic love for Medea. Grades 5 and up.

Lines, Kathleen, ed. *The Faber Book of Greek Legends.* Illus. Faith Jaques. Faber & Faber, 1973.
Itself a noteworthy compilation with tellings from different sources, some of which have been written especially for this volume (Rosemary Sutcliff has written two), this is valuable to the student of children's literature for the historical survey of important children's editions of the classic myths and legends contained in the foreword. Later editions are commented on at the end of the book. Grades 4–8.

Pater, Walter. *Cupid and Psyche.* Illus. Errol Le Cain. Faber & Faber, 1977.
Adapted from the author's longer version in *Marius the Epicurean,* this poetic, graceful retelling of one of the world's most gripping myths is elaborately illustrated in black-and-white Beardsleyesque pictures. Evocative of the *fin de siècle* style in art and text. Grades 4 and up.

Proddow, Penelope, trans. and adapt. *Demeter and Persephone* (Homeric Hymn Number Two). Illus. Barbara Cooney. Doubleday, 1972.
A glowing book. See also Gerald McDermott's *Daughter of Earth* (Delacorte, 1984). Grades 3–6.

Proddow, Penelope, trans. *Dionysos and the Pirates* (Homeric Hymn Number Seven). Illus. Barbara Cooney. Doubleday, 1970.
The cool containment of Barbara Cooney's art is stylistically in tune with the Homeric hymn, which provides the text of the story. Grades 3–6.

Proddow, Penelope, trans. and adapt. *Hermes, Lord of Robbers* (Homeric Hymn Number Four). Illus. Barbara Cooney. Doubleday, 1971.
The mischievous pranks of the precocious Hermes form the story of this book. Grades 3–6.

Sabin, Frances Ellis. *Classical Myths That Live Today.* Classical ed., Ralph V. D. Magoffin. Silver Burdett, 1958.
First published in 1927, this collection shows how myths have been perpetuated in literary allusions, in art, and in decorative design.

Tomaino, Sarah F. *Persephone, Bringer of Spring.* Illus. Ati Forberg. Crowell, 1971.
The story of Demeter and Persephone is well suited to this picture-book format; the illustrations have a poetic vitality of their own. Grades 2–4.

Turska, Krystyna. *Pegasus.* Illus. Krystyna Turska. Hamilton, 1970.

The story of Pegasus is made excitingly vivid in this large, strongly illustrated book. Grades 2–5.

Iceland and Scandinavia (Norse Myths)

Branston, Brian. *Gods and Heroes from Viking Mythology.* Illus. Giovanni Caselli. Shocken, World Mythologies Series, 1978.

An attractively produced collection of Norse myths clearly retold and vigorously illustrated with oversize, meticulously realistic paintings and drawings. With an index, pronounciation guide, and dictionary of Nordic symbols. Grades 4–7.

Colum, Padraic. *The Children of Odin: The Book of Northern Myths.* Illus. Willy Pogány. Macmillan, 1962.

A reissue in new format of a book first published in 1920. Stories of the Norse sagas from the Twilight of the Gods to the Fall of Asgard. Told as a connected narrative in rhythmic prose. Grades 5–8.

Coolidge, Olivia E. *Legends of the North.* Illus. Edouard Sandoz. Houghton Mifflin, 1951.

Famous myths and legends of the Northern European countries. Grades 7–9.

Crossley-Holland, Kevin, ed. *The Faber Book of Northern Legends.* Illus. Alan Howard. Faber & Faber, 1983.

First published in England in 1977, this is a scholarly collection of tales from Norse mythology, Germanic hero legends, and Icelandic sagas. The versions chosen are well told and varied, including verse as well as prose. Grades 4 and up.

D'Aulaire, Ingri, and Edgar Parin D'Aulaire. *Norse Gods and Giants.* Illus. by the authors. Doubleday, 1967.

The D'Aulaires spent years of research on this book, bringing to it their Norwegian heritage and painstaking craftsmanship. Grades 2–5.

Feagles, Anita. *Autun and the Bear.* Illus. Gertrude Barrer-Russell. Scott, 1967.

A retelling of an ancient Icelandic legend first recorded in the thirteenth century. Grades 2–4. See also *Thor and the Giants,* an old Norse legend retold by Anita Feagles, illus. Gertrude Barrer-Russell (Scott, 1968).

Green, Roger Lancelyn. *Myths of the Norsemen: The Saga of Asgard.* Illus. Brian Wildsmith. Bodley Head, 1960.

Retold as a single narrative, from the making of the world to the vision of Ragnarök, the maintaining of an "air of 'Northerness' " has been a prime objective of Green's (see "Author's Note" for sources used). Grades 5–10.

Hodges, Margaret, retel. *Baldur and the Mistletoe: A Myth of the Vikings.* Illus. Gerry Hoover. Little, Brown, 1974.

One of the most poignant of the stories in the Norse mythology, the story of the death of Baldur is the subject of this brief, amply illustrated book. Grades 3–6.

Hosford, Dorothy. *Thunder of the Gods.* Illus. Claire and George Louden. Holt, 1952.

A retelling that captures the stark beauty and simple dignity, the humor and pathos of stories from the Icelandic Eddas. Grades 5–7.

King, Cynthia. *In the Morning of Time: The Story of the Norse God Balder.* Illus. Charles Mikolaycak. Four Winds, 1970.

The central story of Balder's life and death is interwoven with other Norse myths in this contemporary version. Illustrated with dramatic black-and-white drawings. Grades 4 and up.

Picard, Barbara Leonie, retel. *Tales of the Norse Gods and Heroes.* Illus. Kiddell-Monroe. Oxford Univ. Press, 1953.

Strong retellings of Norse mythology and hero tales. Grades 4–6.

Synge, Ursula. *Weland, Smith of the Gods.* Illus. Charles Keeping. Bodley Head, 1972.

A forceful and free retelling, based largely on Andrew Lang, with an altered ending and the interweaving of other tales from the north. Grades 5–12.

Burma

Keely, H. H., and Christine Price, retels. *The City of the Dagger and Other Tales from Burma.* Illus. Christine Price. Warne, 1971. Grades 5–9.

China

Birch, Cyril, retel. *Chinese Myths and Fantasies.* Illus. Joan Kiddell-Monroe. Walck, 1961.

Stories that feature the supernatural; some origin myths and legends are to be found here. Grades 5–9.

Tresselt, Alvin, and Nancy Cleaver. *The Legend of the Willow Plate.* Illus. Joseph Low. Parents' Magazine, 1968.

The ancient legend behind the traditional willow pattern on dinnerware. Grades 1–4.

Egypt

Green, Roger Lancelyn, sel. and retel. *Tales of Ancient Egypt.* Illus. Elaine Raphel. Walck, 1968.

The Egyptian story of creation and the relationship between the Gods and Pharaohs; stories of magic and adventure. The background for all of this material is given in a fascinating prologue. Grades 5–10.

McDermott, Gerald, retel. *The Voyage of Osiris: A Myth of Ancient Egypt.* Illus. by the author. Windmill/Dutton, 1977.

Illustrated in the style of Egyptian papyrus scroll painting, this stunning picture book retells the myth of Isis and Osiris. Grades 1–3.

Manniche, Lise, trans. *The Prince Who Knew His Fate.* Illus. by the translator. Metropolitan Museum of Art/Philomel, 1981.

A retelling by an Egyptologist of a 3,000-year-old Egyptian tale translated from the hieroglyphs of a papyrus manuscript in the British Museum. The story of the prince's destiny is accompanied by the hieroglyphs and colorfully illustrated with copies of Egyptian art work. Notes on the story and life in ancient Egypt. Grades 1–3.

Hawaii

Alpers, Antony, retel. *Maori Myths and Tribal Legends.* Illus. Patrick Hanly. Houghton Mifflin, 1966.

The Maui cycle of stories, mythology of the Maori brought from "Hawaiki" to New Zealand. Meaning, sources, and discussion of treatment are dealt with at the end of the book. Grades 6 and up.

Colum, Padraic. *Legends of Hawaii.* Illus. Don Forrer. Yale Univ. Press, 1937.

Selections from the author's two volumes *At the Gateway of the Day* and *Bright Islands.* Grades 6–8.

Thompson, Vivian L. *Hawaiian Myths of Earth, Sea and Sky.* Illus. Leonard Weisgard. Holiday House, 1966.

Volcano, waterfall, forest, and surf form the setting of these myths where the supernatural mingles with the natural. Grades 4–6.

Williams, Jay. *The Surprising Things Maui Did.* Illus. Charles Mikolaycak. Four Winds, 1979.

Curvilinear, colorful illustrations enhance this legend of the Hawaiian hero who brought fire to his people. The retelling preserves the tone of the myth. No source given. Grades 1–4.

Hebrew

Ish-Kishor, Judith. *Tales from The Wise Men of Israel.* Intro. Harry Golden; illus. W. T. Mars. Lippincott, 1962.

Stories that center around such people as King Solomon, Alexander, Maimonides, various rabbis, and others of no fame, these teach lessons at the same time that they reflect what Harry Golden calls "a literary sense of self-mockery." Grades 5–10.

Ish-Kishor, Sulamith. *The Carpet of Solomon: A Hebrew Legend.* Illus. Uri Shulevitz. Pantheon, 1966.

The "magic" of a carpet that is purchased by Solomon is in the way it shows him his pride and vanity. Only Solomon's newly acquired ability to humble himself before God is what saves his son's life. Grades 4–9.

Singer, Isaac Bashevis, retel. *Elijah the Slave.* Trans. by the author and Elizabeth Shub; illus. Antonio Frasconi. Farrar, Straus & Giroux, 1970.

A simple story of Elijah using miracles to help a poor man is handsomely set into a picture-book format. Grades 3–7.

Ireland

Pilkington, F. M. *The Three Sorrowful Tales of Erin.* Illus. Victor G. Ambrus. Walck, 1966.

Part legend, part myth, these tragedies of the children of Lir, children of Tuireann, and Deirdre and the sons of Uisne have origins in the days of the Druids and the Celtic invasions of Ireland. A poetic retelling. Grades 7–9.

Italy

Davis, Mary Gould. *The Truce of the Wolf and Other Tales of Italy.* Illus. Jay Van Everen. Harcourt, 1931.

Six of the seven stories are told from old Italian legends. The story of "Nanni" is Miss Davis' own creation. Out of print, but may be found in libraries. Grades 4–6.

Japan

Edmonds, I. G., retel. *The Possible Impossibles of Ikkyu the Wise.* Illus. Robert Byrd. Macrae Smith, 1971.

A real person, Ikkyu lived nearly six hundred years ago, but the stories that have grown up about his wisdom and ability to extricate himself and others from impossible situations has made him an enduring folk hero. Grades 4–9.

Hodges, Margaret. *The Wave.* Illus. Blair Lent. Houghton Mifflin, 1964.

Adapted from Lafcadio Hearn's *Gleanings in Buddha Fields.* Strong, dramatic illustrations convey the strength and flow of Japanese art. Grades 2–4.

Pratt, Davis. *Magic Animals of Japan.* Illus. Elsa Kula. Parnassus, 1967.

Legends associated with the animals in Japanese sculpture, architecture, and painting. Grades 2–4.

Latin America

Barlow, Genevieve, comp. *Latin American Tales: From the Pampas to the Pyramids of Mexico.* Illus. William M. Hutchinson. Rand McNally, 1966.

Stories from a number of Indian tribes living in the area from southern Argentina into Mexico.

Bierhorst, John, ed. and trans. *Black Rainbow: Legends of the Incas and Myths of Ancient Peru.* Farrar, Straus & Giroux, 1976.

Sensitive retellings and scholarly notes make this an excellent compilation of myths, legends, and fables from Peru. Grades 6 and up. See also *The Hungry Woman: Myths and Legends of the Aztecs* (Morrow, 1984).

North American Indian and Inuit

Belting, Natalie. *The Long-Tailed Bear, and Other Indian Legends.* Illus. Louis F. Cary. Bobbs-Merrill, 1961.

Animal legends retold from the folklore of many tribes. Grades 2–4. See also *The Earth Is on a Fish's Back* (Holt, 1965).

Bierhorst, John, ed. *The Fire Plume: Legends of the American Indians.* Col. Henry Rowe Schoolcraft; illus. Alan E. Cober. Dial, 1969.

Tales that were collected by Schoolcraft during his travels where Algonquin tribes lived during the first half of the nineteenth century. Grades 3–7.

Bird, Traveller. *The Path to Snowbird Mountain: Cherokee Legends.* Illus. by the author. Farrar, Straus & Giroux, 1972.

Origin stories and accounts of the Cherokee's past told by a Cherokee-Shawnee-Comanche man. Grades 2–5.

Curry, Jane Louise. *Down from the Lonely Mountain.* Illus. Enrico Arno. Harcourt, 1965.

Tales of unusual charm tell of the world when it was new and of the animals that helped shape it. Grades 3–6.

Curtis, Edward S., comp. *The Girl Who Married a Ghost and Other Tales from the North American Indian.* Four Winds, 1978.

A mature collection of nine legends dramatically enhanced by Curtis's striking photographs. Grades 5 and up.

De Wit, Dorothy, ed. *The Talking Stone: An Anthology of Native American Tales and Legends.* Illus. Donald Crews. Greenwillow, 1979.

Twenty-seven dramatically told tales divided by region of origin with informative notes and sources appended. Grades 5–7.

Fisher, Anne B. *Stories California Indians Told.* Illus. Ruth Robbins. Parnassus, 1957.

Twelve how-and-why stories explain the world of nature as the Indians saw it. Grades 4–6.

Goble, Paul, retel. *Star Boy.* Illus. by the author. Bradbury, 1983.

Intensely colored, stylized illustrations based on authentic Blackfoot art give atmosphere to this Blackfoot legend of how the Sun Dance was given to the tribe. Based on the work of Walter McClintock and G. B. Grinnell. Grades 1–3.

Grinnell, George Bird. *Blackfoot Lodge Tales.* Univ. of Nebraska Press, 1962.

Stories handed down for generations by the tribal storytellers. First published in 1892. Grades 5–9.

Harris, Christie. *Mouse Woman and the Vanished Princess.* Illus. Douglas Tait. Atheneum, 1976.

A cycle of six Canadian Northwest Coast Indian stories linked by the authentic character of the narnauk Mouse Woman, a supernatural being. Vividly retold in a western mode. Grades 3–6. See also the companion volumes *Mouse Woman and the Mischief-Makers* (1977); *Mouse Woman and the Muddleheads* (1979); and *The Trouble with Princesses* (1980), which further develops the comparisons between the European Old and Indian New World princess tales.

Harris, Christie. *Once upon a Totem.* Woodcuts by John Frazer Mills. Atheneum, 1963.

Tales of the Indians of the North Pacific Coast from Alaska to Oregon. Brief introductions throw light on Indian customs and traditions. Grades 4–6.

Harris, Christie. *Once More upon a Totem.* Illus. Douglas Tait. Atheneum, 1973.

More stories from the Indians of the North West Coast. Grades 4–8.

Hayes, William D. *Indian Tales of the Desert People.* Illus. William D. Hayes. McKay, 1957.

Retellings of tales that have appeared in several sources. Grades 3–6.

Highwater, Jamake. *Anpao: An American Indian Odyssey.* Illus. Fritz Scholder. Lippincott, 1977.

A cycle of traditional Great Plains and South West hero tales about the mythic Anpao-Scarface sensitively integrated into a single novelistic story that reflects the Indian culture. The poetic prose is enhanced by intense, expressionistic illustrations. Both illustrator and reteller are Indian. Notes on sources given. Grades 5 and up. See also *Legend Days* (Harper, 1984).

Hill, Kay. *Glooscap and His Magic: Legends of the Wabanaki Indians.* Illus. Robert Frankenberg. Dodd, Mead, 1963.

A strong cycle of Micmac legends about the Lord of Men and Beasts, told in colloquial, conversational style, with pointed humor. Grades 4 and up. See also *More Glooscap Stories: Legends of the Wabanaki Indians* (1970).

Houston, James. *Kiviok's Magic Journey: An Eskimo Legend.* Illus. by the author. Atheneum, 1973.

Energetic, lucid illustrations complement this expressive retelling of an Eskimo hero tale by an award-winning author who has lived and worked with the Canadian Inuit. Grades 3–5. See also *Tikta'liktak: An Eskimo Legend* (Harcourt, 1965); a legend of the Raven people; *Ghost Paddle: A Northwest Coast Indian Tale* (Harcourt, 1972); and *The White Archer: An Eskimo Legend* (Harcourt, 1979).

Jones, Hettie, adapt. *Coyote Tales.* Illus. Louis Mofsie. Holt, 1974.

Stories of the trickster who is often tricked himself. Grades 3–6. See also *Longhouse Winter: Iroquois Transformation Tales* (1972).

Leekley, Thomas B. *The World of Manabozho: Tales of the Chippewa Indians.* Vanguard, 1965.

A retelling of the Manabozho tales connected with the Chippewa and Ottowa tribes with whom the author lived. Valuable notes give background. Grades 4–6.

Macmillan, Cyrus. *Glosskap's Country and Other Indian Tales.* Illus. John Hall. Oxford Univ. Press, 1956.

Tales that begin with stories of Glooskap, the supernatural hero of the Micmac Indians of Eastern Canada, and move west over the prairies to the Pacific Coast. This volume brings together stories about Glooskap from *Canadian Wonder Tales* (1918) and *Canadian Fairy Tales* (1922). See also *Canadian Wonder Tales,* illus. Elizabeth Cleaver (Clarke, Irwin, 1974).

Marriott, Alice. *Saynday's People: The Kiowa Indians and the Stories They Told.* Univ. of Nebraska Press, Bison Book, 1963.

Stories of the Kiowa Indians and information about the American Indians are combined in this reissue of two books in one volume, formerly *Winter-Telling Stories* and *Indians on Horseback. Winter-Telling Stories* has been reset and reprinted (Crowell, 1969). All ages. See also *Plains Indian Mythology,* by Marriott Rachlin and Carol K. Rachlin (Crowell, 1976).

Martin, Fran. *Nine Tales of Coyote.* Illus. Dorothy McEntee. Harper, 1950.

Stories about Coyote, the medicine man of the Nimipu Indians, who could change himself into an animal. Grades 4–6.

Martin, Fran, retel. *Raven-Who-Sets-Things-Right: Indian Tales of the Northwest Coast.* Illus. Dorothy McEntee. Rev. ed. Harper, 1975.

Originally published as *Nine Tales of Raven,* this has new illustrations. Raven was the creator, and these stories explain the natural world. Some stories show the vain, mischievous side of Raven.

Melzack, Ronald, retel. *The Day Tuk Became a Hunter and Other Eskimo Stories.* Illus. Carol Jones. Dodd, Mead, 1967.

Ten stories that give an insight into the mood, temper, and customs of the Eskimo people. Melzack carefully cites all sources, saying that these stories have been altered only when it was necessary to make the stories appealing to children in our culture. Grades 3–7. See also *Raven, Creator of the World: Eskimo Legends,* illus. Laszlo Gal (Little, Brown, 1970), and *Why the Man in the Moon is Happy and Other Eskimo Creation Stories,* illus. Laszlo Gal (McClelland & Stewart, 1977).

Metayer, Maurice, ed. and trans. *Tales from the Igloo.* Foreword, Al Purdy; illus. Agnes Nanogak. St. Martin's, 1972.

Stories told by the Copper Eskimos who live along the Canadian Arctic coast. Grades 4–8.

Parker, Arthur C. *Skunny Wundy: Seneca Indian Tales.* Illus. George Armstrong. Whitman, 1926.

Tales from the past of the teller, who says that his versions for non-Indian-speaking children met the approval of his father who heard them "in the days of Deerfoot, the swift runner." Grades 2–5.

Reid, Dorothy M. *Tales of Nanabozho.* Illus. Donald Grant. Walck, 1963.

The adventures of the Ojibway culture hero retold in a straightforward manner. Grades 4–6.

Robinson, Gail, retel. *Raven the Trickster: Legends of the North American Indians.* Intro. Douglas Hill; illus. Joanna Troughton, Atheneum, 1982.

Nine Raven legends of the Pacific Northwest retold with lucid clarity by a Canadian poet. Grades 3–6. See also legends about another trickster hero, *Coyote the Trickster: Legends of the North American Indians,* by Gail Robinson and Douglas Hill, illus. Graham McCallum (Chatto & Windus, 1975).

Rushmore, Helen, and Wolf Robe Hunt. *The Dancing Horses of Acoma and Other Indian Stories.* World, 1963.

The author, in collaboration with an Acoma chief, presents twelve legends of the Acoma Indians, a Pueblo tribe still living in southwestern New Mexico. Grades 4–6.

San Souci, Robert, adapt. *The Legend of Scarface: A Blackfeet Indian Tale.* Illus. Daniel San Souci. Doubleday, 1978.

A classic Blackfoot legend, with strong, precise illustrations. See also another collaboration in *Song of Sedna* (1981), the stark Eskimo myth told in a gentler mode than customary, with compelling paintings.

Scheer, George F., ed. *Cherokee Animal Tales.* Illus. Robert Frankenberg; intro. George F. Scheer. Holiday, 1968.

The fine introduction informs the reader about the history of the Cherokee people as well as the history of the collecting of these stories, which account for the way various animals acquired their important characteristics. Grades 2–5.

Snake, Sam, et al. *The Adventures of Nanabush: Ojibway Indian Stories.* Comp. Emerson Coatsworth and David Coatsworth; illus. Francis Kagige. Atheneum, 1980.

A mature collection of sixteen pungent and flavorful Canadian Indian legends collected from native storytellers, elders of an Ojibway Band. The striking illustrations by a native artist are true to the Ojibway style. Grades 5 and up.

Toye, William, retel. *How Summer Came to Canada.* Illus. Elizabeth Cleaver. Walck, 1969.

A picture-book edition of a clear retelling of the Micmac legend explaining the seasons. Illustrated with vibrant, textural collages by an award-winning Canadian artist. Grades 1–4. This collaboration has also produced two Tsimshian legends: *The Mountain Goats of Temlaham* (1969); *The Loon's Necklace* (1977); and an Ojibway legend, *The Fire Stealer* (Oxford Univ. Press, 1979).

Whitman, William, retel. *Navaho Tales.* Illus. John P. Heins. Houghton Mifflin, 1925.

Stories of creation and magic, originally translated from the Navaho by Dr. Washington Matthews in *Navaho Legends.* Grades 4–8.

Wood, Marion. *Spirits, Heroes and Hunters from North American Indian Mythology.* Illus. John Sibbick. Schocken, World Mythologies Series, 1982.

A handsome, oversize volume in which realistically detailed, colorful illustrations enhance the straightforward text. Grades 3–6.

Scotland

Yolen, Jane. *Greyling: A Picture Story from the Islands of Shetland.* Illus. William Stobbs. World, 1968.

Based on Scottish legends of the selchies (the Seal people). Grades 1–3.

Spain

Irving, Washington. *The Alhambra: Palace of Mystery and Splendor.* Sel. and arranged by Mabel Williams; illus. Louis Slobodkin. Macmillan, Children's Classics, 1953.

The 1953 edition has been reset and has a new illustrator. The legends have been popular since they first appeared in 1832. Grades 7–9.

Jimenez-Landi, Antonio. *The Treasure of the Muleteer and Other Spanish Tales.* Trans. Paul Blackburn; illus. Floyd Sowell. Doubleday, 1974.

Rather sophisticated stories that give the event behind some landmark or another; tales of supernatural and strange occurrences. Grades 5–9.

Switzerland

Bawden, Nina. *William Tell.* Illus. Pascale Allmand. Lothrop, 1981.

This picture-book edition of the Swiss story is told with care and illustrated in a naive folk style that captures the spirit of the legend. Grades 1–4.

Hürlimann, Bettina. *William Tell and His Son.* Trans. Elizabeth D. Crawford; illus. Paul Nussbaumer. Harcourt, 1967.

The moving legend is told from the standpoint of the boy whose courage matches his father's aim. Grades 2–5.

Sacred Writings and Legends

Alexander, Pat, retel. *The Puffin Children's Bible: Stories from the Old and New Testaments.* Illus. Lyndon Evans. Puffin Books, 1981.

Short, simplified retellings in direct, modern English. A strong first Bible. Attractively produced. Grades 1–4.

Bailey, John, Kenneth McLeish, and David Spearman, retels. *Gods and Men: Myths and Legends from the World's Religions.* Illus. Derek Collard, Charles Keeping, and Jeroo Roy. Oxford Univ. Press, 1981.

A mature collection of skillfully retold stories on universal themes and subjects. Parallel legends of creation and good and evil are balanced with the more actively dramatic exploits of such heroes and prophets as Moses, Rama, and St. George. Grades 5 and up.

The Bible. *The Old Testament.* Arranged and illus. by Marguerite de Angeli; preface, Samuel Terrien. New ed. Doubleday, 1966.

An excellent rendering of the King James Version skillfully abridged by Dr. Samuel Terrien and handsomely illustrated. All ages.

Brodsky, Beverly. *Jonah: An Old Testament Story.* Illus. by the reteller. Lippincott, 1977.

A handsome picture-book version of the Old Testament Story with abstract, stylized paintings complementing a first-person narrative. Grades K–3.

Coatsworth, Elizabeth. *The Cat Who Went to Heaven.* Illus. Lynd Ward. Macmillan, 1930.

A Japanese legend of how the Buddha accepts the cat into Nirvana is retold in poetic prose. Includes Jataka tales and the story of Buddha's life. Awarded the Newbery Medal, 1931. Grades 4–6.

Cohen, Barbara. *The Binding of Isaac.* Illus. Charles Mikolaycak. Lothrop, 1978.

A novelistic interpretation of the Old Testament using a framing device of Isaac recounting his experience to his grandchildren. The psychological realism is reflected in the dramatic, colorful pictures. Grades 3–6. See also the gripping first-person account of Joseph and his brothers in Cohen's *I Am Joseph,* illus. Charles Mikolaycak (1980).

De la Mare, Walter. *Stories from the Bible.* Illus. Edward Ardizzone. Knopf, 1961.

A poet retells the stories from the Old Testament with beauty and dignity. The introduction gives valuable information about different translations. Grades 6–8.

De Paola, Tomie. *Francis, the Poor Man of Assisi.* Illus. by the author. Holiday House, 1982.

A picture-book version of the lives of St. Francis and Sister Clare with a strong, graceful text. Quietly eloquent paintings that recall the frescoes of Cimabue perfectly reflect the story's setting and mood. Grades K–3.

De Regniers, Beatrice Schenk. *David and Goliath.* Illus. Richard M. Powers. Viking, 1965.

A retelling of the famous story, for younger children, accompanied by brilliant drawings. Grades 2–4.

Dickinson, Peter, retel. *City of Gold and Other Stories from the Old Testament.* Illus. Michael Foreman. Pantheon, 1980.

A radically original, post-modernist interpretation of thirty-three Old Testament stories. Told not as scripture, but as narrative from a living oral tradition in the time before the Bible, these stories are recited, chanted, and occasionally sung by witnesses of the events or storytellers repeating polished legend. Each tale is set in context by a preface describing teller, audience, setting, and date. Scholarly notes. Haunting illustrations capture the mystery and spiritual power of the stories. Winner of the Carnegie Medal. Grades 4 and up.

El-Shamy, Hasan M., coll., trans. and ed. *Folktales of Egypt.* Univ. of Chicago Press, Folktales of the World, 1980.

A scholarly source book of Egyptian folklore, including Islamic religious legends of the Prophet Mohammed, and the miraculous feats of the Muslim religious orders of dervishes and saints. Grades 9 and up.

Evslin, Bernard. *Signs and Wonders: Tales from the Old Testament.* Illus. Charles Mikolaycak. Four Winds, 1981.

In cadenced, sensuous language reminiscent of King James prose, the author retells stories from the Old Testament and the Apocrypha. The effect of added dialogue and detail is heightened by the dramatic black-and-white drawings. Grades 4–6.

Farjeon, Eleanor. *Ten Saints.* Illus. Helen Sewell. Walck, 1936.

   Stories of St. Christopher, St. Francis, St. Nicholas, St. Patrick, and others, admirably retold by a poet. Grades 5–8.

Floethe, Louise Lee. *A Thousand and One Buddhas.* Illus. Richard Floethe. Farrar, Straus & Giroux, 1967.

   A retelling of an old Japanese legend about the building of a temple that still stands in Kyoto eight hundred years later. Grades 2–4.

Fussenegger, Gertrud. *Noah's Ark.* Trans. Anthea Bell; illus. Annegert Fuchshuber. Hodder & Stoughton, 1983.

   A skillful, intimate retelling enhanced by distinctive illustrations in a tender, naive style. Grades K–3. See also the almost wordless *Noah's Ark,* illus. Peter Spier (Doubleday, 1977), and *Noah and the Great Flood,* illus. Warwick Hutton (Atheneum, 1977).

Garfield, Leon. *The Writing on the Wall.* Illus. Michael Bragg. Lothrop, 1983.

   The Old Testament story of God's awesome message to Belshazzar, the Babylonian king, is told from the child's perspective through the character of Samuel, a kitchen-boy at the feast. The formal, Breughel-like grace and dramatic perspectives of the illustrations add to the power of this original retelling. As poignant and gently humorous as another collaboration, *King Nimrod's Tower* (1982). Grades 1 and up.

Godden, Rumer. *St. Jerome and the Lion.* Illus. Jean Primrose. Viking, 1961.

   Based on a translation from the Latin, this old legend is told in verse with reverence and humor. Grades 4–6.

Graham, Lorenz. *David He No Fear.* Illus. Ann Grifalconi. Crowell, 1971.

   A musical retelling of David and Goliath in the idiomatic African English in which the stories were told to the author in Liberia. Firm, rigorous woodcuts illustrate the story. Grades 1–4. See also four other titles in this series: *Every Man Heart Lay Down,* illus. Colleen Browning (1970); *A Road Down in the Sea,* illus. Gregario Prestopino (1970); *God Wash the World and Start Again,* illus. Clare R. Ross (1971); and *Hongry Catch the Foolish Boy,* illus. James Brown, Jr. (1973).

Gray, John E. B. *India's Tales and Legends.* Illus. Joan Kiddell-Monroe. Walck, Oxford Myths and Legends Series, 1961.

   Includes adaptations of Buddhist Jataka birth stories and the sacred epics as well as other tales from the oral tradition. Grades 6–8.

The Holy Bible. Revised Standard Version. 2d ed. Nelson, 1971.

   A complete Bible with colored maps and photographs of the Holy Land. See also *Young Readers Bible: The Holy Bible, Revised Standard Version* (Abingdon, 1978). Study aids and additional material were prepared by Henry M. Bullock and Edward C. Peterson.

The Holy Bible. New King James version containing the Old and New Testaments. Nelson, 1982.

   An updating of the authorized or King James Version, first published in 1611, which retains the literary flavor of language, but modernizes archaic words, streamlines punctuation, and capitalizes divine pronouns.

Horn, Geoffrey, and Arthur Cavanaugh, retels. *Bible Stories for Children.* Illus. Arvis Stewart. Macmillan, 1980.

   Bible stories from both Old and New Testaments, simply and fluently retold, including quotations from the Bible and handsome, full-color illustrations. An inviting volume with large type and attractive design. Grades 4–6.

Hyde-Chambers, Frederick, and Audrey Hyde-Chambers. *Tibetan Folk Tales.* Illus. Kusho Ralla. Shambhala, 1981.

   A collection of religious and secular stories, retold primarily from Tibetan storytellers, about the Buddha, sages, teachers, and folk heroes. With explanatory notes following each tale and introductory notes on Tibetan Buddhism, history, and oral tradition. The illustrations by a Tibetan monk are in the Thangka style of religious scroll painting. Grades 5 and up.

Jones, Jessie Orton, sel. *Small Rain: Verses from the Bible.* Illus. Elizabeth Orton Jones. Viking, 1943.

   Bible verses which appeal particularly to children, illustrated from a child's point of view. Grades 2–4.

Keats, Ezra Jack. *God Is in the Mountain.* Illus. by the author. Holt, 1966.

   A collection of poetical phrases that show the universality of religious thought. Gathered from various religions. All ages.

Lines, Kathleen. *Once in Royal David's City.* Illus. Harold Jones. Oxford Univ. Press, 1966.

   A simple, fluent retelling of the first Christmas with the Biblical texts appended. Delicate illustrations in muted tones and fine detail. Grades K–3.

Petersham, Maud, and Miska Petersham. *The Christ Child.* Illus. by the authors. Doubleday, 1931.

A picture book of unusual beauty. The artists, who spent several months in Palestine, have rendered the story of the nativity as told by Matthew and Luke into pictures filled with the spirit of the Holy Land. Grades 1–4. See also *The Story of Jesus* (Macmillan, 1967).

Seeger, Elizabeth, adapt. *The Five Sons of King Pandu: The Story of the Mahabhárata.* Illus. Gordon Laite. Young Scott, 1967.

A strong retelling of the sacred Hindu book and dramatic epic, adapted from the English translation of Kisari Mohan Ganguli. Grades 7 and up.

Seeger, Elizabeth, adapt. *The Ramayana.* Illus. Gordon Laite. Young Scott, 1969.

Adapted from the English translation of Hari Prasad Shastri. This is a dramatic prose version of the great Hindu epic which is also part of Hindu scripture. Grades 7 and up. See also the retelling by Dhan Gopal Mukerji in *Rama, the Hero of India,* illus. Edgar Parin d'Aulaire (Dutton, 1930), and that by Joseph Gaer in *The Adventures of Rama,* illus. Randy Monk (Little, Brown, 1954).

Serage, Nancy. *The Prince Who Gave Up a Throne: A Story of the Buddha.* Illus. Kazue Mizumura. Crowell, 1966.

A dignified narrative version of Buddha's life and teachings based primarily on the *Buddha Karita* of Asvaghosa, the Buddhist Sutras. Simply told, with an author's note added. Grades 4–6.

Singer, Isaac Bashevis. *The Wicked City.* Trans. by the author and Elizabeth Shub; illus. Leonard Everett Fisher. Farrar, Straus & Giroux, 1972.

The destruction of Sodom is retold with subtle allusions to contemporary life. Fine, dramatic illustrations. Grades 4–6.

Smith, Ruth, ed. *The Tree of Life: Selections from the Literature of the World's Religions.* Illus. Boris Artzybasheff. Viking, 1942.

A significant book for the thoughtful reader who will gain a knowledge of the spiritual values of the following faiths: American Indian, Norse, Hindu, Buddhist, Confucian, Taoist, Egyptian, Babylonian, Greek, Zorastrian, Hebrew, Christian, and Mohammedan. Grades 7 and up.

Spicer, Dorothy Gladys. *The Kneeling Tree and Other Folktales from the Middle East.* Illus. Barb Morrow. Coward-McCann, 1971.

This collection of folktales includes Christian, Muslim, and Jewish legends. Saints and prophets of the Koran and the Old and New Testaments mix with the ordinary people of the Middle East. Grades 4–7.

Stoddard, Sandol. *The Doubleday Illustrated Children's Bible.* Illus. Tony Chen. Doubleday, 1983.

Endorsed by a board of Biblical consultants, these selections of 108 stories from the Old and New Testaments are retold with drama, sensitivity, and fidelity. Dignified watercolor illustrations capture the sense of time and place. Grades 3 and up.

Turner, Philip. *The Bible Story.* Illus. Brian Wildsmith. Oxford Univ. Press, 1982.

A dignified, rhythmic retelling of Old and New Testament stories. The lyricism, poignancy, and drama of the tales are reflected in the striking graphic designs aglow with rich hues. First published in 1968. Grades 1–6.

Wetering, Janwillem van de. *Little Owl: An Eightfold Buddhist Admonition.* Illus. Marc Brown. Houghton Mifflin, 1978.

The eight Buddhist admonitions leading to enlightenment are presented as an interlinking cycle of comic and touching animal fables for young children. A handsome picture book with expressive black-and-white drawings. Grades 2–4.

Wiesner, William. *The Tower of Babel.* Illus. by the author. Viking, 1968.

The story of King Nimrod and his fabulous tower, retold with simple dignity from the Book of Genesis. Grades K–2. See also the unusual, imaginative treatment of this theme in Leon Garfield's *King Nimrod's Tower,* illus. Michael Bragg (Lothrop, 1982).

Wilhelm, Richard. *Chinese Folktales.* Trans. Ewald Osers. Bell, 1971.

Originally published in German as *Chinesische Marchen* in 1958, this collection includes Taoist, Confucian, and Buddhist stories and secular fables and folktales. Explanatory notes and sources for each tale. Grades 5 and up.

Winthrop, Elizabeth, adapt. *A Child Is Born: The Christmas Story.* Illus. Charles Mikolaycak. Holiday House, 1983.

A dignified, faithful adaptation of the Nativity story from the Gospels according to St. Luke and St. Matthew. The poetry of the King James Version is enhanced by the fine line and rich, somber hues of the watercolor illustrations. A handsomely produced volume. Grades K and up.

References for Adults*

Bett, Henry. *English Legends.* Illus. from drawings by Eric Fraser. Batsford, 1950.

Campbell, Joseph. *The Hero with a Thousand Faces.* Pantheon, 1949.
A classic study of the heroic "mono-myth." See also *The Masks of God: Primitive Mythology, Oriental Mythology, Occidental Mythology* and *Creative Mythology,* 4 vols. (Viking, 1959).

Campbell, Joseph. *The Way of the Animal Powers.* Historical Atlas of World Mythology, vol. 1. Alfred van der Marck Editions, 1983.
The first volume in a projected series, this work of a lifetime's scholarship discusses creation myths of time and the cosmos and the mythic, shamanistic vision of the earliest hunting and gathering cultures.

Chase, Richard. *Quest for Myth.* Louisiana State Univ. Press, 1949.
"The central premise of this book is that myth is literature and therefore a matter of aesthetic experience and the imagination."—Preface.

Colum, Padraic. *Myths of the World.* Engravings, Boris Artzybasheff. Grosset & Dunlap, 1959.
First published under the title *Orpheus.* A scholarly addition to the study of mythology because of the fine retelling of the myths and the valuable discussion of their significance and characteristics.

Crossley-Holland, Kevin, intro. and retel. *The Norse Myths.* Pantheon, The Pantheon Fairytale and Folklore Library, 1980.
Scholarly, eloquent, and contemporary retellings of thirty-two classic Norse myths drawn from Icelandic sagas and contemporary histories and poetry. Informative introductory notes on the Norse world, cosmology, pantheon, sources, and the literary structure of the myths. Notes on selections, a glossary, bibliography, and index are appended.

Dawson, Warren. *The Bridle of Pegasus: Studies in Magic, Mythology and Folklore.* Methuen, 1930.

Egoff, Sheila A. "Indian and Eskimo Legends." In *The Republic of Childhood: A Critical Guide to Canadian Children's Literature in English.* 2d ed. Oxford Univ. Press, 1975.
Analyzes the North American Indian and Inuit legends and the problems in presenting these forms for children.

* See also the bibliography for Chapter 9, "Epics and Romances."

Eliade, Mircea. *Myth and Reality.* Trans. Willard R. Trask. Harper, 1963.

Farmer, Penelope. "On the Effects of Collecting Myth for Children and Others." *Children's Literature in Education,* 8, no. 4 (Winter 1977), pp. 176–85.
Discusses the recurring patterns of creation, destruction, and rebirth in mythologies around the world.

Frazer, Sir James George. *The Golden Bough: Study in Magic and Religion.* Macmillan, 1951.
In this one-volume, abridged edition the author has expertly compressed the wealth of invaluable material contained in the original twelve-volume edition dealing with the development of magic, customs, social practices, and religion among primitive men and women. See also *The New Golden Bough,* abridged and ed. Theodor H. Gaster (Anchor, 1961).

Frye, Northrop. *The Great Code: The Bible and Literature.* Harcourt, 1982.
A monumental study of the Bible's influence on English literature. A definitive work by a distinguished literary critic. See also the author's *Anatomy of Criticism: Four Essays* (Princeton Univ. Press, 1957).

Hildebrand, Ann. "The Bible Presented Objectively." In *Beyond Fact: Nonfiction for Children and Young People,* comp. Jo Carr. American Library Association, 1982, pp. 180–86.

Hughes, Ted. "Myth and Education." In *Writers, Critics and Children,* pp. 77–94, ed. Geoff Fox et al. Agathon, 1976.
A critical essay on the educational value of myth and folklore. First printed in *Children's Literature in Education* (Mar. 1970).

Lawton, William Cranston. *The Soul of Mythology.* Yale Univ. Press, 1923.

Leach, Maria, ed. *Funk & Wagnalls Standard Dictionary of General Folklore, Mythology and Legend.* 2 vols. Funk & Wagnalls, 1949–50.
The richness, vitality, and range of world folklore, mythology, and legend are revealed in this major reference work compiled not only for folklorists but also for the general reader.

Leeming, David A. *Mythology: The Voyage of the Hero.* Lippincott, 1973.

Livingston, Richard William. *The Legacy of Greece.* Oxford Univ. Press, 1921.

Maranda, Pierre, ed. *Mythology.* Penguin, 1972.

A wide-ranging selection of anthropological writings on various theories of myth and folklore, all showing the influence of Lévi-Strauss.

Marriott, Alice, and Carol K. Rachlin. *American Indian Mythology.* Crowell, 1968.

Myths and legends representing more than twenty tribes, told to the authors by Indians, and supplemented by the findings of anthropological studies.

Munch, Peter. *Norse Mythology: Legends of Gods and Heroes.* Trans. Sigurd Bernhard Hustveld. American Scandinavian Foundation, 1926.

Murray, Henry A., ed. *Myth and Mythmaking.* Beacon, 1968 (1959 by the American Academy of Arts and Sciences).

A fascinating compilation of papers from various points of view.

New Larousse Encyclopaedia of Mythology. Intro. Robert Graves; ed. Felix Guirand. Hamlyn, 1963.

See also *Larousse World Mythology,* ed. Pierre Grimal (1965). Both provide rich sources of worldwide myths.

Rolleston, T. W. *Myths and Legends of the Celtic Race.* 2d rev. ed. Farrar, Straus & Giroux, 1934.

Schwab, Gustav. *Gods & Heroes: Myths & Epics of Ancient Greece.* Pantheon, 1946.

Written in German and translated by Olga Marx and Ernst Morwitz, this is a general collection, encompassing both mythology and heroic legends. Told with simplicity and restraint, these tales provide good background for the adult who is reading other tellings for children.

Thompson, Stith, sel. *Tales of the North American Indians.* Indiana Univ. Press, 1971.

First printed in 1929, this is an invaluable source with annotations by the noted folklore scholar; extensive bibliography.

Ullom, Judith C., comp. *Folklore of the North American Indians: An Annotated Bibliography.* Library of Congress, 1969.

An extremely valuable source book with extensive notes and a geographical division of North American culture areas.

Zimmerman, J. E. *Dictionary of Classical Mythology.* Harper, 1964.

A handy reference book that will help to explain allusions that add beauty, truth, and vitality to ancient and modern literature.

9 Epics and Romances

Books for Children

Hazeltine, Alice I., ed. *Hero Tales from Many Lands.* Illus. Gordon Laite. Abingdon, 1961.

An important collection not only for the selections included (many of the original sources are now out of print) but for the introductory notes giving background. Valuable as an introduction to epic literature. Grades 5–8.

Mayne, William, ed. *William Mayne's Book of Heroes: Stories and Poems.* Dutton, 1968.

Raising the question "What is a Hero?" in his introduction, William Mayne states that the hero is larger than life and stays alive in the memories of his friends. ". . . There are all sorts of heroisms here, from Drake and the great sea-fighters of five hundred years ago, to the people of the dawn of time in Finland and the Pacific, from the great beaver-haunted forests of America to the broad steppes between Russia and China, from the Bridge at Rome to the twisted labyrinth in Crete." Grades 4–8.

Uden, Grant. *Hero Tales from the Age of Chivalry: Retold from the Froissart Chronicles.* Illus. Doreen Roberts. World, 1969.

Set against the background of the Hundred Years' War between France and England, these stories of adventure are taken from the Berners translation of Froissart's famous Chronicles of England. Grades 5–10.

Africa

Bertol, Roland, retel. *Sundiata: The Epic of the Lion King.* Illus. Gregorio Prestopino. Crowell, 1970.

Sundiata was a powerful figure of the thirteenth century who built a kingdom where the republic of Mali is today. Preserved in oral tradition, this epic is found in many versions. Grades 4–8.

Mitchison, Naomi. *African Heroes.* Illus. William Stobbs. Bodley Head, 1968.

The author of this book looks at the heroic past as a necessary recognition of a cultural tradition. Grades 6–12.

Babylonia

Bryson, Bernarda. *Gilgamesh: Man's First Story.* Illus. by the author. Holt, 1967.

Gilgamesh is the oldest known epic. It was written in cuneiform 3,000 years before the birth of

Christ. In the nineteenth century a British archaeologist discovered the clay tablets under the long-
buried city of Nineveh. The epic tells the story
of a powerful Sumerian king who undertook a
long, dangerous journey in a vain search for immortality. On the eleventh tablet there was a story
of the Deluge older than the biblical story of the
flood. This discovery started the era of modern
biblical research. The epic served Homer as a pattern for the *Odyssey.* Bernarda Bryson retells this
story in stirring prose accompanied by pictures suggested by actual relics from the time when the legend was current. Grades 7 and up. See also *He
Who Saw Everything: The Epic of Gilgamesh,* retold
by Anita Feagles (Scott, 1966).

Westwood, Jennifer. *Gilgamesh and Other Babylonian
Tales.* Illus. Michael Charlton. Coward-McCann,
1970.
　　Stories that contain fascinating relationships to
classical myths and Biblical accounts: "All the stories in this book were written on clay tablets in
Akkadian, except for *Inanna in the Underworld,*
which is in Sumerian." Grades 6 and up.

Greece and Rome

Church, Alfred J. *The Aeneid for Boys and Girls.*
Illus. Eugene Karlin; afterword, Clifton Fadiman.
Macmillan, Children's Classics, 1962.
　　A dramatic retelling that keeps the spirit of Virgil's epic poem. Grades 6–9. Another version is
retold by N. B. Taylor and illustrated by Joan Kiddell-Monroe (Walck, 1961).

Church, Alfred J. *The Iliad and the Odyssey of Homer.*
Illus. Eugene Karlin; afterword, Clifton Fadiman.
Macmillan, The Macmillan Classics, 1964.
　　The *Iliad* tells the story of the Trojan War, while
the *Odyssey* recounts the adventures of Odysseus
on his voyage home. Classic retellings that faithfully preserve the spirit of Homer. Grades 6–8.

Colum, Padraic. *The Children's Homer: The Adventures
of Odysseus and The Tale of Troy.* Illus. Willy Pogány.
Macmillan, 1962.
　　First published in 1918. The well-known Irish
poet and storyteller skillfully combines the *Iliad*
and the *Odyssey* to make one continuous narrative
in rhythmic prose. Grades 5–7. Also available in
paperback (Macmillan, 1983).

Colum, Padraic. *The Golden Fleece and the Heroes
Who Lived Before Achilles.* Illus. Willy Pogány.
Macmillan, 1962.

First published in 1921. Many strands of Greek
mythology are interwoven into one heroic tale of
Jason and the heroes who lived before Achilles.
Grades 5–8. Also available in paperback (Macmillan, 1983).

Evslin, Bernard. *Greeks Bearing Gifts: The Epics of
Achilles and Ulysses.* Illus. Lucy Martin Bitzer.
Four Winds, 1976.
　　Modern and irreverent versions of the epics.
Grades 6 and up.

Farmer, Penelope. *Daedalus and Icarus.* Illus. Chris
Connor. Harcourt, 1971.
　　The story of Daedalus, his creation of the labyrinth for the minotaur, and his subsequent escape
from the island of Crete by flight. The excitement
of the telling is heightened by the illustrations.
Grades 3–5.

Garfield, Leon, and Edward Blishen. *The Golden
Shadow.* Illus. Charles Keeping. Pantheon, 1973.
　　A strong mood of foreknowledge and foreboding winds around and through the story of Heracles, the main character in this book, which reads
like a continuous narrative. Grades 8 and up.
See also *The God Beneath the Sea* (1971).

Graves, Robert. *The Seige and the Fall of Troy.*
Illus. C. Walter Hodges. Doubleday, 1962.
　　"Homer's poems are by no means the sole source
of the legend; in fact about two thirds of this book
is taken from various Greek and Latin authors."—
Introduction. Grades 7–9. See also *Greek Gods and
Heroes* (1960).

Green, Roger Lancelyn. *Heroes of Greece and Troy.*
Illus. Heather Copley and Christopher Chamber-
lain. Walck, 1961.
　　Told as a continuous narrative from the coming
of the immortals through the last of the heroes.
Grades 6–9. See also *Tales of the Greeks and Trojans*
(Purnell, 1966).

Kingsley, Charles. *The Heroes.* Illus. Joan Kiddell-
Monroe. Dutton, 1963.
　　Kingsley's versions, first published in 1855, retain the strength and beauty of the original Greek
stories. Grades 5–7. See also the edition illustrated
by Vera Bock (Macmillan, 1954).

Lang, Andrew. *The Adventures of Odysseus.* Illus. Joan
Kiddell-Monroe. Dutton, 1962.
　　A classical scholar retells the ancient epic of the
Trojan War and the adventures of Odysseus home-
ward bound. See also *Tales of Troy and Greece*
(1962), which includes the above as well as "The
Fleece of Gold," "Theseus," and "Perseus."

MacKenzie, Compton, retel. *Achilles*. Illus. William Stobbs. Aldus, Golden Tales of Greece, 1972.

Told with the ease of one who is immersed in the literature of the classic tales, this single volume is attractive in both the entertaining style and strong illustrations. Grades 4–8. See also *Theseus; Jason;* and *Perseus*.

McLean, Mollie, and Ann Wiseman. *Adventures of the Greek Heroes*. Illus. W. T. Mars. Houghton Mifflin, 1961.

A dramatic retelling of the hero myths for younger children. Told with simplicity and dignity. Grades 4–5.

Newman, Robert. *The Twelve Labors of Hercules*. Illus. Charles Keeping. Crowell, 1972.

A straightforward telling of the life of Hercules, centering on the twelve feats he had to perform. A pronouncing glossary is at the end. Grades 4–7.

Picard, Barbara Leonie, ed. *The Iliad of Homer*. Illus. Joan Kiddell-Monroe. Walck, 1960.

An excellent rendering of the epic poem. A brief prologue and epilogue give added value to the book. Grades 7–9.

Picard, Barbara Leonie, ed. *The Odyssey of Homer*. Illus. Joan Kiddell-Monroe. Walck, 1960.
Retold in forceful prose. Grades 7–9.

Reeves, James. *Heroes and Monsters*. Illus. Sarah Nechamkin. Blackie, 1969.

Directly told stories of such heroes as Odysseus, Theseus, Jason, Heracles, Perseus, and other myths. Grades 4–8. See also the companion volume *Giants and Warriors*.

Serraillier, Ian. *A Fall from the Sky: The Story of Daedalus*. Illus. William Stobbs. Walck, 1966.

A satisfying presentation of the brief, tragic story. Grades 4–6. See also *The Clashing Rocks: The Story of Jason*.

Serraillier, Ian. *Heracles the Strong*. Illus. Rocco Negri. Walck, 1970.

A straightforward telling that emphasizes the drama of the hero's life and the adventure in each of the twelve labors. Grades 5–9.

Serraillier, Ian. *The Way of Danger: The Story of Theseus*. Illus. William Stobbs. Walck, 1963.

Myths of Theseus vividly retold by an English poet. Grades 4–7. See also *The Gorgon's Head: The Story of Perseus*.

Taylor, N. B., retel. *The Aeneid of Virgil*. Illus. Joan Kiddell-Monroe. Walck, 1961.

The wanderings of Aeneas, the Trojan hero who was destined to find a new home for his people in Italy. An introduction relates this epic to the *Iliad* and the *Odyssey* and gives brief characterizations of the Roman gods. Grades 6 and up.

Iceland and Scandinavia (Norse)

French, Allen. *The Story of Grettir the Strong*. 8th ed. Dutton, 1950.

A vigorous retelling of the Icelandic saga. Based on the translation by William Morris and Eirík Magnússon published in 1869 under the title *The Grettir Saga*. Grades 5–8.

Hosford, Dorothy. *Sons of the Volsungs*. Illus. Frank Dobias. New ed. Holt, 1949.

A retelling in rhythmic prose of the story of Sigurd and Brynhilde based on the two books of William Morris' epic, *The Story of Sigurd the Volsung*. Grades 7–9.

Newman, Robert, retel. *Grettir the Strong*. Illus. John Gretzer. Crowell, 1968.

In the foreword it is pointed out that this saga is based on the life of a man who actually lived in a time when justice and vengeance were individually determined and bloody. Two translations (William Morris and Eirík Magnússon) have been used in writing this book, which is written like a novel. Grades 4–9.

Schiller, Barbara, adapt. and retel. *Hrafkel's Saga: An Icelandic Story*. Illus. Carol Iselin. Seabury, 1972.

This realistic story of a proud man who dealt out his own harsh justice and suffered outlawry is told with a sense of immediacy that brings the tenth-century human quarrels and vengeance into the present. Grades 5–9.

Schiller, Barbara. *The Vinlanders' Saga*. Illus. William Bock. Holt, 1966.

A forceful retelling of the Icelandic saga based on the Vinland Sagas translated by Eirík Magnússon and Hermann Pálsson. Grades 6–9.

Treece, Henry, retel. *The Burning of Njal*. Illus. Bernard Blatch. Criterion, 1964.

"From this true story of Njal's burning, first written down by an unnamed Icelandic author around the year 1280, we can learn much about Northmen of the tenth and eleventh centuries: the constant bickering among farming families; the arrogant pride of men and the bitter taunting of women; the ruthless following of useless feuds; the almost casual manslaughters in ambush; the carefree piratical voyaging abroad; the fearful belief in dreams and omens." Grades 5–10.

England

Crossley-Holland, Kevin. *Beowulf.* Illus. Charles Keeping. Oxford Univ. Press, 1982.

A gripping, memorable retelling in rhythmic, curt prose by a poet and Anglo-Saxon scholar. The sepia illustrations are shocking and cathartic in their nightmare beauty. A remarkable collaboration. Grades 4 and up.

Green, Roger Lancelyn. *King Arthur and His Knights of the Round Table.* Illus. Lotte Reiniger. Penguin, 1953.

Relying chiefly on Malory, Roger Lancelyn Green interposes and fills out the stories with other stories such as *Sir Gawain and the Green Knight.* The result is that all the stories are fitted together to tell the story of Arthur's kingdom. Grades 5 and up.

Hastings, Selina. *Sir Gawain and the Green Knight.* Illus. Juan Wijngaard. Lothrop, 1981.

A stunning book balancing an eloquent, contemporary retelling which retains the eery magic of the tale and magnificent, illuminated manuscript-style illustrations. Careful overall page design, decorative borders, and endpapers give this edition a medieval flavor. Grades 3–5.

Hieatt, Constance. *Sir Gawain and the Green Knight.* Illus. Walter Lorraine. Crowell, 1967.

A modern rendition that retains the flavor and cadence of King Arthur's court at Camelot. The author is not only a medieval scholar, but a good storyteller. Grades 3–5. See also *The Knight of the Lion* (1968); *The Knight of the Cart* (1969); *The Joy of the Court* (1971); *The Sword and the Grail* (1972); and *The Castle of Ladies* (1973).

Hosford, Dorothy. *By His Own Might: Battles of Beowulf.* Illus. Laszlo Matulay. Holt, 1947.

One of the best prose versions of the Anglo-Saxon epic. The heroic quality, the vigor, and the force of the original have been retained. Grades 6–8.

Macleod, Mary. *The Book of King Arthur and His Noble Knights: Stories from Sir Thomas Malory's Morte d'Arthur.* Intro. Angelo Patri; illus. Henry C. Pitz. Lippincott, Lippincott Classics, 1949.

Faithful to the spirit of the original, these stories are easier to read than Malory or Lanier, and shorter than Howard Pyle's stories. Grades 5–8.

McSpadden, J. Walker. *Robin Hood and His Merry Outlaws.* Intro. May Lamberton Becker; illus. Louis Slobodkin. World, Rainbow Classics, 1946.

Stories of the beloved outlaw and his merry men who went forth from Sherwood Forest to rob the rich in order to help the poor. Grades 6–8.

Malcolmson, Anne, ed. *Song of Robin Hood.* Musical arrangements, Grace Castagnetta; illus. Virginia Lee Burton. Houghton Mifflin, 1947.

A distinguished achievement. The editing of the eighteen ballads from the Robin Hood cycle is painstaking and scholarly. Each ballad is given in modern spelling and has been cut without hurting the original story. For each ballad Grace Castagnetta has given the original English music as far as it could be found. The illustrations are remarkable in their exquisite design. Grades 7–9.

Malory, Sir Thomas. *The Boy's King Arthur: Sir Thomas Malory's History of King Arthur and His Knights of the Round Table.* Ed. Sidney Lanier; illus. N. C. Wyeth. Scribner's, Scribner's Illustrated Classics, 1917.

Lanier's version follows Malory's *Morte d'Arthur,* which was published by Caxton in the latter part of the fifteenth century. Grades 5–9.

Malory, Sir Thomas. *King Arthur: Stories from the Author's Morte d'Arthur.* Retold Mary Macleod; illus. Herschel Levit; afterword, Clifton Fadiman. New ed. Macmillan, Macmillan Classics, 1963.

An attractive edition of the Arthurian legends. Grades 5–8.

Miles, Bernard. *Robin Hood: His Life and Legend.* Illus. Victor Ambrus. Rand McNally, 1979.

A simplified version of the standard legend in a large, sumptuous edition. The full-color illustrations create a heightened sense of drama and atmosphere. Grades 3–6.

Nye, Robert. *Beowulf: A New Telling.* Illus. Alan E. Cober. Hill & Wang, 1968.

A free re-creation of the story of Beowulf, this adventure of fearsome dragon slaying becomes part of the story of Beowulf, a human being. Grades 5–9.

Picard, Barbara Leonie. *Hero-Tales from the British Isles.* Illus. John G. Galsworthy. Criterion, 1963.

Tales of the folk heroes of England, Scotland, Ireland, and Wales. In brief notes the author relates these characters to history and folklore. Grades 5–8.

Picard, Barbara Leonie, ed. *Stories of King Arthur and His Knights.* Wood engravings, Roy Morgan. Oxford Univ. Press, 1955.

The editor avoids the use of archaic phraseology,

yet keeps the spirit of the Middle Ages. Grades 5–8.

Picard, Barbara Leonie, retel. *Tales of the British People.* Illus. Eric Fraser. Criterion, 1961.

Marvels and heroic deeds of the different peoples who settled in the British Isles: Iberians, Celts, Romans, Saxons, Danes, and Normans. Brief introductions before each story help place it historically, but the reader may read simply for enjoyment without them. Grades 5–10.

Pyle, Howard. *The Merry Adventures of Robin Hood of Great Renown in Nottinghamshire.* Illus. by the author. Scribner's, 1946.

No other version is comparable to this one by Howard Pyle. Grades 4–7. See also *Some Merry Adventures of Robin Hood of Great Renown in Nottinghamshire,* written and illus. by Howard Pyle, published in 1883. This edition, adapted from his longer work, contains twelve stories while the other contains twenty-two.

Pyle, Howard. *The Story of King Arthur and His Knights.* Illus. by the author. Scribner's, 1933.

First published in 1903, this is one of the best versions of the King Arthur stories. Followed by *The Story of the Champions of the Round Table; Sir Launcelot and His Companions;* and *The Story of the Grail and the Passing of Arthur.* Grades 5–8.

Riordan, James. *Tales of King Arthur.* Illus. Victor Ambrus. Rand McNally, 1982.

Forceful color paintings by an award-winning illustrator enhance this clear, modern version of the Arthurian legend in a large, handsome format. Grades 3–6.

Schiller, Barbara. *The Kitchen Knight.* Illus. Nonny Hogrogian. Holt, 1965.

An Arthurian legend of Gareth, who is knighted at the end of his term as kitchen boy at King Arthur's court. Grades 3–5. See also *The Wandering Knight,* illus. Herschel Levit (Dutton, 1971).

Serraillier, Ian. *Beowulf, the Warrior.* Illus. Severin. Walck, 1961.

The British poet retells the Anglo-Saxon verse epic. Grades 7–9.

Serraillier, Ian. *The Challenge of the Green Knight.* Illus. Victor G. Ambrus. Walck, 1967.

A spirited retelling in modern verse of the medieval epic *Sir Gawain and The Green Knight.* Grades 6–8.

Serraillier, Ian. *Robin in the Greenwood: Ballads of Robin Hood.* Illus. Victor G. Ambrus. Walck, 1968.

Since the story of Robin Hood was told originally in ballad form, this is a form that naturally suits. These are not the traditional ballads, but ones of Serraillier's writing, fashioned closely to the former. Grades 5–9.

Steinbeck, John, adapt. *The Acts of King Arthur and his Noble Knights from the Winchester Manuscripts of Thomas Malory and Other Sources.* Ed. Chase Horton. Farrar, Straus & Giroux, 1976.

An uncompleted version of Malory in forceful, modern English. True to the spirit of the original. Also available in paperback (Ballantine, 1977).

Sutcliff, Rosemary. *Beowulf.* Illus. Charles Keeping. Dutton, 1962.

A distinguished prose version hewing close to the original. Grades 6–9.

Sutcliff, Rosemary. *The Light beyond the Forest: The Quest for the Holy Grail.* Dutton, 1980.

A compelling, novelistic retelling of the grail quest. Modern psychological insight and Celtic mythic overtones create a uniquely original interpretation. Grades 5 and up. See also *The Sword and the Circle* (1981) and *The Road to Camlann: The Death of King Arthur* (1982).

Sutcliff, Rosemary. *Tristan and Iseult.* Dutton, 1971.

The ill-starred romance of Tristan and Iseult is told in a version that is exciting and compelling reading. Rosemary Sutcliff has gone back to the Celtic origins as much as possible, dispensing with the device of a magic love potion, keeping it a story of human love set in Cornwall. Grades 6–12.

Troughton, Joanna, retel. *Sir Gawain and the Loathly Damsel.* Illus. by the reteller. Macmillan, 1972.

Distinctive, colorful illustrations add atmosphere and drama to this sensitive adaptation of the riddle mystery quest. Based on the anonymous fifteenth-century poem, "The Wedynge of Sir Gawen and Dame Ragnell." Grades 3–6.

Ireland

De Paola, Tomie, retel. *Fin M'Coul the Giant of Knockmany Hill.* Illus. by the author. Holiday, 1981.

A whimsical picture-book version of the droll legend in which Fin's wife, Oonagh, helps him match wits with his enemy Cucullin. Grades 1–3.

Evslin, Bernard. *The Green Hero: Early Adventures of Finn McColl.* Illus. Barbara Bascove. Four Winds, 1975.

A contemporary tone permeates this novelistic approach to the Irish cycle of hero legends surrounding Finn McColl. Grades 5–7.

Hodges, Margaret, retel. *The Other World: Myths of the Celts.* Illus. Eros Keith. Farrar, Straus & Giroux, 1973.

Heroes with mythical auras, such as Arthur, Finn, the Swan Children, Dermot, and others are part of the Celtic tales, which are retold with a fine feeling for their sense of mysticism and the poetic phrasing that reflects the Celtic recognition of the "unearthly beauty just over the edge of the world." Grades 5–10.

Hull, Eleanor. *The Boys' Cuchulain: Heroic Legends of Ireland.* Illus. Stephen Reid. Crowell, 1910.

The story of the great legendary hero of Ireland told with beauty and dignity. Out of print, but may be found in libraries. Grades 7–9.

O'Faolain, Eileen, comp. *Irish Sagas and Folk Tales.* Illus. Joan Kiddell-Monroe. Oxford Univ. Press, Oxford Myths and Legends, 1954.

A good introduction to the wonders of Irish folklore. Eileen O'Faolain retells the sagas with a simplicity that retains the majesty of the original tales. Grades 5–8.

Reeves, James. *Maildun the Voyager.* Illus. Rocco Negri. Walck, 1971.

Vengeance spurs Maildun, but when he finally catches up with his father's murderer, the desire for vengeance has changed. Maildun's voyages are filled with events of a marvelous and extraordinary nature. Freely adapted from a translation of an Irish manuscript, dated around 1100. Grades 5–9.

Stephens, James. *Irish Fairy Tales.* Illus. Arthur Rackham. Macmillan, 1920; reissued 1968.

The poet and writer James Stephens has told these ten hero tales and legends with the spirit and style of absolute belief. Grades 5–12.

Sutcliff, Rosemary. *The High Deeds of Finn Mac Cool.* Illus. Michael Charlton. Dutton, 1967.

Fifteen tales of the legendary Irish hero. Grades 6–8.

Sutcliff, Rosemary. *The Hound of Ulster.* Illus. Victor Ambrus. Dutton, 1964.

A retelling in strong poetic prose of the exploits of Cuchulain. Grades 6–9.

Young, Ella. *The Tangle-Coated Horse.* Illus. Vera Bock. David McKay, 1968.

Episodes from the Finn saga. A hero tale magnificent in the beauty of the telling and the magnitude of its wonders. A reissue, first published by Longmans in 1929. Grades 5–7.

Young, Ella. *The Wonder Smith and His Son: A Tale from the Golden Childhood of the World.* Illus. Boris Artzybasheff. Longmans, 1927.

Fourteen tales from the legendary cycle of Gubbaun Saor, a mythological figure of Ireland. Ella Young spent twenty years collecting tales, which were told to her in Gaelic. She has retold them as only a poet can. Grades 4–6.

Scotland

Nic Leodhas, Sorche. *Claymore and Kilt: Tales of Scottish Kings and Castles.* Illus. Leo Dillon and Diane Dillon. Holt, 1967.

Stories that range in time from A.D. 211 to A.D. 1611; they center around such figures as MacBeth, Bruce, Columba. The background of each story is recounted in the introduction. Grades 6–10.

Wales

Nye, Robert. *Taliesin.* Illus. Dorothy Maas. Hill & Wang, 1967.

A story from the Mabinogion tells of the incredible, joyous exploits of Taliesin, a Welsh poet. Grades 6–8.

Schiller, Barbara, retel. and adapt. *Erec and Enid.* Illus. Ati Forberg. Dutton, 1970.

A charmingly told adventure and romance in which one of Arthur's knights rides off to avenge an insult and finds his own true love. Grades 4–7.

Arabia

Davis, Russell, and Brent Ashabranner. *Ten Thousand Desert Swords: The Epic Story of a Great Bedouin Tribe.* Illus. Leonard Everett Fisher. Little, Brown, 1960.

One of the great epics of Arab literature of the Bani Hilal tribe of desert warriors who roamed throughout ancient Arabia, Iraq, and Syria into northern Africa. Grades 7–9.

Austria

Sawyer, Ruth, and Emmy Mollès. *Dietrich of Berne and the Dwarf King Laurin.* Illus. Frederick T. Chapman. Viking, 1963.

The blending of the magical with the historical

makes the book a good introduction to legendary hero tales. Grades 4–6.

Denmark

Crossley-Holland, Kevin. *Havelok the Dane.* Illus. Brian Wildsmith. Dutton, 1966.

The author has retold in a vigorous manner the original story based on legendary material from the Viking period. Grades 8–9.

Serraillier, Ian. *Havelok the Dane.* Illus. Elaine Raphael. Walck, 1967.

A vigorous retelling in prose of the famous medieval poem, *The Lay of Havelok the Dane,* about the son of the King of Denmark who grew up in poverty and kept his royal birth a secret until he was able to return and claim his kingdom. Grades 4–8.

Finland

Deutsch, Babette. *Heroes of the Kalevala: Finland's Saga.* Illus. Fritz Eichenberg. Messner, 1940.

A distinguished retelling of the Finnish epic, by a well-known poet. Grades 6–9.

Kaplan, Irma. *Heroes of Kalevala.* Illus. Barbara Brown. Muller, 1973.

A simple retelling of some of the exploits and adventures of Wänämöinen, Ilmarinen, and other characters of the Finnish epic. Grades 4–6.

Synge, Ursula, adapt. *Land of Heroes: A Retelling of the Kalevala.* Atheneum, 1978.

Three tales from the Finnish epic interwoven to form a single entity. A fine retelling. Grades 6 and up.

France

Baldwin, James. *The Story of Roland.* Illus. Peter Hurd. Scribner's, Scribner's Illustrated Classics, 1930.

Legends of Charlemagne and his nephew Roland woven into a continuous narrative. Grades 6–8.

Reeves, James. *The Shadow of the Hawk.* Illus. Anne Dalton. Collins, 1975.

A collection of courtly love stories and medieval romances taken from the twelfth-century cycle of French narrative poems, the *Lays of Marie de France.* The stories retain the psychological realism and poetic, vivid imagery of the original. Grades 5 and up.

Sherwood, Merriam, ed. *The Song of Roland.* Illus. Edith Emerson. Longmans, 1938.

Based on the Oxford manuscript, this excellent prose version of the *Chanson de Roland* begins with Ganelon's treachery and covers the death of Roland and Oliver and the final triumph of Charlemagne over the Saracens. Grades 7–9.

Williams, Jay. *The Horn of Roland.* Illus. Sean Morrison. Crowell, 1968.

The most familiar episodes from the "Song of Roland" retold for younger children. Grades 4–6.

Germany

Almedingen, E. M. *The Treasure of Siegfried.* Illus. Charles Keeping. Lippincott, 1965.

A retelling of one of the greatest of the German heroic epics. Grades 7–9. See also *The Story of Gudrun,* illus. Enrico Arno (Norton, 1967).

Baldwin, James. *The Story of Siegfried.* Illus. Peter Hurd. Scribner's, Scribner's Illustrated Classics, 1931.

The best rendition for children of the Siegfried legends based on the *Eddas,* the *Volsunga Saga,* and the *Nibelungenlied.* Grades 6–8.

Koenig, Alma Johanna. *Gudrun.* Trans. Anthea Bell. Lothrop, 1979.

Considered a companion piece to the *Nibelungenlied,* this thirteenth-century heroic romance tells the story of the kidnapping, ordeal, and rescue of the beautiful and strong-willed Gudrun. Retold in 1928 by a respected Austrian poet and novelist in a lyrical prose version based on the original epic poem, this German classic dramatizes elements of high romance—love, honor, and treachery—in the tradition of the Arthurian "Tristan and Iseult" and the Celtic "Deirdre." Grades 5 and up.

Picard, Barbara Leonie. *German Hero-Sagas and Folk Tales.* Illus. Joan Kiddell-Monroe. Oxford Univ. Press, Oxford Myths and Legends, 1958.

Hero sagas: *Gudrun; Dietrich of Berne; Walther of Aquitaine;* and *Siegfried.* Several folktales are also included. Grades 5–8.

Hawaii

Brown, Marcia. *Backbone of the King: The Story of Paka à and His Son Ku.* Illus. by the author. Scribner's, 1966.

Hawaii's ancient culture has been captured in this distinguished tale of legendary heroism. Marcia Brown found the legend while living in the Hawaiian Islands. She based the retelling on *The Hawaiian Story of Paka à and Kuapaka à the Personal Attendants of Keawenuiaumi,* of Moses K. Nakuina. More than fifty linoleum woodcuts reflect a strength equal to the epic quality of the legend. Grades 7–9.

Thompson, Vivian L. *Aukele the Fearless.* Illus. Earl Thollander. Golden Gate Junior Books, 1972.
    Aukele, the youngest of eleven brothers, is the favored of his father, the persecuted of his oldest brother. Magic comes to Aukele's aid, not only with his brothers, but with his sorceress wife. This story originated in Tahiti and was brought to Hawaii. Grades 4–7.

Hungary

Seredy, Kate. *The White Stag.* Illus. by the author. Viking, 1937.
    The epic story of the migration of the Huns and Magyars from Asia to Europe and the legendary founding of Hungary. The illustrations are breathtaking in their dramatic power. Awarded the Newbery Medal, 1938. Grades 7–9.

India

Gaer, Joseph. *The Adventures of Rama.* Illus. Randy Monk. Little, Brown, 1954.
    A dramatic version of the great Hindu epic, *Ramayana,* the ancient story of Rama and Sita and their struggles with the evils of the world. The author, well known for his books on the world's religions, explains in notes the various extant versions and the evolution of the epic from the earliest times. Grades 7–9.

Seeger, Elizabeth. *The Five Sons of King Pandu: The Story of the Mahabhárata.* Adapt. from the English translation of Kisari Mohan Ganguli; illus. Gordon Laite. Scott, 1967.
    This is one of the great hero tales of the world. Five Hindu princes struggle to regain their kingdom in northern India. Grades 7 and up. See also *The Ramáyana,* adapt. from the English translation of Hari Prasad Shastri; illus. Gordon Laite (Scott, 1969).

Thompson, Brian, retel. *The Story of Prince Rama.* Kestrel, 1980.
    A fine retelling of Rama and Sita's exile is enhanced by colorful traditional Indian paintings. Picture-book format. Grades 3–5.

Japan

Carlson, Dale. *Warlord of the Genji.* Illus. John Gretzer. Atheneum, 1970.
    Japan's two warring clans, the Heike and the Genji, are pitted against each other in this account of the greatest of the Genji, the young warlord, Yoshitsune. Grades 5–12.

Edmonds, I. G. *The Possible Impossibles of Ikkyu the Wise.* Illus. Robert Byrd. Macrae Smith, 1971.
    The wisdom, wit, and ingenuity of a Japanese folk hero, Ikkyu, are conveyed in these twenty stories, which were collected in Japan by the reteller. Grades 4–7.

Persia

Ensor, Dorothy. *The Adventures of Hatim Tai.* Illus. Pauline Baynes. Walck, 1962.
    An adaptation of a lengthy Persian hero tale about the legendary feats of Hatim Tai. Grades 5–6.

Picard, Barbara Leonie, retel. *Tales of Ancient Persia.* Walck, 1972.
    Rustem, son of Zal, is a continuing hero in these tales of warring adventures of pre-Islamic times, retold from the *Shah-Nama* of Firdausi. Grades 5–9.

U.S.S.R.

Almedingen, E. M. *The Knights of the Golden Table.* Illus. Charles Keeping. Lippincott, 1964.
    Twelve stories about Prince Vladimir of Kiev remind one of the Arthurian legends. The Knights of the Golden Table put duty first, defending Vladimir's palace and the city of Kiev from every invading evil. A good introduction gives background of the Kiev cycle. Grades 6–8.

Serbia

Prodanovie, Nada Cureija. *Heroes of Serbia.* Illus. Dustan Ristic. Walck, 1964.
    Epic cycle of ballads celebrating the heroic exploits of Serbian heroes. Scholarly notes and comments. Grades 7–9.

Spain

Goldston, Robert C. *The Legend of the Cid.* Illus. Stephane. Bobbs-Merrill, 1963.

Told in direct style, this may serve to introduce the Spanish classic to children who are not quite ready for Merriam Sherwood's *The Tale of the Warrior Lord.* Grades 5–7.

Lauritzen, Jonreed. *Blood, Banners and Wild Boars: Tales of Early Spain.* Illus. Gil Miret. Little, Brown, 1967.

Heroic exploits during Spain's long history of small wars and resistance to invaders are recounted by Lauritzen. Grades 4–8.

Sherwood, Merriam, trans. *The Tale of the Warrior Lord, El Cantar de Mio Cid.* Illus. Henry C. Pitz. Longmans, 1930.

A dramatic prose translation of the famous twelfth-century poem that recounts the great deeds of the Spanish hero, Rodrigo Diaz de Bivar, called the Cid, meaning The Chief. Grades 7–9.

References for Adults*

Books

Abbott, Charles D. *Howard Pyle.* Intro. N. C. Wyeth. Harper, 1925.

The chapters "Magic Casements" and "The Middle Ages" deal particularly with his books for children.

Ashe, Geoffrey. *All about King Arthur.* Allen, 1969.

An investigation into the historicity of the Arthurian legends.

Bellows, Henry Adams, trans. *The Poetic Edda.* American Scandinavian Foundation, 1926.

Translated from the Icelandic, with an introduction and notes.

Brown, A. C. L. *Origin of the Grail Legend.* Harvard Univ. Press, 1943.

Bulfinch, Thomas. *Mythology; the Age of Fable; the Age of Chivalry; Legends of Charlemagne.* Illus. Elinore Blaisdell. Rev. ed. Crowell, 1962.

Thomas Bulfinch, the son of a famous Boston architect, was the first to popularize classical myths in America. He published *The Age of Fable* in 1855, *The Age of Chivalry* in 1858, and *The Romance of the Middle Ages* in 1863. All three are found in this volume, which has become a standard reference book.

Colum, Padraic. *Myths of the World.* Engravings, Boris Artzybasheff. Grosset & Dunlap, 1959.

* See also bibliography for Chapter 8, "Myths, Legends, and Sacred Writings."

First published under the title *Orpheus.* A scholarly addition to the study of mythology because of the fine retelling of the myths and the valuable discussion of their significance and characteristics.

de Vries, Jan. *Heroic Song and Heroic Legend.* Trans. B. J. Timmer. Oxford Univ. Press, 1963.

Guerber, Hélène A. *The Book of the Epic: The World's Great Epics Told in Story.* Lippincott, 1913.

Hero tales from all over the world. An introduction giving historical background and indicating sources precedes each tale.

Gutman, Robert W., ed. *Volsunga Saga.* Trans. William Morris. Collier, 1962. (paperback)

The Scandinavian cycle of legends was the principal source of the German epic poem, the *Nibelungenlied,* and of Wagner's opera-cycle, *Der Ring des Nibelungen.* The saga takes its name from Volsung, grandson of the god Odin, and father of Sigmund. The hero Sigurd, or Siegfried, is Sigmund's son.

Hamilton, Edith. *Mythology.* Illus. Steele Savage. Little, Brown, 1942.

Scholarship and imagination vitalize the retelling of these Greek, Roman, and Norse myths. Invaluable both as a reference book and for reading.

Hesiod. *Works, with Homeric Hymns.* Harvard Univ. Press, n.d.

The Homeric Hymns furnish valuable source material.

Hicks, Edward. *Sir Thomas Malory: A Biography.* Harvard Univ. Press, 1928.

Hoffman, Alice S. *The Book of the Sagas.* Dutton, 1913.

Homer. *The Odyssey.* Trans. George Herbert Palmer; illus. N. C. Wyeth. Houghton Mifflin, 1929.

Rendered into rhythmic prose, this is one of the best translations. Anyone beginning to study Homer should read the chapter "Blind Homer" in *The Winged Horse,* by Joseph Auslander and Frank Ernest Hill (Doubleday, 1954).

Homer. *The Odyssey of Homer.* Trans. Richard Lattimore. Harper, 1965.

An eloquent modern translation.

Hull, Eleanor, ed. *The Cuchulain Saga in Irish Literature.* D. Nutt, 1898.

Ker, W. P. *English Literature: Mediaeval.* 6th ed. Thornton Butterworth, Home Univ. Library, 1932.

Koht, Halvdan. *The Old Norse Sagas.* American Scandinavian Foundation, 1945.

Malory, Sir Thomas. *The Morte d'Arthur.* Intro. A. Pollard. 2 vols. Macmillan, Library of English Classics, 1900.

Malory, Sir Thomas. *The Works of Sir Thomas Malory.* Ed. Eugène Vinaver. Oxford Univ. Press, 1947.

Morris, William. *The Story of Sigurd the Volsung and the Fall of the Nibelungs.* Longmans, 1924.
Available in paperback: *Volsunga Saga: The Story of the Volsungs and Nibelungs,* intro. and glossary, Robert W. Gutman. Collier, 1962.

Ovid. *Metamorphoses.* Trans. Rolfe Humphries. Indiana Univ. Press, 1955.
This series of tales, originally written in Latin verse by the Roman poet Ovid, deals with legendary and historical figures. Ovid's retellings of the Greek myths and legends form the principal source of these tales.

Phillpotts, Bertha. *Edda and Saga.* Trans. Arthur Gilchrist Brodeue. American Scandinavian Foundation, 1929; Holt, 1932.

Rank, Otto. *The Myth of the Birth of the Hero: A Psychological Interpretation of Mythology.* Trans. F. Robbins and Smith Ely Jellife. Brunner/Mazel, 1952.

Schwab, Gustav. *Gods and Heroes: Myths and Epics of Ancient Greece.* Trans. Olga Marx and Ernest Morwitz; intro. Werner Jaeger. Pantheon, 1946.
For these myths and tales of antiquity, Schwab went back to source material, taking fragments from Hesiod, Homer, Ovid, and from the Greek tragedians Aeschylus, Sophocles, and Euripides, and weaving them into one continuous narrative. Illustrated with 100 sketches from Greek vase paintings.

Smith, Ruth, ed. *The Tree of Life: Selections from the Literature of the World's Religions.* Illus. Boris Artzybasheff; intro. Robert O. Ballou. Viking, 1942.
Selected writings from the literature of the mythologies and religions of all ages.

Sturluson, Snorri. *The Prose Edda.* Trans. Arthur Gilchrist Brodeue. American Scandinavian Foundation, 1929.

Warner, Rex. *The Stories of the Greeks.* Illus. with photographs. MacGibbon & Kee, 1967.
Three books are republished here: *Men and Gods* (1950), from Ovid's *Metamorphoses; Greeks and Trojans* (1951), dramatic account of the Trojan war; and *The Vengeance of the Gods* (1954), material from Greek plays.

Weston, Jessie L. *From Ritual to Romance.* Doubleday Anchor, 1957 (originally published by Cambridge Univ. Press, 1920).

Woolf, Virginia. "On Not Knowing Greek." In *The Common Reader,* pp. 39–61. Harcourt, 1925.

Articles

Auslander, Joseph, and Frank Hill. "Blind Homer." In *The Winged Horse: The Story of the Poets and Their Poetry,* pp. 19–30. Doubleday, 1927.

Bowers, Gwendolyn. "Legends of the Grail." *The Horn Book Magazine,* 42 (Feb. 1966), pp. 37–42.

Brown, Marcia. "The Hero Within." *Elementary English,* 44 (Mar. 1967), pp. 201–7.

Echols, Ula W. "The Newer Interpretations of Epic Heroes." *Children's Library Yearbook,* American Library Association, no. 4, 1932, pp. 48–56.

Hosford, Dorothy. "Our Northern Heritage." *The Horn Book Magazine,* 23 (Sept.–Oct. 1947), pp. 371–77.

Lawson, Robert. "Howard Pyle and His Times." In *Illustrators of Children's Books, 1744–1945.* Horn Book, 1947.

Oakley, Thornton. "Howard Pyle." *The Horn Book Magazine,* 7 (1931), pp. 91–97.

Sayers, Frances Clarke. "The Flowering Dusk of Ella Young." In *Summoned by Books: Essays and Speeches,* pp. 133–39. Viking, 1965.

Seeger, Elizabeth. "Dhan Mukerji and His Books." *The Horn Book Magazine,* 13 (July–Aug. 1937), pp. 199–205.

Stein, Ruth M. "The Changing Styles in Dragons— from Fáfnir to Smaug." *Elementary English,* 45 (Feb. 1968), pp. 179–83, 189.

Wood, Jessica. "Unafraid of Greatness." *The Horn Book Magazine,* 32, Part 1 (Apr. 1956), pp. 127–36; Part 2 (June 1956), pp. 212–18, 222.

10   Storytelling

Books

Andersen, Lorrie, Irene Aubrey, and Louise McDiarmid, eds. *Storytellers' Rendezvous: Canadian Stories to Tell to Children.* Illus. Bo Kim Louie. Canadian Library Association, 1979.
> See also *Storytellers' Encore: More Canadian Stories to Tell to Children* (1984).

Baker, Augusta, and Ellin Greene. *Storytelling: Art and Technique.* Bowker, 1978.

Bauer, Caroline Feller. *Handbook for Storytellers.* American Library Association, 1977. See also *This Way to Books* (Wilson, 1983).

Bryant, Sara Cone. *How to Tell Stories to Children.* Gale, 1973.

Colum, Padraic. *Storytelling New and Old.* Illus. Jay Van Everen. Macmillan, 1968.

Colwell, Eileen, ed. *A Storyteller's Choice: A Selection of Stories, with Notes on How to Tell Them.* Walck, 1964.
> See also *Storyteller's Second Choice* (1965); *Round About and Long Ago* (Houghton Mifflin, 1974); *Humblepuppy, and Other Stories for Telling* (Bodley Head, 1978); and *Storytelling* (Bodley Head, 1983).

De Wit, Dorothy. *Children's Faces Looking Up: Program Building for the Storyteller.* American Library Association, 1979.

Haviland, Virginia. *Ruth Sawyer.* Walck, A Walck Monograph, 1965.

Pellowski, Anne. *The World of Storytelling.* Bowker, 1977.

Peterson, Carolyn Sue, and Brenny Hall. *Story Programs: A Source of Materials.* Scarecrow, 1980.

Ross, Eulalie Steinmetz, ed. *The Lost Half-Hour: A Collection of Stories with a Chapter on How to Tell a Story.* Illus. Enrico Arno. Harcourt, 1963.

Sawyer, Ruth. *The Way of the Storyteller.* Rev. ed. Viking, 1962.
> See also *My Spain* (1967).

Schimmel, Nancy. *Just Enough to Make a Story: A Sourcebook for Storytelling.* 2d ed. Sisters' Choice, 1982.

Shedlock, Marie L. *The Art of the Storyteller.* Foreword, Anne Carroll Moore. Rev. ed. Dover, 1951.

Wilson, Jane B. *The Story Experience.* Scarecrow, 1979.

Ziskind, Sylvia. *Telling Stories to Children.* Wilson, 1976.

Lists

Association for Library Service to Children. *Storytelling: Readings/Bibliographies/Resources.* Pamphlet by the Association for Library Service to Children, American Library Association, 1978.

Cathon, Laura E., et al., ed. *Stories To Tell to Children.* Carnegie Library of Pittsburgh, 4400 Forbes Ave., Pittsburgh, Pa. 15213. 8th rev. ed., 1974.

Hardendorff, Jeanne B., ed. *Stories to Tell.* Enoch Pratt Free Library, 400 Cathedral St., Baltimore, Md. 21201. 5th ed., 1965.

Iarusso, Marilyn B., ed. *Stories: A List of Stories to Tell and to Read Aloud.* New York Public Library. 7th rev. ed., 1977.

New York Public Library. *Once upon a Time.* Ed. by a committee of the New York Public Library. Rev. ed., 1964.

Articles

Armstrong, Helen. "Hero Tales for Telling." *The Horn Book Magazine,* 25 (Feb. 1949), pp. 9–15.

Britton, Jasmine. "Gudrun Thorne-Thomsen: Storyteller from Norway." *The Horn Book Magazine,* 34 (Feb. 1958), pp. 17–29.

Laughton, Charles. "Storytelling." *Atlantic Monthly,* (June 1950), pp. 71–73.

Mahony, Bertha E. "Guide to Treasure." *The Horn Book Magazine,* 16 (May 1940), pp. 177–85.

Nesbit, Elizabeth. "The Art of Storytelling." *The Horn Book Magazine,* 21 (Nov. 1945), pp. 439–44.

Nesbit, Elizabeth. "Hold to That Which Is Good." *The Horn Book Magazine,* 16 (May 1940), pp. 7–15.

Pellowski, Anne. "Children's Stories around the World." Transcription by Barbara A. Kilpatrick. *Catholic Library World,* 51 (1979), pp. 76–78.

The Ruth Sawyer Issue. *The Horn Book Magazine,* 41, pp. 474–86.

Sawyer, Ruth. *How to Tell a Story.* Pamphlet. Compton, 1965.

Sawyer, Ruth. "Storytelling Fifty Years A-Growing." In *Reading Without Boundaries,* ed. Frances Lander Spain, pp. 59–64. New York Public Library, 1956.

Sayers, Frances Clark. "Enriching Literature through Storytelling." Association of Childhood Education, Leaflet no. 9, "Adventuring in Literature with Children."

Sicherman, Ruth. "Time To Tell an Andersen Tale." *Top of the News,* 30 (Jan. 1974), pp. 161–68.

Spain, Frances Lander. "A Storyteller's Approach to Children's Books." In *The Contents of the Basket,* ed. Frances Lander Spain, pp. 51–59. New York Public Library, 1960.

Storytelling Issue of *The Horn Book Magazinne,* 10 (May 1934); and 59 (June 1983).

Sutcliff, Rosemary. "Beginning with Beowulf." *The Horn Book Magazine,* 29 (Feb. 1953), pp. 36–38.

Thorne-Thomsen, Gudrun. "Storytelling and Stories I Tell." In Memoriam: A pamphlet. Viking, 1956.

Viguers, Ruth Hill. "Over the Drawbridge and into the Castle." *The Horn Book Magazine,* 27 (Jan. 1951), pp. 54–62.

Excerpts from Books

Sayers, Frances Clarke. "From Me to You." In *Summoned by Books: Essays and Speeches by Frances Clarke Sayers.* Viking, 1965.

Sayers, Frances Clarke. "The Storyteller's Art." In *Summoned by Books: Essays and Speeches.* Viking, 1965.

IV Fiction: The Storied World

11 Encounters and Adventures: Realistic and Historical Fiction

Books for Children

Alcott, Louisa M. *Little Women.* Illus. Barbara Cooney. Crowell, 1955.

First published in 1868, this is an attractive edition of an old favorite with drawings made at the Alcott home in Concord, Massachusetts. Grades 5–8. See also the Alcott Centennial Edition, illustrated by Jessie Willcox Smith (Little, Brown, 1968), and the edition illustrated by Tasha Tudor (World, 1969).

Almedingen, E. M. *Stephen's Light.* Holt, 1965.

The fascination of commerce in the fifteenth century is presented with colorful and romantic detail in this novel about one of the few women who took an active role in that century and activity. Grades 7–12. See also *Young Mark* (Farrar, Straus & Giroux, 1968) and other titles.

Armstrong, William. *Sounder.* Illus. James Barkley. Harper, 1969.

The ability to endure and survive against great odds is shown in this powerful novel of devotion. Awarded the Newbery Medal in 1970. Grades 6–12.

Arundel, Honor. *Emma in Love.* Nelson, 1972.

A realistic story of first love deals with the surprise and pain of its ending. See also *Emma's Island* (Hawthorn, 1970). Grades 5–8.

Avery, Gillian. *A Likely Lad.* Illus. Faith Jaques. Holt, 1971.

Young Willy Overs finds his father's aspirations for him a heavy burden to bear in this story of middle-class rivalries, set in the late nineteenth century. Grades 5–9.

Bagnold, Enid. *National Velvet.* Illus. Paul Brown. Morrow, 1949.

A horse won in a raffle wins the Grand National. Grades 5–12.

Baumann, Hans. *The Caves of the Great Hunters.* Trans. Isabel McHugh and Florence McHugh; illus. Hans Peter Renner. Rev. ed. Pantheon, 1962.

A fictional account of an event that did take place: the discovery of early cave paintings in France by four boys. Grades 5–8.

Bawden, Nina. *Three on the Run.* Lippincott, 1965.

The discovery that a boy living near him is the center of a complicated political abduction plot causes Ben, his new friend, and a young girl to attempt to elude the pursuing conspirators. Grades 4–7. See also *The Runaway Summer* (1969); *Squib* (1971); *Carrie's War* (1973); and *The Peppermint Pig* (1975).

Benary-Isbert, Margot. *The Ark.* Trans. Clara Winston and Richard Winston. Harcourt, 1953.

The heroic and human struggle of a refugee family to salvage their lives in post-World War II Germany is made poignant by their sense of the dignity of life and the meaning of celebration. Grades 5–9. Followed by *Rowan Farm* (1954).

Blos, Joan W. *A Gathering of Days: A New England Girl's Journal, 1830–1832.* Scribner's, 1979.

Journal entries provide insight into the emotional life and personal growth of a young nineteenth-century girl during two turbulent years. Closely observed, full of incident and emotion. Awarded the Newbery Medal in 1980. Grades 5–9.

Blume, Judy. *Tales of a Fourth Grade Nothing.* Illus. Roy Doty. Dutton, 1972.

A young boy is embarrassed by the comic antics of his brother, an irrepressible preschooler. Grades 2–4.

Brink, Carol. *Caddie Woodlawn.* Illus. Kate Seredy. Macmillan, 1935.

A tomboy of the 1860s, Caddie has more trouble trying to behave like a lady than she has with the Indians of the Wisconsin frontier. Awarded the Newbery Medal in 1936. Grades 4–7.

Burnett, Frances Hodgson. *The Secret Garden.* Illus. Tasha Tudor. Lippincott, 1962.

Evoking the mood and beauty of the English moors, this story of a disagreeable girl who painfully grew in strength and laughter is told in the romantic tradition. First published in 1911.

Burnford, Sheila. *The Incredible Journey.* Illus. Carl Burger. Little, Brown, 1961.

A Labrador retriever, a Siamese cat, and an old bull terrier go on a 250-mile trek through the Canadian wilderness to find their master. Grades 5–9.

Burton, Hester. *Beyond the Weir Bridge.* Illus. Victor G. Ambrus. Crowell, 1970.

Persecution of Quakers during the years 1651 through 1667 is the core of this story, which also develops the friendship and love of three young people. Grades 5–12. See also *Time of Trial* (World, 1964), which received the 1963 Carnegie Award; *No Beat of Drum* (World, 1967); *In Spite of All Terror* (World, 1969); *The Rebel* (Crowell, 1972); and *Kate Ryder* (Crowell, 1975).

Byars, Betsy. *The Summer of the Swans.* Illus. Ted CoConis. Viking, 1970.

A girl's perceptions of herself and her feelings for others around her become clarified when the neighbors join in a search for her mentally retarded brother. Awarded the Newbery Medal in 1971. Grades 4–7. See also *The Midnight Fox* (1968); *The House of Wings* (1972); *The Eighteenth Emergency* (1973); *The TV Kid* (1976); *The Pinballs* (1977); and *The Night Swimmers* (Delacorte, 1980).

Cameron, Eleanor. *A Room Made of Windows.* Illus. Trina Schart Hyman. Little, Brown, 1971.

The "writer's eye" of a young girl encompasses the lives of people living around her, as the poetry and excitement of the visual world are noted down in her book. Grades 5–7. See also the young writer, Julia, observed at earlier stages in her life in *Julia and the Hand of God,* illus. Gail Owens (Dutton, 1977), and *That Julia Redfern,* illus. Gail Owens (Dutton, 1982).

Carlson, Natalie Savage. *The Family under the Bridge.* Illus. Garth Williams. Harper, 1958.

Three irrepressible French orphans encroach upon the life of an elderly tramp when they move in under the bridge with him. Grades 3–5. See also *The Happy Orpheline* and others.

Cervantes Saavedra, Miguel de. *The Adventures of Don Quixote de la Mancha.* Adapt. Leighton Barret; illus. Warren Chappel. Knopf, 1939.

Dramatic illustrations fit well the Spanish satire of the knight-errant who tilted at windmills. Grades 5–9. See also *The Exploits of Don Quixote,* retold by James Reeves, illus. Edward Ardizzone (Walck, 1960), and *The Adventures of Don Quixote,* illus. W. Heath Robinson (Dutton, 1962).

Church, Richard. *Five Boys in a Cave.* Day, 1951.

An adventure in a cave becomes a life-risking experience that forces to the surface surprising aspects of each boy's character. Grades 4–7.

Clark, Joan. *The Hand of Robin Squires.* Illus. William Taylor and Mary Cserepy. Clarke, Irwin, 1977.

Set off the coast of Nova Scotia in the early eighteenth century, this is a gripping tale of mystery and adventure in which a twelve-year-old boy outwits his pirate uncle. Grades 5 and up.

Cleary, Beverly. *Dear Mr. Henshaw.* Illus. Paul O. Zelinsky. Morrow, 1983.

In this Newbery Medal winner for 1984, Cleary turns from her immensely popular, lighthearted stories of ordinary children's daily trials and discoveries to a more serious theme. Through the epistolary technique of letter and diary entries, Leigh Botts documents his ambivalent emotions towards his divorced parents and finds a burgeoning new identity as a beginning writer. Grades 4–6.

Cleary, Beverly. *Henry and Ribsy.* Illus. Louis Darling. Morrow, 1954.

One of the delightful Henry Huggins books in which Henry and his dog Ribsy get involved in all sorts of amusing predicaments. Grades 2–4. See also *Ramona the Pest* (1968); *Ramona the Brave* (1975); *Ramona and Her Father* (1977); *Ramona and Her Mother* (1979); and *Ramona Quimby, Age 8* (1981).

Cleaver, Vera, and Bill Cleaver. *Where the Lilies Bloom.* Illus. Jim Spanfeller. Lippincott, 1969.

A regional novel with strong, idiomatic dialogue whose narrator is Mary Call, the strong bulwark of a fatherless family. Grade 6 and up.

Collier, James Lincoln, and Christopher Collier. *My Brother Sam Is Dead.* Four Winds, 1974.

The turmoil and stress in a family when, against family wishes, a son goes off to war are the same emotions that exist in 1776 or 1976. An emotional and different view of the Revolutionary War. Grades 5 and up. See also *The Bloody Country* (1977).

Cormier, Robert. *The Chocolate War.* Pantheon, 1974.

A tragic, harshly realistic story of the struggle between personal conscience and social conformity. This parable of power, evil, and free will is set in the microcosm of a New England boy's school. Grades 6 and up. See also *I Am the Cheese* (1977); *After the First Death* (1979); and *The Bumblebee Flies Anyway* (Knopf, 1983).

Cresswell, Helen. *Ordinary Jack.* Illus. Jill Bennett. Macmillan, 1977.

The first in a riotous series about an eccentric British family of geniuses. The episodic adventures of an ordinary boy trying to make his mark in an absurd and brilliant family are told with wry wit and broad slapstick. Grades 4–8. See also *Absolute Zero* (1978); *Bagthorpe Unlimited* (1978); *Bagthorpes v. the World* (1979); and other titles in this series.

Defoe, Daniel. *Robinson Crusoe.* Illus. N. C. Wyeth. Scribner's, 1983.

First written for adults in 1719, this great adventure story has been taken over by the children. With dramatic, painterly illustrations by a pioneer American illustrator. Grades 5 and up.

DeJong, Meindert. *The Wheel on the School.* Illus. Maurice Sendak. Harper, 1954.

A story of the efforts of six schoolchildren to bring back the storks to their little Dutch village. Awarded the Newbery Medal in 1955. Grades 4–7. See also *The House of Sixty Fathers* (1956), a realistic story of China during the early days of the Japanese invasion, told with dramatic power, and *Journey from Peppermint Street,* which won the National Book Award in 1969.

Dickinson, Peter. *Tulku.* Dutton, 1979.

Set at the time of the Boxer Rebellion in China, this impressive novel chronicles the growth of a young adolescent boy. After the death of his father, Theodore joins forces with a dramatic and slightly shady Cockney actress on her way to Tibet. Distinguished by fully realized characters and subtle philosophical speculation. Winner of the Carnegie Medal in 1979. Grades 6 and up. See also the sixth-century Byzantine story, *The Dancing Bear* (Atlantic/Little, Brown, 1973).

Dillon, Eilís. *A Family of Foxes.* Illus. Vic Donahue. Funk & Wagnalls, 1964.

A conspiracy of boys keeps a family of foxes alive on the island where they have been washed ashore. Grades 4–7. See also *The Sea Wall* (1965) and *A Herd of Deer* (1969).

Dodge, Mary Mapes. *Hans Brinker; or The Silver Skates.* Illus. George W. Edwards. Scribner's, 1915.

Written in 1865, this is still one of the best stories of Holland. Grades 4–6.

Doyle, Brian. *Up to Low.* Douglas & McIntyre, 1982.

Winner of the Canadian Library Association Book of the Year Award for Children in 1983, this is a bittersweet story of a teenage boy's journey into Canada's Gatineau hills and the revelations he finds there. Stylized characterization and rolling tall-tale gags are balanced by a poignant tenderness and psychological realism. Grades 6–9.

Enright, Elizabeth. *The Saturdays*. Illus. by the author. Rinehart, 1941.

A highly diverting story of four motherless children, an understanding father, and Cuffy the housekeeper. Grades 4–6. See also *Thimble Summer,* winner of the Newbery Medal in 1939, and *Gone-Away Lake,* one of the runners-up in 1958.

Estes, Eleanor. *The Moffats*. Illus. Louis Slobodkin. Harcourt, 1941.

The Moffat family did not have much in the way of worldly goods, but there was always fun and laughter in the little house on New Dollar Street. Grades 4–6. See also *The Middle Moffat* and *Rufus M; Ginger Pye,* winner of the Newbery Medal in 1952; and *The Hundred Dresses,* a tender story of a little Polish girl.

Field, Rachel. *Calico Bush*. Illus. Allen Lewis. Rev. ed. Macmillan, 1966.

The French-Canadian War serves as a background for the story of Marguerite Ledoux, a French girl who is regarded with suspicion by the English settlers with whom she lives. First published in 1931. Grades 5–8.

Fitzhugh, Louise. *Harriet the Spy.* Illus. by the author. Harper, 1964.

A landmark book in the growth of the new realism in children's literature. The heroine is a feisty, thorny child, a loner and a writer. She explores life on her own, finding her own explanations for matters beyond her depth, and coming to understand the tension in herself between tenderness and ill will. Grades 3–6.

Fleischman, Paul. *Path of the Pale Horse.* Harper, 1983.

Set during the yellow-fever epidemic in Philadelphia in 1793, this is the story of the education and coming of age of a young doctor's apprentice. Grades 5–8.

Fleischman, Sid. *By the Great Horn Spoon!* Illus. Eric von Schmidt. Little, Brown, 1963.

A hilarious tall tale in which Jack and his aunt's butler, Praiseworthy, stow away on a ship bound for California and the Gold Rush of '49. Grades 4–7. See also *Mr. Mysterious and Company* (1962); *The Ghost in the Noonday Sun* (1965); *Chancy and the Grand Rascal* (1966); *McBroom's Ear* (1969); and *Humbug Mountain* (1978).

Forbes, Esther. *Johnny Tremain.* Illus. Lynd Ward. Houghton Mifflin, 1943.

A young Boston apprentice learns to accept responsibility under the impact of war. Awarded the Newbery Medal in 1944. Grades 5–8.

Fox, Paula. *The Slave Dancer.* Illus. Eros Keith. Bradbury, 1973.

A searing story of the degradations on a slave ship. Told from the point of view of a young white boy who was kidnapped and forced to play music for the slaves to dance to. A horrifying and deeply moving novel. Awarded the Newbery Medal in 1974. Grades 6 and up.

Gardam, Jane. *A Long Way from Verona.* Macmillan, 1971.

An intensely self-revelatory, first-person novel about a critical year in a thirteen-year-old's life, set in England during World War II. Grades 5–9. See also *The Summer after the Funeral* (1973); *Bilgewater* (Greenwillow, 1977); and *The Hollow Land* (Greenwillow, 1981).

Garfield, Leon. *Smith.* Illus. Antony Maitland. Pantheon, 1967.

Smith is an eighteenth-century urchin, one of the nimblest pickpockets in London. Grades 5–8. See also *Black Jack* (1968); *The Apprentices* (Viking, 1978); *The Strange Affair of Adelaide Harris* (Viking, 1978); *Footsteps* (Delacorte, 1980); and other titles by this author.

Garner, Alan. *The Stone Book.* Illus. Michael Foreman. Philomel, 1978.

In a late nineteenth-century Cheshire village, Mary, the stonemason's daughter, is initiated by her father into the secret language of stone. This is one of the most elegant and powerful children's books of the twentieth century. Grades 4 and up. See also the following titles, which trace four generations of the family in their pride of craftsmanship, tradition, and place: *Granny Reardun* (1978); *The Aimer Gate* (1979); and *Tom Fobble's Day* (1979).

Gates, Doris. *Blue Willow.* Illus. Paul Lantz. Viking, 1940.

The yearning of a migrant farm worker girl for the beauty and stability of a real home is symbolized by a blue willow plate. Grades 4–6. See also *The Elderberry Bush* (1967).

George, Jean Craighead. *My Side of the Mountain.* Illus. by the author. Dutton, 1959.

A New York City boy decides to prove to himself and his family that he can live for a year off the land in the Catskill Mountains. The book is filled with fascinating details of his daily life and his delight in animals and birds. Grades 5–8. See also *Julie of the Wolves,* awarded the Newbery Medal in 1973.

Gipson, Fred. *Old Yeller.* Illus. Carl Burger. Harper, 1956.

The dangers and events of early Texas hill living are enlivened by the comic and heroic actions of a dog who strays into a family's life. Grades 5–9.

Godden, Rumer. *The Diddakoi.* Viking, 1972.
Kizzy, a young gypsy orphan, has different ways of living from her schoolmates. Scorn changes to wonder, however, when two sympathetic adults get Kizzy a real gypsy wagon. Grades 4–6. See also *The Kitchen Madonna* (1967).

Greene, Bette. *Summer of My German Soldier.* Dial, 1973.
A tragic story of a lonely Jewish girl in the American South during World War II. Alienated from her parents, she achieves a sense of self-worth by aiding an escaped German prisoner of war. Grades 5 and up.

Hale, Lucretia. *The Peterkin Papers.* Illus. Harold M. Brett. Houghton Mifflin, 1924.
A "masterpiece of nonsense." These stories of the Peterkin family and their absurd dilemmas first appeared in the *St. Nicholas Magazine,* 1874–79. Grades 4–6.

Hamilton, Virginia. *The House of Dies Drear.* Illus. Eros Keith. Macmillan, 1968.
The past and present are intriguingly united as a family—new occupants of a large old house—discovers that the underground tunnels that once led runaway slaves into the house still serve a clandestine function. Grades 4–7. See also *Zeely* (1967); *The Time-Ago Tales of Jahdu* (1969); *The Planet of Junior Brown* (1971); *M. C. Higgins the Great,* awarded the Newbery Medal in 1975; and *Willie Bea and the Time the Martians Landed* (Greenwillow, 1983).

Harnett, Cynthia. *Caxton's Challenge.* Illus. by the author. World, 1960.
An adventure story of the fifteenth century revolving around a plot to deprive the printer Caxton of paper. Grades 5–9. See also *Nicholas and the Wool-Pack,* given the Carnegie Award in 1951, and *The Writing on the Hearth* (Viking, 1971).

Harris, Rosemary. *The Seal-Singing.* Macmillan, 1971.
An island haven for seals off the coast of Scotland is the locale for a story with overtones of the supernatural. Grades 5–8.

Haugaard, Erik Christin. *The Little Fishes.* Illus. Milton Johnson. Houghton Mifflin, 1967.
The struggle of three Italian waifs to survive the German occupation during World War II. Grades 5–8. See also *Hakon of Rogen's Saga* (1963);

the sequel, *A Slave's Tale* (1965); and *The Samurai's Tale* (1984).

Haywood, Carolyn. *"B" Is for Betsy.* Illus. by the author. Harcourt, 1939.
The first of several engaging realistic stories about Betsy and her friends. Grades 2–3.

Henry, Marguerite. *King of the Wind.* Illus. Wesley Dennis. Rand McNally, 1948.
The thrilling story of the famous Godolphin Arabian, ancestor of Man o' War, and a mute stable boy's devotion to the stallion. Awarded the Newbery Medal in 1949. Grades 5–8. See also *Misty of Chincoteague* (1947), an equally fascinating story of a wild island pony, and *Brighty of the Grand Canyon* (1953).

Hinton, S. E. *The Outsiders.* Viking, 1967.
A portrayal of boys involved in gang warfare. Grades 6–9.

Hodges, C. Walter. *The Namesake.* Illus. by the author. Coward-McCann, 1964.
A credible story of a crippled boy who was King Alfred's namesake and scribe, told in the first person when he is an old man. Grades 6–9. See also the sequel, *The Marsh King* (1967).

Holm, Anne. *North to Freedom.* Trans. from the Danish by L. W. Kingsland. Harcourt, 1965.
The emerging into life of a young boy who has known only the existence inside a concentration camp. His escape and journey toward Denmark is one of adventure and revelation. Grades 5–8.

Holman, Felice. *Slake's Limbo.* Scribner's 1974.
An urban Robinsonnade, in which a desperate boy seeks refuge in the New York City subway system for 121 days. Grades 5–8.

Houston, James. *Akavak, an Eskimo Journey.* Illus. by the author. Harcourt, 1968.
Facing death by starvation on an icy plateau, an old Eskimo and his grandson merge wisdom and strength in a desperate fight for survival. Grades 4–7. See also *Wolf Run* (1971); *Frozen Fire: A Tale of Courage* (Atheneum, 1977); and *River Runners: A Tale of Hardship and Bravery* (Atheneum, 1979), awarded the Canadian Library Association Book of the Year Award for Children in 1980.

Hunter, Kristin. *The Soul Brothers and Sister Lou.* Scribner's, 1968.
Some of the special problems of being black are dramatized in this story, which is strengthened by an abundance of realistic detail. Grades 5–9.

Hunter, Mollie. *A Sound of Chariots.* Harper, 1972.
A father's gifts to his daughter extend beyond

his early death and give her insights and strength to become what he would have been. Grades 6–12. See also the sequel *Hold on to Love* (1984) and her novel of first-century Orkney tribal life, *The Stronghold* (1974), winner of the 1974 Carnegie Medal.

James, Will. *Smoky, the Cowhorse.* Illus. by the author. Scribner's, 1926.

One of the best books of its kind. Will James tells the story of the smoke-colored cowpony in cowboy vernacular and illustrates it with fresh, spontaneous sketches. Grades 5–8.

Kästner, Erich. *Emil and the Detectives.* Trans. May Massee; illus. Walter Trier. Doubleday, 1929.

A human comedy in which a band of boys organize themselves with great thoroughness and seriousness in order to recover the money stolen from Emil by a train thief. Grades 3–5.

Kelly, Eric P. *The Trumpeter of Krakow.* Illus. Janina Domanska; foreword, Louise Seaman Bechtel. New ed. Macmillan, 1966.

Fifteenth-century Poland forms the background for this story of mystery, intrigue, and courage. Awarded the Newbery Medal in 1929.

Kemp, Gene. *The Turbulent Term of Tyke Tiler.* Illus. Carolyn Dinan. Faber & Faber, 1980.

A feisty and individualistic child at odds with the adult world, Tyke protects slow Danny from the school system. Clever and touching in turns, with a surprise ending. Winner of the Carnegie Medal in 1977. Grades 4–6.

Kerr, M. E. *Dinky Hocker Shoots Smack.* Harper, 1972.

A humorous and perceptive portrayal of the effect of an overwhelming, insensitive mother on her daughter. Grades 5–9. See also *Is That You, Miss Blue?* (1978) and *Little, Little* (1981).

Knight, Eric. *Lassie—Come Home.* Illus. Don Bolognese. Holt, 1940; 1971.

The devotion of a collie dog causes her to find her way home to Yorkshire from the north of Scotland, having endured hunger, injury, captivity, and fights along the way. Grades 5–9.

Konigsburg, E. L. *From the Mixed-up Files of Mrs. Basil E. Frankweiler.* Illus. by the author. Atheneum, 1967.

A refreshingly original story of a brother and sister who run away from home and live, undiscovered, for one wonderful week in the Metropolitan Museum of Art. Awarded the Newbery Medal in 1968. Grades 4–6. See also *Jennifer, Hecate, Macbeth, and Me, Elizabeth* (1967) and *Throwing Shadows* (1979).

Kroeber, Theodora. *Ishi, Last of His Tribe.* Illus. Ruth Robbins. Parnassus, 1964.

Lone survivor of the Yahis, Ishi is portrayed by a writer who also wrote an anthropological study of his life. Grades 5–12.

Krumgold, Joseph. *. . . and Now Miguel.* Illus. Jean Charlot. Crowell, 1953.

Distinguished for its sensitive portrayal of a young boy's yearning to grow up and for its illuminating picture of life among the sheepherders in New Mexico. Awarded the Newbery Medal in 1954. Grades 6–9.

Langton, Jane. *The Majesty of Grace.* Illus. by the author. Harper, 1961.

The conviction that she is really the future Queen of England colors the life of Grace Jones, whose family is caught in the crisis of unemployment during the Depression. Grades 3–6. See also *The Boyhood of Grace Jones* (1972).

L'Engle, Madeleine. *Meet the Austins.* Vanguard, 1960.

A modern story of the family of a country doctor told by the older daughter during the year a spoiled young orphan comes to live with them. Grades 4–8. See also *The Moon by Night* (Farrar, Straus & Giroux, 1963).

Lenski, Lois. *Strawberry Girl.* Illus. by the author. Lippincott, 1945.

A regional story about Florida's fruit farmers, centered around a warm-hearted little girl. Awarded the Newbery Medal in 1946. Grades 4–6.

Levin, Betty. *The Keeping Room.* Greenwillow, 1981.

The haunting power of the past and its relationship to a specific place is explored in this complex story. A young boy working on a school project on the history of his neighbor's land rescues a kidnapped child, uncovers a secret from the past, and grows emotionally as a result. Grades 6–9.

Lindquist, Jennie. *The Golden Name Day.* Illus. Garth Williams. Harper, 1955.

A perceptive story full of kindness and wisdom and enriched with Swedish customs, one of which gives the book its title. Grades 3–6. See also *The Crystal Tree* (1966).

Linevski, A. *An Old Tale Carved out of Stone.* Trans. from the Russian by Maria Polushkin. Crown, 1973.

The fine filling out of a story set in Neolithic Siberia owes a great deal to the author, who is a noted Soviet archaeologist. The story itself is one that transcends time, showing the plight of a young boy whose own reason and logic defy the superstitious custom he is expected to observe. Grades 5–8.

Little, Jean. *Listen for the Singing.* Dutton, 1977.
Winner of the 1977 Canada Council Children's Literature Prize, this World War II story of a young German-Canadian girl's struggles with her impaired vision and wartime prejudice is both warm and honest. Grades 4–6. See also *From Anna* (Harper 1972).

Lively, Penelope. *Going Back.* Heinemann, 1975.
Jane revisits her Sussex childhood home and remembers her wartime experiences, when she and her brother Edward grew up free from parental constraints. The concepts of memory and the passing of time are poignantly treated. Grades 5–7.

London, Jack. *Call of the Wild.* Illus. Charles Pickard. Dutton, 1968.
A superb adventure story with a notable dog character, Buck. First published in 1903. Grades 6–12.

Lowry, Lois. *Anastasia Krupnik.* Illus. Diane De Groat. Houghton Mifflin, 1979.
A lively tale about the day-to-day trials and pleasures of a young girl on the brink of adolescence. The cleanly written story reveals strong, attractive characters and warm humor. Grades 4–6. See also *Anastasia Again!* (1981); *Anastasia at Your Service* (1982); and *Taking Care of Terrific* (1983).

McCloskey, Robert. *Homer Price.* Illus. by the author. Viking, 1943.
Six rollicking tales of the hilarious adventures of Homer Price, a modern American boy. Grades 4–7. See also *Centerburg Tales,* Homer's continuing adventures. (1951).

McNeill, Janet. *The Other People.* Little, Brown, 1970.
As she grows in understanding toward the tenants of the boardinghouse where she is spending the summer, a young girl not only is changed, but helps effect changes for others. Grades 5–9. See also *The Battle of St. George Without* (1966) and *Goodbye, Dove Square* (1969).

Magorian, Michelle. *Goodnight Mister Tom.* Harper, 1982.
A dramatic, suspenseful story of an abused and withdrawn city boy evacuated from London in World War II and taken in by a harsh old widower, who gives him love and hope for the first time. Winner of the Guardian Award for Children's Fiction in 1982. Grades 4–6.

Major, Kevin. *Hold Fast.* Delacorte, 1980.
Strong characterization, close observation of place, and understated humor distinguish this story of an adolescent boy uprooted from his Newfoundland country home on the death of his parents. Awarded the Canadian Library Association Book of the Year Award for Children in 1979. Grades 6–9. See also *Far from Shore* (1981) and *Thirty-six Exposures* (1984).

Mark, Jan. *Thunder and Lightnings.* Illus. Jim Russell. Harper, 1979.
A lively, funny account of an unlikely friendship between two very different boys. Their shared love of airplanes leads them to an awareness of the mutability of life. Awarded the Carnegie Medal in 1976. Grades 4–6.

Mathis, Sharon Bell. *The Hundred Penny Box.* Illus. Leo Dillon and Diane Dillon. Viking, 1975.
The strong sympathetic bond between a grandmother and her grandson is symbolized by their attachment to the box that contains one penny for each year of her life. Grades 2–5.

Mayne, William. *Ravensgill.* Dutton, 1970.
An underground tunnel holds the key to a strange relationship between two families. Grades 6–12. See also *The Incline* (1972) and *Salt River Times* (Greenwillow, 1981).

Merrill, Jean. *The Pushcart War.* Illus. Ronni Solbert. W. R. Scott, 1964.
A witty satire set in New York City in 1986, in which the pushcart peddlers overthrow a truck monopoly. Grades 4–7.

Montgomery, Lucy M. *Anne of Green Gables.* Illus. Jody Lee. Putnam's, 1983.
The first in a series of eight books about the spirited redhead who finds a home on Prince Edward Island and brings warmth and poetry into the life of her newly adopted community. First published in 1908. Grades 5–9.

Morey, Walter. *Gentle Ben.* Illus. John Schoenherr. Dutton, 1965.
A compelling story of the remarkable bond of affection between a young Alaskan boy and an enormous captive brown bear. Grades 5–7.

Mowat, Farley. *Owls in the Family.* Illus. Robert Frankenberg. Little, Brown, 1961.
An account of two owls, Wol and Weeps, and

their antics, personalities, and escapades with the boy whose pets they became. Grades 3–6. See also the survival adventure *Lost in the Barrens* (1956).

Mühlenweg, Fritz. *Big Tiger and Christian*. Illus. Rafaello Busoni. Pantheon, 1952.

A Chinese boy and his white friend, captured in Peking during China's civil wars, are sent on a dangerous mission to the far end of the Gobi Desert. Grades 6–9.

Mukerji, Dhan Gopal. *Gay-Neck: The Story of a Pigeon*. Illus. Boris Artzybasheff. Dutton, 1927.

The author's gentle Indian philosophy is interwoven in this story of a carrier pigeon and the part it played in the First World War. Awarded the Newbery Medal in 1928. Grades 5–8. See also *Kari, the Elephant* (1922) and *Hari, the Jungle Lad* (1924)—tales told with vivid beauty and imbued with the atmosphere of the jungle.

Nesbit, E. (Mrs. Hubert Bland). *The Story of the Treasure Seekers: Being the Adventures of the Bastable Children in Search of a Fortune*. Illus. C. Walter Hodges. Coward-McCann, 1948.

The wit and charm of the author is in the amusing adventures of the Bastable children, whose imaginations result in some original predicaments. First published in 1899. Followed by *The Would-Be-Goods* (1901) and *The New Treasure Seekers* (1904). An incident from *The New Treasure Seekers* was published as *The Conscience Pudding*, illus. Erik Blegvad (Coward, 1970).

Nordstom, Ursula. *The Secret Language*. Illus. Mary Chalmers. Harper, 1960.

The forbidden delights of life at boarding school are shared by two girls of opposing temperaments. Their "secret language" gives them a sense of invincibility and performs an important role in the changes each girl undergoes. Grades 3–5.

O'Dell, Scott. *Island of the Blue Dolphins*. Houghton Mifflin, 1960.

The lonely life of an Indian girl left on an island is one of fulfillment as she learns to turn vengeance into love, and finds her solitary life eased by the wildlife around her. Awarded the Newbery Medal in 1961. Grades 4–8. See also *The King's Fifth* (1966); *The Black Pearl* (1967); *The Dark Canoe* (1968); and *Sing Down the Moon* (1970).

O'Hara, Mary (Mary Sture-Vasa). *My Friend Flicka*. Lippincott, 1943.

A story that involves the faith of a boy in a horse said to be impossible to train. Grades 5–12.

Paterson, Katherine. *The Master Puppeteer*. Illus. Haru Wells. Crowell, 1975.

A time of famine and night rovers makes life unsafe in the city of Osaka. Young Jiro, apprentice puppeteer, becomes involved with a mysterious bandit who aids the starving. Grades 5–7. See also *The Sign of the Chrysanthemum* (1973), *Of Nightingales That Weep* (1974), *Rebels of the Heavenly Kingdom* (Dutton, 1983); and her perceptive novels of contemporary life, which deal sensitively with children's and adolescents' crises: *Bridge to Terabithia*, illus. Donna Diamond (1977), winner of the Newbery Medal in 1978; *The Great Gilly Hopkins* (1978); and *Jacob Have I Loved* (1980), awarded the Newbery Medal in 1981.

Pearce, A. Philippa. *The Minnow Leads to Treasure*. Illus. Edward Ardizzone. World, 1955.

A real treasure, hidden at the time of the Spanish Armada, lures two boys into unravelling the riddle that has been left as the only clue. An intricate relationship between the search for the treasure and the locale is a fascinating aspect of the story. Grades 4–8. See also *The Battle of Bubble and Squeak*, illus. Alan Baker (Andre Deutsch, 1979), and *The Way to Sattin Shore* (Greenwillow, 1984).

Petry, Ann. *Tituba of Salem Village*. Crowell, 1964.

The story of a Barbados slave girl in Salem in 1692 and the slow weaving of a net around her that eventually puts her on trial for witchcraft. Grades 5–9.

Peyton, K. M. *Flambards*. Illus. Victor G. Ambrus. World, 1968.

Growing up together in the years before the First World War, four young people become entangled over their feelings about Flambards, the country place in which they live, and the horse and hunting obsession that has characterized it. Christina, a young orphan, grows, matures, marries, is widowed, and becomes a mother in the four books that comprise the quartet: *The Edge of the Cloud* (1969), winner of the Carnegie Medal, 1969; *Flambards in Summer* (1970); and *Flambards Divided* (Philomel, 1982). Grades 5–12.

Poe, Edgar Allan. *The Pit and The Pendulum and Five Other Tales*. Illus. Rick Schreiter. F. Watts, 1967.

Tales that are properly chilling, told by a master. Grades 5 and up. See also *The Fall of the House of Usher and Four Other Tales* (1967).

Pyle, Howard. *Otto of the Silver Hand*. Illus. by the author. New ed. Scribner's, 1957.

First published in 1888, this is a classic medieval tale of Otto and how "by gentleness and love and not by strife and hatred, he came at last to stand above other men and to be looked up to by all." Grades 5–9. See also *Men of Iron* (1892), which tells how Miles wins his spurs and vanquishes his own and his father's enemy.

Ransome, Arthur. *Swallows and Amazons.* Illus. Helene Carter. Lippincott, 1931.

These lively adventures of six resourceful English children who spend a vacation camping on a small island are noteworthy for the author's detailed knowledge of sailing. Grades 4–6.

Raskin, Ellen. *The Westing Game.* Illus. by the author. Dutton, 1978.

Winner of the Newbery Medal in 1979, this eccentric mystery is a puzzle-solver's delight. Grades 5–9.

Rawlings, Marjorie Kinnan. *The Yearling.* Illus. N. C. Wyeth. Scribner's, 1946.

A classic story of the boy Jody and his pet fawn. In having to sacrifice the thing he loved most, Jody left his own yearling days behind and gained the stature of a man. Grades 6–9.

Richter, Conrad. *The Light in the Forest.* Illus. Warren Chappell. Knopf, 1966.

A government order tears a boy away from his Indian family. Although his skin is white, his feelings and affections have become Indian. Grades 5–9.

Richter, Hans Peter. *Friedrich.* Trans. Edite Kroll. Holt, 1970.

The relentless erosion of one Jewish boy's life during the Hitler years in Germany is told by his friend and neighbor. Intimate details of persecution create a cumulative horror. Grades 4–9.

Roberts, Charles G. D. *Red Fox.* Illus. John Schoenherr; intro. David McCord. Houghton Mifflin, 1972.

First published in 1905, this full-length animal biography is written with sensitive realism and close observation of life in the wild. See also other titles by this author. Grades 5–9.

Robertson, Keith. *Henry Reed, Inc.* Illus. Robert McCloskey. Viking, 1958.

A truly humorous story of the summer enterprises of an inventive young boy and eleven-year-old Midge. Grades 4–8.

Sachs, Marilyn. *Veronica Ganz.* Illus. Louis Glanzman. Doubleday, 1968.

A game of chase and wits dominates the plot of this book about a girl who is a bully and an undersized boy who defies her. Grades 3–6. See also *Bear's House* (1971).

Salten, Felix. *Bambi: A Life in the Woods.* Illus. Barbara Cooney. Simon & Schuster, 1970.

This engaging animal classic tells the life story of a young fawn from birth to maturity. Grades 2–5. First published in English in 1926.

Sawyer, Ruth. *Roller Skates.* Illus. Valenti Angelo. Viking, 1936.

High-spirited Lucinda has a wonderful time exploring New York City on roller skates in the 1890s. Awarded the Newbery Medal in 1937. Grades 5–8.

Schlee, Ann. *Ask Me No Questions.* Holt, 1982.

This exceptional historical novel tells the chilling story of a young Victorian girl who discovers an outbreak of cholera in an asylum for paupers' children. Grades 5 and up.

Scott, Sir Walter. *Ivanhoe.* Illustrations consist of drawings by contemporary artists; intro. and anecdotal captions, Basil Davenport. Dodd, Mead, 1944.

A colorful and romantic tale. Grades 7–12.

Seredy, Kate. *The Good Master.* Illus. by the author. Viking, 1935.

Irrepressible Kate comes to stay with her cousin Jancsi and her uncle on a large horse farm on the plains of Hungary. Hard work, happy holidays, and the wisdom of "the good master" aid in her development. Grades 4–7.

Serraillier, Ian. *The Silver Sword.* Illus. C. Walter Hodges. Criterion, 1961.

Living among the bombed-out rubble of Warsaw during World War II and separated from their parents, who have been told they are dead, three children fasten on a single clue which eventually leads them to their parents. Grades 4–6.

Seton, Ernest Thompson. *Wild Animals I Have Known.* Illus. by the author. McClelland & Stewart, 1977.

First published in 1898, this classic collection of gripping animal stories is illustrated by the author's pen-and-ink drawings. Grades 5 and up.

Smucker, Barbara. *Runaway to Freedom: A Story of the Underground Railway.* Illus. Charles Lilly. Harper, 1978.

Two black girls escape slavery on a Virginia plantation and begin a pilgrimage to Canada and freedom via the Underground Railway. Published in Canada under the title *Underground to Canada.* Grades 4–6. See also *Days of Terror* (1979).

Snyder, Zilpha Keatley. *The Egypt Game.* Illus. Alton Raible. Atheneum, 1967.

An imaginative game, played by two girls in a deserted storage yard, unexpectedly brings them into real danger. Grades 4–7.

Sobol, Donald J. *Encyclopedia Brown Saves the Day.* Illus. Leonard Shortall. Nelson, 1970.

A game, fashioned partly on the riddle and partly on the conventions of the mystery story, dominates this series of short narrative puzzlers. The reader is actively involved in determining the solutions, which are placed at the back of the book. Grades 2–5. See also other titles in this series.

Southall, Ivan. *Ash Road.* St. Martin's, 1966.

How three inexperienced young campers in Australia face up to responsibility. See also *To the Wild Sky* (1967), which won the Book of the Year Award in Australia; *Hills End* (1963); *Let the Balloon Go* (1968), and *Josh* (Macmillan, 1971), the first Australian book to win the Carnegie Award. Grades 6–9.

Speare, Elizabeth G. *The Witch of Blackbird Pond.* Houghton Mifflin, 1958.

Strong atmosphere and fully realized characters mark this compelling story of a young woman swept up in the Salem witchcraft trials. Winner of the Newbery Medal in 1959. Grades 5–8. See also *Calico Captive* (1957) and *The Sign of the Beaver* (1983).

Sperry, Armstrong. *Call It Courage.* Illus. by the author. Macmillan, 1940.

A Polynesian boy, conditioned in infancy to fear the sea, sets out alone in a canoe to conquer his terror. His ultimate victory over himself and his triumphal return make a powerful story. Awarded the Newbery Medal in 1941. Grades 4–8.

Spykman, Elizabeth C. *A Lemon and a Star.* Harcourt, 1955.

A story of hilarious rivalry and intrigue that results in wild adventures, this is a true evocation of the immense freedom of childhood. Grades 4–12. See also *The Wild Angel* (1957); *Terrible, Horrible Edie* (1960); and *Edie on the Warpath* (1966).

Spyri, Johanna. *Heidi.* Illus. Agnes Tait. Lippincott, 1948.

Since its publication in 1880, several generations of children have absorbed the beauty of the Swiss countryside. Grades 4–8. Another fine edition is illustrated by Jessie Wilcox Smith (McKay, 1922).

Stevenson, Robert Louis. *Treasure Island.* Illus. N. C. Wyeth. Scribner's, 1981.

A reissue of the classic story of adventure, with colorful villainy and swashbuckling action. The outstanding painterly illustrations add powerful images to make this edition memorable. First published in England in 1883; originally published in this edition with Wyeth illustrations in 1911.

Stevenson, William. *The Bushbabies.* Illus. Victor Ambrus. Houghton Mifflin, 1965.

A journey to return her pet, a bushbaby, to its natural habitat in Africa is undertaken at great peril by a young girl and an old friend, an African guide. Grades 4–8.

Storr, Catherine. *The Adventures of Polly and the Wolf.* Illus. Marjorie-Ann Watts. Macrae Smith, 1970.

Hopelessly outwitted by Polly, the wolf tries again and again to get her into his pot. Grades 3–5.

Storr, Catherine. *The Chinese Egg.* McGraw-Hill, 1975.

A fascinating blend of spasmodic extrasensory perception and detection in locating a kidnapped baby, this is a story that also combines well-developed characters with a taut, suspenseful plot. Grades 5–12. See also *Thursday* (Harper, 1972).

Storr, Catherine. *Lucy.* Illus. Victoria de Larrea. Prentice-Hall, 1969.

Rebuffed by the boys with whom she wants to play, Lucy has a real adventure and catches some thieves. Grades 3–5. See also *Lucy Runs Away* (1969).

Sutcliff, Rosemary. *Warrior Scarlet.* Illus. Charles Keeping. Walck, 1958.

A crippled arm makes it unlikely that a boy of the Bronze Age will meet the test through which he has to pass in order to wear the warrior scarlet, symbol of manhood. Grades 5–9. See also *The Eagle of the Ninth* (1954); *The Witch's Brat* (1970); *Song for a Dark Queen* (Crowell, 1979); and *Bonnie Dundee* (Dutton, 1984).

Taylor, Mildred D. *Roll of Thunder, Hear My Cry.* Illus. Jerry Pinkney. Dial, 1976.

The powerful story of a black girl's experiences during the Depression years in Mississippi. Her growing understanding of racial injustice and cruelty is balanced by the pride and support of her loving family. Awarded the Newbery Medal in 1977. Grades 5–9. See also *Let the Circle Be Unbroken* (1981).

Townsend, John Rowe. *The Intruder.* Lippincott, 1970.

A threatening sense of mystery and danger builds as a stranger tries to rob a young man of his identity. Grades 5–9.

Townsend, John Rowe. *Trouble in the Jungle.* Illus. W. T. Mars. Lippincott, 1961.

The survival of four abandoned children in a slum hideout has the added complication of an encounter with a gang of criminals who have marked the place for their rendezvous. Grades 4–9. See also *Good-bye to the Jungle* (1967); *Pirate's Island* (1968); and *Dan Alone* (Lippincott, 1983).

Truss, Jan. *Jasmin.* Atheneum, A Margaret K. McElderry Book, 1982.

The eldest child in a poor, chaotic, and crowded family feels overburdened with chores and sibling responsibilities. She runs away to live alone in the Rocky Mountain foothills where she discovers the strength and courage to continue. A romantic survival story. Grades 5–7.

Twain, Mark (Samuel Langhorne Clemens). *The Adventures of Tom Sawyer.* Harper, Holiday Edition, 1917.

First published in 1876, this story of American boyhood is followed by the epic *Adventures of Huckleberry Finn.* Another notable illustrated edition is by Louis Slobodkin (World, 1946). Grades 5–9.

Uchida, Yoshiko. *Journey to Topaz: A Story of the Japanese-American Evacuation.* Illus. Donald Carrick. Scribner's, 1971.

The author has drawn on her own experiences in a relocation center to tell this story. Grades 6–9.

Uchida, Yoshiko. *Sumi's Special Happening.* Illus. Kazue Mizamura. Scribner's, 1966.

The special affinity of the very young for the very old is shown in this simple story. Grades 1–3. See also *Sumi and The Goat* and *The Tokyo Express* (1969).

Ullman, James Ramsey. *Banner in the Sky.* Lippincott, 1954.

The powerful lure of mountain climbing in Switzerland is portrayed in this story of a boy who wants to capture the peak his father died in attempting. Grades 5–9.

Van Stockum, Hilda. *The Winged Watchman.* Farrar, Straus & Giroux, 1962.

The character of the Dutch people is well drawn in this story of resistance during World War II. The Watchman is the windmill in which the Verhagen family lives—at a crucial time it is the Watchman that outwits the Nazis. Grades 3–6. See also *The Borrowed House* (1975).

Voigt, Cynthia. *Homecoming.* Atheneum, 1981.

A satisfying story of courage and determination, strong in characterization and mood. A family of four children abandoned by their mother in a parking lot begin a trek across state borders in search of family and dignity. Grades 5 and up. See also the sequel, *Dicey's Song* (1982), winner of the Newbery Medal in 1983, and the companion volume, *A Solitary Blue* (1983).

Walsh, Jill Paton. *Goldengrove.* Farrar, Straus & Giroux, 1972.

A sense of season and change—painful awakenings for a young girl who was kept from knowing that her cousin was really her younger brother. Grades 5–9. See also *Fireweed* (1969); *The Emperor's Winding Sheet* (1974); *Unleaving* (1976); and *A Parcel of Patterns* (1983).

Westall, Robert. *The Machine Gunners.* Greenwillow, 1976.

A strong, comic, and disturbing story about a group of English children during World War II, who stumble upon a crashed German pilot and a machine gun. They undertake to fight the war in their own way. Awarded the Carnegie Medal in 1976. Grades 6–9. See also *The Scarecrows* (1981), winner of the 1981 Carnegie Medal.

Wiggin, Kate Douglas. *Rebecca of Sunnybrook Farm.* Illus. Helen Mason Grose. Houghton Mifflin, 1903.

The strong personality of Rebecca makes this book continually appealing.

Wilder, Laura Ingalls. *Little House in the Big Woods.* Illus. Garth Williams. New ed. Harper, 1953.

The author has written many of her childhood experiences in a group of outstanding books that form a vivid chronicle of life in pioneer days in the Middle West. This first title (Grades 3–7) is followed by six books, each one a little more advanced, ending with *These Happy Golden Years.*

Willard, Barbara. *The Lark and the Laurel.* Harcourt, 1970.

First in a series of five novels about the families and people connected with Mantlemass, this story takes place during the time of Henry Tudor, when young Cecily comes to her aunt's manor home. Grades 5–9. See also in the series: *The Sprig of Broom* (Dutton, 1972), which combines mystery and romance, also during the time of Henry VII; *A Cold Wind Blowing* (Dutton, 1972), depicting the influence of Henry VIII; *The Iron Lily* (Dutton, 1973), which tells of a woman who becomes master of her own iron foundry when England is ruled by Elizabeth I; and the last, *Harrow and Harvest*

(Dutton, 1975), concluding the saga with the revelation of a family secret kept since the time of Richard Plantagenet. Superior historical fiction, this series was recognized when *The Iron Lily* received the 1974 Guardian Award.

Wojciechowska, Maia. *Shadow of a Bull.* Illus. Alvin Smith. Atheneum, 1964.
    The son of a famous bullfighter is forced to choose between the bullring or the world of medicine. In making his choice he takes his first step into the adult world. Awarded the Newbery Medal in 1965. Grades 4–8.

Wrightson, Patricia. *A Racecourse for Andy.* Illus. Horder. Harcourt, 1968.
    The illusion that he has bought a racecourse is supported by a variety of people who see no harm in "humoring" a mentally handicapped boy. Grades 5–9.

Wyss, Johann David. *Swiss Family Robinson.* Illus. Jeanne Edwards. World, 1947.
    The very improbability of this tale of a family shipwrecked on a desert island makes it delightful. First published in 1814. Grades 5–8.

Yep, Laurence. *Dragonwings.* Harper, 1975.
    Told against the background of Chinese immigrant life at the beginning of the twentieth century, *Dragonwings* centers on the struggle of Windrider and his young son, Moon Shadow, to build a machine that flies. Grades 6–8. See also *The Child of the Owl* (1977) and *The Serpent's Children* (1984).

Zei, Alki. *Wildcat under Glass.* Trans. Edward Fenton. Holt, 1968.
    The playful rivalry of two Greek sisters becomes serious when one is attracted to the National Youth Organization of the new dictator, and the other becomes a messenger for her uncle in the resistance forces. A human portrayal of the disruption and tension caused by the imposition of a set of values. Grades 4–8. See also *Petros' War* (Dutton, 1972) for a story of a boy who found his own way to oppose the Nazis who were occupying his country and a story of Russia on the verge of its revolution, *The Sound of Dragon's Feet* (Dutton, 1979).

References for Adults

Books

Aiken, Joan. *The Way to Write for Children.* St. Martin's, 1982.

Berry, Brick, and Herbert Best. *Writing for Children.* Illus. Brick Berry. University of Miami, 1964.

Blishen, Edward, ed. *The Thorny Paradise: Writers on Writing for Children.* Kestrel, 1975.

Booth, W. C. *The Rhetoric of Fiction.* 2d ed. Univ. of Chicago Press, 1983.

Cameron, Eleanor. *The Green and Burning Tree: On the Writing and Enjoyment of Children's Books.* Little, Brown, 1969.

Dillard, Annie. *Living by Fiction.* Harper, 1982.

Forster, E. M. *Aspects of the Novel.* Harvest, 1956.

Gardner, John. *The Art of Fiction: Notes of Craft for Young Writers.* Knopf, 1984.

Gass, William H. *Fiction and the Figures of Life.* Knopf, 1970.

Haviland, Virginia, ed. *The Openhearted Audience: Ten Authors Talk about Writing for Children.* Library of Congress, 1980.

Hunter, Mollie. *Talent Is Not Enough: Mollie Hunter on Writing for Children.* Harper, 1976.

Kermode, Frank. *The Sense of an Ending: Studies in the Theory of Fiction.* Oxford Univ. Press, 1967.

Lewis, C. S. *An Experiment in Criticism.* Cambridge Univ. Press, 1961.

Lewis, C. S. *Of Other Worlds: Essays and Stories.* Harcourt, 1966.

Muir, Edwin. *The Structure of the Novel.* Harcourt, 1929.

Murry, John Middleton. *The Problem of Style.* Oxford Univ. Press, 1922.

Paterson, Katherine. *Gates of Excellence: On Reading and Writing Books for Children.* Elsevier/Nelson, 1981.

Rees, David. *The Marble in the Water: Essays on Contemporary Writers of Fiction for Children and Young Adults.* Horn Book, 1980. See also *Painted Desert, Green Shade: Essays on Contemporary Writers of Fiction for Children and Young Adults* (1984).

Sloane, William. *The Craft of Writing.* Norton, 1979.

Southall, Ivan. *A Journey of Discovery: On Writing for Children.* Macmillan, 1976.

Townsend, John Rowe. *A Sense of Story: Essays on Contemporary Writers for Children.* Lippincott, 1971.
    See also the revised edition, *A Sounding of Storytellers: Essays on Contemporary Writers for Children.* Lippincott, 1979.

Lines, Kathleen, gen. ed. Walck Monographs. Walck.

Arthur Ransome, by Hugh Shelley (1964); *Geoffrey Trease,* by Margaret Meek (1964); *Howard Pyle,* by Elizabeth Nesbit (1966); *Rosemary Sutcliff,* by Margaret Meek (1962); *Rudyard Kipling,* by Rosemary Sutcliff (1961); *E. Nesbit,* by Anthea Bell (1964); and other titles.

Welty, Eudora. *Place in Fiction.* House of Books, 1957.

Wicker, Brian. *The Story-Shaped World: Fiction and Metaphysics; Some Variations on a Theme.* Univ. of Notre Dame Press, 1975.

Yolen, Jane. *Writing Books for Children.* The Writer, 1973.

Articles and Chapters

Avery, Gillian. "Fashions in Children's Fiction." *Children's Literature in Education,* no. 12 (Sept. 1973), pp. 10–19.

Babbitt, Natalie. "The Great American Novel for Children—And Why Not." *The Horn Book Magazine,* 50 (Apr. 1974), pp. 176–85.

Bator, Robert, ed. *Signposts to Criticism of Children's Literature.* American Library Association, 1983.
See Chapter 9. "Historical Fiction." "Some Observations on Children's Historical Fiction," by Leland B. Jacobs, pp. 267–69; "Problems of the Historical Storyteller," by Geoffrey Trease, pp. 269–72; "What Shall We Tell the Children?" by Mark Cohen, pp. 273–76; "The Historical Story—Is It Relevant Today?" by Geoffrey Trease, pp. 277–82.

Bawden, Nina. "Emotional Realism in Books for Young People." *The Horn Book Magazine,* 56 (Feb. 1980), pp. 17–33.

Bowen, Elizabeth. "Out of a Book." In *Collected Impressions.* Knopf, 1950.

Burton, Hester. "The Writing of Historical Novels." *The Horn Book Magazine,* 45 (June 1969), pp. 271–77.

Edwards, Tony. " 'Stories Not History': The Historical Novels of Cynthia Harnett." *Children's Literature in Education,* no. 9 (Nov. 1972), pp. 24–32.

Egoff, Sheila. "Children's Books: A Canadian's View of the Current American Scene." *The Horn Book Magazine,* 46 (Apr. 1970), pp. 142–50.

Egoff, Sheila, et al., ed. *Only Connect: Readings on Children's Literature.* 2d ed. Oxford Univ. Press, 1980. Part 5. "The Modern Scene."

Enright, Elizabeth. "Realism in Children's Literature." *The Horn Book Magazine,* 43 (Apr. 1967), pp. 165–70.

Fritz, Jean. "On Writing Historical Fiction." *The Horn Book Magazine,* 43 (Oct. 1967), pp. 565–70.

Gardam, Jane. "On Writing for Children: Some Wasps in the Marmalade." Part I, *The Horn Book Magazine,* 54 (Oct. 1978), pp. 489–96; Part II, 54 (Dec. 1978), pp. 672–79.

Godden, Rumer. "Words Make the Book." *Ladies Home Journal,* 81 (Jan.-Feb. 1964).

Gross, Elizabeth H. "Twenty Medal Books: In Perspective." In *Newbery and Caldecott Books: 1956–1965,* ed. Lee Kingman. Horn Book, 1965, pp. 3–10.

Hamilton, Virginia. "Writing the Source: In Other Words." *The Horn Book Magazine,* 54 (Dec. 1978), pp. 609–19.

Heins, Paul, ed. *Crosscurrents of Criticism: Horn Book Essays, 1968–1977.* Horn Book, 1977.
See Section VIII. "Making the Past Understandable." "History Is Fiction," by Jill Paton Walsh, pp. 219–25; "Children and Memory," by Penelope Lively, pp. 226–33; "Johnny and Sam: Old and New Approaches to the American Revolution," by Christopher Collier, pp. 234–40; "Writing about Abraham Lincoln," by Olivia Coolidge, pp. 241–45.

Hodges, C. Walter. "On Writing about King Alfred." *The Horn Book Magazine,* 43 (Apr. 1967), pp. 179–82.

Holland, Isabelle. "On Being a Children's Book Writer and Accompanying Dangers." Part I, *The Horn Book Magazine,* 56 (Feb. 1980), pp. 34–42; Part II, 56 (Apr. 1980), pp. 203–10.

Horovitz, Carolyn. "Fiction and the Paradox of Play." *Wilson Library Bulletin,* 44 (Dec. 1969), pp. 397–401.

Horovitz, Carolyn. "Only the Best." In *Newbery and Caldecott Medal Books: 1956–1965,* ed. Lee Kingman. Horn Book, 1965, pp. 156–62.

Hunter, Mollie. "Talent Is Not Enough." *Top of the News,* 31 (June 1975), pp. 391–406.

Laura Ingalls Wilder Issue. The Horn Book Magazine, 29 (Dec. 1953), pp. 411–39.

McDowell, Myles. "Fiction for Children and Adults: Some Essential Differences." *Children's Literature in Education,* no. 10 (Mar. 1973), pp. 50–63.

Meek, Margaret, ed. *The Cool Web: The Pattern of Children's Reading.* Atheneum, 1978.

    See Section One. "The Reader." "Towards a Poetics of Fiction; an Approach through Narrative," by Barbara Hardy, pp. 12–23; "Psychological Processes in the Reading of Fiction," by D. W. Harding, pp. 58–72; "On Stories," by C. S. Lewis, pp. 76–90; "Kinds of Fiction: A Hierarchy of Veracity," by Aidan Warlow, pp. 97–102.

Singer, Isaac Bashevis. "Are Children the Ultimate Literary Critics?" *Top of the News,* 29 (Nov. 1972), pp. 32–36.

Townsend, John Rowe. "A Decade of Newbery Books in Perspective." In *Newbery and Caldecott Books: 1966–1975,* ed. Lee Kingman. Horn Book, 1975, pp. 141–53.

Walsh, Jill Paton. "The Writer's Responsibility." *Children's Literature in Education,* no. 10 (Mar. 1973), pp. 30–36.

Wolf, Virginia L. "The Root and Measure of Realism." *Wilson Library Bulletin,* 44 (Dec. 1969), pp. 409–15.

12   Thresholds and Frontiers: Fantasy and Science Fiction

Books for Children

Adams, Richard. *Watership Down.* Macmillan, 1972.

    An epic adventure, testing the heroism, loyalty, and inventiveness of a band of rabbits who set out to establish their own warren. Awarded the 1973 Carnegie Medal and the 1973 Guardian Award. Grades 5 and up.

Aiken, Joan. *The Wolves of Willoughby Chase.* Illus. Pat Marriott. Doubleday, 1963.

    An entertaining Gothic melodrama set in a historical England that never was, with stock characters divertingly portrayed and the whole tale written in high style. Grades 4–7. See also *Black Hearts in Battersea* (1964); *Nightbirds on Nantucket* (1966); *The Stolen Lake* (Delacorte, 1981); and *Bridle the Wind* (Delacorte, 1983).

Alexander, Lloyd. *The Book of Three.* Holt, 1964.

    Welsh legend and magic are blended in this tale of Taran, Assistant Pig-Keeper, in the mythical kingdom of Prydain. Grades 5–7. See also the further adventures that follow in *The Black Cauldron; The Castle of Llyr; Taran Wanderer;* and *The High King,* which was awarded the Newbery Medal in 1969. Two books for younger readers, illus-

trated by Evaline Ness, are *Coll and His White Pig* (1965) and *The Truthful Harp* (1967). See also his Westmark trilogy (Dutton): *Westmark* (1981), winner of the 1982 American Book Award; *The Kestrel* (1982); and *The Beggar Queen* (1984).

Alexander, Lloyd. *The Cat Who Wished to Be a Man.* Dutton, 1973.

    Transformed into the shape of a man by his master, a high wizard, a cat ventures into a town where he becomes first the butt of practical jokes and target of villainy, and then the rescuer of a fair maid and the righter of ancient wrongs. Grades 3–7. See also *The Marvelous Misadventures of Sebastian* (1970); *The King's Fountain,* illus. Ezra Jack Keats (1971); and *The Wizard in the Tree* (1975).

Andersen, Hans Christian. *Ardizzone's Hans Andersen: Fourteen Classic Tales.* Sel. and illus. Edward Ardizzone; trans. Stephen Corrin. Atheneum, 1979.

    Andersen's stories were first published in English in 1846. This is a select, handsomely illustrated edition of Andersen's most popular stories. The fluid, light black-and-white sketches and easy water colors are understated complements to the powerful translation. Grades 3–5.

Andersen, Hans Christian. *The Complete Andersen.* Trans. Jean Hersholt; illus. Fritz Kredel. Heritage, 1952.

    Jean Hersholt, the actor, was also a student and collector of Andersen. His translation gives the tales new vitality. Grades 5–7.

Andersen, Hans Christian. *The Complete Fairy Tales and Stories.* Trans. Erik Christian Haugaard; foreword, Virginia Haviland. Doubleday, 1974.

    A translation from a bilingual Danish author who has lived and studied in both the United States and Denmark. All ages. See also the edition for children selected from this definitive translation, *Hans Andersen: His Classic Fairy Tales,* provocatively illustrated by Michael Foreman (1981).

Andersen, Hans Christian. *The Emperor's New Clothes.* Trans. and illus. Erik Blegvad. Harcourt, 1959.

    The delicacy and subtlety of Andersen's humor merges well with the illustrator's fine line drawings and loving portrayal of detail. Another interpretation is given by the artist Virginia Lee Burton (Houghton Mifflin, 1949).

Andersen, Hans Christian. *Fairy Tales.* Ed. Svend Larsen; trans. from the original Danish text by R. P. Keigwin; illus. Vilhelm Pedersen, reproduced from the original drawings in the Andersen Museum at Odense. Scribner's, World edition, 1951.

    An important translation by the well-known En-

glish-Danish scholar, illustrated with pencil drawings by the artist who was Andersen's own choice
as an illustrator of his tales. This edition was issued
from Odense, Andersen's birthplace, under the su-
pervision of Svend Larsen, Director of the Andersen Museum in Odense. See also the four-volume
edition published by Flensted (Odense, Denmark).

Andersen, Hans Christian. *Fairy Tales.* Trans. L. W.
Kingsland; illus. Ernest H. Shepard. Walck, 1962.
    Contains thirty-two stories, some rarely found
in other collections. Grades 4–7. See also the edition illustrated by Tasha Tudor, published by
Walck in 1945.

Andersen, Hans Christian. *Fairy Tales.* By Lawrence
Beall Smith. Macmillan, 1963.
    One of the Macmillan Classics series and an at-
tractive edition, with an afterword by Clifton Fadiman. Grades 5–7.

Andersen, Hans Christian. *The Fir Tree.* Illus. Nancy
Elkholm Burkert. Harper, 1970.
    A luminous use of color and delicate complexity
of line give this edition a jewel-box quality.
The story has been translated by H. W. Dulchen
and, although faithful to the story, is somewhat
more compressed than other translations.

Andersen, Hans Christian. *It's Perfectly True, and Other
Stories.* Trans. from the Danish by Paul Leyssac;
illus. Richard Bennett. Harcourt, 1938.
    Translated by a Dutch actor who was an Ander-
sen storyteller of repute. A conversational tone
is stressed in the text. Grades 5–7.

Andersen, Hans Christian. *The Little Match Girl.*
Illus. Blair Lent. Houghton Mifflin, 1968.
    A New Year's Eve tale of a homeless child who
finds love at last. Grades 2–4.

Andersen, Hans Christian. *The Little Mermaid.*
Trans. Eva Le Gallienne; illus. Edward Frascino.
Harper, 1971.
    This poignant tale of heartache is deepened by
an exuberant use of color. See also the edition
retold by Margaret Crawford Maloney and lyrically
illustrated by Laszlo Gal (Methuen, 1983).

Andersen, Hans Christian. *The Nightingale.*
Trans. Eva Le Gallienne; illus. Nancy Ekholm Burkert. Harper, 1965.
    The superb double-page illustrations with glow-
ing tones reflect the rich detail of Oriental art and
are reminiscent of early Chinese scroll paintings.
Grades 3–5. See also the edition illustrated by
Harold Berson (Lippincott, 1962).

Andersen, Hans Christian. *Seven Tales.* Trans. from
the Danish by Eva Le Gallienne; illus. Maurice
Sendak. Harper, 1959.
    A preface by the translator and one by the artist
add interest to this attractive edition. Grades
3–5.

Andersen, Hans Christian. *The Snow Queen.*
Trans. R. P. Keigwin; illus. Marcia Brown.
Scribner's, 1972.
    The artist has combined in a particularly satisfy-
ing way the mystical and human qualities of this
story. See also the edition illustrated by Jane Atkin
Corwin (Atheneum, 1968) and that adapted by
Naomi Lewis and illustrated by Erroll Le Cain (Vi-
king, 1979).

Andersen, Hans Christian. *The Steadfast Tin Soldier.*
Trans. M. R. James; illus. Marcia Brown.
Scribner's, 1953.
    A favorite story in distinguished picture-book
format. Marcia Brown's fresh, imaginative drawings convey the inner beauty and meaning of the
story. Grades 1–4. See also the edition illustrated
with fine charcoal drawings by Thomas Di Grazia
(Prentice-Hall, 1981).

Andersen, Hans Christian. *The Swineherd.* Trans.
and illus. Erik Blegvad. Harcourt, 1958.
    A young Danish artist interprets the beloved
story of the foolish princess and the wise prince.
Grades 2–5. See also the edition translated by Anthea Bell and illustrated by Lisbeth Zwerger (Morrow, 1982).

Andersen, Hans Christian. *Thumbelina.* Trans.
R. P. Keigwin; illus. Adrienne Adams. Scribner's,
1961.
    Soft water colors enhance the charm of this favor-
ite story. Grades K–3. See also the rendition by
Amy Ehrlich, exquisitely illustrated by Susan Jeffers
(Dial, 1979).

Andersen, Hans Christian. *The Ugly Duckling.*
Trans. R. P. Keigwin; illus. Johannes Larsen.
Macmillan, 1967.
    This edition was printed in Denmark in com-
memoration of the one hundred and fiftieth anniversary of the birth of Hans Andersen on April
2, 1805. The distinguished illustrations are by the
foremost Danish painter of birds. Grades 2–4.
Adrienne Adams has illustrated another edition
(Scribner's, 1965), as has Will Nickless (Penguin,
n.d.).

Andersen, Hans Christian. *What the Good Man Does
Is Always Right.* Illus. Rich Schreiter. Dial, 1968.
    How the "good man" bargains at the fair is sure
to amuse adults as well as children. Grades 2–4.

Andersen, Hans Christian. *The Wild Swans.* Trans. M. R. James; illus. Marcia Brown. Scribner's, 1963.

The sensitive illustrations in soft grays touched with rose reflect perfectly the mood of the story. Grades 3–5. See also the edition retold by Amy Ehrlich and sumptuously illustrated by Susan Jeffers (Dial, 1981).

Atwater, Richard. *Mr. Popper's Penguins.* Illus. Robert Lawson. Little, Brown, 1938.

A house painter's life turns into a wild romp when he takes in a single penguin and soon becomes an impresario for a family of performing penguins. Grades 1–4.

Averill, Esther. *Captains of the City Streets: A Story of the Cat Club.* Illus. by the author. Harper, 1972.

An adventure of two tramp cats who find a new life in another part of New York. Grades 2–5. See also *Jenny and the Cat Club: A Collection of Favorite Stories about Jenny Linsky* (1973).

Babbitt, Natalie. *Tuck Everlasting.* Farrar, Straus & Giroux, 1975.

A young girl's encounter with a family that unwittingly has acquired immunity from death results in her being kidnapped. Knowing the source of their immortality, she has to decide whether or not she will choose an everlasting life. Grades 4–8. See also *The Search for Delicious* (1969); *Kneeknock Rise* (1970); *Goody Hall* (1971); and *The Devil's Storybook* (1974).

Barrie, Sir James Matthew. *Peter Pan.* Illus. Nora S. Unwin. Scribner's, The Willow Leaf Library, 1950.

A beautiful edition with delicate line drawings. This book is part of the Barrie "Peter Pan Bequest," as royalties go to the Great Ormond Street Hospital for Sick Children in London. Grades 3–5. See also the edition handsomely illustrated by Trina Schart Hyman (1980).

Baum, L. Frank. *The Wizard of Oz.* Illus. W. W. Denslow. Macmillan, The Macmillan Classics, 1970.

The popular pilgrimage of the three endearing characters to the Emerald City in quest of a brain, a heart, courage, and Kansas. With an afterword by Clifton Fadiman and the original stylish illustrations. Grades 3–5. See also the edition flamboyantly illustrated by Michael Hague (Holt, 1982). First published in 1900.

Bianco, Margery Williams. *The Velveteen Rabbit; or, How Toys Become Real.* Illus. William Nicholson. Doubleday, 1922.

How the velveteen rabbit was changed by nursery magic into a live rabbit is told in a story filled with the magic of childhood. Delightful pictures. Grades K–2. See also new editions available in a variety of formats and artistic styles, illustrated by Allen Atkinson (Knopf, 1983); Ilse Plume (Godine, 1983); Michael Hague (Holt, 1983); and Tien Ho (Simon & Schuster, 1983).

Bond, Michael. *A Bear Called Paddington.* Illus. Peggy Fortnum. Houghton Mifflin, 1960.

The endearing, mischievous bear from darkest Peru is always ending up in disastrous, hilarious scrapes. Grades 1–3.

Bond, Nancy. *A String in the Harp.* Illus. Allen Davis. Atheneum, A Margaret K. McElderry Book, 1976.

An American boy living unhappily in Wales after his mother's death discovers an ancient harp-turning key belonging to Taleisin, King Arthur's bard. He must return it to the sixth century. A well-observed, sensitive story with strong characters and an engrossing sense of place. Grades 5 and up.

Boston, Lucy M. *The Children of Green Knowe.* Illus. Peter Boston. Harcourt, 1955.

Real enchantment pervades this unusual story of a lonely boy who comes to live with his great-grandmother in an old country house in England. Grades 4–6. See also *Treasure of Green Knowe; The River at Green Knowe; A Stranger at Green Knowe;* and *An Enemy at Green Knowe.*

Boston, Lucy M. *The Sea Egg.* Illus. Peter Boston. Harcourt, 1967.

Beauty and magic of a summer by the sea are captured in this memorable story of two boys and the companion that the sea gave to them. Grades 3–6. See also *The Guardians of the House* (Atheneum, 1975).

Brooks, Walter R. *Freddy Goes to Florida.* Illus. Kurt Wiese. Knopf, 1949.

One of a long and popular series with Freddy the pig as hero. Grades 3–5.

Browne, Frances. *Granny's Wonderful Chair.* Illus. D. J. Watkins-Pitchford. New ed. Dutton, 1963.

These stories told to a little girl by the "chair of her grandmother" were written in 1857 and are still enjoyed by children today. Grades 4–6.

Butterworth, Oliver. *The Enormous Egg.* Illus. Louis Darling. Little, Brown, 1950.

A small boy's hen laid an egg that hatched a dinosaur. Grades 4–6.

Cameron, Eleanor. *The Court of the Stone Children.* Dutton, 1973.

A girl from the time of Napoleon appears to a girl of the twentieth century. Their stories interweave as the puzzle of a past murder accusation becomes unlocked. Grades 4–7.

Cameron, Eleanor. *Time and Mr. Bass.* Illus. Fred Meise. Little, Brown, 1967.

A new Mushroom Planet book in which Mr. Bass, David, and Chuck set off for the Mycetian meeting in Wales. Grades 4–6. See also *The Wonderful Flight of the Mushroom Planet; Stowaway to the Mushroom Planet; Mr. Bass's Planetoid; The Terrible Churnadryne;* and *A Mystery for Mr. Bass.*

Carlson, Natalie Savage. *Alphonse, That Bearded One.* Illus. Nicolas Mordvinoff. Harcourt, 1954.

Out of French Canada comes this robust, rollicking tale of a bear cub trained by his master, the shrewd Jeannot Vallar, to be a soldier. When Vallar is conscripted, he sends Alphonse in his place. Grades 3–5.

Carroll, Lewis (Charles Lutwidge Dodgson). *Alice's Adventures in Wonderland, and Through the Looking-Glass.* Illus. Sir John Tenniel. Macmillan, The Macmillan Classics, 1963.

First published in 1865 and 1872. Critics agree in acclaiming "Alice" the greatest nonsense story ever written. See also other good editions: the Heritage Press edition, with the original Tenniel drawings and a foreword by John T. Winterich; the Rainbow Classics edition (World), with the Tenniel illustrations and an introduction by May Lamberton Becker; and unusual editions by contemporary illustrators, including Barry Moser (Univ. of California Press, 1983) and S. Michelle Wiggins (Knopf, 1983). Grades 4–6.

Chant, Joy. *Red Moon and Black Mountain.* Dutton, 1976.

Three children are dramatically drawn through the power of music into the world of Khendiol, where they play important roles in the struggle against the forces of evil and a wild, primal magic demanding human sacrifice. A brilliantly realized secondary world. Grades 5 and up.

Christopher, John. *The White Mountains.* Macmillan, 1967.

The first in The White Mountains science fiction trilogy, this engrossing story chronicles the escape of three boys from the sinister Tripods, who intend to "cap" them and turn them into mindless slaves. Grades 5–9. See also *City of Gold and Lead* (1967) and *Pool of Fire* (1968).

Clarke, Pauline. *The Return of the Twelves.* Illus. Bernarda Bryson. Coward, 1963.

Past and present are skillfully woven in this captivating fantasy-adventure concerning the set of wooden soldiers once owned by Branwell Brontë and immortalized by him as the famous Twelve in his *History of the Young Men.* Grades 5–7. See also *The Two Faces of Silenus* (1972).

Cleary, Beverly. *The Mouse and the Motorcycle.* Illus. Louis Darling. Morrow, 1965.

A small boy and a mouse share a passionate love for motorcycles in this conspiratorial adventure. Grades 2–5. See also *Runaway Ralph* (1970) and *Ralph S. Mouse* (1982).

Collodi, Carlo (Carlo Lorenzini). *The Adventures of Pinocchio.* Trans. from the Italian by Carol Della Chiesa; illus. Attilio Mussino; foreword, Maria Cimino. Macmillan, 1969.

A welcome reissue of a handsomely illustrated and designed edition of a perennial favorite. Grades 3–5. Other less expensive editions are those illustrated by Naiad Einsel (Macmillan); Charles Folkard (Dutton); Anne Heyneman (Lippincott); Richard Floethe (World); Gerald McDermott (Four Winds); and Troy Howell (Lothrop, Lee & Shepard). First published in English in 1892.

Cooper, Susan. *The Grey King.* Illus. Michael Heslop. Atheneum, A Margaret K. McElderry book, 1975.

The fourth in a five-book sequence in which a continuing struggle between the forces of light and dark is told. Grades 5–9. The first was *Over Sea, under Stone* (Harcourt, 1966); the second was *The Dark Is Rising* (Atheneum, 1973); the third, *Greenwitch* (Atheneum, 1974); and the fifth, *Silver on the Tree* (1977). A fusing of mythological elements with realistic characters and events contributes to the distinctiveness of these books. *The Grey King* was awarded the 1976 Newbery Medal; see also *Seaward* (1983).

Cresswell, Helen. *Up the Pier.* Illus. Gareth Floyd. Macmillan, 1972.

Feeling stranded at a relative's in Wales, a young girl walks up the pier and discovers a family that is stranded in time. Their efforts to return to 1921, where they really belong, depend on magic, the most potent of which resides in the girl herself. Grades 4–6. See also *The Piemakers* (1967).

Cummings, E. E. *Fairy Tales.* Illus. John Eaton. Harcourt, 1965.

Stories that the poet wrote for his small daughter. Grades K–2.

Curry, Jane Louise. *Beneath the Hill.* Illus. Imero Gobbata. Harcourt, 1967.

An ancient evil released in nearby mountains by strip-mining is combated by contemporary children. See also *The Sleepers* (1968); *The Daybreakers* (1970); *Mindy's Mysterious Miniature* (1970); *The Ice Ghosts Mystery* (Atheneum, 1972); *The Lost Farm* (Atheneum, 1974), sequel to *Mindy's Mysterious Miniature;* and *Parsley Sage, Rosemary and Time* (1975). Grades 4–7.

Dahl, Roald. *Charlie and the Chocolate Factory.* Illus. Joseph Schindelman. Knopf, 1964.

Five children tour Mr. Willy Wonka's fabulous candy factory. Grades 4–6. See also *James and the Giant Peach: A Children's Story,* illus. Nancy Ekholm Burkert (1961), and *The Witches,* illus. Quentin Blake (Farrar, Straus & Giroux, 1983).

Davies, Andrew. *Conrad's War.* Crown, 1980.

A uniquely conceived satire on war, violence, and family relationships. Conrad's fantasies carry him, his eccentric writer father, and his dog on bomber flights over World War II Germany and into the famous Colditz prisoner-of-war camp. War is not as romantic as he had imagined. Winner of the British Guardian Award for 1978. Grades 5–9.

De la Mare, Walter. *The Three Royal Monkeys.* Illus. Mildred Eldridge. Knopf, 1948.

Originally published as *The Three Mulla-Mulgars,* this is an enthralling tale of the adventures of three monkeys, Thumb, Thimble, and Nod. Grades 4–6. See also *A Penny a Day* and *The Magic Jacket.*

Dickens, Charles. *The Magic Fishbone.* Illus. F. D. Bedford. Warne, n.d.

A sprightly fantasy of the Princess Alicia and her eighteen brothers and sisters. The illustrations catch the spirit of the story. Grades 2–4. See also *A Christmas Carol,* illus. Arthur Rackham (Lippincott, 1956); Michael Foreman (Dutton, 1983); and Trina Schart Hyman (Holiday House, 1983).

Dickinson, Peter. *The Weathermonger.* Little, Brown 1969.

A future Britain has mysteriously turned back the clock to a medieval way of life antagonistic to machines. Two children in search of the source of this disturbance set out in a silver Rolls Royce on a thrilling odyssey. Grades 4–6. See also the sequels in The Changes Trilogy, *Heartsease* (1969) and *The Devil's Children* (1970), and also *The Blue Hawk* (Little, Brown 1976).

Du Bois, William Pène. *Twenty-One Balloons.* Illus. by the author. Viking, 1947.

Fabulous adventure in the best Jules Verne tradition. The author combines his rich imagination, scientific tastes, and brilliant artistry to tell the story. Grades 4–6. See also *The Great Geppy; Peter Graves; Lion; Three Policemen;* and *Bear Party.*

Eager, Edward. *Half Magic.* Illus. N. M. Bodecker. Harcourt, 1954.

The finding of an ancient coin that grants half of any wish leads four children into many surprising adventures. Grades 4–6. See also *Knights Castle; Magic by the Lake; Time Garden; Magic or Not?; The Well Wishers;* and *Seven Day Magic.*

Engdahl, Sylvia Louise. *Enchantress from the Stars.* Atheneum, 1970.

The first in a science fiction series, this is the story of a space-girl's coming of age as she tries to save a feudal Earth-type planet from invasion by an imperialistic alien culture. Grades 5 and up. See also the sequel, *The Far Side of Evil* (1971).

Enright, Elizabeth. *Tatsinda.* Illus. Irene Haas. Harcourt, 1963.

The author has created a new fairy world, a wondrous mountain kingdom of Tatrajan where lives a race of people with white hair and ice-blue eyes. A many-faceted story written in true fairy-tale tradition. Grades 3–5. See also *Zeee.*

Estes, Eleanor. *The Witch Family.* Illus. Edward Ardizzone. Harcourt, 1960.

A wholly original fantasy of two small girls, three witches, and a bumblebee. Grades 3–5.

Farjeon, Eleanor. *The Glass Slipper.* Illus. Ernest H. Shepard. Viking, 1956.

The fairy play, *The Glass Slipper,* by Eleanor Farjeon and her brother was successfully produced in London. This is the story of the Cinderella play expanded to book length. Miss Farjeon's sense of humor, her gift of poetic expression, and her exquisitely balanced prose give fresh beauty to this well-loved story. The illustrations add their own charm of exaggerated drollery. Grades 5–7. See also *The Silver Curlew* (Viking, 1953); *Martin Pippin in the Apple Orchard* (Lippincott, 1963), a new edition of a collection of tales of fantasy first published in 1921; its sequel, *Martin Pippin in the Daisy-Field;* and *The Little Bookroom* (Godine, 1984).

Farmer, Penelope. *Castle of Bone.* Atheneum, 1972.

The magical properties of a secondhand wardrobe return items placed inside to previous original states. When a boy stumbles inside he becomes a helpless infant. Grades 4–7. See also earlier titles published by Harcourt: *The Summer Birds* (1962);

Emma in Winter (1966); and *Charlotte Sometimes* (1969). Also, *William and Mary* (1974).

Field, Rachel. *Hitty: Her First Hundred Years.* Illus. Dorothy Lathrop. Macmillan, 1937.

A through the eyes of a famous doll, the reader sees America one hundred years ago—whaling days, plantation life, Quaker Philadelphia, and New York in the days of Charles Dickens's visit. Awarded the Newbery Medal. A new edition has been issued. Grades 5–8.

Gannett, Ruth Stiles. *My Father's Dragon.* Illus. Ruth Chrisman Gannett. Random House, 1948.

A refreshingly original story in which a small boy rescues an oppressed baby dragon. Here is fantasy perfectly plausible. The robust text is matched by enchanting illustrations. Grades 1–3. See also *Elmer and the Dragon* and *The Dragons of Blueland.*

Garner, Alan. *The Owl Service.* Walck, 1968.

A haunting tale in which three modern young people are inexorably drawn into the power of a tragic Welsh legend. Awarded the Carnegie Medal in 1968. Grades 7–9. See also *Elidor* (Walck, 1964); *The Moon of Gomrath* (1967); *The Weirdstone of Brisingamen* (1969); and the complex, provocative *Red Shift* (Macmillan, 1973).

Godden, Rumer. *Impunity Jane: The Story of a Pocket Doll.* Illus. Adrienne Adams. Viking, 1954.

Jane is a four-inch pocket doll, neglected by four generations of little girls, who finally becomes the beloved mascot of a seven-year-old boy. Grades 2–4.

Godden, Rumer. *The Mousewife.* Illus. William Pène du Bois. Viking, 1951.

A tender story of a little mousewife whose devotion to a caged dove led to her sacrifice when, moved by compassion, she freed the bird. The story is based on an anecdote in Dorothy Wordsworth's Grasmere journal. Grades 2–4. See also *The Fairy Doll; The Dolls' House; Miss Happiness and Miss Flower; Little Plum;* and *Home Is the Sailor.*

Goudge, Elizabeth. *The Little White Horse.* Illus. C. Walter Hodges. Coward, 1946.

A poetic tale of a tangled inheritance, centuries old, which a young girl first must understand and then find a solution for. Grades 4–7.

Grahame, Kenneth. *The Wind in the Willows.* Illus. Ernest H. Shepard. Scribner's, 1983.

First published in 1908, this new edition celebrates the seventy-fifth anniversary of the ageless fantasy of the little animals that live along the bank of a river flowing through the English countryside, and those that live in the wild wood. There is kindly wisdom, gentle humor, and sheer magic in the writing. All ages. See also the editions illustrated by Michael Hague (Holt, 1980) and by John Burningham (Viking, 1983).

Hamilton, Virginia. *Justice and Her Brothers.* Greenwillow, 1978.

A sophisticated, suspenseful fantasy about a new breed of children with psychic powers and a destiny. Grades 6 and up. See also the sequels, *Dustland* (1980) and *The Gathering* (1981), and also *Sweet Whispers, Brother Rush* (Philomel, 1982).

Harris, Rosemary. *The Moon in the Cloud.* Macmillan, 1970.

A jocular re-creation of the time of the flood when a young animal trainer travels to Egypt for some animals needed for Noah's ark and is caught in the devious intrigues of the Egyptian royal court. Awarded the Carnegie Medal in 1969, this is the first of a trilogy composed of *The Shadow on the Sun* (1970) and *The Bright and Morning Star* (1972). Grades 4–7.

Harris, Rosemary. *A Quest for Orion.* Faber & Faber, 1978.

Set in England in the year 1999, this science fiction story combines elements of mythology and harsh sociological speculation. A group of teenage resistance fighters battle against subjugation by a European-wide neo-Stalinist order. They are helped by the mystical power of Charlemagne's relics and an alien force from the constellation Orion. Grades 6 and up. See also the sequel, *Tower of the Stars* (1980).

Hauff, Wilhelm. *Dwarf Long-Nose.* Trans. Doris Orgel; illus. Maurice Sendak. Random House, 1960.

The adventures and trials of a boy enchanted by a witch. Grades 3–6.

Hoban, Russell. *The Mouse and His Child.* Illus. Lillian Hoban. Harper, 1967.

A multilayered animal fable about the quest of two clockwork mouse toys for home and self-winding. The suspenseful narrative is colored by social satire and sophisticated philosophical allusions. Grades 4 and up.

Hoover, H. M. *The Bell Tree.* Viking, 1982.

Ancient, mysterious ruins on a distant planet are the setting for a battle between human intruders and nonhuman forces. Fastpaced science fiction with strong characterization and vivid description. Grades 5–8. See also *Children of Morrow* (Four Winds, 1973); *Return to Earth* (1980); and *This Time of Darkness* (1980).

Housman, Laurence. *The Rat-Catcher's Daughter: A Collection of Stories.* Sel. and ed. Ellin Greene; illus. Julia Noonan. Atheneum, A Margaret K. McElderry Book, 1974.

A new presentation of Victorian fantasies that have been out of print. The poetic and often mystical tales have long been favorites of storytellers. Grades 4–9.

Hudson, William Henry. *A Little Boy Lost.* Illus. A. D. McCormick. Knopf, 1918.

An imaginative tale of South America filled with that quality the author says he liked best as a child, "the little thrills that nature itself gave me, which half frightened and fascinated at the same time, the wonder and mystery of it all." Grades 5–7.

Hughes, Monica. *The Keeper of the Isis Light.* Atheneum, 1981.

Olwen is an orphan who has lived her entire life alone with her robot guardian on a lighthouse planet. Although she thinks of herself as human, she is shocked by the revulsion at her appearance shown by human colonists who arrive on the planet. A gripping, philosophical story. Grades 5 and up. See also the sequels: *The Guardian of Isis* (1982), winner of the Canada Council's Children's Literature Prize for 1981, and *The Isis Pedlar* (1983).

Hughes, Ted. *The Iron Giant: A Story in Five Nights.* Illus. George Adamson. Harper, 1968.

A contemporary literary fairy tale in which a boy befriends an iron-eating robot who is devouring the machines of the countryside. The innocent monster ultimately proves himself by saving Earth from an alien attack. Grades 3–5.

Hunter, Mollie. *The Haunted Mountain.* Illus. Laszlo Kubinyi. Harper, 1972.

Defying "the good people," a young Scots farmer tries to escape their vengeance but is, at last, captured. See also *The Kelpie's Pearls* (Funk & Wagnalls, 1966) and *A Stranger Came Ashore: A Story of Suspense* (1975).

Jansson, Tove. *Finn Family Moomintroll.* Trans. Elizabeth Portch; illus. by the author. Walck, 1965.

An entirely original population is created for these stories. Grades 3–6. Other titles are: *Moominsummer Madness* (1961); *Moominland Midwinter* (1962); *Tales from Moominvalley* (1964); *The Exploits of Moominpappa* (1966); and *Moominpappa at Sea* (1967).

Jarrell, Randall. *The Animal Family.* Illus. Maurice Sendak. Pantheon, 1965.

A poetic story about a hunter, a mermaid, a bear

cub, a baby lynx, and a little boy. Grades 4–7. See also *The Bat-Poet* (Macmillan, 1964) and *Fly by Night* (Farrar, Straus & Giroux, 1976), both delicately illustrated by Maurice Sendak.

Juster, Norton. *The Phantom Tollbooth.* Illus. Jules Feiffer. Random House, 1961.

A sophisticated fantasy about a small boy who doesn't know what to do with himself. Filled with humor and wisdom. Grades 6–9.

Kendall, Carol. *The Gammage Cup.* Illus. Erik Blegvad. Harcourt, 1959.

A highly creative fantasy of a race of small people, the Minnipins, who live in the land between the mountains isolated from their enemies, The Hairless Ones. Grades 5–7. See also the sequel, *The Whisper of Glocken.*

Kingsley, Charles. *The Water Babies.* Illus. Harold Jones. F. Watts, 1961.

Written in 1862 for his four-year-old son, the author endeavors to teach lessons of nature and ethics in the guise of a fairy tale. Grades 4–5.

Kipling, Rudyard. *All the Mowgli Stories.* Illus. Kurt Wiese. Doubleday, 1954. Grades 3–6.

Kipling, Rudyard. *The Beginning of the Armadillos.* Illus. Giulio Maestro. St. Martin's, 1970.

A colorful, picture-book format of a story that is particularly beguiling in its use of words and rhymed refrains. Grades 1–3.

Kipling, Rudyard. *The Cat That Walked by Himself.* Illus. Rosemary Wells. Hawthorn, 1970.

With black-and-white drawings, much in the mood of Kipling's own illustrations, some in color.

Kipling, Rudyard. *The Elephant's Child.* Illus. Leonard Weisgard. Walker, 1970.

A picture-book format with cool colors. Grades 1–3. See also the edition illus. by Ulla Kampmann (Follett, 1969).

Kipling, Rudyard. *How the Leopard Got His Spots.* Illus. Leonard Weisgard. Walker, 1972.

A sustained mood is set with illustrations on each page. Grades 1–3.

Kipling, Rudyard. *How the Whale Got His Throat.* Illus. Don Madden. Addison-Wesley, n.d.

Light-hearted and humorous, these pictures seem to move with the story.

Kipling, Rudyard. *The Jungle Books.* 2 vols. Illus. Aldren Watson. Doubleday, 1948.

See also *The Jungle Book,* illus. Philip Hays (Doubleday, 1964). First published in 1894 and 1895.

Kipling, Rudyard. *Just So Stories.* Illus. J. M. Gleeson. Doubleday, 1912.

Classic nonsense about how the elephant got his trunk, how the camel got his hump, and other fanciful tales. See also the edition illustrated by the author (1902, 1907); illustrated by Nicholas (Nicholas Mordvinoff) (1952); and illustrated by Etienne Delessert (1972), a special anniversary edition. Grades 4–6. First published in 1902.

Lagerlöf, Selma. *The Wonderful Adventures of Nils.* Trans. from the Swedish by Velma Swanston Howard; illus. H. Baumhauer. Pantheon, 1947.

Nils, reduced to elfin size, travels over Sweden on the back of a wild goose migrating north. Natural history is combined with a delightful fairy story. Grades 4–7.

Langton, Jane. *The Diamond in the Window.* Illus. Erik Blegvad. Harper, 1962.

Dreams become dangerous avenues of exploration with symbolic meanings as two children find they are actively involved in a struggle that may leave them captives in another time and space. Grades 4–6. See also *The Swing in the Summerhouse* (1967); *The Astonishing Stereoscope* (1971); and *The Fledgling* (Harper, 1980).

Laurence, Margaret. *The Olden Days Coat.* Illus. Muriel Wood. McClelland & Stewart, 1979.

In this beautifully narrated time-slip fantasy for younger readers, a ten-year-old girl travels back in time and meets her grandmother when she was young. Grades 2–4.

Lawson, Robert. *Rabbit Hill.* Illus. by the author. Viking, 1944.

An engaging fantasy about a rabbit family and the small animals living on a Connecticut hillside, and how they share in the excitement of New Folks coming to live in the Big House. Awarded the Newbery Medal in 1945. Grades 3–6. *The Tough Winter,* a sequel, is equally delightful.

Le Guin, Ursula. *A Wizard of Earthsea.* Illus. Ruth Robbins. Parnassus, 1969.

A compelling fantasy of wizards and wizardry with an underlying meaning applicable to impatient youth of any age. Grades 7–9. See also the sequels: *The Tombs of Atuan* (Atheneum, 1970) and *The Farthest Shore* (Atheneum, 1972).

L'Engle, Madeleine. *A Wrinkle in Time.* Farrar, Straus & Giroux, 1962.

A provocative science fantasy of two children who, with an older boy, go in search of their missing scientist-father. The adventure takes them through space by means of a "tesseract," or wrinkle in time, to a planet dominated by the Powers of Darkness. Grades 6–9. See also the sequels: *A*

Wind in the Door (1973) and *A Swiftly Tilting Planet* (1978).

Lewis, C. S. *The Lion, the Witch and the Wardrobe.* Illus. Pauline Baynes. Macmillan, 1950.

While spending a holiday at an old estate in England, four children find their way through a huge wardrobe to the magical land of Narnia, peopled with princes, dwarfs, and talking beasts. Grades 4–6. This is the first of seven stories telling of Narnian adventures. See also: *Prince Caspian; The Voyage of the Dawn Treader; The Silver Chair; The Horse and His Boy; The Magician's Nephew;* and *The Last Battle.*

Lindgren, Astrid. *Pippi Longstocking.* Trans. from the Swedish by Florence Lamborn; illus. Louis Glanzman. Viking, 1950.

Pippi's fantastic escapades, in a world without grown-ups, make a story dear to the heart of a child. Grades 4–7. See also *Ronia, the Robber's Daughter* (1983).

Linklater, Eric. *The Wind on the Moon.* Illus. Nicolas Bentley. Macmillan, 1964.

Influenced by "the wind on the moon," two sisters engage in a series of adventures, which include turning themselves into kangaroos; freeing a falcon and a puma from the zoo; and, in their natural form, rescuing their father from a dungeon in Bombardy (a country where Bombast is spoken). Grades 4–7.

Lively, Penelope. *The Ghost of Thomas Kempe.* Illus. Antony Maitland. Dutton, 1973.

A seventeenth-century sorcerer, released from his imprisonment, proceeds to harass a young boy in an attempt to regain his former position of authority. Awarded the Carnegie Medal. Grades 4–7. See also *The House in Norham Gardens* (1974) and *A Stitch in Time* (1976).

Lofting, Hugh. *The Story of Doctor Dolittle.* Illus. by the author. Lippincott, 1920.

The first of the famous Doctor Dolittle books. Hugh Walpole hailed this book as "the first children's classic since Alice." Grades 3–6. See also *The Voyages of Doctor Dolittle,* awarded the Newbery Medal in 1923.

Lunn, Janet. *The Root Cellar.* Scribner's, 1983.

An alienated teenage orphan passes through the root cellar of an old Ontario farmhouse into the 1860s. She finds acceptance with new friends and struggles to understand the cruel realities of the American Civil War. Winner of the Canadian Library Association Book of the Year for Children Award in 1982. Grades 5–7.

McCaffrey, Anne. *Dragonsong.* Illus. Laura Lydecker. Atheneum, 1976.

A young girl on the planet Pern dreams of becoming a harper, a role forbidden to women in her society. She runs away and befriends a family of baby fire lizards, teaching them to sing. Grades 5–9. See also the sequels: *Dragonsinger* (1977) and *Dragondrums* (1979).

Macdonald, George. *At the Back of the North Wind.* Illus. Harvey Dinnerstein; afterword, Clifton Fadiman. New ed. Macmillan, The Macmillan Classics, 1964.

First published in 1871. A rare quality pervades Macdonald's fairy stories. Grades 4–6. See also the edition illustrated by Charles Mozley (F. Watts, Nonesuch Cygnets, 1964); *The Golden Key,* illustrated by Maurice Sendak (Farrar, Straus & Giroux, 1967), a haunting story admired by J. R. R. Tolkien and C. S. Lewis; and for a younger audience, *The Light Princess,* illustrated by Maurice Sendak (Farrar, Straus & Giroux, 1969) and by William Pène du Bois (Crowell, 1962), and the two princess books, *The Princess and the Goblins* and *The Princess and Curdie.*

MacGregor, Ellen. *Miss Pickerell Goes to Mars.* Illus. Paul Galdone. McGraw-Hill, 1951.

A delightful mixture of scientific fact, fantasy, and humor. Grades 4–6. See also *Miss Pickerell Goes to the Arctic; Miss Pickerell Goes Undersea;* and *Miss Pickerell on the Moon.*

McKinley, Robin. *Beauty: A Retelling of the Story of Beauty and the Beast.* Harper, 1978.

Beauty is bright, scholarly, and plain in this expanded version of the classic French fairy tale. Written with psychological intensity in an elegant, contemporary voice. Grades 5 and up. See also *The Blue Sword* (Greenwillow, 1982).

Maguire, Gregory. *The Dream Stealer.* Harper, 1983.

Evocative of Russian folklore, this highly colored fantasy tells the story of two Russian children who, with the help of their dreams and the witch Baba Yaga, rescue their village from a legendary demon wolf. Originally told, with poetic phrasing and light wit. Grades 4–6.

Mayne, William. *Earthfasts.* Dutton, 1967.

A highly original fantasy of compelling drama in which the author employs strands of legend and folklore in crossing the time barrier. Two English boys encounter a drummer boy of two hundred years ago who had gone in search of reputed treasure buried with King Arthur and his knights. Grades 5–8. See also *A Game of Dark* (1971); *A*

Year and a Day (1976); and *It* (Greenwillow, 1977).

Milne, A. A. *The House at Pooh Corner.* Illus. Ernest H. Shepard. Dutton, 1961.

First published in 1928, this is the continuation of adventures begun in *Winnie-the-Pooh* (1926). These stories about a small boy and his toys are contained together in *The World of Pooh* (1957). Grades 1–6.

Nesbit, E. (Mrs. Hubert Bland). *The Complete Book of Dragons.* Illus. Erik Blegvad. Hamilton, 1972.

All but one of these stories first appeared in 1900 as *The Book of Dragons.* Original and humorous, these stories turn traditional dragon lore on its head. Grades 2–5.

Nesbit, E. (Mrs. Hubert Bland). *The Enchanted Castle.* Illus. H. R. Millar. Benn, 1956.

A ring, discovered by four children, has such unusual magical properties that a number of disconcerting predicaments occur before they understand its true nature. Grades 3–7.

Nesbit, E. (Mrs. Hubert Bland). *The Story of the Amulet.* Illus. H. R. Millar. Benn, 1957.

The amazing adventures that befell the children in *Five Children and It* and *The Phoenix and the Carpet* reach a dramatic climax when, through the power of the Amulet, the children are whisked off to ancient Egypt in the time of the Pharaohs. Published in 1906, this is one of the first fantasies written for children that deals with time. Grades 3–5.

Nichols, Ruth. *A Walk out of the World.* Illus. Trina Schart Hyman. Harcourt, 1969.

A brother and sister slip into another world where they engage in battle against an evil sorcerer. See also *The Marrow of the World* (Macmillan, 1972), winner of the 1973 Canadian Library Association Book of the Year Award for Children. Grades 4–6.

Norton, Mary. *The Borrowers.* Illus. Beth Krush and Joe Krush. Harcourt, 1953.

The author has succeeded admirably in creating a miniature world of tiny people no taller than a pencil who live in quiet old houses and skillfully "borrow" what they need. Grades 4–7. See these delightful adventures continued in *The Borrowers Afield, The Borrowers Afloat,* and *The Borrowers Aloft* (the four stories are now available in *The Complete Adventures of the Borrowers)* and the newest addition to the series, *The Borrowers Avenged* (1983). See also *Bedknob and Broomstick.*

O'Brien, Robert. *Mrs. Frisby and the Rats of NIMH.* Illus. Zena Bernstein. Atheneum, 1971.

A highly intelligent and resourceful rat civilization is colonized by some escapees from a laboratory, where they had been injected with a substance to make them the equal of man. Grades 4–7. See also the mature science fiction tale set in a world after a nuclear holocaust, *Z for Zachariah* (1975).

Park, Ruth. *Playing Beatie Bow.* Atheneum, 1982.
Winner of the Boston Globe-Horn Book Award, this Australian time-traveling fantasy takes a young adolescent girl back to the dangerous slums of nineteenth-century Sydney. Emotionally disturbed by her parents' estrangement, she finds strength and love in a family who cares for her. Grades 6 and up.

Pearce, Philippa. *Tom's Midnight Garden.* Illus. Susan Einzig. Lippincott, 1959.
Tom discovers at midnight a Victorian garden that does not exist in the daytime. A quiet, mysterious story, beautifully written. Grades 5–7.

Pope, Elizabeth Marie. *The Perilous Gard.* Illus. Richard Cuffari. Houghton Mifflin, 1974.
Ancient elvish rule permeates the town and Elvenwood Hall, commonly known as the Perilous Gard. Kate, a daring and intelligent girl, becomes entangled with this hidden world in a conflict that engages her entire being. Grades 5–9.

Preussler, Otfried. *The Satanic Mill.* Trans. Anthea Bell. Macmillan, 1973.
A highly dramatic and symbolic story about the hold of evil over men. The climactic scene is an adaptation of the folktale motif in which a prisoner of the fairies is rescued by a mortal. Grades 5–9.

Pyle, Howard. *The Wonder Clock: Or, Four and Twenty Marvelous Tales, Being One for Each Hour of the Day.* Illus. by the author. Harper, 1915.
In his own inimitable way, the author has told these stories based on old tales and legends. *Pepper and Salt* is equally well liked.

Richler, Mordecai. *Jacob Two-Two Meets the Hooded Fang.* Illus. Fritz Wegner. Knopf, 1975.
A farcical romp in which adventure and melodrama combine to tell the story of an unjustly imprisoned child plotting escape from the gothic "Slimer's Isle" with the aid of "Child Power." Winner of the Canadian Library Association Book of the Year Award for Children, 1976. Grades 3–6.

Rodgers, Mary. *Freaky Friday.* Harper, 1972.
When a young girl is transformed into her mother for a day her awareness of others and understanding of herself increases. Grades 4–8. See also *Summer Switch* (1982).

Ruskin, John. *The King of the Golden River.* Illus. Fritz Kredel; intro. May Lamberton Becker. World, Rainbow Classics, 1946.
Written in Scotland in 1841 when the author was twenty-two, this classic fairy story tells how a family inheritance lost by cruelty was regained by love. Grades 4–6.

Saint-Exupéry, Antoine de. *The Little Prince.* Trans. from the French by Katherine Woods; illus. by the author. Harcourt, 1943.
With exquisite imagery, the poet-aviator shares his vision of life through the adventures of a little prince who visited our world from his own tiny planet. Grades 3–5.

Sandburg, Carl. *Rootabaga Stories.* Illus. Maud Petersham and Miska Petersham. Harcourt, n.d.
Unique nonsense stories combine fantasy and realism of the American Middle West. Grades 3–4.

Sauer, Julia L. *Fog Magic.* Illus. Lynd Ward. Viking, 1943.
A richly imaginative story in which the author has skillfully fused two worlds, the present and that of a century ago. Greta is a very real little girl and the 100-year-old village of Blue Cove, Nova Scotia, which she finds in the heart of the fog, seems equally convincing. Grades 4–6.

Seldon, George. *The Cricket in Times Square.* Illus. Garth Williams. Farrar, Straus & Giroux, 1960.
An engaging fantasy of a country cricket transported to Times Square in a picnic basket. Grades 3–6. See *Tucker's Countryside* (Farrar, Straus & Giroux, 1969) for more Cricket adventures. See also *The Genie of Sutton Place* (1973) and *Harry Cat's Pet Puppy* (1974).

Sendak, Maurice. *Higglety Pigglety Pop! or There Must Be More to Life.* Illus. by the author. Harper, 1967.
The rambling adventures of Jennie, a Sealyham dog, who finally finds happiness as the leading lady of The World Mother Goose Theatre. Grades 3–6.

Sharp, Margery. *The Rescuers.* Illus. Garth Williams. Little, Brown, 1959.
A beguiling fantasy about three mice who rescue a Norwegian poet from the grim prison, the Black Castle. Grades 4–6. See also *Miss Bianca; The Turret;* and *Miss Bianca in the Salt Mines.*

Singer, Isaac Bashevis. *Mazel and Shlimazel, or The Milk of a Lioness.* Trans. from the Yiddish by the author and Elizabeth Shub; illus. Margot Zemach. Farrar, Straus & Giroux, 1967.

A contest between good luck and bad luck is told in the tradition of the folktale. Grades 3–5. See also *The Fearsome Inn,* illustrated by Nonny Hogrogian (Scribner's, 1967).

Sleater, William. *The House of Stairs.* Dutton, 1974.

A chilling vision of a future in which five teenagers are subjected to inhuman mind-control experiments. Set in the closed world of an antiseptic, Escher-like environment filled with stairs suspended in space. Compelling and terrifying. Grades 5–9.

Smith, Dodie. *The Hundred and One Dalmations.* Illus. Janet Grahame-Johnstone and Anne Grahame-Johnstone. Viking, 1957.

A melodramatic story of villainy and the mass kidnapping of Dalmations, which is finally foiled by the parents of a kidnapped litter. See also the sequel, *The Starlight Barking* (1968).

Steele, Mary Q. *Journey Outside.* Illus. Rocco Negri. Viking, 1969.

A highly symbolic story of a boy's escape from the underground circling travels of his people and his discovery of the earth outside. Grades 4–7.

Steig, William. *Abel's Island.* Illus. by the author. Farrar, Straus & Giroux, 1976.

A mouse-sized Robinsonnade in which a dandified Edwardian rodent is catastrophically swept away in a storm to an isolated island—there he discovers his true mouse nature in his struggle for survival. The tongue-in-cheek tone is extended through the elegant, droll illustrations. Grades 3–6. See also *Dominic* (1972).

Stockton, Frank R. *The Bee-Man of Orn.* Illus. Maurice Sendak. Holt, 1964.

First published in 1887. Maurice Sendak's period drawings and preface add interest to the story. Grades 4–8. See also *The Griffin and the Minor Canon.*

Swift, Jonathan. *Gulliver's Travels.* Illus. Aldren Watson. Revised and slightly abridged ed. Grosset & Dunlap, n.d.

Published as a satire for adults in 1726, the book has been enjoyed as a fairy story by children for generations. Grades 5–9. See also the edition containing the visits to Lilliput and Brobdingnag, illustrated by David Small with compelling pen-and-ink drawings (Morrow, 1983).

Thurber, James. *Many Moons.* Illus. Louis Slobodkin. Harcourt, 1943.

There is a rare quality of tenderness and wisdom in this delicate fantasy of the little princess who wanted the moon. The sensitive drawings catch the mood of the story. Awarded the Caldecott Medal in 1944. Grades 2–4. See also *The Great Quillow; The White Deer;* and *The Thirteen Clocks.*

Tolkien, J. R. R. *The Hobbit.* Illus. by the author. Houghton Mifflin, 1938.

A rich imaginative tale, with roots deep in Anglo-Saxon folklore, of a hobbit on a magnificent adventure to recover a treasure of gold guarded by Smaug, the dragon. Older boys and girls who like heroic romance will enjoy reading the three books comprising the fabulous allegory, *The Lord of the Rings.* Grades 5–8.

Travers, Pamela L. *Mary Poppins.* Illus. Mary Shepard. Harcourt, 1934; rev. ed. 1981.

Ever since the day that Mary Poppins blew in with an east wind and slid up the banister to the nursery of the Banks children, life became touched with fun and magic. Grades 4–6. See also *Mary Poppins Comes Back* (1935); *Mary Poppins Opens the Door* (1943); *Mary Poppins in the Park* (1952); and *Mary Poppins in Cherry Tree Lane* (1982). *Maria Poppina* is a Latin version of *Mary Poppins from A to Z,* a collection of twenty-six episodes about Mary Poppins and the characters of the earlier books.

Uttley, Alison. *A Traveler in Time.* Illus. Christine Price. Viking, 1964.

Penelope transcends time and history and finds herself in her ancestral home in the days of Queen Elizabeth I. Grades 5–9.

Verne, Jules. *Twenty Thousand Leagues under the Sea.* Illus. W. J. Aylward. Scribner's, 1925.

The story of Captain Nemo's ingenious submarine boat. First published in 1870, it is considered a forerunner of science fiction. Grades 5–12.

Walsh, Jill Paton. *A Chance Child.* Farrar, Straus & Giroux, 1978.

An abused contemporary child slips back in time to the Industrial Revolution in England. He is a silent witness to cruelties suffered by the child laborers whom he befriends. Compelling in the strong characterization, grim setting, and significant theme. Grades 5 and up. See also the author's science fiction parable, *The Green Book,* illustrated by Lloyd Bloom (1982).

Wells, H. G. *Seven Science Fiction Novels of H. G. Wells.* Dover, 1895.

An enduring collection that contains such favorites as "The Time Machine" and "The War of the Worlds." Grades 5 and up.

White, Elwyn Brooks. *Charlotte's Web.* Illus. Garth Williams. Harper, 1952.

Only E. B. White could have written this story of Charlotte the spider, Wilbur the pig, and a little girl who could talk to animals. Grades 4–6. See also *Stuart Little,* illus. Garth Williams (1952), and *The Trumpet of the Swan* (1970).

White, T. H. *Mistress Masham's Repose.* Jonathan Cape, 1947.

Descendants of Swift's Lilliputians are discovered by a young girl who then has to cope with her power as a giant. The issue of human freedom lies squarely in the center of this adventurous fantasy in which Maria and the People join forces to outwit her scheming governess and evil guardian. Grades 5–12.

White, T. H. *The Sword in the Stone.* Illus. by the author; endpapers by Robert Lawson. Putnam's, 1939.

A humorous version of the childhood of King Arthur when he was affectionately called the Wart. His tutor Merlyn magically transports him into one adventure after another as Arthur serves his apprenticeship at being a hero. Grades 5–12.

Wrightson, Patricia. *The Nargun and the Stars.* Atheneum, A Margaret K. McElderry book, 1974.

A primeval monster, almost indistinguishable from earth, moves with relentless destructiveness toward an Australian home as a young boy, and his cousins try to find a way of diverting it. Grades 5–9. See also *Down to Earth* (Harcourt, 1965); *The Ice is Coming* (1977); *The Dark Bright Water* (1979); *Journey behind the Wind* (1981); and *A Little Fear* (1983).

Young, Ella. *The Unicorn with the Silver Shoes.* Illus. Robert Lawson. Longmans, 1957.

In rhythmic prose the Irish poet tells the tale of Ballor, the King's son, and his adventures in the Land of the Ever Young. Wit, laughter, and the wonder of childhood are in these stories, which were told long ago in Dublin for the children of "AE." Grades 6–8.

References for Adults

Books

Barron, Neil, ed. *Anatomy of Wonder: An Historical Survey and Critical Guide to the Best of Science Fiction.* 2d ed. Bowker, 1981.

Cameron, Eleanor. *The Green and Burning Tree: On the Writing and Enjoyment of Children's Books.* Little, Brown, 1969.
Section I. Fantasy, pp. 3–134.

Crouch, Marcus. *The Nesbit Tradition: The Children's Novel in England, 1945–1970.* Rowman & Littlefield, 1972.

Essays Presented to Charles Williams. Oxford Univ. Press, 1947.
"On Fairy Tales," by J. R. R. Tolkien, pp. 38–90; "On Stories," by C. S. Lewis, pp. 90–105.

Field, Elinor Whitney, ed. *Horn Book Reflections on Children's Books and Reading.* Horn Book, 1969.
Section V. Fantasy, Yesterday and Today, pp. 203–49; Section VI. People and Places, pp. 253–90.

Fryatt, Norma R. *A Horn Book Sampler: On Children's Books and Reading.* Horn Book, 1959.
Section IV. What Fairy Tales Mean to a Child: "Cinderella in Ireland," by R. A. Warren; "Animals in Fairyland," by Alice M. Jordan; "What Fairy Tales Meant to a Turkish Child," by Selma Ekrem.

Green, Roger Lancelyn. *Tellers of Tales.* Rev. ed. Ward, 1965.

Higgins, James E. *Beyond Words: Mystical Fancy in Children's Literature.* Teachers College Press, 1970.

Le Guin, Ursula K. *The Language of the Night: Essays on Fantasy and Science Fiction.* Putnam's, 1979.

Prickett, Stephen. *Victorian Fantasy.* Indiana Univ. Press, 1979.

Scholes, Robert, and Eric S. Rabkin. *Science Fiction: History, Science, Vision.* Oxford Univ. Press, 1977.

Waggoner, Diana. *The Hills of Faraway: A Guide to Fantasy.* Atheneum, 1978.

Willard, Nancy. *The Angel in the Parlour: Five Stories and Eight Essays.* Harcourt, 1983.

Yolen, Jane. *Touch Magic: Fantasy, Faerie and Folklore in the Literature of Childhood.* Philomel, 1981.

Articles and Chapters

Alexander, Lloyd. "The Flat-Heeled Muse." *The Horn Book Magazine,* 41 (Apr. 1965), pp. 141–46.

Alexander, Lloyd. "Identifications and Identities." *Wilson Library Bulletin,* 45 (Oct. 1970), pp. 144–48.

Alexander, Lloyd. "Substance and Fantasy." *Library Journal*, 91 (Dec. 15, 1966), pp. 6157–59.

Alexander, Lloyd. "Truth about Fantasy." *Top of the News*, 24 (Jan. 1968), pp. 168–74.

Bator, Robert, ed. *Signposts to Criticism of Children's Literature*. American Library Association, 1983. See Chapter 8. "Fantasy." "Toward a Definition of Fantasy Fiction?" by Jane Mobley, pp. 249–60; "Enchantment Revisited; Or, Why Teach Fantasy?" by Jane M. Bingham, with Grayce Scholt, pp. 261–64. See Chapter 10. "Science Fiction." "Children's Science Fiction," by Margaret Esmonde, pp. 284–87; "Fantasy, SF, and the Mushroom Planet Books," by Eleanor Cameron, pp. 294–300.

Engdahl, Sylvia. "The Changing Role of Science Fiction in Children's Literature." *The Horn Book Magazine*, 47 (Oct. 1971), pp. 449–55.

Cameron, Eleanor. "The Dearest Freshness Deep Down Things." *The Horn Book Magazine*, 40 (Oct. 1964), pp. 459–72. Also in *The Green and Burning Tree*, by Eleanor Cameron. Little, Brown, 1969.

Cameron, Eleanor. "High Fantasy: A Wizard of Earthsea." *The Horn Book Magazine*, 47 (Apr. 1971), pp. 129–38.

Fish, Helen Dean. "Doctor Dolittle: His Life and Work." *The Horn Book Magazine*, 24 (Sept.-Oct. 1948), pp. 339–46.

Eaton, Anne. "Ella Young's Unicorns and Kyelins." *The Horn Book Magazine*, 9, pp. 115–20.

Gág, Wanda. "I Like Fairy Tales." *The Horn Book Magazine*, 15 (Mar.-Apr. 1939), pp. 75–80.

Goudge, Elizabeth. "West Country Magic." *The Horn Book Magazine*, 23 (Mar. 1947), pp. 100–3.

Hand, Nigel. "Mary Norton and 'The Borrowers'." *Children's Literature in Education*, no. 7 (Mar. 1972), pp. 38–55.

Heins, Paul, sel. and ed. *Crosscurrents of Criticism: Horn Book Essays, 1968–1977*. Horn Book, 1977. See Section VI. "In Defense of Fantasy." "High Fantasy and Heroic Romance," by Lloyd Alexander, pp. 170–77; "Realism Plus Fantasy Equals Magic," by Roger W. Drury, pp. 178–84; "The Weak Place in the Cloth: A Study of Fantasy for Children," by Jane Langton, pp. 185–96.

Holmes, C. S. "James Thurber and the Art of Fantasy." *Yale Review*, 55 (Oct. 1965), pp. 17–33.

Lively, Penelope. "The Ghost of Thomas Kempe." *The Junior Bookshelf*, 38 (June 1974), pp. 143–45.

MacCann, D. "Wells of Fantasy 1865–1965." *Wilson Library Bulletin*, 40 (Dec. 1965), pp. 334–43.

McNeill, Janet. "When the Magic Has to Stop." *The Horn Book Magazine*, 48 (Aug. 1972), pp. 337–42.

Merrick, Anne. " 'The Nightwatchmen' and 'Charlie and the Chocolate Factory' as Books to Be Read to Children." *Children's Literature in Education*, no. 16 (Spring 1975), pp. 21–30.

Rees, David. "The Narrative Art of Penelope Lively." *The Horn Book Magazine*, 51 (Feb. 1975), pp. 17–25.

Rees, David. "The Novels of Philippa Pearce." *Children's Literature in Education*, no. 4 (Mar. 1971), pp. 40–53.

Shochet, Lois. "Fantasy and English Children." *Top of the News*, 24 (Apr. 1968), pp. 311–20.

Hans Christian Andersen

Andersen, Hans Christian. *The Story of My Life*. Riverside Press, 1871.

The Andersen-Scudder Letters: Hans Christian Andersen Correspondence with Horace Elisha Scudder. Univ. of California Press, 1949.

Bredsdorff, Elias. *Hans Christian Andersen*. Scribner's, 1976.

Godden, Rumer. *Hans Christian Andersen*. Knopf, 1955.

Manning-Sanders, Ruth. *The Story of Hans Andersen*. Illus. Astrid Walford. Dutton, 1967.

Spink, Reginald. *Hans Christian Andersen and His World*. Thames & Hudson, 1972.

Stirling, Monica. *The Wild Swan: The Life and Times of Hans Christian Andersen*. Illus. with photographs and with reproductions of paper cutouts made by Andersen. Harcourt, 1965.

Toksvig, Signe. *The Life of Hans Christian Andersen*. Harcourt, 1934.

James M. Barrie

Asquith, Cynthia. *Portrait of Barrie*. Dutton, 1955.

Dunbar, Janet. *J. M. Barrie: The Man behind the Image*. Houghton Mifflin, 1970.

Green, Roger Lancelyn. *J. M. Barrie*. Walck, A Walck Monograph, 1961.

Mackail, Denis. *Barrie: The Story of J. M. B.* Scribner's, 1941.

Lucy Boston

Boston, Lucy M. "A Message from Green Knowe." *The Horn Book Magazine*, 39 (June 1963), pp. 259–64.

Robbins, Sidney. "A Nip of Otherness, Like Life: The Novels of Lucy Boston." *Children's Literature in Education*, no. 6 (Nov. 1971), pp. 5–16.

Rose, Jasper. *Lucy Boston.* Walck, A Walck Monograph, 1966.

Lewis Carroll

Carroll, Lewis. *The Annotated Alice: Alice's Adventures in Wonderland and Through the Looking Glass.* Illus. John Tenniel; intro. and notes, Martin Gardner. Clarkson N. Potter, 1960.

Cohen, Morton, ed. *The Letters of Lewis Carroll.* 2 vols. Oxford Univ. Press, 1979.

De la Mare, Walter. "Lewis Carroll." In *The Eighteen-Eighties: Essays by Fellows of the Royal Society of Literature.* Ed. Walter de la Mare. Cambridge Univ. Press, 1930.

Fisher, John, ed. *The Magic of Lewis Carroll.* Nelson, 1973.

Green, Roger Lancelyn, ed. *Diaries of Lewis Carroll.* 2 vols. Oxford Univ. Press, 1954. First edited and supplemented in this edition.

Green, Roger Lancelyn. *Lewis Carroll.* Walck, A Walck Monograph, 1962.

Hudson, Derek. *Lewis Carroll.* British Books: London House, 1954.

Lennon, Florence Beeker. *The Life of Lewis Carroll.* New rev. ed. Collier Books, 1962.
    Originally published under the title *Victoria through the Looking-Glass.*

Phillips, Robert. *Aspects of Alice: Lewis Carroll's Dreamchild as Seen through the Critic's Looking Glass.* Vanguard, 1971.

Wood, James Playsted. *The Snark Was a Boojum: A Life of Lewis Carroll.* Illus. David Levine. Pantheon, 1966.

Walter de la Mare

Brain, Sir Walter Russell. *Tea with Walter de la Mare.* Faber & Faber, 1957.

Clark, Leonard. *Walter de la Mare.* Walck, A Walck Monograph, 1961.

Reid, Forrest. *Walter de la Mare: A Critical Study.* Faber & Faber, 1929.

Walter de la Mare Issue. *The Horn Book Magazine*, 33 (Oct. 1957), pp. 195–247.

Eleanor Farjeon

Blakelock, Denys. "In Search of Elsie Piddock: An Echo of Eleanor Farjeon." *The Horn Book Magazine*, 4 (Feb. 1968), pp. 17–23.

A Book for Eleanor Farjeon. Intro. Naomi Lewis; illus. Edward Ardizzone. Walck, 1966.
    For this memorial tribute to the life and work of Eleanor Farjeon, several of her fellow authors wrote original stories and poems especially in her memory.

Colwell, Eileen H. *Eleanor Farjeon.* Walck, A Walck Monograph, 1962.

Farjeon, Eleanor. *Portrait of a Family.* Lippincott, 1936.

Sayers, Frances Clarke. "Eleanor Farjeon." *The Horn Book Magazine*, 41 (Aug. 1965), pp. 419–20.

Sayers, Frances Clarke. "Eleanor Farjeon's Room with a View." *The Horn Book Magazine*, 32 (Oct. 1956), pp. 335–45. Also in *Summoned by Books: Essays and Speeches by Frances Clarke Sayers.* Viking, 1965, pp. 122–32.

Rumer Godden

Hines, Ruth, and Paul C. Burns. "Rumer Godden." *Elementary English*, 44 (Feb. 1967), pp. 101–4.

Godden, Rumer. "Words Make the Book." *Ladies' Home Journal*, 81 (Jan.-Feb. 1964).

Kenneth Grahame

Graham, Eleanor. *Kenneth Grahame.* Walck, A Walck Monograph, 1963.

Grahame, Kenneth. *First Whisper of the Wind in the Willows.* Intro. Elspeth Grahame. Lippincott, 1944.

Grahame, Kenneth. *The Wind in the Willows*, pp. vii–x. Intro. A. A. Milne; illus. Arthur Rackham. Heritage Press, 1940.

Grahame, Kenneth. *The Wind in the Willows.* Preface, Frances Clarke Sayers; illus. Ernest H.

Shepard. Scribner's, Golden Anniversary Edition, 1960.

Green, Peter. *Kenneth Grahame, 1859–1932: A Study of His Life, Work, and Times.* Murray, 1959.

Randall Jarrell

Lowell, Robert, Peter Taylor, and Robert Penn Warren. *Randall Jarrell.* Farrar, Straus & Giroux, 1967.

Rudyard Kipling

Avery, Gillian. *Rudyard Kipling: The Man, His Work and His World.* Weidenfeld & Nicolson, 1972.

Kipling, Rudyard. *Something of Myself: For My Friends Known and Unknown; an Autobiography.* Doubleday, 1937.

Sutcliff, Rosemary. *Rudyard Kipling.* Walck, A Walck Monograph, 1961.

Selma Lagerlöf

Berendshon, Walter. *Selma Lagerlöf: Her Life and Work.* Adapt. from the German by George E. Timpson; preface by V. Sackville-West. Ivor Nicholson & Watson, 1931.

Larsen, Hanna A. *Selma Lagerlöf.* Doubleday, 1936.

Lindquist, Jennie D. "Selma Lagerlöf." *The Horn Book Magazine,* 20 (Mar. 1944), pp. 115–22.

Andrew Lang

Green, Roger Lancelyn. *Andrew Lang.* Walck, A Walck Monograph, 1962.

C. S. Lewis

Arnott, Ann. *The Secret Country of C. S. Lewis.* Eerdmans, 1975.

Gardner, Helen. *Clive Staples Lewis, 1898–1963.* Oxford Univ. Press, 1964.

Green, Roger Lancelyn. *C. S. Lewis.* Walck, A Walck Monograph, 1963.

Green, Roger Lancelyn, and Walter Hooper. *C. S. Lewis, a Biography.* Harcourt, 1974.

Higgins, James E. "A Letter from C. S. Lewis." *The Horn Book Magazine,* 42 (Oct. 1966), pp. 533–39.

Lewis, C. S. *Of Other Worlds: Essays and Stories.* Harcourt, 1966.

Lewis, C. S. "On Three Ways of Writing for Children." *The Horn Book Magazine,* 39 (Oct. 1963), pp. 459–69. Also in *Of Other Worlds,* by C. S. Lewis, pp. 29–32.

Lewis, C. S. *Surprised by Joy: The Shape of My Early Life; an Autobiography.* Harcourt, 1955.

Lewis, W. H., ed. *Letters of C. S. Lewis.* Harcourt, 1966.

Smith, Lillian H. "News from Narnia." *The Horn Book Magazine,* 34 (Oct. 1963), pp. 470–73.

George Macdonald

Wolff, Robert L. *The Golden Key: A Study of the Fiction of George Macdonald.* Yale Univ. Press, 1961.

E. Nesbit

Bell, Anthea. *E. Nesbit.* Walck, A Walck Monograph, 1964.

E. Nesbit Special Issue. *The Horn Book Magazine,* 35 (Oct. 1958), pp. 347–73.

Moore, Doris Langley. *E. Nesbit: A Biography.* Rev. ed. Chilton, 1966.

Nesbit, E. *Long Ago When I Was Young.* F. Watts, 1966.

Streatfield, Noel. *Magic and the Magician: E. Nesbit and Her Children's Books.* Benn, 1958.

J. R. R. Tolkien

Chant, Joy. "Niggle and Númenor." *Children's Literature in Education,* 19 (Winter 1975), pp. 161–71.

Davenport, Guy. "The Persistence of Light." *The National Review* (Apr. 20, 1965), pp. 332–34.

Eiseley, Loren. "The Elvish Art of Enchantment: An Essay on J. R. R. Tolkien's *Tree and Leaf,* and on Mr. Tolkien's Other Distinguished Contributions to Imaginative Literature." *The Horn Book Magazine,* 41 (Aug. 1965), pp. 364–67.

Helms, Randel. *Tolkien's World.* Houghton Mifflin, 1974.

Kocher, Paul H. *Master of Middle-Earth: The Fiction of J. R. R. Tolkien.* Houghton Mifflin, 1972.

Norman, P. "Prevalence of Hobbits." *New York Times Magazine* (Jan. 15, 1967), pp. 30–31.

Tolkien, J. R. R. *Tree and Leaf.* Houghton Mifflin, 1965.

An expansion of a lecture the author gave on fairy tales in 1938 at Oxford University while he was writing *Lord of the Rings*.

P. L. Travers

Travers, P. L. "The Black Sheep." *New York Times Book Review*, 70 (Nov. 7, 1965), pp. 1, 61.

Travers, P. L. "The Heroes of Childhood: A Note on Nannies." *The Horn Book Magazine*, 11 (May 1935), pp. 147–55.

Lingeman, R. R. "A Visit with Mary Poppins and P. L. Travers." *New York Times Magazine* (Dec. 25, 1966), pp. 12–13.

V Nonfiction: The Real and Changing World

13 Biography

Books for Children

Collections

Archer, Jules. *They Made a Revolution: 1776.* St. Martin's, 1973
   Brief, energetic biographies of some of our founding fathers and mothers.

Berry, Erick, and Herbert Best. *Men Who Changed the Map: A.D. 400 to 1914.* Funk & Wagnalls, 1967.
   From Attila the Hun to Napoleon Bonaparte, this collection of personalities emphasizes the historical impact of each person. Maps by Laszlo Matulay make clear the changes effected. Grades 4–9.

Burt, Olive W. *Black Women of Valor.* Illus. Paul Frame, Messner, 1974.
   Four brief biographies of women who were successful crusaders in their various fields: social work, banking, journalism, and education. Grades 3–6.

Chase, Alice Elizabeth. *Famous Artists of the Past.* Platt & Munk, 1964.
   Pride of place is given the work of each artist; there are twenty-six in all. Illus. with 177 reproductions, 44 in full color. Grades 4–8.

Evans, Elizabeth. *Weathering the Storm: Women of the American Revolution.* Scribner's, 1975.
   A skillful use of direct sources, such as journals and diaries, gives an immediacy and complexity to the adventures, dilemmas, and struggles of the eleven women presented here. A valuable background for history of this period. Grades 6 and up.

Freedgood, Lillian. *Great Artists of America.* Crowell, 1963
   Ranging from Gilbert Stuart through Jackson Pollock, these fifteen brief biographies provide a span of art history as well as a vision of each person.

Goffstein, M. B. *Lives of the Artists.* Farrar, Straus & Giroux, 1981.
   Brief, free-verse poems capture the author's perceptions of Rembrandt, Guardi, Van Gogh, Bonnard, and Nevelson. Reproductions of the artists' works accompany these personal impressions. Grades 4 and up.

Greenfield, Eloise, and Lessie Jones Little. *Childtimes: A Three-Generation Memoir.* With material by Pattie Ridley Jones; illus. Jerry Pinkney and with photographs. Crowell, 1979.
   An interlinked sequence of childhood memoirs by three black women of a single family from the 1880s to 1950s.

Gridley, Marion E. *Contemporary American Indian Leaders.* Dodd, Mead, 1972.
   Brief accounts of accomplishments. Illus. with photographs.

Hayden, Robert C. *Eight Black American Inventors.* Addison-Wesley, 1972.
   Interesting accomplishments make this entertaining reading. An introduction places the black inventor in historical perspective. Grades 4–8. See also *Seven Black American Scientists* (1970).

Kennedy, John Fitzgerald. *Profiles in Courage.* Foreword, Robert F. Kennedy; illus. Emil Weiss. Harper, Young Readers Memorial Edition, abr., 1964.
   Americans who took courageous stands at crucial moments in public life. Grades 6–9.

Meyer, Edith Patterson. *Champions of the Four Freedoms.* Illus. Eric von Schmidt. Little, Brown, 1966.

Stories of the people and institutions that have upheld freedom of speech and religion and freedom from want and fear. Grades 7–9.

Newlon, Clarke. *Famous Mexican-Americans.* Foreword, Dr. Uvaldo H. Palomares. Dodd, Mead, Famous Biographies for Young People, 1972.

Contemporary figures, such as Lee Trevino, Cesar Chavez, Reies Tijerina, and Vikki Carr are given brief treatment. Grades 6–9.

Patterson, Robert, Mildred Mebel, and Lawrence Hill, sel. *On Our Way: Young Pages from American Autobiography.* Illus. Robert Patterson, Holiday House, 1952.

Emotionally significant moments in the lives of Sherwood Anderson, William O. Douglas, Langston Hughes, and others. Grades 5–12.

Plutarch. *Ten Famous Lives.* The Dryden translation revised by Arthur Hugh Clough; further revised and edited for young readers and with an introduction by Charles Alexander Robinson, Jr. Dutton, 1962.

In the introduction Robinson makes the young reader aware of the great heritage bequeathed to us by Greece and Rome. Grades 6–9.

Reed Gwendolyn, comp. *Beginnings.* Atheneum, 1971.

Extracts from autobiographies reveal the enormous significance of childhood. A careful and thoughtful selection. Grades 6–12.

Stoddard, Hope. *Famous American Women.* Illus. with photographs and prints. Crowell, 1970.

A wide variety of times and lives are assembled here with brief, succinct summations. Each of the forty-one lives has a bibliography. Grades 6–12.

Stowell, H. E. *Quill Pens and Petticoats: A Portrait of Women of Letters.* Wayland, 1970.

English writers of several centuries and of various types, all of whom struggled with the handicaps of being women. Grades 6–12.

Sutcliff, Rosemary. *Heroes and History.* Illus. Charles Keeping. Putnam's, 1965.

An examination of the intertwining of legend and fact in the lives of British heroes: Caratacus, Arthur, Alfred, Hereward, Llewellin, Robin Hood, William Wallace, Robert the Bruce, Owen Glyndwr, and Montrose. Grades 6–12.

Trease, Geoffrey. *Seven Sovereign Queens.* Vanguard, 1968.

The emphasis is on color and excitement in these lives, ranging from Cleopatra to Catherine the Great. Grades 6–10.

Triggs, Tony D. *Founders of Religions.* Wayland, 1981.

Biographical introductions to the lives of Buddha, Christ, and Mohammed, including a description of the beliefs of the major religions. Attractively produced with traditional paintings and photographs. Grades 4–7.

Individual Biographies

Adams, Samuel

Fritz, Jean. *Why Don't You Get a Horse, Sam Adams?* Illus. Trina Schart Hyman. Coward-McCann, 1974.

Sam Adams's neglect of his personal appearance and his refusal to get a horse until it is made to seem like his patriotic duty make for a novel and amusing approach to this historical figure. Grades 3–6.

Addams, Jane

Meigs, Cornelia. *Jane Addams: Pioneer for Social Justice.* Little, Brown, 1970.

Even today the social fabric of our times is affected by the vigorous, creative life of this woman. Grades 6–12.

Alcott, Louisa May

Meigs, Cornelia. *Invincible Louisa.* Little, Brown, 1933.

The story of the author of *Little Women.* Illustrated with photographs of the Alcott family. Awarded the Newbery Medal, 1934. An Alcott Centennial Edition with a new introduction and format was published in 1968. Grades 5–9. See also *We Alcotts* by Aileen Fisher and Olive Rabe (Atheneum, 1968).

Aldridge, Ira

Malone, Mary. *Actor in Exile: The Life of Ira Aldridge.* Illus. Eros Keith. Crowell-Collier, 1969.

Famed in England and on the continent, this black American actor of the nineteenth century is little known in his native land. Grades 4–6.

Alexander the Great

Mercer, Charles. *Alexander the Great.* Consultant, Cornelius C. Vermeule III. American Heritage, A Horizon Caravel Book, 1962.

The life of the military genius and empire builder. Grades 6–9.

Lasker, Joe. *The Great Alexander the Great.* Illus. by the author. Viking, 1983.

A picture-book edition of Alexander's heroic life. The simple prose is extended by painterly, epic illustrations. Grades 2–4.

Almedingen, Catherine

Almedingen, E. M. *Katia.* Illus. Victor Ambrus. Farrar, Straus & Giroux, 1966.

The 1874 memoir of Catherine Almedingen's great-aunt has been translated and adapted into English by her great niece. Katia is taken away from her brothers and widowed father at the age of five and raised with other children in a relative's large home. The landscape, the period, and the treatment and education of children are presented in great detail and intimacy. Grades 6–12. Other re-creation of her family's life in Russia are *Young Mark* (1968) and *Fanny* (1970).

Almedingen, E. M.

Almedingen, E. M. *My St. Petersburg: A Reminiscence of Childhood.* Norton, 1970.

The feelings of the author for her childhood in St. Petersburg are summoned up around events, daily occurrences, and the growing climate of unrest in the early twentieth century. Illus. with photographs. Grades 6–12.

Andersen, Hans Christian

Godden, Rumer. *Hans Christian Andersen: A Great Life in Brief.* Knopf, 1955.

A sensitive biography of the beloved Danish writer whose life was poignantly reflected in his fairy tales. Grades 7 and up.

Anderson, Marian

Newman, Shirlee P. *Marian Anderson: Lady from Philadelphia.* Westminster, 1966.

A perceptive appreciation of a great singer and a great woman. Grades 4–9. See also *My Lord, What a Morning: An Autobiography* (Viking, 1956). For very young children, see *Marian Anderson* by Tobi Tobias, illus. Symeon Shimin (Crowell, 1972).

Anne Stuart, Queen of England

Hodges, Margaret. *Lady Queen Anne: A Biography of Queen Anne of England.* Farrar, Straus & Giroux, 1969.

A richly detailed history of a queen and her time. Grades 7 up.

Arnold, Benedict

Fritz, Jean. *Traitor: The Case of Benedict Arnold.* Putnam's, 1981.

An entertaining biography casts light upon the enigmatic character of this complex, termperamental man. Illus. with reproductions. Grades 4–6.

Audubon, John James

Brenner, Barbara. *On the Frontier with Mr. Audubon.* Coward-McCann, 1977.

Using the device of a journal belonging to Audubon's young assistant, the author tells the story of their fascinating journey down the Ohio and Mississippi rivers in search of birds to paint. The boy Joseph sees Audubon as complex, obsessed, and inspiring. Illus. with photographs and reproductions. Grades 3–6.

Bach, Johann Sebastian

Reingold, Carmel Berman. *Johann Sebastian Bach: Revolutionary of Music.* F. Watts, Immortals of Music, 1970.

Objective, informative. Grades 5–9.

Balboa, Vasco Núñez de

Syme, Ronald. *Balboa, Finder of the Pacific.* Illus. William Stobbs. Morrow, 1956.

An action-packed account of the intrepid young Spanish explorer. Grades 4–6.

Beaumont, William

Epstein, Sam, and Beryl Epstein. *Dr. Beaumont and the Man with the Hole in His Stomach.* Illus. Joseph Scrofani. Coward-McCann, 1978.

A fascinating, well-researched presentation on the nineteenth-century army surgeon whose experiments with a wounded fur trader led to important discoveries about digestion. Grades 3–6.

Becket, Thomas à

Duggan, Alfred. *The Falcon and the Dove: A Life of Thomas Becket of Canterbury.* Decorations by Anne Marie Jauss. Pantheon, 1966.

Twelfth-century Christendom seen through the life and death of Thomas à Becket. Grades 7–9.

Beckwourth, Jim

Felton, Harold. *Jim Beckwourth, Negro Mountain Man.* Illus. with photos, etc. Dodd, Mead, 1966.

A larger-than-life hero, Jim Beckwourth was honored among the Crows as their chief and among whites as a great mountain man. Grades 5–9.

Beethoven, Ludwig Van

Jacobs, David. *Beethoven.* Consultant, Elliot Forbes. American Heritage, A Horizon Caravel Book, 1970.
    Use of objective detail firmly ties the musician and his music to his times and contemporaries. Grades 4–9.

Bell, Alexander Graham

Burlingame, Roger. *Out of Silence into Sound.* Macmillan, 1964.
    A vivid story of Bell's life, his invention of the telephone, and his dream to help deaf-mutes come "out of silence into sound." Grades 6–8.

Blackwell, Elizabeth

Clapp, Patricia. *Dr. Elizabeth: The Story of the First Woman Doctor.* Lothrop, 1974.
    Told in the first person, this remains faithful to the attitudes and feelings of the time. Grades 4–9.

Blake, William

Daughtery, James. *William Blake.* With reproductions of drawings by William Blake. Viking, 1960.
    The author, a gifted artist himself, understands and appreciates Blake and his genius. Grades 8–12.

Blegvad, Erik

Blegvad, Erik. *Self Portrait: Erik Blegvad.* Illus. by the author. Addison-Wesley, The Self-Portrait Collection, 1979.
    This is a pictorial autobiography of the respected children's book illustrator from his early years in Denmark to his present life in London. Full of wit, vitality, and aesthetic insight. Grades 2–6.

Brontë, Maria, Elizabeth, Charlotte, Branwell, Emily, and Anne

Bentley, Phyllis. *The Young Brontes.* Illus. Marie Hartley. Roy, 1960.
    A dramatic but authentic re-creation of the known events of childhood in this famous family. Grades 4–7. See also *The Brontës and Their World* (Viking, 1969) by Phyllis Bentley. This is a source book comprising photographs, paintings, and memorabilia of various kinds. Of special interest to readers of *The Return of the Twelves* by Pauline Clarke.

Brontë, Charlotte

Vipont, Elfrida. *Weaver of Dreams: The Girlhood of Charlotte Brontë.* Walck, 1966.
    The rich, imaginative life of young Charlotte laid the basis for her adult fiction. Grades 6–9.

Bunche, Ralph

Kugelmass, J. Alvin. *Ralph J. Bunche: Fighter for Peace.* Messner, 1962.
    The life of the Nobel Peace Prize winner in 1950 is an outstanding example of a man's devotion to a purpose. Grades 6–9.

Caesar, Caius Julius

Isenberg, Irwin. *Caesar.* Consultant, Richard M. Haywood. American Heritage, A Horizon Caravel Book, 1964.
    "This book brings together the facts and myths of Caesar's life with pertinent art, documents, photographs, and reconstructions of significant sites."—Foreword. Grades 7–9.

Carson, Rachel

Sterlin, Philip. *Sea and Earth: The Life of Rachel Carson.* Crowell, 1970.
    The dual interests of science and literature combined in Rachel Carson to make her a distinctive voice in crying the alarm for our destruction of wildlife and natural resources. Illus. with photographs. Grades 6–12.

Carver, George Washington

Graham, Shirley, and George Lipscomb. *Dr. George Washington Carver, Scientist.* Illus. Elton C. Fax. Messner, 1944.
    An inspiring biography of the great scientist and humanitarian. Grades 6–9. See also *The Story of George Washington Carver* by Arna Bontemps (Grossett, 1954); *George Washington Carver* by Samuel and Beryl Epstein (Grossett, 1963); and *A Weed Is a Flower* by Aliki (Prentice, 1965).

Cassatt, Mary

Wilson, Ellen. *American Painter in Paris: A Life of Mary Cassatt.* Farrar, Straus & Giroux, 1971.
    The fascination of Mary Cassatt as a person and the excitement of her development as an artist emerge distinctly in this thoughtful and perceptive work. Grades 6 and up.

Cather, Willa

Brown, Marion Marsh, and Ruth Crone. *Willa Cather: The Woman and Her Works.* Scribner's, 1970.
    A comprehensive account of the main forces and patterns in the life of a woman whose vitality and real living were centered in her writing. Grades 6 and up.

Chavez, Cesar

Terzian, James, and Kathryn Cramer. *Mighty Hard Road: The Story of Cesar Chavez.* Doubleday, Signal Books, 1970.

Slightly fictionalized, moving story of Chavez and his commitment to improving the migrant worker's life. Grades 4–8. See also *Forty Acres: Cesar Chavez and the Farm Workers* by Mark Day (Praeger, 1971), Grades 7 and up. A simplified, picture-book format is given in *Cesar Chavez* by Ruth Franchere (Cromwell, 1970).

Child, Lydia Maria

Meltzer, Milton. *Tongue of Flame: The Life of Lydia Maria Child.* Crowell, 1965.

Involved in the abolitionist struggle, Maria Child discarded the success of a conventional writer to write articles and pamphlets, including a study of slavery: *An Appeal in Favor of That Class of Americans Called Africans.* Grades 6–12.

Chukovsky, Kornei

Chukovsky, Kornei. *The Silver Crest: My Russian Boyhood.* Trans. Beatrice Stillman. Holt, 1976.

The famous Russian writer for children gives a delightful, spirited memoir of his childhood. Grades 5 and up.

Churchill, Winston

Coolidge, Olivia E. *Winston Churchill, and the Story of Two World Wars.* Houghton Mifflin, 1960.

The reader follows Churchill through half a century of stormy, colorful, and courageous leadership in peace and war. Illus. with photographs. Grades 7–9.

Clemens, Samuel Langhorne

Wood, James Playsted. *Spunkwater, Spunkwater! A Life of Mark Twain.* Pantheon, 1968.

A lively account, well-paced, filled with revealing anecdotal material. Grades 6–9. For younger readers, *America's Mark Twain* by Mary McNeer, illus. Lynd Ward (Houghton Mifflin, 1962), is visually expanded.

Cleopatra

Leighton, Margaret. *Cleopatra, Sister of the Moon.* Farrar, Straus & Giroux, 1969.

Known facts of Cleopatra's life are filled out with dialogue and description in a book that brings the famous queen to life as a woman, an astute politician, struggling for her country and power. Grades 4–9.

Columbus Christopher

Dalgliesh, Alice. *The Columbus Story.* Illus. Leo Politi. Scribner's, 1955.

The author skillfully presents the events in the life of Columbus that are most interesting to children. Grades 3–5.

Fritz, Jean. *Where Do You Think You're Going, Christopher Columbus?* Illus. Margot Tomes. Putnam's, 1980.

A provocative and insightful portrayal of Columbus and his voyages for the younger reader. Humorously told and vigorously illustrated. Grades 2–5.

Hodges, C. Walter. *Columbus Sails.* Illus. by the author. Coward-McCann, 1940.

An English artist brings a fresh approach to the story of the great discoverer by telling it through the eyes of men close to Columbus. Grades 7–9.

Curie, Marie

Curie, Eve. *Madame Curie.* Trans. Vincent Sheean. Doubleday, 1937.

A deeply moving story of a woman who steadfastly refused to accept defeat. Grades 6–10.

Damien, Father

Roos, Ann. *Man of Molokai: The Life of Father Damien.* Illus. Raymond Lufkin. Lippincott, 1943.

A stirring story of Father Damien's work on the leper island of Molokai and of how his spirit of love and sacrifice ennobled all who came in contact with it. Grades 7–9.

Darrow, Clarence

Gurko, Miriam. *Clarence Darrow.* Crowell, 1965.

A man of imagination, humor, and heroism, Darrow's life encapsulates significant moments and trends of the twentieth century. Grades 6 and up.

Darwin, Charles

Karp, Walter. *Charles Darwin and the Origin of Species.* Consultant, J. W. Burrow. American Heritage, A Horizon Caravel Book, 1968.

The charming human qualities of Darwin as father and husband are clearly depicted and closely related to the years of work occupied at home with his writing. Grades 6–12.

Dickinson, Emily

Longsworth, Polly. *Emily Dickinson: Her Letter to the World.* Crowell, 1965.

An excellent biography that should lead to the

reading of Emily Dickinson's poems. Grades 6–9. See also *We Dickinsons: The Life of Emily Dickinson as Seen Through the Eyes of her Brother, Austin,* by Aileen Fisher and Olive Rabe (Atheneum, 1965).

Douglass, Frederick

Life and Times of Frederick Douglas. Adapt. Barbara Ritchie. Crowell, 1966.
A skillful abridgment of the great Negro's autobiography. Grades 7–9.

Du Bois, W. E. B.

Hamilton, Virginia. *W. E. B. Du Bois: A Biography.* Crowell, 1972.
The intellectual qualities of Du Bois are stressed; his role as a far-seeing and sensitive person whose conscience and logic led to exile is clearly presented. Grades 6 and up.

Sterne, Emma Gelders. *His Was the Voice: The Life of W. E. B. Du Bois.* Crowell-Collier, 1971.
Presented in a fictionalized, episodic form.

Edison, Thomas Alva

North, Sterling. *Young Thomas Edison.* Illus. William Barss. Houghton Mifflin, 1958.
A sympathetic character study of the complex inventor and scientist. With photographs, decorations, diagrams, and maps. Grades 4–6.

Forten, James

Douty, Esther M. *Forten the Sailmaker: Pioneer Champion of Negro Rights.* Rand McNally, 1968.
A life of adventure and crusading, which began with being taken prisoner by the British during the Revolution and came to a climax when he owned and ran the sailmaking shop. His great wealth was generously spent in the abolitionist movement. Illus. with photographs. Grades 6–12.

Fox, George

Yolen, Jane. *The Story of George Fox and the Quakers.* Seabury, 1972.
The development of Fox's religious philosophy and his lifelong devotion to preaching his convictions provide a story of imprisonment, victories, and almost miraculous events. Grades 5–12.

Frank, Anne

Frank, Anne. *Anne Frank: The Diary of a Young Girl.* Trans. from the Dutch by B. M. Mooyaart-Doubleday; intro. Eleanor Roosevelt. Doubleday, 1952.
The moving and distinctly beautiful record kept during two years of hiding in the "Secret Annexe" from the Nazis. This is a classic revelation of warmth, wit, and humor, the basic stays against depression and desperation. Grades 4 and up.

Franklin, Benjamin

D'Aulaire, Ingri, and Edgar Parin D'Aulaire. *Benjamin Franklin.* Doubleday, 1950.
This picture-story biography serves as a good introduction to the man who played an important part in the history of our country. Grades 3–4.

Fleming, Thomas. *Benjamin Franklin.* Four Winds, 1973.
A lively and careful portrayal, with good use of anecdote. Illus. with reproductions. Grades 4–9.

Fritz, Jean. *What's the Big Idea, Ben Franklin?* Illus. Margot Tomes. Coward-McCann, 1976.
A brief, entertaining biography told with gentle wit and historical insight. Grades 3–5.

Freeman, Elizabeth

Felton, Harold W. *Mumbet, the Story of Elizabeth Freeman.* Illus. Donn Albright. Dodd, Mead, 1970.
A remarkable woman whose courage led her to legally challenge her slave status in the state of Massachusetts in 1781.

Fritz, Jean

Fritz, Jean. *Homesick: My Own Story.* Illus. Margot Tomes and with photographs. Putnam's, 1982.
A fictionalized autobiography of the author's childhood spent in China in the turbulent years of the twenties before the revolution. Winner of the 1983 American Book Award. Grades 4–7.

Galilei, Galileo

Cobb, Vicki. *Truth of Trial: The Story of Galileo Galilei.* Illus. George Ulrich. Coward-McCann, 1979.
An informative study concentrating on Galileo's theories of the universe. Grades 4–6.

Gandhi, Mohandas

Coolidge, Olivia. *Gandhi.* Houghton Mifflin, 1971.
A scrupulously detailed account. Grades 6 and up.

Eaton, Jeanette. *Gandhi: Fighter without a Sword.* Illus. Ralph Ray. Morrow, 1950.
A luminous biography of the great spiritual and political leader. Grades 6–9.

Gehrig, Lou

Graham, Frank. *Lou Gehrig: A Quiet Hero.* Putnam's, 1942.

More than the story of a great ballplayer, this tells of a quiet hero who became a symbol of courage, decency, and kindness to millions of people.

Hamilton, Alice

Grant, Madeleine P. *Alice Hamilton: Pioneer Doctor in Industrial Medicine.* Abelard-Schuman, 1967.

The moving story of a gentle reformer who successfully led a crusade for protective health legislation in occupational diseases. Illus. with photographs. Grades 6–12.

Hautzig, Esther

Hautzig, Esther. *The Endless Steppe: Growing Up in Siberia.* Crowell, 1968.

Surviving the physical rigors of a childhood in a Siberian labor camp during World War II, a young girl experienced a curious mixture of agony and pleasure. Grades 5 and up.

Haydn, Joseph

Lasker, David. *The Boy Who Loved Music.* Illus. Joe Lasker. Viking, 1979.

This story dramatizes an actual historical incident—the impetus for Haydn's composition of his special "Farewell Symphony," in 1772. The presence of Karl, a spirited young horn player, brings this elegantly illustrated study of eighteenth-century Austria to life. Grades 2–4.

Henry VIII

Southworth, John Van Duyn. *Monarch and Conspirators: The Wives and Woes of Henry VIII.* Crown, 1973.

A full historical background is developed in this readable account. Grades 6–12.

Feuerlicht, Roberta Strauss. *The Life and World of Henry VIII.* Crowell-Collier, 1970.

Hitler, Adolf

Shirer, William L. *The Rise and Fall of Adolf Hitler.* Random House, Landmark Book, 1961.

Somewhat sensational, this book focuses on Hitler and his immediate associates. Grades 4–6.

Howe, Samuel Gridley

Meltzer, Milton. *A Light in the Dark: The Life of Samuel Gridley Howe.* Crowell, 1964.

The life of a versatile nineteenth-century humanitarian surgeon, teacher, and founder of the Perkins Institute for the Blind. Grades 5–7.

Hudson, William Henry

Hudson, William Henry. *Far Away and Long Ago: A History of My Early Life.* Illus. Eric Fitch Daglish; intro. R. B. Cunninghame Graham. Rev. ed. Dutton, 1931.

The autobiography of a famous naturalist whose boyhood was spent on the South American pampas; as a boy he was attuned to the beautiful settings and wildlife about him. Grades 6 and up.

Hughes, Langston

Meltzer, Milton. *Langston Hughes.* Crowell, 1968.

A sensitive portrayal of the black poet. Grades 6–9.

Hyman, Trina Schart

Hyman, Trina Schart. *Self Portrait: Trina Schart Hyman.* Illus. by the author. Addison-Wesley, The Self-Portrait Collection, 1981.

The life and art of a picture-book illustrator come fully alive in this unusual autobiography. Grades 2–6.

Ishi, Yahi Indian

Kroeber, Theodora. *Ishi, Last of His Tribe.* Illus. Ruth Robbins. Parnassus, 1964.

The true story of a California Yahi Indian who survived the invasion by the white man while the rest of his tribe died off. Grades 6 and up.

Issa

Fukuda, Hanako. *Wind in My Hand.* Editorial assistance, Mark Taylor; illus. Lydia Cooley. Golden Gate Junior Books, 1970.

A simplified version of Issa's life, concentrating on the haiku he wrote and the feelings behind the poems. Grades 5–8.

Jackson, Andrew

Coit, Margaret L. *Andrew Jackson.* Illus. Milton Johnson. Houghton Mifflin, 1965.

An able historian presents a president who was often misrepresented. Grades 6–9.

Foster, Genevieve. *Andrew Jackson: An Initial Biography.* Illus. by the author. Scribner's, 1951.

Young readers are transported into the presence and times of "the people's president." Grades 3–5.

Jackson, Thomas Jonathan

Fritz, Jean. *Stonewall.* Illus. Stephen Gammell. Putnam's, 1979.

The character of the Confederate general comes

intensely alive in this portrait of a complex, eccentric man who was one of the most brilliant, if erratic, generals in American history. Grades 4–6.

Jefferson, Thomas

American Heritage. *Thomas Jefferson and His World.* By the editors of *American Heritage;* narrated by Henry Moscow; consultant, Dumas Malone. American Heritage, American Heritage Junior Library, 1960.
    Copious illustrations, reproductions of old maps, drawings, documents, personal notes, paintings of personalities of the day, and modern photographs add value as a history of the period. Grades 6–9.

Wibberley, Leonard. *Young Man from the Piedmont: The Youth of Thomas Jefferson.* Farrar, Straus & Giroux, 1963.
    The first of an excellent four-volume work on Jefferson. Followed by *A Dawn in the Trees; The Gales of Spring;* and *Time of Harvest.* Grades 7–9.

Jemison, Mary

Lenski, Lois. *Indian Captive: The Story of Mary Jemison.* Illus. by the author. Lippincott, 1941.
    The story of the twelve-year-old white girl captured by the Indians in 1758. Grades 4–8. See also *Mary Jemison: Seneca Captive* by Jeanne de Monnier Gardner, illus. Robert Parker (Harcourt, 1966).

Joan of Arc, Saint

Boutet de Monvel, Maurice. *Joan of Arc.* Illus. by the author; intro. Gerald Gottlieb. Viking, 1980.
    Originally published in France in 1896, this biography of the peasant girl who became warrior, heroine, and saint is stunningly illustrated by a significant early illustrator of children's books. Grades 3–6.

Churchill, Winston. *Joan of Arc: Her Life as Told by Winston Churchill.* Illus. Lauren Ford. Dodd, Mead, 1969.
    An eloquent telling for younger readers.

Fisher, Aileen. *Jeanne d'Arc.* Illus. Ati Forberg. Crowell, 1970.
    Briefly told, this simple version conveys the drama, courage, and pathos of Joan of Arc's life. The muted drawings are sensitive and restrained. Grades 3–5.

Paine, Albert Bigelow. *The Girl in White Armor: The Story of Joan of Arc.* Illus. Joe Isom. Macmillan, 1967.
    A reissue of an abridged edition of the author's classic two-volume biography. Grades 7–9.

Johnson, James Weldon

Felton, Harold W. *James Weldon Johnson.* Illus. Charles Shaw. Dodd, Mead, 1971.
    Brief biography of a talented, accomplished man, one of whose achievements was the writing of the black national hymn. Grades 4–7.

Johnson, Samuel

Brown, Ivor. *Dr. Johnson and His World.* Walck, 1966.
    A personal and literary biography of the famous critic and author of the notable dictionary. Illus. with photographs. Grades 7–9.

Joseph, Chief

Davis, Russell, and Brent Ashabranner. *Chief Joseph, War Chief of the Nez Perce.* McGraw-Hill, 1962.
    The legendary war leader who fought off the United States Army and led his people to Canada is depicted with respect. Grades 5–8.

Kastner, Erich

Kästner, Erich. *When I Was a Boy.* Trans. from the German by Isabel McHugh and Florence McHugh; illus. Horst Lemke. F. Watts, 1957.
    The writer of *Emil and the Detectives* tells about his own childhood and the people in it, the events of humor, adventure, and near tragedy but, most importantly, the inner feelings. Grades 4 and up.

Keller, Helen

Keller, Helen. *The Story of My Life.* Intro. Ralph Barton Perry. Doubleday, 1954.
    The truly miraculous story of a girl who, though blind, deaf, and dumb, learned to speak and make a full life for herself in serving others. With letters (1887–1901) and a supplementary account of her education including passages from the reports and letters of her teacher, Anne Mansfield Sullivan, by John Albert Macy. Grades 7–9.

Kemble, Fanny

Rushmore, Robert. *Fanny Kemble.* Crowell-Collier, 1970.
    Her sympathies for the plight of the slave in the United States exposed this renowned nineteenth-century English actress to persecution from

her American, slave-owning husband. Grades 5–12.

Scott, John Anthony. *Fanny Kemble's America.* Crowell, Women of America, 1973.

The editor of Fanny Kemble's *Journal,* which was published in 1963, has written a detailed, historical account of the events that lay behind her writing. Illus. with photographs. Grades 5–12.

Kherdian, Veron

Kherdian, David. *The Road from Home: The Story of an Armenian Girl.* Greenwillow, 1979.

An Armenian-American poet tells the story of his mother's childhood in Turkey during the tragic Armenian massacres of 1915. Grades 6 up.

King, Martin Luther, Jr.

Clayton, Ed. *Martin Luther King: The Peaceful Warrior.* Illus. David Hodges. Prentice-Hall, 1969.

A simplified but straightforward account of the outstanding events in Dr. King's life. Grades 4–6.

Koehn, Ilse

Koehn, Ilse. *Mischling, Second Degree: My Childhood in Nazi Germany.* Foreword, Harrison E. Salisbury. Greenwillow, 1977.

Autobiographical memoirs of a German schoolgirl, a member of the Hitler Youth. She does not discover that she had a Jewish grandparent until after the war. Grades 6 and up.

Köllwitz, Kathe

Klein, Mina C., and H. Arthur Klein. *Kathe Köllwitz: Life in Art.* Illus. with her works. Holt, 1972.

The intertwining forces of art and a deeply felt concern for her fellow man are illuminated in this book. The many reproductions of her work allow the artist to speak for herself. Grades 6 and up.

La Flesche, Susette

Crary, Margaret. *Susette La Flesche: Voice of the Omaha Indians.* Hawthorn Books, 1973.

A slightly fictionalized version of a young Indian woman who took to the lecture circuit in order to procure justice for her people. Grades 6–12.

Lee, Robert E.

Commager, Henry Steele. *America's Robert E. Lee.* Illus. Lynd Ward. Houghton Mifflin, 1951.

Written with sympathy, dignity, and respect for the great Confederate general. Grades 6–8.

Freeman, Douglas Southall. *Lee of Virginia.* Scribner's, 1958.

A brilliant one-volume version based on the author's Pulitzer Prize-winning four-volume biography. Grades 7–9.

Leif Ericson

D'Aulaire, Ingri, and Edgar Parin D'Aulaire. *Leif the Lucky.* Illus. by the authors. Doubleday, 1941.

The story of Leif, Erik's son, who sailed with his father to Greenland and later still further west to find the continent of America. Grades 3–4.

Leonardo da Vinci

Williams, Jay. *Leonardo da Vinci.* Consultant, Bates Lowry. American Heritage, A Horizon Caravel Book, 1965.

The story of Leonardo da Vinci, artist, scientist, philosopher, and prophet, who was called the "universal man" of Renaissance Italy. Grades 7 and up.

Lim, Sing

Lim, Sing. *West Coast Chinese Boy.* Illus. by the author. Tundra, 1979.

Dramatic monotypes and fluid pen and ink vignettes illustrate the autobiography of a boy growing up in Vancouver's Chinatown in the 1920s. Grades 3–6.

Lincoln, Abraham

D'Aulaire, Ingri, and Edgar Parin D'Aulaire. *Abraham Lincoln.* Illus. by the authors. Doubleday, 1939 (1957).

An introductory biography and picture book for younger children. Awarded the Caldecott Medal, 1940. Grades 3–4.

Foster, Genevieve. *Abraham Lincoln: An Initial Biography.* Illus. by the author. Scribner's, 1950.

Historically accurate, yet simply written for younger readers. Grades 3–5.

Miers, Earl Schenck. *Abraham Lincoln in Peace and War.* Consultant, Paul M. Angle. American Heritage, American Heritage Junior Library, 1964.

Illustrated with paintings, drawings, engravings, and photographs of the period, which help make history come alive. Grades 6–9.

Sandburg, Carl. *Abe Lincoln Grows Up.* Illus. James Daugherty. Harcourt, 1928.

This classic account of Lincoln's boyhood was taken from the author's *Abraham Lincoln: The Prairie Years.* Grades 6–9.

Mangus Colorado

Cooke, David. *Apache Warrior.* Grosset & Dunlap, 1963.

A great Indian leader of the Southwest who united the tribes in a defense of their lands and freedom, Mangus Colorado is presented with sympathy for and understanding of his and his people's viewpoint. Grades 5–10.

Marco Polo

Ceserani, Gian Paolo. *Marco Polo.* Illus. Piero Ventura. Putnam's, 1982.

A lively and simple presentation of Marco Polo's life and journeys, with full-color, panoramic illustrations. Grades 3–5.

Mead, Margaret

Epstein, Samuel, and Beryl Epstein. *She Never Looked Back: Margaret Mead In Samoa.* Illus. Victor Juhasz. Coward-McCann, 1980.

Concentrating on Mead's work in Samoa, this invigorating biography succeeds in revealing the great anthropologist's character. Grades 4–6.

Rice, Edward. *Margaret Mead. A Portrait.* Harper, 1979.

A sophisticated, well-researched study of the influential anthropologist. Quotations from Mead's own writings give insight into the complexities of her personal life as well as into the far-ranging influence of her ideas. Ages 12 and up.

Mendelssohn, Felix

Kupferberg, Herbert. *Felix Mendelssohn: His Life, His Family, His Music.* Scribner's, 1972.

The genuine love of music in the Mendelssohn home is a charming backdrop for the genius who always remained closely tied to his family. Illus. with photographs and prints. Grades 5–12.

Mozart, Wolfgang Amadeus

Monjo, F. N. *Letters to Horseface: Being the Story of Wolfgang Amadeus Mozart's Journey to Italy, 1769–1770, When He Was a Boy of Fourteen.* Illus. and designed by Don Bolognese and Elaine Raphael. Viking, 1975.

These buoyant, effervescent letters addressed to Mozart's sister recount the fourteen-year-old boy's journeys through Italy with his father. Although fictional, the letters skillfully echo the actual Mozart correspondence and give insight into the mind of this musical genius. Grades 4–6.

Muir, John

Swift, Hildegarde Hoyt. *From the Eagle's Wing.* Illus. Lynd Ward. Morrow, 1962.

Muir's enthusiasm and zest for life shine through this excellent biography of the naturalist. Grades 6–8.

Nansen, Fridtjof

Hall, Anna Gertrude. *Nansen.* Illus. Boris Artzybasheff. Viking, 1940.

An absorbing life of the great Norwegian explorer and statesman who won the Nobel Peace Prize in 1922. Grades 7–9.

Nightingale, Florence

Harmelink, Barbara. *Florence Nightingale, Founder of Modern Nursing.* F. Watts, 1969.

An objective account of this famous woman's life places her accomplishments and personal struggles in an historical perspective. Grades 4–7.

Nolan, Jeannette Covert. *Florence Nightingale.* Illus. George Avison. Messner, 1946.

A well-written, authentic life of the woman who achieved fame as a nurse in the Crimean War. Grades 7–9.

North, Sterling

North, Sterling. *Rascal: A Memoir of a Better Era.* Illus. John Schoenherr, 1963.

An autobiographical record of a year in a boy's life, 1918, memorable because it was the year he had a pet raccoon. Grades 4–12.

Paine, Thomas

Coolidge, Olivia. *Tom Paine, Revolutionary.* Scribner's, 1969.

The historical and personal milieu in which Paine's writings developed. Grades 7–12.

Parks, Rosa

Greenfield, Eloise. *Rosa Parks.* Illus. Eric Marlow. Crowell, 1973.

The historic refusal of Rosa Parks to give up her seat to a white man in Montgomery, Alabama, is the main emphasis of this brief, easily read biography. Grades 3–6.

Pasteur, Louis

Wood, Laura N. *Louis Pasteur.* Messner, 1948.

The story of Pasteur's life, his scientific ideas and achievements, and his tender, tranquil family life is told in a straightforward, simple manner. Illus. with photographs. Grades 5–7.

Penn, William

Gray, Elizabeth Janet. *Penn.* Illus. George Gillett Whitney. Viking, 1938.

Penn gave up wealth and position to become a Quaker. Later he was governor of the new colony of Pennsylvania. Grades 7–9.

Peter I, the Great

Putnam, Peter Brock. *Peter, the Revolutionary Tsar.* Maps and illus. Laszlo Kubinyi. Harper, 1973.

The forceful personality and tremendous energy of Peter emerges in a portrayal that is both colorful and factual. Grades 6–12.

Pitseolak, Peter

Pitseolak, Peter. *Peter Pitseolak's Escape from Death.* Illus. by the author; intro. and ed. Dorothy Eber. Delacorte/Seymour Lawrence, 1977.

A contemporary Baffin Island Eskimo recounts his brush with death on a drifting ice floe in authentically stark detail. Translated from Eskimo syllabics and illustrated in the primitive, simply colored images of Inuit art. Grades 3 and up.

Pocahontas

Fritz, Jean. *The Double Life of Pocahontas.* Illus. Ed Young. Putnam's, 1983.

An absorbing account of this famous Indian princess's life with insights into the complexities of being caught between two cultures. The romantic patina is stripped from her tragic life and the remaining story is one of cruelty and courage. Grades 4–8.

Potter, Beatrix

Aldis, Dorothy. *Nothing Is Impossible.* Illus. Richard Cuffari. Atheneum, 1969.

The lonely, isolated childhood of Beatrix Potter is a prominent part of this poignant "story." Grades 4–6.

Lane, Margaret. *The Tale of Beatrix Potter: A Biography.* Illus. by the author. Rev. ed. Warne, 1968.

Originally published in 1946, this biography for older readers has recently been revised to include information made available by the decoding of Beatrix Potter's journal.

Raleigh, Sir Walter

Fecher, Constance. *The Last Elizabethan: A Portrait of Sir Walter Ralegh.* Farrar, Straus & Giroux, 1972.

The story of a man who was the epitome of his time, this biography brings into focus the color, personalities, and conflicts of Elizabethan politics, literature, and adventurous explorations. This unique man's life is recounted with a fine feeling and regard for authenticity. Grades 6–12.

Syme, Ronald. *Walter Raleigh.* Illus. William Stobbs. Morrow, 1962.

The author shows how Raleigh as poet, scientist, explorer, and statesman contributed so much to his own time and to history. Grades 3–6.

Rembrandt van Rijn, Harmenszoon

Ripley, Elizabeth. *Rembrandt: A Biography.* Illus. with drawings, etchings, and paintings by Rembrandt. Walck, 1955.

"Elizabeth Ripley's biographies of famous artists are never straight biography. She has the selective gift of reaching into the artist's life and work and bringing out those important phases that young minds can appreciate."—*The Horn Book Magazine.* Grades 5–8.

Revere, Paul

Forbes, Esther. *America's Paul Revere.* Illus. Lynd Ward. Houghton Mifflin, 1946.

Vivid prose and striking pictures combine to make an outstanding biography of a great craftsman and patriot. Grades 5–8.

Fritz, Jean. *And Then What Happened, Paul Revere?* Illus. Margaret Tomes. Coward-McCann, 1973.

A lighthearted, entertaining biography meant for young children. Grades 3–6.

Robeson, Paul

Greenfield, Eloise. *Paul Robeson.* Illus. George Ford.

Brief and simplified, this nevertheless gives the spirit of the man. Grades 2–4.

Hamilton, Virginia. *Paul Robeson: The Life and Times of a Free Black Man.* Harper, 1974.

A hero to many people, Paul Robeson's life is sympathetically and objectively portrayed. His accomplishments and espousal of causes are well documented and placed in historical context. Illus. with photographs. Grades 6 and up.

Roosevelt, Eleanor

Davidson, Margaret. *The Story of Eleanor Roosevelt.* Four Winds, 1968.

Emphasizing the emotional side of Eleanor Roosevelt's life, this biography, while brief, presents an intimate view. Grades 5–9.

Jacobs, William Jay. *Eleanor Roosevelt: A Life of Happiness and Tears.* Coward-McCann, 1983.

An honest account of Eleanor Roosevelt's personal life and political activism. Grades 6–9.

Roosevelt, Franklin Delano

Faber, Doris. *Franklin Delano Roosevelt.* Abelard-Schuman, 1975.

Covers a great deal of material in an objective, informative manner. The public life of the man is the focus here. Illus. with photographs. Grades 5–9.

Peare, Catherine Owens. *The FDR Story.* Crowell, 1962.

A complete sense of the man is brought out in this biography, well-balanced in its portrayal and sympathetic in perspective. Illus. with photographs. Grades 5–9.

Sandburg, Carl

Rogers, W. G. *Carl Sandburg, Yes: Poet, Historian, Novelist, Songster.* Harcourt, 1970.

A detailed, objective, and anecdotal portrayal of a many-faceted man. Illus. with photographs. Grades 5–12.

Sandburg, Carl. *Prairie-Town Boy.* Taken from *Always the Young Strangers.* Illus. Joe Krush. Harcourt, 1955.

A shortened version of the author's recollections of his childhood and youth in Galesburg, Illinois. Grades 7–9.

Sasaki, Sadako

Coerr, Eleanor. *Sadako and the Thousand Paper Cranes.* Illus. Ronald Himler. Putnam's, 1977.

The life of a young girl of Hiroshima who died from leukemia as a result of the atom bomb. Her courage and grace have been an inspiration to the children of Japan and the world. Grades 3–6.

Schliemann, Heinrich

Braymer, Marjorie. *The Walls of Windy Troy: A Biography of Heinrich Schliemann.* Harcourt, 1960.

As a boy Schliemann's imagination was fired by reading Homer's *Iliad.* He devoted his life to proving that legendary Troy and its buried treasures really existed. Illus. with photographs. Grades 6–9.

Schweitzer, Albert

Gollomb, Joseph. *Albert Schweitzer: Genius in the Jungle.* Vanguard, 1949.

A splendid introduction to the life of an extraordinary man. Based on Schweitzer's own writings, it is a book to lift the spirit of both young and old interested in helping to build a better world. Grades 6–8.

Scott, Sir Walter

Gray, Elizabeth Janet. *Young Walter Scott.* Viking, 1935.

The unfolding of Scott's genius against the background of his life in Edinburgh. Grades 7–9.

Kohn, Bernice. *Talking Leaves: The Story of Sequoyah.* Illus. Valli. Hawthorn, 1969.

A picture-book format depicting the life of Sequoyah and the Cherokee alphabet devised by him. Grades 2–4.

Serra, Fray Junipero

Politi, Leo. *The Mission Bell.* Illus. by the author. Scribner's, 1953.

Simple text and glowing pictures tell the inspiring story of Father Junipero Serra and how he founded the first mission settlement in California. Grades 2–5.

Shaw, George Bernard

Coolidge, Olivia. *George Bernard Shaw.* Houghton Mifflin, 1968.

A portrait of the nineteenth-century wit and playwright who became a living phenomenon. Grades 6 and up.

Shelley, Mary Godwin

Leighton, Margaret. *Shelley's Mary: A Life of Mary Godwin Shelley.* Farrar, Straus & Giroux, 1973.

Overshadowed by her husband and her father, Mary Shelley nevertheless achieved success in her own right as the writer of *Frankenstein* and managed to support herself and her son after her husband's death. Grades 7 and up.

Siegal, Aranka

Siegal, Aranka. *Upon the Head of the Goat: A Childhood in Hungary, 1939–1944.* Farrar, Straus & Giroux, 1981.

An autobiographical memoir of five years in the life of Piri, a young Hungarian Jewish girl. The spirited, sensitive girl observes the sufferings of European Jews from the ghettos to the trains destined for Auschwitz. Grades 6–8.

Singer, Isaac Bashevis

Singer, Isaac Bashevis. *A Day of Pleasure: Stories of a Boy Growing Up in Warsaw.* Photographs, Roman Vishniac. Farrar, Straus & Giroux, 1969.

Precise and intimate episodes from the boyhood of this masterly writer. Grades 6 and up.

Sitting Bull

O'Connor, Richard. *Sitting Bull, War Chief of the Sioux.* Illus. Eric von Schmidt. McGraw-Hill, 1968.

The qualities of Sitting Bull as a person and a leader of the Sioux are presented against the background of the tragic betrayals of the Indians by the United States Army and government. Grades 5–9.

Smalls, Robert

Sterling, Dorothy. *Captain of the Planter: The Story of Robert Smalls.* Illus. Ernest Crichlow. Doubleday, 1958.

Escaping to freedom with the *Planter,* a steamer he piloted, Robert Smalls not only became a heroic fighter for his own freedom and that of his people, but he also became a force during the Reconstruction period. Grades 5–9.

Stanton, Elizabeth Cady

Clarke, Mary Stetson. *Bloomers and Ballots: Elizabeth Cady Stanton and Women's Rights.* Viking, 1972.

This fictionalized account presents the motivating forces for Elizabeth Stanton's involvement and leadership in the fight for women's suffrage and her long career in it. Grades 5–9.

Stein, Gertrude

Greenfeld, Howard. *Gertrude Stein, a Biography.* Crown, 1973.

Well illustrated with photographs, this work gives attention to Stein's friends and the general cultural milieu in which she lived. Grades 7 and up.

Stevenson, Robert Louis

Wood, James Playsted. *The Lantern Bearer: A Life of Robert Louis Stevenson.* Illus. Saul Lambert. Pantheon, 1965.

A study of the mercurial personality whose sense of adventure was distilled from his own life. Grades 7 and up.

Stowe, Harriet Beecher

Johnston, Johanna. *Harriet and the Runaway Book: The Story of Harriet Beecher Stowe and "Uncle Tom's Cabin."* Illus. Ronald Himler. Harper, 1977.

Concentrates on the writing of the watershed novel. Grades 3–5.

Rouverol, Jean. *Harriet Beecher Stowe: Woman Crusader.* Illus. Charles Brey. Putnam's, 1968.

A succinct, objective account, remarkable for its vivacity and brevity. Grades 3–6.

Takashima, Shizuye

Takashima, Shizuye. *A Child in Prison Camp.* Illus. by the author. Tundra, 1971.

Expressive water colors and sensitive text present the experiences of a Japanese-Canadian girl in a World War II internment camp in the Canadian Rockies. Winner of the Amelia Frances Howard-Gibbon Award for its stunning illustrations, 1972. Grades 4 and up.

Tallchief, Maria

Tobias, Tobi. *Maria Tallchief.* Illus. Michael Hampshire. Crowell, A Crowell Biography, 1970.

Brief presentation of the contemporary ballerina's childhood and career. Grades 3–5.

Terry, Ellen

Fecher, Constance. *Bright Star: A Portrait of Ellen Terry.* Farrar, Straus & Giroux, 1970.

An emotional and affecting portrayal of a great Victorian actress whose human qualities have an immediate appeal. Grades 5–12.

Tolstoy, Leo

Carroll, Sara Newton. *The Search: A Biography of Leo Tolstoy.* Illus. Stephen Gammell. Harper, 1973.

Tolstoy's inner turmoil is the focus of the well-proportioned biography, which shows him both as a unique individual and as a man of his class and times. Grades 5 and up.

Philipson, Morris. *The Count Who Wished He Were a Peasant: A Life of Leo Tolstoy.* Pantheon, 1967.

A factual account. Illus. with photographs. Grades 7–12.

Truth, Sojourner

Bernard, Jacqueline. *Journey toward Freedom.* Norton, 1967.

Sojourner Truth became a legend in her own time in a fight against slavery. Illus. with photographs and engravings. Grades 7 and up.

Tubman, Harriet

Lawrence, Jacob. *Harriet and the Promised Land.* Illus. by the author. Windmill, 1968.

A unique presentation of Harriet and her numerous trips on the Underground Railway, achieved in a series of powerful paintings with unmistakable emotional impact. All ages.

Petry, Ann. *Harriet Tubman: Conductor on the Underground Railroad.* Crowell, 1955.

The magnificent story of the slave who, after escaping to freedom, returned and helped three hundred of her people, in small groups, obtain their freedom. Grades 7–9.

Van Gogh, Vincent

Honour, Alan. *Tormented Genius: The Struggles of Vincent Van Gogh.* Morrow, 1967.

A clear presentation of the main forces in Van Gogh's turbulent life. It should serve as a link to the letters between Vincent and his brother. Grades 6–12.

Washington, Booker T.

Bontemps, Arna. *Young Booker: Booker T. Washington's Early Days.* Dodd, Mead, 1972.

The inspiring story of Washington's heroic perseverance in freeing himself from the shackles of ignorance and the degradation of a birth in slavery. Illus. with photographs.

Washington, George

D'Aulaire, Ingri, and Edgar Parin D'Aulaire. *George Washington.* Illus. by the authors. Doubleday, 1936.

Using the technique of lithography, the D'Aulaires have made the pictures as important as the text. Grades 2–4.

Fleming, Thomas J. *First in Their Hearts: A Biography of George Washington.* Norton, 1968.

A detailed and objective work that achieves power. Illus. with photographs and engravings. Grades 6–12.

Foster, Genevieve. *George Washington.* Illus. by the author. Scribner's, 1949.

Although these "initial biographies" are written for younger children, the interesting text and lively illustrations appeal to older children as well. Grades 4–6.

Whitman, Walt

Deutsch, Babette. *Walt Whitman: Builder for America.* Illus. Rafaello Busoni. Messner, 1941.

An understanding interpretation of the poet and his relation to the times in which he lived. Grades 7–9.

Wilder, Laura Ingalls

Wilder, Laura Ingalls. *West from Home: Letters of Laura Ingalls Wilder, San Francisco, 1915.* Ed. Roger Lea MacBride. Harper, 1974.

With a historical setting by Margot Patterson Doss, this engaging volume of letters transmits the spirit of the author of the "Little House" books. Grades 5 and up.

Wright, Orville and Wilbur

Reynolds, Quentin. *The Wright Brothers: Pioneers of American Aviation.* Illus. Jacob Landau. Random House, Landmark Books, 1950.

Two Americans who kept a bicycle shop and who invented, built, and flew the first airplane. Grades 4–6.

Yates, Elizabeth

Yates, Elizabeth. *My Diary—My World.* Westminster, 1981.

The Newbery Medal winner's adolescent diary begins with her twelfth birthday in 1917 and traces her growing maturity through eight years of enthusiastic passions, dedication to writing, and a tranquil, secure home life. Illus. with photographs. Grades 4–7.

Zemach, Margot

Zemach, Margot. *Self Portrait: Margot Zemach.* Illus. by the author. Addison-Wesley, The Self-Portrait Collection, 1978.

This award-winning illustrator's picture book autobiography overflows with warmth and life. Grades 2–6.

Zenger, Peter

Galt, Tom. *Peter Zenger, Fighter for Freedom.* Illus. Ralph Ray. Crowell, 1951.

A stirring story about the historic fight for the freedom of the press. Grades 4–9.

References for Adults

Books

Altick, Richard D. *Lives and Letters: A History of Literary Biography in England and America.* Knopf, 1965.

Birrell, Francis. *Lives and Letters.* Published for The Little Libraries by Douglas Cleverdon. Bristol, 1932.

Bowen, Catherine Drinker. *Biography: The Craft and the Calling.* Little, Brown, 1968.

Clifford, James L., ed. *Biography as an Art: Selected Criticism, 1560–1960.* Oxford Univ. Press, 1962.

Garraty, John A. *The Nature of Biography.* Knopf, 1957.

Hotchkiss, Jeanette, comp. *American Historical Fiction and Biography for Children and Young People.* Scarecrow, 1973.
   See also *European Historical Fiction and Biography for Children and Young People* (1972).

Johnston, James C. *Biography: The Literature of Personality.* Century, 1927.

Kendall, Paul Murray. *The Art of Biography.* Norton, 1965.

Maurois, Andre. *Aspects of Biography.* Trans. from the French by S. C. Roberts. Cambridge Univ. Press, 1929.

Siegal, Mary-Ellen Kulkin. *Her Way: Biographies of Women for Young People.* Rev. ed. American Library Association, 1984.

Articles

Coolidge, Olivia. "Writing about Abraham Lincoln." *The Horn Book Magazine*, 51 (Feb. 1975), pp. 31–35.

Ellman, Richard. "That's Life." *The New York Review of Books*, 14 (June 17, 1971).

Jurich, Marilyn. "What's Left Out of Biography for Children." *The Great Excluded: Critical Essays on Children's Literature*, 1 (1972), pp. 143, 151.

Lanes, Selma. "On Feminism and Children's Books." *School Library Journal*, 20 (Jan. 1974), pp. 23, 26–27.

Chapters and Commentary

"Biography for Young People" Issue. *The Lion and the Unicorn*, 4, no. 1 (Summer, 1980).

Carr, Jo, comp. *Beyond Fact: Nonfiction for Children and Young People.* American Library Association, 1982.
   See Section IV. Biography: Facts Warmed by Imagination: "What Do We Do about Bad Biographies?" by Jo Carr, pp. 119–29; "Biography," by Margery Fisher, pp. 129–34; "An Evaluation of Biography," by Denise M. Wilms, pp. 135–40; "My Struggle with Facts," by Olivia Coolidge, pp. 141–48; "In Biography for Young Readers, Nothing Is Impossible," by Elizabeth Segal, pp. 148–53.

Field, Elinor Whitney, ed. *Horn Book Reflections: On Children's Books and Reading.* Horn Book, 1969.
   "Biography: The Other Face of the Coin," by Rosemary Sprague, pp. 128–36.

Fisher, Margery. *Matters of Fact: Aspects of Non-Fiction for Children.* Crowell, 1972.
   "Biography," pp. 299–405.

MacCarthy, Desmond. *Memories.* MacGibbon & Kee, 1953.
   "Lytton Strachey and the Art of Biography," pp. 31–54.

14 Travel and History

Travel*

Barker, Felix, with Anthea Barker, Malcolm Ross-MacDonald, and Duncan Castlereagh. *The Search Begins: A History of Discovery and Exploration.* Aldus Books/Jupiter Books, 1973.
   Lavishly illustrated and written in three different sections by different writers, this gives a sweeping, yet richly detailed view of explorations from the time of the Sumerians to the voyage of Magellan. Illus. with maps, drawings, and photographs. Grades 6 and up.

Baylor, Byrd. *The Desert Is Theirs.* Illus. Peter Parnall. Scribner's, 1975.
   The story of the desert of the Southwest, its people, animals, insects, birds, and the elements. Grades 2–5.

Boswell, Hazel. *French Canada: Pictures and Stories of Old Quebec.* Illus. by the author. Rev. ed. Atheneum, 1967.
   A pleasant introduction to French Canada, showing various aspects of the life and describing traditional customs fast disappearing. Grades 5–7.

Brown, Michael. *Shackleton's Epic Voyage.* Illus. Raymond Briggs. Coward-McCann, 1969.
   A shortened account of the heroic voyage made by Shackleton to Antarctica. Briggs's illustrations fill out the brief text. Grades 4–6.

Catherall, Arthur. *Vanishing Lapland.* F. Watts, 1972.
   The customs, people, and way of life are depicted in an informal, immediate style. Illus. with photographs. Grades 5–12.

Clark, Ann Nolan. *Circle of Seasons.* Illus. W. T. Mars. Farrar, Straus & Giroux, 1970.

* See also Archaeology in the bibliography for Chapter 15, "Science."

The inner and outer life of Pueblo Indians follows the seasons in a well-regulated way. What has been permitted for a friend to know is described in this book. Grades 4–7.

Collins, Michael. *Flying to the Moon and Other Strange Places.* Farrar, Straus & Giroux, 1976.

The exploration of space as observed and experienced firsthand by one of the early astronauts. Illus. with photographs. Grades 4–7.

Darwin, Charles. *The Voyage of the Beagle.* Abr. and ed. Millicent E. Selsam; illus. Anthony Ravielli. Harper, 1959.

One of the most significant "voyages of discovery," Darwin's five-year trip around the world resulted in a new way of thinking about man and his past. All cuts in the text are indicated by three dots so that any omitted passage may be looked for in the original. Grades 5–10.

Davis, William Stearns. *A Day in Old Athens: A Picture of Athenian Life.* Biblo & Tannen, 1960.

Depicts the daily life and customs in ancient Athens. Grades 7–9. See also *A Day in Old Rome.*

Dornberg, John. *The Soviet Union Today.* Dial, 1976.

A detailed account of contemporary Russia—its nationalities, economy, government, and cultural values and beliefs. Insightful and objective. Grades 6 up.

Gilfond, Henry. *Afghanistan.* F. Watts, 1980.

An introduction to Afghanistan, its geography, culture, and people, emphasizing its history of conflict and occupation. Illus. with photographs. Grades 4–6.

Goldston, Robert. *Spain.* F. Watts, 1972.

A brief description of the physical aspects of Spain and its political and artistic history is combined with a presentation of the daily life of contemporary people and a view of the country's future. Illus. with photographs. Grades 4–6.

Freuchen, Peter, with David Loth. *Peter Freuchen's Book of the Seven Seas.* Messner, 1957.

A grand compendium about the sea, the travels it has seen, the life it sustains, the stories it has spawned. Grades 6 and up.

Glubok, Shirley. *The Art of the Southwest Indians.* Photographs, Alfred Tamrin; designed by Gerard Nook. Macmillan, 1971.

Art objects, some ceremonial, some made for trade by the Pueblos, the Navajo, the Apache, the Pima, the Papago, and the Mojave. These include baskets, sculpture, sand paintings, kachinas, ceremonial robes, silver work, rugs, and pots. Grades 3 and up.

Hall, Jennie. *Buried Cities.* 2d ed., revised under the editorship of Lily Poritz; intro. Katharine Taylor. Macmillan, 1964.

Excavations of Pompeii, Olympia, and Mycenae. This new edition of the book first published in 1922 includes information about recent excavations and many new photographs. Illus. with drawings and photographs. Grades 6–9.

Heyerdahl, Thor. *Kon-Tiki: Across the Pacific by Raft.* Trans. F. H. Lyon. Rand McNally, 1950.

A thrilling account of how the author, a Scandinavian scientist, with five other men, sailed 4,300 miles across the Pacific from Peru to Polynesia on a balsa-log raft to prove his theory that civilization had come to the South Sea islands from South America. Grades 7 and up. See also *The Ra Expeditions* (1971).

Hirsch, S. Carl. *The Globe for the Space Age.* Illus. Burt Silverman. Viking, 1963.

Early explorers always carried a globe on board their sailing ships. After being unused in exploration for two hundred years, the globe has once more become an important instrument for navigation: A small lighted globe accompanies the astronauts in their space capsules. Grades 6–8. See also *On Course! Navigating in Sea, Air, and Space,* illus. William Steinel (1967).

Humboldt, Alexander von. *Stars, Mosquitoes and Crocodiles: The American Travels of Alexander von Humboldt.* Sel. and ed. Millicent E. Selsam; illus. Russell Francis Peterson. Harper, 1962.

An engrossing account of the German scientist's travels in South America, Cuba, Mexico, and the United States. Grades 6–8.

Huynh, Quang Nhuong. *The Land I Lost: Adventures of a Boy in Vietnam.* Illus. Vo-Dinh Mai. Harper, 1982.

Reminiscences of a childhood in a small Vietnamese hamlet in the central highlands. Grades 4–6.

Jenness, Aylette, and Lisa W. Kroeber. *A Life of Their Own: An Indian Family in Latin America.* Illus. with photographs by the authors and drawings by Susan Votaw. Crowell, 1975.

An intimate and respectful look at Guatemala, in paricular the highland area of Antigua. The reader is taken into the writers' process and the steps involved in becoming acquainted with the Hernandezes, an Indian family who live in the village of San Antonio. A book rewarding for the pleasure and information it gives. Grades 4–9. See also *Dwellers of the Tundra: Life in an Alaskan Eskimo*

Village (Crowell-Collier, 1970) and *Along the Niger River: An African Way of Life* (1974).

Kendall, Sarita. *Looking at Brazil.* Lippincott, 1974.

One in a series about various countries (*Looking at Other Countries*), this is geared to supply the information that a student would need in school. Illus. with photographs. Grades 4–7.

Kirk, Ruth, and Richard D. Daugherty. *Hunters of the Whale: An Adventure in Northwest Coast Archaeology.* Photographs, Ruth Kirk and Louis Kirk. Morrow, 1974.

A journalist and an anthropologist join forces with the Makah Indian tribe in recovering and preserving prehistoric art at the Ozette Indian site. Archaeology students from various colleges and universities learn techniques as they work at the site. Grades 6–9.

Lansing, Alfred. *Shackleton's Valiant Voyage.* McGraw-Hill, 1960.

The gripping story of Sir Ernest Shackleton's ill-fated Antarctic expedition and months of hardship. Abridged from the author's book *Endurance.* Illus. with photographs. Grades 7 and up.

Lauré, Jason, with Ettagale Lauré. *Joi Bangla! The Children of Bangladesh.* Photographs, Jason Lauré. Farrar, Straus & Giroux, 1974.

The story of a new nation is told through the lives of nine children who represent varied backgrounds and classes. Grades 5–12. See also *South Africa: Coming of Age under Apartheid* (1980).

Lifton, Betty Jean, and Thomas C. Fox. *Children of Vietnam.* Photographs, Thomas C. Fox. Atheneum, 1972.

Emotional and disturbing, this presentation of the children in Vietnam, the victims of war, consists of interviews and descriptions of individuals and their situations. Grades 6 and up.

Lucas, Mary Seymour. *Vast Horizons.* Illus. C. B. Falls. Viking, 1943.

A panorama of the development of trade routes to the Indies. Grades 7 and up.

McKown, Robin. *The Congo: River of Mystery.* Illus. Tom Feelings. McGraw-Hill, 1968.

The Congo, its appearance and present life are described, and numerous stories of its history and the men who came to explore it are also presented. Grades 4–8.

Marcus, Rebecca B. *Survivors of the Stone Age: Nine Tribes Today.* Hastings, 1975.

The nine tribes are the Tasaday of the Philippines, the Ik of Uganda, the Bushmen of the Kalahari Desert, the Jivaro of the Amazon, the Mbuti Pygmies of Africa, the Aruntas of Australia, the Onges of Little Andaman Island, the people of Papua-New Guinea, and the Kranhacarores of Brazil. Illus. with photographs. Grades 6–12.

Moorehead, Alan. *No Room in the Ark.* Abr. Lucy Moorehead. Harper, 1966.

A remarkable journey through the game preserves of Africa. Illus. with photographs and map. Grades 7 and up. See also *The Story of the Blue Nile.*

Nance, John. *The Land and People of the Philippines.* Lippincott, Portraits of the Nations Series, 1977.

History, geography, and culture of the Philippines, both before and after American involvement, are clearly presented. This excellent series covers many countries. Grades 5 and up.

National Geographic Society. *The New America's Wonderland: Our National Parks.* Ed. Ross Bennett. Rev. ed. The National Geographic Society, World in Color Library, 1980.

A handsome volume of photographs and articles. Materials appeared in the *National Georgraphic Magazine.* Illus. with photographs. Grades 6 and up. See also *Visiting Our Past: America's Historylands* (1977).

Newlon, Clarke. *The Middle East, and Why.* Dodd, Mead, 1977.

The influence of oil, money, and politics in the twenty-one Middle Eastern countries is examined. Grades 6 and up.

Newlon, Clarke. *Southern Africa: The Critical Land.* Dodd, Mead, 1978.

An incisive and direct review of the colonial history and current political unrest of the Southern African nations. Grades 6 and up.

Parker, John. *Discovery: Developing View of the Earth from Ancient Times to the Voyages of Captain Cook.* Maps rendered by Merrily A. Smith. Scribner's, 1972.

The vital role of geography in the lives of cultures from the times of Sumer to Captain Cook is emphasized. Grades 6 and up.

Perl, Lila. *Ghana and Ivory Coast: Spotlight on West Africa.* Morrow, 1975.

The scenery and people of today are shown, together with a look at their history and speculations about their future. Photographs and details about customs are engrossing. Illus. with photographs. Grades 5–9. See also *Ethiopia, Land of the Lion*

(1972); *East Africa: Kenya, Tanzania, Uganda* (1973); *Mexico: Crucible of the Americas* (1978); *Puerto Rico: Island between Two Worlds* (1979); *Guatemala: Central America's Living Past* (1982); and *Red Star and Green Dragon: Looking at New China* (1983).

Provensen, Alice, and Martin Provensen. *The Glorious Flight: Across the Channel with Louis Blériot.* Illus. by the authors. Viking, 1983.

A stunning picture-book version of the French pioneer aviator's experiments with early airplanes, climaxing in his flight across the English Channel in 1909 — eighteen years before Lindbergh. Graceful, humorous, and inspiring. Winner of the Caldecott Medal in 1984 for the panoramic paintings. Grades K–3.

Rau, Margaret. *Our World: The People's Republic of China.* Rev. ed. Messner, 1981.

A well-organized, objective view of events in China, emphasizing the development of communism, the Cultural Revolution and its effects, and life in China today. Grades 6 and up. See also *The People of New China* (1978).

Saint-Exupéry, Antoine de. *Wind, Sand and Stars.* Trans. from the French by Lewis Galantière; illus. John O'H. Cosgrave II. Harcourt, 1949.

A renowned flyer, who was a poet by nature and a philosopher by virtue of experience, writes of his adventures as a French aviator. Grades 7 and up.

Sasek, Miroslav. *This Is Greece.* Illus. by the author. Macmillan, 1966.

One of a popular picture-travel-book series that captures the spirit of the countries and cities the author visits. Grades 3–5.

Singer, Julia. *We All Come from Someplace: Children of Puerto Rico.* Illus. by the author. Atheneum, 1976.

A simply written picture study of the island from the point of view of its children. Grades 4–6.

Sternberg, Martha. *Japan: A Week in Daisuke's World.* Photographs, Minoru Aoki. Crowell-Collier, 1973.

Fine, natural photographs tell the story of Daisuke, second-grade pupil in Tokyo. Grades 1–3.

Tanobe, Miyuki. *Québec, je t'aime; I Love You.* Illus. by the author. Tundra, 1976.

A Japanese artist observes and celebrates life in French Canada with naive, magical paintings and warmly descriptive text. Bilingual text in French and English. Grades 3 and up.

Thum, Marcella. *Exploring Black America: A History and Guide.* Atheneum, 1975.

A long-needed guide, with background information, to places of historical importance in learning about the black experience in the United States. Especially valuable for teachers. Grades 6 and up.

Toye, William. *Cartier Discovers the St. Lawrence.* Illus. Laszlo Gal. Walck, 1970.

Cartier's voyages of discovery to the New World from 1534 to 1541 are vividly described with quotations from Cartier's own observant journals. The handsome illustrations complement the text. Winner of the Canadian Library Association Book of the Year for Children Award in 1971. Grades 3–6.

Vavra, Robert. *Milane: The Story of a Hungarian Gypsy Boy.* Harcourt, 1969.

Extraordinary photographs and a brief text portray the life of a young gypsy boy and his friendship with an orphaned fawn. Grades 1–5.

Ward, Peter. *The Adventure of Charles Darwin.* Illus. Annabel Large. Cambridge Univ. Press, 1982.

The exciting five-year voyage of *The Beagle* is here retold as if seen through the eyes of a curious young cabin boy befriended and instructed by Darwin. Grades 3–6.

Wolf, Bernard. *In This Proud Land: The Story of a Mexican American Family.* Illus. with photographs by the author. Lippincott, 1978.

The life of a Mexican-American family of migrant workers is treated with sympathy and dignity in this documentary volume that follows them from Texas to Minnesota in their search for employment. Grades 3–6.

History

Alderman, Clifford Lindsey. *The Golden Century: England under the Tudors.* Messner, 1972.

The story of the Tudors, written here in an easy, flowing, clear style, is one that outdoes fiction. Illus. with photographs. Grades 5–9. See also *Colonists for Sale: The Story of Indentured Servants in America* (Macmillan, 1975).

Almedingen, E. M. *Land of Muscovy: The History of Early Russia.* Illus. Michael Charlton. Farrar, Straus & Giroux, 1972.

The early history of Russia from the reigns of Ivan the Terrible to Michael Romanov. Customs of everyday life are also described in detail. Grades 5 and up.

American Heritage. *The California Gold Rush.* By the editors of *American Heritage;* narrative by Ralph K. Andrist; consultant, Archibald Hanna. American Heritage, American Heritage Junior Library, 1961.
Grades 6–9.

American Heritage. *D-Day: The Invasion of Europe.* By the editors of *American Heritage;* narrative by Al Hine; consultant, S. L. A. Marshall. American Heritage, American Heritage Junior Library, 1962.
Grades 6–9.

American Heritage. *The Pilgrims and Plymouth Colony.* By the editors of *American Heritage;* narrative by Feenie Ziner; consultant, George F. Willison. American Heritage, American Heritage Junior Library, 1961.
Grades 6–9. See also other titles in this series.

Anno, Mitsumasa. *Anno's Medieval World.* Illus. by the author; adapted from the translation by Ursula Synge. Philomel, 1980.
Fascinating and original. A picture book that explains medieval theories of life and the universe in clear prose and detailed, handsome paintings. Grades 3 and up.

Archer, Jules. *The Philippines' Fight for Freedom.* Crowell-Collier, 1970.
A portrait of the Filipino people emerges in this history, which reveals the imperialist thrust of the countries that have ruled the Philippines. Illus. with photographs. Grades 5 and up.

Ashe, Geoffrey. *King Arthur in Fact and Legend.* Nelson, 1969.
Archaeology, literature, and historical records are viewed with the purpose of establishing Arthur in time and place. Ashe and Joseph Clancy, both with the same evidence, have come to different conclusions. They make fascinating comparative reading. Illus. with photographs. Grades 6 and up.

Asimov, Isaac. *The Roman Empire.* Houghton Mifflin, 1967.
This companion volume to *The Roman Republic* surveys the five hundred-year period when Rome established her empire and developed two of her great heritages, law and religion. Grades 7–9. See also *The Egyptians* (1967); *The Shaping of England* (1969); and *The Birth of the United States, 1763–1816* (1974).

Baity, Elizabeth Chesley. *Americans before Columbus.* Illus. with photographs, drawings, and maps by C. B. Falls. Viking, 1961.

An absorbing study of American Indian peoples and cultures from the Asiatic migrations to the Spanish conquests. Grades 7–9. See also *Man Is a Weaver* (1942).

Bakeless, Katherine, and John Bakeless. *Spies of the Revolution.* Lippincott, 1962.
History and adventure are tied together in this account of a time when information gathering was the work of committed amateurs. Grades 5–9. See also *Confederate Spy Stories* (1973).

Bales, Carol Ann. *Tales of the Elders: A Memory Book of Men and Women Who Came to America as Immigrants, 1900–1930.* Illus. with photographs by the author. Follett, 1977.
Twelve first-person narratives tell similar stories of passage to America and the struggle to make it a home. Originally from eleven different countries, the elderly American citizens speak of hard work, courage, and perseverance. Grades 5 and up.

Bealer, Alex W. *Only the Names Remain: The Cherokees and the Trail of Tears.* Illus. William Sauts Bock. Little, Brown, 1972.
The Cherokee Nation, with a history dating back a thousand years before Columbus, was forced away from the land of its ancestors. This is their story, told with care and simplicity. Grades 4–7.

Bernheim, Marc, and Evelyne Bernheim. *From Bush to City: A Look at the New Africa.* Harcourt, 1966.
A distinguished book on the emerging Arican nations south of the Sahara Desert. Illus. with photographs. Grades 7–9. See also *African Success Story: The Ivory Coast* (1970) and *In Africa* (Atheneum, 1973).

Bleeker, Sonia. *The Aztec: Indians of Mexico.* Illus. Kisa Sasaki. Morrow, 1963.
One of the books in an excellent series about Indian tribes and cultures, by an author-anthropologist. Grades 4–6.

Boardman, Fon W., Jr. *History and Historians.* Walck, 1965.
A review and questioning of the approaches to the writing of history, this gives the reader a good sense of the field. Grades 6 and up. See also *Around the World in 1776* (1975).

Boorstin, Daniel J. *The Landmark History of the American People: From Plymouth to Appomatox.* Random House, 1968.
The first of a two-volume history of the United States, this is filled with lively detail. An easy, conversational style marks this work of an eminent

historian. Illus. with prints and photographs. Grades 5–10.

Brindze, Ruth. *The Story of the Totem Pole.* Illus. Yeffe Kimball. Vanguard, 1951.

The story of how the Indians, without a written language, carved their history and adventures on giant red cedars. Grades 4–6.

Brooks, Polly Schoyer, and Nancy Zinsser Walworth. *The World of Walls: The Middle Ages in Western Europe.* Lippincott, 1966.

The center of attention is on personalities of renown, their stories and exploits. Illus. with photographs. Grades 5–12. See also *When the World Was Rome, 753 B.C. to A.D. 476* (1972).

Buehr, Walter. *When Towns Had Walls: Life in a Medieval English Town.* Illus. by the author. Crowell, 1970.

Using a fictional town by the name of Norcaster, Walter Buehr describes life in the last decades of the fourteenth century and the first of the fifteenth. His introduction tells how he found the information to re-create this scene. Grades 6 and up. See also *Warrior's Weapons* and *Home Sweet Home in the Nineteenth Century.*

Burland, C. A. *Peru under the Incas.* Putnam's, Life in Ancient Lands, 1967.

The life of the Incas, as revealed through reneairs (artifacts) and written by a noted British ethnologist. Illus. with photographs and reproductions. Grades 6 and up.

Ceserani, Gian Paolo. *Grand Constructions.* Illus. Piero Ventura. Putnam's, 1983.

Cutaway drawings reveal structural details of historical monuments from Stonehenge to skyscrapers. Grades 4–6.

Chubb, Thomas Caldecot. *Prince Henry the Navigator and the Highways of the Sea.* Illus. Laurel Brown. Viking, 1970.

The influence of Henry's interest in navigation was far reaching and long lasting. This story of his time and his role in it is one that places geographical knowledge and change in center focus. Grades 4–8.

Churchill, Winston S. and the editors of *Life. The Second World War.* Golden, 1960.

A special edition for young people prepared by Fred Cook from *The Second World War,* a two-volume abridgment by Denis Kelly of Churchill's six-volume work of the same title. Grades 7–9.

Chute, Marchette. *The Green Tree of Democracy.* Dutton, 1971.

Based on material in the author's book for adults, *The First Liberty: A History of the Right to Vote in America, 1619–1850,* this shows the relationship between political developments in England and the struggles for self-government in the colonies, the uneven and emotionally charged progress of franchisement. Grades 6 and up.

Clancy, Joseph P. *Pendragon: Arthur and His Britain.* Praeger, 1971.

An exploration of sources and historical conjectures about Arthur's actual place in history; his social position, cultural background, and political role bring history and literature together in a tantalizing puzzle. Illus. with reproductions from a manuscript of *Lancelot du Lac.* Grades 7 and up.

Coit, Margaret L. *The Fight for Union.* Houghton Mifflin, 1961.

The brilliant opposition of intellects and personalities in the years preceding the Civil War is dramatically shown as slavery — its morality and economics — became the burning issue in the United States. Illus. with photographs. Grades 6 and up.

Collier, Peter. *When Shall They Rest? The Cherokee's Long Struggle with America.* Holt, 1973.

In a sympathetic and readable account, the author portrays the "long ordeal of the Cherokees from pre-colonial times to the present." Illus. with photographs. Grades 6 and up.

Collins, Robert. *The Medes and Persians: Conquerors and Diplomats.* McGraw-Hill, Early Culture Series.

Discoveries of archaeologists have filled in the story of the ancient Medes and Persians. The author, in writing this history, tells of some of the significant excavations and what they revealed. He also quotes Herodotus's version of certain events. Written in a clear style, this account covers a period from 625 B.C. to 330 B.C. Illus. with photographs. Grades 5 and up.

Coolidge, Olivia. *Women's Rights: The Suffrage Movement in America, 1848–1920.* Dutton, 1966.

Heroines of the women's movement, their characters and achievements, give spirit to this account of the long, determined, and varied struggle. Illus. with photographs. Grades 6 and up.

Cottrell, Leonard. *Land of the Pharaohs.* Illus. Richard M. Powers. World, 1960.

The author, a British scholar, gives a vivid portrayal of everyday life in Egypt at the time of the Pharaoh Tutankhamen. Grades 5 and up. See also *Lost Civilizations* (Watts, 1974).

Coy, Harold. *The Mexicans.* Illus. Francisco Mora. Little, Brown, 1970.

A description of Mexico, its people, land, history, and customs, told in a friendly, informal style. The author has prefaced his book with a fictitious letter from a Mexican youth to his friend in the United States. Grades 6 and up.

Davidson, Basil. *A Guide to African History.* Rev. and ed. Haskel Frankel; illus. Robin Jacques. Doubleday, Zenith Books, 1971.

This simplified version of Davidson's work provides an easily comprehended and thorough overview of African history. Grades 4–10.

Davis, Daniel S. *Behind Barbed Wire: The Imprisonment of Japanese Americans during World War II.* Dutton, 1982.

Clearly and honestly written, this study of the internment of Japanese-Americans looks at the prewar roots of discrimination as well as the lasting effects such suffering has on family structure. Illus. with photographs. Grades 6 and up.

Denny, Norman, and Josephine Filmer-Sankey. *The Bayeaux Tapestry: The Story of the Norman Conquest—1066.* Atheneum, 1966.

The storytelling visual qualities of the Bayeaux Tapestry provide a fine basis for the accompanying text that gives the history of the Norman conquest. Grades 5 and up.

DePauw, Linda Grant. *Founding Mothers: Women in America in the Revolutionary Era.* Illus. Michael McCurdy. Houghton Mifflin, 1975.

This detailed account of women's work in the home and in business, their legal status, education, and home life brings new visibility to women of the period. Grades 4–9.

Donovan, Frank R. *The Vikings.* Consultant, Sir Thomas D. Kendrick. American Heritage, A Horizon Caravel Book, 1964.
Grades 6 and up.

Duggan, Alfred. *Growing Up in Thirteenth-Century England.* Illus. C. Walter Hodges. Pantheon, 1962.

The author gives a detailed description of the everyday life of children in five English households of different social classes: that of an earl, a knight, a peasant, a merchant, and a craftsman. Grades 6–8. See also *The Romans* (World, 1964) and *The Story of the Crusades, 1097–1291* (Pantheon, 1964).

Earle, Alice Morse. *Child Life in Colonial Days.* Macmillan, 1899, 1959.

Illus. with photographs. A new edition of this work has been edited by Shirley Glubok, *Home and Child Life in Colonial Days* (1969). See also *Home Life in Colonial Days* (1898, 1950).

Erdoes, Richard. *The Sun Dance People: The Plains Indians, Their Past and Present.* Illus. with photographs by the author. Knopf, 1972.

Informed and sympathetic, conscious of the tragic position of the American Indian in history, this account moves freely between past and present. Grades 5–12. See also *The Rain Dance People: The Pueblo Indians, Their Past and Present* (1976) and *The Native Americans: Navajos* (Sterling, 1978).

Falls, Charles Buckles. *The First Three Thousand Years: Ancient Civilizations of the Tigris, Euphrates, and Nile River Valleys, and the Mediterranean Sea.* Illus. by the author. Viking, 1960.

The author describes the changing civilizations of the Mediterranean world and tells of their contributions to modern times. Grades 6–9.

Fisher, Leonard Everett. *The Schools.* Illus. by the author. Holiday House, 1983.

A history of colonial and nineteenth-century American schools. Grades 3–6. See also other titles in the author's handsomely illustrated Nineteenth Century America series.

Fleming, Thomas J. *The Golden Door: The Story of American Immigration.* Norton, 1970.

The place of the immigrant in history, highlighted with the achievements of the successful, is presented with a sense of appreciation. Illus. with photographs and reproductions. Grades 6–12.

Folsom, Franklin. *Red Power on the Rio Grande: The Native American Revolution of 1680.* Intro. Alfonso Ortiz; illus. J. D. Roybal. Follett, 1973.

The oppressive rule of the King of Spain was forced out by the Pueblo Indians in a revolution led by Popé. This account is considered from the point of view of the Indians and their culture as opposed to an unquestioning acceptance of the written records left by the Spanish. Grades 4 and up.

Foster, Genevieve. *Abraham Lincoln's World.* Illus. by the author. Scribner's, 1944.

The author discovered how difficult it is for young people to visualize events of a period in relationship to each other. Here she gives a picture of world events during Lincoln's life. Grades 7–9. See also *Augustus Caesar's World; George Wash-*

ington's World; The World of Christopher Columbus; The World of Captain John Smith; and Birthdays of Freedom, 2 vols.

Foster, Genevieve. *Year of Columbus, 1492.* Illus. by the author. Scribner's, 1969.
    Columbus's voyage provides the correlating thread in this view of world affairs in 1492. Grades 2–4. See also *Year of the Pilgrims, 1620* (1969).

Garfield, Leon. *The House of Hanover: England in the Eighteenth Century.* Houghton Mifflin, The Mirror of Britain Series, 1976.
    Under the general editorship of Kevin Crossley-Holland, this outstanding popular history series introduces one period of British cultural life in each book. Garfield takes a vigorous look at the artistic achievements of the eighteenth century. Grades 5 and up. See also *Green Blades Rising: The Anglo-Saxons* by Kevin Crossley-Holland (1976); *A Mighty Ferment: Britain in the Age of Revolution, 1750–1850* by David Snodin (1978); *For Queen and Country: Britain in the Victorian Age* by Margaret Drabble (1979) and other titles in this series, elegantly rendered by well-known writers and scholars.

Giblin, James Cross. *Chimney Sweeps: Yesterday and Today.* Illus. Margot Tomes and with photographs. Crowell, 1982.
    Nine hundred years of chimney sweeps, from live geese to wretched four-year-old boys, are chronicled in this fascinating, informative study. The author records the abuses of child labor in the eighteenth and nineteenth centuries. Winner of the American Book Award for 1983. Grades 4–6.

Glubok, Shirley. *The Art of Colonial America.* Illus. Gerard Nook. Macmillan, 1970.
    A handsome introduction to an era through the spirit of its artifacts and art objects. Grades 4 and up. See also *The Art of China* (1973); *The Art of the Northwest Coast Indians* (1975); *The Art of the Vikings* (1978); and *The Art of Egypt under the Pharaohs* (1980).

Goble, Paul, and Dorothy Goble. *Red Hawk's Account of Custer's Last Battle: The Battle of the Little Bighorn 25 June 1876.* Illus. by the authors. Pantheon, 1969.
    An account that is a composite of individual tellings, both Sioux and Cheyenne, this gives the Indian point of view and is accompanied by paintings similar to those used by Indians on tepees or buffalo robes. Grades 5–12. See also *Lone Bull's Horse Raid* (Bradbury, 1973).

Goldston, Robert. *Rise of Red China.* Bobbs-Merrill, 1967.
    An objective account. Grades 7 and up. See also *The Russian Revolution* (1966) and *The Vietnamese Revolution* (1972).

Goodall, John S. *The Story of an English Village.* Illus. by the author. Atheneum, A Margaret K. McElderry Book, 1979.
    A wordless picture book showing the gradual transition of a typical English village from a fourteenth-century rural hamlet across six hundred years to a modern urban center, prosperous and sprawling. Grades 3–6.

Gurko, Miriam. *Indian America: The Black Hawk War.* Illus. Richard Cuffari. Crowell, 1970.
    Resistance by the American Indians to the efforts of the United States to remove them from their lands culminated in a war that was propelled forward by a series of events that left Black Hawk no choice. Grades 5–12.

Hasler, Joan. *The Making of Russia: From Prehistory to Modern Times.* Delacorte, 1969.
    A clear, comprehensive history written by a teacher of history whose point of view is that of a citizen of Great Britain. Illus. with maps and photographs. Grades 6–10.

Hawkes, Jacquetta. *Pharaohs of Egypt.* Consultant, Bernard V. Bothmer. American Heritage, A Horizon Caravel Book, 1965.
    Grade 6 and up.

Herold, J. Christopher. *The Battle of Waterloo.* Consultant, Gordon Wright. American Heritage, A Horizon Caravel Book, 1967.
    Grades 6 and up.

Hibbert, Christopher. *The Search for King Authur.* Consultant, Charles Thomas. American Heritage, A Horizon Caravel Book, 1969.
    Grades 6 and up.

Hillyer, Virgil. *A Child's History of the World.* Revised with new material by Edward G. Huey. Appleton, 1951.
    This edition has five new chapters recounting the story of mankind up to the end of World War II. Grades 4–6.

Hoare, Robert. *World War Two.* Macdonald/Silver Burdett, History of the Modern World Series, 1977.

Succinctly describes the Second World War, with a detailed reference section, chronology, biographical listing, and diagrams. Illus. with photographs and diagrams. Grades 4–7. See also *World War One* (1977) and the other titles in this scholarly, well-illustrated series, edited by R. J. Unstead and J. M. Roberts and first published in England: *Turn of the Century* by Robert Hoare; *The Twenties* by R. J. Unstead; *The Thirties* by R. J. Unstead; *The Forties and Fifties* by Nathaniel Harris; and *The Sixties* by Nathaniel Harris.

Hoff, Rhoda. *America's Immigrants: Adventures in Eyewitness History*. Walck, 1967.
A collection of writings by immigrants, spanning from the eighteenth to the twentieth century. Grades 6 and up. See also similar collections for Africa, America, China, and Russia.

Hofsinde, Robert. *Indian Sign Language*. Morrow, 1956.
Shows how to form the gestures representing over five hundred words in Indian sign language. Grades 4–8. *Indian Games and Crafts* is a companion volume.

Holbrook, Sabra. *The French Founders of North America and Their Heritage*. Atheneum, 1976.
The important contribution of French settlers, explorers, priests, and others to the development of North America is set forth in a direct and entertaining way. Canada's history, as it is influenced by its French heritage, is made understandable. Grades 6 and up.

Holland, Ruth. *Mill-Child*. Crowell-Collier, 1970.
The story of child labor, told with precise, shocking detail, is brought up to the present with a plea for the migrant child. Illus. with photographs. Grades 4–9.

Hoople, Cheryl G. *The Heritage Sampler: A Book of Colonial Arts and Crafts*. Illus. Richard Cuffari. Dial, 1975.
A book for everyone to enjoy with its recipes for food, directions for quilting, instructions for rug-making, paper cuttings, popping corn, etc. Grades 3 and up.

Jacobs, David. *Constantinople, City on the Golden Horn.* Consultant, Cyril A. Manzo. American Heritage, American Heritage Junior Library, Grades 6–9.

Jacobs, David. *Master Builders of the Middle Ages.* Harper, 1969. Grades 6 and up.

Johnson, Gerald W. *America Is Born: A History for Peter.* Illus. Leonard Everett Fisher. Morrow, 1959.

The first of a three-volume history of the United States. Writing with sharp perception, the author not only describes but also evaluates motives, causes, and personalities of the period. Grades 5–7. Read also *America Grows Up* and *America Moves Forward.*

Johnson, Gerald W. *The British Empire: An American View of Its History from 1776 to 1945.* Illus. Leonard Everett Fisher. Morrow, 1969. Grades 5–8.

Jordan, June. *Dry Victories.* Holt, 1972
Drawing parallels between Reconstruction times and the Civil Rights period, the author uses a dialogue form to bring out the feelings of the black people who, having found victory, have found hollowness in that they still lack jobs, the economic tickets to real freedom. Illus. with photographs. Grades 4 and up.

Kamm, Josephine. *Explorers into Africa.* Crowell-Collier, 1970.
A history of the exploration of Africa from the time of the Egyptians to the Victorians, this gives the adventures of such people as Bruce, Mungo Park, Speke, Baker, and others. Grades 7 and up.

Katz, William Loren. *Early America, 1492–1812.* F. Watts, Minorities in American History, Volume I, 1974.
A marshalling of historic fact that is not ordinarily in history books, this is the first volume in a projected series that will focus on the people who have been forced to fight for their rights against continued oppression. See also *An Album of the Great Depression* (1978). Grades 6–10.

Langdon, William Chauncy. *Everyday Things in American Life, 1776–1876.* Scribner's, 1941.
Grades 7–9. See also volume I, *Everyday Things in American Life, 1607–1776* (1938).

Lasker, Joe. *Merry Ever After: The Story of Two Medieval Weddings.* Illus. by the author. Viking, 1976.
Graceful paintings faithful to the spirit of medieval and Early Renaissance art extend the parallel stories of a noble and a peasant wedding, creating a social history of medieval life. Grades 2–4.

Lawson, Don. *The War in Vietnam.* F. Watts, 1981.
The author describes the economic, social, and political currents leading to American involvement in Vietnam. The aftermath of the war is also examined. Illus. with photographs. Grades 4 and up.

Leckie, Robert. *The World Turned Upside Down: The Story of the American Revolution.* Maps, Theodore R. Miller. Putnam's, 1973.
A vivid description of the circumstances sur-

rounding the forming of the Continental Army, its character, and the battles it fought. Grades 5 and up.

Lens, Sidney. *The Bomb.* Dutton, 1982.
A clear analysis of the historical development of atomic weapons and the possible consequences of the arms race. Illus. with photographs. Grades 5 and up.

Lester, Julius. *To Be a Slave.* Illus. Tom Feelings. Dial, 1968.
A poignant account of slavery in America in the words of the slaves themselves. Grades 8 and up.

Lomask, Milton. *The First American Revolution.* Farrar, Straus & Giroux, 1974.
Cohesive and lively, this historical account reads with the pace of fiction. Fine bibliography appended. Grades 6 and up.

Macaulay, David. *Cathedral: The Story of Its Construction.* Illus. by the author. Houghton Mifflin, 1973.
Step by step, the author takes the reader through the planning and construction of a thirteenth-century Gothic cathedral. Grades 4 and up. See also *City: A Story of Roman Planning and Construction* (1974); *Pyramid* (1975); *Castle* (1977); and *Mill* (1983).

McEvedy, Colin, and Sarah McEvedy. *From the Beginning to Alexander the Great.* Maps, Kenneth Wass. Crowell-Collier, The Atlas of World History, 1970.
Maps and photos of objects from various times are accompanied by concise essays. A clear introduction to ancient history, this is the first volume in a projected series of eight historical atlases. Grades 6 and up.

Maruki, Toshi. *Hiroshima No Pika.* Illus. by the author. Lothrop, Lee & Shepard, 1980.
Controversial and somber, this picture-book retelling of a family's experiences in the nuclear bombing of Hiroshima is straightforward and devastatingly honest. The haunting, expressionistic paintings convey the fear and courage of the people. Translated from the Japanese, it won the Mildred L. Batchelder Award for translation in 1983. Grades 4 and up.

Mayer, Josephine, and Tom Prideaux. *Never to Die: The Egyptians in Their Own Words.* Viking, 1938.
An annotated selection of Egyptian literature—poems, fables, letters, etc.—with illustrations showing the art of the times. Periods covered range from 2980 B.C. to about 1000 B.C. Grades 6 and up.

Meltzer, Milton. *All Times, All Peoples: A World History of Slavery.* Illus. Leonard Everett Fisher. Harper, 1980.
Ten thousand years of slavery are recorded, and the economic and political conditions that foster it are analyzed in this clear, comprehensive work. Grades 5–9.

Meltzer, Milton. *Brother, Can You Spare a Dime? The Great Depression, 1929–1933.* Knopf, 1969.
The human side of the period of economic crisis is presented with particularity and power. Illus. with contemporary prints and photographs. Grades 6 and up. See also *Bread and Roses: The Struggle of American Labor, 1865–1915* (1967); *Slavery: From the Rise of Western Civilization to the Renaissance* (Crowell, 1971); and *Never to Forget: The Jews of the Holocaust* (Harper, 1976).

Meltzer, Milton. *The Hispanic Americans.* Crowell, 1982.
Beginning with the Spanish exploration of the Americas, the history of the Hispanic Americans is documented to the present day. Illus. with photographs. Grades 5 and up.

Meltzer, Milton, ed. *In Their Own Words: A History of the American Negro, 1619–1865.* Crowell, 1964.
Documents, with brief introductions, tell the story of the conditions of slavery from firsthand experience; they reveal attempts at revolt and continuing struggles to prohibit slavery. The second volume takes in the period 1865 to 1916; the third, from 1916 to 1966. All these volumes possess a power of passion that comes from the personal voices behind the writing. Illus. with reproductions. Grades 5 and up.

Meredith, Robert, and E. Brooks Smith, eds. *The Quest of Columbus: Being the History Written by Ferdinand Columbus, Son of Christopher Columbus, Admiral of the Ocean Sea, Who, as a Boy of Thirteen Sailed with His Father on the Fourth Voyage and Heard the Story of the First.* Illus. Leonard Everett Fisher. Little, Brown, 1966.
Grades 7 and up.

Miller, Douglas T. *Then Was the Future: The North in the Age of Jackson, 1815–1850.* Knopf, 1973.
Another in the Living History Library, under the general editorship of John Anthony Scott. Original sources are used throughout. The approach is scholarly but lively, and the bibliography is extensive and presented in paragraph form with occasional notes. Illus. with contemporary prints and photographs. Grades 6 and up.

Monjo, F. N. *Gettysburg: Tad Lincoln's Story.* Illus. Douglas Gorsline. Windmill/Dutton, 1976.

The events of the Battle of Gettysburg are here told from the point of view of Abraham Lincoln's favorite son. Grades 2–5.

Morgan, Edmund S. *So What about History?* Atheneum, 1969.

Attempting to answer the question about the importance and meaning of history, a distinguished historian and professor of history provides a provocative analogy, saying history is junk. Illus. with photographs. Grades 4–8.

Murphy, E. Jefferson. *The Bantu Civilization of Southern Africa.* Illus. Louise E. Jefferson. Crowell, 1974.

The skill and creativity of the Bantu people is shown to have been a major achievement. In this scholarly history, the Bantu people are traced from their origin in Nigeria through their migrations to the great kingdoms they established. Grades 6 and up. See also *Understanding Africa,* rev. ed. (1978).

Nabakov, Peter, ed. *Native American Testimony: An Anthology of Indian and White Relations—First Encounter to Dispossession.* Crowell, 1978.

Told in the words of Native Americans themselves, this carefully documented study records the relationship of Indians and whites over four centuries from first contact to final dispossession. A tragic subject humanely treated. Illus. with photographs and maps. Grades 5 and up.

Newman, Robert. *The Japanese: People of the Three Treasures.* Illus. Mamoru Funai. Atheneum, 1968.

An account of the history and character of the Japanese people, explaining in particular the significance of the three treasures, or Regalia—the mirror, the sword, and the jewel. Grades 6–8.

Nickel, Helmut. *Warriors and Worthies: Arms and Armor through Middle Ages.* Color photographs, Bruce Pendleton. Atheneum, 1969.

The history behind the use of instruments of warfare, from the time of ancient Egypt to the nineteenth century, accompanies a handsome display of objects, all from the Metropolitan Museum of Art. Grades 5 and up.

Perkins, Carol Morse. *The Sound of Boomerangs.* Atheneum, 1972.

An intimate account of the aborigines of Australia. Illus. with photographs. Grades 4–8.

Phelan, Mary Kay. *The Story of the Boston Tea Party.* Illus. Frank Aloise. Crowell, 1973.

The present tense is used to give a feeling of immediacy to events. Grades 5–8. See also *Four Days in Philadelphia, 1776* (1967); *Midnight Alarm: The Story of Paul Revere's Ride* (1968); and *The Burning of Washington: August 1814* (1975).

Prago, Albert. *Strangers in Their Own Land: A History of Mexican-Americans.* Four Winds, 1973.

Tracing the complicated heritage of the Mexican-Americans from the days of the Spanish invaders to contemporary times, this book gives the reader an understanding of present-day tensions. Illus. with photographs. Grades 6 and up. See also *Revolution in Spanish America: The Independence Movements of 1808–1825* (Macmillan, 1970).

Price, Christine. *Made in Ancient Egypt.* Dutton, 1970.

Sculpture, jewels, architecture, and all the finds of the archaeologist are used to illustrate and support this history, which encompasses a period from 3100 B.C. to 343 B.C. Illus. with photographs and drawings. Grades 4–8. See also *Made in Ancient Greece* (1967); *Talking Drums of Africa* (Scribner's, 1973); *Dancing Masks of Africa* (Scribner's, 1975); *Made in West Africa* (1975); and *Made in the South Pacific: Arts of the Sea People* (Dutton, 1979).

Quennell, Marjorie, and Charles Quennell. *Everyday Things in Ancient Greece.* 2d. ed. rev. by Kathleen Freeman. Putnam's, 1954.

Grades 7–9. See also *Everyday Life in Roman Britain* (1952); *Everyday Life in Anglo-Saxon, Viking, and Norman Times* (1955); and *The History of Everyday Things in England* (Scribner's, 1918–35, 4 vols., 1960).

Renault, Mary. *The Lion in the Gateway.* Ed. Walter Lord; illus. C. Walter Hodges. Harper, 1964.

A clear, concise description of three of the most important battles in history: Marathon, Salamis, and Thermopylae. Grades 5–8.

Roberson, John R. *China from Manchu, to Mao (1699–1976).* Atheneum, 1980.

A clear account of Chinese history, emphasizing the events of the twentieth century. Illus. with photographs, prints, and maps. Grades 5 and up.

Roberts, Bruce, and Nancy Roberts. *Where Time Stood Still: A Portrait of Appalachia.* Crowell-Collier. 1970.

Beautifully photographed, the region and the people come through with emotional intensity. Grades 6 and up.

Russell, Francis. *The French and Indian Wars.* Consultant, Lawrence Henry Gipson. American Heritage, American Heritage Junior Library, 1962. Grades 6–9.

Russell, Francis. *Lexington, Concord and Bunker Hill.* Consultant, Richard M. Ketchum. American Heritage, American Heritage Junior Library, 1963. Grades 6–9.

Sancha, Sheila. *The Luttrell Village: Country Life in the Middle Ages.* Illus. by the author. Harper, 1983.
Using the British Museum Luttrell Psalter as a guide, this well-researched and original book chronicles the year 1328 in the Lincolnshire village of Gerneham. The cycle of country life from ploughing to harvesting is rendered as real as the large robust black-and-white line drawings. Grades 4–8. See also *The Castle Story* (1982).

Sasek, Miroslav. *This Is the United Nations.* Illus. by the author. Macmillan, 1968.
A colorful visit to the U.N. headquarters in New York City. Grades 3–5.

Schechter, Betty. *The Peaceable Revolution: A Challenging Inheritance from Thoreau and Gandhi.* Houghton Mifflin, 1963.
A provocative study of the concept of nonviolent resistance as illustrated by Thoreau's "civil disobedience," Gandhi's *sayagraha,* and the Southern sit-ins and freedom rides. Grades 7 and up. See also *The Dreyfus Affair: A National Scandal.*

Sears, Stephen W. *The Battle of the Bulge.* Consultant, S. L. A. Marshall. American Heritage, American Heritage Junior Library, 1969. Grades 6–9.

Sears, Stephen W. *Desert War in North Africa.* American Heritage, A Horizon Caravel Book, 1967. Grades 6 and up.

Seeger, Elizabeth. *The Pageant of Chinese History.* Illus. Barnard Watkins. 4th ed. McKay, 1962.
This excellent history of China, first published in 1934, covers the period from 3000 B.C. to the defeat of Japan. Grades 7–9.

Serraillier, Ian. *Chaucer and His World.* Walck, 1968.
Cultural background of Chaucer's day, with an interweaving of historical and biographical facts. Illus. with photographs. Grades 6 and up.

Shippen, Katherine B. *New Found World.* Illus. C. B. Falls. Rev. ed. Viking, 1964.
South America is presented to young people in eloquent prose. Grade 6–8. See also *The Great Heritage* (1947).

Silverberg, Robert. *The Seven Wonders of the Ancient World.* Illus. Paul Williams. Crowell-Collier, 1970.
Description of pyramids, temples, gardens, etc., are enlivened with historical background.

Smith, E. Brooks, and Robert Meredith, eds. *Pilgrim Courage.* Illus. Leonard Everett Fisher. Little, Brown, 1962.
Episodes from William Bradford's *History of Plimoth Plantation* and passages from the journals of William Bradford and Edward Winslow. Grades 6–9.

Southworth, John Van Duyn. *Monarch and Conspirators: The Wives and Woes of Henry VIII.* Crown, 1973.
This entertaining history of the period of Henry VIII focuses on the family life of the monarch. Illus. with photographs and paintings. Grades 5–12.

Sperry, Armstrong. *Great River, Wide Land.* Illus. by the author. Macmillan, 1967.
The Rio Grande through history. Grades 7–9.

Starkey, Marion. *The Visionary Girls: Witchcraft in Salem Village.* Little, Brown, 1973.
A subject that has a strong appeal for young readers, this is told in a way that gives distinctness to the individuals concerned and the psychological and social pressures that governed their behavior. Grades 4–9.

Sterling, Thomas. *Exploration of Africa.* Consultant, George H. T. Kimble. American Heritage, A Horizon Caravel Book, 1963.

Sutcliff, Rosemary. *Heroes and History.* Illus. Charles Keeping. Putnam's, 1965.
Stories that have accrued to certain British heroes have been examined, disentangled, and put together again so that the reader may find out how these people fit into history. Heroes: Caratacus, Arthur, Alfred, Hereward, Llewellin, Robin Hood, William Wallace, Robert the Bruce, Owen Glyndwr, and Montrose. Grades 6 and up.

Switzer, Ellen. *How Democracy Failed.* Atheneum, 1975.
Interviews with present-day German citizens who grew up as teenagers in the 1930s illuminate the beginnings of the Nazi era. Grades 4 and up.

Tamarin, Alfred, and Shirley Glubok. *Voyaging to Cathay: Americans in the China Trade.* Viking, 1976.
A fascinating study of American commerce with China from its beginnings until the Opium Wars. Illus. with photographs and reproductions. Grades 4 and up.

Trease, Geoffrey. *This Is Your Century.* Harcourt. 1966.
Told with a keen analysis of people and events.

Illus. with photographs, maps, and drawings. Grades 7 and up.

Trelease, Allen W. *Reconstruction: The Great Experiment.* Harper, 1971.

The corruption and confusion, the political and economic struggles arising at the end of the Civil War, told in great detail, reveal a past that has a significant relationship to present times. Illus. with photographs. Grades 7 and up.

Tunis, Edwin. *The Tavern at the Ferry.* Illus. by the author. Crowell, 1973.

A complete and faithful re-creation of a site that was in the midst of dramatic events. The rich variety of life in the area, the domestic minutiae are all carefully particularized. Grades 6 and up. See also *Colonial Living* (1976); *Frontier Living* (1976); and *Indians* (Rev. ed., 1979).

Uden, Grant. *A Dictionary of Chivalry.* Illus. Pauline Baynes. Crowell, 1968.

A fascinating introduction to the Middle Ages, with each entry in the dictionary bearing its own illustration. All ages.

Unstead, R. J. *The Story of Britain.* Illus. Victor Ambrus. Nelson, 1970.

Lively, with a feeling for history as an engrossing narrative, this overview engages the reader and gives a clear perspective on significant events and people. Grades 4–8. See also *Looking at History: From Cavemen to the Present Day* (1955); *How They Lived in Cities Long Ago* (Arco, 1981); and other titles by this author.

Van Loon, Hendrik Willem. *The Story of Mankind.* New and enl. ed. Liveright, 1972.

A detailed outline of universal history from the time of cave dwellers to the present day. Beginning with the question "Where did man come from?" it ends with "Can men work together to preserve peace, the earth and themselves?" New chapters written by various historians discuss developing nations, space exploration, and ecological and economic problems. First published in 1921, it was the winner of the first Newbery Medal in 1922. Grades 5–7.

Vlahos, Olivia. *African Beginnings.* Illus. George Ford. Viking, 1967.

A study of the many cultures that have emerged. Grades 7–9. See also *The Battle-Ax People: Beginnings of Western Culture* (1968); *New World Beginnings: Indian Cultures in the Americas* (1970); and *Far Eastern Beginnings* (1976).

Von Hagen, Victor W. *The Incas: People of the Sun.* Illus. Alberto Beltran. World, 1961.

A scholar's interpretation of the ancient Incan culture. Grades 6–9.

White, R. J. *The Horizon Concise History of England.* American Heritage, 1971.

Illus. with photographs. Grades 8 and up.

Whiteford, Andrew Hunter. *North American Indian Arts.* Illus. Owen Vernon Shaffer. Golden, A Golden Science Guide, under the editorship of Herbert S. Zim, 1970.

A remarkably concise and explicit presentation of Indian arts. The clear depiction of the process and the materials used give a firm foundation for the appreciation of Indian arts. Grades 3 and up.

Williams, Jeanne. *Trails of Tears: American Indians Driven from Their Lands.* Putnam's, 1972.

Five tribes, their trials and endurance during forcible removal from their lands. Comanche, Cheyenne, Apache, Navajo, and Cherokee. Illus. with photographs and maps. Grades 6 and up.

Williams, Selma R. *Demeter's Daughters: The Women Who Founded America, 1587–1787.* Atheneum, 1976.

The vigorous and aggressive activities of women in the formative era of our country set some goals that have yet to be generally achieved. A broad spectrum of women is represented. Grades 6 and up.

Williams, Selma R. *Kings, Commoners, and Colonists: Puritan Politics in Old New England, 1603–1660.* Atheneum, 1974.

Full of incident, character descriptions, and anecdote, this historical view of the complementary and conflicting relationships between the New England colonists and the English rulers is both entertaining and enlightening. Grades 6–12.

Wood, James Playsted. *Boston.* Illus. Robert Frankenberg. Seabury, 1967.

People, places, and events that shaped the character of the city are described with integrity and lively comment. Grades 7 and up. See also *Colonial Massachusetts* (Nelson, 1969).

15 Science

General

Asimov, Isaac. *Words of Science, and the History behind Them.* Illus. William Barss. Houghton Mifflin, 1959.

See also *Great Ideas of Science* (1969) and *More Words of Science,* illus. William Barss (1972).

Aylesworth, Thomas. *Mysteries from the Past.* Natural History Press, 1971. Illus. with photographs and drawings.
    Grades 5–9.

Carson, Rachel. *The Sense of Wonder.* Photographs, Charles Pratt and others. Harper, 1965.
    All ages.

Chinery, Michael. *Concise Color Encyclopedia of Nature.* Crowell, 1972.
    All ages.

Cooper, Elizabeth K. *Science in Your Own Back Yard.* Illus. by the author. Harcourt, 1970.
    Grades 5–7.

De Camp, L. Sprague, and Catherine C. De Camp. *The Story of Science in America.* Illus. Leonard Everett Fisher. Scribner's, 1967.
    Grades 5–8.

Gorvett, Jean. *Life in Ponds.* Illus. Paxton Chadwick. American Heritage, 1970.
    Grades 3–7.

Hyde, Margaret. *Exploring Earth and Space.* Illus. Clifford Geary. 5th ed. McGraw-Hill, 1970.
    Grades 6–9.

Moorman, Thomas. *How to Make Your Science Project Scientific.* Atheneum, 1974.
    Grades 6 and up.

National Geographic Picture Atlas of Our World. National Geographic Society, 1979.
    Illus. with photographs. Grades 3–7.   See also *National Geographic Picture Atlas of Our Universe* (1980).

Rand McNally Atlas of World Wildlife. Foreword, Sir Julian Huxley. Rand McNally, 1973.
    Grades 4 and up.

Ruchlis, Hy. *Discovering Scientific Method with Science Puzzle Pictures.* Illus. Jean Krulis and with photographs. Harper, 1963.
    Grades 5 and up.

Selsam, Millicent E. *Is This a Baby Dinosaur? and Other Science Picture-Puzzles.* Harper, 1971.
    Illus. with photographs. Grades K–2.

Shuttlesworth, Dorothy, sel. *A Sense of Wonder: Selections from Great Writers on Nature.* Illus. Joan Berg. Doubleday, 1963.

Silverberg, Robert. *Scientists and Scoundrels: A Book of Hoaxes.* Illus. Jerome Snyder. Crowell, 1965.
    Grades 5 and up.

Silverstein, Alvin, and Virginia Silverstein. *Metamorphosis.* Atheneum, 1971.
    Grades 4–6.

Simon, Seymour. *Science in a Vacant Lot.* Illus. Kiyo Komoda. Viking, 1970.
    Grades 3–6.

Smith, George O. *Scientists' Nightmares.* Putnam's, 1972.
    Grades 6 and up.

Udall, D. H. *The Story of Life.* Illus. by the author and Michael Udall. Putnam's, 1968.
    Grades 5 and up.

Air and Weather

Adler, Irving. *Weather in Your Life.* Day, 1959.
    Grades 5–8.

Bova, Benjamin. *Man Changes the Weather.* Addison-Wesley, 1973.
    Grades 5–8.   See also *The Weather Changes Man* (1974).

Brown, Billye Walker, and Walter R. Brown. *Historical Catastrophes: Hurricanes and Tornadoes.* Addison-Wesley, 1972.
    Grades 6–9.

Chandler, T. J. *The Air Around Us: Man Looks at His Atmosphere.* Natural History Press, 1969.
    Grades 6–10.

Fisher, James. *The Wonderful World of the Air.* Doubleday, 1958.
    Grades 5–7.

Foster, Doris Van Liew. *Feather in the Wind: The Story of a Hurricane.* Illus. Ati Forberg. Lothrop, 1972.
    Grades 1–3.

Gallant, Roy A. *Exploring the Weather.* Illus. Lowell Hess. New ed. Doubleday, 1969.
    Grades 7 and up.

Jennings, Gary. *The Killer Storms: Hurricanes, Typhoons, and Tornadoes.* Lippincott, 1970.
    Grades 6 and up.

Leutscher, Alfred. *Air.* Illus. John Butler. Dial, 1983.
    Grades 1–3.

Milgrom, Harry. *Understanding Weather.* Illus. Lloyd Birmingham. Crowell-Collier, 1970.
    Grades 5–9.

Navarra, John Gabriel. *Nature Strikes Back.* Natural History Press, 1971.
    Grades 5–9.

Ross, Frank Jr. *Storms and Man.* Lothrop, 1971.
Grades 6 and up.

Schneider, Herman. *Everyday Weather and How It Works.* Rev. ed. Illus. Jeanne Bendick. McGraw-Hill, 1961.
Grades 5–8.

Simon, Seymour. *Projects with Air.* Illus. Lynn Sweat. Watts, 1975.
Grades 5–9.

Spar, Jerome. *The Way of the Weather.* Illus. Helmut Wimmer. American Museum of Natural History, Creative Science Series, 1967.
Grades 4–7.

Stambler, Irwin. *Weather Instruments: How They Work.* Putnam's, 1968.
Grades 5–10.

Stone, A. Harris, and Herbert Spiegel. *The Winds of Weather.* Illus. Peter P. Plasencia. Prentice-Hall, 1969.
Grades 4–6.

Zim, Herbert S. *Lightning and Thunder.* Illus. James Gordon Irving. Morrow, 1952.
Grades 4–6.

Animals

Adamson, Joy. *Born Free: A Lioness of Two Worlds.* Pantheon, 1960.
Grades 7 and up. Followed by *Living Free* (Harcourt, 1961) and *Elsa and Her Cubs* (Harcourt, 1965) for younger readers.

Adamson Joy. *Pippa: The Cheetah and Her Cubs.* Harcourt, 1970.
Grades 1–4.

Aruego, Jose. *Symbiosis: A Book of Unusual Friendships.* Scribner's, 1970
Grades 1–3.

Berrill, Jaquelyn. *Wonders of the World of Wolves.* Illus. by the author. Dodd, Mead, Dodd, Mead Wonders Books, 1970.
Grades 4–9.

Brady, Irene. *A Mouse Named Mus.* Illus. by the author. Houghton Mifflin, 1972.
Grades 4–9. See also *Wild Mouse* (Scribner's, 1976).

Bridges, William. *Wild Animals of the World.* Illus. Mary Baker; intro. Roy Chapman Andrews. Garden City Books, 1948.
Grades 4–9.

Burton, Maurice. *Animal Partnerships.* Photographs and drawings, R. B. Davis. Warne, 1969.
Grades 5–9.

Caldwell, David K., and Melba C. Caldwell. *The World of the Bottlenosed Dolphin.* Lippincott, 1972.
Illus. with photographs. Grades 5–12.

Caras, Roger, ed. *Creatures of the Night.* Foreword, Roger Tory Peterson. Westover, 1972.
Illus. with photographs. Grades 3–7.

Carrington, Richard, and the editors of *Life. The Mammals.* Time, Inc., Life Nature Library, 1963.
Grades 7–9.

Catherall, Arthur. *A Zebra Came to Drink.* Illus. John Schoenherr. Dutton, 1970.
Grades 4–10.

Chinery, Michael. *Animal Communities.* F. Watts, International Library, 1972.
Illus. with color plates and photographs. Grades 4 and up.

Chinery, Michael. *Science Dictionary of the Animal World.* F. Watts, 1969.
Illus. with photographs and charts. Grades 6 and up.

Cober, Alan. *Cober's Choice.* Illus. by the author. Dutton, 1979.
Grades 3 and up.

Cohen, Daniel. *Talking with Animals.* Dodd, Mead, 1971.
Illus. with photographs. Grades 5–9. See also *Watchers in the Wild* (Little, Brown, 1971).

Cole, Joanna. *A Horse's Body.* Photographs, Jerome Wexler. Morrow, 1981.
Grades 3–5. See also *A Cat's Body* (1982).

Conklin, Gladys. *Elephants of Africa.* Illus. Joseph Cellini. Holiday House, 1972.
Grades 1–4.

Cook, Joseph J., and William L. Wisner. *Blue Whale, Vanishing Leviathan.* Illus. Jan Cook. Dodd, Mead, 1973.
Grades 4–12.

Cooke, Ann. *Giraffes at Home.* Illus. Robert Quackenbush. Crowell, Let's-Read-and-Find-Out Science Books, 1972.
Grades 1–4.

Cooper, Kay. *A Chipmunk's Inside-Outside World.* Photographs and drawings, Alvin E. Staffan. Messner, 1973.
> Grades 2–6.

Cosgrove, Margaret. *Bone for Bone.* Illus. by the author. Dodd, Mead, 1968.
> Grades 5–9.

Costello, David F. *The World of the Porcupine.* Lippincott, Living World Books, 1966.
> Grades 5 and up. See other books in this series.

Darling, Lois, and Louis Darling. *Worms.* Morrow, 1972.
> Grades 1–3.

Day, Beth. *The World of the Grizzlies.* Illus. Kiyoaki Komoda. Doubleday, 1969.
> Grades 5–9.

Dixon, Paige. *The Young Grizzly.* Illus. Grambs Miller. Atheneum, 1974.
> Grades 4–9.

Eberle, Irmengarde. *Koalas Live Here.* Doubleday, 1967.
> Grades 1–3. See also *Elephants Live Here* (1970); *Moose Live Here* (1971); *Beavers Live Here* (1972); and *Pandas Live Here* (1973).

Feldman, Anne, and Jeane Ely. *The Inflated Dormouse and Other Ways of Life in the Animal World.* Natural History Press, 1970.
> Grades 3–6.

Fenner, Carol. *Gorilla, Gorilla.* Illus. Symeon Shimin. Random House, 1973.
> Grades 3–6.

Fichter, George S. *The Animal Kingdom: An Introduction to the Major Groups of Animals.* Illus. Charles Harper. Golden, 1968.
> Grades 5–9.

Fox, Michael. *Vixie: The Story of a Little Fox.* Illus. Jennifer Perrott. Coward-McCann, 1973.
> Grades 3–6. See also *The Wolf* (1973).

Freedman, Russell, and James E. Morriss. *How Animals Learn.* Holiday House, 1969.
> Grades 6–12. See also *Animal Instincts* (1970) and *Animal Architects* (1971).

Freschet, Berniece. *Skunk Baby.* Illus. Kazue Mizumura. Crowell, 1973.
> Grades 3–6. See also *The Jumping Mouse* (1970) and *Bear Mouse* (Scribner's, 1973).

Freschet, Berniece. *Year on Muskrat Marsh.* Illus. Peter Parnall. Scribner's, 1974.
> Grades 3–6.

George, Jean. *The Moon of the Gray Wolves.* Illus. Lorence Bjorklund. Crowell, The Thirteen Moons.
> Grades 4–7. See other titles in this series.

Gilbert, Bil. *The Weasels: A Sensible Look at a Family of Predators.* Illus. Betty Fraser. Pantheon, 1970.
> Grades 6 and up.

Graham, Ada, and Frank Graham. *Whale Watch.* Illus. D. D. Tyler. Delacorte, 1978.
> Grades 5 and up.

Gross, Ruth Belov. *A Book about Pandas.* Dial, 1972. Illus. with photographs. Grades K–4.

Hanzak, Jan, Zdenek Veselovsky, and David Stephen. *Collins Encyclopedia of Animals.* Collins, 1968. Illus. Grades 4–12.

Hess, Lilo. *The Misunderstood Skunk.* Photographs by the author. Scribner's, 1969.
> Grades 3–7. See also *The Curious Raccoons* (1968); *Animals That Hide, Imitate, and Bluff* (1970); and *Mouse and Company* (1972).

Hopf, Alice L. *Misunderstood Animals.* McGraw-Hill, 1973.
> Illus. with photographs. Grades 4–8. See also *Biography of a Rhino* (Putnam's, 1972).

Jarman, Cathy. *Atlas of Animal Migration.* Illus. Peter Warner and Tony Swift. Day, 1972.
> Grades 4 and up.

Johnson, Sylvia A. *Snails.* Photographs, Modoki Masuda. Lerner, A Lerner Natural Science Book, 1982.
> Grades 3–5.

Kaufman, John. *Bats in the Dark.* Illus. by the author. Crowell, Let's-Read-and-Find-Out Science Books, 1972.
> Grades 1–4.

Kevles, Bettyann. *Watching the Wild Apes: The Primate Studies of Goodall, Fossey, and Galdikos.* Dutton, 1976.
> Grades 5–9.

Knight, Maxwell. *The Small Water Mammals.* Illus. Barry Driscoll. McGraw-Hill, McGraw-Hill Natural Science Picture Books, 1968.
> Grades 3–6.

Kohl, Judith, and Herbert Kohl. *Pack, Band, and Colony: The World of Social Animals.* Illus. Margaret La Farge. Farrar, Straus & Giroux, 1983.
> Grades 5–8.

Kohn, Bernice. *Chipmunks.* Illus. John Hamberger. Prentice-Hall, 1970.
> Grades 1–3. See also *Skunks* (1973).

Leakey, Louis S. B. *The Wild Realm: Animals of East Africa.* National Geographic Society, 1969.
> Grades 6 and up.

Lee, Nina. *The Bat.* Holt, 1976.
> Illus. with photographs. Grades 4–6.

Livaudais, Madeleine, and Robert Dunne. *The Skeleton Book: An Inside Look at Animals.* Walker, 1973.
> Illus. with photographs. Grades 4 and up.

MacClintock, Dorcas. *A Natural History of Giraffes.* Illus. Ugo Mochi. Scribner's, 1973.
> Grades 6 and up. See also *A Natural History of Zebras* (1976).

McClung, Robert. *Hunted Mammals of the Sea.* Illus. William Downey. Morrow, 1977.
> Grades 6 and up.

McDearmon, Kay. *A Day in the Life of a Sea Otter.* Dodd, Mead, 1973.
> Illus. with photographs. Grades 2–4.

Maxwell, Gavin. *The Otter's Tale.* Dutton, 1962.
> Grades 4–7.

Mizamura, Kazue. *The Blue Whale.* Crowell, Let's-Read-and-Find-Out Science Books, 1971.
> Grades K–2.

Moffett, Martha, and Robert Moffett. *Dolphins.* F. Watts, 1971.
> Illus. with photographs. Grades 4–6.

National Geographic Society. *Wild Animals of North America.* National Geographic Society, Natural Science Library, 1960.
> Illus. with photographs and paintings. Grades 4–9. See also other volumes in this series.

Nayman, Jacqueline. *Atlas of Wildlife.* Illus. Adrian Williams and David Nockels. Day, 1972.
> Grades 5 and up.

Nespojohn, Katherine V. *Worms.* Illus. Haris Petie. F. Watts, A First Book, 1972.
> Grades 3–7.

North Sterling. *Rascal.* Illus. John Schoenherr. Dutton, 1963.
> Grades 8–9. See also *Raccoons Are the Brightest People* (1966).

Oxford Scientific Films. *Harvest Mouse.* Photographs, George Bernard, Sean Morris, and David Thompson. Putnam's, 1982.
> Grades 2–5. See also *The Wild Rabbit* (1980).

Paysan, Klaus. *Wild Animals of Africa.* Lerner, 1971.
> Grades 4–7.

Pringle, Laurence. *Follow a Fisher.* Illus. Tony Chen. Crowell, 1973.
> Grades 3–6. See also *In Beaver Valley: How Beavers Change the Land* (World, 1970).

Pringle, Laurence. *Twist, Wiggle and Squirm: A Book About Earthworms.* Illus. Peter Parnall. Crowell, Let's Read-and-Find-Out Science Books, 1973.
> Grades 1–3.

Sanderson, Ivan T., ed. *Animal Tales.* Knopf, 1946.
> Grades 8 and up. See also *Living Mammals of the World* (Hanover House, Doubleday, n.d.).

Schaller, George B., and Millicent E. Selsam. *The Tiger: Its Life in the Wild.* Harper, 1969.
> Grades 4–9.

Scott, Jack Denton. *The Fur Seals of Pribilof.* Photographs, Ozzie Sweet. Putnam's, 1983.
> Grades 4–7. See also *Island of Wild Horses* (1978); *Moose* (1980); and *Orphans from the Sea* (1982).

Selsam, Millicent E. *Animals as Parents.* Illus. John Kaufmann. Morrow, 1965.
> Grades 4–7. See also *How Animals Tell Time* (1967); *How Puppies Grow* (Four Winds, 1972); and *How Kittens Grow* (Four Winds, 1973).

Shannon, Terry, and Charles Payzant. *New at the Zoo: Animal Offspring from Aardvark to Zebra.* Golden Gate, 1972.
> Illus. with photographs. All ages.

Shuttlesworth, Dorothy E. *Animal Camouflage.* Illus. Matthew Kalmenoff. Natural History Press, 1966.
> Grades 6–8.

Shuttlesworth, Dorothy E. *Animals That Frighten People: Facts Versus Myth.* Dutton, 1973.
> Illus. with photographs. Grades 3–7. See also *The Story of Monkeys, Great Apes, and Small Apes* (Doubleday, 1972).

Shuttlesworth, Dorothy. *The Story of Rodents.* Illus. Lydia Rosier. Doubleday, 1971.
> Grades 4–9.

Silverstein, Alvin, and Virginia Silverstein. *Guinea Pigs: All about Them.* Photographs, Roger Kerkham. Lothrop, 1972.
> Grades 3–6.

Silverstein, Alvin, and Virginia Silverstein. *Rabbits: All about Them.* Photographs, Roger Kerkham. Lothrop, 1973.
> Grades 3–6.

Simon, Hilda. *Partners, Guests, and Parasites: Coexistence in Nature.* Viking, 1970.
> Grades 4–10.

Stephens, William M., and Peggy Stephens. *Killer Whale, Mammal of the Sea.* Illus. Lydia Rosier. Holiday House, 1971.
Grades 3–6.

Stonehouse, Bernard. *Animals of the Antarctic: The Ecology of the Far South.* Holt, 1972.
Illus. with photographs. Grades 4 and up.

Sucksdorff, Astrid Bergman. *The Roe Deer.* Photographs by the author. Harcourt, 1969.
Grades 3–7.

Tee-Van, Helen Damrosch. *Small Mammals Are Where You Find Them.* Knopf, 1966.
Grades 3–7.

Tinbergen, Niko, and the editors of *Life. Animal Behavior.* Time, Inc., Life Nature Library, 1965.
Grades 7–9.

Tunis, Edwin. *Chipmunks on the Doorstep.* Illus. by the author. Crowell, 1971.
Grades 4–7.

van Lawick-Goodall, Jane. *In the Shadow of Man.* Houghton Mifflin, 1971.
Illus. with photographs. Grades 6 and up.

Vevers, Gwynne. *Elephants and Mammoths.* Illus. Barry Driscoll. McGraw-Hill, McGraw-Hill Natural Science Picture Books, 1968.
Grades 3–5.

Von Frisch, Otto. *Animal Camouflage.* F. Watts, 1973.
Illus. with photographs. Grades 4 and up.
See also *Animal Migration* (McGraw-Hill, 1969).

Webster, David. *Track Watching.* F. Watts, 1972.
Grades 3–6.

Wise, William. *The Strange World of Sea Mammals.* Illus. Joseph Sibal. Putnam's, 1973.
Grades 4 and up. See also *The Amazing Animals of North America* (1971).

Zim, Herbert S. *Armored Animals.* Illus. Rene Martin. Morrow, 1971.
Grades 3–5.

Zim, Herbert S., and Donald Hoffmeister. *Mammals: A Guide to Familiar American Species.* Illus. James Gordon Irving. Golden, 1955.
Grades 5–7.

Anthropology

Baldwin, Gordon C. *Inventors and Inventions of the Ancient World.* Four Winds, 1973.
Illus. with photographs. Grades 5–9.

Baldwin, Gordon C. *Stone Age Peoples Today.* Norton, 1964.
Illus. with photographs. Grades 5–12.

Block, Irvin. *People.* F. Watts, 1956.
Grades 5–12.

Borer, Mary Cathcart. *Mankind in the Making.* Warne, 1962.
Illus. with line drawings. Grades 6 and up.

Cohen, Robert. *The Color of Man.* Afterword, Dr. Juan Comas; illus. Ken Heyman. Random House, 1968.
Grades 4–12.

Gregor, Arthur S. *The Adventure of Man: His Evolution from Prehistory to Civilization.* Illus. John Martinez. Macmillan, 1966.
Grades 5–10.

Hirsch, S. Carl. *The Riddle of Racism.* Viking, 1972.
Grades 5–12.

Hoyt, Olga. *Aborigines of Australia.* Lothrop, 1969.
Illus. with photographs. Grades 5–12.

Klass, Morton, and Hal Hellman. *The Kinds of Mankind: An Introduction to Race and Racism.* Illus. Visa-Direction, Inc. Lippincott, 1971.
Illus. with photographs. Grades 5–12.

Lucas, Jannette M. *Man's First Million Years.* Illus. James MacDonald. Harcourt, 1941.
Grades 5–10.

McKern, Sharon S. *The Many Faces of Man.* Lothrop, 1972.
Illus. with photographs. Grades 4–9.

May, Julian. *Why People Are Different Colors.* Illus. Symeon Shimin. Holiday House, 1971.
Grades 3–6.

Mead, Margaret. *People and Places.* Illus. W. T. Mars and Jan Fairservis, and with photographs. World, Rainbow Classics, 1959.
Grades 7–9.

Musgrove, Margaret. *Ashanti to Zulu: African Traditions.* Illus. Leo Dillon and Diane Dillon. Dial, 1976.
All ages.

Nance, John. *Lobo of the Tasaday.* Photographs by the author. Pantheon, 1982.
Grades 3–5.

Perkins, Carol Morse. *The Sound of Boomerangs.* Atheneum, 1972.
Illus. with photographs. Grades 4–9.

Spier, Peter. *People.* Illus. by the author. Doubleday, 1980.
> Grades K–4.

Vlahos, Olivia. *Human Beginnings.* Illus. Kyuzo Tsugami. Viking, 1966.
> Grades 7 and up. See also *African Beginnings* (1969).

White, Anne Terry. *The First Men in the World.* Illus. Aldren Watson. Random House, World Landmark Books, 1953.
> Grades 5–7.

Archaeology

Aliki. *Mummies Made in Egypt.* Illus. by the author. Crowell, 1979.
> Grades 2–5. See also *Digging up Dinosaurs* (Harper, 1981).

Barry, Iris. *Discovering Archaeology.* Time, Inc., Time-Life Discovering Series, 1981.
> Grades 6 and up.

Bataille, Georges. *Prehistoric Painting: Lascaux or the Birth of Art.* Skira, 1955.
> All ages.

Baumann, Hans. *The Caves of the Great Hunters.* Trans. Isabel McHugh and Florence McHugh; drawings and maps, Hans Peter Renner. Rev. ed. Pantheon, 1962.
> Illus. with photographs, plates. Grades 4–9.

Baumann, Hans. *Lion Gate and Labyrinth: The World of Troy, Crete and Mycenae.* Trans. Stella Humphries. Pantheon, 1967.
> Illus. with photographs and maps. Grades 7 and up.

Branley, Franklyn M. *The Mystery of Stonehenge.* Illus. Victor G. Ambrus. Crowell, 1969.
> Grades 6–8.

Ceram, C. W. (pseud.) *Gods, Graves, and Scholars: The Story of Archaeology.* Trans. from the German by E. B. Garside. Knopf, 1959.
> Grades 8 and up.

Clymer, Eleanor. *The Second Greatest Invention: Search for the First Farmers.* Illus. Lili Réthi. Holt, 1969.
> Grades 4–9.

Cottrell, Leonard. *Digs and Diggers: A Book of World Archaeology.* World, 1964.
> Illus. with photographs. Grades 7–9.

De Borhegyi, Suzanne. *Ships, Shoals and Amphoras: The Story of Underwater Archaeology.* Illus. Alex Schomburg. Holt, 1961.
> Grades 4–9.

De Camp, L. Sprague, and Catherine De Camp. *Ancient Ruins and Archaeology.* Doubleday, 1964.
> Grades 6–8.

Glubok, Shirley, ed. *Discovering Tut-ankh-Amen's Tomb.* Macmillan, 1968.
> An abridgement of the three volumes by Howard Carter and A. C. Mace. Grades 7–9. See also *Art and Archaeology* (Harper, 1966); *Discovering the Royal Tombs at Ur* (1969); and *Digging in Assyria* (1970).

Hall, Jennie. *Buried Cities.* Ed. Lily Poritz; intro. Katharine Taylor. 2d ed. Macmillan, 1964.
> Illus. with photographs. Grades 4–7.

Hamblin, Dora Jane. *Pots and Robbers.* Simon & Schuster, 1970.
> Illus. with maps, photographs. Grades 5–12.

James, T. G. H. *The Archaeology of Ancient Egypt.* Illus. Rosemonde Nairac. Walck, A Walck Archaeology, 1972.
> Grades 6–12.

Kirk, Ruth, with Richard D. Daugherty. *Hunters of the Whale: An Adventure in Northwest Coast Archaeology.* Photographs, Ruth Kirk and Louis Kirk. Morrow, 1974.
> Grades 6 and up.

Magnusson, Magnus. *Introducing Archaeology.* Illus. Martin Simmons. Walck, A Walck Archaeology, 1972.
> Grades 6–12.

Magnusson, Magnus. *Viking Expansion Westwards.* Illus. Rosemonde Nairac. Walck, 1973.
> Grades 6–12.

May, Julian. *The First Men.* Illus. Lorence Bjorklund. Holiday House, 1968.
> Grades 3–6.

Pace, Mildred Mastin. *Wrapped for Eternity: The Story of the Egyptian Mummy.* Illus. Tom Huffman. McGraw-Hill, 1974.
> Grades 4 and up.

Pearlman, Moshe. *The Zealots of Masada: Story of a Dig.* Scribner's 1967.
> Illus. with photographs and maps. Grades 7 and up.

Pfeiffer, John E. *The Search for Early Man.* Consultant, Carleton S. Coon. American Heritage, A Horizon Caravel Book, 1963.
> Grades 7–9.

Poole, Lynn, and Gray Poole. *Carbon-14 and Other Science Methods That Date the Past.* Illus. P. A. Hutchison. McGraw-Hill, 1961.
> Grades 5–12.

Samachson, Dorothy, and Joseph Samachson. *The First Artists*. Doubleday, 1970.
Grades 5–12.

Shippen, Katherine B. *Portals to the Past: The Story of Archaeology*. Illus. Mel Silverman. Viking, 1963.
Grades 5–12.

Silverberg, Robert. *Men against Time: Salvage Archaeology in the United States*. Macmillan, 1967.
Illus. with photographs. Grades 7 and up. See also *Lost Cities and Vanished Civilizations* (Chilton, 1962).

Watts, Edith Whitney. *Archaeology: Exploring the Past*. Metropolitan Museum of Art, 1965.
Illus. with photographs. Grade 4–9.

White, Anne Terry. *Lost Worlds: Adventures in Archaeology*. Random House, 1941.
Grades 6–8.

Astronomy

Angrist, Stanley W. *How Our World Came to Be*. Drawings, Enrico Arno. Crowell, 1969.
Illus. with photographs. Grades 5 and up.

Asimov, Isaac. *The Kingdom of the Sun*. Rev. ed. Abelard-Schuman, 1963.
Grades 7–9. See also *Jupiter: The Largest Planet*, rev. ed. (Lothrop, 1976).

Asimov, Isaac. *What Makes the Sun Shine?* Illus. Marc Brown. Little, Brown, 1971.
Grades 4–6.

Bergamini, David. *The Universe*. Time-Life, 1979.
Grades 5 and up.

Berger, Melvin. *Planets, Stars, and Galaxies*. Putnam's, 1978.
Grades 5–8. See also *Quasars, Pulsars, and Black Holes* (1977) and *Bright Stars, Red Giants, and Dwarfs* (1983).

Branley, Franklyn M. *A Book of Stars for You*. Illus. Leonard Kessler. Crowell, 1967.
Grades 1–4. See also *A Book of the Milky Way Galaxy for You* (1965); *The Earth: Planet Number Three* (1966); *A Book of Mars for You* (1968); *A Book of Venus for You* (1969); *A Book of Outer Space for You* (1970); *Black Holes, White Dwarfs, and Superstars* (1976); and *The Nine Planets*, rev. ed. (Harper, 1978).

Branley, Franklyn M. *Darkness in Daytime*. Illus. Donald Crews. Crowell, Let's-Read-and-Find-Out Science Books, 1973.
Grades 1–4.

Branley, Franklyn M. *The Moon: Earth's Natural Satellites*. Illus. Helmut K. Wimmer. Rev. ed. Crowell, Exploring Our Unvierse, 1971.
Grades 6–10. See also *Pieces of Another World: The Story of Moon Rocks*, illus. Herbert Danska (1972).

Clarke, Arthur C., and Robert Silverberg. *Into Space: A Young Person's Guide to Space*. Rev. ed. Harper, 1971.

Gallant, Roy A. *Exploring the Universe*. Illus. Lowell Hess. Rev. ed. Doubleday, 1968.
Grades 6–8. See also *Exploring the Planets* (1967) and *National Geographic Picture Atlas of Our Universe* (National Geographic, 1980).

Gamow, George, and Harry C. Stubbs (reviser). *The Moon*. Illus. Bunji Tagawa; intro. Isaac Asimov. Rev. ed. Abelard-Schuman, 1973.
Illus. with photographs. Grades 5–12.

Gardner, Martin. *Space Puzzles: Curious Questions and Answers about the Solar System*. Drawings, Ted Schroeder. Simon & Schuster, 1971.
Illus. with diagrams and photographs. Grades 4–7.

Jobb, Jamie. *The Night Sky Book: An Everyday Guide to Every Night*. Little, Brown, 1977.
Grades 5 and up.

Knight, David C. *The First Book of Mars: An Introduction to the Red Planet*. F. Watts, 1966.
Illus. with drawings and photographs. Grades 6–8.

Knight, David C. *The Tiny Planets: Asteroids of Our Solar System*. Morrow, 1973.
Illus. with photographs and diagrams. Grades 5–12.

Kraske, Robert. *Is There Life in Outer Space?* Harcourt, 1976.
Grades 5 and up. Illus. with photographs.

Kuskin, Karla. *A Space Story*. Illus. Marc Simont. Harper, 1978.
Grades K–2.

Lippincott, Joseph Maron, and Sarah Lee Lippincott. *Point to the Stars*. Rev. ed. McGraw-Hill, 1967.
Grades 6–8.

Mitton, Jacqueline, and Simon Mitton. *Discovering Astronomy*. Longmans, 1979.
Illus. with photographs. Grades 6 and up.

Moore, Patrick. *Your Book of Astronomy*. 4th ed. Faber & Faber, 1979.
Grades 6 and up.

Motz, Lloyd. *On the Path of Venus.* Illus. Susan Detrich. Pantheon, 1976.
　　Grades 6 and up.

Neely, Henry M. *The Stars by Clock and Fist.* Rev. ed. Viking, 1972.
　　With planet schedules for 1972–1985, comp. by Phillip D. Stern and George Lovi. Grades 7 and up.

Peltier, Leslie C. *Guideposts to the Stars: Exploring the Skies throughout the Year.* Macmillan, 1972.
　　Illus. with diagrams and photographs Grades 5 and up.

Reed, William Maxwell. *The Stars for Sam.* Ed. Paul F. Brandwein; illus. with photographs. Rev. ed. Harcourt, 1960. Grades 6–8.

Rey, H. A. *The Stars.* Rev. ed. Houghton Mifflin, 1976.
　　Grades 4 and up.

Ridpath, Ian, ed. *The Illustrated Encyclopedia of Astronomy and Space.* Crowell, 1976.
　　Grades 5 and up.

Simon, Seymour. *The Moon.* Four Winds, 1984.
　　Illus. with photographs. Grades 1–4. See also *The Long View into Space* (Crown, 1979) and *The Long Journey from Space* (Crown, 1982).

Valens, E. G. *The Attractive Universe: Gravity and the Shape of Space.* World, 1969.
　　Illus. with photographs. Grades 7 and up.

Weart, Spencer. *How to Build a Sun.* Illus. by the author. Coward-McCann, 1970.
　　Grades 6–12.

Weiss, Malcolm E. *Sky Watchers of Ages Past.* Illus. Eliza MacFadden. Houghton Mifflin, 1981.
　　Grades 5–9.

Wyler, Rose, and Gerald Ames. *The Golden Book of Astronomy.* Illus. John Polgreen. Rev. ed. Golden, 1965.
　　Grades 7–9.

Birds

Anderson, John M. *The Changing World of Birds.* Holt, A Changing World Book, 1972.
　　Illus. with photographs from the Audubon Society. Grades 5 and up.

Annixter, Jane, and Paul Annixter. *Trumpeter: The Story of a Swan.* Illus. Gilbert Riswold. Holiday House, 1973.
　　Grades 4–7.

Audubon, John James. *The Birds of America.* Foreword and descriptive captions, William Vogt. Macmillan, 1953.
　　Grades 7 and up.

Austin, Elizabeth S. *Birds That Stopped Flying.* Random House, 1969.
　　Illus. with photographs. Grades 4–8.

Cameron, Angus, and Peter Parnall. *The Night-watchers.* Illus. Peter Parnall. Four Winds, 1972.
　　All ages.

Carrick, Carol, and Donald Carrick. *Beach Bird.* Dial, 1973.
　　Grades 3–6.

Cole, Joanna. *A Bird's Body.* Photographs, Jerome Wexler. Morrow, 1982.
　　Grades 3–5.

Darling, Louis. *The Gull's Way.* Illus. and photographs by the author. Morrow, 1965.
　　Grades 6–12.

Earle, Olive. *Robins in the Garden.* Illus. by the author. Morrow, 1953.
　　Grades 1–4. See also *Birds and Their Nests* (1952).

Flanagan, Geraldine Lux, and Sean Morris. *Window into a Nest.* Houghton Mifflin, 1976.
　　Illus. with photographs. Grades 4–9.

Freschet, Berniece. *The Owl and the Prairie Dog.* Illus. Gilbert Riswold. Scribner's 1969.
　　Grades 4–7.

Gans, Roma. *It's Nesting Time.* Illus. Kazue Mizumura. Crowell, 1964.
　　See also *Hummingbirds in the Garden* (1969); *Bird Talk* (1971); and *When Birds Change Their Feathers*, illus. Felicia Bond (1980).

Gilliard, E. Thomas. *Living Birds of the World.* Doubleday, 1958.
　　Grades 8 and up.

Hogner, Dorothy Childs. *Birds of Prey.* Illus. Nils Hogner. Crowell, 1969.
　　Grades 4–12.

Johnston, Johanna. *Penguin's Way.* Illus. Leonard Weisgard. Doubleday, 1962.
　　Grades K–2.

Kaufmann, John. *Robins Fly North, Robins Fly South.* Illus. by the author. Crowell, 1970.
　　Grades 4–6. See also *Chimney Swift* (Morrow, 1971).

Kaufmann, John. *Wings, Sun and Stars: The Story of Bird Migration.* Morrow, 1969.
　　Grades 7 and up. See also *Birds in Flight* (1970).

Kieran, John. *An Introduction to Birds.* Illus. Don Eckelberry. Doubleday, 1965.
Grades 5–9.

Laycock, George. *The Pelicans.* Natural History Press, 1970.
Grades 4–7. See also *Wingspread: A World of Birds* (Four Winds, 1972).

Litwin, Wallace. *Ostrich.* Photographs by the author. Coward-McCann, 1973.
Grades K–6.

McClung, Robert M. *Ruby Throat: The Story of a Humming Bird.* Illus. by the author. Morrow, 1950.
Grades K–3.

McCoy, Joseph J. *The Hunt for the Whooping Cranes: A Natural History Detective Story.* Maps and drawings, Rey Abruzzi. Lothrop, 1966.
Grades 7–9. See also *House Sparrows* (Seabury, 1968).

McCoy, Joseph J. *Swans.* Illus. Giulio Maestro. Lothrop, 1967.
Grades 5–7.

Peterson, Roger Tory, and the editors of Time-Life Books. *The Birds.* Time, Inc., Life Nature Library, 1967.
Grades 7–9. See also *Field Guide to the Birds* (Houghton Mifflin, 1947).

Pringle, Laurence. *Listen to the Crows.* Illus. Ted Lewin. Crowell, 1976.
Grades 3–6.

Selsam, Millicent E., and Joyce Hunt. *A First Look at Birds.* Illus. Harriett Springer. Walker, A First Look At Series Book, 1973.
Grades 1–3.

Simon, Hilda. *Feathers, Plain and Fancy.* Illus. by the author. Viking, 1969.
Grades 5–12.

Stoutenburg, Adrien. *A Vanishing Thunder.* Illus. John Schoenherr. Natural History Press, 1967.
Grades 5–6.

Turner, Ann Warren. *Vultures.* Illus. Marian Gray Warren. McKay, 1973.
Grades 4–12.

Zim, Herbert S., and Ira N. Gabrielson. *Birds: A Guide to the Most Familiar American Birds.* Illus. James Gordon Irving. Rev. ed. Golden, A Golden Nature Guide, 1956.
Grades 7 and up.

Chemistry

Asimov, Isaac. *Building Blocks of the Universe.* Rev. ed. Abelard-Schuman, 1961.
Grades 6–9.

Berger, Melvin. *Enzymes in Action.* Crowell, 1971.
Grades 6–9.

Cooper, Elizabeth K. *Discovering Chemistry.* Harcourt, 1959.
Grades 7–9.

Faraday, Michael. *The Chemical History of a Candle.* Crowell, 1957.
Grades 7–9.

Gray, Charles. *Explorations in Chemistry.* Dutton, 1965.
Grades 7–9.

Klein, H. Arthur. *Fuel Cells: An Introduction to Electrochemistry.* Editorial consultant, Helen Hale; photographs and diagrams by the author and James B. Laubheimer. Lippincott, 1966.
Grades 8 and up.

Shalit, Nathan. *Cup and Saucer Chemistry.* Illus. Charles Waterhouse. Grosset & Dunlap, 1972.
Grades 1–4.

Silverstein, Alvin, and Virginia Silverstein. *The Chemicals We Eat and Drink.* Follett, 1973.
Grades 6 and up.

Stone, A. Harris, and Bertram M. Siegel. *The Chemistry of Soap.* Illus. Peter P. Plasencia. Prentice-Hall, 1968.
Grades 4–8. See also *Drop by Drop: A Look at Water* (1969) and *Crystals from the Sea: A Look at Salt* (1969).

Conservation

Arundel, Jocelyn. *The Wildlife of Africa.* Illus. Wesley Dennis. Hastings, World Wildlife Conservation Series, 1965.
Grades 5–7.

Billington, Elizabeth T. *Understanding Ecology.* Illus. Robert Galster. Warne, 1971.
Grades 5–9.

Burton, Jane. *Animals of the African Year: The Ecology of East Africa.* Illus. with photographs by the author. Holt, 1972.
Grades 4–12.

Burton, Maurice. *Animals of Europe: The Ecology of the Wildlife.* Holt, 1973.

Illus. with photographs, drawings, and maps. Grades 4–12.

Earle, Olive L. *Scavengers.* Illus. by the author. Morrow, 1973.
Grades 3–5.

Gans, Roma. *Water for Dinosaurs and You.* Illus. Richard Cuffari. Crowell, 1972.
Grades 1–4.

Gordon, Esther S., and Bernard L. Gordon. *There Really Was a Dodo.* Illus. Lawrence Di Fiori. Walck, 1974.
Grades 1–4.

Gregor, Arthur S. *Man's Mark on the Land: The Changing Environment—from the Stone Age to the Age of Smog, Sewage, and Tar on Your Feet.* Scribner's, 1974.
Grades 5–10.

Heady, Eleanor B. *The Soil That Feeds Us.* Illus. Robert Frankenberg. Parents' Magazine, A Stepping-Stone Book to Science and Social Studies, 1972.
Grades 4–8.

Hirsch, S. Carl. *Guardians of Tomorrow: Pioneers in Ecology.* Illus. William Steinel. Viking, 1971.
Grades 5–9. See also *The Living Community* (1966).

Hoke, John. *Terrariums.* Illus. with photos. F. Watts, A First Book, 1972.
Grades 4 and up.

Kohl, Judith, and Herbert Kohl. *The View from the Oak: The Private Worlds of Other Creatures.* Illus. Roger Bayless. Sierra Club/Scribner's, 1977.
Grades 5 and up.

Kohn, Bernice. *The Organic Living Book.* Illus. Betty Fraser. Viking, 1972.
Grades 3–7.

Laycock, George. *Wild Animals: Safe Places.* Four Winds, 1973.
Grades 4 and up.

McClung, Robert M. *America's Endangered Birds: Programs and People Working to Save Them.* Illus. George Founds. Morrow, 1978.
Grades 6–9.

McCoy, J. J. *Nature Sleuths: Protectors of Our Wildlife.* Lothrop, 1969.
Grades 4–7.

MacKinnon, John Ramsay, and Kathleen MacKinnon. *Animals of Asia: The Ecology of the Oriental Region.* Holt, 1974.
All ages.

Mabey, Richard. *Oak & Company.* Illus. Clare Roberts. Greenwillow, 1983.
Grades 1–5.

Marzani, Carl. *The Wounded Earth.* Addison-Wesley/Young Scott Books, 1972.
Grades 5 up.

Miles, Betty. *Save the Earth! An Ecology Handbook for Kids.* Illus. Claire A. Nivola. Knopf, 1974.
Grades 2–5.

Millard, Reed, and the editors of Science Book Associates. *Clean Air-Clean Water for Tomorrow's World.* Messner, 1971.
Illus. with photographs. Grades 5–9.

Müller, Jorg. *The Changing City.* Illus. by the author. Atheneum, 1977.
All ages. See also *The Changing Countryside* (1977).

Perry, Roger. *The Galápagos Islands.* Dodd, Mead, 1972.
Illus. with photographs and a map. Grades 5–7.

Pringle, Laurence. *Ecology: Science of Survival.* Macmillan, 1971.
Grades 5–7. See also *This Is a River: Exploring an Ecosystem* (1972) and *Estuaries: Where Rivers Meet the Sea* (1973).

Pringle, Laurence. *Estuaries: Where Rivers Meet the Sea.* Macmillan, 1973.
Illus. with photographs. Grades 4–7. See also *From Pond to Prairie* (1972).

Pringle, Laurence. *Into the Woods: Exploring the Forest Ecosystem.* Macmillan, 1973.
Grades 2–7. See also *This Is a River: Exploring an Ecosystem* (1972).

Randall, Janet. *To Save a Tree: The Story of the Coast Redwoods.* McKay, 1971.
Illus. with plates. Grades 4 and up.

Rice, Paul, and Peter Mayle. *As Dead as a Dodo.* Illus. Shawn Rice. Godine, 1981.
All ages.

Shanks, Ann Zane. *About Garbage and Stuff.* Photographs by the author. Viking, 1973.
Grades K–3.

Shepherd, Elizabeth. *Arms of the Sea: Our Vital Estuaries.* Lothrop, 1973.
Illus. with photographs. Grades 4–9.

Shippen, Katherine B. *The Great Heritage.* Illus. C. B. Falls. Viking, 1974.
Grades 7–9.

Simon, Hilda. *Partners, Guests, and Parasites: Coexistence in Nature.* Viking, 1970.
Grades 4–9.

Smith, Frances C. *The First Book of Conservation.* Illus. Rene Martin. F. Watts, 1954.
Grades 4–7.

Earth

Asimov, Isaac. *How Did We Find Out the Earth Is Round?* Illus. Matthew Kalmenoff. Walker, How Did We Find Out Series, 1972.
Grades 3–6.

Atwood, Ann. *The Wild Young Desert.* Photographs by the author. Scribner's, 1970.
All ages.

Beiser, Arthur, and the editors of *Life. The Earth.* Time-Life Books, 1970.
Grades 7–12.

Berger, Melvin. *Jigsaw Continents.* Illus. Bob Totten. Coward, McCann & Geoghegan, 1978.
Grades 3–5.

Branley, Franklyn. *The Earth: Planet Number Three.* Illus. Helmut K. Wimmer. Crowell, Exploring Our Universe, 1966.
Grades 5–9. See also *The Beginning of the Earth* (1972).

Clayton, Keith. *The Crust of the Earth: The Story of Geology.* Natural History Press, Nature and Science Library (published for The American Museum of Natural History), 1967.
Grades 6 and up.

Fodor, R. V. *Earth in Motion: The Concept of Plate Tectonics.* Illus. John C. Holden. Morrow, 1978.
Grades 5–8. See also *Frozen Earth: Explaining the Ice Ages* (Enslow, 1981).

Gallob, Edward. *City Rocks, City Blocks, and the Moon.* Photographs by the author. Scribner's, 1973.
Grades 4–6. See also *City Leaves, City Trees.*

Gans, Roma. *Caves.* Illus. Giulio Maestro. Crowell, 1977.
Grades 1–4.

Hammond. *Earth and Space.* Hammond, 1970.
Grades 5 and up.

Heintze, Carle. *The Circle of Fire: The Great Chain of Volcanoes and Earth Faults.* Hawthorn, 1968, 1970.
Grades 6–12.

Hunter, Mel. *How the Earth Began.* Illus. by the author. World, 1972.
Grades 4–7.

Lauber, Patricia. *This Restless Earth.* Illus. John Polgreen. Random House, 1970.
Grades 5–7. See also *Earthquakes* (1972).

Lavine, Sigmund, and Mart Casey. *Water Since the World Began.* Dodd, Mead, 1965.
Illus. with photographs and drawings. Grades 6–12.

Leutscher, Alfred. *Earth.* Illus. John Butler. Dial, 1983.
Grades 1–3.

Ley, Willy. *The Meteorite Craters.* Illus. John Bierhorst. Weybright & Talley, 1968.
Grades 6–9.

Marcus, Rebecca B. *The First Book of Volcanoes and Earthquakes.* F. Watts, A First Book, 1972.
Grades 4–7.

Matthews, William H., III. *The Earth's Crust.* F. Watts, A First Book, 1971.
Illus. with photographs. Grades 6 and up.

Matthews, William H., III. *Introducing the Earth: Geology, Environment, and Man.* Dodd, Mead, 1972.
Illus. with photographs and diagrams. Grades 6–9.

Matthews, William H., III. *The Story of the Earth.* Illus. John E. Alexander. Harvey House, 1968.
Grades 6–10.

May, Julian. *Why the Earth Quakes.* Illus. Leonard Everett Fisher. Holiday House, 1969.
Grades 4–7.

Ogburn, Charlton, Jr. *The Forging of Our Continent.* American Heritage, in association with the Smithsonian Institution (Van Nostrand, distributor), 1968.
Grades 5 and up.

Stone, A. Harris, and Dale Ingmanson. *Rocks and Rills: A Look at Geology.* Illus. Peter P. Plasencia. Prentice-Hall, 1967.
Grades 3–6.

Electricity

Adler, Irving. *Electricity in Your Life.* Illus. Ruth Adler. Day, 1965.
Grades 5–7.

Asimov, Isaac. *How Did We Find Out about Electricity?* Illus. Matthew Kalmenoff. Walker, How Did We Find Out Series, 1973.
Grades 3–6.

Bendick, Jeanne. *Electronics for Young People: Including Automation, Computers, Communications, Microcir-*

cuits, Lasers, and More. Revision co-ed. R. J. Lefkowitz; illus. by the author. 5th ed. McGraw-Hill, 1973.
    Grades 5–8.

Epstein, Sam, and Beryl Epstein. *The First Book of Electricity.* Illus. Rod Slater. Rev. 3d ed. F. Watts, 1977.
    Grades 4–7.

Irving, Robert. *Electro-Magnetic Waves.* Illus. Leonard Everett Fisher. Knopf, 1960.
    Grades 4–7.

Morgan, Alfred. *A First Electrical Book for Boys.* 3d ed. Scribner's, 1963.
    Grades 6–8.

Energy and Power

Adler, Irving. *Atomic Energy.* Illus. Ellen Viereck. Day, The Reason Why Books, 1971.
    Grades 4–7. See also *Energy* (1970).

Asimov, Isaac. *Inside the Atom.* Illus. John Bradford. 2d rev. ed. Abelard-Schuman, 1961.
    Grades 7–9. See also *How Did We Find Out about Atoms?* illus. David Wool (Walker, 1978) and *How Did We Find Out about Oil?* (Walker, 1980).

Branley, Franklyn M. *Gravity Is a Mystery.* Illus. Don Madden. Crowell, Let's-Read-and-Find-Out Science Books, 1970.
    Grades 1–3.

Branley, Franklyn M. *Weight and Weightlessness.* Illus. Graham Booth. Crowell, Let's-Read-and-Find-Out Science Books, 1971.
    Grades 1–3.

Bronowski, Jacob, and Millicent E. Selsam. *Biography of an Atom.* Illus. Weimer Pursell. Harper, 1965. Illus. with photographs. Grades 4–6.

Cooper, Margaret. *Gift from the Sun: The Mastering of Energy.* Bradbury, 1969.
    Grades 4–9.

Ellis, R. Hobart, Jr. *Knowing the Atomic Nucleus.* Diagrams, Susan Stan. Lothrop, 1973.
    Grades 6 and up.

Freeman, Mae, and Ira Freeman. *The Story of the Atom.* Random House, 1960.
    Grades 5–8.

Haber, Heinz. *Our Friend the Atom.* Illus. by the staff artists of the Walt Disney Studio. Golden, 1956.
    Grades 7–9.

Halacy, Daniel S. *The Energy Trap.* Four Winds, 1975.
    Grades 6–9.

Harrison, George Russell. *The First Book of Energy.* F. Watts, 1965.
    Grades 5–7.

Hogben, Lancelot. *The Wonderful World of Energy.* Doubleday, 1968.
    Grades 5–7.

Irwin, Keith Gordon. *The Romance of Physics.* Illus. Anthony Ravielli. Scribner's, 1966.
    Grades 6–9.

Landt, Dennis. *Catch the Wind: A Book of Windmills and Windpower.* Photographs, Lisl Dennis. Four Winds, 1976.
    Grades 5 and up.

Pringle, Laurence. *Energy: Power for People.* Macmillan, 1975.
    Grades 6–9. See also *Nuclear Power: From Physics to Politics* (1979).

Ross, Frank, Jr. *The World of Power and Energy.* Illus. by the author. Lothrop, 1967.
    Grades 6–9.

Valens, E. G. *Magnet.* Photographs, Berniece Abbott. World, 1964.
    Grades 4–7.

Wohlrabe, Raymond. *Exploring Solar Energy.* World, 1966.
    Grades 4–6.

Experiments and Projects

Beeler, Nelson F., and Franklyn M. Branley. *Experiments in Science.* Illus. Ruth Beck. Crowell, 1955.
    Grades 4–6.

Bendick, Jeanne. *Observation.* Illus. by the author. F. Watts, Science Experiences, 1972.
    Grades 1–3.

Caras, Roger. *A Zoo in Your Room.* Illus. Pamela Johnson. Harcourt, 1975.
    Grades 5–8.

Cartwright, Sally. *Water Is Wet.* Illus. Marylin Harner. Coward-McCann, 1973.
    Grades K–2.

Cobb, Vicki, and Kathy Darling. *Bet You Can't: Science Impossibilities to Fool You.* Illus. Martha Weston. Lothrop, 1980.
    Grades 5 and up. See also *Bet You Can! Science Possibilities to Fool You* (1983).

Cobb, Vicki. *Science Experiments You Can Eat.* Illus. Peter Lippman. Lippincott, 1972.
Grades 3–6. See also *More Science Experiments You Can Eat* (1979).

Coulson, E. H., A. E. J. Trinder, and Aaron E. Klein. *Test Tubes and Beakers: Chemistry for Young Experimenters.* Doubleday, 1971.
Grades 5–10.

Fisher, S. H. *Table Top Science: Physics Experiments for Everyone.* Natural History Press, 1972.
Grades 3–6.

Ford, Barbara. *Can Invertebrates Learn?* Illus. Haris Petie. Messner, 1972.
Grades 4–9.

Freeman, Mae, and Ira Freeman. *Fun with Scientific Experiments.* Random House, 1960.
Grades 4–7.

Lowry, Peter, and Field Griffith. *Model Rocketry: Hobby of Tomorrow.* Doubleday, 1972.
Illus. with photographs and diagrams. Grades 5 and up.

Milgrom, Harry. *ABC Science Experiments.* Illus. Donald Crews. Crowell-Collier, 1970.
Grades Preschool–K.

Milgrom, Harry. *Adventures with a Cardboard Tube: First Science Experiments.* Illus. Tom Funk. Dutton, 1972.
Grades 1–4.

Russell, Helen Ross. *Small Worlds: A Field Trip Guide.* Illus. Arline Strong. Little, Brown, 1972.
Grades 3–6. See also *Soil: A Field Trip Guide* (1972).

Schneider, Herman, and Nina Schneider. *Science Fun for You in a Minute or Two: Quick Science Experiments You Can Do.* Illus. Leonard Kessler. McGraw-Hill, 1975.
Grades 1–5.

Simon, Seymour. *Let's-Try-It-Out . . . Light and Dark.* Illus. Angeline Culfogienis. McGraw-Hill, 1970.
Grades K–2.

Simon, Seymour. *Projects with Plants: A Science at Work Book.* Illus. Lynn Sweat. F. Watts, 1973.
Grades 3–6.

Simon, Seymour. *Science at Work: Projects in Space Science.* Illus. Lynn Sweat. F. Watts, 1971.
Grades 2–5. See also *Science at Work: Easy Models You Can Make* (1971); *Science at Work: Projects on Oceanography* (1972); and *Exploring Fields and Lots: Easy Science Projects* (Garrard, 1978).

Stein, Sara. *The Science Book: A Feast for Young Science Explorers.* Workman, 1980.
Grades 3–5.

Stone, A. Harris, and Bertram M. Siegel. *Take a Balloon.* Illus. Peter P. Plasencia. Prentice-Hall, 1967.
Grades 3–6. See also *Drop by Drop: A Look at Water* (1969) and *The Heat's On!* (1970).

Stone, A. Harris, and Robert J. Stein. *Biology Project Puzzlers.* Illus. David Lindroth. Prentice-Hall, 1973.
Grades 2–5.

United Nations Educational, Scientific and Cultural Organization. *Seven Hundred Science Experiments for Everyone.* Comp. by UNESCO; foreword, Gerald Wendt. Rev. and enl. ed. Doubleday, 1964.
Grades 7 and up.

Weiss, Harvey. *The Gadget Book.* Illus. by the author. Crowell, 1971.
Grades 5–7.

Wyler, Rose. *The First Book of Science Experiments.* Illus. Sanford Kleiman. Rev. ed. F. Watts , 1971.
Grades 4–6. See also *What Happens If . . . ? Science Experiments You Can Do By Yourself.* Illus. Daniel Nevins (Walker, 1974).

Wyler, Rose, and Eva-Lee Baird. *Science Teasers.* Illus. Jerry Robinson. New ed. Harper, 1966.
Grades 4–6.

Fish

Aliki. *The Long Lost Coelacanth and Other Living Fossils.* Crowell, Let's-Read-and-Find-Out Science Books, 1973.
Grades 2–4.

Bendick, Jeanne. *The First Book of Fishes.* F. Watts, 1965.
Grades 3–5.

Campbell, Elizabeth A. *Fins and Tails: A Story of Strange Fish.* Illus. Leonard Weisgard. Little, Brown, 1963.
Grades 3–5.

Cook, Joseph J., and William L. Wisner. *The Nightmare World of the Shark.* Dodd, Mead, 1968.
Illus. with photographs and diagrams. Grades 4–9.

Earle, Olive L. *Strange Fishes of the Sea.* Illus. by the author. Morrow, 1968.
Grades 3–5.

Fichter, George S. *Fishes*. Golden, The Golden Bookshelf of Natural History, 1963.
Grades 5 and up.

Fletcher, Alan Mark. *Fishes Dangerous to Man*. Illus. Jane Teiko Oka and Willi Baum. Addison-Wesley, 1969.
Grades 3–6.

Jacobs, Francine. *The Freshwater Eel*. Drawings, Josette Gourley. Morrow, 1973.
Grades 4–6.

Hylander, Clarence J. *Fishes and Their Ways*. Macmillan, 1964.
Illus. with photographs and drawings. Grades 5–12.

Klots, Elsie B. *The New Field Book of Freshwater Life*. Illus. Suzan Noguchi Swain. Putnam's, 1966.
Grades 6 and up.

Morris, Robert A. *Seahorse*. Illus. Arnold Lobel. Harper, 1972.
Grades K–2.

National Geographic Society. *Wondrous World of Fishes*. New enl. ed. National Geographic Society, Natural Science Library, 1969.
Grades 5–9.

Ommanney, F. D. *The Fishes*. Time, Inc., 1964.
Grades 6 and up.

Oxford Scientific Films. *The Stickleback Cycle*. Photographs, David Thompsom. Putnam's, 1979.
Grades 2–5.

Selsam, Millicent E., and Joyce Hunt. *A First Look at Fish*. Illus. Harriett Springer. Walker, A First Look At Series, 1972.
Grades 1–3.

Stephens, William M., and Peggy Stephens. *Sea Horse, A Fish in Armor*. Illus. Anthony D'Attilio. Holiday House, Life-Cycle Stories, 1969.
Grades 4–6.

Stephens, William M., and Peggy Stephens. *Sea Turtle Swims the Ocean*. Illus. Rene Martin. Holiday House, 1971.
Grades 3–5.

Zim, Herbert S. *Sharks*. Illus. Stephen Howe. Morrow, 1966.
Grades 3–5.

Zim, Herbert S., and Hurst H. Shoemaker. *Fishes: A Guide to Fresh- and Salt-Water Species*. Illus. James Gordon Irving. Golden, A Golden Nature Guide, 1957.
Grades 7 and up.

Flowers

Bulla, Clyde Robert. *Flowerpot Gardens*. Illus. Henry Evans. Crowell, 1967.
Grades 2–5.

Crowell, Robert L. *The Lore and Legend of Flowers*. Illus. Anne Ophelia Dowden. Crowell, 1982.
Grades 4 and up.

Dowden, Anne Ophelia. *Look at a Flower*. Illus. by the author. Crowell, 1963.
Grades 6–8.

Dowden, Anne Ophelia. *State Flowers*. Illus. by the author. Crowell, 1978.
Grades 5 and up.

Dowden, Anne Ophelia. *Wild Green Things in the City: A Book of Weeds*. Illus. by the author. Crowell, 1972.
Grades 4–9.

Fenten, D. X. *Plants for Pots: Projects for Indoor Gardeners*. Illus. Penelope Naylor. Lippincott, 1969.
Grades 4 and up.

Huntington, Harriet E. *Let's Look at Flowers*. Photographs by the author; drawings, J. Noël. Doubleday, 1969.
Grades 3–7.

Hutchins, Ross E. *This Is a Flower*. Photographs by the author. Dodd, Mead, 1963.
Grades 6–9.

Hylander, Clarence J. *The Macmillan Wild Flower Book*. Illus. Edith Farrington Johnson. Macmillan, 1954.
Grades 7–9.

Milne, Lorus J., and Margery Milne. *Because of a Flower*. Drawings, Kenneth Gosner. Atheneum, 1975.
Grades 5 and up.

Zim, Herbert S., and Alexander C. Martin. *Flowers: A Guide to Familiar American Wild Flowers*. Illus. Rudolf Freund. Golden, A Golden Nature Guide, 1950.
Grades 5–7.

The Human Body

Asimov, Isaac. *The Human Body: Its Structure and Operation*. Houghton Mifflin, 1963.
Grades 8 and up.

Brenner, Barbara. *Bodies*. Photographs, George Ancona. Dutton, 1973.
Grades K–3.

Day, Beth, and Margaret Liley. *The Secret World of the Baby.* Photographs, Lennart Nilson, Suzanne Szasz, and others. Random House, 1968.
Grades 4 and up.

Elgin, Kathleen. *The Human Body: The Skeleton.* Illus. by the author. F. Watts, 1971.
Grades 4–9.

Freedman, Russell, and James E. Morriss. *The Brains of Animals and Man.* Drawings, James Caraway. Holiday House, 1972.
Illus. with photographs. Grades 5–12.

Gallant, Roy A. *Me and My Bones.* Doubleday, 1971.
Illus. with photographs. Grades 3–5.

Gruenberg, Sidonie. *The Wonderful Story of How You Were Born.* Illus. Symeon Shimin. Rev. ed. Doubleday, 1970.
Grades 3–6.

Jessel, Camilla. *The Joy of Birth: A Book for Parents and Children.* Photographs by the author. Hillside, 1982.
Grades 4–6.

Johnson, Eric W. *Love and Sex in Plain Language.* Illus. Russ Hoover. 3d ed. Harper, 1977.
Grades 6 and up.

Kalina, Sigmund. *Your Bones Are Alive.* Illus. Joseph Low. Lothrop, 1972.
Grades 2–6.

McNamara, Louise Greep, and Ada Basset Litchfield. *Your Busy Brain.* Illus. Ruth Hartshorn. Little, Brown, An All about You Book, 1973.
Grades 1–3. See also *Your Living Bones* (1973) and *Your Growing Cells* (1973).

Miller, Jonathan. *The Human Body.* Designed by David Pelham; illus. Harry Willcock; paper engineering, Vic Duppa-Whyte and David Rosendale. Viking, 1983.
Grades 1 and up. See also *The Facts of Life* (1984).

Nilsson, Lennart. *How Was I Born? A Photographic Story of Reproduction and Birth for Children.* Photographs by the author. Delacorte/Seymour Lawrence, 1975.
Grades 3–6.

Ravielli, Anthony. *Wonders of the Human Body.* Illus. by the author. Viking, 1954.
Grades 5–8.

Silverstein, Alvin, and Virginia B. Silverstein. *The Digestive System: How Living Creatures Use Food.* Illus. Mel Erikson. Prentice-Hall, 1970.

Grades 5–9. See also *The Endocrine System* (1971); *The Nervous System* (1971); *The Excretory System* (1972); *Exploring the Brain* (1973); and other titles by this team.

Zim, Herbert S. *Your Stomach and Digestive Tract.* Illus. Rene Martin. Morrow, 1973.
Grades 4–8. See also *Your Heart and How It Works* (1959); *Blood* (1968); *Bones* (1969); and *Your Brain and How it Works* (1972).

Insects and Arachnida

Borror, Donald J., and Richard E. White. *A Field Guide to the Insects of America North of Mexico.* Color and shaded drawings, Richard E. White; line drawings by the authors. Houghton Mifflin, Peterson Field Guide Series, 1970.
Grades 5 and up.

Brown, Dee. *Tales of the Warrior Ants.* Putnam's, 1973.
Grades 5 and up.

Callahan, Philip S. *Insects and How They Function.* Illus. and photographs by the author. Holiday House, 1971.
Grades 6 and up. See also *Insect Behavior* (1970).

Cole, Joanna. *Cockroaches.* Illus. Jean Zallinger. Morrow, 1971.
Grades 4–7.

Cole, Joanna. *Fleas.* Illus. Elsie Wrigley. Morrow, 1973.
Grades 3–7.

Conklin, Gladys. *Tarantula, the Giant Spider.* Illus. Glen Rounds. Holiday House, 1972.
Grades 2–4. See also *The Bug Club Book* (1966) and *Insects Build Their Homes* (1972).

Davis, Bette J. *Musical Insects.* Illus. by the author. Lothrop, 1971.
Grades 5–10.

Edsall, Marian S. *Battle on the Rosebush: Insect Life in Your Backyard.* Illus. Jean Cassels Helmer. Follett, 1972.
Grades 5–12.

Ewbank, Constance. *Insect Zoo: How to Collect and Care for Insects.* Illus. Barbara Wolff. Walker, 1973.
Grades 3–8.

Farb, Peter, and the editors of *Life.* *The Insects.* Time, Inc., Life Nature Library, 1962.
Grades 7–9.

Freschet, Berniece. *The Web in the Grass.* Illus. Roger Duvoisin. Scribner's, 1972.
Grades 1–4.

George, Jean Craighead. *All upon a Stone.* Illus. Don Bolognese. Crowell, 1971.
Grades 3–5.

Griffen, Elizabeth. *A Dog's Book of Bugs.* Illus. Peter Parnall. Atheneum, 1967.
All ages.

Hawes, Judy. *My Daddy Longlegs.* Illus. Walter Lorraine. Crowell, Let's-Read-and-Find-Out Science Books, 1972.
Grades 1–3. See also *Fireflies in the Night* (1963); *Bees and Beelines* (1964); and *Ladybug, Ladybug, Fly Away Home* (1967).

Hess, Lilo. *The Praying Mantis, Insect Cannibal.* Photographs by the author. Scribner's, 1971.
Grades 3–6.

Hutchins, Ross E. *The Bug Clan.* Photographs by the author. Dodd, Mead, 1973.
Grades 4–8. See also *The Carpenter Bee* (Addison-Wesley, 1972).

Hutchins, Ross E. *Grasshoppers and Their Kin.* Photographs by the author. Dodd, Mead, 1972.
Grades 4 and up. See also *The Ant Realm* (1967); *The World of Dragonflies* (1969); and *Insects in Armor* (Parents' Magazine, 1972).

Hutchins, Ross. E. *Scaly Wings: A Book about Moths and Their Caterpillars.* Parents' Magazine, 1971.
Grades 2–4.

Kaufmann, John. *Insect Travelers.* Illus. by the author. Morrow, 1972.
Grades 5 and up.

Lavine, Sigmund A. *Wonders of the Spider World.* Dodd, Mead, 1967.
Illus. with photographs. Grades 4–6.

May, Charles Paul. *A Book of Insects.* Illus. John Crosby. St. Martin's, 1972.
Grades 4 and up.

McClung, Robert M. *Bees, Wasps, and Hornets and How They Live.* Illus. by the author. Morrow, 1971.
Grades 3–5.

Miskovits, Christine. *Where Do Insects Go in Winter?* Denison, 1973.
Illus. with line drawings. Grades 1–3.

Naylor, Penelope. *The Spider World.* Illus. by the author. F. Watts, A First Book, 1973.
Grades 4–7.

Oxford Scientific Films. *Bees and Honey.* Photographs, David Thompson. Putnam's, 1977.
Grades 2–5. See also *The Butterfly Cycle* (1977); *The Spider's Web* (1978); and *Dragonflies* (1980).

Pringle, Laurence. *Cockroaches: Here, There, and Everywhere.* Illus. James McCrea and Ruth McCrea. Crowell, Let's-Read-and-Find-Out Science Books, 1971.
Grades 2–5. See also *Twist, Wiggle and Squirm: A Book about Earthworms* (1973).

Rhine, Richard. *Life in a Bucket of Soil.* Illus. Elsie Wrigley. Lothrop, 1972.
Grades 4–8.

Ripper, Charles L. *Mosquitoes.* Illus. by the author. Morrow, 1969.
Grades 3–6.

Selsam, Millicent E. *The Harlequin Moth: Its Life Story.* Photographs, Jerome Wexler. Morrow, 1975.
Grades 4–10.

Shuttlesworth, Dorothy. *The Story of Flies.* Illus. Barbara Wolff. Doubleday, 1970.
Grades 5 and up. See also *The Story of Spiders* (1959); *The Story of Ants* (1964); and *All Kinds of Bees* (Random House, 1967).

Simon, Hilda. *Dragonflies.* Illus. by the author. Viking, 1972.
Grades 5–12. See also *Insect Masquerades* (Viking, 1968) and *Milkweed Butterflies* (Vanguard, 1969).

Swan, Lester A., and Charles S. Papp. *The Common Insects of North America.* Harper, 1972.
Illus. Grades 5 and up.

Teale, Edwin Way. *The Junior Book of Insects.* Photos and drawings by the author. 2d rev. ed. Dutton, 1972.
Grades 4–9. See also *Insect Friends* (Dodd, Mead, 1966).

Zim, Herbert S., and Clarence Cottam. *Insects: A Guide to Familiar American Insects.* Illus. James Gordon Irving. Rev. ed. Golden, A Golden Nature Guide, 1961.
Grades 5–9.

Mathematics

Adler, Irving. *Integers: Positive and Negative.* Illus. Laurie Jo Lambie. Day, The Reason Why Books, 1972.
Grades 3–6.

Anno, Mitsumasa. *Anno's Counting Book.* Illus. by the author. Harper, 1977.
    Grades K–3. See also *Anno's Counting House* (Philomel, 1982).

Asimov, Isaac. *How Did We Find Out about Numbers?* Illus. Daniel Nevins. Walker, How Did We Find Out Series, 1973.
    Grades 1–3.

Asimov, Isaac. *Quick and Easy Math.* Houghton Mifflin, 1964.
    Grades 7 and up.

Asimov, Isaac. *Realm of Measure.* Diagrams, Robert Belmore. Houghton Mifflin, 1960.
    Grades 4–9. See also *Realm of Numbers* (1959).

Behrens, June. *The True Book of Metric Measurement.* Children's Press, 1975.
    Grades 2–4.

Bendick, Jeanne. *Names, Sets, and Numbers.* Illus. by the author. F. Watts, 1971.
    Grades 2–5.

Branley, Franklyn M. *Think Metric!* Illus. Graham Booth. Crowell, 1972.
    Grades 3–9.

Charosh, Mannis. *The Ellipse.* Illus. Leonard Kessler. Crowell, Young Math Books, 1971.
    Grades 1–4. See also *Mathematical Games for One or Two* (1972).

Dennis, J. Richard. *Fractions Are Parts of Things.* Illus. Donald Crews. Crowell, Young Math Books, 1971.
    Grades 2–4.

Diggins, Julia E. *String, Straightedge, and Shadow: The Story of Geometry.* Illus. Corydon Bell. Viking, 1965.
    Grades 6–8.

D'Ignazio, Fred. *The Creative Kid's Guide to Home Computers: Super Games and Projects to Do with Your Home Computer.* Doubleday, 1981.
    Grades 6 and up. See also *Small Computers: Exploring Their Technology and Future* (F. Watts, 1981).

Ellison, Elsie C. *Fun With Lines and Curves.* Illus. Susan Stan. Lothrop, 1972.
    Grades 6–9.

Englebardt, Stanley. *Miracle Chip: The Micro-electronic Revolution.* Lothrop, 1979.
    Grades 5 and up.

Froman, Robert. *Bigger and Smaller.* Illus. Gioia Fiammenghi. Crowell, 1971.
    Grades 1–3.

Froman, Robert. *Less Than Nothing Is Really Something.* Illus. Don Madden. Crowell, Young Math Books, 1973.
    Grades 2–5. See also *Venn Diagrams* (1972).

Froman, Robert. *Science, Art, and Visual Illusions.* Illus. Laszlo Kubinyi. Simon & Schuster, 1970.
    Grades 6–9.

Gallant, Roy A. *Man the Measurer: Our Units of Measure and How They Grew.* Doubleday, 1972.
    Grades 4 and up.

Hogben, Lancelot. *The Wonderful World of Mathematics.* Illus. André, Charles Keeping, and Kenneth Symonds; maps, Marjorie Saynor. Rev. ed. Garden City, 1968.
    Grades 6–9.

Hyde, Margaret O. *Computers That Think? The Search for Artificial Intelligence.* Enslow, 1982.
    Grades 6 and up.

Kadesch, Robert R. *Math Menagerie.* Illus. Mark A. Binn. Harper, 1970.
    Grades 5–8.

Linn, Charles F. *Probability.* Illus. Wendy Watson. Crowell, Young Math Books, 1972.
    Grades 3–6.

Lipson, Shelley. *It's Basic: The ABC's of Computer Programming.* Illus. Janice Stapleton. Holt, 1982.
    Grades 2–6.

Ravielli, Anthony. *An Adventure in Geometry.* Illus. by the author. Viking, 1957.
    Grades 7–9.

Razzell, Arthur G., and K. G. O. Watts. *Probability: The Science of Chance.* Illus. Ellen Raskin. Doubleday, Exploring Mathematics, 1967.
    Grades 4–7.

Reiss, John. *Numbers.* Bradbury, 1971.
    Grades Preschool–1.

Rogers, James T. *The Pantheon Story of Mathematics for Young People.* Designed by Will Burtin. Pantheon, 1966.
    Grades 6 and up.

Sitomer, Mindel, and Harry Sitomer. *Circles.* Illus. George Giusti. Crowell, Young Math Books, 1971.
    Grades 2–4. See also *What Is Symmetry?* (1970) and *Lines, Segments, Polygons* (1972).

Medicine

Barr, George. *Young Scientist and the Doctor.* Illus. Mildred Waltrip. McGraw-Hill, 1969.
  Grades 3–7.

Berger, Melvin. *Cancer Lab: Scientists at Work.* Day, 1975.
  Grades 4–8.

Berger, Melvin. *Enzymes in Action.* Crowell, 1971.
  Grades 5–10.

Calder, Ritchie. *The Wonderful World of Medicine.* Garden City, 1958.
  Grades 6–8.

Curtis, Robert. *Medical Talk for Beginners.* Illus. William Jaber. Messner, 1976.
  Grades 3–6.

Epstein, Beryl, and Samuel Epstein. *Medicine from Microbes: The Story of Antibiotics.* Messner, 1965.
  Grades 6–9.

Marks, Geoffrey. *The Amazing Stethoscope.* Illus. Polly Bolian. Messner, 1971.
  Grades 4–7.

Shippen, Katherine B. *Men of Medicine.* Illus. Anthony Ravielli. Viking, 1957.
  Grades 7–9.

Silverstein, Alvin, and Virginia Silverstein. *Cancer.* Illus. Andrew Antal. Day, 1972.
  Grades 4 and up. See also *The Sugar Disease: Diabetes* (Lippincott, 1980) and *The World of Bionics* (Methuen, 1980).

Microscopes and Microbiology

Cobb, Vicki. *Cells, the Basic Structure of Life.* Illus. Leonard Dank. F. Watts, A First Book, 1970.
  Grades 5–8.

Grillone, Lisa, and Joseph Gennaro. *Small Worlds Close Up.* Crown, 1978.
  Illus. with photographs. Grades 3–5.

Jacker, Corinne. *Window on the Unknown: A History of the Microscope.* Illus. Mary Linn. Scribner's, 1966.
  With photographs. Grades 6–9.

Kavaler, Lucy. *The Wonders of Fungi.* Photographs and drawings, Richard Ott. Day, 1964.
  Grades 5–9. See also *The Wonders of Algae* (1961).

Lewis, Lucia. *The First Book of Microbes.* Illus. Howard Berelson. F. Watts, A First Book, 1972.
  Grades 4–9.

Schneider, Leo. *You and Your Cells.* Illus. Henri A. Fluchere. Harcourt, 1964.
  With photographs. Grades 6–12.

Shippen, Katherine B. *Men, Microscopes, and Living Things.* Illus. Anthony Ravielli. Viking, 1955.
  Grades 6–8.

Silverstein, Alvin, and Virginia Silverstein. *A World in a Drop of Water.* Atheneum, 1969.
  Grades 5–8.

Simon, Seymour. *Hidden Worlds: Pictures of the Invisible.* Morrow, 1983.
  Illus. with photographs. Grades 2–4.

Villiard, Paul. *The Hidden World: The Story of Microscopic Life.* Four Winds, 1975.
  Grades 5–12.

Wolberg, Barbara J. *Zooming In: Photographic Discoveries under the Microscope.* Photographs, Lewis R. Wolberg. Harcourt, 1974.
  Grades 5–8.

Natural History

Attenborough, David. *Discovering Life on Earth: A Natural History.* Little, Brown, 1980.
  Illus. with photographs. Grades 5 and up.

Baker, Laura Nelson. *From Whales to Snails.* Illus. John Pimlott. Atheneum, 1970.
  Grades 4–9.

Batten, Mary. *The Tropical Forest: Ants, Ants, Animals and Plants.* Illus. Betty Fraser. Crowell, 1973.
  Grades 6 and up.

Borten, Helen. *The Jungle.* Harcourt, 1968.
  Grades 3–6.

Busch, Phyllis S. *Dining on a Sunbeam: Food Chains and Food Webs.* Photographs, Les Line. Four Winds, 1973.
  Grades 3–6.

Carr, Archie, and the editors of *Life. The Land and Wildlife of Africa.* Time, Inc., Life Nature Library, 1964.
  Grades 7–9.

Carson, Rachel. *The Sense of Wonder.* Photographs, Charles Pratt and others. Harper, 1965.
  Grades 3 and up.

Cosgrove, Margaret. *Seeds, Embryos, and Sex.* Illus. by the author. Dodd, Mead, 1970. Grades 4–9.

Craig, M. Jean. *Spring Is Like the Morning.* Illus. Don Almquist. Putnam's, 1965. Grades 2–4.

Darling, Lois, and Louis Darling. *The Science of Life.* World, 1961. Grades 6 and up.

Durrell, Gerald, and Lee Durrell. *The Amateur Naturalist: A Practical Guide to the Natural World.* Knopf, 1983. Grades 5 and up.

Farb, Peter. *Face of North America: The Natural History of a Continent.* Harper, Young Readers' Edition, 1963. Grades 6–10.

Flanagan, Geraldine Lux. *Window into an Egg.* Young Scott, 1969. Illus. with photographs. Grades 4–9. See also *Window into a Nest* (Houghton Mifflin, 1975).

Hammond Nature Atlas of America. Contributing authors: Gerard A. Bertrand, *Fishes;* Donald J. Borror, *Insects;* George Porter, *Reptiles and Amphibians.* Hammond, 1973. Illus. with photographs. Grades 4 and up.

Hirsch, S. Carl. *The Living Community: A Venture into Ecology.* Illus. William Steinel. Viking, 1966. Grades 6–8.

Hylander, Clarence J. *Wildlife Communities from the Tundra to the Tropics in North America.* Illus. by the author. Houghton Mifflin, 1966. Grades 6–12.

Kane, Henry B. *The Tale of a Wood.* Illus. by the author. Knopf, 1962. Grades 4–6.

Kohl, Judith, and Herbert Kohl. *The View from the Oak: The Private Worlds of Other Creatures.* Illus. Roger Bayless. Sierra Club/Scribner's, 1977. Grades 5 and up.

Kohn, Bernice. *The Organic Living Book.* Illus. Betty Fraser. Viking, 1972. Grades 4–10.

Lauber, Patricia. *What's Hatching Out of that Egg?* Crown, 1979. Illus. with photographs. Grades 2–4.

Leopold, A. Starker, and the editors of Time-Life Books. *The Desert.* Time, Inc., Life Nature Library, 1967. Grades 7–9.

Mari, Iela, and Enzo Mari. *The Chicken and the Egg.* Illus. by the authors. Pantheon, 1969. Grades Preschool–K. See also *The Apple and the Moth* (1970).

May, Julian. *Living Things and Their Young.* Follett, Follett Family Life Education Program, 1969. Grades 3–6.

Menzel-Tettenborn, Helga, and Gunter Radtke. *Animals in Their Worlds.* Foreword, Peter Brazaitis, New York Zoological Society. Grosset & Dunlap, 1973. All ages.

Milne, Lorus J., Marjorie Milne, and the editors of *Life. The Mountains.* Time, Inc., Life Nature Library, 1962. Grades 7–9.

North, Sterling. *Hurry, Spring!* Illus. Carl Burger. Dutton, 1966. Grades 5–6.

Oxford Scientific Films. *The Chicken and the Egg.* Photographs, George Bernard and Peter Parks. Putnam's, 1979. Grades 2–5.

Parker, Bertha Morris. *The New Golden Treasury of Natural History.* Golden, 1968. Grades 4–8.

Platt, Rutherford. *Adventures in the Wilderness.* Consultant, Horace M. Albright. American Heritage, American Heritage Junior Library, 1963. Grades 5–8.

Sanderson, Ivan T. *The Continent We Live On.* Adapt. Anne Terry White. Random House, A Special Edition for Young Readers, 1972. Grades 4–9.

Simon, Hilda. *Chameleons and Other Quick-Change Artists.* Illus. by the author. Dodd, Mead, 1973. Grades 5 and up.

Tresselt, Alvin. *The Beaver Pond.* Illus. Roger Duvoisin. Lothrop, 1970.

Werner, Jane, and the staff of the Walt Disney Studio. *Living Desert.* Golden, 1954. Grades 5–7.

Wiesenthal, Eleanor, and Ted Wiesenthal. *Let's Find Out About Rivers.* Illus. Gerry Contreras. F. Watts, 1971. Grades K–2.

Zim, Herbert S. *How Things Grow.* Illus. Gustav Schrotter. Morrow, 1960.
Grades 3–5.

Oceans and Oceanography

Arnov, Boris, Jr. *Homes beneath the Sea: An Introduction to Ocean Ecology.* Little, Brown, 1969.
Illus. with photographs. Grades 5 and up.

Atwood, Ann. *New Moon Cove.* Photographs by the author. Scribner's, 1969.
All ages.

Barton, Robert. *Atlas of the Sea.* Illus. David Nockels. Day, 1974.
Grades 5 and up.

Berger, Melvin. *Oceanography Lab.* Day, 1973.
Grades 4–6.

Briggs, Peter. *The Great Global Rift.* Illus. David Noyes. Weybright & Talley, 1968.
Grades 4–12.

Brown, Joseph E. *Wonders of a Kelp Forest.* Intro. Wheeler J. North, California Institute of Technology. Dodd, Mead, 1974.
Grades 5 and up.

Carson, Rachel. *The Rocky Coast.* Illus. Bob Hines; photographs, Charles Pratt. McCall, 1971.
Grades 6 and up.

Carson, Rachel. *The Sea Around Us.* Rev. ed. Oxford Univ. Press, 1961.
Grades 8 and up. See also *The Edge of the Sea* (Houghton Mifflin, 1955).

Chester, Michael. *Water Monsters.* Grosset & Dunlap, 1973.
Illus. with photographs and drawings from various sources. Grades 4–8.

Clarke, Arthur C. *The Challenge of the Sea.* Illus. Alex Schomburg; intro. Wernher von Braun. Holt, 1960.
Grades 6–9.

Clemons, Elizabeth. *Waves, Tides, and Currents.* Knopf, 1967.
Illus. with maps, diagrams, and photos. Grades 5–8. See also *Tide Pools and Beaches* (1964).

Cook, Jan Leslie. *The Mysterious Undersea World.* National Geographic, Books for World Explorers, 1980.
Grades 3–5.

Coombs, Charles. *Deep-Sea World: The Story of Oceanography.* Morrow, 1966.
Illus. with photographs. Grades 5–8.

Cousteau, Jacques-Yves, and Philippe Diole. *Life and Death in a Coral Sea.* Trans. from the French by J. F. Bernard. Doubleday, The Undersea Discoveries of Jacques-Yves Cousteau, 1971.
Grades 5 and up.

Cousteau, Jacques-Yves, and James Dugan. *The Living Sea.* Harper, 1963.
Grades 7–9. See also *The Silent World* (1953).

Davies, Eryl. *Ocean Frontiers.* Viking, 1979.
Grades 6–8.

Dugan, James. *Undersea Explorer: The Story of Captain Jacques Cousteau.* Harper, 1957.
Illus. with photos and diagrams. Grades 6–9.

Engel, Leonard, and the editors of Time-Life Books. *The Sea.* Young Readers ed. Time, Inc., Life Nature Library, 1967.
Grades 7–9.

Fisher, James. *The Wonderful World of the Sea.* Doubleday, 1970.
Grades 5–9.

George, Jean Craighead. *Spring Comes to the Ocean.* Illus. John Wilson. Crowell, 1966.
Grades 5–7.

Goldin, Augusta. *The Bottom of the Sea.* Illus. Ed Emberley. Crowell, Let's-Read-and-Find-Out Books, 1966.
Grades 1–3. See also *The Sunlit Sea* (1968).

Goudey, Alice E. *Houses from the Sea.* Illus. Adrienne Adams. Scribner's, 1959.
Grades K–3.

McClung, Robert M. *Horseshoe Crab.* Illus. by the author. Morrow, 1967.
Grades 2–5.

May, Julian. *The Land beneath the Sea.* Illus. Leonard Everett Fisher. Holiday House, 1971.
Grades 3–8.

Oxford Scientific Films. *Jellyfish and Other Sea Creatures.* Photographs, Peter Parks. Putnam's, 1982.
Grades 3–5.

Phleger, F., and M. Phleger. *You Will Live under the Sea.* Illus. Ward Brackett. Random House, 1966.
Grades 1–3.

Polking, Kirk. *Oceans of the World: Our Essential Resource.* Illus. with photos. Philomel, A Global Perspectives Book, 1983.
  Grades 5 and up.

Rogers, Julia Ellen. *The Shell Book.* Rev. ed. Branford, 1951.
  Grades 8 and up.

Shaw, Evelyn. *Octopus.* Illus. Ralph Carpentier. Harper, A Science I Can Read Book, 1971.
  Grades K–2. See also *Fish out of School* (1970).

Shepherd, Elizabeth. *Tracks between the Tides, Being the Stories of Some Sea Worms and Other Burrowing Animals.* Illus. Arabelle Wheatley. Lothrop, 1972.
  Grades 2–6.

Silverberg, Robert. *The World within the Tide Pool.* Illus. Bob Hines. Weybright & Talley, 1972.
  Grades 6 and up. See also *The World within the Ocean Wave* (1972).

Simon, Seymour. *From Shore to Ocean Floor: How Life Survives in the Sea.* Illus. Haris Petie. F. Watts, 1973.
  Grades 4–9.

Stephens, William M. *Come with Me to the Edge of the Sea.* Illus. by the author. Messner, 1972.
  Grades 5–9.

Torchio, Menico. *The World beneath the Sea.* World, The World of Nature, 1972.
  Grades 5 and up.

Williams, Jerome. *Oceanography.* F. Watts, A First Book, 1972.
  Grades 5–10.

Zim, Herbert S., and Lester Ingle. *Seashores: A Guide to Animals and Plants along the Beaches.* Illus. Dorothea Barlowe and Sy Barlowe. Golden, A Golden Nature Guide, 1955.
  Grades 5–8. See also *Corals* (Morrow, 1966) and *Waves* (Morrow, 1967).

Plants and Seeds

Baker, Jeffrey J. W. *The Vital Process: Photosynthesis.* Illus. Patricia Collins. Doubleday, Living Things of the World, 1969.
  Grades 5–8.

Bentley, Linna. *Plants That Eat Animals.* Illus. Colin Threadgall. McGraw-Hill, A McGraw-Hill Natural Science Picture Book, 1968.
  Grades 3–6.

Busch, Phyllis S. *Lions in the Grass: The Story of the Dandelion, a Green Plant.* Photographs, Arline Strong. World, 1968.
  Grades 2–5.

Chinery, Michael. *Science Dictionary of the Plant World.* F. Watts, 1969.
  Illus. with photographs and charts. Grades 6 and up.

Cole, Joanna. *Plants in Winter.* Illus. Kazue Mizumura. Crowell, Let's-Read-and-Find-Out Science Books, 1973.
  Grades 1–3.

Dickinson, Alice. *The First Book of Plants.* Illus. Paul Wench. F. Watts, 1953.
  Grades 3–6.

Dowden, Anne Ophelia. *Wild Green Things in the City: A Book of Weeds.* Illus. by the author. Crowell, 1972.
  Grades 4–7. See also *The Blossom on the Bough* (1975) and *This Noble Harvest: A Chronicle of Herbs* (Collins, 1980).

Earle, Olive L. *Peas, Beans and Licorice.* Illus. by the author. Morrow, 1971.
  Grades 3–5.

Edlin, Herbert. *Atlas of Plant Life.* Illus. David Nockels and Henry Barnet; consultant, Anthony Huxley; maps by Geographical Projects, London. Day, 1973.
  Grades 4 and up.

Fenton, Carroll Lane, and Herminie B. Kitchen. *Plants We Live On: The Story of Grains and Vegetables.* Illus. Carroll Lane Fenton. Rev. and enl. ed. Day, 1971.
  Grades 4–8.

Foster, Laura Louise. *Keeping the Plants You Pick.* Illus. by the author. Crowell, 1970.
  Grades 4 and up.

Grimm, William C., and M. Jean Craig. *The Wondrous World of Seedless Plants.* Illus. William C. Grimm. Bobbs-Merrill, 1973.
  Grades 6–12.

Heady, Eleanor. *Coat of the Earth: The Story of Grass.* Illus. Harold F. Heady. Norton, 1968.
  Grades 5–9.

Holmes, Anita. *The 100-Year-Old Cactus.* Illus. Carol Lerner. Four Winds, 1983.
  Grades 3–6.

Hutchins, Ross E. *The Amazing Seeds.* Photographs by the author. Dodd, Mead, 1965.
Grades 5–8.

Hutchins, Ross E. *This Is a Leaf.* Photographs by the author. Dodd, Mead, 1962.
Grades 6–8. See also *Plants without Leaves* (1966).

Lauber, Patricia. *Seeds: Pop, Stick, Glide.* Photographs, Jerome Wexler. Crown, 1981.
Grades 2–4.

Limburg, Peter R. *Watch Out, It's Poison Ivy!* Illus. Haris Petie. Messner, 1973.
Grades 4–8.

Lubell, Winifred, and Cecil Lubell. *Green Is for Growing.* Rand McNally, 1964.
Grades 2–4.

Prime, C. T., and Aaron E. Klein. *Seedlings and Soil: Botany for Young Experimenters.* Doubleday, 1973.
Grades 5–12.

Pringle, Laurence. *Wild Foods: A Beginner's Guide to Identifying and Cooking Safe and Tasty Plants from the Outdoors.* Illus. Paul Breeden. Four Winds, 1978.
Grades 6 and up. See also *Being a Plant,* illus. Robin Brickman (Crowell/Harper, 1983).

Selsam, Millicent E. *The Carrot and Other Root Vegetables.* Photographs, Jerome Wexler. Morrow, 1971.
Grades 1–4. See also *Peanut* (1969); *Popcorn* (1976); *The Amazing Dandelion* (1977); *Eat the Fruit, Plant the Seed* (1980); *Cotton* (1982); and *Catnip* (1983).

Selsam, Millicent E. *Milkweed.* Morrow, 1967.
Illus. with photos. Grades 3–5. See also *Play with Plants* (1949) and *Play with Seeds* (1957).

Selsam, Millicent E. *The Tomato and Other Fruit Vegetables.* Photographs, Jerome Wexler. Morrow, 1970.
Grades 1–3. See also *Vegetables from Stems and Leaves* (1972) and *Bulbs, Corms, and Such* (1974).

Sterling, Dorothy. *The Story of Mosses, Ferns and Mushrooms.* Photographs, Myron Ehrenberg. Doubleday, 1955.
Grades 4–7.

Waters, John F. *Carnivorous Plants.* F. Watts, 1975.
Illus. with photographs. Grades 4–9.

Went, Frits W., and the editors of *Life. The Plants.* Time, Inc., Life Nature Library, 1963.
Grades 7–9.

Zim, Herbert S. *What's Inside of Plants.* Illus. Herschel Wartik. Morrow, 1953.
Grades 2–4.

Prehistoric Life

Aliki. *Fossils Tell of Long Ago.* Crowell, Let's-Read-and-Find-Out Science Books, 1972.
Grades 2–4.

Asimov, Isaac. *How Did We Find Out about Dinosaurs?* Illus. David Wool. Walker, The How Did We Find Out Books, 1973.
Grades 4–7.

Baity, Elizabeth Chesley. *America before Man.* Drawings, maps, charts, and diagrams, C. B. Falls. Viking, 1953.
With photographs. Grades 7–9.

Baumann, Hans. *Caves of the Great Hunters.* Illus. Isabel McHugh and Florence McHugh. Pantheon, 1954.
Grades 6–9.

Clymer, Eleanor. *The Case of the Missing Link.* Illus. Robert Reid Macguire. Basic Books, 1962.
Grades 5–9.

Colbert, Ewin H. *The Dinosaur Book: The Ruling Reptiles and Their Relatives.* Illus. John C. Germann. 2d ed. McGraw-Hill, 1951.
Grades 6 and up. See also *Dinosaurs, Their Discovery and Their World* (Dutton, 1961).

Colbert, Edwin H. *Millions of Years Ago: Prehistoric Life in North America.* Crowell, 1958.
Grades 5–7.

Coy, Harold. *Man Comes to America.* Illus. Leslie Morrill. Little, Brown, 1973.
Grades 5–12.

Davidson, Rosalie. *When the Dinosaurs Disappeared: Mammals of Long Ago.* Illus. Bernard Garbutt. Golden Gate Junior Books, 1973.
Grades 3–6. See also *Dinosaurs: The Terrible Lizards* (1969).

Dickinson, Alice. *The First Book of Prehistoric Animals.* Illus. Helene Carter. F. Watts, 1954.
Grades 4–7.

Fenton, Carroll Lane, and Mildred Adams Fenton. *The Fossil Book: A Record of Prehistoric Life.* Doubleday, 1958.
Grades 6 and up.

Glut, Donald F. *The Dinosaur Dictionary.* Intro. Alfred Sherwood Romer and David Techter. Citadel, 1972.
Grades 4 and up.

Greene, Carla. *After the Dinosaurs.* Illus. Kyuzo Tsugami. Bobbs-Merrill, 1968.
Grades 3–6.

Holden, Raymond. *Famous Fossil Finds.* Illus. John Martinez. Dodd, Mead, 1966.
Grades 6–9.

Howell, F. Clark. *Early Man.* Time, Inc., 1965.
Grades 6–12.

Hussey, Lois J., and Catherine Pessino. *Collecting Small Fossils.* Illus. Anne Marie Jauss. Crowell, 1970.
Grades 3–6.

McGowen, Tom. *Album of Dinosaurs.* Illus. Rod Ruth. Rand McNally, 1972.
Grades 3–7.

May, Julian. *They Turned to Stone.* Illus. Jean Zallinger. Holiday House, 1965.
Grades 3–5.

Parrish, Peggy. *Dinosaur Time.* Illus. Arnold Lobel. Harper, 1974.
Grades K–3.

Pfeiffer, John E. *The Search for Early Man.* Harper, A Horizon Caravel Book, 1963.
Grades 5–12.

Pringle, Laurence. *Dinosaurs and Their World.* Harcourt, 1968.
Grades 4–8.

Ravielli, Anthony. *From Fins to Hands: An Adventure in Evolution.* Illus. by the author. Viking, 1968.
Grades 4–8.

Sattler, Helen Roney. *Dinosaurs of North America.* Illus. Anthony Rao. Lothrop, 1981.
Grades 2–5.

Scheele, William E. *First Mammals.* Illus. by the author. World, 1955.
Grades 6–9.

Selsam, Millicent. *Tyrannosaurus Rex.* Harper, 1978. Illus. Grades 3–5.

Shapp, Martha, and Charles Shapp. *Let's Find Out about Cavemen.* Illus. Kyuzo Tusgamu. F. Watts, 1972.
Grades 2–4.

Silverberg, Robert. *Mammoths, Mastodons and Man.* Illus. Dale Grabel. McGraw-Hill, 1970.
Grades 6 and up.

Simak, Clifford. *Prehistoric Man: The Story of Man's Rise to Civilization.* Illus. Murray Tinkleman. St. Martin's, 1971.
Grades 6 and up.

Špinar, Zdeněk V. *Life before Man.* Illus. Zdeněk Burian. American Heritage, 1972.
Grades 5 and up.

White, Anne Terry. *Prehistoric America.* Illus. Aldren Watson. Random House, Landmark Books, 1951.
Grades 5–8.

Wood, Peter, Louis Vaczek, Dora Jane Hamblin, and Jonathan Norton Leonard. *Life before Man.* Time-Life Books, The Emergence of Man Series, 1972. Illus. with paintings, drawings, and photographs.
Grades 5 and up.

Zappler, Lisbeth, and Georg Zappler. *The World after the Dinosaurs: The Evolution of Mammals.* Natural History Press, 1970.
Grades 6 and up.

Zim, Herbert S. *Dinosaurs.* Illus. James Gordon Irving. Morrow, 1954.
Grades 4–6.

Psychology

Gould, Laurence J., and William G. Martin. *Think about It: Experiments in Psychology.* Illus. Gustave E. Nebel. Prentice-Hall, 1968.
Grades 5–9.

Hall, Elizabeth. *Why We Do What We Do: A Look at Psychology.* Houghton Mifflin, 1973.
Grades 6–12.

Kettelkamp, Larry. *Dreams.* Illus. by the author. Morrow, 1968.
Grades 4–9.

LeShan, Eda. *What Makes Me Feel This Way? Growing Up with Human Emotions.* Illus. Lisl Weil. Macmillan, 1972.
Grades 3–6. See also *You and Your Feelings* (1975).

Silverstein, Alvin, and Virginia B. Silverstein. *Exploring the Brain.* Illus. Patricia De Veau. Prentice-Hall, 1975.
Grades 5–8. See also *Sleep and Dreams* (Lippincott, 1974).

Stevens, Leonard A. *Neurons: Building Blocks of the Brain.* Illus. Henry Roth. Crowell, 1975.
Grades 5–9.

Reptiles and Amphibians

Bentley, William. *The Alligator Book: Sixty Questions and Answers.* Illus. Barbara Wolff. Walker, 1972.
Grades 3–6.

Blassingame, Wyatt. *Wonders of Alligators and Croco-diles.* Dodd, Mead, 1973.
  Illus. with photographs. Grades 4–8.

Brenner, Barbara. *A Snake-Lover's Diary.* Young Scott, 1970.
  Illus. with photographs. Grades 4–10.

Carr, Archie, and the editors of *Life. The Reptiles.* Time, Inc., Life Nature Library, 1963.
  Grades 7–9.

Cole, Joanna. *A Frog's Body.* Photographs, Jerome Wexler. Morrow, 1980.
  Grades 3–5. See also *A Snake's Body* (1981).

Davis, Burke. *Biography of a King Snake.* Illus. Albert Michini. Putnam's, 1975.
  Grades 3–6.

Fenton, Carroll L., and Dorothy C. Pallas. *Reptiles and Their World.* Day, 1961.
  Grades 4–7.

Hess, Lilo. *The Remarkable Chameleon.* Scribner's, 1968.
  Grades 3–6.

Hoke, John. *The First Book of Snakes.* Illus. Paul Wenck. F. Watts, 1952.
  Grades 3–5.

Holling, Holling Clancy. *Minn of the Mississippi.* Illus. by the author. Houghton Mifflin, 1951.
  Grades 4–8.

Huntington, Harriet E. *Let's Look at Reptiles.* Photographs by the author; drawings, J. Noel. Doubleday, 1973.
  Grades 4–10.

Jacobs, Francine. *Sea Turtles.* Illus. Jean Zallinger. Morrow, 1972.
  Grades 3–6.

Leutscher, Alfred. *The Curious World of Snakes.* Illus. Barry Driscoll. McGraw-Hill, A McGraw-Hill Natural Science Picture Book, 1965.
  Grades 4–7.

May, Julian. *Alligator Hole.* Illus. Rod Ruth. Follett, 1969.
  Grades 3–5.

Pope, Clifford H. *Reptiles Round the World.* Illus. Helen Damrosch Tee-Van. Knopf, 1957.
  Grades 5–8.

Rockwell, Anne, and Harlow Rockwell. *Toad.* Illus. by the authors. Doubleday, 1972.
  Grades K–3. See also *Olly's Polliwogs* (1970).

Shaw, Evelyn. *Alligator.* Illus. Frances Zweifel. Harper, A Science I Can Read Book, 1972.
  Grades 1–3.

Silverstein, Alvin, and Virginia Silverstein. *Metamorphosis: The Magic Change.* Atheneum, 1971.
  Grades 4–7.

Silverstein, Alvin, and Virginia Silverstein. *The Long Voyage: The Life Cycle of a Green Turtle.* Illus. Allan Eitzen. Warne, 1972.
  Grades 3–6.

Simon, Hilda. *Snakes: The Facts and the Folklore.* Illus. by the author. Viking, 1973.
  Grades 5–12. See also *Frogs and Toads of the World* (Lippincott, 1975).

Stebbins, Robert C. *A Field Guide to Western Reptiles and Amphibians.* Illus. by the author. Houghton Mifflin, Peterson Field Guide Series, 1966.
  Grades 6 and up. See other field guides in this series.

Stephens, William M., and Peggy Stephens. *Sea Turtle Swims the Ocean.* Illus. Rene Martin. Holiday House, 1971.
  Grades 3–5.

Waters, John F. *Green Turtle Mysteries.* Illus. Mamoru Funai. Crowell, Let's-Read-and-Find-Out Science Books, 1972.
  Grades 1–3.

Zim, Herbert S., and Hobart M. Smith. *Reptiles and Amphibians: A Guide to Familiar American Species.* Rev. ed. Golden, A Golden Nature Guide, 1956.
  Grades 7 and up. See also *Alligators and Croco-diles.*

Rocks and Minerals

Chase, Sara Hannum. *Diamonds.* F. Watts, A First Book, 1971.
  Illus. with photographs. Grades 4–9.

Cormack, Maribelle. *The First Book of Stones.* Illus. M. K. Scott. F. Watts, 1950.
  Grades 3–5.

Fenton, Carroll Lane, and Mildred Adams. *Rocks and Their Stories.* Doubleday, 1951.
  Grades 5–8.

Loomis, Frederic. *Field Book of Common Rocks and Minerals: For Identifying the Rocks and Minerals of the United States and Interpreting Their Origins and Meanings.* Rev. ed. Putnam's, Putnam's Nature Field Books, 1948.
  Grades 6–8.

Shuttlesworth, Dorothy. *The Story of Rocks.* Illus. Suzan N. Swain. Rev. ed. Doubleday, 1966.
Grades 5–8.

Simon, Seymour. *The Rock-Hound's Book.* Illus. Tony Chen. Viking, 1973.
Grades 4–9.

Wyler, Rose, and Gerald Ames. *Secrets in Stones.* Photographs, Gerald Ames. Four Winds, 1970.
Grades 2–5.

Zim, Herbert S., and Paul R. Shaffer. *Rocks and Minerals: A Guide to Familiar Minerals, Gems, Ores and Rocks.* Illus. Raymond Perlman. Golden, A Golden Nature Guide, 1957.
Grades 4–6.

Trees

Atwood, Ann. *The Kingdom of the Forest.* Photographs by the author. Scribner's, 1972.
All ages.

Baker, Laura Nelson. *A Tree Called Moses.* Illus. Penelope Naylor. Atheneum, 1966.
Grades 3–6.

Buff, Mary, and Conrad Buff. *Big Tree.* Illus. Conrad Buff. Viking, 1946.
Grades 5–8.

Collins, Patricia. *Chain of Life: A Story of a Forest Food Cycle.* Illus. by the author. Doubleday, 1972.
Grades 3–6.

Cormack, Maribelle. *The First Book of Trees.* Illus. Helene Carter. F. Watts, 1951.
Grades 4–7.

Dowden, Anne Ophelia. *The Blossom on the Bough: A Book of Trees.* Illus. by the author. Crowell, 1975.
Grades 6 and up.

Farb, Peter, and the editors of *Life. The Forest.* Time, Inc., Life Nature Library, 1962.
Grades 7–9.

Fenton, Carroll Lane, and Dorothy Constance Pallas. *Trees and Their World.* Day, 1957.
Grades 4–6.

Hutchins, Ross E. *This Is a Tree.* Photographs by the author. Dodd, Mead, 1964.
Grades 7–9.

Jaspersohn, William. *How the Forest Grew.* Illus. Chuck Eckart. Greenwillow, 1980.
Grades 1–3.

Kohl, Judith, and Herbert Kohl. *The View from the Oak: The Private World of Other Creatures.* Illus. Roger Bayless. Sierra Club/Scribner's, 1977.
Grades 5 and up.

Mabey, Richard. *Oak & Company.* Illus. Clare Roberts. Greenwillow, 1983.
Grades 1–5.

Selsam, Millicent E. *Maple Tree.* Morrow, 1968.
Grades 2–4.

Selsam, Millicent E. *See through the Jungle.* Illus. Winifred Lubell. Harper, 1957.
Grades 4–6.

Silverberg, Robert. *Vanishing Giants: The Story of the Sequoias.* Simon & Schuster, 1969.
Grades 6 and up.

Watson, Aldren. *A Maple Tree Begins.* Illus. by the author. Viking, 1970.
Grades 3–6.

Zim, Herbert S., and Alexander C. Martin. *Trees: A Guide to Familiar American Trees.* Illus. Dorothea Barlowe and Sy Barlowe. Rev. ed. Golden, A Golden Nature Guide, 1956.
Grades 6–8.

Appendix:
Children's Book Awards

United States

The Newbery and the Caldecott Awards

John Newbery, the famous eighteenth century bookseller of St. Paul's Churchyard, London, rendered a great service to his age and generation by encouraging the best authors of the day to write for children. It is fitting, therefore, that the name "Newbery," whose owner was the first to recognize that children were a reading public worthy of a publisher, is attached to the medal that since 1922 has been awarded annually to the author of the "most distinguished contribution to American literature for children, published during the preceding year." The donor of this medal was Frederic Melcher, editor of *Publishers' Weekly*.

During the meeting of the American Library Association held at Swampscott, Massachusetts, in 1921, the idea of presenting the medal took form. In an article published in the *Saturday Review of Literature*, Melcher said: "I had been asked to give a talk at the Section for Library Work with Children about Children's Book Week, then a new idea but now the oldest of all 'weeks' and still the most useful. I remember looking down from the platform at all those enthusiastic people from every part of the Union and wondering whether they could not, as a group, take one more job, by helping to assure a greater literature for children as well as a wider reading of the then available literature. . . . These people knew the audiences of boys and girls, knew them intimately, knew what boys and girls really wanted. They could help build a greater literature by giving authoritative recognition to those who wrote well. I conceived the plan of an annual award and offered it on the spot with the suggestion that good old John Newbery's name be attached to the medal.'' Such was the inception of the Newbery award.

The terms of the award are as follows: "The author shall be a citizen or a resident of the United States. Someone living here temporarily is not eligible. His contribution shall be an original and creative piece of work. It shall be the 'most distinguished contribution to American literature for children,' original in conception, fine in workmanship and artistically true. Reprints and compilations are not eligible for consideration. The book need not be written solely for children. The judgment of the voting librarians shall decide whether a book is a 'contribution to the literature for children.' The Committee of Award considers only the books of one calendar year, and does not pass judgment on an author's previous work or other work during that year outside the volume that may be named.'' The medal is designed by René Paul Chambellan and is cast in bronze.

Again, it was at the suggestion of Melcher that the Randolph Caldecott award was established in 1937. The Caldecott Medal, donated by Melcher and named in honor of the great English illustrator of children's books, is also designed by René Paul Chambellan and cast in bronze. It is awarded to the illustrator of the most distinguished picture book for children published in the United States during the preceding year. A picture book within the purpose of this award should be the creation of the artist, the product of the artist's initiative and imagination. The text of the volume need not be written by the artist, but it must be worthy of the book. It is possible to award the Caldecott Medal to artists who work together, e.g., the D'Aulaires, the Hadars, the Petershams.

Both awards are made by a special Newbery-Caldecott Awards Committee of the Children's Services Division of the American Library Association. Announcement of the winners of both the Newbery and Caldecott awards is made early in the spring.

Since the death of Frederic Melcher, his son, Daniel Melcher, has carried on the commitment.

The formal presentation of the medals to the winners is made at a banquet at the American Library Association Conference held in June.

The Newbery Award

1922   Hendrik Willem Van Loon. *The Story of Mankind,* illus. the author. Liveright, 1921.

1923   Hugh Lofting. *The Voyages of Doctor Dolittle,* illus. the author. Stokes, 1922.

1924   Charles Boardman Hawes. *The Dark Frigate,* illus. A. L. Ripley. Atlantic Monthly Press, 1923.

1925   Charles Joseph Finger. *Tales from Silver Lands,* illus. Paul Honoré. Doubleday, 1924.

1926   Arthur Bowie Chrisman. *Shen of the Sea,* illus. Else Hasselriis. Dutton, 1925.

1927   Will James. *Smoky, the Cowhorse,* illus. the author. Scribner's, 1926.

1928   Dhan Gopal Mukerji. *Gay-Neck,* illus. Boris Artzybasheff. Dutton, 1927.

1929   Eric P. Kelly. *Trumpeter of Krakow,* illus. Angela Pruszynska. Macmillan, 1928.

1930   Rachel Lyman Field. *Hitty, Her First Hundred Years,* illus. Dorothy P. Lathrop. Macmillan, 1929.

1931   Elizabeth Coatsworth. *The Cat Who Went to Heaven,* illus. Lynd Ward. Macmillan, 1930.

1932   Laura Adams Armer. *Waterless Mountain,* illus. Sidney Armer and the author. Longmans, 1931.

1933   Elizabeth Foreman Lewis. *Young Fu of the Upper Yangtze,* illus. Kurt Wiese. Winston, 1932.

1934   Cornelia Lynde Meigs. *Story of the Author of "Little Women": Invincible Louisa.* Little, Brown, 1933.

1935   Monica Shannon. *Dobry,* illus. Atanas Katchamakoff. Viking, 1934.

1936   Carol Ryrie Brink. *Caddie Woodlawn,* illus. Kate Seredy. Macmillan, 1935.

1937   Ruth Sawyer. *Roller Skates,* illus. Valenti Angelo. Viking, 1936.

1938   Kate Seredy. *The White Stag,* illus. the author. Viking, 1937.

1939   Elizabeth Enright. *Thimble Summer,* illus. the author. Farrar & Rinehart, 1938.

1940   James Daugherty. *Daniel Boone,* illus. the author. Viking, 1939.

1941 Armstrong Sperry. *Call It Courage,* illus. the author. Macmillan, 1940.

1942 Walter Dumaux Edmonds. *The Matchlock Gun,* illus. Paul Lantz. Dodd, Mead, 1941.

1943 Elizabeth Janet Gray. *Adam of the Road,* illus. Robert Lawson. Viking, 1942.

1944 Esther Forbes. *Johnny Tremain,* illus. Lynd Ward. Houghton Mifflin, 1943.

1945 Robert Lawson. *Rabbit Hill,* illus. the author. Viking, 1944.

1946 Lois Lenski. *Strawberry Girl,* illus. the author. Lippincott-Stokes, 1945.

1947 Carolyn Sherwin Bailey. *Miss Hickory,* illus. Ruth Gannett. Viking, 1946.

1948 William Pène du Bois. *The Twenty-One Balloons,* illus. the author. Viking, 1947.

1949 Marguerite Henry. *King of the Wind,* illus. Wesley Dennis. Rand McNally, 1948.

1950 Marguerite de Angeli. *The Door in the Wall,* illus. the author. Doubleday, 1949.

1951 Elizabeth Yates. *Amos Fortune, Free Man,* illus. Nora S. Unwin. Aladdin, 1950.

1952 Eleanor Estes. *Ginger Pye,* illus. the author. Harcourt, 1951.

1953 Ann Nolan Clark. *Secret of the Andes,* illus. Jean Charlot. Viking, 1952.

1954 Joseph Krumgold. *And Now Miguel,* illus. Jean Charlot. Crowell, 1953.

1955 Meindert DeJong. *The Wheel on the School,* illus. Maurice Sendak. Harper, 1954.

1956 Jean Lee Latham. *Carry On, Mr. Bowditch,* illus. John O'Hara Cosgrave II. Houghton Mifflin, 1955.

1957 Virginia Sorenson. *Miracles on Maple Hill,* illus. Beth Krush and Joe Krush. Harcourt, 1956.

1958 Harold Keith. *Rifles for Watie,* illus. Peter Burchard. Crowell, 1957.

1959 Elizabeth George Speare. *The Witch of Blackbird Pond,* Houghton Mifflin, 1958.

1960 Joseph Krumgold. *Onion John,* illus. Symeon Shimin. Crowell, 1959.

1961 Scott O'Dell. *Island of the Blue Dolphins.* Houghton Mifflin, 1960.

1962 Elizabeth George Speare. *The Bronze Bow.* Houghton Mifflin, 1961.

1963 Madeleine L'Engle. *A Wrinkle in Time.* Farrar, Straus, 1962.

1964 Emily Neville. *It's Like This, Cat,* illus. Emil Weiss. Harper, 1963.

1965 Maia Wojciechowska. *Shadow of a Bull,* illus. Alvin Smith. Atheneum, 1964.

1966 Elizabeth Borton de Treviño. *I, Juan de Pareja.* Farrar, Straus & Giroux, 1965.

1967 Irene Hunt. *Up a Road Slowly.* Follett, 1966.

1968 E. L. Konigsburg. *From the Mixed-Up Files of Mrs. Basil E. Frankweiler,* illus. the author. Atheneum, 1967.

1969 Lloyd Alexander. *The High King.* Holt, 1968.

1970 William H. Armstrong. *Sounder,* illus. James Barkley. Harper, 1969.

1971 Betsy Byars. *Summer of the Swans,* illus. Ted CoConis. Viking, 1970.

1972 Robert C. O'Brien. *Mrs. Frisby and the Rats of NIMH,* illus. Zena Bernstein. Atheneum, 1971.

1973 Jean Craighead George. *Julie of the Wolves,* illus. John Schoenherr. Harper, 1972.

1974 Paula Fox. *The Slave Dancer,* illus. Eros Keith. Bradbury, 1973.

1975 Virginia Hamilton. *M. C. Higgins, the Great.* Macmillan, 1974.

1976 Susan Cooper. *The Grey King,* illus. Michael Heslop. Atheneum, 1975.

1977 Mildred D. Taylor. *Roll of Thunder, Hear My Cry,* illus. Jerry Pinkney. Dial, 1976.

1978 Katherine Paterson. *Bridge to Terebithia,* illus. Donna Diamond. Crowell, 1977.

1979 Ellen Raskin. *The Westing Game.* Dutton, 1978.

1980 Joan W. Blos. *A Gathering of Days: A New England Girl's Journal, 1830–32.* Scribner's, 1979.

1981 Katherine Paterson. *Jacob Have I Loved.* Crowell, 1980.

1982 Nancy Willard. *A Visit to William Blake's Inn: Poems for Innocent and Experienced Travellers,* illus. Alice Provenson and Martin Provenson. Harcourt, 1981.

1983 Cynthia Voigt. *Dicey's Song.* Atheneum, 1982.

1984 Beverly Cleary. *Dear Mr. Henshaw,* illus. Paul O. Zelinsky. Morrow, 1983.

The Caldecott Award

1938   Dorothy Lathrop. *Animals of the Bible,* with text selected by Helen Dean Fish from the King James Bible. Stokes, 1937.

1939   Thomas Handforth. *Mei Li,* written by Thomas Handforth. Doubleday, 1938.

1940   Ingri D'Aulaire and Edgar Parin D'Aulaire. *Abraham Lincoln,* written by Ingri D'Aulaire and Edgar Parin D'Aulaire. Doubleday, 1939.

1941   Robert Lawson. *They Were Strong and Good,* written by Robert Lawson. Viking, 1940.

1942   Robert McCloskey. *Make Way for Ducklings,* written by Robert McCloskey. Viking, 1941.

1943   Virginia Lee Burton. *The Little House,* written by Virginia Lee Burton. Houghton Mifflin, 1942.

1944   Louis Slobodkin. *Many Moons,* written by James Thurber. Harcourt, 1943.

1945   Elizabeth Orton Jones. *A Prayer for a Child,* written by Rachel Lyman Field. Macmillan, 1944.

1946   Maud Petersham and Miska Petersham. *The Rooster Crows: A Book of American Rhymes and Jingles,* comp. Maud Petersham and Miska Petersham. Macmillan, 1945.

1947   Leonard Weisgard. *The Little Island,* written by Golden MacDonald (pseud). Doubleday, 1946.

1948   Roger Duvoisin. *White Snow, Bright Snow,* written by Alvin Tresselt. Lothrop, 1947.

1949   Berta Hader and Elmer Hader. *The Big Snow,* written by Berta Hader and Elmer Hader. Macmillan, 1948.

1950   Leo Politi. *Song of the Swallows,* written by Leo Politi. Scribner's, 1949.

1951   Katherine Milhous. *The Egg Tree,* written by Katherine Milhous. Scribner's, 1950.

1952   Nicolas Modvinoff. *Finders Keepers,* written by Will and Nicolas (Will Lipkind and Nicolas Mordvinoff). Harcourt, 1951.

1953   Lynd Ward. *The Biggest Bear,* written by Lynd Ward. Houghton Mifflin, 1952.

1954   Ludwig Bemelmans. *Madeleine's Rescue,* written by Ludwig Bemelmans. Viking, 1953.

1955   Marcia Brown. *Cinderella,* written by Charles Perrault; trans. and illus. Marcia Brown. Scribner's, 1954.

1956   Feodor Rojankovsky. *Frog Went a-Courtin',* written by John Langstaff. Harcourt, 1955.

1957   Marc Simont. *A Tree Is Nice,* written by Janice Udry. Harper, 1956.

1958   Robert McCloskey. *Time of Wonder,* written by Robert McCloskey. Viking, 1957.

1959   Barbara Cooney. *Chanticleer and the Fox,* adapted from Chaucer's *Canterbury Tales.* Crowell, 1958.

1960   Marie Hall Ets. *Nine Days to Christmas,* written by Marie Hall Ets and Aurora Labastida. Viking, 1959.

1961   Nicolas Sidjakov. *Baboushka and the Three Kings,* written by Ruth Robbins. Parnassus, 1960.

1962   Marcia Brown. *Once a Mouse . . . ,* a fable cut in wood, retold by Marcia Brown. Scribner's, 1961.

1963   Ezra Jack Keats. *The Snowy Day,* written by Ezra Jack Keats. Viking, 1962.

1964   Maurice Sendak. *Where the Wild Things Are,* written by Maurice Sendak. Harper, 1963.

1965   Beni Montresor. *May I Bring a Friend?* written by Beatrice Schenk de Regniers. Atheneum, 1964.

1966   Nonny Hogrogian. *Always Room for One More,* written by Sorche Nic Leodhas. Holt, 1965.

1967   Evaline Ness. *Sam, Bangs, and Moonshine,* written by Evaline Ness. Holt, 1966.

1968   Ed Emberley. *Drummer Hoff,* adapted by Barbara Emberley. Prentice-Hall, 1967.

1969   Uri Shulevitz. *The Fool of the World and the Flying Ship,* retold by Arthur Ransome. Farrar, Straus & Giroux, 1968.

1970   William Steig. *Sylvester and the Magic Pebble,* written by William Steig. Windmill Books/Simon & Schuster, 1969.

1971   Gail E. Haley. *A Story-A Story,* retold by Gail E. Haley. Atheneum, 1970.

1972   Nonny Hogrogian. *One Fine Day,* retold by Nonny Hogrogian. Macmillan, 1971.

1973   Blair Lent. *The Funny Little Woman,* retold by Arlene Mosel. Dutton, 1972.

1974   Margot Zemach. *Duffy and the Devil,* retold by Harve Zemach. Farrar, Straus & Giroux, 1973.

1975 Gerald McDermott. *Arrow to the Sun,* adapted by Gerald McDermott. Viking, 1974.

1976 Leo Dillon and Diane Dillon. *Why Mosquitoes Buzz in People's Ears,* retold by Verna Aardema. Dial, 1975.

1977 Leo Dillon and Diane Dillon. *Ashanti to Zulu: African Traditions,* written by Margaret Musgrove. Dial, 1976.

1978 Peter Spier. *Noah's Ark,* written by Jacob Revius; trans. and illus. Peter Spier. Doubleday, 1977.

1979 Paul Goble. *The Girl Who Loved Wild Horses,* written by Paul Goble. Bradbury, 1978.

1980 Barbara Cooney. *Ox-Cart Man,* written by Donald Hall. Viking, 1979.

1981 Arnold Lobel. *Fables,* written by Arnold Lobel. Harper, 1980.

1982 Chris Van Allsburg. *Jumanji,* written by Chris Van Allsburg. Houghton Mifflin, 1981.

1983 Marcia Brown. *Shadow,* written by Blais Cendrars; trans. and illus. Marcia Brown. Scribner's, 1982.

1984 Alice Provensen and Martin Provensen. *The Glorious Flight: Across the Channel with Louis Blériot, July 25, 1909,* written by Alice Provensen and Martin Provensen. Viking, 1983.

The National Book Awards and the American Book Awards

The National Book Awards were established in 1950 by the Association of American Publishers to give recognition to the most distinguished books of the preceding year. A children's category was added in 1969. This award was discontinued in 1979 and replaced, in 1980, by the American Book Awards (also established by the Association of American Publishers). Unfortunately, the children's book category was eliminated in 1984.

The American Book Awards consider books written, designed, or translated by U.S. citizens and published in the United States during the preceding calendar year. Four categories pertained directly to children's literature: children's fiction (hardback and paperback) and children's nonfiction (hardback and paperback).

Children's books were also considered in six categories pertaining to graphics. The nominees and winners were chosen by an independent body including authors, publishers, editors, critics, and librarians.

The National Book Awards

1969 Meindert DeJong. *Journey from Peppermint Street,* illus. Emily McCully. Harper, 1968.

1970 Isaac Bashevis Singer. *A Day of Pleasure: Stories of a Boy Growing Up in Warsaw,* illus. with photographs by Roman Vishniac. Farrar, Straus & Giroux, 1969.

1971 Lloyd Alexander. *The Marvelous Misadventures of Sebastian.* Dutton, 1970.

1972 Donald Barthelme. *The Slightly Irregular Fire Engine,* illus. the author. Farrar, Straus & Giroux, 1971.

1973 Ursula K. Le Guin. *The Farthest Shore.* Atheneum, 1972.

1974 Eleanor Cameron. *The Court of the Stone Children.* Dutton, 1973.

1975 Virginia Hamilton. *M. C. Higgins, the Great.* Macmillan, 1974.

1976 Walter D. Edmonds. *Bert Breen's Barn.* Little, Brown, 1975.

1977 Katherine Paterson. *The Master Puppeteer,* illus. Haru Wells. Crowell, 1976.

1978 Herbert Kohl and Judith Kohl. *The View from the Oak,* illus. Roger Bayless. Sierra Club/Scribner's, 1977.

1979 Katherine Paterson. *The Great Gilly Hopkins.* Crowell, 1978.

The American Book Awards

1980 *Children's Book, Hardcover:* Joan W. Blos. *A Gathering of Days: A New England Girl's Journal, 1830–32.* Scribner's, 1979.

    Children's Book, Paperback: Madeleine L'Engle. *A Swiftly Tilting Planet.* Dell, 1979.

1981 *Children's Fiction, Hardcover:* Betsy Byars. *Night Swimmers,* illus. Troy Howell. Delacorte, 1980.

Children's Fiction, Paperback: Beverly Cleary. *Ramona and Her Mother,* illus. Alan Tiegreen. Dell/Yearling, 1980.

Children's Nonfiction, Hardcover: Jane Lawrence Mali and Alison Cragin Herzig. *Oh, Boy! Babies!,* illus. Katrina Thomas. Little, Brown, 1980.

1982   *Children's Fiction, Hardcover:* Lloyd Alexander. *Westmark.* Dutton, 1981.

Children's Fiction, Paperback: Ouida Sebestyen. *Words by Heart.* Bantam, 1981.

Children's Nonfiction: Susan Bonners. *A Penguin Year,* illus. the author. Delacorte, 1981.

Children's Picture Book, Hardcover: Maurice Sendak. *Outside Over There,* written by Maurice Sendak. Harper, 1981.

Children's Picture Book, Paperback: Peter Spier. *Noah's Ark,* written by Jacob Revius; trans. and illus. Peter Spier. Zephyr Books/Doubleday, 1977.

Graphic Award, Book Illustration/Original Art: Chris Van Allsburg. *Jumanji,* written by Chris Van Allsburg. Houghton Mifflin, 1981.

1983   *Children's Fiction, Hardcover:* Jean Fritz. *Homesick: My Own Story,* illus. Margot Tomes and with photographs. Putnam's, 1982.

Children's Fiction, Paperback: Paula Fox. *A Place Apart.* Signet, 1982. Joyce Carol Thomas. *Marked by Fire.* Avon, 1982.

Children's Nonfiction: James Cross Giblin. *Chimney Sweeps,* illus. Margot Tomes. Crowell, 1982.

Children's Picture Book, Hardcover: Barbara Cooney. *Miss Rumphius,* written by Barbara Cooney. Viking, 1982. William Steig. *Doctor De Soto,* written by William Steig. Farrar, Straus & Giroux, 1982.

Children's Picture Book, Paperback: Betty Fraser. *A House Is a House for Me,* written by Mary Ann Hoberman. Puffin Viking, 1982.

Graphic Award, Book Illustration/Original Art: Erick Ingraham. *Porcupine Stew,* written by Beverly Major. Morrow, 1982.

Graphic Award, Book Design/Pictorial: Barry Moser. *Lewis Carroll's Alice's Adventures in Wonderland,* written by Lewis Carroll, pseud.; preface and notes by James R. Kincaid; text ed. Selwyn H. Goodacre. Univ. of California Press, 1982.

Australia

The Australian Children's Book Award

The Australian Children's Book Award was established in 1946, and the Australian Children's Book Council assumed the administration of the award in 1959. In 1956, a picture book category was added. From 1974 to 1976, the visual arts board of the Australian Council for the Arts sponsored a competition for the best illustrated children's book of the year. In 1983, a category for junior books was added. The final selection of winners is made by a council of judges.

The Australian Children's Book Award

1946   Leslie Rees. *Story of Karrawinga, the Emu,* illus. Walter Cunningham. Sands, 1946.

1947   No award.

1948   Frank Hurley. *Shackleton's Argonauts: A Saga of the Antarctic Ice-packs,* illus. the author. Angus & Robertson, 1948.

1949   Alan John Villiers. *Whalers of the Midnight Sun: A Story of Modern Whaling in the Antarctic,* illus. Charles Pont. Angus & Robertson, 1949 (published in the United States by Scribner's).

1950   No award.

1951   Ruth Williams. *Verity of Sydney Town,* illus. Rhys Williams. Angus & Robertson, 1950.

1952   Eve Pownall. *The Australian Book,* illus. Margaret Senior. Sands, 1953.

1953   James Henry and William Donald Martin. *Aircraft of Today and Tomorrow,* illus. with photographs. Angus & Robertson, 1953. Joan Phipson. *Good Luck to the Rider,* illus. Margaret Horder. Angus & Robertson, 1953.

1954   K. Langloh Parker. *Australian Legendary Tales,* illus. Elizabeth Durack. Angus & Robertson, 1953.

1955   Harold Arthur Lindsay and Norman Barnett Tindale. *The First Walkabout,* illus. Madeleine Boyce. Longmans, 1954.

1956 *Book of the Year:* Patricia Wrightson. *The Crooked Snake,* illus. Margaret Horder. Angus & Robertson, 1955.

Picture Book of the Year: Sheila Hawkins. *Wish and the Magic Nut,* written by Peggy Barnard. Sands, 1956.

1957 *Book of the Year:* Enid Moodie-Heddle. *The Boomerang Book of Legendary Tales,* illus. Nancy Parker. Longmans, 1957.

Picture Book of the Year: No award.

1958 *Book of the Year:* Nan Chauncy. *Tiger in the Bush,* illus. Margaret Horder. Oxford Univ. Press, 1957 (published in the United States by Watts).

Picture Book of the Year: Piccaninny Walkabout: A Story of Two Aboriginal Children, written by Axel Poignant; illus. with photographs. Angus & Robertson, 1957.

1959 *Book of the Year:* Nan Chauncy. *Devil's Hill,* illus. Geraldine Spence. Oxford Univ. Press, 1958 (published in the United States by Watts). John Gunn. *Sea Menace,* illus. Brian Keogh. Constable, 1958.

Picture Book of the Year: No award.

1960 *Book of the Year:* Kylie Tennant. *All the Proud Tribesmen,* illus. Clem Seale. Macmillan, 1959 (published in the United States by St. Martin's).

Picture Book of the Year: No award.

1961 *Book of the Year:* Nan Chauncy. *Tangara: Let Us Set Off Again,* illus. Brian Wildsmith. Oxford Univ. Press, 1960 (published in the United States as *The Secret Friends* by Watts).

Picture Book of the Year: No award.

1962 *Book of the Year:* Leonard Herbert Evers. *The Racketty Street Gang.* Hodder & Stoughton, 1961. Joan Woodberry. *Rafferty Rides a Winner,* illus. the author. Parrish, 1961.

Picture Book of the Year: No award.

1963 *Book of the Year:* Joan M. Phipson. *The Family Conspiracy,* illus. Margaret Horder. Angus & Robertson, 1962 (published in the United States by Harcourt).

Picture Book of the Year: No award.

1964 *Book of the Year:* Eleanor Spence. *The Green Laurel,* illus. Geraldine Spence. Oxford Univ. Press, 1962 (published in the United States by Roy).

Picture Book of the Year: No award.

1965 *Book of the Year:* Hesba Fay Brinsmead. *Pastures of the Blue Crane,* illus. Annette Macarthur-Onslow. Oxford Univ. Press, 1964 (published in the United States by Coward-McCann).

Picture Book of the Year: Elisabeth MacIntyre. *Hugo's Zoo,* written by Elisabeth MacIntyre. Angus & Robertson, 1964 (published in the United States by Knopf).

1966 *Book of the Year:* Ivan Southall. *Ash Road,* illus. Clem Seale. Angus & Robertson, 1965 (published in the United States by Greenwillow).

Picture Book of the Year: No award.

1967 *Book of the Year:* Mavis Thorpe Clark. *The Min-min,* illus. Genevieve Melrose. Angus & Robertson, 1967 (published in the United States by Macmillan).

Picture Book of the Year: No award.

1968 *Book of the Year:* Ivan Southall. *To the Wild Sky,* illus. Jennifer Tuckwell. Angus & Robertson, 1967 (published in the United States by St. Martin's).

Picture Book of the Year: No award.

1969 *Book of the Year:* Margaret Balderson. *When Jays Fly to Barbmo,* illus. Victor G. Ambrus. Oxford Univ. Press, 1968 (published in the United States by Gregg).

Picture Book of the Year: Ted Greenwood. *Sly Old Wardrobe,* written by Ivan Southall. Cheshire, 1968 (published in the United States by St. Martin's).

1970 *Book of the Year:* Annette Macarthur-Onslow. *Uhu,* illus. the author. Ure Smith, 1969 (published in the United States by Knopf).

Picture Book of the Year: No award.

1971 *Book of the Year:* Ivan Southall. *Bread and Honey.* Angus & Robertson, 1970 (published in the United States as *Walk a Mile and Get Nowhere* by Bradbury).

Picture Book of the Year: Desmond Digby. *Waltzing Matilda,* written by Andrew Barton Paterson. Collins Australia, 1970 (published in the United States by Holt).

1972 *Book of the Year:* Hesba Fay Brinsmead. *Longtime Passing.* Angus & Robertson, 1971.

Picture Book of the Year: No award.

1973 *Book of the Year:* Noreen Shelley. *Family at the Lookout,* illus. R. Micklewright. Oxford Univ. Press, 1972.

Picture Book of the Year: No award.

1974 *Book of the Year:* Patricia Wrightson. *The Nargun and the Stars.* Hutchinson, 1973 (published in the United States by Atheneum).

Picture Book of the Year: Ron Brooks. *The Bunyip of Berkeley's Creek,* written by Jenny Wagner. Longman Young, 1974 (published in the United States by Bradbury).

Visual Arts: Deborah Niland and Kilmeny Niland. *Mulga Bill's Bycycle,* written by Andrew Barton Paterson. Collins, 1973 (published in the United States by Parents' Magazine Press).

1975 *Book of the Year:* No award.

Picture Book of the Year: Quentin Hole. *The Man from Ironbark,* written by Andrew Barton Paterson. Collins Australia, 1974 (published in the United States by Collins-World).

Visual Arts: Roger Haldane. *The Magpie Island,* written by Colin Thiele. Rigby, 1975. Robert Ingpen. *Storm Boy,* written by Colin Thiele. Rigby, 1974 (published in the United States, illus. John Schoenherr, by Harper).

1976 *Book of the Year:* Ivan Southall. *Fly West.* Angus & Robertson, 1974 (published in the United States by Macmillan).

Picture Book of the Year: Dick Roughsey. *The Rainbow Serpent,* written by Dick Roughsey. Collins Australia, 1975.

Visual Arts: Ted Greenwood. *Terry's Brrrmmm GT,* written by Ted Greenwood. Angus & Robertson, 1976.

1977 *Book of the Year:* Eleanor Spence. *The October Child,* illus. Malcolm Green. Oxford Univ. Press, 1976 (published in the United States as *The Devil Hole* by Lothrop, Lee & Shepard).

Picture Book of the Year: Deborah Niland and Kilmeny Niland. *ABC of Monsters,* written by Deborah Niland and Kilmeny Niland. Hodder & Stoughton Australia, 1977 (published in the United States by McGraw-Hill).

1978 *Book of the Year:* Patricia Wrightson. *The Ice is Coming,* illus. with maps. Hutchinson Australia, 1977 (published in the United States by Atheneum).

Picture Book of the Year: Ron Brooks. *John Brown, Rose and the Midnight Cat,* written by Jenny Wagner. Kestrel, 1977 (published in the United States by Bradbury).

1979 *Book of the Year:* Ruth Manley. *The Plum-rain Scroll,* illus. Marianne Yamaguchi. Hodder & Stoughton Australia, 1978.

Picture Book of the Year: Percy J. Tresize and Dick Roughsey. *The Quinkins,* written by Percy J. Tresize and Dick Roughsey. Collins, 1978.

1980 *Book of the Year:* Lee Harding. *Displaced Person.* Hyland House, 1979 (published in the United States as *Misplaced Persons* by Harper).

Picture Book of the Year: Peter Pavey. *One Dragon's Dream,* written by Peter Pavey. Nelson, 1979 (published in the United States by Bradbury).

1981 *Book of the Year:* Ruth Park. *Playing Beatie Bow.* Nelson, 1980 (published in the United States by Atheneum).

Picture Book of the Year: No award.

1982 *Book of the Year:* Colin Thiele. *The Valley Between.* Rigby, 1981.

Picture Book of the Year: Jan Ormerod. *Sunshine,* written by Jan Ormerod. Kestrel, 1981 (published in the United States by Lothrop, Lee & Shepard).

1983 *Book of the Year:* Victor Kelleher. *Master of the Grove.* Penguin Australia, 1982.

Picture Book of the Year: Pamela Allen. *Who Sank the Boat?* written by Pamela Allen. Nelson, 1982 (published in the United States by Coward-McCann).

Junior Book of the Year: Robin Klein. *Thing,* illus. Alison Lester. Oxford Univ. Press, 1982.

Canada

The Canada Council Children's Literature Prizes

The Canada Council established the Canada Council Children's Literature Prizes in 1976 to be given annually to both an English language and French language author and/or illustrator. The categories were broadened in 1979 to include both an author and illustrator in each language. To be eligible, a book must have been published during the preceding year and written and/or illustrated by a Canadian or a landed immigrant with five years' residence in Canada. The judges are appointed by the Canada Council.

The Canada Council
Children's Literature Prizes
(English-language awards only)

1976 Bill Freeman. *Shantymen of Cache Lake,* illus. with maps and plates. Lorimer, 1975.

1977 Myra Paperny. *The Wooden People,* illus. Ken Stampnick. Little, Brown, 1976.

1978 Jean Little. *Listen for the Singing.* Clarke, Irwin, 1977 (published in the United States by Dutton).

1979 *Author:* Kevin Major. *Hold Fast.* Clarke, Irwin, 1978 (published in the United States by Delacorte).

Illustrator: Ann Blades. *Salmon for Simon,* written by Betty Waterton. Douglas & McIntyre, 1978 (published in the United States by Atheneum).

1980 *Author:* Barbara Claassen Smucker. *Days of Terror.* Clarke, Irwin, 1979 (published in the United States by Herald).

Illustrator: Laszlo Gal. *Twelve Dancing Princesses: A Fairy Story,* retold by Janet Lunn. Methuen, 1979.

1981 *Author:* Christie Harris. *The Trouble with Princesses,* illus. by Douglas Tait. McClelland & Stewart, 1980 (published in the United States by Atheneum).

Illustrator: Elizabeth Cleaver. *Petrouchka,* written by Elizabeth Cleaver. Macmillan, 1980 (published in the United States by Atheneum).

1982 *Author:* Monica Hughes. *The Guardian of Isis.* Van Nostrand Reinhold, 1981 (published in the United States by Atheneum).

Illustrator: Heather Woodall. *Ytek and the Arctic Orchid: An Inuit Legend,* retold by Garnet Hewitt. Douglas & McIntyre, 1981 (published in the United States by Vanguard).

1983 *Author:* Monica Hughes. *Hunter in the Dark.* Clarke, Irwin, 1982 (published in the United States by Atheneum).

Illustrator: Vlasta van Kampen. *ABC, 123: The Canadian Alphabet and Counting Book,* written by Vlasta van Kampen. Hurtig, 1982.

The Canadian Library Association
Book-of-the-Year for Children Award

The Canadian Library Association Book-of-the-Year for Children Award was established in 1946 by the Canadian Association of Children's Librarians of the Canadian Library Association "for an outstanding children's book by a Canadian author or an author resident in Canada, for the purpose of encouraging the writing of books for boys and girls by Canadian authors." A second award was given, from 1954 to 1973, to an outstanding French-Canadian publication for children. Since 1975, a runner-up book has also been chosen. The award is given by vote of a committee of the Canadian Association of Children's Librarians.

The Canadian Library Association
Book-of-the-Year for Children Award
(English-language awards only)

1947 Roderick Haig-Brown. *Starbuck Valley Winter,* illus. Charles DeFeo. Morrow, 1943.

1948 Mabel Dunham. *Kristli's Trees,* illus. Selwyn Dewdney. McClelland & Stewart, 1948 (published in the United States by Hale).

1949 No award.

1950 Richard S. Lambert. *Franklin of the Arctic: A Life of Adventure,* illus. with maps by Julius Griffith. McClelland & Stewart, 1949.

1951 No award.

1952 Catherine Anthony Clark. *The Sun Horse,* illus. Clare Bice. Macmillan Canada, 1951.

1953 No award.

1954 No award.

1955 No award.

1956 Louise Riley. *Train for Tiger Lily,* illus. Christine Price. Macmillan Canada, 1954 (published in the United States by Viking).

1957 Cyrus Macmillan. *Glooskap's Country and Other Indian Tales,* illus. John A. Hall. Oxford Univ. Press, 1955.

1958 Farley Mowat. *Lost in the Barrens,* illus. Charles Geer. Little, Brown, 1956 (published in the United States by Atlantic Monthly/Little, Brown).

1959 John F. Hayes. *The Dangerous Cove: A Story of Early Days in Newfoundland,* illus. Fred J. Finley. Copp Clark, 1957 (published in the United States by Messner).

1960 Charles Marius Barbeau. *The Golden Phoenix and Other French-Canadian Fairy Tales,* retold by Michael Hornyansky, illus. Arthur Price. Oxford Univ. Press, 1958 (published in the United States by Walck).

1961   William Toye. *The St. Lawrence,* illus. Leo Rampan. Oxford Univ. Press, 1959 (published in the United States by Walck).

1962   No award.

1963   Sheila Every Burnford. *The Incredible Journey: A Tale of Three Animals,* illus. Carl Burger. Little, Brown, 1961.

1964   Roderick Haig-Brown. *The Whale People,* illus. Mary Weiler. Collins Canada, 1962 (published in the United States by Morrow).

1965   Dorothy M. Reid. *Tales of Nanabozho,* illus. Donald Grant. Oxford Univ. Press, 1963 (published in the United States by Walck).

1966   James Houston. *Tikta'liktak: An Eskimo Legend,* illus. the author. Longmans, 1965 (published in the United States by Harcourt).   James McNeill. *The Double Knights: More Tales from Round the World,* illus. Theo Dimson. Oxford Univ. Press, 1964 (published in the United States by Walck).

1967   Christie Harris. *Raven's Cry,* illus. Bill Reid. McClelland & Stewart, 1966 (published in the United States by Atheneum).

1968   James Houston. *The White Archer: An Eskimo Legend,* illus. the author. Longmans Canada, 1967 (published in the United States by Harcourt).

1969   Kay Hill. *And Tomorrow the Stars: The Story of John Cabot,* illus. Laszlo Kubinyi. Dodd, Mead, 1968.

1970   Edith Fowke. *Sally Go Round the Sun: 300 Songs, Rhymes and Games of Canadian Children,* illus. Carlos Marchiori. McClelland & Stewart, 1969 (published in the United States by Doubleday).

1971   William Toye. *Cartier Discovers the St. Lawrence,* illus. Laszlo Gal. Oxford Univ. Press, 1970 (published in the United States by Walck).

1972   Ann Blades. *Mary of Mile 18,* illus. the author. Tundra, 1971.

1973   Ruth Nichols. *The Marrow of the World,* illus. Trina Schart Hyman. Macmillan Canada, 1972 (published in the United States by Atheneum).

1974   Elizabeth Cleaver. *The Miraculous Hind,* illus. the author. Holt, 1973.

1975   Dennis Lee. *Alligator Pie,* illus. Frank Newfeld. Macmillan Canada, 1974 (published in the United States by Houghton Mifflin).

1976   Mordecai Richler. *Jacob Two-Two Meets the Hooded Fang,* illus. Fritz Wegner. McClelland & Stewart, 1975 (published in the United States by Knopf).

1977   Christie Harris. *Mouse Woman and the Vanished Princesses,* illus. Douglas Tait. McClelland & Stewart, 1976 (published in the United States by Atheneum).

1978   Dennis Lee. *Garbage Delight,* illus. Frank Newfeld. Macmillan Canada, 1977 (published in the United States by Houghton Mifflin).

1979   Kevin Major. *Hold Fast.* Clarke, Irwin, 1978 (published in the United States by Delacorte).

1980   James Houston. *River Runners: A Tale of Hardship and Bravery,* illus. the author. McClelland & Stewart, 1979 (published in the United States by Atheneum).

1981   Donn Kushner. *The Violin Maker's Gift,* illus. Doug Panton. Macmillan Canada, 1980 (published in the United States by Farrar, Straus & Giroux).

1982   Janet Lunn. *The Root Cellar.* Lester & Orpen Dennys, 1981 (published in the United States by Scribner's).

1983   Brian Doyle. *Up To Low.* Groundwood/ Douglas & McIntyre, 1982.

1984   Jan Hudson. *Sweetgrass.* Tree Frog, 1983.

The Amelia Frances Howard-Gibbon Illustrator's Award

Like the Canadian Library Association Book-of-the-Year for Children Award, the Amelia Frances Howard-Gibbon Illustrator's Award was established by the Canadian Association of Children's Librarians, in 1969. It honors "outstanding illustrations by a Canadian for a work published in Canada, whether picture book, fiction, or nonfiction, in the hope that Canadian artists and illustrators would be stimulated." The award was named after Amelia Frances Howard-Gibbon, the illustrator of the earliest Canadian picture book. The final selection is made by a committee of children's librarians.

The Amelia Frances Howard-Gibbon Illustrator's Award

1971 Elizabeth Cleaver. *The Wind Has Wings: Poems from Canada,* comp. Mary Alice Downie and Barbara Robertson. Oxford Univ. Press, 1968 (published in the United States by Walck).

1972 Shizuye Takashima. *A Child in Prison Camp,* written by Shizuye Takashima. Tundra, 1971 (published in the United States by Morrow).

1973 Jacques de Roussan. *Beyond the Sun/Au-delà du Soleil,* written by Jacques de Roussan. Tundra, 1972.

1974 William Kurelek. *A Prairie Boy's Winter,* written by William Kurelek. Tundra, 1973 (published in the United States by Houghton Mifflin).

1975 Carlo Italiano. *The Sleighs of My Childhood/ Les Traineaux de Mon Enfance,* written by Carlo Italiano. Tundra, 1974.

1976 William Kurelek. *A Prairie Boy's Summer,* written by William Kurelek. Tundra, 1975 (published in the United States by Houghton Mifflin).

1977 Pam Hall. *Down by Jim Long's Stage: Rhymes for Children and Young Fish,* written by Al Pittman. Breakwater, 1976.

1978 Elizabeth Cleaver. *The Loon's Necklace,* retold by William Toye. Oxford Univ. Press, 1977.

1979 Ann Blades. *A Salmon for Simon,* written by Betty Waterton. Douglas & McIntyre, 1978 (published in the United States by Atheneum).

1980 Laszlo Gal. *The Twelve Dancing Princesses: A Fairy Story,* retold by Janet Lunn. Methuen, 1979.

1981 Douglas Tait. *The Trouble with Princesses,* retold by Christie Harris. McClelland & Stewart, 1980 (published in the United States by Atheneum).

1982 Heather Woodall. *Ytek and the Arctic Orchid: An Inuit Legend,* retold by Garnet Hewitt. Douglas & McIntyre, 1981 (published in the United States by Vanguard).

1983 Lindee Climo. *Chester's Barn,* written by Lindee Climo. Tundra, 1982.

1984 Ken Nutt. *Zoom at Sea.* Written by Tim Wynne-Jones. Groundwood/Douglas & McIntyre, 1983.

England

The Carnegie Medal

Administered by the British Library Association, the Carnegie Medal is given each year for the outstanding book for children written in English and published in the United Kingdom during the preceding year. The year cited in the following list is the year in which the book was published. First given in 1937, the Carnegie Medal was created to mark the centenary of Andrew Carnegie's birth. In addition to the winner, "highly commended," "commended," and "honour" awards are also occasionally given. The committee of the British Library Association which selects the winner of the Carnegie Medal is also responsible for the selection of the recipient of the Kate Greenaway Medal.

The Carnegie Medal

1936 Arthur Ransome. *Pigeon Post,* illus. the author. Cape, 1936.

1937 Eve Garnett. *The Family from One End Street,* illus. the author. Muller, 1937 (published in the United States by Vanguard).

1938 Noel Streatfield. *The Circus is Coming,* illus. Steven Spurrier. Dent, 1938 (published in the United States as *Circus Shoes* by Gregg and Random).

1939 Eleanor Doorly. *The Radium Woman: A Youth Edition of the Life of Madam Curie,* illus. Robert Gibbings. Heinemann, 1939 (published in the United States by Roy).

1940 Kitty Barne. *Visitors from London,* illus. Ruth Gervis. Dent, 1940 (published in the United States by Dodd, Mead).

1941 Mary Treadgold. *We Couldn't Leave Dinah,* illus. Stuart Tresilian. Cape, 1941.

1942 Denys James Watkins-Pitchford. *The Little Grey Men: A Story for the Young in Heart,* illus. the author. Eyre & Spottiswoode, 1942 (published in the United States by Scribner's).

1943 No award.

1944 Eric Linklater. *The Wind on the Moon: A Story for Children,* illus. Nicolas Bentley. Macmillan, 1944.

1945   No award.

1946   Elizabeth Goudge. *The Little White Horse,* illus. C. Walter Hodges. Univ. of London Press, 1946 (published in the United States by Gregg).

1947   Walter de la Mare. *Collected Stories for Children,* illus. Irene Hawkins. Faber, 1947.

1948   Richard Armstrong. *Sea Change,* illus. Michael Leszczynski. Dent, 1948.

1949   Agnes Allen. *The Story of Your Home,* illus. Agnes Allen and Jack Allen. Faber, 1949.

1950   Elfrida Vipont Foulds. *The Lark on the Wing,* illus. Terence Reginald Freeman. Oxford Univ. Press, 1950 (published in the United States by Bobbs-Merrill).

1951   Cynthia Harnett. *The Wool-Pack,* illus. the author. Methuen, 1951.

1952   Mary Norton. *The Borrowers,* illus. Diana Stanley. Dent, 1952 (published in the United States by Harcourt).

1953   Edward Osmond. *A Valley Grows Up,* illus. the author. Oxford Univ. Press, 1953.

1954   Ronald Welch. *Knight Crusader,* illus. William Stobbs. Oxford Univ. Press, 1954.

1955   Eleanor Farjeon. *The Little Bookroom: Eleanor Farjeon's Short Stories for Children Chosen by Herself,* illus. Edward Ardizzone. Oxford Univ. Press, 1955 (published in the United States by Walck).

1956   C. S. Lewis. *The Last Battle: A Story for Children,* illus. Pauline Baynes. Bodley Head, 1956 (published in the United States by Macmillan).

1957   William Mayne. *A Grass Rope,* illus. Lynton Lamb. Oxford Univ. Press, 1957 (published in the United States by Dutton).

1958   A. Philippa Pearce. *Tom's Midnight Garden,* illus. Susan Einzig. Oxford Univ. Press, 1958 (published in the United States by Lippincott).

1959   Rosemary Sutcliff. *The Lantern Bearers,* illus. Charles Keeping. Oxford Univ. Press, 1959 (published in the United States by Walck).

1960   Ian Wolfram Cornwall. *The Making of Man,* illus. M. Maitland Howard. Phoenix House, 1960 (published in the United States by Dutton).

1961   Lucy M. Boston. *A Stranger at Green Knowe,* illus. Peter Boston. Faber, 1961 (published in the United States by Harcourt).

1962   Pauline Clarke. *The Twelve and the Genii,* illus. Cecil Leslie. Faber, 1962 (published in the United States as *The Return of the Twelves* by Coward-McCann).

1963   Hester Burton. *Time of Trial,* illus. Victor Ambrus. Oxford Univ. Press, 1963 (published in the United States by World).

1964   Sheena Porter. *Nordy Bank,* illus. Annette Macarthur-Onslow. Oxford Univ. Press, 1964 (published in the United States by Roy).

1965   Philip Turner. *The Grange at High Force,* illus. William Papas. Oxford Univ. Press, 1965 (published in the United States by World).

1966   No award.

1967   Alan Garner. *The Owl Service.* Collins, 1967 (published in the United States by Philomel).

1968   Rosemary Harris. *The Moon in the Cloud.* Faber, 1968 (published in the United States by Macmillan).

1969   K. M. Peyton. *The Edge of the Cloud,* illus. Victor Ambrus. Oxford Univ. Press, 1969 (published in the United States by Collins).

1970   Leon Garfield and Edward Blishen. *The God beneath the Sea,* illus. Charles Keeping. Longman Young, 1970 (published in the United States by Pantheon).

1971   Ivan Southall. *Josh.* Angus & Robertson, 1971 (published in the United States by Macmillan).

1972   Richard Adams. *Watership Down.* Collings, 1972 (published in the United States by Macmillan).

1973   Penelope Lively. *The Ghost of Thomas Kempe,* illus. Antony Maitland. Heinemann, 1973 (published in the United States by Dutton).

1974   Mollie Hunter. *The Stronghold.* Hamilton, 1974 (published in the United States by Harper).

1975   Robert Westall. *The Machine-Gunners.* Macmillan, 1975 (published in the United States by Greenwillow).

1976   Jan Mark. *Thunder and Lightnings,* illus. Jim Russell. Kestrel, 1976 (published in the United States by Harper).

1977   Gene Kemp. *The Turbulent Term of Tyke Tiler,* illus. Carolyn Dinan. Faber, 1977 (published in the United States by Faber).

1978   David Rees. *Exeter Blitz.* Hamilton, 1978 (published in the United States by Elsevier/Nelson).

1979   Peter Dickinson. *Tulku.* Gollancz, 1979 (published in the United States by Unicorn/Dutton).

1980   Peter Dickinson. *City of Gold and Other Stories from the Old Testament,* illus. Michael Foreman. Gollancz, 1980 (published in the United States by Pantheon).

1981   Robert Westall. *The Scarecrows.* Chatto & Windus, 1981 (published in the United States by Greenwillow).

1982   Margaret Mahy. *The Haunting.* Dent, 1982 (published in the United States by Atheneum).

1983   Jan Mark. *Handles.* Kestrel, 1983.

The Kate Greenaway Medal

The Kate Greenaway Medal, administered by the British Library Association since 1955, is given for the most distinguished work in the illustration of a children's book published in the preceding year. The year cited in the following list is the year in which the book was published. The award is named after Kate Greenaway, the highly influential nineteenth-century British illustrator of children's books. In addition to the winner, "highly commended," "commended," and "honour" awards are also occasionally given. The committee of the British Library Association which selects the winner of the Kate Greenaway Medal is also responsible for the selection of the recipient of the Carnegie Medal.

The Kate Greenaway Medal

1955   No award.

1956   Edward Ardizzone. *Tim All Alone,* written by Edward Ardizzone. Oxford Univ. Press, 1956 (published in the United States by Walck).

1957   Violet Hilda Drummond. *Mrs. Easter and the Storks,* written by Violet Hilda Drummond. Faber, 1957 (published in the United States by Barnes).

1958   No award.

1959   William Stobbs. *A Bundle of Ballads,* comp. Ruth Manning-Sanders. Oxford Univ. Press, 1959 (published in the United States by Lippincott). William Stobbs. *Kashtanka,* written by Anton Chekhov, trans. Charles Dowsett. Oxford Univ. Press, 1959 (published in the United States by Walck).

1960   Gerald Rose. *Old Winkle and the Seagulls,* written by Elizabeth Rose. Faber, 1960 (published in the United States by Barnes).

1961   Antony Maitland. *Mrs. Cockle's Cat,* written by A. Philippa Pearce. Kestrel, 1961 (published in the United States by Lippincott).

1962   Brian Wildsmith. *Brian Wildsmith's ABC,* written by Brian Wildsmith. Oxford Univ. Press, 1962 (published in the United States by Watts).

1963   John Burningham. *Borka: The Adventures of a Goose with No Feathers,* written by John Burningham. Cape, 1963 (published in the United States by Random House).

1964   C. Walter Hodges. *Shakespeare's Theatre,* written by C. Walter Hodges. Oxford Univ. Press, 1964 (published in the United States by Coward-McCann).

1965   Victor G. Ambrus. *Three Poor Tailors,* written by Victor G. Ambrus. Hamilton, 1965 (published in the United States by Harcourt).

1966   Raymond Briggs. *Mother Goose Treasury,* comp. Raymond Briggs. Hamilton, 1966 (published in the United States by Coward-McCann).

1967   Charles Keeping. *Charley, Charlotte and the Golden Canary,* written by Charles Keeping. Oxford Univ. Press, 1967 (published in the United States by Watts).

1968   Pauline Baynes. *Dictionary of Chivalry,* written by Grant Uden. Kestrel, 1968 (published in the United States by Crowell).

1969   Helen Oxenbury. *Dragon of an Ordinary Family,* written by Margaret May Mahy. Heinemann, 1969 (published in the United States by Watts). Helen Oxenbury. *The Quangle-Wangle's Hat,* written by Edward Lear. Heinemann, 1969 (published in the United States by Watts).

1970   John Burningham. *Mr. Gumpy's Outing,* written by John Burningham. Cape, 1970 (published in the United States by Holt).

1971   Jan Pienkowski. *The Kingdom Under the Sea,* written by Jan Pienkowski. Cape, 1971.

1972   Krystyna Turska. *The Woodcutter's Duck,* written by Krystyna Turska. Hamilton, 1972 (published in the United States by Macmillan).

1973   Raymond Briggs. *Father Christmas,* written by Raymond Briggs. Hamilton, 1973 (published in the United States by Coward-McCann).

1974   Pat Hutchins. *The Wind Blew,* written by Pat Hutchins. Bodley Head, 1974 (published in the United States by Macmillan).

1975   Victor G. Ambrus. *Horses in Battle,* written by Victor G. Ambrus. Oxford Univ. Press, 1975. Victor G. Ambrus. *Mishka,* written by Victor G. Ambrus. Oxford Univ. Press, 1975 (published in the United States by Warne).

1976   Gail E. Haley. *The Post Office Cat,* written by Gail E. Haley. Bodley Head, 1976 (published in the United States by Scribner's).

1977   Shirley Hughes. *Dogger,* written by Shirley Hughes. Bodley Head, 1977 (published in the United States as *David and Dog* by Prentice-Hall).

1978   Allan Ahlberg and Janet Ahlberg. *Each Peach, Pear, Plum,* written by Allan Ahlberg and Janet Ahlberg. Kestrel, 1978 (published in the United States by Viking).

1979   Jan Pienkowski. *Haunted House,* written by Jan Pienkowski. Dutton, 1979.

1980   Quentin Blake. *Mr. Magnolia,* written by Quentin Blake. Cape, 1980.

1981   Charles Keeping. *The Highwayman,* written by Alfred Noyes. Oxford Univ. Press, 1981.

1982   Michael Foreman. *Long Neck and Thunder Foot,* written by Helen Piers. Kestrel, 1982. Michael Foreman. *Sleeping Beauty and Other Favourite Fairy Tales,* ed. and trans. Angela Carter. Gollancz, 1982.

1983   Anthony Browne. *Gorilla,* written by Anthony Browne. MacRae, 1983 (published in the United States by Watts).

The Guardian Award for Children's Fiction

The staff of the British newspaper *The Guardian* established the annual Guardian Award for Children's Fiction in 1967 "for an outstanding work of fiction for children by a British or Commonwealth author." Commended and runner-up books are also chosen. A panel of judges makes the final selection.

The Guardian Award for Children's Fiction

1967   Leon Garfield. *Devil-in-the-Fog,* illus. Antony Maitland. Kestrel, 1966 (published in the United States by Pantheon).

1968   Alan Garner. *The Owl Service.* Collins, 1967 (published in the United States by Philomel).

1969   Joan Aiken. *The Whispering Mountain,* illus. Frank Bozzo. Cape, 1968 (published in the United States by Doubleday).

1970   K. M. Peyton. *Flambards* (the trilogy), illus. Victor Ambrus. Oxford Univ. Press, 1967 (published in the United States by World).

1971   John Christopher. *The Guardians.* Macmillan, 1970.

1972   Gillian E. Avery. *A Likely Lad,* illus. Faith Jacques. Collins, 1971 (published in the United States by Holt).

1973   Richard Adams. *Watership Down.* Collings, 1972 (published in the United States by Macmillan).

1974   Barbara Willard. *The Iron Lily.* Longmans, 1973 (published in the United States by Dutton).

1975   Winifred Cawley. *Gran at Coalgate,* illus. F. Rocker. Oxford Univ. Press, 1974 (published in the United States by Holt).

1976   Nina Bawden. *The Peppermint Pig,* illus. Charles Lilly. Gollancz, 1975 (published in the United States by Lippincott).

1977   Peter Dickinson. *The Blue Hawk,* illus. David Smee. Gollancz, 1976 (published in the United States by Little, Brown).

1978   Diana Wynne Jones. *A Charmed Life.* Macmillan, 1977 (published in the United States by Greenwillow).

1979   Andrew Davies. *Conrad's War.* Blackie, 1978 (published in the United States by Crown).

1980   Ann Schlee. *The Vandal.* Macmillan, 1979 (published in the United States by Crown).

1981   Peter Carter. *The Sentinels.* Oxford Univ. Press, 1980.

1982   Michelle Magorian. *Goodnight Mister Tom.* Kestrel, 1981 (published in the United States by Harper).

1983   Anita Desai. *Village By the Sea.* Heinemann, 1982.

1984   Dick King-Smith. *Sheep-pig.* Gollancz, 1983.

International

The Hans Christian Andersen Award

The Hans Christian Andersen Award, established in 1956, was the first international book award. It is given every two years to a living author who has made an outstanding contribution to children's literature. A committee of five, each from a different country, judges the selections recommended by the board or library association in each country. The award is given by the International Board on Books for Young People. In 1966 the award was expanded to honor an illustrator as well as an author.

The Hans Christian Andersen Medal

1956   Eleanor Farjeon (Great Britain).

1958   Astrid Lindgren (Sweden).

1960   Erich Kästner (Germany).

1962   Meindert DeJong (United States).

1964   René Guillot (France).

1966   *Author:* Tove Jansson (Finland).
Illustrator: Alois Carigiet (Switzerland).

1968   *Author:* James Krüss (Germany) and Jose Maria Sanchez-Silva (Spain).
Illustrator: Jiri Trnka (Czechoslovakia).

1970   *Author:* Gianni Rodari (Italy).
Illustrator: Maurice Sendak (United States).

1972   *Author:* Scott O'Dell (United States).
Illustrator: Ib Spang Olsen (Denmark).

1974   *Author:* Maria Gripe (Sweden).
Illustrator: Farshid Mesghali (Iran).

1976   *Author:* Cecil Bødker (Denmark).
Illustrator: Tatjana Mawrina (U.S.S.R.).

1978   *Author:* Paula Fox (United States).
Illustrator: Svend Otto S. (Denmark).

1980   *Author:* Bohumil Riha (Czechoslovakia).
Illustrator: Suekichi Akaba (Japan).

1982   *Author:* Lygia Bojunga Nunes (Brazil).
Illustrator: Zbigniew Rychlicki (Poland).

1984   *Author:* Christine Nöstlinger (Austria).
Illustrator: Mitsumasa Anno (Japan).

For additional prizes and honors, see *Children's Books: Awards and Prizes,* compiled and edited by the Children's Book Council, revised biennially. See also *Children's Literature Awards and Winners: A Directory of Prizes, Authors, and Illustrators,* compiled by Dolores Blythe Jones (Neal-Schuman/Gale, 1983).

Acknowledgments

Addison-Wesley Publishing Company Geraldine L. Flanagan, *Window into an Egg: Seeing Life Begin,* © 1969, Addison-Wesley, Reading, Massachusetts. Pgs. 28–35. Reprinted with permission.

George Allen and Unwin J. R. R. Tolkien, "Dwarves' Song" and "Riddles in the Dark" from *The Hobbit.* Quotations from *Tree and Leaf* by J. R. R. Tolkien. By permission.

Arena-Verlag Wurzburg "Staver and His Wife Vassilissa" from Hans Baumann, *Hero Legends of the World.* By permission.

Atheneum Publishers, Inc. Dorothy Aldis, "A Letter to Noel" from *Nothing Is Impossible: The Story of Beatrix Potter.* Copyright © 1969 by Mary Cornelia Aldis Porter. Ashley Bryan, "Hen and Frog" from *Beat the Story-Drum, Pum-Pum.* Copyright © 1980 by Ashley Bryan. Susan Cooper, excerpted from *The Grey King.* Copyright © 1975 Susan Cooper (A Margaret K. McElderry Book). Christie Harris, "The Princess and the Feathers" from *Mouse Woman and the Vanished Princesses.* Copyright © 1976 by Christie Harris. James Houston, "I want to laugh . . ." from *Songs of the Dream People: Chants and Images from the Indians and Eskimos of North America.* Copyright © 1972 by M. James Houston (A Margaret K. McElderry Book). Patricia Hubbell, "Shadows" from *Catch Me A Wind.* Copyright © 1968 Patricia Hubbell. Monica Hughes, excerpted from *The Keeper of the Isis Light.* Copyright © 1980 Monica Hughes. Myra Cohn Livingston, "History" from *The Way Things Are and Other Poems.* Copyright © 1974 by Myra Cohn Livingston (A Margaret McElderry Book). Lilian Moore, "Pigeons" from *I Thought I Heard the City.* Copyright © 1969 by Lilian Moore. Myra Cohn Livingston, "74th Street" and "The Way that It's Going" from *The Malibu and Other Poems.* Copyright © 1972 by Myra Cohn Livingston (A Margaret K. McElderry Book). E. L. Konigsburg, excerpted from *From the Mixed-Up Files of Mrs. Basil E. Frankweiler.* Copyright © 1967 by E. L. Konigsburg. Ellen Switzer, Chapter "Paper" from *How Democracy Failed.* Copyright © 1975 by Ellen Switzer. N. M. Bodecker, "Let's Marry Said the Cherry" from *Let's Marry Said the Cherry and Other Nonsense Poems.* Copyright © 1974 by N. M. Bodecker (A Margaret McElderry Book). N. M. Bodecker, "Little Jock Sander of Dee" and "Row, Row, Row" from *It's Raining Said John Twaining.* Copyright © 1973 N. M. Bodecker (A Margaret K. McElderry Book). Russell Hoban, *How Tom Beat Captain Najork and His Hired Sportsmen.* Text copyright © 1974 by Yankee Rover, Inc. Illustrations copyright © 1974 by Quentin Blake. All reprinted with the permission of Atheneum Publishers.

Patricia Ayres "How to Eat a Poem" from *It Doesn't Always Have to Rhyme* by Eve Merriam. Copyright © 1964 by Eve Merriam. "Landscape" from *Finding a Poem* by Eve Merriam. Copyright © 1970 by Eve Merriam. "Windshield Wiper" from *Out Loud* by Eve Merriam. Copyright © 1973 by Eve Merriam. All reprinted by permission of the author. "Things to Be If You Are a Subway" by Bobbi Katz. Copyright © 1970 by Bobbi Katz. Reprinted by permission of the author.

A. S. Barnes & Company Post Wheeler, "The Little Humpbacked Horse" from *Russian Wonder Tales.*

Estate of Jacqueline Bernard "A Slaveholder's Promise" reprinted from *Journey toward Freedom: The Story of Sojourner Truth* by Jacqueline Bernard. Copyright © 1967 by Jacqueline Bernard. Reprinted by permission of Joel Bernard, Executor.

Bobbs-Merrill Company "My Father" from *Meet My Folks,* copyright © 1961, 1973 by Ted Hughes. Used with permission of the publisher, The Bobbs-Merrill Company, Inc.

Bradbury Press Excerpt from Paula Fox, *The Slave Dancer,* reprinted with permission of Bradbury Press, Inc. Copyright © 1973 by Paula Fox.

Curtis Brown, Ltd. "Homework" from *Breakfast, Books & Dreams* by Jane Yolen copyright © 1981 by Jane Yolen. Extract from *Carrie's War* by Nina Bawden © Nina Bawden 1973. "Emotional Realism in Books for Young People" by Nina Bawden reprinted by permission of Curtis Brown, Ltd. Originally appeared in *The Horn Book Magazine,* February 1980. Copyright © 1980 by Nina Bawden.

Cambridge University Press Quotations from Elizabeth Cook, *The Ordinary and the Fabulous: An Introduction to Myths, Legends and Fairy Tales for Teachers and Story Tellers,* 1969. By permission.

Jonathan Cape Text of *How Tom Beat Captain Najork and His Hired Sportsmen,* written by Russell Hoban and illustrated by Quentin Blake, reprinted by permission.

Chatto & Windus "Lone Dog" from *Songs to Save a Soul* by Irene Rutherford McLeod by permission of the author's Literary Estate and Chatto & Windus.

Collins Publishers "My Aunt Jane, she called me in," "Over the garden wall," and "Wall flowers, wall flowers, growing up so high" from *What Do You Feed Your Donkey On?* by Colette O'Hare, published by Collins. Extract from Jane van Lawick-Goodall, *In the Shadow of Man.* Pp. 165–179 from *Prince Caspian* by C. S. Lewis. Copyright reserved, published by Collins. By permission.

Estate of Padraic Colum "Orpheus" from *Orpheus: Myths of the World* and "Bellerophon" from *The Forge in the Forest,* by Padraic Colum, reprinted by permission of Mrs. Maire O'Sullivan and the Public Administrator of the County of New York.

1339

Hilda Conkling   "Weather," "Water," and "I Am" reprinted from *Poems by a Little Girl* (1920–1949 Stokes Lippincott) reprinted by permission of the author.

Constable Publishers   "Plucking the Rushes" from *170 Chinese Poems* translated by Arthur Waley reprinted by permission of the publisher.

Harold Courlander   "Why Wisdom Is Found Everywhere" from *The Hat-Shaking Dance and Other Ashanti Tales from Ghana* and "The Goat Well" from Harold Courlander and Wolf Leslau, *The Fire on the Mountain and Other Ethiopian Stories,* copyright 1950 by Holt, Rinehart and Winston. Both by permission of Mr. Courlander.

Coward-McCann   "The Four Genii" reprinted by permission of Coward-McCann from *The Return of the Twelves* by Pauline Clarke, text copyright © 1962 by Pauline Clarke. "A Lady Comes to an Inn" by Elizabeth Coatsworth reprinted by permission of Coward-McCann from *The Creaking Stair,* copyright 1929, 1949 by Coward-McCann, Inc., copyright renewed © 1976 by Elizabeth Coatsworth Beston. *Millions of Cats* by Wanda Gag, copyright 1928 by Coward-McCann, Inc. Copyright renewed © 1956 by Robert Janssen. Reprinted by permission of Coward-McCann.

London Daily Mirror   "Anger," by Yvonne Lowe, from the *Daily Mirror* Children's Literature Competition.

Guy Daniels   "The Mouse and the Rat" from *Fifteen Fables of Krylov.* Used by permission.

Delacorte Press   "The Old Troll of Big Mountain" by Anna Wahlenberg excerpted from *Great Swedish Fairy Tales* translated by Holger Lundbergh. English translation Copyright © 1973 by Dell Publishing Co., Inc. "Seal" excerpted from the book *Laughing Time* by William Jay Smith. Copyright © 1953, 1955, 1956, 1957, 1959, 1968, 1974, 1977, 1980 by William Jay Smith. Both reprinted by permission of Delacorte Press/Seymour Lawrence.

J. M. Dent & Sons Ltd.   English translation of "Staver and His Wife Vassilissa" from *Hero Legends of the World* by Hans Baumann. "The Silver Nose" translated by Sylvia Mulcahy, from Calvino's *Italian Folk Tales.* "Little Red Riding-Hood," Charles Perrault, *Fairy Tales.* Three rhymes from Roger Lancelyn Green, *The Book of Nonsense.* All used by permission.

Dodd, Mead & Company   "The Sedna Legend" reprinted by permission of Dodd, Mead & Company, Inc. from *The Day Tuk Became a Hunter* by Ronald Melzack. Copyright © 1967 by Ronald Melzack.

Doubleday & Company   "The Peasant's Clever Daughter" from *Grimm's Tales for Young and Old* translated by Ralph Manheim. Copyright © 1977 by Ralph Manheim. "I Am Cherry Alive" Copyright © 1958 by Delmore Schwartz from *Summer Knowledge, New and Selected Poems* by Delmore Schwartz. "Moon-Uncle" from *Moon-Uncle, Moon-Uncle: Rhymes from India* by Sylvia Cassedy & Parvathi Thampi. Copyright © 1973 by Sylvia Cassedy & Parvathi Thampi. Text from "Shimmy, Shimmy, Coke-ca-pop" from *Shimmy, Shimmy, Coke-Ca-Pop* by John Langstaff and Carol Langstaff. Text copyright © 1973 by John Langstaff and Carol Langstaff. "The Bat," "The Serpent," "The Yak," copyright 1938, 1950, 1952, by Theodore Roethke; "My Papa's Waltz" copyright 1942 by Hearst Magazines, Inc.; and "The Meadow Mouse" copyright © 1963 by Beatrice Roethke as Administratrix of the Estate of Theodore Roethke, from *The Collected Poems of Theodore Roethke.* Excerpts from *Anne Frank: The Diary of a Young Girl* by Anne Frank, copyright 1952 by Otto H. Frank. "Summer Night" by Shiki from *An Introduction to Haiku* by Harold G. Henderson. Copyright © 1958 by Harold G. Henderson. "Singing Time" from *The Fairy Green* by Rose Fyleman, copyright 1923 by George H. Doran Co. "jelly in the dish" and "Eddie Spaghetti" from *Shimmy Shimmy Coke-Ca-Pop* by John and Carol Langstaff. Copyright © 1973 by John Langstaff and Carol Langstaff. "The Fisherman and His Wife," from *The Brothers Grimm: Popular Folk Tales* translated by Brian Alderson. Copyright © 1978 by Brian Alderson. "Mice" from *Fifty-One Nursery Rhymes* by Rose Fyleman, copyright 1931, 1932 by Doubleday & Co.   All reprinted by permission of Doubleday and Company, Inc.

Dover Publications   "Baby swimming down river" from Natalie Curtis, *The Indian's Book,* used by permission of the publisher.

Gerald Duckworth & Co. Ltd.   "Overheard on a Saltmarsh" from Harold Munro, *Collected Poems.* Hilaire Belloc, "The Frog," from *Cautionary Verses.* Used by permission.

E. P. Dutton, Inc.   Excerpt from *The Knee-High Man and Other Stories,* copyright © 1972 by Julius Lester. Excerpts from *To Be a Slave,* copyright © 1968 by Julius Lester. Excerpt from *Roll of Thunder, Hear My Cry,* copyright © 1976 by Mildred D. Taylor. All reprinted by permission of the publisher, Dial Books for Young Readers, A Division of E. P. Dutton, Inc. "The Hare that Ran Away" from *Eastern Stories and Legends* by Marie L. Shedlock, copyright 1920 by E. P. Dutton and Co., Inc.; renewed 1948 by Arthur C. Jennings. "The Children of Lir" from *Celtic Wonder Tales* retold by Ella Young. "The Wonderful Tar-Baby" from *Uncle Remus: His Songs and Sayings* by Joel Chandler Harris, copyright 1895, 1880 by D. Appleton and Company, copyright 1908, 1921, 1935, 1963 by Esther La Rose Harris. "Niamh of the Golden Hair" from *The High Deeds of Finn Mac Cool,* copyright © 1967 by Rosemary Sutcliff. Extract from *The Ghost of Thomas Kempe,* copyright © 1973 by Penelope Lively. "Sir Lancelot Fails His Testing" from *The Light Beyond the Forest,* copyright © 1979 by Rosemary Sutcliff. All reprinted by permission of the publisher, E. P. Dutton, Inc. "The March to Lanka" from *Rama, the Hero of India* by Dhan Gopal Mukerji, copyright 1930 by E. P. Dutton & Co., Inc.; renewed 1957 by Mrs. Dhan

Gopal Mukerji. "Ah Tcha the Sleeper" from *Shen of the Sea* by Arthur Bowie Chrisman, copyright 1925 by E. P. Dutton & Co., Inc.; renewed 1953 by Arthur Bowie Chrisman. "The King's Breakfast" and "Happiness" from *When We Were Very Young* by A. A. Milne, illustrated by Ernest H. Shepart, copyright 1924 by E. P. Dutton; renewed 1952 by A. A. Milne. All reprinted by permission of the publisher.

Editions Robert Laffont "Lullaby" from *Poèmes Eskimos* by Paul-Emile Victor, trans. Charlene Slivnick, used by permission of the publisher. Translation © 1971 by Charlene Slivnick.

James A. Emanuel "A Small Discovery" from James A. Emanuel, *The Treehouse and Other Poems* (Detroit: Broadside Press, 1968) © 1968 by James A. Emanuel. Used by permission of the author.

Faber and Faber Publishers Chapter from *The Twelve and the Genii* by Pauline Clark; "Macavity: The Mystery Cat" from *Old Possum's Book of Cats* by T. S. Eliot; "My Father," from *Meet My Folks* by Ted Hughes; quotation from *The Children of Green Knowe* by L. M. Boston, all reprinted by permission of Faber and Faber Ltd.

Farrar, Straus & Giroux, Inc. Excerpt from *Tuck Everlasting* by Natalie Babbitt. Copyright © 1975 by Natalie Babbitt. "Why the Fox Has a Huge Mouth" from *Black Rainbow*, edited and translated by John Bierhorst. Copyright © 1976 by John Bierhorst. "Song of Creation" and "I Pass the Pipe" from *In the Trail of the Wind*, edited & translated by John Bierhorst. Copyright © 1971 by John Bierhorst. Excerpts adapted from *Flying to the Moon and Other Strange Places* by Michael Collins. Copyright © 1976 by Michael Collins. Excerpts from *The Last Elizabethan* by Constance Fecher. Copyright © 1972 by Constance Fecher. "Dance Poem" and "The Drum" from *Spin a Soft Black Song* by Nikki Giovanni. Copyright © 1971 by Nikki Giovanni. Excerpt from *A Wrinkle in Time* by Madeleine L'Engle. Copyright © 1962 by Madeleine L'Engle Franklin. Excerpt from *The Golem* by Isaac Bashevis Singer. Copyright © 1982 by Isaac Bashevis Singer. Excerpt from *A Day of Pleasure* by Isaac Bashevis Singer. Copyright © 1963, 1965, 1966, 1969 by Isaac Bashevis Singer. "Cat" and "Marbles" from *Small Poems* by Valerie Worth. Copyright © 1972 by Valerie Worth. "Magnet" from *More Small Poems* by Valerie Worth. Copyright © 1976 by Valerie Worth. All by permission of Farrar, Straus & Giroux, Inc.

Mirra Ginsburg "The Fox and the Thrush" from *Three Rolls and One Doughnut: Fables from Russia*, by permission of the author.

Victor Gollancz Ltd. "The Fisherman and His Wife" from *The Brothers Grimm: Popular Folk Tales*, translated by Brian Alderson. "The Fall of Man" from Peter Dickinson, *City of Gold and Other Stories from the Old Testament*. By permission.

Granada Publishing Ltd. "Adam and Eve," "Granny's in the kitchen," and "Humpty Dumpty" from Michael Rosen & Susanna Steele, *Inky Pinky Ponky*. Copyright © Michael Rosen and Susanna Steele 1982. Used by permission of the publisher.

Greenwillow Books "Long Gone" from *Zoo Doings* by Jack Prelutsky. Copyright © 1967, 1983 by Jack Prelutsky. Excerpts from *Oak & Company* by Richard Mabey. Copyright © 1983 by Richard Mabey. "Toucans Two" from *Zoo Doings* by Jack Prelutsky, Copyright © 1970, 1983 by Jack Prelutsky. All by permission of Greenwillow Books (a Division of William Morrow & Co.).

Tamar Griggs "I have just taken birth out of dark hot mother," by Luisa Kaye, from *There's a Sound in the Sea . . .*, Tamar Griggs, Collector. Copyright © 1975 by Tamar Griggs. Used by permission of the collector.

Hamish Hamilton Ltd. Extract from *The Keeper of the Isis Light* by Monica Hughes and extract from *A Year and a Day* by William Mayne. Reprinted by permission.

Harcourt Brace Jovanovich "Splinter" from *Good Morning, America*, copyright 1928, 1956 by Carl Sandburg. "Blake Leads a Walk on the Milky Way" from *A Visit to William Blake's Inn*, copyright © 1981 by Nancy Willard. "Fog" from *Chicago Poems* by Carl Sandburg, copyright 1916 by Holt, Rinehart and Winston, Inc.; copyright 1944 by Carl Sandburg. "who are you, little i" copyright 1963 by Marion Morehouse Cummings. From *Complete Poems 1913–1962* by e e cummings. "Macavity: The Mystery Cat" from *Old Possum's Book of Practical Cats*, copyright 1939 by T. S. Eliot; renewed, 1967 by Esme Valerie Eliot. "The Marble Boy" from *Mary Poppins Opens the Door*, copyright 1943, renewed, 1971, by P. L. Travers. "The Talking Pot" from *Thirteen Danish Tales* by Mary C. Hatch, copyright 1947 by Harcourt Brace Jovanovich, Inc.; renewed, 1975 by Edgun Wulff. Chapter 1 from *Rufus M*, copyright 1943, renewed 1971 by Eleanor Estes. "Peculiarsome Abe" from *Abe Lincoln Grows Up* by Carl Sandburg, copyright 1926, 1928 by Harcourt Brace Jovanovich, Inc.; renewed 1954, 1956 by Carl Sandburg. "The Twelve Months" from *The Shoemaker's Apron* copyright 1920 by Parker Fillmore; renewed 1948 by Louise Fillmore. "The Bear Says North" from *Mighty Mikko*, copyright 1922 by Parker Fillmore; renewed 1950 by Louise Fillmore. Selection from *The Borrowers*, copyright 1952, 1953 by Mary Norton. Selection from *The Little Prince* by Antoine de Saint-Exupery copyright 1943; renewed, 1971 by Harcourt Brace Jovanovich Inc. Selection from *Paul Bunyan* copyright 1924, 1954 by Esther Shephard. Selection from *The Children of Green Knowe*, copyright 1954 © 1955 by L. M. Boston. All reprinted by permission of Harcourt Brace Jovanovich.

Harper & Row, Publishers, Inc. "Summertime" from *Little House in the Big Woods* by Laura Ingalls Wilder. Text copyright 1932 by Laura Ingalls Wilder. Copyright

1930, © 1958 by Charles Malam. "I've Got a Rocket," "I eat my peas with honey," and "A horse and a flea and three blind mice" from *A Rocket in My Pocket* compiled by Carl Withers. Copyright 1948 by Carl Withers. Copyright © 1976 by Samuel H. Halperin. "Thor Gains His Hammer" from *Thunder of the Gods* by Dorothy Hosford. Copyright 1952 by Dorothy Hosford. "The Woman Who Flummoxed the Fairies" from *Heather and Broom* by Sorche Nic Leodhas. Copyright © 1960 by Leclair G. Alger. All reprinted by permission of Holt, Rinehart and Winston, Publishers.

The Horn Book   Aidan Chambers, "Letter from England: Talking about Reading: Back to Basics," *The Horn Book Magazine*, 53 (October 1977), pp. 567–611. Townsend, John Rowe. *A Sense of Story*. The Horn Book, Inc. Copyright © 1971 by John Rowe Townsend. All rights reserved. Both reprinted by permission.

Houghton Mifflin Company   "I Met a Crow" from *I Met a Man* by John Ciardi. Copyright © 1961 by John Ciardi. "Dwarves' Song" and "Riddles in the Dark" from *The Hobbitt* by J. R. R. Tolkien. Copyright © 1966 by J. R. R. Tolkien. "A Song of Greatness" from *The Children Sing in the Far West* by Mary Austin. Copyright 1928 by Mary Austin. Copyright © renewed 1956 by Kenneth M. Chapman & Mary C. Wheelwright. "Salt Water Tea" from *Johnny Tremain* by Esther Forbes. Copyright, 1943, by Esther Forbes Hoskins. Copyright © renewed 1971 by Linwood M. Erskine, Jr., executor of the Estate. Selection from *Island of the Blue Dolphins* by Scott O'Dell. Copyright © 1960 by Scott O'Dell. Selection from *In the Shadow of Man* by Jane van Lawick-Goodall. Copyright © 1971 by Hugo and Jane van Lawick-Goodall. "Old Fire Dragaman" from *The Jack Tales* by Richard Chase. Copyright 1943 and copyright © renewed 1971 by Richard Chase. Selection from *Gandhi* by Olivia Coolidge. Copyright © 1971 by Olivia Coolidge. Selection from *Sky Watchers of Ages Past* by Malcolm E. Weiss. Copyright © 1982 by Malcolm E. Weiss. "Alligator Pie" and "Skyscraper" from *Alligator Pie* by Dennis Lee. Copyright © 1974 by Dennis Lee. Selection from *Anastasia Krupnick* by Lois Lowry. Copyright © 1979 by Lois Lowry. Selection from *A Wizard of Earthsea* by Ursula K. LeGuin. Copyright 1968 by Ursula LeGuin. All Shakespeare selections from *The Complete Plays and Poems of William Shakespeare*, edited by William Allan Neilson and Charles Jarvis Hill. Copyright © 1942 by William Allen Neilson and Charles Jarvis Hill, renewed 1969 by Caroline Steiner and Margaret H. Helburn. Quotations from *Tree and Leaf* by J. R. R. Tolkien copyright © 1964 by George Allen & Unwin Ltd. All reprinted by permission of Houghton Mifflin Company.

Hutchinson Publishing Group Ltd.   "Childhood" from *Collected Poems* by Frances Cornford. By permission.

Indian Council for Cultural Relations   "Sleep brings pearly necklaces" from *Folk Songs of India*, ed. Hem Barua, reprinted by permission of the publisher.

Indiana University Press   "Determination of the Seasons," from Stith Thompson, *Tales of the North American Indians*, © 1966 by Indiana University Press.

International Creative Management, Inc.   "My fingers" from *My Fingers Are Always Bringing Me News* by Mary O'Neill. Copyright 1969 by Mary O'Neill. Reprinted by permission.

John Johnson   Selection from Leon Garfield, *Smith*. By permission.

Helen Finger LeFlar   "The Tale of the Lazy People," from Charles J. Finger, *Tales from Silver Lands*.

The Library Association (London)   C. S. Lewis, "On Three Ways of Writing for Children," from the *Proceedings* of the Bournemouth Conference.

Little, Brown and Company   From *New & Selected Things Taking Place* by May Swenson: "The Centaur" copyright © 1956 by May Swenson, first appeared in *The Western Review*; "Southbound on the Freeway" copyright © 1963 by May Swenson, first appeared in *The New Yorker*. From *Humbug Mountain* by Sid Fleischman: "The Fool Killer" copyright © 1978 by Albert S. Fleischman. Excerpts from *The Green and Burning Tree: On the Writing and Enjoyment of Children's Books* by Eleanor Cameron. Copyright © 1962, 1964, 1966, 1969 by Eleanor Cameron. All used by permission of Little, Brown and Company in association with the Atlantic Monthly Press. From *Custard and Company* by Ogden Nash: "Adventures of Isabel" copyright 1936 by Ogden Nash. From *One At a Time* by David McCord: "Blessed Lord, What it is to be young" and "Take Sky" copyright © 1962 by David McCord; "The Walnut Tree" copyright © 1966 by David McCord. From *One at a Time* by David McCord: "Up From Down Under" and "I Want You to Meet" copyright © 1962 by David McCord. "The Master and the Servant" from *Once There Was and Was Not* by Virginia A. Tashjian. "The Eel" copyright 1942 by Ogden Nash. First appeared in *The New Yorker*. "The Guppy" copyright 1944 by The Curtis Publishing Company. First appeared in *The Saturday Evening Post*. "The Ostrich" copyright © 1956 by Ogden Nash. First appeared in *The New Yorker*. All from *Verses from 1929 On* by Ogden Nash. "Was She a Witch?" and "Eletelephony" from *Tirra Lirra* by Laura E. Richards copyright 1932 by Laura E. Richards. Copyright renewed © 1960 by Hamilton Richards. "Cupid and Psyche" and "Demeter" from *Mythology* by Edith Hamilton. Copyright 1942 by Edith Hamilton. Copyright renewed © 1969 by Dorian Fielding Reid and Doris Fielding Reid, Executrix of the will of Edith Hamilton. All by permission of Little, Brown and Company.

Liveright Publishing Corporation   "hist whist" and "in Just—" are reprinted from TULIPS & CHIMNEYS by E. E. Cummings, by permission of Liveright Publishing Corporation. Copyright 1923, 1925 and renewed 1951, 1953 by E. E. Cummings. Copyright © 1973, 1976 by the Trustees for the E. E. Cummings Trust. Copyright © 1973, 1976 by George Firmage. "The Tongue Cut Sparrow" is reprinted from JAPANESE FAIRY TALES by Lafcadio Hearn, with permission of Liveright Publishing Corporation. Copyright 1953 by Liveright Publishing Corporation. Copyright renewed 1981.

Ronald Loewinsohn   "It Is an Outfielder" from *Meat Air*. By permission.

Christopher Lofting   "The Rarest Animal of Them All" from *The Story of Doctor Dolittle* by Hugh Lofting. By permission.

Lothrop Lee and Shepard Books   (Entire text) *Hiroshima No Pika* by Toshi Maruki. Copyright © 1980 by Toshi Maruki. Reprinted by permission of Lothrop, Lee & Shepard Books (A Division of William Morrow & Co.).

Macmillan of Canada   "Alligator Pie" and "Skyscraper" from *Alligator Pie* by Dennis Lee. Reprinted by permission of Macmillan of Canada, A Division of Gage Publishing Ltd.

Macmillan Publishing Company, Inc.   "Who are *you?* asked the cat of the bear" and "Swift things are beautiful" from *Away Goes Sally* by Elizabeth Coatsworth. Copyright 1934 by Macmillan Publishing Company, renewed 1962 by Elizabeth Coatsworth Beston. "The Buddha" from *The Cat Who Went to Heaven* by Elizabeth Coatsworth. Copyright 1930 by Macmillan Publishing Company, renewed 1958 by Elizabeth Coatsworth Beston. "Hansel and Gretel" from *The Golden Bird and Other Fairy Tales of the Brothers Grimm,* Randall Jarrell, trans. Copyright © 1962 by Macmillan Publishing Company. Selection from *The White Mountain* by John Christopher. Copyright © 1967 by John Christopher. Selection from *The Planet of Junior Brown* by Virginia Hamilton. Copyright © 1971 by Virginia Hamilton. "The Seven Ages of Elf-hood" from *Poems* by Rachel Field. Copyright 1926 by Macmillan Publishing Company, renewed 1954 by Arthur S. Pederson. "Early Morning Song" from *Poems* by Rachel Field. Copyright 1924, 1926, 1930, 1934, 1941, 1944, 1957 by Macmillan Publishing Company. "Bats" and "The Bird of Night" from *The Bat-Poet* by Randall Jarrell. Copyright © Macmillan Publishing Company 1963, 1964. "Night" from *Stars To-night* by Sara Teasdale. Copyright 1930 by Sara Filsinger Teasdale renewed 1958 by The Guaranty Trust Company of New York. "Odin Goes to Mimir's Well" and "Sigurd's Youth" from *The Children of Odin* by Padraic Colum. Copyright 1920 by Macmillan Publishing Company, renewed 1948 by Padraic Colum. "Odysseus and the Cyclops" from *The Adventures of Odysseus and the Tale of Troy* by Padraic Colum. Copyright 1917 by Macmillan Publishing Company, renewed 1946 by Padraic Colum. "Atalanta's Race" from *The Golden Fleece and the Heroes Who Lived before Achilles* by Padraic Colum. Copyright 1921 by Macmillan Publishing Company, renewed 1949 by Padraic Colum.

All reprinted with permission of Macmillan Publishing Company. Selection from Paul and Dorothy Goble, *Custer's Last Battle,* by permission of Macmillan, London and Basingstoke. "The Story of the Three Bears" from *English Fairy Tales* by Flora Annie Steel. Copyright 1918 by Macmillan Publishing Company, renewed 1946 by Mabel H. Webster. "The Snare" and "The Devil's Bag" from *Collected Poems* by James Stephens. Copyright 1915 by Macmillan Publishing Company, renewed 1943 by James Stephens. Reprinted by permission of Macmillan Publishing Company and Macmillan, London and Basingstoke. "The Stolen Child" from *Collected Poems of W. B. Yeats* by W. B. Yeats. Reprinted with permission of Macmillan Publishing Company. New York: Macmillan Publishing Company, 1983. Pages 151-171 from *Prince Caspian* by C. S. Lewis. Copyright 1951 by C. S. Lewis Pte., Ltd., renewed in 1979. Reprinted by permission of Macmillan Publishing Company.

McClelland and Stewart, Ltd.   "The Sedna Legend" from *The Day Tuk Became a Hunter* by Ronald Melzack. "Happiness" and "The King's Breakfast" from *When We Were Very Young* by A. A. Milne. "My Mother said that I never should" from *Sally Go Round the Sun* by Edith Fowke. All used by permission of the Canadian publishers, McClelland and Stewart Limited, Toronto.

McGraw-Hill Book Company   "How a Mummy Was Made" from *Wrapped for Eternity* by Mildred Mastin Pace. Copyright © 1974 by Mildred Mastin Pace. Used with permission of the publisher.

David McKay Company   "The Jolly Tailor Who Became King" from Lucia M. Borsky & Kate B. Miller, *The Jolly Tailor and Other Fairy Tales.* "The Wonder Smith and His Son" from Ella Young, *The Wonder Smith and His Son.* Selections from *The Song of Roland,* translated by Merriam Sherwood, copyright 1938 by Longman's Green and Co., Inc. "Three Fridays" from Alice G. Kelsey, *Once the Hodja* copyright 1943 by Alice Geer Kelsey. "Zal the White-Haired" from Barbara Leonie Picard, *Tales of Ancient Persia.* All used by permission.

Julian Messner   "The Two Suitors" from *Heroes of the Kalevala* by Babette Deutsch copyright © 1940, 1967 by Babette Deutsch. Reprinted by permission of Julian Messner, a division of Simon & Schuster, Inc.

Methuen and Company   Selections from Henry Bett, *Nursery Rhymes and Tales,* reprinted by permission.

William and Norah Montgomerie   "Lady, Lady Landers," "A wee bird sat upon a tree," and "The cock and the hen" from *Sandy Candy and Other Scottish Nursery Rhymes.* By permission.

William Morrow & Company, Inc.   "A Poem for Carol [20 Dec 7]" from *My House* by Nikki Giovanni. Copyright © 1972 by Nikki Giovanni. From Pp. 1-30 in *Dear Mr. Henshaw* by Beverly Cleary. All by permission of William Morrow & Company.

Miriam Morton "The Path on the Sea" by Inna Muller, from *The Moon Is Like a Silver Sickle.*

John Murray "The Last March" from Robert Scott, *Captain Scott's Last Expedition.* By permission.

New Directions Publishing Corporation "Fortune has its cookies to give out" from Lawrence Ferlinghetti, *A Coney Island of the Mind.* Copyright © 1958 by Lawrence Ferlinghetti. "Johnnie Crack and Flossie Snail" from Dylan Thomas, *Under Milkwood.* Copyright 1954 by New Directions Publishing Corporation. "The Magical Mouse" from Kenneth Patchen, *The Collected Poems of Kenneth Patchen.* Copyright 1952 by Kenneth Patchen. All reprinted by permission of New Directions Publishing Corporation.

W. W. Norton & Company Rhymes from ONE POTATO, TWO POTATO by Herbert and Mary Knapp, used by permission of the publisher.

Harold Ober Associates "Small, Smaller" from *The Pedaling Man* by Russell Hoban, copyright © 1968 by Russell Hoban. "Poem" by Langston Hughes in *Langston Hughes: A Biography* by Milton Meltzer, copyright 1924 by Crisis Pub. Co. Pages 3–45 from *About the Sleeping Beauty* by P. L. Travers, copyright © 1975 by P. L. Travers. Extract from William Mayne, *A Year and a Day* copyright © 1976 by William Mayne. All reprinted by permission of Harold Ober Associates Incorporated.

Deborah Owen Ltd. Penelope Farmer, "Wayland Smith," reprinted from *The Faber Book of Northern Legends,* Crossley-Holland, ed. By permission.

Oxford University Press From *The Sea around Us* by Rachel L. Carson. Copyright © 1950, 1951, 1961 by Rachel L. Carson; renewed 1979 by Roger Christie. Reprinted by permission of Oxford University Press, Inc. "The Wind Has Wings" by Raymond de Coccola and Paul King from *Ayorama* and "The Golden Phoenix" from *The Golden Phoenix* by Marius Barbeau, retold by Michael Hornyansky, both by permission of Oxford University Press Canada. Text only from *Beowulf* by Kevin Crossley-Holland, illustrated by Charles Keeping, pp. 2–46: © Kevin Crossley-Holland 1982. "St. George and the Dragon" retold by Kenneth McLeish, "Krishna and the Serpent," "Manu and Shatarupa," and "The Night Journey" retold by John Bailey, all from *Gods and Men: Myths and Legends from the World's Religions* retold by John Bailey, Kenneth McLeish, and David Spearman, pp. 112–113, 60–63, 45–48, 136–138: © John Bailey, Kenneth McLeish, and David Spearman 1981. "The Late Mr. Bartholomew" from *Tom's Midnight Garden* by A. Philippa Pearce, pp. 68–74: © Oxford University Press 1958. "The Feast of New Spears" from *The Eagle of the Ninth* by Rosemary Sutcliff (1954), pp. 160–173. "Niord and Skadi" from *Tales of the Norse Gods and Heroes* retold by Barbara Leonie Picard (1953), pp. 35–40. "Unanana and the Elephant" from *African Myths and Legends* retold by Kathleen Arnott, pp. 68–73: © Kathleen Arnott 1962. All reprinted by permission of Oxford University Press, Oxford.

Penguin Books Ltd. Chapter 12 from Leon Garfield and Edward Blishen: *The Golden Shadow* (Longman Young Books 1973) pp. 98–112. Text © Leon Garfield and Edward Blishen 1973. Extract from Richard Mabey: *Oak & Company* (Kestrel Books 1983). Text © 1983 by Richard Mabey. Selection from Jan Mark: *Thunder and Lightnings,* text copyright © by Jan Mark, 1976. All reprinted by permission of Penguin Books Ltd.

Peter Pauper Press Basho, "In My New Clothing." From *The Four Seasons: Japanese Haiku Written by Basho, Buson, Issa, Shiki, and Many Others,* trans. Peter Beilenson. By permission.

Philomel Books "Upright John" reprinted by permission of Philomel Books, a Division of The Putnam Publishing Group, from *The Lad of the Gad* by Alan Garner, text © 1980 by Alan Garner. Rhymes from *Chinese Mother Goose Rhymes,* copyright © 1968 by Robert Wyndham, reprinted by permission of Philomel Books, a Division of Putnam Publishing Group.

Murray Pollinger Extracts from *The High Deeds of Finn Mac Cool* and from *The Light Beyond the Forest,* both by Rosemary Sutcliff, reprinted by permission of The Bodley Head Ltd., Puffin Books, and Knight Books.

Clarkson N. Potter Inc. "Sleep, baby, sleep" and "Hush, little baby, don't say a word" from W. S. and C. Baring-Gould, *The Annotated Mother Goose.* By permission.

Prentice-Hall, Inc. "The Monkey and the Crocodile" from *Jataka Tales:* Retold by Ellen C. Babbitt, © 1912, Renewed © 1940. "The Golden Goose" from *More Jataka Tales:* Retold by Ellen C. Babbitt, © 1922, Renewed © 1950. Both reprinted by permission of Prentice-Hall, Inc., Englewood Cliffs, N.J.

Putnam Publishing Group "Hiding" and "Blum" by Dorothy Aldis reprinted by permission of Putnam Publishing Group from *All Together* by Dorothy Aldis, copyright 1952 by Dorothy Aldis, copyright © renewed 1980 by Roy E. Porter.

G. P. Putnam's Sons Excerpt from *Where Do You Think You're Going, Christopher Columbus?* by Jean Fritz, text © 1980 by Jean Fritz. Excerpt from *Homesick, My Own Story,* text © 1982 by Jean Fritz. Both reprinted by permission of G. P. Putnam's Sons. Excerpt reprinted by permission of G. P. Putnam's Sons from *The Sword in the Stone* by T. H. White. Copyright 1939 by T. H. White: renewed.

Random House, Inc./Alfred A. Knopf, Inc. "Death is like the sleepy door nail" and "Dog, where did you get that bark?" from *Rose, Where Did You Get that Red?* by Kenneth Koch. Copyright © 1973 by Kenneth Koch: "The 1st" from *Good Times,* by Lucille Clifton. Copyright © 1969 by Lucille Clifton. "The Heron and the Humming Bird" and "The Story of the Hungry Elephant" from *Hesitant Wolf and Scrupulous Fox: Fables Selected from World Literature,* ed., Karen Kennerly. All reprinted by permission of Random House Inc. "The Fall of Man" from *The City of Gold and Other Stories from the New Testament*, by Peter Dickinson. Copyright © 1980 by Peter Dickinson: Extract from *Lobo of the Tasaday* by John Nance. Copyright © 1982 by John Nance: "The Deadliest Snake of All" from *The Golden Shadow* by Leon Garfield and Edward Blishen. Copyright © 1973 by Leon Garfield and Edward Blishen. Selection from *Smith*, by Leon Garfield. Copyright © 1967 by Leon Garfield: Selection from *Red Hawk's Account of Custer's Last Battle*, by Paul and Dorothy Goble. Copyright © 1969 by Paul and Dorothy Goble. All reprinted by permission of Pantheon Books, a Division of Random House, Inc. "Recital" copyright © 1961 by John Updike. Reprinted from *Telephone Poles and Other Poems*: "Escape" copyright 1921 by Alfred A. Knopf, Inc. and renewed 1949 by William Rose Benet. Reprinted from *Collected Poems of Elinor Wylie*: "How the Coyote Danced with the Blackbirds" from *Zuni Folk Tales*, edited and translated by Frank Hamilton Cushing. Copyright 1931 and renewed 1959 by Alfred A. Knopf, Inc.: Selection from *The Magic Orange Tree and Other Haitian Folk Tales*, by Diane Wolkstein. Copyright © 1978 by Diane Wolkstein: "Little Red Riding Hood and the Wolf" from *Roald Dahl's Revolting Rhymes*, by Roald Dahl. Copyright © 1982: "September" from *A Child's Calendar*, by John Updike. Copyright © 1965 by John Updike and Nancy Burkert: "Plucking the Rushes" from *Translations from the Chinese*, by Arthur Waley. Copyright 1919 and renewed 1947 by Arthur Waley: "The Frog" from *Cautionary Verses*, by Hilaire Belloc. Copyright 1941 by Alfred A. Knopf, Inc.: "Winter Moon," "Aunt Sue's Stories," "Mother to Son," copyright 1926 by Alfred A. Knopf, Inc. and renewed 1954 by Langston Hughes; "Snail" copyright 1947 by Langston Hughes. Reprinted from *Selected Poems of Langston Hughes:* "Bound No'th Blues" copyright 1927 by Alfred A. Knopf, Inc. and renewed 1955 by Langston Hughes. Reprinted from *Selected Poems of Langston Hughes:* "Dreams," "Poem," and "Youth" copyright 1932 and renewed 1960 by Langston Hughes. Reprinted from *The Dream Keeper and Other Poems*, by Langston Hughes. All by permission of Alfred A. Knopf, Inc.

Estate of James Reeves   "The Black Pebble," "W," "The Old Wife and the Ghost," "Bobadil" and "The Footprint" from James Reeves, *The Blackbird in the Lilac*. Copyright © 1952 The Estate of James Reeves. Permission granted by the Author's Estate.

Alistair Reid   "What is a Tingle-Airey" from *Ounce, Dice, Trice*, by permission of the author.

Paul R. Reynolds, Inc.   "Long Division" from *Long Ago When I Was Young* by E. Nesbit. Copyright © by E. Nesbit. Reprinted by permission of Paul R. Reynolds, Inc.

Penelope Rieu   "Cat's Funeral" by E. V. Rieu from *The Flattered Flying Fish and Other Poems*. By permission.

Routledge and Kegan Paul PLC   "Ladybirds Is Horrid" from Timothy Rogers, *Those First Affections*, London, 1979. By permission.

Russell & Volkening, Inc.   "Song of Weeds" from *No One Writes a Letter to a Snail* by Maxine Kumin reprinted by permission of Russell & Volkening, Inc. as agents for the author. Copyright © 1962 by Maxine Kumin. Extracts from *Gandhi* by Olivia Coolidge. By permission.

Louise Sclove   "What the Gray Cat Sings" from *I Sing the Pioneer* by Arthur Guiterman. By permission.

Charles Scribner's Sons   Judith & Herbert Kohl, "Views of the Oak" from *The View of the Oak: The Private Worlds of Other Creatures*. Copyright © 1977 Judith & Herbert Kohl. Marcia Brown, *Dick Whittington and His Cat*. Copyright 1950 Marcia Brown. Copyright renewed 1978 by Marcia Brown. Both reprinted with the permission of Charles Scribner's Sons. "The Declaration of Independence" is reprinted by permission of Charles Scribner's Sons from *George Washington's World* by Genevieve Foster. Copyright 1941 Charles Scribner's Sons. Copyright renewed 1969 by Genevieve Foster. "The Shell" is reprinted by permission of Charles Scribner's Sons from *The Crows* by David McCord. Copyright 1934 Charles Scribner's Sons. Copyright renewed 1962 by David McCord. "King Arthur and His Sword" is reprinted by permission of Charles Scribner's Sons from *The Boy's King Arthur* by Sidney Lanier. Copyright 1917 Charles Scribner's Sons. Copyright renewed 1945 N. C. Wyeth. Dorcas MacClintock, excerpted from *A Natural History of Giraffes*. Copyright © 1973 Dorcas MacClintock. "The Wild Wood" from *The Wind in the Willows* by Kenneth Grahame. Both reprinted with permission of Charles Scribner's Sons.

Sidgwick & Jackson   "Choosing Shoes" from Ffrida Wolfe, *The Very Thing*. By permission.

Simon & Schuster, Inc.   "It was midnight," "Singing," "This Is a Poem" and "November" from *Miracles* by Richard Lewis. Copyright © 1966 by Richard Lewis. Text of *Sylvester and the Magic Pebble* by William Steig copyright © 1969 by William Steig. Reprinted by permission of Simon & Schuster, Inc.

Smithsonian Institution Press   "I Sing for the Animals" by permission of the Smithsonian Institution Press from *Bureau of American Ethnology Bulletin 61, Teton Sioux Music*, by Frances Densmore, Smithsonian Institution, Washington, D.C., 1918.

The Society of Authors   "Mice" and "Singing Time" by Rose Fyleman. The Society of Authors as the literary representative of the Estate of Rose Fyleman. "Nicholas Nye" and "Some One" by Walter de la Mare from *Peacock Pie*; "Cinderella and the Glass Slipper" by Walter de la Mare from *Told Again*; "Alas, Alack" by Walter de la Mare from *Collected Poems*. The Literary Trustees of Walter de la Mare and the Society of Authors as their representative. All by permission. "The Snare" and "The Devil's Bag" from *Collected Poems* by James Stephens used by permission of The Society of Authors on behalf of the copyright owner, Mrs. Iris Wise.

Ailes Spinden "Song of the Sky Loom" from *Songs of the Tewa,* trans. Herbert Joseph Spinden (published under the auspices of the Exposition of Indian Tribal Arts, Inc., 1933, New York).

Mrs. James Thurber "The Moth and the Star" by James Thurber. By permission.

The University of Chicago Press "Numskull and the Rabbit" and lines from page 21 reprinted from *The Panchatantra* translated by Arthur Ryder, by permission of The University of Chicago Press, copyright 1925 by The University of Chicago.

University of Pennsylvania Folklore Archives "One bright day" from *Trickery and Foolery with Words,* ed. Alvin Schwartz. By permission.

Vallentine Mitchell & Co. Ltd. Anne Frank, *The Diary of a Young Girl,* extract reprinted by permission of Vallentine Mitchell & Co. Ltd. Copyright © 1952 by Otto H. Frank.

Viking Penguin "The White Horse," "Delight of Being Alone," and "Little Fish" from *The Complete Poems of D. H. Lawrence,* Selected and Edited by Vivian de Sola Pinto and F. Warren Roberts. Copyright © 1964 by Angelo Ravagli and C. M. Weekley, Executors of the Estate of Frieda Lawrence Ravagli. "Triolet against Sisters" from *Times Three* by Phyllis McGinley. Copyright © 1959 by Phyllis McGinley. Originally published in *The New Yorker.* Extract from *Letters to Horseface* by Ferdinand R. Monjo. Copyright © 1965 by Ferdinand and Louise L. Monjo. "Crossing" from *Letter from a Distant Land* by Philip Booth. Copyright © 1953, renewed 1981 by Philip Booth. Originally published in *The New Yorker.* "The Loon" from *Under the North Star* by Ted Hughes. Copyright © 1981 by Ted Hughes. Text from *In the Land of Small Dragons* by Ann Nolan Clark. Text copyright © 1979 by Ann Nolan Clark. "The Vikings Find and Lose America" from *Americans Before Columbus* by Elizabeth C. Baity. Copyright 1951 by Elizabeth C. Baity. Copyright renewed © 1979 by Elizabeth C. Baity. "The Poles" from *Vast Horizons* by Mary Seymour Lucas. Copyright 1943 by Mary Seymour Lucas, renewed copyright © 1970 by Mary Seymour Lucas. "Firefly" from *Under the Tree* by Elizabeth M. Roberts. Copyright 1922 by B. W. Huebsch, Inc., renewed 1950 by Iver S. Roberts. "The Prayer of the Little Pig" from

Prayers from the Ark by Rumer Godden. Copyright © 1962 by Rumer Godden. "Dinewan the Emu and Goomble-gubbon the Turkey" from *Australian Legendary Tales* by K. Langloh Parker. Selected and Edited by E. Drake-Brockman. All rights reserved. "The Fox and the Goat" and "The Dairymaid and her Milk-Pot" from *The Fables of La Fontaine,* translated by Marianne Moore. Copyright 1953, 1954 by Marianne Moore. "The Doughnuts" from *Homer Price* by Robert McCloskey. Copyright 1943, copyright © renewed 1971 by Robert McCloskey. All reprinted by permission of Viking Penguin Inc.

Walker & Company Selections from *Figgie Hobbin* by Charles Causley. Copyright © 1973 by Charles Causley. "Wild Geese Flying" from *The Prancing Pony, Nursery Rhymes from Japan* by Charlotte B. DeForest. Used with the permission of the publisher, Walker & Company.

Frederick Warne (Publishers) Ltd. Leslie Brooke, "Johnny Crow's Garden" and Beatrix Potter, *The Tale of Peter Rabbit.* Both by permission.

Watkins/Loomis Agency, Inc. Extract from T. H. White, *The Sword in the Stone* copyright 1939 by T. H. White. © renewed 1967 by Lloyds Bank, Executor and Trustee Company (Channel Islands Ltd.). Selection, Chapter 13, from Frances Hodgson Burnett, *The Secret Garden* copyright 1911 by Frances Hodgson Burnett. Copyright renewed 1939 by Verity Constance Burnett. By permission.

A. P. Watt Ltd. "The Penny Fiddle" from *The Penny Fiddle* and "Hide and Seek" from *The Poor Boy Who Followed His Star*" used by permission of A. P. Watt Ltd. and Robert Graves. "How the Camel Got His Hump" from Rudyard Kipling, *Just-So Stories,* reprinted by permission of The National Trust for Places of Historic Interest or Natural Beauty, Macmillan London Ltd., and A. P. Watt Ltd. "The Stolen Child" by W. B. Yeats from *Collected Poems of W. B. Yeats* used by permission of Michael B. Yeats and Macmillan London, Ltd.

Malcolm E. Weiss Extract from Malcolm E. Weiss, *Sky Watchers of Ages Past,* by permission of the author.

Albert Whitman & Company "Pecos Bill Becomes a Coyote" from *Pecos Bill: The Greatest Cowboy of All Time* by James C. Bowman, and "The Rooster and the Hen" from *Tales from a Finnish Tupa,* by James C. Bowman & Margery Bianco, Aili Kolehmainen trans. By permission.

Yale University Press "How Kana Brought Back the Sun and Moon and Stars" from *The Bright Islands* by Padraic Colum © 1925 by Yale University Press.

Subject Index

This is an index to the content and the themes of the anthology's selections, as well as to the introductory material for each Part and chapter. Under any one subject heading, this index brings together material from all sections of the anthology, including poetry, works from the oral tradition, fiction, and nonfiction. Thus, for example, under SEA are listed two traditional ballads, a number of lyric poems, and two science books. The intent of this index is to help the reader locate writings on topics of interest in a range of types of children's literature. It does not include every work in the anthology, nor is it designed to provide an in-depth analysis of folk motifs and themes.

Titles following subject headings appear in order of their occurrence in the anthology. Page numbers in italic type direct the reader to editorial remarks, roman type to actual selections. In Part VI, topics that are discussed within selections on criticism and creators will appear as pages in roman type.

Particularly with regard to selections in the fiction section (Part IV), note that subject headings may reflect only the content of the excerpt or chapter, not the entire book.

Title, Author, and Illustrator Index

Page numbers in italic type indicate editorial comment; roman type has been used for selections and illustrations. This index includes first lines of poems without titles and the names of persons who have retold, collected, adapted, or translated folk literature in Part III, "The Oral Tradition."